Beyond the Stars

MARY

This One...WAS for You!

LWL
12/25/95

BEYOND THE STARS

The National Library of Poetry

Cynthia A. Stevens, Editor
Nicole Walstrum, Associate Editor

Beyond the Stars

Library of Congress
Cataloging in Publication Data

ISBN 1-56167-273-4

Manufactured in The United States of America by
Watermark Press
11419 Cronridge Dr., Suite 10
Owings Mills, MD 21117

Editor's Note

As one of the judges and editors of ***Beyond the Stars,*** I had the delightful opportunity to review and reflect upon the various poetic selections displayed within this anthology. The poets featured in this compilation artistically portray a variety of subjects and styles, each contributing to the book's quality. However, there are several poems I wish to honor with special recognition.

Sheila Stahl achieved the **Grand Prize** with her poem, "Wounded" (p. 1). An outstanding display of euphony is presented throughout this piece, as in the verse below:

> *Wounded are we at an early age from left-over love and traces of time*
> *dealt out of lips still dripping with wine.*

The poem describes the child of an alcoholic — how the child has been *wounded* from the experience and how the child must reach within to begin healing. A variety of adept images are intertwined throughout this work.

> *And like the onion, we peel and are peeled until the core no longer*
> *lures our tears...and finally peace.*

> . . .

> *We are nurtured like a brook that journeys with life down a mossy*
> *path of pebbles, continually finding breath in kindred crossing waters...*
> *if only for a stone's throw.*

As the nurtured brook, we are pushed along through our childhood, reaching past the decaying wood and pebbles for new life; we find that "new life" as the world opens up to us even though it was always close to home *"if only for a stone's throw."*

A truly solemn piece is "Burial in Rwanda July 31, 1994," by James Koenig (p. 230). With short, direct lines and minimal punctuation, Koenig brings to view the difficult task of trying to live in the midst of a war. The people of Rwanda must harvest their fields in order to grow crops necessary for their survival. Yet, their fields are covered with the dead bodies of their own loved ones.

> *The insult upon injury*
> *of having to cleanup after*
> *And once again it is necessary*
> *to remove the evidence*
> *in order to go on.*

The cleanup for the Rwandans is not only a laborious job physically, but mentally as well.

Another grave piece touching upon the coldness of war is "A Smile for Momma," by Eric Byungchan Song (p. 287). With varied scenic clips, Song allows you to not only feel the loss of a young soldier, but he enables you to picture the soldier. You see him smile.

Demonstrating a skilled rhyme scheme was Michael Wolf's "Worm Turns" (p. 126). Within this work you join a bird on her fascinating journey of fulfilling her appetite. Throughout the main part of the poem, the bird is consuming her share of worms — giving them their "worm turns." However, by the end of the poem, it is soon the bird's turn:

> *crippled huntress, hear her shriek - at nature's twist on hide and seek*
> *for shadows vanish at high noon - she waits exposed, her turn is soon....*

"Hidden Talents," by Debbie McKenna (p. 44), is a very interesting poem which is sure to make you reconsider your outlook upon life. The poem invites you into a man's home — a man named Mr. Lee. Using detailed images, McKenna reveals bits and pieces of Mr. Lee's world.

> *Things like old plastic buckets, some cracked pottery,*
> *rusting and bent fenders off of Japanese cars,*
> *a toilet seat with almost nothing wrong, knobs from ovens,*
> *mop and broom handles,...*

As you'll note by the end of the poem, Mr. Lee may own less than the average man, yet he stands well above the rest.

Pulling you from one line to the next is Joe Waldron's "Slow Siftings of Being by the Cup" (p. 71). This poem is distinctive, both in its language and topic. The poem speaks of several people who are searching the verse of poets and romantics, the theatre and art — trying to make more of themselves than what they believe. In the midst they reach for the word of someone who reads tea leaves as if it is gospel.

> *We sipped on our blood from old battered cups by degrees*
> *From questionable alphabetical tea leaves*
> *In a similarly drained historically empty cafe in York*
> *Waiting upon your pained syllables and persistent look.*

By following the gospel written in tea leaves, the characters of the poem hope to eliminate any faults that make them inferior, but find in the end, they are without identities.

> *All our names now lie discarded upon dirty, ashen tea trays*
> *Survived to tell us of the truth or falsehoods of our clinging ways.*

Angela Francavilla's "Ode for Alice" (p. 80) is a pleasant poem which begins by reflecting intimately upon a woman's younger days:

> *I remember Alice,*
> *Her orange hair of corkscrew curls*
> *Her funny dresses and her shopping bags*
> *The wild blue hat askew upon her bobbing head*
> *She walks amid the rubble and rabble of the city...*

The poem follows with the conclusion that we are all destined to grow old, even Alice:

> *At night with face against the windowpane,*
> *She [Alice] watches shadows dim the candles on her cake.*

"Rib," by Nancy G. Oxman (p. 183), provides a feministic view regarding the Biblical story of Adam and Eve:

> *I am every woman, every woman who believes... Adam did not give us*
> *a rib, we gently "took" it from him when the time was just...*

Two other prominent poems you won't want to miss are "Placental Shells" by David Humphreys (p. 232) and "Fledgling" by James Thompson (p. 55).

Although I do not have the time or space to individually critique every eminent poem appearing within *Beyond the Stars,* you will notice that each verse is well crafted with originality and design. May all of the artists within this anthology be renowned for their talents and efforts in creative writing.

Cynthia Stevens
Senior Editor

Winners of the North American Open Poetry Contest

Grand Prize

Sheila Stahl / San Antonio, TX

Second Prize

Maureen Asfeld / Woodstock, IL

Angela Francavilla / Brooklyn, NY

David Humphreys / Stockton, CA

James Koenig / Los Angeles, CA

Debbie McKenna / San Diego, CA

Nancy Oxman / Havertown, PA

Eric Song / Northridge, CA

James Thompson / Delray Beach, FL

Joe Waldron / Mattapan, MA

Michael Wolf / Arvada, CO

Third Prize

Kelle-Anne Allen / Baltimore, MD

Alan Anderson / Rock Falls, IL

VerNon A. Bingham / Mesa, AZ

Joseph E. Barrett, Universal City, TX

Burke Blackman / Schertz, TX

John Croft Jr. / Houston, TX

Kerry Burroughs / Harford, PA

John Carothers / Mays Landing, NJ

Sofia Cruz / Ashland, WI

Lucy Hassell Davis / Hickory, NC

Janet Drinkovich / Seal Beach, CA

Teresa Duckworth / Pottstown, PA

Dawn Escoto / Farmington, MI

Willard E. Franke / Paradise, CA

James Gilmartin / Rockaway Beach, NY

Katherine Gongora / Forest Hills, NY

Rita E. Gould / Middlesex, NJ

Agnes Griffing / Carson, WA

Dorothy E. Gunter / Port Bolivar, TX

Bret Hardin / Toledo, OH

C. W. Hess / Tucson, AZ

Carolyn S. Hicks / Paris, TX

Jeffrey B. Hodes / Sherman Oaks, CA

Elba Junco / San Antonio, TX

Glenngo Allen King / Brooklyn, NY

Olivia M. Lacson / San Diego, CA

R. Lee Jacobson Houck / Walton, NY

Roger Keith Lewis / Mechanicsville, VA

Eve Lewis-Chase / San Francisco, CA

Darlene Mackey / Waldorf, MD

J. W. Mauldin III / Orlando, FL

Alexander Menke / Pasadena, CA

Richard C. Mikolitch / Nutley, NJ

Chris Miller / Bryan, TX

Matt Mollicone / Highland, NY

Cassandre Novembre / New York City, NY

Jeffery Steven Noesser / Santa Ana, CA

Michelle Oleson / Plano, TX

Romuald Orlowski / Jackson, MI

L. Hawkeye Poole III / Naugatuck, CT

Dean Alexander / Columbia, SC

M. Lanette Ross & John Porst / Clinton, IN

Marjorie Manders Smith / White Plains, NY

Cheryl Stephenson / Huntington, WV

Yvonne Stetter / Dubois, IN

Gregory Owen Thomas / Kirtland, NM

Jennifer Usrey / Denton, TX

Jacqueline Vogelsang / Jacksonville, FL

Bridget Wagner / San Francisco, CA

Staci Waldman / Brooklyn, NY

Jimmy Walls / North Bergen, NJ

Tara Kelly Walworth / Geneva, IL

Chuck Watson / West Babylon, NY

Diana Wheelis / Willits, CA

Jason M. White / Mount Vernon, OH

William K. White / San Antonio, TX

Brian Dale Williams / Westminster, CO

Tisha B. Woody / Deer Park, TX

Congratulations also to all semi-finalists.

Grand Prize Winner

Wounded

Wounded are we at an early age from left-over love and traces of time
dealt out of lips still dripping with wine. With every word and every
deed we latch our hearts and souls and plead to hear for once we are
enough, we are okay, and still...silence. A void that burns and boils
and brews until it bubbles and bursts with bile and bitters we bore
and bear still. With vigor we strive to cleanse our hearts from every
stain of sickness and sour that soaks our soul and saddens our spirit.
For only freedom brings rest to tired eyes and tired aches that no
longer profit from heavy loads of rubbish. Relief we find or it finds
us in ways quite foreign to our finite bodies and yet our ageless
souls cry out for more inviting us to relish in our respite. And like
the onion, we peel and are peeled until the core no longer lures our
tears...and finally peace. Our days and mainly our nights are free
from demons and dreaded ghouls who once plagued our sleep and robbed
our rest. Now, it's spring. It's dawn. It's birth and rebirth.
Like the phoenix we rise with greater strength and dignity and love
for what we endured, for what we learned, and for what we have become.
For now we are wise. We are rich. We are full of healing and light.
We are nurtured like a brook that journeys with life down a mossy path
of pebbles, continually finding breath in kindred crossing waters...if only for a stone's throw.
   Sheila Stahl

e Passing of the Sentinels

r years of school we have finished, we look to the future at last
again we sorrow when leaving all the things we've done in the past.
l now before parting forever, we bid farewell to our class
l pause to strengthen, not sever, the bonds that have kept us fast.

ough memories doorway drifting and down the foot-worn stair
h moving feet a-sounding that trod the hallways there
see as visions passing, the ones that filled the air
h glad and joyous laughter, the days that were so fair.

l now that times are changing as the past we leave behind
unknown future facing, we know not what to find;
e make the best endeavor, there is naught for us to fear
s is but commencement time, so we shall start right here.

w as through life we travel, often our roads are steep
wn with rocks and bramble, before reaching the heights we seek.
ny will fall by the wayside and many the top will not reach
we of the sign of the Sentinel will climb to the top of the peaks.

lay we have gathered together, friends of the senior class,
strengthen what time cannot sever - the ties that have held us fast.
are not parting forever, for many will meet again
en faith and duty shall call them on paths of achievement and fame.

George Samuel Knight

ntitled

n going to write from a place of hope,
eing
tered in God, the interior of me
embers.

ise
hin
ower
hoenix
angel.
fettered wings brighten,
ir unfolding helps me breathe.

velation is an inner illumination.

res gasp
n focus to draw in light,
ich matches and grows in love
ide,
coupled favor
grant from the history of loving
anating.

Elizabeth Drorbaugh

Am.....

am stalking in the shadows throughout the night,
lackened being concealed from sight.
am hiding swiftly in a bed of leaves,
ping with ease the tallest of trees.
am flying over what no one can see,
d escaping bars no one can flee,
am veiled in the sea,
arply submerged where no one can be.

He exchanged my life with death,
d stole the wind from my breath.
He supped a mind of perfection,
en despatched my life with a mortal injection.
He took the tears from my eyes,
d swiped my soul from my demise.
He robbed the beat from my heart,
d planned to acquire it from the start.

All that I have said,
it is conceivable, then 'tis only true I am dead.

Justin Crowe

Why Life?

Life is but a fleeting moment
A brief candle flame in the passage of time.
Some flames burn bright with great portent
Others longer and more sublime.

Still life is but a small thing
Not an item to make great impact.
If this be so, then why sing
the praises of living; an act
so trivial yet all there is?
Me thinks something is amiss.

Man's pretentious self sports ego
and immortality based on long ago
realizations that life is brief.
A non acceptance cried relief.
Thus was invented a creed of surreality
denying all else for immortality.

This belief placed man above all else
saying our flame just goes to another place.
Paradise, where else?
A place of ethereal space.

John Rogers

A Weekend and Lifetime of Love

Let's take a trip to the Colorado Rockies, to the perfect hideaway
A chance for just the two of us, to up and get away
I've reserved a cabin in the mountains, with a romantic bungalow
With a picture perfect breath taking view, to watch the falling snow

The upper deck inside the cabin, has the perfect intimate loft
With cushioned and feathered bed, so nice so plush and soft
The room is filled dozens of flowers, and dozens of candles too
Creating a romantic atmosphere, designed for pleasing two

The candles are layered in circles, completely surrounding the bed
To enhance the many fantasies, that will pop into our head
And just to show my love for you, the surprising gifts I'll bring
I've even composed a melody, it's lyrics to you I'll sing

It's a Best Selling Romantic Novel, filled with heated passion
With plenty of serenity lovemaking, in almost every fashion
Its characters are you and I, acting out our parts
Sharing those burning desires, felt deep within our hearts

Delbert Clay

God's Call For Today

A call is ringing out today for workers
A clarion call, that sounds o'er land and sea.
The fields are white, all ready for the harvest;
The need, so great, now summons you and me.

The world is filled with sin and all its horror.
And yet we think so lightly of its toll.
The Lord of harvest sends us to the lost ones;
He tells us of the value of one soul.

Can you stand idly by while souls are dying?
Can you remain unmoved by Jesus' plea?
Will you not pray, and go, and give, dear Christian?
Your Lord and Saviour now, has work for thee.

Amy Scripture

Untitled

Drugs like food may cost money
As for food you may use to live
As for drugs you may abuse to die
Where in life do you wanna be with the living or the dead

For all points traveled in between continue to put a choice of
the two before you.

Janiece Harrison

Beautiful Memories

A mother's love, a father's love,
A daughter sent from God above.
You count her fingers, check her toes,
You sit and stare at her cute little nose.

She's dressed in pink, bows in her hair,
Her bright eyes gleaming, skin so fair.
It's just a few short years, it seems,
She's changed from dress, to tight fittin' jeans.

Then come the boys, the parties and dances,
You want a phone, know what the chance is?
You can't sleep nights, 'til she's home safe and sound,
Its such a pleasure just to have her around.

The years have passed, and you're getting old,
Your memories are worth more than a ton of gold.
Your heart's so full of love and pride,
Your little girl is his beautiful bride.

Berni Wodrich

On Love Long Lost

You impose upon my dreams -
A dim face that I recognize among
The unrealities my sleep often brings -

How is it that sleep plays host
And allows visions to slip in as thieves -
Bringing to fore - things-

That in our wakefulness we strive
to forget and banish forever from life and thought?

But in sleep, the heart's song grows stronger,
for what my mind wisely dismissed,
my heart has foolishly brought -

Oh - this enigma of life, how
Long will it last -

That while, the dawn brings the morrow -
the nights still host the past

Jeannette Rexrode

The Family

God created families
A family is considered a whole body
Every inch of our body have a purpose or function.
The family is created not chosen
We learn to live together, we laugh together, we cry together,
We were taught to share and to love one another
When a member of the family decides
He/she want to go into a coma.
The living dead- the brain the family becomes dysfunctional.
How can the body function without the brain? It can't body
parts are missing. We the family know longer have a whole body.
The family goes to rehab for treatment, because there is something
missing. The family is created. Not chosen.
When we as a family is headed in the same direction.
We will not have any head on collisions.
God wants us to stay together as a whole body, while we are living.
God wants us to treat each other as we want to be treated ourselves.
We only have one earth. We all have a purpose.
We all have to live on earth together.
So, why can't it be in peace. God created families.

Balinda Olive-Bowman

Love

Wanting love, I searched to find
A feeling to cradle me, my life through
Wrapped up in soul and mind
Yet as years expired, it always grew

What is love, it was here and alive
Two hearts blended, two hearts true
While daily strife you fight to survive
Yet through those years, love would renew

Where is love, now that you at God's side
My heart weighted, filled with pain
Praying to heaven, yet I must bide
Waiting now, knowing we will meet again

Elizabeth Kelly

Tracks In The First Snowfall

A skiff of snow, first of the season,
A film of white blending the landscape
Proving with its surprise visit of jewel-like sparkling crust
That between the colorful beauty of Fall
And the lively green-up of Spring
All manner of homeliness can be blended to form an unbroken line
Of beauty and oneness with nature.

Then the advent of inevitable tracks begins...
With the cross-hatched, close-together feet of birds,
The perfectly placed, but scampering, pads of cats and dogs,
The oblong and deliberate shape of man's heel and sole,
And, finally, the continuous, mechanical mark
Of the wheels of a car.

How much can be told by looking and seeing,
With only one absorbing, examining glance
At the ground, where a complete network
Of one morning's busy inhabitants' activities
Can easily be seen and told,
Just by reading these obvious and informative...
Tracks in the First Snow.

Betty L. Weaver

Possessions

A rich boy, and an orphan boy, was standing by the shore,
A fleet of ships were passing through, at least fifteen or more.

See those ships? The rich boy asked, My father owns them all,
He owns a hundred houses, and the uptown shopping mall.

He owns the bank on main street, with plenty of money to loan,
Then he asks the orphan boy, what does your father own?

The orphan lifted up his head, and said in a voice so sweet,
My Father owns that sky up there, and the earth beneath our feet.

He owns the air we're breathing, and that sun that's shining bright
He owns a million, billion stars, and the moon you see at night.

My Father owns a city, with streets of solid gold,
With walls of jasper, gates of pearls, and beauty to behold!

He owns a million mansions, and He's building one for me,
Yes, your father owns those ships, but my Father owns the sea!

Carl W. Burns

Untitled

When an adults eyes devour the night
    attacking the constellations with labels
    dismissing the shadows and wind with logic
the child is lost
    carried away like yesterday
    concealed by the darkness
    categorized and forgotten.

Jason Gray

t One

nt to be enlightened by every little thing,
ower's petal, a cat's meow, a little bird's wing.

nt to remind others, of harmony and peace,
ind them of the O-Zone and to make pollution cease.

nt to be taught, so that I may understand,
ugh to be of use, enough to lend a hand.

sh I had the power, to judge the wrong from right,
sh I knew exactly, which battles I should fight.

sh I could prove to everyone, that love could be as common
ie brilliant sun,
after all I am just one.

Jessica Valenzuela

Rose In Need

oft tap on my shoulder, and I turned to see,
ail, middle aged woman, looking back at me.

er timid hand, she bore a short stemmed rose,
en from someone's yard, I'd supposed.

ould you like to buy a rose" she said,
eed the money to put a roof over my children's head".

litely said "no", and then went on my way,
king of her simply, as a beggar on prey.

as I garnet home, her presence remained,
suddenly I felt, deeply ashamed.

I had let down my fellow man, in the moment
st, when she had needed a hand.

Denise D'Addario

e Greatest Gifts

gift that goes on giving, through eternity.
gift that knows no limits, has no boundaries.
gift so precious to give, and greater yet to receive.
ne of the greatest gifts, isn't hard to achieve.
ove is the gift I speak of; pure, honest, and true.
reely given, you will find, this gift comes back renewed.

endship is another gift, an investment worth the time.
aring things, the good and bad, that are both yours and mine.
trust and care in high regard, be thoughtfully aware.
treasure golden moments, heartaches and despair.
e magic of this gift, lives on to multiply.
e harvest that we reap, is truly justified.

e gifts that go on giving, through eternity.
e gifts that know no limits, have no boundaries.
e gifts so precious to give, greater yet to receive.
e greatest gifts of all, are easiest to achieve.
ith, Charity, Compassion, just to name a few
ely given, from the heart, these gifts flourish - anew.

Debbie Swenson

Reach!

Reach my brother, Reach!
In a loud voice I exclaimed
Reach my brother, Reach!
This struggle is not in vain
Reach my brother, Reach!
Extend your arm.
I reach for you my brother fear no harm.
The battle was hard but we've finally won.
Just reach for me and all else is done.

I love my brother. We must drive on.
As I reach for you, reach for another
As we journey toward home.

Jahi Omari

The Rose Is No More

A short walk down the aisle,
a gift waiting to be opened.

The rose is but a bud.

Reaching for the warmth of his sun,
devouring his love and affection,
opening my heart to him alone, blossoming under his tender care.

The rose becomes a flower.

Part lover, part wife, part mother,
part here, part there, all at once, so many pieces scattered
about yet he wants it all. Which piece is mine?

The petals begin to fall.

Cold light of day not heat of night,
duties not desires, wants not needs,
wisdom of age not innocence of youth, a trellis too tall to climb.

The rose begins to wither.

Too many questions left unanswered,
too many dreams left by the way,
too much bitterness left to harden.

The blossom has fallen.
The rose is no more.

Ann Marshall

Gift

There once and always will be,
a gift we all held so dear,
this gift couldn't even stay a year.
This gift wasn't of material,
but of a gift much greater than that.
It was of a little boy,
with eyes bluer than the ocean
and a body filled with laughter and emotion.
He filled our lives with happiness
and our hearts with warmth and love,
but then one day, he was sent to special place above.
No one wanted him to leave
but we will all see him again one day, I believe.
We will all remember this cute little boy
that will always fill our hearts with joy!!

Allison Firpo

Endangered

Gallantly tramping in the jungles of Africa,
A gigantic beast exists.
With big, floppy ears and sad, longing eyes,
Gray wrinkly skin and humongous feet.
They're born with tusks of ivory,
But solemnly killed
And their great tusks sawed off and stolen.
For man doesn't care what gets
Caught in his trap,
As long as he gets what pleases him.
The beast tries fighting back and taking a stand,
But is easily pushed aside.
They bravely give up their lives and fall down
And die.

Now the jungles are silent,
This beast is endangered
For a sad reason, too.
They got killed for man's unneeded wants.

He takes someone else's life:
The Elephant.

Amy Saunders

Is This Love?

While walking down the street one day
A girl - just passes by
You do a great big double-take
You give her quite an eye
Is this the beginning?

You ask "What time of day is it?"
You try to hide your watch
You finally look into the eyes
That send you into shock — Is this the start?

You take her hand-into your own
It feels so silky warm
Suddenly she shows her smile
It's like a new spring morn
This must be it!

You feel so light
You could almost float
You don't know where you are
This girl - just passing by you know
Has suddenly become my life!
This is love!!!

Bart Corricelli

Soaring High

As the wind blows and as the clouds soar by,
A great image soaring catches my eye.
As it soars around with power and pride,
This great image goes into a glide.
Just above the tree tops with it's eyes upon the ground,
This great image soars around without making a sound.
With so much majesty and so much grace,
It still has determination all over it's face.
It has the determination to soar high and free,
Because it's the great Bald Eagle that I see.

Eddie J. Thomas

A Castle

As I sit here and gather, it begins with a pile.
A hand full on top, add some more for a while.

Vertically formed, the walls start to rise.
They'll protect you from anything that falls from the skies.

Walls that have eyes and ears to the ground.
Steeples on the corners, a mote all around.

"lower the drawbridge", a cry in the night.
Rescue the fair maiden and live in delight.

Delighted to dream of a day that's gone past.
One that brings joy and happy feelings that last.

A mystical place, that's just in your head.
After construction, it's the waves that you dread.

So when you build things upon unsturdy land,
They will not last forever, like a castle in the sand.

Jon Lee Lauer

Best Friends Forever

Dedicated to Heather Rahn

A shoulder to cry on, a friend to laugh with

Through the years and the tears we have stuck together

Our happy and tearful times have brought us closer

As we get closer the closeness has strengthened our friendship

Although we argue at times I hope we stay best friends forever
because without you I don't know what I would do

Heather Cronk

A Hundred Years Too Late

I once rode fence up in Montana,
A job I soon learned to hate.
I punched cow down in Arizona,
Till that night I slept with the snakes.
The fact that I live my life like this,
Without feeling I'm making a big mistake,
Sometimes makes me wonder;
Was I born a hundred years too late?

I've rodeoed from Cody to Cowtown
and from Dade City to Santa Fe.
Sometimes I ride them to the pay window,
Sometimes I get bucked off at the gate.
Folks often tell me I'm crazy,
There's changes in my life I should make.
I just laugh an tell them hell no,
I was just born a hundred years too late.

Del Cody

Come On In

They're slippin' in to visit me,
A little blue camper I can see.
Coming so slowly 'round the barn,
To spend a day here on our farm.

"Come right on in and sit a spell.
We'll draw cold water from the well.
And make some coffee and a meal.
Tell me, folks, how ya' feel?"

"Has it been cold up your way, too?
Have your days been sunny or blue?
Are ya still comin' the Indiana side?
Like your eggs scrambled, or prefer 'em fried?"

"Come, sit a spell and let's just talk.
Maybe later we'll take us a walk.
We'll see the pit and walk the pike.
It's always good to take a short hike."

"I'm glad you're here. It's ever so nice.
Let's sit right down and have a slice
Of cake I made for just this day.
With a quart of coffee to put it away."

Dixie Edens

Gentle Love

Look into my eyes and what do you see?
A little creation saying, "please care for me!"
The touch of your hand, the gleam from your eye,
Your loving hello, each time you walk by.
The warmth of your lap, holding me tender and true
I could never be happy if it weren't for you.
Chasing in circles, performing just for you,
trying to make you happy,
by touching a sunbeam or two.
Evening tide comes how quiet and secure,
Your loving arms holding me ever so near,
sleep comes so silently, and without any fear,
So leave me not ever, my Master Dear,
cause I'm your loving cat, who God holds
ever so near!

Carol Ann Eigenhauser

Gray Cat

day when I went out to the store
tle gray cat appeared at my door
tood there very plainly for me to see
rove his friendship, he played peekaboo with me
vould stretch on the screen like I knew he would
 make himself presentable and cute as he could

n his style and manners I named him SPORT
ve him food, plus love for his support
ked forward to seeing him everyday
 he vanished suddenly and went away

e things he did reminded me of a child
 made me happy for a brief while
rched and looked everywhere, and all around
little gray cat was not to be found
re is nothing left but his tiny cup
always remember how he cheered me up

Ida B. Seaborn

e Dakotas

ir bones lay there in decay
ving legend of yesterday
 buffalo and old sitting Bull
 was their land, their life was full

n came the White Man, across her plains
change her style and take the reins
un steel rails from coasts to coast
 seed her soil, then watch her growth
 soon there'd be no buffalo
 they'd corral old sitting bull
 ducks and geese soon saw the change
hey would soon not cross her plains

other course they'd find and then
re was the White Man once again
 buffalo no longer stand
 grass is short across her land

 in her eyes a silent tear
 longs again for yesteryear.

Calvin M. Taasevigen

ttle Stitch of Love

ch piece was cut out carefully,
nemory in each one.
 hands, they hurt, but still she worked,
til, at last, 'twas done.

the unknown eye, a puzzle
material piled knee high.
her each piece was memories
special times gone by.

e threaded up her needle and
each piece fell in place,
e magic needle moved along,
e never changed her pace.

e finished quilt lay in my lap
d she gave thanks above,
en said, know each stitch made for you,
as filled with Grandma's love.

Alma M. Spohn

The Hunter's Foe

In the mountains not far away,
A mighty hunter was heard to say.
Give me the very best of luck,
Help me to shoot a great big buck.

So he hiked up hill and down,
But on his face he wore a frown.
He saw lots of fawns and does,
But he couldn't find that mighty foe.

Then he carefully looked around,
And checked for tracks upon the ground.
When he found some tracks, off he trucked,
Hoping to shoot that mighty buck.

Suddenly he spotted a five point spread,
Took careful aim and shook with dread.
That rack looked so big and wide,
"I've got to have it." He did confide.

The roar of the gun echoed through the air,
The deer jumped and ran in the cool clear air.
But the hunter stood with a startled grin,
That darn buck fever and had got him again.

JoAnn C. Hardy

A Different Kind, A Different Me

I am a gift from God to my Mom and Dad,
A more precious gift they've never had.

I laugh and cry just like you, but deep inside I always knew,
I was more different that most of you.

To be different is to stand out,
Jesus was different without a doubt.

All I want is that same love,
That God gives us from above.

My different looks make you stare,
Or pretend that I'm not there.

Open your mouth and speak to me,
For each kind deed I know He'll see.

He's given you a body that moves with grace,
And perfect features to make a beautiful face.

Stop! Stop! This can happen to you!
It only takes a minute and you normal life is through!

It's my prayer you'll never reside,
In a body where your thoughts must hide....

Behind a mask where people see,
A different kind, A different me.

Donese J. Stewart

Pureness

I live in a broken universe shattered by the past;
A mysterious shade of ebony paints a darkened mask.
A single ray of sunlight is shadowed by the wind.
A song is sung in silence of sins not yet sinned.

The moon and all its brightness reflected from the sun
Is forgotten amidst the stars, each and every one.
A haze filled with sadness floats across the wide terrain:
The words of every wise man smeared by the rain.

A figure moves so gracefully, long forgotten, long forsaken,
With nothing left to give - everything's been taken.
A darkness never lightened, a life lived within.
The loneliness of happiness, the pureness of sin.

Amberley Shewalter

Where Dreamers Walk

Again I walk upon the path of dreams
A narrative revealed by the whimsical beams
Of the moon where she, softly above
To an enchanted melody bespeaking of love
A mystical wind caresses the grass
The tree take their bows to an unheard-of cast
A spellbinding night for just such a play
A harmonious greeting for one of the fey

The vistas that I greet with rapturous eye
Are shared by the dreams of those such as I
From my vigil upon this land, this place before dreams
I've seen you dance beneath the moon as she gleams

Beneath the unveiled sky
Across the fields of night-flowers
On the banks of the rivers with unimaginable powers
Through the archaic ruins of legend and lore
In the dreamland near death your spirit has soared

It's time to depart and your gaze touches mine
With a sharing of strength we slip back into time
You fall to your dreams, I fall to mine
Joseph Smith

The Never Ending Poem

A wake up call, a shout from the city, a rooster crow,
   a new beginning.

A new light is shining, yet the old remains.
Which will you choose, whom will reign?

A crack in the night, shines a gleam of light.
Shooting through your soul, all is bright.

Tears seem to flow, yet not one stream.
The door slams, reality hits, the past is but a dream.

Jesus is coming, one might call.
A pair of eyes open, yet another's fall.

Thunder is heard, yet the rain does not come down.
A shadow appears in the sky, as a face with a frown.

The Bible is wide open, yet eyes refuse to look
Fearing that God might speak to them, from His Holy book

The light shines bright, yet the darkness is around.
The hearts of men are looking up, yet all eyes are
   towards the ground.

Satan is here, yet so is God, all men face back to back
A wake up call, a light in the dark, a rooster crow, yet
   all is black.
Hans Westrich

The Right Thing

The dawn is an opening statement,
So awaken in time to its full glory.
Its promise of the new day, its expectations
For some are many,
And others few, and not all come true,
But with the right outlook and a prayer
At sunset you might discover your rainbow there.
If not, there's the moon and the stars
And the milky way.
And if that's not enough, there's
Always a new day, so live life to its
fullest measure, and you will find
your personal. treasure.
Add to this and you will find you are
a major stockholder in this business
called a lifetime.
Joseph W. Pirato

The Thoughts of an Anorexic Mind

Behind the walls sleep the empty hearts,
a pathetic crying rings through the halls-
an endless Feeling of hate...
I scream, being lost in a Flood of memories
No one to cry to, No one who loves you
Trust; only a shallow word, a confined feeling, building hate.
Anger swelling into a tempest Rage
Total loss of control..Screaming-tearing-
Running...No where, you've gotten nowhere.
An open wound that never heals,
A throbbing, timeless scream Floats on our air.
Reaching out For Something to hold,
We find our own hate the only savior,
and as we think we are getting better-
Its only a change, a loss of all Reality, all emotion,
As we become inhuman.
We think the concrete is our confinement,
We are wrong...Someday the walls of
Concrete will be gone, yet we shall never be free of true confinement,
Now that we have been given to a "New Life."
H. Davis

Lullaby

Upon my birth a simple line emerged
A perch for memories, one by one, like birds
Each believing that his song excels.

There, running down the windy street
With tear-blind eyes, perhaps from flying soot
Or else some fear of being late to school.

Here, warming mittens on a ninth floor stove
While icy rain whispers to my window-pane
How far do you suppose before my fall will end.

Or from my roof the eager vigil kept
Of skies beyond smoked glass one summer's day
When the eternal sun paled before our eyes.

Yet I have caged the song that rivals all.
The same that lulled to sleep the listening child
Now lures my word-filled dreams from distant flight.
Anne H. Gibson

Sour Story Of Sweetie

There lived a lady sweetie, she was shrewd and beauty
A pretty cute baby, and parents wished for a doctor sweetie
They gave love and pleasure, she was royal queen in measure
Expected she brings name and fame and give a baby girl of same

Sweet sweetie in high school slasted smoking, ignorant of parents
shocking with diminished pleasure in smoke, shifted to marijuana an
coke cared least parents aspiration and forgot the received affectio
the grades started lowering with late comings hovering.

Parents could not punish, the law forbids child abuse
they forgot the dreams about her and to the fate they left her

Sex education in school and free environment everywhere
made her sometimes high, for sex experience she made and try.
There are many varieties of sex, so some boyfriends became ex
new enjoyment and experience, one day made her to hospital confinement

The cruel doctor declared her positive and the future became negative
Nothing was left to aspire except waiting for death to conquer

So left was only past, has she sticked to parents steadfast
Had she cared studies and had she avoided bad buddies
There would be a doctor sweetie, married to an engineer
Engineering a happy home and getting name and fame
Ashok Mudrakola

A Place In The Sun

Everybody needs a place in the Sun:
A quiet place to be themselves,
To reflect upon the yesterdays and the tomorrows,
A warm place where emotions can express the feelings that
only our hearts know,
A place to come back to when we have no place to go.

Everybody needs a place in the Sun:
A mysterious place so that we may explore the marvels of life
with a sense of awe and appreciation,
A joyous place where you can have fun
A laughing place where you can be free in thought and deed.

Everybody needs a place in the Sun:
A place to bring a very special someone,
A place where you can share and give
with an openness that might not otherwise be there,
A secret place where you can truly love,
A fulfilling place where you can be at one.

Yes,
Everybody needs a place in the Sun.

Come, there is a place in the Sun.

Durand Evan

Monster

Towering over you,
A razor smile cuts my face,
You cower beneath me,
Muttering with fear,
Can see life beat start to race,
My cool blue eyes reflect off the silver blade,
Which I hold firmly in my right hand,
Raising it above my head,
Thrusting down,
Driving into your chest,
Tearing apart tanned flesh,
Until I can see your throbbing emotion,
Reach for your organ,
Dipping my quivering hand into the crimson darkness,
With outstretched talons I tighten my grasp around it,
Tug at the veins until they snap,
Release the pulsing creature to me,
Watch captivated as the beat begins to slow,
A tear slides down my cheek dropping to the dying monster,
Apology seeps from your eyes before they roll towards your mind.

Johanna Youngs

Friends Forever

Here we are at the end of the Road
A road that never truly began.
Set in a young mind
With a torn soul
My thoughts have just been slammed
Though life moves at a lightning pace
This one fleeting moment is
All but disgraced
This memory will stay at the back of your minds
As possibly be dug up at a far future time
For now as we bid farewell
At this bend
Maybe again we will meet
At the End
At the end of the road...

Joshua Hagle

That's All That Matters

In the world you are a rose.
A rose that grows so beautiful and tall
No thorns are around this rose
Because you are all good
But bad can prevail and will if you let it.

You are a rose so proud and strong
That no one can cut through your stem
Your dignity, your wisdom.
You stand tall and always will
Because bad will never prevail
because you are too strong.

You are yourself and that's all that matters.

Evan Cooper

Share It

To speak kind words can start a good day
A simple "good morning" can pave the way;
A hug or a kiss can be a great sign
to feel the comfort of love in mind.

As you travel on through the day
Continue to build on love; it's okay;
There's no harm in being happy and gay
So be careful of what you do and say.

Never forget to add a smile
That facial expression is well-worth while;
A hung down head could be lifted high;
By seeing a friendly smile passing by.

Sometimes it helps just to shake someone's hand
Which could lift their spirit from a burdensome land;
to feel inside that someone cares
Is the beauty of love we all should share.

Faith Lee

The Love Of A Simple Man

From their lips His story was told
A simple man with a heart of gold
Everyday He would preach
With His hands in the air
Some thought He was strange
But most knew He cared
Down on His knees He would pray
For He knew that He would die one day
He said things many didn't believe
That was ok because He'd make them see
When the day finally came
He called out His father's name
Tears fell when they looked upon Him
When He opened His arms
And died for our sins

Heather Foret

Emotions

Emotions give life color
Emotions create in us deep longings
Emotions inspire deep hungers in our soul
Emotions enable us to love more fully
Emotions soften our hearts to embrace love
Emotions create in us a capacity for compassion
Emotions transform us into caring beings
Emotions awaken every cell of our being
to become energized and electrified
Emotions are a priceless gem to be treasured
Emotions are a gift

Doris L. Rock

Snow

In the white snow that covers the ground,
A single bare place will not be found,
The magical frozen raindrops fall in your hand,
With their frost covered peeks, everywhere they land.

They descend to the ground, a white cotton blanket of snow.
They come down in graceful clusters, a constant flow,
They look like sugar atop a funnel cake,
Or perhaps a delicious vanilla topped lake.

The wonders and dreams,
That each snow flake alone,
Holds as it shines in the beams,
Of the new fallen snow.

On the fragile tree tops,
It gracefully drops,
It comes so gentle and light,
Like a dancer into the night.

The sky's a sieve,
And the animals that live,
Run joyously below,
In the new fallen snow.

Alexandra L. Weseloh

Myself

I was a flower all alone - in a field of grass
A sky of blue, a touch of dew, I was waiting for someone to pass.

Cars went by on a distant road as the evening sun went down.
I bowed my head no one to see as I began to frown.

Suddenly I heard a voice so faint and so mild
As I turned my head and tried to look - was this the voice of a child?

A little girl ran up to me and with one pull she sighed,
Then turned around and ran to a house she slipped me right inside.

She said, "Mother, I have a present for you", as she sat down to eat.
She picked me up and gave me away and then she smiled so sweet.

And all the loneliness I felt that day had vanished in one single hour
When I realized how great it was to be just a flower.

Elsie Franklin

He the Master

Terror pierces my fingertips;
A slave bound tightly by my master.
He tears me apart, his pulsing testosterone
unyielding.
Desire drives out reason; Id abounds-
Slithering, groping, lusting a chance to strike;
Controlled by no law.
He passes to it, chained by its waning.
Those damn Christians, calling on a God
To fulfill their emptiness, their inability to
control.
Spare me you meek slug.
Philanthropy is your prayer, strength mine!
Desire is my God. I run with Jesus' brother; such a
wild pack of
gods. He the master, he is me.

Gene Edmiston

Untitled

I know you don't love me
but I love you can't you see
when I'm with you I feel complete
there is no one else I would rather meet
maybe I should commit suicide
then you'll understand I'll always be by your side

Amy Wolfe

Secret Admiration

I look into your eyes seeing emotions hidden behind a smile.
A smile that shatters the dark,
And takes the coldness that's come over my lonely heart.
You sit less than a stone's throw away,
Yet to get close seems like an endless field needing wings to cross
If I had wings, I'd fly into the future
To see us walking on a beach, watching the sunset, holding hands
Sharing secrets, sharing dreams and discovering each other.
We could open our hearts enjoying what pours out.
We could go to the mountains just to scream and shout,
Letting the echoes of love caress the valley.
But these ideas are only dreams
Unless you could open those eyes, awaking from your empty sleep
Open the eyes I wish to keep
By my side to share each moment,
By my side to hear every word
Of praise and glory, of hope, not worry,
Doing my best to keep you content
Because time with you would not be spent.

Cletus R. Mullis

Ode to Songs Unsung

Everyone has a song to be sung,
A song within their soul.
A song that tells their life in words
And they play the major roll.

From the day they are born...
'Til they day that they die...
As the days and weeks and years pass by...
Everyone has a song to be sung...even you and I.

A song of joy... A song of sorrow...
A song of laughter or tears...
A song that tells of today or tomorrow...
Or of the yester years.

Everyone has a song unsung...
From the old to the very young.
Everyone from nation to nation
As this common life we share

EVERYONE HAS A SONG UNSUNG...
EVERYONE...EVERYWHERE.

Gwen E. Ricci

Opening

i am opening for you
a space that you can
climb into and make yourself at home
i give to you the only thing i have
that hollow blackness within me which you inhabit
time and time again but cannot fill

so i remain open and empty
for every creature to thrust itself into me
trying to fill the void
while i scream "yes oh yes" over and over
in the darkness
searching for the tingle of sensation
i always feel with you

but there is nothing
i am left empty
spread open for all the creatures of the night
and waiting for you

Amanda R. Plante

o My Little Girl

⊃ my little girl
spark of hope in such a cruel world
⊃ my little girl
t one so innocent and true
: the age of two with hair of gold
d eyes of blue
⊃ my little girl
⊃ my little girl
niling back at me only at the age of three
⊃ my little girl
⊃w I remember the
; aids has darken our door only at the age of four
⊃ my little girl
⊃ my little girl
⊃pe they find a cure
⊃ my little girl
l see you no more
; I sit sadly awaiting the same fate
l see you in the next world
⊃od by for now my little girl

Bo McLaughlin

hange

∕ant a pen that leaks to roll across my paper.
sticky, oozing, indigo pipe releasing its fluid
nazing stains and shapes that can't be read
nd a clean spot, stretch out and sleep.

∕ant a child flame to dance into my sight.
free little fire, teasing a puddle, my tears
ver a thought or worry, but a spent hope
dash about, leaving a sign that she existed.

∕ant a cat to pounce across my keyboard
rs flicking all directions, sand paper hiss
watch it fill a page or two with crazy words;
tters that don't make sense like zwf or qmy.

∕ant to be woken by a splash of water.
Arctic attack from winter morning pipes
oud, excited, wriggle from its faucet cell
clog my nose; snap open my hazel eyes.

∕ant those things that can't be foreseen.
sappointments, surprise, laughs, shocks
nds in the wheel of infinity creating each moment
∕, different, fascinating; never the same

Jeffery Steven Noesser

e Was Too Busy In Love!

e was young and beautiful,
ure gift from above.
e was a fragile girl,
t someone in love.
e smiled when he walked by,
tried to say "hello".
e wanted a relationship
how was he to know?
e never showed her feelings,
∕hat she felt inside.
night, she would crawl in bed,
there is where she cried.
one knew her life was rough,
felt she had to lie.
greatest smile she would always flash,
worst feeling, kept inside.
regrets she never told him,
now it is too late.
at could've been between them?
s it worth the wait?

Christina Jones

Ole Great Depression

Your birth came when I was only two years old,
A surprise vicious creature you were, I'm told.
At an early age, you took away riches from the wealthy,
And caused them such anguish, they were no longer healthy.
Their minds were so mixed-up, some committed suicide.
And still others even wished they could have died.
For my family and me, we were already very poor,
But you took away from us many necessities and more,
Such as good jobs, clothing and succulent healthy food.
We ate a lot of bread and syrup and potatoes stewed.
You took away many other things, such as daily piece of mind.
Nights were sleepless, wondering what the next day we'd find.
But one thing you didn't take away was our FAMILY PRIDE.
Our heads held high, and on your rough road, we did ride.
MY QUESTION - How were you born in such a great land as ours,
Where symbols of freedom always seen waving from every tower?
And it took a terrible cruel war to finally bring you down,
Where many men's lives were given, and upon you we still frown.
It is incomprehensible, how you lived so long before you died,
But there is one thing, for My Family and Me, WE SURVIVED.

Betty Quisenberry

Graduation

Graduation date is almost here,
    A time for hope and not for fear.
The much awaited date will soon arrive,
    We are doing all we can to survive.

The years have gone by in a flash,
    But memories of the fun, the friends, and the faculty will
    forever last.
Reading, writing, science and math,
    Are subjects needed to pass.

Studying and trying my best,
    Lessons learned were not in jest.
Looking to the future with anticipation,
    Hoping to meet a job's qualification.

David Moody

Your Best Friend

There is a time to be born and a time to die
a time to laugh and a time to cry..
Somewhere in between you blossom into a teen..
When an adult you learn what life is all about..
You learn to love and you learn to hate, if
you are lucky you find an everlasting mate..
For awhile money and possessions become your God
then you learn they can be trampled under the sod.
The real meaning of life as we come to know is love
and compassion and to stop and smell the roses and
in wisdom to grow and grow,
As we are nearing life' end we learn that God is
our best friend..

Dixie Lee Beeson

"Earthbound Stars"

The night like black velvet
    Caresses my face,
    As I slowly make my way through the meadow,
    To my house that warm and loving place.
The only sounds are those of my moving feet,
    And of mice playing in the field of wheat,
    Which stands tall and lighted before my eyes,
    By countless, earthbound stars -
Those beautiful, magical fireflies.

Darius Detwiler

Images

I had a dream of a girl,
a tortured painfilled girl.
Everyone left her so far in life,
so she sits and stares at the butcher knife.
She picks it up and draws it near,
she looked into my eyes, I could feel her fear.
Then her life flashed before me.
A life that soon would just be.
She is getting ready for bed
and she told the Lord what she always said
Then her pain came as quick as the rain.
The pain like to play the touching game.
After it left, here no more,
the pain left and shut the door,
That was just a part,
the pain she felt was just at start.
Then I saw pools of blood.
And the little girl lay in the mud.
I thought how terrible this must be......
Until I realized the little girl was me.

April Hooper

(Just, "One Stepping Stone")

There is a light I see so bright
a voice I hear say come.
And stepping through the veil I see
the one who called me home.
   I pictured not, such majesty in earth my
whole life through.
   Although I lived far God complete, my comforter so true.
   One stepping stone a day I took, knowing
that sometime soon.
   The suffering here would cease, and I would
look upon his face, God seated at the throne.
   We are but little children, we are in the
masters hand.
   We are called to follow, according to his plan.
   Loved ones I must leave behind, but glad
I was to spend the time, to hold each one within my heart.
   But now I'm home where I want to be.
And my loved ones dear will always see.
The love I left behind for them - and will
be, just one stepping stone from me.

Clarissa E. Snyders

Yesterday—

I stare into your soft eyes, searching for
a voice to say our last good-bye.
A hug, a kiss, and a tear or two, still
a part of you is with me, never
letting me free of our memories.
How the pain hurts for me to leave, yet
we must believe we'll see each other
again someday.
Even though I'll be far away, in my
heart you'll forever stay.
So remember me with a smile, as I'll
remember you the same.
But take with you these three words
of "I love you" and cherish them.
And every night I'll pray that we'll be
together just like yesterday.

Connie Martindale

Numb

The razor taps the glass.
A wallflower. Delicately perched, watching.
Hawk claws scrape three lines of powder white blood into the hard
   clear skin.
I count 53 freckles on my left arm.
Pretending not to watch severed Burger King straws
   gracefully glide like ice skaters
      through my heavy lids.
Clogged vacuum sucking sound pulls through my spine.
For years I sit twirling my hair, waiting for him to return.
Cold, numb hands fall like dead fish into my own.
Soft "I love you"s
   and "you're the best thing to ever happen to me"s.
      Come at me like a knife I've felt a million times before.
Icicles form on the tip of my nose, and freeze my heart.
Fists burst through walls, as the magic crystal myth begins to
   extricate itself from his ever-hungry veins.
Pushing cuticles back to my knuckles.
Waiting for sleep to enter those empty blue eyes,
   and happy smiles to return.

Heather Fairman

She's There

   Where ever I am, I know she's near. A sound down the hall,
a whisper in the ear. Her games are childish, but love them I do.
Her smile can brighten any of my moods. Whether it's a shadow
the room, or a flicker by the light... she's there.
   I want to know her... hold her. But she's like the mist,
untouchable, almost unreal. My dreams are only of her as are my
thoughts. How is this possible? Is this love? The reason my hear
pounds and my hands shake? Oh, damn this unthinking emotion! What
do I say? What do I do? These feeling are almost too much to be
She knows all this, because hiding behind a smile... she's there.
   My love for her is without equal, surpassing all in my life.
Still she hides behind her facade, afraid of being hurt. As I
stretch out my hand for hers, I can hear her cry in the dark. I
know her fear... I now know where she is. I can only reach her if
she'll let me. As her hand slips into mine, I finally see her, see
her for what she is... my missing half. The part of me that I've
been lost without for so long. As we embrace, I know now that I'
always know where she is. Here... with me.

Jeffery S. Smith

Woman

She's an angel in truth, a demon in fiction;
a woman's the greatest of all contradiction!

She's afraid of a cockroach, she'll scream at a mouse;
but she'll tackle a husband as big as a house!

She'll take him for better or worse,
she'll split his head open, then be his nurse!

And when he is well and can get out of bed,
she'll pick up a tea pot and throw at his head!

She's faithful, deceitful, keen sighted, and blind,
she's crafty, she's simple, she's cruel, she's kind!

She'll lift a man up, she'll cast a man down,
she'll make him her hero, her ruler, her clown!

You fancy she's this, but you find out she's that,
she'll play like a kitten, and fight like a cat!

In the morning she will, and in the evening she won't,
you're always expecting she will, but she won't!

Jackson B. Sutor

ome At Last

olden arrows from the east shoot into the sky.
bout a field, flattened rainbows lie.
 soft wind and the ruffle of nylon.
 meadowlark's song.
ople mill about, talking in hushed tones;
ie coming of the day brings excitement to the bones
 of those young and old.
nticipation.

ie rasp of metal against metal, the pull of lanyards.
ie rushing breathing of igniting gas.
ue and red flames
llowing.
ainbows fatten and rise toward the sky
here they belong.
imeras click and whir, recording the resurrection
ople cheer with "ooh's" and "ah's."
ppes pull taut.
ainbows and Earth engage in a fierce tug of war.
ppes part and the rainbows rush upwards into the cool morning air.
ome at last.

Brad Anderson

ie Minstrel

 sang of past and thunder,
bout future and silence
at entranced and listened:
e melody enveloped me like a wave.
rung on the clef as notes wafted 'round me,
e voice purred, barely a murmur:
 was wise beyond the present
eming to have lived before,
r he retained knowledge and wisdom.
zing blindly toward him as he whispered his sweet melodies,
atching his yellowish-green eyes cast a mysterious glow
earned to break through the impenetrable facade
aking him like a mask.
 full of simplicity yet comprehending all complexity...
e closer I approached to understanding
e farther he retreated into his metaphoric song.
ached out to stroke his soft back
d I asked him his name, leaning close to hear his answer;
ought he whispered "Jellylorum"
t maybe it was just a meow

Jessica L. Dolce

nely Boy From Far Away

a gonna tell you a story about a lonely young lad.
out the way he lived his life and the hard times that he had.
n and sorrow that would send him astray.
w he's a lonely boy from far away.

ne large oak tree is the shelter for his bed.
d his only suite of clothes is the pillow for his head.
 needs a home or some place to stay.
w he's a lonely boy from far away.

rd times surround him good times never come.
less he'll live his life always on the run.
 needs a home and he needs some friends.
d if he don't find someone his life will end.

 don't they know it ain't easy.
 live the life he lives.
 don't they know it ain't easy.
 live the way he does.

 don't they know it ain't easy.
 live the life that he lives.
 don't they know it ain't easy.
be the lonely boy from far away.

Chuck Heffelfinger

Imago

My fingers ached to intertwine with yours
Across a table where we had newly met.
I've always thought intertwining fingers
Such an intimate display of aphrodisia.

You came into my life that sunny May-fly July
In a room looking out upon the Pacific Ocean.

The mid-day sun played across the waves breaking below us
Sending up sprays of diamonds flying through the air
To sparkle briefly — then evaporate.

Your hesitant smile told me of your fearfulness...
My breast yearned to cradle your head,
To soothe away the worry.

But I didn't touch you...
I didn't hold you...
I never made you mine...

I drove the coast road alone and watched the ocean
Turn into a continent of lush fire as the sun crushed down upon it.

When my thoughts returned to you I remembered I forgot to ask
   your name.
Now I'll never know what loving you would have felt like.....
Or lacing fingers.

Jean Q. Hewitt

Looking Back on a Memory No One Should Have

Hand hard as stone
   across my face many times
Ringing ears colors swirling before my eyes
My body flying crashing into a wall
Stumbling to the bathroom
In the mirror
   see my face puffy terrified
Blood swimming under my crying skin
   bruises forming fast
Gold earrings bent from the blows
Pain shock disbelief horror
   My face healed
   Part of me inside is destroyed forever.

Andrea Lynn Perry

Release from Time

Oh! to walk alone, once more,
   Across the tide-marked sand;
And stand - where waves just break.

To stare, again entranced, almost
   Beyond the scope of eye;
At sky - where clouds meet sea.

Then watch the eager gulls swoop down
   To kiss each restless wave;
And brave - capricious crests

To listen to the muted murmurs
   And hear their timeless singing;
Bringing - yearning thoughts.

Of far and distant shores, where waves
   Once carried ancient crafts of old;
Of gold and sea-washed treasures.

   To be,
   For one brief ecstasy
   Released from time

Jean J. Ray

The Bedoin Shepherd Boy

He sits serenely on a stone and gazes far away,
Across the treeless land.
His eyes are dark as pools of starless night,
His skin is tanned by sun and wind.

Beneath his headdress of purest white,
His thick dark hair is almost hid.
A gentle smile forms on his lips,
As in his arms he safely holds
A wounded lamb who cannot walk.

Oh, happy lamb,
Though of Agnes Deo you have never heard,
To be secured held by strong young hands.
Oh, Shepherd Boy, God loves you well,
For He's a shepherd too.
Janet K. Little

I'll Dance Alone

It's not as though there aren't plenty of partners to be found
After all, "I have a very sweet face"
It's not as though I don't know how to follow
Sometimes it takes a short while
But I'm a quick study as they say

Interestingly enough my free style is much
appreciated and admired even initially
Oh, how they would like to experience my abandon
What then happens?
Why would the shackles come out
and the chain get shorter and shorter.

Why don't I notice when this begins to occur
The truth is I do but believe reason
and love will prevail
That I can "make it" come about.
Wishing does not make it so
So until I find an equal size partner
I'll dance alone and enjoy the hell out of it too.
Joan Schneider

The Plague

(For the millions of Jews who lost their lives.)
Painful screams in the day,
Agonizing cries throughout the night,
Separation,
The loss of God,
Chambers full of poisonous gas
Furnaces that claimed lives
Survival of few
Death of many
Insanity wreaking through every mind
Desperation
Hungry for food, sanity, strength, escape
Hatred raging throughout
Murderous thoughts within
An uncontrollable fate that led to death
Tragedy.
Angie Hagler

Friendship

The warmest thoughts we ever send,
Are those that go from friend to friend.
The happiest wishes we ever make,
Are the wishes made for friendship's sake.
The loveliest memories that we know,
Were made with good friends long ago.
The brightest tomorrows yet to be,
We'll find in friendships company.
Donna Jones

I Made A New Friend Today

Who offers first or do I wait like a school girl
Agonizing over the etiquette of shaking hands
Is it rude if I am wearing gloves
Is my hand too strong or like a cold fish
As we talk and spar sharing the easy laughs
I wonder...Perhaps he thinks I am too plain
Or is he too pretty to be trusted
We volley work and play while looking for hallowed ground
Is he the one...I question me

Could we share secrets, fears, tears
Be private with each other's thoughts
See imperfections as self-made art
And honor each other's dreams
Could we be independent yet dependable for each other
It's a lot to ask in the name of friendship
But I make my request....A small hug when next we meet
We smile and shake hands on it
I made a new friend today
Judy A. Rembacki

Beyond War

Horizons wide, new thinking now beyond the hell of war!
All hearts as one, the eternal sun now the risen star.
The world a whole, all people's role - handclasp serene, sublime
Night now gone, a dream now born, cresting all in song and
rhythm!

The zephyr so gently far, kiss lands from every sea
Joyously, earth's dignity embraces wondrous victory!
The anointed gain, so not vain, forever near and far
The gallant stride, as sanctified, ever none to mar!

Gold banner high, it waves a joy of peace in ev'ry land!
In brotherhood, God's blessed good, as one the loving hand!
Spiritual light, divinely bright, the way the brilliant star!
The nobles dream - core new world theme, beyond the hell of wa
John Pusateri

Untitled

All in jest all in vain
All in love with love to tame
Out of mind out of sight
Gone in foolish crying flight.
Under waves and over stars
Through trained minds in neon bars.
Tripping over trodden streams
Running fast through hazy dreams.
Floating rains up hills sublime
Soaked with light embittered time.
Treated peace engaging home, spraying rabid
frothy foam, X and O in fields collide
Halting truth in all his pride.
Raising answers raising lies
Exalting false with milk-white eyes.
Assorting heavens assorting rot
Taking heed when heed is bought.
Unkind master unkind greed
Earthly goods for which men bleed.
Surface facade surface men, surface beauty suffice again.
Christopher Nelson

"Wonders Of Earth"

Mountains high and oceans low
Canyons deep and rivers aflow
A painted desert, the traveling sands
The greatest treasures in all the lands
These are the wonders of our Earth's heart
They've been this way from the very start.
Chad Littlejohn

otherhood

ely civilization, an atonal world,
is distance.

the rainy street a melody soaks into the
sers-by, each alone, with a barely useable heart.

iny blues," sad flotsam from the past, you sing.
a dark faced Orpheus from the old south.

ies" are not only songs, but the timbre of
ken hearts that seek native souls,
intimacy of brotherhood.

v many nights have you slept on the roadside?
v often have you been hurt by tender love?
return to the distance.

ir mission is to eliminate cruel distance
entwining it with people and forgotten lyrics.

leaves turn to ice, tired people
a night of sleep on the open corner.
h loose coins you made you buy fast food,
s it gently to them.
stand like a candle,
cancel the rainy street of pain.

Han Misyou

t Touches

touches are like a rainbow God painted across the sky
the blessings in our life that money can't buy,
king at daybreak to see dew on the trees,
eautiful sunset or a cool summer breeze,
touches are the memory of Nana's butterfly kiss on my cheek,
istening to my children first learning to speak,
saying "I'm sorry" after a fight,
rayer whispered to Thee in the still of the night,
touches are a baby's tiny fingers wrapped around mine,
stars in the night - how they sparkle and shine,
illow under my head when I lay down to rest,
tching a little bird just leaving the nest,
Touches are God's impressions left on our heart,
y reach our very soul and tell us Thou Art!

Joyce M. Ogden

ide or Out

re they looking inside or out?
the faces looking through glass, most
smiling, some are not, and a few have
ways of looking at you.

re they looking inside or out?
one moves or utters a sound, but some
make you smile or laugh, and few can
ke you cry, either happy tears or sad.

re they looking inside or out?
look at them and even talk to them, but
hough spell-bound the view stays the same.

re they looking inside or out?
ir friends, and their family, their pets you
re, with memories behind frames for you to explore.
re you looking inside or out?

Jackie Haus

forever
a far away breeze brings a farewell song.
from sails that suffer in silence of shadows
and shelters for the insane and fragile
in sighs and in sobs
in solemn
forever

Irina Stepanova

Dying Love

The firm and the frail, the strong and the weak
All walk on this earth, each taking a peek
At love and at life but not thinking at all
That one day He'll meet us and give us our call.
Whatever we do and whatever we say
Will scream forth like rockets on that fateful day.
So think now you sinners and repent your fate
For when that day comes it will be far too late
To change all the habits a lifetime can bring.
So all of us now whether beggar or king
Should start changing places and forget about strife
For this journey on earth is too short a life.

Francis A. Ciminera

The Piper

When the Piper plays his beckoning song,
All who hear him will follow along.
Young and old, weak and strong,
All who hear him will follow along.

Thousands of voices will cry out "No!"
But into the midst of the storm they will go,
Watching with horror the Seeds that they sow,
The Seeds of War which the wild winds blow,
To all the corners of the world,
Whipping the black, black Sails of Destruction unfurled.

When the Minstrel of Doom does finish his song,
Not all who followed will come back along.
Many have gone where no creature may fly,
Although many will mourn, and many will cry.

Aleksandra Darowski

A Mother's Honesty

Dear child of mine, I cry for you
Almost every night.
You think they're true, lies told to you,
"Your future will be bright.
Filled with love and happiness,
Forever and beyond.
Life's lovely fairy God Mother
Will wave her magic wand,
And all your fears will disappear
As night turns into day.
Those golden curls, upon your head,
Will never turn to gray.
You'll meet someone who fills your needs
And find love in your heart.
The ones you love will never die.
We'll Never be apart."
And while the glare from all these lies
Blind you in their light,
I'll cry for you, dear child of mine,
As day turns into night.

Ariella S. Butcher

Eternity

The world is asleep,
All is quiet except for the ticking of the clock
   on the wall.
Is this the quiet of the hereafter — the place our
   soul will journey to when life on earth is done?
Or will we pass over into a deeper stillness, as our
   soul is buried in eternity, like the earth being
   covered in a blanket of snow —
Quiet....peaceful...still...
Forever.

Eileen B. Olson

One Child

One child sitting in the darkness
almost hiding from view,
even though she's a "star"
she doesn't think she's as important to you.

One child forgotten
and alone in her room,
she sits there crying
and thinking only of gloom.

One child working alone
feeling guilty for asking for your time,
worried she might be too dependent
and thinking that's a crime.

One child scared to show her true feelings
for fear everyone will laugh at her,
and use her sensitivity as a lure.
One child scared to let her childhood forever flee.

One child sitting in the shadows
almost hiding from view,
will she ever let her true feelings show through?

Arlette Luta

Just Passing Through

So there you are snuggled up and so warm
almost resembling that humanly form,
about to find out how it feels to be born
so you rest for you'll be very tired and worn.
You push yourself forward through all of that
mess, getting rougher "oh no" stuck forever
I guess. You squirm and you fight, "awh" up
ahead is some light, as you look back and
wonder, why it was structured so tight. You
give a big shove, and in pops a glove, you
just know somehow it wasn't sent from above.
Well finally you made it and out pops your head,
as you're looking around, am I living or dead.
I'm surrounded by white suits with weird gadgets
and knives, oh what a strange place, well I
guess this is life.
There's one thing for certain I can say
with no doubt. It was quite an adventure but
I'm sure glad I'm out!!!

Janice Long-Motta

Silent Witnesses

The brown branches and green leaves reach out majestically
Almost touching heaven
So great is their height

They are aloof from us,
Far above our petty tyrannies,
Conflicts, loves, and hates.

And though my moods are many
I often listen to the wind whispering through these
green sentinels

And if I am near enough, the green leaves and brown branches
stretch out and enfold me,
And I listen to their Silence and Learn

Jennifer Richardson

Destiny

Whispers in the dark, who will listen?
Alone, cold, only the snow is glistening.
Someone, somewhere, you once knew, was kind,
Now you don't know what to do.
Fate, destiny, you sit and ponder, where am I to go,
And how is it I got so low?
Now, home is only a box to shelter you from the cold,
And your once new shoes and clothes
Are now tattered, torn and old.
The only solace you have is from an old book you carry close to
your heart.
And in it, it says, if you believe you'll never be apart.
A glistening tear rolls down your wrinkled, dirty face,
You cry, "Lord, what have I done to deserve this disgrace?"
But you still don't realize it was only greed, an evil seed that
has blossomed and grown, it took over your life and now it has
left you all alone.
And even still, you don't understand your fate, because nothing
happens in God's world by mistake.

Carolyn McCloud

Alone:

Alone with all my memories at last.
Alone with all my dreams of the past.
Separated from all my hopes and plans.
Slipping through distant and foreign lands.

Searching for a place just to call home.
No where else to travel, no desire to roam.
Longing for solitude, peace, content.
Searching my soul for what the past has meant.

Families are scattered from shore to shore.
No one reaches out for love anymore.
Everyone is searching for power, social and financial gain.
We are all tripping over our own personal sin and shame.

Our children are left to pay our dues.
In a tortured world of hopelessness, fear and abuse.
On what is their future, I dare not expand.
What is needed here, is the powerful touch of God's mighty hand

Betty E. Ardito

The Paths We Choose

The paths we choose make up the life we lead.
Along these paths we meet others on their journey.

For many, just a nod as we pass.
For a few, our paths seem to join.

These are the ones we call to for help-
A boulder blocking our way,
A pit that seems too deep.

These are the ones with whom we enjoy our walk-
The colorful flowers scenting the air,
The beautiful scenery we stop to see.

Holding hands around the turns unsure of where they lead,
We know we will make it on this journey.

Together we overcome the uphill stretch,
Knowing that beyond, the view is much better.

At the crossroads where we wave good-bye for now,
Be assured.
There is a connecting bridge easily traveled.

Julie A. Burke

Prayer to God

Each and every night I pray for the sick in pain
   also for the lame
I pray for the rich and for those with fame
I pray that we all will stop passing the blame
I pray we all stop downing one another because
   we're all the same
I pray that we all learn to love, live, and forgive
I pray for the one's that has lost a loved one
I pray for those whom wish they had a son
I pray for those that think they are the one
I pray for those that use drugs for hope and
   that one day they learn to cope
I pray to those that need a friend
This brings my prayer to an end and I must
   say a man to my best friend
    Dyanna B. Greer

How Will I Die?

By my hand — never!
Although I do not wish to live by machine.
By God's hand — yes, in time.
But more importantly, how? Not from what. How?
I pray not whimperingly, nor profanely.
Perhaps with a smile, a sense of excitement
About to visit a new world, a place read about,
a place of peace and joy, far removed from worldly problems.

How shall I die?
I hope knowing that my life was not a waste...
That I made a difference,
Caused a smile to replace a tear.
Made one person feel needed, have new meaning to love,
and perhaps a reason to live.

Have I been the best that I could be?
No, but I hope acceptable in God's sight.
I hope to be missed, not mourned.
I hope all who should know how much they are loved.

How shall I die? At peace and with a happy heart...
Quietly, knowing my life was o.k., maybe even worthwhile.
    Jed C. Alexander

"A Mother's Love For Her Son"

Watch a child grow from day to day
Always acknowledge them when you pray
They grow up so fast, seems like over-night
They're no longer small but of a great height
Yesterday in diapers, tomorrow planning a prom
How fast time goes by when you're being a mom
Remembering the good times as mother and son
The laughter, the tears, the games that were won
All grown up and now out on his own
Now choosing a wife and a new home
There's an emptiness felt within a mother's heart
When it comes time for mother and child to part
Praying that we've done our best to teach him the right way
Hoping he feels the special bond of love that grows everyday
As a mother, knowing that things will never be the same again
But realizing that this is God's plan
With pride looking at the woman he has chosen for his wife
Knowing she has promised to love him for the best of their lives
Praying that the love they share today will only grow stronger
Hoping they know now in their hearts that God has put them
together.
    Annell Carter

A Round

Our world is an attic where many things are found.
Amazing to note how many of them are round!
Round the spinning earth, the full moon and awesome sun,
Our childhood marbles, spheres of glass, just for fun.
Clocks mark our hours with ever-circling hands.
Baseballs crack off bats to please the fans,
And there's the round of basketballs, hoops and hockey pucks.
Alas, bullets too are round.
Birds build their almost round nests when spring comes round.
Imagine the world without the roundness of the wheel,
Coins of silver, coins of gold which we in commerce deal.
We form circles of friends and share a round of drink.
Round too the pipes beneath the sea we sink.
Most cups, saucers and plates are round,
So one can only note - round will be a shape a long time around.
    Catherine J. Greene

Lost to America

Born too late for travel to another place
America has found us all
The waitress smiles her mandarin-american smile
As she takes my british-american order
For very spicy hunan chicken

But what have I said and what has she heard?
Reminding myself she will likely hear my spicy as mild
Deafened by her eagerness to go the American way
Spicy rhetoric referring to toned down reality
I am not an American I say

She smiles at my cross-cultural end-run
But did I succeed?
No

You can do anything in America
As long as you cook it up in the fragile privacy of your
Home

What has the world come to
When success means
Expurgating spice

It makes it hard to have a nice day
    Deryck Durston

On Dew Drop Lawns

   Where shadows slumber in sweet repose, on drew drop lawns of green,
amongst the willow's weeping bows, I'll rest in sleep serene.

   And dream shall I, of times we shared to comfort my stilled heart,
to pass the hours whence from thee, I find myself apart.

   I'll dream of mighty ocean's crash, against the distant shore,
of places we have never been and those we'll go once more.

   Throughout your lifetime travels, companion I shall be,
in joy or sorrow find you, to share your destiny.

   When then your moment comes to pass, I'll gently take your hand,
where shadows sleep on dew drop lawns, beneath the willow's
strands.
    Carlos A. Ascunce, "Charley Potatoes"

A Friend

A friend is someone special,
a person who cares for you,
but to be a friend you must care too.
Friendship is very special,
something you can't find everyday.
You must work at being a friend in your own special way.
A friend is some one who,
well let me put it this way, this friend could be you!
    Christy Spiller

Untitled

Rushed from Eden -
An ancient stream drops deep
To fertile springs
Flows through chthonic caverns
   Pools in fluid darkness
      - boils and distills
   Vaporous deities lift from the mix -
Take shape in evanescent glyphs that
Shift to spirits regenerate
Then soar in infra-firmament -
   They rise through nether flumes
      - quickened to the womb
   The swell of conception
Kindles her icy breast
Cools the bitterness
Fissures through brittle flesh
   And cracks the layer of severance that
      keeps her from living Within -
         Christopher Hassett

The Lobby

One night I dreamt I was on an elevator.
   An elevator leading to the top floor.
When entering the lobby of the top floor,
   I stood in awe.
For the lobby was lined in ivory and gold.
   Portraying pure richness and elegance.
And relaying an atmosphere of perfect peace.

An authoritative voice shakened my amazement.
   Telling me: "I must return to first floor, I am not
   allowed to be here yet!"
My questioning mind wondered, where am I?
   And what was the meaning of all this?

Perhaps the lobby, lined with ivory and gold,
   Is the entrance area to my heavenly Father's
   mansion.
A mansion of pure richness and elegance,
   And the beginning of perfect peace.
      Grace Hulstedt

Venting My Anger

O. J. Simpson:

   HOW DARE you disgrace, disillusion and insult almost
an entire generation of African Americans!
   Most who knew or at least heard of you, and once were
your Loyal Fans?

   WHO do you think you are, that you can change people
or things by the mere force of your fists?
   Let me enlighten you, this earth is occupied by MILLIONS
who feel it a privilege merely here to exist!

   The pinnacle INSULT is your thinking of your race as
a mindless body that is under your control
   We should all think you are innocent and because of our
Blackness, act the same as told.

   Yes, we may have your complexion, and by heritage
belong to your clan
   But our individual, God-given intelligence informs us
we are no longer your diehard fans!
      Jacqueline T. Jett

Spring Crier

Sometimes on rain-washed mornings in the spring,
An old slow-footed wind comes shuffling down
The cobbled sky into my winter world
And hangs around ringing, ringing until
The child behind my womanly guise wakes up,
Remembering herself on such a day
Long long ago, the selfsame wind that way,
And those in whom she found identity
Alive inside the safe warm house and in
The field. And, suddenly, seized by sorrow
And dark unfathomed terror, lost, adrift
In space and far away from home, I cry.
      Grace Roberson Hicks

Daddy's Coffee Pot

Memories often flood my mind, of how things used to be,
And a scene I oft encountered, unveils itself to me....
It's Daddy making coffee in an old stained coffee pot,
While Mama cooked the biscuits on the wood stove, piping hot!

Now, Daddy never "washed" that pot, but rinsed it tenderly,
Whether to preserve the flavor, or from dire necessity!

Though later years the wood stove gave way to electricity,
My Daddy and his coffee pot were still a sight to see....
As he held his "Mr. Coffee" pot, and rinsed it lovingly.

Now, many things from by-gone days are best left behind it's true,
But what I'd give, for just a taste, of Daddy's rich warm brew!

I wouldn't want to go back, though I think of it a lot,
For I realize the magic wasn't in the coffee pot....
Nor in the brand of coffee, this I can plainly see,
But it was the man who made the brew, that made it special to me!
      Geraldine Hulsey

Drought

The sun is bright in a cloudless sky
And a strong west wind blows hot and dry
The fields are as brown as the desert sand
And the voice of the turtle is nor more in our land.

The cattle wander with heads hung low
Searching in vain where grass did grow
The seeds lay quiet in the parchment soil
Indifferent still to the farmer's toil.

What have we done to earn this lot
Is this the land that God forgot
We know we've erred but we want to live
Hear our prayer, Oh God, our sins forgive.

And then one day when all seemed lost
The thunder rolled and the storm wind tossed
And the earth was drenched with blessed rain
And gone with the flood was our grief and pain.

The Lord is my shepherd this I know
And the flower will bloom and the rivers flow
He will ne'er forsake us come what may
He's even there on the darkest day.
      Forrest W. Dunham

Love Petals

Upon the petals, upon this rose, I pledge undying love,
A love as soft and tender as the wing on Heavens Dove.
For many years the rose has been the beauty of love renewed,
That is why my darling, I give this rose to you.

The softness of these petals, like your tender fingertips,
Reflect the kissing sweetness in your rosy lips.
Lovers know the reason God made these lovely flowers,
They hold a love so deep and sweet like this love of ours.
      Frank E. Outcelt

October

October comes with orange, yellow, and black,
And a tiny piece of white,
The orange light a flickering,
In the black of the night,
The eerie whitish glow,
Coming from the moon,
Reflecting on a skeleton,
Makes the light of noon.
But then!
A witch!
Prancing on her stick,
Blocks the eerie whitish glow, coming from the moon,
Say goodbye to the light of noon.
But then,
Yellow light,
Dancing on the lawn
Say goodbye to the witch,
For now it maybe dawn.

Emily Dunn

Dreaming

As I dream when we were just kids
And all the wonderful thing that we did

We roamed the hills and swam in the streams
We heard the whippoorwills and the night birds sing

We chopped the weeds and hoed the corn
On this small farm where we were born

Then we grew our wings and flew away
Not knowing that we would return someday

Now father time knocks on my door
I dream what it would be like
To be a kid just once more

Donald Workman

She Was Always There

With Mother's Day drawing near
And although my Mom's no longer here
Memories of her are still fresh in my mind
For she was so loving sweet and kind
Whenever she spoke, her voice was soft and gentle
In the evening when she reached for the lamp on the mantle
I can still hear her say, in her own quiet way,
"The days are getting shorter now.
Summer has slipped away, too fast so me how."
Sometimes when she tied a pretty ribbon in my hair
She would hug me close, she smelled like fresh air
I remember running home from school
When the autumn days were growing cool
There was always hot cocoa with crackers to share
And the best thing of all, Mama was there.

Helen D. Sullivan

Young Love

You whispered my name
And I felt all aflame
For the word you had hesitated to claim.
You whispered you wanted me
And I felt the same.
We spoke of our love
That nothing can change.
But the words that you uttered
That made my heart shutter
Were "I need you, more than anything."

Dedra Hubbs

"Christmas Without You"

This is the time to come together
and be with the ones you love
But things aren't going to be the same this year
because now my grandpa's up above

I know he'll be there in our hearts
and looking down on us, too
My grandma will be upset, I know
but we'll all help her make it through

If it's not to much to ask
I just want Santa to tell him this
"I love you Granpa, very much
and it's you I'll always miss"

I know there's one thing on my list
that I just won't get this year
because I know there's no way to bring you back
but at least I know you're near.

Grandpa, I hope you know how much
everyone misses you
Even if some of them may not show it
at least you know I do?

Angela Meador

As Told To Wiccan Children

Before there was you
And before there was me,
There was a Great Something
But there was nothing to see.

And then...
Before you could blink,
The Great Something started to think.

The Great Something thought,
"There is only one Me."
And decided to be
Not One; not Two, but Three.

The Great Somethings Day and Night
Became the Sun and the Moon.
The Third, the Earth, exploded with life;
And it was none too soon.

When humans could do so
They said with a nod,
"We can't thank you enough
O, Great Goddess and Bright God."

Geri Cram

"A Mother's Prayer"

Help me Lord, as a mother, I pray
And bless these hands folded in prayer today
May they be ever strong, as they guide
  as they teach,
Being never too far for a child to reach.
May they never, with selfishness,
  try to dissuade,
Nor too quickly to punish, nor too slowly to aid,
May they point out the pleasures
  in laughter and song
And may they show wisely
  the right from wrong,
So that one day I'll know that I've
  helped all I can.
To make him into a strong man.

Cleta P. Garcia

The Dazzling Colors

The dazzling colors filled my senses crisp
and clear as the air flowing in through the
storm window vent.

The full moon was a shining disk reflecting
off the white diamond covered robe the
lake was wearing.

The silver trees held out their jewel covered
arms flashing a display of delicate pink,
pure pale blue, lavender, gold, emerald green
with touches of rose and amethyst and
sapphire to greet the majestic sun.

And are those misty forms moving among
the trees, Fairy Folk about to vanish from
sight as the sun rises higher?

Suddenly the whole earth burst into
breath taking color - then settled down to show
off the diamond covered lake and woods.

Was I dreaming? No! I returned to
a warm bed and kept forever in my memory
that glorious sight.

Ednah Bartlett Himes

A Gentle Man's Fall

I watched the days of fall approach
and clouds begin to form in the sky,
I watched your smile fade away
and the sparkle leave your eyes.
I watched the leaves on the trees
fall slowly to the ground,
Once a man so full of life
I didn't hear a sound.
Every now and again you might look at me
and sometimes squeeze my hand,
I saw a man who loved his family,
and a man who loved his land.
I watched a leaf float slowly,
slowly down to rest on the morning dew,
and at that very moment -
so did you.

Donna L. Unfried

The Angel

There is a light I can always see
And constantly fight to reach
It is never very far away
But try and try, I cannot get there.

I long to be bathed in the light
To feel its warmth upon my skin
To shut my eyes against its brilliance
To bask fully within its glow.

There are times I see the light fade
And shadows close in around me
Darkness threatens to overtake me
To take away my beacon, my driving force.

Suddenly this angel appears
She drives away the dark, restores the light
Her identity she keeps a mystery
But I know, were I ever to see her face...
She would be you.

Adam K. Plummer

I Wish I Was Eileen Vance

To look and be gazed upon
And despair at inadequacy for tradition,
And these would be Ivory edifices,
Stephen, did your flight teach you
to love the marred caress?
What year is it when we hurt ourselves?
Are we somehow oblivious to an apocalypse?
To no avail is help sought
The scars are there
When vision fails
And bruise fades to ivory
I'll never have beautiful hands —

Jennifer J. Vannordstrand

Dreaming Below The Willow

I lay my head upon the pillow
And dreamed sweetly of the night,
All the reckless passion without slight,
Below the soft and gentle weeping willow.
Lustily out the branches billow,
And a songbird takes to flight,
As in comes the moon's soft light,
And I dream on alone below the willow.

Softly, I cry
Whimpering into the depthless night
At the thought of a sad goodbye
Forced at the end of yet another bitter fight,
Edged with angry words and screaming,
I lie alone here and remember as I am dreaming.

Jessica Ann Krcek

No Right to Complain

I sit and complain about all I've done
And even what I still may do.

But all I've done can't even come close
To the grace I received from you.

I sit and talk about how bad I'm treated
And how life is so very unfair.

But would I be willing for just a brief moment
To carry the burden you chose to bear.

What I failed to see while I was sitting
With my eyes slowly drooping to the ground

Was your grace and mercy still shining on me
As the blessings continued to come down.

When I think of all your goodness and love
What right do I truly have to despair?

For you loved me more than I thought possible
And you showed me how much you care.

So, when I feel the need to sit and complain
I should first sit and remember the cross.

I should remember the price that Christ so richly paid
So that people like me wouldn't be lost.

Cortina M. Evans

Ebony Reyes

Ebony the dog and Ebony the person, Ebony the mother
and Ebony the baby. These are all one Ebony, my Ebony she
hops like a bunny, looks like a baby in a diaper and walks
like a lady wearing four high heels. Do not be mistaken
this is not Ebony the wood or Ebony the magazine but the
one and only Ebony Girl Reyes.

Amy Lyn Yeomans

All In Perspective

Toward the west I face my mountains
And gaze through the notch
To keep abreast of the weather
I must frequently watch.

Pink sky in the morning
Red-gold sunset at night
Fill my heart with gladness
And bring great delight.

But beware the great gray clouds of snow
Beware the thundering clouds of rain
For they will crash madly
Against my window pane.

But, oh, on a day
When the sky is blue
White clouds proudly float
Across the sky for you.

So, open your eyes
It is worth the sight,
And no matter the weather
It will be all right.

Jeannette Frantz

Graduate

As a student graduate from school
   and go out to get a job
They must want the job and look
   respectable and respect their employer
And others round them and work hard
   to do the job they're hired to do and to
Earn their own way in life for them
   and their own family in the future
Life ahead as a great citizen in
   the community where you live.

Irene Mary Larson

Regrets

Will you sit there one day when your old
and gray, and wonder where time has gone?
Will the past make you cry for the years
that went by and realize why your alone?

Will voices you hear from memories dear,
make you break down and want to go back?
For all your possession and many obsessions
cannot fix what your children now lack.

When you pick up the phone and your children
aren't home, seems their always 'too busy' these days
For maybe its true, now there's 'no time' for you,
And maybe its your turn to pay.

When they lay you to rest, will they think the best?
Or will they be cold as a stone.
"We didn't know you too well," no time, you did tell,
For you lived, now you've died alone.

Dawn O'Brien

The Whimsical Sink

One day the kitchen sink became angry
and decided to take a long vacation.
It's leaving was not a whole lot of fun
for there were many dishes to be done.
The odor was such, as to cause me great pain.
The garbage, was all jammed in the drain.
With plunger in hand, I attacked with a zest
disposing of all that rotten stinking mess.
The sink it returned from it's vacation
and danced with glee and great elation.

Daniel P. Beckwith

Hopes Dream

Though she strides in beauty
   And her face does shine
Her thoughts are of escape to life.
   And leave misery behind
She is one of the walking wounded
   But her bleeding doesn't show
She longs for strong arms to hold her tight
   And safe secure places to go.
Courage would describe her life
   Though its fear she has for her role as wife.
Her strength may escape your eyes
   If you know her not as a treasured prize.
Fear not my lady for I love you so
   Keep up your head even if I am aware of the show.
Events will evolve to much surprise
   And it shall be me to call you my prize

Clarice Hollingsworth

Mourning

How do I tell you I love you,
And how do I show you I care,
When I'm from the generation of crew cuts
And yours is known for long hair?

Remember when you were just little
And we'd romp and laugh in the sun?
How we'd camp in a tent at the ocean?
Can a bottle be really more fun?

Your eyes used to sparkle with mischief.
Your laughter came straight from the stars.
You used to have fun in the sunshine,
But now you much prefer bars.

Yet, somehow you must know that I love you,
And somehow you must know that I care.
And inside you there still must be laughter.
To hear it again is my prayer.

Helen Gates Pierce

Clouds

Have you ever sat and watched the Clouds passing by
and how the things we see in them can easily make us cry.
The tricks they play within our minds that seem to make them talk,
well I have.

My thoughts these days are ones of love
the way you smile, your gentle touch, the peace I feel when
You are near, and just the sound of your voice.
Can make me smile and watch the clouds.

I've sat and watched the clouds and dreamed of us
the thoughts we share, the goals we've set
The smiles and the tears
and all the happiness ahead throughout the years.

This weekend was just a taste of times we'll have
the joy and love we share
and so I sit and watch the clouds
as they go passing by.

Bruce Schnepp

My view of Heaven is a place...

where Goodbyes are needless and Hellos are arriving
where Friends are coming but never disappearing
where Families are all and Loneliness is nil
where Here is There so separation is unknown
where traveling is Together and Singleness is never
where Distance is close and Closeness is forever...

My view of Heaven is a place.

Donna M. Long

My Gift To The World

My gift to the world is freedom.
Giving to everybody, love one another, care for people.
And help the poor people.
My gift to the world is LOVE.

Brieon Jones

Eclectic

I sit and watch as anger rolls,
and I do not breath as depression deals with deathly games.

Like red, red clouds of doomsday deliverance
with singing swords to perish in gamely names.

Aberration of denial play to tunes Eclectic and mad
Raising voices with glasses of sweet blood and vilest nectar

So I dance a joyful dance
and with praying hands hoping of miracles sung in the sand
praying so patiently
like ever so carefully
to Gods of summer and sand.

David Moore

My Promise to You

The beauty within is something to see
And I have been blessed you've shown it to me
So many times we look with our eyes
And not from our heart where true feelings lie

I could write a small novel and you still wouldn't see
Your a beautiful woman and I want you with me
There's something I think that you need to see
Why I love you so much, what you mean to me

As the novel unfolds as you turn each new page
My loves as a story released from a cage
Like a dusty old chest that's lost and forgotten
Where the wood is all warped and the shackles look rotten

But your drawn to it closer to see what it holds
Sensing a treasure of riches untold
Just blow off the dust hear the creek of the hinge
And I promise you'll find a love without end

Chris McCarty

Senior Citizens

Senior citizen, what a title to behold
And I say so with confidence,
Although it seems I'm being bold
To each of these I'll make some sense.

I believe the term bears in its core
The meaning of deep respect,
From those who want us to leave with them
Experience they'll never reject.

Senior experience includes many times
That of being a father or mother,
And as we who are saved, joyously know
We also become a sister or brother.

Senior saints is a category unique
Which can be found through the nations,
Their spiritual maturity in things of the Lord
Are offered to younger generations.

Though time is about gone for this group we know
Time also is fleeting for all others.
So let us oldsters tell the younger of our living Christ
And they too can become sisters and brothers.

Cecil C. Lawrence

Faith

Put your small hand in mine and lead the way
And I will follow your untraveled path today
Take me where only sweet innocence can go
As you journey into worlds you do not know

If I should but falter, just hold on to me tighter
I promise you that my steps will grow lighter
Your world is mine if only for a short while
Each moment is important to capture your smile

Your heart is so pure, overflowing with love
With soul blissfully serene as the heavens above
Teach me again things that lay far in the past
About memories lost of images that should last

My wish to you is for love and all things good
I'd give you long eternal life if only I could
For now, I'll clear a path for your feet to trod
Oh Blessed little one, beautiful child of God

Judy Caswell

Dream A Dream

Whoever said Dream a Dream
and it will come true

Blow out the wax and wish
but my breath was always too soft

Kneel and Pray and it will come true
but my knees always got too blue

Wish upon a star
but they seem to go too far

If one wish ever came true
a long time ago I wish it would have been you

Julio C. Garcia

Saying Good-Bye to Daddy

My dad is big and strong you see,
And I've seldom seen him cry,
But when it was time for me to go,
I saw a tear in his eye.

To say the least, I was surprised,
It never crossed my mind,
He'd miss me to the point of tears,
It made my very soul shine.

He held me close, and hugged me tight,
I could hardly catch my breath,
I felt a special comfort, upon my dad's chest.

And when he let me go again, I looked into his eyes,
And there I saw the love, the trust, and comfort,
I never realized.

In disbelief the tear did fall,
I too began to cry,
Hugging again, we promised,
To never say good-bye!

Estella Sanders

Nature

Whenever I watch butterflies soar in the sky or
fish swim in the deep blue sea, I watch miracles of
God. Though many take it for granted, I doubt I
ever will, for it has much beauty and wonder for
the eye to see with great love and pleasure. It is
like God sent us a heart filled with love outside our
bodies.
He probably has.

Amanda Tobin

The Dandelion

We should be more like the Dandelion,
And less like the Rose,
"The more it is trampled, the more it grows."

Fragrant and beautiful is the Rose,
But its petals are delicate,
  easily bruised and quickly fold.

Relentless is the Dandelion,
Its head a thistle of gold,
And no matter how tightly squeezed
Its petals steadfastly hold.

Tender loving care is required for the Rose.
But with the least soil to share
  the Dandelion grows and grows.

So though it lacks the Rose's beauty,
  and a lowly place it holds,
The world would be a better place
  if we were more like the Dandelion
And less like the Rose,
"The more [we are] trampled, the more [we should] grow."

Claudette V. Ferron

This Place

What is this place I have stumbled upon?

It has places that man wishes he could stay
  and live a lifetime.

It has an air that will effect the way he
  thinks and acts.

There is a caring and affection all around it,
  covering the walls and floors.

There are vast, open fields and narrow
  thorny places where it is difficult to
  pass without a few bruises and cuts.

There are plateaus that take him to places
  beyond his normal thoughts
  and valleys that are too difficult to
  cross alone.

This place seems like heaven, where no one
  will ever venture.

But this place is the human heart,
  affected by Love.

Chester Schultze

In Memory of My Father

A man has departed from this life.
But, yet he lives.
A man is with us no longer.
But, his presence is known.
A man is dead.
But he lives within my heart and mind.
Yes! He lives.
He is very much alive in my thoughts and memories of the years
past.
He is with me still, just as he was before.
I feel his presence.
I still know of his love; and he is still aware of mine.
Real love never dies because with its birth,
it is nurtured to a degree that could never be obliterated:
not with words; nor with actions;
or in this case death.
Yes, a man is dead.
But, he lives on in my heart.

Debbie C. Gideon

Orthros in the Hills

I climbed atop a woodland hill,
  And looked out o'er a valley still,
  And felt the freshened morning breeze,
  Sweep up the slope and through the trees.

And as I paused to rest and gaze,
  Out o'er the valleys ghostly haze,
  The scene conveyed a peaceful calm,
  That brought to mind a wondrous psalm.

For in this spot I felt his grace,
  And held in awe the healing brace,
  Of sighing winds that murmured low,
  And sang a hymnal to the show.

So seated there on lichen pew,
  Enchanted by the sounds and view,
  My mind was lulled to sweet abstraction,
  Immobile now to all distraction.

And as all nature seemed caressing
  me, with her pontific blessing,
  I knew I'd find no greater thrills,
  Than at this orthros in the hills.

Harry T. Crist

For Amy

When Amy's ill, the birds won't sing,
And mother nature cancels spring.
The little lambs, refuse to play.
And dawn forgets to start the day.

When Amy's well and feeling fine.
Then dawn allows the sun to shine.
The birds will sing a happy tune.
And we all pray, she'll be home soon.

Get well little Amy, there's much to be done,
In your little girls world of mischief and fun.
Your toys have been idle, your doll left alone.
And playmates are eager to welcome you home.

There are ropes to be skipped, swings to be swung.
Games to be played and songs to be sung.
Bikes to be ridden, dolls to be dressed.
Loved ones to welcome you home to your nest.

Anthony Cassoni

Remembering

Country-side where there are many trees,
And musty swamps with cypress knees,
A silence broken by various sounds,
Grass covered knolls called Indian mounds.

As the thoughts return to me,
It is there I long to be,
Where I spent my growing years,
Among those of my peers.

Louisiana was my home,
Until I left to roam,
The world in Navy Blues,
A career spent in those shoes.

Now in retirement and alone,
And Arizona I call home,
The call is ever strong,
To return where I belong.

But time and tide has taken its toll,
And old age has me in its hold,
I cannot keep the pace,
Never again to see the old home place!

Franklin J. Warren

Life

Truth is a flame billowing, pillaring,
And my goal seems far.
My eyes are fixed above the horizon, and
All the jealous little tongues of fire,
Though they burn and char,
Will never force me to another path.

Blackening stumps propel me onward -
Ever swifter -
And are soon forgotten.

For small flickerings always envy the towering flare,
Delaying those who linger to extinguish them,
Disappearing here, leaping out there,
Taunting and eating away,
Until one hears only the sigh.

Frances Tate Presher

A Mother's Love

What perfect hands, I said to myself,
and perfect legs and toes,

It was a wonderful moment while it lasted;
Where did the time seem to go?

I watched you grow from a child of mine,
to a being of your own,

And I said many times to myself;
Where did the time seem to go?

The love that I feel for you
grew beyond my best of dreams,

And I think the Lord for giving me you as a gift,
For you left me with overwhelming gleam.

I also want to thank you dear child,
for letting me watch you grow,

So I could ask just once more;
Where did the time seem to go?

Barbara Keyes

Time In Reflection

I watched the heavenly bodies inching towards west
And pondered the precision with which they made this quest.
For eons their pathways haloed nightly our earth
Like wheels in God's grand clock that synchronize the universe.

Time belongs to the Lord throughout eternity.
But He has granted me a tiny wink of it to be
Master of my domain and of my fantasies.
Some of that time, I've lived with anxieties.

As restless child, I saw time pass with feet of clay.
My elders - having spent much of it - bemoaned its fleeting away.
Then came my spring, I was in love and wanted time to stop awhile.
But there were times of deep despair when I wished
   to relive a better mile.

Time is more precious than all the gems and gold.
Lost fortunes can be regained but never time - experience told.
Yet regrets over moments too mindlessly misspent
Can spawn another chance for being now more prudent.

I always wonder how much of time is still my own
And think it's wise to deem each hour a possible last one.
So I try to live my days with worthwhile aim
That my life will not be wasted, but merits it can claim.

Ilse Wissner

The Lonely Sentinel

The windmill turns its battered wheel
   And pumps forgotten dreams.
Its pipes hold rust, its dry gears squeal
   Like farmers' helpless screams.

The memories of another day,
   Another time and life,
Cling to the windmill's dangerous sway
   And tell a tale of strife.

The drought took hold, the water dried,
   The windmill pumped but dust.
The family moved, the crops all died.
   The pipes began to rust.

The years have passed, but still it stands
   And shakes it lonely head
And looks out over barren lands,
   The guardian of the dead.

Connie S. Webb

A Song for the Hereford-Loving 'Jim'

Today we carried Jim across the field
And put him on a rises of red-oak trees;
He would have rather walked than have us wield
The heavy box we carried at our knees.
He loved to lean against the barnyard gate
And watch his cattle come across the hills;
His pale eyes searched, should any come in late,
The nearest sign of some foreboding ill;
He knew the shape of every bone and horn,
Of spreading rump and giant-shouldered sire;
To these he fed the just amount of corn,
Withholding fat that slows a beasts desire.
He loved to hear white hoofs among the grass,
Swishing through the night outside his door;
He loved to watch the white curled-faces pass
Inside the gate to feed upon the floor.
He loved the years when life was giving birth.
And worked and cared what pure creation spills;
And now he rests; - a little rise of earth
To keep eternal watch upon these hills.

Garland Fisher

The Way I Remembered the Great,
Dr. Martin Luther King Jr.

Rev. Martin Luther King Jr.'s words filled many with hope,
and rained happiness in many hearts.
Mr. King's words were diligently chosen,
that what is said is perpetual and will never fall apart.

Dr. King was like a prophet sent from the Heavenly Father,
contained with words of power and delight.
Martin Luther King was a robust person in every way,
He was ready to nonviolently fight.

In every speech Dr. King gave he included the Lord,
and all words spoken, tremendously affected many.
he was also a great man who had troubles of his own,
and yet still he pursued a dream that finally came true,
not with ease, but rather with tremendous anguish.

This is the way the inspiring Dr. Martin Luther King
should be remembered and also should be known as an honorable man.
Rev. King was a great man, who should not be forgotten,
his words of power and delight many will remember,
and he was surely sent from the Father's hand.

Fitzroy Ward Cawdette

Things That Go Bump In The Night

Did you ever wake in the middle of the night,
And realize you're alone in the house,
And you wonder what awakened you,
For everything's quiet as a mouse.

Not a leaf seems to stir as you peak through the shade,
And the moon casts an eerie light,
It's then that you have a foreboding thought,
For the "things that go bump in the night".

Get a grip on your senses, your inner-self says,
For everything must be all right,
So you snuggle down under the blankets again,
And close both your eyes very tight.

The doors and the windows you know are locked tight,
There's no reason to feel such a fright,
It's only your keen sense of thinking, you hear,
The "things that go bump in the night".

Bertha Hoffler

Hope

The moon talked to me this morning
And said everything is going to be alright.
You see, the moon knows and sees everything
Just like an entity.
The moon was so immense and detailed
Emitting a powerful aura,
Yet not overwhelming.
It gave me a comfortable and warm feeling inside
Just like a loving heart.
It was leading the way, paving a path.
The moon knows I had a downfall yesterday
And it is giving me hope today.

Aniko Molnar

Going With My Emotions

As he rests his hand upon my cheek
and says how much he loves me
I look deep inside my heart
and wonder if I could say
the same to him about me.

I search and wonder in the cave
and then I see a candle, shining bright.
So I walk a little further, and there
I see a treasure right in front of me.
And then something tells me no and I start to fear.

And suddenly I snap out, seems like I woke up from a dream
And I see his hand is still there
And he is moving closer to kiss me
And he is about to do it.
But I step back put my hand across his lips and say no, not with me.

Alla Reyfman

Eagle

The eagle soars so far and high,
His life is a haven in a clear blue sky.
True to the heritage, he was born to live,
Beauty and strength to us he doth give.
Clearly a bird, that was meant to survive,
Is a message to me to be proud of my life.
His movement is graceful, as he slowly flies,
Bringing wonder to my tired old eyes.
And, after each sighting of something so regal,
I thank God for creating the eagle.

Dianne Whittingham

Mirror Girl

(Written at age 12)

I can look into a mirror
and see my outside face,
but I wonder if that other girl has
ever been embraced.
I wonder if she's danced and sang
to melodious tunes afar.
I wonder if she's written a poem
and heard it on guitar,
I wonder how she's feeling
bad, okay, or fine.
I wonder what she likes to do
bounce a ball, shop a lot, or unbraid a rope of twine.
I wonder how she loves to feel,
solemn or filled with glee.
I wonder if she's looking in
and wondering about me.

Creston Hutcherson

Untitled

I look around my house
And see remnants of your livelihood:
A table here, a lamp there,
A photograph on the wall.

Your lives have been reduced
To boxes of linens, doilies, and pictures
Waiting to be rediscovered
By children you'll never know.

My children will know you
Only through stories from memories,
Illustrated by the faces
In an old photo album.

But childhood is relived
In traditions passed on to children,
From pajama-ed trips for ice cream
To sand-filled trips to the shore.

And your presence lingers
In a look on my daughter's face
Or the shape of my son's chin;
You've shared my life after all.

Debbie Spencer

Untitled

Have you looked around?
And seen the things of beauty that abound.
The serene lake that you love.
What about the flight of a dove.
Nature in its best.
The peaceful feeling of creatures of the wild at rest.
To watch an animal with its young is such a treat.
It just makes you feel - isn't that sweet.
Have you looked around? They really do abound.
Just stop and think about the beauty of snow falling.
And how man takes things for granted - its appalling.
With such great gifts as these.
Should we not at least try to please?
The ONE who gave us so many gifts.
Instead people seem to involve themselves in rifts.
Have you looked around?
Think for a minute about a waterfall.
Does it not fill you with awe?
Imagine yourself among the unlimited things of beauty.
To preserve and cherish all of this is everyone's duty.

Judith Kappes

Her Sycamore

The sycamore in her front yard holds fast
And sends beyond her reach its widespread leaves
Across the neighbor's lots in swift reprieves
To lodge in their back yards a shaggy cast.

Wind catapults then in a stormy blast,
Along unchartered paths blows hard and heaves.
Rain pelts them soggy wet into reprieves
To mold and rot in somnolence at last.

She walks around the tree and wonders why
It came to be so troublesome to all
When what she wanted of it was a shade.

Must hindsight like a fleeting dream belie
A ready meaning to the wherewithal
Before the leaves flatten themselves and fade?

Helen Reid Roberts

Mom

Moms can cheer the saddest day
and share the joy and feel today.
Brighten your times of trouble,
and times of happiness make you feel double.
To take your hand and guide your way,
to help you keep from going astray.
She believes in you, in all you do,
she always helps you make it through.
Inspire, believes, listens and cares-
with al her heart, your dreams she shares.
She always knows just what to say-
My Mom, my friend, I love your way.
You're always there to lend an ear,
or a shoulder to cry on in times of fear.
My Mom - my friend you'll always be
you know you mean the world to me.
You give me strength more than you know-
this is just a little something to tell you-
I LOVE YOU so.

Carey Anne Mounts

All About Togetherness

Remember your childhood friend-the one who giggled
and shared your secrets-how you schemed and dreamed
together?
And about the togetherness spanning generations
Grandfathers with grandsons-reliving the years that
were-building castles-
Together-just people-are not mattering-the chemistry
bringing understanding and a bond-just liking each other-as
brother to brother-
That togetherness-just for fun-to romp in the snow, to
play in the sun-
The need for love-a man and a woman to hold someone
special-together sharing, conquering worlds with the touch
of hands and dreams.
That togetherness when you sit and meditate the years
gone-contemplating the past, knowing what's done is done-
And when the eyes grow dim-the need grows stronger
for her and for him to record the years of togetherness

Bryna Schmerling

Heidi

I had many dreams and they did not all come true
Except the ones I had about you
You are so bright, thoughtful and full of laughter
May you never change my darling daughter

Denyse Gatej

Whispers of the Moon

The moon is a ghostly white,
and shimmering all so bright,
The stars are glowing in the night,
But still the moon is twice as bright,
As everything is still you can hear,
The whispers of the night calling sweetly and dear,
Calling from far away,
Sometimes you can hear what the moon wants to say.

Brandy Martin

Half a Second of Time

As children we played in benevolent sun
And slept in the glitter of star light
In youth there were stars in the eyes of a friend
So we danced to the dark of the moon

Faded the stars into withering day
The work of the world growing hot
We buzz all about with differing clout
The market a tippity table
The old people know but move too slow
The young get dreadfully able

Silent the end in drifting night
The stars are there and I am there
Afloat upon infinite space.

Henry Sage Goodwin

A Broken Tradition

Turning sixteen brought the traditional tiara crowning,
and so it was my time.
It sparkled as eloquently as diamonds, the fake cut-glass,
a heady facade.
Who, of my legacy, could wear such glaring hypocrisy.
The tiara glistened boldly, simulating to me the
laborious sweat of beloved slave ancestors.
The elaborate frontal point, the peak of Rosa's courage,
jailed,
all for my societal assimilation.
The death-blood that flowed from tear-stained martyrs,
John, Robert, Martin and Malcolm, mingled within
the shallow victory exuding from the headdress.
It shimmered before me, fiercely gaudy, stale in its appeal.
Still, my hands ached to hold it, to possess it, at last,
the American Dream.
Never.
For to own the tiara would be my consummation;
the ultimate betrayal for justice.

Cindy Williams-Newsome

Gunfighter, Lawman, Or Kid

With an accent or two;
And some sayings of wise.
A little bit o'death
In a big scene where someone dies.
A river of blood under some poor soul,
As, in the street, he lies
maybe the oldest part of the west
Where all the buzzards fly.
As a whore and a wife look on
To the man in the streets, as they sigh.
He looks all around, and then to the sky
And silently, to his life, he says
good-bye...

Jenifer Beverstock

Only Time Will Tell

You put your friends first
  and sometimes it hurts
I give you my undivided attention
I tell you how I feel but you don't listen
You make me feel as if I don't exist
Your woman should be first on your list
My body, my soul, my mind, and my heart,
I gave it all to you now you're tearing it all apart
I don't know if I should trust you anymore
When I try to open up, you close the door
I look at my life now and it's not happy with you
We both know what we should do
It's time to say goodbye. I hope your life is well
I don't know if I could love again, "Only Time Will Tell"

Doniell Holloman

The Dream

I wish sometimes that life was fair
And sometimes wish that someone would care.
But what a cruel and unfair dream
To wake and see it's another scheme.
I often have prayed that love would come
So that my dreams could then be done.
But as always I have failed
And still I dream to no avail.
And so that moon will shine it's light
And I will dream again tonight.

Judy L. Paulik

Sonnet

The summer sun melts softly into eve
And soon will be replaced by barren skies.
As fall arrives I know that you must leave
Why with the seasons change must our love die?
When Old Man Winter comes to chill my heart
I'll close my eyes and drift off like a bird
To brighter days when we won't have to part
And loving words won't have to go unheard.
Until that time the visions in my mind
Will keep me warm on deep, dark, dreary nights.
I'll gaze up at the sky and hope to find
Your brilliant smile amongst the twinkling lights.
  So now I wait with hope until the day
  When springtime's breezes send you back my way.

Amy Krautheimer

Song Of The Fettered Astronaut

If I were free I'd comets race
And sprint across the sky
Then drift in dross of milky ways
As moonbeams filtered by
I'd gathered fists of spangled stars
And keep them in a jar
To light my way, like fireflies,
Across a black hole's spar
With leaps I'd cross the cosmos wide
To watch the planets grow
And see the universe unfold
In one stupendous show
Then to the earth's great blue green orb
Through light or darkness black
Where I would spin and spread my arms
And throw my head far back
And scream to all these wondrous things
That danced for me to see
"I too am part of mystery
See me! See me! See me!"

Barbara Gude

Bridget and George

Hi, my name is George you see,
And that girl Bridget belongs to me.

When I saw her at the pet store door,
My head popped out and hit the floor.

I was holding my breath with excitement you see,
I wanted her, but would she really want me?

I looked up to see her just a bit more,
She smiled and said, "I haven't seen you before!"

I forgot to breathe out, my cheeks must have been purple,
She smiled and she said, "I must have this turtle!"

She reached out to touch me, her hand rubbed my cheek,
I tried holding my breath, but my cheeks were too weak!

And all of that air I'd been holding inside,
Poofed out through my nose, I just could have cried.

She won't want me now, oh what have I done?
She laughed, picked me up and said "We'll have such fun!"

And now we're best friends, my Bridget and me,
We play and she tells me her secrets you see.

To her I'm her pet, to me, she is mine,
And our love for each other just grows all the time.

Irene A. Mussin

Suicide Note

When things don't go quite as plan
and the life YOU live is at a stand still

I have done my best to please everyone, but no one seem to be
  satisfied.

I tried to talk to someone, but an analytical opinion I don't need.

I tried to cry for help, but no one heard me.

So now its time for me to take a stand into that strong wooden chair
with a rope tied tightly around my neck.

Jump down and find me because Dead is where I am.

All I ever wanted was someone to tell me they care or maybe a sincere
"I LOVE YOU" would have made a difference yesterday
but TODAY I'M DEAD.

Deitra Dinkie Foster

The Crow

When darkness falls over the face of the earth
and the light begins to darken,
there will be yet one thing left here on our earth, our world
a bird - the crow
The Crow

Representing the depth of death within us all,
the heartaches and pain of yet man alone,
who and yet every man must bare and see within his own eyes.

But yet through all the darkness in the world
the crow is our light.
The light to our life, lives, loves and death,
yet though man walks over and kills another,
there will always be a crow,
the symbol of death and love.

Brigitte Moreno

STREET LAMPS (and sleepless nights)

We make faces through our eyes
And the moonlight glides our tears,
Motionless they lie
Mesmerized into pearls.

The savage day has died
And the moaning night begins:
Between sheets of nowhere
The guilt hides
Or lies encrusted in layers of remorse.

No sleep, just street lamps.
Millions of people in millions of towns
All lit by lamps,
Their souls robbed by these parasitic glow worms.

The buzz of car dies
And another is born
Only to die as it fades into the distance; dawn.

Let the wind control the blood
As it streams down my face,
There to lie congealed,
Never finishing its race.

Bridget Wagner

Camouflaged

The toad in the road blends into the dark
  and the snail
    stays safe in his shell

The monarchs in the marigolds hide
  while the bees dust their jackets
    with pollen

The spiders look like knots in the wood
  and the crocus holds more
    than a flower

The beetles and slugs and various bugs
  all hide by their
    camouflaged pallor

How nice it would be to step back toward a tree
  and know that observed
    I am not

Or cast off my blight and simply take flight
  and erase me from
    curious eyes!

Jacque Downing

Motivation Is A Ship

The large Galleon of interest doesn't move much
And the winds of motivation do not blow my way
Leaving me to make my own winds
Huffing and puffing till I am the wind
Filling the strong sails and thrusting the ship forward
I find myself pushing the Galleon faster and further along
So far ahead of me that I can't catch up
Falling into the sea of disappointment,
Also referred to as the sea of lack of interest
The cold sea water of reality slaps me in the face,
As I bob and sulk in my failure
The massive galleon slows and stops with out me able to push
- There exists more than just one sail ship in these oceans
And I can board any Ships of interest I want
But I always have to make the wind.

Dustin T. McBeth

Pioneer Farmer and His Barn

This rolling land is a weedy old farm,
  And there stands an old decaying barn.
The farmer is very poor with little money,
  And it makes him feel sick and crummy.

Running out of hay he lost his milk cow,
  And he is in a terrible bind right now.
He raised a big family and they are gone.
  His wife left with a bum, that seemed wrong.

Life has been very long and not very fair,
  But a friend brings him food in loving care.
Being old and lonely he often feels so hurt.
  Expecting he and his barn will turn to dirt.

Harold E. Wagner

So Alone

I sit in my room,
And think about the past,
The things we did together was such a blast,
I look up in the sky,
To see the moon shining bright,
I think to myself what a beautiful night,
Then I think about the beach,
Where we had our first kiss,
That's one day I won't forget,
But I surely will miss,
To hold you in my arms,
Was such a thrill, to me,
But now that you're gone,
You won't be a lost memory.

Lizzy Romero

My Walk

I took a walk this morning
  And this is what I saw.
I saw God's love in the trees
  And every blade of grass.
I saw his smile in the water
  Of a swiftly flowing river,
  But that was not the last.
I saw his tender touch
  On the wings of a butterfly.
I heard his kindness in the song
  Of a bird, as it went flying by.
As I stood there in wonder I learned
  That God's love and care is everywhere.
We only have to "be still" and know that he is there.

Helen Larkin Neely

A Nonagenarian's, Et al, Wake Up Prayer

Lord-thank you for my sleep and rest
and this new day which you have blest:
With life and love and learning habits
conforming to your Sacred Tablets.

Doing Thy will on earth demands
Commitment to your Ten Commands;
These I embrace with heart contrite
I pray God guidance day and night.
Written in stone your eternal law
Universally ordained forever these your immortal words:
"Love the Lord thy God with Thy whole heart, soul,
mind and strength: thy neighbor as thy self:

God- make these words my bottom line
your mind-prints on my sands of time:
And me each day your willing tool
To spread and practice your Golden Rule.

Gene Reiley

Grace

Have you ever gazed into the sky and focused on a twinkling star
And thought about the vision and who lets us see that distance from
    afar
Or to waken in the morning and to see the bright warm sun
To feel its warmth all through the day and pretty sunset once
    again when day is done
Have you ever seen the butterfly with pretty colors on its wing
Or hear the pretty birds in morn with all the pretty notes they sing
And have you ever been outside to let the rain fall gently on your
    face
Then see the rainbow when the sun comes out and know that it's a
    special grace
Have you ever seen a baby born and been a part of that emotion
That perfect child was formed with so much love and much devotion
And when you lose someone you love and you're feeling very low
And a special friend comes by to say I'm here for you — you know
The many times and reasons that we seem to need a friend
Sometimes it is a stranger who will help us in the end
Just think about the miracles that happen every day
Then get down on your knees and pray to Him without delay
For He gives a special kind of grace to everyone in His own way
It's a perfect kind of peacefulness where explanations cannot say
If we open our hearts to another call
He'll give us Himself for His Grace is for all.

Charlotte D'Amato

Untitled

As I gazed into her eyes
and thought of what to rhyme,
my mind went blank and then it sighs
you'll write another time.

But when I left, and kissed her face,
she gave back a warm embrace,
my mind no longer tragic,
from out here hair there was perfume
the fragrance worked like magic.

Why does her fragrance fill my heart with joy?
Why must it linger hour after hour?
Why must I feel just like a little boy
smelling a lovely flower?

I try to erase her face before my eyes
I picture sea and shore and skies,
above all this I see her lovely face
haunting me like a spirit.

Knowing that I am dreaming,
is the only comfort that I have.

Augustine Vicentini

From Roses to Romance

Down the path of life
and through the last day,
Many dreams that we hold dear
are lost along the way.
Hearts get broken while words are left unspoken
we make our choices
and ignore inner voices.
Sending messages we shouldn't send
Finally losing all in the end.
Regretting mistakes, praying to God above
asking why we lost true love.
We had it all from roses to romance.
wishing now we had a second chance.
Losing at last that one true friend,
'Cause we didn't stand by them until the end.

Hector Montalvo

Friendship

We started out as the best of friends
And through the years, we have diminished
    to nothing more than strangers
Our lives went in different directions,
    and we choose to forget one another
We found new friends, not remembering the old
Some of us moved away, and some stayed
No matter how close we were, we became no more
We can't just blame one of us for letting go,
We all had our part
Some of us choose to remain,
    although none of us will forget the ones we lost
We might talk to each other when passing in the street,
    but we know we will never be the same friends we used to be
The friends we were cared for one another
Now we would not know if one of us were dead or alive
We knew life would lead us down different paths
Although we never dreamed our friendships wouldn't last

Amanda Moorshead

Untitled

If you said the moon had turned to doves,
and took to wings away-
then in my heart it would be so
and there would be no more to say

If you said the day was full of stars,
and the night be-filled with shine-
this would be my truth, dear love,
your words would then be mine

So, when next you whisper with sweet breath
words of love beside my ear-
ask yourself: What is her choice but to believe?
For I am all she hears

Chamayn R. Smithey

An Illusion of Freedom

It's interesting as the lights are dimmed.
And tranquility fills the nocturnal air. I
realize that prisoners are dreamers. They dream
of a handful of honest gild, so they can
travel (undisturbed) to the warm sandy beaches
in some far away enchanted land. They dream
of a cozy night by a fireplace, so they can
watch and be engulfed by the warm passionate
flames of love as they dance like ballerinas in an array
of delightful colors. They dream of family and loved ones,
sharing and caring as they reach out through the
veil of illusion and touch one another...
    They play act a perfect part on the
illusive stage of dreams. And as dawn
approaches the subconscious mind grasp so
desperately to play out the final act of love -
But, as sure as day and noise fills our ears.
We watch so clearly, while the sand castles
we build are destroyed on the beaches by
the title waves of reality.....

Gerald Van Hoorelbeke A.K.A. Jerry Van

Untitled

Dancing...
Even hands are capable of this expressive exchange.
A dance of joy, of longing
A dance of gentleness, of coming home
A dance of trust and sadness
Of support, compassion and infinite love.
An intake of breath, a sigh, a cherished moment
And life continues.

Jacqueline De Los Santos

Hidden Treasure

I am like a piece of glass shattered
and trapped within my own frame.
Many look at me and see only a broken picture.
And few, with curiosity, may want to try and
find a hidden art beneath that broken glass.
Some will pick me up, turn me upside down
Perhaps even jar slivers of glass from the frame
only to be lost forever.
Their curiosity has been satisfied.
But the few who take the time to examine
the many broken pieces,
they may discover some value hidden within,
And, if by chance, one out of those few
shall acquire patience,
and the will to visualize all the contents of
that frame not as a broken picture,
but as one creation.
Then, that one shall become the sole owner
of a priceless treasure.

Colleen Medley

The Birds

They sing their song of joy, as they soar high above our head.
And we ask ourselves, "Why? Why must we dread?"

That all things around us, the birds, trees, and air,
Will at one time bring us to despair.

That we were given the world, to watch over year after year,
And yet as years go by, like disappearing clovers,
we are all still here,

Thinking about the things we so - called need, but what about a
little seed?
Like how we wish that someday soon, that seed will be nourished
'til it finally blooms.

And how this seed needs more than technology,
It needs Mother Nature's clean world and cherishing."

So every time a bird sings a song above your head,
Think of the things we all must dread.

Christine Fego

What If

What if I can't get to sleep,
and what if I can't count sheep?

What if, people laugh at me,
what if I fall and scrape my knee?

What if I forget the Pledge,
and what if I fall off the edge?

What if I get a wart,
and what if I don't know the sport?

What if I don't make the team,
what if I fall off the beam?

What if life is not grand!
What if my brother makes the band?

But why worry about all these "What If's"
When life is but a rocky cliff.

Alison E. Cornelius

'Carry A Smile'

1st before you go to sleep —-
And when you 1st wake up ——-
Bring to mind
Something positive — to make you smile

Take a drink — from loves cup
The negativity of the day — it breaks it up

It helps cleanse you
Takes you that extra mile

Let things go
Don't take negativity to bed with you
Carry a smile

During the day — let it radiate
Burn'em —— turn'em
With that beautiful smile

Feel the strength — and warmth of its cunning
It entices opportunity — pursuing it — to keep on coming

It celebrates and stretches for miles
It penetrates yet unpenetrable
Fascinating — sly is the smile

Yes — play that flavored provocative smile

Aaron T. Coleman

Reunification

A family begins with only two souls,
And with those two souls a family can grow.
They can begin a very good start,
The start of a family with love in its heart.

A family grows, a family parts,
But still the family has love in its heart.
The family spreads to the ends of time,
At least that's how it was with mine.

But now and then we get together again,
To share our love with our family, our friends.

Jonathan S. Hendrix

Jennie

Oh so sad, to see the look upon your face,
And yet so awed by God's own grace,
You took the words so hard to hear
Your only time left, just one year
To become an angel in heaven with dad
Ah, but you left me, nothing but sad.

I often wonder if the year was for me
Sometimes I think, oh, God can't you see!
What losing her does to me?
Then He tells me, her star was needed in my sky
Don't you see, that is why.

A life cut short by any means
So very short, it seems
My sister, my friend, apart of me
She always believed, did Jennie

Joyce Procell

Saying Goodbye

I listen to the restless rumble of waves,
For the last time I feel the sun on me
I look around and notice noises,
The time has come for me,
I must now go to the Ocean of Light
Gone from the peaceful waves,
Gone from the warm sure sun,
I say goodbye.

Emily Silver

"I'll Be There"

Sometimes the pain, is so hard to bear;
And you search for comfort, inside your despair.

When you sit and weep, in your dark smoky room;
And the pain and suffering, over your head glooms.

While you wait for peace, in the shadows of dreams;
And cry in agony, with muffled screams.

Searching for someone, who will surely care;
To listen, to hug; and your burdens to share.

At the depths of you longing, at the heights of your pain;
When the walls press closer, until you might go insane.

All is not lost, for your death garments I will wear;
And when all others fail you, I'll always be there.
...He who waits...

Herbert Charles Clark Jr.

Two Tone Love

There are times when the blood runs warm,
And your legs turn soft at the bone,
And your feet start to tingle so violently that it drives you mad.
You start to shake like there is an earthquake inside,
And your hands and arms tighten to stone,
And you perspire so much you feel a large puddle may be forming.
This deep love is a blackish-red,
like the garnet blood that runs fast.

Then there are times when the blood cools,
And your legs stiffen and your arms relax,
The shaking stops and the puddle dries.
You feel lower than the heart that just fell to your feet,
And you feel you will never feel blackish-red ever again.
You swear on your soul that you will never feel blackish-red ever again.
Because the rejection that rings in your ears,
Feels like a scorpion burrowing into your heart.
You cannot afford to feel lower than the slime this blackish-green
   represents.
You may fall in love with another,
But it will never replace the blackish-red felt before.

Ethan Mullen

Untitled

The tiny silver presents that are nestled upon this tree,
are a reminder of the love and strength that come from me.
Each little decoration will remind you that I'm watching in
admiration.
Every red bow tied upon each branch, signifies my love for you and a
second chance
The gold lifeline that's wrapped around this tree,
symbolizes the unbroken love between you and me.
The star will guide the path for you, and show you the right things
to do. The light will show you the way, as it did on our Saviour's
birth that glorious Christmas Day.
The tree that's anchored in this base, symbolizes my love for you
deep within my soul that radiates from off my face.
Alcohol and lies will be a part of our life no more,
because now I know the shame and guilt that you once bore.
Together we will take and conquer one day at a time,
but you must know that I still want you to be mine.
The memories of the music that come from Angle's wings,
will help you to remember all of our favorite things.
I put no lights upon this tree, so you will understand this message
from me.
So in praise I want to raise my cup, and I want you to stand straight
up, strong, proud and SOBER and not lit up!

Jennifer J. Vandermark

Foot-Steps

Babies run, when walking: their toddling little feet
are brief preambles to the lengthy miles they soon must meet...

Childhood steps are longer: running here and there,
the age of sweet discovery of earth and sky and air...

Teenagers dance and gyrate, rambling over town,
too absorbed in self-discovery, to ever settle down...

Then comes the Adult foot-steps: rushing through each day,
running errands - cleaning house - putting things away...
And then - before they know it - they're approaching Middle-Age,
thus ending one life's chapter, and turning a new page...

Things start slowing down a bit, and they look back to see
the steps already taken, and the new steps still to be...

Old Age: a bit unsteady, as life begins to slow,
re-living other footsteps in Mem'ry's afterglow...

And then - one day - the Final Step: a life once busy, filled,
now falters - one last heartbeat - and
   the weary
     feet are
       stilled...

Dorothy R. Cameron

Transformation

The blades of grass with soft green hue
   are silver gray with morning dew.
As Sol comes beaming o'er the horizon
   the droplets gleam as though they were diamonds.
Some heated by the morning sun
   expand to attract the smaller ones.
Gravity's influence on weight and mass
   propels it downward to water the staff.
Dewdrops on flat broad leaf plants
   are drinking vessels for bees and ants.
As Ole Sol climbs higher and higher
   the remaining moisture to vapor transpires.

Ivo Knapp

In My Dreams.....

In my dreams his skin is as soft as a bird's wing. His eyes
are the color of the soft blue sky and the tinted sea when they
   collide. And they glow like stars in the dark. When I
dream he is here, right next to me. I can hear his heart and
   see his smile. His lips like the roses in the garden as
sweet as untasted honey in the tree. In the still dusk my
   eyes burn bright, like fires in the night. The feelings I
have all come tumbling out. So I paint a picture of us with my
   words of love and lust. But even the things I know so well
can never describe the way I feel inside. My heart was caught
   and my mind swept away the moment I knew him. So my
dreams end, as softly as the breezes in my hair, when the sun
   arises to a new day.

Eliza Woody

A Rainbow In My Heart

I have a rainbow that grows in my heart,
And when I am down that rainbow will start.
It's the positive side of all that goes wrong,
and to cover my pain I must feel the rainbow strong.
It is a bandage for all of my sorrows,
and my faith for all the tomorrows.
This rainbow grows as I do,
And the only way it can tarnish is my tears left as thick dew.

Aimee L. Upchurch

The Saddest Words

The saddest words of tongue or pen
Are these four words "It might have been."

"It might have been," said the lover
When the loved one left for another.

"It might have been," said the unfaithful one
When the cheated upon said the affair was done.

"It might have been," said the one who lied
As the words of truth in his evil heart died.

"It might have been," said the one who was shy
As the love of their life passed unknowingly by.

"It might have been," say those who never try
As the challenges of life flow quickly by.

"It might have been," say those who doubt
Salvation not accepted and the light of life goes out.

Sad, so sad, how life could have been
If not for "It might have been."

Al Davenport

Reflections

The world begins and ends with me.
   Are you shocked, displeased, upset.
Don't be, that all the world begins with me.
   And I can change the world, and so can you.
For I am you and you are me.

I smile, the world responds in kind,
   I frown, the world is bleak
and all is misery.
   I listen to the sighing of the wind
That brings to me the words of love
   that say, I care, and I respond, and so will you,
For I am you and you are me.

And if I choose to see the sun
   when storm clouds fill the sky,
Aware am I of glories that can be,
   and storm clouds pass.
The sun is there, and will be there for me
   For I am you and you are me.

Doris M. Bushnell

The Gift

It happened on a sunny April day.
As birds did sing and flowers they did bloom,
a child was born. And those who saw her say
her eyes did shine, her smile lit up the room.

Her parents they did promise her much love,
would keep her safe from harm and always care.
An Angel brought to them from up above,
with eyes sky-blue and curling golden hair.

Her mother oft would watch the infant sleep
and praise the heavens for her baby sweet.
Her father, ever watchful, he would keep
guard o'er the child. No harm would e'er she meet.

And with each passing day they loved her more,
remembered not their empty lives before.

Jill M. Duquaine

Untitled

My life is coming to light before my eyes,
as darkness is replaced by a brilliant light.
This light is a beacon and as I walk through troubled,
often turbulent times,
when the end seems so very far.
I know that I will find the right road,
the road that leads me to my destiny,
my chosen path.

For this road leads me from you and the darkness that is you.
And as I leave the hurts,
the pain, and the difficult paths behind me.....
No longer am I stumbling around in the dark, lost, defeated.

Look at me, for I have emerged,
my head is held high, I am self assured and deserving.
For I am guided by the brilliance of the light in my heart.

Caroldean K. Cummings

Lonely Singer

On that morning, birds boasted their voice
As I glanced at you, I confronted a smile
The paradise was vacant; the echo of birds seemed juvenile
You love life as a fifteen year old girl

That following morning you boasted your song
I saw the birds diffusing their smile
In the garden, plants choked their leaves awhile
I posses your smile as I am touching the edge of the paradise

Winter comes early, you forgot the refrain
I search for the birds; they're all silent
Paradise is vacant; branches bow their leaves as a monument
There is only me, left singing lonely

Ha Luu

Envelop

A thousand nights I've watched myself
As I lie on the floor
My wretched heart trembling
In the hands of strangers
My precious skull crushed
Under your evil tongue
My frantic thoughts
In your dirty hands
And my eyes...
My eyes, they wander
With each blow you cast upon my confidence
My soul soars
To heavens in which I no longer believe and
To heights for which I no longer pray
As your wicked words rush
Across my face
Only to drip
From my mountain of indifference
Forged by cowardice
And raised to the sky
With only these two hands.

Darlene Mackey

I Am An American

The leaf of time is turning; the point is close at hand
For you to see the future revealed through God's great hand.
Desires of heart will quicken and find their place with thee.
Compare they fate with others who mourn but never see.

Remember always one thing that God knows what is best.
Sometimes He beings us blessings and sometimes brings us tests,
But if you'll give to others as you have now received,
You'll hold the key of wisdom unlocking as decreed.

Elyzabeth P. Flecheur

Oak

Cool day as I relax in the spongy grass.
As I look on before me, I see it standing tall.
Tiny beings with more legs than I.
Soft fuzzy creatures invading.
Why do you disturb this precious life?
The tree says, in a deep whisper, do not question them.
I feed them. I shelter them. They are my children.

The blinding sun glistens through,
where the clusters of beautiful leaves give way,
making the sight even more glorious.
It is so powerful.

The strong and weak branches mingle together
rising and falling in a unified motion.
Are you reaching out to me?
No...just the chilled breeze.
Oh, but how I am reaching out to you.
You are magnificent.

Dina F. Argus

Singing of the Little Birds

Praise our wonderful Lord!
    As I sit on my humble little porch, looking at God's beautiful
sun and enjoying the fresh, cool breeze as it blows out of the
treasures of God's stores.... I can not see the wind but I feel
it and it is so satisfying. I see many, many things but the one
thing that catches my attention is the magnificent singing of the
birds that I hear in my ears....

    Oh, what sweet singing! As I carefully listen to each voice,
to my surprise, there is a leader. He has a pitch, a key, just like
an instrument; then all the voices of the birds join in... they sing
to the glory of their king! Oh, such sweet singing! Such sweet
harmony of the bird's singing, working together....

    Their instinct comes from God. In harmony they build their
nests, going back and forth gathering straw, still they sing their
beautiful song! Together they fly away with straw in their beaks,
and as they light upon the trees they are mindful of the others,
courteous, helping each other. When the day is over they hurry
happily to their own habitat for the night.
    Amazing! So amazing is the sweet, sweet singing of the little
birds!

Heady D. Conner

Untitled

Lovely Baby, Lovely Bride
As I stand here by your side
Remembering all that we have shared,
The times we cried, how much we cared.

How I wish for you all that's true
A Love everlasting for you two.

One with honestly and one with pride
As you carry out your promise and agree to abide.

The memories of a life time now come to mind.
Passing from a child to a woman, slowly they unwind.

A gift you were, a surprise for sure
But one we grew to Love and adore.
But grown you have, and we can only remember all those yesterdays,
for now your life is about to change in many remarkable ways.

From today you become a couple, but may your hearts beat as one.
For all that your Love stands for, "this it shall be done."
For in God's house Love means a lot, no matter what the cost,
For today's today and tomorrow may never come,
don't ever chance that loss.

So for all of your tomorrows and all our yesterdays,
may you stay forever so in Love, as you are right here today.

Diana Bonney

The Battles On

The storm clouds rolled across the sky
As if to heed some distant cry,
Up came the wind with all its might
The one great army we cannot fight,
Natures' soldiers the best e'er trained
Came forth from her as a hurricane,
Winds wrath shook ocean and didn't implore
But commanded ocean to open her door,
"Let out your troops, the battles on
We attack the land this very dawn!"
Wave armies came out with a roar
White-caps all, they marched ashore,

What can man do against such odds
When nature wields her staffs and rods,
As yet no certain answers known
Perhaps when all our thoughts have grown,
We'll gentle wind, the wave and rain
And defeat the mighty Hurricane!

Becky Sprague

Fans - 1995

This year sadness looms in baseball town
    As many a fan wears a gloomy frown
They taken our pastime, that once was national
    'Twixt owner and player, they've made it irrational
We, their fans, are losing the thrill
    Of seeing the "Majors"......., maybe we never will!
For when salaries have risen to the level of crazy
    No wonder these guys have turned a bit lazy
The sport is gone, replaced by the dollar
    Feuding with bosses who wear a white collar
So here we are, with the fate of greed
    Rapidly choking away at our need
But let's not abandon our deep down love
    And pray for a miracle from up above
With two out, bases empty, the count three and two
    What do you say guys.....it's all up to you!!

Edward A. Goellner

Pa's Last Goodbye

A lonely tear fell from her watery eye,
As she heard Pa's last goodbye.
There he laid in that hospital bed
With nary a hair left on his head.

She paused and with a sigh
Remembered Pa's first goodbye.
There they stood at that train track.
After the war, he would come back.

Many goodbyes were said through the years,
But only this one would shed the tears.
The two of them had grown to care,
From rocking horse to rocking chair.

Through the goodbyes three loving children were born.
Two girls and a boy, all of who would learn to mourn.
Seventy years have come and gone,
But their love will always live on.

Erica E. Carroll

Star Bright

Star bright, star bright twinkling in the sky at night,
How I wish I were you tonight.
Twinkling high above the world, you show no signs of woe.
Star bright, star bright twinkling bright, I've seen
the death of many a poor soul. All in the name of peace.
Not for the peace of man, but for piece of land.
Twinkle, twinkle little star, what a sight you really are.

Jeffrey S. McKuen

Broken Dreams

Her impassive reflection gazed back from the pane
as she stared at the fleeting fire of a dying sun
The melodic pulse of her hardened heart
was echoed by the rhythm of the train's daring run

Phone poles marked the frames of her life
as one by one the course memories swept by
The trees of her youth swayed in the breeze
gesturing a silent and sad good-bye

Just like a moment that flashes then slowly fades
the house of her childhood gently drifted away
A place she had loved then learned to hate
for now gone were the forts and the frogs at play

Oh, now this is a picture-perfect postcard
was what some would remark upon first view
Yet hidden beneath the artist's placid image
a tear as she thought - If only they knew

It was daddy who said that he loved her best
Then mommy who fought with a vehement scream
Innocence no longer cloaked in a soft pink dress
Now bound for the future - Can she discard those broken dreams

Jeff Lysen

Dear Lady

The world's rage comes haunting
as she waist for the ending
of the new year;
West wind winds through
her wrinkled wretched ways.
The dying of another time
reminds of what was
supposed to be hers
The new man's frost hopelessly tries
to find warmth in her body's young and old.
Cries will be cried tears
wiped gone by the passing of days
while the idolized sun
passes on his way.
The harmony of hubcaps cycling
through time is not nearly enough
to comfort her. But to die once
more in his cold stiff arms
would be all that she needs
to smile once again.

Danny Reley

My Discovery

I've always tried to please the majority
To be what everyone thought I should be.
But it was an impossibility, to be like everyone and still be me.
For there's really only just one me,
Unique and special as can be. I'm not everyone and
They are not me; Thus I must be who I dare to be.
For no one knows my innermost feelings.
Whether I'm surrounded by many friends cheering,
Or alone under a tree, no one can feel what I feel but me.
Now my non-conformity to others expectations,
Is due to my recognition of my own aspirations.
For standardization causes mediocrity,
Subjection to it will cripple my individuality.
For the greatest are those who chose not to
Do what everyone thought they should do.
Who used bright thoughts of their very own,
Who saw the need to stand alone
Thus, my discovery has helped me to see
I do not exist as a majority, that I must be who I dare to be
For wherever I go I'll be with me.

Jacqueline Peters

Silence

She stands in silence
As the cold wind blows
Standing there looking
for what,
No one really knows.

Her ache is deep, pain now growing
Not one more tear will be shed
Only laughter will be showing

Her pain is real
And so deeply cut
No emotions left,
Nothing left to want

She hides herself in a cloak called strength
A cover she wears so well
Life passes her by
She stays silent
Deep within herself

She cries in silence so no once can hear
Alone in the silence
Where the cold wind blows.

Elizabeth A. Huff

Time Of Tranquility

The sun drops slowly
as the lightness subsides,
One by one they appear,
Millions and millions of eyes.

The midnight air seeps in
while the moon plays hide-n-seek,
With the scattering clouds that grip the sky
Until the sun begins to peek.

The fog blankets the morning air.
The birds welcome the day
The flowers enhance the aroma.
To remind that Spring is on the way.

A lover's gentle touch,
His kindness and sincere,
Warm and loving embraces.
A reminder that there is no fear.

A time of tranquility,
When everything is at peace.
No fear, no sadness, just joy,
For the tranquility of each.

Debbie McAllister

Street Made Me Cry

The silence of the night was shattered
as the Street came crashing in.
The insanity of the moment
with its intense violence
brought the pain all around me
into sharp focus.
A dark blue towel mistakenly moved
became the reason for an outburst
that reached to the very depths of the Street,
a hurt crying out for some relief
until the hurricane subsided.
The silence was gradually restored.
I walked and walked
to try to understand
the awfulness of the moment.
Finally I broke down
and sobbed uncontrollably.
No words could be spoken -
A cup of coffee was the only speech.

John P. Nickas

Love's Goodbye

As an actor taking his final bow, so too must we say goodbye.
As the sun sets each evening, so too shall we meet again.
Each bird of flight, and each man doth walk upon this Earth knows
time is but an ever sifting sand, which pours between the fingers.
Love says its solemn farewells, but yet too shall love be renewed.
Love's goodbye is but a farewell to Heaven's gates, whence God
shall hold you close.
In death we must depart, but soon shall I draw close.
Together In God's grace, my dear love, you and I.

Cathleen Murray-Pessolano

Scenes from the Hood

Sitting here watching the sun cast its rays upon the ground
As the wind toss the paper and dirt around and around;
Silence has fallen since the police came thru
At least for a while, I guess this is true.
Sirens ringing in the near-by air
While visions of crime are everywhere;
Tree tops blown by the winds so soft and calm,
While the birds fly high among them without any harm.
Flowers blooming day by day,
Making the neighborhood beautiful, if I must say;
Drug dealers walking back and forth in total jitters,
As life appears to be a gleam of glamours and glitters.
But we all know that this is not true,
At least not in this neighborhood no matter what you do.
Lives being claimed in gang war everyday,
So many of our black brothers and sisters having to pay;
This world we live in so cruel and unfair,
What's our defense? In a world of despair.

Alice M. Green

Heavenly Guests

An Angel slipped into their dreams
   as they tried so hard to rest
   and whispered they've been chosen
   to be heavenly guests.

The angel then stayed by their sides
   until the morning came
   and when she reached out for their hand
   mom and dad were freed from pain.

Their souls then soared to heaven
   where tears do not exist
   although here is this earthly heart
   they'll forever be dearly missed.

Grief shall not be with me
   for they left at Gods request
   I will take comfort in the fact
   they both are now heavenly guests.

For this is not the end
   for when my soul is free
   I will gaze upon their faces again
   when the angel comes for me.

Dorothy J. Fulcher

Untitled

Oh, my frail little flower
How you tremble in the soft breeze
Remain steady and fast
For stronger winds will blow
Take not refuge in the ground from which you sprang
But hold strong in the oneness of yourself
For the sun has moved in the opposite direction
And with it you must grow

Elissa Ryan

Untitled

Hold my heart, it feels cold
as time passes, it grows old.

Listen to my heart, the soft rhythmic pound
hear the sound of it, sinking into the ground.

Look at my heart, it slowly turns grey
the emptiness within it, making it decay.

Learn, from my heart, it holds knowledge of age
ask it questions, turn the page.

Live in my heart, sadness you will find.
Hear a thousand screams, that can't be left behind.

Feel my heart, it was as gentle as a dove
feel it cracking, from the loss of love.

Know my heart, talk to its despair
find its love, tell it that you're there
try to give it happiness, give it your heart,
and remember to be gentle it'll easily fall apart.

Christina Marie Stanley

Plea of Destiny

Dream with me, take my hand
as we travel beneath life's stream
beyond all depths of imagination
close your eyes and dream

fly with me beyond tomorrow, to our castle in the sky
slay my fire-breathing dragons
escape with me, fly

dance with me and destiny, watch the raindrops as they prance
take me past nowhere
run with me, dance

listen to the moon as he speaks, through the stars as they glisten
hear their never-ending fairy tales
through my eyes, listen

stay in the night with me, let your demons run and play
leave your ghosts locked in their closet
disappear in me, stay

live to die with me, take all that give
grasp my soul, don't let go
live in me, live

Jolie Nourse

The Tunnel

Lord I need to see Your face,
As we travel this darkened place.
It is so dark that I cannot see,
Your hand of grace that's guiding me.
Even though I feel Your sweet touch,
I sometimes feel I'm falling from Your clutch.
Then You grab me and hold me tight,
Taking me a little closer to the light.
My ears feel deaf and I cannot hear,
From all the disturbance and fear.
In the darkness it's You I call,
To pick me up when I fall.
You are so loving and faithful to me,
Doing what it takes to set me free.
Slowly and carefully You cleanse me inside,
Getting rid of past problems that I hide.
Thank You Lord for healing my life,
And taking me out of torment and strife.

Jennifer Hendley

The Fragrance of Love

If we would allow love to nourish ourselves.
  As well as the others we meet —-
Not strain after life and the needs there of —-
  But, quietly alert, we'd keep.

For life is here to enjoy and live.
  And when the mind is at peace
Inner energies awake - and work miracles -
  As our restless murmurings cease!

The use of love is to heal from within,
  Without the effort of self.
Happiness radiates like the fragrance
  of flowers.
And even in pain — we find health.

For often we're busy on life's thoroughfare
  And race through life — push and shove -
Never taking the time to enrich our lives.
  With the wonderful fragrance of love!

  Ida M. Lee

Our Second Chance At Love

I first laid my eyes upon you
as you were just doing your job.
My heart could not help but feel something for you.
You were just starting to live your life to the fullest
as I was just trying to live mine.
My mind wondered if you would someday see me as any girl
you looked at on the street.
I wanted to tell you I was more than just a girl sitting in a chair
but before I had a chance to, you disappeared.

Now we are in the same situation as long ago
but under different circumstances.
Each of us have experienced what life has to offer
although we have yet to share one of life's beautiful moments.
With each month that passes by we get to know each other
as best friends, yet our bodies want something more.
You fear loosing your job, while I wait patiently.
As I look up at you and smell your cologne from afar
I think to myself, "Is it other people's opinions keeping us apart
or our own fear?"
Will we give up our second chance to love?

  Jacqueline Parachu

Rain

As I hear the pitter-patter turn into a roaring
avalanche on our roof.
I lie curled upon my bed trying to go to sleep.
The rain soothes my head and relaxes me....

But then I see a streak fly through the sky
then I fear.
Waiting, waiting, waiting for the moment when the
sky will scream its wrath.
Fearing the rumble of the earth.
Then finally, the moment when the screaming begins
I feel as if the earth is shaking but then it quickly
subsides....

In the next room I can hear my baby cousin crying
from the noise.
I close my eyes and try to think of sunny days.
The rain takes away my fears and I fall asleep with
thoughts of summer.

But sometimes the thunder will awaken me again and
if I do not hear someone else wake too
I fear that I am alone in the dark, scary world.

  Erin Rex

"Ethan"

Your empty house atop a hill
Awaits the laughter and the shrill
High, longing voices of kin to come.

I'm your Mattie, you're my man.
Together the two of us shall stand
Someday, silhouettes against the sky.

What God hath joined in Holy blessing
Let no man destroy, all confessing
Their sins as well.

In separate spheres our hearts lie still
Until the reckoning of God's will.
Until then— an empty house atop a hill.

  Carrie A. Schwartzentruber

Always

And I run
away from my fears
to a place where my tears
don't sting.
Where I can't hear the criticism
where I can't hear the laughter.

And I know how I'll feel when I get there.
I'll be free
and powerful
beautiful and
strong.
I will show myself as I knew I could be.
Always.
In my mind.

  Erin Potempa

Hit The Nail On The Head

Like the steel that it implies
Be tough, be strong, be true; be wise.

Bare in mind; and at all cost.
Of who you are - and what you want.

Shed no tears - accept no defeat
Go forward, do not retreat.

For if there's doubt - banish the thought
And God speed on - for all its worth.

Success is obtained, valued, and there -
Only if - you persevere.

Remember - "I am me", I am sure
I can be - what I said.
If - I hit the nail - on the head.

  Joseph L. Reho

Up High

Silver thread jet streamer
beating my sunrise,
Is it your generals that compel you
or a secret you feel inside?

Balloon basket riders
drifting-lulling in afternoon light
you pay a pretty dollar
to soar in wingless flight

Antique bi-plane jockey,
shadowy dusk almost obscures you
save the smoky sputtering your engine sounds
What is it that lures you to the wonders of the blue?

  Carmen R. Gonzales

Winter's Sleep

The falling snow was quietly turning my yard into a
beautiful Currier and Ives winter scene. The oak that
grows near my deck was covered in a blanket of snow. It
was like a mother sleeping peacefully through the night.

She will awaken at the dawn of spring and begin her
chores without delay.

She will give birth to her leaves, and they will cling
to her, and she will nurture them.

She will be a home for the birds and squirrels, and they
will love her.

Butterflies will gaily dance around her leaves and bring
her joy.

In the autumn, squirrels will gather her acorns and
store them for their winter feast.
Beetles will bore into her bark and cause her pain.
Winds will blow and break some of her branches but she will be strong.

Some will pass her and never notice her at all; but I
will sit in her shade and sip tea. I will marvel at her love.

Sleep now, my beautiful lady. Rest well, for the night
grows short and it's almost tomorrow.

Annie Wilkerson

Sunrise

The morning twilight symbolizes the approaching sunrise.
Beautiful rays of morning sunlight transform
the dark, gloomy sky into a vivid, violet twilight masterpiece.

Moments later,
marvelous beams of sweet golden illumination
streak across the morning sky,
replacing the obscurity of night.

The morning star remains twinkling in the early morn sky;
standing defiant against the magnificent sunrise.
Golden beams of brilliant light overcome the defiant star;

The magnificent sun rises form the eternal darkness
like a phoenix ascending from its ashes
with everlasting strength and immortality.

Penetrating through the eastern horizon,
the lovely sun awakens from its sleep.
Spreading its magical, vital glow throughout the vast realm.

Demonstrating its sublime power
with its radiant yellow rays gracing our special land.
Embracing the blue sphere in its sensational warmth.

Dwayne Tunstall

Lily Pods in the Spring

Lily pods in the spring are the most
beautiful thing in my life
Just as much as my children or my wife
Lily pods in the spring
Fill my hart with joy
Just as much as Christmas or Easter for a
young boy
Lily pods are beautiful in the spring
Just as much as my engagement or wedding ring
Lily pods in the spring don't make
me suffer or sad
They don't make me angry or mad
I love Lily pods in the spring
They make me have joy and my heart
began to sing
Lily pods in the spring are everything
to me
Just like a sailor and the sea.

John Albert Britt

Dreams

Dreams are dreams that you can think about and feel.
Because dreams to me can be real.
Dreams aren't fake, nor are they phony.
Dreams are what you can think about only.
Dreams can be a nightmare, sometimes a scare
Dreams can be pleasant and your mind can feel free.
Dreams are what you make of it, bare with me you'll see.
Dreams can be erotic.
Weird, but honest.
Take your thoughts and put them together.
Then close your eyes and see if you feel better.
Once you've created your own feelings.
Picture it in your mind and let it go freely.
That's my understanding of what dreams are about.
If you give it a try I'm sure you won't be in shock.
Dreams are dreams that can come true.
Dreams are me and dreams are you.

Jo Ann Chevelle McDaniels

The Grandmother's Clock

You are in my thoughts today
Because you were in my dreams last night.
I prayed a prayer for you to stay
A friend to those who need the light,
To guide them when the way gets hard
With a kind word, a prayer or card.
In my dream you were visiting our city
And went to an antique store.
I had been browsing, looking at the antiques,
When you came through the door.
I spoke to you but you didn't notice.
A clock had caught your eye.
The most beautiful Grandmother's clock
Hanging on a wall nearby.
I stopped to take a look
As I was headed for the door
And wondered how in all my browsing.
This clock I did ignore.

Elizabeth B. Beckham

The Nighttime Ocean

Large and dark and gently lapping waves
Beckoning and calling.
Bubbly foam licking the sand
At water's edge.
Deep and vast and strong enough
To carry the water spirits to where they want to go
Always large always there
Always dark always moving
Deeply still but always moving
With gentle ripples upon the surface and
Bubbly from licking the sand
At waters edge.

Donna Madison Moore

Festival

Spring has tatted its tender lace of leaves.
Fresh new dogwood petticoats peep coyly
from under winter's long-leaf dress.
Hillsides display their panorama of delicate greens.
Azaleas open hungrily
as forsythias leave sleepily;
tulips frolic at the feet of tired jonquils—
each part expectant, patient, forbearing,
making way for the next.

Beth Cartwright

"Loneliness"

The one you see.... it is not me, I have
been lost for years. For not a soul could
ever find this place I hide my tears. My
hopes, my dreams, my thoughts, my feelings,
aspirations and my fears, all congregate
and rise against me to kill me through
the years. Why do I wear this fair facade,
and where has it led me? I feel as if my
own soul has just got up and fled me.
Aimlessly I wander down the paths I left
unthread. Aimlessly I think about the feelings
left unsaid. Why can't I flee this stupid
path I've tread for all these years? Have my eyes
been blinded by the brackish crying tears?
The one you see, it is not me, I have been
lost for years. For not a soul could ever find
this place I shelter fears.

Brigitte A. Muehlbauer

Celestial Jubilee

Crystal clear,
Before me
Spreads an awesome sight.
Around me I see,
In panoramic majesty,
The dark velvet dress
Of lovely Lady Night,
Adorned with sequins
Of city lights
And lace of feathery trees.
In hushed astonishment,
I look up to see
This lovely creature
Of beauty rare
Wearing diamonds in her hair,
For 'round her flowing tresses
A halo of starry gems
Shines resplendently,
To proclaim her queen
Of this celestial jubilee.

Jane Huelster Hanson

Seasonal Transitions

Beating a rhythm, hail drops from the skies
Before the silence of falling snow,
An eerie quiet over a white carpet lies,
Early flower blossoms no longer show.

Gusting winds whistle through mighty oaks and pine,
Constant rain pounds on window-pane,
Sleeping dog by crackling fire of flames that shine,
Fog swirls around the weather-vane.

Waterfalls appear, splashing over grey granite rocks,
Creeks flow noisily ever on downhill,
Rushing waters rise, through dams and locks,
As rivers, lakes and valleys overfill.

Long-awaited, with anticipation Spring's, timely arrival,
When Nature re-emerges for another years survival.

Jane Gary

Child Unknown

There is a child with eyes of brown.
I saw her in a picture I found
Who is she I asked, but there wasn't a sound.
So on my dresser this picture I mount,
of this small stranger with eyes of brown.

Ann Budge

Paradise

Why? Not now. I want to smile with no worries
behind it. False gratitude, negative smiles,
stale tears. My stomach constantly being tied
in knots for obvious reasons. The ugly duckling
appears. Forever was a stupid fantasy. Nothing
lasts longer than your heart wishes it to.
Change is frightening; more so when the birds
start to peck at your face, your eyes, your
nose, your ears,. Maybe blackness would be
safer than the light I feel now. A neon lava
lamp beating against my brain. I'm so confused
with the lies and pain that creep up so
slowly behind you until they are on top of your
soul, crushing every last ounce of peacefulness
you feel until only anxiety is left. One more
to go and then this journey begins. Take my
weakened personality away to a far paradise
where no one's smiles have traces behind them.

Jenny Pregenzer

Thankfulness for this Thankful Season

Thankfulness for this thankful season
Being grateful that's the reason ,
Sitting at the table thankful for your food
Thanking God you are not dirty or even nude.

Thankfulness for this thankful season
Being thankful that's the reason
Thanking him for that wonderful turkey
Wow! Doesn't that make you perky?

Thankfulness for this thankful season
Full of gratitude that's the reason,
A wonderful family, a wonderful day
After the feast you thank God and pray.

Jamel Huger

Miracles

Miracles are for those who believe, they say.
Believe and see miracles happening every day.
The crocus peeking through the ground—what beauty to behold!
All dressed in their purples, pinks and gold.
A lonely caterpillar hiding in its cocoon,
Will change into a beautiful butterfly soon.
A tiny seed might become a blade of grass or a stately tree,
Spreading its branches for all the world to see.
After the rain —a rainbow is painted across the sky,
A covenant, a promise of hope given you and I.
The greatest miracle is love—a gift for all to share,
Letting others know how much they care.
There's so much we do not understand,
As we see the touch of the Master's hand.
Believe in miracles— the answer is sure to be found,
Because the Master leaves His fingerprints all around.

Blanche Truax

I Miss You

I miss you Oh how I miss you. When are we
gonna be together the week goes by to slow.
When I'm not with you, but when we are together
It only seems so long but I wish it was for
ever I love to be close to you and for you to touch
me like no other guy has touched me before
I want to be with you forever and for you to
never let me go. I love you so and I always want
to be by your side.

Amanda Boreman

Healing

It seems like only yesterday when I walked down the aisle,
Believing all my dreams came true, just with you—just with you,

Wasn't is only yesterday that my heart was filled with joy,
As I held two little baby boys, born of you—born of you?

No, it was not yesterday, many years have passed
And all this time I told myself, sorrow wouldn't last—sorrow wouldn't
   last.

Although it's getting late in life, these dreams and hopes and plans
Still are etched inside of me, like ripples in the sand—like ripples
  in the sand.

I wanted to unearth my hopes and give birth to dreams at last,
Removing all the sadness and those imprints of a past—those imprints
  of a past.

I went to church in search for peace I thought I'd never see,
And there I was reminded that Jesus walks with me—that Jesus walks
  with me.

I heard that in the morning, at noon and through the night,
I have a hedge of angels who keep me in their sight—who keep me in
  their sight.

    Elizabeth Rock

Untitled

My dad is a caring man with a great
big heart, bigger then his hands. I
know I may get flustered at him,
but it doesn't mean I don't care.
He is one of the most caring men I know.
And I love him so. He may talk louder
then necessary but that's just him.
I may not prove it, I may not say it, but
I love so much deep in my heart for this
man. I love him so even though we have a
few differences between us. But I will
always hold a special place in my heart
for my dad, and all the things we would
do together. So give you're dad a chance
like me The Good Guy in the white hat
lives forever, he may not even know how
I love him so.

    Dana Cole

Kisses

A kiss is kissed for sundry reasons,
Birthdays and holiday seasons.
Lovers kiss to show that they care.
Sometimes people kiss on a dare.

  A mother kisses her baby.
  Do brothers and sisters? Maybe.
  Kisses are described in love tales.
  "Let's kiss and make up," seldom fails.

    Reunions prove people are kissed,
    To demonstrate that they were missed.
    Little folk a kiss may render.
    With their gentle hearts so tender.

      Some kisses from lips are but blown.
      Love from across a room is shown.
      Secret kisses, or big and bold.
      Their memories are meant to hold.

Kisses, yes, I've had quite a few.
Kisses, yes, I've given them too.

    Elaine Jarr Schuenemann

Pain II

Pain, agony and grief, where does it come from, where is the open bleeding wound I feel? Blood cascades down my body, but the color of red is not seen. Scalding hot, it races down the inside of me, is that why there is no sign for others to see?

Stifling hot air, void of life giving oxygen I gasp into my lungs and they scream for they die with each breath. Inside I shrivel and the meat loses its hold upon my bones.

I wrap my arms around myself to hold onto me, but even as I do so I feel the sting of air on the raw bleeding flesh as moisture oozes down my limbs.

Naked bones are raised over my head, fingers splayed against the sky, void of tendons and muscles needed to move, there they stay, reaching for the sky.

I stagger as my legs lose their strength, their flesh pooling around my feet, soaking into the desert sands. Dung beetles rise to feast upon my rotting flesh as the hot sun dries my bones.

Bleached bones, standing stark against the sky as the sun fades and the night winds stir and soon howl in the darkness.
The winds topple my bones and scatter them along the sand.
Moving sands creep, soon my bones are lost in their unmarked grave.

    Janet A. Barbour

My Love

My love is the world and still I remain,
  blinded by the call of your vision in dreams.

And you departed.

And I am left with all the worlds of IF we will never share.

All the tropic seas we will never sail.
All the palm fringed sunsets we will never see.
All the dances we will never dance.

With all these words, never to be shared.

All the grains of sand that would pass between our toes,
  as our hands interlock on a distant beach,
    must return unstepped upon, to the sea.

And never our ears to hear the cry of the gull,
  as our hearts smile at our being.

And never the salt wind to taste in each others lips.

Never the playfulness of the Dolphin,
  the freedom of the sailfish,
    the gaiety of the Flying Fish,
      will be ours to feel in our love.

And never the smell of an oceans rain will follow our path.

    Dick Shane

Helplessness

Pain knocked on her door today.
I could not keep it away.

Skilled strangers were attending.
I had to stand idle, wondering,

Why a Dad can't protect his Daughter
For at least a little while longer

Against every threat from no matter where,
No matter who, as long as I'm there.

A fog of despair descended on me.
A damp fear made me want to flee.

From my helplessness.

    Gene Beaulieu

Untitled

My heart is cold,
Blood no longer pumps through the
once vibrant veins.
Body cold to the touch.
Death surrounds.
You can feel my presence within
your soul
Like a cold hatred upon your heart
Do you not see me?
For I am in reach
You once held me in your arms.
I nurtured you and you made me warm.
Your touch slithered over my body,
like a snake after it's kill.
Our hearts pounded together as one
Now all that remains of us is the cold
bitterness you feel in your heart.
Warm me once again.
Awaken my soul.

Jennifer Robison

The Walls Painted Red

Scratch marks and bruises,
Blood oozing from his veins:
Yes! He's gone mad - permanently insane.

As he pounds his head
He rips seams from sheets -
His mind is a place where darkness meets.

The walls are bare white,
Only a cross hung on a single nail -
He rips and tears the room apart
And curses as he yells.

Clawing and scratching at his body,
His life hanging by a thread -
The walls of white are suddenly painted red.

Dana Thomas

Life Is Like A Tree

We branch out here, we branch out everywhere!
Blooming to our fullest beauty
Grow to we shine in the days ahead
Heavenly scent of earth awake us with sweet emotion
Sun shines to warm our hearts thru the day of life
We have our ups and downs come our way like a storm
Our spirit soars to the sky to lift our hearts.
We bud like a tree to reach our goals
Struggle thru storms like a hurricane!
Branches swing thru the wind of life
Someday we reach maturity to find life is so short
Breakaway just like a branch of a tree fallen to earth
Sets ourselves free to wonder thru life alone again!
Always thinking where we came from like a tree!

Joanne Campbell

Mine to Give

If the moon were mine to give
I'd place it in a necklace for you to wear

And if the stars were in my grasp
I'd fashion a girdle to enclose your waist

Then when this was done
I'd place the sun behind your head

Thus I would dress you with the firmament
For you are the radiant image within my life

Byron Abreu

Love

My love is like a rose
Blossoming on a summer afternoon
With each new day it grows
And shines like the moon

I wish you only knew
How much I really care
The love I feel for you
Shows how much we have to share

You light up my life
And fill my heart with joy
If only I were your wife
And there wasn't another boy

You will be my everlasting love
And your symbol will always be the turtle dove.

Cindy Bugajsky

Nocturnes

Eyes, everywhere staring at you from the dark
Blue ones, red ones, each fierce with hunger
Cold shivers run up and down your spine
You wonder now if you'll make it through the night

Howling, growling coming from the dark
Sounds alarming haunting your fitful sleep
Goose bumps appear running up and down your arms
You wonder now if you'll make it through the night

A cold shadow blows through the tent opening
Feel the eerie hush as it creeps closer to your brow
Your hair stands up as you scream in terror
You know now that you won't make it through the night

Cherry Warner

September Nocturne

Summer is waning,
  Blue skies are gray
With clouds of rain prevailing.
  The cold, chilly air fills
One's soul with preparation
  As another winter approaches
And the sun's equinox
  Reaches its destination.

Jack frost comes as a thief in the night,
  Turning bright flowers
Into a black and ugly sight.
  But Alas! In October the leaves
Are vivid and colorful hues
  Winter waits as fall lingers and
Indian summer has paid us its dues.
  For a lingering time summer stalls
In a bright month or so
  As if to ask us mortals
Is it really time to go?

Anita Carlson

Cancion De Los Angeles - II

Just after we met, the full moon
  enveloped our souls together, and I
    never knew that feeling before. A
  new sensation stirred and grew stronger
in my heart, but I could not simply
  forget the peace it would soon rob.
    Every time I think of you, I see you,
      right before my eyes; and the pain lasts longer.

Daniel J. Baker

Ned

There was catfish whose name was Ned.
I threw in my worm and hooked him in the head.
He fought long and hard as a catfish can,
But he still ended up in my frying pan!

Jim Carter

A Place

Rocks, sticks and leaves are just a few.
Bottles, paper and cans are there to.
Bird crap, dog crap and other crap to.
Bags of Trash, broken glass what are we to do?

This place we go to and what we do.
A place made for people like me and you.
We come to play, we come to eat.
I wish they would keep this place neat.

People of all races come here for fun.
It's always crowed when there's lots of sun.
Fires are going, there's a smell in the air.
A family reunion and a birthday over there.

You may have guessed, I'm talking about the beach.
It's never very far, never out of reach.
It's usually about an hour or two away.
So gather your things and go enjoy the day.

James C. Russell

Remembering

I think about you, now and then,
'bout how we had such dreams
yet, now you're gone, and I'm alone.
I've died myself — so it seems.

Your face, I see; those eyes, that smile
a wish that you were near.
But, you have left, cannot come back.
I long for you, my dear.

At times, I think I hear your voice,
and feel the warmth it brought.
That made this heart, now broken — cold —
cherish joy that's now not.

You're always in my heart and mind
so, I shall not forget
how much you loved me; oh, so much —
the moment that we met.

For now until the end of time
I'm sure we'll always know;
'tis true our love won't ever die...
And ne'er will I let go.

Aimee Vicencio

Magic

Life has burned my dreams
branded them to become a murky memory of nothing.
Life has taken its heartless shears to my white dresses
tearing them like the delicate heart of a young girl.
Life has screamed its mindless regulations and
like a merciless thief, has pilfered my hazy imaginings.
Life lines the innocent up by color
turning bright eyes blind and soft words to poison.
Life's calloused palm strikes my rosy countenance
violently pushing away its amber glow to leave only
pale yellows and sallow beiges and faint memories
of interminable youth.
Life crushes magic so swiftly and stealthily
until I am left with nothing
save empty words and paralyzed movement.

Amy Goff

World Reunion

World power over all
Break apart and fall
A little piece of something once big
Gone with a shot, never to return again
Off on a cruise of crisis and crime
Where do we go, war will decide.
Asking for help,
Praying for peace
Democracy win; Dictatorship cease
A battle rages
Conquering the frontier
Setting new boundaries
Our win is near
Making new rules, breaking the rest
Victory has come
The peak of success
It is ours for the taking
We have our own part.
We welcome the world
And the world welcomes us.

Chad M. Forshee

Breaking Through

Just as the sun
Breaks through the night,
You broke out of my dreams
And into my life.

Like a shadow that followed me
And would not part,
You stood behind the wall
That lead to my heart.

Waiting for the moment
To break through to the inside.
You then took my hand
And stood by my side.

From that day on
I knew something wonderful was about to start,
But waiting for you to break through
Was the hardest part.

Angela S. Whitesel

Hannah

Eyes filled with warm dancing light.
Bright but soft, on a hard winters night.
With them to see through all of the ages,
the stages, the rages, the full empty pages.
Hers is the life I've given from mine,
gentle of limb as a soft flowing vine.
Her mother and I to brief intertwined,
lost in our passions, emboldened with wine.
She is our mystery, our legacy, our church.
A strong living spirit to continue the search.
A search for what's truth, what is life, who we are.
A search that still calls me, and takes me afar.

I watch she lays sleeping, and dreams her sweet dreams,
of kittens and bunnies and chocolate ice cream.
I've not known such love as she gives and I feel.
Child of my flesh, an unbreakable seal.

I'll cry when I leave her, my heart will be breaking.
My mind will be shattered, my soul will be aching.
I drift on the wind from Maine to Montana.
When will I see her again... my sweet Hannah.

Christian Fickle

Peaceful Beauty

I stand underneath a cold beaten pine tree
observing the beauty of the country side

A very peaceful feeling passes over me
my body tingles at the sight

See all the small cozy little cabins
smoke gently rising from their chimneys

Rolling mountains surrounding me
small children bustling about in the snow

A stream crackling only a few yards away
steam rises from it's crystal clear waters

Squirrels playing in the branches above me
small birds chirping in the background

A slight breeze ghosting down the mountainside
carrying snowflakes the size of dimes

Am I alive, or died and gone to heaven
this beauty unmatched, and untouched

God, you have smiled upon us
I can only imagine the size of your heart

Your love for us is grander than grand
to allow us the use of this beautiful land

Billy Johnson Jr.

Love's Feeling

Why does my heart feel fulfilled,
but all the same time hollowed?
I feel I've found love so I chased it and followed.
I wonder why love makes you smile and frown?
Is it good or bad since the moments tend to be up and down?
Love also makes you feel pain. This
hurt brings on tears which resemble rain.
Who knows when love make things together or a part?
Sometimes it results what's left of
a broken heart. When a heart's broken
it's shattered. Whether love can fix it is what mattered
love's feeling is the best that's why
it's meaning to me will never rest.

Joseiy F. Garcia

What Is A Kitten?

A soft adorable little fluff,
But full of the most mischievous stuff,
A little mite that is always there,
Chewing your shoe and clawing the chair.

An independent little fellow,
Who eventually makes everyone mellow,
Even though he can't talk to give you any lip,
When you need him the most, he'll give you the slip.

A frisky little fur ball
Who leaves us at his beck and call.
And just when you want to sit down and rest,
Boy, can he ever be a pest!

A little devil who licks his dish,
And, when you're not looking -
Heads for the fish.

At his antics we might all bemoan,
But, alas, before we know it,
He'll already be grown....

Christine Ann Nishihira

A Writer's Lament

As I sit here in my Office of Solitude for a moment of silence, I
attempt to write the great book.

I gaze out the window of my Office with my eyes, the darkness of
night, the stars so bright, that I am compelled to take a look.

The task before me seems so far and distant
But I know to get this task done, I must be persistent.

And when ideas pop into my mind, to write them down, and wonder if all
makes sense
The most of my worries are to the publishers, if maybe I am to dense.

The words flow on a page, like a running stream
but when they don't flow, it is just a dream.

The book is very interesting if you like history, and is non-fiction
but to write this book is with my own conviction.

The seconds turn into minutes, then hours, and days, months, and then years
But time doesn't bother me, as I have no time to fear

And then someday it will all be finished, and I will be glad
But if my great book is not published, and all the time exerted, I
will be mad.

John H. MacArthur

Spirits of the Dark

Here in the forest where the sun sinks down, day dissolves into night.
As the wind embraces, the moon floats up, and the spirits of the dark arrive.

Now the spirits under the wind, wander close to their lost world.
A world in the eye of a thundering storm, a world of barren darkness,
a world of dreams of light, yet nightmares of solid blackness.
Though a light still glimmers, as a star in the sky.

And the call of the hawk still echoes, echoes off the steep valley walls.
Walls that rise to the clouds, and never stop going.
Walls that dwarf the great mountains to the north.
Walls that shadow the wolf's cave.

A shadow where the wolf runs. A shadow where the wolf feasts.
A shadow that belongs to the wolf.

A wolf racing with the wind, racing with the spirits,
racing toward the sinking moon through the terrible dust.
Racing to its stench filled cave, with creatures of the dead.
Racing to its stench filled cave, before light returns again.

Now the spirits of the dark return, return to their lost world.
And now the sun has risen, yet night will come again.

Ian Mason Kennedy

I Wonder

On a hot and humid afternoon, a knock came on our door
A stranger stood there, peering in, he looked so thin and poor
He said, "Could I please have a drink, with a slice of bread to eat?
And could I sit down upon your lawn, and rest my weary feet?"
As he quenched his thirst with cold iced tea, and ate the ham on rye
His soft voice spoke, as he turned away, and brushed a teardrop from his eye
"I've hitch-hiked up the Eastern coast, and picked fruit along the way
I'm heading for New York my friend, I'm going home to stay"
As he removed his old run-over shoes, we couldn't say a word
He had worn his socks through heel and toes, his feet were raw with blood
He winced with pain, as we washed his feet, and softly patted them dry
We helped him on with clean white socks, then he leaned back with a sigh
"May God bless you friends, and give you peace, may good heath always be yours
May the Lord protect and keep you, and let Angels guard your doors
May the good Lord let the sunshine, light up your life each day
Now, thanks to you, I can travel on, so I'll be on my way"
As he walked on up the highway, he turned around and waved
Our hearts were filled with gladness, for the poor man's feet we'd saved
I couldn't help but question, how this stranger happened by
Like a story from the bible, I'll always wonder why

Helen C. Walker

Waiting

I wonder ...
As I watch the jet streams play tic-tac-toe in the cold blue morning
  sky,
I wait and wonder what will be, as each new day goes by.

I wonder ...
Are you a precious baby girl, so sweet with smiles and sighs?
Or are you a sweet new baby boy, with mischief in your eyes?

I wonder ...
Fair haired or dark, with dimples and curls, and eyes of brown or
  blue?
So many choices for God to make as He watches over you!

I wonder ...
With this big new world for you to see, as God trusts you to our care,
Will I be able to show you that you're safe, and I'll always be there?

I wonder ...
Though I carry you with me, my precious one, for only a short time,
Do you know my heart will always hold you close, God's gift,
  this baby of mine.
Darlene Butler

Niagara

I've seen the birds, the trees, the golden leaves cascade in Fall,
  a field of green with morning dew, I've heard a robin's call.
I've seen the moon afloat on the great Pacific, too,
  a shim'ring silv'ry path that beckons 'crost a sea of blue;
The timid fawn at edge of wood; the sunfish in the brook.
Of all the treasured sights I've seen still I'd not had a look.
For now, I say, I've seen a bit of heaven here on earth;
  'twas surely made by hand of God, no man could place its worth.
This raging mass that bobs and swirls along its rocky bed,
  is blue, then green before she hits the precipice ahead.
Now white she'll dash, a velvet roar, to meet the rocks below,
  a rainbow in her veil of mist that tries to hide the flow.
Come fill your eyes with this outrageous beauty and her might,
where scores stand spellbound, as have I, before this wond'rous sight.
Could I but use these meager words that fail to give her due?
Niagara, Niagara... Yes, God did smile on you.
Eledef Rednaxela

The Most Devoted Daddy of the Year Award

To George
For: having chosen to put his work as a deeply dedicated
Brilliant barrister on the back burner for
House spousing-and priority parenting

And: Instead of spending most of his work week
Battling bureaucracy and righting wrongs
He has been bonding with baby Christopher
Changing nappies instead of notices

And exchanging: Defendants for dependents
4:00 meetings for 4:00 feedings
Welfare rights for sleepless nights
Briefs for burps
Clients for colic
Food stamps for formula
Litigation for laundry

And: Spend downs for spit ups
Bettina Chapman

No Regrets

Warm days of spring
  bring vivacious frolicsome
amongst the young and old
Frivol away coats and the helter skelter clutter of life
  Flirt wantonly with the warmth of the sun's ray
Relish the warmth, as if,
    it were the touch of a lover's caress -
    absorb the beauty
    hear the symphony of life
    smell the fragrance
Capture the essence of No regrets -
Jessica C. Van Benthuysen

The Dawning of Spring

The blessed dawn when shadows part
Brings joy of living to fill my heart
The softness of the gentle breeze
Whispering faintly through the trees
The cooing of the Mourning Dove
Affectionately calling his lady love
The Robin's hustling here and there
As if they had little time to spare
The flowers springing from the earth
And squirrels scampering through the turf
With the cold of winter finally past
And the glorious spring here at last
We watch the dawning of each new day
Knowing Earth's beauty is here to stay
Esther Scelonge Janes

The Breath Of Life

Ever so quickly, a tiny infant breathed and
  brought ecstasy to the hearts of her parents.
With God's glorious gift surrounding her
  she entered into her earthly residence.

Ever so swiftly, her life was lived
  flowing harmoniously as God had planned,
Experiencing the joys and sorrows
  which mortal life constantly demands.

Ever so wisely, she used her time
  living her one life given by God,
Using her talents, sharing her love,
  giving of herself as she traversed this sod.

Ever so instantly, a beautiful life ceased
  with the out-flowing of breath, as God planned.
She entered her eternal, celestial home
  walking happily with God, hand in hand.
Joyce Barrett

Untitled

Love is a delicate kiss barely
brushing the lips.
  Knowing there is someone there
to love you.
  Being reassured that you are unique,
  To that one and only person that
you love back.

  Love is a gentle smile that stays with
you all day,
  Reminding you that someone is
thinking of you.
  Filling your day with hopes and
dreams.
  And thoughts of your love in the future.
Brooke Ashley Cook

Burning Flowers

A smoky essence brought into the air
Burning ashes, inflamed eye lashes
Bloody gore, melted skin
Finally lashed out the pain she was in
Alarms sing out, grave is dug
Cigarette burns on a once purple rug
Destroyed as her soul, she's finally whole
Peace is complete, flowers at her feet
The poison can no longer rape her
Clouds are above
Smiling down with happiness and love
Her floral dress is blowing in the wind
No longer scented of a burning fire
Of a distraught desire
She is finally at peace, growing flowers at her feet
A field of pure glow
Reflected of the things she did not know
She has all the power
She's rid the essence
Of the burning flower. . .

Dominique Coppola

When I Die

I want to be remembered, not as a wondered woman,
but a human being who lived her life to the fullest.

I want a simple coffin of earth and sky,
of accomplishments and joyful memories.

I don't want a fancy funeral,
I don't want flowers and black lace veils.

I want my soul to be free,
Free of make up and fancy clothes, free of tears and complaints.

I want to walk out on a cool meadow,
look around and see green fields and grassy hills dotted with spring
flowers,
I don't want to hear a car or a plane over head.

I want to hear mother nature whisper,
There are people in this world who respect natures beauty more than
their own'

She will be sitting next to me looking out upon her last open field,
wondering if her creations will come back after she has died,
or become part of man's artificial world like the rest of her creation.
When I die?

Elane Wright

Hidden Talents

Mr. Lee lives not near to
but actually in a tenement in Harlem
   with old rubber tires lining the living room floor
   - jagged and painted in fabulous colors.

"This is a wonderful place" he says
waving his arms at stripped-down cars and dilapidated buildings,
   because it is so near to a junkyard
where he can go and get things he never dreamed of in China.

Things like old plastic buckets, some cracked pottery,
rusting and bent fenders off of Japanese cars,
a toilet seat with almost nothing wrong, knobs from ovens,
mop and broom handles, a discarded but still living
scefelera tree, and any other thing he can change and arrange

Behind painted windows, through which no light can possibly pass.
Angling a bright orange lamp in a corner
for the sun coming up or the sun going down,
altering the space
observing how the landscape changes,
sometimes crawling on the floor
to see just how it changes from below.

Debbie McKenna

Millions And Me

I'm better off than most, or so they say
but at twenty one I've nothing to toast.
The party is fine, but in the morn
I'll think to crime, for I've not one dime.
I'd like to toast, to my house on the coast
and my lavish roast, but I can't
for I'm twenty one, and I've nothing done.
Ben's got his jag, I've a shirt and fiber in my bag.
I'm sure of nothing, maybe one thing.
My life is rotting. My hopes and dreams
have been shattered by government schemes.
Get out and try, people cry. I've done that
and thrown my hat, keep the faith.
Michael Jackson would say
but he's millions to throw away.
He explodes on stage, before him
A sea of people which swallow me.
Covered by millions, I'll never be seen
but I know one thing, I'll always be me.

Ciaran Lambe

Last Night

When a woman says "no," she means it to the letter,
But compassion they won't show, as long as they feel better.
As her clothes begin to tear, now becoming shreds,
another cross for her to bear, another victim upon this bed.
She can hardly wait to shower, to forget it ever occurred,
but with every passing hour, her nightmares will return.
Who's fault was it? Who is SHE to blame?
She did not ASK for this, but to both men she's "fair game."
Her girlfriend does not worry, she thinks all will be alright,
but the VICTIM wants to hurry, just to get on with this night.
Now the victim is alienated, "girlfriend" calls me a whore.
Because it was me that her man violated,
Was it my fault he found her a bore?
I really couldn't help it - for I DID kick and scream,
But girlfriend can not believe that I was double-teamed!
Despite the woman's pleas when a woman cries "no,"
She is not trying to tease,
As her bruises start to show,
The RAPISTS' abuse is still hard to see.

Jeriesha Williams

Intent

Crystal feelings inside are pure
But feelings of evil should not be.
We are all drawn to adventure,
But by all means, do we really see?
The cloud has descended upon our sight,
In the fog we invent our existence.
We hold onto this belief oh so tight,
Until the world comes into acceptance.
Our mission is for the good,
We believe that we are right.
But in this cloud we never understood,
We just marched into the fight.
When the glory finally becomes ours to grasp,
Will we still view things the same way?
Please undo my personal clasp,
For my beautiful cloak seems to have a fray.

Jeremy Espeseth

Never Meant To Love Me

He never meant to love me
but he does love now
He never meant to love me
but it happened anyhow

When he looks at me
those eyes tell me what he can never say
It started out just as intimacy
now neither can break away

When he pulls me close
it's like the world stop turning
I'd like to shout and boast
he's the man who satisfies my yearnings

I love him! I love him!
This is not just a whim

Will we ever declare
for the whole world to hear
Just how much we care
No — not ever I fear

Alma L. Faulkner

Tuxedo

I never dream I would wear a Tuxedo
But here I am on my daughter Jayne's wedding day
As the father I feel very proud and very lucky
For my dear daughter to marry a macho man

He is tall dark brown and handsome
She looks beautiful beside him
You are looking at a royal couple
The picture makes you think of the cinema

You have read the likes of this in a story book
Lloyd and Jayne are real not a dream
Imagine how happy my daughter can be deep in her heart
I thank God for giving her share of happiness and love

God bless the father and mother of the bridegroom
And everyone in their family tree
God bless all their friends
Who join in to give their blessings

God bless my dear wife Remi and my older daughter Joan
With all their dedication devotion and love
And may God bless me and my shadow
Celebrating with you all me wearing a Tuxedo

John V. Ayson

The Great Escape

The night was dark and silent; no light shone in the cell.
But his eyes had grown accustomed, and now he could see well.

His spirit longed for freedom, for truth, for liberty.
He beat his hands against the wall, he cried to be set free.

But his captors did not answer; his protests were in vain.
So he stopped to plan his great escape from the prison where he'd
    lain.

He could not hope to break the bars; his strength was not that great.
And he lacked the tools to tunnel — he'd have to scale the gate!

With bravery and courage, he climbed the slippery wall,
Then hoisted himself o'er the top, taking care that he not fall.

With nearly cat-like silence he dropped onto the floor.
Then doubt welled up within him as he faced the final door.

But he firmly grasped the handle, and with joy upon his face,
He found it turned beneath his touch — then free, he left that place.

Rejoicing in his freedom, far from that cell he fled —
Until his Mommy caught him, and put him back to bed!

Jon Raibley

Foolish Young Man

I call myself smart
But I am a fool
I try to look tough
I try to act cool

Underneath I am insecure
But I mask how I feel
I can act very good
But do I know me, for real?

It seems very clear
Especially to me
I know what to do
I know who to be

But I cannot do it, I just don't act right
I feel like a hypocrite, very confused, narrow in sight

I try to forget and just live my life
Not worrying too much, not dwelling on strife

But my thoughts they return, figuring out every plan
Am I really thinking deep, or just a foolish young man?

Barry J. Fagerholt

Relationships

Relationships seem to come and go,
But I am not a person who cries like there's no tomorrow.

As long as I live,
Love is what I am going to always give.

People might not realize it now,
But a person as nice as me is hard to come around.

I just pray that I will have success and fame,
And fans who yell whenever they hear my name.

I do not understand why is it hard for me to find a mate,
But nice things come to those who wait.

I am a person who is very strong,
And I am going to move right along.

God blessed me to be very smart,
And to have a good heart.

I know that there's someone who is waiting for me,
And hopefully one day we will have a family.
In the meantime, I will maintain my dignity.

Clarence Easter

Everlasting

Dedicated to Nancy and Tom

I can't touch you,
    but I can feel you presence
My eyes do not see you,
    but your image is etched in my mind
Though your body can never again lie next to mine,
    our souls will forever be entwined.

I know you'd want me to be strong,
    and with your guidance, I'll carry on
When obstacles stand in my way,
    I know all I need to do
        I'll focus on the blazing star
        I've chosen for you
    The strength, the laughter, the power that were yours
        will fall from the sky and fill my soul

I didn't say good-bye, but I know in my heart why
    You will never be away from me,
    our love will never die...

Danielle Kallenberger

Dream Girl

I have wondered, I have thought hard,
but I cannot discard
The thoughts I have in store,
For once I try not to think of you,
my thoughts come more an more.
Yet! Why should I care,
My wants I share,
They are my thoughts of you,
you may not understand me
but yet I think you do.
I think of you as my dream girl,
and I yearn to find a place in your heart,
I know that I may not find it,
I knew that much from the start.
However I didn't know my thoughts
could lure me on,
and make my heart happy and free,
and I didn't know my dream girl
that this could happen to me.

Clinton Henry Eary

Beware Of Dogma

I've heard the story of how we begin to remember.
But I don't know the answer to the question,
"How long should faith last?"
No one talks about the disillusion when May becomes November,
As we rush into tomorrow, learning to forget the past.
Life is a series of trade-offs and silent frustration
Made easier by calling indecision "predestination."
It lessens the price to see life as a gift or a loan.
But the cost is too great when the sacrifices we make are our own.
Maybe it's easier to believe that the dream has died,
To awaken and live, while ignoring the nightmare inside.
But I'm tired of saying I'm sorry for what I'm thinking of;
Tired of making excuses, tired of making love.
So I count the days and the regrets
And measure time with cigarettes.
Running scared and furious;
Trying to kick the dog named curious.

John N. Dornan

All Torn Apart

There is something on my mind
But I don't know what to say
Your in my heart, your in my dreams
I think about you every night...and day

Where have all our good times gone
Please tell me what went wrong
We parted to our separate ways, reality just seems to fade
away I've told you that we're falling apart, but you said
it wasn't so. You gave me a hug ensuring it's true
But after today I guess I.. don't know

The ashes of my burning heart
Have been scattered by a blowing wind
Since the day you took your love away
And said you'd never come back ... again

Living without you is as hard as can be
I'm tossing and turning on a restless sea
Like a jigsaw puzzle you'll see my heart
Stashed in a box all torn... apart

The only leaving I'd like to see
Is you, my love, believing in me

John H. Bosscher

Untitled

I can not express the wonder of God.
But I know He is real and He listens to me.
So all ye who are weary with life's mysteries
believe in God's goodness for He lifted me

Life has not always been easy for me
But God heard my cry and listened to me.
He lifted me up and gave to me
The strength to carry on in spite of tragedies

He'll give you the strength to carry on
The courage to be what He wants you to be
It isn't really necessary to get down on one knee
Let your heart bow down in simplicity

There's only one answer to life's mysteries
It's the faith we have in a God who sees
He'll lift you up and make you free
Giving you the courage to live your life with dignity

He'll listen to you
He listened to me.

Christine Webb

I Am No Longer Claire

I know it's a sin to come here at night
But I know I can't win the battle tonight
I know it is wrong to be here with you
But I am no longer strong and this I must do

If it is forbidden to love you so
I'll keep it hidden where no one can go
I'll remove the ring that brands me his
In your arms I'll cling when you give me a kiss

I'll feel your fingertips doing wonders in me
While your expert lips set my heart free
I'll cry out your name and clutch your hair
I could feel no shame, I am no longer Claire

Claire is another's and that is not me
For I am your lover, a mother is she
Claire is a housewife, a woman just there
She's no more alive for I'm no longer Claire

Elba Junco

"Christmas For Eleanor"

Eleanor is a pretty name, I have no relatives of the same,
But I know of one whom it's done good,
You know who I mean, or at least you should.
She travels all over, here and afar,
It seems like her life is guided by a star.
She's been to Australia and England I guess,
She's getting to be an honest to goodness pest (citizen)
She goes here and there, and then she'll come home,
To stay for awhile, and then again roam.
I've heard it said that right around Christmas,
Santa looked for her, the President's miss'us.
He looked all over, here and there, and no one had seen her,
  hide 'nor hair.
He went to Russia, and England too,
And was off to Japan, but that wouldn't do.
So where do you think the miss'us was found?
Home asleep in her bed safe and sound.
So he delivered the presents he had for her,
The no-good darn scoundrel, the stinker, the cur.
The present that most got her tinker unfurled,
Was a full colored map of the whole dog-gone world.

Genevieve M. Fenwick

Who Defines Culture?

I used to be uncouth.
But I think the trend is to be cultured now.
I'm writing poems and reading the classics.
Who'd have expected it from the "dumb jock?"
I even went to a ballet.
But who says watching Hacksaw Jim Duggan body slam Razor Ramon
while eating a bag of pork rinds isn't cultured?
Maybe art is Snoop Doggy Dogg or Jim Hendrix and his guitar, or a
gang symbol spray painted on the side of the D train in the
New York City subway system.
Maybe Sports Illustrated's swimsuit issue or Archie comics are
  classics
or the Mona Lisa was smiling because DaVinci had belched.
And who's to say that running over another human being with a piece
of old pig tucked under your arm isn't as graceful as women in tutus
walking on their toes?
I used to be cultured.

Craig Carter

Halloween

Halloween is lots of fun.
But I'm sure glad when it's over and done.

Now that its over I can boast.
I wasn't afraid of those goblins and ghosts.

Or skeletons hanging from the trees.
Wobbling, bobbling and bending their knees.

I heard goblins howling and crying.
They sounded as if they were dying.

It made me shiver, it made me shake.
It made me have a tummy ache.

Yes, Halloween is lots of fun.
But I'm sure glad when it's over and done.

Ann Palazzolo

"Don't Worry My Love"

I know we're too close to feel this way.
But it's my heart that's talking the words I say,
And I know you must think I'm a little insane.
Or maybe I'm not using the good part of my brain.

But don't worry my love,
I'm under control.
I'll just love your body,
With my heart and soul.

'Cause you were closest to me,
When you were the furtherest away.
And I'd wake every morning,
And read the sweet words you'd say.

So just hold my hand,
And feel the passion play.
It's the purest foam,
That you'll find these days.

But don't worry my love,
I'm under control.
I'll just love your body,
With my heart and soul.

Brian K. Wedding

Untitled

Truth was on the table
but no one chose to eat.
Some prefer darkness rather than light,
blindness rather than sight.
I shake them off my feet.

Let not my salt lose its savor.
Let me always trust on you LORD.
Melt their hearts with my prayers,
show them what faith is for.

My blood stained hands of many waters,
reach towards heaven with humble abode.
The spirit is willing, the flesh is weak,
His mercy endureth, his grace saved my soul.

Though I pursue you as a chosen vessel,
the strength to do so comes from the LORD.
For men to seek their own glory is not glory.
I'm not at fault if my love is abhorred.

Cecil Moore

No One

I use to think that friends were forever,
But now I know they're no one special,

I use to think you could tell a friend anything,
But now I know they'll use it against you,

You see I use to think that I was a friend,
But now I know that I'm no one, too,

Although I've tried to be real cool,
I have always been treated like a fool,

So now that I realize, it has opened up my eyes,
To see the world, as a big ball,
With a bunch of nobody's, stuck on it,

From the day I was born,
Till the day I can remember,

That special someone,
Was no one too...

Antonio Morales Ibarra Jr.

Riches of the Sea

A treasure one may think would be, that of silver and gold
But one's heart of joy is a treasurer's find, a true jewel of the sea.
Coins clink and jingle when loosely dropped from an open hand
Shells of the sea, jewels... if you will.

The Sound... as it subsides
A beauty lays forth its riches for whosoever to discover.
Its wealth is only to the beholder, but a true jewel of the
sea, that clamors and jingles as if gold or silver.

An echo to the ear, with the sound of the sea
A find that was triumphant in its beauty.
One would think three wishes would be spared, but only to that
one's imagination.
This jewel's beauty is captured in God's creation... of a shell.

A box or container, a now resting place for the treasure...
carried far onto shore for all eyes to witness the splendor.
A true beauty... deep and perpetually embedded,
it shall never tarnish nor fade
an ultimate lifetime. As if a religious faith... forever it is yours.

Joseph T. Hutchinson

Swept Away

She knew there was a Gale Alert
But she didn't heed the warning.
The wailing wind should have made her flee
But she hardly knew 'twas storming

She'd denied the truth as he sailed away
Into twilight, ahead of the tide.
She'd told herself he'd be back again
But she felt so empty inside.

Clouds had been forming for quite some time
She'd thought they were meant for another
Refusing to acknowledge the signs;
That showed he'd found a new lover.

First came the mist, and then the rain
But straight and tall she stood
Watching for his ship to break the horizon
Though she knew that it never would.

For days she stood watching and waiting
With hope welling deep in her heart;
'Til the storm swept the lovelorn lady to sea
With a heart tossed and torn apart.

James J. Jackson

Emotions

She loved him once a year ago
but she has had to let him go
it was when her innocence ran wild
she knows now she was only a child
he was a man of twenty-one
oh what this relationship could have done
she loved him with all her heart
but the signs were true
they had to part
that once young girl has now grown up
the split in her heart
has almost patched up.
She saw him just the other day
and with her emotions
that man can still play
but this time he was not the same
he was now just a man
with perverted ways
isn't it funny
how your emotions can change?

Claire Rooney

Tolerance

In a world where to tolerance is talked about,
but still living in a society that won't tolerate.
Discussing the fact of unity,
with people who will never unite.
Living in a closed circle,
where things go round and round
but no one can find a corner.
What in my world will it take,
when people can no longer hate?
Acceptance of difference is what's needed
but difference is just not acceptable.
Change — the world must find.
But is it changeable - can you alter the mind?

Ashley Dore

Yesterday

"But that was yesterday."
"But that was yesterday."
"But that was yesterday."

We heard the constant repetitious voice
Before we saw her gerichair.
From beyond the present came the words:
"But that was yesterday."

From daytime, deep, unconscious repeat proclaimed
Her heartfelt philosophy.
"But that was yesterday."

Hail hammered corn and beans to soil "But that was yesterday."
Radium treatments came the following March
"But that was yesterday."
Tony totaled the new, red Chevy truck
"But that was yesterday."
The pain and tears are past "But that was yesterday."

"Sun warms the world.
Spring comes in May.
Joy lies ahead," she said.
And heaven, too, for "That was yesterday."

Cecelia Weaver

The Flower

I am yet a seedling covered with the winder snow,
but the warmth of the earth helps my roots to grow.
In the spring of my being I will reach upwards
toward the light, to grow even stronger and blossom
when the time is right.
Then the world may behold a flower
so delicate.
A brilliant multi-colored miracle
with a heavenly scent.
Storms may bend me,
my stem might break.
But with each spring,
I will awake.

Bernice A. Paradissis

Seems Like A Game

People come and go,
but there is one thing they do not know.

What will come of tomorrow,
they do not know if it will be joy or sorrow.

It is all part of the master game,
life is what they call it and it is to blame.

But don't waste time to figure it out,
it is to hard, it is the ultimate bout.

So spend every minute like it is your last,
look to the future and remember the past.

Jason Theriault

Untitled

A sparrow's eggs are cracking open
in a nest high above.

A cardinal's chasing one like him
for a chance to prove his love.

A Robin's singing to everyone
her beautiful song of life.

And all the while there's a family indoors
who will argue into the night.

Christine Clegg

Red And Blue

Roses are red, violets are blue
but these colors are lost when taken from view
of my eyes that have searched for the violets so dark
just to think that these flowers bring changes in heart

Roses are red, violets are blue
but this mixture is bland when looked on too soon
by the eyes that have searched for the roses so bright
just to think that the flowers sing changes tonight

Roses are red, violets are blue
but the petals must fade when seen by the few
sullen eyes that have searched for the violets so long
just to think that these flowers bring changes in wrong

Roses are red, violets are blue
but the moment has come that I must show the truth
to the eyes that have searched for the roses before
just to think that the flowers won't change anymore...

but they will
Carl Warren Fluharty Jr.

Shadows Of My Past

Shadows of my past sometimes darken my days,
  but they are soft shadows, with no sharp edges.
Like those of a tree cast on a lazy, hazy, hot summer day.
  They steal in quietly like a cloud on a spring breeze.

These shadows bring the smiles and smells of childhood.
  Memories of ice cream and kites.
Long walks along shady paths and the security of being a child.
The thrill of just being alive, with the world at my fingertips.

These shadows on my soul leave no darkness,
  they lighten my mood with the brightness of youth.
They leave me with the light of my past to show me
  the way to my future.
Blaire M. Harms

Untitled

Sickness and sorrow comes to us all.
But through it, we grow and learn to stand tall.
For trouble comes as a parcel.. a part of one's life.
And no one can grow without struggle and strife.
The more we endure with much patience and grace...
The stronger we grow and the more we can face.
And the more we can face, the greater our love
And with love in our hearts there's more concern of...
The pain and the sorrow...they live everywhere.
So through our tribulation, we learn to share.
Bob J. Twitchell

Love is a Thought

Love is a thought, if it sees with its mind
But true love's meaning is to start with a sign
To give love is hard, even if you know it
Hopefully, before we die we learn how to show it
We make great progress when we make a start
To see, not with the mind, but only with the heart
A long time loving true heart doesn't make
When we play games with each other and
Feelings we fake
So in order to live life to the hilt
We must not do the things that make us feel guilt!
Julie B. Garrett

The Human Condition

We are all supposed to be made in God's image
but when looking around and seeing all the
evil things we are all capable of
I can just hear our Saviour up above moan, oh no'

Whatever happened to love, kindness, compassion and love
for our brother?
Whatever happened to respect for our father and our mother?

I really don't think God had a hand in any of this
I think the Devil has been working overtime, hit or miss.

What can we do to turn things around
Before we make our journey heaven bound?

I hope I can vow not to commit any more sins
and to think twice before I do whatever to be with the crowd that's in

I hope that when I am making my way up Jacob's ladder that the gates
of Heaven will spring open wide, and Jesus will enfold me in His
loving arms and say, "you made it" and throw all the bad things aside

I can then say, thank God, my earthly journey is over
I have left behind all sickness and misery, my everlasting life is
about to begin, and I can rest in peace with a happy grin.
Jean Campbell

In the Day

In the day a smile is on my face,
But when night comes to fall, I've lost it all.
I lay in my bed, as I bow my head.
Watching those tear drops fall down my cheek,
for now I can barely speak.
I'm all caught up living in a fantasy,
where everybody is what they want to be.
There's no wrong but only right.
There's no hate but only love.
People together living on the beach side by side feet by feet.
Where all their worries are past behind, so they just keep walking
that straight line where you never have to turn back.
The question is why?
It's because I'm living in a fantasy that will die!
Davina Garza

Beck

Watercolor when I think of you.
But where myself is sunk the only hue
is dimness; golden wealth is rich pretense
and treasured eyestrain in opaque regrets.
In clutching tales of what the divers do
my eyes are gagged, my forehead knotted through
by greedy fingers of my arrogance —
I sometimes feel as though I swim in nets —

It is humility to rise to hooks
while fully knowing that the air will drain
your gilded life and bloody-pin your flukes;
but you know grounded prospects are the main,
and brief and breathless stands are worth the view
of silver stars, coral bars, endless arcing blue.
Clare Ximena Gailey

"Soul's Lament"

Speak not to me you ghost of heart's desire!
I care nothing for you can't of sweet revenge
For my soul will ever breathe with burning fire
I cannot accept rejection to avenge.

For I am life, you but a shadow in her mist
And faceless, fade away into the dawn
And sunlight touch the earth. A lover's kiss
The fleeting future lies. I am not gone.
Gloria L. Chabasol

Life

Relationships are played for - longed for
but why do we wish for unhappiness
No one is a perfect friend, spouse or daughter
therefore you always hurt the one you love.

Love, does anyone really know how to love
I know I don't.

Guilt, the left-overs
it lingers like the smell of onions
a potent reminder.

A vicious circle
longing for something
that ultimately brings the familiar odor of onions.

Julie Inman

Lament for Sis (1935-1965)

It's been thirty years.
But you were so much older.
I didn't understand my fears.
You were first - thus, much bolder,
and I didn't know how to be your friend.
Then... You died.

We were of the same ilk -
as coarse as burlap or as smooth as silk,
as sneaky as bourbon or as wholesome as milk -

with a spunk fashioned by similar tailors -
lusting for living, ranting as sailors,
longing for travel (our town: our jailer).

It's been thirty years.
(Seven years isn't so much older.)
I know me now; have shed many tears.
My spunkiness? Not any colder,
and I'm ready to be your friend.
But... You've died.

Donald L. O'Dell

Friends And Lovers

You are what you are and you do what you do
But you will never alter the fact of my feelings for you
I am what I am and I do what I do
That is why I must put these lonely miles between us two

Your deceit and your games and your con man lines
Will play no more with these heart strings of mine
My self worth has been altered and my pride has been bent
But the strength of my mind will never be totally spent

I will never forget your Tennessee twang
As we conversed and we laughed over coffee and tea
Or the passion shown in your lovely blue eyes
As your body gently and greatly moved against me

I know I am totally all woman
And you certainly are all man
But my independence and strongwillness
Has strained your patience as much as it can

And so with these final words I say "Goodbye"
As the tears once again begin to flow
Take care of yourself and those beautiful boys
For at last I must leave you and go.

Diana L. Meyer

O.J. Simpson

I'm not upholding what they say you've done.
But you're a father and you're also a son.
I'm aware that mother Simpson's heart is broken.
But God has a word, that has to be spoken.

There's nothing too hard for God to do.
What He's done for others, He can do for you.
Remember He's opened eyes of the blind.
He has also turned water into wine.

There's so much of this we don't understand.
We will just have to put it all in God's hand.
I can't say what was on your mind.
Just wait on God, He will give you a sign.

Keep your eyes on John 3:16.
Study for yourself and you'll know what it means.
I'll be on my knees for you, day and night.
I'll pray without ceasing, I know that's right.

I'm asking God to keep your mother strong.
Praying that her wait won't be very long.
God is good all of the time.
Keep calling on Him, He's easy to find.

Hortense Anderson

Life

Life is short, it may seem long,
But you're going to have to live a full life, and be very strong,
You've got to live today, like there's no tomorrow,
You want to be happy, and not live in sorrow,
We see people come, we see people go,
We don't want to run, we don't really know,
It seems like a play, the acts and the scenes,
We're all on a stage, what does all of this mean?
I woke up in the middle of the night, I put my thoughts on paper,
I want people to have my sight, right now and not later,
I have a small child, but soon I'll be old and gray,
It may seem a bit wild, but I wanted to have a say,
So it may all seem cruel, we live and then we die,
But we must follow the rule, and try not to sigh,
It will be a good journey, if we take one day at a time,
Don't live life in a hurry, and everything will be fine.

Darlene Dumpit

Our Love

God has shown grace upon an undeserving soul
by granting me a wish of true love to hold
by showing me a path to what is for me true happiness
my gratitude pours down and consumes me
now
all that is me all that I breathe for
all my heart beats for is to cherish our love...

...'til the sun doesn't shine 'til the moon is but a glimmer
'til the waves of the ocean are but a shimmer
'til the sands of the shore
disappear forever more
'til the birds don't sing
when the season is spring
'til the children cease to play
on a bright sunny day
'til the life in my soul grows dark and cold

When the hands of time have whisked me into a memory
below or above
all that is me will still cherish
our love.

Eric J. Quarles

The Pavers of Our Way

The Pavers of our way—the somewhat forgotten ones,
By the children who depended on them for their sustenance
and provision of clothing and education
By the young employees who learned from them and of them
By the government who took part of their wages, supposedly
to be put up for them when they became old and could no
longer work
So that those wages they took from them might be given
back to them to be provided for, to depend on
Nothing that the government would give them, but their own.
And yet, how sad, the government still takes from them
and are penalized for having worked and having laid some
of those wages for the future
And the children—still, when they should be there for
them are not,
too busy, with their own, laying up for what?
Maybe they'll wake up and take notice—-
They, too, will one day become old,
They will be the "somewhat forgotten ones"

Elsa D. Solis

Sea of Thought

Gasp the air and fill thy lungs, I sit down
by the Sea.

The early dawn, all alone;..... my thoughts
and me.

Set adrift, sequestered thoughts, roll out
entwined in tide.

New ones form, on crest of blue, come breaking
to the mind.

The Sea bares gifts through rows of waves,
and cool misty breeze.

The knock is one of thunderous sound,
asking in to be.

Fear not, relent to it's magical rhythm
and breathe deeply into thee.

Disperse old friend into the soul,
the wisdom you behold.

You've shared the thoughts of ages,
the time is now for me.

Dan Farrell

My Home By The Sea

I want to return to my home
   by the sea
To the place where my heart
   longs to be
To feel once again the salty
   breeze
To hear the roar of the stormy
   seas
To stroll on the sand by the
   light of the moon
Like a lover's sweet dream that
   ended too soon
To watch the sandpipers scurry
   away from the foam
Collecting driftwood, sea shells and starfish
My heart cries out for it's only wish
To return to the ocean, the ocean so free
Where wave after wave stirs a memory in me
The memory of where I long to be
Back to my home, my home by the sea

Gerry Wohlfert

Innocence

A child is born with his innocence there,
By the time he's five it leaves him bare.
Only with a curious and mischievous mind,
Goes out into the world without looking behind.
Words mute, intelligence blind,
Only his looks to get by so sweet and kind.
No tongue, no heart developed, not yet,
His play days are here, his future's not set.
As he matures more and more, still with a
Curious and mischievous mind,
There's always an open door—more he can find.
A young man he is and older he'll be,
Intelligence shown, words aloud and a tongue
That speaks clearly.
A graduate, wife and a job that's fair
Soon another child is born with his innocence there.

Dina Futterman

On the Lake

On the lake everything is quiet,
   calm, still.
On the lake the animals are noisy,
   clumsy, hibernating.
While the animals gather food for the winter
THERE! A twig breaks!
The sound of hounds in the background.
In a far distance,
coming closer and closer.
The animals try to find a hiding place.
Suddenly there is a shot.
They got one.
Everything is quiet,
   motionless. Still.
The wind picks up the leaves,
runs across the water, racing time.
All the animals come out.
And everything is quiet again....
   On The Lake

Jeniffer Layton

Can Anybody Help Us?

The children spoke in unison as they began their prayer,
"Can anybody help us, doesn't someone truly care?"

Love is all we ask for, to be safe and well protected,
Though many of us instead confront abuse or are neglected.

The crimes against us children are unfair and so unjust,
For we possess such innocence and are suppose to learn to trust.

The hatred and the violence brings tears upon our eyes,
When we hear on all the newscasts of how another child dies.

We just don't understand why all these things are being done,
For children's lives are meant to be so carefree and such fun.

We need much tougher laws today, as we hope everyone can see,
So many of these criminals still walk our streets "they're free!"

Fearing for our lives each day cannot be correct,
Or to have your childhood stolen along with your self-respect.

Please listen, we are begging and will never stop the pleading,
Help us end this cycle and stop our hearts from bleeding.

We need adults to speak for us, tell the courts just how we feel,
This is the only way to get our emotional scars to heal.

Help us find an answer to this most important prayer,
We promise then, that everyday our smiles with you we'll share.

Debbie Piette

What Have You Done?

What is life but a discontinued story? Is there anything that can be done that hasn't been done? Are we all too ordinary to see the extraordinary? Have we given up hope of ever finding the future by reflecting on the past? Philosophy says life follows a circular path, then why bother breaking new ground? Why wok your bones to dust in a vain attempt to extract meaning from the mundane? When you die, what will you have left behind. Insignificant babbles of a life wasted in pain. We are still young, still capable of looking past the past and through the clouds of the present. We are able to see the bright new future that is still within our reach. But can we achieve it???? Is it just another empty attempt??? Fear not that which has given rise to the question, fear those who have given up without an answer. Life is too short to vainly pursue the pain of the past. STEP OUT! Reach Forward! Take a breath and walk into the light of tomorrow! Seize today for it might be the last chance you get...

James Kammel

Sandman

Sandman lingers at my bedside, legendary elf.
Can he really do much better than I've done myself?

Weaving dreams of ginger kingdoms, ribbons 'round the sun;
Spinning webs of sweet enchantment, never quite undone.

Keeper of the key to nowhere, wizard of the night;
Shapes the image of tomorrow with a silver light.

Painting pictures on the clouds and castles in the air,
Opening the magic door to what stands waiting there.

Ponders just a moment longer, shrugs and softly sighs;
Sprinkles moonlight on my pillow, stardust in my eyes.

Disappears into the shadows, just a brief farewell;
Always one more time for dreaming, always one more spell.

Barbara Siesto

Why Did You Leave?

You opened up my heart with love,
Can't you understand?
You told me that you loved me too,
And we held hand in hand.
Then you told me bad news,
And I thought I would cry.
You told me you just wanted to be friends,
And I still can't understand why.
I love you more and more each day,
And I don't care what people say.
You hurt me bad and I did cry,
I can't believe how much you lied.
The love I felt with you was strong,
I wonder how it went so wrong.
I know you won't open your heart to me,
But I'll search the world until I find the key.

Christine Achey

Since My Last Confession

Lord, rescue me from my evil
calm this bottled steam in my veins
don't let your image haunt me
relieve this God-given pain

Quell this perilous, aching need
to sin against what you command
teach me to extinguish the wild fires
that common aphrodisiacs do demand

Forgive me Father for I have sinned
It's been just a few moments since my last confession...

John W. Lindauer III

The Wind

The Wind blows softly through my hair
Caressing my entire being
clearing the cobwebs in my mind,
showing me reality.

Sometimes it's strong,
its forces pushing me forward;
as if to help me be aware of life.
Yet it circles back, as if to keep me from harm.

The Wind cools my warm body,
and seems to still my trembling heart.
It dances lightly around me
and I feel safe and protected.

And when it stills I am still, too,
Knowing it's always right behind me.
I feel love for this wind
for I know it will always be there.

It does so much good for me that sometimes
It makes me sad, that I can do little in return.
Yet I am consoled in knowing that
it is satisfied with me enjoying it.

Jean Burbridge

When The Last One Dies And You Are Next In Line

Pristine crackling tears spring forth
Cascading down the cheekside.
The heart holds still, the breath benign.
We are next — my cousin and I realize.
My aunt has died at last — the last one.
We are next — the realization pierces the soul.
But turn around and looks the other way.
Children — grandchildren — forging in the mist.
The linear road to eternity and beyond.

Ella Behar

Untitled: "The Blood of Christ"

Only the arm of God could push winds this strong and cause waves to crash upon the shore.

Only the mind of God could give the knowledge to men so that they can build a seaside metropolis.

Only the gourmet of life could recipe the brute strength given to men to pull together a jetty of stone which secures itself to the sand and the waves and the sea can't prevail against it.

Only the breath of God could breathe life into Man.

Only the love of God could give man the ability to be loved and to love. A love that burns and seeps through all the veins of my body can only be part of me because of what I absorb from the Lord. For if love is in the recipe, some love must be evident and Woe to those whom have it not. But if there is one who goes to God and was not recipe with love there is still a chance:

For, only the blood of Christ can forgive man of our sins.

Frank J. Verdi

Tick, Tock - Love's Clock

Each day with you is goodness, joy and peace,
Each night with you is love and sweet release.

Each hour with you is vibrantly endowed;
Each minute, too, is fervently avowed.

Each second's depth of feeling being born
Is like eternity carved into stone.

Julie Griffith Potyondy

Cruelty

It hurts deep inside where you hardly go.
It raises walls of defense to protect the open and tender hearted.
It kills any progress made and tears down trust.
Its rawest form is words of wrath to produce pain.
It leaves a trail of desolation without looking back for results.
There is no escaping its stronghold, only endurance.

Janel Loomis

Old Glory Speaks

If I could only speak - "WHAT WOULD I SAY?" -
Certainly something very worth while -
For I was born with pride and joy with a "Special Unique Style"...

I was made to represent the heart and soul of all...
The BLOOD, the SWEAT, the TEARS that flowed to help us all stand tall.

I am so proud of everyone who stood by me with pride,
And I personally salute each one who fought for me and died.

For those of you who recognize me for who I truly am,
I need no words to utter forth,
For you already understand.

So whenever you salute me and show you really care,
I salute you back, my friend,
With all the pride we share.

Irene Haber

True Romance

   In this world there is chance,
chance that you will find true romance.
   And inside all your deepest thoughts,
you may struggle with each other faults.
   Even though you may somehow want
them to change, it is usually best if
they remain the same.
   And no matter how ones past might make
you feel, if it is true romance you will
know it is real.
   There are just a few things that will
touch you like this, and true romance
has that special kind of bliss.

Dion Johnson

Spring Pray

I want to see, everyday all the
children of the Universe,
to be happy, every day;
that is my great desire.

I want to know, in the world, all the children,
young people, and veterans, to be happy.
I want to see everybody, must be glad;
that is my fervent anxiousness.

For every nation with love,
the best thoughts;
Oh, God, I demand from you,
to bless every day,

every home, every nation,
with their flags;
the entire world,
every new seed;

every new <ERA> (period, age).
I don't know how to pay you, all;
but only I know something.
God is very kind! God is love!

Isamacar Bustamante

In A Christmas Way

Times are changing, yet Christmas keeps its ways,
Christmas shoppers are everywhere, gifts are hard to
   choose,
And come tonight, the watch for Santa's sleigh.

Christmas stockings, a lighted fireplace,
Ornaments hung upon the tree, lots of tinsel, too,
And everything is in a Christmas way.

Snow has fallen, and worlds have knelt to pray,
Choruses of O Holy Night, voices ringing true,
While children's dreams close in on Christmas day.

Anthony F. Neiland

A Glimpse of God

Over in my neighbor's garden clinging to an old brick wall
Climbs a lovely yellow ramble that I've watched grow strong and tall.

Clothed in leafy pale green splendor, harbinger of early spring,
Symbol of the earth's awakening-soon to sparkle soon to sing.

Through the summer golden blooms prolific fill my room with fragrance
   rare
Which no man-made perfume though costly, can in any way compare.

And when doubts and fears assail me, as it seems at times they must,
Just a glance outside my window that restores my waning trust.

A tiny yellow rosebud, a green unfurling leaf,
Miracles of God's creation, there's no room for disbelief.

All too soon strong winds of autumn strip the petals toss and strew
   them everywhere,
Leave the rambler's swaying branches oh so bleak, oh so bare.

Yet I know beneath the surface life though dormant still is there,
To revive another season so I'll wait, I'll not despair.

Gladys M. Fountain

Night

Children gather around the night,
clutching its lingering darkness.
Tender black arms, invitingly wrapped over,
and draped about their starched white bodies.
Eyes gape wide open.
Pupils swollen from the absence,
dried by evil stares.
Their thoughts seem to wonder in and out.
Pale, lifeless minds clouded with fear.
Souls cry in the wind, as the last, rich drop of blood,
is sucked from their still hearts.
It shoots through the veins, and out the stretched fingers.
Blood gathers at the corners of the mouth.
Caught by the dried, sticky, paste of death.
Its tangy, dark, flavor is the last memory of life.
Pulled by the unseen force, taken prisoner in a dream.
The night captures all thoughts and screams.
An emptiness, obstructed from light.
Engulfing all, sound and sight.
  As they become one, with the night.

Cody Young

Forever Love

When I look into his eyes,
I feel like I'm drowning in a pool of sunshine.
When he touches me
I feel like a thousand butterflies have erupted around me.
If I could only get him to hold me forever, and again.
I would feel whole again.
Oh, please, my only one, release me from my tormented dreams.

Heather Lawson

Satan's Plan

Take a moment, I'll be conduit, you see it wrong, what
makes you do it. It's never planned for us to sin, an
outside force, helps you give in. Righteousness is not
forgot, only muddled by an outside plot. The devil's
scheme shows great aplomb, just making sure he's not
home alone.

Francis X. Gould Sr.

A Box Of Crayons

The colors in a box of crayons fill many people with spite,
colors in a box of crayons make people want to fight.
Red, purple, orange, green, yellow, blue,
people will show racism, a fact that is sadly true.
A world full of peace is something there should be,
where everybody in the world lives in harmony.
Prejudice and racism, these things are very bad,
riots, beatings and hate, make many people sad.
Guns, knives, robberies, murders, thieves and thugs,
it should be the opposite, where everybody hugs.
Women and children hiding in fear, men going off to war,
countries that were once beautiful, are now suddenly torn.
Hunger and starvation make many want to cry,
while others do not realize the precious time they have to be nice,
is quickly going by.
People smiling everywhere is something there should be,
and to each other we should give the gift of harmony.
True our lives are filled with many pros and cons,
but most of the problems in the world,
are caused by the colors in a box of crayons.

Ben Srok

Sunsets

As the sun sets in it's radiant splendor,
Colors more brilliant than an artist's masterpiece;
The sky is the easel of God our Master,
Painting His beauty which gives us peace.

The colors, though they are so vibrant and alive,
Are also so tranquil, peaceful and still;
It fills you with such awe and wonder inside,
As it always has and always will.

Sunsets are the introduction into the night,
The first wonder of the night-time sky;
Then comes the brilliance of stars twinkling bright,
After the sunset kisses the day good-bye.

Dorothy Caroline Moody

The Death of a Hero

The flag is at half staff today.
Column by column, row by row,
These once mighty men stand in formation.
Over small hills and beneath great trees,
their columns and rows do not waiver.
Among their ranks: Generals beside privates,
Colonels beside Sergeants.
Soldiers from every war side by side.
On this bleak fall day, my grandfather
is joining the formation.
The rain drizzles and cool October winds
blow the fallen leaves.
Two veterans fold Old Glory,
which drapes his casket,
as a lone bugle cries Taps.
They solemnly present my Grandmother
the flag, so carefully folded.
Tears pour from her eyes...
looking back, I never thought he would die...
But now he has gone... In formation.

Greg Terry

Emotions

Emotions, the essence of our souls,
    come together to make us whole,
    impulses challenging our roles,
    powerful elements on patrol,
    each fighting for control,
    clinging as a camisole.
To follow our minds or our hearts,
    each a dilemma does impart,
    whenever we do, then which chart?
Anger, sadness, love — it seems a zoo,
    all together a tasty stew;
    each has a place, to help renew.
Do we act as an innocent child,
    restrain our feelings, let them run wild,
    guide our passions down an aisle?
As with all of life, we must decide
    how to reveal what we have inside,
    or whether to run away and try to hide.

Gail W. Merrill

Home Again Bound

There's a place that keeps callin' my name whispered long,
"Come up hither my child, here is where you belong."
Full of mothers and fathers and siblings more than few,
Cattails and hay bails, shining spider web dew.
With pigpens and corn fields, smells of soy beans and rain,
Long driveways end at silos.... bright red trucks spilling grain.
Lil lakes with pontoon boats by old rickity piers,
Sunrises and moon glows - they all warrant my tears.
My emotions having reasons as the mist in my eyes,
Sweet displays of each season, and answers to the whys.

Giant pumpkins and cider - sometimes nothin' to do...
Porch swings go with this place like denim goes with blue.
Lord, thy will be done on this earth as in Heaven,
And so it is here - place of beauty times seven
Old clothes lines and roses, "cut them back when they're thru,"
The sweet wisdom of elders telling how their flowers grew.
Smells of soup beans and ham at a place they call "Poe's,"
A senior citizen's discount by a field full of crows.

And so I answer... "Indiana" (like I was singin' a song),
Lord willin' just the same... my return won't be long.

Charles Keith Stanley

"The One"

Endlessly in search for the one perfect
companion and soulmate in life's journey.
Cautious of opportunist whom captivate and beguile their intentions.
This man with whom displays such an assertions.
he appeases my want my need my every desire.
There's no duplicity in his pledge of undying commitment to us.
We are joined before God with vows
to cherish and love each other a lifetime..
In consummating our union, this child is a gift received by all,
as a symbol of this love.
Our children are bonded harmoniously,
as a wholesome unified love for each other.
We rectify in positive harmony,
as a extricate of our being.
The search has ceased I yearn no more.
In adulation and praise to God,
with gratitude for prayers are answered.

Charlotte Sheffield

Fledgling

The possession of life is dark to own.
Complicating all the ballyhoo one has known.
Nurturers charged to feeding full the larder
Feel the onus throes of being solely alone.

Life, he knew, would be different on arrival.
Litter of the herd could test his new armor
When grappling times would bare him sharp rivals.
But he had grit, he was here for survival.

When two track parallels cross for square
Plying unknown ports for scouts immortal,
Sand tides shift this forged earthened fare
And often times gel a portal to share.

Horizons beam we rode to our fair sylvan.
Conquered dreams too fantastic for our visions.
Thoughtlessly love from one to both was given
And by us, unknown, our time cruelly driven.

And scraped the dirt right over my turtle.
I buried him up to the top. Crying love and longing to him.
Letting him know this was our last stop.
Knowing then, we are all this fertile.

James Thompson

"Dirty Parasites"

A dirty girl wiggles her wares on a clammy,
Concrete platter sauteed with pigeons;
Served up stale and spiced with lipstick smudged
Cigarette butts, broken glass, and little
Green gobs of gooey saliva.

A dirty old man with rotting teeth and a black
Conscience pulls up warily to the forbidden
Curb as the stench of poisoned lust
Permeates the muggy late afternoon air.
The dirty animals exchange words...

The pigeons barely break stride as the dirty
Animals drive off to bleed each other's filth;
Quickly, quietly, and very discreetly.
They collect their pride and hide their shame
For, unlike the pigeons who walk in their own shit,

The dirty animals know of their filth.

Daniel J. Lund

Untitled

People fighting in my head,
constantly struggling to be released,
from the gate, that holds their fate
Wanting to be, what the little boy dreamed,
and not just a memory
Is this possible, of course not
Only one in the end will win
The others will be pushed aside,
but never truly die
They'll lie there and wait,
oh, so close to the gate,
'til the boy becomes old
And then they'll escape,
to haunt him again and again

James S. Faries

The Cherub

God in His infinity sat on His throne
Counting His cherubs, one of them gone.
He looked to Earth where one had been placed.
He looked and He saw his sweet, smiling face
For awhile he had been there, three years or so
With those who loved him watching him grow.
God had to call him - He knew he must go
He knew of the sorrow the loved ones would face
When they learned that the cherub had been misplaced
But He called him back to His throne on high
For He knew they would see him by-and-by
Someday in heaven the loved ones shall meet
And behold the cherub who sits at God's feet.

Janet Rasnick

Alone

Why does this happen?
Cowering in a dark corner of an almost vacant studio apartment,
where the light can't touch you, an afraid, suicidal battered
women sobs. What should she do, what can she do?
Nothing.
She can't run, she can't hide... She's trapped.
So she thinks....
The maniac man that is tormenting me should be put away so he can't
make me hurt anymore.
Totally convinced, finally believing in herself and realizing that
she isn't alone...
She timidly picks up the phone.
But she abruptly hangs up....
Her husband just got home.

Bethanie Neth

Storm-Metamorphosis

The black panther of the storm
creeps through the windy night.
Like the shadows that glide across
the moon in its flight.
The soul of the shrieking wind
wails out its lonely cry.
Even the mountainous crags
seem to echo its sob.
All around the intense darkness begins to throb.
And suddenly erupts into the
sound of one huge purr.
Somewhere, on a hillside
the clock in the tower
is heard to strike the witching hour.
The storm-tossed trees wave their
branches like arms on high.
A flash of heat lightning rents the angry sky,
And out of its luminous heart
There appear I, wearing a ring of fire and
wrapped in a cloak of fur.

Eleanor J. Briest

The Stranger

I dreamed of those eyes before
Chased away nightmares of vile gore.
I awoke, held out my rested arms
A kiss awoke me an internal alarm.
I looked for you in the galleries of my mind,
But you were lost somewhere between love and time.
Sublime beauty eye to eye
only in my dreams or perhaps when I die;
But I still looked carried a rotten old rose
Something to give those eyes when they arose.
But here I stand when those eyes that roamed
Pitty though, I left the rose at home.

Jamie C. Lindquist

"The Sickness"

It swoops over the night sky in misty space.
Cry's of pain don't cease.
Smells of death, sickness soar through blackened air.
Children-adults do nothing, just stare.
Eternal blackness comes with a hiss.
It lets out a taste of a sour kiss.
A shrill of horror shrieks out from below.
Death strikes full power with its strongest blow.
People die left and right.
It's too fast,
No time to fight.
The town lies still and silent.
Sickness has gone.
Left are the bones of the young.
Remains of the old.
Once were bold,
Roaming with a dignified grace.
Now Struck down.
"Aids takes their place."

Adrienne Houser

For the Brother

Once I met the lickety slick man _____
Cunning and conniving, dense, but articulate.
He wore no jewelry or rings on his hand_____
But he knew how to lie, steal and manipulate.
Oh, but sorrowful I was that I'd met him one day___
His shroud was glum, no reason to stay_____
But vigorous energy overcome this shadow;
I began to catch on, and a heavenly light shined on my path.
I had a way out____I broke, I ran_____
Leaving him in anger, rage and wrath.
I'm happy to say____I've put him away____
What a joy, what a joy____I'm single today!

Soliloquy Swift

In A Dark Corner

In a dark corner of her room, a little girl weeps
Curled into a small little ball, hot tears stream down her cheek
Her whole body shakes as each scream escapes
Her arms and legs once were tan, but are now
a horrid black and blue
She tries to think of happy past times, that once long ago she knew
A soft old rag doll is her only friend, she holds it tightly
to her for the weeping will never end
She's been locked in her own world
Where everything is dark and full of sin
A world of her own is where she'll stay
Afraid to come out because of all
the violence that's been going on today
Where children like her are getting hurt
and killed and beaten and treated like dirt.

Crystal-Marie Apilado

Feelings

My thoughts are dark as your
deepened heart,
Just knowing you can never catch
it with your grasp,
Slowly trying to hold onto my soul
when yours is rapidly chipping away,
Your endless heart is calling and calling
to be loved for eternity but only getting
rejecting by it's past,
You know now that you can't live
any more, so you become frightened
and scared,
Finally you give up all hope and you
die down for a lonesome sleep.

Jennifer Ragan

Soul Searching

Come laugh with me
Dance and sing with me
For tomorrow I may not be
Laugh with me - for tomorrow I may not be

Give me a day of feeling free
No clocks, no phones, no waiting rooms, no tears
One day without a heart full of laughter
Peace of mind is what I'm after
Give me a day that I can be me
But I feel my time is nearing
To just exist and not live
To die before I am born

Is what I am fearing
I fear no one will know who I am
No one will meet my soul
Now, for me, it is too late
I die before I live

Debra Kimball

Dare to Discover

Dare to discover hidden strengths within yourself.
Dare to be different from everybody else.
Dare to be daring when courage is needed.
Listen and learn. Now have you heeded?

Dare to discover the beauty in life.
Dare to discover the lessons in strife.
Dare to be bold when courage is needed.
Lead, do not follow. Now have you heeded?

Dare! Be and example for others to follow.
Dare to win, always; not victory's hollow!
Dare to be silent when silence is needed.
If you do these things, you will have heeded.

Joyce W. Teal

Dare to Dream

Dare to dream, no matter who you are;
Dare to dream and wish upon a star.

Give all your will power to what you believe;
Stand up tall and honest and never deceive.

Run with the wind and fly through the sky.
Dare to dream; keep your ideals high.

It may take months and it may take years.
Dream of through the laughter and the tears.

Never give up; be steadfast and strong.
Dare to dream and believe that you belong.

Hold your head up high; I know you can do it.
Give it your all and hold yourself to it.

Dare to dream, no matter who you are.
Dare to dream and you will be a Star.

Emily Wright Zavaro

Sadness

I taste the damp walls, as I walk down a
    darkened alley.
The smell of lust lingers as it falls to the
    dark street.
I hear the moans of diseased children in the
    twilight,
I've touched the dreams of our dying youth as it
    slips away,
I know this is not a dream it is our world!

Jill Romanek

56

Independent Self

Beware, young children of what people say
deceitful tongues are set to turn you astray
as sailboats are guided by the winds of the day
their selfish words lead you off course and away

If you let them, they'll make their own plans for your life
regardless of your own dark struggles and strife
they'll mold you like a piece of clay
their prized priceless statue that stands in the hallway

Guard yourself against such use
bend but don't break under the stress of abuse
lead your own determined path
and do not fear their ignorant wrath

Be who you truly are
not a piece of the whole, but an independent part
break the caste with which they have held you down
and bury their lies in holy ground

Society will stereotype and call you names
take their molds and set them in flames

David Anderson

A Lizard's Tale

'Twas lovely hot weather, the lizards did gather,
  Deciding which house to explore,
Said a very long member, "I just can't remember,"
  "Such a wonderful, welcoming door!"
If he'd had any sense, he'd gone over the fence,
  And taken a different way,
He shot for the screen, when a cat very mean,
  Grinned announcing, "You've just made my day!"

He rose in such shock, he ran a full block,
  Then he stood and he bared his front teeth,
He looked so impressive, the cat got expressive,
  Grabbed the chance for his belly beneath!
He rallied once more and raced for the door,
  Sacrificed all of his tail,
He found himself trapped so he closed up his flap,
  And pretended the kitty would fail.

He lay for an hour, the day had turned sour,
  But he knew he'd better stay put,
And then in surprise he opened his eyes,
  When out through the door came a foot!

Arlene Broyles

Ascent

The youth hold nothing absolute, secured,
Decisive death of self they can't realize,
When one caress of Beauty is procured,
To them a fleeting admonition flies!
So as those young appease their peers by feats,
'Tis in this quest that Beauty's glimpse is caught,
To Beauty now denuded love excretes,
Esteem from One is now the laurel sought.
For Beauty then surmounts the ego, wealth,
With less than grand eternal they are bored,
Their lives at Beauty now are aimed, in stealth,
Past joys disgrace them, known by their adored.
  The young in bliss through joyous life careen,
  With Beauty's form divine, that human seen.

Christopher Rogers

The Little Girl

A stream is flowing from shallow to
deep, a little girl steps in the water to
cool off her feet. She wades around and gets
herself wet, her long black hair is now
totally wet.
  She wishes this moment could last but
she has to leave and get home fast. She
wonders what her mother will say after seeing
her this way. She'll probably be grounded for
the rest of her life, but the little girl
guess that would be alright. Because the day
was so hot and the water felt just right, the
little girl wishes she could stay the night.

Angie Faucher

A Stormy Night

Streaks of forked lightening are flashing.
  Deep thunder roars out of heavy clouds,
Banked darkly in the Northwest.
  The cattle moaning and lowing are stirring.
The wind churning and whirling,
  All the brown leaves and debris.

A blinding flash of jagged fire lights
  And brightens the darkness of the night.
A crash of doom careens to earth,
  As we shake and wonder if this is the end
Or an intense graphic warning. Then
  Sheets of hail, rain and fire pour
Out of heaven for half an hour.
  And leaves the earth and air and sky
Clean and fresh and pure;
  A pristine dream.

Maybe we need this wild commotion
  Twice a week to keep
The air fresh and clean,
  And free from pollution?

Billie Perry Pepich

Untitled

Strewn across the verdant floor of a valley lies the
dense fog of uncertainty.
The vapor coils and reacts to bodies passing in its
wake.
It reaches for every bit of the material world, waiting
and wanting to obscure our lives.
It dampens the leaves of the oak and the needles of
the evergreen.
All else is dormant.
Swallowing up the world, and then the memory of
what used to be.
The sun is but a fictitious character now.
A fable to us all.
The ground turns to mush, and sinks from winter's
spit.
And the air stagnates until nature's breath frees us
from the fog's beguiling grip.

Charles W. Eproson Jr.

New Age Dilemma

Add word to word, deduce a wheat-germ dot
of reason, making clear as gel the glue
of knowledge, binding one to one and all
to all. That more makes less, but less is rich
in never-dreamed-of truth, is sleight of mind
to leave us wordless, looking wistful, out
and far beyond the dust of How-Was-That?

Alfhild Wallen

Love Forever

The earthly visit is a moment of illusion
Designed to continue the loving diffusion.

But as the moment goes by and we laugh and we cry,
The purpose may be lost in confusion.

We came to grow and to love and to learn,
The successes to keep on our return.

And if during our stay we can't have our way,
We still have our merits to earn.

But after the ultimate ascension,
The good in our wake is our pension.

Our true love is the permanent compensation.

Jon Stevens

Untitled

I sit here, tears on my face
despair and loneliness, pondering my fate
I feel so alone, so misunderstood
words locked in, struggling to escape.
How do you cope when fear of hurt
builds that wall around you?
You long for tenderness, you long for love
the need to feel arms that love you
hold you, give you peace.
Is there that kind of love? I hope
but loving you has been so painful
and I know you feel the same
I wish I never knew you then I could
walk away.
We are like two destructive forces together
too many bad memories, too many hate filled words
words are like weapons, they inflict so much pain
invisible to others, but you carry every scar.

Joyce A. Bryan

Moon Travel

The magnitude of this feat is too great, too many
Details to relate
But we are finally all going to the moon and its going
To be very soon.
We have often been told "the man in the moon and
His lady love were cold, because they lived on a
Green cheese diet and no one cared to deny it.
Now the race will be to see, who the first vendors
Of Franks and rolls will be.
The realtors will have a field day,
But it will be the earthmen that will have to pay.
All seems to be going well with the task
"But where will I find a parking spot?" I ask.
Was written in 1950 in a home news letter.
I was sec for a group then.

Dot L. Nadler

The Life Cycle

Two separate people united as one;
one day will have a daughter or son.
This baby lives in one but was made by two,
and will soon rest in the arms of parents who are true.
This person will share life with a father and mother
and maybe also with a sister or brother.
Some day this person may find a husband or wife
and together they both will create a new life.
So the cycle continues and the world still goes around.
But without couples in love
life would soon drowned.

Bill O

Magnificent World

God's beauty before us, ever unfurled
Dew dipped to sparkle, magnificent world.

Your mountains and valleys, all of your streams,
Are endless before us, beyond our dreams.

Flowers with colors in multi-array
Graciously dance by our eyes every day.

Trees all a flutter when touched by a breeze,
A haven for birds that nest in its leaves.

Oceans that cover a world of their own,
Ignored by ships, destinations unknown.

And in the heavens you've sown many stars;
My God, the mysteries you've left ajar.

George J. Carroll

What If

What if my son the world as we see, could be different for you and
different for me.
What if we no longer went to airports for hello's and goodbyes,
But had smiles on our faces, not tears in our eyes.
What if our time was not measured in days and in hours, for a
lifetime
together could truly be ours.
What if time had no boundaries, imagine it so, I've missed so much
already in seeing you grow.
For I miss you my son, the smiles and the laughter, not the trips to
the airport, the coming home after,
To a house that is empty, that once held your voice, for your going
away was never our choice.
Though years have gone by, I still break down and cry, but I don't
wonder why, I only ask WHAT IF?

Bill Sturgeon

A Beautiful Woman

Look at me. Am I not a beautiful woman?
Do you see the real me neath the foundation base?
The mascara that darkens the lashes,
The lipstick outlining my lips?
The wrinkles that time has brought?
The deep furrows in my forehead..
The lines around my mouth and eyes
Subtly covered with cream?
The waist that has grown thicker,
The legs slightly bent?
Of course not! What you see is my sense of humor;
A smile that covers the universe.
Skin that is smooth, whiter than snow,
A heart full of love for humanity and
All other living creatures.
The eyes that are myopic yet
Can see deep into your soul.
A hand outstretched to welcome love,
Does this not make me a beautiful woman?

Dorothy R. Gratz

Blue Memory Before Coming Into This World

I had a dream.
I was swimming in the ocean.
The Aegeon Sea, I know.
I couldn't see anything but blue.
I was floating in the blue.
Out of the blue, there came a dolphin.
She took me to the deep sea.
We have returned to the depths of the blue.

Ikuko Yoshida

Dreams

When you close your eyes at night to sleep -
Do you vision secrets you're asked to keep -
Do you see the future or the past -
When you're awake - Does your dream last -
Some people dream of money and power -
Others dream of life being sour -
Some dream in black and white -
Others don't even dream at night -
What kind of things do you see -
What people do you dream to be -
And when you wake every day -
Do your dreams just fade away?

Heather Flicker

Does It Matter

Here is a good question each one should ask
Does it matter because I am?
Answer truthfully take off the old mask.
Listen, lest your life be a sham.

Think, what a beautiful world this would be,
During our little while on earth,
If we would live and love in charity.
This lesson should begin at birth.

True love will conquer any enemy.
It transforms them into a friend.
Lift up loving hearts for our world to see
Then sinful selfishness will end.

The world can be better because "you are"
So fight temptations that occur.
At journey's end beyond the farthest star,
It will matter because "you were."

Joseph Blanchfield

When America Sings

Does America sing the way we want her to?
Does she sing in harmony or sing the blues?
How has her tune changed through the years?
Does she sing a tune of hopes or fears?
It's hard to believe we live in a place,
that discriminates against age or race.
Or lets a man kill time after time
And has no punishment for the gruesome crime.
All over the states this terror began
It's all here dwelling in our promise land.
There's no reason for war of any kind.
If we'll all join together we will find
A song of peace, a song of pride,
A song of beautiful and spacious skies.
We'll sing a song with joy and love
The kind that was meant from above.
"The sooner the better" is what they say
And soon we hope, there will come a day
When once again freedom will ring
And along with that tune we'll hear America sing.

DeAnne R. Tanner

"Grandma's Lye Soap"

"LYE" is an ingredient in your treasure
of today's "DOPE".
Grandma used it in her "SOAP"
Everyone paid the price with loss of hair,
so how could you not care.
Stay clean the "NO" way, so your children
can have their day!

Ann Thomas

Feelings

My heart is overflowing with love.
My mind is overflowing with thoughts.
My eyes are overflowing with tears.
My ears are overflowing with voices.
My hands are overflowing with creativeness,
Myself, I am overflowing.

Jessica Lynn Steele

Cycles

It's hard to trust
Don't know what to believe
When feeling not like other beings
You hide it away
When they laugh and say
It's all in your mind
That's just you
Well maybe that's true
But nothing satisfies you
You're blinded in view
Shaky tremors inside you
Dizzy spells that leave you confused
Lost in deep misery
No where to run, no one, nothing in back
Even yourself aren't able to understand that
Without pills in me
My life is a scary thing
Why is this happening to me?

Gina Maria Luppino

Do We Care

As we travel down life's journey-
Down that often lonely road
Do we always seem to busy
To take time out to pray?
Do we know just where we're going?
Or do we seem to care?
That our souls to him would - be won.

So we must not forget, that old Bible.
and always remember to pray-
Ask our Father in heaven.
To bless us and guide us each day.
Do we know were ready to meet him?
Are we sure the victory's been won
Do we think we can hear the Lord saying;
"Enter in for thy work is well done?"

Alta Price

Fascination

All line up. Across the back.
Dozen of boxes: Stack upon stack
From floor to ceiling. Each in a line.
Inside which a color will find
a special spot in a place.
Hopefully mine.

What is the attraction?
The great satisfaction.
Of conquering each one (and having some fun)
The Colors! The Styles! I can't make
up my mind! For in the next box might be
the right find. To wear while out dancing or
just out and around: hundreds of possibilities abound!

Alas. maybe to think (with a smile) that I could
walk for miles and miles!

But I know deep inside another true fact.
I might put on those shoes and never come back!

Constance Klahn

Yellowstone Prayers

Oat-straw bear grass watching their long winter shadows
Dreaming of springtime and their summer selves

Brown boulder on the horizon   moves and stops   moves and stops
Silhouetted against an azure sky   puff-clouds crown bison-lord
Grazing so peacefully

Like a gathering of quilters each animal
Leaves the pattern of their life-death-life struggle
Stitched in their tracks   criss-crossing the new snow

Geyser steam-fog shroud winter Bison spirits
Shaking their massive heads   clearing snow   eating all day to live
Just to see another spring

Raven came to me for food and I told him
Fly ahead clear a path for us   a safe way
Taking bread from my outstretched hand he flew away

Such a glorious light-filled day cannot be planned
Is not scheduled it must be given
A loving gift to be shared with others

This place holy ground   his presence everywhere
We must find a way to respect it   cherish it   protect it
It is our home our true nature the key to how we will be

   Frank T. Ruggiero

7 A.M.

Electronic shrieks pierce the warming air,
Dreamscape.
Eyelids fight with the anchor of sleep,
Flakes of dust settle through beams of light.
A double-paned shield denies the sounds of morning,
Submitting only to faint images.

The young girl down the street injects death into her veins,
A policeman calls the messenger "niger",
Father beckons to daughter, nobody else is home,
Look to the sun, for there's a hole in the sky,
Heroes fall before the eyes of justice,
Mother cooks meatloaf again, the third time this week.

Is the dream evolving to nightmare?
Quite possible.
Visions flash with each yelp from the night stand,
A desperate yearning for peace?
A heartfelt cry for quiet?
Hit the tiny button,
To make them all go away.

   Bryan Reilly

Untitled

Life is too short to hold a grudge
Either of two sides refusing to budge
A mistake in the past
Held against us forever
Making up it seems will happen never

A part of my history is gone far away
Yet close in my memories each passing day
I've said I was sorry quite a few times
And it doesn't phase your opinions of mine

I can't go on fighting this silent fight
So with thoughts racing on I write and write
My letters go unanswered as do my calls
Another day without speaking as darkness falls

I am sorry once more doesn't do the trick
Someday I believe the right words I'll pick
And we'll become close again
In whatever way we can

This really has to cease before it's too late
And one of us in standing at that heavenly gate

   Elizabeth A. Kocher

One Dove

Birds of a feather, flock in groups together,
Ducks and Geese in formation, apart, Magpies, Robins and Crows.
Most always fly to the warmth, to avoid winters harsh weather,
Where free foods are aplenty, and green foliage grows.

But there was one bird that faced weathers, to fly alone,
When turbulent storms on all the earth had prevailed.
'Twas a quite fragile, small bird, with faith that found home,
Flew through the storms, where other birds would have failed.

For it was one of God's faithful creatures, even though it was small,
That had chosen and sent out, to find safety for all.
For many of humanity were set free from a boat, in a flood,
Because of the reason of love, the faithful bird to trust was a dove.

It's perseverance brought freedom, and escape from the Ark and
   disaster
And the bird that brought an olive leaf to the boat's master,
Was not seen anymore by the captors in ship's safe confinement,
And they same as the dove, were free to live life fully thereafter.

Reliance entrusted to find green foliage and sun, was given a dove,
With wings fully extended, ascended through raging torrents alone,
Returning with living proof, defied elements and made the truth known.
Surely, the creations Creator, in majestic wisdom, approved with His
   love.

   June Carol Isaacson

Seasons To A Child

I wish I could ride a horse with my friend,
During the Spring on a trail that wouldn't end.

What fun would we have? What games would we play?
It's not Spring so I cannot say

Just a few more weeks till Spring will come
Finally I will once more play in the sun.

After Spring will come Summer when I can swim in a pool.
Then I would wish it was Fall when the weather was cool.

Of course, I'd get tired of the forever falling leaves,
Then I'd wish for a cold winter breeze

I'd play in the snow till my lips turned blue.
Then I'd wish it was warmer, so there was more I could do.

I'd wish that summer would come to an end,
and the same thing would happen all over again!

   Aileen Nielsen

With Your Love

Her darkness is as beautiful as the midnight
dusk, as bountiful as the ocean's depths, yet
she has gone undiscovered. Like the mines of
King Solomon, rich with plentiful and abundant
source. Only until I reach the apex of my
being, will the world experience the glory of
her being. I must not be dismayed, while this
time is waiting to happen, for her fruition
must take place. My spirit awaits complete
bliss, for this; has never been, yet it longs
to be fulfilled. I beg not to proceed further
until my angels uplifts, sustains, and purify's
my soul, for I know other's benefit from my
quest to rise. My nature is to soar high above
natures peaks and valleys. For I need not
be kept any lower than what my theme to be
is. Just as an eagle; my nature strives for
nothing less, than to be as I ought to be
for like an eagle my happiness must not fall
short of what my nature is to be.

   George R. Mangum Jr.

Lord

Lord, what a deed you have done;
Dying on the cross for everyone.
You watched us when we split,
But you never quit,
Loving us with all your heart;
You're always ready for us to start
Again and learn your ways;
You don't care if it takes days
Or months or years, if it must,
Because You are filled with love and trust,
In Your creations,
Your operations,
Who really need to live in You,
Because Lord, You have the better view.
Thank You for what You did,
Here's is all my love I have to give.
    Your kid,

Arlene Lemmel Otte

Midnight Spider

The midnight spider spins a web like no other.
Each strand wrought in patient thought,
With darkness as her cover,
Between each tender limb strands fall,
Like Midnight spider tears,
She weaves a story of her own,
Then from the past she hears,
"The spider is alone..."
As morning comes, she goes away,
No sight of her is found,
Except for the dew-mingled web,
and spider tears upon the ground.

Colleen Fleming

To Speak of the Caring Person

Poverty, hunger, prejudice and pain;
Earthquakes, hurricanes, flooding ...endless rain.
Racism, gangs, drugs amongst our kids;
Unwanted babies, unwanted kids.
Welfare, harassment charge;
problems can be small or large.
Lying cheating, hate and guns;
alcohol, fights, some just do it for the fun.
Nobody ever said life would be easy,
but it's true just the same;
there are those who understand you,
and understand your pain.
Suicides, runaways,...
problems can be solved in other ways.
People care... I know it's true,
come work together... the future belongs to you.

Jonelle Malta

Love

There she sits in a meadow
hoping for her love to come and awake her from
her sorrow

She has dreamt for her love many times
but destiny has lead her to be hopeless

So until her love comes and drift her
away from her sorrow into a land of true love
She will sit and dream forever

Belinda Sifuentes

Peace Must Be Now

Have I not waited while suffering the
effects of slavery?
Have I not withstood hurt, pain and
disgrace as I waited for justice and still
today many years after slavery have ended...
I have not been rewarded my rights to freedom,
therefore I question when?

Yes, is it not better than we live in peace
as a nation instead of violence that will
instill fear and mistrust as what we are
today witnessing.

See, I say what Lincoln said, a Nation
divided will not stand, my only question
who will take blame for what is to come?

Bill Goodin

Your Beauty's Beyond Description

Just like the wind you're like a fresh summer breeze who blew
elegantly into my life. Just like pure orange juice you have
been freshly squeezed and strained of all envy and strife.

Just like the sun you shine powerful and bright, stretching your
beauty from coast to coast. Spreading love that so warm in
such a very special way it glorifies that sweet Lord of host.

Just like the stars you're a gorgeous sight your beauty's beyond
description. You're a supernatural cure that I will always endure
I thank God for such a powerful prescription.

Just like the feel of fresh water bouncing of the ocean shore
and rushing all over my feet. You're a beautiful way to add
life to my day, you're a sacred symbol that is truly too sweet.

Douglas H. Tumpkins

The Dark Tower

Behind the desk, a surly old broad
embraces bureaucracy with her flabby arms
all races, racing, under a single roof
the 'Justice' seal in gold!

In this place, I call, "THE DARK TOWER"
where the air is stale and petulant
lawyers display their deceptive smiles
with dollar sign eyes well spent.

Anxious brows and sweaty palms
hopes of the 'American Dream'
papers intact, and I'm sailing free,
but wait, behold a discrepancy!

Come back, we'll arrange a four hour wait
execute your rights to a claim
Did you really think this would be easy?
look, your eyes.....you're going insane!

Nigel Williams

This Single Rose

This single rose before me resembles what we share
A love so unusual, a love so rare.
I love you deeply, with all my heart,
It's always you that will be a big part.
Our love together means so much,
The strength of our words and the softness of our touch.
I give you this rose to show you I care,
And a lifetime together we shall share.

Erica Christina Simmons

A Mother's Eyes

They start out so tiny and small,
Entering a world much bigger than they are,
You try to catch them when they fall,
And protect them from life's many scars.

So often you listen as they play,
Hearing the sounds of joy and laughter,
You wish is that they could always stay,
Happy, carefree and innocent forever after.

Though no one knows life without pain,
Their happiness is your main goal,
And when their tears fall like rain,
It hurts way down to your soul.

They may fail to understand for a while,
Your love and concern for their well being,
That you live for their sweet smile,
And it is an angel that you are seeing.

But one day they will be grown,
And you know that soon they will realize,
Only when they have a child of their very own,
The love that is seen through a mother's eyes.

Brenda Riggs

Listen Please

The future depends on those who listen,
Especially to their heirs not recently christened,
If we don't listen and "analyze" their problems,
And accomplish solutions multi-year prior to post-mortems.
We can all call it quits here and now,
But this needn't happen if our communicators pow-wow.
What a glorious planet this would be,
If all of it's leaders could only see.
That communications and negotiations are needed endeavors,
Not 40 hours per week, but 365 days and all 24 hours.

Gladys W. Farnan

Loving Lament

Don't know the reason why
even though I feel so spry
I feel I soon will die
Oh! How life seems to fly
hope that things won't go awry
please, please don't cry
you won't find one who loves you more than I
but life is short, so please please try
I wish for you a real great guy
one who can keep you on a loving high
life should be a lemon cream pie
to enjoy and not pass by
you were always the apple of my eye
I wish you always a clear blue sky
when they call my name I'll answer "aye"
so when you hear my very last sigh
it will be time to say "good-bye"
doesn't matter where I lie
Oh! don't forget, blue suit, red white blue tie

David Lamont White

What Is A Pastor

A Pastor is a Shepherd of Love. A Love that is pure and comes from above.
One that is Always concerned for His sheep and always know who guides and who keeps.
God has Placed a rod in his hand, to lead and guide at His command.
Thank you Master for sending Our Pastor, who tenderly cares and tenderly feeds.

Angela Santiago

Love

Love is like a rainbow neverending
Everlasting trust so unbending.
Love is like an angel, never betraying
Love sticks in your mind like an old saying.
Love is forever through good times and bad
Love means being there through happy and sad.
Love can be sour, bitter, or tart
Love can sometimes break your heart.
Love means sometimes letting go
Even when your heart is telling you no.

Jennifer Garate

With You, Every Second Counts

I cherish the time I spend with you,
Every second counts;
Whether we spend 24 hours or just two,
Every second counts.

From the first minute I look into your eyes,
Every second counts;
To the time you make my temperature rise,
Every second counts.

Whether we laugh or whether we cry,
Every second counts;
Even if I don't understand why;
Every second counts.

I appreciate your friendship and love,
Every second counts;
I know it's a gift from up above,
Every second counts.

I am sad when you have to go,
But every second counts;
Since I know, I will miss you so,
I make every second count!!!

Harriette E. Bell

Train of Times

It's amazing how fast time goes by
Everyday passes like a speeding train.
We are the passengers on this train of time
And the train carries us through the tunnel of life.

What is time though?
Is it a clock on the wall, a month on the calendar?
We look in the mirror everyday and can tell time has passed,
Where did all the time go?
Nobody knows, it just passes like a speeding train
With occasional stops so we can catch our breath.

The train sometimes jumps the track, when times are tough,
But it will be fixed and will run again.
Sometimes people miss the train,
Running to catch up - wondering where the time has gone.
And one day you won't catch up, your time will come;
The train will bring you upon your final destination.

But only time can tell where the train will take us,
What stops we'll make, which tunnels of life we'll go down,
Because time is like a speeding train,
It's amazing how fast time goes by.

Erika Boers

Family Tree

When our first son, came into the world
Everyone asked, didn't you want a girl?
I answered no! God was good to me,
He knows what's best, then there arrived another three.

We loved all four with all our heart
Then the time came, it was time to part.
They took on wives, that was pretty to see.
They added beauty to our family tree.

We loved them and they loved me.
Now when people ask, no daughter, oh my!
I smile, and sigh, and say don't you see
Our sons married girls who are daughters to me.
God is so good He blesses you see.

Eloise Callin

Love Don't Live Here Anymore

Hurt, sorrow, anger, pain
everything I hoped for was put to shame.
Tears, fear all around
there was no need to be put down.
Abused, confused, accused -
both day and night.
This is not what life is suppose to be like.
Sickness, death -
Why must this be?
People in this world won't let love run free.

Gloria Whitaker

A Lover's Question

Do you love? Can you love? Will you love? Should you love? What exactly is love? Speaking for myself, I do not know if I love, If I've loved, or if I could ever love, simply because I do not know how to love or what it is for that matter. No matter how much I study, I don't feel an input of love, no matter how much or hard I work, I don't receive love, no matter where I travel, I can't find love, than where do I find this infrequent visitor who many claim to have found? Do people think about love in the morning, and decide to go out and find it? Are they prone to catching love, and myself immune to the syndrome?, Have I loved too much in other lives? And this time neglected, to let others have a turn? Am I pardoned from above, saved from the consequences? If any! If I got jealous and curious enough, would it be possible to steal love? Would a friend let me borrow love, for an hour? Could I buy love, and return it for a 100% guaranteed refund?

If I found loves address, could I sent it a letter and ask for it to explain itself? If I write this letter do I act sincere as if to care? Should I send my thoughts and words to share? Should I strip my soul to bear on sight? Reach to the heavens in destined height? Should I open my arms and heart now safe? Unlock the secret hiding place, do I trust and show affection too try not to change, accept, be true? If I tremble when this love I see, will thy comfort, hold, and cherish me? If I climb than fall where will I land, a broken heart, a gentle hand? Well these questions here I'll include indeed, in hopes of blindness soon to be freed. And if I find before receive, my heart to you no longer bleeds!   Love Always, Jimmy

James C. Villepigue

My Mother

She is always there for me.
She keeps everything nice and clean.
You can even see the sunshine gleam.
She bakes all kinds of goodies.
She makes everything from pasta to chicken,
But that is not why I love her.
I love her because she's my Mother!

Christopher Carlucci

Love's Lesson

Day after day the flame burns.
Extinguished by tears or heightened by the light of the stars.
You have the power to reach deep within yourself and strike the cords of wisdom to teach yourself, the ways of the heart.
The feeling is forever. It stares at you through shadows and it can haunt you when you ignore it.
Love can be blind, ignorant and painful and yet.....forever a memory.
When taught, when believed, when held on to, love is the greatest gift.
You grow up, you stand tall;
often creating games, building inner illusions.
The love of prosperity, the love of a friend, your pride, your spirit.
The love of an individual.
Express it, hold it, or at least remember it and the lessons it brings you.
The pain is created for it to heal, but not to be forgotten.
Unexplainable, strange.
Would you bury one of your greatest emotions?
Would you hide your inner reflection?
The world is a strange place and love itself is stranger than that.
Hold tight and watch the ways you walk.
One step closer to growing up.

Diane Riley

"Splendor"

God's handwork is all around us, as far as
    eye can see.
Oh, how beautiful every bird and flower and
    stately tree.
A precious baby with it's little fingers and toes.
the fresh green grass that continually grows.
Each new season with it's wonders to behold.
The beauty in the face of one growing old.
We owe it all to God above, who created it
    all because of his love.
The best thing of all that God ever gave,
    was his precious son, our lives to save.
Let's thank and praise him each day with
    good cheer,
with grateful hearts that He put us here.

Jeanne Marie Tenney

Feeling

Visions of light and dark are contrasted through the pupil of an eye; just as the feelings of the mind are filtered through the heart. What is seen is not the content of what is felt. The inner core of our existence sheds light upon what we feel. A feeling is something cherished by each individual; sacred and divine in its own unique way. Some can be worn on the sleeve and others can be tucked away deep in a concealed pocket. Yet both are what make each individual different and special in their own way. What brings about this eruption of thoughts and wonders we call "feelings?" An answer of any degree provides its own complications and is different in each instance. The one aspect of human nature that keeps america and each individual in it on edge or in suspense, loving or hating, giving or taking,...is feeling!

Without them where would we be? We would all be mindless zombies; prisoners of our own nonaffection towards life and the substances that are contained within it. We would be far from a world of war and crime and distant in efforts of love and worship. Without this one small thing, that is often over-looked by the same beings who embrace them, we would exist in a world of non-existence where emotions and feelings would fill the skies like clouds, as they slowly but constantly, pass us by.

Aaron D. Spears

If I Could Reverse The Hands Of Time

Who wouldn't help a little child with a dirty face and hungered
  eyes, when all around you are wonderfully blessed, plates
are filled, and you're finely dressed.
A plea for a crumb but no one has time...
Oh, if I could reverse the Hands of Time....

A silent whimper, listen! or don't you have time caught up in
  yourself just being a Mime?
A tug on your coat tail, Mr. if you have a crumb, that would
  be fine....
Oh! If I Could Reverse The Hands Of Time.

Harvey L. Grayson

Touch of a Teardrop

Like the touch of a teardrop,
Falling rain on the earth,
For the spirit of hope at our moment of birth
Offers chance that we may
Live in peace with our brothers,
And love will abide if we reach out to others.
Encourage our children,
Envelope our poor,
And strive for the dream of no hunger or war.
Our bodies shall wither,
Our spirits shall fly,
But love is the one thing we cannot let die.
Oh glorious flowing,
Such sweet wondrous love,
Bestowed and envisioned from heaven above
In the still of our hearts,
Through the passage of time,
Endlessly shining through your soul and mine.

Debbie Rawhouser

"Life's Truest Glory"

Physical beauty is a blessing... and can bring you envy, wealth, and fame,
But showing forth your inward charm will give more honor to your name,
Life offers many rewards to us for different tasks and achievements
but what matters more is the path we choose to strive to reap them!

Certainly perseverance, confidence, and beauty are key ingredients,
yet we must accept criticism and occasional failure for security of
  heartfelt contentment.

Realizing when we are deserving of an honor or if it belongs to
  another...
Demands a trial of our heart before proceeding any further.

Whatever life brings you...whether it be success or simple pleasure,
Please remember "eternity in heaven" is anyone's highest treasure.

So be careful and realize my words are delicately chosen to
  encourage your endeavors,
While assuring you I'll be there no matter what you encounter...
  ...For you are a glory of my life.

Beverly Lee Turner

Summer's Day

  Watching the summer's day. I find it
slipping away. The fun it brings me. The
fun and pain.
  Living as a shadow, a dream and another
life, made me think how it used to be.
  I still remember times like these in the
summer.
  To think of that again. I do while I'm in the
classroom.

Carter Mitchell

Female Perspective

She travels alone in the distant land
Familiar terrain, unknown language
Beleaguered by faces that look like her own
Innocent murmur invokes discord
Chance invisible to irascible

She clings to herself and midnight prayers
Desperate thoughts, groping for change
Unheard and unattended
Armor intact, shield clinched to anxious breast
Poised to fray or remove

Indecision born of concern
Break away, turnabout, disperse
Drowning in years of misdirection
Peering out the window from her kitchen sink
She travels alone in a barren land

Janet Beste

Meeting Halfway

She closes her eyes, welcomes the night
  Fantasies so real-could she be wrong?
Her mind narrates of their love story
  Is he listening? Does he hear her song?
The child grown into a woman's body-
  runs to her love when he calls.
Unlike her imaginative youth, in a world so
  great she is small.
Her new literacy in love's ache so piercing
  Great cheer turns sour when he's low.
A smiles so beautiful that he must be wearing
  for their seed to have a chance to grow.
If they two can share a rhythm, hearts adjoined
  composing one beat.
  Their bliss will be eternal!
  Midway is where they'll meet.

Julie Croisetiere

Love Is The Feeling

Love is the feeling that's in our hearts;
Far too deep to be torn apart.
If love is stronger than you and I,
I'll love you until the day I die.

Love is the feeling I have for you,
And I want to show you my love is true.
Deep in my heart, and far in my mind;
I always think of you as sweet and kind.

Love is the feeling shown on your face,
And being close as you say grace.
Your love for me, I love so much;
It grows so warm the times we touch.

In times to come with doubts indeed,
I hope you know your love I need.
The times you comfort me and hold me close,
Are the times I'll say I love you most.

I find that we do make a pair,
For love is found, and love is shared.
Love is the feeling...

Christianne Amouroux

Happy Birthday to You Fearfully and Wonderfully Made

Happy Birthday to you
  Fearfully and wonderfully made;
Chosen by God
  Called by his name.
Today is your day
  Ordered by God.
I'm sure when he made you
  He considered the stars.
Although thousands everywhere
  Share in this day
Only you make it special
  With all you give away.
Love and laughter,
  And a chaste conversation;
Are the main ingredients
  You give any relation
Here's hoping this birthday.
  Is the best birthday ever.
For a person so special
  May you enjoy it to the letter.

    Audrey Davis-Johnson

Forever More

One night there came a tapping, a rapping at my door.
Fearfully I answered, my conscience laden to the core.
Deep within my heart, I knew there would be more.
Should I not answer him, rapping, tapping at my door?
This could be forever more.

As I gazed upon this visage filled with bitter gore,
There was no doubt at all what he was coming for .
His scythe in hand he stood there, looking at the floor.
No longer was be tapping, rapping at my door.
This could be forever more.

Could I possibly escape through a trap within the floor?
Turn out all the lights so he couldn't see me anymore?
Could I search the paths outside, find my way in light so poor?
Or was I doomed forever to this man I did abhor?
This could be forever more.

Running, running, running, the pain within my chest I bore,
Brambles tearing at my feet, I stood stone still in horror!
The path that I had taken led me right back to my door!!
He stood there barely grinning - this was forever more.

    Carolyn Mae Bolander

On Christie Lake

Winds of the earth are calm
Feathers of the trees withhold their song
Rays of the white one reflect in a shimmer
The red eye of a loon can be caught in a glimmer

Scaled ones move beneath with swift desire
By the edge a green one waits with coiled vigor
  For one of Millions to decide to linger

Miles away roars the voice of thunder
All Gods creatures are compelled to wonder

Through the still air comes the crack of white power
Young ones search for mother
  But even she cowers

Heavens let go in the darkening doom
Those dry won't be soon

In grey light the thunder moves on
To give way to natures dawn

With golden tune the birds rejoice
Announce the new fire with their golden voice
In the days new light the cycle moves on
Soon it will be time to wait for another dawn

    Anthony C. Germano Jr.

Poem for My Son

I watch the wind on the flowers on your grave,
Feel morning fog on the back of my neck,
Believe in things I cannot see.

Over there, out of sight, a workman
Runs a machine along the grass.
Above the fog, a jet moves on.

Beyond the trees, beyond the invisible lake,
Cascade Mountains are there, and yet not there.
Through that glass we do see darkly,
We are almost blind.

I sit, and watch, and wait.
Our spirits are at peace and home,
And a million restless miles from home.

    Dr. Michael Little

Angels

Angels watching from above
Fill my world with endless love
Mystical, magical, with crisp white veils
To serve the Lord they never fail

They prance about on heaven's floor
They live in peace and love galore
They're honest ones who never lie
Their goodness and truth will never die

I know that they will always be
Right by my side to comfort me
And when I die, and I move on
My soul will rise above the sun

And they will say, "we welcome you"
And I'll become an angel, too.

    Dana Giese

It's Lonely Being Smart

Oh, it's lonely being smart,
  First one to finish, first one to start.
People always making fun of you,
  Calling you a "goody-two-shoe."
Always getting straight A's,
  Our life is like a giant maze.
Don't know which way to turn,
  People's trust you have to earn.
People use you for nothing but homework,
  When they turn it in, all they do is smirk.
When you say, you're going to tell,
  They beat you up after the bell.
Oh, it's lonely being smart,
  First one to finish, first one to start.

    Amber McMahon

Switzerland

Switzerland has many clocks; they all tell time.
Floors of faces stare at you, their pendulums in rhyme.
The cuckoo sends its brave note out, then goes back in to sleep.
The boy-girl figures dance, retreat, their love tryst for to keep.

The giants jut above the cloud where streams are daily born.
They have good reason to be proud, Mont Blanc, the Matterhorn.
The flower boxes are ablaze with myriads of flowers.
The gnomes of Zurich count their gold while the clocks count the hours.

Cradle of rivers: the Rhine, the Rhone, Danube - here all start,
And furnish the vital life blood of Europe's very heart.
A land of lakes, a land of cheese, of greenery and rock,
Of dreamy clouds and cloudy dreams. Then "cuckoo" says the clock.

    Fred J. Palardy

Beauty

Girdled with gold her beauty
foams like the horizon spray.
The serene touches
of the blithe laurel transcend heaven and home.
And her blossoming vernal rays
dazzle the eye of day.

Her flails float like waves
on a visionary gleam.
Her endless grace emanates like
the chorus hymeneal of a crystal stream.
Her goggling eyes score the sky
and rent argosies of magic sails.
On her cheek and over her Helen's brow -
The perfume melts the evening stars.

Behold those beautiful smiles;
Nature softens its hue from her dreams.
The unrefined sprightly dance
befits soul's immortality.
With tender kisses, beauty infatuates an innocent
brow of love.

Bulusu Lakshman

For All That Will Listen

For all that will listen
For all that do care.
The good Lord has made a world for all to share.
He's given us a chance in this world he has made.
And we've given him back so much heartache and shame.
There's crime in this world and O so much hate.
The love that once was is being overtaken.
The killing, stealing, drugs, and abuse.
The hatred against each other.
And why? There's no excuse.
Were all God's children
For God made us all.
And together we should love.
Before hate kills us all.
So for all that will listen.
And for all that do care.
The world was made for us all to share.

Jan Robinson

Old Age

To let you know I appreciate you.
For all the little things you do.
It is comfort to know that you care.
And that you are always there.

Sometimes I feel cut down and cast away
Then you call and say, how are you today?
Through all the trouble that you see.
But you still have time to think of me.

I think sometime if I got sick.
Who could I call that would be here quick?
So when you have a lot of birthdays, you will see.
Just what these little things mean to me.

Carrie H. Edge

South Central

Gunshots in the light.
Shining down is the streetlight.
The dogs are barking,
And the sniper's marking.
Living in fear all the time,
Because anything can happen, some kind of crime.
The people here don't want your pity,
Since this is life, life in the city.

Harma Turbendian

Rejoice With Me

Wear bright colors, pink, orange and red
For by JESUS CHRIST my life was led
Sing praises, clap your hands and stomp your feet
It's JESUS MY LORD I am going home to meet

Rejoice with me and do not mourn
MY SAVIOUR took me home before the dawn
The joy that I feel on this day
Is because of the glorious beauty I saw along the way

My simple words cannot describe
The golden streets sitting shiny and wide
Angels are ascending and descending all over the place
Something tells me that it is nothing but his grace

Although my body is going back to the dust
My spirit and soul to GOD I safely entrust
So rejoice with me my dearest ones
I am just a saved life away I am not really gone

Live right, put GOD first and let him lead
Your existence on earth that is what you truly need
If you give your life to him you will not miss
This joy, this peace and this heavenly bliss

Angela B. Bottex

Wishes to Fate

There are people who ask their fate
for countless wealth
for rubies and diamonds
and pearl necklaces
There are others who see their future in fame,
voyages, and parties
And there are people who need not
have anything, but the daily bread
and a place to live, to be happy...
But I would like to ask you, my Destiny
to give me one sun ray everyday
and a piece of sky
and a smile of neverending spring

Eva Grzegorczyk

Truth And Friendship

In you, I have found true friendship.
For ever so long I have searched for those that hold
   A passion for living each day as a new beginning.
I have searched and found emptiness in words, darkness in minds,
   Immoral acceptances and weak moralities.
But in my mind's eye, as I pass through this degradation of our
   Humanity,
I see you rise beyond this pessimism with a strength surrounding your
   very being.
You seem to know the weaknesses that make each vulnerable,
And you have walked those dark paths that are better left without
   footprints.
Still yet, you smile when reminiscing those parched memories of a
   bittersweet past.
For it is you that does not judge;
   that does not ridicule,
   laugh or call names.
It is you that will listen when all others have but empty advice.
You feel compassion for the most human of situations,
And these rare and precious qualities in which your soul cradles
   Have drawn my everlasting friendship to you.

Julie A. Linn-West

A Special Thanks

Thank you for all that you've done
For every night until the next mornings sun
You've watched over me, for I didn't have to hide
Through good and bad times, you've stayed by my side
You've given me someone to share my life with
To that someone, my heart I shall give
Taught me how to share, and how to care
Showed me sometimes life isn't always fair
You've always helped me through
Especially when I didn't know what to do
You've helped me make it his far, this long
You've always had me learn right from wrong
Thank you for all that you've done
Now you know it's you that won
This is a special thanks to you
Something I wanted to take the time to do.

Debra A. Baker

Fate

We set our course and planned ahead.
  For forty years - since we first wed
and charted life the way we dreamt
  would be our big retirement.

To sail upon a sparkling sea,
  was all we talked of, him and me.
Let's leave the mooring, hoist our sails
  and gather new and different tales.

But fate would have a different plan
  would want us both to stay on land.
My Captain who has been so strong
  may lose his strength before too long.

We'll take what time is left to face
  still set our sail for distant place,
and both will know when fate won out
  will change our course, and come about.

Anna L. Pearsall

We Live Because Of God's Mercy

It is God's mercy that is keeping us here
For he is ever consoling, ever loving, ever near
If not for God's mercy, we would all be surely lost
We must keep his commandments, regardless of the cost.

He will be our strength in the time of need
If we but have the patience great as a mustard seed
He will fight our battle if we but let him in
He will keep us ever happy if we depart from sin

God's mercy is not reserved for special folk, you know
But for everyone who allows himself to grow
To the christian, to the saint, but to the sinner most
  of all

If you want to be successful
As you live down here below
Just ask for God's mercy, which he will surely show
And, as soon as you should get it
Never let him down: Be merciful to others!
Share what you have found!

Barbara M. Dunn

Reflection

Where oh where have the years all gone?
So many years since I was born.
The golden rule, did I always observe?
Did I do too many things myself to serve?
And as I reflect I feel content
All those years I think were well spent.

Doris I. Lombardi

A Lullaby For Matthew

Cricket Cricket, come 'neath my window.
Sing me a lullaby this lovely night.
Cricket, cricket, come serenade me.
Sing me to sleep till the morning's light.

Jason DeVore

The Message

I've waited for what to me seemed like a year,
For in paradise my thoughts had to be,
If I were to describe a true picture of you,
And the wonders you've done just for me.

A message will come and soon it will be,
Transcribed in my mind, to hold there forever.
A description of you and your wonderful charms,
Your unselfish ways your undying endeavor.

Oh message please hurry, least my thoughts stray,
Oh mind don't betray me and lead them away.
This suspense is unbearable, I tremble with fear,
That my thoughts would be lost, when all were so near.

I'm racking, I'm tearing, I'm purging my brain,
For a message so rare and concise,
Be quiet! and listen for the message is here!!!
And shucks, it just says that you're nice.

Anna C. Bradford (nee) Snesko

My Hand

I'm going to present to you my hand,
For in this hand you'll see how I stand.

For the symbol of peace is present here,
The kind of peace I wish the world to see.
And also the peace and quiet I enjoy, just for me.

This hand tends to hold things inside,
These being feelings and thoughts, who often need a guide.

This is usually a very quiet hand,
But when upset, will take its stand.
For traveling about is a favorite of this hand,
For it has seen parts of the U.S. and some foreign land.

For within this hand, there's a dream in mind,
This being friendship and trust with all mankind.

Wouldn't it be great to shake or hold anyone's hand,
Free of fear in any land.

I hope you see why I take this stand,
And realize it's just a helping hand.

John R. Jones

Be Unkind To Me As It Pleases You

Be unkind to me as it pleases you
For kindness is a truly wretched thing
That demands light be shed on untold truths,
Exposing the lies we are cradling.

Reeking of this predictability,
Falling short of inevitable tears
We two have hidden, unable to see,
The souls of each other these many years.

And yet of all queenly spirits conceived
And impressed upon my petty domain,
Your beauty is in but small bursts perceived
Lest I should forget and alone remain.

Love is easier to feel than to do -
If this is truth then the rest must be true.

David J. Reynolds

My Sister - My Friend

I have a sister we call the glamorous one
For me I felt it wasn't always fun
I always thought that she had the most
And to this day we are still very close
As we get older we try to get together more
But it would be nicer if she lived next door
I love her more year after year
And I happen to think we are just a great pair
So I dedicate this poem to her
In hopes the good times will always occur

Dolores Terhune

March Madness

The tournament consists of 64 teams.
For most of them it was in their dreams
The Wildcats, Tar Heels, and the Hoosiers
Most teams will end up losers
Coach Patino, Krzyzeski, Knight and of course Dean
Their names are not uncommon in the Sweet Sixteen
There's always Dick Vitale's "Unbelievable Baby"
This March Madness thing is totally crazy.
From Webbers timeout, to Jimmy V
You won't want to leave your T.V.
That fade away jumper to win the game
Will bring both player and school, fortune and fame.
Through all the hype, madness and bets
Only one team will get to cut down the nets.
What will the winner be taking?
Why, of course the number 1 ranking!

Brendan Casey

There's Smog In My Valley

Let me sing you a ditty: I left the big city
For my home in the hills far away;
As I came to my valley, folks were rousin' to rally,
"There's smog in my valley," they say.

There's smog in my valley, there's smog in my valley,
Hear the cry of the crow and the jay;
It's time folks were larnin' to hear Nature's warnin';
"There's smog in my valley," they say.

The blue skies are darkenin', the dogwoods are barkin',
The pine trees are fallin' so low;
The Ivy is weepin', no more she'll be creepin',
"There's smog in my valley," they say.

Go pick the last berry for li'l Tom and Jerry,
The mockin' birds leavin' the vale;
Will the birds be returnin' from their long winter's journey?
"There's smog in my valley," they say.

The mill pond is murky, oh where's the wild turkey,
The white wing, the geese and the teal?
I don't want no Diesel, that big city weasel,
Go bring back my ol' water wheel.

Elma T. Cabral

The Brook

Everyone knows the brook babbles in its bed,
For no one has heard it just talking instead.
Plus, few have heard the secrets it will tell,
And those who do are under its magic spell.
It unravels mystery after mystery,
And takes you through stories of history.
Then when it's done,
Away home you run,
Sometimes still wondering what other things it holds
That nobody knows about, except the frogs and the toads.

Evelyn M. Wolgemuth

Come Dear Reader:

Words will be our paint,
For pictures of many a thing.
Pencil will be our brush,
For words that rhyme and sing.

We'll visit many a place then,
Forest, city, farm and woodsy glen.
We'll listen to many a sound,
From rushing trucks, to fairies dancing round.

We'll feel the wind, the rain, and sleet,
The satin softness of fairy feet.
We'll smell the flowers, saltiness of the sea,
And the sweet nectar of the honey bee.

We'll see the sights of harbor and of town,
And ships on rivers sailing up and down.
We'll see the scenes of farm and country,
And of birds nesting in a tree.

What a magic brush a pen can be,
It paints so many worlds for me.
Imagination - what a magic trip,
Better than a plane, a car or giant ship.

Charlott Holck

I'm Grateful

I'm grateful
For rain that falls on ground that's dry
For air we breath and birds that fly
For sunshine warming up the sky___
I'm grateful!

I'm grateful
For flowers basking in the sun
Tranquility, when day is done
For rest, after a day of fun___
I'm grateful!

I'm grateful
For laughter that is full and deep
For friendships that I plan to keep
For children, in the spring of life
Who are free of hate, and fear, and strife.
For life itself is in the living
A joy forever, when it's giving.
The simple things that bring a smile
A life of love, is a life worthwhile!

I'm grateful!

Al Cobine

Notes On The Eskimo

An Eskimo never plays hookey to fish -
For shining's from what he'd play hookey, because
For super or breakfast or luncheon his dish
Is fresh frozen fish without Hollandaise sauce.

An Eskimo dresses in second hand clothes.
(They were mostly worn first by some seals and some bears.)
Just who is inside all those furs no one knows
And nobody much, but an Eskimo, cares.

The Eskimo's sun doesn't set at all right
But it skids all around just above the horizon
And when it goes down for a six month long night
It's the dreariest sight that you ever laid eyes on.

The big polar bears that we think are so cute
When we go to the zoo where the cages are nice
Are the Eskimo's neighbors he meets snoot to snoot
On a slippery slidery small cake of ice.

Howard M. Fitch

Broken Vows

There will always be, a place in my heart,
For so many years, we were never apart,
I feel that you helped me to grow,
What happened now, I may never know.
My memories of you will never die,
Now I must go on, I must try.
Peace of mind is what we both now need,
A new reality, no need for greed.
Let's break away and start a new life,
I know I'm no longer your wife.
Whatever the future holds, we shall see.
For now I know, I must let it be!

Donna Donzella

Mom

I wanted to tell you how sorry I was
for the trouble I caused years ago,
    But I didn't
I wanted to say thanks for raising
me the way you did,
    But I didn't
I wanted to tell you how I missed you all these
years since moving so far away,
    But I didn't
I wanted my family to come out and have a
nice visit this year with you,
    But I didn't
And I wanted to tell you I love you
At least one more time
    But I didn't
Then I thought I would still have my chance
When you got out of the hospital because you
would get better
    But you didn't

Dan Rozsa

I Live...

I live for the sounds that make me dance...
..for the voice that gives me the strength to sing,
yet I cry at night for the days of struggling
that remain...
..for this life threatening cloud seems to
just hang.

I turn to my beliefs and pray for the chance...
to feel like a performer feels when at her first
dance, to return to the peak of my passion
for life...the moment before my song was denied.

Jennifer Rosa Isabella

Memories I Hold

Memories I hold I use to live, feelings I have I cannot give.
    For there is no one to take my love for you - I know it's
dead but it's all I cling to.

Tomorrow I plan it never comes, the song I sing, no one
hums.
I have no joys I have no fun.
...I love memories.

Pictures in mind, on paper I see. Everyone knows you're
no longer with me. I know that fact but can't be free.
...I love memories.

So I say good-bye for the thousandth time and write a
verse that ends in rhyme.
But the death I die, I die each time I have those memories.

Douglas Robert Munves

My Children

O' Lord thank you for my children
For they are everything in the world to me
They are all I could've hoped for them to be
They are such an inspiration
They put feeling into my heart
I cry in desperation when we are apart
I am the lucky one that has this chance to
watch them grow
O' Lord please remind me when they cry
I need to hold and comfort them
Because some day they will have to go
I'll do my best to raise them
I'll give them what I can
O' Lord I'll need your guidance
So please take me by the hand
O' Lord remind me to have patience when
the day seem to go slow
They are so little but through the years they'll grow
When they look back on their memories of me
I want their smiles to glow

Angela Kay Elliott

5-5-2000

The day had come and the day had passed,
For those who believed were the last.
    Those who doubted weren't to be found,
Shrieking cries sounded around,
    As souls body's dropped to the ground.
Innocent children who had no idea,
    Now hiding in corners filled with fear.
The others who were wounded lay there to die,
    As a little girl hovers here mothers body and cries.
Not understanding what had happened that day
    now all by herself, lost, scared, alone.
The Armageddon had come which only few believed,
    As I sat there thinking to myself,
Death had taken millions under it's sleeve.

Jonah Yolman

Key To My Soul

Take me as I am
For thou know not what is inside.
The outside is but a shell with no significance
but the inside radiates with brilliance and heat.

The inside is sheathed from all
except those that have the key to thy soul.
Be aware for thy soul relinquishes great power
Once released it cannot be shut, till that very key closes it
backup.

If the key is not taken out in time
it could be marred by the very essence of this world; evil.
So if thee wish to open the shell
and get to the very marrow of thy soul
make sure thee knows the consequences

Casey L. Maker

Sands Of Time

A golden sunset, an ocean of blue,
Standing on the sands of heartache, thinking of you.

Yesterday's gone and the memories fade,
Tomorrow is the desire of which dreams are made.

Billowing clouds against a horizon of hope,
Praying with each tragedy comes a time to cope.

Life is a journey which we must pursue,
Hand in hand with fate until the journey is through.

JoLynn Foldesi

The Smiling Angels

The Angels must have smiled upon me the day I met you,
for when I first looked in your eyes,
I knew you were my Angel from heaven;

The Angels must have smiled upon me the day we married,
because I knew God sent you to me to share my life,
for I had dreamed of you since the day I turned eleven;

The Angels will continue to smile upon me because I have you
and your love for all the days of my life,
to share through good times and bad;

The Angels are smiling on us now because they know the love
they cast upon us will always be had.

Cathi Hammonds

My Dearest

When I am near you-my soul is at peace.
For you are my dearest.
With my wild heart in your hands-you have tamed it.
For you are my dearest.
When I am depressed-you uplift my weary spirit.
Your smile lights my darken world-and brings warmth
and love into my life.
For you are my dearest.

My love for you holds no bounds.
Happiness-is what you give me.
My life, my hopes, my dreams - I want to share with you.
The sacrifices I make are only for you.
Through life eternal I will always adore you.
For you are my life.
You are my love.
You are my dearest.

Jeffery T. Van Clief

Wishes for Grant

Dream your dreams and make them come true
For your future is the outcome of everything you do
Believe in yourself and hold the world in your hands
Make the best of everything, do the best you can

You'll always be loved whether you're right or wrong
Losing is a part of winning, it helps make people strong
Don't live your life by someone else's opinion
Trust in yourself and build your own foundation

Sometimes you may feel it's a struggle you can't seem to get
through
I hope you'll come to me so I can help you
I see my own dreams in what you'll one day be
Watching you grow and succeed is what sets my soul free!

Anita T. Nouman

Only The Strong

As close as they could be, is what they were and shall
forever be
No one could stop the love is what people would see
Until one night when love went wrong
He wrote a note for only the strong
They met in a forest, on a cold winter night
But only to begin a vicious fight
What happened that night, when his high school ring came off
her finger
Well, all our minds will forever linger
The next night he came to say he was wrong
But the note was only for the strong
Did he place the ring back on her finger is what everyone
wants to know
As they watch her casket be lowered to the snow.

Carrie R. Coram

Always Moving

The earth in its own world
Forever spinning, round and round
People in their daily search of life
Always moving from town to town

Winds of change circle the earth
Chasing sands of time in the sky
Birth, death, love, hate day after day
Burns a tear of joy and fear in your eye

Time to chase your dream once again
Leaving in hope its for the best
Always searching, never finding
Lost in the crowd like all the rest

One day you awake in a pool of fear
Ten years lost, gone, without a clue
Everything lost, nothing gained
Ask yourself "What is left to do?"

Always follow your dreams
Forever guiding your heart
Never looking back
Everyday a new start

Edward A. Galvan

Afflictions of the Soul

Time is unending; it goes on
Forging ahead it leaves its impressions
In its solitary confined movement it scars
Never ending as it goes it marks the unwilling

Just as day becomes night my world strives
toward reality
Reality - not for the eyes of the seeing,
but for the souls of the broken

The outline of the soulful gone,
broken by their reality
They sit a wilting mass
stripped of their identity

The worlds outline fading as the end grows near
it knows the souls of the broken
for its outline, broken by the same sits fading
Death...our reality
Time...our outline
Hatred....our scars

Dawn Bougher

Remembering

Bygone years...now memories,
Framed pictures in my mind.
  I reminisce as dusk draws near,
  Of friendships left behind.

Shared secrets fill a page or two,
With chapters sealed by trust.
  Shared tears paint a rainbows hue,
  O'er feelings 'neath the dust.

Remembering brings back the days,
Of calls made in the night.
  Strong needs to share before sun's rays,
  A real or fancied plight.

In days gone by...time was our guest,
No need to run or hurry.
  Age never put us to the test,
  Sparing us needless worry.

Sometime within these precious years,
Friends slowly grew apart.
  Nostalgia brings them back so dear,
  Cherished within my heart.

Frances Kovacs

A Child's Cry

Where boredom reigns with unrelenting tenacity,
freedom is revolution of the soul.
Grasp it; inject it; breath it; expand!
Distill yourself man—evaporate and condense.
Shed the pretense as a snake sheds its skin—
layer by layer—to reveal a scared, atrophic child within.
Nurture it! Remove the pillow from its face!
Let it scream!
Recognize your own infanticide?
No where to hide?
Face what's inside!
Fight the temptation to lullaby!
[You] ignorant fool—these shackles are made
by you!

James Gilmartin

O Rose, Take Heart

A rosebud sprouted on a dismal day,
from a seed that strayed and survived by chance.
So delicate was the dormant receptacle,
in the gust of wind on its rhythmic dance.
'Twas an enclosed life, shut from the world,
unbeknownst of how it came about, or why,
and what such exposure would be received,
when it opened its petals as time would go by.
Alas, the inevitable had arrived,
when time came for the lonely flower to bloom.
It found enough sunlight, rich earth,
pure moisture from occasional rainfall, and ample room.
Yet quite discontented was the mundane blossom,
for the sunflowers yonder surpassed it in height,
and the lilacs to the left of the unruly yard
seemed splattered by magnificent colors more bright.
O sullen little rose, shut from the world,
unbeknownst of how you came about, or why,
please learn to take heart, for a rose among weeds
begins to choke, and wilt, and soulfully die.

Debra Rivera

"Rhyme"

I do so love the words of rhyme
From poets pens that write like mine,
I'm out of step with rhetoric prose
Whose claim to Art is "Anything Goes"

My youth was with the ones that write
A line of words whose sweet delight
Could easy tell the one who reads,
This is the way that romance breeds.

Without the stimulus of rhyme,
A shallowness invades my wine,
As if there was no strength to pour
A depth of words I could adore.

S. Kahn, Hammerstein and Porter too,
Were members of my learning crew,
Each brilliant song their words supported
Brought such wealth to hearts when courted.

And so; my membership remains,
Amid the vintages and frames
Of those whose feelings spoke like mine,
With words whose meanings were in Rhyme.

Herb Walsh

Slow Siftings of Being by the Cup

We sipped on our blood from old battered cups by degrees
From questionable alphabetical tea leaves
In a similarly drained historically empty cafe in York
Waiting upon your pained syllables and persistent look.

We could only misspell Wittgenstein's non-saying silent game
Heidegger's small hut dug slowly from the ground of the no-name
Auden and Hughes' nearby murmuring for Love's causes,
And Pinter's pettily precise coughing between pauses.

We were never sure how to say our sips meaningfully without bowels
Yet you always uttered to my restive unordered vowels:
"These inconstant consonants matter in soft sighs",
I could only nod into my cup of scattered leaves going dry.

My dissolved dregs seemed like a crumpled deserted Kafkesque beetle;
Then I recalled a meeting in a Parisian cafe between Beckett and
   Wiesel,
They graced through sorrow into holier spaces of silence
Seeing the Being of the world through the swaying of birch trees'
   accents.

We sat amidst soft pausing on ruddy with-drawn old stools
Which could have been made from concentration camp tools.
All our names now lie discarded upon dirty, ashen tea trays
Survived to tell us of the truth or falsehoods of our clinging ways.

Joe Waldron

"Opening Day"

On opening day, baseball arrived, and the stadium filled with sound,
From the crack of the bat to the cheer of the crowd when the pitcher
   walked to the mound.
The first ball hit was over the wall and their team took the lead,
They kept this lead throughout the ninth and one more out was their
   only need.
But we had runners at first and third and my hero was up to bat,
But the ball went past at such a speed that the wind blew off his hat!
The second one was much the same and he was ready for another,
Then the pitcher threw his wildest pitch and the crowd yelled out,
   "Oh Brother!"
But my hero was ready and tightened his grip and swung with all
   his might,
He won the game by hitting the ball out of the park and out of sight!

Doug Pester

Marilyn and the Frog Prince

She is so incredibly beautiful is the only fact he knows about her.
From the curls of her blond hair to the tips of her perfect feet, and
all the luscious sultry curves in between, she's gorgeous,
practically flawless.
One might say, "She walks in beauty like the night." He says from the
flick of her wrist to the twist in her hips he is left in awe. Yet
all he can tell you about her are her looks. For he knows nothing
about her, yet they share a song a rhythm move with me. Of her he'll
tell you only appearance, for its all he knows. Of himself he'll tell
you only feelings, for you could look past him and not see him. To
look at him you might not see that he feels totally unworthy. When
he stands in her presence, he feels like nothing, insignificant but
wanting. Wanting her to take him and like the princess, kiss the frog
and hope for the best. Knowing that he may not turn into a prince
over night, but that inside he is a prince. Down deep where he's
almost forgotten about, but secretly is yearning for the kiss that
will someday transform him.

Edward A. Nason

The Helmet

The helmet lay abandoned a few yards away
From the still young man, who had fallen that day.
He was only one of many to be counted by the squad,
Sent to check their losses, strewn there upon the sod.
They'll look at one another silently remembering those,
Who'd fought beside them yesterday so bravely,
Against their so-called foes.
One cannot help but wonder where all of this will lead,
They say this war must go on 'til everyone's been freed;
Yet they forgot to mention how very much it would cost
In the millions of lives that would have to be lost.
Perhaps these are the free — the ones who fought and died,
Maybe they have found true peace
God knows they really tried.

Dorothy Jeane Renchko

Being In Between

You are in between; you are to old to be called a boy or
girl, and yet to young to be a man or woman. You know to
much about life to be a child and yet to little to be an adult.

It is a strange conforming, non conforming time.
Where you are ready for everything; and prepared for nothing.

It is a time when the lines of love and infatuation cross
and recross than uncross and yet never run together nor apart.

You are in between, not ready to be called mam or sir;
Often just referred to as him or her. Seeking a distinction
of yourself amidst the indistinction of being; because you
are in between.

Germanuel B. Lea Jr.

My Friend

He said every single person is unique,
"Girl, stop feeling sorry about yourself".
He would say in my down times.
"Move on if your best is not good enough.
There will be success as well failure; this way
you shall become wise.
In the meantime wipe up your tears.
They won't let you see the brightness of God.
Do me a favor and don't look back, let me
see your forehead real high and those eyes shining of pride."

Belma Saucedo

Lord My Mother Is Coming

Lord my mother is coming
Give her a helping hand
Don't let her suffer unneedlessly
Just take her to your great land

Lord she's done good for others
I know she'll do good for you
Give her a chance, Dear Father
She'll show you what she can do

She has loved her brothers and sisters
She loved her children and friends as well
She has loved the church that she went to
So please don't send her to hell

She has many elderly friends, Dear Lord
Who will someday be with you too
When they all get together
They'll put on a show for you

Lord I'm begging your pardon
But I must say it again
Reach out your hand to help her
And take her to the Promise Land

Joseph L. Minnella

Freedom

My soul is all of me
Giving me the freedom to be.

All you need is but to listen
And, in time, you'll start to glisten.

Your body is only an encasement for your soul
With no genitals, so I've been told.

So go within and be as one
Now your journey has just begun.

And, in time you'll reach a point
Where love, peace, and harmony
He will anoint.

Brenda Swanson

Swans

They were always two
gliding through the aisles in the grocery store
holding hands
sighing
like twin breezes
of angel's breath
lavender and rose lingered where they stepped
your eyes followed them
watching
precious first-time moments
tiptoe kisses
in front of strawberries and peaches
indecent touches in front of lucky strangers
giggling
making a summer afternoon magic
gliding past through the automatic swinging doors
leaving you breathless
in ecstasy
watching a dream come true
like swans

Ivy Camille Sharpe

March Dreamland

The frost-covered trees
Glisten like crystals.
A mystical, magical March dreamland.

Like some other world,
A forest of legends.
Shining so bright in the heart of my mind.

Yet it is real,
A pure gift from God.
I can't believe I see it, with my own eyes.

Frozen so still,
But it must go away someday.
So glorious, so beautiful, but it can't last forever.

Benjamin Goldblatt

The Wolf

A long grey veil falls over the sun
And there she stands; the lonely one
Her sorrowful eyes look up to the sky
She gives a sharp shudder and starts to cry
A long sad howl; a helpless plea
Making one feel desperate to be free
Again and again she cries on and on
Then, as quick as you've seen her—
  Alas, she is gone.

Diana Toole

Life...Again

Who took my place in the sun?
Glory lay on my face
hot wind held me
strong
I stood in a golden pool
head hanging back
brown to golden orb

My life I saw reflected in the celestial eye...
　　Smiles white as the Everest crest
　　Tears that washed an ocean floor
　　Laughter that tolled a global bell
　　Pain that swept a land from shore to shore

Sheets of gold, my once lived life enfold
pregnant Spring cloud give birth
shower the face
on my head hanging back
in worship

I drank
and my petals opened
and I was reborn
　　Gayle L. Crowell

Between the Tides

Between the tides there lies a perfect place.
Go through the rainbow with sugar cane lace,
Around the sunset and under the sand,
And you will find this most wonderful land.

This place I talk of may not seem so real.
Since it has not been seen by dog or seal.
No other living thing has ventured near.
For this place exists neither here nor there.

Between the tides is where you can reach it.
It can be found in your thoughts and spirit.
Once you find it, it can never be lost,
But you can not buy it at any cost.

This place I talk of makes all things come true.
You can do anything you want to do.
You may jump and run or lie in the sun.
When you are in your imagination.
　　Julie McAskill

The Power of Prayer

Nothing is impossible with God for every hour of fervent prayer,
God sustains us in His divine care.
The solace we find in answer to our prayer,
With the peace of mind we derive with absolutely nothing can compare,
To each of us God gives a cross to bear,
No one is left out, although some of us feel we have more than our
　　share,
It never is because God loves anyone in the world less,
On the contrary, He loves those most, who willingly and patiently
　　withstand each test,
He loves everyone equally, dearly and sincerely I am positively sure,
Because He gives us courage and strength for all obstacles to endure,
Each trial, each sorrow, each stress and each duress,
Graciously within His supreme power He will suppress,
In every possible way, I must convey,
That miracles still happen from day to day,
For every dark cloud, there is a silver lining too,
In many instances God proves that there is nothing He cannot do,
For every hour of sunshine, there is also an hour of rain,
For every loss we suffer, there will be something to regain,
For God is known to always balance everything, to guide and bless,
Bring peace to the World, to always do His very best, to answer each
　　request.
　　Georgia E. Hamil

A Sonnet to Her Lover

What man should be — so you are!
God's echo! Marked by reasoning and mind,
Whose thoughts can outrun time and plan afar;
Who uses facts to cosmic patterns find.

And yet — emotions must the mental process tame.
To create love and warmth within the race;
As rain, when badly need, finally came
To cool the searing drought in some drear place.

And bravery must perforce be in the heart
And gentleness portrayed with every deed;
For man must face the essence of his part
And must give love and, needed, answer need.

Such man should be, and such you seem to be.
Or is desire the glass through which I see?
　　Dorothea M. Eiler

Granddaddy's Chair

Arms high, seat low—
　　Granddaddy's chair.

Rockers short, memories long—
　　Granddaddy's chair.

Within its arms, prayers and hopes wandered—
　　Granddaddy's chair.

Stood before the fire, waiting for the sire—
　　Granddaddy's chair.

Sire's days done, passed to the son—
　　Granddaddy's chair.

Son did magic work, gave old wood re-birth—
　　Granddaddy's chair.

Now it stands, in other hands—
　　Granddaddy's chair.

On log-lit nights, the son's son ponders—
　　In Granddaddy's chair.
　　Charles U. Wood Jr.

Land of Beginning Again

Grief of a lost love will return or be replaced to a
greater height on the wings of a white dove.
Without this courage there can be no trust.
Without trust, there can be no virtue.
If there were only a place where we could take off all
the heartaches, pain, selfishness—all of our mistakes.
Leave them at the door like an old shabby coat and enter
the LAND OF BEGINNING AGAIN.
Where we could hail ones we misjudged as a dear friend
and those we begrudged their victories on earth.
To look at each other and feel in our heart, our love
in new birth. Your question is when?
Kiss my lips, close your eyes, grasp my hand and we
will enter the

　LAND OF BEGINNING AGAIN
　　Carol L. Adams-Kimmel

Wishing

The wishing well, it stands alone, neglected and confused.
No one comes around it now, no one to be amused.

Imaginations long since died, and no one can retrieve,
A solitary wish from it, not even one reprieve.

Hope is fading, love is dying, eyes have all gone blind.
Hearts no more our rulers make, only our simple minds.
　　Holly L. Hampton

The Level

The splinters, all slanted in the same direction,
greet your skin and enter,
accepting the invitation as you crawl up.
Reaching the landing of level ground
the strength of your collapsing body disintegrates.
The sunlight, first so soothing,
begins to stagnate you.
Staying on level ground is never enough.
To you, trying to climb to
higher elevation is inevitable.
But the same conditions salivate for your flesh.
Afraid,
you turn and hang your toes over the edge of the level.
One foot forward and the splinters bow
so you can slide with ease.
Then breaking and crumbling,
your body has hit its cement coffin.

Jill Williams

The Attic Trunk

Oh, frail hands whose gentle fingers on my ancient clasp
Grope, fumbling, for the dreams of youth, held captive 'neath my grasp
Turn hard the key and lift the door to peace for aged mind,
And bid your mistress find within the joys she left behind.

As fingers touch a yellowed gown, entwine a wisp of lace,
A fragment of a sleeping memory, mirrored in her face
Is softly bidding buried dreams to waken and arise,
And paint a blush on faded cheeks, a glow in tired eyes.

How quickly does her trembling cease, her countenance serene,
As she caresses packs of letters neatly tied with string;
And moments, bright with tenderness, imprisoned by the chain
Of time, have wakened to her touch and found her heart again.

Oh, gentle hands, I now perceive your lonely purpose here,
For resolutely she returns the treasures that I bear.
Accompanied by her whispered sigh, you place atop it all
A photo, scribed, "To my dear love" in faint, familiar scrawl.

Bess Sibley

Morpheus

Gloomy, bloodless God in whose hair the bards may hide
grovel hopeful heirs to stars and plummets and horrors
caught by the tendrils in that dewy eye
In oblivious sleep
    carried by force of gentle leading and umbrage o'er-leaning
And when the shadows begin their ominous creep
    This wandering, benighted soul could trip along shores
      with angels teaming

Hang, black-draped, deadly sibling
    And remind us of square white hung with red
    Knots in our structure, stiff in a paler bed
The same sands wherein we've left our print
    Nebulae and fiery winged haunt and call
Milky-orbed grinning
Let me die in the dreaming
For now amorphous form its comfort misgives
    That I may die and in the dying live

Gary Gibson

The Springtime of Our Love

Step by step we walk
Guided by the stars above
Sweet aromas of lilacs and dew surround us
In the springtime of our love.
Birds and crickets begin to sing
Into the blue-black night
As I enter your embrace
To dance in a pool of shimmering moonlight.
While there is no music
But for the song of the birds
Their melody sounds as sweet
As any love song we have heard.
Though clouds begin to filter across
The enchanted velvet sky
The falling raindrops cannot extinguish
The passion between you and I.

Jacci Mohr

Cleo

Thump, thump, thump it walks across the floor.
H-h-ha, h-h-ha, h-h-ha it breaths as it passes.
People gasp,
people ooh,
and people aaah.
Swish, swish, swish goes the tail.
People scream, with surprise as they feel a wet nose
and a rough tongue on their face. Then they say, "Oh,
Cleo you scared me!"

Christine Williams

Half Breed

Half white-half Indian; they call me Half breed
Half cocked-half loaded; my eyes begin to bleed
Cursed by Indians - despised by white
Inner fightings at day - on the warpath by night
Heaviness on my mind - a very troubled soul
So many mixed feelings - taking a reckless toll
Whites and Indians clash in their final revolt
The remaining find is a smoked barrel colt
A stranger finds the colt and admires its flashy spread
Beholding the polished stance - overlooking the dead
Now our story starts - where it seemed to end
Brother against brother - who can you call friend
Don't waste precious time - writing a lengthy will
Prejudice will not rest - until there's another kill
Let it be known to all - this wasn't just a mistake
Man couldn't conquer - a fleshly force called hate

Dennis Anders

A Day In The Life Of A Typical Honors Student

Sitting in front of the computer, my
Hands feel numb, unable to move much more...
Eyes start to droop and I let out a sigh.
You can't imagine how my azz is sore.
I'm groggy, I'm spent and I'm so tired;
But I have so much work ahead of me;
I'm thinking that I need to get wired.
Slapping myself I struggle hard to see,
Focusing on what's in front of my nose
I long dream of a place called Slumberland;
My head starts to nod and I start to doze,
Then I slap myself again with my hand.

Finally I say to myself, "Screw this!"
Then I get up to go to bed in bliss.

Charlie Yen-Chuang Chen

The Break-Up

I don't understand why things
Happen as they do.
Why you told me you loved me,
Then you said that we were through.
All my friends say I'm making a big deal
Out of nothing.
"He's just a guy," they say.
Why can't I look at it
The way that they do?
I feel like a part of me
Has been cut off.
Every time I look at you
A wave of sadness washes over me.
Like sea shells getting swept up
Into the sea,
When the tide rolls in.
You think you did the right thing,
But if you looked inside me
...You would know better.

Heidi Fischer

It Will Be OK

Look out world, there's an evolution in the making
Happiness and clarity are mine for the taking
It's not as complex as it was that first day
by remembering four little words...it will be OK

Judgment and ideas are being turned all around
Hey, guess what? I can touch the middle ground
The tunnel is getting shorter, night becoming day
As long as I keep remembering..it will be OK

These four little words are keeping me on track
Angry words said before now can't be taken back
My world is emerging in colors other than gray
There's those four words again..it will be OK

The words are so simple, If I just listen I'll hear
That the words speak the truth, the meaning is clear
When my defenses seem lost, this voice within will say
Keep hanging on; this too shall pass.. it will be OK

When unfamiliar feeling clash with untamed beliefs
The battle rages on inside with no permit for relief
After it reaches the extreme, I can find a new way
To believe in the magic of four words..it will be OK

Ann Sorenson

The Raven

Raven, raven, of Lenore, hast thou knowledge of the Lord,
Has thou no other cry than this, "nevermore"
Dost know not of that bird of ancient lore?
Who with a cry trice called
Proclaimed the denial of the Lord,
Who by his awakening cry,
Unloosed the tears from those sad eyes.

O, ye citizens of old Jerusalem
Heard you this call so loud and clear?
Heard you not the sound of whips
Amidst the scorn of Jeering lips?

Did you not see him heal the blind
And cast the devils from insane minds?
Did you not see Him raise the dead,
And hasten the lame with quickened tread?

Raven, raven, perched above the bust of pallas,
Raven, raven, bird or prophet.
Know thou not by whom created?
Know not of him who savest?
Wilt tho speak of Him who reignest, "forever more"

Anthony Childs

Stitches of Love

These stitches of love
Have surely come from above
There is just not enough time, I would say!
On their quilt I would work
With never a shirk,
Be it by night, or by day.
When a wedding day they did announce,
Upon the quilt I did pounce
As it had already been pieced
(but not quilted) for that day -
When love would come by
And away he would fly
With his lady, so happy and gay.
The pieces form the wedding rings
And in between, the bells that toll
As angels voices sing
Oh, happy wedding day!
May you be blessed with happiness
And every good thing,
That these stitches of love could bring.

Barbara R. Lee

Pondering Wandering

I haven't thought much about it,
Having been to so many states.
Travel must be my fate.
This land I have roamed,
Calling each place home.
The places an faces,
In a memory all a blur.
Of my lovers and all my friends,
Left behind only to start again.
The love was real and hurting still.
Life is short this we know,
Why must I spend it on the go.
Surely I'm only pondering, wondering.

Bo Strawn

My Lover, My Friend

My lover is so gentle yet so strong, so tender yet so sure.
He allows me to be independent, yet makes me feel protected.
His touch instantly excites me, yet is calm and reassuring.
He tells me so much without saying anything.
He chastises me without loving me less.

He appreciates my strengths and forgives my weaknesses.
When his arms are around me I feel safe and secure.
He is the one I most love and appreciate, but more importantly...
He is the one I respect and trust above all others.
He is my dearest friend.

Jeanne Forsyth

Dear Lord

Dear Lord, let my light so shine,
So that others may not hear me whine.
Dear Lord, the things that I say and do,
May my life show that I'm living for you.
Dear Lord, may the newness of each day,
Bring me to pray for help along my way.
Dear Lord, for all your blessings you give,
May I always be thankful that within me you live.

Deborah Meyers

Pa

I knew a great man once
He filled a child's mind full of wonders
He filled a family's hearts full of love...
   And friend's lives with joy.

He could create treasures from trash
Things with everlasting beauty
   Like stilts... for a grandson's 10th Birthday.

His hard chiseled face smiled at a youngsters pranks
Frowned when the Lions lost on Thanksgiving
And cried... When he buried a son.

His rough calloused hands brought forth life from the earth
A garden of potatoes, tomatoes, lettuce and more
Like the berries... that the children all adored.

People lucky enough to know this man called him Buddy
The wondrous woman who married this man called him Edgar
And three loving children... Called him dad.

To know a great man is rare
But not only did I know one
I called him.... Pa.
    Jeffrey Stephens

Raising a Child with Love

When a child is raised out of duty, instead of love
He goes through life learning how to push and shove
If with his own parents, he doesn't come first
Imagine how he must question his own self worth

As parents we make many mistakes
But a child's self-esteem, we have no right to take
Children are small and joyous wonders
And oh what a strain they can put our patience under

But each and every night, as you place them in their beds
Your hearts so full of love, as you kiss them on the head
Do you sit and wonder? What can be done tomorrow
To have a full day without pain and sorrow

For if this is your final thought of the day
With your own children you can't go astray
Then as you grow old, and your children become adults
And you see them accepting their own children's faults

From that moment on, until your dying day
With joy in your heart, you can sit back and say
That as a good parent, you have done your part
To give to your children, an excellent start
    Carol E. Lutton

Untitled

Off to see the world.
He left her.
Her vision painted on his soul.

A beach front cafe,
Red wine goblet in hand.

Months ago and miles away,
a kiss of passion
oh so strong.

Like the wind, time goes on
Dusk to night, Dawns the day.
A love that lives in eternal gray.

Lost...

A smoke cloud into the dark of the night.
In another time,
another place.
    Alessandro Abaroa

Joey

She would look into his eyes and dream,
He is everything she was looking for, so it seemed.

"I love you," he said as he brushed her hair away from her face,
When she heard those three words it made her realize that she
could run the race.

Without him she would be no more,
His love lifted her; Her soul could soar.

Then without warning he tore her world apart,
He betrayed her, and crushed her heart.

To trust another would be too much to ask for,
She had enough heartbreak, and wanted no more,

One too many times she had fallen for this lure,
This time will be different, she knows for sure.

Only time will tell if he is sincere,
Time goes by, and he becomes more dear.

Alas, she sees that his word is true, he meant it when
he told her that it was her that he wanted, she just knew.

As their love grows stronger,
She doesn't want to hold up the barriers any longer.

Only to risk it all, and go out on a limb,
For life to show that for her it was him.
    April Lynn Hickey

Just A Shot (At A Poem)

He hears the warning shots that bind a country and a soul.
He knows the sound and sees the signs. He must be strong and bold.
While blooming flowers fill the air are carried by the wind.
He smells the sell, but cannot care. For some things time can't mend.
Because often he has thought of life and has but one desire:
To stop the hatred and the crimes that only fuel the fire.
In times of fear and times of doubt he has only himself.
To say something, stand and shout or be put upon the shelf.
He only wants one thing in life, to feel safe and secure.
To end the wars and all their strife that fade and blur the pure.
There is a seed that grows a plant whose happiness is real.
Taking those who claim they can't, it shows them how to feel.
To stop the reign of greediness. Put an end to this disease.
The wealthy and the penniless can all be one through peace.
    Joshua A. Graham DeSilva

The Age of Giulio

From '49 to '67 he toiled to sell the wine
He loaded boxcars, supervised, and carefully pruned the vine.
The people he attracted came from far and wide
Just to listen to his stories and stand by his side.
He told them tales of days gone by when he was just a boy
How he loved his kin and the precious dog who was his pride and joy.
He talked about the job he held far across the sea
Maintaining law and order on the River Yangzi.
It was a time of opulence, of grace, and chivalry,
Of dining out, and dancing slow, and being carefree.
Then came a time of terror and a leader named Mao,
And the opulence and chivalry took their final bow.
So Giulio took his family and sailed across the sea,
To a land of milk and honey where they could all live free.
He found his little winery and a love affair began
And soon the throngs of people came to see this little man.
Businessmen, doctors, and movies stars would call
And while sharing his adventures, he entertained them all.
With retirement came the time they bid farewell to their dear friend
And the age of Giulio reached its timely end.
    Eugenia C. Battistuzzi

Toddler

He's my Rootin Tootin two year old Toddler that can never sit still.

He's my artist that I find writing on the wall, but when questioned he runs down the hall.

He's my electrician that tests the light switch off and on..off and on until he sees me coming and says "Mommie, I'm sorry."

He's my knight in shining armor when daddy and mommie are at play, then he springs to my rescue so that I can run away. But when daddy turns to go after him he shouts "Daddy, mommie went that away."

He's my climber that climbs on the top of the tables, and as sure as sure is, he is very able. When he stands on top with that proud look in his eyes, he turns and notices me looking at him eye to eye.
   Knowing
he's wrong he begins to climb down, because the smile on my face
   turned into a frown.

Although my toddler is always unpredictable, I love him just the same because I am his mommie, proud and never ashamed.

Demetres Joyner

A Grasshopper's Prayer

I once heard a grasshopper saying his prayers.
He said Lord thank you for creating me.

I am proud to be a grasshopper, because I
can hop from tree to tree.

I can smell the beautiful fragrance of
the many flower trees. I can sail along
the stream, upon the lily pad leaves.

And when I am thirsty, I can drink the cool
water from the flowing stream. I can eat the
many berries I find along the way.

My friends and I talk of many things while
we work or play. And now Lord as the
sun sets and it's time for me to find my
nest.

I just want to say, when you created me
you created a mystery, so thank you,
Lord for me.

Eulanhie Anderson

He Seemed So Perfect

He seemed so perfect.
He seemed so perfect when he walked.
And seemed so perfect when he talked.
His great personality and gentle touch,
made me feel loved so very much.
He was always there when I needed him the most.
But now I need him and there is only his ghost.
I want him here to relive,
all of those laughs and happy times he had to give.
His dark complexion and lion-hearted soul,
I will always remember as I grow.
He was so perfect until that day,
When he feel into the hands of god and his life was taken away.
Now I realize though,
that he is still as perfect in all of those same very special ways.
And his soul continues to live on in my heart each and every day.

Charlotte Najar

A Mighty God

Oh what a mighty God have we
He stills the wind
And he calms the sea
The winds and the waves obey His will
When He says to them, "Be still, be still."

The lame can walk
And the blind can see
All manner of sickness too shall flee
When He says,
"Take up thy bed and follow me."
Oh what a mighty God have we.

Oh what a loving God have we
For he gave his son
To die on the tree
That we may be from sin set free
Oh what a loving God have we.

Esther Hjorth

Stroke Victims

When Mother said he died, I didn't cry.
   He was my Dad, I was his youngest child.
If only he had called me, 'his little girl' I
   Would have been so happy.
If I had called him "Daddy" would he have been pleased?
   I wonder — we never spoke!
My questions fell on deaf ears, so I
   looked at his eyes for answers,
Did they say, "I love you"?
   I wonder — but I never asked!
He taught my sister to skate, mom said he loved to dance
   Would he have taught me how?
   I wonder — I never saw him stand!
How different would my life have been
   with him a part of it?
Would he have liked the man I married or
   the person I have become?
I wonder — he died too soon!
   I look back through the years
   and I wonder - now I cry!

Helen Kirkorian

Back Seat Driver

Hopped in my car, put it into gear
Headed down the highway, without looking in the rear.
Road ahead was empty, Fog came rolling in,
Couldn't see where I was going or even where I'd been.
Motor humming lightly, me without a care,
Suddenly a feeling, 'twas more than I could bear.
I knew without looking, that I was not alone,
Swore by all above me, I heard a dreadful moan,
'Scared to turn around, afraid to go ahead,
Kept right on driving though I was filled with dread,
Felt an icy tingle go up and down my spine,
Fog kept getting thicker, could scarcely see the line,
Some one there behind me was breathing down my neck,
Jerked the wheel so wildly, I almost had a wreck,
Heart was pounding madly, breathing was a chore,
Swiftly jammed the breaks on and turning in my seat,
Grabbed the nearest weapon, a flashlight near my feet,
I quickly flashed the light around to see what I could see,
And there sat my imagination, staring back at me.

Agnes Griffing

Conquest

Human ideals put forth by the swaying of ones
   heart through words, this a conquest.
The opponent with his oppressive ways, this is done
   against ideals of truth.
Why slander a repentant man, are thee afraid he
   will find out thy quest.
Great men are not made great on their own, for
   who has founded their ideals of conquest.
The way of peace they know not, for surely a
   conquest dwells in the heavens and on earth.
Some might say the pen mightier than the sword,
   I tell you that which is within lives forever.
For knowledge can vanish away by slight of
   hand, this also a conquest in itself,
Peace and war is put within thyself, this the
   beginning and end of all conquests.

     Frank Florio

Anointed Child

A child is an anointed spirit sent from
   heaven to perform Gods will
They are given a divine mission which
   is to help us change the way we all feel
A child has the ability with their ten
   tiny fingers and ten tiny toes
To cause a miraculous stirring within
   people souls
One look in their eyes or the bright
   smile on their face.
Can instantly change this nation into
   a much happier place
The gifts a child brings us are just
   too great to measure
But they must always be through of
   as this worlds richest treasure
A child is an anointed spirit from
   our heaven above
Sent here to bring us Gods true
   meaning of love

     Cynthia Fox

Windy

A broken wing
   held the bird close to the ground,
A cry over lost freedom pierced the air
   as the bird stumbled upon the earth
I felt the pain from the eyes stare.

Motionless, the bird seemed to have made a decision,
   shutting the curtain, having nothing more to see,
I could not stop wandering
   would I fly if my freedom was taken from me?

The patent chirping of a morning bird
   awoke my senses to a new found day,
Checking the scene I saw his nest
   and the bird in the distance flying away.

     Douglas A. Bly

Far Away

Untouched by my hand but not by my thoughts.
The voice I hear in my darkest hour.
The smile I see in my deepest dreams.
The memories I hold in the chamber of my heart.
And again you will come to bring endless happiness.
Again you will come to bring peace of mind and soul.
Again you will part leaving emptiness with your path.
Again you will be Far Away.

     Heather Holdren

Hell Awaits

Yes he admits he killed many and
he'll do it again you don't understand
what goes on in a mass murder's head,
He guess he could blame it on his
mama or daddy too, it's like a rush
or some type of drug that takes over,
so many families in pain he feel
no pain bloodstains in his clothes
fingernails imprinted in his
skin from the victim's struggling
to get away, yes he knows
what you're thinking he's sick
in the head and he'll awaits
but please understand he's
still human.

     Jermisha Taylor

Contrails of the Mind

She sits on the porch in robe and slippers,
her aged, eastern face, inscrutable.
Though she cradles a cup of tea
for warmth against the morning chill,
solace lies in the cigarette she holds.
Western mores mandate a smokeless space
so her reveries are lonely.
Memories drift to a distant time and place
where the aged command respect
and youth defers.
The smoke dissipates in the air
as do her thoughts.
She rises and accommodates to life.

     Judy Pitchkolan

Arrival

When I carried her for nine months
Her cells multiplied like a drop of red wine
   in a kaleidoscope
Joints and bones formed a partnership
Translucent nails grew like crescent moons upon
   her tiny clutching fingers

She swallowed my breath to fill her lungs
She inhaled the elixir of my blood
Tender and bloated with every powerful twinge
I could feel her pulling against her cord
A gush of water summons her ancestors
They labor through me like wind
   howling through a tunnel
Pushing her out births a loneliness

Aurora Borealis kissed the top of her head
Whorl of black hair wild as a thunderbird
Her soul dwells in the spiral room
Travels in and out from its spinning crown

She danced for a while in the womb
Now the universe sleeps in my Livingroom.

     Elizabeth Mailer

People

People are black, people are white
People are as different as day and night
People are brown, people are yellow
People are strict, people are mellow
People are sad, people are happy
People are harsh, people are sappy
When we hate, what do we gain?
Nothing at all, except for pain.

     Christine Nguyen

My Woman, My God!

Her skin is copper, burnished to golden,
Her face, small and curving, is chiseled for modeling.
She is what people call 'light-skinned.'
She wears a perpetual smile; her eyes smile, too.
And when she smiles, they crinkle at the corners.
Her skin exudes a glow that shouts
Her perfect, well-nurtured health. From where did she get
That perfect complexion? From Black Africans mixed
With white Englishmen, or Americans mixed with
Light-skinned Americans mixed with Brown Americans mixed
With her father's black ebony that came to him
In an unbroken line from Pithecanthropus Erectus
Who got his from God knows what sun-bathing Adam
Who got his from what simian who prowled the banks
And forests along the Ganges, Nile, Euphrates and the Yangtze?
There's a queen's lilting to her throaty welling laughter.
Her breast defy description: all I know is they move when
I touch them and kiss them. They lead her when she walks
That frenetic jungle stride, a quick jiggle to the whole of her.

Burkes G. Greene

Free Will

In stillness
her hands and her eyes move
to betray a voice and a vision
released of God and of hope,
neither conscience nor memory
the siren and sun that reveal and destroy.
Compelled by the word, by the light, by the source,
she looks, blind as she sees,
deaf as she hears, mute as she speaks.
Unseen, unheard and ignored,
she lives now
other worlds as her own.

Frank Murphy

Cupidity Of Evil

Her eyes are windows to her sinful soul
Her heart is a regime of revenge
Her fatal fingers are like sticky thorns on an angry rose
deception lies in her roots

Her tainted psyche sickens
Her sexually ill-fated mind thickens;
thickens with streams of chaos and pandemonium

Her whirlpool of wickedness compliments
Her hellish howls of ecstasy arouses ferment
deception lies in her roots

Euphoria and ebullience covers me
Her evil-ness excites me
Her abominable decree moves me
Her sinister nature is envied by me
Because her roots lies in deception

Chalette R. Washington

My Prayer

Heavenly Father come into my heart
Help me to give this day a good start
Help me to see what I must do
To keep my heart in tune with you
Help me to keep my eyes straight ahead
Passing temptation without any dread
And the day comes to an end
My head will bow and my knees will bend
In a prayer of thanks for all you have done
To make sure each day is a special one
Amen

Edith Cuzzone

Grandmother

As the rain slowly stopped falling,
her life slipped away.
She is no longer here, but her memory
will always stay.
Each time I think of her, tears form
in my eyes, but I wipe them away
and hold my pain inside.
You never really miss someone until they
can't be there, they can no longer say
I love you and show you how much
they care.
There's so many things I feel, but nothing
I can do.
This poems to my Grandmother, I'll
forever be missing you.

Casey Tucker

Mom

My mother now is old and gray
her mind sometimes wanders far away
on things that only she can see.
Her body is slowly bending
like that of a tree in a storm.
The blue in her eyes is fading away
like a flower that's had too much sun.
Now its time for me to be as strong as she,
and do the things for mom
that she has always did for me.

And when the time comes and she goes
to her new home beyond the blue,
perhaps she will look down and say
I taught you well, girl, I taught you well.

Eleanor L. Howell

When'er I Knocked Upon the Door

When'er I knocked upon the door
Her nimble gait through the glass I saw
Her slippers soft against the floor,
A little form I held so dear
With hair so white, I remember clear
A humor quick, a clever mind
A heart so true, a heart so kind

Fun to be with - to share events
To talk of politics and friends
While colorful fabrics she cut to sew
For a dress, a pillow, or door window
'Its all like a dream,' she would reminisce
On the heartaches, the pains, the joys and the strife
The battles she fought throughout her life

But aged and spent, she began to slow
And then, anon it was time to go -
And here am I, the child she bore
That nimble gait to see no more
Nor slippers soft against the floor
When'er I knock upon the door.

Anna Vennitti

Affliction

What is this sadness that I feel,
Does it come from within;
To see all the pain, each has a name,
Affliction of love is dead;
Toll the era once forgotten,
Frenzy is the term;
Mischance of devotion, set back in motion,
Affliction, sit-up and burn.

Angela Llanas

Ode for Alice

I remember Alice,
Her orange hair of corkscrew curls
Her funny dresses and her shopping bags
The wild blue hat askew upon her bobbing head
She walks amid the rubble and rabble of the city
Holding court with other worlds
Of ladies sitting white and starched
Their frilly bosoms hiding purest breasts,
Untouched
Great picture hats adorned with birds
Gentler days of lavender and flowers
Tucked away in books of poems beneath soft pillows
She is the offspring of the bloomer girl
Still primping in the looking glass
Searching for blossoms mid the thorn
Her days now stretched in coffee shops
Or rooms with magazines of bygone days
And bric-a-brac of yesteryears
At night with face against the windowpane,
She watches shadows dim the candles on her cake.

Angela Francavilla

My Cat and I on the Ranch

Along the fence so gracefully
Her paw steps cautiously without a thrust;
Creeping along so silently
Taking no longer than she must.

In the field they fear no name
The little ones who scurry by;
But in the barn they play her game
To catch one low, to catch one high.

Upon the crest of a hill
We see a sunset so orange and bright;
Her meow is pleasant and does so will
That we may stay up into the night.

Shadows leap as the darkness mocks
She can sense their rodent laughter;
Patiently and eternally she stalks
Wary of those she watches after.

Allan R. Smith

Queen of Mirrors

Queen of mirrors, too blind to see
Her sharpened gaze cuts right through me
Her crown of thorns and her endless grin
Show broken glass - another sin

A hole in time bears eternal souls
Throughout its mass, the evil grows
distorted image with which we sing
Can not conceal the demons sting

Queen of Mirrors, hold me tight
Your beauty glows within the night
Your sparkling eyes, they burn so bright
Oh, queen of mirrors, take flight on the night

Queen of mirrors, too blind to see
Her razor edges will put you out of misery
Her cracked reflection and eternal depth
Will steal your freedom - a fate worse than death

As I gaze into eternal depths of dark mirrors
  I just close my eyes....and see you looking back at me

Jon Flanagan

"Him"

Will no one adore me as much as a cat, purring?
Her small skull (that fits in the palm of my hand)
Trustingly thrust back, as if to say, "Go on,
Slit my throat. I am oblivious; I am in ecstasy."

Will no one offer up his taut whiteness,
The speed-bump of an Adam's apple,
A slackened jaw? Will no one say to me,
"Go on, have me. You deserve it. And more?"

I can see myself shaving him with the
Uncertainty of a virgin surgeon, wielding razor
In hand, afraid of hurt, of hurting, HIM me.
One nick and he will surely kiss me goodbye.
My hand trembles and my wrist aches from
The angle, suspended, in time, in place.

I strike a blow and he ducks from my grasp,
Staring, disbelieving. "Just kidding," I say,
A smile as useless and out-of-place as it would be in a mug-shot.
"What would you do to me if I killed you," I ask,
This time suddenly serious. His body rises up to meet mine;
He seals our pact with a kiss, this kiss of death. "I'd kill you back."

Amanda K. Harris

Silent Cry For Help

His anger erupts from within;
  her sorrow burrows deep into her heart.
Objects fly across the room and doors slam
  while the corner is full of tears and sobbing.
Bottles cover the counter and sink
  while tissues and bandages cascade to the floor.
Hands become an arrow cuddling the bow
  while the body becomes a frail strawlike target.

The aftermath reveals the pathetic scene
  of begging and pleading for forgiveness.
His hangovers are painful and troubling;
  her black and blue bruises mar her body's coloring.
Guilt is forced on others
  while fear is brought to a near edge.
Anger becomes the only feeling;
  help becomes the only goal.

He knows she will not leave him;
  Her pride and selfworth keeping her from telling a soul.
She reaches out for a hand to pull her
  but each night the grasp becomes too far away.

Aaron R. Testa

My Grandson and Me

My grandson and me, have a special bond, as many can see.
He's so polite to others and me; I'm as proud as I can be,
I've watched him ride his bicycle, fall down get right back up,
Called him in to wash and sup.
Played baseball with him in our back yard.
To try to catch him is very hard
Grandma can't run as fast as he,
He's as cute and nice as he can be,
He gets good grades in school,
follows every rule,
When in high school he's a graduate,
I hope to be there, and not too late,
Now, he's a boy scout and he is seven,
It won't be long 'til he'll be eleven,
He's growing up right before my eyes.
He'll be a man fast, I realize,
I really love him, I really care.
When I'm in heaven, and he enters there.
I'll say to him, "I knew you'd came, you've been so good."
I'd be so happy, yes I would.

Catherine Boyd

Over the Garden Wall

Sequestered thoughts and dreams untold
  Hide among the poppies gold
  In a cloistered garden,
Where hollyhocks and yew trees tall
  Vie for view
  Over the garden wall.

Mosses intrude on time-worn paths
Conceal thought-prints of loves and wraths
  In a cloistered garden.
Where daisies crowd grasses small
Behind the garden wall.

Conscience searches present and past
For answers and solutions grasped
  In a cloistered garden,
Where seasons progressively crawl
  Behind the garden wall.
        Everett V. O'Rourke

Crown Of Thorns

  The Grey Sky hovers the Earth
His destiny is desire as he is brought to birth.
  His body is frozen and so is his core
Years of decay and she is not sure.
  The Indians inhabit the land of the Free
it has been taken away as you can see.
  They rode the Kings Highway
which has been forgotten to this day.
  They rode the Kings Highway
In which he will lay.
        David M. Budriss

The Lord's Love

I remember a mourning, a deadness of being
His impressioned inner warning, yet I kept fleeing
In this death-walk loomed numbness and darkness and oppression
of soul
Yet His light balanced all, He protected my woe
My spirit was a sea, a torrid black sea
His Spirit was an ocean, a living-waters entity
His light pierced my inner man, what a glorious relief
He proved to me that He can in both mine and His grief
He remembered me so long ago and to this day my peace does show
He petitions me this day I know, I remember Him so long ago
I remember a morning, a bright Morning-star morning.
        Edmundo Oranday

A Poet's State

All was a strain, poetic pain,
His mind a blur with years of lays
Scribbled, scratched, re-scribbled again
On pages torn and yellow with age.

Projected personas lacking life,
Gilded pretense image-rife
With snatches from Hazlett, Hopkins, Homer,
Hoping to seize their power and sway.

Ashamed, afraid of masquerade,
Longing for just one genuine ode,
Prying apart his soul to discern
That strained for vision deep within.

Then, THAT moment came in a rush,
Words gushing like precious streams
Splashing fresh spontaneous grace
Making euphoria worthy the wait.
        Gus Wilhelmy

The Great Game

Before the game, coach told the team about
  his sickly little Tim...
All he asked us boys is that we win the game
  for him...
Coach sent his team of five out onto the wooden
  floor...
He said come back with a victory or poor Tim
  will be no more...
A robust bunch with tears in their eyes, but
  No way were they sissies...
They were playing the Cougars, a bunch of
  wimps and prissies...
The cats played their hearts out in honor of little Tim...
They blew the Cougars away by fifty in the heart of the Bobcat
gym...
When the game was over, the team didn't celebrate...
They were waiting on coach to tell them Tim's fate...
The coach looked his team over and across
  his face there was a smile...
"Don't worry boys! I'm not even married.
  There won't be a Tim for a while.
        Jesse Brown

Maybe Next Time

The thunder of the engine fills my ears.
His strong thighs clutch the machine's frenzy.
The only clue to his feelings stare at me from their
  protective surroundings.
His powerful hands twist the roars out of his steed.
His jacket covers his strong chest offering a feeble
  protection against the whipping winds.
His calves are encased in the latest technology known to man.
I fear for his life, yet am stimulated by his daredevil
  tendencies.
When he returns I long to run up and hold him — but I refrain.
Maybe next time.
        Carol J. Kapustka

"Abe"

  I once saw a man walking,
He was ragged and tired looking,
  His face was deeply etched,
He shuffled in his walk,
  His face gazed at the buildings,
The baggy pants had patches,
  In the morning, his legs moved onward,
A whistled tune pierced the mist,
  Finally, he found his bench,
His friend Ben the squirrel chattered,
  He reached in his pocket and fed Ben.
        Jack Kraai

D.O.B. Considerations

Was I born too late for Tall Ship's crew,
  Through seven seas for this old muse?

Was I born too soon for certain youth,
  Who look at age as Dinosaur Tooth?

Was I born just ripe for World War II,
  With shrunken census of High School youth?

I was born just right for my loving wife
  Whose wisdom could cease much world strife.
        Allan L. Gauntlett

That Child In Me

Many times I wish
I could be younger for a while,
No cares or responsibility
Just that carefree child and smile.

With wishes and dreams
And plans and hopes,
Yet many times it seems -
The older I get, the harder to cope!

I've grown from child to adult -
I wonder what will be,
I cannot stop or halt
Time - it moves endlessly.

So finally I must accept
That which I cannot change.
For with age and yet, I still love
That child in me.

Shirley Sorensen Hinz

259 On Flight 103

In Scotland in the town of Lockerbie
A bomb exploded above the tree's
Year 1988 a jet liner on December 21st
Disintegrated with a loud burst
259 persons on flight 103
There lives are not to be
Eleven more on the ground
Within a mile were found
You have taken their lives at this time
All of them were in their prime
Each of you incognito have spoken
Come out and face us in the open
Keep yourselves hidden anywhere
Sooner or later we will be there
Keep hiding we will be binding
To keep you in hand when we take a stand

Vincent J. Passamonte

Yours!

Intelligent, funny, cuddly and bold
A boxer you can hold.

As you can see by Jake's Pedigree
I'm what you'll make out of me.

So pick a name from A to Z
Which one will it be for me?

Shout it out and make it loud
Let there be no doubt.

Make us proud to be your hound
I promise, I'll stick around.

As surely as you see
Full boxer through Shai's AKC
And one of seven, lucky seven!
Will you make your home my heaven?

Rosemary Reyes

Sea Gulls

They stand on the beach so straight
    and proud
And look out to the sea
Their uniforms are custom made,
    perfect as can be.
Remember, the Lord put them there,
    not you, not me.
To guard the shores, soldiers
    of the sea.

Doris Nieglos

December's Child

December's child came in at our door
A bundle of joy in pink
Everyone standing on tippy toe
To get just one little peek

Soft and cuddly, a breath of fresh air
Sent to us from above
Was there ever in this good land of ours
A child received with such love

This wee bit of sunshine
A treasure to hold
More precious than diamonds
Or rubies or gold

Keeps us all at attention
It's really a sight
Jumping to do her bidding
This child - a mere mite

Our Little Princess is 5 at the moment
And we have descended to earth once again
We see in her, this great love of being
Joys untold and reasons for living

Lillian Smith

The Mask

Once I walked alone down roads
a Cain of modern day
I kept my heart beneath a mask
of finest potter's clay

The mask of clay would block the songs
my heart had yet to hear
the mask of clay would shed the rain
that fell in form of tear

I kept the mask throughout my life
in each and every storm
I swore I'd lift it only when
I saw the rainbow form

But now I hear the music soft
my heart had never heard
the rain of tears inside my soul
now stopped without a word.

The rainbow showed itself to me
because you stopped to ask,
"How much do you love me?"
and I lifted up the mask.

Terry F. Jones

City Streets

Distant rain
A cloud dark with sorrow
A lonely spirit walks into tomorrow
Thoughts of love
And a dream still lost
A child of yours to find at any cost
Dazed and confused
Still sleeping in the rain
A man or a woman not a girl or a boy
A distant voice or a baby's toy
Slowly running across wet city streets
No one in particular to meet
Just waiting, silent, staring
An angel amongst darkness
Just praying
Words just vanish in the air
Without a thought, without a care
A glimmer in the distance
As person lights a cigarette
At that very instance.

Marlene Toledo

He Is...

He is the light of my soul,
a comfort for my pain.
The joy in my life,
forever to sustain.

He is the love in my heart,
the peace I find within.
The grace I receive,
a pardon for my sin.

He is my childhood born again,
the future yet unseen.
The hope of a new world,
the resurrection of my dreams.

He is the blessing of a lifetime,
It's equal I'll not know.
He's angel song from up above
to creatures here below.

To others He's a common man,
in millions He's but one.
To me, He is the breath I breathe
you see "He" is my son.

Phyllis Gossett

Not a Dream But an Obsession

A life of struggle
A dream or two
Not much changing
To make your skies turn blue

You don't ask for much
Just a change of scene
You live each day
With a wishful dream

No matter how bad things get
Always have a dream
It gets you through times
When things get extreme

My dad taught me this
And I'm forever grateful
Not fully realizing
That this would be fateful

A life quite full
With turns and concessions
But my dream came true
With my "Tahiti Obsessions"

Richard E. Davis

Mist

A light wind
A fairy land
A majestic, magical mist
A floating island
in a sea of air.

Always wandering like
a lost stranger
Not really known but yet a friend
A spell of a sort
yet kind and gentle
Always appearing on top of my mantle
Seeming to whisper
through the night.

I say goodbye but we always
meet again—
The last time at my grave.

Michelle Allen

Gettysburg

One Summer morn, a rainy dawn
a farmland was torn asunder
from pounding hooves, and
the cannon roar —
it sounded just like
thunder.
Troops in the hills and
around the trees were
scattered as the cattle
and soldiers riding horses
led them in the battle.
From seminary ridge to the
Devil's den both armies lost
many men.
Forget them not these men who
fell, from the musket bullets
and the cannon shell.
These honored dead who
fought gallantly
July 1863

William S. Cody

Untitled

A hand to firmly hold...
A gentle sigh of relief...
A soft word spoken...
A tender touch to cheek...

To tell all of your secrets...
To embrace you when the world doesn't...
To laugh with and cry with...
To share very special moments...

A new found friend...
A buddy and a pal...
A person to bum around with...
A smile for a lifetime...

To have and to hold...
To understand your innermost thoughts...
To honor and to cherish...
To be with you always...

FOREVER FRIEND...

Tina Minert

Motherhood

Years have passed since youth betrayed
a girl who skipped and sang.
Who thought of simple wistfulness
of dolls and dreams the sunsets made.

Oh happiness was brought again!
The day my babes came forth.
The time was mine to think and do
that nothingness we did back then.

Little years to yet relive
to play and dream just as a child.
To draw and dance with my own babes
whose day pass by as through a sieve.

How wonderful is childhood!
Where from the world we may retreat.
To think the thoughts of youth before,
Oh happy, happy motherhood.

Rebecca T. Carrum

What Am I?

What am I? If not a figment of creation
A grain of dust,
In a world full of nations.
I am but a leaf,
In a forest full of trees.
I am a pebble,
In a river rushing to meet the seas.
I am small compared
To all the greatness,
That fills the world
In all its many spaces,
But I count!
And my voice is loud.
God put me here,
For that I'm very proud.
I form part
Of all this beauteous nature,
Life is the road,
That will direct me,
On a joyous, and great adventure.

Leonor Mora

Love

Did you ever love
a guy and know he
didn't love you did
you ever feel like
crying but wondered
what good it would do did
you ever look in to his eyes
and say a little prayer did
you ever see him walking
with the lights, down low
have you ever whispered I love
you but you'll never let him
know love is fine but it hurts so much.
The price you pay is high so if
I had a choice between love
and death I think I'd rather
die so when I say don't fall
In love you'll hurt before its
throw because you see my friend
I ought to know I fell I love
with you.

Salina Santiago

"Just A Passing Thought"

Just a passing thought
A lingering memory of you
All I have no to hold
Of the days we were two
Love has not grown old
Our youth is ever last
Your beauty I still behold
In a place that is never past
When time together brings
Our lives in joining heart
Again our love shall blossom
Never again to part
Love will always conquer
The woes of worldly wrought
And we shall never be
Just a passing thought

Thomas N. Kirkpatrick

A Smile

As he looked up into my eyes,
   A love I knew, he could not
      disguise,
As he reached out, and
   touched my hand,
Such a wonderful feeling,
   he could not understand,
And as he looked around
   for a while,
My child, so new, gave me
   a smile

Melissa Johnson

The Seasons

As summer closes to an end
A new season shall begin
With the coming of the change
Parts of nature rearrange
Autumn leaves begin to fall
When the trees have none left at all
They lay peacefully upon the ground
A new destiny to be found
Winters moon is close behind
Seeking to be treated kind
And when the snow begins to fall
There is yet another beckoning call
A seed lies far beneath the snow
Awaiting the sun so it may grow
As another season passes by
I sometimes feel the need to cry
To shed tears of love and respect
Hoping that I did not neglect
How much the seasons mean to me
Praying many more my eyes will see

Leisa J. Quintero

Mid-Life Proverb

Autumn days are here.
A pausing between extremes
is this transitional time.
Summer's heat is gone,
soon winter's cold will arrive.

I, too, am at one
in this cycling of the times.
My heat of passion is spent,
but not yet so cold -
Pretty girls can still warm me.

At least I know how
I am now viewed by others
in this autumn of my life.
My lust being dulled,
I am objective at last.

I say to myself:
"They see only their father"
as they briefly glance at me.
I chortle within -
"Old (skin) flint can not strike sparks!"

Richard D. Williams

The Mistake

I will travel over mountains,
   and sail the ocean blue;
When my journey is finished,
   and my days are few—
I will look back,
   and wish I brought you.

Dorothy Novak

Dream Painter

I'll paint on a canvas
a picture of dreams.
I'll use all the lavenders,
the corals and creams.
My brush will be loaded
with stardust, too.
Could I paint a greater
picture for you?

Lowell Connolly

Triumph

To me - you are:
    a pitcher of wine -
        to be tasted and yearned for.
To me - you are:
    a line in a verse -
        to be sung in harmony's world.
To me - you are:
    a picture hung on the wall -
        to be admired for.
To me - you are:
    life's sweetest desire -
        to be made love to.
To me - you are:
    a world of happiness -
        to be taken care of.

T. A. Ferguson

"Happy Birthday To You"

When born you're given
A precious gift
Bestowed unto you -
L I F E
Once obtained, never returnable
But destroyable
Slowly your mind betrays you
How easy to forget
How delicate L I F E is
As the last ray of light
Reaches your eyes
You remember its frailty
Forever shattered
You try to pick up the pieces
Too late
As the last notes are sung and played
One last breath
Your gift is taken away

Melanie A. Milne

The Cycles

Little life
A prisoner within.
Condemned not for love
Lust is your sin.
In amniotic fluid
Your tears are lost.
Not seen as a gift
Only a cost.
An accident they call you
Maybe not to your face.
Always told you are loved
Still in their eyes you see disgrace.
You will grow up yourself
Their sins probably repeat.
Then weep for your mother
Your child at your feet.

Nevin Guglielmi

Reflections Of My Mother's Love

I see in my face
a reflection of you,
You're a part of my life
in everything I do.

A picture of your face
implanted in my mind,
I see how you've aged
with the passing of time.

But each wrinkle to me
represents a time,
When your heart couldn't be filled
with anymore love or pain of mine.

It's love that I see
when I look at your face,
You've touched my heart
with your love and your grace.

Reflections in the mirror
remind me of you,
You'll always be a part of me
I'll always be a part of you.

Sherri A. Davis

Eclipse Of The Moon

Eclipse of the moon
    a shadow crossed it's way
A darkening of the light
    a blossoming of the day

Eclipse of the heart
    gentle inspiration
Enlightening in two people
    a tender realization
Of something buried deep
    far beneath the surface
Causing it to rise
    creating thus a purpose

Suddenly there are no shadows
    everything is right
And for a fleeting moment
    you hold eternity in flight

G. J. Radcliffe

God's Art

A tiger roars,
a small chick peeps,
an eagle soars,
a baby weeps.
A river runs wild,
wind is in the trees,
the air is mild,
soft buzzing of the bees.
A rainbow up high,
plays its role,
connecting the earth and sky,
making the picture whole.
This world - what a creation,
with each and every part,
and what an elation,
living in God's Art.

Robin Ramsey

Cherished Moments

A touch, a kiss, a tender word
A soft contented sigh
Your loving arms, your smiling face
That look that's in your eyes

Cherished moments follow me
In slumber every night
And gently nudge my mind awake
In early mornings light

No words can tell the feelings
That over flow my heart
Or testify my yearning need
Whenever we're a part

To share a touch, a tender word
A soft and gentle kiss
And know that I'm not dreaming
That you truly feel like this

To hold you close and touch your face
And hear you say your mine
And whisper softly on your lips
I love you for all time.

M. D. Burkhammer

The Dance

Whirl and twirl and whirl again.
A step and a half and a cross behind.
A click of the heel and a tap of the toe.
Then, through the long lines to and fro.
Under the arm and around the back,
Not desirous of a drink or a snack.
Meet toe to toe and roll to the right.
Then, back again to defeat the night
Which wanders in with sudden reversals
That are unexpected with no rehearsals.
Each step is taken followed by another
Never responsible to any other,
For the pass or twirl that is made
Causes the curtsy or bow to fade,
And off we go again.

Ric Edwards

Mom's Beauty

My mom says beauty is
a thing in her past, she
said as you grow older
it does not last, she
said as you grow older your
appearance does to, then you
get tired and wrinkled
before your through. Yea,
mom says on beauty age
will close the doors, but
I'm here to tell you mom.
    Beauty is yours.

Sherry Lynn Silva

Untitled

When I run for cover
And my shelter leaks
When my own shield cuts me
And I become weak

When one who gives comfort
Now causes me pain
I build my own fortress
So they can't again.

Jill Abel

"The Portrait Of Life"

Everything you say
And everything you do
Paints a picture for others
Of what's inside of you!

Judith A. Icenhour

UNTITLED

ONE IS A WARRIOR
A WARRIOR OF PEACE
ONE IS HERE TO PROTECT
A DOVE.

ANOTHER IS A MESSENGER
A MESSENGER OF PEACE
ANOTHER IS HERE TO SAVE
A HAWK.

THE HAWK IS A WARRIOR
THE DOVE IS PEACE
AND THOUGH ONE COMMANDS
ANOTHER COMMANDS.

THOUGH ONE LOOKS LIKE A KING
AND ANOTHER THE PEASANT
IN THE END
IT WILL BE THE OPPOSITE WAY.

SO THOUGH ANOTHER WILL FOLLOW
ONE
NEVER DOUBTING ONE'S WORD
ONE, IN THE END
WILL FOLLOW ANOTHER.

Kathleen M. McCarthy

Copper-Woman

Copper-Woman comes to stand
   a white crucifix suspended some
   winter-moon silhouettes on the sand
Where darkness has just been overcome

Spreads her wings in heated hate
   gladly fans a bitter dying fire
   languid with the murky hue of fate
Of yesterday's triumph on the pyre

Moon-dripped shadows on her form
   a running river of nakedness
   welling up in dark eddies to storm
Against man's soft sacredness

Copper-Woman comes to pass
   in a silent and outstretched knowing
   her ashes like snow drifting at last
To where she'd always been flowing

K. David Folsom

Untitled

16: An integer.
A whole number that isn't whole.
It isn't odd,
But it wasn't even.
16 is fractioned.
Perhaps, because it followed 15,
I was hopeful that it would
Have few multiples
And no remainders.

16 came and went.
I was 4 all over again
And it was 4 times as hard.

M. Cirillo

Daydream

If I were a wicked old railroad track
   A wicked old track I'd be
I'd twist and turn and hump my back
   And find my way to the sea

But a wedge of coal in a tinderbox
   'twas cast my lot to be
To stoke the fire on an inland freight
   And never the sea to see

So when I've burned my life away
   and to ashes I resign
Perhaps I'll drift with winds askew
   To rest in a crude iron mine

And some day if I'm lucky
   when the ore is melted down
And cast into a hard cold rail
   within it I'll be found

Though I'll be unattractive
   lying quietly on the ground
I'll be inwardly exalted
   for I'll be seaward bound

N. Dwane Gant

The Concert Grand

I love this three-legged monster,
   A winged, black concert grand -
like a giant earth-bound pegasus
   That takes flight at your command!

I thrill to hear the deep bass chords,
   Man-made thunder at your fingers -
And look down upon a golden harp,
   An immortal something lingers -

To lose oneself in a tone painting,
   In a land beyond I wander -
To break away from earthly things,
   In some higher plane to ponder -

For tones of music give a message,
   Like words - a story tell -
Each composer paints the mental scene
   For your spiritual self to dwell -

Willard E. Franke

Unity

A stare,
   a wink,
     one fleeting glance.

A kiss,
   a hug,
     our true romance.

The love,
   the laughter,
     time goes on.

The tears,
   the joy,
     envied by some.

Our passion,
   our trust,
     never is gone.

Our love,
   our life,
     united as one.

D. J. Louk

Once Upon A Midnight Moon

I couldn't help but thinking
About a certain time
When youth was fresh upon me
And life was there to find.
Gentle was the evening
With stars to wish upon
Unbridled reckless freedom
Like ripples on a pond.
Love was yet a distant land
An ocean to explore
A twisted path into the night
A yet un-opened door.
Visions of her naked flesh
Dancing in my mind
Imagination of a love
Who never would be mine.
Time and its eternal change
Has dulled my varnished swoon
About a dream that I once had
Upon a midnight moon.

Michael B. Castelli

"The Life Of A Feline"

A morning rise is shining,
Above the little cat.
His little eyes are weeping,
Beyond his coat of black,
   Each day a new thing
happening,
excitedly for him.
He'll also do a little scowling,
every now and then.
   Every time I pet him,
He'll purr or scratch or pull,
I hope I'll always be with him,
forever till the end.
   But one day the light'll stop shining,
On his black fur coat.
His eternal rest will be starting,
In cat heaven,
for Bud.

Megan Parker

Men of Reason

To what purpose this searching,
Aching, growing. Slow progression
to life's heart. The ever merging
Of soul with meaning...

Struggle we, the men of reason
For answers. When in truth,
the answers are always near.
So simple, so profound, we gaze
Above their God-set heads
In search of harder clues.
Never seeing ourselves
Reflected time and again
In the glories of sea and sky
Who respond with infinite faith
To the knowing rhythm
Of a throbbing universe.

And we remain empty,
Confused. Our sightless eyes
Agonizing for want of truth.

Sandy Moss-Walker

Oh, What A World

Oh, what a world we share today
Afraid to walk at night
Children taken from us at will
Armed gangs that we can't fight
Drugs flowing across this land
Our courts can't seem to stop
Oil, garbage, and toxic waste
So foolishly do we drop
And we a people are so blind
With racism and greed
That we are one human race
And each other do we need
For if we should destroy ourselves
It's us we have to blame, and,
Because we'll sit and ignore
Is what's really a damn shame
It's only voters that can change
What our laws ought to be
Along with wars, and the taxes
Shared by you and me
Michael D. Wilson

Greenwich Village Seen From Age 7

My coat collar was scratchy
against my neck and cheeks.
I walked just behind
my mother and father.
The cobblestone street
seemed as long as forever.
High above, on a building,
the gaslight blazed.
Outlines of people
hurried past,
bent over,
blurred, in my eyes,
from the frosty cold
and my wonder.
Mitch Persons

Solitude

Ice pellets tap noisily
against the frosty window pane.
I feel a sudden chill as the
crisp wind whips past again.
The snow glistens on the housetops
when the glowing moon is out.
The stars reflect their light on
the icicles dripping from the spout.
Afar I hear the echoes
of the Holy Christmas chimes.
In the icy darkness I am lost,
amid the silent wintertime.
Sherry Ann Smith

War

If there must be war,
Aim an arrow of kindness.
If there must be war,
Fill your canons with understanding.
If there must be war,
Arm yourself with knowledge.
If there must be war,
Drop bombs of love.
Lynne Berghorn

The Baseball Field

Dirt flying
Air blowing hard
Call "Strike Three!"
You're out
Sound of the ball hitting
Sound of the ball flying
People screaming
Sounds of kids stamping
Timothy Falletta

Untitled

You are in the nub of my heart
Alas, we remain apart.
I think of you night and day;
of our life together,
so happy and gay.
Of your warm embrace
and your handsome face.

Are you thinking of me?
You are blind to my love...
You cannot see.
You mean so much to me.
I look into the future and ask myself
what will be.
Together we will stay,
sharing our love day by day.
Lauren Adelson

Can I Call You Mommy?

You left me
All by myself

For other people
To take care of me.

So can I
Call you Mommy?

It's not can I,
It's should I or will.

You walked out on me,
Like you didn't care.

A child isn't
Something to share.

But for some reason,
I love you.

So can I
Call you Mommy?
Sara M. Anderson

Christmas

Evergreen trees
all green and decorated
wrapping all presents
red ribbons and bows
hot fires and santa
hot chocolate is warm
eating cookies and
decorating trees
ornaments
waiting for santa
falling asleep
it's christmas morning
presents galore!
Victoria Lynn Young

Pondering The Thought

As I stand on this cliff.
All my thoughts become questions.

As I stand alone.
I remember all the times I asked
    for help.
Yet, when heard,
I did not accept.

As I stand with the world behind me,
I realize the answer to all my questions.
The answer that will end all
    my worries.

I'm sorry if I disappoint you.
But this is the only way I can be
    happy.
And at peace with myself.
This is the only way.
And so I leave the life
that was not meant for me behind.
Patricia Sandoval

My Mother's Eyes

As I looked back to see
All the pain and agony
My mother's eyes halt for me.

Just like her, it was to be
That I would feel that pain and agony

A war we didn't understand
A war called Vietnam
When he left so young and bold
He came home so cold.

I looked to see, why this was to be
I didn't know this man.
This man that's been to Vietnam
Oleta Johnson

Just a Moment

So much she's said, seen, heard.
All the things she's done,
the long walks she's made;
yet so much she wanted to do
in so little time remained.

There was music in the air
when she's softly saying;
"One more moment for sharing
what's left in me,
one moment for caring
for someone in need,
and never, ever be alone."

Her smile, the warmth of her touch,
her faith, her strength to cope
gave me blessings, always new hope.
"Judge the heart and not the mind,"
mother, how wise was your way!

In any of my remained moments,
(I'll promise) there always be one
I'll dedicate to you -I pray-.
Paula C. Hawk

Waiting for Dawn

Sleep well my child,
All the while not knowing
Of the fears and tears
That have grown
Throughout the years

In the darkness society
Cannot see clearly
The truth and reality
Formed from brutality

Spawned from the darkest seed
The child not knowing sleeps well
Throughout the night,
In a world lacking soul
Blinded from sight

Why should the child awake
To discover foolish mistakes
Created by ancestors past
Unable to last,
So sleep well my child

Michael Yates

I, Hamlet

I, who would serve, suffer for
all your sakes
The spurns which patient merit
of the unworthy takes.

My flesh, exposed to every
unkind stroke and shove,
Bears with calm grace the pangs
of despised love.

My spirit, pure and free from
thought of profits,
Is rewarded by the insolence of
office.

I search in vain for balm in
every clime,
But to be stung by the whips
and scorns of time.

Robert J. Randall

Through A Glass Darkly

My father sits
alone
in the dark,
his hands around a whiskey glass,
his eyes stare
unaware
the light has gone.

Caught somewhere
between my throat and my eyes
a million feelings rise in me
as I watch him fill his glass.

I love him and I hate him
(Did I need him yet betray him?)

Silence all about the room
like shadow,
my father sat
alone in the dark,
and all the memory
I have of him
stares at me from my glass.

Teresa Duckworth

Mother's Love

There has fallen a Mother's tear
Alone, alone, all alone;

She is going my love my dear,
She is going my friend my fear,

The heart cries, "She is gone"
She is gone,

And the red rose weeps
Like the cat at my feet

I close my eyes it seems to me
And open them in time to see

You're going away from me
But my heart aches "this can't be"

I see with no fear
She will always be near

The time has gone
And now I feel so all alone

I know she will always love me
A mother's love will always be.

Mary Sherron

Home

I walk down through the shadows
alone by myself, afraid of the
silence around me.

No one there to hold my hand or
say it's alright.

My voice echoing through the hall
screaming HELLO! Is Anybody
There! I'm Afraid, Don't Leave
Me Alone! But I am alone all
by myself in a deep dark place
called Home.

Kimberly Price

Alone

With us he no longer is
although his chair is not empty
The dog claimed it as his
Many lunches I had with my friends
which was always my treat
My husband a wealthy man
was also very sweet
So many dinners I prepared
No one invites me now as if they cared
As for money he did have tons
It was all left to his sons
My dog and I now sit alone
How welcome a call would be on the phone
With not much money any more
I don't have the friends I had galore
One special friend I have though
My dog Nikki loves me so

Shirley D. Bergfeld

I'm Getting Old Now!

It was the time of year when birds sing,
And for her love I gave my ring.
Now all the trees are grey and bare,
Since I've found she doesn't really care.

Gregory P. Landry

Our Friendship

Our friendship is like the sun,
Always bright and shining.
Without seeing your smiling face,
I would have no silver lining.

When I look at a star,
I think of you.
You're mostly happy,
And hardly ever blue.

You always make me smile,
With your goofy faces.
We have lots of fun,
In all different places.

When I see you cry,
It makes me sad.
When you're smiling,
I'm usually glad.

When you're happy,
I usually am, too.
Without seeing your face,
I would be very blue.

Katelyn Mallard

Grapes Of Love

In her vineyard I shall stay
Amid the blossoms of her love.
Passion builds day by day
Driven by the light above.
Of a kind known to I
Escaping all who cannot see.
A breath of music in my mind
All I feel is she and me.
Entangled in this vineyard I
Daylight shall we never see.
I close my eyes, I hope.. I pray
This dream of us shall ever be.
'Tis season's change and all about
Tiny seedlings drop and sprout.
I am no longer flesh and blood
But leaf, vine, and grapes of love.

Steven E. Jackson

A Quiet Need

Deep within a shadowed soul,
an emptiness had cried.
A need for something somewhere,
refused to be denied.
A need for something lasting,
dedicated, bound and true.
My long nights spent in quiet prayer,
were answered, Dear, in you.
But now my prayers are not for fame,
or fortune soon to be.
I only pray you'll be my love,
for time and eternity.

Laura Garay

I Saw God

I saw God in creation
As I took a walk today.
A butterfly, a robin, a flower
That bloomed along the way.

I talked to God throughout the day
And he talked back to me.
He held my hand and guided me,
For I am his child, you see.

Gracie Black

A Gentle Woman

She was a gentle, loving woman
An honor to have known
For her love was very special
And always filled her home

Time could teach us lessons
On loving from the heart
But this gentle, loving woman
Stood separate and apart

Her love was unconditional
Whether you were wrong or right
She'd say remember good times
And keep them within sight

If time passed without a visit
Or message of news to tell
Her smile was wise and she
Would say, "As long as they are well."

We'll remember all she was to us
As grandma, mom, or wife
For loving wasn't just a word
She brought that word to life!

Kathleen Graviano

The Night After Christmas

'Twas the night after Christmas
and all through the house
every one was stirring
even a mouse.

The stockings were unhung
in boxes without care
with hopes that St. Nicholas
had not crashed in the air.

The children were in their beds
while visions of Game Gears
danced in their heads.

And Mama in her new clothes
and I with my new mink
had just settled ourselves down
for a post=Christmas drink.

Nathaniel Crewe

A Prayer For Existence

Break these binds that bound my heart
   and cause me endless pain
Give me strength to stop this hate
that leaves me - nothing to gain
Help me stop this burning rage
   that dwells within my veins
Replace this all with happiness
   I pray
Before I go insane

Show me how that I can cope
   With all life's cruel games
Give me peace within myself
So that my life's not lived in vain
   And give me love within my heart
      Before my tomb is lain
Please take my hand and walk
   with me
That I may live again

Sonia R. McCarty

Missing You

My mind wanders to you,
   but I can only imagine your place.
My heart is completely fulfilled,
   but there is still that empty space.

Cheryl A. Olenick

Untitled

Darkness,
And despair,
The hall fills with blood.
Everything darkness.
Night becomes day!
Day turns to night!
Things changes...
Total disaster!
With fighting!
And fear!
The dead come back
The world turns to pain and hate,
Thundering with death!
Lightening from hell comes down,
In evil flashes!
Of fire and death!
Spirits rise from graves!
Seeking life,
The fight for life begins.
Until there's nothing, but death.....

Robert Freese

The Best Is Gone

Of everything I know
And everything I don't,
The most painful thing is
A friend who is no longer a friend.

It is said that:
   Friends are forever.
But I have found
Unfortunately this is not true.
Now and then, even
The best of them
Discover their friends is gone;
Discover the best is gone.

If only I wouldn't of —
If only I would of —
Things might be vastly different.
What is done, is done.
It's in the past.
But the memories,
Continue to last.

Stephanie Fier

R.S.V.P.

If constancy is passe,
and fickle is fair-
What kind of magic
will hold you here?
Is it a potion?
Shall I inhale or sip?
Do I simmer, stew or bake?
Shall I cream or ice?
Do I paper, paint and shine,
Devise and scheme?
Laugh or cry?
Give me a sign -
Lest I risk all
and be myself.

Mary Merritt

Garfield The Cat

He's short and chubby,
   and hairy and FAT.
He's a black and orange
   hairball of a CAT.

He eats and sleeps,
   and loves to SNACK.
Lasagna is the favorite
   for this Italian CAT.

His family is weird,
   no doubt about THAT.
There's John, his owner,
   Odie, and Nermal the CAT.

Garfield loves Halloween,
   pulling tricks from a HAT,
But "candy, candy, candy"
   is his best diet SNACK!

I'm sure ... Jim Davis can agree,
   it appears a FACT,
The furry old Garfield
   is America's #1 CAT.

Kimberly Balesteri

The Beetle Prince

There was a little beetle
And he sidled up to me
And he said, "How come you shudder
Every time I'm close to thee?"
So I said, "Now listen beetle,
You and I are friends I know
But you have to keep your distance
'Cause affection I can't show."

The tiny beetle hung his head
And pouted for a while
Until he saw a lovely girl
With bright and glowing smile.
Then off he went to be near her
To bask in her bright glow,
But I heard him say, as she moved away,
I'm a beetle prince, you know.

Myrtle Gartman

"He Is My Savior"

   The Lord is my savior
and I have been saved
   He brightens my soul
like a street that's been paved
   I know that He loves you
and I know He loves me
   Cause He has invited us
to live eternally
   And I feel closer to Him
each day that I live
   And I know in my heart
if you ask, He will give
   For the Lord is my savior
my shepherd and king
   So forever and always
He'll mean everything

Leanora Regan

Untitled

Words can be deceiving
At my age I must say
In order to be respected
I must first lead the way.

Adelino Sardinha

There's A Stranger On My Mind

There is a stranger on my mind
And I think I'm going to cry,
There is a stranger on my mind
And I don't know why.
There is a stranger on my mind
I know he is a man,
There is a stranger on my mind
I love him as much as I can.
There is a stranger on my mind
I don't see him as much as I should.
There is a stranger on my mind
I know him from my childhood.
There is a stranger on my mind
I can feel him in my heart,
There is a stranger on my mind
Every time we are apart.
There is a stranger on my mind
Just can not stop the pain inside.

There is a stranger on my mind and it is
making me sad.
Because he's no stranger... He's my Dad.

Nicole L. Brown

Dream

The night again is drawing near,
And I will dream of you my dear
One day my dreams shall all come true,
No longer far away from you,
Dreams like this must soon come true,
For dreams can make you really blue,
It's just a dream and nothing more,
Until your knocking at my door,
My dream of you someday will be,
When you are face to face with me.
So dreaming on till I shall be,
Standing face to face with thee,
Darling I love you night and day,
And in my dreams I always pray
To bring you back to me one day
Never again for you to stray.

Vivian Ruzecki

Night Time Thoughts

At night, when I retire, —
and lay my body down —
My thoughts, they go spinning —
like an eddy they go round —
Spinning fast and twirling
they go racing by —
I grab my pen and paper
write quickly fore they fly —
Standing on a hill, —
alone against the sky —
The sun warm on my shoulders —
I ask myself why?
Why the grass can't be purple?
Why the sky must be blue?
Why life is short for many?
And long for a few?
Then I stop, and do reflect —
in one single thought —
It's free, it's mine —
and never can be bought!

Peggy Wheadon

The Queen Beheaded

Someone beheaded an iris
And left it here
on the red, red table.
There is a slight wind.
It trembles, wilted, magnificent
three purple-blue petals
Intersect
three snap-jawed calyces
bright gold pollen-lined.
I touch the undercurve of
One languid petal.
It grips my finger
Like a newborn baby.

Stephanie Willett-Shaw

Time Goes By

Live each day to the fullest
and let come what it may.
Do what you want, not what you must,
It is the only way.

Make time for what you desire,
Be on the go and DO
those things you have put off before,
Explore something real new.

Give love and share with others
That which you have learned how.
Keep precious your family ties,
Enjoy, your time is NOW.

Phyllis M. Mollison

The Fruited Paths of Time

I walk the fruited paths of time
And live the moments of destiny
Each separate time.
I kiss the folded leaves of promise
For wed they are to me
Each separate time.
I pluck the blossom from the vine
And see the vision of eternity
Each separate time.
I cross the lighted universe
And reach my hand to thee
Each separate time...

Shirley Friend

In Memory Of Jasmine Noelle Hall

Crystal blue eyes
and long brown hair
Ten fingers and ten toes
I hold her close
as she fades away
To a place that no one knows
whisper my final tearful farewell
as I touch her one last time
Angles come and take her soul
and a part of her heart takes mine
A child I had
A child I lost
With only short memories to suffice.

Malissa Hall

It Is Morning In My Heart

I wake up in the morning
and my heart is beating fast.
I feel the presence of the Lord,
and I know I'm His at last.

His joy fills my heart
as the sunlight fills my room.
I remember what He did for me
when He rose up from the tomb.

He's in control of all my life,
He had been there from the start,
And whatever this day holds,
He is sure to be a part.

He has opened up my eyes,
and He's made me understand,
That He loves me and He wants
me to fit into His plan.

My search for Him will never end
as I seek more of Him each day.
Until at last He takes me home,
to be with Him to stay.

Patricia Elston

I Need A Chance

Conceived in love
and now I grow,

My mother's face
in beauty glow.

Signs shown within
of life secure,

Waiting time
I must endure.

Music, warmth
and loving touch,

Cradled in
my Mother's clutch.

From this warmth
I'll take my flight,

I need a chance
to see the light.

Marlene J. Campbell

Timmy

Timmy was a sleepy boy,
and now it's time for Bed.
He kissed his dolls and soldier too,
and that is when he said -

"I'll be back tomorrow,
and I know that you will too.
But right now I must go to sleep,
so that is what I'll do."

Then Timmy went to bed at seven,
just like every night.
He went to sleep then very fast,
and no one was in sight.

An angel came to him that night,
it happened just like so.
She didn't say a word,
except for that it's time to go.

Just last week his mother came,
and heard something up above.
She looked right above the grave,
and right there flew a white silk dove.

Stacy Talbott

Untitled

Sky so gray get out of my way
and open up for the day
that the angels will say
stay for awhile and don't be afraid-
For the plans have been laid to rest
for the best and this is your test
To see if you can be the very best
and stand your ground until you've
found the peace to seize the pain

Lisa L. O'Brien

To A Loving Mom

You have given me life
And raised me to be
Your son for all time
And all thru eternity
You have given me guidance
To the ways of times
At times I was stubborn
You showed me the ways of life
At times the little I returned
To show my love for you
Did not seem enough
Since I almost lost you
Now I know there is a God above
For I still have you
In thought, in life, and love

Norbert K. Murray

Wind In My Face

When I aspire to higher planes
And seek the topmost place,
I find that I must always fight
The wind upon face.

No vagrant breezes catch my sails
Good luck is not my friend,
The currents never sweep me on
I always face the wind.

But if I someday win acclaim
In life's capricious race,
I'll owe it all to guts and gall
And wind upon my face.

Lois Bramlett

Seaside Dreams

Gentle summer breezes
And soft, sun warmed sands.
The cry of gulls above us,
We look seaward, holding hands.

The surf surges forward
Caressing the shore.
Pulls gently at the sand.
Then recedes once more.

Lulled by the rhythmic sound
Of surf breaking on the beach.
We let the tide carry us
Toward dreams within our reach.

Sue Crisp

Untitled

Myriads of stars
All so very similar
Yet so different.

Jeff McIntire

The Tree

Full of fruit and life,
   a tree grows in a garden,
DEATH upon its limbs.

James M. Roetzer

Love Scenes

There's a love song I'll never write,
and some goings on at night,
that might scare you if you knew,
even though you share my dream.

There's a ballad in my mind,
of a gentle loving kind,
and what we make of all this.
is up to you.

In a story line or two,
we've repeated through and through,
of love not acted out in life,
but just as real.

We've shared an epic story here,
in a life of love that never was,
save the wandering of the mind,
and a dream or two.

Will you simply go away now,
and let me have my say now,
in the most famous of all love scenes,
in imagining's and dreams.

William L. Miller

A Piece of Music

My heart extols in the joy
   and sorrow of your sound
I listen to you and am filled
   with life
I feel a life's energy bursting forth
ready to jump from inside me
I look down below and see me smile
I have attained bliss
The beauty of your sound has sent me
   to the utmost depth of my soul

Mary Perifimos

A Toast To Lost Love

It's time I closed the book my friend,
And start my life anew
For I know you don't love me,
The way I love you.
So I'll drink a toast to our romance
To something that could never be.
Although somewhere along the way
You made me see the woman in me.

So goodbye my love, my dearest friend.
Though it pains me more than you know.
It's time I put the past behind
And see what the future has to show.

So here's a toast to us my friend,
For you have stolen my heart,
But I'll never regret it love
For I knew it right from the start

Yes, here's a toast to all the fun
We shared along the way,
And perhaps we'll meet again
Sometime, somewhere, someday.

Vivian Perillo

The Moment Of Crest

Fell asleep, a clock ticking,
and stirred to its claim.
The sky was brilliant
as if burning with flame.

The sun not yet risen,
just beneath the hill,
I ran to the ridge
to inhale my fill.

The Moment of Crest,
my brief moment of rest,
I was awakened with Aha
at the view of it all.

No longer the clock ticking
would call my name
for a dawning so brilliant
could ever leave me the same.

Theresa Ritterbeck

Please

Sit back, relax
And take a look
What is this world
In which we live?

The defoilage
Of our wilderness
Yet life grows strong
Against man's transactions

A planet full
Of love and laughter
Yet people still hate
And death is so real

Jesus, the Bible
And a love for peace
Yet there is wickedness
Here on earth!

And so, now
That you've looked at the aspects
Please tell me
Why are we here?

Wesley Hicks

Stillness In The Fog

I find myself in a fog
And take my steps slowly.
And then I stop.
The sun will come
and burn the fog away...
and so I wait and wait
It seems never to leave.
My fears grow
and I feel alone.
So I sit
And I find
a blazing rainbow
within me
that has been there
all along.

Steve Haack

Raindrops

Raindrops are Heavenly tears
And that is why, invariably
'When the saints meet
The Heavens weep'
Of course those are
Tears of joyful meeting —
As when the parched old earth
Receives refreshing rain.
Then there are drops of destruction
Such as floods and hurricane,
Best of all are soft raindrops
Just for walking and talking.
The precious raindrop has many moods
But 'Riding Around in the Rain'
Certainly does beat walking.

Mary Pett Barraclough

Widowed By Charity

The toilet leaks, the shingles crack
   and the floor remains undone.
A bag of bread, a rack of clothes,
   a visit to the sick -
The list grows and time dwindles.
And here I sit, alone again,
   a victim of charity.

Where does it begin, the gift of love?

At home with one who aches and
   cries with pain of neglect?
Or with those with no names?

The Parish Outreach beckons
   while I reach out, my needs
bared only to God.
My cries deafen my reason
   as my pleas reach only
the space that exists between us.

Alone, widowed by life.

Virginia A. Petrino

God Love You

God love you, for each kindness
And the patience you have shown,
God love you for each suffering
You've known for me alone.
You lived each day for us
In everything that you did,
Making it easier for us
To do everything that you bid.
God love you for everyone
Whom you have helped to smile,
Thus making each mile of life
A little more worth while.
God love you for each sacrifice
You have ever made for us
Helping us to find courage
Through your Faith & Trust.
God love you for that courage
And for every tear and ache
That you accepted so willingly
For our beloved sake

Lona B. Howe

Things That Never End

When I think of friends,
And things that never end,
I think of gladness,
And sometimes sadness.

The first things that I think of,
Are gentleness and love,
When it comes to friends,
And things that never end.

My friends make me smile,
For a long, long while,
When they're going to cry,
I want to know why.

Friends are kind,
They don't drive you out of your mind,
Friends share,
Friends care forever.

Rebekah Groves

"Longing Just For You"

Longing just for you
and to have you near
seems so heavily

Longing for your kiss
and to have you say I do
just to have your arms
around me forever
would be all I'd want
but until that lucky day
I'll be longing just for you

Thurza McGaharan

Lack Of Word Comprehension

As I write I feel so shallow
and undernourished with words,
my mind seems to recoil
as I try to formulate
the exact phraseology
to express myself.
I often feel dull witted of mind,
absurd you say! oh no,
only the weak of mind
cannot comprehend
the workings of the intellect.
With a little knowledge
we calculate that we can
come out even,
otherwise, we must settle for the crumbs
of the higher echelon of thought.

Marolyn E. Baker

Come the Dawn

Throughout the night I drift
And watch the glint of fire
Of phosphorescent wake.
There is no course to steer,
The tide is running smooth,
No judgments need I make.
When shadows slip away
And mists reveal the shore,
Sun will proclaim the day.
With phosphorescence gone,
I'll pass the port of call
And find a quiet bay.

Wilma Carson McCuistion

This Is The Place I Want To Be

I want to stand by the rocky shore
And watch the wondrous, rolling sea,
I want to thrill to the ocean's roar
That is so much a part of me.

To watch the sea gulls in their flight
Their soaring, graceful ways;
To know such pleasure at the sight
Will last for all my days.

Let me stroll down the beach at dawn
And watch my footprints in the sand,
Let me feel like I've just been born
With the scent of sea air close at hand.

Give me these days of golden pleasures
By the wondrous, rolling sea,
Give me these days I'll always treasure
This is the place I long to be.

Walter J. Pingree

Lost But Never Gone

Why is life so complicated
   and why does it move on?
Why is one minute good
   and the next bad?
Why are we happy
   only knowing we will be sad?

Why is love so complicated?
   Do we ever stop searching?
Do we ever find?
   Is it to all things
Or only that which is under our nose
   to which we are blind?

Why are we so complicated
   and why do we change?
Why do we hide
   and why is it hard
to see that it is only ourselves
   to whom we lied?

And why, above all,
   are those lost NEVER TRULY GONE?

C. A. Thomas

What Christ Has Done For My Life

Since baptism he has been my friend,
And will be 'til the very end.
He always listens when I pray,
There to guide me day by day.

In my hard times, compassion he brings,
And in my sadness he sings,
Of love and joy above all things.

But most of all he has offered me,
A sense of love and security.
And believing that he died for me,
Will bring me into eternity!!!

Lisa M. McCormack

"Tommy Tiger"

Tommy Tiger was a tiger
   and he had no teeth.
He was very, very hungry
   but he could hardly eat.
So he picked some berries
   off a tree,
Then he went home to make
   some soup and tea.

Jenna Vitalone

April A-Fishing Day

With so bright
And wind so soft.
Grass as green as trees.
Me stuck in the mud.
Fish No. 1 to eat.
But back it went.
So my heart so heavy,
Guess I worried for nothing.
For here comes my brothers, Benny!
With fish for a week.
Look out for I intend to eat!

Mary Louise Richardson

"Some Day"

Some day I'll be with you, Sister Dear,
   And you will hold my hand.
And then, I know that God will show
   Me how to understand
Just why He took you far away
   When knowing all the while
The way we'd miss you every day
   And long to see your smile.

You loved to live and work and plan
   And help your fellowmen,
And speak a word of encouragement
   To strangers as well as friends.
And though your life in years was short,
   In service it was long,
So God just thought He'd take you
   Where chosen ones belong.

How sweet to know, when God calls me,
   We'll never have to part,
But just pal along together
   Like we did right from the start.

Virginia Work

Come Along

Come along
   another plane, another wind,
   another star
Bright colors float along the
   outer crescent of the mind,
   waiting to be caught
Come along
The spirit aches that rusted chains
   be cast aside
Come along
Come along with me. Break stride
   before the body dies
Come along
   and the hearth of the soul will
   rekindle and glow

D. Miller

Blue Jay

This bird is blue, as blue
   as the sky can be.
a thief by nature, so what
   else could he be?
He is a planter of seeds.
   A help to man.
The jay is a beautiful,
   helpful scoundrel that nests
   with us all year.

Dorothy C. LaDue

Untitled

I awake—
Another restless nite
my mind clouded
with fantasy
could I, would I, should I
the illusion so clear
but yet so far away
for a moment I slip
away only to be awaken once again
obsession grows stronger
with every day
my heart yearns for
like a new born babe
to its mothers breast
the passion is threatening
as the forbidden fruit
but yet a taste would be so sweet
desire needs to be met
if only in a dream come true
a kiss from me to you.

Sheryl A. Ravel

Candle Light Burns

Candle light burns
Another year turns.

Burning bright
All through the night.

Seasons Change
Burning bright
All through the night

Oh so bright
Burns
Seasons turn

LIFE IS IN MOTION
But, I am asleep
I begin to weep

Starr Golembiewski

Do You Have The Touch?

My skin and bones
are made of soul
and spirit and
my blood and heart
are made of soul
and spirit and
I am here
but you cannot
touch me
unless you are
made of soul and spirit
and I think you are.

Michael O'Shaughnessy

"Restrained"

Broke my knuckles on the steel
Can I get my Christmas meal?
I am strapped to this blue bad
There's a throbbing in my head
Constant lights are blinding me
Lights so bright I cannot see
Trippin' on the Thorazine
Cannot wake up from this dream

J. D. Ardolino

Voices

Voices of the weak
are now an indenture servant

I hear them
blowing across the winds
They're crying from years
of torture and pain

Voices of a culture
that is lost forever

I hear them
in the morning sunrise
After decades of shedding blood
for no benefit of their own

Voices of the young
scare me for eternity

I hear them
as I lay down to sleep
The children who died
cause the color of their skin
The voices continue....

Thierno A. Johnson Sr.

Cats

In my hands
are solemn cats
that gaze at me
their shadows are shooting stars
that are snow-capped in winter.
They are in the valleys
out of the light
then they disappear
into the night.

Ryan Nicholas Hendrix

Volunteerism: Its Own Reward

Don't ever think that volunteers
Aren't paid for what they do;
It's God who writes the paycheck;
He grants them proper due.
He blesses them with caring smiles,
And eyes that warmly glow.
Gentle ways and hopes they share,
More loving their hearts grow.

Words, wise with understanding,
He gives to them, to give away;
Loneliness they'll never know,
For friendship fills their day.
He grants them peace in knowing
This is how He meant us to live,
Joyfully helping others,
We get more than we give.

Miriam Greenberg

On the Eve of Events

With whom did Adam flirt
before he met his Eve?
Was there another skirt?
One hardly can believe
that he, a healthy celibate,
did not find ways to celebrate.
Or do you think he just adlibbed
until he finally got "ribbed"?

Axel Muller

The Merry Shadows Of The Woods

The slow woods of darkness fall all
Around you. The breeziest of life flood
And stumble around it.

It is a dark cold place. You see angels
Appear before you there; they sing songs
Of black and white.

Their blue pieces of wood leap upon you
As they warm you in the darkness
From the darkest night to the light.

You speak to no one for the day will
Bring the dizziest night.
That is held on by light.

Teresa Gilliland

Chasing Black

My thoughts now
As always
Driven by the unknown
I try to do
Only by my will
Things not yet accomplished
The noise, the background,
My life
As real as it is,
Its not happening;
To me, anyway
I call my demons
Please help me, take me with you
But no help comes from shadows

Michael Zasowski

Elusive Youth

Fierce the memories, they live
As flurries strike my wan-skinned face,
Emotions I cannot describe
That reign since times I cannot trace.
Glimpses of a time long lost,
Scents that offer pleasured pain,
Hazy dreams that torture aging
Souls with hopes they can't retain;
Grasping these like surfaced tears
That blatantly refuse to fall,
Clasping at a memory past
One tries to, but cannot recall.
Reliving for split seconds all
Those innocent elated senses,
Wishing to be still so sheltered-
Ignorant defenses.
Inexplicable - such moments
Overwhelm to such degrees
That I stand dumbfounded crying,
Helpless, as my childhood flees.

Marlena M. Esbaugh

The Hermit

An old man rests upon the stoop
And casts a wrinkled smile.
A string of smoke curls past
His face from the old musty pipe
Which he clutches in one slow hand.
And though he looks so out-of-date,
Like an old forgotten relic,
He's not the worse for wear.

John M. Laskos

Do A Good Deed

I saw a beggar one day,
as he sat upon the streets,
His clothes were ragged and torn,
He had no shoes on his feet.

And I began to wonder,
If there would come a day,
when I would have no money,
and would have to go that way.

And as I was wondering,
I walked up to where he sat,
It was then that I dropped,
a five spot in his hat.

And as I turned around,
and slowly walked away,
I felt much better inside,
I had done a good deed that day.

Vernon F. Mundy

Faded Memory

I wonder if I'm dying
as I lie awake tonight
I'm afraid my life will end
before it's ever right.
Someday you'll be happy
your love will be so true.
I'll be a faded memory
it's all the same to you.

I'm afraid you won't be there
when at last my life is done
I want to say I love you,
but I know you can't be won.
I don't know what to do.
It does no good to fight.
Reality becomes a tear
I love you more than life.

Valerie Furha

Where Are You?

A cool breeze blows
as I stand all alone.
"Where are you," I wonder.
Yet, no one knows.
Why did you leave?
Where did you go?
Was it because of me?
I stand and a thousand
questions run through my mind.
To think of how long you've been gone,
as my search for you,
continues on.

Liberty Engelke

As It Melts

There is wonder to be felt
As I watch the butter melt
    Absorbed into the bread
    I feel increasing dread

As with everything it changes form
Turns to mush when it is warmed
    My heart - it can relate
Although we know the inevitable fate

    Deep in the fridge cold as stone
Its demise can not be known
    There is nothing to be felt
As I watch the butter melt.

Linda Jacoby

AIDS

I watch the river
as it flows toward the sea
a never ending circle
My life is not like this river
For I have less to see
I have less to hear
And nothing to fight my disease

If I sleep beside this tree
Will I ever wake
Will I be left here to die
or will I suffer through the years

They say that I deserve to die
They say it's all my fault
But they're the ones who do not know
They're the ones at risk

Mary Zehren

Woe Is Me

Her death was insidious,
As she lay there so hideous.
Casket lid closed,
So no one was grossed.
She'd become very thin.
Like a needle or pin.
Her face shrunk to bone,
How old she had grown.
As she lay there near death,
With her very last breath,
So weakly she said
From that ugly death bed
I must go away,
But I'll be back to stay.
I have to get Dad,
'cause you've been so bad.

Karen Louise Bolander

As We Speak...

My heart is breaking
as we speak,
I feel so lonely
my soul is weak.

Secluded soul
forsaken days,
lonely nights
and weary ways.

Weary ways
a friendship lost,
leads to betrayal
at my cost.

A friends betrayal
a lovers fight,
open and free
like an eagles flight.

The end is nearing
I'm growing weak,
once again this happens....
    as we speak.

Melanie Klinglesmith

The Memory Book

Down through the years
As you may recall,
There was a book in
which memories would
always fall.

The good times and the
bad, your marriage
and the births, the deaths
and grievances seemed to
be the worst.

But now as you
remember how you used
to peek a look,
Here is your own little
Memory Book.

Tanya Bartlett

At Eventide

Father, God, I heard Thy voice
At eventide, call;
In night's darkness even did
Thy Presence befall;
By Holy swords of light
Shewn truly to me;
Thy Holy words upon my mouth
I spoke silently.

From a bed of tears didst
Thy Spirit carry me;
Unto higher ground
To walk with Thee;
Filled with Heavenly Love
Unknown to me before;
At last, at eventide,
Thou findest me, Oh Lord.

Maura B. Vidaure

Hitsville

Oldies got me through today
back to smaller days
far away
that can never be again
unless
of course
I turn my radio on
and then

Old dog's on the porch sleeping
grandma around him
sweeping
big brother fixing that bike too
Dad by the lamp
crossword puzzles no one else can do

Ah those oldies did it again today
those oldies but goodies
take the pain away

Trevor Valentine

The Lord of Love

"Oh creation where wouldst thou be,
But naught in eternity.
For love called out thru
love itself and made a place for all.
As it was in the love
of God that all heard the call."

Ernestine Cantrall

Transition To Metamorphosis

Meadows void of foul cold weather
Bask within their glowing Aurae
Feel each facet's gleaming Glory?
Nasty flaws don't mar this marvel,
For the mortal cruise is over;
Now that earthly phase is ended

Search out an empty Niche aloft,
A Cosmos where Perfection reigns:
The stormless Lair of endless Warmth
This Scene surpassing Beauty leaves...
Perceptions bound in Ecstasy.

Richard E. Smith

The Dribbler

The jumper jumps high
basketball in the air,
knocks the ball to the dribbler
a flick of the wrist with a flair.

The dribbler catches the ball
the goal in sight,
he has to make his moves
with precision and flight.

The audience begins to yell,
"Drive! Drive!"
But the dribbler takes his time
for he knows he must survive.

He dribbles to the right,
he dribbles to the left,
he dribbles past the defense
and hoops it with a lift.

"He is amazing!"
the audience calls,
they call him "the dribbler,"
and he's only four foot tall.

Melissa Bartuska

Circus

Acrobats and animals,
Bears and bobcats too.
Cats are going to be there to
Do some tricks for you.
Elephants with floppy ears
Gorillas and monkeys in cages,
Having a ball and that's not all,
In the jumping
Kangaroo circus,
Little monkeys play with maracas and,
Neat horses jump over people.
The audience thinks its Queen that
Roaring Lions and Swooping birds
Take charge
Usually
Very quickly
Well balanced kids juggle
Extraordinary things
You would think kits magic well it's time
to leave the
Zany Circus right now

Lisa Silver

The Massage (In Winter) For: "A"

I felt his heart
beat
through his hand

I heard his breath
as crystal mist
blew
in icy weather

I felt him breathing
as the mist, hands and heart
touched my skin

He lifted the curve of my lower back
inhaling deeply
his aroma traveled to my solar plexus

The music flooded the room
moving to French lyrics

Outside lights
rushed twinkles
through the windows
bringing the same light
the therapist brings to my life

Liza Scher

Please Give Me A Chance

Please give me a chance
Because I like to dance
Life is funny
Not just honey

A chance to love
Just like that dove
A chance to succeed
A chance, yes indeed

A chance to be free
Not just like a bumble bee
A chance to express
Not just to stress

A chance to compete
That would be neat
A chance to be acceptable
Not just to be connectable

A chance to be the best
That would be the very test
Please give me a chance
If only I just enhance

Michael A. Martin

Untitled

You think you know me, do you?
Because you have touched my body
    your fingers on my skin.
You have felt my lips upon yours,
    my warmth from within.
Because you have looked into my eyes
    peered through my souls door.
You think you know the woman inside,
    a child always wanting more.
Have you ever seen the devil?
Felt her hands upon your face?
Passion is running through you now,
    your feelings can't keep pace.
You've felt my best and seen the worst
    but more is yet to come.
Just because you've seen my soul
you know not where I am from.
You think you know me well,
    Do you?

Trina L. Koester

Untitled

Without my knowledge our friendship and
been tainted.
We shared our thoughts, our dreams and
even our secrets,
We had closeness that was shamelessly
innocent.
One of us was betrayed.

Kaydee Sullivan

Vegetable Thoughts

An asparagus is long and green
Before you cook it
Make sure it is good and clean.

Broccoli is eaten cooked or raw
It is green and grows in a bunch
Some eat it in a salad for lunch.

Carrots are orange in color
And they are good for the eyes
You may even cook them in pot pies.

Celery grows in stalks
But when cut up in salads
You eat it with a fork.

Beets are red and round
And to say it name will make
Many boys and girls frown.

Some onions are white and yellow
And an onion will make you cry
But they are good if you fry.

F. Marion Daniel

Seasons

Summer green and growing still
beneath the sun, the farmers till
the land and larders seek to fill.
Summer days of love, sweeter still.

Against crisp promise of the frost
coming now as sure as time is lost.
I missed you, woman, all my life,
I was, without you, only tied to strife.

The pleasures of the bed not unknown
but loving you has simply shown
another deeper bond for you and I,
and makes the life strands, that tie.

Soon to sleep beneath the winter snow
having lived the fullest life I know,
finding you has made our season send
a love that lives and shall never end.

That seasons matter not at all.
In love there is no spring or fall.
Winter's white is just delight
and summer makes all things right.

J. Clayton Lafferty

When After Comes

What about when after comes
And yesterday is gone again
Tomorrow never lets us know
The road we should be on today
And what will we do with forever
Never really having been
Some would say we hold the treasure
Maybe that was only me
Again

Chris Olea

"Fishing"

If I could only stand
Beneath this willow tree
With fishing gear in hand
How happy I would be.

Away from all the madness
That sets our hearts a whirl
Away from all the gladness
We find when boy meets girl

If you could only try
Then you would surely feel
The casting of a fly
The clicking of a reel

Remember life's too fine
To worry constantly
So go and get a line
And fish a while with me.

Sam Amato

Birth of a Baby

The day you were born was the
best day of my life.
When they laid you in my arms
- oh how you shined with charm.
You father and I were so proud,
in prayer our head we bowed.
We thanked the Lord above for a child
that filled us with such love.
I will always cherish you
no matter what you decide to do.
You will always be in my heart
even if we are apart
you will always be a part
of me throughout eternity

Kelli Finch

The Blind Man Who Could See

Once, when I was walking
between a mountain and a sea,
I came upon a man;
blind - but he could see.
Not one word from his mouth came
until I touched his hand to mine.
He smiled, and in a muffled voice,
sighed "Dividends exist in mind."
I was perplexed, I must admit;
on that clause my thoughts did weigh.
But truth and sight were soon restored
as he lie down across the way:
"We must be one, then, you and I,
yet darkness impedes the human eye."

Sean Michael Furjanic

Untitled

Warmth and friendship
compassion and love.
When most people mention
Grandmother, that's what they
think of.

They live by the rhythm
of a forever going tune,
But out of all this,
I wish you get well soon.

Alec Gillis

Untitled

In silent stillness time does pass,
Beyond this sphere of shattered glass.

Into the bleak with pain untold,
Where dreams disperse in graven cold.

Against these corners behind those eyes,
My laughter ceased with his demise.

Where blackened hopes can not prevail,
Beneath that blistered fairy tale.

Within my paleness darkness streams,
To conjure up these bruising screams.

I kneel upon this desolate ground,
Reflecting vows that hold me bound.

In silent stillness I choose to sleep,
I pray my soul for God to keep.

Where withered hope and vows do break,
Upon this earth I will not wake.

Tana Sramek

Tornadoes

Glowering black clouds hang low.
Blinding flashes
crackle across the sky
as booms of deep thunder
shake the earth.
Angry fingers drag along the ground,
whirling, whirling, whirling,
uprooting trees
and exploding other objects
into assorted debris,
hurling it high,
leaving it behind
to scatter over the countryside.

Ruth Ekstrom

They Come

Out of nowhere, they come.
Bombarding me with their presence
     they flitter like fireflies.
On. Off. On again, they come.
Piercing and jabbing; from all angles.
Weaving webs of wonderment
Lacing desires of fulfillment
Exciting me,
     Embracing me,
          Enchanting me of what could be.
Faster, they come. Drawing me.
Penetrating my very depths.
My soul yearns for them.
Dare I allow myself these luxuries?
Will I be ridiculed, or thought odd,
     if voiced out loud?
Still, they come.
I inhale their existence.
I can not escape them.
They come.

Shirley Reaman

Penguin

Clumsy, black
catching, waddling, diving
Chinstrap, Royal, Emperor, King
sleeping, flying, eating
funny, short
Bird

Grace Assouad

Leaves

We are but leaves
Born from buds
Implanted in a yesteryear.

In spring we stretch
Our lacy fingers
To reach God's nourishing rays.

In summer we bask
In brilliant sunshine
And teach our children
Truth and righteousness.

With autumn's chill
We blush in radiant hues
And pirouette to the earth below.

Winter's blanket of snow
Covers us to fulfill
Nature's divine design.

William C. Brender

A Rose

I was just sitting here thinking
'Bout a gift I would like to send,
A gift to say, "I was thinking of you",
In hopes it never would end.

A gesture of truth to pass the miles
And make it to your home,
To fill a void of emptiness
If ever you're feeling alone.

A symbol of timeless beauty
Yet, not to be matched by yours,
A symbol of sweet anticipation
Behind yet unopened doors.

A sign of strong affections
So daringly revealed,
Words so clear, but yet unspoken
To show you how I feel.

A rose is something fragile
Yet, strong in what it says,
"A rose" is what I've sent to you,
"A rose" that is so read....

Steve Shannon

Grandpa's Treats Not Too Sweet

When he bakes
bowls and pans out he takes
so a mistake
he doesn't make
measures twice, once for you
and once for me
when Grandpa bakes
what does it take?
Easy fixings
not much mixing
Three ingredients are just fine.
So he doesn't miss his nap time
His grandsons standing in the wing
So they don't miss a thing
Maybe Mom and Dad might get a treat
If they hurry and don't drag their feet

When Grandpa bakes
the earth could quake
but he will make
If three ingredients all it takes.

Pat Pitsenberger

Winter Storm

Soggy, soggy, sodden snow,
Branches laden, drooping low,
White fantasies profiled in sky.
Birds in bush hopping happily,
Chirping safe; hidden, carefree.

Peering with wonder, shy and demure,
At people in windows, heated, secure.
Shielded from adversity,
Denied nature's beauty,
Safe in drab, moody sanctuary.

Scurrying tigerish, crumbs to salvage,
Water frozen, useless tho pure,
Cruel winds cutting, fierce to endure,
No chance to rest, driven to rummage.

Life so perilous for puny, tiny,
Heroic and courageous,
Defying destiny.

Marvin A. Rauch

Night Breathing

LORD, bless sleeping, resting,
breathing, dreaming
head upon your chest.
LORD, bless memory, imagination,
mind and choosing,
shadow in light,
bring daylight out of night.
LORD, bless fear, anger,
with healing freedom,
peace and love.
LORD, bless hearing
with your voice,
seeing with your vision.
LORD, bless my soul
with life-giving presence,
day and night, along life's
journey toward eternal life.

Lawrence London

Jesus, Our Saviour

Jesus born so long ago in Bethlehem
Brings good tidings to all mankind;
To rich and poor, to young and old,
To healthy, halt, the lame, the blind.

Jesus was born of God and sent to earth
To live as man, among us to dwell,
To teach us peace and love and joy
And how to live, His praise to tell.

We sing hallelujah to praise His name
And now rejoice because of His birth.
Let's take hold of that bright tomorrow
By being His children upon God's earth.

Margaret Good

Addictus

His searing fingers
Caressed me as a Child —
Slight singe upon my soul.
Embers festering through the years—
Ebriosity, his flaming grip.
A smoldering asphyxiation —
Sly Arsonist,
Death.

Ann Blessing-Williams

Cousin Tamra

Born in my father's island
brought to States
in pursuit of better life.

Life was good for Cousin Tamra
she got lazy, rude and vain
Felt herself bigger than most.

She had man
twice her age
thought she living it up...

Until one day
She lift herself too high
The gal got bold
My father put he foot down.

Next thing we know
the gal butt back home.

Tessa Beazer

The Search

Ringing all the agencies
    but can't get no reply,
Asking all my buddies
    but connection ended all with "Hi",
Using all my business ties
    but inform net gettin' through,
Starting to get disparate
    Is there a job for me?

Reading through the N.Y.T.
    but ad's all seem to same,
Crying to my parents
    but employment was theirs game,
Pleading to my former boss
    but "company's in the red",
Calling up my "soon-to-be"
    and she found a job for me.

Takejiro Kikuchi

Searching For Love

I looked and looked
But could not find
Someone to love
And ease my mind

I searched near
And I searched far
I went by train, plane
Boat and car
Each place I went
I met many
From all I met
There was not any

That could compare
With what I found
Around the corner
In the local dog pound

Rose M. Moulds

A Simple Touch

A simple touch
can mean so much,
but only for awhile
for hearts untold are
oh so bold,
and often in denial.

Amy Tillery

The Shadow

I walk with you
  but I can't see
I'm not a figment
  although I could be
I can't speak
  and I'm not a freak
I'm all around
  with no where bound
I would like to listen
  but that would be a blessing
For I'm one of a kind
  I'm your kind
Sometimes when your there
  I can be here
And at times I'll be gone
  when the clouds are strong
But never fear I'll be near
  Just look around
And I'll appear

Shirley E. Stokes

My Days

My days are long.
But I hold up strong.
My mornings are hard.
It's like I'm carrying
  a pound of land.

I pray to my sweet Jesus.
Before I go to bed at night.
And thank him for feeding us.
He always treats a person right.

I would like to thank him.
For not letting our lives be dim.
I'll be up there to see you soon.
Because my life isn't full of gloom.

Melba May

Bedtime

Today will end in grief and sorrow,
But I will sleep until tomorrow.
Or will my life come to a close?
Perhaps I am the one Death chose
To rest with him eternally,
And he will act paternally,
To care for me generically.

Mortality is understood
By no one young, by no one good.
Only the evil and the old
Obey their knowledge of the cold
And stiffened bodies of the dead.
"Insanity" was all it said.
Now, do not fear. Just go to bed.

Mike Wilson

Grammy

My Grammy's always there
even when I have a nightmare
If we did not have
money. She would find
away to put food in my
tummy. All she have to do is
give me a touch. And I know
She loves me very much.
I'll do anything for her but
I bet shell do even more for me!
I love you, you're the best Memom

Becky Lucrezi

Jodi's Smile

Some days I feel real good,
But it only lasts for a while.
Some days I feel real bad,
'Til I think of Jodi's Smile.
  Jodi's Smile,
Brings happiness to me,
  Jodi's Smile,
It's as Pretty as can be.

When life gets hard
and I feel real down
I think of her smile
and my frown turns around.

She was always there
until the end,
she was definitely my
one true friend.
And to this day
when things go bad
her smile comes to me,
and I'm no longer sad.

Robyn Spears

Where are the Children?

Where are the children?
But it's to late to ask
Be strong, look tough
Where is my mask

The children are gone
The effort was in vain
Oh habits are back
Soon comes the pain

I long to hear my baby
Daddy will you read me this book?
No more fishing with my son
down my the brook

Life without them is driving
me insane
The children are gone
and I cant stand the pain

Richard Greer

Love

Love is like a friend,
But love can also end.
Love is represented by a rose,
Not your stinky toes.
Love can be very grand,
Even better than name-brand.
Love can be very nice,
Just like sugar and spice.
Love is like a little note,
You may get one on the 'love boat.'
Love can be very electric,
Sometimes shocking and symmetric.
Love is also ultra,
It's in every culture.
Love is in every season,
You can fall in love without a reason.
When you're in love,
You're just like a dove.
Love is so sweet,
It just can't be beat.

Nicholas DaCosta

To Destiny — Just Because

Dearest Destiny:

  You are in the TERRIBLE TWO'S
— but none of us who love you
have the blues — you keep us
laughing so hard at your daily
antics and constant line of
chatter!!

  Your a mimic and a doll —
a favorite of us all!!

  Gone are your Baby Mickey
Mouse days — now replaced by
Barney the dinosaur and his win-
ning ways!!

  No child can outdo you in
any way — what else can I say?

Love Grandma Marx

Not Lonely

I watch the sunrise alone
but not lonely

I hear the birds sings alone
but not lonely

You're a thousand miles away
and I'm alone
but not lonely

And I miss you and I'm alone
but not lonely

Because You're here, in my heart
I can feel every beat
I can quiver at the want of every touch

I can hear you whisper that you love me
and I'm alone
But not lonely

Sherry E. Nakoa

Once I Was...

Once I was limited
But now I am smart

I used to like blue
But now I like silver

Once I ate pizza
But now I eat ribs

I used to wear Levis
But now I wear Guess

Once I played baseball
But now I play soccer

I used to watch cartoons
But now I watch shows

Once I was young
But now I am grown

Thomas Bigger

Thinking Of You

Sometimes I see
a bird flying in the sky.
A beautiful eagle soaring
through the rainbow high.
Believing that hopes ad
dreams will come true.
That makes me think of you.

Anne Joy

Love

Love is a special
Feeling that can cheer you up
When you're feeling down.

Carrie Clapper

A Soul's Tear

She laughed
but she wasn't happy,

Inside the joyful exterior,
That had taken so long to build,
piece by piece
The beauty,
The attitude,
The laugh
The lines
The look
It was just a shell,
Inside cowered a soul,
So torn from the world's daggers,
repeatedly beaten by societies ideals,
It was forced to hide
Soul-Sick and Aching,
but too proud to cry at,
It was left, shoved aside, and ignored,

Because as long as you had the look,
who cared, what was on the inside

Katherine L. Arnold

Untitled

I finally found my love today.
But she's 700 miles away.
I see her when I can.
I think I'm still her man.
Even though we have our doubts
I think we can work it out.
She makes me feel all right.
Just have to hang on tight.

I knew right from the start.
Times we would be apart.
Sleeping without her at night.
Is an endless fight.
Goodbye tears and goodbye pains.
Storm down just like the rains.
Sometimes it feels we're drifting apart.
But she has all of my heart.

Matthew C. Pefley

Crack!

Sometimes I just wanna run
But there's nowhere to run to...
Nowhere to hide.
So I run anyway.
So fast I almost feel myself fly
so high
 so high
I can almost feel the wind
from way up in the sky so high...

Crack!
 Snap!
 I think I hear a bird say,
but what it really is
 is the breaking
 of something inside
as I stumble and fall.

Ynnovak Fernandez

Tears

I've never been a little shy,
But wary deep with-in.
Even as a little girl
I kept the tear-drops in.
The tears I cry are not from pain,
Or joy from where I've been.

Frustration is my demon,
That's where my pain begins.
It's wrong to shout and swear about
The things I cannot change.
What would I gain to ease the pain?
To whom would fall the blame?

I've mastered my emotions,
Too well, so it would seem.
To shout instead of crying
Has been my life long dream.
If I could shout and rave about
Without inflicting pain,
The tears I shed would be instead,
Pure joy at all I'd gained.

Kim Capri

Loving Someone Far Away and Near

We are here and you are there,
 but where really is there?
 Is it hell?
Or is it an empty void in-between
 heaven and hell?
Only those of us who are here could
 know this, for we are those that
 stare at death's dark face or the
 loneliness of missing loved ones.
And though we are here and you are
 there...
We all feel the bitterness of lonely
 nights spent wondering if we will
 ever return to the life we once knew.
The emptiness we must feel.
The uncertainty of our futures.
The desire and joy of once again
 being reunited.
The hope that soon, you will come
 home to our open arms...

Mylinda Crane

Inmates Prayer

You can lock up my body
but you can't lock up my soul
because last week I found Jesus
I was half - now I'm whole..

I use to sit in my cell,
so damn lonely at night.
I had no one to talk to,
or no one to write.

Then I got on my knee's
I called for Jesus by my side.
Now I'm no longer lonely,
I was so happy, that I cried...

And now I give him worries,
and he carries my load...
because I ask his forgiveness,
and to lead me straight down his
road...(Man)

He's made this empty heart, full,
I've got a brand new start...
No matter what this world hands me,
the Lord's got my heart.

Mark C. Abel

The Winds of Time

The winds of time
came down on me.
I've turned old and
grey, and can hardly move.

My bones are brittle
And I cannot stand.
I sit and stare out
at my window.

The children are grown,
And I'm left alone,
My sweetheart has
gone before me.
I hear a bird
singing in a tree.

I know it's spring,
And I must go.
Yet, when I do
I just don't know.
The Winds of Time
came down on me.

Kathleen Guyot

This Willow

From atop a willow
Can we observe
The earth's transgression
Toward a fatal curve.

Straight and true
Was the endearing path
Of our existence
And God's Wrath.

Through what we believed
Were noble deeds
Comes a definite judgment
Upon which evil feeds.

This domain shall perish
Sum of a thousand strifes
An event no man foresaw
Sans saints and poets alike

And from atop a willow
We cast an eye toward heaven
And spy three dove...
And a 747.

Michael P. Souther

Measure a Man

Can you measure a man by his age
Can you measure a man by putting him
in a cage. Can you measure a man
by his rage
Can you measure a man worth by the
love he give or, can you measure his
worth by the love he feels
Can you measure a man by how many
lives he saves
Can you measure a man by his sufferings
or can you measure a man by his pain
or can you measure a man by the
love in his heart through God
that's the real measure of a man.

Terry Fernando Newton

The Lights

Sparkling lights in the city
Cars going by so fast
They give off moving strips of light.
Red, blue, white, orange, and yellow -
Colors that show the most.
Sky scrapers taller than any monument -
Each gives off more than one color,
The water reflects all the lights
And ends up showing forever.
Now I see the beauty,
And how great it is!
We are destroying it slowly,
And soon there will be no more.

Sara Webb

My Ode to Life

Bullets rising over clouds,
Childhood dreams begin to drown.
Murdered innocence, forever lost,
Madmen hiding behind political rot.
Alone, I die.

Living young with ancient rage,
Swallow the pill of distrust,
Not knowing I entered the final stage.
Despair growing free, like Maroon Rust
It's nothing but an unholy lie.
Alone, I die.

Fathers teaching dark hypocrisy
Souls nourished on waste and hate,
Everybody knows about the anarchy,
That flows in the veins
Of the leaders of state.

Leaving behind,
My ode to life
Alone, I die.

Noel Cortez

Untitled

All the evil in the world
children forced to be adults
Adults not caring for their own
Everyday people walk past
Not wanting to help
Maybe out of fear
Maybe, they just don't care
We all have to open our eyes
Help the children
Help our fellow man
For if we don't
We shall all perish
In a very cold world
No one to notice our death
No one to even care
Is this the world we want?
This is a question we all must ask our-
selves?

Kimberly Linn

Untitled

During the quiet moments of the day
From the recesses of my mind
I sometimes seek my way
And suddenly I find
You are there
To share
Love

Eleanor L. Lecuyer

The Children's International Song

This day will live in history,
children meet in the land of the free,
to greet new friends across the sea,
    and share the blessing of liberty.

We come from east, we come from west,
and north and south to do our best,
I say to you let us be friends,
because on this, true peace depends.

Oh, troubled world bowed down with pain
we share a common fate, beware,
embrace the virtues, once again,
for a world of peace, love and care.

Vilma Young

Children's Creed

Why, oh why have we made our
    children so sad, for they shall
    inherit the world as we leave
    it.

They, to some of us, are worth
    more than silver and gold, or
    other monetary values of this
    life.

Yet, the children are being
    battered, abused and molested by
    those they call "parents".

If, by chance, they are not wanted
    by loving parents, give them up
    to someone who will love them.

For they deserve a chance in life
    to carry on the family trees
    which stand out like the giant
    redwoods.

Paul P. Lubera

"Little Creature"

The merry little chipmunk
Climbs from his winter home
Under the patio
His bright, beady eyes
Spy goldfinches at the feeder
He stands erect
Paw, jaws unmoving
Until the birds depart
Quickly he snoops in
The seeds dropped
Chomping rapidly on his find
He stares in the glass patio doors
At me!

Virginia Hadley Hall

Guidance

We'll keep our eyes on Jesus.
He'll guide as all the way.

We'll tune our ears toward heaven,
to hear what God will say.

We'll give our hearts to Jesus,
Who never fails to bless.

We'll give him all the glory.
He's the key to our success.

DeDe Short

Dreams

Something to hold onto
close to your heart
deep in your soul
they are shared
they are kept quiet

Sometimes they don't
come true. But the
dream lives on
and on...

As you grow older
and time goes by
you still have your
dream. A little different
a little the same, torn
apart by sadness. Kept
together by love,
close to your heart
and deep in your soul
Dreams...

Kala Haines

Rainy Days

Rain, rain
coating the streets
images of terra cotta
on gray
soothe my mind

Thoughts of loved ones
near and afar
warm my heart
and occupy my time

The world has opened
its arms
and I willingly,
joyfully,
rush headlong into
its embrace

Diamond Deb

Friend of Mine

Low me, no lie
come here, be mine
one smile
lights up the face.

One tear
rolling down
your smile
all dry

Misunderstanding
calm, cool words
upset, nervous
ruffled fur

Pat, smooth
soothing motion
sorry's said
forgiven? You bet

Friends, a while
things unknown
hand in hand
always a friend of mine

Louise Elaine Teasle

Love Light

See my light
come out of the dark
Feel the warmth
your not alone
addictions, handicaps
Ego's needing to win
Acknowledge your feelings
from deep within
Hear the songs of
Unconditional love,
rise above,
out of the darkness-
into Universal
Oneness.

Rose Knight

The Gift Of Friendship

Every now and then one
    comes along our way,
Who cares and truly hears
    what we have to say.

And to be ever so blessed when
    they join with you and pray,
To help keep one on God's path
    so as not to stray.

That someone who comes is
    sent from above,
Because they are filled with
    such caring and love.

You, Dear Friend, are one of
    those many I know,
You're the salt of the earth
    and how your light does glow.

Mary Ellen D. Stewart

Seashores from Afar

The waves splash the shore,
coming more and more.
The sun gleams from a high,
like a light from a castle in the sky.
The sands is like a rough hand,
and there you see a man.
White clouds are to be seen,
but you don't know what they mean.
You can hear happy sounds
there are no bounds.
Then comes the night,
you take a beautiful sight.
The stars shine bright,
and the water flickers in the moonlight.
The time goes by slow,
and you know
life is grand,
you take your friends hand.

Sheelah Lynn Walter

The Nativity

In that holy moment the seeds of
faith were sown;
Angel voice sounded, the world
rejoice unknown;
And hands shall clasp in
reverence for that tiny child;
For Christ lay in the manger
and God looked down and smiled.

Helen F. Gaughan

The Candle

The candle stands straight and tall.
Confidently lighting the way.
Its flame can preserve life,
or take it.

The flame lives and breathes
And loves.
Flickering in the night.

Casting shadows
Transforming reality
Into Fantasy.
Lighting the lovers way
Touching their hearts
Blurring their senses
Bonding their souls.

Randy Holmes

Reality

Scared from life
Confused as a hole
Depending on dreams
Emotions with sole
Vibration from within
Feelings that fall
Grabbed for a string
Pushed against the wall
Eating the pain
Developing a fear
Surrounded by time
Looking through a tear
Lost in a world
Eyes of crystal blue
Space we see
People we knew

Scott M. Downs

Balance

Balancing a rock upon its
corner; a special skill
not had by all.

Stonehenge, rock walls
without cement
standing for ages.

A craft almost lost
like writing a poem
with something for all.

Balanced like a boulder
on side of hill
upon a tee.

Where nature holds
the key; it astonishes
and humbles me.

Ray O'Neal

Fusion

If there's a burning desire
deep in your soul, let it
ignite this incendiary
down in my core. Let us
erupt and become as molten
magma, spreading over and
through each other, until
your beginning can no longer
be distinguished from my end.

George Perry

Untitled

What is behind
    costly sacrifice?

What is behind
    forgiveness
    without conditions?

What is behind
    those risks
    we take?

Love.

Michael Holman

God's World

The sky aglow at break of dawn,
Crystal dewdrops upon the lawn.
The robin's song, so clear and gay,
A flight of geese winging their way.
The scent of blossoms, so pure and sweet,
The feel of earth beneath my feet.
The pounding surf upon the sands,
The warmth of sunlight upon my hands.
These splendors all, are always free,
A gift from God, to you and me.

Robert L. Kurtz

Mother Nature's Portrait

On the clear cold mountain
Crystal shimmering hues
Fragments of the sun stream through
Ice tinsel sails
Blue sky dances
Wild spring thaws
Beauty awakens
Buds sprinkle into bloom
Birds sing in this picturesque afternoon
Artist paints his green eyed view
Mother natures portrait

Marie Roberts

Small Talk About Daisy

"Who is Daisy?" you might ask.
"Daisy is my kitchen Clock."

She possesses hands and numerals
Black as ebony,
A face as yellow as sunshine
And round, as the silver moon.

Oh! I think Daisy has fun
With her incessant
Tick-tock.
Audible throughout
Disturbing to some,
But not to me!

For
Day and night
Dawn or evening
This clock keeps ticking,
Breaking silence that oppresses
In a home
That's seldom visited!

Margaret Feliciano

The End Has Just Begun

Cold winter crossings
dance among the spiderwebs
the door to the red meat
squeaks a welcome
barrels of onyx soot
coat the walls
and a smile betrays the situation.

Limb torn from comfort home
makes a tasty appetizer
the main course
filet of chilled marrow.

Each morsel slithers to the bowels
the vitamin of decay
seeps slowly into the stream.

The dead have the breath of life
(again)
Every tissue, every cell, every memory-
digested.
The eater has become the eaten
and the end has just begun.

Michelle Oleson

Black, Evil?

Destitute of light
Dark, gloomy
Sullen, atrocious, wickedness
Destructive, evil dirty, nasty
Is this what black is?
Is this what blacks are like?
If so why haven't I seen it a lot?
I've seen it on the street
and I've seen it on television
but I've never seen it at home
Joy, love, unselfishness
Light of my life angelic, beauty
Keeper of all my happiness
This is what I see
This is what black means to me
I see this when I walk through my front door
I don't see destruction and evil
If wickedness is what the world sees they
    need to come into
my house and see love like I see it black, evil?
Not in my house not from my mother

Latrice Renee Mayweather

City Of New York

City of New York never sleeps
Day and night for job and tips
Citymen, citizen come along
Build thou city now singing song

City of New York white and black
Homeless shelter trodden slag
Land for world peace love and gay
Birth of a new world, dawning day

Skyhigh buildings, Manhattan
Hanging bridges, wonder fan
World trade, Empire, Statue of Liberty
U.N., Rockfeller grandeur, O hearty

Who says America not whose friend
Righteous stand for serving trend
Worldmen made her immigrants land
Multicolored O bondage band

Skylark, New York wonder state
Fortune seeker's golden gate

Rashidul Kabir Chishty

Once Life, Then Death

Life; once conceived, unable to handle
Death; death once pondered and perceived.
Life; the one great struggle,
Death; the need to breathe.
Life; once thought of as content,
Death; death comes up and pulls you under.
Life; life goes on,
Death; death does not
Life; once life is gone,
Death; death grows longer.

Tracy Lynn McKenna

Candied Apples

Peanuts, caramels, cinnamon glaze
Delicious candied apples
Set upon a bakers tray,
Like colorful little soldiers
Standing in a perfect line
We view them as delicious
Will one of them be mine,
So sweet to the taste
With a crunch to every bite
They come in many flavors
Which one shall I try,
Decision seems impossible
I can't make up my mind
The only way to solve the problem
Is to buy one of every kind...

Wanda L. Schultz

Just Another Day

As I look out at the morning sun,
    Dew upon the lawn.
The quiet of the morning light,
    Will soon have come and gone.

The helter skelter of the day,
    Heard through out the hours.
Hustle bustle and the sounds
    No harm to the beauty of the flowers.

As dusk moves in and the setting sun,
    Quiet comes once more.
Watch the sun set in the west,
    From out our kitchen door.

Soon the darkened sky above,
    And stars that shine so bright.
I'll lie upon my bed and rest,
    And wake to the morning light.

Richard L. Parker

A Rose

A precious bud, waiting to unfold
A precious life, yet untold
Stretching gracefully into time
Growing beautifully in body and mind
Scenting the air with much perfume
Pacing your life with goals to assume
At its peak, a rose is beauty to behold
Look inside, precious child, you're a
rose retold. Grow.

DeMarchia Gibson

The Crime Of Love

Did you need me when you said it?
Did you miss me when you cried?
Did you hate me when you did it?
Did you mean it when you lied?

I never did anything to hurt you;
I loved you with all my heart.
How could you go and hurt me,
Then watch me fall apart?

You said I made you happy,
I was unlike all the rest.
You had me thinking I was special,
While I thought you were the best.

Why did you lie to me, then
Say it all was true?
All the time I made you happy,
Then you treated me so cruel.

Now that I am no longer with you,
I think of you all the time.
You, out of all people, had to
make love such a crime.

Michelle Mendoza

Ing

Pitching pennies, didn't have many.

Skipping rocks,
    didn't want to play with blocks

Looking for the boogie man,
    found him in the garbage can.

Playing hookie, just like a rookie.

Trying to find a place to hide,
    couldn't even get a ride.

Standing tall, thought I knew it all.

Needing pride, taking it in stride.

Seeking grace, fell on my face.

Facing fear, holding it dear.

Seeing tomorrow,
    filled with sorrow.

Crying hot tears,
    heard the jeers.

Thinking twice,
    still paid the price.

Getting older,
    still growing colder.

Monica L. Lewis

Untitled

I sit here and watch the sun
Dip below the horizon.
Another day has come to an end,
Another day is done.
The sky gets dark,
The stars come out,
The moon casts off a light.
The sound is gone,
And all is still,
And once again it's night.

Kevin Oldenburg

Picket Fence

A white picket fence
Divides the street from the yard,
The house, freshly painted,
Overlooking the car.
Dog's barking,
Children playing,
Father on the front
Porch,
Asleep in his chair.
Mother in the garden
Cutting a rose.
Sunrise, sunset,
Day to day,
That picket fence,
It's ramparts
Guarding,
From those who
Would trespass,
The children playing happily
Amongst the flowers and grass.

W. B. Burkholder

View Point

Is life's vast landscape really bleak?
Do darksome shadows fall, and seek
    The stark, discouraged soul?

The restless spirit seeks to know:
O must the platitude be so
    That marks the grave our goal?

No one's just born to live and get,
And then pass on; he still may set
    A goal that's not in vain.

We lay not waste our pow'rs when we
For others live; but someday see
    Them all as heav'nly gain.

Ray Puen

Nature

Nature is about the things we
do, like we look through the stars
at night. Nature is the blue sea
in Earth. The animals hear the
voices of the people in their homes.
God sees us everywhere when
we walk step by step. And the
nights are gloomy. In earth, we
see ourselves in our places.
People are important to earth.
All of us are responsible for our
needs when we do our work.
When we eat it is good enough to
pray. So when you go to bed,
say goodnight.

Sunsary S. Khim

Clothes

Life's three necessities,
Do not include,
What Styles to wear,
For our every mood.
What's fashion?,
No one's the same,
Infinity styles,
Who started this chain.
So much money, invested and lost,
Just for these garbs,
To be worn then tossed.

Kyra Schoening

"Silent Whispers"

Can you read my mind?
Do you feel my hidden smile?
Can you hold it all in?
Do you believe love is a sin?
Will you die with me?
Do you feel the fire inside of me?
Do you want to put it out?
Can you fly?
I'll show you how
Do you feel the pain?
Is my soul inside of you?
I put it there
Now you suffer
But for no reason at all - me too
Do you want to jump?
I will catch you
I have wings to fly
Do you hear that?
He sings to me sometimes
I always listen.

Tricia Topping

Whispering Ways

Hush! I hear the voices.
Does it matter what they say?

I hear the ripple of the water,
and then, the great movement of the sea.
I feel the rhythm of the waves,
as they lash out at me.

I create DISTURBANCE.
A person, who it's said,
Speaks too loud,
Does not follow the crowd.
Who follows a path of her own,
Most often alone.

Yes! I hear the voices, not as
loudly as before.
As I am very busy with the task
left at my door.
There is no time for chatter, so
have your little fun, as
I have taken action, and do not need
your whispering ways.

Virginia Knowdell

Window Seat

The man driving the train
Doesn't want to sleep

For one wink of the eye
And he may miss a view

Of a lifetime that he
May never see again.

Zackery J. Finn

Our Love Is...

Our love is as beautiful
as the nights sky
We lay down together
just you and I
Your kiss is as beautiful
as heaven above
Please God let him
send me his love.

Christina Long

Wake Up America "1956"

Wake up America, and show your-stuff
Don't let the Russians call-your-bluff
You know there laughing up their-sleeve
That is why we're a little-peeved

Wake up America, and be-alert
You know the Russians aren't all-jerks
They have some men that are-scientific
So we will build one that is terrific

Wake up America, and send it-soon
The new vanguard right to the-moon
We have the men to do it-now
And send it right into-moscow

Wake up America, and send it high
Right up into the great blue-sky
It will circle the earth so far and-fast
That they won't know just when it-passed

Wake up America, and do it - right
To send the missile out of - sight
Well make it good and we will come - through
The American flag the red, white, and - blue.

Salvatore A. Giordano

Beyond

My love for you isn't gone,
Don't mistake that for respect.

Love was something that I
Couldn't help but give completely -
Together heart and soul.

Respect you had to earn from
Me, but these days I can't
Say very much for it.

So soft and kind with the lines
That you fed me, but now cold
And empty words are only spoken.

I can't help loving you for
That is beyond my power to change,
But I could never respect you
After the way I've been treated.

Rhiannon Cope

Goodbye Dulcet Tone

Goodbye, oh, Dulcet Tone.
Dost hear me wail and moan?
Euphonious though it be
It is no more for me

Adios, mellifluous voice.
Oh, it wounds me deep
And silently I weep,
Hold back a million tears

For grievous loss to ears.
Yet, must I report
That life is much too short
To continue in this vein.

'Tis sufficeth to retain
The memory in my brain
Of having loved and known
Thy sweet Dulcet tone.

Roslyn H. Taffel

Life In The Desert

Desert sand is wildly blowing
Down the drifted river bed dry,
Mojave Zephyr winds are roiling
The amber dust, mountain high.

Along uneven hard packed roads,
Where drying puddles still play
And there are no human abodes,
Our family car we jounce each day.

The sky is mostly clear and blue,
The greasewood's green is dark,
Yellow desert blooms are all in view
In Nature's bounteous cacti park.

Southern California's burst to Spring
Will be a great and glorious thing
Here in the Mojave Desert high
Where multi-colored mountains touch the sky.

J. Wesley Olds

Dream

Dream a dream of day of night.
Dream a dream of the sun's great light.
Dream a dream of the one you love.
Dream a dream of a beautiful white dove.
Dream a dream of heaven or earth.
Dream a dream of God's great birth.
Dream a dream of the great blue sky.
Dream a dream that you could fly.
Dream a dream without any fear.
Dream a dream without shedding a tear.
Dream a dream of any kind.
Dream a dream within your mind.

J. Nell Brewster

Dreams

I dreamed...
Dreamed that my little world
imagined of hope
arrived at the Planet of love.

I found myself...
With the sun shinning on the horizon
illuminating my thoughts
and on the delight of this moment
my heart fascinated.

I lost myself...
In the skies of my imagination
I saw the Planet of love
bringing the perfect figure of the Human.

I wanted...
But I could not reach it,
in your eternal and sublime splendor
went together with the clouds of the sky.
Here I stayed and my dream was destroyed.

Luzia C. R. Ferreira

I See My Father Crying

My winter months are humiliating
I see my father crying.
I ask Papa, why are we leaving?
He says, we need work to keep on living.
We travel from place, to place
Seeking work, from state to state.
I saw my father fall on his knees
begging a stranger.
please, please, please.

Alice Oros Carrillo

Untitled

I am a salmon,
dredging my way upstream.
Overcoming the obstacles
and swift current,
I press on to my destiny.

I am an eagle
soaring gracefully
in the blue of the sky.
High above mountains, trees,
and plains, in the freedom
I call my home.

I am a rabbit, soft and gentle,
I am not the hunter,
but the hunted.

...I am JUSTIN AUSTIN

Justin Austin

Hawk Sails

Hawk sails
Drops, fails.
Mouse skips,
Hops, scurries.
I walk,
No worries.
Dog tracks,
Dawn cracks.
Sun rises
Through clouds all sizes.
Grass grows,
Dew froze.
Wind blows,
Chills nose.
Buds burst,
Daffodils first.
Spring sings
I have wings!

Nancy Main

Alone Not I

Alone in my loneliness
Dry tears abound me
Embellished insecurities
Stop the music in my soul

Incomprehensible
Cold hearted fools
Unsurmountable
Acts of ignorance

Scarred on the surface
Needless anguish
Selfless indignant
Ruthless to the core

Look ahead regretless
It is I who has won
For those who hath scorned
Are truly alone.

Maryann Sheridan

Untitled

Rain, the sound, the scent, the feeling,
If you close your eyes,
You are anywhere you want to be.
Standing in the middle of the street,
a mad man, laughing,
Drinking the sky,
With his eyes closed.

Eric T. Vogler

My Shadow

From the dawn to the
Dusk, from day to day,
My shadow follows me
In every which way. As
I stride through rustling
Leaves in the fall,
Snow in the winter, grass
In the spring, and
In the bright sunshine in
The summer, my shadow
Patiently, quietly tip-toes
Closely, following me to every
Destination I go to. But
When the sun slips over
The horizon, slowly, without
A flaw, so does my shadow.
Yet, the next day, my shadow
Returns again, following me
The whole day through.
Does that happen to you?

Tracie Leong

Awareness

There were three men.
Each held a rose.
They could not see!
All had a nose
And sense of touch
So they might feel
And let their clutch
A form reveal.
One found the roots
All cast in dirt.
Another a thorn
His finger hurt.
The third found these
But did not cower.
He faced the breeze
And smelled the flower.

VerNon A. Bingham

Tanka For Our Grandchildren

Imagine Planet
Earth, a depleted planet,
Mourning the remains
Of the Industrial World,
Whose bones to Greed we have hurled.

Lo! Our best efforts
To research, and produce pure
Solar Energy,
Will assure our grandchildren
Of life that's pollution-free!!!

Will our grandchildren
Receive from us their just due,
A Solar Abode?...
Or, the aforementioned sphere,
That pollution's hand now holds ...

Martin J. O'Malley Jr.

Teacher, Teacher

Teacher, teacher, teach me now
I'm ready for my lessons now, now, now.
I've got my pencils, I've got my books,
I've got my mirror for good looks.
So teacher, teacher, teach me now
I'm ready for my lessons
  Now, now, now!!!!

Jodi N. Schwaben

Untitled

Life's puzzle is not
easily interchanged.
Daily when pieces are locked
   tightly into place
think clearly, for they will
not be fitted again.
Each fragment chosen helps
To build reality.
Its up to us to choose the
size and shape of the
piece of puzzle.
Finding exactly where it
should be placed when the
day is done. Takes time and
has only assured us the day's
completion has been carried out.
whether or not it has fallen
into place with perfection, is
when placed with the guidance
of the Lord.

Mylinda Campbell

My Guard

Cold iron gate
   enclose my castle
Warmth and beauty
   mark the land
From your distance
   you cannot see
Met by my guard
   but could not pass
Down the road you went
   and mind no more
I ran, but my iron
   bars would not open
I called out to you
   but deaf you became

Vicki Tenorio

Names

I went to visit your names today;
Engraved upon the wall.
You're there for all the world to see
And know you gave your all.

You're over fifty-eight thousand strong,
And you served our country well.
Then came that day you met your fate
As one by one you fell.

You didn't want to fall that way,
So young and in a war so rotten.
I pray each day when I think of you
That your names won't be forgotten.

I want you to know that as I write
Americans have taken a stand.
We want to know, "What was your fate?"
The truth is all we demand.

If you're still alive I pray, "Dear God,
"Please comfort these dear men.
"Release them from their torture and pain
"And bring them home again."

Michael E. Bliss

Misty Morning Flight

A sea of fog
Engulfs
Glittering cities
Hasty decisions
Blue lights met
With pride and precision
Eagles view of the land
Adventure found
Earth at its best
Pure and profound

Lydia Perez

Graffiti

The world is now taking
Europe, America, The Caribbean
Pictures, forms, representing
Said the perpetrators
An other form of expressing
Loneliness, repression
O young! around missing
Not art, not design
But ruined bridge, wall, building
Ugly, hideous, repellent
Images of negative thinking

Marie L. Dorismond

"Austin"

I don't think I have
ever seen a beauty such
as thee.

You mean everything
to me, so handsome,
strong and free.

Your the greatest
husband; "Austin;" in
the world - who
takes care of me.

Shirley J. Crisman

A Special Love

Love is but a feeling
   ever to be cherished,
to grow stronger with
   each breath,
and never cease to flourish.

Love is but a feeling
   to be sheltered deep within,
only to be shared by those
   who feel it without sin.

A special love is saved
   to be felt by just one person,
in solemn hopes of his
   same feelings,
felt by only you.

Linda C. Monastro

Within Reach

How fruitless; chasing rainbows;
   Fleeting moments of happiness:
When there's a world of peace and joy,
   Just waiting, if we confess.
We need more than this world contains.
   Come to know the real happiness
In a life where Jesus reigns.
   ANGELS WILL SING!

Edith M. Beatty

Teardrops

A memory of Gary

In every boat,
every dirt bike,
every tractor,
every wet bike,

I am remembering you,
I know you are there,
yet, I'm not sure where you are.
Are you sitting here beside me?

Are you reading over my shoulder?
Are you holding my hand right now?

I feel the wind blow,
and I wonder if it's you.

I can feel you wiping my
tear drops,
and telling me not to cry.

But I'm missing you,
loving you so much,
and wondering,
why did you have to die?

Kellie Veselka

Inspiring Life

We are in the abyss of nothingness
Every struggle we make for the day,
Will count for a new day
For you and for me.

Life is an open field
Looking for every bit of ecstasy.
That everyone had tried to gain
The very sweet success.

Success, so sweet though small
It gain us self - esteem,
For the little things you get
Will make a big difference.

Little success blossomed for the day
Into myriads of satisfactions,
For whoever strived to get it
Will achieve his wildest dreams.

A bird that fly in the sky
A kite that hoover over me,
A light that shines in every way
Oh! Sweet success, let it be me.

Mila A. Yap

Acrostic Poem

Really good at math
Excellent person
Good student
Intelligent human being
Nice person to have around
Awesome friend

A good problem solver
Neat organizer
Not noisy
Efficient for every task in class

Excellent role model for younger kids
Very interesting person
Always makes A's and B's or all A's
Never tardy in every class
Singer at heart.

Regina Evans

The Tree's Peril

The trees; green and tall,
exfoliate leaves every fall,
Thousands perish every year
and all these humans never care!

Soft gentle tendrils that sway
in warm moist winds...

Young tender leaflets will stay
green until...

Until the Autumn
bares some but few,
And the winter; harsh,
rips on through!

Ascetic rest hung from
branches and chance...

Tears life from limb
and hues that dance.

Marc J. Kulkin

Somalia

Skeletal shadows chase reality,
exploited needs take priority
crumbling playgrounds.

Somber child ignores pain,
makes game out of pauses,
too hungry to dream,
too serious to be young.

Open your roam our soul in search
of understanding,
in need of a reason to smile.

I hear songs on hungry child's lips
as they die,
delicate in their dignity,
too beaten to beg.

Fined the future
by feeding
the children.

Nicole King

Honeysuckles

Memories long gone
falling from dust
and wind

Jesus is coming
again
while I still wait
for my savior

I dance on the
head of a pin
with the demon
called curiosity

And I can't keep
a secret
and I can't tell
a truth

but I smell
sweet honeysuckles
in summer
and I'm reminded

Of a time when I could

Vanessa LaFaso

Untitled

Fading Memories of Childhood Days
Family Gatherings, Christmas Plays

Birthday Parties, Vacation Trips
Class Reunions with Comical Quips

Remembers of Long Ago
Like Making Angels in the Snow

Building Castles in the Sand
Walking Slowly Hand in Hand

Silly Faces, Childhood Games
Friends...you can't Remember Names

"Has it Been that Long Since Then..?"
And "I Can Still Remember When..."
Such Words Like These are Commonplace
And Bring Tears and Smiles to Your Face

All These Thoughts Come Racing Thru
As You Take A Glimpse Into..

The Pictures In The Attic.

Sharon DuPree

"Wondering Mind"

My mind is wondering,
Far beyond my control.
There's no distance between us,
Only feelings.

Feelings of being loved.
Yes, I think I'm being loved.
Or is it just another joke?
I'm strong now.

I can see the road.
Should I take it?
Am I going to get hurt?
I'll take it only with one hope.

The hope I carry with me,
Is the hope of not getting hurt.
Then my mind begins to wonder,
Wonder alone without my control.

Natascha Taylor

Goodbye

Flashing red lights,
Fear grips my heart.
I could tell he was in pain.
Confusion
They said everything would be okay.
It wasn't.
I felt mislead.
Today I feel regret.
I never said goodbye.

Karen Hongola

Report It

He hit you once
He'll hit you again.
Wake up girl
you still have a friend.
If you don't report it
you'll lose your friends.
So report it now
or you won't be around
to report it.

Janet Brown

Endless

As she sits in her room
feeling the aching sorrow
in her heart she knows its
always going to be this way

She can't alter the atmosphere
around her so she convene's
alone crying over something
that's already concluded

When she realizes its
nothing more she can do
she fights a battle that
her heart can't resist
by giving up completely.

Shanna Price

"A Dreamer's Journey"

Carry me, carry me, up to the skies
Fill all my senses
Open wide my green eyes
Over the mountains
Let my spirit give rise
Carry me, carry me, up to the skies

Carry me, carry me, up in the night
Let me drift with the clouds
On their leisurely flight
Caressed by moon's glow
So big and so bright
Carry me, carry me, into the night

Carry me, carry me, through all my days
Let me know rainbows
And the sun's warming rays
Let me fly higher
To God, give him praise
Carry me, carry me, all through my days

Olivia Riker Essary

Stillborn

A new seed is sprouting,
filling my body.
Small heartbeat joined my heart
in a song.
Then one day a sharp jolt
ripped my belly.

You see the emptiness behind
the full.
You feel the despair within
the body full.

Inside in silence my soul is crying;
the happiness
turned sorrowful.

Tear-marked roadmap
is my aging face,
I miss my child
Lord, grant me peace!

Marra Racz

On Bivouac

Here among the pine trees
　Encamping for the night,
Lying upon my blanket
　Amidst the fading light,
I dream of home and heaven
　Of the life that I resigned,
And tears well up within me
　For the girl I left behind.

Arthur Laustsen

Who Shall Prevail?

Walking along a meadow,
finding a pond of clear
water and drinking thirsty.
The doe raises her head
and looks into the cold
eyes of a hunter.
The hunter and the hunted
are frozen in time.
Who shall prevail?
He is looking for sport,
she is looking to protect her young.
She turns to run, he fires his gun.
She does not fall, for he has missed.
She has won but she thinks to herself.
Will she again?

Kelly Cochran

Discovery

Babies discover their
fingers, thumb, mouth, toes,
and feet.

Kids discover
learning, changes in life,
and caring.

Teenagers discover
education, responsibility,
and love.

Parents discover
the beauty in all
three.

Tricia Zamora

The Forest Prime Evil

"To conquer a country,
First cut off it's head;
Then invade the body."
That's what Stalin said.

So fifteen thousand Poles,
Officers of rank.
Were rounded up and slain.
They walked Russia's plank.

Single file, one by one,
All shot through the head.
The green Katyn forest
Turned red from the dead.

A forest prime evil,
Its trees wept tears of blood
That fell on hidden graves
Of dishonest mud.

Within his cell in hell,
The tyrant, Stalin,
Now writes on walls that wail
The curst name Katyn.

Mary Coddington

One By One

The rain that falls on me is mine
I lick it from my thirsty lips
and witness the remote design around me
of the pelted grass....
I cannot sip the total flood
but taste the fracture of a drop
While every river runs to sea
I stand still as earthbound rock.

Betty Litten

The Tides Of Time

Your voice comes to me across the years
Floating on the wind
Soft as a feather
Caressing my mind

I open my heart
And let you return
Memories drifting in on the tide
Washing over me

The years slip away
And we are one again
One with the sand, the tide, the sea
For all eternity

Vivian Lobiak Jester

Untitled

Fly away.
Fly away to be free.

Circle high.
Keep an eye
For the distant shore.

Mariners pass.
Seas build.
The ocean becomes a friend.

Fly away.
Fly away to be free.

Robert L. Tofson

The Bluebird

High above the treetops
Flying so high,
I seek a bluebird
In the sky.

Its perfectly shaped beak,
Its beautiful wings,
It has a cheerful chirp
When it sings.

It is about to rain,
And it tries to find shade.
This beautiful bird
Is a creation God made.

The sky is getting darker,
The clouds are filling the sky,
So I start walking home,
And to the bird, I say good-bye.

Katie Fischer

To Live Again

'Neath me grow the earth,
Folding around my lifeless frame,
Roots of life run through my corpse,
Turn my body into soil,
As it falls from the sky,
I drink from the cleansing rain,
It seeps through the ground,
And washes away my pain,
The warming sun feeds the buds,
And my wanting self enriches the earth,
Giving life from the darkness of my hole,
I bloom from the ground,
And reach for the sky,
Vibrant and bright,
I am again life.

Robert Morgan

America the Beautiful?

For smog-hued polluted skies
For amber ways of crack.

For bare mountains majesties,
Stripped by the wood man's axe.
America, America, God shed his
grace on thee,
But you returned that grace with greed
From coast to bloody coast.

Sagrario Rudecindo

A Child

A new life, a new chance,
for hope.
For peace.

A compact, all-inclusive, package
of squirming, squirting,
cooing, squalling,
hunger,
wonder,
and joy.

A beginning.
A continuance.
And an ending.
All in one.

A new adventure.
And an ancient responsibility.

A gift.
A universe.
A child.

J. Greet

Fantasy

Would you mind if I loved you
For just a little while?
I have no love to fill my heart
To make me dream or smile.

Would you mind if I thought of you
As tho you were my own?
It's only for a little while
That you'd be mine alone.

Would you mind if I kissed you
At night when dreams are free?
There in the beauty of the night
Beside the rolling sea?

For when the dawn awakens
And the world bursts forth in style,
I'll have to give you back to "life"
So may I love you for a little while?

Natalie Smith

My Family Lives In Two States

My life is waiting,
for that call.
I miss half my life
just to say hi.
Why?
My life is in two states,
and I don't know why.
I'll miss graduation,
just to say hi,
for my family lives in two states
Why?

Mollie Carril

September 31

A different day
for some
Who can explain
Septiober 31
Change does occur
summer into Fall
A magic moment
surprised us all
A close friend
trusted and true
Became a lover
we started anew
Our life has
just begun
On this night
September 31

Kenneth J. Violette

Our World of Separation

We once were forced to separate,
for something we knew was wrong;
and were sentenced to a punishment,
unfair for our sin, it lasted too long.

As the years went by,
and our lives carried on;
we remembered what we lost,
in a friendship that was there-then gone.

Then we were reunited,
through a power beyond fate;
a new beginning for our friendship,
we're free now, to no longer hesitate.

It's as if we were suspended,
only a brief moment in time;
all that changed was our maturity,
but together we still do chime.

We share a very special bond,
and what we have, is preciously so;
to each other we remain forever fond,
nothing will separate us; if we don't let go.

Susan J. Wills

Tears

Many tears have been shed
For this human race
They fall on our cheeks
they stain our face
Each one that fall's
Takes it's own place
To help us save
This human race
Do not be sad
When you shed a tear
For it is sent from God
To remind us he's here
He will not leave us
For he promised he'd stay
So let the tear's stain your face
Let them fall on your cheeks
And do not be sad
When you shed that tear
For on your dying day
His hand will be there

A. J. Metzer

Derby

And they're off...
For two minutes or so
Women in hats stop chatting
Men grab binoculars
Julep and popcorn vendors pause
Eyes are on the track.
For two minutes or so
Jockeys hang on tight
Horses fly
Trainers sweat
Hearts are on the track.
For two minutes or so
Bettors clutch tickets
Owners grip wallets
The media aim cameras
Money is on the track.
For two minutes or so
Everyone waits for the winner to cross the line
Step into the circle
And accept the roses.

Tina S. Mackin

Pardon's Plea

Oh come with me and join my cause;
Forget for me disdain.
For it from you, you'd take a pause
Might you just feel my rain?

Oh fly with me and climb my height;
Renounce your even keel.
For if you try, with all your might,
You'd share what I must feel.

Oh opposite we'll always be,
as Foe, you choose the way.
For never will you die with me,
Alas, alone I'll lay!

Laurie Wisnowski

Refuse to Admit Apple Juice

Equality of value, a passing style
France obtained an upper crust
Using a narrow path of evergreen
Negative, elongated men
Impudent slaves
Wobble and have distress signals
Make ready the flowers
Young resist authority
Cause terminates feat of courage
Unhealthy destiny for religion
A faded tale
Refuse to admit apple juice

Michael Langley

Life Is Love

Blue skies and deep sea's can't
keep love from me! I may be fat, but
I will always be glad because life is
love to me.

I have a good family and cute
dog's too. There is not much to make
me blue.

Whenever you are down
and feeling blue, just remember you have
life and love too!

Georgiana Haynes

Freedom Overkill

Dark
Freedom from light
don't want to be free

Denial
Freedom from truth
don't want to be free

Alone
Freedom from friends
don't want to be free

Control
Freedom to destroy
don't want to be free

Death
Freedom from life
don't want to be free

Raymond W. King Jr.

Untitled

Snug and cozy, deep in my afghan,
Friendly pillows, sitting beside me.

A fire, burning and glowing
while shadows dance lively
across my face.

Silhouettes surround me.
Their presence warning the room.
Silent, but cherished.

Reports of snow tonight.
Hmmm...visions of a white Christmas.
Soon....with the ones I love.

Lori J. Moody

Before We Are To Be Bound

True friends are hard to be found;
Friends are few and fine.
Before we are to be bound;
Friends are fond and shine.
Life is costly as accounting
As well mostly as astounding.

True friends are hard to be found;
Friends are few and true.
Before we are to be bound;
Friends are fool and blue.
Life is costly as offending
As well mostly as defending.

True friends are hard to be found;
Friends are few and thirst.
Before we are to be bound;
Friends, but justice, first
As it was in the beginning
And shall never be the ending.

Richard P. Sabatini

I Come to Can't

I come to can't
Is this the chance
To break the bonds that hold me
I fear not to fly
I fear not to fly
Your can't strip them away
It must be me
It must be me

Edmund Mannello

Blossoms

A gentle rain of petals,
From my orchard's trees,
The breezes of spring
Bring down.

Pink and white blossoms float past
My soft countenance.
Their sweetness touches
My soul.

I love the rain of blossoms.
They gently quick-touch
My cheeks, eyes, and lips.
I dream.

Kay Evans

Some Thoughts After Many Years . . .

The past is selected passages
    from our memories
    embroidered and embellished
    to suit our present purposes.

When we carry too much of the past
    around with us, there is no room
    for the present. It preoccupies
    today and denies the future.

Letting go is hard to do.
    Hard to do when we've held on
    so long and so tightly and
    made it the focus of our energy.

The past must be cast upon the waters,
    tossed to the winds,
    so that a broken heart can heal
    and find a new tomorrow.

Patricia Brizee

Agnes

A Yellow Rose, thrown upon
frozen, white ground
so fragile, yet so proud

A Yellow Rose, thrown upon
frozen, white ground
cut from life, vowed

A Yellow Rose, thrown upon
frozen, white ground
the Sun will, come through the cloud.

A Yellow Rose, thrown upon
frozen, white ground
She prayed, aloud

A Yellow Rose, thrown upon
frozen, white ground
died all alone, there so proud.

Mary Ann Mesecher

Punk Lyric

Trendoid verse
Is written in grotesque
Barbwire, brick, and chain-link voices
O so chic with decadent hair
And bathroom similes
Urban, not urbane
It's very poor at
Meadowlarks.

Gail Barton

Dear Sweet Daughter

Sherry was delightful - like a bright sunny day, blue skies, lots of flowers, and happy music. She was fun - like a picnic, a walk in the woods, or a swim in the ocean. She was sensitive - your best friend, and always there for you. And intimate - she knew how you felt, where you were coming from, and what you were thinking, always concerned. She was happy and bubbly like new kittens and puppies, and little children playing. She was beautiful, like a flower shop bursting with fresh flowers and always smelling just as sweet. She was the perfect Mother holding, loving, caressing, kissing, nursing, feeding, changing, bathing, and dressing her baby. And always beaming over this precious new life, her new baby son. A soft breeze arrives...from where did it come? I look around, and look back at my dear, sweet daughter and her new baby son. She is gone! She is gone! Where did she go? Why did God take my dear baby girl? Her dear son is left crying, his Mother has left. No one to hold, love and caress. She was lifted away on the soft flowing breeze. We are left alone — crying, empty, and yearning for the warm, loving Mother and my sweet, little girl. We will never forget her, not even for a moment. A car in the drive! Is she finally home? A call on the phone! "I'll be over soon!" Please! Oh please! Won't another light breeze pass and bring her back home?

Betty E. Andrews

Love and Destiny

The sadness of sweet destiny has past by me. With a little gasp I see him as merely a leaf blown by the wind through the streets of the city. He ponders and looks eagerly about. The twenty-one years he has lived seem but a moment, a breathing space in the long years of humanity. Already, he fears separation calling. With all my heart I want to come close to him, touch him with my hands, and be touched by his hands. If he prefers that I don't, that is because he believes that I will not be gentle, that I will not understand. Knowing that he was the one, I would cleanse him with all the understanding he needed...love. One quivers at the thought of the other; while at the same instant, one loves so intensely that tears draw into the eyes. She wanted to love and to be loved by him, but at the same time she did not want to be confused by his manhood. With all her strength she tried to capture and to understand the mood that had come upon him. They tried to kiss, but that impulse did not last. He took hold of her hand, and when he crept close, she eagerly drew back. Mutual respect grew thin between them. There is no way of knowing what thoughts went through his mind, but she stood beside him in dignified silence. They had for a moment taken hold of the thing that makes life impossible for one another...destiny.

Laketa Gates

Caps And Gowns

Caps and gowns, more smiles than frowns what are you going to be?
A doctor, a baker a candlestick maker, a captain that sails the sea?

Tell me of your ventures, fill me with your dreams,
from deep within your soul the vibrance of life screams.

There is no trick to living, no road maps signs or doors,
The paths are wide and varied the choosing is all yours.

Life's trials will confront you, confusion knocks upon your door,
Take the cards and play them, some of this you must endure.

Oh so many people you'll meet along the way,
All are individual all have things to say.

Take the time to listen while life is fleeting by,
You may gain a little knowledge, it's easy if you try.

Don't ponder on your sorrows, feed upon your dreams,
Though some days are quite impossible it's rarely as it seems.

Sometimes life's rhymes and reasons have no answers why,
One thing I can assure you, don't let it pass you by.

Live it to the fullest, each and every day,
Learning from the lessons that help you choose the way.

Time you can not buy it, no one has it for sale,
It's yours to use or squander, it's life you must unveil.

Ronald Del Mar

Winter Solstice

Day of longest night
gathers foreseeing forces
and speeds to westward sleep.
Burnt sienna reddens the horizon as
fleetingly verdant emerald kisses
the lost sun's sunken burial,
inspiring the great Eastern star
to light the way from death to birth.
Diamond ice fills midnight's eternal blanket
with celestial chanting of solar chimes,
vibrating warmth throughout heaven's cold covenant.
The hosts prepare the Word for utterance,
while three of eloquence are called to journey
the sands of portent and past,
with rich meekness and solemnity,
where the Eastern star's compass point
pierces the heart of prophesy and promise.

Trudy A. Plotz

Shores

Shores denote change and are boundaries
between
non symbiotic states of existence.
Sometimes quite
sharp!
Other times providing a gentle blending.

Usually seen, occasionally merely implied,
their importance exceeds what they divide.

Consider first the direction you cross,
for some are passed over freely,
while others exact a cost.

Some are inevitable, some are obvious-
margins of places: mountain to plain;
between states: solid to gaseous;
or of feelings: joy to pain.

They can be processes of growth,
or entropy...
And there are a multitude to traverse
from birth to death.

Robert A. Basener

MY RESURRECTION ROSE

Oh, LORD, hurry I pray as I watch my father wasting away.
He may not last another day, bloom perfect rose for Dad, today.

You see, I planted a rose seemingly dead; roots carefully spread.
Mulching the soil, ever so gently around the roots I toiled.

How can this dead stick ever be a beautiful rose, is beyond me.
I trust God's promise of sun and rain; His perfect refrain.

I chose a rose with a yellow center; for peace, my loving mentor.
Red petals of love surrounded it as a promise of life from above.

My Dad is dying of cancer, you see; this rose is a gift from me.
I prayed it would bloom before death closed the door, its tomb.

Morning quietly came and took Daddy away. But where's my
bloom?
Tears flowing, my heart broken; hours passing, had he spoken?

Stunning in all its glory, "My Resurrection Rose," told the story.
Gently I cut it and laid it on his quiet, still body; unafraid.

Because today God kept his promise through his son, Dad had won.
Christ is alive, his promise awaits thee too; trust, only believe.

Every year my rose blooms to remind me of His love so dear.
It is my witness, my story; Yes Christ is waiting for us in glory.

Sandra M. Cook

Daddy's Little Girl

I can remember my Daddy as if it was
Yesterday;
I was always there to listen,
No matter what he had to say.
When I was little, Daddy use to put me
On his knee;
And I'll never forget all the other times
When he use to play with me.
Daddy use to call me his little girl every
Time when I was near;
He told me many times before that I was
So dear.
When I grew older, Daddy was so scared;
He thought that he was losing me because
He thought that I didn't care.
Years have past now and Daddy isn't here;
Now I understand, it's so very clear.
I have my own family now, I only wish that
Daddy could see;
I remember hearing "Daddy's Little Girl,"
And that little girl use to be me.

Kristi M. Slusarski

I Know You're Out There Somewhere

I've been searching forever and a day;
Regretting that our friendship has went
astray.
Missing you more than ever before;
Now and forever, there will always be an
open door.
Someday I'll find you and be sure to let
you know;
How much I appreciate you helping me to
live and grow.
A true friend you'll always be;
Never once did you doubt me.
I'll find you someday and then you'll know
How much I care;
Because I know you're out there somewhere...

Kristi M. Slusarski

The New Slavery

From maverick military organizations
to ethnic crime families of every description
to neo nazi and neo communist confabs
the situation is slavery done
to the tune of the truth serums
mind control drugs like Sodium Amytal
psychosis producing drugs
like Naprosyn, Dilantin, or worse
and mind killing drugs like Thorazine and Mellaril

Slaves who do not know that they are slaves
...stolen sperm and seed
fetal experimentation
slaves from conception
for the theft of work and ideas from an individual's sleep
the use of cocaine and other drugs
to produce the violence
which causes civilization's
self destruction
and stroke and heart attack producing drugs
to exterminate the evidence!!!

Les Amison

Vision

I woke up from being still and said I have to do something...
Where am I going? Stepped onto the driving range,
knowing one does not run from the darkness in the light.
Swept with sin, the bitter taste in my mouth, I saw several towers,
but only one way out.

In life you have to talk without speaking, cry without weeping, scream
without
raising your voice. Do this...and you will succeed.

In reality, one takes the poison from the poison stream of life and
floats away.
But one night a vision was seen on the beach with searching eyes,
encumbrance in a black haze under a cloud in the rain.
In through my doorway it brought me white golden pearls,
stolen from the hearts of the sea.

Destiny was ready for me.
Suddenly a storm blew up in my eyes. Destiny called.
The wind and sea of life echoed its sounds,
Singing the thrill of opportunities to be splashed upon me.
Fact, Reality, Truth,
The impossible is possible.

Kathleen Parrish Osinski

Sunrise

A point of light
Filtering through the blackness of the night
Of great significance and wonder to the world
Possessing all the hopes and dreams
Of the past, the present, and the future
What begins as a flickering candle
spreads to an unearthly glow
of shimmering gold
That bathes the earth with its glory

Bringing in its waking hour
A blanket of dew
to cover the ground
And a rainbow
to clothe the sky

Displaying nature's finest wardrobe
Priceless and beyond compare
For just a few breathless moments
We catch a glimpse
of heaven's mystery
in the air.

Kara Hardin

Harvest Moon

How does she know?
The sky is as dark and demanding as the last night of the harvest moon.
The rain is persistent, unyielding to the innocents.
The distant thunder journeys closer to echo with my heart.
And just when I take comfort in the darkness of it all,
lightening strikes, illuminating the emptiness in my eyes.
What an exemplary ambience for a day such as today.
But how did Mother Nature know?
How did she know that I could not weep for your absence?
How tender and loving she is to weep in my place.
How compassionate is she to express to the world my dismay.
So befitting, this storm's arrival,
that one can not believe it purely coincidental.
She knows my sorrow and expresses what I can not.

As I sat upon the rail, your tail lights reflected in a single
tear as it gently caressed my cheek. Should I have had a vial,
I would have placed the tear within, guarding it until I could
return the gift you had given me. A precious drop of salt
water containing all of my hopes, fears, sorrows and happiness.

A gift from the Gods, a gift from you.

Victoria Carrier

How To Create Your Own Well Known Rancher

Needed
1 Great Mind
1 Able Body
A Pinch Of Salt
1/4 Teaspoon Of Money
3 Tablespoon Of Land
1 Good Agricultural Education
Cattle
Time

Mix
   In one bowl, combine the mind, able body, and a good
agricultural education. SET ASIDE. In another bowl combine
money, land, cattle, and time. PUT THIS ASIDE AND LET RISE
FOR
AN HOUR. Add all mixed ingredients together. Put this person on
a GOOD horse and throw a pinch of salt over his left shoulder,
FOR LUCK. Then put him with his cattle and you have the
greatest
accomplishment of all, a RANCHER!!!

Lisa Stroud

"25"

25 blue marbles rolled by as I cried.
25 blue marbles the color of your eyes.
25 round drums banged out a beat.
25 round drums that send a shiver of heat-up my spine.

25 flowers placed in the ground.
25 flowers spread all around.
25 dreams never set free.
25 dreams I'll always keep with me.

25 sand pebbles dug into my soul.
25 sand pebbles that blockade my goal.
25 stars shining in the sky.
25 stars that cover your eyes.

25 moments that we never shared.
25 moments that we had dared-to be together.
25 years that I've a lie.
25 years since you have died.

Karolina Shveytser

Carpe Diem

Think of the days you've let slip by
   a beautiful sunset or a clear blue sky
For time is a treasure for all to share
   we should treat every second as if it were rare
Cherish each moment with all of your heart
   be excited in knowing its a brand new start
Every day's an opportunity for us to grow
   being a warm special person is all we should know
For those wasting time with anger and hate
   the future will bestow an unenviable fate
Choose to see the good in all that's before you
   the choice is yours its what you must do
Why have others passed on and you still remain
   the answer is easy, your life's not in vain
Look straight ahead at what you'll achieve
   the secret of each moment is that you believe
Believe in the Lord and He'll set you free
   and the wonders of life will be yours to see

Philip Weber III

A Angel For My Friend

God give her an Angel, to stay by her side,
a blissful feeling, as calm as a ocean tide.
Make her feel protected, from morning to night,
and keep her days all sunshine bright.

If she is ever alone and feeling blue,
"Her beautiful Angel will see her through."
The melody's she hears are from heaven above
"Its Jesus having her Angel sing about love.

Don't ever leave her, stay by her side,
give her warm breezes, as a kite in glide.
"As she's a travel, away from family love,
give her safe care on the wings of a dove.

Thank you for her Angel, as she has peace in her heart,
she knows, that Jesus loved her from the start.
He gave her the Angel out of pure love,
just like he gave her his blessed white dove.

If you feel a sweet warm air,
tingle up your spine and go through your hair,
Don't be scared, or alarm
It's only your special Angel trying to tug on your arm.

Nancy M. Jackson

Peace Aware

Peace is solely the savior to man's end
A bonding together as one place again
Where across the seas our hands will touch
And what is here is there

Peace can bring us all to one kind
A blending of nations as one race in time
Where colors and sounds will seem the same
And the fear of hate will not remain

Peace will touch us and hold our hands
A judgment of freedom across the land
Where we will live as one as man

Ken Gable

Friends

Sometimes in our lives, there is a moment,
a brief moment when we are fortunate
enough to meet a person who makes
a significant difference in our life,
leaving behind a feeling of well being and caring,
knowing that one human being
could make us feel happy, safe and secure
and who cares about our needs and our fears,
who also takes away all ill feelings
and negative feelings of despair.
I have been fortunate, for in my life,
I have met that one significant person,
who cares enough to allow my mixed up behavior
not to deter the efforts and patience put forth
to help me to become a more stable individual,
and when the time comes
when we must each go on with our lives,
I will remember you,
my one significant friend.

Nancy A. Quinn

Answers

Take time to listen to the world around you,
   Stop running on for just a moment;
Take time to smell the roses;
for you need not search anymore, for all
the answers are right under your nose!

Jennifer L. Hummel

What I Once Was

I used to be a beautiful rose.
A bright red one. Boy, was I beautiful.
I had roots to help me stand tall.
I had red petals to make me pretty.
But then someone came along
And picked me out of the garden.
I no longer have roots.
I can not stand tall anymore.
My petals are faded, they're all dry.

I used to be a beautiful rose.
A bright red one. Boy, was I beautiful.
I once had the sun to meet my every need.
I once had ground and a garden to grow in.
But then someone uprooted me.
I no longer have the sun, I lurk in the shadows.
I now slouch in a clear object.
All alone in misty water.

I used to be a beautiful rose.
A bright red one.
But I'm not so beautiful anymore.

Meghan K. Williams

The Great Joe Louis

The month was June, in Chicago, in the glowing lights in the ring,
A brilliant young boxer named Louis was crowned the Heavyweight King.
It was 1937 when Louis came into his own,
To become the greatest Champion that boxing's ever known.
In the twelve years that would follow, he never sustained one loss.
His left jab was the setup for the power in his vicious right cross.
He successfully defended his title for an average of twice a year,
And endeared himself to millions in his fabulous boxing career.
He steadily stalked his opponents in all of his Championship fights.
With rhythmic combinations of lightening lefts and rights.
From '37 to '49, he was truly the Heavyweight King!
The press labeled him the Brown Bomber for his awesome power in the
ring. He thrilled fight fans by the millions who followed the
boxing game, and turned on streams of emotions at the very sound
of his name. To you, Joe Louis, the Greatest that ever laced on the
gloves, and rose to unparalleled stardom, and sport world honors and
loves. As long as there's a boxing ring and fans to whoop and shout,
the legendary name, Joe Louis, will never be counted out!

Vernie V. Stoneking

For Tom

Tom, our world is bigger now; than a backyard game of catch,
a center-boarded dry docked sloop or a weekend round of chess.
We came so far alone-together from that darkened Christmas light,
through schools and bars and changing jobs and heartache in the night.
You pushed me up to heady heights and swam me out so far,
that now I see your dream for me was to be better than you are.
We talked for years of courage, and the power of the truth,
of wars and bees and flowers and the taste of good vermouth,
through history's great lessons and music's mighty pull,
you led me like a miner and when my soul was full,
you told me there was always more - that I shouldn't walk away...
but that's the place you left me and where I stand today...
"Tom, our world is bigger now," as I was lying on the deck,
I thought of you beyond the stars an enlightened cosmic speck.
It's that the time between us; gets greater every day,
and soft shadows fall in long shafts across our cold spring bay.
I wonder where you are now, and hope you get these thoughts,
of just how much I am you and of the life you brought.

C. J. Evans

A Child Is Born

With God's soft hands, caressing thee
A child shall be born, to you and me
Her hair shall be soft, her skin so fair
Gods sweet love will also be there

With eyes sparkling, and a face so bright
She will bring such happiness and sheer delight
We'll cradle her in our arms, and hold her tight
Knowing that God, has made our life bright

Her tiny hands will hold us
And that will bring a smile
Knowing that we hold in our arms
Our first and new born child

So thank you God for making
This day so full and bright
For a child is born to us this day
Making our lives so right.

Thomas Jackson

Summer Child

What shall I give for a summer's gift...
A cloud of fireflies all adrift in a sea of emerald grass.
Or perhaps a cap of Queen Anne's lace
Picked from my sweet secret place where butterflies and hoptoads pass.
What shall I put in your waiting hand...
Pond pebbles dug from the shimmering sand, gilded and glowing there.
Or a bracelet of clover woven with reed,
Or thistledown puffs studded with seed, afloat in the summer air.
What song shall I sing for a summer's tune...
A piping of crickets serenading the moon, played on the wind in the
   trees.
Or a riff of wren call, clear and bright,
To wake the sun, to end the night, soft on the morning breeze.
What shall I wish in dusk's lavender glow
On the midsummer star hanging low, so near yet so far away...
That as you grow young and I grow old,
All our tomorrows be brushed with gold, the gold of a summer's day.

Lois L. Jones

Martin Luther King Jr.

A successful leader in every way,
A compassionate friend any day.
A role model for everyone,
A person who never thought of using a gun.

A fighter of justice for things that were fair,
A person that no matter what you'll know he cared.
The man that lead the march for us to be free,
A man that strived to be all he could be.

An excellent speech maker with a stern voice,
That allowed us to know we do have a choice.
The man that had a dream that one day we'd be free,
And through his speech he showed us how to open our eyes and
see.

A man that stood up and was sadly shoot down,
But through all of this the black race was found.
A man that tried all his life to break us out of our past.
And to end it off I say to him
"Thank God Almighty we're free at last!"

Nicole Walker

A Beautiful September Day

Today, a beautiful September day,
   A date I had, with a gentleman I married
   an our grand wedding day.
An art show he took me on our way,
   This beautiful September Saturday.

On a beautiful September day, I believe it was
   a Saturday.
My dear love took me away to Bear Creek Farms
   on such a clear September day (I believe
   it was a Saturday).
For a lovely meal he paid on this beautiful
   September day,
You see, it was the last summer Holiday.

Would you believe while we were away,
   Some friends called this special day.
A boating we shall go they say, so
   A boating we went on this special day.
Such an ending on this very Special September Day!

Phyllis Ann Hull

Dreams

I dreamed a dream, that made no sense.
A dream that in actuality is, a dream in itself.
Of faraway lands that do not exist.
Of a sky, that is as blue as water, but in actuality is dark as night.
A dream of battles fought long ago,
and a battle that never existed.
Dreams of the brave who never thought of being brave.
The coward, who thought of being brave.
Dreams of the sea, that you cannot cross, for it does not exist.
Of the mountains so high that man cannot climb.
Or a valley so low that man cannot get out.
Dreams of a desert so hot, that it is full of water,
to quench your thirst.
A dream of the great dreamers,
who wanted a free nation, a united union, and equal rights.
Dreams of life that make no sense, with all the sorrows, happiness,
and of love good and bad.
A dream of dreams is finding out you are awake,
when in actuality, you find yourself asleep.
Dreaming a strange dream.

Ron Wilson

Untitled

As soon as the millions fondle their wisdom
A drought of consciousness and brother's will come
There will be along a cynic fellow of sure
To tell of every to that mame's the cure
I do feel to tell all that mimic's our brute
of a fallen angel fellow whose solemn lute
bring's me to my swallowed breath
As time goes by I have to rest
To all whose coming brought me here
I feel some pity and darkness near
They who flee to tree
   and settle in dainty leaves
Who come's and goes as they please
   and wave your dream's as a trifle tease
Who knows not what each man could
   of what went wrong and what they should
I will realize as soon as the meadow shrink's
That the world is naughty with an uncovered sphinx

Paul Dominick Alleva

Family Love

Love is mother, love is father, love is sister, love is brother.
A family, individuals bound together by flesh, blood and spirit.
Each one absolute yet one.

Like a root in the ground has many legs joining one body. Supports,
nourishes the flower with substances necessary for life and growth, so
is the essence of the love of a family.

Even death not able to disunite the eternal bond created by a seed of
love in the beginning of two lives joined to give the gift of life,
out of love.

Ramon Rodriguez III

Night Mommy

Words of comfort whispered to a sobbing child.
A father trying to explain to his young son,
That mommy isn't ever coming home.

"Is mommy in Heaven with grandpa?" whispers a baby's tiny
voice.
The father nods and softly begins to sing
   his son's favorite lullaby
The one mommy always made sound so sweet.

The little boy kneels quietly by his bed,
Saying his usual bed-time prayer,
   only softly including a special favor
That God give his mommy her usual
   goodnight hug
"In case the wonders where I am."

Nancy Lynch

Walk And Don't Run

As winter set in with a chill in the air
A feeling was stirring, or was it there?
One of loneliness, sadness, and tears
Was it age, or simply fear?

A small voice inside kept on repeating
Leaving, leaving, leaving
Perhaps by leaving, it can be found
A feeling lost and drifting unbound

Leaving is costly, but it's sure to bring
Happiness, security, and the most wonderful things
Among many pleasures, there's a much deeper side
It's lost and gone now, humble pride

When life becomes hard to face with a grin
As age presses on and sets deep within
It's not time, or family that bring on the tears
It's heartbreaking sadness, it's unrecognized fear

And as this day approaches each and everyone
Hold hands with fear, walk and don't run.

Robin R. Werker

The Bore

My husband's friend lacks good humor
Unaware of style or sensitivity,
He continuously plans its content.
Shivering, we know his plan,
And smile as he arrives,
Later, politely, we wait as he moves
Towards us, eyes sparkling anxiously
Coming near, talks to us.
But with close minds,
We await patiently the end of his boring jokes.

Ellen Lewis

Resurrection of a Soul

I feel myself fading out of sight, into the distance without
a fight.
A new becoming is tearing at me, the soul within
beginning to run free.
A feeling of peace has taken the place of a life run
ragged by an age old race.
I've always thought there was more to life than to
hear what is wrong and be told what is right.
But what I have learned of this timeless plight
is the reason behind the endless fight.
You see, the winner is the one thing we all hope to be,
but whether we are remains to be seen.
All you can do is "be true to yourself"
because without you,
   there can be nothing else.

Krysten Torgerson

Life

A trace of a whisper a call to the soul
A fleeting moment of time
A memory, a journey of joy and despair
A prayer, an answer , a life
A conquest, a battle of evil and good
The hand of a fair maiden won
Beginning and endings, seasons and change
The moon the stars and the sun
Sorrow and laughter, pleasure and pain
Days filled with music and wine
Sweet autumn breezes, cool summer rain
Fires on cold winter nights
Dancing and singing, honey and bread
Scripture knowledge and grace
A minute of silence, things left unsaid
The ocean and infinite space
A duty, a motto, hatred and love
Goals, desires and dreams
The devil below us, God high above
Things that have yet to be seen

Mark R. Thomas

Trees

Looking out the window at my old holly tree
A friend gave my spouse and me, it's history.
It was planted more than sixty odd years ago,
Weathering rain, hot sun, cold winters and snow.
At last she grew straight, strong and so tall,
Casting a shadow on my kitchen wall.
We asked her if she needed some company,
How would you like a family of three?
A flowering crab, silver spruce and a pink dogwood,
That should give joy to an old neighborhood.
In September, two trees shed their leaves on the ground,
In the Spring, her berries and leaves dropped down.
Silver spruce shouted this world in a mystery,
They smiled, laughed and swayed in ecstasy.
My spouse and I in our comfortable home,
Talked about the poet who wrote the lovely poem
Who said, "Only God can make a tree."
Yes! He can make everything including you and me
With justice to all and peace eternally.

Salome Shoaf

I Could, I Would

I wish I could. I would.
I wish I could go to c ollege
And get some knowledge.
Just like Dr. Massie.
I think I can I will.

Breyanna Harrison

Watching Within

Behind these eyes is a flourishing sun
A gallery illumined, brilliant in its own society
Corridors of streaming, scintillating rivulets
A countryside of muted fields and sprouting calligraphy

The yearning eyes alone
Eclectic in their knowing
Prolific in their searching

The plum green blooms
In the orchard of the accompaniment
Where eyes are hulled and burst open
In a fugue of understanding
Fruits unplucked and unplundered
Sweetly in their yellow green sanctuary
Ardent in their invisibility
From within the place of their resting
The place of moving waves of poetry
Of watching
Of witnessing
From within the blossom unwithered and still

Nancy Schoenmakers

Untitled

I climbed the mountain with troubled soul, I felt I had no friend.
A heavy heart, a spirit burdened, life's schemes would know no end.

Suddenly I heard the silence, it caused my ears to ring. No phones
or clocks, or honking horns infringed on my domain.

Slowly, slowly, I was aware of soothing sounds...a trickling brook,
a creaking bough; and an eagle soared above.

Then I felt its presence, the peace that I had sought. I was renewed,
my heart was cleansed with the magic Nature brought.

Nancy Lee

Untitled

There is a place no one can see
A hole in a place inside of me
It's a place where love belongs
A place where I'd enjoy love songs
That place exists deep inside my heart
And in my life it plays a big part
For that emptiness keeps me from being happy
And full of grief, sorrow, and especially pity
And everyday the whole does expand
When thinking of my unheld hand
My uncaressed check, my un-gazed eyes
Everyday I submit to the pain with no surprise
Is there no end to my terrible fate?
Will it ever stop? Is it too late?
It never has and never will
That abyss inside my heart will never fill.

Tina Romano

The Eagle

What is an Eagle? He is Grace, Power, A Symbol of Freedom, and
a Majestic Animal all in one.
When you see him soaring through the air, you see his Grace and
Freedom. The Grace within him, is the way he flows through the air
at ease. The Symbol of Freedom is the way he can go from place to
place, and he is not held down by anyone or anything.
When he plunges down to the Earth, that is when you see the
magic, and powerful part of him. The Power is the way he soars
downward to the Earth, breaking through the wind at ease. The
majestic part of the Eagle is the Grace, Power, and the Symbol of
Freedom, all as one and Harmony, for everyone to always see.

Mark E. Swinney

My Jersey's Are My Life

What is a Jersey you might ask?
A Jersey is one of God's creatures who doesn't hide behind a mask.
She looks like a deer with big brown eyes
In colors of brown, black, silver or white.
She accepts you for who you are
No matter how big or small you are.
With names of Arsie, Rosie, Larry and Lennore,
to her it doesn't matter if you are rich or poor.
She has a love which is unconditional
For a human to match it would be unconventional.
I call them my girls and sometimes have to remind them
to act like ladies,
But, after all is said, they are still like my babies.
For there is a trust between the Jersey's and me
Which can only be explained by a power higher than thee.
I have no husband, and have been told, I am not
worthy to be any man's wife
which is why I can say, my Jersey's are my life.

Pat Nichols

Grandfather

Your sweet and gentle ways did show
A kindness tender, warm, aglow.
Did you know we loved you so?

The encouraging words you've always given
Were testimony to your livin'
With pride and honor in your life
And by your side a loving wife.

For your family you did care
And taught us all to share
The things we hold so dear
With others far and near.

You were an example good and true
And made it clear to all you knew
that life is filled with lots of pleasure
But you were our greatest treasure.

LaTonya E. Mallett-McLemore

"The Lord Has Given You!"

The Lord has given you
A little girl to love
She'll bring her charms into your lives
And give your hearts a shove -

The Lord has given you -
An opportunity to share -
All you know about "Him"
She's entrusted to your care!

The Lord has given you -
A precious gift, to shape, to mold -
And gently guide thru life -
Regardless of the problems
Her hand is yours to hold.

The Lord has given you many titles to be earned
You'll be teacher, nurse, chauffeur
Oh, how many lessons to be learned
But better still, the greatest title to be had -
Is when she calls you Mom and Dad-

What a miracle of life! How great the challenge -
How precious the gift! The Lord has given you.

Ruth Ziegler

The Oconee River

From north Lula, to summer hill
A little Oconee River still flows,
Did you know, it is the starting point?
As my foreparents used to talk.

I remember, I was only a child, and
I played beside the road, by the little
Oconee River, out and around an old
Cotton gin.

When the gentle wind would blow
From the huge pipe, of the cotton gin
How the cotton did fall, and cotton
I would gather up, for grand mother
To use for quiets

Through the fields where the beautiful
Wild Daisies bloomed, down beside the
Little Oconee River, on the banks, where
the plum trees grew, sometimes my play-
mates, would join me there, to watch the
Little Oconee River flow.

Ollie J. Bryson

Untitled

On a bright summer night
A man came to bid me goodnight
Looking at me with eyes so bright
Like the ocean on a moon filled night.
The man stayed a little longer
Talking to me softly
Like the leaves of a tree on a wind filled evening.

On a bright summer night
A candle flickered gently
As the man sat next to me
Majestically like a king.
He kissed me gently on my small rosy cheek
Before rising to go.
As he left out my door
He blew out the light.
For the man is my father bidding goodnight.

Rene Aleman

"Bampey"

He lies there quietly, so pale, against the sheet,
A man of courage, kindly, good and sweet.
To those who knew the pain that he endured
Had cause to wonder his accomplishments procured.
Daily tasks that one would take for granted;
Flower and vegetable gardens that he planted,
All in proud array their beauty signified
What he loved and how much he really strived
To keep on going and to ignore the aches
Brought about with age, the body's wearing makes.

One generation goes on for the next to take its place,
Each contributing to the next in grace and face.
Just before he slipped into his quiet slumber,
The sun burst through the rain-filled clouds
Signaling, perhaps, his soul's escape, in bounds!
His gentle wisdom and his quiet teaching helped
Me grow in thought and deed and consternation.
"Mein Kleine Munchen" was his fond admonition.
God bless my grandpa on his journey long.
I thankfully praise his memory with this song.

Nancy B. Ott

A Boy And A Man

A boy will make you cry
A man will be right by your side.

A boy will give you so much pain
A man will hold you in the rain.

A boy will cheat on you every chance he gets
A man won't have you regret

A boy won't treat you like he know he should
A man will stand their and say I would

A boy will get you pregnant and leave
A man will take care of his responsibilities

A boy will not cry or shed a tear
A real man will let you know what he fears

A boy won't think of you
A true man will say I love you.

Shenika Hill

Earthview From Afar

Oh, yes, what a far reaching leap it was —
A milestone for mankind, as fire, or wheel.

Mind and spirit expand, extending us
To the Eagle on the Moon — and beyond.
We, earthbound still, shared wonder and awe.

As Man climbed mast and mountain to see
Sea and plain, so now Man viewed Planet Earth.

We knew and sensed ourselves moving in space,
Part of an ethereal vibration that shall echo
In us all. It was surely a moment of awakening.

Myrna Burkhart McCutchen

Nevertheless

Although the quakes, floods, fatal diseases are spreading like
A mountain fire looking no way to stop here and there on earth,
Yet there is still full of spring scent after severe, cold winter
Around the peaceful pond of a town without my knowledge.
Although no one seems to be able to convert the heartbreaking
Situations of the women and children in Rwanda and Bosnia
Whose eyes are of fear and despair over losing their beloved
Flesh and blood, yet sound of Easter Cantata is leaking out
from the crack of a church where people face tomorrow.

Who were allowed to abuse this beautiful earth?
Who were given the right to misuse of the precious body
Which is the sanctuary of our spirit?
Are we that silly prodigal sons paying the full price?
No. Oh, no. Never!

I know there's a way to go back to old home and share the gifts;
Sweet rain of early spring, heart of overwhelming love, care
And tears of joy and thanks from the bottom of our hearts.
In spite of all the bad news I believe that a good news is still
Alive and working for all no matter who or where they are .
Oh, friends, let's go onward hand in hand saying "yes!"

Myongsu Cho

Faith To Go On

As loved ones pass, so do our lives
We grieve and truly miss them
And life's long struggle for which we strive
Has come to full fruition
For what is life but God's great test
From birth until we die
From pain, to love and happiness
And at the end...is why.

George A. Coons

Desert Hunter

Barren wasteland, arid desert.

Its hunger rising,
A nameless hawk relentlessly stalks its prey,
A forgotten rabbit,
Experiencing terror for the first time.

Burning heat, endless stretch of yellow sand.

Heart beating faster,
The hawk furiously flaps its wings,
Straining to succeed,
Like the rabbit, straining to survive.

Searing, scorching sun, consuming all in its glare.

Closer and closer,
The hawk utters a war-like cry,
Symbolizing victory for the hunter,
And a merciless end for the victim.

Vijay Myneni

What Is A Jewel Day?

I awakened one morning with absolute delight,
A night-fallen snow had left a blanket of white.
A cloudless blue sky was the backdrop for Ol' Sol
Whose beams painted shadows - both intricate and bold.
The sparkle of diamonds would be a jeweler's delight
But it needed one more ingredient to make it just right.
The air must be fresh, crisp, and breathtaking you see,
With a temperature reading of near zero degree.

If I was a snowbird all packed to take flight,
But a jewel day had not come nor was it in sight,
I'd be patient and wait, put another log on the fire
And laugh those to scorn who think I'm a liar.
But when you're down south and enjoying the sun,
I'll be up north thinking jewel days are fun!
All that know me suspect I'm some kind of a freak
Cuz I really love jewel days - and think they're a treat!

Marcia Claire Eklund

The Nightmare's Reality

This reoccurring vision, a terrifying dream,
a paralyzing state too afraid to scream.
The little child listens to their every lie,
with no intent to clip her wings but still she can not fly.
The little one wishes someday she'll be a star,
but they tell her, she won't get very far.
I see the child walking slowly by herself,
her one and only dream lies shattered on the shelf.
The innocent child had one only goal,
and when they stole that they robbed her of her soul,
She looks back at the path she has traveled on,
the road she once took is now forever gone,
She picked her destiny when she chose to join the crowd,
instead of silver lining she culled the dark cloud.
I wake up crying and breaking a sweat,
I look around and realize this nightmare is a threat,
This reoccurring vision, this terrifying dream,
this paralyzing state is worse than it may seam.
This painful reality is what might come to be,
if I let my hopes and dreams slip away from me.

Michaela Stockelman

As I Am

Being as I am, and you as you are.
Two dreams in a mutual desire.
In raptured awe, I drift on eternity.
With the thoughts, that your touches inspire.

Anita Whisher

What Is A Year

A year is but a fragment of eternity
A part of all that was is and is yet to be
A year is but an interlude within
    An ageless span
Ageless in that eternity cannot be measured by man
A year is but a turning point where I take stock of
What I've done, of where I've been
    Of who I am.

Before I enter new year's gate
Some sort of plan I formulate
And as I meditate I find
All of God's resources still are mine
With this idea I now identify
No longer do I question who am I?
Now courage strong and sure erases fear
Joyfully with God I enter the new year.

Pearl N. Sorrels

"Love Is....."

A person who cares when you're down in the blues
a person who likes just being with you.
Someone to hold, someone to kiss
someone to hug and someone to miss.
A person who is willing to share
a person who is always there.
Someone you could always rely on
no matter where you are.
Someone you could always depend on
because he's never too far.
A person who'll love you to the very end
who means more to you than your own best friend.
A person who is only a phone call away
a person who is with you everyday.

Noreen Byatt

Summer Evenings

The essence of time pertains to the realm of reality
A quiet evening, a feeling of sheer tranquility
A time of day. Ecstasy, performing
A mind at rest, on any melodramatic evening
We inherit the gravity of peace instinctively sublime
Designed by God, with nature performing with a plum-line
It is a time to look forward, to the dawn of a new day
Without care you can share time to play
A relevant reminder of a time for romance
Romantic love unfolds, splendor with the evening dance
Benefactors have seen the glory of the twilight sleep hours
There is no secret to illustrate the functional hour
Enjoy a sanctuary, a rendezvous, a heavenly day
We can share in the blessing and a thought of God's way.

Walter J. Lewis

The Best Job of All

What's it like to be a full-time mother?
A more rewarding career, there is no other!
I know that today being a full-time mom,
Is very often frowned upon.
People sometimes turn down their noses,
Thinking that my job is a bed of roses.
From dawn to dusk my job keeps me going and going,
Whether I'm cooking, teaching, chauffeuring, or sewing.
Everyone says that kids grow up too fast.
My job lets me give my kids the love and guidance that will last
And last!

Susan Kay Snyder

Untitled

Gifted life minds power - each scent, sound, shadow assembles
a recall of all time.
Among gentle breeze gale wind, our time - the total acts of
laughter's love to a delicate touch of lips upon finger tips
blends love.
Oh my lady by just laying at body warmth ray's near you - In
slumbers repose - I travel thru gifted life's beauty - that
is you. Breathing a soft heart pulse gentle sweet felt
it be ankle-hips gentle glides or necks scented sweet
nuzzle. My nights travel - hands claps hold you and I
among - emerald forest - lake of jade blue - pure white snow
We rise oh precious lady thru clouds - sky's rainbow hue.
Their among height of such magnificent view - we as one in
life's bonding love flow among heavens rich rich unending view.
But also we as I sense of you a understanding directions
this unpenetrated bond - of childhood love I cherish in
you. So minds unquestionable powers of love and view 'tis it
eternity awaits that I introduce my love as you my Lahoma
Faye. Childhood love - surly I do love you.

Sweet William Snyder

Beware! The Beast!!

Let the sleeping dog lie still. Do not disturb his slumber.
A savage beast might be aroused, your life to put asunder.
...That, "curiosity kills cats", most people will deny.
Nosy felines shriek, "it's true!" as they prepare to die.
Remember ol' PANDORA'S BOX? Dark secrets locked within.
The lid, when it was taken off, released a world of sin.

...Like Adam and Eve and that apple. A serpent told them,
"You'll be wise! Bit the apple in two... soon as you do,
like God - you will have opened eyes."
The serpent was satan, the devil. His wicked deceit lured
them in. One bite and they knew—wrong thing to do.
All God's blessings were taken from them.
They were banished - alone - to work on their own,
as the plight of man's struggles began.

The view from the fruit wasn't pretty - just as God knew it
to be - when He gave man all things in His garden;
but FORBID that one cursed fruit tree.

We pay, still today, for their choices. Consequences forever
remain. Once the beast was aroused —— curiosity, fouled,
and LOST INNOCENCE CAN'T BE REGAINED.

Linda Munro

Wondering of You

Wondering of what to do
  A sea of blue
    And I see you
      Wondering of what to do
  I hear your voice
    Must make a choice
      Wondering of what to do
  Flowers all gone
    And you were adorned
      But now, too, are gone

Days and nights they come and they go
The breeze, the gentle breeze, touches my face
Dries the eyes, so they cry
I mourn a death, the last breath, of my lungs
From city's streets, to country's running feet
I am silent for I am done
I am alone, the unknown
Wondering of what to do
  I'm wondering of what to do

Lawrence Syr Rhodes

Superior Artist

The Lord God painted the earth last night,
A shimmering shining hue.
With mammoth brush and His gentle hand,
He created the beautiful view.
As the shades of evening fell on the earth,
The trees were bleak and bare,
He draped them in an ermine gown,
And put stardust in their hair.
He gave every bush a capelet of white,
A blanket He placed on the ground.
The collected debris of the winter days
Was covered, without a sound.
He slowly and silently started the work
On the masterpiece He would create;
The Lord God painted the earth last night,
I discovered when I got awake.

Violet G. Shirk

International Balloon Fiesta

Colors flying so high and free
A sight well worth a come look and see
Looking and seeing I think golly gee
A myriad of colors and shapes the pleasant sight
The evening glow quite a delight
Dare I say I wish I might
Flying so freely in the air
The warmth of the breeze a special flair
Sailing through the sky really a spectacular fair
The air is in its flair with colors
Soft flares radiating about multi-colors
Multi-colors radiated southwest flavors
I have painted you a balloon
Lofty sights reaching toward the moon
Spiralling about the sky till comes noon.

Robert G. English

Baby

You're about to be blessed with a gift from above,
A small, tiny baby to cherish and love.
A little bundle of joy, to teach and mold,
A new family member to hug and hold.

Life after the arrival, will continue to change,
At times you'll feel life is confused and strange.
There will be many stages this child will go through,
You'll wonder if the quote "a child is a blessing" is true.

As this child continues to develop and grow,
It's important to guide which path and road to go.
To this child try to remain firm, honest, loving, and kind,
A hard task it may be, but a better world this child will find.

As time and life goes on and you grow old,
You'll find each child a different shade of gold.
Always remember, babies are God's gift from above,
Through you, he is bringing the world a new life to love.

Olive H. Cox

The Road of Life

As I walk this road of life,
A little dirt road filled with strife,
There's many potholes, curves, and bends.
I know not where I'm going nor where I've been.
Tell me, to where does this road take me?
Anywhere? Does it meander aimlessly?
If I die now, will it all be for naught?
Will I have reached any goals that I've sought?
Is the most important thing road's end;
Or, how I negotiate each bend?

Robert R. Stallard

A Wounded Bird

Several years past, I first saw her;
  a small, young, carefree cardinal.
The air was billowing with her trilling;
  as she wafted and chirped her song.
Just days ago, I saw her briefly;
  her undulating flight seemingly erratic.
Then I heard her song, low and soft;
  a little less shrill, as vespers aloft.
By concerned compassion, I was moved;
  knowing that I listened to wounded bird.

So I lift up the little wounded bird;
  that by our creator, this prayer be heard.
Now, on through the wooded glade;
  I walk, offering up my prayers.
When to my mind's eye, came a light;
  a glimpse of heaven, hove into sight.
Multitudes and throngs of joyous souls;
  praising God, with song and words.
And, I heard "His" voice to say -
  come - My Heaven's full of - "Wounded Birds"!

  O.S./Rik Teed

The Rape of Beauty

A thoughtless vision, revealed upon
A smooth reflective surface,
Must we comprehend time, in such
A pitiful fall from grace,

Searching vainly for an eternal
moment, in the whisperings of past seasons,
Withering away, to ages of grey,
With not rhyme nor reason,

Open upon unawares, so painfully
Close, so very near, to our mortal lives,
To rise up, beyond lofty clouds,
To a kingdom of such beauty, or so contrived

  Dylan Scott Quebodeaux

Winters Walk

A million stars came out last night, and the stone moon had a ring.
A soft cold wind blew a cloud around,
and I heard an Angel sing.

The cold moon shone down on the snow, and turned dark into light.
Just me, and the moon, and a million stars,
on a winters walk at mid-night.

I walked beneath an old oak tree, undressed until the spring.
With a robins nest still hanging on.
I heard an Angel sing.

"Stillness" had complete control, it covered everything.
I let this feeling take my heart
and I heard an Angel sing.

I still believe no one see's just what tomorrow will bring.
But there's peace inside of me tonight.
And I heard an Angel sing.

Everyone needs time alone, to get away from everything.
And on a winters walk at mid-night
I heard an Angel sing.

  Robert Teall

Untitled

I'll not be proud of my youth or beauty
They'll all wither and fade.
I'll live a good life be honest, and true
And I'll be as pure as a white rose when I'm dead!

  Dorothy M. Cox

From Dusk To Dawn

A touch, a teardrop, a flake of snow
A soft spoken person, feeling quite low.

On a quiet day, in the middle of the night
I grow restless, I begin to write.

Feeling sad, I don't know why
before I know it, I begin to cry.

A touch, a teardrop, a flake of snow
A soft spoken person, feeling quite low.

I write about, the things that I wish to be
A sparkle of good luck to come looking for me.

Maybe one day, when the time is right...
my Good Lord, will show me the light.

On a quiet day, in the middle of the night
I grow tired... I turn off the lights.

I look out my window, and to my surprise!
Dusk is Dawn, and the Sun is Bright.

  Karen Birdsong

Untitled

  A fluid motion is what I desire.
A thought to catch hold, then catch fire.
A poem as bright and as pure as the sun,
a delight in rhyme and lyric sung.
A dancers ease should grace my page.
The smile on my face, the key to my cage.
Loose I run, I am free to roll,
a midnight walk becomes a mental stroll.
No dam should hold my emotions back,
a page once white is now quite black.
I see my pen flowing ever on, a page now full,
another one drawn.
My desire is now quenched, and with these lines
I thee read.
My pen I will bench, and now I'm to bed...

  William Caldwell

"Insomnia"

Toss and turn on bed of rocks; pummel pillows warm with friction.
A thousand eyes gaze down from the darkened ceiling.
The ears of night amplify the creaks and cracks of the settling house.
Soft moans, sighs, chuckles, snores of another's sleep, muffled by the dark.
Endless clouds parade across a clear blue sky, behind my eyelids.
Fluffy white sheep, one by one, leap the creek dissecting the
  meadow of my mind.
Only black sheep remain, mingling aimlessly on the bank,
mocking the futility of the exercise.
The lightening sky lulls me into uneasy rest, to be interrupted too
  soon.
Gurgle -plop- the automatic coffee maker—Gurgle-plop.
Rich roast fragrance drifts through the house.
A quiet click and buzz precedes the soft music from the bedside
  clockradio.
I open burning, frustrated eyes to the sunbeams through the
  window.
And the night is over.

  Margie Sumner

The Rapture

Some say there will come a day
When all the good people will go away
Life as we knew it will be no more
The good Lord has come to destroy, swallow, and devour
For those of us who failed the test
We'll be destroyed with all the rest

Andrew E. Boyer

The Castle Door

A Castle I did build to house and protect my queen.
A throne I did erect to elevate my queen.
A royal family did I have, and all did love and sing.
Now I turn and look around, where did I lose my queen?
The walls to my castle, so tall and slippery,
No knight could just have scaled, to come and steal my queen.
The royal guards, appointed to protect her from all harm,
Still stand attention at their post, unaware that she has gone.
The bad knight to the east, knows not where she may lie,
The bold knight to the west, answers with his jestful cry:
"Sir King, your castle is a virtual fort,
No knight would dare upon you, if he values for his life,
Your doors are way too strong to break an axe upon.
I fear it's not a man nor beast, to that which you do seek.
Your castle doors were opened by her—your royal queen."

Michael Hawkins

Burnside Bridge

At Rohrback's bridge the stand off began,
A tombstone which honors every last man.
Across this tiny bridge of stone,
The men in blue were relentlessly thrown.
Upon the commanding ridge of green,
The rebels vollied into the deep ravine.
The ranks of blue continued to assail,
Their velocity was to no avail.
The crimson swirls filled the creek,
Their dream to possess the ridge was bleak.
The bet of whiskey was finally made,
To any brave soul who'd charge the grade.
The rebels ammo was nearly spent,
They knew they'd never hold the ascent.
The men in gray began to recede,
They'd completed their task to harass and impede.
Now the bridge stands silent and serene,
A place where the souls of the dead can convene.
At Rohrbach's bridge the stand off began,
A tombstone which honors every last man.

Peter A. Gilbert Jr.

Wild Earth

The foliage dark, the jungle hides
  A treasure of earth that heaven prides.
The wild stretches far beyond sight
  Moving in the day, whispering in the night.

No house or road or fence is seen
  To tear and cut the savage green.
No car or scream or fight is heard
  To rise above the most silent bird

Uncut, untouched is the virgin land
  By the fierce cruelty of modern hands.
Untamed, unbridled - Mother Earth
  By silver homes or golden hearths.

Yet deep within a people dwell
  Beyond tax and judicial hell.
The foliage dark, the jungle hides
  A treasure of earth - the Indian rides.

Shane A. Clark

The Legacy

A frozen heart
A trustless mien
  Sightless eyes....
    Thoughtless mind....
All......is your legacy dearest,
All.....
  except for these ears
  that listen to notes....thru' filters
  and longs for that....which it glimpsed
  one morning,
— a gold coin on your creation —
  Yes I know
  It was the light of the morning
  on one of your earthen vessels
But,
  that is mine
  that you took away
  when you asked me
  oh!
    so kindly to go away.

Sharmila Rao

How Is Your Baby?

She came nine months ago
A tumor that was probably benign
To take it off and have it analyzed, no problem
You see however, she was in her last trimester

Look, believe me, I would love to take it out
But we would have to numb it up
It would only hurt a little, that's not the problem
Epinephrine is contraindicated in pregnant mothers

She was told to keep an eye on it
To return after the delivery
To remember when she did come back
Is beyond me

She returned for her six month post-op
Let us make sure there is no re-growth
  Oh, by the way, how is your baby?
  I lost him three days before he was due

C. Scott Combest

Untitled

One little girl, one tortured soul -
A twisted mind, an ugly soul.
Melissa was just a kid
Lovable, cute and dear.
A father who left a mother without care -
What has she now?
Nothing but hate
Dead hate!
A man took her; raped and killed her.
She was only eight, a man three times her age.
What of the guy?
Free as a bird, no burden on his soul.
No man, no woman, no law can help Melissa
Why?
Because no one cared!
Poor Missy - but it's too late!
Tell me what's going on,
What happening to this world?
But more importantly -
What's happened to our hearts?

Mary Bentley

Old House

Weeds grow halfway round about you
A vacant window stars as an open eye

Wonder who once cared about you -
a spent life savings which passed them by

Brick and shingle, all eroding -
ancient shed around the back

Who once lived here - who once loved here?
Cried here - died here - won't be coming back?

Hopes and dreams, fears and sorrows -
expectations of yesteryear

Memories belonging all to others -
echoes ringing in my ears.

You have a look as if heart broken,
those you loved are gone away -

And if I patched you - fixed your surface -
you'd still long for yesterday

Nothing left but to let time take you -
wind and rain and all the rest.

From the ground they will efface you -
then a new house will brave this test.

Suzanne Tzerman

Behold the Dreamer

Is he a visionary,
a waster of time,
a fool?
Do his dreams produce happiness
or intrude on another's life without benefit?
Do his dreams ask profound questions
for the scientist and engineer to solve?
Or confuse an issue with trivia
and impractical ideas,
does it matter?
Creativity is like a chain reaction
resulting in the advancement of society,
even small advances give us benefit,
an individuals creativity
is a step beyond his own self doubt
thus allowing him to grow
in comprehension and
to new levels of accomplishment,
behold the dreamer,
for without dreams this world would soon perish....

Stanley C. Hopkins

Beauty

I saw as the leaves began to inch to the ground slyly,
A young man sitting under a tree.
I soon noticed he was also watching me
I started walking to him shyly.

He told me he thought I was beautiful.
And he said my eyes were blue,
Soft as a cool morning's dew.
He told me my skin was rosy and beautiful.

As I left, I thought,
Am I really that pretty?
No, no, I realized and only I could give myself pity.
He had been looking at my heart, the way he was taught.

My heart told me this fact, the mirror showed it clear,
Yet I wish I was as beautiful as to him I appeared.

Laurie Houck

To Walter

Did you sail a Viking ship?
A wolf's head on the bow?
Which Roman legion fled in fear
at your lapis face aglow?
Flew your standard high o'er Stirling road
that day at Bannockburn?
Slung stinging sleet upon your skin
at Culloden's fatal turn?
Marched you into Yorktown's British guns
to hoist the rebel flag?
Swung savagely, was your sabre red
to boost the Texans' brag?
What bitter tears trudged down your cheek
on Appomattox green?
Did that barricade beneath Canyon's hill
let you evolve again?

Have emerald eyes become ebony?
Has blonde hair turned to brown?
Could Phillip be your name now —
This latest time around?

Landis Munro Land

Fall Comes To West Virginia

At this time of year, West Virginia is just
a wonder to behold -
I call her God's own Master Piece in
hues of red and gold.

It looks as if the master, took a brush
hand painted every leaf -
never have I seen such divine beauty
as I sigh in disbelief.

There are places where, the mountains
just look like they are on fire -
and the sight just gets lovelier as one
drives up on higher.

Every day the leaves up here gives us
an even grander show -
but it won't be long till they're gone
and we see a blanket of snow.

Merry Lynn Lowe

A Heavy Burden To Bare

It pains me, this deep rooted sadness
About life's cruelties, sometimes seemingly like a nightmare
So full of love, yet still entombed in loneliness
This thing called loneliness is a heavy burden to bare

Look deeper than the flesh, take a peek at the man within
He maybe the man that you've been looking for, trying to find
Don't disregard me just because I'm thin
Let my inner beauty be what you see, within mind

Kind, considerate, most of the time too much of a nice guy
Admirable qualities pop out here and there
A gentleman, I think I am, I least wise will not deny
Come curl your fingers in my long brown hair

Come gaze into my eyes, caress me, caress my being
Refresh my soul, bring joy into my heart again
From the realm of loneliness I pray you'll have me be fleeing
Accept my love, allow me to become your swain

I crave an ally, a confidante, a lover, a best friend
Fill the gaping hole in my heart, come satiate me with your love
Come, together let us take the path, see what is up around the bend
Lord, I'm looking, let her find me, let her discover true love

Lawrence Thomas

Spring's First Bell Chimes

I've sung this song a thousand-fold,
about Spring's first bell chimes.
When it's lilt I do behold,
with my heartbeat it rhymes.

Yes, chimes, so slight - March twenty first,
thin, minute note aloft.
Awakes the flower - a petal burst:
echoes notes so soft.

A minute bell - in all ears held,
- a note to start anew.
Ringing echoes: Butterfly unshelled,
a trace of sparrow flew.

I've sung this song - one of the spring,
more than a thousand times.
Bird and butterfly on wing,
echo soft bell chimes.

Mark W. Haggerty

Everything You Need

I heard the way that you talked
About wanting someone real
After so long
Of nothing at all.
Maybe someone was there
But she wasn't who you need.
Next time won't you please
Let it be me?
Let me be the one
To change your heart around.
Let me be the one
To pick your love up off the ground.
I want to be the one
Who let's you soar through time and space...
As long as you let me
Join you in that place.
Please consider me
In your search for reality.
I want to be with you;
Let me be your everything.

Penny Hamstra

Visions Of Beauty

I've admired the colors of the rainbow as they stretched
above the land.
I've enjoyed the motion of the ocean as it crashed towards
the sand.
I've watched the sun rise in the morning, stunningly bright,
topped only in it's beauty, by it's descending at night.
I've seen flowers blooming, trees growing, as nature expands.
I've observed the beauty of a newborn with it's soft tiny hands.

There is a special kind of beauty when brides dress in white.
Certainly snow, as it begins falling, can be a wonderful sight.
Fireworks exploding, with their many colorful displays,
make an evening sky suddenly light up in beautiful ways.
One can only treasure the beauty of an eclipse at noon,
or brightly lit stars, alongside a full shining moon.

Different visions of beauty that have enriched this man's life
yet none can compare to the beauty of this man's special wife.
She's not only beautiful in outward appearance, but inwardly too.
As my friend, wife, and child's mother, she's always been true.
She is a tribute to all that is beautiful in this man's eyes
and I will forever know, in my mind, where true beauty lies.

Ronald M. Majka

We Forgot to Remember

Now the play is over, the curtains been rung down
Actors change their faces, stage props left around
Eulogies said, bells rung, praises sung.
The tragedy is over, applause is done
It's back to reality, back to light of day
The star has gone forever, the audience will say
But is tragedy over or has it just begun?
No! The tragedies, not over the tragedies just begun.
We forgot to remember when the curtain was rung
Oh! We've had tragedies before you see the thing between
Grant and Lee, brother against brother father against son
We forgot to remember and a war was won.
New actors play the parts, a doughboy falls on Flanders
Field, we forgot to remember, the curtains been rung down
Make the world safe for democracy, remember Davehau and
Buchenwald
The stage play is over, the curtains been rung down
We forgot to remember, death is still around
When will it end, when the trumpet sounds?
When we remember to remember the curtain been rung down.

Pierre H. Roan

A Clarion Call to America

O America, land of hope, when first I trod upon your soil
Aghast with strife and violence on my own.
My heart conjured many happy dreams to crown
A life of peace, a reward for sweat and toil.
With my once peaceful country torn asunder to shreds
I admired your unity and fusion, despite the many threads
Of linguistic, religious and racial diversity,
Living harmoniously as one large family.
Sadly within a decade of years this fusion in balance,
Racial tension, disease, gun culture, an irreligious stance,
Marred the spontaneous strains of Hi and Bye,
Once mouthed so freely by all passers by.
Be guided by Moses and his slab of stone
Inscribing the Ten Commandments, their sins to atone.
In your hearts enshrine this time honored teaching,
Love thy neighbor as thyself as a goal worth reaching.
America, land of the free and the brave
Awake, Arise, lest you fall to your grave.

A. Perera

Hope Of An Everlasting Love

Our love is a rising sun
Aglow with the warmth we experience
The rays dance upon our faces
Sparkling, intertwining with hopes of an everlasting love

As the sun rises to its peak and begins to thrust downward
Its kaleidoscope of colors in full strength upon us
We bask in the rapture, the revelation of a
Burning, spreading hope of an everlasting love

Regardless, our restraints are not heeded
The sun diminishes and slips beneath the horizon
Hidden there is our fear
Vanishing, ebbing is our hope of an everlasting love

Pondering our failures, mistakes
Awaiting the night to pass to morn
Our fears grow with the increasing darkness
Mingling, destroying our hope of an everlasting love

The doubts, the trepidation mounts
A chill quivers through our souls
We cradle one another and seek the morning sun
Seeing, believing once again in the hope of an everlasting love

Lynn B. Worley

The Invisible

A little boy asked with wondering eyes, why can't we see the air?
Air is so important we don't see it, still we know it's there.
How do I answer the little one, I'll try, he might understand.
Air has such success keeping us alive, but on the other hand
Air needs the help of all other things that make up our universe
Skies, stars, moon, sun, and the earth
Blending with wind, storms, water, heat and cold
If one failed to work with the earth, all else would fold,
Or refuse to carry it's share of the load, we would feel such sorrow
Don't worry. It was here yesterday, today, and will be here tomorrow.
That's faith, another thing you can't see, but we have it, I know
Faith too, is important to the people on this earth below
And should teach us a lesson, I can see it mighty clear!
All people working together, could change everything we have here.
We need the earth to live upon, we need it all, including rain and
  sun.
We should be like the invisible air, and do good for every one.
Air to breathe, sun for heat, clouds both light and dark is our
  salvation
Earth for the growth of all we eat, and what it provides our nation.
Free things, seen or unseen, sent here for us to treasure.
Heed this lesson, work together in peace, 'twill repay you more in
  pleasure.

Mildred Marsh Ruton

Different Or Same?

Mexican, Haitian Jews, Black or White
All are precious in his sight.
Each has a heart beating in his chest
May get an attitude when under stress.

All people have blood that bleeds red.
Two eyes, a nose and one round head.
They want love, and comfort in their home.
Feel uneasy when their children are gone.

They want food on the table and clothes to wear,
Shoes to put on when their feet are bare.
It matters not what your race, creed or color,
You need to co-exist and trust each other.

Read past history, then you can see
All human being want to be free.
When you look at the picture the facts are plain
We are not that different, but very much the same.

Nadene C. King

Tina The Ballerina

There once was a girl named Tina.
All she wanted was to be a ballerina.
She would dream all day and would try to convey,
I'm Tina the Ballerina!

Now Tina was all of two.
She wore nothing but a tu tu.
She would turn and twirl and make everything whirl.
I'm Tina the Ballerina!

Tina could do more than a sachet.
It would make everyone say,
She's so graceful and sweet someone we'd all like to meet.
I'm Tina the Ballerina!

When Tina put on her taps
She could hear everyone's claps.
She would shuffle and hop and just never stop.
I'm Tina the Ballerina!

Then one day she awoke.
Her crystal ball had broke.
She still had her dream and just wanted to scream.
I'm Tina the Ballerina!

Sharon Infante

What Is My Love?

My love is soft and gentle kind and
all so sweet. My love is like a rose that
has just bloomed in the springtime.
My love is like a wine glass delicate
very easy to break. My love is like a
sunset over the ocean at night calm and
also beautiful. That is what my love is,
also my love is never to be taken for
granted. That's my love!

Lynne A. Mills

Spirits Grown, Spirits Flown

Spirits grown, and spirits flown, my spirit's turned to stone.
Aloft from my window I see a world needing desperately to be free.
Living the world through the mind of a madman,
Its become such a strange place to be.
A boyhood dreams just a country away,
Yet still I smell the salt of the sea.
So walk with me now in a land of dread,
And love me until the end.
Show me the way, and love me today,
And always be my friend.

Maynard

Alone

Sometimes I feel so utterly
alone,
as if I was resting in a flowery meadow on a hot,
summer day,
with the entire meadow vacant except for me and the flowers,
and the birds, and the trees.
No one there caring or loving me in the vacant, flowery
meadow, not even myself, really, just feeling sympathy for my
ignorant tears.
Even if the meadow was full with scurrying children and
couples walking hand in hand, I would still feel
alone.
Feeling so alienated, not a child nor a lover,
as a lady with a gentleman in the cluster.
But alas alone I am with no one to care for, or care
for me.
No father, no mother, no sisters, nor brothers.
I still sit underneath an oak tree in the flowery meadow,
wishing not to be alone but someone caring
for me.

Stacy Updyke-Fennell

The Poet

The poet torments.
Alone, he quiets his noisy mind
To find the words which he must find
To stand for his life.

His paint is black as the blood of his sorrow.
His canvas white, like a light he must follow;
Like hope,
Which draws him to a place outside his dark mind
Where someone waits to read his black letters
Standing like so many war-weary soldiers in the snow.

He belongs not to himself
But to the world,
Where he gives all away and finds no comfort
But for the man in search of words
He himself could not find
To stand for his life.

C. L. Donaldson

First Love

She who sits with ideal passivity;
Alone, with accompaniment from heavens afar
Is the embodiment of the desire which hinders unpleasantry.
Beauty is her life's gift to the stars.

In her smile she brings thoughts to mind.
Gaiety is her nature which carries to thy soul;
Here, hearts discover reality of novel kinds.
Images of eloquence construct a body whole.

Grace be it that she feels affections.
For it is this that burns under candles light,
And warms my heart to enduring satisfactions.
In darkness or light, her grasp thy cherish tight.

The fall of evening souls do not rest,
Eternally her love is the only desired quest.

Michael R. Barclay

Tread Softly, Child

Tread softly, child, and gaze upon the land,
although at times you do not understand
the whys and hows of what this world may bring.
Tread softly, child.

Tread softly, child; enjoy the bird and bee
and love the beauty God has given free.
At daybreak, and at close of day, and more,
Tread softly, child.

Tread softly, child, yet shout with heaven's joy
and pray those prayers which nothing can destroy.
For God will listen when we speak with Him.
Tread softly, child.

Lynn C. Fick

Rapture of Love

That I have loved you, since a child with toys,
Although, I never really saw your face,
I think, you know. But, I have kept the grace,
Of my first dreaming of you.
Other joys, breaking with forward torches,
Through the mist, gives me no sudden sword into my heart,
Which keeps the steel, until I become a part
Of you: bread, wine, my eternal eucharist.
What shall I keep against the worlds cold,
If not the understanding words of your mouth?
Or shall I follow seven swallows south,
That passed me in the morning?
In the fold of your two hands, the seasons seem to keep,
Like four spokes, on an always clicking wheel,
Which ruts no country's road.
With thoughts of you I feel my love to be all waking and all sleep.
What shall I keep then; the slow stitch of birds across the sky,
Or promises you made if I keep your commands of love?
Perhaps it's just a rapture of words.

Wanda Youker

"The Forbidden Castle"

When I open my gates and let forth
A stranger to enter my castle to walk all over
Inside of me I must know at first
This person shall live here forever.
This person soon changes the walls
That were dirty and dingy and knocks
Them out and replaces them with windows
That show me the sea in which love flows.
Therefore this castle will never perish or fall.

Michael Greathouse

What I Would Rather Be

Let them be as snow
always beautiful pretty white snowflakes
but only in the winter.

I'd rather be cold rain
pouring out of thundering clouds like cats and dogs
wind beating rain on hard surfaces.

To have the power to make someone cold
to fall, to feel exposed to the world
of the great mountains and vast plains
to be pushed by harsh winds of the gray sky
carrying my life, my water, to the cold empty world
or into the depths of time?

I'd rather be known, and if shutout by everyone
to be beautiful and white
falling in the most desolate places
where it is abandoned, ignored and never touched
by no one and everyone.

I'd rather smell like wet pavement than of evergreen trees
if I could fall with thunder and lightening
I'd rather be rain.

Molly D. Little

Spirit of the Wind

He must roam,
always in motion he must be
for to stop is to settle down.
This is a abomination to him
and to all he stands for and holds dear and true.

To move is to be free.
Free of responsibility, of worry, and emotionalities.
All and any ties that would tie him to one spot,
rob him of his freedom
and condemn him to a life like a tree.
To be planted within a forest, all rooted to one spot.
No longer to be a free spirit-
a spirit of the wind.

The wind is his guide, his only true friend.
A companion on their long travels
for they travel together to be free.
For like the wind, he has the spirit to roam,
to adventure, to experience true freedom.
To know peace and serenity is their goal.
The spirits of the wind.

P. Joseph Brzezinski

Forever

You stood out like a sore thumb in some cases
Always number one it seemed you were.
You really deserved all the cheering and congrats
Because you were someone with true pizazz.
You weren't a phony-not even a punk
Our lives were lit up by your genuine spunk.
Though your life was short and sweet,
Your memory will be felt in everyone's heartbeat.
You weren't a quitter or a cheater in games.
You always helped us out again and again.
But now you've left us all alone here.
I feel a certain warmth has left- I must shed a tear.
You're gone forever-never to return,
This will be the day when we all shall mourn.
So long, farewell, we all love you forever.
We will cry, we will weep, we will lie down a flower.
The flower will die, but it's spirit shall live.
And so must yours - 'tis it already is.

Miranda Tarnauskas

Parental Guidance

Always caring,
Always sharing,
Always kind,
No one could find...
Better parents than we have,
They gave us love and attention...
And not to mention
The countless other things they did for us.
We'll always treasure,
Their love which we cannot measure.

Sondra Lougee

Thanks For A New Day

   I live each day with thanks
amidst the different ranks
as my joyful heart, beats a sound of praise
to him who gives me days.
   I live each day with thanks
ears listening, eyes beholding
arms enfolding.
Thankful for these wonderful gifts.
   I live each day with thanks
there's power in my hands
to lift some one, to make them smile.
Or cause their world to crumble.
   I live each day with thanks
knowing, that my future's in my hands
for the choice I make will then determine
my today and all my tomorrows.
   I dare not make this choice alone
assist me Lord I pray.

J. Ann Younge

Porcelain Time

Cumbersome hands on galloping time reset blurred visions in
  an agitated mind:
Having, hosting, circular motions entrapped in sculpted day,
With display of pounding hands, confident dominance conquers
  the way,
Refined periods of porcelain revive a smooth soul—-
CRASH, WITH, SAVAGE, HANDS, TO PREVENT, A,
SMOOTH, FLOW.
The structure frail, frightened, and hung, moves prancing
  time, rudely eliminates great tortoise run;
Time's broken hands, numbed, not in vain, forward fragile
  seconds, paused in refrain.
Gathering with might, chipped pieces of time, periods of
  porcelain cheer ticking hands in my mind.

Tanya Rosenbaum

Becoming a Work of Art

We begin as,
  An empty canvas,
    Formless clay,
      Marble untouched by chisel,
        Molten metal, precious, waiting for form

    Open fields, plowed and ready for seed,
   Buds and flowers becoming leaves and shade,
 Cocoons, dormant, then Butterflies,
Open, ready, waiting for the Artist of Life and his
  apprentice — ourselves.

With courage, grace and beauty we are becoming a work of Art.

Marlyn Whitley

Searching

A rusting bike
An empty swing
No childhood laughter do they bring
Untouched toys
Within a room
Hopes and prayers you'll be home soon
One less stop
The school bus makes
One more heart of a parent breaks
Holding your picture
Tears fall upon the glass
Remembering the good times left only for the past
But they'll never stop searching
To bring you home
And with their prayers for you you're never alone
Missing children
All around
Please reach out they must be found

Kristine McKay

Lonely Man

A man oh so simple yet divine.
An image portrayed of father time.
Wise and witty with so much pain.
Injustice decays the fears sustained.
A burden perhaps to others opinion.
Tarnished shoes we have never lived in.
Beneath his heart he keeps his soul.
A life he has lived to some untold.
Goodnight he whispers upon a bench.
A lifetime of despair a pocket of lint.
Peace has arrived to this pale little man.
A heartache has gone a dilemma still stands.

Todd Crawford

Poetess

Write a poem of twenty lines or less—-
an impossible task, I've always written more than that.
Any topic, title or care—-
any subject, whatever I dare?
"Birds of a feather flock together" —-
how's that for rhythm and rhyme?
What shall it be? —-
I must hurry to make it on time.
Two hundred and fifty prizes in all—-
what would I do if they gave me a call?
I'd scarcely be able to hear—-
my heart would be pounding in my ear.
I'd be shaking like a leaf—-
I'd never be able to speak.
Someone would surely have to help me to my feet—-
an amateur poet that's me, best of all this contest
is free!!!

Sandra L. Rober Sharpe

Troubles In The Library

Non-fiction fiction what's the difference?
Why in alphabetical order?
Why index cards? I explained it to the
librarian
She said she would take out the index cards
and mix the books up.
I went next week and I could not
find anything!
she said that is why we need them!
So, I said Oh! now I get it!!!

Angela Orum

Aunt Bama's Slip

While visiting Aunt Bama age 94, she shared
  an interesting story that happened
  seventy-five years ago.
Aunt Bama's mother made her a slip,
  using outing material.

This was before zipper time, and
  The slip was pinned with a straight pin.
All went well for a spell, until
  This group of youngsters
Were on their way to a singing.

The straight pin failed to hold,
  The slip fell to the ground.
Aunt Bama wa sorely embarrassed.
  She picked up the slip and
Threw it under the church house.
  In those days building were set on pilings,
  Two or three feet off the ground.

Mother asked anxiously how the singing
  went. Aunt Bama was so embarrassed
She could not answer. The slip was never found.

Vaudaline Thomas

The Superficial Reality

It came to me as an interruption,
An interruption of my childhood.

I said I'd miss him; I acted sad.
I said I'd feel forever bad.
But can you miss something you never had?

I would cry and listen as she would pursue
To say she missed him; I'd say it, too.
But can you miss something you never knew?

I went through all the stages and said it wasn't fair,
And it's not as if I didn't care.
But can you miss something that was never there?

Tessa Chretien

Whisper Three Words

My mind can see the love we share,
and all I can say is that I care.
For what we have in our hands,
only you and I can understand.

From the depth of your heart I know you love me,
and I love you, though no one may see.
So stay with me awhile, till the sun does set,
and my heart is yours forever, that's my request.

Hold me close and never let me go.
Kiss me gently so I shall know.
Whisper three words that I know are true;
and I'll whisper them back, "I love you."

Margie Meyer

Daddy's Girl

I wish I could stop the hands of time.
When you were young and you were mine.

But as I watch, you began to grow.
Knowing one day I would have to let you go.

To go to the arms of another man.
Knowing one day he would take your hand.

To hold and caress you as I once did,
when you were young and just my kid.

David W. Pearson

Control, Control

"Mother, Mother," their faces call
and all look up at thee
Control, Control, you must surely have
to nurture all of these
For seven years it took you all
to bring forth this great three
And patiently you gathered them
and hugged them lovingly
Control, Control, you must surely have
to sleep so peacefully
For the cries and wails that lasted for days
have vanished silently
And in it's place, made neat in a row
three faces look up at thee
Control, Control you must surely have
covered deeply under a tree

Rachelle Griffin Pasquini

Untitled

It was just before Christmas
And all through your wee house
Creatures are stirring, yes even a mouse,
Alyssa and Sally come quickly and see,
Your family, the darlings, are trimming their tree,
There's a wreath to be hung and cookies to
bake and so many more decorations to make.

I think their nativity scene is so dear
Remember, how you would set up ours here?
We love you at Christmas and all the year through
Merry Christmas to Mommy, merry christmas to you

Now back at the Pole with his feet in a tub
Santa's watching his elves give the rain deer a scrub
We had a good trip, and I don't like to gripe,
but I seem to be missing my favorite pipe.
You know what I think? And maybe it's true,
I think there's a Santa for Doll houses too.
Now this little poem is not meant to deceive but,
if I found his pipe I think I might believe!

Nancy Guarneri

Christmas Ups and Downs

Christmas comes once a year,
and all you ever hear is have you been a good girl this year?
I hate it, I can't stand it,
That's it, I'm gonna have a fit!
And parents are always asking,
"Is a stout little guy with a twinkle in his eye going to come to your
house?"
(Santa)
You tell "'Twas the Night Before Christmas" and go to bed.
And when you wake up your sister says, "I heard thumping over my
head."
You go downstairs (this is the good part!)
You see presents galore scattered all over the floor.
You open them one by one, and then when you're done,
You eat breakfast: pancakes, sausage, bacon, eggs, and more.
You need two plates or even four,
You thank your Grandmother, aunts and uncles, mother and father.
I guess your parents really aren't a bother!

Tracy Palmore

Untitled

Life moves in mysterious ways
we don't always understand.
But if we master these moves we
can turn negatives to positives and violence
to peace.

Jennifer Combs

Worm Turns

It was her nature once to fly - then pause, detached, on ground so dry
and bend to hunt between the blades - which cast both green and yellow
   shades
a quick precise unholy drill - no drop of sustenance would spill
her neck so tight, that beak so sharp - she'd rise beyond this crimson tarp
and in the morning mist would soar - above the holes her hunger bore
and never glance below the wind - until her need returned again
on downward draft with cold black eyes - she'd shed the freedom of
   the skies
in homage to her belly's gnaw - with razor claws and hard set jaw
this dive of death, dispassionate - her mind fixed like some bayonet
the unsuspecting never knew - then once again away she flew
idyllic was this fowl song - until she chose one prey too strong
too buried in the soil's core - and in this struggle, one wing tore
in disbelief she starts and stops - and cries unto the mountaintops
beneath her breast so warm, a shudder - all is lost now, half a flutter
crippled huntress, hear her shriek - at nature's twist on hide and seek
for shadows vanish at high noon - she waits exposed, her turn is
   soon....

Michael Wolf

Downtown

The blanket of darkness is stolen by a myriad of colors flickering
and casting their lollipop hues on the skyline and street corners.

To the distant visitors-observers-watchers this night there is a
beauty not unlike a kaleidoscope-fireworks-a warm fountain—bathed in
rainbows. But come again tomorrow and the radiance will have seemed
but a mask that illusion created, for now the screen of grime and
poverty has become the next act.

It is always there, the assortment of shabby and crowded stores that
parallel each other along the avenues. The cries of the vendors make
music for no one, as they beg for someone to buy their goods. The
homeless in their costumes of rags choose carefully from the trash
cans. The busy executives with their important documents look only at
the ground when passing by—they are wrapped in a cloak of themselves.
The endless conga-line of cars wheeze out their perfumes for the
atmosphere to choke on, creeping only far enough to stop at the next
red light.

They are trapped in the eternal maze of trying to get to their
destinations. But when the lids of the world close once again the
curtain opens to yet another fabrication of colors depicting the
postcard image that exists within the unsuspecting mind.

Melanie Parker

A Spiritual Change

   Let's all start a new
And do the things He wants us to do
   Good life will be not for a few
But beautiful for all races who
   Adheres to His teaching no matter how small
No matter if it is for one or all
   As long as sincerity is the goal
Everyone is welcome to the fold.

   Do not procrastinate from day to day
And find yourself distracted along the way
   From doing some good deed you know
That will help prevent a person to grow
   Stand firm and go forward with a plan
One that will suit boy, girl, woman and man
   Keeping in mind His major concern for all
Lifting up those who along the way did fall.

Mildred Long

Old Age Is Hell!

The body gets stiff; you get cramps in your legs
And corns on your feet as big as hen's eggs.

Gas on your stomach - elimination is poor.
Take Ex-lax at night and then you're not sure.

Go soak in the tub, or your body will smell.
It's like I said folks, "Old age is such Hell."

Your teeth start decaying; your eyesight is poor.
Your hair's falling out all over the floor.

Your sex life is shot; it's a thing of the past.
Don't kid yourself, friend - even that doesn't last.

Can't go to parties; don't dance any more.
It's time to admit you're a Hell of a bore.

Drinking liquor is out; just can't take a chance.
Your bladder's so weak, you'll pee in your pants.

Nothing to plan for; nothing except.
The mailman, who brings your Security check.

If your affairs' not in order and your will's not just right;
On the way to the graveyard, your family will fight.

You feel pretty good and you look fairly well.
Thank God you're alive, 'cause old age is Hell.

Melvin H. Kirschner & Joseph Shorr

"Memories"

Each year as leaves begin to flutter,
and crispness fills the air,
thoughts go back to yet another
time and place; you were there!
It wasn't foliage that caught the eye
nor baseball's fall unwinding.
Not even snowflakes falling from the sky
or turkeys cooked for fancy dining.
No, none of those. Only crosses.
Stark, white and full of memories
of men and families who bore their losses,
forever stored among their reveries.
You're gone from us dear brothers,
gone to that great beyond.
You sleep forever with the others,
the torch of freedom is your bond.
And all we have is memories.

Ralph Ricci

Feelings Of Hog Island

As I watch the clock ticking by, minute by minute, hour by hour,
   and day by day,
I feel a sudden sadness wash over me.
It is a sadness that goes down deep into my heart
and sends a sudden shiver up my back.

For a place that I have mentally become such a part of as well
   as physically
will vanish out of my sight in just a matter of days,
but will never vanish from my heart.

Because this is a place where the ocean becomes part of you as
you stare, the birds fly in harmony above you,
and the trees are the most beautiful you have ever seen,
the animals play gaily in the forest, and the people are all
you could hope for.

As I think about this wonderful place my sadness goes away
and is replaced by the warmest thoughts a person could ever have.
There is only one place on earth that could amount to all this;
this place is Hog Island.

Victoria J. Sloane

Lonely and Despair

I woke up this morning feeling lonely
and despair. Lonely because I couldn't
find anyone there in the house I call
despair. This house use to have plenty of
voices and furniture of all choices. I used
to say "Good Morning Grandma Dear," Get
coffee and read the newspaper, while sitting
in a comfortable chair. Now that Grandma
and Grandaddy are gone I sit here pondering,
Here I am, so all alone! Today, I pray
that I find true happiness and peace of mind
But, right now I sit lonely and despair
Pondering for happiness while sitting
on the living room chair.

Tyrone Ellis

Someone Special

That someone special you meet one night,
and end up loving more than life.
That someone special you love and you cherish,
and make family by marriage.
That someone special you may fuss and fight with,
but you can't wait to make up with.
That someone special you can't imagine not having
close to your side, to enjoy their laughter,
and share their pain when they cry.
That someone special you snuggle up close to
and hold real tight, to keep you warm
on a cold winter's night.
That someone special you love to be around,
who brings you up when you're feeling down,
and with just a smile makes everything alright,
and makes even your darkest days seem bright.
That someone special you would score a "10,"
even if they were less than perfect or ugly as sin,
because you look inside, and see what's within.
So the tears that you sometimes see in my eyes,
is from a terrible loneliness deep down inside.
And once again I've just realized, I'll never find anyone
like I've just described.
It isn't because I'm not a likeable guy,
but mostly because from neck to toes I'm paralyzed.
If only you would stop and take the time to look inside
you just might find that I'm someone special too, just like you.

Randy E. Franks

Blind

It crept upon me like a thief in the night
And even the brightest light or a star on the brightest night
Could predict its time its strength or its destruction
At first it was so beautiful and so wonderful but its power
And its path was just not known
It is all that makes me happy yet is the only thing that makes
Me cry and whine and wonder like a lost puppy
It is the garden of eden and fifty rainbows rolled into me
Short yet all powerful word LOVE
Who could have known it was so sneaky yet so obvious
And that in the end it would crack my heart like a broken glass
But the damage can only be blamed on me
For I saw it coming, but was not looking, and didn't know it was there
But I was blinded by its light and trapped by it tentacles
And from that experience, since it was so kind, I know LOVE IS
BLIND
Next time I will walk the path not knowing what to expect
Where to go and only go with the flow
But with women standing strong and close behind
I can say always and forever, and since the beginning of time
LOVE IS TRULY BLIND

Rahsaan D. Thorpe

I'm Just Another Dreamer!

In the early morning hours - when Mother Nature takes a nap
And Father Time seems to take a coffee break.
If you listen real close you can hear a gasp and a sigh—
And maybe even a shriek, but you must not be alarmed.
For it's just the sound of man, woman, boy or girl—
Engaged in having their own personal dreams.

A young boy dreams of being a lawyer and one day becomes a judge:
A young girl dreams of being a teacher and becomes a poet:
We all have dreams - and dreams to remember...
Dreams are God's way of sharing with us the sweet oracles of his words
Oh what a means!

Even I have a dream
I dream of clean clear water and green pastures
Soil reach in proteins and a land flowing with milk and honey...
I dream of clean air without carbons and sulfides...
I dream of a contamination free neighborhood...
I dream of an industry that can make a profit
Without costing me and my family our lives..
I know we all have dreams, and mine is not the only dream.
But yet and still, I dream because.. I'm just - another dreamer!

Roy L. Malveaux

Ever Onward

He set sail on a quiet day
And for a while was one with the world.
Ever onward, in anticipation of sun and sea and sky.

And that's how it began
With hope of all things good
So young, so full of faith
No question if he could

And he moved ever onward
But as the fickle seas
Began to rise in anger
And taunt and laugh and tease

He knew his fear was welling
As was his will and might
No contest was the sea
Draining his strength to fight

And as the victor, ever onward raged the sea
As it ate up yet another man's hope
As it drank up yet another man's dream.
Yet the sailor mounts his struggle, ever onward
In search of voyages yet to be.

Mary E. Kendig

Mankind

Nature's voice is strong
And forever will it be heard
   by the human heart
But when a demanding generation of mankind,
   armed with a myriad of themselves
   and greedy nature;
Who often choose
   to promote themselves over more important
   issues of reason,
The question is asked: Does their name correspond
   with themselves when such actions are performed?

Sara Pilarski

Tranquility

There are quiet times of peace and love
and friendship in our hearts
there are pleasant thoughts of embracing life
and enjoying brand new starts.
There are tougher times when things go wrong
and worries cloud our space.
But all we need to do just then is bath
quietly in God's grace.
There are rougher times that turn around and
then are not so bad.
And when these rougher times are gone there are
softer ones to be had.
There are people whom are rough and tough but
have a softer side
this side is small, but not for all, and often
hard to hide.
You seem to me to be, I'm sure, of equal
sides its true.
I like you when you're tough, you see, but
I love the softer side of you!

Mark H. Olson

"Shameful Past"

Be little me not, my shameful past;
and haunt me never, lie.

Choices made, so long ago;
may not speak truth, I cry!

Youthful ventures, train us well;
habits hard to break.

Effortless, begins our walk;
thoughtless what's at stake.

With age we learn, embarrassed now;
at what we have become.

Pride stays our change, makes difficult;
our ghosts to overcome.

Try some we may, the venture quest;
Seeking, rid ourselves of blame.

And hope those things, that tried us best;
will try again in vein.

Paul Scott Winkler

Mother May I

I look over and beyond the horizon
and I can see in the near distance
that the Lioness has but one last roar.

The cool serene silence of the night
wills the Queen into existence
never to be misunderstood anymore.

It is her tranquil yet vociferous thunder
that demands the Respect of the earth
thus, this begins the end of an old tomorrow.

Behold the bright light from the darkness
as it becomes lucid from her new Birth
and watch the lioness overcome her lifelong sorrow.

The throne that is rightfully and respectfully hers
has brought Joy, Love, and Peace into our world
Rejoice! Rejoice! Rejoice! for the lioness must finally ask,

Mother May I

Tanya Sweney

I Know

I know at times I stop and glare
And I know at times you see me stare
I know at times I dream of you
And I know at times you know I do

I know of times I've looked at the sky
And instead of stars I saw your eyes
I know of times I've listened to a love song
And all I did was cry, I cried for so long

I don't know if this feeling will ever end
And I don't know if I can go on with you as just a friend
All I know is when you're near
This feeling inside does not disappear

I know if I had one wish to be granted
It would be this
That when you look at the sky
Instead of stars you would see my eyes

Melissa Rolon

Needle and Thread

She was as thin as thread
and I was about the size of a needle, with one eye open
Together we would patch our quilt of life
and mend the tattered edges
and patch the holes
from the wear and tear of our past.

The problem is; we couldn't sew
and never took the time to thread our needle
to patch our quilt of life.

So you see we never started
and may never have a quilt to cover us as one
which would comfort us for life.

J. D. Hall

Or Was It A Tear In My Eye...?

Have you ever had a star, sort of, "wink" at you...?
And immediately, it caught your eye?
Well, listen now and I'll tell you, a wherefore and a why...

He knew where he was going, as he stepped beyond this plane,
He knew where he was going, and there, what he would gain...
So grieve some less, dear family, for there is something, to do...
Just search among the stars each night, and he'll "wink" again, at
you...!

Lance P. Johnson

In Forward Motion

Through the buzz of bumble
and in the midst of tumble
My soul has never fumbled
its true intent

To be at one with two
To find the pleasure in the do
To bang the gong of bliss
To give the sun a kiss
To giggle at the gloom
To fly up to the moon
To anticipate the sate
To sate the anticipate
To spill upon the land
in knots of gems
and grains of sand
To show 'em my true grit
To horseback thunder along the

precipice

Scott LaFond

To Know To See Clearly

I viewed the world through distorted eyes,
And it came to me as no surprise,
That as I would lay at rest at night,
I dreamed a painting of delight,
A world of love, and peace, and care,
The colors spread out everywhere!
And as the night wore on and on,
So did this phenomenon.
But as the sun rose without hesitation,
The dream was torn from its destination,
The day went on, but nothing changed,
Though my thoughts were rearranged,
I wanted to do so much,
But the reality was something I could not touch.
And even though my mind held wonders,
My life was filled with thoughtless blunders,
So, like placing glasses upon my head,
I erased what I had once said.
And clearly saw what I could do,
To get out of my distorted view.

Stephanie Lynn Neifing

Words

Its good to say words that's on your mind,
And it is also good to say something nice sometimes.
Some actions speak louder than most words.
Words can make enemies,
Words can make friends,
And words can accomplish a lot.
So to get something done right give it all you got.

Words can hurt, they can abuse you,
Some people don't think they just act.
Words can make you sad and not know what to do.
Words can make you feel unwanted,
And that's a proven fact.

Words can make friends and they can please,
And they can help you have fun.
Don't listen to words that tease.
To settle an argument use calming words,
Not knives fist or a gun.
The right words will increase your chances,
To see the next rising sun.

Rosa Avent-Snead

A Lucky Penny

I found a lucky Penny
And it was shining just like Gold
I thought that if I wished on it
My Luck wouldn't be so poor
So I wished and wished for a lot of things
But only one came True
I found a Pot of Gold
At the end of a Rainbow's shoe
I carry this Penny with me
And wherever I go I have luck
So never Doubt a Penny
or else you'll get bad luck.

Katherine Kao

Horses

A horse is a beautiful creature,
With glowing skin.
Their delicate mane blows gently in the breeze,
As their muscular legs thrust forward,
Keeping the pace.

Emily Shannon

Dear Emily

When you love someone desperately,
And it's time for them to go,
You can't bear to see them leave you,
You want it to go so slow.

And they lay down so softly,
And their eyes close like nothing happened,
And they say to you before they go,
As they look to God above,
"Every raindrop is a symbol of my love.
My face maybe forgotten but my memories will not."

Rebecca Darke

Mommies Don't Get Sick Do They !

Sissy can skin her knee;
   and Junior can fall from a tree;
Daddy can get the flu, any day;
   But Mommies don't get sick, do they?

Baby can spit, burp, wet and cry;
   And Brother can hit a wall and hurt his thigh;
Little Sis can ride her trike in a reckless way;
   But Mommies don't get sick do they !

Mommies can be Cook; Chauffer;
   Mother confessor; Nurse and Doctor;
   Judge, Jury and the Law, we say;
   but Mommies don't get sick, do they?

God, we three are very small;
   but our Mommy got sick, so we wish to call;
Please help our Mommy, She's all we've got;
   show us Mommies were made from your strong heart;
'Cause, PLEASE GOD - Mommies don't get sick do they !

Leekay H. Bennett

Stand Alone

Stand alone only to be scorned
And labeled as an unconformed.
Rise among kneelers, who worship their
Society, and you're a heathen in despair.
Be different, but harmlessly so, and
You'll feel the touch of critics' hand.
They turn their backs on lone free men
For they need, love the slavery on them.

With gelatin legs and lack of sureness and
A foolish need for others, they all stand
Or none at all stand. They don't know just
What freedom from them is, as they must
Dwell where they are most familiar in.
Pity these people for that they sin
Against themselves, cheating their own
Of a born right to stand alone.

Raymond E. Williams

His Violin

He takes it in his hands
   and makes it sound so beautiful.
   He plays it with a gentle touch.
   His fingers touch the strings
   and with the other hand,
   he takes the bow
   and slides it across the strings.
As the rosin and steel combine,
   it makes the melody sound so soft, so beautiful.
That is the sound of a violin.

Michelle M. Goehring

Change Of The Universe

If man could change the universe,
And no animals were at hand;
Man would not have the food he needs,
To keep him fit to control the land.

If man could change the rivers and seas,
There would be nothing but streams;
Plants would die and boats couldn't sail,
And the land would be bumps and seams.

If man could change the height of man,
So everyone would be medium tall;
Some things would never be reached,
One would have to wait for them to fall.

If man could change the thoughts of man,
And everyone would seem the same;
There would be no Big I's and Little you's,
As no one would be judged by title or name.

But after all it's not left to man,
To judge things by what he sees;
The Supreme Judge of the Universe
Knows what is best for you and me.

Mildred M. Tucker

To Sit For Just A While

Out on a cold and dark windy night
And not a friend or stranger anywhere in sight

Every step taken seemed like a mile
And yet I knew I'd be there, if just to sit for a while

A flickering light was all I could see
And yet the closer I got, I knew it was only just a dream

A shadowing figure, her voice in my head
If I could sit for a while, I could remember my friend

Life's memories before me and more miles to walk
With only my thoughts to amuse me, without words to talk

Like the silent cries of a lost wren in its search
For the nest it had left, where it once had perched

With the wind having shifted and the darkness now gone
I reach for that door that has taken so long

A touch of her face, her warmth, and her smile,
And now a moment to rest, and to sit, for just a while.

Sandy Soucy

The Dance

Well, night finally came
and not even the music can save me now.
I no longer dance
I'm not even sure I remember how.

My life was the dance
as I sought the ultimate melody.
Lost in the moves
Seeking the music to validate me.

I danced through the years
In the background the music began to play,
but my dance was lost
when I heard what the music failed to say.

I no longer dance
I'm not even sure I remember how.
Well, night finally came
and not even the music can save me now.

Seward

Fairy Tale Blue

I think of you when the sky is cold
And on inviting and violet ribbons
Dividing the gray you come out of hiding
You enter my mind mostly in the month of May
When the sky is blue and an old calliope
Plays a love song
I think of you when the scent of violets
and lilac linger in the air I wish you were
Here I think of you when I see the honeysuckle
Vine with its sweet smell climbing between
The Roses Roses
I think of you when a summer breeze softly
Touching my face I remember a place
A soft embrace I can hear you whisper
Your lips look like Roses Roses

Ruth Culver

Quiet Time

Have you ever sat with some quiet time,
And really listen to what is in your mind.
There's no better place than you can be,
Cause this is where we have our history.

A store of memories at your beck and call,
Glad ones, sad ones, short ones and tall.
Let them come forth, let them flow,
Select the ones you want, let the others go.

Think back on times that make you feel good,
That make you smile when you remember.
A picnic, a play, a special Christmas Day.
A first love that was sweet and tender.

A place that is yours, and yours alone,
That you don't have to share with a soul.
A heaven where you can hide if you want,
A place no one else will ever know.

And when you are done you can tuck them away,
To be waiting for you on some other day.

Cause when the urge is strong to escape again,
You'll truly find your memory is your very best friend.

Mary Wizner

Keep the Moment

Watch the moon when it shines down upon your face
And see the beauty in both with a haunting trace
Catch the stars as they shine beneath your beauty
And the sun as it sets for you like a glowing ruby

Smell the air as it purifies the soul of our love
And the way the breeze carries the silent dove
The rustling of the leaves as they part when you walk
And the silence of the world when you start to talk

The lily pads on the pond float gently as you pass by
And mother nature becomes quiet when you sigh
Keep the moment and look around for someone like me
Turn your head, I'm there for you always to see

Glance at yourself as I see you in my eyes
Looking at you truthfully, telling no lies
See if you can feel the excitement that life sees in you
And notice all the magic that only you can do!

Ralph Banks

Through A Glass Darkly

Have you ever looked through a glass darkly,
and seen to the core of your soul?
Are the memories too harsh to be dealt with?
Do you know for whom the bells toll?

Stark visions appear through a gloomy mist
though twisted and cloaked they might be;
images permeate the cloud-filled view,
and the forms become you and me.

In perplexing pattern we dangle there
to come forth and go at my whim.
To stop the vision, I close my eyes tight,
and all becomes murky and dim.

Narrow corridors grotesquely move on
as our sins and foibles come clear.
Beware should we judge others too harshly
lest avenging angels appear.

As you focus your eyes and slowly bring
the accusing finger to view,
and gaze deep in the glass, you soon will see
the finger pointing back at you.

Ruth Warner

Spin a Lacy Web

There was once an arachnid; well really just a spider,
And she wove a silky web, just as soft as fluffy eider.
She was ebony and orange. Argiope was her name,
Which was so hard to say, other spiders called her Mame.

"Oh, my, Mame!" Called her friend from the fencepost down the way.
"Oh, Oh Mame, come and help me, for my web's about to fray."
"Here I come." Mame replied as she loosed her spinneret.
And she wondered to herself how Aurantia could forget.

"Now remember that the warp is just radials or spokes
Made of dry strands of silk as you learned on the oaks.
Then you follow with the woof moving outward in a spiral.
This one's sticky, better oil it, easy...easy, be careful."

Aura tiptoed octopod with the drag line out behind her.
Mame stayed close by her side to be there to remind her.
Aura made one turn around, then a second then a third;
She became so excited that she twittered like a bird.

"Oh look, Mame, I have got it. It is working okie dokes."
Aura spun around in circles as she spiraled down the spokes.
Mame danced around behind her checking each day every cleat.
And the two of them together fairly flew on fairy feet.

Sylvia N. Andresen

Mother

Please come and explain this question dear brother,
And tell why all children love their mother.
She's the heart of the home, and the center of love,
The teacher of faith, from heaven above;
The sweet gift from God, the dearest of dears,
The choice of all children and guide through all years.
She's the best of all gifts and has a heart of pure gold,
They shall always love her, no matter how old.
She's lover of father, of daughter and son,
The nearest to them, the Appointed one.
She's all that she lives for and prays for alone,
That her children will live in the sweetness of tone.
The choice from Creator and no one, no other,
And that's why all children, love their mother.

Lucille A. Lupo

Things Which Live on Departure

The old wanderer moors his flat boat
And staggers up the bank to pluck wisteria flowers.
His arms are long; his fingers are light and knobbed, like bamboo.
The mountain water waves its vacant blue
as he treads on thorns and brambles
pursuing the glint
of falling petals filling the folds
of a mist which hovers
to engulf him
then scatters

green rushes with red shoots

Beyond him lies an eggplant field;
a soft patch of agriculture.
Separating the rows are long stripes of dried mud
five inches high; set on edge.

He stoops to look.

The walls are patted mud
with fingerprints
dried around each root.

Tara Kelly Walworth

Meet Me

meet me at my front door
and take me away from this place.
take me to your world,
that place————far beyond vital flame
and across the unknown seas.
take me to your world of passion and love.
take me away from these modified cities
and cultures and non-active conversationalist logs,
rolling through this eternal river
of pollution and hate.
take me to your pure world
of dreams that will come true....
your world of passion and love.

Tracy Kelly

A Glorious Day

It's a glorious day with the sun overhead
And the beauty of God at our feet—
The rainbows stretching from sea to sea
With the magic for us to greet.

It's a glorious day with the green of the grass
And the clouds with their pillows of cream—
The scent of the flowers and the smiles of our friends
And the magic of power to dream.

It's a glorious day with the love of God's hand
Changing colors of scenes as we talk —
With the labor of love of our dreams that we share
And the magic of Him as we walk.

It's a glorious day when your job's well done
And our rest is well earned at night—
And the strength we've gained for another day
Shows the magic again is so bright.

Roberta Brehmer

Now I Know

I had a dream that I was flying
Above the clouds, beyond the stars shining
Up ahead I saw a mystical glow
A light in which only one would know
In this dream that seemed so true
There's much more to life than what we knew
I was lifted by light and now I know
That everyone's life is a mystical glow

Sasheen Knorr

Steal My Heart Again

You used to be the constant in my day
and the dream of my night.
For so long I could not tell you just how I felt.
What would the elders say.
You knew it too but could not act until the last
and I would not let you.
You already stole my heart, I would not let you break it.
You have chosen to live by Body and Blood,
a force I can not come between.
But you've come back to say hello
and remind us of what we know is there and always will be.
You steal my heart again, I can not let you take it.
I was in love with you and told you it was
just the idea I loved.
What else could I say to comfort myself
knowing you would have me only for a friend.
I will always be in love with you.
But you've come to say hello again and
have me believe that soulmates are just as sweet.
Please steal my heart, I will let you make it.

Leah Gruczkowski

What's To Blame

The sound pounds through the night,
and the one to blame is out of sight.
Constant war is what life has become,
a fight to live free for some.
As one hangs his head in fear,
he sheds a word from his heart as a single tear.
What seems to be wright is really wrong,
and a silent scream is a saddened song.

Mae Gunn

Alone

Until the screaming voices die in her head
And the path of justice is no longer exclusive
She will walk alone

Until men of all color, of all beliefs
Can share a seat with their differences
She will sit alone

Until men are praised for standing up for their rights
And liberty awakens those ingrained with prejudice
He will speak alone

Until men may eat, sit, and learn wherever they please
And can have peace with their fellow man
They will fight alone

Laura Dianne Eschbach

Out of My Hands

Finally the deer is here
And the rest is up to me.

If I shoot it
What shall I do with it?

So I quickly run through my options,
I can eat him or I can mount him.

As he continues to eat
He gives me a look starting from my feet

We stare eye to eye, and I feel I'm in prison
Staring me down, as if he were making the decision.

So I climb down from the tree,
Simply because this deer made up my mind for me.

Neil W. Simon

The Little White Pup

I often think of country and home
And the things we called our very own
A little white pup brought so much joy
to one little girl and boy

The love our little white pup showed
every step we took, he also made
He followed us on the road one day
He was hit by a car, along the way.

The driver said our pup was dead
We walked away, oh the tears we shed
As we walked back toward our home
There set our pup, on roadside alone

We picked him up with love and care
his back legs where broke, we couldn't leave him there.
We fixed a nice basket for his bed
we were so happy, little white pup wasn't dead.

Our Dad said that pup must go
he can't live in Basket, you kids must to
we cared for the pup, the days passed away
Then one day he stood, ready to play.

Rachel Powell

Bury Me At Arlington

Bury me at Arlington, near the Potomac, where the grass is green
And the tomb of the unknown soldier can clearly be seen.

If there is to be a eulogy, let it be said
That I was proud of being a soldier, and desired to be
buried among these dead.

Let it be said that I answered the final roll call, and now I sleep
That I served with the noble, and walked among the meek.

They may speak of the contents of my character,
But not of the color of my face
For men of Liberty and Justice are not bound by race.

And as I lie beneath this hallowed ground
Let my spirit steer by the blast of the bugle's sound.

Tommie L. Davis

I Saw Him Just Today

They thought they had killed Him as on their face they wore a grin.
And they were confident they had killed His power.
But I saw Him just today in the kids at play.
And I saw His face in every flower.

They stabbed Him with a spear and they had no fear
Of this King they had just crucified.
But I saw Him just now as my head I did bow
And earlier I saw Him when I cried.

They took Him to a tomb and though they had sealed His doom.
They all laughed as they walked away.
But I see Him all the time and He's looking fine.
I know cause I saw Him just today.

Never a greater shame has been or will ever be again.
They thought He was dead as they had their way.
But I want you to know that it just isn't so.
For I saw Him several times just today.

They thought they had won but God will never be outdone.
And in eternity they will all be paying.
People still think today Christ is out of the way
But oh I saw Him today as I was praying.

Pat Drummond

Complications

There are things I want to say,
And things I want to do,
But when it comes to you
My voice becomes quiet and my body stops.

Any act seems clumsy and words irrelevant,
So I do not do what needs to be done,
And that helps no one.

I miss the ease which we once had,
And long for the awkwardness to disappear.
I hurt you as I try to recover from my hurt,
And the situation becomes more complex.

How can I tell you I miss you,
When we do not speak?
How can I hug you,
When any touch from you makes me want to cry?

So I sit and wait,
Waiting for the hurt to disappear.
Knowing that it won't until,
I say what must be said,
And do what must be done.

Patricia Jacqueline Scott

A Road We Do Not Know

Time is a mirror, we've seen this all before
  And time is a river rolling, never finding shore
And time is a healer, an always open door
  Time lets us all go home, on a road we do not know

There is a journey, a walk we all must make
  There is a season, when the green does fade
There is a harvest, and then there is a spring
  There is a circle, an ever-present wind

I had a dream, one night she came to me
  She touched me softly, whispered to me in my sleep
She said "don't fear the darkness, it is eternity"
  There is a rhythm, everyone must keep

And there is a bridge we cross, into another life
  Where finally we are equal, even simple men like me

There is a road we go down, that we do not know
  There are seeds we've planted, that will forever grow
And if life is a cycle, we may be birthed again
  Forever ending, begin again....

L. S. Reynolds

Farewell to a Friend

A soul soared free
  and unfettered by pain, suffering, sorrow
Winged back for one last look at love left behind.

My heart whispered, Go.

I would have you here, but I would not have you
  suffer as you have, pain without surcease.
My greater wish is to have you at peace.

Go beyond the vale and wait there for me
  for I will come... in time.
The time will shorter be
  for you than for me.

Her spirit swooped low
  as though she would remain.
Then with a wrenching cry
  She was gone.

A tear glistened on my cheek
  from my eye?
    Or hers?
Goodbye.

Victoria J. Kent-Nistas

Untitled

I look in the mirror
And what do I see
I see a stranger
Right before me

Eyes dark and empty
Your heart so cold
Where did she go
I do not know

I miss her laughter
With her spirit so high
That smile of her's would light up the sky
Where did she go
I do not know

I look at you now
And can not find
That person I knew
Deep inside

Nancy Mickens

Saved By Love

I didn't know it would hurt me; I wasn't even told.
And when I drank it; my parents didn't scold.
For many years I used it; that seemed the thing to do.
I really didn't understand what I was going through.
It made me very happy, or at least that's what I thought.
Until it finally dawned on me; in a nightmare I was caught.
The torment was awful; my health began to fail.
I couldn't keep my mind on work; I even went to jail.
Thank God it's finally over, thanks to a loving wife,
I have now found real joy, in an alcohol free life!

O. B. Harold

DJ

The Rineys had a daughter, they named her Donna Jeanne,
And when she first emerged on earth they knew so by her scream!

Each counted all her fingers, then counted all her toes,
But what they hadn't counted on was jet black hair...who knows?!

She traveled home to live with them, delighting relatives.
Dad took time away from work, for all his love to give.

She went through several birthdays, each one older by a year,
Until she had her Sweet 16...who knew it was so near!

She turned into a lady, almost over night,
And they could not but notice, child - hood had taken flight.

Next year she'll be a senior, at good old Nolan High.
Some future date she'll graduate...let's hope it's not July!

A. Riney

Unceasing Love

I the ocean and you the beach,
together we will always be.
I shall come each day to you,
and cover your heart with love that's true.
Although I leave throughout the day,
I shall always return to you and say;
Don't be afraid, I'm always in reach,
I left my love with you, the beach.

Debby Borrer

Feelings

Have you ever felt alone, like nobody cares?
And wish there was a place where
everyone has smiles and everyone is happy?
Where nobody fought and nobody argued?
Where nobody cried and nobody died? Have
you ever been so mad and nobody understood
that you want to tear up your insides like
nobody would? And wish there was someone
who could understand and would listen to you
not by using their hand? Have you ever
felt so sad and just wanted to burst in tears,
cause of the worries and the fears? And sad
memories and bad memories all cooped up in
your head, that make you feel like you want
to be dead? And you just wish that
someone understood, but no one does, and
that doesn't make you feel too good.

Malitza Rivera

Space

As I looked upwards towards the sky
and wonder to myself the reason why
there's darkness out beyond the light
that goes on into infinity long past night
space the great unknown dark and
foreboding yet tantalizing to the mind
to know what lies beyond the distant stars that
glow like burning ambers in the heavens, as
beacons perhaps lighting the way
to others worlds who's to say
does man's destiny lie in space
the last frontier to conquer, or is this vision
out of place, is it the Creator's will that man
succeeds to spread his seeds of pestilence,
war and greed
all this I ponder as I gaze at that vast
domain that is know as space

Manuel J. Morris

For God, Is Always There

When everyone has dressed and gone
And you are left all alone
Just stand by, with a welcoming hi
For God is always home.

When the world closes in on you
And you find your life's a frown
Hold your head, and smile so wide,
For God won't let you down.

When your heart and soul feel empty and bare
Your skies are gray and you're very scared
Have no fear, don't drop that tear,
For God, He's always there.

Marsha Sockwell-Cox

Can't Sleep?

When the day is done and you're ready for bed,
And you have crazy thoughts running through your head.
Just think of a place that you'd rather be,
A beautiful place that you'd like to see.
A place where its sunny, quite and free,
A place like that you could die to be.

Just think of these places you'd want to be instead.
It will ease those crazy little thoughts running through your head.

Laura Griffin

Untitled

Has our country descended to such depths that people cannot treat
one
   another with respect?
Walk into a prospective employer's office
Take your time filling out an application
Be interviewed by a Human Resources person
Be told your application will be processed and you will be advised
Be called back a week later and sent to yet another individual for an
   interview in your respective area of work

At home you feel you will be selected
They appeared to like you, the interviews went well
You wait and wait for their call
Finally, you phone and are informed they are still waiting to verify
   your employment and references
One month later you are still calling
Now no return calls, no rejection letter, no nothing
Do they think we have no feelings?
Do they think we do not wish to keep our self-esteem?
Can they not realize even a computer generated form letter would
keep
   our dignity intact?
I guess not.

Has the world ascended to that pinnacle where human kindness
towards
   its fellow man has disintegrated?
If so, where do we turn?
Dare we even contemplate the twenty-first century?
I think not.

Patricia Anne Quigg Lynch

Retreat

No longer does the sloshy rain
Any artistry dare acclaim
For splatter-painting ochre polka dots
Over unkept yards and empty lots;
No longer awkward need to puddle jump
From slippery mound to sliding hump,
On paths flanked knee-high by weeds and grass
Slapping wetly at you as you pass

No longer inch deep water-mirrors show
Huddles of coy dumpling clouds below;
The winter rain has lost it's will.....
For everywhere the daffodil
Has caught the sun within it's cup,
And so the rain
   just plain
      gives up!

Virginia E. Wagner

Golden Angel

Her world shines for it is hers to wrap in golden sunlight.
Any spirit that can bask in that eternal light will see through
deception of the abyss that is night.
She is an angel in lives' masquerade, and I have seen through her
disguises.
You cannot hide a purity of spirit for it will shine through.
It will lead you to what your essence knows to be true.
I have made positive identification through observation.
I have spent endless days and nights in a dreamland of
contemplation.
All of the love that there is in the world,
and all of the love that will ever be,
that is what she means to me.
She is an angel with a celestial body.
Eyes with eternal starlight shine.
What passions hide behind the glowing orbs?
The mysticism of women is hard to define.
They burn themselves into the consciousness of the universal mind.

R. Dale Smith

Dare to Discover

Dare to discover magical things, things that can fly without
any wings.
Dare to discover things that can scare. Boo Bang Bam
Do you dare?
Dare to discover magical tales under the sea, or even whales.

Dare to discover water or land or even things that fit in
your hand.

Dare to discover the great Outerspace, for someday soon,
we may leave this place.

Dare to discover songs with rhymes, music to enjoy all
the time.

Dare to discover a magical book, set your mind to it
and take a look.

Sarah Kuhn

Baldness

For a head of hair, I would gladly pay
Anything to rid myself of this ugly toupee
I want hair to call my own
Hair to brush, hair to comb.

Hair recedes from the front and falls off the top
When will this shedding ever stop?
Massage the scalp - hair follicles need blood
Take a shower - hair down the drain on soap suds.

Hair combed from the sides and the back
All because of the hair I lack.
Hair fall out - on the pillow, sink, and floor
I don't want less, I want more.

Minoxidil my bald spot
Rub some Couvre on my scalp
Cover my head with some hair
Like snow atop the Swiss Alps.

With age my hair gets thin and fine
Please God, give me hair I can call mine
Pills, creams, hair plugs will make me poor
When will doctors find a lasting cure?

Mark L. Taff

First Sight

Long are most days and hard are the hours within when you
are alone. There are times when love is easy to find, it is
like a feather in the wind which rises and falls and finally
dips and clings to your clothes, it has found you and you're
stuck. Others times, you're the feather but, the winds play
tricks with your flight and, other times, it is the object of
your clinging desire which turns and blows you off and away of
whatever reason. That rejection in your face works like Mace:
it turns you nauseous, brings tears to y our eyes and leaves you
disoriented. Still, the worst scenario of all is the floating
feather which hovers close by, at times doing twirls for you
attention but goes unnoticed until too late— or worse yet—
never noticed at all.

Michael A. Barros

Our Parents

You are our candle so bold and bright
You shine in the morning and still in the night
There are times when we smother and cause you to choke
You start to flicker and throw out some smoke
There are times when your light becomes dim and low
Just think of good times and watch your light glow
In each of our hearts you gave us some light
An eternal flame, that burns big and bright

Annette Schau

Under the Mimosa Tree

The nocturnal winds beneath the stars
Are blowing west from the sea,
And sunrise is waiting in the wings
To illuminate the branches of the mimosa tree.
How small seems the universe.
Should we grieve in summer our haunting vision of solitude,
Our names spelled in the pink petals of the mimosa tree?
Should we lust for silence,
A secrecy for the paltry self,
Bathed in the colorings of Eden,
Earth-stained, tear-stained, fire-and-water stained?
As those who understand the empty void,
Ought we give advice to the somberness
And honor the eagle's sweep?
Must we continue to submit to a twelfth-foot of this and that?
The universe is as blanket and, for now, I unfold it beyond my space,
And the day after I will double it in my fingers
Until it is all white in my hands.

Roger Keith Lewis

Mirror Image

I, for one, have no doubt she is ugly both inside, and out. Her eyes
are dim just as her life, she will never marry and be a wife. She
is an error of Yours, Your first, she is a sin and of course will
never amount to anything. And yet, You are always there to hold her
snug in Your arms, tight, never far from Your reach, not even Your
sight. You serve her as You would a queen and yet she does not even
deserve the privilege of being seen. You make her problems Yours as
if it is a part of Your chores. The question should not be why I
cannot just leave it be but why You choose not to face reality. Why
do You tend to her every need? Why do You hear her cries? Why do
You listen to her false pleas and her constant lies?
Your mental presence has provided stability but all she has to offer
is the destruction of Your very own credibility. You have given her
so many gifts, and still she believes that You do not exist.
Why did You create such a being? Is it possible that You were
incapable of seeing clearly, or did You merely give her the breathe
of life for the sake of giving? I know I should not question Your
authority. And it is quite obvious that You know more than me,
but You must also remember that when she says I, no matter how much
I do not want that to be, she will always refer to me.

Melissa Abrahams

An Ode to my Grandmother

I often sit and wonder, as I gaze upon her face
are those frowns of toil and woe are those frowns of age?

This woman who has been so kind who has a heart of gold,
who has labored long and hard and conquered feats untold.

This woman whose wretched body has grown so frail and old
whose mind dwells in senility, for nature's taken it's toll.

This woman who bore so much pain, in such an artful way
whose strength and soul grows weaker with each passing day.

This sweet and gentle woman who took me in her home,
who reared, taught and loved me as though I were her own.

The joy and happiness that she gave can never be repaid
if all the worldly riches were bestowed upon her today!

I'll be as good and kind to her, as she has been to me
when I grow old and feeble, myself in her I see.

I hope someone will sit and wonder and gaze upon my face
and think of me in gentle terms of kindness and loving ways.

Wylene Cooper

Stalker

He watches her and she knows it.
Around every corner, she peers
Hoping he isn't there waiting for her.
In class she feels his presence,
But is unaware of who he is.
She feels his cold eyes piercing her as she talks to others.
Never does she walk anywhere alone.
She fears even in her own dorm.
The phone is an enemy itself.
Her roommate screens all calls,
Worrying, too for her friend's safety.
Cautious of every move she makes
And every person she talks to.
Fearing for herself, from someone she doesn't know.
Tear streaked cheeks, from crying after each uneasy feeling.
He tells her he doesn't want to harm her,
But she doesn't believe his notes,
Or his eerie voice that she hears on her voice mail.
His haunting voice constantly professes-
"All I'm hoping to do is steal a kiss from my Goddess in pink!"

Shannon-Elizabeth Kelly

The Writer Sits Alone

The writer sits alone
  Around three in the morn
When most of the world has gone to bed
With thoughts of stories, going around in his head
Taking shape of a song or a poem
  The writer sits alone
    At his desk, in the corner of his home
Each time on paper, a new adventure is born
Using a eraser, that's old and worn
But he is or will be, the author that's well known
The writer sits alone
  For him, stories published in the future ahead
Or poems sold, money coming in instead
All the staying up late, effect and time he does
  get his rewards
But in his mind, there's a thousand, more waiting
  to be told
The writer sits alone
  Around three in the morn

Mary Foucault

The Night Of The Tornado April 3, 1974

Darkness came early that long dreary night,
as clouds hid the bright setting sun.
Tornado warnings were sent over the air,
this dark Wednesday night of gloom.

The lightening was flashing, the thunder rolled loud.
Over the Daniel Boone mountains that night.
While thousands were wondering as the twister drew neigh,
is it possible it may pass me by?

The hills of Kentucky, the valleys and plains.
The cities and towns by the score.
Set helpless in the pathway of this monster of death,
that cares not for rich or for poor.

So wild and so angry, so swift and so strong,
that tore, ripped and scuttled the land.
These ruthless tornadoes, we all must agree,
have actions and deeds just like man.

Sam Davis

Untitled

The smoke made circles in the air,
As did his words.
My head felt too heavy for my neck
So I propped it against my sticky palm,
And watched the gray clouds
Curl toward the ceiling.
It was much too late for me.

I couldn't understand what he was saying anymore
But I don't know if the mud was in my ears
Or in his mouth.
The garbled sounds reaching my brain
Made me sleepy
So I closed my eyes.
Though I still smelled the smoke
And I felt his hand touch my face,
It was much too late for me.
The sleep I fell into was inevitable,
But I wish I could have watched him
Snuff out his last cigarette
And listened to the end of his story.

Robin Allison

Celestial Symphony

Darkness gently sweeps across the sky,
  as dusk prepares for evening's symphony.

Faint, twinkling stars; the mellow flutes
  of heaven, take their cue as wispy clouds
  stretch overhead - God's stringed section
  taking center stage.

Orion in all his majesty rises in the east
  as a baby grand piano and the heavens
  swell with rich, harmonious resonance.

Bright cello stars chime in while dancing
  planets pirouette with graceful elegance.

Maestro Moon in shining splendor does his thing
  and then,
As tho by magic dawn's faint lights appear
  . . . another day is born and Heaven's Rhapsody
  concludes.

Rose M. Juneau

Willard McGraw

There once was a man named Willard McGraw,
As fine a man as you ever saw,
And all were cheered by his friendly smile
For he took the time to sit awhile.
He told them jokes and their troubles shared
And everyone knew that Willard cared.

As the years went by, their struggles done,
His good friends passed on one by one,
And faithful Willard his comfort gave
As he stood and wept at each open grave.
But later on, then Willard, too,
Grew old and weakened, as people do.
So when it came time for his life to end,
Though he'd been at the funeral of each dear friend
When he'd buried them all, and his dearest Liz,
No one was left to come to his.

Lucy Hassell Davis

The Kiss

Her beauty radiated an almost warm glow
    as he entered the room to wake her,
    the one he had held all night
    with her naked body next to his.

So silent was she in her slumber
    that he only knew she still breathed
    by the rising and falling of the silk sheets
    that lay upon her unclothed bosom.

He felt the air that passed from between her lips
    softly waft over his own,
    as his lips neared her slowly,
    so to be sure they touched gently and passionately.

At first she lay, lips unresponsive,
    but gradually begins to press hers
    against his when her arms stretch
    around his back pulling his body next to hers.

So blossomed the kiss that she awakened to
    in the most blithe of spirits.
    So painful is his memory of this first kiss,
    of the last day he was with her.

Shamus Patrick

Feast

Rinds and acid drippings fade,
As I feast upon the pulp of my youth.
I lick the core and taste the sweet of your skin,
Smooth, golden, and pure - ripe for the picking.

Hung above my head, tempting my thirst,
You were untouched by greedy fangs and grubby hands
    and I worshipped your shine.

As I blessed your beauty, I ate the serpent's head,
Tasting the bitterness of regret sweep through my veins.

Now with mellow age, I gulp the juice
    as it dribbles down my chin,
A witness to a grand harvest.

Susan Cataro

Midnight

The moon shined bright across the trees,
as I knelt upon my knees.
    By your grave, I sat and cried,
why was it you that had to die?
    I knew one thing that would bring us close,
so I reached into my coat.
    Out I pulled my trusty knife,
and with it made one quick slice.
    Down my wrist I watched the blood flow,
now I'll be with you wherever you go.
    My life was yours, and yours was mine,
now we will be together throughout all time.

Michele R. Biddle

"Ship To Shore"

I was floating from wave to wave,
overlooking the island right in front of me.

I finally landed on the island;
on the outskirts of the land.

I hope I am able to travel to the center of the island,
where the pounding of the heart of the earth will be so warm,
I will feel safe and secure.

Diane Rogozinski

My Grown-Up Valentines Wish

Mom and Dad - I speak to you through my eyes
As I see through my eyes
I endure the silent thoughts that I wish I could say
To you from day to day.
You have loved me from day one
And I want to tell you affectionately some
Of the feelings that I, as a young woman harbor
For the parents and all parents as devoted as you are
Through my eyes I tell a story for everyone to see
But you are the only ones who really know me
Through the good and bad; the happy and unhappy
You've stuck by me through thick and thin and
    I appreciate it so endearingly
And though I am unable to tell you with words
I hope you will know that the gift you have given me
    I am forever grateful for
Life as other people know it is different than I live
And I don't know why I've been chosen to strive
So intensely for so many "taken for granted" tasks
But I know in my heart something I want to ask -
Will you be my valentine for the 21st year in a row?
I would be grateful and honored more than you know.

Leslee Renee Nance

An Indian Cannot Die

The warrior raised his trembling land
As if to cast aside this evil spell
The warm red life ran fast from out
That spear-pierced, bronzed, brown side

The warrior watched with steady eye
His own life sink below the prairie sand
His faltering breath came quick and dry
His fixed eyes dimmed and glazed

Oh Manitou, take not that war like soul
That youthful, high cheeked cruel challenge
An Indian cannot die!!!

Nancy Johns Kent

The Girl on the Seashore

With grace and beauty she adorns the shore
As, lazily, she strolls along the beach,
Collecting shells. The wind against her dress
Reveals a supple figure, slim and lithe,
And whips her dark brown hair against her face.
Her lips are pink as coral, full and sweet;
The hue of setting sun glows on her cheeks,
Kissed now and then with lashes dark and thick
As she stoops down to see what curious gift
The ebbing wave has washed up on the sand.
Her eyes mirror the deep blue of the sea,
Dark'ning as it drifts out to meet the sky.
Is she a jewel upon the seashore's breast,
Or does she wear its beauty as her crown?

Pat Boardman

War

The rain fell with all
Its might on that dark dark night.
The thunder crashed and the lightning flashed,
Making children shriek with fight.
The wind whirled round tearing everything down
Not stopping for innocent lives.
Everyone cries as everyone dies as they slip into the light never to return
But never forgotten.

Ben Shaw

Sailing Into Night

Another day turns into night,
as my ship sails on this peaceful sea.
My nights are filled with dreams of you,
as my ship sails on this endless sea.

Another day passes into night,
As my ship sails on a darkened sea.
My heart is full of our hopes and dreams,
as my ship sails on this silent sea.

Another day retires into night,
as my ship sails on this restless sea.
My heart cries out your name this night,
as my ship is tossed on this stormy sea.

Another day turns into night,
as my heart sails on the open sea.
My dreams of you I will always hold,
as my heart sails on an unforgiving sea.

Another day passes into night,
As my soul sails on this eerie sea.
My love for you will always endure,
as my soul sails over the deep blue sea.

Mathew G. Young

I Heard You Coming

Beautiful white moons are scattered here, everywhere
As pearls under the tree
And the tree picked up a branchful of beauty
And branched it out to me
This morning I heard you coming
And a little blue sky dropped out of my eye
And your hand picked up a handful of me
And handed it out to the tree
This morning I heard you coming
And it sounded like a hundred days of you
This morning I heard you coming
And my dreaming hands went gathering
Little blue skies, little green mornings...
Eye could possibly drop here and there
In my impossible dream. I heard you coming
Here, take, put it around your neck
I made it out of those little tiny blue skies,
White moons, black nights, green mornings
And my impossible dream as a string
I heard you coming

Shez Riff

You Are My Life

You are as exhilarating as a brisk, December wind
as pure at heart as a freshly, fallen snow
the warm fire that keeps my heart glowing
You are my Winter

You are the calm after any storm in my life
as gentle as a fresh, April shower
your eyes sparkle like the early morning dew
You are my Spring

You are the mountain stream coursing life thru my veins
the sunshine that illuminates the very depth of my soul
your passion burns deeply into every fiber of my being
You are my Summer

You are more breathtaking than any autumn landscape
being with you is a blessing I'm always thankful for
your spirit invigorates my entire world
You are my Fall

You are the reason for every breath I take
for every single second that I live
you put every beat in my heart
You are my Life

Martin Distelhorst

The Silence

The silence lingers around the room,
As she prays her life will make a change soon.
The silence is blurred through her murmured cries,
As thoughts race around through her burning eyes.

The silence roams throughout the halls,
As the wrath of death is making his calls.
The silence grasps and takes her mind,
Promised salvation that she'll never find.

The silence talks in cold whispered words,
And only the pain is softly heard.
The silence creeps in a motionless stride,
In thoughts of sadness; in echoes that hide.

The silence preys on her frustrated brain,
But nothing can take away this pain.
The silence remains and never goes away,
In the depth of the night or the height of the day.

The silence is shameless and has no fear,
It has no feeling and sheds no tear.
The silence continues and never leaves.
It has many faces, but never deceives.

Kimberly Cope

Elite Solitude

The day, laden and methodic, sighs relief
as stressors lessen and night breathes full...
listless whispers in the dusk
calm the spirit, enliven purpose spent...
Without hesitation, I surrender reason
and bestow my gifts to you, while others begin
their exchanges, their hearts belie their truth,
with hesitation and clouded judgements
they again summon courage,
suppress their desire and engage,
baring wearied bodies,
seeking love without giving,
discovering coitus without fervor,
encouraging freedom confined...
the world resolves to continue,
as I welcome the rhythmic adventure
that is ours...

Kellie Gibbs

A New Day

A new day awakened
As the dawn crept in
It's silence gently broken
By bare feet worn thin
From crushed pebbles on the path
That were taking their usual morning bath
Soaking in whatever came-
Be it sparkling sun or spattering rain!
And feeling neither joy nor pain.

Then close by - a wild flower awoke
Glanced about but never spoke
Her petals moved as the dew drops fell
If she were bothered by this - I could not tell

All nature suddenly seemed in a state of mirth
As the great shinning sun came in to warm the earth

I too smiled as I went on my way
My heart ever grateful for this another
New and glorious day!

Margaret Byassee

Deletion

It cuts like a butcher knife... to sever in pleasure
as the sinew crunches... and the last utterances die
to take another piece of meat...
off the grappling hooks of populace
and devour flesh-word cannibal
not bothering to close their mouths
    CHOMP CHOMP CHOMP
more creations wasted
on... if nothing else... blood shedding eloquence
sever prose with lightning quick taloned descent
come on... I know how ya love to...
    CHOMP CHOMP CHOMP
make mince meat my verse
come and shatter a decaying corpse
and feed it to the back of your hearse
to be laid in some unmarked grave
Phantasm smoky grin and electrocute me
with your byte
what control do I have?
But to believe you.

Kandy Carter

Untitled

You are dead to me.
As the tears of mourning
Roll down my face,
I remember your face,
Your arms around me,
Your lips on mine,
Your body next to mine.
A tear for each memory
Slowly rolling down my cheek.
Even though your body still walks the Earth,
Your soul is dead
And you are gone from me.
All I have is a few photographs
And the memory of us.
I mourn for you.
You are dead to me.
The tears fall gently like rain
As I whisper three words to your memory,
I Love You...

Michelle Golden

The Woman I Cannot Have?

To count the times I dreamt of the touch of her arms;
As they drove the loneliness from my body;
One would need to dedicate their life to figures and numbers.

To describe the satin touch I perceive in her lips;
As they communicate their feelings for me;
Limits created by our language render my thoughts indescribable.

The pain I must endure when I see her smile, talk, live, breath,
    exist.
I am helpless, in a cage, created not by me, but by my society.
There are rules I must follow, yet rules I hate.
There are no utterances of man I can use to describe this pain.

Yet, I do know the soother of my pain.
Like an antiseptic for my torn and bruised heart there is and will
    always be hope.
Hope that someday I can be held in her arms;
Be kissed by her lips; Be free to speak my feelings true;
All the while not having to endure the scorn of the ever watchful
    eyes.

As now, as much as it goes against my being,
I will deny my feelings and fear her look,
As I know she is the woman I cannot have.

J. Lawrence Kolb

To the Memory of Franklin D. Roosevelt

I saw old glory hang down her head
    As though she trembled and cried
When our dear president lay down his load,
    When our dear president died.
I see her flying half mast all day
    A symbol of sorrow and grief
Of a people who are mourning the loss
    Of their brave commander - in - chief.
But I shall see old glory raised higher again
    By hands that are strong and brave,
And millions of voices rise up to say,
    "Old glory shall ever wave!"
When she's proudly flying up there again,
    To his name let's send up a cheer,
For the man who gallantly fought to the end
    For our freedom from want and fear.

Lois C. Shepherd

Mother Earth

Mother earth.
As we move each day, she breaths.
She seeks a period when she shows her fear.
When the day begins to grow her thoughts expand.
As the day grows upon us, she shows an itch for excitement.
She thinks about what dangers might come for when she expresses
her feelings.
She feels our pain when we are in danger.
Mother earth doesn't have to worry about the pain of herself.
Having to hold it in, not expressing it to others.
She lets it out on the earth,
knowing full well that we can handle it.
As the day grows to an end,
Mother earth spends special time with her family planet,
keeping a hold of it as best as she can.
As she puts her west to bed she awakes her east.
Knowing full well that her day cycle is about to begin with a new
group of humans who believe in her.

Sarah M. Phillips

Someday...

When you put me away, someday,
    (as you really might have to do)
Remember my love of blue sky and green grass,
    And give me a room with a view.

And if I no longer can speak your name
And I watch blankly with unfocused stare,
Remember the caress of a mother's arms,
Say you love me, tell me you care.

Don't carry the grief of the choice you must make,
Be strengthened for what you must do,
But remember my love of blue sky and green grass,
And give me that room with a view.

Marian A. Hufnagel

Souls of the Dark Side

Crying through the nights of
darkness, dying through the depths of
tears. If you try to touch my eyes the saint
of death will soon arrive. If you try
to touch my eyes to see what
death will soon be like, touch
my eyes come in and see why
that death is inside of me.

Angela Crivello

Making Love

Making love to you
would be like eating dainty little flowers
with strange powers
that need no words to chew.

Danny L. Weiss

Generation X The Awakening

Will to change, but lack the boil of blood that sets the clay
aside from the soul that yearns to live. Ashe call ashe to
regather itself, reform, revive, no longer disconnected from
the purpose for which it was planted. Float like feather upon
the sour breath of change, blown from the sneeze of Father Time's
ruthless red nose. Up and down, drenched in the pus of apathetic
sores, open wounds left to fester in the shadow of aimless
revolution. Hear me not, see me not, touch me not with plastic
gloves, and polyester sport-jackets. Green hair and black silk
stockings, sharp fanged teeth that suck the nectar of past
purpose with no fresh vein of its own. Neon signs, aimless
rhymes, rusted dimes, in desperate times, echoes of the
disenchanted, homeless dwellings of an unknown people until
. . . THE AWAKENING.

Thomas J. Bradwell III

Reality

What can I be?
Asks the inner city child
With head held high and big toothy smile.
Don't aim too high the system reminds,
I'll always be there to keep you behind.
Public School oppression.
Slum livin' depression.
Concrete walls.
Piss in halls.
Crushing dreams, the children scream
Frustration.
Grab your bootstraps and pull them hard,
still you'll never see an ivy league yard.
College costs.
Borrow and beg to get higher knowledge in your head.
Then try to get a job but the market is tight.
Factories are closing and you can't sleep at night.
Still hold your dream of a white picket fence.
With goals out of reach,
the situation is tense.

Martina Bridgetta George Jackson

Reflections

A little girl stands in front of a mirror; her long golden hair astray.
She frivolously searches how to get in
She finally replies, "Can you come out and play?"
"Well I guess. But first I must tidy myself up." "Oh, me too!"
She goes to her mother's room to explore the closet.
Later, she returns looking like a princess
Dressed in the finest clothes and decorated with rich jewels and
    makeup.
"My! You look beautiful!" "Thank you. So do you!"
They sit down together and mother their dolls while drinking tea
Talking away with secrets and laughter.
As the day wears on the toys become scattered about
    along with the clothes and jewelry; make up smeared.
The little girl yawns, rubbing her eyes.
She jumps when her mother calls her for dinner.
"I'm sorry, I have to go now," she says sadly.
"Will we ever play again?"
"Oh yes! Don't worry about that. What great memories we now have,"
    she winks. And I find myself standing in front of a mirror.

Kirsten Weaver

One Without

Without a doubt, there will always be
At least one without - maybe for a lifetime?
Let's hope not! even for a blink-for it goes
On and on - so always without a doubt, there
Will be at least one without. Promises is
A promise - one accord a is rhythm, different
Sounds strange beats, lyrics heard, just can't
Seem to comprehend? Or won't - you know
The vision, now the quest - someone's journey,
One odyssey or all - for without a doubt, there
will be one without. The trapeze takes longer
for a once spectator - giving into the terror
that it's not optional - all aboard! - Opening,
And closing in the same paragraph - almost
Typical, or expected fate? - but the end may
Justly be - enough to ponder, anyway, for
Without a doubt, one's without. Reoccurrence,
More than just a breath - sure is natural,
to reply, to wonder or even to sort, but final
destiny comes to rest in favor of, for within
Now - was no doubt, once without.

Vera M. Wilson

Night Knight

The Lady of the castle has a beast in her dungeon's midst.
At night, the beast invades her sleep,
                              kidnaps,
and escapes with her to his lair.
One night an invitation she bestowed,
an invitation my heart would not miss.
Her mind, was troubled by her dungeoned demon.
My heart I conveyed to ease her dreaming.
The beast...
he went prowling
with a taloned fist, took the lady in one hand,
and my heart in the other.
My soul attempted a rescue.
Weaponless, human efforts futile.
On my knees a wounded wreck,
hearing her cries below the stone deck.
Her mind is strong; she will endure.
My heart I gave to ensure.

Terry N. McDowell

True Life Mystery

In search of ancient history a tragic true-life mystery.
Back through time tunnels of the past
A stirring prelude to the aftermath
of the way things are going to be.
Open your eyes and see repeated history.
There were heroes, Great battle stars,
When trumpets blew their fearful charge
Many would die before the days end,
Death and destruction one cannot comprehend.
Damn those who thoughtlessly kill
for the pleasure of their will,
And the treasure and the plunder.
For who can stop the cycles of war.
Who can justify what killings for.
Women and children starving once more,
Why can't man live without war.
is there no justice in mankind's heart,
Where in the world do we start,
Why can't man live without war
A son sacrificed, what for.

Thomas Seaman

Shadow And Sunshine

Tall, dark shadow, casting life's gloom
Bad times, black luck, aura of doom
Gleaming, bright sunshine, no worry, no care
Glowing within her, joy she will share.

Opposite worlds, like night and day
Shadow and sunshine pass on their way
Bold, heavy glances, light, feathery touch
Substance from the other, needed so much.

No shadow, there's no sunshine
No sunshine, there's no shadow
Together, one makes the other.
Linda L. Chandler

Balances

Balance of power,
Balance of trade,
Balances due, for the debts I have made.
Balance your freedom,
Balance your checks,
Balance your cards, are you stacking the deck?
Balance of reason,
Balance in rhyme,
Balance your interests, keep an eye on the time!
Balance is wisdom,
Balance your wits,
Balance your foot, in the shoe that it fits.
Balance of power,
Balance of trade,
Balances due, for the debts I have made.
Steve L. Grant

Threads of Steel

Threads of steel across the land as far as eye can see,
Barbs that rip and tear the flesh of cattle, horse and me.
Not long ago this land was owned as far as one can see,
By God and the government, and myself made three.

We got along real peaceful, no fence to mark our lot;
We understood each other, respect was ne'er forgot.
Then hooves and wagons charged across our still and
Virgin land; buffalo were slaughtered, it grew out of hand.

The red man lost his hunting ground, he had no place to hide.
Bereft of all his heritage, he fought hard for his pride.
Then came the scourge of settlers to settle on our land,
And with bloodthirsty fences made their stern demand.

Mile after rolling mile threads of steel were strung;
The death knell of our freedom was slowly being rung.
No more could deer or antelope graze as was its right;
Here on a rider took his mount with caution in the night.

Tho' it was sad to see all this, 'twas nothing we could do
But sit and think about the time the west belonged to you.
So now a way of life was gone, no freedom could I feel;
The open ranges that I loved have died from threads of steel.
Merle W. Kinne

Untitled

Lion's roar is an echo of an angry heart.
Baby birds squeak, tears a cry for help.
A dolphin's song calling upon the heart to smile.
Giraffe feeding on a tall tree.
Graze on hope, and stand proud.
Flamingoes dancing in the water.
Just be and create your divine salvation.
Conformity is for the birds.
Zebras galloping towards the sun.
Lisa Hofrichter

"Imagery"

A glimpse of light...
Barely seen and never heard
Softly sublimating the malevolent darkness
Slowly transcending the mystical bed of waves.

Rampant, it ascends with arrogance
Flaunting its beauty and power
Growing ever so fervent and bold
absorbing the insipid dark.

Its shape fatefully inveterate
the intangible form consoling
A glimpse of light...
Another day is born
Sergio Pineda

An Update of "Casey at the Bat"

Casey at the Bat - an updated ending: it begins with no two outs, the bases loaded and the nighty Casey coming to bat.

Then all heard Casey say,
"I demand a raise in pay."

The mayor stood before the anxious crowd
and said in a voice that was clear and loud,

"For all the hits we have Casey to thank,
so we're giving him the Mudville bank."

Then the umpire shouted
words which no one doubted,

"Not another pitch will be thrown
until my salary too has grown."

In unison the fans shouted, "Enough,
we don't want any more of this stuff.

To us it is quite plain
that you are all insane.
We're fed up with this new breed,
and with your terrible greed.
That's why we're not going to stay
and watch another play.

So you can take this game and stuff it.
Besides, the mighty Casey will only muff it."
Ray Sindermann

Knights Of Today

Hours come forth, fronted by duty's need,
Battle boundaries incised within our street.
Right and wrong turn face citing conflicting creed,
War upon morals once again shall meet.
Cloaked by armor's badge do tour take,
Weapons of choice being wit and will.
Force of good only few we make,
Against evil armies seem growing still.
Fights are fought with dragons slain,
Wounds are lanced as crimson flow.
Tears of sorrow and pain's scars remain,
Casualties survive lacking peace to bestow.
Vice's vengeance beset love's kind of heart,
Swords and white flag fall a world apart.
N. B. Schlepp

May No Child Live In Fear

If you're ever called upon, to raise a little child,
be kind and understanding, and loving all the while.

A child's the richest blessing, sent from God above,
and He has put His trust in you, to nourish them with love.

Children born into this world, have God's love deep within.
Help them make this love grow. Don't plant the seed of sin.

Show them by the way you live, a love that's warm and pure.
This will build the confidence, to make them feel secure.

May no child ever know the pain, that comes from child abuse.
To teach a child this way of life, there's never an excuse.

They're with you such a short time, so while they're still at home,
give them all the love they need, to make it on their own.

Have patience in correcting. Do so with loving care.
But never out of anger, for it only brings despair.

A hand is raised in anger. A child's eyes fill with tears.
A child learns to replace God's love, with hate brought on by fear.

So be a fine example, in all you say and do.
Show them love and kindness, for your child learns from you.

Of all God's many blessings, can any be as dear,
As precious little children? Lord, may no child live in fear.

M. Lanette Ross & John Porst

My Broken Heart

I knew when I first met you: That you would
be the one. No one had ever made me feel
the way that you have done.

When you gazed into my eyes: My heart began
to pound. I closed my eyes, and held my
breath, I could not make a sound.

You took me in your warm embrace: And held
me to your chest. I never knew such love
before or gentle happiness.

I thought our love would never die: You said
we'd never part. But here I sit in my room
just me and my broken heart.

Why did this all have to end: And the tears
have to start. What happened to the love we
knew: The promises we embarked.

Although your gone, your not forgotten. My
memories will never fade. Your in my heart:
And on my mind, for yesterday, to-day and
always.

Kay Wallace

Ocean Doth Beckon

The ocean doth beckon - the waves reassure -
be they short and sharp - or a gradual unfurl.
Sometimes quite prominent, strong, and a lash;
low the arrival, so rhythmically cast. Coolness
and strength, the current doth feel; a
dimension of coolness, yet uplifts one still.

The breeze so caresses, salty scent so
real; it's quite effervescent, the way one does
feel. A song of oneness, with God above;
the ocean and its peace, strongly beckons
all ones. In troubled times seek such,
rejuvenate life's plane; return then to life's
tumult, much peaceful for the same.

Lorraine A. Allard

Wall and Window

Not my eyes are blurred by the rain
Beating on the window, But the window is
Blurred because of tears standing in
My eyes, and yet, again and again, I cleaned window,
Because , the window is hazy and blurred,
All day long, I rub the window, as I would erase
The three words of a name, written on a paper.
A window-cleaner who knows how to repeatedly
Wipe a window can clean a rain swept window.
But my hand can not clear away my window's blur.

Even now, If I can wipe away the tears
Standing in my eyes, I will be able to
Comprehend why the window has seemed so
Blurred to me, the window, a soul of the wall,
Is opened towards the clear sky, and I see
The nature of living love which is sleeping in it.
For the body without the soul is dead, man is
Living inside the wall and its window, continually
Wiping the blurred window without cleaning away
The tears which stand in his eyes.

Young Sook Park

Stop The Killing

Beautiful ladies, coke and dope, don't forget, the liquor and beer.
Beautiful cars, and lots of money, please don't forget the diamonds, and gold. Shooting and killing for all these things, you will sure, serve your life in jail. Courtrooms, prisons, and jails are full, don't forget the ground, as well. Brothers and sisters, can't you see, all this killing, don't have to be. Old and young, those who kill, how can your heart, be real. The world will soon end, its the only way, all this killing will end!

My city, your city, the streets are not safe, drugs and guns, are here to stay. Jackets, shoes and sweaters, people are getting killed for them things, in all colors. Brothers and Sisters, watch the news, you always see a killer, on the eleven o'clock news. Old people, young people, crying, because they have lost a love one before their time. White people, White people, what's the fuss, your people is just like us, we all are going back, to the dust. There is none to blame, people doing this killing, don't have a brain. Courtrooms, prisons, jails, they all are full do the ground have room, for one more killed. Brothers and Sisters, this killing must stop, do I'm going to call, the Heavenly Cop, when he comes, it will be the end of all this killing and sin!

Robert L. Barham

Erin

When I think of her, beauty comes to mind.
Beauty that is like a rose but undying.
Beauty so great, that even the sight of her makes you happy.
Her face is as gentle as a babies touch
When she walks in room; it screams "I'm so happy your here."
When I'm sad she makes me glad just by being near me.
When I look in her eyes,
All I see is beauty;
In the way she walks,
How she talks;
The way she looks,
And how she acts, all I see is beauty.
To me she is all things of great beauty.

Ken Wagner

A Memorial To Mel

One day not long ago, the heavens rang with a song and a shout;
because a Saint of God, Mel McConnell, had come home without a
doubt.

In his robe of righteousness how beautiful and radiant he must be,
for Christ has promised to clothe all of his children in this robe
of immortality.

Through the veil this must suffice for you and me; Although,
at times it's difficult to just let things be.

He stored his treasures in heaven, where safe they would be;
This the Holy Spirit reveals with spiritual eyes to see.

Mel studied God's Word, and applied it for all to see. He not
only talked it, he walked it—a blessing to me.

He placed his faith in God and humbly followed his Savior by
the path he was led; Always with the knowledge that the Church
is the body and Christ is the head.

With sin Mel was not without, a man with feet of clay was he.
But, mercy our Lord did show as with Peter so long ago.

Mel has left us with a legend, a legacy I'd say, too fight our
battles valiantly and to share of that we have, each and every day.

Rebecca McConnell Peeples

Untitled

I am all alone,
because you're so far away,
but the love we have inside us,
I know it's here to stay.

When you are here beside me and I'm looking into your eyes,
our love it surrounds us, like the heaven and the skies.
When you look at me that way, I don't know what I should say,
but I think it would be all right,
if we let our love be the words tonight.

It's hard to live,
these lonely days without you,
but someday we'll be together,
because our hearts are true.

When you are here beside me and I'm looking into your eyes,
our love it surrounds us, like the heaven and the skies.
When you look at me that way, I don't know what I should say,
but I think it would be all right,
if we let our love be the words tonight.

Victoria S. V. Collins

Remember

Death by the doorway
Beckoning silently.
Tears steaming, I slowly nod.
My warm tears fall on his cold ashen face.
I whisper, "Remember me".
Staring at his bed,
Sweaty sheets clinging,
Twisted around his pained body.
Death finally looms, claiming him.
Carefree days since departed—
Days of love and joy.
Eyes closing, I remember...
..Hint of dawn, streak of blue, birth of day...
..June sun, soft swaying green grass, laughing carelessly...
..Ocean roaring; red, orange, crimson unfolding in sky, night
approaching...
Never forget, my love.
Death beckons all;
Someday I shall not stand alone.
Until then, sleep and remember.

Katie McCormack

What Would Jesus Do?

Lift high the Cross. Lift Jesus banner higher,
before neglected beings of earth's sinful social sty,
completely left alone and wasting time and money.
What would Jesus do? Let that be your theophany.

Behold, shyness shall depart at each forward advance,
the perfect answer comes quickly in every circumstance
to speak with enthusiasm, transforming interest
from your no purpose in life to spiritual existence.
The redemptive work begun by God's Holy Spirit
shall have effect on all displeasing resistance:
upon all men, all women, and all sinful nations,
brutality, squalor, hunger, and degradations.

Pledge to do what Jesus would do in joyous suffering.
all shall feel his touch not knowing how the changing
of old habits and certainly the antiquated view.
God's precious Holy Spirit will guide all the way through,
when you faithfully ask—"What would Jesus do?"

Shirley B. Rodabaugh

Ego

Journey far to the illusion hidden
behind thousands of screaming crimson masks
seek reality where pleasure is forbidden
screaming what hers, what yours, what my heart lacks
search the lonely black flame looking for death
entertaining life, seducing spirit
crawl to the eyes that will reveal green wealth
so maybe love's black center can taste it
paint the questioning whispers in your head
that try to intoxicate and promise
there is nothing here the master is dead,
but do not worry I gave a notice.
The sane voice of a dancing madman's tears
the fatal loving of a dead man's fears.

Kimon Yannopoulos

The Cry "Behold He Cometh"

It should be realized by the cry,
"Behold He Cometh"

With great zeal it should be proclaimed,
As we herald His mighty name.
"Behold the Lord Cometh"

It has been told long ago
By the ancient prophets of old
"Behold I come quickly"
"My reward is with me, for
My name sake I will up hold."

"Behold", the greatest of all event
For this cause He came into the world
For this cause was He sent.

He has made a supper as a token there of:
"Till I come do in remembrance of me".
His return is nigh even at the door
With wonders all the heavens shall see.

Thomas Miles

A Mother's Lament

To hold you again in my loving arms,
To feel the nearness of your enduring charms,
To change you, to bathe you, and dress you in pink,
To hold your little body while I give you water to drink,
To love you, to kiss you, to nurse and caress,
To tell you I love you, all this I confess —
Confess this to be my insatiable yearning
For my departed baby, my heart is burning.

Doris Stegall

Life

To be an angel you must have a lot of love in your heart,
Being an angel means doing your part,
Wouldn't it be nice to just fly away,
But we can't so we have to stay,
Wouldn't it be nice to live in a place where there is no hate,
And to all evil they just close the gate,
Wouldn't it be nice to just fly up above,
And all you'd feel was lots of love,
But here we are,
And heaven is yet so far,
But just wait,
Soon the angels will take you up to that golden gate,
But life takes so long,
Is it just me or is something wrong,
You live it day after day,
Sometimes you wish you didn't have to stay,
But we're here now,
Even if I don't know how,
And here is where we'll stay,
And watch ourself get older day after day

Samantha Star

"What About Me?"

When you found out I was going to be born,
Being my father you said you were not.
Of course that was sixteen years ago,
I still remember; you've probably forgot.
Now when you see me you ask,
"How's my daughter?"
I am still upset, now confused,
All of a sudden I have a father?
You will never be able to make up for all those years,
Just the thought of that brings me to tears.
Sometimes at night I cry out your name,
but you don't hear, it's not the same.
To my heart, Dad, you hold the key,
so I ask you this question,
"What about me?"

Tia Armstrong

Fifties Children

Are you part of the generation raised on fairy tales?
Believing in Prince Charming,
and castles
    and happily ever afters?
Did you Love Lucy and dream of being Queen for a Day?

Are you a Fifties child living in a sad world?
Where Prince Charming never comes,
and castles always crumble?
A place where happily-ever-afters
never stay happy... after?

Are you part of the generation raised on illusion,
who no longer gropes for security,
depending instead upon eternity?
Are you a Fifties Child, weighted down
with fairy dust on your heart?

Susan Prince

Sunset

    As I watch the colors dance in the sky and
the sun had just started it's descent on the evening, the
uneasiness of night, the fear and anxiety slowly crept into
the depths of my mind. Ironic how a time of such beauty can
give away to such blackness and man's mind created of such
innocence and love can give way to the sinister evil that
lies in the recesses of the human mind.

Evelyn McGovern

Soulmate

The air has an unusual freshness about it.

The young couple walk hand in hand along the path
beside the quiet pond.

Passing beneath a willow,
the wisps with their new pale green leaves
caress their faces and pass over their shoulders.

A fish jumps.
The splash pulls them from their private thoughts.
They watch as the concentric ripples emanate out
and pass across the water.

The pond is still again.

They turn to each other and pause.
Something unspoken passes between them.
Suddenly they know they love each other more than life itself.
They embrace and kiss tenderly.
A second kiss, again.

Arms around each other's waist,
her head resting against his shoulder,
they continue along their path.

The air has an unusual freshness about it.

Roger Engebretson

The Gunslingers

Said the baby grizzly to the sleepy little skunk:
    Bet I'm quicker on the draw—-
But that little sharp shooter precisely hit his mark,
    Before his challenger could even lift his paw!

I'm going to tell my Dad that you don't fight fair—-
    You turned your back as though to leave.
How could you take aim with your back to me?
    I think you had something up your sleeve!

He didn't fight fair Dad— I stink as I've never stunk.
    I'm a lot bigger than he; and I'm a grizzly bear!
When you gunnin; little champ—-
    You can't compete with all this modern warfare!

Now let's go down to the river, and while I fish
    You will scrub and scrub till you'll wish you hadn't fought him.
This salmon is a whopper; your mom will sure be happy.
If you don't get clean, your Mom, I know, will paddle your bear
    bottom.

Isn't Teddy kind of young to have B O? Seems strange to me—-
I've told him not to play with anything that might be black and white.
Where's your Avon underarm Dad, there still could be a trace.
I'll never challenge anyone again, till I have his face in my sight!

Walter V. Conklin

Between The Crosses

The war is over! But is it, though?
    Between the crosses, row by row
Are dreams and promises for young and old
    Buried before they could unfold.
Atrocities took place, too bad to relate
    Where humanism and love did separate.
Now bring forth the criminals at any cost
    Their privileges as humans have been lost.
Plaster truth with pamphlets instead of bombs
    Until truth is known, we are not done.
Bless those who only stand and wait
    Some were rewarded, some too late,
Perhaps in the quiet of guns now resting
    Love will come forth with God requesting
An inner peace we need to know
    To understand those crosses row by row.

Mary Loa Mathes

Ode To The Land

I look across the green field,
Beyond the creek with spring deep waters
and see the hill which rises ahead.

On that hill is a forest of pine trees planted by my Father,
as a boy scout, how long ago?

I walk the pipe line to the top of the hill
and can see the highway, a ribbon of black across the land.

Once killdeer nested there, driven out by the road makers.
And below I can watch cars of many models zapping past.

Ahead, I walk through the pine trees
over a rivulet and multitudinous rabbit holes.

On the other side of the hills is a valley, untouched by humans—
yet.

Pat Farr

Ancient Lessons

A luminous light bleached my tepee
Bidding me to seek its source.
Stepping through the opening I was greeted by infinity
Wanting to teach its course.

The sky was black, the air was crisp
The stars shown diamond bright.
They wanted to instruct me on simplicity:
Blindness vs. sight

I stood in hushed wonder
Beneath a hundred million stars.
Seeking their wisdom to open my vision
From beyond city shadowed bars.

The skies taught me volumes
As I watched with silent intent.
I then turned to the tepee with lightened up steps
My heart having been opened to the lessons star sent.

Rachael Singer

Woman

I am night and starlight, a spun silver dream.
Bitch Goddess, Queen of Night,
Ruler of the shadowy unknown.
Hecate is My name.

I am afternoon and sunshine, full flowing with emerald soul.
Earth Mother, Queen of Harvest Fine,
Ruler of the radiant here and now.
Demeter is My name.

I am morning and twilight, shrouded in pale aquamarine.
Queen of Death and Rebirth Rite,
Ruler of the exhilaration of springtime.
Persephone is My name.

For I am Nyx, First Daughter of Chaos.
And I am Inanna, Queen of Heaven.
I am the Snake Goddess and the Snake,
For I am Alpha and Omega, beginning and end.

For as I was there at the creation of the Cosmos,
So will I be there at it's termination.
And they that believeth in Me shall not die,
But live again and again!

Lori M. Temple

Arms Length Plus One

laying on a mattress streaming with sun.
Bittersweet ray drops fall on my face.
Tickling the moon with Iridescent fingers.
Stroking its check with the back of my hand.
landish desires far in my mind.
Forgetting my fears, my gloveless desire.
Laughing with urgency at absolutely nothing.
Tossing and turning, no desire to be held.
The thought of a touch sends shivers up my spine.
Tongue kiss my soul with lips so divine.
Closed marbles an altar of prayer.
Watch at a distance but always too far.
Tenacious mouth shaped like an "O"
Awaiting your bite to cleanse me pure.
Disguised with silver pennies in my eyes.
You'll never feel my breath on your breast.
The hot tears stinging your sleep.
Virgin pillows alone to hold arms length plus one.

Stephanie Burchard

Whisper...

I knew a girl with hair as
Black as night.
She had a soft, white face with an innocent smile.
Like a princess in a fairy tale.
She was beautiful.
We used to sit on the cold, giant steps of her house
And tell secrets. And laugh.
I don't know her anymore.
She has been charmed by popularity and swept
Off her feet.
Her smile no longer innocent now, but as cold
As the steps we sat on.
And it blends with her thick, black hair like a mask.
Her laugh has faded to a whisper.
She doesn't tell me secrets now,
She keeps them.

Lindsey Egge

Grandchildren

God made children little and tall
Black, white, yellow
And he loves them all,

He made us parents
To worry while our children grow
He made us know happiness
Far beyond what we'd ever know

He let us care, share and be there
To see them become a woman or man
And now, the magic moment came
When your child say's "mom were expecting"

Now again you worry and wait
It seems like just a moment ago
The Dr. Handed them to you
Now your pacing, waiting and finally
God has completed his miraculous chore
He's outdone himself in every way
Because finally comes that wonderful day
The Doctor says "Grandma, Grandpa" right this way!

Rachelle LaVine

Death's Call

Castle peaks reach in the night,
Block built walls keeping out the light.
Emaciated bodies lean on the gate,
Corpses lie in ghastly wait.

Strewn about, sheets where they have bled,
Women and children on blood soaked bed.
Coming in droves, filling the court,
Bury the dead, empty the port.

The air is taken from one man's lung,
Another lies molding in another man's dung.
Tunics of dead men, they lie in a pile,
The stench of the dead is like that of bile.

Skin covered corpses, piled so high,
Lifeless shells hurled up to the sky.
Bones of some lying, attached pieces of skin,
Some still alive, their lifeline so thin.
Now it arrived, man has answered death's call.
It has come. It has conquered. It has taken all.

J. W. Mauldin III

Storms

Storms come in many forms and fashions,
Blowing everlasting like our passions.

They are the seasons of our lives,
Changing our course forever.

They come and leave a path of destruction,
Torn deep within our soul.

So many storms exist,
Each unique in it's own way.

We pass through storm to storm,
We grow stronger all the while.

Ever changing, ever growing,
Our person and soul forever.

Kathleen Vacik

The Beauty of Nature

This is one beautiful and special day for me.
Blue skies with fluffy white clouds floating by.
Later when I went to toil in the garden
this faint sound came to me from the north.

Being very attuned to nature-
I knew in a moment it was the joyous honking
of wild geese
So very high above my head.
A sound that always lifts my heart.

Immediately the garden went on hold-
This pleasant occurrence must not pass me by-
so I watch and listen with reverence.
To the amazing grace of a flock of geese
sailing across the wide blue sky
in a zigzag pattern of a lazy Z.

Watching, I revel in the sight of it all.
The lead goose...how does he know...the direction,
time of year...how to keep the flock in route.

Holding onto nature's world of beauty
makes me feel fulfilled, happy, wild and free.

Melba Hollister

Seasons

Born in the Spring, she knows no Summer.
Born in a time of unpredictability,
Of sunshine chilled by lingering gusts
And pink plum buds bitten by bitter frost,
She cannot predict the coming of safety
When she will not need a blanket for protection.

Snow is the only blanket she can remember;
The time of waiting, enclosed in the
Cold, dark, wet waiting place,
The small light so far away.
She does not venture out with excitement,
But with caution and much coaxing.

She cannot believe in the Summer warmth.
She sees the sun and is told it is warm.
It should be warm, she thinks.
But, unable to feel it, she knows herself to be
Too frozen in the spring-chilled quilt
To feel the promise of the sun.
Born in the Spring, and the Summer never comes.

Priscilla Hardin Munson

Unique

Love, interests, and motivation planted in seed
Born with special talent and the ability to succeed.

Family and friends may influence you, so it seems
Your unique design within, is the key, to all your dreams.

Focus your mind on life's many challenging tests
Achieve personal satisfaction, doing your very best.

Keep a positive attitude when making decisions along the way
Consequently, affecting your life each day.

As you grow through life experiences, you'll surely see
You're becoming the person you were meant to be.

Never will there be, another like you, near or far
That'll make a shining difference, bright as, your star!

Toni Scott

Living Free

The eyes are the key to your soul, you can reach a level of spiritual boundaries that are not reachable in any other means. You can find someone's weakness, find the truth, the hidden past, and sometimes even find the answers that you are searching for, that you are desperately in need of. Searching for life and the great meaning of it, searching for truth in yourself and in others. Life tends to have a meaning all it's own and we are not bound to those answers, nor will we find them out there, because there are all inside of us, hoping to be discovered, if we only dare to look and to listen. Speak and yet hear the words that follow, strive to understand the meaning of each thought. Build life on dreams that are steps above your standing, even though there may by some dreams that you never catch, but you may
find that there are things that you never even thought about wishing for and yet discover that you have not only caught it, but you have conquered it. Take the flames of life and dare to live by your rules and not theirs. Believe in your dreams and fight to keep them alive.

Sandra L. Brenk

My Son

When I look at my son I still see a boy
All curled up and cuddled with his favorite toy
Memories a mom has stored away in her heart
With each of them having their own special part
But when I look again I know the little boy's gone
Replaced by a man who's grown handsome and strong
His body ripples with the strength of three men
And I know I will never see my little boy again

Judy Parag

There Is Time...

In our seventies, there is time to:

Savor the taste and texture of each bite,
breathe deeply the cool air of the night,

Hear the crickets, an owl, a distant train,
Faure's Elegy, the whisper of rain,

Think about each loved one, far and near,
recall the ones no longer here,

Remember the good times, not the bad,
dream a little, don't be sad,

Read a book without a pause,
call a friend, just because,

You're lonely and you want to talk,
or ask the friend to take a walk,

Note each leaf, each tree, and flower,
mountains, clouds change every hour,

Relax, let moments flow away
with no accounting for the day.

    Mary Wolff Gamble

The Wolf Has Risen

The air moves slovenly within the hands of time
  Breathing changing, chills upon your spine
You can hear the howling fill the skies
  You can hear the pain within his cries
The world has unleashed its greatest beast
  As astonishing predator looking for the feast
Lightning is striking and the thunder does roll
  Now the ancient scrolls will start to unfold
He's not afraid of elements, divinity or man
  He will come to your door and demand your hand
The gates have opened at the immortal prison
  You know in your heart that the wolf has risen
The prophets have warned of the impending reign
  The tables have turned and the hunters the game
Quickness of thoughts fly with lightning speed
  He will use his power to stalk his feed
Betraying the Gods, he has rebuked his claim
  The wildness is unearthed and no longer tame
He won't quit stalking until his aching is through
  The wolf has risen and he is coming for you

    Shirley Bolstok

The 39th Day of Rain

The earth was created and man from its dust,
breathing the winds of the wild.
It's he who gave birth to the evil within,
and birth of the indolent child.
A generation of wicked ruling the land;
the destruction of life became clear.
Lucifer's army yells at the rain
as the flood to drown evil draws near.

Pouring from heaven as death fills the air,
forty days worth of pure genocide.
The people stop running as they see no more land,
"Shall I drown or just take my own life?"
All that will die make plans to avenge
their death on the 39th day.
The dust of the dead remains on the earth
and evil is here to stay...

    Robert R. Uribe

Washington, My Home

Silence is pleasure so is my home.
Breeze through the trees is like opera on gold.
An artists picture, real to the touch.
The artist has taken a natural scene added real colors,
  topped it with green.

Over my shoulder a wide mass of blue.
American lake is the name of this marvelous view.
Brownest of brown, greenest of greens, is the vision I'll remember
  when I leave the scene.
The sound of a car is rarely heard, yet the chirp of a bird
  is valued by her.

She is the mother of all that I see.
Mother of nature has planted her seed.
State of Washington is approved by far, for the peace and
  fulfillment it hold in its arms.

Satisfaction is achieve by just looking around.
For the beauty is hold is overwhelming to all.

    Kathryn Y. Lewis

Behold

Beautiful sunshine on birds so red!
Bright blue skies just overhead,
Lovely little flowers bursting thro' soil,
Wonderful rest, after our toil.

Sweet little children full of play,
Without a care in their childhood day,
Happy my heart as I behold
These precious pictures of silver and gold.

Time changes so many things—
But not the song of birds on the wing,
Or the laughter of children happy at play,
Nor the beauty of flowers on a warm spring day.

Grateful my heart that I can see—
The miracles of God surrounding me!
Hopeful my soul of a home up above,
Always encircled by beauty and love.

    Sarah Frances Furlow

Lost and Found (He or She)

I lost my child - won't you help me
Bring my baby home - where she should be

She's out of sight - now filled with terror
Please bring her back - be an angels bearer

We have searched the fields - and river beds too
Long stretches of roads - and where eagles flew

We start early morning - until late at night
Not a clue found - no where in sight

My wife is terrified - and I am too
Volunteers stay with us - until wet and blue

The flyers we posted - have now become worn
Please bring her back - where she was born

Our house is empty - no longer a home
Our hearts tore apart - the day she roamed

God will forgive you - and we will too
Mend our broken hearts - as you should do

We beg your compassion - please turn faith around
Give back our child - our "lost and found"

    Samuel T. Felicia Jr.

How Deep His Love!

How deep this infinite Love from God,
    How thorough! Supreme! How pure!

        How immense! How great! SO intense,
            How perfect! How sublime! How sure!

I cannot begin to comprehend,
    No way do I yet understand -

        The Earth is filled! Even rocks obey!
            Over All is His loving Hand.

Ah, yes - I can see the opposite come,
    There's envy, and hate, there's greed,

        There's SO much evil! Consider ITS source!
            But that Love is still here we need.

Our Lord and God is in control,
    HIS purposes He WILL fulfill,

        I cannot lose hope, I KNOW His Love,
            I smile! as I feel it, still.

I have a personal testimony,
    I KNOW that He loves ME

        It's there no matter WHAT I do,
            And some day - HIM, will I see!
    Ruth W. Graves

Untitled

Within
Hot steamy days, causes me to glisten,
With memories of her, my heart beat quickens.....

How long can these memories, stare off the rot,
This rejection I feel, is causing a blot.....

My tormentors know, it's no secret to them,
These memories of her, are stored deeply within.....

I know what they plot, have tried to get in,
To steal her away, away from within.....

Careful I am, when I see her inside,
My tormentors wait, they know where she hides.....

Won't they give up, she's all that's within,
I'll not let her go, I'll not let them in.....

Tormentors again, they're always around,
Bringing memories again, how she put me down.
    Roslynn E. Lofton

My Dad

How can I ever tell you,
How much he means to me?
The gratitude and love I feel
No one will ever see.

I know that life is oh so sad,
Since Mom has passed away.
He longs for the day,
When once again side by side they will lay.

His strength has always helped me
Through my days of pain and sorrow.
If only I could turn back time
And give him my tomorrows.

Always will I thank God,
For the man who is my Dad.
And wish that everyone could share
This closeness that we have.

    Rose Mary Goodson

Death By Surprise

I was looking out the window when a bullet caught my eye when the
bullet hit my forehead it took my by surprise. I fell down on the
floor with the blood gushing out. As I lied on the floor my hand
came up onto my face to feel the gap between my eyes. My Mom, she
cried, my sister too, my father tried to scoop me up. I knew then,
it was too late.

I found myself floating on air. Then looking down at myself as I
was floating high above I saw some people pick me up. They put me
in a body bag. I floated out to sea...where they would put my dead
body. I was put in back of a wagon that read Mortuary. All of a
sudden there came a man dressed in black. Calling my name. I was so
afraid. I was so unsure. Because, this man in black was taking me
for sure. I seldom thought of the event of death until the shadow
fell across my path. So antagonist is life, that death flows through
like a transparent host.

I stood firm, and calm as this man in black, led me through a passage
that was dark. I noticed a change that was so new to me. The eternal
dark was getting extremely clear. I wanted to ask this man, a
dreadful question...about the fields...and streams that flow forever.
I wanted to ask about the stars whose fields of blue now raised my
spirit. Now I know why my youth was sacrificed. To fate, I felt so
dumb, as I gazed upon my face, I knew that my death would bring love
eternal to those who saw me fade from life I know that today will
disappear, and that the great law dooms us all to dust.
    Nelva Concepcion

Mirrored Carriage

Dear father of my only child,
How precious that gift, the rewards never mild.

I want to thank you for that young man, who has inklings of your face.

And on reflection from a higher place...

I ask forgiveness for the pain and blame of our failed marriage,
For I have learned, you came to me on a mirrored carriage.

A reflection for me to view,
All the work on self, I wished to allude.

You are a man of values, that I admire.
My prayer for you is that you obtain your every desire.

The blessings you brought to me,
Will be cherished for eternity.

God bless,

Your Only X
    Terri Scott

Poetry In Motion

Golden warmth shines through graffiti windows
as the B train cradles its passengers to Coney Island.
The sleepy rhythm of the tracks creates an atmosphere for naps
and one by one we close our eyes, release our fears and our disguise.
An Asian family lays across from me with remnants of their shopping spree.
Father holds foreign papers in his hands, and reads with smile of distant lands.
Two Hispanic children cling to their mother's wedding ring as they
watch the rooftops
bleed into each other. They add to the flavor of our sleepy cradle soup.
The Spanish spice upon their tongues begins to slur as their heads droop.
I also with my Irish eyes bring a pattern to the quilt
under the blanket of the sun, within the city we have built.
We sit together side by side, free from fear through our short ride.
Never before have I felt so secure within the belly of the beast
which streams its needle through the tunnels and screams above the city streets.
As we reach our destinations, the train crawls into familiar stations
at which we awake from our subway slumber,
standing and stretching above to the number of ads,
like bedtime stories, which we occasionally read while drifting off to sleep.
Above our beds they hang while the soothing sounds of the train are humming
to the "Poetry In Motion" by E.E. Cummings.
    Tara O'Grady

My Mother

Mother, you are as beautiful as a rose,
but as it seems nobody knows.
You live a life of sadness,
in the end turns to madness.
Cancer, is what you had
we all got through even without a dad.
Don't leave us in your time of need,
say you'll stay for another day indeed.
We may not have much,
but we just need a tender touch.
I know what's right and wrong,
there's no need to be so strong.
You can admit your body's weak
as your children are here for you every week
allow yourself to take that last dive
love will keeps us all alive.
Until that day we must say goodbye

Ralicia Gugliotta

The Gift of Life

I gave you birth
But I do not know your name
You were not desired
Nor were you a necessity
Yet, bearing you in shame,
And scorned by superficial friends,
You were not deprived of the gift of life.

In the present
As in the past
A hauntingly curious wonder of you
Overturns my pattern of thought
Is this true of you as well?

Is your life rich? Full?
Of the genes who chose your fate?
Nonetheless my deepest longing for you
Is not to have borne
A life without meaning
Without purpose
In the one whose name I do not know.

Patricia M. Scharfe

Why I Love and Hate Him

I say I love him cause he's got beautiful eyes,
but I hate him cause he always lies

We usually have our good days,
but he gets mad when he don't get his ways

I say I love him cause he's real nice,
but on days he could be as cold as ice

I love his hair which is long and brown,
but I hate it when he looks real down

I love him and hate him, yes it's true
how else could I really say, I love you!

Stephanie N. Tamayo

The Black Rose

Here I sit all alone,
Deep within my broken heart,
Guarded by the barriers of depression and despair,
My body is an empty shell,
Driven by sorrow and pain,
Walking endlessly through life,
Looking for the Black Rose,
  the rose of eternity...

Clayton Onnen

Clouds

The clouds move I can see
but its not them that move but we
all different colors across the sky
because the suns rays are beginning to die
the clouds turn orange, pink, and purple,
then they become grey and dark
soon to be leaving it's mark
of stars that twinkle
and a moon that glows
waiting until dawn
when the sun will show
the clouds still move I can see
but its not them that move but we

Kathryn Martinuzzi

Send Us Your Verse (But Keep It Terse)

Your contest seeks new talent in the field of poetry,
But makes it clear there is a rule that mandates brevity.
'Tis difficult to woo the Muse; our talents you suppress,
When you tell us we must show our stuff in twenty lines or less.
What deathless verse can one construe in twenty lines at best?
Yet this is what you'd have us do - forsooth, you surely jest!
My creative bent does atrophy in facing these constraints,
For in lieu of composing poetry I merely rhyme complaints.
How could Edgar Allan Poe quoth the Raven "Nevermo'","
Or ponder Night's Plutonian shore, in twenty lines and never more?
And could Oliver Wendell Holmes, he so skilled at writing poems,
Tell the tale of a one hoss shay which performed for a century to the day,
And then collapsed into a heap, if this strict rule he had to keep?
Could Whitman give us "Leaves Of Grass" if that twentieth line he
  dar'sn't pass?
Wherefore his paeans to Old Inverness if they told Bobby Burns "Twenty
  lines or less?"
Could Homer's tale of the Trojan War be told in lines not exceeding one score?
To conjure up that deathless verse, twenty lines I say is just too terse,
Hardly more than a juvenile scrawl you'd find inscribed on a men's
  room wall.

Ray Smith

Stone Heart

I've shed a thousand tears.
But now I shed no more.
Blocking out the pain and anger.
That knocks upon my door.

My heart has slowly hardened.
To one that's made of stone.
I will shed no tears.
I prefer to be alone.

Alone to deal with sorrow,
Pain, and agony.
No tears will moisten my face
No remorse shall I ever seek.

My lips will never speak of foolish things.
Feelings from deep with in.
Because my heart is made of stone.
No one shall ever see me cry again.

Randy G. Frazier

Untitled

Love we all want, we all find.
But there is a love we all must find.
For that is the love we can't give to one another.
For without this love we are not strong.
For this love is the love that we have for ourselves.
For without this love we can't love another.
For this love makes us strong, when we are alone.
For this love is what most people love about us.
So the love we must find,
is the love that can't be given to another.
But we must find it to be strong,
for this love can be found just by saying "I love myself."
For you can never find the love you want.
If you can't find love in yourself.

Michael Logue

Karen

I see the beauty from and beyond her face
But where her heart should be, there's an empty space
I want to share the dreams that we dream
And conquer together, almost anything
We both have loved and lost before
And felt the emptiness, we can't ignore
If we use the knowledge from the past
We'll see our love through and make it last
I want to give her all I can give
And make her happy, as long as we live
I want to see a twinkle in her eye
Not the pain, that makes her cry
I wish I could take away her sorrow and pain
If I did, could she tell a loss from a gain
I believe all things happen for a reason
Like the dying of leaves, in the fall season
So let the heartaches that's fallen to the ground
Nourish the new beginning, that we have found
The love that she holds so distinct and barren
In time will shine, from this women named Karen

Quinten Adkins

"Friends"

Some friends are small, short or tall
but will always be there through the
good and bad.

Some friends are there to shed every
tear drops with you and there to say
"Lean on me."

Friends are weird, shy, funny, or just plain
lazy. A true friend will not put
you down, but lift you up high as the sky.

Friends come in many different ways or
shape. Sometimes here or there and some
will leave without a sight or even keep in
contact, or writing once or twice a week.
A true friend will last forever
till the end.

Michou Joseph

Untitled

These words I say are simple
These words I say are true
These words I say come from within my heart.
I'm in love with you
would you be willing to share all
in love and life?
Cheryl, would you be my wife?

Jerry A. Brown

Mother

It was such a long time ago.
But, yet I still can't let go.
I remember my mother calling my name.
Telling me that it was all a shame.
Yelling at me because the house was a mess.
Calling me names and saying she couldn't care less.
She told me leave and never come home.
She said go I need to be alone.
And so I left not looking behind.
Trying to avoid all that could remind.
So that was it I never returned.
But there are so many things which I have learned.
I know new troubles come with every day.
But things will always work out some way.
I will never again love no other.
Never love anyone like I loved my mother.

Maggie Kaczmarek

Guardian Angel

You have an angel over your shoulder
But you'll never see they're there.
They're just a running shadow
Or gently blowing air.
When you seem to have a problem
And you don't know which way to go
Just close your eyes and ask your Angel
Is there a path that they can show.
The peace and comfort that follows
Is all that you will need.
So when you feel you need some help, pray
And let your Guardian Angel take the lead.

Peggy Michel

Innocence of the World

Babies and children, innocence of the world.
by far, are not to be blamed for what their
parents are.
They bring joy to some parents and anger to others
but what ever they bring, they are not to be
blamed.
Don't let these angry parents take their abuse
out on them.
Don't let them break their spirits, if you can.
Some children are ornery, who need attention,
Some are slow and need your love.
Have fun with them while you can for they
are the innocence of the world.

Virginia L. (Trevillian) Lane

Easter

Easter is when our Lord
gave His life and rose again.
He suffered a cruel and awful death
All because of the sin of man.

He spent His time on this earth
without a place to lay His head.
And yet, He was victorious,
our blessed Lord rose from the dead.

Jesus was an humble man
no beauty was there to see.
But now, His beauty is everywhere,
may it ever shine in you and me.

Marvelle Hobbs

Fear

The fears of things that are supported
by the fears of what may be, yields endless
acres of rich soil.

Soil that is worked and seeded by thoughts
and imagination.

Years of harvesting such crops over loads
the mind with fear, resulting in a form of
depression.

A continuous increase of fear nurture depression,
blinding the mind and allowing fear a free
hand in all areas of life.

Depressed, blind and over loaded the mind's
grip on life is threaten.

Blind and unaware, skillful hands supported
by concern, reach beyond intellect, breaking
the soil in an effort to root up fear by its root.

Hands that leave resins of concern,
that is watered by sweat from the effort.

Michael E. Ayers

Most Precious Dearest Wife Dorothy

Dedicated to my departed "Love of my Life"
Dorothy, who, as God's guest, is impatiently waiting
for that bright day of our Souls' Reunion in
the presence of our Lord, Amen.

Your eyes my sweetheart were the windows to your soul,
By time unaffected, for this purpose their goal.
Their glimmer remains as a brilliant diamond,
Revealing youthful joy, loving thoughts and a true friend.

An affinity to times of the past,
Spent together for forty-seven years in joy, that lasts.
When you were in need, I loved you the more.
There isn't anything I wouldn't have done for you anymore.

You remain as I first knew you.
Your soul never changes, I could see right through you.
Dear GOD, allow me to hold onto her LOVING MEMORY for ever...
May THIS PRICELESS GIFT entrusted to me, never sever.

Victor Silzer

Beaten Body, Triumphant Soul

Docken bottom and pickled sight
came stumbling over in the light,
reeking with saliva in fouled mouth
I passed quickly away to the south.

Away and away but yet it came
always so near me running the same.
All was left to plead and beg
for it to leave for a leg.

My leg I gave and I hopped on
coming to be bothered again at dawn.
Not the same, yet still so similar
I gave my arm less familiar.

By the time the sun came only my head
lay upon the ground crying, almost dead.
There had been too many who came and took
never staying to love, never minding my look.

Kaya Marek

Rejoicing

A wee little girl, and a wee little boy
Came to live in our beautiful world,
Little did we know one summer day
Wee little boy would claim little girl.

Parents nurtured them in spiritual growth
Pastor Bill would teach them in God's ways,
Together they were baptized in church
As they grew and went separate ways, one day.

On a spring afternoon, Cristie went shopping,
With her mother for a new vacuum belt,
All of a sudden, there stood Troy!
This was someone special, Cristie felt!!

Soon Troy would come calling
Bonding began early on,
Phone calls, visiting, and dating
In their hearts a new love song.

Soon this bonding will be complete
The two shall be as one,
Praise God, in His wonderful plan
We rejoice, God's will will be done.

Ruth Crisp

What Is A Man?

A man, a man, is that what I am?
Can I do what a man can do?
I really don't know; what should a man do?
If a man is kind, I am kind.
If a man is understanding, I am understanding.
If a man is intelligent, I am intelligent.
If a man is responsible, I am responsible.
But is that really a man.

If a man is courageous, I am courageous.
If a man is strong, I am strong.
If a man is loved. I am loved.
If a man loves, I love.
But is that really a man.

Can I say I am a man?
Real men have no fears, or do they?
I have fears of life and fears of death.
Real men admit their faults and weaknesses
And I have; but...am I a man?

Kevin L. Jernigan

To Whom You Love

True love comes through anywhere, anyplace, anytime;
Can make all look from dark into the light.
Love makes all that is written come to a rhyme;
Makes dawn break through to destroy the evil night.

Can love be left to one alone, who knows?
For love is there so all may live in peace.
If love were gone, sorrow would leave many woes.
Love is everywhere, so partake in a piece.

Love can become anything to anyone's love.
Pure love is great and powerful, yet mystical;
It stands up through all, and always above.
Unlike all things, true love, is immortal.

True love will always come through bright and bold;
Let love shine bright to whom you wish to hold.

Noel J. Kukucka

What Kind?

This kind of love that I have
can't be bought at Kroger's for $ 9.99 on sale;
buy one get one free.

This kind of love can't be put in a
pawn shop for a little while and then
taken back when you want it back.

This kind of love is my love and can only be bought
by YOUR love.
Something that all the money and power in the world couldn't
buy!!!

This kind of love is what YOU call
A daughter's love.

Rebecca Garcia

Paintings in the Clouds

Make me happy, make me sad; paranoid and then I'm glad;
Can't quite figure out the plan, but I like the game.

Though I do not understand how you're going to play your hand;
I sure want to be there when you lay your cards down.

I hear music all around. I see paintings in the clouds.

If we were to share love tonight, tomorrow you'd still be so right;
And it would be such a delight to be loving you.

I hear music all around. I see paintings in the clouds.

Inside me there is a child who thinks that life is so worthwhile;
I also think you've got the style to take me as I am.

Something from inside, you see, is telling me we're meant to be;
I know you'll say "let's wait and see", and I think that's okay.

I hear music all around. I see paintings in the clouds.

Thomas Sparks

Taking Time.....

Can't you see me ..... a still, small voice floats from the distance....
Can't you see I want to achieve...
Can't you see I'm trying...
Can't you see I ache to hear the words of praise...

One shaky step after another.....I step towards you.
I want to believe in you, but the hurt is fresh and raw.
Failure lies outside my doorway.

Please catch my hand; I don't want to be lost...
My eyes are dull with confusion.
Clear the doubts....I will shine.
Hope is laying deep within me.

Trace the pathways of many who have gone before me.
We are the forgotten generation.
We seem unreachable, but its only a protective layer.
Keep searching for who I am; I will surprise you.

Don't dig a deeper tomb of apathy for a child who strains
to stay focused.
Take the time to appreciate the gift of trust a child gives to you.
Know that you are shaping a life for the future.

Susan Burfeind

To "Buddy" With Love

The sun is setting in the West.
It is the time of day your loved best.
The breezes are blowing through your trees.
It brings back so many memories of your evenings with me.
Although on this earth we are apart,
you will always be present in my heart.
I send you my love on the wings of a dove.

Dorothy A. Wilder

Her-Story

It's her-story. She's strong, full of great strength and she's quite capable.
Full of energy, determined, unyielding, yet, so lovable.
Over the years, she has suffered hardships, has always taken a back
seat.
She seeks little recognition; she's caring and overcomes great defeat.
She's unwavering; she's brave, and she's blessed with fortitude.
She has a kindred spirit, and has love worth a multitude.
She gives encouragement — yet shies away from the limelight.
A great woman — an African-American - brown skinned and a
beautiful sight.
We're blessed to have her among us and she's grateful to be.
It's her-story. She's my idol - can you tell me - who is she?

Pamela F. Bax

Capture the American Eagle.

The great armies of the Eastern world will never
capture the American Eagle.
He will fly high in the sky, over seas, and
soar over mountain snow.
Like a streaking comet he will strike
with wings and rod edged with steel.
Soaked in blood he returns to his land of
Freedom and gold.
Scanning the earth with keen yellow eyes
he sees field of golden poppies glittering in
the sun.
He bends his wings and legs rigid
with power, he lands in the gold to heal.
The American Eagle a war hero, born
of heritage is home.

Lidi Mary Kyle

The Calico Chameleon

A Calico Chameleon is creeping through your cranium
Carrying a crucifix of a crazy Jesus Christ
He's headed toward his heaven on a helping of hypocrisy
Harassed by holy harlots and a hateful fear of hell
Relentlessly rejecting all the reasoning and ridicule
Reluctant to release the written dogma of his rape
He instinctively insinuates incredible injustices
Insidiously influencing the id of imbeciles
He's shit-faced with stupidity from a singular source of slander
Screaming slogans and a sermon saving someone from himself
And trusting not to pass unnoticed
    through your twisted neural networks
The two-toned tinted lizard tests the hinges of your tomb and says
    Don't think for yourself
    It's easier that way

J. A. MacDonald

Jade

Exquisite Chinese Lady
Carved from priceless jade
Were you a treasured concubine
Or a high bred Manchu maid
Your tiny hands cup a lotus bud
Thy lips curve secretly
Holding the promise of man's delight
Sought eternally
Who was thy love so long ago
Who gave thee ecstasy
Did you drum in the blood of a coolie man
Did an Emperor sigh for thee
Or was thy Lord a dark skinned moor
From across an alien sea
Where is the man whose master hand
Carved thee so tenderly......

Veronica Anderson

The Dark Between the Stars

I sweep the nightly skies...and embrace the stars,
Cascading glory 'cross the awesome, endless dark.
And I ponder... perhaps they too, gaze upon me afar.
For space alone hath ne'er eclipsed the hungry heart.

These stars... long have I known them as my friends.
They judge me not in their march along our skies.
Thus I failed to see the gentle dark that never ends.
Where, perchance, dwell those with whom to harmonize.

Now I reach for them that may outward gaze and yearn.
I comb the night b'twixt the beacons blazing bright,
In search of those with dauntless candles yet to burn,
To cherish equal dreams... "Behold! My lifted light!"

By God, I crafted thus more than just stuff of dreams.
Amidst these exalted stars, I came! I blazed! I went!
If my small candle amends no vast, Eternal schemes,
However brief the glow, the Dark has thus been rent.

Attend me, you where night beclouds most eyes aloft.
Many, many more than I hold up hopeful candles slight.
Seek on, and beckon long, for torches small and soft.
We may forever thrive... do we salute each tiny light.

Stu Ladue

My Friend the Bottle

Can you burn a million candles and light fire to my sky.
Cast the night as bright as daytime, though this light which shines
  can die.
Can you extinguish the fire which has consumed me from within.
Help to ease this pain which scalds me hot against my skin.
Introduce me to the daylight, make my darkness disappear
I'm trapped beneath that midnight sky, my torments hidden there.
Convince me life holds meaning there's room for more than pain.
Can you tell me my long journey has not been in vain.
When I hold you close with each euphoric sip
all my doubts, my worries they seem to fade so quick.
When I hold you close I feel like I could fly
in you I drown my troubles my inhibitions die.
Once without you I am lost, a veil of sunlight gone
without you my black darkness triumphs over dawn.
So can you love me now if only for tonight.
I promise not to leave you for I'm just too weak to fight.

Staci Waldman

One

One
cat in a research lab, tested for sleep deprivation effects,
kept awake in its chamber by temperatures below freezing,
head bolted in a steel clamp, metal rods in its ears and mouth,
bones exposed around its eyes, screws threaded through holes
drilled behind its eyes, holes cut in its windpipe,
blasted with ammonia hydroxide so it drools and its eyes burn
if it doesn't hold its breath when a tone sounds.
One cat like this is one too many.
One.

One
cat, full of supper, dozing on a porch rail
superbly appointed for observation of coquette pigeons
who strut fat, rise above death when a bell laughs
from a neck whose fur shines thick with love.
This cat dreams long, slow dreams in the sun of the whole world.
The huge-standing giants in the house
know this cat is a gift of grace, their salvation.
One cat like this is not enough.
One.

Sarah Smiley

Cattle Drive

As the trail winded down toward the creek.
Cattle running like lightning in the hot
summer heat.
Cowboys in trail, hoopin' an' hollerin'.
Cows win to no avail.
Water which can quench a thirsty soul.
Weak and listless they lay in the heat of the
night on a knoll.
Cows and men sharing the same starlight.
Dreams of home, women and dangerous plight.
They awake hungry and alone.
Cowboys on the trail,
or just rolling stones.

Kathryn Odom

Inside Looking Out

I don't have to worry about burglars
'cause I've got burglar bars
I'm looking through bullet proof glass
at an interstate full of cars.

There's beans and greens three times a day
I was set up for money, they want me to pay.
I won't go home unless they say
"A-T-W" which means "all-the-way"

My clothes won't be stolen
I wash them out in a pail
Cuz I'm inside looking out
of the mobile metro jail.

The drinking water is hot, the showers are cold
Sleeping on cement floors, is getting very old
Line up for the phone, "I love you honey."
I need some soap, please send "a lot" of money.

The only thing to look forward to
is a visit or some mail.
'cause, I'm inside looking out
of the mobile Metro Jail.

Virginia Banks

Chase The Comet

Comet hurtles through cold darkness.
Chase the comet.
Scorching white hot center,
mysterious and deadly.
Streaming tail glowing golden,
reassuring and safe.
Run too fast and you may plunge into fire
engulfed by flames of shattered hopes.
Run too slow and be left in the cold
searching for the last light of old dreams.
  Always, always
  chase the comet.

Katherine Johns

Stardust Memories

Careless whispers on the radio
Bring silence to the bottom of my heart
I've spent so much time trying to forget you
But not enough
Trying to let go

Maybe I should wait until tomorrow
Before I say goodbye
To all the dreams we shared
And the quietness of sweet memories

Karen Kitral

The White American

I am cherokee, Irish, English and Jew by adoption.

I have not been through the pain and troubles that my
Cherokee brothers and sisters have been through
Will you accept me?

I have not seen the troubles of my Irish brothers and
sisters. Will you accept me?

I have not seen what the English have gone through.
Would you accept me?

By adoption, I am Jew. Your pain and trouble. I have not
felt. Would you accept me?

I am known as a White American. Will you accept me?
I apologize for any pain that a part of me, caused to
another part of me so many years ago, and will you
forgive me? Will you accept me?

I am Cherokee, Irish, English and Jew by adoption.
My creator will accept and forgive all of me.

Rhonda L. Gregory

Snow

Who in the world likes snow anyway,
Children of course who likes to play.
The working man is the one that knows,
That snow is hard on fingers and toes.
The mailman on his daily round,
Would much prefer walking on ground.
The retiree is anxiously awaiting spring,
Looking forward to what good things the earth will bring.
The housewife gazes out the window in sheer delight,
As flocks of birds are stirred to flight.
The farmer patiently takes it all in stride,
With a hope and a prayer that God is on his side.

Robert G. Miller

What's Going On

Parents on drugs and in the street
Children with guns that can't be beat
Drug dealers making deals by telephone
All I need to know is what's going on

Children are crying everyday
They can't find their parents nor a place to stay
The parents have gone and left them alone
While HRS is trying to find them a home
The kids are reaching for help, but its all gone
Will somebody just tell me what's going on

When parents make their kids go to school
When everyone follow that one golden rule
When we can get the devil out of the church
When welfare people get out and work
When all parents listen to what their kid have to say
We can make tomorrow a better today
When we can stop teenagers from having babies
When we can get men to stop acting like ladies
When kids stop coming home right before dawn
We will then know what's really going on

Yolanda Kay Womack

Tractors

I like tractors, they are neat.
They dig up roads and make new streets.
I see an old house that needs knocked
down and along comes a bulldozer
and knocks it down.
I love to watch everything that tractors do and
hope someday when I get big I can do it to.

Donald Newsome

Smile Now, Smile Forever

The warrior drooped in silent despair
Clenching his spear in a bloodied hand
His history lost in the realms of the war
Fighting to keep his family's land
That forbidden tear embarrassed his cheek
For as a boy he was taught a man does not cry
He kneeled in disgrace to his sacred soil
Stared deep into the gray clouds storming the sky
"I must die!" he screamed to his God
His eyes drowned in sorrow, his heart full of hate
He raised his left fist to challenge his God
Throwing his spear as to surrender his fate
Then through the dark sky a bright voice spoke out
"My son, don't give up, for your people are few;
Be proud, be strong and rebuild what you've lost,
Be grateful you've survived, for your bloodline shall continue."

So today here I stand with the blood of a warrior
Who's destiny to live, everyday I'll remember
I've learned and I've taught to those who cry lonely
You must smile now, so you can smile forever.

Rene V. Alarcon

Peacemaker

I am following you;
Clouded visions of light — I see nothing and everything at once.

Fleeing from the lies, the injustice and the hate,
Watching you as you weave your web of truth.
My head is spinning.

I am following you;
Dancing and twirling in circles as you lead me to safety.
I am the dove;
From above I see the river ebb into a deep, blue delta.

I watch the spinning wheel.
A thousand eyes beckon to me; a million voices tell me it's alright.
I hear nothing but my hand opening empty.

I am following you;
I see only my outstretched hand reaching towards you —
You who are spinning farther away from me every second.
I try in vain to cry out to you.

I am spinning out of control — back towards my world and
    away from yours.
Only when I am completely lost in the cold mist which
    envelopes me do I know that I am safe.
I am following you.

J. Schanbacher

Memories

My brain is like an attic
cluttered from years of use.
Its contents are precious memories
from when I was a youth.

As I sift and sort through piles
my mind drifts back through all those miles.
And slowly as some order comes
I see my life before me.

One box contains my summer dreams
all those wishes and far reaching things.
Another bursts open at the seams
and out spill laughter and happy scenes.
An open drawer displays quite willingly
all those treasures that are so heavenly.

The further I go the better I feel
as cautiously I tuck away all that's revealed.
I stack and label with tremendous care
knowing that when I need them, my memories will be there.

Sarah Anderson

Us

Come out, do not be afraid
Come, welcome us even if your father forbade.
I know we fascinate you,
just the sight of us.
the sight of him,
Makes you tremble,
a glance makes you obey his every whim.
I understand the position you are in,
I once stood in that door,
Listening to the sweet music our kind makes,
but that was so long ago.
Come, join our perfect posture and alluring stance,
Come join the children of night as we sway to our exotic dance.
Run, into the dark, until you lift off the ground,
And up you will soar with the rest of our kind, skybound.
Come into my arms,
let me love you with all I have,
what ever you do, don't fuss.
Soon, you will roam the skies and stalk the night.
Soon you will be one of us.

Toni J. Parmentier

Wake Less Hours

Blackness overpowers the light
Consciousness is pulled to my inner realm
Where the dark and hidden secrets are
and the images are formed in my mind
They are not there
They never were
A movie I've never seen
And no one else ever will
The Horror of it all!
I'm searching for what I can not find
Oh! The pain of memories and hopes
I can not run
I can not hide
Trapped within myself - me!
Of flesh and blood I am
And a spark in the midst of my mind
That spark that is so hard to find
But time slips away
Then time slips away
And the dawn of the light must return.

Steven C. Banks

The Response

Once I was strolling freely
Content as I can be
And then they ask the question
About this wonderful me
Conceited I am not
But self confidence I often boast
My style is tighter than dred locks
My vocabulary shuns most
Prim and preppie does not describe me
Queer and eccentric does not either
Stupidity was not desired
I prefer being intellectually leisure
Common sense is a gift I have
Like a battery always charged
If they measured the knowledge my mind hold
It would too vast to be called large
But I shall not answer the question
I'm sure they already know
Contentedly I will continue to stroll
And let this wonderful me show

Tamika S. Magee

What's Inside?

Are things what they appear to be?
Content, pleased, full of glee.

Never, never I do believe,
Too many are out there to deceive.

What's down is up, and what is in is out,
So confused and full of doubt.

Lies become truth and truth becomes lies,
The soul becomes smothered and slowly dies.

"Time heals all wounds" I've heard them say,
Instead, the wounds leave scars that don't go away.

Reminded of feelings that you're nothing but dirt,
Nothing ever seems to relieve the anguish and hurt.

How do you reach these desperate souls?
To give them hopes, dreams and goals.

Come on people, you tell me!
Have we all become deaf and can not see?

We are all to blame,
In the big shame game.

Let's teach our children love, respect and pride,
Instead of hate, misery and "keep it all inside".

Sharon Lynn Most

The Roller Coaster

Heads bobbing, hearts throbbing.
Corkscrew coming, always running
Over loops, hills and swoops.
Tossing, turning, whirly whoops.
Up, down, up and down again
Hats fly off hair in the wind.
Over and over through rings and springs
All blur by, such marvelous things.
The squeaking of rails, ringing of bells,
And oh, a real menagerie of smells.
All fly by at twice the speed
Your stomach turns, that's all you need!
Yet suddenly all does halt
Right when up-rise fries and salt.
A bar lifts and you stand with a gulp
The ride is over, you need to throw up!

Yet something holds you back right then
And you look at me saying, "hey, again?"

Lisa Neal

Mother's Day

Many said the smile Mom had, the laughter that she spread,
Could fill a room with warmth and love, without a word be said.
The admiration I had for Mom, the love I also shared,
The strength she showed me way back then, today could not
compare.
No tea parties, no dress up time, bike rides or such,
And I remember feeding her, what I had fixed for lunch.
No summer walks, no baking tips, no dresses to be sewn,
These things I did, I did myself, I learned them on my own.
Mom would share her many hugs or give a teary kiss,
Knowing soon that these would be the things we'd always miss.
She loved her life as I do mine,
But nothing on this earth will find,
The emptiness I feel each year,
When times like this should be of cheer.
It's the strength, it's the love, it's the fight that she fought,
To give to her family, life's gifts to be taught.
Dear God, who took my Mom away,
Give me strength to live each day.

Norma Briggs

Changes

Time passes - Never to return
Barren trees - With new life coming
Glistening snow - Going back into the Earth
A wave crashing on pieces of sand - Moving, swirling
A smile, a Touch - Never to be seen or felt that way again
Our deepest heart - Sensing change, slowly accepting -
   yet knowing it must!

Mona L. Doyle

Somewhere In Time

If a time of one's lifetime
could have been brought nearer,
to find that certain someone
no matter how far away.
A happiness with no end
would also be found.
But even though that time is lost
never to be found again,
there will always be a tomorrow
with a never ending dream,
that maybe....just maybe, today is the day.
My love is there, my feelings real
showing my affection only in touch.
But with that touch a thousand heartbeats
with only one meaning, yes, I do love you,
Today, tomorrow, and forever.

Lee Beckwith

The Greatest Gift of All

Not store bought, nor hand made;
Created by love
Opportunities never ending,
Passion and hope as bright as fire.
It's future unbound with each new breath...
Thank you for this gift of life.
A chance, a hope, a flicker of light,
You are the one who bestowed this gift.

No you, No life.
Joy and aspiration running like a river;
my blood.
Each beat of my heart your creation.
My vision, hands, arms and legs,
unattainable but only by you.
My thoughts and dreams as sharp as morning cuts night...
Thank you for the greatest gift of all,
My mother;
My life.

Robert Louis Pastore

"My Love For You"

I do believe that God above
created you for me to love.
He picked you out from all the rest,
because he knew I loved you best.

I once had a heart, so brave and true,
but now it's gone from me to you.
Take care of it, as I have done,
for you have two, and I have none.

If I go to heaven, and you're not there,
I'll paint your face on the golden stair.
Then if you're not there by judgement day,
I'll know you've gone the other way.

I'll give the angels back their wings,
and also many other things,
To show you that my love is true,
I'll go to hell to be with you.

Tina Willard

Crispy Crunch

He sits and waits for the lights to go out
crouched behind the ice box, between the tile and grout.
He ventures between the cracks,
searching, probing for tasty snacks.
The empty dark kitchen is open ground,
I see him and creep in without making a sound.
He tinkles across the floor and stops at my big leather boot,
he probes, and twitches his head and ponders another route.
Turning and running he finds some cookie crumbs by the door
his dirty little legs move back and forth in search for more,
He grabs the crumb, brings it to his mouth and begins to munch.
With a ferocious stomp I smashed that roach with a crispy crunch.
Now on the floor all squished and squashed in colorful blobs,
maybe next time you'll know not to be such a slob.

Lauren Campbell

Daddy

For as long as I can remember
Daddy, you've always been there
Going out of your way
To show me that you care

It wasn't always easy
I've caused my share of pain
But Daddy, you always found it in your heart
To forgive me again and again

I know that you love me
I've known it all along
Over the years I've come to learn
A Daddy is seldom wrong

Now that I am older
With children of my own
I appreciate, Daddy,
All of the wonderful things you've done

Maybe it wasn't often said
Maybe we rarely touched
But you'll always be my Daddy
And I love you very much

Michaeline Jones

Care Free

Ha ha ha you laugh and sing, ha ha ha you shout and
dance, with never a care like kittens and pups, who love to
jump and prance.

Who taught you so well to giggle, with whom do you have
so much fun. It beats my imagination to fathom the thoughts
you toss around.

Let's go out this evening, before it begins to dark, and
don't forget girl to come prepared, the boys will be chilling
in the park.

They come home heavy eyebrowed, slow foot steps laden
deep, and sneak to lay their pleasure filled souls, like old
folk seeking sleep.

Wayne Bynoe

Year Around

My love is so strong it never dies,
   as a leaf falls into a pond it never dries.
Your always in my mind- not news that old,
   especially in winter during the cold.
Dream of your touch and laughter you bring,
   while the Red, Yellow and Purple Roses bloom in spring.
Call to talk to you in the hot sun,
   right when summers begun.

Tracie Trevino

Spread

Spread the guilt of June
Dare to chase the moon
Blessed innocence is doomed
Killers fountain springs youth
Use your life for food

You can't lie what you can't hide
Every life is a life lived dangerous
You can't waste a tasteless spirit
What smells like children feels like Jesus

Plastic people hurt to
You mistake our youth
Angels dawn in time
They steal what is not mine
Lemon eyes take sight with pestilence love

Miracles are dreams shot twice
Wish upon a life of secrets
Legends are story's bottled and sold
Green makes peace with mothers a filth
Strange is strange, glaze is a glare
Timeless counts, reverse insight out.

    Ryan Taylor

Never Alone

I sit alone as grey skies gather to cover what might be
dark clouds build to majestic mountains in a far away
corner.
Brown leaves born by the breeze skip across my feet
I sit alone and watch the leaves crowd against the cold
grey stones, rising from the earth.
Lettered in print to mark the passing,
Restless leaves that pay homage to the past.
I sit alone while muttered voices heard only by the
wind tell of things that used to be.
I sit alone as leaves slow to rest, as rain drops pin
them in there place.
I strain to see as rain forms blotches upon the leaves,
while muttered thunder in the far tell me its time to
leave.

    Ken Clemons

The Cello

Asleep
Dark, shining potential magic.
Awaiting the inspired, the Master's touch
bringing life and expression.

Lifted from velvet closet
cradled and stroked, I sing

Warm, amber, honey-hued melodies
I sing!
Deep colored songs of love, mystery, and sadness.
I sing!

To hearts bound in agony's chains,
I send bright, gold-flecked joy.
To minds in chaos, peace.

Till at last I am at rest, for the moment, spent.
Yet yearning to sing again, for only then do I live.

    Thelma E. Montara

Obsession

The resonance of days gone by has once again ambushed my quiet
daydreams, leaving me here in desperate concentration, trying to
fight off old demons intent on annihilating my existence. Sudden
images of colorized sound materialize inside my mind, serenity
comes dancing through only to be ravaged by the sinister musing.
Will it ever cease? Trepidation ensues and I'm tossed about
like a raft in a typhoon, engulfed in waves of emotions I never
thought existed, pummelling me and leaving me defenseless, STOP!
STOP! I hear myself crying into a vast expanse of nothingness. I
begin to perceive a sense of solace, however perverse, luring me
into bewilderment, but wait! could I be contemplating surrender?
Ah! sweet surrender, relinquishing my hold on my own destiny, I
discover the paradox of ages, I comprehend strength and
reconciliation with myself and God. Serenity dances passionately
and I am free of the torment called, obsession.

    Michael Russell

White Fog

The moon was peeking through the
Dead oak and maple trees, peering down upon the three swans
Who were peacefully gliding
Across the silver river like a wooden raft.
Their charcoal-black beaks breathed in
The seclusion of the lake. The swans' belly's feathers,
Peeking out of the water, showed proudness,
And were fearful of the night.
The midnight fog suddenly appeared from nowhere and was
Spying beneath the trees.
Scornfully whispering to the family of swans,
The white shadow shrouded them meaningfully,
A tiger stalking its prey.
The terrifying fog made it difficult for the victims
To paddle their way like passing through a ghost,
To the moon's light of safety.
All become peaceful as the luminous beam zig-zagged its
Light through the trees and
Shrouded the lake in a gentle way,
Like a bear club cuddling in its fur coat during hibernation.

    Marie Rosemary

Cycles of Life

An old oak tree stands in the meadow.
A sentinel to time and weather,
Its branches reaching heavenward,
Its gnarled knees bowed to the earth;
Attest to its ancient age
When long ago the acorn was buried
By some hapless creature or winged jay.

Each season clothes it in new array.
Spring hails, bursting forth its swollen buds
Pregnant with life;
Until a shaded silhouette catches every
Languorous breeze and hurls it through the
Balmy morn, drying drops of sparkling dew.

The autumn air whispers through the golden leaves
As they wait in respite for the wind
To sail them to the dank humus below.
The old oak tree shivers as it stands unclothed
And barren; stripped of its bowered beauty,
Silently it waits for its blanket of snow.

    —Rebecca R. Odom

Following Without Knowledge

What did you learn from your friends today,
dear little son of mine?
What did you learn from your friends today,
dear little son of mine?
I learned that you should never question authority,
I learned that adults are never wrong,
I learned that kids are never right.
And that's what I learned from my friends today,
That's what I learned from my friends today.

What did you learn from your friends today,
dear little son of mine?
What did you learn from your friends today,
dear little son of mine?
I learned that advances in technology are always good,
I learned that every thing in life is safe,
I learned that school is too hard and I should not try,
And that's what I learned from my friends today,
That's what I learned from my friends today.

M. J. Rivett

I, The Ocean

When I want to rest I go
deep deep down under
its dark night, so much silence
it's unbelievable to my eyes
I, the ocean I see an eel swim towards
all my beautiful flowers
amazed at everything she sees
she sniffs my flowers
taking in the aromas
all the reds, green, orange, purple and blues
the colors dazzle her
as if seeing colors for the first time
the orange corals seem to pull her
around and around she swims
she was having so much fun she was getting me dizzy
straight she stood, looking for something to do
she sat on my rock, as if tired
to smell the beautiful flowers
I was so rested, I decided to move on
to see what else was going on in my waters

Milagros Cabrera

The Fervent In Spirit Are Ready

The fervent in Spirit are ready to go
  Deliver the message of Jesus the King!
They do not suppress it they just let it flow!
  This message do they speak, and heartily sing.

But the fervent in Spirit will also wait
  In prayer, seeking His will to know.
For God is the Author of their spiritual state.
  He cleanses their hearts so they're white as snow.

The fervent in Spirit are eager to be taught
  Thru preaching and teaching they learn to share.
Their wisdom increases as battles are fought,
  Victories are won by warriors who dare!

The fervent in Spirit live the Christian life,
  Loving the unlovely, the sinful, the lost.
Battles aren't fought by gun or by knife,
  Repentance comes when sinners count the cost.

The fervent in Spirit have been thru the fire!
  Young or old, facing the battles that have come.
They love their Redeemer, they obey His desire
  Waiting to see Jesus in their Heavenly Home!

Weldon Munson

Loving Thoughts

Our timeless hours together were many,
Depending upon each other - we are one.

I live in two persons - and two
persons live in me. He fills my life
with love and security.

I pass from moment to moment
seeing his smile,

When he leaves my soul is with him,
for alone never will he be,

Our souls are intermixed in a mist of love,
that fills the emptiness in us both.

There is so much, I don't know how to say.
But I'll learn - just listen long enough.

People say God sees me. Through him
  I see God.

Kathy Dianne Duborsky

Reflections

Looking out of my window I feel what I see,
Desire to express the beauty surrounding me.

It is morning and the sun is brilliant in its duty,
Shining upon trees, accentuating their beauty.

Gold, green, brown leaves that just seem to glow,
Reflecting in a lake of gentle, soft flow.

The background of all is a perfect blue sky,
Not even a cloud, only birds that soar by.

Sounds soft and pleasant, all part of the features,
Wind in the trees, songs by feathered creatures.

The geese float serenely across the lake,
With barely a movement to create a wake.

There is something of morning brilliance so strong,
That awakens my heart with an internal song.

To realize and appreciate every beautiful sight,
The work of God's hand, His power and might.

The warmth of God's presence in all that I see,
Reflections of His love given so generously.

Sharon L. Courey

Paradox Of Being

Darkness envelopes the contours of my soul
Destined forever to revert to the core
A point ambiguous, an environment volatile
Each attempt to overreach the definite
  bounds of my being
Doomed to failure, once again precipitating
  a return to familiar yet nebulous confines
Familiarity itself fathering doubts concerning
  well-established precedents
Certainty destroyed, the core implodes,
  collapses upon itself
United with the haze of the periphery
  and the beyond
All is one — everything accepted, nothing known —
Another lost spirit in society's senseful march
  to a summit aspired by the many, understood
  by none.

Nasir Malik

Possibilities

Dark, lightless lifeless night
Devoid of warmth, Devoid of color.
Dark, lightless, lifeless spirit
Devoid of love, Devoid of friendship.
A perverse parody of Moon and Sun
One beautiful reflection of brilliant splendor
One a desolate image of empty despair.
Love is the true Light of Life
Friendship the true color of Love.
Darkness, emptiness, is all that is here.
Searching for something, Finding Nothing.
As the eye tends a points is fixed:
As the mind tends a difference is noted:
Not light-not the graying of dawn.
Not dark-not the void of doom.
A Possibility
of things that might be,
of change that could be.
Light
love.

Walter Reindl

"Children"

I know children are fun.
Did you ever notice them run?
Haven't you seen them play in the sun?
I have noticed children as they grow.
I like to watch them in the snow.
Children, children, they bring joy.
I have seen them play with a toy.
Mighty, mighty children sing.
As the school house bells ring.
Tic Tac Toe and hop scotch, they did play.
computerized games have come today.
I have seen them as I walked their way,
as I watched them mold the clay.
Standing, sitting will they stay?
Believe it if you may.
I hope they will continue to pass my way.
I will keep them in my heart today.

Marcia Sevier

The Princess and the Knights' "War Horse"

Early morning haze obscuring the meadow view,
Dimming the perception and memory of budded complex petals,
Making the princess yearn for the spectral steed,
Galloping amidst the gray curtain of fog,
Gilded harness and bit resounding in the stillness.

Iridescent droplets clinging to your braided mane,
She longs to interlace her jeweled fingers in your weaved hair,
To feel your reacted muscles shudder to her touch.

That tell -tale, blithe wind carries her scent,
The bracken attacking your flank as you wallow indulgently,
She leaps and you rise, you rise!
And they, together, went wetly through the rift.

Your perked ears and tense slowing to a trot,
Alert her to the approaching pounding of other hooves.
The barbs of the earth pull at your fetlocks, causing you to cry out!

Sunlight gleams from the advancing knights' drawn sword.
You, the "War Horse," Vegard, recognizing "your" knight, rear and fell the princess,
The princess sobs as the knight mounts "his" shared, excelled, borne support.

She was now the past tense of Vegard's present goal,
His trained destiny...and he fearlessly increased his gait to the battle!

Kathleen Lorraine Carrithers McCombs

Rage

Lifeless dolls with painted smiles and vacant eyes
  dirty water and a rusty faucet dripping
 never know how much it hurts until it happens
and it's all true
  bloody knives long forgotten
the wounds never heal
meaningless words and fake kisses
  it was all a game to you
    you-you-you it always was
nobody else mattered
this time around the game can't be found
    dark nights up all hours
  the little cafe on the corner
only sells black coffee at half price at three a.m.
black lipstick smeared and torn
  the cracked mirrors hold the memory of
    the blood
good-bye

Nicole Leary

Wandering Thoughts

Sitting in here all day makes me wonder what I'm doing.
Disillusioned thoughts make me go crazy
as I ponder on how much longer I will be able to last.
Not knowing kills the human mind
destroying it till there's nothing more to say.
Covering the feelings of one's self-being unable to understand
the meaning of interaction with more than one person, yourself.
Crazy counterparts try to relieve the strain of everyday life,
but not believing what they're actually doing.
Threatening but in a weird way
interesting as we look at the person next to us not
in the strangerous way but differently too different,
eerily a mess our mind becomes.
Vivid shadows evolve until we can't take much of it anymore.
Then we wake up, wake up from the bitter sweetness of comfort
and security unaware of what I've become.

Kelsi Blasingame

Terminal

Waiting areas lined with chairs like soldiers standing inspection.
Disinfectant permeates the air like formaldehyde fills a lab
Music broadcasted into unsuspecting minds while
People in various uniforms scurry to their appointed duties.

Wheelchair victims dodge people pacing, waiting for new arrivals,
Some ponder what it would be like to leave this earth,
Others gripped with fear of dying while children laugh and play,
A few search for concessions while others seek solace in chapels.

Behind restricted doors, operations seem endless;
Watching of gauges and scopes, concentration on instruments.
Safety and comfort is on every attendants' mind
As they begin to announce who is next.

Security checks for passes while people move forth in order,
Knuckles whiten on many as they are strapped in, some read.
Like the roar of a hungry lion, engines come to life
As the aircraft leaves the gate and begins its taxi to the runway.

William J. O'Brien

Conversing

The cat said meow, the dog barked loudly.
Along came the horse whinnying softly.
The woodchuck chucked trying to sound fanciful.
The Blue Jay modulating his cries of delight
No matter how it was said it all
came out as what a beautiful morning

Mary Jane Fronk

Untitled

Heavy heart, blue and wide like the ocean.
A trickling tear; so familiar from the many
times before.
They let me down.
An overwhelming feeling of unimportance.
Forgotten.

Shannen Legere

Home Of The Beast

Through the towering dungeon doors, on a path of cold stone
Dispiriting, dark decayed thoroughfare still to walk
Time, unheard-of, no hands on the clock
Yet thine hour glass sits of sand of powdered bone
For in the distance I hear a faint groan
An odor of perfume noisome an intense
Gauntlets; a rapier art ready for defense.
Closer and closer thee come for the fateful sight
Thine last days may anon become night
At the corner thou turn; stand.
She dreams of her past, the Beast sleeps fast
Never to awake, this day's her last
Beheaded with no warning or delay
This deed is done, without betray.

Paul George Meckes

The Soul's Journey

Embraced by the waves, far from the shore
Diving deeper and deeper,
    into blackness below.
Closer and closer the center becomes
    soothed by the coolness, lost in the core.
    Twirling and spinning a dance with the heavens.
Then, from beyond the darkness a storm rises.
The wind, like a whip, strikes out,
    and waves, with angry hands,
        pitch and toss the soul to the shore.
Drowning, gasping and clawing for air,
    desperately aching for solace within.
Frantically searching for a fulcrum in the storm -
    a light from below,
    a hand from above,
To calm the waves and quiet the wind.
    But just as peace returns and the dance begins,
        the storm will rise to scatter the soul into the wind

Searching and waiting for the seas to still.

Tracy Carreon

A Mother's Assurance

My child asked me mother can this be really true,
    do angels watch over us in everything we do?
I answered yes, my darling, in this be rest assured,
    angels are so close to us they hear our every word.
So if I'm frightened mother and you're no where to be found,
    will my angels protect me from everything bad that comes around?
I wish that I could tell you no bad will come to you,
    but already your angels have protected you more then you ever knew.
Just call upon your angels, they will guide you through the day
    listen when they talk to you, you can hear the words they say.
They're the words that tell you wait until the street is clear,
    when you were just about to cross it, but you didn't see
    that car that was coming near.
How you shivered when it passed you because you knew it
    could have hit you, but you listened to that inner voice that
    told you what you should do.
So close your eyes my darling and sleep, sweet dreams tonight
    your angel is watching over you, everything will be alright.

Kay Woitha

Mommy Sonata

Mommy:
Do they take care of you now
    the way you once took care of me?
The house that you once filled,
    now rattles empty, only with me.
Your shadows still are everywhere but....
    gone are "you", put away by me.
That tiny red bird I saw you watch,
    Now watches, quietly, over me.
Those linen towels you once embroidered,
    Now hang, on a rack, near me.
Your wedding bedspread painted with angels,
    now drapes, gently, over me.
Your 56-year-old wedding band I took,
    and now, is worn lovingly, by me.
The "you" I love so much is disappearing,
    agonizingly, witnessed by me.
Mommy:
    I never told you as much.... but...
    your life did matter to me.

Terri Rachelle

To Whom Is So Greatly Loved...

I would Like You To Know

If there was anything humanly possible that I could
do to make you feel better "I SURE WOULD BE THE ONE
TO DO JUST THAT.." If there was a way that I could
pick you up and take you to the mountains in the
Holy Land that spills with the Holy Waters of Christ..
"I SURE WOULD BE THE ONE TO DO JUST THAT.."
Michael, I would like you to know I sat beside Jesus
and I said Jesus we all have a journey to fulfill. But
I need you to prepare us for Michael's journey and
prepare Michael, Lord, by giving him courage and
strength and ease his suffering, help him walk
through this journey in peace.
Jesus answered me: FOR HE NEED NOT TO WORRY FOR HE SHALL
NOT TAKE THIS JOURNEY UNPREPARED FOR HE SHALL
BE CLEANSED
WITH THE HOLY WATER OF CHRIST," FOR SURE CHRIST
SHALL DO JUST THAT."
MAY YOUR SUFFERING EASE....

Renee Bye Thomas

Always And Forever

My heart is in your hands
Do with it what you may
Promise me forever
And forever my heart will stay.

Few words cannot express my thoughts
Perhaps thousands per page
Even more they may speak,
But are locked in my heart's cage,

Those three words could never express
The feelings wrapped inside
Ready and waiting to be said
But in my thoughts they hide

Always and forever race round my thoughts
As someone mentions your name.
How my heart does shudder
No feeling could be the same.

Melissa Bruce

The Bottle...

What do you see at the bottom of the bottle my friend?
Do you think once you reach it your pain will end?

The drink is just a game of hiding seek.
The more you drink the deeper you can hide.
But my friend, it's alright to be weak.

Often in one's life the path may turn grey
And a place of refuge is needed.
But at the bottom of the bottle is only a darker day.

Can't you see that the more you drink the more you'll hurt?
Sure, you may feel on top of the world for a while
And you may feel that you can fly-
But you're only letting yourself die.

I care too much about you to let you drown yourself in sorrow.
Please, remember there's always tomorrow.

It won't be easy to face your pain
You may feel that you're souls' on fire
But let it all go, release a thunderous rain.

Eventually that rain will wash away all the flames.
The clouds will break away freeing a beautiful sun,
And that's when you'll know, the bottle is done!

Lori Anne Merchant

Cousins

Our minds have traveled down a volcano of time
Dodging the slow larva flow born by hidden
Explosions of feeling exposed by family
Forced thinking brought on by the death of a cousin
Not brought on by us.

Our family connection inhibits handling our own explosions
Shields the innocence of our forgetting
Protects our own asking, our own identity.

Finding it was so open, not empty
There were people to trust, respond to us.
Now we recognize the scary thoughts of that explosion
The slow of larva tells us we no longer want to mingle
With people who live within their own frightening terms.

Peter Merrill

Friendship

Friendship
    does strange things,
arouses arguments, MEANS HAVING DISAGREEMENTS,
    but at the end...
            it's love!

It's like a butterfly
    spreading its color-stained wings
for the first time as a young adult.

Friends start out as caterpillars
    that are motionless and ordinary
    but as you grow,
        friendship grows
and soon you'll be a color-stained adult.

Vanessa A. Forcina

Untitled

What virtual reality?
Alive, enscreened totality?
Puffing vanity, tempting sanity,
"Come play", the small green Lorelei sings,
"To Oz, the land where you'd be kings."
And so, to inner space we flee —
But who'll be pulling all the strings?

Norine Casale

Plea for Harmony

"This tapestry of faces
enrich our lovely land.
This melody of languages, a symphony of sound.
Blended together, as cultures finally are,
can't we be harmonious
on this, our special star?

Susan D. Otto

My Master

My master is taking me out for a walk! I am just like a dog, except I can talk! My master is taking me out for a ride! I should be happy! Instead, I just cried! My master went shopping; he brought me some food! Hey, this says, "Alpo," what's wrong with this dude! Okay! It got chilly, I needed a coat! What's wrong with this man? He brought a new boat!

I thought I'd make him happy. I'll do a trick! You know that man hit me! He used a big stick! I said, "I know, I'll beg - May I have a quarter?" He said, "You're really pushing it. I am boiling a pot of water!"

I really needed a few dollars so I went and asked my son. Why did I ask Master? I knew. He had a gun! Oh sure, I get his slippers and I lay down at his feet! I even like his friends, Bow wow! Bow wow! That's Mr. Pete!

Christmas is coming, maybe, he'll let me chew on my Bone! You know he took that away from me! And, he's on the telephone! I try to please my Master and do the things I should. But master doesn't try to please me back. He's not a good master! I wished he'd gotten a CAT!!

Sharon Anita Jackson

Poem

Father don't tell me what you know...
Don't say that it will be alright, and then walk away from me.
It will never be alright again because you've lost your love for me.
I cry for you Daddy.
You never notice the tears on my face, because you fail to care.
Well daddy, I can't love you anymore either.
There is no room left for me to do so.
So I'll say goodbye without shedding a single tear.
But I want to ask you one question before I go...
Will you remember me?

Nora Wojtanowski

Taking A Stroll

I took a stroll a while back
Down an old abandoned Railroad track
It went thru the woods and across the bridge
Down thru the valley and over the ridge
Debris was scattered along the way
Looking as though it was meant to stay
The ties were rotted, the nails full of rust
The dust atop the cinders, had somehow formed a crust
It reminded me of way back when
I watched the train come round the bend
It's whistle an Blowing, smoke shooting from the stack
It's long line of cars with he caboose at the back
The engineer waving as he passed me by
They called it the Flyer, but it could not fly
That iron trail is quiet now, there's no whistle, no click clack
From those many wheels of iron,
As they rolled right down the track
AS I stop and stand in silence
There's a void that's left within
I am left with only memories, of those day's way back then.

Merle L. Ray

How Do We Know

Like rivers of great, flowing- always flowing- up and
down, sometimes rough and sometimes calm, deep and shallow,
depth unknown in parts; as life is, reminds one that inside
of us all are peaks and valleys, joy and pain; dark inner parts
of the soul, undiscovered; struggling to survive and reach a
medium.

How Do We Know
Can one ever see, or come close dwelling together,
reaching a point of contentment, so as to exist without
fear and terror. All is not vanity. Moving beyond the
dark shadows of lost hope; to grasp and hold on to peace
and happiness. Pain is pain, love is or isn't - Time is
seemingly endless - yet person to person-

How Do We Know
Touching, the reality of it all is, do we really ever
touch - other than the surface, a fleeting moment
of joy, holding on tightly to all the in between's, bits and
pieces of a brief moment of closeness. Through space
and time there are limits; yet, the sun still shines
on the good, and the Bad. For now, and
perhaps tomorrow too. How do we know

Mamie L. Pace

The Hefty Shepherd

That winter eve the bust crept slowly
Down the frozen, snow-buried avenues.
The seats, old and tattered, shook vigorously
Vibrating loudly from the over-taxed coach.

The squealing of old, worn brakes
Brought the bus to a creeping halt.
Raising a clatter, the rusty doors opened
Letting in gusts of sub-zero winds.

A haggardly woman, looking bizarre,
Clumsily climbed aboard with her Hefty bag.
She plopped heavily into a ragged seat
Emitting a grown and a rude-sounding grunt.

Five or six others of similar stature
Sullenly occupied the bedraggled bus;
Travelling nowhere as the rode and rode
Down street after street.

Yet all were safe and well-protected
From winter's bite and the terrors of night.
Yes, the scenario did seem more than odd;
Little did I know that their driver was God.

Ty Kaufman

Thinking About the Rain

Picture a little mountain stream that suddenly comes alive and rushes
down the mountains side to add new life to the lakes and rivers below,
the trees and stones washed clean leaving the appearance of a fresh
coat of paint, and the air is filled with the scent of wild flowers
blooming somewhere not so distant. I see rain drops hanging on
leafless branches as cut glass prisms on costly chandeliers.
I see a farmer, head bowed holding a straw hat while the rain fill the
cracks in the sun baked field and with the rain comes a promise that
the crops will grow.
When I am walking it is a comfort to know that I am not alone, for I
can feel and see it all around me, and the city lights reflecting in
the hundreds of rain pools on the streets and sidewalks, they depict
to me what one would find in an art gallery.
The twilight hours of a rainy day are set aside for the melancholy a
quiet time for personal thoughts, to think about the past or what to
do in the future.
The steady gentle pat of rain on the house roof is but a symphony to
sleep by or for that occasion when two people have something
special
to say to each other.

Ken Ruggles

The Discovery (Alaska 1994)

A song sings from Mount Hess, permeating the earth's scent
Dreams upon the breeze extend to the horizon
Gently whispering toward a field of fire
Midnight sun — dancing through the sweet grass

Searing across the enormous sky, on a cold charcoal morning
Rooted in a memory of a kiss that once enveloped
Carried on the wings of white wind, a hidden trace of passion
Lies dormant — sleeping beneath the birch and aspen

The sun reaches to caress, melting arctic snow and ice
A lone gray wolf pauses for a moment
To drink from the Chena, awakening a primal hunger
That devours — and cannot be denied

Raven comes to rest on silken shoulders,
        with talons that rip at virgin flesh
Painted clouds framed in crimson, blanket the cutting desire
Piercing the very instinct that draws inward,
        while learning to walk on stars
The moon — hypnotizes and steals the sacred soul

Carefully encircling glacial peaks, a veil of fog and mist rises
Deftly the once-scarred smoothed stone falls from fathoms deep
To pristine crystal waters and the lands created by time and motion
Uncharted latitudes — pure, untouched and waiting...

Lisa Y. Eskin

Dark...Light

The time of darkness is full of fantasies and
dreams. When daylight breaks, the secret love
must vanish from the human eye. During the
time of light, the hatred comes from underneath
denying what it witnessed the night yonder. Under
the cover hides the love two people shared with
compassion and understanding of each one's
needs. Until the fatal flaw when one drifts
away into solid brightness. The other stays
behind with another in the opaque darkness. The
two are now lost forever, but hold the other in
their heart forever. For love after love, the
feeling is still there. Until that day when darkness
disappears forever. Her heart leaves from within
him as he forgets his first forsaken love. But yet
the hole is there, and as it widens, the man
turns forever in the eye of hate and soon
realizes he is lost from her heart forever
which he banished.

Kim Geisthardt

Rain

Walking down the sidewalk, her face in my mind,
Dusk had just settled and traffic grew high.
The rain becomes drizzle, the street lights only glare.
A giggle of happiness were her kinds of days,
Playing with the rain as her nose wrinkled raindrops.
Continuing down the people lined city,
Depression beside me holding my hand.
Wish it were hers to keep warmness there,
Now its the cold wetness that sets in.
Forgetting her is impossible as asking the rain to stop,
For both are inseparable as sounds remind me.
A truck in the distance comes screeching to a halt,
The memory of rain and my daughters last cry.
It pulls from my heart the last of the pain,
And leaves me walking by the rain.

Marie Beck

Steps

Long tendrils from mind-sight continuum
drew me to ivory-clad figure undulating
to lone rhythm of white cane
across geometry of parking lot-street.
A stranger's "may I help?" roused her.

She turned her body half a circle." I had to see you
but my left brain has a large tumor."
I didn't take her arm, but stayed close to her touch
as together we essayed red-green light.
"I live on the corner. Everyone around knows me."

"What do you do?" "Play and teach music." "I played piano
at conservatoire. But it takes two hands" - here
she lifted left hand to crush down upon crystal
piano in the sky - "two hands to play Chopin!"
Swift she turned from landscape of despair.

Ocean-at-dawn eyes-luminous-blazed her own truth:
"I can still teach! The university uses me to teach
French over the phone to students with AIDS.
...I'll be all right now."
I live on the street of man.

Vernez Olshausen

The One and Only ... The Lonely

My heart is lonely,
drowning in the pool of forsaken feelings.
There are deserted days,
where I am alone always.
My abandoned soul weeps so,
desperately grasping for someone to hold.
A single tear descends from my eye,
but no one's there to see me cry.
I feel so empty and withdrawn,
suffering from years of pain and rejection.
Look at me with your incriminating eyes.
I am the one and only.... the lonely.

Kimberly Lutz

Love Lost

  Girl, I love you more
Each and every day, but I
can't tell you because I
wouldn't is now what to say
  I tell myself tomorrow
But tomorrow never comes I'm scared of being
Rejected but tell myself this
Could be the one
  But I know I'll never tell
You, that's the way I am
  I've been that way all my
Life I hope you'll understand
  I wish I could forget you
But every time I try something
Always happiness
  Makes me want to cry
I know you'll never see me
The way that I see you
  I can't get you out of my
mind and I don't know what to do

J. Lozen

A Portrait Of A True Friend

A true friend isn't afraid to say how much they care.
A true friend isn't afraid to promise they'll always be there.
A true friend will stick by your side
until those feelings of loneliness and insecurity subside.
A true friend loves you with all of their heart
and you both hurt whenever you're apart.

A. Edwards

A Road

A road on the left; a road on the right.
Each of which roads will lead to a fight.
A road on the left; a road without pain.
Only a road like this has no lanes.
A road on the right; a road with no strength.
A road such as this contains no such length.
A road in the rear; a road of the past.
A road such as this shows your life lost.
A road you are on; a road with some wrongs.
A road that must always build and stay strong.

Mark Anthony Ortiz

The Past - The Future

As I turn the pages of my life
  Each one is filled with joy and strife.
Ah, such a mixture of brass and gold
  A perfect blend of hot and cold.
I found a page that looked so grand
  My grown up men-their baby hands
Had filled my heart through all these years
  With happy days and gentle tears.
I turned the next and smiled with glee
  There was a lady just for me!

We laughed and cried as women do
  And saw each others troubles through
The last page faded as I looked
  I saw beside it - another book
A brand new story - old but new
  Of babies and ladies and how they grew!!

Mary E. Austin

Precious Trials

Life is precious
Each time a hand reaches out in love
  angels rejoice and praise God
Man in made in the Creator's image
  to fellowship, to do what is pleasing
  to one who is pleasing
When suffering begins to manifest
Which part of the heart cries out -
Is it the hurting or the appeased?
Many trials are endured
Yet so many are wasted
  because the worth is not realized
God grieves for us - this creation called human
Each soul in its portion is a testimony
Will the tender Care of truth overcome self?
Gradual resolution to bend to His will
  makes perfect the spirit.

Susan Cunningham

Bills

Bills, bills, bills; everyone in the United States has
bills to pay. This is almost everyday.

This I know for a fact is true, if you're late it's
going to be late due.

Every time I turn around there is a bill to be found.

It's not a thrill to be paying all these bills.
Light bills, gas bills, telephone bills; I wish they
would chill on all these bills.

Takeisha Austin

Whereabouts

The forest is surrounded with a dew of unknown mist,
Echoes of a dew drop ever so silently exist.

An archaeological wonder a story so untold,
civilizations are arising breaking all the mold.

Rustled needles hug the ground go undisturbed by the breeze,
as the sunlight passes down through the holes atop the trees.

A place of sanctuary sanctified from all the rest,
Human interference is only an unwanted guest.

Spores of energy just awaiting ready to explode,
symphonies about the treetops are easily bestowed.

With no walls to protect it embraces all as a friend,
once one gets inside has no beginning or has no end.

We all try to duplicate it but simply we cannot,
the genuine lasts forever the counterfeit does not.

We try to make it better a mountain we cannot climb,
lets stop and realize, mother nature is doing fine.

Thomas Casey

Courage

Courage, I have often heard, the word said
echoing waves through out my head
the strength of power, strength through pain
like a rolling ocean again and again.

I close my eyes and hope to see
the illusion fade into reality
and when I ask, and question why
courage, courage is always the reply.

From my slumber, I awake
the first step I must take
and boldly I begin to climb
through the recesses or my mind.

When I reach the final stair
the weight I knew is no longer there
then my laughter echoes down
courage I have finally found.

Kristin Mull

The Wedding

They sent out 200 invitations and there were
endless preparations. The Church was filling up
with all her friends, and her Mother was in a
tizzy. Her Father was standing there "much poorer"
and He was about to escort his daughter in.

Mary Ellen Robert's, was about to change her
name forever, and she too was in a flutter. The
fragrance of the flowers, the photographers at
the ready, the wisp of smoke from the candles,
the tense anticipation of the audience, were all
at their very peak. Now the organ peeled out
loudly and The Minister stood there smiling.

Richard, starched and sweating was waiting and
his best man stood beside him. The solemn
march to the alter was over and now the
Minister spoke. "Mary Ellen Do you take....?"
She looked deep into the eyes of Richard and
she knew she hadn't made a mistake!

Bill Davidson

A Brotherly Portrait

Free spirits, rare breeds on earth,
Enervating lives with soul and mirth.
Live and let live the music they wrought,
Visions of tomorrow free of prejudiced thought.
Relishing dares of life's mocking faces,
Filling their pores with life's bountiful places.
Offering drink from their spirited cup,
They'll forever share their gift to sup.
Don't clip the wings of these delightful souls,
Leave them intact, complete, and whole.
Impugned by societal constraints, unable to fly,
They will plummet to earth,..... and die.

Kathy J. D'Antoni

Drifting Dreamer

Shifting patterns of dizzying light
Enter through my windows tonight.

I close the blinds of overworked eyes
And escape into worlds where vision flies.

In dream, I float as light as air—
Fearless and strong but helpless and bare.

Quick thoughts dance wild rhythms unknown
Revealing connections, relating what's shown.

But sight joins sound with scent felt sweet.
I capture its essence while details retreat.

Evasive truth, my experience teaches
Arrives in moments one seldom reaches.

The mind is body when thoughtfully felt
In memory of lessons God randomly dealt.

Awoken by daylight in jumbled belief,
I splash out colors and smile great relief.

Mike Salis

In My Arms

Come to a room that's warm and inviting
Enveloped in perpetual sunset—the sun's blush,
Cuddle a baby in soft, fuzzy jammies
With the sweet smell of Spring in his hair.
Warm lips against a petal-soft cheek
Drink in fragrance like nectar,
Tiny laughter mixed with yawns
Fills a yearning soul.
All too soon this too will fade
Like the blush on the face of the sun,
The child will grow leaving longing arms
Wishing for Springtime again.

Susan R. Woodward

The Power of Poetry

The power of poetry is hard to deny
Even when fate steps in, and we're about to die
It seems words are so powerful, they cut right through
The heart, mind and our being
Without leaving a clue
Poetic thoughts and words may bring solace and tranquility
Although some words defy sensibility
Poetry can be passionate, sorrowful and cruel
And we use the words and feelings as a sorrowful tool
Finding comfort is a complex emotion to all
We look, and seek, and sometimes we create an imaginary wall
As a poet I feel compelled to say
I become more enthralled with the mystery of poetry each day

Sandra Glassman

Forever Knowing

Every tear I've cried,
every thought I've thought are from inside.
As each tear falls from my face, I think of what I have done.
For just being human I have killed people.
I've ripped out their hearts and torn it with my thoughts.
Fearfully I face a world unknown to those who feel pity for
confused, lonely, and sad me's.
I'm not alone, so I've been told, but where are the people
who cry at night?
Where are the people who are scared to awake in the
morning, and face a friend?
For I am alone, and either I die not knowing their are
others, or wait knowing I won't be alone forever.

Kathryn Rowton

Common Sense

The question of why seems to enter my mind
every time I see them whispering.
The question of my seems to enter my mind
every time I hear them snickering

Why don't they know their ruining their lives
every time they do it.
Why don't they know their killing themselves
every time they abuse it.

I like them for who they are
but not what they do.
I like them for who they are
but they must not have a clue.

You and I were smart
I would rather be shot.
You and I were smart
maybe they'll get caught.

The question of why seems to enter my mind
every Friday after school.
The question of why seems to enter my mind
knowing that the stuff just isn't cool.

Katie Bell

All Through The School

Give self directions all through the school.
Everyone will love you and think you are cool.
Making good decisions will help you keep the rules.
A positive self image will make you stay in school

Your peers will look up to you, teachers will be impressed.
By your way and actions, everyone will be blessed.
School will be a better place, learning will be a ball
This attitude will be enjoyed by all.

Each day you will see, there is no better way
Than controlling yourself, and out of trouble you will stay
This philosophy can be used in school or home
Direct yourself and you won't fear answering the phone
The proven result will fill you with glee
If you begin now, you can use it endlessly.

Sandra E. Thomas

Creatures Of Beauty

They have cast their spell over our imaginations for
countless centuries. Most deadly beast of prey, the guards
of treasure magical and golden alike. Steadfast in time
and history. With their impenetrable skin grown armor they
make the bravest man run in fear. Steal muscles and sharp
razor teeth shred anything in their path. The dying out
race which once engulfed the skies with terror. The winged
fighter with fire as breath. They are the monarchs of the
sky, they are DRAGONS.

Michael Schulze

Wanting You

My heart is full of joy, when I think of you Oh boy!
Everything is so bright, and its going to be so right
My heart aches and aches, I feel like it's going to break
Being away from you I can't hardly bare
But I know in my heart you really care
You're such a beautiful light
You make my life a wonderful sight
I know where I want to belong
So I'm sitting here all alone
Lying here at night, wanting to hold you tight
When I'm thinking of you I get the chills
But it gives me so much thrills
My heart is not in a dream-I want to hold your hand and things
For when the time comes, I know it will bring
I want to be in your arms
That would be such a charm
I've been hurting for a long time
Wishing you could be mine
I'm so very lonely
Oh, I love you only

Linda Gambino

The First Time

I could tell the first time I saw your face
Everywhere you go I would have to follow
I trailed from here to there, place to place
When together, I was free as a swallow

As we walked hand in hand on the beach
Beneath the glittering moon and the stars
You could hear the gulls overhead shrill and screech
We part leaving deep emotional scars

Thoughts of you are what I could be proud of
As you walk slowly away I feel remorse
If only you could feel the heat of my love
You feigned your love in every course

As deep is my heaven made love when together
When you die my love will remain forever

Robert A. Pavolka

The Poetic Ploy Boy

As a poet I write about
experiences, persons, places and things.
Some make me cry,
while others make me sing.
Yet, this is my joy
and ultimately my poetic ploy.
For I shall not be outwitted!
My emotions have been acquitted,
by reason of the rhyme,
my heartfelt efforts being sublime.
Anything short of love has no guarantees
and loneliness can be a wretched disease.
But as for me, I cannot release
those and that which touches and does jolt
these inner workings within me.
Let it be for the sake of expression
that I learn these lessons.
Nothing and nobody can bring me down or make me blue,
cause my utterances, words, slang and writings
release me from captivity and always renew!

Paul Davis

11 O'Clock News

The News is a half-hour commercial,
exploiting the most hideous crimes.
Life blows-up in our face,
and we're asked the same question —-
"You've just lost everything,
how does that make you feel?"

They highlight sports and fighting,
scientific blunders, and religious perversions,
expanding their media coverage,
to exclude - all that is "good".
Focusing on extremes,
exemplifying freaks! —-

They reinforce a tolerance for madness,
as the main thrust of our existence.
They tell you, "it's going to rain", it snows.
Tell you, "It's going to be fair", it's cold.
Tell you - what they want you to hear.
But they tell you, what you don't want to hear!

The News is a travesty, systematically - dehumanizing.
But tell me, "how does it make you feel?"

Michael Blaine

Father's Day What Does It Mean?

Father's day, what does it mean?
Eyes are sad, no happy gleam
Father caused so much pain
Have you ever wondered why you're the blame?
Father stole my childhood, confess
Eternity filled with so much stress
Father, please don't open that door
Your footsteps covering the floor
Father is a wonderful word
But it rings of terror being heard
Father's image stays in the mind
So peace is very hard to find
Father's day, what does it mean?
Day light, dark night, silent screams.

Sharron Wright

Watch The Angels

Did you see the lightness in their
eyes, eagerness in their faces.
They look at you with awe and
admiration your the greatest king of queen.
Their hearts swell with love and pride.
They love the simple things, the kind
words spoken, the gentle touch.
The simple songs you sing lulls them
a drift into some other realm where all things
are beautiful.
All the wonderful you've done for
them will return like a ripple in a pond.
You'll look back someday and wish
you could get that loyal stare.
You'll long to hear the sweet melodies
sung in harmony by you and that sweet
little angel.
Take care of those little souls entrusted
to us to care and love. One day you'll
get back ten fold all the love and time given freely!

Robin Olivero

Seamless Transitions

Dark, only stars, trees outlined by horizons,
Eyes, search for definition but fix on nothing,
Sky, in the distance the only noticeable fixture in sight.
Light, slowly filters into the space once filled by nothing.
Stars, fade away, giving up their luminescence to the solar king,
Bursting, into your gaze, pastel colors coat and fill the air.
Lost, without a trace, the darkness gone you wonder
if you blinked too soon.
Horizons, now in view, the branches of the trees can now be seen.
Seamless, was the way, the darkness of the night slipped through.
Transitions, of time and space, melt together days to fill the years.
Gone, is the moment never to again be seen this way.
Forever, on this will, continue before you notice the years
have now slipped by.

Paul Vincent Longo

Gotcha

Let me out I say to the stranger. He has locked me in a room where
eyes stare through flickering candlelight. Propped up in a
corner, your lifeless body gloats and I feel the silence of the
laughing heart from within a cold, pallid being. And these eyes
know my secret and they shine as I tell the stranger lies from
behind the door. But he continues to sing the song of a lifetime.
Reaching for those ethereal high notes, the notes sung only by the
noble and gold-throated martyrs of old. I stand shaking and
listen, and listen no more. Pounding fist to the wall, I try to
escape from your suffocating gentle grasp, still void of life but
still fierce and loving. And the shadows dance on the wall,
slipping forked tongues and dripping hands down my throat, reaching
for my story. Outside, the stranger sings and sings.

Sofia Cruz

The Dragon's Gold

Sometimes you must go through fire to find love.
Facing the dragon may earn you the dragon's gold.
Joy of joys follows desolation of desolations.
When your vessel is packed with pain, empty it so that it may be
    filled again.
You'll find before you break, relief will be granted.
Never give up and impress your enemy with your obstinacy, at
least.
Offer, kindness in the face of ill will,
Peace in the presence of destruction,
Sorrow in the company of sorrow,
Joy quietly at all times.
Life is of your making,
Knowledge is the key to life,
Variety is the spice.
Realize that love is gained slowly like the making of a diamond.
And rejoice when at last love is given to you.

Marianne Cline

The Second Day of the Latest Year

He questioned the fault for dying leaves

and shrank from the heat of candle flames.

He remembered the taste of warm plum wine

and the pain of last year's labor.

He told himself secrets to stir his blood

and wrapped my hair around his hand.

He recited the names of tyrants and kings

and named the color of my softest skin.

Katherine Gongora

The Master's Bouquet

Satan had plucked me from the Master's bouquet
Faded and dying in a dark corner I lay
My roots, uprooted, my petals turning brown
All alone and forsaken I lay on the ground
Guess who planted me back in his bouquet
And came and revived me with his holy water today
Who could have believed a dying flower like me
God could revive and plant again for all to see
With bright eyes skyward I praise Him all day
Because now I live and grow in the master's bouquet
I grow for his glory and I bloom in his love
Just for him only, my master in the sky above
I stand in his garden head above the rest
Because He is my master I give him my best
I show Him my true colors each day of my life
And in His garden of love my prayers are rife
He waters and feeds me each day with his word
And above the others, my praise to Him can be heard
Never again will Satan get a hold on me
Because in the master's bouquet I will always be.

Patsy Thomas

Inviting A Vision

I stood and watched from afar, she appeared to me in a mist of falling rain, for I could see within her eyes, that each crystal raindrop fall reflects a beauty to reach beyond non-comparison.

A sudden vision raced across my mind just as fast as my heartbeats, as I gazed at what I thought to be the most precious thing, though this was no ordinary vision, for my mind had created the utmost extraordinary exultation.

A vision far beyond a fantasy, one to believe that only she can be the one to take me there. From just a few seconds ago, I've come to discover, that I know not of a place on earth I'd rather be than in her presence, if only I could perceive a simple touch from her, my destiny is well more than considered found my destiny I will be living at that very moment, and my heart and soul shall surrender every sweet emotion. A time or two in my life I've experienced love yes I've had

love and I've learned that love is not at all an easy task. Due to the fact that love is a very delicate agitation of the mind.

I would go beyond any point to convince this darling angel that the love I have is nothing more than true.

Straight from the core of my heart I cry out helplessly, Please let it be that she will give the same to me, please let her be Mrs. Me!!!

Walter Tucker

So Distant

As the wing-beats fade into the
    far lands of moonlight,
And the dense leaves overhead
    quietly seek their places of rest

I - almost breathless with your being so close -
    failing to satisfy the unfilled pages that
    rustle softly as if kissed by the wind.

You - absorbed by the water's edge -
    with hazel eyes intent upon your
    half-drawn poem.

To think of all the faint jesting,
    yet secret, earnest plans we made
    about coming here - never really thinking
    it ever would be, or it ever could be.

Moments ago, Syros seemed so distant,
    but you said, "Just trust me."

Sherry L. Gleason

A Dinner For Two

A dinner for two with candles all aglow, your favorite music on the stereo, a table spread with lace so fine, a feast fit for a king to dine, a single rose sits in the midst of this grand array — as if it knows — this is a special day.

A prayer of thanks to God above for sending me someone to love, a glass of wine — lifted in anticipation — to toast a future filled with great expectation, a beautiful evening, filled with rapture and bliss, ends with a single kiss. A goodbye is said, a door is closed, and a tear is shed.

C. A. Howard

The Learning Tree

Tears are shed to those who are born
Fearing of the misery of this world of terrible scorn
We try our hardest to teach.
Values of life and one's purpose;
With reason they can reach
Some taught to be earnest, respectful, and to appreciate
While others are taught to be cold, ruthless and, to hate
Once fully grown we understand
To each his own is the way it's planned
Live and let live principles we preach
But what comes down to it, is the sad part
That goal in life will we ever reach?

Michael L. Jones

I Am Like

I am like a blind man
Feeling his way around a room
Searching for meaning
And things to do.

Then I stumble upon a table
Which is like a problem to overcome.
Or go around just as the blind man would.
If I could.

Just see that filled-up room.
That's why God is my seeing-eye dog.
I hold His leash tight but sometimes it slips.

When it slips, it's hard to find.
When I do, I grab with all my might.
Because without Him I am confined.

To an unknown area where I am lost,
Then find His leash and grab on tight,
Like the bind man would.

Torrey Steven Moss

Heaven's Gate

In a quiet, darkened room - tired, weak, dying, a woman lay.
Family and friends were told to leave. She motioned one to stay.
The dyer said, "I can tell you. They would not understand."
Her eyes danced excitedly. "It's going to be grand.
I'm standing in line before a great big gate.
I can't go in just yet. My turn I have to wait.
If I stand on tippy toe I can see inside.
It's true what we've been told!
Heaven's streets are paved with glittering, glimmering gold."

L. Janeene Versfelt

Our Forever Love

Last night I dreamed about you;
Felt your arms about me tight;
And I trembled in blissful agony,
As you loved me through the night.

I saw your face above me;
The love shining in your eyes;
Heard the sweet words you whispered to me,
Just before the sun began to rise.

Then I woke, and it was over;
I remembered that you were gone;
For my love lies buried in a foreign land,
And forever I'll be alone.

My darling, I still see you;
As if it were only yesterday;
And the love that we knew then,
Sustains me through each new lonely day.

When the blessed night comes,
I'll dream of you again,
And maybe I'll awake in another world,
Where love like ours will never end.

Laura J. Robinson

People

People
Fight, is it right, weak against the strong
Is it wrong?
Children starving, the aged screaming day to day
How will tomorrow be?
Mother's grief and sorrow,
Is it right
Father's depression
Is it wrong?
People, how long before we understand
That to live for ourselves,
And not for one another, just makes it even longer
The rich live's to die
Is it right?
The poor die to live,
Is it wrong?
We see it does not work, but for how long?
The stripping of people's pride, and taking of self respect
Why can't we live as one, before we are all gone.
I ask... Is it right or is it wrong?

Steven Milo Squires

At Day's End

Soft light of dusk when day is done,
Fill me with the warmth of the now gone sun.

You are somewhere between the day and the night,
You are somewhere between the dark and the light.

Soft light of dusk when the day is done,
You bring a calm such a peaceful one.

I sit and stare at your musky hue
and gaze about at your veils of blue,
I audit the things I accomplished this day
And contemplate the tasks I've let go astray.

Soft light of dusk I stop and savor
replenish my soul with your mystical flavor,
Then quietly day transforms into night
and peacefully blue turns away from the light.

Till the soft light of dusk
is no more,
And the frosty night
chills my bones to the core.

Sally Morris Tonks

Together Forever

Let me be the one to hold on to your dreams.
Fill you with pleasure, love, and beautiful things.

To hold you in my arms by the sea of deep blue.
Together at last, together as two.

Together forever and never to part,
your love will live forever and grow within my heart.

Your love to me is more precious than gold,
the love that any other was never told.

Every night I dream of you and things
that lovers do.

But these dreams are reality,
because forever in my heart will be you
    and me.

Misty Blair

Beyond The Pall

My life is covered with the stench of failure
filled with aborted dreams shattered like
cold glass in the arctic twilight of my
solitude
One step after the other falling on
the unforgiving earth, as the yearnings
of my heart dance in droplets of
frozen mist before my eyes

Lurching from side to side circling
footprints made only moments ago
I watch the drifting grains of cold
sweep over them
I am filled with a numbness that admits
neither doubt nor certainty as I pitch
forward to kiss the earth with my cheek

I say hello to the pale tranquility
that greets me with silence

Paul B. MacRae

Secrets

You come to me at night in a dream it seems at first, but the
first touch quickens my heart to fear.
My imagination runs away as the night goes on.
Why are you here! What do you want! My spirit asks in fear.
When will morning come, why isn't it here yet?
Before daylight can make its way into my room, your shadow
appears at the door. I hear the screeching of the door, your
footsteps are drawing near,
I hear your breathing clearly as you are close. I smell
the stench of your body, you are there.
I am afraid, what do I do or is this the secret between us two.

Wishing I was dead, I pull the blanket over my eyes; hoping, you
don't realize, I'm alive. It's too late!
You reach to unveil my face; but to your surprise, I have slipped
away. Under the bed, I hide away from your
wicked eyes. Praying within for you not to
take me again. I am saved from that hour you came to cause trauma.
I am afraid, what do I do the secret is escaping between me and you.

Years and years have gone by; and no one has heard my cry.
I can't forget the eerie and restless nights. Still, the pain lingers inside.
My soul cries out to be freed, so please tell me? "Why! Why! Why
did it have to be me?"

Marlene Huffman

Ship Wreck

Dragging himself to the nearest splinter of drift wood,
Floating until, Alas!
Land,
Getting closer and closer,
Noticing men carrying long sticks with pointy ends on them,
Sticks came flying towards him,
Hitting him square in the back,
He sunk.
With his last ounce of energy,
Making a failed attempt to stay above water.
He died.

J. T. Fisher

Marriage

Expecting marriage to be a perfect bowl of cherries, is pure
foolishness, one has to come into a marriage with an open mind,
knowing that there may be differences, challenges and changes
ahead. It takes two to make a good marriage, just as it takes two
to break it, no one person is totally at fault. To make a good
marriage, one has to be willing, first and foremost, and put aside
all senseless anger that can do more harm than good.
Communication, no matter what, is most important in a marriage,
without communication, a marriage can have more problems than
necessary. Life is a constant challenge for whatever goal or
mission, this is also true with marriage. People have their
problems, their differences, faults and failures, we are all on
different levels of thinking and knowledge, specifically, men
and women. It is interesting to know that some people are hard
at work to keep their jobs, and hardly working to save their
marriage. However, there are those who are willing to take the
challenges, and make changes, to do what it takes to hold on to
the marriage that once meant something in the beginning.

Ursulla M. Streets-Jones

Moment Of Escape

For a moment of escape my soul cried out
For a moment of escape my body reached
Soul and body unite forces as they ride
the waves of torment endeavorsly preparing
for Siege

Riding the stormy waves of torment— Hoping
to deviate the tragic course of destiny

Only to come to an unruffled state— As my
soul mate emerges out of the midst of the
stormy waves— reaching out with emotion
guiding with illumination my being to
liberty

At liberty reaching for the body
Embracing the soul that cried out for a
moment of Escape

Only to give with predilection a promise of
Eternal Escape

So, I am free for Eternity

Marisol Hammers

Sparrow's Flight

Through the darkened night, the sparrow flew.
Bound by fear but destined he knew.
His courageous attempt for freedom he'd fly.
With strength in his wing's he soared to the sky.
With nothing ahead and nothing behind.
He flew for himself, at ease in his mind.
For he was the last, the last of his kind.
But now he had made it, his freedom he'd find.

Scott Thomas

Shell

Rolling, tumbling through this world seemingly forgotten.
Broken, battered and abused it comes to rest upon the shore.
It has found its sanctuary and it will survive forevermore.

Melinda F. Powell

Let Us Think!

Every time I wake up I thank God
for a new day. For the whole day
ahead of me is filled with dangerous
and fear. I pray to God to direct my path.
Every day before I go to sleep at night
I sit up and listen to the news, I hear
a lot of murder and young innocent little
children being abused. It just makes me
want to cry.
"The United States of America" we all say
with proud and strong! The land of freedom.
"Freedom", kind of makes me want to laugh
just thinking about it. How can we say
we're free when we can't even cross our
own streets? The world is changing, the
world is cruel. It's time to stop and think,
people! It's time to stand up strong and say,
"Let's make a difference!" Lets show what
"The United States of America" really is!!!

Summer Soberanis

A Life Wasted

The strays slowly file in
For a night of wasted time
Wasted words and cheap wine
Oh! That cheap wine
gives you that glow every time

Do they come in for that barmaids smile
Or to dream of what they could have had
Or come in here to forget
What they regret
A life wasted

They fill the dens up day and night
The one's who found that dead end street
And exchange fantasies of I could have been
What a sin
A wasted life of I could have been

And before they know it their time has come
To die without anyone to care
Just those who say they knew them well
What the hell
A life wasted

Robert J. Tomasso

Family

There lives a man who's soul is so glad
For all of the wonderful things he's had.
A fine full life with blessings so great
An ever loving wife who is his soulmate.
Four children who treat him like a king
He loves them more than anything.
They have spiced up his living so much
It is a miracle, they all have that tender touch.
Thanks to you, my family so dear
For filling my life with a cup full of cheer.
The man who is so glad is
Your very grateful Dad.

Tom McCollum

Heaven

There's a place up in the sky,
For all the good people who die;
It's a place called heaven,
It's really nice.

In a dream, I visited heaven.
There I saw angels dancing
And other peculiar things,
It's kind of unique,
A new way of living,
Where all people are free.

The angels were calling, they said,
"Come on in."
I was led through a pearly white gate,
Where a sign state, "Heaven waits."

I danced with the angels and I was pleased,
I loved it in heaven,
What a great place to be.

Lisa Marie Cassels

A Narrow Path

For all your time and consideration;
For all your work and determination
For every effort shown from you,
You'll reap rewards your whole life through.

You toil and fuss and moan and groan -
You work your fingers to the bone,
But never giving up you see
Will bring you where you want to be.
So give it all you've got to give
Each and every day you live.
And sure enough you'll come to see;
You CAN be all that you can be!
The road ahead is hard and long,
But once again you must be strong.
Just keep it straight and see it through
Is all you really have to do.
And keep that dream you have in sight -
Just work real hard with all your might.
And in the end I know you'll see,
You ARE what you set out to be.

Patricia T. Wiggs

Rage Called Life

Give me your hand. Reach out and hold on.
For I shall lead you through this rage called Life.
Reach out far enough so you can follow and I can lead.
Do not fear where I'm going to take you, for I know the way.
Do not fear the unknown, because in the darkness you will find
your future, your destiny. I will help you.
We all will fall sometime, but it shall not matter because we shall
rise again.
Though some times it may seem like we are lost in our journey,
Trust me, for I know the way.
I follow in the footsteps of the ones before me.
Did they finish the game called Life? How did it turn out?
Only one knows for sure...
Is it me? Or is it you? Who is leading who?
Maybe it is neither of us.
But maybe we know all we need to know but
maybe we just don't realize it.
But trust me, for I know the way. I see what others do not see.
I hear what others do not hear. I know what others do not realize.
This is the journey of Life.
Listen closely, for you shall hear the Earth speak.
It can only be heard by those who listen.
It tells you what you need to know.
Do not be afraid. I will help you. I will lead you.
Do not be afraid.

Kandas Burnett

Kids Of The 90's

Innocent victims of vengeance and violence.

> Anxiously opening their young little arms
>   for love, warmth and acceptance;
>   Welcoming a new day, a new dawn
>   Waiting for a gentle touch, a kind word, a soft heart.

Only to be ignored

Then kicked away into the cold and left,

Abandoned and Forgotten.

Innocent victims of vengeance and violence.

> Tied down and helpless while
>   they are bruised, beaten and burned;
>   Hung 'til the death or drown.
> Their bodies mutilated, minds annihilated

>   THE CRIMINALS GO FREE!
>   No Consequence.
>   No Repercussions.
>   No Punishments.

Only the children

Innocent victims of vengeance and violence.

Shannon Morgan

"Night"

As the sun sets the earth is blanketed by a velveted darkness.
For many a time of romance and rest, for others a time of terror.
Away from the lights of the city, night took on a new dimension.
In the jungles of Vietnam, night was a time uncertainty and terror.
A time controlled by the enemy.
So dark under the canopy, as if engulfed by a black hole.
Unable to see your hands in front of your face.
To lay down your head in an attempt to rest.
Suddenly! awakened by the roar of rockets or the thumps of
mortars.
Screams of incoming, the eruption of small arms fire.
You'd hug the darkness at your feet as if it were a woman.
Trying to burrow like a mole to its protective den.
Flares plummeting to the ground, through the smoke.
The brilliant light gave the land scape an eerie 3-D effect.
Red tracers dancing in the darkness, in search of victims.
Screams of pain, medic, air support and medivac fill the night.

Victor Karcz

Are We Really Free

We were bought and sold
for money and gold
given labors because we were thought to be nothing
just because of our skin color
we were thought to be incompetent
so they continued their sales until
Abraham Lincoln came to our aid
then we thought we had it made
but little did we know what the future would bring
for Abraham Lincoln didn't do much of any thing
we were free in body and soul
but the chains of slavery still hold
the chains are loose but we are still not free
because of prejudiceness in our society.

Tamilia Reed

I Need Your Love Dad

Help me please I need to be set free,
For my dad could be calling me.

I'm in need of your love and help dad,
I'm missing the love that we once had.

My friends and I try not to get in trouble a lot,
Mom always wants me home on the dot.

Dad, I need your love more right now,
How could you die, just how?

Without you, I feel all empty inside,
Sometimes at night I've just sat up and cried.

I miss you so much, I don't know what to do,
Dad, please help, I need you more than I used too!

Lindsey Caraker

Retirement

The best time of life can be retirement years,
For one can reminisce o'er both smiles and tears
And look back o'er those years with fond memories;
Some of tribulation, some of apparent ease.

A tribulation of old brings forth a smile,
And the mere thought of past joy can still beguile.
The thinker, o'er remembrances will often muse
While contemplating the reasons for changing views.

Tell me true, what better period of life is there
For me, for you, to reminisce o'er smile and tear?
It seems a waste that just when wisdom is so great
Our physical attributes begin to dissipate.

But can we not ever be glad
    For the lives we've lived
        And the times we've had!

Shirley Artley Earnest

Welcome Autumn

In New England I like fall the best
For she knows no prejudice.
She has no concerns of what is said
If you are black, white, yellow or red.
Autumn cares not of what wel(l) you are,
Welfare or well to do,
Only that a welcome comes from you.
When she arrives everyone knows
Flashing everywhere, her glowing wardrobes.
Autumn blankets colours in the Ghetto and Suburbs,
Not being the colours of a gang or klan.
Her beauty the colours of nature man.
And when you look as far as the eye can see,
Autumn has taken her colours
And painted them, not just for you,
Not just for me.
But for everyone rich or poor to see.

Martha Walker-Dawkins

Meant To Be

In my heart, in my soul
I believe that two people are meant to be.
In my dreams and thoughts
that's how it was meant to be
the two people that were meant to be
The two people you and me
Together we should be
If we were meant to be.

Tina L. Melvin

"Pretend"

To love is to say I am sorry
For the way I have treated you
To love you is to say I am sorry
Because there is nothing that I can do
I have failed to make you happy
I failed to fill your heart with love
But most of all I have failed to give to you
What he has given to me from up above
The times we were together
I took for granted and lied
The times we were together
I carelessly put them aside
I do not know how to care
And fill your heart with love
I just pretend to be fulfilled
Like the flight of a loving dove
It is time to hang my head in sorrow
For the shame that I have caused
It is time to face tomorrow
And make peace with the Lord above

Shenial St. Amant

Sharing

"Who am I?" I say as I wonder today.
For there is so much to say,
there is so much to do,
when I touch the heart of a dying soul.
When I touch the hand, when I feel the pain,
when I see the fear in eyes so scared.
I share my life.
I share my love.
I give freely of myself only hoping to share,
hoping to comfort in the long days of despair.
Loss you see is the hardest fear, for those we lose
and those they leave behind.
I give comfort again a second time, hoping only
to ease the pain for those that are left behind.
The mother, the child, and the spouse,
I give of myself to ease the pain.
It doesn't seem as if the words are right,
so I give a hand, a hug, and even shed a tear.
Oh God the pain of being here!

Sharon Heath

United

Sweet are the kisses of your mouth
    for they are more delightful than wine.
I wish to fill my cup overflowing with them
    and drink until I am drunk.
I am fevered with passion.
My heart burns for you. I long for your embrace
    and the gentleness of your touch.
I am faint with love.
I want to run away with you to a place where time stands still
    and make love to you.
To have my king carry me into his chambers
    to a world I have yet to uncover.
Let me stand before you in all my splendor,
    before my king, my master, my lover.
I dream of the day
    when our hearts will beat as one
    and our love can be united.

Mandy Pouliot

My Brother's Birthday

Fifty years ago on March 3, 1938 a new life began,
For unto Marion and Evelyn was born a son.
They named him Roger; he had black hair, brown eyes,
In his early years he was an artful dodger,
Thus being constantly chastised.

He loved the outdoors, and often went to the river,
Causing him to neglect his chores, thus making
Mom and Dad with frustration to shiver.

But when Roger'd return home with a catch of fish,
Then all was well; Mother would cook a fine dish,
And the eating was swell!

At age 18 we nearly lost this man,
An accident in his Ford car,
But it was, thankfully, in God's plan,
To let Roger aim for a star.

He's a son, a brother, a father, a friend.
A grandfather and a husband,
How lucky are we all,
For his family Roger will never disband.
And, to us, he's Redwood tree tall!

Mary J. Daugherty

Through the Head

Black History, here we go, our ancestors sang spirituals;
For us to get back to meaning, it'll take a miracle.

It took bravery, liberation from slavery;
The fight for equal rights has me.
Think of the way it used to be.
Brothers and sisters working as a family.
But the criminal-minded were blinded and had to see;
We're not a family anymore, we need to face reality.

Mandela spoke the word, but he wasn't heard
By the brothers in the States, who ignored their race.

For trying to educate your people, they claim you're too Black.
They don't understand the intention of a message in Rap.

Tell them where it's at, explain the facts.
Tell them the effects and that it's more types than crack.

Kids always play the outlaw, that's a sign;
He had a pistol made of plastic - it looks worse than mine.

'Cause our young brothers and sisters are constantly being misled;
WE HAVE TO GET PEACE "THROUGH THE HEAD."

Ray Marcel Scott

Ethereal Love

I'll tell you what you know within your heart,
For who would know it more than you, my love?
A man could sooner hold the tide, than bar
My trust, devotion, faith. The One above,
And Him alone, has strength that can deter
My loyalty, my steadfast love. It's far
Above the earthly sound-it's strong and true.
Mere words cannot express the feelings known,
For Heaven placed them deep within my breast.
And none could steal that gift from me, and none
Could keep me far from you: I'd never rest
'Til I returned to stand beside your love.

Kristin Schweitzer

Silence Is Not Golden

Our tears are but a survival from the blatant absurdities of life.
For years we have died with dreams unfulfilled and hopes shattered.
Still we do not hide behind masks but continue to share our hurts,
Our sorrows, our worries, our dreams, our angers and our insights.

Our veins pulsate heavily
    ...and our hearts ache...
        and the sweat from our foreheads continues...
            to irritate our eyes.

We no longer have the strength and therefore will not...
    remain chained to the subservient roles placed before us
    nor will we burden ourselves with the guilt that has allowed us

        ...To drag our swollen feet... behind us
        Kicking dust in our faces

We will not remain mere statistics supplying endless facts and
information ...about the injustices of the world...

To you our eyes are swollen
    To us they're not
        To you they're just beginning
        To tell a story
            To us it's Ancient History

Maritza Meadows

Forget Him

Forget the boy who made you cry,
Forget the boy with big blue eyes.
Forget his arms that are so strong,
Forget his legs that are so long.
Forget the time that you loved him so,
And never wished to let him go.
Forget the day when he said hi,
Forget the way he made you cry.
Forget the time that he was next to you,
Forget you wished that he loved you too.
Forget the gentle look that he gave to you,
When you were sad and feeling blue.
Forget that he did not love you too,
Why was this so untrue?
Forget when his friends weren't around,
He wouldn't act like a silly clown.
Forget your love for him was real,
Because his love you would never feel.
Forget the sparkle in his eyes,
And forget the day that he said goodbye.

Melissa A. Hawke

I Have Woken

I have woken up to sing new songs,
Found the long lost words and broken bonds that go beyond the time!
With new might I bring to light
The wordless tales of fairies and the sprites!
New streams of power keep growing louder.
The sleepless dreams grow tall like towers!
New hopes will bloom and flower, new avenues with open yonder!
The silent songs fill kinder spaces and through the ages
The wisdom of old sages unlocks the gilded cages of the time!
The power of your voice sped through my space,
New winds blew across my sleepless dreams buried in the moss -.
With new hope I sing of wordless promises, new morrows,
Of futures bright, shared love and life -.
I have woken up to rhyme,
To sing the songs, to ring the chime!
I have broken all the bonds,
I have woken up to sing new songs!

Pia Baltzar

Free

Free your mind
Free your soul
Free your spirit
Reach your ultimate goal

Stop talking about the things you want to do
Make every effort to make them come true

Free the land
Free your heart
Free everything
Give life a new start

Let's all come together
Set things right once and forever

Free yourself
Free your brother
Free your neighbor
Give a hand to help one another
Rosalie Hill

God's Changing Seasons

The white clouds scud in two directions looking
friendly as well as fierce.

The horses throw their manes and seem to
listen for man's unheard sounds.

The silence of the birds bear a strong hint that
they have broken their lease and flown to more
promising climes.

The grass that has been warm and embracing
now has grown cold and uninviting.

Yes, the Fall is about to walk on stage and be
the current hit of the dramatic season.

Only later to give way to beauties just as
temporary, as winter descends.

And this has been repeated for an eternity.
Wendell Reid

Celebration Day (Wedding Sonnet)

Gather'd together on this special day
Friends and family and memories made
To each other you give your hearts away
Radiant moments that time can not fade
The marriage of two joins their hearts as one
For hearts set afire together belong
Sacred bonds can by no man be undone
Lifelong as love is eternally strong
Honour and cherish in sickness or health
Giving absolute love without measure
Knowing love is always your greatest wealth
In each other find richest of treasure
Share your lives as one anothers' best friend
Happiness eye in a world without end
Paula J. Wilkum

Challenge

Life without a challenge is life without a goal
If you haven't found it, better search your soul
Measure time on achievements - not in utter waste
On you will have no destiny or influence on your fate.

Conflict is the birthplace of the struggle and despair
Yet without conflict-there'd be no "bill-of-fare"
There are wins and losses in all the scheme of life.
Life would have few thrills without the strife-of-life.
Robert J. Menten

A Special Friend

Friends together means friends forever.
Friends who share are friends who care.
We listen, we laugh and we cry,
We may even bicker,
when our opinions may differ,
but our friendship still flickers inside.
We my even distance in times of our hurry,
looking for a few extra minutes in that day.
But, we always remember those people in our lives,
Who's faces don't ever fade away.
Their words are from honesty, openness and love,
And their presence is one that is dear.
They collect all your misery and surprise you with joy,
And lessen some of life's greatest fears.
Sometimes we have one, two, maybe three people
who act in this way,
But, all it takes is that very special one,
to tell you today you're okay!
Marni Beth Gerstel

The Duel

He wore his scar upon his face,
From cheek to chin it lay in place.
He wore his saber at his side,
Sharp, shimmering, lethal and wide,
He wore the smile of victory upon his lips,
A cunning and obscene smile was it.

He wore the scars of his defeat,
Under granite, crumbling in the noon-day heat.
He wore his saber at his side,
'Twas dull, rusting, and rotting with time.

She wore her scar where none could see,
Oft after rising from on her knees.
She wore the scar that never healed,
For her memory of the duel was tightly sealed.
Mary Kay Uraga

The Rose

Who dared to pluck you, red, red, rose?
From God's lovely garden of song and prose:
Where bees hummed and raced to be first fed
With rose-gold nectar from your petaled shed.

In a crystal vase I now behold
Your radiance dimmed by captive hold:
No rain your soft, soft cheek to brush,
No night birds song breaks evening's hush.

Sad rose, I will take you back and root you deep
So your seed may fall, then rise from sleep-
And color the garden with strokes of red
Multiplied forever from the tears you shed.
Mary Merrill Greco

In Other Words...

The spring winds come and take me away
and in affect, your smile the same.
The summer sun spurts back once anew,
to behold your reflection in the morning dew.
Fall leaves dance in the wind like a prom,
The vibrations of our strings play their song.
The winter sun holds the night like I hold you,
in other words...
I love you!
Stan Davidson

If Help I Could Others

If help I could others, could diversify time
from gold refine wisdom, then turn wisdom to wine.
Become drunk in it's teachings and create a new lust
bend reason a little, while instilling a trust.

For a moment a salesman, a trickster of sorts
and poor souls make wonder, at the awesome reports.
I'd ask not for millions as the elected oft do
but cup overflowing, I'd offer to you.

I'd close down the vinter that watered the wine
and the teachers of temperance, I'd give a hard time.
To play on their passions, to fulfill their desires
I'd build in their souls the hottest of fires.

If help I could others, no tolerance I'd show
I'd serve the wine freely, their cup I'd o'er flow.
An addict I'd make them, to wine they'd be sold
then turn wine back to wisdom, and wisdom to gold.

Robert Freeman

Psalm Of The Super Mom

The lady is strong in her beliefs,
From her convictions, she does not waver.
She possesses a courageous spirit, a will not easily broken
Even by the strongest bonds of oppression.
She stands firm against the tides of hatred and intolerance
Which threaten to drown the entire race.
And though she might be swept beneath
The initial onslaught of the suffocating waters,
She fights, and regains her footing to once more brave the storm.
In her thoughts, she is selfless,
Forever giving to those nearest her heart;
In her soothing embrace,
Fear is banished, failure forgotten;
And in her eyes so gentle and as endless as the evening sky,
The forsaken are found.
Go to her when the world seems too cruel to bear.
Cling to her when the dreams
Of childhood's innocent grace are shattered.
From her draw the strength and will to live on.
She is life, she is love, she is woman.

M. E. Pike

Love Is Like A Volcano

COMPRESS LOVE IS LIKE A VOLCANO, In which molten rocks
from inside the earth that has been melted by heat, compressed
heat that erupted from inside the earth and burst through the
earths surface and breaking out into a rash of lava,

LIKE THE VOLCANO, Our pains that we suffer is like the
compressed heat that our pains are melted into tears like the
molten rocks that were melted into lava, from inside our hearts
we try to hide our pains, but only to have our pains to erupt
into tears that we're suppressed so long within our hearts.

LIKE THE LAVA, Tears like lava that flows from your eyes
down your cheeks like the lava flows down from the peak of the
volcanos mountain top reaching to the bottom of your cheeks
like the lava has reached the bottom of the volcanos mountain,
Tears that we wipe is warm like the lava is hot,
COLD we are not when we cry the tears of LOVE,

Terry Laster

The Loner

For she has no one. This person and her self. Alone
in the dark, alone by herself. Where did all the people
go. Where did she go, all by herself. Alone on a big
world, by herself. No one but no one is here. Upset
and frustrated, by herself. All good all evil, all by herself.

Taylor Workman

The World from My Treehouse

As I look down at the world
from my little treehouse, I see things
I've never seen before. Things I never
knew existed. At a distance, I see a
wild wolf and a man together, but the
wolf is not growling. I see a child
being punished, but she is not crying.
I don't understand. Where is all the
hatred I've learned to live with?
It was like all of a sudden it disappeared,
like magic. I didn't want
to get down from my treehouse,
because I was afraid the hatred
would start all over again. But then
I saw my parents, and I knew I
couldn't stay up here forever, because
in our family, we all love another.

Valerie Vickers

Piercing The Heart

The severity which echoes
from the chambers of the heart
can only be seen through the faint glimmer
which the beholder finds edging its way
across the face of affliction
as the breaches of love fall oppressively
within the tears of a fool
to shatter it self upon the shelter of the Earth
only to be scattered abroad
beneath the soles of the unforgiving.

Terry Joe Adams Jr.

Untitled

Father, protect our children
from the pitfalls of this day and time
Help them to see drugs and alcohol
as slave bondage of another kind.

Let them see there's another high
where they'll never have to come down.
A high that's free and will linger on
and can no where else be found

Lord I ask thee, please be nigh
for with thee Lord comes a natural high
It's hard to describe a high so great
One that makes you love instead of hate
A high that makes you laugh when you want to cry
Makes you want to live, when others want to die

Lord you know you're my all and all
Please heavenly father hear my call.
Take our children in your hand
Bring them back Lord as only you can.
Lord hear my cry and hear my plea
Hold them in your hand, please, just for me.

Marie Henry

Call Me Back Lord

Please call me back, Lord, when I wonder away
From The road which you want me to take.

Sometimes, I'm like a little child,
Picking wild flowers for awhile,

And fail to realize how far I have gone
Away from the path which leads to home.

Do call me back, then, Lord; take hold of my hand,
And plant my feet firmly on the right road again.

Marie Dudley

The Raindrop

I sit in my chair looking at the raindrop on the window,
it can not run, it can not dance, yet it is free.

I can not run, I can not dance.
The raindrop is a tear in my heart.
Megan Timbie

Hear My Dream Arlene

A country field.
Frozen dew melts by noon.
Horses pull a wagon, carrying me and you.

Enough leaves left on trees, shades the angels view.
Warm North-East wind, circles a picnic for two.

Magical land, replying canyons delay.
Carving into dust.
Hide en seek we play.

Pure truth is love, heart in heart.
Surrounding crystal rapids flow, over the cliff of rock.

Untold miles, mark ancient trails.
Tears from laughter scream.
After turning veils.

Forever forms, be-tween hands.
Time loses value, over again.

A quarter moon. lanterns brightly shine.
Blackness fills the rest of night.

Toward home we glide.
Soon fast asleep.
I have never had, this much needed peace.
Lenie D. Burch

Moon

Dedicated to Jon Murdock
No matter if you are out
full and glowing in the sky.
Or being shy, hiding behind the clouds.
You always seem to be around.
To watch out for me.
I watch you as I go to sleep
Shinning down on my face.
I feel you with me.
As if you left part of you with me.
It makes me not be afraid.
I feel your strength and love all around me.
Patzi Howells

Full Moon

So big, so bright, a passionate delight
Full moon

Romance, mystery, just look and you shall see.
A magic, gorgeous, miracle,
All you want for free.

I often wonder, gazing up and staring at the sky
What is this magic wonder that he gave to you and I?

Sometimes its so bright it leaves us in amaze.
Others times its twinkling beneath a misty haze.
It never seems to let me down, I look its always there,
Looking right back down at me, almost as if it cared.

I'm sure this might sound crazy, so I say this with dismay.
When I see that big full moon, everything's ok!
It makes me feel so peaceful. It's always gone to soon.
Nothing can compare to a big full moon
Mickey Moore

Little Sunshine

A little ray of sunshine has been sent us,
    full of love,

She's precious, she's beautiful, and she's a
    gift from God above.

Sent to fill our lives that were so heart-broken
    and sad,

She makes us laugh, she makes us smile,
    she makes our sadness turn to glad.

A little girl who can be precocious, with big,
    bright shining blue eyes,

Her name is Breanna Marie who smiles an angelic
    twinkle that money could never buy.

God above has lent her to us to love and
    be so proud,
So, thank you Lord, you'll hear us sing
    so joyfully out loud!
Rachel Rupert

I Ask The House

The last time I visited her empty house was when she died, after the
funeral. It's been three years. I remember how it rained and snowed at
the same time, as the casket was lowered into the dark muddy ground.

There's a little ritual I go through
here at grandma's house, inviting like a familiar friend.
I look through all of the dusty photo albums grandma kept on a high
shelf. As if at a museum, I view all of grandma's sisters, the
relatives I never knew:
Aunt Basha, Aunt Tzillie, Aunt Marie —the ones the Nazis got to know.
Their eyes glow a faded sepia; they stare as if they know me,
as if they know I'm looking, eavesdropping on their lives.

I feel guilty as I pass each smile, page after page;
they never could imagine being taken away
naked in a cattle car - I want to warn them.

I close the album, walk down the long hallway,
touch the fading blue and gold wallpaper.
This is what's left of them now, a stale shadow of their lives.

Will I become a withered photograph in some distant relative's
forsaken album? I ask the house.

Peering into the hallway mirror, I see Aunt Marie's smile.
Meri Harary

The Rose

From a stem of thorns a bud is born,
gathering strength from the sun, and the dew of morn.
It swells in such beauty; virginal and fine,
protected by sharp prickles where the blooms entwine.
Pure as a babe it is gently unfurled,
each petal unique, and beautifully curled;
the fragrance breath-takingly sweet to behold,
their lasting beauty strong and bold.
Like a bride on her wedding day in satin and lace,
or a child in a garden with an angelic face.
Each flower is lovely, where-ever it grows,
but there is nothing so exquisite as the bud of a rose.
Ruth Shillito

Many True Poets Revisited In 1995

"The world is too much with us"! Sooner or later,
Getting and spending we lay waste the world,
We trash the Universe. And history?
So few know it that they think their thoughts original,
Creative, I've heard it before and better.
So we wander, empty-headed, in soulless bodies,
Politically correct, while the blinding Desert Sands
Blow freely into our dry eyes.

Great God, I'd rather sit in Church and pray,
Thank you for the roof over our heads,
The simple food, on our table,
The children running barefoot through our home.
I pray, Thy will be done... Thy will be done...
Thy will be done, Father, in the cool damp
Of the Cathedral, Temple, Synagog, Church or Chapel
Amid the sounds and scents that remind us
That we are only part of time- Not owners,
Just children learning lessons- Not owners,
Each learning lessons-essential to eternity.

Patrick C. Davis

Untitled

Give me a smile, I'll smile back.
Give me a hug, I'll hug back.
Give me a kiss, and I'll gladly give back.
Tell me you love me, and I'll tell you the same.
When we married, we said forever.
So why do I feel lonely?
Does your heart no longer think of me?
Tell me what it is?
I keep reaching out for you, but you're never there.
Where have you gone my love?
Where have you gone?
The flowers no longer bloom.
The sun no longer shines.
The birds no longer sing.
As my heart no longer loves.
Just as you no longer exist.
Now I can say I have once found true love.
It too has vanished.
So tell me is it just a dream.

Sheila Tucker

Autumn

October, gentle breeze, trees dressed in their vibrant leaves.
Giving the last magnificent farewell to summer past.

I too can feel the Autumn of my life rushing in.
Some bright colors of happy wonderful days past.
Youth that slipped by quickly, childhood days of wonders sadness.
Teen years of never fitting in, there were many winters.
Bright colors of learning and winter shades of lessons
never learned. In some of these winter hues are
sadness that we glean happiness from.

Autumn reds and yellows of friends, sweethearts, marriage
and my child. Winters of sickness, sadness, and death of loved ones

Autumn always comes on earth as in life.
Hold on, hold on, to the last rays of warm sun.
Indian summer is short. Till the last leaf flutters
to the earth, until the last breath goes out of
this body, the trees wait as my soul, for spring.

Wyn Garrett

The Revenge of the Damned

Bloodless skin of pasty white.
Glowing like a ghost in the moonlight.
Venomous fate by mortal men,
Keep me away. Always running,
Malicious attacks from the living.
Saying I am a lifeless being.
So, I hunt them down like animals,
And slit your through as sacrifice.
"Join my army of the damned," I'll invite.
"Or die a slow and painful death."
"For I hold your future in my teeth."
"Eternal life or death of the damned?"

Roxxy Suicide

Don't Give Up

You've been told to give it your all.
"Go for it!" They say
But are they there if you should fall?
Disappointments you will face.

When you go into the world, they cry and say "good luck"
You miss them in that big, cold world.
No one to depend upon as much.

Are you prepared, if you should fail, to pick up every piece?
Who to run to, when you're frail?
Do all your troubles simply cease?

So, when you fail, do not give up as hard as it is to do.
You must not think you're not good enough.
You must see - that isn't true.

In the world, disappointments strike, on everyone now and then.
And if you give up without a fight,
You'll lose again and again.

If you still have a shoulder to use for your tears,
Go ahead, let the comfort sink in.
Because when it is gone, you'll remember it well,
And be able to lift up your chin.

Samantha Gingold

My Baby

A toddler died in a fire today
   God, please protect my baby
Infection of Aids is running rampant
   God, please protect my baby
An eight year old was raped on her way to school
   God, please protect my baby
A three year old drown in a pool nearby
   God, please protect my baby
Kids are bringing guns to school
   God, please protect my baby
A boy of ten died of an overdose
   God, please protect my baby
My daughter starts school today
   God, please make my baby strong

Mary E. Nasca

Unrequited Love

He holds my heart within his hands,
But his hands must not know what they hold,
Because my heart remains undaunted,
Despair rises in my soul.

My love for him so pure so true,
Makes death seem far above.
The single thought that what I feel for him,
Is simply unrequited love.

Lori Janner

Mona

31 years ago you were born
God smiled and gave you a kiss,
And all the angels knew that without you
What the world would have missed

"Beautiful" everyone would say of you
A happy and loving child,
With dark curly hair
You always had a smile

A young lady into you grew
Still beautiful in every way,
With loving and caring thoughts of others
Is how I see you today

And into my life you brought
Four other persons such as you,
They have given me love and joy
And blessings like these are few

So, if I should die tomorrow
I know the world is a better place,
Because 31 years ago
God created an Angel with your face

Kathy Klassen

Friends

We were the best of friends
   going to the mall, fishing, hunting and just hanging
Doing what good friends do
   Why did it have to end?
You always seemed to be happy
   having a smile from ear to ear
But I couldn't hear your cries for help
   I know I should have been there
for the time when you needed me the most
   that split second before your final step
Did you think of me?
   I hope so

Scott Kaminkow

All Dressed Up And Nowhere To Go

Ain't I pretty, all dressed up and nowhere to go.
Got on my Sunday best, my high heels, my dress. AND
my hair is combed. Got on my mama's locket, even got
some money in my pocket. Lookin' good. Feelin' good.
Gotta smile on my face.

A country gal, that what I am. Just me and my o dog Sam.
Living many a miles from nowhere, nobody else. No
city, no town, not even a store close round. Ain't got no
car, walk...to where...that's too far.

So here I am, standin' in the middle of this o dusty road.
Um..a dead toad, thinkin' life is just a song, like the
water in the branch, rollin' along. Can't imagine where it
go. Seem like nobody else no. Once I asked a fella
and he say - it depend, somewhere down the road, it
end.

Come on Sam, let's go back to the house, and sit for a
while. Turn on the radio, listen to the top-ten show.
We've been out here now for two hours or so. All dressed up
and nowhere to go.

William H. Smith

Soldier's Detail

When hefting the cadavers onto the truck
grab the arms or the legs and then swing
The corporal in charge of the detail must shout
grab the arms or the legs and then swing
"Break your backs not the bodies, that's
men and not meat"
Grab the arms or the legs and then swing
But to you who must do it and not throw your gut
grab the arms or the legs and then swing
You know that it has to be meat
grab the arms or the legs and then swing...

William K. White

"The Waters Trickle Like The Mind"

A gentle brook trickles through blue
grass, miles away you can hear it
calling, pure waters flowing over shy
aqua crystals. Innocence rolling down
hillsides of life splashing into pools
of pisswater and sewage...So like babies,
angel eyes awake to a world undeserving
of their purity, midnight eyes close to
a world that engulfed them - closed
forever....sounds of purity deceiving all
those that hear creeks trickling over
sterile rocks, plummeting into puddles
of wasted energy.

Stephen Eric Ketzer

On the Finches' Farm in Manville

The tall grass scares me, open to insects,
grasshoppers, sunned and muted, leap on weeds
above my head, my eyes shut. Fright infects
with spiders, spotted feathers freed
from black and white pheasants by the half-breed
German shepherd who chases bees and wasps.
Pink flamingos swarm trees beyond my grasp

Mimosa buds, I thought were pink flamingos.
The winding road, only a private drive
which rests at this land, lost imagination close
without the devoted dog — fetch, and dive.
Some stalks step and dance, the grass alive
and crickets glisten black under the moon
hidden in waist-high grass, the bugs plead June.

Kerry Burroughs

Sh-Sh-Sh-

As I look out I see one in a long Darkish
green long flowing dress, with shoulder length
Black hair as of a raven. Talking and whispering
to another. No one seems to know -sh-sh-sh-
can you see there standing in front
of a mirror-look- one is writing and thinking
for many hours. One is tired. One is
whispering to another - can you
see - as I look out I see myself looking
up -to-to see one another a whispering and
telling secrets of the lady in the
Darkish Green dress. I looked up to
see -see the (secret) myself. Let me
introduce myself as I look out to see one
My name is Edgar Ellen Poe - I see again
   Sh-sh-she

Patsy Smith

The World, Our World, God's World

The Sun, the Sun gives us our light to see and to
grow our crops. It warms us, gives us energy. The Sun
is God's soul, it's Heaven. With out it, without God we
cease to exist. No man will touch or reach the sun. Only
when God calls us up. "For the Sun is Heaven."
The Stars, they are Gods eyes, they are God's ears.
They are up in the Heavens. This is how God is able to
see and hear the multitudes of us. As we pray and go about
our everyday lives.
The Earth, it's very gravity holds us while we are
mere mortals. It supplies us with our every need to live
and breathe. We breathe, we bathe, we drink, we live.
Thank God for everything.
The Light, it's bright it draws me, it pulls me.
Closer I go, further and further. Till I reach this light.
The light is the sun, God's soul. It's heaven. God is
everything. He is our world. He is our every being.
God bless us. God forgive us. God have mercy own our souls.

"God" the word that means the world to me.

Robert B. Winstead Jr.

My Family As A Rose

My family was like a plant
growing slowly from the ground.
And in a few short years the plant was grown,
with two red buds so round.
God dearly, loved those roses,
and put faith in the plant to bare more.
And from time to time, as they burst forth.
He gladly opened his door.
And 'one' of them, we know
Dear Jesus, must have been as gentle as a Dove.
It was your will and our wonder,
that you took him, safely home to his place.
As we drop from the bush Dear Jesus,
may we enter your open door.
And all be tied in the same 'bouquet'.
And dwell there, forevermore.

Rolene Lancaster

Mirage

The morning air felt so-o g-o-o-o-d! Never before
  Had it been this crisp and invigorating!
There was a sense of something different from other
  Dakota prairie days. But what was it?

The familiar blue fleece lined dome overhead had
  Changed to an azure sky reaching into infinity;
There was an unreal absence of all sounds of farm life,
  And not a hint of movement of air. The mood was eerie.

The neighboring farm - WOW! Only dots on the
  Horizon yesterday, today it is red and white buildings
That can be counted. It's as though I had slipped
  Into a Kodachrome photograph.

Tension and anxiety mounted; the silence and
  Stillness seemed to wrap itself around me.
Had the world been trapped in some vast vacuum? Was God
  Punishing me for some misdeed? But I was only eight!

Slowly, the spell of this montage dissipated with
  The gentle and soothing "Co-o-o; Co-o-o; Co-o-o;"
Of the mourning doves restoring normalcy.
  The magical reality of that first mirage lingers.

G. Calvin Tooker

Untitled

Sand slipping through an hourglass.
Hands ticking on a clock.
Everything that is loved,
has it's moment to be unlocked.
Precious thoughts and feelings
are memories to withhold inside.
But it all seems too hard to bare,
when all of reality just died.
United we stood as friends.
United we'll stay in spirit.
I'll tell you I'll love you forever,
while wondering if you'll hear it.
My tears all fall for you.
So catch them if you can.
For when it rains, it's me you're thinking of,
and I'll catch you in my hand.

Nicole Stadnitski

Dreams

A phenomenon of night, or a goals journey of
happiness and fright.
A dream of the mind can wander furiously while
a dream of achievement doesn't.
Set your mind to it and work for it, disaster or
contentment. More than you expected or a
feeling of disappointment.

What is your dream?
Mine is a fantasy island with clear sparkling
water and horses dancing on tip-toes up on the highlands.
A unicorn or two to make things light-hearted
And a faithful lion and leopard to stand guard.
A castle built of multicolored stones, and in the
most beautiful room I sit in a throne.

My dream may never be reached,
but give it love and it will teach.

Lorena Bajer

Fifty Years Of Wedded Bliss?

There were good times and bad times,
Happy times and sad times.
A multitude of memories that make us laugh or cry.
Patience, faithfulness, honesty, dependability,
Being forgiving, thoughtful and polite
Are what make a marriage work,
Even during a rousing fight.
Having mutual interests (music, art, gardening)
is very important too.
And a sense of humor is absolutely essential,
When things do go askew.
Our children were a blessing we accepted and loved,
Even though, sometimes, they were none of those above.
Grandchildren are dear, but, as we oversee them grow
And make their own mistakes,
It's like seeing life anew again, or watching double takes.
But, to hold a great grandchild in our arms.
We are really grateful.
Our love and persistence have truly worked
To make our lives so fateful!

Mary J. Kesling

My Friend That Walks With Me

My friend that forever walks with me
 Has made a solemn promise his words will always be.
He watches me from front and behind,
 He is truly the best friend of mine.
He corrects me when I am wrong and
 He's made me sing a joyful song.
Two thousand years ago He walked this land;
 He died for the sins of every woman, child and man,
He died with no remorse or refrain and on the third day
 He rose again, so our prayers for forgiveness would not be in vain.
He makes Lucifer stop cold in his tracks
 And since my friend walks with me I'm free from vicious attacks.
I hear his spirit speaking from deep within, thank you Jesus
 For the forgiveness of sins and accepting me whole and born again.
Step by step, side by side, you, my father, are the only perfect guide
 We're doing the two step you and me, thank you God, for setting me free.
You have opened my eyes and made me see
 That this life, Lord, with you is the life for me.
Thank you again, Jesus, for walking with me.

  Kevin Ray Bergman

What Goes Around Comes Around

What goes up, must come down.
Hate not to be their friend.
All Around, talking behind my back.

Goes around, and comes around
Expecting, they would not do it.
Seeing, them do it.

At home, or at the store.
Ruining, our friendship.
Over, the whole school.
Under, every note passed.
Never expected, didn't know it was going around.

Comes unexpectedly, over reacting.
Must, come around sometime.
Expecting, it to be really mean.
Suspecting, they did it.

At school, or out of school.
Ruining all, the fun.
Old and young,
Under and over, never your friend.
Deciding between them.

  Kelly Soleau

The Man I Love Is Named God

Let me tell you about this wonderful man I
have in my life!
He's the best man in the WORLD, this is
one man that I would be willing to share
with other women because he would love
us all the same.
You see, this man gives me money to
put clothes on my back, food on my table
and keeps a roof over my head.
He accompanies me everywhere I go, showers
me with blessings and NEVER tries to harm me.
This man loves me whether I'm rich,
poor, fat, skinny, good, bad, black or white.
When I lift my voice to praise his name,
I know in my heart I'll never let him go.
You see, the man I love so much is
named God. You should love him
too, for he's worthy to be praised!
He's one man who won't let you down!

  Pamela Jones

My Longtime Companion

  We have gone through so many changes in the years that we have known each other. Each day I ended up thinking of only the good times that we shared.
  Our companionship had bad day's where we never spoke to each other. Sometimes I regret this decision of not talking about our problems. No matter how many fights or arguments we had, we could always count on each other.
  We look to our friends for comfort when the other person is not around. That is not often since we know each other better than most of our friends.
  We see how many of our friends have passed on or moved away from our lives but, we still call them friends. What I guess I am saying is, "I have enjoyed the time the two of us have shared...My
Longtime Companion."

  Michael J. Haskins

Untitled

  The time has come to move on through the webb of destruction I have set up for myself. Another day of living a lie that I knew is the truth. Will he ever give me what I need? Will he ever be you? Do I want him to be you? The pace is quick; my head is spinning; Is this the end or just the beginning. Of this game you take no prisoners and the winner will always be you.

  I am following you down this dark tunnel you call your life where the only person who sees the light is you because you carry the torch . "Can I hold the torch for just a minute?" I knew when I asked you would give it to me to see exactly what I would do with it in my possession. I blow the flame out and struggle with the thought of not knowing where to go. Why should I trust you, you have never given me security before. I trust you, I do. I always have. That is why I remained. I always stayed the same. Through thick and thin I committed a sin, every time I thought of you.

  Stacy Mini

Nuevo Commies

Feeling almost stupid, they easily starve today
Having no food leaves them with nothing to say
Feeling almost silly, citing interesting stories tearfully
Yet, hiding their doubts and going along most fearfully
Feeling about shoulders, he is only now
This massage in her lonely chow

Take our daily angst: Yes
Take some more or take some less
Take help innocently saying
Hey, mac, thought we were playing
Place arguments gleefully everywhere
Look real hard but do not stare

Talking on my microphone only relays our words
Shooting off my mouth is for the birds
Alone
A phone
Buy our odd killer
Can't move any stiller

  Zixi Q. Abaca

Swept Away

The river tumbled and rolled lazily along the river bed while
gurgling and whispering the sweet nothings of my name.
My heart softly answered its beckoning.
My body was drawn to the river as a moth is to a flame.
The very essence of myself longed to become one with the river.
At first I gingerly touched the glass edges then lowering my body
in its wholeness into the stream,
I let the water sweep me away until I blended with the ebbing,
flowing, endless currents.

  Natalie Carter

Untitled

There was a young man that grew up on the coast,
He became a fair logger, but did not boast.
He worked through the 70's and most of the 80's,
By then he had married a couple of ladies.
He had 5 kids by wife number one,
Thank God number two ended with none.
He met number three, got tired of the fog,
So he moved to Shingletown to cut another log.
He logged about four years and cut some trees,
That's where he left wife number three.
He's on unemployment raising a 14 year old girl,
He met a nice lady, why not give her a whirl.
He works pretty hard, wears out his heels,
But he logs more timber in a place called Big Wheels.

Richard A. Easter

The Old Man

His youthful skin and withered, into wrinkled, age-old flesh.
He combed his grey-hair to the side, as if to look his best.

He shut the gate behind him. Walked slowly down the path.
Yet, no-one wondered where He went. They knew He would come back.

Dead leaves had fallen on the stone. He brushed them with His hand,
and scraped from the letters, the bits of dirty sand.

Sometimes He sat for hours, recalling things they've done.
How life had changed in Forty years. Since the time, when they were
   young.

The path has since grown over, with weeds and bristled thorns.
The gate has Ivy on it's locks. The old man walks no more.

Now two stones lie together. No one knows, how His got there.
Perhaps she too was lonely. 'Twas Her that placed it there.

Lorraine Smith

Profile of a Freedom Fighter

This man has died before. Dallas was a resent demise.
He died with farmers and city people, laborers and
businessmen, rich and poor — Northern and Southern, fathers
and sons, friends and neighbors.
He died in the Boston Massacre, Valley Forge, Normandy
Beach, Okinawa, Chosun reservoir and Viet Nam's iron triangle.
He died with four children in a church in Atlanta, with Martin
in Tennessee and Bobby in California.
He will die again and again as long as threats and violence,
hate and tyranny rise up in countless ways to test all men's
yearning for freedom.
His deaths will not have been in vain as long as we carry the
torch of liberty he has passed to us who remain on the
battlefield.

William J. Gough

Thoughts

Many years of turbulent storms
Have engraved and etched
A beauty for which there is no form.
Life with you is never dull,
And God in His infinite mercy
Makes it ever so full.
Each turn and curve in the road we take
Gives life a challenge
For which plans can never make.
All of these things are the essence of dreams,
And love cannot be measured but by the years,
Never by the amount of tears.

Dee

Untitled

As he stands alone
He dreams about his younger years
The smell of freshly cut grass
The noise of the crowd
The crack of the bat
He dreams and dreams
Just thinking how good he could have really been
He dreams more and more
Remembering every play and every hit that he ever had
The smell of the grass
The crack of the bat
He dreams and dreams
Just thinking how good he could have really been
He remembers back when the wind whistled through the grass
And the crack of the bat was the only thing heard throughout
the ball park
He was going to be the best there ever was
He dreams and dreams
Just thinking how good he could have really been

Nathan L. Washington

New Interpretation Given, Go En Receive

A thorn in man's side causes him great pain
he has not the strength to pull it out; his cries never wane
in constant mourning, his life has become one of torture
the body once so vigil is now the condemned structure
wise men tell him he is in pain and is fatally ill
a face painted with the colors of torment begs for death's saving pill
open mother Earth and receive your crying babe
comfort him, soothe him, allow him to forget his life's plagues
lo there stands a stranger, his face I cannot see
with hands adroit, he removes the thorn; the pain cease
O how happy the man is he; as whole as others
the strangers, his savior, does it matter his color?

Theron D. Marshall

A Toast to Heartache

I would like to propose a toast to Heartache;
He has proven to be a good friend.
Sometimes, I won't see him for months or even years
But, when I least expect him he always appears.
He'll stay by my side as true friends will do
And if times were hard I'd bet he'd stay with you.
He's an inspiration and a very dear friend.
He is known as 'a fighter 'till the end'.
He accomplishes his tasks with the utmost perfection
And never gives up when faced with rejection.
So, raise those glasses high.
To Heartache, he is the one!
I couldn't imagine life without him;
It would probably be too easy and less fun!

Monique R. Walters

The Man

There's a man out there who takes away all my worries
He never seams to get in a hurry.
He's gentle and strong, but he can do no wrong.
He's tall and lean but could never be mean.

His smile makes all my days worth while
He knows just what to say to make me smile
He makes my heart skip a beat because this man he can't be beat

There's a man out there I wish were mine but only in other time
Only in my dreams will this man be.
How I wished that he loved me.

Mary M. Rogers

A Fine Fellow (Franco Newman)

There is a fellow that is so sweet
    He is also very neat.
Has a lot of laughter as he goes,
    To show you how to be on your toes.

Has a lot of energy that flows,
    So much happiness he doeth show.
Through out days with many faces,
    Which will bring you through the races.

He is so wonderful to be around,
    When we've gone out in town.
To show him you do share,
    As he shows you he doeth care.

Joy of laughter rings in my ears
    As he whispers so I hear.
All the wonders of his voice.
    That has given me a choice.

To say that I feel the same about you
    As we carry on in our shoes.
While were on our way a sailing
Lots of love will be a trailing.

Margaret Desmond

The Gander

The goose becomes ill - she can no longer keep up with him
He knows not why
She struggles and falls in the brush
Her loyal mate, faithfully by her side
His presence comforts her as she slowly dies
The call of the south beacons, still he refused to leave
He is driven away by the fox, no longer can he protect her
He calls for her in the lake
She does not answer
The flocks converge, his wings take flight
A departure of glorious mass darkens the setting sun

Michael Silvey

Moments

Although God gave me many crosses to bear,
He made sure there was ever someone to care.
That's why, in this world, I ever did see,
So many moments of purest ecstasy.

If we grow up, we must truly realize,
That life doesn't fathom a sweet surprise
Which each of us has forever dreamed of,
But only gives each one, sparingly, moments of love.

These are the moments that brought our hearts pleasure;
These are the moments we shall treasure - forever.
then, when we're down and need to separate,
These moments remain - we continue our fate,
Waking us to feel sublime - just living on earth,
But making us know - it's time to be showing our worth!

Cherish the moments that are good;
Delete the moments that are bad and could
Mar our thinking, till we can't carry on,
Rescinding the sweet promise of each new dawn!

Lorraine K. Johnston

A River's Splendor

Crystal clear water runs nearby.
It runs between the mountains that are oh so high.
It matches the sky that is sapphire blue,
and is filled with trout, some old and some new.
Its bottom is covered with many colorful rocks,
and rivers run forever just like clocks.

Pierce James Brossett

The Designer

The Lord's will is best for you.
He made you and molded your very being,
The very essence of your character, too.
A masterpiece like none has ever seen.

Too much evidence of design, it's true,
Gives evidence of a designer at work.
So why wouldn't He know the real you,
And all of the appropriate and deliberate quirks.

Those quirks, so that we may always and evermore,
Lean on the underlying hand of our maker.
He is our refuge when we run through His door.
His masterpiece He will protect from the breaker.

A designer/maker that loves His creation,
Who cares about the condition of His people.
For He is the King of all the nations,
The most high of the highest steeple.

Robert A. Perez

Ballad of Friendship

"Can I try to save my friend?
    He may be near life's end!"
The Captain replied with a sigh:
    "It's hell on the beach, but you can try!"
The sailor dashed ashore that D-Day, dodging
    bullets coming at him 'long the way. Soon he
    was brought back with a blood-stained neck.
        Now dying himself on the PC's deck.
The skipper looked down on the hapless lad, as
    a wave of regret made him extremely sad.
He knew he'd erred when he okayed the trip, and
    allowed the brave, young man to leave the
    ship. "It was worth it, Sir! Didn't you know?
        Seaman Ryan was my best chum!"
You see, Bill's last words were:
    "Sure is hell on the beach...but...
    I knew you'd come!"

Raymond E. Goin

PATIENCE

God teaches us PATIENCE daily, if we open His Holy word;
He speaks of it over and over, if we but let Him be heard.
He ALLOWS us to weep and to struggle, to reach what we've set for our goal;
He TELLS us to ask for His comfort when there's misery deep down in our soul.
Sometimes we IGNORE the great Master and think we can make it alone,
But He gives us a nudge to remind us to come and beseech at His throne.
And though we ENTREAT without ceasing, He reminds us again and again,
That joy will come in the morning, relieving the night of pain.
He'll NEVER give us what we ask for as long as we worry and fret,
We must CEASE thinking life has betrayed us, and never look back with regret.
With ENDURANCE, faith and thanksgiving, we must live our lives day by day;
And give thanks to the Lord for His PATIENCE each time that we kneel down to pray.

Shirley Carter

The Dark Recruiter

Evil wants me
He waits behind opportunity
Waiting beyond light and hope...
my predator
Always pushing towards the easy way
locked in battle with love
Like my mother's dream
They're both pit bulls
tenacious
Teeth sunk deep
Each has an ankle
Refusing to let go...
I'll fight evil now that I've seen his face
He may win someday
For I have no illusions or delusions
However, he'll repent on inspection of his prize

J. J. Johnson

Our Dad

Our Daddy was born in 1916 -
He was a man full of self-esteem.
Times were rough in those days.
He grew up and had some very special ways.

There was nothing he couldn't do.
If you needed a hand, he would be there for you.
We remember him as being kind, patient and strong.
But, he would let us know when we were wrong.

He showed us what love and understanding was about.
He was the greatest without a doubt.

Golf was the game he loved to play.
That's where you would find him every day.
He got a hole-in-one three separate times.
Boy, he could hit that ball on a dime.
He was going for his 4th on the very day
That God decided Heaven was the place that he should play.

We gather here with love today,
As our Daddy reunites with our Mother so that
They both can play.

Linda Burns

The Little Old Man

A little old man passed my house one day,
He was thin and old and awfully gray,
He lived in a house down the street from me,
I loved to go climb his old oak tree.

His house was old, small and white,
But he kept it up with all his might,
He had a little brown dog, that barked all the time,
The neighbors complained, I'm glad he's not mine.

Now my little gray friend has gone away,
His house was torn down, I wished he'd have stayed,
I loved his tree, his dog and his smile,
Now I still go and visit him once in a while.

Kathleen Sorte-Goranson

Night Falls

Night falls, the shadows lengthen o'er the land.
I feel the majesty and the touch of God's hand.
Our trials and our troubles are behind us,
tomorrow is another day.
God in His mercy pulls down the shades of sleep and
we hear Him say as we nod,
"Be still and know that I am God."

Peggy Martley

He Was Still and Quiet

I came across a Black man, lying on the ground-
    He was very still and quiet, speaking not a word.
"Are you sleeping? Are you resting?", I said unto the man-
    But he was very still and quiet, and answered me not a word.

"Get up Black man!", I shouted. "Can't you hear my voice?"
    Yet he lay very still and quiet, and he spoke not a word.
"Someone, somebody help him!", I screamed and yelled so loud.
    Cause' he's very still and quiet and speaking not a word.

I looked and saw a Black boy, walking swiftly away.
    "Young man", I called, "Can't you help him, don't you see?", or
    "don't you care at all?
        No madam", he said, with hatred in his eyes,
    "You see, I left him still and quiet, he'll never speak again."

Linda F. Haynes

Officer

It seems all you ever
hear about is the Food Shortage,
the Homeless, nothing but ugliness.

Nobody talks about the beauty anymore.
I mean our police officers are one of the
unspoken beauties of the world.

Have you ever noticed how a police officer
talks to our young children, or see their
smile when they get a baseball or football
card from that police officer?

Or heard that child say Oh! Wow! I don't
have this card; and that child says thanks.

Next time you meet a police officer no matter
what the reason, stop and tell them what a great
job they are doing and wish them a safe day.

Melodie B. T. White

Later

I sit in the beach house, alone
Hearing the refrigerator and my own heart beat,
Captive to the beauty.

Did some masterful Artist
boldly brush a deep blue acrylic across an easel
or is that the ocean?
A sea gull soars above the sands,
Dribbling an irregular line of white,
Momentarily splitting the splash of color.

The houses are stark in the November sun,
Their pilings go deep
And the empty porches and battened shutters
present a unified front to approaching winter gales.
The sea oats and briny hedges bend low
and huddle together.

Lengthening shadows now darken the beach,
Covering the very spot where I stretched my sun-screened body
In the month of July.
If I close my eyes, perhaps the sounds of summer surf
can drown out the refrigerator.

Rachel C. Wilson

Untitled

Listen to the rustle of autumn leaves
heart the wind whistle through the trees.
See the frost on the window pane
see the sun setting across the plain.
Let me tell you a story of days gone by
I'll tell you a tale of pudding and pie.
Time goes by so quickly
savor the spice- savor the life.
Chimes echo through valleys in your mind
remember the mirror, remember the lines.
When what you think you fear starts drawing near,
you begin to learn what you really fear is not what's coming-
but what already here.
If the suns setting on your dreams
consider now the moon it beams
Never say never, its never too late
recognize your limits and then exceed them.
You are the beginning, the middle, the end,
my pen is yours now you fill it in.

Lisa Rawlings

Hearts

In life you'll find,
Hearts that are warm and sincere,
Hearts that are cracked - if not completely broken,
You will find Hearts that are cold and have no feelings.

The heart you will find in me,
Has warm and caring love for those close and far from me,
My heart has understanding for the pain that others have suffered,
You will find the Lord - which is most important to me,
You will find Children, Happiness, Kindness and more which the eye
   can't see and many can't understand,
You will also find a hole that is being filled by you.

So, while your in this Heart of mine,
Please treat is as if it were your own,
Love it, Hold it, and never drop it,
Water and nurture it,
And let it grow within,
To see the best in me,
Is knowing how my heart can be.

Nannette Ary

Suicide

His life was a mess and he knew it
He'd had a chance and blew it
And though he'd moan and curse and cry,
He didn't really want to die
He called for help, but no one came
He cringed and slouched with growing shame
But he continued to hope and try,
Because he didn't really want to die.
He hinted to peers day after day
Sensing weakness, they turned away
They were afraid to be nosy, afraid to pry,
Yet he didn't really want to die.
And when life had lost all trace of fun
When he stared down the barrel of a gun
His hopes had flown, his tears were dry,
But he didn't really want to die.

Valerie Hajdik

Rib

I am a woman obsessed
Heliumed full of dreams
Sometimes gassed by life
Oftentimes not
Existentialism powered by idealism is my brain
Cushioned by foam rubber to ease the blow
I am a woman lost
Lost in matters not to be solved
Only to be thought about, toyed with, arranged and rearranged again
I am womankind and unkind deeply touched by babies and other forms
of art, vane for lack of anything better to do
And find trivial the dailies of "domestic engineering"
I'm a woman more spiritual than you might think by looking at me
and far less superficial
I am an antique-laced tulip pollinated by the birds and the bees
One with nature and Este Lauder
I am every women, every woman who believes... Adam did not give us
a rib, we gently "took" it from him when the time was just
And stood firm in the righteousness of what's called the "intuition"
of the "species"... woman

Nancy G. Oxman

A Letter to Bizak: The Destroyer

Dear Nobleman with warm regards I wish to send my fond
hello..... 'Tis missing you this cold and wintry night snuggled up
here all alone.
   Felt......a note in private may be just what's needed to
pass the long night. So here I am knocking at your far off door
hoping you may open it if not tonight than in the morrow.
   And know that you were being thought of as I lay upon my
bed and dream of all the fantasies we have shared.
   A smile upon my face and a warmness in my heart I hope
you feel and know...... will always await you any time you knock
upon my door or lift the flap upon my tent.
   Hearken to it at your leisure, I will be there.....to greet
you with an open arm and a drink or two. There is one called wine
and a second that we must grind,...and both I will share with you.
   Until the time that we can meet in time and place......
Remember fondly all that we have shared.
   My short hot breath and tongue upon your neck. My naked
breast pressed hard against your chest. The smell of my sweet
perfume permeating the air, as you take me there......where ever
it may be. Our bodies one, for all eternity.

Mary J. Rotner

Soul Mate

If you would be my love, I would need you to:
Help me learn to trust again, and then be trustworthy.
Let me be weak and afraid sometimes, and not make me
   ashamed of my fears.
Let me be strong and fearless, and not make me ashamed
   of my strength.
I would want you to be weak and afraid sometimes,
and trust me enough to let me see that you are afraid.
I would want you to be strong and fearless without
   being a bully.
I would want you to accept my intelligence and be proud
   of the things I know,
and not feel that I am a threat to you.
I would want to rejoice in your knowledge,
and be happy that we can learn together.
I would not want you to ogle other women when I
   am with you,
Nor will I flirt with other men. Period.
I will promise you constancy and respect.
I will expect the same from you.

Ruth Schwarzbach

Untitled

I walk the path to a place I may return to once again.
Helpless eyes staring at me, looking out through the panes of glass.
These people long forgotten by society.
These doctors, these lawyers, these teachers
These husbands and wives
Mothers and fathers, role models and heroes.
Hardly given a second thought.
This is where they come to die.
Staring at the same four walls
Anxiously awaiting their nightly programs on TV
Only seeing the beauty of life when it briefly
comes by for a snack at the feeder,
Then watching it gallantly fly away to explore the world.
An occasional visitor brightens their day,
Only when we have time of course.
We go through our lives, never thinking of
those who long ago experienced it.
Those who are now alone and in solitude. Those who we will
someday
be. Not looking into our future.
But looking out to our past.

Kristin M. Black

Sand Box

Playing in her box
Her mind is at ease
No thoughts of before, just feeling the summer breeze
Playing in her box
Her mind thinks like a child
No feelings of before, toys so many piled
Playing in her box
Her hands make castles
No pain from before, no marks from their tassels
She asks herself why, what has she done
Her eyes start to cry, skin burning in the sun
Playing in her box
Her thoughts are so dirty
Only thoughts of before, they're not trustworthy
Playing in her box
Her mind slips to dream
Thoughts of the future, she starts to scream
Playing in her box
Her feelings are severed
Only thoughts of escape, a life only better.

Marc Fitts

Brown Baby

Creation of a beautiful queen
  her personality flows like a stream

Rippled dark skin appears at birth
  skin smoother than a silk shirt

As a moment passes by you hear a cry
  doctor try to save her before she dies

Crackle of life causes a flat line
  the death of a child so divine

Knowing that this baby wasn't coming back
  beautiful brown baby was born on crack

Lawrence M. D. Williams

God's Sufficiency

Though I have not a dime oh God,
In joyous celebration I give myself to Thee
For all my needs, wants and hopes are met in Thee
For all my needs wants hopes are met in Thee
My every fancy is supplied by you
Who gave your life for me!

F. Schaeffer

Songs of Shenandoah

Many songs have been written about the Shenandoah Valley
Her serenity and beauty of world wide renown
But to little has been said for the ancestry
Who toiled and there died and handed it down
The calloused old hands that built the stone fences
And hued out the big timbers for the stately old homes
Were motivated by a heart and a God fearing mind
To create this wonderful heritage and leave to mankind
Without even the aid of a midwife
Many pioneer wives suffered the pain
Of child birth in a lonely log cabin
And many there were who suffered in vain
The mothers and wives of first settlers
Who proved so loyal and strong
Should be held in highest esteem and in reverence
And forever be honored in song
If the cold gray granite used for markers
Bearing only the dates and a name
Could relate all their hardships and actions
I'm sure we'd thank heaven they came.

C. A. Hockett

Eulah

It's rare to find a friend who will devote
Her time to teach without reward in pay.
Each night from nine to twelve you phone, I quote
My lessons till you tell me, "it's okay."

Our likes and wishes have the same appeal.
The game of life is filled with tales and jokes;
We both put in our share with hearty zeal,
As I correct my work with rapid strokes.

At last I learn! The glory's yours. We share
A joy in concepts, beautiful and true;
Because I love new words and work with care.
This drive imbues my will in all I do.

  With versatility your knowledge glows;
  Our precious tie that binds this friendship grows.

Mary Isabel Dale

Untitled

No more hate, no more sorrows
Here we can only live for tomorrow
Love them to death is read clear on his face
Souls caught up in an iron embrace
But don't worry, big brother loves you
He gives us happiness, can take away all the pain
Little do we know, to him we're just a game
Lies turn to truth, the truth, well to lies
Slowly but surely each one of us dies
But don't worry, big brother loves you
We had to believe him, his word was his bond
Next thing you know, we're all dead and gone
Lurking somewhere in the corners of his mind
Memories of us all, so trusting, so blind
But don't worry, big brother loves you
Love's fruit is bitter more often than not
And once you have eaten, you're eternally caught
In a world of anger, lies and deceit
An end like this we're all destined to meet
But remember, Big brother loves you

Nikki Wright

The Pilgrim

Somewhere the cloud drops at the end of sunset light.
High sky a lazy swan slides on the end horizon.
Trail...Trail after trail the pilgrim shuffles his life.
Where will he go? Where does he come from? God knows!!!

The dark night promptly submerges the whole world!
Oh! My motherland! My home! My love! Nothing exists?
The North wind blowing, why did he stay there?
Alone! Is he awake? Is he dreaming?

The past, the angel, young time he could not find.
Does he dream to discover a new Heaven?
Is the murmuring wave calling him to a new world?
In this life, being or no being are so indifferent!....

Mai N. Luu

My Cloud

Today I watched a cloud be formed,
  high up in the sky.
As I looked on, in wondering awe,
  a tear fell from my eye.

From a wisp of white - there it was -
  growing bigger all of the time.
I knew in my heart, beyond any doubt,
  I could claim that cloud as mine.

For never before had I seen such a thing
  and the beauty of it made me cry.
But, alas, as quickly as it came
  my cloud disappeared from the sky.

I wasn't sad to know it was gone,
  for the beauty was etched in my mind.
There it will grow from a wisp of white
  and get bigger all of the time.

Phyllis Shaffer Caudill

Silver Hill

A quiet calm comes over me when I remember the old days of Silver
  Hill.
The laughter, the old gang, and the crazy antics we played.
Memories unfold of the front stoop where I gazed upon my playmates
romping through the streets, playing dead block, dodge ball and catch
  a girl kiss a girl.
The good old days.

The good old days, when Mr. Moody moved out of the house,
and relocated in a truck on the corner with no hot or cold running
  water;
or a ice box to keep food cold — but the neighbors loved him.

Silver Hill when you could go to the corner store called Doc's
and buy 2 for a penny candy, a hoagie, and a soda for $1.50.

Things has changed pretty much since then.
but the memories will linger forever in my heart.

Maria E. Lamar

View From My Back Door

Near my backyard, a huge majestic tree
It held a home for the blue jays
That huge majestic old tree
Maybe the beautiful blue jays will go away
For the tree fell over and took their home
I hope they don't have far to roam
So the beautiful blue jays I'll still see
Only maybe in another huge majestic tree

Yvonne G. Casey

Crucifixion of Christ

He lay on the cross with arms spread and hands nailed.
His head dropped with inability to hold it up on his own.
With spikes surrounding the skull, only he can describe
the agony for which his temple is suffering.
Nails pounded through the feet of many holy miles.
No strength left to hold his large frame up to cease
the tearing of his muscles.
He watches the rising of the sun and the descent to night.
With no food nor water, he goes for many a day.
All for your sins and mine.
Christ's suffering was for the evil's we have spoken and
physically committed, not only for the past but for the
present also.
What love he has for the children of God.
Jesus died for our sins, not His.
Isn't that reason enough to live heavenly for our Lord?

Michael A. Wiggs

Untitled

  Twisting stems of pain shoot through
his heart,

  One thought running through his mind,
how could she, oh my God how could she

  No reason left to live and every reason
to die

  He won't go to sleep for she dances
through his dreams

  All he can say is...
.....she cheated on me

Lisa Wynn

Sweet Memories

I had a cat named Jacque Pierre.
His kitten tricks kept him in the air.
His heart was made of purest gold.
I loved him dearer as he grew old.

He'd come to greet me at the front door.
I'd scoop him up off the floor.
I'd pet his beautiful beige and white fur,
And always, magically, he would purr.

He had the sweetest disposition,
But sometimes he'd make a mischievous transition,
Like clawing the carpet or the back of a chair,
Or escaping outside with a wild hunter's stare.

He loved to roll on the rough cement,
Or loll in the grass, ah, time well spent!
Sometimes he'd rub gently against my knee,
But mostly he liked to cuddle with me.

He'd snuggle, nice and cozy, up on my lap.
He'd turn a few circles before taking a nap.
He was the "sweetness" that made my life bright.
I'll miss my dear friend as I bid him "good night!"

Marianne T. Gajewski

Slow Death

Death climbs slowly up my spine.
Fear grips my heart, still beating in time.
A whispering wind, a quiet creak,
And comfort is all my heart will seek.
Death will takes its arms and wrap them around.
Then by its shovel, we'll be buried in the ground.
The silence that follows isn't a good thing.
Death will take us all, it will take everything.

Karin McWhorter

"Down Will Come Baby" (For Laura)

Mother's blood the purest pusher,
his mother's womb was "Needle Park".
This newborn screaming...screaming!
The tiny body jerks like some marionette gone mad,
in a rabid retreat of withdrawal;
each cell writhing in heroin agonies,
toy veins no virgin to evil inhabitants.
No cradle of arms, no soft bears, no untainted milk
Will sooth this maimed "mommy's boy"...
This baby's powder was cooked in spoons.

Karen L. Costello

My Husband (My World)

I have a beautiful and strong minded husband...
His thoughts are as solid as a rock...
Steadfast in his beliefs, as dependable as a winding clock...
A man of not many words, yet his actions speak loud and clear! ...
A man of no sense...
A man of limited fears.
He's the king of our castle...
I'm the Queen of his throne...
Perfect our marriage is not...
But with communication...
We can't go wrong.
I thank God for a man as splendid and unique as this.
Quiet, meek and strong...
At times as gentle as a loving kiss...
Yes, I have a beautiful husband...
Considerate...kind...and true.
Yet sound...distinct...and definite...
A true man of virtue.

Theresa Howard

An Age of Greatness

The pied piper of Harlem...
His tune is so sweet...
He tells it like it is...
On one hundred twenty-fifth street...
There's a new day in this land...
Revolution stirs the souls of the young...
Like pieces of old newspapers...
Swirling by to the tune of...
'The times they are a changin'...
Great men die, the world spins round...
And babies cry... a generation of youth...
Refuse to go to war.....what for they say...
Love's better than hate anyway...
Hippies clinging to Pacific shores...
Chanting, "NO WAR, NO MORE WAR,"...
An age of greatness passes by...
Going up in 'jaded' smoke...
In the California sky...

Tobi Kumar

My Child, My Child

Can I touch you one last time?
Hold your tiny hand in mine?
Soon you'll be gone, far far away.
Let me hold you if only for today.
   My child, my child how you have grown,
and because of all the love you have shown.
We will never ever be apart
I am you, and you are me,
forever together in our hearts.

Michelle C. Watson

He Walks Alone

He walks alone with a brown paper sack
Holes in his shoes and wrinkled clothes on his back
He stops to rest on a bench in the park
Sipping on his wine as the light turns to dark

He used to walk alone with a suitcase in his hand
Leather shoes, He was a sharp dressed man
He used to stop and chat with the coffee shop clerk
Conversation and laughter before he went to work

   So long ago this memory seems
   His company folded, and so did his dreams
   He lost his home along with his wife
   And now this is the story of his life

All huddled up against a tree
People pass by, but none of them see
A man that was once so full of pride
Now a stranger among us, like he died...

Sandra Rogers

Substance

Tears drip from the seems of my window eyes.
Hopeless drops of confusion cascade into the pool of
my soul.
Laughing, laughing at the void in that terrain,
laughing.
Laughing at the shimmering meadows of knowledge,
there faces stare back at me.
Pushing to pierce shields of thought,
I enveloped the echoing of fire.
My mind screamed.
The cold rod entered my heart.

William F. Groves Jr.

The Dollar Message

   "Annuit Coeptis" - Thirteen words in all
   Horizoning over the all seeing eyes of Horus
   "God favors our beginning", was the faith, the faith
   of the founding fathers of the Great American Nation.

A faith that moved them
to inscribe
These eternal words like the Great Shema
over the Dollar Bill

   A top and Ancient Pyramid, Thirteen steps in all -
   A number that meant, a new beginning for Egypt of old
   Horus watches over a Nation in search of a new order
   "Novus Ordo Seclorum", 'a new order for the ages'

With a resounding creed, IN GOD WE TRUST
Binding on the thirteen colonies and beyond
The mighty Eagle looks away from thirteen arrows of war
To face the thirteen peaceful leaves of the Olive Branch

   The Dollar Bill a summation of our creed, summons all,
   To turn from the thirteen arrows of self destruction
   And hate, within our midst, in pursuit of peace, to build
   A stratum that makes our pursuit an authentic one.

Tom S. Ebong

Grown Up Tree

Pick, pick, who are you?
I am the one that helps you, the tree says.
I hope there are some for me to keep growing
pick, pick, pick;
It's all gone by a strong wind blown away
But just take what's left, I had in mind.
Green, green tree, now that I can see

Kenneth H. Hunter

Endless Love

A single tear falls
How I longed to hear your call.
I remembered what we shared
And can't forget the way I cared.
The pain I feel deep in my heart,
I ask myself if we could have another start
This broken heart will take time to heal
But what I felt was very real
Why must all good things come to an end?
My heart is torn and can't be mend
I can't believe your really gone
Living life, trying to hold on-
How can innocent love end up like this?
It's all apart of growing bliss.
The touch of your hand and the kiss of your lips made
   me weak in the knees
This was all just a part of your tease
Memories of you haunt my mind, how can love be so blind?
Thinking back of how much I cared
I can't forget the weight of your stare.

   Karen Aquila

My Wedding Day Prayer

Oh, my dear God, here at last is my Wedding Day.
How I wonder what future will come our way.

Oh, my dear God, this wonderful man you have given me,
With complete and total devotion, is my husband to be.

Oh, my dear God, please keep him ever close to my heart.
Let our love be eternal, let us never part.

Oh, my dear God, give me understanding as a new wife.
Give me strength and compassion thru daily strife.

Oh, my dear God, bless us with children to have and to hold.
A family bound together with love as we grow old.

Oh, my dear God, this special day is like a dream.
The colors are so lovely, all peach and cream.

Oh, my dear God, let me always remember how it felt,
To be a beautiful bride so in love I could melt.

Oh, my dear God, let me always remember the look on his face,
As I walk down the aisle all in white satin and lace.

Oh, my dear God, hear the music played so sweet.
The notes echo abiding love as two hearts meet.

Oh, my dear God, all of my thanks I give to you.
For I see true love in his eyes as I say to him now...I do.

   Paula Mackey Geeteh

Sisters in the Lord

How many times you've been on my mind
   How often your thoughtfulness has been the kind
To nurture me on my path to heaven
   Even though you may not know how much you've given.

Your warmth and caring are truly heaven sent
   As you demonstrate God's love in willing to be spent
For others concerns and burdens to share
   My heart is now full and doesn't feel bare.

As the years go by and ties grow stronger
   My heart replies in love much fonder
To realize I do have a sister, yes many sisters indeed
   Who, for me, have met my deepest needs.

   Sherlyn Bryant

Over The Hill

Many know the poetry "Over the river and through the woods to Grandfathers house we go".

Not so many know of the poet who at 65 broke his first bone and the femur bone it was.

   Falling through the air from 12 ft. up was shocking; however the sudden stop, alas, was bad and sad.

Two years later the "Over the Hill" male poet crashed with his bicycle and broke his collar bone.

   His feelings were hurt as well as the bone; however he was perturbed more by the "accident prone" name that he was gaining, for why should two bones broken in 67 years be considered a "proning."

So now "Over the Hill" he may be with one leg shorter and one weak shoulder the greatest sign of his "Over the Hillness" is his compliant of the "accident prone" label by folk who are just concerned for his welfare.

He joyfully serves in "Mission" with his spouse in Haiti, the "accident
prone" reputation, and the "you say you are serving where?" remarks
Blessing others and being blessed one day at a time.

   Tom Counts

Fantasy

I dream of you
holding me in your arms at night when I'm scared
keeping me safe and warm from all of the harm the world can do
let me love you
let me have you
be with me until you can stand it no longer
I feel so strongly for you
everything about you is unreal
I remember your touch
I long for your body, your soul, your heart
I need you now
love me now and forever
just as you have been since we last departed
why is love here now, so early?
answer if you can
do you love me?
will you love me?
touch me, hold me, caress me, love me
I love you

   Julie Watson

"Message From the Angels"

I sent my message of love over a bright rainbow,
Hoping it would touch your soul on its way to Heaven.
Memories of our time together filter in and out of my mind;
Memories that started the day you left.
Life is painfully quiet now that you're gone;
Days once filled with bright colors,
Are now tinged by the grey skies of loneliness.
I used to hear the angels sing when we were together,
Now all I hear are the songs of broken hearts being played
on broken harp strings.
The angels frolic above you,
I wave to the dancing stars in the eastern sky;
They are happy to be near you,
Just as I was.
Twinkling stars;
Angels smiling,
Telling me you are safe.
Message from the angels;
Life isn't the same without you,
Wish you were here.

   Anthony Failla

Ash-Man

I am a stranger now in the town where my children were born.
Houses and churches are so many tombstones that I must somehow
climb over.
And I have fallen, and become covered,
with a black soil that they can not see.
I am the ash-man. It is hoped that I will blow away.
   The people are angry at me because my blood
runs through their streets, causing them to slip,
thereby tasting their own disgust.
   I come to the waters, and small animals lie
wounded in my footprints.
When I would heal, they fly or run away.
My soul goes after them, but may not catch them.
   A young man with an earring offers to help,
but he is weak, and tries to turn on what is already running.
   An old woman smiles, but she is afraid, and
waves good luck.
   I hop over fences, but snow is in the garden.
   I will eat the dark embers and warm my belly with the blackness.

David Stanfield

As Night Falls

The sky is so blue.
How blue the sky is.
White puffy clouds, making intriguing figures.
The suns streak trying to get through the big clouds.
What it would be like to fly sky high, so fast.
As night falls the light goes out, darkness is my enemy.
It takes over the day.
The moon watching over me;
My guiding light down the dark, dreary path ahead of me.

Ami Drogo

My Love

How can I speak my heart and not frighten you?
How can I ease your fears?
How can I relieve any pain?
I want to. I love you.

Can I speak my heart in my eyes,
   or shall I close them?
Can I ease your fears with a kiss,
   or shall I keep it?
Would it relieve any pain if I hold your hand?
   I'm here. Guide me.

D. L. Sharkey

Black Is A Crayon

Black is a crayon in the coloring box of life.
How can this simple color be such a source of strife?

Old westerns distinguished the cowboys by how they were clad.
White hats meant the good guys, black hats the bad.

Black is associated with loss, superstition, pain.
Yet this color brings us rest at night and clouds of
needed rain.

Black can be as soft as a shadow, or hard as a lump of coal,
often it is used to describe a wicked, sinful soul.

If a blind man were rescued by someone with a skin of black,
would he berate the hero's color and gratitude lack?

Perhaps if all were blind to the color of another's skin,
we could look past the different hue and find the
brightness within.

Bonadine Fausnaugh

Feelings

How do I feel living in a world marred by contempt?
   How do I feel being shunned by society?
      How do I feel as an outcast in their minds?

      I am trapped as an outcast in their minds forever-
      unless the ignorant, blind fools set me free.
      And when they do so,
      I will not judge them as they have done me,
      For I have no right to do so.
      Hence, I will not become one of them.

   Why should I be shunned by society?
   Because of my race, my gender, my beliefs, my differences? Hah!
   Society will not ignore me for I am here.
   I am not a nobody, I AM SOMEBODY!

I want to be indifferent, but I cannot be so.
I can only wonder why this is so primitive
and why diversity cannot be tolerated.
I can only dream of a world where hatred and injustice are extinct.
A world where the words of Martin Luther King fill the air proudly.
I know together we can make this dream reality.
So let's get together and make a difference.

Anh Dang

Can't You Hear My Cries?

Can't you heart me cry, or don't you care? I have tried to tell you
how I feel, why don't you care? When you were sick wasn't I there? I
took care of you till you was well. Where were you when I needed you?
To help me through the times I couldn't do, is that asking too much of
you? Couldn't you hear me crying as my heart broke into? The tears I
shed, I felt so alone as I often do. Do I ask that much of you? As
my tears fell in front of you why didn't you care? Why do you always
make me feel blue, is a kind word too much to ask of you? A simple
word of kindness is all I need, can't you find one kind thing to say
about me? I guess I'm not as special as I try to be, since you can't
tell me. I try so very hard to be what I need to be but, I guess I
can't be what you need me to be. The tears and pain will never go
away for since I needed you, you went away. Away in spirit, your mind
miles away, to a place I want to be. Why can't we go together, it is
me? I see the different look from years gone away, why can't you see
me like I used to be? I'm a little older and heavier you see but, my
heart is still like it use to be. I care for you enough to set you
free if you want to be. I hurt all the time can't you see? One day
I'll be gone and you'll see. Why can't you hear my cries while I'm
here and let me see how much I mean?

Dianna Dickerson

"Reminiscent Friend"

A time in my life I like to review,
How special you made it for me.
Many hours we spent sharing, caring,
Never tiring of one's company.

A big laugh, a silent cry,
Long talks we had, you and I.
How special a person you've been to me,
In times of trouble and sheer folly.

A time in my life I like to review,
Those days past I spent with you.
A friend I'll always hold close to my heart,
With great admiration I've had from the start.

And as I sit here thinking of you,
I will thank Our God for past days to review.

Alice Thomas Cambron

Tim and the Squirrels

I have never been able to figure at all,
How Tim guards the house because he is so small.

He watches the fenceline, both day and night,
If he sees strangers, he puts them to flight.

A stranger comes around without looking up,
He would think Tim was a ferocious pup.

The squirrels play on the fence and jump in the sand,
Tim is right there and in full command.

They try to gather food for winter,
Tim stand poised, forbidding any to enter.

He weighs only about eight or nine pounds,
Quite fast and a challenge to any hound.

He is very nervous and extremely rude,
Especially if you try to take away his food.

Now Chihuahua Tim is growing old,
An interesting pet, and still very bold!

James Stephens

The Love Experience

I always thought love was easy to define
I always thought love would sparkle and shine
I always considered myself a decent kind of man.
I always thought love would take me by the hand.

I never thought love could disguise itself so well
I never thought love would go down an unknown trail.
I never considered myself as a man of uncertainties.
I never thought love would leave me on my knees.

I once thought love would sweep me off my feet.
I once thought love would make my life complete
I once considered myself as a man prepared for such.
I once thought love was dependent on just your touch.

Anthony Owens

Dearest Mom

I gave you all the hugs I could
I always told you how much I loved you;
I acted the way a daughter should
And I gave you a grandson too.
I felt it was not enough when you died.

I know you loved me with all your heart
You never doubted how much I loved you.
The years have been so painful being apart
Living without my Mom and my close friend too.
I have felt so empty inside since you died.

People tell me we should learn from the past
Yet we must set all of our painful scars free.
Your death won't change and your love will last
Because I am a part of you and you are part of me.
It's still hard letting go and I struggle without you.

I forgot that it was you that died and not me
Still, I allowed much of myself to die inside too.
It was very short sighted of me not to see,
I am the part of life that lives on, instead of you.
Passing on your love, stories and wisdom to my son.

Denise Splan

My Only Fear

My will is gone,
I am all alone.
I am fighting for a lost cause,
I fear when I'm done I'll hear no applause.

My will is gone,
I'm all alone.
I feel like a lost fawn,
That can't find it's way home.

Will someone show me the way,
Do I go left or right,
Is it night or day,
Is my home in sight.

Before I came here,
I had no fear.
Let it be known,
My fear now is to be alone.

Jenny Southard

Sega

I see things in black or white
I am either wrong or occasionally right
I can talk my way out of a sticky situation
But putting it on paper is a hard expectation
I am as loyal as a puppy who loves to play
And as sneaky as a roach in the light of day
I express the sound of a piano as it awakens and soothes
Even in troubled times like Magic Johnson I have the moves
Academics may never come with ease
Although my talent for sports is a breeze
Action, adventure, music and sports are all big parts of me
You can call me Sega or a Big Screen Color TV

Joshua Mintz

Fire

Oh come ye dear people and hear what I say,
I am telling of an old woman burned to death today.
She was smart and loving but too old to run, and
The child played with matches — now she is gone.

Did she scream? Was she scared? Do you even care.
The poor old woman was burned and charred, as they
Carried her away and I knew she was going home to stay.

The spoiled child with a match burning bright
Caught fire to the house and it burned in fright
The firemen tried bravely their best to save
The little old woman who died today.

Two days she suffered while her family looked on.
Lay in a hospital bed, with all hope gone.
And I, the outsider, my heart in my throat.
Still shedding tears because I miss her so.

The child's not to blame, it is the parents who taught
Him to strike the matches for the fireworks they bought.
So now she is in heaven, no pain will she feel.
But will the child with the matches will he ever heal?

Glenda Spears

The Real Meaning of Life

What is it that mankind wants out of life?
Is it possible that we want love?
Hah, Hah, No.
Is it possible that we want success?
I think not.
Could it possibly be money we're after?
Of course, what else?

Tiffany Lawrence

Wisdom's Eye's

I am the Sun dancing in the wind.
I am the Skies covering the Earth with warmth & breath.
I am the Mountain; Crystals singing; I ching I ching.
I am the Brook whispering strength flows
 over craggy gray rock warm smooth by ancient years.
 Past muddy grassy banks, water and wind flows.
 Neither dawn nor dusk shall not blossoms bloom.
I am the Tree that bends as the wind dances me
 Whispers crying in sigh and moans.
I am the caress of lovers hand, below the saddened eyes.
I am the Tears that fall as lovers hug and part.
I am the Stars that twinkle gladly dance.
I am the winds caress that dries your eyes, then dies.
I am all that is and was, Eternally on forever, to be,
for I am Love.

Jonathan Eric Hawke

Yesterday

As I sit here all alone
I ask myself could I be wrong
I think of the way it used to be
has time changed or have you and me

We fuss and fight everyday
we just don't have time now to sit and pray
people we need to go back to yesterday
because time is slowly passing away

The Lord has brought us form a mighty long way
but yet still we forget to say
thank you Lord
For the things you have done
for the many blessing you have thrown upon

People we got to come together
and it don't need to be long
God is going to sweep down
and take his earth
and then it will be gone

Clift Bell

Ruben

Ruben was young and He couldn't see,
I asked him; what do you want to see?
And he said: "I would like to see
The stars on the sky, the moon when it brights
The clouds, the flowers, the trees, and the mountains
The water, the fields and the fountains
The sun, the sunrise, the sunset and the lights
The colors, the horizon and the fishes of the sea
The birds, the flies and the bees
The people, the train and the planes
The cars, the houses and the buildings on the street
The eyes, and the smile of a child
My brothers, my sisters, my mom when is with me,
 everything I used to see."
I asked him; did you use to see?
And he said - yes fool of me
I hurt my eyes, now I don't see
We cried loud "Lord, please let Ruben to see"
a month after this, He died
And now from Heaven: Ruben can see!

Jose M. Ramirez

Forever Thinking Of You

When the sun slowly rises upon the brilliant morning sky
I awake with a wonderful thought of you,
As the day goes on and the sun passes across the sky,
I think of you,
Your smile,
Your eyes,
Your strong hands.

As the sunsets and the day ends
I dream of you,
your face,
your voice,
your presents is always in my dreams,
It all seems so real.

Then I awake and realize that my dreams of you are not real,
And the tears begin to fall,
They fall often when I think of you.

Every day I pray for you,
Every night I dream of you,
Every moment I think of you,
All I can do is love you.

Jan Renee Shoultz

Summer's Gone

In the last days of summer,
I become melancholic and serene,
From the absence of Robins.
The squirrels' nests are complete in the trees,
as they excavate for hidden nuts,
gather during the summer days.
The planted fields have become barren,
and the Tourists have left for home,
in symbolic of an ending seasons.
The forest discards their leaves,
leaving behind a translucent views.
Yet, I recollect the succulent days of summer.
But, behind lies the seacoast dunes,
to indoctrinate the emerge of Fall.

Dorothy S. B. B. Robinson

Good Friday

I stand, my body pressed against the cross
I bend my head against the thorn,
Look down and see his Mother's face,
Look up and see the envious scorn.

I feel no pain; I am not he.
The blood dries on his face, not mine.
I have no wounds on hands and feet.
I cannot taste the sour wine.

My heart beats wildly in my breast,
Then stops, then beats, but he is gone.
I follow slow on splintered feet,
Rest at the tomb, then follow on.

Anne M. McBride

Morning Glories

Do you remember, mother, the morning glories
I brought you, so fresh and wild,
And placed them by you while you slept,
When I was just a child?
Youth is like morning with eyes wide and bright,
But both grow old and face the night.
Perhaps when morning comes again to open sleeping eyes,
I will find you, mother, waiting for me,
Then I will bring my gift once more,
And climb upon your knee.

Joan Jones

Image of Life

The Image of her clouds the Sky
I call out her name, yet there's no reply
She left me that day
To fall behind
Now the memory of her fills my mind
I reach out to touch her
And there's nothing there
But the cold chill of midnight air
All I can Hear is the Sweet laughter
of the one I loved
That is no longer here
I wish there was another way to Say goodbye
To the one I loved
And left behind
Now she haunt's my dreams
I'm riddled with guilt
from the day she left me
upon that hill
Now I fall to my knees, And begin to pray
That Soon I shall See her again... Someday

Jason Zimmerman

Sea Breezes

Walk along the seashore,
I can hear a whistles,
It is the winds.
It is blowing quite hard.
I can smell the salt air;
It smells so fresh;
Just like a Rose Blossom;
On a hot summer day.
Oh what a breeze;
I still hear the whistle blowing in the wind.

Cindy Thoman

Lost

Where has he gone, this man I call Daddy?
I can see him and hear him and touch his soft fingers,
But when I look in his eyes, I know he's not there,
Yet I sense that some part of him lingers.

How I yearn to crawl in there, to feel what he's feeling.
If it's dark on the road, I would turn on the light,
If he's weary and hurting, I would carry him gently,
If he's frightened, I'd say it's alright.

"It's alright," I'd lean close and whisper to him,
"I'll miss you but it's OK to go without me,
For the part that still lingers I now claim as mine,
And I'll try to become as you want me to be."

They call it Alzheimers, for want of a name.
It came and it stole him away in the mist,
Before I could tell him how special he is,
I was left with his shadow, so I'll bend and I'll kiss

His sweet forehead now furrowed with problems unknown,
By the rest of us left on the outside to grieve,
For you see, he's still with us and I long to hold on,
Yet I want to see peace and his pain relieved.

Jean Brody

It's Spring

Spirea blossoms. Skies so blue;
Pansies and petals of every hue;
Rainbows above and rain falling down;
Icicles gone - ideas abound for
New things to plant and watch them
Grow in gardens and fields and even in town!

Mary F. Grau

Where Is My Love?

I can't see her face or even the color of her hair
I can't tell you her age or what size dress she'll wear

The color of her eyes are a mystery to me
The complexion of her skin I can't see

I don't know how she'll act, I don't know how she'll talk
But I'd bet my bottom dollar she'll have a very special walk

She'll hold herself with dignity, she'll hold herself with pride
She'll hold herself aloft and have no one at her side

She has her own dreams, she knows her own mind
She's a very special woman, she's one-of-a-kind

She's had a lot of experiences but she's learned from every one
There's nothing new to her, nothing under the sun

She's seen most of the world and she's not easily impressed
Power and money mean nothing, she's been courted by the best

But something is always lacking, something is not there
She thinks about it each morning as she brushes out her hair

Then out into the world as a bright new rose
She creates quite a stir no matter where she goes

She's strong and independent but gentle as can be
I know she's out there waiting, she's waiting just for me

Joe Fry

The Old Magnolia Tree

I stood beneath the old Magnolia tree.
I could hear the buzzing of the bees.
As they nestled among the leaves
I could hear the whippoorwill calling to its mate
I pondered a while, and wondered what would be my fate.

The aroma of the magnolia blossoms was all around.
As they fell slowly bur gently to the ground
I stood amazed, at all I could see.
As I stood beneath the old Magnolia tree

The old tree stands straight and tall
As the evening shadows begin to fall,
When I say good-bye to that old tree,
I'll just have to let things be,
As I slowly walk away
I hope I can come back again some day
And stand under the old Magnolia tree.

Grace Upchurch

Naked Apes

I was a baby, and You were a baby.
I could hear the sound of wind, You could smell the nature in the air
I was a pure, and You were an honesty.
We were born in this beautiful planet.
We used to wake up with the gentle sunshine.
We used to go home with the tender sunset.

I was naked, and you had no make-up.
Too many sound, too much smell
Can you remember the smell of earth?

Desire, Ambition, Money and Science
Real Wisdom was gone.
Hurt each other and kill the nature
Destroy this planet.

Open your eyes, Humans Humans
Look into your arrogant mind

I was a baby and You were a baby
We, Humans are just only naked apes
Only naked apes

Asayo O. Thomas

Loan

We never know how fate is going to work in our life
I do believe if everyone would always think
before they react, that they would not have so much strife
If we agonize in defeat, fate will take us as
far as we allow it to take us
This happened to me until God gave me someone I could trust
I really believe this man was a Guardian Angel
put on earth for hundreds of people far miles around
This man had a soul as pure as a dove
He thought me the true meaning of God's love
But what ever road that life takes us on
We should always think of our life as a loan
Always with love doing for others, help us to grow
And God's grace, love and mercy in our lives
will always show

Joyce Hazel Pitts

The Drifter

I once knew a cowboy who was called by "Old Gaffer."
I doubt if he knowed the name really was his.
And all that he owned was a rope and a saddle
And even a horse, on occasion, that is.

Once, durin' roundup when wind was a saber
And water as scarce as the chips for our fire,
I saw 'im walk up to a starvin' old piebald
That some said was his'n and others 'for hire.'

He took out his flask and poured down the holler
Of that hoss who would never see mornin's first light.
And whether he died wasn't really what mattered.
He just couldn't bear not to do what was right.

It was talked about lots over long winter evenin's.
Oh, some called 'im crazy and some couldn't talk.
But it seemed after roundup, when I got to thinkin',
There was more human feelin' went into our work.

I've thought many times of the sweat and the trail dust
And the blisters that made us put pride on the shelf.
But it all seemed so little and so unimportant
When they buried the drifter who thought last of his self.

Jewel Estes

Valediction

I strove with science for science was worth my strife.
I endured the vicissitudes of my life
because science was my refreshment.
I overcame the boredom of routinement
because science was my enthrallment.
Everyday I unlocked my lab door
with the expectancy of discovery or of new lore.
Impatience against ennui or non-recognition
was neutralized by the thrill of cognition.
Though too modest for a Nobel in hand
nevertheless novel enough to ban
the dejection of any scientist of the land
so take heart my colleagues in science
together we constitute much, much more as a Nobel alliance.

Donald E. Pearson

Ponies

Ponies running in the wind,
Ponies playing and jumping again and again,
They are so beautiful, so bright,
You should see them in the sunlight,
At night in their stalls, they look so peaceful,
But sleeping and dreaming of the day they're full,
Of running restlessly in the wind,
For tomorrow another day begins for them.

LaTasha Payne

Separated From You

When I'm separated from you,
I feel a need to cry.
That need is because I love you.
The love I have for you is like no other love I know.
When I'm separated from you,
That is when this special love really hurts.
I can feel my heart ripping and tearing in many pieces.
For two long years I have waited to see you,
But the distance that keeps us apart is great,
But of the distance that keeps our hearts apart-
There is none.
When I'm separated from you,
I think back to the times I spent with you.
The good and the bad; the happy and the sad.
Mom, I really love you and nothing can ever change that.

Crissy Campbell

Peace "In The Forest"

I look East, then West. I glance North and South.
I feel peace all around me.
  In the forest, In the forest.
A little squirrel gently cracks a nut
  In the forest, In the forest.
A calm wind gently blows the high treetops
  In the forest, In the forest.
I spy a raccoon comfortably lying in a hollow log
  In the forest, In the forest.
A little ladybug quietly climbs up my leg.
  In the forest, In the forest.
I sit still, motionless and enjoy its beauty
  In the forest, In the forest.
A beautiful butterfly untroubled flies overhead
  In the forest, In the forest.
Secluded in a nest, I hear a baby robin chirping.
  In the forest, In the forest.
I feel no violence, just tranquility and peace all around me
  In the forest, In the forest.

Jordan Ulfig

In My Heart

In my heart I feel many things,
I feel the warmth of your hands, your sparkling ring.
Your caring smile, your warm embrace,
Your beautiful, gleaming, beckoning face.
I feel your heart as if we are one,
beating in rhythm as we laugh and have fun.
In my heart I feel taken over by the love I have for you,
I search deeper and I find it to be true.
I find that your love is addictive like a drug.
I must have it soon or I will die.
in this warmness and love I shall soon begin to fry.
Please give it to me my dear, please don't deny,
I still hunger for that love, if it not be mine, then I cry.
I cannot bear not to be near you, this I cannot stand,
I cannot live without holding your hand.
So I ask you this time, I ask and I plea,
Do you love him or do you love me?

Jeff Hackett

Winds Of Change

The winds of change blow swiftly now —
On a day that I thought would never come to be.
These winds that I speak of stir quietly at first,
But soon build to leave the soul in a state of unrest.
Quickly tomorrow arrives,
And with it one wonders if the winds will cease,
Or if they will remain to unsettle what was once laid to rest.

Tamara Hill

Looking Back At Those Four

As I leap into the lane of youth,
I feel uneasy as the trigger is pulled.
Taking off into those years like an unguided rocket.
The first lap is unchallenging, but different from the familiar.
Making my turn into the arena, the eyes of my peers burn.

Again on the back stretch, which seems an eternity.
I feel like a feeble kite blowing in the wind-
With no man, nor spirit, holding the string.
Half way there - have I made a difference?
There is no scale of measure for the distance I've run.

Thrice I've gone, and thrice I've repeated.
When will the change come - so I can beat the clock
Success is measured by my desire and will.
On the last straight-a-way, my confidence strengthens.
No one can feel the victory I do as I pass my opponent.
She at my heels, and my heart in my hand.

I glide through the finish line and
through a different arena of existence.
He as my shepherd and my spirit as inspiration -
Now to compete in the next arena.

Damon Hilary Mock

My Angel

She is there within my dreams, she shares my hopes and fears
I find her when I least expect.
My angel, My friend.
Through sorrow, joy and tears, I find my friend in thought.
Sometimes when life is full of doubt, a simple song,
a shining star.
These are signs of hope in sight. A second chance to
make things right.
My angel, My friend.
Guidance and unconditional love, a touch seen to be sent
from above.
My soul and my pain have purpose, the life I have has reason.
I look above and not in vision, but in my heart I feel
My Angel, My friend is there.
To guide me and to always be there.

Debra Bierbauer

My Garden

One day to my garden I went to weed,
I found that many flowers had gone to seed.
Seemed like 'twas only yesterday
the flowers were blooming in fine array.
What happened, I thought, to cause such a mess?
It was I who was careless, or lazy - I guess!
With weeder in hand, I got down on my knees,
and all I could see were wee maple trees.
The big trees, you see, had seeded this year
and the wind had scattered them far and near.
The cool rains that fell had been their cultivation,
and the warm summer sun had nurtured their creation.
As I marveled at the sight, I thought, what a shame -
to destroy natures wonders; but its all in the game.
With that I began uprooting without pardon,
For who wants hundreds of maples in their flower garden?

Elaine C. Barta

Time Is Precious

A waste of time is a thoughtless sin.
Never knowing where to start or how to end.
Accomplishments are few and success is none.
For the time we wasted, our job wasn't done.
And time is something we shouldn't throw away,
So let's not waste it each day after day.
For time is precious.

Tony B. Jordan

Overcoming Maturity

Aghast at such a revelation:
I have come of youth, dear age!

Respect having lost its lustre
wisdom I have often craved rendered whimsical

Jubilance, a more fitting dish
for those who grow inversely
innocence, a better charm

I can now chirp with mirth
things are as they ought to be, see

From wounds flows blood now
instead of wind
and I, a gentle boy, now feel
instead of understand.

Burke Blackman

Something Wrong

Things I wish to change
I have no control over,
Things I should change,
I don't,
why is it that the things in this world that need changing,
never do,
and yet the things in this world that are fine the way they are,
are always changing,
We can change a policy or a law,
but we cannot change the fact people are going hungry,
We can change our minds at any time,
but we cannot change the minds of the people killing each other
on our streets,
We can change our names to whatever we want,
but we cannot name all those who have been hurt or killed in
mindless
crimes,
We can change our point of view,
and yet most people don't or won't view the homeless people
on the streets,
We can even change our sex if we are unhappy with it,
and I cannot change the fact that half the people who read this still
will not care or try to change anything,
Something's wrong with that...

Brian A. Ploszaj

Unborn Love

I want to write, but the words won't produce sentences
I have so many feelings, yet nothing to say
I feel teardrops falling from my heart, yet I cannot cry
I want to think of nothing, but heavily reality weighs

Emptiness fills me, yet I am surrounded by love
Thoughts run through my mind, yet none complete
Hurt is the only emotion I possess, yet I cannot feel the pain
The decision breathes strong, but weakened, I cannot stand on my feet

My body, where you are cradled inside, feels lifeless
My love, by which you where conceived, has no place
Pain shoots through my heart, where eternal love for you stems
Tears flow through the same eyes that can picture your face

The words, the feelings, the teardrops, the thoughts
All sit within me where reason is sought.

Emptiness, incompleteness, pain and weakness
Fill my present state with such bleakness.

My body, my love, my heart, my eyes
Must recover to keep your memory alive.

Emiko L. Schlette

Pictures of Spring

In the quiet of morning as I watch the sunrise shine.
  I have visions of some pictures that my thoughts now bring to mind.

There are trees so tall and stately with buds now bursting through.
  And the birds return to branches with their songs for me and you.

The crocuses and daffodils will soon be in full bloom.
  All these bright and cheerful colors help dispel the Winter's gloom.

The trees, the birds, and flowers help remind me Spring is near.
  Yes, it brings a smile of pleasure to enjoy this time of year.

Connie Kessler

Letting Go

I have waited and I've loved your ways,
I have watched you deny me day after day.
Alone am I with total obsession.
Treating your cruel acts with not one ounce of aggression.
Yet loving you more and knowing all to well,
That this pain inside me will become a lonely hell.

I am letting go of ways of old,
With feeling and emotions for you so bold.
Alone am I without you still,
Aware that I can't hide from feelings I feel,
Staring at your face only in mind.
In my fantasy to me you are nothing but kind.

Upon a pedestal so high safe from flooding tears I cry.
Knowing to well that about my feelings I cannot lie.
From feelings I feel one can't run or hide.

Alone am I in utter pain,
You hold the sword for my heart has been slain.
For the reason the River of tears from my eyes flow,
I cry...Alone
Because I am letting go.

Brandon K. Carman

The Stranger's Presence

The rain gently falls to the ground
I hear the gentle rapping at the door
I open the door a crack to see who lies on the other side
And to my surprise, I see you standing there
All wet and cold, I invite you in
You take off your coat and shoes and try to dry off
As you stand in the hall, I wonder who you are and
why I let you into my home
I have never seen or heard of you before, so why do I trust you?
Is it those big brown eyes that seem to be flooded with innocence?
Or is it the way your lips form that smile that makes me melt?
I show you the way to my living room
Your face glows in the light radiating off the fire in the fireplace
The wood crackles as you sit down in front of the fire
I never want you to leave
For some unknown reason, I am so drawn to you and can't take my eyes off you
You feel the penetration of my eyes, searching for something deep in your soul
As our eyes meet, I sense a certain restraint causing me to realize that there will be an eternal Bond
Yet those very steps that led you through my threshold would once again be walked upon
Only this time leaving a void that was once filled by your presence

Charlene Goodwin

Wild Wind

I heard the wind, it was more than a whisper.
I heard it years ago when I was wild as a twister.
A long time ago but the sound never died.
A time when thunder roared and could not hide.
A way of life this wild wind,
It would grab your heart and pull you in.
Young or old it will never let go,
Strong as steel, fast or slow.
The wind's still blowin'.
The fire's still there.
It just moves a little slower
Through my salt and pepper hair.

David B. McEuen

A Wolf In Sheep's Clothing

It's night now and I tell my children a tale,
I hope that they can't see, I'm not coping too well,
I guess I'll explain to them when they are grown,
About why we're at grandma's instead of at home.

A wolf in sheep's clothing has stolen my life,
A wolf in sheep's clothing has made me his wife,
now after 2 children and after 4 years,
I see now that my sheep has awfully big ears.

He huffs and he puffs and he blows my house down,
he thinks that I can't see through that white granny gown,
good-bye picket fence and good-bye childhood dream,
my husband is coming home lying to me.

He smiles like a lamb and oh how my heart hangs,
Yanked the wool off my eyes now I can see fangs.
Oh, where's the brave hunter that he used to be?
and why does it hurt when he's looking through me?

A wolf in sheep's clothing has stolen my heart,
A wolf in sheep's clothing just tears me apart,
It's not hard to reason why I feel so blue,
'wore wool for a veil - when I said, "I do".

Amy C. Nguyen

Stop the Clock I Wanna Get Off

Stop the clock; I wanna get off! time's just racing on by.
I just can't seem to slow it down, no matter how hard I try.
Spring arrives and, before you know it, winter's around the corner.
Yep, you guessed it, time rushes on and this year's another goner.
They talk about daylight savings time; they give to you and I,
But, try as I can, I just can't find it, no matter how hard I try!

It seems your kids are all grown up in just a year or two.
If we could only stop the clock, but there's nothing we can do.
You to try to fill your mind with memories that will last,
But you just can't stop that blasted clock from going by so fast.
Months turn to years and soon you see that the future is now the past.
So stop the clock; I wanna get off! times going by too fast.

Harold L. McClusky

Fulfillment

When we wake up in the morning - to a bright or cloudy day
Do we consider the effect we have on other's - in the things we do or say

Is our greeting always cheerful - do we extend a helping hand
Do we show an earnest interest - with a smile they'll understand

Do we lend words of love and comfort - to all whom we chance to meet
That may help to lift their burdens - and make their life seem more complete

But no matter what encounters - that may cross our path each day
Let's extend to all good wishes - and God's blessing on our way

Dorothy Whitlock

"Unborn"

...To see daylight and You Mommy,
I just can't wait anymore .
I've got my head, hands and feet
I've got my heart, it beats
I have a small nose and big blue eyes.
I'm your baby, beautiful as you are.
I want to be born,Mommy!
But I can't, I'm chocking in here.
Please, Mommy...Don't eat bad medicine!
I'm still inside You, but it's not safe anymore.
It gets worse and worse, my skin is tearing into pieces...
Mommy, don't kill me, it's not my fault!
I didn't come of my own free will,
I didn't ask for a life, but You gave me one!
Promise, I will be happiness and joy,
The sense of every day
Mommy, Mommy! ! !
It hurts so much.
Good bye for ever!
I'm dying now.

Beata Piotrowicz

Sound Of Spring

I heard a lot of noise outside
I knew not what the reason
When I looked out the door
It was a brand new season.

The air outside is really clear
The birds have started to sing
Their songs are both loud and sweet
As they announce, "It's spring!"

The flowers have poked thru the ground
Their buds are ready to bloom
They look up toward the sky
To ask for a little more room.

The trees are starting to get their leaves
In all the shades of green
If you listen you'll hear them say,
"We are the prettiest you have seen!"

The birds and trees and flowers are here
With all the noise they made
How can you possibly just lay there
And fall asleep in the shade?!

John Hunter

Door Ajar

I looked and saw a door ajar.
I knew not where it went.
I stepped inside and there I saw a world of great content.
The people there did not despair, their faces full of hope.
No tears to shed just peace and love
They did not have to cope.
The streets were made of purest gold and flowers did abound,
And wondrous music filled the air, there was no end to sound.
The purest light shown all about, no human eye has seen.
I wondered could this all be real or was it just a dream.
I think God must have given me a glimpse of the unknown
He knew that in our human way, to accept, it must be shown.

Betty Dean

Vanished Love

I know it's my fault that we are no longer together,
I knew we wouldn't last forever,
But I thought my feelings would still be strong,
I'm sorry our love didn't last that long.
I am hurting so much inside,
That my feelings I just can't hide.
I didn't think I loved you so much
Till I no longer could feel your touch.
Now because of me,
Our kisses are just a memory.
I already miss your voice and smile,
I would call but it's to hard to dial.
Knowing that we are no longer a couple brings me pain,
All these feelings are driving me insane.
I guess I will attempt to move on,
I have to realize our love is... gone.

Becky Butler

I'll Let Him Go

My God I have to ask you this.
I know I shouldn't though.
I was taught to never question you, but I really have to know.
Why does he suffer so much? Why does he hurt so bad?
He never did a single thing to make somebody mad.
He's just a little angel. Sent from you to me.
So why do you want him back so fast?
My Gods he's only three.
At times I see him dying, in my arms I hold him tight.
I'm praying and I'm hoping, everything will be alright.
I try to think of something else to get it off my mind.
But deep down in my heart I know, its just a matter of time.
Dear God I'd like to tell you, I'll fight you everyday.
To keep him down here with me, to watch him run and play.
I know I shouldn't say that.
But it hurts to watch him suffer.
After all, my dear God, you made me his mother.
So if you take him from me, before my life is thru.
Please don't let him suffer long.
I'll let him go with you.

Donna Damiano

Dear Father

Dear Lord, I hope you hear me.
I know it's been a long, long time.
But today I'm really hurting
And there are answers I need to find.
Dear Father, just please tell me
The reason for my tears.

Let me know there was a purpose,
Please help erase my fears.
Dear Jesus, come and help me.
Let me know he's safe with you.
Help me understand what fate has brought
And give me strength to make it through.
Oh Lord, I'm so, so sorry
That it took this for me to see.
I keep wishing I could close my eyes
And you would give him back to me.
Dear Father who Thou art in Heaven,
Please listen to my cry.
Just tell him one last thing for me;
I'll love him forever, and good-bye.

Cynthia Bortz

Southern Style

I like ham hocks in my greens,
I like hot sauce on my beans.

I like lemon in my tea,
I like Miss Marie and she likes me.

I like fried chicken every day,
I like comfort when I lay.

I like my lemonade served in canning jars,
I like Hank Williams and Ray Charles.

I like butter on my bread,
I like stetson hats on my head.

I like my hometown and that ain't all bad,
I love my mother and my dad.

Ike Hoover

Thinking Of You

At one time in my life, I needed you so much.
I lived for your smile, and dreamed of your touch.

My heart would start to melt at the sound of your voice, and when I looked into your eyes, my soul would just rejoice.

Your laugh made me happy, your tears made me blue.
You said that you loved me, and I thought it was true.

Sometime things came between us, and bent your beautiful smile.
Your thoughts left my dreams, but the pain stayed a while.

It took lots of time, tears and repairs, but my heart stayed to mend.
I think I love you more now than ever, for you're my closest friend.

I'll hold you in my arms forever and a day, and all I can do is hope in return you love me the same way.

Even though my heart is broken, no more tears shall I shed.
I've gone on with my life, and there is nothing more to be said.

If you happen to look up one day, and see that the sky is blue, you'll know its going to be a good day, because, I AM THINKING OF YOU.

Deirdre Jerelon Alexander

Loneliness

Just me and the loneliness of the night
I look at the sky with no stars in sight
And nothing around me seems to be right
When the will to live is always a fight

I think of my life these past few years
No longer having strength to hold back tears
When the end of my life seems so very near
I'll tell you why if you'll only hear

I was happy once - so long ago
Before this world I came to know
With lies in disguise people put on their show
And away from this world I finally would grow

There once was a time when I tried to see
What the meaning of love could really be
And you couldn't know what it did to me
When the girl that I loved didn't love me

Just me and the loneliness of the night
I look at the sky - there's no stars in sight
When nothing about me could ever be right
My will to live fades into the night

Jack Beacom

Yesterday And You My Child

As I sit and watch you play,
I look back to yesterday.
It was then you were so new and it was me who had to do
all your playing and your caring,
now you stand so brave and daring
reaching out and holding on,
yes those infant days are gone.
And though I anxiously await
baseball games and your first date
I'm not quite sure I can give up
your diapers, blocks and training cup.

As I rock and watch you sleep, I smile and I weep
for I know this little hand,
that's holding mine will soon demand
to be set free so as to go,
so as to learn, so as to grow
and I will know I helped to mold
one who is loving, brave and bold
then I'll look back calm and mild,
to yesterday and you, my child.

Dawn Diamond

Dream to Her

The moon shining so incredibly bright,
I look up at thee, and wonder if she might,
Be studying such a romantic sight.

Knowing how I long for her
Holding, caressing, feeling, that loving purr.
Now I pray she does concur.

That we can be so heavenly,
To her I will give all of me,
Cause we were made so perfectly,

Distance so far apart,
All I have is my beating heart,
But Mystical powers force clouds to part

And they bare down to my open skin
Now I know, she's my eternal twin
Together through life we will swim

Past obstacles of jealousy and greed,
So come to me, and take no heed
Cause together our souls, will soon be freed!

Craig Gambino

Our 7th Deliverance

When my job seems like a task
I look up to the sky and I ask,
Dear Lord above when you gave to us,
These children both to me and Gus
How did you know, How could you tell,
That he and I would serve you well.
We do the very best we can,
Till they grow up and take a hand,
I hope the love that's in our heart
Will always be a little part of everything they
think, say and do.
Dear Lord to you they always will be true.

Irene P. Young

Failure

Doesn't it hurt when you've tried and you've tried?
Nothing went right so you sat down and cried.
When you finally realized it did you no good,
You got up and said that this time you could.
If you failed again, then you'd just start anew,
Because no one is perfect, not even you.

Regina G. Capelli

Explicit Content

When she's been bad
I love her so
Takes my hand puts it all over the place
Drags her nails across her face
Closes her eyes
Listens to me
Tales of extreme
Suffering in sexuality
One sick little girl
We saw Natural Born Killers on Valentine's day
I spank her hard
'Cause she likes it that way
She says she wants to hurt me
Well I want to hurt you too
Whips or chains or handcuffs
all the same to you
Oil or hot candle wax
Loves it rubbed upon her back
Tortures so much fun with you
There's so much more that we could do

Benjamin King

'Palomino'

As I straddle the horse, heading westward, trotting at a mild canter,
I loved the smell in the air, the humidness of the weather, sticking
to my skin. I love it out here where the horses run and play, where
the horses ride together in great herds, and where friends sometimes
take me.

I stare off into space as the horse carries me off without me even
guiding it (such a tame animal). Such a peaceful time. I try to
down out all the other shouts from the people next to me, so I can
just think... Think of what...? ...Nothing at all.

I wonder of what I want to voyage off to next? A fun place, yes
indeed... The horse I'm riding is saddled up to be a show horse,
looking its best. The horse canters slowly on the inside of the
pack, running with no effort, as we turn circle-like.
I love it here!
As I step off my palomino, as it slows to a stop, I pat the wooden
saddle, and smile, as I step off the carousel.

John Young

Description of an Elephant

An elephant is grey, if you know what
I mean, they're not black and they're not
green.
An elephant is tall, higher than a wall.
So, when you get on one, make sure
you don't fall.
An elephant has as trunk, longer than a
skunk.
An elephant is nice like sugar and
spice.
An elephant is wide, and when he tries
to hide, he can't really hide, cause he's so
very wide.
An elephant has ears, bigger than your
head, and if they so big, why don't they
come off his head?
An elephant is heavy, heavier than
glue.
So, if your feeling sad, he'll pick you
up and carry you.

Ashlee Forte

Lost Friend

Once I had this friend,
I never thought our friendship would end.
We had a relationship that was heart to heart,
But why all of a sudden did it fall apart?
Was it because of the things she said,
Or was it because I didn't want to see her dead?
One day I found out what she thought about me,
Now I see, just how much she cared for me.
A lot of the time things were okay,
Then we went our separate ways.
She had a real problem;
All of a sudden she hit bottom.
I would change her if I could,
But I know she never would.
There are some things I really miss,
Then again, I guess you have to get used to this.
Every night I sit down and cry,
And I have to ask God, "Why?"
There's one last thing I have to say,
No matter what she did, I love her anyway.

Crystal Graham

The Promise

I never asked for more than you could give
I only prayed that you would live
Your hand held so tranquil in mine
Our thoughts unspoken, yet intertwine

I made the promise to be strong
Not to grieve for very long
Or let Sadness be my guide
Nor let yet Another leave my side

We walked miles together
Past fear, past trouble, past loneliness, Past pain
Through sun, through chill, through snow, Through rain
The years ran away, the seasons sped by

At the end I asked why,
The only answer my faith in Life wouldn't die.
Because love keeps a promise.
So dear, so treasured, in ages past and to be
That Nothing can erase my memories, and what you gave to me.

Ailegra Millman

Our Legacy

I owe my children to do my best
I owe them more than I have, not less
I sometimes cry when I think what their inheritance will be
A dirty and violent place, from sea to shining sea
Please tell me, what can I do, what can I say
Why do I feel so powerless, helpless in every way
We must stop our greed, the things money can buy
We have to have everything, I wonder why
These material things come from the earth
When the earth is barren, what will our camera be worth
Why can't we see, why can't we stop
Of all our priorities, our children must be on top
In Town Halls, tax dollars are more important than clean water
Money before water, is our love so out of order
I love my children, yet I rape their world
I am a terrible dad and my shame lies unfurled

George Schultze

Selfishness Spelled Defeat

Thirty seconds left in our most important game.
I passed the ball but was out-smarted by their guard.
  She stole the ball, dribbled to the side, jumped
and dunked the ball inside.
  "They are up by two," the crowd roared! I did
remember the many points I had scored.
  Twenty seconds left and the coach said, "Take it
upon yourself!"
  I dribbled a while to wind down the clock, preparing
to make the final shot.
  My teammates scrabbled and were open for trays,
but I nodded my head thinking, I will win this my way.
  Fake left, right, spinning left, my quickness was
called a travel by the ref.
  In disbelief, I challenged the call. No change in
possession, my opponent had the ball.
Will you shoot the tray, or try taking me for the lay? "Neither," she
said. "I can pass to FOUR and be quite certain of adding TWO more."
  We were out of time and had lost the game.
I knew in my heart, I had SELFISHNESS to blame.

D'Shawn D. Watts

Dark Angel

In the magical, dark blue sky,
I placed my warm hand
  within your icy grasp.

As a backdrop of twinkling
  stars appeared behind us,
we began to dance upon a zenith of clouds.

"My dark angel, bring me into
  a life where there is no pain, no suffering.
Dark Angel, bring me into a
  life that has no heart break, no loneliness,
oh please, my dark angel."

As you turn and look upon me
  with your crystal green eyes from an expressionless face,
a tear rolls down my cheek.
  For I know that you see into my soul.

As you turned away
  I knew that you were leaving without me.

"In time, my love, in time," the darkness replied.

"Goodnight, my love.
Goodnight, my Dark Angel."

Angela Hansen

Mother

I regret the things I said to her.
I regret the things I did.
If I could do them all again, she and I would simply live.

We would cherish every moment.
We would talk about our dreams.
We would grasp what holds tomorrow, for now my eyes can see.

When she was there, I would hold her.
When she smiled, I looked her way.
But, my thoughts were not my actions.
Which was greater? I can't say.

How I miss her like no other, and I hope to make amends.
She's my friend, my heart, my mother.
I shall love her till the end.

If God should grant me mercy, I will honor all these words.
I only have one mother.
My sentiments must be heard.

Dawn Williams

Grandmother's Final Day

I went to see you in the hospital your last day,
I realize now that you were pleading to be let go
for these artificial means were not your way,
this proud woman who left us not long ago.

I think back to the scribbled notes you wrote
what you were trying to convey as you held my hand,
"tell all I love them" was the only understood quote
words not often heard from this strong woman from Ireland.

I looked at you, longing for more time to get to know you
to understand the thoughts on your face,
if anyone did there were only a few,
but we all knew you always exemplified such elegance and grace.

I sometimes see the sadness in my mother's eyes
who felt cheated of your love,
even with a family of your large size
your innermost thoughts and feelings were kept between you and
God above.

When I returned home the telephone rang
My heart began to race,
Nothing but heartbreak and sadness this message brang,
Nana, no one will ever take your place.

Cheryl Clark

Fairy Tale Dream

I was dreaming.
I saw you in a velvet gown near the castle walls;
They started tumbling down.
You were thrashing
The billows of your satin cape, and you picked yourself a thorny rose
And tossed it toward the lake.

It landed on the peacock who threw it to the lamb,
And then it landed on the grass and turned into a man.

Then he stood up
And leapt into the evening sky where he turned into the great Orion
And you began to cry,
But I consoled you,
And told you all wasn't lost, but you ran right toward the lake
Where your thorny rose was tossed.

The lake would not uphold you; the sky would not comply.
Orion reached out for you so you wouldn't die,

And he grabbed you by your satin cape, and shook you out to dry.
The lamb and peacock danced and I began to fly.

Yes, I began to fly! But, I was dreaming...

Cynthia Geary

The Mirror

Look into the mirror, what do you see?
I see a stranger looking back at me.
Someone I once knew well now has seemed
to change;
Bitten by life, now dreams are rearranged.
Look into the mirror, what do you see?
I see the trace of where a smile used to be.
Years roll by, dreams unwind,
Time echoes its mournful call;
Staring in the mirror I can see it all.
Look into the mirror, what do you see?
Reflections now are not so clear;
Worn with time and cracked with fear.
Look into the mirror, what do you see?
Far beyond the mirror is where my dreams
are free.

Bea Tullis

Star Light, Star Bright

In the dark night sky surrounding my heart,
I search for one glimmer of light.
Perhaps a star, perhaps a glimpse of the moon
To pierce the cloudy gloom.

Then one eve, while wrapped in memories of song, laughter and a
    margarita,
The elusive star appeared.
A thin light, yet strong enough to creep through the clouds
To touch me...and bring a smile to my eyes,
    my face, my heart.

Bit by bit that night sky has brightened,
Bringing the dawn of a new day that I thought was never to come.
Amidst a friendly crowd and swelling music,
Came the light of the midday sun...
And the heat of a summer day from the warmth in your eyes,
    your smile, your arms.

Now that light has been eclipsed by doubts and confusion,
And the air grows cool...and soon so will my heart.
The sun will set, the sky will grow dark
As our day draws to a close.

All I ask is will the starlight go as well?

    Dawn Jameson

My Reflection

As I sit and I reflect on myself today
I see dark spots that need fixin' in a godly way

For I know that the demons want to submerge and take their place
To hold them down is hard - let me tell you of my case

For when you're born an angel you are
But as life goes on your heart becomes scarred

For people don't care, or you don't feel
It's a place in life you just learn to deal

A child learns what their parents do
A world of hate and prejudice just for you

You see people in a different lite
that all you want with them is to fight

As you become older and wiser you'll see
That people are all the same to me

For respect is earned with the deed you do
For what you do with others they will do to you

So sit and reflect the person deep inside your self
And place all your anger up on a shelf

For when love's lite begins to shine inside your heart
The world is a better place each day when you do your part

    Darlene Gunes

The Ring

Time to go run 3 miles
So if I get hit on the chin, I don't end up in a pile

Hit the heavy bags, skip some rope
So in a heated exchange, I can cope

The life of a boxer, is a lonely one
But to hook off the jab is a lot of fun

To win the fight the feeling is grand
Standing in the center of the ring, the victor I stand

    William Murphy Jr.

Beauty In Tomorrow

I see no beauty in tomorrow when today is so bland
I see no beauty in tomorrow when today is so plain
I see in tomorrow no sunshine
when today all I see is rain
I see no happiness in tomorrow
when all today I see is pain
I wish tomorrow to be bright
instead of being blue like today
I wish tomorrow to be sunny
unlike the skies of today
I hope to be happy tomorrow
leave all my sadness in today
I hope to be able to forget my troubles
drown them in the rain from today
My one wish is to meet GOD, my Creator
The one who created ALL
I cannot await tomorrow, I must go today
I want to leave my belongings to you, my bestest friend
with hopes that I'll see you again
in another sunny tomorrow

    Christie Diane Franklin

Hand In Hand... In Heaven's Land

As the golden sun glows from the eastern skies,
I see the beauty of a brand new day 'bout to begin.
There, I see a child of golden hair and bright blue eyes
With her warm smile, tender touch, and silky skin.

As a lass, together we would play and walk hand in hand
Sharing un-pretended tender moments unrehearsed.
And why God's children must soon die, I don't understand.
Dying young or dying old, I've questioned, which is worst?

Time's elapsed and blooming flowers create petals in the sun.
Motherhood soon teaches lessons never to forget.
I now see, and time and time again, recall the never ending fun
Sisterhood once was, and as I dream, I now regret

The things I didn't say when time was on our side.
Once, life and total joy was in her eyes, and I recall her smile
That now haunts my aching heart as these tears I cry and cannot hide
Yet, I know we will be apart but only for a while.

And when I die, and laid to rest next to your side,
In spirit and in soul, we'll both recall our childhood days.
And, hand in hand...in heaven's land we'll walk, and both maintain
A watchful eye, and wait to reunite us all again someday.

    Jose Luis Gonzalez

'Companions'

I hear the shrillness of the soundless scream.
I see the brilliance in the sunless beam.
I know that things are not what they seem.
There is no repartee in my mindless dream.

My dream of a land so fresh so new.
My dream of a land laden with morning dew.
My dream of a land that belongs to me... and to you
In this adventure so fresh so new.

I hear the footsteps as we walk the walkless mile.
Suddenly, I see the repartee as we wait the waitless while.
The 'ups' the 'downs' make life's potential aisle.
Giving to this couple all the worthiness life can beguile.

As with Adam and Eve, we try to express
Our virtues, our excellence, our righteousness.
As HE did with Antony and Cleopatra, let HIM bless
My partner and I as we caress.

I sense the joyfulness from the joy we have learned to accept.
I vision the bottomless bottom of our two lives' depth.
We have conquered our land for which we had wept
As companions we lie...in our eternal crypt.

    June K. Vargo

Utopia

I see a beauty beyond my reach.
I see the mornings are cool and crisp as the first snowfall of the
    season.
The sun is as bright as a light entering into a dark room.
The mountains are covered with snow, as fresh as a new store bought
    diamond.
The lake sparkles like stars in a cool summer night.
The hills are alive with life.
The grass is as tall and green as an evergreen tree reaching toward
    the heavens.
The trees reach for the sun like a small child would reach for candy.
The clouds drift like a small boat upon the sea.
The birds sing joyfully all day long.
The animals run free and undisturbed.
The sunset is as colorful as a painting, and beauty abounds from every
    direction.

Jenniffer Coomes

A Farmer's 23rd Psalm

The Lord is my farmer,
I shall yield abundantly.

He plants me in fertile soil,
and lets me grow to glorify Him.

He cultivates my soul and lets my leaves
flourish to spread His good news.

Yes, when the devil's drought
is around me I will fear no evil,
because the rains of heaven
will fall upon me.

He sprays me with the Holy Spirit.
He sends sunlight to warm me.
He lets my growth stand out
in a field among sinners.

I shall mature in Christ and
as I am harvested he will say
I will use your seed for
another crop.

Claude Harper Jr.

The Bells

Sounds of temple bells ride on the breeze
I sit folded up with my feet on my knees
Closing my eyes I prepare to go for a ride
Off to explore the vastness inside

Remember when it use to give me such a scare
So frightened to find out what was waiting there
Worried that it would be a big black hole
To my delight it was a smiling soul

Seemed so odd it would be that way
Always so happy and wanting to play
From our first remeeting it was plain to see
This wonderful soul really cared for me

Now together we travel each day
It helps me see things in a different way
All that happens to us isn't always good
But that's how their supposed to be is now understood

It's like having all the time you want with a best friend
Day and night it's only love that it will send
Gladly now I listen to it's voice, I hear it in my heart
Here's to you my soul in all my life may you take part

Gloria Johnsen

Oblivion

I woke to a mosquito sucking my life away.
I smashed it with a slap.
The sound of gunfire in the background—
I don't mind it anymore.
I open a can of beans and ham
Rations form World War II, the beans white from age.
I shave with my bayonet,
My reflection from a polished brass shell.
I pack up and move out with my platoon
To the awaiting killing field.
As we approach, rounds whistling by,
I see men laying about bloody stumps
Where limbs once were.
I pass without remorse
Nerves dead from war.
I load a clip and chamber a round.
I saw my best friend go down.
I step over his limp body into battle.
I fall with a hole in my side
There to stay forever to abide.

Daniel Barker

Out of Touch

The labor for freedom is exhausting, commanding work.
I somehow feel for those whom I shall never know.
I am just a minute part of this world;
spoiled, but starved from the hunger of life.
Those who fought to live - died,
and those who craved death adequately survived.
The backwards being of our dwelling place
is the depth of the moon we can not reach, but can see so clearly.
Those who have lived so long ago
have gone through tragedies far worse than I.
For I, in the small role I play,
can change the world...

if I choose.

Jessica Wurzelbacher

The Way It Really Used To Be

I realize that you care no more, that you wish we'd never met.
I 'spose I'm sorry for ever coming into your life,
But maybe I'm not the one who should apologize...

I'm not stupid; I know, you see,
About all the many cruel and heartless things you've said about me.
I remember when I thought we'd always be good friends,
Always be so tight, and I begin to cry...

I ask myself nearly every hour,
"I wonder what he's doing...I wonder what I did?..."
I think of you, and I try to see what I ever did,
What happened to our perfect little world?
I still have the letters you wrote me, still stare at all the
    pictures...

Do you remember how it was-or are you still so naive?
Do you still think it was never how I say it was?
I hope not-because I hope you realize that,
Even though you maybe fooling them-and probably yourself, too,
I'll never forget-I'll never be fooled
I'll always remember you and I-the way it used to REALLY be...

Emily Harris

I Am An American

For I am an American.
I stand proud and free.
I won't forget the men and women who died for this country.
For there is no slavery.
So I am proud to be part of this country.
I wish this was a gang-free country.
For I am proud to stand straight for this country.
Our country has freedom like know other country.
For I am an American proud and free.
I am an American.

Elizabeth Stroup

Dysfunctionality

I prolong the torture:
I stay in your presence,
I don't resist your wearing downgrading.
Your words slowly erode my soul
Ripping at the construction of my existence.

You chisel my foundation with your daily barbs.
I must drink in your abuse and revel in it.
And convince myself it's only love.
I rub your sweat in like lotion nourishing my skin.
I warm myself with the heat of your temper
I open my arms with invitation to your callous heart.
I invite your wrenching language.
My body absorbs your disgust and packs it away in my Heart.
My anger flows from my pen like blood from your veins.

I inhale the vapors of your annoyance
And breathe out air of determination.

Cheryl Stephenson

On Passion and Pain

Was early spring when robins sing and young ones yearn to fly
I stopped beneath an evergreen to watch one's struggled try

Persistent, Patient, Plodding, he tried throughout the day
The longing in his little soul allowed no rest's delay

Undaunted by the struggle, driven for the cause -
Echo of our human passions - longings lingered on

I'd hoped to ease his burden and teach him what I knew -
Was not so much the flying but the trying he pursued

For with each challenge rendered and those as victor claim
Comes yet another passion a restless soul attains

I left him with his labor but longed to ease his way
Yet none could bring him peace save he who seeks the same

Returned again next evening as robin's songs soon fade
and found my lifeless friend whose passions made his grave.

Diane Palm Creager

Paradox

I laughed, I cried;
I succeeded, I failed;
I was sick, I was well;
I remembered, I forgot;
I liked myself, I disliked myself;
Money was important, money was unimportant;
I hoped, I despaired;
I was tormented, I was peaceful;
I grew up, I stayed a child;
I stood still, I moved forward;
I used my talents, I wasted my talents;
Life was real, a dream and a nightmare;
I was filled with love, empty of emotion;
I learned the taste and feel of life,
I am still in wonder - at life!

Diana Fabiani Suplee

Bipolar Depths

As terror surpasses the essence of being,
I succumb to madness.
Death is imminent, time is irrelevant,
As the madness drones on.

Dreams and reality have no meaning, as terror surpasses them all,
A bipolar existence captures my soul,
As I destroy with little regard.

Delusions are secondary,
Paranoia is prime,
As the cell door is locked, leaving me behind.

A voice cries out as the hallucinations begin,
Where is my sanity?
When will it end?

An element named Lithium, makes an offer of peace,
Four times a day, in hopes of relief.

The madness is conquered
The healing is done,
The soul is together,
The battle is won.

Joanne B. Rasche

Being Different

What makes someone different?
I suppose it all depends.
It's what's peerless in each of us
And we can still be friends.

You can be my neighbor or sister
And learn a different philosophy, too.
But each of us are different,
Including me and you.

You can live in New York
Or in Chicago or L.A.
She can frown and look ugly,
But you can smile and look nice all day.

She wears pants;
You wear skirts.
They go to one school;
While you go to another and are diverse.

So you see we are all different;
It really all depends.
We can still stay opposites,
But at the same time remain friends.

Ilana Simkin

Mnemosyne

Oh Mnemosyne, your gift is bliss...
  I taste again the joys I knew;
in solitude I reminisce...
  the past parades in fond review.

Oh Mnemosyne, thou faithful friend...
  You grant my troubled mind surcease;
what happiness and love attend...
  Your memories which bring me peace.

To live again in happy halls...
  remembers scene the years contain;
the Love and Loved the mind recalls...
  to ease my lonely world of pain.

Oh Mnemosyne, You give me Leave...
  a refuge from such days as these;
a haven where I will not grieve...
  but dwell, content, 'midst memories!

Jimmy Walls

Jealousy

Seek you here to sit upon thy knee
I tell tales of love lost and thy jealousy.
Be alert and listen well and thy moral thou shall see.
A man to which his love was thine own atrocity
The woman he loved, her love, did not meet
And in return has created a monstrosity.
His love hath grown cold without thy woman's heat.
Hurt followed confusion, hath bore a hellish creation.
Jealousy was thy name and thy entrails is thy seat.
It hath turned thy love into aggravation.
With envious ivy clinging to thy mind
And thy soul left to abomination.
The green eyed monster to which loneliness shall find
A clouded heart and a stomach to feast
With an endless appetite devouring all of mankind.
My friends, be not thy vessel of the emerald beast
Be strong in mind and undoubtful in heart
And thy mortal love shall never cease.

John G. Orozco

Godiva No More

Her name was Godiva, she said she was mystic.
I tend to believe her, disposition ballistic!
She stood by a mark and she dared me to cross it.
I gave her my heart and eventually lost it.
With the soul of the redwood, tall and so proudly
Displayed all her glory, quietly, loudly
Proclaiming her presence, one could not doubt her.
Something quite moving and striking about her
Alone in her wonder, released inhibitions
Radiate outward, celestial dimensions.
Night disappearing, morning she's gone.
I knew in an instant I couldn't go on.
Dead in the spirit, Godiva no more.
I weep in my solace, collapse on the floor.

Barry Sisk

Summer and Twilight

Now that winter is almost ore,
I think of summer more and more;

The mornings are so fresh with dew,
The sun bursts through the sky so blue;

The songs that birds so sweetly sing,
Just makes your heart with joy ring;

You can feel the cool and balmy breeze,
Beneath the big green leafy trees;

The fragrance of flowers in the air,
Makes one happy to be alive, without a care;

But what I like most of all,
Is when the twilight begins to fall;

You hear the sounds of the crickets nearby,
And see the lights of the tiny firefly;

Now don't these things paint a picture for you,
And make you long for summer too?

Billie Devins

A Gift Never Forgotten

Here is a little kiss from me to you.
It's not white or blue for it is red,
each time remembering you dancing in my head.
Only the rose that needed no pose shined in the light and
grew so pretty, for nothing but love was given to it. You
are my rose no needing to pose for I shall do the same
to you.

Mario Gil

Life On The Clock

Before the first eyelash begins to flutter
I think of waking and begin to shudder
The handless, red-faced, demon bites my ear at five
His little reminder that I live though not alive
For no matter what my day hold in store
It shall remain all to similar to the one before
I jump into my carriage of painted steel
To join the thousands behind the wheel
Lines of giant ants moving in slow motion
or lemmings on a cliff towards the ocean
I punch a clock that has never done me wrong
To start my dreary day eight hours long
I do my work like a prison sentence
Five days of Hell is my penance
No great discovers or grand inspiration
It's only formula, 12 parts stress to 8 parts perspiration
Slowly fades the dreams of Art and Silence
As I meet each day with much defiance
As another day passes my escape is planned
and the curtain closes with time clock's hand

David R. Bennion

Tomorrow, Yesterday, Today

As I take in each breath and count how many times
I think of what will happen tomorrow.
I realize that tomorrow will be just the same
or maybe worse...
Tomorrow isn't just a word to me, it has a
meaning, a meaning of what I will wear,
Where I will go who will be there
and who will not.
Tomorrow just happens to come and go, but
sometime I feel that mine never ends.
As I sit in my room and cry or as I laugh,
I wonder how I will feel in the
morning.
Will I be the same as yesterday or will
it be as weird as today.
I can only sit and hope that as I grow
and become a person my-
Tomorrows will never be yesterdays.

Brandy Johnson

To My Brother

I light a candle, and watch it burn,
I think of you Frank, I watch, I learn
Then August 3, 1990
The flame is gone, into the air
All I see now is smoke lingering in the air
I remember the good times, and the bad
I remember growing up together, we had so many laughs
We were the best of friends and sometimes the worst
I miss you Frank, so very much
You were always there for me, no matter what
I learned a lot from you, but now I am on my own
I wish you were still here, to help me grow
But God had a place for you in heaven, it is your home
I will always love you and I will always miss you
I will never forget you and please don't forget me
But for now it is time to say goodbye and take care
I will always carry you in my heart!

Love always your sister and friend,
Coralee Boyd

Memories

Although I never felt you touch...
I thought Id never grieve this much
You past away on a Saturday
Your last words to me have slipped away.
I don't think I'll ever forget the day
they put you in your resting place,
For you to finally waste away.
Memories of time, you are starting to fade...
And now I find myself forgetting exactly how you look.
Like the way you always did your hair
How you have left me in faint despair.
What color were your eyes...
I hear a little voice inside
Asking green, blue or maybe they were brown
If only I were more perceptive when you were around.
And now today I can hardly recall...
Any fond memories of you at all.

Christian Trinity Pichnarcik

Love Between Us

As I was walking late that night
I thought of all the things that
went wrong between us that night.
I try to erase the memories
but they won't go away. Now there is love between us.

I know sometimes we didn't care but
there was love between us then.
There is love between us now.
There was love between us all the time when
we was together but now we are in
different places there is still love between us.

You always said I love you but you
never said there was love between
us a lot of love between us,
when you called me that day and
told me you was leaving. I lost
my life knowing there was still love
between us to keep me alive, so just
remember there will always be love
a lot of love just between us.

Amy Trump

My Best Friend

(To my daughter Lori)

As I picked up an old album today,
I turned through the pages of time.
I found the memories of yesterday,
And that best friend of mine.

As I leafed through the years.
Again I watched her grow.
I remembered the joys and fears,
And all the good times we know.

Not one regret or bad memory,
Of all the years that have past.
The infant, the toddler, the child she would be,
The young lady, and a woman at last.

We've shared sweaters and ear rings,
And good times that will never end.
And love that being a mother can bring,
My daughter, and my best friend.

Dorothy McMurray

Bare Bulbs And Lace Tablecloth

When I was young and striving for ideas grandiose,
I visualized a world of wealth and wanted no repose.
I thought that happiness would come if fancy things were mine,
A great big house with three car garage and pool for summertime.
Education was priority and my degrees meant expertise,
It would guarantee my dream and hopes for "material" increase.
But one day I was "awakened" to a different world of gain,
Not based on mere externals for prestige, or wealth, or fame.
Still saving for our "special" home we called upon some friends,
To share our meal and chat awhile about life's current trends.
The basement served as our "domain" - unfinished and so plain,
Bare bulbs overhead and lace tablecloth, set with no disdain.
I suddenly realized the important things that gives us an access,
It isn't money, fame, or prestige that add to our daily success.
It's the depth of meaningful relationship-a magnifying wealth,
It gives us a sense of belonging, and nurtures mental health.
I may not have position that once was my ultimate goal,
But the ones I love are my source of wealth that satisfy my soul.

Diane S. Stouffer

A Romance

Everyday as the sun reaches high
I wait at the place you daily walk by
I watch you go your usual way
and I memorize you, day by day

I wonder if you see me stare
Often, I wonder if you know I'm there
I don't want to talk or have a chance
Watching you is enough romance

Afraid if it were maybe more
A long walk on the ocean shore
Scared, that by chance, you were not true
Scared my heart would be broke in two

If some day soon you notice at last
Maybe the day Cupid's arrow is cast
I'll wait by just so we can talk
and maybe some day we'll take that walk

Joanna Carman

The Sound of the Sea

I walked alone, at The Sound of the Sea
I walked alone, cause you've gone from me
The wind in my face
The tears in my eyes
Such a lonely place
And I realize
I'll walk alone at the Sound of the Sea
I'll walk alone till Eternity
I call your name in the ocean's roar
It tells me, you're not here anymore
I walk alone at the Sound of the Sea
I walk alone cause you've gone from me

Gertrude Kirkbride

Ode to a Cup of Coffee

Ah my friend, how your sweet aroma lifts me from my slumbersome
state beckoning me to join in the world of reality.

Your warmth shaking off the cruel coldness that the darkness
of the night throws over me.

Your hotness tingling my lips- rescuing me from that ever so
haunting world of dreams.

And as I take your being into mine, I am some how made whole
again and able to greet the sunlight of the day.

T. Leli

Untitled

There is nowhere to run, nowhere to hide
I want to live in the dream where I fly
To tell the story or keep it inside
If I wake up from my dream I will die.
My spirit soars above me as I look
I float higher now then you ever will
My soul is here but my spirit they took
I awoke, did not die, but was lost still.
If night was longer could I escape the day
Reality chases me as I run
My soul is wandering, can't find its way.
When all's over and we return to dust,
Who will be my judge, which one do I trust.

Julie Rosskam

Freedom

Lord, in some small way,
I want to say,
Thanks for loving me
and setting me free.
I know I can never repay,
Nor the cost can I defray,
For the love you so freely gave
By hanging on that cross so I could be saved.
You are the Way, the Truth and the Light,
Anyone who searches can find you day or night.
You are always near and never sleep,
You even hear when we laugh and weep.
You hear our every plea
For a better person to be.
With hands that are nail scared and torn
You reach down and touch us when we've been scorned.
You embrace us to your breast
And say, "child, come to me for rest."
Oh, what a joy it is to me
to Honor, Praise and Worship Thee.

Jane G. Breland

For You

My name is Troubles
I want you to put me on your shelf
I'll carry the load, when there's too much to hold
so you have the time to get touch with yourself
You can look me in the eye
I'll not look away
I'll form opinions before I reply
we will talk another day
Only you control me
and you are the master of your own mind
also the heart and the soul of me
with all the power to leave me behind
I can take the pain away
and let you feel relief
or you can choose to let it stay
I choose to let you breathe
You can hold me in your hands
and make me disappear
then only you will understand
if I was ever here

Debbie Wood

Untitled

Cold, harsh winter,
The remnants of myself,
Bitter winds blow through my soul like a whirlwind,
Leaving only sketches of yesterday,
Frozen are the tears as icicles now hang from my eyes,
Night falls early in the winter of my life.

Kimberly Sierotowicz

My Sister

This is your BIRTHDAY, your very special day.
I wanted to say "I LOVE YOU" in my own way.
You are my sister, you are like no other
So very special, more like a Mother
Since Mother was in my life a very short while,
it was you who helped me through so many trials.
You taught me what was wrong and what was right.
Even though, sometimes, I resisted with all my might.
Then ever so softly you would take my hand,
somehow, you could help me understand
that life is not always what we want it to be.
I knew in my heart how much you loved me.
Thank you for being there whenever I'd call
Gently pick me up when I'd stumble and fall.
The words of encouragement were so loving and kind.
Sincerely, you searched for the best you could find.
May God bless you richly as only He can do.
I wish you a HAPPY BIRTHDAY, I'll always love you.
Love always

Ginger Cox

Runaway

I'm a runaway person, who was treated wrong
I was a runaway person who lasted so long
With marks here and there
To me it was not fair
But I was a runaway person, who needed some care.

My life was at risk
Something had to be fixed
Then finally I had a chance to be free
But I was thinking if they caught me
Well it's worth a try so let it be.

There I saw myself
With special care
And wonderful health
I took my chance and then I realized
That when I looked down
I was still alive
There an exotic miracle passed me
and then I was finally free!

Jessica Velazquez

The Silent Scream

No one heard my silent scream as I lay naked on the bed.
I was ashamed of my helplessness, the cries existed in my head.

The words that escaped my trembling lips, only he could hear.
But no means little for he was strong, and I was filled with fear.

His kisses burned, smelled of wine and smoke, while his body
    made its intrusion.
Taking from me all that was mine, my mind engulfed in confusion.

He spoke to me as if we were lovers knowing each other for the
    first time.
I question myself everyday and if what he did was a crime.

Was a whispered "no" and streaming tears enough to say "I resist"?
He said he knew I wanted him, on my desire he did insist.

They asked "Why didn't you call for help if what you say is true?"
I couldn't answer honestly because I felt that way too.

Late at night; although years have passed,
he has control while I am dreaming.
I live my life day to day, all the while, silently screaming.

Jessie Thompson-Kelley

And You Whispered, "I Love You"

I was full of life and in your arms.
I was drawn in by your wonderful charm.
My face was more angelic than a beautiful dove,
while my heart was fulfilled by your undying love.
My hand wore a band of your promising care.
For the future ahead, as one, we would share.
  -and you whispered, "I love you."

Then my life seemed to fade near our once special place.
And I lost my true angelic face.
For there you stood, with your arms opened wide.
But only to hold someone else there inside.
As my body grew numb with a harsh dreadful fear,
I saw your lips gently lean close to her ear.
  -and you whispered, "I love you."

Jennifer Dargan

"Sugar And Spice"

As I walked our girls down the aisle.
I was feeling so sad, managing a smile.

Many many memories, flashing through my mind,
There they stood, so gentle and so kind.

Remembering the moments, when the snuggled on our laps,
So full of life, and no generation gaps.

The years have flown by, and they have grown,
to handle life's problems, all on their own.

Today they are married and quite the young ladies
to us they will forever, be our babies.

Alice Golebieski

What My Heart Can't See

Lately when my thoughts move toward her
I weep because she is already gone.
Memories of her life are buried under
rooms of sorrow that years of pain built on.
I try to unearth a happier time,
remembering her pain-free days,
when her heartbeat was the same as mine,
how her love touched me in so many ways.
But a sad longing crowds into my heart
covering her joy with it's black pall
and, though I know her death was just one part
of her living, it's what I most recall.
If only she were still here with me
she could show me what my heart can't see.

Cathy Carolus

Airman Of Honor

I am dedicated to my subordinates and loyal to my superiors.
I will, at all times, present an image of competence, integrity,
and pride.
I am, and will continue to excel at all I do.
I will earn respect based on my morals, principles, and leadership —
not by the stripes on my arm.
I am, and will continue to motivate those around me; creating an
atmosphere of high morale and esprit de corps.
"I will never forget that I am an American, fighting for freedom,
responsible for my actions, and dedicated to the principles
which made my country free."
I am an airman of honor.

Darrell Natoli

Image

If I could only see myself in the mirror
I will see a woman/man,
With a rainbow of questions.

If I could only see myself in the mirror
I will mourn for death
I will understand Aids.

If I could only see myself in the mirror
I will reason with you
I will appreciate you better.

If I could only see myself in the mirror
I will ask, why this world is such a mess?
Why the children are dying?

If I could only see myself in the mirror
I will be able to help you,
I will be able to help me.

If I ever see myself in the mirror
My problems will be solved,
My worries will be lifted.

And if I see myself today
I'll be a better person tomorrow;

Cecilia Pitcher

The Void In My Heart

You can come out now, it is okay.
I will unlock the doors, you will be alright.
I feel the same way. Do not ignore me. I do not hate you.
I would kiss you, but, I do not have the might.
  I am interested in your thoughts,
    And all of your beautiful parts.
I took you away from your misery.
I took you where you could be loved.
It is not going to be bad, you will be happy.
  I am interested in your thoughts,
    And all of your beautiful parts.
Try not to break my heart, I do not want the pain.
Listen to me — Do not start, I will do the same.
Be with me and you will see.
Please will you tell me.
  I am interested in your thoughts.
    And all of your beautiful parts.
For you are the void that filled my HEART.

Brian Cortus

Two Worlds Apart

Sorrow and misery following me, pain and isolation is all that I see
I wish I was OK but I'm sure you can tell, this loneliness and
suffering is truly my hell
Bleeding and crying in total bliss, wanting only your one last kiss...
Saving me from my torture and doom returning me to that safe little
room, inside my head, inside my heart; all I wanted was a new, fresh
start, but I crushed you and tore you apart.

I see now all the mistakes I've made
Admitting I'm lonely and very afraid
Please hold me and tell me it'll be alright
Can't stand to be alone and caged in fright
Wanting to scream and tear out my heart
Please forgive me and make a fresh start.
Don't know what I'm saying - don't know what I mean
Feeling lost, like all mixed up in a dream
As usual I'm all mixed up and in shock
But whatever you do just please don't mock
These words I'm saying, these words I feel
Reach out your hand and start to heal, my bleeding and dying heart
Before we're thrown two worlds apart.

Caleb Nathanael Brickman

Dedicated to Aunt Myrtle

See the world, feel the happiness.
I wish this wasn't true.
I miss you so much.

If you were here, I'd feel better.
I miss you so much.

I wonder what's up there.
Are the streets paved with gold like the Bible says.

See the world, feel the happiness.
Just remember, I love you.

Jennifer Cook

I Am

I am an intelligent boy who loves airplanes.
I wonder how they can go so fast.
I hear their sonic booms.
I see jets doing rolls across the sky.
I want to fly them someday.
I am an intelligent boy who loves airplanes.

I pretend to be shooting down enemy fighters.
I feel the sadness and sorrow for the pilot's family.
I touch his face and apologize.
I worry someday I may be in his place.
I cry when pilots die in crashes.
I am an intelligent boy who loves airplanes.

I understand we must shoot down enemy planes.
I say we negotiate hard to try not to kill each other.
I dream about world peace.
I try to understand why we can't have it.
I hope we do not kill each other off.
I am an intelligent boy who loves airplanes.

Jeremy L. Waller

Faces in a Picture

As I gaze upon the faces
I wonder what deep thought are in them.

Some sad, some joyous,
some deep, some weep.

In that little three by five
I sit and wonder it's great to be alive.
There are friends, there are family,
They're at weddings they're at parties,
they're at picnics eating hearty.

In the mountains, in the plains,
by the streams or near the ocean,
I look at those faces,
and I see so much emotion.

I sit and wonder, it's great to be alive.
Holding hands, hugging friends.
Just dreaming someday this never ends.
It maybe just a picture,
But its a time in space,
you could never replace,
because someday, you will miss, that face.

Bruce A. Baker

Vision

Your name echoes thru the valleys of my mind,
  For its origin I search, but cannot find.

I smell the trees and listen to the wind,
  But a cry from a hawk is all my ears do lend.

Spring is here, on leaves grown from trees of old,
  And the warmth of the sun releases the flowers from the cold.

Roby Matson

Tears

As I walk through the valley of tears,
I wonder why no one else fears,
The loss of a friend,
Departing to his end.
I'll never forget,
The swings where we use to sit,
Time has gone and so has he,
But I couldn't forget our amity,
Death had taken him away,
But the sadness in my heart would always stay.

Angela Perry

If

If I were a bird I would fly my way out of here;
I would not chirp or beep - but I would sing
  "free, free, free"
with a tilt in my voice - flutter those wings way, way high.
And nigh let you be.
For I will leave a trail behind like a sting from a bee...
In other words,
Try to catch me!

Francesca De Graff

Without These Thoughts

What would my world be without these thoughts?
I would see only shades of grey
I would hear only monotones
I would scent no perfumes

What would my mornings be without these thoughts?
I would recognize no birdsong
I would taste no sweet fruit
I would notice only light

What would my afternoons be without these thoughts?
I would detect only sterile heat
I would sense only road noise
I would have no wishes for rain

What would my evenings be without these thoughts?
I would recognize no sunset
I would extol no purpose from the day
I would only fear the coming darkness

What would my dreams be without these thoughts?
I would not dream

Dale B. Johnson

The Letter

Dear Lord,
  I write this letter on behalf of a good friend. A friend
who's life is turned upside down ad coming to an end.

  He needs from you dear Lord — direction, love and care.
He needs to know from you dear Lord that you will always be there.

  This friend dear Lord is so confused, he's holding on to
his past. Each time I look into his face I can see just how far back.

  I've prayed just as you have taught me Lord and I put it
in your hands. Please save this dear friend of mine from Satan's
evil plans.

Candy R. Geeter

I Write

I write with a closed door;
I write with an open mind.
I write through a silence filled invisible wall.
I write whatever I feel, even when I feel nothing.
I write speedily, or careful and slow.
I write no matter where I go.
I write when I'm dozy or wide awake.
I write whatever I get;
I write what I can take.
I write very seriously, or silly as can be.
I write when I feel loved or when my heart feels ripped apart,
because writing is in me.

DeAndra Riki Mack

Tapestry

Before snow-runs and
Icy rills of winter bring
Deep sleep to still the land;
With summer vanishing
Into mist and maze of memory,
These spurning winds steal honey from the comb,
Paint with silver frost
Mountain woods in trailing
Saffron robes and scarlet veils.
They mix with copper beech and aspen gold, to
Blend with purple wine and
Berry bitter-sweet,
Cinnamon, nutmeg and winter brown.
This ever returning
Tapestry of fall
Drapes an autumn mantle
Of paisley across the hills
And lies sleeping in eternal keep of mind.

Jessie F. Lewis

If I Could Build You A Sand Castle

If I could build you a sand castle
I'd compose it of the finest grains, one from every beach
The sand deposited by ten prize elves from Santa's Workshop
A sand castle that would stretch as far as your eyes could see
If I could build it for you.

If I could paint you a picture
It would mirror paradise, painted on stain glass windows
The sun illuminating if for all eternity and
With it's radiant glow, would lift your spirit upon a single glance
If I could paint it to for you.

If I could tell you a story
I'd encompass it with your tender thoughts, centered on your fears
I'd stretch the truth until you hated to hear it, so that
When I'd finish telling you the story, your fears would disappear
If I could tell it to you

If I could sit you down for ten minutes
I would tell you my feelings towards you, how I cherish you,
Desire you...ah, but how silly I can be sometimes,
For to sit you down, to talk to you without hesitation
It would be easier to build you a sand castle.

Jay Abramson

The Mother

If death should over come me in the eyes of the sun
May my body return to the soul of the earth
Let the shrill of the Hawk sing the song of the living
And the sound of the dark sing the song of the dead
Let the sister of the earth and her brother the sea
Twist and turn as one as siblings should be
Let the seed of our people join together with hands
And keep the beauty and soul of their mother the land

J. D. Sholey

Untitled

My wish for you-
    I'd like you to light a candle
    and let it burn.
    And with each drop of wax-
        See and feel the tears flow.
    Tears of the hungry, the
        homeless, the sick.
    Tears of the children, the aged,
        and of the hostages.
    As it slowly burns,
        pray these tears turn to tears
        of joy and happiness.
    And that their world becomes brighter.

Jean M. Miller

Regrets or Maybe No Regrets

How often say that I have no regrets?
    I'd live my life again the same old way!
It has to be my troubled mind forgets
    The self inflicted woes I wish away.
We half-live life, in fear we'll go wrong,
    We hesitate to grasp the nettle prize,
Lest we should later on, regret en-song
    And suffer for our greed, to agonize
Our lives in some deep rut or private hell
    Where skulls and bones, death's skeletons are found.
Negativity's influences tell,
    "Don't try, don't think, beware it's too profound.
Content yourself, you'll never better find
Than what you have or are, a state of mind."

John Gerson Davies

Just Me

If I were an eagle,
I'd soar through the thick, glassy sky.
If I were a snake,
I'd slither through the long, thin grass.
If I were a fish,
I'd swim as far as I could go.
If I were a lion.
I'd roar as loud as an echo on a tall mountain.
But me.....
I'd like to see as me.
Not an eagle or not a fish.
And not a snake, or a lion.
Just me.
Plain old me.

Emily Stearns

My Love

Sitting here all alone, wondering where you are.
If I were to see you for just one moment,
just one chance to see you by far.

If I could hear your voice, my love,
speaking to me, like you use to do.
The one who made me so happy, the
guy who made me weak, my love, it's you.

You are the one for me, my love, the one who
filled me up with happiness, the one who made my heart alive.
You, are the one who made my heart beat race,
you, my love, are the one who made my heart
take a deep dive.

You, my love, will be mine.
May it be tomorrow or in a different life time,
You will be mine, my love.

Christina Brown

Why I Cry

When sadness looms over my head I cry
If life seems but a passing phase I cry
When pain devours my very being I cry
If things begin to overwhelm me I cry
I cry not just because I know I can
But because I can't begin to understand
The feelings are so overpowering
And nothing I do will over shadow them
They come like a thief in the night
Taking my mind into a state of fright
Sometimes I cry over things I dread
But sometimes crying clears my head
If crying helps to relieve my soul
Then I'll cry and cry and let the tears flow
Then next time I cry it'll be with great anticipation
For knowing why I cry helps relieve the aggravation

Audrey L. Johnson

Our Roots Are Our Pride

Do you know where you're from?
If not, go ask your mom.
Our roots are our pride.
Buried deep down inside.

We put this on the wall.
So we can show you all.
Where our roots are strong.
But where our hearts now belong.

If you follow the colored string.
That is where you'll find me.
Around the world, we all make a ring,
And stand together, one, we will be.
(Cleveland Middle School, Dorchester, MA)

8th Grade Students

Know Me

If only I could know you.
If only I could reach beyond
The confines of a touch,
To feel you ... understand you ...
Must out senses lack so much?

If only I could know you.
If only I could see inside
With gentle spirit's sight
And share with you your hopes, your dreams ...
Your pain and your delight.

If only I could know you.
If only I could see your world
And all you have to give.
But we're separate souls. Alone, so close ...
Will I know you while I live?

If only you could know me.
If only you could see my heart
As God can from above.
You'd find there's nothing there for you ...
Nothing there for you but love.

Bob Kuplin

Sincerely Yours

Since the foundations of the world were laid bare
there exists a garden splayed beyond compare.
Amidst the high walls a glimmering furrow
blossoms like a flower, the bouquet of a girl.
For a boy cannot live upon bread alone,
but upon the honey which drips from the comb.

Marc A. Sabo

Time

Time.
If only there was more...
If only I didn't waste it...
What happened to it?
Time.
Each moment flies by.
With each breath taken,
with each tear falling
Time.
Can't be bought.
Can't be sold.
Yet is squandered as if unlimited.
Time.
In one moment
someone is born
someone dies
Time.
Why waste it?
Cherish each moment of it
Time.

Jennifer Moore

The Highest Honor

You've of'n heard the question, "Who do you admire the most?
If you could choose a man and woman, who'd receive your highest toast?
For me, the answer's simple for I was truly blessed -
My dad could not be beaten - my mother was the best!
Both of them had faults - to that I'd agree;
    But they gave the best they could to the other kids and me.
Mother taught me right from wrong, and not from work to run;
Dad taught me how to live, yet have a little fun.
'Twas hard for Mom to show her love, so hugs were pretty rare
But, if you ever needed her, you'd always find her there!
Dad was full of tales and lore - he knew an awful lot
And 'twas he who'd hold me tightly 'til troubles were forgot.
Dad advised to live each day as if it were your last -
Looking ever to the future - building on the past!
Mom could do most anything her irish mind conceived,
And, anything she told you could always be believed!
Mom and Dad have passed away - they didn't need a will;
For every gift they gave me is living in me still!!
So if you'd ask me who should receive the greatest honor had,
I'd tell you with the greatest pride - "It Goes to Mom and Dad!"

Betty Mason

Do For Me What I Do For You

I'll be there for you, please be there for me.
I'll remember you, please remember me.
I'll think of you, please think of me.
I'll defend you, please defend me.
I'll pray for you, please pray for me.
Whatever you wish for me, I'll wish for you.
I'll care for you, please care for me.
Remember I'll do for you what you'll do for me.

Edith Dickerson

You Are My Lighthouse

Carefully watching....in your leisurely way,
scouring a wide view both night and day;
safeguarding my course like a guiding light,
affording protection as complete as a waveless night.

Your spellbinding glow, like satin and pearls in the skies,
is radiant, as the gleam of first love is in my eyes.
Intrigued by the unconditional surrender of hope you aspire,
I am soothed, as if by voices heard from an angels choir.

Sherry Blanchard

My Country Home

Quiet are the days and nights
I'm all alone
In my place of solitude
My country home.
Faraway into the haunting, dark woods it stands
Amongst the beauty of God's gracious good land.
My country home is my sacred place
Where I have traveled far to get away
Worldly cares and woes I leave behind
Searching for some understanding
Searching for peace of mind.
In my garden of earth's good food I till
Rejoicing in gratitude for each daily meal.
From soothing waters of the spring well
My thirst is quenched, my body cleansed
And my troubled soul is healed within.
This country home is not a fancy place with a fancy name
It's just old-fashioned, simple and plain
But it is my country home, my sacred place
Where I have traveled far to get away.

Bernace Eady

This All Came Out of the Earth!

As I look about at myriad things,
I'm filled with wonder and mirth
At the vastness of all the material wealth -
This all came out of the earth!

Just think of each thing that's before you
No matter what the worth
It did not come out of thin air, you know,
This all came out of the earth!

Have you counted your tangible blessings,
Your gems and possessions since birth?
Wherever you live, just look around,
This all came out of the earth!

Look at the flowers and see the trees,
Remember God's creatures of worth -
Even we mortals and all living things,
They all came out of the earth!

Alice Meissner

A Peaceful Place

Not much time left to do what must be done.
I'm heading for the light,
my day is soon to come.
Searching for the peace to end these painful
dreams.
Nothing feels the same as it used to be.
The days seem so much brighter now.
So much clearer somehow.
The shadows that used to surround me have
all disappeared.
The light is my guidance, there are no
more fears.
So much beauty and joy surround me now.
The peaceful dream I have finally found.
So much warmth and love inside the light.
There is no wrong.
There is no right.
A peaceful place for you and me.
A love for all.
Unity.

Alina Garcia

Your Love Is Like An 'Expensive Perfume'

It is very much possible for me to love again,
I'm just thinking about that as I sit in my den.
Your love is like an expensive perfume,
The fragrant is left in every room.

Yes, I enjoyed my stay in San Diego,
I've never felt like that before.
So helpless I said, I'll, I'll, I'll, soon return,
I'm grateful that you show me so much concern.

You shower me with much care and bathe me with much love,
Thanks for the lovely pair of black leather gloves.
Your love is as refreshing as a summer breeze,
It protects me from the deep winter freeze.

This morning is at an early stage three (3) O'Clock,
My love for you just won't stop.
I can tell you this even at high noon,
Your love is like an expensive perfume.

Yes, yes, I can definitely love again,
What I feel isn't just every now and then.
Darling the fragrant is left in every room,
Your love is like an expensive perfume.

Ella Smith Dixon

After the Rape — Goodbye to Who I Was

Can somebody help me?
   I'm lost and I can't find my way back.
Nothing looks the same
Nothing smells the same
Nothing seems the same
Can somebody help me?
   I'm lost
Nobody looks the same
Nobody sounds the same
Nobody seems the same.
Can somebody help me?
   I'm lost and I can't find my way back.
I don't look the same
I don't think the same
I don't feel the same
I don't sound the same
Nothing seems the same.
Can somebody help me?
   I'm lost!

Jane P. Wuest

The Last Reunion

As I'm traveling halfway across the Pacific ocean,
I'm sitting here in my plane thinking of our teenage years.
Every Saturday morning we'd run along the beach,
The wind whipping back our hair,
The sun beating on our backs,
The sand glittering like the glitter in your eyes, your eyes
radiating happiness and excitement.

The last year,
The last year of our senior year we ran along that beach.
The wind was whipping back our hair,
The sun was beating on our backs,
But the glitter in your eyes was no longer there.
As the last glitter faded from your eyes, I promised to return.

It's been four years since I made that promise,
But when my plane lands,
I will run out into the open, wind blowing, sun beating,
To see the glitter in your eyes return.

Carolina Reyes

Conscience

"What was that?"
"I'm sorry, I wasn't listening."
No reply...silence...
But, I'm sure I heard someone...something...
indistinctly...oh so softly...
Yet, somehow, insistent, demanding to be heard!
Was it a warning? A reprimand? Counsel? Advice?
Opportunity? Something that could change my life?
I rise...eagerly now...
But nothing is there...no one...
Only the stillness, the silence.
I am alone.
Next time...I promise...I will listen!

Deborah Pietrantozzi

Empty Shoes

Mama I'm hungry
I'm sorry, You'll just have to wait
Why, I'm hungry now
Because I don't have a job yet
What does that have to do with me being hungry
Tell me, Who use to bring food home
Daddy, He always did
When was the last time you saw your daddy
I don't know, I forgot
So did he
When is he coming home
I don't know
Where did he go
I don't know, stop asking me these questions
Mama, Don't he want to be my daddy anymore

Alvin Horhn

Rejection

My ship has left without me and is sailing far away.
I'm standing on the weathered pier, coping with my dismay.
I'm trapped inside my cruel world to fight the war alone,
and quickly walk across my mind to flee the dying's moan.
I can walk up to the edge where the barren landscape ends,
but my ship has sailed away, and will never be back again.
I could try to trace her path by her footsteps in the wind,
or follow her trailing ripples that she never ceases to send.
But, I fear I dream of an impossible task, for she travels with no
    anchor.
And if, by chance, I'd catch her up, I'd fear someone had sank her.

David M. Long

A Time Of Your Own

To be what I want, to do what I want,
    in a world of my own, to be all alone.
The wind in my face, my heart full of grace,
    the faith from above, the flight of a dove.

A bright starry night, a miracle in sight,
    a warm blue lake, just for my sake.
A forest of green, a stone with a gleam,
    a beautiful chime, a glorious time.

To be able to think with thoughts so meek,
    a time of my own, just to be all alone.
It's a beautiful time to use your mind,
    and to think your own thoughts————
        that's been hidden behind.........

Debora Horton-Green

Remembering

My eyes open slowly, everything is a gray haze of memory.
    Images flash and fade everywhere, happy ones, sad ones.
        Colors blend, washing together before my crying eyes.
My breath is heavy, labored.
    I have worked too hard, too long.. I can't breathe.
        The smell of roses, the lovely fragrance lifting me into a state
        of ecstasy.
        I don't want to leave, I don't want to forget.
With my textured, dry hands, I reach out and feel the warmth of the fire.
    Soft, subtle changes in temperature warm my spirit, and
        Bring me out of the cold, unforgiving snow, into the safety of
        my mind it is here where I have trust in myself...
Holding a mug of hot chocolate with both hands, I carefully take a sip
The liveliness that left me years ago returns with this one mug of
hot chocolate.
    It has made all the difference and I am revitalized.
The quiet crackling of the fire lulls me, carrying me into a deep,
far away sleep.
My eyes, once crying have now stopped, and I can see clearly once
again.   My breath, once labored, is now free and strong.
My hands, once textured and dry, are now young and smooth.
I have left this old, frail body and with all my senses, I remember.

Eric Hwang

The Birth, Death and Resurrection of Jesus

On a day we now call Christmas, He was born,
In a simple way, our lives to change;
And after living only thirty three years His life He gave
On that erratic day, our future to arrange.

He did not grumble or complain, but died an unusual
Death at the hands of angry men.
The righteous for the unrighteous, to provide an extraordinary plan,
By which all mankind could be saved from their sin.

He was placed in a borrowed tomb,
And the leaders of that day thought they had sealed His doom;
But He in the grave would not remain,
He arose victorious for evermore to live again.

Because He came, died and from the grave arose,
We can, through Him defeat all our foes.
Because He lives, you and I may also live,
If to Him our hearts and lives will truly give.

A gift from God, the Father, He was the Son;
That voluntarily paid the price for all our sin.
So that when the Christian's life on earth comes to an end,
Through all eternity, with Him, a new life we can begin.

Edw F. Redmon

Today

Help me to live today,
In a very special way;
To hold my head up high,
As I'm looking toward the sky

Help me to love today,
In a very special way:
To treasure each moment,
As I travel down this road.

Help me to pray today,
In a very special way;
Grateful for worthwhile things,
Laughter, tears, joy.

Help me to stay today,
Always in the presence of the master,
Help me to avoid disaster,
Please give me the strength
To cope, to hope, today!

Jennie W. Brantley

My Wish For You For 1995

May you find serenity and tranquility
In a world you may not understand
May the pain and conflict suffered
Allow new strength to take command
May you always walk in certainty
Facing new situations all around
May courage lead to greater heights
Where enthusiasm will abound.

May you see enough goodness in this world
To believe in a future peace
May a kind word, reassuring touch
Be gifts that never cease
Teach love to those who tend to hate
By the Life you live each day
And remember when storms seem unending
There will be sunbeams on the way.

Ibera B. Garner

Desert Seed

The howling wind sends raindrops drumming against my windowpane
in cadence with my thundering heart. Awake I realize that I
am alone.
As the rain pours down the gutters in its race to join the
loam, In silent anguish my eyes search the shadows,
You are gone.
Lightning flashes like arrows straight into my soul, above
me the darkness gathers under the cloudy foggy bowl.
Across the room a mirror shows a ghostly face as cold as stone
Beside me sheets stay taut unwrinkled dry as bleached bone.
No lover mussed these sheets nor left his seed.
Dry, forever dry the stream bed stays after the stream has gone
Never to grow weed until the stream gushes forth again to fill
its dry need.
The rivers and the streams must go where they must go and so
do you. But try not to forget me in the sweet waters you come
upon. I will be here yearning for I am like a desert
until you come.

Jacqueline Vogelsang

Written Because Someone Said Clams Are Uninteresting

Hide your delicate bodies
In carapace armor
Against enemies hidden
In crystal sands
Beneath the rolling waves
Of aquamarine
Gathered in clans
To witness death
By invaders from
An alien world
Who spoil our tranquil haven
Let us sway to the
Gentle, rising rhythm
Of the mermaids song
While we wait
And listen

Cathy Reedy

Yours And Mine

The hands on the clock continually spinning
The essence of time seems to be winning
This battle between us and the sky
It seems to me we never did try
The hole in the ozone is still growing
The cancer is still quickly flowing
A painful, stinging, burning sensation
A slow death of our own creation

Kristen Rose Schwary

Untitled

I look toward the hills of Arlington and I see what appears
  to be phlox to me.

As I look closer, I realize it isn't phlox as all
  -but the FLOWER OF FREEDOM.

Karen Bryan

Leaves

Brittle, cracked, yet still more beautiful
in death than ever in life,
Reflecting hues of auburn and gold
More radiant than woman's hair, I'm told
Blowing, falling, dying with sensual grace
They form aged yet gorgeous lines on nature's face
Another year slips by, burned by light, buried in mist
Another face of joy too rarely kissed
Are all my days to thus unfold
With never another's heart to hold?

Brian Yothers

What Is Real Love?

Real love is patient, it waits quietly
in each of our hearts. So not to be destroyed

Real love takes time
So not to be fooled

Real love takes understanding
So not to be explained

Real love takes giving
So not to be taking

Real love takes touching
So one can be touched

Real love takes tears
So the soul can be cleansed

Real love takes care
So not to be ignored

Real love takes a lifetime
So not to be taken for granted

Real love is not a mystery
It wants to reveal

If you ask me what real love is?
Real love has the power to heal

Catherine Valdez

Springing-Out

Spring sings it's arrival, day by day,
in its wonderful "crescendo" way,
yellow, white, and purple crocus,
suddenly come into focus,
orchestrated wind, sunshine, rain soaks us,
as God does His botanical hocus-pocus.

Birds romantically chase one another,
and then nest in a nearby tree,
lawns desperately need raking,
to remove the unwanted Fall debris,
shedding of winter is everywhere,
awakened by mother nature's tear.

Zombie-eyed hibernating neighbors,
exit their dwellings, dazed; half-crazed,
instantly become unpossessed,
magically, their spirits are raised;
as if freed from prison, profoundly amazed,
and very glad to be outdoors again!

Joann G. Kuebler

Loving You Forever

I want to let you know
In just the perfect way
How much your love does mean to me
But I don't know what to say
You've always stood beside me
Through the good times and the bad
I never thought that anyone
Could make me so happy, even when I'm sad
You've see me at my worst
And you never tried to leave
Instead, you showed me the importance
Of dreaming, and to just believe
I never thought I
Could ever let you in
My heart has been through so much
I thought that it would be a sin
You have shown me I was wrong
That love can and will always prevail
No matter what anyone may say
Some special people do live in a fairy tale!

Debbie Henderson

Ode to a Brown Leaf

Tossed and turned
    in Spring's restlessness
Still
    in Summer's calm
Now you tumble
    brittle and torn
A mat for Winter's down.

I could pick you up
    and I might
In your turbulent travail
Tuck you gently into my pocket
Eventually pin you to my peaceful wall
Where live my view and occasional dusting.

There you tell
    what you know well
That which eludes the surface glance:
Beyond repose and
    apparent darkness
Renewal eternal
Abides the passage.

Hylda Clarke

When It Comes To Sweethearts

When it comes to sweethearts - I love you most of all,
In the dark of night - YOU, I sometimes want to call.

Just to hear you sweet voice - just to recall,
All those lovely phrases - left lingering in the hall.

In the hall of memories - when I am alone,
I even hear them - just looking at the phone.

All the bright tomorrows - just borrowed for awhile,
Lost somewhere in sorrows - some day, no more your smile.

My special sweetheart - the best that can be,
Holding me so tightly - understanding my plea.

My plea of just wanting - love that is so true,
Oh, just what will I do - when I no longer have you.

I already feel lonely - even though you are still near,
That pain of loneliness - that sometimes lingers here.

That fear of departing time - when I no longer see,
My special precious sweetheart - still just holding me.

When it comes to sweethearts - the best that can be,
'Cause you are my little pal - made especially for me.

Evelyn Ruth Taute

The Streambed

There she lay
in the muddy bank of the streambed
letting a flood of the earth's
tears
wash over her,

Feeling her form being
lifted,

Over the rocks that had held her there-
over the rocks stained with her own blood-
over the rocks that had held her a prisoner-

And
letting her body gently float down
life's waterfall
she felt her spirit
rise.

Emily Barron

In The Name Of Progress

What have we done, what have we lost,
in the name of progress,
in the name of technology,
in the name of God?
What have we given
that we can't take back?
What have we lost
that can never be found?
We say it's for the good of all of mankind.
But what of the men who were left behind?
The ones here first were quickly destroyed.
The animals were killed.
The trees were chopped down.
The sky of blue
is now turning grey.
The oceans full of life
are dying each day.
What have we done
and what price will we pay,
in the name of progress?

Dana Hurleigh

Final Farewell

I see his face so close to mine
In the soft day light
We share a kiss as I make my final wish

I hold on tight as the seconds go by
I know he sees the sorrow in my eyes

I see in my mind all the men that will die
I fear that he will be one that will never come home
That I will never feel his arms around me
To keep me warm

I see the others lining up
As the bus snakes near I feel my heart beat speed
As I fear the worst

As the others board he promises to return
Then he wraps me in his arms
In a protectful embrace

I know the time is near as we share our final kiss
Our hands slip apart as he boards the bus

And with one last wave the bus pulls away
And he does not see the crystal tear
That streaks down my cheek.

Amanda Lee Smith

That Wind

When you walked into my life from out of nowhere you were just someone in the wind. I was introduced to you and you became another face with a name and a friend. Then with that wind of the introductions, the time we began to share, you turned out to be someone that I can't seem to remove from deep within my heart. With my many disasters and
roller coaster rides, I suddenly had fallen into a state of needing passion, love, and warmth. That was when I let myself go into your open arms. I then realized you were still the same unique person with a name, someone that became a true friend, and then you became my soul. When I remember your touching embrace, your warm words, your unforgettable smile, this is how I'd like our friendship to grow. A touch of softness if either of us need it. Maybe a "Hi" or "Hello" as we pass over each other's path.

But truly — you have given me myself, passion for life, and a great deal more. All because of "that wind!"

Christina M. Husley

America

See the sunset feel the cool breeze
In the wind there blows many autumn leaves
Feel the warmth of your loved one's
Reach out and touch the sky
Just say "I Love You"
But never have to say "good-bye"
Watch the tall grass grow
Hear the dogs bark see the birds fly
And the singing of a lark
Just forget about all your worries
And fly to the highest mountain
see the snow - covered tops and
The water like a big fountain
Watch the blazing fireworks
Think of the fourth of July I hear
"Freedom" ringing in my ears
I think of America and sigh follow
Your greatest dreams!!
And make them come true
Nobody else can do it, the only person who can is You!!

Celeste Tapper

This I Hope You Know

In this room full of sadness,
In this room full of tears,
I lay in this hospital bed,
Fighting cancer and not fears.

I remember when I was so active, so alive, and so young.
Now I can barely move my tongue.

I struggle to hold on just a little while longer.
But I can't, I just can't, I've got to be stronger.

My body is so limp, so lifeless, and so weak.
I've got to tell my family I love them.
Oh, if I could only speak.

I can feel myself drifting off and fading away.
No, not yet, I've got to stay.

I can hear a voice and a hand on my head.
The voice is my mother's cry, "I wish it were me instead."

I'm so sorry mom, I don't want to leave you.
I'm so sorry mom, but there's nothing we can do.

I've got to go mom, so please let me go.
I will always love you mom, this I hope you know.

Gina Ramsey

Manchild

Manchild, my son,
in your eyes burns the anger
of innocence stolen from you, never to be returned,
of changes far beyond your years, forced upon you,
of life, unfair, out of your control.

Why you; all you did was arrive, clean, untouched
by the hurt, by the pain, by the shame of your protectors.

Be strong, manchild, my son.
Do not extinguish, but cool the fire
that burns in your eyes and has spread to your heart.
The flicker of the flame will keep you alive,
but the fire that burns in you will consume you.

Survive, manchild, my son.
Find balance between the fire and the water,
between the anger and the love,
between the debilitation of the pain and the exhilaration of the love.

Grow, manchild, my son.
Soon you will become the protector.
You will know; you will write,
to your manchild, your son.

Judith A. Wilson

Judge Not

Judge not, your fellow brother.
Instead, let's try and love one another.
Once you judge things fall apart.
You find it hard to trust ones heart.

It's not our place to lay the blame.
We all make mistakes just the same.
Let's just try and do our best.
And leave to God to do the rest.

Judge not, the things others may do or say.
Mind your own business and for them you pray.
Having the power to judge is not in you.
But praying for everyone is something we all can do.

To judge is wrong and that's a fact,
When we ourselves are not in tact.
All make mistakes and fall short of glory.
In the last days, we'll hear the whole story.

Judge not, for time is not long,
We'll soon met together in our final home.
The judge of all judges will judge us all.
He'll be the one to make the last call.

Barbara Furlow

Stay

As I look
into your eyes,
I see the flicker of a flame.
I look deeper, my mind opens
and I see the real true you,
locked away with a key lost long ago.
The flame consumes me. The heat begins
to rise. I look again and see the lies
you have been told, the fear and
the pain that has loomed
over you for so long
And the flame fills my body with its
presence. A mirror appears, and begins
to cry. The mirror is not me, and as it begins to
change and take shape, I finally begin to see, that
the mirror is you and you are like me. A lonely
spirit looking for something to help fill its void for
eternity. I'll fill the empty, if you'll make me
whole. We'll be forever in love
body and soul.

Christopher Burnette

Insight

'Tis said that the love of a man and a maid
Is a beautiful thing to view -
But can anyone see what must needs only be
Apparent to only the two?

It's not outward, but inward, that we find love,
And whom else can inward see
Deep into the heart of a man or a maid,
Excepting just he, or just she?

Henry Lyndon Despard

Dear Brother

As your time with us here on earth
 Is coming to an end,
We just wanted you to know dear brother,
 You've been a special friend.
As we grew up throughout the years
 Our bonds grew very deep,
Through love and laughter, tears and joy,
 There are special memories to keep.
The feelings we have for each other,
 No one will ever know,
Words need not be spoken,
 It's a feeling that doesn't show.
Though apart in our lives
 We will always be,
Together in our hearts
 For all eternity.
So now as we stand together
 With sorrow in our hearts,
We know we'll heal in time
 In years after we part.
Love,

your brother, and sisters.

Judith McCurdy

The Sound of Silence

The sound of silence
is harsh and loud...
Sitting alone in a large room. Hearing
a ringing in my head. The ringing of
silence. Thoughts ponder and pass through
my mind, different ones. Ones of laughter
and cheer, ones of sadness and ones of
fear. Echoing and banging, softer... louder, Louder,
and Louder, but still the sound of silence lingers.
A creek here, a settling there, but all
to remain is the endless hum of silence.
Deeper in thought and deeper in concentration,
being alone and free listening to the sound
of the crackling ceiling, and the endless
ring of silence that lingers on and on and on.

Audra Robin Weintraub

Heaven's Playground

Sitting on a cloud and dreaming away the day
Is how we see the oldsters passing time away.

What about the children so early from us gone
Shouldn't we be happy that their life is now a song?

They'll never have arthritis or lose their minds to age
Their lives shall e'er be happy like playing on a stage.

Imagine clouds with pockets for playing hide-n-seek
Or shooting stars to ride on for those who aren't to meek.

And what about the infants too young to do all this?
They're rocked in the arms of Mary for all eternal bliss.

Alice S. Guzay

Poetry

For what is it?
Is it yet a word?
Or possible a definition!
No, it must be an idea.
Perhaps we shall never know.

Find your slightest feeling.
Is that poetry?
Perhaps!!
Yet we write it, therefore we should know it.
Perhaps we shall never know...

Erin Elizabeth Johns

To Say Goodbye

For me to say goodbye to you
is not an easy task to do.
If I were to say different, it would be untrue.
It would be easier to wear a mask to disguise
the hurt that is eating me up inside.
I have nowhere to hide these tears that now fill my eyes.
All I see now is cloudy skies.
I see no silver lining, but this pain is terribly blinding.
So as you prepare for your tomorrow
I will be here remembering all our yesterdays.
I welcome tomorrow but without you, I must say
brings great sorrow.

James Harris

"Peace"

"Grant us peace," we all chant.
Is not peace different to many:
Security to the needful,
Victory to the competition?
Where's the peace when famine strikes or love is gone?
Peace is when the children sleep,
but how can they sleep when there is no food
Is it peace to muggers when they
roam looking for the price of a fix?
Peace is no violence to the streets or
screaming is silent at home;
To some its just to be alone so they
can contemplate and meditate.
Is peace and love in disunified religions
or killing in the name of God?
The dead have no peace for they cannot enjoy it.
Can there be peace in immorality or disease?
Who is at peace without the wisdom of God?
Tell me truth, teach me faith and I shall make peace.

Griffin Ferrell

The Words I Must Say

When we wake each new day,
Is Thank you Lord the words we say?
For a good nights sleep,
I say, "Thank you Lord."
For the very air I breathe,
I say, "Thank you Lord."
For the sun shining so bright,
I say, "Thank you Lord."
For my family before me, they are all right,
I say, "Thank you Lord."
As I go out to begin my day,
I say, "Thank you Lord."
For the job I have to earn my way,
I say, "Thank you Lord."
When day is over and I am home,
I say, "Thank you Lord."
I completed the day, but not alone.

Joyce Hebert

Hallucinations

Is this music or just noise
Is that a pen or a fountain of dreams
Am I here or an illusion
Are those clothes or a suit of armor
And is this a picture of you and me
Or am I all alone again
Is there a God or is it a lie
Is this the beginning or the end of it all
Do I exist or am I a thought
Could this be love or is it called lust
And are we having fun
Or is this just a passing moment in time
Am I a man or a machine
Is that noise or is it music
Is this a song or is it a poem
Is this being normal or am I insane, again
And are you as heartless as the rest
Or could I really love you

Charles E. Stephenson Jr.

Untitled

Being Anorexic
is to be dead to the world
And dead to life.
Only wanting to live from within,
Deep down wanting more, but not being able to reach it,
hurting within to the point of letting go.
And letting death take control,
Too weak to fight to live, but not wanting to give up,
for you know there's hope somewhere,
Confusion overrides the sense of peace,
the peace and hope you're wanting,
but having trouble reaching,
So you continue on until that hope arises once again,
wanting to reach out grab hold and not let go,
Hoping you'll have a second chance at life,
To live, love and cry
once again!

Colleen Collins

The Enigma — Who Really Understands Love?

Its cheaper than copper, yet more precious than gold;
  it blooms in winter, summer, spring or fall.
Its prejudiced against no one, neither young nor old;
  one size fits all.
Its fair to the best and to the worst;
  its not partial to kings or queens.
It puts no one last and no thing first;
  even the indigent knows what it means.
It has no color or smell or taste;
  though often shown by a diamond ring.
It has patience and no need to make haste;
  this intangible but beautiful thing.
It has great power, one man laughs while another cries;
  the outcome, no man can foresee.
I know its awesome when I gaze into your eyes;
  I hope you'll always love me.
It is more timeless than the sky above;
  its deep and its vast and its blue.
And through the ages, I think you'll find;
  my love is a special gift for you.

Harold L. Patterson Jr.

Our Mother

"Mother" is a word - known around the land
It brings to mind, someone stately and grand
The Queen of the household - she runs the show
Her husband and family - make her heart glow

Our Mother, has devoted her entire life
To caring for others and being a wife
Two grown kids and grandchildren too
For these five people - there's not a thing, she wouldn't do

She's there when we're happy - she's there when we're sad
To share in our lives - the good and the bad
The backbone of the family - she keeps us together
She's strong, when we need her, through all kinds of weather

Never once in our lives - has she turned her back
With words of encouragement - she never lacked
She taught us love - and all about God
And in which direction - our feet should trod

A "Mother's Love" is beyond all measure
And for all of us - she is our treasure
Forever and ever - our hearts will be true
So from all us kids - we love you too

Angela Redman

Our Fear

It lingers over me like the hot summer sun,
It cascades over me like the crashing waves of an endless waterfall

The near thought of it makes me cringe
with unquestionable pause,
For it will engulf me quickly
with no warning

Like the lioness guards her cubs,
my soul guards it's desires

It hinders me from continuing
my journey for greatness,
And causes me to falter in my quest
for the unparallel realm of finality

What I must realize and make myself believe
is that I can overcome the force which holds
tight onto me
Like the wind and the rain hold tight onto
the land

Mine and yours incompacitated fear of which we
do not always know
But feel in every breath we take

Julie Conway

Thanksgiving Dinner

There was a turkey who wanted to have a nice and long living.
It did not want to be a part any Thanksgiving.
Since it had a lot of money in its pocket,
It bought a large rocket,
And went very far away.
So far no one had anything to say,
But a cow jumped over the moon,
And the turkey fell down with a spoon
Next to its breast
In our plate for its final rest.
Its meat was tender and sweet,
We never had such a fine dinner to eat.

Helena Shaskevich

Loneliness

Loneliness is the worst companion on earth.
It creeps in where its not wanted,
And stays long after it has been dismissed.
With loneliness around, many tears are shed.
Each new day is always a dread.

If only my door bell or my telephone would ring.
Then loneliness would go away, you know.
But days have passed,
No voice to be heard.
Oh what I would give for just one word.

I lay down in silence,
I rise with the same.
This loneliness is sure to drive me insane.
With no one to love, and no one to care,
I'll go far away, somewhere out there.

I'll take a walk down by the shore.
No one will miss me or care, you know.
And when I wake up, it will be all over.
And I'll never be lonely, again you know.
I will be with my creator forever more.

Hilda M. McMahand

A Poets Daydream

Joy, it is a feeling like one other,
It drives a person on, when one can go no further,
Joy, it is a rainbow; after a rain,
One cannot have it without some pain;
Joy, it is a smile on anyone's face,
It cheers one up no matter the place;
Joy, it is a laugh from a friend,
Any problem; trouble it can mend;
Joy, it is a hug anywhere,
It solves on pain, all cares;
Joy, it is a cool breeze on a sunny day,
It is a bright flower along your way;
Joy, it is a happiness; a feeling,
It is an answer; a problem worth dealing;
Joy, it is a walk worth every mile,
It is your laugh, hug, and smile;
I've waited all these months,
Smile and laugh, just this once;
for me.

Ben Graham

Rough Stuff

Schizophrenia takes you apart. A piece at a time.
It employs the worst of mental inventions.
Oh, to weep. Lost my wife.
This is rough stuff to read.
So get braced or get lost.

Schizophrenia breaks your heart. At least it did mine.
It destroys the best of gentle intentions.
Oh, so deep. Like a knife.
More than enough to bleed.
The waste makes more the cost

that must be paid
by he who would love her.
No matter what.
It's rough to write, too.

Bobby Stillwell

Summer Breeze

You came to me, like a man from my dreams
it felt like a fantasy, as true as it seemed.

You took the scattered pieces of my life and made it into one
who would've known you were just using me for fun?

You told me that you loved me, and I believed it true
for you were my god, and I loved you too.

I believed you when you said you'd never leave
you took my heart and soul, but something else I tried to believe

You ripped out my heart, and let it there to bleed
and blew out of my life, like a cool summer breeze.

Jaime L. Garbisch

On Politicians

I thought I heard a tiger roar, 'twas a very impressive sight
it filled the air with tumult, and rabbits ran with fright

Roars of thunder echo around, and sparks of lightning flew
our ears are filled with promises only correct and proper too

Then all at once it's over and the losers fade slow away
to practice roaring in a closet for new contests, another day

The tigers pack their travel bags to take the winners seat
too late we find our tiger is really rather meek

You see, the roaring sound of thunder that raises up your hair
is only to win the magic contest, to win the princely chair

For the roar so correct and proper, is simply only a token
to sounds we're really used to, the sounds of promises broken

Fred Pettigrew

Something In Everyone

Fear. It started. It swelled.
It gradually consumed my life. Fear.

The inescapable dream of hell.
That dream was myself. That fear was myself.
It was conceived, but unknowingly, in an act of ignorance. Fear.

It began as a tiny speck on the horizon.
For a while the entity never grew, nor vanished or even faded.
It was ignored, but then it was not.
Its recognition fed it more power, so it slowly began to metastasize
like the disease it was.
It bred insecurity and more offspring.
They veiled my thoughts, distorted my voice, and always controlled my
Actions, which define me. Fear.

The battle began. It started as fear pitted against myself,
But just as it initially grew from my thoughts, I grew strong from its
oppressive presence.
I made it retreat. The raging was reverted to myself against fear.

And here I am, myself. Not fear, just me.

But then I'm not. I am fear itself.
Myself.

Jeremy Katz

The Meaning of Love

Love over-rides all of the hurt and pain.
It fills your life with sunshine,
Without the rain.
Love can mend a broken heart,
Restore the lives that have been torn apart.
Love can fill your life with joy,
Bring happiness to every girl and boy.
Love is a peaceful, wonderful word,
It's the sweetest one ever heard.

Chantell Uhl Sanchez

Justice

Is justice blind, or can it really see?
Two souls committed the crime-
Yet, they both will not do the same time.

Same Judge, same crime-
Yet, one will serve more time-
So is justice blind, or is it numismatical?
Raul G. Torres Jr.

My War

The war I fought it had no soldiers
It had no generals, guns or tanks

Just an enemy to big to fight
A war fought alone in the dead of the night

The only cease fire came with the day
when memories of war were hidden away

Pain and blood no one noticed
No doctors to stitch my wounds

I heal myself through time and space
Strength and courage come in their place

Scars still carried tell the story
Of the war I fought in silence

No screams or bombs or blasts or dead
Yet still a war filled with violence
Deborah Armitage

Midnight in the Hen House

Once I heard a tale they said was so.
It happened hereabouts some time ago.
It was late at night, early in the Fall
When, all at once, the hens began to squall.

John heard the ruckus and jumped out of bed,
Grabbed his shotgun and to the hen house fled!
His nightshirt flapped with each step he took.
Ole Spot stretched and yawned, then went to take a look.

John saw the chickens with their heads stuck out
And there sat a 'possum, sullen in a pout!
John's gun was cocked, his hand on the trigger.
"I've got you now, ole 'possum, I figger."

Then up from behind came friendly ole Spot.
His nose touched John and he jumped like a shot!
Bang! went the gun and how the feathers flew!
John got the 'possum - - - and fourteen hens, too!
Annette B. Jackson

"The Desperate Hour"

It has come once again in the mist of the hour.
It has found the way up to the top of my tower.
The hour it tells me to open my door, my strength
is no more, I sit and I cower, at the top of my tower.
The door knob spins fiercely and shakes the whole wall.
The hour wants in, but my tower holds strong.
The hour is silent, but soon will return.
My time here is questioned? My thoughts are all wrong.
How then to fight it when it is so strong?
Why was it put there to tangle our minds?
Why desperate the hour?
Give praise to the seasons, for shot they may be.
Hold fast to your tower, for in there you'll see.
Time goes to swiftly to waste it with fears.
Take hold of your hour, and face all the shadows.
Let the rain wash the pain from your face.
Make happy the hour!
Jeannie Jason

Life Is...

Life is like a rolling stream
It has its ups and downs.
It sometimes flows along straight shorelines
Then goes round and round
In confusion trying to find its way.
And even though it stumbles over rocks and then falls down,
It seems to move with meaning,
But know not where it's bound.

Sometimes in its swiftness,
It carries in its grasp
A tone of indecision
Which somehow seems to last
Until it finds a solution
Within its own strength.

When life is as its calmest
Like the slow flowing streams
That creep ever so quietly
Upon their bed of many things,
It seems so content, in any event,
To be flourishing in sobriety.
Clara E. Hund

Procrastination

What is this thing they call Procrastination?
It has three lanes leading to its destination
There's a fast, slow, and a no budge one.
And how do we know which of the lanes to follow?

The inner, little worker nudges all the time,
But its messages received, can be so deadly wrong
Only because we fail to listen intently.
But when our channels are opened wide
We can hear the constant nagging
Of the little, inner worker,
Pleading for us to heed its visionary warnings
Which in the end, come a Blessing in Disguise
If only we would listen, to that little, inner worker.

Now, tell us little, inner worker,
Which of the lanes to follow?
"Just get to know that nagging voice
And learn to listen more intently
Because it will tell you when you should, and shouldn't
Ride the fast, slow or no budge lanes leading
To Destination, Labeled, Procrastination."
Joan E. Gettry

Love

Love is like a flower, in many, many ways,
It is begun with a thorn, so deep in to your soul,
It reeks havoc there, until one morning a bud begins to show,
And as days go by, the bud grows, larger and stronger,
Till one day it begins to bloom,
From all corners it begins in the morning, exposing beauty inside,
Branching out all over, reaching tenderly out,
It grasps the hearts of mortals, making them realize,
That love is growing in there, larger every day,
But yet, as days go by, the flower loses beauty,
And begins to wilt in spite of itself,
Clinging on to memories, and hope it has inside,
But eventually the blossoms have all fallen,
Leaving just the thorn, pricked inside the wound,
Causing pain and shadows on the love,
That grew inside the thorns tomb.
Heather Groghan

Butterfly Song

You cannot catch a butterfly, you cannot hold it tight,
  It is by God's divine intent designed for spacious flight.

You cannot place a butterfly in cage, or box, or jar,
  It must with artist's wings unfurled dance blithely near or far.

You cannot mold a butterfly or tie it with a string,
  Its wings you'll mar, its spirit crush, it's such a fragile thing.

A butterfly can't be a moth or insect dark and gray,
  It must a touch of flavor sweet bestow upon its way.

A butterfly is meant to glint on leaf or bushes fair,
  To brush a painter's dash of bright on flowers here and there.

A butterfly's a miracle sent from the heavens above,
  Small and frail, yet free and fair, a gift of God's great love.

No, you cannot catch a butterfly, can't hold it in your hand,
  It is by God's creation wise designed to be more grand.

Evelyn Dahlke

Spirited Away

I turn and catch a glimpse of the holiest of holies.
It is everything, it is nothing.
It is my name, it is your name, it is no name.
It defies description—more a feeling, a sense
Of white hot colors bringing light and peace
To the darkest caverns of my spirit

It is strong and overwhelms me with its power.
And, for a moment, a lifetime, I am afraid.
I stand, frozen in time, afraid to look upon the spectrum.
Afraid to look away.
I don't know how I know this is all things—all nature, all knowledge.

I am swallowed up and, at the same time, set free.
I cannot speak and, yet, communicate in all tongues.
I can see the tiny buds within tree limbs—and I become those buds.
Waiting, with patience, for the bursting time, the blossoming.

I taste the dew, and taste in it all the tears of birthing and dying.
I am spun out into the dark sky
Trailing a thousand million sparks of light and color.
Yet held safe and warm as if against a mother's breast.
And I am everything—and nothing.

Judith Karlson

My Journey

I walk on a path,
It is filled with many,dips valleys and cliffs,
I know that I must brave them all on my journey along the path.

I walk and walk,
sometimes people stop and laugh at me for trying,
But they know nothing, nothing at all.

As I walk, I see the paths of others,
Others who must walk the path too,
Sometimes we talk but mostly we just walk,
Always intent on our own journey.

Sometimes I see paths that have stopped abruptly,
These are the paths of people who have ended their journey,
Someday I too will end my journey,
But for now I must continue on.

Night has fallen upon my path,
The stars shine down on me in all their brilliance.
If I look closely, the paths of loved ones reach up,
Up into the starry sky,
Loved ones that have finished their journeys,
They watch me as I walk, walk on the path of life.

Andrew Yang

Universal Growth

There is a light that shines in me —
It is my "inner light."
It guides me well throughout the day,
And brings me peace at night.

I've journeyed through life's many streams -
What joys and tears I've known!
But like the little bird in flight,
Each one of them has flown.

My life flows swiftly through the years,
And the years have taught me much.
I've listened, learned, experienced
From the "Universal Touch!"

There is no "right" or "wrong" I've learned -
One learns this late in years.
Whatever "was" - was meant to be —
The joys, the work, the tears.

So live your life in "sweet content,"
And know that "all is good,"
For whatever you've experienced
Is exactly what you should.

Bunny Geller

Gray Is A Blend Of Black And White

The sky is so gray today...leadfoot gray
it is not so much a color as a feeling
it is kinda like being on the edge of blue
it's no dismal or otherwise better reason...just gray

Today under the sky so gray
I saw a man digging a hole in the ground and putting
the dirt in a wheel barrow and another hauling it away
I wonder what the marker will say when they so neatly cover it?

Across the county on the other side of the world
a wedding is planned
I suppose that that couple won't see gray today
maybe just a fleeting glimpse and then laughter and gaiety

But the neatly trimmed sod is waiting
under the gray for it's marriage with the grave
and the loved one who will be borne to this last address
given a farewell and covered with gray

All things considered it's a pretty good trade, I think,
two ceremonies of finality, two deaths, two new beginnings
and the sky won't see a difference in either spot
I wonder what the grave diggers are talking about?

David N. Wilkins

Purple

Purple is a flower, soft as felt,
It is the cherubic face that makes you melt.
It is the pixy dusted wing of a fairy,
It is the secret that you long to carry.

Purple is the dimness of a glow at twilight,
It is the essence of a spirit by night.
It is the rainbow with an angelic spark,
It is the spirit of a star, emerging from the dark.

Purple is new life, a joyful tear,
It is the mother that holds you near.
It is the feeling of loss, a pain in your heart,
It is the true experience that makes you smart.

Purple is the depression you feel deep inside,
It is the fear from which you hide.
It is the warm embrace you long for at night,
It is the angel that guides and shows you the light...

Jaime Carbo

Always Work

In my head thoughts of work..
It just won't leave me, always there nagging
Yes. That's a cute idea.
Boy... My that would be great for me... No. My class.
The rustling of papers and the ever grating whimper of the
pencil sharpener.
Sometimes I feel, if I ever hear,
"Can I go to the bathroom?"
again, I will screeeeam.
The endless droll of "He did this."
Then the classic response, "No. I didn't do anything."
Pulled this way and that. Always juggling
and jumping to the beat of all the various dances.
Sad so sad all the pathetic, desperate faces.
Hope already gone at six... It usually happens at 35.
So young... Always in my head... Following me Haunting me.,
Fair... Care... Share... Qualities... Pressing down.
Care so much. I must be the best for them.
Set the alarm, 5:30 comes early.
Always in my head, thoughts of work.

Diane E. Dieter

Rainy Days

The rain, wet subtle drops from an endless sky,
it keeps us from the scorching sun, as we complain of being dry,
as the rain glides on God's standing earth,
there is always a new birth,
of growing and budding flowers, trees and plants that divulge like
towers, we need the rain to help our survival,
to fill our streams and rivers — oh! what power!
The effect of nature's good ole' juice,
helps quench our thirst,
keeps our bodies lean and loose,
sometimes though, it causes us to sit and listen,
as it makes a popping, yet soothing sound,
it has its own rendition,
keep on pouring from the source of grace,
I like it leaping on my face,
the rain has a familiar taste.

Janice E. Williams

Your Love

Your love surrounds me like the warm summer sun
It kisses my eyelids, and holds me tight

Your love keeps me warm like the flame of a fire
It flickers, grows, and fills me with light

Your love embraces me like a gentle breeze
It flows all around me, and kisses my cheek

Your love humbles me like a big thunderstorm
It rumbles and crackles, it makes me feel weak

Your love has touched me in such wonderful ways
It took you and I, and made us into one

Your love can be seen in a little girl's eyes
It sparkles as we watch her play in the sun

Ginger Ditton

Birds

Birds are very special.
Some are gifted with song.
They sing songs of melodious tunes as they fly along.

High amid the skies they fly, without boundaries or restraint.
Soaring mountains of varying heights as they fly away.

Listen to their solos, and duets too,
And the chorus sounds they chirp, as they sing songs for you.

Naomi Slay

Life

Life is a merry, merry-go-round.
It lifts you up then lets you right down.
You feel as though you were out on the town.
But, you've only been on life's merry-go-round.
You find that life is give and take.
You never know till you make a mistake
That what goes up is sure to come down.
Just watch your step on that merry-go-round.
There's always a brass ring that you can catch
Or the brass ring can catch you.
So, be careful on that ride of all the things you do
Life is a merry, merry-go-round.
It never leads you where you can be found.
It never helps you when your luck is down.
You are just out on the merry-go-round.
You get the notion that life is profound.
Wish that you could travel around,
Wherever you go and whatever you found,
You'll always be on life's merry-go-round.

Catherine Shea

Love Brings Comfort

Love comfort us in rain or snow,
It make us feel good whether you go.
Love comfort when a little baby cries,
With love, God light up the blue skies.
Love comfort when there is pain and sorrow,
You will have a better day tomorrow.
Love comfort when rich or poor is in need,
It will help both of them to succeed.
Love comfort's when we need tender care,
It is good to have love to share.
Love comforts when there is a disaster,
God is there before and after.
Love and comfort is all one should know,
All of us should spread love wherever we go.

Deanie M. Carter

Love Invention

"Love" is an ingenious invention
It makes you forget all the stress and tension
Love is so precious, so dear
It will make all you aches and pains disappear
Love is so glorious, so extraordinary
Everything else seems secondary
When the chemistry is just right
You may be wide awake for many a night
You are overwhelmed by lots of joy and satisfaction
By lots of happiness and lots of action
Diamonds may be a girl's best friend
Marriage without a love connection may have an unhappy end
Love is the best thing anyone ever invented
It should definitely be patented
The inventor must have had a brilliant mind
He must have been a genius and one of a kind
Inventing love is superior to diamonds and gold
The inventor must have thrown away the mold
Let's all bless and thank the Love inventor
For surely he is our divine mentor

Henry Friedman

Death

Why must we all die so soon?
Is it true that over a hundred people die by noon?
Why are people shortening their lives by taking drugs?
Also, why does our neighborhood have so many thugs?
Are you really scared to die?
Sometimes I am scared to go outside!!
I'll tell you that I am afraid to die....
and that is not a lie!!!

Gabriel Macias Jr.

Raindrops

From the dark blue clouds it falls;
It may be in the winter, summer or fall,
It dances on the ground as if at a ball.

When it reunites;
It runs with sheer delight,
It may stop birds in flight.

It flows from the highest to the lowest places;
Small puddles form in most cases,
Puddles may overflow its bases.

It enlarges the streams;
The water will reflect the sun or moon beams,
As the puddles and streams form a team.

Ira W. Briggs

Peace

Peace-according to webster's dictionary,
it means, a state of tranquility, quiet, calm
Like a soft running brook, or a verse
or Psalm
It means, an absence of war, a pact
to end a war, and freedom from
worries and fears
No more listening to quarreling
children, or impudent dears
Peace, brings, exemption from private
quarrels, and silence to a weary heart
Oh, or a hidden sanctuary, away
from it all
Miles and miles away, from anyone's call
Lost in a maze of never ending peace
Is it possible, that in our time we will see
A better world for you, and a better tomorrow for me
Somehow I'd hate to think, that
the word peace; will always be
Just a beautiful passant, in Webster's dictionary —-

Germaine A. Tavares

Wagon Ho

As the wagon train rolled on its way
it seemed like it rained most everyday
the rivers they passed were out of there banks
the cowboy was watching as there wheels sank
the horses were straining with each pull
the whip it snapped it seemed so cruel
but soon the wagons were moving again
with two miles to go somewhere 'round the bend
soon they reached a place to camp
they circled the wagon it seemed so cramp
the women they cooked men played their fiddles
couples were dancing in a circle their kids in the middle
soon darkness had fallen on those brave pioneers
the homestead they dreamed of was oh so near
and the hardship they faced along the trail
they knew they would make it they could not fail
no matter what happened there dreams would come
true, because they were great people their name was blue

Darrell Blue

Loneliness

Loneliness such a bitter sweet sorrow;
It seems to drift in like a song longing for a listener.
As if a hand comes through my window and
steals my heart away until somewhere
somehow I forgive it;
Loneliness has the sensation of a triumphant sun-beam
breaking through a sorrowful
cloud;
Only to meet the great sea or land like
a partner longing for its fellow friend.

David Foxley

Dawn

As the sun peeks out from behind the trees.
It seems to smile at the sight it sees.
The drops of dew slowly drip.
Pip, pip.
The morning flowers stretch with a yawn.
Exposing their loveliest beauty in the dawn.
A sweet aroma fills the air.
Alluring effulgent butterflies from everywhere.
The vivid color of the rose.
Its luminescence strong with pose.
The most beautiful of nature is only seen at dawn.
Only a few hours later, it is gone.

Carrie Simpson

Continuity

As dusk encompasses the setting sun
    it shines more beauteously than when on high;
when darkness reigns complete the sun's not done
    but blazes on in antipodal sky.

So live that more your sands of time re fled
    your inner light shines thru more plain;
when shallow man — and even church — think "dead",
    your subtler form lives on a fairer plane.

Think not as fools life comes from form of clay,
    life is of God, and life the clay does fire;
and when with heat it cracks ... you now can play
    thru fresher fields and to new goals aspire.

More fast, more clear, is played the melody
    within the pulsing realms of space and time;
man's strings vibrate with greater harmony
    more near his rise to orchestra divine.

Again sun lights and warms this half of earth,
    again your star will seek this darkened shore,
with vows to brighter shine you'll come thru birth;
    to live a perfect life, you'll try once more.

Benson Boss

Autumn Flowers

The leaf that fell was a bright red
It fluttered down past my head,

Landed down by my feet
By the flowers that smelled so sweet.

The tree before was a bright green,
The most amazing thing I've seen.

To see it change day by day.
From green to yellow as golden hay.

The mountain are a colored blaze,
That stay bright through the autumn days.

Emily Radwich

Alive

Death walked by as I stood and watched
It shook its ugly finger at me
And rushed right on by

I felt its eeriness
I saw its ugliness, smelt its destroying ways
I closed my door and forgot

Later I awoke to a feeling
I felt an emptiness
I needed the past
Something of the future ended

I felt my brother's hand on my shoulder
I saw him smile
I heard him whisper, "I'm alright"

I walked by his casket
I let my right hand move along its side
The tears flowed

That day it seemed he had died
But, death, you lied
Someone you loved NEVER dies

Death you're sly.
Jeannie Pierre

Life

Life, one day I told to myself
It should be the happiest thing on earth
Life should be always a summer day
But life is the abandoned human being.

Life is hungry on an empty stomach
It is desolation of a cry in the street
Life is heavy rain or dried season
But life is war or peace.

Life is the rich or the poor
It is a politician or a humble man
Life is the rotten law or the human prayer
But life is also you and me.

Life is a selfish human heart
It is thunder, cloud or ocean wave
Life is the pretty sunset
But life is also my love for you.

Gladys Ortiz

Untitled

There is a beast feasting on my death.
It slurps and nips at my gut.
My vain attempts to escape the clutches of it's claws
Leave me with a profound disinterest,
Helpless and empty.

In the dark soul's distance, the nightingale sings of rest.

I am wrenched by the mechanics of a life that lies
Between my being and its true home.

I long to penetrate that blinding star
That imitates light;
To abandon all hope
So that God may move within.

Hannah Robinson

A Stranger From Afar

Nature is wonderful
It spreads its beauty throughout the world

From the ice blue color of the sky, to the majestic flavors of fall

Nature is all around us
Its mystery and wonder are within you

From your cascading locks of silken hair, to the flowing curves of
   your face

Spreading through you is the wonder of nature,
   the beauty of the sky,
     the wonderment of the earth

To be able to view such a creation, is to be filled with awe

Your soft and pristine nature
   makes you untouchable to a simple, humble man

You have an incredible power
   to awe struck any person

An innocent man can only sit in the shadows,
   and watch nature pass him by

But every once in awhile,
   he'll get the courage
     to say hello, and then...life will go on
James Karom Jr.

Confusion

Confusion can never grow old,
It stays deep inside like a story untold,
Your mind keeps on spinning but the pieces aren't fitting.
Like the poet who's writing but his poem stays unwritten.
You dig deep to find what is it you seek,
But the deeper you dig the more you find out you are weak,
If our mind could bear us a sweet or sour fruit,
We could harvest and eat it, maybe then we'd find truth!
On the outside we're happy and show a face that will glow.
Yet on the inside we're burning, and there's a pain they'll
never know.

We seek advice from great men, and they give us their best,
But what of their advice when at night you can't rest,
There are so many questions we ask of ourselves,
But the answers are hidden in a cupboard that's locked on
the shelves.
So what is peace of mind, if our lives we can't bind?
And where do we find it, in front or behind?
Arthur G. Bredin

It Takes A Whole Village, To Raise A Child

No one should be alone, left to grow wild.
It takes a whole village to raise a child
That means all of us, to light the way
Pick them up when they fall, hear what they say
Encourage them to strive, even help with their math
Be their guiding star, help them stay on the path
No one's born hard, mean, or just bad
Cause it that's what you believe then we've lost what we had
Maybe long ago, there was no one there for you
Reach down in your heart, see what I say is true
No one should be alone, left to grow wild
It takes a whole village to raise a child
Kids were never meant to grow up all alone
Unfortunately many grow, start to flower yet
No one is there to behold the bloom.

Jocelyn Renee Creech

Innocent Heart

I saw a sight.
It was happy and clear.
It made me feel a peacefulness
   never felt before.
I heard its soul whispering into my ear
I saw, too, that the sight was sweet, tender,
   Charming and Young. It's dazzle
     gave an immense happiness
      in my inner most.
   Then I felt in fondle.
Its dazzle reflected a dream
   translucent, pure and full
     of love. I still remember
      that sight of passion and faithfulness.
Its friendly, beautiful,
   world conquered my own.
    I saw, a honest, fleeing
     sight, a free wondering
      One. It was the image
       of an innocent heart...

   Angel Sanchez

Adventure On Green Street

I have broken the ice, that lays arctic thick,
It was in the basement of the upside-down building,
If I can push through, I will touch the sky.

Clouds will appear on the never-bleak horizon,
Where stepping stones play like rain chimes,
In streams, where consciousness flows.

Where constellations fuse with the sun,
One for every day, even the apple tree,
Forbidden fruit, making God's labor of pies.

Answers are love, to the mind's questing heart,
Lullabies for tired babes, where fast droop the eyelids,
Night nannies, for nightmares, in night's looking glass.

Hunger and thirst, the flowers of righteousness are pure and free,
Lamenting illusion, as love in perfection flows forward,
Old age and death, the welfare of happiness is comfort and joy.

   Harold Schultz

"True"

Our love was like a flower.
   It was raining. It was a shower.
A shower of love, that is what our
love was.
   And it ended, just because.
Its like a flower, because it finally died.
   But the love I still have for you, I hide.
The love for you is there.
But your life you did not share
You did not share it with me.
I just couldn't make you see.
I wish I could get over you.
But I can't, because its true.
True as the day I meet you.
True as the wind blowing on the sea.
True our love was meant to be.
But true that together we'll never be.

   Celestia Graham

Even in the Dead of Winter

Even in the midst of summer
   It would be a cold and dreary day,
If I had to do without you, Darling
   If you had to go away.

O, I know that life must have its partings
   And closest hearts do separate.
And, yet your absence, but for God,
   My heart and soul would devastate.

And so I pray, if God be willing,
   For many days, yea, many a year,
Before the time of parting comes
   That I may have you ever near.

For even in a cruel world
   Your love and kindness still abound,
And even in the dead of winter
   It seems so warm when you're around.

   Jerry Church

You Are So Beautiful To Me

Beauty is not just a pretty face.
It's a quality from within that somehow fills an empty space or
otherwise lonely place from deep within.
It's a treasure sometimes called memories you can't buy or sell.
Something you can't always see or touch.
An unseemingly quality you possess that is loved so very much.
It's not one reflection in a mirror but a look into or through
another's eyes.
Beauty had endless individual meaning and sometimes wears a
disguise.
Children have it all the time, something they're not aware of.
It's innocence and honesty and unconditional trust.
Beauty is a way of looking back with love.
You see, it may be all of the above.
But certainly and most important to me,
It's how you make another feel, "Loved."
"You" are so beautiful to me.

   JoAnn Geoghegan

"The Hole, A Blessing In Disguise"

The hole is a blessing in disguise, the day it will make you realize,
It's all Gods will from up above, sent with all of his love,
never doubt, instead, in happiness just shout,
shout out so loud, that you make God proud,
don't despair, because you don't think it's fair,
but remember, God is always there, because He really does care,
Jesus will lead you through the trail of death,
just take a deep breath.
Because Jesus is coming to your rescue,
from the heavens that he made so blue,
so have faith and pray, that's when you'll have your day,
of eternal life at hand, because God is in total demand,
our God the Alpha, Omega, Supreme Ruler of all,
take a minute and hear His call,
because this is the hole, a blessing in disguise.
After reading this, it will make you realize,
it's all God's will from up above.

   Dennis J. Reed

I'll Bough Out

When I studied the roots of my family tree,
What I found really made me wince.
The chances those branches took have me,
Way out on a limb ever since.

   Kathleen Gibson

The Dependable Friend

A rainbow appears every time the rain falls.
Its beauty stretching across the evening sky.
Despite its beauty there is something missing,
It looks so lonesome all day until nigh.

It happened upon me one quiet rainy day,
That I myself was becoming lonesome and gray.
As the day ended the rainbow appeared,
This depressing scene led my thoughts astray.

So I sat thinking of the rainbow,
And how dependable it would show.
Why was I so lonesome and dreary,
When it's the same God we both know?

Jeremy Aragon

Something's missing... could there be a leak

Some small escape hole into darkness
It's dying... could something be wrong
Even a flower can get too much water
Dripping... from the faucet of my heart I feel it weakening
Weakening to the point of non-existence
Love never dies... It just fades away like the note at the end of a
wordless tune
Perhaps the line between love and hate is more than just fine
maybe it perforated... so one can leak into the other
slowly eliminating one or the other
creating something mush less equal, less tangible, less there
until finally pain and happiness no longer matter
and the void can't ever be filled again.
So I step back and let you see what you would see... and hope all is
not lost.

Carmelina D. Marin

Fear

There's a word called fear we need to know
its forever constant as we grow
we learn to fear at an early age
it starts in cribs known as the cage
we fear the things we do not know
as we grow that fact remains so
fear keeps us in our mothers arms
where in all the world the fears not strong
fear of falling won't let us walk
fear of words won't let us talk
and when we do its at a slow pace
for fear of losing won't let us race
when fear takes over all hope is gone
for when you fear nothing carries on
if you fear fear put fear on a shelf
cause there's nothing to fear but fear itself

Chikeisha Taliaferro

Gettysburg

Great-Grandfather,
   What spot of ground here nourished by thy blood?

Your form, your face I never knew
   Yet cells of you, in me, now wonder o'er this place.

How many men and boys your freedom gift has and yet will embrace?

A severed nation stitched cruelly by your gift of life.

And many yet pass by, who also ignorant of your special grace
   Gratefully-stop
   Pray,
And bless this hallowed place.

William Saladin

My Easter Wish for You

In case you've forgotten what Easter's about
It's Jesus the Saviour, of that there's no doubt.

Eternal life is His offer to give
Accept and believe that He does still live.

Into your heart He asks to come
Setting you apart just for His Son.

Our life here on earth so very short
But by His death, good news to report.

There's a life in heaven with family galore
If only we accept Jesus as our Lord.

Please make up your mind, don't be left behind
A decision is due, He's calling you!

Your sins He'll forgive by His grace alone
Eternal life to give, can't make it on your own.

Whatever role in life I've had that you see
It's not just this life that I want you sharing with me.

A love so full of sacrifice that you find so rare
I beg of you to listen and BE THERE!!!

Berlinda C. Ogas

Time

When we're together
It's like being in a city of gold,
The weather is always for the best
And the time with thee is to be told.
Never want to rest for time does fly
And the moments are always of riches.
I hate to leave your presence for inside I cry
The time away from you must have been created by witches.

To be from your soul
Is like being in a storm of doom.
The weather seems to be as black as coal
And the day is ever-lasting gloom.
The chills I shall reel
Shall compare nothing
To the loneliness I will feel
To death I would dare,
To collect a few more seconds with you.

Harold Guidry

Jennifer

Her heart is not like yours or mine,
it's like the grape without a vine.
Her fingers are clubbed and lips blue.
But she tries so hard to be like you.
She laughs, she loves, she tries to play,
But her struggle for life is everyday.

She has so much courage in her heart,
Constantly hoping for a new start.
Hoping someday for that final repair,
Knowing sometimes life isn't fair.

She sees the beauty in everything,
I wish I had that song to sing,
But when she looks at me and smiles,
I know everything is alright....for awhile.

Geri Lyn Jones

The Pathway Of You

My ears can't stop ringing your voice,
It's more than just a memory of us.
Just knowing that I will always
love you, tears my heart with fear.
Like rose peddles dancing till
the end of time.
That's how long I'll wait for you.
Forever.
In time I'll try to forget the
love I hold for you.
But will always be hoping to
see you walk toward me once again.
My heart can feel the loneliness
and my eyes can feel the tears.
But if wishes do come true,
in the end, I'll be with you....

Holly Ellis

Watching From Above

It swallows itself in a life of production.
It's motive being money, evils greatest seduction.

Forgetting to cry for the strength of it's mother
It continues to layer the pain it must suffer.

It ignores our voices, our tugs at it's heart
It would rather buy minds and tear souls apart.

We're calling you America.
You hold the world by a thread.
Stop thinking of yourselves
And live for each other instead.

We only want to help you
By giving eyes to see
The world needs a change.
We're here to set it free.

Jennifer Lento

The Gift

I want to give you a gift, my friend; but its not of silver or gold..
Its not of satin, silk, or lace and it can't be bought or sold.
It isn't dressed in glittered wrap and there's no expensive scent
To try to disguise what's there inside or how much one has spent.
It doesn't come in a fancy box tied up with bows and ribbon.
There are no strings that bind this gift, because its freely given.
Its not of chocolate or confection and it will not melt in heat,
But enjoy it as a "spice of life"...the rewards are just as sweet.
It will not wilt and fade away like a single yellow rose;
Yet it strengthens as the roots are set and everyday it grows.
It has no certain form or shape...it can't be caught or held.
It can't be touched by flesh of hand; yet is something truly felt.
It can't be put out on display like a book of thought or rhyme
Or a trophy set upon a shelf to be viewed from time to time.
For its made of things not seen with sight
Like trust...respect...and love...
A true and lasting friendship
Is this gift I'm speaking of.

Carolyn J. Barnes

In Search for the Primrose Path

The subtle mind, that of man
In futile efforts to command
The life he lives, that is at hand
He strives to learn to no avail
The price he must pay to find the trail
The path is certain, the way unsure, till the
knock at devils door
Now the path has come to an end
For he has failed, making no amends

Brian Oyague

Untitled

There is a lock latched onto my heart
with only one key to spare.
The key has always been in your hands
you just never knew it was there!

Monica Smith

Imagination

There is a place, where I can go, to get away from people;
It's not underground or in the ocean or upon the highest
steeple;
But a simple place in my mind;
It's called an imagination;
I can go here, when I'm behind;
And start an investigation.

I am Sherlock and you are Watson;
And we're tracking down a thief;
Or I can be a mean old shark;
And smash a coral reef.

But then my teacher will wake me;
And say that I was drifting;
But between you and me;
Tomorrow I'll be;
A body builder lifting!

Casey J. Kennedy

Alone in the Crowd

Can't you see
It's only me
Alone in this great big world.
A little company
Would cheer me
And your smile would warm me.
So cold is this world.
But I don't want to be alone in the crowd like so many
others.
They could always "make talk" with their mothers.
But with me that could never be
Because I'm alone in the crowd.

You I like
Remind me of a kite.
Free as the wind that blows over
And sweet as the wind under.
So fly away to the sky.
Don't worry about me
I'm always alone and will always be.

J. J. Louis

The Fool

See him walking down the street,
It's raining hard, upon his feet.
His head, bowed sad and low,
As he wonders, with no where to go.
For who is he, but a broken man,
Who once loved, and no longer can.
People stop and look, with long hard stares,
But, no one ever-really cares.
For a man with no love, has no respect,
He is lost and alone, with nothing except,
His mourning, and his regret.
Of a love well lost, from neglect.
Life was hard, and taught him well,
He carries his cross, can't you tell?
Love is sweet, and the world so cruel,
Especially for ones, like the fool.

Joel Galindo

"Never"

The feeling in my body can't described,
It's something great and makes me feel alive.
  When I'm with you my heart is filled with joy,
You show your love and don't treat me like a toy.
  You say we'll be together forever and to say
Goodbye I don't think so never.
  I wanna be with you always.
Your passionate kiss gives me shivers,
A kiss on the neck gives me quivers,
Your touch gives me chills down my spine
then you slowly whisper "your mine".
  I want to be with you forever
  So baby please don't leave me
  NEVER
  Jane Obremski

Gnome

It's very late, late in the night
It's them I hear am I all right?

In the covers I turn around
Open my eyes not to be found

I fall asleep and drift away
Away from home and there I play

They're playing tricks that's what they do
I'll see them soon and hear them too

Through the forest and in the trees
I see them there down on my knees

I saw their cap and it was red
I'll see no more cause I am dead

They dug my grave I'll never roam
Or see no more a gnome or home...
  Charlotte Siracusa

Invisible Prison

This prison that I'm locked within they'll never understand;
Its walls are made of hatred, reinforced by fellow man,
And though I walk beside you now, pretending to be free,
I'm locked within my suffering, and searching for the key.

The loneliness I've felt at times seemed more than I could bear,
Wishing to share feelings with someone who'd really care,
Wanting to be honest with the world and not retreat,
Yet not knowing what reactions to expect from those I meet.

My emotions can't be justified as though there was a cause;
They are as much a part of me as with any one who loves.
To keep them locked within my heart, and hide them from full view
Creates a wall between us all that only few break through.

They are right that a disease has made this evil come about,
But the evil is not what they think, of that there is no doubt.
For the evil is not what I am, but what they say and do,
The disease's name is prejudice, it destroys both me and you.

Why can't they just comprehend, there isn't any reason they must force
me to defend. If they'll accept I'll cause no harm, they'll find
  that in
the end, there isn't any reason why we all just can't be friends. So
open up your mind, I'll show you how we can begin; set me free and
you will see that I can be your friend.
  Charles R. Balgenorth

The Haunted House

And though the haunted house is growing old,
its walls still hold a magic tale,
The romance, hope and joy that once it knew,
brought bliss and warmth to hearts that beat as one
and every room and every stair within
held whispered secrets, touches, glances, memories and more,
Passions that were shared behind the door.

And time encompassed this,
for time had seen it all before
but never quite so beautiful as this,
the haunted house now creaking in the wind,
Deserted, empty, seemingly alone.

But stay awhile and listen well
for this abode remembers,
and ghosts who dwell here
may have stories yet to tell.
  John L. Eaglesham

Tall Tales And Bold Faced Lies

Sit down and I'll tell you tall tales and bold faced lies.
I've been there, seen it, done it don't look at me with surprise!
Give me enough time and you'll hear what you want to hear.
I'm not one to tell too many facts, and that's the truth, dear.
The mountains I've climbed, might be just mole hills.
And the big falls that I've taken could be small spills.
Let me tell you about the one that got away just yesterday.
That's just the way I tell 'em, what more can I say.
How 'bout stories of my lost youth full of vim and vigor.
I'm not telling lies, I just tend to remember bigger.
I'll tell you of lost loves, life experiences, and places I've been.
Stories go on and on, it's hard to know where they start and begin.
I've got all the answers, the whats, whens, wheres, and whys.
Sit down and I'll tell you tall tales and bold faced lies.
  David E. Rollins

Painless Day

Dear Lord, thank you for all that
I've gained

Thank you more for this day without
pain

My body feels so light
and so free

It's been so long,
since I felt
like me

I feel so young I can stretch and bend
it feels like my body is on the mend

The headaches have all gone away
oh the joy of this painless day

I can lift my arms to give you praise
it's been so long since they've been raised

My legs feel strong I didn't realize I was so tall
Can't seem to remember when I wasn't afraid to fall.

And I've eaten today and my stomach isn't sour
Did I hear you correctly Lord?

It's only been one hour!!!
  Jessie Colon

When I Grow Up

I don't know what to do now!
I've got seven kinds and no husband,
And I'm bored out of my mind.
I miss my life, the old one,
   The one I left behind.
I don't know what to do now!
An abundance of bills, yet a scarcity of money.
I have too many to support!
And they always cry and scream
   When I fall a little short.
I don't know what to do now!
My life is coming to an end
Before it's even started.
And I didn't realize, until now,
   From all hope I have parted.
I don't know what to do now!
Can't be reborn?
...Be a little girl and say...
"When I grow up I want to be..."
... And then turn out that way.

   Cristie Grissmer

To Mom

There's a story from my childhood you've never heard before;
I've kept it deep within my heart, someday to restore...

There was a time before we "met" that you know nothing of;
When God and I walked hand in hand, as He taught me to love.

He led me to a mountain top; we watched life pass before—
He held me once more in His arms as we walked through life's door.

He smiled gently as He said, "My Child, our moments now are few—
A woman now will give you life, I give the choice to you."

I looked at Him with tear-filled eyes and spoke with One so dear,
"Someone with the kind of love that you have shown me here.

Strong, yet tender, arms as Yours to guide me day by day;
She'll remind me of Your endless love...my choice is this", I prayed.

I awoke in new surroundings, but the love I'd known was there;
I looked up at you, Mother, and I knew He'd heard my prayer.

The eyes of God's own angels were shining from that face—
that smile was as my Father's, with a touch of God's own grace.

And to this day, Dear Mother, I pray to God above...
and thank Him for that special gift—
my answered prayer, your love.

   Jeanne L. Murphy

Oh, Foolish Man

Oh, foolish man
I've laid out my plan
My promises to Abraham I'll keep
The blessings through Isaac will seep
Though you've been scattered about
You will be called home with a shout
Listen to He that was sent
Jesus words are free and won't cost a cent

Oh, foolish man
Walk with me everyday that you can
For I breathed eternal life into that day
Eternal life you must stay
Trouble times lays ahead
Please don't be mislead
He's coming to take you to the kingdom you see
To worship me with glee
Those who are left
Will know the Son's power is deft
To the heavens they will scream
Tears will flow like a stream

   Clarence Edwards

Wait For Me!

The year has been long since you went away!
I've searched the corners of my mind trying to find you there.
I call your name- and look behind the shadows of yesterday.
Where ever it is that you have gone- let me join you there.
I hear your voice echoing through the halls of time-
In the darkness I seem to see your outstretched hand.
The days and weeks go by without reason or rhyme.
I am alone in a dark and dreary land.
Oh! how I long to see your dear face again,
Long to walk through fields and forests again with you.
My heart would never be so lonely then.
Oh! please wait till I can come and be with you.

   Bethel E. Capron

Company

Last house to water
Jo and Jack in Florida
Comforted in warmth these winter months
I am cold, tired
It's been an endless workday

In the kitchen
Loved ones enfold me
Their presence is everywhere

Daily voices
"Oh, you must have something to eat!"
"How's business?"

Holiday rhythms
Three generations each pursuing their own agenda
Food, gifts, football
What have you been doing lately?

I water today's plants
While yesterday's events swirl about me
So real, I must blink
The house devoid of visible bodies and sound
Is tangibly, comfortingly alive in spirit

   Betsy Lytle

Lady Libra

Of worldly things, like gold and silver rings, that have not life or
joy to bring.
Existing is a loving Mother, in this world that God alone can suffer.
A multitude, of children I seek, large or small, strong or weak.
The time is now, that I declare war on the seed of Satan and His snare
Of the hell that His seed has sown, stealing Our children, to be His own.
Let us get the hell out of them, before they are consumed by Him.
Now is the time, Amen.
There is no time or place, equal to Our Father's Grace.
I ask my God, "Where do I begin, the children to gather in?"
Especially, the ones who have lost their way.
Tell me not tomorrow, but today.
Hear me children, calling you?
The Lord God, He is calling too.

   Evalee Gray Gibson

"A Price To Pay"

In this world of joy and pain
   We're constantly searching, searching to gain

We search for freedom, we search for love
   We search for happiness a step above

The sky's the limit, or so we're told
   We are constantly searching to find the gold

Perfection and power, glitter and fame
   How much do we lose to win the game?.

   Thomas J. Sboto

Christmas In Stalag II

What good could I possibly say about that first Stalag II Christmas Day?
It was a day I'll never forget; yet one I'd not like to repeat.

We'd saved and stolen materials each day in our desperate plan for a play
To lift the spirits of fellow habitants, lonely, cold, sad in that camp.
If only for a single day!

Where stage wood came from, who knew; frozen hands had nimble fingers
that flew. Ever present was fear in our hearts, we'd be stopped, punished, and apart.

Still, with incentives, hearts of hope, to fulfill wishes on that wintry slope
for a Christmas celebration, barring none, in a place run by the evil Hun.
If only for a single day!

Christmas morn arrived at last, with homemade Christmas pudding as a repast.
Plays performed each hour on the hour; Christmas songs filling the cold air,

By prisoners, recalling home, family times, forgetting pain behind enemy lines.
Depressed men raised voices and smiled, a first time, in respect for the child.
If only for a single day!

Much to our unimagined surprise, Hun visitors made us all fearfully rise.
With a wave of hand to continue, down sat the Commander, men in tow,

Enthusiastically, grins on faces, took part, clapping in all the right places.
We were as one, enemy and prisoners, that day, celebrating our Christ's birthday.
If only for a single day!

Rose M. Kuter

The Abuse of Blackness

The color black, or blackness, has been greatly misused and abused
down the ages in every sector of life. Scientists, economists,
religious leaders, politicians and lawyers are among many that have
referred to blackness as bad, evil, unfavorable, helpless, diseased,
poor, mention just a few.

Here are some of the stark truths to this claim:

In naming one of the worst practices in a given economy, the Economist
said "black market". This "market" can be defined as an illegal
practice of selling goods at unreasonable prices. Would this imply
that black people are unreasonable? Why name it a "black market"?

When the religious leaders met, it was agreed upon to paint the devil
black and Jesus white. Nowhere in the Bible does God say that "the
devil is black and Jesus was white". Little wonder that Europe was
once the "father of light" and, by implication, Africa the "cradle of
everything evil".

In a family, the basic form of society, a person who is regarded as
unrespectable or degenerate is called a "black sheep". Why not a lost
sheep, but a "black" sheep?

Consider the field of employment. A person who is denied employment
is placed on a "black list". Why not call it a denial employment or
not-worthy list, but a "black" list?

To indicate that one has something unfavorable in one's record,
lawyers use the term "black mark". Why not a red mark? When
unexpectedly lights go out, it is explained as a "black out". Why
not lights out? Does it always have to be black-something?

In light of the views propounded above, it should not cause any ado
when an individual prefers to be called an "Africa American" rather
than "black" American. Notwithstanding, this should not suggest
that one is not proud of being "black." It is only the misuse and
indeed abuse of the name that bothers us.

Michael Kiyaga

Tears

We made love and she wept
I asked her love why do you cry
She said some secrets are best kept
I said dear love please tell me why

She placed her body in my arms
I felt her heart beat strong
I tried to soothe her with my charms
She sighed there's nothing wrong

I kissed her face and held her tight
She moaned so soft and sweet
We made good love all through the night
Yet still her eyes did weep

We made love and she wept
My heart cried out to know
And after love she dreamed and slept
Her face a smile did show

As time passed I watched her face
The secret it had kept
And as I watched it fell in place
Why during love she wept

Donnie Williams

She's Gone

She's gone, she's gone.
I am. I am alone now.
Why do they sing songs?
Don't they know how,
how dark it all is now?

Love's gone, love's gone.
No sad or happy feelings,
just dark instead of dawns.
No strength for reeling,
when everything, she's stealing.

Life's gone, life's gone.
Six feet tall, all below now.
Under the lawns, the lawns
that she walks while she avows,
avows her love for that one gone now.

Jason C. Clark

The Sounds of Home

As I lie in bed;
I can hear,
All the sounds of home;
That are so dear.

I can hear beside me;
My husband of eight years,
Who makes me feel so secure;
And evaporates all my fears.

In the room across me;
I hear a whimper, not quite a cry,
And in yet another room;
I hear a peaceful, calming sigh.

Down the hall I hear my oldest son;
Breathing ever so slight,
Dreaming many wonderful dreams;
All through the night.

My second born is the last to hear;
Laughing quietly in her sleep,
And now I can rest peacefully;
For all my sounds are now complete.

Doraine Stines

When Memories Were Born

Remember me-
I am your memory
to stay-until we meet
again. That I am sure of!
No ill can cloud these precious
times together, when memories
   were born.
Give thanks to some of life's
great treasures, to share, to feel
innermost thoughts, when
beauty reveals itself to us
in harmony and goodness
especially, when we are
"Together!"

Elisa H. Lucksinger

Memories

In my Rocking Chair
I can go slow or fast
I can go anywhere
Memories are made to last

I love to travel
North, South, East, or West
Worlds wonders to unravel
Don't know which I love best

It might be Oregon
Or off to see the Falls
A quick look and then be gone
Memories to recall

Oh, I am getting bold
To the North I shall see
Wonders to behold
What is to be will be

The ground covered with snow
What a beautiful sight
I've rocked to and fro
I am tired so Good Night

Doris L. Kearton

"When I Look Into Your Eyes"

When I look into your eyes,
I can see some hope ahead;
It's the light that shines in you,
That helps dry the tears I've shed.

Even though I am hurting,
And feeling nothings right;
Just know that I love you,
And that love will be our light.

When I look into your eyes,
I can see relief from my pain;
I see the love you have to offer,
I see the sun shine through the rain.

When I look into your eyes,
I know that you'll be there.
When I look into your eyes,
I know you'll always care.
Let me look into your eyes.

Charlie Gobeille

Tunnel of Question

So many days spent traveling down this dark, lonely tunnel - no light in which to guide,
This journey that continues on - waiting for a sign - an end that I may find
Familiar voice I thought I heard-yet it seems so far away.
As I move closer, his voice I hear once more as he tells me to come near,
Trying to move, I long to feel the warmth of his breath upon my skin-frozen by fear.
Questioning the direction I may seek an end - an end to this tunnel in which I live,
He holds a lantern so I may see - he allows me light - however freedom he cannot give.
A grip of my hand, pulling me in - I see his face so clear - that face I know so well,
Blue eyes that pierce into mine-screaming to be freed-strength that holds me still.
Awareness sets in - I was so blind for he is also prisoner within this tunnel.
Scared to move any closer to the end - he stands beside me-intrigued to what we may discover.
Suspended in time-I whisper his name "follow me - trust me - we'll find it together."
Determined to conquer this maze, we must accept what fate has planned,
Shall we walk out as one, we may separate once found - nevertheless - I will always hold your hand.

Diane Marie Steele

I Have...

I have borne the beginnings of mankind and sown the path of existence.
I have raised Pharaohs, Princes, Kings and Queens and advised them to greatness.
I have commanded armies and armadas and had continents discovered in my name.

I have bridged many worlds together and signed my blood in their treaties.
I have braved the worst that nature has given and tamed the wildest of frontiers.
I have spoken my words of wisdom and been seen as a founder and prophet of what was to come.

I have discovered the causes of diseases and fought to find the cures.
I have beautified the world with my talent in the arts and enlightened
the people with my acts of kindness.
I have started revolutions so that all could have freedoms and cried
at the graves of our fallen heroes.

These are my accomplishments set forth without want of praise or acceptance.
They are what bind me to my sisters to the past and my daughters of the future.
This is a part of what I have been, am, and will be,
Forever-more.

Dameron C. Moch

The Rose

The rose bud emerged as the bombs did explode, so was the start of a Rose;
as the World War's door slowly came to a close,
all in a day of a Rose.

Then the Rose petals blushed to a deep shade of red, when the love of
   her life came along;
from a far away land, there to ask for her hand,
like the tune of a nightingale's song.

Soon the Rose moved away with a bud of her own
to a new garden, Red, White and Blue;
to the land of her love, blessed of God from above
with more buds she could glamorously shew.

The Rose prospered and grew as the days came and went
with each day blessed by God's loving hands:
Some of her bud's took, on a new kind of look,
ornamented with little gold bands.

There were some gray days in the garden so fair, as a Mother Rose far away past;
yet God's grace it prevails, His love never fails,
two more "Roses" God planted steadfast.

More happiness and dreams lay ahead on life's road; so goes the path of a Rose:
For the pathway of God, is the pathway she chose,
so blessed is the life of this Rose.

Anita M. Downs

Celestial Bodies

Oh how radiant you are
Miss Moon,
staring back at me
shining unabashedly
with absolutely no concern
that the Sun is still in his place.

Innocent to the idea
that it is perhaps a little risque
and maybe even inappropriate
for one of your age to act this way.

You are like an overeager lover
who cannot wait to show herself
so she rushes in
only to wait
for the darkness
to surround her
making her
even more
beautiful.

Justine McClimon

My Momma Said

My momma said,
to walk like a lady.
talk like a lady,
and act like a lady.

To always look good,
Always smell good.
Always feel good,
And always be good.

To walk straight and tall,
Never slumped over.
Always speak proper,
Never uneducated.

I love my momma,
I honor what she says.
And I will continue to do,
What my momma said.

Joi K. Burgin

Dragons

Loneliness
a silent samurai.
Sneaks up behind me
a willing assassin.
He lays his icy hands upon me.
a chill runs up my spine.
I can see only his reflection
he raises his sword high.
And I cower as he brings it down
the single blade slashes
Through me, almost as
if it were the tooth of
a Dragon.

Brooke Shewmaker

The Beauty Of Love

The beauty of love,
is so exquisite,
It brings out the joy,
in every soul.
It's a wonderful gift,
to be given and see,
and it's a gift,
that never gets old.

Colleen Ann Jaros

Rhyme of the Ancient Writer

Warm autumn afternoon
A child content at play,
Building sand castles
To pass the time.

Her father calls,
"Come, go with me
New wonders await,
Trust your hand to mine."

Castles forgotten,
Toys cast aside,
She runs to him
Eager to go.

Content, I wait my father's call,
With fragile words
I build sand castles
Of my own.

Dawn Clutter

The Winding Road Of Life

A baby's toddling steps go on
A child's laughter, in fun
A first day of school
Hopping in the swimming pool

I learned my ABC's today
Gosh I did better than Ray
Arithmetic is hard to do
I can take away, can you?

High School and Latin to learn
My college degree to earn
Rockets rumble skyward fast
Army fellows marching past

My girls hug and wave goodbye
Leave for training, my mothers sigh
A trip thru hell and strife
A freedom fight for life

Cheers greet us, as we land
Laughters, tears, a helping hand
Hugs and kisses from my wife
On this winding road of life

Jewel Haehnel

"Coming Home"

As I sail the sea, sitting out here on
a cold and lonely night.

I look out over the moon lit sky,
As a shooting star passes by.

Wishing to be near you so beautiful
as you.

I see your eyes in the sparkling stars
high in the heavens.

The glow of your hair off the
shimmering sea.

Your aura in the moon light, brightening
my way home,

To where you are tonight and always
be.....

Jerry W. Hartzler

The Things That Might Have Been

I saw him in the restaurant
A dear old friend was he
I never did quite understand
Just what he thought of me

But here he was, my handsome friend,
Momentarily our eyes met.....
On seeing him my pulse quickened
My heart did not forget

He gave my hand a gentle squeeze
I melted at his touch
It's funny that I never knew
That I had cared this much

We exchanged the usual pleasantries
And then we said good-bye
And as he disappeared from view
I sadly breathed a sigh

I wish I hadn't seen him again
(My big, but gentle friend)
I think I'll always wonder now
The things that might have been.

Ginny Kopf

To Dream

On a sailboat out to sea
A dream of a sailor me to be
Land and places that I would see
If it were to be

A cool breeze blowing the sails
Billowing forth a ship gliding through
The froth

Harbour lites left behind glowing
Dimmer and loosing there shine
What land will I make mine to be
As my ship glide through the sea

What ever the future will be
There is so much to see
For in a dream it is not what I am
But what I can be

Edward David

Dreams

I dreamed a dream last night -
A dream of love and peace.
I dreamed that you were mine again,
That our love would never cease.

I dreamed that dream of you again -
That dream where we were young.
We were so happy then
Before life snapped its ugly tongue.

In my dream, there was no one,
No one to tell us we were wrong.
Before I knew what to do,
I noticed you were gone.

I cried myself to sleep last night
As I saw the sun's first beams.
I knew that I had to sleep -
All that's left of you is dreams.

Jill Harris

A Farmer

A farmer, an environmentalist
A farmer, a horticulturist
A farmer, a computer operator
A farmer, a mechanic
A farmer, a veterinarian
A farmer, a chemist
A farmer, strong-minded
A farmer, physically strong
A farmer is an honest,
sincere, loving, and caring
human being.

John Frederick

The Game

Life is just a game,
A game that we must play.
And some of us will make it,
While others pray for another day.

There will always be the winners,
While the rest will all take last.
And no one seems to notice,
That love never seems to last.

For some the game is never fair,
But everyone must play.
And some will always find,
That hurt never goes away.

So, while people keep on playing,
Even though they may get lost.
There still must be the few,
Who will dare to pay the cost!!!

Alicia Powell

Afterthoughts

The thunder of the guns is still.
A gentle hush falls o'er the hills.
The scattered dead lie on the fields,
Victims of those whose power wields
The force to send our sons to fight,
For matters not concerned with right-
But only an image of greater might.
While we pay tribute to our honored dead.
Let us not forget the greed for wealth,
The lust for power
That look them from us
In their finest hour.

John B. Rogers

Island

The island grows dark against
a hot sky.
The sea is now calm, as the earth
heaves a sigh.

It floats on the heart of the blue
world below,
and the dusk grows still as the
beat gets slow.

One cannot imagine for what this
is worth,
this one passing link between
heaven and earth...

Ashley Mastio

Discrepancy in Nature's Plan

The funeral that kindles a
a joyous spirit in all mankind
is the festival of dying leaves
In awe eve view their
shimmering brilliance of
Red and gold
As each leaf flutters to eternity
When the day grow cold.

So unlike man -
also a product of
nature's plan -
Who often die alone
in murky light and
in wretched pain...

Dorothy A. Grant

Too Young to Die

A bright sun a blue sky
a life too perfect to live.

When the happiness is gone
comes a life hard to live.

Knowing that tomorrow could
be my last day.

I think about
my past and my future.

I realize why me
what did I do wrong.

My life just began
now my life
is at its end.

A dark sun a gray sky
A life too hard to live.

My life is limited to a bed
and a closed in room.

All my thinking tells me that
I'm too young to die.

Amie Martinez

Smitten

I turned to see you look my way.
A look of wonder crossed my face.
Before I knew just what to say,
There stood an archer in your place.
I felt the arrow from the start.
The shot you made was a kiss to blow,
Opened up my aching heart,
Let the love I held there flow.
I have waited here for only you.
The pain I feel, you know.
Cupids arrow has run me through.
In your hand you hold the bow.

Andrew B. Honaker

Untitled

My mind lets go a thousand ways
Thinking of you; still in a daze
And yet recall the very hour
I fell upon this beautiful flower
The wind comes briskly up this way
The leaves are falling, my flower's gone away
So I await a new season, another year
Hoping the sun and my flower will reappear

Thomas L. Starace

Burial In Rwanda July 31, 1994

It was a grim harvest
a planting incomprehensible
roots to earth
limbs reaching to eternity
a child's hand outstretched
to a stone
an abyss decorated
with the fabric of lives
calico...crimson...denim...blue
a null and void that could not answer
the question in death-glazed eyes.
And this field's furrow—
a cleft landscape beyond despair.
The insult upon injury
of having to cleanup after
And once again it is necessary
to remove the evidence
in order to go on.

James Koenig

Our Darling Little Gal

She was our little angel,
  A present from above.
Brought down to this earth,
  On the wings of the Dove.
Her face shone with glory,
  Not marred by a tear or worry;
She was perfect in every way.
  Although she could only stay,
To touch our lives for a day.
  We love her dearly -
And some day we'll see clearly,
  His purpose manifested.
When our presence is requested,
  To sit at Jesus' feet;
And have the privilege to meet,
  Our darling little gal,
God's precious little Angel.....
  ABIGAIL

Brenda Fox

Regret

Once Christmas meant
a shining tree
and Santa Claus and presents
just for me.
Soon I learned
that starry skies
and crunching snow and candles
are as nice.
Later on
my heart would sing
at carols, dancing feet, and
sleigh bells' ring.
I found too late...
and all alone..
that Christmas means the love and
warmth that's home.

Edith M. Scheid

Wind Song

The vagrant wind swirls
Memories like so many fallen leaves
Over the land of my mind,
And sings sweet and sad
Until the rustle ceases
And the song ends.
Then comes the wondrous silence.

Gerald W. Adams

Daybreak

A tinkling, a timbre
A soft sighing breath -
dawn is approaching - skies aglow
Rosy light shining - sun kissed streams
Shimmering with a golden light:
A brightness is everywhere
Mountain waters rushing, rumbling-
tumbling downhill-
Companions in this life,
Even if there is strife.
Each day is created anew...

Cynthia L. Vernon

Waiting at Richland

A precious gift was given to me
A taste of life and what it could be
Sweet, tender warm and kind,
so much unlike mine.

I've been here ten years before
sitting on this very bench
contemplating these same thoughts
  of what needs to be.

A dreadful decision occurred back then
Now my life is empty again
No one to love and hold me dearly
An empty house, pretty furnishings,
  hollow angry people.

Make it right! Do it! Decide!
Take a chance on life.
All our wealth cannot buy
wistfulness, laughing sunshine, and love.

Carole Pepe

Wisdom of the Mind

In our life times
  a truth that must be told,
Of fear and greed as in our minds
  Does a passion try to hold.

When righteous acting of the day
  emits a dazzling light.
'Tis in our hearts the time
  for knowing what is right.

A succinct day away
  the anger can be kept,
If in our souls
  our emotions are not inept.

Remember this the glory
  of ever be the knowing,
That care and love
  forever must be growing.

Harlee Vageline

My Lord's Touch

To live and love was all I planned
A wedding ring upon my hand
Three children came to lift my heart
My family was a special part
Then they branched out and gave me more
Six grandchildren to adore
My life is full and blessed so much
Because of the love in my Lord's touch

Caroline Smith

The Empty Hole Inside Of Me

What is this empty hole inside of me?
A vast dark hole is all I see,
Is an endless nothing awaiting me?
What will fill this endless hole,
Is it the love of one I know;
Or a simple friend to be with when
I'm alone.
Maybe all my life I'll be alone.
To never feel the touch of love,
Or be with one you yearn to hug.
This empty hole is far down deep,
But still it's a secret hard to keep.
This dark hole is easily found,
It hurts so bad I can't make a sound.
Even though I'm big and tall,
This empty hole brings me down!
From head to toe I feel so alone.
If I ever fill this hole,
You can be sure,
I won't be alone.

Josh Bobbitt

The Few

I share my room with Spiders
A very lucky few
They nibble at my toes at times
But keep me safe from you
For when at night the darkness hides
And nothing left to do
The spiders dance upon my chest
And make me feel a new

The lightness of their touch is warm
Warmer than the night
I take them with me where I go
But keep them out of sight
For any who might dare to glance
would shiver out of fright
Yet when they dance upon this chest
They make me feel alright.

Floyd Collins

Natures' Contrast

Maple trees produce
a wide color range.
When Autumn arrives
nature orders the leaves to change
from green all year long
maple comes on strong.

Red, orange and yellows
then it mellows the leaves fade
put on a big parade
while they drop to the ground
Pine trees are stately and tall
sturdy and up-right
proving their strength and might
no change in color all year long

Yet, nature wheedles
telling pines to drop
it's cones and needless

Pines don't swing and sway
they just obey and stay
where planned by nature.

Joy E. Stone

Jesus

One who was smitten
About whom is written
The greatest of pages
Throughout all the ages
Has given us all
The hope not small
To live throughout eternity
Despite our flesh's paternity
In his lovely mansions
Built on his stanchions
Above the pearly portals
Too lovely for mortals
To gaze upon with
Eyes full of pith
His sacrifice made possible
What had seemed impossible
Man could now live
Because God could forgive

Bob Bell

Mommy's Angel

Here I sit and stare
Above me at it's wonder
Arms reaching through the air
The blossoms fall around me
I begin to ponder
The reason for my despair
Your vision I still see
Engraved upon my memory
I know not why this had to be
Some came to say there is a reason
Still I search...
I come here for my strength
A gift you give me, for through
all these seasons you are here for me
As I wipe the tears
From your plaque, In loving memory
Will always stare back.
Eric Nicholas Marrero
(6-18-93 to 7-6-93)

Donna Marie Marrero

Memories with a Rosy Glow

Memories from long ago
Acquire a kind of rosy glow
That filters out a bitter taste
(Regret I felt at my own waste)
I want to think of only good
Of you and the time we stood
Together, against the odds
That threatened us, and pounded us
And as I dream it happens thus
Beauty yours in frozen time
Diffuses through my memory mind
Blue skies, stars, and candle flame,
Perfume you wore, and champagne
Lips on lips, and hand on skin
In a sun of love and sea of sin
and how I loved! and how I love
How I love
Memories with a rosy glow
Of you and I, so long ago.

Josh Poage

Playing a Game

Sitting at the bar
admiring strangers from afar.
Catching the eye
of the cutie driving by.
Working out at the gym
wondering if that could be him.
That's me, always looking for love.
Searching for someone to fill
the hole you left in my heart.
Finding love these days is a game.
I just can't win
No matter how many times I play.
I keep on searching
thinking he has to be the one.
But in the end I lose again.
Then I am back to the start with an open heart.
If only I knew I was a winner with you.

Jennifer Iapalucci

Wicked Smiles

The tender smallness lies peaceful
After mounting a fierce joust with
The darkened shadows that lurk
Inside the minds of all
At one time or another.

The battles rage ongoing
Second by fragile millisecond
Freedom condemned by stranglehold
Breath of life swallowed.

Wicked smirks of the crescent
Mock my very being
Hiding will do no good
As the line will be crossed
Yet once more
And the crescent grins to all
Its blood red smile
Hovering low on the horizon.

David B. Rhind

My P-Pose

Life is for one purpose, pose to a dream
aim for the stars
how funny life may seem,
Seem to be one purpose
I will never figure it out
Doubt, without
a thought
in the world, I scream
for I not know, what I scream about
what is life,
about
a p-pose, a dream
deemed impossible,
p-pose, it together
what does it mean
life is filled with one
Purpose
to live
for all to see.

Charisse Riley

The Credit Cardsharp

While you enjoy your credit card,
All he's got is a debit pad;

Yeah, yours is a laden bank card,
While his is a fading blank wad;

He gambled much with the jet set,
And ended up with the debt set;

He sure is a decrepit card
Since he owns a you-name-it card.

Captain August Okpe

Another Chance

Yesterday has passed and gone
All mistakes and failures too
God tender mercies forgives us
so we can begin anew.

Today is a new and precious gift
God has allowed us to embrace
Learning from all yesterdays
and giving God the praise.

Lord, teach us how we should
live in a world so filled with sin
Knowing you Dear Lord is the answer
We can always begin again.

Ernestine McCreary

Argyle Socks

An open dew covered field
Alone
Then accompanied.

Unable to move
I'm speaking
Yelling
Yet not heard.

All is green
With white polka dots
Metallic zippers
Falling from the sky.

Little people
With argyle socks
Pushing
Pulling
In every direction
Red beady eyes
They laugh and laugh and laugh
And stare.

Jaime L. Thone

Children's Gifts

In my passing
Don't forget
The things you see
Wanting
Or in wasted space
The prized possession
That might have meant
The most to me

Jana M. Phillips

"Halloween"

Soon trick or treaters will be marching
Along our city streets
All dressed in halloween finery
Behind masks and peek-a-boo sheets

Remember the day when you were young
And your spirits halloween gay?
What happened to those wondrous years
That seem so far away

Leave off the tricks that hurt and maim
Think twice before you spite
And join in making this special time
A safe and happy night

So offer the season's goodies
With warm cocoa to quench their thirst
And welcome the little hobgoblins
On O-C-T-O-B-E-R 31st

**Christopher Ors and
Dorothy A. Whitlock**

Placental Shells

I used to come here
along the tundra's river,
rattling antlers and snorting steam
beside the ice bound torrent's edge,
fog rising from the water.
We came to this crossing
year after year,
all of us in our grey fur,
caribou in the northern lights.

Then I took the wings of a goose
and learned the currents of the sky.
The winds of a wider map and compass
carried me beyond the sound of hooves
and the crash of antlers.

Now I am cut free.
My wet head bobs and nods unsteadily
above a placental bed of broken shells
and I thoughtlessly suckle,
knowing that this cannot be.

David Humphreys

Good Night, Good Friend

The moon arose with all its glory
    amid its delight.
It rose to meet its morning
    its day is the night.
Beaming down its power of
    just how much it shown.
No one could say it didn't try
    for it was all alone.
The minutes past; the hours flew
    its color turned a bright.
Shining down upon the earth
    to see with its own light.
Time moved by, towards a new morn,
    the moon began to fade.
I woke to greet a new day
    the moon had just seen made.
Walking through the morning light,
    I said, "good morn; adieu."
The moon looked down and smiled at me
    and said, "good night to you."

Bill Barton

Time Passes Over Rusting Leaves

Where is the path of his dream?

Yellow crocuses bubble out
among tree roots, trembling down banks
and lust of bees drinks
honey in cherry blossoms.

Summer is straight ahead —
merging into golden tasselled corn.

And the hour of tender white desire —
surrender, surrender, surrender.

Vineyards cascading down the slopes
and sweet melons laden the fields,
and a humming bird drinks the dew.

Hawks cluster on leafless trees
and there in the dark ravine — fear.

Time passes over rusting leaves —
silent as falling of snow flakes.

His path and dream goes on — and on
and it will be April again
and blue iris
down where the river bends.

Emma Crobaugh

Heaven's Hands

When the time has come for us to leave
an angel takes our hand,

showing us the way to go
to God's promised land.

Our guardian angel holds us close
guiding us step by step.

Comforting us with words of love
and reminding us we are blessed.

There are times' we don't feel ready,
we try very hard to stay.

The Lord knows what is best
and he takes us gently on our way.

As our souls enter heavens door
we feel love and kindness everywhere.

Security surrounds our being
we are in our Lord's care.

Shed not one more tear
for those whom have gone.

For each spirit that has passed our way
is a new spirit being born.

Catherine Harris

Untitled

Love me not with sympathy,
    Love me not with shame,
Love me not with empathy,
    Love me not to claim,
Love and nourish
    And you'll be blessed.
Love me, this fool,
    Who loves thee best.

Donna D. Harris

Untitled

There was an emptiness in my heart,
An emptiness that could not be filled.
Always with a pain at each heartbeat
To the torment I was subject to yield.

Then the Lord God himself intervened
As He sent down an Angel of Light,
To chase away the shadows
And fill my heart with pure delight.

The pain which life had brought me
At that moment ceased to be,
All was erased as your radiance
Shown brightly about me.

Yet on that wonderful day
To a new fate I fell,
I really didn't have a chance you see,
For Cupid knew his target well.

At first the nerve failed me
Yes it's true,
So in this way I had to say,
With all my heart, I love you!

Christopher M. Pendley

Thanks

For all your tender loving care
And always being there.
For all your words of wisdom,
The freed me of my prison.
You gave me the wings of a dove,
And the ability to again love.
For the understanding and the patience,
And the magic fingers touch.
For that really special smile,
That warms me.
And the shirt......One of a kind,
To caress me, when your not here.
That sweet, first kiss,
And the concern.
You are and always will be,
Truly cherished and loved.

Jacqueline Barat

Untitled

When you awake in the morning
And God's wonderful world comes to view,
Do you say a prayer, "I thank you God,
Now what can I do for you?"

Or do you frown and shake your head
Over all those things to do-
Those very very important things-
But just from your paint of view.

Now God has a plan for each of us,
But waits for us to say.
"I'm ready God, to do the work
You have for me this day."

Please let me be your hands to day
And help someone in need
"Please let me be you feet today
And do a kindly deed."

Then when the day is over
And looking back you'll pray.
"I thank you God please let me do
Your work another day."

Florence M. Gallagher

Love Again

If I ever love again,
Let me love as a soft breeze
 blows —

Gentle in its caress
Then gone where no one
 knows.

Hazel C. Schreckengost

Untitled

Don't mistake my flaming mane
and golden eyes that glow
for the Tiger.
Don't mistake when you feel
the claw's close in,
But a passionate need.
The golden circle around my eyes glow.
GIRL/WOMAN

Cathy Monroe

The Race

I lie awake, aware of the consequences
And I accept my share of the blame
But don't deny me this one last chance
To truly understand the game

I refuse to stand without action
That's been a burden all along
Just go and chase the dream
And wake me if I am wrong

There are times when simple existence
Makes me shudder to the bones
This is only my response
To open wounds I feel at home

There is no clear chance at healing
The scars which security leave
If the dreams which cut into your soul
Are left as pain you won't relieve

You cannot mask a man's obsession
You should not bet against his will
As I take the next strong stride
As I awake with my dream fulfilled

Joe Gerani

The Perpetrator

I am the governor of your life
And I am never changing
By all I am feared
And to all I am ruler

I control your life
As I shall be your death
I rule your world
As you willingly follow my periodic beat

If I didn't exist
There could be no future
There was no past
And there would be no present

I am God's invention
Without me nothing would exist
I am Satan's Hell
And Heaven's bliss

I am like a perpetual river
I flow forever
I will end at eternity
I am the perpetrator known as time

George T. Ferrell

I Do Not Want To Quit

At times when I grow weary
  And I feel I want to quit
When living is a burden
  And I just don't seem to fit...
When nothing seems to matter
  And my dreams have fallen through
When doors refuse to open
  And I don't know what to do...
I take a look around me
  At the torment that I see
And I am soon reminded
  Of how thankful I should be...
I do not find my comfort
  In the grief of any man
But when I count my blessings
  I just do the best I can...
I gain an understanding
  And I gather bit by bit
The strength that keeps me going
  And I do not want to quit...

Helen E. Dodge

I'll Remember When

Another nightshades falling
and I have made another day.
Things that I had never thought
of, came to my mind and wanted to stay.

Like San Francisco skies in summer
And white sands on Barbados Isle,
Island drums in sweet Jamaica, and,
swimming on Bermuda's Nile.

It seems this was not long ago
and yet I fear I'm dreaming.
It could have happened - was I there?
Or do my mind betray me.

The years are many, and have passed
And not returned again.
But as long as I have memories left
I'll always remember when.

Evelyn Carter

Untitled

Now you say you love me
And I just laugh
Why do you tell me that?
Do you think I can believe you?
I'm not even over your leaving
(even though you're back)
But don't tell me you love me
What is love?
A big show?
It looks nice on the TV
But it isn't real and it will stop
And then you're still who you were
(or who you've become)
But after you tell me a few times
I say "I love you too"
And now you think you're a big man
Because your friends think I have a nice body
But I guess in a way I do love you
(I wouldn't take this from just anyone)

Allison Gant

Quietness!

Be still and know that I am God;
And I will work for you,
Just put your trust in me, dear one,
And I will take you through.

You must not fret and be afraid
Tho' dark may be the way;
Just lean upon my arm, my child
And trust me and obey.

Be still and know that I am God,
You've heard me often say,
Remember that I never fail,
As you read My Word and pray.

When at last the Victory's won,
And Satan flees away;
I know, you'll Praise me then, dear ones
For the clouds have rolled away.

Clyde Jones

Waco

I'm thinking 'bout Waco.
And if you hear me cry,
I've been gassed
by the F.B.I.

They weren't satisfied
just to see him fry.

They had to hush him up.
They had to burn his book.

And with it, they put
our bill of rights
    to burn
    as an incense
    on an alter
    of an icon
    of an eagle.
      (It is bird of prey.)

Let's all cry!
We've all been gassed
by the F.B.I.

Evangeline Tartt

Growing Old Artificially

When I awake each morning
  And it is time to rise,
To better see what I am doing
  I put on my artificial eyes.

A couple artificial teeth
  Help me when I eat.
They fill the empty spaces,
  And help me chew my meat.

To better hear what's being said
  I wear artificial ears.
But unless you face me when you speak
  It's difficult to hear.

My heart works on a battery,
  And it's doing very well.
Will I need an artificial knee?
  Only time will tell.

But my memory is fading.
  some brain cells must be dead!
So maybe what I really need
  Is an artificial head!

Florence T. Robinette

I Love You, Friend

When someone is taken from you
And it seems hard to bear,
You feel no one understands,
They don't seem to care.

It may be a dear one,
So very close to your heart.
How can you go on,
Where do you re-start?

The other side of living
Is dying, I guess.
But seems no preparation
Can relieve mental stress.

Before it's to late
And life has come to an end,
Tell all close to you,
'I love you, friend.'

Eddie C. Barnett

My Dream

I have a special desire
And like to be free
If I could fly
Looking up to the sky
Leaving all my care
Soaring about and high
Circling in the air
If only for a spree
I could be free
Have you heard
I like to be a bird?
And fly, fly fly
High up in the sky
Now would you like to be
A bird with me?
And be free, free, free
Look up high and see
And come fly with me
Together we will see
How free we can be.

Helen Evans

'To You'

A love of yours is barred within,
And lonely cried my soul.
Dear God in heaven keep her close,
Lest hell should take it's toll.
For prison cell and prison stone,
Hold not the anguished cry,
It echoes in hearts chambers,
That space cannot defy.
Oh give me hopes and give me dreams,
To heal the dread despair,
For night is dark and hell is deep,
Before the morning air.
And wise men in their heart of hearts,
Know love is healing balm,
So echo love through darkened cell,
God speed the breaking dawn.

Charles L. Spencer

Less Than Best

When life has dealt me less than best,
I don't give up and quit.
I take the less than best I get
And make the best of it.

Blaka Y. Abee

Untitled

Moonlight on the waters
Of a lake enchanted
Where each mermaid loiters
for a second granted.

C. D. Higgins

Blessings of Springtime

This morning when I first awoke
And looked beyond the screen;
The sun was shining in the East
The meadow field was green;
And in the yard, a little lamb
Was frisking in the sun;
I stopped and breathed a little prayer;
A new day had begun.
A new day! Dear God me grace
To live it all for Thee;
For thou in thy great goodness,
Hast done all this for me.

Dorothy Kline Dolick

Untitled

Fading faces
and lost memories
always come back.

They come back
to get you by another day.

They leave you
standing in ah-
over how fantastic life is.

And they Hurt ya!
torturing your soul,
making your heart bleed
for everything
that made you once live.

Fading faces
and lost memories
always come back.

Just wish
that for once
I could get past them
and finally move on.

Brian Gilbert

My Final Day

When life is full,
And love is now.
My heart can reach,
The outer space.
Eyes are bright,
My step is sure.
I can laugh in Winter's face,
Young or old,
Doesn't matter.
Future and past,
Can only tell,
That this is my time,
At long last.
So I say my,
Farewell to all.
Friend or foe,
It is the same.
Come what may,
On this,
My final day.

Betty Bishop

Emptied Pockets

Odds and ends of this and that
And miscellaneous too
All found on your dresser
And all put there by you.

I could brush the whole thing off
But only to my sorrow
The things that I brush off today
Would all be back tomorrow.

So I've come to this conclusion
And you'll agree it's true:
This little idiosyncrasy
Is just a part of you.

Helen Mansheim

My Mother's Hand

When I'm feeling lost and alone,
And no one understands
I know I have a home,
In my mother's hands.

When life becomes a storm,
And clouds threaten my skies,
I know a place safe and warm,
In my mother's eyes.

When I feel there's no place for me,
And I seem to fall apart,
I know I'm welcome completely,
In my mother's heat.

When I follow others, blindly,
And I soon lose control,
I know again, I'll learn to see
Through my mother's soul

Eliza Marie De Rade

Fireman's Day

A piercing sound, a cry for help
and now their on their way

The rush, the lights, the sirens, blare
no time to delay

A roar, a flash, caboom, cabash
fully involved they say

They grab their gear, and disappear
beyond the smokey gray

The hoses roll, the pumpers pump
water blasts the blaze

The smoke then thins, the fireman wins
the crowd then shouts in praise

Ashened face and reddened from heat
he smiles and walks away
all during a fireman's day.

Cheryl Blackburn

"Freedom"

Oh, to run naked in the wind
On sand swept beaches
Bathed in moonlight-
Soft and white as an egret's wing.

To plunge wildly in the pulsing surf,
Swept by starlight-
Kissed by island winds
Warm and sweet as love unspoken.

Gene Fisher Kosich

Untitled

"As we travel onward
And our steps turn homeward,
Toward that mansion in the sky,
There'll be no more sorrow
In that new tomorrow
When we reach our home on high."

"If we've had to borrow
From life's grief and sorrow
And our self esteem is low,
If we'll just remember
When we reach our life's December
There'll be a better life
To which we go."

"All will be peace and gladness
With no more grief or sadness
And no more we'll have to roam,
We will enter singing
With all our heart bells ringing
When we reach our celestial home."

Hughie Dale

Handicaps

Strength reached for me
And placed my hand on power
I did not question why
For I hardly knew what

Fear grasped my screams
And made me be still
I thought I knew who
But rejected my answer

Guilt caused me shame
And forced me to be silent
I wanted to tell
Yet couldn't find the way

Time eased the pain
And showed me I was a victim
I thought of it less
While burying my anger

Love replaced hatred
And searched for the truth
I was finally a person
Challenged, but free

Connie Amandeo

The Choice

Shadows pass
  And seasons too.

But, never shall
  My love for you.

If the world had
  One choice.

I would surely help
  It voice.

I know it would
  Be you.

Your love is
  Ever true.

Charlotte B. Bowlan

Why I Know God Is Real

When I get up in the morning
and see the beautiful sunrise
like a smile from God "God is Real"
When I see the blue sky all
day until evening sunset
God is saying goodbye to
another day. "God Is Real"
I see the stars and the
shiny moon in the sky
"I know God Is Real"
Then I see the black clouds
and hear the thunder and
see the rain drops fall
and hear the rippling water
run and maybe see a
rainbow "God is Real"
Then there is nature
sparkling everywhere and a
soft wind blowing in my face
"I know God is Real"

Earl Neiss

Zombies of the Green

Justice take off your blindfold
And see the corruption
Going on in the land of freedom.
Your scales are unbalanced
Made so by custom made laws.

Justice take off your blindfold
And see the suffering of children
With parents lost in the dream.
Your scales are unbalanced
By men of greed and a lust for power.

Take off your blindfold
And see into the hearts of men
Who have lost their spirit
To become zombies of the green.

Anita Jones

God Made an Angel

God made an angel from up above,
and sent him down for me to love.

He made his lips for me to kiss,
So I can give him eternal bliss.

He made his feet for him to come,
to my arms on the run.

And best of all; he made his hand,
So he could wear my wedding band.

He's that angel from up above,
and I'm the one who fell in love.

Now you know how I feel,
"While I" at your feet do kneel.

Janet Vaughn

Monstrosity

We preempt the lives
Of millions of children,
And the world sleeping
Does not weep—
But a mother cries,
And billions of tears
Resonate until at last
The earth shatters.

Deborah Beachboard

Untitled

I hold you in my arms
And stare at your face
I'm glad you're mine
and know this is my place

I love your smile
and just plain you
Feeling a strong bond between us
hoping it's always true

Please don't you cheat
and don't even lie
for you know how I am
and for sure I will cry

Today's life is very scary
I worry for your life in every way
What if a rival comes for you
This is something for what I pray

One day we will unite as one
Leave the gang so you won't die
For I love you so much
And never want to say goodbye

Diana DeFaria

Loving Is Understanding

When the leaves are dried
    And the birds left their nest
When the river stayed calm
    And the sea stopped to wave
When the sun ceased to shine
    And darkness started to spread
When your heart no longer beat
    And your love has faded

I will gather all the dried leaves
    And clean the lonely nest
I will let the river paddle
    And encourage the sea to wave
I will urge the sun to shine
    To skid the spread of darkness
I will always treasure the time
    When your heart was still beating
I will always cherish the moments
    When your sweet love was still present

I have no regrets with the time I spent with you
    All because I truly love you....

Camila Esteves Tacto

World's Greatest Grandmother

You always hold my little hands,
And wipe sway my tears,
With your special magic,
You turn away my fears.
You have the patience of a saint,
And even when I'm bad,
You always sun to give me love,
Which makes me very glad.
God knew what he has done,
By putting me on earth,
To receive your special love,
That started at my birth.
Each night before I go to bed,
I thank the Lord above,
For giving me a grandmother
Who fills my heart with love.

Darlene Locker

If We Could Resow

Oh the webs that we do weave
And the marks that they do leave
As we journey through each day
Taking chances along the way

If we could see through another time
Another path we may have tried to find
To lead us through another phase
To another time or another age

So now while our thoughts do linger on
We soon find we've been struggling along
Don't seem to know where we have been
Of if this road will ever end

So if by chance we've looked again
We might have seen the light within
Waiting to Help as it does lead
Down the path that we so need

Then as we see the webs that we now do weave
We learn to watch where we scatter the seed
And watch it weave its love through toil
As we plant it's roots beneath the soil

Josephine M. Perren

En-masse

I am en-masse
And the scents and musks—tart
Combine in androgyny.
The sexless sway simmers
With a paradoxically chaotic focus,
Moving, moving, moving.
The sky and the air
Juxtaposed with the edges of
The amorphous body
Press and crush its edges
Into diminutive ants
With burdens of consciousness
So that the lone struggle
For Identity
Or Meaning
Or Purpose
Is but hopelessly lost
In the tide of its brothers.

Chris Miller

Let's Talk About

Let's talk about our big blue sea
And the statue of liberty.
Let's talk about what's right and wrong
And the people who traveled
Near and far
To this land we call the USA.
It stands for freedom in every way.
Let's talk about our freedom
Not some ruler in a kingdom.
Our president is good, really fine,
But I'm running out of time.
So what I want to say
To all the land,
The kids, the moms, the dad's
Is really true.
Take care of the land
It will take care of you.

Jenny Nessel

Doomsday

The day is dark,
And the wind howls,
Whispering the end,
There is no sun,
And the time is unknown,
the structures are empty,
The streets are full,
For this is where the bodies lie,
Is it really Doomsday,
Or just a bad dream.

Chris Dasanjh

To Be With You

My feelings for you are so strong
    and they run so deep that
in one lifetime,
    I wouldn't be able to show you,
    just how much I love you
I would give anything and everything
    just to be with you
the bond we share,
    can never be broken
it is so strong and so true
    that there's nothing in this world
    I wouldn't do
    just to be with you

Jennifer Jones

Fire In The Sky

He lights the match
and watches it fall
a small flame forms
"pretty color!"
Soon the room is engulfed
then the house
"a fire in the sky!"
He hears screaming
but cannot move
only watch
soon the screams fade
and so he will grow

Angela Etherton

The Mirrored Truth

I looked into the mirror
And what did I see?
I saw the reflection,
It wasn't really me.

I looked into the mirror
And saw what others see;
If they could but see deeper
They'd see the real me.

For I am inside the image
Behind a facade, you see.
I know what truths I hide,
You must look deep to find me.

Allen L. Binns

Life's fragile web

Tears with the force of time,
redirecting paths,
no longer to connect,
leading nowhere — everywhere,
circling back
to weave a new web.

Antonia Pisciotta

Happy Springtime

Well faith and begorra
And what have we here.
Why it's March seventeenth
That time of the year
When on lapels
The Shamrock is seen,
The day of the Irish,
The wearin' o' the green!

The day of the Irish,
The beginning of spring.
The time when new life
Makes one want to sing.
So smile and rejoice
There are great times ahead.
May God grant you blessings
As you stay in his stead.

Eileen M. Taylor

Late Winter Ice Storm

A cheerful sun awakened me,
And when I looked around,
There-a magic ice land,
That glistened sky to ground!

Each blade of grass sharp sword became,
Each branch a crystal wand.
Where was a dull gray forest,
The trees all silver stand.

Each cattail and each hollow reed,
Each pond with prisms shine,
Reflecting brilliant points of light,
From groups of ice-spiked pines.

Fleeting Borealis,
Played as an icy song,
Mixed with the blue of Heaven,
I will remember long.

Swollen buds all sparkle coated,
Twinkling gems each one,
Till kissed by sun and southern wind,
Soon all the jewels are gone!

Angeline Lauricella Jenness

Power Play

When I want to go out
and you don't
and I stay home
you win

When I want a drama
and you want a ball game
and you have the remote
you win

When I want seafood
and you want steak
and I just have a salad
you win

When I need attention
and you want a nap
and I walk out for good
you lose

Billie Harding

Life

God did not make
    Life so easy
That it would never want
    To say goodbye.

Jimmy D. Bautista

Daydreams '94

The wind will sing my songs
And you will dance to them
Your spirit
Is free
I will feel it.

Sunshine will kiss you tenderly
As you caress green leaves
Softly-
As soft as raindrops
Falling on your grave.

Buds will wink and bloom into petals
To find you touching them
But you will leave
Caressing more green leaves
The blossoms will stay.

The wind will sing my songs again
And you will dance to them again
Then you will leave
But - in essence, you will stay
To dance to all my songs.

Elma Diel Photikarmbumrung

To Edgar Allen Poe

Now that the opium dream has ended,
And your life on Earth has wended
Far into the Great Beyond,
Memories both strange and fond
You have left us in your wake,
Praying hard for your sake.
Today I stood at your grave,
Opining in the church's nave,
How your talent, brave and true,
Spun tales and poems we never knew.
A century apart we two were born,
But when I hark to Gabriel's horn,
We two shall meet some brighter morn.

Barbara W. James

Untitled

When walking seems hard
And your mind fades in and out
You don't know where you are
Or what your life is about
To others you are alone
But to you, you have yourself
You dwell without a home
Rest in peace you are myself
Live life the best you can
Walk with all your pride
Help your fellow man
And take each step in stride
Be all you are
Even though you are poor
Free life's scars
And the pain that you bore
Let your feet wander
To where you may roam
Take yourself yonder
And find myself a home

Cari Caldwell

Safety Valves

There are times when beset with trials,
And you're tired of all the riff-raff,
And then, for no apparent reason
You break out in a hearty laugh.

But there are other times, it seems,
When in none you dare to confide,
You'll open up and let the tears flow,
Then peace comes in to abide.

Man is quite a complex creature,
One thing isn't always the cure
For all the things that happen to us,
And this fact we know for sure.

So whether it's laughing or crying,
Give vent to whatever is best;
Then go on your way rejoicing,
And you'll finally pass the test.

We need the moments of sunshine,
And we need the tears, it is true.
God made us all with safety valves,
So let's do the things we should do.

John F. Brand

Life's Melody

Sing a song to tell of love,
Another to praise God above.
Hum a tune when feeling blue-
Whistle one-that's soothing too.

Listen to a mocking bird,
Sweetest sound you've ever heard.
Whistling winds can be a song;
Sometimes playing all day long.

Thunder's like a big base drum,
Bull frog's croak-a banjo strum.
Crickets on a summer night—
Form a symphony alright.

Parades are led by big brass bands,
Thrilling people in all lands.
Clocks tick with a rhythm too;
Again there's music just for you.

A note to sing, a note to play...
Music going all the way.
Everything in life is song-
Remember this and sing along.

Clarice H. Dionne

Winter

The sounds of winters' winds
Are murmurings of ancestors
Long dead.

The infinite spirit lives
To communicate forever
With those who want to hear.
Listen to the winds.

Life goes with the winds —
Everywhere. Could it be
That we will someday become
A wind?

Donald G. Baker

Next Generation

They say the children
Are our future
Tomorrow is in their hands
Some of the children are
Too violet killing each other
Can't make a decision by themselves
Not going to school-dropping out
Hanging with their peers
Selling and taking drugs
Babies having babies
Others are gang-banging
Involved in drive-by shooting
Showing no fear of the law
Having no respect for themselves
For others, just doing their thing
So what kind of future
Will the next generation have?

Cynthia Wilson-Du Bois

Not Forgotten

Gone but not forgotten
are the times of long ago.
The soft caresses,
the gentle words.
Gone but not forgotten
are the romantic nights,
the early mornings.
Gone but not forgotten
are the times shared,
the memories made,
the love that was there.
Everything is gone
but not forgotten.

Gail Lynn Beving

Kisses

Kisses
are to cherish

Long
and tender
memories

Emotions
let loose

Passion
Love

Brought to
the surface

Through
Kisses

Andrea Catherine B. Sybinsky

Are You There

Somebody call me and say,
are you there.
Somebody call me and say,
I miss you, if you're there.
Somebody call me and say,
help me, I need you,
Are you there
Somebody call me and say,
I love you, are you there.
Somebody call me and say,
if you're lonely, are you there.
Somebody call me, are you there?

Billie McKiernan

Why Are We Here?

Armed with his army of soldiers,
Armed with the Book' unread,
He marched them into battle,
Until his last man was dead!

Dry-eyed and numb he stumbled,
He ran, he screamed, he bled,
Until he couldn't show his anguish,
Except to hang his head.

Why are we here, he wondered?
As he viewed mountains of dead
Could it be, he pondered,
Because of what somebody said?

Animals kill for hunger,
Man kills for Gods or plunder,
But most likely of all,
The world shall fall,
Because of what somebody said!

Jeanne Jay

Night Breeze

I walk in moonlit darkness,
as a cool breeze caresses my face.
For its touch reminds me of yesterday,
when I had nobility and grace.

Now I am evil,
a beast that is called undead.
But I can still fill the fall breezes,
as they blow about my head.

I am alive,
I can take a deep breath.
After roaming for two centuries,
overpowering the grip of death.

So as the wind surrounds,
my dark brooding soul.
I take my vampire existence,
wherever the night breezes may blow.

Charlie Lynn Mowery

The Wind Is Passing By

The wind is passing by.
As clear as the sky.
Blades of grass dance.
Flowers prance.

The wind is passing by.
The wind slowly howls.
Feathers from owls.
Float through the sky.

The wind is passing by.
The tails of horses blow.
The wind is on a flow.
The wind is passing by.

Catherine Kegher

Untitled

My reflection hits the waters edge
As I gaze into my eyes
I sink unto a glittered dream
And laughter hides my cries

I've searched for happiness
Security and love
Under small stones
Clear to heaven above

And what I've found
Is in a simple place
It hides behind my soul
And my very plain face

Aubri C. Pearson

Teddy Bears...

Teddy bears have feelings too,
As I hope that you do.
I sit on your shelf all day,
Watching the dust mote flows,
As you are out at play,
And my heart to sorrow goes.

But now the night comes,
When you are away,
And a lonely tear runs,
Down my face to say,
"I miss you, I need you."
Please, for me, say the same is true,
For teddy bears have feelings too.

Gary Lee Moore Jr.

Sometimes

When everything goes wrong,
  As it sometimes will;
And you are not feeling strong,
  As you sometime will;
Just reach out your hand,
  And God will understand.

When you are feeling sad,
  As you sometimes will;
And nothing makes you feel glad,
  As it sometimes will;
Just turn to God in prayer,
  And He will always be there.

When there seems to be no hope for you,
  As it sometimes will;
And the sky seems black, never blue,
  As it sometimes will;
Just ask God to turn on the light,
  And He will make everything right.

Doris J. Bailey

In Remembrance

The day was dreary, dark and gray
as though all nature mourned.
Her passing left us naught to say;
with grief we were adorned.
The son shines brightly far above
beyond earth's shadows here;
as she looks down in perfect love
on those she held so dear.
Her pain and suffering far behind
with burdens at an end;
the joyful memories left through time
sustain us as we mend.

Burton Sherrard

A Second Chance

Your gentle love has touched me,
  as nothing else can, or ever will.
It has sheltered me in tenderness,
  and helped me heal.
It has awakened my sleeping heart,
  and taken it down from its shelf.
Now all things seem possible,
  for my children
  and for myself.
It has restored my faith in God,
  and given me a second chance.
It has filled me with the courage
  to do this loves dance.
It has given me strength,
  as I struggled with each task.
It has granted me hope
  that all my gray dawns, are past.
Dearest friend,
  you have brought summer to my soul,
  and I will always.... love you so.

Christina Keenan

Aging

Aging, is not a process,
as you've been lead to believe...
to age, is truly a blessing,
that many do not receive...

To age, is not a penalty,
as you must really know...
to age is God's nourishment,
which enabled you to grow...

Aging, is not a process,
it really is a skill...
for wisdom makes you executor,
to carry out God's will...

Now that you are older,
some may say bolder...
remember, for your servitude,
God will reward you...

The many hours you've surrendered,
he definitely will remember...
so wear your years with a smile,
and carry His cross a few more miles...

Judy A. Johnson

Untitled

He looked in the mirror
at a monstrous image
his face he no longer knew
it was his reflection
but
he was a stranger
among himself
a violent man stood
looking
at a child
seeing his anger
scared
of what it was
not quite understanding
where it came from
or
how to stop it
putting his fist through the mirror
to stop the monster
only making it stronger

Heidi Kraus

UNSCH

ELLIOT WUNSCH
ATE HIS LUNSCH
TOO EARLY FOR DINNER
TOO LATE FOR BRUNSCH
HE HAD A CARROT
I HEARD IT GO CRUNSCH
HE DRANK IT DOWN
WITH VODKA AND PUNSCH
THEN HE HAD GRAPES
HE ATE A WHOLE BUNSCH
WILL HE EAT LATER?
I DON'T HAVE A HUNSCH
BUT I BET IN A CRUNSCH
HE COULD MUNSCH

Eric R. Greenberg

The Struggle

Always the same
Attack is swift and strong.
Onto my back
It clings silent, unseen.
I spin, shrug, shake,
Wrestle with human form.
Beaten, I fall.
The struggle is over.
I stand and see
My attacker is me.

Diane L. Casavant

Away

And in the streets I'll dance
Away - That burns with life's
Desire.
And the time has come to
Me - I'll burn in flames of
Life's new desire.
And when I get there I'll see
The force of you - outside -
Ascending to the sky.
And my hands of flames -
I reach to you and say
To you good-bye.
And I never looked back -
I never ran from life,
But still I search for
Peace of mind.
And I looked for you, but you
Were gone - so far away -
You, I'll never find.

BIAS

Loneliness

Quiet and dull,
Blue and empty
Dark as the night.
An overwhelming sadness.
Brings many tears,
That fall like raindrops.
Silent as the moon,
Passing by.
Blue as the night sky,
As bright as the stars,
As dull as the sea.
All of this is going on inside me,
When I am lonely.

Charla Heibel

Up And Away!

I love to fly in an aeroplane
Away up in the sky,
And watch the buildings grow so small,
And see the clouds go by.

As up above the clouds we soar
Like sleds on drifted snow
Billows of white stretch endlessly
The earth hidden down below.
Then the clouds all melt away
And rivers and lakes appear
Checkerboard fields of green and gold
The sky above so clear.

How God allows us to come so high
I'll never understand
But I thank Him each time I fly
For such a beautiful land.

Garnett Daly

Fantasy

I am your fantasy
Beautiful and perfect
This moment is all that exists
My hands touch your body, caressing
And memorizing the feel of you
I taste your kisses, savoring
Each sensation
Intensifying the sensuality
Until you are lost in my touch
My love fills your soul
And I hold you in my arms forever.

Janet Baltz

Untitled

Becki Nuttal (inspiration)
Along comes true beauty
that is hard to explain.
You know it's from Heaven
as sure as Aprils bring rain!
Her presence makes me tremble
like a leaf in the wind;
But what I would have missed,
If I dared not seek out;
the HEAVEN sent rain!

Jace Caywood

A Christmas Meditation

Rough-hewn the manger—
bed and table—
where beasts do noisy
eat their provender,
and Christ, the Babe,
is Host and Guest.

Rough-hewn my heart,
in need of grace,
and I am sore bestead
to keep the Yuletide feast
until the Christ come in,
Himself, the Host, the Bread, the wine,
and I, the guest.

Dora M. Monson

Smile Awhile

If you tend to worry or fret,
Been anxious or worried for a while.
Remember this and never forget,
Give the world your greatest smile.

When your day seems all out of tune,
When nothing you do seems worthwhile.
Don't pucker your face like a prune,
Give the world your greatest smile.

When you're tired of stops and starts,
As you trudge along each weary mile.
Why spend time throwing angry darts,
Give the world your greatest smile.

If all you do turns ugly and sour,
And your temper turns ugly and vile.
Don't let unhappiness grow by the hour,
Give the world your greatest smile.

James E. Hodges

Kiss Me Good Bye, My Darling

Everyday and every morning
Before I step outside
Kiss me good bye,
Good bye my darling.

Every time I go away
I hope you do not forget
In the middle of the day,
To kiss me good bye,
Good bye my darling.

If a minute it will be
For a moment I am not here
Kiss me good bye,
Good bye my darling.

I will always remember
No matter where I am
Kiss me good bye,
Good bye, my darling.

Juan A. De La Rosa

Celestial Jubilee

Crystal clear,
Before me
Spreads an awesome sight.
Around me I see,
In panoramic majesty,
The dark velvet dress
Of lovely Lady Night,
Adorned with sequins
Of city lights
And lace of feathery trees.
In hushed astonishment,
I look up to see
This lovely creature
Of beauty rare
Wearing diamonds in her hair,
For 'round her flowing tresses
A halo of starry gems
Shines resplendently,
To proclaim her queen
Of this celestial jubilee.

Jane Huelster Hanson

A Child's Tomorrow

A child is but a picture
Being painted day by day
Each stroke a new experience
Absorbed along the way

Dry paint upon the canvas
Colors bold, soft hues and shades
Brings the picture into focus
Or causes it to fade

True art reflects its artists
Whether living or the dead
All hope comes to humanity
When paint and worth are wed

Andrea Maillett

They Are Not Gone

They are not gone who pass
Beyond the clasp of hand.
No, they are come so close
We need not grope with hands;
Nor pause to look, or
Catch the sound of marching feet.

For they have laid down their arms,
They have put off their boots,
To softly walk by day
Within our thoughts, to tread
By night our dream-led paths
Of sleep.

Arthur L. Sorge

"Right Wing Idiots"

Judeo-Christian static
Bible thumping automatic
Irrational nut, erratic
Evangelically ecstatic
Religious procedures
More like Kant's epileptic seizures
Stupid restrictions
Boa constrictions
Red tape, stifling bureaucracy
Hidden communism, propaganda democracy
No justice from the lawyer
The warrior was Tom Sawyer
The Roman Catholic Pope
Hung on a rope
He's another egalitarian dope

Jeff Jison

About Face With Plastic Surgery

Crow's feet become neat,
Big wrinkles - small crinkles,
Thin lips get bigger,
Big hips get trig - er,
Dewlaps don't lapse,
Lyposuction means,
Great reduction,
Everyone looks younger,
Therefore the hunger,
Women love it,
Men aren't above it,
Plastic surgeons do well,
And they won't tell!

Dorothy Durkee

The Blae Lock

Blae you're not fleshy for my wit.
Blae you're not fleshy for my gift.
Blae lock drift into a stiff nit and
Crow crow crow with your tiff spit.

Blae crow flutter away today and
Forever fritter into a jay maze and
May your crow days always be blae.
Crow flit away with your nip nixs
and bow out it and be a gay twit.

I don't want a blae crow, not a bit
So don't ask me for a maize whit.
Bonita L. Andrade

The End

A leaf fallen from autumn
blew through the air
suspended
indefinitely in the breeze
it swirled
in its own personal hurricane
around and around
dancing
and happy
until the wind
decided to leave
Amy Bowden

Mary Dear

Sweetest little granddaughter,
Born July of eighty-eight.

A big eyed, smiley firecracker,
We named her Mary Kate.

Pop and Mom-mom cuddled her,
and kissed her small sweet face.

Took pictures, to keep for memories,
Tied them up with lace.

We buy her cards and dated gifts,
Pack them away with care.

Maybe someday she'll open them,
and wipe away a tear.

Sorry she missed meeting us,
But knowing we had no fear.

That her adoptive family,
Loved and raised our Mary Dear.
Alyce C. Weeber

And Then There Was One

Conceived by the Holy Spirit
Born of a virgin
The Son of God chosen to die
Betrayed by a kiss
He hung on the cross
Between two villains
He died for us
His Mother wept
Tears of joy and of pain
Her Son will save us all
Emilie Campbell

Christmas Time

Caring during the holidays
Bringing Christmas cheer,
Families coming together
Just like every year.

Hanging decorations
Putting up the tree,
The joyous time of the season
Fills me with glee.

Hearing christmas carols
Children on their sleighs.
Filled with the joy of knowing
Santa is on his way.

Receiving lots of presents
With many thank you to say,
Many wishes, many kisses
It will soon be Christmas Day.
Jill Eisnaugle

Untitled

Dirt sodden
broken dreams
of a picture
I'd seen in a magazine

The perfect image
of who you're suppose to be
white picket fences
2.5 kids and a shiny new limousine

Sleeping dreams
haunting me
of faces in the past
that I used to see

Resemble now empty scenes
milk gone sour
stomach curdling
unraveling at the seams

Left standing alone
on the shores of an angry sea
rain pouring but not washing
this slippery mud from me
Julie Greason

Flicker of Passion

Flickering candlelight
brushed
by a shadowed caress
dances
upon moonlit walls
smothering
the darkness
with
dusky light

Amber embers
distort
reflections of desires
imprinted
upon a contoured wall
surrounding
a hidden love
revealing
the flame of passion
Coreen Spencer

I'll Be There For You

this world may be harsh
but all you have to do
is call on me
and I'll be there for you.

If you need a shoulder to cry on,
always remember,
I have two.

I'll always be your true friend,
and if anyone hurts you,
I'm there 100 percent.

I've got your back,
so, remember that,
I'm always for you.
Colleen Ann Pugh

Lost And Alone

Mystery brought us together,
But fate tore us to shreds.
Time welded us as one,
But time slips away.
Please hold me tighter,
Your grip seems to loosen.
I kiss your tender lips,
They begin to fade away.
I reach out for you,
But your pillow is empty.
I call out your name,
Just an echo returns.
Lost and alone —
I carry your picture,
Searching for something that's gone.
Debra-Ann Paul

God's Love

I never knew how much God loved me,
But He sent His Son to earth
To be born of a girl named Mary,
Who in Bethlehem gave birth
To a babe whose name was Jesus;
He'd redeem us from our sins,
And would bring us our Salvation
If we'd only ask Him in.

When we believe and come to know Him
We'll have peace and love within.
Let's just lift our eyes to Heaven
And thank the Lord and worship Him.
Oh, yes, Jesus is so wonderful
And to have Him for my friend
Is such a miracle, so beautiful
And of His love there is no end.

If you haven't asked Him in as yet
Please don't wait another day,
Because that "other day" may be too late.
Why don't you ask Him in today?
Beverly Lane

Reminder Of You

A butterfly I saw today
Reminded me of you... so beautiful
But when I tried to pick it up
The butterfly flew away.
So I sat down and thought about
How much I love you
And how I wish I could hold you forever.
John F. O'Hara

Meant To Be

Good-bye may seem forever
  but if it's meant to be
Somehow, somewhere we'll find it
  If God will let us see
I cannot explain
  The reason we must part
I'm so sorry I can't change it
  But I'll see you in my heart
If it's in God's plan
  For us to be together
I'll wait for the day
  We can begin forever
Time is just a measurement
  That keeps us far away
Counting every second
  Turning minutes into days
I'll miss you every moment
  And keep searching all I see
Somehow, somewhere we'll find it
  If it's meant to be

Cara C. Ward

Alone

I'm all alone there's no one around.
But I'm sure I hear footsteps thumping
against the ground.

I also saw a shadow floating
across the wall,
and I thought I heard some voices
coming from the hall.

Maybe it's a stranger or maybe
it's a friend,
Maybe it's for real or maybe it's
pretend.

I think it's my imagination that
there's someone else in my home,
or maybe it's that I'm afraid
of being all alone.

Brandy Lee Grajeda

Angelic Vision

I saw you once so long ago
But only for a minute.

You smiled at me, your face aglow
With heavens starlight in it.

Your face expressed a happiness
No human could portray.

You looked around and smiled once more
And left without delay.

There are no words that can express
The hope you gave to me

That there is life beyond this life
That holds utter ecstasy..

Sometimes, I think this life I lead
Is all that there can be

And then the memory of your Angelic face
Comes back to visit me.

Eileen Cannizzaro

Her Petals

I scream for her name,
But there is no answer.
Her rose,
My weed.
Her man makes me peeve.
I need her petals.
He's Hansel,
She's Gretel.
I want her,
I need her.
My weed can still grow.
Why is the weed not mixed with the rose?
My leaves are too big,
Her petals so small.
Nor happy, nor sad.
Nor anxious,
Nor glad.
My weed is still,
Yet urging to grow.
Why is the weed not mixed with the rose?

Corey Faircloth

The Ventriloquist

I move my lips
But utter not a sound
I blink my eyes
But see nothing around
You confine me to a box
With a padlock lid
You pull me out
Every now and then
To show me off
To all you big time friends
Well I'm tired of being
Your sweet little doll
I'm tired of having no choice
In the matter at all
Well now I'm breaking free
And speaking my own mind
You shall no longer rule me
Time after time.

Cristina King

Divided By Man-Made Law

Your scent is all around me
But your not here

At night I call out to you
You comfort me in my dreams
You reassure me

I can see your eyes
Filled with hope
Compassion
Tenderness

Yearning to be loved
Appreciated
Respected
I am here

We were two, yet one
My thoughts were yours
Your ideas were mine
Our ambitions were one

Physically divided
But one in mind, soul and spirit
I am with you

D'Anna Dettore-Keeble

Life Beyond

Your body is weak,
But your spirit is strong,
Goals you may seek;
But dreams are not wrong.

Outside may be as dark as night,
Your body is soon and sure to die,
Dreams and wishes that's gone away;
Will soon come back another day.

No one knows where they'll go,
Heaven or hell, or as a soul,
Heaven and hell are places to find;
But both may not be what you like.

Earthly items that we may have,
Money, a mansion, and artifacts,
These things stay here when you die;
Your spirit can't carry it as it flies.

The enemies you hated has already died,
Leaving you with no one to fight,
Trying to find him day and night;
Not even knowing, he has left your mind.

Janice Chen

Lonely and Alone

Stars hang
By sight so close
But so far away
Alone in reality.

The moon hooked to the earth
By the eyes of you
But so far away
Alone in reality.

Love sometimes seem so strong
But actually
Alone in reality.

Chris Ellis

Entrance To Oblivion

Grim reaper, angel of death
calls to me as I take my last breath

As I lie here now, in limbo void
to face, now, what no man can avoid

Life's journeys, past and gone
death's ascension, fast and strong

His bony hand around my soul
does strip from me all I've been told

Lips of eternal life I have kissed
my physical form will be missed

As I ascend towards the light
will I die or will I gain flight

I stand in judgement, infinity waits
do I go through hell or pearly gates

Fear now gone, I've done my best
life's just been another test

Pass or fail, I do not know
as life and death casts their shadow

David Haber

Where Are My Friend's

My friend's are gone from me.
Can it be,
that since he died
they must hide
their shame and sorrow,
and some tomorrow
they will awake
and say to me
"Friend's we'll be
for we did not know,
we hurt you so."

Elizabeth Ann Fetta

Eye (I)

Eye
Can Sea
U
With My
I
By the...
See
With Your
I
What you want
In my
Eye

Albert S. Ruiu —Away—

Forever, Love

The winds of time brought you;
Carrying you into the void of me,
Filling my shattered life with
Crystal clear breaths of love.

Clouds full, shedding droplets of love
Into the arid desert of my heart,
Brimming it over with joy,
Growing flowers of peace at my feet.

Sunshine, to evermore glow
From your lips in a quiet smile
And bringing bright moonbeams
Brightening my darkened sky.

All this in so short a time -
Making for the future, a promise,
To love, honor and cherish
Simple words, spoken in truth - everlasting.

Elizabeth A. Green

Today

To live for the moment
caught in reoccurrence
the plain and dreary
dismal blunders
that darken cloudy skies.
The day no longer,
for as time chimes away;
the body toils for no reward.
But thine be cast aside,
the narrow minds that
spread men too thin.
On shall sleep dreams
that problems fade away
when all things laid up for tomorrow
are being lived for today!

Dideshe Young

Man's Greatest Desire

Release all homes,
cars, relationships,
egotism, pride and greed.
Anger and hate can have no place
if God it is you seek.

Do not ask for love
that comes and goes,
for human are we.
Earthly things never last
so trust in these no longer.

To find true happiness
you must go within,
only there can He be reached.
And your cry can not be a little one,
it must be unceasing.

Day and night,
night and day,
allow your cry to be heard.
When your desire is for only Him,
you will find He is there.

Debbe

M.I. Morn

The Willows' purring kitten
caught abroad dew from the ground
and pussy willow nods her head
for sun to shine around.

The meadow morning sweetness
a fresh breath of Northern air
the earthy smell of forest floor
the milkweed bursting there.

Salamander red and orange
slips 'tween the rocks and twigs
winter's berries, pink and rosy
near wild spearmint sprigs.

A dreamy haze hangs overhead
the leaves fall burning -
amber, red.

Peninsula of wondrous beauty
kissed by humid winds off lake
my mind soars to you reeling
for my heart begins to break.

Brian Dale Williams

Hovering Harlequin

Skepticism
    Circling her pursuits
Scrambling her sentiment
She leans uneasily beside her shelf
    Containing and preserving all she
    has retrieved, the shelf of memory
    and derivation
Her trembling, right hand lifts the
    disheveled mask
    Why?
    That is simple.
    Disguise.
She is worried only about invasion
    and loss
Few decipher her.
The harlequin visible to the
    trivial eye.

Elizabeth A. Robbins

Ode to a British Night Fighter

Up through the cold still air of night
Climbs this demon seeking fight.
It's metal wings of dull colour
Follow close it's motors roar.
Then speeding swiftly through the sky
This man made comet leaves the eye
And then is heard no more.

It goes each night to join the fight
For country and for King.
It's purpose is to guard the rights,
For which free people sing.
It's vigil watch has made the minds
Of many souls rest lighter
May I in my small way salute
The British Night Fighter.

Bernard W. McGinnis

Helping A Child

I looked at the child all
    cold and pale
As if in prison with no bail
    Eyes filled with sorrow,
    tears and so cold
Shivering with fear and
    skinny with bone
I set down the blanket and
    some warm food
Hoping that others wouldn't be rude
The child looked up with a
    spark in her eyes
And whispered "Thank You"
    with quite a surprise
Watching the objects with
    curiosity in mind
Not used to someone being so kind
As I walked away tears filled my eyes
For I knew I had helped a
    child's strength rise

Angela Gruber

Tea With A Japanese Angel

Little Japanese Angel
    come and sit here beside me.
How lovely it is in the garden,
    where the cherry blossoms bloom.
A prayer unfolds
    from your little heart,
as you bow your smooth dark head.
    Let's have some Jasmine tea
served from these delicate blue cups.
    This tea is such a delight,
little angel of the Rising Sun.
    It's so peaceful here,
that time seems to stand still,
    for you and me.
Your lovely almond eyes
    speak of serenity.
You have made my heart lighter
    than thistles blowing in the wind.
Now that I have met you,
    may I come for tea, again?

Dorothy S. Melton

Untitled

A friend with a simple mind
comes upon a lustrous field
a field of sickle and rain
In my soul I hold the key
to the awakening of everything
and my heart sits
encased in glass
only broken by your leaden hand
and opened by your simple looks
your looks of love and hate
your looks of fear and godly attributes
and I wait for your blissful rain
to come upon me in gentle drops
but nothing comes
and I feel no joy
and so comes the rain without a drop
upon my head or hands
but I'm still wishing I could feel your touch
I'm still wishing I could feel

Christopher Schuh

"On Being Free"

I am not bound by the chains of
conformity
Nor am I caged within my soul
I am the breath of summers yet
unborn
Whose fragrance fill the earth
I am the thundering hoof of
wild horses
Racing sunset across the plains
I am the wild geese, heading southward
through a flaming sky
Who may change the seasons?
Or redirect the course of a star?
And what of this body, soon to
crumble?
Neither chain nor dungeon may
confine the spirit
As it sets sail upon the wind.

Ashley Bertrand

Fire of Life

Blazing roaring fire,
Consuming and consumed
By it's own desire.

Creeping, leaping flames,
Out of bounds
Yet self-contained.

Glowing embers, warm and gentle.
Things remembered,
In the chill of November.

Ashes feathery and white
Blowing in the
Timeless night.

Emma P. Turner

Ode To My Wild Humming Bird

Little bird you make my day
Perched upon my balcony
Sipping nectar all day long
Life for you is one big song

Free to go or free to stay
I'm glad you choose to share my day.

Clare A. Shannon

Searching

Somewhere in a dark
Corner of my heart,
I found a longing..
An empty part.

I needed someone
To warm my soul,
To embrace love;
Keep out the cold.

God, grant that I
(Just one more time)
Shall a soul-mate find,
To share this life of mine.

Parting the curtain of time,
I found my gentle spirit,
Passion and love and grace.
Bound by God's merit.

We walked hand in hand,
We heard the angles sing.
I laid my head upon his heart
And found a place to dream.

Bobbye Tubbs

Vanessa

A gray sadness
Cornered in my yard.
Is filled with myriad memories
Of that time...

Once filled with fluffy kittens,
That casually relaxed
On the tip tops of fences.

And in that corner of my yard
One purred while I pet her
(In the morning breeze).

She smiled
Like an angel
So sweet,
So kind.

Not like her two sisters
Who hissed and clawed.
She
     was
        an Angel
From the day I found her to the day she
died.

Inga Markstrom

Broken Heart

Lost the one you loved all your life
    departed forever
Broken hearts never heal easily
  . putting it together
is a very difficult task to complete
    full of sorrow
breaks it farther apart
    never hide
if you have a broken heart
    never run
that will never heal a broken heart
    but joy
slowly connects a heart together
    fully healed
then you found your love again.

Christopher Tran

The Past And Now Tomorrow

How many years ago
Could we walk our street
Look up at the sky
Glance around and hear laughter
And the look down
Finding a gun pointed your direction-
What do you want?
Fear in the face of the victim.

Laughter from the children
Playing on the porch with Momma
So innocent, unknowing, wanting
Only to run into the sunlight aimlessly
Now do what you're told
Don't look at me!! Look away!!
Give me everything
Look down, look away, it's over.

This is where I lived
Grew-up, grown-up, moved away
Some old house, now
New memories replaces old fears.

Joseph G. Poulos

Mother

   Mother you were there when I
cried my first cry,

   Mother you were there to
dry my eyes,

   Mother you were there when
I walked my first step,

   Mother you were there when
I rode my first bike,

   Mother you were there when
I scraped my knee,

   Mother you were there
for every little thing, so here's a
"Thank You" to you from me.

Candace E. Pack

An Ode to an Expressionist

Brown,
dark haired fingers;
the twist in his wrist,
those ornate blue veins...
His hands massage up my thighs,
whisper down my back.
I will write sonnets
of the way they hold his pen
and epic poetry
of them running through his hair.
In my lonelier times,
I will recall the texture of his touch.
I will forget the awkward silence.
I will forget my fears of rejection.
I will remember
the beautiful things:
his voice,
his love,
his hands.

Jenni Lotman

The East Bay Fire Storm

The sky was red, then mauve and black.
Day had turned to night.
You could not see the jet in the sky.
Huge bats went into flight.

The fire spread so rapidly,
it was: Get out or die.
An old man barley saved his life.
No time to say good-bye.

When he looked back towards his house,
its windows filled with glow,
he knew his life's work was destroyed.
A huge fire storm was his foe.

It was three days when he returned,
and found his house in ash.
But there in the chimney was his cat,
with singed ears, but oh, not dead.

He picked it up and looked at it.
Tears streamed down his face.
"I'll build a house for us again,"
he said, "with courage and God's grace."

Carmen Bedell

Safety Zone

STOP
deafening tortured strident sounds
and frenzied writhing motions
and psychedelic shapes and symbols
surging out of electronic limbo
to drown the senses
in medium's mindless messages

LOOK
up and out across those
dead-end roads going nowhere -
beyond the reach of put-ons
make-believe and cynic fancies
lie steadfast green draped heights
and lofty pristine peaks where
sunlight holds the night at bay
for sullied flesh and jaded spirit
to recapture lost perspective

LISTEN...
still sounds, thought sounds
soul sounds, God sounds

Irene Prater Dell

Faith

If I took your eyes,
do you think you could see?
If I took your ears,
you think you'd hear me?
If I took your nose,
you think you could smell?
If I took your soul,
do you think it'd be hell?

If I took your life,
you think you'd be dead?
If I slashed your throat,
you think it'd flow red?
If I snapped your neck,
you think you'd live?
If I did all this,
you think your "God" would forgive.

Abdalla Awwad

Faces of the Fire

Laughing, crying, bending low
Destroyed, alive, dancing bright
Keeping alive the warmth for all
The faces of the fire

I need your warming, giving love
To last forever - not like you
What form will you take next
The faces of the fire

I feed you, care for you
Stroke you warm and full
But you die like the rest
The faces of the fire

What can I add to give you life
You have hickory, cedar and ash
And all the sweets of the forest
The faces of the fire

You change, different from before
From solemnity to wrath
Your hunger never ends
Maybe you want me

James P. Chovan

Untitled

What do you see
Distaste
When you look at me
Contempt

My clothes torn
Ratty
My hair unkept
Dirty

My face worn
Grime
My hands black
Germs

My body unhealthy
Cough
My legs sore
Tired

My soul lonely
Desperate
My heart breaking
Unloved

Brenda Cleary

My Dad

Take one day at a time and make it count
don't dwell on your woes and sorrow.
Look around you my friend, there's much
  to enjoy
and no one promised you tomorrow.

Look around at the trees, the grass
  and the sky,
and see what God had done,
to make your world a better place.
Now wait for the rising sun.

Tomorrow can be good, my friend,
but there is no guarantee.
So live and love and laugh and learn.
Whatever will be, will be.

Delilah Stranch

Hated Skies

Mourning sun,
Do you like the scent of Death,
Like the hatred on your breath?
You offer life,
But give only pain,
Sprinkling, expected,
Like the April rains.

Foolish Moon,
Can't you see faith is dead?
It died when a child fell down,
And bled.
Broken hearts, cast aside.
Love devoured by foolish pride.

Vengeful Stars,
Do you drink the blood of man
So you can send Hell's fury
To the promised land?
Silly people kneel to pray.
It's never stopped the hatred,
Why would it today?

Emilie Anne Hruzek

Cirque

Are you flying in your dreams?
Do you sail, soar, swoop?
Do your feet savor sawdust
  while your head caresses clouds?
Do you sense crescendo melodies
  that tease and tear
  and haunt?
Do you cloak your brazen beauty
  in a mask of porcelain gold
  even as you plume your spirit
  so it too shall soar aloft?
Do you tutor feats of witchcraft
  as your children torture bodies
  into tiny tents of dance
  and prayer
  and praise?
Are you flying in your dreams?
Do you sail, soar, swoop?
Do your feet savor sawdust
  while your head caresses clouds?

Isabel R. Make

A Dream

Beaver coach with three axils is a
  dream for retirement;
Living in a dream even before,

When you are lower then low income,
  a dream it shall be maybe for always
who's to know for sure.

Beaver coach O' Motor home
  is a dream of travel to
see our country's highways
  and by ways.

It's a dream that might and
  might not come true.

Dream on dream on as
  dreams are what makes
life cycle go round;

So dream on O'dreamer
  it could become your home yet.

Delores Rice

Rose Scent

The sweet fragrance
embraced my nostrils
with an eternal addiction
to the delicate scent
of a rose.

The perfumed rose
is natures way
of sweetening the earth
with only a faint
but enchanting scent.

Brenda Faye O'Neal

Untitled

Life is a joy
Enjoy it

Life is a present
Open it

Life is fun
Be it

Life is abstract
Unravel it

Pay close attention to criticisms
So you will avoid subversion

Strive for the best
Ace all tests
For you are the greatest

Life is a mystery
solve it

Life is wild
tame it

Life is not created
Until you create it.
Learn form your past with all it's mistakes
Take hold of your present which you make
Along comes the future which will be great.

Delondi Kintaud

Why The Silence?

The building heat of fury
Enraptures mind and soul

The rage that grows inside of me
The rage that makes me whole

It used to let me get away
It gave me time to sleep

Now it has control of me
Now I can't escape

My body is devoured
My thoughts are turned to dust

I used to know emotions
Emotions that are crushed

But still I am an entity
But still I am a man

My spirit is held prisoner
Crucified and damned to obliteration

Charles Lee

Beauty

Your beauty like a warm wind
enveloping me, comforting me

Your presence like a tiger
strolling through the city streets

Your knowledge of life
as fresh as the most beautiful rose

Don't stop growing
else your beauty be lost

Take off your mask
and experience life

Life as it's meant to be
here in grand utopia

Ed Slivinskas Jr.

For Someone Special

You're always on my mind.
Even in my sleep,
Thoughts of you aren't left behind.
You I never want to lose.
I hope I never have to choose.
When you have to leave,
With you my thoughts will always be.
Because although it's hard for me to say,
I love you in a very special way.

JoDell Smith

Money

You can find ways to spend it,
Even when it's not yours.

You will look and you've lost it.
No satisfaction for your chores.

You will never have enough.
Can't! Always wanting more.

No matter how wealthy,
You want what is next door.

You do not see the sadness.
It is easy to ignore...

The material things it gets you,
Really leaves you rather poor.

Deanna Chmelik

Metaphors

Every plane is you
Every boat is you
Every dream of flight or fancy
Every ca - rou - sel is you.
(Ev - e - ry Ferris wheel too)
Every move that might be dancing
All the music's you,
(All the drummers too)
All the rhyme and much of reason
Every summer's you,
(Spring and winter too)
All the joys of every season
Rainy days are you
And all shades of blue
Sea and sand and blazing skies,
Silver rings are you,
(Toy-like things are too) and,
Every pair of Spanish eyes.

Angelina Coluccini

Untitled

"I see more of me in you
everyday."
Is what you used to say.

How do you think that makes
me feel today,
Since God has taken you away.

It's because of me your life
came to a halt,
The whole thing was my fault.

I carry the guilt everyday,
It's tearing my heart away.

I can't just live with it,
Soon I will break down or
have a fit.

I want you to know,
I would have never let you go.

You waited till I left that day,
You waited till I was gone
before you let God take your
life away.

Deborah Young

One Mind, One Body

The shattered mind
Explodes in a disarray of
Splinters- the brain
Sizzles in its casing.

The trials of the day
Spiral in each ear,
And nerve-pulses
Pound dents in the core.

Limbs falter
Numb as the dead,
A body trapped
In its own spores.

The heart grinds
In rhythm unknown.
Trapped in the shell
Of the mangled structure.

Jamie L. Barajas

Mary's Life 1897

Little Mary, orphan child,
eyes of blue, gentle, mild.
Adopted many years ago,
by Emma, during winter's snow.
Adoptive Father took them south,
to land of dust, wind and drought.
Left them penniless down there,
traveled home without a care.
Finally suffering from remorse,
begged to borrow some resource.
Sent to Emma far away,
funds to start them on the way.
Now, able to return with Mary,
Emma left with haste and hurry.
By train they traveled on the way,
as Mary's life slipped fast away.
Little Mary, ill with fever,
age of seven, the Lord received her.

John P. McReynolds

Traditions

A child in the south
faces much joy and pain
A lifetime that's more
than a long lasting stain.
The traditional things
that we must look at
like a smooth southern drawl
and a dried out straw hat.
We face now a future
full of promise and hope
leaping over a barrier
of severe crime and dope.
The shining horizon
lighting our darkest times
brings technology upward
as the old church bell chimes
As we look to our leaders
We believe what they say
Our children can look forward
to a much brighter day.

Dale Julio Rosado

The New Life

Let not a trifle worry you,
Fear not a single thing.
But joy in the presence of My love,
To you my gifts I bring.

Your mind will be mine,
Your eyes will see,
What you didn't see before.
Your actions will be mine
and mine alone; once you've
opened up your door.

Yield yourself to me and I'll
give you a life brand new.
Receive my blessings and graces of love,
forever abundant for you.

Connie Moran

Dirge (A Funeral Hymn)

Laying on my back
  feeling joy to purge
    why do in the distance
      I hear the sound of dirge

In a wooden box
  Half up open wide
    Why are all these people
      Staring down inside

I know all these people
  relatives and friends
    Some I treated poorly
      did they come for mends

Everyone oh gather around
  why have all you cried
    the way you act around me now
      You'd think that someone died

Brad Dezek

His Promise

When you have those days,
  Filled with worry and pain,
Look for sunshine and rainbows,
  Beyond the rain.
In the gloomiest day,
  Or the darkest night,
God is always with you,
  To show you the light.
If you put God first in the morning,
  And the last thing at night,
He will show you the way,
  To do everything right.
He will always be beside you,
  To guide your way,
Whether it is the dark of night,
  Or the light of day.
God will lead you,
  To his promised land,
Where there's no more pain or worry,
  Sitting at his right hand.

Elouise Collins Mason

Kaleidoscope

Round and round it goes,
Fills up dreams when it glows—
See the colors; warm and bright
Put it closer to the light.

Round and round it goes,
What is the symbol when it shows,
Many circles, shapes and size—-
Pick them out with your eyes.

Round and round it goes,
Designs dance and also pose.
What's the mood when you see,
Different flow of tranquility.

Round and round it goes,
One last turn by the nose.
I like the green and the blue
Tell me now; how 'bout you?

Jaime Colonna

Don't Be A Frog

A slimy frog on a Lilly pad
floating on the lake,
or a lovely monarch butterfly
drifting with the breeze.
A joy in its own world
but a stranger in the other.

Try as it might the frog can't fly.
But a butterfly on a Lilly pad
is surely out of place.
Just like some folks I know,
Trying to be what they aren't,
And yet not happy where they are.

The frog is dumb to the ways of life
But happy in a world of its own.
So don't be a frog on a lily pad,
Just lift your voice in prayer
And you like the butterfly can soar
above the sea of trouble into the air.

John F. Tucker

Spring

March winds blowing,
flowers growing.
Spring is back in town.
Bees are buzzing,
I tell you cousin.
Spring is back in town.
I'm not lying,
winter's been trying,
to really get me down.
It's cold did show,
leaving all that snow,
white upon the ground.
But, I finally won,
here comes the sun.
Spring is back in town!

Betty Stuart

Our Love

Our love is like a river;
Flowing through the earth
Our love is like a rose;
Opening at the sign of light
Our love is like a bird;
Spreading it's wings in air
Our love is like a mountain;
At its highest peak
Our love is like an angel;
Strong and sweet
Our love is special;
Better than ever
Our love is us,
Let us never part

Elizabeth Marie Shull

Up North In March

Pussy willows are
  fluffing their fur,
Curious flowers are
  poking noses through earth...
Days lasting longer
  awaken to sounds of
  cardinals and robins
  singing in rounds....
The first signs of life are here...
After a long, trying winter,
  spring hovers near...
Like a warm, teasing lover,
  she slowly uncovers beauty
  and secrets...
to charm our new year.

Connie Harding

Fight Of Freedom

Blood of the innocent
for freedom and worth
they fought for their rights
defending their earth.

Their armies were few
but their hearts were strong
Unified and together
they would right the wrong

They died for their country
and when justice was done
Their freedom was given
and the war was won.

Jenna Gathje

Narragansett Bay

Watching ships leave the bay....
fog settles on the water,
like a cloud in the sky.
Forms are but mere shadows,
against a sullen sky,
moving as if in slow motion,
knowing they are about to die.
Rising comes the sun,
burning off the fog, revealing life anew.
Busy people work on the docks,
loading and unloading who knows what,
simply working for one's pay.
The sun sets and work begins to stop,
slowing down,
the day has been long enough.
During the night all is quiet and still,
channel lights flash,
distant bells are heard.
Morning will be here soon,
and I'll watch ships leave the bay....

John A. Racine

Untitled

God did not promise you a rainbow,
For every time it rains.
Nor promise you a field of flowers,
As you look across the plains.
He did not promise health or strength,
Nor purses full of gold,
Or sturdy limbs or shining eyes
As you are growing old.

He promised you abiding love
And strength to bear the load
For there are many shady lanes
As you trod the dusty road.
The days will never be too long
The race too long to run,
For when the last long day is o'er
He'll call and say "well done."

Henry Schendel

May An Angel Love You

It's the sound of her voice,
For her words, we rejoice.
May an angel love you.

There is soul in every part,
For these are feelings from her heart.
May an angel love you.

See the glow that's in her eyes,
Every time she says, "I rise".
May an angel love you.

When she spreads her love around,
There can be thunder in the sound.
May an angel love you.

I am so thankful that she shares,
Her way of showing that she cares.
May an angel love you.

Yes, she is a blessing from above,
And she is flowing in God's Love.
May an angel love you.

Andrea Hockenhull-Shepard

I've the Right for the Fight

My poem is to honor the cat.
For his friend is not the rat.
His life is opposite of the bat.
The bat as blind as can be!
The cat, even in the dark, can see!
To meet one another.
They need not bother.
They might fight each other.
Friends, they may never be.
The cat will eat the rat.
Did it taste good?
Yes, I bet you wish you could,
Be like the cat.
Not very fat.
Just, solid muscle.
It's worth the hustle.
When he needs to tussle.
Yes, observe the cat,
For he will show you where its at,
In cleanliness, survival, and the nap.

Lonesome Crow Feather

Untitled

To live in peace is but a dream
for so events do make it seem.
For mankind strays from ways divine
and is pre-occupied with time
spent chasing wealth and foolish
things that discontentment
only brings.
This earth could be a better place
devoid of this the human race.

John Longbottom

Thank You

For the birds in the trees,
For the air that we breath,
For making me.
I say,
Thank you, please.

For the beautiful land,
For the touch in my hand,
For the white grains of sand.
I say,
Thank you, please.

For the clouds in the sky,
For the mountains so high,
For the sight in my eyes.
I say,
Thank you, please.

For all you have endured,
For the cross that you bore,
For the life that you gave.
I say,
Thank you, Dear Lord.

Becky Knight

Model

She twisted and twirled
Down the runway she whirled
Music blaring Wildly

Bedecked in black with
plunging line
Sleek tights — Utterly divine!
And, in the finality
Showing off her sexuality.

Elizabeth Valicenti

Yearly Token

Robins on parade
Red vest uniforms perform
Celebrating Spring

Colleen Bingham

Forgive Me

Please Lord, forgive me,
For what I have done,
Give me some patience,
I know I have none.

Forgive me again Lord,
I get so upset,
Lord, I am sorry,
I haven't learned yet.

Lord, I'm asking once more,
To please forgive me,
I just don't understand,
Why I get so angry.

My Lord, I beg You,
Let me get this straight,
It could have been okay,
But I just wouldn't wait.

Thank You, my Lord,
I'm slowing down now,
I'll use my new-found grace,
To You, I give this vow.

Bobbie Allen

Why?

Why must a love be
Forced on me?

Moments of lust and passion
Have impounded me

A cry for freedom
is never heard

Responsibility crushes
Every nerve

Oh, lust and passion
without a word
You have been heard!

Arnold Joseph LaSota

For You The Pain Is Gone

Our last time together,
forever in my mind.
A doorway to the past,
I'd almost die to find.

If I could find the key
to open up the gate,
I could ease the pain,
and change our tragic fate.

But you never let me in.
You never let me know.
You hid behind a mask,
the pain you couldn't show.

You could've run to me,
but now it's all too late.
For you, the pain is gone.
For me, it's just as great.

Cara Burrell

248

The Hourglass

The sands of time
forever pouring
while we struggle
to keep from boring

Always in search
for something new
out of the way
for just a clue

All for a taste
the fruit of the vine
but never forgetting
the sands that chime

Edward J. Rohr Jr.

Peace from the Night

Fear of the shadow
    framed by shame
Surrounded by the same
    nameless
faceless presence that has only form
Just a familiar posture,
    that same weighted pose
Abysmal fear...
    that left me forever froze

Endless terror—this dread of night
Emanating from deep within
    beyond any light

A wounded nauseous center
    from a scar hidden from view
Totally unknown,
    but all too familiar to be new

Desperate search for comfort from within
    or anyone who might
Care enough to bring forth
Peace from the night

Barbara Joan Zaha

Nova

"I would be free," you said.
"Free as the sky and sea,
Entangled only by the wind
And tides of destiny."
Yet there is a freedom
In the studded skein
Created by the spider
Torn, but spun again.
Each star holds to its galaxy
A free wanderer as such.
And are you then the star I see;
The star I must not touch?

Gertrude M. Taylor

Friendship

Friendship is a silver ring
Friendship is a lovely thing
Just beings and has no end
doesn't even need to send
messages on paper;
knows all is well and right
lives on thoughts and true affections
now and then has its objections
time is swell and meetings are few
so this brings my love to you!

Fatima C. Matos

Flow

Let it go river flow
from
crimson hallowed cavern

Rusty sea forever
be relentless flood unaltered

Red moon tide
dare not hide what life expels
with wonder

Can it be I shall see
the coming of blood's mother

Ann Poyas

True Legacy! A Guardian Angel's Bliss

Mother's love reaches
from beyond the grave,
the little girl
she had to leave,
so very young at age.
Trying to shelter her
from all the hurt,
with hope that love
would fill her little heart.

To keep a loving bond,
through dreams and prayers
reaching far beyond.
That she may always feel,
someone way out there,
still watches over her.

There is no one, of any kind
could ever take away,
the motherly bond
that reaches from beyond.

Eva Croci

Winter

Snows, the soul of winter, fall
From murm'rous clouds upon, in mains,
The midnight milky shawl;
Hoary forms but whiskered grains
Down glimm'rous swells of hours worth.
Itself the wintry silver veil,
White once more and over earth,
Her burrowed flesh asleep and pale.
I watch within by spelling vein,
Wrapped in word and wool, at how
Here zagging pinions trace the pane.
I'm growing warm and tired now;
Time dusts the hushing year again.

Benjamin Deardorff-Green

Secrets

On tip toe they tread,
from one to another;
to maybe a sister
or perhaps a brother.
They sneak past parents,
to a best friend.
But once they get there,
should their journey end?
A secret to hold close
or one to impart?
To know the difference,
follow your heart.

Jean A. Farr

Night Songs

As the sun silently sneaks away
from sight,
Making room for the moon
the night owl calls out
"Goodnight, sweet dreams, goodnight"
I lie there in the dark
And listen to the wind and trees
talking to each other
They are saying how beautiful
they sound together
And I agree.
I listen to the night time singing
its song
Making me sleep
Making me dream.

Amanda Welty

Finding My Way

Once again I've lost my way
From the narrow path I stray
Footsteps falter as I go
Over rocky ground I do not know

I look for someone in the dark
To bring me back to my safe mark
I stumble, fall, and rise again
While struggling hard to find a friend

Then light is shown me after all
I'm back on path and walking tall
My chin held high, my heart is light
My footsteps steady, my life is right.

Frances Parnell

Chamber Of Fragmented Shards

A chamber is fragmented,
Full of crystal shards.
Sharp words, life's blows.
Heartfelt desires, unfulfilled.

It splits the central vessel -
Broken.
Scattered....
In bits of life!

All shards - picked up,
repaired and learned from.
Strong glue!
Strength of my soul.
Soundness in mind with body

Whole, once again!
A beauty - as fine crystal.
I radiate from this vessel.
The central essence....
Full of iridescence,
as sunshine catches - light.
DAZZLING.

Elaine M. Sawyer

The Barn

Come with me to the barn.
See all the horses galloping
With their manes flowing in the wind.
Hear the horses neighing wisely.
Smell the fresh hay in the barn.
Taste the air damp from the frost.
Feel the soft fur of the horse.
So come with me to the barn.
You'll love it very much.

Carolyn Godfrey

Hummingbird

Drinking in the sustenance
   gaining energy from the nectar.
Wings beating rapidly, coming close but
   fleeing from advances.
Luxuriating in the surroundings
   but not touching.

No baggage.
   No compromises.
Now.
   Not tomorrow.

Delicate frame and wing.
   A joy to see, not to hold.
For the spirit,
   A fortress, bold.

Alice Higgins

The Angel's Dance

Far above the flowing water
Gliding through the sky
On a wind swept adventure
Until the day we die

Sounds of joy about us
Sun rays on our head
Clouds forming their pretty pictures
But what if we were dead

Then we'd see the angels
A sure sight to behold
Gliding through the heavens
On golden wings to fold

Come and dance the dance
Of the sea gull's flight above
Come and fly with us
To join our everlasting love

Carmela Straccione

Who Am I?

I want to be, the very me,
God wants, me to be.
I don't know how,
I just know this, I must try.

I want to live for Him,
how do I do this?
I have been lost for so long,
God show me the way.

Who am I?
I am your child.
Please love me, I pray!

I want to laugh,
I want to love,
So much.

I've never known that
anybody cared for me.
Now I know that it's true you do!

Gayla Fuemmeler

Poems Calling

I want to sleep
But poems won't keep
Safe in my mind
If I go to sleep
Write them I must
If I'm going to at all
When, at night, a poem calls

Carol Candela

The Breeze

I can feel you cool on my face
Going through my hair and
I close my eyes
When you stop I feel sad
I want more
It touches my skin and feels good
The way a lovers touch feels
Only you and you lover
Know how you feel
Its special something that's yours

Becky Adams

Summertime Ecstasy

Summer night—-
   golden bright—-
Air heavy set
   with dew so wet
On leaves of trees
   and shrubs of jet.

Sparkling diamonds bright
   in the night—summer night—-
Still—still—misty light.
   No leaf astir.

No cold, wintry scene
   can here occur
In silken-soothed mind
   mid midsummer's lure
Of golden sheen.

Gwendolyn Yvonne Walker

Woodsmoke

We drift from our moorings
   gradually
just as the summer
   turns to autumn.

To wake
   weighted wanting
the secure shore
   we no longer see.

Aimless tunes
   darkened sky
and early fires
   mix in the air
the most restless of fumes.

Now vulnerable to
life's fickle sea
we learn to navigate
midst falling stars
   and fate.

Ann Skiold

On Growing Old

I am in the Autumn of my years
Spring is just a hazy memory
And summer has ground past,
Time is slower, the air colder.

Oh I know winter is coming
And life is slipping away,
The light is clearer, the shadows longer
And God! the colors, the colors

Are brighter now.

Don Moore

Untitled

Sky is green,
grass is blue.
In heaven,
my living colors
become secrets shared only by;
The flowers are sun,
leaves are red.
Come to my world,
down like beams of wavelength crayons,
swirling, narrow and wide,
slow tilt on this ball of mud,
then slide.
Spikes zip past on invisible planes,
Time warp speed.
Never have I seen the day,
when I could float away on a distant cloud
of brilliant gold.
Forever with my Maker,
and my colors, bold.

Jennifer Erb

Perfect Person

She was blessed with a very
grateful life.
To her husband, she made a
great wife.
Becoming closer and closer to God
every year.
She was with you to shed
every tear.
Her family meant the world to her.
Her heart was weak, but always
pure.
Everyday of her life she helped
someone out.
In her mind there was never a doubt.
God put her here for a reason.
she celebrated every season.
Hopefully she found out why
she was here.
Before the day she was faced
with her only fear.

Jennifer Sackenheim

Yellow Tree

Yellow tree against a
gray-blue sky
always bending, yet I wonder,
did you ever try
just once to hold fast
when swirling winds rush past?
To stiffen your limbs
that they not give way
to an angry gust?
You must enjoy the storm
as you stand amidst great harm.
Should you not be strong?
Tell me, why dear tree
do your branches bend?
"A simple truth, dear friend."
Said the tree, "My Creator
crafted me to know when
to give and when to take,
and to praise and thank Him
that my branches don't break."

Gordon Newton Smith

Just A Door Hinge

I'm mostly colored white or black.
Sometimes can't I be orange?
But then, of course, alas, alack,
I'm only just a door hinge.
Anthony Gutowski

Who

Who greets you in the morning, whether
grumpy or bright

Who stays every evening to see that your
letters are typed

Who screens your calls and protects you
from the pests
Who remembers your wife's birthday and
anniversary no less

Who knows all your faults and never
complains

Even though sometimes she would like
to entrain

If you wish to be told who this person
might be

I'll let you in on a little secret
it's your secretary
Helen P. Sassaman

Untitled

Walking
hand in hand
upon the road,
with the sun at our backs,
and a song in our hearts.

You turn to me
smile,
I am so happy,
so content.
Your smile is the key
unlocking the door to my heart,
the journey has just begun....
Deborah L. Swiss

Footsteps

The tracery of one's footsteps
Has very often swept
Above, beyond and over
The yearnings we have kept
Just like the blink of
A tear drenched eye
What's done, is done, is done.
There is no eradication
An inventor could conceive
To ease, assuage or pardon
This foolishness we grieve
For racing headlong, step after step
In ceaseless mortal acts
There is no other way to say
Nor get out of this trap, except
To let our humbleness be that
That is our faith, then we will see the
constancy
And understand our place
For by our hearts he'll take us
And forgive our sins with grace.
Frances B. Akins

Case Hardened

Our children, yours and mine
Have taken our support for
granted, almost every time.
Luxuries were not the made-of-the-day.
Shelters, food and space
paved the way.

To journey up ward and onward everyday.
Privileges taken for granted
While they set there pace.
You and I, we provided the
firm foundations for base
Do they comprehend the American
Life Race?
They could call or visit
And remember why?
We have learned to hide the tears.
Sometimes with laughter to
suppress the aches and fears.
Sharing with good friends sustains,
While heirs scorn our cares.
Holly Carol Harvick-Ward

The Gift Of Peace!

He sent his love from above,
He gave us the choice,
To ignore or to rejoice.
  He asked to believe,
  An thou shall receive,
The gift of peace...
  If your love is true,
  The pain we grieve,
  One day shall leave...
Patience is the key,
To open the door,
To a world that is free!
  The Lord is our soul,
  We need his love to survive,
  Be thankful your alive,
  And the Lord will help-guide!
Debbie Compton

The Frog

When the frog rises out of the mud,
he hops around with a thud.
His legs are big and very strong
and at night he sings his song.

He eats bugs in the pond,
and to his tongue they always bond.
He likes to lay in a pile of grass
and watch the deer as they pass.

The frog is ever so very smart
and once you meet him, you'll
never want to part!

You will love the frog of the lagoon
and I hope you will meet him soon!
Joseph F. Simpson III

life

popularity yet shyness
strength and weakness
beauty, ugliness
giving but always looking to take
happy yet filled with sorrow,
mirrors are the windows to ones soul
eric anaya

Does He Know

Does he know
He is always on my mind
Every day
Every second

Does he know
He is always in my dreams
Every night
From when I lay down
Until I wake up

Does he know
I am always watching him
Every time I see him
From the first sight
Until he walks away

Does he know
I go out of my way to see him
All the time
No matter what it costs me

If this isn't love what is it?
Elizabeth Beasley

Some Say

Why marry an old man, some say,
He is so worn out and raggy,
His hair is grey and gets dirty,
And his pants are awfully baggy.

Then you wonder also don't you,
Does he ever take a clean bath?
As an alcoholic over the years
Made his facial skin so saggy.

But then, don't you wonder,
What this man's got to offer?
So you set and search within him
And you'll find a hearts much softer.

He may have been whipped or beaten,
And have taken many very hard raps,
Then, it's no wonder at all, is it?
How his energy got worn and sapped.

But brush him up a little bit, "please,"
And take time to see him come clean
From all of his old, old, bad habits,
He's like a mother's baby, just weaned.
Eileen Corey Norwood

The Lord's Ways

The Lord hears what I do not hear
He sees what I do not see,
He guides me on the straight and narrow
Where ever I may be.

But I must listen to his voice
Where ever I may go
The road may be rocky
On the strait and narrow.

I must walk behind him
In his footsteps
No matter how hard the climb
For Heaven is waiting at
the end of time.
Benedicta Bunek

Stormy Weather

Whitecaps flash on Alsea Bay
Headlights catching wild waves spray,
Gulls huddle on a bayside lawn
On one foot, keeping cold in pawn,
Beaks tucked to eyes in downy feather,
A Christmas tree in a little park,
Flamenco dancer in the dark,
Sequins shimmering her costume,
Bowing, writhing in winter gloom,
Romping with wind and weather.

Clyde A. Beakley

Her

I see her
her eyes
as beautiful as the sea
her hair
so shiny, so shimmery in the breeze
her skin
pale and soft as a white, sweet rose
her body
oh her body
with every step, every twist,
every turn sets my heart, body,
mind, and soul on fire.
Heating every inch of me

How I want her!

Chelsea Figgins

Heavenly Love

It was all around us,
Here, there, everywhere we
were together. The aura of love.
Yes, it was there, everywhere.
   There was only one love,
and that was our love,
soaring higher and higher.
Approaching heavenly love.
   I know I can't have that
without you, please, I want
you to stay, so we can
perfect that heavenly touch.
   I want to be with you,
night and day, and there
ain't no way we can say,
we didn't create that
special touch, heavenly love.
Created by us!

Hank Kersey

My Dreams, My Life,

Our Dreams, Our Life

Here we go
here we go
here we go, again
is this a dream or reality
I don't know why.
I don't know where.
I don't even know how.
But I do know that
to give up on your dreams,
You might as well give up on life.
So always remember that our dreams
is what our life is about.
because if we give up on our dreams,
we might as well give up on life
because our dreams are our life.

Gale Davis-White

The Sadness of Speaking

Secrets running here and there -
   hidden rumors in the air.
How the ears do strain to hear
   what the private things do bear.

Is it truth or is it not?
   Hopefully they won't get caught.
Lies are sour, lies are sweet.
   Liars tell without a thought.

Gossip flows with bitter tales.
   Hope is gone while heartache trails.
No one cares how mankind feels
   if they aren't the one who fails.

Through the grapevine they must talk;
   speaking loud they scream and squawk.
Looking in, they take a peak
   just to find distress and shock.

They should mind their own affairs
   if they want to clear stares.
Holding back the pain and tears
   people find what really scares.

Brett Leabo

Untitled

She looked down
High heeled shoes
The floor squeaking
Her breasts were full
Her mind bursting
The baby looked at her
She tiptoed out
It was all for the best
The war was over

She knew sorrow
Her chair became her comfort
Deep and soft
Until time became future
And a letter arrived

She had found her destiny
Her baby came home
Years had gone by
There eyes met
Like a mirror image
The milk was gone.

Inge Smentek

"Forever Friends"

The time which we have spent,
Has gone by very fast.
I never would have dreamt
That it would never last.

I've heard some people say,
That guys should never cry.
Then do not look my way,
As we now say goodbye.

And as we now must go,
Unto our life's next space.
I think that you should know,
You will not be replaced!

Joseph Marshall

Birds

Birds fly place to place
None are the same
But all are beautiful

Elizabeth Mann

Against The Wind

Simply spread your wings and soar
higher than the highest
life yourself
above yourself
and now you are the mightiest

Freedom from your hell below
escape from all of torture
tear you mind and body
and soul away

and fly against the wind

Blind your weakness
bind your strengths
and soar
simply soar against the wind

Believe it now, not later
for now is when it occurs
it's your own escape
your own Utopia, your freedom
your flight, your strength
against the wind

Jagoda J. Gillis

PAPA

His hair is thick and silver
   His face has wrinkles of love
His eyes the color of the sky
   He's an angel from above.

His open arms, his cheerful smile
   His wisdom for all to share
And in each passing moment
   His love is always there.

Ninety-three years in the light of God
   He's lived a lot of passing seasons
With few regrets to speak of
   And all with very good reasons.

I see him in my Mothers eyes
   And in her Brothers too
In all the things they share with us
   In all the things they do.

My dearest Papa, I want you to know
   That no matter what we may endeavor
Your legacy of undying love and courage
   Will live in our hearts forever.

Deborah K. Brown

"Nowhere To Be Found"

   I recognize his body, but not
his face. I should look closer but he
needs the space. I think he is hurt
bad, also very sad.
   Something has happened
what should I do. I looked all
around but there's just me and you.
I want to touch him and see
what he will say. But I'm afraid
he will just walk away I think I
should leave and come back in an
hour, maybe he will have more
power. As I was walking, I turned
around, I stopped to look and he
was nowhere to be found.
Wherever you are, whatever
you do, I'll be right here
for you.

Amanda Shaw

Saudi Arabia

I see an Arab riding hard
his horse as white as snow
his robes flow with the wicked wind
to tell tall tales of woe

He is Mohammed of long ago
high upon his steed
warning warriors down below
the folly of their deeds

Blood and oil mix very well
on the sands of burning hell
the desert shows no mercy dear
to those that do not know

See deep into the sea of sand
where lies the foul dark oil
there will appear the son of man
when earth is at a boil

Allan H. Lambert

Stormy

The wind is at war tonight
Hissing, spitting rattling
Like angry lovers quarreling
The trees are bent like a bow string
Pulled almost to the point of breaking
But Cupid's flown from here
And a siren screams in the night
The wind chimes on the porch sang tunes
While the wind gathered up things
Like lovers when parting
Again the wind swooped, as if trying
To catch someone
They were once lovers
And the wind chimes ended their song.

Diana Dolhancyk

Garden Of My Life

Flower my garden!
Hold back the swirl of passing time.
Let me lie in your welcome shade
And contemplate my future life
Surrounded by your beauty
And serenity.
Flower my garden,
Garden of my life.

And the garden of my life replied:
"Dear Nature's child, so sweet and mild,
I cannot make time stand still,
That's not God's purpose or His will.
Dedicate your future years
To stamping out this Earth's tears.
And when your life is through and done
You'll come and join me in the rays of the sun,
Shining and smiling as my wife
Onto the garden of my life."

Flower, flower, flower my garden,
Dearest garden of my life.

Daphne Gulland

Haiku

Old house of sorrow
Mortised with fear and anger
What axe can fell you?

Alice Faye Singleton

Surrender

Take my hand
hold it loosely
keeping your distance
Lay your head
near my shoulder
but not to close
Put your lips
across my cheek
ever so softly
Lend me your heart
but not so quickly
Surrender your soul
HOLD ME TIGHTLY.

Deborah L. Sherrill

You Called Me Your Friend

Thinking about those happy days
Hoping they would never end,
Remembering your kind ways
You called me your friend.

Keeping those you love
Close to your heart,
Always room for another
Willing to help them make a new start.

"I know I can help him,"
You would often say
They did not realize,
What a treasure had come their way.

Holding us secure in your love
Never letting us fall,
Remembering your courageous ways
How you lifted us all.

Cherishing our happy days
And, all the love you would send,
Remembering your kind ways
You called me your friend.

Cynthia Leyva

The Little Tree That Stands Alone

I smile an say, good morning my friend;
How are you today?
Its always good to see you, as I travel
along the way
Looking up high upon the tracks;
To let you know I will be back.
I see you every morn;
Don't be sad, but be glad, that someday
you'll be grown.
I thank God along the way,
that you bring sunshine to my day,
Your bristle sometimes wet with dew
don't forget I love you too.
I hate to leave as I turn the bend;
And hope our friendship will never end;

Gladys Paris

Passing

Each morning I walk into the bathroom,
Open the medicine chest,
And fumble for the toothpaste tube.
"But isn't it strange?" I say to myself,
"I thought I just bought a new tube
And this one looks almost empty."
Yes, isn't it strange to see one's
Life pass so quickly
Through a tube of toothpaste?

Edwin R. Hamilton

Lonely Anyway

I'm thinking....thinking
How do I go about this
Is it all about dreaming
Or is it just hit or miss

Words on paper
Thoughts in my mind
It's like pulling off a caper
Leaving everything else behind

I love when it flows
A mystery being solved
Like fighting with no blows
A new energy is evolved

My body must relax
Though it wants to sing
My mind is in contact
With its very being

Loneliness must be the answer
I always knew it was so
It is like a hidden treasure
I always knew it was gold

Bobby Joe Fischer

The Face Of Darkness

Oh, Night!
How passionate is thy rage.
Thy face so cold.
Thy breath so still.
And yet, thy calm,
Is as soft as a summer breeze.

O' Darkness,! So strong!
Like death,
Consumes both soul and spirit.
To its grave, its destruction falls.
Darkness fades.
Into its own shadow it escapes.
Light!
Emerges in its majesty,
To reclaim the soul and spirit lost,
Reliving its dance of joy on earth.

Genevieve Chevrez

The Eerie Cry of Death

The eerie cry of death
How pleasant to the soul.
No more sorrow, no more joy!
The soul is torn between life
and death.
To travel forward.
To meet one's mother
But wait- leaving behind
the child
The very soul of the one
departing.
The eerie cry of death

Elizabeth Klumpp

About Love

How do you know if you're in love?
Do you have a special feeling?
Or is love blind or does love blind you?
How does love work?
Does love work?
Will love always work?
Is love good or bad?
Someday answer me before I die!

Cintra Carolina Dacosta

If

If along life's highway
I can some kindness show-
If I can, with tenderness
Lift a heart that's low-
If I can bring a hopeful smile
Where now there shimmer tears-
If by showing courage myself
I can ease another's fears-
If I can lift a discouraged soul
To a little higher plane,
Then dear Lord perhaps 'twill be
I have not lived in vain.

Edythe Wouters Cline

Battered Thesaurus

Lover of words that I am
I cast them aside
  Book
  Tome
  Volume
All useless to me
in my need for coherence
in my need to articulate
in my need for you.
I cannot utter a single
syllable which would
  encapsulate
  consummate
  placate
that which flows within me
under the expansive bridge of vocabulary
beyond the muddy banks of words
to the river's silent, impotent mouth.

Angela C. M. Cox

Sculptor

I am the Master.
I command
and the clay bows before me.

I can exemplify my heart,
my mood
through every line
in three dimensional thought forms.

With awesome precision,
I sculpt the direction,
the path it will take.
Obediently it begins to breathe.

Every work,
expresses my creativity,
diversity, and skill.

And in my power
I hold the unsuspecting
breathless
and awestruck.

Belinda J. Wilder-Snider

The Fire

A fire sang between us
So lovely, warm, and bright!
Some said we could not keep it
Beyond the morrow's light.
Still the lyric binds us
Though many years have passed,
And cynics are astounded
To see our singing fire last!

Alice Lynton

In A Room Full Of Thought

Is where I sit, The reason for my thoughts? For my window shows much
in what I write. a room full of wonder... a page of tears... a book
filled with memories...a mind full of pain. how can I explain?...
Examples on how lost my world can be, as my pen writes what my heart
bleeds for ever so often!...

Lost in a light,...a light that shines through the narrow shading of
my window and still, I hear the rough breeze ease its coldness
through the cracks. for there now I lie listening to the shattering
rain as it bounces harshly upon my window, and still a young man
writes how he sees and feels the changing settings,...changing words
being said to him....

He writes...He writes only to find a question, questions that he must
find with the answer of the pen,...and then if I must,...if I shall
wait a while to stand to say a simple prayer..."a hand full of wishes
is a dream full of time...dreams I spend with you,..now dim the light
and wish I might share moment with you".....

Till pen meets paper,"GOOD NIGHT..."
always,
"WONDER"
"ONE "X" ONLY"

Michael Snider Jr.

Have Faith

Blessed art I your Lord your God who giveth and taketh away.
I create and I destroy. In this particular case, you have no say.

My grey, ashen clouds are billowing. You sense My swelling power.
The darkness of death is sweet to me. You experience it solely as sour.

My rain that falls mixes with your tears. I grieve the loss of your
rudder. I quake the earth that resonates with your loss, I can feel you shudder.

I can see that My act makes you crimson with rage. I can see it in
your face. The sunset I bring to you reflects the scarlet of My shame and disgrace.

With David, you had plans, things you had hoped to accomplish.
With an unacceptable act I made your dreams completely vanish.

Your loss is My gain. I maketh you now to lie down in green pastures.
No longer can you hike mountains together as you did these past years.

So, you fear the future without him to guide you, show the way. That
is My role, it is not to your friend, David, to whom you need pray.

As you listen to it, My wind will tell you things. Things you need to
know. In My ocean, the surf, the current will bring messages to help you grow.

  My snow covers your earth, blankets this death like a white shroud,
  I shed frozen tears to cover My mistake.

  He's climbed a taller mountain, you cannot hike it, it's unplowed.
  He rests in My peace; for you, never to awake.

Milt Davis

Endless Destiny

Long, lingering endless days of existing life are seen deep in your
saddened eyes with a flow of a tear as you are in deep thoughts, my dear Mother.
As, I gaze at you in hopes that you would return as you were, and
would speak to me once again with all your helpful knowledge offered throughout the years.
I wonder what deep thoughts are milling in that once so brilliant mind, my dear Mother.
How could such a strong woman capable of tailoring, knitting,
crocheting, baking, cooking and dealing with the struggles of a hard
life in the early 1900's of Europe have succumbed into this cocoon of no response?
Your frail, tiny body with such physical, strong strength, now
frustrated with a weakened confused mind that no longer permits expression.
I pray daily to God to open His arms and allow you to enter His
Kingdom to reunite with your loved ones who are long gone, my dear Mother.
I feel I am dying with you each day as I see your saddened eyes with
empty thoughts just lingering endlessly day by day with no destiny in sight.

Frances Peters

Unseen Illusion

Time is but a false memory in my mind:
Just a way to bind
What was...with what is ...
A way to devise a future:
What will be — for others — not for me.

Time etches out longings in my heart,
And I cannot depart
Their illusion:
Sometimes joyful — sometimes sad,
A way to keep what I once had.

To never let go — yet it must be so.
Time goes quickly... yet, slow:
A dichotomy of illusion — causing only confusion.
Will it go quickly, so I can reek gain? ...
Or crawl so slowly, I'm mired in pain?

Oh, time — what is your secret?
  You ARE — yet I cannot see you ...
  You are mine — for a while.
And, yet, when you no longer belong to me,
What will the results of my existence be?

  Faye E. Branhof

Prayers

As I wake in my bed each morning
Just as the day is dawning
My friend who has cancer comes to my mind-
I speak a prayer softly, "Please, Lord, be kind
And give her a body renewed,
And help her to keep a good mood."
Then I think of my friends who are totally blind
And I ask the dear Lord, again, to be kind.
And my nephew needs prayers to stay in A.A.
"Please, Lord, do not let him wander or stray".
There are many others for whom I seek
The Lord's kind blessings, in hopes He will speak
To each person's needs with His wonderful love.
Then one more prayer I send up above-
To thank Him for all the wonderful things
That daily, into my life, He brings.

  Helen M. Shea

The Ozarks

I stood at the foot of the rolling hills
just observing the beauty around me,
the sunlight sparkling off the rocks and rills
the profusion of flowers astound me.

I see a momma cow and her calf
under a tree she is licking it clean,
while watching a baby colt I laugh
the ozarks are a beautiful scene.

The dogwood trees are all in bloom
the sheep sorrel and the clover,
oh the beauty here can drive away gloom
yet the ozarks produce many a rover.

A young buck leaps over the rill
a red squirrel chatters from the sycamore tree,
it gives my heart a wonderful thrill
the ozarks are still wild and free.

Oh the rolling hills their beauty has stayed
around a little cemetery fair,
where at may family's graves I've prayed
and I know I'll someday be there.

  June Wiley

That Wind

When you walked into my life from out of nowhere, you were
just someone in the wind.
Suddenly I was introduced to you and you became another face
with a name and a friend.
Then with the wind of the introductions and the time we began
to share, you turned into a special friend that I can't seem to
remove from deep in my heart.
Even with all my disasters and roller rides, I seem to have
fallen into a state of needing passion, warmth, love....that,
was when I let myself go into your arms.
At that point I realized you were still the same person with
a name, someone that's a friend, someone that became my lover.
But with all that I still can't get you out of my heart. With
your embrace, warmth, and smile I would just like to let you
know, that this is how I'd like our friendship to grow.
Just with a touch of softness if either of us need it, and
maybe a "Hi" or "Hello" as we pass over each others path.
But truly I just wanted you to know that you have given me
myself, passion for life, and a great deal more with just that
gust of wind.

  Christina M. Hulsey

Why Do I Grasp So Tight,

When There's Isn't Anything There?

Don't rattle on about such, life is too much.
Just take my hand my friend, we shall walk together, you and I
There are seven days in the week, each day made for our scrambled
  emotions.
We shall cry, laugh and swallow all the pain there is too bare.
  Then in remission, rest.
I am free, I can soar. You have to take the first step, so you can
  be like me.
People will pity you for a day, then they will become angry that you
  were selfish.
Turn off the T.V., they only want you to watch, so you will fill their
  polls and ratings.
Now I had enough my friend, get out of bed, or you shall be alone
I'm not one for waiting again and again.
The pain is becoming you. Fight! Fight! Fight!
Life is a game, only the ones that play will win
in the end, the ones that didn't even try will be crushed by the rest
Take wind of what I tell you, I am running out of patience
The toll of time is near. Thank you for getting up.
Now we will have some wine and dance a jig, you are truly a friend
because you listened

  Jill Sue Wion

Never Mind The Broken Wing Of A Dove

Never mind the broken wing of a dove, dove, dove,
Just think of love, love, love
Two wings you should think of
So you can soar, soar, soar
Above clouds that roar, roar, roar
Two wings: that's the sense, sense, sense
You can fly and never think of anything dense, dense, dense

Two wings will make you free, free, free
As long as time doth flee, flee, flee
Two wings to fly, fly, fly
Out of the desolate sky, sky, sky
Never mind the broken wing, wing, wing
It's one of the desolate things, things, things

Remember to always think of God, God, God
Who made the burning sod, sod, sod
And never turn back, back, back
Keep your eyes on the track, track, track,
Always pray to HIM, HIM, HIM
And he will fill your cup to the vim, vim, vim
Praise God, Praise God, Praise God from whom all blessing flow.

  Helen E. Ritter

Life

Here I sit watching the sun rise,
just waiting for some surprise.
Here I sit thinking again
What it would be like to live in a den,
A place far away to plan my daily plots.
and hours of writing my forget-me-nots.
   To talk to nature is my pleasure
There's only a few things that I treasure,
Animals, nature, a roof over my head
Oh, how life pulls together like a spool of thread
Somehow it all fits together one link at a time,
Sometimes it storms, sometimes it shines
   Here I go again
A new day is about to begin
To tell you the truth,
All life is like a big chore
And it don't take much to open the door.

   Breanna Schreck

It's Me Again Lord

GOD watch over us again tonight,
KEEP us safe within your sight.

AND again tomorrow when I rise,
THROUGHOUT the day walk by my side.

GIVE me the strength and the vision,
TO always make the right decision.

SHOULD I falter and let you down,
GIVE me the knowledge to turn it around.

HELP me to resist all of the temptation,
THAT'S put before me by the evils of SATAN.

AND when my days on earth are through,
WATCH over my family I beg of you.

THESE things I pray to you tonight,
FOREVER and always keep us in your sight.

I'LL close now and leave you alone,
THANK you again for being in our home.

   Jack Sheffield

My Children

If you want to be intelligent, cool
Keep your mind and time on school.
Don't let books fade away for anything,
try to get a moment for everything.

If you want to be young again,
try to be polite even on the train.
Don't put money on fire by smoking,
don't drink alcohol, a drug in hiding.

If you want to be successful,
as long as possible stayed in school.
If you want to make some friends,
learn to give without expecting from them.

If you want your marriage to be happy,
take time, don't choose a lover quickly,
don't choose only the face, the cover;
marriage is never happy, never ever

Successful by meanings or by chance.
That your marriage keeps its importance!
Your children will be obedient moreover!
That world will be under your feet forever!

   Eddy Damis

1994

The city streets are heartless and cold.
Killing our young and beating our old.
Bums beg for a buck to buy them some booze,
Kids getting shot over a pair of shoes.
Drive-bys, carjacks and guns in our schools,
Children being raised by alcoholic fools.
They beat them, starve them, and sometimes molest,
The cops need to come and make an arrest.
Mothers selling food stamps to buy them some crack,
They don't feed their babies, only the monkey on their back.
Young girls being bought and made into slaves,
Their pimps need that money that they crave.
There's a rapist living in your neighborhood,
He'd still be in jail if our system was good.
We need to stop the killings, the violence, and pain,
Because these young lives are something to gain.

   Dani R. Augustine

J.T.R.

Crack
Kills and you're next, in a world of denial
How I hate to watch my neighbor struggle
Like a rat in Monty's mouth

Crack
Kills and you're next, have you forgotten who I am
Has my character lost its meaning
like a lizard lost its tail

You
Can't grow me back I'm no longer a part.
Like a chameleon without a tongue
A bird with a broken wing

Crack
Kills and you're next, on a sleepless night
At 24 west Sidle street- The red lights a blur
through my tears

Crack
Kills and you're next on your back under the sheet
All our memories gone for you, but not for me
Yes I will miss you

   Jonathan Smither

Image of Mother

I saw a face I used to see everyday.
Kinda like an image of me.
The only difference you can not tell,
Is her complexion that was so well.
At thirty-nine she was a woman very divine.
A feeling only she could know.
Past down to me as my story goes.

A mother that bared seven.
Each so different as nite and day.
Through thick and thin she fought a battle,
That was hard to win.
Her faith was in heaven her hope in hand.
She took life like a grain of sand.

She taught me right from wrong.
She gave me love and made me strong.
She gave me faith and hope to live by.
When I had a tear she wiped it dry.
To this day she is my Mother unlike any other.
I love her in every way.

   Brenda Kaye Jones

Whispers Of Color

Color fell;
Kissing time good-by.
Loves past whispered secrets to the passing breezes.
Promises kept.
Stillness lay among the grass; burning desire into flesh.
Echoes rose from the hillside.
Restless passion.
Time stirred.
Passing breezes gave rise to a halting first breath.
A blush of color kissed the morning dew.

Debbie Visnaw

"Alone I Thought"

Sometimes I feel so encapsuled, to be where it seems few,
know, no one else has been.
Like the clam a pearl's entrapped in, the glove a hand
was never felt in, the steeple the bells were never rung in,
a puddle I alone have fallen in,
a new year never brought in, a wish from a star never fallen,
a hope, a thought, that ought, but has not;
a lesson yet to be taught, or something, I alone just thought.
Oh Lord, oh God, let it be not, something, alone,
I have got, something, I stand alone in, which I have sought.
Some part of I, alone I love, alone I try, alone I give,
alone a lot - alone - the takers seem to be in short.
Though alone! May be in this thought, for what this is,
is a thought, not what is, in fact it's not,
explore it, I ought! Alone was with, the love I've got?
Alone was with, a world filled with people I thought?
Alone was with, those people I love a lot?
Alone - I thought? Alone! Why how universal a thought -
of course we're not!!!

John J. Gervais

What Is Love?

A special feeling, shared between two people that care
  Knowing no matter what happens, the other will always be there
Through thick and thin, happiness and pain
  The love shared with one another, will always remain.
It may be a struggle at times together
  But if it's really love, it will last forever
When they need a shoulder to cry on, you'll be there
  When they need someone to talk to, let them know you care.
When they are feeling down, show them the light
  Be there for them each and every night
If they're wearing a frown, make them smile
  Be with them every inch of the mile.
When they need some love, hold them tight
  Squeeze and love them with all your might.
And if, their heart needs a mend
  Don't act as their lover, but as their friend.
But most of all, be faithful and true
  And they'll live their life, loving you.

Cheryl Bell

Mistress At War

I've been at war.
The battle to win his heart.

The enemy does not know she's in a battle,
but we are.

I've tried strategy but I'm hit.
I don't think I can get back up.

After all she's got the strongest weapon.....

"His Daughter"
Tamoa Martinez

The Forgotten People

Unto themselves they live,
knowing not truth from lie:
blaming others, for life's failures,
OH Yes! Another day has passed them by.

In mob like fashion,
followers of the blind:
what will it be? A drink or hit,
OH Yes! Another day has passed them by.

Having contributed nothing,
yet! Crying aloud, for share of humble pie.
Expecting silver platter service,
OH Yes! Another day has passed them by.

Refusing life's knowledge,
state of oblivion sure;
knowing not what happens next,
OH Yes! Another day has passed them by.

With toys of ignorance lie,
destruction await their lives;
slipping yonder to other side,
OH Yes! Another day has passed them by.

Andrew S. Rolle

Late Twentieth-Century Absolutes for U.S. Citizens

Republicans reactionaries, democrats incompetents, and independents
  kooks,
you suffer political nausea.

Public debate mere spleen, leadership and conformity terrorist
  targets,
and dissent a scapegoat you feel the temptation of silence.

No consensus in sight, no norm, no center, but plenty of centers,
you see the void in which they drift.

Ethnocentrists, hate groups, hate crime, and race riots,
you wish you were somewhere else.

Misogynists denouncing misandrists, misandrists misogynists,
  heterosexuals and homosexuals,
you wish you were something else.

Dystopias, diasporas, deracination, dismemberment, disfigurement,
  no destination,
dementias, diseases, and destitution you grieve for humanity.

Death,
you grieve for yourself.

Cletus Keating

Untitled

As I walked the earth, the road of life,
laying one foot in front of the other,

I will kick aside the stones of hate
and make the road clear with love
my brother,

I hope to walk towards love with a
quickened pace, I don't want to walk
alone, for company, the human race.

If for some reason I should start walking
in reverse, I must stop an help myself
first.

But then I will turn around and continue
straight ahead and walk the road of life
towards peace and love until the day
I'm dead.

Fred Allen

Untitled

Live for today, and for you and you alone.
Learn from the past, and mentally you have grown.
Only you can be you, no one else can.
You make up you, whether woman or man.
Follow your heart, and you will have pain.
Ignore your heart, and what do you gain?
Seize each moment, and each time.
For the next sound, could be the final chime.
Stop for a moment, to look around.
Everything you seek, is easily found.
Don't be one to let life pass you by.
Laugh each laugh, cry each cry.
Absorb each moment, happiness or sorrow.
For it may be, your last tomorrow.

Christina Miller

Winter

The wind blows swiftly across the way
Leaves go dancing in disarray

Frost buds tip the bushes and lawn
Dark clouds form quickly and summer is gone

Comes thunder — lightning flashes across the sky
A burst of rain falls from the heaven on high

This is the announcement that winter is secure
We accept it with optimism and hope we endure

Comes the snow and a beautiful sight one sees
When snow is like frosting all over the trees

We witness a period of turmoil and flood
A heap of problems with water and mud

We look forward to the sun and warm air
To dry up the area that caused us despair

Winter is a time when the world cannot rest
It prepares for springtime and the time we love best.

Evelyn C. Nevis

Two Sides

His endless defeat with immaturity,
Left him to be a kid with endless
dreams.
A kid who sees something new to discover,
and tries to discover it.
A little boy who still asks shyly for a helping
hand or advice.
He's a little boy who can't wait to help
his dad with the car.
A new flower waiting to be admired.
He loves attention.

Then,
He turns into someone who cares about
living life to it's fullest.
A working man who can't wait to see a
welcoming bed for him to rest.
A husband who cares more for his family than his own life.

He'll still be the little boy.
He'll still be the working man.
But which ever one he wants to be, I'll never love either one more.

Cristy Nicol Caylao

Inner Conversations

Living with no communication
left me in a desperate situation.
Feeling isolated and so alone
sometimes I felt I couldn't go on.

While looking for someone to confide
without raping me of my pride,
I began listening to my own words,
feeling openly that I wasn't heard.

Inner conversations have helped me heal
to release my anxieties and the way I feel.
Forever grateful I will be
for this God given ability.

Janis Jagaczewski

Desolation

Little children everywhere, little children everywhere,
left to wander here and there, children all alone!
Conceived in haste without a care...burden soon to great to bear,
products of society, living fast and fancy free, then running scared,
no time to weep, leave 'em on a garbage heap, little children gone!
Home is prison, filled with fears, keeping secrets, hiding fears,
wearing smiles and living lies, different families in disguise.
Welfare lady's at the door, come to take them off once more.
Daddy has come and gone again, mommie found another man,
they seek solace in the street with every stranger that they meet.
Runaways, and unaware of other dangers waiting there,
still, no way to go back home, unwanted, kindness never shown!
Growing up so hard they find, growing up can blow your mind!
They turn back in time and cry, curse their own and wonder why!
Objects of frustration pay, broken toys thrown away,
hand me downs to grief and pain, what goes 'round comes back again,
Little children everywhere, children all alone!

Eunice Putnall

Eluding Inevitability

If someday I must go, (for all lives end, they say),
Let it not be in spring! No, not in spring
when life renews itself with hope!
Let it not be in warm and lazy summer when the whole
world pauses to view its self-created beauty.
And, please, do not let it be in icy wintertime
to sink alone within the cold and distant crust of Mother Earth.
If I must go, I'll try to leave with grace.
Become a falling leaf amid a forest of radiant hues as leaf
on leaf descends.
These bits of nature's whole, in seeming death are still alive.
Their altered state performing yet the mysterious cycle of life.
If I could, I, too, would be a leaf, evolving like a miracle
from green to gold to red to brown...falling ...falling...
Then, one with the earth, I still would exist...part of a useful
quilt to warm the earth and thus eluding death.

Jean Weston

As Though A Dream

With warm surroundings and warm embraces
We dare not open the door of regret
As candlelight dances upon our faces
And softly paints our silhouette.

To express unspoken thoughts and feelings,
To perceive the love that flows between,
Is to curse the night for time adrifting.
And suspend our thoughts as though a dream.

Keith Steen

A Sea Called Life

On the shores of life's tumultuous sea I stand
Letting the sands of time slip through my hand.
Watching the driftwood as it drifts aimlessly by;
Saying to them, we're alike driftwood you and I.
We drift with the tide and are tossed to and fro,
Caring not for the time nor whither we go.
Wondering who careth for us as we go drifting by,
Not uttering a sound or heaving a sigh.
Oh driftwood, what cut you from life asunder,
Satan's satanic power or a deep rumbling thunder?
Life has given to some a glorious retreat,
But to us each day brings a heartache we have to defeat.
Knowing the depth of an anguished cry, signal of distress,
Until we have conquered all our soul shall know, no rest.
Then hidden deep in the depth of time—forevermore,
We'll drop anchor and live on Life's golden shore.

Agatha Jordan

Precious Ways

Touching, hearing and a sweet verbal "Coo;"
   Life awakens on this day.
Growing and learning everything new,
   Changing in every way.
Thoughts transpiring from deep within,
   Shine through the wondrous eyes of a child.
Asking, pleading softly with a smile;
   Who can resist the thoughts of a child?
Filling the air in a musical way,
Sounds of excitement and laughter ring loud and clear.
It's the hustle and bustle of a child filled with joy.
   Are you listening? Do you hear?
Children with eyes filled with tears;
   Will touch your heart in all their growing years.
These precious ways will be here to entwine;
   With all our lives till the end of time!

Joan K. Walker

A Prayer Of The Cherokee: The People

OH, GREAT SPIRIT of the winds, waters, earth, and skies.
LIFT YOUR VOICES so that I may hear them! I am weak and need
To hear you speak with mighty strength and ageless wisdom.

PERMIT ME TO be ever aware of the beauty of the trees and
flowers; of the mountains and of the misty valleys; of the
rushing waters and of the still pools; of the sparkling
dawn and of the glowing sunset.
ENABLE ME TO appreciate the handicraft of your magnificent
creation; the world, and let me ever hear your voices in the
music of the winds and of the rushing waters.
OPEN MY EYES and my heart so that they might see and understand
all things necessary for the good of my people.

PROTECT ME FROM the evil spirits that walk the earth seeking
to destroy me and my people. Let me be strong of heart and long of sight.

LET ME RUN with the sun and soar with the winds, so that I
might have the strength to overpower the weaknesses in me.
ENCOURAGE ME TO be ever ready to appear before your with steady
eyes, clean spirit, and courageous heart.

Juanita Arrowood

Sky Eyes

I am a cloud
with no real form
whisping along in a furious storm
I may turn black but I'm not really mad
I am just a cloud who is very sad. So when it
rains from the sky those are my tear drops
for when eye cry

Shane Lines

Note to Myself

Look with what care he picks the meat from the bones,
lifts his wine glass and sips,
curling his tongue around before swallowing with a smile.
He lifts a manicured hand and signals for his check.
I respond, nervously and quickly (as I'm sure he expected),
eyes reluctant to meet his - still the timid schoolgirl
serving him night after night
yet knowing
I'll be here again tomorrow sunk
in the dark martyrdom of my corner booth just
to feel this hatred this betrayal this longing.

Debbie McDonald

Bird's Eye View

Through sheets of bullying white clouds
Light pierces its way toward the land
Revealing schematic designs
Untouched, unmolested by hand....

   "A bee's only arbitrator
   Over which posy to hover,
   Was the presence of sweet pollen
   Not the crimson on its cover!"
   "Beached turtles did not need knowledge
   Concerning their sandy shore's shade!
   Watch them nestle under moonlight
   Tucked in beds Poseidon once made."
   "Rainbows cast no light of hatred
   Forming arcs of spectral kissing.
   Love's embrace maps a rich pattern
   With earth's disdain clearly missing."
   "See those erect walking mammals?
   Heaven holds them in low regard."

   Pandemonium has no sun
   Just burning crosses out backyard....

Jason Allen Black

Our Love

As a cutlass clips through sheaves, or
Lightning bursts flail through skies,
Bolts penetrate my heart again,
To a remembered glory of past love,
From a desolate nothingness of present...

Yes, down avenues of sky we stroll,
Arm in arm above imaged clouds,
Our eyes speak our undying hearts,
Speak of times to come, a dire omen,
Yes, we know a love beyond the now,
We know an all transcending love,
Beyond temporal mortal improvisations.

We are gods in our own right, my dear,
Rule our own domain as it were,
You, in your elegant garland of flowers,
I, in my crown of lost memories
Recall that perennial oneness,
Only you and I have ever known.

Anthony Trent

Deadly Ignorance

   The smell of the hot apple pie cooling on the window pane
while the poor homeless man dreams of feeling the hot pie touch
his cold, chapped lips.
   Everyone passing, wishing they could help him, but feeling to
awkward to do so. Little did the passers-by know that their
ignorance and awkwardness of seeing the homeless man would soon
kill him; not because he starved or froze to death, but due to
the man's broken heart.

Loretta L. Bodine

The Bind

The inversion winds swept through the Argentinean night,
like a Russian tsar seeking a nom de plume that seemed right.
The bear like the raven fought on, but this fiend took only
one thing-my mothers arm.
They flew to the site that separated them by the spanish
night, that the fiend yelled, "who gave the mystics the right?"

The right that Lucifer ranted about, was that this
dimension lacked entropies battled scouts.
Why did this fiend take my mother with him, to a place that
seemed only fit for a gauchos whim?
THIS SITE! Whispered the savage, is the perfect place,
especially if I am to fall from your mothers grace!
DAMN IT, entropy again has found its mark, that the only
answer lies in a physical spark.
What spark would dissolve that fiends bind? I know-the one
that Aristotle conceived in his mind.
If his mind conceived and produced such logic, why then are
there so many devils breeding such deathly magic?

> *Juan E. Carrera*

Savannah-The Lonely Lady

As the dark hours engulf our city
Like a shade that is slowly drawn.
Our freighters slip silently up the harbor,
And we hear their weary moan.

Savannah is never the same at night
It's really a most enchanting sight.
The fog drifts in like magic
With shadows surrounding the light.

We hear the murmur of a police car
The lights give an occasional, blinks.
Listen! there's a noise in the darkness
It's the alley where the stray cats slink.

This is a seaport which has slumbered
Through many thousand's of nights.
It looks as if it were created, for
Motion picture lights.
City of parks, squares, azaleas and trees
She sings in the darkness with the gentle breeze.

> *Gena Dickerson*

Gnosis

Mama fades
Like Breath surrendered, into a place
I cannot enter.

Only misty Self remains
Not able now to filter Shadow.

Shadow, long-repressed, unknown,
Veiled behind Self's Light,
Now will have her say and loudly! Now demand
Her recognition! — That's she's
Embodied one with Self!
And so affirmed, be ever gently led to Love's embrace.

.........And thus a lesson's brought to me.....
That I should cherish Shadow, embodied in Self's Light...
For each is not itself alone,
But only in the other.

> *Anne Marie Gentilini*

That You May Change Your Mind

To know the time of ones death, what a bliss.
Like David prayed,
The words of prophesies I kiss,
And then to you, O! Lord I pray,
That you may change your mind.

I am but flesh.
Like Hezekiah and Nineveh cried —
So I cry unto you, O! God of all flesh,
Esther and Jehoshaphat too cried,
And you did change your mind.

My brother! I love you,
October, from coming if I can stop you,
Dear Lord, my hands I spread out to you
That with heavenly intervention,
You can change your mind.

We will all one day die.
Great times we have had.
Six months, to say good bye!
In October, the farewell to have,
If God changes not His mind

> *Edith N. Chuta*

Happiness Is...

Happiness is so many things
like feeling good, being satisfied, and trying your wings.

Happiness is a mother's delight
in a beautiful child, or one who struggles with blight.

Happiness is a wife's special feeling
of husband's support when her world is all reeling.

Happiness is a neighbor, a pal or a friend
who offers to help you or simply to lend.

Happiness is that peace in the soul
when storms rage around and your faith still upholds.

Happiness is the grandchildren God gave
to comfort and help, brag on and rave.

Happiness is here, happiness is there
Happiness comes when we work and we care.

> *Gloria Hearn*

To Louise

My dearest love, my life with you has been
Like heaven on earth; each day has come to be
More precious than the last; your gifts to men
Are great and kind, the best you give to me.
A loving warmth, an all-embracing glow,
A noble purpose, and the signs of thought
Come forth in one array; those near you show
The happiness and peace your strength has wrought.
How glorious is the world through which you move!
And where you go mankind is borne along
Within the stream of life; by grace you prove
To be an able leader of the strong.
And God himself has led you to delight
In all the good of man and moral right.

> *John W. Leist*

About Rosary Peas

The girls in Madras wear them on their heads
like little queens and play in lotus gardens,
dreading the trucks that tow the sacks of hardened
seeds. In export ships, men pack these red

and prune black-spotted seeds that merchants spread
across the seas like Calico cloth for women
of India's sashes and sheets. The ports in Venice
wait with open arms embracing the beads.

Two sets of arms lifting a sack. One pair
of hands crafting a sequence of ancient words.
So much is said and placed upon the skeletons

of rosaries. Sicilian widows wear
them carrying hybrid tea roses toward
new graves. In India, mantras sing loud and rotund.

Helen B. Thomley

Painful Memory

Memories disappear to come again
Like sun
Like moon
Pain dwells deep inside of me
Takes root

Tragedy of that day haunts me
The wound half buried is resurrected
Like salt thrown on a healing cut
Feeling the burning hurt

Let go
Live again

Darkness is my place now
Stone cold heart of gold weeps to be free
The weight of the wound over powers me.

Adrienne J. Hullum

My Child

Like the tinkle of a fairy's bell,
Like the ripple of a brook;
Like the robin's trill in shady dell,
Is my child's laugh.

Like the down of a tiny duckling,
Like the petal of a flower,
Like the summer's breeze in the evening,
Is my child's touch.

Inborn with God's unfailing love,
No worldly fears can conquer,
Like the shining glow of the stars above,
Is my child's faith.

Audrey Hansen Winland

Forever Together

On this day I will marry my best friend.
Someone in whom I know I can always depend.
The one who fills my life with love and laughter,
and whom I will be with forever after.
Together we will walk the path of life
disclosing all it's joys and strife.
Yes, forever together we will remain
counting on the love we do obtain.

Theresa Zipprich

Twilight In The Midst Of Life

Twilight, in the midst of life,
like watching the rain forest on fire,
and we are just one small leaf, on just another tree.
Someone should be looking for the rain, where is the rain?
This never-ending dreading of uncertainty,
this ever-present struggle to find fortitude
where there is only a faint hint of hope.

Midnight, from here it can only be a start.
A new day? Or nightmares of an old one...
being or not being, who gives a damn anymore,
existing or living is now the puzzle to walk through:
Where do we go to ease the pain of not living?
How do we insure the existence of our dreams?

Twilight, heaven help us!
To wake from the lethargy that poisons our spirit,
or plunge into darkness for relief, head first,
with a last smile of defiance, covering our pain. But wait...
Oh! The failing eyes, is that a hand reaching for our souls...?
Dear God, oh dear God...!
I think it is...another dawn!

Albert Jimper

Raindrops

From dark clenched clouds burst darts of light.
Lines of rain stab staccato rites
on leaning laurels, dropping drips
in puddles below, plopping blips,
bubbling up echoes—bright delights
of dancing days, of sad song nights,
of dreams rising and bursting,
like rockets to the stars, thirsting
streaks of hope, that then arch down
to the sea's muffled mist and drown.

As whispers weep and descend the air,
huge fists of waves pound the white stir
of water retreating from shore.
We curse the course and damn death's door,
but life flickers in fiery flash
and looks back only in cool splash.
From cloud to earth each particle
shines, a prism of light—of soul,
and merges one cell with the sea,
an instant with eternity.

Gerry Heinz

My Shining Knight

It wasn't very long ago, I was a
little girl. My mommy always tucked
me in and told this fairy tale. She told
me of this shining knight and how he
always looked so bright.

Through all the years my hopes,
my fears, I can't bring back her words.
So as I rest my weary head, I gaze out
at the stars. I see their twinkle in his
eyes the moon beams in his glow.
Then slowly as I drift to sleep, I pray
for him to have and keep. But, in the
morning when I rise and slowly open
up my eyes, I search for him and find
he's gone without a clue to what went
wrong. Now as I go from day to day
for you, my knight, I'll always pray.

Harry Fullerton

Mommy and Daddy

Mommy and Daddy always in a fight
Little girl alone caged in fright

Mommy's had to much to drink
Daddy needs his time to think

Mommy stumbles down the hall
Daddy's backs against the wall

Mommy says "It has to be my way"
Daddy walks down a long lonely highway

He makes it home, he knocks on the door
Mommy tries to make it across the floor

Little Girl lies in her bed
So many thoughts running through her head

Jay Leno Blares on the T.V. screen
Why do they do this? They say they love me.

The bedroom door slams muffled voices

They talk over all their different choices
They scream, They yell

17 years shot all to hell
Mommy jumps in the car speeds into the night
and leaves her little girl caged in fright.

Amanda Elam

My Sin Has Caused Your Pain

My Father God in heaven
Long ago upon a tree
You allowed Yourself to be nailed to the
    cross and bled and died
For the sins I've committed against Thee.
You willingly laid down Your life
You bore my sin and shame
I come to you and humbly bow
And just magnify Your name.
As I live on earth today
Lord, give me grace that I
Do not inflict more pain on You
As You view me with Your eyes.
As You listen with Your ears my Lord
May You be pleased with me.
May my life and words reflect
Your love and grace in me.

Gayle Johnson

Probably Possible

Look at the world so confused and so vain,
Look at the people so bemused and insane.

Look at the tiny tots with their eyes all aglow.
Then ask yourself calmly, "Where did it all go?"

Where did the laughter go the smiles on their faces?
Where did the joy go the quaint little places?

Ask where the love has gone, the love of all men?
Then ask is it possible to start all over again?

Is it possible to trust a man, if he a different race?
Is it possible to respect him if he has a different face?

Has the anger gone so far that it cannot be retrieved?
Have all truths become lies, that nothing is believed?

Is it possible that two children, one black and one white,
Might actually like each other meeting at first sight?
And if the adults do not get involved when they have their first fight
They might forgive each other and hug and make everything right.

Anything is possible, or so we have all heard.
So if it is possible, it is probable with just a kind word.

Deborah J. Rojas

"Take A Look"

For just a minute look around
Look at the trees, flowers, and ground

Look at the beauty of a deep blue lake
The canyons that took years to make

Pick a rose, sniff it's scent
Watch an eagle in dramatic descent

Look at the grass that grows so green
Inspect the trees, some fat, some lean

Even the rocks are special and rare
Just like animals such as a bird or bear

So just for a minute look at the sky and ground
Because if we're not gentle we won't be around

Christy L. Thom

Prayer For A Black Male Child

Gentle Jesus meek and mild
Look upon this Black male child
Keep him save and sound today
Away from guns and drugs we pray.

Protect and guide him in his school
Give him wisdom to obey the rule
Steer him away from any fight
Bring him closer to your guiding light.

And when his day at school is done
We thank you, Lord Jesus for another day won
For this Black male child was not alone
For your guiding light brought him safely home.

Carleen Adams

A Wish

I sat as I watched the kids stand right,
Looking at the stars at night.
They wished upon the stars so bright
To bring hope and happiness in their life.

All they wanted was to have a home.
All they wanted was a room to sleep in.
All they wanted was to have some freedom,
Without people staring at them.

I watched these children night and day,
Wondering where they might play.
They had no friends to keep them gay;
They only had each other night and day.

We are all one,
In our hearts and in our bodies.
We're all connected
So if one suffers, so does the rest of us.

I sat as I watched the kids stand right,
Looking at the stars at night.
They look so full,
But inside they're starving for life.

Christine Aspiras

Home

Home, my thoughts take me home;
to that stack of lumber, that place of rest,
to my birth, to where my heart sits,
and were love was born,
marriage, fellowship, and children's laughter.
Where I now grow old, where I soon will die.
It all begins where it all ends.

I head home to complete the circle.

Tim

In His Presence

So I brought my sinful soul to the house of the Lord
looking for repentance,
But I found the Altar tainted by the prophets of hell
Whose sole desire was the dollar
And to them it was a force deemed as almighty.
No souls to be saved today - Oh no souls!
Only heaps of money to be gained.
After all was it not divine right which dictates
the preacher should afford: An air-conditioned dog house
For Fido's eccentric delight?
And expensive manicures for his cat
Given weekly by Pierre de France.
No souls to be saved today - Oh No Souls!
Only our desire to rake your money,
And when it hurts the most;
to leave you flat most especially when you
need the hope.

Frank Cadillac

Looking Beyond

Looking beyond our daily needs
Looking instead to do good deeds
So many around who need our care
Someone to talk to someone to be there

Looking beyond life's hard times
Looking to Sunday when church bells chime
When all get together to thank our Lord
And keep pressing on to our just reward

Looking beyond to what we have on Earth
Looking not just at our families worth
But leaving something worth while behind
To be used and enjoyed by all mankind

Looking beyond to the end of the road
Looking when there will be no load
For no more will we be alone
Finally we will have made it home!

Helen Carswell

Ed Jr. 1994

Ed Wood is dead wood, but Ed Wood stood
lousy stinking, crazy so
The world's a lesser place without Wood's goods.

Cheap silly wrong, the world is still a better
place without Ed Wood, understood?

Crummy, misguided drunken loser
doesn't anyone see an idiot, even an earthman
could make a better movie than Ed Wood could!

But the world is still a smaller place without Ed
someone Shirley said.

Awful addled pompous prose, redundant to a tee
too many spaces to fill in, even Beach Blanket
movies had more goods than Wood's.

Ridiculous, boring bad, every other flick was better
than a Woodian shitter.

Passionate loving alive, no one ever even wanted to be
like what was in Ed's head.

Unique, wonderful different, Karma impossible to begin
to duplicate, some kind of genius, Ed Wood really could.

That he was once hear was good!

John F. Kundrath

Endless Love

To me you mean everything, you are my endless
love.
You are what keeps me going, you are all I'm
thinking of.
You take me in your arms and show me that you
care.
With passionate love and kisses that keep me
in a stare.
I look into your eyes and all I ever see.
Is all I ever wanted it's where I want to be.
You take me to a place where I don't want to
leave.
You shower me with love I'm ready to receive.
At times I know you wonder what I am thinking
of.
I think of all my happiness I think of you my
Endless Love.

Jessica Mercedes

Older Love

Over the years our
Love has grown stronger and stronger
Day by day you have been by my side
Enriching my life with your love and laughter
Ready to face anything that comes our way
Life long I know it can't be wrong
On good days and bad
Very much in love side by side.
Each day as we grow older we look at
   each other and know there is no
   other love. Stronger than ours
   for each other.

Barbara Golz

Remembrance

So far apart, so close together,
Love is strong under covered.
Distant feelings are spoke in secret,
Kindness and truth the words will make it.

Speak so few, understand so much,
Strong relation cannot touch.
Truth is tardy will never show,
I'll travel to Hell, where you will go.

Truth and love rejected,
Pain is suffering, never detected.
Lust and trust confused to be clear.
The soul of suffering will always hear.

The hell I see, the heaven you live
The hole for you. I will dig.

Chris Doty

Malcolm And The X

Malcolm X the name commanded respect
Malcolm X the name created fear
Malcolm X the name of the man
The X was a symbol of a past you could never know
Mighty warrior beloved prince you are gone
But your X is still with us
X how will I make ends meet
X where are the jobs
X what's going to happen to the neighborhood
X future future future

Allen F. Burks

"Love"

Love is a feeling, you both have to share,
Love makes you happy, because you know you both care.
Love is for all times, even if your not always together,
Love is one thing, that's not governed by the weather.
Love is knowing, that each others problems, you both have to share.
Even though your own problem, seems to be, all that you can bear.
But you know it will work out, with loving care,
Because you both work together, with "God" in your prayers.
Remember the vows you made, to each other, as you became
  husband and wife,
How you would share each others problems, regardless of strife?
Because it was there you made "God" a promise, as husband and wife,
That you would share them forever, which is the rest of your life.
Our "God" is "Love" which we all adore,
And this is sufficient, we need not ask for more.
You know, he showers us with more love, than we accept,
Therefore we need never fear, for "God's promises are kept.
So let's all build a better world, and to all, our love express,
For we know that by so doing, "God" forever waits to bless.

John Bentley

Love Was A Stranger

Love was a stranger
Love was never here
Hate took over, and brought many tears

Love always hurt
Love was a waste of time
Hate was so much easier, the revenge was always mine

Love brought you
Love became real
Hate went away, cause I began to feel

Love is so beautiful
Love I hope will last
Hate is just a memory, it's all in the past

Jan C. English-Fredrickson

Time

Time is and always will be a man
made limit. Time is used to limit
the day and to limit the night and
to limit our lives. To find the beginning
and end to everything. But
time is not a limit in the soul of
us. We can soar as high as an eagle
above the clouds passed our galaxy
into another. To live life after life
and to see Heaven as it is. To find
God. And to be one with God's physical
and spiritual world. To love and to
be loved. And to remember that we live
on forever.

Amy Manchel

Broken Promises

You're moving to begin a new chapter in you're life,
  Leaving old friends to make new ones.

You promise them you'll write, but you never write.
You promise them you'll call, but you never call.
You promise them you'll leave them something
  to remember you by before you go.

Only you don't leave them anything, except Broken Promises.

Jennifer Haneke

Life Is Your Own

Create a path in life, and don't be led astray,
Make your own decisions and let nothing stand in your way.
Walk to the beat of the music you hear,
Don't let them control you year after year.
If you always live your life to please everyone,
You, yourself will never have fun.
Who cares what they say,
All they have are opinions anyway.
Always stand up straight and tall,
Your true friends will be there if you happen to fall.
Don't let yourself get discouraged,
Hold your head high and face it with courage.
Look to nature and God above,
He will guide you with strength and love.
Live for today and not for tomorrow,
Don't always dwell on the grief and the sorrow.
Put the past behind you and move on today,
For this really is life's true way.

Julie Lemery

Free To Be You and Me

No beginning, No end, No boundaries, We are free whispering breezes
making their way over glistening bodies, etching road maps leading to
paradise. Follow me, Follow me, We are free! Spirits that are wild,
tame, mysterious and shy. They are at home here, They are free.
Just like you, just like me. For an hour, for a day, Forever. Is
this not as it should be? Here you cannot hide. Not you body, not
your mind. Breathe deep, listen to your heart beat. Let your soul
ride the wind; For here, you do not have to pretend. There is no
shame, no envy. We face equality in this kingdom, Far away from the
big city lights and frights. We see only deep starry nights and a
stairway leading to heaven along the Milky Way. We belong, finally,
a home, A longing, a hunger now satisfied. We are free to laugh, to
play and to roam, Maybe shed a few grateful tears in awe, Of this
Shangra La. As we again return, but hesitate. We're here, please
open up the gate. No, wait; Please come in, don't look back.
We will ride Eagle's Wings to unknown heights and walk forests
floors as if on Wolves velvet paws. We are finally free.
This was means for you and me ...... for us.

Ellie Hetman

It's What's Inside That Makes The Man

Down through corridors of endless time,
Man has trampled others, to self a slave,
Forgetting, that he too was made from dusty slime
That regardless of rank, all inherit the grave.

Some, like Burns, rang a warning knell,
Seeing through the foolish pride and sham,
Telling us tolerance is not an empty shell,
It's what's inside that makes the man!

For all that and all that,
They may be black and all that.
Have you time to choose the donners stat,
When all bloods the same for all that?

Oh forego that foolish haughty pride!
What has it gained worthwhile or grand?
So many have fought and so many have died,
It's what's inside that makes the man!

Yes, my friend, our time is short,
As we travel through this land,
Let neighborly love show your worth,
For it's what's inside that makes the man!

Jack Rutledge

Putting It In Perspective

A flower is an amazing thing.
Man is an amazing thing.
A flower starts out as a seed before it begins to bloom.
Man starts out as a tiny egg, buried in his mother's womb.
A flower waits for the perfect time to sprout up from the earth,
A baby knows by instinct when it's time for its birth.
A flower grows and shows its petals, growing stronger every day,
Man grows tall and expands his knowledge, changing all the way.
A flower grows old and wrinkled and soon begins to tilt,
Man grows old and tired and he too begins to wilt.

Jessica Hadamik

Twilights

Somewhere near the line that marks the end of the day a
man rose and faced what was left of the falling sun

... and mourned the passing of time.

The spectacle of the evening heavens before him brought
tears to blur his vision

...and he wept for a soul that was lost.

Much had washed away before his eyes, including himself,
in a tide too swift to hold back

...and he was left in the orange glow of life.

Twilight was a step away from the shadows he walked in the
days beyond his dream

...and he remembered the faded years of his dawn.

A small child took his hand: "Come on Grandpa, Mama's
waiting," as he turned and walked away from the bluff

...and her soul waited in the winds with the fading
light.

Fred Campbell

My Mother, My Friend

There are so many dreams I've had,
Many of which you alone made happy not sad.
Talk about seeds - growing miracles,
With Gods help, your green thumb could grow circles.
You've stood by and hugged me through my fears,
What would I have done without you through the years.
You've been my nurse, body guard, companion and teacher,
Never once acting like a preacher.
Now once again you came through,
With open arms, a loving smile, not a kick with your shoe.
Lord, why didn't I listen to her,
I guess I was young, blind, but oh so sure.
You are a mother oh so rare,
No others could even compare. Thank you for always being there.
When I was born. You didn't realize,
It was me. Not you, who won the prize.
I love you Mom.

Bette A. Bodenhorn

A Twist of Fate

The victim with the dagger deep within his now still cold body
lies looking as if asleep. Gulping down the stale night air, the
murdered prays for his life, falling on the ground, crawling all
around. The snoring sound has started now, buzzing from the nose
of death. The tickling whispered breath of the wind brings the
crow; the raven of death. Sounds of panting animals grow louder,
their tails twitching with each movement. The lights grow dim as
the candle burns out. A life for a life thinks a man as the kiss
of death descends upon him.

Penny Lea Ruth

Life Styles of the Wind

In Spring, the pine tree happily hums and dances with the
March breezes, clouds play tag and the sun plays peek-a-boo.

In Summer, a hot searing brilliance burns your dry parched
skin under the relentless rays of a blinding hot sun, with a
touch of the wind burning more than the scorching sun.

In Winter, the blustery wind whistles 'round the corners of
your house, and whines away to dance and twirl in space with
a powdery mound of snowflakes, then gusts yonder to ruffle
poor sparrow's feathers.

Offshore, a constantly blasting storm flaps the sails of the
seagoing ship and pummels it to and fro through mast-high
waves that pound the deck with oceans of salt water washing
over all the ship's gear.

The refreshing dew-laden breeze of daybreak is heavy with
perfume of wild violets and pungent of mushrooms.

A cool evening zephyr whispers through the leaves of the
aspen tree, touching each leaf and getting a soft whisper
from each one.

An evening breeze wafts gently, caressing your cheek as
softly as a kiss.

June M. Carlson

"Saguaro's War"

Through the Valley of the Sun
  March the armies of Saguaro.
Mighty bivouac in the desert,
  'Long the hills and through the 'royo.

Grim guerrillas fighting nobly,
  In a warfare with the weather;
Grizzly giants still unbeaten,
  Beards of spine and backs of leather.

On they struggle for existence,
  'Tween the rocks and sandy trenches;
'Til reward for triumph's given,
  And the ground the freshet drenches.

David S. Bishop

Love Story

You loved me well!
May call you any time just to say hello.
Made me feel the comfort you were there for me
  and this was reversible.
Shared your time as much as possible.
Closeness no one would or could understand.
We could talk about anything and everything
  that was on hand.

I loved you well and you are missed so much.
It was more than friendship, marriage
  or chance encounter as such.
A once-in-this-lifetime good experience, can't ask
  for more than this - here and now.
Swiftly you were gone, so suddenly
  leaving me breathless - and how!
Tear drops come and go, and for whatever
  reason, your ascension will find
  you in beautiful gardens you did not heretofore know.

Anna Daines

Young Men: Too Big For Your Britches

The young men who have no honor
May end up in the ditches
When they are being led - and by drugs are fed
And have grown - TOO BIG for their britches

The young men who fail to obey
Commands of their fathers and mothers
Are shortening their days - by their wicked ways
And may soon end up in the gutter

Too big for your britches can cause many stitches
You're laid up in a hospital bed
You're just too hot - you're Johnny on the spot
And end up with gunshot wounds to the head

So young men, I admonish you now
Take stock of yourselves today
If you're distressed - can't find peace nor rest
Just get down on your knees and pray.

Say "Dear Lord, I'm growing up too fast!"
I'm too big for my britches a bit
My heart's icy cold - restore any sin-sick soul
From condemnation - so my britches will fit.

Evelyn L. Minor

"Paddy St. Patrick"

St. Patrick, may the Angel of luck, be with you -
May you enjoy, your strong irish tea, too -
Each year, on March seventeen -
It is normal, for everything, to turn green -

The luck of the irish shall continue to be -
Celebrated on March seventeen, as it has been, historically -
In old county cork, in Ireland, you see -
Is where the Angel of luck, was born, that is no mystery -

She wears a green bonnet, to match St. Paddy's hat
As St. Paddy drinks his green beer, she sits in his lap -
What could be better, than being irish today -
That is exactly, what, St. Patrick would say -

So on the special day, of March seventeen -
When the entire world, is wearing green -
The beaches in Ireland are the most picturesquely seen -
As each wave strikes the beach sand, which is ever so green -

Paddy, oh Paddy, the toast is only for you -
In county cork, the green beer is flowing too -
So put on your top hat, the best ever seen -
For today, round the world, "Tis the wearing of the Green."

Harry B. Sherr

Sweet Hours

I knocked on the door and what did I hear?
"Mommy, great-grandma is here."
The door opened wide than what did I see?
Sweet children's smiles welcoming me.
After kisses and hugs, a giggle or two
The words then came "What can we do?
"Play with us please, great-grandma come see
"What mommy and daddy bought for me.
"Let's play with my toys, come sit on the rug."
And so we did and played, laughed and hugged.
We colored pictures; I read a story or three.
What a warmth, doing this, came over me.
To be so close to such innocence
Touches this heart and ever since
I have felt happier than I'd been before
Sweet little children opened the door!

Ethel M. Sturm

Waiting for Dawn

Maybe I believe
Maybe I have some faith
Maybe I'm staring at the window
Or standing at the gate....

Great golden moon in the distance.
A calm, clear twilight.
I witness a shooting star.
Do I wish, as it's still in flight?

Who am I, forget for a while.
Shining star is sinking so fast.
Maybe I've reached my true love.
Maybe we've come together at last.

For a brighter tomorrow, I make a swift wish
to reshape a world gone wrong in the light.
As it explodes in the sky
my shooting star slips away, out of sight.

I'm left naked and soul alone
neath the willow at the edge of the lake.
The end of another silent night
waiting for the red dawn of life to break.

Anne Pipenhagen

The Search

I must be a cradle - I lived in one...
Maybe I'm an extension of the two arms that held me.
Am I the smile, the coo, an apple in the eye?
Or was I the — not a boy — but yet another girl?
Not sure who I was where I came from... confused...
I must be a teen — that's what I'm called!
Not into that music — or even a movement,
I still don't belong, I didn't fit — into a clique!
As I painted the mask on my face, I asked "Who was that
in the mirror?" Not who I saw —I had to belong, for
how else can I IDENTIFY, who am I? — where am I from?
I must be a wife — he says "my wife"...
I must belong now, I find I am owned by him, and by others;
they call me "My Mom." Who am I where did I come from?
How can I be owned? Slavery is dead!...
An "ex wife" now, children grown - I'm still called mom.
I find my concepts have bound me.....
Into the quiet, — not identifying with person, place or thing,
I know now, Infinity, the "where I came from," my destination —
That one source — unowned, unnamed...... "I Am"...."Am."

Diana Forest

The Beginning Of Hope

I can hear the heartache of a crying world in the rains falling about me.
I can see the world's despair through the eyes of a hungry child.
I can fill death's cold hands while listening to an old man's dreams.
I comprehend the painful loneliness of the Mother anew.
I sense the anger in a Father as he sees his son's shame,
And the Mother's pain as she turns to look the other way.
Though this world is filled with such emotions, there is one that
stands above them all.
And this I have found in the heaven, and within the windows of your
soul.
I understand the concern, I delight in the love I feel when you come near.
I sense the joy that you release at the sound of a job well done.
I hear the excited laughter as you make aware of a world yet beginning
I see the love you project.
I realize that someone does care, thanks for being part of my world.
For taking the time to hear, to feel, to sense, to see.
I feel I'll always have you as a friend.
Thanks my friend for the beginning of hopes anew.

Darlene Adalay Moore

Men Who Are True Friends

Men who are friends never need to say it.
Men who are friends never take friendship for granted.
Those men who assume their friendships, do not really have it.
Those true friends that are men know each others anger, pain
and joys.
True friends, that are men, can express friendship with a common
handshake or a simple hug.
Men who are friends will never need to say it.
Men who are friends never need to deny it.
Men who are friends just have it.

Jim R. Williams

Ellen Elizabeth

First child of my last child — long waited; with your
Midnight hair and wide eyes of dusky blue.
On a morn when spring surged on the edge of bloom
You arrived at last, albeit somewhat overdue.
Your spirited entry was muted by the strains of Motzart
And heralded by the rays of an upcoming sun.
It was a new day, a Tuesday, and tho the earth
Did not cease it's spinning, you were the only one
To fill the minds and hearts of those who loved you.
Welcome sweet Ellen! May the world long be your domain.
Reign gently, little princess. Your realm, tho not unlimited,
Will grow by your grace, and overflow what it cannot contain.

Gerry Leavy

Beyond Robert Frost

Robert Frost once waxed so eloquently about a
minor bird, who sang out of key.
My lament to you will be of a different theme
I like to sleep and I love to dream.

No problems with sheep passing me by, just a wink
a nod, and I'm off with a sigh.
Visions then come to mind, some of them new, some
left behind. A journey to a place where poets are kind.

James Rzezniczek

A Phenomenon of Colors

Colors of the rainbow, so alive, so blue
  Missing you...
Yellow, how the sun rises
  Missing you...
Pink for the days swept under the dew
  Missing you...
Green, for thoughts of winning that finish line
  Missing you...
Silver, Oh how those coins plunged deep in the slot
  Missing you...
White, Those linen napkins-how crisp
  Missing you...
Black, The day when how much I tried-couldn't cry-
  To cry when alive my belief
  Missing you...
Red, Always so bright, what a change
  Missing you...
Plum so sweet, we two are alike, some ways not all
  Missing you...
Sand your color and shells to echo your voice — Remembering
Colors.

Jan Seaman

A Little Piece Of Heaven

The dew kissed roses glisten in the early morning light,
Morning glories open after sleeping through the night,
Hummingbirds are busy tasting the sweetness of the flowers,
The frogs begin retiring after all their late night hours,
The water glides on effortlessly along the winding brook,
Chipmunks scurry along the cliff, checking every curious nook,
Butterflies dance their random waltz, hopping to and fro with ease,
The aroma of the flowers ride adrift upon the breeze,
The cat, it stretches lazily upon the old stone wall,
Bluebirds perch on the weathered fence, singing freely to one and all,
I've seen these things so many times but they always seem so new,
It's like a little piece of Heaven open there for me to view.

Diane Hall

The Mountain Top Where The Man Of Wisdom Stands

I'm trying to make it to the
mountain top where the man of wisdom
stands. It's as easy as making a
wish but you have to rub dirt on
your hand. I see the man of wisdom with
a question mark on his back.
I guess it represents what do
you want or need, an answer or a fact.
He now wears a velvet cape
that says, tell me what you need.
Just one thing at a time, is
that a deal, do you agree?
The man of wisdom now wears a blue and gold dashiki
This outfit says if you want any info or facts etc; all you have to
do is come and see me.
I've finally reached the top of the mountain where the man of wisdom
stands, He said, what's your request,
I said oh, I forget to put the dirt on my hands.
I come all this way to prove to people who didn't understand
That way on the mountain top a wisdom man stands.

Jennifer Alexander

And The Lady Is The Winner

I went from being an iron maiden to a platinum princess in one swift
move. I feel no bitterness, emptiness or loss. The game is over.
And the lady is the winner.

You my vagabond lover with your lies, infidelity and deceptions gave
me strength instead of weakness. You my vagabond lover are now a
part of my past.
And the lady is the winner.

I thought it would be a six day war,
but in less than a flash the battle was over.
Without a lift of my hand you were gone, returning to nothingness.
And the lady is the winner.

As the light of dawn appears, love flourishes again.
Confidence is my keynote. Love is my portion.
And the lady is the winner.

The sacrifice I was willing to make is unnecessary.
My pride is intact; my self-esteem high.
And the lady is the winner.

The past came full circle one year to the day.
The game was played to the fullest, we both reached a draw.
And the lady is the winner.

Audrey Kathryn Bullett

Voices

I walk along in total nonexistence,
Mumbling voices racing thru my head.
if only I could make them clearer,
But still the words I cannot understand.
I wonder is it my inner soul trying to reach out,
Or just my conscious trying to speak.
They hush when I come close to believing,
Just to start again when I'm unable to trust.
I know they are there I hear them laughing,
But they have not the courage to let me in.
For what, right do they have judging?
If not for myself I'd not gotten this far.
Still I wait in total silence,
Wondering about those words they try to speak.
And what if their not voices at all,
Just the passing scars I've tried to forget
And if those scars where to go away
Would my existence go to like
An unignited flame?

Jane Clayton-Cornell

A Promise To A Child

Escape... somehow... when opening eyes to skulking shadows that
murmur admonition behind the drapery of dark corners...hiding
from the playful fingers of moonlight as this glowing orb
beckons as you are waking.
Celebrate... the childhood blanket warmth of dawn's hazy
innocence... the sun has soothed the "beast...within"...for now.
The click...and rusting of a brainless working day and fruitless
solitude while saints burn for the hope of something greater than
they can scar themselves to be.
Blind eyes...can't see...the infant light yawning Nature's sweet
milk breath on the naked forms of starving "men" as painful black
turns to nourishing grey...and groping fingers
shield virgin eyes that were seared and now perceive...
a strength... A vow...to keep a promise to a child who wakes from
the soundless terror of a shadowy nightmare and needs the
tenderness that lulled you once upon a time.
He gently leans...upon your arm...and frantic breathing...
slows...and the nights preoccupied lullaby sighs tenderly
through the screen...and you both sleep...
Two infants in the comfort of each other's insecurity.

Debra Grossano

Into The Darkness

Words without color, words without meaning,
Music without harmony, music no ear can hear;
Feelings only my own that are not mine,
Being nowhere and painfully lost;

That which is, that none can see,
Occupying different places, I don't even want to be.

My vision of hope and glory from her eternal flame,
Vanished into the darkness,
And again I'm lost between joy and sorrow,
Forever until tomorrow.

Lingering memories that fill my mind,
And things to fill my empty heart;
But there's no escaping my troubled soul,
And all the beautiful moments shared with her;

So I'll just think it out, and write it down,
Pay my dues, and leave this town.

My vision of hope and glory from her eternal flame,
Vanished into the darkness,
And again I'm lost between joy and sorrow,
Forever until tomorrow.

Jose Rodriguez

An Aging Single's Prayer

When, dear Lord, will I find my true love ?
Must I wait 'til I reach Heaven above ?
I just would like someone to care
and to share with, and always be there
To laugh with and cry with, to work with and relax with,
Someone who doesn't mind middle aged spread
or slightly graying hair.
Someone to have and to hold and with love enfold.
Someone to cuddle with when we're sad or cold.
Someone whose gentle smile lights up my life
And on whose shoulder I lean during strife.
Someone whose presence makes me glow
And who I can learn with and personally grow.
While sharing makes the good times even better,
And lessens the pain of the sad the bitter.
While together we are one, yet separately whole,
Giving love not just from our body, but from our soul.
Someone whose hand feel so right in mine,
With principles and character, admirable and fine.
When, dear loving Lord, will I find my true love ?
Must I really wait 'til I reach Heaven above ?

Carol Marie Brewer

Untitled

Race, what does that word really mean
Must we be defined by Red, Black or Green?

How did the world become so full of hate?
They say times are changin', but that I debate.

Through the eyes of a child, Color can't be seen
Just another playmate to share in their dreams.

Until an adult with a heart full of hate
Fills the child's head with prejudice waste.

Why must we fill our youth with ignorance and pain
Haven't we learned there is nothing to gain?

Dr. Martin Luther King said, I have a dream
that one day all God's children will be treated the same.

Somewhere along the line his dream faded away
I pray to our Father in Heaven that it's not gone to stay.

Instead of hatred try teaching the Bible sometime
Then maybe you will find the OUR GOD IS COLOR BLIND.

Gaye Beasley

My Angel Is My Friend

My angel is there for me.
My angel is something that is special to me.
My angel loves me and cheers me up.
My angel is something that I can have with me.
My angel helps me.
My angel has a big smile on her face.
My angel is the most beautiful thing in the
whole world God has given me.
My angel is next to me and...
My angel loves me and...
God gave it to me!

Jeannette Di Muont

I Find Out I'm In Love

When the wind whistles through my ear;
I can feel you coming near.
When flowers start to bloom;
I can sense you within a room.
When I run with the wind and sing in the morning dew;
I find out I'm in love with you.

Samantha K. Bossard

Untitled

I sit in depression sad as can be.
My broken heart shattered that I can see.
As I cry, and tears fall down my cheek
I think of the way we once were and now I'm weak.
I am sitting in despair because my love I cannot share.
My anger inside I try to hide,
the guy I love and I always will
even though my broken heart cannot be filled.
One last cry that's all I ask for,
because my love is waiting at your door.
I just sit and wish about our faces,
and think about all of our special places.
Every time I walk a mile,
I think of your wonderful bright SMILE!

Christina DiMatteo

I'll Put My Rainbow in the Sky

I'll put my rainbow in the sky,
My covenant; I'll tell you why.
My heavens declare a holy vow:
Perpetuity I will endow.

I'll splash some red, orange, yellow, too—
From green to violet every hue.
I won't enhance one color more.
I'll take my stance, for I abhor
Your preferences, your color ban,
All prejudice conceived by man.

'Twas not your Master who devised
A separate dwelling. Observe the skies:
The prism's palette He designed,
A pattern shaped for all mankind.

Adjacent let their light abide.
Let none his neighbor's glory hide.
For each has beauty all its own—
Celestial gift, terrestrial loan.

Dawn Escoto

Like A Mountain

I walked along a pleasant trail one afternoon;
My drooping spirit to renew.
The sky above me was clear and blue.
I gazed upon the path ahead to see the view.
Behold! What I saw was awesome.

There was Mount Rainier with its white crowned dome;
Firmly planted, in regal majesty it stood.
It overlooked everything like a vigilant guardian,
    watching everyone, the bad and the good.
Its position was solid and immovable, where it stood.
There it was rooted strong and sure.

It seemed to be watching, waiting, and protecting.
Then, this thought came to me as I pondered what I saw.
When difficulties enter my life and I can not see You,
    Lord, You are always there; correcting any flaw.
Like this mountain, You are strong, solid and
    protective and this leaves me in awe.
You told me that afternoon, "See! My beloved,
    My love for you is strong and forever."

Joanne Marie Lake

Black Butterfly

I was born a black female with short, curly hair.
My eyes are not blue; my skin is not fair.
I learned all too quickly that long hair and light skin,
are much more important than what lies within.
So I had dreams at night of long flowing locks,
and envied light skin-I followed the flock.
I was living my life in fear of the sun.
My fight with racism hardly begun
And then one clear day, I don't recall when
and then looked at my sisters dark skin
she was pretty and regal, she seemed like a queen
her color had beauty that I'd never seen
so I painted that mirror in my own direction
for the first time in life, I saw my reflection
not that of the media or society.
That Regal black Queen now best describes me
That regal black female who turned butterfly
I an now a black queen crown shall not die.

Jessie Dunbar

Gracie

Gracie, a woman I have known all my life.
My friend, my mother, my father's wife.

A rare commodity, a precious stone,
keeper of the house that we call our home.

The painter, the plumber, cook and maid.
Precise and stunning as a newly cut jade.

Always seeking perfection she will never find.
Mysteriously sad with little peace of mind.

Bitterness to sustain the anger inside,
A diary in which all her hurt she will hide.

Jackson was her given name.
It never brought fortune, it never brought fame.

Three children, some pictures, an unfinished house.
Heartache and laughter shared with a spouse.

Undeniably a lady with class.
A mother first, a person last.

Understand her, I probably never will.
Important to me is the love I feel.

God has blessed me in so many ways,
By sending Gracie to love me each and everyday.

Deborah Wyatt

Stiff Sentence

At the first sight of you I kissed
my heart good-bye.

Now, it's you and no one else for
me.

With our first embrace you imprisoned
my heart and there is no escape
from the sentence imposed from your
warm and tender kiss.

I stand guilty of the charge of loving you.

For this, my heart seeks mercy. For
it has fallen victim to love in the
first degree.

My sentence-life without the possibility
of parole.

Donald Washington

Times of Trouble

I walk in the midst of trouble
My heart is full of anxieties
But I don't need to know where I'm going
For God is leading me

Times of trouble, are times for trust
God's presence comforts me
I don't need to know where I'm going
For God is leading me

I thank the Lord for trials that sore
They taught me how to trust Jesus more
For when I found no other way
I learned to lean on him each step of the way.

Yes my friend, through eye's of faith
His glory will be seen
I believe in Jesus, Saviour and King.

Frank Greeson Jr.

Lost Love

Your eyes and smile drew me to your flame
My heart skipped when I heard your name
You held me to you with a silk thread
But - that thread broke when you were wed

I didn't want to believe we'd ever part
I fell for you and gave you my heart
Maybe a part of me knew we'd never be
My heart wouldn't listen to what my head could see

So go love, be happy, I'm setting you free
Tomorrow - you'll be a memory
Today - I'm sad for dreams lost
As I think, I wonder, was the pleasure worth the cost?

You'll never know the tears I cried
The hurt I keep hid inside
Soon - I'll be happy and when I do
Then I'll know - I'm over you!

Emma L. Hamm

Mothers Cry! "What, Did I Do Wrong?

Since the day my baby was born, he brought Joy and Happiness into
my life and when he would smile, there was always, lots of Sunshine
and as he grew up he was well mannered, polite, kind and caring.
My Son, my Delite.
All I ever wanted was the best for him and to be a kind, caring and
responsible person. But, "WHAT DID I DO WRONG?" For suddenly, he
changed, we couldn't communicate anymore, and there seem to be the
lack of Love, Oh! "WHAT DID I DO WRONG?"
He wasn't my Son, he was a completely different person and I felt the
Love lost between us, OH! "WHAT DID I DO WRONG?"
He was another person, a stranger, not the son I raised, who told me,
he loved me so much, like all the stars in the sky and all the birds
that fly, OH! "WHAT DID I DO WRONG?"
ALL I WANTED was for him to have a happy and secured life. Whatever
happened to my SON? OH! "WHAT DID I DO WRONG?" I love
him so, but,
where is he? Where has he gone? My heart cries for him! Oh God!
"What did I do Wrong?"

Baroness Angela R. La Rosa

Spring Time

As the flowers bloom,
The trees grow back their leaves
    that they had before the cold
    winter came.
As the birds sing,
The mornings are filled with beautiful songs.
I know that it is spring time again

Laura Lee Matson

Mom

For is she not wonderful?

For is she not beautiful? Truly God has walked with her.

For he has sent his angels to guide her steps, for she trusts in God.

Has she not believed in me? For has she not blessed any being?
My life has been molded by her. For I am lost without her, for
she has prayed for me.

For she is strong. Her independence has set her free. She has
not fear of life, but receives it as it comes. For no one shall be
her teacher, except for God. For he is true and so too she, the
foundation of my life.

For she is gentle and her words are calm. Her touch has given
me peace. I receive her words, for they are wise. Truly they
are from my God.

How blessed am I to have known her. How blessed am I to have
loved her. How blessed am I to have held her. How blessed am I.
Amen.

J. Bomma

Being Old

The time has passed like a shooting star
my life is almost history, for some it has just started
    Being old, really clears my thoughts, and my mind
goes back as far as it can.
    Trying to remember the time when I was young
when I was a kid, a baby, in my mother arms.

    But it is not working, because I can't remember
those things, those moments in my life.
    My life that runs thru my fingers as a sand
that I can't hold in my hand
    This really makes me sad, this really make me scared,
because that was I, that was part of my life,
that I can't remember.

    Maybe I'm already old
and my mind is gone.

Aurelio Fernandez

The Windsock's Smiling Face

One day there in my chair I sat
My life with recent tragedy met.

Sapped of life, full of sorrow
Hoping hope would come tomorrow

Lingering memories of times gone by
I sat in my chair and began to cry.

Then I lifted my eyes to my backyard eve
And a windsock hung there-smiling at me.

With a great big face and a great big smile
I sat and pondered this awhile.

A message, I thought, from God to me -
"Get off your chair and on your knees!"

I prayed the Lord would give me strength,
And new hope and life renew in me.

And when I stood, I knew that God
Had really been there all along.

And now I have new hope embraced,
Thanks to God and the windsock's smiling face.

Andy McClain

Mutual Respect

When I walk into thy presence, with an ego times three
My lust is fed, copiously, yet insatiably, when I see you
Taking a stance, of your desire, for my to inquire, I want you
To receive me, welcome me, wet me, like you want me

When we converse, there's a certain amount of Mutual Respect
To make us impishly smile, and loathe, both say no
To an erotic attraction, where our physique can not go
And indulge in greed, to which others would surely object

Can avidity, be so wrong, that our hearts shall only long
For the goods held inside me, to flow warmly, deeply within thee
To taste, of the unseen, to feel as one has secretly dreamed
If only there were common ground, I'd lay you down, on me, gently

And share with you, parts of me, known to be satisfying
Even when thy mouth, thy heart, and thy confused mind
Struggle in conflict, loving what words and action are denying
Our Mutual Respect has a treasure, one day I wish, we'd find

Harry W. Tatum Jr.

My Song Of Praise

Oh Lord, when there isn't much I can do,
  My mind, heart, and soul sing praises to you.
I know you are near all the time,
  Your presence and my praises cause our song to rhyme.

Oh Lord, ruler of the sky, sea, and land,
  With such a powerful and yet, gentle hand.
Power to cause the earth to lurch,
  Yet, sooth an aching pain with a soft gentle touch.

A voice, much louder than a thunder's roar,
  Cause towering waves on the seas to sour,
And yet, soft whisper in my ear,
  Telling me the things that I surely need to hear.

My God, full of mercy, so kind and true,
  Help me always sing praises to You.
I feel your touch, hear your voice low,
  Plant seed in the rhyme of our song and let them grow.

Oh Glory, Hallelujah, praise Your holy name,
  Yesterday, today, tomorrow, You'll always be the same.

Beulah R. Brown

From The Darkness

The essence of nature is accommodating
my open attention....
providing opportune reminders, respecting
the birth - death custom of change.

The sun rose with thundering vitality
and with equal vigor,
it disappeared. Dark clouds rolled in -
thick, black, ominous, they
pushed the light away.

The impact of some sudden change can
indent and empty all spirit from my chest
My heavy heart and soul are then again
refilled with the inexhaustible promise fulfilled
through faith and hope.

live being. Live. Be.

Charlotte Preston

Untitled

The rain comes down, the tears freely flow
my secret's inside of me, no one can know
the wind blows fiercely, my heart beats fast
I am leaving now, it's over at last
the doors are locked, my soul is free
my body is broken, no one can see
the raindrops slow, the tears they stop
I look at my reflection, my heart rate drops
the rain picks up, the wind begins to roar
my knees buckle, I fall to the floor
I rock back and forth, my mind knows no time
the mind is forever gone, the body is no longer mine

Beth Hofstad

My Sweet Emily

How do I describe thee
My sweet Emily?
A work of art?
A beautiful dream?
Or a kind deed?
Engraved in mine memories
Is thy picture perfect contouring
Bathed in pure sublimity.
The fragrance of thy scented locks
And the succulence of thy full bloom lips
'Twas a veritable loves treat.
And now thou standst before me
I all thy youthful glory
Reminiscent of the violets
In my garden tree.
Truly my sweet Emily,
Thou art a fantasy
Etched in mine everlasting memory.

Aparna Mukhedkar

Untitled

As the radiant sun shines through nature's glass,
my thoughts escape with the slow moving current.
No longer are the bleak memories of recent days past
  blazing through my consciousness.

It is the cold air that refreshes my need for new thoughts.
The pureness of the white snow clears my passages, and
the majestic sight of such creations settles my heart.
I realize there is so much more going on around me.

This feeling of new beginnings encompasses me.
Never again will I be dragged through such dark loneliness.
I know now that ultimate peace can be obtained,
But only when I release the fears that bind my soul.

From now on I will allow the sun to shine,
  I will allow the snow to fall, and
  I will allow my fears to show themselves...
  but, I will never again allow them to encompass
  my life.

Jenny Pelisek

Spring

Spring came in on moonbeams, with robins at her feet.
Nature's band applauded, cold winter's late retreat.
The crocus shyly peep their heads, not sure old winter's gone
But Spring's conductor leads her band, of all the birds in song!
She spread her bright green carpet, dropped violets by the brook
Woke up the sleeping daffodils, every where you look!
Oh! Spring you are so welcome
Please take your time and stay
It is such a great relief
to feel your warm, bright, day!

Elizabeth Bolick

Will You Still Love Me?

Will you still love me, when our time grows
near, if our love seems weak, and our souls in fear?
Will you still love me, if I grow sick or grow old,
if you seem alone, with no one to hold?
Will you still love me, when there's no one that you
know, when forever is near, and my heart beats slow?
Will you still love me, if I love you more, if
love is a rock, and heavens my door?
Will you still love me, when feelings fly high,
when I'm weak, alone, or just want to die?
Will you still love me, when I'm bleeding insane,
when I'm lost in fear, and dying in pain?
Will you still love me, if love is a flame, if my hearts
on fire, and impossible to tame?
Will you still love me, if I love you too, if there's
no one between us, just me and you?

    Brent N. Lord

Feelings

Loneliness is a friend of mine,
Never failing to descend on me, whenever I'm alone,
Hurt, depressed or without someone
To hold on to, to pour my heart out to.

I guess it's destiny
That there's no one around, no one to trust,
Because that's just what I am -
A nobody, a loner in this big, cruel world.

Love has no meaning to me,
Nor does friendship or company.
Why? Because I've never experienced it.
Never felt it's joy, it's comfort,
The laughter that it brings along.

A heartbreak hotel, that's what I am.
Hurt and pain rule my emotions,
My feelings of jealousy and envy,
Take control of me wholly.

Will this ever end? Will there ever be a time
Where I can laugh wholeheartedly? Experience the real joy of
friendships and relationships? Only time will tell...

    Gillian Alexander

Together

Your eyes sending messages
never heard before
My eyes showing pain
not wanting anymore
Tears spilling over my powdered
cheeks proving sincerity
Brawny hands gently wipe them away
accepting acceptance
Falling slowly away here no more, I'm gone
My eyes sending messages
never heard before
eyes peacefully close
Your eyes showing pain
Knowing there is no more.
Tears spilling over your cheeks showing sincerity
No hands to wipe the tears away
no more to accept
Eyes peacefully close
Falling slowly away
here no more you're gone

    Jennifer Huston

The Seasons of Life

Spring is the season of renewal
Newborn children pristine as jewels
Life unfolds into a delicate flower
Youth attains their inexhaustible power

June ushers in the onslaught of heat
Asphalt oases sear our naked feet
Hot sultry air kisses our cheek
Nudging mankind to its ultimate peak

Autumn enters the retirement of our life
Crimson colors reflect on our strife
Daylight hours dwindle very fast
As we contemplate feats of our past

Leafless trees rake the winter sky
Colorless birds cease to fly
Icy cold winds steal our breath
Drawing us nearer to an inevitable death

    David J. Audia

A Prisoner's Dream

A prisoner's dream is short and sweet.
No cuffs on his wrists, nor shackles on his feet.
But if you dig deep, down into his heart.
You'll find very soon, that's just a start.
It might take a minute, or even two or three
He'll tell you the truth though, I know, cause he's me.
He wants the world to be a better place.
You can tell by the lines, cut deep in his face.
These lines come from worries, deep in his head.
They also come, from the life that he's led.
He worries about the kids, he wants the best for them.
'Cause his biggest fear, is that they'll end up like him.
So, to all the kids in this land, far and wide.
He says to them all, "look at me and decide."
If you value your freedom and like where you're at,
Then just do what is right, and leave it at that.
If you make some mistakes, and want them to end.
It's time to look to God, 'cause He's your best friend.

    Jeff Bistodeau

The Shape Of My Heart

My love is endless it has
no end my love is boundless
there is no distance it cannot travel,
death cannot ever extinguish it's flame.

The shape of my heart is not
made of emeralds and is more precious
than diamonds or gold, no money on
earth could every buy it's mold.

The shape of my heart is more like
a dove loving and peaceful like God
would have created from above,
serene and gentle like a smooth flowing
stream more beautiful than anything I could
ever dream.

The shape of my heart is like the sun
it rises in the morning to greet a
new day, then embraces the glorious
sunset at the end of the day.

That's the shape of my heart,
a true work of art carved from God's own heart.

    Gregory S. Peters

Kennedy, King, Kennedy

Now the drumming is over,
No longer a parade in America's Heart.
Love once again lie in the field of clover,
A few more great men did part.

Buildings were dedicated, a Holiday Observed.
Epitaphs and streets to be seen.
Instead picture their lives as an Oasis in the desert,
So their memories will forever be green.

Commissioner's reports were needed.
The evil deeds could obviously be seen.
Remember President Kennedy's Words?
"What we can do for America",
And Dr. King's unfulfilled Dream?

Kennedy, King, Kennedy, everybody will say.
Their initial point out K.K.K.
Hate groups and Racism, a sickness in the world today.

Let us strive for unity through understanding.
Equal opportunities for all, not charity.
Security will then be in our hearts.
Living in America, the home of the brave and the free.

John E. Lynch

No Longer

I will no longer allow myself to wither rather than grow. I will no longer permit myself to remain in a pit of deep stagnation, to let my potentialities go uncultivated, to let opportunities go by without my concern. I will no longer.

I can no longer retreat from my responsibilities, to myself and to the world. I can no longer indulge the fear of failure as it contaminates my spirit, idly accepting mediocrity, pathetically forsaking greatness I can no longer.

It occurs to me that, no longer will abundant time avail itself, is I tarry. No longer will resources flow plentiful, as I waste. The whole world stands before me and anything in it could be mine, but no longer must I hopelessly accept defeat as long as success is a possibility.

No longer must I allow my vision to be blinded, to let my ingenuity be stifled, to let circumstances dictate my destiny. My determination is substantial and to all these things I say - NO LONGER!

James Edward Williams

If You Continue

If you continue, you will loose the sun,
no longer will there be any fun.
Only unhappiness will last, the only sound you will hear,
is your heart beating too fast.
When you look up, you will see the blue fall from the sky,
your life is nothing more than a lie.
If you continue, you will not see the flowing river,
inside, you will only quiver.
You will not smell the fragrant flowers in bloom,
all the days ahead will be an endless doom.
You will not hear the birds sing,
you will not even hear a bell ring.
If you continue, your mind will be lost in the wind,
and your body will be lost in a world of sin,
All your days will run into one,
everything in your life will be lest undone.
You will only be wondering in endless time,
sweet little girl of mine.
If you continue.

Carolyn Thorsen

My Son James

Compassionate and cute,
Not at all shy.
He has the brightest eyes
As blue as the sky.
He makes me laugh
And sometimes cry,
But he always says he loves me
When he says his goodbyes.
Sometimes he can get on my nerves of steel,
But that is all very much part of his deal.
Cause when he pesters you
Just like a bug,
He will turn right around
And give you hug.
He plays a mean trumpet and loves to sing.
His voice is as clear as a bell when it rings.
He tries to act tough even though he is not.
He is my son James
And I love him a lot.

Cheryl Ippolito

The Beauty of Love

At age 50 you will remain beautiful
Not for your physical perfection
The dark locks of hair
Large light eyes of gold
Lips and teeth so aesthetically pleasing
When in a smile they blind

The sparkle of your eyes
The mischievity of your smile
The tilt of your head when
Pondering a thought
These will remain when the physical exhaust

I find you beautiful each time
I look in your eyes
My knees quiver and I want to cry
For happiness seizes me that
I know you ... so beautiful

Jennifer Rosinski

Gifts

For gifts I pray
Not gifts of gold, for my hand to hold
To rattle in another's ear, and shout to them see here, see here,
I have coins and you do not, so I may say what is the plot,
And you will step the way I please, as I do thank God on my knees.

Yes for gifts I pray
But not the beauty of this shell, in which for this time I do dwell,
To prance about in showy style, and be admired all the while,
Expecting eyes to follow me, enchanted by the form they see,
And thinking such a comely face, shall hold with truth in beauty's
    place.

These gifts I pray,
No greater gifts then these; no finer fortunes found would please,
As an offered cup of faith to me, and this I pray, I pray it be,
To be endowed with an open heart, that lets all in and none apart,
With ample room for the self to stay, in love's bounty,
    the faithful way.
I Pray

Dee A. Roche

Colors

My mind whirls and whirls as I see the many colors.
Not just black and white, but reds, yellows and browns.
All of these colors make up the most beautiful thing of them all,
The world.
But as I start to look around, I can see that the world is not a
beautiful place to live.
Even though there are many cultures and colors and variety
whirling
around, there is nothing else besides that.
But when the colors of the world mix, many bright different colors
will arise from them.
But when we do, there will be a radiance of blue,
both for the sky and sea.
A majestic green for the land for our human eyes to see.
And of course, there will be that mixture of colors from all over
this world.
All of those colors are made up of those people who are courageous
enough to widen their eyes, and take a good look at the world.
Then they will see the most beautiful color of them all,
The clearness of everything

Aneesa Sataur

From Me To You

I miss you more than words can say
Not just now but everyday
You feel the warmth of my arms around you
I likewise can be sure to feel your warmth too
We may be many miles apart
But good feelings come from within the heart.
Close your eyes a minute and open them to skies of blue
Because you know that I am thinking of you.
No matter where we are
We still have a shining star.
So keep good loving thoughts every day
Love is forever here to stay.

Jean Visockis

"Things In Life That Count"

Not what we have, but what we use;
Not what we see, but what we choose.
These are the things that mar or bliss,
The sum of human happiness.

The things nearby, not things a far,
Not what seems, but what we are
These are things that make or break
That gives the heart it's joy or ache.

Not what seems fair, but what is trust;
Now what we dream, but the good we do.
These are things that shine like gems,
Like stars, in fortunes diadems.

Not what we take, but as we give,
Not as we pray, but as we live.

These are the things, that make for peace
Both now and after, time shall cease.

Goldie Christensen

"The Ode Of An Infinitive Friend"

"... We met each other as strangers,
And time has made us the best of friends...
I pray, (each day and every night), that
we stay as close, regardless to times' end...
This ode is from one, on whom you
can depend; please! Take heed in me always,
for I am; your: INFINITIVE FRIEND..."

Robert L. Wright

A Woman Waits

A woman waits, unknowingly, for me.
Not Whitman's woman, but a modern
breed, needing different satisfactions.
Her attraction is to pocket sized
physical representations of trust.
Silent among the pulsing bass sounds,
beneath the loveless grin of our neon downtown,
she waits. Dancing, swinging beads to that
trystic honking beat, the woman inhales ash from
a GPC. She slaps a skate punk wearing big
pants and blows rings to hide her face, her
inescapable shame.

Our cancer filled, city wind slashes the smoke
and dashes through hair, unveiling light eyes.
Oh, the look of interest, the sound of her cherubim
voice beckoning me. Smacking those redundant red
lips, she sings out, "Seventy-five." In loosened black
lace, on the sidewalk, she waits.
Alone for a while, then not.

Corey Kingsbury

Virgil the Closer

There's a saying around most coffee shops
"Nothing happens ' till something is sold,"
'Tis the potion that greases the wheels they say,
Selling Bibles or African gold.

Now should you agree with this theory of things
I've a story of valor to tell,
About a man called VIRGIL THE CLOSER
Out serving his country well.

Passed over, some say, years ago,
Top brass was he left to serve,
No Bachelor's degree ever graced his walls
And age had tossed him a curve.

A hundred yeahs, a thousand nays,
Talking to folks wasn't hard,
"Good things happen if you keep on Truck'in"
On the back of his calling card.

Yes, the CLOSER knew where the secret lay
To accomplish his fruitful task,
With your order enclosed in that old leather case,
For starters, you FIRST have to ASK!

Grant Halsne

My Life

In everyday, nothing seems complete
Nothing that I do seems to matter
  nor does it seem right
I try my best but it all falls down
  my life has fallen down.
I reach for help,
  but no one listens, no one cares
    my parents pick me up
    and let me free
But I am still alone
  frightened by my thoughts
  and scared of the future,
Of what lies ahead for my life.

Jennie Bender

Autumn

The towering rods of corn, their asexual reproduction
notwithstanding, swing seductively in the gentle
wind, scented like old dirt and slippery leaves.
I listen, fascinated, to the sound of that old wind
slithering itself through the dried stalks. The sound
makes its own irregular rhythm, scuffing up its floor
with unpracticed feet. The realization of isolation
overtakes my senses for a moment, and suddenly the wind
is heard even more so, adding a plaintive whine to
that of the lonely rustle of leaves and branches.
From overhead, the autumn clouds, that perfect shade
of grey, float serenely across this field,
covering it slowly with a blanket of shadow,
I know it's getting late and that I should go, but the
sound of the rhythm of the season
will not release my hypnotized mind so I stand still,
and become a cornstalk, lost in the wind,
and dying of degrees.
        Frances Knott

Remember Us: To Dead Comrades On Veterans' Day

We loved our land, heeded its call,
Now among fallen comrades all,
Here we lay and forever keep
A freedom vigil, a well earned sleep.

The bugle blew, the charge begun,
All hell broke loose, no place to run.
No turning back, we must plough on,
Only praying to see another dawn.

There may have been another way
To settle the strife and save the day.
We did not vote, we were not asked,
Only learned to fight and die at last.

On Arlington's hillside, under the sod,
We lay with comrades, known but to God.
Warriors from many battles past,
Our country free, we rest at last.
        James R. Hinton

Untitled

My best friend and I parted today.
Now I must sail alone around the Bay.

The times we shared we'll have never more -
If I travel alone now will I ever reach shore?

Some days will be stormy - some will be clear -
I'll keep the shore in sight to sail on without fear.

I'm on my own now - that's the best way -
Perhaps we'll sail together some spinnaker day!

I must sail the Bay on a ship all alone
Without the best skipper I have known.

Will I return? I don't really know -
It's too hard to leave when I can't let go!

I'm off to sail around the Bay -
My best friend and I parted today...
        Bonnie Frank

Dream...

Cross the path of immortal soul
leap into the eyes of the wondrous poles
look at the moon so crescently light
look at your imagination as a wondrous sight
let the fire leap through time
and eat away at your soul
till you think of a dream so unpleasantly untold...
        Christina Kendall

Falling Sickness

I have returned again against my will.
Now I will blink my eye of solitude
and wonder why? Wherefore? Must I sentence serve?
Sentences do not serve me but enslave,
wind a chain about my neck, whispering:
"This is now the beginning of thy end.
Thou art The Half-Man, all the rest is lost.
Half of thee is done and gone, half thy sight,
half of thy mind, all of thy innocence.
Your rhymes scheme wickedly. Thou verse is blank,
empty and alone." Sentences do speak.
Sometimes I understand and my world weeps,
waxes and wanes and finally it ends
endlessly for beginnings are begone.
I lost an eye, sickened, now fall and fall,
failing for I forget to hit my ground.
        Ashton John Fischer Jr.

God's New Angel

For many years you told me I was your precious love
Now I'm in heaven with my Father up above
You always made me feel I was your special little one
Now I have traveled far beyond the sun

No need to worry for I am safe and free
For many great ones came to greet me you see
My heavenly Father, angels and all
You must carry on until you get your call

From the Father to one day join me
Live life spiritually for that guarantee
To have your name put on that heavenly scroll
You must accept the saviour, keep the faith, that's the only toll—
        Arlene M. Swilling

"Across The Prairie"

I see the black cat as it walks across the prairie,
Now that everything seems so dreary,
It makes me wonder why I am giving,
He makes me realize, that just yesterday,
That life was worth living.

Yet, he sets me free,
Free from my pains,
He fights to be,
Like a pulse in my veins.

Now he runs,
Like he is scared,
Now he awaits,
Something he feared.

Closer, and closer,
It comes to him,
He crouches down,
And his face looks grim.

This is it, and I must know,
Why this noble creature,
Was afraid of his own shadow.
        Jennifer Wilson

Happiness

There are a few things in the world living for,
    That of sunshine, happiness and your smile
        I long to see your smile again
            The happiness of my world
I question if your world is fill with the same happiness
    I found to make everyone happy,
        Your give some of your happiness to them
            And I give my happiness to you.
        Laura R. Murphy

What Happened to Us America?

We once were the "Melting Pot" for all Nationalities
Now we are the "Boiling Pot" for all our Realities
We once were America, Land of the Free and Brave
Now we have become Unamerican, digging our own grave

We once used to be a family oriented society
Now we are dysfunctional units without roots or gravity
We once used to trust society by leaving our doors unlocked
Now we are a society with doors bolted and guns cocked

Remember the good old days, before materialism and credit
Homemade cooking touched our senses, and security was a habit
Remember when children had responsibility and chores to do
Accomplishment, pride, and discipline were instilled in us too

We have fought hard for our standards and the American Flag
A country of "Mutts" we are, who would let nothing lag
We had values, ethics, respect, and pride in our country
Responsibility, hard work, sacrifice were found in our pantry

We have the basic foundation to triumph and revise
If we give up selfishness and greed we might be surprised
That in this wonderful country of ours, we are one family
United, with common goals, hopes, dreams and American Reality

Janice Schindlbeck

"Life Is Just A Number"

Life, it seems is nothing more than a list of dates and
numbers. The day I entered the world I was given a number. One
of the first things I learned in school was how to count numbers.

My mind and ability are graded and turned into numbers. If I
break the law, I'm jailed and given a number. If I want to get a
job, I need a social security number. When I want to prove I'm
worth something, I need a credit card number.

When I'm old and wrinkled, I'll be told my days are
numbered. When I die, my gravestone will bear the numbers that
have symbolized my life...

Clara Smith Ford

The Last Refrain

Behold the fires of night come forth,
O'er barren trees of autumn woe,
The fallen harvest of the north,
Where lifeless limbs await the snow,
Of winter's cold eternal flow.

Soon come the shadows dark and deep,
Lost years within a timeless stream,
For autumn takes what heart's would keep,
What bears the gold of Virgo's gleam,
The glory of one's fondest dream.

Now falls the scythe's all ending pall,
That shant the love of May sustain,
Like tears the withered petals fall,
Though try the heart their fate restrain,
No hand may stay the last refrain.

Craig Richard Lysy

Gone

He leaves me and now I feel my cold, bitterly cold blood
rush through my veins in a whirl of disorientation. Each moment
I am not with him, my mind, my life, and even my own sanity are
overpowered by a peculiar sense of solitude. As I recall the
conversation that took place when the room was filled with much
more than myself, I start to feel the loneliness take control of
me. All my hopes fade and my dreams go away. Now, full of sorrow,
needing a companion to release my suffering, I do the only thing
that appears possible. I end it all.

Zeyneb Kazimov

The Cowboy's Midnight Dream

The Cowboy always dreams at the midnight hour
of a beautiful lady with golden hair, with
dancing heels that can dance on the winds of
time at the midnight hour. He sees her in the
silhouette of the dream world, but he knows
that she is and her beauty is beyond compare.
He can only hope the winds of the ages will
bring this love of a lifetime, unto him. He
bows on bended knee before his Creator and
prays to the Lord above to send him the lady of
love. Even though he is now old and broken, he
still dreams of the beautiful lady, and he still
has a whisper of hope in his heart, that the
graciousness of the Lord that before his eyes
grow dark that he may see the angel of the winds
for she is the very creation of beauty.

"The Old Cowboy" Charles E. Chancellor

Heaven

Heaven is a place
of glorious grace.
Where flowers will bloom and trees will grow.
No sadness, no unhappiness, and no sorrow.
There'll be no sadness,
there'll be no madness.
And will be glad,
and never be bad.
We'll hear David play on his harp every day.
We'll all be happy and our hearts will be gay.
So, I hope to see you in Heaven, I hope to see you up high,
where we'll meet again and never say good-bye.

Jill Withers

Kitchen Warmth

Microwaves are the black pot bellies
    of kitchens in the 90's
Warmth and glow is not one of their mightiest.

Breadmaking machines decorate the
    most fashionable counters.
But carbohydrates are one of those
    ingredients that cause mounters.

Toasters are gathering dust in the pantry
    as table top ovens make their entry.

Crocks pots simmer all day while your
    labor makes way for evening ease.

Black iron skillets now replaced by
    cords to the teflon contraption
Makes the kitchen not the same
Warm, inebriating smell, or conversation
    and exchange of ideas the same
Meeting place of the family.

Dominga T. Esquivel

The Cotton Fields

I've lived in Alabama for about fourteen years,
On the lake, I've sat at the end of the pier,
I've seen cotton fields that stretched on for miles,
I've seen it picked, and up in piles.
And on the ranches so wide and spread out,
I've seen horses run so fierce and stout.
I've seen little kids play in the hot summer sun,
They play and run until mom declares it done.
So I guess you could say I've seen Alabama, in bad and good,
And it's raisin' me right, the way that it should.
One day when I'm grown,
Thanks to Alabama, I will have shown.

Jennifer Danford

Inside

You press yourself against the walls on the inside
Of my body - a liner to my frame.

Your voice - like one hundred perfectly carved arrows,
Pierce echoes in my blood.

You breathe - with the warmth of flesh and
The coolness of soft water, molded together by whispers
Of concrete.
You breathe - weaving hints of magnets,
Heavy through my chest.

We are sculpted and your promises sail through the wind,
Navigated by your breath, into layers of paintings of dusk

That hang in full view... only on the walls, on the
Inside of my body.

I touch you and I feel vacant air scolding my fingers.
It scoffs as I study the sailboat entering the bottom
Of the black of my pupils; through a mirror.

A crisp white sail cradles the wood of our words,
Growing smaller and more unknown, as it enters the walls
On the inside of my body.

I look at my skin where I know you have touched me.

John Arce

Visions

Light, startlingly bright, comforting and warm in the midst
    of the darkness of our world and our thoughts
Whiteness, pure and simple, clean amongst
    the dirtiness that surrounds us
Gentle sounds of the surf pounding gently at my feet
    as I stroll slowly down the beach
A vision in white approaches in the distance,
    with his arms outstretched
I stop to ponder the ethereal feeling of harmony,
    love and togetherness that surrounds me
I feel a gentle push,
    as though an unseen hand is guiding me
We move cautiously into each others arms and
    gently sway to the sounds of the surf and the crying of the gulls
A perfect fit, destined to a life together,
    blessed by the unseen forces of goodness
Kindred Spirits being guided together by the
    pure and simple surrounding of nature at its finest
PERFECT HARMONY IN AN IMPERFECT WORLD

Deanna Knutson

Foothills of Tennessee

Oh, how I would love to be, back in the hills of Tennessee.

In the ridges and hollows lightly sprinkled with snow.
of the mighty and beautiful cumberland plateau.

A touch of orange, brown, and green
help make up the beauty of the mighty scene.

Where the squirrel, raccoon, fox and hare,
all scamper at the roar of the big black bear.
To hear the trickle of the mountain brook
as it rushes to feed life in every cranny and nook;

And then in the darkness and still of the night,
hear the call of the wild geese in their southern flight.

A day hath passed and at the early crack of dawn,
a mother deer licks her newborn fawn.

Feel the warmth of the early morning sun,
as all the little animals play and run.

When my day comes, I hope they bury me,
back in the foothills of Tennessee.

Hap Inman

Just Me

Of the fathoms of the oceans....... I am just a drop.
  Of the sands along the shore...... I am just a grain.
   Of the lands between the seas..... I am just the dust.
    Of the powerful, mountain range.... I am just a hill.
     Of the lilies of the field........ I am just a petal.
      Of the graceful butterfly......... I am just a wing.
       Of the mighty, blowing wind....... I am just a whisper.
        Of the giants of the forest....... I am just a leaf.
         Of the most melodious song........ I am just a note.
        Of the language of all men........ I am just a word.
       Of the opinions of the heart...... I am just a voice.
      Of the millions of the world...... I am just one.
     Of the earth from up above........ I am just a speck.
Of the universe so grand........... I am just me.

Danielle Ivane Gerrish

Untitled

These eyes have seen the glorious sights
Of the wondrous earth that has reflected
them back
Infinitely precious, yet deceivingly porous-
Yes, it was you, walking alone
Strangely hopeful, I thought, to
think it was someone else
My heart quivered some——
....a lot, when I saw you.
Of all these, the trees, sky, earth,
and fire, you were isolated-
Not unlike before, when we were in love,
walking alone, together.
And for all this, a wave of anxiety,
a life's worth passing before them,
these eyes saw you:
I subtly wish I had blinked for a second.

John Prieto

Reflection

What is this pain in these eyes I see,
    Of this tormented person in front of me?
Unwanted, unloved, uncared for, and hurt,
    I read these things in these eyes I see.

What is the pain in these eyes I see?
    This hate-filled person in front of me.
The screams, the yells, the hurt never stops
    So near the bottom, so far from the top.
I read the pain in these deep green depths,
    What is the secret this life has kept?

What is the pain in these eyes I see?
    This hated person in front of me.
A tear rolls down at a slow, taunting pace,
    Like so many others have touched this face.
What is the pain in these eyes I see?
    This person is a mirror staring back at me.

Joshua Pezzullo

Prayer

I love you, Jesus, Sweetheart.
How I loved seeing you, Darling!
Jesus, do you love me, Dearest?
How much, Christos?
So much, Sweetheart.
I look at you and smile, Dearest.
You are forever young and handsome, Darling.
I am your fan, Christos.

Virginia C. Sullivan

A Simple Poet

A passion for Truth and a dead end...
  of which of these now do you befriend?

Awake and rise so you may see
  just what is manifest destiny.

Luck and Providence are quite apart...
  The answer is written on your heart.

Someone waits for you, you should know,
  And toward them only love should grow.

I offer now a simpler line
  So that you will not be left behind.

Treasure your name above all things,
  And see what happiness it brings.

John Mark Carver

Coo Baby

Coo Baby, was a wild white dove
of whom I came to love.
  Coo Baby, Coo Baby, I miss you.
In the summer of the year she became so dear.
She was wild but with my love she became mild.
  Coo Baby, Coo Baby, where are you?
I taught her first to eat from a spoon,
shaped like a moon, then she learned to trust
as though she new she must.
She ate from my hand on command.
  Coo Baby, Coo Baby, I miss you.
Then one day came coo two, as all wild things.
They both flew any, to my dismay.
  Coo Baby, Coo Baby, where are you?
  Coo Baby, Coo Baby, I miss you.

Betty Lee Muse

Untitled

May the Smiles
of yesterdays
Carry us forth
and shine through the fog
of unpleasant tomorrows.
For friendship is a shelter for our sanity
And a source of strength
That stands irreplaceable.

Jamie McCartney

Memories Of Life

The change has come upon us like a blink of an eye
Oh how quickly the years have gone by
Sit back and remember what was then
The wishing we could do it all again
The distance in years, if not in miles
We hold in our minds the lasting smiles
The sharing of childhood dreams
The laughter and crying as a teen
How long has it been, just a moment ago
The thought of a time last week or so
So many things we thought we forgot
When we looked back we remembered a lot
Why are so many dreams left behind
Along with friends we will never again find
Each of them leaving a lasting memory
With everyone having their own story
It's nice to remember with a smile
And look back if only for a little while
Many miles we have walked to get here
Many miles still to go and more dreams to share

Janice A. Wilder

From Within My Prison, Kneeling

Like a river, swiftly flowing,
Oh, my precious life is rolling -
Rolling, rolling....quickly to the sea.
On the icy waves I'm riding -
My fleeting time abiding—
'Til the darkness shall protect me
From the cruelness of the sea.

As the mighty waves keep flowing,
And my life's blood's slowed, I'm knowing
Every sin committed in the tossing
And the turning of the soul within me.
Still I continue rolling...
Rolling, rolling.....and lost...
Upon the waves of the cold, cold sea.

James D. Warwick

My Long Forgotten Childhood

I used to be a kid once, you know.
Oh - those were the good old days.
Each day. I'd leap out of my bed just to watch the sun kiss the sky.
I'd run through the vast fields to feel the vibrant rays of the sun
upon my baby soft skin. I'd sit under an old sycamore tree for hours
watching the hard-working bumblebees buzz from flower to flower
as the soft gentle summer breeze danced through my silky hair.
And at night, I'd sit under my porch and stare into the limitless sky
as the blazing sun slowly descended leaving the sky fiery red.

Yes, those indeed were the good old days.
I, now, wake up each day hoping that the sun will rise
just an hour later, so that I may sleep a bit longer.
I, now, run through the bounded fields not to feel the warmth
of the sun, but to catch my bus to school.
I no longer sit under a sycamore tree
for I think it's a waste of my time.
And at night, I sit on the couch and stare into the meaningless screen
of the television set while, outside, a land that is now far, far away
from me, the sun slowly descends from the sky leaving the sky filled
with the redness of blood...the blood of my long forgotten childhood.

Danny Choo

Fond Memories

A memorable childhood I'm lucky to recall
On a Staten Island farm with trees so tall

Grandma and Grandpa were very special to me
Fond memories of them shall forever be

A religious upbringing was important and then
Receiving Holy Communion and Confirmation by ten

A High School graduate I was in '44
Then on to a job with the British Army Corps

At the age of twenty one in '47
My Prince Charming arrived from Heaven

A Navy man with so much pride
I said "I do" and became his bride

In '49 baby Pat made us three
And in '54 baby Pam came to be

The years have passed and the girls are grown
Both with families of their own

And today Prince Charming and his wife
Are happily enjoying our retirement life.

Evelyn F. Ryan

The Old Bachelor

He has so little time to think,
Once in awhile, in town, a drink,
He's reminded he's alone, no wife or child,
Never took the time to marry.

Everybody knows him, miles around,
Said "Best neighbor to be found."
Lifelong county resident, but,
He never took the time to marry.

Been a quiet guy all his life,
Kept to himself, raised his stock,
Enlarged his place, gosh, several times,
Never had the time to marry.

Hired men, a cook on the rampage,
Calvin', brandin', hayin'. shippin',
Fences to mend, ditches to clean,
Couldn't take the time to marry.

An old eccentric? Well, maybe so,
A kinder pard his horses will never know.
His dog, the barn cats, part of his soul.
Just never found a gal to marry.

Barbara J. Fleming

Wishing Well

The reason I was there today,
  One could truly tell,
Was to ease my cares and heal my dreams
  Within the Wishing Well.

The old gray stones were cracking
  And the wood held rusty nails
But, yet, it seemed the answers laid
  Within the Wishing Well.

And as my eyes eagerly searched
  For some relief, they fell
Upon a phrase of wisdom great
  Scratched on the Wishing Well.

"Look not within these depths for peace
  But let your praises sail
To the Maker of the maker
  Of the Wishing Well."

Cathlene Morrow Sampson

My Sweet Love

There is but one I adore so much,
one I think of all the time;
She is lovelier than anything
I've ever seen before.
  I feel so wonderful to know
she's mine.
  She is so beautiful, so kind, so
pleasant to have around.
  I know this is the one person
to whom I'm bound.
  She fills my life with such
sweet happiness.
As God gives his eternal sweet bless.
My love for her is brighter than the brightest sun.
For eternity my love shall surround just this one.
  It is the work of the heaven's that I was led to her.
  I thank so much from the center of my heart.
And I know as God is true, we will always be as one part.

David Tolley

Love's Sacred Song....

Love wants to show the world to live in unity
One is for All and All for One in perfect harmony
In every child we see the spark, it brought along to light
Reflecting spirit's sacred vow for Love's eternal right
The food of life is only good if love is in the name
the color of each others skin, in Love is all the same
Love mirrors our world as One from eye to shiny eye
Love... as it is, lights every star in mind's creative high
The warmth you feel in close embrace, is love in tender bloom
Let's All hold hands and dance away the darkness and the gloom
Love cultivates the seeds of thought and plants them wise and free
With faith as root, hope as growth, love as perfect tree
Love breaks away the shell that dims the purity of light
Let go the past, release the now, let Love be future's height
The love we are is here to stay, the binding...
it's all gone
The circle is renewed again
We are the sacred song...

Gertraud A. Nelson

Untitled

With one more step away from the cradle —
  one more toward the grave,
Our mine of time diminishes...
  there's little left to save.

With one more page torn from our lives,
  one more chapter ends.
The final draft has been played out
  the Author of Life commands.

Daily erosion of this, our life
  takes place each passing year,
Until it takes its final toll,
  it yields not to our fear.

At last our journey home is ending,
  we bow to destiny -
For twilight's final call has sounded
  and beckoned us to history.

Janice Poirier

Be Strong

  Be Strong

When lifes' circumstances throw us for
one reason or another into a state of
stress and depression...

  Be Strong

Think of beauty - that which life has
given us - with nature. Share laughter,
and smile; to enlighten our thoughts.

  Be Strong

While smiling on the outside...the
natural beauty of life smiles with us:
and all around, so...

  Be Strong

Laughter: uplifts the spirits of all
of us. With laughter... comes smiles!

  Be Strong!

...In your thoughts - of the mind.
When some of life seems again;
impossible to bare...

  Be Strong!!

Deborah A. Register

As I Looked Out My Window

As I looked out my window
one scraggly rainy day
behind me stood the highway
Above me stood the sky
In front of me was the horizon
stretched over the fields far and wide
I got up and went outside
and ventured across the railroad tracks
I opened my palm to observe a nickel
I opened the door to observe a smile
I opened my mind to observe a moment
that otherwise would be forever lost in time
The trees were stained with scarlet
rose and amber leaves fell
I could hear many different sounds if I strained my ears
but if I concentrated
all I could really hear
was the sound of my own heart
beating slowly over and over

Ian B. Lande

Francesca

Hearing of her illness a part of me died
One so vibrant, filled with fire, brimming with laughter
One so giving, loving and forgiving.

Hearing of her demise, Oh! the phoenix began it evolution
Was hard to describe, the hurt felt inside
Was this justice for all the good done?
Whom am I to judge, whom am I to relate?

Hearing of her death, Oh! the phoenix rising from the flame
Spreading it's wings, free of hurt, free of pain
Spreading its beauty, in freedom for all to see.

Hearing, Francesca in the wind
Knowing she rose from the fire
Surrounding us forever on the wind
Never to be forgotten, never to die.

Always a breath of vibrant, dazzling color
Always a gust of vibrant, warm air
Surrounding us... Francesca.

Colleen M. Browne

All I Want For Christmas Is A Pot-Bellied Pig

All I want for Christmas is a pot-bellied pig
one that's cute and cuddly
that I can teach the jig

With black floppy ears and a great big snout
"What a cute little pig!" all the kids will shout

He'll have a yellow summer bonnet
and booties for winter too
and everyone that sees him will want a pig too

With a curl in his tail and a twinkle in his eye
He'll be a classy little pig from a clean pig sty

I think I'll name him "Spanky" and he'll be real smart
He'll feed on fruits and berries if they're not too tart

I'll proudly take him walking down the city park trails
He'll strut and grunt and snort a lot and wag his curly tail

Everyone that sees us will smile and say
"Hope I'm lucky enough to own a pig some day"

Connie Jacobs

Mi Amor

Mi Amor is a love that is endless and true
One unmeasurable, one only imaginable
With every sunrise there follows a sunset
Which each shall possess a beauty within
Mi Amor, Mi Amor, what am I to do?
Since my love for you is all too true

My days are long, my nights even longer
As reality strikes, I begin to ponder
My clear blue skies became so pale
As our distance grows to no avail

As time goes by, I see a light
which emanates from only inside
It reveals a time, a time so right
That neither one could ever fight
'Cause in the end we both shall see
A love so true for you and me

Abigail Cruz

Don't Regret the Path that We Take

Don't regret the path that we take
Only know, you don't travel alone.
Never doubt the choices you have made
Nothing more can ever be done.
Always look to the future for all that you seek
Knowing some answers still lie in today,
Ask not what may be, revelations aren't free, and
Tomorrow will come anyway.
Whatever will happen, can never be changed
Only which decisions we make,
Our future is ours, we can win if we try!
Don't regret the path that we take.

David A. Hoppe

My Shadowing Image

So alone am I, here's my time to cry
 Only then will I wake up, stronger then
I intended to be, sorry to have shown my needs

When will I learn, to handle on my own
 Why cry, I should have known
Got to finish what was started, tho not
 Finished just departed

Holding on for dear life, I realize it's
Worth the fight, yet shut my eyes
There's no light, I only wish the fears
 I felt you could've seen

For all the wrong I've done
The price was paid, no need for
Answers the question lies within
 our heart

From our lips, truth will not depart
 No one cares what's in your heart
Unless it's what they want to hear
In other words, I was never here

Darlene McFarlane

Autumn Gold

A tree cannot a miser be
That freely gives its gold.
The leaves that flutter to the ground.
Are more than purse can hold.
A robber wind will find his way,
This treasure to purloin.
And gather up in gusty arms,
The last bright, golden coin.

Dorothy Tilley Wike

I Swear

Expiring in death
only to die by exhaustion of life

Divorce of living to extremes on length
always to tire of destinations to come

Eyes on truth of heart
to deny that love would force you to quit loving
forever......
do you hate me that much??
Do you?

That you would deny your love for me by substituting it
with disillusions of happiness and pain free ease
that only leave you later with all that hate and sorrow
and then some more to be added with every disillusion

Do you care what belongs to this love
of friends forever

Do you SWEAR to be loved no more?
If you do make it so, if not come to me

For I shall love thee
ever for and to eternity!

J. D. Jackson

Imagination

I thought I heard the door bell ring,
Or a key turning the know within.
I opened the door, you were there -
Rays of sunshine on your hair.

"Oh how I've missed your presence dear,
It's been long since you were here.
Our secret messages, your smile and humor
Whether alone, or across a crowded room."
A sorrowful sigh, and to my dismay
The sunlight, and my love, had disappeared.
How I tried to keep the dream
Of tender love that I had seen!

Alone again, and through my many tears
Remembering our love, fun, laughter, and fears,
We have had throughout our married years.
How I wish you were really here!

Caroline J. Todd

Yellow Rose

Yellow Rose...

As I watch you on a blossoming bush
or in a delicate crystal vase
My hearts aglow and a warm smile is on my face

Yellow Rose...

As I watch the magnificent and wise transformation of your beauty
from young to old
I love the glance we exchange
And the everlasting magic you hold

Yellow Rose...

As I watch the inevitability of your perilous petals
Drop one by one,
I know a new day has begun
And although I will miss you with an intensity I have never known,
I know it won't be long
Before I will see you... in a world I can not wait to belong.

Desa Wade

Circa 1995

Do you see behind your eyes
or in your soul, above the lies?
Do you answer when a heartbeat cries,
or do you close yourself in your own circle?
Love hears pain, can't bear the sound,
but tomorrow doesn't believe the world is round.
If it was, couldn't hope be found
just by linking love in a circle?
Spinning, spinning, lost in space, peace breaks to
pieces every place. What goes round, comes round, in an
endless race: Ground zero is a deadly circle.
Can you feel inside your brother's skin,
knowing every other mother's son is kin,
or do you live for power, like the dying men,
turning their covered wagons of greed and hate and sin
against us in circle?
Spinning, spinning, lost in place, tears rain down from
heaven's face, could today be a gallows trying our case,
tightening the noose in a final circle.

deni nipps

Endless Thoughts

I wish that words could really tell,
or perhaps even say how I feel
When I'm thinking of you;
And lets you understand how much
it would really mean to me if there
were a chance of seeing you to....
But, my words continue to linger on,
in search for that precise certain thought;
So that I may express what these empty
feelings of missing you so much have
painfully brought....
And though, there may be many miles
between us, that's keeping us away and
So very far apart;
but you will always be here within me,
in every thought and in every single
beat of my crying heart....

Benjamin Andujar

Foolish Pride

Foolish pride becomes a heart breaker, if it controls the inside
or perhaps it becomes a soul wrecker, that awful foolish pride

Lord, just the other day, when we were having our conversation
talking about troubles, trials, and tribulations

I failed to realize, while we were talking
satan was working over time, he was stalking

And Lord Jesus, I made a mistake
probable the worse, I could make

There were lots of people, gathered all around me
but with pride in control, I failed to bend my knee

Father I am so very sorry, I used your name insane
don't know what come over me, I must have yield to insane

Truth is, I hadn't done this, in a long long time
oh, oh, Lord, wish I'd kept you stronger on my mind

Praise the Lord I was reminded, I was still under God's protection
but not to practice sin, and I could feel his love and affection

Now my heart and soul is perfect, and spiritual clean
and I no longer worry about that, self-righteous thing

Friend, don't let your hearts be broken, by that awful foolish pride
please, don't let your souls be wrecked, pride must not control
inside

Dennis E. Moore

Without a Trace

Wind ruffled on this tiny no-name lake is no distraction.
Other night sounds blend, for they are natural, and belong.
A scrap of canvas is enough against the early morning dew and chill.
No tent, it would shield me from the glory I now see.

Overhead a limitless vault of stars reaching to infinity.
Starshine outlines the mountains, the walls of my cathedral.
It is a time to turn inward, to examine, to ponder,
To consider if to others I have left a worthwhile mark.

An insignificant dot of blue on the map of the Sapphires,
Not an easy place - one way in with hairpin steep trail.
It is worth it. No shod hoof or wheel will mar this place.
When I leave there will be no mark, no reminder of my passage.

Bob Metcalf

On Growing Older

Each day we dutifully take our pills
Our food is definitely "no frills"

We see our Doctors on a regular basis
Sometimes we just hate to face this.

The list of "eulogists" is never ending
We expect them to do our major mending

Cardiologists, Rheumatologist, Dermatologists, too
They're standing in line - waiting for you

Exercise takes up much of our week
But we want to feel we're at our peak

We wouldn't be caught dead - sitting and rocking
We're better off just quietly talking

But - there are many moments of happiness and bliss
Seeing grandkids grow up - we wouldn't miss.

So - in spite of the pitfalls, complaining and such
We don't want it to end - we savor it too much!

Betty B. Fink

Wedding Day

A wedding day is a beautiful thing,
Our friends and family all join in.
The day you exchange that special ring,
And a brand new life will begin.
The day is filled with flowers and joy,
Festivities with food music and dance.
The vows exchanged you never tov,
Looks of love you trade at a glan e.
Before you know it your Mr. and Mrs.,
as the warmth of happiness enters your heart,
given to each other are tender kisses,
knowing now you'll never part.
Now at last you toss the bouquet,
in hopes you pass on your good luck.
This blessed event makes a beautiful day,
The memories away you will tuck.
Off you go on your honeymoon,
some intimate time for you two.
The most glorious day you'll remember in June,
while tonight you're both still anew.

Jeanette J. McAdoo

Young Today, Grown Tomorrow

Just today, I'll let you be,
To search and wonder, let you see
To be on your own to frolic and play
Decide on your own what to do or to say
Just for today you will be on your own
To show me at last to see if you've grown.

Joanna Szeto

And Sometimes A Rainbow

There are times in our lives when
our souls are battered
by storms.
Cold, bitter winter-dark days
that bring the sting of ice and snow.
Fearsome summer storms, flashing, loud,
violent, damaging.
Never-ending, day-after-day weepy rains
which threaten to drown the spirit.

But just when you think you'll never feel
warm or dry or happy again,
God always send the sun
-and sometimes a rainbow.

Gloria Ziemienski

Our Daily Walk

Up in her arms she carries me upon our daily walk,
Out passed the barn so we can see the circling of the hawk.
Along the creek we stop to watch the muskrat swimming by,
And frighten the blue heron who takes off for the sky.

"Dear Lord," I hear her softly say, "I thank you for this place,
For fields, the trees, the birds, and dogs, the creek, and all this space.
How wonderful you are to me, I look to you above,
And thank you for your mercy Lord, your grace, and peace, and love.

My heart is oh so full today of joy and its content,
To sit here by your side and hear the words that you have sent.
I hear them in the rushing water of the meadow's creek.
I feel them as the wind blows the grass against my cheek.

They say, 'I love you, child and never will I leave,
For I have bought you with a price that you can not conceive.
It was my Son, your Sacrifice, they nailed upon that tree,
So that my Love can heal your wounds what ever they may be.'"

We sit there till the sun goes down, a wondrous time we spend,
That quiet hour loving life so that her soul can mend.
She picks me up so carefully, her shoulder's where I ride,
Our daily walk together, Lord, down in my heart I'll hide.

Joyce A. Bostwick

Bear Patch

There once was a bear who wore a patch
Over his eye because of a scratch.
Around his neck was a red bow tie
That made him a really classy guy.

His fur was soft and when given a hug
He felt like the pile on a very soft rug.

No den for him, he lives in a house
With two other bears and a VERY cute mouse
Who also wears a plaid bow tie,
That makes him a very classy guy.

So if you're sad and you need some cheer
Always have a stuffed animal near.
They're great to hold and in a little while,
They'll turn your frown into a great big smile!

Donna L. French

Sunsets

Just like the clouds
   that may float away;
These buildings pass the word...
Since I am now gone,
   you may reign...
Just like the clouds
   you may rain...

Christopher DeManss

A Tribute

Brunswick Georgia claims a famous tree
Over looking the "Marshes of Glynn."
Under its shade Sidney Lanier wrote one of his best,
A living monument to one that's gone on to rest.

This great poet blessed others with his talents from above
His works describe his life, his ideals, and his love,
It has been said of him, he lived in "sweet sounds"
With a flow of music and melody all around.

Seldom does the world produce a genius as Sidney Lanier
His kind is not born every day of the year,
In silence he suffered with an incurable disease
But he never stopped writing about the sun, the stars, and the trees.

With his last and greatest poem "Sunrise" finished
His soul crossed over on the other side,
Now he is walking on streets of gold where the
Sun never sets, and where we will never grow old

Aletha C. Middleton

A New Day

Fog — obscuring everything;
    Over the village, over the trees, over the man-made
    office building,
Over my understanding.
Fog — Smothering the morning.

The sun — a glimmer of light within,
    Struggling to break through,
    Suddenly emerged, through the fog,
Focusing the village, the trees, the office building;
The sun — an end to night, always returning.

O, fog: shroud of transient uncertainty —-
    My doubts.

O, Sun: Beacon of faithful clarity.

The truth within burns away the doubt beyond.

Alfred Muller, M.D.

A Terrace View

I sit and look out at the wonders of nature,
overtaken by its simple beauty,
The silence so peaceful,-
Feelings of serenity,
Warmth permeates my soul,
Soaring birds dot the blue sky,
My heart is full,
Below the sailboats adorn the spectacular view
Amidst the ripples in the bay,
Infinity is the horizon - such clarity,
Quiet meditation - happy thoughts,
Stress is overcome,
Peace - peace - almost a dream.

Arlene Windmiller

The Circle

The big grit wheel is spinning around;

The dull-edged axe is being ground,
Prepared to make the thudding sound.

The sap encroaches on the axe;
Defiant chips move to defense,
But miss the blade and strike the hand
That turns the wheel and swings the axe.

The trees are toppling to the ground;
The dull-edged axe now makes no sound.

The big grit wheel is spinning around.

David L. Hyde

Star Bounce

My God took the earth and bounced it off the
palm of his hand and said, go out and make a
light and the light twinkled all night a star
so bright what a tremendous and radiant sight
with so much hope and care no love beyond
compare for he knows what it is right. My
God so wondrous full of great concern, love
faith and gentle kindness somehow I've missed
Oh! God forgive me my life full of laughter
joy, sadness and pain will continue to be
within me until the last day. I love you!
My father so promised strong and true lead
me to that bright star twinkle I wish to be
bounced too!

Darlene Collier

Death Is Beautiful

Dry your eyes, child, for Death is Beautiful,
Parting becomes an unknown journey.
Traveling the road of life is endless,
Eternity is around the corner.
Dry your eyes, child, for Death is Beautiful.

Lift your head, child, for Death is Beautiful,
The aesthetic path toward heaven is brief.
Beauty is once again restored
And love still remains.
Lift you head, child, for Death is Beautiful.

Smile to the world, child, for Death is Beautiful,
All pain has ceased on an airy cloud.
Peace arrives at last in heaven,
And there is no better place to be.
Smile to the world, child, for Death is Beautiful.

Live once again, child, for Death is Beautiful,
Light seems to emanate from above.
Gloom is erased and the shadows depart,
Eternity resides around the corner.
Live once again, child, for Death is Beautiful.

Candice Pelkey

Wisdom Of The Wise

Hear the wisdom of the wise
Past footsteps have tread our way
Paths to choose where the future lies
Are made smooth by what the old say

Take a step in the distant past
Reconstruct what how has been
Make a pattern of days to last
Replace bad with good as life descends

Hear the wisdom of the wise
Listen as the old softly speak
Lend a graceful ear and sympathize
Words are strong even tho bodies are weak

Hear the wisdom of the wise
Where we go they have been
Take a look through their eyes
To make it around life's early amens

Edgar Williams

Life

We sit and sit until
we are mellow
And all our muscles turn
into jello
I can't sit another minute
If this is life there's nothing in it

Alfreda Harvey

Wish Poetry

I wish I were a wall
that could stop any
machine that could pollute or
cut down trees just to
put up a store.

Jason Fischer

Ode To Emily

The rain is about to clear the pungent sent of yesterday
peace is on the horizon for the children of the black widow

Time is the only healer of Prince Albert and the Victorian
Matriarch, who has carried the crown of three generations
to now be buried to the sea of Manhattan.

It is far from an Irish Diddy... a lake of currents and
bitter Jams... a son of a different color... daughters of a
storm of a turbulent fire...an angry branch of the old oak,
who has no connection to it's own watering hole.

It's truthful face is to the sky... to the clear blue
powder of the baby's bassinet... to the heart beat of ones
own pulse.

A dive to the inner coral of one's ocean... is the adventure,
to be lost at sea, only to find the buried treasure...
brilliant, detailed, baroque, and that of remarkable value.

Oh sleep in the calm of your own decision
be of the time where souls can fly...
dance to the big bands with the lovers you create
rest in peace in the comfort of this universe.

Donna J. Elia

Stay? Yes! Recycle? No!

There was a little bird sitting up on a hill.
Pecking at a worm with it's little yellow bill.
As he pulled it from the earth it said, "Oh no.
Don't leave my family all alone below."
The bird said, "Yeah! Well, up in that tree
my hungry family is waiting for me.
They want to eat 'till they get their fill,
and I'm tired of pecking on this hill.
You know you're no good if you don't fulfill
your role in life like the others will.
You'll be recycled and returned to the earth
to help make the flowers grow.
Now just think what you're worth."
The worm said, "Yeah! If I had my way
right here at home is where I'd stay.
And your hungry family could go fly a kite,
or sing for their supper if they wanted a bite."

Betty B. Mahair Holmes

White Easter Lilies

Awake and rise from your wintery grave,
Peek out from beneath the earthen clay.
Let us know that you are coming forth,
to remind us of the Savior's re-birth.

He rose from the dead as the stone rolled away,
From the dark, and damp tomb in which He laid.
He rose with a Heavenly body, though He was not known,
To show that his body would never decay.

Remind us that He still lives from your beauty
To our hearts,
That we might realize the purity of your blossoming petals
are symbolical of His love for us.

Jean Nickles

Teenage Pain

Pressure, pressure, pressure;
Peer pressure, peer pressure, peer pressure;
Motorcycles and dirt bikes;
Go fast, go fast, go faster;
Riding over his head;
Broken arm;
Pain, pain, pain;
Emergency room;
Pain, pain, pain;
Surgery;
Pain, pain, pain;
Hardware in elbow;
Pain; pain; pain;
Healing, healing, healing;
Pressure, pressure, pressure;
Peer pressure;
The pain is not his.

Harvey R. Levenson

Fallen Nation

Once there was a country of beauty and more.
People from all countries, flocked to her shores.
Searching for freedom, hope for despair,
In this nation of peace and justice so fair.

One day this country; past two centuries old,
Began to change; love waxed cold.
Courtrooms were mockeries of justice and truth.
For the right price, evil could rule.
Blood covered her lands and shores.
Value of human life was no more.
Shivering people behind doors locked so tight.
Crime, greed, and violence controlling with fright.

Gone are those who fought for right.
Screams of pain and terror ring through the night.
Gone justice and liberty.
Acceptance given for horrible deeds.
Parents moaning and crying,
Young sons and daughters lay dying.
In this fallen nation.
A nation under siege.

Janice S. Hensley

Norway Tour

Trip to Norway, Sweden and Denmark
People we met happy as a lark
Hamar, Bergen, and Oslo we went
The time we used was always well spent

More beautiful scenes we see each day
In colors of green, blue, and grey
Churches of wooden nails and slats
Farmers fields without much flats

Wood country houses with roofs of grass
Door hinges of wood and knobs of brass
Unusually made rain gutter drains
They do their job well made of just chains

Mountain tops covered with ice and snow
All streams bring water down below
Mountains roads blocked with rocks and white goats
Rivers filled with most beautiful boats

On the bus fourteen days we did roam
Now we are thinking of our own home
Souvenirs bought and money well spent
For months now we'll dream of where we went

John A. Strommen

Candy Bars and Cigars

He was beaten senseless in his little store
People were sitting outside in their cars,
The storekeepers face showed a beating took place
All of this for candy bars and cigars.

The elderly huddle in their shacks and tents
Too afraid to go out in the night,
'Cause the gangs emerge with their drugs and guns
Then terrorize everything in sight.

The world has evolved in so many ways
Its decline is quite painful to tell,
I think it shows as cruelty grows
That morality has gone to hell.

So where will it end I think no one knows
For humanity already shows many scars,
Like the beaten storekeeper by his register he lay
Shot to death for candy bars and cigars.

Julian S. Genet

Sketches for a Masterpiece

The canvas is primed by the master of crafts, with outlines for a perfect draft. Capturing the essence of space and time, creating a picture one of a kind.

Colors are strewn in dark shades and light, casting shadows of dancing delight. Mistakes are rare and none by chance, undetected by a glance.

Images emerge happily and gay, forming contrasts along the way. Figures adapted to nature's plan, each stroke bowing to the artist's command.

A composition arranged harmoniously, echoing the existence of you and me. Signed and sealed with a special identity, destined to hang throughout eternity.

The painting of man is a wonder you see, only a copy to hereafter be. The miracle you've witnessed will never cease, yes, we are sketches for a masterpiece.

Bettye L. Holland

Perhaps

Perhaps a smile is a promise of a kiss to come.
Perhaps a sigh is a wistful thought.
Perhaps a tear is a river of sorrow.
For the dreams that have come to naught.
Perhaps a grin is a remembrance of a long-forgotten joy.
Perhaps a wrinkle is what the passing years have wrought.
Perhaps a laugh is a catch in one's throat
For the dreams that have come to naught.
Perhaps a smile, a sigh, a tear, a grin a laugh
Are but outward signs of emotions we have sought
To cover the pain and anguish felt
For the dreams that have come to naught.

Joseph Hoffman

Life

Life is a theater, the world is the stage.
Played with emotions, bravery, fear, happiness and, rage.
We are the cast, actors are needed not.
It is ours to unravel all the twisted plot.
Predestined are our lives, I renounce this today.
I didn't always, what a price I had to pay.
We all have choices, on what paths to follow.
Make the wrong one, you can't just sit and wallow.
Pick yourself back up, chose a better one now.
Pride starts to return, you give yourself strength somehow.
There is more story to tell, than what's on this page.
Life is a theater, the world is the stage.

Butch Mize

The Ruler

The ruler stands
The blue shines
The numbers look out
To see what they
Can see

Elisha D. Appleton

My Sunday Night's Prayer

"....Dear Lord, high in heavens above
Please send me somebody to love.
Someone whom I can love and who will love me, too
Dear Lord, that is what I ask of you.

I do not ask for riches, for money is meaningless to me
Someone who is deeply loved is whom I want to be.
I do not ask for fame, or nothing of the kind
I just want somebody to love whom I can call all mine.

My life feels so incomplete and you may wonder why
I'm longing for someone to love, someone to be my guy.
He need not be handsome or fine, for looks come and go
My love for him will be true, that's all he needs to know.

I ask of him to have a tender kiss and be kind to heart
Oh, will this true love I seek ever even start?
I've been so very patient but how my loneliness lingers on
Oh, will this heartache of mine ever be gone?

For as long as I, Gina Marie Martinez, am upon this ground
I'll search for my one true love who has yet to be found.
So, please Lord, keep my prayer in mind
And pray for me from time to time...."

Gina Marie Martinez

The Intercourse Of Fire And Ice

It slips faultlessly through the fingers of time,
    portrayed of beauty and love
    haunted by it's ominous tendency to dance in the dim shade
    of two wooden hearts.

A silent passing through minds, not completely halting, but a
    soft pause, mimicking the salty heir to which it was bore.

Opposite identical pairs of micro-organisms threading wombs of
    generations together by a single double axis of obvious
    empowerment.

An array of competitive choices, battling for your purity...
    the satin petals of Eve slowly blooming and forever withering
    away... and when the battle is over,
    The war will have just begun.

Jessica Leopold

To My Children

I have eight gems that are unsurpassed by anything this world can
    produce.
Eight gems of matchless beauty that as I sit here and muse,
Have brought me untold moments of happiness, joy and pride.
And have filled this mother's heart with a love that shall forever
    and ever abide.
There have been moments when I have wondered, "what if this had
    not been?
What if I had pursued another way of life, when, as a teen,
I was on the crossroads of deciding what path my life should take;
Could any other road have led me to the satisfaction and
    fulfillment that this treasure gave?"
I know in my heart that, in spite of disappointments and heartaches
That must come our way when so very much of ourselves is given,
No amount of wealth or fame could give me the peace and contentment
That God, in His infinite love, gave me through these priceless gifts
    from Heaven.

Ila Diamond Marta

The Fall Of Night

Shades of dusk drawing near;
Purples hues, dark, yet clear.

Twilight's coming night shall fall.
Dark animal sounds hear them all.

Stars parade in the skies.
Up it comes, the moon shall rise.

Smothered clouds around it spent;
But they shall leave, away they're sent.

Ghostly winds, shiveringly cold.
Wolves shall sing the songs of old.

An unearthly palace, a different realm;
So different from when the sun's at helm.

The murky shadows, sounds, and sights,
All come to life, at the fall of night.

Julia York

Eve Of Disaster

Waters calm, sand still,
Quiet, for now, 'til morning we kill

Staring at my pictures wondering if I'll see them again,
Wanting to hold them in my arms once more before the killing begins

Mixed emotions surround me
Stand tall, be strong, protect your country,
Scared of the unknown, wanting to flee

I'm forced to protect myself and my country
Doing the opposite of what I've been taught,
Unlike oil, our lives cannot be bought

Lord, I'm ready to meet you if that's your desire,
Because you're the one to whom I aspire

Be with my family and friends
Make them strong,
Help them pull together
In hopes this won't last long

Realizing how little I've done since the day of my birth,
We'll meet again in heaven,
But hopefully, on earth

Cynthia Bomar

Quiet Waters

The night is fast approaching, yet she lies motionless, waiting...
Quiet waters don't make waves.
A slight wind makes small ripples, but she doesn't move...
Quiet waters don't make waves.
Lights flash. Dim, and he has yet to arrive, but...
Quiet waters don't make waves.
Clouds scatter throughout the sky. Their day is complete but...
Quiet waters don't make waves.
Jasmine closes her eyes and bids a due and still...
Quiet waters don't make waves.
Out of the shadows he appears. Shining, glowing, full, complete.
Ready to push the wave to its highest peak creating endless motion.
Lights flutter, then go out. Midnight has come and it's time to surrender.
Tomorrow the clouds will gather and the light will shine bright.
Everything will begin anew, but for now...
Quiet waters....make waves.

Jennifer Eddings

The Child / The Woman

As a child I lived in a nightmare,
Quietly I walked through my youth,
taking each step in fear.

As a woman the nightmare I relive,
Each night I walk the same path,
every step takes me back a year.

Slumber threatens my peace,
Stripping me of my womanhood,
intruding upon the night.

Sleep contrives with evil purpose,
Directing my mind, resurrecting the child,
and ineffable fright.

With absence of sound the child enters,
A definite existence in my mind,
Into a repeated role am cast.,
Is the child a token of remembrance from my past.

I'm incapable of separating the two,
THE WOMAN / THE CHILD.

Darla J. Smith

Sometimes

Sometimes at night when I'm in my car, a tune on the
radio will bring your memory back.
I can almost hear our voice and it brings a smile to my face.
I can almost feel your touch and my heart trembles.
The thoughts are of your love and hopes we had. They
put a twinkle in my eyes and brightened my smile.
The scent of your hair I can almost smell, and I
reach out to touch only to come back empty-handed,
but not empty-hearted.
The spring in my step was put there by just thinking
about you.
The rush of my heart, the tremble of my hands, are
because of you.
Sometimes at night you guide me, you hold me, you
love me.
Sometimes at night....

Herman M. Perkins Jr.

Cold Eyes

The glare, piercing a mind with aggression
Raw hatred, boiling with rage.
Pure rejection, shuddering with fear.
An affliction to Mother Earth,
Deep, hostile wounds within her generous bosom,
Turning generation against generation;
They separate the ages without mercy;
Their icy, stinging stare slaughters the soul;
Children are nabbed from Mother's womb
   and Father's teaching hands.
With natures bondage broken they learn to reflect
   stone, cold eyes.

Amanda S. Colwell

Fall Time

So many colors
Reds, yellows, oranges, and more
There're colors galore
The air is nice
The water is like ice
When you look outside you see everything from:
The clear blue mist
To the feel of:
A crisp, cool wisp

Christina Tucker

Graceful Deer

The tall graceful white
Tailed deer wounded across the
Daisy filled meadow

Julie Marie Smith

The Redwoods

In the deep, deep valley lays the forest of the
Redwoods. Your hands get tickled, then your run
them through the soft pine needles. You like the
smell of the red bark. You lift your head to see
them move with the wind. Next to the redwoods
is the river they drink from. The roots take a gulp
of water and you watch the river sink. The fish
in the river quickly rushes to safety under the
rocks. The sun in the distance slowly sinks in the
west and the moon slowly lights the sky. The stars
dot the sky and you see the redwoods have stopped
drifting in the wind and begins to rest. You know
that it is resting because it's smell is gone and the
bark is now brown.

Alex Michael Johnson

Devoided Wedding Vows

Cleansing scent of lilac, in the spring,
Refreshing her memory, of when they touched.

Noise and confusion, outside their realm,
Deft, and quite, melancholy now.

Believing in the one, she's chosen,
Years of one's life, true with devotion.

Watching so many, gaze deep to each other,
Aching to enhance, the eyes of her lover.

No more shimmering, moonlight nights,
Nor strong, gentle arms, holding her tight.

Upon, removing her wedding band,
Her eyes, brim with tears, her future ends.

She's empty, confused, and hopeless now,
Circumstances, devoided, their wedding vows.

The loss of her loved one, has cut of her air,
All senses, are dying, in mournful despair.

No more strolls, with matching footsteps in time,
Lover's embrace, has withered and died.

Deft and quite, melancholy now,
Circumstances, devoided their wedding vows.

Cherlyl E. Ralph

That's Life

Although the clouds are dark and gray;
remember the sun will shine another day,
If life seems bleak, unfair, unkind,
you'll feel much better when you see the
    sun shine.

We all have problems; we all have woes;
but always remember, that's how life goes.
You're never alone, no matter how down;
replace with a smile, that terrible frown.

Smile with sincerity, laugh at your ills
Take what life offers - enjoys the thrills.
To be alive and to see the sun rise,
Is, in many a life, the reason to survive.

Eleanor E. Whelan

One Great Sound

We are the skins of drums, on which the world beats out it's
    rhythmic pattern of life.
Even within a great symphony orchestra, when the swelling sound
    fills the air, reducing and resounding again.
The harmonious music meets our ears, now not so great, not so
    dignified, comes the blast of horns to swing in jazz.
Watch or you will rock, you will swing, with these sounds.
Oh, what noises you do hear
Sadness, yes—Mournful woes come from the longing comfort of the
    blues.
The trees, the birds whistle and sing with the music.
Solace they will try to find.
But, when all is quite and music there is no more, they will
    melt together, the great the small.
Every sound fills its space and the skins of the drum are worn
    thin.

Anne Dearing

Ridin' Her

I'd been checking the cattle in country real wild,
Ridin' gently along like an innocent child, but
We started down a mean hill and things came unglued;
I felt like a beginner, a green eastern dude.

Now I'd been a bronc buster for near twenty years,
But ridin' this critter brought me some strange fears.
Sidewindin' don't tell it and whirlin' won't do,
The moves comin' at me were totally new.

My neck got snapped back, I bit my tongue 'til it bled,
My ears rang so loud it was splittin' my head.
The dust was a flyin' so I couldn't see much, but
We'd soon know how this cowboy would react in a clutch.

I dug in with my spurs, hung on with one hand,
Lost my new stetson, saw it roll o'er the land.
I heard a weird noise comin' from the dust cloud,
Then realized that I was screamin' out loud.

Of a sudden it was over; we came to a stop.
I was one surprised hombre...still up there on top.
I've ridden wild horses of all sizes and shapes,
But nothin' I've seen...beats a Ford truck with no brakes.

Allen A. Hill

A Smile For Momma

Ice shards frozen before they can
Roll down the gentle yellow-peach
Curve of your cheek and
Into your mouth: Salty, tastes like the
Sea and open fires burning and
Home cooking: Could it be a
Smile on your face: Unadulterated and
Pure? But no; it's gone and the
'kerchief on your head blows as a jet screams by with its
Cargo: Death
And you remember to walk - left, left right left
Tho' tomorrow you will fall in a ditch to be
Hit by the bullets from a
Young lad's rifle - pat plop pat -
crimson rising to your
shirt: The shirt given to you by your
once beautiful
Momma: And now its
certain: A
smile.

Eric Byungchan Song

Untitled

I fell like a driftwood being tossed by ocean waves.
Rolling deep within the sea.
Lonely, weak and full of sorrow.
A hidden deep song.
Rolling, rolling, rolling along.
Sometimes over come.
Seldom existing wished.
    With the rhythm of the waves.
A driftwood in this wonder of wondrous world
More sacred still.
Eternal Father save.

Dolores Wills

Memorare

Living our memories each moment every day
Rolling in like the fog and then drifting away
But why so uncontrolled must they remain
These fears and flaws under another name

Had I let these pass me by
Would I secure an expanding eye
Soul-searching toil
These dreams and thoughts foil

But are these thoughts really free
If they become as real as reality
So deeply submerged and so intense
Regardless of our intelligence

When only through these can I grasp
Although no contact a tighter clasp
Falling from grace with borderline thought
Then how unimpeded and free is the lot

Yet only in thought may we leap without a chute
Shedding our skin like an uncomfortable suit
Distressful thoughts which expand in the night
Masquerading at approach of dawn's early light

Jill S. Ward

I Lie Awake

When the first rays of light creep into my
room and the darkness turns to light, I lie awake.
When the never ending silence is broken and the
sound tumbles in, I lie awake.
When that blue bird sings it's enchanting
and peaceful song, I lie awake.
As the horrible war sounds thunder into
my room, I lie awake.
As the hungry man begging on the street
collapses, I lie awake.
As the abandoned little child dies in her sleep,
I lie awake.
As the lonely woman cries with her broken
heart, I lie awake.
Even though I wish not to hear the
sadness, I lie awake.
As the sorrows cancel out the pleasant, I lie awake.
All I have ever done and can ever do
is lie awake and listen.

Becky Bonfey

La Vie

Life is a mystery for
everything comes and goes.
Like the howling winds of the north.
The little babes that are born.
The little birds that learn to fly.
All in all, once again,
Mother nature has left us in AWE!

Stella Mavrophilipos

Trap Door Roses

Abe Lincoln borne away to Springfield
rustling railroad tracks and misty grains
of shadowed purpose
sunk like the galleon with the treasure
and the legend still to grow
His killing conspirators shackled at McNair
breathing dank within canvass hoods
Hearing the birds whose cousins sang the Emancipator home
The hourglass through which they sank in time
was interrupted by the seamless refrain of
the Military Tribunal
while outside the wooden gallows rose and sand bags filled
arrogant, majestic, confused, scuttled
all men but for a single woman
holding the harp of innocence in an iron cage
Abraham resting and watching
as the hooded sacks of humanity dropped
and they split the gallows for kindling
and souvenirs
where roses now grow sweet beneath the hanging trap doors

John Carothers

The Longing

What once was beautiful, now seems
sad. Memories of simple pleasures,
never to be lived again, bring
tears. Songs of long ago, songs I
sang to,
danced to, now I
cry to...since I may not sing, nor
dance to these again...A reverie of
colors, sounds, and smells assaults my
mind and I am filled with
joy of these; and I remember
sensuous things; and I remember
love. And every cell of me craves all of life
again, as I am now. Yet
who may know of what I yearn? And
who is there to listen? And
who is there to share with me, this
sweet, but fated dream?

Gloria Valenti

Requiem En Arborea

The forest sleeps. Rest here my love.
Sad yellow leaves float aimless down
To earth-whose color turns warmly brown.
Stone gray limbs, quiet, cold, tell the syc'mores grief.
Gone the glitter and rustle the deep hued golden leaf..
Soft white a wooly gift of snow stills the ground.
Between old trunks icy breezes blow,
And whistle sorrow's tune of lost colored leaves.

God gives love and color. He also bereaves.
Take solace from this wooded dream that nature keeps.
Rest here my love. The forest sleeps.

Alexander Menke

Untitled

We look at each other
With hurt in our eyes
For it's this hatred filled world
Which has made us despise
The ones that we love
The friendships in which we share
For the people of the world today
Are simply objects
In a game of unreal play.

Heather Petersen

Pain's River

Doubled in witchcraft, written in blood,
satan's children killing death, starts the flood.
Dreams of darkness, wishful for death,
seen in the beast, blood on his breath.
Mind starts to wonder, icy blood chills the veins,
wonder about life, rules of the game.
Fear shows his face, wind howls cold,
confused yet calm, cowardly yet bold.
Stare into empty eyes, soul starts to shiver,
go for a swim, wade in pain's river.

Heard God calling, chose to ignore,
bad mistake, he opened the door.
Walked up the stairs, top of the tower,
preacher turns, demon now comes his hour.
He tries to repent, begs to forgive,
pleas have no meaning, he's lost the right to live.
lightning flashes, bodies scatter,
soul is still cold, teeth start to chatter,
good is crushed, evil takes the stand,
then all is made pure with the wave of God's hand.

   Heather Moore

Only Love

What is gained with hatred taught - brave men have gone to fight
Save the children - Save the soldiers
Can there be a light?
Love must be taught - wars not fought - stop the killing
Souls cry for peace - cry for oneness
See a light?
Tears burn hot for the lost ones - whatever the cause
Black, white, yellow - color is nothing - only love
Can there be a light?
Dear God, we need a light.
Save our people - Save our land
Dear God, we need a light!

   Genia Corne

Making a Difference

Some people do just enough to barely get by.
Saying "It really dose not matter how hard we try."
Some people's effort is boisterous, their way is to yell it aloud.
They feel yelling is what it takes for them to be heard above the
   crowd.
Some people move in silence making no waves as they go,
thinking still water runs deep and every ripple will show.
Since life is but a fleeting moment and we get only one try,
do not waste your unique special moment, reach for the sky.
Do not be discouraged by those gone before.
Remember, boats without oars may never reach a shore,
and like a dot from an ink pen still leaves it's mark,
it only takes a tiny flicker to show light in the dark.
So grasp and treasure your precious moment and say
"This moment is mine,"
and like the bright evening star your moment will shine.

   Dympna Murphy Taylor

Geriatrics

Buttons pop, and zippers stick
And problems get so numerous.
With aches and pains, and broken bones
We often mend up bloomerless!

When ankles swell and wrinkles tell
We could become quite humorless
But one thing we can count on tho,
Our Doctors bright and gloomerless!

   C. G. Pulse

Love's A Blaze

At twelve such a tender age
A pounding thunder rage
We laughed and talked
Held hands and walked
Looking into each others eyes
What a great surprise!
How could you and I know
That love would blaze

   Henrietta Hopkins

Dusty Dreams

My dreams are all shop-worn,
Seat-sprung or counter-tossed,
Like some old suit in a thrift shop
What has held them together so long,
Is now slightly soiled or lost.

But like the clerk in the thrift store,
I'll piece, patch and try to restore,
See what there is I can salvage,
Redeem, make over, make do,
As I sort through them some more.

I have to pick the pieces up from the floor
And knock off some of the rust,
Trim off all the ragged edges,
And get the best of my dreams
Up out of the dirt and the dust.

   Helene Carnello

School

First grade perfect,
second great,
third was okay,
fourth always late.
I'm older now and feel like the worst.
I think I may have been wickedly cursed
My mother says, :just study more."
But really, I find that a total bore.
My father says, "read more books."
When really I should be checking out my coolest looks.
It's Monday now and I'm back in school.
Everybody's laughing,
and I feel like a fool.
But now that I see,
they're not laughing at me!

   Christina Guzzo

Time...

The carrier God provided to
Securely take us through life
It has no physical appearance
Only a viable mystical presence

Aging rapidly minute by minute
Humans are summoned along for the ride
For without it, there is no existence
No defined meaning to life

Having no perception between night and day
It recognizes only the commands of God

In it's condescending way, it keeps us alive
While consistently consuming our precious lives

Color matters not, for we are all God's children
As it quietly devours us, one by one

And, so, time moves on
Waiting not for anyone!!

   Burnette Geddis

Reflections

I look in the mirror and I
see a child content with just a
doll and a teddy bear she
hasn't a worry, she hasn't a care.
I look in the mirror and I see
a young woman staring back at me,
surprised at the salubrious reflection
I turn and look away for that is not the way it always is.
She works intricately on her
appearance to look pleasant on the
outside, but this is just a mirage.
She is usually depressed and down hearted everything upsets
her and gives her fears. She is torn and upset.
I look in the mirror and I see
a successful woman. She is beautiful
and wise and lives life to the fullest.
This is the way it should have always been.
I look in the mirror and I see a girl desperately trying to get
from adolescence to adulthood. She will get through it somehow,
she will find a way.

Grace Schehr

Mirror Pond

I once played there so wild and unrestrained,
Seems like I recollect a lonely song,
Sounds like an old familiar refrain,
One to which I must sing along.

Come back, go back, complex affair,
My brain and emotions clog up my recall,
'Tis hope for past events I despair,
For nothing clears up my past at all.

Complex, difficult as it must be,
I search my thoughts, my past events,
To flip through the pages of my revere,
To browse through my emotions to my heart's content.

But, yeah, I muster all the courage I can,
I notice that life's accelerated to a fast pace,
Perhaps I'm left to destiny's plan,
To mourn the past, or come face to face.

It's not my choice to pick my will,
For God sure knows what's best for me,
He makes it all, it fits His bill,
God, oh God, I give in, set me free!

Darrell J. Palombo

Celebrate Jesus

You come willingly to planet earth,
Sent by Your Heavenly Father
To let us know the "why," the "where," the "when,"
  the "how."
All questions we could gather
To get the answers for our "now."

Because of our human duplicity
We shun Your Blessed Simplicity
And cause snares to mar our ways.
But You've had here and there
An anointed one, a lover of souls,
To point us to You, to gladden our days.

Thank You for sharing Your gems with us:
Your Holy Spirit, Your written Word,
And those anointed ones by whom
  we've heard
That You are alive and seeking the lost
For whom You've paid the ultimate cost.

Borgny Bakke Sorensen

Baby's Gifts

A baby is joy with dancing feet,
Sent from the Heavens to make life complete.
And on the descent that baby dear
Caught pieces of song to fill us with cheer.

The babbling brook reflecting for miles,
Gave Baby's sweet face those endearing quick smiles.
The glimmering stars shared their own soft light,
And gave to the baby eyes sparkling so bright.

Arms that gently hug, hands that softly cling,
Once were held by angels on Heaven's golden swing.
Of all things gathered, the most precious is love,
Brought here by the baby from Heaven above.

Juanita Gerling

How Wars Are Absurd

Ordinary men turn into heroes overnight.
Sent to a land far away and out of sight.
Fighting in a war to keep us free, I'm not quiet sure if they hear our
  plea,
"Come home to us safe. We love you all."
While they fight a war, there are some just having a ball.
Taking for granted life as we know, our freedom to come, our
freedom
  to go.
We live for tomorrow, they live for today, waiting to hear what our
  President will say.
Do we dare hope?
Do we ask why?
It's so hard to cope, so easy to cry.
And now it's tomorrow, and still there's no word.
We just go on thinking how wars are absurd.

Crystal Hinch

The Pursuit Of Wisdom

It is an undeniable fact that a formal education
Serves as an impetus for the acquisition of knowledge
But this same knowledge becomes a sham
If it is not tempered by objective analysis
Which is conducive to understanding the complexities of life
For as we make our way into the real world
We often find out that all the answers to our problems
Are not always in the books
Because books were never meant to contain all the answers
Yet if we continue to use objective reasoning
Predicated upon common sense
Only then will our formal education help us
In the pursuit of wisdom.

Henry T. Sarnataro

In the Corner

Reality strikes me here, where two walls meet.
Shadows stand in silence,
Fearing I might discover the life in them
Which they do not understand.
I find my eyes focusing on the line formed here-
Separating dark and light,
Always believing this line to be a bend,
Never questioning why.

Once, as a child, I crossed over the line
For only a moment in the shadows.
As I cautiously stepped forward,
A hand withdrew my fragile state from indecision.
I was placed away from either side
And made to sit before both.
As a child, I chose the side which darkness fears,
Though I did not understand temptation.

Ellen Caldwell

Butterflies and Burdens

A woman has certain burdens
  she carries as her load
Life has not been kind at times...
  the sea, swiftly surging as her road.

But the little things she does
  bring out the love inside
Her family is all that matters...
  It fills her with precious pride.

She takes what life hands her
  in sickness and in health
From the womb 'til ever after...
  It's warm in a mother's wealth.

Her butterflies are coming...
  on wings of words I wrote...
She'll have a sea of silk
  and a velvet vessel as her boat.
  Barbara Clark Holladay

Loneliness

She hates being all alone
She despises hiding out
If only she had the courage to face them
Bravery and confidence is what it's all about

If they'd give her a place
If they'd give her a home
She'd be happy and wanted
Instead of living in a solo dome

If they'd accept her for who she is
Instead of the way she used to be
If only they'd open up their eyes and hearts
If only they could see

She changed into a real person
Someone who could listen and understand
Someone who opens her eyes and mind
Someone who doesn't always demand

She's changed into someone who people can respect
If only they could see her now
If only they would forget the past
If only she could come out somehow
  Erica Joy Lenard

The Pain He Didn't Share

She didn't know what was happening
She didn't know what he did
How could he hurt her like that?
She was just a kid
After he had his pleasure
She realized what he had done
Why did she let it happen?
Why didn't she run?
Would anyone believe her?
Would anyone really care?
She still feels the pain from the incident
The pain he didn't share
He didn't think anything of it
Not one bit of guilt did he feel
He could care less weather he hurt her
To him it was no big deal
Maybe he'll get the punishment
That he deserves someday
It would be nice to have justice
But her pain will never go away
  Angela Summers

Corn! Fresh Corn!

The farmer's wife, she's great indeed;
She dries and salts the pumpkin seeds!
She also shucks and cooks the corn
The stalks, shucked fresh, scent of earth and chorn!
Why, what is chorn? You may request?
Well it's the state of smell fresh corn suggests
Between the just picked and prepared to eat stage
Newspapers catch corn strings that fall on the front page!
It's the raw vegetable smell, so fresh and natural
But, don't get me wrong- with dripping butter and salt,
It still makes ALL tongues loll!
  Annie McFarlane

Destiny

Day and night, night and day.
She is in his thoughts, in his dreams.
He has only met her but once.
He has envisioned her into his mind forever.
He will not forget, he cannot.
She has a power, a power of love and passion,
of beauty and of strength.
She has drawn him in.
He is always reminded of this woman,
like when a gentle but cool breeze
whispers her name through the treetops.
Or when He walks in the midst of night
with the stars shining so bright, her eyes
sparkle like the ocean, as the full moon shines upon it.
Her power is strong.
He will not forget, he cannot.
If destiny awaits, she will come.
And he will be there.
But for now, he walks alone.
And there is, no other.
  David J. Bailey

The Sorrow of the Senses

In the bed of the wagon
She lies
Arms cast overhead
Exhaustion of the day streaming from her limbs
Head to one side
Labor's creases folded into her face

Climbing in beside her
I fit myself about her body
Leg hooked around her thighs
Arm burrowed beneath her back

Longing for sleep myself
But for now, shielding her
Soon to wrench her from this catalepsy
Into the confusion of consciousness
The sorrow of the senses
  Judith Evind

What She And He Like To Do

She loves oil.
She loves to boil.
She loves foil.
She loves to plant in soil.
She wired a coil.
She loves math that is why she takes a bath.
He loves roses and noses.
He was born to eat corn.
He loves to cook and read a book.
He likes to look and go by the brook.
He has a hook.
He also is a crook.
  Alice Aluko

Grandma

She was always such a lady
She never would turn you away
To greet you with loving eyes and out stretched arms
was always her way-

Her life was hard, not many frills to aid in the
long journey ahead of her, yet, she never was heard to complain

The times were hard for all and some needed a home or food
No matter where they came from or who they were she only
cared that they were safe and feed-

My memories of her are very vague, we were not close in miles
My mind has only good thoughts of her and no one has a bad word
to say of her-

I'll miss her, because somehow I know she and I were thinking
of one another often-

All my grandparents are gone, I knew them so little or not
at all as I was growing up-

I feel the loss of their presence even now
I will be thinking of them often
God is taking care of them until we meet again.

Gloria Jean Mason

He Said, She Said

He said that she needed to bring in money
She said that she already did her work
He said that he meant a real pay check
He said "You really are a jerk!"
He said her worth was really nothing
She said her children were the best
He said "I'm staying at the office"
She said "I'm having empty nest!"
He said he thought she could be thinner
She said "I work out all the time"
He said "Perhaps it's more your age, dear"
She said "But I'm just entering my prime."
He said "You don't please me any longer"
She said "Are you referring to our bed?"
He said "Maybe it's just mid-life crisis"
She said "I wish that I were dead."
He said "I don't love you any longer"
She said "Have you found someone new?"
He said "Find yourself a lawyer"
She said "I've already contacted two."

Gay Klearman

The Shower

Her legs wouldn't hold her any longer.
She sat down in the shower and let the water
fall over her like a warm summer rain,
mixing with her tears.
She prayed to God
   to wash away the dirt and with it, hopefully,
   the night before.

There was no anger in her shower,
   only fear and hate.
The hot water left marks of red on her body
   where they hit her skin.
Just like the marks he left on her in the darkness of her room.

Who could she tell of this and how could she go on?
It would never be over.

Jennifer Bucco

Earth

Earth is dirty
So clean it up
So lets do some
Work on the Earth
The world is round
So lets not frown

Corey Wall

Oceans of Time, Never Enough

Where seas of gold meet oceans of blue,
She stands waiting before the setting sun.
I call, but she cannot hear.
I reach out to her, but she is too far away.
I walk toward her, my legs full of lead
The sun sinks farther, and I walk faster.
The sun sinks, and I run.
The sun sinks, and I fly.
The sun dips, not enough time.
The sun disappears behind the horizon,
And I am too late.
The darkness hides my weeping face.
I have lost that which I love,
Yet never knew.
Tears coarse down my cheeks.
Without her I weep.
Without her I die.

David Madsen

Mother

In the dead of night his infant cries awaken her dreaming slumber,
she stumbles out of bed as tears well up in her
blood shot eyes and I
Begin to feel her frustration, rage, the doubt of her own sanity
And the lifestyle she has chosen for herself, and the green envy
of those who are able to take such things as sleep for granted.
And yet through all this, I see
The great determination planted deep within her strong being, not
to cry,
Not to give up, to prove to others and herself her motherly strength,
her willpower not to give in to the inhumane thoughts that surely
race through her mind.
And as the moonbeams cast eerie shadows on her face,
I know my prayers have been heard,
for the infant lies cradled in her arms...
unharmed and asleep.

Jessica R. Gomez

The Silent Cheer

The first cheer came when I arrived.
She told my Dad - was he surprised!
Whether it's a boy or girl they didn't care.
All I remember was everyone's stares.

The silent cheer came once again
I spoke my first word, how proud I made them.
And when I took my very first step,
The silent cheer I certainly did get.

With report card in hand, I had no fear.
All those A's and B's deserved the silent cheer.
And since I loved music, I wanted them to hear
Me playing my instrument - yes, the silent cheer.

Now I'm grown up and I love my parents dear,
For I realize how hard it was to give the silent cheer.
I owe it to my children to praise them when I can,
For I know that in my parent's heart, they were my biggest fan.

Frederick J. Leone

To My Sister

Whom I think of every day
she was so different than the woman of today.
She met the wrong man and got into
drugs, then went on her way.
Leaving three children along the way
My mother and father all they do is pray
That she'll come to her senses and come home some day
They can't understand what they did
To make her change this way
They blame themselves till this day
But this much I have to say
That we choose our paths and live our lives our own way
We can't go blaming people everyday
The blame is ours wouldn't you say
So live up to your mistakes each day
Because we have to live with ourselves everyday
So stay away from drugs is all I can say
Because some day your family can all go away

Debbie Montelongo

Missing You

It's been a few years since you've been gone.
How time and life just keep going on.

I still find myself wishing you were here.
It's hard missing someone who to me was so dear.

The tears still come and the pain does too.
'Cause I know there'll never be another like you.

We had our bad times along with the good.
We were both very stubborn, as only we could.

And even though we lost a few years,
We got back together and worked out our fears.

And just as it seemed we were on the right track,
The Lord stepped in and wanted you back.

I didn't feel it was fair, I didn't feel it was right,
To take someone I loved at the end of the night.

And though life goes on and time heals the sorrow,
I'll still always wish I could see you tomorrow.

I just wanted to say these feelings I had
I just wanted to say, I miss you a lot Dad.

Susan E. Murray

Inner Most Thoughts

Do you ever wonder who you are?
How you feel, the way you feel.
Do you ever wonder how you became this way?
What made you; you
How did I become to be the person that I am?
Was it my parents, was it my friends?
Do you ever wonder how you were dealt your hands?
Not that you want to change it
Because you love the way you are and who you are
It is just so confusing, I don't understand
I believe it was God, who has his ways and reasons
For everyone and everything in life
There will always be something you don't know
But life is a mystery, life it is a risk
I guess to never risk is to never live
I have to live my life to the fullest
Always learning something new about myself
Their are so many questions left unsaid, things
I do not know, but underneath all my insecurities and all my doubts
Lyes a young women who knows herself more than she ever lets
out!

Kimberly A. Moniz

Night's Song

She sits in the darkness, her sorrows cured,
Humming a song that she's never heard.
Vast seas of ebony high above,
are whispering tender words of love.
Angels dancing from star to star,
spreading hopes and dreams to the world afar.
Night's shadows extent to the morning's edge,
and the moonlit land to the ocean cliff's ledge.
As the morning star over the horizon soars,
the maiden appears from beyond closed doors.
A lark's song gently caresses her ear,
a sweet song, she was longing to hear.
As day begins to hold hands with night,
trouble and burdens are far from sight.
She sits in the darkness, her sorrows cured,
Humming a song that she's never heard.

Stephanie J. Craven

So Long

How can I live without you, when we is all I've ever been.
I always felt our souls were united in a bond shared only by a twin.
I still expect to wake one day and find that you've come back to stay,
but when I open my eyes and it's tomorrow,
I realize you're really gone and my heart sinks with sorrow.
How will I find the strength to carry on
without my sister to make me strong?
I'm blessed with family and friends that care
and yet my life is so empty without you there.
I miss your eyes, your voice, your laughter,
and when our paths cross once again in the 'ever after,'
I'll hug you close and never let you go,
and tell you I've missed you more than you could ever know.
For now, I'll have to travel through life as one, instead
of you and me against the world, like I always thought it'd be,
but I know you're watching from up above and that
somehow you're still taking care of me.
So I won't say goodbye, but only so long,
until I see you once again, your memory will forever be with me,
as I find the strength to carry on.

Maria Stincer Llambes

The Fullness of Being

To experience the FULLNESS OF BEING
I am become PRESENCE
Energy   NOTHINGNESS   the spaces between quanta.
To experience the FULLNESS OF BEING
is TRANSFORMATION   EXPLOSION the
    TRANSVALUATION OF VALUES
Suns exploding in my brain
Illuminating pathways to my heart.
Aeons ago I left this one-dimensional
    corporeality
Never, never to return again though I must
    from time to time if
I am ever to take the hand of another
    gently
To become my realm as I momentarily become
    hers or his.

Victoria Kokoras

Molly Dog Rudlong

As Molly lay there still and quiet
wind blows threw her thick black fir,
When the birds they make a riot
calm she stays and does not stir.

Becky Rudlong

I Am But...

I am but a human, solid and alive.
  I am but a person, for goals I strive.

I am but face, innocent and fragile as porcelain.
  I am but a silhouette, of a mind devoured by sin.

I am but a vampire, afraid of the day.
  I am but an animal, seeking my prey.

I am but an orchid, with petals untouched.
  I am but a rose, whose thorns are much.

I am but a piece of land, with decades etched into me.
  I am but a grain of sand, forever victimized by the sea.

I am but a drawing, by an artist, wild.
  I am but an outline, sketched by a child.

I am but liar, known only to a lover's heart.
  I am but a fire, that may never see a start.

I am but a sound, not heard by any.
  I am but an emotion, not felt by many.

I am but a wind, through which flies a kite.
  I am but a whisper, heard only in the night.

I am but a vision, in a mind so keen.
  I am but a silence, still and serene.

Lillian Lujan

Without You

All that I have desired can now be achieved,
I am no longer lost and I can't be deceived,
my dreams are manifesting themselves in my life,
after all the confusion, sorrow and strife,

I am no longer weak because now I am strong,
after all I have suffered and endured for so long,
I've passed the test of time standing all alone,
now I stand victorious through efforts of my own,

I am like an unfinished sculpture forever in progress,
as I strive to fulfill my concept of love and happiness,
my trials and tribulations have not made me less but more,
and I am now approaching all that I have always longed for,

I ask you now my love for the very last time,
to accept your place in my heart and mind,
once I move on looking back is something I never do,
if you leave me no choice I'll go on without you.

Tina Marie Klinkhammer

I Am

I am me
I am the girl who longs to be loved
I am the one who is searching
for a way to end the confusion
I am the one who is protecting
herself from getting hurt
I am the girl wondering about life
The girl who wants to explore every option
like a tiger explores the jungle
I am the girl who's angry
at everyone like a mother
who's lost her child.
I am the one who needs understanding
like a baby needs love
I am the one who wants to
please only herself cause
I am the only one I'll have forever.

Nicky Burg

God's Power

As I kneel before you God
I beg of you to give me grace

To keep me pure
And keep me safe.

To keep me from the devil's grip
To keep me from the stain of sin

To give me courage to do what's right
To give me strength to win life's flight.

To help the soul that he has made
I asked the Lord for your aid.

As I stand before God's throne
A place of beauty I stand alone

I know not fear
For God is here

A love so great
That one can hear

The angels singing
In the night.

Peggy Johnson

The Flower

(To my wonderful brother Wayne, who died 2/18/95)
  While walking in the woods one day,
I came upon a flower. It was so full of
nature's love, I sat there for an hour.
  I was just watching it flutter in the
wind, like a happy butterfly, and then the
sight of something else that quickly caught
my eye.
  A tiny little kitten, was creeping in
the grass, and then it looked up at me, and
quietly walked on past.
  I thought about that kitten all the
rest of the day, and the very special
reason why, I wished that I could stay.

Patricia Jamison

True Friend

Why did you leave me?
I can barely stand on my own
It's been two decades. And I've no one left

You left a vacuum
A child that still mourns
Your son in your shadow knew
And helped fill the gap
That did not last. He joined you

There are no friends
Not in the real sense of the word
Not the spouse nor child

I cannot bare my naked soul
Not for anyone
No one will ever know me as you

You knew and loved me just as I am
No mincing words
That was a waste

No plan was imagined
It's just there
To change naught

Ruby Corbin Courey

Who Is In The Mirror?

Who can hear the crime, Who can see the crime, Who can feel the crime?
"I can," says the Mirror's reflection.

What? What? Speak up Mirror, I didn't quiet hear you.
What did you see, hear, and feel?

"I said, I saw the crime and more—a little girl, with blue eyes as
dark as the sea, and sandy brown hair,"
said the Mirror's reflection.

Go on! Go on! said the Something..

"I saw a tear as shiny as a diamond fall not far from her eyes,"
said the Mirror's reflection.

Go on! Go on! What did you hear? asked the Something.

"I hear only the sobs and whimpers that come from her mouth,"
said the Mirror's reflection.

Go on! Go on! What did you feel, of crime? said the Something.

"I felt her heart pounding until I wanted it to stop; I felt her tears
on my reflection, and I felt her pain again, each moment passing,"
said the Mirror's reflection.

All of this? What caused it? asked the something.

"It was caused by feelings," said the Mirror's reflection.
I am sure glad I don't have feelings, said the Something.

"I am glad I only have to reflect the feelings," said the Mirrors
reflection.

Stephannie Sorrick

"You'll Never Even Notice"

You'll never even notice, how much I need your smile,
I can't relive the moments, you gave to me awhile,
I'll gaze upon your picture, it's what I have for now
I'm grateful for the memory, it please's me somehow
No, I'm thinking it won't last, so now I'll have to stray,
You'll never even notice, how much I wanna stay,
I'll pass your way real gently, don't look me in the eye
I'll love you in the midnight, as stars do in the sky.
No you can't regive the moments,
    Still they're written in my soul
You'll never even notice
just how you've made me whole
So I'll pass your way real gently, don't look me in the eye
I'll love you in the midnight, as stars do in the sky
Yes, I'll love you all the midnight, as stars do in the sky!

Leah K. Wiley

A. J. (Another Joke?)

What happened to our love?
I can't remember when it changed
From love and passion to hate and revenge
But I know that it did.
How can something so beautiful become so ugly?
The power of our love lit the sun,
But our bitterness caused the eclipse.
So little time we have actually shared.
Then why do I feel we have loved a lifetime?
I once promised you the world,
Believing that I, little old me,
Could possibly have been your world.
All you ever needed or wanted
Was what I wanted to give to you, and be for you.
Is that too much to expect?
No, just enough to cause disrespect.
I've always just wanted you, nothing more,
But all I got was nothing less.
How do I deserve you?

Lara P. S. Eastman

A Prisoners Dream

Am I alive?
I can't tell my hair is gone.
My body...it's thin, like a toothpick.
I'm hungry!
The smell...I can almost feel it.
Bodies...everywhere.
I can't take it anymore.
I have to let myself go.

To be free...people say that its just a feeling.
But its a lot more than that....
To be free its like a dream come true.

Lisa Czerniecki

Daydreams In My Rocking Chair

I daydream a lot in my rocking chair.
I close my eyes and travel everywhere.
When I'm feeling depressed or sort of low,
I travel some in the valley below.
If I feel peppy or ever so spry
I will travel along the mountains high.
On a hot and dry day I go to Spain
So I can enjoy the "rain on the plain".
And sometimes I sail on the China Sea,
But not often, I get seasick, you see.
At times I go to somewhere in England
Then I will travel to snow in Greenland.
Still other times I travel to Peru
To enjoy all the fun things that they do.
If I don't know exactly where I am
I just might be in the land of Siam.
Now and again I will go to Brazil,
Then from my daydreams I return at will.
When I open my eyes I am back home
And no one but me knows I have been gone.

Ruby Byrd

Someone Cares

When my heart is heavy - weighted down with woe-
I close my eyes for a moment and to my heavenly Father I go-
He soothes my troubled body and takes my trembling hand-
And in my mind He leads me to a bright and untroubled land-
He speaks to me of someday when all my pain is gone-
Then He gives me strength I need to bravely carry on-
He says now lean upon me heavily I'm strong beyond compare-
And tho' you sometimes forget it, I'm always there and I care-
So call me when you need me, I'm never far away-
Just close your eyes for a moment and take the time to pray-

Katherine Walter

Good To Me

The Lord sure is good to me,
I communicate with Him each day,
You may wonder how I talk with Him
Well, I kneel down and pray.

It sure is a joy to know
That He is there with me,
And, oh, the blessings I receive
When that light shines down on me!

So, I'm watching and waiting for His return
To take us where we will forever be
To be with Him in that city four square,
The One who shines His light down on me.

Stella M. Coffey

The Wind

The wind blows softly against the trees,
It blows the tall grass along the prairie,
On a hot summer day, the wind can cool you off,
You can not see the wind, but you can hear it,
Sometimes it sounds like a wolf howling in the night,
The wind blows flowers,
The wind is just air,
But I know that the wind will always be there!

Kaitlin Barry

Dream

Our love was like a dream.
I couldn't believe I was whom you had chosen.
Every time we were together, I couldn't believe I was with you.
The way our laughter sounded .....so happy.
The way you kissed me .....so gently
The way you held me ......so softly.
It just didn't seem real.
It was just like a dream.
It was
  and sadly
  I woke up.

Kristel Losiewicz-Ramonis

The Wedding Gown

Years ago when we stood before God and said "I do,"
I couldn't have chosen a better partner than you.
We shared love and joy and have been up and down
And I felt like a queen when I donned my wedding gown.

We never knew what was around the bend
We were not only lovers but each other's best friend.
Two rubies, a sapphire, and are emerald are the
  jewels in my crown
One for each child we had after I removed my
  wedding gown

We travelled the pathways of life side by side
And look at our accomplishments with pride.
Settling now as senior citizens in a small town,
There in the closet still hangs my wedding gown.

Keeping all our memories close to my heart
Always remembering the words "till death do us part."
Though the years have turned my gown slightly brown
I still feel like that young girl walking down the
  aisle in my white wedding gown

Rosie Reese

Ode To A Life Without Christ

My life was over I was at the end of my road.
I couldn't seem to carry the heavy load.
I'd tried my hardest I'd done my best.
I just couldn't seem to get ahead of the rest.
My mother had tried to raise me right.
But without a father it was along hard fight.
When I was young I looked to the LORD.
But as I grew older I became bored.
There were so many rules for a young man to follow.
That by doing for the LORD my life would be hollow.
Then I sinned greatly and had no where to turn.
And then my heart began to yearn.
For the days of old when I was young.
And for my mothers touch when the day was done.
And the prayers we said beside the bed.
To the LORD in HEAVEN not enough could be said.
I returned to the LORD and prayed his forgiveness.
I'll for ever work now towards doing his business.
The work of the LORD is life's great reward.
And trusting in him you will never be bored.

Russell K. Malloy

The Box

It was smooth and shiny.
I didn't like it.

No one looked at me, for no one could.
I was staring at the box.

I hated it. I wanted to scream that so loudly that
  it would ring in everyone's ears.

They closed the lid.
I wanted to cry out and tell them to
  leave it open, just to let it be.

When they rolled it past I cried.
I hated it, but, I reached out to touch it.
  It was smooth and shiny.

When they lowered it, I pleaded.
Inside I asked them not to do it.

I hated that box. It scared me!
I wanted to lift it up. To pry it open.

I wanted it open.
For it was not the box I wanted to touch.

No not the smooth and shiny surface of that horrid box.
What I wanted to touch was you.

Kimberly Lovitt

A New Belief

Last night I had a strange dream going through my head.
I didn't understand it but music played softly.
There were many candles lit.
I was in a strange land, didn't know where to go
then I saw a man approaching was he an angel or a ghost?

I started to run but something in my head said, "don't go, stay."
He came up to me slowly and said you must not be afraid
He took my hand in his I realized then
I needed to be calm, I needed to be brave.

That night we went to a special place, full of wonders,
softness and grace.
He looked at me and he smiled and said, "you're in God's house now,
so come child and let us pray
for all he has given in so many ways.

Now, my life has changed, but only for the good.
I took Jesus as my Savior and he's touched my heart,
somehow I knew he would.
So give your life to him everyday
and it will shine in every way.

Laura York

Where Is My "Tootie"?

Where is my "Tootie" with the braids in her hair?
Running and laughing without any cares.
Sharing Moms money with the neighborhood kids,
Or taking her skateboard out for a spin.
Basketball, dances, acting and more
Music and driving and phone calls galore.

So, as I walk in her room expecting to find
A young girl in pigtails with stars in her eyes,
I find a woman with remarkable grace
Talking and smiling, a glow on her face.

Now she is a mother of a beautiful girl,
She'll put her hair in pigtails and show her the world.
She will hold her hand and guide her, only so far,
Then she will step back and let her explore.
Where is my "Tootie", my heart wants to know?
Right here in front of me, loving her own.

Carrie Cole

I Couldn't Make The Game

I couldn't make the game today
I died, you see, I passed away
I have a bad heart, you know
Oh yes, I never told you so

I couldn't make the game today
An ambulance took me away
And though they tried to save my life
Using shocks, paddles, and a surgical knife
It was all in vain

So mark your time and measure it well
For the future, who can tell? Enjoy your game,
enjoy your day, enjoy your life in every way
Enjoy the present while you can
The future is uncertain to every man

For who shall live and who shall die?
How and where and when and why? Who shall stay behind to mourn?
And live to see another dawn?

I couldn't make the game today Or work or
rest or breathe or stay I died you see.
I passed away. I couldn't make the game today,

Robert Leshen

The Roller Coaster

Some people like the roller coaster —
I don't.
Too many ups, downs, loops and rushes.
Some people say the roller coaster is like life,
but I like life.
Some people need that constant rush in life,
Maybe to forget about the past,
or maybe they think if they go so fast
   they won't have to think about what
   is going on around them.
I'm satisfied on slow and relaxing rides.
I don't need those big thrills.

Stevie Koller

My Best Friend

Why do I remember the things that hurt the most?
I don't want to forget, but I hate to remember it more.
It happened so long ago, yet it seems like yesterday.
The beginning is a blur, but the end is clear as day.
She never wanted to go; I persisted until she came.
Now I wish she had stayed home that day.

We got there early, she stayed very late.
It was dull but soon picked up pace.
A boy came with a present;
The fateful gift of death that I hated the most.
I never even tried it; she had to see the glamour.
That glamour is what I must forget
   And is the reason for the hate.

She started to act strange, so I said "Let's go!"
She was having too much fun, "You go!"
I left with sadness and dread in my heart.
When I awoke the next morning I knew I should have stayed.
When I read the headlines I fell to the floor.
And now I remember the glamour that never should have been.

Kari Aurbakken

The World Outside

Moonlight creeps, and while the Palace sleeps
I dream I fly beyond the walls of Taja.
Far and wide, I see the world outside;
I see the crowds and hear them pray to Allah:
   Loving King, hear our voices as we sing,
   Far and free, from the desert to the sea!
What can it mean, this haunting dream?
Showing me a world that my eyes have never seen...

Sister moon, why do you run so soon?
Why do you leave me lonely in the morning?
Cold as death, the midnight's sighing breath
Blows down to me a bitter wind of warning...
   Sometime's wrong, and I know I must be gone.
   Far from home, to a world I've never known,
I'll make my flight into the night.
I'll find a new life far beyond these walls!

The desert is calling, the Earth is wide...
I'll find my Oasis
Within the world outside.

Michael A. Hienzsch

A Dream of Rachel

I dream of Rachel all night long,
I dream of Rachel while I sing this song,
I dream of Rachel while my life slips away,
I dream of Rachel all of the day,
I dream of Rachel as the day goes so fast,
I dream of Rachel as my life goes past,
I dream of Rachel standing right there,
I dream of Rachel for she is so fair,
I dream of Rachel when I'm out at sea,
I dream of Rachel and what could come to be,
I dream of Rachel knocking on my door,
I dream of Rachel, then I dream some more.

Robert R. Delgado

Silent Cries

I feel so lonely,
I feel so gray

My life is passing by
each long day

I feel much sorrow
I feel much pain

What is wrong with me?
Am I going insane?

The day fades away as
the sun goes down and soon darkness will play
its sorrowful sound

I lie awake in my comforting bed
that gives me shelter from
the dreams that wait ahead

As the shadows grow larger
on my walls which they lie
Soon will begin my silent cries
My anger and pain pour out from
my heart so weak

Until I drift into my little land of sleep

Shannon Gilmer

The Devil And His Mother

Amidst the dandelions in the grass,
I fell asleep and thought to ask,
The man in the back room,
Whether he is alive or dead.
All he would say is, "the rain has gone and come again another day."
The rain that cleanses, washes away dirt, makes new.
Rinsing off the lies and making them true.
Walking over hills of green, I had a vision of a coming dream.
The dream was abundantly filled with pieces to the maze,
The maze that leads you to the land away,
Away from man, away from the confusion of this idle land.
Sitting in the dark, I lost my face.
Searching for it in a stranger place.
I found it under the rising sun, with fire burning from within,
A blaze of tragic light, blinding man from its sight.
Close your eyes to see, the meaning of life in its entirety.
Listen to the river's cry, underneath the endless sky,
The river that holds the voices of nature's tongue.
Revealing the earth as a land of green, instead of a land of misery.
The devil and his mother...man and earth

Kevin W. Coombs

Susan Rochelle

I tore my tunic late one day, as on the battlefield I lay,
I fell so hard flesh shifted from bone, a bruise for me I now did own.
The cut was clean on my garment there, and now my lining it did bear,
My friends did notice my injury and voiced their sympathy to me.

I now disclose the remedy, for it was so clear for me to see,
For the injury became opportunity for something with meaning deep
   and dear.
I wrote the name Susan Rochelle upon my lining hem,
I showed it to her one fine day, then bound it up again.

Only she and I know it's there, a sweet secret we now share,
But now comes the analogy, the story of a different injury.
A previous day I fell so hard my soul and emotions then were jarred,
A loss of love was my injury that became the precious opportunity.

My heart was torn I now do tell, but the opening was made for
   Susan Rochelle,
Being written on the lining of my heart, from that interior it shall
   not part.
For the tear has now been bound up tight, within me I carry her both
   day and night,
As her name in my garment I do bear, her name in my heart I likewise
   share.

No one else knows how deep and dear,
That name to my heart I tell.
No other name within it dwells,
Than that precious name Susan Rochelle.

Robert M. Pecoraro Jr.

Untitled

One wish I hold in my heart for you
Not that all of your dreams come true
though surely I hope for than a few
Not that you may never know a care
But oh never more than your heart can bear
Not that your life may hold happiness only
Or that you may never be burdened or lonely
For life without sorrow, a life without giving
is but half that is truly worth living
No my wish for you encompasses more
May there always be something for
you to wish for
So if its comfort you wish, even just some
you can call me anytime of day

Donald T. O'Hagan

Maine's Summer Coast

On a gray and misty morn
I gaze upon the black becalming sea
A gull upon the wind upborne
The shoreline, the trees as one, embracing me.

Ghostly islands, three, four, maybe more
Shrouded by a delicate, ever changing mantle so fine
Waves, white, frothy, lapping upon their rocky shore
Each a jewel, waiting to sparkle in the suns later shine.

Boats moored in the harbor, here, there, scattered round
Spars stark and thin reaching for the sky
A peaceful, quiet, calming beauty I have found
Made surreal by the haunting cries of a soaring gull passing by.

Afar, granite cliffs, steep, sheer, falling to the sea below
Shaped and smoothed by the battering waves through endless time
Here and there, a crack, a ledge, a fissure for a tree or shrub to grow
Thus Maine's summer coast, a reverie, an inspiration, a scene sublime.

Philip C. Furber

Dawn Meditation

In the pre dawn mist
I go into the woods, my heart's turmoil to release.
Breathe deep the perfume of earth and pine and oak
quietly now, disturb not the peace.

In this sacred moment I watch,
as His creation wakes. For this I did rise early from sleep.
Listen, past bird songs, beyond crickets praise,
to the sound of wind within my soul, deep.

Come to me,
and from seeking in your own strength cease.
Come to me,
my beloved daughter, I give you peace.

Now the sun chases the mist,
and I was here to greet a new day.
Now back to the path of becoming, back to the journey,
but with peace. I must be on my way.

Patricia Barnard

Summertime

Summertime is what I like
I go outside and ride my bike

Sometimes I go out to swing
or just play ball or other things

When it gets real hot outside
My mom takes us for a ride

She sometimes take us to the beach
Or for an ice cream or a treat

When it rains I stay inside and bug my mother
she says to me why don't you play with your little brother

When it stops I go back out
to jump and play on run about

When dad gets home from work we eat
we cook outside and that's a treat

When it gets dark I still have fun
I catch lighting bugs one by one

Yes summertime is what I like
but most of all I like my bike

Meghan Ferron

Below Bug

So, Mr. Mafia
  when you see bug,
    you know,
    you below!
  Adam Meredith Dash

Not Just Another Day

I just had my 30th birthday
I got an early gift: a head injury
What is a head injury?
No one knows what to say

When ever I ask that question
I feel I get nothing but lying
But I will keep trying
Hey you go another suggestion

Tell me the truth about my injury
Come now be honest with me
I might be slower now but I can still see
Your nonsense answers are making me crazy!

What did this accident take from me
My girlfriend, job, and a degree
But I will come back you'll see
That is if God allows it to be!!!
  Virgil Lundberg

Songs Unsung

There was a time when very young
I had a dream of songs unsung
That I should write in all their splendor
Inspired by God for all to render
To put into words for all to sing
About love and birds and pretty things
Of boys and girls and fun and games
Of holiday joys and things mundane
Of family gatherings, of friends and laughter
To enjoy today and for years ever after
A little boys dream has all come true
Beholden to God and a wife like you
  William H. Jones

"Lost And Found Love"

Life is beautiful when you are around.
I had never looked for true love;
but in you is where it was found.

  My mind is blank,
my days are clear.
The more I think of you,
the more I want you near.

  You have pulled me out of my past,
not so easy, nor so fast.
But, you never gave up,
And, at last, you have put my mind to ease.
Now in my future, you are the only one I see.

  How did I earn someone so gentle and sweet?
I had never imagined someone like you
I'd never meet.

  We're so close and never far away,
In my life I always want you to stay.

  Never leave me, and I'll never be blue.
Because, in my heart I know,
the love I feel is forever true.
  Thomasina Williams

Heaven On Earth

Wandering down a country lane,
I happened across a pure delight.
An old wooden gate was straining in vain,
To hold back the garden that came into sight.

The wilderness was trying to reclaim;
An abandoned homestead of long ago.
Birds sang loudly to proclaim,
Their ownership to friends and foe.

Rose bushes were tangled in blossoming trees.
Pansies and daffodils peeked thru the weeds.
An old rotted tree was home for some bees.
A fragrant soft breeze rustled tall reeds.

The closeness of God enveloped me.
Can anything on earth be so heavenly,
As a garden of flowers man has set free,
That our Father still tends so lovingly?
  Lila Peeters

Family On Pecos Street

Days gone by...
I have changed,
but not my relatives on Pecos Street.

I like visiting because I can have a family
reunion without going anywhere.
My cousin Flora lives one house down from my aunt Rita,
y mi otra tia Nacha lives two houses down from her,
y los otro cousins live in between.
So when I go visiting we just all get
together at my cousins house... in the middle.

Some people wouldn't like it this way,
they say that it was to close for comfort.
Families need to learn to stand on their own two feet.

All I know is that mi familia on Pecos Street, likes it...
and wouldn't have it any other way.
  Maria J. Fernandez

Untitled

We see each other...eye to eye
I have desire - you want to try
And get something you think you've never had
I want to ease the ache I have
I desire you, I want you to know
that when I look at you
my heart just soars
Because you have something
that I need
And I have something, but your need
is greed; for something that is
forbidden......
Something that has no logic - just lust
And desire is gone in one forceful thrust
And mine, well there's more to behold
Pure desire to me is like a pot of gold
Something to be treasured; something destined to last
Real desire that reaches from present to past
Desire that seems to have no end; I desire you, love will begin
  Reba M. White

The Last Time That We Talked

I was talking with my mother, in a dream I had last night.
I heard her softly say, I want you to know that I'm alright.
The last time that we talked, I told you Jesus held my hand.
And I went with Him, to His promise land.

He took me to my home in heaven, and I could not believe my eyes.
Beautiful flowers all in bloom, throughout this land,
  where nothing dies
I walk through the meadows, see the grass and trees so green.
The curse of death can't touch them, and will never again be seen.

No more sickness, pain, or sorrow, my eyes never shed a tear.
Joy fills my heart, overflowing, and never again to fill with fear.
I drink of the living water, and eat of the tree of life.
And in all God's promise land, there is no sin or strife.

The wall of the city, has foundations twelve in all.
Garnished with precious jewels, many I have never saw.
The sun and moon, and the stars won't shine, to give the city light,
for God in all His splendor, will illuminate the night.

I live in a beautiful mansion, Jesus built, many years ago.
I never clean or dust, you won't find that here you know.
My table is set in splendor, with silk linen made so fine.
And I will be here waiting, for you to come and dine.

Norma Jean Owens

My Swing

I swing upon my swing, I swing so very high
I jump, I hit the ground, gee I wish I could touch the sky
My friends jump too while we laugh and play
Come to think of it we swing most every day
I swing to reach a certain height
So I can jump clean out of sight
I don't know why I swing to jump, I don't know why I do
Most every one swings to jump, don't you do that too?
I jumped so very high I could see the entire town
"I'm in the air!" I screamed. THUMP! Now I'm on the ground
I'm swinging on my swing today and having lots of fun
But I'm not jumping today, just swinging till the day is done

Samantha Ciccimaro

Lost Love

I have gone through this pain a lot before,
I know I should move on and not care about you anymore,

But I love you too much to turn away,
I wish you felt the same way.

I know you don't love me,
  but I wish you could see,

You hold the key to my heart,
  that's why I can't stand us being apart.
I wish you would hold me in your arms forever,
but we'll never be together.
Now that I'm trying to hold
  back the tears in my eyes,
I wish you would give us one more try,

I would change all my ways,
  Just to have you here day after day.

I really do care about you,
and I hope you care about me, too.
I know I need to find someone new.
I just want you to know
that there's always a place in my heart for you.

Kim Hemmens

The Beginning

Inside my mother's Catholic womb
I learned the forbidden secrets of a 32 year old woman
And the immaculate morals of adultery.

I want to run naked in the grass
And let the feathery foxtails
Tickle my sensitive skin. As
My mother begins again
To preach about the solitude of purity,
I kick her.

That stops her mumbling lips and
Allows me to get back to my dreams of the future.

I've come to the conclusion that
My mother is on temporary loan
From the stuffy Renaissance.
She would never dream of stolen nibbles, and lazy caresses
Or lust after a wild frolic on an old, faded rug.

Maureen Asfeld

Rain Cover

Cellophane-wrapped thoughts and a puddle of dreams —
I lie awake at night wondering what I mean.
People ask me what I'm looking for
But what I can't find is me.

It's raining and my feet are cold.
I need a goodman so I can grow old.
I need some comfort, a gentle touch,
Maybe some love, but not too much.

So I paint my face, I do my hair,
I spread my legs, there's no one there
To comfort me when it's raining.
But I'm chasing something
        somewhere.

And maybe you have the answers.
Tell me, who should I be?
But you don't know —
  You don't know me.
It's just raining
And I'm chasing something
        somewhere.

Sarah E. McDaniel

The Details of a Storm

As I lie in bed on a rainy night,
I listen to the thunder, and I watch the light.

The leaves blow around from the howling wind,
And the birds snuggle close on a dead tree limb.

As I watch the candle light dance on the walls,
I think of scared little girls hugging their dolls.

A tree cracks loudly and falls to the ground,
And after that I don't hear a sound.

I think of when I was young and how I was scared of storms,
And now they make me feel so complete and so warm.

Slowly the storm in weakening and things start to calm down,
And in the morning the grass will be all dewy and everything
safe and sound.

As I start to get tired and my thoughts begin to drift,
My eyes close tightly shut and the clouds persist to lift.

I will always memorize the details of a storm,
And I can't wait to hear another so I don't have to mourn!

Lorrin Anne Marsh

Growing Love

I am little, My body is very small, I am a baby.
I look to you for touching, bathing, feeding, and communication.
You are my protector for medical procedures, and are my secondary
parent.

I like to be cuddled and massaged, for I am a premature infant.
I know my parent's voice but I'm not allowed to visit with them as
much as I would like.

So hold my hand through the porthold of my isolette, brush my hair,
    call my name
and I will turn my head to your direction for human contact.

I will gain weight and enhance my lung capacity and will be ready to
go home by my delivery date.

I will not remember your assistance, but I will grow and develop to
be a normal infant because of your dedication and your loving care.

Thank you to all the nurses in the NICU.
"Baby."

Lori Sobczak

The Winds Of Westend

The moon stepped out from the endless nothing and dimly lit the night
I looked down at the world and only saw the shadows of our sorrows
flowing within the darkness
I had reached in my soul a state of peace I had never encountered
before, and for one second I truly believed I was flying
Before me laid a road made of black stone and dead thorns
I walked barefoot through the road, hence my feet began bleeding,
but I felt so calm inside that not one bit of pain could ever hurt
me again
The road then ended and all I could see was the still silence of the
night breathing hard against everything
The breezes blew as strong as they could
I placed my legs together and opened my arms,
stretching them horizontally from the floor
I then closed my eyes, kept my mind free of thought,
and let myself go.
For the first and last time, I found myself completely free
    and then I fell straight into the arms...
        ... of the dark winds of Westend.

Sergio Gato

The Wrong Turn

As I walked down life's highway past signs long since weathered out,
    I looked hard at those others on the road walking in the opposite
        direction,
And 'twas then I realized that someplace along the line,
    I had made the wrong turn!

But neither spurned nor dejected, I turned and trod deep in the dust,
    And as it swirled to a fog, then cleared
'Twas then I saw no one around me and realized,
    I had made the wrong turn!

When finally righted and believed heading correctly,
    I looked to make certain those nearby were with me,
But so intent was I on assurance that without realizing,
    I had again made the wrong turn!

My journey had taken me near and far, to where I had no idea,
    But seeing people, I followed, and 'twas to a church and thru the
        doors
I walked, and looked and felt good, and 'twas then I knew at last
    I had made no wrong turn!

Robert H. Wyatt Sr.

Divorce

I was falling into a chasm of darkness
I lost all track of time, place, my very being
I was lost and afraid.
But I saw a glimmer of light and reached out to it
I grasped this shred of hope, my safety net.
I am hanging on
I am on my way
    up—-
I am wounded
I will arise.

Maryanne Fair

I'm the Girl

I loved hard
I loved strong
I loved many
I loved wrong
They say, it's only one true love in this world,
Where's the boy? Because I'm the girl.
Tell me, about this love, how will it be?
Will it be honesty? Will he be true to me?
Is he somewhere just as sad as me?
How will I find him? Where will we meet?
I'll go to the park hoping he'll touch me on the shoulder,
Or maybe I should be a little bit bolder.
I'll go to the ocean, swim in the sea,
Do something unique hoping he'll see me.
I loved hard
I loved strong
I loved many
I loved wrong
They say it's only one true love in this world,
Are you the boy? Because I'm the girl.

Patricia Robinson

God's Winter

Winter is not my favorite at all.
I much prefer Spring, Summer or Fall.
But seasons are not created by man;
as we know, God is the only one who can.
His hand is seen in snow and rain,
ice and sleet, at times causing pain.
Intricate designs appear on trees so tall
after an ice storm or the very first snowfall.
God surely made Winter a special season,
the beautiful white snow could be a pure reason.
While Spring and Summer bring rain and sun,
beautiful Fall colors appear when they are done.
But Winter sends chills up and down the spine
and footprints distinguishable as yours and mine.
So while Winter has exquisite beauty, it's not for me,
for I'm just a warm-blooded southerner, you see.

Rosa H. Nemes

Haiti

I dreamt a dream of death last night.
This island black within our sky.

This sign of death surrounds us all.
The wives and children, all will fall.

Ebony arms raised to fight.
But cannot stop the bullets flight.

A people's will cannot be crushed.
A freedom's voice will not be hushed.

History's shown its well worn face.
But lust for life fills this place.

J. Edward Kernan Jr.

The Life You Save May Be Your Own

Darkness and destruction, it follows me all around...
I need sometime for peace of mind but none is to be found.
Where does it say its a crime to love someone?
Sitting here and waiting for my test results to come.

I've found a man who wants to do me right...
I need protection but there's none in sight.
I try to wait but I need me some love...
I heard a voice from somewhere above,
It said hold on my child, hold on...
The life you save may be your own.

Ladies of the night not even love is for free...
I've got my good time in my pocket, it's talking to me.
What would I do without you here by my side?
You take me places I've never been here inside my mind.

I'll be your lover when you don't have one...
I'll be your only friend, no questions.
But when you come back to reality,
Nothings changed, the problem still remains
You've got to hold on my child, hold on...
The life you save may be your own.

Sandra F. Herring

Friends Not Forgotten

When I think about the past,
I often wonder why.
Why did all my childhood friends,
go to war and die.

It seems like only yesterday,
that we were all in school.
All young boys just having fun,
we thought we were so cool.

But then one day a letter came,
and took us all away.
They taught us how to fight and kill,
there'd be no time to play.

Nothing that was ever said, could ever answer why.
Why such good and loving boys
had to fight and die.

Life since then has been a mess,
it never has been calm.
For all of this I have to thank,
a place called Viet Nam.

Robert L. Kramer

Walk On A Cape Cod Beach

Today I was a millionaire and walked my vast domain,
I paced along its rolling edge and watched it wax and wane.
I glimpsed the canopy of blue with white ships set a-sail,
I heard the cries of flying gulls that wheeled and then turned tail
When, finding on their spot of land, my person there alone;
With graceful sweep and plaintive cry they wished that I be gone.

But I became a millionaire and owned that stretch of sand,
I plucked my wealth and held it, glistening, in my hand.
The dunes were mine, the floating clouds in blue sky out of reach,
The water spreading lacy frills all up and down the beach.
My wealth was sight and sound of changing changeless sea,
And shore dunes stretching endlessly in glorious panoply.

Lorraine E. Mitchell

A Prayer for Peace

Each and every race has so very much to give
I pray we will all soon learn to live and let live
There's so much good in each person under the sun
If they learned to love they'd send hatred on the run
We all come from different ethnic backgrounds
This thought can put discrimination out of bounds
If we all would live and let live and do not cease
This would bring our sick world permanent peace
Now we know this could not happen overnight
But if we try others may see the bright light
How wonderful to see the good in each other
and to realize every one is our brother
Their lovely costumes, their dance, music and art
Should bring the world together and never apart
Each race in the world has so very much to give
Our world would be richer if we live and let live

Mary D. Price

Doll's Tears

I woke up in a clear plastic box, I recall,
I realized I was in a front window mall,
Fingers, big and small, would point as you see,
There were others, in clear boxes along side me,
It won't be long, I thought to myself,
Before I was bought and pulled off the shelf,
Being placed in a bag - Oh! so very dark!
Once opened, I felt myself being almost torn apart!
I heard laughing and chattering all day,
I couldn't believe fun is being treated this way!
My facial expression stays the same during abuse,
My feelings weren't considered, Oh! what's the use!
A doll fairy came, made me human, gave me a name,
I find that being a human, the abuse is the same.
Fingers, big and small, would point as you see,
If they could not keep a control on what my life to be.
I've learned this from co-workers, relationships, friends
I've heard, read it happens to others, on all of earth's ends.
Deep in thought, doll's tears and all,
I realized the safety, I had in the plastic box at the mall.

Marlene Lambright

The Parkway Rabbit

On a cold winter night while driving home,
I saw a rabbit on the parkway grass.
It was under the streetlight, all alone.
No cottontail; it was a bigger mass.

Yes, a tame brown rabbit someone let go.
Did they know it might not survive the day,
In this location all by itself? So-
I tried to catch it, but it got away.

When I got about ten feet close to it,
He would hop swiftly to the bush cover.
I'm trying to save your life, Dear Rabbit!
I'll try tomorrow. You'll know me better.

The next day, with great anticipation
Of seeing the Parkway Rabbit again,
I saw the worst of my expectation.
A car victim, on the road he was lain.

A tear welled up for my parkway friend.
I moved him to the side of the road.
Little did he know where his life would end.
Dear Rabbit, you're with me as I grow old.

Ken McCambridge

302

Untitled

I walked down the stairs into the basement
I saw a sight that I could not believe
It was so strange that I wanted to leave
I wanted to retch because of the scent
Then I saw the blood dripping from a vent
The red bloody floor almost made me heave
All the dinner I had eaten that eve
I wanted to run back, but down I went.
Oh how could I cause such an awful thing
Pain and torture to all those around me?
Oh How could I be so selfish and mean?
Leave them alone, they're all human beings!
They think I don't care but they do not see
The things I have felt and things I have seen

Melissa Bailey

Sitting By A River

Looking into the river, flowing so free,
I see a photo, a picture of me.
I look a little closer, the view comes clearer,
I see a little girl, looking into a mirror.
I put my hand in, the water starts to stir,
I sit behind and watch and think of her.
She drifts away, all alone,
To start her journey, on her own.
Why did she leave, why did she go,
Oh my Lord, I love her so.
Now she's seventeen, with a baby on the way,
The father not there for her to lean, And no place to stay.
She sells her body, for $15 or less,
And does lots of drugs, her life is a mess.
Now think back, to the river flowing,
That little girl, was her life worth throwing.
All she needed was a little love,
Like the kind from up above.
So next time you're at a river, look in and see,
And hope to God the reflection of you, is not of me.

Shaunna Wentworth

When I Look In The Clouds

When I look in the clouds I see a dragon shooting out fire
I see a raging whale talking to a liar
When I look in the clouds I see a sleeping lion
I see a golden Pegasus a flyin'

When I look in the clouds I see a hunting boar
I see an eagle that can really soar
So what do you see in that cloud
Maybe you will tell me out loud.

Michael Birchfield

Looking At Life Through Winter's Eyes

The first flakes of life fall from the sky,
  I see my past unfold on the ground before me.

Each moment touched the earth.
  One by one,
  Before I realized,
    A layer of my day's lived was before me.

Some melted away.
  Yet others remained,
    Not one second alike.

I look to Heavens to see what my future holds.
  I am unable to forecast.

This I know,
  Like life there will be storms,
    But I never forget the sun will shine again.

Lisa Thomas O'Brien

Untitled

Sunny outside and all is fair
won't you be my Teddy Bear

Dan R. DeGruttola Jr.

Blind & Paralyzed

I am blind and paralyzed by choice
I see nothing of the problems in the world.
And I stand motionless to violence and hatred

Yes, I stand blind and paralyzed just as most
Why is not an optional question for the
  answer is self evident.

I need nor want any involvement in problems or
  solutions
I don't need any other complications.

But even though I give no help to the
  generation of today
I share my heart with the children of tomorrow.

I as well as many others will see and
  walk again when a cure comes.

The cure is a light
A light so bright I see it
A light so powerful it moves me.

A light so innocent that my first sight
  will be that of love and unity
But, until the day I shall not move or see.

Richard Hubbard

The Street's Hush

As I walk up and down the downtown street
I see the pain of poverty as a tear gliding down
  A clown's face to his feet
The hush of the street is inevitably missed
The fierce growl of the dog and the alley cat's
  hiss
The drip of the last drop in the bottle of the
  homeless guy
The prostitute's abandoned baby's cry
The yell of the people fighting in a gang
The moan of the one shot when off goes a bang
This may not be all the streets downtown
As I walk up and down the street I am wearing a
  frown

Kandi Begeman

As Time Goes By

As I approach the autumn of my life
I seem to see the past a weary strife
Yet looking forward nothing much will change
My life as always has been prearranged
For me the future like the past
Will quickly move along
And as it travels into winter I'll learn
To sing a lovely song
I'll sing of youth and love and happiness
I'll sing of work and love and loneliness
And then I'll sing of you
You not in spring I loved
But you who in summer I loved
You in winter is all I want for me
I thank the dear Lord above
For bringing us together to share our love.

Mary Morgese

Untitled

One never knows what is around the corner-
I should be content, but have become a mourner.
I mourn for the happy times that are now gone-
I mourn for the love that I know now was wrong.
I believed in all the truths and lies,
And now my love, I must say good-bye.

Please don't humiliate me with further ado-
I have tried again and again to explain to you.
It's over, no more, I am drained of strength and life-
I must start once again, clear without strife.
I felt weighted down, dull and nearly lost-
You almost won, but I have become my own boss.

Supported by family and friends you tried to divide-
I find myself moving once again on life's ride.
You will suffer and grieve your most sad fate-
I am sure you will look at me with anger and hate.
The answers you seek you will find in the mirror-
For it is you, not me, you will come to fear.

Vicki Lynn Looper

Now and Then

Now and then I sit and wonder why
I sit alone and cry
How could I face life without you
Now and then I ask myself what went wrong
I felt you and I belonged
Our life was like a song together
Now and then I recall that day
That day you went away
And all you had to say was so long
You left me standing in the dark
You should have heard my heart
I thought I was going to die
All the thoughts that ran through my mind
I never had the time to ask you why
Now and then I sit and wonder why
But now my eyes are dry
I found somebody new, I'm happy that's true
But he'll never replace you.

Luba Becker

Fear For The Future

As the clock ticks on the wall
I sit and stare
As time passes on
I wonder what will be

I see the past
Its memory like the yellowing
pages of an old book,
Telling me it is gone;
"Don't dwell upon the things that are past."

I fear the future. I see decay and turmoil.
Unhappy thoughts of what may or may not be.
Like a spectre in the dark, wearing
a black hooded cape - beckoning
me to come and look at what lies ahead.

Mary J. D. Steinhauser

With This Prayer

With this prayer to our Creator, I welcome you.
I stand with you before all those I love, to invite you
into the most Sacred place I know...my soul.
Until today, I have kept these words hidden deep in my heart...
Now they are fully grown and I am ready to give them away.
With these words as my gift, I honor you and ask you to hear.
I will protect your dreams, doing the best I can to give them life,
through all our days as husband and wife...
I will have courage through whatever tests we face,
I leave my old self in this place-
A new person comes to you, singing a new song in a joyful voice.
We will learn to talk with each other, and take time to be quiet...
We will make love our strength and triumph.
The truth will build our faith, provide us light-
to keep our Road of understanding bright.
I will teach you how to learn from me, while I am learning from you,
we will open the doors of Mystery together from now on.
With this prayer to our Creator, I welcome you.
I stand with you before all those I love, to invite you
into the most Sacred place I know to take you to...my soul.

Patricia A. Dean

My Albert

Although he's gone to heavens above
I still see his sweet smile in my mind's eye
His aura surrounds me during my daily tasks
and I still wonder why
God gave him to me for ten short years
and I've since been left with flowing tears
Just once in a lifetime one meets his soulmate
Nevermore to see again
Alas, only dreams are left to remember the moments
The laughter, the tears, but most of all the sad goodbys

Goodbye my love
I'll keep you in my heart until once again we meet
When my days are done I'll see you above
Once more to cherish and greet
For it is only in the hereafter that lost hearts can reunite
Then we can fulfill our dreams and be forever bright

Marie L. Vooris

The Compassion of a Bystander

Withered in sorrow, on that hot day.
I stood and watched. The flies swarmed 'round the wounds,
In the stale heat as their sickness rotted in my heart.
No longer able to speak, I stared, unblinking,
at the torturous image before me. The heat. The heat,
burning his skin and peeling the wounds.
Oh how those nails absorb heat. How quickly blood dries in the sun.
The smell of suffering rots in my soul.
I cannot react to all the pain. People laugh in the heat, the
    wound-peeling heat.
People mock in the heat, the blood-drying heat.
I can't keep the flies out of my eyes. They suck on his wounds.
I stood withered in sorrow, on that hot afternoon.
I stood and watched. A man's life slips into the heat.
Into the fly infested heat. To watch where he gazes makes thick
sorrow in my gut. To wonder what thoughts pass deep behind...
the eyes that know inescapable death.
Oh the heat.

Philip Martin

Hold On To Autumn

Looking in the mirror today,
I think if only the hand of time would stay.
So in the beautiful, easy days of autumn I could lay:

Safe, well past the wild storms of spring,
That forever in my heart will ring.
And the sweat and toil of summer days,
That my best did take and pay:

But time seems faster now that I would have it slow,
With what's left of life in sure tow.
Time now for thoughtful reflection,
And questions of past direction:

Now with each autumn leaf that falls,
Time trudges onward toward the call,
Of cold and winter days,
When it finally drags me on no more,
My body sore,
And leaves me here to stay:

Norma J. Ramsey

Feel Like Wearin' Glasses

I can see more clearly, the way you're loving me
I think it's gonna make me, the best man I'll ever be
Bleary eyed and foggy, 'til you came along
Proud and I'm so happy, I'll sing it in my song

You make everything seem, clear comin' into view
Like glasses fit the picture, I know that I love you...

No more double vision, I'm focusing on you
New light has arisen, I'm seeing what to do
I dreamed I'll never ever, saw more sleepy wood
Telescoping better, you make me think I should

Near insighted future, shining all the way
Break all previous records, every single day
You have really shown me, clearly what to do
Ah, lets see here...I'm sure glad eye met you

You make everything seem, clear comin' into view
Like glasses fit the picture, I know that I love you.....
And I feel like wearin' glasses....feel like wearin' glasses,
Feel like wearin' glasses all day long.

Michael J. Finn

As I Sit On My Porch

As I sit on my porch, I watch the roses bloom.
I think of last night and that full yellow moon.
I think of its beams—how they danced in your hair.
And then on your skin so soft and so fair.
As I sit on my porch, I watch the clouds move toward us.
I think of our children—how else could God reward us.
As I sit on my porch, I look at the sky blue.
I thank the Good Lord for my young ones and you.
As I sit on my porch, I see the mountains around us.
They are big and majestic but nowhere near the love that surrounds us.
As I sit on my porch, I see the growth and the green
I see all around me from Autumn 'til Spring.
All in all, I think what a wonderful life
But it would be nothing without my kids and my wife.

Tim Michael

Come Back (A Tribute To My Friend, Ryan)

One Spring morning, I listened to the birds sing.
I thought, I heard your name.
Then I heard the distant toll of church bells ring.
The feeling was the same.

On the grass, a million drops of diamond dew.
Do you see this treasure?
In the sky, white puffs on a bright sea of blue.
Beauty I can't measure.

I wonder if its you when the sun shines bright...
Telling me you are near.
Are you the brilliant star I see each dark night,
that takes away my fear?

I must die a little with each tear I shed.
On earth, your years were few.
Please. Please come back from where you walk with the dead.
This world really needs you.

Rebecca Lynn Rzeszut

The Halls of Time

I walked the halls of time today,
I tread the creaky floors.
I studied faces hanging there
of those who'd gone before.

I read the eyes of hopes and dreams
of conquests (large and small).
I heard the shuffling and the laughter
resounding in the halls.

I smelled the chalk, so flaky and white,
and the books with tattered pages,
and the soft faint smells of erasers and ink
still lingering thru the ages.

The tears welled up and overflowed
with sadness in my chest,
when your eyes met mine like they used to do
before you went to rest.

O memories of faded past,
that's all I have of you.
I walked the halls of time today
on creaky floors of our old school.

Patsy K. (Harold) Spaulding

Where Am I?

I dream, yet there is no Vision
I walk, while the earth is empty of footprints
I work, but there's no job to find
I think but, my mind is never present, where Am I?

I plant over land, yet it remains seedless
I build, but the house of Dreams never show it self.
I hurt, but there's no Pain.
I cry, yet my tears are without wetness, where am I?

I sing, but Remember not why there's no music.
I smile, without the benefit of laughter.
I understand, but have never known
wisdom or knowledge
I write but there are no words where Am I?

I Desire, yet have no emotion
I kiss without lip to kiss.
I embrace, while lacking Arms to hold
And I live yet have no Heart to feel. Where Am I?

And when morn becomes nigh, and
Dawn whispers no more in the angles of
Love and life, Where Am I?

William J. Walls

I Wanna...

I wanna be beautiful
I wanna know joy
I wanna live in Paris and speak french
I wanna be free
I wanna feel, dance, laugh and sing
I wanna have peace
I wanna know desire
I wanna know you
I wanna have you look into my eyes
And read my spirit
I wanna make love
I wanna outline your essence with my tongue
And touch the outer most limits of your galaxy
With my kisses and caresses
I wanna love you the way a man needs to be loved
By a woman
I wanna be loved
The way a woman needs to be loved
By a man
mmmmmm I wanna.....

Kyoto Lagundi Walker

"Just To Be Me"

I want to be emotionally free
I want to cry when the wind blows
I want to be emotionally free
To laugh with the rain, and smile at the sea
Please let me be emotionally free
Let me be sad, when things aren't right
Please let me cry, when I want to at night
I just want to be emotionally free
I want to love the colors in the sky
The light of the stars as the moon passes by
Please let me be emotionally free
I don't want much, but just to be me!

Vivian Alice Burnau

Alexandra

When she speaks I feel a joy... like no other joy there is
I want to laugh and sing and dance... my life is full of bliss
There was a time when things were sad...and often I would cry
I'd turn around and see her there...and then I'd smile inside

She gave me strength to carry on, to live from day to day
Her laughter rang the bells of faith, together we would pray...
Bring Daddy home to us anon, his safety we implore...
In your name we ask, watch over him, there's nothing we want
more

Our prayers were answered and all cried out- "A SONG FOR
PEACE TODAY"!
The worry, grief, and apprehension we felt was lifted all away...
She's growing fast now and learning well about her toddler world
The war is over, and all is well; she's "Daddy's little girl"

Hold on to faith...forever sweet; the strongest trait you'll possess
Be forever empathetic my love, and try to put resentment to rest...
You mean to world to both of us, we never will forget
The love, sacrifice, and faith in God, we never will regret

The sands of time fall gently now upon the morning dew...
Each day awakens a brand new life for us to share with you
Our love for you will never end as long as there is life...
and someday I know you'll feel the same...As a mother and a wife.

Sandy A. Quispe

Untitled

I do not want to live 'til I am old;
I want to leave when life is at its best.
If in the prime of years I am content,
Then do I want to lay me down and rest.
If all the joys of life I have possessed
And all its sorrows, all its cares and woe;
And then at last I know some peace of mind,
That is the time when best I'd like to go.
But if my life is destined to be dull,
Quite void of love, though it bring joy or pain
At twenty-one, then let me go to bed,
And close my eyes and never wake again.

Thus spoke I with the tongue of youth
Those many, many years ago. And at the time I spoke the truth
For there was much I did not know.
And although poets long have sung
That living's sweetest for the young, I cannot in my heart agree
For it has not been so with me for every year is bringing more
Of pleasures never known before
Now few are more content than I. Oh, no, I do not want to die!

Sarina Salerno

My Love

My love, I want you to ravish my quivering body.
   I want your desires to be filled.
     I want others to know that we are as one.
I desire you to be my-
   Passionate lover,
     My school-boy pal,
       A stranger.
My soul longs for a soul mate-
   I long for... YOU.
The empty lonely heart only feels,
   only aches, when we are apart.
My love, I want...

           You!
Stacy L. Hitchcock

A Love About Ten Years Ago

When the wind blew,
I was floated.
When it rained,
I was soaked.
Sometimes I found myself lain
just like grasses.

The memory of the softness I still remember
while being floated,
while being soaked.
But it should have been something aching
which can not be now easily restored:
it might be an innocence, a passion, or a tragedy,
holding the curtains of doubtful silence.

The other night
on a dog-eared page which I happened to open
a tomb I saw
which used to lead the corridors of my life.

It was a love?

Young K. H.

The Letter

I received a letter from an old friend today.
I was glad .... and excited.
My first thought: "I'll bet Jack and Wanda are coming to visit us!"

Our friendship goes back a long way.
Back to college days ... newly married ... fellas in school...
Wives working to put them through.
I tore open the envelope.
I wonder how soon they will be here?

"God loves you", the letter began.
An unusual beginning - although I knew that in recent years Jack
and Wanda had become deeply religious.
I remember the last time we saw them .. can it really be five
years ago? ... they seemed very happy with their new-found faith in
God.

"And I love you", the letter went on.
I really should write them more often .... from now on I will do just that.
"Jack went to be with our Lord on October 1."

Good-bye, Jack.
Sylvia Huecker

Skeleton's in the Closet

My husband was in his easy chair, nodding off to sleep.
I was in my rocking chair when he began to speak.
"My dear," he said "I know you've been a good and loving wife.
You've been through thick and thin of things the total of my life.
I've loved you every single day you've stuck there by my side.
I know some days, I've failed for you, and walked a faltered stride.
I have something that pains me, buried deep within my chest.
And I would like to tell them, Dear, to get some peace and rest."

I put my book down gently, to rest it on my lap.
And wondered what had brought this up, to interrupt his nap.
"Good husband, there are things, I do not wish to know.
Of all your little skeletons that bring you all your woe.
Tell me of your troubles, when your time is drawing near.
When you have heard, IT'S TIME from God, whispered in your ear.
Tell me on your death-bed, such pains that you've kept hid.
And skeletons in your closet, love, that you would like to rid.
So I will know, where your ashes go, to watch my gardens yield,
   Or across the fence to watch the cows, fertilize the fields."
Raven Feaster

Your Love

I never intended on falling in love
I was just having fun
But just one night and I knew
A new life had begun

Through all the days that followed
We grew closer, and closer
I felt something I had never known before
A sense of love had blossomed

You tended it with parts of you
And fertilized it with warmth and kindness
As the blossom of love grew, time became endless
Melody A. Jennings

Untitled

Why is there so much fear in love
   When all we have is honesty?
Why are we so afraid
   When all we've ever been is true?
What causes us to be so humbled
   When words are spoken simply?
What makes us shake an tremble
   When we speak our love anew?
Jonathan Hemphill

Friends

Rain poured upon my face.
I was running for some reason in the field out back of my house,
naked.
As far as I could see were blades of grass, various lengths.
The rain continued.
What had gotten me up so suddenly?
The dream. The abandonment.
The old woman's face. Each line a scar, containing lines,
years, friends, months, days?
They were appearing so fast now. Minutes?
She just smiled and pointed a bone in the direction of a bucket.
A perfectly formed web was there. The spider asleep in the middle.
Do spiders dream I thought. No matter.
She speaks. Choosing her words with care, composing her
sentences.
"Everyday", she said, "He's there asleep."
"I wake," her voice fading, "And shoo him away."
As she told me this, she started to force the web from inside the
bucket.
The spider scurried and scampered away.
"He'll be back," she said. "We're friends. He leaves me presents."
"Every time a new design to start my day."
Mark E. Lancaster

Falling

You said you were falling, and would I be there
I was there waiting, but you did not care.
Your head ruled your heart and you wouldn't let go;
My heart ruled my head, and I told you so.

Now a pain deep within continues to stir;
It reminds me of Christ's love and the pain he did bear.
For he loved us all and we put him aside
In search of a love that cannot abide.

And though our closeness has drifted apart
Our friendship will remain always, close to my heart.
Kathleen Bittner

Strong Love

My Nieces and Nephews,
I watch you soak up life like a sponge..
So little, so frail,
wadding pools and pails.
Preschool and direction
smiles and reflection.
You are the best gift my brothers and sisters could give,
for you my life shines and believes.
The love you send off,
stronger than a tornado.
Through the years, heartbreaks and tears,
remember, remember your Auntie will always be there.
Buses and backpacks,
letters and phone calls.
There will be a day, you will be mad,
many years down the road you will be glad.
The word is so big, but yet so small,
make the best of it and you will have it all.
My words of wisdom are only because I am older,
so hold your head high, sending your love stronger.
Mary E. Curnell

"Time Is At Hand"

For time is at hand. My time that is. My time has passed for I watched as it whisked by. I had but a simple question, and for a moment time slipped by. Wait I had said, but it was too late. Why has my time gone by I ask. A quiet voice spoke saying You are not of this time so that is why time has gone by. Time I hear has a swift white horse. For it's mission is of a pure heart. Why can I not answer this soft voice. Each night I see the white horse ride in my dreams. Again I hear the faint voice say to me. Time has passed you by. You are no longer of this time. You will pass soon to the time that you so deservedly belong. Wait and behold for patience is for your time to come. In the dreams I see a time of long ago for you said the voice. A peaceful time. I do not belong for time has truly passed you by. Take heart though says time in a soft faint voice during a dream while riding the white horse. For your time is at hand.

Tod E. Jackson

I Am...

I am a young girl living in 1995
I wonder about the world's fate
I hear the sounds of death
I see the pain throughout the world
I want peace and no more suffering
I am a young girl living in 1995

I pretend not to hurt
I feel pain when I watch the news
I touch the hurt everyday
I worry about young children's death
I cry when a gang shooting takes place
I am a young girl living in 1995

I understand the bad condition of the world
I say things that hurt others
I dream about dying young
I try to ignore pain and suffering
I hope to live to see my 20th birthday
I am a young girl living in 1995.

Sarah Jane Davis

I Am

I am a wonderful girl who loves the ocean.
I wonder if there is a dolphin being born right now.
I hear the whales talking to each other.
I see a school of fish swimming by.
I want to one day ride on a dolphin.
I am a wonderful girl who loves the ocean.
I pretend that I swim with the whales.
I feel safe with a school of fish and fear the sharks.
I touch the crabs that walk down the ocean deep.
I worry about the fish that are dying today.

I cry when a whale is dead.
I am a wonderful girl who loves the ocean.
I understand that I won't be at the beach everyday.
I say let the fish roam free, not to be caught by fisherman.
I dream that I will play with the sea horses.
I try to be considerate with the fishes homes.
I hope in heaven there are fish like the ones on earth.
I am a wonderful girl who loves the ocean.

Melissa A. Scharfe

Star Gazing

As I lie awake gazing at the vast night sky
I wonder what I'd see, if ever I could fly.
Forgetting the expanse 'tween me and the starry sky,
I reach for a star, and sigh, remembering I cannot fly.
If e'er I may, I'll pass those specks of glowing light
To see a wondrous creation that proves God's awesome might.
Those tranquil stars that float 'cross Heav'n and fade away
Are roaring trillions of miles, unnoticed, night and day.
O'er the Earth an occasional bat flutters by
Not aware of the Heavens above, although it can fly.
Ne'er do I tire of the splendor of it all,
Exceeding the grasp of our mortal minds, yet without flaw.
Mighty heavenly bodies obey God's wise direction.
Each glorious star He calls by name, without exception.
Galaxies are as common as fish in the ocean,
How I do admire the creator who sets them in motion!
And as I drift off to sleep under the vast night sky,
I cannot help but smile t'ward that endless black space
For I feel like I can fly!

Karen Lemon

Surprise

After seeing the doctor
I wouldn't feel like this,
if I hadn't taken my annoying list.
He begrudgingly listened,
and to my surprise
upon awakening this morning,
my eyes opened wide.
I held my breath in disbelief,
for I had slept all night. What a relief!
I could think because my head was clear,
for the very first time this year.
I could taste what I ate,
and thank goodness I had no headache.
As I breathed through my nose,
I felt air going clear down to my toes.
Now I can smell the coffee brewing,
the fragrance of roses at the back door
and all the perfumes when I walk through the store.
Feeling so full of vim and vigor,
never before can I remember.

Margaret G. Poole

Criticized

I watch you have the same thoughts that I have every day:
I write and it's wonderful,
read it the next day and it's horrible,
back and forth,
time and time again,
and all because I have all these things inside my head,
wandering around, trying to find a place to rest.
Some are simple little thoughts,
that would solve all the world's hurt.
I can never just sit and do nothing,
arrive at a thought and stay with it for more than one second,
expand on it,
derive peace by locating
a point of reference
beyond my small skull.

Michelle Long

Promises

If bright stars were wishes
I'd give you the sky
If clouds could be kisses
I'd not say good-bye
If raindrops were tears
And the waves were my fears
I'd walk on the beach, gather up every shell
With the shore in my reach, and my fears hidden well
I would kiss you so softly
And hold you so tight
My heart would burst open
And the world would be right
If the winds were beginnings
I'd start with you
And if sunsets were promises
I'd promise to
Always be honest and loving to you.

Susan M. Tobiens

One More Day With You

(To Pansy)

If I could spend just one more day with you
I'd pick a day in early spring when everything was new.
We'd walk through fields of fresh bloomed flowers
Talk non-stop for hours and hours,
If I could spend just one more day with you.

If I could spend just one more day with you
I know each place we would go and everything we'd do.
We'd laugh about those yester years
And how we struggled through
If I could spend just one more day with you.

I wouldn't let your hand slip out of mine,
I just couldn't waste a minute of our happy golden time,
I'd say those words I always meant to say,
If I just knew...
If I could spend just one more day with you.

Rosemary Chandler

A Woven Ring Of Friendship

A poem you ask of me.
If a pen could launch a thousand ships,
an odyssey I'd write for you.
But the words I long to write
just get tangled up in the emotions
that my heart weaves.
Sometimes I catch myself falling
and I fear that you'll see it burning in my eyes.
So I'll ask of you
to breathe me a song of friendship.
For it is all your heart can safely give.
Allow me to hold you
in the comfort of my wings
until you're strong enough to fly.
For friends as well as lovers
require rhythm as well as rhyme,
and a woven ring of friendship
outlasts the sands of time.

Shannon M. Moon

For My Boss

A trunk to pack your troubles in,
And for your health, a vitamin.
A clock with hours for you to gain,
And aspirin to ease your pain.
A cigar to relax and end the day,
And flowers to smell along the way.

K. T. Boyd

A Letter to God

Dear God,
If I may, can I please take a few moments of your time?
You see, I have several questions that have been lingering in my mind.
They took me from my family when I was only four,
Then I was five, yes mom still alive, they placed me behind
    this strange door.
For days I just sat there, not really knowing why;
They left me with these strange people, and said goodbye.

Who were these people, that took me away?
Who were these people, with whom I had to stay?

Everyday for one very long year, I have awaited to come forth
    this special day;
For my mom to come and rescue me, for the pain had to be relieved...
To only have waited for the worst birthday present I have ever
    received...
Was to awake that morn being told, my mom had just passed away.

I was forced to stay with these people, and call them Mom and Dad,
I said no the mom part, then asked, "What's a dad?"
Not wanting to stay, but I had no choice,
For in the eyes of the law, a kid has no voice,
For we young and naive, and do not know what we say.

Well God, If the courts would have listened to my cry when I was
    young,
I could have had a normal childhood; and instead of
    crying, I would have sung.

Margaret M. Ehrmann

Victory Leigh

Her child's life was wasted, her soul was taken away.
    If it wasn't for a drunk driver, she might still be here today.
Because of his stupidity, she had to pay for his mistakes.
    I never thought a three year old could cause so many heartaches.

If you want to know the story, I'll tell it all from my heart.
    Just bear in mind as I tell it, that a family was torn apart.

They were walking along a sidewalk, on a hot summer's day.
    The sun was high in the sky, it was the 24th of May.
The little girl said, "Look, Mommy!" as she looked her in the eyes,
    "Look at the pretty colors of the clouds in the sky!"

She was suddenly knocked from her feet, she looked like a tiny ball.
    And as the car sped past them, mommy heard the final call.
The little girl landed in the road, mommy heard not a sound.
    Her daughter, "Victory Leigh", was dead when she hit the ground.

Now mommy has these nightmares, and she wakes in the midst of night.
    She hears her baby's voice saying, "Don't worry mommy I'm alright!"
Now you know why it's so important not to drink and drive,
    'Cause if it wasn't for that reason, Victory Leigh might still be
    alive.

Melissa Jo Harris

Starting Over

Maybe "good-bye" does not mean forever
if I wait for you in the shining light
I know you will say "hello" and come over
then, we'll start again at a fresh sparkling sight
with our clear minds, I know we can get through
blank mind albums, let's fill them with a dream
we can achieve all, 'cause our feelings are true
brightness of our future shines with a beam
we have the strength to fly over any hurdles
so God, please, please, give us another chance
what I'm writing isn't meaning less doodles
I'm serious, anything bad, we'll enhance
let's not give up, let's start everything over
maybe "good-bye" does not mean forever.

Mari Sakai

The Promised Land

Oh what a dismal world this would be
  If we had no hope of immortality,
No assurance when we reach the journeys end
  We should someday meet with our loved ones again.

Christ's death on the cross at Calvary
  Proved the truth of immortality;
For when He died to rise again
  He proved that death was not the end.

Because Christ lives, we too shall live,
  Is the promise our Heavenly Father gives;
And if we live by His holy plan
  We shall meet again in the Promised Land.

A land that knows no grief nor pain,
  A land where we never part again;
Where with God and loved ones we may be
  There to dwell through all eternity.

  Lennel A. Stutler

The Mirage

Beautiful it was, in retrospect,
Ignorance - no chequered doubts.

The sinister fluorescent smile on the Venus, that perished winged
creature I envy,
Free of pain - for temptations for them only a moment last.

The daily routine of the sun, it leaves in my mind many a doubt,
Like shadows which symbolize reality, when transient and unreal
itself is.

Eyes given to see, so other senses for that function we use not,
I wish we were so very blind, so the light we would see.

Relative the truth is they say, but the truth remains no matter what
the perspective; money, fame, power - we see but untrue,
the truth we see not, and yet the only thing that is true.

To the vacant, unwise the wise seem - bathing in milk they prefer,
Their destiny like that starved dead beast would be, whose flesh
would always keep the vultures' mouth full. For,

Momentary pleasure - it is you these credulous fools seek,
Temptations it is you they have succumbed to,
Weakness - it is you they revere,
Disillusionment - it is you they will gain and
Desires - it is you they have made immortal.

  Sachin Sheth

Awareness

Though awareness can bring fear and pain
I'll live each day aware
Knowledge learned and feelings felt
More alive than that old blank stare
For in the past, I've know the absence of light
I've existed in that bland/colorless snare
Where I denied all feelings and most all facts
Not acknowledging my needs or my cares
I now know the value of struggling through the pain
Now with courage, the pain I'll gladly bare
Awareness of reality, I'll choose every time
That old existence doesn't begin to compare
So I'll continue to break through the walls that I have built
Knowing more light and awareness are to be gained
I'll embrace that light of reality with newfound trust and joy
And its peace and its vibrancy I'll strive to maintain
For to me reality is simply this:
I AM A CHILD OF GOD
I AM A WORTHY WOMAN
And I am ALIVE and AWARE!

  NaVena Carol Foor

Goodbye My Best Friend

The day you left me and we said goodbye
I'll never forget 'cause it was the last day you were mine
I know it's over I know for a fact
We finally broke our sacred solid pact
We had it all and even more
Now my heart is broken, scarred and sore
So I search for a new best friend
But no one can compare
I still don't think 3 years was enough we had time to spare
So I leave you with these words of love
So you will remember me
In your hopes, in your dreams, in everything you do
"You really are my best friend and I truly do love you."
Someday I know you will be my friend
But until then I wait and just hope
The good times and memories won't ever end

  Phyllis Rehling

Candle

The candle sits upon the hearth,
illuminating my mind.
Sending rays of light
to open the darkest corners of my soul.
The flame licks the unfriendly air,
as the fiery wax drips on earthen brick.
The fire is like the thoughts
that burn up my intelligence.
Residue from the candle is like my brain,
some thoughts must be melted away,
to see something new.
As the wick reduces into nothing,
so does my life.
With the many hours it has given warmth,
as so did I.
Me as the candle we burn flicker and die.

  Mindy Smith

Father Time

I've been walking down the street with Father Time
I'm getting old, I can see the signs
my hair is grey
my skin is wrinkled
But Father and I have a love that even time can't stop
we took the vows many years ago
The children who were once little,
are now full grown
you can love them
you can miss them
you can cry at night
Father Time will progress and make everything alright
as time goes on
so must my life
so I will love you now
and for the rest of my life

  Karen Mosqueda

Lonely

My heart is lonely,
I feel so bare, drowning in my despair.
Forsaken feelings, deserted days,
Secluded soul; and weary ways.
Trapped in my reclusive life,
Fear cuts me like a knife.
In a quite place, waiting to pull the trigger,
I cry a single, neglected tear.
Isolated, the one and only,
Scared, lost, and lonely.

  Nicole Martina Underhill

Untitled

I knew you once and now I wonder why you aren't there
I'm seeking out that sheltered place, looking everywhere

There in many dreams of mine I ponder how you went
Days and years in quick success have known how you were spent

I hold within a tattered piece, it warms me when I'm cold
So wondrous how that little bit can magically unfold

On and on it spins a web that wraps me with its thread
So I am safe and sleepy as I rest my weary head

Guardian of those who passed in silent reverie
So the strength to look for you is given back to me

Know you haven't failed us for I'll always hold it tight
The puzzle keeps me waiting but I feel that it's all right

When scattered by an angry wind, some think you're nevermore
Fragments meant to bind as one are destined to restore

I'll see you stand before me with your light upon my face
And I will know the love we knew within your firm embrace

Oh you are missed dear family and the days seem very long
When I think of how you slipped away - not knowing you were gone.

Laurie Kendall Saylors

Dragons, Fire, Frost and Snow

Silvered mist upon its heels the hull runs low
Immersed in a mirror of blue
Broken only by the tears of a dragon's eye
Sleek in the line of a fighting lady
Hold pregnant with rapine, fire, plunder and war

Always there, always watching, surf caressing her fur-clad feet
Snow capped peaks ivoried crown, tawny hair golden as winter dawn
Only a woman knows her joy, home and safe comes her frost giant
Blood lust drowned in the booty he holds
Home comes the dragon, winter comes in a rush of life

Impassioned visions burn with life, winter runs on feet of youth
Love plays its tune in dawn and dusk, two find love becoming one
Comes the spring that wakes the dragon, from a winter's peace
Clinging arms and stinging tears claim not
The heart of a dragon's rider

Tar-pitched keels bind timbers of war, sun beams dancing on weapons
Hum broadswords to Brimstone tune, prayers to Odin
A voyage of luck, spring's warmth dies there on the strand
Surf suckling her naked feet, gone now the frost giant
War once more, mirrored blue reflects fire in dragon's eyes

W. G. Claunch

Direction

Direction found at last
    Impulse gives way to new precision
Symmetry between my dreams and past
    Gives focus to a boundaried vision

My fate now firm settles to the ground
    I take my thrills from profound prediction
Values lost are suddenly found
    Conformity my new addiction

Destinations now seem clear
    Old lust for life
        Now new born fear

Richard W. Hubbard

Ode On The Possession Of Immaterial Things

I have the soul of a poet,
In a bottle on the shelf.
I pour a little dollop,
When I want a muse myself.

I have the heart of a dreamer.
I keep it in a jar.
I take it out on holidays
To take me near and far.

I have quite a collection
of things immaterial.
Most of them came
In boxes of cereal.

Richard L. Parker

"Ode To Elliott"

There is a beagle named Elliott who lives
    in a condo in Ohio
He is only two - full of vim and vigor
He would bring you his toys and baby
    stuffed bear
To throw for and near and he would
    fetch it from anywhere
One day he sat on the couch very still
His sad little eyes moving from side to side
He would look at you - his illness trying to hide
His tail would wag back and forth -
He would try to play or all he was worth
To the hospital he went for five days
A very sick beagle was he
Now he is at home trying to make a
    recovery
Four little pills he takes each day
Once again he is starting to play
We wish you well little Elliott
    because we all love you so.

Mary Dellovade

A New Beginning

This ice-bound winter will soon come to an end,
In a few short weeks a new spring will begin.

No more waking up to a weather so foul,
That we greet each day with a groan and a growl.

We look forward to the sun and it's healing powers.
As mother Nature brings forth all her spring flowers.

We can enjoy our work from nine to five,
And thank our God for just being alive.

Life is precious, but it too must end,
so make each day count, make a new friend.

Give of yourself, make your heart sing!
Rejoice in our world as we greet a new spring.

Ralph H. Pilgrim

Altar

There is an altar that I know of
In a place which is far from here
Maybe across this alter
We can look into the eyes of each other
Could the hatred and accusations die away?
Whether we believe in the Divine of the sun
Or the Divine son, or absolute biology
There is still an uncertainty to it all
Perhaps within this doubt we can still
Find the humanity, the questioning in each of us.

Sherry A. Teerlinck

Watch Your Step

The devil is out to get you
in any way he can
if you are not very careful
he will have you eating out of his hand
just tell him no and mean it
give him a kick right in his pants.

He is a very smart old cookie
he will trick you if he can
he get his pot on boiling
mixed with all kind of roots
if he can get you to taste his mixture
he know then he got you hooked.

You watch him in the alley
and watch him in the street
he comes in so many fashions
he can almost trick you in your sleep.

Laura Kate Brown Keen

Johnny Reb

He struggles across the field
In his suit of butternut gray.
He's already wounded twice,
But that won't keep him from the fray.

They call him Johnny Reb
And that's what he's proud to be.
He'll gladly give up his life
To keep his pride and liberty.

He stumbled and he fell,
Yet rose again to climb the hill.
The courage within his heart
Is more abundant than the blood he'll spill.

He lets loose one last rebel yell
And falls upon his hated foe.
Another ball takes his life,
But he won't go alone to that home of the soul.

Just like his rebel spirit
That rises to live again on high,
The South will rise once more
Because it's spirit will never die.

Ronald E. Shultz

Isaiah 55:8-9

God showed me these words
In Isaiah one day, in chapter 55:8-9
How his plans are not what I would work out
'Cause his ways are higher than mine

He said he would teach me
How to write all these poems
To tell of his love, and to share
All the things he has done, of his miracles and love
And truly how much he does care

Ruth Knudson

Poverty

Poverty is hunger; poverty is sorrow.
Poverty is knowing that you have never had
Enough of anything.

Poverty is crying; poverty is despairing.
Poverty is knowing there's nothing to wear.
Cannot go places.

Poverty is freezing; poverty is dying.
Poverty is knowing you can't get warm inside.
There is no fuel.

Helen M. Martin

The Window

I stand here
In my cold, dreary room
Looking out the window as the lights play.

Born dark
I am not welcome there
So I watch as the come and go till the dawn of day.

Sitting here
Myself to blame
Why wasn't I born of life's preference?

No answer
But one day
I will crack the unbreakable glass of ignorance.

Raquel Ellis

Shredding the Moon

I shredded the moon on my cornflakes today
in my pillbox hat and velvet navy shoes.
It tasted so delightful.
I ate it up without analysis,
just sugar and milk.

I want it back! I want it back!
It's much too black, I want it back!

Too late! Too late!
You fool, you ate the moon
And now it's gone forever.

I shredded the moon on my cornflakes today,
and now, I dare not look at the sun.

C. G. Shevchenko

Breaking Free

I remember my child
In my womb, soft and mild.
She was a part of me.
I was her and her personality.
Soon she came out and was separate from my body,
But she was still me.
She grew fast, full of thoughts of her own.
At that time I had no clue as to what was ahead, if only I had know.
She began to want freedom and demand her rights.
Soon emerged a relationship between us of constant fights.
Rebellion was in her blood, she wanted change.
She was growing apart from me, that fact was plain.
She got allies in her friends, willing to hide her away.
When we had awful fights, communication between us would cease for
days.
Now my child considers herself motherless, completely free
And I have lost power; there is no longer an extended part of me
Don't you feel sorry for me,
The Mother Country?

Liesl English

Live Life

You hold the knowledge,
one that no one but you posses.
Teach it, share it, but dear God
don't let it go to waste.

Life withholds a message, it is your duty
to find this message and use it as a key,
to unlock the magic of the world.
The key to happiness lies within your heart.
Learn to love and unlock this happiness.
Laughter is the key to all humanity.
Reach for the stars. Do what you can,
live life to the fullest, never let it end.

Danielle Cardillo

Where I Found You

I found you in the gentle morning breeze,
in quiet, easy places,
in placid, turquoise seas.
I found you in a thousand starlit nights,
in happy glowing faces,
and in a ray of moonlight.
I found you in the strength of autumn trees,
In a little pool of rain
and in happy memories.
I found you in the snow's purest white,
in a careful, well placed smile
and in the spring's newborn leaves.
I found a little of you in all of these,
and I found a piece of you in me.

Patrick Potter

Grass Circus

This morning I saw a stout robin land
In search I thought of a wiggly breakfast
Not twenty feet from where I sat smoking,
Gazing at what some thought an unkempt lawn;
But somewhere Red saw a circus bandstand
Whose silent fanfare I could not hear blast;
Then, foregoing plans of wormy poking,
Nodded to my porch bleachers and moved on,

Bicycle pedaling across the grass
Till, perched on the dirt wall at the drive's edge,
Wings umbrellaed, he bore his bike across
And, disdaining applause from nearby hedge,
Whirred his stems on ground again, then soared away
To the high wire act of a boastful jay.

W. Russel Gray

Will There Ever Be Peace

In everyone's heart there lies a place of eternal love and peace.
In some, this place is larger and more visible to those around them.
In others it is hidden by repressed anger longing to be released.
In our society, all people long to be free of all the troubles of
the world around them. Each and every individual wants to be
respected as an equal and everyone wants to be loved and accepted by
one another.
There is a place in all our hearts that wants to reach out and
help. We each want to be part of a peaceful civilization. We all
long to be united in friendship with one another.
Each of us needs to reach inside ourselves and find the strength
to help one another. For without each other's help, there will be no
peace and we will be forever at war with ourselves and others. Unless
we learn to overcome our own inner wars, we will never find peace for
the entire human race.
That only leaves two questions to be answered. Are we willing
to lend a helping hand and if so, will there ever be peace?

Maria Bush

Jambalya Jam

A soft, warm veil ripples my face
pressed in layers of sun brilliance.
Spilling over neck, shoulders, chest
   legs, toes.

Stirring embers flame my inners,
Warmth brings rest to a tired, aching flesh.

Sweet, sensuous sleep
washes the turbulence of days spent.
Songs of lavender blue contentedness.
Ah soul! All is well.

Barbara T. Davis

Beyond the Same

We were there in Bangladesh, when wind and water came
in swirling bands of whirling death, eliminating land and breath,
consumed in tempest destiny,
and nothing was the same.

We were there at Wounded Knee, like ghost shirts of the plain,
where eagles fly and bison roam, in blood-soaked memories of home,
a page torn out of history,
and nothing was the same.

In White Star splendor we were there, when waves could not restrain,
then frozen death came in the night, invincibility took flight,
Titanic conquered by the sea,
And nothing was the same.

In vain we look within ourselves, and ask "who is to blame?"
when nature wields its sovereign hand, and man kills man to take
   command
and death awaits both you and me,
and everything's the same.

In faith we look beyond ourselves, for healing from the pain
for hope restored, and heart reborn, with visioned eyes above the storm
the face of God we see,
and nothing is the same.

Richard A. Goldsmith

How Does God Speak To You?

God speaks to me through the birds that sing,
In the flash of color on a butterfly's wing;
In the rustling leaves, as a summer's breeze
Riffles the branches of the trees.

He speaks to me in rolling hills,
In majestic mountains with fast flowing rills
Cutting their way through ravines so steep,
Dropping into the valleys that lie at their feet.

God speaks to me through a friendly face,
Through a helping hand when I fall from grace;
An encouraging word from a stranger's lips
When I'm far from home, and my world's amiss.

He speaks to me through those I love,
For surely such bonds are from above.
In so many ways I hear God speak,
In the splendor of nature and in human speech;
But to me, the most precious way of all
Is the still, small voice within my soul.

Margaret Plenk

So October

When the leaves fell from the trees
In the gentle autumn breeze
Natures beauty surely shone
While silent hearts sit all alone
Bright sunlight glaring through the trees
An array of colors sure to please
A ray of hope in a favorite season
To question a thought that yet has
to reason
So is the gleam in an eye of a past
Brings tears in the present of that
which is vast
The winds silent whispers of stories
unclear
Collective clouds show visions
imagined as there
A falling of truths found on ones own
To emancipate love engraved in a stone
An ending of something that never began
A moment of triumph in the palm of whose hand.

Kristen M. Arcovio

Sleep Little Cloud

The little cloud that fell asleep
In the purple hues of night,
Drifted into the shadowy valley
As the sun slowly dimmed its light.

The little cloud, asleep so tight,
Had been having quite a day,
So he floated to the valley for a rest
As he glided along his way.

A very short rest was all he'd planned,
He seemed to have so far to go,
But the valley was quiet, safe and warm,
And looked inviting in the evening's soft glow.

So the little cloud settled comfortably
Onto the hills and tops of trees
And with a contented sigh,
Was rocked to sleep by the soft evening breeze.

Sleep little cloud, sleep so soft,
As the sunlight fades away,
Tomorrow as the sun's rays brighten again,
You'll be riding the breeze of a brand new day.

Wanda Sigler

Young Fisherman

If you caught your catch
In the red seas of want and take
Might the winds blow in your favor?
Stronger and brighter,
The sun shines down on your kill.
Face like snow, white and weak,
Hands bound at the base of your boat,
The mind slows and movement ceases,
The sea is ever so close.
Thrown back, still different, still dead,
Staggers away,
Thrown back, done with, no longer needed.
Might the winds blow in your favor?
Young fisherman,
The winds blow east and you sail west.

Keith Robert Filaski

Untitled

I caught the cold blue rhythm
In the slick black shiny street
Where broken glass there glitters
Then in trampled under feet
That walk on shattered spirits' dreams
And evaporate mid-air
Midst smiles of fleeting so-called friends,
Pretending that they care...
I hummed it and then sang it
As I swung into the gravel
With a longing on the inside
That began there to unravel
And tear my hopes to pieces
With the notes of this same song
In the black and hungry evening
Surely didn't take too long...
And I was void of visions
And empty too, of pain
Luckily for me, there came the rhythm of the rain.

C. S. Base

Mama's Rocking Chair

Mama's rocking chair sits in my parlor
In times of stress, often proved a harbor
When my mind went floundering like a ship at sea
In vain I searched for a place to flee
I turned around, and then I stared
There sat my mama's rocking chair

I raced to it fleetingly just like a deer
Hoping that suddenly it would not disappear
I sat down and rocked and soon fell asleep
Safe and secure from that cold briny deep

The memories that old chair doth hold
Are worth more to me than diamonds and gold
Sweet memories of scenes that can ne'er be forgotten
Sweet songs that were sung, stories told at twilight
Then the Bible was read before we said goodnight.

Marjorie C. Peyton

Raindrops Fall Slow To Bring Fell Earth To Bear

Raindrops fall slow to bring fell earth to bear,
in tribute, airy wisps of light weave through;
creating me as surely from midair.

E'er heaven be rent from those receding fair,
belie sweet fruit, to scourge the sun anew;
raindrops fall flow to bring fell earth to bear.

So man to desert God must build with care,
archaic two score thunder flash ensue;
creating me as surely from midair.

Lone dove, to home, with sunlight wing you there,
no desert sand to blight his drowning crew;
raindrops fall slow to bring fell earth to bear.

One olive branch should guide your bearing where
new sunlight beamed, would guide the flame anew;
creating me as surely from midair.

So loved, the legend wings to here from there;
both Son, and wind and fire decry the view.
Raindrops fall slow to bring fell earth to bear,
creating me as surely from midair.

Susan Blake-Caldwell

Late Winter Storm

Late winter wind comes howling 'cross the plain.
    In vicious gusts it sweeps the arid land.
Dust laden air, that choking man and beast,
    Leaves everywhere a film of sifted sand.

Like London fog it hovers 'round for days,
    Obstructing view for countless miles around.
Then slowly filtering to the famished earth,
    Its blanket brown, it spreads without a sound.

How blest to breath the clean, fresh air once more!
    Then in the night, the sound of falling rain
Comes softly, not to wake when sleeping world.
    Ah, welcome to the ear, the sweet refrain.

When softly comes the breaking of the day,
    The world appears in sparkling ermine dressed.
In fluffy muffs it's wrapped in pure delight
    As to the thirsty ground its blanket pressed.

How beautiful the sight of new laid snow!
    What welcome moisture to the barren earth!
And man with grateful heart, bows down in prayer,
    To Him who plans for every Spring, New Birth!

Mary I. Widney

Broken

The machine is broken - it grinds the bones of
innocence to dust.
    The machine is broken - it fuels its flames with greed and lust.
    The machine is broken - heed the call to run away.
    The machine is broken and the record will no longer play.
    What shall we do with this machine? We built it with
our blood.
    Can we throw it by the wayside-wash it away amidst a flood?
    Will we allow it to devour us-our minds no longer strong?
    The machine is broken - hear me crying - it will blow before to
long.
    It's claimed the freedom we all craved - we are bound by many
chains.
    The locks are heavy and enormous-our body ridden with
it's pains.
    It exists because we formed it - many years we labored hard.
    The machine is broken - you must forsake it - and cleave only
to our God.

Kim Starlene Graham

Lord Let Them Play

They killed another child today,
Innocent and trusting, just out to play.

Mean, not caring, violence and crime,
From strangers and playmates and parents —
No time.

Children not given a chance to grow,
Children deprived of their right to know.

In this world of non-conformity,
Victims of moral senility.

Guns and blades and left alone,
No time to nurture, provide a home.

What will it take for all to see?
Without our children, we cannot be.

They are the light, God gives them grace,
To make this earth a better place.

How can they learn, when they do not live,
To develop the talents, their gifts to give.

They killed another child today,
Innocent and trusting,
Lord let them play.

L. Lowry

Self-Deception

Tsistu tricked me
Into believing
That your eyes
Only listened to
My smiles
That your heart
Only tasted
My tears
That your soul
Only danced to
My lifebeat.

*Tsistu is the Cherokee trickster figure who revels in causing
chaos and disrupting assumptions.*

Kimberly D. Taylor

Mommy O' Mine

I'm twenty two years old now. To the woman who brought me
into this world, I will forever remain a baby.
Sometimes, I call her mom. When I'm mad, I call her mother.
When I feel affectionate, I call her mommy.
Some might say that at my age, it is too immature, too
childish to still be calling her mommy.
But to be honest, all I've ever known her as is ma-ma, Mom, Mommy
to me, she's just Mommy o' mine.
You see, I was two when my grandma died. So I don't remember her
nor will I ever know her.
That will always be one of my heart aches because- to hear my
Mom talk about her Mommy
makes me feel cheated for I will never know this incredible
woman named Grandma o'mine
Whom, to this very day, Mom still calls mommy
This shining, warm, soul my mother smiles when she speaks of, I
will never meet.
But, I have a part of her for keeps in me, for her blood is my
blood-and thanks to the woman my Mommy still calls Mommy-
I have my sweet mommy o' mine

Nicki Hardwick-White

The Fire

In your soul
is a burning fire
to fulfill an unquenched desire,
Hold my hand and walk with me tonight,
you'll not get lost for I'll show you a light,
Don't be afraid for you're on your way,
Happiness is the dawn of a new day,
Let's walk on clouds and leave the world behind,
Pleasure and joy are ours to find,
Let's do cartwheels and dance on air,
There is so much that we can share,
When you wake, you'll forget I was here,
you'll smile and laugh without any fear,
Sometimes I wonder when I'll know who you are,
I'll close my eyes and wish on a star,
not it's in my soul
a burning fire.

Lisa Durfee

"Try Again!"

"If I had my life to live over again!"
Is an idle wish, I know.
For we pass through this world but once, and then
We reap whatever we sow.

Opportunity knocks of often in youth,
But we waste those precious years.
We look back and wish we had known the truth,
And we weep such bitter tears.

Oh, why do we spend our time on dreams
While reality passes us by?
The future is endless in youth, it seems,
And we give up before we try.

Then one day we realize that "what might have been"
Has passed us by, somehow.
But it's never too late to start over again,
For we still have the blessed Now.

So square your shoulders, and hold your head high!
Try a new road today, my friend.
There's a great shining light up ahead if you'll try,
For God patiently waits at the bend!

Sue Dick

Saying Our Goodbye

The pain in our hearts today,
Is for a friend who has gone away.
He shared with us how to live and believe,
He lived his beliefs for all to see.
He was to all a friend indeed,
Always there for us, when we were in need.
Remember him with love as he gave to all,
He has now answered God's heavenly call.
A better place he has gone away to stay,
A place where no pain will come his way.
So in our hearts let us remember him,
Even if our eyes are full of tears to the brim.
Our hearts are sad,
But for him we should be glad.
So let us mourn and shed a tear,
Saying goodbye to someone so dear.
On with our lives he would want us to go,
With love and kindness always to show.

Ruth A. Winter

Daddy

What does Daddy mean?
Is it a man who is there when his
    daughter is growing up?
    To show her how things are done?
Is it a man who shows no prejudice?
    Gives everyone equal love?
    And teaches his daughter to love everyone?
Is it a man who is there for his wife?
    Gives her the love and support she deserves?
    And is there to hold her up when she falls?
Daddy is all these things and more!
    But most of all Daddy is the person,
    his little girl calls him when he tuck's her in at night!

Mark E. Davis

Hurt

When I come home, I don't know what to think
Is it going to be good, bad or just in between
If you were a person who would come home to my life
You'd get hurt from the bruises, the fighting and lies,
But your not me and you don't know how I feel
I feel like I'm alone and nobody cares
I wish I could tell you what your doing to me
But I'm really not sure what your reaction would be
Would you hurt me with your words or your fist instead
I wish I could hit you hard or maybe hit you dead
I wish I could love you as a mom, like other kids do
But that seems impossible when you can never be true
What I'm really asking is a plea for help
Because my pain is to hard and it will never stall out

Sondra Elham Barker

Alone

I stand alone in a room with no light
I walk forward and see nothing
There is no sound except for the beat of my heart
No one stands by me
I am alone
I look forward and see nothing
This room has no length or width
There is no place to go
I am lost in this darkness
My eyes are open, yet I see nothing
There are no doors before me
I see a small glimmer of light ahead
But I can't seem to find it

Phillip C. Voneichen

Follow the Leader

What does leadership mean to you?
Is it something that comes from the heart?
Does it take much nerve to step forward?
Should a leader be assertive and smart?

We all are divided into two groups,
The leaders and the followers, you see.
It takes both for any kind of success,
Which one do you choose to be?

The followers wait for instructions,
And then expedite them with ease.
It's their nature to be soldiers,
To remain behind the scenes.

Leaders plot the plans of action,
Making decisions both large and small.
We pray that they have divine guidance
In their schemes that affect us all.

Leadership is a valiant art,
To be treated respectfully,
But without those diligent followers,
Where would the leaders be?

Kathy Nesiba

The Real Me

Singing and dancing and the music plays on.
Is it the real me that's having fun?
Deep down inside I'm lonely and sad;
I've nowhere to run, on my own I can't stand.
It's hard to hold on when there's nothing to grab.
I reach out my hand, but there's nothing to have.
Loneliness lurks in the shadows of my heart,
And the sadness threatens to never depart.
The hurt and the pain continue to build.
There's a numbness inside that I continually feel.
The people I love hurt me the most,
Over and over the daggers are thrust.
The pain rips my soul and cuts like a knife.
What's left is a hole that drains all the life.
The tears start to fall, a continual stream.
I gaze at the wall, left only to dream.
The darkness surrounds me, it closes me in;
My fears have all found me, they won't let me win.
As my eyes close with sleep my journey will start,
And my pain for a time will slowly depart.

Vicki Zamorsky

Priceless

Fear of the future for what it holds
Is lack of faith from what I'm told
I must look to God for courage and strength
If I wish to accelerate and go the full length

With God at my side, nothing's to fear
Feeling invincible when the almighty appears
Surrendering my ways, I seek out His will
Expanding horizons for my life to fill

I look for the truth, in the words He's spoken
As a treasure I guard this priceless token
The token of life is priceless indeed
Looking no further I've found what I need

The choice is now mine to follow His route
For living is what life is really about
Looking no further I plant this seed
The seed of life which sprouts a new me

Michael Grennan

The Shortcut

Walking in the dark across an open field
Is nothing more than a shortcut home
Darkness and unseen things, confidence is your shield
It can't be helped you wonder, are you really alone?
You pick up the pace
Sweat starts to pour
The heart begins to race
Your imagination makes you see more and more
Eyes open wide, feet moving fast
But somehow you miss that open hole
Your head hurts as it hits the ground last
Boy do you wish you could kill that mole
That shortcut you thank so very much
Because of it, you're now on a crutch

Mark Morris

Life

I wonder of life
Is really the same
For the poor, the middle class, and the people with fame

The poor have there problems with money so there shy
and the middle class have there problems with just getting by
the people with fame are always to blame
but it seems like they always die

Although, I really don't know what it's like to be poor
thank GOD up above I'm in the middle class door
and I really don't know what it's like to have fame
But if I had my choice
I'd probably pick the same

Marc Bellman

The Empty Chair

Is there anybody listening?
Is there anyone who knows what's going on?
Every day I sit alone.
All I can do is think.
I am empty; surrounded by space.
The noises manipulate my mind,
sweet melodies put it to rest.
I am alone.
Ignored by love.
Ignored by simple thoughts.
Ignored by logic.
You can know me.
I can be understood.
Listen to me! Talk to me!
You can think about me, I think about you.
I am tangible too.
But every day I sit alone.
I feel empty.
I sit... I sit... I sit...
I sit alone.

Meredith Grasso

The Parting

The old woman said, "I am ready to leave.
I really must go now 'tis my time.
I will miss your all sorely,
But know always that I will be near."

With that she departed,
A little of her leaving each day,
Till one day, she was no more,
But for her scent, which lingered in the house
And her memory, which lingers in our hearts.

Maggie McFadden

Sea Gulls

The song of the gulls, when you live by the sea
  Is truly nature's symphony.
Great white wings spread in God's free flight,
  they soar and chant to man's delight.
The rhythm coincides with the roll of the wave
Never losing their agility and always brave.
Graceful and charming they fly in with the tide,
  and go out on the waves, just for the ride.
God's feathered creatures which form this band
Can be observed from a quiet walk in the sand.
Thank you Lord for letting me stroll by the sea,
  No greater sight will ever be.
Just as it were in the days of Yore and it will be
  forevermore.

Mary Helen Hall

The World Is Changing

The world is changing, and I'm afraid of the way that people feel...
It doesn't bother them to know that, they can kill...

There is not much of caring left...Fear and hate have took their toll...
The world is changing, now its hearts beat cold...

I love the world I grew up in, but my kids don't stand a chance...
What kind of world have they got, it will be gone in a glance...

The world is changing, and love is fading fast...Nothing left to do,
  but Pray and Hope, till the last...

Martha Sue McPherson

Hate is a Deadly Disease that We Can Cure

It is wrong to hate our white brothers for the atrocities of slavery.
It happened a long time ago — we cannot turn back the hands of time.
But we can just choose to be color blind.
Dr. Martin Luther King believed a man should be
judged by his content of character not race, color, or creed.
We can stop the hate, no longer to let it breed
for racism in our nation is the deadliest disease.
So much is decided in our world
based on whether your hair is straight, kinky or curled.
Respect me for what/who I am not my ancestry.
We must stop somehow this deadly catastrophe
of the battle of the races.
Place a smile in our hearts and on our faces.
For when we are wounded we all bleed red.
If we don't stop the human race will soon be dead.
We can start with respect for each other
don't let race or ethnicity define your brother.
To just be friends is a way we can start
we can later share desires of the heart.
If still unsatisfied, again we can part
we can work together — in time we can play too
we can decide individually what we would like to do.
We can move into the next century hand in hand
equally sharing resources and responsibility for our land.

J. Harris Jefferson

My Little Girl

I know a little girl with eyes of brown,
Pretty golden curls and a funny little frown.
You ought to hear her talk and see her turned-up nose
Her sexy little walk and crooked little toes.
She makes such silly faces and has the cutest smile
Whenever we go places she's always dressed in style.
I know she loves to sing and play a little rough,
She's just a little thing and I guess that makes it tough.
Soon she will be four and always in a whirl,
I could never ask for more, 'cause that's my little girl.

Barbara J. Stevenson

My Heritage

It is like something that comes person to person.
It is like a shooting star.
It can shoot place to place.
I think it is like a meteor.
I think it's like meteor man.
How something came out of nowhere and hit him right there at his house
Then, he became very powerful.
Something handed down from one's ancestors or the past,
as certain skills or right, or a way of life.
It is like something handed down from my grandmother, like a quilt.
It is like something handed down from my grandfather, like his love.
My mom and dad put a roof over my head.
My grandmother taught me not to have a messy room.
My grandfather taught me how to cook.
When I was little my dad taught me how to wash dishes.
My mom taught me how to tie my shoes.
This is my heritage.

Leslie Bacon

Miracle

A miracle is something there is no preparation for
It is the impossible known to man
But far beyond the most magnificent imagination
It happens o'er and o'er across our world wide land
It can happen suddenly like the blinking of an eye
That man alone could not ever accomplish
Not even in the wildest of dreams
There's no way to even try
Until it happens to you
Can you then fully understand
We are part of the most miraculous miracle
There will ever be
Until the end of time
Forever and a day
In any form or any way
In our heart and soul
We hold the key

Wanda Owen Meier

The Highway Of Dreams

The highway of dreams is a well worn road
It is traveled by the restless, the young and the old
A place where human dreams reside
As strong as the wind, as sure as the tide
Dreams of honor, glory and fame abound
Lost dreams and broken dreams can also be found
The highway of dreams never ends
When an old dream dies a new one begins
For without dreams there would only be sorrow
There is always the dream of a better tomorrow
As long as there exists someone with a vision to be seen
They will travel down this highway of dreams
For dreams are of hopes and goals and strife
The highway of dreams are the dreams of life

Marilyn Church

The Meaning of Christmas

The meaning of Christmas isn't money and toys,
It's Christ being born giving out his special joys,
It's about being with family and sharing love,
The true Christmas meaning comes from above,
Above like I said is beloved Jesus,
Sharing and caring every step of the way,
Until we realize how good he's been to us on Christmas Day,
And when that day comes he's smiling and gleaming,
Because he knows we know Christmas's true meaning.

Lori A. Calmbacher

I'm Sorry

I'm writing this to let you know
It isn't your fault, I had to go.
I don't want you to take the blame,
My reasons didn't have your name.
But still I wish that you'd been there
When what I needed was someone to care.
But you weren't home and that's okay,
You just had somewhere else to be that day.
Don't worry about me, I understand.
I've been gone when you needed a hand.
Please keep me there in your memory,
And when you need me there I'll be.
I have regret, don't think me cold.
I love you more than I ever told.
I just wish you'd been there when I raised the gun.
You might have saved your only son.
That's the end, there's no more to tell,
For now my soul burns bright in Hell.
Please forgive me for the way I died;
I never thought I'd succeed with suicide.

Samantha Hill

Untitled

Following a trail through a petrified wood
It led to a river called Styx where I stood
I there met an angel who gave me a sword
Scuffed my sneakers on the ladder to heaven
  On my way to challenge the Lord
Snuck past the gates while St. Peter was sleeping
Passed several children wrapped in clouds, all weeping
Tamed a dragon to ride, its fire my armor
Took a rainbow for a shield, its colors my guarder
And when God almighty and I finally met face to face
He challenged me to trivial Pursuit...
  I came in second place

Matthew E. Kalland

Wind

Wind...
  it makes a lonely sound at 5 a.m.
I wonder if wind thinks?
Does if know that it whistles and moans?

Wind...
  it makes a happy sound on a late March day,
For it blows easy and gentle and keeps the children's
  kites dancing in the sky.

But November's wind at 5 a.m. is icy and it's cold,
  without the promise of a hot cup of coffee
  and a Danish with melted butter.

Late March's wind flutters the curtains and
  gently sways the trees.
November's wind creeps howling through the window
  pane and under the door to chill us even
  when we're warm.

But November's howling gale holds a promise for us,
The promise of March's gentle breeze.

R. Guy Slater

Helios

The rotund, luminous ball
ascended his perch and smiled on all.
Then the tulip's patron saint,
the jovial, glowing blob of paint
left us with our squinting eyes
to go and kindle other skies.

Kathryn L. Ackley

Rain

I can't stand my life during the rain
It makes me more aware of my loneliness and pain.
Depression mounts, and drops start to fall like tears
Suddenly I'm vulnerable, and so full of fears.

The thunder crashes, the wind blows,
And my blue sky turns to gray.
Leaving me to wonder where goes the light of day.
Will I see tomorrow? Will it ever come?
Happiness is only a memory, now I'm down and glum.

My love is gone and dreams are shattered
Where did they all go?
Will I find some peace of mind? I hope I'll someday know.
I'm all alone, no end in sight, with nothing else to gain.
Oh please God tell me, why does it have to rain?

Ruben

Never Want To Leave

You listen so intently to my heart
It says so many things
Going slow is the way to start
Your beauty has so many meanings

With your gorgeous face on my beating chest
You hear it, I know you hear it
That's my heart trying to pass the loving test
It cannot give up, it will not quit

Your face so smooth and creamy white
Hands so soft, yet so strong
Your elegance is what I need at night
Don't complicate the love, if nothing is wrong

Your seductive lips are so voluptuous
The lips of silk and lush
The touching of our lips so sumptuous
The affection for you will always gush

From my body into yours
Like a flying kite in the sky
The passion soars
Must I never say good-bye

Shannon Brown

The Heart of a Friend

What a beautiful treasure is the heart of a friend...
It Sees...beneath the surface
  far beyond what is visible to the eye
  where so many others have not the vision to see.

It Hears...more than the spoken words
  far beyond what is audible to the ear
  where so many others have not the capacity to hear.

It Feels...more deeply the agonies and joys
  far beyond what is merely expressed
  where so many others have not the compassion to feel.

It Understands...more thoroughly the shared thoughts and memories
  far beyond what is easily grasped
  where so many others have not the ability to understand.

It Touches...the very depths of the Soul
  far beyond what is a simple meeting of two
  where so many others have not the willingness to tread.

And the joy of being
  seen...heard...understood...and touched
  "far beyond what is"
  is the beauty of the heart of a friend.

Sharilyn S. Klahn

Change

The world today is full of selfish greed
It takes a criminal in politics to lead
People lie and people steal
They say to everyone. What's the big deal?

Give me the days when people were honest
Everyone worked and always gave it their best
There are people today who really don't care.
It's easier to lay around all day and collect welfare

People today cheat and lie to get things free
The system will not check, its easier to let it be
The welfare way is spreading fast
Working people will only be known of in the past

When will people finally open their eyes and see
The world we are making today can never be
Children today need to learn how to work and have pride
And not the easy way out by taking a free ride.

Karen Schamburg

Easter the Resurrection of Life

Easter is a wonderful word to me.
  It tells that the resurrection of life sets one free.
All nature has been asleep in its winter beds;
  Time tells all nature to raise its little head.

Parks are filled with people seeking fun.
  Children fly kites, skip, hop and run.
The smell of spring puts joy in their steps.
  Winter has gone and suddenly, in spring has crept.

Easter bells ring as many go to church,
  Seeking the word as they diligently search.
Music fills the air about the Resurrection morn;
  This soothes the ears and none are forlorn.

Birds fly in flocks seeking new homes;
  Bees search for nectar as they buzz and roam.
Little lambs bleat as they skip and hop,
  Baby calves moo as they graze and stop.

Blue-bells paint pictures on the hillsides with blue;
  All wild flowers spring up with vibrant hues.
Then what is better than a day in spring -
  A day which Easter, a resurrection brings?

Ruth Golson

Charlie Chicken

Ah!!! Caught ya! I bind its feet and chop off its head.
It thrashes around and I pick it up and bang it on the ground.
Life still squirms under its clammy skin but I dunk the bloody
corpse in the bubbling black cauldron. Stir Stir Stir. Herbs
and spice and everything nice....plus the blank stare on its
stone cold head go into the pot. Hours of simmering and wafting
of the carnage in the fresh summer air...
I lay out my towel and don my shades. It's a lovely day, isn't
it? Two hours pass. The dog waits patiently beside the fire.
It's ready. Water makes a hot muddy stream over my sandal. I
brush away the feathers and devour it whole. I go back to my
towel and lay down. Gnats stick to my sweaty oily skin. Two
hours pass. My stomach starts to turn and I reach for my Rolaids
that aren't even there. It's annoying. Oh my God it hurts!!!
A twisting and turning and knotting and clotting!
A scratching and clawing...a snapping a gnawing!
More rugged than a knife, more jagged than a saw, looking down at
my stomach there emerges a claw. Peck Peck Peck...Slurp Slurp
Slurp Old Charlie's revenge happens here on the ground, so all
you remember, what goes around comes around!

Lorna Larson

The Inner Smile

We search
It turning every stone I choose

This constant tender stream and I
Spreading my eyes, smoothing my forehead
Like a dry wrinkled sponge turned soft and moist again

Its warm healing hands
Melting my jaw, parting my teeth
Like pebbles in an icy stream just before spring

Its gentle tickle and buoyant bubbles
Lifting the dimple place in effortless flight.
Ahh...Here I am...
I am..
I...
Teresa Barton Balistreri

A Whisper of Love

This was going to be our last mothers day
It was a beautiful day: the sun shining so bright
We had a tea party with light hearted conversation
Mom's favorite music playing and she wearing her favorite
nightgown
We knew this was our last...
Oh, she was so strong, yet so fragile - oh, I'd
Cherish this day .... this beautiful day.
With tears not shown, but hidden inside - Mom
was so filled with love.
Sadly, another day came and took her away
My heart broken, my eyes filled with tears
I look up at the dark sky to find the brightest star
I say "Goodnight Mom — I love you"
I wait, I hear a faint whisper say "I love you too"
I close my heavy eyes to drift asleep to dream
Of "Mother's day our last"

Love your daughter,
Lynda Cestare

The Hero

This isn't the first time that you've been here,
It was not so long ago, only a few years.
You were a strong brave woman the first time around,
Determined that nothing would bring you down.
You struggled and fought this deadly disease,
hoping your body and mind would soon be eased.
A miracle had happened, we thought the worst had passed,
but as the saying goes, "good things never last."
And even though the news has not been the best,
your love, faith, strength, and courage have passed our test.
You never gave up, that's all anyone asked,
You've accomplished one of the most difficult tasks.
So, if the time should come that we must part,
I want you to know that you'll always be in my heart.
I love you dearly and I want you to know,
that you, my grandmother, are my hero!
Kerri L. Maletto

Untitled

The world seems so unfair
Seems that no one cares.
Murder, disease, and crime,
These are bad times.

But I know it'll get better,
Someday, somehow
By everyone pitching in
The world will survive
Crystal Wilson

Window Of Opportunity

Computers, atomic bombs, the space shuttle
It's all enough to make a body shudder.

O.J., Clinton, Saddam Hussein
Really America it's all so insane.

Exercise, brussel sprouts, mud baths, acupuncture
Have you ever known such adventure!

Nintendo, Rosanne, AT&T
Could it get any better for you and me?

Limbaugh, Sununu, Connie Chung
Let me tell you my friend I've just begun.

Football, Dancing, School studies too
Oh, so very much for a person to do!

Elvis, Sinatra, Pavarotti, Beethoven
It doesn't get any closer to heaven.

Frost, Thoreau, Edgar Allen Poe
Hark! Opportunity knocks I must go!
Marie Gillette

The Old Patch Quilt

The old patch quilt of Grandma's day has now grown obsolete —
It's been replaced by "touch controlled" electric blanket, sheet;
They're soft and light, in pastel hues, for modern day decor;
But for an album of the past, the old patch quilt means more.
The warmth it gave to many a soul was not from weight alone,
But from the tender memories that threads of love had sewn.
This teal blue, in diamond shape, was Mother's wedding dress,
This dainty print of "Teddy Bears" once held our little Bess,
And, oh this pink—I loved it so! It made me feel a queen;
I stood so tall to graduate——I wanted to be seen.
Yet heartaches, too, this quilt relates—like this small stripe of
grey,
It was the gown that Grandma wore when God took her away.
Each piece of cloth means much to me; it represents my life—-
I go to rest upon it when my days are full of strife.
I seem to hear my Grandma's voice as she knelt down to pray
And little Bess, with doll in hand, laugh loudly at her play.
My graduation speech comes back; the lump still in my throat,
Sad memories of our class song, caused by that sour note.
Yes, happy times and somber times, in grey and pink and teal,
But reminiscing on that quilt, makes life's gifts rich and real.
Wanda Lasseter Kiesel

Wind Song

Do you hear the wind?
It's calling your name.
It's calling for truth, justice.
Those who are innocent and those to be blamed.

The wind has a song that's like no other.
It calls to all people;
mothers, fathers,
sisters, brothers.

It calls for pride, strength, and peace.
It calls for a loving, tender world.
It calls for all struggles and wars to cease.
It calls for all man's cries to be heard.

This wind song touches my heart.
It touches yours too, I know.
So tune into the wind song, now and then.
Listen to it blow.
Mina Madison

The Love I Lost

He sits like clockwork with a love,
it's destined to ruin me.
Each time his eyes meet with hers,
I wish that I couldn't see.
She's all he'd want - a body to hold,
a smile to greet his tears.
I gave him all I had to give,
I've lost my love I fear.
He sees in her all I'm not,
she has style, poise, and grace.
He touches her and feels the fire,
her flame can't be replaced.
He looks at her the way, I feel,
that lovers should from the start.
He's proud to be seen with the beautiful one,
not the one who would give him her heart.
So I sit and wonder what I did wrong,
He wants beauty at every cost.
I guess we never truly had love,
but he'll be the love I lost.

Wendy McCoy

I Can Smell The Rain

I can smell the rain,
  it's falling somewhere, somewhere;

I can smell the rain,
  it's close and moist, somewhere out there.

With eyelids closed, I smell the rain,
  a delight to my nose;
an invisible curtain hanging in the air;
  I cannot see how far it goes, but,
  I can smell the coming rain.

I can feel the rain, while it clears the air.

With intimacy it will freshen away the dust and haze
  that lingers everywhere.

How cool and clear the day will become
  from the blessing of the shower to come,
as it patters in the dust to soak down deep,
  this sweet sound, as is the smell,
  offers its rejuvenating refrain;

Ah, the sweet smell and feel of the rain...
  washing and renewing that day again.

June 29, 1994 Wed 11:11
Sandra Winstead

My Ego

Farewell, you fiendish foe; you lifelong mate of mine
It's finally time for you to go; I'll get along just fine
In fact, I will be better than I've ever been before
That phony self esteem of yours is really such a bore
You caused me grief — I lost my one true love
It was such a price to pay
because you were thinking for me every minute of each day
But now I'm on to a better world to do the things I should
I look at life so differently now
Perhaps I'll do some good
So, goodbye mate; it is time for us to part
And after all I found you are really not that
smart!

Robbie Miller

The Blue Jay

I saw a little Blue Jay,
As blue as blue can be,
He peeked into my window,
He was free as he could be.

Marie J. Kowalczyk

Hard to Believe

I don't know exactly what to say
It's hard to believe you died yesterday
If only someone knew what I'm going through
It wasn't too long ago, I was in love with you
I remember when we would take the horses and ride
It's hard to believe someone so young has died
At one time I thought the world of you
But I doubt if you ever even knew
And it brings tears to my eyes
Because I didn't get to say any good-byes
Although your time was up and you had to depart
I'll always carry you around in my heart

Kelley Simmons

It's God's World!

God's world is so Great, our minds so small
It's impossible to really grasp
How this Wonderful God who made it all
Will listen when we ask!
To all our problems, big or small,
He lends a willing ear
How Great and Perfect is His love.
We Know He's always "here"
It's so sweet to rest on His promise
Of His Presence every hour
For, "Lo, I am with you Always"
Are golden words that are really ours.
These last words of Christ our Savior
Give us Faith to walk along
Because of His many teachings
We know "to whom we belong"
So never fear what comes your way
No matter what it is!!
God is there to care for you
He bought you and you are His!!!

Martha Sheppard

My World Of Imagination

I go into my world of imagination
It's like an enormous garden with beautiful flowers
With birds singing their merry tune
With bees flying from flower to flower
And in the middle of my garden is a large meadow
There I can sit on the grass and watch the unicorns grazing
There I can think and relax
In my world there are no troubles or worries.
Everyone and everything lives in peace and perfect harmony
There are no wars, there is no hate
Everyone is nice and kind
In my world everyone loves and no one hates
That's because no one knows how to hate
They only know how to love
But when I come back to reality
Everyone hates and only some love
Why can't our world be like my world of imagination
Where we don't know how to hate
But we do know how to love

Ursula Humienik

The Christmas Lamb

Chrissy had a little lamb, it followed her to school.
It's name was Missy dog. But all the kids were fooled.
Grandma had shared her like a lamb, so she could show her off.
She didn't know it was time for the Christmas play,
and they were at a loss.

The Bethlehem scene was ready, the kids all knew their lines.
But a little lamb to lay by the manger they could not find.
The kids all laughed with glee, when Missy came that day.
There she was so wooly and white.
Please! Please! can't she lay by the manger? "they cried!.
So Missy was the little lamb, she did her part just right.
She laid down by baby Jesus, oh what a sight.

Missy helped the kids put on the show, that told the story of so
   long ago.
When Jesus was born in a manger, on that Christmas morn.
We all know that a little lamb's breath kept baby Jesus warm.
So Chrissy and Missy went home that night knowing they had done
   their part. To tell all the friend's and family whether we
   are great or small. Weather we are man or beast.
That God loves and keeps us, and will cherish us for eternity.

   Lillian Reed

"In My Pocket"

In my pocket I carry a word of encouragement if
its needed,
   In my pocket I carry a little optimism in case I
feel defeated.

   In my pocket I carry some heart felt hope,
   In my pocket I carry lots of faith to help me
cope.

   In my pocket I always carry some laughter and a
smile or two,
   In my pocket I have enough to share with you!

   In my pocket I carry also good will and love,
   In my pocket....is so heavy with God's blessings
from above.

   Patty Hadley

"Brothers And Sisters"

We are brothers, we are sisters holding hands in a bond -
it's only right I don't sit and just watch you bomb.
Thousands out there living in a simple cardboard box -
reach out and give them a house solid as a rock.
It hurts my heart when I see a child with no father or mother -
reach out and let's help one another.
The old folks with little money sick and alone -
reach out to them and let your love be shown.
To live in a world where there's no hate, war or crime -
that surely would be the best of time.
The men that gave up their jobs and left their family to go fight the
war - hold them, tell them it won't happen no more.
The junkie on the street stealing to feed his habit -
be a friend and tell him there's a better life if he'll just have it.
We all have problems in our single daily lives -
but we can't stand by and watch friends take a dive.
We are brothers we are sisters holding hands in a bond -
it's only right I don't just sit and watch you bomb.

   Tricia Joly

Merry Christmas Mama - 1994

It's Christmas 1994, but it's hard for me, Lord.
It's the first without my mother, and the future holds many others.
I try to live one day at a time,
I put on a fake smile and pretend I'm just fine.
But inside, my heart is shattered, and my world is totally tattered.
Christmas should be happy and gay, for it's your son's birthday.
Lord, thank you for giving us the greatest gift of all.
Please forgive me, but I feel a sadness this fall.
I miss my mother so much.
Her warm smile, twinkling eyes and such.
I miss her hands - how gentle but strong.
I miss her voice - singing a little song.
I miss her words of wisdom and advice.
Oh! the way my mother would sacrifice.
I love my mother and I miss her too.
But Lord I know she's happy with you.
Dear Lord, please do one thing for me,
Tell my mother "Merry Christmas" - from me.
Would you tell one more thing to my mother,
Tell her one day she and I will be with each other.

   Pam Rountree

The Ultimate Warrior

Feel the everlasting sea
It's treasures of knowledge in its' touch
It knows and roars our answers loud
Intimidates and laughs but carries the truth

Smell the unforgiving sea
It has no patience for ignorant fools
It devours weakness and carries the strong
It's infinite passion forever moves on

Taste the ever limitless sea
It provokes your failings but ignites the answer
Enraged at blindness in careless men
Gives hope to women and children

Listen to the fearless sea
Never hesitant, world without end
The ultimate warrior that inspires us all
And sets us free, our eternal friend

   Lisa Dominique

Hope

Desolate Nomad
I've been waiting for you
take me to your shadows of grey
celestial bodies in agony-crying over time

Endearing entities in my head
spitting out bitterness to the dead
singing torturous songs to the air
beholds the completeness now in their souls

I was once pale you know
but I've grown dark inside
life's like a circus do you care to take a ride?
or let it rip thru you like a serpents tongue

The angels wing is dripping a tear
as she clutches us to her breast
heart beating a thunderous song
she devours us with prayer.

   Mary Monismith

My Feelings For You

My feelings for you come from my heart
I've felt something special from the very start

My feelings for you are controlling my mind
I'm not sure whether to laugh or to cry

My feelings for you are so very true
I find myself always thinking of you

My feelings for you are making me strong
They make me feel right instead of wrong

My feelings for you I can't explain
When I think of you I feel no pain

My feelings for you are like none before
As every day passes I like you more and more

My feelings for you increase by the day
I'm falling in love, what can I say

My feelings for you might come to an end
But it will not be now, and it will not be then

So I need to know your feelings for me
If I'm wasting my time or it was meant to be
Matthew Trigg

Thoughts Inspired By A Rural School Building

Uneven stones,
joined by rivers of stained grey mortar.
And those windows, ahh those windows;
small glass panels in a framework of dark oak,
so very tall.

They tilt outward,
reaching to the ceiling and the ceiling to the sky,
allowing refreshing breezes to come in
and sincere, longing glances to go out;
dreams of playgrounds.

And the smells—
ripe apples and crayons in a cardboard box,
chalk dust and hardwood floors polished and gleaming;
down the halls the smells of lunch and cobbler;
the morning wears on.

Ten minutes more;
the earsplitting bell closes the day
and opens the doors of waiting yellow buses;
green vinyl seats and paper wads and secrets,
the ride home.
Ron M. Buck

Lost In The Night

I love to sit here and stare at the stars,
Just allowing my mind and thoughts to go so far.
It's only me and the sky and the stars and the moon,
I can tell them anything; they will listen until noon.
I tell them my problems and they make it all right,
They never turn away from me, never yell and fight.
They watch over my life far from common sin,
They watch over me and I look into them.
I could lay here for hours staring at the sky,
always will be together; even if we die.
No matter what; I never want to sleep,
Because the stars won't forever keep.
It's not a big hustle or even a struggle,
It's the bright shiny stars that I want to smuggle.
Safe and sound tucked away in my pocket,
or I could carry them around my neck in a locket.
It's so beautiful here, such a wonderful sight,
It's so glorious to be lost in the night.
Loree Wardwell

Just Because

Felt at first that I knew you.
Just because I liked your style.
Sometimes I'd stop and think about us.
Day dreaming with a sigh and a smile.

Just because we sometimes argue.
It's only because I really care.
I know "sorry" sometimes means so little.
But baby, I will always be there.

I know you're wondering what I'm trying to say.
I wanted to share with you how I feel.
Just because I really need someone like you.
Full of life, love, and sex appeal.
Victor R. Rodriguez

Inspiration

One day, you stepped into my life-
just like that, out of the blue.
There you were, making things right that
I had made so wrong.
You bolted in like a streak of lightning,
bringing with you a brand new song
of Peace, of Joy, of Love and Happiness
that had long since been forgotten.

Because of you, my outlook on life has
changed. My feelings, my thoughts—
every idea rearranged on a different level.
The impact that you have grows deeper every
day, as I sit remembering the old me and my
old ways of doing things. I love you.

I can only hope that I touch someone's
life the way you have highlighted mine.
Thank you for your inspiration, your love,
for giving me something new to call my own.
Thank you for stepping into my life-
just like that, out of the blue.
Shalanna D. Bell

Untitled

Hello, I need to be clean.
Just like the earth, I have been stuffed with junk.
Junk that should not be in my system.
Only what cannot service the earth without me,
should be in my system.
I have covered many grounds, and I have many friends
who adore me, use me, and pleased with me.
But there are some, who have made it bad for those
who really appreciate the good in me, and the good I do.
Now... I call onto you earth... to put your hands together
and help clean my system. I need you.
I am the water that you swim in... the water that keeps these
beautiful fish alive. I am the ocean... the sea that you
sail your boat and ships on.
I am crying for help. Help! Help!
I have been storing your junk!
Help clean my system before we lose each other.
Help! Help! Help! I need your hands.

I NEED CLEANING,
William Edwards

Frozen Time

A moment frozen in time,
Just so I can remember.
What happened that night,
No matter how insignificant,
Was the best night of my life.

Being with you,
Talking to you over dinner,
Time seemed to stand still,
Holding your hand and kissing your lips,
I wish time would have stopped.

We stood at the door,
I needed to leave because the hour was late,
A kiss good night turned into many,
We both knew I had to go,
But each kiss made me stay even later.

Time caught up with us,
All I have left is this picture,
A picture says a thousand words,
And every painful word tears my soul,
As time rolls on.

J. Alan Derry

What Is My Mother Made Of?

Love and warmth that fills me with joy.
Kindness and understanding that leaves me secure.
Confidence and security that allows me a choice,
and a sense of encouragement to let me be who I am
    She is as beautiful as a summer sky,
    As bright as the sun does shine,
    And as wise as the Bible says,
The mothers of the world should bow to my mother to day
Because they could learn something from her in each and every way.
To you, mother, I will say I love you more and more
with each passing day.

Lisa Johnson

"My Prayer"

Heavenly Father, this is my prayer
Knowing how much you truly care,
    please take the evil out of my mind
    Allowing me to always be kind
    please take these chains surrounding me
Allowing my heart to be set free
please put goodness in evils place
Allowing me keep a smile on my face
Please take the woods that I curse
Allowing me to live for you first
Please take the ignorance from my soul
Allowing me to be completely whole
Please take this sadness completely away
Allowing me to be joyful
In your love everyday

Marie Hammonds

My Magic Yardstick

I have a magic yardstick a gift from Auntie to measure only me.

It helps me know I've done my best and ne'er to worry 'bout the rest.

Other people's yardsticks are very nice indeed; but mine is truly magic made for only me.

At night before the "Land of Nod" my magic yardstick says, "In all the world magic yardsticks come from different trees." And thus I know the same is true for me.

Marjorie Pilote

A House

Looking back I see the joy and laughter, I created.
Knowing that the house is quieter since I'm gone makes me feel missed.
Remembering the silliness and rough-housing, I can almost touch it.
I know I am loved.

Looking back I see the pain I caused.
The hurtful words which burned in the heart.
Painful memories, memories which I caused, linger.
I know I was wrong.

Looking back I see the good and bad times, I was a part of.
Holidays, normal days, rotten days, you were there to laugh, cry,
    tease, or to help.
I know who really counts.

Looking back I see a house.
A house where I used to live.
A house where my family lives.
A house where I know I can always come home to.

Ruth Miner

Till Death Do Us Part

As I lay here alone, thinking about you
knowing that tomorrow I'm doing something I said I'd never do
Feeling a little nervous now that the time is near
Wishing my Mother and Father could be here
I've led a weird kinda, life, Now I'll share it with kids and a wife
Bringing joy to three smiling faces
making love to one in all type of places
I hope we don't change in the coming years
I never want to see your tears
Just the smile on your face and the love in your heart
If we have that together, we'll never part
Believe in us and we'll conquer anything
Even the horrible sounds you make, when you try to sing
If i had to do it over again, I wouldn't change a thing
Well maybe, I'd buy you a bigger Diamond ring
So come tomorrow, I'm single no more.
All the Black and White girls I'll have to ignore
So after I say I do, I truly belong to you
Then we can start to make all our dreams come true.

Keeneth Powell

God Painted First

God's the one who painted first, used colors of all kinds, on land, and sea and in the sky.

After the rain God paints a rainbow in the sky, it's a sign of hope and a promise made to all man kind.

In the evening darkness, God put into the Heavens groups of stars that come together forming picture of humans, animals and dippers right before our eyes.

God gave us all seasons, Sun rises and Sun sets, colors of all kinds coming together, oranges, reds and blues in the sky, what a beautiful sight.
Trees and flowers of all colors, and designs, shades of green in the trees, soon turn, red, orange and even brown, then soon drop to the ground.

Snow flakes falling more then one of a kind all pure white, and glimmering in the night.

In the sea God put fish, plants, and flowers with all different colors.

God painted it and put us here to see it all, and then sent, His Son Jesus, to die for us so we could go on to a more glorious painted sight.

Margaret Matyok

An Angel

Swaying midnight when she walked,
Laughing torches when she talked.
A fallen angel, an earthly saint,
A loving spirit, a village quaint.
She loved many, she loved few,
She rose with beauty, just like you.
One day soon you will see,
That she will leave, just like me.
Love her true, love her long,
Maker her stay, make her belong.
She is strange and very new,
But wait awhile, and you'll see her through
Love's toils and love's hate.
Right or wrong, just wait.
She will go and you'll regret,
That you ever touched her, ever met.
Viola Park

The Old Lion Meets His Mother

in the Shape of a Hyena

She came closer, the great grinning female,
leader of her pack.
  He could barely manage
the pretence of a growl.
  The deadly paw
twitched useless in the dust.
  He felt her breath
tickling his whiskers, but he hardly felt
her teeth.
  It was
His mother carrying him.
  Her month
was wonderful on his nape.
  Great
and merciful is God.
Richard R. Korn

Life

Puny human, trembling in fright,
leave now before I delight
in consuming your entire essence.

No, wait mortal; before you go,
I demand that you show
your thanks by giving me presents.

For moments you stand confused,
as I stand amused,
because you can't think of something worth giving;

then almost by reflex,
you turn and let knee flex,
and beg of me to be forgiven.

With your head bowed low,
I deliver the blow
that sends you to your grave;

how worthless the man
who refuses to stand,
and would rather become a slave:

For resistance was present enough.
Richard Beirne

Translucent Shade of Dark

Flourishing to the amber of dawn
leave of absence ever prolonged
terminally ill with mnemonic device
love foreseen nothing o' nothing will suffice
stabilize the hunger which burns
watch the ocean's tides as it turns
there your patience must lay
as it washes all the pain away
sand crystallizes, elusively befriends
water rushes through sewing broken mends
birds peacefully sing their melodic hymn
we all must bear the test of time
insurmountable mountains await our strength
our overall good will measured in sarcastic length
fear the fury of a destined mans' wrath
we are all drowning in a horrific visual bath
Matt Mollicone

Domination

Chosen life by the Hierarchy
  Leaves only happiness within self
  Unhappiness in the living life
  No real love, only loneliness
  Must obey to be loved
  But one mislead step equals disappointment
Chosen marriage by the Hierarchy
  Wanted only for the body, not the mind
  Children borne unto the world
  Out of love or just duty?
  If love, the children will be life
  If duty, the children will be pained
Chosen death by the Hierarchy
  Life has passed before the very eyes
  Unimportant now, just death awaits
  The Hierarchy with another, in love
  Children moved on, to forget their past
  Alone, but happy for there is no more suffering
Melinda Yang

Oh, If I

If I be but so small a glow
let me be your light

With my eyes I'd see for you
then let me be your sight

Should my lead be wise enough
let me be your guide
for where the tides of life take you
we'd float within its stride

  If I could pave your unsure steps
  through darkened roads on unseen depths

  And through insipid pains of life
  where toiling task meet frequent strife

  Then lift your weights borne in despair
  and make then easier to bare

If I could put at ease these plights
and render meaning to your life

Hence, there would be no need to sigh
such wishful words as OH, IF I
Vernell Walden

A Whisper

I hear a whisper in my ear
as my eyes shed a tear.
My bones tingle inside as my
great-grandmother is no longer
here.

Kristofer Manulla

Sail On

Take me away on a Tall Ship
Let me see the sky meet the sea
Together as one that we may be
On this far away mystical trip

I hear the wind against the billowing sails
Far overhead, so strong, so sure
On decks that long gone heroes were
The Tall Ship is alive, it's strength still there

Though the heroes are forever gone
Might I share some memories past
Then I to shall forever rest
While the great Tall Ship sails on.

Sally A. Peto

Life's Mystery Road

Let me show you the moon with all of its light
    Let me show you the stars that glow in the night
We let them guide us from heaven above
    But not all understand the message of love
The stars try to tell us what heaven may hold
    But not to believe all we've been told
The moon tries to guide us on mystery roads
    Past forests and swamps and croaking of toads
Thou night be not day and day not be night
    We may not listen to those who are right
This road of travel is full of surprise
    Till we open our eyes and see the sunrise
We may not understand the stars and the moon
    As opposite as they are from our own high noon
Watch if we may as close as we can
    For our very existence, it's where we began
Our journey of life as we know it now
    And answers to questions, do we know how
To share life with others, not borrow or lease
    For our guide be above us, let's live in peace

Walter Kielbowicz

Love's Love

Rest yourself on the wings of a cloud
Let's begin a journey through love
Close your eyes breathe with me
Lay yourself next to me
Fly with me - slide into love
Feel my heart soft as a dove
Tell me now is this romance
Then join with me in a sensuous dance
Your love with mine our souls will rest
It's waiting for us wanting the best
I look at you I realize
A passion shines in the mirror of you eyes
My love lies still - waiting for you
Wanting to hear - I feel that way too
When I do you'll see me cry
It will be a love - that will never die
Seal my dream with a seductive kiss
I'm so happy I've gotten my wish

Michael Derscha

River of Forgetfulness

Drifting in the Lethe
letting the current take me home
to peacefulness.
There is no one here,
I am by myself,
and this is the way I like it.
There are no distractions, no objections,
as I feel the slight tingle
of the Lethe's magic.
Forget all the days of crying
over a shattered, broken heart
and a love so lost;
forget all the pain, humiliation
of the past couple of weeks,
of my life.
Drifting in the Lethe,
letting the pure waters rebaptize my soul...
the river of forgetfulness,
the Lethe.

Niki Barkley

Demonic Angel

Demonic angel, the world is but coming to an end,
Life will be over soon and guns will blaze upon the graves;
Demonic angel, fear not of the darkness,
For after you will see the light;
They say we're doing it for peace,
But there is no peace in war,
And war doesn't bring peace,
Only death; and in the darkness,
There then is a blast of bright light,
And Demonic angel, death is begged not to come;
Now from a war of peace,
Your dear sweet life is gone;
Demonic angel, life is sweet and dear,
But now, its too late to hold on.

Larry Rosen

The Four Horsemen

    The leading horse is white, he holds a sword that gleams by the
        light of the sun.
He brings war to the people, as they rally to fight.

    The second horse is red, he holds a bow tightly to his chest.
He brings strife to the people, as they try to rebuild that which was
        destroyed.

    The third horse is black, he holds a balance that measures the
        destiny of man.
He brings plague to the people, as they try to fight the infection.

    The fourth horse is green, he rides upon a horse of bones,
        carrying a scythe.
He is the pest, and brings death to the people, relieving them of the
greatest diseases that has been brought to this land, that which is
mankind.

Karl Schuchardt

Trading

Somewhere a crow flies
its wings reflecting the world with moonlight
its song piercing my ears and mind
the flapping of its wings creating a pattern
that seems to control life and death
and I have to wonder if this creature knows me
because maybe I know what its feeling
maybe one time our places weren't so defined
and we weren't so different...
maybe

Leigha Franklin

Lightning

Lightning strikes... with intense light
Lightning strikes... with intense power
Lightning strikes... setting the forest ablaze
leaving a thick shroud of smoky haze
The hungry flames lick up the trees with endless yearning
leaving behind a path that's burning
Can't stop it
can't put out the fire destroying everything
Forests, cities, nations
plants, animals, and large plantations
Dealing nature a crushing blow
putting on its arrogant show
Fire believing it has won
has just handed over it's own gun
Burning itself out with no fuel
leaving ashes as nature's tool
After the flames have ended their purge
life begins to slowly emerge
Creeping upward to the crust
to do what it must to survive

Taylor Hughes

Untitled

Walking into a prepared room
Lights of a metropolis
Candles of a quiet city
A crucifix in every shadow
A sun closed in every window
Adopted in the sacrifice
You should be here
Shining....the sign can never be there
Wasting and peeling the face from skin in peace to a sin
Name of God cut so fine
The angel of passion lost in you
Alive a flow to kill you
In a cycle over a mind
Back to innocence on knees
A sexual iron disease
Bleeding colors around the way
Hurting to follow on shallow days
A slave to the devils reality
Masturbating to a sunshine of the soul
Establishing a pain inside a dream for all

Scott L. Silver

My First Love

His heart is filled with love
Like a colorful rainbow up above
His eyes are so different and bright
Which blinds me when I see him in sight
His lips are so soft and kind
Which make me want to kiss him all of the time
He has so strong but gentle hands
Which makes me think of walking together in the sand
His hands, his lips, his eyes, his heart
Only time could tell if we will be together
Or if we will be apart
He has touched my life in so many ways
I look forward to spending each and every day
With the man that means so much to me
Having him near is all I want him to be
I wish he would look with his heart
Instead of being blinded
With what else he will see
But only time will tell if we will be
Together or if we will be apart

Renee Nicpon

The Freudian Dance

Feral humans dance unsheathed round the hell fire's light;
Like animals they howl in the deep, dark night;
Primal screams - acts of delight;
A ritualistic caper - untamed spirits unite.

Conflicted souls allured by the roaring blaze;
Insanity inspired by the luminous haze;
Personalities altered by the raging heat;
The circle unbroken - a barbarous feat.

An attempt to satisfy sadistic savage desires;
Humans jump through flames like ethereal vampires;
Selfish pleasures are consummated in the shadows
of the full moon's light;
Graceless feelings are on the rampage this turbulent night.

Like hungry wolves they rally to feast;
Humanistic desires - or satan's defeat?
Hearts untamed - souls unleashed;
The Freudian dance;
A ceremonial gathering - the "id" released.

Sherrie Stevens-Newcomb

A Symbol Of Love

I light the candle knowing it's just
like love.
The flame burns bright.
It reaches it's highest peak.
But like love the fuel soon runs out.
It seems to last long,
But it can't last forever.
The flame loses energy, and soon dies
out like a young lover's heart.
The smoke floats away like lover's lost dreams.
There are always more candles to burn
like there are more hearts to love.
So you can never lose love as long as
you carry that match inside of you.

Lindsay McWilliams

I've Been There

Listen young girls to what I'm about to say, so you might not end up like me one day. Oh, yes, I've been there with a guy I thought cared: He left me standing at the end of the road, to carry the extra load. Yes, I've been there, and it just doesn't seem fair. I was carrying a new born all alone.

For so many miles, I had to carry his child, yes I've been there as a teenage mom. I didn't mean any harm. Take some advice, and think twice: Make something of your life. I'm telling you young girls. I've been there because I really care.

Girls, get your education so you can look forward to graduation. If your man loves you like he says, He's going to be there because he really cares. Yes, I've been there, a teenage Mom, with a guy I though cared. He's gone and I'm all alone, to make it on my own. You see I have his baby and he found him a real lady. I've been there and I care, because I was a teenage Mom. Girls I've been there, don't become a teenage Mom. Take my advice, think twice. Make something of your life.

Maggie King

Dreams and Reality

Dreams
perfect, beautiful
remembering, riding, charming
fantasy, images — truth, quality
living, loving, dying
imperfect, complex
reality

Lindsey Albritton

Changing Seasons

Clouds are slowly drifting by,
Like patches covering holes in the sky.
Soon flakes of snow come floating down,
Till one no longer sees the ground.
A blanket of white everywhere,
As the wind picks up piling drifts here and there.
Birds looking for shelter fly low,
Too find a safe place out of the snow.
Soon southward they will be bound,
As the weather changes and food can't be found.
Before the weather interferes with flight,
Call of ducks and geese can be heard flying by day and night.
On their way to their winter home they go,
All the way from Alaska to Mexico.
As Spring comes again up North,
It is time for flocks of birds to go forth.
From Mexico to Alaska bound,
To raise their young at their nesting ground.
As they increase their flocks each year,
By their flight we know a new season's here.

Pete Mosbrucker

The Loner

He braved the cave alone
Like so many times before
He said "I'm going to do some digging
I should be back around four.
When he returned he was muddy and
from the expression on his face. He had
almost exhausted himself, from digging
in that place.
But he seemed well pleased, with what he
had accomplished while down in that hole
To me, with that small shovel he was
digging like a mole.

I gave him supper, he thanked me as he
left with a grin.
He said one of these days, those caves
will run end to end.
Just think how great that would be to walk along that ridge.
Other cavers who come to explore will say
It all started by a "Lone Caver."
Who made his first dig.

Marie Bowers

Love's Seasons

When love is fresh and innocent,
Like Spring, with flowers blooming,
There is nothing to compare
The excitement in the air
Of days spent wide-eyed dreaming.

When love is in full bloom
Like Summer, with petals open,
The feelings of excitement wane,
Wide-eyed dreaming becomes mundane,
Replaced by society's responsibility token.

When love is in the golden hue
Like Autumn, with brilliant color,
Wide-eyed innocence is remembered fondly
As hands are held, and new dreams are pondered,
And memories are a pastime wonder.

When love is in the final stage,
Like Winter, and snow-capped crests,
Love depends not upon the time or depth
When this closing chapter is laid to rest,
But so, to grow and accept the death.

Sue Marsh

The Moon

Around the dark skies,
Below the amazing clouds,
There!
Right there is the moon!
Shining with a cheerful gleam.
Smiling down gratefully.

Mecha Bennight

You are Precious, Perfect and Whole Like the Universe

Like the light that makes the stars twinkle.
Like the ever changing tides.
Like the seasons with its hot and cold -
bleak and sunny you are precious, perfect
and whole.

Like the Universe with its mysterious and
never ending search for your own personal
truth you are part of this mystery unfolding and
becoming part of this cosmic puzzle.
Like the planets you have a special place.
This place is precious, perfect and whole like
the Universe.

Lucianna Basile

Steel Drum Song

A small native girl on an island beach plays her steel drum.
Listeners are filled with the rhythm;
with each of her tappings, her heart pounds to the same count —

keeping time.

Little feet dance as she sings songs made of wondrous rhyme.
Little feet dance on the silvery sand, as songs are sung of
wondrous rhyme.

Sometimes her little head throbs from the sound, from the sun.
she taps out the minutes of her life for curious onlookers,
and is rewarded at times with a smile, and once, a golden coin!

The sun sets, the melodies subside. Tomorrow is another day.

We are all players on the steel drum, beating out the moments
of our days and nights. We too bring smiles and sometimes,
even a golden coin!

One could do worse in life than to be a player on the steel drum,
and dance all day on the silvery sand,
and dance all day on the silvery sand.

Nancy Gavin

I'm Only Sixteen!

It was six o'clock, a party at seven,
Little did I know, I'd soon see Heaven.
It was just a party like the one last week,
One of a gathering, from popular to meek.
Friends of all kinds gathered around,
To laugh, to drink, and to paint the town.
No one took the slightest hint,
As the party was over, and off we went.
We didn't think to designate someone to drive,
Although if we had I might still be alive.
But instead I'm dead. Dead as can be.
Because we lost control and our car struck a tree.
The E.M.T.'S came and took us away,
And I passed on the very next day.
My parents and friends cried so much,
and oh how I longed for just one last touch.
I kept hoping and praying that this was a dream,
And all for the fact, I was only sixteen.

Sherri Hanlon

William of Argile

A handsome, freckles, fair brave laird,
Lived, loved, fought, in old, argile,
For King MacBeth's banner prepared;
Tough, William of that land, could smile!
When, then bold English Lord, went North,
With three of his sons, tall, brave bold,
With a cousin, captain, Martin, Morth;
Some of these, not destined to grow old!
King MacBeth, with King Duncan's kin did fight,
The English Lord Siwerd, did them help,
Then William of Argiles fierce raid at night;
In that battle, fierce cries, then a dying yelp!
The English Lord's oldest son, there slain, fell,
Religious men, Scotch, English, lay still dead,
On bold William of Argiles form, rang, 'death's bell'
No more, he the invaders, hard to dread!

Raymond Bradburn

Stepping Out of the Darkness and Into the Light

I have been traveling on a long and winding road
Located in a vast and very dark space
Encountering many lessons dealing with negativities
And not knowing what new situation I would need to face.

There were times when I could not see any light at all
I just had to rely on my perseverance and will
And believe I would eventually see some illumination
Perhaps around the next bend or over the next hill.

I kept thinking the light was a destination
And my journey would take me to this place
I realize the light is not "somewhere" I go to
But a consciousness I can choose to embrace.

What does my road now look like?
Imagine — There are many beautiful flowers to enjoy
  and pick along the way
I daresay, when I decide to end this mode of travel
I will have collected an exceptional and wondrous bouquet.

Karen A. Meyerson

Screams

Screams...my screams are strangled within me.
Locked within my mind, is their intensity,
  and the horrors that formed them.
Where is voice to the screams I hear in my head?

I hear them, as if afar,
  Echoing from the depths of a dark chasm.
They tumble towards the surface,
Only to be strangled there.

With all my energy, I force them out.
Yet, all that emerges...is their fading echo.
As if screamed long ago,
And deep within...the chasm of my soul.

  Please, free me of my screams...
  Return my voice to me!

Virginia Henriksen

Believe

I shall believe
Believe in me
My believe is in two
Two on two
True love that last forever
Thy will believe

Lawrence Earl Dorr

Still Small Voice

The stillness within the quiet chambers deep within my
lonely heart, whispers softly its tender message, "Seek
the One who will not depart!"

The pain I feel, the hurt I've caused, the broken dreams
I've torn apart, fill my mind with endless mourning. Still
I hear that quiet whisper, "Don't be frightened of dark!"

Night has fallen all around me and all I have is yesterday.
Memories of that special season - Why'd I throw it all away?
Yet that still small voice reminds me, "Son, I love you anyway!"

The guilt and shame of all I've done, the lives I've ruined
because of sin, leave their wounds, their scars, their sorrows!
I find myself alone again.

How can I repair the damage?
Is there any hope for me?
Then I hear Him gently whisper, "I did it all at Calvary!"

G. Stuart McCain

Beyond The Silence

Look beyond the silence of the room.
Look at these children who do not speak.
At first glance you may feel pity and doom,
Be patient, look beyond the silence of the room.

You will discover a secret which they silently keep.
If you win their trust, they will provide what you seek
You will find a human being no different than you;
with emotions, thoughts, feelings; no different than you.

They may be restricted in what they can do
They are called disabled, with limited I.Q.
But look closely, beyond the silence of the room,
you will see the individual emerge and begin to bloom.

Suzanne Love

Eyes Dark And Sunken In

Covered by the green moss that in fact keeps them alive.
Look past today and wander aimlessly into tomorrow
Forgetting time, but feeling the restraints
A body sanctimoniously rises and sleeps over and over.
Awaiting the day that it will finally be awake
And discover the life it was meant to live
This mind was not meant to be feeble
It was given to him as a gift
To store knowledge, to teach others
While still learning all the white
Hands strong and warm strain to touch the sky
To embrace life and feel what he only imagines
Hair warm and dark hides the face
Chiseled carefully, that expresses the feelings,
The joys, the pains
The experience felt by us all.

Kelly Phillips

To Be Little

Little daughter.
Little sister.
Little pocket.
Being little...protected...safe...gentle...
When I am little, God has more room in me.
To be a little pocket of God's love.
To be a small reserve of God's breath.
To be a tiny spark of God's fire.
Pockets are convenient,
  not necessary,
  not noticed
    except by absence.
Lord, teach me to be a pocket...

Kay Thompson

Even Though

Love, my heart beating inside.
Love brings out all I try to hide...
my fears, my joys, my tears, my love, my hate,
and all I can ever take.

He, He changes every feeling.
He calls them out while kneeling, at my feet
to endure the swell of my love's forbidden hell.
I give it all, in Him I rest. He is who I love best.
My anger turns to sweetness, and strength
is drawn from my weakness.
The man He is changes me so. To only let Him know...

It's tragic words cannot play all the feelings I want to say.
He is my ever good all; at His feet I fall.
When life is filled with despair and disdain,
He, He kisses away the pain.
I can only write, and write for what?
For mere words expressed my feelings not.
I give my life to Him to show,
even though, the greatness of my love He will never know.

Melissa Day Stotler

Yesterday

There was a time of happiness...
Love embraced us, with a kiss...
A look, a caress...
Love of our youth...
The beginning of hope...
The dreaming of dreams...
Yesterday...
Where it all began...
To only have our yesterday...
Would it be different than today?...
For there is no tomorrow...
Our yesterdays have sped away...
There is nothing worse than wasted years of silence grown so cold...
Waiting too late to show your love...
Feelings that have gone untold...
These were my thoughts...
As I touched your still cold face...
Our yesterdays gone forever...
Forever gone ... with you...

Mary R. Jackson

Love

Love is an open heart
Love is an open door
Love can make one smile; multiply if shared

Love ties us together
Love can be contagious
Love can be habit forming
Love can bring heartache

Love can bring laughter
Love can bring joy
Love can bring peace
Love speaks all languages

Love is control of anger
Love is biting your tongue
Love is freedom, not containment
Love is life

Love is truth
Love is grace
Love feeds the hungry
Love quenches the thirsty
Love helps....

Patti P. Deese

Love Is

Love is understanding, love is caring, love is kind.
Love is opening two hearts, through the channel of two minds.
Love is taking time to know and accepting good and bad.
Love is appreciating and sharing happy times and sad.
Love is helping one another with whatever they have dreamed.
Love is being patient when things aren't all they've seemed.
Love is being two, together, but also being one.
Love is being needed, giving more when there is none.
Love is being faithful, loyal and sincere.
Love is being all of this, loving you my dear.

Phyllis Sassano

Forever, Being

The Swing
Life is so exciting!

Highs
  Lows

dragging my feet on the ground,
by my toes.

Lean back,
look up at the leaves, the sky, the birds.

Feel the rush of evening air
upon my face and on my curls.

Motion

  Motion

I can be anything I want to be.
I fly,
I am free,
and so are you, watching me.

Susan C. Buttimer

Bridges

Was it the dancing beauty of the fire
Lured me to burn the bridges that I crossed-
The golden, writhing flames that lit the pyre
Of faded dreams and older loves long lost?
Was I the fool who saw lush green valleys
Beyond the burning bridge I left behind?
Were mine the wild dreams of golden galleys-
The rich and pleasant life I hoped to find?

Now in this wide expanse of desert sands,
Here is a point that joins the roads away;
Could I go back? God! I'd give my hands
To go! But forward, will the path betray?
... Will there be a bridge I cannot burn?
Will there be a place I cannot spurn?

Norman M. MacLeod

The Paraguayan Harp

There's sea coming to shore in that music
luring and bouncing me back;
sand dances in that music
and rubs my footprints with silver and gold;
a cliff points to eternity
breaking an opening in the ribs of the wind
each drop of time,
there's an unborn flight in that music -
wings spread inside and flutter
beating the void into becoming.

Lavinia Jennings

Plumbs In An Apple Orchard

Suffusion of Yellow
luscious pushing lumpy
dimples into skin,
to fill,
to fill.
Tart and Tart and Tart,
thin skin.
Plucked, two purple plums
plumbing and Apple Orchard,
and falling into baskets,   into lips,   into widened hips,
supple skin is wrinkling,   flexing,
tingling. (Gently sloping, arching tummies.)
Sunken, tasty navels
are doing something entirely of their own accord.
All around red ripened apples are
thud-ludding and lump-bumping two the earth, Thud, thud-ludd
Lump.
No more plums will plumb   or pluck
Today,
The sun is orange like the inside.

Macky McCleary

The Wonders Of March

The snow covering the hill.
Lying so very white and still.
Look farther down, underneath.
There is a hidden beauty that does not cease.

Daffodils shedding their coat of brown.
They are so eager to get up and around.
They are bursting at the seams to take a peek.
Up comes their head through the snow to look and seek.
To the sun their heads do arch.
They know without a doubt, this is March.

Oh, the beautiful birds of all kind.
Coming to the feeder, hanging from the vine.
They hop with joy on the limbs and spread their wings.
They are saying this is March and start to sing.

There is a stirring in my soul.
At all the renewed things I behold.

You can have all of Paris with their fountains.
God grant me March in the Blue Ridge Mountains.

Virginia Tipton Hollifield

"Magic Is"

Magic is .. God creating the heaven and the earth
Magic is .. A woman giving birth
Magic is .. You evolving from a young girl into a grown woman
Magic is .. Asking you for a date, with all the courage
      I could summon
Magic is .. The very first kiss we shared
Magic is .. The knowledge that you'd always be there
Magic is .. The twinkling stars up in the sky
Magic is .. The love between you and I
Magic is .. The day you became my wife
Magic is .. Letting the whole world know, you are my life
Magic is .. Nature showing us humans, how things are really done
Magic is .. A family living for the moment and just having fun
Magic is .. A simple, powerful force called love
Magic is .. Something that always will be supplied by the man
above

Walter McMehan Jr.

An April Morning

A bright spring morning in Florida time
   Makes me write this poem of rhyme
As the sun comes up on a sky so blue
   A new day dawns and takes it's cue
      God's gift of beauty seen by few

The water's warm, the air is cool
   It makes ole mother nature drool
She drools her dew on roof and dock
   So quiet, peaceful, stop the clock
      But time moves on tick tock tick tock

It seems a shame all those in beds
   With silent dreams up in their heads
That they should miss this wondrous sight
   This sky so blue and orange bright
      Because they stayed up late last night

They miss the fish who jump so high
   They want the sunrise, they reach for the sky
Why don't I take this time each day
   Before this beauty fades away
      How should I answer, what do I say?

Larry J. Breault

Rereading Crossroad Signs

As if, in dreams, a mirror to mind's eye
Makes plain the arid pathways that we wend,
We turn about to face a different sky...
Convinced that life shall have a worthy end.
Ahead, the valley lies... a fruitful plain...
A scene wherein we'll reconcile with hope.
Our footsteps sure, we face our friends again,
Resolving to accept what comes... to cope.
   The homage that we pay to worthy cause,
   And guiding principle that's just and fair,
   Deserves a careful look and thoughtful pause...
   A recognition one's life's worth a care.
The thorough thought, to make a second choice,
Can give both faith and love a welcome voice.

R. Wayne Crews

Night Dream

Papa smoked a cigarette
Mamma smoked a pipe,
Junior, took a nip or two,
Grampa, he got tight.

Papa, coughed the whole night through,
Mamma, spit a whale or two.
Junior's head was floating high,
Grampa cursed till I thought he'd die.

Me, I sat and watched the mess,
Tried to be, and act the best.
But good gosh, it's lonely here
wish to heck I had a beer!

I took a nip, I drank some rum,
I smoked a pipe with the devil's son.
Screaming pink elephants danced 'round my head
I woke with a start and fell out of bed.

Marie E. Pethick

Life's Masquerade

Just another member of life's
Masquerade.
Playing the part in my latest
charade.

Only scratch the surface when
you look in my eyes,
To see in my heart is the real
surprise.

You think you know me,
but He only knows me
and He is not around.

Just another member of Life's
Masquerade.
It seems rain keeps falling on my parade.

No one can see through these lies.
To see in my heart is the real surprise.

Just another member of life's
Masquerade.

Tiffany Zandes

Innocence

Innocence stands
seeking experience

fragile as china
free as the sky.

Born to depend
relying on trust.

Innocence unnerved
as force is applied

Uncertain as the aged.
Hides like the deer.

Innocence once deep
deflates against age,

and cries out in anguish
as it lay down to rest.
Sometime later innocence dies.

Jane E. Fuhrer

"Without You"

Why should I be so blue.
Maybe it's because I'm here "without you."
It was always you, who wiped my tears
away.
Since you've been gone, they're streaming
everyday.
I still recall, how you used to say
Babe every cloud has a silver lining,
yours will show through someday.
"Without you" there's no merry in Christmas,
there's no happy in New Year's.
"Without you" there's a broken heart on
Valentine's day.
Mother's day is just another day.
"Without you" the 4th of July can pass me by.
On all of these days
you've shown me the love, and wonder
in each, and every one of them.
But you see, they're all nothing without you.

Veronica Boscini

Oh Mother of Mine

Oh Mother....Mother of mine,
Me a product of your nurtured vine.
I now know of your struggles and your fears,
But with head held high ... holding back the tears.

As I take hold to your vine and continue to grow,
A clear look, into my life ... it's you that I owe.
You placed in my heart, to share what I had,
See the goodness in all people, and not the bad.

Taking me into the house of God......
Giving me guidance and not sparing the rod.
How to work hard, for nothing in life is free,
That the successes in my life — lies deep within me.

Though you're no longer here, for me to see,
It's the you-in me, that sets my souls free.
I wish I had said sooner, how I feel,
God came...he offered you a better deal.

I thank you father, for a mother so dear,
Who's words.. I can often still hear.
I'll continue with mine...nurturing your vine,
In remembrance of.. oh Mother, Mother of mine...

Rachel A. Coleman

Help Me To Remember

Help me to remember that I am not chasing time but learning to
manage it better.
Help me to remember that I am not losing ground with the
difficulties but using them to move forward.
Help me to remember that the fear, pain, and the nightmares can
be turned into trust, joy and dreams of a better tomorrow.
Help me to remember that the small setbacks will lead to great
accomplishments.
Help me to remember that one smile and the sound of laughter
makes it all worthwhile.
Help me to remember to meet the children in their darkness and
step-by-step, together, walk into Your light.
Help me to remember the changes I am able to make and except
the things I cannot.
Help me to remember when it is time for them to leave, that I have
done my best with the tools You have given me, and my rewards are the
children You have let enter my life.

Kevin James Howe

In the Heart of the Matter

The snow comes in silence. It dances a silent waltz with the wind as
it catches the first light of the evening moon.
I watch this silent ballet from my place in the window.
The moon catches the snow; it does not catch me. I silently watch on.
The pure and tranquil beauty around me begins to blend into the coming
night as the world outside my window fades to black and white.

I will leave this window eventually for another.
One can never sit at a window too long, I have discovered.
Time will keep gently pushing me, even when I do not want to go.
But, for now, I will sit here quietly and enjoy the moment.
I allow myself to settle into the silence; I need to regain my center.
I feel myself coming into harmony with the night; the peace will come.
It invades my soul gently without pretense.
The return of the calm comes again as it has so often before, in that
moment when I almost lose myself to the chaos that surrounds me.

The moment is not lost; I treasure it forever in my heart.
Perhaps I will never return here; there will be other quiet windows
that will share some of their serenity with me.
I remain, and yet I go, the moment goes on.
I am the moment.

Suzanne Seider

My Hungry Years

When I was young and always broke
  I dreamed of things I'd like to buy
A house, a car, perhaps a boat
  Or maybe something in the sky.

I'd let my fancy run amok
  I'd keep my dollars in a pile
My clothes were made of finest silk
  And of the very latest style

  travelled to exotic lands
  And dined with shahs and ranas
And even had my picture snapped
  With haughty prima donnas

I sailed the ocean in my yacht
  Each mountain climbed was higher
I showered gifts upon my friends
  Their wishes my desire

I call those days "my hungry years"
  With dreams to hide the pain
Yet now with extra change to spare
  I wish them back again

Georgette Noble

Unknown Vengeance

Thinking through my often dreary past,
I find things that I cannot explain.
The unidentified anger that swells,
It drives me out right insane.

Questions of which I cannot answer,
Plague me night and day.
Dreams that are not fulfilled,
A silenced person I portray.

Grief is changed to resentment,
Standing beyond the throne,
Of which sits the creature,
That makes my spirit unknown,

To all who wonder why,
I am so full of resent.
There are no words in the world,
That can describe this kind of torment.

Ann Christine Brechbill

Once Upon a Time

Once upon a time I made a little rhyme.
I gave it to the world,
So all the world could see.
I want to give it all I can,
As a writer, plain old me.

Stories end "happily ever after,"
That's never true with life.
Life has lots of happiness,
But also pain and strife.

This world is all one family,
Each person we should cherish.
Those people, who do not respect,
In their cruel hearts they'll perish.

Life is dear, life is short.
And to all the people of any sort:
"Enjoy life, make of it what you can.
'Cause you only have one chance, not ever
again."

Erica Belitzky

Without You

It has been so bad
I have been so sad
Since you went
I have spent
My life with no-one
Waiting for someone
But it seems you were the only one

You won't let me spend
So I must mend
My heart

I will cry
And I will try
To say good-bye
Or I will die

Jessie Halberslaben

Momma

I love you Momma.
I have yet to make
a formal appearance,
but we already share
something very special.

I feel you happy,
I feel you sad,
I feel you work,
and I work to wake you.

Our worlds are intertwined
by a miracle,
and they will be
for all our lives.

When I arrive
I will meet many people,
and even call one daddy,
but now I know
only you.
I love you Momma.

Eric S. Towe

Mother, Father

Life took a turning and I am lost.
I hug tight to those that I can touch.
Reassure me; give substance to my being.
Those that knew me longest are gone.
My cloak of childhood shelter,
questioning, but all accepting love,
gone.
What was I as a child,
forerunner of what I am?
What did I lose as I
climbed through years?
What did I dream
that now I don't even long for?
Who can tell me?
Who will sing the praise of me?
Who can love my beginning?
Who can second my past?

Diane Infante

knowledge

i know of no distortion
i know of no normality
 i know i have no one
in this stagnant reality

i know of no pride
i know of no sorrow
 i know of no one to thank
for granting me a tomorrow

i know of no peace
i know of no fight
 i know not of this fool
with whom i must act polite

i know of no person
i know of no place
 i know of only myself
i know recognize his face

James Hearn

Thoughts On Centipedes

Come with me
I know the way
I can show you forgiveness
And the hell that's to pay.

I can reach through the stars
And throttle the moon,
I can juggle the months
And make the years come too soon.

Come with me
I know what to do,
I can restore what is old
And surpass what is new.

I am the scorn of surprise
I am the minutes in hours
I am the keeper of time
I am the change it empowers.

I can keep you awake
As you lie down to bed,
I am the thoughts in your mind
I am the brain in your head.

James A. Watson

"Attorney Clause"

Common presents I've dismissed,
I know what I want for Christmas;
Not a diamond or a tree,
I REALLY WANT A BANKRUPTCY!!
A Chapter Seven, if you please,
No more collection agencies;
Calling me at dinner time,
Calling me a piece of slime;
Free and clear from doctor bills,
Hospitals and other ills...
No credit cards or such involved;
This bankruptcy is not my fault!
Sick too much, so I was canned,
Sick without insurance plan;
COBRA costs were high as hell,
"Not sick enough" for Medi-Cal.
Sick and broke and so depressed -
Physicians and psychiatrists...
Which brings me back where I've begun,
My Christmas wish is only one:
Six Hundred plus the filing fee. Enough to
buy my Bankruptcy!

Diane Kurnick

When Morning Comes

I go to bed and close my eyes
    I look into the darkest skies
Sometimes the nights are calm and deep
    I wonder why I cannot sleep

I dream of pleasant things gone by
    The darkest things and wonder why
I awake and scream into the night
    When morning comes, I'll be alright

I think today I will forget
    Tonight must come and here I sit
To wonder why I cannot sleep
    My dreams and fears to myself I keep

I know that God must know my fear
    In my heart I know he's near
Tonight I'll sleep and see his light
    When morning comes, I'll be alright

This morning fills my soul with peace
    My dreams of darkness all released
I feel the calm and deep of night
    All my fears have taken flight

Betty D. Shirey

Together Forever

You looked at me
I looked at you
Just one kiss
and we both knew
we'd be together
me and you
together forever,
until you
had a change of heart
and our love grew
into something less beautiful,
now I'm just hoping
we can get back together
and start anew
and be together forever
just me and you

Angela Spranger

How Much Do I Love Thee?

How much do I love thee?
I love thee o' so much,
I carved it on a tree.
I want to tell the whole world
How much you mean to me.
I think my trusty pocket knife
Has made my message plain
And best of all it won't wash off
In case we have some rain.
My love will grow as years go by
And when we're old and gray,
We can come back and look again
At what I've carved today.

Cheryl Williams

A Daydream

As I close my eyes
I see your face
The one I love
With your sweet embrace
The sound of your voice
Flows in with the wind
The love I feel is so strong
With in

Julia Gillette

Who Am I?

I am Self!
I move in a sea,
A microbism of bone and flesh,
Heart and mind.
Cut from the umbilical cord,
I am solitary in worldly space.
Nearby are You and He and She,
Them and They.
All are passers by in
Flashes of sun mist
And moon drift.
Wrapped in your arms,
With your passionate giving
I am Self, I am self, I am self.
I live in a window of time
Less than the forests
Less than the whales of the sea
Less than seeds of bright flowers
I am mortal, I remain into dust.
I am Self!

Charlot Hentz

Where Are You, God?

Where are you, God?
I need you so bad.
I need you to help me
From feeling so sad.

Where are you, God?
I'm trying so hard
To make some changes
And get out of my yard.

Where are you, God?
As I cope with each day.
Am I making any progress?
Only you can say.

Where are you, God?
You've sent many friends.
How is it then -
That's it's lonely I've been/

Where are you, God?
Oh! You're right here with me.
Just like you've always been
Only I simply didn't see.

Janet K. Baker

Mother Earth Cries

I turn around each and every day.
I provide life and comfort in
numerous ways.
For hundreds of years I've
turned around
To see myself being abused.
I'm neglected now and being ignored.
I'm crying out to you for
help, to save me before it's too late.
I'm now just wondering, do
you care to live?
I'm dying inside and I don't
have very much left to give.
I'm asking you to consider
the terrible state I'm in,
I'm pleading with you to take care of me.
If you can't love me and think about my life,
Then why am I still turning around each
and every day?
And why do I still provide you life and
comfort in
numerous ways?

Jodie Day

Flower of Love

In the garden of emotion
I see a lovely flower,
Possessing unique beauty
Symbolic of the hour,
When cupid spies two lovers
With overflowing hearts
Waiting to be united
By cupid's magic darts.
Gazing in speechless wonder
I feel my senses stir.
At last a dart has struck me
I know what they infer.
Lift up with tender sweetness
Your petals to enfold,
And keep within your chambers
The love I wish to hold.
Entreat me not to leave thee
Flower of love to be,
And guide me to the altar
Of blessed unity.

Ferol Elizabeth Lake

America "Let Ole' Glory Fly"

When I look at this dear ole' flag,
    I see a symbol of freedom.
"America" the land of the free!
    One nation under God.
Every time I walk by this flag
    it gives me the chills,
    to know what it represents.
Now it gives me a chance to serve
    my country...
To know that my fellow man gave
    his life for you and me.
"One nation under God", I love you.
    So unfold your flag and
    never let the ole' glory
    down!
"Let ole Glory Fly!"
    America.

Charlotte Voldarski

Somebody Special

I know somebody special,
I see her every day.
She gives her love to me,
In many different ways.

She is very very special.
She even has a special day.
It comes once a year.
It is in May.

When I am ill,
She stays home,
And gives me a pill,
So I am not ill.

I still love her,
Even when she is not around.
If you want to know who this person is,
Look down,
My mother

Donna Lindsay

A Tumultuous Day

Deep inside a thunderous cloud,
I see her face
drenched in ceaseless rain
Not knowing why
on this tumultuous day
she is there, a weeping statue
I begin to weaken
in silent desperation
not knowing anything
Her arms reach out
pushing aside the clouds
I know now as the sun breaks through
filling my body with warmth
My soul on fire, I know now
why she is there.

Abdul Rashid

Her

Even though she does not exist
I see her figure now and then.
I wonder where she came from,
And I wonder where she's been.
I talk to her when she's not there
And she answers in the breeze.
Often times I see her shadow
Out beneath the trees.
Her form is light and simple.
Her hair is colored by the night.
Her eyes are sad and lonely,
Yet her looks are plainly bright.
I see her almost every morning .
She brings in every day,
And right at sunset she appears
To welcome night this way.
But as the sun sinks down behind her,
I wish again for dawn
For as the sun blinds my eyes,
She fades, and then she's gone.

Brandon McGarrah

At Last

As I look to you
I see me,
thoughtless, but carefree.
You see my faults,
When I am proud.
Like an avalanche
You cascade on me.
Smothering my hopes
Smothering my dreams.
My thoughts are not mine.
Experiments forever will fail.
As I run,
You say walk.
I fly-
And finally I am free.
Circling above,
Where I can look down,
Look down and laugh.
And hope you are proud of me.

Casey Schlaybaugh

The Naptown Scene

Every time I see this town
I see what's going down
Every time I go downtown
I think it's my town
Every time I go to work
I see enthusiasm and not jerks
When I talk to my friends
I'm by their side to the end
The reason why I'm here
Is to do good far and near
I love this down-to-earth town
A town we call "Naptown"

John R. Jones

Loneliness

This feeling has conquered my soul.
I shall not fight it anymore,
for I am inferior to this power.

Drained and weakened, my heart beats
only to pursue the lonely days
I have left in this wicked world.

I cannot find love, for my heart
has been cheated more than once.
Now a master at this game
It shall not be tricked anymore.
I will live in unhappiness
For it is the only thing I now feel.

It is what I know and
what I shall return to my gives.

A young dreamer, I am
with an unloving heart and all I have now
is the loneliness that tears at me.

How I wish just once
I could find peace and love
that is waiting for me.

Jennifer Trotter

I Will Climb This Mountain

I'm climbing this mountain
I started at the bottom
When I was half way up
You pulled me down
But I continue to climb
Because in my heart I know
I will climb this mountain

The more I climb
The more luggage you throw me
All the burdens you throw slow me down
But in my heart I know
I will climb this mountain

The trail I'm taking
Is not at all easy
The further I go up
The more burdens I must take with me
But in my heart I know
I will climb this mountain

Alicia Trusty

"Alone"

I woke up from the silence
I stepped outside
Now I see the world
Through different eyes

I wish someone could find me
In this place of fire
Where all I see is hatred
Crossed with burning desire

Why can't someone tell me
That I'm not alone
I wish someone would show me
The right way home

Lost in this place of danger
I can't find my way
I guess I'll just go on
With another day

There's a place along the way
A place that I call home
I wish someone would tell me
That I'm not alone

Jeff Perrot

Time And Age

When I was young and time so slow
I tried so hard to make it go
To speed it up and make it fly
Please make me older I would cry

My mother's shoes I'd often wear
Her skirts - to long I'd always tear
Her lipstick smeared upon my face
I tried so hard to win the race.

Of time and age and glory be -
It's flown so fast - just look at me
With hair so white and wrinkles deep
The time has gone it will not keep.

Now little one don't fret and frown
It won't be long before you've grown
And be a lady aged - like me
I promise you just wait and see.

Alice D. Stermer

Sleep

Sleep eludes me
I wake with a start
No particular dream
Rises to my thoughts

Peace pervades
The lateness of the hour
Restless stirrings of my soul
Pilfered my dreams

Aimlessly I wander
The clock ticking away
Seconds of my life

The fatigue in my bones
Not yet communicated
To my churning thoughts
I wait

I drift away
Floating
In the half-asleep, half-awake worlds
Not granted entrance
To either.

Barbara Read Voss

My Sweet Nick

I need you
I want you
I crave you

I'm dying for you
I can't bare to be apart from you
To feel you against my lips
Giving me that ecstasy I so desire

I need you
I want you
I crave you

When I don't have you
I feel my world is about to end
I can't eat, sleep or concentrate
I desire you so much

I need you
I want you
I crave you
My sweet nicotine

Ashwantie Maraj

Life's Lesson

There was such joy when I was born
I was showered with warmth and love
My parents always told me
You're a gift from God above

As I grew up, and went to school
A change entered my life
Some of the children were so cruel
Hurt stabbed me, like a knife

They pushed me and they mocked me
I said, what did I do?
Your skin is black, your hair is kinky
That's what's wrong with you

I ran home crying and afraid
I thought my heart would break
I told my mom what they had said
She said, there's no mistake

Your skin is black, you have kinky hair
You know these things are true
But you are smart and beautiful
There's nothing wrong with you.

Joan R. Smith

My Son

Not long ago at the close of day
I went to the grave where my son lay
And as I knelt there to pray
I heard a voice that seem to say
I am not there daddy, I am far away.

Then in my mind I saw a light
Shining radiant clear and bright
I saw his mother dressed in white
Weep not daddy, I am all right.

Then as I slowly turned away
To face yet another day
Again the voice that seemed to say
I am not here daddy I am far away.

Alvah W. Futrell

A Tribute to Mother

If I was just an artist
    I would paint with utmost care,
A picture of my mother,
    In her quaint old rocking chair;
In a dress of rosy gingham,
    And dainty flowers pressed
I would paint in favorite colors
    And drape it at her breast.
Then, I'd paint a ray of sunshine
    Across the sill and at her fact,
And her face would be so patient
    And her smile I'd paint so sweet.
Her hair would look like silver
    Beneath a lacy cap;
She would have her well worn Bible
    Open in her lap.
Yes, if I were just an artist
    I would paint with loving care,
A picture of my mother
    In her quaint old rocking chair.

Helen Bolton

My Life

When I was a little boy,
I would play with lots of toys.

I could run and jump real high,
Once I thought I could touch the sky.

Now I go to school most every day,
Sometimes it makes me want to run away.

I am 8 years old today,
And celebrated a great birthday.

Now I am a teenager,
And a McDonalds' manager.

I love the taste of their lemon lime,
And eat a Big Mac every time.

Now I'm going to college as you can see,
And I'm working on my P.H.D.

God has given me a family and a wife,
Now God's will is in my life.

Brandon Fowler

Empty

If a hand could go but anywhere,
I'd reach inside of me,
And pull out all the feelings,
Like doves I'd set them free.

No tears to cry,
No fears to face,
Nothing there,
But empty space.

Nothing could matter,
For nothing could care,
Nothing could hurt,
For pain isn't there.

No anger is formed,
So no remedy sought,
I can't control feelings,
That I haven't got.

But with all of the bad,
Would go all of the good,
So my feelings can stay,
In me, as they should.

Allison Cohen

If

Penny have a nice birthday,
    If I had a dollar,
I would not want it.
    If I had fifty cents,
I would not want it.
    If I had a quarter,
I would not want it.
    If I had a dime,
I would not want it.
    If I had a nickel,
I would not want it.
No if's or an's about it.
    I want my penny,
My million dollar baby,
To have a very special,
    "Happy Birthday"
    "I Love You"

Gladys E. Walker

Our Love

You will always be mine
If not in body or soul
You will always be mine in mind.

I will always be yours
If not in body or soul
I will always be yours in mind.

We will always have our love together
Even if we have found another
Even if it is stronger.

Debbie Meese

"The River's Journey"

River, river, crystal clear
If you listen closely, you can hear
Rushing water and whistling wind
Where do you end?
Where do you begin?
Flowing down into the sea
This is where the waters meet
They merge together
And become one
With the earth,
And with the sun

Amanda Denise Moshier

A Waiting Child

When the time is right
I'll put up a fight,
It may be day
It may be night,
In relief my Mama will sigh,
I'll be so happy, I know I'll cry,
I'll need a bath,
But Mama won't care,
As she presses me close,
To the breast we'll share,
In Mama's womb
I got my start,
But my permanent home
Will be her heart.

Irene J. Priester

You Reject Me

If I'm a beggar,
I'm also a
    drunk
that holds on to his addiction
and drinks
memories of you.
(Even if I have never had them).
And when I dream with things
that have never happened (or existed),
I'm also called crazy.
Insane, just because
    I still haven't
        given up hope.
Weak and blind, I am,
Since I don't want
    to open my eyes
to see...
    that the night,
        the dream (you),
            has come to an end.

Joao B. Soares

I've Had It...

I've had it,
I'm through,
with you and your lies.
You say what you think people want
to hear.
But you never say what you
mean.
You hurt me.
Yet you don't care.
You said you loved me.
And I believed you.
You said I was the best thing that
ever happened to you.
And I still believed you,
but not anymore.
So the best thing that
ever happened to me was
breaking up with you.

Adina Munger

Dream

Close your eyes, take my hand
Imagine me until it seems
That I am standing now before you
Asleep I visit in your dreams

Pick yourself up out of bed
Follow me into the light
I breathe your name and lift you up
Together we'll explore the night

Hand in hand we fly away
Into the depths of painted skies
Below our shadows disappear
In cold dark seas, where my soul lies

Return to your unconscious body
Step through your mind's open door
My spirit rests its golden wings
Until you fall asleep once more

Cling to me, ignore the dawn
When you awake I will be gone
But in your thoughts and dreams I wait
Where memories of me live on

Craig Pyter

The Dark Mask

My parents still don't know me.
Impossible without a deity, then again
omniscience could be hysteria.
From this I glimpsed an eternity
in the MAKING,
which unveiled the dark mask
of a mad, shadowy past
sending a yellow flame to
unity and reality.

Amy Quist

Beauty No Where

As an artist, I used to see the beauty
in each and everything, when we met
the world seemed new, and the beauty
I saw was focused on you.

I remember looking into your eyes,
and seeing places and things of beauty,
clearer then I've ever seen before.

In your eyes, I saw blue skies,
waterfalls, children playing, the city
lights at night, and the sun setting
on the horizon out to sea over the
softly rolling waves.

But since you left me, it seems
I can find beauty no where, for all
I see is darkness and shadows
sadness and tears.

So love me, or set my heart free,
so once again, the beauty I'll see.

John Chetuck

Glorious Springtime

As I open up my door
    in early morning hours,
God's world is smiling at me,
    through singing birds and flowers.

With spring around the corner,
    a fresh newness comes to light,
Green buds bursting on tree limbs,
    chase shadows left from the night.

The air is quiet and still,
    as birds rustle in a tree,
A day is just beginning,
    a new one for you and me.

We thank Thee Lord for this day,
    for another time to start
a new hope for better things,
    New courage for soft hearts.

Casting away the winter,
    and dormant time of rest,
Opening eyes and windows,
    to greet a day God hast blessed.

Ethel Krause Johnson

Borrowed Gifts

Lay very still my precious love,
in fields that soon will bloom.
Winds of change from high above,
will bring new life very soon.

Blue diamonds sparkle in the sky,
while darkness creeps along the lane.
Shadows come to where you lie,
to share your earthly pain.

Playful moonbeams will kiss your face,
while stardust falls to earth.
Your emerald eyes soon will gaze,
upon the miracle of our child's birth.

The hush of night will soothe the grass,
while smells of violets ride the wind.
I watch the dew caress my lass,
and pray for tears to end.

Hold my hand precious dove,
cry for joy and sorrow.
Although our gift is from above,
it is only ours to borrow.

Guy Walters

The Meaning Of Retirement

Retirement means an easy chair
In front of set - without a care.
The snacks are near - devoured at will
The figure goes - you're o'er the hill.
Retirement means a life of ease
Sleep late or rise at hour you please.
Retirement means a life of fun
And sometimes getting odd jobs done.
Unpleasant tasks are put on hold
Until the days you feel so bold.

Retirement means you must admit
That years have passed it's time to sit
And watch while others toil for you
At jobs you really should not do.
Retirement means some calm for nerves
Excitement too - with Dow Jones curves
Retirement means those trips for mail
To find full boxes - without fail.
Retirement means a splendid thing
A smile, a laugh, a song to sing.

Elizabeth J. Blake

Love's Blindness

He reaches out to hold me
in his protective embrace
whispering loving words
that fill my heart.
Though if I look hard enough
into his beautiful eyes
I see the deceit
buried deep within.
He tries to hide it
from even himself
that the love he believes in
is no longer alive.
Now looking in those eyes,
the truthful windows into his soul,
I wonder if that love
ever burned within him.
His once strong embrace,
that I ran to when afraid,
no longer holds my fears at bay
and I now see the love is gone.

Fonda Christians

My Mother

With a sad heart I write this poem,
In mem'ry of she who has gone home,
To be forever with her Lord
As promised in his Holy Word.

In God's own House she loved to be,
She worshipped Him on bended knee,
Her faith in Him she did retain,
Her life on earth was not in vain.

My mother taught me how to pray,
And read His Word from day to day,
I know she's in Heaven above
And sharing in God's Holy love.

Elva E. Howell

"The Secret"

I have a secret
  in my hand.
I placed it there
  to keep it mine.
My place has been
  to react.
I don't do that now...
  I decide my good.
My secret isn't big
  others will see
  But not know it.
I don't have the
  same value on
  other's secrets.
I have a secret
  in my hand.
Do you belong
  in my secret?
It is mine.

Dianne Skalnek

Sam Cat

The cat was the jewel
in my tapestry.
All other creatures and things
were necessary furniture.

Not so the cat.

He came and he went.
He soft padded
in and out of the warp
of my mornings, wove
himself into the woof
of my days, tied up
the skein of my evenings.

And when of a sudden he left
- it was like being shut up
with nothing soft
in a cavern of stone -
and I was alone
in the silent night,

Without the jewelling star.

Fern-Rae Abraham

Sarah's Poem

I like the sound of the
butterflies buzzing with
the bees, and I like the
sight of flowers and the
budding trees, all of this
means spring to me.

Sarah Ruby

To Eve

How many times have we, my friend,
In some past life, in some gone day,
On some path starting to ascend,
Found one another on the way?

In some new life, in some new time,
By great design and not by chance,
In some amazing circumstance
We are to meet, new hills to climb.

I know, dear friend, that you and I
Find more to life than just to die.
Love is forever. Love survives.
Love is the essence of all lives.

Genie Grimmett

Insomnia

The stars are all a shimmer
In the dark blue midnight sky,
Because I'm not too sleepy
I'm watching the night pass by.

The crickets are making music
As the leaves gently keep time,
Because I'm not too sleepy
I'm hearing the night pass by.

The east is getting brighter
The sun is beginning to rise,
Because I'm not too sleepy
I still haven't closed my eyes.

Carole French

Sounds of a Storm

In the silence of day or night,
In the flash of lightning so bright,
Be as silent as you can be,
Hear the rain coming towards me.

I hear the rain so far away,
I know it won't be able to stay,
It's on a journey and has far to go,
When it leaves, nature will grow.

With summer's heat the ground is dry,
Without the rain, the crops will die.
All the farmers pray for rain,
When it doesn't, they loose their grain.

So, when you see a cloudy day,
Listen for the sound that's far away.
Be as silent as you can be,
Hear the rain coming towards me.

Bonnie Curtis

Quantum

Particles that buzz
in the floor beneath your feet
are holding you up.

The spinning atoms
composing your flesh and blood
moor your spirit here.

We move through the world
in our orbits, colliding
with fellow beings.

And this gravity,
this *spiritus* incarnate,
fuels the human tide.

Jeffrey B. Hodes

Orchestra

The wind played the trees
And then settled, so we called
For an encore

Scott Gainer

Hiawatha's Old Age

In the lap of the Hill Country
In the path of screaming war birds
By the dry creek called Cibolo
By retirement from the Air Base
Deep into the heart of Texas
Deep down beside the Alamo
Came an old dog Face and his brood
Came a Dog Face an Old Soldier
Old and useless as a soldier
Old from fighting his country's wars.

Sat he down beside the dry creek
Sat he down to watch the kids grow
Up they grew and sought their fortunes
Up they grew and fast departed
Seeking, searching far overseas
Seeking ever the chimera
Fickle fame and fabled fortune
While he sought to forget his years
While drying his old soldier's tears.

Joseph E. Barrett

Untitled

Her eyes glance at me
  in the reflection.
Questioning,
haunting me still.
Her pain
now mirrors my own.
I turned from her
  angry and defiant;
not knowing
  that my last glance
would only become a
  memory of those eyes
Never to be seen
  on this earthly plane
again.

Donna Sherman

Red Velvet Sings the Blues

Hazed in the eyes.
In the room with the eyes
Of beholders.
In the sweat,
In the hot sway of the Juke,
The SmokeHouse seduced.

Beauty on the breath,
Sweet with sorrow.
The bass touches the lows.
Beat brushes time.
The lead picks out pain.
The harp wails why.

And the light;
Red gel
On the light,
On the spot,
On Red Velvet.

Alex Ledger

No Man's Land

Shots can be heard
In the streets
Where no one walks
No one has for years
Gangs have moved in
Children caught in the cross fire
Walking home from school
Buried in white
Caskets closed
To hide
Bullet holes
Target practice
Was good that day
David Jonas

The Fear of God

Elijah was right,
In what he said,
As he stood on the rim,
Of my present ego.

The movement of my behavior,
Sets the pattern for the matrix.
I change without changing,
My imperfections repeated endlessly.

He said that I am tested,
Tested because God cannot trust,
What His fear creates.
I am made of unstable stuff.

So I am made of fear,
An illusion of personality,
Wrapped around God's terror.
Think on it... an eternity alone.
Elizabeth Maurer

The Thistle Weaver

Weaver of thistles
In youth was I.
Mis-use of mind the thorn.
Raging at God
To heed my cry,
By my own garment torn.

Thistle weaver,
Mind the loom,
The key, unknowing, hold.
Thinking, the shuttle
Thought, the yarn
For Tapestries of Gold.
Jeanne Barnett

Lovelorn

The hollow hallways of my heart are bare.
I fear no one will ever tread there.
I need someone who can fill my soul,
With jewels and song and pots of gold.
The days are long and nights are longer,
For all I do is sit and ponder.
Why has love passed me by,
When all I do is give and try.
Everyone says to wait and it will come,
But I have to ask, when do I succumb.
Cherish Dorman Shreve

Process of Elimination

Complex minds above, charged my
inner-most thought.
Timely progression enhanced,
still all has not been caught.
Deathly experiences close, yet
none have gone so far..... as
to see the light beyond, this
well-wishing star.
Dark tunnels searched, still nothing
has been found. Someone has
returned, have I previously searched
this ground.
Unrehearsed movements, my hands
are not my own. I have lost all
control, I have passed through the
unknown.
My life as I know, does not belong
to me;
My life is as a parallel, foreshadowing
another man's destiny.
Jeff B. Newton II

Center

It is bleak
    inside
tempers flare
ugly red nostrils
as smiling mouths
spit venom
    alone
I sit plugged
into the air
listening
for the sounds
of pain
or blood
rushing through
my veins
ready to spill
I scan
copying my regression
fetal proper
10-8a insanity
Barbara Lee Jewell

Sky Quilt

I've never acknowledged the sky's burst
    into gray and white from
    clouds and rain
    and, yet combined like a painting
    that I cannot draw
    the pink and gray and dark of
        olden times
        and shame and
        fear for what we
        hold inside

I walk on wet grass
    to see the red I cannot
    paint but only write
    in words so incomplete as to say
    BUT...for this one day...
    this gray on red that
        mixes, blurs and
        disappears to rain
        a comforter of mauve,
        deep gray and light
Carol Scott

Without A Prayer

A voice without a meaning,
is a ship without a sea,
A thought with no expression,
Is a leaf which knows no tree

A soul with no desire,
Is a life without a heart,
An idea which sees no action,
Is a finish without a start,

A growth with nothing gained,
Is a bird without it's flight,
A love without a truth,
Is a wrong without a right,

A friendship with nothing shared,
Is a plant which had no seed,
A life without direction,
Is truly nothing indeed.
Jeffrey L. Mayer

My One Wish

My one wish is peace, is love,
is babies, kisses, and
lots of hugs.
My one wish is happy not
sad, I hate to make
others feel bad.
But peace and love, and
happy not sad is not
all this world needs,
It needs to unite and
learn not to fight,
and that is ...
My One Wish.
Jen Gosselin

Ode To The Poet

Poetry, a man once said
Is foolishness from out the head,
But think I now, how can this be
When I find they love in my poetry.

How now do I explain a kiss?
A shallow stream of rippling bliss,
A sigh caught fast, now blushingly
Thy gentle hands and a fierce plea.

How now do I explain my scorn?
I'm loved to leave, then feel forlorn,
I sit and fast, I hesitate
Then blind am I in warm debate.

How now do I explain success?
I prance your favor to happiness,
In sheerest black and tender peach
To find you breathing at arm's reach.

How can we say a poet's lost
When tenderness of heart is boss,
A truer mate, no need escape
For the writer ne'er leads to interrogate.
Charlotte Liebel

Untitled

Once upon a time
is how
the story starts

A pair of eyes
meets yours
and the arrows hit their mark

You want to speak
You want to touch
but he just turns away
then here comes the pain

Never again you say
but you know that's untrue
You gave your heart away
but it came back to you

How many hours
How many days
Until the hurt is done

Just pick up the pieces —
and then move on.

Janel Oshinski

His Only Sonnet

Every word in verse,
Is like a brush stroke,
That paints a picture
Seen by common folk.
With lofty ideals
As tall as a tree,
Giant Sequoia
Are nothing, you see!
Only a desire
To move hearts of men,
Makes one an artist
With paper and pen.
And one who paints God,
A poet, my friend.

Barry K. Brahe

.38 Caliber

Cradling a loaded gun
is like cradling a man

Sleek, smooth
to run
desperate hands over

Built strong and solid
as impenetrable as steel

An element of risk
constantly hovers

I'd rather cradle a gun
than a man

At least a loaded gun
won't give you aids
won't get you pregnant
won't walk away

I'd rather cradle a loaded gun
than a man

Amatullah Bahria

Untitled

My mental creation of women
Is my da-ja-vu of you.
Through the thick life giving
Wave of your hair
Down through your sleek
Peach body
Curved with its own unique dimensions
Silhouetted against the green, black,
(Back drop) of the essence of life
Which life lives in you,
To feel the very essence of life
Trickling down the spine
As if a feather
Being led up and down
The back of the memory's
Once lived, in the midst of doubt,
In the love of life,
Let not life be short lived,
But awake it with a gentle squeeze,
For doubt has no place to dwell in our
hearts.

Cal B. Colin

A Plain and a Paltry Pot of Clay

A plain and paltry pot of clay,
  Is nothing gracious to behold.
Yet be not deceived or dismayed,
  For a treasure it could hold.

Among the varied pots of clay,
  Found by the Master Potter's hand,
Are the precious few that lay,
  Humbly waiting midst the sand.

Could you be like a humble pot
  And accept the Master's care?
Can you yield to Him or not?
  Will you let Him make repairs?

It's not for the pot to say
  Just how or if it will be used.
For the potter made it the way
  He wants it, so let him choose!

Betty J. Follis

Fears

Our fears of aids,
Is our parents fear of cancer.
It makes you count your days,
It happens to an athlete or dancer.

It's a plague,
Inflicted upon us,
That we cannot stop,
With a jump, skip or hop.

We can do research,
We can take precautions,
It will still hurt,
And we'll still feel nauseous.

Becky Youmans

The Essence of the Rose

The essence of the Rose
is pure love and tenderness;
a maternal gem in repose.

Velvet petals reveal its heart
beautifully basking in the sun
curling each one apart.

God's love is entwined
in the essence of the Rose
by its unique presence of design.

Josephine C. Henson

Life Mixed with Death

Life mixed with death,
Is the greatest tale,
Either you go to heaven,
Or straight to hell.

Death is a mystery,
Life can be grand,
If you make somethin' of it
And take a stand.

Life is a broken heart,
Death is like the healer,
But when your mind breaks up,
It could be the killer.

Angela Zito

Tao

What is the way?
Is there a way?
The way is what we see
the way to see without sight
Understood without vocally
not explainable,
attainable
just do
fluid as a wall
walked around
need not take the straight path
meander down the way
no hurry
stay awhile
without thought learn
your way
to meet on the way
Could this be Tao?

James O'Meara

Grandma's Chick

Who says the loss of a chick
isn't felt by the mother hen?
The idea that her chick is forgotten
as if it had never been.

But the hen is much like a shepherd
who fusses and prods and tends.
But feels the loss immediately
the moment a lamb leaves the pen.

Grandmas, like the hen and the shepherd,
regardless of how our lives bend.
Always have in the back of our hearts
our chick can come home again

For me that love is forever.
This ache in my heart never ends.
The hope is always that somehow.
My chick will be back again.

Doris Wattenbarger

Peace

What is Peace?
It comes from within
Taking everything to Jesus
Leaving it all with Him

At times we're too busy
Our thoughts go astray
We end up just fretting
All we need, is to Pray

How hard it is to understand
The freedom we do have
In easy access to His throne
The Peace so near at hand

When times get so rough
We're at our wits' end
Just walk along with Jesus
On His road, there is no bend

Believe in His promises
Have no fear of the day
It's been taken care of
That's Peace, His way.

Esther Nixon

Silence

Silence is not golden
It is dark,
It is gray,
Like a torture chamber
Resonating cries and screams
  of helplessness.

It will never comfort me to know
That the silence within me
Must be toned down,
Must remain quiet,
Like a mouse,
Hidden safely in
  its
    hole...

Howard Marr

The Coming of the Storm

The storm is coming.
It is rushing at us,
Like an army of gallant knights.
The clouds are rolling toward us,
Like the waves of a gentle sea.
The rain is upon us,
In a torrent of rushing water.
See the lighting flash and,
Hear the thunder roar!!
Boom! Boom! Boom!
Then all is quiet,
The storm is over.

Aaron Phillips

Books

Books are, Oh, such charming friends!
I stand mine in a row.
I love to see their shiny backs
And titles all aglow.
I like to hold them in my hands
And leaf their pages through:
Some day I'll have to take the time
To read their contents, too.

Harry Bartron

Age Is Just A Word

Dedicated to Anna Mae Bergren
Age is just a word my friend,
It matters not to me.
I love to hear of things you tell,
Of things I'll never see.

The wisdom that you have inside,
Is softly, gently shared.
The strength you show from day to day,
There's nothing to compare.

You tell me of the days gone by,
Of things back in your past.
Enjoy each day, you say to me.
Memories are all that last.

You tell me that you're old and gray,
You've nothing more to give.
To me, my friend, you give much joy,
To the world in which we live.

Yes, age is just a word my friend,
It matters not to me.
You're among the rare and special few,
Someday, like you, I'll be.

Ann E. Willcut

Parents Heart Thoughts

To say how special you are,
  it need not be said
To say how smart we think you are,
  it need not be said
To say how proud of you we are,
  it need not be said
To say how missed you are,
  it need not be said
But until the time we can
  no longer think it,
  nor can we feel it,
  We will say it,
    Every day,
      Every day,
        Every day.

Carmella DeGidio

Foot Prints in the Snow

I was visited this snowy day
It occurred while I was away
If you should ask me how I know,
I see the foot prints in the snow.

Three turkeys came strolling by
I can see them in my mind's eye
Feather stitching as they go.
There are foot prints in the snow.

A pair of deer crossed the drive
Moving as though they were quite alive
Their haste doth truly show
By their foot prints in the snow.

Tracks proceed to and from my door
Someone was here, I am sure,
Trailed across my patio
Are the foot prints in the snow.

If you are careful to discern,
Really see and want to learn,
There is much that you can know
By the foot prints in the snow.

Doris E. Bitting

Innocence

When the flower comes to bloom
It often finds there is no room
Crowded by the first in line
To feel the warm rays of sunshine

It's petals withered, edges bare
Who knows in youth it was so fair
The virgin in a small clay pot
Then thrown amidst a thorny lot

The rains were comfort, watered fears
Now only drops like lonely tears
If God created things to grow
Then why's the soil so shallow?

All flowers need some space and time
A loving hand, a nursery rhyme
A smile, a touch, some confidence
To bring back long lost innocence

Barbara Robertson

Nature

Nature is a beautiful thing,
It sometimes makes you want to sing.
As the waterfall fall's,
dusk turns to dawn.
Bees buzzing by,
while butterflies fly.
There are many things in Nature,
some are even endangered.
Rain forests, whales,
and maybe some snails.
Animals are endangered because of us,
and they can't even make a fuss.

Candice Irvine

Unexcelled Choice

No trivia
  It was an anniversary
Coming oblivion
  Unexcelled choice

Costumes
  Edel and Benois
Story of exlimet chime
  Unexcelled choice

Reflection
  Dramatic and subtle
Positive image
  Unexcelled Choice

Harmony
  profile flattered
classic unique
  Unexcelled choice

Immerse
  inspired view
fun and commerce
  Unexcelled choice

Isabelle Hunter

Behold Love

Reverence the mystery.
Withhold your curious mind.
You strip not petals from the rose
Its beauty sweet to find.
Behold the mystery of love
As you the rose behold.
Let love its tender secrets
To your heart unfold.

Edna Price

The Rose

I had a rose that would not bloom
It was but a small bud
I nurtured and tended it
And then gave it to God
Sometimes it grew big thistles
That pricked at my heart's door
And brought such tears into my eyes
And still I loved it more
One day I saw the wee small bud
Peeking from 'neath a thorn
So carefully I placed it
So that the light of morn'
Would fall upon the little bud...
No let it die away
I'd had it such a short time
And I wanted it to stay!
My life's not had much pleasure
And of roses there's been few
but how I love this rambling rose...
My precious son, Andrew

Janet M. Burns

Can You Hear The Music

Can you hear the music?
It's calling to me from hone,
And those I turned my back on,
When I started in to roam.

Can you hear the music?
It's a tune we used to sing.
I'd forgotten all about it,
Upon my traveling.

Can you hear the music?
It makes the feel so sad.
I haven't seen my family,
Not since I was a lad.

Can you hear the music?
Or is it only in my head?
I wish I never saw the road from town,
And wondered where it led.

Joe Leach

The Game

Life...
It's hard
Can you survive
Be a success
Reach Nirvana
Succeed in your goals
Conquer your fears
Make many friends
Create few enemies
Have a family
Relax
Take vacations
It's all a game
Can you reach the end
Win the game

Jason Lee

Sorrow for Love

To the touch
It's petals are smooth and soft
To the eye
It is beautiful and inviting
To the heart it is warmth:
For it is a symbol of love
Blooming for all to see....

The rose will comfort and show care:
But embrace it only if you dare
For the rose has its dark side
As all things do
It will prick you with its thorns
For it hurt to be picked
From its home in the earth.

But when it finds it is loved
It will forgive but not forget
For it was happy
But now it is done
Not to be changed
And so the rose lives on...

Destiny Schwartz

You Enter My Dreams

When you enter my dreams
it's your whisper I hear
telling me you love me
and it's me you hold dear

I feel your arms around me
holding me close to your chest
you tell me to close my eyes
for it's then I sleep the best

I feel the warmth of your body
as you pull me in tight
the only thing that I ask
is to make it last all night

Please don't let me wake up
and find you're not here
just let me keep my dream
of having you ever so near

Cindy Tran

Simple Extravagance

You can have your fine cars,
jewels and furs,
Your Caribbean cruises
and fancy hor' doerves.

Give me instead
Fresh fruit and flowers,
A nice hot bath
I can soak in for hours.

Content happy noises
Of Children at play,
A good book to read
(Please give me all day.)

A kind, loving husband,
Friends true as can be,
And a big, cozy house
Where I can be me!

Cynthia S. Wright

Sifting Through

Sometimes ideas
Just get lost
Among the busyness of life

Who can find
The gems which glare
Among the papers and the dust

We can sift
Through all that's there
And we will find among the piles

Hopes and dreams
Of life gone by
And things once thought worthwhile

David A. Nesbitt

Brown

So soft, so cool,
Just like a cloud,
But not. More like a herd,
of funky cows.
When I talk to brown,
I cover my eyes,
with a smile on my face,
because she's so cool but funky.

She'll remind you of Woodstock,
a clam chick brown bell-bottoms,
and loud clogs.
When irresistible,
the way the post holds her up,,
at this moment,
everything is completely unreal,

her bouquet, makes her perfume,
taste like a box of chocolates,
and her contact, is like hot fudge,
melting through my fingers,
and before my eyes

Adrian Grays

Just Friends

Your life touched my life
Just several months ago.
I felt a door had opened,
You were someone I should know.

We laughed, had fun, enjoyed ourselves,
In fair and rainy weather.
Made love, and your words
So sweet to hear,
"Such beautiful music together".

What went wrong, and why the pain
Of longing to touch you again, in vain?
Maybe some day
You will find your way to say
"Hi, I need you again."

Anita E. Fraiman

The Promise

Here, cold white cover
Where a rose will be
Leaf and lawn so long gone
Waiting patiently.

Then, a warm bright aspect
Touches everything
A rite sublime in nature's time
The advent of the spring.

Charlotte B. Jefts

The Sea

Walking along the deep blue sea
Just strolling about so peacefully
Splashing through the bubbling waves
On the shore, there are several caves.

Walking on the grains of sand
People strolling hand and hand
Walking through the sea so blue
Gazing over the beautiful view.

Sitting on the sandy shore
Fish are swimming on the ocean floor
Looking over the deep blue sea
Makes you feel so peacefully

Erika Vella

I Love Thee

Oh, to say I love thee!
Just words upon the wind
Yet, how far they carry,
to the ear
that yearns to hear.

Let not death
take your words unspoken
and ashes make.

Rise up from the grave
and loose thy stingy tongue.

Winds! Blow strong!
With the force of a gale,
seek every corner and nook,
until thy rightful ear rings
with the blessed sound
of withheld love.

Let the balmy eyes of the moon
be witness,
and the stars
thy gentle guide.

Elizabeth A. Cornele

Alone

I'm the girl with the hidden life
Kept inside, locked up, and put away
for no one else to feel the pain
and cast a shadow on their day.

But when I find the time to spare
I take the key and silently go in
to try to understand my hurt
And justify his sin.

I cry alone in the dark
And wipe my countless tears
The pain's depth is never ending
Because I enclose my fears.

But when I return to the busy world
I am again happy, content, and strong
so no one will think twice about me,
My feelings being right or wrong.

But there is a problem I now face
My cell is getting full
There is no more room to hide it
And it's about to take it's toll.

Johanna Murphy

Marbles, Marbles

"Knuckles down"
  "Knuckles down"
    Goes the yell —

"Cat's eyes", "aggies",
  and "Milkies"
    all jell —

"Marble bingo",
  "Shoot-a-loop" —
Marble lingo's
  Hula-hoop!

"Handy candy"
That's just dandy —
"Corner the cow"
Jeepers and wow!

"Groundhog"
"Ducks in the pond" —
Zip, zap, and pow!

There they go across the floor —
Happiness in that big ring
Not just now, but evermore!

Joan Paulus

Untitled

Give yourself to me, love
Lay down your defenses -
Be still ....
Like water I shall envelop you,
Surrender all your senses!
Forget yourself, my love
In my arms do return
To the beginningless time
When you and I were one
Undivided, sublime!
Give yourself to me, love
Your fears lay down
Be still....
Like water I shall envelop you.
No longer apart but one
Not mine but one

Joanna Adams

Historic Tree

On a pathway
leading
through the edge
of a history
from
the rain
it camouflages me
made a
shelf
itself
like me
seeking protection.

Cheryl Felder Scott & Blair Cameron Scott

Icicle

Sparkling
an iceberg
a sword when it's upside down
frozen waterfall over a tree
sword
frozen
diamonds.

Corrie N. Hillman

Unsmitten

Strung along,
led on
to look like
all the others.
Stuck now
between identical symbols
of creamy stability
only to be ground
against someone's teeth,
making the sound she makes
in her sleep when having a nightmare
about him.
Yes, I am real
he squeaks
just before
being bitten.
Like all the others,
he must
prove
his worth.

Donna Ahrens

The Realm of Dreams

Sleep now my dear, the moon is high
Let go your fear and troubles, nigh
Give in my love, to night and dream
Of far off lands where it would seem
There is no hatred, death, or war
Where children play as once before
Where roses bloom in fields of gold
Where lovers swoon, and poets, bold
Tell tales of worlds beyond the sea
Of kings who ruled in harmony
Of dragons, fought, and bravely bested
By knights whose honor the fire tested
Of maidens their beauty unsurpassed
By that of the heaven's starry cast
All these things, I promise thee
Lie beyond the reach of society
So close your eyes, the night is young
Sleep now my dear, the time has come
Give in my love, for in my care
The Realm of Dreams awaits you there.

Frank Marsh

Giving Thanks To The Lord:

Giving thanks to the Lord,
Let us stop and heed,
The blessings that are stored,
For He knows what we need.

His infinite mercy and love,
Shines through the day and night,
Like the pure white dove,
He shows us the guiding light.

We ask with humble care,
Like little children on a whim,
That through the power of prayer,
All things are possible with Him.

He is with us in our toil,
He is with us in our affliction,
Like the untrodden soil,
He is there for our contrition.

Giving thanks to the Lord,
Let us walk in the sands,
Thinking of our daily accord,
We leave everything in His hands.

Jerry Senatore

From Our Eyes

Friends,
let's gather here, in this circle,
where we have never been deceived
and look into each other's eyes,
like in an innocent childhood game,
to see how little we know about
each other,
but most of all,
how much we miss each other,
how deep our eyes can reach,
how much our words can hold,
how strong our hands can be,
how deep our footprints,
how alike our shadows,
when we touch the light,
with steps like hopes,
under the forever expanding sky
from our eyes
as big as infinity.

George Bajenaru

Heart Of Cries

Heart of gold
lies of steel
Dreams are sold
nothing is real
Minds of sorrow
paths to lead
yet nothing to follow
Hands in need
people greed
And no one can see
That a mind can try
A heart that dies
A dream that flies
and a cry that sighs.

Dawn M. Peleska

Confusion

Lost in a world of confusion,
Life is just an illusion.
My world flashes gray then red,
I suddenly feel dead.
The ground rushes up to me,
And I start to laugh hysterically.
Laughter turns to tears,
As I am overwhelmed with fears.
The fear controls my body,
Someone help-Anybody!
Fear takes control of my mind,
My sanity I will never find.
Out of control I scream,
This all seems like a dream.
The world flashes gray,
Then I fade away.

Amanda Kendall

Dreaming

Picture on the wall,
Make me grow tall,
Teach me a way
By making a new day,
Show me just one thing,
That should bring
Me a pretty dove,
Could it be love!

Brandi Bennett

Rain Drops Like Tear Drops

Rain Drops
like
Tear Drops
on spring day
Fall on
silky daisies
and
Green meadows
Thunder rolling
wind blowing
How I like
the rain
Today.

Carrie J. Scott

Sadness

Gray and damp
Like a rainy day
Sadness comes my way
Tears wash away the hurt
As daylight slowly fades
Like raindrops against my sill
The tears trickle down
As I try to stop the hurt
From deep within my soul
I hide among the shadows
Not wishing to be seen
Till all the tears are shed
And all the pain takes leave.

Debra L. Sheets

My Hero

He was a knight,
Like a shinning light.
He would ride into the twilight,
Until we could unite,
We would ride through the night,
Until it became daylight.
It was a beautiful night,
Under the moonlight.
He was a charmer,
In shinning armor,
He was my knight,
My hero.

Jennifer L. Trimble

Little Boys And Little Girls

Frogs, spiders,
Lizards, worms.
Muddy, grubby,
All those germs.

Frilly dresses,
Curly hair.
Wearing makeup,
Skin so fair.

Nap time.
Snack time.
Bed time.
Play time.

So different,
Yet so much the same-
Little Boys
and Girls.

Brittany Fitzgerald

The Exodus

Time swept through a distant pasture
Like a spreading disease without a cure
Capturing a tear
I live in fear
As I fall to my knees, unsure

Dampen wind blows dust in my face
Wondering forward, behind my disgrace
Limitless mission
Imagination
Praying to the heavens, I chase

A journey I have just began
With a touch of a hand, I was mistaken
Trembling inside
I lost my pride
Not able to hide, I make my last stand

Coming undone, images appear
Cold steel in hand, stroking the trigger
A flash of bright light
I gaze in spite
Toward Eden I head, with the wind's
whisper.

Garrett Beget

I Wished On A Star

Like a bluebird in the sky
like an arrow floating by
like a horse by the bay
I'd be riding everyday
easy being on the go
like it was gonna snow
I wish on a star
I rode in my car
to school on a day
where I just sit and play
I wished on a star

Heather Marie Downing

Sin

Satan dances before my eyes
Like Hannibal Lecter on a bad acid trip.
The blue flames rise higher and higher,
Almost reaching the ground.
His minions chain me down
On a bed spikes
Made of human bones.
An anguished scream
Echoes through the walls.
Another soul has been torn apart
By the merciless angels of death.
Perhaps if I had not sinned so often
During life,
My fate could have been different.

Anna Chan

The Hunting Trip

I shot a bear
It roared so loud
It gave me a scare
It fell to the ground
Without a sound.

I checked to see if it was alive
But I was to late it had died.

It's lifeless body moved no more
Then to the sky it's spirit soared.

Casey Sutton

Regrets

Regrets lie in the mind
Like printed words on the page,
Indelible, permanent
Scar tissue.

Looking back,
We have to stumble over them
To get to the good times,
Like a blockade runner through memories.

At times we plunge ahead
Through the open mind-fields
Toward forgiveness.

Then, lest we forget,
Ahead (always just ahead)
Stand our children,

Unwitting reminders
Of yesterdays beyond forgetting
And tomorrows beyond regretting,

Guardians of a future we cannot reach,
And a past we can't release.

Diane Harrelson

Coming Home

I see them going by
Like whispers materialized.
The past realized,
Years later, the time is nigh.

The jovial children of parents proud,
And surrounding dismal geometry.
Yet infant, infantry,
They turn and stare, their yell loud.

Loud like a life I never lived,
Rebirth, the dream.
Realities scream,
Time goes by, images vivid.

If I could be like them someday,
If they could be like me someday.
Till death do us part,
Like this from the start.

George Earle

Keep Practicing

If you would like to play
Like your neighbor next door,
Or your friend, or friend's friend
Who plays Bach, rock and more,
KEEP PRACTICING.

When, at the recital,
You made a big mistake

And kept right on playing,
But felt your heart would break,
KEEP PRACTICING.

At least one hour a day
Is not too much to ask,
On your choice instrument,
If you'd master the task.
KEEP PRACTICING.

On the piano, the horn,
Violin or guitar,
You'll have more friends, more fun;
You may become a STAR.
KEEP PRACTICING.

Harrison L. Frye

"Listen"

Listen to the raindrops.
Listen to the wind.
Listen to the silence.
I'm missing you again.

Look at all the gray clouds;
Where has my sunshine gone?
Watching raindrops falling
Can make a day so long.

Remembering yours laughter,
I see a rainbow form.
From out behind the gray clouds,
Sneaks the sunshine, bright and warm.

Now I see you smiling,
The raindrops cease to fall.
I feel you close beside me,
But you're not there at all.

So I...Listen to the raindrops,
I listen to the wind,
I listen to the silence;
And I'm missing you again.

Criss Moore

Dear Ola: A Letter To Gdansk

Another
Listening to your words
Enchanted by the beauty
Keeping at heart
Swirls of unknown ecstasy
And with sudden passions
Never straying too far, A
Dedicated friend holds your hand
Reminiscing of a time gone by
And of Gdansk in the end....

Jerry D. Abuan

Noemi

Fountains of light
Live in your eyes.
San Juan night
Starred skies
And the rose that
Is white
Both dream of Noemi,
Her hands are
Kittens, lazily
Purring in the sun.
Her smile, ah that
The secret of the Holy Angels,

Barry B. Blander

I am the Monster

Blackened skies match their feelings.
Locked door create a prison
Junkies cover the cold streets.
Children's cries fill both my ears.

Dripping blood seeps into gaps
Their empty eyes close tightly.
No one escapes the monster.
Useless cars line the sidewalks.

I stand back without much hope.
What have I done to help them?
"Food for the monster." I scream.
And then I break down and cry.

Brian Nollner

Spring

Coo goes the lonesome dove
Living in Maine

Calling to a lark in the redbud
In Spain

The flowers are all swaying in the
Cool gentle breeze

Which floats past us all with comforting
Ease
Moo said the milking cow
Grazing in North Carolina

Bellowing to the sleepy Panda
Living in China

Rhuuu said the mighty elephant
Living in chad

Trumpeting to the camel
Living in bagdad

All these animals around the world
Are very happy to say

Get ready here it comes spring is on
Its way.

Jessica Crim

Untitled

Today I saw a child,
Lonely, roaming the streets.
I went to lend him kindness,
Asked to walk him home.
Tears filled his eyes.
He had no home...he was abandoned.
We spent the day happily together.
I noticed a twinkle in his eyes
And a smile gradually formed.
When the day finally ended,
I asked him to stay with me.
He had a friend to stay with,
Now he had to leave.
I believe his friend was God.
For that night he went to Heaven,
And left behind a lesson to be learned.
How a child's life was touched
By one day of love,
But scarred by the many days without it.

Janet L. Greenhagen

Reminiscence

Rust eroded shopping cart squeaks
More every year, and the plastic
Bag that holds the laundry stains
Springs a few more holes.
Around the aged head a cartoon bubble
Hovers like a swarm of bees.
She plods along, the words still clear,
The dream of youth, of Azulejo
and Bougainville, the terrace
And Tequila sunrise,
Plaintive mariachi, birds that sing
At midnight in Amate tree....
Tug that cart, hold that dream
While the spirit fades
Surrendering to death.

Doris T. Marks

O Dandelion

O dandelion on my lawn you
look so handsome young and
strong.

Your yellow hair is fair to
view and you have so much
to do.

As time went on and fleeting
fast , you changed overnight
it seems, aweless.

Your hair turned white,
you look so wise,
I bet you can tell great
stories and not be lies.

In the air your silver hair
flew swiftly like time on my
lawn, then thousands like you
came along.

O dandelion on my lawn you
look so handsome, young and
strong.

Joyce Walter

Early Morning

I'm sitting on the back porch,
Looking across the land
Sitting in a rocking chair
A cup of coffee in my hand.
The sunrise is pink and purple
As the darkness slips away
We are going to have another
Bright and beautiful day.
I see a hungry gray cat
Looking up at me
I hear a beautiful song
From a bird in the apple tree.
The smell of baking bread
Floats thru the back door
A lovely Tennessee morning
Who could ask for anything more.
I say a prayer, "Thank you, God
For all that you give to me...
The beautiful world around me
Love, friends and family."

Betty McGlasson

Love Ever True

What face do you have
Love ever true
Will you recognize me
And I, you
How does one know
Is it as if a stake
Where driven through
A beating heart
Do our souls see
The others light
Does true love
Feel like a half
Of a solitary part
I am searching
But I am blind
Or is it that
I would not see
Simply put
I do not know
Who you will be.

Ellen Gallagher

Ode to Our Ancestors

They once were children dreaming
Looking up to find their star,
Their hearts welled up restless
Reminding us who we are.

They grew up to wonder
How in this life they fit,
Their hearts welled up restless
Reminding how souls are lit.

Their gaze stretched out further
Beyond the ocean blue,
Their hearts welled up restless
To make their visions true.

Now we seek the wisdom
Of far flung dreams of old,
Our hearts welled up restless
Their stories no longer cold.

We observe with awe and wonder
Lives gone but near abide,
God's heart will well up restless
Until we join them at his side.

Harvey K. Bue

Make My Face Lovely

Here am I, Lord.
Lord, come into my being,
Stay with me while I remain here
Come with me as I move about.
Let others see that I spoke to you.
Make my face lovely before them;
As your countenance rests upon us.
For where two or three are gathered,
Your spirit is among us.
Let me speak kindly,
Lest they miss Your grace in me.
Your Being in me may be all of Christ
  they shall ever see.
Oh Jesus, there is such calm between us,
As I sit here with you.
Let us share our Peace with the world.
Let us go forth to shine on Life.

Dorcas

Trust

Trust, that's what real
love is, based on, it has,
to be, this in order
for love, to grow, strong

True love, has a cost
if not, then, forever, love is,
lost, hearts, must be, opened
with care, and hope being there

Trust, for love, its, truly,
the key, for now, and always, it,
shall be, this, is true, its, no
fantasy, for great love, wait patiently

Love, must have, honesty
if, its willing to always, be
this thing surely, must be, applied
if not, love is deftly, to have died

Keep hold to feelings, that are
shared handle them, with tender
love, and care, true love, is, a must
and its all based on, trust

Dexter Long

Love

When you look at me
Love is what I see
When I see your face
Love is what makes my heart race

When I'm in your arms
Love brings me no harm
When you are by my heel
Love is what I feel

When I feel your touch
Love is what I want so much
When we kiss
Love is my wish

When we are close
Love is what we share the most
When we are away
Love still comes our way

Idonna Graham

Love Me

Love me for what I am,
Love me for who I am,
Love me for what I can give,
Love me for what I think,
Love me for what I feel,
Love me for my honesty and loyalty,
Love me for loving you,
Love me to love me,
Love me just love me.

Carlos Tapia

My Diamonds

Diamonds are beautiful and
  lovely to see
Necklaces, bracelets and rings
  for a fee
Formed and shaped by
  artisans
Designs exquisite, dazzling,
  and brilliant
But I must tell you the
  best of all
Are my diamonds by the
  shore
The sun shining on the
  sea
Beautiful, radiant,
  sparkles galore
Gorgeous to see these
  diamonds are free.

Dorothy Schaedler

Truisms

Chickens scratch and children splash,
Monkeys swing and birds hate cats,
Snakes slither and dogs slobber,
Music soothes and kites amuse,
Rain falls and bears love honey,
Tans in June and flannels in Winter,
Wisdom sticks on refrigerators,
The sun is in the East again,
Ice cream melts and bills come due,
Lovers cuddle, and touching you
I always seem to smile.

Bob Stevens

Right or Wrong

As I roam through life,
Love's stabbing me with a knife.
The pain is so deep and true,
It seems nothing can pull me through.

Then a new one comes along
And I wonder "right or wrong"?
The answer that I do not know
Blinds me like the light of snow.

Yet something keeps me going,
Maybe it's the not knowing
What is to me "right or wrong",
For I know I must be strong.

Tomorrow is another day.
To this I must decide, leave or stay?
This day I know it won't be long,
Till I know what is "right or wrong".

James R. Perry

Peace

Mister, I deserve better than you.
Low morals,
No values,
Lies,
Deceit!

Mister, I deserve better than you.
Love of self,
Love of family,
Love of God!

Mister, I deserve better than you.
It is my choice.
It is God's will,
That you be replaced with
    Love
      Honesty
        And
          Happiness
Mister, you don't deserve me,
And
I deserve better than you!

Clariece Morris

Unconditional Love

With you he sleeps
Makes you feel good under sheets
Tenderly gently supplies the heat.
From the neck onto your feet.
He then nips at toes and head
Dragging blankets off to shed
Such performance on the bed.
Tries to wake you, but dreads.
Anxious patience, with no hate,
Puppy dog knows, he must wait.
Wagging tail to say you rate,
Sitting up in final state.

Eleanor Kral

Indian Summer

Gossamer moonlight
    Marshmallow cloud flight
      Narcissus dancing
        Indian summer passing
Innocent symphony
    Secrets beneath peppertree
      Maidenhair laughing
        Indian summer passing

Holly Sweet Thayer

Eight-Legged Harmony

Toothpicks
Match sticks
Twigs
Eight legs loosely fastened
Clatter knee to shin
Grasp a shiny thread and drop
Eight leg
Free-fall
Gig

Georgia Jones

My Friend Jesus

My friend Jesus
    Means everything to me;
To know He loved so deeply
    And died at Calvary.
My friend Jesus
    Is the greatest friend of all;
He's always there to lift me
    Each time I fail or fall.
My friend Jesus
    Puts peace within my heart;
Having the assurance
    From me He'll not depart.
My friend Jesus
    Is faithful kind and true;
And my friend Jesus
    Also died for you.

Janet Lee

Flying Lessons

Potions and lotions and spells,
    methodically made at eight.
We jump and jump from tree stumps
    until our feet are blue.
And then at nine we see the light
    and learn we cannot fly.

But then again at seventeen
A dark and windy afternoon
    beckons with a wonder.
An Ansel Adams picture,
    haunting, yearning, calling.
The open window taunts.
    A wild and wondrous autumn sky:
Food for dreams
    in our young minds.

Ajayne M. Bryant

Untitled

Chimes sing
Middle path
Middle time
Middle day
Chimes ring
Bring change
Change bring
Middle day
Chimes flow
Valley music
Valley magic
Magic music
Chimes
One
Magic
Center

Charles Anthony Bufalino

Peaceful Remembrance

Snowy night's quiet blue haze
Multi color twinkling days
Fires warm with glow
And hopes of more snow
Shall we wish for gifts galore
Should we think and be thankful for
Love and joy
To each girl and boy
Jingling bells ring again
Beneath the tree see the train
Remember Christmas's beauty and fun
And always be young.

Beverly Jean Blain

Music And Noise

Music is a clock that chimes
Music is a poem that rhymes
Noise is a wine glass breaking
Noise is someone heavily raking
Music is a fairy tale
Music is a slapping sail
Noise is the stomping of a hoof
Noise is rain on a galvanized roof
Music is shells washing up on a beach
Music is a star just out of reach
Noise is the buzzing of a bee
Noise is a bear scratching a tree
Music is a horse in motion
Music is a child's devotion
Noise is the slamming of a door
Noise is the sound of a lion's roar
Music over comes all strife
Music is a way of life

Ginger Lee Coon

Black Is

Black is...
My cat,
So furry and fat.
Attempting to cry just,
A little meow,
That comes out as high,
As a squeaking mouse being chased.

Black is..
The taste of fur flying,
As the same cat runs,
Out the door,
just to slam into a screen door.

Black is..
The crashing rain,
That my poor cat runs into.
a car smoking,
As it turns on,
Including the pollutants it lets out.

Black is... All of the above.
And a lot more, that just wouldn't fit.

Bryon Nuttall

Life

After a while I finally see
just what life means to me.
The changes, the stages,
the feelings, the ages.
Life comes day by day
no one knows how, why, or which way.
After awhile I finally see
just what life means to me.

Heather Hamilton

Around

You are special, sweet.
My darlin' very neat.
When I look in your eyes.
I see a wonderful guy.
Loving you is so great, knew.
You are always their when I'm blue.

Take me in your heart,
never let me go. Just
think of me. Let your love flow.

If you ever are down.
Call me I will be around.
Trust me, hold me tight.
I love you, goodnight.

Bobbie Lynn Floyd (Kerwin)

My Meagan My Michael

My Meagan my Michael
My dear grandchildren
My Meagan sweet and pretty
My Michael full of joy
You give me joys of laughter
You give me full of tears
I give you hugs when in fears
To see you grow all these years
Makes my life worth while
I give myself a smile
My Meagan My Michael
Now you left to a different State
While I here in sunshine State
Miss your voices day to day
But then I call you every day
My Meagan My Michael
My love is loved by me
And will ever be

Dolores C. Sespene

The Crow

Suddenly I hear a rapping on
my door. I look east. I look
west, but it was nothing more.

Then on my window sill
there sat a crow. Seconds later
a man's face as white as snow.

He comes closer, I'm hoping
nothing happened. He shouts boo!
And secretly disappears inside his
jackets.

For I awaken, it was only
a dream, or was it? There on my
window sill sat the same crow, and
every now and then I can see the
man with the face as white as snow.

Jennifer Lee Johnson

Sunshine

The sun is vast,
a ray from the sky.
It shines on the water
and makes me sigh.
It warms the earth
from heaven above.
Because God created
the brightness
I love.

Alex Webster

God's Verse

In the mid of night
My eyes behold;
Wonders, words would leave untold;
A tapestry of moon and star
Cast their light on planets far;
Shinning on the beaches sand
They brighten up the darkened land.
While patiently
The blackened earth;
Sits waiting for the suns rebirth.
The darkened sky
Holds mystery
Hidden in its history;
Of galaxies so vast;
So old;
Of stars that dim while growing cold.
The universe existed here
Before man, or even beast appear.
Time alters slight the universe;
For that its God's own living verse...

Jackie Belkiewicz

God Is Love

God is love God is Joy
My God is much much more
God is Strength God is power
Every second, minute, and hour
God Is Peace
When our doubts of Him are
released.
God is greater than material
things you see
God is everything to me.
Jesus died upon the cross for you
and me
Away on the cross on a hill called
calvary
Much can be done
So little is said
But I been inspired to tell
you God is not dead

Carol L. Horsley

Your Friend

When I was down and feeling low
My Lord looked on me below
He said "Look up and see my face"
For you, all troubles I'll erase.

The tears you shed will be no more
Since I am now your open door
All cares and troubles leave behind
The grace of God be on your mind.

Laugh and smile instead of cry
Don't worry about the other guy
When all is over, said and done
You will be the winning one.

Look now to God so far above
It's all in those who know his love
From this day on, and to the end
He's always there "Your loving friend"

Delores G. Snyder

Lullaby

While I lay me down to sleep,
My loving heart condemned to weep,
I pray to God your love to gain
To mend my heart and ease my pain.
As I sleep this dreary night
I pray to God to Aid my plight.
As my poem comes to close
My love for her surely grows,
For now I must say good bye.
This is the end of my lullaby.

Chris Speight

I Am Yours

So often when I think of you
    my mind goes back in time,
To when the skies were always
    blue, I was yours and you
    were mine.
I remember the loving way we
    shared each day and minute
    of time,
And wish so much it will
    once more be, I am yours
    and you are mine.
This heart I'll give to no one
    else through out eternal
    time,
For only you shall hold the
    key to this heart, that's yours,
    of mine.

Dennis Millam

For One Brief Moment

My heart soars
My mind is free
I feel the love
Surrounding me

I do not know
When this will end
The wounds I have will
never mend.

But for one brief moment
I have found this place
of blood red roses and
elegant lace

With silken dresses
and petticoats fine, how
I wish I could keep
this place as mine

But for one brief moment
a glimpse I get
of the past I know
and the future yet...

Breanne Rowe

I Am!

Times stands still,
While flowing on.
Past, present, future,
Rolled in one.
I am what I was,
What I am,
What I will be.
I Am!

Carol Johnson Nelson

Seasonings

Gentle, she was;
my Mother,
Gentle as the rains of Spring.

Warm, she was;
my Mother,
Warm as the winds of Summer.

Giving, she was;
my Mother,
Giving as the fruits of Autumn.

Soft, she was;
my Mother,
Soft as the first snow of Winter.

Gentle, she came to us;
my Mother,
Gently, did she leave.

Dagney Marie Johnson

Mother's Day

In Memory

Mother, mother, dear,
My Mother from yesteryear,
From my birth on the farm,
I was guided by your charm.

Yes, you had problems with me,
But you always managed to see,
The bright side,
Always forgiving me of my faults.

Teaching me from cooing to talking,
Then step by step to walking,
Teaching me good from bad,
The patience you must have had,
You got me through this plight,
Ever guiding me from wrong to right.

You had taught me,
"To love thy neighbor as thyself,"
"Abiding by God's Laws first,"
"To love and honor thy Father and Mother,"
Because you'll never, never have another

Harold L. Sargent

Love's Armor

I have so much patience that it hurts.
My patience is a suit of armor.
How I long to take it off.

I look upon impatience with lust.
I wish to embrace her.
To take her to bed.

I want to make impatience my companion.
To rendezvous with her.
But I know that I must not.
Give up the love that I have got.

I will not take my suit of armor off.
Nor will I lay it down.

Said I'd always keep the faith.
Said I'd never let you down.
Then I wrote it in my heart.

Gwendolyn Davis

My Leader

In the paths of righteousness
  my Shepherd leadeth me
If in weakness I digress,
By His love and tenderness,
  From my fault and fear set free,
Where the strain than strength is less
  He leadeth me.
All the way is safe and light,
  My Shepherd leadeth me.
As the noontide shines the night:
warded by His love and might,
  Undismayed I well may be;
For, in paths where faith is sight,
  He leadeth me
Not that I deserve His grace,
  My Shepherd leadeth me
out of sin and danger's stress,
In the paths of righteousness;
  Unto Him the praise shall be,
For His name's sake I confess, "He leadeth me."

Gladys Copeland

Thoughts On Valentine's Day

Lovers need no urging
Nature takes it's course.
Everything is joy and bliss
Sealed with an endearing kiss.

Spouses may be more sedate,
They've had the test of time,
They know the joy of sharing
With each other - really caring.

The most unselfish love of all
Is a mother's for a child
No other feeling is as strong
You're a "Mom" your whole life long.

On this date that's set aside
Across the country far and wide
Express your love and you will find
It takes in everyone - mankind.

Jane Reeder

Untitled

May your hopes
  Never fall to the ground
    like autumn's leaves,
  Nor melt away
    like past winter's snows.
May your fears
  Never darken the skies
    like a threatening storm,
  Nor hold you back
    like the ocean's tide.
May your dreams
  Never get left behind
    like a childhood toy,
  Nor ever be forgotten
    like an overgrown garden.
Instead...May your successes
  Come in conquering the challenges
    of life's mountains,
  And reaching the highest peak,
May you always, Soar like an Eagle.

Amy Sappingfield

Cocoon

Mind bound earth crawler
Never rose into the sky
Walk the world with no desire
Blindness till I die
Feed on guilt and pain
The end will come too soon
Sunk into the lowest low
Into self - cocoon
Therapy of solitude
Transforming all alone
Sins of past life fade away
Inner light has grown
Aspiring for success
The binding chains ripped off
Once a beautiful caterpillar
Now a hideous moth
Heavens are wide open
Have the world to prowl
Previous life had anchored me
But try to catch me now

Bret Hardin

Which Way To Go?

Mother sun shining bright,
nine planet children
within her sight.
Only one, full of life.

The blue one's special,
but has much trouble.
Its' God-like creatures
waste trees and water,
pollute the land
they hadn't oughter.
To mend their ways
or end their days.
What path we take,
the world we make.
A desert scene
or lots of green.

George W. Pekar

Just You and Me

A place to be pressure-free
No duties persist
  It's just you and me

Faint lyrics mingling
  with the mist
Jacuzzi bubbling near

Tall candles flickering
  reflecting the sheen
of smooth satin sheets

Fresh flowers dew-kissed
  aura sweet
Warm ocean breezes
  caressing the lace

Steaming Jamaican java
  in dainty cups
Crystal-dipped raspberries
  afloat in fresh cream

A place to be pressure-free
No duties persist
  It's just you and me.

Elsie C. Snook

The Price

There is no honeycomb without the bees.
No fruit will grow without the trees.
No garden grows without the rain.
No healing comes without the pain.

No fragrant rose without the thorns
If there is no pain, no child is born.
No rainbow without the storm
Without the darkness no bright morn.

No love at all, unless we give
Share this love each day you live.
Remember, Jesus paid it all
So share this love and heed His call.

Judie Robinette

Picnic Land

Oh, life is grand in picnic land,
No indoor life for me!
I love the air, wind in my hair,
The feel of being free.

Oh, life is grand in picnic land,
The brooklet bubbles by.
The bluebirds sing, while on the wing,
And soft clouds pad the sky.

Oh, life is grand in picnic land,
And what good things to eat —
The pies and cakes that mother bakes,
And wieners — what a treat!

Oh, life is grand in picnic land,
But somehow, after all,
When twilight's near and stars appear,
Home seems a welcome call.

Diana A. Todaro

Love

Love is a mystery to all.
No lies are considered accurate.
Only true hearts will stay together.
If it is only a crush,
Do not use it for
An excuse for a shot of love.
You cannot understand the
Questions and pain of heart breaks,
Until they happen to you.
Do not let love conquer your life
So please, excuse "Love"
From you vocabulary.
And from someone who knows
Do not try it.
Love will break your heart.

Jessica Vanderweide

A Broken Heart

Like the leaves fallen from a tree
my heart is torn
only to be blown away
by the wind.
As we talk
I begin to gather
the scattered pieces
to put it back together.
Your words mend the cuts.
Your smile stops the pain.

Amanda Joy Marbach

The Return of the Paper Clip

I'm aboard the CHALLENGER,
No one saw me,
I'm the sole survivor
I know what happened
We were on our way to Mars
Suddenly everyone started screaming
I know what happened
One loud explosion
Another and Another!!
Everyone was falling
heads jerking
arms, legs flailing
Deathly Silence!
We plummeted down
Piece by piece we hit the ground
Metal twisted into all shapes
People gathered
Yelling, Crying, Searching
I AM THE PAPER CLIP!!
I KNOW ALL!!

Carl Holscher

Empty

Whispering windows
No ones' home
Empty house
All alone

Saddened shadows
In a lonely space
Raining tears down
Upon its' face

Winding webs
Silent fame
Lulled laughter
Forgotten names.

Denise J. Clynes

What Hope?

Torn clothes, bare feet
No place to call home
Sitting, laying, crumbling
To the door of a fancy place

Inside, the finest food
Wine, scotch, other spirits
Outside, the wind is cold
The homeless makes his nest

Inside, much, much abundance
Bitching about the food
Outside, there is sadness
Now it rains; No one cares

Life has such disparities!
Why do we have such tragedies?
Will I ever have the courage to,
Open my umbrella and stop the rain?

Dennis Borges

About Angels

How do little angels grow
Do their halos ever show
Does some fairy lead the way
Keep them sweet and neat by day
Do their wings fold out of sight
As their eyelids close at night
If I knew how angels grew
I would like to raise a few

Pearl Wainshal

Raped

Not a single garment removed,
nor a hair out of place

Yet all mental and emotional serenity,
the peace of mind known by most -
Are stolen senselessly, for eternity.

One mind, one soul
Raped.

Not by touch,
but rather,
By words and images -
which over time
Have robbed a life
of its meaning and purpose.

Anne Marie Sterling

"Stone Statue"

She stares into the night
Not a soul around-
Her soft, sad whimpering
Is the only sound

I want to comfort her
But she's too hard to reach
Too stubborn in her ways
Too smart to teach

Stone statue
Chiseled frown
Remnants of life
In tears falling down

She sits on her dark throne
Safe in her bad ways
Nobody has the right
To tell her she'll stay

Stone Statue
The path is hers to find
No one can touch her
It's all in her mind

Andrea Castro

Ride the Wind

I ride the wind on silver wings.
Not knowing what tomorrow brings.
I search the skies and earth below,
I wonder when I'll meet my foe.
I ride the wind as within I fear,
that as I fight, my death is near.
But when my Foe has fought in vain,
they paint his emblem on my plane.
I ride the wind in Dawns light.
Again I search for foe to fight.
The emblems increase as I soar.
These men will ride the wind no more.
I feel a sadness when I see,
these painted emblems caused by me.
A star-circled emblem is my sign.
And someday they'll be painting mine.
That day I will be free to soar,
I'll ride the wind forever more.

James A. Capsalis

Tears In My Father's Eyes

Drop! Drop!
O sweet warrior! Let your tears drop!
Undefeated in all your battles,
You have conquered me too.
All your tears
On the floor
Blood that gave me life,
Floor weeps with you.
So wet.
All the sun in the heavenly sky,
Can never wipe away
Sea,
Flowing on your cheeks.
Noble Niaba* !
Man as I am
I sob and weep.
My own tears
Will choke me.

Ido Babou

Illusive Treasure

If there be a jewel
Of brilliance and beauty,
Sought by many
And seen by few;

If there be a blossom
Of tenderest petals,
Grown in a garden
Obscured from view;

If there be a perfume
Of heady aroma
A scent of temptation
To tease and elude;

If there be a virtue
to speak these treasures,
Let it be known
As gratitude.

Ellen Lucas Mahoney

Web of Handsome

God wove a web of handsomeness
Of clouds and stars and dew,
But made not anything at all
So wonderful as you.
You shine around our simple earth
Our lives such joy you bring,
And every common thing you touch
Glows bright like angels wings.
There's no one poor or less than you
When you are here to care,
Your hands work hard your touch is soft
Our problems you will bare.
Your as pleasant as a flower bloom
You outshine any star,
And I am rich who learns from you
How magnificent you are.
I'll stand without at anytime
My hands are poor my heart has love
I know that fate sent you to me
As did our King from up above.

Betsy Fewell

Time Marches

An impression
    of embrace
Releasing my amour
And casting the warm
    empowerment of love.
The soul flies free
    woundless
    and time marches.

The goal is set
    for what I had
        is left unconquered
And the mind plays tricks
For I hear you call
    in a muffled hymn.
I see the way
    you pranced before
The smoothness of your skin.
I watch the silhouette
    painted to the door
        and wait...as time marches.

Barre Blake

New Ways

I'm learning to make myself aware
of feelings that put me in a flare.
I really, really don't like to wait
But, I'm learning patience as a trait.
I'm learning not to portray hate
But, of my feelings to relate.
I'm learning to dispel the rage
that keeps me locked inside a cage.
I'd like to be more tolerant,
My way is not the only operant.
I'm only human and will err,
and if I do, I won't despair.

Carrie L. Walker

Autumn Leaves

Today I walked among the leaves
    Of gold, red, green and brown
And as I stooped to pick one up
    My mind just raced around.

Why must these pretty little leaves
    Grow ugly and turn brown?
And as I went to bed that night
    I tossed this thought around

I woke up early in the morn
    About 5 A.M. you see
For I had to have an answer
    To this question, facing me.

I thought how God has formed these buds
    So perfect on the tree
And in due time, which took awhile
    They sprang forth brilliantly.

The purpose of the leaves you see
    Is to glorify the tree
And once its task on earth is done
    Then they become brown leaves.

Ginny Shrader

Gathering of Butterflies

It is loss
of green and of warmth, a cold
shock of change and death. Wind
and rain. Wind
and rain, a letting go that brings
us to this spot again
and again. As if this dark
soil could warm us.

Drawn to some one thing
to feed on. We've gathered.
Drawn to some one
thing they lift, circle around,
circle through leaves to land.
Here, I sit to watch.
Any one thing too close
we rise up.

James A. Veloski

Unfinished

Rotting memories
of happiness
Wash ashore
with thought's tide
Waves break
upon my beach of hopes
And drown them all
inside
Shifting sands
of time and space
Erode reality
here in this place
Mummified deep
within the debris
Rots the corpse
of my sanity

Brett Wiedecker

The Final Chapter

After the loving comes the past tense
of loved.
After the grief comes the realization
of acceptance.
After the memories comes the picture
of a blank screen.
After the feeling comes the thought
of something once felt.
After the hope comes the truth
of what will never be.
When you finish the final chapter,
it is time to close the book.

Deborah A. Tackett

Loves Lost Memory

Life is but a flashing glimpse
    of loves lost memory
Traveling through that space
    and time to gain eternity
Eternity is but a summary of
    life's good and bad
To make known the goodness in
    life we shared
It cannot be life will not exist
    after loves lost memory...
For love goes on forever, and life
    side by side with Eternity.

Blanche McLanahan

Life Goes On

Within may be a stormy anger
Of past experience dead
Confusion, hurt and struggling linger
Reaching out to be led.

As a river flowing onward
Softly moving round the bend
Awakes faint hearts to new beginnings
And with gratitude will mend.

No experience can restrain
A purpose and a reason
As the river's inner cleansing
Strives to move each in its season.

Bernyce Rutherford

Interlude

Far from my world
of sleep
I wander
restlessly
seeking the elusive keeper
of my dreams,
Vagabond on dark, silent highways
Traveling the sharp edge
of thought
up and down both sides
of midnight,
Captive to the journey
of my day
and the unfolding of tomorrow,
Tugging down taut webs
of consciousness,
Free at last
and drifting slowly
into the soft cocoon
of night.

Helen Sand Schaeffer

Poetry

Poetry is the friendship
of spirit, heart and mind.
It is the perfect ending
to your fondest dreams.

It is a colorful collection
of the sympathy in our hearts,
and the immortal expression
of compassion for mankind.

It is all the love you imagined,
but didn't know how to show,
and the courage and wisdom
that allows us to cry.

Poetry is the strength we feel
when we laugh and smile,
and a very long rest
after a long life's work.

Poetry is the hand of God,
and while it flows through you,
if you let it in your soul——
Poetry heals.

Deborah Stoeckel

"Mindscape"

He stands on the edge
Of the cliff he just climbed.
Not caring for where he is
The place or the time.
He reflects in his subconscious
The windy place of his mind.
And feels what he never
Expected to find.
A world full of hatred
Destructive and frightening.
A world of desire
Thunder and lightning.
He looks toward the sky
Not knowing what he will see.
And sees a vision of you and
Falls deep into serenity.
Not knowing exactly what He's supposed to do
He starts walking back.
To the world where he came from,
Which is dark and black.

Brian L. Miller

The Darkness of the Shadows

It's the endless staircase
Of turning nothingness
It's the empty room
The surrounds the pain
The walls close me in
Trapping my twisted thoughts
Wrapping them in darkness

The brick face mutilates
Your pounding fists

Sentimental objects
Fill the memory
Of the time you lost
In your never ending journey
Through the unknown

Christa Dillon

Grandpa

I think back to the distant years
   of when you were alive,
and the happiness that you created
   in so many peoples' lives.

And of how you could have left
   the children of four,
that I know you must have
   loved and adored.

In the present day and time
   they try not to bring up your name,
but when it does, a sadness occurs
   that can never make things the same.

I never personally knew you,
   but I will always wish I had
a chance to see -
   what now makes people so sad.

We wonder even unto this day
   what made you possess
the dreadful urge that caused you
   to put yourself to rest.

Angela M. Murphy

My Little One

God sent you from above,
Oh little one it's you I love.
A father blessed with such a gift,
This precious love will never drift.

I talk and teach, you learn and yearn,
Goals and dreams you yet to earn.
My desires and your thoughts,
Together we will fire our best shots.

The joy you bring me is the best,
Far ahead from all the rest.
A love like yours is mine to keep,
For without it, I'll forever weep.

Principles and values I have given,
You strive to apply them in your living.
Overcome your challenges one by one,
For success will be there to take and run.

O little, my little one,
Remember me while we have fun.
For one day, you'll have a little one,
And one day, me, there will be none.

Jose R. Serrano

"Delicious Jewel"

Jewel you are to me,
Oh so sweet and mellowly.
Happily I watched you grow,
Not breaking from the cold.
Nodding at the wind that blows,
You made it through the ice and snow.
Apples you bear bounteously,
Pleasing to my eyes they be,
Presenting themselves deliciously.
Looking at your fragrant bouquet,
Each year brings joy to my soul.
Seizing fruit from your limb,
Eating the pulp that's within,
Enjoying the nectar filling my mouth,
Dropping the core, I pick one more.

Judith Anderson Meeks

Ode to Sara Teasdale

Strike right to the heart.
Oh, Spark!
Like lightening
Light up my life!
Send me the dart
That hits the mark-
Do not let me flounder
In elements not my own,
I seek the fire of the muse
The delight of a lark in flight
Take me to the height
And breadth of joy!
Oh Beauty!-the song
Sung from the heart -
How I wish the words were mine -
And on my chart the praise.
Sleep well, Sweet Spirit,
You've earned your rest
"Carved from the stones
of agony".

Bernice Davis Brigham

Untitled

While exploring my grandmother's attic,
    Old books and letters and such,
I found the tattered old ragdoll
    That's come to mean so much.

It was very torn and dirty
    And both it's eyes were lost;
I thought I must repair it
    No matter what the cost.

I washed the doll, sewed new eyes on
    Made a dress for it to wear
Of pretty floral yellow,
    Matching ribbons for it's hair.

Once I was like the old ragdoll,
    I was almost torn apart,
But in a way no one could see,
    My hurt was in my heart.

Then Jesus came to save me,
    He gave me new sight too;
Behold, old things are passed away,
    All things are become new.

Glenda Sue Prince

Gently By Nature

Through a rainfall,
    on a star lit night,
And by those dreary places-
    You are there.
Caressing me; in that great,
    depth of silence,
        I shall never understand.

You sprinkle sweetness -
    on all the bitter illusions.
Oh, you big, wonderful,
    bundle of love.

Protection and care -
    through every triumph,
        and tragedy.

So priceless, so eternal, so good.

Audrey L. Telthoester

Bright Hope

    A rainbow is a smile from God
on dark and cloudy days
It shows me that He's always there
    To guide me on my way.
    Though others try to hurt me
And sometimes they may succeed
I know my Friend will help me
    If I'll only let him lead.
    When troubles over whelm
me I know the clouds will part
for the symbol of God's rainbow
Nestles deep within my heart.
"Brightly Beams our Father's Mercy"
    Is the hymn that I recall
When I think about a rainbow
    And the meaning of it all.

Barbara Gil

"E"

I turn my head, then I feel your eyes
On me
Like a lock a snooper's trying to pry

Open
Your eyes are like golden lasers
Blue hot
My soul's being cut with a razor

And laid out
For at least one person to see
I break out
What are you doing to me?

It's disturbing
You radiate raw emotion
Unnerving,
Stronger than some death potion.

I escape
class is a good place to hide
From your gaze
No one else has tried to come inside.

Althea Bryan

One Matter of Being

The tipple and smack of rain,
On my page,
The fire elemental burns,
Recollections of bygone days,
Pulpous smells of intriguing novels,
Lying amidst the grass of summer,
Heavenly dew drips,
The ink blurs,
The words merge,
Helpless and uncaring,
The reading never stops,
Incomprehensible and shapeless,
The page of a novel,
Blatant and stupid,
Words and ink once divided,
Now, one matter of being,
Comprehensible, yet unreadable,
Was it just a fantasy,
Or, must I die too?

Jonathan Fleischman

Pretty Brown Face (The Sun Shines)

The sun shines
on my pretty brown face
the same face
that society frowns upon
and says will not amount to anything
but I relish the thought
knowing the sun
doesn't feel that way
So I smile...
knowing the sun
shines on my pretty brown
my pretty brown face

Carlos L. Roan

Rapid Fears

White river rapids
bashing against rocks
Causing fears which
no one blocks
As tears go rolling
rolling rolling away!

Sarah Gregory

"The Girl And The Woman"

Looking through a window,
On my soul,
I see two people,
At play,
And at odds,
One a Girl,
The other a woman,
The girl wants to laugh and play,
The Woman wants to be free,
One will go,
The other will stay,
But does it have to be this way?
Always in conflict,
Yet in harmony.

Cynthia Post

Ninety-One

Who doles out my remaining days or years
on this earth?
Is it the moon, the sun, the stars
or a higher being up above,
Once I could bend, twist and turn
at my will
I could even run in races never won
Now when even the hearing
is fading, I must just be
thankful for memories before
I was 91

Elvira V. Connerth

I Can't Look Back

One day hot, one day cold
one day young, next day old
at times I'm glad, then times I'm sad
It's not the same from day to day
But I try and try to make my way.
Life passes fast, I then think why?
How come I didn't harder try
A little late now I kind of fear.
For here it is another year,
Kind of late now for me I guess
I should have tried when I felt my best
To old to start, to young to quit
Should I just say this is it.
I believe that fate plays its hand
I have to accept where I stand
Oh well!! The cards did stack
I guess I just can't look back
My life seems wrapped in one big sack
Again, I say "I can't look back."

Anne Soehngen

The Journey

Against the wind I stand
Onto my problems I go
Below my future I am
Inside I'm feeling lonely
Outside I'm looking tough
Beyond is a long, hard, journey
By myself I go
Towards the light
After, I will feel confident

Anika Stevenson

Someone's No One

Am I just a drunken fool
or a stoner on the street
Begging for a dime or two
something please for me to eat

Walking with someone's no one
floating on my fourth cloud nine
Selling to the Mayor's son
Digging in my buried shrine

And they say are you worried now
dying deaths and the weird effect
You ask me why, what and how
the only reason is reject.

Gabrielle Graham

Identity-Crisis

I've known of myself
or at least I have for the
last few years as a —
person a role model.

And now I've come to
realize that when I was
young I was a sick young
man, person...

I've grown, through the
stages, been around the
bend....

And I've come to a fork
in the world where I'm
questioning myself...

Why do I exist? Is this
hell on earth? Or is this just
plain hell? "Why am I here?"
"Who am I?" "Why am I?"

I will search my soul to
establish myself, for I have done this.

Gerald Sakata

The Guardian

Never will I see defeat,
Or beat a dead horse.

I know you can make it;
You can run the course.

Like a Phoenix from it's ashes,
Someday you will rise.

For I have touched your soul
As I've looked into your eyes.

You are a gift of nature
From your hair down to your toes.

And you have opened up my heart
Just like a budding rose.
I will always be beside you,
For I will never rest.
I will watch you take control
Pursuing out your quest.

And when my time has ended
As I walk over the hill,

I will look back longingly,
And I will love you still.

George S. Francis

Dorothy

Were I a king or stately Lord,
    or prince of great sobriety,
With my bare hands or by my sword,
    my life I'd stake for Dorothy.

It matters not the pains of death,
    'though I suffer eternally,
The bitter torture will be blessed,
    for you, I'll bear it Dorothy.

But I'm no king, nor stately lord,
    nor prince of great sobriety,
Still no girl can be more adored,
    than I adore you, Dorothy.

And for your love I'd gladly die,
    or live my life in infamy,
I can't exist without your sighs,
    your sighs of love, my Dorothy.

Please speak the words I long to hear,
    sweet syllables of ecstasy,
soft words that say "I love you dear",
    because I love you, Dorothy.

Edmond E. Colletta

Untitled

Of all the songs of wind
Or strings or birds
Above a murmuring sea
And hers is the fairest.
And hers is the fairest.

Whenever she speaks
In love or in anger or
She breaks my
Heart confessing her fears

Her voice is the
Song that binds
Creation and

She is everything
to me.

Daniel Chambers

Time Spent With You!

You are the man I never knew
Or, was too blind to see that
every moment spend with you,
brings out the best in me.

I see a smile in every raindrop
a blessing on a leaf, I feel a
woman burn with passion each time
you're close to me.

Time spent with you is priceless
to me worth more than gold, your
precious words, and loving kindness
for you might make me fall.

Second and minute of every hour
that we have spent together I
pray to God that it might last,
I wish it was for ever.

Aidee Ramirez

Meal - Ease

It's packaged this and packaged that
Our worth is done in nothing flat
No more kneading dough
    That's too slow
We buy a box and break the seal
There stands exposed a pre-cooked meal
In the mike a while
    Turn the dial
No more a slave to stove and pot
Cooks mealtime stress is eased a lot
How we find time stands
    On our hands.

Emma Lloyd Belcher

Our Love

Swallowing water drips
over the edge of time.

Slowly draining our
love of all its newness.

Reveling our trusting
and caring side.

This is not the end,
but the beginning.

Our relationship is no
longer drips of passion,
but showers of love.

Darlynn E. Bovidge

Poem of the Wind

The wind moves through the trees,
over the old church,
cascades down the white washed wall
onto the grass
and ripples across it
out onto the river
to the channel
to the sea.

Jefferson S. Barlew

What Is Time?

Time is one thing we can't hold
Over time we have no control
God is the keeper of time
We must keep this fact in mind
There's a time for living
And a time to die
A time for happiness
And a time to cry
A time to give a time to keep
A time to wake a time to sleep
A time for caring a time for sharing
A time to love a time to be born
A time to get old weary and worn
And when all our time has past
God will take us home at last
To a place where there's no time
Only peace love and beauty sublime

Georgia Rose McLane Collins

Together

May the Lord keep watch
over you and me
when together we can't
always be.

May He guide us
safely on our way
and bring us home
to each other everyday

May He always
allow us to be
together forever
you and me.

May he never
cast doubt on our love
and keep his light shining
towards heaven above.

May the Lord keep watch
over you and me
when together we can't
always be.

Jayelee M. Stone

But Then Tomorrow

Here I stand on a mountain top
   overlooking the raging seas
Thinking of my homeland
   And its glorious memories

But yet today the world stands still
   With sadness everywhere
My God! What's happened to our land
   To cause such great despair

Today it seems as if the world
   is coming to an end
We've lost him, what a tragedy
   He was more than just a friend

For on this dark November day
   The whole world mourns and weeps
The silent words in each ones heart
   Our hero forever sleeps

God rest you Mr. President
   Your task was at death's door
But then tomorrow someone brave
   Will lead us as before

Breda Gallagher Cunningham

Pardon Me While I Cry....

I should have felt something,
Pain, guilt, remorse, sadness,
Anything, anything at all.

It was like I was the one
Dead and buried, all I could see
Was the whiskey and beer
At the end of the food line
And oblivion, no feeling, no thing.

Charley read from the bible
As we sat by Dicks lake,
I cried violently for hour's on end
And he's a young child frightened
To see his father crying for his.

Pain is a real two-edged sword
That allows us to grow
Even if it is a little late
To start acting our age.

Jeffrey L. Seger

"Our Buffet"

Our Buffet has played an important
part for a good number of years
In days gone by and even now
it carries happiness and tears
The mailman makes his daily rounds
and when we have a letter
Mom places is on the buffet and
the whole room looks much better
When there's a word of gladness
oh Buffet your so shining and so bright
When there's a word of sadness
your legs tremble with all their might
It's not that they wanted to go, the
job had to be done.
Soon the war will be over and
victory will be won
Then the sun will shine again
and the whole world will be free
My brothers three will come
marching home to Our buffet and me.

Barbara Hy

The Four Seasons

Flowers
Peeking their heads
Above Mother Nature's
Winter mantle of downy warmth...
Awake!

Yellows,
Lilacs, Ambers,
And sprouts of blues and whites
Bursting forth to greet sunny skies...
Gardens!

Chilly!
The air grows cool;
Trees compete for grandeur.
It's time to close down now for rest
And sleep.

Gale winds
Bluster about.
Glittering snow covers
The earth in stillness and beauty
'Til spring.

Bonnie Gottermeyer

Descriptions

Feelings - sad
People - confused

Friends - listeners
Lovers - ignorant

Time - out
Life - dead

Streams - meaningful
Maze - lost

Hell - heaven
Heaven - hell

Nights - dark
Days - gone

Money - wasted
Birds - soaring

School - learning
Death - approaching

Chrissa Roessner

Shadows

There are shadows quite fantastic
Playing here upon my wall.
Large ungainly friends of darkness -
Some are squat and some are tall.

For long hours at a time they remain
Each in their place,
Until someone disturbs them
Then they change their shape and space.

I have known them all my life,
These dear friends upon the wall,
And I still am making friends
For I haven't met them all.

Jane Martin

Untitled

They tell me my reasoning's poor,
Premise to conclusion not sure.
   Well, I work on a flicker
   Of what makes me snicker,
I love a good non-sequitur!

          like

There was a young man from Kilkenny
Whose relatives numbered too many.
   So with great self denial
   To give mayhem a trial
He raffled them off for a penny.

With me it's becoming a habit,
Limericks increase like the rabbit.
   If so much of the time
   I give birth to a rhyme
Should I smother it, choke it, or stab it?

Anne K. Rowe

Promises

Promises made
Promises broken
Promises kept as love's sweet token

Promise me all the stars above
Promise me I'll always be in love
Promise me all the precious jewels
Promises made to oh, such fools.

Promise you I'll never lie
Promise you the blue, blue sky
Promise you I'll never say good-bye

Promise you there will always be.

Promise made
Promises broken
Promises kept as love's sweet token,
forever, for an eternity.

Angela Carol Brooks

Jimmy and Brenda

I pray you'll walk a beautiful road
Rich in trust and love
Sprinkled with success and happiness
Sent from God above.

Set your goal together
And work to make it come true
Walk shoulder to shoulder - hand in hand
Your love will see you through.

Agness Hamilton

Priceless Old Friend

Time is our teacher
Proven wise thru the years
A wealth of life lessons
As the curtain draws near
Reminiscing of days
Filled with colorful hues
Would enlighten us all
Given what they've lived thru
Shining memories like diamonds
Once flawless and clear
Cascading away
Lost in sorrowful tear
Who are we to pass judgement
Discriminating on age
The final chapter yet written
When life leads us off stage
Take heed in this message
There's a means to its end
Such wisdom is golden
In your priceless old friend.

Joy Neff

Tickled

Shake, shake,
Quake, quake,
Oh my.
Jiggle, jiggle,
Wiggle, wiggle,
Giggle, giggle,
Oh me.
Snicker, snicker,
Quicker, quicker,
Oh no.
Tee, hee,
Ha, ha,
Ho, ho,
Hee, hee,
Oh dear!

F. C. Dean

Losing - My Mind

Trapped in my own world
Reaching for my mind
Floating around fear
and I am blind.

Shutting every door
Keeping the answer away
I don't know if I can stand
to live another day.

Between the truth and lies
There is a guiding light
But I have given up
Because I can not fight.

The past is not remembered
only what's ahead
Oh where's this pain inside me
that's leaving me dead.

My words will fall like soldiers
with everything I block
so my only escape
is the hysteria that does not talk.

Jaime Eisenschmidt

Wherefore

The pattern of chaos
Reduces the pond drop
To the cosmos
That our universe encloses.
In this water world
The dew on our lashes
Turns to tears,
The magic of the firefly
Becomes mundane
With the day.
Yet violets bloom in the concrete,
Of the mean streets,
The blossom assured,
Of its place in time.
If you hear the silence.
You will hear the wind whisper,
And the face of woman,
Upturned to moonlight
Is beauty in earth and sky.

Ida Maxey Scott

Manna

Autumn's flaming, glorious dress —
Rehearsal for future happiness.
Beauty recorded in the memory,
Brings joy, hope, and trust in Thee!

Bleak winter may peacefully sleep,
Or rage furiously, to keep,
A balance on account bearing
Simple beauty born of suffering.

Early spring heralds newness of life,
Crocus heroically push through snow.
Angels signal end of strife,
And forsythia point way to go.

Butterflies emerge from their cocoon,
Free to dance among the flowers,
Spreading nectar like a gospel tune.
His coming may be in hours!

Emma E. Glynn

A Touch Of Culture

The professor from abroad
Related this one day;
How impoverish nobles
Saw fit to come your way
And borrowed money from you,
For you, the right thing to do.

Then, later, when you met them,
Cordial was their greeting
And kind words were sent your way
(Which showed their good breeding)
With a good mood, you were left,
But your money, it was kept.

Art Ernest Juntunen

Untitled

Ethics
Do not
Sign
but defend/what is right
And suffer
Be prepared/to the end
To win

Constance DiFiglia

An Epitaph

What matter that the last communique
Reports the beach is held
Or mortar fire has reeled the foe
Back to his shattered hill?

What good to your broken body
Burning in the sun
While the golden grains of sand
Drink up the coursing blood
From your sad wounds?

They will say that you were brave,
Gave the full measure of your youth
In valiant stand
To hold the beach
Where others dauntless, true, and young
Died with you.

What good the cold regrets,
The little trinkets they will send?
They all spell out your epitaph—
A word so cold to wear upon my heart
Once warmed by your young love.

Freda S. Plummer

Untitled

These tiny incarnations
rest moments from the surface,
echoing shape,
while others remain distant
in the boughs
of the infinitely opening sky
yet to burst
with sudden approach
and pause on fingertips
as these
inviting the earth
to take that leap
that tiny yet miraculous
bound
toward
that something
returning her voice
with an ever deepening resonation.

Daniel J. Tarrant

Rhyme

Time heals all pain
reverse that axiom -
time pains all heals,
driving one insane.
We can say "I am"
comprehend "feel"?
Man can conquer the sky
-never mention
the "love dimension"-
and I ask, "why?"
Opposite sex-
understanding one's mind?
There is not time.
Mysteries perplex
each to his own kind
   rhyme.

Jordana

Magnificence Of Spring

The cool wind surrounds me-
rustling the leaves,
lifting the flowers and birds in song.

The music of the spring is
quiet, soft timid.
The chickadee gently calling,
the pine boughs humming.
all to the tune set by the wind.

I can felt it in my soul
the warmth growing steadily,
the freshness slowly unfolding
from inside my winter's heart.

A fly lands on this page
and I greet a kindred spirit
and rejoice in the magnificence of
spring.

Josalyn E. Rasmussen

Desolation

The ache within in my heart
sags my shoulders in sadness

I try to smile, feebly
To stop my quivering lips
But alas,
The tears caress my cheeks
And fall gently on heaving breasts

The pain of this moment
Takes away my breath
My body heaves with sobs
My heart is bursting
I cannot speak

Is this not more than I can bear?

Barbara Phillips Munson

The Race

One day we watched hawks,
　Sailing—
On air currents,
　Wheeling—
Above the brown - edged river,
　Diving—
Out of sight.

Now it's your turn,
　Shifting—
This way and that on icy edges,
　Taunting—
The gravel wind.

Your skis whispered
Through the flag labyrinth,
　Racing—
Against time, time,
Speeding like you,
　Blurred—
Blue against white.

Carolyn d'Entremont

Daniel

A day feels like a week
A week becomes a year
Hope stands on the edge
　of time
Beneath the gaze of fear

Lisa Copenhaver

Love, Lost And Found

I lost my love,
Sent from God above,
I did not know,
What the experience would show,
What I was to learn,
From that fateful turn,
On the path of life,
I walked on in strife.

I see now,
Through the tears that I shed,
I found the answers,
In the Bible verse I read.
Love is given
And taken away,
To teach me and strengthen me,
Bound by Faith I must stay.

Much I have lost,
But much I have found,
I feel inspired now
By those in the ground.

Cynthia J. Henrich

Changing Seasons

Misty, hazy
shades of autumn
hush the swaying
of dancing trees,
strip them off
lusty leaves
as the earth
starts to rustle
and life...
succumbs to death.

Wintry, whistling
winds of winter
hugs the whole
horizons bare,
gogs the chirping
of a robin
with the shrouding
frozen, frigid,
fluffy veil...
everything is silent and still.

Jerry E. Uy

"My Friend"

Unwanted and unloved,
She came into my life
Not by design, just luck,
And stole my heart that day.

Oh, how we roamed and trod
The city parks and streets
With restless wanderlust,
Every day, year after year.

Time passed and we grew old.
How come? We have no zest!
Our pace became a crawl
Is this the very end?

Yes, pal, indeed it is.
For days and days I wept
When I put her to sleep
She was my dog, my friend.

Frank De La Rosa

One

She wanders the streets alone
She has no one, no home

She cries herself to sleep
She lives in an alley, hers to keep

She dreams of a time, a place
Where everyone is one race

One race of love, no hate
One race of people, no gate

No gate to shut you out
It's you everyone cares about

No one cares of your color
Everyone is a brother

Now her dream is not there
Now no one seems to care

She wanders the streets alone
She has no one, no home.

Brooke Neiger

Untitled

My angel has eyes of stone,
She looks down upon me with crimson
　empathy.
Her dawn has long since faded,
　grown cold in the stale winds
　of indifference.
She has left me.
Gone is the life in my eyes,
　the carefree days of my youth.
Empty is my soul, for I am one
　who sees yet is blind,
Who lives yet does not,
Who hurts but feels nothing.
Soon I will join her inside her
　kingdom in the sky,
And embrace her with lifeless
　arms.

Jim Meeker

My Best Friend

I whisper a secret,
she never tells.
She'll be my friend,
it will never fail.

We talk on the phone,
and share our clothes.
She's very caring,
and sweet as a rose.

We do our homework,
while listening to music.
She'll always be there for me,
even when I lose it.

We get into fights,
and still remain friends.
We're as close as sisters,
best friends till the end!

Danielle Easterday

Anything...

Anything...for her I would do anything. The way she holds
me and looks into my eyes is enchanting. She holds the
Key to my heart, she is my emotion, everything I do
contains a part of her in it. When you look at the most
beautiful priceless artwork and are held captive for
a moment, this is the hold she has on me. She controls
my destiny, in her eyes lies my fate. Those big,
beautiful, sensuous eyes are like a magic mirror. I see
No reflection, only love from the depths of her heart.
She is the reason for my state of unconsciousness. With
her in my mind nothing else is evident. I am impervious
to pain, not knowing of the passing of time, and reluctant
to speak when she is near. My only wish is to gaze into
her eyes and be held in her grasp for eternity. Knowing
that this is an improbable wish I cherish the times at
which I can indulge in her stare. She is the reason
I live, love and continue. Shannon is my one
and only love for the rest of time.

Marcus Arens

Why Now?

Why now, after so long do you want to shelter
me with your arms when for so long it was your fists that
put me to sleep at night?
Forgive and forget are the only words that I can hear
murmured from your lips, even they don't sound sincere.
But for how long do I forget, until I meet your dark
side once again when the world seems to give you the cold
shoulder?
How long will this be? You make me fear my own presence,
how dare you make me fear what is inside longing to be free
from the hatred that is within you.
Unable to let another close to me, I sit here alone.
I will someday repay the favor.

Kelly Stein

Bahama Mama Blues

Slowly descending on to a small busy runaway, Hearts pounding,
minds spinning with the anticipation of what's to come next.

Rapidly walking through the Airport terminal following the
lead of the other passengers as they go through customs, while
all the time quietly rejoicing in the fact that I'm finally here.

Willowy trees, winding roads, complexion kissed by the God's
If this isn't Heaven, then what is?

Cool, clear, clean blue water slowly caressing my ankles,
while easing away the cares of the day
Sandy white beaches sparkling under the rays of the Sun, beckoning
my feet to come and take a relaxing walk back to the Hotel.

Sunrises that show an Island completely encompassed by water,
shimmering in the first rays of the morning sun, castings
it's blessings on man and beast.
While Sunsets are filled with the sound of Island rhythm's

How I miss thee my peaceful Island retreat

Sharon T. Myrick

Untitled

Red, white, black, brown and yellow
mix and swirl together in USA's melting pot
are we a rainbow-color jello
or a frozen dinner store-bought?

No, we are a home-cooked meal
where all the ingredients blend
into a seven-course dinner with appetizing appeal
for freshness, everyday, add to the pot - a new friend.

Melida Ojeda

The Man In The Mirror

As I look back, I watched and waited to see that Man in the mirror
Puberty was fairly easy, not many disappointments or questions
    but there was still a quest to see a man in the mirror
The Marine Corps, marriage and fatherhood all came and went-
    they were easy and the boy still looked for the man.
Many years passed with hardship, joy, sorrow and sacrifice
The professional achievements were many, the personal strife
    huge and the peace the man longed for gone
All to quickly a man's face looked in the mirror and saw a boy-
    naive, unsure and timid-full of questions about life and
    what it is all about.
The pain was intense, a hundred times that of the first broken heart
The memory of that first love long gone, but the emotion, pain,
    hurt and disappointment of the present far too real and personal
The man who now looks in the mirror sees a boy and longs for the
    days that he did not recognize
The days he saw the man in the mirror

Mark P. Hines Sr.

Votre (Yours)

Words, thus engraved in a simple tree,
Misshapen lines that stab,
Uneven distorted shreds pressed,
Uninterpreted feelings flowing,
Stopped only by the ceasing of a pen.
For the machine will continue churning,
will the paper ever burn only to be
shredded like the bitterness of one
simple leaf.
Leave
For the words must stay, for they are thine.
Time
do not carry the ignorance of your own accord.
For the truth lies within the roots,
Ever bound and mangled within one great book.
Eyes, continue to play,
closed and the words remain for even the
devil will speak.

Molly Voges

Love Is A Four Letter Word

It is often misused, misplaced, misapplied, distorted, ignored and
    misnamed.
Often what is called love is not.
There is love and absence of love - that is all.

Love cannot turn into hate.
Hatred is not the opposite of love, rather a focus of suppressed
anger.

Lust is not love, but emotional excitement
related to power, control, pleasure, and gratification.

Love is the creative energy, the dance of light within;
the quiet warmth of being - acceptance without conditions;
an inner calm, the still small voice;
the physical world, and the spiritual world;
awareness of unity with each other;
the essence of all.

Love flows, never still, always in motion.
Love cannot be held or contained, only experienced and shared.
It is the living expression of source, in, around, and through us all.

Your are love, I am love, God is love;
We are love.

Stephen Ruback

Death Valley at Night

Sand dunes spotted with scrawny trees.
  Moon-lit spectres on hump-back seas.
Oceans spilled out through burnished days.
  The night now tells of a primordial haze,
With huddled stars, a ghostly breeze,
  The crush of nature in silent sleep.

All this does seem a surrealist dream.
A still-life wild with inanimate schemes.
The God of Zen here reigns supreme.
  Paul York

Little Girl Within

The full moon rises as darkness falls
Moonlight shadows dance on the walls
In this house she feels trapped and alone
No one is around, everyone is gone

Not one person understands the way she feels
Could not possibly know unless, until...
Until they could touch her anger, fear, and pain
That started as a little girl and will always remain

The abuse of a child is confusing to all
"How did you get those bruises... did you fall?"
"Yes, I fell." That's what little girls say
But that little girl's bruises grow deeper each day

She becomes independent, and everyone says, "She's great!"
But she can't get close to boys who she has learned to hate
Now that she is older, her past is hidden within
She's as good an actress as there has ever been

Has struggled through Depression, Anorexia, Low self-esteem
Behind closed doors, nothing is ever as it seems
All these things have made her strong, yet forgiving
The only thing to do now is find happiness within and keep living!!!
  Tina Marie Lufkin

Complacency

Ships docked within the harbour,
  Moorings taut and quite secure,
Sit with delight upon calm waters
  Ne'er drifting out to ocean's lure.

Yet just beyond the harbour bar
  Sea billows roll and toss
Souls desperate for the placid calm...
  But most at sea are lost.

Shunning undertow of current,
  Swelling waves and rising tides,
Schooners tethered to their boat slips
  Sit in the bay to hide.

They could go out on the rescue
  To battered skiffs in storm-tossed seas;
Yet they choose to sit serenely
  While others are lost eternally.

But storms have a way of brewing
  And venture inland to the shore,
Irrespective of the souls there
  Who naively wait to be destroyed.
  Micki M. Padgett

Present or Past

Why wait with yearning for tomorrow?
More desirable things might come with sorrow.
Why waste one's time and think your doomed,
Throw away the danger that may depress,
Hark! Live your life. Guard your happiness.

To be alive one must face everything
With modest grace; for being joyful
When times are tough. For caring
When the road gets rough

Through the years of heartache and dismay
one may grieve but
When you reach the autumn years
the world indeed will appear to be gray.
Do not let this make you sad;
But indeed be glad!
Turn this to praise
Hark! So many things to be
How few the days.
  Lorna M. Lassick

Cirrus

Oceans
    more than one
    stretching farther than I can see
    layered one on top of the other
Mountains in the distance, castles of the sky

marshmallowy fluff
    at one moment
        the next-roaring
        choppy waves rolling away underneath my wing
    dense and white
    a billion chameleons
        of shape and form
  Sally Hartzog

I Remember

Times were different when I was little.
Mother stayed home making peanut brittle.

It's really a shame our children miss out
On the fun filled moments that life's all about.

We came from school and Mother was waiting
With cookies and milk or apple pie baking.

Then run to meet the kids out back,
Red rover to play, hide and seek or jacks.

Our lives were active in body and mind.
We had no T.V. to steal our time.

No grown up guns, no violence, no hate,
No kids killing kids, no fear of rape.

We had no malls for hanging around,
No useless waste of time was found.

We had fun being kids, but youth of today,
No longer have childhood, it's stolen away.

Our life was complete with family and friends.
Oh, that our children could be children again.
  Norma McClain

Memories

I sit by the window all alone,
Motionless like a ruin of years forlorn,
Gazing into space early at dawn,
Waiting for the new day to be born,
And wondering about days long passed and gone,
Also of those coming up with things unknown.
Those passed still stand fresh in my memory,
With minutes like honey sweet,
With emotions and feelings that mingled in harmony,
Will remain cherished in my heart with every beat,
Also dreaded times with shadows and fears,
Empty triumphs, painful regrets and sad defeats,
Some ups and some downs, few smiles and few tears,
Unnoticed scratches and deep scars barely concealed,
Bitter wounds of a soul that cannot heal for years,
They neither faded away nor disappeared,
But are all there deeply engraved in the chamber of
    MEMORIES.
    Regina D. Moshe

The Mountain Of Love That I Have For You

I, have this
Mountain of love
Deep inside my heart
For you, and you only.

As, the years
Have gone by,
My mountain of love
Has grown larger and larger
Gradually melting its snow caps away

So, will you
Please come climb
This mountain which has
Been cleared for your passage?
Reaching the highest point is the hardest
It's an accomplishment which will take great
Amount of thought, time, and preparation for survival.
So, start gathering your hiking equipment and begin climbing.

Just, know that, I'll be waiting
Patiently and open-armed
To greet you and never let you down
    Katherine Papadimitriou

Symphony of Autumn

Golden leaves dancing in the autumn breeze,
Moving in rhythm with the swaying trees.
Autumn's fresh sweetness pervades the air,
With the smell of burning leaves everywhere;
The restless birds of summer take flight,
Putting an emptiness to morning light.
Autumn's skyline stands out a little bleak;
A reminder, that the sun has grown weak,
And all too soon winter's wind will blow,
Whistle and moan through boughs hanging low.
All creatures huddle in Mother Nature's arms,
To find warmth before winter's many charms.
Meadows once lush green have turned brown,
Faded flower petals one-by-one fall down.
No emerald green grass, but auburn instead,
Covered with leaves, orange, gold and red.
As the last dry leaf falls, cymbals clash;
The "Symphony of Autumn," over in a flash!
    Margaret E. Hill

To Alyssa, My Daughter

With your big, bright eyes full of blossoming love;
My beautiful baby, so innocent and so pure;
You are God's Perfection, of this I am sure.
That cold January day you were sent from above,
My wonderful angel, on the wings of a dove.
You are truly a gift, and I do assure
you that your life is protected — my faith will endure,
And get stronger through time, for you are my true love.
But what of the Hate of the generations past?
He turned mother against daughter, friend against friend,
And broke the true bonds that were to hold fast.
Do not worry my dear, this is where it will end—
To past mothers and daughters we will contrast;
For our lifetime of friendship is about to begin.
    Sandra L. Lopez

Why Me

The room was cold,
My body, it looked so old,
I hear a soft whisper,
And then, a low sniffle,
I fought with all my might,
My death, it just wasn't right.
I served proud and strong,
I think, there going to miss me after all,
I think, I see it starting to snow,
Then my door, slowly goes closed,
I still wonder, why did I have to die,
I wasn't that, bad of a guy,
If you asked me to do it again,
I'd look at you, like I didn't understand,
I wish, everybody could of seen,
How much life, really meant to me.
    Robert Lewis

Seeing the Sunshine for the First Time

I'm in a hole full of dirt
My clothes become stained of this black soil
And I can't shake it free.

I'm in a hole full of dirt
Sinking into the despair I feel
And I remember you, your kindness.

I want to be rescued from this hole, yet
I wish I could erase all the pain I've caused.
I'm helpless.

I want to tell you I'm sorry, and I love you
But I'm scared of your reaction.
I'm lonely.

Then, I see a light, a ray of hope
That illuminates my dark hole until
I can see the bright sun.

Only then do I realize
I can have faith, and I arise.
I shake the dirt off my clothes,
And I walk into the world.
I'm ready.
    Katie Windett

Forever Memory

Missing you I shed a tear.
My cries of love you do not hear.
Your beautiful image pervades my mind.
A wonderful memory I'll always find.

When I place my hands upon your hips,
I can hear a silent whimper escape your lips.
When I stare deeply into your charming eyes,
I am controlled with a power I'm unable to deny,

As we tremble underneath each other's hands,
As I sweep you off to another land,
As our bodies get nearer and nearer,
My vision becomes clearer and clearer.

I wonder from the weakness of your embrace,
From the expression upon your face,
From the comfort you don't ask for,
That you don't love me anymore.

As I protect you within my arms,
My love for you is still unharmed.
Even though I sense your heart growing cold,
It is you I will forever hold.

Peter Yen

The Most Precious of Images

I reached out and touched you
My fingers enfolded you, and your cool exterior delighted my senses.
You sent me travelling to another time and place.
You are my escape from now and today.
I went with my feelings, and felt the strain leave my mind.
You're my friend and peace of mind, - you are my unicorn.
Oh sweet creature, why is there such peace and joy when I touch you?
Travel with me through the meadows covered in the brightest color,
let me walk holding your mane.... Let's run together to the sparkling
brook, and drink of it's fresh clear waters, then lie by me in
the coolness of the green in the forest; let us be friends for this
life and the next.
You are my Unicorn.
The most precious of images.

Victoria Lynn Mulcahey

As My Eyes Fall Upon Myself

As my eyes fall upon myself I see the glitter of my personality
my good humor indulges myself in laughter
as my romance finds myself weeping
my faith carries myself up to sit with God
my kindness reaches to fill my hungry stomach
my generosity put the separable money in my poor hand
my love unused waiting for my acceptance
as I sit in a dark corner waiting to learn how to use my gifts
if only I knew who I was
if only I knew who I'm going to be
if only I knew the answer to all my problems

Todd DeJong

Learning

As we make our way in this
School we call life we experience
the dark and the light. In the
process of learning we may find
ourselves yearning for something
that seems so out of reach. But
the knowledge we acquire could lead
us to our desire and what we
learn we shall teach.

Joan Doranzo

Autumn

Whenever I see
my grandmother's house,
it is in an old Cleveland suburb,
fall has just begun,
many children play in the park.

I sit in the kitchen,
while the autumn breeze blows through
the window,
sweeping away the smoke,
as my grandfather sits across the table,
and puffs on a cigarette.

But this is not my story.
My story is seeing an empty hospital bed,
silently sitting in the living room,
after the funeral,
the death caused by his precious addiction.

Meighan Hargreaves

To Justin

Oh my love, my fair one,
My heart and my delight,
You shine like satin in the night.
You glow golden as the day. Golden!
Oh my handsome one,
You are my all, my own true love. My dove.
You touch my heart and soul.
Come to me now.
My knight in white satin,
Has wisdom come to you? Has love?
Then come to me and see what we can be together.
My love for you is never ending,
I want to warm your heart and life
Oh my love, my heart's desire is toward you, for you alone.
Won't you let me love you?
Oh my sweet and golden boy,
My own true love.
My desire is toward you.

Talis Turner

Beyond The Sun

Each day goes by the pain is there
My heart can not find peace

I wait for night to close my eyes
To sleep and rest my soul
But once again the morning comes and with it brings the hurt

My thoughts go back to days of love
My son just you and I
I look for you as each day begins
At night as each day ends

I search to find the reason why
I seek my heart to mend
The wind calls out to let me know
To make me understand

You soul has reached a better place
A place beyond the sun

I feel you reaching out for me
I hear you call my name
And soon my Son I'll reach out to you
In that place beyond the sun

Shirley G. Richmond

Tom

When this handsome man Tom came into sight.
My heart grew wings and took flight.

I knew I would marry him, but not too soon.
Eight years later - We wed in June.

We lived thirty-five years as husband and wife.
It's as though I've known him all my life.

There were good times, as well as bad.
We've laughed, we've cried, been happy and sad.

God blessed us with one girl and two boys.
All grown now, with their own tears and joys.

My friend, my spouse, my lover and more.
He's leaving us now, through a different door.

Time is fleeting - Oh so fast!
Not yet. Dear Lord - Make the moment last!

The sun is setting on this lovely day.
It's time to say "Lord, have it your way!"

Lord guide Tom to your heavenly gate.
He'll wait for me - 'Cause we have a date.

My Tom, with the dancing eyes so blue.
My love, my darling, is only you!

Mary Ann Corcoran

Restless Heart

Like an angel fallen from grace
My heart is feeling out of place.
For once I learned that love was a lie.
My heart jumped up and said "goodbye."
And though to say this gives me great pain.
The search for my heart has been in vain.
I looked under tables - I checked under chairs.
Even under the rug - but my heart was not there!
I ran through the neighborhood knocking on doors.
I searched under the hat of the wino who snores.
On the back of milk cartons, I made my plea.
"For a runaway heart who belongs to me."
I even appeared on the T.V. talk shows.
But where my heart is - nobody knows.
Now I'm forever doomed to be heartless and alone.
While 'round the world, my restless heart roams.
I heard my heart is searching for someone to hold.
Someone whose love won't be forced or told.
My heart's in hot pursuit for a love that's true.
And it will never give up - until it catches you!

Stephanie Rochester

Sweet Love

Hold me in a gentle embrace
See the passion upon my face
Kiss me with your full lips
Squeeze me tight upon your hips
Love me now and thru the night
Then again in dawns light
Silken skin, beaded sweat
Passion that has been met and met
Whispering sweetly of our love
Birds singing in the trees above
Listening to each other sigh
While we lay thigh on thigh

Christine J. Felten

I Desire

Where do I begin to Voice these pent-up feelings of mine?
My Heart whispers your name and visions of you Ebb into my Soul.
I gaze into your Loving eyes and feel your radiance Enfold my being.
I am Branded by the Sensuality you embrace.
Oh, is there Anything under the Heavens
that I would not give to Touch you once
like no one else ever has?
I not only want to Caress you as a lover,
or to take in your sweet smell;
but I Desire to merge with your Soul
to mold us into One,
to Touch your Heart as softly
as flickering butterfly wings would.
I Desire to take all of you in,
to Taste your life,
to feel your Spirit take Wing.
I Desire you,
and I Desire to know that we have said
"I Love You"
Without Words.

Kathy Hicks

The Majestic Ride

I am a carousel horse on a merry-go-round;
  My life filled with laughter and musical sounds.
Lights and mirrors fly past me, as I journey along;
  With my head lifted upward, I waltz to the song.
Prancing to the music, I take children for a ride;
  I move in perfect rhythm, other animals at my side.
The tiny child, on my back, is clutching my reins;
  Her father is beside me, caressing my mane.
My golden mane is swept with a magical wind;
  My tail flowing proudly, showing strength within.
My bridle and saddle are brilliantly jeweled;
  By the finest wood craftsman, I was tooled.
My majestic body is brushed with gold;
  Children want to ride on me, so I am told.
The children in front reach for the brass ring;
  Laughter and cries in the air, loudly sing.
For years, I have rounded the mirrored drum;
  The crowds around me, a deep, steady hum.
Feelings of strength and majesty, I hope to inspire;
  For providing joy and peace, I will never tire.

Patrice Thomas

The Working Maid

I was born poor on a farm without an education
My life was hard, I know not of another nation
I went not to school for there was none
Worked sun up to sun down till the work was done.
This was done through fourteen years of life.
Until I got married and became a wife.

My husband died leaving me with three tots
I had to move for I wanted them to have lots.
From the farm to the city I became a maid
I knew I would do good, 'I promised God', I said.

My children finished high school and oh, I was glad!
I told them I wanted to finished college or I'd be sad.
I took another job to help them you see
For I wanted them to have everything better than me
I worked until all the three finished college, I was so proud!
'I done what I promised god', I yelled out loud.

My children became a doctor, lawyer and teacher, you see
For I was there to see each one receive a degree
Now old without any help; my children's gone I've not seen.
God knows what I said and He knows what I mean.

Stanley Williams Jr.

Lisa

Although so many nights have passed
  My love for you has far from died
    And though I might appear held fast
    In darkened chambers I have cried

Random thoughts pass through my mind
  Can't sleep; my eyes are opened wide
    As I drag through the daily grind
    From pain and loss I can not hide

Another seasons holiday
  Will pass without you in my arms
    I'm close to you; you're far away
    Immune to my effects of charm

It seems there's nothing I can do
  In bringing your love back to me
    But you should know that I'll love you
    And hope that always
      You'll be free.

    Mark A. Phaneuf

My Love

To grow to love a woman like you;
my love has to be complete and also very true.
  It's ways in which to show
emotions and words from the heart;
  But in your mind you must know the
right word to start.
  I'm not saying there will always be
happiness in days to come;
  That's why it's two people in a relationship
instead of one.
  I must say from this day after
and years to come by;
  That my love is with you forever
and even in every tear drop that you cry!

    Ralph Vashawn Footman

Monsters

  There's no such thing as monsters
my mother said to me,
But there is one thing in this world as
monstrous as can be.
It is not gruesome to the eye and as you
think all hairy.
But its a dangerous threatening thing and
to you should be scary.
It's face is not all green and scaled as you
might tend to think.
But soft and clean with undertones
of lovely orange and pink.
It makes no sounds like grows or howls and
does not have big teeth yet it is mean and
wicked and means harm underneath.
It has all of human features I hope you
can understand the monster that I warn
you of is just a simple man.

    Kim Baxter

Our Narcissus

In form of a bulb thou gave to me
  My narcissus then quite wee.
And now a sturdy plant has bloomed
 .With green shoots that nature has groomed.
A flower white and undefiled
  Natures own most beautiful child.
Pleasures that arise from a simple thing
  Becomes a sweet memory to the heart will cling.

    Mildred E. Stacey

The Sycamore

Though my body be bare, yet I do not rot.
My nakedness embarrasses me, but that be my lot.
Just wait and see when spring comes around again,
I'll stand majestic and resume my reign.
I'll give beauty and grace to the surroundings terrain.
And moisture and nutrient to the parched plane.
Appearance aren't all. I'll still stand tall.
Autumn! That's when I'm at my best,
With hues that outshine the rest.
Jack Frost is the least of my worries,
For I've cradled many young lovers and listened to their stories.
I still have many, many years before losing my stature,
Then I'll have done my duty: to serve Mother nature.

    Kenneth A. Campbell

Please Hold My Baby

Daddy, I wonder, have you seen my child,
  my new beginning which was cut short -
Daddy, I wonder, was this life allowed to bloom in heaven,
  with looks which do not distort -
Daddy, I wonder, if this life had been granted its blooming on earth,
  would it look like you, instead of abort -
And Dad, I wonder, are you truly there, or was life merely a sport -
Did you meet God with open arms - did he retort,
My son, my son, you've reached your end,
  and now a new beginning is about to unfold -
Dad, I wonder, would you, for me, hold my baby, rock it
  in rhythmic chimes of love, and only unto God allow it to be sold
-
Could you, would you, Dad, do this for me -
I feel you do owe me this much you see,
You left me too early in history -
I was never given the chance to let you get to know me -
I never was given the opportunity -
So instead, Daddy, instead of holding me,
I wonder, Daddy, would you please hold my baby,
My baby, Mine, you see.

    Katie Brickman

Role Reversal

"There's no chance of your going to Saudi?"
My question was more of a plea.
Because
I knew what the answer would be.

My sister's blue eyes avoided my stare.
"I don't think so," she smiled and said,
"Because...
the active troops will go instead."

We both knew we were kidding ourselves.
How could they take my baby sister
When
Surely they knew I would miss her?

All our lives I watched over her.
I protected and provided care.
When
She needed me most I was there.

As the deadline came for her to go
I was helpless to keep her around.
How?
Why? A man over 200 pounds!

    Kay Lohner

The Birth and Death of a Dream

A dream born brightly in my soul.
My soul is ablaze.
It is engulfed in an euphoric stupor.
The fire shoots through my entire being,
Until I feel my skin tingle.

Dream slowly changing.
Fading from my grasp.
My spirit is plummeting to earth with a crash.
My hope light is flickering.
Getting dimmer until it glows by embers.
Tears streaming down, drowning my spirit.
My spirit asks, "why?"
My dream is slowly dying is my reply.
My hope light is extinguish, surrounded by darkness.
I have lost my way.
I have settled!

Nedra L. Coleman

Little Zane

This morning I woke up and thought of you.
My tears flowed down for, maybe an hour or four.
I could not forget the day, in that old empty house,
When you looked at me and said, "My mama doesn't ever
  come here any more.

We fell in love when you were only a day or two.
I picked you up from your bassinet and held you.
The world around was yet warmth and light,
We didn't know then that there would be a dark "night."

I kept you all day for a year or two.
You sat up close to me and clung to me to sleep.
You were one of a few sent from heaven,
Oh, why does this earth have to make us weep!

I cannot live if my tears continue to flow.
I want to sit beside you and feel your smile.
But life has changed for us all,
And your little heart may get hard with each mile.

But someday, a man, all grown you'll be:
And I shall be gray, old, and wore.
But in my heart, I'll still hear you say,
"My mama doesn't ever come here any more."

Patricia H. Barnhill

Veteran's Day

Dad...
My time like yours, has finally come
War is here, its finally begun.
Life or death, is either or.
What might happen, what's in store?
Throughout my life, your stories you've told,
The courage of men, the young and the bold.
Each one I'd listen to, with interest at hand.
Who knew years later, I'd be fighting in sand.
At night I lay here, listening to sounds.
Hoping and praying, no incoming rounds.
The sounds of war, is an unpleasant noise.
Destruction of land, and dying young boys.
I'll admit I'm afraid, and the job won't be fun.
But America's been called and the job must get done.
Just like you, we were the first at the scene.
Just like you, I'm a U.S. Marine
When this job is all over, we all be glad
I'll come home a veteran, just like you Dad

Sean Cowan

Change of Season

Ah! Autumn is suddenly here!
My very favorite time of the year.
Once it was Summer—before that, Spring;
But now, to me, Autumn's everything.

Our Wedding Anniversary and Harvest Moon;
Autumn leaves (that familiar tune);
Halloween's coming with costumes and fun;
Thanksgiving's soon, then THE BIG ONE.

Yes, Christmas is special
With memories ever dear.
There's nostalgia and excitement
At Christmas, each year.

Time performs wonders.....
It mellows each creature;
With age comes a deepening
Insight into Nature.

In the Autumn of my life
I often pause to ponder:
Do the tools God has given us
Prolong this awesome wonder?

Peggy Walker Cozzi

My World

If the stars and heaven were to both fall today,
My world would not end.
If God destroyed man in a fit of anger,
My life would not be over.
If pleasant dreams no longer visited me,
I could still sleep.
If the sun saw fit never to shine again,
I would still see light.
Even if hope, the reason for living, disappeared
I could still live.
Friend of my body and spirit,
do you not see, don't you understand?
You are part of my world, my life, my
dream.
You are my light and my hope.
But, how can I tell you this?
How can I let you know how
I feel?

Krist Peterson

Traffic

Two ways, two way streets that ends nowhere,
near and far, we try to pursue one way, here or there.
Can we succeed, or do we have to fight,
can we turn away, and answer the next man polite.
Africans we are, but Blacks we are called,
be proud, be loud, bear it, we will prevail all.
Down the road we travel, back and forth and yet the same spot,
what can it be? Why can't I see? That this place
wasn't created to hold me.
Society itself, passes us by, they cry equal, but
we know it's a lie.
We build their schools, we build their penitentiaries,
they succeed, while we fall in their territories.
But I along with my fellow brethren, are a few who
didn't got trapped.
But our destiny is far, and there's more trouble ahead.
So teach us well, don't turn your head,
cause this is life, it's not the end...

Victoria Scarlett

Yesterday, Today and Tomorrow

Before today there was yesterday. Yesterday is over now and will
never come again.
After today is tomorrow. Tomorrow will always be a new beginning.
Before tomorrow comes there is today, take it slowly, there is always
another day.
After the sun goes down, the moon and stars will shine, lighting your
way in the darkest of times.
Forget about yesterday, live for today. Tomorrow will soon be on its
way.
Remember today and yesterday with sadness if you must, anticipate
tomorrow, as it will be here soon after dusk.

Lori Harris

My Grandma

She was so happy, always full of laughter,
Never complained.
She didn't have a single fear,
Oh, I loved her so dear.
She was my own flesh and blood
I was very happy sitting with her and talking.
Then, through gray, still eyes I looked at my Grandma
As she breathed a tired sigh
She was in pain it was easy to see
And the tear in her eye had touched me
I realized that someday
We'd be sitting here talking as usual
And again in her eye I would see the tear
She would start crying,
Or maybe be silent.
Then,
She would stretch out her arms,
Breath her last sigh
And slowly, but willingly
Leave me and die.

Michelle Hamilton

Never Give Up

No matter what may happen.
"Never give up"
Even thou our days are not always spent together.
"Never give up"
(On me or us) no matter if you can not see your way
"Never give up"
Rain may come, snow may go, always believe in your dreams.
Only you can make your dreams come true.
"Never give up"
Life has so much to give you. All you must do is keep
Walking in the light.
"Never give up"

Laura Ann Gibson

Rain

Just a small child,
   never understood why.
Dad's hitting mom, sister always cries.
Woke up every morning
pretending everything was great.
Soon as I saw dad, my mind was full of hate.
I remember thinking, I just
   wish he would die......
Leaving us forever, ending my sister's cry.
Never understood him, never
Asked him why.
   Now it's all over, I've said my
Last good bye.
Memories of childhood so full of pain.
All forgotten now.
Washed away by the rain
   "washed away by the rain."

Shane Risley

The Reader

Books, Magazines almost everything.
Newspapers, backs of the cereal boxes.
Contracts, billboards anything the eye can scan.
Poems, prose, horoscopes, the Bible.
Read for pleasure.
Read for information.
Read to discover.
READ, READ, READ.
Read the small print
I love to Read!

Lois Elain Darrington

Dawn of Hope

The sun comes up in the morning each day;
no different for them than for you or for me.
Then each evening, of course, it gets dark and it's night;
they to bed, and to sleep and dream.

So why, if their days and their nights are the same,
if they eat and they drink and they live and they die,
why do their hopes live with greater assurance;
their fears all diminish with time?

Can it be that some small thing that started in childhood
has left an impression as deep as the heart?
Can it be that just one thing has made all the difference,
has let them look forward with joy?

Their hope started long before they can remember.
Their mothers, it seems, had been taught that it's best
to sing their babies awake in the morning
instead of to sleep at night.

Theodore J. Cullen

Earth's Soul

It has a history of its own
No hatred can bequeath
So many stories to tell
So many years to live
Not knowing its future
But knowing only novelties of the past
Our forefathers it's seen
Harsh wars it's bared
Many a child born into its world
Many a man lost in its despair
Though through our greediness
We may override the bareness of its structure
No barterer shall reveal
It's mixed emotions and untouched exposures

Nicholas L. Cooper

The Last Rose

The last rose of summer, so beautiful to see,
My love picked it from the bush and handed it to me,
I took it and smelled it and pressed it to my heart.
We swore to love forever and never ever to part.
He was a perfect lover, all I hoped that he would be.
We married in the spring time, no couple happier than we.
The years have passed, I knew they would,
We made our love last, I knew we could.
I opened an old picture book, and there between the fold,
lay that beautiful rose, my love had given me to hold.
The petals are all faded now, and as the years flew by,
the rose is my favorite flower, now you know the reason why.

Sara E. Stone

Dear Old Al

It could not happen - "not to me!"
No memory of short - but long
And then one morn - the sun a bright
My thoughts of yesterday - had taken flight

In fright and alone - "Where am I now?"
This place, this dwelling - "I do not know"
"My family gone?" and "Who is she?"
Or, "He?" — and day or night - "I crow."

"My mother is alive you know"
and I, myself, am ninety - three."
My husband, wife, or child, I see.
But cannot remember - did they visit me?

"What do I do each minute think — I'm told — and repeat — repeat a
toil its wheel chair now — feed me too or clean me — when I soil

Wash my face and wipe a tear and now a prison — this bed
I am hot, or cold, then laugh or smile
This life with Alzheimers — most dread

I do remember — the college days of past and all I did for fun
But today — and tomorrow — woe unto me
A new life's cycle — has now begun

    Val Kohlman

Geese Of The 90's

Geese of the 90's they swim across the sea,
no need for arithmetic, they do whatever they please,
cause they're geese of the 90's they swim across the shore,
try and look for the fish that they might store.

No need for a pencil and paper,
they fly where they can caper,
look around all the rivers,
OH my gosh there's some beavers,
no wonder geese are cool,
they don't have to go to school,
all they do is look for food,
that's why they have a good attitude.

They can fly and they can honk,
hope they don't go kerplunk,
stuck there into the sand,
Uh Oh! Let's give 'em a hand,
they eat fish and they eat trout,
that's why they wonder about,
they can run but they can't hide.
when they get wet they always get dried.

    Lauren Lee Lipshaw

Love

There is no age for burning love,
No segregated youth for heart's desire
Not only for you, dear girl and boy
To feel the depths of the soul on fire.

The heart never ceases to jump with joy
When a special one comes into sight,
And vibrate with ecstatic emotion,
Making eyes twinkle like a star studded night.

Earthly beings must succumb to age
Love of the spirit is heaven sent
The budding of love will never cease,
The function of its amorous motion never spent.

Ageless are poets great works on love
By snowcapped lovers, love songs are sung
Love, yes, love is without an age
The rapture of heart forever young.

    Mary E. Smith

Young Future

When I was a teen-aged youngster
No one could tell me a thing.
This whole wide world was my oyster,
I was going to have myself a "fling."
I would step right into that future
That offered so much from the start.
Not thinking there'd be any changes,
Not knowing I'd follow my heart.
Oh that future offered so much to me,
Education - travel and fun.
But that first step led me straight to you
And my traveling alone, was done.
The road we have traveled together
Has been filled with detours, but yet
Through the years we have found our future
And we have no cause for regret.
Today our children stand on that threshold
And if they should ask where to start.
I'd tell them, "Have Faith and Courage.
Step out and Follow Your Heart."

    Mavis L. Selby

Alone

I am alone, I stand by myself, no where to hide,
No where to go.
I listen to my inner voice, fearing I'll make
a wrong choice.
I go with my mind leaving my fears all behind.
I wonder what will happen next, no one knows on what to expect.
I pray that I'll meet someone along the way.
I can't do it by myself, for now I know I stand all alone.
I am afraid to walk this path alone.
So please come with me, guide me,
for there are too many unwinding paths to face all alone.
There are many twists and turns along the way.
I try alone to face it everyday, but I can't do it.
So please reach out your hand, so I can at least stand,
Knowing that you're right behind me all the way,
I know I don't have to face the world all alone everyday!

    Stefanie Sileo

Universality

Judge me not by the color of my skin,
Nor by the clothes my body travels in.
For I too, was born under the sun,
And just like you, I am but one.
Forgive my ancestors for what they may have done,
And accept me for what I have become.
We've all tasted bitter pain,
Chewed and swallowed our pride.
We've digested all emotions,
And liberated the awful hate inside.
Both of us breathe the same kind of air,
Whether you're here, or I'm over there.
Our commonality is mortality,
And fear of the unknown.
And if history is a teacher,
Let us learn what has been shown.
Here's a toast to peace,
And its cup of redemption.
Drink up humans!
And let's become one.

    Sylvester Sibert

Without Eternity?

Together not once more spiritually we two?
Nor forever, best friend, sweet incense
No more to enjoy with you?
To know that I could never more feel
Your hand in mine in spirit, as on
Earth before, rests not well upon
My mind
My soul would have no peace at all
(My earthly life knows little now)
If it knew it couldn't ease the call
To join you there somehow
While looking towards the skies above
Talking to you day and night
I'm seeing through sad eyes of love
You smiling - sending light
A light I know that will never fade
A light that forever will be
Mama, love I send back to you
Through all eternity.

Melany Slane

Sweet Mysteries Of Life

Of the heart, there can be no explanation
Nor of the spirit or the soul
Mysterious things drive them,
unbridled, unknown, even to myself
With my mind I force my body
to do the things that give me purpose,
that give me goals
Yet strange and wondrous things take hold
as passing loves and passing times
bring me moments of great joy and pain
but, all things pass, both good and bad
only to start through a cycle again
Sweet mysteries of life how dear I hold you.

Augusta March

Elements

The forest cannot speak
nor tell us of the sunlight and the rain
save in an alphabet of leaves.
Our words fade to the measure of distance
and silence chases round our little hill.
The geography of time
tilts us over a horizon fresh with stars.
After air
after fire
after earth
after water
a fifth one most sublime
elegant, eternal, and divine.

Milton Patterson

The Kite

The kite flies high
Not a single bird can touch it,
Not a single thing can touch it,
The kite flies around the world,
The kite touches the sun and the moon,
The kite goes into space,
Then the kite comes back down,
You get a good grip,
Then it slips away and you start to weep and cry,
Your kite has an eagle picture on it,
Your Mom and dad say to you "Do not worry",
We will get you another one!

William D. Hall

Sometimes It Hurts

Sometimes it hurts to see.
Not in a physical sense, but mentally.
It hurts to see how some people act.
Sometimes it hurts to see the truth.

Sometimes it hurts to speak.
Sometimes you shouldn't say a word.

Sometimes it hurts to feel.
It hurts to feel the pain in my heart.
It hurts to feel other people's hate.

Sometimes it hurts to think.
It hurts to think about how much I love you
and you don't love me.

Sometimes it hurts to care.
It hurts to care about someone who doesn't feel the same.
It hurts to care for someone who doesn't even know my name.

Sometimes it hurts to be.
It hurts to be a teenager.
Sometimes it hurts just to be me.

Melissa Gunter

To Whom It May Concern

I was born on a bleak and dreary day,
Not in the merry month of May.
I am a baby so soft and serene,
With a life to live so full and supreme.
And on my first birthday it rained and rained.

Four years old now and full of joy.
My life right now is based on a toy.
Not thinking to much but from day to day.
I wonder if I can go out and play.
And on my Seventh Birthday it rained and rained.

I'm in my teens now, with few cares in my life
Not thinking to much about a wife.
I sit in the classroom, watching the girls,
Play around and fiddle with their curls.
And on my Fifteenth Birthday it rained and rained.

Nearing my twenties, and out of work,
Because the employers think I'm a jerk.
Sitting in a court room blank and pale
I robbed a bank and I'm on my way to jail.
And on my Twentieth Birthday it rained and rained.

Tommy Earl Camp

This Is My Story

I was wondering all around, lost deep in sin
Not knowing my Savior, I couldn't ask Him in.

There he was waiting all the long time,
for me to stop running, Oh! He is so kind.

One day I grew weary and paused for awhile,
I heard a voice saying "Come to Me, my child".

Those words so simple that fell on my ears
were resounding from down through the years.

My old life was forsaken as I answered his plea
and a gush of living water washed all over me.

The peace I received I had never felt before.
It passed all understanding and flooded my soul.

The joy of knowing Jesus filled my heart with glee,
and I was so thankful, I dropped to my knees.

There I gave my heart to Jesus and I'm no longer the same.
I'm now a new person for I've been born again. Amen.

Sarah Thomas

The Singer

The Singer's touch is like a sweet caress
notes so beautifully sung expressing God's
eternal love.

His passion for music brings a melody to life
His special touch anointed with love from
the heavenly dove.

No one can move me like this special one, his
soulful haunting melodies echoing God's love
from above

He's no ordinary singer; he's a treasure
Molded by God Jehovah, who brings
pleasure beyond measure

To his mother he's the little boy she cuddled
To his wife he's friend and lover
And to his brothers a helping hand
And to his sisters he's their baby brother

And to his children the hero they call Dad
But to me He's the Singer who soothes me when I'm low
who lifts me up when I sigh, his music has been my
bedtime lullaby.

LuAnn Allen Sides

Time

If nothing had ever existed,
Nothing, not you, not I,
Still there would be time,
Forever passing by.

Like a brook with no beginning,
Or a road without an end,
Time is that certain constant,
Whose intervals one cannot lend.

It's never been early or late,
Nor can it ever be delayed,
It's the clock that's always been running,
But whose gears were never made.

With as many tomorrows as yesterdays,
Too numerous for mortals to gauge,
We reckon its relentless passing,
By an inappropriate term called age.

Lawrence A. Baur

My Final Advice

Do not cry!
Now that darkness falls upon my face
For my soul basks in heavenly light.

Do not be sad!
For I am in a better place, even though you
can no longer see me, I am there.

Do not forget!
Remember I always loved you and if you
keep me in your heart I never left.
Look back at our good times and laugh for me.

Do not be angry!
There is no one to blame. My time has come.
Here is where the train stops, the conductor
has called my station.

Do not have regrets!
For I never did and never will.

Do not stop!
Because I have gone. There is no reason
for you not to go on. Live, love and let go.

Leslie Paterson

Autumn

Apples, trees, golden leaves,
Now, that's the beauty of autumn.
We're picking pumpkins and the leaves are crunching,
That's the beauty of autumn.
It's getting cool in the country,
And we're thankful for the food in the horn of plenty.
That's the beauty of autumn.
No more bumble bees, but time to rake the leaves,
That's the beauty of autumn.
Cool nights, stars are bright,
No more wind to fly a kite.
Now, that's NOT the beauty of autumn.
Seeing your breath means snow's coming soon,
It will start getting chilly under the moon.
That's the beauty of autumn.
The ice will soon be freezing,
Soon the hockey players will be breezing.
That's the beauty of autumn.

Leesa Vogt

Untitled

Once we were children, our lives full of hope
Now we've grown older and learned how to cope.

Once we had dreams for our daughters and sons
Instead we are coping with violence and guns.

Once we were certain we could do as we please
So now we are coping with drugs and disease.

Once we envisioned great wealth and success
In order to get it, we're coping with stress.

Once we were children, our lives full of laughter
Now that we're older, it's things that we're after.

Now that we're older, our goals got distorted
Our childish dreams somehow got aborted.

Now that we're older, we still have to cope
But let's think like children, and focus on hope.

Shirley Shephard

To Ms. Anupama Mary Eapen

Alas my friend! I know not why, that I should write these lines
Now, when my moods are nots so goods and also nots too fines
Unless it is that urge so bad, to compete with a friend,
Perhaps to confuse readers so, and make their minds just bend!

A time was there when I too wrote, and won prizes at my school
My lines were crisp and thoughts were clear and could just anyone fool
Around some decades back I wrote and wrote the words in cores
My prose and verse - and worse too were read by savants and bores

And how they laughed and loved and swore and wept their eyes so red,
Releasing all their hearts with me, taking my books to bed,
Yet take a look at me right now!!... My memories! ... That's all!...
Even my memories make me sad, as I have had my fall.

And now, my friend, to change the mood which has become so sad,
Please look at all the first letters of all the lines! Be glad!
"Expect" they say "the unexpected" -and I believe in that
Now tell me friend, doesn't my back deserve at least a pat?

R. Raghu

Mother Nature Holds Me Dear

Thunder and lighting is my fear.
Numerous raindrops are my tears.
Cold, gray days are my sadness; as I feel the pain of something near.
Mother Nature holds me dear.
A land of green grass, rushing waterfalls, big trees for shade,
  a nice spring day is my happiness.
A hot summer day is my smile.
A Weeping willow is my hair.
The soft, blue sky is my eyes.
Mother Nature holds me dear.
A gloomy, cloudy day is my weariness; as it slowly drifts away.
A pastel butterfly is my mind, as it flutters into the air.
The song of the bird is my voice.
The whimper of a dog is my scream.
Mother Nature holds me dear.
The wind of a tornado is my confusion, going every which away.
The prick of a thorn is my pain.
The soft peddles of a rose is my skin.
The meaning of this song is my heart.
Mother Nature holds me dear.

    Kelly Bauchmoyer

Ambrosia

Greedy jaundice leaves drink
oblivious to tiny eruptions on neighbor's sill.

Rivers flow from downspouts chattering
muffled onto buffalo boxes
buried below.

Pools collect,
running, sliding, pointing fingers
at man's uneven world.

Heavy droplets
crash on cement
birthing bubbles that drift
down sidewalk gullies
behind soggy cigarettes
sliding on a surface of hydrogen bonds
holding hands — storing entropy.

    Tara Kelly Walworth

A Thousand Tomorrows

How I distrust these sensations
  of 9:30 success
We've packed it in for the night
Away from our diurnal masks
And post-its of retribution
Scattered about office floors;
Here, within myself, with you,
One from two
Away from hubris and disguise.
How I distrust these sensations!

  For at this moment, I believe in a thousand tomorrows.

I imagine some day,
  Not yet near enough to hurt,
When these shreds of success
Weave shrouds of regret,
Will you still be there
To answer the question
I cannot forget;
To question the answer
I did not remember.

    Ryder E. Smith

A Horse Named Dammit Or A Bit Of History

Listen my children and you shall hear.
Of a horse named dammit and Paul Revere.
The signal they awaited would come
Like a light - and dammit he knew
They would ride hard all night.
They would slow for a village
An Paul he would holler - to arms
Dammit "The British are coming."
For a scene like this, there is only
one solution - Paul, his horse dammit
that's right, a revolution.
They rode hard all night, and part of
the day - warning the villagers along the way.
At the end of the ride, they really had
had it. So Paul said to his horse stop now dammit.
His work, it was over - his job he
had done they retired him to pasture no more would he run.
In the books of our history His name they won't say.
They put him to pasture and Dammit he stayed.

    Robert West

"Dawn"

It came out of the night like the beginning of
of a year. It awoken like the beginning of life.
Rising to the beat of it's peak. Out of the dark
dust of night.

Therefore, awakening itself to the morning of each
day. A rising to it's peak so unique, so bright is
this light, shining throughout this day.

Sunlight so bright shine through my life. Up then
down within my sight. "Flash past" although you may
not share this light through my sight. "Shine so
bright so that we may see.

Come! "Dawn" so that we may feel the warmth of your
touch passing through the days and nights of time.
shine throughout years, bright as a bird in flight.

Guiding the waters of the sea's to the shores, guide
them, oh sunlight throughout the days and nights.

    Marvin Gresham

Patience

Being patient means not being in control
of another person or a situation.
It suggests the idea of "chilling out"
and not responding out of frustration.

At times it can leave us feeling helpless
and bring to mind a word we often hate.
Since there's nothing we can do to rush things along
we have to just sit back and wait.

And while we are waiting for a change to come,
relaxed and content we are to be.
Realizing the situation's out of our hands
and getting upset won't make it happen more quickly.

    H. Calvin Cunningham

My Comedy

I have a situation comedy
  Playing in my mind,
I'm the director, and the producer
  At times, I write the lines.

There's always more than just one plot
  No certain characters exist
Its just the events that happen each day
  To show how funny life is.

    Asia Roberts

Land of the Midnight Sun

WINTER is short days of cold temperatures, glistening snow with hues of blue, frosted trees, Aurora Borealis and long dark nights with snow falling or clear nights of the moon and stars shining brightly. The shortest day is less than six hours on the first day of winter.

SPRING is break-up of melting snow into puddles of water that flows to the rivers, lakes and oceans to make the land turn to a lush green. As it warms, the trees and bushes begin to bud. The sun is shining twelve hours a day or there are days of snow and rain.

SUMMER arrives with twenty some hours of daylight and the rest is more like twilight than night. Days can be sunny or misty rain. Wild flowers bloom in the primary colors of the rainbow. The grass grows rapidly into a rug of green velvety carpet. The birch trees and bushes are full of green leaves. The spruce trees dress up with sprouting cones. Later the winds of fall will blow the cones to the ground.

FALL starts with a frost when the leaves curl and turn into colors of red, orange, yellow and brown. As the winds of winter come, the leaves will flutter to the ground, scattered here and there. The tree and bush branches are bare and ready for the snow of winter to start again. The days will shorten and the sun sinks into the horizon as each day goes by.

LaVonne Mebust

Artist Unrestrained

When you hear someone speak of artists what do you say?
Of course you think of Van Gogh, Rembrandt and Da Vinci right away.
But do you ever think of the greatest artlist of all?
He who painted the sunset over the cascading water fall
The beautiful winter scenes, and the snowy mountains peaks
The glorious desert and burning sands, the miracle of God speaks
The country lanes in autumn, the meadow with its bubbling spring
The trees in their green finery and the birds on lifted wing
From the "blue" grass in Kentucky, to the Rocky Mountain chain
You can almost see the brush in his hand when you see the western
    plains
The sunrise on the ocean, the pounding surf shivering against the
    shore
The beauty of the grand canyon in all its pristine splendor
The orchards blooming up in Maine
The lush Virginian valleys

With our eyes we can see His work
For the whole worlds 'His' gallery

B. L. Dahl

amiss

the days are broken like the white lines
of daily highways broken
into mornings leavings packing children off in all the vans
receiving them back settling
the same safe life—
but dull as dull knives deceptive
knives that cut away in a deadly manner
not sharp so you know they are there
but slow and dreadful
like the empty complaints that catch like fish hooks in the throat
before they can get out and turn
the once bright eyes now hollow
into cruel cavities—
never to see a difference
i have neither the lines nor the fortitude to walk away

s e stewart

The Sight of Early Dawn

When first we see the sight,
    of dawn's soft glimmering light;

How it silhouettes the trees,
    in the skies passing night.

we see the fluttering of the birds,
    the eagles majestic flight.

The scurrying of a hare,
    as if escaping in great fright.

The dew that forms the teardrops,
    that sparkle oh so bright.

The lakes still waters,
    that mirrors the fog's drift, to ever greater height.

The nocturnal deer on the lake's rocky shore,
    looking for cover, before the days plight.

As the days early dawning
    comes clearer into sight;

How we revel in nature's beauty,
    in this new born light.

Louis O. Bruneau

On Seeing the Love of Children

Oh I would think the very walls
    of earth could not the joy contain;

That rushes forth from way down
    deep inside.

And I would guess that all man's books
    could not the mirth retain,

Nor could the jungles hide,
The heights and depth and width and length
    of warmth and thanks and pride

Within my soul when children smile
    with glee and sing their love refrain.

Paul H. Hahn

A Story Of Jesus

There is a story I heard long ago
Of God and His wonderful love.
Since then I've learned it is really so,
And I've started for that home above.

The Father so loved all people on earth.
He provided a beautiful plan.
That plan all started with a miraculous birth.
God's son was to live as a man.

His boyhood was spent in a carpenter shop
This meant He worked with His hands.
I believe He knew someday He would stop,
And be a leader issuing commands.

Jesus was in the temple when very young.
He felt He had a task to perform.
He later urged people to hold their tongue.
And once on the sea stilled a storm.

There's lots of miracles contained in the Book.
That Jesus performed where He went.
Many people followed Him to have a look
They learned from His lips to repent.

Shirley Shepard

Untitled

I heard the Marines song today you know the one "from the Halls
of Montezuma "Great tune catchy isn't it just the kind of song
you can sing all day without thinking about the words but I have
to think about the words I've been to Chapultopec The last
Mexican Fortress to surrender the real Montezuma's hall mentioned
in the song and I've seen the statues of the Men and boys who
died there I heard that when the ammo was gone one man wrapped
himself up in the Mexican flag and threw himself from
Chapultopec's high walls just so that the Americans could not
claim that anyone had lived to surrender The boy lived a few
minutes after the fall The American commander saw that he was
just a boy and said that I never would have fought If I had known
that the soldiers I was fighting were so young. The boy said that
if I had one more bullet left you would not be standing here
right now I wonder why the Marines never mention their opponents
bravery in their song? Maybe because if our Marines thought that
their opponents were nobel and brave and that they had both a
mother who loves them and a girl back home waiting for their safe
return just like our Marines do Then maybe none would ever go to
war and of course we can't have that now can we.

Manuel Oropeza Jr.

Lavender Lover

The plot outside
of my window
Blooms regularly,
reds, pinks, and whites.

Daily, humphrey sits by the window;
Watching mother nature
as she spreads love
all around.

Humphrey loves the plot,
He loves the different colors; reds, pinks, and whites.

Today,
Humphrey looks at me,
He looks at the plot,
He arches his back, He
leaps in joyful bounds!
I look at the plot, and what I do I see...
A lovely, little lavender flower
Blooming for humphrey!

Sheila D. Lewis

The Answer

Ah...So you speak of dreams. But what is a dream, than a mere stage
of reality - the unconscious quest for answers to the questions that
are to feared to be asked, or to silent to be heard? Your visions are
lovely; illusions of grandeur, yet, would they be so grand if realized?
Would I measure up to the persona you have depicted in your mind,
or become a disappointment to your heart?
In your dreams all I request is a kiss and all you seek is true love,
but, should the tide turn, and should you awaken, what the
expectations then?
Should we meet one another's willingly or shall we rebel with animosity?
For in dreams you have the power of God to mold me into any form you
desire, while in existence only the simple hope that I shall form the mold.
Is it worth the risk of trading fantasy for factual when all is well?
Or do you wish to conquer morning's turbulence instead of concur with
nighttime's dreamy mist?
Who am I to question your intent?
For as nighttime engulfs the harrowing day, I sleep, and all the
unresolved questions form a sea of illusion around me as I dream.
With morning's glare I awaken to the realization that once again——
I've dreamed of you.

Rhonda L. Tubaj

Painful Love

My eyes were fixed on the legitimate bond, staring at the showers
of shame drop from it. My ears heard a voice that sounded so
distant and faint, but seemed so real and acquainted.
My heart knew how so much it owned, but couldn't explain the
cruel passion that cracked my neck from side to side.

The ignorance was ready for the time, but there was no one else
to trust but me; so I secluded myself from the fantasies of
glory, driving the bitterness of sudden pain into a lonely heart;
That burned, and hurt, and stole away all pride in the ability to
love and to cherish that love; the ashes of which were left
behind in undefined but painful memories, with wishes of the hope
of a fantastic rejuvenation, blemishing from a heart so deeply
wounded to blame.

But still wanting for it to be the way it was or should have
been, fearing only to retire by saying fare ye well to the broken
pieces left of it. And dreaming that open eyes see the dream that
was forever meant to be, but in a battle of lose without weapon,
passion was taken for granted by a sense of black humor; And by
instinct, great pride was lost and buried in terrible
fascination, bringing out the victory that would always be wrong.

Kafain Emmanuel Mbeng Sr.

The Lost Key

The key to this door is in the heart and the unspoken language
of the eyes. Try as you may, only one can open this door. Only one
send shivers down my spine, as he looks into my eyes. Puts that
smile on my face with a word. Having my mind in overdrive, yet I
still have this door locked, it's getting harder to hold shut, but
silence is my key. Silence is this locked door. I can't open this
door by myself, I need the key, like the last piece to the puzzle.
Don't give up, have patience, the silence shall be broken. Look into
my eyes, what do you see? Intuition tells me you hold the key but
something's missing, something was over looked. Lost words in the
   night
creep back, dreams led the way. The key is in the fantasies. Close
your eyes, what do you see? Remember fantasies are never fulfilled
once and never forgotten, let down your guard, open your eyes. The
hazy nights clear as stars shine though. The key doesn't lay far, but
for now, silence is the locked door.

Nancy Burns

Still Proud and Strong

Osage Hills, ancient stamping ground
Of the proud nation to whose name you are bound.
You hear the mournful cries of this great nation
That never waged war against the growing population
Pushing them from Missouri to Kansas with what they could carry,
All else left abandoned in cabins, now cold and dreary,
To be taken by land-hungry immigrants longing to be free.
The starving Osage left more than bloodstains along the trail.
Rock covered graves stand witness to their trevail.
As they walked so painfully to their new "forever" home
Until short memories allowed the conqueror's memory to roam
Revealing covetousness for Kansas, too.
The continuing story contained nothing new.
That is how, Osage Hills, you became our home,
Your sky our sacred dome.
Your red clay has formed and shaped us — still proud and strong.
Our weakness you challenge, for we belong
To the present and the future — as surely as to the past.
You have cradled the bones of our dear ones, land of our birth,
A witness to Great Mystery that we still inhabit the earth!

Lela Mae Fenton

The Serving Poem

Cookies and cake and ice cream too,
of these types of snacks I'll eat only a few.

The milk group provides me with calcium, you see,
so I'll have 2 servings, or even 3!

The meat group gives me lots of protein;
I'll have 2 or 3 servings, but I'll keep it lean.

Vegies and fruits, I can eat a lot more,
3 to 5 and 2 to 4!

The bread group allows servings from 6 to 11,
this will surely keep my heart muscle revin'!

If I eat from all food groups, I'm sure to feel great.
This will also help me stay at the proper weight!

Sharon Saputelli

Without Form And Void

Somehow your silent expectation for a violent explanation
Of this splattered, sprawling shambles on my desk and on the floor
Makes me mumble, start but stutter, and then stumblingly mutter
That the system's sacred order's not immediately apparent from the
  door.

Is it really admiration or some other, strange, sensation
That gasps away your breath and makes your eyes grow wide?
When the winter wind increases just before the snow storm ceases,
I pray tell me just how tidy are the drifts replete and mighty
That are dumped upon the driveway: unquestionably the work of God
  outside.

But no matter how I chatter, like the Wonderland Mad-hatter,
I fear your halting hesitation shows some inner reservation.
Yes, this utter shameless clutter makes ME shiver, makes ME
shudder,
Makes me shrinkingly abide by your judgment—mortified.

Max H. James

Ly-Tong, The Hero Of The Space Flown Into History

Oh, Vietnam! The beautiful multicolored one
Oh, Autumn! The very deep blue homeland
Your words echoed in every direction
Waking up someone, still fast, sound asleep

You returned in the middle of the autumnal falling leaves
A petal of shooting flower, hanging in the air
A million hearts, awaiting quietly
Write your name, it made history

OH, Ly-Tong! you're the immoral one
Not disheartened with difficulties nor dangers
Your work is rescuing your fatherland
Leading people up to the bright sky high

You're the gracious heroic airman
The unique one in this world
Are you. A genius?
Famed in the world over

Your work commands respect
Like angel of the 20th century (20th generation)
Written in verse, eternally bearing in mind
Composing a symphony for loving Ly-Tong.

Tri Nguyen

Time Flies

A wise old woman once said to me,
Oh child, time flies why can't you just see.
She always said, with a heavy sigh,
Do something now while the sun is high.
You can't see it now, for it hides in illusion.
The present is not future in youth's confusion.
Yesterday I was young, and could not see,
What this old woman was telling me.

They say, everything goes around comes around.
Perhaps—past into future can indeed be found.
That time has no meaning in the youth of our day,
Viewed by young and old, it is just the same,
  Nothing different I say.
So I become that old woman,
seeing things almost the same.
Warning those young ones, time flies,
But knowing, it is only a game.

Lois L. Haase

Jennifer

She told me there is nothing
Oh no, one more time around me
There's someone else she's holding
She never saw me see
And now that there is nothing
I know, that pain is always truthful
Never been given to lying, I should have been more careful

She never saw me see the distance in her eyes
The beautiful face, the beautiful smile
The beauty beneath the beautiful skin
Is making me cry

She told me to be friendly
Oh God, I just want her to be near me
Then I will not be as lonely
As a man who cannot see
I am not one for crying
You know, the years have made me harden
But now that there is nothing
I have something that I did take part in
And it's not like I didn't know

Matt Smith

Siempre Como Ayer (Always Like Yesterday)

I took the piragua from the
Old man, and he made me
Feel displaced...
I tasted the sweetened ice,
Trying to keep the cold chunks
Away from my sensitive teeth,
But they froze, and my
Head was quickly heated....
I was now in a world where
Actions are committed, without
Reason, necessity, or feeling,
Everyone runs red lights and
My family suspects me,
No one knows the answers, so
Questions are never asked,
But if they were, you
Would be mislead....
The old man asked if I wanted
Seconds, but I said I knew
How that flavor tasted before.

Manuel Rodriguez

The Little Grey Rock

(Written at age 11)
I was sitting at the bay,
On a cool, but quiet day.

I thought, as the wind whipped through my hair,
How a day like this is very rare.

The clouds were white, as white as snow,
they were big, but moving slow.

Suddenly, I felt a drop,
I felt two more, they didn't stop!

Not far away, I saw a tree,
Whose long, thick limbs could shield me.

The rain stopped, and soon afterwards,
The sky was filled with squawking birds.

Then as my glance fell on the ground,
I saw something that wasn't quite round.

It was grey and covered with sand,
I picked it up and held it in my hand.

It wasn't great in the world's eyes,
No robber would steal it because of its size.

So it doesn't need a key or lock,
Still it's special to me, it's a little grey rock.

Katie Schenk

Tippicanoe

And where the rock the Prophet stood,
On a dire November day,
I alone did stand to look
Out upon the prairie bog
Where on that night his singing did carry,
Where the many braves did lay
And on the bluff, the dark and bitter fight ensued.

And where the rock the Prophet stood,
On a dire and rainy November dawn
I felt the spirits pass on their way,
And so I tried to sing his song,
But they, remembering all the wrongs,
Passed on, and over the air,
And, alas, forgot me there.

William R. Ford Jr.

In Retrospect

A mind does curious things
on a February day
when the sky clears to a friendly blue
and sun shines warmly through the crystal air
washed clean by rain the night before.

It's snug again in some forgotten cove
touched by the turquoise waves of some far sea
and we're together, now,
wandering the reefs, exploring them,
lying on coral sand and loving there.

Brief the illusion, short the interlude,
bright the slim paradise that's glimpsed and gone.
Quicksilver clouds run fast before the wind;
the sky is dark. Once more
I am alone, and winter lingers on.

Phyllis W. Reinauer

Untitled

In an empty desert,
on a lonely road,
worn heels carry an equally worn soul.
His old jeans are faded, his shirt robbed of color,
and the wind has stolen the blood from his face.
His purpose is gone,
his task is done,
nothing binds him any longer to the earth.
His home is in his boots,
his laughter lost in someone's eyes
down the road, left far behind.
Occasionally he stops,
and takes a sip from his canteen,
but not too often
for the water tastes of tears,
tinged by the taste of lost hopes.
Mostly he walks
in the empty desert
on the lonely road
to the sound of his groaning soul.

Omair Ahmad

Remember When...

Remember when the yellow sun shone long
on meadow grass that grew so strong; and bold
were life's true mysteries. Dreams like a song
surely to you true friend were gladly told.
Amidst life's rushing sounds, obscured was the light
and wondrous dreams became so hard to find.
The secrets were disclosed, you weren't in sight,
lost and alone, certain I was felt behind.
In darkness was searching, you were there all along.
The clouds seem to lessen, the gentle breeze
touched my heart, yes, with you I belong.
You hear my cries and grant me rest and ease.
The sun still shines on meadow grass and me,
through darkest secrets you have set me free.

Kathleen Hillary

My Kangaroo

My Kangaroo goes hop, hop, hop!
On the floor I don't want him to drop.
Because he's so cuddly and pale,
With two big feet and a big long tail.
I like to play with him everyday,
He makes me feel happy in a special way.
I like to hold him by his ear,
And whisper secrets for him to hear.
When we have a boxing contest,
We like to see who boxes the best.
My Kangaroo doesn't have any special name.
With him I have fun playing each game.
And when I take him to bed at night,
I really like to hold him tight,
I don't know what I'd do,
If I didn't have my Kangaroo!

Pamela K. Walczak

Empathy

Hush... Do you hear them? They're crying
Precious little hands reaching out
Cold, wet, hungry, and dying
Babies born without love, no doubt.

Find them...don't let them suffer
Look around you, they may be next door.
Protect them, they need your comfort
Don't ignore them...
 We can do more

Joan Morris

The Morning After

Gentle as the fallen raindrops
On the petals of a red rose
Some slowly slipping, sliding down the stem
Plop. Plop. Into a puddle
As the crisp, October breeze
Swaying the trees with its leaves
Dropping down to the ground
A blend of orange, red, and brown
Its messy pile covering the cold earth
The skies, what a sight
The birds, how high they fly
Singing a new song for a new day
As you step onto the balcony
Wrapping your arms around me

Roy Vu

A Lover's Whisper

Come let me take you into the night,
On the wings of a raven, a soft gliding flight.

Come dance with me to the sounds of the sea,
And the music you hear will set you free.

Come walk with me through the forest of life,
You will never grow weary - whatever the strife.

Come and gaze at the stars - they are in my eyes,
The images you see will tell no lies.

Come sit by my side in the warmth of the sun,
And feel my touch - for life has begun.

Come and wander peacefully as the days begin to pass,
I will guide you safely through the looking glass.

Experience with others what you have found -
For life is rewarding, puzzling but sound..

Michele Cassano

"Each Day"

Each day is like a golden thread
On which we string our deeds
Whether good, or whether bad,
Shows where we sow our seeds

God gave us day, he gave us night,
And all the beauty we can see
But what I do with every day
Is strictly up to me.

God leads us through no darker days
Than he has known before
He did not say, 'twould easy be
To enter through his door

Count up the good deeds you have done -
at end of day,
And list each morning things that you should do
If you do wrong, joy fades away, but not the pains,
If you do good, the pains will fade away
And only joy remains

Pauline Longnecker

Endlessly

Name of a girl stirs my head
Creamy mixtures pour from eye sockets,
tunnel vision thaws to exploding tides
breaking on her alluring shore,
lovely beach my form dissolves,
birthing in exquisite gold,
alive, dousing love for her
name I'll never dry

Paulo G. Acosta

Seasoned Love

Come now with me through the vestigial garden of our life.
Inhale
once more, the sweet fragrance of our budding youth.
See again the vivid colors of the bloom of awareness and feel the
caress of the winged moth of vitality against your cheek.

It is no more, however————-
We are together still.
If I leave this mortal realm first, I will not forsake you.
I will weep with you from my place. I will hover near on nights in
your time of trouble, think on your problems and rejoice
in your solutions.
How far away can I be if you remember love?

Phyllis Adam

Those Empty Eyes

Those beautiful eyes so sad and empty
Once were filled with joy, laughter, and knowledge.
Eyes full of brightness and sparkle, now filled with confusion.
Eyes once filled with knowledge and wisdom, and so much to share
Now there is nothing, nothing to spare.
Beautiful eyes that once danced with love and joy
Now remain still and no longer glow.

I'll never forget the love your eyes showed
Pain in my heart but memories afloat.
I love you Papi and I'll never forget
Those beautiful eyes that once danced in your head.

Zoraida Flores

Friendships

You should treasure friendships.
One and all,
Don't sit alone just plain and tall.
Those who are true,
Like navy blue,
They will stay from winter to fall.
Years coming so quickly and quietly,
Just how friends leave you so silently.
When a crisis comes upon me,
Friends will be there and they will guide me.
I trust in them that they will help,
And not beat my spirit to a pulp.
Guiding me and staying with me throughout the years,
I just hope they'll never have tears.

Pamela Konwinski

"To Laugh"

I love to laugh - I love to smile...
one cannot change what is his style,
nor should one whose fare is such
that others lives he may reach and touch
with a part of him that will brighten days,
and show his care in caring ways.
Be it a spark of joy - a bit of wit..
just something no one might soon forget.

I love to hear the laughter gay
of others who live in joyous way..
or to see the smiles on smiling faces
radiating brightness to darkest places.
If my life is spent bringing joy through laughter,
then I'll leave traces of the love I'm after...
And this could be my epitaph...
"Here lies a man - who loved to laugh."

Rudy Butler

Dual Illusion

There are two sides of one face
One is kind; the other is not so gentle;
One is loving; the other is unloved
Perhaps, one is curious, the other is cautious!
One holds faith; the other cannot trust;
One is happy; the other is sad.
One has forgiven; the other seeks revenge!
One cares, the other hurts.
One accepts; and the other changes.
Yet, I can only balance one face with courage;
Restoring spiritual strength by faith,
And walk on... and on again...
As I've chosen...as I choose....
With all, or most, of my memories.

Monika Arnett

One Perfect Rose

One perfect rose is said to be me
One more perfect rose I'm saying is thee.

Petals fall off flowing gently in the breeze.
A form of renewal, a way to be free.

A thorn for a sorrow, as a pain in your heart.
A leaf for a tear, it's a symbol of thought.

The days cease and night always falls.
You wither away with no substantial cause.

I want you to know light will appear.
And when you rebloom, I will be here.

Kathryn Peterson

"Fantasy"

I have an anniversary fantasy,
One of only you and me, hand in hand
By the sea, sitting beneath a coconut tree.
Your moonlit silhouette is all I see.
As we converse very intimately.
"Come sit closer you're still to far,"
Then our skin sticks like melted tar.
In your eyes, the reflection of a shooting
Star, our bodies come together like a
Lid and a jar.
Maybe someday this fantasy will come
True, but until then the rest is up to you.

Thomas Anthony Estrada

Three Kids and a Baby

this here's a story about three kids and a baby
one says, "hello," and two say, "maybe"
green Dodge Dart on an open highway
the baby's thinking that they're all crazy

no dust and diesel just mountains and tree tops
Indian summer cool water can't stop
quite a distance from a cluttered bedroom
climb and climb until body says drop

standing on the edge you just know
when the man says, "go," you gotta go
you think it's over well it's just beginning
ultimate rush like everyone said so

sell you a tee shirt so you can say
how brave you were on that one day
nothing compares or could be so grand
face to face and fear gave away

Nick Romer

Wind

The wind gushed by me with a loud misty sound my hair flew to one side of me my eyes became glossy and tears rolled down my face.

My bare feet became warm with the gush of wind and my white flowing dress began to flow further and further away from me.

As my thoughts followed my dress my mind became blank and I was filled with no feeling but with lots of thought I wasn't sure if I was going insane or if I was going to die, the thought of dying didn't bother me as much as insanity. Then I noticed how cold my hands were they felt like ice and they hurt when I bend them kind of like I hurt all inside but only the wind knows my pain.

Michele Jungwirth

Untitled

An armored conquistador, lion-clothed brave;
One to win, the other to save.
Helmeted and uniformed soldiers world wide;
Young widows how they cried.
Young men, some hardly boys;
Never to experience life's little joys.
By their country sent to die,
On foreign soil they came to lie.
The old men made the wars,
Why must the young even the score.

Ronda R. Ross

A Tribute To Larry

God gave me a very special true friend,
One who stayed with me through thick or thin.
We had a great life, he and I
Until one day God said, "It's time to say good-bye."
Now he's been gone over a year,
I feel him sometimes, oh so near.
I have days when it seems I can't go on,
but then I hear them play our song.
The one that said, "We'd always be,
right next to each other through eternity."
I must go on and live my life,
even if it is as another man's wife.
I'll always remember, the times that we shared,
when times got tough, but you weren't scared.
You stood up to life, right up till the end.
But now you are gone, my dear special friend.
I'll love you forever, in my own unique way,
I'll think of you often, though maybe not today.

Nancy S. Boerger

What Have We Reached

I use to think that the best would
    only make me happy.
Then I realized my hand was
    forever reaching.
Learning to love the good in
    people.

Times got better, but always
    ended the same.

As time passes through us, we become hard
    hearted and our minds not so simple.
To many scars for our minds to handle.

How do we get back to the beginning
    when love was given.
When our hearts and minds were in
    sync with each other.

Now I don't reach - for anything
    for my scars have won!!!!

Toni M. Guynes

A Daughter To Her Father

Unto you I was born, without a decision or choice,
only to listen, trust in your decision, and not share in a voice.
The growing years came, and with them the plea,
for what I thought were growing pains,
you would highly disagree.
The school days, the boys, the not so intentional "annoys,"
all seemed to take their course,
and as I didn't always understand you,
I knew you were the "Boss."
The endless nights you'd lay awake,
to hear the key at the door,
only to tell me you were on your way,
to that bathroom on the same floor.
How as we grow, things do change,
Life has a tendency to certainly re-arrange.
So as I've grown older now and look back on the years,
the thought of you being gone, brings nothing but tears.
You see Dad, our trials, tribulations, and sometimes
shaky relations, wouldn't be traded for the world,
as I now have a choice and it is to use "Your" voice,
to the children in my arms,
as they are curled.
I love You Dad!

Karen L. Jerro

What Do You Do?

What do you do when you can no longer think? What do you do when the only vision you can see is the vision of his tender smile? What do you do when the only scent that you can smell is his scent? What do you do when you find yourself missing him and he is only in the very next room? What do you do when your arms feel empty they are not holding him? What do you do when his kisses are all you can feel even when he is not kissing you? You do the only thing you can do, you give into love and follow your heart and that my love is what I have done!

Lorraine Asencio

A Song of Loneliness

Serenity, long lost memory drifting through the air for a grasp onto reality. Death has hath wakened the living. A silent whisper of what is left. It is gone, loneliness...... a song.
The play of life. The soul of everyone being played by Marrinet strings. A joker struggling up and down and for what death the sorrow kings. The time has come and the strings hath broke.
Just another quiet choke, recent worry and loss, when everyone plays impatient boss. Untimely frost upon the keys of life play the song... loneliness. Bold life has struck to the artillery of hate.
Gaps fall through the many brave boundaries of the sick, twisted world. Peace has come to pass the mind of one and all. A tree the only thing that can stand tall. Lame to the eye. Shadows of yesterday, to which one must spy. To see an idle world the way it is. Determined by the pleasing and lascivious. Maybe about a song. Stern eyes turn to desperate wrongs. Victories has hath lost with a sigh. The few triumphs to last, to possibly grasp as long as you can. We all have these to caress but me in my world has lost it all, to the song of loneliness.

Patty Carambot

Perfect Mate

Through living life, and the work of fate,
Mother-nature brought to me my perfect mate.
He is genuinely sensitive, perfect in every way.
If I had my choice, I would be with him every hour of every day.
He holds my heart in the palm of his hand. I know he won't let go.
He is the true love of my life, and I love him so.
Forever will I love him, and be there 'til the end,
Then when I die, my love, to him, I will send.

Michelle D. Post-Evett

An Ocean of Love

Love should be like the ocean,
open and free
yet holding its own boundaries.

Each wave, as it breaks and disturbs the calmness
adds to the beauty of the water
and makes it appear to be
growing.

Sailboats seen crossing,
leave their peacefulness
for those who reach for it.

Fish stir confusion
yet add life.

In all, we can love and the happiness it brings
as long as we are able to flow with the currents.

Pamela A. White

Dolphins or Angels At Sea

Are dolphins really just mammals at sea?
Or could they be angels quite possibly.
For they swim to and fro
Helping people as they go.

Have you not heard the stories on T.V.,
Of dolphins helping people who are stranded,
Floating along aimlessly?

And please believe me
They don't just play games.
They are now helping people
Who live daily in pain.

And isn't it strange how easily they are trained.
Marine Biologist seem overwhelmed by their brain.

Dolphins bring cheer and happiness
No doubt.
Is that not in part what angels bring about?

If angels walk the earth
And look like you and me,
Maybe angels swim the sea
And dolphins they could be.

Kathryn Ann Thornburg

Obiter Dictum

Are there not gods watching us from moon mountains,
or hidden greenly in the leaves we touch
when grass is crushed by shoddenly winged feet?
And are their birds not oracles:
sibling summers, springs, riding
sweet as sylphs living on air?
Then do we not dare look to where the Gods sit:
on ivory white thrones set deep
in an azure stone setting;
and become Hellenic, drifting past countless Aegeans
that flux through the veins - which keeps us from shore-stepping
(gracefully in a half shell with dolphin reins)
after our wombing seas, to wonder the greater mystery
of ourselves - and of flowers after they lose their will?

Kareen Szabo-Hillman

Imagine

Imagine me as a drop of sap as I rise inside a tree;
Or maybe as a grain of pollen as I stick to the leg of a bee.

Or imagine me as a speck of dirt as I cling to the face of a child;
Or imagine me as the influence that changes the wild to mild.

Imagine me as a dewdrop as I lay upon a leaf;
Imagine me as the answer that would stop all pain and grief.

Imagine me as the changer of all the wrong to right;
Imagine that I was a comfort that came to all each night.

Imagine me as a leaf being blown by the wind.
Imagine that I was a child at play and the day would never end.
Just imagine!

Kyle Harrison McKinney

The Beauty of Nature

I love to listen to the birds sweet call.
Or the gurgling sound of a water fall.
I imagine the water flowing to the sea,
The sounds of nature fascinate me.

I watch the flowers after a rain
lift their faces up to the sun again,
Butterflies sailing so wild and free,
The sights of nature fascinate me.

The sweet smell of roses fills the air,
The fragrance of honeysuckle is everywhere.
There's no place on earth I would rather be.
The fragrance of nature fascinates me.

I feel close to God as I walk o'er his land,
I feel I can almost touch his hand,
Nothing seems as eternal as a mountain or tree,
And all things of nature fascinates me.

Mary Bridges

Suspended In Time

Did I hear a few words strung together in a rhyme
Or, were those the church bells that at last did chime?

A paean to human endeavor and pain
or a praise in submission to God's reign
Which of these do my songs call upon
Or are they just an account of loss and gain?

On every step in life, they tell me I learn
as they show me a 'Joan', whom on the stake they burn.
The quest to surrender in the 'Mother's Lap' does not die
Though I have been betrayed at every turn.

That which lives today, shall perish tomorrow.
Laughter shall end in tears, and joy in sorrow.
Only the soul shall thrive, and give life to the aching heart,
As all barriers shall be torn apart;
And all shall hear the melody of the rhyme -
When I surrender in the 'Mother's lap' and we become
Suspended in Time.

Parmeet Grover

Untitled

We read not only for a quest for knowledge and false sense
   of experience.
But, also for sanctity from our own mundane and incorrigible
   thoughts, feelings and ideas.
Thus, submerging ourselves in someone else's mind we forget
   our own faults.
We try to delve into literature land and hide from our
   homeland.
It is a cowardice which fuels this quest to pretty life with
   pavonian descriptions and ideas.
Thus, we admit our incapabilities to ourselves.

Patrick Jules White

Little Billy Badass

   Little Billy Badass while at school one day, went with all the
other children for recess out to play. But as the kids each took
turns, and played their schoolyard games, Little Billy Badass would
push them down and call them names.

   As he grew his deeds got worse. He went from stealing candy to
stealing someone's purse.

   He was known to every cop. But to Billy jail was just a joke. They
couldn't make him stop.

   Then one day he thought he'd really have some fun. Little Billy
Badass bought himself a gun.

   He knew how to make an easy score. In and out, smooth and quick, he'd
rob the liquorstore.

   But he didn't figure on a clerk like this. From behind the counter
both barrels blazin! He wasn't about to miss! Lead and blood were
flying! Billy hurt and crying was knocked back through the door.
Scared, and bleeding he staggered toward his parent's house. They
had been his only source of refuge many times before. He reached
their stoop that night. Then collapsed as she turned on the light.

Little Billy Badass run wild in the street!
Little Billy Badass lay dead at Mother's feet.

Robert P. Parsons

Prayer IV

In Him we trust, with faith long last
Others aside to Heaven fast!
Before it's closed and they try to sell
Us passage down the stairway to Hell

Righteous defenders in the name of the Lord
With word and faith, a double edged sword
The attacking sword, defend or flee
Or be blinded by grace of the almighty three?

When and where The Rapture will be
to set the souls of Heaven free?
And the souls of Hell (born again in the nick of time)
Will soon visit death, and call it crime.

Steve Kruse

Easter

Easter is the day Christ arose!
Our church has early Sunday Morning Services;
   With children all dressed in their easter outfits:
We sing joyously; Hallelujah Christ arose!

As we sit down to our Easter dinner;
   We shall all say Gods grace.
And now that we are finished;
   Let's all go out together:

We will laugh and talk and have a reunion;
   As we watch our children.
Look for their easter bunny and baskets!
   With his easter baskets full of goodies!

The children go hunt for easter eggs.
   To see who finds the prize egg first;
And to see their eyes light up!
   when they hear what the prize might be!

Linda Marie Grizzle

Where Wildflowers Grow

Our eyes were red with rage
Our hands were blue with strength
And our minds white with pure pride
As our ships set sail for the Normandy Tide.

As we jumped onto the cold dark beach
The cliffs were just in our reach
Remember our Hawaiian Pearl rang in our minds
And even though different, we're all the same kind.

It was loud, it was bright, and it was long
But we remembered and we were strong
Our pride in our land never left us
And in our anthem we put our trust

Many still lie on this field, friend and foe.
In Normandy where red, white, and blue
Wild flowers grow.

Kiely Velez

Untitled

There they go off to fight Hussein
Our men with numbers instead of names

Off to fight another war
Some still wondering "what's it for?"

Some say oil, others greed
While soldiers have mouths at home to feed

Some of these mouths they'll never see
Except in pictures or occasional dreams

For most young men, their day will come
To eat Saudi and instead of bubble gum

My 18th Birthday in the 5th of June
And yes, I realize it could mean my doom

Other men my age wonder uninformed
Of the conflict at hand, the brewing storm

I hope what I've written makes you stop, take a breath
And think of the people, for their country, give death.

Mike Erickson

"Through Their Eyes"

We look past the sallow eyes of
our nation's delinquents,
As we try to envision the evils
they eagerly frequent.

If we were sincere about wanting to
learn, we'd look into their eyes, right
Into their souls, and witness the crater
into which a searing pain has burned.

We'd see the pain, the anger and the rage
that forcing them into projects, ghettos
and slums has caused.
If we'd just take the time to look, we'd
find the reason they feel they are lost.

Permissiveness of our decadent culture has
picked their fragile bones and drained their
Lives more effectively than a ravenous vulture.

We can return their childhood to them if we
make the sacrifice.
It can be done if we only would see their
lives through their eyes.

Larry K. Pilgrim

The Real Sweethearts

Parents, Educators and Community are the Keys to the future success of
our young generation, for this is the generation which will one day
govern our nation. But who is responsible for educating our children
to their fullest potential? "The Real Sweethearts" in a shared
commitment, provide this essential.

Who instills in our children that they are wonderful creations -
instructs them that there is no limit to their success with
imagination, hard work, and deep concentration?
Psychologists, Lawyers, Teachers, productive citizens they can be.
"The Real Sweethearts" take on this mammoth task — you see.

"The Real Sweethearts" are the ones who give students that extra shove
when they need special attention, improved test scores, discipline,
and a little love. Their kindness and graciousness always come from
the heart because they are constantly sacrificing themselves to give
our youth a new start.

Yes, Parents, Educators and the community are "The Real Sweethearts."
Although different, yet working together to do their parts.
By working together to make success happen, they are a symbol of
   peace,
like the dove displaying knowledge, and fiscal support,
but most of all.... Overwhelming Love.

Vera Thompson

The Willow Tree

There it stands at the end of the field,
Out near the black-topped road.
Growing taller and fuller each year,
Adding more shade to its heavy load.

Grown-ups bring a blanket or chair,
Neighborhood children bring a ball.
The old willow tree doesn't seem to mind,
It spreads its shady arms for all.

Comes afternoon, it casts its shadow,
Casts it wide and long.
Comes evening it welcomes all birds,
That come to sing their song.

It never seems to mind a bit,
That it stands and takes the heat.
It's only too happy it makes the shade,
Where people can come to meet.

Yes, it stands out there at the end of the field,
Where it's stood for all these years.
But why is it called a weeping willow?
I've always seen smiles, never tears.

Walter A. Tymerson

Perseverance

Crazed white foam spilled out
over jagged rocks,
lashing its way to shore.

Thundering and spitting at the floor of the cliff,
robed in rich lavender flowers.

Climbing upward along carpeted crevices
Clutching vainly toward the cliff top
Strewing crystals against its amethyst crown.

Spent and exhausted, the white rage retreats
to gather strength from its ocean floor
Returning in fury to beat once more
at the lavender carpet lining the shore.

Valencia Cacciotti

To "The Infinite World"

Oh! why cannot I see an angel passing through
over the high green pines, deep in the sky so blue —
as I feel so tiny...yet, my hopes are many
for the skies to unveil to me their mystery?!

Then comes another night, with all it's majesty —
and I gaze into it, with such intensity!
The moon like a Goddess, seems to show me the way —
To the "Infinite World" and it's mystic glory!

Why do men always want to discover a star...
or to see some angels, so close, and yet, so far?
And yet, I know at times, like on a silent sea —
during some restless nights, they are calling for me!

Monique M. Kroll-Gallocher

The Snow

The snow was like a big, comforting blanket
  over the lush green grass.
It was like dusty baby powder
  and fog floating by.
It was like a lamb's fuzzy fur
  and soft, silky satin.
It was like a ball of cotton
  or newly bought socks.
It was like baking powder
  and packaged up paper.
And I was at peace.

Lori Welch

Waiting For The Rain At Fourth And Spring

"We live in
Paradise, don't
Destroy"
Mouths the midnight bus that
Slices like a suicide scar
Through downtown's abandoned skin
Like a phantom murder express,
With the hieroglyphics
Of lost conquered tribes
Cutting bloody stains on its side
Its laboratory light casts
Cold neon stageset shadows on the
Four phantoms chosen for this role, who
Huddle, staring isolated
At the forms of the departed;
Like the dead their breaths tread
Past each other's eyelids,
Crusted mouths,
Cold calloused feet sheltering
The cockroaches of Eden.

Maya Pressnall

Sweet Little Angel

One of Your sweet little angels
  passed through our life today,
We had hoped to keep her...
  to train her up in Your way.

We know one day we'll be with her
  and hold her close once more,
Till then we count on You
  to care for this one we adore.

You've never made a mistake Lord,
  and You'll not start with us;
Though our hearts are torn with grief...
  in You, Oh God, is our hope and trust.

Margaret Campbell Riddlebaugh

Destination Moon

Another Apollo is due to be launched, its destiny the moon.
People all over the world watch, some thinking they're crazy as a
  loon.
The astronauts are thoroughly trained to go out into space.
Leaving behind them loved ones, praying again to see their face.
The journey takes them out beyond our sky oh so blue.
Sometimes there are many that go, sometimes only two.
Regardless of the number, we should all stand up and cheer.
For the astronauts are brave as they leave our atmosphere.
They go outside the spaceship and float around in space.
And all the while that danger lurks, a smile is on their face.
Their purpose is to gather facts of what lies beyond our sight.
Bless all the astronauts who have and are yet to make these fights.

Shelby Jean Aldridge

The Flag Resting

The flag said, "I am resting today
people come by to see me flying in the
breeze.
The wind makes me a little tired
so I am resting today

I like the breeze, the lovely breeze
makes me say hello to everyone

No wind or breeze today so I am resting today"
said the flag.

Sure the best I love to say hello in the
summer breeze, the flag said

But I am resting today

Phillip Kottal

Friendship

What is friendship someone often wonders
People sharing secrets every time it thunders

Exciting information to share with a friend
Or a letter packed with gossip you want to send

Lying for a friend to cover a mistake
A dollar you lent for a burger and shake

A hobby or sport you enjoy together
Playing football in the backyard no matter what the weather

Friendship is a lot of things
But together and closer it always brings

Roslyn Lea

True Friends

People who are there in good times and bad,
People who listen with both ears, and just don't hear what they want,
People who care with loving hearts,
To laugh with
To cry with
Are called Friends that we hold dear to our hearts.

Friends are like the lonely star, on a dark and stormy night,
Friends are the rainbows after a summer storm,
Friends are the cool breeze on a hot and humid day,
True Friends are one in a million,
And that's why we should cherish them each and every day.

Nancy Kromrey

Remembrance

The blatant sound of blasting music
Playing havoc with sensitive ears
Unlike that tender tune we danced to
That diminished our every care
We made that melody our very own
When you whispered the words in my ear
For me it was a rhapsody
I'll remember through the years
My darling I'll dearly miss you
And no new love will I embrace
For another can ever take your place
I'll remember, remember through the years
Yes, I'll remember - remember with my tears.

Lillian Drake Carew

The Parade

People dressed in the uniform of life
Playing loudly and differently from each other,
But the crowd never seems to notice.
...And the band plays on.

At each crossroad a member is lost
One steps out silently, slowly muting his horn.
One stumbles, never to get up again.
...And the band plays on.

A member is lost while wandering one day,
And one gets violently yanked away,
While yet one more is embraced by disease.
...And the band plays on.

When the parade comes to my town I'll grab my drum
And rat - a - tat - tat my way along,
Then bid farewell to friends I've made.
...And the band plays on.

Sarah Millslagle

Hypothalamus Hiccup

Ah, discovery swims in a familiar darkness it
plays in the shadows rubbing backs and burying noises against
the deep curves and undeterminable lines longing to
trespass far beyond the perimeters of unknown worlds echoed
by tender a.m. lovers dilating in the blink-blink of soft throbbing
light, tips of fingertips explore the imperfect-unsheltered soles
tremble on the unleavened ground of this comfortable crust where
secret passwords are quietly tucked away in the binding of
heavy books and hidden in the crossings of uncharted maps that are
unfolded then refolded but never relaxing in the initial bend
rather incessantly enfolding immersed within the body wave the
love serum back behind the hills of black silk curtains.

Olivia M. Lacson

Earthshine

Hovering over dark sleep, primordial mother of young,
of old, of winding form, reaches up, up through pools of
faded light, breathing forth ancient wind out of hidden
places. Working the old sap of some essential root cut off
from it's original source.

Muffled laughter, streaks of broken song echo from
those distant worlds, as shadowed figures reenact a mythic
dance before they gather skirts, and scatter in the dim night
of hush and swirling dust.

On the horizon, a pale erosion of the darkness. Trees bend,
lifting weary arms toward the face of a shrivelled moon.

Vivian Dillard

"The Fool And The Wise Man"

Sometimes sunshine, sometimes rain, the very fine line between
  pleasure and pain.
Should I tell you goodbye, are ask your name, like the fool
  and the wiseman, their one in the same.
A little girl laughing makes a little boy cry, it can't be the truth
  then it must be a lie
The cat in the hat, a mouse or a rat, Dr. Zuess on the loose and
  the little red caboose.
Going up, coming down, either through or around, I've floated on air
  and I've fell to the ground.
A beggar, a thief, an indian, and a chief, don't says you believe,
  then stare in disbelief.
You can't take it with you, but you can't let it go, seems like
  by now, all this you would know
You pay for this, but you settle for that, and when it doesn't fit,
  you take it right back
You've worked all your life, now you have a sore back, but the
  slightest of touches will make your eggshell crack
You opened your heart to empty ears, your joys, your sorrows,
  anxieties and fears.
Too much to this, too little of that, look at the years
  you'd like to have back.
With a frown or a smile, take an inch or a mile, your pride
  or your shame.
Like the fool and the wiseman their one in the same

Timothy E. Rider

Untitled

As I lay on the ground, I can not understand what is happening to me.
Police cars all around, fire trucks, and ambulances are all I see.
I look up at the sky, and I wonder what is going on.
  I can not feel any part of my body.
I look at everyone, but they do not seem to be looking back.
  I see blood, but I cannot believe that it is my own. There is just
  to much of it.
I see the car, but I can only see a little bit.
  I then realize what is going on.
I had left the party just before dawn.
I was drinking and driving, that's all that I remember.
  My last hours will be spent dying on the street on this cold
  morning of December.
I begin to cry, but I produce no tears.
  Everything is gone, my dreams, my hopes, even my fears.
I wish I had been more careful and that I had thought about what I
  was doing.
Maybe then I wouldn't be laying here, all my blood spewing.
  I should not have been so stupid to drink and drive.
If I had thought about what would have happened I would probably still
  be alive.

Nicole Rinaldi

The Artist

Captured quickly as my eyes dart about
pressing brush to canvas as it turns out
like flowing rivers the picture appears
there remaining through the years.

Painting portraits, landscapes or assure skies of blue
silent sunsets of a golden hue
soft roses in gentle ladies hair
sunlit faces without a care.

Little children with love for laughter
silenced in stillness ever after
captured in time of life indeed
captured on canvas forever to be.

Rick Douglas Smith

Finally/Fire

Black and sorrowful, the smoke rises,
Polluting the chimney's brick walls.
With layer after layer of dark resin,
it decays the cold stone.
But now, finally, the smoke starts to clear.

Gray and burned, the ashes of past relations lay,
Hidden under the shadows of a
happy, humoristic front.
I am a drop-out in this God-forsaken game.
But now, finally, the ashes start to clear.

Red and hot, the fire has been denied
any residence in this fireplace.
Sparks extinguished too soon to show full potential.
It has been tedious.
But now, finally, the fire starts to burn.

White and intense, the fire builds,
expunging the smoke and ashes from memory,
laying bare the defenses.
I am vulnerable; I am petrified.
But now, finally, I am happy!

Robert Tatroe

Patience

Patience is Trusting and Believing that God will Answer your
Prayers. Going one day at a time Praising his name through
Good and Bad days.

When your Prayer still seems like it will not be answered,
is a test of your Faith and Trust in the Lord. That brings
on more Patience. Just continue to Hold On and Strive and
do what God wants us to do in his Commandments.

The way is hard you often want to Give Up, but don't Give up
keep Holding On, that is more Patience. I know you wonder
why it is taking so long to see your way through, but just
Wait on the Lord; he is always on time. He may not come
when you want him, but believe, the wait will turn out to be
worth the while.

God knows what is Best. So through the times of Trials and
Tribulations ask the Lord to Grant you more Patience to Hold
On, Trust to Know that you will make the Right Decision,
and Faith to Believe he will Deliver your Blessing on Time.

Tammie Derran Barnett

My One Rose

Sitting here talking to GOD
Praying for my son to be free,
I hear GOD saying, do you not have a Rose?
Is there more that you need?

At first I did not realize
What those words would mean to me,
Until I looked at a plaque on my wall
Then I knew my son would be free.

The plaque says — A Rose is GOD's autograph —-
A plain and simple line,
To me it meant so very much
For GOD has made him mine.

My heart was full —-
For I knew HE had heard my plea,
HE was telling me to truly believe
And soon my son would be free.

So if it's true that a Rose is GOD's autograph
Then with that sentiment I will close,
For in my heart forever and always
My Beloved son — YOU are my ONE ROSE.

Ruth Helen Price

Images

Images of Yesteryear
Pressed within a Scrapbook
As the book is opened
the yellowing pages
hold many dear and loving memories.
The photo of a small child appears
thinking back to when...
he was born, each year that so quickly fled by.
Hoping and wishing this child
will always stay small and
precious but inside he will
always be very special
no matter what his faults or
achievements may be.
Love him endlessly
for this tender-loving child is You!
Deep within the heart
searching, seeking for a new place.
Forever treat him dear
for he is today's image and tomorrow's future.

Katherine Agents

Pressure

Sometimes there is pressure:
Pressure to do things never intended.
Walk the tight rope of life.
Leave the ones most loved,
To hold what doesn't want to be held.
To make certain of what your going to do,
Ten years down the road.
To accomplish the unseen, the unheard.
Make do with what you have,
Live on the inside not the outside.
Who can we really help?
The unfortunate, the poor, the addicts?
The pressure to walk on even though
They are still there.
Look on, don't look down.
Look up, but just don't look down.
Can you see the world in endless light,
Or eternal darkness?
Do not overlook, but look into.
The Pressure Of Life.

Katie Russell

"Memories Of Dad"

The gentle arms you held me with,
Promises you always tried to keep.
Always turning to you, in times of doubt,
Knowing you'd be there, to help me out.
And now I'm left with my memories.

God came and took you so suddenly,
I never got to say good-bye.
To tell you how much I loved you.
My heart is hurting, all I can do is cry.
And now I'm left with my memories.

When I was growing up, you were a hero to me,
But as I grew older, I felt a need to be free.
Now I realize how much you cared,
You only wanted the way best for me.
And now I'm left with my memories.

So I'll take my memories, I'll hold them near
The good and the bad, the happy and sad.
I just wanted to let you know,
How very much I loved you.
You meant the world to me, and I miss you Dad.

Mary L. Logsdon

Life In A Fish Bowl

Willowing, wallowing
Quickly swallowing
The very water they stir.
Repeatedly realizing, they have no future.

In a cage,
Somewhat in rage,
Always in motion,
Wanting to return to the ocean.

Tiny, precious, living things!
"Set them free", my heart sings!
But, I, too, am trapped like you, alas.
Trying to escape and bumping into glass.

Kathy Assouad

Love Day

O'what a beautiful good day
  Quickness fresh air banner's flying
Celestial blue skies and white clouds
  Peace on earth golden Sun
Wintertime cool living evergreen trees and park
  Church Bells my right Ten Commandments
Oceanic Seafaring ships Nautical Ocean
  Planet heavenly body remember aquarius

Nighttime hot black room studio one
  window view of utilities illicit
Snow white dress yankee O homeda
  Peaceful possession home ownership
Rightful mother and child window literary

Quiet white crescent moon and stars
  Remember Ancient light
Great dark blue sky supremacy
  The universe thy truth!

Joan D. Bancroft

Untitled

You have left me with lips inflamed, unkissed,
Raised passion to trembling, burning heights, unquenched.
This, the Exquisite Torture you plan
Touch of hand to face, heart to heart
Fingers drawn across my soul.
Briefest of interludes leaves an ache within my being.
Leave me not suspended between earth and sky
Weakened by this consuming need.
Breathless, burning -
The Uncommon desire you cause to rise in me
This Exquisite Torture, the drowning fire

Karen Abston

Harden Lake

giant, white, skinny, knotted trees
reach toward a solitary cloud.
and except for the leaves rustling and dancing brilliantly
  (the way that sunlight shimmers off the lake)
it is still.

and except for the buzz buzzing dragonflies
  (carrying a kaleidoscope of iridescent colors)
that dart close and inspect my toes
it is beautifully silent.

and except for the water caressing the rocks
  (as the breeze pushes it rhythmically toward shore)
it is absolutely quiet.

Only here can I truly believe that God exists.

Myrna P. Cisneros

I Am Humbled

Here I sit at the end of my day,
Reflecting on what I've accomplished today.
Exhausted, upset, and ready for bed,
So many things running through my head.

I get on my knees and pray,
Thank you God for this beautiful day.

Did I thank you God for the day of my birth?
You know it's hard to survive here on earth.
Without your guidance, I couldn't do what I do.
And did I tell you I know I wouldn't survive without you?

I get on my knees and pray,
Thank you God for this beautiful day.

Counting my blessings to you I see,
All the wonderful blessings you've bestowed upon me.
Goodnight then God, and thank you from me,
For the beautiful day it's turned out to be.

Vivian F. Scholes

The Cycle of Life

Life is a miracle that begins when a love seed
Rejoices in passions pollen
Then germinates into a tiny spirit
And when the time is right,
Blooms in the garden of life.

In time,
Muscle, bone, and teeth mature to full glory.
At long last, the miracle is a man.
Years go by unnoticed.
What was once perfection
Becomes a gnarled stump.

Death is a dark shadow
That passes over a restless soul
And brings with it the gift of mercy
That sets the spirit free.

Terri L. Dodge

After the War

Many hearts will be rejoicing, many tears will be shed,
Rejoicing for the living, weeping for the dead.
Thousands of soldiers will be marching back to their homes with joy,
Into the outstretched arms of mothers, waiting for their boys,
Brightening darkened homes with their presence once more,
After the battles are over, after the war.

Many a sweetheart will marry many singles remain,
Their beloved lost or dead, never to be seen again.
Many children will hug their Daddies, remembering them from a picture
  in a frame.
Many children will never know their fathers, left only with his
name,
But the honor and glory he leaves, they'll cherish forevermore,
After the battles are over, after the war.

Thousands of ships will be sailing, over the ocean blue,
The rails lined with soldiers, waiting for a glimpse of the homes they
  knew,
Their hearts filled with gladness, together they'll sing,
Thanking God once more for the peace he brings,
And after the ships reach land once more, our boys will touch
  America's shore,
After the battles are over, after the war.

Marie Dippong

Lighten Up the Load

When life gets so troubled, and more than you want to bear,
Remember God still loves you, and always will be there;
He'll take you through the rough spots, and guide you down the road
He knows your load limit and will lighten up your load.

When you've reached a darkened crossroads, and can't see the light of day,
The times it is difficult to determine the better way;
Just put your faith in God above and let him lead you on,
The journey through the valley will end at rising dawn.

The trip gets rough and rugged, and seems will never end;
But the peace and calm of His great love will all the sorrow mend.
It's hard to make it by yourself, and carry all the load.
Remember He knows your load limit and will see you down the road.

We often don't seem to understand why life's a difficult quest,
It's not our place to question Him, or doubt He knows what's best;
Just trust His love and keep the faith that all will turn out right.
It will be better after time, through God's power and His might.

When you see a friend in need of just a kindly word or two,
Tell him, "God can solve your problems, His love will see you through;
He will smooth the rough spots and guide you down the road,
He knows your load limit and will lighten up your load.

Ted Blevins

Faces And Names

As you travel the road back to where you came.
Remember those you leave behind
all those different faces and names.

Remember those who made you laugh
and a smile will light up your face.
Remember those who made you angry
you'll wish there had been a better way.

Remember those who tried to make your day
better then the last,
by teaching you new ways for a difficult task.

Remember those who shared tender moments,
even the one's that didn't last,
and those who cried tears from the past.

So...when you're safely back to where you came
remember all those who touched you in a unique way.
For they gave you their friendship,
which is something that can't be framed.
Your life and theirs, will never be the same
all because of those... different faces and names.

Lee D. Stewart

Last Prayer

Sometimes at night I just sit and stare
   remembering my past and getting nowhere.
All I wanted in life was a crazy little dream
   Instead I find emptiness that wakes me in screams.
My childhood was sheltered in a loving home
   stepping out in the world shattered that dome.
People take, causing such pain.
   Walking on others, what can be gained?
I wanted to live and spread my love,
   Create some beauty like the snow white dove.
But when they knock me down out of the sky,
   breaking my wings makes it hard to fly.
Being cold and bitter is not in my genes.
   But in order to survive I'm learning their schemes.
The world has changed me I feel for the worst
   How much more hate will it take before I burst?
As time goes on, I die more each day.
   I ask you Lord, please take me away!
Leave this world to the ugly and cruel
   I'm a child of God. I belong with You.

Lyric

Why?

Why do I think back on the moments we shared,
   Remembering a time when there was no doubt that you cared;
Why do I keep trying to pull you away from your fears,
   When all I can do is just be near.
Why do I kneel down on my knees every night,
   And pray to God that you're alright.

Why must everything remind me of you;
   The sun, the stars, and even the moon.
Why should I cry, and why should I keep trying;
   Knowing that each day, inside, I am dying.

Why do I remember the way we used to dance;
Why do I even think we have a chance.
Why do I remember the clothes you used to wear;
Why do I close my eyes and see you standing there.
Why do I remember Christmas and all the good times it brought;
And, what about Valentine's when you held me close to your heart.

Why do I remember ALL the times that we shared-
And,
   Why does it now seem,
    I'm the only one who cares?

Sonia Y. Odems

Once Again

Come sit here and talk of the days that are gone,
Remind me again of the joys and the tears.
Tell me of friends, and of dreams that live on.
Tell me of wisdom that comes with the years.
   Come sing to me softly a song or two, maybe,
   Remember the songs that brought tears to the eye?
   Sing me the lullabies you sang to our baby,
   Sing the old songs, the good songs, the tunes that don't die.
Come kneel here beside me and pray once again.
Ask the God all goodness to hear and forgive.
Hold my hand firmly as you held to me then
As we vowed to keep loving just as long as we live.

Merceda Ruth Pond

Blowing A Kiss

She kissed him on a haunted moon,
removed his scars removed his wound.
She danced before him naked and free
she danced before him with pleasure and glee.
He pushed her away into the night.
She faded fast with greater height.
He pushed away his nightingale
So now he's here to tell his tale.
My nightingale - whom I once loved.
Is but a star into the sky she so
   fast, she flew so high,
I miss her now - her diamond tears
   only to be seen when rain appears
The night has a moon - the day has
   a sun, but my languid life has just begun.

Keziah Dillow

The Challenge

Drink from the well of challenge,
Fill your goblet to the brim.
Climb the heights of canyon walls,
And scream out from it's rim.
I have faced the fear before me,
And harnessed the power deep within.
I have made friends with limitations,
With desires and a will to win.

Ronald C. Douglas

By Your Grace Lord

By your grace, I am set free.
By your grace, you've chosen me.
By your grace, please let it be,
That I will know your will for me.

By your grace, I can serve you,
in everything I say and do.
By your grace, your light can shine,
through and in these eyes of mine.

Stella Blake

Egg Frying

With snapping and sizzling sounds
  Resembling angry fireworks,
The yellow liquid smothered the gold and white egg.
Here and there a white bubble burst
  And splashed its liquid contents
  In the strong black pan.
The Golden yolk whispered noisily
  To the intense heat.
With swaying motion it scattered
  Over the white of the egg.
This white liquid, evidently disliking
  This turn of events,
  Spit and sputtered loud and long.
Echoing on all sides of the pan
  It uttered a soft sigh.
Covering itself with a golden brown coat
  It rolled over on its back
  And fried itself to sleep.

Sara Drew Sweeney

night in my town

My town has cool, blue, silky
rivers running down the roads,
sleepy and sinuous.
Nothing is more quiet than my town;
nothing ever happens in my town.
My town wears dark blue nights like a tent-dress:
big, bulky, unwieldy.
Nights can be a heavy pressure of fear 'cause
light pools around the sodium bulbs of street lamps.
Outside the circles the rivers flow and balloon
into blue shrouded night. In my small town,
if you don't see it don't know it fear it. Stay in the light
avoid the night. My friend Rachel said small towns are
insular. Insular. People in my town are trapped in their
little pools of light, like moths hypnotized. Scared to leave
and surrounded by the dark, the unknown. and me?
I always was a night person.

Rita E. Gould

A Fist

He hugs his knees to his chest.
Rocking to calm a fearful unrest
Of a fist.

He utters a call that no one hears
He lifts up his arms but no one is there
And he cries.

He becomes a man, a petulant stone
And in a room down the hall he hears the call
Of his child alone

As she hugs her knees to her chest
Rocking to calm a fearful unrest
Of a fist.

And he cries.

Tracie O'Neil Saunders

Picnic

They prepared a basket for their stroll, jelly cookies, home baked rolls, a book by Burns and when they dined, some fine old elderberry wine.

They walked along a path that led to the forest pond ahead, where croaking frogs and bluebird tweets, lent rustic music to their feast.

Where imagination made it appear that woodland elves were waiting there, but their thoughts were only of this life and their roles as man and wife.

They ate most of the picnic food and in that relaxing attitude, no words of love had to be said, it was in their shining eyes instead.

Not often found in modern times, it was love, the real old fashioned kind, and readers of this poem can tell, Dan Cupid did his job quite well.

Norman Rasmussen

Life's Golden Treasures

Listen to the wind, my child,
rustling through the trees,
and hear the music of the birds who sing sweet melodies.

Look up at the moon, my child,
hanging in the sky,
like a great white spotlight o'er the land where shadows lie.

Breathe in the mountain air, my child,
the aroma of the sea,
and smell the fragrance of morning flowers opening tenderly.

Taste the berries from the vine, my child,
the fruit which on the tree grows,
savor the goodness of each planted food in Granddad's garden rows.

Feel the bitterness in the air, my child,
as slowly winter creeps in,
and touch the bare limbs of the trees,
where soft leaves once had been.

Hold fast to the world, my child!
Life's treasures around you lie.
But seek with the inner eye of your heart, or you may pass them by.

Misty Leigh Butler

U.S.A I Love You, I Owe You

U nited peoples on this planet seen here
S ince centuries they are all closed Dears,
A merica, America, what attractive sound

I n times around, everyone feels proud,

L ove and freedom the priceless things of the United States
O ver all, justice and civil right, a real human shade,
V iva freedom of worship always exists
E vertrusting believers of West East, religions indeed,
Y ou and I, we have no right to be indifferentists
O r careless dummies with nothing to be contributed,
U. S.A., without your help I couldn't have achieved my wish

I n completion of all what I am in need,

O n both physical and spiritual viewpoints
W ith knowledge, self-confidence and mutual assistance,
E veryone can be proud to live in this promised land

Y es, also a most enthusiastic community with hands in hands,
O f course, you have really made my dream become true
U. S.A., thank you so very much but I have already owed you too...

Le Minh Duc

The Hanging Tree

Sagging black teardrop swaying from oak limb;
Sad weeping wood bears the burden of sin.
She colors the Alabama clay red.
Strange lacrimal nectar this tree sheds.

On American nights she's not alone.
Obeying white sheets; her innocence gone.
Only limp black torso and limp black feet
Offer solace for quilt - so sour it's sweet.

Bound by life granting roots; betrayed by same.
Black teardrop swings in a breeze of shame.
Bare and dripping a briny crimson sap,
Blood rooted oak sleeps an eternal nap.

Kevin Jones

Battered Hearts

Echoes of fear are perceived through his ear.
Sadness lurking will not depart.
This man upon the mountain top
wants all madness to stop.
I warned you, said he,
of what would be
if I found battered hearts.
Why is there fear?
Am I needed here?
I told you this and
now you fear.
All I can see are battered hearts.
This maliciousness is pitiful.
I thought more of you than this.
How then, can you disappoint me?

Lauren Dey

Golden Heart Be Still

I hold you quietly, warmly, with tenderness.
Safe am I from the depths.
The gentle waves of our love wash me ashore
tattered, bruised and beleaguered.

Soft clouds fondly touch the moon.
The caresses at hand calm my angst.
Our embrace submerges my fear.
The rapture of our passion soothes me.

I spent years upon Neptune's realm.
Heartache and despair filled many
days and nights at sea.
Now, in a sequence of swells we bathe
in the moonlight.

Pixies dance upon a black sea riffled by the
wind and once again I feel one with you.
We peacefully lay on speckle of pearl.
Serene in your embrace I sleep calmly,
free at last.

Tender is the night
Patrick Severne

First Love

Adonis with curls,
all blue-eyed, twinkling smile.
Silent, strong,
with knowing ways.
Locked in a corner
of my heart, he stays
forever young.
Because he loved me.

Mary Boufis Filou

A Grain of Sand

The waves of memory come crashing through my mind-a bleached, parched
sand-land.

White froth purges itself of treasures that tempt
the light of sun or moon to expose their hiding places.

Afraid, another wave reaches out and quickly recaptures them.
Returned to Coral Castles guarded by half-shadowed sentries of the deep....

...and they wait, for the next storm-the next shoreline...to surface.
A piece of glass, weathered by the elements-worn down by time.

Is it a treasure? Did it gain it's value only as it became lost to
us? Or was the value always there?

What heart can endure the storms? Will a hand offer freedom? Or
casually toss it away?

Lost forever.

Finally, to return-unnoticed-as a grain of sand among many.

Lynn Gallagher

"Reverences Apathy"

Walking through a pit of needles;
scarred down to my soul,
starvation makes me full,
I am being eaten by snakes and beetles.

My tear does not fall,
my heart has wanted it's wounds to bleed,
I can not let go and for me there is no need,
my life is being written down on the wall.

But an obstinate mortal I am now;
ignorance makes me numb,
intelligence makes me dumb,
for as I kneel through motions of rituals,
being an anti-christ embellishes through my other half;
and to God alone I do not bow.

My mind is smothered and beaten to no return,
I can not go back to that life of abound
for I am paralyzed in plentifulness and do not walk upon their ground;
in Reverences Apathy I become endured, abolished, and I start to
burn.

Merry Elizabeth O'Brien

Innocence

I hurt so bad, is it life that drives me mad?
Seed me with knowledge, oh life.
Seed me with experience, oh life.
Seed me with acceptance, oh life.
I cannot have, nor will I accept less than but to try and do my best.
Is it enough? Will anyone care, that I cry tears of grief?
I pleased not he nor she nor them nor they, even though I try every
   day.
For years I've tried, for years I've died,
inside my mind is where I hide.
It's here where my mind was once free
to make me happy and motivate me,
now so clogged with life's realities
it sometimes brings me to my knees.
For it's in my mind where I pray, hoping for a better day.
In my mind, life's innocence's may still be at play,
this life with hope and joy I still do pray.
Hoping that these thought's are not mere toys,
please, please of life bring me back,
to innocence where imagination was a true fact.

Myron R. Ward

On Line Connection

The wedding was set for Saturday night.
Settled down at their keyboards were guests
Anxious to witness this couple unite...
Would on-line vows pass the tests?

I can't say if the bride dressed in white
Or what the groom and his best man had worn,
But I know that their love began at first byte
By the ever-green monitor glow in the morn.

Some graphics plotted their trek up the aisle.
Joe and Ann keyboarded vows without fail.
Proceedings slowed at one point then, while
They read congrats from their E-mail.

While each at a keyboard, champagne glass in hand,
They poured out the bubbly...then taking two sips...
They hastened toward log-off, their PC's still manned
They ran not through rice but through showers of CHIPS.

This on-line happening really is true.
The accounting needs no one's correction,
If you don't believe, I'll give you a clue...
'Twas LOVE made this on-line connection.

Ruth Kassner

Feelings Of The Quilt

Lives brought together by one common bond, memories
sewed together to always live on.

Babies, children, men and women a like, never in my
life was I overwhelmed by such a sight.

As I walked along, the many quilts I did see, thinking
ordinary people who were just like me.

Each quilt had a signature of that person's being,
as I wiped my tears their lives I was seeing.

A rattle of a baby not even two, the undershirt of
a little boy the color blue, the cut braid of a singer, and
a Grandmother of such, as I bent down I yearned to touch.

As I came near the end a special quilt I did see,
anyone could sign it, so I did, to Robert from me. He was a
good friend, and he gave my life meaning. Another aids victim
so many I'm seeing.

Tears, anger, sadness, and loss. This disease takes
it's own course. The patches that make this quilt a sight,
tells us all who care not to give up this fight.

Kim Johnson

Lost Horizons

Off in the distance, upon a sunny morn,
shadows of the day birds shown, months after born.
Up aloft the hillside,
the mighty bear once fought.
In the far off meadows, baby deer just learn to walk.
Under the ground, a gentle shove,
a small ground squirrel sees the sun.
Watch the forgotten horizon,
long since gone.
Feel the pride of the earth,
long since gone.
See the freedom of the deer,
long since gone.
Witness man's mark,
forever scarred.

Tom Nelson

Thunder

It starts as a muffled sound, as it rolls and grows as it
shakes the ground, I like thunder it's an old friend a
thousand voices talking again, riding a chariot they call
the wind. Old soles living again, riding through the night
on there chariot, the wind. Through flashes of light
each living again, old soles that once were earthly
friends, oh the calling the thunder and wind. Saying hello
to their earthly friends some day ride with us in our
chariot of wind. We ride so far but never to the end.
For God has given us the eternity to send the messages
too our old friends. As we ride chariots of wind. Oh,
the calling the thunder the wind letting me know I'll
live again.

Timothy O. Casey

Chained

Seconds turn into hours
Shattered glass upon the floor
Thoughts submerged, conquered, and swallowed
   to be buried in barren soil
Minutes blaze into days
Time can never be defeated
The mad escape, the sane explain
As they grasp, the thunder rumbles

Seasons turn into a lifetime
The days of play are forever never
The smiles we wear remain the same
Hidden echoes of innocent laughter
Decades fade into a grave
A cradle of relinquished love
The tears of pain seldom change
   chained to an endless shower of hope

Sometimes, I laugh at breathing
An illusion, a masque, a disguise
Sometimes, I dream of screaming
As I dance through the mist of ocean tides

Kevin A. Butler

"Sorry"

A beautiful lady is like the winter's first snow.
   She comes in a soft pristine flurry of delicate flakes.
They swirl about and envelope your entire life and capture your
heart
   and soul.
   You think you have found your one true love.
And as the relationship warms and grows;
   She melts and disappears.
All that remains are the bittersweet memories of what might have
been.
   The flower is wilted the scent has flown;
The night is over and you are alone.

Peter R. Hines

A Viking He'll Stay

He sailed into the sunset, and off into the night,
Seeking battle and war, and an awful fight.
He's a viking, you see,
And a viking he'll stay
And by now he's reached another land's bay.
The dragon comes first, but he doesn't get the worst,
For the viking steps out with proud horns on his head.
(His wife is at home with the dread that he's dead.)
The battle is on as the vikings intrude!
The other land is now being pursued...

Wendy Van Fossen

The Touch

As Anna walked to the garden
she could see that the roses were in full bloom
like magnificent red suns in the hot summer heat.
But there was one little rose behind all the others.
It was shriveled up
and beginning to lose its color.
This rose was the only one Anna noticed.
This rose was beautiful in Anna's eyes,
and she bent down on the soft soil next to the rose.
Then Anna reached out and touched the rose.
Feeling its pain, Anna lightly swept her face close to the rose,
soft like the brush of a cobweb against her arm,
and the rose was healed by the touch, the touch of a small child.
For the touch of a young one is special,
the small hands just beginning to explore the world outside.
The little rose lived on, longer than any of the others,
all because of a child, a very special child.

Stephanie Berry

Power

He feels the need to have power-he will have none.
She cries. She wants to be a victim. She cries because she is not a
    victim.
There is no real hate. I created the hatred you think you feel
But you will listen
Man is home. Home is the power. Man is homeless. He has no power.
There is none. No power his worthlessness envelopes him. Why does he
shake? He has become the victim. She kills him. She wanted to be
the victim. Even though he wants her, he can not. Stop stop stop he
says. I can't do this. She is a child. But she is reflecting the
innocent light that he can not feel. He takes her anyway. The light
slowly goes out. Now she is the victim. She laughs, after all, the
victim has the power. He takes her again. She cries. She is wrong,
the victim has no power. She wants to end it all. Suicide is the
most selfish of crimes that someone can commit. No no no - I am not a
victim. I will rise. I am not weak. You think that you know.
Knowledge is all we have. Man has taken away my innocence and
    crushed
it with my own hands. Man has the power-the power to steal and
destroy my innocence in order to achieve what he lusts for most.
Power.

Sarah Gillespie

The Girl Next Door

There is this girl her name is Sherry,
She likes wine coolers-premium berry,
I think she is pretty and really smart,
If only she knew she has a big heart.
My next door neighbor is the girl next door,
She makes me laugh and is never a bore.
Only a neighbor you see-I'm just a guy,
When I'm around her I get really shy.
I'd like to get closer but don't know how,
She's probably reading this and raising her brow.
Sometimes I'd like to just call and say hi,
But my heart begins to race and I wonder why.
A volunteer paramedic both proud and true,
She did all she could to save my brother's life,
And she would do the same for you, I'm not really sure if
this poem is for her, maybe She's wishing this was all a big blur.
I have felt this way for a very long time,
I'm lucky just to get all these words to rhyme.
If she never knows how I really feel-it's o.k.,
Tomorrow is just another day, another day to feel unreal.

Tony Klein

Who Is She?

She wakes every morning to the gentle sound of her slumbering family,
She shuffles to the coffee pot and begins her routine.
Silently her house places a cloak of safety and peace around her,
Sitting at her kitchen table she sips her first cups of coffee and
    ponders,
Softly recalling the past when she only had concern for herself.
Solitary shadows drape the lawn in shrouds of early morning shimmer,
Seeing the squirrels and chickadees going about their ritual of
    survival she feels akin to them.
Showering and luxuriating as the warm steam encircles her,
She hastens on to meet the challenges of her day.
She emerges from her warm haven to find her children and husband
    waiting,
Simultaneously she pours milk on cereal and juice in glasses,
Smoothly she braids her daughter's hair, runs a comb through her son's
    and jabs at her own.
Sophistication and power enfolds her as she hurries the children into
    the car,
Solitude is a far off vision as she backs the car from the garage.
Solicitors, harsh decisions, high pressure are the things that await
    her day
Shifting mentally from mom to competent executive as the children
    leave the car,
She eases herself into the transition of the rest of her day.
She is you and I—sister, daughter, mom, lover and wife —
She is wearing many hats and wearing them quite well.

Nancy L. Berkompas

In A Rocking Chair She Lingers

In a rocking chair she lingers,
She stretches her aged and careworn fingers.

The springtime of life which to soon passed her by,
now has only the witness of a gleam in her eye.

Her only wish to recapture her youth,
has only unveiled the bitterness of truth.

"Come see me", "come see me", an unending plea,
as the fruits of her labors fall far from the tree.

The darkness and cold that arrive with this winter,
bring along discontent, through the heart do they splinter.

In the twilight of her day she is forgotten, alone,
in her quiet room at the nursing home.

Victoria Rashid

A December Day

It was a dreary December day, when my mom faded away.
She suffered for so long. Why did everything go wrong?

A woman of great stature, no one could ever match her.
A woman with a heart of gold, she could never be undersold.

A woman of remarkable strength, one who taught me to go to great
    lengths.
A woman who concealed her pain, just not to let me feel the strain.

A woman who helped me in the past, one who always put herself last.
A woman who shined so bright, I am sure she followed the Great Light.

And even though I prayed each day that the Lord would let her stay,
I knew she wanted to let go, she said, it was time for me to grow.

It's hard for me to understand, what is in His Glorious Plan.
To take someone so beautiful;
I pray, He holds her in the Palm of His Hand.

Theresa Palladino

Profession's

There was a girl who couldn't be cuter
She was an expert on any computer!
But quick as a whistle,
She slipped on a disc;
And unfortunately, they had to boot her!

Her pencil was always poised in a arch
To take dictation ever so fast;
But her job didn't last
Because of her past...
Now she's a white collar girl - minus her starch!

She was as thin as a rubber band
And twice as flexible
She could twist and bend
So that in the end
Her figure was completely undetectable!

Having a child
Is really wild!
A feeling like none other
Unless it's being called, "Grandmother!"

Olivia Deutsch Jacobs

Gerry's Song

I knew an unsung hero.
She was "just" a daughter, mother, grandmother, friend and wife.
Yet she gave so much to everyone -
everyone who touched her life.

She was a kind and compassionate person.
Her trademark was a great big smile.
And she was never, ever too busy
to stop and talk a while.

She used to give me pep talks.
Inevitably, it was on a bad day.
But she had a way of lifting my spirits
and making the clouds seem less gray.

I should have thanked her for caring.
It's too late - hope somehow she knows.
For the most I can do now is visit her grave
and leave there a fresh cut rose.

I knew an unsung hero.
She was "just" a daughter, mother, grandmother, friend and wife.
And I thank God everyday for having known her -
for she was "just" a friend - who changed my life.

Mary Cooksey Wilks

God's Greatest Gift

Many years ago, on a chill wintry night
Shepherds beheld a glorious light
As angels proclaimed the virgin birth
Of a babe sent from God to dwell here on earth.
In swaddling cloth the new-born baby lay
Tucked down to sleep in a manger of hay
When there dawned on this earth THE FIRST CHRISTMAS DAY!

The Magi rejoiced with exceeding great joy
When the Star led them to this tiny new boy.
The gifts they brought were treasures of earth,
The GOLD signified His Royal birth,
FRANKINCENSE symbolized His deity on earth.
MYRRH spoke of His life crushed and poured out
In a crimson stream from Salvation's fount.

He was the LAMB OF GOD from the foundation of earth,
Yet angels brought tidings of His humble birth.
Isaiah called Him MIGHTY GOD, PRINCE OF PEACE.
From bondage of sin He brought release.
What gift can we give that could e'er repay
That wondrous GIFT OF GOD on that FIRST CHRISTMAS DAY!

Ruth Mills Grant

Tears of Joy

I am a symbol of unspoken joy yet many are ashamed of me.
Shiny, clear, natural, chilled to perfection still you fight me,
I have won the battle dancing around your nose and mouth.
Like glistening rain in the sun I fall to cleanse your soul.
Each drop of me is needed to help dissolve the pain into a smile.
The salt in me is the magic dust I spread upon you
to burn away the evil so that again you will have reason to cry
and shed a stream of happiness, in a tear of joy.
My journey is ended by an embarrassed hand but I will never die
I am the crystal of life forever existing within your eyes.

Maureen Christopher

Which Way To Go

Can I undo what has already been done?
Should I just grab my bags and run?
Can I go backwards in time?
Or is it my turn to wait in line?
Like many others before me, they just took their chance,
Hoping, wishing for just a glance,
Of what might have been or what could be,
Is that right, truly for me?
I stand here afraid, all alone.
Wanting to call him on the telephone.
What should I say, think or do,
It's not for "I" to answer they say,
It's all up to you!
I know not where to turn, which way to go,
I feel like dying, crawling into a hole.
I've shed many tears, that shall always be,
Because my love for him will last thru Eternity!

Sheila Ann Eichacker

Misty Morning

Misty, rainy morning,
Showering drops of fluid crystals
Upon our graceful forms,
Saturating every pore with pure scintillating love
Flowing freely from distant heavenly bodies.
We journey quietly down a winding path,
Searching the innermost recesses of the soul,
To discover our true Self,
Breathing in the sweetness
Of perfect love that engulfs us,
Breathing out the ignorance of
time that had us bound,
Moment by moment
Step by step
We settle in a serene place
Only to rise in the mystical
garden of the heart
A sacred place
Where no one can exist
But you and me.

Onondaga Lake

She Knew Not What

She knew not what was to become of her once he laid his bite.
She knew not that she was to become his mistress, but only at night.
The day sun burned through their skin and turned them to ash.
They roamed all night in search of blood.
They were hungry and did not care.
Many joined them.
Many did not dare.
They, the creatures of the night, those in search of love.
All I can say is that I want to be loved.

Shylla Cotten

The Meaning of Life

Sunrise and first morning dew,
Shows early sign of a day anew.
See this as a sign from above,
Bring in it bright smiles and love.
For the meaning of life is around us all,
Still there, even if we fall.
Living isn't about possessions,
Or needs, desires, and obsessions.
These are the downfalls that lead to strife,
And take away the meaning of life.
The meaning of life isn't about things,
Only about the joy each day brings.
A baby's giggle, a newborn kitten,
The feeling you get when your smitten.
For isn't the one who reaches the top of the ladder,
The same one who makes room for us also to matter.
The sooner this lesson of life is learned.
The quicker everyone's cheek will turn.

Paula M. Borkowski

May the Good Lord have Mercy Upon Your Soul

Condemned man's thoughts lived over in minutes
Signifying dwells in every limits;
Fictions form, wishes untrue,
Societies welcome, not for you;
Right they have by appointed laws,
Also satan's embedded claws;
Money and power, 'tis all you knew,
Friends bought but never true;
Chamber, chair, and seeping gas,
Solemn spectators peering through the glass.

"In the name of the Father, Son, and Holy Spirit"
Amen

Malejo

If the Shoe Fits

"We're a brand new pair of patent leather shoes,
Size 7-C, Navy Blue -
Cooped up in this shoe box such a long time,
Hope the salesman puts us on view"

"What lovely feet we have here?,
Our shoes fit her just right -
She's pleased and so's the salesman,
We're comfy and not too tight"

"That day had come, one we had feared,
Her feet began to swell -
And now our shoes were ever so tight,
Her feet would never get well"

"This little old lady had problems,
With bunions and corns galore -
We never knew our shoes would fit,
Her toes were terribly sore"

"Once again it's back to the shoe store,
We did our best to please -
How can you fit a 7-C shoe, into size 8 feet?,
Just squeeze, and squeeze, and squeeze."

Marty Rollin

From Searching Seasons The Stripped Tree (Autumn)

Behold the caterpillars, in furs so soft and bright,
    Skimming up the autumn trees, to vanish from our sight.
They tell the tale of new birth—from crawler to butterfly,
    And now they've had to be transformed, and look like they did die.

They've had to give up their warm garment, and sleep in just their skin,
    Hanging in faith awaiting, for their transformation to begin.
Yet, all that time of expectancy, through winter's deadly cold,
    Simply dangling in suspense, 'till Spring calls them to unfold.

Hardened in slick death cases, the butterfly grows it's wings,
    To soon break out in splendor, amongst new growing things!
Wings of breath-taking beauty, lift the sleeper from it's rest,
    Into a world of sun-light, on earth at nature's best.

New life! From fuzzy creeper, to high angelic flight!
    This jeweled wonder brightens God's child, with a holy God's
insight! Dancing ballet of warm days —— mummy of the Fall;
    Symbol of Christ's resurrection, given to us all!

Roseanne Steyh Dooling

Quiet As The Night

Quiet, as the night settles for yet another darkness...
Sleepy as a child our eyes close.
With the faith...
Of yet a never ending moon's glow,
A light begins, a vision show...
Through the silence and goes the night,
Fables come real as dreaming is right...
A whole new world is brought to your feet.
The visions that only is seen in your sight.
So sleep in child...
Until you awake,
Sleep for your dreams another day make.
Dreamy, dreamy, dreamy one.
Awake my child to see the sun...
Awake my little dreamy one,
So...
Sleepy eyes sleepy will see the night fun.

Kathryn Wolfe

The Chess Board

My life is like being a pawn on a chess board
    Slowly moving across square by square;
Awaiting to be picked off
    By some greedy rook or knight
    Seduced by some intellectual queen,
Or knocked off by another lowly pawn
    Trying to cross no man's land.

I may have gotten a late jump into the game
    But in this game, the first out of the block
    Is usually the first consumed in the peril and danger.
I may die in the first exchange of fire,
    I may sit in a corner,
    But maybe, just maybe I'll make it to the other side
Where the grass is greener....And BINGO!
    I might become a knight, a rook, a bishop
And be able to move more than one square at a time

But one thing I do know-even a pawn
    Can take down an unsuspecting king or queen.
I often wonder when the game is over-
    Do the pieces get set up again?

R. Scott Nemzek

Alone With Another Broken Heart

I liked you so much I could go thru eternity with just one of your
smiles my way. Your smile warmed my heart and kept me happy all thru
the day. I gave my heart and soul and you left me standing here with
nothing at all. You were the light of my life until that one day that
you left me alone with another broken heart. So now my heart was
a wall built around it. I can't let you in. I think about you
sometimes, thinking about how fast you made my heart beat, how just
by you saying hi I could go for a week so deliriously happy. But then
I remember that one day that you left me standing alone with another
broken heart. I don't think you meant to hurt me, you didn't know that
I loved you that much. I sometimes get those old feelings back, but
I must push them aside, for I do not want to be left standing alone
with another broken heart.

Kristina R. Shuda

Watch the Looking Glass

All the water is a musky brown.
Smoke fills the air three feet thick.
A broken heart lingers like a constant nightmare.
Shades reality.

Lost and alone, pain comes in repeating monotone.
Wander down a familiar hallway to find a locked door.
Drift into a sea of better - forgotten memories.
"Please, someone, wake me!"

So run to the shore.
"Free!" She cried.
All everyone ever wants to be is free.
Nonsense.

Sometimes I feel like I'm chasing rabbits.

Miranda Shropshire

A Mountainous Thought

From the foothills I can see, the tip of the peak—all white and snowy.
Oh, how I want to climb, to the top of that mountain—so large and fine.
Never mind those treacherous cliffs, nor possible
risks—embroidered in blue all blissful and true.

From way up there, sitting in this chair, I don't believe I'd have
a care. Nothing could tear my eyes, to initiate these endless sighs.

No more nurse to push me around—and put me on exhibit like a
pathetic clown!
And I know my siblings mean-well, but I too get embarrassed—oh,
why can't they tell?

If I could escape from those faces of pity and sorrow—it just might
bring on hope for a brighter tomorrow! No more cruel, cruel,
mockery—or ones who pretend they don't even see me.

Then God's love would shine so bright, he'd take me away from
this misery, and fright.
You know, maybe, I am special after all—perhaps in God's eyes I
already stand tall!
I've never really done any wrong, I can't even walk, talk, or,—sing
out a song.
So, I guess I'll just remain right here, until God finally
shows—and takes me out of this chair...

Lou Megyeri

The Tears of God

The clouds drifting along the blue heavenly
sky. The rain falls softly upon the green meadows,
into the valleys, flowers humbling themselves
to the great storm. Up in the air, the winds
rolling by, quivering over the trees and sending
ripples through the water. Hearing the pidder
patter of the rainfall, whispering the pain
to me. I continue to watch in tears...

Nicholas Sky Hopkins

A Breath of Life

O'Lord give this statue a breath of life.
So beautiful is she, created merely to see.
Made from gifted hands and clays bond by the finest sands.
Just to look at her beautiful face is to see an earthly
display of heaven's grace.
So the angels envy her mere face of stone.
Much too beautiful to become skin and bone.
So beautiful is she that even the light of day would shine
her way and at her sight, the stars of night, spontaneously ignite.
She is but a miraculous sight to see, if only she were alive
and alone with me.
But she remains mere stone, yes, mere stone.
While my fantasies continue to live on.

Otis Wilson

My Mothers Walk With Me

As the eagle takes flight.
So did the two most important women of my life.
It has been now 19 yrs. and one!
I ran all my life because I felt abandon
But today I can rise above my pain.
Remembering the love we shared.
So many times, oh, how lonely it was
Not having the hug of my mothers.
As time goes by, as it is sure to do.
In the eye of my heart, they are there.
When sickness falls upon my weakening body, they are there!
As I sit at my table, writing about their hopes
And dreams for me, Yes! They are here.
All my life my mothers taught me about God.
In time past, I'd reply, "Yea right."
So much anger at God, the world and myself!
When I cry silent tears, due to many years of fear, they are there!
As long as I live, through and in me, they will be here!

Monica Raymo Ladet

Not Special

Beautiful you beautiful me
So different sharing life
loving hating so different.
Not special
Just touched by an angel with love
and magic to make beautiful
you beautiful me. God what
work would it have been
with out the love and magic
not special not special an angel not special
Who am I to say what is special
What is normal a way of life to you
my love with us no answers
just dreams and fantasies to
share a reality
The hardest game of life
not special
not special

Marsha Lemmo

Silence

Silence please from those noisy days.
Silence from your obnoxious ways.
Silence please right from the very start.
Silence, so I may be able to hear the beat of my heart.
Silence please from the opinionated view point.
Silence from the crowded dance hall and music joint.
Silence in the noon day and quiet still night.
Silence, so I may meditate to God and do it right.
Silence please from the media and its glorified violence.
I am not asking for much just your sweet and justified silence.

Robin M. Cole

Untitled

My heart is heavy.
So full of fear of
all that happens thru
the year. The burdens
of life sometimes overbear.
The things least expected.
That aren't prepared
But as I count my blessings
And the love I share,
With my family for whom I care.
My prayers and faith come shining thru.
And I know my Lord helps me live my life true.

Who is the man in my life.
The one who made me his wife.
He's the man I love I treasure
and the man who gives me pleasure.
He's my strength, my joy, and
my dream come true his arms are strong
as they hold me tight.
And with him by my side I know everything's alright.

Terre Smart

Chicago

Chicago, Chicago, the Windy City
So full of life and mystery
With buildings that climb to the clouds
No wonder the people are very proud.
Lake Michigan as far as the eye can see,
Inviting us all, come visit me.
Chicago, Chicago, with her hand held out
Come and I will show you what life is about.
One time around is all it will take
To see and enjoy and also partake,
At night she will open her heart to you
For all who are willing to make dreams come true.
Chicago, Chicago, in all your splendor
Just waiting for all to come and surrender
With beauty and fame and so much to see
Sometimes the thought just bewilders me,
Why thousand of people have not come to see
Chicago, Chicago, the Windy City.

A. J. Barlotta

The Girl Who Stands In One Spot

The girl who stands in one spot,
so full of passion, so full of grace,
The center of attention, but no smile upon her face.
Is she really lonely, or is it just a plea,
to get a needed kiss from you, or from me?
Love is an instance where fate plays by chance,
Courtship of our hearts, with a wink and a glance.
I know she reads my mind, and I pray this isn't so,
True love is different colors, somehow I've got to know.
Our souls will never happen,
Our lips will never meet,
Is it love or passion in my heart
when I see her on the street?
The girl who stands in one spot,
Is she really true to me?
Or is her heart with another, is this my fate to be?

Larry D. Hunt

Prenkha's Prey

'Tis been a few cold hours shan't I feed.
So I begin to hunt my prey with pain.
O' may these sins make I be washed by rain.
Now you will play that role of prey and bleed.
But it shan't hurt, I guarantee indeed.
My way of loving is harsh yet not sane.
I, Prenkha, of centuries walk with no cane
And look younger than la lily's new seed.
Closer to you I glide as Devil's Ghost
And kiss thee neck below thy beauty face.
Soon, rivers will drown me without a dam.
But you are thoust first victim I loved most.
My teeth, so long, sink in your skin of ace.
Forgive me... for now you know what I am.

Salvatore Barone

While Wondering

I asked—dear guardian angel, why have I lived on earth,
  so many years?
Good friends have gone before me
  leaving me in tears.
She answered—you are right. I have been with you
  forever and a day.
I will ask our consulting angel.
  She has the final say.
Her reply was—she is a gentle sort,
  As near as one can tell,
Not good enough for heaven,
  Nor bad enough for hell.
So, just keep taking care of her.
  That is your assigned duty.
She's living on the garden isle,
  A land of wondrous beauty.
Her home is near family and new friends
  She has met.
And that's as near to paradise,
  As she can get. Yet!!

Mary Agnes Usher

Storms in the Mind

Honey, I know that you have loved and been loved
so much more than I.

Even so, my love for you could have been deeper
than the ocean and higher than the sky.

I know that there is a storm brewing of which
will soon be quite and still.

And the hurt I have caused by loving you will
be no more for you to feel.

Now if you have bade me good by, just remember
that I would have loved you until the day that I die.

May the one who's arms cradle you now be as
strong and the happiness you find be your life long.

I am sure that you must have been looking for
some one so much better than I.

But the little time we spent together was such a joy
to me, I just wish that I could have had a little more time to try:

If my foolishness has caused you to decide that I am not the
one that you want by your side.
Then honey, may I just say thanks, for the
time you gave me, God knows I tried.

Robert H. Stowe

If the Flowers Could Talk

(They'd compare themselves to a deteriorating human.)

We have pollinated and nurtured them
So that they could mature into
Healthy happy blossoms, with brightly
Colored futures of their own, fulfilling
A potential fitting to each personality.

We are thankful to be in this
World even for a short time and yet
Our guilt ridden hearts and souls tell
Us we could have done more.

Maybe we didn't give our little
Buds enough space to spread out
Into full fledged blooms.

Perhaps we have crowded our hearts
And protected our offsprings from
Distasteful situations a little too much.

Once we were distinguished and
Handsome.

A beautiful thing cannot last
An eternity.

Lorraine Berenson

I'm Your Conscience

I know the pain you feel inside,
so there is no reason for you to hide.

See, I'm your conscience, I dwell deep in your soul.
You know together we will both grow old.

Through the years, I've seen you go through so much pain.
A person of lesser strength would have gone insane.

So it's time to get the monkey off your back
and get your life on a brand new track.

Search just a little deeper and you will shine,
and leave the ghosts of the past behind.

The power you need comes from deep within.
Just open your heart a little more and you will have an everlasting friend.

You can't change the past, but you can live for today.
And with hope for the future you will have your brightest day.

So take this advice from your conscience, I won't steer you wrong.
I will make you feel like you have been reborn.

And years from now when you're old and gray,
the heavens will call and I'll hear you say:

"I didn't try to change the past, I just lived for the day.
I had hope for the future and today is my brightest day."

William D. Salley

Memories of Her

Her voice gentle as a summer nights breeze,
softly whispering through the trees.

A kiss so passionate, so divine;
how I long to make her mine.

Time spent together;
now for apart;
keeping the memories in my heart.

Can I see her once again?
Or will love come to end?

Passing days seem forever;
knowing soon we'll be together.

If the need to say goodbye;
memories of her will never die.

Rosario Piraino

Him And Her

He was two and so was she, both forbidden to leave their yard
so they stood at the edge
separated by the dirt road between them

Each day little hands longed to explore
but when the sun went home at rest
small footprints remained awaiting their return

When they returned it began all over again
with her begging softly from her yard
"come across now, no one is looking, you won't get in trouble,
I'll tell when someone comes"

Finally she had won
his eyes told her so
her smile, she tried to hide
he was on his way one foot in the road

Suddenly he stopped
didn't she know he was just teasing
he couldn't come

his Grandma had one leg and WHO
would help if he should fall?

Linda Clay Garvin

Inseparable

Take flight O great and wondrous one
Soar into a blissful twilight night through the windows of your soul
Rise freely above the limitations of the day, the excessive
distractions
Causing detained intents of the heart, away from the darkness of the
noonday mania!

Behold the brilliance of the Master Key
Opening countless doors to exquisite light. Glide with graceful wings
above all
Mountains, valleys, forests, and troubled waters
Drawing nearer the distant flame forever leading you homeward to your
beloved.
Shed the cumbersome cloak of winter's gloom, the useless veil of fear
Disrobe all outer garb as you lift your face upward. Stand in
confidence,
Clothed in the magnificence of heaven's glory.
Reach out, touch, receive, and share the fullness of our anticipated
embrace.

Behold the radiance of our perfect union.
As the painful emptiness subsides to a memory of worthwhile growth
Come, my beloved.
Let us blend together in the completion of our ecstasy...

Virginia Louise Pitale

When I Think of You

When I think of you, my love, my heart takes flight and
Soars to unimaginable heights. My eyes behold a billion
Bright lights. It brings back fond memories when I was
young, when life was always fun and I enjoyed the
Warmth of the summer sun.

When I think of you I can hear the strings of a thousand
Violins as they play our favorite song. I think of you
Holding me gently in your arms. When I think of you I
Think of the day we met. Suddenly I am overcome with
Deep emotion; but at the same time I feel the peace and
tranquility of sailing alone on a vast ocean.

When I think of our love I am instantly transported to
The stars above. It's such a thrill when love is real,
Etched in stone and sealed. When I think of you I think of
A love that will endure until life ends and death wins.
But until then, when I think of love I will always think
of you.

Lessie M. Kelly

Lady Montana

Who is she? Whose majestic curves tantalize the sky, whose sweet
soft rolling hills channel warm, pleasing Chinook breezes that
whisper of a winter's thaw and shout promises of a playground
bleached with her long nuptuous strands that invitingly waves to
the wayward wanderer
Who is she? Whose mountainous crannies spew tearful falls of water
that rainbow the jagged horizon, whose pelican dotted skies open wide
across drifting mesas which cargo the mighty ram and long lost buffalo
Who is she? Whose mood whimsically changes from gray blustery
typhoons of angry white snow to crisp golden, brown sunsets that
nestle blissfully in the white peaked pillows of evening shade's
purple lake Vista
Who is she? Whose seductively wild beauty has long since hypnotized
the adventurous settler prompting calls of divorce because of her
harsh coldness and perpetuating everlasting marriage proposals just
because of the elegance, grace and stature she poises over the mind's
eye as her harvest green locks turn cinnamon and sashay across her
rolling mounds that backdrop the panoramic stage
Who is she?

Orrin Keith Loftin

Innocence

Freedom beacons in the night.
Some day you will be able to stand up and fight.

I can hear the silent dripping of your tear.
Along with the subtle tremble from your fear.

You ask "why" and I can not answer.
This disease is worse than any cancer.

Greed is the cause of our disaster.
I just wish it would not speed any faster.

I can feel their sadness and their pain.
But no one seems to be able to explain.

It's the innocence that I cry for.
I wish I wouldn't have to cry anymore.

I wanted to save you, but I was too late.
You were already on someone dinner plate.

Can I stop that lonely tear, my friend?
Will this world ever mend?

I will not give up this fight for you.
Our friendship will forever be true.

Animals will one day be free,
you can just wait and see.

Michelle Annette Haller

Daughter of Duality

Passion unending, lust for living;
Soothing quietude, peaceful existing.
I'm created from love of Mother Tradition and Father Novelty.

Spicy kisses, scalding embrace;
Delicate whisper, icy caress.
I am fruit of Desire nourished by self-denial.

Warm tones of felicity, enigmatic night;
Cool shades of serenity, cleansing beacon of light.
I am exotic flower tipped with dulcet dew.

Music, poetry, Flamenco flavor;
Reality, technicality, docile behavior.
I am Latin love-child of Mother Tradition and Father Novelty.

Leslie Ann Rodriguez

The Grandkids Were Here!

Today's the day the grandkids are coming,
Some past occasions have been benumbing;
But I try hard and think of whose they are
'Cause they're better than most kids are by far.

How grandma's love for these kids would abound,
If only grandma could still be around.

They're here but too soon they must cease at play,
Their mother has come to whisk them away,
Announcing she's due for another date
And she can't wait 'cause she's already late.
If only she hadn't shown up so soon —
Perhaps 'til later in the afternoon,
We'd have enough time to put stuff all back
In its rightful place on grandpa's toy rack.

I had thought, at least, we would undertake
To wipe clean the smears of ice cream and cake;
But suddenly the dear rascals are gone
And the house is as still as early dawn.

Then looking about, when the coast is clear
Somehow I still know the grandkids were here!

Wayne R. Kelly

What I Feel For You

What I feel for you is
something I've never felt before,
Just thinking of you makes,
Me love you even more
What I feel for you is,
deep down in my heart,
I have a feeling we will never part
What I feel for you won't end too fast,
I have a feeling my love for you will last
What I feel for you is true love and I
meant everything above!

Mayra Delucas-Santana

Small Happenings

Something in her has been taken away,
Something she had yesterday but doesn't own today.

But something has been given,
A small package of love, dependence, and innocence.

It is an end, yet a beginning.
It is the start of a new king of living.

A miniature of something larger,
Growing, developing in a home inside her.

A heartbeat, a foot, a nail, a wrinkle,
All seem so ordinary, yet it is a miracle.

Stephanie Cavanaugh

Escape

Sometimes it's planned, but mostly not.
Sometimes a little, sometimes a lot.

I take a little time to escape for awhile
and think about things that make me smile.

So when problems arise or I'm feeling blue,
I know just what I have to do.

I take a little time to escape for awhile
and think about things that make me smile.

Mary A. Hall

As the Days Go By

With each day that goes by, you're with me just like you said
Sometimes are tough, some days are bad, but mostly times are
like you said they'd be
As our love for each other grows day by day I learn to love
you in another way
Slowly you're becoming like my soul, guiding me each step I take,
in my thoughts each moment that goes by
My dreams are that of you and me, together is how we'll always be
Taking the days as they come, we can dream together of times to come
We can sit and remember the days that have gone, old friends, family
and things that we've done
As we sit and watch our dreams come true
We enjoy each moment just me and you
Times will be rough, some days even sad, but mostly they'll
be good, just like you said
As I sit and think of our future to be, I sit and think of you and me

Thomas R. Malanga

Emptiness of Loneliness

Life's mysteries. The known and the unknown.
Sometimes I think it was mean to be, to be all alone.

What would it be like if we were able to foresee our destiny.
There would be no disappointment, no heartache to make you
search for some meaning and understanding. There would be no
confusion in our mind to lead us into self-pity. Or into despair
that no one cares or understands. No real discovery of the self.
How will the fears inside come out to reveal that it's up
to us to "shake it off" and say,
"Cry if I must, but I need to go on and seek the truth behind it all.
Am I really alone or was it me . . . I was searching for."

The "moment of being" will only occur
when one lets go of that frustration that she can no longer take
anymore ....Letting the memory of pain in the heart ease little by
little, like tears slowly gliding down your troubled mind and soul.
To vision that all this build up of mass-confusion was meant to be in
order to break free. To create a new tranquility in yourself. A new
discovery of yourself, your inner strengths, your mind and soul at
peace as one.

Rosa Maravillas

Why

Why do people hate me? What have I done wrong?
Sometimes it just a different key, where have my true friend gone?

They've gone, they're left me in a place where happiness is unknown,
the place I used to know.

I wish they'd come to get me, to never leave me there again.
Then to leave me alone, just let me be with just my real true friend

I wish they'd come to get me, I wish they'd tell me why,
they left me without a single wish, they left me there to die.

Whey must the world be this way? Why must it be so cruel?
For people to be hurt and cry, to even worry at school.

A friend can be as nice as a rabbit, or as cruel as a shark.
Pretty son, life becomes a habit. If change comes, sneak up
and grab it.

Don't worry if they like you, don't worry if they care.
For its you life they're doing harm to, they could care less
if you were a teddy bear.

Its time to think it over, its time to take a stand.
Its time to leave your worryful life, for a better one without demand

They won't always like you, they won't always care.
Now its time to say good bye you don't really care.

Nicole McKivitz

Winter

Snow, sleet, ice and more
sometimes your not able to get out of the door
With the snow on the ground
and the ice on the trees
It's a beautiful site for all to see
With valentines day and your friends b-day
You know that summer's not that far away
But when summer gets there and
There's no snow on the ground
Nothing but grass to play ground
All you see is the grass ready to mow
But no more ice and no more snow!

Kim Schwartz

Winter Is Almost Over

Winter is almost over, and spring is about to begin.
Soon we will start our summer vacation,
And run and play with our kin!
We might have some water-balloon fights,
And snowball fights will stop.
Spring is the time to climb a tree
From the bottom to the very top!
So...winter is almost over,
And spring is about to begin.
We won't worry about the snow,
We know we'll play in it again.

Sarah Rossol

Seasons of You

I thought you stepped out for a little while and
    soon you would return.
You forgot to shut some shutters down, and there are
    summer flowers in urn.
You said you loved me, as you walked out the door,
Then smiled and winked and promised even more.
That was in the autumn, and winter's come and gone.
I'm still awaiting your return and feeling so alone.
Now spring is starting to birth anew, and I am looking
    forward my dear for just a sense of you.
I know when summer comes along I will be just fine,
To walk with you on greening grass between the rows of
    lofty pines.

Mary V. Mogle

Who Is In Control?

What happens to a man when his conscience will no longer listen to
    his soul?
Does that man struggle to stay in control or was he ever in control?
And what happens to his soul?
Does that soul of that man wonder endlessly like a breeze and where it
goes nobody knows?
Or does that very soul seek refuge in the core of the heart of that man?
And when that poor shell of a man no longer has control over:
Rage, anger, hatred, violence, and love.
The devil comes in and steals the soul from the core of the heart of
that man because the windows were all left open by the conscience.
But does the devil have control of the devil?
Or is he to trotting to and fro to the ends of the earth trying to
find a heart, a soul, a body, and a conscience?

Pedro Dennis

A Star Falls from Heaven

Brilliantly shining in darkness of night
Sparkles of hope at its best
Calm and peaceful in moonlike glow
The face of a child at rest

Awakening innocence dawns another day
New mysteries of life unfold
A developing mind anxious to learn
Seemingly harmless facts untold

Our children are stars precious gifts from heaven
Not to be abused or neglected
A star that falls increases darkness
Abandonment diminished hopes broken dreams reflected

A star falls from heaven
without option
A child falls from life
with throw-a-way adoption

Pat Smith

Keyless Door

How long ago it seems that my heart held a name that my lips dared not
   speak,
The unkind bond of friendship locking it within me, while trying to
   soothe another's tragic moment -
Never letting the stronger feeling gain a foothold within, the battle
   rages on -
Yet could it have been one act in the play, the beginning - not the
   end?
Somewhere in the darkness an ember was glowing - once and again
   to light,
How hard it was to still the soul's despairing cries, yet it was done.
Once - for a moment - our eyes had gazed, one upon the other, only
   to turn away.
But the truth had been undressed and ran through my dreams - ever
   beckoning.
Yet this too was locked away, ever to wait at the mind's keyless door;
Though the soul has no such fortune and is left open to all that is
   pressed upon its memory.
And it was there that the truth found it's calling and remained,
Waiting - so quietly growing stronger - until it could no longer be
   contained.
It was then that the soul burst open wide the walls which had for so
   long held it back -
Vowing, swearing never again to be content in the self-imprisoned
   darkness
But to run - strong and unafraid - intimate with the sweet fire of truth
And to, at last, find peace in your quiet accepting strength.

Patricia G. Sylvester

Tonight

Speak to me of love she said
  Speak to me of faith
Speak to me of things unknown
  Your heart-your head-your soul and home
Of poetry and words alive
  The sun-the moon-the stars-your eyes

You hold my heart within your hand
  A soft caress from you my friend
You shelter me from wind and storm
  with love, sweet love, and nothing more
And from this love that you supply
  I draw my breath and am alive

and so, my friend, lover and life
  speak to me of you tonight

Steven Leslie McNichols

Fall Rites

Nestled on the earth in quiet repose
spent and awaiting the winter snows.
The autumn wind rising and settling,
Gathering up all it touches, on the way
to its invisible theater.
Brown and curled the dead lift,
swept playfully along in an ensemble
of dance, choreographed by the swirling
gusts across the ground.
Together and apart they perform this
dance of fall.
The wind searching for more fragile
dancers, whirls through the tree.
The tree clings to its last curtain of summer.
Wind and tree engage in momentary
struggle for possession of its participants.
The curtain parts and all is motion.
The gray sky looming speaks of winter's approach,
The conductor winds demands this graceful
farewell of them.

J. D. Harper

Waiting for Spring

From whence the laughing water flows
  splashing, gleefully, to and fro
  upon the banks of the river, sits
The wide-eyed dreamer, wispy light feather,
  flying high as a kite; glimpse
  of trials and sorrow, drift away.
  With every lapping wave that hits
  the inlet shore
  upon the bay.

Dreams of sunny days; of scarlet night.
Where flowers grow; wild
daintily tilting
  basking in the golden glow.
One of the wondrous gifts of spring
  emerging after the powdered snow.
More than that
  Only God does know.
Unless my dreamer's smile
  betray my lips, and my mind,
  in a joyous show....

Shannon Amber McHenry

Morning Draped

Watching the sunrise, two sisters sat still.
Staring into the orange sky, one felt a cold chill.
As morning draped itself, sun shining upon her,
she looked at the grave and tried to remember.

The guilt she felt, she couldn't explain.
Deep in her heart regret will remain.
"Why didn't I go ahead and say something, gone ahead and told
someone?
Then maybe I could've saved her from doing what she's done.

But no, I couldn't do it, I was too afraid,
and now look where I'm at, sitting next to her grave.
All those drugs inside her body finally did what I said they would.
She never thought it'd ever be her, she never thought it could."

Twenty years had passed since that God awful day,
they lowered her into the ground and that is where she lay.
Orange sky was no longer cast upon the stone.
Just like her sister, the sunrise was gone.

Stacy Michele Milam

Untitled

I am open about my feelings but sometimes I choose to keep them to
    myself
I wonder why the sky is blue
I hear the waves crashing and I wish I was at the beach
I see the world so big and think, "Wow!"
I want World Peace but know this will never happen
I am open about my feelings but sometimes I choose to keep them to
    myself

I pretend to be far away from it all
I feel that everyone is equal
I touch the sky with my feelings
I worry that the world is over crowded
I cry when I see the homeless
I am open about my feelings but sometimes I choose to keep them to
    myself

I understand that life isn't always fair
I say everyone has rights
I dream about being older
I try to be fair to all
I hope that someday everyone will have equal rights
I am open about my feelings but sometimes I choose to keep them to
    myself

    Missi Wiley

Our Flag, the Stars and Stripes

Our flag has stars,
Stars of the 50 states,
Colors of our nation,
That shine so bright.

The shine of men and women's eyes.
The shine of their courage,
That helped make our flag shine,
So beautiful and bright.

We remember the men and women as our brothers and sisters.
When we look at the stars on our flag,
We see their faces.
When we look at the stripes, we see their souls.

When we look at the colors,
We see their hearts,
That loved our flag,
All 50 stars and stripes.

    Lindsey Jung

A Military Child

As a military child, you very often hear the news..."And our new
station will be...." You listen, but you don't really hear. You
refuse to believe it. "Live for today" you tell yourself. Forget
about it - It's not now. You say "I'll see you later" to all your
friends, because "good-bye" is too scary a word. It hurts too much to
say. So, you're driving away, and you see nothing familiar in front
of you. Everything familiar behind you. It's easy to look back.
Looking ahead is the hard part.

You start over new, and you begin to realize some things about yourself.

You realize how important your family is to you, because when you're
somewhere new you thank God for their familiar faces. You realize
that you're lucky to be able to see so many different places, and meet
so many different kinds of people. You realize that real friends will
always be your friends- no matter how far apart you are.

You need to mourn a little, and always keep memories in your heart,
But you have to live for Today.

And finally, you look back on everything you've done,
Look at yourself now, and realize that everything you've gone
through...
Has made you that much Stronger.

    Mary Kate Blaine

Lighthouse

The old Lighthouse - a replica of the past
Still stands for posterity and may it's symbol last
It gave guidance and help to those in distress
As the stormy seas did not it's walls caress.
It was a beacon of hope a haven to reach
Many were grateful to land on it's beach.
Some dozens of them now unused stand
As computers and robots dot the land
But they do not shine whit compassion and care
To let a frightened voyager know someone is there.
We can show gratitude to havens of by-gone years
By helping others overcome fears
Assuring them any life storm will abate
And that love is more powerful than hate
Thus making ourselves tiny beacons of light
Helping to make darkness become bright.

    Pearl E. Hubbart

Mother Earth

Beneath a sleeping world, my kiss
stitches seeds through an empty forest.
Beneath my skin, ferocious tenements
sign names in languages that never answer.

God evades me, thundering in the distance.
I punish the leaves with a deliberate step.
My shadow trembles in the furnace of the moon
with the milk of human invention.

I inherit a crystal world where days harden
into spellbound eyes, unmade beds, breaths
without origin, and a wilderness of atomic syllables.
A visible chemistry of change disappears

into crimson skies and silent seas.
An invisible poverty blows ignorance
from cloud to cloud, and face down
in a hounding rain, my black, butterfly lips

murmur against a serious life.

    Baloian

Forever

Won't you come and save me, help me get to sleep
Stroke me clean of heartache, and lies I just can't keep
Watch me till I'm lucid, and pray that I don't wake
The screams that dwell inside me, I'm sure you just can't take
Hum softly in my ear, try to calm the fire
Read me scriptures from your book, before my mind goes drier
Feed me shadows, tell me secrets, make me want to see
Crush the thoughts and sins, that make up all of me
You speak in tongue that's foreign, move my lips to teach
Call my name and moan obscenities but I'm too far out of reach
No more pain or fear, nor any signs of life
Peel away the old skin, and throw the rusty knife
Race me to the finish, beat me to the end
If you leave me now, my heart will never mend

    Tisha B. Woody

Child

Round palms clutching a scribble,
Standing with in the orange and pink trees,
    under a white paper sky
The crooked yellow sun, with its cheshire-cat grin,
    gazes down upon this figure,
Geometric shapes,
Triangle dress,
Circle head ... too many fingers,
Holding so tightly to something,
    that one day will fly away —

    Shelby Graves

Love's Rose

Held together by a common bond
Strong as an iron rope, too thick to be frayed
Our hearts are joined together as one;
The pain and sorrow of you is also felt by me.
An eternal flame glows within,
Never to be extinguished only to occasionally flicker.
Our passion that we feel for each other
Increases day by day.
A smile which brightens your face
Brightens mine too.
Far apart we sense each other's sadness,
Until we meet and are again filled with joy.
Our love has bloomed like a rose
And with loving care it will never wilt and die.

Rebecca Schack

Life's Eyes

Through my three year old eyes, I see a big,
strong man. One whom I trust, love and adore.
One who understands me, along with every sound
and movement I make. A man who takes the time for
whatever I might have in store for him.

Through my thirteen year old eyes, I see a man
who doesn't seem to understand the changes I'm going
through. Who doesn't understand the thoughts I have.
A man who listens to what I say, but doesn't seem
to hear me anymore.

Through my twenty one year old eyes, I see a man
with tear filled eyes whom I'm leaving to marry another.
A man who watches quietly as my wedding day lingers on.

Through my thirty one year old eyes, I only see a
man's memory of how he gave his heart and soul to me
in everything we did together. How he really did
understand through my life and what a wonderful
father he was.

Tracy M. Federoff

Him

His voice is more gentle than snowfall,
Stronger than death, yet as still as incense rising.
  In Him,
    I pour out my yearnings and invocation,
    My sadness and sorrow.
  From Him,
    Flows joy and compassion,
    and we are quiet together.
    Like candle flame, intense and pure.
  And after our exchange,
    We are still. . .
    No thoughts,
    No sounds,
    Placid and mystery,
    Barren and replete,
    Lovers.
  As I go,
    He gives His words,
    I am loved,
    and, I love.

Miguel Landes-Schlosser

"Apart"

Why have you gone away?
  Since you left me there is no dawn to my day.
I loved you dearly with a full and free heart.
  Now look at us - here we are apart.
My heart is empty as can be.
  And my head echoes with your memory.
Did I take for granted your warm embrace?
  Is that why someone else is taking my place?

Myrna Lou Kinzler

Moonflowers

For days and days I walk,
Stuck in a world of isolation.

I walk through fields of flowers that seem to be singing to me,
And at night the moon comes out speaking to me,
Saying the time will come.

As the months go by,
Every night I cry,
Thinking of the future without forgetting the past.

Now that I am back,
Every night I lay outside on thy grass,
Adjacent to flowers,
Staring into the sky.

I hear the moon again,
Now whispering "It wasn't your fault,
It was never your fault."

Mike Daoud

The Wind

In this essence, I have grown to acknowledge
such a silent grace, a splendid element in our
ambiance, yet silent and often never seen, your
reticence, is always a graceful captivating
prospect.

As I sensibly, feel your gale upon me,
around me, and above me, thus never
below me, yet such a mystery, you
proceed from no where, and yet
your breeze is Universal.

Wesley Alexander

Untitled

As the night slowly creeps up on me, I watch the stars
Suddenly appearing... one by one
A chill goes up and down my spine, as the wind blows heavily
around me
As I sit on the cold hard steps, I wonder....
What brought me here? How did I become as I am?

The blue moon stares down on me, and everything becomes silent
I begin to think, I think of crazy things, beyond human understanding
My thinking becomes louder and louder
but quiets down as my heart beats faster
My arms and legs become stiff and cold, almost numb
I feel a trickle on my cheek
It is a tear...
A simple drop of water that means so much
The stairs I am sitting on seem never ending, as if....
Even if I were to try them, I would reach nowhere
I could never escape
All I feel are chills, numbness, and that trickle on my cheek
I know now that I cannot escape
For it will always be with me
This feeling of loneliness

Vicky Marlow

In Memoriam

Laughter came to him as easily as warm, golden sunshine on a
summer prairie.
Gentleness, kindness, not mere words, but the style of life he chose.
Blue eyes sparkling, with delight, with mischief, with the inner
joy of walking in the Light of God's favor.
A warrior - Challenging the forces of darkness, bearing witness
to Goodness. Showing by example the simple wonder of enjoying
the Lord's Bounty.
His duties complete, lives enriched of all he met - His journey
continues. A few short of preparation for an eternity of
joyful new experience.
His ready laughter and bright smile now await us as we travel
our own path.
Remembering the examples, and always, always, remembering the
love!

Katy Jo Miller

Quapaw Tribal Pow Pow

Bold painted faces, grimaced expressions, heads bow then look to the
sun. Head dresses of color, of bear claws and teeth, of eagle
feathers snatched from the nest. Remnants of deer hide draped the
bodies, trimmed with accessories of leather, silver, turquoise and
beads. Original creations that came from the land not the sea.

All keeping time to lamented tones of flute and the simple beat of
the drum. Gestures telling old, old stories with arms in movement
of the great hawk, feet beating the path of the wolf.

There is mumbling, chanting and sharp shrieking cries, reflecting
their inner most beings. The spirits are present and shared by
the tribes, dwelling in all things, the fire and the wind.

Fire intensifies in the tent to the side, where cedared smoke is
ascending. It is fanned by the elders to cleanse and clarify the
inner most wanderings of the mind.

The arena is soaking in tradition and homage is given to those
gathered and to ancestors of time gone by. There is a sanctity
about this place and all who dwell in its midst.

Sadness fills the air as they depart from the old, yet they're ready
to return to the new. Mixed emotions encircle them, but they turn
from the inner longings focussing forward to ensue.

Lou Ann Tipps

The Wind

The wind can be a friend or foe,
Surely as it mightily blows.
How the wind blows the clouds away,
To bring a beautiful sunny day.
Sometimes the wind blows in strong gusts,
Or in a quiet hush.
The wind is crystal clear,
And it is always near.
Oh! Wind surely you make a tree limb snap,
Or to blow off my hat.
In the fall the wind shakes the leaves to the ground,
As they twirl around and around.
In the Winter the wind is cold,
But during the summer cool breezes unfold.
The wind can help with a sailboat on the lake,
It can be nice to us for heaven's sake!

Phil E. Huebner

Three Little Words

Silently and secretly, I waited for those words,
Sweeter than the singing of a thousand humming birds,
Grander than the glory of budding in the spring,
More wonderful than all the joy of all that gold could bring.

Precious jewels, and rare perfumes.
Moonlit nights, exquisite tunes.
All of these could not compare,
Or even want to make me care.
About a single thing I do,
But just to hear "I Love you"
Yes, I waited long, it's true,
Sometimes teary eyed and blue,
Happy moments there were few,
But not after hearing "I love you."

At last it came, that glorious phrase.
For it waited months and days.
Sometimes, I wondered was it worth the pain,
But then you came back to me again.
Bringing me the sky so blue.
With just three words. "I Love You."

Shirley Hill

Natures Bounty

Good Morning Lady Columbine and you Miss Morning Glory!
Sweetpea's peakin' ore the fence to tell us all her story.

Lovely little Violet has barely even risen.
Poor Ms. Daffodil and Tulip are tryin' to keep from frizzen.

Petunia's in her garden hangin' out her clothes.
April showers bring Spring flowers don't ya know Miss Rose?

Iris and Daisy are baskin in the warm sunshine.
Lady Bug is cleanin' house, on aphids she will dine.

Humminbirds are busy rehearsin' on their hummin'.
Ms. Impatien's tired a waitin' is Springtime really comin'?

Little Johnny Jump Up's playing leapfrog in the garden.
Nasturtium's crowdin' dandelion, Oops! I beg yer pardon.

Mrs. Pansy's family's all lined up, showin' off their bonnets.
While all the little chick-a-dees are singin' natures sonnet.

Sharon L. Richter

Untitled

Beautiful gulls with silent wings
Take me for a while with you

To sail in free bird flight
Over waters and in the heavens

I'll touch your wings gently
As we pass all below

We'll dine on clams and muscles
And rest upon the sand

When it's time to depart, I will let you go
To your world beyond my own

Until a time when we meet again
And in friendship's silence will know

That I may join you
In a world beyond my own

Sally Jackson

Escape

Dreams help me escape.
Takes me away from all this misery
and hate.
   I seep into the shadows of my mind
where I can find happiness all the time.
   I rest my eyes to get away from
all these crimes, and constant cries.
   In my dreams there are no screams.
I feel as though I were a clown wearing a
smile to cover my frown. My upside down
smile lets me believe I am out of denial.
   I am happy here, faraway from any
fears. It's better than it seems, if I could
only take you to one of my dreams.

Rebecca Devine

You Own Nothin' Here

A mummy on an assembly line.
Taxes on time; never a day behind.
Pay the sitter and rush to the bank to save a dime.
Not enough left to pay the rent.
The grocery bill cut down ten times ten.
Free breakfast and lunch save many a child.
We all turn in when the sun goes down, lights much too high.
Children asleep on the springs of the bed.
Shoes are nice, but sandals are cheap they last a long time.
Savings plus interest bought us a home; the house we have is truly
   our own.
No fear of the Grocery, Water and Electric Bills; mortgage is cheaper
   than rent.
The fridge is full, our shoes are shiny and new; these treasures are
   not for long.
Property taxes, flowers and fraud on the hill become our new bills.
Poor once more, our home no longer our own; our Uncle takes more
   than he gives.

Mildred Hobson

Treasure Hunt

You hear IT speak to you
Teasing you with a warm whisper

You see IT'S shadow
Spreading across someone else's face

You feel IT touch your soul
As your dreams carry your heart

IT says, "Catch me — if you are able!"
So, you run like a madman
Stepping on IT'S skirt tails,
Trying frantically to pin IT down

But, just as you think you've won
IT wiggles free and disappears
And leaves you feeling lost

Truthfully, IT is not hard to find
IT is right beside you waiting to be discovered

Look — dig deep into the soil of your heart
Unbury your treasures

Follow your heart, your spirit
You will then capture IT...

—HAPPINESS—

Stacey Sharpton

Tell Me What You See...

Look up at the sky,
   Tell me what you see...

Is it an enchanting man looking down on you in the night?

Is it a sea full of white, puffy creatures and objects
   aimlessly floating?

Maybe it's a friend to turn to when no one listens to
   voices spoken by you...

A rainbow of colors streaking across the sky, just
   before the dark blanket of night falls upon the
   Earth.

Thousands of tiny twinkles... so far away,
   yet every one you see is a part of History.

Look up at the sky

   Tell me what you see...

Maybe you see seven sisters and two dippers... or just
   a big game of connect-the-dots!

Do you see another world, filled with mystery...
   possibly another land...another people?

What a marvelous place of wonder and phenomena!

"Look up at the sky! Tell me what you see..."

Kristin M. Scanlon

"Love Of My Life"

If love is the answer, to what I'm feeling,
Than I'm glad I'm feeling, it for you,
'Cause no one makes me happier, darling
The way you always do.

I don't know where you came from,
Or who sent you from above,
I'm just glad your by my side,
To care for, hold, and love.

Your love is very special to me,
It's something I've never known,
And now your happiness means more to me,
Than my very own.

If there's such a thing as heaven,
And if wishes can come true,
Than I know my wish was answered,
'Cause I found my heaven in you.

Sandra L. Esposito

Growth

A path is laid for us when we are born
That few may change or alter as they may
With happiness and sorrows we are torn
Until with wisdom we walk into the day.

For those who linger too long at their youth
Forsaking all the lessons offered them
With clutching fingers cleave and are aloof
And offer little until their lights grow dim.

We pity those who wander through their life
And never see the joys of older minds
But at the same moment be cry our griefs
Of times when we were crushed and left behind

To never face these sorrows or these joys
To shiver at the thought of forward strides
To hide behind a veil of childish ploys
Is someone who with fear just runs and hides.

To live a life as children all your days
Is to lose true life, and live in only haze.

Lisa Finney Doss

Sleep Walker

I was watching sunset with my family on my penthouse.
That evening was beautiful
With sparkling bright color all over the horizon
Just like an artist drawing wonderful scenery.

Suddenly, I heard a distant voice for help,
I was sure it was my sweetheart
The one I loved once more than myself.
Oh God! now, she is in the street,
Maybe her parents have thrown her out again.
Somebody is hurting her, I am hearing outcries for help,
They are multiplying.

I felt all over my body
A sudden electric impulse to rescue her
To jump down instantly from the third floor,
But before jumping I held the window for a moment
My head spinning like a propeller.
Moments later, I looked down:
The people were floating as usual.
I was whispering to myself,
My family stared at me as if I were a sleep-walker.

M. Abdul

I Walk in the Rain

I walk in the rain to disguise the tears
That fall from my eyes to my trembling lips.
The people I pass...I pray they mistake
The moisture on my face as ...rain...
I pray...don't look inside me to see my pain.
I walk in the rain...

I reminisce about the first time I saw you...
A crowded room...your spirit touched mine...your
Presence surround me...you stood behind me...
You spoke. It shook me from my daze.
We made the connection.
Now...I walk in the rain...
A voice...taunts with the question...
Did...I...fall in love too soon?

When you said...."You're not the only woman in my life".
My heart...a stab...a knife...
My spirit sighed. I soul died.
It hurts... It hurts..so bad...emotional pain.
I love you...I love me...
I walk in the rain...

Lena Teagarden

My Little Boy

It seems long ago, but still so clear,
that first moment I held you near.

I didn't know what to do,
yet this little boy in my arms was all I knew.

He, so small and frail, brought instant joy.
Tears fell when I saw you, my little boy.

Time could never change they way I felt,
I loved you the same then as I do today.

I can only say what I feel in my heart,
you are my life the biggest part.

You've grown so fast and it doesn't seem right,
I still remember my little boy who held me tight.

Many beautiful years have passed and I know
there will be more. But I always look back
to that day you were born.

You will always be my little boy,
playing with his toys.

Marcella C. Diaz

Baby Within My Walls

There is this little baby within my walls
That forever likes to move and kick.
I pat my tummy when she calls.
I wonder what makes this little gal tick.

I often like to think you'll look like me
Instead of your dad.
But if God makes you look like daddy, my little honey bee
I promise I will not be mad.

I got to see your teeth and your cute tiny face
As well as your leg and your itty bitty spine.
There is no doubt without a trace
That soon you'll really be mine.

Your big sister Emilee is waiting to see you
Because she wants to play.
I know that she loves you too
Because she really wants you to stay.

Tammy DeBeck

Rain

Rain is the pain in my heart,
that happens when I think we are going to part.

The lightening isn't very frightening to me.
You see, I like the rain. To me, it's just like
a long train ride, to a beautiful mountain side.

Thunder's rumble makes me feel humble.
It shakes the ground, and makes it hard to walk around.
It's very loud, and you can see it through the clouds.

As the wind howls, a cat meows.
Is it cold? I want to deny it, but I've never tried it.
Blowing in my face, making me feel like I'm a disgrace

A tear falls from my face as I close this sorry case.
I am crying, trying, denying. But with the rain it looks
like many tears, all washing away my fears.

Coming down fast or slow, who would know?
Just watch, wait and anticipate.
You can never bet you won't get wet.

Will it rain tomorrow? Only if God feels sorrows.
Because rain is heaven's pain.
You an feel it too, if you listen softly to it like I do.

Melissa Humphries

Passage Of Time

There is nothing like the love that lasts to the end;
    That love is the love I give my best friend.

We travel through the years, the happy and the sad;
    We soar through the months, the good and the bad.

We run through the days, together man and wife;
    We walk through the hours, together the rest of "our" life.

We sail through the minutes, standing side by side;
    We glide through the seconds, this love we cannot hide.

Through the passage of time, may our love grow stronger;
    And may it last until we go on no longer.

Robin Engberg-Maluvac

Peace

It wasn't many years ago
That peace was all around us
We prayed together, hand-in-hand
To end the war in a far-off land
In God, we then, did trust

Since that time
The rate of crime
Has steadily increased
An evil force has been released!

A force so strong, it breaks the bond
....between the husband and his wife
...after promises to love each other for life.

It turns the children into beings
..unrecognizable and without feelings

The unknown force deposits strife
...in everybody's life
We must defeat the enemy
To recreate the family.

Nancy Louise Timko

My Love For You

You are as fair as the spring breeze
  That rustles through the trees.
You give me feelings of joy
  Like a lollipop does a boy.

Your every move is of swan-like grace
  That makes my heart race
and my blood run like steam
  Like no man could dream.

All day, everyday, no matter what I do
  I'm always thinking about you.
So even if your feelings for me are tart
  I'll always love you with all my heart.

Travis A. Birge

There is Life Between the Waves

There is life beneath the waves
that which belongs and that which is out of place.
Stuffed together in a long black tube
traveling together captain and crew.

United they must stand or divided they'll fall
when comes the time to answer duties call.
The foes they fight cannot be seen
they only appear as dots on sonar screen.

Oft times though, the foes are not flesh
but loneliness, and loss of trust.
Worries about loved ones left at home
the fear that mates might start to roam.

Yes the submarine life's hard to understand
one that an outside never really can.
A compact ship and a close knit crew
the path of career chosen by few.

Yet if hateful war's trump doth sound
then at the front subs will be found.
Fighting and dying to keep us free
though their wars we will not see.

Norman Caughel

To A Friend

Good friends, are hard to come by these days
That's why I'm so amazed
That a nice person like you would be my friend
And I can depend on you through thick and thin

I may not be your best friend but you definitely are mine
And whenever you're in trouble I'll be there for you anytime
You're someone I can share my secrets with and really talk to
And say anything else that's on my mind because I trust you

When I'm around you I can really be myself
Instead of acting like I'm someone else
And if we shall ever go or separate ways, I want you to know
I wish you the best at whatever you do, wherever you may go

And I'll always remember the times that we had
Some were happy others were sad
But no matter what, I'll remember over and over again
How you were my very BEST FRIEND

Rashida Colbert

Seasons

The leaves are alive with green
The air is still as the sun beats down
We fan our faces and sip our lemonade
Reminders of the season.

The leaves are turning gold and red
The cold wind blows them on the ground
We rake them, pile them, jump inside them
Reminders of the season.

The leaves are gone now, the trees are bare
An icy wind, blows the snow
We shovel it, pile it, slip and slide in it
Reminders of the season.

The leaves begin to grow again
The gentle wind blows the cold away
The daffodils bloom and robins play
Reminders of the season.

May He who has established the seasons-
He alone, who changes not,
Be the source of our strength and encouragement,
in the changing seasons of life.

Kathy Temple Scott

And So It Goes

Through the eons of ages this earth has existed
The billions of people who have lived
  and died remain unlisted.
No doubt we all, today, are a combined
  mixture of everybody that's lived.
That comprehensive evaluation will very likely give

Cause for great concern to those who
  place such value on
Their recent ancestors who might have been well known-
Famous for various reasons and some
  worthwhile deeds.
We need not forget them but we're another seed.

This earthly visit is gone before you know it.
We're only here a little while.
To those who understand the soul lives
  on after earth's last mile —
Have much more reason to fulfill life
  because they understand
That their soul will live on with yet
  another set of plans.

Lucile I. Burke

A Wonderful Day

The sky is blue. The grass is green.
The birds are singing.
The children are all swinging.
Oh, what a beautiful day it is.

The sun is shining. It is not raining.
The cows are all grazing
While the sun is blazing.
Oh, what a beautiful day it is.

Thy sky is dimming. The moon is shining.
The night has come.
The crickets are chirping. The frogs are croaking.
Oh, how peaceful it is.

The moon is out while stars are all shining.
The children are in bed.
Their eyes are all closed.
Oh, how peaceful it is.

Melissa Thompson

Flowers....

The sun will shine on another day;
The birds will sing their song once more;
And a flower will bloom in the morrow beside the springs of
eternity.
A flower so beautiful blooming,
Stays unforgettable... always in memory.
Yet, someday it will wilt away and die, in reality.
People may laugh and tease;
Yet, no human will contain the beauty, it withholds.
People may pick at its fragile peals,
And watch as it slowly glides to the open ground.
Yet, no-one may glue together,
The ruins that once contained life.
A flower will bloom in the others place;
And the captured beauty lies within,
A poet's morbid mind, only to be seen through his darkened eyes.
The sun will shine on other day;
The birds will catch, their joyful refrain;
And a flower will bloom in the morrow beside the springs of
eternity...

Melinda Marie Smith

Winter In Wisconsin

With snowflakes floating softly down,
The blanket of white will soon cover the ground.
It's nature's way of changing plant life,
The leaves have fallen and stems lie flat.
Most birds have gone south to beat the cold,
But those left behind are searching for food.
The ice on the ponds and lakes freezes hard,
Making ice fishing and skating a good drawing card.
Deer and other animals move around
Forging for food that is hidden and brown.
Skiers and snowmobilers race for trails and slopes,
Hoping to enjoy winter's frozen white coat.
Snowplows are out clearing the roads,
Many are out with snow shovels and blowers,
Removing the snow from driveways and walks
In hopes that the mailman will bring them written talks.
Soon bright sunshine will lengthen the day,
Snow will melt, fields turn gray,
Birds will return, full streams will run,
For winter is passing and Spring has sprung.

Lyle J. Campbell

The Presiding Olympia

On Tuesday night in 1992
the bluest political moon
was torn apart. America,

it's your new day! (Mosley-Braun)

Her microphone equally surprised
woke up the angry white men
Enough; two hundred years today
the US Congress passed a fiscal
to be responsibility act, the toothless
tiger to guard human appetites
tempered by a loony chap
of evil parts: On its deathbed
capitalism shall ask for the cheapest
rope to effect suicide.

Four trillion red dollars choke every male
his working wife, the unborn child.
And yet, Senators Byrd, Daschle, Nun
are more concerned with correctness
of noosing than with real plight

Romuald Orlowski

Pains

I HEAR the pains of the world
the children cry
the homeless beg
I SEE the pains of the world
the poor starve
the rich search
I FEEL the pains of the world
my heart aches
my soul hurts
my arms can only reach so far for the world
but I TOUCH
and I PRAY

Richard Fredrickson

Brothers

I see an inner grace in them....
the children of my youth....
now men.
I've walked within the shadow
of their triumphs never seen
yet held with pride and tenderness
all I hoped they've been
now...as the jackals and the clowns parade
in colors dimmed by winters snow
I wave my flag
and sing my song
for those I've loved and do love still
and those I've never known
for my heart holds true the promise made
by the dream that calls me home.

Ruth A. Williams

Spring Eagerly Bursts Forth

Eager buds can't wait to burst.
Struggling crocus for dewdrops thirst.
Heaving through the sod that holds them fast,
Buttercups hurry, they must not be last!
Evergreens chuckle as they watch the scene,
They don't have to worry, they're already green.
Run-off swells the rivers, days are longer too.
Frost on the ground each morning turns into dew.
Soon the final evidence is in place.
The robin's cheery song resonance through space.

Naomi Wiltse

Spring Is In The Air

Each dawn begins another day,
 The cold north winds no longer sweep.
Our furry neighbors in their dens,
 Have risen from their long nights sleep.
The rippling streams hidden from view,
 Have given up their frozen sheets.

Each twilight leaves a greener coat,
 Upon the fields and meadow land.
Young saplings in the forest rise,
 Through mother nature's mighty hand;
With clothes of leaves upon their boughs,
 The towering timbers o'er them stand.

Upon their shaded earthen floor,
 Sweet beds of colored beauties lay.
Beneath the bright blue sunlit sky,
 Our singing, feathered friends so gay;
Into their camps from exile land,
 In pairs and flocks have winged their way.

Orman Berres

Changing of the Seasons

Spring gives rain so things can grow
The colors of life really starts to show
grass turns green, fragrance fills the air
Birds sing their songs, squirrels stand and stare

Summer gives sunlight we feel so hot
Children play all day and don't stop
Summer break from school is just another way
To learn about life freely exploring the day

Fall is the chill you feel in the air
Keeping warm and sung in a nice lair
The leaves on the trees changing with the weather
Birds fly south after ruffling their feathers

Winter is cold winds that blow in the night
The beautiful white snow reflecting the light
The frolicking sled riding, the snowball fights
Keeping us cheerful, joyful and bright

CHANGING OF THE SEASONS IS LIKE GIVING BIRTH
A RENEWAL OF THE CYCLE OF LIFE
THE LIVING EARTH IS GOD'S GIFT TO US ALL

Tenna Faison Catlin

An Angel Must Be...

An Angel must be...
The Comforter I cannot see
The Source of Strength and Wisdom
When I am weakened and troubled

For those who've gone on before me
Were Comforters I could see
Those whose hands were stretched out to me
To catch me before the fall

And God Himself had called them all
To do that for Him...
Which He has always done for me
In His Name,...and...by His Grace

The most beautiful Comfort I know
Is the kind I'll always know
As long as I believe
No matter how many...should drift out before me

I'll Always have their Comfort
I'll Always have their Strength
For God has made them Angels
To keep their Watch over me

Sheila M. Lansing

Windmill

Old and tall they stand against
 The Darkening Sky.
 The windmill—
Sentinel of the West
 Silhouette against the
 Texas Sky.

Time and time I've tried to photograph
 You, but I haven't captured
 The feeling yet.
Ever faithful you remain, standing, watching,
 Waiting for me to come back and
 Try again.

Or, perhaps I've captured your feeling
 On film, but just
 Not mine.
Are you teasing me, leading me on until
 I give up? Leaving you the
 Victor of the Texas skies
And me—the Silhouette?

Linda L. Autry

Enslaved

I once was a master, a master of the trade,
The decisions for many people I have made.

While all the time my course I had stayed,
Never realizing that it was I who was enslaved.

My work was fulfilling and I had fun,
But the prestige usually given to masters I never won.

Although I was good and some may say the best,
The other masters never allowed me to pass the test.

The test was given on a daily basis,
But I could always see the doubt on their faces.

I tried real hard and gave it my best shot,
But once again it was revealed that I could not.

So here I am not quite the same,
My hunger for money and power has definitely changed.

Today I smile and have inner peace,
Because the test I did not win but the "Race" I did beat.

Shirley A. Barnes

The Signs Of Day And Night

Sneaking up through the mountain peak,
The early visions of day is still weak.
But uncovered by the hands of the grazing plains.
The shine of dawn still has its light to strain.

Then in a blink of an eye
The sun bursts out of the ground and brightens the sky.
The dew on the grass and the misty air
Awakens the animals, insects, and birds; they stare.

What is that they see?
Is it the sparkle of a lake or an apple tree?
No, it's the birth of a bud growing into a rose.
Pollen dangles in the air and tickles your nose.

Then quickly and rapidly the night caves in.
Silence takes over and daylight is thin.
Suddenly, a bitter, cold breeze sheaches over the land.
Gradually, it echoes through ears and howls so grand.

The clear opening of a vast purple sky
Lets fireflies know that it's time to shine.
As the day camouflages into the night,
Little birds soar through the silver clouds and vanish out of sight.

Melissa G. Dela Cruz

A Life Worth Living

The shouts, the screams
The endless scenes
The pain, the sorrow, there's no tomorrow

It's now or never this life,
Whatever...
The Buck Stops Here!!!
No fears, no cheers.

Look back in time
That once was mine
But life for me now, is how to learn, to live, to give

Strong of character
pure of mind, in search of love
I look to the divine,
A future maybe I can find...

No end in sight, I see the light.
Mira Patterson

The Hidden Island

I wish that I were watching
The evening sun from that amber shore
Sliding down the sky to touch that Eastern sea
From that hidden summers island
Of sun-warmed rocks
And wind-tossed trees
Where we watched the silent flight of owls
And listened for the whispers of the past
On windy nights
While the rain fell gently in the sea
And clouds raced across the moon
While the moon cast its patchy light
On old graves hidden beneath the trees
With you, my life-long friend, walking
The hills and marshes
And chalk-white cliffs with me
Patria E. Danielson

Movement of Time

The hands slowly, yet continually do their work.
The face is still, showing no emotion.
Yet the power it has is immense.
There is no stopping or controlling time.

Each second, minute, hour we get older.
The years pass; the generations come and go.
Creations are made; diseases are cured,
But life itself still grows old.

The years do not stop nor rewind.
Though time seems to stand still or fly by,
The movement is constant and only forward.
The future always a second ahead, we a step behind.

Through all our inventions of making miracles,
One power man has yet to behold.
Time is our controller, ruler of man
And too persistent to be grabbed by human hands.
Shannon McNamara

Angel's Wing

The call come - a voiced asked, "Mom?"
The feeling? I know it "what is wrong?"
My heart, pounding, I cannot hear
Then I recognize it, fear!
I listen then I cry, He's too young, don't let him die,
At his bedside, I bargain and pray
Don't take him, take me, I say.
We wait, we hope, and we feel the pain
Will things ever be the same again?
Another challenge he had to face
Open heart surgery was the place
A second chance to live his life
Maybe a future with babies and wife
Life has gifts wrapped in odd color and sizes
Opening and discovering some pain, some prizes
Remember the fear of that late night call
The pain, the joy, the relief of us all
The life given back, a beautiful thing
My son's return on an Angel's wing
M. Patricia Hanson

Window View

I look outside my window, but I do not see
the filth and trash of the big city,
Instead I see green fields that roll on and on,
the isolated trees sway gently with the wind, the
leaves rustle softly as the wind flows between them,
Beyond the fields the ocean glitters and crashes on
the rocky shore...
A blaring horn brings me back to reality and the
meadows turn to roads and the trees are no longer
rippling and whispering, there is only the wind moaning
between the buildings.
The majestic roar of the ocean turns to the dull roar
of traffic,
my image of peace is gone, for the moment...
But wasn't it beautiful, the wonderful scene that I
didn't see when I looked out my window?
Wasn't it beautiful?
B. J. Long

Undertow

As darkness falls and darkens the eyes
The fitful dreams leave you like a motherless child
The water breaks and envelops the hell
The silence shatters and then collecting itself

Wait for the pull, wait for the undertow
I gave you my hand but you just let it go
I struggle in deep waters and I may drown
But you chose to drown
To go with the pull, go with the undertow

Behind the heart, behind the brain
A distant hum where the angels fall like rain
The water breaks and swallows the past
The silence shatters and finds the freedom at last
Lugene Chicks

Spring

It was a long harsh winter, the kind that chills to the bone
The arctic air has moved out, the snow and ice is gone,
in its place the soft drops of rain
Outside my window a tree stands naked
I ache for the first signs of spring, green grass,
birds chirping, a scampering squirrel
I long to feel the warmth of the sun, to see longer hours of daylight
Come to me spring, don't dillydally
The sooner you come the sooner you can go
And then bring on glorious summer
Kathleen Sorensen

Drops Of Pain

There I sat idle almost in a trance-like state
The flame from the candle could be seen dancing in the mirror
Of my eyes almost extinguished by my vast blue sea
Then I noticed it raining outside
Drops of rain began forming on the window
Running down the clear glass as they sped up and changed direction
They knew there destination but not how to get there
Yet they still trickled down as the blood did from my arms
Feeling so warm as it ran against my skin
Only to collect in a pool on the floor
Suddenly my sense's became very acute
I felt each heartbeat as they began to slow up
The sound of each drop landing in the pool was deafening
The echoing in my ears seemed to last for minutes
The slight draft in the room soon felt like a fierce wind from
The east then the glow began to set in
My field of vision slowly clouded with light
The sensations through my body went numb
Now I would finally answer all of life's questions
Till at last eternal darkness captured my soul and my heart went cold.

Mark M. Jarvis

Rock'er Don't Knock'er

In the corner sat an empty rocker, on
the floor in a heap was a frail small figure

Clothes tattered
Body battered

The reflections in the mirror brought unkind
memories of days gone by.

Beside her stood her small child - tiny and frail,
with tears in her eyes,
with pain in her heart,
she stooped to pick up her child,
walked over to the rocker.
As she sat down, a voice in her heart said,

"ROCK'ER DON'T KNOCK'ER."

Nancy Newger

God Is Love

How marvelous is the splendors of thy love.
The gentle breeze, the crystal rain,
The enigmatic forms of a cloud.
The symmetrical perfection of a snow flake.
Thy bounty is our's to have,
Given freely, with no demands.
How may times, on the early morning rays,
Is thy love so evident!
And so many times,
On a starry night
Is your presence so overwhelming!
And you are there.
Past, present and future
Your love is there
Given freely, without demands
That, little man, is God love for us.
So mote it be.

Ray Molino Myers

The Sparrow's Last Song

The sparrow's last song, when to be sung
the greens all to be gone, from man's earthly wrongs.
The hole up above, the widening gap
he once spoke of love, as he drew out his map.

I'll first build a tower for my mother, the earth
and I'll pull all the flowers to splice a new birth.
He took all the gifts freely given to him
and he started to sift until they all became dim.

The children all asked, "Where can I see the sky blue?"
The man answered so fast, "I'll show pictures to you."
And the album it showed only a memory to gaze
of sunsets that glowed with the sun's gallant rays.

His hand held to his brow,
"What have I done!"
Could he change it all now
before the last song is sung.

Patricia Ann Mayorga

Winter Morn

The trees are bare,
The ground is covered with snow.
Even the sea gulls, so far from shore,
join the blackbirds, starlings and sparrows galore.
All waiting for their kind old friend,
to open her door and throw out some bread.
Alas! the small sparrows have no chance whatsoever
to even pick up a crumb,
for they are outnumbered by almost twenty one.
Luck came their way when the others had gone
For children going to school dropped a cake on the ground
and left it there for the sparrows to take.
In no time at all not a crumb could be seen,
And the old lady returned to her chair by the window.
Awaiting the next visit from her feathered friends.

Margaret McCord

Gentle Rain

The night is cool and misty.
The ground is moist with rain.
The breeze blows gently through the trees.
The sky is brimming with rain.

No stars can be seen up in the sky.
The clouds have blocked them out.
A sheet of gently falling rain
splashes in the puddles without.

I sit quietly by my window
and gaze out at the rain.
The cool, damp air blows softly in
and whispers the words "gentle rain".

The rain continues falling
soaking the once parched earth.
A blessing from Heaven, I would say.
A gift from God to Earth.

Again, the moist breeze blows
and I gaze out at the rain.
The cool, damp air blows softly in
and whispers, "gentle rain".

William J. Swenson

I Never Dreamed.....

I Never Dreamed.....last winter when,
 the "ICE STORM" was upon us,
 that something "special" was in the making,
 that I would love, oh, so.

I Never Dreamed ....the awaiting months would quickly pass,
 ultra-sounds, monograms, questions to be asked,
 summer heat, a faded memory,
 October leaves all aglow.

I Never Dreamed....You, dear Easton,
 would arrive (three weeks early),
 the long awaited boy child,
 diapers, burps, and tiny toes.

I Never Dreamed... this Christmas of 1994
 would hold such treasured memories.
 as with God's own Son,
 born so very long ago.

 Marvene Twisdale

Innerself

The thoughts that run through one's mind;
The idle moments of one's time;
The joy that comes with each passing day;
The peace that holds and never goes a stray;
Serenity of knowing your day is near;
The fear that comes with each waking day;
The turmoil that erases a tranquil state;
The mind and soul will do it's best;
Until the body is put to rest.

 Paulette M. McGee-Jones

Reality Of Living

What kind of darkness comes after night?
The kind that blinds you with all its might.
When the sun is down everything seems calm,
And we can lie to ourselves reading good
 fortunes in the world's palm
But when dawn comes wiping away false hope
We see the world's real face
And with the true darkness we must then cope.

What kind of nightmare comes after a bad dream?
The kind that leaves you without a voice to scream.
When the eyes close imagination is what we see,
And deep inside we know we can easily be set free.
But when eyes are open and there's nowhere to hide
We see the world is a cradle of dread
And in the nightmare we must learn to reside.

 Magdalena Laska

The Last Sonnet

No longer shall I write poetic verse
The last Romantic on the hill top cried
This gift of mine has turned into a curse
Surely you can see that true love has died
Along with Chivalry and truth and prose
Lay buried deep within some sacred ground
Like the dead petals of a lover's rose
Or all the poets no longer around
These friends left me one hundred years ago
Alone to keep their dream of love alive
But love is dead and fed on by the crow
And all that's left for me to do is cry
So alone on this hill top I will stay
Wishing that love had never gone away

 Rob Liddle

All Hallow's Eve

No one's home, you're all alone.
The lights blow out, to the window you turn, open it's thrown -'
Walk to the chair, look down the long grey room.
You see a shadow, over the Count's picture it looms.
Call out to see who's there.
No answer, no movement, behind you the curtain tears.
Night has come, sharp wind, a storm.
The shingles drop, the shutters are thrown.
Windows rattling, doors banging, walk through the kitchen, find your
neighbor hanging. A scream escapes while falling to the floor.
Your mind is with pain, the knob turns on the door.
The shadow appears, points the finger at you...
laughing and moaning, but what can you do.
Find a candle, put it quickly to light.
Must see who it is, then live you might.
Too late! Its got you now! Pulls out a knife, and lets out a howl.
Gotta get away you've got no more time.
Out the door you run, it shuts with a whine.
Yes, gotta get away to live through this night,
for it's not for living -only the dead.

 Linda Shema

The Elements Sing Thy Praises O Lord

O' Lord, how great is thy name, reaching far above
 the limitless sky.
The elements sing thy praises, with their voices lifted high.
O' wondrous stars of heaven, that twinkle bright and glow,
Signal praises to their creator, so quietly no one would know.

Break forth or beauteous sunlight! And usher in the morn.
Your face shines with all His Glory, as the crack of day is born.

Slowly, silently the moon rises, to dispense the sun's bright light,
Then whispers its praise towards heaven. As calmness declares the
 night.
Tempestuous winds, with it's mighty breath, blows praises loud and
 strong
And lifts the gray clouds higher, while whistling a happy song.

A blanket of snow covers the earth, from heaven it fell with grace,
With beauty and such majesty, only this God could appreciate.

Raindrops fall, to water the land, and abundantly replenishes the sea,
And taps a melody, understood by God. But enjoyed by you and me.

I believe the elements sing thy praises, in a voice not heard by man!
Lord let me now sing, such a worthy praise, Only you can understand.

 Larry Moyer

Crossing Beyond Jordan

One day at the waters of Meribah,
The Lord gave Moses advice
To smite the rock, as at Rephidim,
But Moses struck the rock twice.

The Rock was Christ,
So the second strike was a fallacy.
It implied Christ's death on the cross
Was lacking for time and eternity.

Crossing beyond Jordan was refused.
Only from a distance could Moses see.
He and Aaron had doubted God's mercy
In showing forth His sanctity.

God's will is nothing more, nothing less,
Nothing else, at any cost.
If Moses had followed it that day,
His vision would not have been lost.

Obedience to His will is foremost
For all of us to adhere.
Proceeding in anger, doubt, or haste,
Deters blessings which may appear.

 Mary L. Jordan

To Daughter With Love

When you were born, you gave to us
the love, from God, of a heavenly child.
We watched you grow from child to adult
With grace, compassion and full of love.
The joy we found as each day progressed
can never be fully expressed.
But we can say with truth from our hearts
How lucky we are that you came to us.
The kindness you show to young and old
Is remembered as you travel each path and road.
Your inner beauty shines as stars at night
Reflecting a soul with a spirit so bright.
May your life continue with light and truth
And to always remember how much we love you.

Mary O. Schaefer

Beyond the Grave

We all know what lies beyond the grave.
The loved ones we lost.
    The lives we prayed they'd save.
All the tears we've cried.
    The tears we believed could bring back those who died.
Beyond the grave and in our hearts,
    Will always be the love for he who departs.
We're forced to stare blindly out windows,
    Searching for answers no one knows.
We try day by day to go on with our lives.
    But there's the memories that cut our hearts like knives.
The hope that it's all an awful dream,
    Should bring them back it would seem.
When we wish they could have just one more year,
    Remember it's worse for those still here.
The tragedy is not just for the hearts that have stopped beating,
    It's also for the hearts who must go on bleeding.

Sandra Kay Komendo

Poison Pen II A Time For Healing

Today the sun is shining upon a crisp white page.
The marks that I make on it reveal an altered state.
My poison pen lies silent.,
alone in the shade,
awaiting my hand to hold it,
seeking the child of rage
but the memories are now sleeping and autumn is so far away.
The time has come for healing as the anger turns back to pain.
The spring rain flows from my eyes,
the child begins to age,
a world of color comes to life
and laughter soothes the ache.
Growing ever stronger through the summer days,
peace of mind lasts longer as love transcends the hate.
Russet leaves begin to fall, the fear begins to fade,
the seasons have taken me over the wall
and brought me back to stay.
The winter's snow is on its way and I seek my loyal friend.
The child has grown and I have gained.
Tamed, my poison pen.

R. Lee Jacobson Houck

If Only I Could Talk To Goldie!

Since death was here,
    I fear
the loss of many things:
    the songs, the laughs
    the memories they bring.
My solace is
    you graced our lives
    and love survives.

Robert Ribakoff

"Bonnie"

She's gone to heaven free from pain.
The memories she left are sweet and dear.
Her poems written with so much love, to mark special
occasions, so fondly thought of.
The special glow that lit her face when the little one's were near.
Little hands clutching bags of sweets like special
treasures, from "BONNIE" with love.
Memories of days gone by, some sweet, some sad, some funny.
Of a peppery little woman who said what she thought.
Of her vegetable gardens tended in the hot sun, with
a floppy hat on the head.
Or with a broom in her hand, chasing Oscar the goose.
All of these and so many more are the "BONNIE I KNEW."
Her children, grandchildren, great grandchildren,
and great-great grandchildren were "BONNIE'S TREASURES,"
there were forty-two in all.
Even though the rocker is empty, "Bonnie" lives still,
through the wonderful memories we all have of "OUR BONNIE"

Susan R. Mitchell

Graveyard of My Mind

Just yesterday I buried you, in the graveyard of my mind,
The memory of your face, your scent, I left it all behind;
The touch of silk that was your skin, the fire that lit your eyes,
Nevermore a part of my world, so I said my last goodbyes.

It's been so long since we kissed, or I held you close in my arms,
When I was captured by your smile, you beguiled by my charms;
Together we were so happy, and our lives were made of dreams,
But there were times of revelation, as nature often deems.

We began to see more difference, than things that were the same,
Though I wanted to keep on trying, you wanted back your name;
Because you left without a word, to me it was like you died,
And in the weeks that followed, all the real reasons I denied.

At times the grief unbearable, made everything seem so lost,
The price of our relationship, paid at a terrible cost;
A broken heart and a shattered soul, left here alone to heal,
And only with the passage of time, they learned again to feel.

So yesterday I buried you, in the graveyard of my mind,
No matter what lies beyond for you, I pray that it is kind;
One more tear watered your grave, where laid the flowers of my
youth,
I will visit there again one day, when I can face the truth.

L. Hawkeye Poole III

Lost Love

Now alone on the shore, he watched his love walk away.
The mist wrapped itself around her, it covered like a veil,
As he sought to find her again, he caught a glimpse of a figure at
the
    water's edge.
As he moved closer, he could see her, she had begun to move into
the
    water,
Her motion was so graceful and gentle, she did not create even one
    ripple.
Farther in she went, with no fear or hope, to stop her.
He could only watch her, his love, forever she was out of his grasp.
The terror built inside him, like a mad dream,
He could not move as her figure disappeared into the darkness.
Beneath the waters, he knew she had gone.
As the veil began to dance away with the breeze, he could see her.
Her graceful figure just floating there as if lying on air,
Her face at peace as if she were asleep
But he knew he would never be able to wake her.
Yet he could still hear her whisper
    "I love you, I will always love you."

Suzanne M. Dick

Nothing Is The Same

The sun rises and the darkness goes away.
The morning has come,
It is time for everything to wake up.
The sun warms the earth,
It makes life grow.
The trees grow taller and the flowers bloom,
And children play outside.
Soon the sun goes down and darkness sets,
And it is now time for the world to rest.
For tomorrow is a new day,
And nothing will be the same,
Now that it will be daylight.

Kathleen Cramer

The Morning After

Even though it's morning
    the night is still here
lingering in my mind and in my essence.

The warmth that you gave me
    is a feeling that I will not soon forget
You relax me to the point
    that I lost track and concept of time.

I enjoyed the evening so much
    that I hope we can share another
one tonight.
    It amazes me,
that hot chocolate can do so much.

Brame

Friend

The heart, love does scar, beats rapidly;
The pain shows not and cries secretly.
Love does not mean to frighten nor demand a toll,
But to comfort and make whole.
Fear not the love for no harm is meant.

Time will peace bring, when loves a wonderful
Memory or love stands nearby. Life's greatest fear
Is to be forgotten by one held dear,
The one reflected in her vanity mirror.
Fear not the love for no harm is meant.

The greatest measure of one's love is friendship,
For who can weather life's despair with a hidden tear
And attempt to calm the fear,
But the friend who cherishes and holds you dear.
Fear not, love, for no harm is meant.

William D. Simo

Just Once More

Reaching across, the summer grasses stretched over the sand
the path to our house now fades into a pale history
a painted stallion father rode, standing tall above the land
seasons wax and wane creating things that, which used to be

Iris by the road, once tenderly sown, now forsaken
their beauty yielding for the mind alone to see
and the road, once bustling with wagons and coaches heavy laden
now an avenue for snakes and lizards, the searching honey bee

Amidst the cactus of the past one might have seen
not our rusted tin roof, nor its midday reflection
but an ancient soul, now as then
already a man, though not yet a teen
with hands above his brow shading the light of sun
horizons of the past he scanned, to recast a simple memory
would that this sunset host more than just a vision
yet sensing not, until he too is that, which used to be....

Laurence J. White

This Old House

The doors are squeaking,
The paint is peeling,
The moss now covers the roof.
The place, is badly in need of repair, to tell you the truth.

As I look out my window, I recall the past.
No trees, shrubs, or flowers 50 years ago, time goes fast.
Now each budding flower, shrub, or tree,
Brings back a most fond memory.

A gift for Mother's Day, Christmas, or birthday with love.
Each sharing it's special beauty, with God's touch from above.
One by one the family now has gone,
But the happy memories continue to linger on.

I see so much to please me inside too.
Pictures of loving family and keepsakes, quite a few!
As I see the polished piano still standing there,
I can almost hear the music, as singing fills the air.

No other place, shining bright or new,
Can fill me with memories, as this old house can do.
No matter the age, to me it's still home.
With the memories that linger, I'll never be alone.

E. Pearl Silverthorne

Untitled

Like deep, black waters
The panes reflect my World-
Shadowed and dim,
Luminously unstable,
Forever shifting like the
Fretful Tides of my soul.
I remember the shimmering Sands
That were once mine-
Soft, warm, inviting to the touch,
But sodden and cold now
From the pounding Waves.
The loving words writ in the Grains
Are all washed away.
Will I ever forget my Shore of happiness
Or how the perfect Summer Sun
Shone down on my World?
Never.
Beneath this roof, within these walls,
Behind these panes of glass I sit,
And remember.

Melissa S. Green

The Horrors Of The Past

I ventured back there many years later.
The place where the tank tracks
scared the land like angry teeth.
The crumbling buildings, the broken glass,
the Earth trembling under the weight of bombs,
the corpses rotting in the hot sun,
the smoke that burned my eyes,
the place where a soldier stood
with a gun to the head of woman
pleading for her life, and the life of her child.
I can still see the look in her eyes
as she saw the flash from his gun.....

The grass grows tall by the river now.
Honey suckle flowers attract swarms of bees and
birds flock to the trees. Couples walk,
slowly and romantically. Silence abounds —
the wind blows around me kicking up the sweet smell of lilac
and I leave the place I had been so many years ago
and wonder —
if I'd ever been there!

Steven Tseki

The Robbing Hood

Popular guy this pickpocket from the deep dark woods,
The poor think him benefactor and accept the good,
Though the rich folk do not care for him too much,
It's their purses he seems to like to touch.

He is not alone committing these dastardly deeds,
His is a fast gang which leaves behind no leads,
His victims wish their own arrows to shoot,
But about capture this hood does not give a hoot.

This legendary mugger even has a maid at hand,
She too plays a part in his merry band,
She eggs him on as swords cut into wealthy flesh,
She shares in the loot, he brings her flowers fresh.

I fear time will make this woodsy worm hero to admire,
The telling of his wicked tale will never expire,
But, for me, I would see this pointy-toed crook forgotten,
I am the Sheriff of Nottingham, and I am not rotten!

Lawrence J. Murphy

The Scapegoat from the Orient

I felt the raging anger of their wrath,
The pounding waves upon the distant shore,
the mounting passion of their vengeful lust
set high amidst the throng filing past
the prostrate, ashen, cold spectre of despair.

I felt the grief poured heart and soul
for this fragile creature and humble grace,
who was tossed adrift in some forsaken land,
victim of murderous, vile, fantasies,
gentle and innocent gem of our motherland.

I kept on asking while I heard their cries,
why did you suffer this woeful fate
for a mere pittance of earth's supply?
No, you did not have to die
to cover up the web's tarnished truth.

Violeta Barleta-Jamero

My Christmas Song

Our Songs of Christmas' Herald bring
The praises of our newborn King!
Outward burst the joys of blessedness
As we sing in communion, in holiness!
Our songs upward flow in harmony,
In gratitude for the Babe Most Holy.
Peace, Peace on earth! Be Still! Be Still!
Christ has come . . . our hearts to fill!

With The Newborn comes joy and love,
Gifted of the Father . . . His son from above!
Upon Him the light of the world is shone,
In the shadow of the Manger it has grown...
In reverence, with love and honor,
Gladness, tidings of greatest favor!
Our shouts and songs Heavenward ring.
Thanking thee, God for Christ our King!
With the advent of this Birthday Yuletide,
This is our Prayer and this our Song...
May the Love of Christmas be made strong!

A. Charles Swanson

Mourning

My whole world mourns your death.
The rain falls not gently,
But straight down in driving tears.
The trees stand stark, lifeless,
Lamenting the loss of leaves.
Even the grass is brown, withered,
Trampled with the heaviness of life.
Acorns lie decomposing,
Worm-eaten holes marring the smooth, brown exterior,
Exposing the soft, inner core to rot and decay.
Even the people I see are thinly disguised decay:
Rotting teeth, fetid breath, creaking joints,
Unseen hideousness hiding behind every mask.
Nothing will ever bring you back
Or take your place.
But today I did see a picture of a ladybug
Alit a green leaf in the sunlight.
And it reminded me of life and you.

Lorna Root

Christmas Poem

A time to show the one you love,
the real gift from God above.

The gift of peace of love,
and sharing, the time to tell someone your caring

A time for peace, for peace on earth,
a time when Mary just gave birth

A day for joy,
for friends and family,
a time when we should all live happily

I wish to you all gathered here,
the very best of Christmas cheer.

That peace on earth will come to you
and all you love the whole year through

Katy Crunk

Night Dreams and Day Mares

A dusting of starlight and the velvet caress of
The rich evening sky entice the moon to appear,
To slip her silvery shadows into the minds of the world.
Night dreams dance through their souls,
Ensnaring them in visions of Fantasy;
Fears borne on the wake of a distant reality melt.
Dreams belong to the Night.
The luminous sprites release their gentle hold
Of the world to allow the sun's beams to penetrate
The comforting darkness within the hearts of the slumbering.
With a peaceful sigh, nightdreams dissolve into daymares.
Reality's grip shakes comfort and security from dreams.
Heartless and cruel, daymares rob the night of her magic;
Memories of a dream are abandoned within the Day's embrace.
Terrors of the Mare belong to the day.
The balance between dreams and mares are a confused blur.
Yet, Humanity makes the transition unknowingly.
Close your eyes,
And walk the line.

H. M. Adams

Untitled

The monkey bars are gone, as is the sliding board
   the sand has hardened to asphalt

As I swing, I hear the echoes of
   pageants, picking sides, squeeze the lemon, tag you're it

Strongly I swing trying to feel the child within
   sadly realizing she's not there
I try to recapture the gaiety, the hurt and skinned knees
I beg you please, don't make me grow up.

I walk away with the swing slowly swaying, I'm praying
Amid the broken glass
   of broken dreams
   I hear screams

Bits of paper fly by, like me, only stationary

I start across the empty field and turn to look back
And as I stand there,
   I know
   How much changes hurt.
         Regina G. Makem

I Love Trees

Trees are very fun to sit under.
The shade is very comforting on a hot day.
Sometimes I sit and ponder.
It is cool when you play on such day.

The trees are so so pretty to see.
Trees are kind in a way.
The joy is wonderful to me.
Sometimes I will stay and stay.

When the cool breeze hits my face.
The sun wouldn't touch the tree.
While people run I take the pace.
When I sit there the world is free.

While the birds are chirping.
I try to stop and listen.
I see all the bees working.
When it snows the snowflakes glisten.

When I see a tree the world changes.
All the animals nesting and hibernating.
I found out that I like these changes.
Because trees are so beautiful when it's snowing.
         Kenneth James Franklin

Together Again

She stands on the street on a cold winter night
The shopping cart before her holds her whole life
The clothes she wares are tattered and torn
The shoes on her feet are shabby and worn
She begged money from passersby on the street
Trying to get enough so that she can eat
She'll spend the night sleeping on an old heating grate
Leaving herself open to any kind of fate
As she lies sleeping, dreams fill her head
Her sweet husband is beside her in bed
He wraps her up in his big strong arms
Saying he'll protect her from all harm
He tells her that she has nothing to fear
That he will always be hovering near
She tells him how she misses him so
That she feels it is her time to go
To leave behind this stress and strife
And to live with him in eternal life
Together again they stroll hand in hand
To enter eternity with family and friends
         Pamela Ketcham

Anxious Change

How rapidly the seasons change, how fast the year goes by
The signs of Autumn once again, prompt my reflective sigh

I watch trees fade in splendor, all their colors mesh and blend
Their leaves once buds of promise, now fulfilled aptly descend

Up above, big cloudy pillows, join to fill the vacant skies
Turn my lonely thoughts to pictures, daydreams captured in my eyes

In the dusk, as clouds are cast aside, and the day comes to a close
I can see the sun lose fury, yet in auburn skies it glows

And at night the world looks diff'rent, as the harvest moon appears,
Big and bold and more apparent, lying in the stratosphere

All the stars in radiant beauty, shine against the twilight sky
Hung there just to welcome wishes, or to dream on by-and-by

Underneath...the sounds of Autumn; I can almost always hear
That a time of "change" is anxious, as the old shall disappear

While outdoors, the winds do rustle, safe inside we both shall be
Cozy, cuddled by a fire, life transforms for you and me.
         Lynn Homisak

Carnival At Midnight

At night Nature visits the carnival.
The silvery moonbeams dance gaily
On the steel bones of the once noisome rides.

The odors of cotton candy and popcorn
are replaced by the sharp salty air of the sea.

The roar of the ocean takes the place of
the murmur of humanity and the sand, borne
by the wind, clusters in small dunes about
the booths, rising high to obscure the writing there.
While above, a lone gull glides gracefully
on the currents, seeking a choice morsel.

In the morning, humanity will return,
and nature will be pushed back, like the
tide going out.

But one day, nature will roll in like
the tide and not go back out
         Paul Popiel Jr.

The Actor

I had a dream last night.
The sky was blue, the clouds were white.
The breeze blew cool, and the sun shone bright.
On a ledge a pigeon cooed.
The leaves rustled, the pond rippled.
Rollerblades invaded space, fun exercise.
I stood on a bench, and reached out across the lake.
With voice I reached, with words I filled the air.
I practiced like this, I prepared for the day.
For the time my performance will count the most.
The time I have been working for,
The time that brought me far from home.
The time that will be bittersweet,
For I have lost all the charms of innocence along this trek.
A trek so unwanting of me...
I wake up to the sound of car horns.
Buildings so tall shield the light. I am left in their shadow.
I must prepare for my audition...I don't care about the sun.
         Michael Straka

Unchained And Wild

The glory of the wind
The song of the sea
The air is free of sin
It breathes life into me

The early morning sunrise
The crisp daylight break
I open my eager eyes
I find myself awake

I wonder where the day will take me
I quiver with prospect and anxiety
For my soul is now out and free
Unchained and wild, my life will forever be

The sun's charm has just begun
It's going to be a majestic day
My liberty I have now won
Unchained and wild, my life will forever stay

Kevin Cess

All Give Thanks

The eagle soars far above the clouds.
The sparrow frantically flaps its wings through
the smallest breeze.

Whales enjoy the deepest of oceans,
while the bluegill is content in a farmer's pond.

Lions of the jungle command respect of all the
other jungle animals.
While the docile house cat asks just to be
loved.

From the tiny mustard seed to the great trees
of Yellow Stone National Park.

All give thanks unto He who has created them
and He is God.

Wendell T. Kinney

I Would Speak Of Love

I would speak of Love,
the starry flights and mountain climbs.
Immersed in you, I surface within and find myself.
Essence blending and separating,
the taste remains giving strength to purpose.

I would speak of Love,
but only you would understand me.
You who are there, when I am.
Paltry the language, vain the attempt to convey what is.
Yet I drink in your thoughts with abandon.

I would speak of Love,
when memory flash's, berthing pains.
Powers forging new channels.
Muscles taut, rippling in the wake of ecstasy.
Not a reminder, but re-living!

I would speak of Love,
joining spirit and soul, to travel this mortal path to rebirth.
To you I give, and keep my responsibility.
I hear and I obey, and I am free. My net. My prod. My goal.
I would speak of Love, To You.

Stephen M. Burzi

Crystal Teardrop

Within a crystal teardrop lay the pages of a book and
the story of a mortal soul and the many paths she took:
Some pages are filled with happiness others stories too painful to
tell for though she had felt the love of God she had walked through
the depths of hell:
Within the book are many pages some lined with silver lined with gold
and some with the black of sorrow and too many tears to hold:
Yet through the many tears came one that one could explain
except the soul who shed it with love for those who caused the pain:
This one small crystal teardrop so pure so rare so clear
and radiant with the soft glow of love was free from all pain and fear:
Someday in time the story must end and the book will slowly close
only then shall it be revealed the final path she chose:
And then this tiny teardrop, that no one could explain,
shall return with love to the soul who shed it and free her from
  sorrow and pain:

Patricia A. Ellsbury

She Touched Me

She was staring through the window of the old bookstore,
   the street was empty, except for her;
I approached her gently, and asked how she had been,
   she said, "I'm making it" with a toothless grin.

Her clothes were soiled, and she smelled of wine,
   she nodded, again, and said, "I'm just fine";
and for a moment, time passed before me,
   and I remembered my friend, as she used to be.

A perfectionist in her field, with a world of knowledge to share,
   I knew she had seen hard times, by the chance in her there;
I asked where she lived, and if I could give her a ride,
   she said, "I live just down the street, over on that side".

With a saddened heart, I watched her walk away,
   shuffling off so slowly, I was left in dismay;
and suddenly she turned, and asked if I had some spare change,
   and the poverty of our times touched me in my friend's old age.

Pat Poole

The Wall

Sand was added to the mix.
The strength of his arms folded the mixture together.
Water lubricated the powder.
He turned the mixture, producing the mud.
He took the trawl, like a knife,
Forming wounds in the mud.
The mud was spread evenly over every brick.
One by one the bricks were hit,
Causing them to be shaped to his desire.
He used the mud to smooth over the cracks,
Hiding the brokenness within.
Breaking, Hitting, Smoothing,
The process went on for years,
Until at last, the wall was complete.
He was a bricklayer,
She was no more.

Kim Smartt

Kristen...........

Kristen, what a fine young lady!
Helps Mommie take care of baby.

Sets the table and helps with cakes -
Folds the clothes and likes to bake.

Decorates the outside tree -
And likes to play games with me!

Gives me kisses and lots of smiles -
Kristen, a real life doll!

Zelma Moorman Hunt

The Island

The night is quiet except for the ocean wave,
The strip of moon moves in and out of the clouds
As the dawn is aware of the day.

The big sea oaks lean over,
I guess with age from all the years of wind
And nature within it's great limbs.
They hold onto life by bending and always giving in some
To all the elements around and in them
Maybe if we could be like the oaks
And lean over instead of breaking into with each new day,
We would all be able to find our way.

The blinking lights from the ships at sea
On the horizon they beckon,
As to let me know they are there for me,
How I love the sound of the sea.
The solitude and the feeling of being free.
How dark it is
Just the white of the waves, coming in at me
The morning will break soon,
The quiet will be gone and I back to reality.

Jessi Louise

Education

Education is the space ship.
The student is the astronaut.
Education takes us into the interior of the atom.
It takes us around the world, in the air, on land, and in the sea.
Education is capable of time travel.
It takes us into the past, shows us the present, and tells us what the future may be.
Education can travel faster than the speed of light.
It takes us out to the stars.
The space ship education builds our minds, exercises our imagination, and peaks our curiosity.

Norma Rait

"It Must Be Spring"

I sat beside my window,
The sun came peeking in;
I saw a crocus wink at me,
I think he knew 'twas spring.

There's a violet in a sunny spot,
A little wren sang "hello"...
A dandelion raised her golden head,
To see that last flake of snow.

A little stream went chuckling by,
With diamonds on her face,
A gentle breeze reached out to me,
With fingers soft as lace...

The birds, the flowers, the gentle breeze
Each have a song to sing;
And even I am smiling,
I know it must be spring.

The birds, the flowers the gentle breeze
The warming rays of sun;
Be still and listen, you will hear
God's voice in every one.

Nell M. Tipton

Cat Company

The wind was whispering it's secrets;
The sun was kissing my nose;
The violets were telling beautiful tales;
The birds were practicing concertos;
The butterfly was waltzing with the sweet-smelling air;
The cat came purring her greetings...
And because I delighted in these visits from Spring,
I never did finish my flower-bed weeding!

Twila Joy Payne

Spring

The winter snow had melted and Spring is finally here
The sun is always shining and the sky is blue and clear.

The trees are all in bloom now and full of birds' nests
As they are getting ready for the arrival of their newborn guests.

Now the sun shines longer, kids can stay out late and play
Yard work is even easier with these longer days.

The buds that once were dormant are now open to the sun
Showing off their vibrant colors to each and every one.

The grass is finally green and growing at a fast rate of speed
Time to dust off the lawn mower and go pull those blasted weeds!

It's time to do Spring cleaning, time to make things fresh and new,
It's just so amazing what some soap and paint can do!

The coming in of Spring makes the world a pretty place
The changing of the season puts a smile on every face.

Kim Rainey Bradshaw

Magic Is Not Magic

The Rainbow is a letter from the sun to the moon.
The Sun is the universes big golden eye.
The Moon is a powerful wizard's crystal ball.
The Stars are Gods endless dot to dot, but...
Thunder is not thunder,
it is the sound of bodies falling to the ground in the middle of a war.
A Hurricane is not a hurricane, it is the breath of a dragon.
Dew is not dew, it is the foot print of magic.
Magic is not Magic, it is the heart of God.

Bonner Stave

The Wilderness

The sky was blue
The sun was out
The wind was lazily blowing about

He saw a farmer making hay
As he slowly made his way
To the middle of - nowhere

One side of him there were mountains steep
The other side a brook danced at his feet
And under the trees the birds sang sweet

The day grew warmer as the sun climbed the sky
And as he passed a snake he heaved a sigh
As he made his way to the middle of - nowhere

Pondering over what life meant
He tripped over a branch that was bent
And headlong into the brook he was sent

The sky was dark
The stars were bright
The trees were whispering good night
And then and there the old man knew
That this was — the middle of - nowhere

Kaushiki Rao

May 12, 1936

The streamlined train was swift and serpentine.
  The sunlight glimmered on its silver side
As it went past. The passengers inside,
  Beguiled by speed, their sense of travel blurred,

Ignored the scenes of wretched poverty
  Outside the windows of the shiny cars.
The great depression roved the woeful land
  That day the Super Chief began its run

Across the West in nineteen thirty six,
  Chicago to L.A. The tracks were laid
By Chinamen and Irishmen, the poor,
  Their labor limitless. Infinity.

(We left our pony carts along the shore
Of Ireland to board the ship to here.)

Richard Brennan

My Valentine

I'm so delighted that our paths connected.
The sweetest nectar, I have ever consumed.
You are, by far the sexiest man alive.
Your smile is toes.
That body is a virtual cornucopia of delights.
Your love has conquered all my secret spaces.
Wherefore do you doubt me?
We are so much in likeness.
You should know by now you are head of this realm.
And invaluable to the interior in which we live.
Together we are excessive at best.
To you I give mine heart, and soul forever.

Sherri Brown

Our Flag

There it waves, its broad stripes and bright stars.
The symbol of Victory from so many wars.
The blood that was shed to prove its, great might.
The peace it brought to make all things right.
The sky so blue filled with so many stars,
Beaming down on a world filled with so many scars.
People so greedy, more money they crave,
So the entire world, they would make it their slave.
Homes ruined, so many lives lost,
But they care not for this mighty cost.
Their fortunes, their mansions, their vast real estate,
All this the world must stop, before it is too late.
Bring to an end to all this ungodly hate.

Pauline B. Kuhn

How Sweet The Memory

How sweet the memory of your touch
The tenderness I relished so much,
The warmth of the sunlight upon your hair,
The pain of your loss I now must bear.

How sweet the memory of your cheerful laugh,
The smile that was your personal autograph,
The haunting memory of your caring for me,
The loss of the smiling face I can no longer see.

How sweet the memories I cherish in my heart,
The warmth of your kiss so welcome from the start,
Of joyous music that filled up our days,
The deafening silence....my newest phase!

And yet....to change one precious day, my love,
Would be to deny the stars up above,
Would I ever regret the treasures of special you?
How sweet the memories......the regrets so few!

Peggy Creedon Barrie

What Will You Do?

There's rioting in Africa, there's murder in Detroit
The taxes that you're paying, they're using to exploit...
The money is used for "defense," at least that's what we're told,
But, a bomb can't feed a child, or shelter all the old!
The suffering, the violence; the hatred and the greed
The poor keep getting poorer, no one listens to their need!
The KKK is in Georgia, and other places too
The Africans are starving.....is there something you can do?

Or...will you simply shrug your shoulders, as you turn and walk away?
Will you just ignore the problems that confront the world today?
There's people 'killing people: There's hunger in the land...
It only makes me question, the "Brotherhood of Man!"
The murder of the harp seal...the raping of a nun
The child in the ghetto, trying to steal a gun!
There's people hurting children, the innocent and small...
It really makes me wonder...if there's sanity at all!

....So...what will you do to help it end?
What will you do to ease the pain?
What will you do to help the planet mend?
What will you do, my friend?

Lady Cat Powers

Discovery

As I reflect upon my life, my senior years recall
The things I would do differently and others, not at all
Some times were harsh, some times were sweet and some were
  tints of gray
And still I count the blessings I'm reaping yet today

Who's to say what lies in store, we only know of "passed"
In looking back, like those my age, the years have gone too fast
The wisdom "then," as I know now, could have shown the way
Which road to take, which choice to make, how not to go astray

With tired brow, bent still in prayer, I thank the Lord above
At last I've found the secret true, the staff of life is "Love"
For "Love" is trust and "Love" is faith and "Love" is being kind
And "Love's" the greatest legacy that we can leave behind

Vernetta Ann Neuroth

Vampire

The hunt, the chase the death, the sweet blood, the taste the feel,
the thrill the seal!
The rising and waking, the picking and choosing. So much for one
to decide. It's hard
for one of us. The smells, the tastes, the sights, the bright,
bright lights!
But the Power, the feeling, the immortality. The times the lives,
the past is Alive!
Its the hunt, the chase, the kill, the blood, that keeps us young,
to wonder the earth from dusk till dawn.
Good and evil, fight night by night, Ultimate Power the key, for
mortals near and far.
Life and death. Day by day. We live for the thrill, we live with
with pride. To kick up our heels, and stride amongst them.
Those who hunt us will die, those who praise us too. We hunt to live,
live to kill.

Strong as twenty men in the day stronger still within the night.
Children of the night, we love to hear. Raise our voices for all to
fear. They guard well by day and leave by night. No mortal dares our
domains are near. Our lives are full of lust. Power is high the
night is young. We sleep by day gather by dusk. In the light of the
new full moon once a year. We are among you, so don't fear, insanity
is near and any one who dares ... To cross paths with immortals such
as us. Vampires do not deal, we steal, your very souls.

Molly Allen

Far From The Zodiac

This worry that I have is gradually getting stronger
The time has arrived, can't put it off any longer
This lump I can feel, I'm sure's getting worse
So a call to the doctor, then thoughts of a hearse.

My appointment's at ten and now it's nine, I'm just pacing in my room
Positiveness has still not arrived, my room is scented with gloom
So I leave my home and crawl around, I'm oblivious to what's around
And think back to the day... hour... minute, of when the lump was found.

Destroyed nails as I sway in my chair, as the patients arrive and leave
Another name is called out, and inside I shake and heave
And then my name is mentioned, and there's a thumping in my chest
One last chance to chicken-out, and stay home like the rest.

I'm rigid in my chair, as my rehearsed words rush out
And the look on the doctor's face, leaves me in no doubt
I tell myself to calm down, I've come here for the answer
But I again land on the fact, the fact that I have cancer.

Paul Conchie

The Time of Your Life

As the earth moves forward and time marches on,
  the time of your life is so quickly gone
so while you are able to greet friends and foes
  let me tell you how to more sweetly smell the rose.

Whether you know it or not, God made other ones.
  He made many daughters, likewise many sons.
After every production, he threw the pattern away
  so he wouldn't repeat what he made yesterday.

God gave us our guidelines, ten commandments on stone.
  Said if you abide by these I'll never leave you alone.
As sure as the night will follow the day,
  your maker is waiting to hear what you say.

W. De Loss Murphy

To You I Return

To you I return
  the time we spent together,
  the few days and the many nights.
I return the smiles you gave,
  the smiles of your own free will
  that you once intended for me.
Along with those is everything
  of yours that made me smile,
  your jokes and games, your laughter
  and happiness, your touch.

To you I return my sense of pride in myself
  and the strength to hold my head high,
  for you were the one who instilled them in me.
I return the laughter and light in my life
  for once again
  they came solely from you.
Along with those is the one gift
  that I want you to know that you gave
  and the one that you couldn't,
  my life and my love.

Michelle Berger

Feelings

You are the reason of my songs
The topic of my dreams
The beginning and the end
Of a temptation in peace.
You are the smile of my strength
My blanket and my warmth when I'm cold
The pillow that I lean on when I love
The sensual touch of pleasure in my heart and soul.
You are the sin that makes me blind
The place where I can always my peace find
The friend who always heals all my scars
The one the brings me a loving sincere smile.
You are the rhyme and rhythm of my voice
The ups and downs of what I always do
The whispers of your shadow when I'm yours
The one that wrote our love in many books.
You are the one that makes me write love songs
The one that gives me always so much joy
The one who does not expect nothing in exchange
And the one who I will always... always love.

Patricia Maldonado

Untitled

The cries go unheard, the voices in the dark
The unbearable pain, makes it make
Not too much, I want to take
So much sadness, is at stake
Ease my suffering, I've had enough
It speaks for itself, I'm not that tough
A big empty space, a big lonely life
This is what I am, a double-edged knife
Stabbed in the heart, stabbed in the back
The pain is unreal, what do I lack?
A little help, a little love
Some understanding, is what I dream of
The taste of anguish, the smell of fear
There is no escape, I am trapped here
So, the cries go unheard, the voices in the dark
The unbearable pain, leaves it mark.

Stephanie Uhlman

I Hate "Hate"

I propose that you start to eliminate
The use of the four letter word, we call "hate".
When ever you want to communicate
Just take your time and contemplate.
Listen for words your mind will create.
Let both your head and your heart motivate.
But if an idea starts to irritate
And gets you upset and makes you irate
And in your head there's an angry debate,
'Cause you think there's something you can't tolerate,
Then stop yourself and make your voice wait.
Take a deep breath and at least count to eight.
Clear your mind and alter your state.
Relax for a while and meditate.
Then just before you pontificate,
Think it through so you don't exaggerate,
Or unfairly judge or discriminate,
Then express yourself clearly, elaborate.
My goal's to persuade and to educate.
So choose a more accurate word than "hate".

Beacon

As Eye See It

As I look out of my house in P.A.
The view is spectacular, I really must say
Nature has really outdone herself here
The serenity and beauty of watching a deer
While the streams run free and so do the brooks
It's indescribable how it really looks
The birds like to sit in the trees for awhile
Just looking at them, makes you smile
In the morning, when I open my door
There are some turkeys, twenty or more
Then I'll take a walk, and what do I see
A couple of rabbits jumping so free
As I look by the lake, watching for trout
Suddenly their popping up and about
Nature can give you a natural high
No need for drugs, they can make you die
Our eyes are the cameras for us to see
No need for film, they are kodak free
What God has put here for us to enjoy
We shouldn't take for granted, we shouldn't destroy!

Linda Protus

Thank You

My heartfelt thanks to you is made of many special things,
The warmth and happiness your valued friendship brings,
The little things you do to me, that mean so very much,
The way we are especially close and always keep in touch.

My heart felt thanks to you is for things I cannot chart or measure.
Just knowing you has brought me joy and hours of untold pleasure,
The way you look with a real happy smile,
The sparkling eyes like diamonds, make me want to stay a while.
You are a special and loveable friend who grows more dear,
With every birthday and every glorious year.

C. H. Reeve

Opportunities Lost

The fire dissipates and along with it the light it provided.
   The warmth escapes and leaves a subtle chill in the air.
A new dimension has chased away reality as we knew it,
   And looking back on the light of day is a challenge we share.
The fire in the sky must be our source for energy and aspiration.
   If not, then why is our gaze cast with such intense wonderment.
The power to illuminate and transcend the bounds of creation,
   graces our existence but for a brief moment.
We must grasp this illumination and use it quickly,
   lest we discover the air is cooling, the shadows growing.
Time is the enemy who weakens the flame,
   an enemy ignored by those unknowing.

The fire dissipates and with it opportunities lost.
   As the light fades our soul likewise soon forgets.
The importance of a single day has been disguised.
   Alas, it is gone, the sun has set.

Lena S. Pierce

Memories of You

The soft silkiness of your hair
the warmth of your smile, and
the joy and laughter of your
heart are like rays of sunshine upon
my memories of the short time we
spent together.

As memories fade away
   only one remains;
      The memory of you holding me close,
         as the love in your heart overflowed.
         You said goodbye with tears in your eyes
         as though you knew the end was near.

Tracy Hall

Desolation

The bridge was narrow and high,
The waters deep, and deadly cold;
Each time that she passed by,
She shook, 'n almost lost her hold.

She cursed the luck, and cursed the road,
That led her where no kind being
Could come to lift the heavy load
That kept her soundless and unseen.

One dark and lonely night,
She approached the bridge in pain.
The sounds were echoes of her fright,
Never disguised, always the same.

Quietly now, she wanders there,
No more pain, and only a light
To lead those away from where
She once suffered from such fright.

Nelida Rios King

Prayer Meeting Night At North Cove Baptist Church

The attendance has been good, considering
The weather.
It is a good fellowship, when we
all get together.
We enjoy our selves and sing a few songs,
Then someone leads Bible study, it's not
too long!

The book of Proverbs contains great
wisdom untold,
We learn about the fool, the coward,
The wise and the bold.
Every one gets a chance to speak,
We are all there to learn, God's
knowledge to seek!

God is so great and we are so small,
We know when death's angel comes to call,
Glory hallelujah, there will be nothing to fear,
As our faith in God makes all things clear!

Ted R. Braswell

Different Life

I sit and wonder what I could be.
The whole world to explore, but nothing much to see.
Everyday I do the exact same things.
Waiting for what the normal day brings.
I stare out the window, in a great daze.
I wish for a new life, in many ways.
The one I have is so boring and so very bland.
I wish for someone to take hold of my hand.
And take me away to a place that is new.
To travel the world, and have lot's to do.
Or to sing, having a wonderful voice.
With celebrities, and an agent, and having no choice.
Or maybe to act, and to have lot's of fame.
My boring life is driving me insane.
Even if I were to take up a sport.
Showing what talent I have up and down the courts.
I wish to have a different life, no matter how.
Cause anything is better than my life right now...

Lorie Muszynsky

Not Alone

The sun beats down on my hot crimson cheeks,
the wind whips my hair.
And they,
they stand sheltered by a tree
from the sun,
and from the wind -
laughing and mocking me.
Their eyes dart from me to their protected circle
as I stand in plain view -
unsheltered, unprotected.
Tears tumble down my burning cheeks.
I pray to my Savior...
the wind calms to a soft breeze
which dries my tears.
A cloud covers the sun,
my cheeks are cooled.
They walk away,
bored.
As they leave a snow white dove lands in the trees,
and coos softly.

> *Nicholle Reinhardt*

My Heart's Compass

Through the canyons and passages of my mind -
The winds of emotions swirl.
My memories of you consume my being,
Your presence surrounds my soul.
The breezes stir before me hidden paths
Where I have never ventured to travel.
But I am following my heart's compass
In the search of a true love to follow.
When I find in your face a reflection -
Of my journey as such,
I will know and not guess,
How strong your love is, and how much.

> *Meredith Hughes*

Robert Tyler

Time has not worked its miracle for me,
The wound is not healed, nor will it ever be.
How can it be, after thirty-two years,
I haven't yet learned to hold back the tears?

Did God have some special plan for you,
Something no other in His Kingdom could do?
It cannot be that you left my womb,
Only to fill an empty tomb!

Was your mission so special that it had to take,
Your mother's heart and make it break?
For this broken heart has paid a price very dear,
A child I can never touch, or see, or hear.

Whatever the task for which you were born,
Do it well, Dear One, lest I forever mourn.
Let me find peace, knowing your race is won,
I love you and miss you, Robert Tyler, my son.

> *Ruth Ward*

When Mom Is Upset

When mom starts to frown, the whole world seems upside-down
The sun stops shining, when mommy's not smiling,
but when the frown goes away, she brightens our day.
When mom gets down-hearted, a bad day has just started.
It darkens the whole sky, when mom starts to cry.
Rain stops getting things wetter, when mom feels better.
When I feel agony, I know mom is angry........
And when mom is upset you can bet, we'll try with all
our might, to make things alright.

> *Kathleen Wisneski*

"Insomnia"

Evening is climaxing downstairs
their laughter cascades fitfully
down the moonlit lawn
all the way to the whispering lake
of white ducks beyond
the woods.

Yes, it must be ending
the door slams and slams
like a poor clapper from the bells of hell
rejected by satan himself.

Now and then
The lights of automobiles
project geometrics
radiating and sweeping ceiling and walls:
Some appear as swords.

> *Tommy Richardson*

Time

How do you really define time?
    Then can you make it kinda rhyme?
Between sleep, meals and work needed done
    can you budget your time and still help someone?

On this ranch we have wheat, milo, cows and calves
    and sometimes a few taters.
But the grains all go to the Utica,
    Laird or Beeler co-op elevators.

Do you enjoy a grandchild, relative,
    a friend or even a flower,
Youth and ballgames, back deck,
    a parade or even a leisure hour?

Do you attend church or
    read the Holy Word.
Does your time include a
    little prayer to the Lord?

If that durn ol grim reaper told
    us when we'd take our last breath
You know of course, that would
    surely scare us to death.

> *Lee Norton*

The World Starts With Me

I look to see the beautiful sun.
Then, I sit down to plan a day of fun.
The more I plan the more I do.
When I do, I begin to renew.
I become so confident and brave
That I attempt to rant and rave.
As things begin to change in my favor,
I begin to feel good and savor.
Looking through my mail I become deplored.
The bills amount and I become gored.
Reading through letters, newspapers, and books,
I search for answers and looks.
As I read about starving kids,
I become outraged and get bids.
My bids from Childreach supports those in need.
It's hard to understand the articles and letters I read.
How can people be so mean.
Is it right to kill an innocent baby or teen?
Let's reconsider our goals.
To make earth the best place to save lost souls.

> *Timothy E. Becker*

True Love

Deep on earth my love is lying
Then I softly began crying
My heart is gone and full of pain
My feelings shower down like the falling rain
When you fall in love, you take in the pain and sorrow
With the glad times and bad times
Your memories to me are solid gold
Even if there new or old
If you should ever die
Then inside so would I
If that rose I gave you wilted away
My sunny days would wither away
For better or worse
Till death to us part
You know you'll always be in my heart
With this ring I thee wed
Then she said I'll always and forever
Love you

Travis Primeau

Just So I Could Be With You

If angels are allowed to roam on land,
Then that was you, floating upon the sand.

If angels are seen in white and purity,
Then that was you, I saw glowing brilliantly.

As you touched the moist soil, your toes,
Would curl inside, strickened by the cold.

As you stood silent, facing the ocean,
The moonlight danced around the upon,

Your rose petal face,
Such fullness and grace!

I saw your footprints etched so firm,
I wanted to follow them with every turn,

Just so I could be with you...
Oh! Just so I could be with you!

As I hold you upon the sunset's smile,
I wish how this could last more than a while.

But forever is how long I want to be with you.
But forever is not long enough, I always knew.

If I could capture such a picture in my grasp,
And keep it forever, for I know it will always last.

Steven Kirkpatrick Mudge

Highways Of Life

If the gains in life are not worth the cost
    then the price was too high, and
    therefore you have lost.

Thoughts can make you happy, sometimes sad,
    but would you be better off if
    thoughts you never had?

When people talk of oceans
    but all you see are streams.
It's time to move on, if only in your dreams.

Dreams can make you happy, even if they are sad,
    but would you be better off, if
    dreams you never had?

The highway of life is like an hour glass filled with sand
You cannot turn around as you travel toward the end

But would you be better off, if
    the highway never began?

Mike Spedden

The End of the World

The thunder rolls as the lightning flashes!
Then the sky turns dark as ashes.
It's the end of the world, I anticipate.
What's going to happen? What is our fate?
The war has raged on and many people have died,
because they wouldn't repent of their pride.
Before all life ended and the world burned,
God said "Enough!" The Lord had returned.
He destroyed all evil, and wiped out sin,
making the whole world, beautiful once again.

Lillian Graves

Friends

There are good friends and also false friends
There are fair weather friends too.
That stay with you when all is fine.
But when it's not they're through.

Old friends are the best,
The ones you come to trust
And know you can depend upon
If ere it is you must.

Not all new friends are bad.
For once the old were new.
In time the new friends
Will prove if they are true.

There is a friend that never fails.
He's a friend that's ever true.
You can trust in Him completely.
What He promises He'll do.

Jesus is the friend that
Sticketh closer than a brother.
You can depend on Him
When you can't depend on others.

Nora Shutt

God's Gift

As we open our eyes to a breath-taking sunrise,
There are many beautiful things to see,
Like the brilliant sky at twilight and all its heavenly mysteries.

The moody oceans with their restless waves,
The imposing mountains standing firmly in the haze;
Harmoniously, welcoming the soft touch of the sun
As it regally approaches the horizon.

The moon's loving gaze upon the streams and hills,
Rivers running rampant across the meadows;
The soft whisper of the breeze singing harmonies
Through the window of our souls.

How magnificent are these entities, which brighten each person's life;
And I realize I am blessed each day
As I begin to see the world through God's eyes.

Alas, with these treasures each day should be special, but we often
miss these spectacular wonders of God. Taking for granted their
timeless beauty; A free gift from the one above

and though it seems in this world everything has a price,
Nature is free; though it costs nothing, it is priceless
And I know that it is God's gift to me.

Melissa Marie Tijerina

The Road to Me

I am what I am, not what I will be,
there are still turns to take on the road to me.
I feel myself moving, spinning with life,
Days filled with laughter, loving and strife.

I am grateful for knowing all that I know,
but yearn for direction, which way will life go?

I feel great excitement, mixing wonder with fear,
Where will I be when I am no longer here?

I hope my history has taught me well,
The Lord only knows, and with time he will tell.

Susan Buechele

Untitled

You're my wife, my friend, my lover
There can be no other.
I know I'm quiet, and sit and stare.
But have no doubt, I really do care.
I wish I could show you all the things
That your love and patience brings and brings.
I know you don't understand my ways,
But it's easier to write than it is to say.
I wish you could see in my heart
Then you'll know we'd never be apart.
As we continue to build our love and home
And I can't find the words, I'll write you a poem.
But if it's only one thing you must believe
Then my promise to you is I'll never leave.

Randy Mitterando

Just Us Two

In solitary quiet, we sit upon the beach, knowing that
there has been no contact with company-pet or phone.
Our night's and days are disturbance free-except for the
sounds of the incoming tide, engulfing sand and stone.

Our ears strain, to hear the crashing of a wave - a boat
horn or a distant bell.
We stay busy with yard work, flowers and sometimes at twilight
a funny story one might tell.

Without motion, we can remember the past with children playing
a game of street hockey or hopscotch - then to end up
with chalk pictures on the asphalt that's hard.
A game of hide and go seek way after dark all around the
yard.

Though we feel, we have done no wrong - the children had love
and warmth - we have nothing to hide.
Now we sit alone here on the beach, hurting inside while we
watch and listen to the outgoing tide.

Wayne D. Barton Sr.

Dreams of Love

Among the dreams and the hate, the faithfulness, and love,
There is a ray of one other thing set from above.
Jealousy is it's name.
And crying is it's game.
It loves to tear you apart.
It loves to rip up your heart.
It loves to come down and make you cry,
One little tear out of one single eye.
But you can over power it and make him stay,
All you have to do is push her away.
With the love you and him built.
With the love she almost killed.
With the love that will always be there.
That is the love you and him will always share.

Kristen Richardson

Shopping For An Answer

Walking down the streets of any average town,
There is graffiti on the walls everywhere to be found.
Violence on our streets and drugs in our schools,
We've broken our eternal law, our ten commandments and rules.

God promised us he wouldn't flood us one more time,
but what if this keeps up, what if we can't stop the crime?
Where will we go and what will we do?,
Life is so precious and it can be snapped in two.

When a life is taken away we can't replace it with more,
we cannot bring that person back, it's not like shopping in a store.
For sitting on the shelves of that very store are people with
        different characteristics, right down to the core.

Each one of us is different,
unique in their own way.
But in the end we realize,
no one is here to stay.

Sara Halle

Winter

Now that the ground is covered with snow
There is no place I care to go.

Except to get the necessities,
For postal and commodities.

The ice is too thin to skate on.
And the windchill too cold, long after dawn.

January's thaw will tease the trees.
Then February and March winds continue the freeze.

But the rhythmical rhythm of the hands, creating lace,
Crocheted, Knitted, or Tatted will satisfy taste.

For when the winds howl and snowfalls,
It's best to sit low and not stand tall.

And as the days of long darkness lessen,
The lace being made will lengthen.

When buds swell and sap flows,
Created lace will steal the show.

Linda L. Busse

Where Will They Go?

As progress continues to grow,
There is one question that most people ask,
What about the wildlife and where will they go?
We are taking over their territory,
But progress doesn't care
And they cannot say a word nor tell their side of the story.
People complain about the wildlife invading their homes.
But man took theirs away,
So where else do they have to roam?
Progress says that the wildlife will relocate
And the way that they are going.
It could mean their fate.
Does progress really give a damn about the wildlife? Answer, NO!
I ask one very important question - where will they go?

Keith D. Peeler

Speak Well

The spoken word, once said, lives on in memory tucked away,
There to repose, patiently, to be used again some future day,

Semantics, grammar, spelling, are all of infinite use,
As we construct our daily speech, with its patterns of abuse,

The "ands" we use quite freely, the "ahs" are a special case,
Our "you know" is perfect, for filling in empty space,

"And uh" is nice for some, while "umms" issue forth,
Lets not forget the "eh?", for our Canadian friends up north,

There is something we should use, its value high indeed,
The silent word bridge, best of all, fills an urgent need,

Just a pause between the words, a minor verbal dwell,
Articulate, enunciate, we urge you all, speak well.

William D. Tighe

Music-in-the-Air

There was always music upstairs,
There was always music in the air.
This old house stands silent and tall,
For now there's no music at all.

Her room is empty, the phone doesn't ring.
In my memory, I still hear her sing.
I want her with me, I love her so.
I cannot hold her, I must let her go.

She spread joy, sunshine and fun,
Like gentle rain, that falls on everyone.
I watched her grow, from a babe in my arms,
To a lovely, young lady, with many charms.

Why did she leave, why did she go?
I'm left here now, with a heart so low.
She's still my baby, just seventeen,
Guess she has to try her wings.

I must look forward, to things to share,
I know our love will always be here.
There was always music in the air.
And, one day there will be music everywhere.

Ruth Rossi

Friendship

Amity is great to have
therefore, be a friend and pal.
Don't be mean be real keen
find a friend that's not to mean.
They'll be really neat
and they'll act mighty nice...
just like sugar and spice.

I had a friend named Mary Anne.
She was really nice,
and said she'd be my friend for life.
One night she went to town and found a shop.
She bought some spices to make a pie
just for me because she was kind and nice...
just like sugar and spice.

I had a friend named Sarah Lee.
She was really mean.
She dyed my hair green!

After that I found a friend that wasn't mean.
I mean my husband Dean!

Tracy Bowersox

Walk With Me

To reach the Goal at the end of the way
There's a path I must walk a little each day
Sometimes its rough and sometimes hard
And sometimes impossible for me to trod
So walk with me Lord down the pathway of life
With its long narrow road of toil and strife
But let me walk this path no matter how hard
For I want to make it no matter how tired
For to see its Beauty we all must seek
So help me Lord my faith to keep
Walk beside me Lord and lead the way
Help me Lord not to go astray
Help me choose the path that's bright
The one Lord that I know is right
Your Heavenly face I long to see
Beaming with Love for you and me
We'll walk the streets hand in hand
For you see I've made it to the
Promised Land. "Thank you Jesus"

Lennie T. Hale

"I Just Like Talkin'"

Get up off that couch, a potato you're not
There's room at the spa; come fill the spot
Exercise with machines, they'll keep you arockin'
But as for me... I just like talkin'.

I hear the old pitch to keep physically fit
But before I get started, I'm really to quit
Exercise machines bore me, I shouldn't be knockin'
But give me a phone and I'll exercise talkin'.

They say you should choose something you like
Jogging or weights, perhaps riding a bike
Do some aerobics? You're kidding of course
In those leotards, I feel like a horse.

Walking someday in heaven, God'll say to me
Come let us sit down, beside the Crystal Sea
"Lord, it's so much fun to be with you walkin'"
But let's do sit down, I just love talkin'

Ruth A. Amato

With No Goodbye

Why did you have to go?
There's so much I don't understand.
There's so much that I need to know.
You've slipped away just like sand,
Like sand through my hand.
I dream of you night and day.
I miss you now that you've gone away.
You left and nothing did you say.
I try to think of what I could've done
As I sit and watch the setting sun,
But that only makes me think of when
We watched that same sun together and then,
And then you would kiss me so softly and slow.
And then we would go.
I did not know when you drove away
I would never see you again or say,
"I love you, always."

Kody Lynn Anderson

FRAGILE

Whenever I think of my dead son
I go so far from this world
I'm not even in it.
Don't touch me please,
I may break.

Rose Mary Mann

Friends

Lord created special people
They are called your "friends"
When you need them they are there
    for you
If you need support of prayer
    they are here for you

The Lord is a special friend, too.
He's there if you need Him
So, if you need our Lord
Just call on him in your prayers

I have those special friends
They are my church families
And I know I'm a friend of there's
So, if you need a friend call on the Lord
But friends should be loyal and forever true.

Rhonda Powell

People Are Very Capable

People are very capable.
They are capable of hatred and violence.
They are adept at hurting each other as well as themselves.

They are capable of gossip and slander.
They are practiced in the art of unjustly judging one another.

They are capable of malice and spitefulness.
They find such evils particularly natural.

But hatred breeds hatred.
Violence is answered with violence.

No good ever come from gossip.
Slander is repulsive in the ears of God.

Malice destroys the heart that holds it.
Spitefulness darkens the soul who is lost in it.

I lament to admit that I am also very capable.
But Lord help me to be different.

Let me answer hatred and violence with your love and peace.
Let me answer gossip and slander with your kind words and tolerance.
Let me answer malice and spitefulness with your grace and forgiveness.
Help me Lord because — in so many ways — I'm not so very capable.

William H. Campbell

Daughters

Because they are they and we are we...
They are the colorful fruit snuggled in the leaves.
They are the shiny jewels gently placed in our lockets
They are the soft breeze rustling through the trees.
They are the memories planted within me.
Once captured within a picture frame,
A monet they commence to be.
Not quite defined, their colors entangle with alacrity.
Their presence takes us back
Where beginnings were demanding and dependent on thee.
But now as they grow, we face what must be;
They are our daughters - FOREVERMORE.
For they shall have our blessing and guide,
As within our heart, our love, we provide.

Lisa Frye

Your's

What can you possibly do without them?
They are your all in all tools.
Assisting in your every emotion,
    desire and need.
Never left alone to "fin" for themselves.
But will pioneer into the deepest
    parts of ones soul.

What can you possibly do without them?
They fix the wrongs of mankind.
At times causing sorrow and pain.
Exalting the world with creativity and flare.
We must care, appreciate and applaud them.

Your hands, my hands, their hands.
What can we possibly do without them?

Olivia Frazier

Untitled

The city- A city- All cities
They attract me - repugnant
Cities there- I'm there- cities stay
I leave- Some day I'll remain
Beauty- ugliness- culture- ignorance
Stability- decadence- wealth- homelessness
Cold buildings in this city- their city
All cities
Peoples from everywhere- frustrated- preoccupied
Efficient- attractive
Capital cities- destruction- no one goes anywhere
Man moves to the city- running from starvation
To the city- a city- all cities
The moon shines when you look up- everyone
Looks down in the city- backs hunched- noses
On the ground- eyes on the ground- minds on
The ground- if man looked up to the sky he
Would not go to the city.

Nancy Portal

The Yielding

We got bored so we counted the stars,
They became broad circles into the night sky.

The dreamers passing their earth-bound lovers,
Fighting the elements, trying to fly.

Drowning violins and dusty wings,
Waiting for love, dormant I lie.

Draining the solitude from the girl in the window,
Too young to speak. Too weak, now, to cry.

The beckoning and calling of those dizzy spirals,
No other choice except to comply.

Rachel Fisher

Untitled

If in a dream is the only way I can be with you,
    then I hope I will never wake up.
If in the past is the only way I can see you,
    then I wish I will never forget.
And if in my prayers is the only way you'll hear me,
    then I will never stop praying.
And even if I can't always touch you,
    I will never let go of your hand.
And if forever never comes,
    You will always have my heart.

Lisa O'Donnell

Downtrodden

The downtrodden sit in their rusty cage.
They cried for help but there was none.
The downtrodden speak in many tongues and vary in complexion.
They are your neighbor, your teacher, your brother, and your friend.
They seek to find a better way, but for the downtrodden there is none.
They spend their eternity in their rut until somehow
the cycle is broken.
You will hear them call out in the night, calling you to them.
Some seek them out and what they find they wish they would have left
well enough alone.
The downtrodden do not feel pain, they live it.
The downtrodden rot and deteriorate, yet survive just enough to
realize and revel in the anguish they classify as an existence,
however in the covenant, it is said that one day the downtrodden
will arise, join together, conquer, and overcome.
The weak will become strong and goodness will abound.
It is written that this day is to be the beginning of the 2,010th year
after the beginning of recorded time.

Rob Fraundorfer

Owls

Owls are predators in the night,
they hunt and hunt with all of their might.

Watch out below you poor little creatures,
you must be sure to hide all of your features.

They fly through the air with their big feathery wings,
they are like flying kings.

Scurrying away out of sight,
only trying to do what is right.

Swooping down for the kill,
getting much more than their fill.

Watching, waiting, is he gone?
No one knows until dawn.

Katie Metcalf

My Wife, My Life

They held each other close in sorrow.
They knew his plane would leave tomorrow.
It wasn't something to believe,
that at that time she would conceive

The desert sands were far away.
He did his job and sent his pay.
He wrote to say, "my darling wife,
you are the purpose of my life."

She answered back in a hurry,
"I'm just fine. Please don't worry."
Then with some pain came great joy.
For God gave her a baby boy.

The Gulf behind, he's on his way.
He met a friend with this to say,
"I met your wife and her new young man.
Looks like you need to change your plan."

"Oh no, she can't be through with me."
With heavy heart he went to see.
He got a kiss and then she smiled,
as she placed in his arms his very own child.

Nina Anderson

A Sight For Sore Eyes

As the week goes on by, my vision gets so strong
They long for your beauty and charm
Wherever you go, your image lasts so long
To ask your name would do no harm

While headphones play music in your wonderful ears
It soothes the most savage beast
Your hair in a pony tail, it might last a year
Or maybe even longer, to say the least

Please take my hand, and I will take yours
Walk together, side by side
A stroll through the forest, or out on the shore
I can imagine if your were my bride

In a castle in the sky, we'd live together
Candlelight dinner every night
All and all, I want it to last forever
It will start when the moment's right

It will happen right now, my watch says it all
Seconds that pass as minutes to do
If I'm not careful, in love I will fall
The woman who I'll love is none other than you

William Ebert

Mothers

Mothers took care of you when you were young.
They sat you in their lap and sang you a song.
Mothers would comfort you when you were sad.
And cheered you up when your day was bad.
Mothers cleaned you up when you scraped a knee,
and they got you quiet when you were stung by a bee.
Mothers cooked you delicious foods.
They made your favorites when they could.
Mothers took care of you all of your life.
Their days were filled with pain and strife.
Now you are grown and you have found.
That it is all turned around.
Your mother isn't the same anymore.
So, now it is your turn to take care of her.

Lezlie Griffin

Why Does The Lady Cry?

As she stands in the New York Harbor, times go from hard to harder.
They say it's getting better, but that's just a lie
She holds the torch up so high, as the tears trickle from her eye.
Why does the lady cry?
The politicians talk of building rockets, but the money just lines
their pockets.
The youth to them are just slugs, drinking their booze and doing
their drugs.
The more you work the harder you sweat, just to cut the deficit.
I wonder when I look in the sky, when feeling oh so high
Why does the lady cry?
Sending your money to a foreign country, while you watch your neighbor
go hungry.
Polluting the rivers and stripping the land, as we contaminate our
fellow man.
The flag is battered, tattered, torn and ripped, as our freedom is
being stripped.
But can you tell me as the Eagle falls from the sky
Why does the lady cry?
It's up to you America's youth, these words I speak are the God's
honest truth.
The future is in your hand, so stop vandalizing and polluting the land.
Wipe the tear from her eye
Pull together, we've got to try
Why does the lady cry?

Scott Safford

Your Eyes

Your eyes are like diamonds, on a ring of gold,
They sparkle and shine, with a brightness so bold.

Your eyes are as pretty, as the flaming orange sun,
That sets in the west, when the day is done.

In your eyes there's an effervescence that glows,
Like stars from above, that reflect down below.

Your eyes are like nothing I've ever seen,
They dazzle with the brilliance, of an emerald so green.

Your eyes are like spectacles, of beauty to behold,
Yet hold secrets and mysteries, that remain untold.

Your eyes are just something, I can not explain,
But to get too attached, would just cause me pain.

So I'll say goodbye, with I guess no regret,
But the memory of your eyes, I will never forget.

Ron Harast

What Happened To The Chrome?

What has become of the Great American Car?
They used to be oh so grand.
A big and bold workhorse, a beautiful treasure.
A finer auto not found, in any other land.

Thoughtfully planned and designed with true flair,
The smallest had seating for ten.
They had real big engines with power to spare.
They were made from real metals and made by real men.

Today, cars are made to be tiny.
Good on fuel, but their small motor's so tame.
They're made out of tin foil and rubber and plastic.
And everyone's car looks the same!

You can keep your toy cars of this chromeless era.
Zipping here and there, and impatient to pass.
I'd much rather cruise, in open spacious comfort,
and I will... when I get some more gas.

Ronald L. Uetz Jr.

Spring

The days were slender
They were filled with joy and beauty
You could see the glimmer of
the snow on the trees and bushes
Everything was still
As winter passed the snow melted
the beautiful flowers bloomed
and the trees grew back their
lovely dark green leaves
The blue birds began to sing and tweet again
The animals which once were
sleeping awoke to the warmth of the sun
on there body and face.
The days grew longer with each passing week
The weather was warm and
the wind no longer blew freezing air.
The days were happy and
filled with joy and much beauty
the still look of winter soon disappeared
Prays spring has finally come.

LaNette Spadt

The Unborn Child

While curled up here in my mother's womb
   They've decided my fate and sealed my doom
That I'll not be born and shall never see
   The life and the love that was meant for me
What gives them the right to throw me away
   It's unfair, unjust but who am I to say?
I wish I were a whale way out in the sea
   At least then there would be protection for me
Or maybe an eagle flying high in the sky
   At least maybe then I could live 'til I die
Well I guess it's for certain that I'll never know
   A soft gentle kiss or feel the wind blow
If I had a wish, I'd wish they give me
   A chance to be born and someone adopt me
The thought of it all just makes me cry
   Oh dear GOD those strange noises, it's time now
Goodbye

Ron Kirkland

Heart Bank

I've got a bank, if you're afraid of a broken heart.
This bank will hold your heart so deep inside.
It's a safe, and warm deposit box so locked up
that no one could get to it.
Not even with tons of dy-na-mite!
So trust in me, put your heart in my bank.
It'll cost you nothing, but a chance.
You'll reap all the rewards and benefits.

The benefits are so special, one of a kind.
The rewards are as sweet as A & W rootbeer.
All you need to do is take the chance.
Trust in me forever more!
My heart bank will hold your heart warm and close.
My bank's empty, until you make your deposit.
The sooner you deposit, the sooner the rewards are reaped.

So trust in me, put your heart in my bank.
I'll never throw your heart away so we'll toss the key away.
Then no one else can get to your heart to break it or steal it from me

Trust in me, give me your heart!
My bank's empty until you make your deposit!

Nancy Ormsbee

My Sweetie

Your anatomy is a fascinating work of art.
This is my rendition of your incredible parts.

Your brow is furrowed with intelligence lines-
With you I can explore the limits of my mind.

Your chest is massive and appears so mean-
With my head rested there- I have the sweetest of dreams.

Your arms are powerful and so very strong-
Being held between them is where I belong.

Your hands are callused, yet gentle with touch-
I love to hold them so terribly much.

Your back is composed of muscle and bulk-
I have my own personal incredible hulk.

Your bum is perfect with incredible form-
Walking behind you is a real turn on.

Your legs are defined underneath all that hair-
Where ever they venture- I want to be there.

Your feet are imperfect-they've suffered abuse-
I want to care for them-restore them to use.

Your anatomy is a fascinating work of art-
I want to take care of those incredible parts.

Tracy L. Porter

Weather In The South

Cool crisp mornings, with radiant warm afternoons.
This is Spring in the South.

Hot and sunny, humid and bright.
Scattered showers throughout the night.
This is Summer in the South.

Warm and comforting, just right for walking.
Cool and brisk, fine for night stalking.
This is Fall in the South.

Winter is moody, who knows what it will bring.
It is cool and windy in the morning, even cooler in the afternoon.
But when the sun comes out, it glows like Spring.
And midmornings so clear, you can still see the moon.

So you see, the weather in the South is quite a varied delight.
With it's sun that shines bright,
and it's just right climate at night.
Once in awhile, at different times of the year, you may even see a
  little snow falling light.

That is the Weather in the South.
   Wanda Cook

Baby Free

A child a gift from Heaven above
This special gift needs only my love.

A baby a life with eyes to see
In need of protection please help me be free.

The free I need is a decision from you
A choice to make I depend on you.

To decide for me to be drug free
See, I'm a special gift, you choose to conceive

So let me be your baby drug free
I'm especially for you, your choice should
be for me.

Please Choose...
   Baby drug free.
   Lori Lacey

Our Love Story

In this love story; we give God the glory.
This story tells, of wedding bells.

With our God; we found each other.
Thank you God, besides you, there is no other.

Dad and mom, we do leave.
To each other, we will cleave.

God is the head; of my life.
And I thank him, for my brand-new wife.

God lives inside of me, and I thank him, for blessing me.
With a brand-new groom, who makes my heart swoon.

For our wedding guests, we ask God to bless.
You've traveled far and near, came to bring us love and cheer.

We thank the Lord, for you today.
We thank you, for witnessing our wedding day.
   Minette Smith

Fate's Friend

I don't recall that day we met so many years ago,
Those old High School days in the corridors I'd always say hello;
Out Pathways kept on crossing I'd see her here and there.
Her kindness and her love of life went with her everywhere;
As time rolled on our goals our dreams, were found in separate ways.
The sunrise came and sunsets went as we lived life day by day;
And then I found my friend again, through material acquaintance
Our friendship grew, fun times we had, we came to close the distance
So she met her knight in Armor, her soulmate, and to him, she wed
And just like her I call him my friend, down life's path choppy life
  they led
Through Auld Yang Syne the seasons past, the in-laws I all met
Along with all their other friends, there was not one regret.
And as my life comes to the winter, the reflections Bittersweet.
I find that I've been blessed, by that old friend, that fate called
  me to meet;
But today I yelled and screamed at God to ask the reason why
This wasn't fair, not old was she and why did she have to die.
   Tom Sheedy Jr.

Night

Ah, night!
Thou dost encompass us with thy vestments of darkness.
Yea, when dusk becomes invisible, long strides wilt thou take.
Candle power dots the landscape, as an artist does with a brush.
A last locust call, hark! A cricket echo —
A whisper of ice- wind, a solitude of peace and emptiness,
All accompany thee on thy evening whirl.

Jet black background for city great,
Blacker yet in country wide.
Iridescent moon, glow in glory and fog this night,
Stare as a lonely sentinel o'er shadowy landscape,
Dormant flower, dew-dropped and limp rest from weary day.
Lovers in shadow, pine and sigh — but lo! Time interrupts
this multitude of tender feeling.

Tiny leaf on birch tree white, reflect and wink at shaft of light.
Light! God-made and warm to touch, seems to embrace thy
graceful
     trunk.
Red sun, peep o'er yon' hill and fill in shadows deep
with thy intruding light, as dew-drops evaporate from night's sight.
Escape night! Away with you! 'Tis daylight's turn!
Wait till eventide — then come and fall again.
   Michael J. Gallo

Together — For Life

Two souls together from the very start,
Though total strangers they lived heart to heart.
Yes two separate souls created by God,
And both intended on this earth to trod.

Being together was not of their plan,
But more important than how it began.
The first could not see through the hurt and fear,
The other's first sight was God waiting near.

One heart rejected touch of the other,
Plans didn't include that of a mother.
Ignoring truth in a whispering voice,
So much was lost under the veil of choice.

Separation pains were felt most by one,
Still both did suffer before all was done.
All earth and heaven shed many a tear,
For the lack of love for a life so dear.

Hope is not lost though it can't be undone,
The power of prayer can reach anyone.
The small heart now knows only perfect love,
Praying for its mother from up above.
   William H. Hopwood Jr.

Ode To Provider

You are so regal; the symbol of man-kind,
Though we still viciously hurt you.
    You are the reason we live, we prevail,
Though we still treat you so terribly.
    You are our mother, and we your children,
Though we destroy each other, our brothers and sisters.
    You give us everything we need, we want,
Though we never show our appreciation.
    I only we had a second chance, but alas,
We can't, for it is far too late, unless we work together.
    But, if we could save you,
I know I would treat you so much better, my Mother Earth.

   Sara Zeigler

The Poet

To many I recite of dreams of love and fear
Thoughts of yesterday and now
And those still yet to hear
A rhythmic entourage of words
Each chosen by the poet
A symphony of verse and voice
Please listen while I sow it
As gently as I started verse
I take it to the limit
Like crescendos in a symphony
I forge myself into it
As pounding words of verse and rhyme
Rise quickly to its peak
The throbbing rhythmic climax
with a literary beat
Falls quickly to its gentle verse
I lay them at your feet
To ponder on by thoughts of man
A poets poem complete

   D. Bruno

Why Try

In everyone's life there is cause for some strife,
through all of the tumult, insults and loud shouting
and sorrows that cause you at times just to pause
and think of your problems and the joys they are routing,
    why try?

When banks all foreclose and cause you new lows,
your life is a battle and nerves start to rattle,
your furnace won't light and your kids want to fight,
always they prattle and constantly tattle,
    why try?

What's really the use of staying all loose
when the roof starts to leak through holes you must seek,
you've run out of food and the kids are all rude,
you've never found work that you seek — and booze makes you reek,
    why try?

I'll tell you without prying, never start crying,
you might put your foot in the fire place soot
or try to escape from a life full of strife
when it doesn't solve problems in your's or my life,
    that's why you must try!

   Terry Roberts

Angel

By her love, I came into this world,
Through her care, I am here today.
God put an angel here on the earth.
I'm so glad He let her stay.
Through her voice, I've heard sweet melodies;
Through her eyes, I've seen rainbows bright.
Her hands have often soothed my brow
While she tended me through the night.

With no weapon, save undying love
And no shield except her faith
She has many times stepped forward
From harm to keep me safe.

I've defied her and I've said hard words
That have left her dear heart to bleed.
And still...she has always loved me
No matter how awful the deed!
She's been steadfast, forgiving, my strength,
My guardian angel on earth.
God gave me a miracle.....
He made her my mother at birth.

   Mary P. Sayman

Goodbye Daddy

There was a man, big and strong; he believed in us, all along
Thru the shadows, and suns that shined; he loved us deeply,
all the time. The lessons we learned, weren't always nice
But they were necessary, for us to survive
He'll suffer no more, and feel no pain
He's passed thru the door, free from the game
We musn't be selfish, this we should know
We'll mourn his passing, but we must let him go
onto the great, world beyond
He'll be with us in spirit, from now on
Yes! It hurts, to see you part
But you'll be with us forever, in our hearts
You be proud, you did us right
You loved us dearly, you gave us life
Don't you worry, we'll take care; of matters that need to be settled here
We'll meet again, on the other side; we'll all be there, by and by
Thank you for being there, when I needed you most
I'm here today, because of those
I can't believe, it's really true
Goodbye Daddy, we'll miss you

   J. Michigaus

Winter Night Sky from the Hill Top

Sprawled on my back in the tall wet grass
Tickling the soles of my feet
I'm contemplating the vast night sky above me.
I am not the first to gaze at the white hot pinpoints
Suspended in perfect contrast to the blue black ceiling-
Nor am I the last to be moved by this eternity.
    The moment is cool an crisp- focused
    I wish I could stretch it out
    And extend it into eternity as well-
    A moment as endless as the star swollen sky.
What would it be like tomorrow
If I chased myself dizzy in a circle-
Spun out until the horizon blurred
Black fused to green
With the hills above my head
And the clouds beneath my feet?
    If I was to be alone evermore
    I would ask only for a wide field
    And a smooth bare limbed tree
    Held stark against the clear night sky.

   Natasha North

Christmas Time

It's Christmas time but once a year
time for parties gifts and cheer.

A time for missile toe and holly
a time for carols and being jolly.

But let us set aside some time
for the real reason of this Holy Season.

Today the Christ Child has been born
to share our pain and sorrow

To give us peace and happiness
and sunshine for tomorrow.

To help us share the good and bad
in life's path that we all walk

For all we need to comfort us
is a little prayer and talk

You need not say you standard prayers
in a church or in a temple.

Just speak to him right from your heart
words plain and sweet and simple

Lorraine Slaby

"Time Is..."

Time is like a river that sometimes flows too wide.
Time is indeed a fact of life we should not
keep hidden inside.
For it is in my "crazy" world that time comes
in different forms;
Where the hours dissolve into the night
and the minutes fade into the morn.
There are perhaps some moments where I wish that
time would stand still;
Then my life one day, might become fulfilled.
Unfortunately for me, life does rear its ugly
Head and begins to convince me that time goes on,
and to accept that fact instead.
What a world, what a world it could be if
time were like the human race longing to be free.
Will the clocks in my life ever remain the same;
Or will I continue having nothing ever to regain?
Time is like a river, that fact remaining true,
For life can indeed be happier, because dreams will indeed
come through for people like you.

Lauri Sullivan

My Rainbow Girl

I came home from work just the other day
Tired and worn out then I heard you say
"Hello Daddy-O" and I felt like new
With a great big smile and a hug from you.
The storms they come - sometimes they're strong
But weather them out, they won't last long.
And if you look, you'll sometimes see
A beautiful rainbow like you are to me.

Purple is your Royalty, a child of God are you,
Blue it is your Loyalty (and favorite color, too!)
Green is life and Growing, like creation all around,
Yellow's your Light Glowing, in Jesus' love you've found.
Orange is the Caring Way you act each day that's new,
And red it is your constant Love for those that surround you.

Don't lose those vibrant colors, don't let your rainbow fade...
For the Pot of Gold God blessed us with is you who He has made.
And as you turn a teen today and your life you do unfurl,
You'll always and forever be your Daddy-O's "Rainbow Girl".

Lee Melton

"Sweet Reminisce"

Memories - a mind full of thoughts and moments
    To appreciate what life gives and means.
Memories - times to share and never forget,
    Only if one could put them in a bottle and save them forever.

But to lose them would be such a terrible thing to waste,
    Memories - things to keep, love, and cherish.
When one could pass them down to future generations,
    Memories are like roses; things one could find beauty
    And dignity in.

Memories - times when people assemble to reminisce
    A thing to value and preserve.
Memories - it brings laughter and joy,
    What magnificence can one have more than a mind full of
    Memories.

Shaliza Parsons

Reflection Pools

Memory is satiable, accessible and sweet,
to be brought forth in times of darkness and heat.
Thoughts of past beholds an inner light that cools,
so refreshing and peaceful like glass reflection pools.

Hot waves of torment and strife come into life,
pushing down, pressing, dulling the senses,
cuts like a knife.
Focus on the memory of good and the appeasing,
reminiscing does not depress,
it is enlightening and pleasing.

Serene and absolute solitude, shimmering with insight,
the reflection and revelation in the flash of a light.
Sparkling water that mirrors the heart and soul,
ripple the everlasting eternity of love as a whole.

The deep and dark waters decline from the conscious depths,
wanes to a world of wonderment that waxes on the water.
The surreal images show on the surface of this sentimental
sensation.
Glowing...and living.
The glass gleans in the glory of life.

Victoria Kieffer

Free To Be Me!

FREE to be what people don't expect me to be.
    To be myself not what people think is me.

FREE to walk on hot coals.
    To dance, not feel inhibitive.

FREE to fly high.
    To do things to make myself a better person.

FREE to build a wall around me, so I'll know if you take
    time to tear it down that you must really care.
        Too many pains of the past. I need more time to
    trust and get to know you.

LET me, be me!
    I'm still growing and developing who I am.

Patricia Ruth Wissert

New World?

One by one they pass me, pausing for a moment
　to bow down their head, then moving on past
　my up raised bed;
Through my closed eyes I see their eyes crying,
　as they bow their head I wonder if they how
　in sorrow or bow in happiness;
Someone shut my door to the outside world, my
　communication has been cut off to all
　foreigners to my new world, no matter how
　hard I try they seem oblivious to my voice;
They are lowering me down to my new world home and
　everyone is walking away with their head
　down, I am being drown to a bright light
　beyond the dark tunnel which I stand now;
My new life that sits beyond my old is where
　I am to be, no one can follow it it's not
　time, my mission is done and my time has come;
My purpose to walk has faded and my new purpose
　awaits me.

Kristine Meklune

My Gift

If I could choose for you one gift, of beauty without measure,
To carry in your secret heart and in your memory treasure,
I'd turn aside from wealth and power, I'd choose not jewels rare,
One thing alone I'd ask for you - that you would be aware:
Aware of beauty in the things surrounding you each day,
To greet the opalescent dawn, portending skies of gray
And still lift up your voice in song, with joy that life is yours
To humbly walk in brotherhood as long as life endures;
To be aware that for each joy there is a touch of sorrow,
Those you've loved and lost today will still be yours tomorrow.
To be aware of God's great love enfolding you each day
With love and sure direction, to guide you on life's way.

Nellie L. Truxal

Appreciate Simplicity

If I could soar above the earth and rise to a magic place
To close my mind to problems, stress and tears.
What would tempt me back again
And bring a happy smile to my tear stained face?

The sunlight on the water as it quietly ripples in the stream,
The laughter of a child as he takes his very first steps
A happy song that makes your senses reel
The softness of the moonlight; the quiet peace of a happy dream

A friend who offers you his hand to hold
And gives you strength when you feel you cannot cope
A tender look of love, exhilarating and fulfilling
From a lover - warm, understanding though never too bold.

Then I would appreciate and really come to understand
That what I have from day to day is all I will ever need.

Valerie Meyer

Puppet

I once was a puppet with many masters at the strings
They dress me in colors of camouflage and green
They taught me to function as a war machine
They moved me from my country and left me in the stream
They brought me back home but didn't cut the strings
They tied up my spirit said it didn't belong to me
They gave me a heart of anger for many many years
I found a special lady who picked up the shears
As she snipped the strings my eyes filled with tears
It took a lot of courage to do this sort of thing
I know when she is done my heart will finally sing

Robert Greenlief

One With The Sky

Aspiring to fly with the eagles,
　To float majestically in the skies,
To soar among the windswept cathedrals,
　To have no earthly ties.
To call the wind my brother,
　And the clouds my home,
To live among the mountains crags,
　Forever, among them I would roam.
To perch upon a mountain top,
　Waiting until such time
That I would spread my wings,
　And into the sky I would climb.
To feel the wind rush past me,
　Beckoning me forever on,
To be witness to the birth of every new day,
　In the early morning dawn.
I would ascend to the very threshold of heaven,
　Become one with the sky,
And death would never catch me,
　It would only hear the echoes of my cries!

Michael J. Fredde

The Garden

I sit on my porch in the fading sunlight,
To gaze at the place where I've spent hours of delight.
Bees buzz merrily over the rainbow of color to get,
All the sweet nectar my flowers will let.
Butterflies flutter happily throughout,
As though they wanted to sing and shout,
"What a wonderful day, to be winging about".
Fluffy grey clouds sail by overhead,
To bring gentle drops of rain to my quaint little bed.
The little seeds I planted grow into plants big and strong,
And give me a sense of peace and serenity, I know I belong.
Early morning is my favorite time
To look at my garden and watch Ladybugs dine.
While little drops of dew glisten and shine,
Wetting the leaves with luxurious grace.
My eyes wander to the Queen Ann's Lace,
The beauty fills my soul and puts a smile on my face.

Marie E. Martinez

Rocky

A Sapling sprouted some years ago
to grow into a big strong tree.
He had to fight for sun and rain
and room for his roots to run free.

How good he grew, so straight and tall
A beautiful picture he'd take.
His branches long and leaves spread wide
cool shade for his offspring he'd make.

Three saplings sprouted at different times
and room for them he made sure of.
So they could grow in the sun's warm glow
and his love his son's were sure of.

The wife he took was also strong
but her branches stretched a little farther.
To surround them all with God's beckon call
for they were the Mother and Father.

Vonciel Fordham

Goodbye Sox (My Friend, My Cat)

You left so suddenly, I never had a chance,
To hold you close and receive your glance.

You've been so very special since you arrived,
Down there in Fallbrook, so much alive!

You were so clever, I thought you could talk,
At least you survived that dreaded hawk.

As time went by we grew very close,
You nurtured my needs when I needed them most.

You accepted "Silly" and she accepted you,
By eating together your friendship grew.

Everyone that met you, loved you from the start,
All thirteen pounds, and most of that...heart!

You played with the birds or they played with you,
But, when you were hungry, one less of them flew!

A hunter you were, always stalking your game,
The gophers disappeared, as fact as they came.

Now you are free, you can do as you please,
And I hope where you are, there are no fleas!

I feel so much better, that I've said goodbye,
I still love you dearly, so I need...one more cry.

T. W. Sutton

Night Fireman

I work in a power house of night,
To keep a fire, hot and white,
To furnish steam that make the power,
To run the mill, hour by hour,
Watching the needle, rise and fall,
From six to twelve, best shift of all,
Whenever the water drops a bit,
Speed up the pump to replenish in,
And when the pressure falls too low,
Into the fire the shavings blow,
Recharge the water softener,
Once a night, and sometimes oftener,
Then with lubricant, I fill the oiler,
Of the pump that feeds the boiler,
And when all these jobs, at last, are done,
I check them over, one by one,
But only to find I have one more,
I clean forget to sweep the floor!

H. A. Dick

The Sparrow

A sparrow came to my window today
To let me know my Mom passed away
Moments later my phone began to ring
It was my Dad calling to tell me the same thing.

After hanging up the phone I went
back to the window to see
That the little sparrow was
still sitting there waiting for me

I sat at the window and cried most of the day
He sat on his side of the window never flying away

A few days later I returned home
from the funeral to see
Once again he had returned to comfort me.

Many people ask how could this all be
But that is between the sparrow and me.

Margy Ahnen

Special Love

Slowly I'll awake and then slowly I'll arise
To look at this world straight in the eyes
I'll try to overcome a fear I once believed
That there is not a woman that will accept my seed
When I see her I'll know she's the one
Because she will be as beautiful as a white winter sun
My fear is I won't be able to find her soon
So I can love and hold her beneath our big bright moon
This is something that I am longing to do
The people that long this more has to be few
I just wish that this is what one woman would see
But the women think different and no longer is that me
Some day soon please let her be mine
I want her to be my everlasting love of a lifetime
Because the last thing I want out of my life
Is to have this special love become my wife

Larry M. Wade

A Blackwoman

Love? I want to love.
To love, and be loved.
I love my black man. His dreams,
Fears and desires, they're all mine to share.
His love? Oh yes! It's mine.
And me? Girl, I'm open like a window
With warm sun rays, leading straight down to my soul.
He knows my inner being, my purpose,
And my self is his to belong.
Take me and undress me, kiss me and caress me.
Mmm...
Love me over and over and over.
I'm here and I'm yours
Hurt me? Please, oh please! Don't hurt me.
I'm your black woman
Just let me love you - yes, that's it baby
Take my hand, don't be afraid
I'm a black woman
Love me.

Michelle Alicia Collins

Walls I Have Built

There once was a time, when my heart was free,
To love one and all, and the same be towards me,
But it wasn't to be how I expected at all,
Cause my heart was there, always taking a fall.

So, I had to protect the one thing of mine,
To let no one in, expect the warm sunshine,
It was a fortress to protect me from pain,
And the only thing soothing was to hear gentle rain.

Many things happen as the years go by,
As they sometimes are difficult, to be explained why,
I've always believed that there's always a reason,
For whatever happens in whatever the season.

Since I've found you, I knew things would change,
My feelings are different, it's all been so strange,
How lonely I've been and so lost in the world,
I would escape to a place where together we curled.

Your existence brought back the hope I once lost,
Which I vow to cherish, at whatever the cost,
Now the pains are gone, along with the sorrow and guilt,
No more do they stand, are the "walls I have built."

Raven

Untitled

"Drunk again!" I hear myself say
To make a joke of the lurch and sway.
That's a gift of Parkinson's to me
And one that all can see.
Others are known only to me.
Better to smile and talk of other things.
Think of the blessings that life brings.
I have reached the age of eighty-two.
Something I thought I'd never do.
That span of years was not in my view.
Children and grandchildren
Show me love and respect.
As I love them back I know that
My love is all they expect.
That is the "silver lining" in my dark cloud.
It shines clear and bright and thunders loud.

Lilly Appel

The Downfall Of Winter

Winter.
To many it is a season of joy,
the cold and dark days it brings,
that can brighten someone's days,
and nights.

Winter promises a new year each time,
some are ready for it,
and some could wait a bit longer.
Either way the year begins and ends,
cold and dark.

The snowflakes fall from overhead,
each its own shaped and size,
none alike,
covering the ground with a white blanket,
and waiting for the spring sun to beat down upon it.

This whole season,
nature and its beauty are at rest,
waiting for the right time to blossom,
from season to season,
there is always, The Downfall of Winter.

Michael Lavine

Sights and Sounds of Blackness

To all black nubian kings and queens.
To Martin Luther and his dreams.
For cotton fields and plantations.
A time of pain in our South African Nation.
In '95 the first black man walks in space.
A large strive for the Black American race.
We left afro puffs for curly weaves.
Well, quite frankly I am pleased.
We must move ahead, but still look back.
Let's never forget the sights of black.

The Apollo Theater is a black musical landmark.
For those who made it big, that was their start.
"What it be sweet thang?"
A '70's phrase from our own black slang.
A jazz band on the New Orleans streets.
Playing for quarters, pennies, and dimes
You give a dollar, they'll play one more time.
We must move ahead, but still look back.
Let's never forget the sounds of black.

Nelley Ridley

Trouble

Sounds of warbled guitars strumming
to my heart, pulsing
against her soft, precious chest. My eyes
through the smoky walls of beer and dance
prey on another female,
and another.
Distracted I was by hairspray,
afraid - to die
so moonstruck.
Carpe Noctem. Pull
the trigger for the other wishes.
Her warm mouth of condensation nibbles
my neck
while alcohol scours
through my
anxious veins. For
my soul's sake,
Good-night, good-bye
would be
in order.

William Hayes

Promotion

Practice acts of constant civility
To offset random occurrences of hostility.
Ensure that you maintain a level of positivity
To avoid mental apathy leading to early senility.
Attempt to indulge in the "rich fruit of peace"
To refrain from ingesting the "meat of the evil beast!"
Gorge yourself in the fluid of fantasy
So that you never fall prey to the "clutch of inability."
Bathe your body and mind
In continual happiness
So that they don't become paralyzed;
Thus, regress!
Pamper your eyes with sites of beauty
So that your daily activities won't seem like
A "Tour of Duty!"
Do all of these things to keep your mind, body, and spirit
Young, challenged, and free from strife.
For these things promote Good Mental Health
Which in turn.......Promotes Life!

Nicole M. Jackson

Going Home

It is my prayer for you this day
to peacefully go upon your way.
With outstretched arms, may you soar
on wings of the Dove forevermore.

Leaving a tormented spirit below
of toil, strife and woe
release your soul; embrace the light
in a Heavenly Father take endless flight.

If I could, I would go with you hand in hand
to the Promise Land
and bask in the glory
of God's great story
where tears and sorrow
no troubles will borrow.

Cross over Jordan, precious one let the healing waters flow
now in your heart you know the infinite love of God, and His Son.

Go in love, that will never cease;
fly away home, drift into peace.
Embrace your father on the other side
and may eternal rest with you abide.

Nadene Perry

Love Yourself First

I tremble at the thought, but love is on my mind
To portray love on paper, what a foolish waste of time
On shoals of love, our greatest poets flounder and fail
Why then should I try to thread this treacherous trail

Poets are all who love and feel great truths
And love is the truth of all truths
Like a magnet it attracts anyone who takes pen in hand
To make sense out of love is every dreamer's plan

If love is such that no words can describe
And fools like me nonetheless stubbornly strive
To have love understood by all mankind
Know that I'm tuned more to my heart and less my mind

One thing is certain, a truth beyond question
The key to love is in one's own reflection
You must love yourself first or else
How can you hope to love someone else?

William L. Heinz

Kissing a Cracked Mirror

Whenever the opportunity comes to pass,
to re-evaluate a mans' worth, under glass.
Inventory his soul for direction and reason,
to anticipate change, like the month and season.

Differences and distinctions set all men apart,
none more revealing than the size of a mans' heart.
Any mind can discover cures, formulate the law,
pencil a child's' face from memory, hollow fingers draw.
Accepting love from this soul, warmth and flesh appear,
to animate desire, tragically a dream so few hold dear.

Tony Sacco

Rita Bard

God made Rita special,
to reach out and shelter the living.
Her star shone bright,
to lead the young and old, along the path of light.
Teaching Moses' law with a song,
that God knows our deeds and thought all along.
Through cancer and sorrows, her example set fast,
showing God is always first and last.
When my friend Rita died,
the angels must have cried.

Mary Tragus

Your Friend

If you find that you need a friend sometime
To share your troubles and ease your mind
To hold your hand to comfort thee
Then you can always call on me.
To sit with you in times of sorrows
To be there for you for today and tomorrow
To share with you everything I have
To guide you right in never doing what's bad
To help you in prayer to the Lord above
To fill your life with peace and love
I'll be there for you when you're in need
I'll prove to you I'm a friend indeed
I'll keep you warm, I'll wipe your tears
I'll laugh with you in times of cheers
I'll love you too with all my heart
If ever I'm given this start this part
This life I live is just for thee
Only you can fulfill my destiny
On this my love you can depend
I being your friend to life's very end.

LaToya Natasha Stoll

Advice

Mother-like, I often wished
To shield my children from tears,
Somehow to wave a magic wand,
And wipe out hurts and fears.
But, luckily, a wiser voice
Said, "No that would be wrong,
To grow and learn, they need
A blend of sorrow and of song.
To really help these dear ones,
Teach them to meet each day
With unfailing kindness
To those who share the way,
Of course, they must have faith and hope,
An added dash of mirth,
Then their trip will be a real delight
On this wondrous place called Earth."

Kathryne Hitchen

Come the Morning Rise

Silver silky, moon beams, cleaving yet to tree leaves - giving way
to soft golden rays of light - striking mountains high;

Come the morning rise, now come the morning rise

When creatures of the darkness have taken final glance,
and sleepy beasts awaken trading haunches for a stance
Busy notes of earthy ways tingle early air,
the crispness of the first cut breeze - a day to promise fair;

Come the morning rise, now come the morning rise

High held heads of prairie dogs, in roadside groups abound
first flight feathered young ones take the launch
    freedom facet now is found.
Guarded colors of flowers are shown - to heaven high, with pride
Kids of antelope and deer are leaping - flying into sky;

Come the morning rise, now come the morning rise

Now usher out the lazy night and satisfy the search
for light - Heavens' hopes, our planets' size:

Come ahead the morning rise
    So come the morning rise.

C. W. Hess

My Overnight At Grandma's

I tried and I tried for what seemed like year
    To stay overnight at Grandma's.
I'd pack my bag and Mom would drive me over
    To stay overnight at Grandma's.

With a smile on my face, I'd run into the house
    To stay overnight at Grandma's.
I'd give her a hug and tell her I couldn't wait
    To stay overnight at Grandma's!

Mom and Grandma would talk a bit—while I waited
    To stay overnight at grandma's.
Then Mom would hug me and tell me to have a fun time
    Staying overnight at Grandma's.

As mom walked out the door to leave, I was so excited
    To stay overnight at Grandma's.
I ran to the big window to wave Goodbye—ready
    To stay overnight at Grandma's...

But at the car slowly backed away,
Tears would start streaming down my face.
Grandma would run outside and wave Mom back—and I realized
I had to wait just a little longer to stay overnight at Grandma's!

Lori Radecki

My Friend

To the friend who always listened to what I had to say,
To the friend who stood close by me, when others turned away,
You've treated me like a sister in so many ways, throughout the
years,
You often made me smile, while wiping away a tear,
You helped me find my inner strength, that was lost along the way,
It was your friendship I often turned to, that helped get me
though each and every day,
And now that we're so many miles apart,
Your friendship I cherish and hold close to my heart,
So wherever you go and what ever you do,
If ever you need me, I'll be there for you,
A friend is someone who listens and cares,
I'd like to say think you for always being there.

Kathy Hamlin

What Happen's When The Lord Needs You

Do you turn and run,
To think, few could get the work done,
Or do you stay and pray,
To have thy Lord, get you through the day.

What will he do for you now
you need to pray, and see how,
his love will ever show through,
in everything you do.

How he will give strength a new.
He will show how you grew,
Through his holy words divine,
that they give grace, glow, and define.

Linda Hughes

The Pale Horse

Death comes to us all, sometimes lingering, sometimes swift.
To those in the city, or on the ocean set adrift.
It comes for children, adults and seniors alike,
Whether you own a car, or only ride a bike.
Gender doesn't matter, men, women, boys and girls.
Neither does hair. Long, blonde or black with curls.
Race is not an issue, nor the color of your skin.
Whether you're European, or American Indian.
It comes for the rich, it comes for the poor.
One day it will come, knocking at your door.
*This morose poem was inspired by the untimely
death of my beloved Fiancee, Darlene Munoz.
Whom I love, and will always cherish our short
time on this earth together. It is to her this
poem is dedicated.*

Rudy R. Moreno

Searching For Self

A whole life time it may take
To understand and really see
Who and what and why you are
The way you are.
The truth, so often hidden from youths eyes
Is rich and deep, yet it's been known
To make one weep.
Children! Do not hide yourself in fear.
Many family members long since gone
Are near—inviting you to share
Their circle of accomplishment and love.
So, take the time to seek them out.
Do not ignore and NEVER doubt
Their love and hope for you
Is to win life's often grueling race
With courage, spirit, wit, and grace.

Lee L. Pierce

My Creator

My life's book my creator planted firmly in my hands.
To understand the thoughts of heavenly pure wonderment of delight.

Old time maketh new again.
Seasons change in a voice from near.
Afar the trumpets sound; my heart hears the beginning anew;
   treasures beyond belief....
Glorious times wait for their moment, surely father
times motionless hour-glass; steadfastly I count my time.
Monuments of calendars, timeless thought they seem;
I've never forgotten.
At last I'm aroused to feel for my first moment,
   truly a gift of love.
Jericho's Soul being I,
   loveth not frightening despairs,
fashioned envies, nor taketh council with transgressions
which destroyeth the heartwalking beams
   of mine heart felt labour.

Paul Gamer

Why I Write

I write because it relieves my mind of tension.
To visualize life simple and carefree, Is my favorite vision.
Writing puts me in situations, I'll probably never be.
To put experiences down on paper also, let's me share my memories.
Be they good or bad, without them, I wouldn't be the me I am.
I encourage you, pick up a pen or pencil and write when you are tense.
Just write what comes to mind.
You will often find your worries are right there on the lines.

Pamela D. Jones-Dukes

Don't Give Up

As I walk life's narrow road each day, I seem
to walk to close the edge, I begin to look at the
world around me and this I pray, "Dear Lord, guided
me back to the center of the road please, I pray
do not let me stray." Jesus then simply replies
"Life is a tough road but you can Survive, my
child see your faith and Don't give up."
As my burdens increase. I feel as I can't go
on, the load is just too much. And this I
pray," Dear Jesus my burdens are heavy, forgive
me Lord Jesus help me to go on." Again he
Just Simply replies "Life can be a tough road, but
you can survive my child see you strength
and Don't give up."
Then its all so clear my faith and strength
are really there, now I have the courage.
to go on. And this I pray" Dear Lord I
thank you for reminding me of you love,
this road can be so tough but Jesus because
of you I really can make it, sweet Jesus I won't give up."

Victoria Hughes

Flowers

Flowers are pretty to your sight;
They make Congratulations right.
Flowers Compliment a tender touch;
Saying, "I love you very much."
Flowers are sweet to the smell;
Expecting everything to be swell.
Flowers, with words you like to hear;
Will bring big smiles and good cheer.
Flowers, with candy show good taste;
And true love will not go to waste.
Flowers, are for the human race;
Looking for that perfect place.
Flowers grow almost everywhere;
Let's have Love and Freedom without Fear!

Victor S. Wallace

Untitled

So beautiful it is
to watch
nature take its course
throughout the day
We take it for granted...
that the sun will shine, rise and set
that the moon will glow
the rain will come
that leaves will fall, flowers will bloom
and the birds will sing...
We take for granted
that this earth is forever
even as we consume all of its splendor
cultivating a land of waste
we sit back and watch
the currents shift, the tides wave
the mountains roar, and the winds
blow....everlasting change.

What Ever Happened To...

  "Keep America Beautiful"
  D. S. Bell

To Rosemary ...And (To Sara Grace....Who Died)

Dear Rose, I have this great need inside of me
To write to you.....But you are dead!
And I cannot input this "Death" thing into my brain...
Not FICTION now....But FACT....based upon....finality!
  Rosemary, the Novelist. A unique and talented writer,
  Who gave birth to her character. Sara Grace, until
  'Sara Grace' became a human being. That DIED too soon...along
  with you.
You were the fine, gold thread with your smooth, enunciated words
That taught us much with your soft spoken wisdom.
  Your bitter marriage to Bogie! Oh God! Life was hard for you!
But Bogie, who preceded you in Death still held you captive in
His old abusive prisoned World...And now that your door
Of Freedom had swung wide....IT CLOSED!
  WHY? Rosie...Why did you have to die?
  Never having shown the world how rare your talent,
Waiting, Lying knurling, there inside your mind
So disciplined...Hungry to spread its wings and SOAR.....
Among the Greats...But having died, Bogie still clutched
  your fragile gown,
Soaked in patience, wrinkled, torn...and thin, threadbare
From awful years with HIM!...still snatched at you,
And you, too weak to fight again.....still held you tight
  and pulled you in!

  Lucille Milburn Wall

Love to Understand

There are many different words, expressions, phrases people put
together to explain this feeling, love.

Everyone is promised love because love is forever. In the day or
night, sleet or snow you don't have to ask or question it.
The father we all share said so.

For the one you share this feeling, there's nothing you wouldn't do.
For as you do for them, they will gladly do for you.

Love is a short and simple word so seldom used or even heard.
I love that car, or I love money.
Now you hear that each and every day and that's quite funny.
How can you love something that can't love you back?
Pause — take a moment and think about that.

  Murphy Dwayne Ewing

Too Young

Too young for wilted flowers,
Too young for deserts
That explode in the eyes
Of a newborn child crying out in the night
For relief of a tortured stomach.

Too young for mortal wounds
Brought on by knives,
Cars and booze;
Too young for rejected minds
Silenced by venomous oppressors
Who repress benign victims of scorn
With ruling belts.

Too young for torture;
Too young for scars of the BODY,
Of the MIND
And of the SOUL.

Too young for demolished flesh
That withers away into dust;
And most of all,
Too young to DIE.

  Kiki Stamatiou

Transcription

Shorthand into a document translating,
Transferring someone else's thoughts so clear,
Translucent thoughts disturb my concentrating.
My keyboarding transports through the veneer.

Transfusions of ideas are awaiting.
Fleeting and transitory, they appear.
My hopes, transcendent, reach to heights elating.
My mind in flight, a transverse course I steer.

Letters transposed and grammar abdicating,
All my transgressions change the atmosphere.
My eyes transfix on errors I'm creating.
I'm now aware of what's transpiring here.

Business transactions must have regulating
Transparent codes to which I must adhere.
Transplanted back to routine punctuating,
Mind's reverie transforms to souvenir.

The room transmits a mood intimidating.
Transmuted doors, blocked windows instill fear.
A transient vision is illuminating.
The open transom beckons as I cheer.

  Margaret Bebble

Driver

  As I try to forget my past, my past keeps haunting me.
  Traveling the highway of my destiny searching; searching for
someone to be.
  Moving up the road and rolling back down, to young to know
to young to turn around.
  Riding the rails of fantasy, I hitch a ride looking for my
destiny.
  Danger comes and danger goes, a warrior nobody knows.
  I've traveled near and traveled far, lost in the sands of time
fighting; fighting for who you are.
  Nobody to show me, nobody to point the way, fighting to survive
another day.
  The winds of change are mean and rough, some can't stand it
some ain't tough.
  A warrior in reality never knows where he is going or what
he will be; or will he ever stop searching for his destiny.

  Mike Jeanquart

431

Khazaria: The Forgotten Empire

They came from Central Asia,
  Triumphant Turkic horsemen of the steppe.
   Hun Avar Bulgar Pecheneg
Great trading center of the medieval world:
  Silks and furs, jewelry and coins.
Refuge for persecuted Byzantine and Persian Jews.
  Menorah, cross, crescent - tolerance for all.
King Bulan's angel appeared to him in a dream:
  "Create a tabernacle and convert your people,"
   Tribe of Simeon, Togrul Messengers of God.
Cyril evangelized to Khazar rabbis, but failed;
  Judaic stronghold on Khazar consciousness.
   Wise men Isaac, Avram, and Pesach.
Khazar swords sharpened on only one edge,
  Their power relentlessly crushed by the Rus.
   Assimilation. Judaization. Slavicization.
Hear the voices long since retired -
  Ashkenazim, Szekely, Kumyk, Karachai:
Children of a Vanished Empire,
  Tengri worshippers of the Sky.

    Kevin Alan Brook

Coping with a Problem

Sitting up at night
trying not to cry.
You're asking yourself why.

You're coming up with reasons that will stop the pain,
but you know the reason why.

Talking on the phone;
going to a friend.
They say it will happen again.

You say the line was disconnected and you couldn't get through,
So you hung up and tried again.

Going to a shrink;
come back another day.
Try when you can pay.

You say taking these pills is the only way,
and you collapse while you pray.

    Zach Nix

Feelings For You

When I smile at you it's my disguise
Trying to hide the pain in my eyes
I know you won't open your heart to me,
But I'll search this world till I find the key.
Maybe someone has hurt you before.
Now your afraid it will happen again,
But I'm not trying to hurt you,
Its your heart I'm trying to win.

I won't be happy until you are in my arms.
And I know you're really mine.
But I'll keep hunting until I find your love,
I don't know what you think.
I don't know what you want me to be.
I just know that I want you and wish you wanted me.

    Kenn Pate

Summer Was Over

There they stood speaking their silent sighs,
Trying to word their lonely good-byes..

Summer was over, it was time to go,
They fell in love more than anyone could know..

Days on the beaches, nights in the town,
They were so proud of the new love they found..

They both knew it would end on this day,
There was nothing to stop it, what could they say?.

This page in their lives, would stay in their hearts,
Their summer was over, now they would part...

They thought of how it could have been,
How much they wished it would happen again...

He clinched her tight and got ready to leave,
Summer was over, as her tears rolled down his sleeves..

She walked towards the plane that would take her far away,
Only to stop, turn and wave...

As she sat in her seat, she reached in her coat,
Pulled out a piece of paper on which he had wrote...

You are my dream, I've longed for sought,
Summer may be over, my love, we are not..

    Rob Casale Jr.

A Tribute To My Dad

December, the month of the miracle birth,
Two great people came to this earth,
One person was a likeable lad,
He married mom, and became my Dad.
As God giveth, he taketh away.
Which makes for one very sad day.
It leaves the three of us most sad.
The sorrowful day, God called dad.
You were near, and now you're far.
We'll watch the sky for the guiding star,
For it matters not on the earth, or heaven's above
To you dear Dad, you have all our love.

    Marguerite Weidenhaft

My

Impossible to conquer, easy to know.
Two minds as one, will always grow.

I am I, as no one see.
The hardest part of life, was learning me.

Know thy will on what can be done.
Mental satisfaction is the meaning of fun.

Be yourself, a natural - fact.
Anything beyond is only an act.

The sun shines, while the moon glows at night.
What's reality and who said it's alright?

To avoid worry, you must seek new goals.
If thought about, it's still a role.

From beginning of birth, until we die.
Life isn't perfect, can anyone tell why?

"I THINK I'LL BE MYSELF"

    Sherry A. Pinkney

Love Is Something That Is Shared

Love is something that is shared between
two people from their inter-most being.

The beauty of the birds as they sing their
love songs to one another.

Love is the sound of children's laughter on a
bright sunny day.

Love is something that this world needs
plenty of.

Love is God's creation for all humanity.

Love is forgiving one another, and making
peace within.

Love doesn't have to be a dream because
loves comes from our inter-most being.

For we were all created to love.

Sheila Johnson

Brother

One Apache, One Navajo,
Two tribes, one land.
The days were countable,
I was first, then you.
You were my battery, as I was yours.
Tempers flared as moons passed,
and the battle for the edge would always last.
Though it was the day you reminded me of our name,
that broke the glass.
Since its our name that will remain the same

Simon Gislimberti

You'll Know Where To Find Me

Hide me away under my bed
under a blanket
in my closet
Sheltered away from the cruel world
until
destiny spins round and fate knocks at my door
Cover me from the everydayness of life
the bills, the calls
the misfortune of man on the nightly news
Wake me when peace is at arms reach and dreams can come true
and hope
can be picked from trees like
multicolored leaves
Find me when good fortune is present
and despair and frustration is nowhere
in sight
Reach for me when the sun shines yellow
and happiness pours from the sky in its rays
When disappointment is unknown
you'll know where to find me.

M. O'Brien

Getting Out Of Bed!

My mom said she called me five or six times
to get out of bed and be ready before nine
She didn't know I had long been awake
since the clock on the wall said "ten till 8"
I threw out my arms and stretched my legs
'Cause I knew she was down there fixin' my eggs
But my eyes were shut tight and just wouldn't open
So I simply relaxed and kept on Hopin'
For a few more minutes of peaceful sleep
the first I'd had in nearly a week
Suddenly I heard her heavy steps on the stairs
so I "jumped" out of bed and started brushing my hair.

Martha Robinette

Forever Asleep

Forever asleep,
under the ground, 6 feet deep.
There your body lay,
every long and peaceful day.
The golden streets of Heaven will your soul now roam.
Forever asleep in your eternal home
so wise, yet so much like a child.
So strong, yet so tender and mild.
A life full of pleasure and peace,
your life-long, built-up energy you now release.
Never again will you hurt, or feel the dreaded gain.
Never again will you feel the pain.
So guarded by this scarlet blanket,
in a bed of roses you will make it.
Make it, while never moving a limb,
make it in the strangest hymn.
You're open, full, and free.
Not a single, care or mortal worry.
Forever asleep,
playing in Heaven's green fields, so deep.

Rachel Martin

A Treasure

Search you needn't do - but to
unpack, let go and exhale.
You will find - peace be unto you.

It is with you during the light of day
surrounding you during the uncertainty of the night
bringing you warmth - peace be unto you.

It is everywhere you go
in everything you do
you needn't be unsure - peace be unto you.

Peace be unto you,
now that you are who you are
and not what someone else wants or expects you to be.
Peace be unto you - now that you are you!

What a treasure to behold,
Peace, now that you've found you.

Maxine D. Thompson

I Thought I Knew, But I Didn't

The madness and anger was concealed cleverly,
until it had the painful grip it viciously was waiting for.

I knew it was not what it showed itself to be.

I felt the dangerous potential it had, but instead
I foolishly ignored it.

It was hunting all this time, it was waiting patiently
for a perfect time to strike.

Now as it viciously tears away, I desperately try
to fight and cling on to the little unity there is.

It sits there in triumph, it knows it can win if nothing is done.

But I alone will triumph over it.
It sees me as an obstacle, but little does it know that I
am the power and strength that will cast its malevolent
presence back to the evil it came from.

Paola Quinones

Lost Love

I'll love you forever or until my dying day
Until my life is over and there's nothing left to say
When I remember the days when our two hearts were one
And know that I loved you second to none
Even when life's over, I'll still feel the pain
I tried to go on with life but only in vain
You tried to forgive me, but you weren't to blame
Even in the end, I'll still feel the shame
I woke up with hope in each new day
You were first in my thoughts as I bowed my knee to pray
There's no way to describe how long my love will last
Forever and a day will at some time come to past
You were my only true love for so many years
I loved you through the good times and even through the tears
I wanted to forget you after many years past by
But I never stopped loving you no matter how hard I tried
My heart is filled with sadness and my eyes are filled with tears
You're still my love of a lifetime after all these years
Now as my life is over, I'll take this love to my grave
I'll still hold the memories and heartache of a love I couldn't save.

Tami Jo Johnson

Tears Not In Vain

The raindrops fall slowly on a dreary day,
Until the dark grey clouds make their way
Through the storm they float, hovering above
Your only umbrella.... the ones you love.
Praying for clear skies you beg Him, please
As the weight of the clouds bring you down to your knees
Your heart a bit weaker until the storm is past,
Only sunshines and rainbows are in the forecast.
The calm winds set in to keep pushing away,
Those dark grey clouds that infringe on your day
When the windows are finally clean and dry,
Start to move quicker and push on to get by
Take in the beautiful sunsets and skies,
And when the rain returns just close your eyes
At least let the tears wash away all the pain
So you know that your struggle was not all in vain.

Patricia Ann Mora

"A Wild Flower"

I was just another flower growing in the wilderness
until your shower of love fell upon my pedals and
I became a breathtaking rose full of radiance. As you
walk up to me and touch my pedals I'm delighted in
your inspired smile as you ponder in thought. For a
moment I lavish in splendid thoughts of you uprooting
me and taking me to your own little garden. Your
delicate hands carefully moving over my stem and the
ground surrounding me, making sure no wind will carry
me off in the dead of the night. I will gladly open
my soft pure pedals for your love and the beauty within
my soul will be for your majestic eyes only. I will
have no fragrance until you appear in my view and will
only then shine open with gratification. I'll thrive
on your loving heart, your exquisite smile, your tenderness,
your every move. Just never leave or my pedals
with fall off to blow in the wind and once more I'll
be that flower you saw in the wilderness.

Stephanie M. Wright

How Heavy the Cross

The weight of the cross I must feel
Upon my back, the burden's so real.
JESUS my Lord suffered for me,
As He bore the cross of calvary!

Heavy, by far, it must have been-
Carrying the sins of all men.
He was so strong compared to me...
WHY OH WHY, did this have to be?

His love is so GREAT, mine so weak,
Love so divine... I daily seek.
His love shining through all that I do-
As I struggle and toil this life through!

Loving, caring and hurting you see,
As He bore the cross of calvary...
Never concerned that He might fail,
Trusting His Father, whose love did prevail!

Louise Crenshaw Mobley

Sonnet To Joy, My Love, My Wife

Fragile and precious is my love for you.
Upon the branches of life we are perched.
Into nature's wind, rain, snow, and sun, we must fly.

The tree of life and grace is our shelter.
By its nurturing river, we are cleansed and refreshed.

Love's height is a crystal delight;
It desires simplicity and solace.
Love's branches, like its roots, grow day by day.
We, too, must exceed the bounds of the season's sentiment.

In the rising and down pouring of the waters of life,
May we in confidence abide.
In the stillness of God's peace,
May our vision and wisdom be held in love's rich soil.

Strong and secure is my love for you.
You are a reflection of my desire to grow more in the image
of bold and redeeming love;
To be an authentic giving, creative force;
To be like God in my presence with you.

May our wings of joy, peace, and forgiveness find strength and
security in each other and in God, everlasting.

Vergel L. Lattimore III

Love

A mysterious experience, a new feeling, a new sensation.
Two living being's drawn together by an unexplained force.
Two being's sharing the same unusual mood.

This strange new wonderful feeling can bring us so close
And yet tears us apart. It has the power to create and it has
the power to destroy.

Like the whisper of the wind lost in a mindless storm love is
forever searching for a home.

The experience is like quenching a thirst...then you are
satisfied...then you are thirsty again.

What is this thing called love anyway?

Michael Clarke

A Virtuous Woman

A woman of God.
V irtuous in nature.
I ntegrity upheld.
R ighteousness is the key.
T ruth in seeking God.
U nsual is this woman.
O ut of the world is her style.
U nique style of living.
S piritual guidance from the Lord.

W ifely duties are adhered to.
O ffends the world of Non - Christianity.
M ankind is of the image of God.
A cts of christianity are done willingly.
N ever worships anything or anyone but God.

Lynette E. McCall

Winter Walk in the Lost Valley Glencoe

Gullies shadowed by black, dripping rocks,
Vertically descending in rough staggered blocks.
Crisp, fresh snow consolidating scree,
Dripping, wet icicles hanging free.

Shimmering ice curtains on windy wet walls,
Solidified flutes, formed by the falls.
Blue, ultra violet in deep trodden snow,
Merged with the spectrum of a waterfall's flow.

Beauty is shown in bursts of sun gold,
Shadows grow long as the weather turns cold,
Colours retreat to black shades and grey,
The winter night comes, gone is the day.

Martin Musson

How Can I Aid My Sister?

Her flirty, feisty, funny ways seep, creep through my mind like a
vibrant flash. And I ask, how can I aid my sister?

Her voice laughs with me as it always has, at jokes too corny to
repeat. But when I listen the echo is only mine. And I ask, how
can I aid my sister?

So much love flourished between us—yet my soul feared to
reach out, to touch. Why? because thousands of keep-you-
informed articles failed to prepare me and reality hit home.
Ouch! And I ask, how can I aid my sister?

The laughter, fun, and feistiness may be gone, but AIDS...
...still wraps its cruel arm around our blacks, challenging,
"if you don't educate your sisters, why should I? —"I don't discern,
and don't care that I'm seizing blacks, I'm a mouse that roars."

AIDS is real!

Who else must succumb to it's devouring grasp before we wake
up and admit, yes, AIDS has us all by the b——?

So I ask. How can we aid our sister?

Love her, befriend her, support her, touch her, educate her,
pray for her....

For it may be your sister today, but it may well be you tomorrow!

Menrose Killion

Promoting Baby Doe

Congratulations you've got yourself another
victim of circumstance. There's gonna
be plenty enough adrenalin pumping
throughout baby Doe. Excuse me mothers
and fathers. The planted traditional
complex is perceived. As a result,
baby is displaying over the speed limit
adrenalin. Who's monitoring those
thin lines there treading with the
quaritine like complex? Excuse me to
who's reading this. Are you monitoring
baby doe? Or are you just seeing the complexion?
Outside looking in or inside looking out,
are you keeping an eye on those thin lines
there treading with over the speed limit
adrenalin pumping? Or all in favor of
the finger pointing game?
You can run but you can't hide from
baby Doe.

Angie

Traditions

Generations of life, perpetual learnings,
Victories, defeats, kudos and yearnings.
Small windows of time, just glimpses of living,
We make our traditions, and remember our giving.

Valentines, mistletoe, fireworks, picnics,
Brass bands, egg hunts, sleigh rides and car trips,
Staples we choose to bind our existence,
Clinging to love with strength and persistence.

Let's make this our light, while we are still here;
Let it shine on our times for our children to share.
So they may retrieve them again and again,
Adding their lights and re-singing the hymn.

So rare are the moments when we touch heaven;
When we are just people with no labels or pennants.
When in battle or in loving we rise above clouds,
Traditions are those times we make our God proud.

Robert J. Klesko

Hello....

It's been a long time my friend, since I've heard your
voice that is. And now that all of my pain is over, you
come along with all of your sorrows. As usual I reach out
to grasp your hand to pull your back to reality. But just as
you catch your balance I fall into the mystic array of where
you've been. Finding no one there to pull me out again. Each
time I come to your rescue, will I never learn? I've
recreated images of us in my mind time after time
wondering how I could have gone wrong. Knowing how close we
we're, and how close we've been, how could I ever let you
fall again.
You were never there to hold my hand or share my pain.
You always seemed to be miles away. I could never understand
why your pain hurt you less than I, or why it hurt me so bad
to see you cry. I've always been so trusting, maybe even naive.

It's been a long time my friend next time you call I hope
I'll be in.

Melissa R. Rupe

War Is Hell

"War is hell" McArthur said. Now thousands of soldiers are dead.
  War is not for the weak or the strong.
  Not to prove which one's right or wrong.
  War is to prove who's got the brain,
  And the one who loses is left with pain.
  So many words can describe this battle or war.
  I can write it on paper and give you more.
But as I sit in my chair I can hear the cry of people in despair.
I hold nothing against the war, as a matter of fact I could ask for more.
  But, we would lose more soldiers of kin,
  And who would know who's gonna win?
I can think of better things we can do instead of fight.
But unfortunately somebody in command is not that bright.
  And so I leave you to decide.
  Men or Mice? Pick your side.
  Protest or support, I don't care.
  It's your choice of the pair.
  But remember this good and remember it well.
  War is not good, War is Hell!

   Katherine Jones

How Bright the Light

How bright the light that caresses this day,
Warming my soul with each golden ray.
Absorbing its glow while rejoicing in life,
Yet full of the knowledge that the world lays in strife.

Children molested while their parents kill,
Gang wars erupting, corpses lay still.
Maniacs on subways, uzis, and dope,
Silencing happiness, passion, and hope.

Presidents menacing, machismo, be men,
Your country's like mine or begin to defend.
Greed forcing hunger, people are dead,
Because there's no food for them to be fed.

Goodness survives, saints keep on trying,
Creating a balance to deny the dying.
Often it seems like a hopeless task,
The devil is dancing behind the lamb's mask.

Oh bright light which envelopes this day,
Pierce the darkness that humans portray.
Send forth the message into this rift,
That life is so precious, a cherished gift.

   Michael Keshigian

Prince Of Darkness

Coming out of the night your shadow looms over me like the
warmth I have always searched for.
Your presence builds a longing urge in the depth of my soul.
I find myself drawn into your eyes with a passion I have
never yet felt before.
Your smile soothes my aching loneliness.
Your touch takes away the sorrows that have built up inside me.
Your velvet voice is wrapped around me like a warm friend
on a chilling night.
If I could kiss your lips but, once I would be satisfied
for the rest of my days until the end of time.
You will always be my Prince of Darkness.

   Michele Tesch

Child of Divorce

The biggest hurt I ever had —
  was not to know my real dad.

At Christmas time, a simple toy —
  from him would have been the greatest joy.

No one to hold me with a big strong arm —
  when it was dark and I feared harm.

It makes me feel 'Oh so sad' —
  never to have walked hand and hand —
  between Mom and Dad.

Life is not a wonderful game —
  when you grow up with nothing but his name.

He wasn't there when I fell down —
  he wasn't there, he was never around.

He wasn't there the day I was married —
  he wasn't there when his grandchildren I carried.

I wonder —
  will he be there, the day I am buried.

   Mary Moose

Seasons Of Love

In the Spring of life the love we shared,
Was reflective of our years,
The dreams and plans of tender youth,
Seem shed like angel tears.
Life's Summer brought a special love,
That again will never be,
Our lives were shared with precious mates,
That gave us families.
With Autumn's chill the lives we knew,
Were slowly torn apart,
The ones we loved were taken,
Though we've kept them in our hearts.
And now with Winter comes a love,
More than a passing thing,
So the life ahead will be fulfilled,
With the one we loved in Spring.

   Vicki Cler

Ripples (When Beauty Seems)

Standing among the shadows of the weeds - the child me -
Watching trance-like the now stilled quiet center of the pond.

Out rolled - a moment ago - the at first clear struggling waves
From the murky under pull of a weight now hidden at the center.
Where something precious selfishly thrown now shrouded pulled down -
In even rhythms reversed the circles cascaded away
As they fought against the secret of the water's fall.
The line of each circumference softly stretching smooth
With each expanding motion to near transparency;
The spreading of each ring's diameter
Evoking lines so delicately subtle eyes alone no longer see
Their definition between the dry golden stalks of grass
On a yellow-bright sun filled day in fall (or is it early spring?).
The surface water too cloaks sapphire blue - a day sparkling clean.
Me myself - not tall at all - watcher of this sad memorial's memoir
Of a day openly adorned in nature's beauty hiding secrecy now unseen.
Night terrors and shades hold no candle to the truth a moment past —
Seen in daylight's dress a silenced child's scream - a poet's dawn.

Now secret silence suits itself in emotions through my dreams -
A quilted web of confusion's scraps sown together when beauty seems.

   Sidona Marie Hunsberger

Before

So many oceans breathe between us, deeper than what I could swim
Waves that seem forever crashing stealing me away from him
With every silent moment passing, allowing little time to feel
It shares with me the time I need to let my lonely sorrow heal...

For all the silence brought between us, memories begin to die
Sunless days and dreamless hours float among a crimson sky
Holding me with burning passion, fires burn inside so deep
Crying not to leave his presence begging me forbidden sleep.

Smiles that were true with loving, lips that couldn't stand to part
Two shadows that were bound as one but never had the chance to start
Feelings full of ecstasy alive with innocent desire
Growing in a world secluded, suffocating flames of fire...

It seems so long I've felt his fingers caressing every hidden curve
Roaming where my innocence would burst with every tingled nerve
I want so much to taste his juices, to swim inside his swirling pools
But time has stolen all our love and drowned us like forgotten fools.

Sherri Weiner

The River Of Life

If I were a river, I'd flow on and on,
waving goodbye, till I'm gone;
passing my friends, from shore to shore,
hoping to see, many many more;

I'd make my friends, swimming in me;
as happy as, happy can be;
I'd revive the things, I want to see;
the things growing, along side of me,

I'd be a part of life today,
in my own, little, special way;
there's much need of things, like you and I,
to take the place, of our friends that die;

Then I'd flow on and on, out to sea,
and make it a part, a part of me;
beginning a life, of something new,
is what I was made, made to do.

Robert A. Gagliandi

Tesfia the Village of Hope

In this village we are held together by a thin rope.
We all kneel down as one and pray and hope;
that the dryness doesn't parch our soul,
so we can watch our children grow and see their lives unfold.
We all need so many things: Food for body, food for thought,
we need to provide clear liquid to an idea scorched by drought.
These needs eat away at us like some plague or disease
Sending us down on scabby knees;
to pray, to yell, to curse, to cry, to scream
for someone to help us replant our dream
so the water will flow blue again
and we can rid our bodies of this ugly sin.
Yes, in this village we are one,
sharing shade under the same sun.

O. H. Burbridge Jr.

Good Memories

Good memories we keep, to others loan or give
True riches from infancy, each day we live
Our lives are embroidered in memories.
Threads different, as patterns, design decrees,
True riches to recall, feel, smell, hear, see
Once again years, moments, people, youthful glee.
Cogitation glorious jubilee, when all else flees
Memories' rich embroidered wrap warms, frees
Us from cold, pain, poverty that is, might be
Today or tomorrow, what's left for, or of, you and me.

O. Emily Williams

Special People

There are Special people in the world
We all know some.
We just want You to know
You are among them.

In time of strife, or bitter woe
You are always ready to go
To give time, support, whatever is needed
Your help and support are unimpeded.

Words are small and do not do justice
For what is in our hearts
For the love you have shown us.

God comes first
Your Family comes next
This is to say
You are the BEST.

Sandra L. Lowe

Penelope and Me

There's an affinity between Penelope and me,
We awaited our husbands' return from their Odysseys.
Penelope's wait longer, by many years, than mine.
Ancient travellers, contextually slower, needed time.

The life of chastity celebrated faithfulness of heart and hearth,
Unknowledgeable of the duration of lonely separation,
Placing the heart on the altar of faith, hoping to behold again
The hero's tender face, with fatigue lines, grown old in vain.

The traveller's quest is a sensitive uncertainty of time and space.
We imagine the time frame while at home arrayed in lace,
Whilst the fires of the heart and the passions of the soul
Are masked by comfort of attire, shrouded in time, we grow old.

Ulysses's quest, ended in decision, enjoyed a homecoming triumph.
Penelope's welcome: a hearty meal of body, soul and mind, he never
    more to roam!
My tired corporate warrior's quest stretched time ever so thinly,
Incurring a hero's breaking point, the sorrow of indecision;
Thanatos
    welcomed him.

Rose M. Guatelli

"The Ride"

The road feels fast under our feet
We can hear the hum from our tires.
    As the sun slowly sets on the path we ride
We can almost see the stars

    Sometimes we ride just as fast as we can
And sometimes we coast along slow
    The sun has now set on the path we ride
Now we will see the stars glow

    The night air is caressing our faces
We wish we could ride forever
    We must have ridden a thousand places
But to the darkness, we must surrender.

    So we turn our bikes, and start to ride
Back down the path we've just ridden
    The stars have lost there nightly glow
For behind the clouds they have hidden.

    Now we are back at the end of our ride
But tears we shall not shed.
    For we'll have the memories, of our ride
tonight as we lay in our bed

Vance G. Horton

What Will It Be?

One morning while hiking with my sister Peg,
We found a giant purple egg.

We tried to lift it, but it was too heavy.
We'll have to haul it in Daddy's Chevy.

Then we'll watch and wait awhile,
To see what hatches—bird or reptile?

Will it have feathers or leathery skin?
And who will be its next of kin?

Will it be herbivore or carnivore?
And will it always beg for more?

Will it be a friend or foe?
Only its mother could know.

Will it live on land, water, or up in a tree?
I hope Mom lets it live in our house with me!

Will it walk or fly or crawl?
I really hope it's a dinosaur most of all!

Lisa Tompkins Matta

The Power of Love

Love, with all its mysterious facets.
We hunger for its magic.
Its ability to elude us.
Its appearances and disappearances.
Its ability to inflict pain and
Its ability to soothe all the hurt.
Its ability to take us to an ultimate height,
as well as a devastating low.
Its excitement and its disappointments.
Its ability to give and take away.
Its pleasures and its cruelty.
Its ability to die and not die.
Its ability to live and not live.
Its ability to steal our hearts and
at times our mind.
Its ability to blind and confuse us.
Its ability to bring out the passion in us as well as the hate.
Its ability to create fear in us as well
as provide security for us.
Its ability to mend as well as to destroy.

Milagro Stella

You said you loved me, more than I know
We laid in bed, imagine the snow
    pelting on the ground
    sleeting on the pane
You said you loved me, and I prayed for the rain

Of Spring when time could validate
The pace of your heart, the sound you make
    my face in your hands
    our legs intertwined
You said you loved me, and I dreamt of sunshine

Beating down on our bodies, a red healthy glow
We'd lay 'til evening, like lovers who know
    sand on our backs
    beads on our skin
You said you loved me, and I tried to breathe in.

Laura Davey Solomon

Sleep

Welcome my friend
We meet again once more
I knew you'd reach me
For not once since the day I were born
Have you not met me with open arms.
I trust you complete,
Your warmth,
Your passion,
The adventures you hold in store for me,
-Always secret, only between us.
I know sometimes I've battled against you,
Although I've never despised you for winning.
Your my friend, with you I feel safe.
So with the moon and stars above,
Come take my hand, kiss me softly,
Take me to paths of new,
For always, it will be me with you.

Kaz J. Barker

Where Children Lead

Where children lead
We often have need.
Whether toward merriment
Or a place for anger to vent.

A child's way is quick,
Direct, unassuming, and slick.
Laughter is so easy for a little one,
And fright can quickly be turned to fun.

Without sidesteps or roundabouts to tarry them
Children can lead us on a whim —
A whim that is a place in the heart
Where children and men must often part.

At times we guide them, but when they lead,
The children fulfill a very real need,
To restore our faith and show us the present —
Where life is accepted and the moment is pleasant.

Bill Brand

Unshaded

Absence can make this poor ole beaten heart of mine yours

You should always know that you're the one to heal my abrasions

We state these things, yet knowing our true deep feelings.

One mind, one accord, that's how
we solve our differences.
Bubble is our true habitat.
Sharing keeps us truthful, let's
stay this way, we say.
If you see my light, run to it no questions
Come to me opened armed

Lust is not what we become of, nor end of

purity ripens heart, soul, mind
Our problems will only be problems, if let
Eternity could we become
come to me opened hearted

Listening could build answers, questions
Questions that could be unquestionable God know this
He gives us this long chain of mercy
We withhold this, we die together eternity
Come to me open minded

LeAnn Caudle

Earth Prayer

The delta earth and sky were one
We sometimes talked of heaven
And when the twilight hid the sun
Survival was our leaven

Gods and goddesses were many
They showed us all the way
When searching for true love, there wasn't any
We always had to pay

And we continuously pay
With pain at the end of a day
With thoughts to comfort
With thoughts to stay

With thoughts that understand and
thoughts that motivate
The two are suitable mates
They dance and undulate

And when the night is almost o'er,
And these two are happy, hand in hand
They will not go gentle into that good night
They will live on and preserve the land

Susan Spivey Freydl

Birds In Sunlight

Slicing the air they catch fragments of sunlight;
we watch what these tiny shapes do,
celebrating distance. We know they are birds,

but at that height we don't see them as birds —
rather as some kind of effect. What the sunlight
and the sky itself have decided to do

this morning! And what wonderful things they do—
the flickering, the flashing — identifiable as birds
only in brief moments; more often chips of sunlight

or of sky. The birds (giddy, out of character) do
improvisations. Sunlight approves, and we smile, too.

Wayne A. Harriman

If Only...If Only

If only....If only....
We would nourish and protect all around
And leave a place better that when we found
And teach our children to do
What we have done too.
So our earth may be
A lovely place to be.

If we would plant more trees
And protect our lakes and seas
Put trash in the right places
To be recycled by all races.

If we did not waste water
And would protect its source like we ought to
And would protect the birds and bees
And all wild life from sky to sea.

If only...If only...
We would do what we've said
So our earth will not go dead
And will continue to furnish our every need
It'll be a special place indeed!

Margaret Pate

The Dance

I bowed, you curtsied, then we clasped hands.
  We'd made our choice, and the waltz began.
Life was the music, the stage was the world.
  Each step brought us closer, as we danced and we twirled.
At first we were clumsy, through the first thirteen years,
  With sore feet and hurt feelings, and many shed tears.
And all through the dance we thought it'd be best,
  If we called off the dance, and gave ourselves rest.
But, we had chosen each other, and we just couldn't hide
  The feelings we carried for each other inside.
With these thoughts in mind, to the world we would show,
  We were partners for life, and would give it a go.
I notice a change now, a lot fewer stumbles,
  Many more smiles, and a lot fewer grumbles.
Now dancing with you seems like dancing on air.
  We move a lot smoother; we make quite a pair.
Though we may not be perfect, it doesn't matter you see,
  Because I'm so happy, that you're dancing with me.
And now as I dance with you on through life,
  I'm still glad I chose you as partner and wife.

Ricky Crawley

A Daughter's Thoughts

Thoughts of one gone 'round the bend today
were fluttering through my mind.
Not the ones I refer to as free-floating
anxiety - them's the kind that bind.
These were fragrant, thoroughly refreshing,
like a spring-shower in the mist of a summer's heat.
I remembered violets, wind song, soft-breezes
of a melody... a light-hearted beat.
She cared not for fashionable cloth, but possessed
raiment far more shimmering than the sun's heat.
Gentleness: a quiet strength, meek,
unencumbered by conformity, emptied of self.
Ambitious? Only for those who wanted,
instinctively willing to care for those
unnoticed, shunted and shelved.
Can I hope to reflect one so
chosen? To ascend to the mountaintop,
to rejoin my earthly root, and
share again the kinship of our spirits.

Karen Ann Wolfe

Love Flight

A little girl of three and me,
were sitting in a summers breeze,
watching clouds and tops of trees,
and sweepers in the sky.
Leaning back in a lounging chair,
with her blue eyes in an upward stare,
She said: Daddy do you know what?
Look up there! Do you know we can fly?
I asked her how, and she said: Just try.
So I lifted her up closely,
and as we danced in circles,
I noticed heaven in her eyes.
And when I moved my arms like wings,
her laughter lifted me,
and daddy's do you know what?
I took a love flight.
Do you know we can fly?
Just try.

Lance Butler

Spring Morning

The sun is rising across the sky with tones of gold
What a lovely sight to behold.

The birds are singing their songs and bustling around
as they look for food upon the ground.

The dew shines likes diamonds from the morning sun
as a new day has just begun.

The blooms on the trees swaying in the breeze as the
sun shines on each and every leaf in the spring morning light
what a wonderful sight.

The meadow with its new green grass looks
like a looking glass.

As the blue sky slowly shows its face,
you can tell God has created a beautiful
spring morning place.

Lynn Hoyle

Mean Things

So many voices, so much time
What did they all mean?
Were they lies? No, I doubt-
But perhaps things unclearly seen.

Love? Hard to know-
Puppy love, the need for love, but all incomplete.
The search continued, a thirsty heart
tried to drink from all it would meet.

Now I find truth, sincerity
to quench me with every new day.
I am beautiful, I am loved
And you mean what you say.

Promising not to leave-
You mean this too.
Revealing your fear and your happiness,
Exposing a heart that's true.

No more guard or hesitation,
I'm quite willing to tell
These things that you mean
Are what I mean as well.

Marie A. Pettit

The Eyes

Lying in darkness, where I am I don't know,
what do I do now, where do I go?

Then out of nowhere, all I could see,
were these eyes, these eyes, so wild and free.

I could then see a person, without seeing its form,
it was all in their eyes, unusual, yet warm.

I knew I understood them, for me it's easy to know,
because most people don't realize, the eyes are the
    windows to the soul.

So then I knew their purpose, all I needed were the eyes,
it was time for me to go, time for me to rise.

They'll take me to a better place, where I'll finally be free,
of all worries of this world, someday you will see.

Monica L. Little

Between Yesterday And Tomorrow

Is that disappointment in your eyes dear?
What has stole the sunshine from your day?
Surely there must be a way to set things right.
God willing, you will find the way.

Between each yesterday, and tomorrow.
Theirs a brand new day too live, Yes! to dream.
Keep your dreams bright and new,
You'll find before your through,
The worlds needs dreamers like you.

Between each yesterday and tomorrow.
You must make the most of each new today.
To your dreams be true. Always see things through.
Always hoping, that someday, success will come to you.

Fames frosted stars may never come your way,
Still each new dream will bring you joy you'll see.
Till then work, plan, and scheme,
Until the dreams you dare to dream, come true.

Ruby May Juillerat

What Is Life

What is life, but a sorrow that everyone must face.
What is life, but a war between the human race.
What is life, but a struggle to survive on this Earth.
What is life, other than just a woman giving birth.
What is life, but a game that nobody can win.
What is life, but a world always full of sin.
What is life, but a problem, a complicated matter.
What is life, but a pitch always striking out its batter.
What is life, but a path that has no way out.
What is life? What is it really all about?

What is life? Well, it also can be fun.
What is life? Is it t he love for everyone?
What is life? Is it a gift from the man upstairs?
What is life? Is it someone who cares?
What is life? Is it the joy of having friends?
What is life? Is it the happiness that it sends?
What is life? I now know what it can be.
What is life? Well, it is simply you and me!

Rebecca Chaisson

I Wonder

Wondering what to do, about this confusion between me and you.
What should I say, if anything at all?
Wishing you would hold me in your arms just for another day.
I wonder where you are tonight, and what you're thinking of.
I wonder if you're in the arms, of the one you love
I wonder if you think of me, the way I think of you.
I wonder what to say to you - I haven't got a clue.
Could it be possible, that you feel the same?
Or am I just fooling myself? Are you just playing a game?
If this is just a game you play, don't ever tell me so.
I'd rather wonder forever, than to let my heart just go.
I wish it could be true, that you love me as I love you.
I wish I could relieve that night, to hold you in my arms so tight.
I'd cherish every moment together, make every second lost forever.
But now there's nothing I can do but wonder,
Wonder how you feel.
And hope that someday,
We will have a love that is so real.

Kristin Davis

The Keeper of My Heart

There's no denying
  What we are in.
Love has gotten under my skin.

Our meeting
  Was no accident.
Someone had a hand in it.

I wasn't looking
  For what I found,
But now my wings soar Heaven bound.

When the world outside
  Had taken its toll,
You became the soothing music for my troubled soul.

You've touched my life
  With love and joy.
I feel like a child with a new toy.

Now I've got what
  Took me so long to find,
And its in the way you say that you're mine.

You are the keeper of my heart.
  Nothing can tear what we have apart.

Sanya A. Brown

Memory

Many Questions torture me to which there's no reply:
"What were his thoughts? Was he afraid? How can this be? Oh why?"
My son is dead. The words ring false. Can I do naught but grieve?
  Can I accept what I cannot believe?

Bewildered yet I stand inside the room where he should be;
  I see his bed, his desk, his chair,
  His books, his games-he's everywhere-
  His favorite records, model planes,
  School compositions, railroad trains-
    The void he's left is deepened by
    Such things as these that do not die.

For nine short years I watched him grow, and in him saw myself.
  I felt with him his hidden fears
  His hopes, defeats, his laughter, tears.
  With joy I sensed that as he grew,
  His dreams were dreams that I once knew.
    He is not gone; there's memory.
    While I still live, then so shall he.

Pauline H. Kammet

My Painful Tears

My life wasn't over I was only beginning to fight,
when all of a sudden I, transferred all my anger
threw my writings
and each time I swallowed my tears fell.
I could feel my heart pain.
And from the pain my heart swelled.
I continuously wept and hurt.
Trying to block it out of my mind.
But I had such an awful taste in my mouth.
It was bitter yet kind of sweet.
I was drenched in sweet and I shivered all over.
So scared I was inside. My heart, voice, and sanity
became stagnant when my mother died.
still I am young and wet behind the ears
I have no parents yet and still my smile
is bright and clear.
I hurt so much I can't even begin to explain
My tears still fall like drops of rain.

Martha Southern

Home to Stay

There shall surely come a day
when all of us shall say,
"How wonderful and glorious Heaven is today,
now that the griefs and sorrows
of earth have all gone away.
Gods' blessings are upon us this very day."

There shall surely come a day
when all of us shall say,
"How wonderful Gods' grace is today;
for all the things we had on earth have gone away
and our peace of mind and eternal life is here to stay."

There shall surely come a day
when all of us shall say,
"How wonderful the Glory of Heaven is today;
for now we're finally home to stay.
All of our earthly sufferings have finally gone away.
No more suffering shall come our way-
only peace at last for all eternity."

Rhonda J. Nycum

Life's River Flows On

As we struggle and climb life's tall ladder.
When all you really loved seems gone.
It seems no one cares or loves us anymore.
The waters of life's river flows on.

Everyone says, Oh don't worry about that.
You couldn't have change it, it's done.
We try so hard to keep going ahead.
The current of life's river flows on.

I'm not everybody, I'm only somebody
Everyone is a daughter or son.
We're all a little different not nearly the same
The waves of life's river flows on.

So remember, if there's bad there's good.
And through all strife better will come.
Hold your head high life won't pass you by.
Remember life's river flows on

Larry W. Kile

Yet Another Tear

There is no peace for the broken heart and mournful soul,
when day by day, month by month, and year after year, it can not
reach it's inner most goal, and in the already red rimmed eyes,
there forms yet another tear; and the inner man calls out in
despair, Lord why?! Why do all my thoughts, plans and dreams
go awry, and these tears in my eyes never be dry?

For what comes the pain and wherein lies the end?
Is there nowhere in this retched world and parched land, where
I can find a place or person some comfort to lend? Lord, how
strong do I have to be, before the pain and suffering flee?
How much firing and beating can this steel take, before it is
no longer strong, but becomes weak?

Father, I know you are near and when needed most your
help will appear, but I need YOUR strength until that day is
here; I know I don't always bring things before you, solve
things myself is what I try to do; I always forget and wander
too far, from the warmth of the protection of your dome, and
you have to come and bring me home;

Help me not to forget anymore and stay home, with my
Father, Savior, and Lord.

Mary Birchler

A Long Been Forgotten Dream

A long been forgotten dream.
When dreams use to be so sweet.
Oh those dreams so wonderful, filled with bliss.
A walk on a beach, a tender loving kiss.
A dream to be loved a dream to be missed.
Now as I wake with a heart of despair
Eyes open wide, fighting a side of me
I never seen and never knew.
Knowing what was in my heart.
My perfect dream was past do.
A long been forgotten dream.
Taunting my spirit, they were overwhelming.
A mist about them so dreadful and blue
I opened my heart with a desperate prayer.
"Oh God let these dreams be long forgotten
Let me have peace!" I cried Amen.
My long forgotten childhood dream
Reappeared
It was a heavenly place and I've forgotten.

La Shauna Clanton

What Happens to Old Cowgirls

What happens to old cowgirls when there jeans no longer fit,
When grooming colts and cleaning stalls tires them a bit?
What happens to old cowgirls when they just can't sit a buck
and hope the roughest ride today is driving that old truck?
What happens to old cowgirls when they just don't have the strength
to stack up all those bales of hay or mend a broken fence?
There calloused hands and weathered skin begins to show the
age from all the work they did in there younger days.
What happens to old cowgirls who no longer can horse show
at least they have the trophy's they won so long ago.
What happens to old cowgirls? Well this I know is true, they
thank the Lord for what they had when each new day is threw.
What happens to old cowgirls when there wild days are done?
They smile and say oh what the heck at least I had some fun.

Suzanne Ferchak

Wanda's Son

He hurt's my heart, and makes's me cry.
When he's drinking and telling lie's.
When he's in trouble and on the run.
I still Love Him, Cause he's my son.
When he's in jail, and calls for bail.
We pretend we're not home.
We don't answer the phone.
It hurt's my Grandson and make's him sad.
When he see's what's going on with Dad.
I know someday when, he's sober
and stable.
I'll be sitting with my children at
the Dinner table.
I'll be proud to say" Greg you've
come along way. Your my Son."
Your my only one.

Lara Bullman

Lost Love

The unfortunate sacrifice to love is pain
We once shared sunshine, now there is scattered rain,

Our hearts have grown apart, I am not sure which path to take
Is letting you go the right choice, or is it a mistake?

Our love is hanging by a thread, once the love was strong
How could we let this happen, what went wrong?

If we were meant to be, our hearts will see us through
I want to find happiness again with you.

Pam Holtzman

Pleasures

I was out walking where the tall trees towers
when I came upon a field of wild flowers,
if I could I would like to say
their beauty just took my breath away.

They were prancing in the breeze
on a hill beneath the trees,
as many as there are stars
they seemed to stretch as far as Mars.

Happily jogging without distress
they dipped and tossed around,
as if to say their soul caress
within their roots beneath the ground.

I must confess how much I enjoyed
while my eyes watched with delight,
the spiritual way they toyed
Oh! What a beautiful sight.

I stayed there until dark
to soak up all the pleasure,
I got more than I expected from the park
there is just no way to measure.

Margie Lynn Scholl

My Life With You!

From the elementary days of childhood,
When I counted the petals of the daisy;
From those days in early teen years,
When my love for you was "crazy" —
    My life wouldn't go on without you!

In those early days of marriage,
A teen bride I was at your side,
You meant the very world to me;
Planning my life with you to abide,
    And my life couldn't go on without you!

We struggled along the way together
Through all the years of child-rearing.
Today we enjoy, looking toward tomorrow
As each day to older age we are nearing.
    And my life can't go on without you!

May God give us many years yet
With a love that he keeps strong
As we grow old together and enjoy
Our many children and their young.
    May he grant I won't have to go on without YOU!

Sharon Matson

Gifts of the Heart

When I was lost... You showed me the way
When I felt lonely... You gave me your hand
When I became unhappy... You brightened my day

You gave me... Your courage, Your strength,
    Your kindness, and Your generosity

Now for every hurting soul I meet
    ...I am able to show them
      there is a happier road to destiny
    ...I can extend my hand in friendship
    ...and I can show them
      how the sun shines through the rain

For You see I can do all these things
    through my heart, mind, and soul
    -Only because You taught me the
      most important thing of all
    ...You gave me the gift of Love.

Tina Marie Lovitt

My Teddy Bear Blues

What will happen to my teddy bear blues
When I look around and can't find them
I love to hold and squeeze them so tight
And leave all my problems behind them

Wouldn't the world be more inviting
If your teddy bears could do all the fighting
Peace would come and flood this place
As long as my teddy bears could have their space

It is my fulfillment in life to achieve
A teddy bear kingdom for all to believe
Black ones brown ones white ones you'll see
Will all live together as one and be free

Maybe someday if we look watch and listen
We might just learn a valuable lesson
As for me and my bears I always will love
My teddy bear blues and a white turtle dove

Thomas F. Mattive Jr.

I Fell Into The Ice-Cream Soda

A soft white cloud held me high in the air
when I lost my balance, I was no longer there
As I merged deeper and deeper my silky skin felt cold
and I looked outside the glass to see a boy with hair of gold

The silver spoon spun round
The bubbles got fizzy
And I got dizzy
And all at once I didn't hear a sound

All the ice-cream eating and soda drinking
Had come to a stop
And there I sat alone at the bottom
A little cherry from the top

Trudi Tropp

From the Past to the Future

I sit and think of my past years.
When I sat alone with only fears.
The people I thought I loved,
Had little faith in me and no love.
They had their fun as the days rolled past,
while I was doing hard time away down South.
A thousand days and a thousand nights,
My thought in life were only of fright.
So here I now sit in this gloomy cell,
with my thought of only hell.
But my future plans in life,
are of spending time with my beautiful wife.
She's the one I really love,
for she was God's sent from heaven above.
I look forward to my days of age,
For they'll be with her and not in this cage.
  I love you!

C. J. Bailey

Mirrored Reflections

Look deep into the mirror.
What kind of image begins to appear.
Does it show joy and happiness or sorrow and tears?
Only you can reflect those past and present years!
Beware of becoming so engrossed with the mirror,
that you can't see beyond the tip of your nose.
All that matters is what's reflected in our hearts and souls.
God is the only one who really knows!
In heaven, Our spirits are who we've become
each entwining into one. Invisible to any mirror!
What then, My friend, Do we have to fear?

Leslie Rosenberger

Candle Light

I feel this now and I've felt it before,
When I think of you, my heart ends up tore.
Tonight I sit by the phone
Waiting all alone.
I keep telling myself you'll call
But you don't and my heart falls.
I think I'll die,
But instead I start to cry,
I will wake at dawn, wishing you here.
I sit by the dim candle light;
Thinking maybe just might;
And then tears of love roll down my face
Remembering your warm embrace.
There's nothing I can do but patiently wait.
Could we come together? Possibly by fate?
I pray you love me every night;
As I put out the dim candle light.

Krystal Masterson

Perfect Love

It's times like this
When I wish you were here
When I am all alone
And nothing seems clear.
I long to touch your face
Or just to feel your touch
Seeing you and feeling you
Forever is never too much.
Will you promise to love me
Tomorrow as much as today?
Will you promise to stay with me
When everyone else goes astray?
Forever isn't long enough for me to be with you
People search a lifetime to find a love to true.
I used to dream of how my life might be
If I loved him and he loved me.
I'll never love another
As much as I love you
True love is so hard to find
And perfect love is so few.

Paola DeBartolo

"A Special Message"

Violence, racism, prejudice, hate.
When is this going to go away?
I can't believe my eyes about what's going on.
"Jew, spic, nigger"
I can't go on.
These hatred words are such a scare.
My child, my slave, there will be no more.
The voices are calling,
they want to be free.
Come on and give them their dream.
The children are crying,
the teenagers are fighting,
the parents are saying, when is this going to end?
The K. K. K. is going on.
Let's stop this war.
Make peace throughout the land.
You get my message,
let's stop this hate,
before it becomes or turns to fate.

Tanya J. Davis

In Tune With God

The symphony is suddenly out of harmony
    When just one musician strikes a wrong chord.
But the conductor, with patience, will proceed with his program...
    Now isn't that the same way as with our Lord?

When a Christian's life is out of harmony with God
    Our strings of moral conviction will tug at our hearts
We must look to our Conductor for new directions
    And pleadingly ask Him to grant a new start.

For when our hearts are out of tune with our Savior
    We soon will forget the joyous notes of our song
Our prayer life will suffer with neglect from rehearsal
    In His symphony, we will no longer belong.

A musician must stay in tune with his instrument
    Then the symphony, with pleasure, will be heard
As Christians, we must be in harmony with our Conductor
    With daily prayer and reading in His word.

    Sybil W. Becker

How Society Stole Christmas

I once heard of Christmas so holy 'twas told.
When man did not worry of silver or gold.
Where gifts that were given were truly from heart.
And Jesus of Nazareth still had a part.
For man made Christmas meaningless you see.
For Christmas right now, is a big shopping spree.
Society has played a mean mean old trick.
Instead of Jesus they gave us St. Nick.
Some worship and praise this man with a beard.
And wants us to believe in his flying reindeer.
Don't let society steal it away.
For Christmas is truly the holiest day.
So praise God in glory for what he has done.
For his gift was so special he gave us his son.

    Michael Smigiel

My Brother

My whole life changed one dark night,
when my brother was hurt driving home that night.

I got a call, that's what changed my life.
I couldn't bear the pain inside.
It felt like a knife so deep inside,
I closed my eyes and started to cry.

I walked outside and looked up to the sky,
I saw a star so far and high.
I prayed to God to make him fine and with a sigh I felt fine.

I saw him late the next day.
His eyes were closed, his body was numb.
I held his hand and prayed to God, but deep inside I knew too much.

It's been seven years since and he's still here.
His eyes are open, sometimes wide,
his body though seems stiff outside.

He can't eat nor can he talk, he may never even walk,
but deep inside I just don't know.
I've seen him smile, I've seen him cry,
I've heard his moans many times.
I pray to God to make him fine.

    Laurie Ann Fante

Get Out While You Can

I was talking to my girlfriends just the other day
when one of them had something juicy to say
She said "Girlfriends I just can't take it no more
last night he threw me once again down on the floor
he said I made him feel like a fool
I said to myself girl remain cool
I knew he had been drinking
but this was not the only time I had seen him drunk
I remember the smell
that alcoholic funk
he said women think they know it all
this was something he chose to start
a brawl
I called myself being smart
I saw it coming right from the start
today I said it's gonna end
that's right I left him girlfriend!!!

    Tracy Simms

Old Memories

She thought about when she first walked.
    When she saw her father and mother smiling at her.
She thought about when she got her first bike.
    When she fell off of it and hurt herself.

She thought about her first birthday.
    When she grabbed the cake with her little hands.
She thought about the first time she went to school.
    When she cried because she didn't want to leave her mother.

She thought about when she got her first boyfriend.
    When she kissed for the first time on the lips.
She thought about her only husband.
    When she had her first baby and five more to come.

She thought about her first grandson.
    When she had waited so long to be called "Grandma".
She thought about when her husband died.
    When she thought she would be alone forever.

She thought about all these things that had happened in her life.
    How she had lived a long life and was now 97 years.
She then closed her eyes as her heart stopped beating.
    Leaving her life behind and leaving this world forever.

    Veronica Herrera

Moonlight Of Winter

There's beauty as far as the eye can see
    when the cry of the wolf
    echoes through the trees
Haunting melodies
    drowned by the frigid wind
In the wilderness
    it's winter again

The full moon of mystical glow
    shines delicately on the virgin snow
Brilliant shadows dancing alone
    tranquility and peace among the unknown

Aurora illuminates the sky
    the timber wolf calls to a pack nearby
Again another day is done
    here in the land of the midnight sun

Listen to the season
    as it enters
Hear the cry of the timber wolf
    at the moonlight of winter

    Mary Naik

Am I My Brother's Keeper

Am I my brother's keeper?
  When the homeless ask for help,
am I suppose to do it?
  When the sick ask for mercy,
am I suppose to do it?
  When the old ask for help, or the young ask for my time,
am I suppose to do it?
  When there are too many to help,
  When it all seems so hopeless,
  When so many die,
  When all I see is despair, and loss, and more and more needy,
am I suppose to do it?
  How much can one person do?
  How much can one person give?
  How much difference can one person make?
    Only as much as they can.
  Am I my brother's keeper?
    We all are.
    Susan Scott

A Clash of the Titans

There used to be a time
When the mighty trains would roar
And the cloth sails of the huge clippers would flap in the breeze

The pirate ships loaded down with gold
Plundered from an english ship
That same ship does not exist today
For it was sunk on the spot by a peg legged thief full of greed

A train with clothes and food
Huffing like it has asthma
It is trying to get up a hill
When it has gotten over the hill, it whistles merrily

But alas the days of old have passed
Never to be seen again in all its glory
Only to be remembered by in a trip to a museum
    Nathaniel Emers

Searching for Solutions

What has become of our so-called, Generation x.
When the only thing on our minds, is violence, drugs, and sex.
Tell me, just tell, me how far back did this problem begin?
When we tossed away our principles, and lost our souls to sin.
What was it that broke our spirit, was it what took our pride?
Was it a pre-planned conspiracy, was it a genocide?
How do we go about saving our nation, saving our youth's souls?
What part do we play in society, tell me what is our role?
Tell me how much longer, will our nation last?
When our population, is dying out so fast.
Everyone is a victim, even you and I.
If we don't find a solution, all of us will die.
We don't have to worry about, the threat of other nations.
The enemy is right here before us, lacking in education.
How do we get our children, back on the right track?
How do we get our lives back in order, securely back in tack?
If we have the intelligence, to send people to the moon.
Why can't we use that same ambition to find a solution soon?
We have no more time to wait, no more space or room.
If things keep going the way they are, we'll all be heading for
doom.
    Rose Cole

Always

Always waiting for the time to come
when the strings of this perplexing universe come undone
and the world as we know it will fall into a bliss,
blown away with a smile and a kiss.
Always singing and dancing in the rain
until someone doesn't notice its horrible pain.
I can see it coming,
maybe I'd better start running.
Always striving to be the best
When we know we are just as bad as the rest
for we all know that man's a perfect race,
just not enough to call it to our face.
    Phil Hart

The Only One

From the first time his loving eyes met mine
When the sun glistens off his golden hair
My feelings could not find words to define
The future times together we would share.
His personality so appealing
Every image of him builds emotion
The thought of him sets my mind to dreaming
Inside rapidly growing devotion.
A sight of him makes my heart skip a beat
His voice so deep, yet enticingly sweet
A loving promise to him I would make.
Although he may not feel the way I do,
For all eternity my love is true.
    Stephanie Bates

These I Love

I love the first few silent moments of morning
when the sun shyly slips inside my window.
With the softness of a cloud, morning rays
drift and fall, and fill my room
with the radiance of sunlight.
My eyes and ears open in unison.
I am aware of a crisp new day
that contains all the freshness and beauty of Spring.

I love the magic in the beginning of a flower
and the mystery of a velvet sunset.
Soft pale colors entwine themselves around a stem
and are also splashed across the sky.
A fascinating spell is cast over those who dare to watch
as orange, pink and blue combine to form the prettiest picture of all.

I love to run, to laugh, and feel the eagerness of my youth.
I love the strong, fresh scent of mountain country,
and the delicate smell of an on-coming rain
but most of all, I love to hold in my arms,
all the beauty God created in a child.
    Sandra Neubauer

Secret in the Woods

I saw them. I was the only one. Necks bent,
trying to find grass under the cold Wisconsin snow.
Only for a moment, I saw their unyielding grace.
Me, speeding along in the back of a van.
They came and went like a spirit on the wind.
The does in their natural morning splendor.
My secret, mine alone.
The memory seems almost a whisper in my mind.
But in that moment I knew that I was the intruder there.
I was not welcome in their peaceful bliss.
My eyes were the witness that did not belong in this natural world.
A world were humans no longer seem to belong.
    Mariah M. Schaper

Retirement

Retirement is a very special time in our life
When we relax, and rid ourselves of stress and strife.
We can pack up our bags now and get away
To have fun and stay, as long as we can pay.

No answering the alarm while it is still dark,
Or getting to the office, with no place to park.
We've become our own boss now, we set our own pace,
As a retiree, we now are the majority of the human race.

Time to visit our Grandchildren, and go for a walk
And share with them some real personal talk.
Telling how we became wise in such a short time,
Also how we could buy so much with just a dime.

No more racing to stay in the fast lane,
Cause we're not trying to keep up with Jack or Jane.
It's time now for hobbies, and doing our own thing,
And we're all still young enough to learn a new swing.

Retirement years go fast as we all know,
Let's make ourselves useful, and wear a special glow.
We need to volunteer to help our fellow man,
And keep healthy and happy as long as we can.

Lucy T. Brockette

The Things You Could Do

The things you could do in one lazy day!
When you do absolutely nothing at all
There are possibilities that are not far away
If you'd only start rolling the ball...

Clean the house, sing a song
But don't stay cooped up for too long
Smile and laugh, read a book
Buy a wok and learn to cook.

Learn to type without looking down,
Look for those car keys that just can't be found.
Pore over pictures of your days in the park,
Go on a hike, an adventurous lark.

Confess your sins and go to church
Beat old rugs with some birch
Make new friends, but keep the old
Go live a life that could only be told!

Now look at all you have to do-
How can you say, "I'm bored"?
There's all this, and lots more, too
So...what are you waiting for?

Michelle Rose Lau

Emptiness

When you look down a barren, bottom less well
where a blinding darkness dwells
you feel something you knew very well
it causes a blinding spell
and sucks you into the obscure world.

Heart jumps up to your throat
you perspire, go pale and choke
with fear that you will be lost
forever without a hope, without a cause
into a well of obscurity and blinding spell.

But always, there is a light in the heart of darkness
in which you search and read your own mind
and slowly curtain of blindness winds
up for you to suddenly find
your self looking into your own emptiness.

Shakil Haider

Free Popcorn

Those walls came a'tumblin down
Where a church fell all broken to the ground
It had deteriorated weary with age
Except not God's word from its page
That church is alive today
Because its people had learned how to pray
They purchased a building once used to peddle porn
Where sin abounded and the Gospel scorn
Now the message of Christ is viewed on big screen
And needy sinners washed holy and clean
Christian love welcomes where glowing smiles are worn
Come see where God turned crumblin' walls into free popcorn

W. H. Shuttleworth

My Cousin Vera

One of my Mother's brothers lived on a farm
Where Buena, Flossie, Orvid and Ovid and Vera were born

Vera, my cousin, grew up as a country girl, you see
and on all my visits, she was a real friend to me

She taught me country ways, poetry and songs
and how to live our life without too many wrongs

When they left the farm, and family moved to town
Vera took care of step-children which did then abound

We had fun living, learning and always seeking to find
A different way, a smarter way, to improve our searching minds

For years, as we grew up, I heard her often say
When I move out on my own, I'll create my own way

'Twas then we lost close contact and went our separate ways
And I went off to College, wars, and other times and days

But time goes by- tomorrows come and always go
and we never see the ones we love and know

A phone call comes saying "your cousin died today"
you then remember the best events you shared along the way

Although a life has been "spent" and called home to rest
Of my memories, my cousin Vera, was one of the best

Norval M. Lock

The Fisherman

I picked a site by the river's edge
Where deer had trod and perhaps fed,
The sun was bright upon my face;
I thought I'd found the perfect place.

The bugs on the water danced and played;
The fish in the murky waters stayed,
I waited and watched and sometimes prayed
Till I finally drifted off in a daze.

Then out of my revelry I was shook,
Something was on the end of my hook.
I started to pull: he decided to play;
Tugging he flopped and swam away.

His belly was white in the bright sunlight;
His body was simply an anglers delight.
If I live to be a hundred and one
I'll never be certain which of us won.

Don't feel too bad on a "no win" day
For you only keep what gets away.

Nina L. Brady

The Dream

"He has shown me the high place,
where Earth, Nature and Spirit are One.

The Buffalo observed my approach
from the ashes of the sacred fire.

It is an island unto itself, surrounded by the high plain.
The trees form a circle through which you can see the world.

I have seen his face and I smiled.
The Guardian holds the key for the one who is yet to come.

I toasted my find - as the four direction soared above me
on Red Tailed Wings.

I go to the mountains to be healed -
I will see this place once more."

Mary K. Foster

Sonnet

Wandering on a crimson cosmic shore,
Where every swell cast flow'rs of mystic flame,
I heard a voice (my own?) in muffled shame
Plead with its love to enter the Dark Door;
Not louder nor more thunderous was the roar
Of climbing, bursting surf; and still it came;
"Enter the Dark Door, Love!" no voice could tame
Its wild insistence, ringing evermore....
What spirit moved in anguish to erase
My anguish, I know not, nor understand
Yet suddenly I viewed my Love apace
In darkened wells of light, dim on that land,
And lo! there came an angel, with his hand
On mine, and there was quiet in that Place.

Mary Burg Whitcomb

American Astray

America, my country, what has happened to you?
Where is the pride in the Red, White and Blue?
Where is the teaching of the "Golden Rule?"
Where are the principles of faith we were to be taught in school?

Somewhere along the way "We, the people" went astray.
We closed the Good Book; we forgot how to pray.
Our choices of leaders to govern and protect our great land
Were not based on the Rock, but on shifting sand.

Shaping a New World Order is well under way—
The wave of the future, America 2000 and OBE, are sheer American decay
Taking control of our children, redefining morals and what's right,
Downgrading standards of education, holding back those who are bright.

The future of America can be held in one hand,
All answers are here to cure our great land.
Let's ask for God's help, open the Bible and read.
We'll find life in abundance to fill every need.

America, my country, don't hide your pretty face.
If together we seek it, we'll find God's sweet grace!
With the power of God's people America will not fall,
Our Red, White and Blue will wave above them all!

Ronald Blacklock

Heritage

Nor I walk the gardens of childhood
Where more than half a century ago
Violets were set among the rocks by a man
Because a woman had cherished his first gift.
Those violets are gone but in the path
Where sharp white stones hurt a child's bare foot
From green crowns of leaves I see
Diminutive spots of purple sprouting
and covering those stones.
Violets in wild profusion overflowing past pain
Spilling down to the pool:
Children of love reflect a woman's
Warm essence and a father's love.
Rich in my heritage I turn at my daughter's step
To catch the violet flash in her eye.

Mary K. Sweeny

Spark

At Rider's (Writer's) Point did I dare fall
  Where no one could bear witness
There I lay, head in arms
  This sweet and bitter justice

There I sat for hours,
  Riding on past oceans
Facing them, I cowered
  These painful blistered emotions

With my mind I stabbed my soul
  So that I could share my pain
With a touch, felt marble cold
  And my soul cried out in vain

After all this time
  My mind still draws a blank
A stubborn fool, this mind he is
  I gave up, with none to thank

A final thought, a spark ignites
  That could lead to others
For sparks can ignite fires
  Than can heal or scar forever

Woong-Sae "John" Jung

Where Once a Wild Rose Grew

I know a place where fields were, not far from here at all
where now there is a parking lot, and bright new mini mall

I knew it well because it was a tranquil place indeed
a wild rose bush grew out there, in the midst of all the weeds

On and on for hours and hours I would take my share
of sunshine, light and breath, in that wild rose air

And I might pray to the God of change to stay his busy minions
to hold at bay the juggernaut increasing in dominion

A sorry thing it is to see a bit of beauty gone
bulldozed to oblivion as "progress" marches on

Now I'm lost when I go there, where singing birds are few
you see the work is nearly done where once a wild rose grew

W. Woodland Hastings

Imagine That

Imagine that the world is united, and nations are joined as one.
Where people are free to do or to be, anything under the sun.
Imagine that the world has no violence, no wars, no crime, or hate.
Where people want peace despite different beliefs,
    and no one decides another fate.
Imagine that the world is of people neither brown, nor white or
    black.
For nobody cares what color each bears, now can you imagine that!!!
These dreams that I see I leave up to thee, the future, the youth
    to come.
For you are still free, to imagine it to be, and now, you have begun.

Mark Kessler

The World In Which We Live

Once a plenish garden, now canals of sand and hollow.
Where sparkling waters turned to sludge and shallow waves of dust.

A victim she's become, trapped by packs of vicious K-9.
Who's savage hunger's ripped away the richness of her meat.

And lurking in the caves and tunnels, vultures swarm for prey.
Invading with their tubes of iron, draining every vein.

But standing in an unseen shadow, clouded by the eyes of beasts,
her prince awaits his moment to come free her from her pain.

Her pain is his. His gain is hers, as victory is their freedom.
The gnashing of the grinding teeth of enemy destruction,
and endless mourn will be their sentence, then will be forgotten.

New seed will scatter, rain will fall, and good fresh fruit will grow.
Her broken heart, he so will mend.
His love will make her whole again, and then the end no more.

Robert Tassone

Bridget's Grandma

Look deeply past her sunken eyes,
where the wrinkles on her forehead lay.
The hair color she'll now despise,
her teeth are crumbled with decay.
Her joints hurt with every move,
her speech stutters every verse.
Her life's been full, no more to prove,
but her later days are quite perverse.
The children blind to the person within,
read not a book but only a page.
The way they laugh is quite obscene,
for her eyes are the windows of my heritage.

Richard C. Mikolitch

Dream Skies

Soft is the light from dream filled skies,
Where thousands of stars glint and gleam,
Like jewels in the queen's finest crown
Of rubies and sapphires
And emeralds
And white-hot diamonds,
In unending lakes of iridescent purple ink,
Clear and vibrant,
With deep jet black stripes and blue-red patches,
Where hides the moon's soft milky glow
Of finely spun silk.
On nights such as these our dreams are held
High above
In the silken strands of the Milky Way,
Suspended in Never-Never Land—
Real and living,
Vital, breathing giants
That fill our souls and lift our spirits.
On nights such as these it is not difficult
To believe in possibilities.

Merry G. Woodard

Shalom Bayit

Where there is peace. A home.
Where you can find refuge from trouble or danger.
A sanctuary
in its own right.

Where you can live, love, laugh or cry.
Where you can meditate, create, and fly.

A place so beautiful:
It can be anywhere
it can be in heaven or on earth
it can be an entire country;
a temple or any structure
it is inside of you
and me
Where there is peace. A home.

Simcha Ponce

Labor Workers

Laborers that go unnoticed
Which work through the wee-hours of the morning,
Battling the muscle fatigue and weathering the loneliness,
Waiting to hear the irate sound of the cock's crow,
To usher in the sun in the line of the eastern horizon
I am, but for now, one of these workers,
Taking the cross before the crown,
A youth aspiring to attend college soon
More willing to wear a smile, than bare a frown,
I realize that many who have gone before have travelled this path,
And afterward, the vanquished path that I once followed,
Will one day, be followed by another
Thus the proverb will prove true,
Humility comes always before Honor.

Phil West

Untitled

He shuffles along between the cracks in the pavement
While all around the city swells and devours him.
Never does he pause at the windows along the boulevard
For what he does not see, he cannot desire.
And he knows that they all stop to speculate and whisper
And in silence they pass by, eyes burning into his skin.
Still they deny this breathing monument to modern times.
Maybe one day this heartache he feels won't matter.
He draws a ragged breath of bitter cold air
and holds tight to those treasured pieces of tonight's blanket.
Pieces of cloth and cardboard, fished from gutter and can.
Maybe someday he will once again sleep through the night
not waking from fits of violent coughing or from simple fear.
Ignoring the burn, he drinks in long steady gulps
From the half-empty bottle of cheap whiskey.
And on some forgotten park bench, he fixes his bed of paper.
Into the darkness around him he whispers his terrors
And dreams of a tomorrow that, perhaps, shall redeem him.
Where the cold and the pain and the fear will no longer be.
And as every night, he folds his hands and prays.

Vicky DeMarco

Solider's Lament

I don't want you to worry.
While, I am far away from you,
I don't want you to fret and pine
A-wondering if I am true.
You should know I'll always love you, dear,
And that I'll miss you, too.
And I'll be home, my darling
When our job over here is through.

Mavis Helzer

Tomorrow

We think about tomorrow
While today is not yet gone
Enjoy today and all it brings
Then tomorrow, we'll carry on.

Time is short and precious
So live with love and faith
Today will soon be yesterday
For tomorrow we all must wait.

The future is truly important
But still, it may never be
Plan what you must and live while you can
Soon we're all just a memory.

"The land of the free" has meaning
There's nothing you can't do
Remove all doubt and give it your best
Quite simply, it's up to you.

Pretend I have all the answers but
You're the only person I can show
If you ask and ask me nicely
TOMORROW, I'll let you know.

Patrick W. Ingram

Time

Must the sands of time run through the clock,
While we each remain alone?
May I hold you in my arms,
And turn your heart from stone?
Could you love me - just a little;
Soothe my fears and take my heart,
Inside the walls where you are hiding.
Holding me, never let us part?

I have loved you, it has been forever,
Though I tried to fill your shoes.
In my heart, I knew I would never
Find anyone I loved as much as you.

You were my darling first love,
You will be the very last.
If you can't love me just a little,
Then I shall dream of the distant past.
Because I still love you like no other,
There can never be another.
Let us love each other just a little,
For our remaining years are precious few.

X. L. Goff

Tears of Freedom

I sit here shedding tear after tear,
While your in a bar drinking beer after beer.
I'm not on your mind right now,
You don't care if I'm feeling down
You walk in the door midnight or so,
You never did this when we were girlfriend and bow.
The vows you said don't exist,
To love and to cherish when up in a mist.
I wish I knew the real you back then.
There would be no Mr. and Mrs. to put an end.
These tears are shed,
For a marriage now dead.
Freedom at last,
Tears now left in the past.

Michelle Twining DeVatt

Grandpa Dear

Wish I had chatted with you more
    While you were living and could speak
Of facts and tales of 'yesteryore'
    So I wouldn't have to search and seek.

But now I must ferret information
    Of where you lived and were born
Before crossing the Atlantic to this nation
    To raise Iowa and Missouri corn.

To libraries, maps, and relatives I go
    To uncover events of your past.
Reading and interrogation—it's so slow;
    It seems an almost endless task!

But, oh, how thrilling when I find
    Some bits and pieces of history
Unlocking the puzzle in my mind—
    Helping to solve the mystery.

Grandpa, it's true, I've just begun—
    There's much more work to do.
But I wouldn't stop now—I'm having fun
    In my genealogical search of you!

G. A. Schnakenberg

Angels

Mighty pinions, feather soft, magnificently white,
Whispering touches tipped with gold, a glorious heavenly sight.

Golden locks and burning eye which turns a look away.
Power unleashed, yet infinite in gentleness to pray.

Robes that float around the forms of creatures undefined.
Reverent servants of all good from God's loving mind.

Guardians for each battered soul, always watching over
the precious flock, the little ones who seek for heaven's door.

Calling, calling to the lost, their presence guards us well,
shielding with their mighty wings even into hell.

Rejoicing when just one is saved, their songs light the skies;
and a child of God can see His works with new and opened eyes.

Linda Russell

Lost At Sea

The wind on an adventure
Whispering with the breeze
Seeking the love I lost
Somewhere out at sea

The tedious days pass on
As I lay beneath a great oak tree
Gaping deep the ghostly air
Hoping the tide delivers it to me

With one quiet blink, a noble appeared
He was probably thirty-three
Caring, generous and charm
Who identified himself as "Larry"

His compassionate eyes fulfilled
The empty eyes that were once possessed by me
He promised a lifetime devotion
And endowed me a novel vitality

Hand-in-hand with my eternal memory
Stunned slightly . . .
Forgetting the love I lost
Somewhere out at sea

Kendra Bendowsky

Snowflake

Little snowflake from the sky, you make the ground so pretty and
    white.
You shine abroad in the morning sun and glitter in the evening
    moonlight.
When the earth is calm and laid to rest, you come calling once again.
For this is the time of year for you, you've only one chance and then
    you are through.
You lay your blanket down to rest, so white with beauty at its very
    best.
The earth is warm for you today and, little snowflake will melt away.
You say goodbye to me for now, I know it's time for you to go.
When you return to me again, I know it will be time for snow.

Patricia A. Canty

Winter Muse

A relentless onslaught shapes and blows
    White caps on a sea of snow
Landmarks familiar disappear
    Into a barren snowscape here

The harshness of the arctic drear
    We keenly see and feel and hear
But yet there is a gentler face
    Amidst this desolate time and place

A fantastical scene of opalescent white
    Under a clear full moonlit night
Is a special beauty to behold
    Much more precious than silver or gold

In the pregnant stillness of the night
    When snowflakes fall so soft and light
You can almost hear the mountains sigh
    To feel soft kisses from the sky

And beneath the evidence of storms long past
    Lie the patient beginnings of a new forecast
Eagerly awaiting the promise of spring
    At one with nature — our awakening!

Lori Hoyt

Ultraviolet

Proud of a color that's not even a color
White, lack of color, uncolor
I'm going to be purple
I'm proud to be purple
I'm going to dance in the rain
Reborn, baptism into chronic purpleness
Elementally colorful and substantially subsonic
I'm subterranean, I'm underground
I'm purple and tameless from this human whiteness
Knowingly red and unconsciously blue
The purple in me is the hatred in you
Colors, life in my eyes
I'm going to shine wild and purple
Dancing under the sun
Ultraviolet
Smiling, a purple kind of feeling
Color me, color me purple
As purple as I can be

Kelly D. Kenson

Lonely

Hey is someone out there
Who can hear my voice
My heart is breaking
Because you see.
I feel like a woman without love,
How I search and search looking for love.
And finding it in no one.
Or any place I've been
When people see me laughing and joking around
People swear to themselves
Man, she's such a happy person
It's so good to have her around
But no one truly realizes
That when I go home at night
And lay my head down
On my pillow,
I cry myself to sleep.
Because deep inside.
    I'm so lonely.

Rosalina Plaza Guadarrama

Standing Naked In A Full Length Mirror

When you look in the mirror
Who do you see
Is it you
Or another's reflection in you

Can you see the past in a living soul
Or are you blinded by it's existence

How does your future read?

Do you see someone marching
to the tune of an old man's perceptions
Do you see the incarnation
of a young girl's dreams

Can you admire what you see
in this crystal Wall

Did you ever have the feeling that you're damned
Because you don't accept the notion of hell
Or that heaven is one emotion away
Did your mother warn you about people like me

When you look into the cheval glass
Can you uncover what it reveals?

William J. Green

Fifteen And...

There was a girl of Fifteen years,
Who had lived a boring life.
And as the days began to pass,
Her spirits would not revive.

It appeared there was no reason,
To be sad the way she was.
She had her health and family.
But she was sad just because.

Maybe it was her boyfriend, no,
She was sure there was not one.
Maybe it was her classmates, no,
"This is our cliche, you can't come."

Her friends from before found new friends,
Her family seemed to stray.
A distorted world it looked to her,
That just wouldn't go away.

And that is when she decided,
The power was in her hands.
"This is for my well-being"
She thought, and...

Kim Falinski

Come Together Beautiful

Black, white, yellow, tan
Who knows the face
Come together beautiful, who cares the race

Cut you and you bleed
Cut me and I bleed
That is the color of our seed

Come together beautiful, we all have a need

Flowers of the field
different species, different kinds
That don't seem to matter
They don't seem to mind

Come together beautiful, now is the time

White clouds and blue skies
Purple mountains share the highs
Rainbow colors touched by light
stick close together an awesome sight!

Come together beautiful, we can make it right

Things in nature, as you can see
work well with colors, why can't we?

Come together beautiful, and the light we'll surely see!

Willie T. Mack Jr.

Distinction

There are some
Who possess color determinant minds
That wish to prevent the touching of our bodies
The melding of our intellect
By placing barbed wire fences of segregation
And spikes of racism between us.

As we hold hands
Each on opposite sides
Along the path of oppression
The barbs rip the thinly veiled ligaments of our hands
The spikes gouge the tender fleshy soles of our feet
And we both begin to bleed.

Our pulsing blood is crimson red
And when this thick scarlet liquid
Meets in the folds of our tightly clasped hands
Even you cannot tell the difference.

Leigh Ann Hudson

They, Them, What About Me?

I read a story about a child abused
  Who was severely beaten and grossly misused.
I read a story of people who choose
  To end their lives 'cause they have the blues.
I heard on the news where people have said
  If I don't want this baby, I'll just make it dead.
I read a story about freedom of speech
  If it's not about God, it's okay to teach.
I know in my heart that this is wrong
  And they need to do something before too long.
They need to teach about morals and love
  About the God who made us from heaven above.
The world is full of hatred and sin
  If they don't fix it, then evil will win.
So I went to call them to let them know
  "I'm fed up with things, so get with the show."
And as I searched, for them in the book
  It became clear to me don't bother to look.
They don't exist can't you see
  because they isn't them, they is ME!

P. Spencer Kingsbury

Tit for Tat

There was sleek slick Lizard,
  Who was a bit of a wizard.
While sunning himself quietly on a rock,
  He watched his dinner out for a sunlit walk.

With one eye lid he raised,
  The distance between them and him he appraised.
By night fall his belly was filled!
  And into the stream his swollen body spilled!

But he too was a tasty morsel, you bet,
  For in this streams his enemies too were well kept.
What for him was to be leisurely swim,
  Turned out to be something terrifying ... something grim!

His enemies circled him with jaws wide open,
  Who would get him first,...they were all hoping.
Some Lizards though have a special way,
  Of wiggling and snapping when 'they' are the prey.

Rudely.....he was snatched from the stream like a rocket!
  And into the darkness of some strangers pocket!
Now he lays stuffed beside book and candle,
  In a game of Tit For Tat he was snatched,.... On this he didn't
  gamble!

George-Alicea Heinze

Darika

  Once upon a time there was a girl
who was dying to fit in...Did
Darika know or did she care? Was
it her mother's fault for not making
her aware? I wonder what she felt
as she went to sleep. So now at a
hole in the ground her mother weeps.
To the invisible girl she cries why
Darika? Why? Darika was just
out for a cruise on the town.
How was she supposed to know
it would be her last round?
When her friend offered something she couldn't
refuse. She never imagined it would be her to lose.
At first it felt great but then
came the fall. By the time the ambulance came she couldn't
feel anything at all. The bright flashing lights and
the low droning sound. She cried as she realized she
wasn't home bound. She slipped away as she heard her Mom cry.
Why Darika? Why? And no one live happily ever after

Renee Slone

Daddy?

Daddy? Asks a little child
Why do we have war?
Will I have to fight
What is it for
The father looks down
in his sons questioning eyes
With a lump in his throat he tells his son lies
Why is this happening is there no better way
Now there's nothing you can do but hope and pray
Be strong for your country
you can't let her down
You'll fight to the finish
you'll stand your ground
We gave Hussein a beating
but he's not a dumb man
To not back out now he must have a plan
Innocent people are killed in the streets
when, if ever, will the terrible war cease
Young men are now leaving and preparing for war
Daddy...I have to fight and I don't know what for

Kristin Acker

Forever Love

Two hearts entwined on this life's highway,
Who would believe they would meet this way.
So many things on which they both agree,
Wishing to add a limb to their family's tree.

Want to know each a little bit better,
Have tried to do this with many a letter.
Each once came with a fragrant air,
No doubt in their minds of who put it there.

Many a visit they planned and spent,
So now things can get a little more intent.
Look for the place to put their possessions,
No doubt their will be many a session.

One little boy to build their love around,
He'll keep them together with his love abound.
When they run out of things to talk about,
Drew will pick up the pace I have no doubt.

The only advice we parents can give,
Make each other happy in this world where we live.
Always show your love each has in their heart,
A love story forever that won't pull apart.

Marty Shea

Goodbye Daddy

They say I look much more like you,
  who'd guess I hardly knew you.
Your love for children I possess too,
  yet I hardly knew you.
Your outward strength I well display,
  my heart's as big as yours,
Your smile, your voice, I have it all,
  though I hardly knew you.
I hear them tell of who you were...
  your personality, character, and traits.
It's strange, I see so much of me,
  it's to bad I hardly knew you.
I am your daughter, that much is true,
  amazed I hardly knew you.
Tons of love I hold inside,
  because I hardly knew you.
  ...goodbye daddy!

Shelly Werfelmann

Why?

Why can't the flowers always bloom?
Why can't there always be enough room?
Why can't a smile always stay on my face?
Why does the world move at such a furious place?

Why can't I ace every test?
Why is everyone else always the best?
Why can't I be perfect in every way?
Why is there always a price I have to pay?

Why can't everyone always get along?
Why can't life be one happy song?
Why can't we always agree?
Why can't life be perfect for you and me?

Why do people leave me to be sad?
Why am I sometimes so, so mad?

Why, why, why so many questions without an answer?
Why do I think of all these whys?
And why, why, why can't I fly?

Michelle Cole

Why Oh Why God

Why oh why can't they see just how much they're hurting you and me.
Why did they send us away, was it because we were in their way.
I ask the Lord from up above, why is it they couldn't show us any love.
Why was it that they abused us so, I've thought and thought and I sure don't know.
I used to cry every night, pray and hope that they'd stop their fights.
God please take all this pain away, for now I'll close, because that's all I have to say.

Lynn Boothe

Star Speckled Sky

As I look at the star speckled sky I ponder.
Why does man fear death?
For it is a doorway that he must pass through to feel complete and whole.
Why does he fear a God?
One that he has never seen, felt, tasted, or heard.
Why can't man enjoy the better, more finer things in life?
Peace, love, empathy.
Instead of fearing, fearing, until death comes and frees him.
Why can't man become Godless and be free from the fear?
And enjoy life while he can.
Why?

Markus Edgar

My Grandma Lost It

  My grandma is in the loony bin,
Why? I don't know. Maybe it's cause she put
rocks in the apple pie or cause she
chewed the gum out of her purse
without her dentures on.
My grandma went to the loony bin,
Why? I still don't know.
Maybe cause she chews her
toe nails or picks her nose. Why?
I still don't know. I got it!
She's there because she saw Henry with no
clothes, No! What could it be? Mmmmm
I know she couldn't fit finger in her ear
No! I give up besides it's time for my pill so silly
story come to an end but, I still don't know why I am in here.

Kathy Ross

Live To Ask Why

I know the answer to the greatest question of all. Why?...
Why there are stars, why we are here, why short, why tall. I...
I have conjured up an answer from the deepest part of my soul. Try...
Try to understand, to comprehend this idea, try to see it whole. Lie...
Lie underneath the stars, question what you think. Tie...
Tie the boundaries together, connect the final link. By...
By the edge of the earth, by the horizon of your mind. High...
High above is the answer, but here the clues you can find. Fly...
Fly to your destination, see the food on which you've dined. Sky...
Sky and mind, stars and thoughts, truly are combined! Pry...
Pry open your soul, see heart and universe perfectly aligned. Die...
Die to be it, live to see a glimpse and wonder what's behind.

Kirsten Hopkins

In God's Hand

Oh Lord please help me, I just can't understand,
Why there's so much pain and suffering here within my hand.

Her grip's so tight, a quivering cold.
reaching within my heart, she grasp's my very soul.

I stand here now with my hand by my side,
As I look down she brings tears to my eyes.

The pain's so great, but she shows no fear.
She knows the times coming, God's son soon will be here.

We all hate pain, this we know,
but this is one pain that's hard to let go.

The pain's left my hand, it did depart,
but the pain's forever within my heart.

Although she lived with pain, for oh so long,
those memories died and the best live on.

I thank you Lord, I now understand,
you now carry that pain within your hand.

    Richard Lee Visbal

Emptiness

Slowly she crossed the bedroom thinking, "I have to get dressed. How will I get through the day at school?"

Last night her world came to an end... Very quietly he explained, "I can't live this way any longer. I have to go."

A part of her being stopped, flash -frozen and quite dead.
A cry rose in her throat and died, like a clock painted by Salvador Dali.

All through the night the digital clock performed while tormented bodies tossed and swollen eyes peered... one o'clock... three o'clock... four twenty two...

Picking up her stockings she repeated the thought, "How will I get through the next few hours? How will I get through the rest of my life?"

Her identity - wife - is gone
Her residence - home - is empty
One child - away - at college
One child - gone - in prison
Her faith - only - in God.

As her nightgown fell to the floor, he walked through the bedroom door to say, "I'm leaving for work now. Take care of yourself."
She was stripped bare of everything in that moment of utter emptiness, standing alone in the middle of the room.

    Margaret M. Beard

Finding Yourself

Do you know your true identity
will you search for infinity
can you reach deep within yourself
to find, to learn, to see your heart
will they carry you off on a cart
do you want to know
will you be ready to go. Do you even care
has it been to long to bare
you can honestly say that time is ticking
away. How much bolder will you get
as you grow older or will you just
get colder will you need a shoulder

    Rufus Lloyd Boggs III

What Am I?

"What am I?", asked the child of the butterfly.
Wings of china
Understandably quiet
Sing about tragic beauty.
Birds flying clouds
Eyes hearing softness.
"What am I?", asked the child of the grasshopper.
Seeds are sown
Explode into muscle
Sweat until work pours off.
Bees of the earth
Hands smelling sweetness.
"What am I?", asked the child of the wise one.
Child of beauty and muscle
Dance until dawn.
Taste the colorful sea
And salty honey of work.
Love the earth and sky and self.

    Peggy Loevner-Sloane

I Mourn the Loss of You

Raindrops fall like the tears I shed.
Winter's distant in the moonlight.
Thoughts of you fade to blue.
In the twilight's morn,
I mourn the loss of you.
My lover's cries echo through the forest that is my mind.
Crimson is the color my broken heart bleeds.
Amber saturates the sun setting,
for my soul's sake,
and the sea swells for each time I weep.
I'm broken, embittered and blazen with loneliness.
In the twilights morn,
I mourn the loss of you.

    Stacey Edison

Life Is A State Of Mind

So very often I wasted time just thinking about the past
Wishing I could change some things and make the good times last

So very often I wasted time just thinking of tomorrow
Planning only happy times not wanting any sorrow

So very often I disappeared in dreams that I knew just couldn't be
Planning all the days ahead to be a comfort zone for me

So very often I tried to blame my childhood and my past life
For all the pain I feel inside that cuts just like a knife

Too often I let the memories that saddened my younger years
Creep back in my mind and just re-surface all my tears

The years kept passing by and still so much time I wasted
Searching for that perfect life I think somewhere I tasted

Then one day I met a friend who found something special in me
And I was taught to forget the past and let bad memories be

This person made me like myself and I bloomed when I was with him
And I learned to live each day with the motto... "Carpe Diem"

Forget the past don't get lost in the future just live from day to day
Love yourself... trust yourself... and don't forget to pray

Face each day with a positive smile and you will surely find
Life is beautiful, life is precious and life is a state of mind.

    Martie Velardi

The Price Of Time Is What We Paid

She said she needed time, time to roam for a while.
With a broken heart I gave her a yes, and a smile.

Like a beautiful bird I set her free,
hoping deep within she'd come back to me.

As time went by I could still feel her touch.
My love for her, she could only imagine how much.

Then one day I saw her face, she caught my glance.
The one thing I stopped hoping for was a second chance.

We hugged and began to cry.
We should have never said goodbye.

I said time had been a friend to her, this I saw as sure.
She said time made me distinguished.
Our flames had not been extinguished.

She was with hers, and I was with mine.
We both realized, there would be no second time.

Each of us knows we must act as friends, if we meet again.
For this is the only mask we have to cover and hide our pain.

Decisions about our lives we have all made.
The price of time is what we paid.
Scott W. Dias

Carving a Dragon

You put around my neck a gold necklace
  with a charm of a dragon carved with jade.
"I see the wind," I said, "it flies like imagination.
  His head rides on its wings, his tail cleaves through the speed."
"That's style," you replied, "the style of a dragon
  instead of a phoenix."
"I see the bones," I said, "the substance of his form.
  He prances with all his might."
"That's essence, the source of his power."
"I see his spirit, it carries his thoughts
  soaring above the clouds, diving under the sea."
"That's the soul, the center of his being uniting a whole."
"I see his emotions, daring colors and clarion tones
  shake the mountains, vibrate the universe."
"That's gloss, lustering the sentiments."
"I see his splendor, illuminating like lightening."
"That's conspicuous, from his uniqueness."
"And I also see his beauty." "That's recondite,
  hidden under his grandeur, beyond appearance.
  And that is the secret of his magnificence."
Wang Wei

The Christmas Angels

There are beautiful angels on our Christmas tree
With ethereal countenance, and they number three.
They do not shine forth as a colored light,
But assume all the sphere of Christmas night.
They reflect not the glow of each colored ball,
But their poignant being, I humbly recall.
Tho' they were cut from plain white paper,
They stand on the tip of the branch as a taper.
And tho' their faces were drawn with a pencil
They're more animated than the shimmerin' tinsel.
Each angel's gaily crayoned dress,
Was fingered with love, through creative duress.
And she deemed her efforts quite artistic,
As she fashioned the angels so realistic.
They came into being, a few years ago when,
The angels were carved by a child of ten.
Poignant! Ah, yes, I recall with a sigh
As the colored lights fuse through a tear in my eye.
For the child who created these angels for me,
Is now an angel herself, on God's christmas tree.
Virginia E. Peterson

Unto All

Unto all was born the marvel of Christmas Day,
With gift of the blessed savior to lead the way.
Let peace reign on earth as a symbol of the dove,
That is among blessings showering from above.

Unto all is a feast of the nativity,
Which remains constant in all the festivity.
the message of the manger is recalled with grace,
To greet the holiday by a sincere embrace.

Unto all praise, love and joyful acclamation,
Throughout the light of the world's entire creation.
There's an ecstasy of delight in faith of thee,
By the purity of spirit in hearts set free.

Unto all is the seasons wondrous bestowal,
And the sound of voices are echoing Noel.
Nothing in life could be more excitatory,
Than to give the source of God all of the glory.
Mary Rosine Chable

Beautiful America

O, beautiful America, land that I love,
With majestic mountains towering above;
Mountains of grandeur, rugged and high,
Ever reaching upward to touch the sky.

O, wonderful America, land of my dreams,
With beautiful rivers and sparkling streams;
Rivers of splendor, deep and wide,
Ever flowing onward to the ocean's side.

O, glories America, land I adore,
With valleys and plains from shore to shore;
Valleys fertile, long and wide,
Ever reaching onward to the mountain's side.

O, Marvelous America, land of the free,
With millions of people just like you and me;
People with faith in the God up above,
Ever marching onward in the spirit of love
C. T. Taylor

Did You Ever?

Did you ever walk down a busy street
With never a friend chance to meet
And felt that you were all alone?
No, my friend, you were not. God was there.
Did you ever hike a country mile
With your thoughts a wandering all the while
You were happy one minute, sad the next?
Yes, my friend there was an answer, God was there.
Did you ever climb a high old hill
And look out over the earth so still
Thinking that you were all alone up there?
'Twas not so my friend, God was there.
Did you ever ponder about life and living
Were you taking more than you were giving?
You cannot hide your way of life
Because dear friend, God is here.
Did you ever feel that you could not cope,
That all was gone, even hope?
Then remember the "everlasting arms"?
Oh, dear friend, you did know, God was there!
Virginia Thelen

I Am One Of A Kind

I live with Multiple Sclerosis; it's a miserable diagnosis.
With no cure in sight; to live with joy, I must use all my might.
For some days I'm afraid to touch, for fear my grasp may be too
strong. I'm afraid to speak, for my words may came out wrong.

People I know have a need to point out each wrong turn; They don't
notice that their comments makes me burn. Only I know what I can do,
and yes, some days I am blue. But this is my life; I am in charge. I
may not always know which path to take, but the path I choose is mine
to make. Life is up and down; it matters not what happens, but if I
smile, or if I frown. It's how I react; do I allow myself to grow, to
expand on what I know.

When my face is frozen and my hands go dead, my vision is blurred
    and my legs are like lead...
What do I do, so I don't turn blue?
I reach beyond the physical and strengthen the spiritual.
I expand my intellect; I reach inside my mind.
For this I know, I am One of a Kind.
Learning through troubled times has made me strong.
Some days I can do no wrong. For you see, I dare to be..
Happy to be me.

Yvonne A. Fischer

The Reality Of A Dream

Loves of all the lovers that ever were
With sizzling passion-flames of fire,
Within my breast could never stir
Even embers of my heart's desire.

You are near to me deep in my slumber state.
Seductive siren love songs sound.
Warm robes of rapture seal my fate,
As angels dance with wings fluttering all around

In this mystical time and enchanted place
I know that though this a dream might be
As I gaze upon my dear heart's face,
There will exist no other love for me.

Marjorie Foster Fleming

The Maiden

Among us, there was a maiden fair
with smooth ivory skin and strawberry hair.
She wore a white gown, elegant and long,
and hummed the sweet melody of a romantic song.
She sat perched on her white steed, regally high
her head tilted up toward the beautiful Spring sky.
Long tapering fingers sparkled with emeralds, rubies, and gold,
on her face she wore an expression of one very bold.
She had won many a distinguished male suitor's hand,
which made her the wealthiest lady in all this great land.
Chastity among her virtues was not,
if an offer proved promising, she would seduce the local sot.
But not once in her life did she have to do this
she married a gallant knight and they live in complete bliss.

Serena R. Saxton

Untitled

I have never met anyone
Who compares to him that I love,
With hair so brown,
That even the taste of chocolate can't surpass,
And the shine makes me
Want to run my fingers through the sunbeams.

His eyes are the same delicious brown,
But contain a spark of fire
That shoots right through you like lightning
When he stares.
Filling your ears with the sound of the sky.

Lesley E. Martin

Conscious Awakening

"O Beautiful for Spacious Skies" is where all this began,
With spoken words of truth on how " God Shed His Grace On Thee";
Our country has been blessed in more ways than we can see,
If only we would allow our eyes and our heart to lead the way,
Instead no, ever since the beginning of time people have gone astray,
Is this right or is it wrong,
They just could not decide,
Their faith in God washed ashore as temptation became their guide,
Temptation of the wrong kind took over like a river without an end,
Envy, selfishness, hatred and wars became man's closest friend,
Now the question of our future lies in our own hands,
Is this the way we chose to continue or so we take a personal stand,
We all know we are not perfect, it wasn't intended that way,
Although each of us has plenty of good to offer, like love, peace and
    caring
Wash away the wrong and bring in the right,
Open those eyes, have it finally become clear,
Life's abundance of goodness is all around us,
For starters yourself, because it's a blessing that your are here.

Ruth Olsak

Untitled

If when we walked together in the rain,
With tears and raindrops mingled in our eyes,
And talked of foolish things to ease the pain
Of panting which we thought we could disguise.
Our feeling in the light of stolen joy.
And hand in hand determined to enjoy
These last few moments we were soon to lose
We walked in silence owned by shrouding mist,
And wondered at the silent wilderness,
Of moor and mountain and the moon above,
We laughed awhile and sometimes kissed,
Did neither of us see that this was love.

Lillian Bilka

Untitled

Atop a valley essence abides
with tears that vow to always subside,
In quiet patience beneath the stars
grace embellishes my heart from afar,
As majestic mercy blooms a vision
my soul smiles in sacred decision,
For tonight I clutched the pearl of truth
the heavens holy angelic youth,
Whispering a promise that reveals the way
to help me prosper throughout the days,
But miracles befall when faith perceives
that love and life retains eternity,
For tonight I saw God's spirit arise
atop a valley essence abides.

Lindsay Gentry

Handicapped People

So you're handicapped you say,
Well what a shame,
I mean for us, not you,
For we are the fools,
Because indeed we cripple ourselves,
Through our own weakness.
That leads me to believe,
If you took and put us all in wheelchairs,
And told us to walk,
That handicapped people,
Would be the first,
To walk among us.

Kevin R. Cooper

Secrets from the Past

As the sun submerges, thoughts from my past emerges
With the passage of time, I now realize I'm a victim of crime
My mind is crystal clear, though my heart is filled with fear
Through my tears, I recount the years
My childhood horrors, has left my life filled with sorrows
I can't tell, it would lead to a living hell
Many nights of sleep I lost, just weighing the cost
The incidents were many, the consequences are plenty
I relive it day by day, although I'm afraid to say
To save face, I pray daily for God's grace
The constant threats, I will never forget
Whether real or not, I was only a tiny tot,
My innocence was taken away by my brother, how could I tell mother?
For sexual abuse, there is no acceptable excuse
To begin to recover, you must uncover
Recovery is slow, but you can learn to grow
To acknowledge the pain, strength you will gain
If you continue to hide the facts, it leads to self destructive acts.
Let the abuser know, to the police you will go
A life restored at last, will relieve quilt and shame from the past.

Susia Smallwood

E.M.H.

Just like the soothing whisper of a summer wind,
With the promise of a storm
Just cause there's no shape or form of emotion
I will always love you
Out of the closet and into the light,
I'll tell the whole world that I love you
While rivers run deep, I challenge the depths
My thoughts are of you with the pass of each breath
On the steps of the truth I admit to the fact
That I am a prisoner of your love
The stars in your eyes leave the sky a pitch black
I politely refuse to be lost in the mist,
How many ways?, I'm counting the gifts
For my darling, I promise
I swear, for the rest of my life,
I will always love you

Ramon M. Maisonet

Yellowstone

Yellowstone is beautiful in many ways,
With their trees, lakes, geysers, and bays.
There goes old faithful, it's erupting again
It's spouting real tall I'll give it a ten.
"Click" I got a shot of a buffalo big
Doesn't it look like it's wearing a wig?
"Ooh!" That waterfall is really pretty
I like it just like a newborn kitty.

The mud volcanoes stink with sulfur,
They make me quiver and really shiver.
The mountains are tall and they're tough
The rocks on the mountain are real rough.
Above eagles fly, below swim the fish
A man catches one placing it on a dish.
I enjoy the lake so shiny blue
I hope that you come and enjoy it too.

Tania B. Talaid

Mother's Prayer

Dear Master, we come to you with humble hearts,
With this question most sincere.
What kind of mothers are we
to those little ones so dear?

Bring up a child in the way he should go
And when he is old he will not depart.
These words we read in God's Holy book.
And hold them dear to our hearts

Help us to teach them thy ways, dear Lord.
By our actions, our love, our prayers.
So they may travel life's pathways
Knowing there is one who cares.

When we cross through those pearly gates.
To join the heavenly band.
May we hear "Well done little Mother."
As he gently takes our hand.

Ruby Deidel

To Love

I left my heart in Stone Mountain
With this wonderful girl that I met.
I may not remember Stone Mountain,
But the girl I will never forget.

We found there was love in Stone Mountain.
Respect and desires were there, too.
Kisses were tender with passion restrained,
'Til our old love blossomed anew.

I may never go back to Stone Mountain,
I'll cherish those memories, it's true.
Just remember until our next meeting,
I'll be thinking of no one but you.

William V. Rush

Daughter

In the beginning I had a name for one, but I was blessed
with two. One is gone now, but God left me the strongest of
the two. I saw you grow from a little fragile girl, to a
beautiful young woman. I wish much for my son, but you my
Daughter are all and more than I ever hoped you could be.

When you walk into a room it's like a breath of spring,
you are charming, witty and have wisdom and grace beyond your
years. I will always cherish the fun times, with the laughter,
the sentimental times that brought us closer together as friends,
and the quiet sad times just knowing you were there for me without
question.

I wish for you all the songs of happiness filled with love,
and when sorrow appears, know you're not along for God and I are
walking by your side.

My Daughter, my Friend, my Love is with you always.

Lorraine L. Chrone, "Lady Blue"

Wake Up Call

When I woke up it was twice as cold,
When I woke up I was twice as old,
When I lay down I had a gnawing ache,
When I lay down my heart had started to break,

When I woke up I could hardly feel,
When I woke up my heart was made of steel.
It took a mystery to fashion new flesh,
It took a marriage to build a nest.

I swallowed unknowing and faced despair,
I accepted commitment and found life there.

Steven B. James

A Dream's Reality

I lie in my bed
with visions of us in my head.

Dancing together into the night
there is no music, no sound, no light.

Gold dust on rainbows pave our way
I look into your eyes with nothing left to say.

We lay together on the tops of tall trees
we make love to the rhythm of the summer breeze.

In this world of the mystical turtle dove
the only magic we need is in our love.

But now I feel fear
for the dawn is coming and you might disappear.

I hold you tight, not wanting you to leave
but my grasp is lost and I can only grieve.

I scream in anger, I'd give my life instead
but it does no good for it is all in my head.

Now the sun has risen and I must awake
was it real, a dream, or just a mistake.

Lawrence L. Romo

Colors of the Rainbow

Rainbow -
With your promise so true;
Rainbow -
Blue, red, orange, green, yellow, and violet too.

Blue -
Found in the sky above;
Red -
The color of new-founded and eternal love.

Orange -
Symbolized by the pumpkin so round;
Green -
Like the grass carpeting the ground.

Yellow -
Is the color of the sun so bright;
Violet -
In the rainbow not far from sight.

Colors -
The portrait of life they trim;
Colors -
There's no escape from them.

Marchele Wilbanks

Joni

It was once said that a castle
without a beautiful woman is like
a spring without the rose.
So too is it with my life,
for it is the absence of your smile
and ever present beauty
that gives testimony to its truth.
In a world that abounds
with things of beauty
from the common to the rare,
I can find not one that can ever compare
to the beauty of the rose.
You will be forever my rose
and I have seen too springs without you.
Will I ever again see the rose in spring
or will it remain forever just another memory?

Richard L. Walton

The Sentimental Soldier

Falling in an eerie black space
Without the beauty of lights
Like a roaring roller coaster off its track
Knowing not where his destination lies
Not caring

Feeling whirlwind of emotions
Like a newborn gasping for breath
Wanting the darkness to envelop him
Still trying to cling to the womb
But eventually never caring

Feeling a suicidal sadness
With an uncontrollable urge to cry
And the tears flow from its ducts
Not sure whether to drain
Not caring

Heading towards a place unknown
Leaving sacred love behind
And filling one's self with emptiness
Unknowingly filling the void with hatred
But in his heart, starting to care.

Wendee Ulmer

The Sun

The sun rises early in the morning
    without very little warning

The air smells so fresh and clean
    it makes such a beautiful scene

The morning dew makes the grass
    wet and cold
It feels so good between my toes

The flowers are budding, I see a bloom
    they will be pretty very soon

I like to be out in the sun
    getting a tan can be real fun

I'll get my radio and play some tunes
    and sip on lemonade until I see the moon

The sun is warm
    the sun is bright

Evening comes soon
    then comes the night

Rosalee Wilson

Back to God

In fitful slumber I dreamed, and
Woke with flooding eyes to write
Of the grim visions I had seen
That broke my heart throughout the night.

A cemetery of children so very small -
Wee Phantoms in lonesome graves -
And with tiny voices that rose from all
They wailed a mournful tune of pain.

I walked amongst the weeping souls,
All of them pleading to be taken, and
In their song of bewildered woes
They begged, "Oh, why were we forsaken?"
With sorrow I had not the word
To deliver them from their darkest plight;
But the one who did had heard
And called them home into the light.

So, one by one, each little soul stood,
Spreading tattered wings so frail, and
Took flight toward heaven, back to God,
From the wretched hands of betrayal.

Maree Stoehr Colwell

Beyond the Fire

Beyond the fire stands a
wolf, his eyes glowing, his fur
shining, his muscles tense
  He stands there beyond the fire
looking at you, you control his
destiny and the fire is a boundary,
yet we break this boundary daily,
like putting out the fire we are
putting out the fire of life that
once burned within the eyes of the wolf
  Beyond the dead coals lays a
body, the wolf, so we go on never
looking back, the air grows cold
just like the heart that once beat within the wolf

Shanna Owens

The Dreamer

  Beyond time there lived a dreamer who seemed to
wonder about the world and the power of violence
with a caring need

  There is a fancy of a wonder that prevailed the
dreamer who experienced so many tragedies that
seemed to make its presence known throughout all times.

  As wonderful as life has been given, why do we
take it away so hastily?

  Why fight the hard times when you can only
dream of a nicer life that you have only wondered
about all of the time?

  My dreams are not fake: they are the real thing
compared to the world we live in today.

  I am a dreamer who seems to rely on hope and
prayer with a pondering mind about a drum major
who was a dreamer so long ago.

  My dreams are for a peaceful time.

  What we long to have someway in this dying,
loving world where peaceful water flows

  So let the good times begin.

Leon Hodge

The Hurt In The Dark

I sit in the dark and stare at the phone
wondering why I'm depressed and alone.

I face the fear that lingers inside,
there's nowhere to run, there's nowhere to hide.

The anger inside me can not be controlled,
I'm trying so hard to be patient and bold.

He might say he's sorry but the truth is he's lying.
He can't understand why inside I'm crying.

He's torn me apart in every which way,
is forgiveness the answer.....
maybe someday.

According to him, he's done nothing wrong
why did he make me suffer so long?

Kate Smith

My First True Love

His muscles glistened with sweat as he chopped
wood for the fire.
He would give me a wink, he would
only be a moment more.
His constant affection and approval I desired.
His charm I adored.

I dream of his laughter, his smell, the touch
of his hand on my face.
I dream of how his hands have molded
and shaped my life.
I dream of how I used to lay in his
arms, and the lines of his muscles
I would trace.
Sometimes the jealousy would be to much he had a wife.

He is gone now, he's in a place of constant peace.
Someday's it is to much to bare-
I picture his spirit soaring on the wings of snow white doves.
And I dream the two of us hand in hand
walking barefoot on golden streets.
You see, My Daddy is my First True Love.

Susan Kay Lindsey-Brown

My Babies

Tiny hands with the best of intentions, little voices with innocentwords,
Little legs that are so quick. How often I lash out with angry words
And your world comes crashing down. I forget you're just beginning,
you're new, you're fresh.

Patience is a hard thing to find after a long day of coddling grown
ups and badgering coworkers. Love is so far away coming home to the
realities of bills in the mail box, getting the same old dinner that
no one will eat.

But there you are...wanting to share what a great day you've had;
Showing me pictures you've drawn and the letters you've learned to
write. You're so happy to see me that you squabble with each other to
see who gets my attention first. You are so full of life and trust.
You are my two bright stars on a cloudy evening.

When the day is over and you're all scrubbed clean, I tuck you between
the covers and kiss you good night. After the "I love you's" have
been spoken and you've drifted off to sweet dreams, I come to watch
your even breathing, your healthy and content faces, and I think what
a lucky person I am to have you. My life wouldn't be complete without
you.

Kelly M. Snyder

The Mad Woman

She shuffles along, hoary head held low
Worn out by Time, Life's enemy,
Defeated by Fate, Man's foe.

Once she had a family,
A husband, loving daughters two
Living together in domestic harmony

Happy were the days she knew.
Why did they have to end?
Away from her daughters grew.
Her husband left her for herself to fend.
Loss of home, of heart, of mind.
Results of hurts too deep to mend.

She shuffles along, deaf and blind
To life's harsh unwavering decree:
Love flees, loved ones are unkind.

Still she imagines herself to be
(Reason abandoned her too, poor thing!)
Where together they laugh and sing
In a warm world only she can see.

Kelle-Anne Allen

Eulogy

I wonder if there would be a change if I went. We all would like to think that we would leave this empty space. A hole or void that could never be filled. An opening in life that would be there through all of eternity. Never to be filled because well, there's only one me.

Or is it like taking a teaspoon of sand from the beach? The hole is quickly filled by the crowds of other sand and if not, washed away by the tides of time.

I wonder if I leave any remembrance. Any importance. After a year or two or so. Would a name be called? My name? Or would it vanish? Like the echo down a mountain slope.
Can I mean so little to life? Did I somehow miss my purpose?

We start out life so furiously. I'm gonna, I will, I am. And then as time passes, those declarations fade to I wanted, I would've, I can't.

I want to leave something to keep the hole open. I want remembrance. For in the end it's all there is.

Lola Knapp

Would You?

Would you miss me if I was gone?
Would you miss me if I passed on?
Would you come to visit my grave?
In memory of me would you love, honor, cherish and save?
Would you remember things of the past?
Would my memory even last?
Have I made an impression on your heart?
Would you cry if my soul did part?
Upon my death would you wear red?
Would you shed tears upon my bed?
These are all questions I need to know,
before it is my time to go.

Lynn M. Wood

To Hell With Willows

Willows will grow and take all for it
Wringing out of the land, and who knows
For quenching of one is death to another
Birth of a life may be death of a mother

They take and do not offer
Wringing out of the land, and who knows
Consume all there is, no beckon to give back
For one to have plenty - two others must lack

A calling is coming, the willows are falling
Wringing out of the land, and we will know
That, for the sake of one there must be others
Yet, for the sake of all - we all must be brothers

Peter T. Hanson

Isolated Heart

Her heart feels so isolated,
  without him near.
Her heart feels so cold,
  without his stare warming her soul.
Her heart feels so limp,
  without his strong embrace.
Her heart feels so empty.
  without his incandescent smile.
What is this pain and sorrow worth,
  for absence makes the heart grow fonder.

Nancy Massaro

Success Or Failure?

There's a restlessness within me that seems to grow stronger as the years go by.
A feeling of something unfinished or possibly an act yet to be done before I die.

Even as a child, I sensed there was a reason for my creation and felt very odd.
Now, I know that before ever being in my Mother's womb; I had made a
  pact with God!

My days are haunted with the thought that maybe I have failed, and will feel God's wrath!
On the road of life, did I make a wrong turn? Follow the wrong path?

There were so many times when only blind faith and trust seemed to make me strong.
It would have been so easy to give up, yet I still kept trying, whether right or wrong!

Are the days left too few to accomplish the one thing written in my "Book of Fate"?
Or will it be so obvious I will know at once that my job is done: it wasn't too late!

Louise M. Tanderes

The Great Equalizer

Life made me dance the dance of desire,
yet death has ravaged me and I am so cold.
I am now a shell of the person I was.
The soundless beating of my heart
as I felt the icy hand of death grip my mortality.
Limbs growing cold and limp as my life blood slows.
Oh, the lack of oxygen to my brain...
The synapses failing to connect the energy of dreams and ideas.
Clouds of confusion as the world fades from view.
Muscles once full of strength,
now full of decay.
Just a carcass of flesh remains.
No gender...
No wealth...
No social status.
Just another body in the Great Equalizer's valley of pain.

Marilyn Campiz

Untitled

As I reflect my life today, I am thankful and most happy,
yet I feel the need to pray.
What a perfect world this could be. Unfortunately, it will take all of us to believe.

I am very afraid for my children to grow. It will be a long, hard road for them, this I know.

If only this world could be violence free. No more hunger, just love, what a vision to see.

I think it should be obvious, a new direction needs to be taken. A world of hope, love, faith and prayer, in the making.

And so I pray to God, for your family and mine. For He alone possess the power of all time.

Sandy Kaye Smith

A Tribute to Mom

From the time we were small and we needed your love so much,
You always knew the right words to say and how to show your love.

It really didn't matter what child wanted your attention the most,
You found the time for all four of us.
We often hear, "There are no supermoms,"
But your bountiful energy often left us amazed and stunned.
There was never any obstacles or walls to high for you to climb,
no problem to tough that you couldn't find a solution nearby.

As we matured and thought we were smarter than you,
You would smile and say no words because you knew what all mothers
knew. It took wisdom, courage, strength, and patience and also a few
punishments to allow each of us to grow, and sometimes we may have
wondered if you really loved us so.

But today, there is no question, no doubt of your endless love.
We know you were the greatest Mom who will always watch over us.
We will forever cherish and love you, and never will we forget
The values and morals you taught us. We will continue to be a loving
united family even though you are gone,
And we will remember and cherish the words of wisdom you shared with
each one of us.

Samella Burse

You and Me

You've changed as far as I can see
You always know just what to say you are such a sweetie.
I'd love to be the one you love, but for now I can only imagine,
what it feels like to be touched by you.
A kind of electricity flows through
me thinking of your honesty to me, I'd like to be the one your true
    to,
but I know it could never be so I wish I could have just one kiss.
I know you'd be true to me. I do so desire thee.
I know you'd be true to me.
I love to dream of you and me holding hands,
holding each other, kissing each other, making love, and being
loved.
You touching me would make me know everything's okay from
the vibrations you send me. I wish you'd look
at me, oh how I wish it to be. I'd say I've
fallin' in love but I don't remember what
true love is or what it's like to be in love again.
But if this isn't it, what is? All I
need is for you to say you'd be happy to love
me anytime of day, baby we can do this make it work,
you and me together love will make us both happy

Lorrin Carson Adams

You Are to Me,

You are to me, pleasant and intelligent possessing respectful ways
You are to me, a bright spot bringing sun to cloudy days
You are to me, (in the physical), handsome with an attractive frame
You are to me, a strong temptation causing ignition of a flame
You are to me, a gentle male-a gentleman; sensitive and caring
You are to me, an overachiever with time on occasion unsparing
You are to me, a positive factor within the equation of my heart
You are to me, like a new hit single, rapidly climbing the charts
You are to me, what my music is: an enjoyable variety of flava!
You are to me, still.. a good person during moments of ill behavior
You are so many gifts to me, what I want you to comprehend:
You are to me, which means so much, a very special friend

A. Benjamin

Oh My Puppet

Oh my puppet
You are unable to disobey
We pull the strings to command you
You satisfy our every need

Oh my puppet
You follow orders from us not the people
When they summon thee, we tell you how to respond
This keeps them happy

Oh my puppet
You always smile as if in control
Tell the people what they want to know
But you are never to deliver, what you speak

Oh my puppet
You are here not for the people
Only along to assist us
Try to resist and your downfall will come

Oh my puppet
Only around for a short time
Here until they realize you have failed them
Then they find us a new puppet

Salvatore Pino III

Dare to Discover

Smoking is bad as we all know,
You can get cancer from head to toe.
Why buy cigarettes, you know you should stop,
I would make you feel at the top.
All smokers always puff and puff,
Stop right now and you'll become hot stuff.
Second hand smoke effects others too,
It kills all that grew and grew.
If only you'd look at your lungs and watch them turn black,
You'd not want to smoke like a chimney stack.
I think stores should stop the sale,
And put all cigarettes in the pail.
Tobacco companies move away, we don't need you- do not stay.
Though tobacco pays lots of taxes, when you're gone all relaxes.
The world would have cleaner air,
This pollution— it is not fair,
The ozone layer will not stay,
Cigarettes helped that in its very own way.
Cigarettes, I must say no!
I want my generation to live and grow

Lindsay Plotkin

Give It To Me Child

Give it to me child,
You can't do it alone.
I'll give you the strength and the courage
That will help you along.

Start trusting in me, I won't let you down.
Believe I can help you; I'll lead you around.
Give me your troubles, your hurt and your pain.
Don't take it back or you won't make any gain.

Your path is filled with troubles; you stumble through the day
Darkness is in front of you; you do not see the way
Despair overcomes and you feel you're at your end.
That's when I come to tell you I will be your friend.

The path won't be so rocky and you won't fall so far.
Just come to me, I'm bright shining as a star.
Give a little; I'll give a lot. There's Peace, Hope, and Love.
Ask and all things shall be granted from above.

Kim Ivy

A Blanket

I have this blanket, it was made for my son
You can't find one like it, it's the only one
It was made with nothing save love and care
By someone I knew that's no longer here
It's beautiful to see as well as to touch
But that's not why we love it so much
It was made by hands he never would hold,
By a heart that somehow grew too old
One simple blanket, nothing more to see
To keep my son warm as she did me.

Thomas O'Connell

The Player

You said you would be here for me until the very end,
You claimed that you and I would always be good friends.
You told me that you cared and I really mattered to you,
You said I could call when I just needed a friend to talk to.

But I was just another game for you to play,
And when you grew bored, you tossed me away.
You always had me at your beck and call,
I had no mind of my own at all.

You see, I've always known things you didn't think I knew,
But I set the hurt aside to start our friendship anew.
When the hurt came back and I needed you most,
You walked away and continued to boast.

You boasted of how another girl fell for you,
And how you led her on and pushed her away too.
I hope I am not a trophy won in some macho game,
Because those sort of games will grow feeble and lame.

No one will fall into the spider's web you weave,
They'll recognize you as a player and turn to leave.
I know we may never be friends, but take heed,
I hope this is the only warning you'll ever need.

Shelly Bryant

Untitled

I limp! You don't.
You cry! I won't.
I am dark! A grudge you hold.
You are light! For this we fight.
You tell me that I am poor.
Though my strength you still adore.
Your fame and fortune I'm taught to envy.
My fortune lies within my family.
Only a child seems able to see, the beauty in the world,
the way it should be.
Please open your eyes as only a child would do.
Try looking at the world as if it were new.
Only then will you be able to see all the love that's in the world.
It's inside you! It's inside me!

Marquise C. Wood

Joy

Softly...a voice cries out to
  you during the night.
    disconcernment laid bare in a body
      new to the world...
        endemic to new father who
          yearns for the joys of youth, not knowing,
            that this, his new
Love, is ironically what it is he longs for.
  yesterday, a zeal for pleasure in his own life...
    now, selfishness laid aside, his new love...his
      new life.

William J. Johnson

Anchor's Away

You had calmed the seas of unsteady waves
You had slain the serpents grasping your ship
You had hooked the fish brought to the galley
You anchored the ship safely in it's slip

You had been the leaf that fell from the tree
Shaken from the chill of autumn's calling
Your crumbling spirit could no longer hold
You let go too quick to keep from falling

Unanchored crew as you jumped off the plank
Weeping willows try reaching blades of grass
Searching for the lighthouse to guide them back
Branches crippled by the storm that did pass

Now in the corner of the wishful eye
A captain in a ship just passing by.

Ken Partch

Life Without Dad

You have heard the song about Daddy's hands.
You have heard the song about just like my Dad.
You once were a little girl and now you are grown.

You helped all you could to keep him well and at
Home.

You woke up one day and your Dad's life had changed.
And you were sad for this big change.

The years went by so fast, needless to say, that life
Had past and the Lord had came.

So don't be sad for all has past. The best has come
for your Dad at rest.

He smiles among you every day from the heavens so far
away. Continue to live your life today, for one day
you will be on your way.

Karen Crusenberry

David Of My Heart And Soul

Oh David of my heart. How much I love
you. How much I care. I prey on God every
Day and night. That one day we will be
together once again. And I can tell you at
last how much I love you and stop hiding
my feelings for you. And how much I need to
be with you.
Oh David of my soul. Without you in my
life is like an endless day. Without you I feel
like a piece of my heart is gone. I know that I can't
live any longer without you in my life.
Oh David of my heart. My love for you can be like
a bolt of lighting in my heart. My love for you
is line singing. It fills me with joy. When I am
with you my heart needs to sing to your heart. You
are David of my heart and soul.

Stephanie Culpepper

The Poet

What can I rhyme with this?
Will my thoughts come across or miss?
Most poetry is lovely and pointed.
Mine seems senseless and disjointed.
I only wanted to convey
A good message for today.
What joy working with words in verse
Making them come out to not be terse!
Thinking of nature like birds or flowers of beauty,
Nothing compares to words assigned to a duty.

Louise Childers

Let Me In

Let me in
You keep trying to stop me
Let me in
This is my world too
Let me in
Have you no shame
Have you no empathy
Get out of my way
Move back ... move back, before I walk on you
Let me in this is my life
Let me in I will get involved
Let me in I'm not stepping back
Get out of my way
Move back...move back, because here I come
You don't know me, have you tried
You don't know me, will you try
Oh No! Let me out, let me out
You don't understand
You don't understand
Your world, my world...you'll never know
You will never understand, until you have GOD in your life.

Serena Penn

You're Open Heart

You give me sight into your heart, you let me feel what you think,
You know my loves, my hates, my thoughts and dreams.

You see me -
A young gentle rose blooming, waiting for the sun to
shine on her so that she can open up her petals of beauty.

The emotions inside of me, the love that I feel
you have brought this out of me, the way no one else can.

You have touched my heart and made it dance upon the moonlight.
You have touched my soul and have made it yearn
for the love I have found - wanting to grasp
every second, every moment I am in your presence.

Mary Beth Dohoney

Friends, Above All

Of the olden days, I can recall
You looked out for me, because I was small,
And you were my big sister, through the years
You cared for me through laughter and tears.
The friendship we had, the best ever known
Just grew and grew into love, full blown.
Like a rose it blossomed, and gave full measure
Of the caring and kindness I'll always treasure.
Now in these "golden" years, I've reached eighty two
And you share in my troubles, are there when I'm blue.
So I look back, all these years through
And know you're the best friend I ever knew.
Your heart knows no guile, and no arrogance
My very best friend - my sister, Florence

Luella M. Knutson

The Candle of Love

I am a dull candle waiting to be lit.
You are a flame ready to light.
We meet — the candle and the flame,
Both of us working together, as one.
Without you I am dull, having no glow;
However now, I glow and flicker with delight.
Jointly we continue to burn,
Until someone interferes and blows you out;
Leaving me nothing but your ashes for my
memory,
I again am a dull candle waiting to be lit.

Layna Smith

A Young Soul

I must make you aware of something I've found,
You must be tolerant of others as life goes around.
This path that you walk is yours, that is true,
But to make others walk it is wrong to do.

The right that you ask for is to be your own man
So the right that you give must be the same my friend.
No person on earth is exactly like you
Your values are yours, unique only to you.

So don't try to change those that you know
Their path is theirs don't judge how they go.
Accept who they are, the good and bad,
Learn from their life, that's why we cross paths.

As you walk down your path, where ever it goes,
Be tolerant of people for there's no way to know
Those lessons we must learn we cannot foresee,
And the teachers in life are the people we meet.

Oralie Spink

Untitled

All the pictures that hang on her wall,
You only look once and you think you know all.
A beautiful woman so tall and so lean,
her hair is so blonde and her eyes so green.
She's celebrating her daughters wedding in her
beautiful home,
Seven years later she'd have three grandchildren
of her own.
But life can be cruel and have a sad twist of fate,
For just one motor vehicle accident and then it was too late.
Now her life is confined to a bed,
Tubing runs through her stomach for that's how she's fed.
So tiny, so fragile and so very weak,
She can only smile but cannot speak.
But I can see her tell me to enjoy everyday,
Because you never know, your life can be taken away.

Kimberly Muller

Rich Man

You look at a rich man, what do you see
You say money defines him, but to me family
All the money in the world, can't buy you a heart
Take the love of your children, that's where you start

I am a rich man, with my girl and boy
Each precious memory, brings a lifetime of joy
They are my fortune, and all that I see
And I know I'm a rich man, when they smile at me

Diamonds and gold, money and fame
Yes I am the rich man as I call them by name
Josh and Kristina, and my loving wife
A fortune of love, for the rest of my life

Night has now fallen, as I kiss them goodnight
Please dad read a story, before you turn out the light
The story's half over, but their fast asleep
So I close the cover, but these memories I keep

The trust of your children, is something you earn
With the time you spend sharing, all the lessons you've learned
I just can't be take for granted they say
Be honest and caring, every day

Ron Ingraham

The Gifts (Two Conquests)

Roses
you sent her roses
twelve of them
deep red ones
long-stemmed too
with a love note
handwritten
she glued them in a Scrapbook to remind her

Once
ah but once
oh inadvertently I know
your cool capricious lips
brushed ever so briefly
against my flustered brow
And now
whenever a light wisp of air
whispers even very faintly
across that sacred spot
my Heart throbs anew

Kathryn J. Matthiessen

In Search of Dreams

As you grow and travel along life's winding path
You tend to experience frustration.
You hurt,
You feel defeated.
You want to give up - to quit.
You want to turn away and pretend that
    disappointments don't matter.
But you won't walk away because
    you're not a loser -
    you're a fighter...

We all have defeats and losses before we can win.
We all have to cry sometimes before we can smile.
We all have to hurt a little before we can be strong.
We all have setbacks before we can move forward.

But if you keep trying - have faith and believe
    that you can do anything,
You will have victory in the end.
You can have all your dreams and more than you ever
    thought possible.

Linda C. Boyer

Untitled

Just like an angel, whose arms hold off my fears,
you walk ever near me protecting me from the sky.
It's falling down upon me like a nightmare as I scream.
Crying out your name so loud, you are my only dream.
Never shall I upset you, for I hate to catch your tears,
Your eyes as gentle as the fallen snow, so bright, so wide.
So open to your fears they draw me in.
I am your creation, so make me what you will.
Promise just to keep me and hold me ever still.
Sleeping softly beneath the stars I sit and watch you breathe.
Walking just beside you, I wander through your dreams
We come across a rippling stream, new colors on its shores.
We could dare, of course, to wade...
but your shoes are made of precious jewels,
and my tan will surely fade.
Thoughts of future days to come run rampant in my mind,
just rolling by the clouds of my eyes and clearing up the sky.
Coffee... cream and sugar, keeping me awake.
Your consciousness growing near.
Go ahead and open your eyes, I will always be here.

Nita Jackson

The Wedding Poem

When did you know
You wanted her in your life
When did you know
Was it after your first date
Or was it after your first kiss
Or maybe it was after you first held her hand.
You knew you wanted her to wear your wedding band.

As you got to know each other
Something was taking place
You where seeing more then a pretty face

You where trying to be bold
Love was taking hold of your heart
Then you knew the two of you must never part.

Now the time is near for all to come together
The church Bells will ring
The birds will sing
You'll be happy for the rest of your life
With your new wife

Paula Hursh

My Most Precious Son

I felt you inside my body for nine, long months
You were kicking me all the time and doing your stunts
You were such a wonderful blessing to us
You were not willing to put up a fuss
You were a great dream come true
You and your wonderful eyes of shy blue
Your white blond hair as straight as a board
I felt like you were surely a precious
gift from the Lord
I counted each one of your fingers and
toes
I realized then and now how much your
personality shows
You have given me so many wonderful
moments
There is not a day that goes by I
don't require your solace.

B. J. Guthrie

Keeping The Faith

Keeping the faith will be tough,
You will take roads that are bumpy and rough.
Everything must happen one day at a time,
For sin is the biggest crime.

Keeping the faith is no longer rare,
Because all it takes is a prayer.
Following Jesus has become the new craze,
So join in, raise your arms and begin to praise.

Keeping the faith puts a smile on his face,
All you need is Jesus and his grace.
He tells us to be a living witness.
To share all of the greatness.

Keeping the faith is a service that is free,
Without Jesus what would I be.
For he parted the sea and walked on water,
Your salvation to him make him the one and only father.

Keeping the faith is part of your will,
Since he has been known to heal.
He made the blind to see and gave hope to the lame,
Now you know keeping the faith is no game.

Ronnie Fox

You Are Everything Special

Your eyes are like fingers on the braille of my heart,
  Your arms, the shelter from the storm.....

Your smile is hope and light like the sun on a rainy day,
  Much desired, always warm.....

Your voice the whispering of the tree that blows in the breeze
  on a hot summer night.....

You, are my foundation the rock I am built on,
  Your heart, the ocean..... deep and inviting.....

You are the stars in my life, dark as night,
  The way it's been since you've been gone.

Me, the sheep that is lost from the herd,
  Until we again can be one.....

Lisa Michelle Dukes

Our Morning Jog

With labored thought and breath, I watch
your back move away from me.
My mind and body, exhausted a mile ago,
ooze a wet, Crayola-colored pain from my side.

You circle around to me, to ask what is wrong.
If only I could explain.

What to say? Our lives have become a deceitful joke?
That our callow infidelities and childish games destroy us?
Or that we are left only with the angry pallor of sex?

If I could explain,
old wounds would someday scab over, the rage subsided,
We could retract our claws, repair our armor, fight no more.
If only I could explain.

Instead, silence betrays me,
my demons remain locked away,
taunting me and the smile I feign
when I assure you that everything is fine

And I keep running, with a pain in my side

Scott Carpenter

My Science Test

Momma told me— "Just do your best,
Your brains and hard work will do the rest."
And with that she hugged me and patted my back,
And I leaned over, picked up my sack,
And went to school.

And it came time-after lunch,
To take the test-I had a hunch,
Walking out-that I did well,
It's one of those things that I could tell.

That evening Momma asked — "How did you do?
I said I was certain I'd made a ninety-two.
And Momma smiled- "You tried your hardest-
  I'm happy for you;
But I'd still be happy if you got a thirty two."

The very next day my test was handed back to me,
I was so disappointed with only a forty-three!
"But Momma," I pleaded, "you said you'd be
  happy with a thirty-two."
"A forty-three," she yelled at me, "deserves
  being grounded for a month or two!"

Shira Amdur

Little Dove

Little dove with blue eyes,
your eyes are more blue than the bluest,
blue sky.
Your scanning the sky and flying high.
Holding you seeing you and loving you turns me on
to the highs of all natural highs.
I love you like I love a May day
just like the Red Rose and Yellow Tulip
budding on this clear, warm, spring day.

Mike Runfola

Babies

Babies are so precious but, they'll steal
your heart away.
Even though they fuss, and cry at night,
and want to sleep next day.

When morning comes, they awake afresh,
They'll kick, they'll coo and smile,
To make you forget the night before, and make
it all worth while.

There's feeding time and bathing time
There's much to do all day,
Yet when you hold them in your arms
They'll make a sad heart gay.

They'll bring much happiness through the years
  to the home, in which they live
A softer bundle, you'll never find
  A gift only God can give.

You watch them grow all through the years
  There's joy in everyday
There's sorrow too but, when there's love,
  It smoothes the roughest way.

Nora Whitaker

Comforter

How I hate to see the pain on your face, the tears in your eyes;
Your illusion of paradise shattered by endless lies.
You run to me not knowing what else to do,
Confident that my gentle touch, my soft words will comfort you.

Alas! To restore your happiness I'm useless,
Because your sorrow serves to feed mine naturally.
But I try my best nevertheless,
For just being with you is pure ecstasy.

Thus, I console you to the best of my ability
Because that's what true friends are for.
But how can I tell you I desire so much more?
To be your humble servant I feel is my destiny.

However, this isn't the time to address the issue;
Restoring your happiness is my priority, it's the least I can do.
Just remember when it seems there's no one to turn to,
These open arms and undying love will always be here for you.

Peterson Pierre

Easter Visit

Easter morning, bright and warm, a beautiful day to be adorned.
White clouds sailing two by two, across the wide expensive blue.
The long white ribbons of the interstate,
rolling hills and wooden gates.
The farms and trees go swiftly by, the cars in a hurry seem to fly.
Everyone is on their way, to greet someone or a day of play,
The city soon comes into view with all its winding roads so new.
The houses nestled side by side, the jets are circling in the sky.
Then the happy moment to greet everyone you love
and a silent thank you, to the one above.

Virginia J. Fitz-Gerald

My Shiloh

If my voice were to be silent for one hundred years,
your name would be the first sound out of my mouth.
If in those same one hundred years, my eyes were unable to open,
I would still try many times every day;
just in case you would be passing my way.
If in those same long one hundred years,
I were restrained from touching,
I would trace your silhouette over and over again in my mind
'til the end of the time.
If in those same dragging, and long one hundred years
I were denied my ability to hear,
I would surely long for your voice to tenderly call my name.
If in those same dragging, and long one hundred years
I were robbed of all feeling,
I would instantly die from lack of your love.

Laura L. Gross

The Moment

You met him a an awkward age, you 17 and he, slightly older
You're not children but not quite adults
The moment when your eyes met was magic
He took you for a fast ride in his car
The freedom he gave you was amazing
You felt like a colt running through a field
Throwing caution to the wind
The sun was at your back
But it's a feeling you can ever have again.

One day everything seemed to change
You adored him even more than before
But he was different
His bright blue eyes were no longer brilliant
But a dull gray
His warm, friendly smile
Now a frown that could turn you to stone
You wonder who could turn him around
But you knew it was you
Your words stabbed him like a knife.

Melanie A. Chapin

Your Time

Your time is near,
  you've heard their cries,
    you've seen their pain,
      but still, you continue.

You were warned once,
  and you won't be warned again,
    but you don't have to worry,
      'cause, your time is coming.

No longer will she be beaten,
  nor will she see her daughter in pain,
    I will not allow it any longer
      you are not a true man.

I hate you so much
  that I despise your every breathe
    but don't you worry,
      your time is here.

You've heard my words
  you've seen my madness
    you've tasted your own fear
      now feel your undying pain

Kristy Atwood

If You Only Knew

Honey if you only knew how happy you've made me feel

For things I've only fantasized about
you've somehow made them real

My love for you goes far beyond any
words that I can speak

But if my heart had its own voice
it would say "I'm yours to keep"

The compassion shared between us
is strong and here to stay

And the love that you have given me
I never would betray

In you I find a special man who's turned my life around

Within myself I finally know
that true love I have found

The closeness that I shared with you I've never felt before

And the eagerness to spend my life
with you I can't ignore

To stay the man that you are now is all that I am asking

For I am confident our love
will be one that's everlasting

Pipkin

Labels

"You're too skinny"
"You're too fat"
"You're too smart"
"You're too stupid"
Who are you to say these things?
Who am I to question you?
I am Frank and you are Bill,
but what gives us the right to label a person.
We are all too skinny,
    fat,
    smart,
    and stupid.
We should look at ourselves and label our self.
For who knows Frank better than Frank, and Bill better than Bill.
So before you start to label someone look at yourself
and maybe you are just the same.

Sara Olivares

Common Ground

Ask nothing in return except the knowledge that my life is yours and
yours is mine believe we are one
Our feelings, our hopes and our dreams, a single vision of the future
We are all connected you and I and together we can create what seems
impossible, a better world for us all.

Where love is the ideal, hopelessness, anger and bitterness seem surreal
The true test of humanity, have we learned the lesson
That true love, selfless love determines whether we rise or fall

When will we learn that everyone has a place
The black, the red, the yellow, the brown, the white, in other words
the human race
We share this world and need to learn that for every child born a
vision is revealed
The children of the nations must stand together side by side
No prejudice, no bigotry, no intolerance only a sense of pride

Though diverse we share common ground
We can learn from each other, understanding can be found
The experiences we share creates a bond
Mother to child, woman to man, nation to nation

Linda Wilson

It's Just Me

It's just me. It's just me.
I say just me. Hello I am
right here. Hello are you deaf?
There you are it's just me.

Kristen Frolich

Mom Is Dying

Mom is dying. Cancer. Inoperable.
She turned 84 last Sunday.
84 years seems like a long time.
But it isn't.
When it's your mother
There are never enough years.
I don't want her to go.
She doesn't want to go.
But her body isn't cooperating.
No appetite. No energy
Dehydration.
I would give her some of my body
If it would help.
But I can't.
So I sit here and watch.
Watch as she tries to eat, but can't.
Watch as she wastes away.
I want to hold her, and rock her
Like she once did me.
Mom is dying. I am overwhelmed.

Beulah Eastman

Touch Me Touch Me Not

Touch me touch me not says
she who laughs.
Touch me touch me not says
he the one who cries.
Touch me touch me not says
the girl who plays.
Touch me touch me not says
he who is lonely.
Touch me touch me not says
the one who loves, laughs, cries, plays
and the one who is lonely till the
end of time. So touch me touch
me not...

Cassie Strong

Winter Silence

The grayness of winter
Sheds little light
With it's coldness and solitude
And stillness of night

The snowfall brings enlightenment
So white and pure
It brings with it hope for the future
So for now we will endure

It is a time of reflection
Silence and grace
Of quiet times passing
At a less hurrisome pace

As we remember times past,
And contemplate what has been done
Winter keeps its silence
Of the future yet to come.

Donna Dixson

Kitten

A little kitten as white as snow
She's really a lot of fun you know
She loves to run and jump and plays
Especially Frolicking in the hay
She has a pink little nose and big
yellow eyes
When you look at her she seems so wise
She's soft and cuddly and oh so sweet
Isn't that the kind of kitten you
would like to meet?

Barbara Griffin

Life

Life runs with the wind
shifting like sand
changed from the roar of the waves
opportunities, fleeting
but ever present
love, elusive
but a necessary chase
Attack life with a vengeance
drink from it till you are drunk
with its beauty
live life full with the intent
of returning for more

The thought of coming back
may just inspire you
to create something good
and leave behind a legacy of love

To argue with life
is to celebrate the grave
the enemy is not life
but those who refuse to enjoy it.

Jon Alexander Daye

Like The Fallen Rain

Through every turbid mist,
  Shines some sunlit rays,
Sparkling on the morning dew,
  Along the traveled ways.
Falling under many footfalls,
  Across the passing days.

There're days of freedom,
  days of glory,
There're days of sadness,
  days of pain,
Like the fallen rain.

With every sensation,
  We become aware,
We see each other's waking life,
  The circle that we share.
Wrapping around every person,
  The burden we must bare.

Jeffrey Bain

Vision

In a vision of loveliness
  I see the flowers sway.
In the whispering wind
  I hear them say.

You must like yourself
  To be liked by others.
You must love yourself
  To be loved by your lovers.

Martin J. Bonner

Untitled

The ocean behind her
shining through the window;
her back to its majesty,
her blue blouse melting to eternity...

My eyes caught sight
and realized the moment:
my mother sits dying
so beautifully, we grieve
together as the waves pull
back to their vast fullness, I
would hold her close and not let
her go if I were as strong
as the waters that birthed me.

She was lovelier in that moment
than my grief can ever be,
but I will take her gently
with me, as I wander these wetlands
more alone...

Diana Wheelis

Flight Fantasy

Soaring around in my airplane,
Sight-seeing and flying about;
I thought I saw a familiar face
Beckoning me around.
I turned and banked, and to my surprise
saw an angel on a cloud.

Smiling at me I heard her say,
"You'd better get your feet back
on the ground —
That flying machine, which flies you
around — bothers me."

Bothers you! I cried in alarm.
Hell, I said, stow your wings,
Give me your arm;
We'll fly by heaven's gate,
And if that hanger in the sky
is opened wide,
We'll land this craft; step inside
and have a drink. Hic.

Henry R. Correa

Visions

Anticipation has got me
Since I first saw your smile
Untold stories of the future
Imaginations running wild

Messages I send to you
Both beautiful and bold
Reaching deep inside you
For secrets yet to unfold

A selfish man like I
With an eye for style and grace
Sees you as a classic wine
And would surely take a taste

Have you any idea of
What this world has in store
Nights of love and passion
Ecstasies and much more

A spell has been cast
That challenges my mind
But it won't be complete
Until your lips meet mine

Charles Arnold Jr.

Little Unknown

Little unknown baby
Sleeping so snug and warm
Nourished by your parents love
As bones and limbs do form.

Will you be blonde or dark of hair
Your eyes be brown or blue
Suits or dresses will you wear
When you make your first debut?

Will Rhonda's charm or Michael's grin
Shine rampant from your eyes
You're bound to be a beauty
Whatever God decides.

Of one thing I am certain
You must be very wise
To have picked the finest parents
In this whole world wide.

Little unknown baby dear
I wait with open arms
To hold you to my waiting heart
And know your many charms.

Irene Coombs

My Son

Little feet and fists curled into balls
Small feet to climb the wooded paths
Barefeet leaving wet prints from
    pool or baths.
Sneakered feet to roam learnings halls
Booted feet to climb life's hills
All echoes resounding off memories walls
Adult feet a mother's pride to fulfill.

Judith Smith

Experience

Wisdom is born of experience
So don't be afraid my lad
To put your shoulders to the wheel
Or to sort the good from the bad.

Work your very best through life
Don't be afraid to carry your load
Many good things can be learned
Even with the wild oats you've sowed.

Good things can be found in a book
But if they've never been tried
They can be lost in the shuffle
They need to be used and applied.

By using the two together
You can have a successful career
Whatever it is you try my lad
The solutions will soon appear.

Cherish all the knowledge you learn
Whether by reading or by toil
You can have the same satisfaction
In an office or tilling the soil.

Francel Rietz

The Loss

I have been alone before.
I will be alone again.
But, I will be far loner then;
Because I have known and
Loved you now.

Roswita B. Davis

The Little Heart I Hold So Dear

My little heart that I hold
    So safely in my arms
Is it any wonder that I'm a
    Captive of her charms

We are like one as we gaze
    out to sea
Our hearts are happy
    And our spirits are free

The world is our playground
    And together we dream
Of sand castles and shells
    And just maybe ice cream

The shadows lengthen
    And she nods her little head
Grandpa, I'm tired
    I'll take my dreams to bed

Joseph G. Milnes

My Life

My life has been arranged,
So the hard times are lacked,
But not so the change.
I sing and I dance,
And let the day pass,
And watch the stars,
Witch hold my salvation,
And look to the moon,
For my guiding light.
I feel sober and unfulfilled,
Though I have my relations,
For whom I do not have to plead.
I am deserted,
Though not enriched.
Not understanding
Wish to be switched.

Brandy Adler

Since You Were Little

Your smile's my sunshine
so warm and so bright
Your hugs are uplifting
causing my heart to take flight

Your chuckle is honest
it brings on my laughter
I'm bonded to you
Forever after

As I sit and I listen
to hear what you say
I realize how lucky
I am on this day

I see in your eyes
my hopes and my dreams
and even in strife
my heart always screams

Love for my child
what more could I ask?
The answer: God's help
in life's biggest task!

Janette M. Wehrley

How Much?

Question me.
I shall say "I love you"
More than yesterday
Not as much as tomorrow
But with all I am today
I love you

Marianne Sickle

Love Is

Love is like a melody,
    Soft and sweet.
Notes of joy spread on high,
    With tunes of laughter.
The way of love can be seen
    In kisses, tears, and words
The words of love are many
    Soft whispers of glowing truth
The touch of love can be felt
    As tender loving caresses.
The smell of love is variant.
    Sweet perfume and sweeter souls.
The thought of love is simple.
    Deep in the heart it is found.
Yes love is many things.
    Laughter, sorrow, and eternal joy.
Love can be defined as a question.
    The answer is in your heart.

John Fitzpatrick

Shadows of the Past

The door swings open and the
soft voice within my heart cries
for your touch each night

As I stand at the crossroads
buried deep within my soul of
wasted youth, stolen innocence,
faded hopes and long forgotten dreams.

I slowly reclaim all the
misplaced memories of you
that I threw away long ago

The love that I once adored
now and always endlessly will
wander through the corridors of
my heart and soul until finally
I can set you free

Beth Downey

I Wish I Was Wind

I wish I was wind,
Softly blowing through the trees.
Making everyone feel cool,
On hot summer days.

I wish I was wind,
Blowing the storm clouds away.
I'd keep the sun close by,
And the rain a million miles away.

I wish I was wind,
Blowing the tops of water.
Making everyone hear the slight crash,
As the water collides with the shore.

I wish I was wind,
Soaring far away in the sky.
Far away from the earth,
Like an eagle in flight.

Christina Poling

Black Cats

Some cats are mean,
some cats are lean,
some cats meow,
some just prowl,
some cats don't like you,
some will just bite you,
but some are black,
and that's a cat!

Black cats are cool,
they totally rule!
Some just like to stay
under your bed all day.
Some are lazy,
some are crazy,
some like to play,
some runaway,
black cats are freaky,
and their real sneaky!!!!!

Alisha Streitmatter

If I Had A Friend

If I had a friend
someone to share
my hopes and my dreams
my fears and my cares

She'd be a good listener
and never to judge
who always understands
and never holds a grudge

If I had a friend
she'd have to be strong
someone to help me
when I'm right and I'm wrong

If I had a friend
with the knowledge of life
I'd trust her enough
to ask her advice

And with this friend
I could laugh with and cry
she could answer the question
of when I ask why?

If I has a friend
I'd cherish her like no other
I do have a friend
and she is my mother.

Francine Kowalski

I'm Gray, Leaping Dolphin

I'm a gray, leaping dolphin
splashing playfully
daydreaming lifelessly
A slick and sleek pyramid of life
skimming across the sphere of water
blindly devouring fish
The fiery blue water around me
full of explosive energy
reaches for the sky
vegetating wildly on
a lazy Saturday afternoon.

Alvin Poon

It's His Poetry

God shines on all age,
Split with night's curtain.
Right on each new page
Is time that we're in.

Those old pages turn
And curtains will rise.
Someday people learn,
But must realize

Mortal life will end,
Still time will go on.
An ear may you lend
Before you are gone!

God created love
That we're a part of.
His word made it known
That His light has shown

Straight on from the start,
Deep inside my heart.
His love's part of me.
It's His Poetry.

Gary Neer

Beware!

Blade of grass,
   standing straight,
tree of God,
   born to wait.
Bird of sky,
   flying, winging,
insect small,
   buzzing, winging.
Reptiles supple,
   gliding, waiting,
woman quiet,
   loving, waking,
man of earth,
   fighting, working.
Shrouded figure,
   shadow lurking.

Caryl R. Pearson

Power Poet

Adventure woman,
standing tall upon the
shoulders of two muscular men,
tan, naked, oiled men,
reined in finest leather,

Seeking today's conquest
or supplication.
cruelty or kindness,

Riding before the winds,
hair flowing free,
bodice of crystal steel,

Liquid words
are thy weapons,
thy caresses,
thy torments,

Unsheathed arrows
of indescribable beauty,
causing thy victims
to cry out in glorious pain,
shoot me, shoot me!

Gene A. Blinde

The Gift

On the table
Stands a box.
Buried beneath layers of tissue
Lies a treasure
Waiting for me.

I've passed it
Oh, so many times.
My mind teased
By the endless possibilities
Of what is hidden within.

I am torn.
By all rights,
Wrappings should be torn away
And this very special gift
Unearthed.

And yet, I hesitate. Could it be that
Anticipation is everything
And satisfaction a mere will-o' the wisp?
Perhaps I will
Just walk away.

Anita L. Fogg

Untitled

Friendship is a tree.
Starting out tiny,
But with care,
Love, and consideration,
It grows strong.
At first needing work,
Attention and time,
It grows into something you can lean on.
Branches to give shade and comfort;
Trunk to give support,
Falling leaves to remind of times past.
If neglected, the tree dies;
If forgotten, the leaves wither,
If abused, the trunk bleeds sap.
Wounds that don't disappear,
And are never forgotten.
Always there to remind
That nothing is perfect;
Or forever.

Elise Irving

Farmer's Work

Oh, the smell of summer's heat
   stirs us to rise
      to the day of work.

Early hours of coolness,
   kept us quiet in our rest
      without concern to agonize.

While life and breath continued on
   and gave us time to build
      for the coming day.

Clover's odor rides
   the early morning breeze
      sweet to each who does partake...
each separately.

No time for other else,
   to re-supply the dinner's store.
      No trip to town...
or thought of later day.

Rise to the day's work,
   farmer's work....
      dry stiffness of muscles sore, still of
yesterwork.

Carl Schoelkopf

Passion

Circle, my blood, pulsate,
storm, o pulse, rage,
blow, wind, coolness
around my burning brow;

Beat, o my heart, burst,
swell, my breast, breathe deeply,
fly, o hair, and fall
upon her twitching shoulder.

Nod, treetops, and lash,
smell, flowers, unbend,
tremble, you grass-blade,
and strut around our rhythmic bed.

Flow, my blood, founder,
then darken, o world, disappear,
flee life, and stream
into our flaming death.

Henry Orland

Untitled

The world flows by me,
Such wonderful things,
I guess it's the time, to not
care what tomorrow brings.
I just follow the world,
not making plans, just do it
how the next day lands, sometimes
it seems like there's no
point to life, we just live it
because that's the intention
right? A lot of questions with
no answers, there's millions
of ways, to live life it occurs.
No one knows why as we are
what we are, but there is an
answer, somewhere, out far.

Hannah Redfield

Lagoon Haiku

The lagoon mirrors
surrounding trees, now plate glass
smooth, then wind-rippled

images of shades
of green - setting off floating
flotilla of ducks

crossing the lagoon
from the sunny, peopled side
to hidden places

in the brush, where trees
bend over the water with
branches dipping low

beneath the surface -
playground for ducks and squirrels
and a place of rest.

Edda Hackl

Butterfly-Way

Wanna have your way
like the summerday
of a butterfly?

But what,
if at noon
you're still a
cocoon? - - -

Euge Abel

The Darkened Room

Traveling along in a padded wagon
Sweeping down the path of doom
Attacking like a hideous dragon
Leading me to my darkened room

Eating away at my fragile mind
Beating like an ominous clock
Seeing others in the same bind
Feeling the stranger fasten the lock

Confusing me with all their might
Pretending to be there in my need
Clouding the essence of my sight
Growing as rapidly as a weed

Going to an early grave
Grasping for days gone by
Remembering one in which to save
Wishing I knew the reason why

Hoping I will find the answers there
Knowing that the end will come soon
Needing the knowledge of knowing where
Leading me back to my darkened room

Donna M. Sample

Shadows

It's there Lord, standing between us,
Tall and dark, this shadow of sin
     upon my soul.
     I won't let go -
          I can't let go.
Something deep inside me holds tight
To this thing within me that I despise,
And tho' I try with all my might to
     confess it,
     Turn it over to you
          Yet there at my feet it lies.
Oh Father don't turn away -
This specter of shadows won't let me be.
It haunts me night and day.
     Will anyone tell me how to make
     him flee?
Where are your children Lord that could
     speak to me -
          of thee?

Betty Lee Rhodes

My Most Precious Gift

All her warmth,
tenderness and love

She wipes away
my tears, like
the sweep of a dove.

With all her beauty
inside and out,
never raised her voice,
not even a shout.

God knew what he was doing
when he made her
that way.

She's special to me
in every way

I'm proud she's my mother
that's easy to say

And I thank God
she's my mother
everyday

Carolyn Thomlinson

The Party In Front Of The Mirror

Good looking
Thank you
Good temper
Why not
Without drink
Without jealous women
Without men
looking for right answer

Only for herself
In front of the mirror
She cuts her smiles
Before midnight comes
So she is dancing
Through the party
Alone
In front of the mirror

Jarmila Furmankova

Light of Life

Gazing at the rays of light
that dance ever so brightly
on the cool morning waters
of spring
I travel slowly through many
memories that are reflected
in this mirror of life. A life
I've led, another yet to be lived
just as my eyes are to close for
a moment, they see a glimpse
of a gull. Chasing the breeze,
freely brushing the tips of his
wings over the light.
It's time to breathe again,
     time to live.

Christopher Meads

Forever My Child

Sweeter than rain
that falls on my face
forever my child.

Pure than snow
that covers this place
forever my child.

Born unto me
rapid and wild
forever my child

So tender so sweet
no other pain has made me complete
always and forever my child.

Dawn-Marie Tomlinson

Shadows From My Past

Canoeing in the twilight,
A picnic for two,
A candle between us,
Smiles,
A memory,
Flickering on the water,
Shadows from my past.

Jennifer Roizen

You Are the Answer

"To be or not to be,"
"That is the question."
"Life is what you make it."

Life can hold many mysteries,
Life can hold many sorrows,
Life can be what you dream,
Life can be what you are.

That is the question!

You can give, you can hate,
You can wish, you can want.

Turn hate into love
To those you come in contact,
Give, what you can
To those around you,
Want, but to an extent,
Love, everyone you see
For you are the answer.

Candyce C. Arlitt

Touching the Heart

Sometimes I feel so sad
That it makes me cry

Tears so strong
They burn the human eye

The tears are sharp and cold
They feel like needles and pins

Hoping many of times
I wish this would all end

My heart is strong
Filled with love and desire

Longing for someone to touch me
And set my soul a fire

I deserve a chance to be happy
In body, spirit, and mind

Touching the heart for any reason
Touching the heart any time

Jimmy Antoine

Nature's System

There's a fly in my room
   that keeps buzzing around.
And I can't sleep
   with that buzzing sound.
My desire is to kill it,
   but I'd feel too much guilt
for breaking the system
   that nature built.
So, I test my patience
   and try to ignore it,
as the fly buzzes 'round
   my room to explore it.
I hope soon, the web
   in the corner, he'll find.
I'm sure that my
   eight-legged friend won't mind.
He'll hog tie that buzzer
   and have fly mignon dinner
while I sleep well,
   knowing I'm not the sinner.

Carroll W. Jourdan

Mom

For you are my candle
That leads me through this life
of darkness
For you ease my fear of the unknown
by lightning my way with your
courage and wisdom
The everlasting glow about you
has given me the sparkle in my eyes
to know that I can rise above all
and shine in the eyes of others
as you shine in mine
Thank you for giving me
The light of your ways.

Cassandra Ryan Lim

Untitled

It's just having you here with me
that makes me want to sigh
'cause I'm a part time father
and one day you'll ask me why
but I love you child, really
for God knows I've tried
and someday you'll be with me
as the ocean shores its tide
so please just call me Daddy
and put your hand in mine
'cause together we'll share many
my love for you you'll find

John Di Cristofano

My Special Love

You gave me love in a special way,
That no man has ever done;
You made me feel like a woman,
Now my heart is what you have won.

You know how to treat a lady,
And all the right words to say;
You even sent me red roses,
Every single day.

You never seem to get upset,
Over the little things I do or say;
That's why I love you more,
In a special kind of way.

Now that you have captured me,
Mind, body and soul;
I give you all my love,
Forever etched in gold.

You made my love shine brighter,
On all my gloomy days;
You are my special love,
Forever and ALWAYS.

Delores Spight

Reef (for Cole)

Gardens, rodeo,
an ocean—
void of matter pulses
with threatened

metaphors, your
doubles tremor
taut
barometer, corral.

Erik Ulman

Redemption Yet

Dear Youth, how angry is your way
That takes from you by night and day;
What hurt does waywardness reveal
As power lust makes grim appeal?
Your life borne now on winds of chance,
Manipulated as one in a trance
By vengeance taking murderous toll
When life has neither love nor goal.
Know, Once-Child, we bear such grief
No hopeful heart gives you relief;
No noble promise can you give
When in festering hate you live.
Fanciful and filled with grace
Mask intent peers sought to place;
Child-Yet, will you ever see
Life your gifts would let you be?
Come, return to well-worn trail
Trod well by souls who would not fail;
Come triumphant! Come to share!
Each milepost holds a promise there!

Bill Kimmey

Summer Breeze

The summer breeze touched
the arctic soul of the cynic.
Eternal hope and spring gave
the man, a new charge, a life
which had left with youth
but returned with wisdom.

One is not alone nor is the
death of man, one of physical
denial, the heart, the soul
can speak of youth and reflect the
power so hidden, which does not
appear unless cajoled by a
stream of energy.

Dan McCarthy

Mom's Greatest Love

Mom you've given me
The best years of my life
I know you had to suffer
And you made some sacrifice

But mom you'll never know
Just what you mean to me
These are words on paper
But they mean more than that you see

Mom your love goes far beyond
The imagination of the mind
With all the love you shared with us
Was so rich and so kind

The tender years of my life
You showed how much you cared
By asking God to bless us
And saying a simple prayer

When my time on earth has ended
And life has faded like the setting sun
I pray my children can see
All the good things I have done

Eva Thompson

Life

Life has bought about strings of changes.
The birds in the trees
This mornings breeze
Without the insight to see the light
These things of life would not be

One morning I got arrested
Something that was not to be digested
Strings of things to behold
For all the alcohol and dope to be sold

I thought, for what I sought
Only today I seek the meek

Now I know life is too precious
of a gem to give away.
While there's not that much time
to stay.

Connalita Stewart

My Last Goodbye

My heart is now broken
The birds won't sing again
There are no more rainbows
Our dream has come to an end

You said you'd never leave me
But you went anyway
To a place that is so peaceful
So far, far away

I look above to the heavens
And still don't know why
You left me here alone
Without you by my side

I want to tell you something
Since we couldn't say goodbye
I'll always love you
Until the end of time

Debra Gonzalez

Internal Journey

Walk with the sun to your back,
The cool breeze in your face.
Carry all your thoughts within you,
Don't leave behind a trace.

Walk as far as you must,
To reach the silent land.
Lay your body down softly,
Rest your head upon the sand.

The thoughts you so ponder,
Begin the game of chance.
As you gaze up into the sky,
Let it draw you into a trance.

Reach deep to study intently,
Mysterious questions of all kinds.
Powerful weapons to win the battles
Lie deep within your mind.

Jeffrey A. Wolff

The Visits

I quietly approached
the crib in which she slept,
then to my knees I fell
and silently I wept.

It seemed as only yesterday
I held her so sublime,
but now my arms are empty of
this Blessing that was mine.

Her sweet angelic face
with skin, so soft and fair,
her 'Visits' I shall cherish
in each and every prayer.

One day we'll be together,
I'm sure it's meant to be
when our little 'Visits' last
for all eternity.

Dennis Herrmann

Responsible for Me

It was the day before yesterday
The day I put my childhood away.

It was not the loss of Childhood dreams,
But the facing of what life means.

It was the day I began to see,
The purpose of responsibility.

A child I would no longer be,
As I became responsible for me.

No longer blaming the other man,
For what has happened at my hand.

That's the day I began to grow,
To live, to love, and to glow.

Things that I could never see,
Until I accepted responsibility.

Today I again began to grow,
What it's called I do not know.

Today my responsibility,
Is for everything I see.

If responsible I stand,
The glory will be more than that of man's.

Charles E. Houser

Old? No!

As the years keep passing by
    the decades just unfold.
My birthdays seem to come and go
    and friends think I'm growing old.

I do the things I want to do
    and still have lots of fun.
I have seen plenty of time pass by,
    as I'm going on eighty one.

When I was going to grade school,
    if I should tell you more,
before us kids could get inside
    we chased dinosaurs from the door.

I am not really growing old,
    that I know for sure.
But as the years keep passing by
    I'm just getting more mature.

George E. Keller

Women

I live in hell
The demon fiends
keep flashing back
haunting
screaming
I try to fly
but fire grabs my wings
melting limbs to stubs
I beg to die
hang me high by
fishhooks in my   wrists
till flesh recedes from my body
leaving icicle covered bones to hang
tangled
twisted
like wind chimes
singing in the gallows

Jeff Rose

Lost In New York City

Amidst the roar of traffic
The dirt and dust and grime
A homeless body's sleeping
To while away the time
Manhattan in the morning
Another faceless day
The privileged are working
But have they lost their way

So few can see the sunshine
The mighty dollar calls
Trapping them forever
In a prison with no walls
They do not smell the flowers
Or care that some don't eat
Their luxuries are foreign cars
And Gucci on their feet

Anita Calicchio

The Edges

Why oh why cannot I see
The edges of reality?
It spans so far
I'm on the brink
I lift my cup to take a drink
What if I could only see
the edges of reality?
Would I lift away the veil?
Would I trod the untrod trail?
I know not where
I know not why
The edges reach beyond the sky
I cannot reach the edge-I think
I lift my cup to take a drink

Ardys Edstrand

Rudi

The man and his sensuality,
The element of surprise,
The danger,
The adventure,
The soldier,
The gentleman,
Casting impressions,
Forever
On my life.

Cynthia Hoskins

471

Untitled

The saying of vows
The exchanging of rings
The symbolization
Of so many things

They promise forever
They both say I will
They'll stay together
When time stands still

The love is shared
The two become one
The life they live
Will not only be fun

They'll laugh together
They'll sometimes cry
They'll love together
And never say goodbye.

Danielle Upton

Untitled

The dried brown grass,
the fallen trees beneath the sky,
are proof that at some point,
every living thing must die.

The fish in the ocean,
the dog in your backyard,
the people you wave to,
the child you've raised to work so hard.

The horse in its stable,
the raccoons in their huts,
the hamsters in their cages,
and the cheap little street corner sluts.

The ozone will break,
the Earth will blow,
and with all that shit,
every living thing will go.

People hate to face it,
but I will not lie;
Sooner of later,
YOU will die.

Elissa Green

Simple Pleasures

The trees in the meadow,
The flowers atop the hill
As quiet as a whisper
So beautiful, so still.

The river in its bed,
The newly fallen leaves
Tumbling down its path
Stirring in the breeze.

Little birds chirping
Their sweet melody,
Little pups being
As playful as can be.

Tree frogs singing
To the sound of pouring rain.
Many bees buzzing
Without a single strain.

Little children playing
So loud, yet happily.
Many people working
To be the best they can be.

Alicia R. Pack

Time

Today it is your wedding day
The happiest "time" of life
Thought it may seem strange at first
You will be man and wife.

Life is so fast today
Rushing here and there
How can you find the better things
If you don't take "time" to care.

So don't rush through your life so fast
Looking for material things
Take "time" to smell the roses
That mother nature brings.

"Time" is a precious thing
That people try to buy
But that is something hard to do
No matter how you try.

So when little things seem all wrong.
And life seems on the brink
Take out a little "time" with God
He will never let you sink.

Gertrude Smith

Summer Dance

And so begins her summer dance
  The heart's design is left to chance
And such assiduous romance
  For sun and wine and circumstance
The harmony, the graceful rites
  Of sultry summer days and nights
Capriciousness nothing may sate
  Content only to aestivate
And be forgiven all her sins
  And so her summer dance begins

David W. Sjoberg

Memory Highway

Some days I drive fast, some days slow
The highway long
When I look into the rear-view mirror
My reflection is distorted

I turn the radio on
I tune into memories of yesteryear
I try to sing
I try to smile
Reality oblivious

Some days are sunny and pleasant
Some days are dark and cold
The highway long
I turn the radio on
Memories come in sharp and clear
Reality oblivious

Some days I drive fast, some days slow
The highway always long
While songs sound the same
My reflection is distorted again

John T. Carroll

Summit

The far is near.
The hot is cold.
The sheep are milling
Around the fold.

The shepherds smile
And make pretense
Of mending holes
In the fence.

More than the holes
The woolies fear
The awful staff
Which one was dear.

Dumb as they are
The fleeced things know
Pretentious work
Is just a show.

The shepherds have changed...
Relationships rearranged.
They are no longer sheep-keepers
But Fleece-reapers.

Chuck Hunt

Nature's Great Gifts

The wind outside is gently blowing,
the leaves are falling without even
knowing.
Trees are swaying from side to side,
the squirrels and birds are trying to
hide.

They scamper in the autumn frost,
gathering food, at no cost.
The dawn of day is here,
the squirrels and birds are near.

There is an owl hooting in the tree,
as the little mouse scurries rather
free.
Lying under the brush,
a doe and fawn are hushed.

The wind outside is raw,
waiting for the snow to fall.
The earth is covered winter white,
the tracks will then be forever bright.

Crystal Lickliter

My Child

As I look upon
The life I have led
I wondered If I've done
Everything I said.
Did I forget,
to kiss you goodnight,
Or whisper I love you
And sleep tight?
Did I give you the tools
to learn what you need?
Did I give you the praise?
Did I nurture the seed?
Did I teach you as well
As I could have done,
To enter life's gambit
And still have some fun?
Did I give you the wisdom
Of my experienced years
As the age of young womanhood
Quickly draws near?

Elizabeth A. Collins

Heavens and Earth

The darkness of the night descends
The light of day appears
While the stars are saying goodnight
To the earth below that hears
The moon just catches sight
Of the sun beginning to rise
And the sun compliment
The moon's glowing size
They said farewell and then they went
To their positions in the sky
They continued this routine
Watching the earth go by
But they only met twice a day
At dawn and nightfall
And although they would like to stay
They are commanded by God's call

Joie Gibbons

Untitled

Soft! The clock strikes midnight,
The li'l one cowers in fear,
In darkness she cannot fight,
For light she holds too dear.
Her creamy white complexion
Reflects her ill beliefs,
Is she the true perfection,
All others lowly thieves?
Is she destined for glory,
Though most fail all too much?
And is she any smarter,
Than blacks, or reds, or such?
The answer to these questions,
Will doubtlessly be nay;
For night, without exceptions,
Is no worse off than day.

Jessica Bruesewitz

Life

The sun is bright,
The moon is dark,
My life is just about to start.

In October,
I will turn ten,
I wonder what will happen then?

Will I see things differently,
Than I did just recently?
Life is so confusing
But sometimes quite amusing!

School will be going so smooth,
Then they throw in something new.
You have to try to retain,
While you are trying to retrain.

Will life always be this confusing way,
Or will I come to understand one day?

April Prentice

Masked

The double face of "I don't care"
Is oft' misunderstood
The tiny threads that bind them there
Are "Yes, I know I should"

The first are feelings left unborn
That haunt the darkest night
The other shields against forlorn
That stains with tears of fright

Kerry French

Caleb

To see your life begin
The most exciting thing I've seen
So fragile and pure
A greatness I never knew
The joy and happiness
Your mother and I share
To see you grow and learn
To know the magic of your birth
Is far more than I thought it would
Far more than anyone could
Our love joins together in you
Dad

James Evans

Revelation

A palm tree above me
The ocean spread before me
The fishing boats sparkle
As the sun blazes its orange twilight
The moon shines silver
As palm trees bend to the breeze
The waves lap the shore
Ending their sojourn from distant seas
And the cloudless sky
is illuminated with stars
And promises a clear vista
When the sun breaks the horizon
And I will be here to witness
Yet another triumph of nature
And I will be here
The subject of yet another
REVELATION
Under a palm tree
With the ocean as my horizon

Joseph H. Daas

The Last Sigh

Each time I fall in love I sigh,
The passion died as time went by.
When I met you I gave a sigh,
Now I will sigh until I die.
Your green eyes are all that I see,
When I'm with you my heart is free.
Theresa, will you marry me,
And be my wife for all to see?
I want to feel your soft, tan skin,
And know that it is not a sin.
Heaven will smile on our love,
Marry me under God above.
Your hair feels like a summer breeze,
It always throws me to my knees
Your charm is timeless like the sea,
Together we're in harmony.
Your patience is shelter in the wind,
Open your heart and let me in.
My love for you will never die,
It is true you are the last sigh.

Carol Bauman

Golden Silk

It blows like the wind
It shines like the sun
It smells like a slice of pie
Soft to the touch
To look so fine
I love the way it sways
your golden silk hair...

Rochelle Woodson

Forever, Come What May

The times are tough.
The questions abound.
You are lost in life's uncertainty.
Let me help you to be found.

There seems to be more times to cry,
than there are times to smile.
Let me help to carry the load,
for you for just a while.

The pressure from all,
is coming down upon you.
The weight is much lighter,
when divided by two.

Always know that I love you,
and that I'm here to stay.
I'll help you through tomorrow,
and forever, come what may.

Jennifer A. Wheeler

Where Is God

Where is God, they say
The scoffer insists
blind faith is, not enough
to prove that he exists

I should offer reason
if it's reason you should ask
who formed the universe
who's equal to the task

A million stars strewn to and fro
each with its own clarity
planets spinning is unison
man knows no such regularity

And if, by now my friend
you've still not seen the light
do this one more thing
and then I think you might

Look into a young child's eyes
and you'll be on the brink
see the trust they have in you
and you'll see God, I think

David Duvall

Yesterday's Treasure

A beautiful sunset
The smile of a child
The grace of a deer
As it runs in the wild
The things we remember
Slip swiftly away
Yesterday's treasures
We cherish today
Each day is a gift
Full of sadness and pleasure
Sweet hopes for tomorrow
Build yesterdays treasure
The gift of tomorrow
Too soon on its way
Yesterdays treasure
We build on today.

Gayle R. Wheeler

Where Love Has Been

So sweet the life that flows within,
the smile upon your face;
to touch my heart and fill my soul
forever with your grace...

In darkest times I see your light
that shows the way to go;
so time and time it guides we back
to place that I know...

Of carefree days and loving ways
that brings you happiness;
to hold again those feelings deep
that filled your life with bliss...

Where love has been it leaves the glow
of warm days from the past,
and though sometimes it cannot stay
sweet memories will last...

David F. Weaver

Please Don't

Don't look at the chubby cheeks,
The sparkly eye which peeks.
Don't look at the pinky toes
Or you will call her Rose.

Call her Jasmine, call her Pansy,
Call her Violet, call her Daisy.
You may even call her Chrysanthemum,
But please don't call her Rose.

She is an angel full of joy,
Do not her path destroy
And such a name will I oppose,
So please don't call her Rose.

Call her Marigold, call her Zinnia,
Call her Daffodil, call her Virginia.
You may even call her Chrysanthemum,
But please don't call her Rose.

A rose's beauty our faces light!
A joy to have, the heart's delight!
In beds of thorns roses repose
So please don't call her Rose.

Agnes L. Aikins

Hearing With The Heart

My world is filled with silence
The spoken word I cannot hear,
My latent loss of hearing
Has been my lot to bear.

But I was given other values
And I have been enlightened,
By hearing through silence
Cries of animals who are frightened.

I hear the silent cry
Of the homeless dog and cat,
Of the imprisoned circus animal
And the laboratory rat.

I hear the silent cry
Of the furred animals whose skins
Are torn from their bodies
To clothe human manikins.

My ears are not for hearing
It is only within my heart,
I hear the cries of animals
Whose silence must never be forgot.

Florence Levine

Untitled

Heart, why this mad behavior?
It's only her showing her face.
The very one I've assured you
we no longer care for.

Michael Morganson

Streetrooms

Today is a good day,
The steam is on,
The warmth from the grate
Protrudes as the Sunday comics
Hold my shoulders warm.

The dumpster is my source;
The cupboard will be the walls and roof
I found some garage clothes-
I'll make due in my booth,

Spring is near; only forty days away
Food and shelter is what I'll pray.
I feel so ashamed, with my cup in hand
I'm not a bad person; just a poor man.

I'm quite lucky; others don't make it.
The bite of night steals its victims.
The box is small, as streetrooms will be
To shelter me as the snow does fall.

Harold Williams

Red Rose

A dove is in the sky,
The sun is melting the clouds.
The sea is running by,
The sun is blocking the clouds
  of silver tears,
The wind is chasing the stars.
Red rose - oh, red rose.
Snow falls like the twinkling
  sounds of the stars.
Rain falls like golden tears off
  moons dancing on rainbows
  and shadows of love.
Red rose, oh red rose.
Summer comes again as
fast as the humming bird.
Oh, rose you are still alive.
oh rose- oh, red rose.

Chelsea Turnbo Hardin

The Beautiful Day

On this beautiful day
The sun is shining bright.
The sky is blue,
Not black like the night.

The horses are grazing
Out upon the grass.
A loud noise startles them,
And they gallop away fast.

Out on the lawn
I see a cardinal of red.
As he is picking up seeds,
He has nothing to dread.

The bird flies away,
But I wish he had not.
I wish he had stayed,
"But that's okay," I thought.

Emily Ingle

Rock Roof

The roofers come.
The sun isn't up and already
my forehead throbs with boots
clumping overhead.
I almost shout an angry Quiet!
when I remember to weigh pools
of rain on my floors against
the devils prancing on my eardrums,
and hold my tongue.

Every flood year the roof
undergoes another transformation.
Each time my bones shrink a little
more, my flesh condenses
in the hissing tar, my ears slowly
giving up the sound.

Claire Mirakentz

Silent Tears

A silent tear rolls slowly down
the surface of my heart
as quiet as the passage of the sun
But loud inside - a cry of agony
Pounds inside my heart
And leaves me weak and trembling
like a young colt newborn.

I wonder as I look around my world
How many people cry these silent
tears?
....The breezes whisper to me as
they curl around my head
and whisper ever softly in my ear
"Dear one - all of us - you are
not alone!"

Charlotte Likens

Favorite Companion

My favorite companion,
the thorn in my side.
The fun times remembered,
the secrets we hide.
For every adventure,
we share a new smile.
The simply put signal,
that makes it worthwhile.
We share all our free time,
together 'til end.
She's my favorite companion,
my very best friend.

Farrah Osterberg

Can't You See

Why can't I have a friend,
that's true.
One that love's me,
as I still love you.
One that say's its okay.
I will always love you anyway.
Why can't this be.
Can't you see.
All I want is a friend,
that loves me.

Jessica Antoinette Thompson

Dreamscape

The middle of the night
The top of the darkness
The blackest blackness
That our senses can touch

Deep in the night
We reign unconsciously
With such perfection
While the dead endlessly play

The sea of darkness
Swallows the earth
Concealing our secrets
That only daylight can reveal

From dusk to dawn
It is nonstop
And only if we awaken
Will it cease to exist.

Jason Robbins

Image of a Mountain

I Had Never Before Seen
The true image of the mountain
The mountain looks like a man
Holding a child in his arms
Now I know the feeling of things
The Mountain that looks at me is
A father too
And in the evening the fog plays
Like a child around his shoulders
And about his knees
Now I Remember a crevice in the valley
Between two mountains, in its deep ravine
A stream went singing
Hidden by a tangle of twigs and bushes
I am like that ravine
I feel singing deep in my heart
Within me a little brook
And I have given a bit of flesh
For a cover of twigs and bushes
Until it comes up to the light

Johnny Cuesta

The Player

The player he treats people
...The way he wants to be
But he sets expectations that
They'll do the same you see

He plays with his emotions
...And even plays with fate
He tries to paint a picture
Of a life that will be great

Try and fix you if you're broken
...Put you way up on a shelf
Fill you up with high esteem
...And forget about himself

Someday maybe he'll grow up
...And stop being such a jerk
Realize no matter how hard you try
That some things just won't work

The player he must understand
...Finally stand up and toast
The person that he plays with
Seems to be himself the most!

Charly French

Dinosaurs

One murmur woke up
the whole valley
and they called that a play

A child can have as much fun
watching snails
with an iridescent trail
the indifference is not between
mollusks
and the prehistoric

Something too selfish to mention
be worthy
of a therapist's couch

Powerful, awestricken
ugly (yeah, but who cares)
and envied beyond age and gender

The questioning why dinosaurs
disappeared
will likely end in a very
private silence

Clayton Chou

Summer Scene

Softly blowing -
  The wind.
Gently swinging -
  The hammock.
Now all is quiet -
  Hush!
James is curled up
  Asleep.
When the wind whispers
Leaves answer tenderly.
Still he sleeps.
Summer has come.

Carabelle Monfort Stitt

Reflections from the Heart

The night creeps in.
The wind blows free.
My lonely heart
Keeps telling me
As I lie here in my bed that
Happy days are just ahead
Around the bend
And my broken heart will mend.

Life at best is not good.
But I never thought I would
be lying here so all alone.
But I will neither cry nor moan.
I'll pick up every little part
and rejuvenate again my heart.
And vow until the bitter end
"My heart will never break again."

But that's not true.
Its destined to.

Ann Davenport

Autumn Shadows

Beneath the wintery autumn sky
the winds across the valley high
The clouds cast shadows dark and long
reflecting change as seasons song

Then just as winter's deep frozen cold
Consumes life's empty chilling hold

A crocus shoots its arm
of green
against the grayish barren scene

And life again begins to creep
and shadows run away to sleep
For in the wind the seeds do blow
the sun begins again to glow

New days of sweet and fragrant scents
the past is gone, is done, is spent
And now the earth must stretch so high
and turn its face up to the sky

For now a new time has arisen
which life can use and God has given

Dennis Charles

The Wings of the Wind

Soaring gently over the land,
the Wings of the Wind glide
softly and surely over the Mountains
and Plains.

Rushing by the leaves on the trees,
the wind awakens the world.

Reaching high into the sky
the wind whips the clouds
swirling them lazily.

Whether in the sky's above or
close to the ground, the wings
of the wind will carry you endlessly.

Christina A. Caruso

A Riddle: "Never Look Back?"

For once upon a time
there was a mighty warrior
the master of the warrior
was he who broke the camel back.

The camel was the mighty warrior
who vowed to never quit
he climb the trouble mountains
and cross the raging sea.

The camel was a mighty warrior
his master was his guide
the foolish camel never saw
his master lagged behind.

The camel was a mighty warrior
who carried his master treasures
yet, the camel never saw
his master treasured him the least.

And once upon the moon so bright
the master shadow grew
Then the camel wisely saw
the straw that broke the warrior back.

Diane Bryant

At First Sight

And so
there you were, simply existing
before I ever had time to prepare
for the effect you'd have on me.
Tall, lithe, a comfort to the space
you occupied.
I wanted you
to notice me... did you?
I wanted
to entertain you, dance for you,
wear pearls for you and nothing more.
I have long legs, did you see them?
The air adores you
I wish to have you move through me
in much the same way.
Twice
when you looked at me
I could not breath
so taken was I by your presence,
I want more.

Jane R. Walker

The Old Bean Bag

It's a hot and lazy morning
There's just no fun at all
We can't play jacks today
Donny lost the ball

Tabby's got new kittens
Hidden somewhere in the barn
Don't know why she won't trust us
We wouldn't do them harm

Mother's at her sewing
She's sorted beans for soup
No time to read us stories
We haven't got a hoop

Then she called us to her
I've something new for you
It's made from stained and broken beans
And scraps of fabric blue

There's really nothing better
When the chase is on in tag
For loads of fun and laughter
Than our favorite old bean bag

Elnore Smith

These Old Hands

These old hands have begun to tremble
These old hands have no time to waste,
These old hands have raised this family
These old hands have worked this place.

These old hands will tell a story
These old hands are old and weak,
These old hands have never harmed you
These old hands will fold in sleep.

These old hands will leave this bedside
These old hands deserve a rest,
These old hands will climb to glory
These old hands Lord you have blessed.

Edna Boldridge Cornett

Reflections

From near and far away places
They come, walking slowly along
A dark, polished granite wall —
The Vietnam Memorial — where America
Consoles its grief and its loss.
Through their ever-enduring pain —
In the midst of their sorrow —
They search for a name
To be etched in their heart —
Forever in their prayer!

I stand there in silence
With my hand on the wall —
I tremble with emotion —
I grieve for them all!
Take time to remember
Our Sons, Brothers, and Friends.
Let's all come together
To honor them — in a spirit of love —
And let's never forget
The Freedom! We are so blest!

Donald D. Dunlap Sr.

Untitled

The clouds
They darkened
The sky
On this day
The green of the grass
Lit up the earth
As the shadows of the heavens
Scattered showers
And the world around me
Was washed clean
Tomorrow the sun
Will shine upon
The day's pure
Smile

Jennifer Louise Lutz

Cemetery At Normandy

Lo though
they westward face

from their high mown bluff
of a resting place,

they can not look,
they can not see,

the endless ocean,
the restless sea,

that lies between
them and home;

sea gulls, water, ships
and sea foam.

A rift it grew
and held them back.

It kept them from
continuing their attack

on land and now
they're up above.

Gone with the speed
of a loosed white dove.

Daniel James Ocharzak

Relations

When someone shows love
They're put to a test
Beyond the limits
Brought forth by stress

Sometimes our words
Just aren't enough
A relentless exhibition
Of all the right stuff

It's so easy to say
I told you so
Rather than blend together
As one should you grow

A passage through time
To play these games
When the effort put forth
Shows little gain

As tomorrow comes
A new day shall begin
For just as we love
So shall we sin

DeJuan Blumbery

Transcendentalism

Think about life
think about it
look around
gaze into the visuals
listen not to sound
sit a top a dawns daylight
and get a taste of day
transcend into a spot of time
reality no say
relax inside a ripple cloud
float inside a dream
taste the blue you never knew
of what it all should be
stroll on down a
bow of light
cascading colors slip
in your sight
imaginary yesterdays
makes it all inside
someway

James Defilippis

The Rain

I see through the bleak rain
though it stings my soul,
and it brings tears to my rusty heart.
I shed soft, white tears in my mind
that rain from the black,
diminishing cloud in my soul,
and it shows me what the rain brings;
and what it washes away.
This soul has bled
these tears for so long.
They take the mind and spirit,
and pull and twist them forever
wringing them clean
of doubt and sorrow
while I remember it all.
And when the bleeding stops,
the pain returns again
to sting my soul
as I see through the rain
once more.

James Harper Moffitt

Thirty-Five Years

To this day we celebrate
Thirty-five years to commemorate.

At the beginning of that road
We have heard of many things told.

The fun times you had
And unfortunately the sad.

When two people wed
There are sometimes things said.

A doubt; will they make it?
or the question; they break it?

Now, we're here to say
Oh this very happy day,

That along through life's struggles
The blessings and troubles;

Our parents have shared;
Have loved and cared.

And although things got rough
They pulled through and got tough!

A marriage to endeavor
From now until forever....

Beverly J. Gooding

Play Ball

We drove to the ball park,
This game we must see -
The plan was all wrong,
It was backwards to me.

They batted wrong handed,
Took off for third base-
We laughed and laughed,
As they fell on their face.

Then get up and run,
Second base and then first-
Then off to home plate,
He's worked up quite a thirst.

The game was exciting,
Such a change of pace-
Old habits die hard,
When you run to the base.

Sometimes they forget,
And run the RIGHT way-
The object is to go around,
Backwards to play!

Joyce Keeler

Boundaries

So
This is the something that
Is the nothing
So
This is life and that is death
              Tell me
Where is the instant/the sliver/the
Quiver   Who is the Shadow?

   When is the change?

When did it happen that life became
Death
And nothing became something
Became Life

Where is TIME?
              On the edge?
Deanna Joy Taylor

Haiti

I dreamt a dream of death last night.
This island black within our sky.

This sign of death surrounds us all.
The wives and children, all will fall.

Ebony arms raised to fight.
But cannot stop the bullets flight.

A people's will cannot be crushed.
A freedom's voice will not be hushed.

History's shown its well worn face.
But lust for life fills this place.
J. Edward Kernan Jr.

We'll Remember

We'll remember her cakes,
those biscuits and pies;
Those Saturday meals of
hamburgers and fries.

We'll remember her stories,
of day's gone by;
Sitting on her lap, and
hearing her sigh.

We'll remember her kindness,
The love that she gave;
Even remember how she
made us behave.

We'll remember our Grandma.
She'll always be in our minds.
We'll remember those switches
We felt on our behinds.

We were all "special," in Grandma's eyes,
Never forget this, and never ask why?

We love you Grandma,
Good-bye....
Carla Casarez

Those Eyes

When I look into those eyes,
Those eyes that show you care;
I just can't help myself
And all I do is stare.
Staring deep into them,
Makes me wonder why...
Why you said you loved me,
Then you said good-bye.
When I look into those eyes,
Those eyes so filled with love;
I dream of all the greatest things
And pray to Him above.
I pray that one day you'll return
And be with me again;
I pray our love will last this time,
This time it will not end.
Angela Rogers

Help

Somebody help, anybody please
These are the words you would hear,
if you were inside of me
You would not hear how I hate people,
You wouldn't hear about my love life.
You would hear one small, but BIG
voice day...
   Help, Help me Please
Jessica Renee Hamner Wood

Faith

Oh tree, oh tree!
Thou art to me
A tower of strength
A symbol of eternity!
Though now you seem so old
And very very cold
Deep inside
A spark is glowing!
Fanned by him.
Who is all knowing!
And so I watch
And wait and seek
He who says
Not dead but asleep!
Edith M. Ricchio

Comet

There was nothing I could do.
Though it wasn't my anticipation
To see what I saw
I'd gaze up in the horizon
And see again...
The magnificent comet
At first I thought it was there
Then it bolted out of my view
The constant arrival and departure
Make me agitated every time
I couldn't adjust with it's routine
Nor was there any intention
For some outlandish reason
I'd always be the little boy
In search for the glistening rays
Every time it caught my eyeful
I would have an emotional revolution.
I would remain distracted because
That little boy had no one
To tell his observation to, then it struck me
that I was a comet.
Charles LaRocco

In Your Eyes

In your eyes I was nearly perfect,
though you seldom said it.
Perhaps so that I wouldn't
become obnoxious or haughty.

But I knew-
I could see it in your eyes.

The unconditional love,
the pride and joy when
greeting me was always there,
shining in your eyes.

I think that is what
I miss the most.

I hope that somehow you knew
that in my eyes,
You gave me the
greatest gift of all

In your eyes.

Joyce B. Doane

Spring

I took a walk one clear Spring Day
Through a fresh green country side
The sun was shining bright above
The sky was blue and wide.

A gentle breeze brushed past my face
as I picked daffodils
The grass was like green velvet
Spread across the rolling hills

I walked along an old rock fence
That had stood for years in style
It had dressed its self for spring
With roses blooming wild

I heard a bluebird singing
Its song seemed just for me
I listened to its concert
'neath a weeping willow tree

I wandered on and found a brook, so quietly
it did run
The water rippled gently, like silver in the sun

I sat beside the little brook, just filled with
perfect bliss
I'm sure if God lived here on Earth, it
would be in a place like this

Flossie Shackelford

"Trust"

"Oh" how could one live
   Through a single day,
Without God leading
   Each step of the way.
Only He knows and understands
   The anxieties and pressures,
The world demands.
   Only to Him can we go
In times of despair,
   And knows He will help
With just one little prayer.
   So when life looks real dark
And there is no one to care,
   Just run to him
As He's always there,
   And say, "Lord take my hand
Tell me what to do,
   Because I put all my trust
   In You"

Josepha Mitchell

As A Friend

As a friend I will be here for you
Through good and through bad
As a friend I will be here for you
Especially when you're sad.

As a friend you can count on me
To help you through it all
As a friend you can count on me
To help you up when you fall.

As a friend I will help you
Through all the ups and downs
As a friend I will help you
To keep your feet on the ground.

As a friend I will always love you
Just because you're you
As a friend I will always love you
Because our friendship is true.

Jillian Angela Brick

I Wish

I wish I was soaring,
through the clouds, and the night.
I want to be there,
no problems, no frights.

It's the only place,
I'm afraid I can go,
to escape the pressures,
and the pains,
found below.

I wish I was walking,
through the mountains,
way atop,
to hear myself think,
where the chaos has stopped.

For now, I guess,
dreams will have to do,
but someday, I wish,
to be there, above all of you.

David L. Carter

What Is Love?

Is it a phase, that people go
through, to make up a life? Or is it
a dream, that's only bound to die?
Maybe it's a curse that makes you
cry. It's a roller coaster in motion,
that leaves you heart broken.
   You wish that it lasts forever,
you turn around, and you're no
longer together. Maybe it's miles
that set you back, maybe your lives
were on a different track, maybe
you loved, and they never did, maybe
you had nothing to give.
   The reasons are so very wide,
but love comes to pierce you in the
side. Yes you bleed because you
hurt, and your heart lies in the dirt.
   The hardest part is after
some love is gone, because the
love still lingers on.

Arianna Sikes

Atlantis

Into your deep pools of blue, I dive
Through your visions, I drift
In a sea of heaven
I feel your waves wash over me
With breathtaking ecstasy.

I'm caught in your warm current
It pulls me under,
And out to sea I am taken-
Without a struggle.

Though I am beneath the surface,
Still I breath.
I will not drown in your ocean,
But simply
Live in Atlantis with you.

Abbey Lynn Marterella

Time and Love

Time flies!
   Time changes!
      Time heals!
         Time silences!
Yet, what difference does time make?
Is love constrained by time?
Does love belong to
   Time of acquaintance,
      Time of youth,
         Time of years?
Is not time in the mind?
   And love,
The meeting of minds?

Althea Evelyn Cordner

My Wish

For the people of the world
To change.
Like the oceans tide
That returns and returns
To kiss the shore
Changing every grain of sand
So can the people of the world
Change.
For as long as the sun sets
And hides beneath the oceans rim
Time, patience, hope, compassion
And love
Can touch the hearts of the people
Changing them and the world
For the better.
This is my greatest wish.

Dorothea Pogue

A Prayer For A Gift

Oh for the knack or knowledge...
to create, instill, impart;
to compose a work of beauty,
an articulate form of Art.

Oh for the gift of glibness...
to be blessed with silver tongue;
to paint, with words, a portrait,
or sing some song, unsung.

To draw, with flowery phrases...
a picture, ever clear;
give voice to lilting lyric...
the world would love to hear.

To visit with variable image...
with love and ecstasy;
with the metered, magic music...
of the Muse of Poetry.

Deny the gift I ask you...
deny the prize I seek;
but let me learn the language...
I know I will never speak!

Jimmy Walls Jr.

To You

Do you know
How much I love you
The question is?
How much, do you care
If our emotion, it
Can be equal
The world would be
The same again?

J. L. Sas

Tiger!

I acknowledge my respect
to frustration
a God given emotion

Frustration is the I
the tiger of the soul
reaching into the heavens
for the farthest star
reaching for the dawn
of a new world
seeking the justification
of existence

Deon

Shout It

Love, such a difficult thing
to fully comprehend.
For some, love is something
they can not do.
Because past experiences make
it hard to stand.
But when it comes to me and you,

Well, I can say it,
louder than ever.
Shout it from the
highest mountain top,
Because in my heart
I will sing it forever.

Danielle Neemann

Love

An abstract
To give and receive
Reject or accept.

Rejection hurts
Try again
Rejection hurts more.

Forget it, impossible
Look for another
Interfered by remembrance
and hope.

That a change of seasons
Will bring a change of mind.

Arthur Gallant

On Turning Fifty

In this world
To have only one,
One, who cares,
A firecracker!

To have three,
Four, five....
The fourth of
July!

Those who have no one
No one who cares,
A black silence!

Find one!
One who has no one!
Light a firecracker!
A string of firecrackers!
Let the silence explode
With a celebration
of LOVE — LIGHT!!

Carolyn Haynes

Mother

She climbs the highest mountain,
to help you get down,
She jumps into the river,
not to let you drown.
She passes through a fire, to
save you from the bad,
She does all the impossible,
to show you that she cares.
She never says I can't, when
you need her help.
She never does a thing, to
make you be sad.
She does the best in all.
And everything she does,
shows her true love.

Alina Tigu

A Special Gift

I am preparing you
To learn about life
And love
And at the same time
You are teaching me about love
A love that is special
And one I have never experienced
It is of joy and celebration
Not of fear or distrust
I often wonder who is the teacher
And who is the pupil
It really doesn't matter does it?
I only know what I experience
In my heart and in my soul
You have given me a gift
A special gift
It is your heart
That is now entwined with mine.

Herlinda Rojas

A Guardian Angel

A guardian angel was in the dell
To protect a person who had fell
The person's spirit and broken heart
Was all a splattered and torn apart
The angel lifted high the form
And bathed it soft and golden warm

Renew your faith and spirit dear
You have nothing else to fear
A rescue band of angels soar
Upon the clouds and sky will tour
For fallen spirits near and dear
The angels bring us tidings here

So laugh and sing and be aware
That angels fly within the air
A calm and loving heart will bring
An angel message in a ring
There is nothing on this earth to fear
When we believe in angels here

Rejoice in sorrow and learn the way
As angels come and go today!

Donalda Klippenstein

Release

A place to go
to release
the fears forgotten
in awoken hours
the outside world
a place to dream
and fear the time to lay to rest
I lay to rest in restlessness
to reach
unconsciousness
afraid asleep
afraid awake
never escape this dread I make.

David Lam

Pretty Dolly

I'm only a pretty dolly
to set upon a bed,
I'm made of silk and satin
from my toes to my head,
My eyes are big and bright
and a beautiful sparkling blue,
My lips are bright and shiny
a beautiful color too,
I'm not made to play with,
to toss around or hurt,
I like to stay my shiny clean
without a speck of dirt,
If you wish to look at me
Please handle me with care,
cause I am special in every way,
with all my wear and tear.

Judy Harrison

Time

Oh! What a lovely feeling
To sit in the morning sun.
Listening to the sweet music
The birds have always sung.

Has the world given up treasures
That are around to see?
To spend our time in search
Of what cannot be.

We hurry to make the rush
While noise crowds our mind.
The world of madness
Is in control
As static reaches our soul

Reach out and you can capture
A little bit of time.
Enjoy what is about you.
It doesn't cost a dime.

Eleanor M. Wanosik

Desiring You

If you would let me kiss you
then I would stop as much missing
the lips that called my name
With the candlelight blown to darkness
there is now only one way
to start again this summer flame
Your dress is as fragrant and sweet
and the new moon hides
The lingering taste of your breath
to drown in its tides

Anthony J. Burns

I Fly Out

I fly out from this balcony
to the desert where you lie
in a place I know you stay
alone and oh so shy

You are miles and miles apart from me
a second by my mind
give to me an answer
if you would be so kind

Unsure why I am drawn
to your soft and tender smile
could it be your difference
could it be your style

Talking to you each day
helps me ease my mind
for I'd rather make this call
than not be in touch at all

So I fly out from this paradise
to a place I know you live
and I send to you my thought
which is all that I can give

Jeff Sanks

Press Close

As you enter the door
to the glories of God
don't stand on the threshold
in shadows of past.

Come all the way in
to the presence of God
let the light of the Lamb
flood over your soul.

Press close to the throne
stay near to the Lord
keep out of the shadows
that linger behind.

Keep moving onward
press closer to God
and the light of the Lord
will fill your whole life.

Jacqueline F. Totten

Love

Love comes naturally
to those whom are genuine,
and to those whom are sincere.

Love is more
than a spoken word
just for folks to merely hear.

Love seeks not
what it can get,
but seeks to give
for no selfish reasons.

Love shines brightly
with warm devotion
without need for holiday seasons.

Love rejoices with successes
not with failures
a heart holds near.

Love grows stronger
from the trust it earns
with each and every passing year.

Jolie Fuselier Sibley

Ode to a Memory

I felt your lips so soft and yearning
Touch mine with gentle sweet caress
And fill my empty longing heart
With emotions long suppressed.

I felt your hand as it reached out
And folded into mine
A bond of measure as though forever
When two souls inter-twine.

Perhaps I'll never feel again
The same gentle lips or hand
But in my heart and memory burns
What love, sweet love commands.

I'll carry this where ere I go
And when my heart is aching
I'll recall your lips so soft
And feel my hand's been taken.

Perhaps it will be just a thought
A memory deeply treasured
But the love we shared a day
Will bring eternal pleasure.

Joan Renn

Listen to the Warm

Listen to the warm.
Touch the silence
my friend,
and be not afraid
to search your heart
to find the truth.
Laugh,
cry if you must,
for pain is one of
the greatest teachers.
Especially do not
be afraid
to enjoy what is beautiful,
and believe
that as you
give to the world,
so the world
will give back
to you.

Ellen Dostal

Silence

How long, Oh God, how long
Trapped in a silent world
Somewhere between life and death
The days, the nights go slowly by
No one will let me die
This was not meant to be
Oh please, set my spirit free.

She comes again into the room
She leans down and gently kisses me
She connects the tube that feeds me life
Doesn't she hear my silent plea
Please, please let me be
She pats my hand, I see her cry
Why doesn't she help me die

Betty Breding

'Tis Spring

"Look up" look up at the budding
trees there are some robins to see three
Look down look down the grass is
green I see some dandelions in between,
The earth is awakening for spring
is here, sometimes I see a baby deer,
Whether you are young or old there's
so many things to behold the
little kittens that I love today I
heard a mourning dove
so when you feel alone and blue
just look around it will cheer you,
There's so many things to behold
far more precious than silver or
Gold, don't shut your seek out
from life's greatest joy's
whether it is spring or fall
the Lord God made it all

Audra Riggs

Untitled

I'll never forget the ride
Trying to reach my arms into the sky
Seeing the light so soft and peaceful
As the tears rolled down my eyes.

Cry, cry, cry,
Never going to say goodbye
You've left me here and now I find
My arms reaching into the sky.

Day after day
Living with this pain
Oh God! How it aches!
How do I stay sane?

Sometimes I feel your hand
Wipe the tears from my eyes
Saying don't be sad I'm here,
We'll meet again please don't cry

Cry, cry, cry
Never going to say goodbye
You've left me here and now I find
My arms reaching into the sky.

Cindy Booth

Majority Whip

Majority whip
trying to rip
the family apart.
Man without heart
wanting to do
out of the blue
what others don't dare.
Heaven's great care
on mother and child
not one beguiled
by fortune and fame
playing the game
of the elite
planting the seed
of fear and distrust.
Celestial disgust
resting on him
recording the sin
closing the gate
to one irate.

Gerda A. Saul

The Little Prayer

With your heart and soul on high,
Turn your eyes toward the sky,
And with your heart so full of care,
You say a little prayer.
With your soul and eyes of tears,
In a vision, God appears,
So full of love and tender care,
He says to you, you will get there.
So some day when I die,
I will also, be on high,
Because my heart and soul of care,
Also said a little prayer.

Charles M. Reeves Jr.

"Mattie"

In a store, on a shelf,
    two teddy bears were.
One was very pretty,
    the other; matted fur.

One day a little rich girl;
    who thought much of herself,
bought the bear of beauty,
    the other, left on the shelf.

When the store was sold one day,
    all the toys were taken away.
Never sold; in years unkind,
    the matted bear was left behind.

One day a wealthy lady,
    stepped through the broken door,
there to see the matted bear,
    had fallen to the floor.

"I was wrong in leaving you,
    but now I'm so elated,
You can now come home with me,
    I'm so glad you waited.

Bruce W. Smith

Doors

Doors to where we wish to be,
Uncharted waters, fantasies.
Brushed gently by the dust
Of time, to map our destinies.

A flash of life, captured by a
Memory, somewhere, so elusive,
So rare, awakens our desire to be,
Outside the door, free.

If in this life we but seek
Only one path to explore, may
It so graciously await us, at
Some point beyond the door.

Jean D. Clements

Tall Ships

Let me go to sea in ships,
Whose billowing sails strain mast and line,
And rudder and keel guide her flight
As bow cuts the wind-tossed brine.

Let me breathe the fresh sea air,
See the glory of day change to night,
And listen to sounds of a creaking hull
As sails bathe in moonbeam's light.

Yes, let me go to sea in tall ships.

Raymond J. Shallbetter

Freedom

Blistered Earth
under a fire red sky.
That tar on my wings
won't let me fly.
I just want to get out
to escape the bliss,
of flashlights and fire-bombs,
and a dream of the kiss.
Sun drenched seaways
don't tell the tale
of pavements broken down,
all part of the scale.
I can't understand
the backwards of the now,
and as people depress,
I can't imagine how.
Stop me as I dive
into the deep blue sea.
Grab me, hold me, and tell me,
am I prisoner or free?

David Conforti

In Remembrance Of Christal

Christal shimmers with
unparalleled beauty,
lightning up the lives
of those fortunate enough
to have gazed deeply into her heart.
And though more fragile than
the impervious diamond,
when shattered—
her soul became liberated—
set free to sparkle in infinite numbers,
like the stars that brighten
the night sky.
The forms may change,
but the light lives eternal.
Remember her light
as you gaze at a crystal.
And remember—
she is not gone,
but merely free to shine
far brighter than before.

Barbara A. Bolek

The Other Side

Those impoverished children,
Unplanned and unwanted.
Void of the love
That only a caring mother can give.

Nurtured in the promise
Of a quick fix,
Sirens prevent serenity
In this urban maze.

Michigan Avenue welcomes Cadillacs,
But the other avenues
Hold no dreams,
For anyone.

And as they grind incessantly
They know they can't beat the system.
Fading in reality
Is the great American dream.

Dennis A. Arrichiello

Unto Us

When I truly feel
unpresentable
    dusty, drafty,
        discouraged
Unready (or unable?) to meet
life
I find I am truly glad God
chose to be born
in a stable...
He looks at my
shabbiness and sees
possibilities
And by his grace
transforms my straw into
gold...
No longer a habitation for
despair,
I am become a temple
where God himself
resides...

Betsy Virnelson

The Time has Come, for Us to Part

The time has come for
us to part.
    We knew it could happen,
right from the start.
    No late night movies
till morning dawn.
    We knew it could happen,
life goes on.
    No afternoon soaps
to share on the phone.
    I must watch them now, all alone.
    Life goes on, so they say,
but I'm just counting the days,
when I can go away.
    To hear your voice means
more to me, than anything I could
hear nor see.

Denelda DeWitte

Questionable Thoughts

What are we to do
us working parents?
When summer comes around
and our children are out.
We ponder the thought
of where? when? whom
with? and how?

Can we survive the two
months they are out?

As the summer days go by
and by
we ponder the thought
of why, why was
I not able to spend more
time with my child?

Banomatee N. Yaghmour

The Boot

Through the mire I've been trudged
used by others for themselves
I'm falling apart, slowly
from their constant use

My leather has been dirtied
through the toil and dust
through kick after kick
I took punishment and pain

Can there be no redemption?
For my sole is surely cursed
I ask for someone to remember me
before I last trudge upon this earth
Daniel B. Rego

Sax

It taps reason, with its sinewy
vibrato and carnal attitude

a jaded spirit of night

a guttural, smooth voice
that hints some absurd wisdom
performing a random subtle probe
gentle understatements
and soft improprieties
spontaneous thoughtless advances
and teasing withdrawals

a dangerous slut who offers a respite
of madness on these antiseptic streets

Swirling viscous sad legato
the horn squanders tones
cheats of satisfaction

till memory finds it
Later
Shadowed resonating in a hollow
corner of mind
now and again and Later
Jay Berglind

Standing at the Wall

I was standing at the
  Vietnam wall one day,
When a little boy happened
  to say.
See the big man crying
  Ma Ma,
It's as if his heart is far
  away,
See the big man crying
  Ma Ma,
Why is he so sad this
  day.
Bert A. Meiners Jr.

Love

Two people
One heart
Inseparable
Never Apart

Two stories
Together told
Two people
One soul.

Cheryl Quimba

Conquest

Roses are red
Violets are blue
Spring is here
Why doesn't anyone make their bed?

Orange are round
Apple are eve
Spring break are over
Why don't you go to School?

Dog are Men
Women are reproduction
Don't get mad, get even
Can we all get along?

Armed forces are people
Forget are bulls eyes
New seeds so stay off
Can anybody take a joke?

Happy are hour
Have fun while you're young
Sad are you
Set-up causes time goes by.
Edwin N. Tupas

Flora's Song

Don't go away, hill.
Wait for me, tree.
Be in your place still
When again I am free.

Child that I am,
I do not have your knack
For staying in one place.
But I'll be back.

For I must come and go
As I am told to do:
Go, stand, eat, sleep,
Before I can play with you.

Don't go away, grass.
Wait for me, winds.
I'll be back as soon as I can
To run with my outdoor friends.
Flora B. Schereck

Irresistible

Extra large shirts
Warm fuzzy slippers
Loose flannel shorts
No buttons, no zippers

Flushed dimpled cheeks
Half crooked smile
Shoulder length locks
It's all your own style

Arms of a gymnast
Body of a model
Legs of a cheerleader
You really look wonderful

Humorous and sensitive
Athletic and gentle
You just can't help it
You are irresistible
John Richard

Yesterday, Today, and Tomorrow

What was,
  was.
What is,
  is.
What's going to be,
  is going to be.
So let's always do the best,
For it will make today
  a cherished yesterday.
And——
turn an unknown tomorrow,
  into a beautiful
  and wonderful
    today!
Felisa L. Buensuceso

Ode to Sappho

In your keeping the divine spark
was brought to flame
As with your stylus you writ
On blocks of moist and willing clay
Of Beauty, of Earth, of Sky
And of the painful longing
For the love he failed to give.

Clothed in the island's mist
You reached the highest rocky cliffs
And cast your life
Into the wild and spuming sea.
  Yet, still you live.
Jeanne Hastings

"As I Walk"

  As I walk, I wonder why!
Watching birds spread their wings
against the sky - yet I walk
upon the grass only to see
another pass -
  As I walk yet another mile
knowing soon I'll end this trial.
  For as I walk I sense no fear -
for today was all so clear.
Now I know my heart within ...
for as I walk I found a friend ...
Jami Abdul Sabur

Sea Shells

Sea shells screaming for air
Water so calm and pure
No rough edges or wild wetness
For tonight they dance
In the water so deep
Making love between the whispering waves
Crushing sand dollars
Peace unfound
Only blissful meditation
Pure existential lust
Sea shells screaming for air.
Anne L. Walton Ramirez

"Precious Memories"

Thy sweet lips, how I
  miss, thee let me
Count the ways, how I blundered
  please forgive me,
give me another day.

Robert Forsyth

A Picnic On The Beach

Little children dancing 'round
Way up high, then touch the ground.
In and out, then out and in
See them jump and run and spin.
On their hands and on their knees
Asking Mom for ice cream, please.
A hot dog, a hamburger on a bun.
Everyone has so much fun!
Waves and sand within their reach
Hooray for a picnic on the beach!

Dianne D. Bartunek

Miles Apart

Although we may be miles apart,
we are right beside each other
in our hearts. The distance
sometimes seems insurmountable,
but the many thoughts I have of
you are very countable.

You are what I think of when I
first awake and the last before
I lay down. My dreams are of
you because you cannot be around.

But there will come a day when
we will be together; everyday,
every week, always and forever.
This is the day that I am looking
forward too. I am hoping
in my heart so are you.

So until that day comes, I have
only one thing to say; the love
I have for you will make those
miles just seem to fade away.

Drew A. Fenical

Memories

  Memories are a treasure
We carry within our hearts,
  They are of greatest value,
We must never let them part.
  Forever we are needful
Of values of great worth,
  But some do seem so useless
That we care not to unearth.
  So even though we err
In so many of our ways,
  We know we're only human
And memories seem to stay.
  We learn by our experience
And God's eternal love,
  That the bad as well as good ones
Bring a new strength from above.
  Every day that brings new learning
With it's countless trials and strife,
  Is only the beginning
of a long and wondrous life.

Alma Barnes

Influenced

Throughout our lives
we encounter many people.
Many faces come and go,
Like long lines
at a grocery store checkout.

But every now and then were stopped
by that special someone,
a unique face that we think back on.
We remember their words,
their actions,
the little things they did
that forever shaped our own future.

Their powerful influence
was not even understood,
not even realized,
as it was taking place.

It's only after days turn into years,
that we realize
just how powerful they were,
in shaping our lives.

Darin B. Scism

Where Are The Answers?

Where are the Answers?
  We say now and then.
We wonder and we wonder
  Again and again.

Where are the answers?
  I think we all know.
We need to look inside ourselves -
  Down deep in our souls.

Where are the Answers?
  You know for your self.
They're your inner knowing.
  Not in a book on a shelf.

So we all have our answers -
  We all know the way.
So let's begin listening.
  On this very day!

Carolyn Dawley

Things I Miss

Burma shave signs, warm wool shirts
Well-mannered boys and girls in skirts

Drug store phosphates, trolley cars
Home-made bread, free lunch in bars

Sunday picnics, chestnut trees
Scent of lilacs in the breeze

Romantic songs with catchy verse
The silence of a passing hearse

A cool, green park that's litter free
Someone to kiss an injured knee

Blocks of ice and lumps of coal
And naked boys in a swimming hole

A baseball game when I'm at bat
I surely do miss all of that

The milkman's horse, the corner store
Those things that aren't there anymore

I miss my friends who've passed away
Oh, how I long for yesterday

Harry W. Michel

The Tree

  High on a hilltop of
West Virginia stands this
lonely old tree.
  Why was it put there
if not for me to see.
  It must be a lonely
old tree with its branches
all splint and worn,
  It must have had a lot
of years swaying in the storms.
  As I sit here and gaze
upon it, I think to myself.
  You must have someone
to share your life with each day.
  So we can learn to sway
and fight our storms away.

Charlette Kirk

Tommy In The Tree

Tommy, high up in the tree
What do you see?
Oh, Grandma! I can see so far
Is it Daddy coming in a car?
I hope he's coming back to stay
I miss him since he went away
No, its Mommy coming home from work
Trying her duty not to shirk
Being both Mom and Dad to Chris and me
And making a home for us three
When I grow up I hope in time
I'll never leave any kids of mine

Ellen L. Reich

Shadow on the Sand

A beautiful day in January
what I wanted to see
was God's creation.
The ocean, the sun,
a day for relaxation
the fresh air
little did I know
what came near!
evil lured on the shore
O God don't let be a victim once more,
while I was laying in the sand
I pray'd to God
don't let it be the end.
Somehow I escaped
without realizing
that I was raped
raped of body-mind and soul
my body healed
so did my soul
but my mind won't let it go.

Heidi Plomteaux

The Boogie Man

They say the Boogie man
Is very spooky.
But I say that
He is kooky.
Hearing this he jumps,
But I run.
And now my poem
Is all done!

Meredith Reid

The Blanket

Oh, maiden whose hands have created you.
What was on your mind
As you wove the threads together
To create a grand design?

It must have been a great love
For the father and the child
Who played and laughed together
Away out in the wild.

Did they toss the moonbeams and stars
Into the skies of blue?
While clouds of white rolled overhead
And the grass lay wet with dew?

Your love is free and giving.
Your tears are filled with joy.
The weaving is now completed
And warms the baby boy.

Dorothy Rathje

Honor

Heap no bouquets on my cold corpse
When all my life has passed away;
Send me roses while yet I live,
Give me the praise and honor today.

Sing then no sad songs for me
Nor weep the false or useless tear;
Sing sweet, happy songs with me today
And keep your true heart ever near.

Let us walk a way together;
Let us enjoy life hand in hand.
Give me love, truth, and honor
And let not our lives be damned

And if the fates should so decree
It's time for one of us to go—
Both of us shall rest easier knowing
That we loved each other so.

So today let us stem the tide,
Let us make life so good to live;
Begin anew and forget all the bad,
Before it becomes too late to forgive.

Jean E. Hackett

Oh Tenebrous Day

Oh Tenebrous day
when day became night,
and the sun veiled its face
from the terrible sight.

From the horror and madness,
oh how could it be,
that the Lord of Creation
should be nailed to the Tree?

A day when the darkness
ruled as the light,
and evil prevailed
though deceived by its might.

It demanded a payment
a ransom, a fee,
so the Lamb interceded
to pay it for thee.

Donald Thomas Kelly

When?

When did we stop loving?
When did it turn to hate?
Was it something we created
Or was it determined in our fate?

When did we stop trying?
When did laughter turn to tears?
Are we living out our destiny
Or are we living out our fears?

When did we stop caring?
When did happiness turn to pain?
Must all these years be for nothing?
Must our hearts always bear this stain?

When can we go on living?
When will this agony end?
If we cannot stay married
I beg you please, let us be friends -

Cathy D. Myers

Katie's Day

I was just a kid at heart,
when he and I were torn apart.
A minute doesn't go by
each and every day
when I don't think about him
and that dreadful day.
Crying and holding me in his arms,
for five years he kept me from harm.
But he and Mom did not agree,
deep in his heart he wanted to be free.
I kissed him and said goodbye,
he kissed me and said don't you cry.
I'll always be here,
as he pointed to my heart
I'm off on my own,
to make a new start.
As he walked out the door,
he turned around and said,
I love you Katie,
now off to bed.

David Conrad

To My Children

No need to shed a tear for me
When I am dead and gone
I've cried enough in my short life
To fill the seas and shores beyond

The tears I've dropped were not in vain
I've cried for all of us
But happiness, you've all attained
In you, I place my trust

Remember, you are not alone
Enjoy your family
For life is for the living
It just wasn't right for me

I've cried with tears of happiness
And sobbed with tears of sorrow
Tears of dread were shed again
When faced with my tomorrow

But life goes on, or so they say
Then too, so must you all
Remember, I am where I want to be
At rest, at peace, beyond your call

Elinor B. Kowalski

My Cabin By The Bay

I dream of the time,
When I am old and gray,
That I will rock on the porch,
Of my cabin by the bay.

The morning sunrise will delight me,
And help me through the day,
At night I'll watch the sunset,
With its reflections across the bay.

When the end of my days approach,
And it most surely will come,
I hope that I'll be able to say,
Just take me to my cabin by the bay.

Donna M. Coffman

"Fighting For Love"

How can I love you
When I'm trapped in this body
That won't let me live.

Every day a struggle
I must fight for every inch
that I gain.

Closer and closer
Maybe I'll reach you
this time.

Then with one single word
Someone knocks me
back down

And I start again
fighting this battle
that I'll never win

Jennifer Powers

The Nightly Walk

During the night
When the moonlight
Shows down
A dark shadowy figure
Strolls through
The night.

Eyes as bright as the moon
He opens his wide jaw
To show his teeth
As sharp as knives
The moon puts a spotlight
On the furry creature
As it runs swiftly
On its four legs.

Determination in his eyes
Determined to get where he
Is going
At last the shadowy figure
Is on a patio in a little bed
Fast asleep.

Amy Kotowski

Sorrow

Sorrow fills my lonely, empty heart,
Knowing we are now far apart.

Choking on the lump in my throat,
I feel like my body is about to float.

Through blinding, hot tears,
the world is blurry, and fears
Overcome my troubled soul.

Marcee Ekstrum

Where Are You?

Where are you?
Where are you, my love?
I know where I am,
but, my love, where are you?

I'm here at my house
just waiting for you.
And I'll wait for a lifetime
to prove I'll be true.

For I want you,
I need you,
I love you,
but, my love, where are you?

It's true what they say about home,
that there the heart is too.
But my love here will stay,
'til maybe someday, you will return to me.

For I want you,
I need you,
I love you,
but, my love, where are you?

Donna L. Taylor

My Specialness

I am an Angel
Where Jesus lives
And before I die
I want to rise up to heaven
I come from a bad world
I then go to a better world
Jesus is inside of me
I am inside of Jesus
Everything is love and happiness
Everything is correction and life
And everything is like a dream
Before death is life.

Jodi M. Ward

One Love

Lighting life from piece of mind
Where there's love I cannot find
Undying pain from my heart
My love and I just had to part

He spoke soft words
true at best

They run through my
mind and I cannot rest

By a river to sit
and talk

Or through the woods
on a peaceful walk

My life was there
right by my side

My thoughts were open
deep and wide

There was nothing
there no touch or kiss

But it's those talks
that I will miss.

Erin J. Rodriguez

Where Trailing Arbutus Grow

I must go again to the North Woods
Where trailing arbutus grow,
With pines all around to protect me
From sun, the cold wind or snow.

Stars peek through the tree leaves
When gentle breezes blow,
With moon shadows making magic
Of dancing lace below.

Picnics by the lakeshore,
Hiking in the fall,
Waterfun in the sunshine,
Winter sports for all.

Crab apples to eat or make jelly,
High bush cranberries, I recall
Berry picking in the summer,
Gathering hazel nuts in the fall.

I cannot squelch the longing,
My heart will ever know
That home is in the North Woods
Where trailing arbutus grow.

Florine Doris Gilligan

Mother

A Mother is a smiling face.
Whether you have won or lost
the race.
A mother is a guiding hand.
When things happen that were
not planned.
But most of all a mother's
love.
A cherished gift from above.

April Lawson

The Clock Maker

Jolly old tinker,
White hair and mustache.
Glasses propped up on a
Red nose.
Screwdriver tucked behind
Left ear,
Pipe firmly in mouth.
Apron pockets hiding loose
Gears,
Springs,
Wheels and
Cogs.
His hands going around,
Pipe ticking on grinding teeth.
Eyes winding,
Oil dripping
From a still face.
Always looking out,
As time
Goes by.

Carrie Smith

Musical Days

I was listening to music
It was hot and it was new.
It's fun for me and you.
Although it made me tried
So I'm no longer wired
I kind of wish I were,
Because time is passing
In a blur.

Melissa J. Jean

Let Us Have Peace

The Lord sent his son
Who gave his life
So we might be one
And not live in strife

Where is our world going
Don't we care anymore
As men fight their brothers
And go to war

The Lord sends the dove
As a sign of peace
Let's lay down our weapons
And let the fighting cease

God gave us this earth
To make our home
Let's not destroy it
And the creatures thereon —

Jim Brogan

Listen to Him

God is a miracle
Who gave us, this earth
From the time he made Adam
Until he gave us, birth

He, is our master
To him, we obey
He is always with us
Through the night and day

Whenever we need Him
He's always there
He listens to what we say
When we say, a prayer

He, gives us strength
Whenever we are down
He tries to make us happy
When we wear, a frown

God was crucified
Because of our sin
And now I think its time
For all, - "To Listen To Him"

Eva M. Moore

An Ode to Robert Frost

Here is to all those poets
who made sure
with all their might
that their poems rhymed
not withstanding history
which judged them trite
or our English professors
who showered the poets
having no sense of meter
with undue praise
we can make a case
that a great wrong has been done.
Oh but how Robert how
frosty the winter is
and I see lovely woods so deep
but now Robert now
You would rather not pick apples
but go to sleep.

Harsh K. Luthar

With a Wink and a Nod

I know a little man,
Who's as nice as can be,
And every time I see him,
His winks and nods at me.

He has a little house,
Which has a little door,
And every time I go in it,
He winks and nods some more.

He has a special tea time,
When he drinks his tea,
And every time he takes a sip,
He winks and nods at me.

When it was time to go,
I walked out the door,
And I turned around to see,
He winked and nodded once more.

Amanda Jo Huskey

Untitled

Steven found a little dog
who's fur was all white,
it followed him into the cotton fields
and disappeared out of sight!

Steven found a little cat
who's fur was all back,
when the stars come out that night
it disappeared,
and he cried, come back!

Steven found a little skunk
who's fur was black and white,
and when it raised it's tail,
Steven ran out of sight!

Steven found a little duck,
who's feathers were all gray,
his mother saw it too,
and guess what they had
for dinner that day?

Barbara Markel

Forgotten Finally

Why can't I be pretty
Why can't I be smart
Why can't I be skinny
Why can't we be apart

How do I forget
Our times of the past
Maybe for a little bit
I thought it would really last

I've forgotten you
You've forgotten me
I found someone new
But I wish you'd see

We can still be friends
Like we used to be
Things don't have to end
Please, don't forget me

You have something, a part of me you stole away
I have something, a part of you and you only say...
Good bye forever, and walk away

Amanda Petersen

Untitled

Oh lonely one
Why do you not smile
Oh passer bye
why do you not wave

Has the world been cruel to you
in some awful way...

How do I help
How do I change
A world inflicted with such pain

Should I cry for you
Should I die for you
Maybe a simple "Hi" would do

Oh lonely one
Why do you not smile
Oh passer bye
why do you not wave

Has the world been cruel to you
in some awful way...

Elaine Emmett

Why?

Why is a tree called a tree?
Why not call it a shrub?
Why is a shrub called a shrub?
Why not call it a bee?
It seems to me
That everything is not what it seems.
Even though a tree is a tree,
Even though a shrub is a shrub,
Even though a bee is a bee,
Everything is not what it seems.
When someone says no,
They really mean yes.
When they say they don't know,
They really mean guess.
Why is the world this way?
Why can't it just be simple?
Why is an ear called an ear?
Why not call it a pimple?
Why?

Anna Bergdall

Running Spirit

Running spirit
  wild as the wind.
A broken heart
  you cannot mend.

See it running,
  running wild.
Across the pasture
  like a child.

Try to catch it.
  Do you think you can?
I think not,
  your still the same man.

All you will do
  is break my heart,
and leave me
  just to fall apart.

Running spirit,
  run as fast as you can,
and never stop searching
  for the right man.

Cristin Colston

Moonshine

The moon is a balloon

That floats so high, and I wonder
Will it ever float away
Without ever saying good-bye?

The sun is a star

That shines so bright, and I wonder
Will it ever run out of fuel?

The sun rises in the morning
The moon comes out at night

But when morning and night collide
And they both look
Down at the earth together

What a sight!

James M. Filoso

Missing Link

One faded image,
Will it let me know?
Will it help me gage
the essence of you?

You look so strong,
Your face is fair,
Your legs seem long,
Quite a gangly pair.

Did you possess humor
or were you drab?
Did you flash temper
like a hostile crab?

Did the printed page
give you pleasure;
Or did pursuit of wages
rob you of leisure?

Your life's reign
preceded mine,
But in my veins
runs your line.

Jean Whitaker

Weeping Willow

Weeping willow swaying in the wind,
Won't you come and be my friend?

No one will come out and play,
And if they do, they never stay.

I want someone to play with me,
I'm so alone, can't you see?

We'll play all day and sleep all night,
And wake-up with the morning light.

Weeping willow, is this the end?
So tell me, will you be my friend?

Allison Emrick

Another Beautiful Day In Paradise

As I wake up in the morning
Wipe the sleep from both my eyes,
There beyond the shutters,
Is a beautiful surprise.

The sun is up and shining,
What a glory to behold.
The doves are cooing softly,
Another day unfolds.

A beautiful day in paradise
Surrounded by olive trees,
Prairie dogs and sunsets,
Now and then, a breeze.

Palm trees, cactus blooming,
Mountains all around.
God's touch is everywhere.
HIS love for us abounds.

Betty Winn

Vicky

An angel sent to this world
With a hole lot of Love.
The most precious angel
sent from the heaven's above.
Her eye's like sparkling diamonds
and hair like silk which I
long to touch.
And a smile so bright it
lightens up the darkest night.
An angel I call vicky
sent to this world to give
me all her Love.
Which I prayed for from God
Almighty from the heaven's above
my beautiful Angel Vicky
whom I love.

Jimmy Calderon

Prayer at Dawn

Awaking I see your face
with a ray of first light of Dawn.

You are my life, my light,
my early rise at Dawn.

We walk together each day
in mind and spirit at Dawn.

I carry your memories with me
everyday from Dawn to Dawn.

Your stories will be shared
through the years, each day of Dawn.

The body is gone but you
are with me your light of Dawn.

May God Bless and keep us with
your love from Dawn to Dawn.

Dawn Shiree McGaha

My Cabin

I have a little cabin
nestled in the country hills,
and at night I like to listen
to the singing whippoorwills.
In the morning I awaken
to the songs of many birds,
and I lie there quietly listening,
sweetest songs I ever heard.

Ruby P. Garvin

Untitled

She looks out the window
with a tear stained face, the
moonlight shining softly on
her face, she looks out over the
ocean for miles and miles there
is nothing. A slight breeze comes
and gently lifts her hair off
her shoulders. The rain is pouring
down similar to her tears, never
stopping, her mind wonders
not knowing anything of what
the outside world holds, she's
a prisoner of love. Always hurting,
never believing, she's always
believed if you love someone
set them free.

Angela Schuler

The Hiding Mask

Your arms spread out
with a welcoming smile.
Everyone's joy and laughter,
You are the happiness
in one else's lives.
But to your own self
you are the misery in the sky.
You are your own soul's killer,
the hunger in a starving child.
Why is the world still laughing,
When your name turned wrong.

Efaat Yossifor

Butterflies

It arrives the spring
with a whirlwind full
of butterflies
A million painted ladies flutter
lost as I,
pinned to pure white cardboard
encased in glass
waiting for the spring to pass
hear
too late
again
again?

Jere Earlston

My Sister

You stand there
With angry eyes
Looking down on me.
Mouth quivering,
You cuss me
With sharp,
Cutting words.
You pledging your hate for me.
I strike back
With spiteful words.
The monotony
Of this vicious circle
Makes me
Turn my back
And walk away
From our friendship
And you.

Allison Abernethy Higginson

Springtime

Spring is like a fairytale,
With beautiful birds singing for you
Colorful flowers appear in the vale,
This all reminds of our lady in blue.
A time for children to laugh and play,
A time to put skates and sleigh away,
The trees take a look of splendor,
While rain and sun their service render
Spring, indeed, is wonderful.

Elizabeth Ann Leick

Mother's Shy Little Girl

A shy little girl, who looks like you
With big blue eye's so shiny and true
A funny like smile, on her face
Just tells you at times
No one can take her place
She seems at times
To be carefree and gay
That's how I know, you cannot look away
A peek from the corner of her eye
Just seems to tell you, that she is shy

You want to hold her
And squeeze her real tight
To let her know
How much love is in sight
For at times she seems puzzled
When she looks at you
But then, she will say
"You know, Mommy"
I love you!

Bill Verdon

I Warned You

As He entered the cave,
with evil thoughts in mind.

With every step he takes,
he sends shivers down my spine.

The vampire come closer,
what a gruesome sight.

He has been chasing me
throughout the entire night.

And from my terror,
He does get delight.

For running into this dead end cave,
I feel like such a dud.

And when he bites into my neck,
I feel the gushing...BLOOD

And I hate to say it but....
I WARNED YOU!

Dustin Bunch

A Perfect Spot

At a lagoon,
where the loons swim,
dive, and fish all day.
A lagoon lined on both sides
with ornate and picturesque homes.
A lagoon gemmed with a silver moon
reflected at certain times.
A lagoon, long and narrow,
whose background is Mt. Tamalpias.
Where the mountain meets the sea.
Where the sea comes to rest.

Bernard J. Kennett

Such a Crime

No more waiting in the cold
With fear of growing old
Our better days behind

Only panic in the streets
We steel what we must eat
Survival on our minds

Fire's burning in the breeze
No safety from disease
It's really hell this time

No emotions we can't cry
The week ones they must die
We've left them all behind

It's extremely cold tonight
We're strickened by frostbite
Though pain's not on our minds

No more animals or rain
Just violence, death and shame
Of what we did this time

Such a crime
John Paul Beniamino

To Help One Child

Children are little people,
With feelings, opinions.
  They are the future!
Guide them, protect them.
  Treat them well!

Abuse leaves a mark,
  On a life for life.
The scars run deep.
  The trust is broken.
The pain is hidden.

  Children do count!
Love them unconditionally.
  Listen to them, teach them.
They want to learn;
  Be there for them.

To help one child,
  Is so rewarding.
Think what this world
  would be like,
If we all helped.

Annette Rodriguez

The Beautiful Birds I Love

Once on a cold and stormy day,
With leaden skies above.
I saw a flock of honkers,
Those beautiful birds I love.

Out of the cold grey north they came,
Their ranks so straight and brave.
Making their way to the southland,
And the sunshine that they crave.

Oh, that we could have the power,
To follow the seasons change,
To summer on northern Lily bower,
And winter on southern range.

I wonder if we truly are so great,
With our struggle for money and fame,
God gave the honker and his loyal mate,
A life that few of us can claim.

Elton Carlson

My Island

I was left on an island,
with no-one around.
No-one to talk to,
not a soul to be found.
I wish you could help me,
oh where could you be?
For I'm all alone here,
surrounded by sea.

Come take me away,
to a place with no fear,
and I promise we'll be happy there.
Just one more chance,
to make romance.
A dinner with candles,
or maybe a dance?
In front of the fire,
that's my only desire.
For it's then that ecstasy,
will lift me up higher.

Chris Johnson

Still

The sun still rises
with skies so clear
It is not uplifting
You are not here

Flowers still bloom
and dance with grace
It is not breathtaking
I can't see your face

Raindrops still glisten
as they hit the ground
I can't feel their cool mist
You are not around.

Snowflakes still gather
White blankets will enfold
all of the world, except me
It's you I need to hold

Hope still exists
that in heaven I'll see
your beauty once again
instead of just your memory

Debra E. Carcich

Chubby Little Fingers

Chubby little fingers
wrapped around my heart,
golden memories in my mind
even when we are apart.
Cherished mementoes
from each and every year,
treasures wrapped in love
ever cherished, ever dear.
And when the time comes
for me to set you free,
the memories will forever remain
an eternal part of me.
For from the time that we
were bound together as one,
you've been my greatest love
my little boy, my son.

Beth Bender

Bundle Of Love

Beautiful baby girl
With tiny smile so sweet,
You bless our lives
With each and every heartbeat.

Precious bundle of love
With eyes of deep blue,
You light up our world,
Making troubles seem few.

Lovely skin soft as silk,
Hair dark as night,
You fill hearts with pride
And make burdens light.

To each day, comes joy,
As lonely lives you touch.

A lusty cry, a quiet sigh,
We love you so much!

Beautiful baby girl,
You bless us with love —
Creating visions of hope.
For you, we thank God above.

Dorothy A. Wallace

Significance

It's not the speed
  with which I rush to your side
  which signifies that I love you;

Nor the numerous times
  I've scratched your back
  or rubbed your feet
  or brushed your hair

Or done all those things
  which lovers are meant to do
  but seldom have the chance.

But lying there
  under your quilt,
  with eyes turned inward
  toward some distant dream,

I can't help but notice
  how much those little things add up,
  and provide the meaning
  that your soul,
  departing,

has for me.
Allan N. Guberman

If You Would Know Me

See me
  with your heart;
Weigh me
  by my deeds.
Hear
  my soul calling
For help
  to be all that I am;
For light
  to find yet more
Which lies there
  unperceived.

Alma Garrison

Senior Year

Last year of freedom,
    Without a care in the world,
Before you're all grown up.

Memories of your friends,
    Run through your head,
While you wish you could receive them.

Some you'll stay in touch with,
    But will slowly drift apart,
With only the memories remaining.

The last night you're all together,
    Sadness becomes quite clear,
While others are glad to leave.

Your friends and you,
    Are glad to be finished,
But wish it would never end.

Adrianne Heist

People Without A Heart

Oh Lord there are people
without a heart. Oh God
people are unkind to the
elder, people. Oh mine
Lord knows.
People lack generosity,
Oh Lord.
    How can it be,
Some people are so
mean and spiteful.
Oh Lord he knows
People don't have a heart.
    People really don't
care. They don't have
a heart.
    Oh Lord Lord people
have no heart. How can
it be.
    Oh how great it is
that Lord got a big heart.

Christine Phillips

Nature's Magic

The whole world changed
    without a sound
So softly, so gently
    the snow flakes came down
Covering the ground
    with a blanket of white
Keeping the flowers snug
    through the long winter night
To sleep, to rest, to renew
    to he awakened by
April Showers and morning dew.
The age old magic of nature, ever new
That brings the flowers back to you.

Alice M. Hutt

My Mark

I do not leave my mark upon the sand
Nor is it carved in stone,
But in the guise of song
It journeys on the wind,
And thus, by sound and echo,
I leave my mark forever.

R. Bernice LeClaire

Commitment

Ella Kissed me where she stood
Leaning o'er the balustrade,
Soft lips pressed against my own
Love's commitment freely made.
Ella kissed me!

Norman L. Parks

Without

How dark a room
    Without light
How dreary a day
    Without sunshine
How long a night
    Without dreaming
How useless a life
    Without purpose
How hollow a soul
    Without "GOD"
How cold a heart
    Without love
How lonely my days
    Without you

Francis Hoffman

Where My Road Ends

Standing where my road ends
wondering what it holds,
beyond the depths of seclusion
to where nobody goes.

The road is an obscure warning
on what my future holds.
This road means more to me
than I can ever show.

Confronting my own mortality.
Is it worth this scorn
to weaken every bone,
a reflection of my self, well known?

This road to me is more than life
so clear and bold,
paved my way to today
where the earth grows cold.

To my eyes a beautiful world unfolds
more radiant than a woman's love; comfort
triumphs over cold.
As I abandon my road
I can see what the world holds.

Jeff Parcheta

The Forgotten Tears

Of all the pain, through all the
    years
There has come to past the forgotten
    tears
I weep no more for my eyes have
    dried
The pain lies still, deep
    inside
Stir not the emotions to create those
    fears
For my heart will bleed and shed more
    tears
My mind's eye refuses to see many
    things
Yet my heart tells the story where the
    sorrow still rings

Allysan F. Drew

Untitled

Need I go on and on?
Yes! I could
But I think you get some
ideal of what love is
or at least I think you should

Love is a smile
even if you are not
feeling the best

Love is putting your best
foot forward, and God will do the rest

Beulak Hill

Have You Ever Been In Love?

"Have you ever been in love?"
"Yes! Once."
"What was it like?"
"Painful."

"Have you ever been loved?"
"Yes! Once."
"What was it like?"
"Sad."

"Why was to be in love painful
And to be loved sad?"

"The one I loved was not
The one who loved."

Inez M. Kirby

Valentine

So far away
Yet close to my heart
I just can't be happy
When we are apart

Think of me when I'm gone
Keep the flame alight
It will be thoughts of you
That get me through the night

Keep your chin up high
For soon I'll return
When I'm finally in your arms
My passion will burn

I love you so much
In each and every way
Oh no, I almost forgot
Happy Valentine's Day!

Emie Bailey

Love

Vain, arrogant,
Haughty, proud.

Noisy, pushy,
Showy, loud.

Timid, doubtful,
Humble, bowed.

Love is candid;
Love is vowed.

Nancy J. Richeson

A Baby's Tiny Hand

So tiny is a baby's hand
Yet so much does it hold
Memories of those happy days
Mean more to me than gold.

So helpless yet so fearless
So precious and so dear
It only takes a little love
To wipe away a tear.

A tiny smile can bring the sun
Through the darkest cloud above
She says "I love you" with a coo
She borrowed from a dove.

Soft blue eyes look up to me
She does not understand
She holds the future of my world
In her tiny baby's hand.

Dorothy Myers

Reflection On Weeds

We do not plant, we do not sow,
Yet the delightful flowers from weed
plants grow.

I gazed on a "weed field" of beautiful
colorful flowers.
Nature was having a Flower Show and was
showing off Her green thumb powers.
Purple, yellow, pink and white, 'twas
surely a blue ribbon sight.

Such a pleasure was the view, I lingered
long enjoying nature anew.

Angeline Lopatka

A Tall Tale

Did
You
Ever
See,

A
Poem
To
Be

Tall
As
A
Tree?

It's
Probably
A
First,

Hope
Not
The
Worst.

Dale T. Stewart

Life

Life is a shamble
Life is a gamble
Life can be crumble
When ever we stumble.
Life is not always a rumble
even through we mumble.

Martha Bazemore

Emergence

For a brief time
You became a butterfly,
Emerging from your chrysalis,
Showing the world
Your bright intense colors
And enjoying the feel
Of the power of your wings.

How beautiful you were
Soaring above the others!
Thrilling in the magnificence
Of your new-found strength,
And revelling in the joy
Of your freedom.

But all too soon,
Frightened by the immenseness
Of the world around you,
You disappeared into the darkness and
confusion
Of your chrysalis again,
Depriving all the world
Of your beauty and splendor.

Carolynn E. Metz

The Voice of a Skeptic

When there is golden silence,
You can hear my heart beating.

If you listen closely,
You can hear the echo.

The echo.

The echo,
Of the songs it used to sing.

Such sweet melodies are merely memories
Carried to the sky on a bird's wing.
There is no bitterness in my tone.

My breath is e-e-even,
And cool.

My shoulders back;

My head held high;

I walk with confidence,
And grace.

"Your heart will sing again,"
Is what "they" say.

But I live carefully;
My guard up at all times.

Daniele Williams

Catharsis

Angry lava churns
Floods the mind
Scalds the soul

Molten dreams
Ashen roses

Purge the anger
Crush the doubt

Blossoming dreams
Vivid roses

Nancy F. Karr

Hell

No key out
You can yell
You can shout
Nothing can undo,
the things,
done to you

Black and gray
all around
from the heavens
to the ground

snowflakes pound
in my head
not caring
who you dread

the battles fought
bloody and cold
bang bang
out with
the loud

Isabelle Johansson

Desire

What if
you cried
in the night
and wanted
your friend to come
comfort, console you —

Would you
let her into
your heart?

Could you
then come
to terms with
desire?

Debra L. Woodruff

Dinosaur Dinosaur

Dinosaur Dinosaur, what will
you eat for dinner?
Dinosaur Dinosaur, will you
eat me for dinner?

Dinosaur Dinosaur, where do
you go to walk?
Dinosaur Dinosaur, do you
walk to the Park?

Dinosaur Dinosaur, do you go
swimming?
Dinosaur Dinosaur, will you
wade in the water?

Dinosaur Dinosaur, where do
you sleep?
Dinosaur Dinosaur, do you
live in a cave?

Dinosaur Dinosaur, will
you play with me?

Beau Daly

Merry Go Round

Life is like a merry go round
You get on and can't get off
You go up and down
Round and round
You think it will never end
It takes you into dream land
Everything bright and beautiful
It takes you into night mares
With hellish freight
You grab for the brass ring
You think if you get it
The world will be at your feet
But the brass ring is just out of reach
So you keep on
Going up and down
Round and round
Lost forever on that MERRY GO ROUND

Elizabeth Davis

Just Do It!

Life expects the very best of
you. Give it up and turn it
loose. Every one is of some
use. The best in you will
light your way. It will lead
you to a better day. If
at first you don't succeed,
let this be your final plea.
Let us see the best of
you. We wish you well and
life will too.

Carrie Bedden

Candle

Candle, candle, burning bright,
You give such a lovely light.
In the window shining clear
For the traveler wandering near.

Through the night by baby's bed,
Throwing a halo 'round his head.
In the church you vigils keep
Over dear ones gone to sleep.

Like life you start with flickering glow,
Burning steadier as you grow;
'til life's flame sinks out of sight
And God's hand puts out the light.

Betty Mandt

Jordan

You don't know how much
you love him, 'til he's gone.

You hate yourself for
letting go but you'd
only get hurt holding on.

So you let go, you
think you're as hurt as you ever
will be for letting him go.

You wish he'd come
back, but he says we're only friends.

Amanda Yarnall

Untitled

When love has hit
You make it fit,
When love has gone:
It's like a dawn.

For love to last the day,
It is this, I have to say:
Be sweet, loving and kind,
And love will be there to find!

Jose A. Gonzalez Jr.

The Argument

You act as if I have no feelings,
You talk as if I have no fears.
Sometimes I wonder if you notice
behind my smile, there are tears.

The fight we had didn't phase you,
You are always in the right.
So, our anger seems to continue,
Day after day, night after night.

It's time to put this to an end,
Communication is the key.
We'll try to be the best of friends,
I for you and you for me.

Jolie Abbott

God

I used to think
    You were in the sky,
So far above my head

Amongst the clouds,
    The moon and stars,
And left me when I'm dead.

But now I know
    A different truth
Far greater than before—-

You're by my side
    And deep within
Abiding near, evermore.

Claudia Stuart

To Grow A Tree

To grow a tree
you will see,
    The joy that it will bring.

The birds fly by
and soar real high.
    How beautiful the song they sing.

When the rain comes down
to soak the ground,
    You will surely know it's spring.

The kids will play
all night and day,
    And all because of your tree.

They'll build a fort
of some sort.
    It will truly bring them glee.

They'll climb real high
to the sky.
    Oh the sights that they'll see.

David Kephart

Sunburn

Down by the sea,
You will see me.
On a hot summer day,
Late in May.
The waves, they will crash
I'll be there in a flash.
With my bathing suit on,
You can see me at dawn.
To soak up the sun,
And have lots of fun.
I look down the shore,
All I want, is more
Of the gorgeous white sand,
Now I hear a band,
On the radio playing.
And over the noise my mother is saying,
Put on more lotion,
Then I get the notion,
That I will learn,
After I get an awful sunburn.

Heather Zawalick

Only in God's Time

When you carry your own cross
You won't burden it alone
You won't have to cry or worry
Just believe and trust in Him.

He'll be standing right beside you
Pick you up when you fall down
Give you rest when you are weary
Help you fight when you're worn down.

He'll keep watch as you lay sleeping
He'll strengthen you each day
And the price He paid to save your soul
Has been repaid this day;

By asking Him into your life
And wanting Him to stay
By teaching others of His word
And teaching them to pray.

Even though the body dies
Your soul remains with Him
Like the precious, fragrant flower, that
blooms softly on the vine
Keep praying, things will happen, but only
in God's time.

Gwen M. Young

True Advice

Advice well taken,
your words well spoken,
and your mind well understood,
but what is my mind,
and what are my feelings?
What shall I do,
and why shall I do it?
Who will help me,
and how will I decide what's right?
Is it you,
the one with the answers,
can you help me,
and make my life easier?
I really hope so.

David L. Kemmerer

Eulogy for Manuel Cabrera

My moist, wet lips embraced
your cold, lifeless body.

Did you feel me?

Your eyes were closed as
if angels were whispering
sweet nothings to you.

Did you hear them?

Your face was tanned.
Your tension was gone.

Are you leaving?

My tears dripped on
you in a fruitless effort to
warm you.

Did you know I was there?

"Ave Maria Ilena eres de gracia"
I chanted for your eternal salvation.

Did she hear us?
Are you there?

Domitila Hilerio

Untitled

Now, that you have found
your cosmic twin,
there is no reason
for me to stay around.
I can no longer
be of service
so I might as well
just disappear.
I'll always need you
but I must let you go.
The time has come
to follow your destiny.
All I ask of you is
remember me
and read my poems
to the world
so I may continue living
long after my death.

Christina Rogers

Martha, My Mennonite Friend!

In your dress so very different,
Your hair pulled back in a bun,
The little white hat that covers it
Is not too keep off the sun.
It's to be so very humble,
Because of your beliefs, you opened
Up your heart to me, it makes me look,
And understand, that there is no
Difference between us. We both believe
In his great healing hands.
And that he lives with in our hearts.
And that he once walked among man.
So when I see someone who dresses,
Different I'll try hard to understand
That we are all created by his hand.

War Kloud

A Light

A light
went on in my
head; I think I
get it now. A light
went on in my head I
got it. Yes! Oh wow!
The light is on in
my head; this one
I'm going to
get. I'm
raising
my hand;
"yes what
is it? "Uh,
darn, I
FORGET!

Matthew Gist

"The Alarm Clock"

Its fiery red digits
are just a blur to me
I forget them all at 11.

My eyes are shades
that have been pulled down
But, by imagination, another is drawn.

In this land of a wanna-be life
my bee, the box, is not there
To buzzzzz for me at 7.

Then, "Buzzzzzzz!" I'm up like a shot
this bee's not gonna forget me
It won't let me snooze at dawn.

Dana Celeste Holler

Peace Is.....

Praying for
Exactly what you need
And getting
Courage and strength in
Every endeavor.

Anita Raup

Untitled

I saw the rain begin.
First as one dark splotch
on the garden gate
and then another.
Each icy drop hurting earthward
on a 45° slant.

So my tears began.
First one, then another,
then a seeming neverending torrent.

The fence is all wet now-
the ground soggy-
but the rain has stopped,
the heavens spent.

Someday too shall the tears stop
pain spent.

Sandra L. Achterman

Real Eyes - A Love *Like Answer*

A lone
inner wish

These feelings
come - it meant
nothing?

In different paths
she wished to travel
Yet knowing the trail I'd chosen

Her cue lay in
my journey down it

So words from her pierced a
nerve on a numb body

Lighting these pains
which continue on -
ensues idle torment...

Not *deep rest*
lying
in my lonely bed

Jason Monday

Quarter Moon

Silver
   sliver
      shining
         through
            hazy
            veil of
               passing
                  cloud
                     shed
            nocturnal
               peace
               upon
               weary
               workers
            homeward
         bound

Sandra D. Miller

From One Vet to Another

To all the troops in far Kuwait
To see you home we cannot wait!
All for one and one for all,
To see him gone that was your goal.
The word was given, the time was set-
good luck to all!
A KOREAN VET

Aurelio Avilés Sr.

Untitled

  'We touch each others' lives
so briefly,
  We touch each others' souls
so deep,
  But this I say to you,
  Take care friend, take care,
for one you have touched now
remembers you.'

Kathleen Smiley

Us

As the moon glows brighter
We grow closer
As the wind blows harder
We grow closer
As the sun grows warmer
We grow closer
As the river flows faster
We grow closer
As the fishermen row faster
We grow closer
As the clouds cover the moon
We draw apart
As the wind dies down
We draw apart
As the sun slowly sets
We draw apart
As the river begins to calm
We draw apart
As the fishermen take a rest
So do we

Leesa Beirold

Courtney Blake Eberhard

"Chris and Jill Eberhard
are proud to announce the
adoption of their daughter."
Welcome to the family
welcome to the world
we're all just beaming
to have a little girl!
She arrived in a special way
on a bright and warm spring day
April 21, 1994
7 lbs. 9 ozs.
20 inches long
10 little fingers, 10 little toes
so sweet, soft and perfect
one tiny little nose
a song in our hearts, lots of love too
little girl.....all because of you!

Jill Eberhard

Loss

Sad,
   yes, oh so sad.
The feeling strikes hard,
   Cold,
   like ice flowing,
      through warm veins,
   drives deep,
      like the knife,
         put through your back.
Deeper,
   an' deeper,
   the feeling grows.
      Stronger,
         an' stronger,
         as sorrow grows.
Tears form,
   in blood shot eyes,
      as the pain starts to flow.
Tearing away at the inner soul.
As the sadness comes and goes.

John W. Hudson III

Just A Thought

Has there ever been a day,
When I have been your friend?
I think about it night by night,
It is a thought that never ends.

Has there ever been a moment,
When you have really needed me?
Why must I pay to life.
A never ending fee?

Has there ever been a time,
When we have laughed together?
When will my gloomy sky
Exalt its stormy weather?

You have told me many things,
Both hateful and truly,
But, there is one thing,
You have never said to me

"I need you", and "I love you.

Kristina Helb

Somewhere Up Ahead

How do I know where I'm going,
when I haven't been there yet?

How do I know when I get there,
if it's where I really wanted to go?

If I go back to where I've been,
will it be the same as it was?

In a space where time was,
in a place man never knew.

In a zone where all living things;
are nothing but bones.

From this place, on the return trip,
can I be with you?

Or will I be alone in this place;
where all things belong?

Among the places, somewhere in a space,
between being and dying.

If I find my soul, in part, or in whole,
can I be with you, right or wrong?

Royce Earl Whiddon

Unkind Times

To each of us there comes a time
when life is not so very kind.
We close the door and seal it up
in hopes no more pain will erupt

Soon we find the cell we made,
is a prison full of rot, decay.
Keeping out the world we find
can only bring torment of mind.

All closed up the spirit dies,
it must be free for it to fly.
Throw open the door and let light in
only through sharing can new life begin.

In life there's times both good and bad
a learning experience we've all had.
Let go of all your doubts and fears
make the most of all your years.

Linda Sprouse

"Gone"

Once upon a time
When life was but a dream
Nothing really mattered
Except for you and me
Now you are gone
And I remain
Can you hear our song
And feel the pain
I think of you
You think of me
Our love is true
Though they can't see
I'm feeling very empty
Though others call me friend
My spirit tangled in a tree
No flowers did they send
I know that we will meet again
Before the stories over
Remember how it once had been
A love as sweet as a clover.

Richard E. Poerio

How Do You Say Good-bye to a Friend

How do you say goodbye to a friend
When love is at its very end
When friend is not to blame
You just want your life re-arranged
How do you say goodbye at love's end?

How do you say you no longer care
And want to divide possessions you share
Affections of a child...
Some things equally will not divide
How do you say goodbye at love's end?

How do you know when it's time to go
Before overtly feelings show
Friend may even know
May not care if they stay or go
How do you say goodbye at loves end...?

Lonnie Fitzgerald

Hidden Nest

Who can say what's right or wrong,
When love stands in the way?
Was it you who lit that candle,
Making my agony go away?

Could it have been that long ago,
When you touched me in the night?
Or was it only yesterday,
I knew our love was right?

Only now that yesterday is gone,
Can there be no turning back?
Had our love not come undone,
I know we could've made it last.

I hold an image of your smile,
With the softness of your eyes.
In my heart you'll always stay,
Despite the many lies.

So here's to you my love,
And I wish you all the best.
The key's within the fisted glove,
In the heart of the hidden nest.

Maryann Viverette

Adult Puberty

Is there such a thing?
When one changes,
moves on to other things.
Adult Puberty
When you no longer know
what to do.
Adult Puberty
I always thought I would
be with you.
Adult Puberty
Emotions run wild.
Adult Puberty
I feel like such a child.
Adult Puberty

Kathy Richardson

The Reality of Pain

Look out among the shattered sea
where all good and evil breed.
For what you will find is pain
and the pain you feel will free your soul.
Everlasting life is why we live,
for now I die but you can not.
Moonlight falls in darkness so bright,
never again shall I see this sight.
Falling figures make their mark,
across the night sky,
from which they came.
They look to me,
and all my shame.
Oh please, oh please,
just turn away.
I'm not all there,
can't you see.
She loved me, she loved me,
please let me be.

Matthew McNelis

Looking Out

Looking out of my window
Where did the time go!
Years have passed by.
What a beautiful blue sky!
Leaves are turning different shades.
My memories of the past fades
away - no complaints from me!
For the first time I feel glee!
Life is fair - it is true
Since I discovered love with you.
You helped me ease my pain.
Your love was pure like the rain.
God must have sent you to me.
As time passes by we will see
What our destiny holds.
Hopefully we will be shielded by the cold.
But do not worry and pout
Because I am looking out.

Nadia Ballas

Thinking of You

As the telephones poles pass
One by one,
And the slender wires
Connect them all,
So do my thoughts
Appear and pass by
And you are ever in them.

Nancy Barraclough Thomas

Keltic Dream

Come dance with me on sacred oak hill
Where druid charms of mistletoe fill.
Sweet perfume of sea mist and heather
Will not ask us how, when or whether.

Sad bramble thorns have torn my life
Yet affinity sounds a responding fife.
Now I sleep a transit eggshell peace
In thoughts of you that do not cease.

Reviving feelings, rhymes and cadence
Keeps all bitterness in far abeyance.
Your kind words have warmed my heart
Morpheus, guard these dreams not part.

Rosalie Kidd Lopez

Land Of Lost Souls

There is a plane
Where few may tread
It's graced with souls
Too weak to mend

There's Janis and Jimi
And Mr. Mojo Risin
Too weak too strong
Too pure to survive

They used any means
Any way to escape
Did they succeed
Without being raped

We all have a soul
That longs to belong
Alone and abused
Battered and bruised

Will he remain
A pure little boy
Who finally came home
To the land of lost souls

Valerie Klingenhagen

The Legend of the Daisy

Amid the brambles and the briers
Where filth and wreck were flung
Upon a lowly mound of clay
A little daisy clung.
Its heart was heavy; clean for spent
Its head was bending down.
From dew that gathered in its eyes
Fell teardrops to the ground.

It saw the rose in glad array
'twas loved by all it knew
But underneath, the daisy saw
The unkind thorns it grew
So strength again, the daisy felt
And from the lowly clod
It humbly raised its weary head
And turned its eyes to God.

And God, He saw the daisy there.
Its lonely heart He knew
And Lo! About, with simple grace
Ten thousand daisies grew.

Lola Garren Lance

The Homestead

I want to go back to the homestead
Where I lived so long ago.
Let me roam the grassy hillside
Where the wild flowers grow.

I fancy it is summer,
I can feel the gentle breeze.
I can hear the red-winged blackbirds
Singing in the trees.

I can see the cooling rain clouds.
I hear the thunder and the rain.
I can hear the chirping of the crickets
In a field of golden grain.

Let me wander through the coulees
Where cattle used to rest,
And view the golden sunset
As the sun sets in the west.

And perhaps an old acquaintance
That I knew may live there still,
Who can share the many memories
Of that house upon the hill.

Rose Matross Noteboom

To Whom It May Concern

Is this the world you're dreaming of,
where money takes the place of love?

Where peace is nothing but a word,
that has no meaning when it's heard

Where people live each day in fear,
'cause love and peace ain't welcome here

What's in it for the children when,
so many die before they're ten?

Have you ever tried to do,
for those less fortunate than you?

You see the anguish and despair,
then pass it by like it's not there

Nose up, chest out! - with foolish pride,
could such a cold heart beat inside?

What makes you think you're better than,
your sister or your brother man?

When will we see what life is worth,
when nothing's left of this old Earth?

Dear God when are we going to learn?
This goes to whom it may concern.

Sharon Allen

Wishing Well

I wish, there was a wishing well,
where only good wishes come true,
and everything you wished for me
I wished back to you,
and magic would only be found in
good,
and bad would soon be gone,
for the well won't work, alas
for the jerk,
who isn't wishing someone well.

Richard A. Granholm

King of Starless Nights

Below the empty silent skies
Where shadows conquer light,
Where distant are the angel's cries,
Stands the king of starless nights.

My pain is an abysmal wound.
My sorrow, cut by winter's knife.
My sun is the pale dead moon.
Blackened death haunts me in life.

As my crying soul withers dry
I howl to the frozen breeze.
Winter fire burns in my eyes.
My heart drowns in arctic seas.

Blind to the sun's radiant gold
My darkness swallows light.
Upon my throne, I sit in bitter cold.
I am king of starless nights.

Below the empty silent sky,
Where demons dance with grace,
When the king of night shall die,
Will he and light embrace.

Mark DeSimone

Somewhere in the Far Arctic

Somewhere in the Far Arctic,
Where the twisting Gulf Stream
Coils and faints and dies,
On an unmapped shore
Where the great floes grumble unheard,
And groan and crash and crack,
Lies the bottles' graveyard.

In drifts, heaps, piles,
They lie, dislabelled,
Hinting still of
Tabasco or whiskey,
Or bearing sallow,
Faded messages
Begging for rescue,
Deep-buried,
Frozen,
Lost.

Richard Persoff

Life Makes Circles

Comes the coolness of the day,
which has made birds fly away.
South they journey to their home,
above the Earth they float and roam.

Tiny body with spanning wings,
I listen to the song he sings.
Delightful tunes and merry song,
he'll fly away, his road is long.

Over speckled landscape, golden leaves,
the last of summer he retrieves,
He swoops and dives in playful ways,
as in the long, hot summer days.

I bid so long to my old friend,
and my best hopes with him I send.
Come back to us in spring once more,
for you'll be welcome at my door.

And as he makes his final pass,
he notices the browning grass.
With promise spring will make all green,
this withered land and grayish scene.

Peter E. Metropoulos, D.O., M.P.H.

The Butterfly and the Rose

Sing to me, oh butterfly,
Which landeth on the rose.
Sing to me of whence you came
And whither you shall go.
Will those lovely wings of yours
Float on evermore?
Or will they rest for me to see
And evermore adore?
Sing to me, oh butterfly,
That you are soon to go,
And I shall cry a bitter tear
And wish that 'twere not so.
But yet, oh butterfly, if you may sing
Of the many joys that you shall bring
   By staying by,
      And clinging to the rose,
I shall dance and leave my stance,
Sing the songs of sweet romance,
   And live the life
      The love god only knows.

Tim Larsen

"Pondering"

It seems as if this life is going nowhere
While I sit outside in the dark,
Writing by a street light
As if I were trying to be smart.
The rest of the world
Goes by while I speak,
Just like another day
Turns into another week.
As I look across the sky
I wonder if there is another,
Who thinks as I do
As if I had a brother.
I've lived here for a good while
So have many more,
People with dreams also
That somehow get pushed back down
   to the floor.
It's kind of cold out here
The windy breeze is a bit cool,
That's why I must go inside
Before I get pushed back down too.

Terry Lee Green Jr.

Michael's Mid-Air Float

It is a curious thing. You stare!
While Michael floated in mid-air.
Tongue hangs-out as he rises to the hoop
Two more points in one quick swoop.

There is power in the liftoffs
Passes, dunks and finger rolls
How he hovers elevated.
Only he and Nike knows.

Is he astronaut sans spaceship?
Is there lineage to Gengis Khan?
Is he extra terrestrial being
Martian special, heavenly born?

No mystic powers hoisted Michael
Or unseen hands empowered all.
Courage, grit, determination
Made him king of basketball.

Viola F. Hill

A Seasonal Smile

Your budding smile, recalled Spring
While toying with April shade
Was held with roots of love
As you listened and obeyed
Summer vowed she'd seen it too
My smile full grown by June
Adorned by your acceptance
Came a brilliant hybrid bloom
The fruit of your forgiveness
Was the smile I still remember
And no harvest matched your bounty
Autumn said of my September
Then Winter reminded gently
How the dark December earth
Always cradles fragile seeds
And nourishes them till birth
So with quiet faith I ponder
This smile now gone to seed
And the lessons we must learn
In the season of our need

Sharon B. Ethridge

Sunday After Easter

Lost! A crowd of people
   Who came to church last week,
In fellowship to sing and pray
   And ministry to seek.

Lost! A very happy throng
   All dressed in finery,
But now that Easter's come and gone,
   We ask where can they be?

The message "He is risen"
   Brought faith and hope and cheered
A multitude of worshippers
   Who now have disappeared.

Lost! But not forever,
   The words "A Child is born"
Will bring a glad and cheerful host
   To church on Christmas morn.

With hopeful hearts and willing feet,
   They'll hasten to the door.
With mistletoe and holly wreath
   The crowds will come once more.

Yvonne Orman Trull

Gabye

If there was one person
who could always share
the things that happened
here and there
it would be you
that I would pick
even if a million people was
standing in line
waiting to meet Rick.
You will always be
in my heart
you and me hold the key
so you will never depart
and if you do I swear
there will be another time
and place that I will meet you up there.
when I found out you had cancer
I didn't understand but all I know
is that my love for you
will never end.

Patrick Arnett

Lady's Limerick

There once was a maiden fair,
Who had the ugliest hair;
She sang a song,
As she skipped along,
For she was without a care.

She soon met a man named McGee.
His legs were as stiff as a tree.
McGee would blunder,
As the girl stared in wonder,
For his brain was the size of a pea.

When she had passed this man,
She stumbled over a can.
Inside was a puppy
That looked like a guppy.
'Twas in horror the fair maiden ran.

Kristin Ankney

To The Almighty

Our Fader
Who in Hebbin be
Dare I be invisible
An say that it be me?
It be me who no one hears
It be me who disagrees
It be me who can create
It be me who writes the truth
It be me in my aguish!
Yes, I am minority!
The media say me be animal
Business say me be fool
The Arts say me be jester
Politicians say me be beggar.
But Out Fader
Who in Hebbin be
Who say you I am?
That I know I be.

Lillian P. Jennings

Untitled

I have someone very special
Who is always in my heart.
I owe her for so many things
I wouldn't know where to start.

She always has looked out for me
From the time when we were young.
But I couldn't always see back then
All the wonderful things she'd done.

Now that we are big and grown
I turn to her even still.
She always knows just what to do
I guess she always will.

And if I ever forgot to say
A thank you or sorry
Along the way
Just know that I've treasured you every day
My sister, my friend, my wonderful "Kay."

Sally Balsmann

Angel Eyes

Dark and mysterious;
Who knows what they see?
Full of pain;
How could this be?

Inside them a hidden story
Of fear, loss and destruction;
A never ending nightmare,
When attracted use caution!

Their innocence has been torn
As the years went by
From unfortunate experiences,
But they are still "Angel Eyes."

Tina Marie Mullins

When

Who makes us talk so much
Who makes me say so little
Who are our friends in time of need
Who is a friend I'll let them be

Why do we run away from intimacy
Why do I run away from pain
Why do we hold onto our feelings
Why do I mask them with a smile

How can anyone know what we're feeling
How can I show you what is deep inside
How can we tear down walls around us
How can I break this suit of armor

What are we doing with our lives
What am I holding onto to survive
What are we...as we do so much
What am I when I do so little

Where will we go from this time forward
Where will I go from this place down here
Where will people unite together
Where will I let him hold my hand

Kat Seiple

Ode to America

There's hardly one in the human race
who wouldn't go at a faster pace
if it weren't for the shoes they lace
and the other's hand on mace.

And is the day already black
who for the color of their skin they lack
a way to free their bending back
and keep clear of the wayward track?

And are we so right as to be
the only ones in the planet free
to take our leave for tea at three
and tell the others they cannot see?

For if we do not heed and master
the machine that goes much faster
next time we meet the Caster
we'll wish we were the church's pastor.

Tim K. Fitzgerald

Friend

A friend I have met
Whom I've not heard
One's voice nor seen
His luscious body
For I who wish
    to dig beneath his soul,
To learn the truth
    behind the mask—
For I am a friend
Who wishes to communicate
And understand one's emotions.

A friend I have met
Whom I wish to know better
To hear one's voice
And see one's body
For I shall soon
Meet my friend.

LeAnn Cruz

Dancing Tree

Little tree outside my window,
why do you beckon so?
Can't you see I have work to do?

Ah, this is spring, a time
to treasure. I see your many
wombs about to give birth

again. Yesterday's children
are gone, taken by a cold
and heartless winter.

For months you mourned, a gray
and broken lady. But I see
you coming to life

again. I see you dancing
in the spring breezes,
happy because you know

you will have new children
soon. Yes, you look so
happy I stare in awe.

Little tree outside my window,
I know why you beckon so. You
want me to share your joy.

R. F. Sanchez

Interrogating Love Beneath the Glare of a Bare White Light Bulb

Alright! I want to know where you reside?
Why don't you come my way?
Am I being punished or what?
How much more debt is there to pay?
Will my searching ever find you?
Are you trying to find me?
Can't you tell I need you too?
Don't you know I'm lonely?
Did you know I've been waiting now
for quite some years?
Have you listened to my sobs at night
and sympathized my tears?
Why don't you feel warm and passionate
when it comes to me?
Or feel devotion and tenderness
and other things you're suppose to be?
Does being elusive please you
as obviously does my strife?
Aren't I entitled to know you too
if for only one time in my life?

Michelle Corbitt

Sweet Sorrow

You wanna bet that tomorrow
will bring me sorrow
you wanna bet I'll be here
Not that I wanna be; but that sorrow,
that brings me near is bitter sweet
fills my lungs with air
makes me breathe and feel
As I can feel my heart beating,
through my chest
every time I sense his presence
it scares me, frightens me
So that I am as pale
as the golden sun
at night with the
light of my rays
leads you right to me
Always time after time
Tomorrow on to the next
That sweet sorrow keeps me here
And brings you near

Melissa Coughlin

Untitled

I see her with long, dark
wisps of hair, flowing in
the breeze of life.
Blue eyes weeping to summon
more time to run barefoot
in the sands of time.

But she had to appease the
goddesses, so they gently
led her soul to the heavens,
there to reside with them
where the sands of time
are endless.

Laurie Brace

On Wings Of Joy

I look upon the Universe
With eyes that clearly see
The marvel and the magnitude
Of creativity...
And find within its sacred depths
A rhythm made apparent,
The tempo of the Song of Life...
Eternally inherent
In all that ever was
Or is to be in God's creation
Revealed in soaring melodies
Of love's illumination;

Oh, look upon the Universe
And learn of wondrous things...
In search of all that's beautiful,
Each heart shall find its wings!

Thelma Hull

Understanding

We may not always have a choice
Of circumstance or wealth
Nor can we choose a time
To have the best of health

But we can express the hope
That each new trial may bring
A strength and understanding
In almost everything.

Nelda Robertson

Colors

I saw this great big fish tank
with fish of many colors.
Most ignored their color
and went to hang with others.
They swam and play all day and night.
To watch was such a magnificent sight.
If only the world could be so smart.
That awful hatred just might part.
And if that worked,
it would be so great,
But if we don't hurry,
it might well be too late.

Kelly Huntington

"Grandson"

A little boy comes riding by
With his arms out his head held high
Look grandma, look at me
I can ride a bike, I can climb a tree

He's growing up too fast it seems
But he still looks up at me and beams
He'll always be my little boy
And he's really been a delightful joy

Sometimes my nerves might get on edge
I might be a little bit cross
But my love for him I solemnly pledge
If he ever moves I'll be at a loss

He looks to me to give him praise
For the things he does and his good days
I love to see his little smiling face
No one else could ever take his place

Lela Mae Hubbs

A Mother's Poem

The morning woke to a quiet breeze
with mist upon the leaves.
Mind and eyes embraced a solitude
and heard a silent new beatitude
of my serendipity.

Days and nights in years of hope
were dreams of strength for me to cope
for loving duties and worries, too,
for precious offspring as they grew
to their serendipity.

Pat McInerney Slapinski

"Can't Live Without You"

I can't live without you
Your love is so strong
Why won't you stay
I did nothing wrong

I can't live without you
I bet she pleads that too
She's lying but I'm not
I truly love you

I can't live without you
Your love has touched me
Why can't you understand
Your love sets me free

Crystal Rohr

Contentment

Alone,
With my thoughts again.
Only one emotion,
allowed within today.
I revel in its bland intensity.

No sadness or despair,
No rush of fear,
Today here.
Just a relaxed
Soothing stillness,
of contentment.

No Future, no Past,
No Dreams that never last.
No Expectations not met.
Just this beautiful suspended Reality
Animated freedom, of Contentment.

The children play with languid cheer,
Soaking the sunshine of their will
Teaching me to stop and see,
The beauty of the day and of me.

Mininder Kaur

"Dreams"

The ideas you hold dear
With never any fear.
Feelings no one will ever know
Because you never let them show.
Dreams are what you make
And nobody can never take.
Think of what you do
To make people believe in you.
What ever are in dreams,
There always seems
To make you who you are
And carry you very far.
A thought all yours
And a will to make it more.
Without a dream,
You are on a losing team.

Leanna M. Doe

Living Memories

You passed so quickly from our lives
With no chance to have a family or wife

Though we will never let you go
All of us are healing so slow

It seems as though just yesterday
You were here to laugh and play

We lost a part of our lives that night
And though you are not in our sight

We love you still with undying devotion
And we will as long as there are oceans

In our hearts is where you'll stay
Alive as just the other day

When you where here to touch and see
The memories are so dear to me

And though you are not still around
I long to hear the joyful sound
Of your voice saying
"It's all right, we won't go down without a
fight"

Oh darling brother, son, and best friend
Your memory lived on though the tragic end

Rebekah Evans

Events Of 2-4-94

In a cage
With no where to go.
Lay your head on the desk
And watch the water flow.

Ignore your surroundings
While you hide.
See the puddles forming
Since you lost all your pride.

Questions enter your mind
What is life worth?
The pain seems endless
Why was I given birth?

I raise my head up
And my emotions flow.
Why is it,
That I feel this low?

Help is what I need
And that is what I will seek.
I need serenity
To end this week.

Von Moody

Untitled

Black as the board
With no writing
Just a layer of dust
And standing lines
To light my way
And I write
Though it falls anyway
The truth just powder
On the surface
A tribute to my fight

Matthew J. Harke

Left Standing in the Snow

The day's beginning was clear and cold
With not a hint that we could know
That you'd depart for realms of gold
And leave me standing in the snow.

For there you fell, no more to rise
My frantic heart cried out, "Don't go"
You were even then beyond the skies.
You left me standing in the snow.

Your eternal home was prepared
He called you to Himself, and so,
You left this place we loved and shared.
Alone I stood there - in the snow.

By and by, dear one, we shall meet
Where all is glory, all is light
We'll humbly bow at Jesus' feet
All sorrow will have taken flight.

The heartaches of life - all past.
Disappointments, failures, every foe.
Safe forever, home at last
No more standing in the snow.

Veva M. Alleman

The Lamb Of God

Upon the cross they laid him,
With painful nails they pierced him.
And hanging there they let him be,
For all his friends and foes to see.

The veil of the temple tore,
The earth tumbled and shook
And the sun hid.
Earth a darkness bore
And God his son to heaven took.

He promised he would come again,
To claim his own another day.
To wash the pain and tears away,
So we could live within his reign
Where men no longer war and fight
But love the Lamb with all their might.

Mary L. Holden

"Once Upon A Winter's Day"

Once upon a winter's day
With spring lingering not far away
A robin at my feeder rest
He sang his song, his bright red breast

This winter's day was crisp and bright
Old Mr. Sun put out his light
The warm ray fell upon the ground
Melting snow that lay around

A crocus with it's flower bright
Was poking through the snowy white
I looked upon this beauty rare
And thanked God, for He was there

He was there, His mighty hand
Stretched out and over all the land
In winter, spring, summer, fall
God's the one who does it all.

Spencer D. Nave Jr.

My Refuge

It's been said "you can't go home again"
With this I disagree.
My safe harbor from life's stressors
Is home for me, you see.

That one brief time I visit,
Be it every year or so.
Rejuvenates my spirit
And creates an inner glow.

There are no expectations.
I don't have to be the "giver"
I'm accepted and loved for who I am,
Not what I can deliver.

"You'll always be our little girl"
I hear my parents say.
How comforting to hear those words
As I tackle these "middle aged" days.

That's why I know you can go home
And cleanse your soul and mind.
It's home that brings a peacefulness
That nowhere else I find.

Linda Ann Black

Wise Old Man

Take heed old man the day begins
With you your time to spend
In ways of wise through reflect
Broken thoughts you can now mend
A life time of experience
A worldly view to tale
To give us all a meaning's worth
Some wisdom to inhale
Smile old man as you will see
The lessons we all must learn
You let us go with your own eyes
Sharing with taught concern
I smile with you old man this day
For all that passes through
I thank the heavens for your touch
For life and how you grew
As now my teacher I have lived
A piece of life with thee
And known a man I can respect
And hope to see in me

Margi Pongritz

Erotica Earth

Put me in touch
With your forest, your trees,
let me sway in your branches,
eat the fruit that you bear
— sweet and juicy cool and firm;

Brush my quivering limbs
around your trunk;
My fresh milk will drench your roots,
And nectar from flowers,
I'll drink with red lips;

Sprout mangoes from the earth
avocados and eggplants,
orange blossoms, grapes,
lace my arms with vines;
Together, our veins flow;

Let me sing, let me dance,
Let me roll, with you

Then,
I'll come —
Alive.

Susan McConnell-Celi

I Can't Imagine

I can't imagine a day
   without your charming smile
Nor can I justly convey
   how much I love your style

I can't imagine a week
   without your warm embrace
Nor the absence of your pleasing form
   and lovely, flawless face

I can't imagine a year
   without you near to share
The times that do endear
   or the moments of despair

I can't imagine a lifetime
   without you at my side
For if I want a love divine
   I need you as my guide

I can't imagine eternity
   without the love I've known
My spirit would wonder helplessly
   in agony—alone

Jason Fischer

Deliverance

"Thoughts of a Hospice Volunteer"
Wondering, Watching, Waiting,
    When? Why?

Questions invade my mind
    about life, now about death.

Holding her hand, soothing her brow
    talking in soft tones,
    hoping she'll hear.

"Everything is fine here,
You can leave when you're ready."

Then, with a deep breath and
    a soft sigh,
She slips away to another realm
    PEACEFULLY.
Suffering subsides,
    All is well,
    A new beginning.

Louise Ann Todd

Reward for a Long and Patient Wait

I waited there alone;
Wondering what the end would be.
The throngs had disappeared.
Now, there was only me!
    Fearful — no!
But pleased - and thrilled - hoping
That the end would be a joyous one;
And not with disappointment fraught!

Then — it came!
My wait, alone, was o'er!
And there before my eyes was my reward —
For patient and uplifting thought!

The uniformed man approached —
Holding it in his hand.
Yes! There it was! For me alone!
The flavor — strawberry!
The reward —
My ice cream cone!

Ray Leland Caley

Won't

Won't read what I write,
won't hear what I say,
Won't even notice me
or look my way!
Why don't won't want to cope
with problems that won't don't?
Won't probably don't want to read this,
cause Won't don't read what I write!
I'll never get a chance to say this,
Cause Won't don't want to see my sight!
However I am Can, and I can so I must
and if I can't then I don't
and if I don't then I just won't!
Won't + Won't = us.
Will we or won't we be friends?

Marc B. Lewis

Depth

What have I done?
Words that erupted from my lips.

RECANT!

Suppress my ill feelings,
to save our love.
My opinion means naught,
and strength is weakness to you.

UNLEARN!

Everything that this life has taught me,
hide my self in a shoe box,
and sell it in a rummage sale.

SUBMERGE!

Like the sun at dusk,
disappear into the horizon'
bask in that dark night,
blind night.
There is depth in darkness.
Depth is nothing to you.

Paul Lawrence Cline II

Born To Die

Have you ever though about why our God
Would send his son to earth
To learn, to teach, and then to die
So that we might have new birth.

Our Lord was sent to show us all
That death is not to fear,
There is eternal life out there
For all he holds so dear.

God let his son be born to die
And take our sins away
He only asks that our hearts be pure
And with him always stay.

The cross that Jesus bared that day
Was so heavy with not just a tree,
But with the sins of all on earth
Just so our hearts could be set free.

A death so cruel in all our eyes
Was so that he might live
In all of us who praise his name
And our life to him we give.

Scott L. Justice

Journey

While change through the
    years is emanate

Toward the end there is
    only sentiment

Your younger blissful,
    careless days

Turn into lonely cloudy
    haze

You struggle to avoid
    getting caught in the
    mire

Hoping in the end not
    to glimpse hells fire

Kathleen Mangan

Living, Loving and Learning

Yes, and...
Yes, and...
I loved you poorly,
I know now.
My eyes were dimmed by fear.
The price paid was high for me.
The cost to you most dear.

I release...
I release...
I release you freely.
Please go now.
My vision has been made clear.
What's suffered is valued high for me.
The cost for you most dear.

R. J. Van Fleet

"The Girl Is Holding A Balloon"

She stands alone
yet in a crowd.
Clutching contentedly to a big ball
Floating above her,
People swarm around this
Peaceful and serene creature,
Possessing wispy, golden brown hair and
Toffee colored eyes with -
Flecks of green and blue,
Sunshine radiates up
From the warm pavement as
A slight breeze, sways
The balloon cherished in her grasp.
Freckles dance across her
Cheeks and her lashes brush
Them with each new blink
Into a new direction. Softly
Spoken are her words as
She turns to a clown near her
And whispers, thank you.

Norel Honey

Loving An Alcoholic

When you love an alcoholic,
    you can see their mind going...
    their body too.
    Their terrible need....
    torment and torture
    for them and for you.

You've tried closing the door.
    That wouldn't do.

    Your loving heart
    wouldn't let you see it through.

You can shake your head,
    wondering why.
    Hoping and praying
    that they'll at least try.

But......all you can really do
    is be there for them,
    for if love could cure......
    there would be no problem.

Patricia A. Hagy

Lonely Hearted

When you left me
you left me so broken hearted
you never showed your face
I never heard your voice again
And now your back
I see your face
I hear your voice
I wish for you to come back
But you say you love someone else
So were suppose to be like friends
But when I told you I had someone
I don't hear or see you
You won't even give me the time of day
Why, your making me feel...
Lonely hearted in this lifetime
of which I've earned from you
till you took that away from me.

Marie Shain

Through the Eyes of the Cross

Sorrow, and Suffering, I hated you -
You never fit my point of view.
Others knew you, and I would cry -
Never understanding why.
Then JESUS came and stood with me.
I watched Him nailed upon a tree.
He touched my eyes, and I began to see -
Sorrow, and Suffering, you're not my foe,
but with your help, I can grow -
To be more like my King.

Sandra J. Walleman

The Black Sheep

The thing about the prodigal son is
you never know
if he ran off again.
Tired of doing the right thing-
tired of trying-
tired.
Did he stumble over pride
shunning mercy's embrace
and God?
Did echoes of his wild nights
deafen the sleeping farm
and did he have to learn again
the hard way?

Stacy Dry

Life

Some people think
You only live once.
That life's only purpose
Is to win the big hunt.
Some people think
You keep coming back.
You only live once,
And that is a fact.

Some people think
Life means nothing at all.
You keep messing up
And stumble and fall.
But the whole point in life
Is not what you do.
It's how you live it,
And if it's lived true.

Mike Seewer

Reality Check

Sweet innocent angel
You seemed beyond belief
Frequently I'd ask myself,
   Is she real?
So precious
So pure, so unique
You tempt the boundaries of reality
Overanxious and wondering
I just had to find out,
   What is real?
Everything about you is real
It's obvious now.
With just one touch of your face
I could feel your warmth
Warmth from your embrace
Warmth from your heart, your love
Your touch is like magic
Putting a smile on a once saddened face.
Don't ever change
My heart knows your real!

Thomas Ryder

Sweet Embrace

I see your soul,
you shadow
outstretch a hand to me,
and beg me come
and somewhere between
magic and miracle
we two again
become one.

Somewhere between
night and morning
our spirits
to Heaven's height soar
and our glorious love
is reborn
forever
are we in sweet embrace
captured to be entwined
if nothing more!

T. Aurora Alexander

Bum

I am that man
you skip around each morning
as you make your way
to the 7:55 train.
Today you wore those shoes
with the harsh soles —
stomp stomp stomp stomp!
The rest of you as always
looked immaculate.

I think I saw your eyes once.
They were green and unforgiving.

"Happy Birthday, Mam!"
Remember? That was me.

I, though you choose not to look,
have fallen down in life
or life has fallen down on me.
But that's O.K.

I will soon be swept under the carpet
when cancer takes me.

You've never given me a penny.

Trevor Carr

Untitled

Curiosity meandering among
   Your emotions and illusions
Opening your doors to insight
   And your windows to confusion
Plunging young minds into the waves
   Of your pseudo-intellectual cappuccino
Curious, she asks about the game
   "How may I play?"
"We are all players," he answers
   She doesn't know that
She is the pawn

Victoria Hart

Steven

Live each day as if it was
your last day,
then you'll see things in a
new way.
With me standing by your
side,
and the stars shining bright
up high.
The smell of romance is in
the air,
and I just know we could be
the perfect pair.
So let the hurt of the past
go free,
and you won't regret it for
choosing me.

Michelle Smith

You

I wish I could carry,
Your smile in my heart.
At the times when my life,
Feels as if it's falling apart.

You're a dream so perfect,
And a light so pure.
You're my sun on a rainy day,
The one I've been searching for.

You give me such happiness,
Something no one can ever take away.
And there is just something about you,
That is special to me in every way.

Nicole Cena

To God

In a life of misconceptions and dreams,
Your the light in my window.
Shining bright your love gleams,
And shows the path like a rainbow.

I am yours so take me at will,
And shape my life like a mountain.
In my heart my devotion will spill,
Pouring out like a fountain.
So be with me and touch me within,
Seems I'm a man with no reason.
With you there I know I can win,
And share my life through every season.
Your blue skies up above,
Your the leaf in every tree,
Your the smile in every child,
Your the love light inside me.

Noel Orlando Olivarez

A Cry From A Lonely Oak

If you never intended for her to be mine, why did you send her to me like an angel from Heaven?

For so many years I have stood alone without bending against non-sympathetic winds. Then one day you decide to bring this most precious love into my heart, without giving me a chance to embrace and protect it with my strong limbs. Taking away my need to embrace and protect, you turn my strong Oak exterior into a Weeping Willow, which hangs lifeless in the wind.

Hanging limp, I cannot survive the strong beautiful storm of love that you have blown into my lonely existence.

This love surrounds my world and engulfs my very soul of eternity. This love nourishes everything that surrounds me, and helps it grow to the very height of ecstasy.

Why after so many years of standing alone and strong, must you send me a love that belongs in another world?

My whole life, I never knew what my human heart was for. Now you give me a taste of something so sweet and divine that it would cause anything to bend in it's wake.

What were you thinking of Lord when you did this to me? Why give me a taste of something so sweet and so divine, then take it away from me?

If it was a reward for being strong, then please let me belong to her.

Weeping Willow
Gary L. Davis

It Hasn't Happened Yet

You know it's in the future but you never know how far
you wake up every morning and it's amazing there you are
it hasn't happened yet
as you move on through the day you look around and see
then say out loud to yourself no it won't be me
it hasn't happened yet
a minute later you look again and notice you're not there
now you're on the outside looking in whoever said life was fair
yeah it happened
Eileen McMenamin

Homeless But Human

Constantly I am watched, as I struggle to pull my weight.
    Discouraged by society's rejection the street is my current estate.

Going weeks at end, without a good nourishing meal.
    Praying for a change in fortune, asking myself, "could this be God's will?"

Cold nights I huddle in a corner, sometimes lying slouched in a cart.
    Afraid to sleep for fear of not awakening, I plan a fresh start.

I am trampled upon even threatened, if I refuse to vanish from sight.
    People wishing to cause pain to me, because I am homeless, and too weak to fight.

I pose no threat to you, I merely wish to survive from day to day.
    I live on the street, not by choice, for me it is the only way.

I beg not for food, but for time to get my life together.
    I didn't become homeless over night, and I will not be homeless forever.

I am not standing on the corner, I am not holding out my hand
    I do not expect you to know what I am going through, so don't pretend to understand.

I once possessed those same possessions that today you hold so dear.
    But life can sometimes throw you a curve ball, and possessions do disappear.

But I don't ask for your sympathy, I will not tolerate your pity.
    All I want is to be treated humanely, like a citizen of this great city.

The next time you see me, don't beat me, but instead stop and speak.
    Although I am homeless now, I have yet to reach my peak.

Fernando A. Green

Untitled

Forbidden.
Your touch.
So tender.
So sweet.
I melt.
Captured.
Oblivious.
I am puzzled as I indulge.
Absorbed.
My breath stolen.
You encompass
and envelope me into a
secret private interlude.
Uncalculated.
Unknown.
I am rhapsodized,
tantalized.
Intoxicated
by your essence.
I close my eyes and enjoy.

Kathy Davies

My Best Friend

Through thick and thin
you're always there
It's without words you show you care.
A gentle nudge, a wagging tail,
Just reinsures you're my best pal.
You listen when I need to talk...
When I feel alone, with me, you walk.
And when I'm happy,
or even sad...
A truer friend, need not be had.
And if I feel I'm left behind...
I just look down, you're by my side.
It's through devotion, love, and trust...
You're friendship is, I feel,
a must.
And with that friendship throughout the years...
You've help ease the pain and dry my tears.
A friendship that'll never end...
My thanks to you...
You're my Best Friend!

Karen A. Kowalik

Primordial Spring

Frogs, and dogs, and cats awake
'Mid lusty mating chorus...
But true love ne'er did move nor shake
Like the amorous brontosaurus.

Thomas D. LeFevre

My Sun Flower

How captivating you are,
    Your tall green stem
Climbing proudly to the sky;
    Sporting a glorious head dress
Of yellow sun soaked petals.
    Your dark core seems to obscure
The woes of a troubled world.
    And as I stand in awe
Feeling drawn by your radiance,
    I can hear you boldly saying,
"Be happy world."

Ann-Marie O'Raidy

The Good Old Days

We dressed up as monsters, giggled through our dates
and shared our most intimate secrets with each other
we cried, we sang and danced together and nothing
or no one dared come between us
we learned from each other, sharing our cultures,
languages and our dreams, we served as the support
system each of us so desperately needed
separated by the conventionalism of a mere blood line
we were closer than Siamese Twins

and then one day . . .
like the ruthless and ferocious hurricane which attacks
without warning, taking all . . . you were gone

and I no longer giggle.

Gloria E. Pérez-Ramos

Toward Nirvana

As the curtains close on a man's lifetime,
a woman appears, standing naked in a gentle stream,
the wavy reflection of her breasts trembling on the water,
undulating in and out of the eye's view, like untouched
angels, inside the walls of his every dream.

And as the sunlight warms her goose-bump flesh,
blackbirds fly overhead in perfect circles,
against a stark, azure sky,
suggesting the full moons of breasts,
or fresh blood splattered across virgin snow.

All the while, he stares with great amusement,
on how perfection washes itself clean,
appearing lost until caught in her gaze,
whereupon she moves closer, into shallower water:

an angel stolen from the chaos, the tranquility
of dreams, holding forth a key,
capable of releasing the darkness
behind every locked door: you know,
the one rubbing the shadows, between her thighs,

the one that says, *there's a wound*, it's time it healed.

Frank A. Mastropaolo

Early Impressions

I scuttled over floors of silent seas,
And used my ragged claws to gain the shore.*
I crossed the rugged rocks on bleeding knees,
Invented Time and God and so much more.

I fought the awesome bear with club and spear,
And built the roaring fires before the caves,
But late at night I still can sometimes hear
The constant crashing of the distant waves.

* CF "The Love Song of J. Alfred Prufrock" T.S. Eliot lines 73, 74.

T.S. Eliot "The Complete Poems and Plays" Harcourt, Brace & World,

Inc. New York (21st Printing) 1971 p.5

DeForrest A. Penley

Goodbye

Memories flaunt my mind.
You're in everything I find.
You don't know I really cared.
I remember all we shared.
I pray and hope for you.
May your life be happy and true.
I must go on with my own.
I realize how much we've grown.
I hope to see you again someday.
And in my heart you'll always stay.

Kimberly Huetsch

Autumnal

Autumn,
　　　　falling in step
　　　　behind summer,
　　　　yet always aware
　　　　of impending winter,

　　　　　　　waiting like an archer
　　　　　　　who shoots cold arrows of ice
　　　　　　　at autumn's messy carpet;

　　　　dead leaves
　　　　earnestly awaiting
　　　　to be warmed by
　　　　cold blankets of snow.

Peter G. Brown

Touch

How many kinds of touch are there?
Five, maybe six, or more, there is
touch of air, touch of earth, of sea,
of rain
Touch of this
of that
of eyes
and yes
even tears;
of ears, of nose.
Touch of lips
some warm, some cold.
Touch
of cheek, of skin,
of breasts, of hair,
even - touch of mind
but
of all the tactile things there are in this world

I choose touch of
Y O U.

Robert Rougé

The Collector

To live, is to dream of objects yet unattained.
For my life abounds in ethereal beauty.
Something is missing though, somehow, somewhere.
Perhaps another, to share my passions and treasures?
Lonely is the heart of the collector, pursuing exquisite beauty.
To explain, is to destroy its endless and inherent meaning.
Carefully sought out, then thoughtfully displayed.
In a harmony of personal and individual regard.
A pride like none other, a rewarding ownership.
Unlike that of another, of which no one can own.
Which should I choose, a permanent or temporary possession?
That Sèvres figurine, just to the right, I shall gladly take instead!

Thomas H. Dodson

Faded Thoughts

A faded memory fills my head:
　　Of the last time I saw your face:
A faded memory fills my heart:
　　With you warm embrace:
A faded memory lives within me:
　　of days I wish to be with you:
A faded memory holds on:
　　Until the day my faded thoughts
　　Are through

Lianna Garcia

S. A. D.

I killed a little boy last night
He was only two years old
I'll kill his parents next
And then I'll move on
They can't stop me
They can't control me
I run wild and free
And strike where and whom I please
I could easily kill your mother
Your father
Your children
And there's nothing you can do about it
I love to kill
It's what I do
It's all I do
You'd better watch out!
You'd better be careful!
Because I would be happy to kill you next
My name is AIDS
Catch me if you can

Richard I Merrell

Will You Marry Me?

Within the realm of my mind your silhouette appears before me...
I am speechless...
Looming in my subconsciousness is the epitome of my desire...
Levitating far above my dreams, my wishes, my goals.

Yesterday, I had the same thoughts, emotions, visions
Only this time the feelings were a little stronger...
Unprecedented by anything I've witnessed in the past.

My life lacks nothing...
All my wants and needs are fulfilled...
Reality, with you, is a living paradise
Rich with joy, peace, satisfaction, and contentment...
You are the essence of my love.

Most men can only fantasize what I now acknowledge...
Eternal bliss....

Michael Warren

"Let me See Graceland"

If I have to sleep and work,
If I have to carry on a load-
Let me go to Memphis
Let me see Graceland;

If I have to eat and cry;
If I have to laugh or die,
Let me go to Memphis
Let me see Graceland;

If I have to sing for joy;
Or see such sadness around this world-
Remember that there's always "hope"!
Let me see Graceland -

For Graceland's where King Elvis lived;
A place where friends just love to meet -
Where marriages nearby take heed;
It's home to everyone in need -

So dear Lord, please hear my prayer,
If I can be a better person somewhere -
Let me go to Memphis to prepare,
Let me see Graceland, Please "Take Care"!

Mary Alice Peña

My Love

To the steps in our dance, our hearts beat as one,
In the puzzle of life - you filled it with great fun!
The road of experience, threaded with sadness and
    joy - we shared.
No one but you could have so nurtured me or cared.
At a time too soon, the master from above.
Came, and took you, before our dance was completed -
    my love.
Nothing in this world - for me - will ever shine as bright.
But with your spirit entwined in my memory and life,
    I'll be alright!
Our souls will surely meet
And again you'll sweep me off my feet.

Julia Szöke Tallerico

Only Your Love

It's only your love what can make me cry.
It's only your love what will make me die.
I look up to the sky and I can see
my life coming through the deepest
cloud, and even though you're not here,
I can still feel your love, I can still
see the light of your body.
Body to body, face to face I would
like to see you.
Time and place? I wouldn't care if
I could just see you.
In my dreams I search my way.
In my dreams I can see the day.
But in this dream, it's only your love
what is killing my love and faith.

Azucena (Suzy) Pena

A Call To Arms!

A call to arms. A CALL TO ARMS!!! I request of you my separated people. We must close our ranks, unite in to a fist. For we are at war, my brothers and sisters. We need our fist to protect and to defend.

But first, we must stop our petty bickering, let us stop our squabbles and our fights; our killing each other on sight. This keeps us vulnerable like five separated fingers in an open hand.

I sound this call, because the weaker finger is in danger, the one called **Sickle Cell Diseases**. Our enemy wants to rip us right out of our family hand. By using narcotics, to poison our bodies, bending our minds, all this to keep color on their welfare lines

We are your friends, your cousins, nephews and aunts. We are some part of your family hand; immediately remembered or not. We are your bloodlines, flowing from Africa ever on, and never apart. We stand so quietly, hurting in pain, right next to your heart.

Please proud people, separated and distraught. Unite our talents together, make our differences one. For we are your heritage finger, surround us, protect us, for your daughters and your sons. For if no fist is available to defend us, a slave we shall be and freedom will be no one's.

Gerald W. Corprew Jr.

Two People in a Crowd

Two people in a crowd
Really one.
He, being jostled, never unfixes his gaze,
Never looking about, seeing first her eyes,
Then her lips in a glance, and up
Again to her eyes for a lingering, longing stare;
Devouring yet preserving at once.
She, looking up, a smile
Of contentment that says *yes;*
A tacit blissfulness,
A blink - it sustains him.
Why is it that
You can always tell
The look of the lover?

Paul M. Eckstein

HINDSIGHT

Looking back now - with **hindsight** - I see
That kind guardian angel who's looked after me:

For years more than sixty she's tempered my dreams,
And helped me prove worthy of crossing rough streams;

When deluded I've been by my own wishful thinking,
Into despair and self-pity - she's kept me from sinking;

When remorse laid me low 'cause I couldn't do more,
She soothed with an insight on how to keep score;

Her thoughts became mine in decisions I made,
When things worked out fine, 'twas her plans I had laid;

My good deeds for years seem done at her bidding
To brighten tired faces with warm cheers and kidding;

But one face I can't see is that angel's in heaven,
She's **my mother** who died when I was eleven.

Carl C. Tinstman

Daddy

You may not have been there
the day I was born,
the day I began to grow.
the day I came into this world,
it was quite a surprise, you know.
But the day our lives became intertwined
My daddy you became.
A daddy is a special man and that
Not all can be.
You've touched my heart through
out the years,
You've helped me to learn and grow.
For this you are my daddy.
and I always hope you'll know,
  I love you daddy!

Barbara Lund

Jesus

Someone who cares about every facet of your life,
  whether things are going well or not.

Understands your ways, even though
  you may not always do right.

Someone who can look on the inside,
  knowing how to bring peace and comfort.

Entrust your life to Him—the One
  without a wrinkle or spot.

Jesus is the One who can make
  everything all right.

Tammy D. Saunders

"Red"

Red is for anger, the hatred, the blood of man
The Irish hair, that red, the candles burning flame
Ruby's glow - the red of Love
The red of a fox, their eyes
The bright red of embarrassment
Cherry red, the red of winter cheeks
The eight sided red, telling one to stop, look, then go
The red of robins breast, a glass of fine rosé
The flush of excitement, of what is to be
Red of teachers correcting ink, making its mark
The red of hearts, the flowing red in the veins
The scorching red of peppers, their spicy, burning glow
Red roses, glorious bloom
The red of Santa, red lips, and glowing nose

Courtney Comack

Nature Speaks

Earth's breath   frees fettered leaves
tree thoughts drift   speak.

Autumn rain   a soft mist blankets
feeding needs   of thirsty earth.

Wet humus   tempts hungry nostrils.

Deadfall snaps beneath a cautious step
  wildlife scatters into windblown leaves   rain
forms a trickle   a torrent   lake.

The solitary thinker   contemplates
human heat   dissipates.

Again the forest   alone
in a darkness   of intangible thieves.

Ryan Austin Cox

Dreams

Come young ones, leave this world and enter Mine.
Shed your heavy veil of trouble and fear,
To surround yourself in my warm embrace.
Lay back and fall into the dark Abyss.
Look at it, with all it's innocence and ignorance.
Step into it, with the hope and want of every man.
Share with me all of your heart and feelings.
But I warn you tell all, for as you look into the Abyss,
The Abyss stares into you.
We feel your resentment, we see your vulnerability,
And we hear your shallowness. But please fear not!
For we see you when you are most completely you,
And still want to accept and shelter.
So open your self to us and stand with me on the edge of forever
Grasp what can never be held in a conscious mind.
Look past your graveyard of buried hopes to see what can be yours.
Learn to open your heart and share your richness.
Realize that yesterday never comes back,
And if today is dark with clouds, seek and conquer tomorrow.
When you find tomorrow, hold tight,
Don't be left with a fist full of ashes.
So now comes the dawn, and you must wake, but take heed to what was
    said.
Remember us, your dreams as you emerge from our deep.
Then share with the others, our dreams, as you swim up out of sleep.

Julie P. Wells

Lands Lure

The morning sunshine spills over the horizon
Shedding golden light on the churning sea:
Rippling, glittering like jewel, the waves roll,
Reflecting the world behind them.

The waves hide under the salt foam -
Faster and faster they roll,
Reaching a peak of momentum;
Then toppling over, piece by piece,
One by one each drop of water falls
Into a rush of white.

The waves crash onto the beach like thunder,
Gripping the shore with wonderful force;
Rolling, reaching for each tiny grain of sand,
Then slowly shrinking back,
Bumping into another wave.

Catie Rideout

Love of a Daughter

She's our Daughter
She's our Girl
There's no one like her in the whole wide world
Her smile, her greeting, makes for delightful times
When we are meeting
She's so positive so upbeat
She makes our lives so complete
She's petite and very sweet
It's no wonder we think She's neat
She radiates joy and lots of style
She generates happiness when she flashes her smile
She's our Daughter
She's our Girl
There's no one like her in the whole wide world.

Evelyn J. Roach

Frank

Smiles rain down on him at work.
Shine and light spill in through his window
at home. Even with the warmth of the glare,
he feels the harsh whip of winter cracking.
Tunnels of no light, no hope.

With two children, one crying on each shoulder
and a hungry baby in his arms, Frank measures
the impossibilities. His spine is breaking
from the weight, the burden. These suffering children
miss their dead mother so badly. Forever crying.

In a faded denim jacket, he thinks:
I hate this town, I have no car, no money,
no woman. I hate my job,
the idiots who think they know my life,
my hardships. All I've got
is the kids and a little too often I
hate them too.

Jessica C. Kearns

Memories

Memories
of the shadows of the night,
indifferent to the cries of dawn
still hold me tight.
But life at its best
promises to release me tonight,
just in time to dance the last waltz
with midnight.

Yanick Lalite

Ode to the NRA

Buy a gun.
Shoot your son,
Accidentally.

Continue the slaughter.
Shoot your daughter,
Accidentally.

Waste life.
Shoot your wife,
Accidentally.

Do not end.
Shoot your friend,
Accidentally.

You're not done.
Shoot everyone,
Accidentally.

No one left.
Shoot yourself,
Accidentally.

Jesse O. Bankston

Infinite Patterns

Flakes of snow strike the frozen ground.
Silence yields their threshold of sound.
A rhythm embraced by the creatures they surround,
A rhythm reflective of creatures abound.

Each snowflake, a moment, distinctively complex -
Drifting, falling, impacting the rest.
A memory, a memory, a memory, lest,
The transcending moments of snow fall desist.

Charles Stampul

Fugue

Lovely theme,
simple and unadorned in youth,
sings its song in the face of destiny,
goes forth to meet unkind counterpoint,
to travel through foreign keys
and surrender itself to myriad variations

never guesses
that when the journey ends,
its closing cadence
will speak a selfhood
more glorious than the original
could ever have become
in solo
flight.

Dolores Barling

Friends

You are the same, you say
    Since he died;
Of course you look the same
    And smile the same
We talk, as friends,
    Of literature and dance and art
Each others interests known,
    Yet behind the flimsy screen
Of smiles and words
    I have seen
The pain, the truth, the sacrament of death.

Felicia Cotich

The Visitor

I've come to see you again at the gardens of stone
Since you've gone away I've felt so alone.
I long to once again hold you near and say loud and clear
That I miss you so much and love you so dear.
I know that while you were here
We sometimes had harsh words had days and tears
But the good days we had allays all my fears.
I know you've gone to a better place, and even now gaze upon
Our sweet saviors face, someday I'll join you by God's heavenly grace.
I'll swim the crystal waters 'till I reach that golden shore
Pass through those pearly gates, then I'll weep and hurt no more.
Then like you I'll gaze upon God's face
And hold you tightly in a loving embrace.
I wait for that day but until then
I'll be back to visit you
At your final earthly resting place again.

John W. Williams

Tree

Alone among mix master highways,
single tree,
you drag my eye to your dusty dress.
Somehow time swells enough,
Shooting past,
To admire your unsupported tenacity.
Not even a wildflower sprouts near you.
You grow not as tall
as those clustered in a group
down that way.
Your limbs, though, have pushed out in all directions—
You've grown a savage density
and a thick, crusty bark.
I imagine your scraggledy roots
wrapped round rock.
I wonder your secret,
how you manage budding, getting leafy, giving shade,
dropping it all, enduring
winter's bite,
summers drought.

Barbara Emmert-Schiller

In A Box, Upon A Shelf

In a box, upon a shelf
Sits a doll all by herself.

A lovely doll with soft dark hair
A pretty smile and face so fair.

Big brown eyes that peek
From above each rosy cheek.

She dreams in her box, upon the shelf
Of a little girl just for herself.

A little girl with whom to play
To laugh and sing with everyday.

A little girl to hug her tight
To keep her warm all through the night.

Still she dreams in her box, upon the shelf
Of a little girl just for herself.

From the shelf the box is taken
By little hands it is shaken.

Wondering at this treasure found
Opening the box without a sound.

Is the little girl herself
Just as the dreamed while on the shelf.

Jinx Walker

The Pub

At the square at noon
sitting here wanting to moon

I am drinking alone but I won't moan
I have all these folks around to look and see
what my pen can do for me

Everyone is having a beer
so they won't sneer
when they go back to work
and act like a jerk

The line for food
puts everyone in a bad mood
it is such a long wait
for such awful bait

The waiters are in such a hurry
to prevent everyone
from being in a fury

Lots of men sitting alone
but none I would be willing to phone

I am happy being solo and saying no
To just any Joe who happens to be just so.

Judy Knoll

What Is Loneliness

Each one has had his...her own experience.
Sitting on a bench in a busy place watching others' lives pass by.
Driving past an airport with no one's face to search for.
Passing through the holidays with no gift to receive...no one
    thinking of you.
Watching as suitcases are packed, closets are closed, dreams are
    doused, doors are shut,
    tail lights disappear into the stark, naked morning.
Having time to reflect over useless words, unsaid praises, unused
    hours... wasted days, months and years of your life.
Grieving over missed opportunities and goals...now realized,
    that were unknown at a time they could have been.
Rolling over in a bed too large for one, smelling a lingering scent on
    cold, mussy sheets.
Being left alone in the dark of night, turning, curling into a ball,
    grasping a pillow, holding on tight...
    as cries of anguish drop in the dead darkness.
Having everything you thought offered security taken, step by step.
Being stripped until there is no covering for the body or the soul.
Having every belief ripped open...exposed to strangers.
Looking with total disbelief into eyes you have known as they coldly
    deny your very existence.

Denise Hughes

The Hitchhiker

He was a hitchhiker
Sniffling with cold
Not very old....
Yet, he carried in his pocket
A rare sort of gold
He made his way with a poem or two
And left before his story was told....
Perhaps that is the way it should really be
For those who dare to be free
Not many dare the path he chose...
For fear of bandits along the road
Yet life "bandits" our costumed life
No matter how carefully it is sowed...
I could not restrain a tear or two
For I believe in each of us
There harbours a secret you...

Jeanne Aya Chapman Duncan

Untitled

i miss seeing my face in the morning;
   sleepy eyes, a mouth and a nose,
  hair that has become its own nightmare.
rolling over into the single sunbeam
   that dares thread it's way into
  my, now our bed.
i don't see my face anymore
waiting for his naked arms to warm me;
   curling into a small lump,
  pulling all myself in requires too much effort.
small mental pinpricks of tears begin;
  as the constant sunlight grows
  and i wish for rain.
i can't cry salt anymore
burrowing my toes free of the blood covers;
  fleeing the warmth, the safety,
  wanting the fresh new morning air on my skin.
and now i see my feet,
because they are all that support me
  anymore

   Georgina E. Ruff

Do Snails Burp?

One day I observed a little snail,
Slither leisurely across my path
It left a rather sticky trail
I wonder. . . do snails take a bath?

It appears it has life easy
Though perhaps it just doesn't know
(The thought of it makes one queasy...)
To think it could be Escargot!

It seems to be happy and has so little to say,
A rather content little slug
When it sees its family after a long day
I wonder. . . do snails hug?

When the day is done and its finished its roam
Does its family get a kiss—or a slurp?
Then does it announce: "Honey, I'm home!"
And after dinner, I wonder. . . do snails burp?

   Deena Briggs

Regrets

'Tis a bride well, collagenous and dank.
Smells of death hang foul and rank.
Keeper of thine own institution gate,
But this, alas, is realized too late.

Upright anthropoids, all envenomized.
A nebulous of holocaust envisioned.
Thru never ending intervals of time,
Without bravado, or rhythm or rhyme.

Clandestine games make up your sphere of play.
Living in bulwarks, void from orb of day.
No ardor, no martyrdom and no one cares.
Family nom de plume no scion bears.

Cosmos of darkness, void of cosmic rules;
A cosmos made especially for fools
Hails a life of caliginosity,
and quietly ignores my anguished plea.

   Alan Anderson

God's Beautiful Creation

The mountains, so majestic, towering so high,
  snow capped, reaching up to the sky.
Tidal waves, crashing, with tops so white,
  ten feet high, what a fantastic sight.

Music that a bubbling brook makes,
  as over the rocks, it's journey it takes.
Wind whispering in a tall pine tree,
  has such a calming effect on me.

The twinkling stars, my what a sight.
  A comet streaking, down to the right.
Glorious beauty of the mighty rainbow.
  A sign of God's promise, I well know.

Holding a puppy in the hollow of your hand.
  A mother cat with her kittens, so grand.
The wiggle of a bunny rabbits nose.
  The bucking of a colt, as it runs and grows.

I hope you see what I'm trying to say,
  you can enjoy what God has made, every day.
They are such a thrill, and they are free.
  A message from God, for every one to see.

   Grace Wimberly

The Edge Or End

I can see you in my mind standing on the cliff's edge,
So close, so dangerously close to the narrow ending line.

I can see you in my mind looking out into the beyond,
so still, so far away on this clear, blue day.

I can see you in my mind, and I ask, "was it a pause; a
picture you are recording in your mind, or a cause to
ponder and reflect?"

I see you there on the edge so often in my mind,
especially when you are now so far away.

Is this my final memory of not having you here to carry
me thru my day?

Where were you on that edge—was I paramount in your
thoughts, or were you going back to another, or having a
time warp?

Were you using the edge for your heart's wedge?

I still see you there in my mind.

Dare I ask and cross or push you over and bring you focused
to my presence and time?

   Bobbie J. Cooper

Love's Place

As I journey within the core of this place I feel a warmth that has
so gently covered me. It has given me a feeling of security and
calmness I cannot easily explain. It is as if I had entered a new
place where it glitters with a resting calmness I have never seen or
felt before. A place in its infancy!

Oh! How beautiful it is to behold its innocence and eagerness to
reach out and share its total self so completely. It has no feelings
of losses for it searches for no gains! How is it that I have not
seen this place before? As it begins to grow from its infancy, the
warmth becomes more intense and passionate. I have begun to
  flow with
its intense feeling and have come to trust its every move. I feel an
eagerness to give of my self. The everyday fears of life have left me
and I no longer feel sadness and despair. I only feel joy and
happiness within me and yearn to share all of the feelings I have
found. Is it that this place is a place of dreams or is it the inner
core of mankind opening up and sharing its most prized possession!
The birth of love is surely the birth of life at its best.

   Deborah K. Richey Kelley

Searching For Love

As beautiful as a golden dove,
so I believe your full of love; you'll always
be wild and free, and always the way you want to be;
Life is for love not for hate, remember this when
you pick your mate; See not just the body and face,
but also see a person's style and grace;
I sit in the shadows of the night, searching for my guiding
light; I see her standing in my sight,
and all my courage takes to flight;
Oh my love, my love, come here to me,
but at last I know I'm a shadow she can not see;
Oh what must I do, Oh what must I be, Why do I torture
myself by still gazing at such beauty?
So I watch her like she's a golden dove, and as she flies by
she takes my heart and my love; and so I pray to God above,
to have with me the one I love:
Tonight and forever my love.

Joseph R. Kenner

"Echoes"

I thought I heard you calling,
So, I turned my head to see;
Your whisper rose above the wind,
And made its way to me.
It touched my ear so softly,
And brushed against my cheek;
My heart began to race inside,
As we played hide and seek.
Then, you place your hand in mine,
And walked with me awhile;
My heart is filled with butterflies,
Each time I see your smile.
Together we picked flowers, in the fields along the way;
You always loved the colors of a windy summer day.
Then you turned to kiss me with the lips I often crave;
And love's embrace was lifted as you left me with a wave.
So...I kneel down beside you,
Where they once lay you to rest;
And gently placed the flowers,
where I thought you'd like them best.

Carl Wilkinson

Paranoid

An art gallery during day,
so innocent
An art gallery at night,
that's a different story all together,
the paintings become portals that lead
to evil places; places that are so scary,
horrible, and gruesome that you don't know
what's real and what's not.
What comes out of the paintings?
Evil
   creatures
     bent
       on
         destruction

Unfortunately not all janitors
come back from the art gallery.

Jeremy A. Luttrell

Solitude

Fly to a cave.
Sleep by the edge of a cliff.
Dive under water.
Scream for anyone that will listen.
Be quiet for a lifetime.
Wake-up it is over.

James C. Williamson

Snoring!

This poem is about my husband's snoring!
So loud - comes on with no warning.
Then our Terrier joins in barking, purring, and snorting.
Now that's what I call SUPPORTING!

When stated — to HIM is so boring.
But for me — restless till morning
Making sleep so UNREWARDING.

So in my mind I have some sorting,
As to the solution of curing?

Hate to get bed wet with a down pouring!
Shall I make a recording?
Hearing that — off to Doctor for reporting?

Knowing HIM — he wouldn't do according,
So I guess - it's off to SPARE ROOM for sleep FORWARDING!

Joann Knapp

Silent Cry

In the distance the rumble of thunder,
So near the flash of lightning,
Crackling through the night sky,
Shattering darkness into a thousand
  blackened shards,
Like a precious vase broken.
To the ears of fools it brings fear,
To the wise man's eye it brings a tear,
And the sky, she cries,
A million billion tears, that
Washes the earth and seas.
Like a lost child cries for its mother,
So nature cries for her children,
Although we've chosen not to hear,
She has cried for a million years,
And for a million years more
She will cry - unheard -
  Unheard until forever
    Is no more.

Dolores DeCola

A Tragic Story

She was once so happy, so joyous, so bright.
So what makes a sweet girl to take her own life?
Is it sadness, selfishness, stress, or grief?
Is it lack of friends, love or belief?
We watched her grow up, such potential she had.
Now she's cold in a grave, the story so sad.
As she sat alone with a gun in her hand,
What flashed through her mind, what did it demand?
Would she regret her actions, if alive today?
Would she apologize to family? What could she say?
Though the story is tragic, the fact is true.
It was someone so young, it was someone I knew.

Jacquelyn C. Turner

Flora

The flute of love can
play no song
that can reach to higher peaks
than this
that when I am in your arms
the worlds apart
I find swept deepness in
your kiss

Thaddeus Marczak

Soaring

Soaring to heights above the clouds
Soaring to heights above the rain
Gliding on the air currents that flows thru my wings
Gracefully and motionlessly.
I come to a sudden stop.
Caught in an air pocket; A violent descent.
10,000 (Ten Thousand Feet) I drop.
Then upward, again, soaring, soaring.
Oh so high like a giant roller coaster in the sky.
High above lofty peaks and towering castles.
Rising above ordinary levels of bound.
Until finally I have disappeared from sight
Escaping from my mundane life.
I am the mighty of my species.
And this is my flight of fantasy.

James C. Polite Sr.

A Poem for Patty

Like the bud of a crimson rose,
Softness surrounds you as your pedals,
and fragrant beauty lies beneath.
From a distance I gaze at what years have refined,
Hoping one day to see you effloresce.

But the arcane splendor of the rose lies hidden,
And needs patience and care for its graceful bloom.
An enchantress veiled by subtlety,
Its beauty is engaged by poise.

It captivates my heart, the Rose,
Its depthful charm a provocative affliction.
Drawn towards its mystery, defiant of thorns,
My enduring confidence. Express awaiting delight.

Eddie Correia

My Basketball Game

Some people say it's just a game
Some people say it's only a sport
But some people have not played my game or sport
My game is a pure intensity of running, rebounding,
   defense and offense
My game is made of emotion and feeling
My game started when I was two
And my game will never end
That's why
It's not just a game
It's what I do
It's who I am
This sport lives in me
And it howls to get out

Amber Richgels

Someday

Someday the stars will shine.
Someday the world will always rhyme.
   For this is God's world
   Yes, this is God's world for you and me.

Someday the flowers will always bloom.
Someday the world will have no gloom.
   For this is God's world.
   Yes, this is God's world for you and me.

Stars that always shine,
A world that will always rhyme,
Flowers that always bloom,
A world with no more gloom.
   For this is God's world.
   Yes, this is God's world for you and me.

Carol Jean Mack

Someday

Plagued is my heart with loneliness, as tears fall frequently;
   Someday there will be happiness, someday, someone for me.

Stilled by silent thoughts at night, my heart cries out for love;
   Wanting, waiting, to hold tight, that long awaited one.

And as I dream of things that only two can share;
   This answer, oh God bring, will someone ever care?

To care, and not be cared about, Oh God, why must it be I
   To always live in doubt that someone will need me.

Forever to be lonely, is this to be my fate?
   You know the love that's in me; this heart which holds no hate.

Oh God, if you shall ever hear my long unanswered prayer;
   Then send a love, remove this fear, that no one will ever care.

Deep within my soul there are tears, but yet there's hope, I swear.
   This hope will last for more than years;
   Someday, someone will care.

Geraldine B. Schmidt

Untitled

My Love, I want my life to be shared with
someone I can appreciate sharing
it with, and someone who will appreciate
sharing their life with me.
Someone with whom I can enjoy the
beauty of all the "God" given things upon
this earth. Someone with whom I can share
a relationship of togetherness, but putting
"God" first in "our" lives, by being all that
we can to each other, by letting God's
love be the foundation of our relationship
and our life together, by learning and
growing as we become one in our
love for each other, by sharing the
blessings of knowing that "God" brought
us together, and by giving thanks to "God"
for our life, love and happiness.........

Eugene Morrison

Sonnett #1

As he jogged to the mound, all became quiet
Someone shouted, "Oh no, here comes the Ace!"
He heard the other coach plead, "Sam, try it."
Sam went to the plate with sweat on his face
The home side murmured and started the wave,
The visitors moaned and slumped in their seats.
The whole crowd knew that Ace would make the save,
The visitors knew too and smelled defeat.
Ace rubbed the ball and glanced from side to side
He went into his wind-up and let loose.
The ball hurled towards home and Sam took his stride
His swing came through with the power of Zeus.
As the ball sailed out, where once Ace stood proud
He now was the target of the wild crowd.

Danny Vibert

Heart Of A Friend

Someone to trust,
Someone to care,
Someone who will always be there,
Someone to talk to and understand,
Someone to take up for you.
Someone who is kind,
Someone who cares with their heart, not only their mind.
Someone to depend on right to the end,
All of these lies in the heart of a kind friend.

Jessica Lynn Gross

Empty Love

We search for someone to love all our young lives.
Someone who can make us complete.
Maybe if we had never tasted love,
There would not be such a craving for it.
Broken hearts, trials and error,
Has left many empty.
The days go by like turning pages of the book.
It doesn't seem fair that you can't turn ahead;
Or go back and rewrite the past.
If love heals, nurtures, and inspires;
Why is this a world so filled with hate?

Amy H. Nutt

Light Catcher

The light catcher —
    sometimes blue as the deep still waters,
        yet with strength apparent.
The palm tree —
    hiding the blossoming soul of a flower,
        its growth and regeneration.
You look deeply.
    You see clearly.
        You are my Light Catcher.
What am I to you?

Jade Archer

Sometimes...

Sometimes we win
Sometimes we lose
Sometimes we sin
Sometimes we choose.
Sometimes our lives spin out of control
Sometimes we're criminals on endless parole
Sometimes we're lost in thoughts from afar
Sometimes our hearts are shattered and scarred
Sometimes we want to run so far away
Sometimes life's games aren't ones we want to play
Sometimes we meet people who change our whole life
Sometimes they induce the epitome of strife
    they take our world and tear it apart
    a demented souls depiction of art
Sometimes life grabs you in the games we must play
Sometimes, regardless of outcome, there's a price to be paid
Sometimes I dream of murderous revenge...
Sometimes dreams don't satisfy this binge
Sometimes I wonder where my life must go
Sometimes its greatness... and sometimes death row.

Donald E. Traves III

The Flower

I feel a tear run down my spine,
Soon the sun will start to shine.
My arms are folded cross my face,
As I unfold to show my grace.

Then I feel a shower of rain,
But soon the sun dries me again.
As a dance on balmy breeze,
I feel so small among the trees.

I hear the singing of the birds,
I think there's one who's lost the words.
For as he hovers round my bloom,
He can only hum the tune.

It's time for me to go to sleep,
Another day my bud will keep.
As the sun begins to fall,
I close to wait another dawn.

Denise Ann Swanson

What is Wrong with Our Children of Today

What is wrong with our children of today?
Sorrow and pain is the price many have to pay.

Our children refuse to go to school and study,
Instead they turn to drugs;
And make their parents worry.

Many of our children cry out, please help, please help.
Their parents won't listen instead they take up the belt,
And then they start to pelt.

There are so many children committing crimes;
And when they get caught,
Their parents start to pine.

Their feet are so in a hurry to do badness,
Why don't they try to do
Some good, and show kindness.

Why are they so in a hurry to grow up?
Why can't they listen sometimes, and hush up?

whose fault is it that the kids are this way?
Some turn to the streets and kill, and even get away.

What is wrong with our children of today?
Parents did you give up? And let them have their way?

Ivonne Delancy

Feelings

When I look in your eyes and hear the
Sound of your voice, I wonder
I wonder who is this person?
I see caring in your eyes
I hear understanding in your voice
But who is this person?
When I kiss your lips I feel warm inside
When I touch you I feel safe inside
But who really is this person?
How can something feel so right but
always in question at the same time?
Is it the laughter in your voice, or the
look in your eyes, or the beating of your
heart, or the touch of your skin I miss the most?
No, for what I feel is deep inside me
For what I feel may only be a memory but
never forgotten.

Debra Biechy

Gravity

Youth is flame with naught to burn,
Speed, falling weights and hearts that turn,
Seeking as a river finds the sea
A means to live, a way to be.

And when the force has found a route,
It meets its course less resolute.
Where once horizons seemed so wide,
Challenging a giant's stride,
Now it's small and tight and mean
Unrelated to what might have been.

The flash, the flesh, the flush of dreams subside
Into the bone, hard as stone, they coincide:
Their weight is pain old age must try to hide.

Betty de Sherbinin

Beyond the Hills

Beyond the hills the evening sky turned red,
Stained by the blood some dying God had shed,
And through the flood there swam a ragged cloud
Who, to the wind, for succor cried aloud.
The north wind paused and took a deeper breath
And called, "You must swim on... perhaps to death.
I only sing, but listen to my song,
That it may strengthen your resolve as long
As breath shall last. I die with coming night,
So do not tarry. Summon all your might
And ride upon the billows of my voice
And, when you gain the shore, we'll both rejoice!"
But then the spreading darkness nearer drew
And, in its blinding depths, the lone cloud knew
Both it and its fair windsong could be lost
Among the stars...horizons left uncrossed.

The moon appeared. By then the wind was still.
The cloud raced on to find more Gods to kill.

John H. Dolloff

"My Eyes Have Seen It"

Standing on a moon of light
Staring at a beautiful gem
Blues, white and green
fill my eyes
The greatest site a man has ever seen
and in this great gem
I see a nation form
a place of freedom
where dreams are born
But in time
The nation begins to slip and fall
enter a place powered by fortune and greed
Forever lost is the seed
a seed of hope swept away with the wind
ripped out of the hearts of humanity
it becomes a place of insanity
The sees are gone, never to return
And I watch with pity and dismay
as my eyes watch this world burn

Brad Wareing

Lonely Nights From March To June

While the cool March winds blow in the night and the
stars are shining bright, I lie here dreaming of June
when you'll come home to me.

The April nights are long and warm from fresh rains
that came in the morn. And I lie here alone dreaming
of June when you'll come home to me.

The fresh flowers of May are in full bloom and sweet
in the air while I lie here alone dreaming of June when
you'll come home to me.

The moon is full and bright on this hot and breezy
June night with the sweet scent of flowers that
whisper thru the trees, I love you, and I'll never be
lonely again because you came home to me.

Julie Granger-Palmer

Perils

Running in circles, swerving around the same bend
Starting at a beginning that never comes to a end
Doesn't get better, just stagnate in one course
Trying to make it fit while it rebels against the force

Drops in a ditch that makes it even worse
Only to return repeating the same old verse
Like a roller coaster stuck in a continuous loop
Not scoring points because you can't reach the hoop

How did I get here, doesn't matter look for a way out
Just have to leave, make it stop, can't stand and pout
Wasn't me, wasn't you was every one's and no one's fault
But to stay is like a open wound searching for the salt

Andree M. Crushshon

Summer Pastures

My quiet ascent to undulating hills
Startles the bare and piques whippoorwills.
Rivulets well from the entangled deep
And criss-cross the path far from the neap.

Gowans and feathered flowers spot the heather
And lend a cast despite foul weather.
Even when gathered in armfuls to preen
They timidly, searchingly peek from the green.

My shoes are thin. I feel the rocks.
The remain from sojourners cast a pox
Of gum wrappers, cigar butts and tissue,
The spore of despoilers with whom I take issue.

And I stray beyond where there's no trespass
And spy a hoof, not that of an ass.
The cloven foot leads me quiet as death
Beyond church bells that toll Sabbath.

Aging patriarchs with gnarled root
Bathe their feet and charm the newt
And wiggle their toes in the silent pool.
It's not protocol, but it's certainly cool.

John W. Ceder

Quickly Comes The Night

Quickly, quickly comes the darkness,
Stealing colors from the day;
Sparing not the crimson sunset,
Chasing children from their play.

Gone, all gone the light and laughter,
Empty benches in the park;
Bolts and locks and wooden shutters
Attempt to push away the dark.

So like the heart, bruised and battered,
Cold and barred, afraid to give;
Reds and golds all cloaked in blackness,
Where embers glowed, now ashes live.

Touch a wounded heart to heal it,
A voice within me seems to say;
Passing, fleeting are the moments
That turn the chestnut hair to gray.

Ocean waves are weeping, sighing,
A sea gull cries in lonely flight;
They mourn the death of light and color;
Quickly, quickly comes the night...

Jan J. Jireh

A Better Tomorrow

Illusions of problems today
Steer some to an evil way

Hear their cries for only one creed
They have a need to re-plant the wicked seed

The righteous stand and wave their banner proud
Intending to incite the restless crowd

The plastic puppets ride the wave
Gaining the power they so crave

We can vote to stop their lead
And write letters for all to read

Be the first to extend a friendly hand
Communicate to help understand

Teach our children to stand tall
Because hatred affects us all

Settle not on vantage unfair
See the truth and beware

On an ocean of uncertainty we set sail
With persistence and strength we shall prevail

Resisting the assaults which cause sorrow
We live and hope for a better tomorrow
Joseph A. Lopez

Still Crying

   Still crying since the day he left,
Still trying to ignore the feeling I feel,
When I hear his name, my heart fills
with shame.
   There's not much to explain, and there's
no one to blame
I brought this upon myself
   Still crying from deep in my heart
I try to hide my feelings, but I'm falling apart
   what should I do
   I can't make another start
So I sit at home and cry,
The tears roll down my face, as every
moment, a special part of memory
of him will die.

Erin Kessler

Time to Fall

Tightly embraced and clung to a wall
stood melancholy and depressed a proud waterfall.
Hurt was impossible; somehow it cried only pain.
A foggy, separating shield hid its pouring rain.
As an audience praised how sturdy it appeared.
Some leaves blew past the shield discovering puddles of tears.
The water pressure rose forecasting a healthy flood
but the explosion was suppressed deep into the murkiest mud.
The powerful, crystal water pushed but could not be seen.
Aching to burst, it attempted a reach for the sea.
Growing longer, it did not increase its unstable height.
The indifferent waterfall began to feel familiar fright.
Tipping and bending, it was finally ready to fall,
And a branch cries merrily for the first crack in the wall.

Debra Shansky

Lend a Helping Hand

Lend a helping hand to all who are in need,
stop the selfishness and that awful greed.
It's time for peace and for love,
so send in the peace bird, that lovely white dove.
It doesn't matter what color the face,
we're all the same, the human race.
This awful, mean war has got to stop,
we've got to clean up so grab a mop.
There are guns and bombs and even knives,
we're killing each other and losing our lives.
Our planet is lovely and quite clean,
but with violence everyone is becoming mean.
If only someone would stop and help out,
reaching out a hand is what it's all about.
Caring and sharing is the way,
to make the people of this world happy and gay.
Children can't even go out and play,
because someone innocent might have to pay.
We're trying real hard to make this world great,
so the children of the future can have a nice fate.

Erin McMurry

Untitled

Emotions unknown
Stories untold you don't know me
Nor do you owe me a dime
Though, I owe thee a million of mine
Supported by you for 20 years of my life
Through smiles and tears, joy and strife
A lot of problems and almost a wife.

But now... I don't know how
I can stay at home
When my heart wants to roam
Arguing everyday
Driving us further away
I don't want to leave and yet I cannot stay
There's no alternative, simply no other way.

I love you both, can't you see
But inside the boy you know
There's a man trying to break free
Strong independent and mature
It is time for me to leave
Time for me to stand on my own two feet.

Adam Cain

The Bluebell

A field of roses; an ocean of scarlet
Stretching beyond the unending eye.
The dew burned off; nary a droplet.
Please tell me why does the bluebell cry?

The ocean it rises; an infinite high tide
Straining itself toward the deep azure sky.
Drowned in the shadows, meekest in pride.
Please tell me why does the bluebell cry?

Under the surface, violent choking;
Sharpened green thorns each scraping by.
The prayer of one flower, silent evoking.
Please tell me why does the bluebell cry?

It's head is bowed, quiet with fear
In awe of the presence of the golden eye.
With dew does it shed, one crystal tear.
Please tell me why does the bluebell cry?

Cale Dempster

Dandelions

A field of clover,
Such a wonderful sight,
So green and lush,
But what's that way out there
What do I see,
A lone dandelion
Swaying in the breeze.

It just sways like a string puppet
In that cool spring breeze,
The wind is like the puppet master
Making the yellow flower dance.

Soon the yellow petals fall to the ground,
And send many parachuting little seeds drifting
In the wind.

I was sad until before my brown eyes
Sprung hundreds of tiny yellow dandelions
To sway in the breeze.

Jennifer Meek

Revelation

"The grace of our Lord Jesus Christ be with you all. Amen!"
Such states the very last line
Of The Bible.
Mystery books are always resolved
At the very last ending.
So the meaning is clear!
The Holy Spirit be with each and every one of us.
The love of Jesus,
He who carried and He who carries our weight of guilt,
And He who reigns,
Holy Spirit extending, reaching, loving,
Awaits the time, lovingly,
Whenever all are safe within His fold.
He patiently endured and endures our sin, forgiving,
And loves to the very end...
The end whenever all are pure,
And wickedness in no form
Any longer exists...
Jesus reigning in each and every heart.
God complete.

Irmgard Elizabeth Spirk

The Four Merry Seasons of the Year

The four merry seasons of the year,
Suddenly became very undear.
They argued which one was the best,
And each fought against the rest.
They didn't make sense for a while,
But that actually made people smile.

The four merry seasons of the year,
Couldn't believe what they were about to hear.
Spring said, "I'm the best,
'Cause I bring flowers for every fest."
"No your not," said Summer, "the beach is a lot funner."
"No, it's not," said Fall, "your season's too hot for all."
Then Winter yelled, "Who cares about all of you, Winter's the best
   too."
And they kept going for some time with a sensible rhyme.

The four merry seasons of the year,
Had nothing to fear.
They got tired of the fight and slept for more than a night.
Then they had a lovely day and decided
That ever season is special in its own way.

Alexandra A. Nienart

The Voice

And so the voice, from whence it came
summoned me to my conscience
through the mirror of remembrance
that I had all but forgotten
I had no choice but to observe
to right the misguided wrongs
that I had revealed in
oft times being a bed of deceit
clothed of negligence
unmindful of what tomorrow would bring
and so the voice, from whence it came
questioned my conscience
regarding my values of what life is about
I felt my nerves tingle under close scrutiny
I felt the tentacles of hindsight
grip my heart deliberately
and with that, insight was born
so the voice, the voice of wisdom
had summoned me

Jane Solberg Smith

The Lure Of The Trees

How can one express their glory; how can one describe their
surreal presence through the minds eye where all becomes
cluttered with man's insatiable conquest for the concrete pinnacle
where the tree is only observed in a small pot.

Remove yourself for a moment from their God given stature and
try to imagine a world without their song on the windy eve or their
cool caress in the noon day sun or their laden branches supporting
crystals of ice for rainbows sake.

Find their beauty again through the eyes of your childhood
remembrance; the days spent climbing their perfectly placed limbs
to heights never reached before to view your world in those
colorful days of yesterdays brief embrace.
Thank you Father for the lure of the trees...

Andy Parrish

My Child

Take my hand and let me show you the way.
   Take my heart, please don't throw it away.
I've been where you are going, listen child of mine.
   The way is dark and sorrowful and certainly isn't kind.
Let me hold you close as I whisper, "Everything is O.K."!
   "The Boozy Man will go away".
It isn't easy, the road is rocky and narrows as we go,
   But rewarding as we travel, reaping as we sow.
There is a light to guide us, call it what you may.
   A power so great and loving it takes the pain away.
Teaching us to deal with our own created strife.
   A power that needed loving and so He gave us life.
Alcohol, cunning and deceiving, it loves to possess.
   Destroying because we are obsessed.
I love you, dear child of mine.
   You helped me, when it was my time.
I'm here, reach out and surrender!
   Life, with love, is so sweet and tender.
God is love!
   Your mother, an alcoholic

Beverly G. Maloney

Thistles and Weeds and Me

My soul grew full of thistles and weeds,
Tap roots sapping the life from me,
Not one - but Generations old,
Whose deep, dark secrets were never told.

If I would live a life that's free,
I must destroy those weeds from me,
Not one - but Generations old,
Whose deep, dark secrets were never told.

Once the thistles and weeds I removed,
I found the Re-Generation of me,
I found I lay in a rich man's grave,
Not one - but Generations old,
Whose deep, dark secrets were never told.

I return the rich man's grave to thee,
Whose thistles and weeds I had nourished
'Til my soul was all but perished.
I plant new seeds not known to thee,
To find the Truth and Origin of ME.
And now - I pray for thee.

Dorothy S. Rice

Moral Ethics

Oh moral ethics, why aren't you around?
Tell me where thou can be found?
Show yourself soon, if not we are doomed.
If you stay in hiding who can we confide in
Oh save this nation so we can have
a next generation

I remember yester years
We never had any fears
We were companions being everywhere
Woe unto us should you stay away too long
How could we survive on this land
Lost we would be, that's what I see
Come, come return to us and let our light. Shine
So as a nation we'll be fine all the time.

Henrick Patterson

For Me A Sailor, For You My Love

This is my life pondering the sea
Tending the lines of my ship I set free
The waters have a power over me so vast
The sun in my eyes they overcast
Drop the anchor in the harbor, people of the trades
I tell the acclaimed story of flying snakes and mermaids
Set my sail once again for distant coves
For I am just a poor lonely sailor looking for my homeport
The water calls me out to be cradled once more
So let me set the sail, and put on my cap
Have no need for your compass and map
Say goodbye to your loved ones, due to this fact
I have this strange feeling
We won't be coming back

Jacob G. Johnson

Significance

The caterpillar -
small and insignificant to the forest
until stopping to recognize,
the ladybug
beside him.

Karen R. Gravlin

Neighbor

There's more to being a neighbor
Than them lending you, something they've got
It's more than living next door to you.
Or maybe on the next block.
It's the way a neighbor shows you love.
Even though they're feeling low
They'll give you the last thing that they've
   got, and never let you know
They'll come to your rescue at
   midnight, if it's help from them you need
And do their best, without any rest
   to help you to succeed
They'll give you their last dollar, and never, ever complain
The rich folks that live around them, think they must be insane
But God in heaven, see's all.
And knows their hearts are true
He gave them a heart of love, to help their neighbor through
Dear God above with your great love
Please make me a neighbor too!

Faye Brewer

Love

Once in a lifetime, you feel a special pride
That comes from someone else, not from inside
The pride is from love, from someone near
Some say love is golden, some run from the fear

I have found love, and at first I was weak
But out of the love, came what I did seek
I sought for happiness, that feeling of joy
That comes from a child, when he gets a new toy.

I sought for life filled full of song
And to always see hope, when there is wrong
To look at the sky, and see beauty above
And this is all possible, when there is love.

I never saw colors, in the sun's setting shine
Just a bright light, that can make you blind
I never saw shapes, in clouds full of rain
I only felt wetness, and hurt and pain.

Now I see beauty, in everyday that comes
Pain it now has strength, it no longer numbs
Love is more than just a word, it has a new sound
Thanks to the woman, the one I love I have found.

James D. Merwin

My Heart Has Wings

Today there's a feeling in the air
That even yesterday wasn't there,
It's a promise of spring.
My heart's near to bursting inside of me
Like the swelling buds on the maple tree,
And I must sing!

My song goes forth in a glad refrain,
Comes floating back to me again
From out of the blue.
A robin has captured my song of cheer
Is singing it now for the world to hear,
He's singing to you!

So I go about my daily tasks,
My heart has found expression at last
In the song of a bird.
Today my happy heart has wings,
It soars on high with the robin who sings,
And is everywhere heard!

Helen F. Mitchell

Miracles

Oft times I think of the miracles
that God has done for me
He created the beauty of Heaven and Earth
and He gave me eyes to see

Today I watched and eagles soar
high above the plain
and stood in awe as flowers smiled
when it gently began to rain

I saw a mother with a newborn child
and the joy I saw on her face
makes me to know God's plan is real
and miracles still have their place

I stood beside a mighty river
and watched as it headed toward the sea
and marveled at all God's creation
for it all seems a miracle to me

Dave Ivins

The High Mountain Trail

There's a trail I see by the old pine tree
    That goes winding up o'er the ridge,
And the rocks and shade stands o'er the glade,
    As it winds on down to the stream.

My horse's hoofs ring on the rocks by the spring
    As she pauses there to drink,
And the whispering wind seemed to calm the din
    That was caused by my passing through.

Tamarack trees stout and tall, made me feel small,
    As I rode 'neath their branches green,
It's certainly fun to see the wild deer run
    As I surprised them in their leafy bed.

There's music sweet that can't be beat
    Not even in the halls of fame,
That is made by the leaves of the tamarack trees
    On the slopes near the timber pine.

Florence Campbell Horton

A Teeny, Tiny Town of Ralph

There's a teeny, tiny town of Ralph just off interstate fifty nine.
That is where I live and a lot of friends of mine.

The traffic is not noisy, hence, no streetlights to obey.
In the stillness of the morn, you can hear the farmers baling hay.

Across from the teeny, tiny post office is the fire department painted
    red.
The services they provide, can't enough be said.

The many churches about help us prepare our soul for eternal bliss
Because the road to calvary we surely don't want to miss.

The busiest place is the corner grocery, our only store.
Where the retired gents chit and chat and tell tales galore.

Ah yes, just a teeny, tiny town of Ralph just off interstate fifty
    nine
Where we share our joys and sorrows knowing God is watching
    over us and everything is just fine.

Annie L. Windham

About Life

Everyone knows in this crazy world
That it is a struggle either boy or girl
The simple fact of life all around
Will seem to go up and down
One person in life will touch your heart
Whomever it be, it will be from the start
Some of us were born with fashion and fame
Others were poor with no one to blame
Some of us will never find who we are
Others will be admired as a super-star
Those who are poor will find hope
Others will find life too hard and just can't cope
Some of us will make it and some will take the fall
Others take the easy way out and end it all
Whatever road you take in whatever case may be
It will all end the same, we will all rest
    In Peace!

Dominick Piernas

Pumpkin Moon

Risen over the here, the there, and all
That loosely draped in cloudy gray
Of stone to mark each ebb of day
Of one year are one Celtic new
There, skybound for eons, having often flew
In torrid eyes filled a cold Hades Fall

Luna, toned as rust abright in sun
Whence glistened, darting hills and dales
Bestowed the chill entrenched by gales
A heatless torch from high in rule
In new, crescent, half, three quarters, full
All suitable shining to a Spring harvest done

Forked by trees stripped barren, true gloom
Displaying shrouds, she glows on
Bestial hopes gazed out, incognito, anon
Like the lighted candle, a spectral light
Concordant to that which she this night
Shall kindle Autumn's orange nocturnal sun in loom

Chuck Watson

Seasons Past

What causes nature does so subtly bend and sway
That mankind can only humbly obey.
To stand erect and never falter
Is to live within an ageless time
Where there is no renaissance;
Where nothing is ever altered.

Oh, the seasons do so swiftly flow
Wearing ceaselessly upon the heart and soul.
We must accept that eroding feature
As through this travailed course we go;
For things have changed from that youthful future.
'Tis the affect of life's time worn teacher.

David R. Chaffee

Untitled

All alone she waits
Surrounded by broken fairy tales
All alone she weeps
No one to dry the trails
Of tears shed for him
The one who never came

Melinda Mencin

Memories, Hope And Sadness

He was a boy with a round shining happy face
That never seemed to be filled with sadness
And seemed to always be filled with a grace
But as he grew to a man he seemed full of a madness
A rage in himself that never seemed to have peace in any place
And with his own hand he took himself to a place of no madness or
   sadness
A place to shine and find peace in Gods own grace
To those of us he left behind with a dark hole of blandness
Recanting and chastising ourselves for not helping him find his place
And for the son, brother, father, and friend his lasting grandness
In our hearts and minds will always be a boy with a round,
   shining, happy face

Barbara A. Martucci

Restored

I've swallowed bitter, burning cinders of despair
that scorched the empty pit.
Flames assailed the ardent dreams wrought from my bosom,
guarded intimately within my soul.
I, in anguish watched them seized,
as an infant wrenched from it's clinging mother
and thrust into a deep abyss.
Tears preserve my sorrow with their pungent flavor,
lest I forget.

The whirlwind encircled me.
Spoke the still small voice within,
before the earth and sky existed
I named you as my own.
Tender whispers in my ear inspired fortitude.
His soothing oil, like a satin sheath embraced,
healed this stricken spirit.
Mighty hands raised me up, emboldened.
I called out to the crypt and claimed my young,
forever it stands empty.
Restore did He a steadfast faith, everlasting hope.

Anna L. Carrera

Heavenly Feeling

Do you see, boy
That there's a girl who cares always about you
I follow you in my heart
Can't hold back to tell
You're my ideal thing

Do you see, boy
Even when I see you walk by
You just lift me up
If I was God wanna let all your wishes come true
Because I love you

It's only you
Only you can give me such a heavenly feeling
The way you live keeps me moving on
It's only you
Only you can give me such a heavenly feeling
All of you is my passion

Aska Hirose

Bloody Tears

Suddenly jolted by a fierce force
Stunned by an unknown source
Echoing screams and pleading cries
Bloody tears stream from innocent eyes
Swirls of color distort their lives
Turning dreams to hopeless lies.

Sonja Eklund

Untitled

The winds of change are often violent gales
That threaten tiny vessels with their rage.
The Tempest's tirade batters homespun sails
And gives to Life's weak fiction a fresh page.
Some wrestle with the rudder, curse the tide
That sweeps their chosen fate beyond the curve,
While others simply hold on for the ride
As cautious indecision eats their nerve.
How quickly we assume our only choice
Lies twixt a futile fight and fearful flee;
How sweet to hear, within the gale, a voice
That urges us to strive for what could be!
   For when the storm seems worst I meet the gale
   Head on; my pen as mast, this page my sail.

James D. Malone Jr.

Courage

Courage and power don't come out of a bottle or from a pill for
that ultimate thrill which only brings a cold, cold chill, subtracting
from your till. You may laugh and you may cry for your portion of the
sky. But there is no genie in a quick fix, teach yourself some new
tricks. Learn your letters and your words. Express your thoughts,
feelings and dreams to humanities cultural stream. Be a builder of
the family, city and town never a destroyer of infamous renown. Use
your energy and your mind for the good of all mankind. Look with love
and not a sneer, to smile at others will endear, helping to tear down
obstacles, barriers, fences and frowns.

The image of beauty and strength can be created by sculptors from
the resistance of granite, marble and stone. And your profile shines
from that throne. Your family gives and instills love, beauty and
peace to build upon that foundation of character from stone, mortar
and brick-that won't be beat by any stick. Your brilliance and
strength, kindness and peace will withstand the raging elements of
wind, rain, hail and storm-not for you to be torn, for you are adored.

You may yearn, mourn and cry for the strife-ridden and suffering
kind. Emotional chaos is their lot. Sadness and pain should not
sustain let's beat back the emotional rain. Let that be our refrain
for our ultimate gain to fame with no shame. This is as it should be,
let us work for plenty and peace for all of thee. Let that be our
spree.

James Toler

Night - November 1981

Dreaming - She was there but seemed unaware
  that we were there
   She was aware but seemed
  not there - reflections from opposite window

Awakening - Talking tracking the mind

Listening - Moving sounds, cars speeding
  freeway in distance
   can something be done about that
  two yelps from dog, nothing to be done about that

   One lone whistle, voices, screeching rails
  Four strong blasts without fail
   signaling train's approach as it nears
  Is this soothing to the ears

   Birds a chirping - rooster crowing
  Night time ending leaving
   We were there, aware
  Thoughts from the bed side.
Remembering.

Jewell and Joel Lewis

The Hero Within The Friend

There is a Hero within you, my friend.
That will be there until the end!

You always have known the right thing to say;
Those words have helped me on my way.

My tears you've dried each time it rained;
You've made me smile and eased my pain.

Together we've shared the times of happy and sad;
Together we've been through the good and the bad.

So very many memories we have shared,
Just to know how much we care.

You've always been there for me,
Urging me to be all I can be.

We could always tell each other everything,
Without a worry about anything.

Since so much love and gratitude fills my heart,
I wish that we would never ever part.

Though my gratitude I can never extend,
You will always be my Hero within my Friend!

Jacqueline A. Jones

The Window Of Memory

I know of a window in your mind,
that will help you when you're in a bind.

It will help you when you're feeling down,
it will help you when you wear a frown.

I know the pain will sometimes be deep,
and during these times you want to weep.

When the pain becomes too much to bear,
reach for the window of love and care.

It is there in the back of your head,
ready to release you from your dread.

Open the window and you will find,
all the cherished memories of your mind.

The memories will help you through the bad,
they will set you free, and make you glad.

The window is always there for you,
to keep you happy, to help you thru.

So whenever you start to feel low,
open that window and find the glow.

Christine Klekman

A Mothers Prayer

Wherever we may be, as long as your with me dear,
that's heaven today.
As long as the children are near, and they have nothing to fear,
that's heaven today.
What makes life really count,
and gives happiness in small amounts,
to be together is the reason for you and me.

We have our hurt, we have our fears,
and we've had our problems throughout the years.
We've had our sorrows and shed our tears,
yet through it all, we're still together dear,
and that's heaven today.

When our children are each fully grown,
and venture out to be on they're own,
we'll have these memories to keep as our own,
and that will be heaven today.

Anna A. Mann

Empathic

Whenever I hear someone
Speak of a "great love",
I finger my scar,
(still tender),
And marvel that I recovered
From so great a wound.

Mary Jacks

Ed Was My Friend

But before Ed was my friend, Ed was my father's friend.
That's how Ed became my friend, because my father loved Ed first.
It would have been hard not to love Ed, but still, there were not
many who loved Ed.
I knew Ed before I met Ed, I loved Ed before I met him, Ed was dad's
favorite subject. "We've read all the same books." Dad would beam.
I used to tease dad about Ed, mom did too.
Then I met Ed, after that, Ed was my favorite subject.
"We've had all the same thoughts," I would think.
It would have been hard not to love Ed.
My dad got a taste of how hard a few years later.
He stumbled into the house, fell past the door, crawled into bed.
I stood in the doorway watching him sleep, and my mother whispered.
"Ed's dying. Ed's dying of AIDS." Ed died for five years after that,
his body, but not in us. Ed could of died of anything, he's still gone.
I'm sorry Ed, for you and me, I should have known you more,
I wanted to.

Angeline Roan

Knocking On Board

Knocking on board - body of bones
That's how you are
If you don't eat
Your body won't carry you far
Eating disorder for me
Stop judging me, please

Nobody knows - don't understands
Look at you, certainly look like a samalian
My God! Have you been eating?
Ribs peeking, sure is sad
So skinny, you don't eat
Sure will die
Wish it was so easy, as I sigh
I've tried, but it takes time
As my not eating, became a crime
Not eating, started somewhere in my youth
In those days, in the shortness of food
Became a habit
Over many years - became my way of life
How can I change it in one night?

Jasmine White

Infinity

....The circle of life keeps revolving around.
The answers to its riddles are yet to be found.
Where does this leave me?
Desolate and alone....
Surrounded by darkness,
my reasoning overthrown.
The voices of my heart that call out from inside are what guide my
    way;
by them I abide.
I rely on myself, my thoughts, and my desires which burn in my soul
    like raging fires.
No one is there to extinguish the flames.
Gazing deep into the shadows I see no figure, no name.
The fire keeps burning, our world keeps turning
Until that one day my ashes blow away....

Amy Yerkes

Her

The second guessing,
the betrayal of herself
it is all ludicrous.
One that should be strong and have no worries,
can do nothing but wonder,
not know that she is great.
Idolized by many,
yet the silent nature of these wantabes
will not show their longing.
Unknowingly these followers talk of her,
wanting to be as pretty or as personable as she.
But at this same time she wishes,
wishes she were more like them.
Never happy with anything concerning herself.
Always wanting something different,
she does not realize how perfect she is,
how everything about her shows greatness.
Being the caring individual that she is,
it is hard to believe,
that she can not find the time to love herself.

Dennis Mooradian

Old Wood Stove

I remember our old tar paper shack,
  the big ditch that ran by the railroad track.
I still smell mama fryin' that old fat back,
  sweatin' over that old wood stove.

We had good times when I was a kid,
  we worked hard, but then everybody did.
The summers were hot and the winters cold,
  as we warmed by that old wood stove.

It's been 20 years since I've been back,
  they've torn down our old tar paper shack.
And weeds have grown over that railroad track,
  but what happened to our old wood stove?

They've made changes in the land,
  we get our peas out of cans.
Neighbors just nod now, and don't shake hands,
  but what happened to our old wood stove?

No hickory grows in the grove,
  the creek is dry where we swam and dove.
And guess what,
  the junkyards got our old wood stove.

John Cleveland

In My Eyes

I see the dawn peering through a tree
The birds are singing for they are free

I see a squirrel run across the lawn
Running along with a young fawn.

I see a bee buzz around the porch
The lightning bug with it's torch.

I see old friends walk down the street
Making new friends as they meet.

I see the moon shining into the night
The stars looking down with their light.

I see memories of loved ones gone before
As they walk through heaven's door.

Joan L. Green

Pain Of Departure

I could have tolerated:
The bitter freezing Siberian winds
Penetrating my outer protection
Fiercely besieging my frost-bitten skin
Whilst I turn pallid in my complexion

I could have endured:
The heat of the desolate Death Valley
Dwindling at every moment my strength
Condemning me therefore to atrophy
Abject suffering, indefinite length

I could have brooked:
A typhoon of the western Pacific
Bringing intense gusts in its deadly path
Thus unleashing waves likewise horrific
While letting loose its unrelenting wrath

However, I can not bear:
The torture that our parting has produced
This distress haunts me even while sleeping
The cause of a joyful person reduced
To sullen moods and impulsive weeping

Jonathan Hughes

The Boy

The air: A deathly chill it had.
The boy running to Catch up;
"NO! STOP DON'T GO!"
The bus driver never suspecting,
not even braking - it was too late.
Fear was the look on the boy's face.
Horror, the look on the crowd.
The body - lifeless - laying in the street,
blood seeping out of every pore
spreading over the black top like
a relentless monster in pursuit of its prey.

Hysteria

Baris Konur

In The Womb Of The Great Mother

In the Womb of the Great Mother,
the child- protected and warm.
Ancient stone cities tell of tropical Divinity
where human souls entered this scared earth.

The child is born and the mother heals,
for she has more love to find,
She would sacrifice her body, her mind or soul,
and rise up to the spirit to save her child

All of the material things she would forbade,
travelling through darkness.. conquering fear.
Birth is eternal, that she has found,
as death is the power of regeneration.

Great Mother..we feel your discomfort
the bonds of all love come from your pain.
You nurture and feed our hungry souls,
your child born in spirits is the only goal

Jonathon Ray Spinney

Ocean

Ocean so pure and clear.
Surrounding land and people,
Shallow or deep.
On the special floor many
species creep,
So that women and men can
explore the ocean floor.

Naeesa Aziz

Untitled

My heart spoke words only
the chosen could understand,
patience, kindness, to be content.
My heart saw a vision,
On a clear Indian summer night,
The second sun glistened its
Luminous light, the waves spoke
A language of their own,
how their tongues can soothe one's soul.
The other dreams envisioned in
This scene, to die and become
one with the sea. Lovers hold
hands to become one, their
footprints embedded in the
grain of sand, washed away
By the lonely hearts that dares
to come ashore, to prove nothing
last forever, not even the false
stories told by the heart,
centuries old.

Antonia Digregorio

Untitled

One day while I was walking, I looked up in the sky.
The clouds were moving all around and birds were flying high.

The sun was trying hard to shine, I stood and gazed in awe.
Such wonders we all fail to see just walking to the mall.

A flower was gently swaying to the rhythm of the wind.
I bent to smell of it's perfume then up to go again.

Life does have a hurried pace as we all surely know.
We need to stop and take the time to share love as we go.

I finished all my shopping, to work I had to go.
Rushing here, racing there, the day it flies by so.

We need to steal some minutes from each and everyday,
to stop and smell the flowers before they fade away.

Betty T. Eaton

Spring Fever

It's the beginning of spring
The cold winter is dying
The earth is warming
The sun is shining
Awakening to spring showers here and there
Plants starts popping everywhere
The grass is changing from a yellow to a green
I then start to feel
That listlessly restless feeling that I feel
When those first warm days of spring steps in
   It's the fever

Audrey Adams

Dare to Discover

   Dare to discover the oceans blue,
the colored fish and dolphins too,
the killer whales that swim all day,
and seals that bark and like to play.

   Dare to discover the oceans below,
the sea shells, the coral, and the seaweed too,
the jelly fish and octopus catching their food,
the big bolder rocks that lie on the bottom,
the sandy gravel, and big tidal waves,
this is the ocean, the ocean below, filled
with creatures we all know.

JaKell Farnsworth

Life

Behold, the Book of Life is open.
The Course of ages is like a parable,
and in the passing, each may burst in flame.
I see the future clearly now,
as if the world has come to a Stop,
and I can prophesy events,
Like an ancient Sibyl in a trance,
"In a world of chaos, we Stand, unprepared"

One Star alone
Shone bright on the way to Bethlehem
One star alone
I am who am

Felix Navidad = Happy Nativity

Frederick Witt

The Miracle of Birth

Looking around us we can admire
the creativity of mother nature,
the way she works and without help to hire
continues tireless a superb nurture....

The flowers, the birds, the green world,
on the land and in the sea,
it's something admirable and very old
and we are lucky to be around and see.

But the crown of the universal creativity
is the mystery and miracle of birth.
What more superb can exist than nativity
the best lovable present for humanity on earth.

The infant's mumbling; majestic symphony
and the precious eyes; tranquility of the universe
Oh, that sweet smile; celestial harmony ...
and, the face of innocence and purity, what else?

God's with nature's best creation,
what happy home, having gained a baby.
It gives joy, and life worthy valuation
when a toddler says the word like "daddy!"

George G. Katsampes

Realization

In perfect dreams, curious souls strayed....
The day before eternity began.
And the Angels were silent high above the world....
The day the dead began to speak.

So when God whispers your name,
Breaking the silence of centuries,
Turn to see his face reflected in the blazing sun....
And stand in the light that shatters all but your soul,
And know that there is no where for your heart to hide.

Turn to see a new horizon,
Where the baby blue sky smiles,
And the wind plays melodies,
And the softest rain is falling.

Bridge the abyss and go where you are always welcome....
The realm of the spirit,
And listen until your hear your own soul's voice,
Like a whisper in the sand....
And know that God hears it too.

"Welcome home, dear child..."
Welcome home."

Heather Dawn Skelton

The Gift of Life

So tired.
The day too long.
Limbs aching, mind numb, fatigue oozing from every pore.
I struggle to cross the threshold,
My soul heavy with the worries
of this Old world.

So young.
Her day too short.
Legs strong, energy exploding from every cell.
A mop of blond curls running down the hallway,
Her spirit as light and sweet
as a robin's song in the summer air.

I stop, amazed
at the wonderment of this being.

Our souls collide.
Twisting, turning, tumbling into one.
She is too strong for me.
And I eagerly embrace the warmth of her light
Until, once again, I am filled with hope,
And happy to be home.

Bridget A. Reynolds

Untitled

With all the world comes a mystery
The days come and go wondering
What will ever come of me?
A different path chosen by each one
Though really just the same
No real choice or plan to win the game
Everything being equal and seemingly not
To be part of all though an individual slot
Twist and turn - understand
Sent for a loop on a midnight ride
Breaking such our rule which we abide
By the time it's over penalty takes place
Which time to face - conclusion of reality
A secondary rush of excursionary thoughts brought from within,
Alas a sought for end - so it does seem
On to the next dream
With all the world comes a mystery
The days come and go...
On to the next show -

Frank C. Pusateri

Down Deep

Trapped in the depth of hate-
The Devil will soon call me waiting for our date.
I slowly burn my heart weighing heavy,
My spine is ruptured and my body saying why?
The eyes can see through me and hear my cries.
I don't know why all this fear..spinning in the rages of burning Hell,
Never knowing what will come next...maybe, my burden of sorrow-
Will be figured out tomorrow- we will never know.
My soul is closed and echoes oh so hallow,
Drowning in my misery and self wallow.
The sun is endlessly burning-imitating my soul and,
I'm down deeper than the deepest hole.
Hell- what a word, a burning sword,
Hell- what a sight, the Devil won't bite,
Only, I have fear the Devil just might.
Vicious demons nipping at my toes,
Telling me just how much the Devil knows.
Chills race up and down my spine.
And... all's it takes is a little time,
To be down deeper than the deepest hole.

Jessica Paulos

As Distant As Echoes

Blistering sun that dreams with
The distant clouds,
Wakes the mornday dew, that
Ensweeps the mysterious shrouds:

In crimson clouds, the answer is within,
Burrowed deep in the depths of
Looking glass skin.
Ice let eyes gleam, as the yearning flesh
Furrows,
Deep within whispers, of yesterdays
Tomorrows:

Amongst snowflake sheets
Satin to the touch,
Beauty lays still.
As coral coolness swims
Amongst our eyes, this one night of truth,
Is worth A lifetime of lies.

A. Angel Andy

Tribute to Imogen

"Cunningham is the artist's name,"
The docent informs standing by;
While we savor photos frame on frame;
Insights often missed by our eye.

Pain and toil are caught in a stance,
Alongside a peaceful mother.
Mischief peeks through a twinkling glance,
Love's pathos weeps from another.

She sought not to gild or flatter
But illuminated what's found
Amid the brocade or tatter
Where essence alone is profound.

Human character was the quest,
A Grail in a portrait that's true.
Our heritage dwells in the best,
Or the worst of life in her view.

Inspiration, her muse, or God
Guided Imogen to that goal.
My viewing self feels a quiet nod,
Affirmed by the shiver of Soul.

Eve Lewis-Chase

Springtime Rhyme

The tranquil glow of Springtime moon
The eerie sound of the peepers tune
The rippled brook with waters high
From winters snow the sun made cry
The evening breeze like feathers soft
The greening fields neath geese aloft
The shedding coat of the whitetail deer
The crimson shield neath the pheasants ear
The golden crowns of daffodils
The rising clouds o'er maple hills
The angered crows in owls' tease
The lazy buzz of honey bees
The new life born a gift of spring
The fulfilling joy of each new thing
The daylight hours now long and bright
Soon guide the way to summers' might

Bert L. Snyder

Eagles Prey

Spiraling softly overhead
searching by the break of day
vision sharp, the hunger great
searching for the knowing prey

Melissa Domey

Untitled

You and I;.... distinctly a couple.
The epitome of togetherness,
Two halves that form a whole.
Perfect and complete in every way.

You and I;.... redefining our relationship.
Searching for something to fill
the empty places inside.
Going round in endless circles
Dizzy and confused.

You and I;.... separating ourselves.
Painfully tearing open wounds
in what once was smooth and unmarred.
Savagely possessive and insanely jealous,
Making a mockery of a love affair.

Heather Leigh Smith

Untitled

The love that I feel is too strong to say
The feelings I have can't be written down
Emotions I go through everyday
They all seem to spin my world around

You've been in my life for quite a while
I just never seemed to notice before
Though now when you come, all I do is smile
And I'm ready to open, to my heart, the door

Just say the word, and I will be there
To be with you would be everything
All you must do, is show me you care
I don't need a rose or even a ring

Throw caution to the wind and just close your eyes
Cause with you and me, the limits the sky

Christianna Rognstad

Graduation

When I saw you go across
the field, my heart so full of pride,
I had flashback of memories coming from inside.
I saw the baby, I held in my arms,
Who made my life worthwhile with her many charms.

Then I saw the little girl, I love so much,
Who touch my heart with her tender touch.
The little girl with so much love,
That's why I thank the Good Lord above.

A teenager girl always on the
phone and always on the go.
God! How I love her so.
Through the years with her many friends,
I hope she knows I will be there till the end.

The day has finally arrived
and I see a young woman and no longer a child.
Who still makes my life worthwhile

I will have my memories and a few flashbacks to recall
If the future is as good as the past then I know it was
worth it all.

Dolly Kilgore

It Was You, Mother

It was you mother, who taught the world to sing. You heard
the first sounds of the day and the resounding of the seas.
It was you who heard the siren song, that stirred the instinct
within—the yet—unborn Chanter.

You heard the sound of the wind, and the rain dropping;
melodiously to the ground. You hummed to sooth the germ
inside, and patted your feet, while the Diva bounced in the
womb, to the beat. It was you, who taught the world to sing.

It was you who sat on some distant hill—ten million years
ago—and cried out in pain, as the Minstrel broke free, and
uttered the first sounds of life. It was you who taught the
world to sing.

You watched the flames dancing, and heard a melody in the
firewood crackling; while the Musician suckled at the breast.
It was you mother, who taught the world to sing.

It was you, who first heard the earth sounds, and saw the
stars of the darkness night. You watched the trees swaying in
the wind, and the leaves falling —a metamorphosis of
harmony—an inspiration to the Bard inside.

It was you mother, who taught me the world to sing....

Ivory J. Webb

Eagle

O, victim of Christendom's god-murder,
the first time ever I saw you is etch'd
forever on the back side of my eyeballs;
a black star soaring in an azure sky.
We've touch'd clouds wingtip to wingtip;
together, we've seen tops of verdant forests
and streams and rivers like arterioles.
I've watch'd sunsets brilliant through your pinions;
and terrified, your glittering eye stalk
your poison'd prey. When it was over,
I, all alone, wept and reverently buried
your cold feathers, talons and bones.

David Thomson

A Mother's Joy

The first time they smile.
The first time they cry.
The first time they coo
and you wonder why.

The first time they giggle.
The first time they grin.
The first time they look at you
innocent from sin.

The first time they sit.
The first time they talk.
The first time they crawl.
The first time they walk.

The first time you hold them,
your new baby girl or your boy.
The first you kiss them and whisper goodnight.
All of these special things add to a mother's joy.

Darlena Evans

Choice

Choices you'll make,
Mistakes you'll survive,
Prices are high,
Families never die.

Linda D. Rhodes

'Tis Spring In Virginia

Though the winter may be harsh with much ice and snow,
the first warm sun gives a signal to grow;
as the oft brilliant rays hit the side of the hill,
the Crocuses bloom from roots sleeping and still.

Then the Forsythia gives forth with a startling array,
to be followed by Japonica without hesitation or delay;
soon all the trees awaken with a profusion of buds,
and the Dogwood sends forth blooms like a woman with new duds.

And while all this transpires without a time table,
the most elegant blooms are yet to fulfill this fable;
for now spring breaks forth with Azaleas in full dress,
while awaiting the Roses as the seasons progress.

We look forward to each spring with it's thrilling events,
and are mindful of the joy mother nature invents;
to think all this beauty awaits us each year,
gives us pause and due thanks to the Lord we hold dear.

Glenn A. Swanson

Transition

Signs all around me verify
The fullness of age
As the days go by.

Colored leaves swirling
Through the Autumn sky.
Splashes of color around me lie.

Snow on the mountain.
Covering the green,
Patches of white are everywhere seen.

Movements are slower,
Eyes gone dim,
Crumbling and cracking of many a limb

Only one part
Resistant to change,
Peacefully sheltered, regardless of range.

Nestled inside, never to die,
The spirit immortal, just waiting to fly.

Dorothy E. Gunter

Comatose

Life itself is a mechanical machine
The gears of evolution changing with time
Dreams tucked away beyond tomorrow.
The precious gift of life therefore,
Can also be a death sentence, awaiting for.
Time passes, hope dies,
Only the love that once was, keeps us alive.
Please love me enough to let me go.
When living has ceased, love lives on,
The memory of what was will never die.
If it be Gods will the machine of life, will run no more.
Talk to me hear my plea,
I can not speak, only in my mind.
If this is my destiny, please be kind.
Your gentle care and concern will be with me ever more.
Remember this could be you that lives on!
Will there be a tomorrow? For you I am sure
I have accepted my destiny with peace and grace,
It is now time for this worn machine to rest
And rely solely on love and faith.

Christine Seaholtz

MY Elusive Butterfly

Today I emerged from the winter of my soul
The gentle touch of your wings warmed my heart
If you'll light for just a moment, I promise not to
Hurt you. Perhaps I'm dreaming, let me touch you. I know
That your wings are very delicate, and you must be handled
With care. You are unique, your beauty is rare and a joy to behold.

Where are you off to now? I have just begun to enjoy the velvet
Softness of your wings, and the splendor of your dazzling colors
My heart is made content by the graceful movements of your body.
Is it fear of capture that sends you on instant flight? Or could
It be that you find a strange delight in this endless pursuit....??

The summer is drawing to a close. Once again you have taken flight
I should not complain; I have enjoyed your beauty for another season
I must allow you to return to the place from whence you came.
I no longer fear the winter; For winter gives way to spring; you
Will emerge more beautiful than before. I await your return...My
Elusive Butterfly.....

Bettie Barney McMillan

I Will Wait For You:

The blue waters that gently moves in the bay.
The green grass in the fields that will soon turn to hay.
This is where my love and I once walked.
This is where my love and I once talked.
The gentle words we once whispered.
The tender kisses we once shared.
The pain since then, that I have endured.

Now I walk through the fields with great sadness.
Praying for the happiness that had my heart singing
With gladness.
Why did he go away? Who made him stray?

Oh my love please return to me. I want happiness
So bad. Let us share the love that we once had.
I want you to hold me in your arms, and whisper words
Of love to me from your heart.
And I will pray that we will make a new start.

The grass has turned brown where we once talked.
It is no longer soft and green where we once walked.
I will walk through the fields every day whispering a prayer.
And someday I hope that you will be waiting there.

Janice Haugabook

Dad

The greatest man I've ever known lived just down
the hall, he came home every night from work,
I knew he gave us his all.

We'd sit down to eat our dinner, then watch the
old T.V., we never spoke too much back then, or
mention words of love, we'd go to bed without a
prayer, not inspired from God above.

Years went by, and times were hard, but he held
us close together, then the holy spirit came and
made our family life better, Jesus Christ came
in our lives and tore down the heavy walls, now
words of love can be spoken, to the man who
lived just down the hall.

Jan Marie Briggs

Narcotic Illusion

Impetuous passion, pale naked virgins relinquish
The hallowed plastic altars of salvation.
Easy seductions in subtle decanters of
Vampiric ambrosia.
Temptress, quiet Morphine queen, Pallid Wanton
Lady of velvet venom, misguided tyrant
Of heady decadence, usurper of guilded
Graveyard Idols
Enslave me in elaborate enchantment of
Aching arsenic agonies, incestuous illicit gluttony,
Taunted by the turgid gangrene guilt
of desire.
The damned betrothal to idle lies,
Narcotic illusion

Jonathan Ball

An Hour of Fantasy

When first I hear his fond "hello"
The happiness within me starts to flow
I cannot wait to feel his arms
Making me succumb to his fatal charms

His red hot kiss upon my lips
Makes me want his fingertips
To explore my body in gentle fashion
That takes me to heights of fiery passion

An hour of loving from within our souls
Our minds creating the perfect roles
I cannot touch him, but yet and still
I can feel him, and I always will

To please me is his first desire
I, too, want him to feel the fire
But now he's gone, and I'm alone
Because all of this has been by phone.

Eileen K. Oeky

Grandmother

Grandmother can lessen every burden
The heavy as well as the light
Her strength is made perfect in weakness
In her there is power and might.

Grandmother can bear most sorrow
In her there is hope for tomorrow
No matter how great the affliction
She will tell you what's best.

Grandmother can solve most problems
The tangles of life we endure
There is nothing too hard for Grandmother
There is nothing she won't do.

Brenda L. Fulton

Spring Joy

April showers are over
The hills and valleys are covered with flowers
Spring is here and birds all over
Are chirping and singing their best.
Step out and see the beautiful scenery
That covers the earth from east to west
come one, come all
There's room for all
This heavenly scenery is free for all

Julio S. Zamora

From The Depths Of My Soul

What does it take to fill this deep hole
The hours of despair thinking I'm all alone
there's no one who cares
Searching searching day after day
to find the right way
Where oh where is my peace at last
so weary of biding my time in a cast

There as I languished in my own black pit
In the vacuum I heard a voice calling my name
From this day on I shall ne'er be the same
I'm here take my hand be not afraid
together we will travel life's road
You alone will no longer have to carry the load.

Doris Naughton

Footsteps

Footsteps - through the forest
The hunter leaves no trail.
Following where the path takes him.
The animals respect him, for today he is not looking for them.
His people survive on instinct.
He has no fear, only pride and courage.
His culture - all but lost;
The dawn of civilization was
The dusk of his existence.
The earth that he protected,
The land that he occupied,
Handed down to us.
Evolution, taking him as a testament
To our pure, unbridled form.
His spirit has been quenched by
Our desire for more than just life.
The nomad, hunter/gatherer,
The first phase in our evolution.
One of the simplest, most pure forms
Of the existence of mankind.

Joseph Deeken

The Spring Pageant

Water trickles as the sun tickles
the last of the wint'ry snow.
'Twill soon be spring when cardinals sing
and nature begins her show.
Toward the end of fall she had a ball;
many seeds she had to sow.
And now she waits and anticipates
the flowers she knows will grow.
As days turn warm and honeybees swarm
these seeds she sprinkled with care,
will plant their feet and begin to feast
on nutrients buried there.
Then they will sprout for a look about
as their buds unfurl and flare.
And so will unfold her tale retold —
this pageant of life we share.

Frieda D. Klotz

Untitled

How do we live?
Why must we die?
Why do we mess up our life?
Why do those kind of people comment suicide?
Why because we love.
Why do those kind of people comment suicide?
Why because we love,
those who can not love themselves
Love for them who can not love no one else.

Shelby Allen

523

The Perfect Day

Picture a beautiful sunny day.
The leaves are falling down.
Their colors of yellow, orange and red.
Lay upon the ground.

Across the meadow is a brook.
And the water flows gently by.
As I sit beneath the trees.
I watch the world go by.

Over on the hillside, among the trees.
The pretty flowers grow all around.
As the gentle breezes blow.
My heart just wants to sing.

Sing of the beauty of the earth.
That God made so perfectly.
He has given everything that perfect place.
Even you and me.

Just like the tree that stands so tall.
And the flowers that smell so sweet.
I want to be everything,
God created me to be.

Janet J. Anderson

Loving A Soldier

Loving a soldier isn't all play
The life it enforces isn't so gay.
It's mostly the having and not to hold.
It's being too young and feeling too old .
It's the life of skimmed milk without any cream,
It's being in love with a wonderful dream.
It's a lonely letter from a far-off camp
With a "free" in the corner, instead of a stamp.
It's hoping for a furlough that never can be,
And making the plans for a future you see.

So you work and smile each hour of the day,
And the victory that's near will be plenty to pay.
You're lonesome, you're tired from doing your share;
But you're helping your soldier win over there.
So loving a soldier is bitterness, tears,
It's loneliness, sadness and ungrounded fears.
It's working and hoping for freedom of living,
With a reward that's immense for what you are giving.
No, loving a soldier isn't much fun
But it's cheap for the price when the battle is won.

Alkus Ward

Whispering Willows

As the wind goes by and the willows sway,
The light shortens, and so does the day

From the golden sun in the afternoon,
To the low sweet holler of the black and white loon.

Now listen to the whisper that rings in the trees,
And hear the hum of the birds and the bees.

Alas comes the mist over the ocean,
Silent with movement, silent with motion.

To feel the warmth of a soft pillow,
Will always remind me of the whispering willow.

James Lanman

Untitled

If ever did an auburn tress catch the eye of great Achilles,
(The locks that spilled down a porcelain face,
Lightly touched by spring-time lilies,
And even spread in perfect shape 'round a lovely chin,
Made Hades glad to part its maw
To accept those warrior's spirit of kin),
Or if ever the scop on his lyre did play in warm mead-halls
The tune of Taliesen's love,
And how that Angel of Song
Bonded the blood of men in harmony,
Made pleasant a savage kind,
And if ever did Keats' Fair Star give warmth to a cooling body,
Keenness to a dulling mind, or a thousand intangible treasures
To a man's poor spirit
———These also do I see, hear, and feel as the west wind
Now blows in leaves crisp red and brown on the fading sun,
And you stand in the midst of this all.
Why do you let that gale push you onward?
For it travels on to an ice-berg'd sea and that is the end.
Tarry. Stay awhile with me.

Jason M. White

"Who Can Say"

When you're in "Love" - why do they say -
"The love you feel will fade away?!"
   That you're too young or not to smart-
   To know the feelings in your heart!?
Why can't they let you live your life -
And face the world - wrong or right?
   So they say, "You're not so cool,
   To let your heart make you a fool!!"
But say perhaps, that they were wrong -
You turn your back, you walk alone!!
   Could you know or could you say -
   that you were "right" - to turn away!?
Those who say, that love is bad -
Do so only, cause they are sad!!
   But I can say, "I'm truly glad!"
   For it's your "love" that I now have!!
Love is hard - but so is life
Each one has a "wrong or right"!!
   But this is living and live we must -
   To learn to "love" and learn to "trust"!!

DiAnna Wolf

Untitled

Murder... an ugly and yet noble word!
The masterpiece of human life is oft'
Compromised by schemes of those who know all;
Those who know all and are all. What is life?
A human life is nothing but a "one";
A number that, with zeroes behind it,
Spells doom to our comfortable living;
Something innate within us tells us so.
And yet we suddenly, over the years,
Develop a strange numbness to this fact;
When numbers seem so cold and far away,
And only seem to clutter up some page
Within some newspaper we choose to read;
That over time we grow to welcome it
As solace for those troubled minds abroad;
Even those too close for us to notice.
Where does the answer lie? I do not know.
Since Abel fell under Cain's heavy staff,
We have lived in a state of constant strife.
Perhaps we must feel it to understand.

Anthony J. Aschettino

The Forest

As I looked yonder into
   the mist of the forest
I could barely see a
   single tree

By thunderous noise and falling
   trees the inhabitants will surely leave

No more will I hear the birds sing
   like golden strings of a violin
So much in harmony
   sounds like a symphony

The pretty butterflies will surely die
   rare bees ascending towards the sky
like if looking for a place to hide

The forest is gone now
forever lost - the ground covered
with simply dust, and fallen moss

I've lost my friends forever
   I cried in vain
will I ever see them again
   Ashami Lewis

The Passing of Moments

Our days of living are comparable as to a Grandfather clock,
The moments pass ever so quickly with each sounding ticktock.
To keep our ticker ticking we should not wind it too tight,
For the best of our plans could, and do, cease to be overnight.

Of course, we in being perfect, easily find faults in our fellow peers,
In our tensioned thoughts we cast upon our once loved ones our sneers.
The provoked dislikes and shunning of one another, how sad it be,
When all this hatefulness destroys the once closeness of a family.

The once cherished love of a sister, the treasured closeness of a
   brother,
The moments, the special times, that you've shared with one another,
The laughter of good times along with the shedding of tears,
The closeness of each other in sharing the hurts and the fears.

Now as the hands of time silently tick away to a final end,
The family ties are no longer...my brother, my sister, my friend,
Share your love while your clock still ticks and you both are here,
Instead of trying to convince the undertaker of your love with a tear.

I remind you my friend......
Ticktock, ticktock, .. tick....................?
   Frederick J. Pretak

A Desert Paradise

I live in a "Garden of Eden",
The most wonderful spot on earth.
I'm surrounded by beautiful people
Most of whom have proven their worth.

The coo of a dove here awakens me
The quail entertain all day long.
A robin will chirp a sweet melody;
God, are you sure 'tis where I belong?

Where else can I go to be able
To see so much beauty unfold?
From the break of dawn in the morning
'Till our sunsets all melt into gold?

Oh God, give me just one more hour...
One more day... One more year is my plea!
I want to enjoy all this splendor you gave us...
I just can't believe it's all free!
   Anne Koepsell

Free Spirit

When I first met you, I knew you would be
The most important part of me

You've taught me so much, but now you must go
I know if you stay that you will not grow

You're longing for freedom
I can't keep you here
If I hold you back
You won't persevere

It hurts deep inside
That you have to leave
But I will not cry
And I will not grieve

Instead I will keep you
Dear in my heart
And know that in memories
We will not part

Don't ever forget me, and what we have shared
Remember I loved you, remember I cared

Perhaps in another place in time
You will again be mine.
   Barbara Grapes

Jazz

The music for the moment, the music of the time,
the music that makes you think, the mood, the rhyme.

Listen and Hear, the beat, the pound.
Relax and Enjoy, the melodic sound.

Words can not explain the feelings felt,
Thoughts can not relate to the sound that melts.

Rhythm and blues is alright for some,
But I need the music that's on the one.

Sometimes I sit and furiously sought,
through the sound that doesn't need words to convey its thought.

It moves me, it soothes me, it helps my see;
then when all is at war I have the peace within me.

Grover; and Sandborn; the list never ends,
Najee; and ole Miles, I miss you my friend.

When I'm sitting with my buddies, just hanging around;
For hours we kick that Bee-Bop sound.

From the "J", to the "A", to the "Z", and the "Z";
Jazz in its many forms is shear poetry.

Next time you're alone, waiting for time to past;
put you feet up, dim the lights, and enjoy the jazz.
   Danette C. Tucker

Dangerous Weapons are Constant Reminders of Violence

What's inside of you certainly does matter.
The negative 3's and 4 letter words do penetrate.
Your explosiveness, assaults and attacks do invade.
Death, paralyzation and scars can't be retracted.

Violence, hate and prejudice is the world most dangerous weapons.
Visual expressions is the minds constant reminder
Isolation and distance does not render a cure.
Obedience to oneself to be honest is great power.

Learned experience of kindness and peace is your greatest teacher.
Evolving to practice patience and endurance will break the cycle.
Passage of life conquers denial, apathy and pain.
Consciousness within must balance with perception and method.
   Beverly A. Johnson-Finley

The Dark Path

The land is dark, black and cold.
The night is frightening, very bold.
I walk down road near barron ground,
The land is lifeless, there is no sound.

I wish to see a bit of light,
A tiny morsel for me to site.
I fear the darkness will steal my soul,
But wait not yet I have some hope.

I see some light beyond the hills,
It shines so bright, the skies' revealed.
I see life forming in fields of green,
The land is but a luxurious scene.

With trees swaying in the wind,
Creatures gathering deprived of sin.
And birds with happy chirping sounds,
In rays of sunlight shining down.

Although it's now a brighter place,
I keep on walking to my dull pace.

Jason Barry

One Night

Starlight spreading over big black sky,
The night's promise is deep with the darkness laughing.

Into the gully with the pale moonglow,
Skipping over rocks we know exist, yet cannot see.

Down to the meadow where the tall grass sways,
In the expansiveness we run, tripping
over each other's shadows until they meld.

Daylight is flooding our resting eyes,
We stare, at what we knew better not seeing.

Candace Nadon

Rose

I look at and remember the rose,
The one I laid down beside him.
The one that meant good-bye.
I remember how I felt
When the rose was handed to me,
How I didn't want to let it go.
I knew that if I put it down,
That my world would be gone.
A blur of love and hate,
Life and death.
Oh how I hate the word death
And now, the word rose.
Though it may smell of sweetness,
It means the end,
A way of saying good-bye differently,
A way of showing love to somebody
Who cannot feel it anymore.
A way of saying I care and
I will love and miss you forever.

Jennie Dominic

The Miracle

Last night a miracle took place on earth
The miracle of miracles called birth
Tucked down below the bosom of my wife
Lay still inside of her the miracle of life
A message came to her from up above
A message of the miracle of love
It said; "Now is the time for
you to bring upon the earth
The miracle of miracle called birth"

Alton Lander

Prayers For A Mental Breakdown

Why can't she slay the invisible demon,
The one she doesn't know she's fighting?
Why can't she say what's in her heart,
even though she can't look inside to see what's there?
And why does she try so hard to hide
What she so desperately wants someone to see?

Could it be she was too young to know
When her innocence was taken from her;
Or was it the mind that mercifully
Blocked what it knew the soul couldn't beat to see?
For how could she stand to look into the gaping
crack in the earth? The chasm of emotional depth.
Or worse, perhaps, to see what's on the other side,
the possibility of what might have been.

For when the flesh is cut, it bleeds a brilliant red,
a passionate call to action.
But the soul bleeds an invisible blood,
its cry for help goes unnoticed.
Even, perhaps, by the soul itself —
the soul of the invisible warrior.

Carol Pendergrass Caster

God's Rose

The roses that bloom in our garden,
   The ones that you tended with care,
Have a beauty and wonderful fragrance
   That to nothing I can compare.

They stand so proud and majestic,
   Their blooms reach up toward the sky,
The colors so vibrant and glorious,
   People exclaim as they pass them by.

I believe you were one of God's roses
   That he saved and nurtured with love,
Then he plucked you from his earth's garden
   To brighten his heaven above.

In a land that knows no sorrow,
   No more tears or bodily pain,
God placed this rose to bloom forever-
   Earth's loss was heaven's gain.

Juanita Weston

A Lightening Before Death

The clouds of night were falling fast,
The pain of the victim could not last.
The light of day was long since past
The turn of the evening tide.

The eyes of the young man were distant and vague,
His sand colored hair was moistened and bathed,
His dreaming dark eyes are far from land,
The nurse knew that death was soon at hand.

The clouds of night were distant and dark,
As the ship moved in full sail towards the approaching land,
His trembling voice calls, "I hear the song of the Lark!"
Its song a vestige of his native land.

The approaching strange land is not his home,
His footsteps have taken him far from there.
But his yearning heart would back again roam
To what in all his travels is still past compare.

The captain shouts for more speed in the sails,
The ship comes nearer to the approaching aid.
But the anxious father meets the nurse, who wails,
"The Star has fallen. But it fell, unafraid!"

Angelique Warner

"Car Accident Heart"

Your Mother's heart is broken
The pieces scattered all about
Every memory, every thought, every dream
My son, it's unbelievable
They should fit so easily
And yet somehow
With every piece I try to place
The space between is always wide
Will these spaces ever mend?
Never + this is the way
They will stay.

Irene Koziol

The Rose

The time I set eyes on you, and how my time had froze. Of all the pretty things I thought. A flowers what I chose.

I saw your face so plain, and beautiful, and precious like real fine meadows, and so I reached into my heart and gave to you it's petals

And then I saw your eyes, and how they showed no grief, so then I reached into my heart, and gave to you a leaf.

So then I saw your body, and I pictured many gems, so then I reached into my heart, and gave to you the stem.

And then I took my loving hands to protect your heart from being torn, and reached into this heart of mine, and gave to you the thorns.

So now my flower is complete. This one that I have chose. I look into the heart of yours, and see a precious rose.

Daniel P. Crockett

Daybreak

The cool stillness of morning.
The quiet opening of day's door.
The silent increase of lights intensity.
The murmuring of nature's voices.
The soft push of early breezes.
The still click of life's locks releasing.
The rising mists of day's yawning.
The red sky searing the dark crust of night.
The blinking eyes of early morning children.
The footfalls at day's silent birth.

Carney B. Jackson

In the Sky

The rain, the birds that always seem to fly.
The rainbows, the burning sun are always in the sky.
The days and nights that always go by
are all results of what's in the sky.
Why there is moonlight, we wonder why
because of that wonderful, beautiful sky.
Why there are stars way up so high
because of that glorious, elegant sky.
Those beautiful clouds so precious to I
are way up there in that lovely sky.
The amazing things I see with my very own eyes
are nothing compared to the things in the skies,
That shooting star, that comet, and that beautiful butterfly.
You can see all of these up in the sky.
To view the world, to see the world, to be the world.
If your up in the sky you'll see so much more.
You'll see so much more to die for.

Alexander William Bowers

Untitled

The reality of a lion killing a dear
    the reality of a bird in flight
the reality of the warmth of the sun
    the reality of the tides of the ocean
the reality of death ever present
    the reality of all that is meaningless
the reality of time as sheer nonsense
    the reality of history and its distortions
the reality of hate and the price paid
    the reality of love and its misuse
the reality of the past and its distance
    the reality of the future and how it controls
the reality of the genius who realized life passed them by
    the reality of dreams lost
the reality of dreams fulfilled
    the reality of never experiencing true silence
the reality of truth in its purest form
    the reality that nothing does not exist
the reality that its all been done before

Jeff Procida

To Know Our Frailty

"To know our frailty" causes pain,
The resurrection, someday our gain.
God, on the throne where He belongs;
Welcoming His sheep to His heavenly home.

"To know our frailty" we decide,
In who we wish to confide;
A christian friend will abide,
To the rules a church, sets aside.

"To know our frailty" leaves us weak.
My tomorrows, uncertain, completely bleak.
As a strong oak tree, I must remain meek.
When I look at "you" I want submit to defeat,
Our ministry together, is not complete.

"To know our frailty" leaves room for change.
This world a big wide open range,
We don't have to feel completely strange;
The Holy Spirit, God's terrain,
Christlike. I must remain.

Bonnie L. Hurt

Truth I've Learned

Truly the truth shall set you free,
The revelation of truth stands so beautifully.
Oh if "I" could die enough to stand in "true",
with compassion to myself felt through and through.
Giving birth to peace, birth to love,
freedom's birth by graces above.
Then I could stand alone; naked with God,
all could look on and we'd not seem odd.
Truth lived and spoken in the highest degree,
stands straight alone for all to see.
In joy I'd cry and God would smile,
For ego died at long last while.
This born of truth that's been taught to me,
is the infant truth I wish to be.

Gabriel B. Santiago

What Love Really Means

Sometimes on this road of life,
The road gets rough and long:
It is loved one and friends like you:
Who keep our faith and courage strong

Sometimes we fail to mention,
Seems that words just will not come:
To express our thanks and gratitude
For deeds of kindness you have shown.

Please try to understand
What I really want to say:
Friends are more precious than silver and gold
When you can call upon them night and day.

Many thanks to you,
May God bless you over and over again:
I know what love really means,
You have shown by being such a friend.

Antoinette Young

Christmas

With armor bright and saber's flash
    the Roman Legions came.
To conquer world with sword and lash
    in Augustus Ceaser's reign.
On that beautiful night of long ago,
    when angels sang their best.
To the greatest power the world would know
    held there at Mary's breast.

Brave men have died for loved ones fair,
    for country, home or wife.
But never could their deaths compare
    to God great sacrifice.
Born of man as the star shone bright
    among his earthly foes.
God greatest gift to man that night,
    lay wrapped in swaddling clothes.

Yet now as then, the world endeavors
    from his gracious ways to part.
Is Christ within you, safe forever
    in the manger of your heart?

Arthur McCrea Johnson

Loss

An overload of negativity fills my soul,
    the shadow of loss hangs above me.

Hope still exists in my heart,
    but my mind can't handle the chaos.

It shuts down.
All that is left is my love to hold on.

Is it enough to carry through?
The answer will soon follow.

If sorrow shall overcome,
    my mind may remain shut off
    for my heart need not exist any longer.

To pray for happiness is all I can do now.

It's not in my hands any longer,
    it's all up to you.

Edward P. Sinnett

Only A Dream

The time has come
The signs have been placed before my eyes.
I have been invited to be woken.
Surroundings have become delightful.
My skin has taken to its ways.
Air is no longer frigid
hands are no longer numb.
There is hope for me
There is such a thing as opportunity.
I have hibernated in long sleeves,
All the while my mind had been swept away
With the snow flakes and frost.
I have almost awoken.
As I look down inches above the paper.
I can see my many reflections
Almost accepting their truths.
As my ice melts I feel the sun like no other time before.
The time has come to grow beyond
My supposive limitations, to live my dreams
At last, but first I must be woken

John Daley

The Promise

Nature passes over time.
The sky mists by the mountain
As thunder echoes in the distance.
A brilliant light pierces through the clouds,
And the solitude of His beauty shines.
Graced by what seems an eternity, Spring triumphantly
breaks man's doubting belief of infinity
with answers strengthened by all present.
Just as an eaglet tumbles ridged-rocks through space,
the wind cradles his solo flight to soar high
over the mountain top.
By believing we come to understand.
For age is a witness of time allowing
wisdom to flow true.

Denise Worner

Have You Ever

Have you ever wanted to see,
The sky open up and deposit your dream?
Have you ever sat and thought,
Wished you had one thing, neither you got?
Have you ever drank and danced,
Enjoyed yourself and found romance?
Have you ever made love so right,
That later on you got in a fight?
Have you ever been so scared,
To let yourself go to someone,
and found out they didn't care?
Have you ever been caught in a dream,
To, barely escape the night's domain?
Have you ever been hypnotized,
By the cool of the air, and a rain so light?
Have you ever listened to a train's whistle blow,
Just to fade in the distance ever so slow?
Have you ever?

Herbert Randall

Silence

Silent, hear the chirping, hear
the sound of the wind
blowing against the trees
and leaves that have fallen.
    You hear nothing but
the wind carrying the
chirping of crickets.

Criket Ursry

50 Years

Fifty years of better and worst of times,
the songs our hearts sang.
The Beauty our eyes could find,
helped overcome the bad that came.

The walk along the path of life,
brought back memories of our strife,
a newborn we held in our arms,
picnics, games and work on the farm.

Remember the fence we built,
that the kids used for a swing.
Milking cows and the milk spilled,
couldn't cry, had a duck with a hurt wing.

The year of chicken pox and storms,
we faced them with determination.
Help came in all forms,
Because we held God in our meditation.

Edna Mae Norton

Painful Memories

Lying beside you, so close at your side,
The sound drifts in of the sea at high tide.
I reach out and touch you, your skin is so warm,
A breeze softly blows and you're moving your arm.
Away from me now, you roll on your back.
I slowly get up, I quietly pack.
I'm leaving you now, I'm saying "Goodbye."
Don't ask me explain, you know the reasons why.
This whole scene's a nightmare, I cry, you cry, too.
I walk out the door, don't look back at you.
I saw you again, just the other day,
I turned my head and walked away.
Like a ghost from the past, your face haunts me still.
And I supposed, my love, it always will.

Jill M. Bacott

"Teen Love"

If you only knew how I feel inside,
the tears and pains that I can't hide.

I would do anything in the world for you,
with hopes that you feel this way, too.

When I look at you my heart just pounds,
with fears that you won't be around.

I've never felt this way before,
and I never want us to ignore.

You've heard my cries in the night,
longing for you to be in my sight.

I know we're always going to have bad days,
words might come out that we don't mean to say.

These are the days to don't listen to me,
just shut your ears and let me be.

It makes me feel happy knowing that you care,
it gives me feelings I can hardly bare

If you only knew how I feel inside,
You would never, ever, want to say goodbye.

Cherie Taylor

In My Garden...

In my garden grow only the rarest and loveliest flowers:
The tender ones that extend passionate petals to the warmth of the sun
   and the glow of the moon;
The kind ones that support and defend even the unworthy from the
   thunder and the rain;
The princely ones that grace the simplest of gardens with their
   radiance and exquisite form;
The spirited ones that refresh the seasoned with their vigor and
   vitality; and,
The intriguing ones that delight me and endear themselves to my
   very heart.

But in the garden of life, thrive other flowers
   that endanger the delicate blossoms I so lovingly nurture and grow:
The impenetrable ones, difficult and uncompromising;
The cruel that abruptly disrupt the peace and harmony I have
   painstakingly sowed;
The evil that derive pleasure from inflicting pain and suffering to
   those around them; and,
The devious ones that mislead even the most virtuous and pure.
Let me sustain my garden with love, warmth, and compassion,
So my blossoms may eternally thrive, prosper, and grow.

Carmen A. Vazqueztell

The Thing

The thing is, we misunderstand;
   The Thing is not born of a gland.
The Thing is walking hand in hand;
   The Thing is "footprints" in the sand.

The Thing is, lyrics often lie;
   The Thing is not "pie in the sky."
The Thing is reticent, it's shy;
   The Thing is naked to the eye.

The Thing is, people "drive" too fast;
   The Thing is, we hate to be last.
The Thing is to prevail upon the caste;
   The Thing is to correct "color contrast."

The Thing is, "Things" lead us astray;
   The Thing is just to please the day!
The Thing is, "thought" gets in the way;
   The Thing is, love is risque.

The Thing is quite misunderstood;
   The Thing is like seasoned firewood.
The Thing is called "intrinsic good;"
   "The Thing" is peace and brotherhood.

Curtis C. Lundbeck

Fishing and Resting

When I'm tired and need of rest.
The thing that I like to do best, is get my
Fishing rod and creel and sharpen the hooks
Made from the finest steel and go fishing.

To many people fishing is a waste of time.
But to me, I relax when I wet a line.
To see the trout rise to my fly. to see
The eagle in the sky. To hear the bird call
to its mate. Lets me know that I'm not
to late to let my spirit rest and
get my troubles off my chest.

As I return from my fishing,
I never find my self wishing,
That I was some place else.
All my troubles have ceased,
and now I enjoy my inner peace.

James A. Sprigler

Ageless Moments

These are times when we conceive,
The thoughts, and do the things that
we've wrought.

They may have seemed impossible,
they may've been awkward too; but deep
within our ageless mind a stirring did occur.

We thought of times when we could
do, from the ridiculous to the sublime.
so off we'd go to do what we do;
forgetting the age of the mind.

'Tis there that the moments we use,
are never subjected to age; because as
we ponder our thoughts, the moments
remain in our hearts.

Clarice L. Williams

Sounds From A Sleeping City

The mournful echo of a passing train,
The ticking of a clock in an empty room,
A lost voice calling midst the falling rain.

The piercing of a bullet through a stagnant brain,
The snuffing of a candle in the gath'ring gloom,
The mournful echo of a passing train.

The cry of a soul in mortal pain,
A child born dead from a mother's womb,
A lost voice calling midst the falling rain.

"An eye for an eye" — and another is slain
As the condemned await an unknown doom
Listening to the echo of a passing train.

Why should I live? Is life in vain?
Or am I merely a soul for whom
A lost voice calls midst the falling rain?

The ending chord in life's old refrain:
Raindrops falling on a silent tomb,
The mournful echo of a passing train,
A lost voice calling midst the falling rain.

Frederic De Feis

What A Game!

The score stood 20-19 with two minutes left to dread.
The Tigers were down, but driving quickly down the spread.
One score and the Tigers would dance with glee.
But this would not be easy because of the Lions, Tommy D.

The first pass was thrown to big Pete.
However, it was incomplete.
The second and third plays went the same,
Which caused the team to go insane.

With twelve seconds left, it was fourth down.
The Tigers had to go for it, or else they would frown.
As fourth down had begun, all the Tigers wished for was 23 yards.
Once again, who saves the day? It was mighty Johnny Cards.

With 1 second left to play,
The Tigers brought in big Gary May.
If the field goal was good, the Tigers would win.
But if it was missed, there would be team chagrin.

So Gary stepped up to kick the ball,
And the whole crowd exclaimed, "Don't fall!"
Oh, he wished for the ball to go in,
But he did not have that kind of luck. The Lions win!

Joseph Tursi

Thirteen

It was 1961, dreams of Camelot had just begun.
The times were lean, but not a boy's dreams.
He awoke to the sound of cries, tears from his
Momma's eyes, and he knew things would never be
the same.

Thirteen, when his Daddy died,
Thirteen, when the child inside him died,
Thirteen is too young to be a man.

The rifles cracked the air, as his family stood in
prayer, but a folded flag was all they had to share.

Thirty years have come and gone, but those memories
linger on; of a childhood lost and a life forever
changed.

Thirteen, when his Daddy died,
Thirteen, when his Momma cried,
Thirteen is too young to be a man.

The time has come at last to let those memories pass,
for a child is born again inside a forty year old man.
And with the grace of God, he can learn to dream again.

Ed Jerome

God Sees You

Every heartache that you feel;
The times you think love's not real;
God sees you.
Every lonely tear that falls;
And in your heart you've built up walls;
God sees you.
God sees every trail and every pain;
He wants you to see that there's much more to gain.
We cannot look with human eyes;
For only by faith can we realize,
That these lonely times of intense pain,
Are given to us that we may gain;
The knowledge of God's saving grace;
And the joy of seeing His face.
We have this peace in knowing;
That God's grace is always showing.
And that no matter what you're going through;
God is right there beside you.

Eric Mackey

The Titanic "A Survivor's Story"

It was a clear but gloomy night,
The Titanic sank in the pale moonlight.
As I heard a cry ring through the air,
I hung my head in despair.
Women and children first I heard,
All the sudden I heard not a single word.
Everyone began to flee, that is everyone except me.
I calmly walked toward the bow, not knowing what to do now,
They said the Titanic was unsinkable,
But for some reason that seemed unthinkable.
The Titanic seemed to be losing float,
So I decided to climb aboard a lifeboat.
As they lowered us into the sea,
Everything seemed so blurry to me.
When I finally realized what was going on,
The Titanic was almost gone.
When I saw the ship's stern go down,
I thought of all the people who drown.
Today the Titanic is at the bottom of the Atlantic Ocean,
Far, far away from all the stress and commotion!

Coleman W. Vestal

Forever Mom

As the sun goes down and the moon appears, the wind blowing through
the trees, I see a shadow following me. I hear a voice calling from far, far away, it's echoing back from above. I feel my foot prints being lead by a hand. I can feel her spirit guiding me, helping me with all I have to do. She left me behind with only a thought, "Do all that you can and do all that you can do, you can only accomplish what you set out to do. Follow your dreams for that's all that you have and remember the good things and not the bad." I never thought I'd miss her so much but I know she's better off. I can't help but think of her, for she will always be in my heart, my thoughts and in my dreams. No one will ever take her place. I loved the way she made me laugh and the patience to listen to me when I needed an ear. Her heart was filled with so much love it's hard to think she's gone. But now when I need to talk to her or tell her some exciting news all I have to do is look up into the sky and talk to her like she were there with me. I will miss her so much and keep her so deep in my heart. The memories of her will never be forgotten, I have so many of them I will cherish them forever and forever and share them with all who loved her. She taught me so much and helped me in so many different ways. She gave the gift of love and she gave me the gift of life. For she is my mother and I will love her forever.

Jo-Ann (Rahn) Losson

Pleasant Rest

Pleasant rest my love. The night is yours to slumber.
    The trials are troubles of tomorrow will try to take you under.
Pleasant rest my love. I'll watch you as you sleep.
    For while you're gone, I know for sure your soul is his to keep.
Pleasant rest my love. A new day has begun.
    Close your eyes and you can see all the treasures you have won.
Pleasant rest my love. I'll keep you close in mind.
    The friend in you that now is gone, again I'll never find.
Pleasant rest my love. May you drown in gentle dreams.
    May the love and strength that you possess put your mind at ease.
Pleasant rest my love. May angels carry you home.
    The wisdom and love you've shared with us will never be unknown.
So pleasant rest my love.

Arlene Richards

Slack

If I could, Id take it all back,
the true love that I gave , and give it slack
If I must, Id back away from you,
leave myself and think of what I could undue.
To kill true love that I gave to you,
you tore it up so there wasn't us two.
To kill true love I treated so bad,
now I love you, is that so bad?
As I sit and watch the rain,
I feel the love, I feel the pain.
How can I forget all the past,
the love we had, I thought Id last.
I know you can't help but say goodbye,
but you do see, the tears in my eyes?
Open your heart and let me in,
have faith in us, and just give in.
I can't bare to be just friends,
cause the candle burns both ends.
I'll change for you to get you back,
will take the time to give it slack.

Jennifer Ann Ball

Christmas Tree In The Snowfilled Yard

He lay six foot stretched from head to toe,
The twinkle long since passed his eyes,
The clock and spring his dearest foe,
With a forest smell in green he lies.

In his day he was the envy, a fine spruce,
The sickle felled his seasoned roots,
The corpse fell a short fly from the noose,
Silent cheers, alone, from the "Humbug" brutes.

I'd like to remember him as he could light the room,
Promote a childish grin,
Mothers eyes to God as she pushed the broom,
And he'd be jolly through thick or thin.

I refuse to mind his pining later days,
I'd rather strike them from the page,
I'll record him from his gent like sways,
And not in death the bloody rage.

A wake I shunt think they'll provide,
Soon forgotten all he'd done,
Though I'll never forget the day he died,
Prideless priceless memoirs won.

John P. Malone

My Little Sister Bonnie

When I think back and remember
The very first time I laid eyes on you
I just knew I'd love you forever

Together forever, as sisters I knew it would be

Then you were sick for so long
And fighting for your little life

The pain you went through — it definitely was not right
I'd never believed in a million years you were going to go

When I remember your little laughs and little smiles
The tears begin to flow

I want you to know that I miss you so very much
And my love for you — no one will ever know

Bonnie, our love is a love only sisters share
No one will ever take that love away

No one will ever take my memories, they are here to stay

You are with me every day — right here in my heart
And you'll be here, Sister as long as we're apart

Then one day I will come and I'll see you again

Together for eternity as sisters in heaven
Until then, I'll always love you "Sissy" "Little Bonnie Bear"

Jennifer C. Tipton

Two Families

From the elegance of life through
the walls of doubt a shimmering
voice is crying out.
Two families put together as one
and half of this family has just begun.
With a mother not really a mother,
brothers only half brothers,
and a father who could not be of bother.
Although half of this family
remains the other half will never be regained.
So we suffer with agony and pain.

Jennifer Parcell

Love And War Even The Score

Achilles hung fierce Hector from the high tail of a horse;
The war's outlandish sleight of hand
Could not alter the downhill course
Of action, which began upon the kidnap of the wife
Of Menelaus, whose honour required all that dirt and strife.

The worst were saved; no lecher was a man enough to slay-
Each soldier wanted heroes' hides to be his valiant victory.
A hero could not hero be, unless he'd slain the best;
And that is why the best were slain,
And left were all the rest.

So, now, the greatest, bravest men
Are fighting many wars;
The best are planning ways to take
Lives of the best on other shores.

As lovely woman stoops to folly, hearty man swoops in for war;
Now as her passion rises, mounting, his horse dies, and he's no
more.
The two of them are star-crossed loves, the stuff of Shakespeare,
that's for sure;
A love can never be requited when its lover are at war.

Catherine Mizgerd

The Perfect Poem

I want to write a poem
  The world will want to read,
I wonder what to write about—
  A topic's what I need.

It seems each thought that comes to mind
  Has been set down quite well,
What else is left for me to say?
  What more is there to tell?

In everything I think about
  I always hear a rhyme,
But someone else has heard it too—
  It happens every time.

So I'll keep searching every day
  For just the words I need,
I'll write the perfect poem
  The world will want to read.

Fern Herrington

Why Can't The Lonely Get Together

Oh why can't the lonely get together
The world would be a brighter place
If the lonely men and women got together
Everywhere we would see a smiling face

There's a man sitting in his lonely room tonight
Just wishing he had someone he could love
While somewhere across town a woman is crying
She's so lonely as she gazes at the stars above

The pain of loneliness is a special kind
You feel as if there's no one who will share
Your lonely life you need someone to hold you tight
Someone who thinks you're special who will care

We're just human and we all need someone to love
Someone to be there when we're feeling blue
There's so many lonely people oh why can't they meet
One alone just can't be happy it takes two

So all you lonely people listen to me now
It's not hopeless there's a lot of us out there
We can beat the loneliness together if we try
We can win this fight don't give up in despair

Edna Kreiter

The Scattered Stars In My Life

Fireflies party in the meadow
Their disco lights shine on my shadow
When the dancers go away
I rest in a carpet of hay

Diamonds burn on the black curtain of mother earth
I wish for touching them
But they are just too far to reach
Like a goal that you can never achieve

I think about the road ahead of me
There is still along journey
But those diamonds are still encouraging me
They are my destiny
I promise myself and say
"I'll catch you someday"

Esther Huang

The Rose

The petals are soft and the thorns are so sharp
Their looks have much beauty, as the sounds of a harp
They're given with care to cure someone's woes
That's the main reason God created the rose

They're a sign of devotion and a sign of goodwill
The feelings they deliver can't be found in a pill
They come in all colors, even sent to our foes
But with a much different meaning, God's creation, the rose

They are good for the mind and they're good for the soul
And in the fine art of love they play a huge role
They're given in friendship and they are good for our lows
Our Creator was thinking when He invented the rose

The softness of petals and the contrast of thorns
Are held by the stem and the leaves it adorns
The scent is translucent and sweet to the nose
There's no greater beauty than that of God's rose

Donald L. Foster

I Am Here

One day I was walking
Then I began talking
Not knowing who was stalking
But peace in my heart began balking.

The voice I heard, that was stalking me
Caused me to look up in the tree
I began to wonder
As the voice began to sound like thunder.

Then the voice began to say
As my heart began to sway
My son, you are the apple of my eye
So in my heart I began to cry.

The voice then began to say, be of good cheer
So, my heart began to fear
Again I heard, "My son, my son, I am here,
I am here, I am here"

Everett H. Scruggs

My Father

When I was little we used to hug
then I grew a little and he would just shrug
Can't he hear my silent plea?
Don't say he stopped loving me
I would sit around and cry
He walked out the door and didn't say good-bye
I tried to make it the way it used to be
Please, somebody say he still loves me!

Jennifer Graham

Unbounded

I glide into depths of mighty oceans
  Then surface upon moonbeam lighted shoals
I float above the breath of angels
  Free from within anger's incipient goal
I rise to view our fertile sphere
  From a Nebula atoll
Then fall softly as a petal into
  This hortensial bowl

I stride the earth discovering the ancients
  Footprints in the sands
As one by one they stepped to be entered
  On humanities roll -
From before the beginning to
  Beyond the end
  Linking past and future with
  Every unbounded soul
  Joseph Binder

Homecoming

I searched for a peace that I could not find
Then the precious Lord Jesus said child you
Are mine
I know of your hurts, the tears and the pain
But thru all your trials, my truth still remains
I'll never forsake you nor leave you alone
And a day will come when I will call you home
Oh what a joyous time your homecoming will be
As we welcome you there, my father and me
The streets will be paved with the sparkle of gold
And there in my home you will never grow old
No tear drops from sadness will fall from your eyes
There will be no more sickness and nobody dies
Be strong and be faithful as the time dwindles down
For my Father awaits you with your robe and your
Crown.

  Barbara A. Bailey

Morning Walk

Early each morning if you take a long walk
Then you and the Lord can have a little talk
At this time the air is clear and your mind is too
So it is not very hard for Him to get through

Words don't really have to be spoken
because each thought He will surely know
If your mind is not filled with yesterday's cares
Then many new things with Him you can share

Things that happened yesterday are just memories
Some will be remembered a lifetime through
Then others will shortly disappear
Just like the morning dew

If we hold on to everything
Then new thoughts can't find a way through
But if some things are pushed away
We make room for a brighter day

There might be times when we almost have to start life anew
If we put Him first this He will help us to do
He will make us a pathway, it might not always be bright
but if we will follow it leads to the light

  Claude Carter

Poem About Children

If you don't know straight up,
then you're like a child who had no bringing's up.
You'd follow the leader into a pit
and easily deceived, you'd laugh about it.

Is there a secret to the fountain of life?
I assure you so, as day will turn to nite.
Do we all have a guide when we are alone?
Partly in knowledge of right and wrong.

The children know there is peace of mind
and a peacemaker is thankful many a time..
The clever talebearer may say to you,
"Where once went something wicked now is new."

A child's imagination need not be cast down
and the gift of love can turn a frown.
Their capacity for learning will never end
once they learn how to read and understand.

So kiss good night and tuck them in
most worthy of a peaceful grin,
The sweetest sleep I wish for them
and to all who care for little children.

  Douglas K. DeVine

Iliad and the Odyssey

'Twas a time long ago in ancient Greece,
there dwell great King Agamemnon,
he hath such passion for one lady,
she but was called helen of troy,
this lady caused a mighty war,
Ulysses the bravest warrior
there ever could have been,
he bolted with great fury,
his strength and bravery won the war,
for twixt the achaeans and the trojans,
this battle raged for many a year,
twenty years hence Ulysses returned,
he had encountered the many creatures of the sea,
he had fought the evil cyclops single handedly,
and upon his heroic homecoming,
there was hesitation, forgotten passion,
too many years had he been on this
long, mythic, and legendary odyssey,
for he alone will be remembered
this ancient hero of Greece.

  Celine Rose Mariotti

Ever Love...

There is always a feeling we keep so very deep,
there is always a word, we never could forget,
the soft whisper heard in some phrases long lost,
bringing closer the memories have been saved behind.

Like to have all the world locked up in your chest,
looking at the Universe giving birth and reborn,
to hear the weak moan of any grieving bird
and heal the bird wounds, to see it fly again.

But it is also love, the soul that gives console
when dries some tears shed, or relieving a pain,
the merciful smile of a sincere friend
by offering your love, expecting nothing else.

The nostalgia your soul have concealed so long,
the most precious illusion in your passion repressed,
it will be compensated with something even purest,
some almost sublime, but very human too:
To see in other brother, the smiling of the Lord.

  Esther Ortega-Lage

Weeping Willow

Weeping Willow dry your tears
There is something to calm your fears
Weeping Willow please don't die
Just because people lie
Weeping Willow please don't go away
Just because you do not want to stay
Weeping Willow please don't go
Oh, Weeping Willow I love you so
Weeping Willow dry your tears
There is something to calm your fears
Are you crying because he could not stay?
Are you crying because he had to go away?
Oh, Weeping Willow can't you see?
How much the pain of you leaving will hurt me!
Oh, Weeping Willow I love you so
Promise you'll never let go!

Joanne Bayer

"Queen Beauty"

There is beauty everywhere for the eye to see.
There is the breathtaking beauty of the sunset.
The strong rolling waves of the seven seas.
The first heartfelt kiss that you never forget.

The majestic horse running perfectly in stride.
The eagle soaring overhead on high.
The reflection on the ocean's night tide
Of the stars shining above in the sky.

The classical music of violin.
The soft and tender sounds of a singing swallow.
The light breeze of the summer wind.
The winding forest path that is a joy to follow.

These beauties are fabulous and hard to beat.
There are many things that cannot contend.
But with these beauties, you do compete.
This sincere message to you I do send.

After looking deeply into your eyes,
I viewed a beauty which made all others seem inferior.
And the thing I want you to realize
Is that, compared to all other beauty, you are superior.

Joseph Gatto

Johnny B.

A family was moving away
There was a party that same day
Jaime was looking for him
If he didn't show up she would be grim
He walked in the door expecting to be fed
His blond hair draped over his forehead
His eyes shining like a starry night
We stared with all our might
I was dying to kiss his cheek
But I felt too weak
I watched him play a game
Hoping some day he would have fame
He was standing with his back to me
His name was Johnny B.
When we were leaving
My parents thought I was grieving
I wasn't but I was crushed
The car ride on the way home was hushed
Hoping to see him just out of the blue
Wish I knew

Jennifer Denault

The Big Boom

Into darkness and empty space,
there was nothing, nary a trace;
not a dust speck, not a sound,
until an explosion turned time around.

Then came planets, moons and stars,
followed by gravity and motor cars;
rockets and spaceships, a curious crew,
adventuring outward, seeking the new.

For many years further out they went;
traveling forward on a galactic bent;
observing nebulae and watching old suns explode,
new sights did greet them where ever they rode.

If only they'd known, when they began the space race,
as they worked their way forward at a feverish pace,
that the universe they lived in and wondered about,
was inside a mason jar, with no way out.

Gale Toller Rowell

Sign of a Bad Year

Where there should have been happiness
    there was sadness
Where there should have been laughter
    there were tears
Where there should have been birth certificates
    there was sad lettering
Where there should have been cigars
    there were wilted flowers
Where there should have been cribs
    there were graves
Where there should have been blue or pink
    there was nothing

Ashley Miller

I Promise...He Would Have Said, Is Saying Now

Dear, I know I wasn't always there for you,
There were times I let you bear the hardships all alone,
But I promise now that I'll never leave you.
In your heart I've made a permanent home.

When you first said "Daddy" I was there to hear it.
Later you may have thought I wasn't listening
But I promise that whenever you call me now
Every word I'll hear within my very being.

It's true I may not have seen your first steps
But when you take these first steps to healing
I promise I will hold your hand
And all your pain in my heart I'll be feeling.

Now I know you think you weren't there enough
But a stranger there every moment could not have outdone
I promise that every moment was like a thousand,
And it was more than enough; no guilt, my son.

Candace Olivia Hardin

Memoirs of a Heart: Note Book Stories

My heart couldn't bear it.
The sorrow you put me through.
When I wrote your name 1001
times, I thought "What else can I
do?" I'd tell you my feelings, I'd tell
you my life, someday I'd be your wife.
And the next day you'd act so
suave and cool when no one was there.
But, when you stopped talking
my heart stopped hoping, I knew
it was to much to bear.

Areina Cabezas

The World In Angel's Wings

If I could encompass the world with angel's wings,
There would be no hatred and prejudice seen.

Only sun shining off golden wings,
Would warm heart and souls of all human beings.

No shadows of doubt or guilt would show,
For all would be seen in a golden glow.

Our skin would shine and appear to be,
The same as the person standing next to me.

We all could then, get on with our lives,
Less quick to blame, now to harmonize.

For hasn't mankind spent far too long,
Finding excuses to hate and not get along?

With excuses gone, a calm atmosphere,
We can stop and see why God put us here.

Beth Reelhorn Hawley

Changing of the Guard

This could be the day
There's a changing of the guard
Life is at stake
The last card to drop.... Drops hard

We've been fighting from the beginning
And to deal with the end
It takes Making...Bending...Breaking rules
The circle's soon to start again

This could be the day
There's a changing of the guard
Life is at stake
The last card to drop...Drops hard

Babies now are finished
That never got a start
From a Mother and a Father
With love in their Hearts

This could be the day
There's changing of the guard
Life is at stake
The last card to drop...

David Jones

Hangin'

I can't give up on my brother man
There's a king which lies in him
But deep inside, his mind is tide
To a world that has no end.

I won't let go of the spirit and soul
That bore my nature of kin
I can't give up on my brother man
Cause he needs my helping hand.

I won't let go of my brother man
There's a mighty warrior waiting to come out
But in his head his will is dead
And hope has been tossed about.

I can't give up on the flesh and bones
That's able to roar like the sea
And through my fight and pressured nights
My brother man best not give up on me.

Cinetrea D. Grace

What Do You See?

I see you watching, but what do you see
There's a picture in my mind, it's a picture of me
Sometimes I'm so brave, and in others there's fear
The future looks cloudy, and then it is clear

Is it the money we're after, or the thrill of the game
Those who have faith, are happy just the same
So why all this fuss, over retirement ahead
Why not enjoy life, and not worry instead

I guess it's the unknown, and it scares us clear through
We don't know what we need, or what we'll have to do
We just know we want it, and have this great need
We're blinded by want, and ignore our own greed

And there lies the answer, to the puzzle of life
Greed choking out faith, and causing us strife
The pain gets so bad, and our ego soon dies
In our picture of life, we soon filter out lies

Now we know the answer, but no one believes
The louder we tell them, the less they receive
My final conclusion, that makes me feel good
Let's all lead by example, you know that we should!!

Bud Dauphin

Why Did You Go?

I write this poem for you today
There's just too much I have to say
You were always there when I needed you
Now you're gone, I don't know what to do
I have feelings that you are near
I hear you whisper in my ear
Telling me that it's okay
That's not all I have to say
I miss you grandma, as you know
Tell me grandma, why did you go?

September ninth was the day
I did not know what to say
They told me the news, I did care
I got so mad, I had to swear
I locked myself in my room
I hit the wall and broke the broom
I blamed myself, I don't know why
All I could do was sit and cry
Tell me Grandma, I don't know
Can you tell me, Why did you go?

Jaclyn E. Thomas

I Am But Human

I am made of HEART: that love possess and pumps through my body and soul
I am made of a BRAIN: the mind that tells me what I know.
I am made of EYES: which can see the earth's beauty that surrounds me
I am made of a NOSE: which smells the fragrance of nature.
I am made of a MOUTH: that can express my feelings.
I am made of WORDS: that communication is based on.
I am made of SHOULDERS: to hold the burdens of the world and its children.
I am made of ARMS: which reach out to hold and to be held.
I am made of HANDS: to caress and touch.
I am made of LEGS: which carries my body where it is willing to go.
I am made of NERVES: that scream to feel touch.
I am made of EMOTION: which want to feel acceptance and love.
I am made of a SOUL: to wonder with during the night.
I am made of ANCESTORS: which created this world.
I am made of STORIES: of past and present to tell.
I am but a mere HUMAN: with which I will care for all the same
    but differently.
I am not PERFECT: for which I will make mistakes
I am ALIVE: so I will live.

Jenny Allen

The Defeat of Love

How do one as I, begin to love one so dear?
There's many of reasons to love and one so dear
Only if I had the courage and words to tell thee

When close to thee, love is so clear
There's none as beautiful as thee

Thy eyes blue as the sea
Thy hair so long, so beautiful
Thy body the finest of all

Only If I had the courage and words to tell thee
When face to face courage seem to vanish

The words I dare to say, defy the mouth
The hand so eager to write the words
I love you

If thou knew the heart of mind
thou would know my love is true

Since this can not be
thou must trust the words I write
The words I write is from my heart

The heart of mind is full of love
My heart belong to you.

Gary Chatman

Precious Jewels

Given by God to nourish and guide,
These jewels of life we cherish with pride;
Fruits of our love, the future will see,
For them to grow, we must set them free.

These wonderful gifts were placed in our trust,
Polishing these gems was an absolute must;
They grew and flourished with love and care,
Their beauty now shows with each special pair.

Placed in a setting - these jewels now shine,
Shaped and polished in such a short time;
Working together and blessed from above,
Held together with threads of God's love.

These stones so cherished by both you and me,
Their future unknown, only God can see;
Yes, with such beauty their lives unfold,
More precious to us than all the world's gold.

Clifton C. Schmitt

The Seasons

The seasons go in order,
they follow one by one.
Each three months are different,
its really lots of fun.

There are four all together.
One season is what we call spring,
were everything is reborn.
When mother nature does her thing.

Summer is next in line;
and the sun is hot, hot, hot.
It could get so humid,
sometimes you would think you'd rot.

Fall is really pretty,
when the leaves get red, orange, or brown
Animals are busy storing food,
while the leaves fall to the ground.

The winter is very cold,
when the rains turn to snow.
The sun hardly every comes out,
and the temperature goes down low.

Janelle Bonanno

I'm Sorry

I'm sorry for all the things I said.
They hurt you so much, I wish I was dead.
The pain I caused by getting mad.
I probably lost the chance with you,
    what little I had.
You hate me, despise me, or do what you may.
But I know the only thing that keeps me alive,
    is I love you anyway.
You probably hate me and don't want to see my face,
    all I know is I want out of this place.
To rid you of all the pain and suffering I gave.
I just want to loose my self in a maze of caves.
To hide my face from this world, spinning 'round.
But when they find me, I'll be ash on the ground.
With them thinking of what happened,
    but not knowing what's true.
The only thing they'll know is,

    I'm sorry and I love you.

David Shane Sutton

Birthing Field

Alone among the dewdrops fall the tears of broken dreams;
They issue forth from mountains tall and carve out mighty streams.

Within their courses wash away the hopes of all the ages,
The anguished cries of yesterday: The wisdom of the sages.

And yet the might rivulet bears softly on its shoulder
Two blossoms that cannot forget a knowledge that is older.

Though strong and swift the current be that rushes them along,
Beyond all rivers lies a sea which sings a sweeter song.

At last adrift on timeless waves, one entity combined,
They both recover from the staves of lands they left behind:

Eternal are the flowers twine, who to no deluge yield
And though they're neither yours nor mine, we are their birthing field.

John Croft Jr.

Yellow Marching Jonquils

The yellow jonquils came marching up my street today.
They marched right up to my door as if to say,
"Won't you come out and enjoy the day."

They marched next door to Miz Joy's gazebo and went all around and about it and then, they marched across the street and into Mr. Jim's little window seat.

Oh how wonderful it is to see the marching yellow jonquils swaying in the wind as they march down the street, over the vacant lot - making it look like a big bowl of sunshine.

Then they marched over to the church yard and gave it a golden halo hue, and up the block they marched and out of my view.
But I know the marching yellow jonquils are now marching up your street to you.

Joanna Moses Hughes

Untitled

On Summer nights I lay and watch
The twinkling stars that shine
I sail away on moonbeam ships
To other worlds I find

When I return by early light
A peace with me will stay
Because I know when darkness fall
Again, I'll sail away

Louise Harden

Untitled

The wise sit in circles around the fire of the night.
They read the flame of the mind.
They search the flame for more truth.
They hold to them the knowledge they possess. And use the fire as a mind sedative.

After the fire has burned and dawn creeps over the still land, the children come running by two and by three to gather the embers for the next generation.

They give to the land the bones of the dead and in return the land gives them their final resting bed.

Gathered in boxes are the embers of fires from generation past and though the children see no meaning their ancestors minds hold all the reason.

Corinne Marie Sandy

Postscript

Through high design or chance the amoeba's birth,
They say, took place some billion years ago.
This was the tiny spark upon the earth.

From which mankind at last began to grow.
As the planet cooled and the waters drained away
His hands and brains were shaped through ages slow

That left their marks on rocks and banks of clay.
Through dreary aeons at length he climbed to where
He stands and views the universe today,

The seeming master of the earth, the ground and air,
And now the final veil is opened wide;
The secret of the atom is laid bare.

Mankind, beware, the earth you stand astride
May be a flaming pyre for your suicide.

Edward Abbott

Pictures

The pictures keep falling onto my tear stained face.
They scatter around me like rockets,
returning from outer space.
Each holding a special memory,
a time, a place, a face.
I try to push them away, but this only brings them closer.
Then I realize how special they really are,
I then discover that I should not cry over you,
not wanting me I should be happy,
that there is another love to be.

Jessica Nachole Rayburn

Mother Africa

I am Mother Africa!
They stole us from our motherland,
   stacked us into slave ships,
     deep, deep down in the hulls,
       let us pew as we sat huddled in shackles,
         whipped us, if we dared to protest.

Days, months went by
   as we travelled over the oceans,
     separated us from our Mothers, our Fathers,
       our brothers, and our sisters————
         Until we reached the shores of America.

Generations have passed,
   We have made our contributions—-
     Now we are part of this land,
       We are African Americans.

Judith Grant

Last Lullaby

After years of trying to bring you life
They tell me you can never be
But you have been forever mine
And now I have to say good-bye

From the first time you would have kicked
To the first tear you should have cried
I can feel who you could have been
I know everything you are

I know the soft sound of your laugh
I feel the smoothness of your skin
I see your smile mirrors mine
And your eyes dance like your father's

You're the child I can't bring to this world
But you have been—you are—my child
And I am losing something precious
I am not sure how to live without

So as I find strength to let you go
And you become a child of dreams
Know of all things that should have been
Mommy loves you very much

Jeanne Bell

Mother's Day

When you get down on your knees to pray
think of mother on this day.
Times of good, heartaches and bad, with
mom none were sad.
Food on our table, clothes on our backs
mom washed dishes with a flour sack.
Our big family worked hard from day to day.
On sunday, after church wed all get to play.
Dad would be our pitcher as we played ball.
Mom would take care of our bruises if we
should fall. With us, this was a special
day, mom would have it no other way.
All of this and so much more, thank
God for our mom, she didn't seem to
mind that were poor.

Fay Guthrie

Eliza's New Path

I stand out in the graveyard, I stand out in the breeze.
Thinking a terrible thought, I turn and freeze.
I see my mother's stone and under it, rests her bones.
How she got there I don't know? But, I wish I did so.
I'm so sad, but I do not cry. Sometimes it makes me want to die.

But there's a little voice in me that I really cannot see.
It tells me I have to go on, but before, I did not respond.
It says "Eliza your mother's OK," so now, I calm down and,
Pay my respects everyday.
I say a prayer that she shared when she was around and loved me.

I remember the days and now it seems like only hours,
That we spent together at the England Tower.
And when she played football in the English grass,
And on Christmas Eve...to midnight Mass.
Now she has passed away and it isn't so happy and gay.

I think of the day I shall see her again, without any pain.
I put a flower on her grave, look at the words all engraved.
To her I talk "GOOD-BYE MAMA," then I walk away.
I am taking a news steps, and carving a new path for myself.
Turning to new beginnings, new beginnings.

Eva-Marie Tanner

I Sent My Son

When distressed and feeling down
Thinking my life is such a bore,
Thoughts of loneliness and being afraid,
Feeling that in my life there should be more,
Self pity enters into my thoughts,
AND I can't see my way through,
I hear my Fathers words,
    "I sent my Son to die for you."
There are power in those words,
That walks me each day through.
So when in great need, I hear God say,
    "I sent my Son to die for you!"

Barbara Seward

Ballet Of The War Monkey

Monkeys beat each other with stones
Thirty million years ago.
They scream in bloody tones
They are too young to know.

Humans kill each other with swords
Their false natures they show.
They swear their lives to ungrateful Lords
They are too young to know.

Homo Supra, speed through the sky
In chrome helmets, through the stars they go.
To always fall for the same lie
They are too young to know.

No one is here now.
The only sound is from the wind that blows.
All the world in burned.
They were old enough to know.

Brendan McGuire

Tomorrow After Today

Weary, weary, weary, that's the way
    this day had been,
my thoughts are muddled and upside down,
feel like a frog wearin' a crown.
Keep thinkin' about a hundred things,
like roses, and corn, and lima beans.

Should I do this, or
should I do that,
sing like a bird or
purr like a cat.

Oh, tomorrow, tomorrow will soon be here,
    and the sun will come shining brightly.
Don't take everything so seriously.

Lay down, sit down, stand up or swim,
    decisions, decisions, work or play,
what will the choice be, I wonder.
Why to ride a horse to heaven of course,
over a rainbow, on a lightning bolt of
    thunder.

Jean Eckery

Blue

The color of a new born boy,
The color of pants worn to school,
The color of an infant's toy,
The color of a swimming pool,

The color of the outward sky,
The color of the morning dew,
The color that makes people cry,
The color we know as blue.

Steve Hightower

Clever Poet

I am a poet
this is surely so
rhythm and rhyme
and all that flow
Tickled by pink
enticed by green
If you could see what I mean
Know that there is life in all that exists
Find the quality in everything
    Remember
    Tickled by pink
    enticed by green
    fickle to nothing
    Awake from a dream
If you could see what I mean.

Ava Malazian

It's You!

Times aren't getting better for me,
This room so dark I cannot see.
Now I've opened my eyes, and I've realized
What's missing in my life.

It's you, that made my dreams come true,
It's you, the one that I see when I hold someone
else close to me
And it's you that I find in the back of my mind
waiting for me to dream
things ain't always what they seem,
It's you.

Since the days turned dark, and my heart turned cold,
I've been waiting for you to see,
that the only thing that I have left, is fantasy.
And if you hear what I'll say, then I'll see what you do
in your special little way.
But if things were any different
would you be with me today?

Curtis M. Carter

Joy Eternal

A sister named Joy went home to her room in the sky.
Those are tears of joy that come from the eye.
The stars, the universe, is it all imaginary?
Look up to heaven and see Joy's luminary.
That bright new star shines from her cell;
She has her wings, hear the ring of the bell?
The star of Joy is giving off her light;
You can see her up there on any given night.
There's a sign you are able to see;
That is, in Christ, Joy shines for eternity.

Jeph "Servant of the Lord"

Untitled

Yesterday, I had walked through the forest,
    smelled the cool autumn air and wished for winter.

Yesterday, I had walked through the knee deep snow,
    breathed in the cold air and wished for spring.

Yesterday, I had walked through the park,
    watched the children and wished for summer.

Yesterday, I had walked along the beach,
    swam in the ocean and wished for fall.

Today, I now sit quietly in awe of their passing,
    and am somehow made content by the memories
    of my yesterdays.

Chriss Crouse

No Time For Mom

"No time for Mom", so softly she said
Those precious four words still race through my head
For only a short visit, she did say
Can't you find time in your busy day?

Those are words that really cut deep
And coming from Mom can make you feel cheap!
But she really meant you no harm
Cause she could win you over with her charm

Moms are very dear, we all know
They take the time to clean, cook and sew
She'd send us off to school with hug and a kiss
And usually a lunch box filled with heavenly bliss

She would read us the Bible and teach us to pray
And count our many blessings every day
For she knew the day would come when we'd leave the nest
But we always loved Mom, cause she is the best!

So as life goes on, "Take Time For Your Mother"
Because in her eyes, there is no other
Don't ever let her say, "No Time For Mom" again
Cause she will always love you through thick and thin!

Barbara J. Schnadinger

Pinesnow

Snow glistens on the pine,
Those white green mem'ries of winter linger in my thoughts,
Too beautiful to behold;
A breath of sweet, snow scented air,
A wisp of wind, and back to truth I am.

Yet winter's truth I love,
Its beginning, it's story, it's life;
Its graceful body again beckons before my eyes,
And ever a picture of winter's rain on pine returns,
Unheeded, welcome.

Be it Sun's rays, Moon's shine, starry heaven's splendor;
It matters not which light on path it shines,
Each one celestial, without zenith,
But my body and mind, a pinnacle have reached,
And from the ground no earthly force could stay me.

And if one with me will stand,
Together we on wings of passion will soar,
Flying an evergreen world; Iced with white,
Flying to a place, crowned by our happiness,
Named Forever.

Chris Martin

Untitled

To speak the art
Thou shall not kill
I speak my words
Thou shall not kill
To a place of worship I pledge
Thou shall not kill
Now as I step over his battered body I mutter
Thou shall not kill
But I can't escape the truth of
Thou shall not kill
And I fall to the ground
Dying inside as a result of
Thou shall not kill

April Cates

Earth's Journey

Oh heart, why fear earth's journey?
Though you may grow feeble and old,
God will provide your every need
From the storehouse of His riches untold.

Why think on tomorrow, dear heart?
Why struggle with sadness and stress?
Think not things that are uncertain
Just follow God's road-map to happiness.

Dear heart, why are you weary and heavy?
why carry an unnecessary load?
God promised he'd be your burden bearer
Giving you strength for life's road.

Why worry about prestige and opinion?
Why worry about that at all?
God's direction is all that matters,
Or whether from God's path you fall.

"Be strong!" Oh heart, "Be of good courage!"
This promise in the Bible you know....
"Be not afraid! For I, the Lord your God
'Shall be with you where-so-ever you go."

Inis Danley Ray

Lady Angela

Lady Angela, Princess far from home,
Though you seek a Knight in Armor,
Even now, you're not alone.

For the King you serve is with you, keeping you within His sight,
In your distress, I too with serve you, though I be no honored Knight.

For your friendship is my motive, and my reward to see you smile,
for these treasures I would suffer many along and arduous mile

Because you helped me when I'd fallen, when no solace could be found,
Fair Maiden I will love you and to your service shall be found.

For if beauty were a river, both within as well without,
In your presence should I thirst no more, though the land be wrought
with drought.

If by chance our lives were fantasy, such as in this fairy tale,
then we should live forever, and in perfection, never fail.
And though life seldom copies day to day this storied scene,
I will try to be a Knight to you and love you as my Queen.

Brad Miller

Ocean Serenity

As the wave begins to break on the endless shore,
Thoughts of childhood pass once more.
As I walk on the beach of the endless sea,
Thought's seem to roam frantically.

As the crab burrows itself in the sand,
I find myself trying to understand.
As a piece of wood has drifted in,
I know my journey is about to begin.

As a dolphin swims swiftly without regret or goodbye,
As does the sea gull into the sky.

As the ocean water barrels the surf,
Brings forth in myself, a sense of rebirth.
As the under tow carries away the pollution,
There's only one way to find the solution.

As I dampen my feet in a watery grave,
The children of the earth are what we must save.

For the future of all is in their hands,
The earth, the sky, the water, the land.
We must teach them well in the way of the spirit,
So future generations the earth can inherit.

Justin Gabor

The Weeping Widow's Tears

The widow stands with her head bowed.
Thoughts of no tomorrow and the end
race through her mind.
Her glazed, sunken eyes stare with sympathy
as she stands reminiscing the times
with her loved one.
Her tears blended with her running make-up fall
slowly finding a rugged path through her many wrinkles
like her journey to cope with death.
Each tear falls containing a year of life and memories.

Adam Ionakana Eslinger

Utopia Bound and Gagged

As I looked out to the world before me,
  thoughts ran though my head:
Why all the anger in the world?
  Why are some unfed?
How can one hate a person
  he does not understand?
Why instead of pointing a finger
  can't one extend a hand?
Let us stop focussing on what we want,
  and give to those what we can...
Help the one's who need it,
  every child, woman and man.
Do not just turn your back
  on a stranger at your feet,
Remember that stranger huddled in the cold
  was not born on the street.
Take the time to appreciate all you have and be glad
Then take the time to ponder what others do not....
  and be sad.

Colleen Miller

Soul Mate

I came all this way to find you
through all the years of my lonely youth...
through all the tears of sad goodbyes to men who never stayed;
who were not meant to stay.
I came all this way, across hours of learning foolish things
in foolish schools
across all the miles of useless journeys
through the dust of crumbled dreams.
I came all this way, pulled by the mysterious electric currents of
your mind, by the cosmic cries of your solitary heart.
All this way I came as I had to come
For you stood still, locked in time and space -
not moving, tied to places of Eastern earth
while your soul searched me, stalked me, drew me near,
through all the years and hours and miles and dust.
I came all this way so far, so very far.
And when I stood before you, knowing I was home
believing my heart could rest at last,
You looked at me from your stillness, and did not see me
and did not know.

Cynthia Norris

In Retrospect

The perfect mother, I wanted to be, I'm not
The dreams of becoming an artist, I forgot
The beautiful books I've written, in my head
Were never finally published, to be read
I thought of becoming a doctor healing the sick
Perhaps a scientist to see what makes us tick
A very fine actress of greatest renown
Picking up an Oscar, in a fancy gown.
Time waits for no man, so if the truth were told
I really did nothing, but just grow old.

Helen Wurn

Sunshine

As a ray of light shines
through the curtains of a room
in early morning,
she begins your day
with a glow on your heart.

A sparkling laugh, a radiant smile;
the room brightens
as she chases the shadows away,
where they will wait to reappear
as she is leaving.

If you are down, her smile
shines through the windows of your eyes
and melts the snow from your heart.
If you are up, she will make you believe
that the feeling will never end.

Having her near is like the summer sun,
massaging your shoulders with a warm silence.
As the sun shines on flowers and helps them to bloom,
her warmth shines on your heart
and allows love to grow.

Donald E. Smith

A Child's Sunrise

Have you ever seen the sun rise
through the eyes
of a little child who sees it for the first time?

Have you ever seen the sea
in the way that he sees it,
from the cool wet sand at dawn?

Have you ever wondered at a rooster...
a field of dandelions... a pine cone...
a boulder... a tiny brook?

Snow... gravel...an oak leaf?

When was the last time you walked in the woods,
sat on a stump, touched a pussy willow,
saw a frog?

Have you ever seen a miracle?

Here is a recipe for a miracle.

Take one small child,
a meadow or a seashore, a dawning sun,
fold in your heart,
mix slowly for one hour.

Dwight A. Johnson

One Day You'll Realize

One day you'll realize that the stars aren't as bright as they used to be.
And your smile takes a little more effort than before.
You'll realize that trust and devotion are a little harder to come by.
And confidence is almost nonexistent.
You'll realize that love,
REAL love, is almost unattainable.
And your once ever-ready climax is suddenly unachievable...
You'll realize that everyone won't put up with your childlike idiosyncrasies
AS I DID
and everyone won't put your needs ahead of their own.
So think of me when the tension mounts and your heart aches for
something like we once had.
You'll realize then that you made an irreconcilable mistake.
For opportunity only knocks once, my friend,
and you left the door unanswered....
This, my dear, will be the day you regret leaving me.

Gayle Bowman-Randall

Season Love

Season love goes on and on
throughout the seasons of the year.
Seasons love is a summer rose
blooming through time's ebbs and flows.
Though time is relentless, in winter snowfall
the river of frost still flows.

Season love sparkles like dew
and it blooms like a tulip
when Spring is new.
The change of the season opens your eyes
and the beauty you see makes a tired heart sigh.
It opens to others, making you care.
And like Mother Nature, leads us to share.

But season love can break a heart
If instead of a hug, it becomes a dart.
If love isn't used in just the right way,
the seasons will fade;
their beauty won't stay.

The seasons's joy
is completely destroyed.

Aaron M. Elliott

Love Then, Love Now, Love Forever

They say the minuet is all the rage, come dance with me my love
Thy beauty stirs my very soul, my heart is yours my dove

My Antoinette, my Antoinette how beautifully you dance
In Louis' court I wager you'll be the toast of France

For you my lamb the rarest jewels, gowns of satin and lace
No powdered wigs, no gaudy paint to mar the beauty of your face

Now my search has ended, I have travelled far and wide
I've found the love I yearned for and you are by my side

Marry me my darling, I'll cherish you for ever
I'll worship you 'till life doth end and I will leave you never

You will, you will, you love me too, Oh happiness divine
My Antoinette, my Antoinette now you are truly mine.

Diane Abichandani

The Consummation

It is time to let the truth spin from within;
Time to watch it twirl around the crowd to finally
    settle without great disturbance.
I watch as you take it in, and you understand.
Regardless of the circumstances, you understand.

The room was warm and comfortable, and impulse was power.
It controlled us both.
Laughter from the occupied space around is heard;
    and gasps, and the looks.
I can hear the looks of disbelief;
I can feel them, the eyes upon me.

I am uncaring.
I continue to touch and feel the simplicity of you,
    as a small laugh escapes my lips.

I looked, then, at you.
I watched you smoke.
I watched you smile at me; at all the craziness.
And then you came to me and surrounded me until we were
    both far away from the looks, and the laughter,
    and the predictable surprise.

Jennifer Usrey

Follow Your Heart... To A Land Of Dreams

Go down the road and up the street,
to a land of dreams come true.

It's a land of chance, of light, and of beauty,
this land of dreams.

It's not hard to find,
you can find the way in your heart.

For your heart knows the way,
to find the dreams you want to come true.

So follow the desires of your heart,
to find this land of dreams - it's for you!

Elena Wright

April Thirteenth

Drive south on any sunday afternoon
to a sudden city seldom without
faces. Slowly summer begins to loom
in the abandoned bathhouses and shouts
with the bungalow hospitality
above the seaside sewage mosquitoes
and the spectacle of night buoyancy.
The superficial sidewalks seem shallow
when the taverns empty and the fish cakes
stomach the evenings meant to mellow.
The concrete jungle muscle integrates
with the strip tease gypsies' dark afterglow.
As the sea gulls stagger on slippery rocks
the season belches like pandora's box.

Glenngo Allen King

A Summer Song

A summer song past across my mind
To a time when we were young....
The song came back to yesterday
To the song that we had sung...
So young the birth of first love
Buds like a new red rose....
Although the rose turned black
With time
Treasured memories froze....
And once the thorn pierced at
My heart
Now lies amongst the dead...
Yet it is brought anew
When the melody
Again beats in my head....

Jessie L. Paulsen

Truth and Reality

Our destiny is written in the book of life.
To be born is to live and then die.
Life is supremely beautiful.
As beautiful as a garden of roses.
Life is more beautiful and divine
when you have someone to love.

I have said it before, and now say it again.
You don't have to love in presence only.
True love can be felt in the distance.

Love is for the heart as the dew is to flowers.
Love gives the heart life and happiness.
The dew gives flowers life.
That is why I want you to fill my heart
with the delicious dew of your love.

Auxiliadora Taleno

Deep Inside Of Me

Deep inside of me, a lonely girl wishes
To be free
Hiding from her deepest fears, God knows
she's shed a lot of tears
Isolation's been her way, every night
and day she'd pray
Won't somebody set me free, joyous and happy
I long to be
Deep inside of me, Happiness I'd long
to see
A little girl who never grew, find the love
she never knee
Where's the family she never had?, Tell me
why the girls so sad
Won't somebody set her free, that little girl
Deep inside of me.

> *Avery Gee*

Building Memories

Each day I plan to plant a memory,
To be inside my heart a summary.
Of all life's elegant events,
    Sadness and loneliness to prevent.
One memory is the loving hugs of my grandchild,
    Keeping love at the center of life so in style.
One memory is the tail upright of a deer,
    In the pasture, it's Bambi, coming my brother to cheer.
One memory of the time sitting around a table with family and
friends,
    Each other's ear we always seem to bend.
A memory of words said gently, "I love you".
    Yet simply stated yet so true.
Remembrances of sitting in church looking at the stained glass
windows
    aglow,
    Memory of the times we kissed under the mistletoe.
So plant each day so clear in your mind,
    Those memories of those things sublime.

> *Howard B. Childs*

That's Why I Love Her

I'm in love with Yasmin. She knows that I'll be in
To be with her, always forever.
That's why I love her.

I know Yasmin loves me. That's what I always see
When I'm with her, always forever.
That's why I love her.

The tears in her eyes makes me realize
That I do have true love.

She has no other love for she has just one love
Who will love her, always forever.
That's why I love her.

Bad times that we may have, our love will always last.
Yes, I need her, always forever.
That's why I love her.

The tears in my eyes makes her realize
That she does have true love.

We're both truly in love and that is just enough
Being together, always forever.
That's why I love her.
Yeah, that's why I love her.

> *Eric A. Faiz*

Why Me

The mornings are hard sometimes too hard
to bear, but my face must show the world that
I don't have a care. I see the suicides and
overdose death of stars, I wonder is this what
fate has in store for me. I have so much, yet
live for so little, and all I ask is why me.
The nights are long, I lay sleepless dreaming
of what's next, something good, most times
bad. Wondering if I'll get through the next
day and all the time asking why me.
If this is how my life will play out, I'm not sure
fame or fortune or anything will make that
big a difference, as I lay and think of all that
will be, all I ask is
Why me
Why me
Why me

> *Greg Broderick*

What Is Life?

What is life, if not a chance to grow,
to bloom, mature, accomplish, and to show
what feelings that there be within us hid,
and give back to the world the things we know?

What is life if lived for self, alone,
with no regard for others that we meet,
no caring smile to brighten someone's day,
nor words of comfort, no love have we shown?

Life is in vain when we have naught to give,
and we should search our hearts for what is wrong,
for we were all endowed with some good thing
to share, and when we do, we'll learn to live.

> *Annette Weems Naramore*

Life Reasons

What shall be my reason for life
to breathe, to eat, sleep, care,
and avoid the knife?

Is there a cause
so deep, true, alive
to justify another pause
another look at the day.

Where is the passion, the glory
the get up and go?
Is it asleep - waiting for the right moment
to push me from this deep
slumber and discontent.

Shall I just wait and hope for
a nudge, a spark
or should I ascend back to nature
to what is real.

By my own capacity to stand
shall I again live and
If yes again I pose
For what reason?

> *Brenda Lujan*

Untitled

It's not easy to unravel
the Intricate patterns of the past
when all that's left to cling to
is the slender fibre of
the future.

> *Pamela H. Gramlick*

In Quest Of

Oh God! We're striving from our birth,
To capture in mind and verse,
The illusive secrets of the Universe.

The time, distance and the space,
That fused to produce the Human Race.
The purpose of which escaped our grasp,
Though we ponder blindly, to define the past.

Our feeble efforts, seemingly in vain,
Yet we endure, with hunger, hope, and pain.

We're born, we die, and somewhere in between,
We should know the truth, or myth, or so it seems,

Of that Seclusion, whether near or far,
Which states, "Why and Who We Are".

Herman Wheadon Jr.

In My Eyes

I looked upon the open field,
to find the beauty that it yields.
With every step that I take,
I think of that one costly mistake.
The one that made you very sad,
and cost me all I ever had.
I should have known better than to cheat on you,
It was only one night, but somehow you knew.
I know it was wrong, but what could I do.
When I looked at her I thought of you.
I don't know if I can live with this pain I feel,
Somehow I need my heart to heal.
Can you ever forgive me for what I've done?
Cause in my eyes you're the only one.

Joey Williams

Precious Little One

Eyes of blue,
Skin so fair,
Button nose and twinkle toes,
And everyone knows he's my special rose,
For he's my Great Grandson - -
Austyn is his name,
And to me - - he is simply awesome!
He's God's amazing creation,
So fearfully and wonderfully made
And my heart is filled with glad adoration.

I thank and praise you, Lord
For this precious baby boy,
Who is bringing so much joy,
He's a perfect gift of love,
Sent from heaven above.

Dear Lord, bless and keep this little one,
Make your face to shine upon him,
Be his guiding light,
And may his life be pleasing in your sight

Jean Knight

The Sight

I've seen a bird fly through the skies,
yet see it never with my eyes.
I have no sight of these fair lands,
but I see them with my hands.
Colors I have never known.
Blackness is my eternal home,
and in this dark I dwell alone,
For the fates have me confined,
to have the sight, and yet be blind.

Kelly Harris

The Mommy Lair

Where is this mommy lair the curious do ask.
To find the place is no hard task.
It is the spot where small children race.
A wonderful locale in which none feel out of place.

The mommy lair has a warm fuzzy air,
To visit, is like a day at the fair.
It's walls are filled with big brimming smiles.
Smiles that will carry you over very long miles.

The mommy lair is full of loud hearty giggles.
They flow all the way through, to make toes wiggle.
A warm sunny spot overflowing with love.
If you wish, you may ride upon the wings of a dove.

The mommy lair travels with you everywhere you go.
It builds up and up through the years as you grow.
The foundation is firm, made solid with heart.
A frame nailed with happy memories which from you,
    never will part.

Becky A. Kramer

I Wish I Were An Angel

I wish I were an angel
to guide you on your way'
to help you when your lonely
Although your far away
I'd like to be there always
to help you with the fight,
The days, the weeks the months,
That you fight for what is right.
Now that you must leave me
And work for Uncle Sam
I keep wishing and thinking
"I wish I were an angel and not what I am!'
But when this war is over
And you come back to me
I'll know you had that angel
to keep you safe for me.

Vianna M. Currier

My Life Long Promise

Fifty years ago I made a promise.
To have and to hold, till death do us part.
This promise has paid me dividends in fold.
We grew together and so did our love.
Watching our children grow and get married.
Then one day we were grandparents.
You made me smile and when I could not smile,
You made me understand.
You were my life, my love, my best friend,
But nothing made me prouder than the day I called you my wife.
Fifty years have past with no regrets,
But now, today, when we celebrate our 50th anniversary.
I ask you to help me renew my promise to you.
I ask, will you marry me just one more time?

Edwin Henry

J. B.

The winter sky is dark and grey,
The time has come dad can only say,
I miss you J.B. and can only pray;
That God will let me be with you, again one day.
We rode my bike and had much fun,
The days were beautiful in the summer sun.
You said faster daddy and laughed so loud,
If the sky were grey we'd see no cloud.
This poem is for you J.B.
For together again we'll be, you'll see.

John Byron Davidson

My Gift from God

God gave you to me, for a little while,
To hold you near and know your smile
He gave you to me the best that He could
He knew I wanted a man of perfection
One who could warm me with the deepest affection
Yes, I think He has made a very wise choice
When I think of you, darling, my eyes grow moist
And though you'll only be mine for a little while,
When we part, I know I'll smile
But please, never leave me, never say you must go
Because I'd die without you, because I love you so

Dee Espinosa

Friendship

To have a friend is to inherit a gift;
To keep him is to honor his ways!
Like sands in an hour glass;
Time does sift;
Like a friendship from day to day.

Friendship; you are an honest spirit,
As lasting as the day is long!
Your echoes of love, I choose to hear it,
And to let your kindness to remain strong.

Forever friends, till the end of time;
We'll help each other if the need arise.
Friendship, I have now, yes it is mine,
As limitless as the skies.

Gary Alton Waltemire

"Conceive Thoughts"

Conceive thoughts dwell in my head.
To look inside and see they're red,
With anger and frustration for me to try,
To figure our, and then to lie,
To myself and to my friends,
And follow the fad, to follow the trends.
Set before me as a trap or snare,
To sit and wonder, to sit and stare,
At the light shining brightly, at the wonderful glow,
To see it come towards me, and watch it flow,
Completely around me and to the side,
Wanting it to me, wanting to confide,
To the wonderful person that's so close, so near,
To never watch her shed the tear,
For me never to leave, and never to go.
But it's okay for me because I know
That inside of me it will always show,
That inside of me I have that glow.

Carrie Anne Feague

Untitled

Being a black child, I was born to excel.
To see defeat as a challenge not a failure.
To breathe the breath of life and fear God
    not man,
To be a beacon of light in my community,
    my neighborhood and in my home.
Let the light of Jesus shine all around and
    through me.
To be a leader not a follower,
To show someone I am a child of a King ...
    Jesus,
To stand tall and strong,
To be accepted for who and what I am.
T L C
    This child Loves Christ.

Diana Havard

The Sounds of Silence

To meditate with God
To look into one's soul
To sense your being
To feel the warmth of the sun
To smell the aromas around you
To see the beauty of a butterfly
To look at a cloud caressing you
To sense a divine presence
To feel the love around you
To smell a log on the fire
To see the outstretched arms of a tree
To look at the character lines in your face
To sense him almost being there
To feel the softness of your chair
To smell the one rose in your vase
To see the wonderment of silence
    Silence is golden

Helen Penn

If I

If I'm the dark,
to me you'd be the sunset
the horizon bursting into a frame of colors
showing how beautiful you are to see
If I was the ocean,
you'll be the moon
reflecting your beauty
showing your every movement
half and quarter moon
represent the many moods of a real woman
If I was the sand,
you'd be the stars
with people all on me
making a crowd
making it hard for us to see each other's eyes
then you shoot down to be closer to me
when you hit the sand
you set off sparks
disbursing the affection between you and I
If I....

Carltouis Stevenson

The Forest: Our Everchanging Home

Towering stumps, giving homes
    to new animals all around.
Invisible fortress undergoing attack,
    seeking new enemies from the jaws of eternal life.
A hobbit drinking from the stub of a tree.
    Next to him a bottle of ginger; he's making tea!
The spongy, green moss is the roof of the hobbit's home;
    please don't step on it!
    Forest:
        Always
        Giving
        And
            Taking
            Life.

Aaron Herman

Her Love

Her eyes, were as green as
the Jamaican waters.
Her lips, were as red as
the ruby gem stone.
Her kiss, was as sweet as
wild flowers in a multi-colored meadow.
Her love, no one could match.

J. Brian Towle

Learning of Truth and Trust

Loving parents welcomed him and promised
  to provide the best of everything.

He learned to trust without question
  and to accept everything his parents told him as truth.

Then he came to realize that parents could not always be trusted
  and "truth" was sometimes not the real truth.

One parent would use him as bait against the other,
  Arguments were just discussions,
  Santa Claus, Easter Bunny and Tooth Fairy didn't exist,
  Yes meant no and no meant yes.

And so he decided to use caution and not to accept what he was told
  as truth; he would test everything before believing.

His last fleeting thought as he pulled the trigger was that
  this time he should have trusted his parents;
  they were telling the truth.

  Jean Malick

Toot! Toot!

A tree sat on a railroad track
To see if it could,
Along came the 515, Toot! toot! firewood.

A pig sat on a railroad track
And gave little snort,
Along came the 515, Toot! toot! cooked pork.

A banana sat on a railroad track
Just to get fed,
Along came the 515, Toot! toot! banana bread.

A tomato sat on a railroad track
Trying to be a boss,
Along came the 515, Toot! toot! tomato sauce.

A carrot sat on a railroad track
And didn't have a clue,
Along came the 515, Toot! Toot! carrot stew.

This poem sat on a railroad track
Since it looked like fun,
Along came the 515, Toot! toot! it's done!

  Julianna Bulina

A Far Cry From Help

I try to unlock the door to my dreams
to see if my future will be what it seems
Wanting to grow up, but not grow old
The present, something I try to keep a hold
Not wanting to ever die
But know I will and wonder why
Death soon comes to us all
So why try when in the end we Finally Fall
What difference will I make
Why should I take the chances I take
Why do I need to be here
living a life filled with Fear
I don't need to live as far as I can see
Why should I, nothing will become of me.

  Jessie M. Howe

Sadness

Loneliness brings on a world of darkness
Thoughts of desperation
Wickedness to the unknown
Acts of envy
But learning to love one self
Is the healing of sadness

  Wendy M. Wiley

For Bill

When I can't see, you are my eyes.
When I can't hear, you are my ears.
What I lose, you find.
Whatever I need or want, you provide.
For all these, I'm grateful.
Besides, I love you.

  Elizabeth W. Coan

Untitled

To be free from gravity, what utter joy
To see majestic mountains at a moment's whim
I would not be afraid of soaring heights if I could fly.
Just to free fall for 60 seconds I would pay
five hundred dollars.
The first time I jump out of a plane,
I would be scared, of course screaming like a banshee.
Would I live, would I die, what a natural high
It's probably a feeling matched when
astronauts go into space, free from Earth's gravity
floating on the moon, taking that first step.
The parachute would open right?
Saving me from the clutches of death
It acts like the wings of white doves.
Free at last, free at last.

  Emily Y. Shinsato

Send Me Roses For Valentines Day

I want to watch them get old, wither and die;
to see the stem weaken, bending under the weight of its own bloom.
Like an old man, straining to lift his head,
which over the years, has become so polluted by knowledge,
that it weighs as much as a bowling ball.
Send roses, because I can do nothing to preserve them.
They will eventually get thrown out, or if I were a romantic,
hung upside down from the wall. Like some satanic monument to morality.
Roses, to remind me that life boils down to nothing more or less than
itself; and joy it temporary.
It wilts with time and exposure to the elements.
Anyone who sees them will think I'm loved; when, at their simplest
form, they're merely a part of the cycle.
But send them anyway, so someday from now,
I can say that at least I got flowers for Valentines day, once.

  Cynthia Wish

I Close My Eyes

I close my eyes on this unfair world.
To see, to touch, to breathe the unspoken fear.
To hear a bird's song, or a child's cry, is to
hope for a renewing of faith and unpromised life.

I close my eyes on this unfair world.
Not knowing what the wayward tide may bring.
Will it be panic, devastation, heartache or death?
Is this my plight to go through my unwilling and
unprepared life as an outcast, an unsightly blemish?

I close my eyes on this unfair world.
Whispers on the wind clear my mind.
Shadows haunt my dreams as visions.
Piercing like a knife into the night,
my laden heart cries no more.

I close my eyes on the unfair world.
Never to be noticed or seen.
I close my eyes on this unfair world.
Never to be held, not even in fleeing.
I close my eyes on this unfair world.
To die without ever being!

  Costella Harper-Snapp

Follow The Sun

One day you will look,
To see who was the one.

So until that day comes,
I could only follow the sun.

There is no way to ever tell,
Who was right or wrong but, I know it is done.

While we shared the times, we both had some fun.

So until that day comes,
I could only follow the sun.

The past is behind and what lies ahead,
We may never know but, hopes and dreams.

Endure for the future to realize that
All is not lost until there is nothing to dread.

So until that day comes,
I could only follow the sun.

If you and I were to part,
The biggest part of me would be gone.
My love for you, with all my heart.

Please let's stay and not go, we will take it very slow.

To live as one, we can only follow the sun.

Chuck Sapp

A Sinner's Prayer

To love you, Lord, with all my heart, my strength, my mind,
To serve you, Lord, with all the zeal my aging heart and body find,

To become a helpless little child and realize that every blessing I
receive comes from you,

And nothing I can ever do will make you love me any more—or any
less.

To know that in Your Father's heart Your love is there to bless
and keep and guide my way,

To show me as you light the days and nights ahead
That the way that I am being led is by Your will and not by pride.

To know the lives of those I passed will not be quite the same

Because in passing I may have breathed Your Name in reverence,
Or did some kind deed in Jesus' Name.

And when my remaining days are done, I pray that I will leave this
foreign land with head held high,

And approach that Gate of Pearl and will hear my Saviour cry,
"Well done, my son! Welcome home!"

Charles F. Bybee

Fallen Sand Castles

Man as a species must learn to see
To sit silently observing ever after
The great grey years tide in and out.
Stifled power lapping the sands of eternity
With less sound than a whisper
More emotion than a shout.
If through the current's passage
He finds the wisdom to watch, to wait.
Wastes no fear on his sandy destruction;
But with open hands takes their message.
The waves of time will draw him out; creating
on their shoulders, his resurrection.

Esther Mann

Mom

To the one who brought me here -
To the one who's helped me through so much,
The tears, the laughs, the boys the friends,
Through so many decisions and such.
The times I've needed you most,
Were times I needed to cry.
Times you always understood,
Times you didn't ask why.
When my heart had been broken
by my first true love,
you wiped my tears to dry,
Like an angel from above.
I can only hope
What you have done for me,
I can do for my kids,
My kids that'll someday be.
To the one who brought me here,
To the one with the special touch,
To the one who's always helped me,
To my mom, I love you so very much.

Christy A. Benedict

Valentine's Day

Is there a day that hearts can be completely satisfied
   To welcome the good, and also the bad, yet take it all
   in stride?
On one such day it's possible to find everyone in good cheer
   The smiles are many, on the fourteenth day in the
   second month of the year
A certain feeling hits its peak on this most precious day
   Love is the one that I'm talking about, which each of
   us shows in a special display
Some may buy roses, others get candy, but this is only a start
   Nothing is truly a Valentine's gift unless it comes
   straight from the heart
Everyone of us needs to be loved, by one person or another
   It can be by a husband, a wife, or a teacher, or even a
   sister or brother
The love we feel inside of us is almost too much to bare
   Valentine's Day is the most wonderful time to show how
   much we care

Brian Wardrip

Forever Bound

Two souls, as pure as the white sands in fabled untouched lands, come
   together in a magnetized embrace of pure love and trust.
Thoughts of "live-ever-after" dance through their heads as they gaze
   into the windows of their souls. Like celestial thieves on the
   prowl for life's inspiration, they steal heavenly flashes of inner
   strength from each other like a newborn infant suckling the
   innocence from his mother's swollen breast.
Slowly the tension and raw energy builds as their lips touch for the
   first time in unbridled anticipation.
All that surrounds them fade to black as they are left standing naked
   to each other with their walls of emotional self-protection in
   rubble at their feet.
Mistrust and hurt are empty words that were shed with their first
   embrace, like the skin of a snake.
Nothing exists now but pure truth as the passion begins to swirl in a
   torrid storm of lust and love, want and need. In a crescendo of
   mystical, feral rhythm, excitement builds like the raging force
   within Mother Nature's wondrous volcanoes.
Together they reach the apex of absolute surrender as the two souls
   become one, forever bound.

Jared I. Lenz

My Guest

I had a guest at my home—Topsie T. Bear.
Topsie came to show me that others really do care.

Topsie came because I was successful last week.
Losing weight is what we all really seek.

Topsie gave moral support and friendly advice.
Hungry? How about some diet pop with ice?

Every time I want to eat, Topsie says— "chew gum,
Be Topsie smart—not dumb."

Losing weight—that's what it's all about,
When we lose, we're so happy we could shout.

Thank you, thank you, Topsie T. Bear,
For your help and showing me that others care.

Topsie and I just want to say,
We hope everyone has a happy Valentine's Day.

Joyce Leonhardt

Childhood Memories

Furnace-like graveyard monument, reaching upward-
touching lavender skies.
Reflections of past childhood memories with heart
throbbing—pulsating visions of why such a place
was nicknamed—Snake Hill, as I pass by,
Echoing cries bursting forth from the ruins, of poor
withered—tormented SOULS—with locked minds of lost
YOUTH and unfulfilled DREAMS.
Decaying bodies of those-who belonged to the yesterdays
have been released through eternal time—no longer held
earthbound. But what of their soul/minds—are they
still wandering in a Dante's Inferno or have they found
their Paradise Lost through—DEATH'S IMMORTALITY.
Black pavement—yellow lines—rolling wheels, twilight
shies homeward bound—FREEDOM of heavy-laden thoughts.
Leaving —the now city dwellers with the mark of past
time. But Laurel Hill State Mental Hospital will always
"BE" a memory of city life and struggle, of old familiar
places with intriguing names for childhood play—
ringing—Snake Hill—Snake Hill, now I KNOW WHY.

Anna Theresa Pierro

Mother Earth Celebration Earth Day

Be grateful, O people for the earth we live in,
Towering mountains, clear skies and deep blue seas,
Golden waving grains on the wide verdant plains,
Everlasting hills where flowers bloom and birds sing.

Then let us make everyday an earth day
Let's rally on, make it a reality,
Protect our environment, plant trees, clear the air,
Let the earth bloom for the coming generation.

Be grateful, O people for the earth we live in,
Let's love and preserve it and never defile,
It's the only world God gifted to mankind.
We'll pay dearly if we do not help and mind.

Let's protect our seas from chemicals and wastes,
Protect our zone from thinning out,
Protect our environment from gas and fumes,
Recycle plastics, papers, bottles and cans.

Be grateful, O people, for the earth we live in,
Let's rally on, protect our environment,
Love her, keep her for the coming generation,
Let's remember, earth's future is in our hands.

Herminia Layson

Cabrini And The View

Merchandise Mart, so long, bold and strong.
Towering over is, Sears tower, for all the world to see,
Mr. Hancock even beckons at me.
Is it an ocean! Is it a sea?
No it's lake Michigan staring at me.
How beautiful to enjoy Chicago's most precious view,
In the Dawn of day I feel the dew,
at my window I even see you!
Black woman your struggle is not in vain,
Just enduring every days lite with its pain.
Feeding our children, Clothing them too,
And for shelter we thank Cabrini for such a marvelous view.
If it weren't for you Cabrini would we do?
We thank you for the view.

Diane Davis

The Best Time Of The Day

Today's flowers grow brightly in the meadows,
traces of morning dew drip gently from their petals.
Majestic colors of blossoms so serene,
Proves once again that Mother nature is indeed a queen.
Bees hover ever gently in the breeze,
while birds sing softly high up in the trees.
Great white clouds float freely in a sky of blue,
as rays of periodic sunshine evaporate the dew.
It is indeed the best time of the day,
a time to think and a time to pray.

James R. Rodman

The Mighty Denver - Alaska

On the White Pass train you must start up the narrow track to the
    trail head,
If the weather is warm, you are sure to have all the beauties of
    nature looking back at you,
The wild strawberries, the logan and the blue, the birch, hemlock and
    spruce, they all display colors of red, green and blue,
The tall trees are showing off, growing fast, so to stave off Winter,
Glacier waters racing down, eventually to Skagway River,
Birds in flight sing their song, making you wish there were more,
Mushrooms in various colors, begging you to take them - caution, one
    must gather only those you trust,
After climbing in the bog and on the rock, gazing at the fern
    reflected by long streams of light, you find serenity seldom known,
Visualizing the might glacier just ahead, I must not overlook what is
    at my side - maybe a bear will scare me, or a flower will take my
    mind,
All of a sudden I am made quite aware the Denver Glacier is just in
    sight; as I look to watch my footing, the mighty Denver gives of
    herself to save life below......

David A. Johnson

Baltimore Street

His creviced hands
tremble under the gray chill of the night.
Able-bodied arms that used to
embrace frail bodies, used to
feel needed, used to want to live—
now only grasp
weary knees nearer to his broken heart.
Shivering toes peek out of ragged
tennis shoes. His body sways
restlessly under the dim moonshine
on the corner of Baltimore Street.
You and I walk by, averting our eyes,
pretending not to see.
His misery.

Amber Sharp

Candlelight and Moonbeams

Candlelight and moonbeams
trespass the nether-reaches of my nostalgic soul
haunted by memories of a small, studying boy.
(the neighbor kids never studied; they had electricity)
(and TELEVISION!)
he learns by the light of a single, dim candle
and a moonray weakened by the pane
in passing the window
shaded by dirt-road traffic.
Presently...
that's "NOW" to an educated-by-deprivation
adult son of the child-father...
the T.V. sits dark in the corner as I read
"THE WIFE OF BATH'S TALE"
by the soft miracle of florescent light.
Candles, these days, keep company with strings, tacks
and other etceteras in the etcetera drawer;
and no responsible adult, of course,
would ever overconsume
the paraffin moon.

Bryan Seelye

Sugar Melt/Salt Lump

Use to shelter myself,
Tried to in all situations.
Faded away in the mist of things,
Died to come out, guess you thought I was crazy.

You just try to run between two drops of rain,
and see how worn you become.

It really wasn't the down pour I feared, that would
melt the sweetness away.

It was the sudden lump in my heart that just seem to lay,

Left there by the little melts that continued to grow a part.

Carolyn L. Arrington

Comin' Alive In '95

It's almost that time for the world to see the
    true inner peace,
that steps to the beat; even in the hottest heat.
It's all quite unique... to know in which row
you must go...in order to show the meaning of
life throughout which you strive to be alive.
    The strength is in the mind; where in you
will find, all the thoughts that do refine your
treasures so they too can shine. All the way
from the back of your mind.
    So I do say that it is time .....
to come alive ..... yes... in '95.

Let the spirit be a wine as your heart inclines,
    to the discipline and love from the man above!

De'Anginae Holt

Can't Love: Can't Hate

Fly high I say
Try to touch the sky
Escape the demons that are holding me down
Darkness within my soul,
Haunts me like a nightmare
Captive in my own heart
Loneliness surrounds me like a cold winter's wind.
Can't touch the world
Can't love; can't hate.

Jody Cappiello

Rewarding Cycles

Looking out across my hay field,
trying hard to guess my yield.
One bale, two, three and four,
oh, at times, it is a chore.

I cut, I rake and then I bale,
stack on a trailer past the top rail.
A trip to the barn, it's pitched real high.
Safe in a loft to cure and dry.

How can hard work bring such reward?
Year after year, always working toward,
feeding those cows as much as I dare.
No one but the herd would hardly care.

They're happy and fat, jolly and round,
waiting for those babies to hit the ground.
The cycle continues, it never stops.
Year after year it's hop, hop, hop.

Carolyn F. Teegarden

Life Missing Love, Missing Life

I'm trying to see what it is that you feel;
trying to sense where you are.

  In this place, at this time
  reality scored,
  yet our hearts and our souls
  reign sublime.

There's no need for transgression.
Our Love will survive
each day's slight, gentle touch of despair.

  We now know the difference
  life makes without Love
  through this Love that we've found
  with each other...

Life missing Love, missing life.

Dawn Iris

Can You Feel The Cold?

Crisp and Sparkling flakes of white,
Twisting turning in mid-flight.
Brisk and blowing in the wind,
Winter's here; time to settle in.
Pops and sparks from the fire,
Sleepy solemn, I could retire.
Warm socks and a comforter please,
Oh no, I think I'm going to sneeze.
Chicken soup in a cup,
Steamy warm, I drink it up.
Excuse me please, I've got to go.
My nose is running, can you feel the cold?

Annette Good

silently she sits;

a whisper on the wind,

complacently perusing thoughts

of a love she can't rescind-

tolerant of his many faults,

accepting what has been-

expectations will soon reveal

a passion that knows no end....

Steve Huygens

The Actor

Up there, on the stage, suspended
'Twixt heaven and hell,
Dawn and twilight, truth and fantasy,
He gesticulates, and speaks the oft-repeated lines
That before were dead black words
Tracing lines on virgin paper....
All silent till he speaks,
And suddenly, they leap alive, afire with meaning -
Trembling hope, quiet despair,
And tender-whispered love;
He becomes two other men, himself submerged
'Neath the creation and its creator,
So that which he was born to give -
Imagination - which is his substance,
Is spent, purchasing for those who watch
An hour's respite from reality.

This is his offering upon the Altar of Ambition
He makes a commoner of a king,
And of the lowly beggar,
Prince Charming of the Realm.

Carolyn S. Hicks

A Nation of Trapeze Artistes

Performers abound as my attention is directed to a Circus.
Under a tent, seated and waiting to be Entertained,
Proffered for my view, I observe animals in Cages.
Also clowns, outlandishly dressed, directing Foolishness.
Now lights, spotlight the stars of this Tent Society.
The Trapeze Artiste disregarding Danger, swings and somersaults.
Overcoming danger, Disciplined is he.
Media-Controlled to heights of Fantasy
Disregarding the signs of their Dissipating Society
Transposing Images; the viewing, not Disciplined.
Grasp their Own Trapezes and swing individuality
As children into oblivion.

Joseph Wojtech

Culture

Speaking of culture, and not keeping silent,
Under harassment, not knowing what to do
Face to face with dismay, or what to say,
For difficult it is to hold one's ground,
Or tell which way to go with a thumping conscience-
To make a swift departure for seas unknown,
Or stay on the muted shore and watch in anguish
The things you loved and hoped for passing by
Like boats indistinctly sailing in mist
And fetched by a wayward wind- speaking of culture,
Where are the gifts, the skillful accomplishments,
The words of wisdom, the competence, discretion;
Where is the praise, the happiness, the value?
All I see is the wilful compromise
Of a wonderful life, our heritage on earth.
A ripple of laughter beside me is predisposed
To recognize the changing times, and I
Ask if anything grows cut off from roots,
Remembering that throughout this whole concern
Are all degrees of presumption- speaking of culture.

Carolyn T. Abbot

You

You are You
What makes You, You
Is what You do.
So do what You, what to do
And You will be who You want to be.

Phyllis Cimaglia

Eternity Is Calling

It's voice rings across
the void in my soul
and I whisper your name
to stave off the loneliness
that follows.

Lynda Ferrell

This Death of Mine....

Crimson waters the eyes do see,
Upon the stones of hypocrisy.
Coldly crushing carefree clasps,
The hatred blackens death's sweet grasp.

Calmly, teardrops whisper why,
Another's fate must soon reply
To wantonness is shadow's mist
Majestically marching up the list.

Clinging, hopes repress sweet pain.
Yet, ravage darkness remains unchanged?
Calling, coaxing, cooing loud,
Lightning's thunder looms so proud.

Yet, all is not lost this morrow's eve.
Because love's lonely lariat can deceive
The ominous darkness within our mind,
And the passionate pleasures known in time.

Then, the crimson waters will flow bright,
Hiding charcoal dreams in the pale moonlight.
Ending mundane madness in a mirthful time;
Why must I hurt, this death of mine?

Gregory Owen Thomas

Another Time of Forgotten Space

Dreams of escaping the limitless lash of sorrow
Used by the beast to control your every move,
Fearful of your invisibility by the sunrise of tomorrow.
A weapon to the white skinned man, indescribably powerful
Speaking not of his lash but of ignorance possessed within,
Within slaves whose future is potentially doubtful.
Endless drips of blood blend with your tears in a moment of dismay
To express your thoughts of retaliation will only make matters worse,
Or so they say.

Anthony Coloneri

On This Day

On this day to my Valentine,
"Valentine's day", we would say
Is for couples who are in love.
Why don't we give thanks to God above
For sharing with us, his precious love?

We give thanks to one another,
Sometimes that is our father and mother.
Give thanks to the highest, He can also
Be our brother.
Sister, brother, mother, or child,
Give thanks to God, He is worth the while.

On this day, did you take the time
To pray?
Remember God. He made this day.
He made this day special for you
And in our hearts, we know that this
Love is true.

On this day: To my Valentine,
God bless you.

Alice Briggs

"Absent Dad"

Recollection of dad and I
very small, probably shy,
Flashes of a huge oak tree
towering high over me.
Taken on a picnic we sat upon a shawl
playing in the warm sun "daddy" I would call.
Fun and laughter all around
In the woods no other sound.
Not many memories are for me
as dad left when I was three.
The growing up years did pass
questions sometimes I would ask.
Only a photo I would keep.
sneak a look, sometimes a weep.
Now a woman old and grown
with beautiful children of my own.
Does he ever think of me
or of those days when I was three.

Carol Whitaker

Viola

Violas fifteen eyes of green
Viola dreams of beautiful things
her mothers a drunk her father smokes crack
he comes home to tell her eye on your back
he touches her she knows it's fowl
Viola does what she told
she wishes she didn't know how
She hears the battle drop mommies out cold
to get away she closes her eyes
to dream of loving parents in her demise
when always done its back to the crack
Viola knows he'll be back
She must leave no turning away
She prays to God, but somehow she stays
to the gun she goes, she trigger gives away
Viola knows she won't be back
not for a while
not today
Violas lives her dream, now
For forever starting today

Dawn Tully

A Secret Society

There are people whose main objectives are to destroy historical
  vision.
Some are educated and well read, its their long life ambition.

To deceive a people into believing their culture doesn't matter.
As it relates to history, and the messages get even sadder.

It's alarming to see how the poison spreads throughout the African
  Nation.
People of color always forget we are the pillar of civilization.

We built our African society with continual patience and care.
Our civilization was taken away by an enemy, who does not share.

Our dreams and ambitions to further our cause
to be a people with pride and distinction, who have mastered
  ancestral laws.

Daniel Mason

Desire

Lying here......
Visions of you intoxicate my sleep
My passion rages as I pull you close to me
Your exquisite eyes reflecting a desire
begging for release

Wanting to taste the sweet nectar of your full lips
My skin coming alive with your caress
Wanting to lose myself in you

Hearts racing, minds melting, souls joining
Our bodies becoming a single life
You answer my dream with a single word
YES

Becca Houston

Nevermore....

Sitting alone you start to imagine sitting on death row,
waiting for the big day.

Nevermore is the sun.
Nevermore is the stars in the sky.
Nevermore is the smoke filled cells.
Nevermore am I shy.

The gas filled chambers with colorless walls.
The electricity running throughout my veins.
The liquid shooting through your skin going to your heart.
The afterlife will soon begin; but when?

Life is adventuresome,
but is so the lighted trip to the heavens in the sky.
Waiting. Waiting. Waiting.
Nevermore am I.

Dawnetta K. Trott

Dream's Fortune

Summer's here and I'm still
Waiting on a distant hill,
A hill that guards a love so true
And takes the sadness from the blue.

I'll stay here and a long time wait
Till you come knocking at my gate,
You'll hold me close; I'll not protest
'cause I've waited long for that great test.

Hark! Do I hear a knock?
Or only the sound of a falling rock?
Could I mistake that sound so clear
For only a rock that fell right near?

I'll open the door and see a light
That's shining brightly in the night,
Please walk right in and close the door
To shut out sadness that will come no more.

Calvin W. Haywood

The Silence

I looked out the broken Window,
Watching the wind and rain,
I blamed God for everything.

Closing my eyes
I could hear the waltz,
A razor blade began dancing.

Bring on the silence.

Tweed Banister

The System

Sitting in the county welfare office,
Waiting on my check.
People all around me,
Waiting to break their caseworkers' neck.
Tension in the air, nerves balled up tight,
The System says you have a few more days to wait,
Although your last meal was ate the other night.

The System says to fill out these,
And then you got to fill out those.
Your shoes don't have no soles on them,
And there's holes all in your clothes.
You really didn't want to come to this,
But you had no other choice.
Now that you sit across from this worker,
You don't even feel like you have a voice.

I'm very sorry I had to call you in, but,
I need one more signature,
Then you go back home and wait a few more days,
And you'll get your check for sure.

    Diane Jacob Green

The Anvil

There it sits, that time worn mass of steel.
Waiting to help mold a horseshoe, a plowshare, or the rim for a
wagon's wheel.
The blacksmith, next to it with hammer in hand, his foot on the fiery
forges pedal.
Removes from the fire a glowing brand, and on the anvil, lets it
    settle.
He strikes with a mighty blow that makes the anvil ring,
The anvil is his helper, a tool they are creating.

There it sits, that time worn mass of metal, waiting silently on its
oaken pedestal,
For young lads, their strength to test by trying to lift that mighty
anvil and its oaken rest.
The one that passes that weighty test, becomes "King of the Hill."
He has proven that he is stronger, and the best, and admired for
lifting that anvil.
Or they sit and listen to the hammer blows, that make that anvil sing.
To their young hearts, a desire it does bring. To be strong like the
blacksmith!
And like the anvil, steadfast and useful in their daily living.

Tho many years have passed, and brought progress through
mechanization, to our land, now a modern nation.
The anvil will always be, remembered in our history as a tool that
helped mold and create an easier way of living in a land that is truly great.
Nor is that anvil thrown on the scrap heap, to be forgotten and
covered with rust.
It sits patiently in a corner, covered only by memories and dust.

    Cliff Guinn

Our Joy and Our Sorrow

When a friend loses a loved one so dear,
We feel so useless when we can't be near.

So we send you our love, and our prayers each day,
And we hope that it helps in some small way.

God loans us our loved ones such a short time it seems,
to give us their love, and share in our dreams.

But oh aren't you lucky because you knew,
Someone so special, who really loved you.

    Gayla Crum

The Loved Ones

At eighty five the old man still
Walks up the stairs with subtle skill.

He moved into the upper room
When loved ones thought him near his doom...

But that was over five years past
No loved one thought this long he'd last.

Less often was he spoken to
Except when given things to do.

To occupy his idle days
And keep him out of others way.

The loved ones shared some common thought
The old man's welfare each one sought.

Perhaps his room is just a cage
Shouldn't he be with those his age?

They shared this with the ancient man
And spoke of several different plans.

Dwelling on each idyllic place
The old man turned his weary face.

And felt his knotted hands grow cold
All at once he felt so old.

    Felix Hernandez

To Be Somebody

To be somebody, yes that is me, means I can be what ever I
want to be.

To be somebody, I will use my mind, perfect my ideas and wisely
use my time.

To be somebody, I will work real hard, stay focused on goals buried
deep within my heart.

To be somebody, I will fast and pray, for I want God's blessing upon
my achievements each day.

Whether a doctor or whether a lawyer, a teacher, businessman, or
policeman of law and order.

Whether a scientist or astronaut, or a photographer that takes great
shots.

Whether an athlete with incredible fame, a writer or poet with an
unknown name.

To be somebody, that you can be, takes putting your mind to it you'll see.

    Derek L. Braxton

Crumbled Cookie

"You're an Oreo," He said.
We both laughed at that.
Oreo: Black on the outside and white inside.
How was I supposed to know that I should
have been offended? Coming from a white boy's
mouth it should have hurt, but it didn't.
I mean that is how I felt. God must have made a mistake.
He made me black. Big lips and big hips. Black.
Hair so nappy it could break a comb. So, who or what was
trapped in this dark vessel? My heart?
It had no color, except the red blood that flowed to keep it
beating. I was not an Oreo. I was neither black or white.
I was child. I was sister. I was lover.
I am human. I am mother.

    Cassandre Novembre

And Sometime You Cry

Making your way thru life one way or another,
wanting to go back in time and not at all bother.
They talk about equality, but when faced with reality,
you realize, that in that rush to the top,
it's still mostly men who beat you to the job.
With more money that you'll ever earn,
when will these men ever learn, that women,
without threatening, can be partners equal to them?

As you get older, time passing by, men flying high;
and you just getting by. Taking care of family,
home and a job too, with a sigh:
You are so tired and just want to sleep,
but problems you're facing are just so deep.
Each day such a chore, you can't take much more.

You then turn to God, who is always there,
as lots of people with promises failed to appear.
The comfort of prayer gives you much hope,
as in the earthly darkness you continue to grope.

And then you cry.
Anne P. Dickson

Things We Say Today

Often our tongue betrays our heart
Wanting to say "I Love You" with good intent
We often react and speak concerning the moment

Moments of stress, hurt or anger
We say things to protect ourselves
Hoping that problems will pass

What is meant to be a helpful word
Can easily lead to a deep scar
Not that we meant it, but it is done

It is not easy to take back words that cut
And the "Love You's" don't seem to help
All we can do is wait

Waiting can be a healer
It can either let one leave
Or sometimes bring love closer

I am hoping for the latter of course
Hoping you know how much you mean to me

So heal your heart from pains of past
And scars I've given you to, soon, I hope, I'll hold your hand
Knowing this time love is going to last
Jon Lewis

Lost Beaches

I remember when beach front
Was almost free........
Now, people come from Norway
To purchase our dreams
The cool breeze's and gentile waves
Offer them sanity and peace
I pray these industrialists respect
And care for our eden
Building houses 3 tiers high
Obstructing our view of virgin beach
A concrete jungle on our white sands
God will send a "cane", then:
Their venice will be valhalla again......
Crystle K. Italiano

And I Wait

And I wait, here in the waning twilight of these many years,
Watching, listening all alone, blinking back the tears.

Is that a familiar footstep on the pathway to my door?
Will I hear joyous laughter and be embraced once more?

But no, it is no one coming up the lane.
My expectant heart slows to once more feel the pain.

And I wait.

Remembering small smiling faces, some needing just a hug,
While others, slightly naughty, giving my heart a gentle tug.

Guiding and preparing each for the adult world ahead,
Loving words of wisdom, as I tuck them in their beds.

They're gone, grown up, with busy lives of their own.
Such a hurried pace of living, there's no time to even phone.

And so I lay my head down for another lonely night.
Pulling covers to my chin, smoothing them just right.

Staring out the window at a sliver of the moon,
Praying, hoping, wishing they will all come, one day soon.

And I wait.
And I wait..
And I wait...
Bobbye J. Inman

A Spring Vision

The leaves and limbs, newly bright,
    Wave farewell to the damp dark winter.
Flowers push through to the light,
    Bound by the call of spring, "Enter!"
"Come forward and paint the day."
    "Bring joy to those at play."
The long shaded night melts away,
    To the now eternal spring day.
This most glorious yearly delight,
    Gives to this watcher a special sight.
I view the greatest gift
    Without moving from where I sit.
Let the balance of the year come now,
    I will be able to face it somehow,
With assurance that what I survey,
    Will be with me every day.
James H. Harper

July of 1985

How I long for those endless afternoons,
waves singing and dancing,
salt stinging my tongue,
tickling my teeth, golden rays
speckling my flesh,
minute grains of sand mounting my body,
to hide in my bathing suit,
as sweat glides down my temples,
my hair flying upon the breeze,
silky lotion glistening on my skin,
and delicate castles housing me, the princess,
dressed in a flowing gown caressing the granite floor,
holding my magic wand,
I command the world,
queen of the sun and moon,
with a sky full of stars to wish upon at night.
But as darkness appears,
the waves no longer graceful,
roll over upon the land,
and wash my dream away.
Alison J. Dwyer

America

In this world of crime and corruption
we all strive to make it somehow;
To work hard at getting things done

We try to love one another
To live in this world
As brothers

But, there are times when race, creed, and color
Get in the way
And brings frustration
That often stays

We must learn to live as equals
And help each other out
For, in America, living, learning
And loving, is what it's all about!

Camille R. Burns

Sailing Life's Sea

On life's sea, we rarely get a tailwind.
We almost always sail into a headwind.
Occasionally, unexpectedly, the wind blows
  violently against our port or starboard.
Confused, we drift, searching for direction,
  wondering what course to follow.

Who is the Captain of our ship?
Surely, it is not you or me.
We would chart a course of certainty,
  smooth seas, and gentle breezes.

But would we tire of tranquility,
  become bored, and slow-minded?
Would we choose to alter our course,
  seeking a challenge?
We will never know the answer
Because you and I will never be Captain,
  no matter how mutinous we become.

Barbara J. Doddridge

Jr's Friends

I once had a florist friend by the name of Wilson,
  we always called him Joe
He said if you give a plant affection,
  it will surely grow.

He told me just talk to them,
  that they will understand.
Now as I look back on his words of wisdom,
  I can see the results firsthand.

These little friends don't eat very much, they don't talk back
  They are always there for you.
And every day as they continue to grow,
  They show you something new.

As the sun goes down, it's watering time
  I can hear them calling out.
Thank you, they are saying,
  They were mighty thirsty, there's no doubt.

Clara can hear me talking in my backyard
  When no one else is there.
No, I'm not talking to myself, but to my friends,
  Because they are everywhere.

Frank Walker Jr.

Stop

   We are people, not animals. We go to school, we have knowledge,
we have feelings and we should not be treated differently just
because of the color of our skin is black.

   We do things the way others do. We all have blood in our bodies.
We know when something hurts and we can feel pain. We all know
suffering is not something that anyone wants. It does not matter
the color of your skin.

   We have made life easier for others and their families. We have
built the streets where others drive their cars, we have planted
the food where others find to feed their families each day. We
clean houses and we wash clothes for others. We are human. We
deserve better than that. We are human and we refuse to be
treated like animals.

Junie Clauther

Thanks

Thank you God for everything,
  We have had upon this earth,
Thank you for our children,
  From the moment of their birth.

Thank you for our life together,
  From the time that it began.
Thank you for the gifts of feeling,
  That speaks to our heart again.

Thank you Lord, for being you,
  And sharing your love with us.
Thank you for letting us reach this goal,
  And keeping our faith and trust.

Thank you for the warmth and love,
  We share with our family and friends,
But most of all, we thank you God
  For Jesus Christ, our friend.

Jenny Adams Cooksey

Gone

We have come to the parting of the way.
We have said goodbye and shed many tears.
I wonder if she understands I still love her?
Can she perceive the torment I felt
Loving her, but fantasizing I held another?
Torrential waves, peaked with white, would roll over us
As I buried my face in her bosom, drowning me.
The hand of death would grip me as I wandered
Aimlessly through the motions of touching, holding, kissing,
Welcoming my landing on the shore, as lunging, ejaculating,
Meant the end of another nightmare.
I close the door, bags in hand,
Peter, my new lover, awaits me.

Estelle Sirkin

Boundaries of Love

We are trying to be good friends, but we want much more,
We heal each other's hearts every time they get tore,
We both know what to say and we know what we feel.
But we can not give each other love like a four course meal.
The boundaries I feel are more than I can bear.
Every minute of the day I say it is not fare.
I can only share my feelings to a certain amount,
The times I share them are less than I can count.
We can both read and understand each other's actions,
We have a lot more love then those other attractions.
I know our love will always stay strong
But me having to stay away, I can not take it for long.

Anna Sanchez

Nexus

In all the trials and tribulations of life
We must tell ourselves
There is a greater reason
For our suffering and distress.
I believed that
Loving someone was enough
We both know that isn't true;
The obstacles were relentless.
I know how hard you tried; we both did.
It has been said that
If you truly love someone
You must be willing to let them go.
As difficult as it was,
I want you to know that
I don't regret one moment.
Overlooking this spectacle
I see a stronger bond that will now and forever be
A special love between us
Linking our hearts together.

Jason Miller

"Tortured Souls"

The wombs are opened and the spawns are born.
We never suspect mal-adjusted forms.
It begins with minute steps as we look away.
Only to open our eyes and find they have gone astray.
Precautions are taken to correct the chaos.
But, defiance has never taken a day off.
Nothing ever seems to prevent the frost.
So all of creation must pay the high cost.
Problems continue to be created.
The ones in charge quickly negate it.
The pebbles have grown into boulders - too late to stop the avalanche.
Realize, we all shall suffer until the lambs are
returned to the ranch.
Yet, we must console ourselves with the prospects who
will lead us to a brighter future.
Lest we destroy our humanity completely with consistent temporary
suture.
The universe is an infinite place and is the home of our mother
We are all tortured souls at one time or another.

Henrietta Beavers

My Love, My Life

Her rich pillows pressed closely on my chest afire
We paused for fears and doubts then submitted to our youth.
I entered the sealed chamber exhibiting my desire
Hoping our love each to each was not the mirage of truth.

A girl of fears, a woman of compassion, a lady of beauty,
Made of me a man, as we talked and shared our days
Nursed on the weeping violins of Jewish tradition and duty,
She helped give meaning to every Godly phrase.

I love her purely and without regret,
For if we end a tear will find my eye
But I will always bless the fateful day we met
For she lives in my heart till I die.

Alvin Miller

Children of the Darkness

Yes,
We are children
Hidden in a corner of darkness
Until someone shines a
Light
On us and sees that
We're here, too!

Lucy Ann Herschman

Benediction

Without any purpose, reason or rhyme,
    We roamed a deep valley, which is ancient as time.
Great mountains arose, piercing the sky -
    The home-place of eagles we saw passing by.
Silence pervaded the heart and the soul,
    An unseen benediction, which made us feel whole
We sensed a great presence - a spirit of love,
    In the blue of those skies so far above.
We were quite alone in that pristine place,
    Removed from the furies of our human race.
Within the sweet solace so deep and profound
    We felt that right there, the Lord could be found!

Dorothy L. Black

Unveiled

Meet me at the masquerade my puppet.
We shall wear the un-masked masks,
Dance beneath the shrouded shadows,
Smile our crystal sly smiles.
We will fool them all
With our tie dyed eyes.
Oh yes, my whimsical warrior,
We will mock their illusion
more honestly than even they can embellish.
And as the stars succumb to twilight,
We shall lift our veils,
Reveal our facets and our double tongues,
As our eyes unfold ebony
To a porcelain masked menagerie.

Jenna L. Atkins

YOU Became A Stranger

We were once so close
We shared everything
We told each other our deepest and darkest secrets
We were inseparable
But then you went away
I did not hear from you for awhile
When you finally came back
I did not know how to act
I did not know what to say to you anymore
It was like meeting you for the very first time
What happened to you
What happened to us
Because
YOU became a stranger

Feona Sharhran Huff

Shells In A Jar

Each time we arrived at the ocean blue,
we tasted the salty water, it is true.

Still the ocean is blue, and the water is salty,
but all I have are memories of you.

This jar holds more than just shells,
this jar holds memories of which I will tell.

The sea the cottage, the shore,
even the old hat you once wore.

The walk down the beach and over the dunes,
a whiff of beach fires, the rise of the moon.

Walk to a seaside eatery,
where the seats are old and teatery.

Then to order a fine boiled lobster,
and attack it as if it were a mobster.

Alice Elek

Dear Grandson

In the olden days when I was a child,
We walked to school, well over a mile.

My Brother, Sister and I walked each day
To our school house which was far away.

In school I learned to read and write,
After school I learned to fly a kite.

Oh I did my homework every day
Even before I went out to play.

I also did many chores
Inside my house and out of doors.

I fed the dog
Then fed the hog
Put out the cat
And hung up my hat.

I loved my father, mother and teacher,
And when I went to Church I respected the preacher.

I hope this tells you something about the olden days
Because I am still learning about your ways.

Amanda Davis Wallace

Untitled

Goodbye my love
We will never meet again
Once this endless love was sworn to never part
Yet thru the years our love has grown apart

Goodbye my love
We will never meet again
No more the yearning, the passion, the pain and the tears
No more the tenderness we once shared

Goodbye my love
We will never meet again
Love has gone into the skies above
Will we ever remember the sweetness of love?

Goodbye my love
We will never meet again
Not true the yearning, the passion, the pain and the tears
Are still present
We weep for the memories of the past, can we forget?

Goodbye my love
We will never meet again
Parting of our love is now gone forever

Celia Chu

To A Poet

Poor poet!
Wealthy man!
Whose heart and soul must always be
Open, like a tender wound,
To all life's beauty and adversity.

To whom rain is seldom rain,
But tear drops falling, fey voices calling,
Storm wings spreading, or, God's voice fading
Across a mountain top or plain.

And how often you shall seek to find
A kindred feeling, a friendship healing,
Eyes that speak of bonds you seek;
And how seldom find the sign.

Lonely poet!
Lucky man!
Whose happiness, and sorrow too,
Will reach those depths
Reached by so few.

H. Inez Thomas

Let Him In

Do you feel lost or sometimes confused
Well the Lord will help if you wear
the right shoe's — He'll fill you with
hope and light through the day — He'll
even be with you at night when you
pray...for day by day and week by week
the Lord is your shepherd for whom
you seek — so open your heart and
let Him in He's always with you through
thick or thin — so what more could you
want in your life each day knowing
that Jesus is leading the way....

Debra A. Griffin

"I Love You"

"I love you,"
Well, what the hell is that supposed to mean?
Love, does it have a meaning?
I really don't know,
I thought I knew, but what I do know is,
I know it causes pain.
For it hasn't made me happy yet,
Well, maybe it's not supposed too.
Does it come to you in the night?
If it does I better leave my window open.
I better get ready for it,
Pretend I'm not waiting for it.
I hope it comes soon.
For my patience is small,
But my heart is big,
And it yearns for you,
So, I better prepare for love,
And so should you.
Because if it has any meaning,
Then "I love you."

Heather Palczynski

Hope

The roses that once blossomed around you
were as vibrant as a spring morn.
The gentle early light put diamond in their ruffles
Their thorns were just delicate prongs for dew drops

But today is night
Tender buds wilt with the dark sickness
Petals curl with the fear of each passing moment

Yellows to browns
Red to black

Rigid thorns battle the evil unseen
They, like you, are rooted to an unyielding earth.
Void of love
Void of light

Will the vicious black swallow their souls?
Where is their Hope!

Christine M. Donahue

Tomorrow

Tomorrow is another day to laugh, run and have some fun.
Tomorrow you and I would have spent time together you and
I forever.
Tomorrow the sun will shine and with the shine all of people's
spirits will rise.
Tomorrow the grass will be greener and the sky bluer,
tomorrow flowers will bloom and spread across the land.
There is only one thing wrong about tomorrow what I can see,
tomorrow will never come again for me.

Christine Ramos

The Language Class

Ten little children in language class,
Were seen, but seldom heard.
They laughed, cried, ate and played,
But they never said a word.

Some were dark, and some were light.
Each came from a different nation.
They brought their culture, while learning ours.
At best, a strange situation.

Their language no one understood.
It's true, not even their teacher.
But each one was a special delight,
For each one was God's creature.

Days went by before there arose,
A constant buzz of chatter.
When each could tell things went wrong.
Or when something was the matter.

Ten little children in language class,
Are now heard, as well as seen.
They chatter all day in work or play.
And everyone, knows what they mean.

Faye Teague

Choice

Oh my baby, oh so lovable,
What did I choose for you?

Conceived in weakness or in wanting,
what did I choose for you?

Racked with fear, torn with worry,
What did I choose for you?

Breath unbreathed, sight unseeing,
What did I choose for you?

Smothered, ripped from a womb life -giving
What Did I choose for you?

Gifts unique to a world denied,
What did I choose for you?

Oh my soul, Oh my God, forgive me,
What I did choose for you!

Hal Andrew

Song Of The Zodiac

As you gaze at the heavens
What do you see - a vast endless sky
The unsolved mystery

The planets in orbit - sun, moon and each star
That affect and direct us
Be they near or afar

There's a zodiac wheel - twelve houses in all
It's a blue-print of life
Tells of man's rise and fall

Celestial mechanics touch all that we meet
From Aries the Head - to Pisces - the feet

The stars may impel - if you let them it's true
But they cannot compel - when you're Master of you

Each house has it's memories
Of tears, smiles and song
They are lessons we learn
As we move along

There's much to accomplish before you are through
In the Zodiac House - designed just for you.

Jenny Travers Bouza

Love Is Red

A sonnet
what is a sonnet
putting to words a feeling
a feeling that eludes words
therefore a creative trick
somehow coerce the feelings into words
or symbols
paint a picture and pray
that the viewer sees
all the subtle shades and nuances that reflect the feeling

Words are colors interpreted differently.
Love is red, and pink, and shades unimaginable.
I will paint one very specific variation,
    and you will never see it quite like I do.
Therefore, you will never know exactly how I feel.

Be content.
When I feel,
    everything was red
Today,
    it pales in comparison.

Dwayne Kiefer

Questions

Why were we put here on planet Earth?
What is the meaning of existence and birth?
Why is the sky blue?
How high is up?
Why does the tail wag on a happy little pup?
What causes weather?
Why is the grass green?
Why when you need help is no one to be seen?
How good is perfect?
What kind of creatures live at the bottom of the sea?
I don't have the answers,
So don't ask me!

Joseph L. Closson

Memories

Where do memories come from?
What is their worth?

Spring brings happy memories of awakenings,
Easter, new flowers, new buds, new grass, newly tilled
soft black velvety earth bring forth life.

People are made of memories. Memories spew forth
like a passionate volcano, hot and fiery;
or steady and purposeful like a bright yellow sunrise;
or calm and cool like an azure blue-green bubbling brook...

A memory is like a person, it has breath, a pulse,
it needs nourishment to survive and it is dependent on its
creators for meaning and value. If ignored or forgotten
it will wither and die.

Memories need to live to keep bygone events and people
alive in our minds.
We need more than realism, virtual reality, movies and TV
to keep the past alive for better tomorrows.
Memories are the key to our past and our future.

Judy K. Kane

"Yesterdays Flower"

The flower that smiles today tomorrow dies
What is this worlds delight when even lightning that
Mocks the night, such a sight
We are born and later we will morn from the cradle
To the grave someone so dear is approaching so near
Yet why do we fear
The seed you sew another reaps while the wealth you
find another keeps
The robes you weave another wears and the arms you
forge another bears
Life is short. Plans are mislaid, and dreams
start to fade.
Look within your soul and you will behold
When you start in believing you will end up by receiving
To unlock the heart and let it speak
Are even lovers powerless to reveal to one
Another what indeed they feel
when you let it grow than you will know
The flower that smiles today
Might be here for tomorrow to stay

Jonas Laurinaitis

Works And Deeds

While people toil under the sun, what is their goal?
What would they gain with riches of the earth?
While lost and hungering for filling was their soul?
What would they have when they were just from birth?

Can a man takes his worldly treasures to the place beyond normal
    man's sight?
What has man at his birth at which was his own?
What has man at his death can he help in his might?
Will a normal man reap worldly treasures,s after his life,
    what he has sown?

Can man occupy every single place in this universe at once?
Can man see what is on his head with only his eyes?
Can man be satisfied in work of the world after months?
Can man keep his worldly possessions after his life as hard as he
    can try?

Hark! What will you do if the things of the world are worth nothing?
Lo! Trust in the one who has already died for you on the cross.
Yes! Trust and obey the LORD for he has more than of the world,
    everything.
Hear! The one who has created everything is the one who is the boss.

The one who lives and reigns forever is the one you should be
    living for!
What, at the end you should truly trust, obey, and fear?
Why, God Almighty who reigns forevermore!
So trust, obey, and work for the Lord Jesus Christ now and here!

Edward Tsai

Angie

When I feel no one cares,
When I feel no one is there,
When it seems they're all lies,
I sit back and close my eyes.
I dream away to the perfect place,
My dress is white with pretty black lace.
The people there are so nice and so kind,
I'm in their hearts not just their minds.
No one there screams or yells,
The loudest sounds are pretty bells.
When I think happiness and I are about to meet,
I'm back at home getting beat.
What can I do? Where can I go?
Who will help me? No one I know.
I wish I was cute little Bambi,
But instead I am five year old Angie.

Jennifer L. Portschell

Where Do the Children Go

Where do the children go?
When black meets white,
and they become kin.

Where do the children go?
When the red young brave would
fight the wind to see his fair true love again?

Where do the children go?
When oceans cross and slanted eyes,
are seeked by men of other skies.

Where do the children go?
Is it the end?

Or did we just begin; to make,
one race, one nation strong!
All alike and on our own.

One race, one nation strong.
Is where our roots trace back so long.

Debbie Clark

Love and Death

The nebulous fog waivers in the pale light of the full moon
When he awakes to the need of that sweet life giving fluid
To begin the hunt of one that is pure and virtuous
He rises slowly out of the earth that gives him power accursed.

Again he roams to ease the agonies of his existence
His thoughts on his soul's deprivation of happiness
Requisitioned to live damned eternally, he must hunt
Until the finds one to take from so pure and helpless.

His mind jolts back to the task upon him set this night
When he sees her wandering and singing in the gardens below
He is stunned by the beauty of the creature he has spied
And tears fill his eyes as in his heart love begins to grow.

She is everything he ever wanted to have in his life
Her aura radiates her serenity and her voice her contentment
And in her eyes and her song, her happiness flows freely
And in uncontrolled fury he attacks, beginning the defilement.

He pauses distraught, not wanting to violate this love he feels
But his desires take control; he drinks and then homeward embarks
As enmity comes and in bitter defiance he turns for one last look
Moonlight finds her milky white neck and on it the devil's mark.

Brian A. Little

Forget-Me-Not

I am the last of a long line of those who came before me.
When I am gone, there will be none to follow. There will be
no one left to remember me.

My path of life will be forgotten.
My footsteps will be erased.
My dreams will fade like yellowed pages in an old volume of
words.

Only fragments of myself will remain,
Fragments that leap off the parchment before you.

Will someone keep a lock of my hair, tied with ribbon as a
possession of worth?
Will someone keep a picture of me framed beside their bed?
Will someone slaughter my speech or quote me with care?

I merely wish to be remembered when my time comes. I want
those who come after to see who I am and to understand me.

I don't want my birth to be seen as a crime or an end, but as
a beginning. A beginning of someone who has chosen not to
forget those who have come before. A beginning of someone who
will carry on the name that should die.

Alice Schaefer

"The Love That I Would Share"

If the time should ever come
When I can hold you close to me
I would welcome you with open arms
And the love I have for you within my heart
We would share it all together as one!

Our lives would be filled with joy
For all the time to come out fear
I would hold you close, and comfort you
In all your sadness, as well as happiness!

So until that joyful day arrives
I'll always think of you with pride
If only in my thoughts and dreams
I shall always be near you dear
If only in our hearts, it's clear!

You put the laughter, and song in my heart
When I think of you, on those lonely nights
As I wish you were here to hold me tight
As I would tell you things, like it's all right
And give you all my love, both day and night!

Frank L. Stanley

In Hope to Grow Weak

I was lying in my bed;
when I heard the house begin to creek.

I was beginning to grow weak;
as tears started to roll down my cheeks.

Then I heard someone speak;
"I am God, and your soul I shall keep".

And hopefully one night;
we will all grow weak.

So that God will take our souls as we sleep.

For God will never grow weak.

Captain F. Stines Sr.

And Nettles Too

The Old Man, my brothers said; My time with him short; He did not die
When I was young. My Mother took us; left; I was six or seven,
And never really understood or was told the reason why.

This I know. My father was the one who taught me how to read.
In my memory lurks the fascinated absorption I fell
Into, as I curled within his arms, while he read to me
The Sunday Comics; not just read them, but brought them into life
With chuckles, gestures, tone of voice, and with green and smiling
    eyes.

I was not sent to school 'til I was six and long before that
I was reading everything to be found in a working home.
My brothers brought a magazine-type book, called Western Stories,
And, in a chill, forbidden parlor, replete with leather chairs,
I found adult books; not in the sense the word today is used.
Grown-up would be a better term; no obscenity or lust.

In our short time, he taught me other things as well; Deep breathing,
Exercise, for physical well being; and, for the heart and soul,
A love of flowers and all growing things; respect for nettles
And their sting; a love for animals, respect for fang and claw.

But the greatest gift he gave, the world that nowhere else is found;
The magic world that between the covers of a book is bound.

Janet Gorman

To Have And To Hold

When he puts his arm around me I get hot
When I'm away from him I get cold
It doesn't matter if he's near or far, he's still mine
To have and to hold.
We don't have fortune, or we don't have fame
But I still love him just the same
After all is said and done
The years have already told
When we married and became one
I'd be his to have and to hold.

Janie Reed

To My Love, Paula, On St. Valentine's Day

Love....What's in a word?
When it is spoken is seldom heard.
A thousand years in the blink of an eye,
this word holds, when to you I sigh.
Sometimes is uttered without a thought,
but the feeling is there, always in my heart.
I honestly love you and I always will,
my heart is yours until the earth stands still.
We have loved each other for just a few years,
our time is filled with laughter and tears.
During all this time I've had no fears,
our love will continue throughout the years.

Gino Howard

Our Melody

We cause a melody every time we meet,
when our hearts sing together and start to beat.
The band starts to perform music in the night,
as our love for each other attains new heights.

With the words "I love you,"
there is so much there,
yet still too much is very unclear.

Trumpets gleam as we touch,
when our eyes meet and say so much.
Drums burst into vigorous sounds,
as our hearts begin to pound.
Violins sigh, as you look in my eyes,
and tell me there will be no lies.

Until the last notes that our hearts are sending,
travels off into our happy ending.

April Neese

Looking Back, In Memory

Looking back on that sad day
When our Lord took you away
Heartache we thought we could not bear
But those who loved you, our sorrow shared.

Many years have now passed by
We no longer ask the reason why?
For all things done, are in God's plan
Hearing, believing, God's word, we
    now understand.

Adeline Hubanks

A Christmas Prayer

Christmas is that special time of year,
When people have renewed hope and show good cheer.

It's a time of giving and thanking God for his love,
It's a time of praise and blessings from above.

But most of all it's the gift of God's son, Jesus, who was born
  on this day,
Long ago in a manger in Bethlehem far, far away.

Thank you, God, for the love of Jesus and His tender care,
Thank you for Christmas and the joy we all share.

Bless us, dear God, throughout the coming new year,
Give us peace and prosperity and shield us with your tender care.

Watch over us, dear God, as we each go our own way,
Watch over us in our work, at home, and at play.

Love us, dear God, and keep us in your care,
Keep us mindful of Jesus while we feast on good foods, and presents
  we share.

But most of all, dear God, thank you for Jesus who provided the way,
By being born on the very first Christmas Day.

    James R. Tanner

It Was All A Swift Moment

It was all a swift moment
When the Sky bent down to kiss the Earth,
Giving new life to grow in her loving depths.
That time fell on the verge of Autumn
Where now I stand at the door to Spring.
And though so much is about to break
  (up through the soil and out of Sleep)
It is the Rose for which I wait,
Opening to Summer's sweetest month
When that dear flower would be God's earthly messenger....
'Calling out to the tiny one within my being
To emerge and be counted—
To open its innocent eyes to the wonders of procreation—
Viewing all from the safe perspective of my cradling arms.

    Elizabeth L. Bowling

That Special Night

'Twas that special night so long ago.
When the star shone bright o'er a stable low.
The shepherds rejoiced and leaped for joy.
As the angel told of a small baby boy.

  The heavenly host in a choral
delight, sang GLORY TO GOD on this
Holy Night.

  The animals quietly turned their
head, and just sat and stared at the
small manger bed.
  As Joseph and Mary knelt silent
and still.
  GOD'S SON had been born to do
His will.
  The world lay in slumber and
cared not that night, that a KING had
been born in such humble delight.

  But now, just as then, to all
who receive, the CHRIST will still
enter a heart that believes.

    Donna June Chearney

Untitled

A firefly sits on
my nose I sneeze hard it smiles
like mom like a rose!

    Reynaldo Encina Jope

Untitled

Before, your hands were rough.
When they held mine they shook.
My eyes cried out a river,
Yours' were as dry as a desert.

We held on so long and so tight.
And at times you showed no comfort.
Both my heart and mind were opened,
Yours' were closed with a lock.

But it wouldn't go on forever.
I shared my feelings through laughter or tears.
My soul had trust in yours,
Yours' was just beginning.

Now, your hands are a blessing.
When they hold mine they comfort me.
My eyes cry out a river,
Yours' cry out a sea.

    Cathryn Samarco

The True Meaning Of Christmas

Christmas is that wonderful time of year,
When we are light-hearted and full of cheer,
With gifts to buy and wreaths to make,
After grocery shopping, goodies to bake.

Everyone is smiling and full of glee,
For in just a few days, the time shall be,
When families will gather to share their gifts,
There's magic in the air that gives us a lift.

Then comes the time when we should pause,
And remember who is the real Santa Claus.
Not the fat, jolly man in the bright red suit,
With a white beard carrying a bag of loot.

The real Santa is often left out in the cold,
While wild parties, expensive gifts seem to fit the mold.
When not far away, just around the bend,
A soft voice calls like the sound of the wind.

"The greatest gift of all is LOVE,
Sent from the Father up above."
Just look around and He's always there,
His wonderful creation is everywhere.

    Jane Hardeman

God's Love

God loves us all the time,
When we fall....
He takes us by the hand to help us along,
Now is the time to live just for Him,
Giving up our worldly sins,
He forgives us when we hurt Him and loves
  us at our worst,
God's love outshines the sun,
Each day is good when we love Him with
  all our heart,
It takes a great while to know Him,
But God is love and in His love we can shine!

    Glenda Rae

Full Moon

Look at the moon, so bright, so clear,
When you are full, why is there fear?

You have a purpose for shining so bright.
I wonder what I will find by your guiding light?

If you look closely, inside there is a scene,
but only true hearts and eyes can understand its theme.

Once you are out, the night has begun,
but when you go in, then out comes the sun.

With you comes mystery, light, and romance
to add to the love that has begun to enhance.

When all goes wrong and you feel a little doomed,
just take a look above at the sight of a full moon.

Your troubles may be many, your worries may be few,
but in the eye of the moon, you will find a new you.

You are gone now, the sun is shining bright and I
will look forward to seeing you again, perhaps maybe tonight.

Angela Lynn Aycock

"Life X 2"

Where life ends and begins,
when you step out of a world

Onto a platform of faith,
no desire to look back,
spiritually, psychologically
emotionally inclined, never
to look back at a life left behind.

The pain, the suffering, the turmoils
of life are steps leading toward another life.
Once you step across line,
Never again to look behind, where
Old life ends; and new life begins

Eunice Williams

When You Were Young

Oh how to recapture the glory days
when you were young
And the world was yours
for the asking?

A whim took you around the world
and a fancy gave you love.
Everything was easy when you were young
and sunshine was for basking.

A handsome lieutenant was in his glory
when a pretty maiden ran to him
On the other side of the world
where even a war was just a tasking.

Oh how to recapture the glory days
when you were young
And the world was yours
just for the asking?

David J. Seigle

True Conviction

Priorities, like love, pulled tight
Until we loosen reins, in plight
Things, we thought in life, a must
We tend to leave in Blinding Dust

And as we gallop, gasping breath
When feel weakened, close to death
We stagger back, to our dismay
All the fragments have Blown Away.

Lynn S. Feld

Beyond Our Tears

Where are the evenings of warm, Summer winds....
Where are the mornings of Spring..Where are the
days so full of love, they made our young hearts
sing! Where have they gone..those memories..of
sharing joys long past? Where are the lips that
promised..happiness would last?
Often, I have wondered..what we'd find beyond our
tears..when all the dreams were wakened and we'd
gotten on in years..with no journeys left to savor
and no love songs left to sing..no mountain tops to
soar to as we mend life's broken wing!
How can anyone survive, a tattered, broken heart..
a spirit without vision..a soul that's torn apart?
Now that voice that was great within us, as we reached
for the stars so bright..is but a fading whisper heard
crying out at night!
Yet..all must face the future...the winter of our lives..
It is the final season..that comes as no surprise..I pray
that when my time comes...and I am called above...that
I'll be carried home again..in an angels arms of love!

Jaime Shockley

My African Place

Take me home to my African place.
Where I can walk around proud,
Because of my race.
Eye-to-eye and never looking down.
For, I am equal to everyone around.
Take me home to my African place,
Where I am looked at without disgrace.
Take me home to my African place,
So, I can say, "Yes God, I am proud of this place."
Take me home to my African place.

Angela Yvonne Terrell

Oasis

I want to be in a place where time does not control me
Where life is not surrounded by fear and circumstance
A place of unkept beauty, by no means any lesser
Untouched by human selfishness, for anyone to love
Flowers never cease to bloom, the sun is always brilliant
Even in the darkness, the stars don't lose their way
Where rivers run on endlessly, not halted by construction
Where trees grow as old as time, unharmed by a corporate race
The air never so sweet as now, the wind never overpowering
The mountains strong and majestic, never crumbling to the sea
It's hard to find this rarity now, but still it does exist
although it is a wonder, it's been spared so long
For others gone before me, without consideration
banished all new wilderness their greedy hearts could grasp
Now learning from their errors, it's not too late to find it
the place that not so long ago was common on this Earth
A dwelling I only dream of now, but someday may I find it
And never take for granted the beauty of this place

Dana L. Reid

Mankind's Quest

Where doth on this dusty road I travel
Where my fate in life shall unravel
That path which has already been chosen for me
That place which faith will bring me to see
When the meaning of my life should at once be surpassed
When the knowledge of my place in life should come to me at last
As the aimless wondering of my place in life begins to come to an end
As this never ending quest brings to me mine our message to send
Then my heart will have found purpose and my mortal being shall be
thrilled
Then my mind may be at rest knowing that my life hath been fulfilled

Cory L. Overton

The Wound that Bleeds in Silence

It's the wound that bleeds in silence
Where no scar is ever seen -
    That turns to rigid firmness
A face where smiles have been -
    It's a wound that drains the happiness
No more does laughter ring -
    There are no sounds of merriment
From lips so wont to sing -

    SO,
Let's all share, - let's be aware
    When someone hurts inside
He may not ask -
    He'll wear a mask
    His pain he'll try to hide
Oh, MAY I HAVE YOUR SPIRIT, LORD
    THAT I WILL SENSE THE NEED
AND WITH COMPASSION, FAITH, AND LOVE
    BIND UP THE WOUNDS THAT BLEED

   Iola Fisher McNutt

Life In The Slow Lane

Somewhere there exist kinder, gentler places
Where people are content with less,
    without hi-powered cars, color TVs and VCRs.

Where they don't worry about getting into the right college
So they can qualify for a high pressure job
So they can earn more to spend more.

Sure they have their problems. Don't we all?
One thing they don't have to worry about is dying
    when their time has come.

It's called life in the slow lane,
    and it does exist;
I can show some places to you.

They're just over the rainbow, but don't settle in;
    you may never want to leave.
Perhaps such a place in paradise lost...

For once we've tasted our way of life,
We can never go back to paradise
    except in memory, or for a short vacation.

   Joseph Desloge Jr.

Dreams

'Tis often said that life is a dream,
Where reality can vanish as water to steam.
But what is real and what is not,
Is easily confused and too soon forgot.
To be able to sleep, to sleep like a child,
See visions of flowers and animals wild.
And of all visions mere mortal could find,
To spy with the eyes the divinest of kinds.
With eyes like a spring day, as dark as the sea.
A face with the beauty of simplicity.
And skin as soft as a feather of down,
A voice so light, the sweetest of sounds.
But this is a dream that must we remember,
Like the crispest of days in the heart of December.
To see what is real in the realest of sense,
And dream of our wishes to our heart's contents.
And if in dreams all wishes come true,
Then in all my dreams, I wish for you.

   Andrew B. Newberg

I Dream Of A Beach

I dream of a beach....
    where sea gulls fly and children play
    where feelings are bright
    and love is the breeze

    Where the sand is soft
    and its warmth is like a heart
    where sandpipers roam like lost loves
    and people build lasting memories

I dream of a beach....
    where families are created
    and nature is the mother
    where the clouds serve as pedestals
    and God is the speaker

    Where the sea is as blue as life
    and the waves are unavoidable obstacles
    where the sun is a ray of hope
    and the warmth of all

If only in my dreams
    this beach appears;
    then this must be life and my holy home.

   Jennifer L. Matheny

Untitled

Take my hand and we shall go where the forgotten forest lies
Where the peaks soar, scraping the sunsets, uniting heaven and earth
There the river is life and it touches all who dare to take a drink
This is not a myth
There is no cause to fear, for man has laid no hand here
The smells soothe the soul, intimately relaxing the mind
Submission and union are inevitable, we all long for such paradise
This is where it began and where it all must end
Where illusion, dreams, desires, and fantasy all become truth
Here you shall not be judged or harmed
Here you may live and take shelter, this will never fade away
Here you shall finally be safe and cherished beyond understanding
This is where you shall be found and rescued from the lost
This is where there is heart beyond measure
Where there is love that is true, lasting, boundless, and infinite
Just believe
And take my hand

   David Hutchinson III

Woodland Forest

I know of a woodland forest
    Where pine trees grow straight and tall,
And green branches cast their shadows
    On ground where pine needles fall.

There is a peaceful silence there
    Which fills the soft sweet air,
But for the singing of the birds,
    That can be heard most everywhere.

One stands in awe and wonder
    At the beauty the scene conveys,
And knows that God, the Creator,
    Is the artist it portrays.

   Gloria Andersen

Untitled

Heaven is a place
Where the temperature is seventy degrees.
Nobody needs money.
Because everything is free.

There is no hate, no lust, no greed.
All people is of one race
The human race, indeed.
Jessie M. Eady

The Light Of God, Forever Shines

There's a time and place for everyone
Where there's love, a joy and peace of mind.
Where angles sing of glorious things
And, the light of God, forever shines.

Stars will sparkle like diamonds.
Butterflies will fill the sky.
Flowers will bloom, sweet perfume.
And in life, no one ever dies.

No more pain or sorrow.
No more sadness or grief.
All there is, is happiness.
And in all hearts, belief.

Children will laugh and play there.
And, the child in all will come alive.
If we walk His way every day.
We know we have arrived.

There's a time and place for everyone
Where there's love, a joy and peace of mind.
Where angels sing of glorious things
And, the light of God, forever shines.
Mark Amel Travis

Still Waters

To still waters I did go
Where upon Geometry was found
Made by sceeters all around

With their dance of circles they performed
Patterns true with form

And all the while I gazed
I could not help but be amazed
That still waters could reveal
Such busy Geometry
Always perfect and so real
Gloria Mary Rodriguez

Venice

In a west coast beach town
Where yesterdays linger on street corners and in shanty alleys.
Where sunken eyes look out from tired minds
Which once housed dreams of love and bright tomorrows.
And faded jeans and dirty sandals pace the sidewalks -
And "hip lives on" sprawled across buildings forming questions
As to their real meaning.
And sunrise and sunset mark time by the steady beat of an ocean
Who thrashes in angry response but cannot stop.
I rest my body - but my spirit finds little repose
And nightfall carries disappointment
And resignation settles into sleep -
But a stubborn seed refuses to be crushed,
And nourished by the morning sun it sprouts a tiny fetus of hope.
Janet Drinkovich

Ode To Marian

Marian, O Marian!
Wherefore didst thou flea?
Me thought thou wast contented
And engrost with love for me.

But something stirred thee from without
Pray tell me what it be.
Unless, alas, I die from doubt
of the love thou hadst for me.

Aphrodite could not change thee from within
For I know thy heart is stout,
From the love I gave to thee and then,
Thou returnedst it only now to walk out.

If I could reach with mortal hands
I would bind the Pleiades,
And loose Orion from his bands
Then smile, and give you these.

Were I Pygmalion or the living God
This one thing I would do.
As all men must return to sod
I would return the love that's given you!
Dewey L. Duncan

Looking Back

A smile comes upon my face
Which no one can erase
As I think of the days
And also of the nights
That my true and only real love
Held our hands together
Our clasp was warm and tender
The look in our eyes would shine forever
The old man in the moon
Who knew us so well
Whispered, never have I seen
Such a love for one another
But, my love's mother
Could not see that we
Were in love with each other
Sad, but true
Never will he and I
Ever love another
Although we part from each other forever and ever.
Alice Oates

Alike

The world is like a little toy top,
    which spins and goes around.
It's sort of like the human life,
    which has its ups and downs.
The rule of earth and living lives,
    must clarify themselves.
To engineer the future near,
    we must learn to represent ourselves.
We correspond with one another,
    and lecture how it's done.
To solve our problems in a fashion,
    brings hope to everyone.
To set our goal within our life,
    and strengthen all our needs.
For human life and earth alike,
    will balance and achieve.
Catherine C. Mondragon

A Stray Baby Skunk

Silky snow was gracefully falling in whispering silence,
While a Michigan's February morning was just slowly dawning.
All of landscapes were covered in the thick gray languidness,
The frozen ravine was winding as appearing and disappearing.
When pairs of ducks were intimately ducking into darkened cracks,
Unexpectedly a black spot popped out of a drooping thicket.
Oh, what a surprise; the unseasonable visitor was baby skunk,
That started to fuss around with sniffing at the ground snow.
Suddenly squirrels playing on the ground climbed up trees,
And watched over the skunk with bated breath while wagging those tails.

The tiny creature's movement was nimble as if battery-powered,
Its overcoat so well-designed in black and white stripes.
After pursuing a round of food hunting, but without a catch,
The poor skunk vanished back in the shadow, where it came out.
Squirrels cautiously hiding in the high branches leapt down again,
Then hopped toward me begging for food at the glass door.
My mind wandered to my grandchildren hugged in their parents' love,
While silky snow was still falling in peaceful dreamy silence.

Esaku Kondo

The Storm

Over head we see the dark the clouds that black the sky
While all around we feel the fright and watch our children cry.

The winds begins, the big trees bend, there's noises neath the ground.
While right before our eyes we see, those big trees tumble down.

Then in the distance near the hills, we see the rushing waves.
Of water from torrential rains, some captured in the caves.

Again, the fear of what to do, to save our house and home.
Again, we wait for strength to show where strong folks seem to roam.

Then as we look for some relief, we see the water stopped.
The only small signs of the storms are where our people mopped.

Oh how fearful is the sound of storms when passing by.
Oh how fearful we still are, when spellbound by the sky.

Fred J. Vague

Reincarnation

Wild wind roils grass to a reedy green sea.
While great hawk circles, turtle suns a lee.

Ashen black sky frames a radiant sun.
Each in their element, in their element none.

In sameness and contrast time pulls asunder.
There my love and I walk in silent thunder,

Of men on great horses and armor's harsh clang.
Fear in my nostrils and heart's burning pang.

Caught for an instant in time's chasm rift,
Shunned by reality in ether adrift.

A treacherous journey cross a bridge of dark mud,
Baptized for centuries with witches' spilt blood.

When the luminous sword from my own hand to his,
Healed the great gulf in time, closed the abyss.

Just a man and a women, not two and not one.
Each in their element, in their element none.

Christine M. Jewell

Fall

The leaves fall to the ground like an evening star,
While I was walking through the woods, it seemed so far.
The fall wind blew so seemingly,
As if an old man's eyes were watching me.
I looked upon the sky and saw, the white clouds dangling by.
The pond's water shiver,
The ducks quiver.
I walked slowly through the woods,
Tripping over stumps that stood.
As I was walking a squirrel passed my by,
Gathering nuts in his pouch to supply.
When to the end of the wood I stopped, and stood.
My weary mind looked and saw four angels from the heaven's far.
They looked upon the fall's dropping leaves,
When they left I felt the cold winter breeze.

Eileen A. Fleming

Spring

One morning when I first awoke,
while no one in the house yet spoke,
I rose and from my window saw,
that winter soon would be no more.

The trees which seemed to be quite bare.
would soon have leaves of green to wear,
and later on the fruit would come,
then 'round the nectar bees would hum.

A little sparrow and his spouse,
conversed about our new bird house.
While now the breeze still seemed quite cool,
Our bird bath soon would be their pool.

I knew all this was done by God.
The trees, the birds, the smell of sod.
only he, such good could bring,
this was the first sweet day of spring!

Carol Kaszubski

Whispers at Night

Soft cold whispers pull me out of peaceful sleep,
Whispers are my heart's release of secrets that I keep.
The moment passes, the voices cease and leave me to myself,
But the feeling lingers on and gives my soul the creeps.

I stir from bed to see what calls to me from there outside,
And find there's nothing there because my senses, they have lied.
To calm my quaking nerves I pull myself to by the window.
My mind begins to wander and I think of tears I've cried.

Again to bed I wander and I fall to restless slumber,
And wake throughout the night again so much I've lost the number.
I fear the fitful dreams that will remain here though I wake.
As morning comes my fear is none and the dreams have gone asunder.

Deidre Stacy

The Road

Love is a road that must be
    Traveled every day.
To keep unwanted temptations
    From getting in the way.
Keep this road traveled
    And you will surely find.
That love will last forever
    Until the end of time.

Matilda Pace

Serenity

The sky is azure blue
  white clouds drifting by,
The beauty of the mountains
  in the distance greets the eye.
The rustle of the leaves
  as a soft breeze whispers through,
The nodding of a flowers head
  a small bird comes in view.
I wish that I could share today
  the riches I've been given—
Gold and silver none of these,
  only this gift from heaven.
Man cannot match the things I see
  nor make the peace that brings the calm.
The quiet stillness of the day
  is like a healing balm.
I am so grateful at days and
  for each new day I see
And that my God does send his love
  to keep and nurture me.

Allian L. Eddy

Tale of the Winter Blahs

There once was a gal from Westminster,
Who dreaded the coming of winter.
It brought on the blahs,
Not the ha, ha's,
On this poor Westminster spinster.

She said to herself, "This must stop!
These winter blahs I must now pop."
She thought for awhile,
Got a plan and smiled,
And demolished those blahs from bottom to top.

"How did she do it?" You ask,
It was definitely no small task.
She did deeds of kindness
To her neighbors, no less,
With a heart that was true and not masked.

This plan can surely be done,
By everyone under the sun.
Get out there today,
With kind deeds, don't delay,
And you too can put the blahs on the run.

Edwina March

Don't Light My Dark

Why does this light intrude upon my dark?
Who gave it permission to break into my night?
I close my eyes trying to hold onto my dark,
but the light refuses to surrender.
My night brings me comfort,
the comfort I cannot find in the light.
My dark is calm like the sea at night.
My night is a soothing dark sky,
yet it is still adulterated by flecks of light.
The light shows all of the anger and hate.
The night contains the peace and love
that I always seek.
The light unleashes danger in every corner.
The dark bathes me in safety at every turn.
Stay away light... I need my night... I need my dark.

Hendrix S. Boags

Waiting for Reasons

Staring is easy if you are one
who is inclined to stare.
I've only met two
who could make me blush and drop my eyes.

Looking through people
into the depths of oceans, rivers—
we are all liquids, really.

Only
we do not flow by ourselves,
so tonight
I sit at my keyboard
in a glass.
Think

wind, tremors,
rain.

Jennifer Jenkins

Woods And Streams

I am a man of the woods and streams
who loves the feel of autumn leaves
to look at he morning sun
as it rises above the trees
to see the frost upon the ground
oh how I love the feel of autumn leaves

The streams are cool and flowing so slow
to see a small stream entice's my soul
to look to God for riches untold

I am a man of woods and streams
who loves the feel of fresh fallen snow
and the trickle of rain across my brow

The God above who made us all
but I love the woods and streams
He gave to us all

The Deer abound in meadows so clear
I love to see them all
I am a man of the fall

David R. Evans

"L'Adieu"

Here is, gentle people, the ballad of lovers
Who once, so eagerly, did care for each other.

"George, I beg you, remember Valdemosa..."
"Please, Frederic, forget Valdemosa."
"The grand Monastery, wedding dressed in the light..."
"Shrouded in the mist, as a widow in white."

"Silence and peace, a sweet and living harmony..."
"Silence of hearts, a slow and subtle agony."
"See again the dew-drops on blooming almond-trees."
"I see the rain weeping on bitter-sweet memories."

"Can you still hear the bells singing in the mornings?"
"I hear the knell mourning eternal love endings."
"But your heart was beating, in those times, wasn't it?"
"Only a last echo, the drum beat of retreat."

"George Sand and Chopin, love and life for ever..."
"War and death, Frederic, the voyage is over,
The vessel, from now, is called Nevermore,
The blue note dies away in fading yesteryear."

Tell me, gentle people, why the winds of winter
Tonight, in minor cry and sigh and whisper.

Fanny Rougeot

Blessed

This morning I awoke to the sound of a chirping bird
who took liberty in imposing on my secret world.
His songs placed magic and praises in my heart
and moved and inspired me to another start.

My feet united with the tiled floor...
while my hands made contact with the bedroom door.
I dressed hastily, for this was a special day,
God had blessed me with one more day.

Off to work to start the day's task,
of rendering God's work at my very best.
Exalting his name and glorifying him in praise
for I was thankful he had blessed me with another day.

The sun had gone and the evening had come,
but I knew my work was not complete and done.
So as I kneel at my bedside and begin to pray
I ask the Almighty to bless me with just one more day.

Diana Wilkerson

A Dog With A Certain Problem

There once was a dog named Sam,
Who was as cute as a new born baby lamb,
He could snuggle and hug ya to pieces,
his problem he had 39 leashes.

What to do with leashes amount 39,
Sell them for a dime?
Sell them for a penny?
Who we kidd'in we ain't gonna sell many.

But soon people from every place,
Came and took them out of Sam's face,
Jump for joy hip hip horray,
Those people really saved the day.

This puppy has no more stress,
He's sittin' in money, more or less,
Wow this hound,
Sure can get around.

SAM with 39 leashes!!!!!!

Jessica Slater

Virtual Reality Is Our Andie

We once had a daughter named "Andie"
Who was born with sparkling brown eyes and hair
When she was two or three she'd sit on your knee
For another ten, blessed were we, life was fair

At age thirteen life's lessons taught humility
Witty and clever jokes were a cover for smoke in the air
At fifteen studying was for jerks and to her friends she'd flee
Several years of counselling: our souls were stripped bare

At seventeen our teenage queen worked and drove a Camaro 280 Z
Mom and Dad were stupid and dull, and driven to despair
The counsellors said NAY: they had no answer to our plea
Now eighteen is at hand, and tired are we, Andie has energy to spare

Immortality and beauty has she, to offer to society
A warning to the wise: lookout and beware!
Andie is now free to practice her magic on you and me
Her disarming smile can beguile even those who are aware

Cecile MacIvor

Untitled

I walk down my street, watching and weary. Looking for the boys
who yell my name, they always say how pretty I am, and how soft my
skin must be.

With my head held high I keep walking on by. I know what their
really saying. "Come on, go with me girl, I want to show you my
side of the world."

No thank you I reply. I'm gonna see the world, and all the
wonderful things in it. Things that a girl like me could only dream
of, I want to see the places that ancient men and women danced and
look at the same night sky, they gazed upon so long ago.

They laugh, "Girl you sure are crazy, ain't no way a girl like you
gonna ever see something like that, don't you know that by now?

I hold my head high and with every ounce of pride I own, I tell
them boys. I won't live in this city all my life, and before they
plant me in God's green earth I'm gonna see all them places, my heart
wishes to see.

And when I do finally set foot on that sacred ground I'm gonna
dance, and sing, and yell.

Brook M. Chaffin

Ideals

Ideals flow like roaring mountain streams
Whose waters pass sharp crags and dreams.
Crashing against each critic's canyon walls
Our glistening thoughts approach the Falls.
Cavorting, flashing like rays of golden darts
Confused by mindless boulders' hearts,
In time uncertainty exacts its tolls
As cascading waters torment all mortal souls.
The waters slow by Nature's descending rules
To flow into soft swirling middling pools.
So hopefully all moments stand expectantly.
Only to ebb downcast and unrewarded to the Sea.

Donald Steinberg

Why?

Everyone is crying, they say there's a hole in their heart,
Why?
They say there has been a death,
They say that my Papa is gone,
Forever.....
Where is he? Why does he not come back?
I wish for him to be there, to sit me beside him, for me to hear
him say, just once, that all will be well again....
I wish for him to coax me, to plead with me not to cry, I wish to
see his wise old head turn to me and say...
Do not cry, all will be well again. They say to me, soon little
one, all will be forgotten. Why did my Papa leave us, what is this
death they speak of? They say that soon, they too, will leave,
why?
Hopefully, I ask them Why do you cry, did you fall, do you feel
pain? Tearfully, they tell me, no, little one, I did not fall,
but my heart is torn to pieces, and never will heal again, I ask
them, why?
They say there has been a death, they say that my Papa is gone,
Forever......

Jessica Leah Gilchrist Callinan

"Why Am I Here?"

Have you ever wondered when you were full of despair
  "Why am I here?"

When the world around you seemed to be falling apart
and you asked, "What can I do and where do I start?"

You wake up in the morning and whisper: "Still another day,"
and the face reflected in the mirror looks lifeless like clay
and you find yourself asking: "Why am I here?"

Then suddenly, out of your despair a light from within,
seems to appear and you wonder perhaps I am here to lead,
or to guide, for to do my best will fill me with pride

To be a glowing example for those who have lost their way
Would surely be the answer to a better day.

To wipe a frown from someone's face and put a smile in it's place.
To ease another's heart felt pain will let me know
my efforts were not in vain.

When you can set an example by your good deed
and the people around you take your lead
and the world becomes a better place and the people around you
begin to cheer, then, you will have the answer to,
  "Why am I here?"

Ann Heinz

The American Indian's Plight

Haven't you done enough? Why can't you leave them alone?
Why are you making it tough, for them to have a home?

You've taken away their land, you've made them live in shame.
You think that you're so grande. How can you in God's name?

They're the natives of this soil, not me and all the rest.
It makes my blood boil, to see them in this mess.

How can you be so insensitive? You know that you are not right.
It is all so very vindictive, the American Indian's plight.

But, someday all will be judged, and you'll have to pay what is due,
and God will remember that grudge, and the same will happen to you.

So think let your conscience be clear. You have what you deserve.
Listen, please open your ear. Show that you have nerve.

Geri Cooper Shorter

What Went Wrong?

Why do the years seem so long?
Why do the days go on and on?

Why does pain hurt me so?
Why do tears always flow?

Why do dreams not come true?
Why do dark days make me blue?

Why does my mind spin 'round and 'round?
Why do my cries make no sound?

Is it just rumor or is it just fake,
That my whole life is all a mistake?

What can be deceived cannot be learned,
For all my sorrows have left me burned.

Now I feel that life is gone,
Oh dear God, what went wrong?

Debbie Louise Dement

Thousands, Thousands Of People May Wonder

Thousands, thousands of people may wonder.
Why does it seem as if nobody cares?
Why does it hurt when we do surrender?
Why do we always need to put on airs?
Time no longer has the power to heal.
It's easy to fit in when we do sin.
So we break hearts and cause sorrow and steal,
Until love captures our hearts in a spin.
Your body and soul can again be true.
To keep your sacred love pure you will lie.
Sudden love can make you heartbroken too.
Risking yourself for a fancy you may die.
Time will no longer hide and forgive crime.
The answers are fading away with time.

Astrid Avedissian

Why Is It?

Why is it that you make me feel this way?
Why is it that you make me want to say?
I LOVE YOU, I LOVE YOU!

I love you, but I don't know why it is,
I want to be with you and start to kiss,
ALL OVER, ALL OVER!

All over you I want to be tonight,
Why is it that you make it feel so right?
WHY IS IT, WHY IS IT?

Why is it that you make it grow inside?
This thing I have for you I cannot hide,
I LOVE YOU, I LOVE YOU!

Why is it that you make me feel this way?
Why is it that you make me want to say?
I LOVE YOU, I LOVE YOU!
WHY IS IT? I LOVE YOU! WHY IS IT? I LOVE YOU! WHY
IS IT?

Gary C. Peeples

A Wildflower

She wasn't like the other flowers,
Wild, tempting, and beautiful to the eyes.
She was a flower tamed by the wind,
Innocent, sweet, and living alone.

She watches the others dancing in the field
And wonders why she isn't like them.
She hears the wind whisper,
"So you are different, is that so bad?"

It says she is free,
Yet she remains on her own.
She is a stranger of love,
Though she wants to be loved.

A man sits in the field now.
For the first time in her life she feels love.
His eyes pass her.
He is looking for a wildflower.

Nobody has seen her and she believes they never will.
Is it fair for someone so special to go unnoticed?
She waits for the wind, but there is no reply.
The night is still.

Alisa Cohick

Does Anybody Truly Care?

One of these mornings I
will arise and sing,
of the turnabout nature
of the human being;
Jails overcrowded with
no room to spare,
But, does anybody truly care?

Conceive them, birth them,
and kill like a flea;
Sometimes they don't
make it to even see.
We say this is something we all must bare,
However, does anybody truly care?

To rise and sing seems far for me,
The human being is
too near sighted to see.
Changes are rare, and
do we really dare;
The question still is,
does anybody truly care?

Ernestine Green

The Bride Wonders

As I start this wondrous day, I wonder how things
Will be? Will our plans go right or will they go wrong,
I wonder...how things will be?

As I start to put on my gown, my shoes, my veil,
I wonder what people will see? Will they see a
Beautiful bride, a handsome groom,
I wonder...what people will see?

As I enter the church, where friends and family
Wait, and my fiancee as nervous as me, I start down the
Isle, with my dad at my side, and again...I wonder....
How things will be? Will everyday be a new adventure,
For my husband and me, or will it be quiet and loving as
Can be? I wonder...how things will be?

I wonder, and I wonder, how things will be, but the
Only thing I see, is hardwork and loving and
Everything left to my husband, my family, and me.

Jose R. Garza

Stealing Sanity

A whispering voice, deep inside;
Will not let me free.
Echoes tension, rips you apart;
It steals your sanity.

A mindless laugh, the laugh will kill;
An evil thought, my mind goes still;
It gets your eye, and drives you mad,
A mindless laugh your mind now has.

An evil clown, the clown can be;
To watch your dreams - shatter!
It crushes you, and blanks your mind;
Leaves no thoughts for you to find.

Thoughts rush toward, a frightened train;
A mindless thought, an evil insane...

Joseph Benden

Friendship

If I tell you the meaning of friendship,
will you agree or disagree?
It has many different forms, limitations,
depths, and degrees.

The miracle of friendship can happen anytime.
It forms within a moment,
and can change your life and mine.

It happened in the moment
that you gave your heart to me,
and I will always keep it close,
and know it makes us we.

The miracle of friendship is truly a gift from above,
and He has blessed me doubly with the sharing of your love.

He's made us friends forever,
and of that we'll never part.
For friends are friends forever...
When the friendship's from the heart!

Donna S. Smith

The Lovers

Below, midnight ripples under a net of shivering light.
Wind sighs through trees standing sentry in the night.
Above, diamonds twinkle in a black satin sea.
Time stands still, perfect, for he and she.

Fingers dance through hair black as night.
Brown eyes sparkle, with anticipation, at the sight.
The touch of a hand against all she can see.
Broad shoulders, muscled arms, no one more perfect than he.

Breath, taken away, dwindles to sighs.
Passion glows in soft, velvet eyes.
Soft caresses, breathless whispers, a beginning to all they can be.
Everything, forever, perfect for he and she.

Gail Davis

Thoughts of Home

Memories like a river flowing through your heart.
Winding through bringing thoughts of home, parents,
special times together that will never depart.
Sweet memories of by gone days.
Where my sisters and I use to play.
The big oak trees where our swing use to be.
A metal rod between to close trees
were we hung down by our legs
and laughed with glee.
The old windmill that stands upon a hill
with it's rhythm like music we can still hear.
Pumping water at night making sounds
that's forever there like a life line through the years.
Golden moments of memories that are treasured so dear,
become more precious with every passing year.
They say, memory is one gift of God
that death does not destroy -
If this is true — these things we have stored up
in our minds will be there to help us make it through...

Dorothy Jo Jurney

The "Love Game"

Love used to be a game
winning was everything
risking all I had to win the "love game"
then I met you
and suddenly the games rules changed
winning doesn't matter to me anymore
as I look into your baby blue eyes
I know I am going to lose,
but I don't care
all I can think of is your smile
and it's all that matters now
I've lost the "love game"
I've given you my heart-not willingly,
but now I've lost it forever
to the "love game"

Alicyn Blackman

Aesthetic Truth

Here we are assembling a circle and stomping at its core
    with a cadenza of shouts in reprise without a word
    of caution
Here we are disregarding sticks using only fingers and thumbs
    to shape a true feeling
Here I am so shall I cry, beg, seek, love, want?
    Yes, all this and more
Digesting a greater portion of earth than others may seem
    excessive in a small man's eyes, but I justify my
    appetite by presenting you

Dean Alexander

Goddess Of The Sky

She glides through the endless blue sky,
With a keen sense and watchful eye,
She dominates the heavens for that is her domain,
Unlike the vulture, she is proud of her name,
She flaunts her style with a patented mark,
Creatures are helpless out of the dark,
Her shadow is cast down from the sun,
As fear by all animals respect her, as the one,
She swoops down quickly, deadly, like an arrow,
No hope for small prey such as the sparrow,
Her wings span out as the wind passes by,
As she soars up, up and away over mountains so high,
A sight to be seen for God she is blessed,
She settles so gently into her nest,
So beautiful, graceful, unlike the sea gull,
Ahh the goddess of the sky, the bald headed eagle.

Frank J. Mirabella

Lamentation

Where are you, Lord?
Why did you leave me in a shadowy place?
Where were you when I consumed my own?
Am I inspired or judged by you?
Where were you when I sought freedom?
Where are you?
I am here.
Your allowance lets me plunder my soul.
It is a constant sacrifice of me and mine.
I in me, thee in me?
Unfortunately,
There is more of me, than thee.

Frank Offner

The Price

You do have the right to do as you wish,
with a license to drive, and a permit to fish,
another to marry the mate you wish.
Ain't that nice?
Freedom is your for a price!
Strap on your gear and utility belt,
Don Chromium P. Js so you don't melt.
I think it was burning flesh that I smelled.
Don't think twice!
Freedom is your for a price!
The arms of the law beat down on your back.
The man has your number and cuts you no slack.
Trust me, you don't even have to be black.
Ain't that nice?
Freedom is your for a price!
Your not even safe way out in the sticks.
We pay the price for their dirty tricks.
They whitewash their crimes, it's all politics.
Ain't that nice?
Freedom is yours for a price!

Danny Wayne West

The Forgotten Soul

There's a thousand miles that face him now
With a thousand in his past;
And he walks on 'cross the lonely miles
In search of a love to last.

His forgotten soul roams near and far
With his hopes and all his fears;
He calls out into the dark of night
For the one to dry his tears.

He walks on through the coldest of nights
And down burning summer roads;
The forgotten soul will always roam
In search of someone to hold.

There's but one last mile that lies ahead
And is carried meek but brave;
This forgotten soul now roams no more
But, lies silent in his grave.

Charles R. Taylor Jr.

Old Friends

In the evenings after supper when I can sit and rest
With a warm fire dancing around the logs
And my cat curled on my lap.
When my dog lays dreaming by my side
And the silence settles in,
It is then my thoughts turn to my old friends
Whom I have known for low these many long years.
Like Jacob's coat of many colors my books wrap around the walls
Softly reflecting the dim light stemming from the fire.
It is then that I revisit my old friends waiting on the shelves,
Each one with a different tale, each one a story to tell.
Sometimes my friends will take me across a storm tossed sea,
Or maybe through a jungle where mighty emperors dwelt.
We may cross the highest mountains or plod the desert sands.
We may chart the depths of oceans or explore far distant lands.
I never tire of the tales they have told so many times before
And only Morpheus will make me put them back upon the shelf.

Diana Forrester Newhall

Changing with Seasons

Every flower holds stories untold,
With every blossom that blooms in spring.
Miracles take place when petals unfold,
With two tiny leaves unravelling like wings.
The stem grows stronger and sprouts with ease,
Having mystical secrets to grow tall and stout.
Shining from dewdrops that fall with the breeze.
Yearning to break free, the petals cry out.
Petals drop, looking like fairies in flight.
Falling through air to replant their seeds.
Darkness comes, they will sleep through the night,
Needing the dampness from the ground, they plead.
When dawn arrives there are few remains,
Patiently they await next year's embrace.
Then comes a few months where time sustains.
When spring arrives once more, they find their place.
The circle of life repeats, once more,
Gently adjusting to the change of each season.
An exquisite aroma lingers, as never before,
Helping us enjoy life, without question or reason.

Elizabeth Melinda Marie Wilson

Endless

If every moment could be a life worth living
With every glance a smile worth kissing
Then nothing would seem dull in recollections light
Nothing would need righting
I would stop all inner fighting
And all that surrounds and confines
And all that enshrouds and defines
Would yield to expectations pure and bright
The land awash, the hills alight
On such a scene my eyes would never close
The point of past remembrances would fade in blithe repose
And at that height my senses would fully wake
And in that life I give, I cannot take

Charles P. Salerno

A Mother's Eyes

I think of then and feel my tears
with eyes that remember her there.
And the crying is everflowing ere
remembering the one who cared.

But the days passed by so fast and clear
that I knew and wanted before.
I looked by my side and still standing there
the mother I forever adore.

I say that I love you forever, I do
for you answer the questions I need.
It's a feeling of crying and smiling for you
and you feel the same feelings for me.

Looking at her with tears in my eyes
I remember the forgotten regrets.
Then she gazes into me and wipes my tears dry
for with her there are no regrets.

John Taylor Biggs

The Essence of Man

A man who makes no effort,
usually has no dreams.

A man who makes no effort,
will never succeed.

A man who makes no effort,
is NOT a man!

Shaun P. Kelly

Friendship

Friendship is like a garden
With flower that bloom as they grow
It take care to cultivate a good garden
There are special folks who make it so.
One must enjoy the beauty of friendship
A new friend is like a precious seed
Tend it carefully and enjoy happy results
Discard any ill thought like a bad weed!
A good friend may sense the mood of another
And may suggest a ride or a walk.
The silence or perhaps a problem shared
After helps when friends begin to talk.
Share problems or joys in friendship
Some are short, other friendship don't end
A favorite sentence in life brings happiness
When one says "I want you to meet my friend!

Bonnie Joudrey

Apprehension

The old man opened the door and shut it with a bang
With furrowed brows, he let out an unusual "dang"
The blizzard, the wind, the fast blowing snow
With this awful storm, there was no way he could go
His wife Sue wondered what happened to Gus
It had to be dire to make him want to cuss
He fussed the evening away as they looked at television
Sue noticed and watched with alarm and apprehension
As Sue slept, he lay listening to the wind outside
Early morning, the silence told him it had died
He crept out of bed to find the warm clothes he'd hidden
And silently prayed the bag had not been lost or stolen
When he got to the car and opened the door
Thank goodness, the bag lay on the back seat floor
Later Sue awoke and looked around with a start
Gus was gone, the bed cold, she could hear her heart
Under the lamp on the table an envelope greeted her eyes
She ripped it open with shaking fingers and to her surprise
Read "Happy 50th Anniversary, I thank God He created you for me"
As smiling, Gus walked into the room with her morning cup of tea.

Elsy Tessier

Life's Circle

The thunderous waves come crashing down,
With half arched bodies and foamy white crowns
They leap, they swirl, in the dark blue sea,
As they continue their guest tirelessly.
Wedged in between these ever moving forms,
Are less vigorous waves who no longer belong.
Their voice silenced after years of roar,
Are beckoned home to the awaiting shore.
Where life is easier under the blazing sun,
And they are warmed by the ground until they are one.

Betty Biruboum

Southern Love

Southern hearts and southern moons
  Why does the hurt come so soon?
I loved you with all my heart
  like I always have right from the start.
I've trusted, I've cared, I've understood
  I've always given what I could.
But the tears always come so very fast
  Why doesn't love seem to ever last?
Was it you was it me that couldn't walk the line?
  Or was it that we just never made the time?

Gloria J. Snyder

He Knows Not

He knows not how she sits in sorrow
With heavy tears hazing her vision
She may sit and weep until tomorrow
Still, from him, she receives no reaction.

He knows not of the daggers he twists through her heart
Nor of the bloodshed bursting through her veins
Of hurting her he knows not he's made art
Turn her inside out and discover the red stains.

He knows not of the quiet darkness in which she seeks shelter
The nothingness surrounds her— inside and out
He doesn't know her. He hasn't felt her
Pain— the pain that conquers without a doubt.

He says he is different an that he'll take actions
She still believes this to be true
He knows not of his contradictions
She still waits for his words to bloom.

He knows not of the feelings he brings to her
These two the love bug has bitten
Without love such emotions could not occur
Without love this poem could not have been written.

Nahrain Gewargis

Middle Age: A Season of Life Lost

How did November come so fast
with its avalanche of dry leaves
and dusk shrouding homebound traffic?

I thought it was August
when I frolicked in the waves of heat,
pumped with the exuberance of timeless summer.

What happened to autumn?

I missed the robin's flight—
I wasn't wearing glasses then.
Fresh corn on the cob was still sweet in my mouth
when I got my dentures.
Like leaves of oak and maple,
my hair turns another shade day by day
and breaks and falls away
leaving a barren crown.

And while I lost myself in summer's toil and sport,
September crept by into October
which fluttered me into November,
spent and aching, naked, cold,
and still hungering for summer's fruits.

Hal Howard

The Life I'm Living

Here I am in my life still
with my empty heart that no one can fill.
I feel so useless, I feel so weak
I have another side that my eyes can't seek.
Why is my life one big fear?
Why can't I just disappear?
In my soul I have no hope but,
In my mind I learn to cope.
In my heart turns the knife
As I officially declare "I'm at war with my life!"
Will God forgive me for feeling this sin?
Or will he give me courage to find love within?

Andrea Butler

Thank You Mother

I remember the first time you held me, I was too young to see you with my eyes, but I knew then that you loved me, because I could feel the warmth in your heart.

I knew that you could be trusted, as I felt secure in your arms. I knew that I would never have to worry, because I knew that you would never be too far.

You picked me up when I felt, you dried my tears when I cried, and you comforted me when I was lonely.

You let me grow up so slowly, and you taught me how to survive. You gave me all your knowledge, your strength, your heart and your soul.

Now that I am a grown women, I will never worry needlessly, because I know that you dear Mother, have always cared for me.

So, I want to thank you dear Mother for loving me, our children will thank you too, because if it were not for you, we may not have made it this far.

I love, and respect you very much, and I will always remember, 'the first time that you held me.'

Diana L. Yoakum

Time

She moves too fast.
With my fragile grasp, I cannot hold her.
She does not wait.
I dare not stop to smell a rose
Or pause to watch my children grow.
On and on she goes
Like a thistle in the wind,
Never interrupting her stride.
In my vane effort to keep up,
I am faced with reflections of the past.
It is forever gone.
I cannot call it back.
I can only shed a tear and ask forgiveness.
Oh time! Why were you not on my side?

Jessie C. Murphy

In My Dreams

In my dreams I was drowning in a sea of despair,
   with my last hope I looked up in the air.
Down from the sky came a pure white dove,
   and she sat on my arm, with eyes full of love.
She said, "You have to believe in yourself and in me.
   If your love is strong, it can set you free."
I started to go under, but remembered what she said.
   I believed, and I loved, through my mind filled with dread.
Then this little white dove picked me up from the sea,
   and with strength unimagined, I was in the air and free.
She carried me through bad times, through thick and thin.
   Through times of sun and times of wind.
Then she set me on a grassy plain, and sat on my arm once again.
   She said, "I have to go now, and I'll never be back,
but if you believe in love, you'll stay on the right track."
   Friendship, trust and caring, always use this as your bearing.
Then she took off, and left me, and with tears in my eyes,
   I watched this great dove take off to the sky.
When I woke up and thought things through,
   that dove was my friend, and that friend was you.

James R. Clair

The Rolling Hills and Fields

The rolling hills and fields abound
With nature's wondrous wild sound
  And in the tumbling waters roll
Can yet be felt all natures soul.
  The outdoors calls to you and me
And beckons us all to be free
  Of all our daily trouble and care
And let our hearts with nature share.
  The way which nature shares her wealth
Shows in the richness of our health
  As each relaxing hour is spent
In joy of nature that's heaven sent.
  Nature really holds the key
To total peace and serenity
  If we could only learn to love
Nature, on land, on sea and above.

Don Peloubet

Untitled

This world we lived in is full of hatred and violence
With no one to help or stand up beside us.
They say there's a God way up in the heavens,
When we mess up all our sins are forgiven.
If this true, which I do not believe.
Then why are our hopes trashed like fallen leaves?
Why are the children molested and beaten,
Is it something they deserve or am I mistaken?
Racial disputes separate our people into gangs,
Innocent people are being shot everyday.
Rapes, homicides, felonies, suicides, everyday they're reported.
What kind of drug has the people of this world so distorted.
Graffiti and destruction has been through the streets,
With words of foul language and many more treats.
Mistakes we have made hidden deep in the past
Are crawling up behind us but this time too fast.
We have screwed up the world for the new generation,
They believe not in God but the new Lord of violence, Satan.
This is the future of our children, we've made it this way.
Violence overrides peace, is it right that for our mistakes they are
    to pay?

Christina Bocock

A Tale of Folklore

He walked out from the blackened forest;
With not a glimpse of what he sought.
His chain mail dampened by the forest leaves.
His sword in it's sheath as he stood and thought.
A tale of folklore ran through his mind,
Of the one horned beast, so gallant and benign.
The god's gave our mother an animal of virtue and wisdom
Of innocence and a single spiral horn so divine.
So all would know that from which the creature came
Was the gates of heaven and our Father's domain.
Evil could try but would not succeed,
To extinguish the magical, single horned breed.
And so our valent knights search ended in vain.
Let him who hath understanding, reckon
Unicorn by name.

Corey W. O'Keefe

HomeSick

There once was a boy from Rome
Who was oh, so far from home;
he missed home so much
That he cried up a muck
and decided to go home with an gnome

Sandra Vasquez

Snowfall

The leaden February sky hung low
With only now and then a glimpse of sun -
Extinguished, like a moon when night is done;
Imparting neither warmth nor cheer below.
In spits of frozen sharpness came the snow.
Uncertainly at first, it whirled and spun
Before the quiet beauty was begun
With luxuriant flakes descending, feathery slow.

What artist hand has painted such a scene -
This vast expanse of tranquil, shimmering white
That glorifies each form from three to clod?
No lowly thing is common now, nor mean.
Now small and great are equal in our sight,
As every soul is precious to its God.

Ferne Eikenberry

Mother Nature

Mother Nature dust our Earth
  With shining sleet and snow so white,
She adds some crispness to the air
  As Winters moon lights up our nite.

She always gives a new tomorrow
  Our Earth she decorates for Spring
The hills she plants with flowers
  Gentle sun and rain she brings.

She gives hot days of Summer
  With searing sun she cloaks our Earth
Thirsting fields of wheat look upward
  With pleas for rain to quench their thirst.

She paints our Earth in golden hues
  Each stroke of brush has special reason
She dresses trees in yellow, orange and brown
  To usher in her Autumn Season.

Ann Burton

The Day Time Stood Still

(When I Decided Not To Love You Anymore)

I feel to the earth and lashed her soil.
With tears falling from my riven face,
I moistened the ground and asked why?

I looked to the stars, and they ceased to glisten.
The moon glow failed to flush my mother earth,
I prayed for dawn.

Then I realized,
I need not wonder why - I just did.
Suddenly the sun burst in.

John C. Frankhouser

Guinea Pig

I eat carrots, lettuce, and anything green;
When you feed me don't be scared, I am not very mean.

And on that occasion I'm given a fright;
I'll run like mad, or I'll turn around and bite.

I'm not quite a rabbit, I'm a rodent you see;
But I am so cute even moms will like me.

When I hear the fridge door, I'll let out a squeal;
Cause I know, yes I know, here comes my meal.

I'm short and fury, and oh so fat;
And when you rub my nose, I purr like a cat.

John Clark

Together Forever

Friends are forever with everlasting love,
With the help from the good Lord above
He has made it possible to live forever,
So once again we will be together;
You really meant a lot to me,
I just wish that somehow I could see: -
Your smiling face,
That can not be erased;
You were a good and trusting guy,
Whose love and companion will never die.
Our friendship should never perish,
    Because my memories of you shall be cherished;
For with God we will meet once more,
Through the gates of the open door,
So just remember me,
    my good and faithful friend -
Because our love and friendship,
    Shall never end!

Jennifer Black

Untitled

    Her lovely features glowed
with the wonderful radiance of youth.
    Her eyes sparkled like purest diamonds.
Her smile was so bright that the sun sent
a ray of sunlight from the sky to kneel at her
feet in homage.
    Her hair was black as the night, and in
it's fullness was as a young forest in all it's glory
    Her warmth, kindness and genuine love shown forth
in the (living christ) who dwelled within her tender heart.

Gregory Walton

Ode to Our Minister of Music, Earl

Oh! Where do I start?
With this heart felt tribute
To a man who sings like a lark —-
In the daylight or in the dark.
And lo, he strums perfectly on the guitar -
Why, he's been known to play a tune —-
While looking at the stars!
This maestro has conducted our choir
When tired and sick,
He "waves his arms" to make us tick!
Yes, again I tell it to you one and all —-
An extraordinary gentleman has been at our beck and call.
An' I shall sorely be devoid of joy and a song in my heart —-
When this genius and his nice, faithful
Peggy doth depart!
But, alas! All good and great things
Must come to an end —-
This is no different, so my very best wishes
And love I send!

Frances Jeane Davis Branon

Ocean High

We gathered on the shore,
with trembling waves forming battalions against us.
And the pushing current struck us with a cold, sudden
blow, together with wind carrying billows of hot sand.
Sauntering slowly down a vacant beach,
rocks jagged under water's cruel caress.
Seals bob up and down, chase each other through silvery waves.
And we laughed with insane jubilance,
joyous paranoia gathering within us in kindled ecstasy.

Ben Priest

Grandmothers

Old wrinkled short little ladies
With very big hearts
You know
The ones who give money on birthdays
The very first ones
To greet you with hugs kisses and heys
And when everyone else leaves you
She'll always be the one who stays
And she'll always love you with all her might
And no matter how tired she may be
She'll always read to you at night
Yes now you know who I'm talking about
The one who will never kick you out
The one who buys you the little teddy bears
The one who always loves you
The one who always cares

Justina Lynn Melloch

Ode to Mount St. Helens

Oh, alluring Mount St. Helens
    With your slopes so snowy white;
What a surprise you gave us
    When you turned our day to night.

Now they say that you've lain dormant
    For one hundred forty years;
Suddenly you cover us with ash and sand
    And we try to smile through our tears.

But the heavy grayish covering
    Is just everywhere you look.
It dries out and blows in the wind.
    You wish you'd just read it in a book.

They say in time this ashen material
    Will be a blessing to us all;
That living things will flourish
    And you will again stand very tall.

Oh, alluring Mount St. Helens
    We hope you rest in peace;
Settle down and be majestic,
    For a hundred years, at least.

Betty L. Beverly

The Greatest of These is Love"

Within the mind, there is Hope.
Within the soul, there is Faith.
Within the heart, there is Love.

Your mind can ponder.
Your soul can move mountains.
Only your heart can love.

It is said "Abide in these, Faith, Hope, and Love;
But the greatest of these is Love."

It is possible to know all things,
It is possible to believe in all things.
But to do it without Love, it is nothing.

Love within your heart is not Love,
It only comes from your heart.
For it is not love until it is given away.

True love is from deep within your heart,
It is a treasure waiting to be given away.
Receiving true love is to receive a gift from far beyond.

Treasure the Love that is given to you,
In return give out the Love due to all.
"For the greatest of these is Love."

Courtney Lee

Life To Eternity

Without life there is no death
Without death there is no reason for life.

For death is the passing on to eternity
And the bringing of new life.

For when they are dead, they are not gone
For eternity surrounds everyone completely.

If you do not forgive, forget, and move on
You will remember and live in pain.

Remember life is short and eternity is forever
Live your life the as it is the last moment.

Edward Tully

Soul's of Flame Set Free

The Birth of Love, Never can man know.
    Without the Love of Christ, to touch our inner Soul.

Courage is Our lack, Our Blackened Soul's Blood Stained.
    Our shame burned and branded, Consumed our Heart in Flames.

Our sorrows or our fears? Which take root and grow?
    Man so weak by nature, Tis our silent screaming Soul.

No power or strength alike, Will we refuse or even try.
    The Spirit's rolling Thunder, To soar the black of Night.

His Spirit He released, Search for Souls in fear.
    It devours all the flesh, Then dries His children's tears.

The majestic stars that guide, Or moon of Visions dream.
    The glow that sparks my Soul, I'm drowning in pure peace.

Mystified I speak, my world lost in flight.
    When the soul illuminates, I'm imprisoned by His light.

Seek Eternal Life. Break cycles and change paths.
    Have Faith in Jesus Christ, Elude the circle's trap.

Tabulated, summed and totalled, North, East, South, and West.
    I've searched my life in vain, for Christ has always led.

Mortal men or mere, so flawed dark and vile.
    It's truly God's own Son, Jesus Christ that holds the fire.

Deborah Lopez

Sheltered by the Blood

Sheltered by the Blood of Jesus, safe from peril and storm; it is
wonderful to know our Saviour is
near, and will keep us from harm: For all who will trust and believe
him. He has promised to
guide them along; though weak and frail we may be, in Christ, we can
be made strong:

Sheltered by the Blood of Jesus, what a Blessed thought; oh what a
price to pay for our
Redemption, by his Life's Blood we are bought:

It was on Calvary's cross, Jesus suffered and died for us all; and in
trusting him only, he will not
let us fall: If we are Sheltered by the Blood of Jesus. For that is
the only way that we can be sure of seeing our Blessed Savior some
day.

Dessie Anne Seigler

A Night In the Student Union

I sit at a table and glance into space,
Wondering if anyone notices my face.
I sit here alone with everyone around,
Noises and bustle but I make no sound.
Dreaming of things that seem to never be,
I wonder if anyone thinks like me?
So much pressure and sometimes no time,
What do I get from walking this straight line?
So much I could do but don't seem to care,
All because I take pleasure in things that aren't there.
These people I see, they are not like me,
It is like them I hope to never be.
Here I sit but I cannot stay,
For me there will be no end to this day.
Facing the cold, the dark, and the wind,
Forever searching for an ear that will lend.
But I will go on and face the night,
And conspire a way to make things again seem right.

Jason M. Leete

The Heart of Friendship

The heart of friendship is a deep feeling
words could never express,
though many have tried.
It's a feeling of anticipation
in the morning,
And a feeling of comfort
at night
It's a chance to dream wildly and
A chance to laugh twice as much at life.
It's the right to agree to disagree
It's the freedom to hold the other's hand
without conditions and
The freedom to say I love you
without turning red
It's a special type of heart
so few are lucky to find
But most of all the Heart of Friendship
are two souls speaking a language
all their own

Deborah De Steno

Daddy

Daddy what do you do all day, I listen to the
work whistle blow, my boss hollars and you know,
Daddy what do you all day watch the ships sail on
the river and the tug's pull away.
Daddy what do you do all day, think about you
And Mommy and wish the time away.
Daddy is that really what you do all day.
No I try to work to keep my bills almost paid
but Daddy do you think that's right, I mean
If you do that always. Daddy what do you do
All day, cry a little bit and hope you'll never
have to go this way. Daddy you know what
I do all day, what's that son? I play.

James T. Gallon Jr.

Reach Across Barriers

Could she?
Would she touch me?
So that I might break apart,
Into little pieces,
That only she would understand.

Tijuana R. Watssen

Between Life and Life

Fallen spirit, pierced soul, a life of broken promise, I see a hidden
world with nothing but destruction, approaching destruction. I'm
alone with destruction that's approaching to destroy me. A malignant
demon caught me terribly. Caught all of me.

Agonizing existence, love and hope are foolish shadows. With an
anguish of desire for all I've been given, yet may not have, nor ever
know again, I look upon despair and am afraid. I'm mortally afraid.
I long for more bodily pain to blot this other anguish out.

Tortured, desolate, swept away from all my anchors, great tides of
destiny bear me beyond the dark, concealing wall of greater mystery.
A shaft of love and knowledge like a light pierces a way to me,
There, across the barriers, between life and life.

Peace beyond peace, tremulous joy, the cold, crude gleam of sorrow
and pain flickers, then fades and I'm free. I'm totally free.
   Suffering
is but a moment in this paradise of bliss. Seduced by the sacred
caress of eternity, I look no more to that life I loved so well.

For potent Mystery knows my name and calls to me. In matchless
ecstasy it fastens the life I know to the life I have yet to know.
A hunger greater than any desire for this life replies as freedom
enters on eternal wings and I know union with a Spirit Divine.

Dorothy Okray

Just Once

What would life be if I couldn't be with you?
Would the trees die or will my heart just disappear?

   Just once, I would like to hold you in my arms.
   Just once, I would like to tell you I love you,

But when, will it happen.

   Just once, I would like to carry in my dreams.
   Just once, I would like to hear you say I love you,

But when, if you are so full of pride and integrity.

   Just once, would I want you to love me the way I
   love you.
   Just once, would I want you to suffer the way I
   have suffered for you.

But when, if you are so cold with girls like me.

   Just once, would I like to hate you, but I can't
   because I truly love you.

Imelda C. Ulloa

One Nation Under God

Remembering that our forefathers, inspired by Providence,
Wrote a Constitution for our own mighty, fair land, we remember
that our destiny includes the "blessings of liberty for
ourselves and our posterity."

Thomas Jefferson, with the Hand of God on his shoulder, and
The aid of many with a similar dedication, created the blueprint
For greatness, eternal purpose an integral part of each process
In development.

Of the future of a world without our deity, no value system or
rhetoric can evolve constructively so deprived.

An ideology, even one that produces heroes, has no noble
Purpose, never Eternal Purpose, without the advantage of Truth.
True Americans, those whose faith is Eternal, sing with
Undying devotion that immortal prayer to the "Author of
Liberty": "Long may our land be bright with freedom's holy
Light; Protect us by Thy Might, Great God, Our King."

Jane Banks

Grey Ballerina (for Hurricane Andrew)

Aged leaves dance in circles,
yellow waltz, for whose time have come.
At the outcasted beckons o' weathercocks
from thy early breeze; whose death fragrance hath some.
Outcrying thine braggiest dateless eve.
Nature's Pivot; fourthly comes grey.
Sullen destruction itself is Thee, so naive!
As the dew laid by night's kiss yesterday.
Misglanced ruins recall nostalgic memories o' mine
as my hard'st trials to hold, seasonal tears that tear.
And not to fear for my seasonal life; neither thy tearless eye.
But unchanged remains this morbid me!
As time from time subsides to time,
as wind from wind subsides to Thee.
O' suffer forth; as grey as the wolves.
Mind not the beweeps o' widows.
And play orchestra, with cries o' the world,
a prelude for the wind's whistle!

Ivo Romel Freitas

A Question

Daddy, Daddy, answer a question for me?
   Yes, sweetheart, how hard can it be?

Daddy, is moon light when God is sleeping?
   Yes, sweetheart, it's God's dreams for us.
Daddy, is sunshine when God is smiling?
   Yes, sweetheart, it's God's happiness for us.

Daddy, is thunder when God is talking?
   Yes, sweetheart, it's God's words for us.
Daddy, is lighting when God is raging?
   Yes, sweetheart, it's God's energy for us.

Daddy, is wind when God is whispering?
   Yes, sweetheart, it's God's wisdom for us.
Daddy, is rain with God is weeping?
   Yes, sweetheart, it's God's tears for us.

Daddy, is hail when God is hurting?
   Yes, sweetheart, it's God's pain for us.
Daddy, is snow when God is freezing?
   Yes, sweetheart, it's God's love for us.

Daddy, Daddy? Is that last answer true?
   Yes, sweetheart, when cold, Do I hug you?

Gary G. Swancey

Inside Your Eyes

I may be looking into your eyes,
Yet, blue is not what I see.
I see much more than face value.
Your soul is there somewhere;
Somewhere deep inside.

There is a little child looking back at me,
A boy who doesn't know what to do.
He thinks he is in love,
And wants to make it true.

As I look inside your eyes,
I see you looking back at me.
You have no clue what to do.
But please, for me, say, "Yes, I love you so."

I look inside your eyes,
As if I am reading a book.
It is written that you love me too.
So come with me and together we'll go,
To a place inside only we can find.
A sacred home where we can hide,
Inside your eyes.

Caroline Swensen

Light On The Ice

The World is frozen, and cold this dark night,
Yet bright in the center shines one gorgeous light.
Emotions run wild, the fear and the pride.
On razors of steel this precious light rides.

A weapon of wood held tight in its hand,
Its only friend in this bone-chilling land.
With a head full of fury, and a heart of desire
The blood of its youth is fuel for the fire.

It stands tall on its ground to hold and defend,
And the cool arctic air shows its breathe in the wind.
To win or to lose makes no difference tonight.
The issue at hand is how brave is the fight.

If on this cold night the enemy should win,
The light will still shine. It burns deep within.
And living forever in the eyes of a fan
Is that night on the ice when boy became man.

David C. Jacks Jr.

Frozen Tears

I saw you standing there apart,
Yet reaching out and trying to belong,
Hiding behind a mask of smiles and bravado.

Big, Bony.
Hair pulled back,
Unruly strands of brown mixed with gray.
Old jeans and shirt.

Deep are the scars embedded in your heart and soul,
Products of cruel ignorance and abuse.

You are so hurt, angry, and confused,
So starved for love,
Seeking validation of your worth.
Like a lost child you search for connection and identity.

All I could do was listen to your wounded soul with love,
And later cry the tears you cannot grieve.

Emily K. Uptegrove

Your Eyes

Trying not to stare and cause suspicion,
Yet still gazing across from you with deep admiration.
Wondering what thoughts daily cross into your mind,
Hoping that someday my aching heart you may find.
Were we brought together by reason or by fate?
Will I ever have a chance or am I years too late?
Of all the people on this earth why have you touched my heart?
Has my life already passed by or could I make a new start?
Years ago we both made choices of our own,
Husband, wife, and children make up our separate homes.
Daily responsibilities keep our paths going straight,
Living my life as others choose is really what I hate.
Why can't I just touch you and open up to you?
Why did someone else find me before I could find you?
Are we only given one chance for true love to find?
Will I be left with only a dream of you in my mind?
Brown eyes that pierce right through my very soul,
Melting away my beating heart and leaving just a hole.

Brenda DeRienzo

Lost Loves

Lost loves, never intended to be.
Yet they were, however brief.

Born of hope, need, the longing of the soul
the never ceases to reach out to another.

Wished they never were. Yet without them life
would be an empty space with no experience,
no breath, nothing to remember.

Sad loves, not destined to last.
Like comets, they came and went.
Wished they could have staid.

They were lost loves from the start.

Filippa Leone

Only Time Can Tell

Time can only tell how much
you are loved.
You touch my heart each and
every day of my life.
Only time will tell if we're
meant to be.
Only time will tell if we
say farewell.
As far as I know we will
always be, forever you and me.
Each and everyday I hope you
know I'll stay.
Please don't ever go away!
Only time will tell if we're meant to be.
Only time will tell if we say farewell.
Come with me and we will
be very happy for the world to see.
Only time will tell if you and me will always be.
I hope we never say farewell, but only time will tell.
My love forever will you be?

Cheryl King

Mom, I Love You So

I watch your frail body, and I look at your face,
You are somewhere in time, in a much different place.
I miss you, Mom — and I love you so,
Where did you go?

Your thin body is bent, and your hair is so white,
I remember past times, when your face was so bright.
I miss you, Mom — and I love you so,
Where did you go?

When Dad passed away, your life became dim,
And often I would see your dark eyes gently brim.
I miss you, Mom — and I love you so,
Where did you go?

Our family was happy, boisterous and full of life,
We were fortunate in never suffering much strife.
We were always together — a unit of one,
What happens, when one considers her life is done?

You were always there for us, a love undaunting,
Now your thoughts are strayed, and your face is haunting.
I miss you, Mom — and I love you so,
Where did you go?

Beverly J. Johnson

Like a Goddess

Like a goddess that slowly discovers herself
you ask for the moon to shine on your path
and the moon listens

the ways of the world offer you pleasures and luxuries that are
yours upon asking

but love
love is waiting for you

restless

knowing it will surely die without you

Ildemaro Martinez Jr.

Advice from a Father

My daddy always use to say, "Son,
You can tell a lot 'bout a man
By the way he maintains his shoes.
Look to see if the tongue is loose,
If the heel looks downtrodden
Or the toe, stumped and scuffed.
Have the eyes shifted? Are the laces firm?
But most important, is the sole sound?"

I've thought about my daddy's advice often
And noticed lots of men's shoes:
Sneakers, loafers, ropers, walkers,
In man-made leathers or genuine calfskin
Stitched soles or soles glued
But parting at the bend
After getting soaked. There's
A difference, though, between looking at them
And wearing them —
            "Shoes aren't
The whole story, Daddy,"

James A. Grimshaw Jr.

You Don't Know My Name

Say Dad!
You don't know my name.
I'm the son you left behind
When you ran off in shame.

You made a promise.
Mama bore a son.
Not long afterward you were off and gone.

Say Dad! Did you ever think
If the son you left behind
Would live or die or rise and shine.

What would he eat, where would he live.
For his occupation...would he work or steal.
How would he make it alone with his mother,
Would they survive...or have an endless struggle,
Just to live and survive.

Was it the responsibility you were running
From...or rushing toward many more mistakes because you
Didn't learn from the first one.

Promises made, no promises kept
This your fate a man in a hurry to procreate.

Everlena Hemingway

To Be Free

To be free
You find yourself running away
You dream of a place far away
and threaten to leave
You think of a wonderful place
where you can run with no rules
You get out and there's nowhere to go
You keep walking on...then you're LOST!
No one can help you and now
you're suffering.
To be free
Is it worth it?

Jennifer McWhorter

You

You fill my heart with joy
You give me strength to grow
You make me feel happy
You make me glow
You make me feel wanted
You make me feel loved
You are my joy; You are my love
You show me how love can be so wonderful
In each and every way, how caring and
Gentle a person can be.
You are tender and you are kind
You are my love, I believe for the very first time.

Bonnie E. Demarsh

Daddy's Little Girl

War just broke out,
You had to go fight.
You left me tonight,
That's why I'm sitting here crying myself to sleep.
When you left,
You kissed my cheek and said,
"I love my little girl".
I won't see you,
Until the war is over.
I don't know how I'll live without you.
You and I did everything together,
Skated, swung, swam, danced, and read.
Now my sixth birthday is coming,
And you won't be here to celebrate.
I don't know when or if,
I'll ever see you again.
You're so perfect,
I want to be just like you when I grow up.
Oh, Daddy,
I love you!

Elizabeth Lanier

I Am

I am not Soix or Crow or even Choctaw,
    yet I am.
I am not Chinese or Japanese or Korean,
    yet I am.
I am not Scottish, Irish, Welch or Dutch,
    yet I am.
I am not African or European or Asian
    yet I am.
I am not any of these, yet I am all.
I am American.
Therefore, I am.

Andrea L. Cooper

You Know I'm Alive

You know I'm alive, when you feel me inside,
You know I'm alive, when morning sickness arrives.

You know I'm alive long before you begin to show,
You aware of my existence, when people begin to
notice your glow.

Please make no mistake, of my not being born yet, as though,
I can not hear, think or be, because make no mistake what's
inside of you is ME...

If I could talk aloud, I'd shout, don't let them make me out.
Give me the time I need to grow, the body I need to survive.
In a society with laws that let potential mother's make a mistake
that will burden them all their lives.

A society that enables oppressed decisions of not being
fair to these Babies, or giving them their chance at
living, loving, and to grow up to make decisions they would
be totally opposed to, had they had their chance to survive.

Christine Chandler

The Desert Storm

They are from every part of this land
You know their faces like the back of your hand
You see them when you walk the streets
You watch them go, as your heart beats
And tears pour down out from your eyes
As the planes go up into the skies
And here you are hoping, praying
Watching them sit, hoping and praying
Under the stars in the land
Somewhere in the desert sand
Awaiting to come home to see
You, in the Land of the Free.

David Vogt

That Special Someone

Every once in awhile
you meet someone
that really cares and makes you smile
When you're next to that person
they make you feel that life's worth its while
A simple touch
A simple smile
Makes one feel so grand
Just having that someone next to you
holding on to your hand

Heather Diane Lang

Oppressor

Control is what you're all about.
You rant, you rave, you scream and shout,
If someone disagrees with what you say.
The truth you know not from a lie.
So will you see before you die,
Your black and white have mixed to give you gray.

Somehow I just don't fit the mold.
I'd rather stand out in the cold,
Than lie unto myself to gain your grace.
It angers you that I'm this way.
I just won't yield to make your day.
Disgust is what I see upon your face.

I'll never be much in your eyes.
Whatever I do you despise.
It's hopeless to believe you'll ever change.
The things I see I have to tell.
I see the truth and speak it well.
Ironic though it is you think I'm strange.

Daniel S. Williams

Birthday Rose

You are like a rose, its beauty never fades.
You remind me of the sweet smell
of its fragrance and its petals
blowing in the wind.
The rose always represents love,
kindness, and happiness.
I give this rose to you because
this is the way I see you.
Always giving of yourself and
with a tender heart to go along
with it.
I give this rose to you, as God
has given you to us, as a treasure
of love,
May this birthday rose be a
token of our love.

Connie Varner

On the Question of Life...

"Life," Grandfather said, "Is like hot-dog on a stick.
You roast it till it's good and hot and then you eat it quick.
Alas my Oscar Meyer has collapsed into the flame.
Live for each moment, Sonny Boy, or yours will do the same."

"Life," my Mom assured me, "Is a weekend at the Beach.
Lay back and let it tan you like a juicy desert peach.
You'd better wear your sunblock, it's a lesson that I learned.
'Cause I forgot one afternoon, and Kiddo, I got burned."

"Life," my Sister told me, "Is a poisoned throwing dart.
It stabs you in the back and then it sticks you in the heart.
You men are scum; it can't be helped. Your destiny's to die.
You won't avoid your wicked fate. Not even if you try."

"Life," my Dad lamented. "The elusive trophy bass.
I've followed him for twenty years, but never caught his ass.
Fight him hard and reel him in. Don't waste a scrap of time.
For if you lose a second you'll find a broken line."

"Life," my English teacher crowed, "The conjugated verb.
The fairy tale, the limerick, the epic poem superb.
Read it, write it, sing it out. Express, Expose, Make known!
It's the passage you'll remember when your mind and heart have
grown."

Adam Bakker

Memory

Why'd things have to end this way?
You said we'd always be together
even if that meant we had to run away.
Now you're gone, and I have no clue...
if you still love me the way that I love you!

When you left I had tears in my eyes
Wondering why they made you say goodbye.
But memories last forever and yours will always stay.
Close to my heart, every waking day.

So please don't forget, the times we shared,
the fun memories, the long soft glares.
For I won't forget any of them.
They're so important to me.
They're all I have left of what is
now called a memory.

Bethany Kessler

"Proud Mary"

We've got proud Mary
you say she's through,
remember my family
she was tougher then you!

So don't remember Mary this way!
her proud mind will return again some day,
it will be in heaven, with oceans so blue
she'll be smiling at sea gulls
that are staring at you!

With her bonnet, fishing pole, and so tanned,
we will follow proud Mary to the tide to stand
it will be such a beautiful remembrance,
O' so grand", to talk with proud Mary, hand and hand

With Mary's proud mind we loved so true
together, forever!
we will never be blue
thank you proud Mary for seeing us through.
we will continue to always love you!

Chris V. Curry

Stamp Upon That Tear

I sent flowers and a card that said I love you.
You shed a tear that said I feel the same of thee.
And then you placed a stamp upon that tear dear.
And sent all your feelings back to me.

When I came back we kissed, I said I've missed you.
I stepped inside and took my shoes off at the door.
You said the soles showed cheating circles.
And when I left my heart was so for-lorn.

When I sent flowers and a card that said I'm sorry.
You shed a tear that said I feel the same of thee.
And then you placed a stamp upon that tear dear.
And sent all your feelings back to me.

The next few years we both dated others.
I'm so pleased we went on to finish school.
You said I've matured and was more fun to be with.
You had grown from being a jealous teenage fool.

I brought flowers and a card that said I love you.
I held your hand and went down to one knee.
You shed a tear that said yes I will dear.
And now we two are making plans of being three.

Jack T. Freeland

Sitting at a Desk with Pale Light

Three lines of pale light rest on a darkened wall.
You sit, letting your eyes swallow that light.
Rest your body on me;
Look through the curve of this glass bowl,
She lets the sorbet slide through her lips.
Through the bowl, lines protrude
passing through your sight.
Lick at your spoon again;
What the sun provides for
you - you flaunt it with perfection.
Darkness slips into me and steals my light away.
She lets her arms fall on me.
Fingertips slide over concave skin;
She asks- "How can we prepare for death?"
I lap up the sweet raspberry
juice from her cheek and
reply - "How can we prepare for life?"
She smiles and swallows again.

Greg Evangelista

Untitled

It happened on a traveling road
you spoke your heart and filled my soul
with belonging, laughter, joy, and pain
I await time spent with you again
Like Heaven awaits a missing angel to return.

In sleepless darkness I think of you
with warming smile and eyes of blue
a soldier's strength and handsome youth
a poet's heart and a soul of truth
Like an angel fallen to earth in lovely form.

I do not know what happens now
but give my honest all, I'll vow
to never speak dishonest words
your joys and fears they will be heard
Like an angel's melody you speak to me.

Jennifer Arnold

Untitled

Sinking slowly into the shadows of you
You stand on your platform staring down at me
You look away, can't stand the pain
sinking into the shadows of you
I hear you screaming your death wish for me
try to obliterate me
don't want to see me
don't want to hear my words
It all doesn't matter anymore
The sun has set on the world
It's cold all alone
But I have a fire burning in me to keep me warm
I can get through this
I will get through this
"It can't rain all the time"
Sinking into the shadows of you
free of control
free of the suffocation
It all doesn't matter anymore

Eva Shumicky

All Good Things

When all had been better than ever before,
You told me our nights would be no more.
The nights that were filled with tenderness
Are replaced with nights of emptiness.
And the warmth of two bodies that was shared before
Will be shared no more, no more.
"All good things must come to an end,"
Said the one I'd considered my closest friend.

I don't want to give what you don't want to take,
For that would be making an awful mistake.
And I don't want anything given to me
If it's given as meaningless charity.
I tell my eyes that the tears I've cried
Were wasted and not really justified,
But my heart tells my eyes that the hurt I feel
Spews forth from a void only time can heal.
And maybe someday I'll be more forgiving
If I find a new lover and start again living.
I wish you much love, as I wish it for me,
And a friendship that's ours for eternity.

Jay E. Boyd

The Voice Of A Child (From Beyond The Grave)

Why did you hurt me? I'm just a child
You took more than my life, you took my smile,
You really hurt me, you hurt me so bad,
You left those who love me, heartbroken and sad.
How can you live? How can you sleep?
When you threw me in the river, It was cold and dark and deep.
I guess you hoped they would never find me,
You'd keep your dark secret, and forever be free.
You deceived so many people, but God had a plan.
He cradled me in his arms, and kept me close to the land.
Your rage and your anger, no one understands why,
My casket was closed, my Mommie couldn't kiss me goodbye.
Me and my Dad won't play ball or fish.
Or walk through the woods, look at the stars and make a wish.
My Grammie and aunt and all those I love,
Can't buy me a bike or a new baseball glove.
You've never been sorry, your face is so cold
But now it is time for the truth to be told.
You are so evil and you'll never win
You'll burn in hell and pay for your sin.

Della Populis

Speak to Me Softly, Love

Speak to me softly, love, with your loving heart
You touch me deep within and heal my heart
Speak to me softly, love, in your loving way
I'll give my love to you and never be far away

Speak to me softly, love, let me hold you next to me
My loving, peaceful friend, who knows the soul of me
Speak to me softly, love and you will see
Just how much that you mean to me

Speak to me softly, love and our love will be
Your's, my darling, for eternity
I know that I've found that one true heart
That keeps me near to you, never apart

My love, you are a star so bright
You light the night with love
A kiss I have for you tonight, my love
We'll light the night with love

Speak to me softly, love
Joseph Paul Voros II

You Were There

When I was a child - afraid of the dark
    you were there
When I grew to a woman, to become a mother
    you were there
When I doubted my ability to raise my children
    you were there
When I turned my back on you
    you were there
When I turned my life over to you
    you were there
Always waiting, watching, caring, loving
    you were there
Thank you God for always being there
    and being here.

Frances L. Winters

Faith

Faith is like the stars you see
you wonder how could this be
faith you hold onto inside
to believe to see how can we decline
that faith is in the mine
faith we ask this question
Oh I don't know I just make the suggestion

Faith, faith, faith
Oh if only I could see before
To see before is not faith
to see you will just have to wait

Wait you say before I see
I wonder how could this be

Faith is like the seasons we do not see
we believe it's coming year after year
we have faith and it appears
faith is God's way to say just trust in him
No matter what you see
It is because you believe in me
faith is like the stars you see

Annette G. Cooper

Memories

These four walls are closing in around me.
Your beautiful body and thoughts seem to surround me.
"Oh" if only I could escape this prison of pain.
And no memories of you would remain!

I would be the happiest one alive,
and for this I will strive.
To remove you from my mind,
to remove your memory and escape this bind.

For your memory drives me insane
And tangles up my brain.
But to erase you from my thoughts.
Would keep my mind from being caught.

Judy G. Hodge

The Abyss of Desire

I awake only to find
your face embedded in the abyss of my mind

And what burns deep down inside of me
are your words of heartache and misery

Oh yes, you're wild, wicked and cold
it's only indignation that dwells within your soul

For you've cast your spell of passion and desire
and turned my heart to ashes from the fire

So say goodbye to what could of been
now is the beginning of dispiriting end

Once consumed by your web of lust
I now renew my heart of dust

And what now burns deep inside of me
is a flame of hope of a spirit set free

Oh yes, you're wild, wicked and cold
it's only indignation that dwells within your soul

And you awake only to find
it's my face that is now embedded
in the abyss of your mind

Deborah Meyer

Lord, Make Me Like You

Some call you, the saviour; some just say: Oh, Lord
Your magic is shown as freedom as an eagle soars

Some know you as the courage in the mighty lion
Some know you as the enemy of hypocrisy and lying

Some see you as tenderness in a mother's hug
Some feel you in the mercy and security of love

Some see you on a cross, so loyal and brave
Treated like a common, disobedient slave

Some shed a tear for your ultimate sacrifice
Some feel a deep sense of gratitude, once ore twice

Some hear your message in the preacher's voice
Some ignore your instruction, that's their choice

Some read the bible, and quote verse after verse
They feel that keeps them safe from Satan's curse

Life is a road, with many twists and turns
On one highway, you reach heaven; on the other you burn

I'm proud to proclaim my loyalty to your crusade
Its the wisest choice, I've ever made

I'm but a teenager, as spiritual beings go
The more I mature, the more about you I get to know!

Harold Charles Lobb

Last Writes

Don't cry for me with tears of sorrow
Your sighs of sadness are unwelcome here.
My struggle has ended for all tomorrows
My peace has come without fear.

Why sob for me with eyes of pain
Continue in strength with joy for living
All risk is worthy, despite the gain
My pleasure came from the spirit in giving.

Keep your condolences at my departure
Lament is wasted with burdensome release.
Know my body enjoyed this short adventure
I am no soul tortured in grief.

No ritual to end in mourning, wearing black
Children of the stars are we on this Earth.
Remember the seasons revolve to come back
Be joyful in miracles, our human birth.

Have life with more tears cried in excited happiness
And say goodbye with ease today.
I swear in death, as God is my only witness
My love from family, friends, myself, in memory is to stay.

Giovanna Burleigh

Untitled

I wandered lonely by the sea
Your spirit came and walked with me.
Side by side upon the beach
Closer in death than we were ever to reach
  in life.
Bound together with ties of love,
Strengthen and solaced
  by God above.
I wandered lonely by the sea
Your spirit came and walked with me.

Juanita Roese

Of Seasons and Tears

I watched a winter's pale sun rise
Your sweet face amidst, my prize
A gem so pure, so truly rare
A silver thread between us lays bare

I felt a springtime shower
Your strength, my climb towards that tower
A desire to attain
A degree of your gain

I saw a rose abloom
Your memory a delicate room
A broken though grateful heart
A place we shall never part

I smelled a fall fire burning
Your joys, your trials I'm learning
A gentle, beloved teacher
A longing somehow to reach her

I brushed a tear upon my face
Your life one of amazing grace
A time again when we shall ever be
A season of oneness, you and me

Dyeanne Koller

A Mother's Love

Your there for me when others aren't
Your there for me when were apart,
Your like the wind beneath my wings,
Your love for me shines like diamond rings,
When I stumble on my own two feet,
Your hand reaches out to help me meet my tomorrow.
The tears that fall from my face you catch with distinct timing -
And grace, when God seems to just not care and friends have no-
shoulder to share, I know that you are always there.
Your the Mom any - other can't be,
Your the perfect and only one for me.

Angelica Acevedo

Words

Your words have the power of death or life.
Your words can heal or they can cause strife.
Your words represent power, make them work for you every hour.

Whether it's in the morning or when you go to bed,
Don't ever speak negative words, but positive words instead.
Let every word from your mouth be, the words of God and you will see,
Each area of your life get the victory!

By your words you can set free, those held captive by the enemy.
Send God's Word like an arrow into their life,
His words will penetrate the darkness like a knife.

When others judge, curse, and speak evil of you, I will tell you
  what you should do:
Bless them back with a word of love, hot coals will be heaped on
  their head from above.
They will feel ashamed for their action, and you will see that God
  stopped the faction.

Your words can bring death and destruction, they can cause others
  not to function,
Or they can bring life and health, it all depends on how you use
  your mouth!

Don't ever let the enemy use your tongue.
Guard against speaking negative words, and every battle will be
WON!

Judith A. Reno

Tribulations

When your life is chaotic and it seems to crumble;
You're brought to your knees. You learn how to be
humble.

When interrupted by life's tribulations, you seem
to crack in two by the trying situations!

A death makes you feel like your heart is going
to burst. Then all you think is that your life has
been truly cursed!

So; Stand firmly on solid ground when facing your
tribulations. You will not fall because of your
strong foundations!

If you fall, brush yourself off and continue to
fight. In the end you'll have a future that is
prosperous and bright!

Remember the pain you've suffered and felt and
fight the tribulations you have been dealt.

In the end, you will surely sit high! You only
thought life had truly passed you by!

Do not be interrupted by life's intrusions.
Instead: Be aware of life's tribulations and
their many illusions.

Gaston B. Langston

Just You

Please don't ever change who you are
You're close enough to perfect for me
You are my shining star.
All my love to you from me.

We started from nothing and found our love
From yesterday filled with pain and sorrow
We were blessed by God above,
Because we have each other to share every tomorrow

You're gentle, loving and, you really care
I believe we'll always be together
As far as leaving you, I wouldn't dare.
I've looked for you forever.

Frances R. Glennon

We Are Death

You drift into the night,
You're leaving out of sight.
You'll never be seen again.
People say you'll live to see the end,
But we all know that is a lie.
The reason we live is to die.
We actually have nothing to live for.
Look, look at this horrid planet.
We are all hypocrites.
We say we're going to keep this planet clean,
But we all know we trash it.
We say we're going to stop the violence,
But here we are killing our own kind.
We say our children won't use drugs,
But we use them ourselves.
This is not good and is not right.
Soon enough we won't have a world,
Then we will still all die.
Have you ever thought about how the world will end?
It is because of us....human beings.

Heather Reasonover

The Tangled Heart

My heart is whispering your name,
You're my longing, a stain in my memory like the crying rain.
I need you, though you don't know,
You're my destiny, the one flame I let go.

I loved you more than I could've ever said,
For then I was young and my heart rarely bled.
For now my heart bleeds for your soft, gentle touch,
Your satin sensitivity that warmed me so much.

You taught me how a bind can begin,
You loved me although I didn't realize then.

I've grow up now and I understand what we had,
It was something true, poetic, and in some ways sad.

I wish you knew now how I loved you then,
For I'm beginning to feel that love once again.

A secret in my mind, no one can know,
I love you right now, and can't let you go.

I'm with someone else, but my dreams are of you
I wish I could explain, for my love's torn in two?

Jennifer DeVolld

Black Thursday: Or Whitman's O, Captain, My Captain,
A Personal... Tragedy

For my fifth grade class day, Miss Goodwin selects solemnly a student
to perform in the Flag Day Program,
I, the token immigrant, am chosen to recite a classic and immortal
poem.
Each day her fleshy cheeks bend over my faded text as I practice and
flawlessly recite the meaningless words.

One rainy day she is satisfied.
She licks her lips as I commit the words to memory.
I enviously watch my classmates playing. They are barely visible
through the grimy windows.

On Thursday she whisks me from my seat.
Her black, pointy shoes accompany me to the auditorium.
Her thin, veiny hands push me through a fading curtain,
I am told to speak loudly.

People are sitting in chairs and light hits my eyes as my stomach lifts.
My voice refuses to cooperate
Miss Goodwin's hissing and prodding can not produce the result she wants.
I am a disgrace to her and my country.
I hate Thursdays.

Anna Dea Diotalevi

Moving On

Feeling a breeze but not hearing it
You turn and feel alone.
Deep in the desolate forest
You try to move forward, but you can't
For something is holding you back.
You can not push this object down
For then you will be pushing yourself
For it is part of you.
Your feeling for the breeze is trying to set free,
But the trees will always keep you from going.
Too scared to go into the dark depths of the underground
forest, but too scared to stay and be alone.

Caitlin Kaplan

The Mall

It makes me laugh, it makes me smile,
Going to the mall to walk my mile
At all the different shapes and sizes.
The parade of walkers take the prizes.
The jogging suits so well filled out
The designer jeans with so much clout
Babes in strollers on parade,
While Mommy dons her favorite shades.

Candy shops and ice-cream cones,
Department stores and public phones
Lovers strolling hand in hand,
Store windows show their favorite brand.
The seniors walk each day it seems
Helps their heart and lungs and dreams.
Of all the things that come and went
Think the mall was heaven-sent.

Phyllis Brunt

A New Beginning

Meditate on what we take for
granted.
The sun's continuous
rise and set.
Realize what is,
and what will never be known.
Birth and rebirth.
There are no mistakes in this
concept of time
Life.
Always remember,
there are no endings;
Only
New beginnings

Kyneesha Dew

Untitled

A glazed eve waves confidence through,
Grey although of magical charm,
A member a communal grace,
As shadows appease more of solitude.
Situation as before a rain,
If playful stroll intuitive gain,
While arches the drifting sun,
Shall mark of leaves never undone.
Change of color ages partake,
Never by nature have seasons forsake,
Her light figures of Autumn trace,
As if a goodness had shown her face.

Michael Price

August

August—rain is cold sky is dark
grey and wind would howl but is
soothed by mighty trees that are so

Close—touch but cold and close but
cold and far away and hearts beat with a
passion never to be realized in the

Rain—fear and want never to let go
but time is slow; so slow that one can
never, never know the

Love—love for an innocence that smiles
and flows like a fountain and
flashes in deep brown eyes but now

Turning, leaving,

Goodbye...

Matthew Loverin

Grace

As I lay in a huddle
Grieved and lowly bent

Sins heavy hand upon me
In tears and sorrow spent,

Lost in fear and failure
Until your spirit came,
O sweet love, sweet precious blood
My soul in grace proclaims,

There is none as sweet my Lord
Who never condemns or blames,

O sweet love, sweet precious blood
Intimacy does console,

When love comes as a healing flood
Pouring o'er my soul.

Pat MacLeod

Simply Complex

A very special moment
happened with my friend.
She wouldn't tell me her problems
until I agreed,
to be with her until the end.

What she told me was disturbing
but I didn't care,
and because of what I promised
whatever happened, we shared

Our friendship
made a great team,
even though she was an adult
and I was just a teen.

To her I'd like to say

Because I'll never forget
All the things we've been through,
now you're gone forever
and all I do is miss you.

Melinda Peterburs

The Universe

I live in a body whose color
happens to be black.

I am looking out through eyes
that see a rainbow of colors.

I see you — yet, you're neither
black, brown nor white.

You are beautiful-without flaws.
Without hate.
Without prejudice.
Without jealousy.

You are a tall redwood tree reaching
up toward a cobalt sky.

You are a stream with crystal clear
water.

You are the delicate petal of a
radiant red rose.

You are me — I am you.
We are the Universe.

Raquel Fuller

Consent

A just and perfect right
has he
To look into a company
Of birds arranging
to go south
Avoiding winter's chill
and drought
Who sits upon my window sill
In summer sun and warms my heart
But he has left on fearless wing
Who wishes for a wider view
Of ocean span, hilltop and glen
In warmer climes with feathered
friends
So who am I
To wonder why
A bird will shun my winter sky
When all I offer him to be
A boarder in my pepper tree.

Margaret Ann Cole

His Guidance

He holds me close,
He holds me dear.
Embraced in his arms,
I have no fear.
God's ways are right,
His ways are true.
Blessings of wisdom,
To get me through.
Each day that passes,
He's by my side,
As my Lord God's child,
I will always abide.
His amazing grace,
And miracles abound,
I have been so lost,
But now, am truly found.

Sherrie L. Clarke

"My Billy Bear"

In the middle of my pillow,
he is there.
In the middle of my pillow,
hidden there.

All the trouble I'd be having,
if they knew that I still had him.
In the middle of my pillow,
he is there.

Stained with tears, dirt and snot,
he is there.
I love my bear a lot,
he is there.

They think that I've out grown him,
so I dare not ever show him.
But in the middle of my pillow,
be Billy bear.
"MY SWEET LITTLE BILLY BILLY
BEAR."

Misty Akers

The Greater Load

'Twas not alone a heavy tree
He journeyed with up Calvary
'Twas not alone a cross tho' rude
He bore, amongst the multitude;
Much greater was that other load
He carried on Golgotha's road
His leaden steps made heavier still
As on He trod up Calvary's hill.
He carried to that evil place
The sins of all the human race
Of those unborn and those who died
And those alive, when crucified.
Not just alone a heavy tree
Like others borne to Calvary
Not 'neath that tree alone He fell
He could have borne that burden well;
But with that cruel cross He bore
With crimson sweat, my sins galore
If to my Savior I will pray
Jesus will wash my guilt away.

R. Geo Thompson

Endearment

I tell him "I love you",
He says "I love you more",
He's my guardian Angel
He's the man I adore

He calms my fears,
He's my pillar of strength,
And the good Lord knows
I've used it to length.

Our love is so deep,
so true with out measure,
for he holds my heart
like a precious treasure.
My husband, my family,
the time I've been given,
I thank you dear Lord,
for the life I am living.

Victoria Vanderstine

Jesus' Love

He lifts me up when I am down.
He shelter's me in His love.
He clears my mind when it's fuss.
He loves me when no one else does
The thought of His love makes me smile
When I am sad.
And it is He who sends me a rainbow
To let me know I am not alone.
He gives me special people to love
Because He loves me.
He gives use precious children
To love and raise.
All because He love us so
And to show that love
He give us all to see a snow dove.

Lorine Young

A Fact of Life

The lens sees
The film records
The print will tell
anyone
anywhere
What the lens once saw
in a click of time.

Ruth Marie Colville

Hypocrite

To save the spotted owl,
He stood at the gate
Locked arm and arm
He made the loggers wait
He drove his boat through the tuna nets
Saving dolphins from sure deaths
He blew up a dam
So the mud fish could swim
Now happy and proud
He made love to his wife
When she got pregnant
He put the fetus to the knife

William E. Queale

Doggy Froggy

There is a little frog.
He thinks he is a dog.
He likes to chase cars
And he sleeps on a log.

He howls at the moon.
He likes to chase the cat.
His best friend is a mouse
Who thinks he is a rat.

He likes to chew on bones
And bury them in the dirt.
He wears red tennis shoes
And a big, floppy shirt.

You may think he is silly.
He's not like any other frog
Because he likes to run and play
And thinks he is a dog.

Michael Godwin

Tale Of Night (Silence-The Guide)

Silence surrounds me now
Hear in security of darkness
What was once unheard is loud

The scratching of an unattended pencil
The sigh of a lonesome animal
The splash of a misguided tear
The beating echo of a broken heart

Candlelight dancing upon the walls
A rivulet of emotion a waterfall
The time has come to remember it all

Hey you, my friend
I've been waiting
Take me to the end
Pull up a chair and
help me to begin

Matthew Beebe

My Destiny

When young. I blissfully
played by your shores
now old I wearily
play no more

Come to me, wrap me
in your foam
take me out to sea
and home.

Phyllis K. Fitzgerald

Trapped In Reality

Feel it coming,
hear its scream.
Understand the sorrow-
trapped in a dream.

Vast black waters
roll across the sky.
Listen for the wails-
a forlorn cry.

Know the pain;
you cannot run.
Breathe the suffering-
when Darkness has come.

Katrina Sun

Shepherd of the Hills

Serenely I come to the house of the Lord
Hearing His word is a must.
Each day of the week has
Placed at my door
Hard choices I cannot ignore.
Early and late I commune with my Lord
Reveling in His presence.
Daily I seek His help from His word
Often receiving new insight
From old familiar phrases
To ease a troubled heart.
Hearing the Master's promise
Each day can turn into joy.
Holding His hand as
I-forge on
Living has purpose and pleasure,
Loving Him always
Serenely, I go, hopeful without measure.

Lois W. Orr

The Shooting Gallery Duck

Back and forth she glides each day,
Her movements without fail,
Smile fixed, and posture plumb,
Anchored to her bumpy rail.

Her life is like a carnival game,
Loud music, gaudy lights,
A colorful shooting gallery duck,
He keeps her in his sights.

With deadly aim he narrows in,
Cruel words go whizzing by,
She rests a moment as he reloads,
To make another try.

For in the end, ducks always lose,
A sharpshooter wins the prize.
Back and forth, she accepts her fate,
As over and over she dies.

Melsyne Montgomery

To Grandma

Her smile was my sunshine.
Her sadness was my pain.
Her love was my reason for living.
Her death, it brought the rain.
If I could touch her one more time
If I could have said good bye
If I could tell her what she meant to me
Grandma please don't cry.
Thank you Grandma.
I love you.

Kim M. Zaker

If I Were A Skywriter...

If I were a skywriter
  here's what I'd do,
I'd display to the world
  all my love for you.

One bright, sunny morning
  you'd glance up high,
to discover your name printed
  across the clear, blue sky.
You're the inspiration
  who caused me to be proud.
for I've expressed affection my way
  through symbols of cloud.

Except, lacking a plane
  and a gifted pilot's art...
I've written your name
  all over my heart!!!

Leilani Lim

My Dog, My Friend

A dog, indeed, is man's best friend.
He's faithful and loyal, from
beginning to end.
He guards and protects, his
love does not fail,
and for a kind word his
smile is a wag of his tail.
He doesn't ask for much
and in return,
He's a lifelong friend, a
lesson we could all learn.
Be kind to him for you
have him not long,
but for the undying love
you share it makes you
strong.

Rebecca L. Davis

Andy

My son's name is Andy
He's my pride and joy
The only one I've ever love
That's my little boy.

Your father left us long ago
Before you were even born
I guess he didn't care for us
Leaving our hearts to be torn.

That's ok - we'll get along
I'll be both mother and father
I'll do the very best I can
We'll always help each other.

It's all a very sad sad story
But the ending will be happy
Because you'll never be alone
You'll always have your mommy.

When I say - I love you
You'll know it to be true
Every minute of the day
I'll be reminding you.

Robin K. Bell

My Little Guy

My little guy is suffering,
his grades are going down.
Because of all the teasing
and constant fooling around.

The other kids are on his back
because they know he's meek.
They always take advantage
and make him feel so weak.

They all gang up on him
and tease and make him cry,
because they all know
that he's the one so shy.

This story is not only about
one boy who stands alone,
but about countless others too,
that are not allowed to grow.

Dear God let me find a way
to help my little man out.
To pull him out of his rut,
a situation he can do without.

Robert L. Macchia

Medical Betrayal

You trust and then you give your all
Hope and health

Stumble and fall

From a silver tongue, plated in gold
Came wondrous warm words

That leave life cold

You start again, have need to believe
A wise decision?

Should you leave?

How do you know? Will the axe fall?
This time, next time?

Not at all?

Rita Kurgan

The Flower and the Sun"

A flower reminds me of the sun
how each wakes and shines each
morning
and closes each night
how they both shine their beautiful
bright colors
and bring joy and happiness
to many
how they warm the heart of and
show their cheerful faces to all
each is beautiful

Sara Wohnrade

Untitled

Walking the sleep.
Pulling the candle.
Consummating the darkness.
Holding the break.
Feeling the edge.
Plunging the clock.
Gripping the cold.
Burning the night.
Ending the color.

Kathy Goodman

I May Never Know

I may never know,
How great it would feel,
To hold you, so close,
I'd know it was real.

I may never hold,
You close to my side,
Like squeezing you tight,
And turning the tide.

I may never kiss,
Those beautiful lips,
But can always just wish,
As my heart, seems to rip.

I may never hear,
From the chuckle inside,
The words, sought for,
As I always, cried.

I may never be,
What you'd want me, to dear,
But without really trying,
I'll just, still always, want you near.

Shelton McGraw Sr.

"Remember"

Remember when we started and
how it ended

Remember me with kindness and
love in your heart

Remember me as the one who
loved you well

Remember the trust that we
both shared

Remember the promises that we
made and the love we shared

Remember I'm here if you ever
need a friend who cares

So good-bye and good luck with
the future you hold, for I can't
hope to be apart of what later
unfolds

Remember me with kindness
and not with woes.

Wanda Grice

Betsy

Betsy, Betsy boo.
How we all love you.

Just a little over three years old.
Fisty little tease and very bold.

Sweet sweet little honey.
Worth more than all the worlds money.

Lovely and full of fun.
She loves to be out in the sun.

Loves to play and tease the cat.
She sure puts him on the scat.

Pretty and very smart.
She's been given a real good start.

Wonderful grand daughter of mine
In life I know you'll be just fine.

L. L. French

My Parents' Poem

Do I ever tell you
How much you mean to me
You open up my eyes to things
I simply do not see

My growing up is hard
For both you and me
But no matter how I change
We're still a family

I know there have been times
When I have really hurt you
With words said out of anger
And rude things I do...

But I realize my mistakes
And I just hope and pray
That you will find it in your heart
To forgive me someday

Without you in my life
I don't know what I'd do
And writing this is just my way
Of saying I LOVE YOU

Michelle Mijewski

How Rich

How rich has the voyage been, traveler?
How studded with stars?
And how much of a lifetime was wasted
with strangers in bars?
How far did you wander?
How deep did you wonder?
What dreams did you follow?
How many reject?

Was it money or marriage or family
that stood in your way?
And isn't it true
that the roadblock was you?
For the stars never captured
are still there to explore...
a perfume, a voice and a brilliance!
Is there time to walk backwards
and open that door?

Mel Freedman

Who Am I, What Am I?

I am girl.
I am boy.
I am spirit.
Filled with joy.

I am woman.
I am man.
I will grow
Because I can.

I am love.
I am life.
Filled with passion
Not with strife.

I am body.
I am soul.
I am spirit.
I am whole.

Karlene Valadez

A Seedling

When I pass thee,
I am but a small breeze with a soft sent.
When I admire thee,
I am the warm blood traveling through
your kind heart.
I see you when I lay to sleep,
you say not a word—
You only stand in the mist.
Your beauty shines like the stars above.
Is this but a fantasy?
Or merely our destiny?
I know of the other that you love,
I wish that thou would love only me.
Out of my hate for thee,
love has risen and taken over my soul.
For give me for letting a seed of hate
grow into a rose of love.

Natasha Dea Briggs

Untitled

My shadow is lost, and know
I am lost, lost in the mist
of no where.

Walking through the path of
illusion and there's no sign of
direction and no one to ask
question, the atmosphere dimmed
to darkened cloudiness.

Being alone in the mist is
an unthinkable unexplainable
existence foreseeing sight that exist.

I will try to explain where
I was and what I've seeing,

And they would listened but
never understand what he is
trying to say about the mist of no where.

Now you know every man has
is own shadow that can be
Lost in mist of mystery
my shadow is lost, and know I am Lost.

Paul Morgan

The Pines

The pines tower above.
I breathe in their awe.
The silence is like a blanket,
Will I hear a tree fall?

The needles beckon unto me.
They are as soft as the finest down.
I lay on nature's bed,
Sleeping on a cloud.

The world is all around you,
But you never hear the call.
The pines were sent by God,
To protect us from it all.

I awaken,
The silence is broken.
God has sent his messengers,
And yet a word is never spoken.

The pines tower above us,
Giving solace to the meek.
God has made this sanctuary,
So every living thing can learn of peace.

Trina K. Hixson

My Mind's Eye

In my mind's eye
I can see,
a babbling brook
that belongs only to me.

A beautiful spring day
with a gentle breeze,
I can hear the leaves
rustling on the trees.

I just have to relax
and think of this place,
that can be seen with my minds eye
and dream at my own pace.

This is my own special place
that can never be taken away,
I can see it whenever I want
either by night or by day.

Maryellen F. Payne

Thank You, God

I cannot walk like others -
I cannot talk like others -
But, I can write and pray -
    Thank you, God

I cannot visit with others -
I cannot sing with others -
But, I can visit with God -
    Thank you, God

I can smile at others -
I can shake hands with others -
I can show love to others -
    Thank you, God

Mavin Houlihan

There's Something in My Closet

There's something in my closet,
I can't explain at all,
At night while I am sleeping,
It's banging on the wall.
There's something in my closet,
My closet is its lair,
And I swear when I'm not home,
It eats my underwear.
There's something in my closet,
What, I do not have a clue,
Until I saw it on my bed, gnawing
on my shoe.
There's something in my closet,
I wonder what it eats,
So I slid some mashpotatoes under
the door for several weeks.
There's something in my closet,
With short and spiky hair,
I guess I do not mind it,
As long as it stays in there.

Richard T. Balsavage

Skippy

Skippy the frog,
Sat on a log
Told the bird
He was single.
He came from here
And too far from there
To dance around in
The rainbow.

Wareetha Habeeb

Remember Me God?

Remember me God?
I come everyday
You taught me how to pray
You really taught me a lot
it's nothing money could have bought
You made me feel welcomed,
You reached out Your hand,
I need never explain
for You understand
I came to You frightened
and kept You close to my heart
it was really nice to know
that we'll never part!

Natasha Monique Porter

Myself and My Identity

(Why Am I the Way I Am?)

Why am I the way I am?
I could blame it on my mother,
   or my father, or my heritage.
But, that wouldn't be the real reason
I am who I am.

Many people I come in contact with
try to act like someone else
who they are not
why I ask myself, why?

I am proud to be who I am.
I have learned that to love someone
you must learn to love yourself first.
I know who I am.

I am an American who is free.
I am one who will stand up for
   all I believe in.
I am one who realizes my flaws
   but works to make them less
   noticeable with my strong points.
I am who I am.

Sarah C. Ward

Love Gone

After all those years of living
I couldn't believe you were gone.
Inside my anguish was screaming
NO, I can't, I just can't go on.

I could shed no tears with crying
My eyes were as dry as could be.
I felt that my heart was dying
Dear God, have mercy on me.

I laid my head on your cold hand
And cursed all the powers above.
Of all the ones in this cruel land
Oh, why did they take my dear love?

I must go on, I kept saying
But the words seemed only a dream.
Somehow I just kept on praying
For God to take over the scheme.

With time God gathered my heart strings
And helped me to know I could live.
He showed me the beauty that life brings
When a person can learn to GIVE.

Sarah Andrews-Stark

My One and Only

To my one and only,
I do have to say,
Because of you,
I'll never be lonely.

Without your love
and without your strength,
I am just a lonely dove.

Your smiles and wit
comes so naturally,
so does your silly side
just a bit.

I love you with all my heart,
and remembering our vows,
till death do us part.

Monica Dykes

Untitled

You got my heart in an uproar
   I don't know what's going on
My, its in my sleep, it tosses and turns
   the knife it cuts even deeper more
And I sit and I cry,
   and I hurt and wonder why
Yet the pain grows strong
   I wonder who's right, who's wrong
And I feel all by myself
   sitting here all alone, in a room
That's so cold and dark
   this lonely room in my heart.

Tony Anthony Partee Sr.

Could I Live Without You?

Could I live without you?
I doubt it very much,
I'd miss your tender smile,
Your warm and gentle touch.

I'd miss your hearty laughter,
Your anger and your tears,
I'd miss the understanding,
You've shown me through the years.

I would be so lonely,
Without the love we've shared,
Through all the good and bad,
You showed how much you cared.

If ere the time would come,
That we should have to part,
I wouldn't live without you,
You'd be there in my heart.

Linda Rincon

Me

I am black-yet
I am White-
because someone-
Someone said so-
and you tear me apart-
because of your
unknowingness
I am not Black
I am not white
because I say so
I am Me-

Leon R. Smith

Feast of Earth

I eat the oceans and the sun
I drink the rocks and luscious hills
The silver night is my dessert
The creamy sunrise is my fill
In this paradise I live
Many times I sit and wonder
Who else gives their sweet surrender
To the stars and singing thunder
Tasting of the flight of eagles
Shivering in the roar of the bear
Is there none who find the joy
Of windsnakes rustling in their hair
My coats are rich velvet sunlight
And silk of rippling ocean green
Seaweed dancing are my shoes
Glassy eyes of fish their sheen
I eat the earth and all its splendor
Freedom day and night swept by
Entranced I sit and do remember
Words to the dancing of the sky.

Melanie Tormos

A Last Goodbye

The mist of time is closing in
I feel it closer day by day
That's why I want you dear
To pray while I slip away

I see the reef just ahead
It is waiting there for me
My body is so very tired dear
My spirit now is ready to flee

Parting is not very easy
That's why I shed my tears
The only thing I wanted in life
Was for you to be always near

So, in this very last moment
The last thing I want to see
Is your loving smiling face
So I can carry that image with me

Please, don't leave me with a stranger
When I draw that long last sigh
For I want to go with dignity
Wishing you my love, a last goodbye

Kathleen R. Jazwienski

Here It Is

Sin is the worst enemy
I have ever known
It robs, kills, and destroy
The children and the home
If you have not been born again.
It have the upper hand
The death grip will not, let you go
It is distraction, woe!
It's every generation curse
Worst than atomic bombs
Destroying not only where you are.
But all over the world.
The damage has and is being done.
In hearts, homes, and churches.
On every job, school, and business.
Friendships, marriages and families.
Repent and believe the gospel
Mark 1:15
His love for us is infinite
I am a living witness to this.

Katie S. Gamble

The Victorious President:

I have heard of wars,
I have seen war.
I have known of wars,
and it scares me to
hear or see war for if
there be war there will
be no peace.

Which country goes to war
without firing a shot, and
to what honor gave the
commander?
The man who loves peace
in command, he never fought
a battle, but with victory
came he home.

Prince James Awah

"Healing"

Let me be, I am healing
(I have to collect my feelings)
I am a crystal, I am a rock,
I am my mother sweet and tender
and the angel by my side
or the soldier that surrenders...

The darkest night,
the deepest pain,
will go away, will go away,
but let me now search for the light,
that always filters
through my life...

To soothe the pain,
to light my night,
now that I am healing,
just give time, just give me time...

Vicky H. Vargas

A Kiss

Here's a kiss from me to you,
I hope that all your dreams come true.
But when I look into your eyes,
I get lost among the rhymes.
I want us to be together all the time.
'Cuz when I'm with you I don't need a dime.
All my life surrounds only you.
And if you leave me, I'll feel so blue.
From the bottom of my heart,
I hope we never part
'Cuz if we do I'll cry all night.

Tina Wallace

Sad Souls

Tortured souls
Bleeding in a hell of anger and resent

Too weak to try again
Too strong to repent

Wishing they could find a way
   To share a simple smile

Come here my child
Sit down my friend

Let's sit and talk awhile.

Stacey V. Butler

The Tempest

A tempest is coming.
I know it.
I feel it.
Everything grows quiet,
So quiet and still.
Shadows form
And with them
That feeling of
Despair.
It prevails.
It fills the air.
And then,
With no other warning,
It breaks
And
Tears fill my eyes
And cover my face.

Laurie Zuelke

Byways of Life

The road is so familiar,
I know it's path so well.
Yet each curve and windy bend,
Have secrets still to tell.

Should I wander to the left,
And bare my soul anew?
Or stay the straight and narrow,
Though days and years pass through?

The best of paths of follow,
Is to the right, you say,
The dark shadows of the night,
Will lighten with the day.

The curves are dark and calling,
All those who enter there,
"Open up the darkness here,
A new light, if you dare."

The road is too familiar,
Go out and grasp the bend.
For all to soon it is gone,
Never to come again.

Pat A. Kiger

By the Light of the Moon

By the light of the moon
I long for you,
your touch,
your smile,
your voice in my ear.
But miles away are you,
with another love
touching her,
your voice in her ear,
your smile only for her.
By the light of the moon
I weep for you,
as you smile at another and forget.

Vickie Zello

Baseball

More than a field
of sod and clay.

It is the joy of
boys who play...
the game.

Thomas W. Maynard

Silence

As I stand here oblivious to time
I look out towards the sea
and feel oh so free.
Your presence brings the joy
and allows for me to be me.
Blessed am I for I can love
not just you but all in view.
Be it the sky, the sea, or the land
I can wander in all places
shining forth through all phases.
You have led me down a path
of which there is no return
and to you I can only say
it is love that compels me to stay.

Sela Pearson

Suicide Dream

In a place I dwell
I met a boy I loved so well
He came and taught that love from me
Now he's willing to set me free
I even know the reason why
The other one is prettier than I
I went right home
Laid on by bed
Not a word spoken or said.

My dad come home
Searched for me left and right
Up the stairs; the door he broke
Found me hanging from a rope
He caught a knife
Cut me down; in my jeans a note be found:

   Dig a grave, dig it deep
   marble and stone, from head to feet
   and on the grave, place a dove
   to let the whole world know
      I died for...love

Kelly Hudson

A Man Of Good Times

Once upon a long, long time,
I met a man who used one eye,
For in the other, he was blind.
His face was covered with fine lines,
And his hands shrivelled up like vines.
He sat by the store of nickel and dimes
And whistled a tune, that was fine.
People listened to him all the time
As he spoke good of all mankind.
Whenever I seem to be in a bind,
His smile would work, like a chime.
Then one day, as I sat at his side,
he fell asleep, but I didn't mind.
I began to look at him for a sign
And the only thing I seem to find
Was his life had ended, as had mine.

Kerri Stembridge

March

First Robin.
Crocus.
Sixty-four degrees.

Twelfth day.
Spring?
Agreed!!

Sharon Sharp

I Am Free

My body is subject to your laws,
I must behave in accordance;
Civic rules for personal action,
you may censor my movements.
You can control what I hear,
You can control what I say,
You can control what I see.
You can control what I taste.

YOU CAN NOT control WHAT I THINK.
My thoughts are untouchable.
My thought are free,
My thoughts are pure.
You may capture my body;
my mind will be free

RobT. Gutkin

Resolution

Many times alone at night
I often wondered if I was right
To love someone with all my heart,
Knowing soon he would depart.

Wishing so that it would last
Oft I lingered in the past,
Until I sensed it's not to be
There's someone better out there for me.

Patricia J. Alford

Those Words

Will you ever say those certain words,
I pray so long to hear?
The words that say you love me too
and fill my heart with cheer.
I need to hear those words from you,
those words that mean so much.
Those words that could also be said
in a look, a smile, a touch.
Those words are as important as
the beating of a heart.
Those words that will make us stronger
for the times we are apart.
Those words will help us overcome any
questions, doubts or fears.
Those words will always be used by us
through out the coming years.
For two that will love as you and I
can start our lives a new.
And always face each other and say,
"yes I love you too"

William R. Muller

A Sad Face

Looking in the mirror
I see,
What a sad pathetic mess
he has made out of me.
No more will I let him
get away with that!
No more will he take
the two parts of me I
need to survive,
My soul, and heart!!

Shannon Lopez

Onward

Portrayed in all the things I see
I see a light, and give it to you.
Just like the song I try to sing
You're a song to me.

Onwards - through the night.
Onwards - through the night.
Onwards - through the night.

Just like the words I could not find
You bring the words to me.
Just like the man who always tries
You bring life at the end of the day.

Onwards - through the night.
Onwards - through the night.
Onwards - through the night.

In tears of pain so dear to shed,
You wound and heal my soul
With time I grow to understand
Love conquers all.

Onward thought the night.
Onward through the night.

Nicholas W. Zubko

Sky-Blue Delphinium

As down my garden path I trod
I sense the presence of my God
And in a blue Delphinium
I see the handy-work of Him
Stately, tall, it's color blue
of such a deep and lovely hue,
Reflects the color of the skies
therein I feel it's beauty lies,
As the heaven's declare the
glory of God,
Even so this earth, this sod,
Through the blue Delphinium
Here reveals the glory of Him.

Suzanne Weidendorf

A Talented Fly

As I walked by a lonely pond,
I spotted an oversized black fly,
skating in his knee-highs.

He looked me straight in the eye,
and said,
"What are you staring at?"

"My name is Fred,
let me show you how to play dead."

He sailed through the air,
and sat upon my hair.

"Do you mind if I come along,
to buzz you a song?"

"I will do you no wrong,"
explained the talented fly.

I nearly died at the sight of
that amazing fly.

Margaret Marshall

A Spring Day

When I think of spring,
I think of the Birds that sing.

The smell of fresh cut grass
a gentle breeze that may pass.

To lay in a field,
to look in the sky,
to watch the clouds slowly go by.

I write this so others may
see through my eyes,
what life means to me as a
spring day passes by.

Tim Aievoli

Running Out Of Time

With the setting of the sun
I think of things I've never done
And spinning in my head
Are the words I've never said
So, let me try to say
Each and every day...
I love you

Lorena Pankotai

Like An Elephant Upon

A Spider's Thread

Like an elephant upon a spider's thread
I tread, and though my mind
Can be clothed in a pea's skin,
I still remember your faces
Staring through the bars of my cage.
Your eyes waving sticks
And throwing stones,
And your words lodging themselves
In the great folds of my ears.
You couldn't understand my tears
That were older than my bones
And the stones that caught them.

There was a call and a charge,
And your faces fled with fear,
But I found them underfoot
And not in the clear.

I still remember, though now
Your faces are the colour of dust
That covers my path along the spider's
thread.

J. X. Francis

Five

I've seen the future
    And it's big
I've tasted the rushing
Torrent of knowledge
I've felt the escalation
    Of technology
Heard the siren song
Of virtual reality
And smelled the burning brakes
    Of humanity

Steve Hyde

The Voice

Can you hear me?
I want to get out!
Don't smother me
In moments of doubt.

Share me with life!
Let me help you feel.
We're a pair, you and I,
Like a banana and its peel.

Why keep me inside
To fester and ache?
Do you think I'm not worthy
To icing your cake?

I have to be heard
To give you a chance.
This world needs me
To know you can dance!

I'm the voice inside you!
Don't hold me in!
Together we're strong,
Through thick and through thin.

Mary Atkins

My Children

I look at you and my heart overflows
I want to touch, hug, feel
Don't feel so much!
My superstitious thoughts say
To feel is to hurt
But can loving hurt?

I look at you and my heart sings!
I want to jump up and dance
Don't joy so much
My guardian self says
For every joy there is a pain
But does joy hurt?

My children! How my heart smiles
No matter what the pain!
No matter what the hurt!
You and only you
Bring everlasting love,
Joy, laughter to my soul.

Melva C. Lewis

I Was God

Before my Mother birthed me;
    I was God.
Before my Mother conceived me;
    I was God.
Before the Doctor smacked me;
    I was God.
Before the coming of Christ;
    I was God.
Before the Heavens were made;
    I was God.
Before He breathed His breath in me;
    I was God.
Now I'm a living soul, a man of flesh;
    I am just a temple for God!

Samuel Rudolph

Untitled

At the water's edge
    I watch my reflection
Every movement I make
    distorted ever so slightly
    as the water flows swiftly
    over pebbles hidden
    beneath the surface
As my tears drop
    the image is obscured
Rippling
Pieces floating outward
    in
        ever
            widening
                circles

Kirstin Cummings

"I Will Help Your Heart"

If your heart begins to tumble
I will catch every piece
If your heart begins to crumble
I will fill every crease

I will help your heart heal
I will try to feel what you feel
If you feel sorrow
I will try to follow

Can't you see me trying to help thee
If you don't then I won't

I will help your heart see
And be all that I can be
There's no road too long
For me not to be along

If that road shortly ends
And we become just friends
I will help your heart find
Another place in mind

To help your heart see
That you mean the world to me

Patti J. Flowers

Secrets

Confide in me,
I will not tell a soul.
Place your trust in me,
I'll hold faith with you.
Take up your pen
And tell me what you will.
I know the secrets of ages past,
For I knew Voltaire and Shakespeare,
Chaucer, Tacitus, and Homer.
I will not divulge your secrets,
Save you allow it
Or care no longer.
I will not break this trust,
Save it be broken
By force and violence.
Confide in me,
I will not tell a soul.
Place your trust in me,
I'll hold faith with you.
Confide in me.

Wade Tokumine

Looking in the Mirror

When I look in the mirror
I wish I could see
A vision of someone
I've always wished to be.
Someone who's smart,
Funny and kind.
Someone positive and brave,
With a creative mind.
I wish to be someone
Everyone else could see
As someone who's got it together
And is really happy.
I wish to look and feel
Like someone full of life,
And to grow up to be
A mother and a wife.
If I care for myself
And ignore all of the hate
Then maybe someday I'll get
What I deserve from fate.

Kelly Marie Watson

I'm All Confused This Christmas

I'm all confused this Christmas
I wish I never grew up
Is it false or is it true
Is there one and is it you?
I'm all confused this Christmas
Can he be all around
In the stores and in the town?
Jackie told me it's not true
My Mommy told me to believe
I don't know just what to do
Is it false or is it true?
If I say I don't believe
They'll be nothing on my tree
I don't know just what to do
Is it false or is it true
Is there one and is it you
Is it you Daddy?

Nancy Lejuez

If I Could Be An Angel

If I could be an angel,
I would give God a horse
    of a different color.
If I could be an angel,
I would give God a flower
    of a different smell.
If I could be an angel,
I would give God a bird
    with one million songs.
If I could be an angel,
I would give God a color
    of all colors.
If I could be an angel,
I would give God the heart
    of all hearts.
If I could be an angel,
I would give God the spirit
    of all spirits.

Michaela J. Polster

Untitled

If I saw you today
I would try to smile
I'd look thru your eyes,
And search for the cure.
I'd take a deep breath,
And then ask you "why'?

Why did you leave -
When you knew it was over?
Where did you go -
With my blood on your hands?
Did you forget how I cleansed
Your wounds, of transgression -
And how I washed your soul -
Of all of its sins?

To me you were perfect,
My light in this world;
My endless obsession.

Next time invite me
to my own crucifixion.

Wm. Scott McCall

"What Will I Be"

If you saw clouds
I'd be your sunshine.

If you were in pain
I'd be your cure.

If you were thirsty
I'd be your water.

If you had sadness
I'd be your joy.

If you had no one to love
I'd be your friend.

If you were dying
I'd be your inspiration to live.

If you had tears
I'd be the one to wipe them.

If you had a frown
I'd be your smile.

But if you had nothing
I'd be your EVERYTHING!!

LaToya Banks

Vocal...

Words come saying . . .
What, people do—playing.
Oh! Thou sweet—bray!

Marcus Nelson

Untitled

Hard
To
See

A
Child's
Education
Need

And

Kneed.

Ronald Perron

A Christmas Bit

If I were Santa Claus this year
I'd change his method for the day.
I'd give to all the children here,
But there are things I'd take away.

I'd enter every home to steal;
With giving I'd not be content.
I'd find the heartaches men conceal
And take them with me as I went.

I'd rob the invalid of pain;
I'd steal the poor man's weight of care;
I'd take the prisoner's ball and chain,
And every crime that sent him there.

I'd take the mother's fears away,
The doubts that often fret the wise,
And all would wake on Christmas day
With happy hearts and shining eyes.

For old and young this is my prayer,
"God, bless us all on Christmas day,
And give us strength our tasks to bear,
And take our bitter griefs away."

Lawrence G. D. Wertz

Distance

Alone in the room I stand
I'd never thought I would be this calm
without no one to hold my hand
without you holding me in your arms

We met for only a short time
I hated to hear that you had to go
you were the only thing on my mind
but it was better for me to know

Distance may keep us apart
distance may keep us away
but you'll never leave my heart
no matter how far distance will stay

Sherrina Annette Eddins

The Artist

If I could paint a robin's song,
I'd paint one just for you.

If I could paint a breeze so soft,
I'd paint that for you too.

If I could paint the fragrance of
a rose or a tender word or a
gentle touch,

I'd paint them all for you because,
I love you so very much.

Shirley Hammonds

What If...?

What if they gave a war
  ...and nobody came
No one to fight
No one to blame
No one to lie
No one to shame
No one to cry
No one lame
No one...to die?

Vickie L. Vanderhoof

One Extra Prayer

If I live one minute longer
If I breath one second more
If I do not leave before
my loved ones all have gone
I have lived too long
If I see one extra rainbow
If alone I walk the meadow
If I only see my shadow
and by myself I watch the sea gull
touch the ocean shore
after my loved ones all have gone
I have lived to long
if I sing one extra song
If I cry one extra tear
if I hear one extra thunderbolt
after my loved ones yield their hold
I have grown too old so if I say one extra
prayer
if I love them every moment that I'm here
and if I say one extra prayer
they will never leave me here

Ute Dahmen

Emptiness Craving

Ah, sweet tenderness of passion,
if I could but know thee.
all tortuous hours are mine,
but of love, nay, I know not.
Would not my wrung heart drink,
and saturate in the fountain of love?

Loneliness.... and again that loneliness.
'Tis this, my faithful companion.
If, with but a small morsel of love
destiny would but serve me.
Would I then not hold up my head
and sing forth, I, too, know of life!

Vassili J. Mirsch

Unabridged Love

My body is longing for your touch.
If I could just see you
It would mean so much.
Just to be near you
And to hear your voice,
Would make my lonely heart rejoice.
When I am with you
My life is complete.
When you look at me
My heart skips a beat.
We share our thoughts
Of today and tomorrow,
Tho' it be happiness
Or tho' it be sorrow.
We can face life together
Whatever may come.
We can face life together
As we walk slowly toward home.

Polly L. Spainhour

OOO, La La, Ma

You love me,
  You say
Love me,
  You may...
Who knows?
  We know...
I love you.
  "Stinky" stank

Cornelius (Neal) Thomas

If I Only Can Stop

If I only can stop the time
If I only can stop the day
If I only can stop the grieve
If I only can stop the pain

If I only can stop the sadness
If I only can stop the tears
If I only can stop the madness
If I only can stop my fears

If I only can see my future
If I only can live without you
If I only can stop the rupture
If I only can stop loving you!

Lorena Justin

A Plenitude Of Pulchritude

When we were young and slender,
if this old mem'ry serves,
I spent much time caressing
your very lovely curves.

The passing years have changed us,
so now I take delight,
Expressing adoration
by fondling cellulite.

Willard V. Roberts

Soul Whispering

I know someday
I'll fly away.
I'll fly into
A bright new day.

A day where there
Will be no night.
Where all is bathed
In dazzling light.

Where brilliant sun
Projects its ray
Into God's
Ethereal day.

And in that distant
Time or stay,
Bonds hinder not
My wingéd way.

Lucille R. Glasscock

Puppet In The Rain

Once long ago,
In a place with no snow,
A puppet named pal,
Lived long long ago,
He was never cold,
He was never hot,
He was never warm,
like a boiling pot.
He could not feel happy,
He could not feel sad.
Because he was just a
plain puppet left out in the rain.

Marty T. Durkin

True Side

I believe there is a part
In everyone's heart
That's the true real side
of your face.
It's something you can't
change.
You can't even rearrange.
That you can't peel off or
erase.
It was there from your
very first cry.
It was there from that
vision in your eye.
One day it might change
your life,
And it might even cut
through it like a knife.
It, you might try to hide.
Your one and true side.

Nicole Saxton

Still The Flowers

As a little girl I played
In fields of flowers.
People looked at me
And shook their heads.
I wondered why. Still
The flowers heard my songs.
As a young girl, I pressed
These flowers between
The leaves of my diary.
They ornamented the words
Of a young girl. Still
The flowers heard my songs.
Oh but when love entered
The diary of my heart, a poem
Rose from each petal
Pollinated by questing bees.
My rose opened to a bee with
A golden jacket buttoned
With a doubled heart. Still
The flowers hear my songs.

Knarig Boyadjian

Saying Goodbye, I Lie

In her arms, I reach for her.
In her sight, I look for her.
By her side, I long for her.
In assurance, I hope;
In a promise, I wish.
Everything is never enough.
Nothing is ever enough.
With her, I miss her.
Saying goodbye, I lie.

Peter Edward Burch

Neverlasting Light

It's like a firecracker
Shooting up in the sky,
Anticipation high.
What a sucker.

Burst of color and light.
Briefly the sparkle stalls,
Then glitter falls
Leaving dark night.

Sue Duvall Beck

Special Friend

The thought of you. I have
in my mind, are pure as
Day light and bright sunshine.
I look in your eyes, so
Perfect and blue, when I see
A crystal blue lake, I'll
Be thinking of you.
When I'm down and Depressed
and at my "wits End"!
I'll smile and think of my
"special friend."
Time and Distance will
tear at my heart.
But fires of hell can not
Keep us apart.
So too you "My friend"
I have one thing to say,
I'll love you tomorrow
as much as today

P. Schroeder

Peacefulness of the Moment

I went alone to the river today
In order to find some reason
For some unsettled feelings
I may have not found the cause
But as the tide continued
Beating against the shore line
A special thought came to mind
Life, with all it's problems
Can also be like a surfs tide
They too can crash into us
We can stand firm or be swept away
One thing for sure though
Each problem leaves something new
Whether it be a new friend
A smile from someone you don't know
Maybe a new dream or perspective
Or the "Peacefulness of the Moment"
Which we all need!

Vicky Lynn Teichert

On the Sunny Side

As he walked the street of life,
In such a happy and carefree way,
Who ever could guess that strife,
And grief were his lot each day.

He's a type seemed favored to be,
Of impunity from worry and care,
On the brighter side he could see,
The hope and the happiness there.

With a manner the most debonair,
Called the happy go lucky kind,
He fought both pain and despair,
With fortitude seldom you'll find.

Though his troubles grew every day,
And it seemed he'd fall in defeat,
He'd rally and then manage to stay,
On the sunny side of the street.

What a wonderful life it would be,
If every day Those that we meet,
Could walk in the same way as he,
On the sunny side of the street.

Kenneth P. Sery

591

Looking Through the Afternoon Shade

Reflections of grapevines
In the afternoon shade
Casting images of childhood
Memories once made.

We had apple, cherry,
And blueberry pie.
With a crisscross crust
To please the eye.

There was sweet golden honey
That is to most,
Good for spreading over
Crunchy buttered toast.

In my mom's red velvet or
Butter cream cake,
There was a recipe of love
She worked hard to make.

I could taste her sweet smile
And smell the pleasant aroma of her
affection.
I can still feel her warmth baking
In every confection.

Mark William Jacques

Smile

Smile
In the face of disaster.
Smile,
till your cheeks are sore.
Smile,
till you can't stop smiling.
Smile,
and then smile some more.

Smile,
until your teeth drop out.
Smile,
until your eyes go blind.
Smile,
until your face falls off.
Smile,
until you lose your mind!

Kim Whybrew

The Glow I Feel

I see your face
In the windows of my mind
And your eyes tell of tenderness
You'd try to deny.
You speak to me.
Through echoes of memory
And your soft, warm tones
Wrap around my soul.
The years have not worn away
The glow I feel;
Your presence is so real
It's yesterday.
Yet,
If I never see you again,
Or you never write to me,
I won't grieve.
I believe what I hold of you,
In my heart,
Is enough for a lifetime.

Shirley Hutchinson Allen

Your Heart

Inside you there is a space
In this space, your heart goes

Some hearts are small and black,
Cold hearts
These hearts think of no hearts except
Themselves, and the pain they can cause
Other hearts

Your heart is unique,
Inside, it lights a special path
For lost hearts to know
Your heart is there
My heart always wants a place in
Your heart

Tamara A. Hacker

Desert Storm

God bless our boys and girls
    in uniform
Be with them one
    and all
Please walk with them
    each step they take
As they march so proud
    and tall
May the day quickly come,
    when all fighting's will cease
And our boys and girls
    come home again
And the world will
    be at peace.

Wanda Spicer

Basement Sanctuary

I listen to you talk
In words that make no sense
About children not here
And an upstairs
That never existed—
Except in some recollected time
And place of your childhood.
In search of sanity
I sadly seek some
Basement solitude.
There, among treasured rocks
I collected long ago
And favorite clothes outgrown,
I find order
In the way things used to be.
Perhaps we are not so different
After all.

Mary Swanson

A Time Passed

Where we walk to school each day,
Indian children used to play.
All about our native land,
Where the shops and houses stand.
The trees were tall, there were
no streets at all.
Not a church nor a steeple,
only woods and Indian people.
Wigwams circled on the ground,
and at night, bears prowled around.
What a different place today,
where we live and work and play.

Rosemarie Burgess

Valen-Times

Your eyes convey a deep desire
inside me burns your flame.
I feel the heat of your hearts' fire
our passion is the same.

I see you glowing in the dark.
Your light is all around.
I want to touch the parts of you
that no one's ever found.

Your total beauty I absorb
you touch me deep inside.
I want that secret part of you
you've tried so hard to hide.

The way your soul and body blends
is such a work of art.
I've never seen such gorgeous work
in any human part.

Your pleasure opened all the doors
that were inside of me.
I give to you my secret joys
with you I'll always be.

Michelle Dwinell

Individual

All at once I am alone,
Inside my head the echoes drone.
Out to you, they seem to call
On through the night,
As the rains fall.

Then all at once there is a change,
The echoes ring to a different range.
Not out to you, yet not to another.
They call to me,
Go no further,
And

So all at once I've realized
That I must live as I surmise
No more out to you shall I reach.
I've found myself

Kathryn M. Lynch

Post Meridian Vision

While sleeping she jerked and turned
into a fuzzy gray lightness. She
rounded a corner in her mind, and

Found herself at the edge of her life—
looked out, and saw her body fall
from her body, surrounded by fields

Of younger bodies, falling from their
shells—bent running—hands clutching
hands. They were mouthing words she

Could not hear. The purity of fright
gave birth to enlightenment, by the
guardian of fear, and the hand that

Sparked the vision, and shot them from
darkness to sight.

Marjorie F. Burr

Fright!

A frightened rabbit
Racing across the green field
Dodging coyotes

Terry McEvoy

First You Are My Friend

We have chatted on for hours
Into the darkness of the night
Telling jokes and poking fun
At all that brings delight

We've also shared some secrets
And discussed our painful pasts
Heard with hearts of understanding
Where no judgement's ever cast

We are building the foundation
On which all true friends will stand
'Cause it's made with bricks of honesty
Instead of drifting sand

And who knows where we'll go from here
Or if love will ride our wind
In my heart you'll always stay
Because first you are my friend

Robin A. Creglow

Beckoned Call

Beyond the skin of color
Into the hearts of others
One for one
All for all
Heed the beckoned call

A rainbow of many colors
Is proof enough
That we are brothers
Stand together
One for another
Heed the beckoned call.

Side by side
Together blending
The strength of beauty
The Lord is sending
A message from above
Heed the beckoned call
Of Love

Pamela Y. Mann

Listen...

Listen... how softly the rain
is falling on my window pain...

I look around my silent room
and watch the dancing silhouettes
on the wall for awhile,
from the candle light.
I hold my pillow tight,
and feel your lips on mine...
Your hands playing with my hair
your eyes bringing peace to my despair.
Then, I fall asleep again,
feeling your love with me there...
Listening to the soft falling rain,
murmuring sweet loving words
soothing my heart from its pain
as it softly falls on my window pane.

Roma

Time

Indeed, the time of a man
is like unto a feather
sought by a breeze,
Like a spirit tickling a thought
in the mind,
A seed planted to mature,
with the soil holding tightly.
And in a moment
a sprout of life begins,
a dawn into eternity.
At noontime, strong and secure.
Then the seed carried on the feather
floats into flight again.
Time, a breath taken in!

Pearl Nickerson

The Final Journey

Lift your head and look at me
Is what he said to thee.
I'll take you to my home on high,
Come fly away with me.

They strolled through the deep valleys,
They walked the lakes and streams,
Beside a house with cherry trees
Among a field of dreams.

Across the windswept prairies,
O'er hills, and to the sea,
To oceans, lands, and fairy tales
Is where he walked with thee.

They walked upon a snow-capped peak
The chariot stood of ivory,
And embarked upon the journey
Toward immortality.

Wendy Hill

Silent Love

It's a silent love.
It cannot be expressed.
Like the spirits of your soul,
it's like a secret kept.

It's a silent love,
So never do you show
the true touch that's there
    to give,
the one that you love most.

It's a silent love.
It is within your heart
like the key that opens it
but which cannot be found.

It's a silent love.
You just don't seem to care
that I yearn for your caress
so dormant does it lie.
It's a silent love.
It's what I need so much.
Please let go of your today
so no more must it be —
    a silent love.

Kathleen Joanne Parsons

Frog Wise

You put a frog down in a well,
    It doesn't seem to matter.
He'll eat the bugs that come along
    And continue getting fatter.

And bugs there are, a plenty he sees,
    They float by him a spell.
And all the water in the world,
    He thinks is in his well.

There are some people like that frog,
    In winter and in summer.
All the wisdom they suck in,
    Just seem to make them dumber.

It puffs them up just like a frog,
    They sit around and smell.
And all the wisdom in the world,
    They think is in their well.

Warren E. McDaniel

Always a Tomorrow

As the light shines through my heart,
    It fades away so each part of me
    falls apart.

My soul feels empty and alone,
    And I have realized,
    there is nothing to be done.

Each love that I thought I had,
    Just disappears and leaves me sad.

"I just want to be friends" they say,
    Have they thought of how I
    feel with each passing day?

But oh no! They must stand proud,
    "I never loved her" they tell aloud.

And so, the pain will never go way,
    I will live my life in sorrow,
    there is always a tomorrow.

Kelli Birchfield

By The Side Of Me

With you always by the side of me
it is not difficult for me to be
the happiest guy alive today
please don't ever go away.

With you always by the side of me
the whole world can easily see
that you and I will never part
that our love comes from the heart.

With you always by the side of me
we will forever and ever be
two sweethearts so happy and gay
as we live our lives day to day.

With you always by the side of me
and giving your love so faithfully
fate has smiled upon my life
by giving to me, you for a wife.

Willard H. Weiss

Besse

Besse, it is your birthday
It is your 90th year,
cards overflow your mailbox
You are loved that's very clear.

We gather here this evening
to help celebrate your day,
We pray that the Lord above
sends many more your way.

Your interests are so diversified
this keeps you young at heart,
So each day when you arise
It seems like a brand new start.

We have no gift for you dear friend
we didn't even try,
You deserve more than our worldly goods
so there is nothing we could buy.

But we wish you many happy days
and good health for every one.
And next year at this time again
we'll celebrate number 91.

Marlynn Starring

I Never Meant to Love You

I never meant to love you.
It just up and happened one day.
I never meant for anyone
to over my heart hold sway.

I never meant to need you.
I only wanted to touch.
Oh! how could I have ever known,
It would come to mean so much?

How could I have ever known,
When I looked into your eyes,
That I would lose my heart that day?
Well, such is my demise.

How could I have ever known.
When I gazed upon your face,
That the sun would come to rise and set,
In oh so small a space?

I guess that I'll just live with it,
This love that I have found.
Thank God that when you look at me
I know our hearts are bound!

Lynn Taylor

Take Command

If trouble beset you from all sides,
It maybe simpler than you think to
stem the tide.

Choose an attitude that is confident,
And take a good look at how your
energy is being spent.

Are you the biggest prayer moocher
in the land,
simply because you have refused to
take a stand.

Be your own broker to a degree,
quit askin' the Lord to spoon feed thee.

Paul B. Tucker

Summer

Summer, Summer coming near,
It only comes once a year.
  Get ready,
  Be steady,
It'll be on time,
For soon no more snow,
And the sun will shine.
Won't it be great,
Fishing with bait,
Or eating a pumpkin pie?
But let's just wait,
Summer won't be late,
For it will come,
By and by.

Sarah Klewicki

Untitled

The end year
it seems.
There is a place kept for you
in me
always
inspiration
assurance
a mother's love
instilled
in me
you.
The end year,
it seems,
creates new beginnings...

Michele D. Lewis

Talkative Heart

I've got a talkative heart
it speaks too loud at times.
It tells of love and broken hearts
with endless words and rhymes.
I fall in love at least once a week
my heart can vouch, it's true.
But this time I have fallen hard
one week has become two.
Love can be one-sided
ask me I should know.
Cause if you decide you don't love me
then I shall let you go.
Maybe I'm in love with love
or maybe it's just you
I don't care cause either way
there's nothing I can't do.
So a word of warning to the cautious one
if you love me play your part
Cause more than two weeks is stretching it
for a silent..talkative heart.

Paige Leigh Brown

The Light Within

Within us is a light.
As bright as a star at night.
The light shines through,
As others can see,
It shines bright and clear
in you and me.
As the moon gives off the light at night,
And the sun shines in the day,
The light within us shines the same way.

Zelma D. Cagle

The Sun

The sun.
It's a bright fiery red;
  to show its anger.
It looms in skies of blue;
  to show its tears of sorrow
It slips through clouds of white;
  to show its purity.
It rises in the east;
  to show its achievement.
It sets in the west;
  to show it surrenders.
Its rays glow around it;
  to soak up the differences.
It can not be seen on some days;
  to show it gives up.
It comes back on other days;
  to show it will keep trying.
It's our life.

Melissa Pennell

Moth to a Flame

Softly the moth circles the flame.
Its lovely wings are singed and are
lovely no more.
Premonition of danger; yes, I think it
was a sign.
I should have noted it and kept away
from you,
You spelt danger, you radiated danger,
you are danger!
Softly as the moth, you circled me and
then my wings were singed.
I was broken, dead, and you were gone,
ready to circle again.
Like a moth to a flame, and you are the
flame!

Kelli White

Appreciation

A word which means so very much,
It's needed more and more.
For every sweet and gentle touch,
It opens up a door.
Appreciation for each little word,
Each kindness large and small.
Love of flowers, life a bird,
For trees both short and tall,
For mountains high, valleys low,
For country's state or nation.
Are we too proud, to bow our heads,
In pure appreciation?
I've looked through the almanac,
Encyclopedias and such,
And all the words, from front to back,
None should be used so much.

Lillian E. Scott

Books And Poems

Books are worlds
Within themselves.
A universe can be held
On wooden shelves.

Poems are music
In the air.
The ageless dreams
Of those who care.

Robert L. Laumeyer

My Family Tree

The years have come and they have gone
It's time to pass this info on.
So all our family may now see
The members of their family tree.

If at sometime or another
Searching may not be a bother,
The information on these pages
Will start your searching thru the ages,

I give it to you with much pleasure
To read and scan at your leisure
As I have lived thru many ages
It helped me to compile these pages.

As your families grow and you get older
Perhaps you will be a little bolder
And tackle the job when you are free
To continue the search of our family tree.

Kathryn Heinke

Trinity Oaks

For all you folks
It's Trinity Oaks
For an experience
To go through
Which was meant
Just for you
Forget all your sadness
Come back to gladness
We are here to stay
One large family
Who have come to
Love each other
Like sister and brother

Michael F. Breit

Fear Of Growing Older

My face withers
I've felt it, in my soul.
I've seen it in the dying leaves
My face will go.
My body sighs,
Like the last breath of autumn,
Winter will come and
wrap a blanket round me
I will walk through woods
Where sacred snowmen dream
And candles will burn
in my window,
into another spring.

Patty Kay Badgett

Untitled

Sometimes when you
feel like giving up,
you find a friend
who will lift you up.
There will be days
your feeling down,
just know you have a
friend who won't let
you down.

Susan L. Jecmenek

Untitled

I always was a hunter
I've followed many a track
My legs carried me over the ground
As I roamed to hell and back

I always was a hunter
And I always was a rover
Something urging me on and on
Always another hill to go over

I always was a hunter
But now I am getting older
The sunny skies can warm my bones
But the north winds getting colder

Now I am sitting in my easy chair
When I move I am moving slow
I soak up the heat in my living room
And I let the north wind blow

Lyle D. Jensen

"This Love"

There's a secret "Love" in my heart
I've kept always in the dark
This "Love" that I can't show
Gladly wanting all to know
"Love" I hold, and can not share
Knowing it won't go anywhere
I could give this "Love" in vain
But, don't know about the pain
Knowing, well, from the start
I would never win her heart
This "Love" that's for her only
Kept, in my heart, forever lonely

Manuel Barros, "Manny Love"

Untitled

The love and hate of being
    Jamaican and American
Is the love and hate
    of two parents
Which one is love and which one is hate

    Love and hate

The love and hate of
    one child in the middle
Is the love of the mother
    Love or hate
Is the love of the father
    Love or hate
Which one is love and which one is hate

    Love or hate

I ask of you, Lord
    Please help me to decide
Is the parent I love the parent I hate
Is the parent I hate the parent I love

Shantae Ridley

Who Has Seen The Wind

(Written at age 8)
The wind is very strong sometimes.
It blows everywhere.
North, South, East and West.
It blows the trees right and left.
It blows the leaves on the ground.
And blows my hair, it blows my hair.

Paul Michael D'Angelo

Untitled

  They say ones heart
just can't
be broken
  well,
my hearth aches
from its emotion.
  It hurts
to see
just what goes on
  and people seem
so unaware
  They just stand back
in awe
and stare.
  Why can't they share
what their hearts feel?
  For then love comes
right back
  to you.

Lori Suglia

Untitled

When the times get really hard
just go and dream away
Things will soon get better
There's nothing you can say

The dreams will help you relax
Troubles will float on by
Your life will be much better
You no longer have to cry

Dreams are something great
They're things you always share
No one will think they're stupid
Especially the people who care

Your dreams are your thoughts
Of what you want to be
Everything will be perfect
Will you forever stay with me?

Lisa Fritz

Wind

You whistle
Just like a man off to work
You comfort
Those who are feeling sad

You blow away
My troubles and tears
You kill
The ones who are tired and hungry

You brush away the summer days
And bring in winter
You are the core of life
And the crust of death

You are stronger
Then the strongest being
And yet through your virtues and vices
I do not hate or love you

You are wind, blowing in the distance!!!

Blair Bodine

Untitled

Half broken I rose
just over my toes
to stand
once again from falling
In a distance I see
a shadow of me
What once was
now is belonging
To a time of when
what's now will be then
To the future
my past keeps calling

Millard Sadler

Will There Be A Next Time

I know we started off bad,
Just remember the times we had,
We cried together
We laughed together.

We had so many memories,
All I think about is you,
And only you, who knew,
That love could feel this way.

I know what I did was wrong,
I know I can't make it up to you,
But what am I supposed to do,
I miss the way you felt in my arms.

I was there before,
I'm here now,
I'll be there till the end,
You'll always be my man.

Michelle Huling

Christmas Cinderella

Cards, greetings like bright ribbons
lace the globe into a tight ball
that glitters and glows in the
purple blue void, delighting
studious white stockinged angels
propped up on billowy clouds
until the sound of the 26th blow
when the ball suddenly fades
the ribbons pop and underneath
the glitter styrofoam shows
as pale and cold as the porcelain
white faces of the silent
unsmiling angels.

Vera Kistler

The Cycle

There is a girl in the yard
Laughing -
Smiling - yet crying to be loved.
Outside - she's peaceful -
A brook bubbling -
Over rocks - calmly.
Away from this -
She is like the rolling clouds -
Across the fields of swaying grass -
Stirred by the wind.
One day the laughter will end.
Others will take her place -
Laughing in the field -
Smiling - yet crying for love -
The cycle will go on -
   Forever.

Kate Gadberry

Untitled

Rock upon rock,
Lake upon lake,
Tree upon tree,
Mountain upon mountain,
Valley upon valley,
Fjord and fjord,
My soul is triumphant.

Snow, ice, sleet, rain -
A ray of sunshine -
to much delight.
Winds howling - blowing - stirring -
Lightning flushing -
Yet she stand - unmoved.

Saluting the path of ancestry,
I, too, stand.
The rock of soul.

Oh mountain, O rock,
Your strength unsurpassed.
Press on Oh wind,
Perfect the mountain.

Tordis Hilger

The Lumber Man

There was a old man, on the timber
Lane, He was cutting timber for
his plain, The tree cutting was
for his entertainment, but it was
Not to be. Man were cutting the
tree it fell striking The old man on
The head. He did not live but 8 hrs.
His son called the timber wagon for
The hospital trip but he never lived
To see his plain fulfilled, his son
was at his side in a stride, but he
couldn't get much pride because his
Father was not at his side for the
plain he had in a stride.

Tim G. Mack

Joy

Joy can be happiness and
laughter, it can also bring
life ever after. Joy can
come whenever we want,
in the morning or in
the evening, it doesn't
matter what. We can
have joy in our life as
well as pain. With joy,
our days can produce sunshine,
it can also produce rain.
Joy can last forever, until
the days of yore. With
joy, you can be happy
forever more.

Roy Collins

Unfair

When he died,
   fair ladies cried,
Placed pretty flowers
   by his side.

But when she died,
   died of grief,
Upon her grave
   was placed no wreath.

Oleto L. Daniels

Parting

Let there be no word of parting
Lest precious tears should give,
And win the sympathy of Heaven
Above all else who live!

Let this night a testament be
enchambered in thy heart -
Hold fast that key forever,
Let it never more depart!

Give me thy kiss, lend me thy sigh,
To keep me company
And lighten all my burdens
Till thou again I see.

I leave thee to the Nightingales
And the song of Mourning Doves
For when ye hear them, think of me
And this, our night of love.

Will Anderson

My Son

Come my son, in from the rain.
Let my love and my warmth;
shield you from the pain.

Let me hold you
until the storm subsides.
For I know the efforts
of your strides.

Stay with me until the sun
comes out.
Let me erase those clouds
of doubt.

Together we'll watch
for the rainbow.
For it means love;
my son don't you know.

Rossiland R. Harris

The Cycle Of A Safari!

A Safari will suffice,
lice can provide no taste,
a lot of porridge,
can get old and hard.

To sight an animal in it's wild,
can stir the fear in many.
How bars in a battered cage,
gives us peace to watch the beast.

The miles traveled to hook to a Safari,
only shows how far freedom is.
Sleep is scarce as many will tell you,
and rest is fleeting while in the wild.

The beast, best the antelope,
the slow snare the hare,
no amount of feed fed,
can keep them from falling a prey.

They kill to survive,
we kill for reasons other,
we would survive if we never,
willed the life of another.

Walter Tomalis

Untitled

Intertwined with intangible pleasures
lies the materialistic reality.
Altered beauty and vivid pureness
break from the grasp of the unkempt.
Our disposition admonishes us
as we carelessly toss it away.
Entranced by the passions novelty
assures us only from the terminal sun.
We sweep our lives with vengeance
and become one with our own innocence.
Relying on embellished fabrications
and treacherous verity,
we corrupt what we have not yet created.

Sana Okab

Improvise

Mothers say, "Don't do as I,
lift up your hands and touch the sky."
But I say, "Mother, you are wry!"

You fondle us on every page.
You smudge our ink. You flaunt your age.
Deny! Deny!

I stare from hidden inglenook
into flame that dapples fair
from aging eyes and graying hair.
I see a girlish groper there.
Despair! Despair!

Burn the book!
What should it matter, baby girl,
the truth I scatter?
Turning pages clang and clatter.
Improvise!

Thelma Bergman Sawczuk

Miraculous Things

The clouds spread thin
like a coat of paint
spilling across the sky.

The clouds grew orange
and bluish grey
as the night gave way to day.

The sun rose high
in the bright orange sky
and life as we knew it began.

Michael Morse

Hiding

The building rose in the sky
like a giant who died standing
while doing battle.
Lifeless soldiers stretched their arms
over the yard to refuse sunlight from
my eyes.
Glassless windows and torn shades
crowned the giant's head.
In the yard, I stood, imprisoned by
a clothesline fastened to a tree.
Shredded glass like moss cover the
ground.
Bathed in dirt, the silence was
my playmate.

Sandra Sacco

The Shadow

You've captured my heart,
Like a shadow in the night.
And though we're apart,
Our love's never out of sight.

As the light starts to fade,
Does the shadow grow weak?
Or in the darkening shade,
It's true meaning you seek.

A shadow can't be seen,
Until the light of day.
What our love means,
You've found your own way.

You can try to run,
And you can try to hide.
But when you're done,
The shadow's by your side.

What is this shadow,
This mystery in life?
It's the never dying love,
Between me and my wife.

Steven D. Wilson

The Salty Wave

Heat of the sand,
    like lust.
After a while,
    you must journey
    into the ocean.
At first it's cold,
    even though your feet
        are the only part submerged.
When you look out
    it's big and open,
        there are so many possibilities.
Then, you look again
    and there are so many hurdles.
Slowly, as you move deeper
    it becomes more difficult.
You make it past the little waves,
    and come upon the real ones.
You can turn your back to them,
jump up and try to avoid them, or
dive through and take the chance.

Linda Mielcarek

Hate, Love And Sorrow

Hate,
Like poisonous acid,
Eroding the mental capacities and
Weakening the physical capabilities.

Love,
Like melodious chords,
Floating on fleecy clouds
With companions of trust and faith.

Sorrow,
Like a rampaging stream,
Spilling tears of grief
Along the streets of pain and woe.

Wallace W. Price

My Mother's Place In Heaven

My mother has always been there
like the bright and shining star,
that led the Wise Men to Bethlehem
from their homes in lands afar.

She's tender, kind and so gentle,
like Jesus' mother must have been;
her heart is surely made of gold,
just as the temples were way back then.

The way a shepherd knows his sheep,
my mother knows me too.
That's because she's right behind me,
in everything I do.

It's because of this and so much more
including God's good grace
that makes me know without a doubt,
in Heaven for Mom there's a place.

Linda D. Constable

Awakenings

Coming out of winter
Like walking from a cave.
The tease of spring
Giving hope
For new beginnings.

Farewell to endless nights
And the slow marking of time.
Anticipating the freshness
And the beauty
Of color and scent.

The warmth of soft breezes
Rekindling my spirit.
Giving birth
To renewed faith
In all things good and living.

Marsha Meave

The Essence

Eyes meet
Linger
Dive deep
The beginning of it all

Hearts beat
Stop
Race
Ache from it all

Minds seek
Ponder
Dream
Analyze it all

Bodies feel
Caress
Desire
Discover it all

Souls reveal
Align
Entwine
The essence of it all

P. Deneane Hart

Front Porch

Sitting on the front porch,
Listening to the wind blow.
The sun shines through the trees,
With a bright bronze glow.

Sitting on the front porch,
Thinking of friends long ago,
While the neighbor down the road
Is getting ready to mow.

Sitting on the front porch,
In the middle of May.
When infants are bringing delight,
Everything is joyful on this day.

Sitting on the front porch,
Just listening to the birds sing.
I enjoy the simple pleasures
That only country life can bring.

Stephanie Charmin Husky

Untitled

It's all a part of nature,
Little girls grow up too fast.
Oh, the treasured years of childhood
Very quickly become the past.
Even though I face the future,
Years gone by are in my heart.
Over obstacles and through victories
U have been beside me from the start.

Stacy Robinson

Passing

Many important people
live upon this earth,
with lots of wealth and power
and reputations of worth.

They are of all descriptions
and live in every town,
and when their time on earth is done
it seems the world slows down.

People everywhere pay homage
with words of sweet refrain,
praise and honor for their gifts,
the heights their lives attained.

There was a recent passing,
the world did not take heed.
She had no fame nor riches,
no great gifts nor noble deeds.

An ordinary woman,
her life lived quietly.
She was my beloved mother.
She was the world to me.

Sandra Adell Sheridan

Roses

Rise little one,
Look around,
See the world,
You give it's beauty,
See the empty field,
Like the empty heart you once
   thought you had,
See the sky,
Up above,
It's like heaven on earth.
Isn't it?

Samantha Patterson

Angels In Heaven

The Angels in Heaven,
Look down on us with grace.
They watch our every move,
And the smiles on our face.
The Angels in Heaven,
Look down from the clouds,
They watch when we are proud,
They watch us when we have hard times,
And our good times too,
But most of all,
They don't want us to be blue.
For the love they have is very true.
These Angels in Heaven,
Watch over you.

Sheryl Lynn Meyer

Memories

Sitting empty, sitting still
Looking pitifully alone
Stood Grandma's big old rocking chair
The kids had now outgrown.

Grandpa made this handsome chair
With all the love he knew
And it's two broad outstretched arms
Seemed to welcome you.

The seat was hard, the spindles loose
It's dark wood squeaked with age
And the memories it held within
Could fill more than one page.

It once knew joy and laughter
The children made this so
How quick they made the time pass by
WHY DID THEY HAVE TO GO?

Lois Le Mottee

My Country

Lag in step, low on pep,
   losing rep, need of he'p

Debt is deep, babies creep,
   young girls weep,
     life's held cheap

Taxes rise, old not wise,
   theorize, exercise

Little boys, men's play toys,
   crime destroys, truth annoys

Nations prod, aliens trod,
   ban the rod, ignore God

Late in day, mend our way,
   time to pray, my country.

Lila J. Muno

I Have Five Friends

I have five friends, there names
I won't tell
One byes
One cries
One gives me a five every time I walk by
One tries to fly
One even lies
I like them all the same except the one
who lies.

Rachel Harder

A Lifetime

I'll love you forever
Love can last a lifetime
Through arguments and pain
Through bad times and good

Love can last a lifetime
All one has to do is try
And it will continue on

Love can last a lifetime
The harder one tries
The longer it lasts

My love will last a lifetime
I will love you
With all of my heart

My love will last a lifetime
I won't doubt you
Don't ever doubt me

My love will last a lifetime
It will never fade
It will always get stronger
And I'll love you until the day I die

Lindsay Sitko

Love Is...

Love is soul
Love is when a boy like's a girl
Love is giving sweethearts
Love is each other
Love is roses
Love is valentine's day
Love is kisses
But out of all
Love is your heart

Natalie Bustamante

Father's Day

Wanderlust and water lure
Love like daily bread
A healthy focus on today
and living in my head.

Horses in the summer
space to swim and run
Islands in the winter
chasing down the sun.

Trips to Carolina
strolling by the sea
support and strength and caring
wings for living free.

You've given me so many things
they give you just one day
not enough, my soul mate,
who loved me all the way.

Rebecca L. Larson

"Youth"

The beginning of time
   where goals are set;
To learn what we know
   to feeling regret.
The youthful days
   the family we shared-
The legacy we lived
   was our youth
     we remember....

Kim Trebing

Kiss My Love Good-bye

I ain't going to give you my
love no more,
And I am not going to show
you my tears,
I gave you my love,
And my soul,
My love was here,
You never thought I would find you
out,
You know,
You and the other woman,
What you both were about.
Kiss my love good-bye anyway
you like,
You were just taken care of
yourself,
That one night,
oh yeah never mind now,
just kiss my love good-bye!

Misty Williams

You Will Never Know

You will never know how I once
loved and no one loved me back,
or how I've cried because of
broken hearts.

You will never know how
different we were in the past,
you were in the light and I was
in the dark, you were a person
when I was just a shadow, you
had someone when I had no one.

You will never know how we
were strangers back then, how
I thought about you and
wondered if you were with
someone new.

You will never know that from
the first time I saw you, I
wished that we would meet so
that we could make things
complete.

Tanya Chong

Ecstasy In Full Flight

Flowin' my arms - limpid lithe -
Love's river of delight -
Ecstasy takes full flight.

Melt damp and warm into my thighs -
Exult in my lupine cries -
Read the message of love in my eyes.

Mellow as fruit ripe -
From the melon, draw clean the knife;
Leaving not a dripping slice.

P. Pierritz

True Love

True love is more than a feeling
It is a touch, a smile, a smell,
or a memory
True love is always with you
In good times and in bad
True love is never forgotten
But always cherished

Marie Busse

First Snowfall

Midnight came a storm.
Luscious winter melody: A milky spray
of silent white shrapnel,
chanting and frantic.

Frigid blanketing chaos;
its power to blind
appeasing some,
oppressing others.

Life's whisper lustfully stifled;
whose every chime
once amplified
as delicate music box symphony.

Nature's virginal earth suffocated,
that had bloomed innocent: Simple
yet intricate.
Like peace...like love.

Veins frozen, essential blood stopped;
violated of growth,
the warmth of summer long faded,
the rebirth of Spring distant.

Laurie McQuade

Christmas

Sound the trumpet
Make a joyful noise
with the horn,

For on this day in Bethlehem
a child was born.

A child so fair and full of grace
Who came to us in his father's place.

He came to bring us peace and joy
Healing and comfort was the mission
of Mary's baby boy.

His name is Jesus, our Lord and
Savior, our King.

And today on this quiet Christmas morn
Sound the horn and let the bells ring
to greet baby Jesus,
Prince of Peace, and our king!

Mae R. Gerardi

Jesus' Mary-Nature

In your Mary-Nature, Lord,
   make me like Mary be.
Draw me in with your good Word
   that I be human me.

Your glory is a live new man
   through Mary's Nature born,
A birthing through that first New Man
   with Mary's Nature born.

Our Mother's Mary-Nature taken
   by God's Begotten Only One;
Eve, by whom the tree was shaken,
   saved from sin through Mary's Son.

Uniting all the human race
   with Heaven once again,
We all see in Mary's face
   what Eve had lost through sin.

With your Mary-Nature, Lord,
   make me like Mary be,
A brother of New Adam, Word,
   who truly dwells in me.

W. E. Knickerbocker

The Mark

A playful tinkering in the mind
Making putty from the tears
Which drop to form the marble slab
Raised letters, only indentations
Of an artist's mind
And talent gone to waste
At the looming door.
Weeds cover life
As immortal memories die
And marble turns to ash
And a mind ponders
Forever dripping putty from the soul.

Mary Grether

Birth of the Optimist

The Almost Inconceivable
Married the Unbelievable
And, as they mated
They created
An end to End,
A new Beginning;
With wheels of progress
Ever spinning...
An end to No,
A new direction;
With endless faith
In true perfection...
To strive for better,
Never tired,
To good devoted,
God-inspired...
Then, as they saw the babe
They kissed
And named the newborn:
OPTIMIST.

Stephen A. Zoldos

Unrequited Lover's Lullaby

Do sleep well, my love.
may death be on your door by dusk,
slumber touch thy tired mind,
love break thy frozen heart.

Close your eyes, m'darling.
taste poison on your tongue,
feel thy mind go quickly mad,
feel thy heart stop at my touch.

Live the night, my baby sweet.
dream of love confessed, of me.
I sing for you to sleep, my love,
I sing for you to never wake.

Patricia Cheng

Hope

The years roll by and take their toll
Must I admit that I'm growing old?
I look in the mirror and what do I see
But a gray haired old lady looking right
back at me
Is she eighty four and going on five?
Just how many years has she been alive?
Maybe she's not as old as she seems,
She has a heart full of hope and a
head full of dreams.

Mabel Parsons Phelps

My Name Is Hope

My name is Hope,
　May I come in?
I thought I'd happen by
To chase away your cares and woe
And set your spirits high.

My name is Hope,
　Am I in need?
I guessed so by your face.
Allow me just to step inside
And brighten up the place.

My name is Hope,
　Did I work well?
If so I hope you'll see
When things go wrong, anytime
All you need is me.

Terry May Luke

Here With Me

Though you are not here with
me physically.
You will always be with me
mentally.

I cannot hear your voice in
my ear.
Although the words you have
spoken to me are in my mind
so clear.

I cannot feel your arms around me.
But, I can feel your strength
within me.

Though our bodies are not
lying beside each other.
I dream of us making love
together.

It may seem as if we'll always
be apart.
But, I know you'll always be
in my heart.

Patricia Murray

Me Oh My, That's Only Me

Me the only one,
Me the one who's name
is my name
The only goofy girl I know
Who thinks on my own
Me oh my, that's only
Me
My hair black and sandy brown
My eyes brown like a
tree branch
My nose shape like
the McDonald's arch
I could go on and
on about me
Cause
Me oh my, that's
Only me!

Takeishia DeNee Denkins

Message of the Hawk

Oh Hawk!
mighty red-tail hawk.
As you stand
so boldly before me
I hear your message
loud and clear.
As the Indian legends ring true
It all unfolds before me,
renew your faith in me
and I shall release your soul.

Sally L. Duncan

Untitled

You know we can't go back and change
Mistakes made in the past
We have to live and learn from them,
And they to face the facts

To think about what might have been
Is just a waste of mind
It's time to think of what will be
Not what me left behind

Take a look at future goals
And you might realize
To leave the past back where it was
Is starting to be wise.

You'll make the future joyful
And make sure it will last
Cause sorrow felt just yesterday
Is already in the past

Karen Fiscus

Untitled

The computer
Modern essential
Life less tutor
Celebrity with credential

No brain - no head
No life creature an instrument
Like manna demand spread
Giant affluent patent

Dream to the moon
Even to not discovered star
In time - not soon
Distance not far

All creations not in vain
In search - in mind
No trouble, no pain
More progress to find

Reproduction by religion
Human power to advance
G_D in heaven on earth a decision
By people for people the chance

Nathan Solomon

Birthday Greeting

At times I find it hard for me -
My feelings to you impart
But these I'm sure you'll realize
Are coming from my heart.
I wish you peace and happiness
As you travel life's highway,
But most of all I wish you love
On this your special day,
　"Happy Birthday"

Monica Berei

Why Arbutus?

Consider the scent —
　more sigh than syrup,
　more fresh than full.

More of the plant
　than of the perfume,
more of the source
　than the echo;
borne well by the air,
it is scarcely there.

Long abiding and almost buried
　in last year's leaves
it breathes
content to meander
　in low recessed green. . .

Gazing from starlets
　a few days per year.

H. Joseph Breth

"Sometimes"

Sometimes
　mothers are for gotten
Sometimes
　when we hurry
Sometimes
　we misunderstand
Sometimes
　we forget they worry
Sometimes
　they seem a burden
Sometimes
　we feel ashamed
Sometimes
　might be today
Sometimes
　we really miss you
Sometimes
　we really know
Sometimes
　why mothers cry

M. J. Ondricek

"Enlightenment"

Breathing in the fresh
mountain night air,
looking up at the stars,
all purpose now is clear.

A vision of a world,
that was always meant to be,
but which is for so many,
the hardest thing to see.

Open your eye,
its not hard if you try,
seek the truth within,
and you shall find no lies.

The truth has been there forever,
written among the stars,
when you begin upon the path,
you'll realize its not at all far.

Once you hear the call,
you will be shown how,
and understand the meaning.
of the eternal now.

Penny Rollins

Mother

When I think about you
moving away, it tears my heart
in two,

I can't remember a day when
I didn't think about you.

I've been with you every
day of my life, you are always
there to give me advice,

You've been without a doubt
the best mother, I could never
ask for another,

I know I've let you down
with some of my decisions in life,

But the thought of you
leaving hurts me like the stabbing
of a knife.

Mother I guess what I
am trying to say is, I love
you and I'll miss you if you ever
move away.

Kerry Toomey

Graveyard Dreams

Hollow speculation
Murderous eyes
Sheets are dingy
Can't rest

Collect the pieces
Of the end
Arise once more
Sterilize the sheets
Imagine tomorrow

Capture sleep
Dream tonight of
Rose gardens
Waterfalls

Stop! Cemetery is crowded
With the forgotten ones
In a profound drop
Absent from the pain

Walk companionless
And admire the fog
Settling on the graves.

Stacey Burnett

Grit

Though tragedy afflicts me
my head remains unbowed.
I shake my fist at heartbreak
"No victory to you!" I vow.
The very nature of this life
is one of constant change
and though no guarantee prevails
that blessings will remain
'tis folly to give up or fear.
I must see through the pain.
For I alone can guide me
to set forth on trails unknown,
experience all my feelings
but venture on when shown.
The path I take is up to me.
And so I purpose
shall it always be.

Melissa Treadwell

The Return Home

As the time gets shorter and shorter
my anticipation
Seems to overwhelm me.
The thoughts of returning home
Brings excitement to my heart.
The longing to be near her
Is becoming so unbearable.
So to keep calm
The urge to shout
In knowing I'm almost home.
The time is spent
Waiting, doing work alone.
The conversations of
Plans and arrangements
That I've shared
With my wife from afar,
Will make this return home
A joyous one
With tears of peace and love.

Lorenza Harrell

Creative Silence

Night uncovers
My creativity,
Unleashing torrents
Of words
Lost in the dazzling darts
Of day.
Silence speaks softly,
Awakening my pen
To march
Into eternal quest
For a place
In your memories.

Samye Hill

Inner Cycles

My palms sweat
   my eyes glisten,
   you hear me though
   you do not listen

Under the carpet
   too often swept,
   this silence marks
   my rage unkept

Preying upon the
   resistance I lack,
   flashing sequences
   beckon me back

Amidst the rubble
   my conscience lies,
   taming the beast
   as it slowly dies

Kristina M. Diossy

Shade

No swifting nor shaking
No sounds is it making,
No bright light enhances,
Under the branches,
The tree blocks the light,
Oh what a sight,
A quiet place to read,
There are no bad deeds,
You know it will fade,
My dear quiet shade!

Lauren Wolf

A Father's Masquerade

My God your smart
My God your brave
Don't you ever feel afraid
You never have the fears I have
or show your tears when you are sad
and so it should be no surprise
that your a giant in my eyes
I'm small, I'm weak, I'm insecure
Won't you protect me just once more
If you were me you'd find a way
to keep the demons far at bay
What's that, your not the things I say
It's just your job to act that way
Oh what a burden it must have been
to make me so secure and then
to never let me know it's true
that when I'm scared
you may be too.

Ronald J. Kress

To Elizabeth

I think of you my dear
My heart goes soft, it feels a tear.
Dear God, an angel gift
A touch of heaven here.

The smile form your sweet face
Reveals soul's gentle grace.
Such goodwill overflowing
My cup fills up all empty space.

The strong oak in the field
To perfume of rose does yield.
Strength with beauty flow
At oneness the seeker kneels.

In bed you lay beside me
I touch and feel so warmly.
We never can be pulled apart
For in my heart you live inside me.

I thank you God for wife
Whose touch is source of life.
The feminine tender
Calms all inner strife.

Manuel J. Vargas

Lost

I'm lost in this world without you
My heart is always in pain
I do nothing since we parted
But walk in the darkness and rain
I know I'll never find you
Yet I see you wherever I go
I picture your loveliness near me
But forever your lost I know
I think of the times together
And all the things we have done
Now my life will end in teardrops
Cause love for me, there is none
When I'm old and feeble
And my life is gone from me
I'll look upon our love
As a love that never could be.

Robert G. Barzilay

When

When you look in my direction
    My heart melts,
Like a snowflake
    Upon the ocean.

When you speak to me
    My heart soars,
As though the sky
    Cannot limit it.

When you touch me
    My heart sings,
With the harmony
    Of an angel.

When we kiss
    My heart burns,
As though fire
    Has enveloped it.

But, when we love
    My heart stops,
So as not to miss
    One moment of our touch.

Sandra K. Adams

When I Look Into Your Eyes...

When I look into your eyes
My heart skips a beat
I see a reflection of my love
That no one else can defeat.

It's like looking at stars
When I stare into your eyes
Their so beautiful and mysterious
Like a fire that never dies.

When I stare into your eyes
Oh what beauty I see
And what stories they tell
When they look back at me.

When I look into your eyes
I always try to see
An answer to my question
What do they see in me?

I hope your eyes can see
That my love is true
My eyes never lie
When they are looking at you.

Narciso A. Coello

Grandmas Wedding Ring

When I think of this ring of mine,
my mind goes back to another time.
The Gold Rush days and the 49ers,
the early rugged west, America
at it's very best...
This ring must come from around
1910, when 14 K. Gold was pure,
But its worth more to me in 1995,
Somehow it keeps my Grandmas
memory alive...
How I cherish this inheritance
of mine, I will wear it always.
It's so beautiful, this wedding
Band so fine...

Shirley Hurst

My Home Town

In my dreams I gaze from
My open window out over
The oceans blue water
Of lovely horseshoe bay.

I see the towering cliffs in
All their splendor as the
Waves crash against them
On this wild and windy day.

Through the misty haze I can spot
The rock they say looks like
Georges head. As they skim across
The waves I can hear the haunting
Curlews call.

I see the old strand line walk
Where we strolled on summer evenings
Long gone by. Those beauty spots and
Happy hours I an exile still recall.

Patrick Doherty

Age And Youth

My youthful days are over;
My remaining days are few.
I sit and dream of bygone times,
And curse my age anew.

In my jealous reverie
Of youth that's long since spent,
I feel that every waking hour
Is one long, sad, lament.

When was that fateful moment
That my youth first ebbed away?
Was it washed away by hardship?
Or when first my hair turned gray?

No—when age began to replace youth
'Twas on the very day
That I began to peer the past
And shun my present stay.

Nancy Razanski

Unfinished Business

Oh, Tiananmen
My soul aches for you
flower of promise
Seed of despair
Tears are shed
Which you are unaware
That which you cannot hear

Refrain not, from this press
for liberation
for nothing is the treasure
of idle time
Red, bitter, wine, is the blood
of lives lost,
But, oh, so sweet is the fruit
of victory

Venita M. Miller

The Ocean

Beautiful yet
mysterious
in its own sort of way

Searching for
answers
standing on the bay.

The mist
spraying my face
from time to time

Hoping and praying
that I would find maybe a sea shell
or even a dime.

Questions asked,
mysterious untold,
waiting for the answers
of the Ocean to unfold.

Sarah Ray

One

Today we shall become one,
Never again will be alone.
Will always be together,
For now and forever.
Our love we shared,
For will never be scared.
Will live with Love,
The Love we found above.
We found each other,
For will never need another.
The time we spend together,
Is always happier then ever.
The Love you have given me,
Is the Love I will give to you
    Will always be One.

Mary Gull

On Letting Her Go...

He lost what he'd
never had and much more,
The world became an empty church
until finally, it was the hate
that sustained him.

Driving in anomic circles with a
gun in the car,
her beautiful loveless eyes imprinted
like a fossil in his mind.

In the giving, there's the losing,
this time permanent,
and now he's dying as the
hate wears thin and the nothing
swells into every breath.

When you let something go
it might not come back
and he forgot to consider this.

Sara Kelly

Springtime Celebration

Springtime is a celebration of
New life seen many ways,
Baby animals in their
Frolicsome play.

With spring also comes
New leaves and flowers that bloom,
And birds with each season
Seem to sing a fresh tune.

God shows us his love
In all this celebration,
So we can share in
The joy of his creation.

Kimberly Faust Bowley

Animal Plea

(Wood Land Creatures)

Did you see a human, go by today?
No I was on my way, to work said
The beaver,
Piling up twigs and mud to build a damn
The river waters are getting high.
And all of us are protecting our
homes with eager.

Did you see a human, go by today?
No I was collecting berries, and
nuts, said the squirrel.
Winter will be here early said the
ground hog,
As all signs of an early winter is
on the way.

Did you see a human, go by today?
Yes I did he was looking at the trees,
Some are bare, and have no leaves
Our homes are getting destroy by drought.
No food now what will I do
Let's hope some kindness will see us thru.

Rita R. Jamialkowski

"Luck Of The World"

There is no point
No justice
We all have hearts
Everyone has feelings
People may act different
But are alike
Race, skin, religion
Everybody feels for the struggle
Even though there shouldn't be one
Ignorance is the luck of the world
Equality is the key
If all men are created equally
Why are there stereotypes
In a world of difference
We should try to be the same
Fight as one
Treat this like a war
Kill the problem.

Mickey Carey

Children Of Silence

Children born with silence,
no knowledge of sound,
must struggle through life
to find what is to be found.

Each day they face
challenge after challenge
to be understood and
to understand.

Yet through struggles
they are made strong,
and through motions
they are found.

Through motions they
are heard and through
motions they hear.

Through knowledge and power
they become strong and
no longer are
children of a silent land.

Michelle Hopkin

"Look Up And Live"

You are always in God's hands,
   no matter how you feel,
Just look up to Heaven
   and God will always heal.

No matter how you are troubled,
   be it body, mind, or soul,
you can always believe in God,
   to touch and heal you is His goal.

So don't look down in troubled times,
   hold your head up high and give -
give you faith and love to God -
   above all - "Look up and live"!

Marguerite Isenberg

Reminiscence

I walk alone in memory
No one can go with me
To the grassy banks of the stream
Where fish played. A butterfly
Tasted a crimson flower. Scents
Of grass, honeysuckle and mint blended
Delicately. I heard the symphony of
A birds love song, babbling water, and
Children's laughter. Kids on bikes
In the dusty road, waved to us, then
Joined the others in the yard of the
White farmhouse across the way.
No one can feel the warm handclasp of
A trusted friend which etched this
Moment upon my soul forever!
Motel lights flash where the farmhouse
Stood. A paved highway has replaced
The country road.

Ruth Batton

Untitled

Since no one knows the cause of Love
No one knows the cure
The taste of Love can be so sweet
It is the greatest lure

Without Love there is no life
No reason to awake
The quest for Love we all must join
And any risk we'll take

Love can fill the heart with joy
It makes the sun to shine
Loss of Love can break the heart
The pain can be divine

The risks of Love encompasses all
Yet any price we'll pay
Love, itself, the great reward
This anyone will say

To find a Love is the great prize
For which we all must strive
Without a Love to call our own
Is our soul alive?

Richard C. Foster

Hatred

(Written at age 11)

   Hatred is a thing with wars,
no peace, and violence.
   Bloodshed is here, graves are
there, you can never trust love
here or there.
   The wars in Bosnia, the taking
over in Kuwait. I can't believe
peace has to wait.
   Why do we have to have this, so
strong and mighty? I just don't
get it.
   People say in the distance they
find friends and all countries shall
be on their own. No invading, nor bombs,
no guns, just us as innocent little
elves.
   I just think one day hatred will be
no more. God can help us but we must
make a difference on our own.

Kyle Harder

"No Reason"

No reason to live
No reason to give
No reason for trying
No reason for fighting

Since you left
I have had no strength
I couldn't eat
I couldn't think

And still I miss you
I always will
The memories will never fade
In death's lonely shade

No reason for trying
No reason for fighting
No reason to give
No reason to live

Rachel Barker

Untitled

I was born a seed in a world of trees;
No roots to hold me to this earth.
Always different from the rest.
Who am I?
Where did I come from?
Who am I?

Always searching,
Sometimes just pretending.
Drawn through the forest to other seeds,
Comforted by their sameness.

But someday a child will be born.
A miracle will happen.
You look like me.
You're part of me.

At last this seed will grow roots
To hold it to this earth.
The roots will grow deep, the branches tall.

No more lonely seed to blow through time,
Lost but not alone.
And the search forever over.

Kelly A. Holder

"Good Ol' Days" "Little Ol' Shoes"

Go bare-footed, from spring to fall,
no shoes, for me at all,
wait until, school begins,
I may get, a new pair then.

"Be Careful," don't scuff the toes,
I will need them, when it snows,
"One Pair," is all I get,
winter has barely started yet,

Walk for miles, through ice and snow,
to the school house, I do go,
soon my toes are saying hi,
to the north-wind, sigh oh sigh.

Sole is flapping in the wind,
griefy, grief, I fell again,
skinned my knee, tore my socks,
must have landed on the rocks.

Spring oh Spring, when you arrive,
I will be lucky, to be alive,
I want to feel that southern air,
these little ol' shoes, are beyond repair.

Norma M. England

Sister

A sister is special,
no one can deny
When you're happy she'll laugh,
when you're sad, she will cry
She wants all the best,
in the life you will live
All that she has,
she gladly would give
She's there in the good times,
she's there in the bad
She's also the best friend,
that you've ever had
You go through so much,
as you march on in time
So feel very blessed,
if your sister's like mine

Michael D. Larson

My Dream

Searching to find that one bright star,
Not knowing where it leads,
To care about one thing,
And that is how to achieve.

To help people through their woes,
Although you may need the help most,
Encouragement so obsolete,
Still believing I can conquer my dream.

To understand failure might come,
But rising above it all,
To understand the great difficulties,
Wanting to prove I can show them,
Only inside a touch of hopelessness,
Reaching for that one hope or dream,
Still uncertain to where it may lead.

I keep reminding myself no one can break
my dream,
And deep down knowing only I can make
my dream come true.

Sara Beth Rzeppa

That Day

We all go our separate ways
Not knowing where we are,
Or where we're going
In Life's unruly plane.
We trod where we please
Doing what we will
Until that fateful day,
When all the world
Will follow the same path.
What a day that will be!
A time of uniformity,
A time of conformity,
What a day that will be!
Everyone doing the same thing,
No one caring one way or the other.
When that day comes,
What a dismal day,
That will be.

Steven J. Polasik

Wish I Wood

Woodscapes and landscapes
Occur to maintain,
An abundance of life,
I've again to attain.

What they show me-
Their story they've mold;
They will show more
They show when its cold.

Blossoms rebloom,
For summer's sake.
Though the cold takes from them,
All that they make.

When it's my wish,
To feel life again,
That's when I know,
How I've admired them.

Kevin Manzon

Thoughts of a Posy from My Lovers

The beginning, thought a poet,
Of a Romance in Bloom.
As I glanced, your bouquet move
they follow me room to room
A Love New
A fresh lovely posy grew,
Opened to the World for the first time
Never to close up, you're mine
Never to dry up, cease time
through out to the day your gleam

Our souls dream
Romantic thoughts they send
My thoughts of you begin
Your thoughts of me within
Your flowers sweetly scently
Fragrant with love
Days passed slowly
Dried are your posies
Fresh are our thoughts.

Karen A. Saffa

Remembering

The falling leaves remind me
  of a time so long ago
And the one I loved so dearly
  for you see he was my beau
We strolled beneath October's sky
  thru leaves of red and brown
So much I can remember
  and the color of my gown
Some burning leaves gave off a scent
  that perfumed all the air
If I close my eyes I see it
  it's as if I still were there,
Then he took my hand and kissed me
  I recall the moment well
Beneath the soft October sky
  as the leaves around us fell
Yes I think God made October
  with it's colors bright and hold
To create such special moments
  that leave memories of gold

Mildred Rex-Snyder

Jaded

Childhood pictures swirl in my mind
of all the wonderful and glorious times
only to grow up and soon see
they fade like raindrops in the sea.

Long ago I stopped the dreams
of things I always wanted to be
and grew into a daily routine
and existed that way for many things

Somewhere past I lost the urge
to keep on dreaming of the future
and put up with what was there
only to find it wasn't fair

Watching children live a life
of childhood dreams and the like
and waking up to discover
There'll be more days just like the other

When did I grow old inside?
When did I start to die?
Seasons change and so can I
Where did I lose my love for life?

Susan Mary Murphy

Things Not Meant to Be

It's time for us to talk, my love,
Of empty nights and sunless days,
And shining stars above.
And of the us that's you and me,
Of life, and love, and fairy tales,
And things not meant to be.

As have you, I've seen my death,
And suffered, too, my private hell.
There are the things I can't forget
And those you can't forgive of me.
So let's talk, my love, of futures dark,
And things not meant to be.

Sometimes love is not enough,
Or so I've heard it said.
Now the past is far too rough
And we've lost whatever made us "we,"
So now, we'd better talk, my love,
Of all the things not meant to be.

Maureen L. Sheler

The Pain Within

The turbulence of restless images,
Of grossly exaggerated,
Grotesquely disfigured,
Shadows of dreams
Of an unquiet past.

The child within
Cannot scream out in pain,
Will not acknowledge to the world,
The unsettled truths
Of her immobilized reality.

The fear of recurrent nightmares
Only serves to justify their existence.
Giving power and life to their presence.
How desperate is this need
For the peacefulness of contentment?

The struggle continues in wake and sleep.
And each small triumph
Must be rewon, again and again,
For the dragons immortality
Has unrelenting power over me.

Mary Sheehan Martin

Melissa's Nails

My fingernails have grown; they're
   not itty bitty!
I'll paint them, while they're
   so long and pretty.
My nails are splendid and I'm
   proud to show;
I'll change the color, before I go!

I'm thankful for their length, at last
How long will they stay to flabbergast?
I know I'll break one, doing a chore,
Scrub and clean and soften them more...

I just shutter at the thought, to see
   them go,
Cut them all short, then a long wait,
   for nails to grow.
I wish they would grow out to be
   heavy duty,
I'd have more time, with all their
   beauty!!

Linda D. White

Lamentation of a Dreamer

Oh the pain, the pain!
   of my deprived heart
Hear its cry of mourning
   feel its song of grief
For I have lost my love
   by waking from my sleep.
My lady, I did find her
   within a dream one night
But barbarous reality
   has caused my grievous plight
It tore me from her embrace
   It shook me from my sleep
And left it up to fortune
   it twice our hearts should meet.
And now I quest the dream worlds
   and other realms thereof
In constant grief and anguish, in search of
my true love
And if I intrude your dream, excuse me if
you will
But, tell me, have you seen my love?
   pursuing me as well?

Karl Hiller

Love Vagabond

I've roamed through acres
of pubic things
always seeking my
Raison d'etre
thinking each encounter
each conquest
the prize, at last.

Love, a word never upon my lips
affixed only to ending
of letters and postcards.

What perversion within
rejects Eros' gift
so often sought
so seldom found.

I am destined, it seems
to endless phallic spasms
leaving emotions empty of resolution
leaving me forever asking
Why? Why? Why?

Wilbert D. Fisher Jr.

Untitled

I was ready to say
okay—start again my friend
And then you walk upon my private space
With no regard
It is hard to recognize
   you are simply
      ignorant of other's rights

Sorry but I do not
Wish to live beside you
When there is no limits...division
No regard for property...or feelings

So long-I am ready to say-goodbye
   I may be ever prepared to be alone
      For I have no desire for sharing my
      life as I am today

Nancy Ehrenreich

One Flower

It stands there in the coverlet
of snow.....alone.
Its petals long ago dispelled as
stripped to its bone.

A once surrounding foliage has
given up...dried and crumpled.
But it still survives tho' wind
and cold have pushed and pulled

Its very roots in an attempt to
force its submission...
The elements having no concept of
its strength and obsession

With life, survival, zeal to
overcome.
Adversity through tragedy - in
that range is quite a sum.

That single flower exudes a
strength - a will to survive
and to bloom again, to expel its
fragrance - vibrant and alive.

Marjorie Ann Renspie

Desert Love

Eternally lashed by the heat
of the bright afternoon sun
Her peaks and hills of shifting sand
were being caressed by none

Loneliness kept her company
only one to console in
Death devoured her visitors
though she committed no sin

Longing for someone to hold close
yet frightened to hold too tight
She strained to hear loving footsteps
in the coolessness of night

Day after day brought no lover
Nor did the dry wind bring hope
But the raindrops fell upon her
and pleaded with her to cope

She is tired now from waiting
she will look and care no more
In her breathless abandonment
It is she that she'll deplore

M. Cathleen Macshane

Sun

Years ago when I was young
All I looked forward to was the rising
   of the sun;
To laugh, play and run.

As I got older I looked forward to
becoming a Nun.

Then I became an Adult
And looked at life a little different;
I saw that life was not always Pleasant;
There were wars, prejudice, poverty and
Life that never begun.
I just wanted to run.

Maybe by the time I'm old,
I'll find a way to return the Sun!

Martha-Mary E. Scherer

Alone At Sea

The dappled shadow
of the setting sun falling
across the limp sails.

White birds in the sky —
billowing sea swells rising
stir up memories . . .

Anchored, she's below
Good smells rise from the galley
She smiles up at me.

Coffee in our cups
side by side in the cockpit
we sit together.

A distant bleak shore
my boat at sea, now adrift
without my Sonya Lee.

A star glows brightly
like her smile those shining days.
The sea consoles me.

Robert Tralins

Twice Burned

Now a charred memory remains
of the time you first came unto me
in all the splendor of your youth
Your love pervaded my spirit
leaving only an empty shell
of what once was.

Never to find an earthly sensation
to wet my lips
that were left parched from
the burning fever you left
in my limbs.

Is my devotion only passion
that leaves a lasting memory
burned into my flesh
or was it love that
surged through my veins.

Leaving a glow in my eyes
and a memory that
always pierces my mind...

P. C. Schneider

Life

Life is one long journey, that each
of us must make, with countless new
adventures, Down every road we take, the
pitfalls they are many, rewards are
small that's true, we have no say when
it begins, or know why, when it's
through, we hope to learn by past
mistakes, our own and those we've seen,
For down each thorny road we walk
Another soul has been the actions that
we take today the things we've done
and said could change the patterns of
our lives before we go to bed our
parents try to keep us
From the pitfalls they have known
To ease a bit the road ahead When
we are on our own We enter life
with nothing but if the fates are
kind We leave it taking with us a
treasure - peace of mind

Lorne D. Veale

Untitled

I sing the ballad of castles
    of vampires and created lore.
I sing the heart's desire,
    of love and pain no more.
I sing a song of sunshine,
    of unicorn dreams in mist.
I sing to thee an epic, love,
    of the stolen night we kissed.

Shijii, my dear heart
    I do long to hold you so.
Shijii, heart of hearts,
    Such dreams you'll never know.
I lay my wearied head, dear,
    upon thy silken chest.
I close my eyes to reality
    and pray that I may rest.

Reyth E. Salvaje

Untitled

Upon this planet earth
of which I and millions live
this is what I have to say and give...

I think the seeds of life
have always been planted
I think a child thinks not,
but takes life for granted.

Life is like the budding of spring
giving of itself... unto every
living thing.

To hear, smell, touch and see...
these are wonderful gifts,
but the giver beyond me...
I think life should be...
loved, lived, and wanted
that life should go on and on
undaunted.

Wilbert F. Edwards

I Cared

If I had known
Of your deep grief,
Those troubled nights
Of restless sleep;

If I had known
Of the tears that fell,
Silent hours spent all alone,
Cheeks that slowly paled;

If I had known
I would have taken time
To show you that I cared —
So often you were on my mind.

But I didn't know
So I was not there.
And you died alone
Thinking no one cared.

Lynne Garren

Untitled

(In loving memory of Amy Louise Crain)

I saw a beautiful flower die
Oh how I cried
When this flower died.

But when I look around
at all the beauty of the world,
that God has made for us to see
the tears go away
as I look and see,
all the beauty he made
for you and for me.

So I cry no more
for the flower that died,
as God has let us behold
and see its beauty.

May E. McCurnin

Spanish Eyes

Spanish eyes...
    Oh how they woe me
Tease me, unfold me, do me...
Spirit fires, beams of light
    Capture our sight...
Raptured hearts soar -
    Minds on fire
Desire...
    Morning' mist
Reminisce...
Love's first kiss
    Our's in bliss -
One in spirit, love's song...
Your spanish eyes woe me on...

Rosalinda Lara

Untitled

A barren tree stands, solitary,
On a bracken-clad hillside.
Birds weave in flight
Through the bracken.
But the trees stands friendless,
Untouched by the wings of happiness.
The tree is surrounded
In an aura of darkness, undisturbed,
Until the sun bursts through
The mist and spotlights it.

The tree can either flourish
In the sun's nourishing rays,
Or wither and die, blotting
Out the sun forever.
Every flicker of life so far
Has scarred the tree.
It can grow and once again
Lead a normal life,
But only of its own accord.

Lesley Alison Fraser

Country Memories

Country is a place of trees
Of shady lanes and cooling breeze.
Meadows warm with waving grass
And butterflies that flutter past.
Where roosters crow to wake the dawn
And dew is fresh upon the lawn.
This is a place where you can rest.
And fishing is the very best.

Mildred Diane Rice

Father's Hug

Still as calm lake water
　on a summer evening . . .

Quiet as a resting dog
　in the shade . . .

Comfortable as young birds
　safe in their nest . . .

He rested in his father's arms.

But only for a few moments

Alive as a colt and playful as a puppy,
　He was off to explore.

And sure to return.

Rob Boschetto

Remember Me?

Have I made an impression
　on anyone?
Does anyone remember me?
Did I bring about any changes
　that anyone can see?
Have I left anyone with memories
　that bring a smile to their face?
Have I left any thoughts
　in anyone's mind
That I made life a better place?
For while I was seeking my
　happiness
And searching for peace of mind,
I tried to help whomever I could
And tried to be loving and kind.
I wasn't always a good guy.
Sometimes I wasn't so great.
But I'd like to have made an impression
　of LOVE, rather than hate.

Margaret Heller

Glowing Velvet

Sweating beautiful
on my blanket
c'mon and share it with me

We'll force a smile or two
until it gets easy
Passing the time
with the near by

hear that tenderness
that's coming from me sometimes
ease your shoulders
on my blanket
turn it over if it suits you
turn me over if it suits you
it's early August anyway
have a holiday on my blanket
treat yourself to another
let the colors bleed
it's always as I said
"we'll always have Oklahoma in August."

Micheal Wood

The Dancer

I was born to be a dancer
On my toes since birth
People always marveled
I always doubted worth

Too busy to hear the voices
Shouting warnings from within
I tap danced round the clock
No one knew just where I'd been

Filled my life with umbilical romance
First my mother then my son
Momma's moved to southern Utah
The boy has left, my job undone

Alone I dance on starlit nights now
and I cry when I get blue
Scour mail for letters from the boy
Reading old ones as if new

In retrospect I wonder
If I'd left my life to chance
Would my memories still be littered
with the casualties of the dance

Sue A. Roby-Dinenno

"Glenda And Me"

Two for tea Glenda and me
On the sofa, we used to be.
Nana's biscuits and honey
Sugar cubes to stir.
We were the party
For our family.
Curls on our head
Of red and gold.
Nana used to brush
And tell us to hush.
Dressed in our finery
Of ruffles and lace -
Big taffeta bows
In our hair was placed.
Mama ironed our dresses.
Nana sewed them up,
Papa worked for money,
For Glenda and me.

Norma Jean Brenneman

Happiness

Happiness is too elusive,
one day here, then far away.
Why won't it last much longer
than an hour, or a day?

Surrounding it with fences,
allowing it no freedom,
We'll put it in our hearts
and keep it in our kingdom.

We'll barter it for money
and suddenly be fated.
Our product so desirable,
it can't be overrated.

If we can learn the secret
then patent it exclusively,
we'd lease it out to everyone
now, wouldn't that be silly?

Sadness would be in demand
happiness too common.
The nature of the "Beast called man"
Would need a new phenomenon.

Louise Connors

Character Defined

There is a word we use most time -
　One hears it frequently -
It's meaning now - we shall define -
　And see how it fits thee!

Repeated acts - habits become!
　Habits produce things too!
Dispositions - they're called by some -
　Becoming part of you!

Dispositions then - I surmise -
　Form the Will - inside man -
The rightly formed Will - no surprise -
　Gives what no other can!

The word that I now give to you -
　I need not to infer -
One plainly sees how clear and true -
　'Tis called - your CHARACTER!

J. L. Shaneyfelt

Foreclosure

Dust bodies happily settle
on palletized clay pots
loneliness resounding as
the banker snaps the lock.

Calmness blankets the dark
as the quiet swoops down
smug laughter echoing
through the keyhole.

Blackness snuggles the pots
in their catacomb shelves.
One soul jumps, cracking
but the others just wait.

Kathleen A. Muja

Shattered Dreams

Take a bowl and place the following;
　one cup of fear,
　one pint of despair,
　one pint of hate,
　two spoons of death.
　One cup of fate,
and all other feelings left.
Simmer on a fire of night,
cook till the break of light.
Serve when your lonely heart screams,
and now you have Shattered Dreams!

Penny Bryant

Endangered

Endangered means
Not usually seen. It is
Dangered, usually by humans
And pollution.
Not good, right?
Good news! People are trying to save
Endangered animals.
Run! Go help them!
Everyone help. They are
Dying out.

Lief Liebmann

The Sky

Forever changing.
One minute covered with clouds,
The next minute clear as water.

Forever changing
Never the same
But, always amazing.

Forever changing.
So untouched,
So unreal,
Always forever;
Forever changing.

Nazima Kathiria

My Special Joy

You are a special spirit,
one that is so true,
the joy that you give
to others will come
right back to you.

Your spirit is like the
sun that shines
and the moon which
radiates the pure
heart you are blessed with.

Your mom needs you and
loves you with all of her
heart. I love you as
your big sister and your
friend. You can always
count on me, and talk
to me any time.

Kathleen M. Carr

One Kiss

One kiss - that's all.....
One zephyr'd touch upon my brow
Yet do I feel your lips
As though you placed it there e'en now.

One kiss - just one.....
A spirit moment out of time,
Leaving an echo in my heart
That throughout eternity is mine.

One kiss - no more........
I would that time could but erase
All else around but leave
The memory of that one kiss upon my face.

Lee Bradley

God's Grace

Oh God, our King in ages past,
  Our king in life to be,
Raise up this child from out the dust
  to live eternally.

When from my lonely spot below,
  I lift my hands to Thee,
My knees are bent, my heart bows down;
  Thy light is shed on me

I would not be a child of God
  If Jesus had not come;
He took my sins and set me free,
With His shed blood at Calvary.

Lela M. Miles

For Only Time Will Tell

I know the clock, is turning and
only time will tell. About each
passing minute, that everyone
knows so well.

A time, a season, for everything to
change, for only God knows the
reason of what this world reigns.

Winters nearly over and spring is in
the air, summer's around the
corner and everyone wishes it was now.

For there hot summer days of basting
in the sun and everyone having picnics
up until the day is done.

Happiness and laughter is the sound you
hear, as the clock still keeps on
ticking through another coming year!

Viola Kathy Bates

Thoughts Of A Love Lost

Our days were warm and full of joy
our lives were quite delightful
Until the day we got the word
The word that was so frightful

We had to cry, we had to cope
Embrace, the only answer
Two sets of eyes, so full of tears
The doctor's word was cancer.

Through many months, so full of pain
Our love, it grew much stronger
This love, our love, I now enhanced
With prayers to keep her longer.

Although I never understood,
the reason she was taken
I thank God every day I wake
My love was not forsaken

For she's with Him, her mum, and dad
These three prepare the way.
My love, her love, we'll meet again
And God will pick the day.

F. J. Galligani

"An Easter Poem"

In a land that seems so far away
Our saviour died that day,
Upon the cross of Calvary
Our debt He had to pay.

Who can ever comprehend
Or understand the pain,
The agony that He went through
For our eternal life to gain.

Who can even fathom
The rejection that He knew,
When His Father turned His back on Him
Because of me and you.

We'll never have to carry
The burden put on Him,
He took it all upon Himself,
The punishment for sin.

So when you feel discouraged
Or like you need a friend,
Just lift your heart to Jesus,
And ask Him to come in.

Mary Johnson

The Styxx

When I was fifteen we hung
out in the cemetery, he was sweet
to me, but he couldn't hold me.
  When I was seventeen we hung
out in the cemetery; he made love
to me, but he couldn't hold me.
  When I was nineteen we hung
out in the cemetery; he was good
to me, but he couldn't hold me.
  Passion between the stones of
death, embracing lovers rotting
together.
  Shadows of the tattered dreams
creep up.
  They could touch me, but they
couldn't hold me.

Melanie Brown

A Dead Night It Was

Alone she stood
  out there in the dark,
  where no bird sang
  and no dog barked.

The coldness wrapped
  around her tight,
  but no one was there
  that dark cold night.

The clouds
  drifted slowly by,
  as the moon showed through
  and the dead lie.

Howls could be heard
  as the cemetery floor creaked,
  and grave diggers
  so slowly peeked.

A dead night it was
  with no life around,
  no wind at all,
  not even a sound.

Tamara Gilson

My Thoughts

My thoughts..... floating...
Over and under...
Up and around...
Blocking out all other sounds...
Hearing no one as they speak...
Seeking memories..... beyond the deep
In the bleak somewhere...
Buried in the past...
So dear...
Ever so near...

Vivian Kasakov

Silver Moon

When the moon shines
Over the trees
It seems to paint the trees
Silverer than a coin
And as bright as the sun
Especially when it is full
The light of the moon
Will paint your paths
As bright as the sun
Like a flashlight
It will guide your trails

Samuel Denison Taylor Steyer

"Keys"

Passion and Rage
Passion the key to love
Love the key to life
Fear of Death
The end of life
Rage against death
Live life to the fullest
Live it with passion
Live it with a reckless abandon
As if death is a heartbeat away
Love's end is death's away
Love's end is death's prelude
Love is the key to life
Death is the end of life
What happens to those whose love dies?
What happens to those who never love?
The key to life
The prelude to death

Walter Stemberga

Heartstrings

Heartstrings that bind me
Passions that run deep
Ruler of my emotions
As our hearts meet

Your presence demands my attention
Devotions without compare
A burning kiss upon my lips
From a loving heart that cares

Love is created
By a heart that is touched
Reason is lost
When a heart loved too much

Bondage sweetly accepted
Imprisoned by fantasies of you
Feelings suspended in time
As love begins anew

These heartstrings that bind
With a love knot too strong to sever
How can I be free
From a knot tied to last forever

Patricia Ann Lackey

Untitled

Alone for a while
Peace at last
I've been waiting for time
But the moments pass

Past the tulips
Deep in a cave
Devour the berries
So long I've craved

One morning I'll wake
Pick up my guitar
Sing a new melody
Play for the stars

The words that flow
Wash my lips
The freedom I need
At my fingertips

Alone for a while
Peace at last
I've been waiting for time
But the moment has passed.

Tammy Zirbes

Outlook On Life

Mountains or molehills,
   Peacock or Sparrows.
Where the path widens,
   Again where it narrows.
These are the things
   You encounter each day,
The way leading home,
   Or going away.
Don't take them lightly,
   Rise up to the tests.
Be glad you're alive,
   Be thankful you're blessed.
Walk your path daily
   Accept every trial,
Keep looking forward -
   And be sure to smile.

Shirley A. Landstrom

A Friend

A crutch
   perhaps could be
As reliable as she
No more though,
   the good friend
That she is
Always there
   to answer the phone
To hear
   my cries
And complaints
Not only listening
Advising
Suggesting
Helping
   me to get through it
Never alone
She's always there
   and always will be
In my heart.

Kim Kempton

Clothes Pins

The clothes pins were strung
   Pinchered together
Fun in storm
   And in fair weather,
The mile long freight
   Or the short passenger train,
What fun they had
Pulling their clothes pin train
Everywhere!
From kitchen, to dining room,
   To living room,
Under the table
   and over the chair,
The happy hours woven
Around these pincher clothes pins,
No dime store toy
   Could match this fun!
And the hours they spent
Playing in rain
   or sun.

Myrtle M. Gamroth

Reflections

Reflections of a trellis
Pink blooms flowing down
A slowly swaying palm tree
It's arms stretched to the ground.

Reflections of the sky above
Fringed with clouds of gray,
A buzzard circling overhead
Searching for its prey.

Reflections of a thousand smiles
On faces I adore,
A million cherished memories
Of times that were before.

Reflections of tomorrow
In clear waters shining glow,
The sunshine of the future
I see within her flow.

Reflections most amazing
Like teardrops running cool,
I even see reality
Deep within my swimming pool.

Shirley Carlotti

Secrets of My Heart

This heart of mine has a special
place, yet to be touched
It waits, a secret
A magical space in time
Locked inside my mind, I see your face
Etched so warm an tender
Is sparks a glow, I long to know
Love's sweet surrender

I dream one day your eyes will say
What mine have told you love
Secrets, awakening
Passions for you alone
Secret passion cast it spell
The time is here, Love me now
Love me now!

Mary Ann Wear

Ode From A Vegetarian

Little fishes in the sea
Please don't be afraid of me.
I don't eat meat and I don't eat fish
I think that veggies
Make a tasty dish.

Just yesterday I overheard
Scientists say something most absurd
That veggies have thoughts
And feelings too.
I don't that it's really true.

For if they did
I would have heard them say
"Please don't eat me"
As I dined today.

With all my being will I deny
That vegetables can think
Well, that's a lie.
If I accepted what scientists say
Then what in the world
Could I eat today?

Phyllis Fort

God's Creation

As you travel down life's road,
"Please," take the time to Look,
Listen, and See all of Mother
Nature's Beauty - Doesn't Cost
anything. It's all free.
Beautiful Mountains, Valleys, and Trees
The many Lakes, Rivers, and Seas
The animals, Large and Small
Beautiful Birds, every where you go.
Look up into the Blue Sky, Soft
Clouds, Floating by - Beautiful
Sunsets and at night, pretty
Moon and Stars, shining bright.
Look at the People and Homes,
Children playing, Happy and Free.
What a Blessing for you and me.
For we are "all" one of God's
Creations, Don't you See?
"Smile," God Loves You.
P.S. So Do I.

Lucille Burke Imel

Hungry Children

Tear stained faces,
Pot-bellied kids,
Reaching for a morsel,
Or even a crumb.
What can you give me?
What can you spare?
A full coarse meal is really very rare.
Give me a nickel,
Give me a dime,
Mister would you like a nice shoe shine?
Dreams of the future,
No longer come to past,
A life nearly over,
Never going to last.

Sarah Y. Goodman

The Last Memory

The morning sun,
poured through the church, window.
Its flowing hair,
warming my body.

Pine and wood,
danced together,
making a fresh smell.

My grandma,
was a lost soul,
crying in despair.

Tears hugged my eyes,
like a storm,
without rain.

I glanced in the casket,
the last memory,
of my great-grandma.

Nicole La Verne Knight

Tendencies

Tendencies to happen-
prayers do move that way...

Through faithful efforts of belief-
each wave is also sea...

Virtual, potential, actual-
blossoms from the seed...

As with forms about us-
as with you and me...

Nature can reflect us-
meditations mirror divine...

We glimpse the omnipresence-
eternal in space-time...

Sensing, knowing- all is well-
beyond what words can speak...

Surrender to the mystery-
and grace we daily seek...

Lynne Riedy

Forbidden Kisses

The warmth of your presence
pressed against my mind,
engulfing me with surges
of pleasure, assuring me
of erotic and exotic fantasies.

Secret invitations that only we share.
Thoughts entangled with desire
and fear. Uncertain of this seasoned
emotion, shared by even the most
toughened hearts.

Frustrated by the magnitude and
intensity of this savage fullness
that boldly left us without refuge
from the restrictions of the
larger group.

Delightful, passionate mental kisses,
tounging and tickling my inner most
sanctioned place. One moment expunging,
the next, enforcing all of unnecessary
yet, obvious insecurities.

Monique Fenn-Haydel

The Speech

As a boy, I heard him speak
pressed between the elders' elbows
where I strained to get a peek
to see this noble soldier
with a face the color of night
representing all that was good in us
representing all that was right.
With a stiff lip and clasped hands
he spoke at length
of a life so grand.
He spoke of the winters
and all the hatred he'd met
He spoke of pain, of war
and finally of death
I remember the old man
and of all he used to speak
Alone in my barracks sometimes,
I'd think of the words
and sometimes I'd weep.

Keith Gillespie

Journey of a Soul

In the abyss of darkness my soul
Proceeds...
Towards purgation and release
And letting go confirms that peace

But first the trepidation of dusk
On stones of sin
This is where the battle begins

Midnight wraps my being
Doubts prevent my seeing
God helps me I am so afraid
So prayer becomes a woven braid

Faith and hope are intertwined
God's grace is seeping in my mind
And then a light so softly glows
Spraying rays of sun laced
In my soul

Now - Throw me wise and powerful One
Into the arms of Your Loving Son

Nancy Lauer

Cues

Final curtain
Proscenium silent
Strike the set - -
Tomorrow

Stage whispers
Vocal - ghostly
Walls tremble from applause
"Bravo's"

Footlights dimmed
Backstage
Greasepaint
Spectrum colors
Costumes rustle - impassioned
Emptiness in shadows

Play book open
Act 3 - Scene 3

Lock up
City streets
Cacophony

Rita Lurie

In Admiration Of Colonel Mere

O noble sire
Proud and strong

How didst thou stand
Ever straight this long?

Thy back never bent
Thy brow yet uncreased

Upholding those beloved
Till the end without cease

Dost thy burden toll heavy?
Do thy shoulders grow weary?

Thy countenance would not tell
Thou hast weathered well

Kelly Loden

Hate

Roaring like a hungry lion,
   Raging like the sea -
Hate is ready day and night,
   To devour you and me.

A needle put into your eye,
   A knife right through your heart -
The swords of hate are clanging still,
   Will they ever part?
Rose Graham

The New Eureka

Enticing sirens
Rarely affect
The motion of the sea.
Only now and then,
They can sometimes
Be observed to fly against
Red sky on halcyon days,
Or disappear
Inside the cargo ships,
Which gradually,
Unexpectedly,
Lose control—
Drawn by the loads of
Scientific arguments,
And yet
Safely guarded by the smell
Of plastics and steel—
Hidden under the ship's strong deck
They patiently await
The new Eureka.
Robert Baginski

Dew

Sparkling diamonds of dropping dew.
Reflecting the sun each morning is new.
So small so fragile, it can't be touched.
The smallest wind can hurt so much.
It's first stand in the pure sunlight.
Looking at them there is no fright.
For once it gathers all its prestige.
It falls to its death upon the weeds.
But this diamond of sun dropped dew.
Feed the plants that become anew.
Stacey Link

"I'll See You Again"

Oh my dearest sweet one.
Rest your soul. The angels
have come to take you home.
The fight is over, there's no
more pain. But don't you
worry, I'll see you again.
Everything is okay, I finally
understand. God only sends
the angels down, to get the
best of men, I know you weren't
afraid. Because your face showed
no fear. You told us all
goodbye, because your ride
to heaven was here. Now
you have your wings,
and your soul and spirits are free!
Rolynda Gould

Dear Little Jackie

Her Immaculate voice
Rings out from the dark cavern
Beneath, between
The waterfalls of gold
Which frame the angel's face
Uncharted territory
Lies ahead
For our little lady of the altar
Lady of innocence
Her presence is peace
Her voice is bliss
Her body too fragile
For a world such as this
She is pure innocence
She is our dear little Jackie
She is Heaven incarnate
She is our dear little Jackie
Steven I. McCormack

Washed Away

The water flows downstream
Rippling with waves
So go my lost dreams
That nobody saves
Away they flow down the river.

The wind catches a leaf
Fallen from a tree
As when you thief
The innocence of me
Away it flows down the river.

And what do I have left
When all has washed away
Into the depth
Of the past day?
Away I flow down the river.
Kelly Parkes

My World

Every person has a world
Round which their lives evolve
Our problems often easy
And not too hard to solve

Sometimes our world's perplexing
We don't know what to do
Often things, turn out right
While other problems brew

I'm thankful for my world
Please let me tell you why
I'm surrounded by some people
Who will love me till I die

A precious wife and children
Who think that I'm the most
Grandchildren and some friends
Of whom I proudly boast

No, my world's not perfect,
Nor indeed will be
But I'm the happiest man alive
Because my spirit's free
C. S. Upthegrove

Drummer Man

Drummer man play for me
   Rumm Ta Ta Tumm
Bring forth the Christ in me
   Rumm Ta Ta Tumm
For those who died for me
   Rumm Ta Ta Tumm
   Rumm Ta Ta Tumm
Starting with the Christ in thee
   Rumm Ta Ta Tumm
For God, Country and Liberty
   Rumm Ta Ta Tumm
Let's march on for them and thee (we)
   Rumm Ta Ta Tumm
   Rumm Ta Ta Tumm
   Rumm Ta Ta Tumm
Drummer man play for me
   Rumm Ta Ta Tumm
   Rumm Ta Ta Tumm
   Rumm Ta Ta Tumm
Kay M. Johnson

July

I like to watch the tide
rush in from canyons of the ocean
and blanket footprints in the sand
washing away all evidence.
Timid sun addresses
the water still brisk and rustling -
I approach the shoreline

misty morning
curdles curiosity, threading desires
planting roots
into the hopeful wake of
an integral sea

leaving behind a feeble stride
let the sand soak up my past;
I swim in order to breathe
Matthew J. Iannucci

Christmas Season

I listened to the Carols of Christmas
Sang along with every note.

Went shopping, reluctantly
With every package to tote.

Even went up to cut a tree
And hung up lights for neighbors to see.

Sent Christmas cards
To friends far away.

And baked many goodies
To give Christmas day.

Altho Christmas isn't fun anymore
I hung a wreath on the front door.

Alas, I'll be glad
When the holidays are gone-

But next year I'll be singing
The same old song-

Merry Christmas and a
Happy New Year!
Nina Crawford

Chemical Insanity

Scream to release the pressure
Scream before you explode
Can't live another day without it
Your veins are getting cold

What have you done to deserve
The fix that you're not in?
One more line, one more time
One more deadly sin

If you'd rip your own eyes out
Then maybe you would see
That every day you are dying
From chemical insanity

You destroy the lives of children
They would rather pay than pray
The devil sends a thank-you card
Every Christmas day

So as you die now slowly
There rings a final bell
Take all you live for with you
You'll need a high in hell
            M. J. Roland

Time

Seeds develop into flowers
seconds becomes hours
uncertain whether I live or die
a dreadful disease time is to I

A child is growing
not even knowing
what time has in store
as he gaze behind that vast door

Life grows with time
wasteful to mime
in a crystal ball
the future holds for all

Stars to sky, moon to sun
no time for fun, I have to run
so fast is time
never having to rhythm

Such a beautiful day
never able to stay
suddenly comes the moment
there is no more torment.
            Madeline Dawson

Untitled

Know what hurts; feel the pain,
    see the shadows through the rain.

Gone for now the flowered fields,
    beauty for a while yields,

To empty holes like empty wells
    waiting for the magic spells.

Quiet are the lonely nights
    yet loud the voices of the soul,

Ancient rivals still at war
    wrestle deep within the core.

Believe the One who cannot lie.
    will one day color blue the sky
Taking the winners higher than high.

Until the hurt and pain subside
    You know each day how hard you tried.
He knows how many tears you've cried.
            Marilyn R. Heller

Love Lost On The Trail

We headed west
Seeking the best

Her name was Sue
But now I'm blue

She was my dream
She was my gleam

There was a quarrel
Now there's sorrow

Why did she go
Where did she go

Never known a night so blue
As the day without Sue

What trail she take
Can I cure this heartache

Is she riding the rail
Love lost on the trail
            Lowell Kirchenwitz

Tick Tock

Listen to that old clock
    Seems like it ticks faster,
Faster, tick tock, tick tock.
    It really is the master
Telling you when to do,
    Ordering you to go.
The days become too few
    It's impossible to say no.
Please God, give me more time,
    How can I get it done?
Two of me would be sublime
    But I am only one.

The tick tock keeps repeating
    And the minutes are past.
Life can be so fleeting
    No one can make it last.
But do not hurry your pace
    Work to your own inner clock.
It has its own set face
    And hands, tick tock, tick tock.
            Patricia M. Sharp

Seem

Angels seem to hurry by
Seems that one has forgotten me
Once again I sit alone
Waiting for my turn to come
Angels in front, Angels behind
I seem to fall further
Life in my mind?
Angels seem to touch my shoulder
Energy absorbed through me
Slowly I seem to live again
I seem renewed as a part of life
Life is my playground
My mind seems just a piece
            Katherine Jones

A Day's Cycle

Dawn, a beautiful morn's coming,
Serene, free as a bird in the sky,
Hopeful as a child staring,
Looking up for a star so high.

Learning, diggin' up the unknown.
Knowledge, the sun's greetings to all.
The best a man has ever owned
Is his way to top the roll.

Noon, the highest point of man,
Brighter than any time of day,
Vigorous as the wind blows can,
A chance that happens only in May.

Sunset, another phase to see.
Dusk, the sand in the bottle spent,
Nature's wisdom has made thee
Recumbent strength and back bent.

Nightfall, a recollection of time.
There is something in every strand...
A phony along the line.
These and more we must understand.
            Victoria Ignacio

Shadows

When the shades of night are falling
Shadows lean against the door
They creep up o'er the door sill.
And cross the earthen floor.

They steal among the corners,
And creep along the wall.
They make the ghostly figures,
Seem short, fat and tall.

They run along the windows,
and out into the night.
Back again across the table top.
To shatter the shaft of light.

All night long the shadows play,
Hide and seek with one another.
All day long they skip about
And do not look for cover.

They never tire of playing pranks,
As they dance and skip away.
And take no time to even sleep
But continue their tireless play.
            Virginia P. Sampson

"Grandma"

She had so many things
she gave up when she died.
She was so full of life,
and she was so alive.
She knew that we loved her,
and that she loved us.
Nothing could break that love,
not even a wicked cuss.
It is sad that she left us,
but she had to go.
The time was just right,
even if the answer was no.
To see her laying in that bed,
breathing was so hard.
Her heart just stopped,
that was the last regard.
Even though we miss her,
the only thing left to do is cry.
But I guess you have to accept it,
and just say good-bye.
            Maegan Sankey

"I Dream Of Her"

As I pass by her with a sigh,
she gives no "hello" or "goodbye."

She has no knowledge of how I feel,
if she broke my heart it would never heal.

I dream of dreaming
me and you,
all alone
I hope I'd be true.

Then one night my dream came true,
but if only you knew...
I love you.

Omar Meza

Queen Mom

My Mom is a queen.
She has a ruby crown of wisdom
With emeralds for eyes that show
compassion, dignity, and conquered pain.
She has a Mother of pearl smile,
skin speckled with garnets, and a
Soul of amethyst that makes her
the most royal of them all.
The queen protects her castle and
is good to her kingdom with love
She brings just by her presence,
And her kingdom has loyalty and
Love for her so.
My Mom, the queen, the most
precious jewel in the world.
My hope diamond.

Penny A. West

Kermit

Who is she now,
she's not real sure.
Her path has changed,
into one big detour.

Everything is different,
nothing the same.
Some call her a poser,
but that's not her name.

She knows not if
she's happy or sad.
There isn't a day,
where she's totally glad.

She can't determine,
the wrong from the right.
She can't tell the difference
from darkness or light.

It's gotten to where,
so many abuse her.
She feels as if,
she's just a dumb loser.

Lindsay Aaron Smith

Braces

Iron jaws and metal clasp,
rubber bands are wired.
Fruity mold that makes you gasp,
X-rays make you tired.

Endless pain and suffering,
tortured to the quick,
that's what bright new teeth will bring,
until then I feel sick.

Kelly Ferguson

Spring?

Diamonds glistening, dancing rainbows
Shining in the sun.
Emanating halos, each and every one.

Branches, bushes, biting cold
Encased in icy grasps.
Beauty shining, danger hiding
How long will it last?

Yesterday those heavy ladened branches
snapped and crashed.
With a flurry, sparks and losses
Lights went out so fast.

Now restored, we all can see
The wonder and the grace.
One last bow from winter,
Now we start the race.

March has begun, attention getting
Roaring like the lion.
Where is spring, those soft warm breezes
And the shining sun?

Maureen T. Kaniewski

The River Tree

His roots stem from Mary
Since she agreed to be
Mother of Jesus, King, to set free
Us, His children, from slavery.

She welcomed the Spirit, most Holy,
In perfect humility,
Became the host of the Trinity
And the hope of humanity.

Tree of crossed compassion,
From lifted-up position,
Present, Living Expression -
Leave in our hearts, Your impression.

As members of Your wounded trunk -
We ponder Your passion in love!
We accept our cross as a chunk -
of Your role as King of our love.

Peace flowing divine,
Enrich our life in earth's planet;
Temper our efforts in line,
With You, as our goal, implanted.

Sr. Margaret Ann Kelly S.C.

Memorandum of a Mother

It's been a year
since you died
dear Mother
Oh, what sadness
is in my heart
Oh, how I yearn for
yesteryear
When we did not depart
I have a lifetime of
remembrance
that brings a sparkle
to my heart
It's your gift of love
to be remembered
forever
in our hearts

Marcia Dunning

"Friendship"

Sharing secrets, telling stories,
Singing songs, playing games,
Friendship, friends for life.

Writing notes, talking out troubles,
Building bridges, knocking down walls,
Friendship, friends for life.

Climbing mountains, sailing the seas,
Riding the waves, walking on beaches,
Friendship, friends for life.

Laughing, joking, caring,
Hoping, liking, loving,
Friendship, friends for life.

Kathy Anne Tanton

Treasure the Memories

The old house in the small town
Sits abandoned and empty,
And precious memories left untouched.
Treasure the memories.

The teddy bear in her room
Sits alone in the corner
And yet is still smiling.
Treasure the memories.

The picture on the wall
Shows her first car.
She was young and smiling.
Treasure the memories.

The old yearbook in the attic
Is filled with loving farewells
And old familiar faces smiling.
Treasure the memories.

The family Bible she once read sits on the table,
Which tells the story of her Savior
And the heavens where they live, and
they're smiling.
Treasure the memories.

Kristin R. Lamb

Easter Memories

Flowers are blooming
Skies are so clear-
All signs are showing
That Easter is here.

Look in the eyes-
And look in the hearts-
See all the joys-
That Easter imparts.

New gaiety lightens your step
And spirits are high-
For Easter is here-
Lets shout to the sky.

And you in your bonnet-
With me by your side
We'll be envied by others
Who watch our gay stride.

Let's always remember-
This beautiful day-
With love and affection
Come trouble what may.

Mary Walter

To My Unborn Child

A tiny person,
Slowly grows inside of me.
A promise from God,
of the wonderful thing to be.
I will do my best,
to be the perfect mother.
That's a promise from me,
That you'll never hear from another.
I'll nurture and guide you,
as you continue to grow.
My love for you is strong,
Stronger than you will ever know.
I'll be there when you laugh,
I'll be there when you cry.
I'll help you to take your first step,
I'll be there until our final goodbye.
Times may sometimes get rough,
but I'll always be there to see you through
these, my unborn child,
Are the promises that I make to you.

Kelly Blubaugh

Expression

Depression of bright blue skies
slowly wilting in your hands
gripping them as fragile lace.
Watch in gruesome fascination
as they fall,
under the sea and sink together
into bottomless spilt ink.
What is left
watching o'er us?
Vague misty fogs
dancing somberly the cycle of life
and death.
Hesitation of pain-filled tears
aimlessly searching your blank stare,
holding them ransom
for a peaceful end.
Spotted in the distance
soaring in jubilation,
a serene beginning
of expression.

Melanie F. Heston

Burning Trees

Clouds of grey
Smoke of guilt
Float away in mother's milk

Burning hopes
Burning dreams
Burning thoughts
Burning trees

Children cry
People cough
Complaining souls have no day off

The sky's now black
The sun's now gone
Sunburnt grass and bright red lawn

Broken glass
Boiling seas
All along they're burning trees

Megan Pickett

Untitled

Lay down trouble
smooth in cool water
and rest furled brow
under fire gently pulsing
let breath of wind sweep sand away
close strained eyes
and let blood flow away
in the river
become a cloud of summer
for loving sun to lift the mist
hands guiding each other
we clouds of summer
do float along above the river
we clouds of summer
do forget the river
for sky forever

Mark Esser

Patience of a Mother's Love

Patience is a virtue
So blessed and so strong
It makes a mother
Feel she's right
Even if she's wrong

It makes a mother weep
When she finds her
Son gone astray
To have him back
As a little tyke
She always seems to pray

To take this drug
From his taste
So that his life
Would not be a waste
And wonders upon
A new sunrise
If her only son
Will still be alive

Ruth Jane Thornton

Those Little Hands

My sweet little boy
So hard at play.
I watch through the window
And remember another day.

You were a baby
So precious and sweet.
I rocked you, cuddled you,
And sang you to sleep.

Now hugs are embarrassing
And a kiss I have to steal.
But nothing will ever change
The way that I feel.

You act so grown up
My big, little man.
But no matter how much you grow
I will remember those little hands.

Kammilia K. Townsend

Love Is

Love is so painful,
so hard to express.
The fussing and fighting,
God only knows the rest.
Tears come to my eyes,
and you wipe them away.
Just tell me you love me,
and I will be okay.
It's so hard to believe that,
you really care.
When there's so many just
waiting out there.
But when I gaze into,
your sparkling eyes.
I can feel my quivering,
heart as it starts to fly.
Because I know now,
Our love will never die.
It s the type of love that,
can still reach the star's in the midnight sky.

Kami Prieto

Vision of Life

When I was just a little girl. Not
so long ago. My Mom would sit and
talk about. How it was when she
was young. She said candy was a
penny. A nickel brought a pop.
Radio was their T.V. And they
danced in their socks. You didn't
sass your Mama. You minded your
p's and q's. You didn't go out on
a date. Without a curfew. They
looked out for one another. The
way it's meant to be. They filled
each other with pride and love.
That make strong families. Now I
sit and wonder. Where did we go
wrong? Every one seems so selfish.
Other things have come along. With
babies having babies. The sex,
guns and drugs. Have taken up the
spaces. Where there use to be such love!

Norma J. Williams

"Senses"

I see your eyes,
  So lovely and true -
Disparaging days I live
  Are the days without you.

I feel your love,
  So warm and tender -
Every beat of your heart
  Fills my life with splendor.

I hear your voice,
  So soft and sweet -
Without you by my side
  My world will never be complete.

I detect your scent,
  So stimulating and sensual -
With every breath I take
  Your redolence becomes more essential.

I savor your lips,
  So moist and luscious -
The intense, passionate seconds
  Give me a sense of unconsciousness.

Sang Lam

Generation X-plained

Imagination of four year olds
So many dreams
of when "they're grown"
to feel
and believe
and hope
and wish
upon a reality
of twenty years gone
and bitterness
now only an "X"
so meaningless

Michelle Kane

Trans-Dimensional Pause

The petals of the rose,
So soft, so delicate, that,
When touched by Winters harsh frost,
They wither and darken, falling,
One by one to an unforgiving,
Earth, such a shame, and,
Yet so inevitable, to be born, to,
Live, to die, even things of beauty,
Must one day cease to be, yet as the,
Unbreakable circle of life and death,
Makes yet one more revolution,
The rose is born again,
Another rose is brought to,
Life, with the warmth of,
Spring, the circle is complete.

Robert Charles Sadlier

No Longer

When no longer your love I received,
So vivid your intent to deceive.
Heavy heart, tortured soul,
Mostly, I don't feel whole.

You tried so desperately to achieve,
Tainted words, I cannot believe.

My eyes grow cold from wretched tears,
A friendship vacant after all these years.
Magnitudes of surfaced fears.

Confusion and disillusion I be-friend,
What exactly did you intend?

I wonder what more proof,
You knew my earnest search was truth.

Time be my friend,
When you no longer can.

Lisa Camme

Inside Cage

They say the child in me
Shields the woman from the pain.
The pain has a life of its own,

Uncontrollable, unrecognizable,
all consuming.

Must the woman feel the pain,
To kill its life?
The pain is Victor, it is obsessive,
The woman is the child.

Denise A. Bell

Song for the Dead

Send a promise in the wind
So we can meet again.
Time is what stands in the way
To force me through another day
Without you.
It's the enemy of the living
And the savior of the dying.
Don't cry
You'll die too,
In time.
It drinks the tears of the crying
And the blood of the dying.
It took me too;
It will take you.
Don't cry.
You'll die too,
In time.
All that matters is
Time.

Marci Segars

The Crane

Watching all its gracefulness
soaring high in the sky

with such precision
swoops down low to grasp
then slowly rises
with it's catch

swaying back and forth
correcting its position
placing its subsistence atop
a collection of metal like itself

now it's lunch time
and all placements halt
workers fill up with energy
to continue the pursuit

awaiting its next catch and placement
the crane hovers in the sky.

Robin Guthrie

Creatures Of The Night

Creatures of the night how
softly they glide, with the
moon light so bright and
star light in sight.
Gazing at the sky
wondering how bright it is
so very bright the moon
lit sky how can it fly
across my mind with it
all I feel the creatures of
the night.

Susann Pickard

The Waves

The waves rushed in fury
Showing its violent ways
Making the bathers to scurry
In hopes of a calmer day

It thrashed and tossed its body
Sending debris to the shore
Its anger finally spent
To calm for a day or more

Kathy Hockey

Untitled

Some forgot, some never knew,
Some didn't even care
But regardless of all
Some still went there
Some came home smiling,
Some came home crying
Some came home in a box
But regardless of all
"Some are still there"
Some want to go back
and get the rest that are there
But some of us forgot
Politics are in the Air
So when it's your time
and you have the courage to stand
in front of many to say
what you will do
I hope that you will go
back and get them
"The one's who voted for you"

Paul G. Cassell

The Chain of Life

Here we are!
Some people screaming
and never heard.
Some fighting but
wanting to give in.
Some people running
to the sun!
Some, just walking in
the rain believing
the lie that they
are the ones to
Blame.

Here we are placed
in a world we will
never change .
We are all victims
of each other's pain!
As long as this continues,
life will remain one big
cruel game.

Lorraine Randt

The Quilt of Friendship

A friend is someone special
Someone honest and sincere
A friend is there for you
each day throughout the year
They laugh when you are happy
And cheer you when you're blue
Their shoulder's there to lean on
if the need is there for you
A true and special friend
is a greeting to the heart
A bond is formed as well
Which should never break apart
It's like a quilt of friendship
That makes you feel secure
It's woven through with love
To have forever more
Each patch is made with care
and when complete you'll see
Forever you have found a friend
to last Eternity!

Lori S. Pittmann

I Am Alone

I am alone inside my head
Sometimes I feel as if I'm dead

I am not sure I'll ever come out
To sing to laugh to folic about

In here there is no pain no fear
Only memories of those I hold dear

In my dreams I hear a shout
Please oh please you must come out

Perhaps I'll fling the door out wide
Forgetting I have a place to hide

I should have stayed behind the door
This pain I can stand no more

I am alone outside my head
I just found out I'm really dead

Shari Cummings

Confused

When a person seems hard, and mean,
Sometimes we need to see the core,
Realizing the pain that has been felt,
Feeling the purpose of the hurt.

When we draw on emotions,
All situations grow intense,
The hurt will be inflamed,
Sorrow will be felt by all.

If we give love freely, without clause,
Continuing even when resisted,
The hardness will soon crumble,
And trust will be able to grow.

Many times we label each other,
We reassure others, what we disbelieve,
But, the hard truth is to open,
When the fear still hurts inside.

Kathy Barker

Cheers

As her body moved
somewhat rhythmically
to the swaying force
of the noise,
her hands nurtured
the cup
that filled her soul.
The sweet taste of cranberry
had long since departed
and the warmth of what is Absolute
seduced her mind.
Scanning with numb senses,
she took notice to the door:
    His arrogant stature trapped her;
    for the evening,
    for a moment.
Smiling only to herself
she raised the empty glass
and toasted
what she knew was nothing.

Marie Sarita Gaytan

Mowing

Cheddar smell of gas
spills into the air as a sharp tug
brings the motor smoothly in existence.

Willfully we walk
around the field
scything wide swaths.

Crowds of bugs flee
before this deviant of nature
outside of their knowledge.

Great towering caves
of man will fill this forest
and field where I stand mowing.

At the sun's respite
the life mists of the grain
rise to the moon.

Robert A. McNamara III

Field Of Daisies

The feeling of your soul,
spinning, spinning, laughing, giggling,
in a field of daisies.
Your secret found land,
ALONE.
Finding yourself,
hangin' with the daisies,
No matter what color their pedals are.
You spin, spin,
spin so hard it feels like ecstasy.
An incredible power,
NAIVE.
Within each and every one of us.
FORTUNATE.
There are no worries,
We live in ONE, Harmonious world.
No racists. No segregation.
TOGETHER.
One race-the human race.
That field of daisies!

Lauren Marie Williams

Brooke Manor C C

A wispy cloth of mist
Spreads over fairway and rough,
Rising as one hits.
Somewhere life is tough.

The second shot gets up
To the green, smooth and shaven.
Next stroke's in the cup!
This course is surely heaven!

Green and manicured grass.
Ponds and trees galore.
Geese graze and ducks sass.
While traffic snarls down the road.

But reality looms one day
Bulldozing ponds and sand.
Houses replace fairways.
A tragic of the plan—

To us who are displaced
Seeking another spot,
But we'll remember with fondness
The place that golf forgot.

Mary S. Walthall

Spring Showers

Spring showers come and go.
Starting with a plit, plit, plit.
Going to a plop, plop, plop.
Then, all of a sudden -
Silence.
Except the
Whistles and chatters
Of the birds. And
Everything is clean
And new again. The
Air is fresh, cool, and
Clear. The grass is moist,
Green, and bright.
A soft, gentle breeze
Caresses the trees as
The scent of Spring
Falls around us.

Suzanne Pointer

Inspiring Shimmers

Glance upon glance,
    Stirring of sweet light;
Passions in dream,
    Enchanting first sight.

Glimpses do seem,
    Flittering hearts of dance;
Sweetness a nimmer,
    Daring eyes dare chance.

Touching of shimmer,
    Dreaming upon dream;
Quickened to passion,
    Though glances may seem.

Keith P. Sargent

His Sea

By stillness ever boding,
stood time itself, ever rolling.

Crouched, weathered, bent and old,
The man of ages, wrinkled gold.

Within a salty shack he abides,
in a life liken to a sea gull's cry.

The sea a mistress and his food,
changing weather his only mood.

Alone to gaze across the waters,
the wind a son, the waves a daughter.

Waiting for one ethereal wash,
uniting his lifeblood with his cause.

Living to hold her windswept hair,
beneath her pulsing mystery.

One is one till two will be,
swallowed forever, her lips, his sea.

Karen Galley

Friends

Friends are like clouds reaching out to
    the sky,
They come and they go, as life
    passes by.
The true ones will stay,
    while the others will leave,
And those few who remain,
    are the ones that we need.

Sandra Silberstein

Stop Dreaming

If you're not going anywhere
Stop bumming and do something about it
Life won't get any better
If you are laying around doing nothing
Get off your ass and change your life
It's time to grow up
Get on with your life
So stop dreaming
Start doing
Stop dreaming
Start living
You can wish upon a star
But if you don't help that wish
It won't come true

Nancy K. Kerr

Stray Cat

Stray cat roaming the
streets what are you searching for?
stray cat out on a stormy night
where are you heading?
so beautiful stray cat you are
how could anyone destroy you.
Stray cat crying a lonely world.
Stray cat drifting, floating through
a dark twisted life, will it ever
get better?

Nahla Ramadan

Earthly Fury

I love the sound of the rain
striking against my window,
driven by the wind
in the midst of a storm.

I love the sound of the wind
whistling through the trees,
as the leaves swish with laughter
in defiance of the breeze.

I love the sound of the waves
crashing onto shore
as they tumble and race each other
in competition of play.

I love the sound of the house
creaking with age,
as the walls groan and shutter
in fury at being disturbed.

I love to sleep on nights like these
when nature combines her forces,
pelting rain against house
wind against sea.

Rosalie A. Brockert

Stillness

Distant white
Space shimmers through
Thick chocolate pines

Up slope to the hoodoos
Where mists hang
In the morning

And cold
A lake sits pearl
And smooth

In the stillness.

Wes Gibbs

Sunshine

Sunshine is special,
Sunshine is wonderful.

You sit down under a tree
and feel something hot,
cold,
wonderful,
special,
lazy.
You see something beautiful,
colorful,
bright,
dark.
You can imagine the sky,
birds chirping,
sun,
clouds,
trees up so high.

Sunshine is special
for you and for me!

Rachel Rizer

A Lover's Toy

Life has shown me quite a lot
Sure of much — I'm really not
I've had love — I've had sorrow
I'm not too sure about tomorrow

Will it bring sun — will it rain
Will it hold laughter or more pain
I've shed tears — I've worn smiles
Do good things last more than awhile

Can life give me what I need
Where on earth will the next road lead
I have given — I have taken
Is this a dream — Will I awaken

Is it raining — no, it's a tear
My life is a fog — nothing is clear
Do I know love — does it destroy
Is life just a lover's toy

Marcella Samson

In My Dreams

I saw you in my dreams last night
surrounded by a golden light
You were so calm and understanding
when my questions became demanding
"Tell me what happens when you die."
"Do we really need to cry?"
You just smiled at me and said:
"I know someday you'll understand"
Now my fears have gone away
about what happens on the day
When my heart no longer heats
from the body my soul retreats
To that plane where you now stand
Will you then reach out your hand
To be my guide and my friend
Or just be my big brother once again.

Mary L. St. Cyr

She Walks By Silverlight

She walks by silverlight
Surrounded in a misty veil
In her hand she holds a candlelight
To guide her feet along the trail

Swiftly drifting by
The starlit midnight sky
Slowly, with unerring grace
Smooth and soft
as gentle as her face

Softly now her lips
Sweetly waken him
With a kiss
Quickly now she flees from him
To blend into the pale morning light
To wait and soothe him back asleep again
Upon the approaching of the night.

G. R. Preiss

Spring

The canopy of a weeping willow
Sways green.
Blooming irises can soon be seen.
Enchanting perfumes rise from
The ground.
Nature plays a sweet, peaceful
Sound.
Robins hatch from their eggs.
Bears come out to stretch their
Legs.
Sparrows cheerfully chirp and
Sing.
With winter far away nature has
Brought us spring.

Patricia R. Ireland

"Powerless"

As I ride this wave of obsession,
swiftly rolling-aimlessly denying.
Unconsciously lying,
growing stronger,
lasting longer.

I wonder...
Should I pray about the consequences,
I have to weigh.
In this game, only GOD will know.

As the tide rolls in...
Is it low or is it high?

GOD help me -
as I pray,
why does it have to be this way?
compulsion fills my heart and mind.

GOD I pray,
grant me that it takes
to ignore the voices so real
in what we know is fate.

G. Philip DeMuth

Help Away

Help me fly
Take me away
Push me high
Teach me to say
Words that are true
Words that are real
Words that express
How both of us feel
Kiss my lips
Hold my hand
Tell me you love me
I know that you can
Keep me sure,
Guard me from harm
Hold me close
Let me die in your arms.

Kristin Carson

A Friendship Lost

Pain and suffering,
Tears and frowns.
Who can you turn to
When you're feeling down?
Your best friends are turned against you,
Your heroes are gone.
No one is around
So you're left all alone.
A friendship is lost,
So what does it mean?
Was it really worth
All the fights and the screams?
As you look around,
You see that you're not alone.
Without the others,
Your true colors are shown.
So say goodbye to the tears and the pain,
Because one friendship lost
Is more friendship gained.

Lisa Iris Scarbrough

Love Is

Love is a rock that rolls
Tears are loneliness calling

Love is a sunny day
Tears are sorrow's rain
Love is a tender kiss
Love is remembering the ones you miss

Love comes and goes
It never lasts forever
But the pain endures
'Til the twelfth of never

Lust does nothing for me
I have no faith in love
Yes, I am a spirit roaming free.

Teresa Dawn Calvert

Golden Trees

I saw a ray from the sun
touch a tree when day was done.
It left it's gold upon the leaves
to make them look like sun-baked trees.
So all can see when skies are gray
the golden color from the ray.
It's beauty mocking cloudy skies,
the brilliant color dazzling eyes.
On dismal days, dark and cold,
I look upon these trees of gold.

Virginia Costa

Save Me

The darkness
That I have dreaded for so long
Has found me.
It slowly and silently snack up
Behind me - Then
BAM!
It exploded; encircling me
And started attacking
From all directions.
Now I am drowning
In the evilness of it.
I am being smothered
By its cold, lonely sheets of black.
This darkness is destroying
My being. Help.
I need you.
I need you to come and save me.

Lori Mull

Memory of the Navajo Tale

Riding and fearing
that it shall come
the Skin-Walker
a creature who walks only by night
protector of the reservation
coyote, but somehow human
we drive beyond limits
60, 70 miles per hour
if not more
you can feel his eyes watching us
garish blue, gleaming, shining
he draws closer and closer to us
we can sense his presence
running close to our car
as fast as we can
we flee the terror.

Melissa E. Laser

Hidden Secrets

There are so many things
that just should not be known;
It just awakes the ailing hearts
of those who are alone.
There are so many things
that just should not be said,
Because some secrets should
be matters, that are kept
within the head.
If details were kept hidden
pain would be no more.
Tears would only exist inside,
and only behind closed doors.
There are so many things
that one just should not see.
All the love one has inside
and cannot share with thee.

Shawnta Renae Williams

With Each Day

If today was forever
    then tomorrow wouldn't matter
Only the past with it's memories
    would thoughts gather.
But we live for today
    Working, sharing, loving,
and look forward to tomorrow
    as we live today.

LoRaine L. Allen Setterberg

Life

Like a sightless force
that manipulates our soul,
effectuating our ups and downs,
she is a firm ruler
who dominates our seasons
with her on-going plans,
while controlling our senses
with a will of iron.

A look of determination
is etched on her stout features,
while she watches us suffer and toil.
To be held in her power
by greed and want,
one of her devoted fans.
The game of survival
being in great demand.

With a little creativity
she can become our fan.
Like a deck of cards,
to hold the upper hand.

Sylvia T. Wilensky

Dare to Soar!

It's quite humorous to me
    that the beauty of an oak tree
lies in the intricate way
    in which it proceeds

And man in his simple mind
    feels he can unwind it
and strap it to a base
    forcing it to grow straight

Isn't that how life is?
    We dare not move too far
to the left or right
    We brace our feet to the ground
yet reach for the stars

It would be so glorious to fly
    but the fear of hitting ground
prevents us from the try
    therefore we stay grounded and watch,
as those few brave souls who dare

    SOAR THRU THE SKY!!!

Wendy Bernal

Toys for Christmas

Christmas is here
That time of the year
For girls and for boys
Fulfilling dreams
Of snow, sweets and toys

He wanted a train
With steam from the top
Its one of the toys
He never got

He wanted an auto
You wind up after stops
Its one of the toys
He never got

Thoughts of Christmas
With all its joys
About songs and trees
And about toys
The ones he never got

Sebastian

Grandson

We know that you—have things to do
That's far, far more exciting
Than spending time with two old souls,
Who just keep on inviting.

But Pa keeps wishing ev'ry day
Hoping and a praying
You'll come and spend a whole weekend,
And Pa just hates delaying.

Then, I just smile and say, "That child
Can never spare a minute.
He's busy trying to excel
His class and all that's in it."

There'll come a day he'll come our way
When it won't be a bother,
If we can just hang on until
He too, becomes a father.

Rozella Dunaway

A Witness For Jesus

A witness for Jesus,
That's what I long to be,
Oh, that he could love,
Someone as low as me.

A witness for Jesus,
Some of his love to show.
Lord, through me forever,
Let your love lights glow.

A witness for Jesus
Lord, help me hold out my hand,
Some how in this world to be,
A help to my fellow man.

A witness for Jesus.
While on this earth I dwell,
A witness for Jesus,
to save some lost soul from hell.

Shelia Smith

Spring Time

It's Spring time, it's Spring time,
The buds are appearing
The birds that migrated
Are coming to roost.
The animals that hibernated
Have all been awaken.
It's so beautiful to experience
A season so pure.

O Welcome, O Welcome,
Spring season, Spring season,
Pretty tulips, red roses
We're glad you have come,
Cool breezes, fresh showers.
It's Spring time, beautiful season
God made the flowers, the rain, the sun
For you and me.

Miriam Lawrence

Dance of Death

Dancing, twirling, leaping,
The cadence kept my feet.
Flickering lamplight, leering eyes,
Yet all was flowing and sweet.

And did I dance?
Oh yes, I danced!
Delight of my own mother's eyes!
Deftly displayed
For Herod's men,
Her moment of glory and pride.

And did I know? How could I know?
Daughter destined for fame!
'Twas the dance of death
I danced that night,
And she was the one I blamed.

Now the flickering lamplight's died,
The murderous deed's been done.
The blood of the holy man
Stains her soul,
Yet I, I was the one!

Kim Skivington

Best Friends

We've had our times of laughter,
  the campouts, the parties...
We seemed so close then
  the best of friends.

We've fought our share of fights
  hurting words, evil thoughts...
But we have now forgiven
  And are still the best of friends.

We've cried many tears
  frustrations, the stress...
But someone always lent a shoulder
  proving to be the best of friends.

Through everything we've all grown,
  matured, we've grown together...
To look back upon the memories
  we see ourselves; the Best of friends.

I will hold you very close to my heart,
  loving, caring, remembering...
That all the while I believe
  that you are my Best Friends.

Leigh Ann Allen

My Favorite Color

What a beautiful color!
The color I believe
The color I love
Is blue
My mom said the color
I love is Blue.
Because I am loving
I love the sky
Because He loves me.
It could be my eyes
Sometimes the ocean
gives me the water
I enjoy the water
It give me the
forgiveness
What a beautiful,
loving and joyful
Earth I can see.

Monica Bennett

So Shall We Dance

In the silent night
the cool wind rushes
seeking someone to touch.
Hopeful eyes and fallen tears
search through the magnificent sky
for an answer.
What shall be the meaning of me
when all is complete?
"In Me is the fullness of all
you can be.
Nothing that is, is without.
As My frosty breeze touches with you
the waves of the sea
So they dance
It will soon be warm
once again
And so shall we dance."

Ni R. Burnett

"Questions" (I Ask Myself)

What could heal
the crippling sound
of cries throughout
the night?
Who holds the one
key, that could unlock
the only light?
Where is the peace
that each soul tries,
so desperately to find,
And
when will it arrive... if
there should be
a given place in time?
Oh love... it's you...
Love, how strong!
"Are you in me?"
For, if ever, hate could feel
your true strength...
would, than, hate let us be?

Kemberly Jo Duckett

Solitude

Deep in solitude
The curled tendrils
Of my soul unfurl.
They creep about
Seeking sustenance
Smoothing, polishing
The sharp stones
That have breached
And torn the inner walls.
They gently mend and
Leave the sanctuary
Tidy and firm.
Ready now to go
Into the world again,
Where pain may devastate
And crush the walls anew,
But here, hope is renewed,
Laughter rings, joy abounds
Beauty beckons, music
Surrounds and love awaits.

Verle Nichols Higgs

A Flower

I was a flower in
the dark and now I am coming
out, trying to see why did
I stay, in the dark so long.

What kept me there, who
made me stay, Guess what
it is time for me to bloom and
be pretty, and show my beautiful
colors, to live, to breath.

Hum...The Rain feels good
On my leaves I can even
wave my long stem back and forth,
I am a pretty flower full
Of life ready to be seen, I am a
Flower, Come look at me!

Linda Hughes

I'll Be All Right

As you look into my eyes, I see
the deep concern you have for me.
But I'll be all right.

As you hold my hand, I feel
the passion I did the very first time.
But I'll be all right.

As you run your fingers through my hair.
I sense your not wanting to let go.
But I'll be all right.

When I gathered my things, I remembered
the tears you shed as I first told you.
Yet, you'll be fine.

When I held you in my arms, I heard
you gasp for air as if there was no more.
Yet, you'll be fine.

When I tried to sleep last night, I kept
thinking of the time when I'll see you again.
Yet, for now, I'll be all right.

Stephanie M. Erickson

Jean and Kathe Kollwitz

I never really felt
the depth of pain
and despair
in Kathe Kollwitz

- until
I watched my wife
strain,
turn and twist,
distort and suck air
with it
through tight dry lips
as the cancer spread;

And all I could do
was helplessly brace,
stand by,
cringe,
clinch my fists
and see her drawings
etched upon
Jean's face.

Robert J. Saunders

Love Alone

Though night wind strikes
The dying coals
They cannot light
The darkened soul

The empty ache
Of love now gone
Or never known
But greatly longed

Cannot be stilled
By goals or gain
No accolades
Can ease the pain

Love gives alone
That we all need
And only love
The heart has freed

Love forever
Will by those stand
Who stand for love
The great I AM

Patrick S. Williams

America's Prayer

Give us light, the sun light,
The fields, and golden grain,

Let us walk, on lands of clover,
Let us climb the hills again,

Let the wind go, round about us,
Flinging loose
The cares we've borne,

Let the ocean
Take, and cleanse us
Of the sorrows we have worn,

Let us scale the worlds above us,
As we watch the stars appear,

Or let the rain
Fall down upon us,
Giving peace defying fear,

Let us know that God is with us,
Just as he is there above,
And may our flag
Hold high his honor,
Sending peace good will, and love!

Virginia Mackenzie Schilling

Country Roads

A straight line is
    the finest way
to get from point to point,
    they say —
except,
    for butterflies
        and me;
    for, somehow,
autumn brings
    a little love
        of country things
when country roads
    go winding
        through the fields!

Rilla Black

The Golden Orange

At the close of a warm day;
The golden orange is suspended.
Momentarily, then paints the heavens
With a luminescent panorama of rosy,
Sunkist hues, floating between
Cotton puffs and blankets of blue.

Melting slowly, ever so slowly
Into the cool blue sea. It spills
Colors like rays of rosy ripples
Cascading over the foamy crested waves.
And then it fades....onto
the glistening sands; making the
sea and sky one.

Vera Strong Anderson

Lessons In Eating A Turkey

When eating a turkey, first eat
    the head.
But first make sure that the
    turkey is dead.
Then eat the neck,
So that you know how to peck.
Then you eat the drumsticks,
So that you could use them for
    toothpicks.
Last of all you eat the feet,
And now my lessons are complete!

Rose Bertorella

Saturday

There's so much to be done now,
the house to clean and all -
that laundry in the basement...
and I need to make a call.

I start out in the kitchen -
do the dishes - sweep the floor.
Then take something to the bedroom
to put in a dresser drawer.

But the drawer, when it's opened,
reveals such a motley mess
that I start to rearrange it,
make it neater - more or less.

Before I know what's happened
they've been added one by one
'til I've got so many projects
I can't ever get them done.

If I could just get started
and do one thing at a time
'til I got through the whole house
then things would be just fine.

Musa Knickerbocker

Sonnet in an Antique Style

I cannot say "I love thee"
Of love I little know.

I shall not say "I want thee"
'Twould sound too course and low.

I dare not say "I need thee"
For thou could'st hurt me so.

Instead I'll cry, "Reprieve me!"
Pray let my heart strings go."

And if thou should'st believe me
Truly thou must nothing know.

Lisa Tietjen

Birds of Prey

Barn Owl shaken from his sleep into
the light of day.
Red Tail Hawk from power pole,
pursuit is under way.
Over fields of grapes where men half
seen, pluck the fruited vine.
No one lifts a head to see.
This drama is all mine.
To watch as both birds of prey
soar to lofty heights.
I wonder will this bird of day
catch this bird of night.
I follow, trying to keep up.
The journey is not long.
Barn owl finds a place to roost.
Red Tail Hawk continues on.

Stan Harris

Falling Feathers

Now we are gone.
    The long days of peace
And the longer days of conflict
    Are behind us.

The trails we marked
    With our moccasins are
Grown up with trees
    We never lived to see.

The skies we watched . . .
    There was the rising of the sun
And the coming of the moon
    And there the blossoming stars.

The lives we lived,
    First in bountiful peace
And then in savage warfare.
    There seemed no middle ground.

We were a Presence
    In the beautiful land,
A land we loved
    But never claimed. Now we are gone...

Peggy Bancroft

The Love I Feel For You

    The love I feel for you is
the love you will never
understand because deep
down in my heart, I feel
for your love and affection
to keep me moving in the
right direction.
    When I'm at home at night, I
feel I want to take you in
my arms and feel you with
all my love and charms.
    There will always come a
time when we can make a
moment of a dream come true
but just remember these last few words.
    Just knowing your
love is always there means
more than you will ever know.

Patricia Walker

A Symphony

We have a symphony to play.
The music is before us
but we have not practiced it.
And the world laughs.

The Master taps His baton.
He wants to direct
but no one listens.
And the world mocks.

We all have our parts
but we're trying to play it alone.
We all want a solo.
And the world ridicules.

We think we know how it should sound
but we have not yet played it.
We have not yet heard it.
And the world ignores.

We have a symphony to play.
A portrait of the Master,
a symphony of love.
And the world waits.

Larry Vosters

A Friend In You

One day I was lonely,
the next "sad and blue."
Until the day I began to smile,
was when I found a friend in you.
You gave me confidence,
and made me strong.
To finally be happy,
after being sad for so long.
Although my sadness is something,
that will never really go away.
At least it doesn't bother me,
every single day.
Because today I will not be lonely,
and tomorrow "sad or blue."
Ever since the day I began to smile,
The day I found "A friend in you."

Regina Lee Stout

The Wreck

Why did it happen?
The pain is now yours
Physical pain,
Mental grief.
The glass crystallizes
Metal like paper,
Fumes prevalent.
The vehicle creaks
Screams heard,
Pain felt.
The suffering surges
Eyesight blurry,
Visions of past.
The lighted tunnel,
Why did it happen?

Matthew Dillingham

Notes of Time

The door is closed
The past is done
Tucked away like dreams
Remembered only in murmurs
Each whisper cherished
Each piece linked to another
It is a symphony

The door is there
Each moment
a million thoughts
Each second a thousand choices
The present is but an instant
a single note

The door is open
Tomorrow is beckoning
A realm of endless prayers
A region yet untouched
but the paths are worn
It is the future
a song still to be heard

Maria Lee

Ordinary Man

How I will love you,
The person I am to meet.
For you I will care the strongest,
And forget the stereotyped elite.
Their depth is shallow,
While yours will be deep.
My eyes will look into yours the longest,
And capture your warmth from within.
My knight in shining armour
You will not be
For he has been,
Once, twice, thrice, maybe four;
An ordinary man you will be
And nothing more.

Sally Ezell-Daniel

Tidal Wave

Cement walls surround
the raging sea
of feelings unexpressed,
with only the smallest trace
of moisture beading on the outside.
We talk
and the walls slowly transform
into fluffy pink masses
of cotton candy...
melting
unable to keep their form
as the once confined tide
begins to trickle through
leaving a winding pink trail behind it.
The trickle builds to a roar
as the sea escapes
causing the ground to tremble
in time with my hands.

Kirsten Boye Herman

For the Love of a Child

For the love of a child,
  the rent is due.
For the love of a child,
  what can I do?
For the love of a child,
  I would stand in the rain.
For the love of a child,
  I would run in front of a train.
For the love of the child,
  I do what I can.
For the love of a child,
  some don't give a damn!
For the love of a child,
  we don't have time to play.
For the love of a child,
  put it off another day.
For the love of a child,
  what can be done,
  to make this world better for everyone?

Stacie Mertz

Together

The sun is on my face
The sand between my toes,
You are beside me
With no cares or woes.
Your hand in mine,
Mine in yours,
The love we share
Is deep in our souls.
So as we lay
Out in the sun,
We think about our future
Together as one.

Kimberly Tate

Song of the Earth

The mountains in their majesty
The sea in silent pageantry
Evoke an inner melody
That causes me to dream.

The sound of swelling tympani
From sea and rock in symphony
And lute of robin brings to me
The music of the spheres.

My soul is lost in wonder
As silently I ponder
On the mystic beauty under
Stars and sun of holy light.

Margaret D. De Yong

Hope

Though I have seen,
the many perils of life,
there is one,
who causes me to see good,
amidst Strife.

It is only through,
His tender love and care
that it is possible,
for me to love and share.
All those things,
that only the love of God,
can bring!

Michael D. Vogle

Untitled

A gust of wind, blows out from
  the sky
Brushing its hair back into the
  breeze
Gracefully racing through gardens
  of flowers
Frolicking until the very
  black of night
Through the sands and fields
  of flowers
When the cool air changes
  direction
The beautiful horse stops
  to look around
As it hears a loud, starting
  sound
Taking off into the darkness
The beautiful horse
Galloping with freedom.

Valerie Sings

The Drowning Child

The lake looked up in terror at
the sound of a crying baby's screams;
unable to save the baby's life, it
moans in anguish pain. How
could this be? It wonders silently
to itself as the child sank further
into its embrace. Then as if the
conductor stops the music suddenly,
silence fills the air. The Lake
grasp in horror as the thought
occurred, the sweet Laughter of this
child will be heard no more.

Rema Flowers

First Warm Day Of The Year

It is a lovely day outside
The sun is warm and shining.
Clouds are few and some abide
Yes, it is time for outside dining.

Grill is ready to be lit.
Meat prepared just right.
One will have time to sit,
Odors a wondrous delight.

Patio places are set.
An umbrella furnishes shade.
Soon food on the grill we'll get
Our appetites this day are made.

The taste of food in the fresh air
Just seems to be much better.
Thank you God for this affair
A day like this couldn't be better.

Mary Ellen Brown

Mental

In the house all alone
the light on but no one is home
locked away from it all
by myself I can have a ball
in the house in a room
you can assume
that I'm all alone in my head
I feel miserable and dead
no way in or out
that the way it will always be
without a single doubt

Tasha Nelson

My Prayer

God gave me grace to overcome,
The temptations of the day,
Help me to lend a hand,
To others on life's way.

Help me to be more patient,
As I live with my fellowman,
Help me to lend an ear,
That I may understand.

Open my eyes that I may see,
The weary and the downcast,
Then, dear God, open my heart,
That I may help with their task.

Help me to be a little kinder,
With those I meet today,
Guide my lips from unkind words,
In all I have to say.

Lord, let me be more humble,
As I live with friend and foe,
If you should call for me today,
Help me to be ready to go.

Lila Coats

Battle of the Mound

The Bear, Dragon, Stag, and Hawk,
Their spirits gleaming in their hearts,
Bestowing passion for a mission sought,
Sung in part by the winded Bards.

Tempers mount bellowing the song.
Shields raised to protect the soul,
Claymores arched, poised for long,
Straining, waiting, wanting the goal.

Morning stars shooting the heavens,
Wielding forth the mighty mace,
Battling back the Baron's seven,
Breaking the barrier of time and space.

Nay, they spy that mountain crest,
Never claiming what they sought,
Drinking from their gloom of rest,
Laying waste to all they fought.

Sailing North to lands of hymn,
Leaving behind the great gold mound,
Tasting glories that might have been,
Save the one that was not found.

Kathryn Saunders

The Bride of Christ

First comes happiness.
Then comes pain.
And sometimes I think,
I'll truly go insane.

But there is a divine plan.
That's comes from far above man.
That's not always easy.
For him to understand.

Take comfort in knowing.
That the hour is approaching.
That the glorious one will soon appear.
And the Bride will be joined with Jesus.
And all those that are dear.

Wayne J. Fulmer

Lesson From Hellen Keller

Perhaps if folks were blind
Then they could truly see;
For they would have to look around
To other parts of me.

Instead of looking outside
At the color of my skin
They'd have to go much deeper
To the qualities within.

This concept, if extended forth
Could make all people wise.
Instead of seeing handicaps,
Sex, faith or body size

We'd notice things more carefully
With more discerning mind.
Like is the person helpful?
Is he tolerant and kind?

We would then need rely on
What we feel within the heart.
For to perceive true beauty
People only need that part.

Karen Griner Smith

Falling Awake

It's raining golden sunshine
There beneath the trees
As the last of summer
Flutters to the ground.
I'm drenched in scarlet leaves
And Mother Nature's breeze -
Her gentle whisper
Now the only sound.
Inhaling crisp fall air
I quickly close my eyes
A mental picture
In my mind to take.
For the first time in a while
My soul begins to smile
As my sleepy spirit
Slowly starts to wake.

Peggy Pape

Untitled

I visit the depths of my conscience
There I see strangers and friends
The existence of mind over matter
The knowledge of means without ends
Expansion of truth's overwhelming
The degree of my love really shows
As for hate it's there in abundance
The extent that nobody knows
And the wheels of eternity's spinning
For a cause we know nothing about
The visual facts are before us
But the secret will never come out
And I float in hypnotic explosion
To places that I've never seen
Much like a thing we call Heaven
Or a paradise I'd never been
I slowly awake to awareness
And try to remember the past
But all I can see is a conscience
That's mine only mine to the last.

Larry Ramirez

Romancing A Theater

With the enrichment of fine arts
There is a play writer with a script
The auditorium relishes a heart
And there are balconies which to sit
The intelligent and physical acts
Where characters portray the mood
The embellishment of emotional facts
Where transformation of actors elude
Preview of performances on Broadway
Giving to the audience such grace
Rather enticed by Opera or a play
The theatre is a captivating place
But through my idea of mental image
The figmented romance of my vision
As to taste a softness of vintage
Came a phantasm inspired decision
The story unveils with great triumph
When the fantasy of emotions redeem
There only heard is the deep silence
And the lighting of an empty scene
Where an excellent performance found
Was to find the evening but a dream
The inspired audience comes around
While I romanced a theatre not seen

Yvonne Stetter

This Time Around

This time around
there is no pretense-
no image to project,
no persona to uphold;
just fighting hard to be
authentic and serene,
cause serenity
will keep me
from a heart attack.

This time around
I am honoring my fear
and the courage it takes
to risk
going out among strangers.

Marva C. Edwards

A Burden Called Love

Many times you have said,
  "These burdens are too rough";
But I have brought you through,
  and it has made you tough.
You have been as a ship,
  wading upon troubled waters;
But don't forget, my child,
  I can clam those raging waters;
And make thee the watchman,
  I have called thee to be;
The burdens that you go through,
  are because you love me.
Look not to the things here,
  but look to things above;
And the things that I give,
  because the burdens I give you are called
love.

Tina R. Dearing

Trophy Hunter

Death and decay;
they are companions to life
Few are the revelers in such
though they be many
Only one
worships and treasures it
For "His" vanity they are sought
and shot
Red are "His" hands
diseased are "His" thoughts
For some, the morbid is life
disease is their pallet
only naturally given
They are not sick to the soul
having no soul
But "He" builds his home
on their suffering and torment
"He" displays it for ego and sells it for gold
"He" is the only one that is dead.

Kevin Kirkpatrick

Parents

Parents are people we need.
They are fantastic people indeed.

"Do this. Do that." they say,
in almost any way.
You look, you try, you find.
You're getting a smack on your behind
But that is only when you're bad
and when they are really mad.

Parents are really fun
till the day is done.
That is the time I dread.
When I lie down my head.
I don't like it in anyway,
when I have to say
"Goodnight Mom and Dad"
until the next day I had.

I think parents are really fine
I thank all parents, especially mine.

Samantha Martin

"Moonbeam Dreams"

On midnights clear
They hold hands and stroll
O'er glistening beaches
To listen as the waves
Caress the shore
Seeking familiar treasures
In the sky
As they count stars and meteors
Wishing they could shanghai
A ship and sail away
To forget memories of a world
That exists no more
Yet they're still young and
Can start over
How and where they're
Just not sure
So they ask God to send them
Visions on moon beams
To guide them through a future
That seems very insecure

Linda D. Johnson

Untitled

I have no love for words
they stick to my tongue
like ticks on a dog
growing fat and lazy
I grow weak and crazy
trying to spit them out.
    If I cut off my tongue
    would I grow strong again?

Or would parasitic words
slaves to appetite
crawl up into my brain
and drive me insane
with the sound of smacking lips?
    I'll cut off my head
    the weight of a lifetime
    lifted from my shoulders,
    cut out my heart too -
    only my fingers left behind
    curled in pain
    like question marks.

Leonora B. Rianda

Grandma's Treasures

They pull my hair, they scratch my face,
They throw their things about the place.
They chase the dog and tease the cat.
They're out of this and into that.

They have a hundred fights a day
About the things with which they play
They bang the tables, walls and doors
And scatter debris on my floors.

Although they almost drive me mad
These precious things cannot be bad,
They're my pride, and pleasure too.
This girl age one, this boy, age two.

They've won my heart with winsome ways
And bring bright sunshine to my days.
The dimpled girl, and brown eyed boy
Have filled my world with greatest joy.

Of all the gifts one can possess,
Few give perfect happiness.
I thank the Lord for what he's done
To give these children to my son!

Mary Kimball

Untitled

She comes and goes
This friend of mine
only able to exist
in between

Time spent
together
is pure...
Refreshing as summer rain

Like the finest diamond
she radiates...
Drawing me in as the sirens
Once did the sailors so long ago...

But once I'm near she withdraws
like a snake...
leaving me only with the promise
of her presence...
Yet another day

Mykal Carns

Angels Among Us

"They are there but we can't see them,"
they watch us while we sleep,
they've been sent down to protect us,
"we may even pass them on the street."

"I've been told that they have wings,"
and wear a halo on their head,
but yet I've not to see them,
"that is just what I've heard said."

"In those times when we are in need,"
and a miracle occurs,
it may be that they were there,
"for in need we surely were,"

"In their hearts kindness you'll find,"
for that's the reason that they're here,
God trusted them to help us,
"to wipe away our tears."

"The truth is that they are real,"
and believe that you surely must,
for if look around you'll see.
there is angels all among us.

Natalie Thomas

Winter

They're coming down
They're coming down
Snowflakes are dancing all around

In the Street, in the Yard
Winter is now all about

Trees and Rooftops dressed in white
Soon there'll be a Snowman and his Bride

Mr. Frost did cast his spell
On the Creek and Pond as well

Town and Country changed it's scene
To Winter Wonderland supreme

Maria Blaha

Untitled

Tempt me! Look at me! Speak with
thine lips so luscious the words my
ears beg to hear. Indulge me with
thy kiss that will leave me with
desire to seek thee. Why do you
not look at me, I know your eyes
can see. Why are you so afraid that
thy breath will become one with mine?
Do not close down at the near touch
of my skin, for you know now long
yearning can become. I hear your
fantasy, I feel your caress, do not
try to hide, your desire is too
aware of my presence. It will stand
alone, waiting. Tempt me to look at
thee! Kiss me lusciously, long and
crave me. For my fantasy surrenders
to thee.

Karla Salvador

Dad

Listening to his old records,
thinking
of times in the past we shared.
Looking at pictures,
seeing him in my sister,
wondering
why did our father have to die?

Watching home movies,
remembering
when my father was alive.
"You would have liked your father."
My mother said.

Mother, you don't know
how much I am like him.

Kimberly Hendricks

My Mind Wonders

My mind wonders everyday,
thinking of what say.
Everything seems the same,
playing your head like a game.
Problems come and problems go,
day by day taking it slow.
Solutions never found seem lost
    in time,
like a soft wind blowing a beautiful
    chime.
Always there, just silently waiting,
while your mind sits desperately hating.
Knowing nothing is changing in your life,
cuts deep into your heart like
a bleeding knife.
So as my mind wonders, my heart bleeds,
praying to God, he'll fulfill my precious
needs.

Lyn Stroud

The Ingredients Of A Mother

Mother's are special
This you must understand
The blended ingredient
God did with His own hands

Flour He used
To enrich her soul
Sugar is her sweetness
That He mixed in the bowl

Butter was added
For the creamy taste
Of the love she shares
With a smile upon her face

Nothing can take the place of a mother
They are beautiful and nice
God's has specially seasoned them
With His own heavenly spice

Marlon Ray Hill

Mother's Care

In our grief when we cry
there's someone who says
there's no need to worry why
when our sighs are enough
for the world. She comes
with love better known as
mother care. For her love
there is no limit just a
ticket in which we all share

LaQuita Sanders

Only A Look

This look you give me,
Those eyes I thought were vacant,
Are now open windows to your soul.
A glimpse of pain in the glass,
Then the curtains are drawn.

I blink, and turn away.
I close my eyes,
And deny what I saw.
But eyes don't lie.

So I turn back,
And your eyes are as they are always.
Did I really see what I saw?
Or was the pain in your eyes
Only a reflection of the pain in my own?

Katherine Zane Fee

Blank

Mindless abandon
thoughts left to rot
never picked up
as yesterday trash
just ME
alone
watching YOU
walk away
as my brain
is raped
some more

Mario Mezzacappa

Voices

I carry with me voices of
    thousands and thousands
    gone before

I hurry to trace their words,
    feelings and emotions.

The time is set, the place is now
    if only I could do justice somehow

These loves, fears and dreads
race through my mind like soft
spindles of thread weaving the
cloth that none can ignore

Those voices of thousands and
thousands gone before.

Rose Radley

Train Whistle

From far away
through the dark still night
the loneliest sound in the world.
From the cars behind
it's a bugle blast
a triumphant message hurled.

To ride on a train
is to conquer space
while on level ground propelled
to another time
to another place
momentary worries quelled.

Marjorie Weichal

Nature

The brook runs serenely,
    through the trees,
While the leaves,
    make love with the breeze.

The mountains ascend,
    majestically to touch the sky,
And thunder clouds roll in
    to have their daily cry.

Nature's aromatic scent,
    fills the air.
While squirrels gather,
    nuts without a care.

The sun is setting,
    the animals have all retired.
Wouldn't it be nice to live,
    where only survival's required?

G. L. M. Szekely

Untitled

Finding life in sadness, falling
Through the weight of ponderous years
Lonesome, longing, stifled laughter
Bursts the soul with untold fear
Fragments at the feet of gladness.
Washed a shore by pounding rain
Silence now, the wind still rushes
Blowing free all joy and pain
Empty headed, empty handed
Nothing left to do or say
One more passive, watching, waiting
For the next new life or day.

Melania Lancy

You're My Everything

I wander by the river,
Throw pebbles in the stream.
Travel every highway.
Climb mountains in my dream.
The fragrance of the flowers,
Dances in the air.
How sweet are the moments,
When you are here

The sunshine in the morning,
Shines in your eyes.
The promise of the rainbow,
Paints up the skies
In summer or winter
Autumn or spring.
I want to be with you
You're my everything.

Verrol K. M. Ebanks

Taking Life for a Spin

Around and around you go,
The longer you stay on the faster you go,
At first your head begins to spin,
But naturally you fit right in,
When it's time for it to come to an end,
No matter how bad or good it's been
You don't want to stop
Whether your at the bottom or the top
Life is something borrowed
Giving it back brings such sorrow
Remember the joy of jumping in
And taking life for a spin.

Kathleen Haag

Time

Time is seconds
Time is minutes
Time is hours
Time is days
Time is things I must endure

Time is being born
Time is being young
Time is growing old
Time is all these things
Rolled into one

Time is you
Time is me
Time is moments spent together
Time is moments spent apart
But, most of all
Time is things we (endure) together

Kim E. Perry

I Wish...

I wish I knew the answer
to all life's ills and woes,
And I could bring a happy smile
to every friend and foe.
    Alas! I cannot do it
so I'll just go my way,
and watch what I am doing
every single day.

If one man makes a difference
then I must do my best,
while living, ever learning
so I will pass the test.
    I wish that I could tell you
which way for you to turn,
I wish ... but I can't tell you
you'll have to live and learn.

Louise Brooks Snyder

In Heaven

I have no words my children
To describe the beauty here
Such peace and love surrounds me
There's not a hint of fear

No one here feels heartaches
No one suffers or feels pain
No clouds are here to hide the sun
There's not a trace of rain

I do not regret my leaving
And I do not miss the earth
For I've seen the glory of my Saviour
And experienced New Birth

The only thing I long for
As I look upon Gods face
Is the day when all my family
In heaven I'll embrace

So my children when you think of me
Remember this one thing
I want for nothing - I feel no pain
And I am with the King

Marilyn Thisse

St. Patrick

You don't have to be "all Irish"
to enjoy 'St Patrick's Day'
although it helps a little
if you're Irish in some way.

And though you proudly wear the green
and a shamrock on your chest
the 'truly Irish' are plainly seen
for they're happier than the rest.

Here at dear ST. PATRICK's
although our kith or kin
may not have all been Irish
one wishes they had been.

For God saw fit to give us
a Patron Saint so dear
who deserves sincere thanks every day
and not just once a year!

Loretta M. Hanneman

Sometimes

Sometimes you must go through sorrow
    to find yourself again.
Sometimes you have to loose
    too learn how to win.

Sometimes you've got to hurt
    to find a way to heal.
Sometimes you must tear down
    in order to rebuild.

Sometimes you've got to fall
    to learn how to stand.
Sometimes you must reach out
    when you need a hand.

Sometimes you've got to cry
    to learn how to laugh.
Sometimes you must loose your way
    to get on the right path.

Sometimes you must go through matters
    which appear somewhat strange.
Sometimes you must go through a storm
    before things ever change.

Ronald Lampkin

My Son

To that child I had and love
To him give all my thought
Day and night without a doubt
In him I'll put my faith
And he should not know hate
For when he makes a mistake
He'll realize its ok!!!
For he is now a young adult, handsome
And a lot to give
And many years to live
Son don't forget what you learned
For the years come fast and many
Things turn, for wrong or right
Do all things you know best
With love and pleasure
Its not a test
I'll love you son
For what you are
Baby, child, teenager, young adult
And man, that is my son.

Veronica Buzo

Life's Fulfillment

Another year has almost gone
To join the ranks of others past.
The pace may change, but time goes on
Our lives are frail and cannot last.

The time will come when life must end,
We'll wonder where the years have went.
The only question for us then
Is "Were they very wisely spent"?

I cannot answer for the rest,
But as for me "I can't complain"
For though my life was not the best
I saw the sunshine more than rain.

So if the master calls my name
And from this earthly life I leave,
It will not bring me too much pain.
I feel I have no cause to grieve.

I have seen more joy than most.
My life is full, there's no remorse,
So as I part I'll drink a toast
To life's fulfillment, you, of course.

Robert F. Fischer

To My Love

I long to have you in my life,
To love and cherish as my wife,
All my treasures belong to you;
I give them all, though they are few.

I ask to see your smiling face
Under a virgin veil of lace.
I swear to be a faithful man,
To always love and hold your hand.

Through the park we will walk all day
Smelling the scents that come with May.
Flowers I pick to grace your hair,
I will place without great despair.

As the bright sun begins to dim,
Birds chirp gently on a tree limb.
This background scene accents the most
Beautiful woman, I must boast.

As we touch under the sunset,
I still recall the day we met.
Now days spent apart are but few
Because I will always love you.

Sandi Klein

Mike

Our brother
There'll be no other
He was always there
and seemed to care
He was chosen first
It seems the worst
He is here
some how, somewhere
So I'll remember the best
He is laid to rest
Our friend
  Our brother
There'll be no other

Peggy Barney

The Blessed Trinity

It clearly takes three parts
To make the Blessed Trinity
If a single part were missing
It plainly would not be.

If the Father had not sent His Son
To die for you and me.
The Holy Spirit would not have come
To make the Blessed Trinity.

For the Father is the Son
The Son is also He
The Holy Spirit within them
Making the Blessed Trinity.

It clearly takes the Father
And His Blessed Son
Along with the Holy Spirit
To make the Three In One

Now we have the Three In One
And it's so very plain to see
Not a single part is missing
From the Most Blessed Trinity.

Sharon Y. Federico

Untitled

I scream aloud, in silence.
To release the beast,
My silent childhood.
Nobody knows the pleasure
of such pain.
It feels so good.
It feels so good,
to be raped of my childhood.
Secret innocence,
Child's secret.
Innocenced.
Trusting, naive mind of pleasure.
Feels so good to be
Raped of innocence....
Raped of childhood.

Kristen Rose Dagenais

To Stand Before a Class

As a child I had my dream:
To stand before a class.
Yet, it began to fade
For no chance to see.
I never saw a glimmer of hope
And no need to tell.
Some would only smile and say
I can't believe it.

As time went on,
My dream became clearer:
To stand before a class.
For maybe there can be
A solution can be discovered.
A plan to put to work
With the help of self-esteem.

I only expected the young, but was sur-
prised.
There was young, old, and older for it had
only just begun.
Two years later I am on my way to a more
promising career.
Maybe three more years and I will have
achieved a dream: To stand before a class.

Teresa Lance

Never Lost

There are times I feel the need
To stretch my hands above my head,
To reach into the great beyond
Where lost hopes are found.
With open hands, heart and mind
A renewed charge I seek to find,
The spark Mother gave me at birth,
That binding force of love and truth.

I must expand to share with all,
To answer life's pulsing call.
Joy fills every chamber of my being
With lasting confidence in living.
Of my maker I am fully aware.
Life's force is everywhere.
Within myself I need to know
Live's force is an eternal flow.

LaRee Fleck

If I Had One Wish

If I had one wish
To take and explore
I'd wish me a wish
Like never before

It wouldn't be simple
Or too hard to grasp
But I'd wish the wish
That would always last

One not self-serving
For everyone to share
From it, we'd grow closer
And learn how to care

This wish would move mountains
all violence would cease
'Cause this wish that I have
is simply for PEACE.

Takaylla L. Gordon

Untitled

Through the trees on Monday morn
To the sky where dreams are born
Over rooftops far and wide
Always pausing on this ride
Riding raindrops in the air
Jumping moonbeams not with care
Eyes half lit from waking sleep
From a night of restless sheep
Over glen and gale and nook
Dreaming's better than a book.

Vincent Edward Frick

Almost Yesterday

What happened
   to yesterday
Did I close my eyes
   and I flew by me
Was I even aware of
   being in it
And why am I wondering
   about it now
Is it because today
   is almost
      another
         yesterday

Sylvia Gordon

Now

Today people snap.
Today guns fire.
Today fists hit flesh.
Tonight children cry themselves to
sleep. Tomorrow parents apologize,
it won't happen again they say. By
that night the children are crying again.
Today children turn around in the
rain. Tomorrow they can't because of
acid rain. Yesterday people said we
have to save the trees and recycle.
People today say they were paranoid.
Yesterday the police said crime went
down. Today we are going to our
friends funeral. If you don't give
a rose what it needs today it
will die tomorrow.

Susan E. Boyer

Temptation

Underlying thought — Reincarnation

If I had died four years ago
Today, I'd be three...
Waitin' for daddy to take me out
There's so much to see.

If I had died three years ago
Today, I'd be two...
Crawlin' and walkin' around
With so many things to do.

If I had died two years ago
Today, I'd be one...
Playin' with mommie and daddy
At times, they can be fun.

If I had died one year ago
Today, I'd be three-months old...
Suckin' on my momma's breast
Not knowin' care or cold.

If I should die today...?

Robert Chinn

She Walks with God

She walks with the clouds
today, in the most cheerful way.
Is she talking with Grandpa? Is
she getting her angel wings? When
will she be with us again, she's
watching over us, helping us
with whatever trouble were in.
We may cry, but she will know
that she is in our lives. She used
to follow in God's footsteps, and
now she walks beside him. She
was a wonderful woman, I
say, in the most unusual way.
But now I see that she will
be in heaven, and watching
over me. Oh, walking with
God how wonderful it must
be!

Kendra Salfer

The Gift

One day God called all the angels
Together
He wanted them to create a gift
for all on earth
A gift of beauty that would be for
all the people to see

The angels came up with one idea

They took the dark of night and
made eyes
From the clouds they made a soft
smooth skin
And from the brilliance of the stars
they made a smile

They put it all together and you
were born
You're that gift of beauty for all the
people to see
May your beauty be like artificial
flowers

   Ever lasting
Mario De Vincenzo

From a Confused Old Man

I'm too old to play games,
too dumb to play smart.
But, I know now for sure,
I still have a heart.

I stopped thinking about love,
and the games people play,
and, I thought it all,
had just went away.

I quit running around,
I never go out.
I thought I had forgotten,
what it's all about.

Then, I met this lady,
we became friends.
Now I find myself wondering,
just where friendship ends.

I now see her different,
she has made my life aglow,
I want to keep my friend,
but, I think she should know.

Ray Usher

The Bee

Into the lobby, flew a bee
Totally confused was she
She banged herself against the glass
Through which she could not pass
We watched her efforts in despair
For her welfare, we did care
For she could not comprehend
If offered help from a friend
If on my hand, she would alight
I feared that she may bite
Next morning Heather reported to me
The death of the brave Bumble Bee
If there is a bee's afterlife
May she find a garden fair
With space to fly freely there.

Lillian A. Spector

A Path Chosen

He walked when silent darkness stared
Treading to where no one had dared
Between the twisting pillars of fire
On moving rock where heat expire

On yet he marched into the thick
Of razor thorns and oozing stick
And blinked not he when faced a Snake
Dared He to strike, the fiends mistake

He held his prize a triumph there
The tossed the beast aside in air
Without delay he went again
Toward destiny where he'd amend

But just as soon resumed his trip
He came across another quip
Among the sucking sliver grass
An infant child he could not pass

So down he stooped to look at Him
And noticed how like a cherubim
He picked Him up—Then in light stood alone
"My child," said He, "Welcome, you're home."

Michael Turnbull

A Deadly Freedom

Like a see saw up and down
trials and tragedies all around
like a swing set back and forth
a lifetime of grief and remorse
could it be only me
fed up with the land of the free
America the beautiful
home of the brave
land of opportunity
violence filling graves
politics and hollywood
now one and the same
"should we fight"
"I think we should"
as if life were a game
to resort to violence for compliance
that idea must die
if a gun in hand makes a stronger man
the weakest of men am I.

Scott Schneider

Be Not Jealous

Be not jealous, my husband.
  Try hard to understand.
I've pledged my love to Another
  and given Him my hand.

Be not dismayed, my husband.
  I've given Him my heart.
I vowed to love Him forever;
  from Him I'll never depart.

Be not angry, my husband,
  when to His arms I flee.
'Tis there I learned of faithfulness,
  my dearest gift to thee.

Be reassured, my husband.
  My joy is being your wife.
I'll bring you honor and loyalty
  all the days of my life.

Be not jealous, my husband.
  Our lives are richly blessed.
Because His love I did embrace,
  I love you more — not less.

Linda Wright

A Puzzlement

If I ever get to Heaven,
Two things I want to know,
For I've thought in vain about them
As I've journeyed here below.
God has said, "In the beginning -,"
But before that time —what then -
For when God spoke the beginning,
Then, what came before, and when?
And, if when this earth is ended
It shall be the end of time,
Whatever could come after
Except a lot more time?
I've heard about eternity,
But that's too much for me;
If there's no end and no beginning
Just what would the future be?
I'm sure there is an answer,
Therefore, I can hardly wait.
Yes, as soon as I reach Heaven,
I want to get all these things straight.

Mary Leah Blake-Miller

Friendship

I lie awake this nite
unable to sleep.
My heart embracing your
kindred spirit.
Only so brief I see your face,
then gone again and
returned to my thoughts.
A happy but lonely
tear emerges, wiped away
by an unsettled content.
The flickering flame lights
my confusion.
The question so strong,
I sense the answer.
Even boundaries
of time cannot keep
the love of a true kindred spirit.

Nicole Peltier

Manatees

Out by the riverside,
Under a willow tree.
On a soft patch of grass,
Is where I want to be.

Sun shining brightly,
The water has a soft glow.
Manatees are playing,
They're putting on a show.

Ripples appear in the water,
Where they surface and dive.
So gentle, calm and peaceful,
Even more begin to arrive.

Now on the endangered list,
I'm glad I've been able to see.
An animal that one day,
May possibly cease to be.

Michelle L. Mientek Solocinski

Broughton

He is and was My man,
Until Dear God decided he belonged,
To his heaven from above,
How could it be said "I to me."
Where are days that were,
When he and I, did believe,
That we would achieve, all the dreams
That filled our hearts and love,
But now are gone to above eternity,
My soul just aches to feel a touch -
Hear his voice from there and here,
And have his spirit reach my daily
Wish and longing,
Today from land and sea, my thoughts,
Must remain is disbelief,
"How could this be."

Marie B. Williams

Losing

Where did they go?
Up and gone us the wind blows.

Not a word to anyone.
What has this world become?

Not an answer at the door;
What am I knocking for?

Not a light was turned on;
We had a strong bond.

Tire tracks in the drive;
I just started to cry.

No more friendly play,
I just don't know what to say.

Leaving me behind;
Our friendship was so kind.

I don't understand anymore
Why my heart is so sore.

As it slams in my face,
It's never an open and shut case.

Mary Hirschenberger

The Rolling Ocean

I am the rolling ocean,
Vast, green, and blue.
The sun glistens on my waters,
As it shines on you.

I am angry when a storm is near,
All the people swim in fear.
I am happy in the sun,
I love children having fun.

All the sharks, dolphins, and whales,
All the jellyfish, flounder, and snails,
They all swim in me
They all live in me.
I lap the beaches and the shores,
I am never, never ever bored.
There are boats, scattered around,
There are people on islands, homeward
bound.

I am the rolling ocean,
Vast, green and blue.
The sun glistens on my waters,
As it shines on you.

Maire O. Malley

Retirement

Stripped of reason to arise,
View the world with chalky eyes.
No more battles, no more fights
For power, money — sweet delights.

Tucked away with tapes and books,
Banned to quiet, leafy nooks.
No more talk of plans and schemes
Hatching plots for corporate dreams.

This the goal so long awaited?
Death of vital, pulsing life?
Give me back the rush and fury.
Give me back the noise and strife.

Though my muscles may be slower,
And my vision needs a guide,
Though I cough and wheeze a little,
I am still a lion inside.

Caged and comforted with pillows,
A Goliath bound in chains.
Put me in a final pasture
Where the ticker tape still reigns.

Marjorie Manders Smith

"The Commuter"

Standin' on the platform
Waitin' for the train,
Waitin' for that 'lectric horse
To take me home again.
Nothin' much to do here
Nothin' much at all,
'Cept read bizarre graffiti
Written wall to wall.

Can see my horse she's comin'
'Bout half mile down the track,
Lights gleamin' from her eyes
Determination she doesn't lack.
As my 'lectric horse gets closer
Her whistle sounds that familiar tune,
I climb aboard, I still feel bored,
But I know we'll be home soon.

Robert C. Korenic

Depending On Dad

"I'll take you later."
   Waiting.
"Quit bothering me!"
   Crying.
"What's your problem?!"
   Yelling.
"Leave me alone!"
   Screaming.
"Just one more."
   Drinking.
"I can drive myself."
   Crash!
He's okay.
He didn't hurt anyone.
   Physically.

Michelle Huguley

The Encounter

Collided with my inside,
Walking down the road of life

Crashed head-on into the reality
Of whom I was taught not to be...myself

Gathering the crumbled pieces
Of my soulless shell
I ran from me, scared to see
The honesty, of my being

Chased
By the deafening laughter
That followed my retreat
I blocked my ears — ran
Scared to be what I truly am...myself

Afraid of the storm, if I don't conform
So I remain the empty frame
For of myself I am ashamed...

And the berating laughter
Pursued my hollow carcass
As I turned...saw my inside
Beckoning me home

Novel-T

Time Passes By

My mother sits alone
Wandering if I'll ever come home
My father left her long ago
The grass has yet to be mowed

The house needs many repairs
Especially the hallway stairs
The light shines in the parlor at night
She sits staring at the walls
Hearing echoes of familiar calls

At night sitting in her rocking chair
She knits to pass the hours away
The house is infested with mice and rats
Not caring, but only for her cats

At midnight my mother is sound asleep
Not even to hear the slightest peep
The howling of the wind keeps the house
alive
Only until dawn when the clock strikes five

For this is the hour she will not rise
For the closing of her eyes
Life has passed

William D. Simpson

Owed to Women

Gentle creatures!
Warm, understanding, kind.
Blessed with features
wondrously designed
to comfort man.
   And, by the creator gifted
   with the miracle of motherhood.
   With love by nature graced
   for all things young,
   the weak, the unembraced.
   With attributes so perfectly
   befitting man's society,
   it's true, that you
   have become, unwittingly,
   the victims of your virtues.

Thomas William Curran

Gaze of a Winter's Dawn

Horizon of gold
Warms blistering cold
Light voids dark
The doubtful one love does embark
Crystals of ice
She melts to entice
Out leaks the salt
Of hope held in the vault
Tree dressed in white
Stands tall with the light
Decorated by her life
They live together as man and wife
A rose near by
Blooms in her sunrise
Cold winds brush through
Singing a song of joy to view
The cloudless skies
Are seen from her sunrise
Out flies the jay
Signaling the Dawn of a new day

Richard S. Fitzpatrick

Wind Dancer

They say her soul
Was from the winds
Her eyes were from
The waters
Her hair was spun
From strands of gold
She was the chiefs daughter
And when you see the fields
A moving from the winds
Like waves a swaying
To and fro
'Tis her spirit still
A searching for white buffalo
She is the spirit of the kin
Of the souls from way back when
The west was wild and full of game
When the land was still untamed

Mable Jean Johnson

"My Daughter"

The little hand she placed in mine
was full of love and faith divine
"come walk with me", she softly said
"don't wash the dishes, make the bed"
and so we walked
the things we saw
My child and I were filled with awe
a robin's nest
a new born rose
a puppy with a turned-up nose
a happy toad
a painted sun
I soon forgot my work undone
when we returned our voices
sang of all the beauty
God proclaims
in Nature and
in all we do
   Ask a child to walk with you.

Kathleen T. Cheatham

Past... Present... and Future (Love)

The beginning of our Love
was so divine... my heart
was soaring on cloud nine.
As months went by, our
Love grew strong... with you
I felt my heart belonged.
Now we've been steady over
a year... I want you to
know my Loves still dear.
We will be married some
coming May... I want
you to feel on that special
day. Not only is my Love
deeply true... But yes my
dear I'm still in Love
with you.

Susan Shapley

The Old Oak Tree

The old oak tree in our front yard
was such a sight to see.

If only it's rustling leaves could talk
they would tell you about me.

Of how it sheltered me as a child
when I would romp and play.

It kept the sun from kissing me
I'll never forget those days.

It was there I hoped and there I dreamed
as I lay in the grass beneath it.

I'd gaze at the moon and wish on a star
as it's branches waved and fanned me.

I always said some prayers right there
and knew that God was listening.

My childhood friends and family too
I've seen them all around it.

The old oak tree has been cut down
how very sad you see.

I cherish the memory of all we shared
that beautiful tree and me.

Patricia McClure

That Which Remains

He shattered my porcelain mask,
watched it fall,
and scatter
across clean tiles in broken time,
allowing me to see with unlocked eyes,

He sucked the fire out
of my hardened heart,
left me with a transparent head
and empty glass bottles.

He stole myself from me,
licked my marmalade soul,
and smiled.
As I felt the weight of my emptiness,
The cold of being see-through,
My insides disgorged,
My veil ripped away,
as I felt the remains of my evaporation,
I smiled,
knowing I had nothing left to feel the ache.

Stephanie Lee

Autumn's Lady

Tranquil lake amid the pines,
Waters cool and deep,
Silence rims your silvan shores
That soon in winter sleep.
Tranquil lake aflame with color
Dropped from autumn's nest,
Shadows steal across your waves
And presage coming rest.
Tranquil lake caressed by wind
Ripples stir your face.
Peaceful is your placid smile
That softly bears a trace
Of woman's constant grace.

Robert Oliver Shipman

Sometimes

We all have troubles
We all have pain
But if we try a little harder
We all will gain

We all are down sometimes
We all may cry
But we'll succeed in life
If we give it just one more try

If we just work together
And make it right
We'll all be positive
And see things in a different light

Sometimes you're down
Sometimes you're not
Sometimes things hit you
Right on the spot

Always be happy
Never be sad
'Cause in the end
You'll turn out glad

Sean Harrington

summer lightning

though no word's spoken —
we are apart —
we cannot share a life, we two,
yet this i know
you know it, too:
you have my heart
and yours i keep
though you are far and fast asleep
i know it, feel it, evermore
it's grown into me
knowledge felt
like summer lightning
shows a storm
to blind men
stirring in their sleep
so, dear love, if you blindly stir
and wake to think of me this night
lie quietly and know and feel
our summer lightning
yet may strike

marci l. pinkard

Pure Love

As God grants us each day on earth
We carry out his plan
For even before our very birth
His blood was on our hands

For as we sin and all men do
His son has died for me and you
To cleanse us of the wrong we've done
And put our name among his son

So when you hear salvation's plan
The time for you is now at hand
Ask him now into your heart
Never more from you to part

Rejoice the angels up above
As you've accepted God's pure love
Your life to never be the same
As Jesus Christ writes down your name

Tom Roberson

The Other World

With a loud cry we came upon this earth
We cry for life of fate and myth
Gently we were fed and loved since birth
But a violent reality we must face with
We have been earth bond ever since
Longing for a different world in space
With a broad smile we left the earth
We are children of everlasting faith
Softly we soared into the High Heaven
With God we dwelt in a peaceful Haven
It is the other world we dreamed
It is the secret Eden we pursued
Birth and rebirth merged into one
This and other world also became one

Micah W. Leo

"Feelings"

Love is a special feeling
we have for a certain person.
Whether it be family or a
dear friend.
This feeling comes from the
heart-
There are many different kinds
of love.
We feel and share in our
lifetime.
All special and memorable in
their own way.
Two hearts that share one
love, one life will always know
true joy.

Virginia Raymond

Frustration

The robin came
to herald the spring
and catch the early worm.
With rosy vest
and suit of brown,
his cheery songs to sing.

On leafless bough
he sits today
with ruffled feathers cold.
From baleful eye,
the early worm
lies safe beneath the snow.

Philenese Slaughter

Walls

We all have walls we've built inside
We keep our feelings there
So we can hide
Keeping pain and love blocked from view
Hurt can't get in
Love won't shine through

Like countries divided
Walls must come down
So love is shared and spread around
The peace that brings
We need to live
Feeling love helps us to give
That sense of sharing
Makes us whole
So we can reach our inner goals.

Richard H. Parson

Joy Cometh in the Morning

Death is a final thing
We mortals seem to feel,
We often fail to realize
That it is only relative

Take heed- Joy cometh in the morning!

Weep only for a little while
Some day we will meet again
Death is not the end
But, the door to better things

Remember - Joy cometh in the morning

I know that you will weep and mourn
But, only spend a little while
I am where I have always strived to be
I am finally, truly God's Child!

Thank God - Joy cometh in the morning!!

You should really be happy for me
I have truly made it through
I will be waiting somewhere up in Glory
Waiting for each one of you!!

Hallelujah!! Joy cometh in the morning

Lois King

God Blesses Through Special People

God blesses us in special ways
We never know when it will be,
Just like the day when God used you
To send special joy upon me.

I will never forget that day
When with tears you did touch my heart,
God has brought us both together
A friendship that day He did start.

We never know whose life we'll touch
Or when God will bless our life,
He promised to never leave us
And give strength in our daily strife.

Thank you God for sending a friend
Give Jennifer blessings each day,
Lead her always with your power
As you guide her upon her way.

Walk through life with a special goal
One God gives to everyone,
Shine with the glory of Jesus
Our dear Savior and God the Son.

Royce E. Leonardson

Someone

Through eyes,
We see today and tomorrow
With friends,
We live through joy and sorrow

What would this world be,
with no one to share,
our feelings so deep,
with someone who cares

For me there are few,
who give me such joy
To lesson my pains,
To fill my life's void

When someone this special
takes a part in your life
Be thankful and always be true
As I do each day I'm so warmly reminded,
The someone in my life is you...

Ren Daellenbach

Reunion

Cotton candy memories
weave cobwebs through my mind
As visions of our yesteryears
now surface and unwind
Some make us laugh,
some bring a tear, but,
all are ours to keep
And we must face the
seeds we've sown and
brave the crops they reap
Some of us have
touched the wings of eagles
as they soar
While some have faced
the lion and braved
his chilling roar
Now echoes sound from
two-score gone reclaiming rank again
Reminding us the years
command from what we've placed therein

Vickie M. Duckworth

"Willow"

Willow, willow, why are you
weeping? Your branches always
hang so low. Is it because you
long for springs soft breeze
and gentle rain? Or is it
because you long for winters
snow and glossy white? Willow,
willow, why are you weeping?
Your branches always hang so low.

Susan R. Cramm

Spanish Colonial Revival -

When We Return

"When we return to our ancient land
That we knew not here.
And speak of all things,
spoken briefly here.
We will walk holding children
By their hand, and listen
To their voices, and live
The life we lost
Here."

R. Elisabeth Swayne

Canis Lupus

And here's a health to these
    well-met fellows; arrayed in
    ballistic nylon and angst.
I never met Catullus, but tarried
    in the wilderness waiting for
    the echoes of our brokers'
    rhetoric to bounce off the
    marble.

Did you hear something out there?
When we started out nobody could
understand each other - the accents
were that bad! Now we all
sound the same...I read once
wolves howl to communicate
Only humans like to hear themselves
talk.

"And Carthage must be destroyed"
Swear to God I heard something
    out there...

Matthew Barker

My Soul Reached Out for More

Through the mortal window
Went my screaming feet
Into mortal darkness
My head kept up the beat
And as I walked on further
I saw the living door
That leaped out to the future
As my soul reached out for more
So further on I journeyed
Grasping for the handle
Of the door to everlasting life
Surrounded by twelve candles
My hand did touch my heart
To find the eternal light
As one candle it did blow out
Leaving me in fright
As it was the candle
To light beyond the door
So I could see forever
As my soul reached out for more.

Tom Penaskovic

To Ellen

For fifty-one years
We've shared a goal
We've given all -
Which took its toll.
We tried to rise
Above the flow
Of life we saw
As down-below.

But then we jumped into the stream.
The current took us to things unseen.
We lived to the hilt-took time to play -
And savored life in every way-

I'm proud of us
And what we've done
I'm proudest now
Of what we've won.

Marilyn D. O'Neill

"Forgiven"

At the cross
What a cost
To be forgiven.

Blood shed
Jesus bled
To be forgiven.

Lord, I cried
Not denied
To be forgiven.

Sins of the past
Gone at last
Now forgiven.

What a cost
To save the lost
Forever forgiven.

His life He gave
For all to be saved
All sins, FORGIVEN!

Madene L. Keefer

Retirement: What It Means To Me

Retirement is here
What does it mean —
A time to reflect
And collect a dream

A backward glance into the past
To view the work now done -
A look into the present
And feel a victory won

Another mile stone passed in life
The rocky road smoothes out -
The challenge has been met
And now, there's very little doubt

Work must continue even though
A slower page is set -
There's still move time to give of self.
Until the need is met.

Retirement then is slowing down.
And living from day to day -
To capture all the little things
One missed along the way.

Rita Marie Cloyd

Imagination Or Reality

Close your eyes so very tightly
what does your imagination see
a rainbow, spots, or a fantasy land
or maybe just all three

Now open your eyes slowly
think about what you saw
maybe it just wasn't your imagination
but reality is all
maybe this means your imagination
holds your true destiny
so close your eyes tightly
and next time think about what you see

Rebecca Smith

Death. Death Who?

Who are you death
what enables you
to clasp your hands
around life's candle
burning bright.
Who allows you to take
the light.
What gives you the right
to take a mother
in the night
and leave the children
crying and alone
wailing with their dreadful drone.
When will you be satisfied
when everyone
has cried
or
died.

William Evans

Black and White

Great Great Grampa,
What have you done,
You fought a war, you won
From the north,
You were white.
For all of mankind,
You gave your life.
You helped pave the highway
to freedom for all.
For your country,
you had to fall.
You faced your cousin,
He shot you dead.
Yes, you won the cause
You led.
On the T.V.
You were Black and White.
You turned to color.
Never knew you were white.

Mark Edward Mondroski

Parents

It's very easy to see
what those birds mean to me
In their perspiration
I have found much inspiration.

They protect their young at night
With a shriek to cause some fright
No matter what their plight
Those birds, will put up a fight.

In their endurance to the mark,
Those birds showed quite a spark.
Birds have not just begun
To show us how to protect our young.

Their chicks they do lick,
As the clock doth tick.
The time passes by,
Without relief or even a sigh.

Birds just live to be,
A safeguard, don't you see.
They work hard to feed their young today
So that their chicks can play and play.

Michael Alexander

Architect

Architect, architect,
What will you build next?
What were you really feeling,
When you painted the ceiling?
So high above the ground,
Did you ever see anything when
You looked around?

After all your work is done,
Do you drive by your finished
Building for fun?
It must always be a great
Feeling for you to know that
The building may still be
Standing when you go.

Robert Hoover

Leaves at Night

Listen late at night
When all is still
To the sound of
    leaves falling.
Lonely, by themselves,
    before the sun
Can light their golden
    flame one more time.
People die lonely too
    in the still of the night
With no one to say goodbye
Before the morning sun
    could show
They were the light of
    someone's life.

Mary Eileen Grutza

My Prayer

I pray Dear Lord that
when I die you'll let
my paint the butterflies.
You'll send them out at
night all white and
arabesque, I promise to
stay within the lines,
I'll do my very best.
When the mornings
blush is dew and the
suns radiance is cast
anew, the butterflies
with their gossamer wings,
amongst them their mighty
king, the Monarch with
the most vibrant shades and
hues will display the
Lords grand view.

Ruthellen Hallahan

Contradiction

Lovers beware.
The night is ending.
Lovers beware.
The day is coming.
The day bares all that is ugly.
Lovers rejoice in the night.
The night harbors all that is precious.
Lovers beware.
The night is coming.
Lovers beware.
The day is ending.

Michael Alpha

Remember the Horses

Remember the horses, he said. Remember the horses.
Sometimes I forget. I get too caught up in life wondering what it brings.
And then, I remember the horses, a young boy's promise to his grandfather.
A young boy's dreams remembered, never forgotten.
Remember the horses, he told me. Remember the horses.
Six beautiful white horses he said someday he would buy.
I thought someday sometimes never never comes, then I remember the horses and think
Maybe, the horses aren't for sale. The horses were a young boy's promise, a dream.
The purest kind of dream - unselfish, for they were to be a gift.
What he doesn't know is that they have already become a gift - the gift of a dream.
Remember the horses, he said. Remember the horses.
The promise has been fulfilled - no the horses aren't here.
But they are with us, in our dreams, waiting to become real.
For you see, as long as we remember them and pass the dream along, they are alive
Alive for the grandfather, the young boy, and all of us.
So keep dreaming and keep remembering. will become reality.
For you see, dreams are made of the best and most beautiful things in life.
And, if you try hard enough, you can grab the reins and ride your dreams.

Elizabeth Ann Edwards

Baby Jim

Dear sweet little baby Jim, Oh how we all loved him.
Tho only here for just awhile, never will forget that precious smile.
Born in April on a warm spring day, only to lose him in the month of May.
To be able to hold and love him so, without any warning have to let him go.
Holding him close was such a treat, with eyes so big, a smile so sweet.
Everything about him filled you with joy, what a special little baby, what a cute little boy.
How God chooses which one he takes, hard to accept the decisions He makes.
Especially when their taken so small, hardly enough time to know them at all.
My heart goes out to my little brother, he loved baby Jim above all other.
For him the pain and heartache will lie, it was his little baby who had to die.
You rock-a-bye baby at the end of the day, not knowing God's coming to take him away.
Morning is here, how we'll all weep, for he left our lives when he feel asleep.
But life goes on and memories will last, of that sweet innocent baby now in the past.
So we ask you God to hold Jim dear, for our arms are unable to hold him near.

Catherine Gass

What's Beautiful To Me

There are cold wars, culture wars, race wars all around,
    not only in metropolitan cities but also in country towns.
We are bombarded with negativity and a whole lot of mess. Why not
    think of the beauty around us and give positive thoughts a chance.

The golden sun rising in the early morn. The cries of a newborn baby
    just being born.
The dryness of the desert and the dust drought plains. The rolling
    hills and valleys low the liquid sunshine we call rain.

The brilliant colors of the flowers, the extraction of pollen by the
    bees. The animals in their fur coats, green grass and shady trees.
God's nature and all its wonder is so beautiful to me.

The pillowy, fluffy, white clouds in a sky so blue. The night with
    twinkling stars and a full moon for lovers true. The snow capped
Covered mountains, the wetness of the dew all of this for the
    enjoyment of me and you.

No matter who you are, or what you possess you see. It's what inside
    the heart that counts, there is no doubt, sharing, caring, loving
Of all God's glory that's so beautiful to me.

E. Chapman

Life With Death

I came into the Valley,
Unknowing,
the crack of bullets,
the color of life expended;
the anguished song,
of mothers mourning.

I departed the Valley,
Humbled,
by the pain of friends lost,
by their fragile heartbeat;
Resigned to the Paradox,
of life, precious yet cheap.

Robert T. Jensen

In A Dream

In a dream
there was solid ground
beneath me
and I knew I would never
fall again.
In a dream
the girl in the mirror would
protect me
rescue me from myself
take me
far away until I become
someone else.

Virginia Kroger

"Witness"

Witness the witness taking
The witness stand now
Your a witness, what does
it take to be a witness,
To be some place at the right
time. To see the right thing,
do you remember what you
saw yesterday, if you do
Then you may be a witness,
But if you forgot then
your a bad witness.

Michele Schafer

Symbols

A crystal tear
    the ultimate symbol,
So pure and clear,
    Thoughts of that tear
falling from the eyes
    reflections of what once was.
Thoughts of what was had.
    Imagine that tear
frozen in time.
    Think of that lone tear
as the ultimate symbol
    of what was there.

Tom Riser

A Mothers Love

A mothers love is so very strong
like a river, it runs deep, forever, and long.
She cries the tears of joy.
when she holds her baby girl or boy
She cries when it takes its first step.
in her heart, that memory is forever kept.
A mothers love is so very strong
She sings to you a comforting song
She's there to tuck you in at night
In her eyes your the most beautiful sight
She's always there to chase away any fear
She's always there to let you know she's always near
A mothers love is so very strong
In her heart you'll always belong
No matter what you do
A mothers love is forever true.

Michelle Sanders

Forever Beside You

I chose long ago to be with you,
but everyday I make that choice -
when faced with decisions that matter,
being with you is the one I treasure most.

You are so much a part of me,
it seems like I'm beside myself.
To be with you forever,
is where I want to be.

Some people search their whole life long,
to find their place in this world,
but I found mine early on,
forever beside you.

The world may seem like a very small place,
when compared with the love I have for you,
but in the heavens,
    the world still has its space,

    And now we do too.

Donovan Arch Montierth

I Ask You, Why Him?

Why am I in love with someone that will never be mine?
Why do my emotions run wild every-time I think of him?
Like a child, I write his name every-where, time after time.
Why do I give all of myself, only to end-up out on a limb?
Should I trust him?
I feel something dying, I know he is lying.
But yet, I commit myself to Mister slim.
My heart, body and soul, are crying.
I'm like a tied up slave, being stabbed with a knife.
Why do I only want to share my life with him?
He's not my husband, nor I his wife.
My candle is burning bright, but it's starting to become dim.
For a man and woman there stands a strong and passionate
affection.
Why is his love going in the wrong direction?
Lord, is this love? or am I INSANE?
Why does his heart drive down the wrong lane?
Why doesn't he turn around?
He was to make a {right}, but instead he {left} me.
Know who's looking like the clown?

Lillian Baldwin

Our So Called Rights!

Freedom of speech, it's our right!
What we hear, what we say,
What we wear, why do you care?

Why can't I a "person" of 16,
go to see a movie, listen to music,
or even take a drink?

Who are you to tell me what I can
and can't do? Or what I can and cannot say?

Teachers, parents, people everywhere
tell us what to hear, or say, or play.
We have rights, too!

Just because were 15, 16, 17 doesn't mean
we don't care, share, or stare
when things aren't right

Why can't they see
we're humans, too?

P. A. Stinson

This Is Love

It was meant to be
Especially when love holds the key
And realizing what was found
Lets one know it will always be around

When love tends of cease for even a day
The heart wonders astray
And one just can't deal
With that which isn't real

Therefore, it can't be wrong
To possess such feelings of which love is strong
How great for the heart
To have to never be apart

And while back together
It's going to be forever
Cause to leave once more
Would only make life a bore

So love has returned
And shall never be burned
These words are to stick
For there will exist no more conflicts

Rita R. Callahan

Love And Trust

Love is what you know is real
Trust is what you've found in someone
Love is what you feel with your heart
Trust is what your heart tells you
Love is what you feel with every part of your body
Trust is what you feel when you're around him
Love is like a passion that runs deep in your soul
Trust is more valuable than pure gold
Love is what every person should have
Trust is what every person should get
Love is something that can't be bottled
Trust is something that can't be taken for granted
Love is something that makes our hearts grow
Trust is something that grow's very slow
Love is something that should be expressed
Trust is something that needs to be known
Love is something that can't be hidden
Trust is something that should come from within
Love is something that should be trusted
Trust is something that will turn into love, Trusted love....

Della Clouse

Aliens

As I sit here thinking of cattle,
aliens cross my mind preparing for battle.
Missiles shoot here missiles shoot there,
not one of these aliens willing to care.
Destroying the universe bit by bit,
and none of these aliens give a #@*!

Mark D. Beveridge

Join My Now

Come join me in the gladness of my now!
Why smother now with fear and past despair?
The past does leave its mark for us to learn
A better way to know to safely care.

Come join me in the heaven of my now!
Why threaten now with ire of moments gone?
Each task we face has momentary worth,
Forgotten when the work is quickly done.

Come join me in the feeling of my now!
Why color now with shades of darkened gloom?
Paint bright the final outcome of your dreams,
Give time a chance to let its flower bloom.

Come join me in the sadness of my now!
Why pamper now with time enough to share?
The future has its mystery to give
To all who dare to take the chance to care.

Come join me in the future of our now!
Invest your now with love and faith of heart.
Joy also leaves a memory trail of smiles
To comfort you when happiness would part.

Carol L. Thompson

From Spirit

From spirit to a tangible being am I?
To return to free form someday by and by;
For into the clouds I stare and sight —
God's up there and He's the reason why.

Helen Marie Brooks

LIFE

THE TREE OF LIFE IS EVERLASTING
SEEDS MAY FALL TO THE SEA OF GREEN
SHELTERED BY THE TENDER BLADES
FOREVER REPRODUCING LIFE

OTHERS FALL BUT NEVER RISE
FALLING ON THE SHADY SIDE
ON EARTH REFUSING TO PRODUCE A BUD
UNABLE TO SEE THE LIGHT

THE TREE OF LIFE IS TORN
BETWEEN THE DARKNESS AND THE LIGHT
UNABLE TO CONCLUDE OR CHOOSE
WHICH IS MORALLY RIGHT

AND IN ALL THE FURY
THE TREE OF LIFE IS STRUCK
BY A BOLT OF INDECISION
AND IT WITHERS TO THE GROUND

THE DARKNESS DID NOT FLOURISH
NOR WAS IT ENLIGHTENED WITH HOPE
AND THE LIGHT SIDE LIVES IN DENIAL
THAT THE DARK SIDE EVEN EXISTS

Melissa Hilgeman

Inside or Out

Are they looking inside or out?
All the faces looking through glass, most
are smiling, some are not, and a few have
silly ways of looking at you.

Are they looking inside or out?
No one moves or utters a sound, but some
can make you smile or laugh, and few can
make you cry, either happy tears or sad.

Are they looking inside or out?
You look at them and even talk to them, but
as though spell-bound the view stays the same.

Are they looking inside or out?
Their friends, and their family, their pets you
adore, with memories behind frames for you to
explore.
Are you looking inside or out?

Jackie Haus

The Lament Of A Soldier

"One man's glory is another's shame,"
Was the phrase that rang through his head;
"One man's courage is another's pain,"
But the brave man's soul is dead.

He charged forth like a bolt of bright light;
His eternal mistake was done.
The killed mortal now clearly calls out,
"For whom was this battle won?"

The mortal is now dead in the grave,
And his oppressor wonders, "why?
I did not know this unlucky man,"
And he turns his face to the sky.

War! What a mad and cursed ordeal!
One man loses his soul and dies.
The other? His heart is frozen stone;
He utters lamentable cries.

"One man's glory is another's shame,"
Was the phrase that rang through his head;
"One man's courage is another's pain,"
But the brave man's soul is dead.

Lindsay La Mancha

The Farmer Of Wisdom

The warm sun had tanned his hands dark.
They were tired from all the work they had done.
He had worked hard
   every day beneath the sky above,
And each crop he planted
   had received his love.
He cared for everyone and everything,
It seems his good will
   never ceased to be done.
He had gained the respect
   of his fellowman,
   and had a distinct understanding
      with his land.
And when the time came
   for his last breath of life,
He knew he had not been forsaken.
His eyes went shut
   with a look of rest,
      and God took his hand
For he had done his best.

S. A. Segraves

Heaven

I found myself on a street of gold
Where even the air was seen
It was big white fluffy clouds
And everything was clean

At the end of a path there stood a throne
My Lord was seated there
Before him lay the book of life
He handled it with care

There were many many chapters
But soon he found my page
It did not have a number
Nor did it list my age

It did not state my color
It only gave my name
And it was not important
That I'd achieved no fame

I had no wings and wore no crown
But in my heart I had a gem
I knew why my name was there
'Cause I believed in Him
Mary Still Webb

Part III

As I lie here waiting for you to dry
   Your body off
I can only pray that you will come with
   Me. And when I become
A ball of vulnerability that you
   Will let me whimper in your arms.
Glenda Gracia

Abused No More

Rolling rage
richly ripening
resting rigidly
rarely roped.
rendezvousing.
realigning reality.
residing rarefied rage
untethered in man unkind
unwavering in its intensity
unresolved in its etiology
unwilling in its relentlessness
undulating
uprootedness.
un-healed.
unwanted relationship:
unkempt marriage.
Rolling Rage
Not Mine.
Lethal.

Victoria Menzies

On Viewing Ancient

Ruins at Midnight

Here in this world of night
Their marble columns taper a moon path
Somber halls with fine illusion
lead enticingly on to nowhere,
You may step in shadows
Or persist your length in silver time
Beyond all questioning doors
The hood of space folds,
obliterates.

Madeline Waldron

Through Someone Else's Eyes

It's hard to see through his own eyes
It's only he who tries and tries

And days are lost and none are found
Amongst the perfect of renowned

We just go on and see through eyes
of those so perfect-tell no lies-

The thinking moving living done
It says so much but no one's won

Days go by and days get lost
Night time turns from warmth to frost
Seasons change and time goes on-
Once again-no one's won

Sometimes life is such a game
And nowhere found is all the fame

Except for he who tries and tries
to see through someone else's eyes
Sherry L. Musil

My Mother The Hero

My hero is my mother,
so strong and brave.
May my God bless her soul,
as she rest in her grave.

I love my mother,
though we've never really met
But her memory,
I always have kept.

You see,
if it weren't for me,
She would still be here,
ever so near.

Cancer took my mother,
I can blame it on no other.
She could of had chemotherapy
but that wasn't to be.
She had to carry what she wanted more.
And that she did when she bore,
a tiny baby girl.

Heather Holm

The Birth

Fumble, tumble
on the ground.
What is walking?
What is sound?

His fingers jelly,
his legs rubber bands.
What are fingers?
What are hands?

His hair stringy,
all in his mouth.
What is North?
What is South?

Water falls down,
heavy rain.
What is pleasure?
What is pain?

Colors, objects,
bright and nice.
What am I?
What is life?

Dawn T. Ishizaki

All Alone

You don't think about it
till it happens
Close to home,
You think of being, alone
You realize you need your
Friends, you need you family
You don't wont to be left, alone

Short periods of time are
fine to be alone
but you need people
and if they leave you
you are left, alone

You lose you soul
You have lost you spirit
Your heart-cruised
You are left, alone

You cry, you weep, you
Are in sorrow, you lost your
life, you are left, -
all alone
Jennifer Ann Hyde

Rose, My Love

She sits alone,
   swaying in the cool breeze
   of the blue moon's glow

   chilled and closed
   yearning for His touch.

He slowly comes,
   His gentle, soft warm hands
   beckon her in all her elegance

   to burst open and expose
   her beauty layer by layer.

She lays in splendor.
Denise M. Weir

Youthful Reality

You read it in the newspapers
So devastating and true,
It's everywhere - senseless murder
It always presents itself to you,
They are our youth, our future
Caught up in so much crime,
We need to guide them straight
So they don't end up doing time,
They're not just hanging out
They are forced to be in gang's.
All it does is destroy their souls
And cause their family pains.
Come on young Americans
This country's here for you,
So take control for what it is
That you have chosen to do,
Make America livable,
For generations to come,
Instill those family values
Make it safe for all, not some.

Rosette Marturana-Johnson

"Being Born"

I'm sure we were meant to be
with each other before we met,

And that some measure
of what I am and want to be
will come from you.

You gave me honesty
I gave you laughter

You gave me humility
I gave you strength.

You gave me courage
I gave you hope.

We decided to take a risk,
a chance, a gamble.

We hitched a ride home
on the same comet,

but we touched earth and separate times.
And like electricity giving up sparks,
we grew in character until we approach
being born.

Tony Lashea

Indian Girl

Early on a September morn
Her Mother ask, "Please pick the corn."
She did as bid, but with a sigh,
The corn stood nigh — Six feet high.

The corn was spread out on the ground,
A crib was built and hung up high,
A shelter made to keep it dry,
The husks were strewn upon the floor,
The husk no good any more.

An Indian girl picked up a husk. She
Formed a doll with silks for hair.
A beaded dress for her to wear,
Tiny moccasins for her feet, her little
Doll almost complete.

Only eyes upon her face —
Least bad luck on her befall,
If she painted a face
Upon her doll.

Pat Flowers

The Black Ribbon

He wore it in memory,
He wore it in love.
I hated it for the memories,
I hated it for the lost love.
He wore it in respect,
He wore it in honor.
I dreamed of it.
I dreamed I hated it.
I dreamed I loved it.
Then it was gone
And I wanted it back.

Jennifer Philips Jordan

I Am....

I am a snowflake
I wonder when I will fall
I hear the children calling out to me
I see the ground but just can't reach it
I want to fall but I don't know how
I am a snowflake

I pretend to be the most beautiful even though
I know there are others as beautiful as I
I feel the wind arise to carry me down to earth
I touch the hearts of children
I worry I won't be there
I cry out to those that never get to see me
I am a snowflake

I understand that it may not be time
I say please don't let flowers bloom
I dream of a place were snow will never stop
I try to wonder how it would be to fall in such a place
I hope that some day I will fall to the ground
I am a snowflake

Sara Hart

Sea Song

It didn't take long - for a song
to enter my mind.
And it reminded me - of the raging sea
I'd left behind.
As the tune lapped - about my shore
I suffered more.
For I wished to see - just how far I'd come,
swimming toward the sun - searching the sea.
And the song told more - 'bout my nearing the shore
and swimming a calmer sea.
And how I spied a man - standing in the sand
with arms stretched out to me.
And a voice rang clear - as I drew near
to this man.
He said, "Welcome son. - I've waited long
to take your hand."
So now I wait and listen - whilst the sea glistens
for him to come.
So that I may reach - for him to teach.
He who will be - my son.

James A. Rosa

WAKING

Dark decreases over growing glare

Line leads line
Corners define
Colors splash as have been

Lazily   all   that   is   sails into my head
tugging covers bound baggage
From the unmade bed

I am lying in

Voyaging another day to nowhere...

Ralph M. Alley

Homeless Drift

As I walk through New York City,
I see no friends, I feel no pity.
Looking down a lonely street,
There is no one that I could greet.
No one wants to look at me,
I wonder why they can't see,
That I'm in a world all alone...
Like a dog's buried bone.

Alan Karmin

The Answer

My silent cries
from out of the dark void
wasted on the fog and
wind shrouded shore.

I hurt and you were not there,
afraid of being seen
even in conversation,
Your unsure heart told the tale,
of love with convenience
a woman's silent sorrow.

Barbara Griffin

ABBOTT, EDWARD E.
[pen.] Ed Abbott; [b.] December 18, 1907, Franklin, MA; [p.] Dr. C. Edson Abbott, Mrs. Lillian F. Abbott; [m.] Beverly Abbott, February 13, 1983; [ch.] Carol Montgomery, Margaret Herrick; [ed.] Dartmouth College, AB George Washington University, Law Georgetown University Law School LLM; [occ.] Retired; [memb.] BPO Elks Lodge 1787, Big Bear Masonic Lodge, Big Bear Shrine Club, Big Bear Order of Eastern Star, Big Bear American Assn. of Retired Persons; [hon.] Honorary Mayor Big Bear City 1978; [oth. writ.] "On Mountain Tops"; [pers.] I have been influenced by writing of William Blake and Walt Whitman; [a.] Big Bear City, CA

ABBOTT, JOLIE
[b.] June 28, 1971, Germany; [p.] John and Carole Lorenz; [m.] Keithly Abbott, September 22, 1990; [ch.] Alicia II, Jennifer, Holly, Eddie, Caitlin and Gregory; [ed.] G.E.D.; [occ.] Housewife; [oth. writ.] I've had three other poems published in a local newspaper.; [pers.] My poetry mainly reflects how I am feelings at the time it is written.; [a.] Greenbrier, AR

ABEL, EUGE
[occ.] Literature, Painting, Music (Opera, Symphony), History; [oth. writ.] His fields comprise environment, society and life. He writes to the very point condensed with suggestive words... In poetry, he works with rhymes "for condensing and easy remembering." "Also, rhymes are fun in themselves." Euge knows literature from Homer etc. on, over Shakespeare etc., the 1920 expressionism etc. Yet he formed his own style to meaningful terse expression. In poetry - well founded by his historical knowledge - creates modern rhymes, the lines loose and free.; [pers.] "Give your life meaning and live joyfully".; [a.] Spartanburg, SC

ABEL, MARK C.
[b.] December 16, 1950, Akron, OH; [p.] Robert and Elaine Abel; [ch.] Emmylou Melinda, Joshua Paul, Travis William; [ed.] H.S. Manchester High School Franklin Township - a world of travel U.S. Army 4 yrs.; [occ.] 100% disable Vietnam Combat Veteran; [memb.] Member of Vietnam Veteran of America-Chapter 199 Canton, OH. Several poems published since 1969 during the Vietnam War. Poetry able war - duty love people emotions. I write from my heart.; [hon.] I've written and recorded a song called "P.O.W and M.I.A." it has been played all over the country. (Prison of War, Missing in Action.) decorated four times for heroism silver star - 2 bronze stars - Army Accom. "V" for valor.; [oth. writ.] Story published in book titled "Headhunters" paperback pub. Ind. under military history sold in all book stores, Author "Matt Brennon" my single story published within this book.; [pers.] Wounded twice in Vietnam - 100% disabled veteran travelled all over the Eastern US. speaking to students about the Vietnam War. Patriot of the U.S. lives to write poems and music dedicates my life to the Vietnam Veteran; [a.] Saint Petersburg, FL

ABRAHAM, FERN-RAE
[b.] Grimes Territory, OK; [m.] James Rolla Abraham, 1935; [ch.] Eric Abraham; [ed.] Kansas City Art Institute Kansas City, MO, 1924-1931; [occ.] Fern-Rae Abraham passed away May 6, 1995. She was an Artist and writer for the major part of her life. (Early 20's to the week before she passed away.); [oth. writ.] Mrs. Abraham has had numerous poems published in the Christian Science Monitor. And many other publications. She authored a book on "Tim Craft" published by Sunstove Press, Santa Fe, NM.

ABRAHAMS, MELISSA
[b.] March 12, 1977, Jamaica; [p.] Eudith and Noel Abrahams; [ed.] I will be graduating from Mephon High School this coming month, and in September 1995, I will attend New York University. I will be majoring in Journalism-Communications; [hon.] I won the Coca-Cola essay contest. I also received a certificate of accomplishment from the superintendent of schools.; [pers.] I have everything to lose if I do not pursue my dreams, but everything to gain if I strive for them.; [a.] Bellmore, NY

ACKLEY, KATHRYN L.
[b.] February 10, 1973, Covington, KY; [p.] Randy and Linda Barlow; [m.] Doug Ackley, December 30, 1994; [ed.] University of Kentucky, BA in Chemistry, BA in Science Education; [memb.] National Forensic League, American Chemical Society; [hon.] National Merit Scholar, High School Valedictorian; [pers.] I have been greatly influenced by flowers, sunsets, and the love of others.; [a.] Lexington, KY

ADAM, PHYLLIS
[b.] May 3, 1931, Chicago; [p.] Helen Leonard Wiese; [m.] Douglas Adam, October 1, 1949; [ch.] Brian, Brenda Palmer, Christopher, Courtney and Eric; [ed.] Central High School, Briar Cliff College, St. Joseph School of Nursing; [occ.] Wife, mother, grandmother, part time writer; [oth. writ.] The Operculum (book); [pers.] "If you don't stand for something you'll fall for anything"; [a.] Yankton, SD

ADAMS, CARLEEN
[b.] Georgetown, Guyana, South Africa; [p.] Carl Hooper, Lorna Hooper; [ed.] Howard University, B.S. in Electrical Engineering. Currently pursuing a Masters Degree in Telecommunications Management at the University of MD; [occ.] Systems Engineer, TRW Government Information Services Div., Washington, DC; [hon.] Tau Beta Pi (Engineering Honor Society), Dean's List; [oth. writ.] Several unpublished poems; [pers.] I have been greatly influenced by Maya Angelou. My favorite poems (written by Ms. Angelou) are "Still I Rise" and "Phenomenal Woman"; [a.] Bowie, MD

ADAMS, GERALD W.
[b.] May 9, 1908, RI; [p.] Samuel and Lillian Adams; [m.] Dorothy (deceased), April 18, 1942; [ed.] East Providence High, 1 Year Brown University; [occ.] Retired and writing; [oth. writ.] Editing my own novel. Compilation of short stories (ready and in search of an agent); [a.] Warren, RI

ADKINS, QUINTEN W.
[pen.] Quinten W. Adkins; [b.] December 16, 1960, Ravenna, OH; [p.] Fredelene and Maxine Adkins; [ch.] Angela Yvonne Adkins and Tanya Marie Adkins; [ed.] Graduate of Buckeye High School; [occ.] Employed by: Owens Corning, (roofing plant); [oth. writ.] Several poems I have writing for people who mean a lot to me. I also have written a few to express my own emotions.; [pers.] Try to always look past the flaws of people and things and you will always look at people and things in a positive way. And try to bring at the goodness in everyone.; [a.] Akron, OH

ADLER, BRANDY
[b.] June 12, 1985, Denver, CO; [p.] Craig and Karen Adler; [ed.] Will be a 5th grader next year at Sandburg Elem. in Littleton, CO

AHMAD, OMAR
[pen.] Tanvir; [b.] December 29, 1974, Aligarh, India; [p.] Mr. Zamir Ahmad, Mrs. Raihana Ahmad; [ed.] Woodstock School, India, Aligarh Muslim University, India; [occ.] Student; [memb.] National Cadet Corps, WOSA Member; [hon.] Cassinath Writing Award; [oth. writ.] Poems published in my campus magazine and Woodstock Alumni magazine; [pers.] "Why tarry on unhappy thoughts and in grim halls of learning? Time flies like a taunting ghost, and the wick of life is swiftly burning!"; [a.] Albuquerque, NM

AIKINS, AGNES L.
[pen.] Agnes Aikins Dormon

ALEXANDER, DEIRDRE JERELON
[pen.] Deege; [b.] April 1, 1980, Albuquerque, NM; [p.] Angela Burrough and Keith Burrough; [ed.] 9th Grade at Wilson High School, Long Beach, CA; [occ.] High School Student; [memb.] Chess Club, Orchestra, and Pep Club and St. Matthews Baptist Church Sunday School Dept; [hon.] Presidental Achievement Award, Black History Award, Honor Rolls Award; [oth. writ.] You Never Love Something, I Was The One, and Broken Hearts. Published in school newspaper.; [pers.] I am greatly influenced by Maya Angelou and Langston Hughes.; [a.] Long Beach, CA

ALEXANDER, JED CHARLES
[b.] July 27, 1926, Dublin, GA; [p.] Jed and Evelyn Alexander; [m.] Penelope P. Alexander, December 28, 1991; [ch.] Michael Avery, David James, Patrick Charles; [ed.] Dublin High School, Georgia Military College, Jacksonville J.C., Florida State University; [occ.] Retired; [oth. writ.] Other poetry, nothing published; [pers.] Always live your life in a way that if you had the opportunity to live your life over, you would gladly.; [a.] Atlanta, GA

ALLARD, LORRAINE A.
[pen.] Lorraine A. Allard; [b.] December 13, 1958, Hartford, CT; [p.] Maurille O. (deceased) and Georgette M. Allard; [memb.] Society of the Little Flower (St. Therese of the Child Jesus and the Holy Face); [oth. writ.] Some College Newspaper Editorials, Articles, graphics, cartoons. Two books of poetry spanning ten years (unpublished), letters of multiple facets (i.e. condolence, sympathy et al), gifted with language via many means; [pers.] Never question God - trust in him blindly. Expect the unexpected - you're sure to get it regardless.; [a.] East Hartford, CT

ALLEN, JENNIFER
[pen.] Jenny Allen; [b.] September 11, 1975; [p.] Paul and Sandy Allen; [m.] Charles Kibbe, October 12, 1996; [ed.] Ogemaw Heights High School, West Branch, MI; [occ.] Hostess at Forwards Convernse Centre West Branch, MI; [memb.] H.O.S.A. (Health Occupations Student of American.); [hon.] This is my fifth year being in "The National Library of Poetry" books. 2nd place in Medical writing for Health Occupations Students of America.; [oth. writ.] Other poems "Untitled," "Dance With Me Oh Enchanted One."; [a.] Prescott, MI

ALLEN, LEIGH ANN
[b.] November 6, 1974, Lufkin, TX; [p.] Wesley and Barbara Allen; [ed.] Graduate of Central High School Associate Degree from Angelina College; [occ.] History and English tutor at Angelina College; [memb.] National Honors Society, Fellowship of Christian Athletes, Phi Theta Kappa, (Angelina College) A.C. Singers, Future Teachers (T.A.F.E.), KYSSED (Knowledgeable Youth Stand Strong Eliminating Drugs); [hon.] Who's Who in Drama, Miss CHS, Fine Arts Scholarship, Who's Who Among American High School and College Students, Deans List, All star cast (Vil one act play) and honorable mention all star cast.; [oth. writ.] Selected poems; [pers.] "I can do all things through Christ who strengthens me." This poem is dedicated to my friends in the A.C. Singers.; [a.] Pollok, TX

ALLEN, MOLLY
[pen.] Michelle Lewis; [b.] April 13, 1979, Samaritan; [p.] Joyce and Charles Allen; [ed.] Freshman-Hillsdale High School; [occ.] Student; [pers.] I try to keep an open mind every day of my life; [a.] Jeromesville, OH

ALLEY, RALPH M.
[b.] August 23, 1935, Lewiston, ID; [p.] Ralph M. Alley, Louretta H. Alley; [m.] Virginia Hines Alley, June 6, 1971; [ed.] B of Architecture, Univ. Of ID. 30 years self-employed business man; [occ.] Registered Architect; [memb.] Sigma NU Fraternity, Past Corp. Member AIA, NCARB Certified, CSI, and ASID; [hon.] Past Anchorage Chairman, AIA, Alaska State AIA Chapter President-Elect, member Anchorage Planning and Zoning Commission-vice chairman, Chairman and Borough Liason-Anchorage, Beautification Commission; [oth. writ.] Numerous published articles RE: Architecture Land Development, comedic routines for performances and stage presentations for theatre productions; [pers.] From sudden deafness to some resigned normalcy, a ten year road was taken along a life scape reconciled aboard this vehicle of poetry.; [a.] Temecula, CA

ALLISON, ROBIN
[b.] July 17, 1975, Morristown, NJ; [p.] Michael Allison, Susan Allison; [ed.] Housatonic Valley Regional High; [occ.] Philosopher of various things of minor importance; [pers.] Deep and serious philosophy must always be countered with overt and rampant silliness. It's the only way to live.; [a.] Northville, MI

AMANDEO, CONNIE MARIE
[pen.] Connie Clark; [b.] July 3, 1963, Gaithersburg, MD; [p.] Charles Clark, Marsha Cornett; [m.] Leonard Amandeo, December 7, 1990; [ch.] Christina Amandeo; [ed.] Concord High, University of Delaware; [occ.] Senior Records Manager; [memb.] ARMA; [oth. writ.] Published article for Records Management Newsletter.; [pers.] Always accept adversity as a challenge to grow.; [a.] Philadelphia, PA

AMATO, RUTH A.
[pen.] Ruth A. Amato; [b.] December 28, 1941, Lorain County, OH; [p.] Howard and Genevieve (Beck) Riffee; [m.] Larry J. Amato, July 2, 1971; [ch.] One Daughter; [ed.] Harding High School-1959, Marion Business College; [occ.] Secretary at United Transportation Union; [hon.] Special religious study, no big awards nothing significant; [oth. writ.] Poems locally; [pers.] Christian - involved in church praise and worship band. I play guitar and sing. Daughter and I sing together.

AMISON, MR. LESLIE S.
[pen.] Les Amison; [b.] March 12, 1945, New York, NY; [p.] Mr. and Mrs. Samuel L. Amison; [ed.] Cornell U., Moravian College, Northampton C. C. Hutztown Univ. - Now, I attend classes to check my premises; [occ.] Prisoner, writer thinker, inventor, slave; [memb.] I hope to join the International Society of Poets when I have spare money. The Planetary Society.; [hon.] First-1993 PA State Prison Poetry Competition, Golden Poet-Silver Poet Awards, Certificates of Merit, Dean's List; [oth. writ.] Cinder Earth, The Buck, published in newspapers and small presses. Over 90% of my literary output has been stolen by relatives and Lehigh Co. Pros. office, PA; [pers.] If we honestly care about one another, we won't kill one another or die from indifference. Human hate guarantees the destruction of the world and science makes it final. The middle east didn't listen to Christ about loving or caring in Christ's new commandment, now much of the Middle East is a desert.; [a.] Bellefonte, PA

ANDERSON, DAVID A.
[pen.] David Sheridan; [b.] June 13, 1971, Columbia, PA; [p.] Robert Anderson, Martha Anderson; [ed.] Columbia High School Columbia, PA, Indiana Univ. of PA, Indiana, PA, Millersville Univ. of PA, Millersville, PA; [occ.] College Student at Millersville University; [memb.] Cut and Thrust Museum Kutztown, PA, National Rifle Association; [hon.] Beta Gamma Alpha Indiana University of PA, Army Commendation Medal, 2 Army Achievement Medals, 3 Army Certificates of Achievement; [oth. writ.] None published; [pers.] Life is a struggle of endless proportions and it is the duty of a writer to emphasize and illuminate on both good and evil emotions. A poem should draw an emotional response from a reader that feels authentic; [a.] Columbia, PA

ANDERSON, HORTENSE
[b.] March 31, 1926, TX; [m.] Winfred R. Anderson, May 11, 1946; [ch.] Gregory Anderson and Deborah Hollinguest; [ed.] Fred Douglas High School SC, Sam Houston College; [occ.] Housewife retired; [memb.] Second Baptist Church Monrovia, CA; [oth. writ.] I've written several poems but have not published them yet.; [pers.] I strive to reflect the goodness of mankind in my writing. I have been greatly influenced by God. Most of my poems are about personal events. Wedding, funerals, social events etc.; [a.] San Dimas, CA

ANDERSON, JANET J.
[b.] May 24, 1941, NC; [p.] Edmond and Jeanette Clark; [m.] Jimmy Anderson, August 3, 1956; [ch.] Pamela Hayes, Penny Norris, Dale Anderson, David Anderson; [ed.] Went back to school at age 52 and graduated; [occ.] Broyhill furniture factory; [memb.] A member of the South Lenoir Church of God, Sunday School Teacher, Ladies Auxiliary; [hon.] Mother of the Year Award in 1988 at North Lenoir Church of God; [oth. writ.] I have written many Gospel Songs this could be the day and heaven our new home. Recorded by Rainbow Records. I sing my songs in my Church. I also have written many poems; [pers.] I strive to let people see the beauty of the things God has given and to feel his greatness in my songs.; [a.] Lenoir, NC

ANDERSON, SARA M.
[b.] April 23, 1978, Grosse Pointe, MI; [p.] Warren and Nancy Anderson; [ed.] South Lyon High School; [occ.] Pretyel Time; [memb.] 4-H, South Lyon Soccer Club, Girl Scouts, South Lyon Sea Lions Swim Team; [hon.] Student of the week at Oakland Technical Center Southwest Campus; [oth. writ.] A personal poetry book, and numerous articles published in the Oakland News.; [a.] South Lyon, MI

ANDERSON, VERA STRONG
[b.] August 5, 1931, Mound Bayou, MS; [p.] Will C. and Charlotte C. Strong; [m.] Arthur R. Anderson, April 21, 1955; [ch.] Arthur R. Jr., Lisa A. Word; [ed.] Tennessee State U.-B.S., Meharry Medical College - D.D.S.; [occ.] Pres., An-Strong Symbols, Inc; [memb.] Delta Sigma Theta Sorority NAACP, AME Church; [hon.] Cert. of Recognition CA Legislature Assembly, Commendation - Alameda County Board of Supervisors, Citation from Gary, IN City Council; [oth. writ.] Recollections of My Birth (First Memories); [pers.] To live a full life. To try to understand is complexities, to enjoy its simplicities, to embrace its beautifulness, to avoid its profanities, and to accept its inevitabilities.; [a.] Albany, CA

ANDERSON, WILLIAM P.
[pen.] Will Anderson; [b.] December 29, 1957, Dallas, TX; [p.] Charles L. and Kathryn Anderson; [ed.] Graduated Central High, Marlow, OK Class of '77, other than a few thousand books and years of traversing the US, no other formal schooling; [occ.] Free lance artist-cartoonist; [memb.] Marlow Jay Cees, Marlow's "Good Old Boys" Network (Charity Organization); [oth. writ.] Unpublished for now.; [pers.] Each generation shall produce it's great leaders but it shall be the leaders influenced by the poets, the artist and the philosophers who shall create the next golden reinassance.; [a.] Marlow, OK

ANDRESEN, SYLVIA N.
[b.] March 5, 1929, Colorado Springs, CO; [p.] Julian and Sylvia Nichols; [m.] Glen W. Andresen (deceased), February 10, 1945; [ch.] Three sons and one daughter: Kent, Mark, Vern and Gayle; [ed.] B.A. English, M.A. Management University of California, Fullerton Redlands University, Redlands, CA Graduate "Institute of Children's Lit" Current student "Long Ridge Writers"; [occ.] Retired Executive, Secretary, Garden Grove, CA Police; [memb.] Past director, current member, St. Joseph's Choir. Wedding Soloist. Editor Senior Valley Views, Past Ed. Busy Bears Quilt Guild Newsletter, Member, Big Bear Valley Writers' Group, Member Spellbinders (sic): a writers' group.; [hon.] English Honor Student; [oth. writ.] PCT Magazine: "Backpacking the Pacific Crest Trail". Kid stuff: "Snowflakes". Farm Wife News: "Dough-Pretty Projects from your Oven." "Geology of Old Saddleback" Santa Ana "Defensive Steps to Educate Merchants Against Fraudulent Check Writers"; [pers.] Expose youth to the best in literature whether imaginative or factual. Give them something to aim for, not just in literature, but in life as well.; [a.] Fawnskin, CA

ANDREWS, BETTY E.
[b.] November 8, 1938, Oak Park, IL; [p.] Louis and Elizabeth Andrews; [m.] July 28, 1956; [ch.] David E. and Sherry L. Zipprich; [ed.] Attended Oakton College; [oth. writ.] Poems published in the Compassionate Friends Newsletters.; [pers.] This poem is written about my daughter, Sherry L. Zipprich, who passed away at the age of 30 leaving a son, Jack, four months old. My dear sweet daughter is loved, missed and remembered.; [a.] Des Plaines, IL

APILADO, CRYSTAL MARIE
[b.] January 4, 1981, Vallejo, CA; [p.] Yvonne and Emil Apilado; [ed.] Vallejo Jr. High School, Winters Middle School; [occ.] Student; [hon.] Editors Choice Award, Honor Award for Highest Achievement in Written Language; [oth. writ.] Blind; [pers.] Our world today is being shattered by the influence of violence. We can only stop and realize what we are doing to each other before we can attempt to change things.; [a.] Winters, CA

APPLETON, ELISHA
[pen.] Elisha D. Appleton; [b.] May 18, 1981, Chicago, IL; [p.] Eydie Appleton, Roy Rusch; [ed.] High School Freshman; [memb.] Member of CTAFC (Christ Temple Apostolic Faith Church) Jr. Credit Union Broad Member; [pers.] I press for the mark of the prize in Jesus Christ my Saviour and Lord; [a.] Chicago, IL

ARAGON, JEREMY S.
[b.] March 21, 1981, Houston, TX; [p.] Judith and Jacinto Aragon; [ed.] 8th grade student at Park View Intermediate; [memb.] History Club (Treasurer), Youth for Christ, Newspaper Staff, Yearbook Staff, (NAL) National Academic League (Team Captain); [hon.] DAR Citizenship Award, (2) Presidential Academic Awards, Numerous for academic achievements including: Math, Reading, English, Science, and History; [oth. writ.] Stories: The Next Door Neighbor, One True Friend, A Trip to Remember (unpublished); [pers.] Nobody will care how much you know, until they know how much you care.; [a.] Pasadena, TX

ARCE, JOHN CHARLES
[pen.] "Arce"; [b.] July 31, 1973, Brooklyn, NY; [p.] Mr. and Mrs. Arce; [oth. writ.] Anti-drug related poems, short (short) stories, poems on the subconscious way of life.; [pers.] "Through divinity and death, this poem holds its worth in blood, money, and magic."; [a.] Dumont, NJ

ARDITO, BETTY E.
[b.] April 20, 1937, TN; [p.] Willie and Nettie Allgood; [m.] Vincent Ardito Sr.; [ch.] Vincent Jr, Rita, Brenda and Gwenda; [ed.] Greenbrier High TN, OCC. NJ; [occ.] Retired; [memb.] Arthritis Foundation Scleroderma Foundation, First Assembly of God, Point NJ Deborah Heart Association; [oth. writ.] Two poems published in Springfield Herald, TN; [pers.] I plan to write a book of poems have written aprox. 40 to date my poems are written about people and things that I feel very deeply about.; [a.] Toms River, NJ

ARDOLINO, JUSTIN
[pen.] J.D.A, J.D. Ardolino, Braindead; [b.] January 2, 1978, Hackensack, NJ; [p.] Raffaele Ardolino, Noreen Ardolino; [pers.] "The greatest influences on my writing are Stephen King and William Butler Yeats. My three month stint in Elizabeth Medical Psychiatric Unit had a great impact on my poetry. I love you Kizzy."; [a.] Springfield, NJ

ARGUS, MS. DINA F.
[pen.] Dina Fleming; [b.] April 13, 1969, Chicago, IL; [p.] James and Thelma Fleming; [m.] Robert J. Argus, July 4, 1993; [ed.] Lockport, IL High School; [occ.] United Airlines, Chicago, IL; [oth. writ.] Poetry, currently writing a novel.; [pers.] I endeavor to paint honest and beautiful pictures through lyric. Some of the most exquisite views are those created by way of the imagination. This is my way.; [a.] Des Plaines, IL

ARNOLD JR., CHARLES
[pen.] Mr. Quicksand; [b.] February 1, 1966; [pers.] "My life has been a classic struggle of one man searching to find the purpose of his existence. After years of searching I have come into the light only to find that the journey has only just begun".

ARROWOOD, JUANITA
[pen.] Mahala Fox; [b.] May 3, 1930, Towns Country GA; [p.] Carey William and Lillie Mae Bernard; [m.] John Floyd Arrowood Jr. (deceased), August 16, 1955; [ch.] Lillian Chloe, Herbert Edge, Theresa Ann Arrowood; [ed.] Education specialist-University of GA. Master Arts in Education Western Carolina College, Bachelor of Science in Education-North Georgia College, Towns County High School; [occ.] Nurse Aide, Retired Teacher (40 years of expression); [memb.] NEA, GAE; [hon.] Susan B. Anthony Society; [pers.] To leave the world a better, greener, more beautiful place because I walked this way and to teach others that birth, life, death are only adventures to be experienced, savored, and remembered; [a.] Blairsville, GA

ASFELD, MAUREEN A.
[b.] May 23, 1974, Elgin, IL; [p.] Ludwig Asfeld, Arlene (De Morett) Asfeld; [ed.] Woodstock High School, Winona State University; [occ.] College English Writing Student; [memb.] Grub Street, The Loft, Forensics; [hon.] Honor Roll, Academic All-American Scholar, ACA Recognition Award; [oth. writ.] Literary reviews for the Winonan, poetry published in the Satori, a regional literary magazine, articles published in the McHenry County Business Journal; [pers.] I have been greatly influenced by my parents, my college poetry professor, dreams, and lifetime experiences.; [a.] Woodstock, IL

ASPIRAS, CHRISTINE
[pen.] Tin Tin; [b.] October 8, 1981, Seattle, WA; [p.] Henry and Gloria Aspiras; [ed.] Currently, I am receiving my education at Bonita Vista Middle School and I am in the gate-honors program there.; [hon.] I've received some awards for my citizenship and scholarship.; [oth. writ.] I have one other poem being published in the book anthology of poetry by young Americans.; [pers.] I would like to thank my parents who has always been there and supported me. I'd also like to thank my sister, Crystal, and all my friends who has always been on my side through good and bad times.; [a.] Chula Vista, CA

ATKINS, MARY F.
[b.] August 18, 1955, Houston, TX; [p.] Johnnie Krezinski and Dorothy Zabawa Krezinski; [m.] Jack Douglas Atkins, June 13, 1985; [ch.] F. Andrew Goodwyn, Dustin S. Goodwyn and Jaclyn Atkins; [ed.] St. Pius X High School; [a.] Houston, TX

AUDIA, DAVID J.
[b.] March 15, 1960, Torrington, CT; [p.] John and Rita Rufenach Audia; [ed.] Lewis S. Mills High, Waterbury State Technical College; [occ.] Design Engineer; [hon.] Golden Poet of the Year 1991, World of Poetry Association; [oth. writ.] A poem published in a local daily newspaper; [pers.] The enigma of life isn't just what we might have been, but what we may or may not become; [a.] Torrington, CT

AUSTIN, MARY E.
[b.] February 25, 1916, Beaves City, OK; [p.] Dora and Charly Francis; [m.] Ralph Austin, January 4, 1936; [ch.] Robert, David and Barbah; [ed.] Amarillo High School Commercial Art School; [occ.] Retired; [memb.] Reporter for Lancaster Woman's Club, Antelope Valley Emblem Club, (Part President) Jushua Till Grange (Past Master) Volunteer at Antelolpe Valley Indian Museum and Lanc City Museum; [hon.] Many awards for water color, oils, acrylic and crafts and poetry; [oth. writ.] Short stories, and articles for local paper (Valley Press) poems in the local paper; [pers.] 1. "The more you give of yourself the larger you get" 2. Learn to accept the things you cannot change, 3. Look on the Sunny side, 4. Laughter is loving and living; [a.] Lancaster, CA

AVEDISSIAN, ASTRID
[b.] November 22, 1979, Europe; [occ.] Student in 9th grade in Adrien Block; [memb.] Member of Arista Junior Honor Society; [hon.] Citizen of the best country in the world, member of the female sex and an eccentric dreamer; [pers.] The three things I hold closest to my heart are: my family, the study of Science and the constant strife for improving humanity. All of us have to keep in mind that we soon will be just a speck of dust in this wide hole called Universe.; [a.] New York, NY

AWWAD, ABDALLA RAPHAEL
[b.] April 28, 1975, Detroit, MI; [p.] Patsy and Raphael Awwad; [ed.] St. Angela Roseville High; [occ.] Furniture Delivery; [oth. writ.] 20th Century, Another Life Sign on the Dotted Line, Question of Sanity, Midnight and Predator, I am Life, Presidential Promises, Depression of Laboratory Mice and Men, Death Once More, A Bleak Future, Test of Strength, etc.; [pers.] If genius is not used for the right cause, a lunatic is born.; [a.] Roseville, MI

AYCOCK, ANGELA LYNN
[b.] December 16, 1966, Clinton, NC; [p.] Robert L. Aycock, Hilda O. Aycock; [ed.] Clinton High School, Sampson Community College; [occ.] Secretary - David L. Best, Attorney at Law; [pers.] I express my feelings and thoughts through the words of my poetry. My

poems seem to have a special effect on its readers. Poetry is an expression of the mind.; [a.] Clinton, NC

AZIZ, NAEESA
[pen.] Nancy; [b.] November 7, 1984, Norfolk, VA; [p.] Lateefah Aziz and Keith Tally; [ed.] Preschool-5; [occ.] Student; [memb.] St. Louis Childrens Choir; [hon.] Honor Roll; [oth. writ.] Several poems and stories; [pers.] I was inspired by my aunt.; [a.] Saint Louis, MO

BABOU, IDO
[pen.] Ido Babou; [b.] November 10, 1964, Abidjan; [p.] Niaba and Liahon; [ed.] Master of Arts Degree The City College of New York, 1993; [occ.] Educator, community servant, entertainer; [memb.] Association for supervision curricular development. National Council of Teachers of English. American Globe Theater.; [hon.] NYC Board of Education, partner in Education New York City Public School volunteer award. New York Public Library second place winner - Essay Contest.; [pers.] I'd rather attempt to do something great and fail, than attempt to do nothing and succeed.; [a.] New York, NY

BACON, LESLIE
[b.] August 1, 1985, Los Angeles, CA; [p.] Carol and John Bacon; [ed.] Hillcrest Drive C.E.S. 4th grade; [memb.] Girl Scouts, member of Lynwood Christian Center Choir; [hon.] School attendance awards; [oth. writ.] Various stories for school; [pers.] I try to do my best in everything I do, including writing; [a.] Los Angeles, CA

BACON, PATRICIA J.
[pen.] Landis Munro Land; [b.] July 7, 1930, Plainview, TX; [p.] Henry G and Cora Land Robinson; [m.] William Bartlett Bacon, Jr., October 28, 1971; [ch.] Walter Munro Miller (dec.), Mary Scott, Lowell Land, Anne Boston; [ed.] Panhandle High School, '47, U. of Mary Hardin-Baylor, BA West Texas State U. '91, MA West Texas A and MU '95; [occ.] Retired, Quality Analyst, 30 years, fr. Eng. teaching ass't, 2 yrs.; [memb.] Sigma Tau Delta, Phi Alpha Theta, Confederate Air Force, Civil War Society, St. George's Episcopal Church Bishop's Committee, Virginia Country Historical Society; [hon.] Who's Who in American Universities and Colleges, 1992-93, Pres. Sigma Tau Delta, 1992-93, Dean's List, 1990-91, Dean's Round table, 1991-93; [oth. writ.] Short story awards: "Betrayal," U. of N Texas, 1992, "Bricks," Baylor U, 1992, "Where the Wild Sumac Grow," Texas A and M U, 1993 (presentations at Graduate Literary Conferences); [pers.] Never let obstacles nor people thwart you from following the deepest desires of your heart, no matter how impossible your goal may seem.; [a.] Canyon, TX

BAHRIA, AMATULLAH
[b.] August 15, 1971, Montana; [ed.] Life experience - ongoing; [memb.] Director of Publications for the Organization of the Islamic Ummah (community), Volunteer Publications Consultant and past talk show host for KUCB 89.3 FM in Des Moines; [oth. writ.] Extensive local publishings, AIM magazine, editor and chief writer for an international Islamic publication (in English); [pers.] "By the token of time through the ages, surely man is at loss. Except such as have faith, do righteous, deeds, and join together in the mutual teaching of truth and of patience and constancy." - Holy Quran Surah 103; [a.] De Moines, IA

BAILEY, BARBARA
[b.] October 4, 1947, Tulsa, OK; [p.] Bob and Chloe Garroutte; [m.] Ancel Bailey, August 6, 1966; [ch.] Gregory, Sheree, Donya; [ed.] High School, 1 yr College; [occ.] Administrative Assistant; [memb.] Profes-

sional Secretaries International; [oth. writ.] Poem published in book compiled by local Church in Kansas City; [pers.] Writing poetry helps me to put thoughts and feelings on paper that perhaps can help others by reading them. A lot of my poems were written when I just needed to be closer to God.; [a.] Conveyers, GA

BAILEY, ERNIE
[b.] June 12, 1974, Louisville, KY; [p.] Gary D. Bailey, Wanda A. Bailey; [ch.] Christopher D. Bailey, Ernie Bailey; [ed.] High School Graduate 1 year college. Attended Sheldon Clark High School Inez KY. Angelo State U. in San Angelo, TX.; [occ.] Services Specialist U.S. Air Force; [hon.] High School Speech contest, 2nd place High School wrestling Awards; [pers.] Life has no limits; [a.] San Angelo, TX

BAIN, JEFFREY V.
[pen.] Jeffrey Wheeler; [b.] December 11, 1979, Memphis, TN; [p.] Richard Bain, Stella Wheeler; [ed.] Idlewild Elementary Gateway Baptist, both in Memphis, TN; [occ.] Student, Gateway Baptist School, Memphis, TN; [memb.] Society for the preservation of Film Music, National Geographic Society; [hon.] 3rd place in local poetry contest for city Beautiful Committee, Presidential Academic Fitness Award, Principal's List; [oth. writ.] One poem in the local newspaper; [pers.] To my family and friends, My Shadow and my Sun, ever changing, but always there.; [a.] Memphis, TN

BAJER, LORENA MARGARET
[b.] January 4, 1982, Los Angeles; [p.] Steve and Tina Bajer; [ed.] St. Rita's School; [occ.] Student; [hon.] Musical and many scholastic awards; [oth. writ.] Short stories and poems; [pers.] I write for what I believe in!

BAKER, BRUCE A.
[b.] February 21, 1963, Colorado Springs, CO; [p.] Ronald and Marie Baker; [m.] Tami J. Baker, June 20, 1992; [ch.] Mallory Jane Baker, 1 yr old; [ed.] Pomona High School University of Northern Colorado; [occ.] Wholesale Apparel Sales Representative; [oth. writ.] The adventures of Howie and Alan, 4 books for children ages 5-12. I also have 25 other unpublished poems.; [pers.] Life is too short not to enjoy it. I am at my best when I am writing. The romantic in me comes out in my poetry and a flood of childhood memories come forward in my children's books.; [a.] Denver, CO

BAKER, JANET K.
[pen.] J. B. Riling; [b.] May 14, 1930, Huntingdon, PA; [p.] Fred King, Helen King; [m.] Floyd Baker, October 14, 1964; [ed.] Huntingdon High, Harrisburg Polyclinic Hospital School of Nursing; [occ.] Registered Nurse; [memb.] Friends of Huntingdon Co. Library, Central Pa. Humane Society, Salvation Army Women's Auxiliary; [hon.] 1993 Quorum of Excellence Award for Employee of the Year at J. C. Blair Memorial Hospital; [oth. writ.] Several health articles in 'Standing Stone Senior Citizens' monthly newsletter; [pers.] I have always treated others as I would like to be treated, laughed frequently, be a friend and counted my blessings. These have sustained me through my life. Greatly influenced by Mother.; [a.] Huntingdon, PA

BAKKER, ADAM
[b.] January 25, 1978, Munising, MI; [p.] Kim and Bunny Bakker; [ed.] Currently Student at Superior Central High School; [occ.] Student, Superior Central High School; [hon.] Attended National Young Leaders Conference, Multiple Year "Who's who in American High School Students?"; [oth. writ.] Numerous Political Essays, 2 Satirical Plays, one Screenplay; [pers.] To observe the world around you is to be entertained, to influence the world around you is to be an etertainer.; [a.] Chatham, MI

BALESTERI, KIMBERLY
[b.] April 24, 1980, San Diego; [p.] Vincent and Louise Balesteri; [ed.] Scripps Ranch High School; [occ.] High School Student; [pers.] Poetry is a form of 'art in words'. I enjoy creating poems that entertain and paint a picture of humor.; [a.] San Diego, CA

BALGENORTH, CHARLES R.
[b.] May 18, 1962, Detroit, MI; [p.] Thomas and Goldie Balgenorth; [ed.] De La Salle Collegiate High School, Wayne State University (B.S.E.E.), University of Michigan (J.D. and M.B.A.); [occ.] Intellectual Property Attorney; [memb.] American Bar Association, Institute of Electrical and Electronics Engineers, Engineering Society of Detroit, Los Angeles County Bar Association, American Civil Liberties Union, University of Michigan Alumni Association; [hon.] Tau Beta Pi, Eta Kappa Nu, Merit Scholarship and Dean's List - Wayne State Univ., Benton Scholarship - U of M Business School; [pers.] In our struggle to advance, we have left behind the simple truth of life. My poems reflect glimpses of the truth that I have felt, peace that I have found from within but that is to be shared. My hope is that others feel the truth and begin to find their peace through the words that have been shared with me by the spirit that joins us all.; [a.] Long Beach, CA

BALSMANN, SALLY GLUECK
[pen.] Sally Glueck Balsmann; [b.] September 20, 1960, Cape Girardeau, MO; [p.] Orville and Rita Glueck; [m.] Keith Balsmann, April 13, 1985; [ch.] Dane Joseph Balsmann, Lacey Rose Balsmann; [ed.] Major in Management Minor in Journalism, Southeast MO. State University; [occ.] Sales Tax Auditor for State of Missouri; [hon.] Editors choice Award from National Library of Poetry, Dean's List; [oth. writ.] Was published once before in last book of poetry. Journey of the mind; [a.] Cape Girardeau, MO

BALSAVAGE, RICHARD
[b.] October 28, 1980, Reading, PA; [p.] Eric and Deborah Balsavage; [ed.] Student at Kutztown Area High School; [oth. writ.] Several different poems for school contests and one printed in local newspaper.; [pers.] I enjoy using my creative talents to come up with my own writings.; [a.] Lyons, PA

BANCROFT, MARGARET V.
[pen.] Peggy Bancroft; [b.] November 30, 1919, Oakland, PA; [p.] Claire and Paul Thomas; [m.] Fred F. Bancroft, June 28, 1941; [ch.] Richard L. Bancroft, Joan C. Bancroft, 7 grandchildren, 5 great grandchildren; [ed.] Whitpain Twp. H.S., Norristown Business College, Mansfield University, Ohio Unversity School of Journalism, East Stroudsburg University (summa cum laude); [occ.] Magazine Advisor, Editor, 38 years; [memb.] La Anna U.M. Church, Administrative Board, Pike Co. Historical Society, Greene Twp. Hist. Soc., Newfoundland Area Public Library Board of Directors; [oth. writ.] 10 books: includes "Ringing Axes and Rocking Chairs", "Tales from Pawdaddy Farm", "Journey By Lamplight", "This Mountain Land", "Of Rabbits, and Rain and Rhode Island Reds", "Unto the Hills", "This Land of Promise" "A Feeling of The Heart", "All Roads Lead Home", "Monroe Co. Women in History"; [pers.] Most of my writing deals with history. The sound foundation of historical truth is important and must be preserved. American Indians, early settlers, people and places that made a difference should be remembered.; [a.] South Sterling, PA

BANCROFT, MS. JOAN D.
[b.] Providence, RI; [ed.] Professional University; [hon.] Caucasian white race I'd respect civil code moral laws; [oth. writ.] Christian Ten Commandments; [a.] San Rafael, CA

BANKS, JANE
[pen.] Jane Christian Barnes; [b.] February 12, 1933, Tahlequah, OK; [p.] E. J. and Marion Green; [m.] Ex-husband C. B. Banks, March, 1953 - February, 1972; [ch.] Marian Sue Banks and Paul Randolph Banks; [ed.] Plainview H. S. - 1950, Texas Tech BA, English 1953; [occ.] Retired teacher, poet, writer; [memb.] AARP, Republican Party of Texas, Baptist Church, International Society of Poets, Past Member - TSTA and NEA, TAACE; [hon.] 1950 Journalist of the Year-Plainview H. S., 1977 - Teacher of the Year-Lubbock I. S. D.; [oth. writ.] "Identity: Red, White, and Blue," anecdotes submitted to Readers Digest, other unpublished patriotic poems, Biblically based poems and romantic verse; [per.] I have been much influenced by the writings of John Keats and other romantic poets. John Milton, as a writer is also an influence; [a.] Lubbock, TX

BANKS, STEVEN C.
[b.] February 28, 1966, Englewood, NJ; [p.] Veronica Marie Costa, Robert Whitehead; [m.] Monika Rosemarie Meyer Banks, November 23, 1993; [ed.] Monroe-Woodbury High Orange County Community College; [occ.] Student; [memb.] M.A.T.C. Alumni Association; [oth. writ.] The Face of the Falls (1993), Protracted Reality (1995), Hundreds of poems and short stories awaiting a publisher at the time of this publication.; [pers.] When we tune the mind so consciousness and conscience work in harmony and are guided by the silent rhythms and feelings of the heart, then we know true serenity and peace. When we allow the God our own understanding to direct the whole living being, we understand unconditional love.; [a.] Greenville, NY

BARAJAS, JAMIE L. SCROGGIN
[b.] August 16, 1966; [p.] James L. and Barbara M. Scroggin; [ch.] Brent A. Barajas, Barbara M. Barajas; [ed.] Bremen High, Moraine Valley Community College; [occ.] Divorced, single-parent mom/student; [memb.] President of the Alpha Lambda Chapter of Phi Theta Kappa International Honors Society '94-95 distinguished member hall of honor, Vice president '95-96; [pers.] Following the heart can be scary, but this is where truth is found.; [a.] Markham, IL

BARAT, JACQUELINE
[b.] May 20, 1948, Ontario, Canada; [p.] Mrs. Marion Barat; [ed.] Associate Of Arts; [occ.] Cosmetologist; [oth. writ.] Poems: Completely Todd's Lesser Road Travelled, Sunrise Sunset, Keeping Faith, The Sensitive Man, He Loved Flowers, Listen To The Quiet, Marie, Silver; [pers.] May I always remember that love is a gift, not a possession.; [a.] Phoenix, AZ

BARE, MAMIE ELIZABETH
[b.] November 15, 1920, Gary, WV; [p.] Arthur-Maude Bare; [m.] (1st marriage) Peter Danison, September 1947, (2nd husband) married November 16, 1974; [ch.] Daughter Shirley Suzanne Danison, November 28, 1951, (deceased),; [ed.] Studied Violin 1928-1940 Private Tutor Roonoke, VA. Graduated Jefferson Sr. High School 1940 Roonoke VA. Six Months Training Photo Artist Philadelphia PA, Six Months Training Film Etcher World Color Inc., Ormond Beach, Florida, 1958 - Employed 10 yrs, Novel to Mesa, Arizona 1968 to Las Vegas, Nevada 1968; [occ.] Retired, over years build variety jobs during travels Sales Girl, Typist, Receptionist Cashier, Billing Clerk Typist, Photo Artist Chemical Artists Seamstress, Drape Make and other; [memb.] Spouse and I were Host and Hostess for Silver Square, Dance Production - Silver Bird Casino, Las Vegas till Club closed. Member after required starly-of Swinging Stars Square Dance Club Las Vegas, Nevada, 1974-1988. Also member of Dancing Shadows Round Dance Club, Butterfly Square, Square Dance

Club and NCHA Camping Promenaders. After required study became Clag Dancer and Member Silver State Daggers 1977 to 1779.; [hon.] Greatest invited Violin Soloist for graduation class banquet at Radford State Teachers College, Radford, Virginia June 1935. Same year entered Yoyo Bedspread I made - in Hobby Fair Roonoke, Virginia won ribbon 2nd place. In 1979 - designed and made as requirement Square Dance Costume for spouse and I. Entered same in Fashion Show sponsored by Jackpot Squares, Square Dance Club, Las Vegas Nevada. Won 1st prize - a beautiful trophy. December 1989 - entered contest sponsored by Meadows Park mangers, for most beautiful decorated Mobile Home. All decorations - won a beautiful plaque as 1st place.; [oth. writ.] To date have written 121 poems. My favorite "Mother You Came To Me" was written and dedicated to my adopticie Mother Julia Paule after her death. Other favorites include my Dream Castle, Teen Age Baby, and Two Baby Shoes written for my sister in dedication to my namesake niece Elizabeth Sward who died at age 2.; [pers.] I put my faith and trust in God. In Him all things are possible. I try to show love and understanding to all I meet and I hope my beloved daughter in Heaven is proud of her mom.; [a.] Gary, WV

BAREFORD, SUSAN
[pen.] Susan Prince; [b.] September 16, 1941, Wilmington, NC; [ed.] B.S. - Political Science; [occ.] Health Care Administration, State of Virginia; [memb.] Poetry Society of Va.; [oth. writ.] Several poems published in poetry magazines.; [pers.] Writing helps me know how I feel about things...; [a.] Richmond, VA

BARELA, CARL SAMMY
[pen.] Lonesome Crow Feather; [b.] May 19, 1958, San Luis, CO; [p.] Ernest and Julia Barela; [ch.] Ambrose Nathan Barela, Daphne Diane Barela; [ed.] High School graduate from Centennial High San Luis, Colorado, MTA Truck Driving College graduate, UCCS Senior; [occ.] I'm a tandem and bobtail truck driver for Pioneer Sand Company.; [memb.] Bally's US Swim and Fitness Club; [hon.] Colorado Springs Police Department Smart Driver Award; [oth. writ.] My "Donny" Poem, "Jesus Cries and Satan Laughs!", a few other poems.; [pers.] I believe Jesus is the Christ, I believe in the Power of the Holy Spirit, and in the Wrath of God. I'm gifted in writing, spelling, and poetry. I only write poems in rhyme.; [a.] Colorado Springs, CO

BARHAM, ROBERT LEE
[pen.] Big Wolf; [b.] June 18, 1950, Franklin, VA; [p.] Edward and Susie Mae Barham; [m.] Ora C. Barham, March 29, 1986; [ch.] Pearr D. Barham, Antoinette Council; [ed.] GED, Cabinet maker Commercial Arts; [occ.] Leadman State Enterprise Woodshop; [oth. writ.] I'm writing a book about my past. Paying a big price, for the love of money; [pers.] I write about life, things that's real. Each day I experience something new, learn on live. Big world of dreams, not always the way they seem.; [a.] Jarratt, VA

BARKER, DANIEL H.
[pen.] Dark Poet; [b.] May 14, 1976, Phoenix, AZ; [p.] Jack H. and Sharmaine Barker; [ed.] Graduate of Prairie Grove High School in Prairie Grove, A.R.; [occ.] Enlisted in the U.S. Air Force; [pers.] I have been greatly influenced by the works of Edgar Allen Poe, and I leave you with a question. Why can't we all just get along?; [a.] Prairie Grove, AR

BARKER, MATTHEW ADAM
[b.] September 28, 1970, West Chester, PA; [p.] Kenneth and Joanne Barker; [m.] Pamela Lynn Barker, June 25, 1994; [ed.] West Chester East Senior High, George Washington University '92, Graduate Work in Space Studies, University of North Dakota; [occ.] Air Force Officer; [memb.] Tau Epsilon Phi Fraternity, American MENSA, National Rifle Association, Air Force Association, The army and Navy Club; [hon.] Air Force Achievement Medal, Combat Readiness Medal, Golden Key Honor Society; [pers.] When everyone on this page becomes obscenely wealthy and renowned, let's get together and throw a party of epic proportions.; [a.] Grand Forks AFB, ND

BARLING, DOLORES
[b.] San Francisco, CA; [p.] Howard and Mildred Barling; [ed.] MA in Music Univ. CA Berkeley, MA in Pastoral Ministry Univ. San Francisco, BA Holy Names College, Oakland, Theology-Psychology, Rome, Social Justice, Washington, DC, Spanish, CA and Mexico; [occ.] Pastoral Minister Mission Santa Ines, Solvang, CA; [memb.] Sisters of the Holy Names of Jesus and Mary; [pers.] In our brief moment on this planet, let us embrace the joy and pain of existence. May we serve one another, striving for unity, celebrating beauty. And while bowing down before the great mystery of life, may we be lost in worship.; [a.] Solvang, CA

BARLOTTA JR., ANTHONY J.
[b.] June 16, 1941, Newark, NJ; [p.] Anthony Barlotta, Sr and Lyda Barlotta; [m.] Sandra Barlotta, November 29, 1970; [ch.] Anthony J., III and Christopher Paul; [ed.] Bloomfield Tech; [occ.] Night Manager, Weis Markets; [oth. writ.] A Tribute to Robert F. Kennedy, A Tribute to the Western Open, A Tribute to Ellis E. Paul; [pers.] The Poem to Robert F. Kennedy I wrote the day after his association. A tribute to the Western Open and Chicago were written when my wife and I were in Illinois on vacation the summer of 1984. Lastly, a tribute to Ellis E. Paul, my wife's grandfather whom I loved very much.; [a.] Dingman's Ferry, PA

BARNES, SHIRLEY A.
[pen.] Lady, Inc.; [b.] October 29, 1962, Philadelphia; [p.] Janice Slaughter, Donald Barnes; [ch.] LaToya Barnes, Brittany Barnes; [ed.] John Bartram High, Temple University, University of Penn. Writers Conference, varius Writing Courses; [occ.] Paralegal; [oth. writ.] Wonder, Wander, Wonder (book) other spiritual writings; [pers.] You are predestine to meet your destiny, so be prepared.

BARNETT, JEANNE
[pen.] Jeanne Barnett; [b.] January 8, 1924, Fresno, CA; [p.] Zona and Elwood Letson; [m.] Jack Barnett, March 30, 1952; [ch.] Penny Cooper; [ed.] Laton High School, Visalia College of the Sequoias; [occ.] Artist also Residential Design and Drafting; [memb.] Kings County Art League; [oth. writ.] A lifetime of poetry - unpublished, "How could you print a piece of your soul" Emily Dickinson; [pers.] At one time I wrote poetry as a means of survival. Now I write out of joy and amazement at the incredible guided path to enlightenment that is available to us all.; [a.] Laton, CA

BARRIE, PEGGY CREEDON
[b.] May 5, 1943, NJ; [p.] Betty and Patrick Creedon; [m.] Frank Cooper Barrie, Jr.; [ch.] Erin Elizabeth, Tara Siobhain, Brendan James; [ed.] M.A. New York University, B.A. Pace University, A.A.S. Pace University; [occ.] Junior High School Teacher, Immaculate Conception School, NYC, Principal: Donna E. Vincent; [pers.] I have been given a temporary writing talent from God which I strive to turn into a permanent writing talent for my students. Music is my exhilarating force.; [a.] New York, NY

BARRON, EMILY BETH
[b.] July 16, 1983, Boulder, CO; [p.] Molly Elizabeth Barron/Eric James Barron; [ed.] Easterly Parkway Elementary School - K through 6; [memb.] Centre County Harp Assn.; [oth. writ.] Free Air, a novel entered in the local library contest nature of character a poem written for personal pleasure.; [pers.] I really try to reflect a lot of feelings into my poems rather than just writing. Feelings help to reflect something of human nature.; [a.] State College, PA

BARROS, MICHAEL A.
[b.] February 15, 1995, Brockton, MA; [p.] Mary Barros and Alice Bullock; [ed.] Brockton High School, Massasoit Community College; [occ.] Dialysate Sieve-Perpetual; [pers.] "Take care of those you call your own and keep good company"; [a.] Brockton, MA

BARRY, JASON
[pen.] Jay; [b.] October 3, 1980, Brooklyn, NY; [p.] Terry and Rob Barry; [ed.] Pocono Mountain J.H.S. 8th grade; [occ.] Junior Ski Instructor; [memb.] S.A.D.D., (Students Against Drunk Driving), Newspaper Club Chorus; [hon.] Karate, Pool, Baseball; [oth. writ.] Articles for School newspaper. Other poems not published yet.; [pers.] At times, life can be harsh and cruel, but it can also be happy and bright especially if you have someone to share it with.; [a.] Long Pond, PA

BARTON, GAIL
[b.] December 13, 1944, Gallup, NM; [p.] Mr. and Mrs. Redlingshaefer then adopted By Billie and Robert Barton, Billie being my birth Mother's sister; [m.] James Jackson, October 27, 1978; [ed.] Arvada High School, Colorado University, Tufts University and C.U. Postgrad, Colo Inst. of Fine Arts; [occ.] Artist, and (of course) Housewife, Poet by involuntary Inspiration; [memb.] Denver Area Science Fiction Assoc. National Space Society (off and on) Denver Zoo, Denver Museum of Natural History, Denver Botanical Garden; [hon.] 1st place Miletticon Art Show 1982, 1986, 1977, 1972, Artist Guest of Honor KingCon 3, 2nd place Astronomical Art Division Westercon in San Francisco, Golden Poet Award 1989 (World Of Poetry) Hon Men. (World of Poetry) 1988; [writ.] Paper Shadows in Publication Shadow Shifting, Verses in publications Ambrov Zeor, and A Companion in Zeor, Between Galactic Arms (self published anthology) Guy-Wire Time, Verses in The Periodical Lungfish Songs published in...High Wings Thor Records; [pers.] I try to give you what I see when I perceive an event, place, being, or thought.; [a.] Lakewood, CO

BARTRON, HARRY
[b.] December 26, 1917, Van Etten, NY; [p.] Margaret Crammer, Fernando Bartron; [m.] Inez Lee Fortner, June, 1942; [ch.] Stephen Bartron, Liz Pittenger, Carol Furtick; [ed.] B.A. in English, M.A. in Speech, B.A. (Equivalancy) in Theology; [occ.] Actor, Singer, and Writer; [memb.] Screen Actors Guild, Secular Franciscan Order (Catholic), Equity, American Federation of Radio and Television Artists, Dignity, The I Am...Foundation; [hon.] Who's Who Among Students in American Universities and Colleges, Dignity Archangel Award; [oth. writ.] Poems: Book of poems entitled "Poems of Protest." A novel entitled "Drummer Boy. "Book of Poems: Entitled "Quite Another Place"; [a.] Los Angeles, CA

BARTUNEK, DIANNE D.
[b.] May 17, 1975, Parma, OH; [p.] Gayle Wilcsek; [ed.] Maple Hts. High School, Institute of Children's Literature; [occ.] Manager of Dessert Manufacturer; [pers.] My goal is to make children everywhere happy by my writing.; [a.] Maple Heights, OH

BARTUSKA, MELISSA
[b.] September 8, 1958, Tachikawa, Japan; [p.] Arnold Nita Lahti; [m.] Gary Bartuska, November 7, 1981; [ch.] Misty Dawn, Alicia Hilja, Aaron Dale; [ed.] High School; [occ.] Housewife; [pers.] Life is too short. Live everyday to its fullest.; [a.] Jefferson, TX

BASILE, LUCIANNA
[pen.] Lucianna Basile; [b.] July 26, 1932, Bronx, NY; [p.] Antoinette and Joseph Pisano; [m.] Peter Basile, October 14, 1950; [ch.] Catherine and Frank; [ed.] Walton High School - 2 yrs of College, Leahman College in Bronx, N.Y.; [occ.] Tutoring English and Astrologer (Hobby); [memb.] Local Community Assoc. and clubs, book clubs, poetry society of America; [hon.] High School Award in Languages and Art Class, Honored in School Plays for written material; [oth. writ.] As a teacher-some articles in school newspaper; [pers.] I believe that our mind is like a garden. The cycles of both seeding ideas and weeding out outworn ideas are needed to achieve personal inner happiness.

BASKS, MARK DION
[b.] March 6, 1963, Claremore, OK; [p.] Leon and Helen (Minor) Basks; [m.] Single parent raising daughter; [ch.] Lara Elizabeth Geneieve Basks; [ed.] Catoosa High School, Catoosa, OK; [occ.] Miscellaneous Machine Operator, Burgess Norton, Claremore, OK; [memb.] Hilldale Baptist Church; [pers.] Through my writing, I hope to be a spiritual lighthouse to guide other men to the Lord; [a.] Claremore, OK

BATTISTUZZI, EUGENIA C.
[b.] January 31, 1948, Shanghai, China; [p.] Sir Giulio and Eugenia Battistuzzi; [ed.] Graduate: St. Helena High School, June 1965, Gen. Secretarial Course, Empire College, Santa Rosa, CA, February 1968, Assoc. Arts Degree, Santa Rosa, Junior College, January 1974; [occ.] School Secretary, Robert Louis Stevenson Middle School St. Helena, CA; [memb.] California School Employees Association, Chapter No. 287, Women Missionary Union, First Baptist Church of St. Helena; [oth. writ.] Various other poems. I am currently working on my autobiography entitled On Eagles Wings.; [pers.] I will strive to share with my readers the presence and mercy of God and the goodness of the people who have come in and out of my life.; [a.] Saint Helena, CA

BAX, PAMELA F.
[b.] June 3, 1954, Chicago, IL; [p.] William and Elizabeth Nunley; [m.] Paul A. Bax, November 21, 1981; [ch.] Paul William Dion and Patrice Tiffany; [ed.] Bachelors of Science Masters in Guidance and Counseling, Doctoral Candidate, Ed.D. Program Northern Illinois University, DeKalb, Il.; [occ.] Professor of Counseling Governors State University; [oth. writ.] Just You Hold On published by Quill Books in whispers in the Wind, Volume VI., My Unselfish Prayer Published by World of Poetry Press, 1991; [pers.] I believe that all humans are born with an innate desire to be loved, recognized, and to achieve. I believe that this discourse cannot be realized until every member of society recognizes the other person's uniqueness and individuality. Moreover, the world cannot grow, reproduce cultural, and achieve self-actualization until respect for diversity is acknowledged. We must as a diverse society, join hands and form an alliance that will create and maintain unity, peace, harmony, liberation, and justice for all mankind.; [a.] Country Club Hills, IL

BAYER, JOANNE
[pen.] Lucia Summer; [b.] August 25, 1980, Southampton, PA; [p.] Dennis and Irma Bayer; [ed.] 8 years at Our Lady of Good Counsel School; [occ.] Student; [memb.] O.L.G.C. Yearbook, O.L.G.C. Youth Choir, O.L.G.C. Counsel Gazette, National Library of Poetry; [hon.] Winner of Upper Southampton Drug and Alcohol Advisory Counsel, International Society of Poems, Editor's Choice Award; [oth. writ.] Several other poems printed in Counsel Gazette and Reflections of light; [pers.] We have to tell everyone what's happening in the world and through poetry I do my part!; [a.] Southampton, PA

BAZEMORE, MARTHA
[b.] Hilton Head, SC; [p.] Arthur and Mary Lawyer; [m.] Thomas Bazemore; [ch.] Gary Bazemore and Lawanda Bazemore Kelley; [ed.] B.A. Education-City College, M.A. Education-Adelphi University, M.A. Science-City College. Certificate In Reading-Bank Street College; [occ.] Teacher; [oth. writ.] I wrote a poem for my senior class in high school. "Oh High School Days" The poem was put into music for the senior class graduating song.

BEACOM, JACK
[b.] December 18, 1956, Minneapolis, MN; [p.] John Beacom and Charlene Beacom; [ed.] Coon Rapids Senior High Normandale Community College; [occ.] Writer, Student; [hon.] Certificate of Excellence from the Division of Rehabilitation Services, 1994; [oth. writ.] Short stories, poems and essays; [pers.] Never let the world get old; [a.] Chaska, MN

BECKER, SYBIL WRAY
[pen.] Sybil W. Becker; [b.] August 10, 1925, Reidsville, NC; [p.] Ruth and D. F. Wray; [m.] Widow, October 26, 1946; [ch.] Sybil Joanna Becker, Kivett; [ed.] Reidsville, N.C., 11th grade; [occ.] Retired; [memb.] Woodlawn Baptist Church, Conover, N.C., (Sunday School Teacher); [oth. writ.] Inspirational poems; [pers.] I pray my poems might be a blessing to someone.; [a.] Conover, NC

BECKER, TIMOTHY E.
[pen.] Tim Beckel or Tim Beckey; [b.] December 30, 1964, Norfolk, NE; [p.] Neil W. Becker and Anne Vera Becker; [ch.] I raised two foster kids Dan Larsen and Carl Lollar; [ed.] Harry A. Burke High School, University of Nebraska at Omaha, University of Nebraska at Lincoln (BS College of Continuing Studies); [occ.] Writer, paper carrier, and student; [memb.] Holy Ghost Church, UNO Alumni Club, Writer's Digest Book Club; [hon.] Royal Patronage from Hutt River Province (1994-1995) recipient of Elmer C. Rhoden Scholarship for six semesters; [oth. writ.] I am currently working on the Changing Kid, a detailed book about the needs of kids, articles for Omaha World Herald; [pers.] It's always best to reach for the stars, excel at everything and be yourself.; [a.] Omaha, NE

BEDDEN, CARRIE
[pen.] Nina Cardinal; [b.] January 23, 1954, Faunsdale, AL; [p.] Mr. and Mrs. David Nathan; [m.] John L. Bedden Jr., February 14, 1980; [ch.] Elaine Bedden; [ed.] Johnson High, AL. A and M Univ. Temple University; [occ.] Physical Science Teacher; [memb.] Science Resource Leaders NOBCHE, NSTA; [oth. writ.] "Nothing Can Take Me", "Love or Fight", "Come on Now", "To Be Run by a Mule"; [pers.] It costs one nothing to do the right thing.; [a.] Camden, NJ

BEDELL, CARMEN
[pen.] Ellinor B., Conrad Bedell; [b.] Carmen Bedell, West Germany; [m.] First: Robert Conrad, Second: William Bedell; [ch.] Marlene; [ed.] Lyzeum, Wiesbaden, West Germany, Associate in Arts degree in Business Admin., Golden Gate University, San Francisco, Five semesters of creative writing, Skyline College, San Bruno Calif. Also: Palmer Institute of Authorship, Los Angeles, CA; [occ.] Retired as legal secretary. Also worked as bond underwriter and foreign language Teacher in S.F. prep school.; [memb.] The International Society of Poets, Alumni Assoc., Golden Gate University, San Francisco, California, Retired Employees of the City and County of San Francisco Assoc., AARP; [hon.] Two Editor's Awards from National Library of Poetry, 2nd prize in Awards Edition, January/February 1993 "Lines in the Sand", a S.F. Bay Area Literary magazine; [oth. writ.] Remarks: I wrote a full length novel in 1952. Arco Publishing turned it down after keeping it for nine months. I never submitted it again. An entire collection of short stories which I wrote as assignments for my creative writing classes. Two stories have been published.; [pers.] I feel that intellectual endeavors keep me young. Poetry is a wonderful outlet for creative energy.; [a.] Oceanside, CA

BEEBE, MATTHEW
[ed.] Linton High, Schenectady County Community College, Union College; [occ.] Student; [memb.] Staff of The Idol Literary publication; [hon.] Phi Thetta Kappa, Presidents List, Best Poem 1994; [oth. writ.] Numerous poems and lyrics. Published in Rhythms literary magazine, The Idol literary magazine as well as songs with local artist.; [pers.] For me poetry and lyrics are a journey to an inner parallel world. The challenge is to unlock this world to others, to allow those outside to touch, taste, see, smell, hear and feel what I discover. Writing is the extension of my hand for anyone to take to follow me in the exploration of this world.; [a.] Schenectady, NY

BEESON, DIXIE L.
[pen.] Dixie L. Beeson; [b.] September 28, 1925, Frisco, CO; [p.] Faye and Joe Korthius; [m.] Ray B. Beeson, April 15, 1944; [ch.] Ray II, Sandra Lee, Nancy Lynn, Jesse Overman; [ed.] Associates Degree in Dietetics; [occ.] Retired manager of school work as volunteer in Vancouver, WA, lunchrooms in Denver, CO 33 yrs.; [memb.] Hazel Dell Grange American School Food Service Association, Denver Public Schools Retired Association, Vancouver Baptist Temple; [hon.] Colorado School Food Service Association Caring Center Denver, CO, RSVP (Retired and Senior Volunteer Program), President of Denver School Food Service and State President of Colorado School Food Service; [pers.] Through poetry I can express my innermost self.; [a.] Vancouver, WA

BEIROLD, LEESA
[b.] November 25, 1968, Los Angeles; [p.] Howard and Marie Mull; [m.] Paul Beirold, Jr., March 20, 1993; [ch.] Justin Howard; [ed.] Providence High School; [occ.] Homemaker; [oth. writ.] I have my own book of poetry, none of which has ever been published before. I have written my thoughts and feelings through poetry since I was fifteen years old.; [pers.] I feel my life as a whole is such a blessed wonder, I thank God every day just to be alive. An inspirational thought to me is by Ralph Waldo Emerson: "What lies behind us and what lies before us are tiny matters, compared to what lies within us."; [a.] West Lost Angeles, CA

BELITZKY, ERICA
[b.] December 7, 1982, Brooklyn, NY; [p.] Tanya and David Belitzky; [ed.] Currently attending Junior High School in East Brunswick, NJ; [hon.] East Brunswick Public Schools Excellence Award Contest, Certificate of Creativity awarded by Child's Play Touring Theatre; [pers.] I like my poems to give the message of peace, love, and happiness. Many people have encouraged me with my writing, my family, my sister, my friends, and my seventh grade ILA teacher, Ms. V. I wish everyone could live in a peaceful world, and my poems show that.; [a.] East Brunswick, NJ

BELL, BOB
[b.] July 20, 1946, Wilmington, DE; [p.] John And Erma Bell; [ed.] BA in Church Business Admin., Southwestern Assemblies of God College-1991. Attended Gordon Connell Theological Seminary-1992.; [occ.] Auditor with the Commonwealth of Virginia; [memb.] Co-Founder "Laymen for Jesus"; [pers.] I desire to be the most effective witness I can be for Jesus Christ, by expressing His love for all mankind whether they are Christian or of other faith.; [a.] Alexandria, VA

BENDEN, JOSEPH W.
[b.] September 19, 1976, Fairview Park, OH; [p.] Vicki M. Benden; [ed.] EHOVE Career Center, Milan, OH Major: Electronic Engineering Tech.; [occ.] Midway Deli, Catawba Island, OH; [memb.] Vocational Industrial Clubs of America; [hon.] 1st place Regional Electronics, and went to State Level (3rd place), Student of the Year (junior and senior year), Award of Excellence Academic Award of 3.5+; [oth. writ.] Oak Leaves, A publication sent out by the Giving Tree of Port Clinton, Ohio; [a.] Marblehead, OH

BENDER, BETH
[b.] September 30, 1954, Harrisburg, PA; [p.] Bruce D. Krecker, Mary Beth Krecker; [m.] Stephen G. Bender, June 26, 1976; [ch.] Matthew Stephen, Adam Garrett, and Mitchell Bruce; [ed.] Susquehanna Township H.S., B.A. - Allegheny College, M. Ed. Indiana University of PA; [occ.] Part-time Secretary and Baby sitter; [oth. writ.] Feature articles about DeVry graduates, poem published in a local newspaper, stories written as gifts for my children and other children.; [pers.] Poetry is the easiest form of written expression for me because it comes straight from my heart.; [a.] Ephrata, PA

BENEDICT, CHRISTY ANN
[b.] September 5, 1972, Oswego, NY; [p.] Carl and Marie Benedict; [ed.] G. Ray Bodley High School, Onondaga Community College Psychology major; [occ.] Student, and a Drug clerk at Fay's Pharmacy, and an Assistant teacher at Doreen Lockwoods dance studio; [oth. writ.] Several poems and drawings for close family members.; [pers.] My close friends and family members have greatly influenced my poetry; [a.] Fulton, NY

BENIAMINO, JOHN PAUL
[b.] October 21, 1964, NY; [p.] Carolann and Armando; [m.] Robinann, April 5, 1986; [ch.] Erik Vincent and Matthew Robert; [ed.] John Bowne Vocational H.S.; [occ.] Country Club Greenskeeper; [oth. writ.] Unpublished poems, songs, and short stories; [pers.] Praise and love the children, relieve life through their eyes.; [a.] Bushkill, PA

BENJAMIN, ANTOINETTE LETTICE
[pen.] ALB; [b.] May 18, 1970, Washington, DC; [p.] Cornell Benjamin, Phyllis Benjamin; [ed.] Largo High School, Salisbury State University; [occ.] Public Information Specialist; [pers.] I thank God for my talent-Larry Martin Jr. family and friends for their support.; [a.] Temple Hills, MD

BENNETT, LEEKAY H.
[b.] September 13, 1939, Seattle, WA; [p.] Samuel J. Hutchinson, Ruth D. Hutchinson; [m.] Divorced; [ch.] Tammy Lynn, Teresa "Tess" Michelle and Timothy Earl; [ed.] U.S. Grant H.S. - Portland, Oregon Washington State College, Columbus State College and Lifetime Career Schools, grad.; [occ.] Manufacturer/Artist of Custom Miniatures - in one inch scale and smaller.; [memb.] N.A.M.E., Ohio Arts and Crafts Guild, Ohio Historical Society; [hon.] Chosen Ms. Congeniality at the 1988 Ms. Wheelchair Ohio pageant. Winning in 1993 and again in 1994, the honor of reading my poetry at the Columbus Arts Festival.; [oth. writ.] Several

poems published in the Delaware Gazette, local newspaper. A children's story "Packy the Poke - a - dot Pachyderm".; [pers.] I would like my poems to be enjoyed for their rhyming quality about everyday subjects, not because I'm a disabled person - even though seeing and experiencing life from a sitted position has given new meaning to the phrase, "Perspective gives the beholders eye, a season, a unique Point of View, thru Rhyme and reason.".; [a.] Delaware, OH

BENNETT, MONICA L.
[pen.] Monica; [b.] March 1, 1967, Thomasville, GA; [p.] Earl M. Bennett, Loette Kennedy; [ed.] Model Secondary School for the Deaf, Washington, D.C. North Florida Junior College, Madison, Florida Graduate with honor roll; [occ.] I am looking for employment, volunteer; [memb.] 1st Baptist Church, Taekwando, Columbia House, William Shatner Connection, Naval Institute, Star Trek Communicator, Pen Pals Clubs; [hon.] 1st Degree Black Belt, Deaf Women of the Year, Poet of the Year (nominated) Miss T.E.E.N., Honor Roll Student, National History and Government Award 1995 North American Open Poetry Contest; [oth. writ.] I was a writer Digest Student, I received diploma in the school. Poems 'The Out and On Moon'. 'Love is my Favorite Emotion' I am thinking of writing a novel for Bad Burt.; [pers.] I love to write in what is in my mind and my heart spread the realities I like people as well as things. I like politics as well as arts. Please stay in touch!; [a.] Knoxville, TN

BENNIGHT, MECHA ANN
[pen.] Scrambles; [b.] July 8, 1977, Warren OH; [p.] Mr. and Mrs. Daniel Montgomery; [ed.] High School Senior; [occ.] Student; [memb.] Future Teachers, Future Home Makers; [oth. writ.] Several poems in local papers; [pers.] This poem was my first and is my father's favorite.; [a.] Youngstown, OH

BERENSON, LORRAINE
[b.] November 15, 1924, Philadelphia, PA; [p.] Rose and Samuel Pollock; [m.] Albert Berenson (Deceased), March 20, 1949; [ch.] Kathy Bonfig, Craig Berenson; [ed.] High School Grad. West Philadelphia High Phila., PA, Bucks County Tech. School Levittown, PA; [occ.] Retired Nursing Assistant; [memb.] Lower bucks activity center, Bristol, PA Bristol Township Seniors, Levittown, Levittown Seniors, Levittown, PA. Bensalem Seniors, Bensalem; [hon.] Woman of the tears - Deborah Heart and Lung Center Certificates for volunteer work in Galilee Villrof Village and in Bristol Townwship Elementary Schools; [oth. writ.] I write a column entitled "profiles in the news" in the Galilee Gazette I also send in poetry to this publication; [pers.] I have been writing from the bottom of my heart for years and would love to be recognized as a poet. It would be gratifying to see my poem published; [a.] Levittown, PA

BERGER, MICHELLE K.
[b.] November 13, 1973, Coldwater, OH; [p.] William and Janice Berger; [ed.] Marion Local High School, Maria Stein, OH. Xavier University, Cincinnati, OH; [hon.] Xavier D'Artagnan Chapter of Mortar Board, National Honor Society, Dean's List, Special recognition in 1990-91 Lucille Loy Kuck Ohioana Award for Excellence in Creative Writing; [pers.] I would like to thank my family and friends for all they have given me in life and my teachers for showing me the writer I can be.; [a.] Osgood, OH

BERTRAND, ASHLEY
[pen.] Ashley Bertrand; [b.] January 5, 1932, Detroit, MI; [p.] Lilian, and Ashley and Bertrand; [m.] February 21, 1960; [ch.] Two sons; [ed.] High School; [occ.] Retired; [memb.] A.A.R.P., Local 898; [oth. writ.] I have many writings Accumulated over the years.; [pers.]

I have been influenced by Kahil Gibran. Mostly, I try being original. I have to say a thing, my way.; [a.] Detroit, MI

BEVERLY, BETTY L.
[b.] July 26, 1928, Wenas, WA; [p.] Roy and Coral Longmire; [ch.] Rita Uber, Carol Ashworth, Richard Addington; [ed.] Selah High School; [occ.] Field Office Manager for a fruit cannery; [memb.] VFW Auxillary; [a.] Yakima, WA

BEVING, GAIL LYNN
[b.] November 30, 1976, Wisconsin; [p.] Darrell and Charlotte Beving; [ed.] Terril High School; [occ.] Full-time student; [memb.] Lakeland Raider 4-H, National Honor Society; [hon.] Academic All-Conference Minor letter in choir, 3 pins in journalism National Honor Society pin; [oth. writ.] Articles for the school newspaper, poems published in the Anthology of poetry by young Americans and a poem published in the High School Writer; [pers.] I like to write about love and friendship because they've both played important roles in my life.; [a.] Dickens, IA

BIERBAUER, DEBRA ANNE
[b.] October 11, 1972, Oil City, PA; [p.] Ted Bierbauer Jr., Mary Anne Bierbauer; [ed.] Oil City Senior High, Mercyhurst College Erie, PA; [occ.] Student; [pers.] My poem is dedicated to my deceased sister.; [a.] Oil City, PA

BIGGS, JOHN TAYLOR
[b.] July 10, 1976; [p.] David and Maggie Biggs; [ed.] Raceland High School Shawnee State University; [occ.] Student; [memb.] First Baptist Church; [a.] South Shore, KY

BINNS, ALLEN L.
[b.] July 29, 1928, Scott City, KS; [p.] Sam and Inez Binns; [m.] Divorced; [ch.] 8; [ed.] High School, Selected College Course; [occ.] Retired, Self-employed; [memb.] American Legion; [hon.] Several-Relating to sales and management; [oth. writ.] None published; [pers.] All poetry that I write is spontaneous-covering wide field of subjects; [a.] Moore, OK

BIRCHLER, MARY
[b.] March 27, 1949, New Buffalo, MI; [p.] Joseph Carpenter, Verdon Carpenter; [ch.] Terri Dawn Faucett, Aaron Owen Steenson; [sib.] Chester High (GED), BAC (Red Bud Campus), Currently NRI Writing School; [occ.] Associate for AFLAC - American Family Life Assurance Company; [hon.] 3 - with Highest Honors Awards - NRI, Sales Champion Tournament of Champions Certificate; [oth. writ.] Murder Mystery-Short Story, Suspense Romance-Novel - Both as yet unpublished, currently working on: Cult Thriller Novel; [pers.] Always remember no matter how dark the clouds, the sun is just on the other side, and never forget no matter how deep the trouble, despair, or fear, peace is as close as the heart; [a.] Sparta, IL

BIRDSONG, KAREN
[pen.] Tippi; [b.] April 13, 1953, Muncie, IN; [p.] Shirely Simmons; [m.] Alex Birdsong, September 19, 1987; [ch.] Carlos Wilkerson, Carletta Wilkerson, Feather Birdsong; [ed.] Roosevelt High School finished up to the 8th grade; [occ.] Homemaker; [memb.] Third Baptist Church; [oth. writ.] Several poems "Forgive Me O' Lord", "Peace", "I Dream", "A Kings Castle", "It Doesn't Figure"; [pers.] Even though I haven't finished school, my greatest inspiration were my children, they have given me my strength to become the writer that I am today; [a.] Xenia, OH

BITTING, DORIS E.
[pen.] Dew Marletz; [b.] March 31, 1924, Blain, PA; [p.] Frank J. Wohletz; [m.] Eleanor S. (Martin) Wohletz, September 11, 1948; [ch.] Richard E. Bitting Jr., David W. Bitting; [ed.] Blain Vocational High; [occ.] Homemaker retired; [memb.] Matamoras Community Church, Halifax Historical Society; [oth. writ.] One poem published in local newspaper; [pers.] I attempt to tell a story with my poems, and relate some interesting facts that others might enjoy.; [a.] Halifax, PA

BLACK, GRACIE
[b.] March 14, 1915, Hickory Valley, TN; [p.] Charlie and Leona Smith; [m.] James Black (deceased), May 15, 1941; [ed.] Grand Junction High, Memphis State University; [occ.] Retired School teacher; [pers.] Since retirement I spend time during volunteer work at Church, The Senior Citizens Group, tutoring slow children, (etc) I believe I serve God when serving others; [a.] Grand Junction, TN

BLACK, JASON ALLEN
[pen.] J. Allen Black; [b.] October 31, 1969, Redwood City, CA; [p.] George W. Black Sr, Jo Evelyn Pounds; [ed.] High School: Bellarmine College Preparatory, San Jose, CA College: Loyola Marymount University, Los Angeles; [occ.] Reservations Agent, Hyatt Regency San Francisco and Singer/Guitarist; [oth. writ.] Several unpublished short horror stories; [pers.] Words and music are precious gifts. Playing with them demonstrates our appreciation of the giver.; [a.] San Bruno, CA

BLACK, LINDA ANN
[b.] September 11, 1946, Conneaut, OH; [p.] James and Bessie Green; [m.] Don L. Black; [occ.] Registered Nurse; [pers.] The emotions I feel, in response to everyday experiences, provide my inspiration.; [a.] Fullerton, CA

BLACK, PATRICIA
[pen.] Pat Black; [b.] April 25, 1966, Arkansas; [p.] Mary and Curtis Robinson; [m.] Ulysses Black, January 27, 1993; [ed.] Graduate of Wyandotte High School 1984, also attended Kansas City Kansas Community College; [occ.] Customer Service Rep. for a utility company; [oth. writ.] Self poetry for personal use. I also write for people indifferent types of situations.; [pers.] My writing skills are from different types of experiences, and situations to shed light on reality. To ensure and help others; [a.] Kansas City, KS

BLACKMAN, BURKE
[b.] January 20, 1976, San Antonio, TX; [p.] Barbara Blackman, Barry Blackman; [ed.] Samuel Clemens High, Incarvale Word College; [occ.] Telephone operator, U.S. Long Distance; [memb.] International Thespian Society; [hon.] Distinguished Presidential Scholarship - Incarvale Word College, Dean's List, Editor of high school literary magazine, Quixote; [oth. writ.] Unsubmitted, unpublished poetry and short stories; [pers.] Instead of heavy usage of word fool my, which seems the modern trend, I put my faith in word play. Truly good poetry manipulates the established constraints of the English language, not avoids them altogether.; [a.] San Antonio, TX

BLAINE, MICHAEL
[pen.] MB; [b.] August 20, 1961, Detroit, MI; [p.] Albert and Shirley Blaine; [ch.] Danielle and Amanda Blaine; [ed.] Troy-Athens High, MSU, MaComb Community College; [occ.] Custom Decorating Consultant; [memb.] DIGNITY Catholic Church (Detroit Chapter), American Bowling Congress, Fitness USA Health Spas, Bally's Vic Tanny Health Club, Down River Social Club; [hon.] Dean's List (several years); [oth.

writ.] Many unpublished works!; [pers.] Number one Hero: Yoko Ono, "Life is a quest leading back to your dreams....." MB '95; [a.] Belleville, MI

BLAIR, MISTY
[b.] October 23, 1980, Greenville, SC; [p.] Molly Blair; [ed.] Am attending Richland High (going into 10th grade); [memb.] JROTC (Jr Reserved Officers Training Corps), Science Fiction Book Club; [oth. writ.] I have wrote many poems in my spare time. Me and my friends are in the process of making a book of poems.; [pers.] The world in my eyes need more love. Everyone should show more love for there fellow brethren. A world without love is a world dead and desolate.; [a.] North Richland Hills, TX

BLAIR, TRACEY
[b.] June 3, 1967, Welland, Ontario, Canada; [a.] Victoria British Columbia, Canada

BLANDER, BARRY B.
[b.] November 19, 1952, Brooklyn, MA; [p.] Bernard H. Blander and Esther Anne Blander; [ed.] B.S. Emerson College, Boston, MA 1974; [occ.] Free-lance writer; [oth. writ.] Author of 3 plays, Forgiveness, (performed in Boston, October 1984), The First Snow (revision of Forgiving), The Abolitionist (An Historical Drama), I like to dabble in poetry; [pers.] Currently being represented by the Bertha Klausner International Literary Agency of New York, New York; [a.] Boston, MA

BLISS, MICHAEL E.
[b.] May 31, 1952, Wichita, KS; [p.] Dale E. and E. Jeanne Bliss; [m.] Kathleen A. Bliss, May 4, 1979; [ch.] Myki, Mandi, Matt, Melissa; [ed.] Maize High School (1970), Military Electronics Schools, Electrical Apprenticeship School (1981); [occ.] Electrician, Instructor at Wichita Electrical Training Center; [memb.] Veterans of Foreign Wars Post 4664 Maize, Ks (life member), The Ark Church Maize, KS; [hon.] Various awards from service in the Marine Corps including Republic of Vietnam Cross of Gallantry, Outstanding Apprentice 1981, All-state Team of Quartermasters 1993 (VFW).; [oth. writ.] Other poems and short stories; [pers.] I believe that whatever we accomplish in this life is made possible only through the grace of Jesus Christ and He should receive all the glory.; [a.] Wichita, KS

BLY, DOUGLAS ALEXANDER
[pen.] Taz, Captain, Doogie; [b.] December 12, 1968, Mount Holly; [p.] Gisela Juliana Bly, Robert John Bly (deceased); [ed.] Montclair State College 1991, National League Baseball School for umpires graduate with honors in 1992; [occ.] Psycho-Social Rehabilitator, Certified NJ State Umpire; [memb.] Tau Kappa Epsilon Fraternity, South Jersey Umpire Association; [hon.] Moorestown High School Hall of Fame; [oth. writ.] College newspaper columnist; [pers.] Learn yourself all the time and remember where you come from. Appreciate others for what their abilities allow them to do, not what they cannot.; [a.] Moorestown, NJ

BODENHORN, BETTE ANNE
[b.] February 8, 1955, Detroit, MI; [p.] Glenn and Doris Mutter; [m.] Lee A. Bodenhorn, May 25, 1985; [ch.] Beth D'Amico, Lisa Kott, Wendy Valente, Jason Oody, Justin Oody; [ed.] Redford Union High School 1973 Livonia Business Institute 1973 The Academy of Hair Design - 1979 Master Barber Stylist Degree; [occ.] Rectory Kitchen Supervisor and Cook for Sacred Heart Catholic Church; [memb.] Roseville Historical Society; [pers.] This poem is dedicated to my Mother who was an excellent role model. The love we shared was my inspiration for this poem and life. Surround yourself with loved ones.; [a.] Roseville, MI

BODINE, BLAIR DILWORTH
[pen.] Blair Dilworth Bodine; [b.] January 24, 1984, Philadelphia; [p.] Barbara Carty Bodine and Lawrence Dilworth Bodine; [ed.] 5th Grade Student at German town Academy; [occ.] Young author and student; [hon.] Blair has won numerous awards and recognition for her talents. This includes a poem about Peace called "Battlefield" that was published in the Peace Action Newsletter and a Philadelphia Contest sponsored by "Chilis" Restaurant. Her work appears in student publications and she is a talented young voice.; [oth. writ.] "Battlefield", "Nigthmare", "Sorrowful Soldier" and "Things Inside of Me."; [per.] "I believe that all voices make a difference in this world ... young or old"; [a.] Ambler, PA

BOERGER, NANCY S.
[b.] September 12, 1949, Coshocton, OH; [p.] Kenneth and Betty (Dixon) Bercot; [m.] Larry S. Boerger, January 11, 1975 (deceased); [ch.] Rebecca L. Boerger, Brian S. Boerger; [ed.] 1968 Coshocton High School Real Estate at COTC, Computer Intro. JVS. Presently attending MATC Zanesville, OH; [occ.] Homemaker, student at MATC Zanesville, OH-foster parent; [memb.] Church of the Nazarene; [hon.] Dean's List; [oth. writ.] None published; [pers.] I love the way poetry can lift you up and make you smile or touch your life in some unique way. My desire it to some how touch my fellow man.; [a.] West Laffayette, OH

BOGGS III, RUFUS L.
[pen.] R. L. Boggs III; [b.] October 3, 1961, Greenville, SC; [p.] R. L. Jr. and Mildred Boggs; [m.] Single parent; [ch.] Jonathan L. and Joshua J. D. Boggs; [ed.] 12 grade at Parker High School; [occ.] Auto glass installer; [oth. writ.] Several poems and song's not published; [pers.] I strive to make one think of they're life and maybe change it for the best or to simply make them smile; [a.] Simpsonville, SC

BOLEK, BARBARA ANN
[pen.] Banshee Shadow Wolf; [b.] April 19, 1957, Detroit, MI; [p.] Anthony Bolek, Amelia (Mikosz) Bolek; [m.] Alan Toubeaux, November 18, 1981; [ch.] Brandon Bolek-Toubeaux; [ed.] Osborn High School Wayne State University - B.A. Journalism; [occ.] Library Search Analyst; [memb.] Salis - Substance Abuse Librarians and Information Specialists; [hon.] Dean's List; [oth. writ.] Poem accepted for publication in the Metro Times 1994 summer Fiction Issue. Writer and Editor of Crow's Cause: News, Comment and Controversy, a newsletter. Typesetting: Moving Out: A Feminist Literary Arts Journal - 1995 issue. Contributing Writer to Wayne State University student newspaper, The South End.; [pers.] The journalist in me is revealed in my poetry. Poetry is an eyewitness account from the eyes of the soul.; [a.] Hamtramck, MI

BOLICK, ELIZABETH STOWERS
[b.] May 23, 1930, Pearisburg Giles Co., VA; [p.] Ernest and Hallie Stowers (deceased); [m.] Robert Kelly Bolick, September 24, 1983; [ch.] Jay Butler, Tina Cline and Jeanne Beckner; [ed.] 2 years Radford College Woman's Div. of VPI-Va.; [occ.] Retired, Housewife; [memb.] Baptist Church, Historical Preservation Society, American Heart Assoc., Audubon Society; [hon.] Graduated with honors Blacksburg High School-Va. Beta Club; [oth. writ.] Many. Local newspapers - National level poetry winner-Great American Poetry, Anthology - John Campbell Editor and Publisher 1988; [pers.] Since grade school I've been writing poetry about my true life experiences.. My love of nature...sadness or joy..my faith and heartfelt love.; [a.] Gastonia, NC.

BOLTON, HELEN DELANEY
[pen.] H. D. Bolton; [b.] March 9, 1910, Olympia, WA; [p.] Emma Holland Levi Holland; [m.] 1943; [ed.] Grade School 1-8 State Exams; [occ.] Retired Cook; [memb.] U.F.W.; [oth. writ.] No more published, but lots of scribed of my own written for my own good and bad. Lots of pretty ones, some silly, always make up for my own Christmas, and holidays; [pers.] I wrote this for my mother pluring good friday earth crock in Alaska in 1974 Shehlied before I could get home June 6, 1974; [a.] Tacoma, WA

BOMAR, CYNTHIA B.
[pen.] Cindy Bomar; [b.] June 20, 1964, Halifax, VA; [p.] Mr. David Booker and Ms. Betty Booker; [m.] Mr. Tim Bomar, January 23, 1988; [ch.] Morgan Brittany Bomar 4 yrs. old; [ed.] William Campbell High School, Central Virginia Community College; [occ.] District Loan Technician, Special Emphasis Program Manager for USDA, Rural Economic and Community Development; [memb.] National Association of County Office Assistants and Clerks, Brookneal Baptist Church; [hon.] Graduated with Honors, Appointed to serve as Chairperson of the National District Office Committee; [oth. writ.] Several poems published in local newspapers, article for The Union Star; [pers.] I write poems concerning topics that are emotionally moving and by sharing then with others will hopefully trigger positive thinking.; [a.] Brookneal, VA

BOOTH, CINDY
[b.] July 9, 1964; [p.] James and Shirley Boaz; [m.] Cpt. James P. Booth; [ch.] Jessica, Michael and James David; [ed.] Beauty Consultant with Mary Kay; [oth. writ.] I have written over 100 poems never seen. This is my first poem submitted.; [pers.] This poem is in dedication to my brother who was killed in a car accident in 1990. James David Boaz, ascended into the sky at age 24, March 3, 1990; [a.] Chesterfield Township, MI

BOREMAN, AMANDA KAYE
[pen.] Mary Poppins; [b.] May 14, 1980, Hazel Crest; [p.] Walter and Brenda Boreman; [ed.] Freshman Bloom Trail High School; [occ.] Student; [hon.] Basketball, Softball, and Bowling; [pers.] I like to write poems and go roller skating. I would like to work with killer whales in the future. I like to read.; [a.] Sauk Village, IL

BORGES, DENNIS
[pen.] Diniz Aurelio; [b.] October 20, 1958, Acores-Portugal; [p.] Jose and Albertina Borges; [m.] Niveria; [ch.] Steven Vincent and Michael Dennis; [ed.] Finishing Bachelor of Arts at Chapman University; [occ.] Sales, Teacher, Journalist; [memb.] Cultural director at the Portuguese Center for Evangelization and Culture. Coordinator of the Cultural Radio Show. Dimensao 2000. Organizer of an Annual Symposium on Portuguese Literature- "Filaments of the Atlantic Heritage"; [hon.] Deans list at Chapman Univ., Medal of Honor from the Portuguese Government; [oth. writ.] Maintains a regular column in the Azorean Newspaper "Correio dos Acures. Writer for 4 Portuguese-American Newspapers. Collaborates with a couple of literary supplements in Portugal.; [pers.] As I write, I cannot close the door to the world.; [a.] Tulare, CA

BOSCINI, VERONICA
[b.] January 12, 1957, Brooklyn, NY; [p.] Veronica and John (deceased); [m.] Thomas Boscini, May 15, 1976; [ch.] Thomas and Elisa Boscini; [ed.] Finished High School; [occ.] Disabled S.S.; [oth. writ.] "My Guardian Angel", "Just Say You Still Care", "Forbidden Love", There's Nothing Stronger Than Our Love, Come Be My Man Take My Hand, I'm So in Love with You; [pers.] In 1976, I wrote a song titled "My Love" which was stolen from me by voice instructor. Which was later to become known as "You Light Up My Life." With no way of proving I wrote it.; [a.] Winter Park, FL

BOUGHER, DAWN
[b.] February 19, 1977, Marion, IN; [p.] Terry and Kathy Bougher; [ed.] Senior at Jefferson County High School in Dandridge, Tennessee; [occ.] Employed by Philips Consumer Electronics; [memb.] Beta Club, National Art Honor Society, Pep Club, Academic Imentire Program (2 years); [hon.] Presidential Academic Fitness Award, Honor roll, many art awards, academic incentive program honore; [oth. writ.] Poem published in school literary magazine voices and visions; [a.] Dandridge, TN

BOUHAMIDI, CHERIF
[pen.] Shez, Riff; [b.] May 1, 1950, Rachidia, Morrocco; [hon.] Readings and Lectures Locally and Abroad; [oth. writ.] "Le Lezard", Poetic autobiography "I do not I", poetry book "The Title Is Up To You", humorous book (no submissions yet); [pers.] 25 years of writing M way out of circles, of notions, of nations... I am home. I am a citizen of the world.; [a.] Palm Desert

BOUZA, JENNY TRAVERS
[b.] March 10, 1915, New York City; [p.] Michael and Bertha Travers; [m.] Anthony Bouza - (Deceased); [ch.] (5) 4 sons, 1 daughter, 12 grandchildren - 6 boys and 6 girls; [ed.] Drake's Business Institute; [occ.] Home maker - time dedicated to raising a family; [pers.] My interest are varied nutrition, creative writing and astrology poetry is my hobby which I hope to have published in the near future. Know that "Life is the greatest teacher and love conquers all.; [a.] Greenwich, CT

BOWMAN, BALINDA OLIVE
[pen.] Balinda Olive; [b.] November 9, 1953, Portland, OR; [p.] Herbert Olive (deceased), Martha Vanarsdale Olive; [m.] Ronald Bowman (deceased), May 6, 1989; [ch.] Muhammad, Lashonti; [ed.] John Adams High School, Oregon State University; [occ.] Member Services Liaison Blue Cross Blue Shield of Oregon; [oth. writ.] I have written dozens of poems. I am working on my novel, "I saw a vision, but I was diagnosed crazy."; [pers.] I enjoy writing my thought son paper. I try to focus on the way I see this world. I am inspired by the truth.; [a.] Vancouver, WA

BOYADJIAN, KNARIG
[b.] Beirut, Lebanon; [p.] Nazar and Alice Nazarian; [m.] Noubar Boyadjian; [ch.] Hryr, Zareh and Sera Boyadjian; [ed.] Beirut Women's College, Humanities; [occ.] Poet and Composer; [memb.] National League of American Pen Women, Santa Monica Branch, National Federation of Music Clubs, World Congress of Poets, The Manuscript Club of Los Angeles, Southern Calif. Motion Picture Council; [hon.] International Dove Award, For Poetry, (1994) Australia, Gold Medal (Poet Laureate Int'l, Bangkok, Thailand) For poetry, Gov't. of India, Hon. Doctorate, Lit., World Academy of Af Arts and Culture, Taipei, China, Poetry listed "Who's Who", Cambridge, England Hon. Doctorate, World University Listed "5,000 personalities of the world" India, Grand Dame of the Order of the Knights of Malta; [oth. writ.] Published books - The Pink World, (poetry), The Music of Crystals, While Seagulls Climb, The Daunted Swallow, Love, There is no Time, The Lighted Broom, In Search of Life, From the Beginning to the Beginning (3 titles published in translation); [pers.] "In the rainy moments of this world, let me shelter you with my umbrella and let it pass from hand to hand until the rainbow reveals its promise."; [a.] Van Nuys, CA

BOYD, CORALEE
[b.] September 9, 1975, Chehalis, WA; [p.] Gordon and Dorothy Boyd; [ch.] Amber Nicolle Boyd; [ed.] Graduated from W.F. West High School; [occ.] Veterinarian Assistant, Receptionist, at The Chehalis Vet Hospital; [pers.] I express my thoughts and my feelings in my writing. I can escape this way, and then I turn my writings in to poetry. It means more to me, (all my poems are about people); [a.] Chehalis, WA

BOYD, D. H.
[pen.] George Alicea Heinze; [b.] Santa Monica, CA; [p.] George and Alice Heinze; [m.] Deceased; [ed.] High School, Otis Art Institute, Art Center (LA), Private writer's clubs, Adult School in writing. 7 years Comm. of Nothrop's Art Club. Studied music. Also people and Photography contest awards studies in nature.; [occ.] Retired from 'Creative Design Artist'; [hon.] 14 Suggestion work awards, Tech. Ill. awards, Pub. poems in Adult School papers. Photography 1st 2nd prizes in contests.; [oth. writ.] Children's fantasy stories. Story poems, Fiction stories.; [pers.] I write in honor of my beloved parents, who worked so hard to support my creative interests and humbly what I do is their memory, their love. And faithful friends Roy and Mazzie Holes. "If we give all we can, better would life be for man"... thoughts.; [a.] Thousand Oaks, CA

BOYD, JAY E.
[pen.] Jay E. Boyd; [b.] May 6, 1950, Baltimore, MD; [p.] Jay M. Boyd, Jr. and Margaret Culler Boyd (deceased); [ed.] Friends School (Baltimore), West Virginia Wesleyan College (B.A. 1972), The Catholic University of America (M.A. 1974); [occ.] Computer Specialist/Systems Analyst; [hon.] Hatfield Fine Arts Award (W.V.W.C., 1972), Omicron Delta Kappa (Leadership Honorary), Kappa Pi (Art Honorary), Alpha Psi Omega (Drama Honorary), Mayor's Citation (Baltimore); [oth. writ.] Poem published in "The Mock Turtle" (Friends School Literary Publication). I'm currently in the process of writing a book - A multi-generation Saga about my ancestors.; [pers.] We can accomplish so much if we can learn to work together instead of working against one another. Diversity is the spice of life. It's what makes us different from one another that makes us interesting to one another.; [a.] Reisterstown, MD

BRACE, LAURIE
[b.] February 9, 1927, Chicago, IL; [ch.] Robert Haynes and Judith Haynes; [ed.] College (Humanities) Merritt Jr. College; [memb.] People for the Ethical Treatment of Animals; [oth. writ.] Other poetry, Awaken My Soul, Oh Inner Child etc.; [pers.] My writing commenced after the death of my daughter, Judith Ann Haynes, March 7, 1992. This poem is in her memory.; [a.] Berkeley, CA

BRADY, NINA L.
[b.] November 9, 1913, Wyandot County, OH; [p.] Isaac Myrtle Brewer; [m.] John A. Brady, June 14, 1932; [ch.] Carol Ebert, Bradford Brady; [ed.] High School (Harding);· [occ.] Retired; [memb.] Poetry day in Marion Association Federation of Women's Clubs, Lydia Chapter #83 O.E.S. White Lily Temple #273, Timothy Lutheran Church; [hon.] Second place Poet of the Year 1994, first place Poet of the Year 1995; [oth. writ.] Two books, yesterday and the day, before I and II, wrote articles and poems for several newspaper and church bulletin

BRAND, JOHN F.
[b.] May 1, 1912, Opekiska, WV; [p.] James M. and Virginia Brand; [m.] Susie M. Brand, June 7, 1947, Evelyn H. Brand, February 12, 1983; [ch.] Freeman C. Brand (by No. 1); [ed.] Completed 8th Grade in one

room school at Opekiska, WV; [occ.] Minister in Church of God 49 yrs. Also was truck driver to supplement salary, Retired from Pastoral Work; [memb.] Church of God (62 years), Senior Citizens; [hon.] Poems published in 4 books; [oth. writ.] Random Recollections (a 414 page scapbook written from memory), other books, The Cream Of The Crop: Evening Bells: The Last Straw: (I printed these on a mimeograph and bound them myself). Plus smaller books of poetry, verse and prose, (4).; [pers.] I just wanted to add that the name on my birth certificate is John Freeman Brooks, Alvin Rand. (There's a story behind that!); [a.] Nutter Fort, WV

BRECHBILL, ANN CHRISTINE
[pen.] Ann Christine Brechbill; [b.] December 14, 1976, Chambersburg, PA; [p.] Daniel and Patricia Brechbill; [ed.] Graduated from James Buchanan High School in 1995. Went on to Sawyer Business College in Pittsburgh.; [occ.] Still deciding; [oth. writ.] This is the first of my poems published. I have over 13 others that I have written in the last 2 years.; [pers.] Every poem that I have written is a description of an experience that I have had in my life. I try to include myself in every word I write in my poetry, and I try to make people feel my own experiences through my writing.; [a.] Greencastle, PA

BREDING, BETTY M.
[b.] July 17, 1929, ND; [p.] Delmar Dahl, Bertha Dahl; [m.] Vernon Breding, June 10, 1948; [ch.] Robert Breding, Steven Breding; [occ.] Licensed practical nurse, home health care; [memb.] Ladies Aux VFW, Civic Club; [hon.] 14 yr Service Award Tioga Medical Center; [oth. writ.] Letters in a daily newspapers; [pers.] Ultimate Happiness is found in a life of service to others; [a.] Powers Lake, ND

BREIT, MICHAEL F.
[pen.] Michael F. Breit; [b.] September 29, 1918, Beaver Falls, PA; [p.] Michael and Sara Breit (deceased); [m.] Dorothy Woods Breit (deceased), February 14, 1947; [ch.] One daughter - Deborah Ann Breit; [ed.] High School - Beaver Falls H.S. graduate class of 1936 - June; [occ.] Retired Steel Worker Beaver Falls, at Bobcock and Wilcox (McDermott); [memb.] A.A.R.P., S.O.A.R. (Retired Steelworkers), National Council of Senior Citizens, The American Legion Post 0261, St. Paul's Evangelical Lutheran Church in Beaver Falls; [hon.] World War II Veteran Good Conduct Medal, Bronze Star (Germany) European Theater for Operation 330th Harbor Craft Company - Army of the United States - Technician 4th grade. Thank you letter from President Truman for serving in the Armed Forces; [pers.] Writing helps me to relax and reflect on life and the people I meet. As a Christian I strive to share with others my feelings of what is truly important to myself and mankind.; [a.] Beaver Falls, PA

BRELAND, JANE G.
[p.] Mavis and Ferrel Greer; [m.] divorced; [ch.] Angela and David, Jr.; [ed.] Graduate of Linn High School, 1961; [memb.] Hernando Baptist Church, Hernando Chamber of Commerce, Christian Singles Network, Solo's Square Dance Club; [oth. writ.] Many poems and short stories; [pers.] My talent is God given and my desire is to share His Greatness, His Love and His Mercy with others.; [a.] Hernando, MS

BRENNAN, RICHARD
[b.] January 4, 1929, Moline, IL; [p.] Clarence and Alice Brennan; [m.] Judy, February 15, 1962 (deceased); [ch.] Lawrence W. Brennan and James R. Brennan; [ed.] BA in English Composition with a minor in theater, University of Illinois, Champaign, Urbana in 1952; [occ.] Retired Daily Newspaper Bureau Chief; [hon.] University of Illinois English Department Poetry Prize 1949; [oth. writ.] About 100 poems, three full-length plays and two novels; [pers.] Not even a newsman can write correctly without being a poet. I know.; [a.] Geneseo, IL

BRENNEMAN, NORMA JEAN
[pen.] Jeanie West; [b.] Birmingham, MO; [p.] Glen West, Violet Heater; [ch.] Gregory Frederick, Todd Frederick; [ed.] Jarbalo High School 2 yrs Dental Therapist School - U.S. Dental Corp. Ft. Leavenworth, KS; [occ.] Ret. D.T.A.; [memb.] Leav Garden Club Natl. Board of Dental X-Ray Radiology.; [pers.] Writing is like the wind - grasp it quickly for it is gone.; [a.] Leavenworth, KS

BREWER, CAROL MARIE
[b.] August 30, 1942, Dayton, OH; [p.] Ralph and Clara Brewer; [occ.] Former Reg. Nurse, hypnotherapist, now disabled by Disseminated Lyme Disease; [memb.] I am an opinionated, yet questioning, member of the human race; [oth. writ.] Two poems published in Treasured Poems of America by Sparrow grass Poetry Forum, Inc. (to be out in Dec. '95); [pers.] In our fast-paced society, many people do not take the time to sit and converse with others, and get to know each other well. In my writing, I feel it is a way for friends, and loved ones to gain insight on my own personal philosophy at their convenience. Journals and writings of any type are valuable insights into family history.; [a.] Dayton, OH

BRICKMAN, CALEB NATHANAEL
[b.] March 17, 1978, Garland, TX; [p.] Les and Twyla Brickman; [ed.] High School, Music School; [occ.] Musician, investor; [oth. writ.] Melodic Agony; [pers.] Always remember: Something beginning so beautifully can end so deadly... pain = knowledge, knowledge = pain; [a.] Jupiter, FL

BRICKMAN, KATIE
[b.] February 14, 1961, Painesville, OH; [p.] Ray and Dorothy Jylanki; [m.] Daniel A. Brickman, August 7, 1992; [ch.] Thomas Allen, Matthew Daniel; [ed.] Mentor High School, Cleveland Institute for Medical Assisting, Cleveland State University; [occ.] Medical- Psychology, Pediatric University Hospitals of Cleveland; [hon.] Cum Laude; [oth. writ.] Several poems published mentor in High School literary booklet; [pers.] Writing poems in a release for me, of my innermost thoughts and feelings. They remind me that life is a constant learning experience-one worth striving for.; [a.] Euclid, OH

BRIGGS, ALICE LEE
[b.] May 29, 1957, Columbia, SC; [p.] James and Ruth Ann Briggs; [ch.] Tykiesha Nieovie Briggs; [ed.] C.A. Johnson High School; [occ.] Laundry Assistant; [memb.] Young Adult Choir - Young Adult Choir for Emmanuel A.M.E.; [pers.] He that desires, endures. He that endures, rules the world.?; [a.] Columbia, SC

BRIGGS, DEENA
[pen.] Goldie Christian; [b.] July 9, 1952, Upland; [p.] Mikki Lewis and Frank Moats; [m.] Divorced; [ch.] Cory "Ric"; [ed.] Fontana High, Chaffey College; [occ.] Judicial Secretary; [memb.] California State Employees Assn., Calvary Chapel; [hon.] Dean's List, Pioneer Club Leader/Guide/Camp Counselor; [oth. writ.] Poems published in school newspapers; [pers.] My inspiration comes not only from my own son, but all the children I have worked with. I strive to create and bring to life the child in all of us and use my God-given talent to reflect and bring joy to others.; [a.] Running Springs, CA

BRIGGS, IRA W.
[b.] January 14, 1939, Post, TX; [p.] Ben, Wynama Briggs; [m.] Myrna, June 18, 1960; [ch.] Timothy, Brian; [ed.] Lamesa High, South Western College, San Diego State University; [occ.] U.S. Navy Retired, Master Chief Petty Officer; [memb.] Knights of Columbus, Fleet Reserve Association Naval Enlisted Retired Dental Technician Association; [hon.] Dean's Lists, Meritorious Service Medal, Navy Achievement Medal; [pers.] Success Through Dedication; [a.] San Diego, CA

BRIGHAM, BERNICE DAVIS
[b.] July 8, 1912, Macon, GA; [p.] Deceased; [m.] Harry S. Brigham, October 21, 1930; [ch.] Cherie Brigham Hanson; [ed.] Polytech High Long Beach, CA, Jr. College Bahersfield, CA, L.S.U.N.O. Tulane, LA; [occ.] Retired; [memb.] International Society of Poets, National Authors Registry Iliad Press, The Academy of American Poets; [hon.] A recipient of literary awards she is published in Anthologies and in the periodical "verses"; [pers.] Main thrust of her life has been world wide travel 65 countries and two trips around the world Bolstering her study of the masters, in Art Painting, poetry and History of Mankind.

BROOK, KEVIN ALAN
[pen.] Kevin Brook, Khazar; [p.] Joel Brook, Marjorie Brook; [ed.] Danbury High, Bryant College; [occ.] Undergraduate Student; [memb.] American Marketing Association, Libertarian Party USA; [hon.] Dean's list, National Honor Society; [oth. writ.] Newsletter editor for a computer club from 1986 to 1992, design editor and contributor to The Nutmegger (a high school literary annual publication), computer bulletin board directory published in Board watch Magazine, Internet electronic publications; [pers.] I seek to publish a non-fiction history book within the next few years. The book is currently in manuscript form and is a comprehensive overview of the history of Khazars, Sorbs, and other eastern European Jewish ancestors.; [a.] Danbury, CT

BROWN, BELINDA MCCRACKEN
[pen.] Rudi Blake; [b.] May 21, 1962, Regina, Saskatchewan, Canada; [p.] Mrilyn Walter Hodel; [m.] Robert Brown; [ch.] Teigan, Ryan, Chelsea, Tayler, Ainsley; [occ.] Homemaker; [oth. writ.] Previous poems published locally and in anthologies [a.] Strasbourg Saskatchewan, Canada

BROWN, BEULAH R.
[pen.] Mae; [b.] December 23, 1930, Pollocksville, NC; [p.] Henry and Dolly P. Riggs; [m.] Harold E. Brown, May 25, 1951; [ch.] Harold E. Brown Jr., Harry C. Brown; [ed.] High School grade 12 Maysville-Pollocksville H.S. Pollocksville, NC; [occ.] Retired Fed. Civil Service; [memb.] Tabernacle Bapt. Church New Bern, NC. Young at Heart- Sr. Adult Club; [oth. writ.] Several poems and a child's story. (Not published as of now); [pers.] I believe every one has a God-given talent to share and use to help and enrich the life or lives of others. We have to want to use it before it can useful.

BROWN, BRENDA
[pen.] Roxxy Suicide; [b.] October 5, 1970, Fort Dixie, NJ; [p.] Karen Lemster and George Brown; [ed.] High School, Valparaiso Vincenes University (1 year) State College of Beauty; [occ.] Musician; [hon.] Chestertorn Art Show 1st place '89 4-H Fair - Reserved Grand Champion - 89; [oth. writ.] Several unpublished short stories. Song writer for my own solo project.; [pers.] "If you have a dream, no matter how obscure, follow it until it becomes reality." "One voice is that of 10 people. If people don't like your work. Fine. They aren't one of the 10 year trying to reach."; [a.] Valparaiso, IN

BROWN, DEBORAH K.
[b.] December 30, 1955, Smyrna, TN; [p.] James W. and Beulah I. Hicks; [m.] David A. Brown, October 21, 1978; [ch.] David Thomas Brown; [oth. writ.] Short stories for local newspapers, other poems my poem "Papa" is dedicated to my late grandfather Sim Morton, and his children, especially my Mama.; [pers.] May your spirit soar on the wings of intelligence, and know the world is as close as the nearest open book.; [a.] Middleburg, FL

BROWN, MARY ELLEN J.
[b.] October 10, 1928, Wheeling, WV; [p.] Mr. and Mrs. James Russell Brown Marie Rohlog - mother; [ed.] Master's Degree, St. Louis University and Webster College/ B.S. WV University OVGH Nursing School/ Wheeling High School; [occ.] Retired RN AWO, Retired Lt/Col U.S.A.F. N.C.; [memb.] Westminster Presbyterian church, Air Force Association, The Retired Officers Association, American Diabetic Association, Red Cross, AARP, and Beta Ziama Phi; [hon.] Air Force Commendation Medal Lou Meritorious Service 20 May 1967 - 6 May 1969 (Vietnam) Air Medal - 21 Aug. 1968, Honor Graduate of Nursing Service Administrative school - June 1970 Air Force Commendation Medal (1st Oak Leaf cluster) Nursing supervisor - 30 Sept. 1974 - Sept 1978; [oth. writ.] New to writing presently writing autobiography; [pers.] I strive to write about observations in nature and the blessings given to us by God.; [a.] Fairview Heights, IL

BROWN, PAIGE LEIGH
[b.] November 17, 1975, Williams, AZ; [p.] Carolynn Louise Lyons, Peter Kim Brown; [ed.] Saugus High, College of the Canyons; [occ.] Student; [oth. writ.] An unpublished notebook of poems; [pers.] I miss you mom love forever, Paige Leigh thanks Jeffrey; [a.] Valencia, CA

BROWN, SANYA G.
[b.] May 18, 1971, Scranton, PA; [p.] Wayne and Elaine Mertz; [m.] Harold "Skip" Brown, Jr., July 14, 1992; [ed.] Central Baptist Christian Academy, Binghamton H.S.; [occ.] Policy Secretary; [pers.] Words touch the soul and sharing our innermost thoughts and feelings through written words makes them valuable to those whose lives they've touched.; [a.] Yuma, AZ

BROWN, SHANNON DANIELLE
[pen.] Thumper Davis; [b.] December 5, 1980, Phoenix, AZ; [p.] Kirk and Carmen Davis; [ed.] Marina High School, class of '98

BRUCE, MELISSA
[pen.] Melissa Bruce; [b.] July 18, 1977, Waco, TX; [p.] Knox and Cindy Bruce; [ed.] Community Christian School; [occ.] Full time student; [hon.] Who's Who Among American High School Students, American Scholastic Award, Physics Award, "A" Honor Roll; [oth. writ.] Several unpublished poems; [pers.] I hope to become a known poet by my portrayal of emotions. I love the early works of Emily Dickinson; [a.] Mineral Wells, TX

BRUNEAU, LOUIS O.
[b.] January 11, 1920, Cambridge, MA; [m.] Eleanor (Flaherty) Bruneau; [ch.] Stephen L. and Mark O.; [ed.] Rindge Technical High School, University Extension Courses, evening classes; [occ.] Formerly, Manager of Machinery Engineering Dept., Polaroid Corp., Cambridge, MA, retired 1976; [memb.] American Humanist Association; [hon.] Eight United States Patents for mechanical inventions and manufacturing processes; [oth. writ.] Book of personal quotations, Book titled "Uncommon Sense", a philosophical treatise advancing the argument that moral values can be based on reason and enlightened self-interest.; [pers.] My interest has always been with the wonders of nature, and, the complexity of human behavior. If you like labels, I think of myself as a rational pragmatist, philosophically and as an independent, politically.; [a.] Weston, MA

BRYAN, ALTHEA PATRICIA
[pen.] Althea Bryan; [b.] March 9, 1978, Bronx, NY; [p.] Alton And Viletas Bryan; [ed.] Walter Panas High School; [occ.] Full time student; [memb.] Panas Players Interethnic Club, Panas Track and Field, Tutoring at Van Cortlandville Elementary School; [hon.] Credit Roll, Certificate of Excellence for Lakeland Education Foundation Art Logo Contest; [oth. writ.] Several poems, English papers, 4 page Spanish essay (en espanol) other private stories; [pers.] I hope to be in college by Fall 1996. I would like to thank everybody who used to their positive influence on me. I'd like to thank "E" whom I wrote this poem about.; [a.] Cortland Manor, NY

BRYANT, MEREDITH M.
[pen.] Shelly Bryant; [b.] August 14, 1979, Smyrna; [p.] Carol Bryant, Perry Bryant; [ed.] Junior at South Lake High School; [occ.] Student; [memb.] National Honors Society, Bible Club, A.C.E., Key Club, Environmental Club, FEA, Honor Roll; [pers.] I always try to go by the saying, "Expect the best, but prepare for the worst."; [a.] Clermont, FL

BUCCO, JENNIFER LYNN
[b.] September 5, 1973, New Jersey; [p.] Carol and Anthony Bucco; [ed.] Millersville University BA English; [memb.] International Society Of Poets; [oth. writ.] Published poem in Reflection of Lights, several other unpublished poems; [pers.] You stand between your lesser self and your whole self.; [a.] Millersville, PA

BUDGE, ANN
[b.] December 19, 1970, UT; [p.] Eldon and Deanna Budge; [ed.] I graduated from High School in 1989. I'm now attending Mesa Community College; [occ.] I work at Comet Cleaners Dry Cleaning; [hon.] I have played several instruments and have been given awards for my performance. Ex: piano, accordion, flute and clarinet; [oth. writ.] I have written several poems, however this is the first to be published. Poems include: Broken Mirrors, The Love of a Friend, and others.; [pers.] I believe that you get out of life, what you put into it. And if you love have a goal never give up tell you've reached it. I attribute what I've learned in life to my dear friend Rhea.; [a.] Mesa, AZ

BUECHELE, SUSAN
[b.] May 3, 1956, Buffalo, NY; [p.] Paul, Jennifer Baumeister; [m.] Divorced; [ch.] Casey Lee Monahan, Jennifer Lynn Monahan; [ed.] Studies at U.S.M. Communications; [occ.] Broadcast Advertising; [memb.] New Covenant Ministries; [hon.] 1994 Jacor Broadcasting Sales Award; [oth. writ.] Casey's Angel, Men's Works, The Fool that I Am; [pers.] I feel that writing is my purpose in life. I wish to bring glory to God that will last through time; [a.] Orange Park, FL

BULLETT, AUDREY KATHRYN
[pen.] Kitty Hill; [b.] February 12, 1937, Chicago, IL; [p.] Louis Hill and Eva Reed Hill; [m.] Clark R. Bullet, Jr. (Deceased), September 18, 1965; [ch.] Iris J. Hill daughter, Stanley Arron Hill, Grandson; [ed.] Ms. D. Metaphysics Currently Pursuing B.S. Ferris State University P.A., A.A. Ferris State University; [occ.] Metaphysical Minister, Consultant, Counselor, Retired Public Administrator, Reiki Practitioner, Aromatherapy Practitioner; [memb.] First Baptist Church of Idlewild Uriel Temple of Spiritual Understanding, Inc. Idlewild Lot Owners Association Life Membership Lake-Newaygo Branch NAACP Volunteer Fire Fighter, Yates Township Fire Department; [hon.] Certificate of Recognition Yates Twp Police Dept., Twenty Year Fire service Award YTFD, Victor F. Spathelf Leadership and Service Award FSU Robert F. Williams Memorial Scholarship of Merit, FSU; [oth. writ.] Lake County Star, Column Crystalline View, Newsletter; [pers.] I walk in the direction that God's leads me, seeing the beauty of the earth and listening to the rhapsody of life. My writing is an expression of the Christ within me.; [a.] Idlewild, MI

BUNCH, DUSTIN W.
[b.] April 17, 1983, Toledo, OH; [p.] Arnold and Brenda Bunch; [ed.] 6th Grade; [occ.] Full time student; [memb.] Zen Ryu Martial Arts Club; [hon.] Academy of Scholars, 1995 - (In Achievement of Academic Excellence), Honors Bands; [pers.] I like the rhythm of writing poetry. Most of my poems are about frightening things and feelings of despair; [a.] Washington Court House, OH

BUNEK, MRS. BENEDICTA
[b.] January 25, 1922, Wis.; [p.] (Deceased); [m.] Deceased; [ed.] 7 years grade school served in the First Women's Army Wacs. Have an honorable discharge.; [occ.] Retired and have a garden where I raise my own vegetables.; [memb.] I am catholic and go to St. Sylvesters Church in South Milwaukee Wis.; [a.] South Milwaukee, WI

BURBRIDGE JR., OLIVER H.
[b.] May 27, 1955, Saint Louis; [ch.] Nicole E. Burbridge; [ed.] Vashon High School. St. Louis MO, Univ. of Missouri-Columbia; [occ.] Therapist; [pers.] My poetry reflects my soul. And my soul longs to soar.; [a.] Houston, TX

BURCH, PETER
[b.] January 7, 1968, New Brunswick, NJ; [p.] Marjorie Lee Case and Chris Charles Burch; [ed.] Bachelor's Degree in Business from Wayland Baptist University, Pursuing a Masters of Divinity from Golden Gate Seminary; [occ.] Youth Pastor, Valley Church of Moraga, Moraga, CA; [memb.] Southern Baptist Convention, Southern Baptist Minister; [hon.] Dean's List; [oth. writ.] A small collection of poems and sermons, none published; [pers.] I try to reflect upon the great motivations of the human heart.; [a.] Mill Valley, CA

BUREAU, JESSICA
[b.] March 17, 1979; [p.] Ed and Chris Bureau; [ed.] High School (Currently in 11th Grade); [memb.] New London Presbyterian Church and Youth Group; [hon.] Honor Roll, Honors Band, American Music Abroad; [oth. writ.] Published in church newsletters and numerous unpublished poems; [pers.] Poetry delights and enriches the imagination. My poetry reflects many different aspects of life: Nature, religion, dreams, aspirations, hopes and failures.; [a.] West Grove, PA

BURFORD, SAMANTHA STAR
[pen.] Samantha Star; [b.] April 15, 1981, Whittier, CA; [p.] Colleen and Rich Thornhill (stepdad), and Mike Burford; [ed.] 8th Grade; [occ.] Young writer; [memb.] Club Live (inspire and help keep students off drugs), Church Youth Group; [hon.] Honor Society; [oth. writ.] "What I should've done, "Fears", "Release the Pain," "Always Stay in my Heart," "I didn't Ask for This, "Through the Eyes of Pain" "Eternal Pain", and many more; [pers.] I write my poems, to express my emotions, with high hopes it will later help other people deal with their emotions.; [a.] Moreno Valley, CA

BURG, NICOLE
[pen.] Nicky; [b.] February 5, 1979, Wauwatosa, WI; [p.] Donald Burg, Diane Burg; [ed.] Now attending Milwaukee High School of the Arts as a Junior; [occ.] Student; [hon.] I got a (letter) for my dance major.; [a.] Milwaukee, WI

BURGESS, ROSEMARIE
[b.] February 14, 1943, Bridgeport, CT; [p.] Joseph and Theresa De Profio; [m.] Robert; [ch.] 3 children and 3 grandchildren; [ed.] High School and Medical background; [occ.] Dental Assistant; [pers.] I dedicate this poem to my Lord and all native Americans who inspired me.

BURKE, JULIE
[b.] January 3, 1969, Des Plaines, IL; [p.] Rita and John Albrecht; [m.] Joseph Burke, August 27, 1994; [ed.] Northern Illinois University and St. Francis Hospital School of Nursing; [ooc.] Registered Nurse; [a.] San Diego, CA

BURKE, LUCILE I.
[b.] December 16, 1922, Macon, GA; [p.] R. E. Thompson and Myrtle Thompson; [m.] R. E. Burke, 1941; [ch.] Charles Byron Burke; [occ.] Retired; [oth. writ.] A few anthologies. Personalized poems for others.; [pers.] I've spent all my life sowing seeds and giving care. Now the harvest will appear. One of my poems says, "Please Grant The Time That I Will Need to Plant My Garden With The Seeds of Love and Peace and Understanding."; [a.] Iola, KS

BURKE, SHAMUS PATRICK
[pen.] Shamus Patrick; [b.] June 6, 1978, Toms River, NJ; [p.] Barry B. and Deborah Burke; [ed.] Junior Year at Toms River High School East; [occ.] Student; [memb.] Peer Leadership, RAP (Resolving Arguments Peacefully), S.S.T.O.P. Team (Students Solving Their Own Problems), Toms River High School East Soccer Team, T.R.A. Soccer Team-goal keeper; [hon.] Symposium on Violence Prevention, Conflict Management Workshop for Teachers, NJ State Special Olympics Competition Are 6 Ski Coach, Peer Problem Solving and Conflict Management; [pers.] I try to write of subjects which cause "conflict in the human heart" (Faulkner) in a manner that provokes thought in my audience.; [a.] Toms River, NJ

BURKHAMMER, MARCIA D.
[pen.] M. D. Case; [b.] November 5, 1951, Sidney, OH; [p.] Virgil and Roseann Case; [m.] Roger D. Burkhammer, August; [ch.] Jon Mitchell, Sherry Mitchell; [ed.] Anna High School 1969, Edison State Community College working on a degree in Computer Science; [occ.] Service Representative Sprint-United Telephone; [pers.] I think each of us posses the potential for profound insights on life. Only our limited thinking and inability to express ourselves holds us apart from the truly great writers and poets.; [a.] Quincy, OH

BURNETT, NIRAL
[pen.] Ni Burnett; [b.] October 8, 1973, Brooklyn, NY; [p.] Russell Burnett, Yvonne Burnett; [ed.] John Jay High, School, Regents College; [occ.] Bookstore Clerk; [memb.] Exousia Ministries Fellowship in Brooklyn, NY; [hon.] Mayors Voluntary Action Award City Council Citation; [oth. writ.] Several poems such as: The Lamb, Many hearts one blood, and other Christian literature to be published in the future; [pers.] My desire is to be sure that the Lord Jesus Christ is glorified in all that I write. Jesus is Lord!! Phil. 2:5-11; [a.] Brooklyn, NY

BURNETTE, CHRISTOPHER C.
[pen.] 12:02, Christophe, Shadow; [b.] June 5, 1976, Petersburg, VA; [p.] Chastine Burnette and Patricia D. Booker; [ed.] 4 years of High School; [occ.] Student (Graduate year of 95); [memb.] Explorer, Scout, Mercy Ambulance of Richmond; [hon.] Outstanding Band student '95, Alumni of Saint Vincent De Paul H.S.; [oth. writ.] Poems of all natures published for 4 years in school (St. Vincent de Paul Literary Magazine); [pers.] Take the small things and appreciate them, then the big problems that come into your life won't seem so bad.; [a.] Petersburg, VA

BURNHAM JR., MR. JEANE W.
[b.] March 10, 1925, Gratiot Co., MI; [p.] Jeane W. and Lyna May B.; [m.] Diana Bell Burnham, April 15, 1966; [ch.] Jacquelyn, David, Susan, Kim, Richard, Isabella, Bruce; [ed.] 1-12, Okha. A and M. 1943; [occ.] Retired January 1, 1990 Mich. Dept. of Transportation; [memb.] WW-II, VFW, American Legion, Military Order of Purple Heart, AARP, VAVS, Member of St. Aidans Episcopal, Ann Arbor; [hon.] 1994 NL of P, Editors Choice Award for the "Evergreen". First poem to be published.; [oth. writ.] The Evergreen, NL of P., after The Storm 1994., The Butterflies 1988, unpublished; [pers.] Everything is Beautiful, even the Ugly!! The Lord Jesus is my pilot.; [a.] Ann Arbor, MI

BURNS, ANTHONY
[pen.] Anthony, Tanaka-Burns; [b.] April 30, 1964, Pittsburgh, PA; [p.] John J. and Rita K. Burns; [ed.] Santa Monica College, California State University Northridge, UCLA Extension; [occ.] Writer, Computer Analyst, Poet; [oth. writ.] A book of poetry called "Stranger Dreams Than I ever Imagined"; [pers.] There are many forms of poetic expression, box the most important box the most important reaction is the creation of an emotional response in the reader. If she can find some kind of common-cover

BURNS, NANCY
[b.] November 14, 1977, Milwaukee; [p.] Joseph F. Burns and late Patricia Burns; [ed.] Nicolet High School; [occ.] Student; [memb.] Our Lady of Good Hope Church; [hon.] Editor's Choice Award 1994 from The National Library of Poetry; [oth. writ.] Poem published in The National Library of Poetry - Seasons to come; [pers.] Laughter is a key to happiness. Ignorance, stubbornness and madness won't achieve this. Be happy with yourself then happiness will enter your life but to have a life you need to live.; [a.] Glendale, WI

BUSSE, LINDA
[m.] Richard J. Busse, December 12, 1975; [ch.] None; [ed.] High School Graduate; [occ.] Homemaker; [memb.] Ring of Tatters; [hon.] Previous issue Journey of the Mind and tape, the sound of poetry. While in high school I was in an all female singing group called The Girls Glee Club which won in state wide competition against other female groups for best pronunciation, and ability to reach high tones and maintain them.; [pers.] I was taught the basic stitch or stitches to knit, crochet, and tatting. From then, I applied my knowledge to read the instructions and created knitted hats, mittens, Afghans sweaters, crochet doilies and table cloths, and tatted mofits, edgings, and candy canes working with three shuttles.; [a.] Lansing, MI

BUSTAMANTE, NATALIE
[b.] August 14, 1981, Houston, TX; [p.] Germen and Gloria; [ed.] I'm going to 8th grade; [occ.] Baby sits, likes to act, likes to skateboard.; [memb.] I was in my school's club to tour new kids which is called pier helpers.; [oth. writ.] I had a poem published in elementary years in a poetry book that they sold at school.; [pers.] Poetry to me means love, friendship, peace. I

admire Shakespear's excellent work of art.; [a.] Alpharetta, GA

BUTLER, MR. KEVIN A.
[pen.] Kevin A. Butler; [b.] November 12, 1967, Bronx, NY; [p.] Mr. Edward Butler and Mrs. Anne Butler; [m.] Stefanie Butler, July 15, 1995; [ed.] B.A. English Literature Rutgers University, New Brunswick, NJ; [occ.] Warehouse Employee; [pers.] Now is today, today is tomorrow tomorrow forever always...

BYASSEE, MARGARET FOLEY
[pen.] Margaret Byassee; [b.] January 17, 1922, Newport, RI; [p.] Edward and May Foley; [ed.] High School - Newport R.I. 3 1/2 yrs Wheaton College, Wheaton Ill. graduate B.A. University of Tenn. MA - Ed University of Tenn. at Chettanooga, Knoxville, TN; [occ.] Retired art teacher- 1981, Professional Artist- (new poet); [memb.] President - authors and artists past president - Civic Arts League, Ariel Gallery-Soho N.Y. -(not at present time) 1990 Art Expo NY, several Galleries-Chatt. Area-work now displayed, Hunter Museum of Cest. Chatt.; [hon.] Art Awards from any juried shows - cubist painter many one pesos shows - Tennessee, Maryland, California, Kappa Delta Pi - honor society in Education; [oth. writ.] Poetry - 3 given 1994 on local tv station - Ch. 12 or 13 cable other poems done on different programs "Alabama Tornado". "Flogging in Singapore", "Veteran's Day" poem about my 2 sisters and myself as veterans of WW II; [pers.] Wisdom commeth in knowing who we truly be!; [a.] Rossville, GA

BYBEE, CHARLES F.
[b.] May 28, 1920, Iowa; [p.] Peal and Cecil Bybee; [m.] Frances Mehann Bybee, June 10, 1954; [ch.] Robert Douglas Bybee; [ed.] Moulton (Iowa) High School Capitol Radio Engineering Institute, Washington, D.C.; [occ.] Retired/Free-Lance Writer Bible Teacher; [memb.] St. John's U.M. Church; [oth. writ.] "One Man's Family," a geneological history of my line of the Bybee family.; [pers.] My poem sums up my philosophy!

CADILLAC, FRANK
[pen.] Frank Cadillac and Frank Savage; [b.] April 9, 1958, Bronx, NY; [p.] Louis and Adele; [m.] 1981; [ch.] Two; [ed.] Graduate of Bronx Community College spent 1 year at Columbia University NYC; [occ.] Leader of a Hard Rock Band - The Relix; [memb.] Broadcast Music Inc.; [hon.] Dean's List at BCC; [oth. writ.] I am a song writer and performer I am releasing a CD album on Black Hole Productions entitled I need mercy; [pers.] I've already made it. It takes me one day at a time to catch up to it.

CAGLE, ZELMA D.
[b.] September 30, 1963, Richmond Heights, OH; [p.] Walter A. and Myrtle V. Cagle; [ed.] High School graduate Trade School; [occ.] Cashier; [hon.] Editors choice award for poem entitled "Angels"; [oth. writ.] Angels, I Am Near; [pers.] My poetry is based on spirituality and life. Life is the most precious gift of all.; [a.] Medina, OH

CAIN, J. ADAM
[b.] October 27, 1971, Decatur, GA; [p.] J. C. Cain Jr. and Marilyn M. Cain; [m.] Dana Lynn Cain, May 6, 1995; [ed.] Redan High Furman University; [occ.] Programmer/Analyst, Trax, Inc., Atlanta, GA; [oth. writ.] Currently compiling a book of my poetry and artwork; [pers.] Art whether written or drawn is half inspiration, half arrangement. I strive to find this balance in all my artistic endeavors.; [a.] Lithonia, GA

CALDWELL, SUSAN BLAKE
[pen.] Lillian Daniels; [b.] November 29, 1958, Friona, TX; [p.] Mildred and Spencer Blake; [ch.] Anita Brett Caldwell; [ed.] Canyon High School, WTAMU - West Texas A&M University; [occ.] Student; [memb.] Canyon Cares Bd. of Dir, Vice Pres. - Friends, Canyon Public Library, Editor - Legacy WTAMU, Secy - WTAMU Literary Forum, Advisory Board for Lutheran Social Services of the South, Aid Association to Lutheran's, Treasurer, St. Paul Luth. Church; [hon.] Alpha Chi Honor Society, Sigma Tau Delta, English Honor Society, Panhandle Professional Writer's Association 1994 Poetry Contest, 1st Place, Pres. List, Dean's List; [oth. writ.] Various Poetry published in the Legacy, and other short stories; [pers.] I strive for a focus on the nobility in mankind. As a Christian writer, I believe that, while recognizing the ignorable, it is my responsibility to illuminate the honorable, loving creation.; [a.] Canyon, TX

CALLIN, ELAISE
[pen.] Elaise Callin; [b.] June 14, 1927, S. Georgia; [p.] Mr. and Mrs. Thomas Edenfield; [m.] Glenn J. Callin, October, 17, 1953; [ch.] James, Arthur, Thomas, David; [ed.] High School and Business School at Atlanta GA; [occ.] Housewife and Grandmother; [memb.] Downey Church - C.M.A. The National Library of Poetry; [hon.] Editors choice award for poem "Creation"; [oth. writ.] "Creation" "A Song in the Storm", "Family Tree" I write for the Douglas Enterprise and coffee county progress. A recipe column and Society News.; [pers.] My family is very important to me. I have 5 grandson three granddaughter. My husband and I do some traveling and I enjoy poetry. And hope to publish a book; [a.] Chuluota, FL

CAMBRON, ALICE JUNE
[pen.] Alice J. Thomas Cambron; [b.] June 10, 1947, Tulsa, OK; [p.] Glenn C. Thomas, Waunetta M. Thomas; [m.] Harold F. Cambron, June 10, 1983; [ch.] Autumn, Alesha, Andrea Lisko; [ed.] Central High, Tulsa, OK, Rogers State College Claremore, OK, Claremore Beauty College Claremore, OK; [occ.] Unisys (State Of Oklahoma), Walmart, Cosmetologist; [memb.] League of Women's Voters, National Wildlife Assoc., Tulsa Blues Club; [hon.] National Deans Honor List; [oth. writ.] Short story and recipe published in, Oklahoma Cooks; [pers.] I write to bring pleasure to others and myself. My goal is to transform, arouse, stirrings feelings or imaginations through my poetry, songs and short stories. Robert Frost and Helen Steiner Rice are an inspiration to me!; [a.] Claremore, OK

CAMERON, DOROTHY R.
[pen.] Rebecca York; [b.] June 28, 1922, Saint Louis, MO; [p.] Rebecca and Russell Hibner; [m.] Deceased, December 31, 1977; [ed.] High School Graduate (Jefferson Davis Sr. High of Houston, Texas); [occ.] Retired Long-Distance, Switch-Board Operator; [memb.] Utah Poetry Society, International Society of Poet's (very new!); [hon.] 'Editor's Award' from (The National Library of Poetry), Nominee as 'Poet-of-the-Year' for 1995 (International Society of Poets), 2 poems accepted for two anthologies: Seven Who Dared - "Reflections of Light" and Foot-steps - "Beyond the Stars"; [oth. writ.] Poems published in various magazines (ideals) and newspapers (salt lake tribune) two poems published in "Utah Sings" - (published once every 10 years); [pers.] To live on (when I am gone) in the poem I have written for the 1995 Poet's Convention Symposium: "I, too, had a dream" - but it will never be judged, as I am unable to attend...it is my dream of what such a gathering means (to me) and what it would have meant to me, to have been able to come.. and to have met you and Jeff Franz and Elizabeth Barnes...in person...I weep for that...; [a.] Salt Lake City, UT

CAMP, TOMMY
[b.] January 26, 1962, Cleburne, TX; [p.] Bobby and Jean Camp; [m.] Divorced; [ch.] Preston, Foster, Tosha, Bobbie Jo; [ed.] Cleburne High School; [occ.] Automatic Transmissions; [memb.] Sons of Legion Address Post 50 Cleburne Texas; [pers.] Power and wealth leave something to be desired. Don't you think J. C.; [a.] Alvarado, TX

CAMPBELL, CHRISTINA L.
[pen.] Crissy Campbell or C. L. C.; [b.] December 1, 1980, Harrisburg; [p.] James Campbell and Jackiline Hetrick; [ed.] Cumberland Valley, Eagle View Middle School 7th grade; [occ.] Student; [memb.] Cumberland Valley Valateen, I play violin in the 7th/8th Grade Orchestra; [oth. writ.] 404, for a teacher that could not stay with the class for the rest of the year because of a sickness; [pers.] I'm a foster child. I come from a loving mother and a brothers. I wrote the poem for my mom who lives a few states away. This was my way of telling her I love her.; [a.] Enola, PA

CAMPBELL, EMILIE M.
[pen.] Emilie M. Campbell; [b.] March 24, 1977, New Albany, IN; [p.] Elaine Basham and Kennith Campbell; [ed.] Lanesville High, Lanesville Ind. Purdue University; [pers.] This poem is dedicated to my grandmother Juanita Campbell. Her faith in God and strength of will, has influenced me greatly.; [a.] Lanesville, IN

CAMPBELL, FRED
[b.] February 23, 1945, Dothan, AL; [p.] James and Gwendolyn Campbell Sr.; [m.] Beverley Campbell, August 17, 1968; [ch.] Philip Daniel and Jamie Rae Campbell; [ed.] Lakewood High School, University of Idaho, Sawter College; [occ.] Test Technician; [pers.] Life is not always easy, but it is always beautiful - live a life!; [a.] Agoura Hills, CA

CAMPBELL, JEAN
[b.] October 26, PA; [p.] Walter and Lucile Carter; [m.] Randolph, August 5, 1951; [ch.] Ten, 7 Boys - 3 girls; [ed.] BS in Nursing, Penn State, Masters in Education University of Pittsburgh; [occ.] Guidance Counselor, Registered Nurse; [memb.] PSEA-NEA (Education) Association, PA. School Nurse Assn. NAACP, Notary Public for PA, PA State Education Assn, National Education Assn.; [hon.] Award from American Intercultural Student Exchange, Proclamation from Reaver County, PA Commissioners for program sponsored; [oth. writ.] Poem published in Tap Root Literary Society of Am Bridge, PA book of poems to be published under title of "Reality Bites"; [pers.] I hope that through my poems, I can offer hope and encouragement to people. I wish to make this world a more hospitable place for all mankind; [a.] Freedom, PA

CAMPBELL, MARLENE JOYCE
[pen.] M. J. C.; [b.] March 19, 1946, Pittsburgh, PA; [p.] John Leffler, June Bittner Slaton; [m.] Ernest D. Campbell, July 24, 1985; [ch.] Carla, James, Tonya Gardner, (stepchildren) John, Danny Campbell, 6 grandchildren; [ed.] Gateway Sr. High, John Lesko Beauty School - Penna./Weaver Airline School Kansas City, MO; [occ.] Cook - Community Care, Milan, MO, since October 17, 1994 - Clerk/Treasurer and Tax Collector - Osgood, MO, since 1991; [memb.] Distinguished Member of International Society of Poets May '95; [hon.] For outstanding Achievement - Editor's Choice Awards December '94 and May '95 International Society Nominee as Poet of the Year for 1995 and Induction as International Poet of Merit for 1995 - August '95 Sparrowgrass - Poetic Voices of America; [oth. writ.] "Untitled" - Oct, '94, "My Heart's Desire" Feb. '95 - National Library - Editor's Awards "Memories of My Son" (Echoes of Yesterday) and "God is Watching"

(Best Poems of 1995). "Salute to all our Veterans" (Between the Raindrops) - all 3 on Cassette. "I need a chance" this issue. 3 self-published books - saluting Sullivan Co. - 1845-1995-, poetry by Marlene Campbell and poems by MJC, out for sale March and April, 1995.; [pers.] Start each day with a smile. Kind word and love in heart for everyone. Believe in yourself and God will show you everything is possible.; [a.] Galt, MO

CAMPBELL, WILLIAM H.
[b.] August 12, 1955, Germany; [p.] William and Elfrieda; [m.] Kate, October 7, 1982; [ch.] Jessa and Heather; [ed.] B.S. Central Washington University, Ph.D. Montana State University; [occ.] Chemist; [oth. writ.] Working on a novel; [pers.] The Lord is my shepherd, and I try to follow.

CANDELA, CAROL COUGHLIN
[b.] October 28, 1953, Saint Louis, MO; [p.] Victor Pius and Thelma Coughlin; [m.] James Candela; [ch.] Michael Candela; [ed.] Cleveland High School, U.M.S.L. Musically educated by the Sisters of St. Joseph of Carondelet; [occ.] The "neighborhood piano teacher"; [memb.] Nottingdale Civic Association Weight Watchers, Spa World Fitness Center, Hylton High PTSO; [hon.] Chosen for the May 1995 issue of Weight Watchers Magazine as a "Before and After" story. Semi-finalist in 1994 American Open Poetry Contest; [oth. writ.] Poems, family histories, "Mrs. Candela and her students, Write a Beginners Piano Book" (this is a current project with my students); [pers.] God gives everyone gifts and talents, May we all find our's, and put them to good use.; [a.] Dale City, VA

CANNIZZARO, EILEEN
[b.] June 30, 1935, Larchmont, PA; [p.] Albert and Gertrude Snyder; [m.] Joseph Cannizzaro, June 1, 1957; [ch.] Joseph, Melissa, Paul and Ann-Marie; [ed.] Mother of a set of twins, a child at age 40 experienced cancer; [occ.] Merchandiser of Greeting Cards; [memb.] Legion of Mary, Ministering To Inmates in Maximum Security; [hon.] Gift of Holy Laughter, honored to identify angels; [oth. writ.] Letters to Editor on integration and love of neighbor; [pers.] I like to write about my true experiences. And woe to us when God loses His sense of humor.; [a.] Willingboro, NJ

CANTRALL, ERNESTINE J.
[pen.] Ernestine J. Cantrall; [b.] August 15, 1925, Alvarado, CA; [p.] John and Olive Lemas; [m.] Omar J. Cantrall, February 28, 1943; [ch.] Patricia, Ava, Bonnie; [ed.] Four months short of finishing High School 12th Grade - World War II prompted us to marry early; [occ.] Housewife; [memb.] 1. Third Order Carmelite Catholic Order, 2. Catholic League to defend our faith, 3. S.C.D.E.S. Society Of The Crown Of The Divine Holy Ghost; [hon.] 4th award and honorable mention on oil painting - called "Sea of Galalie" also honorable mention on oil painting "Red Sea at Dawn."; [oth. writ.] Many inspired - poems, writings - I am hoping to put out a book called "The Lord of Love" spontaneous - no effort to rhyme poems - or writings - a gift from God - since 1975; [pers.] My writings are to reflect to others our great God of mercy - beyond human imaginings.; [a.] Vallejo, CA

CAPPIELLO, JODY
[b.] March 5, 1974, Illinois; [p.] Clark and Nancy Jenkins; [ed.] Harrison High, North Arkansas Community/Technical College, University of Central Arkansas; [occ.] Student; [oth. writ.] Many other poems that have not been published; [pers.] I would like to give a special thanks to Kevin LeBlanc for finding a door in me that I never knew existed. I would, also, like to thank J. D., A.H., B.B., P.R., and T.B. for their friendship and support.; [a.] Harrison, AR

CAPRON, BETHEL EBERT
[pen.] B. E. C.; [b.] December 19, 1914, Cody, WY; [p.] Fred and Coral Ebert; [m.] William A. Capron, May 29, 1937; [ch.] Coral Nancy, Mary Louise, William A. Jr.; [ed.] High School Graduate, 1932; [occ.] Retired Homemaker, Mother, grandmother, and great grandmother; [memb.] High School Glee Club, 2 yrs. Presbyterian Church - U.S.A. Two Memberships in Home Extension Clubs; [oth. writ.] Seven other poems that I feel are right, all non-published. Biography of my father.; [pers.] The poems that I have written seem to flow from my pen as though there was someone telling me what to say.; [a.] Powell, WY

CAPSALIS, JAMES A.
[pen.] Jim Capy; [b.] August 20, 1925, Ayer, MA; [p.] Apostolos Capsalis, Rose Capsalis; [m.] Shirley A. Capsalis, August 6, 1976; [ch.] Sheryl J. Capsalis; [ed.] Bartlet Junior High School, Lowell High School, Center College Danville, KY, Scott Field Ill., Radio Tech. University of Lowell Engineering; [occ.] Retired; [memb.] P-51 Pilots Association St. Michaels Church, Veteran Of Foreign Wars; [hon.] Honors PSI Delta F1, Presidential Citation with there Oak Leafs Silver Star, Purple Heart with floor Oaks Air Medal. Pastel Drawing, 1st Award (Baby in crib); [oth. writ.] "Earth", "Wrinkles Of Time", Auto Biography of WW II; [pers.] When I write, I live it. I become a part of it. I write from the heart and it affects me in such a way that I write as though I lived it. I capture what I feel and put it on paper for others to enjoy.; [a.] Lowell, MA

CARAMBOT, PATTY
[b.] November 14, 1982, Long Island, NY; [p.] Patricia H. Mannol Carambot; [ed.] I am in 7th grade, 1 year left of junior high; [memb.] St. Margaret of Scotland Catholic Church, Center Stage Academy of Dance, Selden Middle School Band; [hon.] Award for - ABC quilts (making quilts for babies with AIDS) and Trim a Tree Program (for people with Cerebral Palsy) others vane with school activities and classes. Honor Student; [oth. writ.] Have written more poetry, but nothing has been published; [pers.] I like to focus on the possibilities and the depth of imagination. I have been greatly influenced by Shakespeares writings, his tragedies have inspired me the most.; [a.] Selden, NY

CARDILLO, DANIELLE
[b.] December 6, 1979, West Islip, NY; [p.] Pat and Frank Cardillo; [ed.] Student at West Babylon High School; [occ.] Student; [hon.] Honor Student Academic Excellence in Social Studies and Science; [pers.] Be true to yourself. Have fun, dare to be different; [a.] West Babylon, NY

CAREY, MICKEY
[pen.] Mickey Carey; [b.] September 28, 1982, New Rochelle, NY; [p.] Ernest and Debbie Carey; [ed.] Columbus Ave. Elementary Valhalla Middle School; [memb.] Whitney M. Young Society; [a.] White Plains, NY

CARILLO, ALICE
[b.] June 20, 1947, Casa Crode, AZ; [m.] Pete H. Carrillo, February 4, 1966; [ch.] David O. Carrillo and Adriana Carrillo; [ed.] B.A. in Child Development, San Jose University, plus 2 yrs. toward the Children's Center Permit; [occ.] Founder and President of License Home Provider Support Group and Owner of Love N' Care Daycare Program; [memb.] 1. Founder and President of the License Home Provider Support Group, 2. Member of the Monterey County Family Daycare Assoc., 3. Member of the R.O.P. Advisory Committee, 4. Member of the Ladies Auxiliary Club; [hon.] 1. Received a plaque for President from MCFDA, 2. Received a plaque for Founder of the License Home Provider Support Group; [oth. writ.] Just published a

book called "How to Become a Home Provider and be Successful"; [pers.] I relieve my life as a migrant child through my poetry. I hope that all the migrant-children in the world can rekindle their memories through my writings. For we must not forget when we come from!; [a.] Solinas, CA

CARLSON, ANITA L.
[pen.] Anita Carlson; [b.] February 18, 1930, Wisconsin Rapids, WI; [p.] Edward and Lillian Carlson; [m.] Clifford Mineau, November 19, 1990; [ch.] Linda (43), Barbara (42), Nancy (40), Mary Rose (36); [ed.] Graduate High School - 2 yrs. in Journalism - 2 courses at Bay College in Creative Writing 4.0 Gr; [occ.] Retired Secretary; [memb.] All Saints Catholic Church; [hon.] Grade School poem published Field and Stream. Wrote Fictional Book age 13, wrote various poems during WW II picked beans to buy a typewriter (age 13) to type my story.; [oth. writ.] I was named Poet Laureate for Escanaba School's for my poetry during 60's. I was grand prize winner this past Christmas for my story, and poem "The Key of Christmas"; [pers.] I present my optimistic view of the world in my poems and stories. I want people to smile as much as possible. I feel nothing is so bad that we can't ask the Lord for help.; [a.] Gladstone, MI

CARLSON, GWENN
[b.] May 18, Texas; [ed.] Home schooled during High School; [oth. writ.] Publication in Alternative Arts and Literature magazine, Issue #15 ("As the Writer Marries the Written"); [a.] Pasadena, TX

CARLSON, JUNE M.
[b.] August 13, 1921, Niles, MI; [p.] Mary and Armin Pawloski; [m.] Widow; [ch.] Ralph A. Wilks; [ed.] Graduated Niles Sr. High School; [occ.] Asst. Office Mgr., Smith Storage, Niles, MI; [memb.] St. Mark's Catholic Church; [oth. writ.] Three poems published in other poetry collections; [pers.] My love of nature helps me write sensitive poems.; [a.] Niles, MI

CARLUCCI, CHRISTOPHER
[pen.] Chris Carlucci; [b.] September 8, 1981, Plainfield, NJ; [p.] Tom and Madeline Carlucci; [ed.] I am in 8th grade at St. Joseph's School North Plainfield New Jersey - I have attended St. Joseph's since Kindergarten.; [hon.] 1994 and 1995, 2nd and 3rd place in Science Fair St. Joseph's School - 1994 and 1995 won awards in Art Shows St. Joseph's School; [pers.] This is my first poem, my first love is art. I love to draw and work with day. I also play soccer and roller hockey.; [a.] North Plainfield, NJ

CARMAN, BRANDON KENT
[pen.] Brandon K. Carman; [b.] July 14, 1978, Beckley, WV; [p.] Kent and Charlotte Carman; [m.] Not Married; [ed.] Still in High School entering senior year, Woodrow Wilson High School Beckley. WW; [occ.] Student; [memb.] Spanish Club, Band, Art Club, Science Club, Hollywood Missionary Baptist Church; [hon.] 1993 Raleigh County All County Band (Timpanist). 1994 Tennessee Honors Band. Honor Roll Student; [oth. writ.] Personal Collection of Poetry; [pers.] "Life is not understood truly without the power to create one with pen and paper".; [a.] Beckley, WV

CARR, KATHLEEN M.
[pen.] Kathy, Kaytee; [b.] June 6, 1957, Cartland, NY; [p.] Charles C. (deceased), Mary Carr; [ed.] Fabius - Pompey High School BOCES, International Correspondence Schools; [occ.] Sub position Teacher Aide at Salvation Army and YMCA Daycare; [memb.] International Society of Poets; [hon.] Six Honorable Mentions, Poet of Merit, Who's Who In Poetry, several Golden Poet Awards; [oth. writ.] The Sunset of Tomorrow, The

Touch of an Angel, now in the process of being published; [pers.] The Lord is my strength and the best friend a person can have. He will never let you down.; [a.] Syracuse, NY

CARREON, TRACY
[b.] February 4, 1968, Vero Bch, FL; [p.] Barbara and William Hoskins; [m.] Benny Carreon, January 15, 1994; [ed.] BA from FSU in English Education. Currently working on MA in Counseling.; [occ.] Full time graduate student (former teacher); [memb.] Sigma Chi Iota - Honor Society of Counselors; [oth. writ.] One other published work, "Child Wise" in AIM (American Intercultural Magazine); [pers.] My poetry has always been an inner reflection of my own emotional and spiritual journey. It is my doorway and mirror of growth.; [a.] Oviedo, FL

CARRERA, ANNA L.
[b.] June 6, 1952, Puerto Rico; [p.] Luis Caraballo and Benilda Caraballo; [m.] Leonardo A. Carrera, March 19, 1988; [ch.] Joanne Rivera, Rene Rivera, Leonardo L. Carrera, David Carrera, Rebecca Carrera; [ed.] Passaic High School, William Paterson College 2 1/2 yrs., Fairleigh Dickinson Univ. 1 yr.; [occ.] Medical Secretary; [oth. writ.] Poetry, Short Stories, Articles for College Newspaper (Fairleigh Dickinson Univ.); [pers.] My desire is to uplift and inspire hope in those who read my writing.; [a.] Clifton, NJ

CARRERA, JUAN E.
[b.] August 9, 1960, Washington, DC; [p.] Eloy E. Carrera, Adela Carrera; [ed.] McLean High, Northern Virginia Comm. College, Georgetown University, U.S. Navy 1979-1983; [occ.] Engineer - Georgetown University; [memb.] ASME - American Society of Mechanical Engineers, SME - Society of Manufacturing Engineers; [hon.] Received U.S Navy Expeditionary Medal for Persian Gulf Duty - 1981 Aboard U.S.S. Independence CV-62; [oth. writ.] Poem published "Man and the Humanoid" in the Amherst Society American Poetry Annual; [pers.] I have dedicated my work to my mother who passed on October 7, 1994. My influences include Poe, Frost and the philosophical writings or Ayn Rand, especially objectivism.; [a.] Arlington, VA

CARRIER, VICTORIA
[pen.] Tory; [b.] October 5, 1958, Rochester, NY; [p.] Charles and Muriel Gill; [ch.] Kenneth Scott; [ed.] Penn Yan Academy; [a.] California

CARROLL, GEORGE J.
[b.] February 19, 1924, Bronx, NY; [p.] William and Margaret Carroll; [m.] Florence Carroll, July 27, 1946; [ch.] George, Martin, Janet, Barbara, Patricia, Therese; [ed.] Cardinal Hayes High, Adelphi Business School; [occ.] Retired; [memb.] Knits of Columbus, Joseph Barry Council No. 2520 Hicksville NY., Holy Family R.C. Church Ministry of Praise Friendly Visitor to the Home Bound, Holy Family Church; [oth. writ.] A number of poems published in local Catholic Bulletins and periodical; [pers.] Childhood acquaintence with, Kiemer Longfellow and Poe in grammar school moved me to express my thoughts in verse.; [a.] Levittown, NY

CARTER, ANNELL
[b.] August 16, 1953, Booneville, AR; [p.] Clayton and Gnell Weaver; [m.] Raymond R. Carter, June 19, 1983; [ch.] Claye Carter and Sherri Shryock; [ed.] High School Graduate, Booneville Arkansas Valley Vo Tech Graduate with degree in Licensed Practical Nursing; [occ.] Office Nurse for Dr. Fred Feder, Urology; [oth. writ.] Gospel songs which I sing in our small country church in Natural Dam. I have written other poetry too. When I get an idea in my head it usually takes 5 minutes to write something.; [pers.] I enjoy writing very much,

if I'm "Uptight", writing is soothing for me, usually everything I write mentions God because he is so important in my life. I give him the "Thanks" for my being able to write. My poem, "Watch a child grow from day to day" was written before Claye got married this year.

CARTER, DAVID L.
[b.] October 26, 1974, Brockport, NY; [p.] Kenneth Carter, Nancy Carter; [ed.] Brockport High School, Elmira College; [occ.] Full-time Student; [oth. writ.] Several poems and short stories; [pers.] My ideas try to convey my inner thoughts on every day life. My inspiration often comes from my best friend, who is also the love of my life, Julie Rochelle Robords.; [a.] Hamlin, NY

CARTER, DEANIE
[b.] March 23, Skipper, VA; [p.] William Show Mamio Snow; [m.] Willie Carter Jr., August 31, 1963; [ch.] Lang Carter, Samuel Carter; [ed.] High School Graduate. I took a course in poetry how to write novel, Beauty College, Nursing and a Modeling Course; [occ.] Home Health Aid; [memb.] A Former member of the tide water writers Association of Hampton VA. Christian writers guild of California the world of poetry; [hon.] Mert award, Silver award, A Golden poet award in 1987; [oth. writ.] Warren record the creative record songs for little people the songs are being sung in Africa I was told; [pers.] I like to express my love to all I meet because there is so much hate and I has so much love when I was growing up I want to give what was given to me. I have been writing for many years; [a.] Littleton, NC

CARTER, SHIRLEY
[pen.] Shirley Carter; [b.] Sycamour, IL; [m.] Harold E. Carter, February 3, 1977; [ch.] 2 children, son and daughter; [ed.] B.A. degree; [occ.] Retired/Writer; [hon.] Volunteer Award, Mary McCann Award; [oth. writ.] Had a book copyrighted in 1992; [pers.] My poems reflect my interest in people and my love for my fellow man. In addition I enjoy writing humorous poetry.; [a.] Rockford, IL

CASAREZ, CARLA
[b.] October 19, 1948, Memphis, TN; [p.] Wilford L. and Francis Smith; [m.] Robert V. Casarez, June 5, 1970; [ch.] Robert L., Michelle L. Casarez; [ed.] Joliet Central High, Joliet Jr. College Pt. time; [occ.] Homemaker, part time student; [memb.] Anxiety Control Technique Co-Facilitator of a Support group for individuals with Anxiety disorders; [hon.] Roll of merit-Joliet Jr. College, Certificate of achievement in Cardiac telemetry; [oth. writ.] Book in the making about anxiety and how it feels, when a loved one dies, to a person with Agoraphobia; [pers.] Follow your dreams, never say I can't; [a.] Joliet, IL

CASAVANT, DIANE
[b.] April 20, 1956, Lewiston, ME; [p.] Simeon and Lorraine Labonte; [m.] Gerard Casavant, April 20, 1979; [ch.] Sarah, Jeanine, Hillary; [ed.] Lewiston High School, University of Southern Maine - BSN; [occ.] Homemaker, Freelance Writer; [memb.] St. Kathryn's Church, Wordsmiths Writers Group; [hon.] National Honor Society, Top Ten graduate, Dean's List, Magna Cum Laude; [oth. writ.] Several devotions in various publications, book reviews in local newspaper, letters to the editor, article in New Hampshire Challenge; [pers.] I write for personal development and spiritual growth. Writing is an opportunity for self-discovery and a form of prayer. Know God and self first then you can communicate with others.; [a.] Hudson, NH

CASEY, BRENDAN
[b.] April 28, 1981, CA; [p.] Eamonn and Colleen Casey; [ed.] Currently in 8th Grade at Neuhart Jr. High, Mission Viejo, CA; [occ.] Student; [hon.] Presidential Academic, Fitness Award 1993

CASEY, TIMOTHY OWEN
[pen.] Timothy Owen Casey; [b.] September 5, 1956, Nashville, TN; [p.] Sarah E. Casey, Owen A. Casey; [ed.] High School, Glencliff High School 1975; [occ.] Furniture Company Owner; [oth. writ.] Have now Book of Poems and philosophy I have been writing sinse childhood. I also write children's books I hope to have published; [pers.] Youth is a great time to be care free. But start as soon as your mind will let you to make your mark. With age life is very short. And let know man kill your dreams or say they're stupid; [a.] Nashville, TN

CASSELS, LISAMARIE
[b.] September 1, 1969, Brooklyn, NY; [p.] Ted and Alice Reynolds; [m.] Thomas Cassels, August 24, 1991; [ch.] Thomas Joseph Cassels Jr. (T.J.); [ed.] Sheepshead Bay H.S., Kingsborough Community College; [occ.] Homemaker (I'm also editing a fictional novel); [memb.] Softball Team - Jims Marine Inn. - World of Poetry, Book Club, C. D. Club, Lucille Roberts; [hon.] World of Poetry Honorary Mentions, Silver Poet Awards and Golden Poet Awards; [oth. writ.] Poetry Forever, Hiroshima, That's Me, etc.; [pers.] I'd like to publish my own collection of poetry. I feel you can accomplish anything you want in life, if you really want to. There are no limits.; [a.] Brooklyn, NY

CASTRO, ANDREA MICHELLE
[pen.] Lacey Van; [b.] May 6, 1971, New York; [p.] Graciela and Jacky Castro; [ed.] Spanish River High, Palm Beach Community College; [occ.] Sales Coordinator, Brothers Coffee, Boca Raton, FL; [hon.] Creative writing award at spanish River High School; [oth. writ.] Some of the many poems I have collected since I was 15 yrs. old: "Tears That Stain", "The Optimist". "Blessings". "Healing", "Living On the Edge", "Cobwebs"; [pers.] I like to reflect upon the small miracles of everyday life that make the world a more interesting place to go to.; [a.] Boca Raton, FL

CASWELL, JUDY
[pen.] Judy Caswell; [b.] August 9, 1940, Alexandria, VA; [p.] Anna Lee (file) and Frank Horton; [ed.] Sarasota High School, Charles County Community College (CCCC); [occ.] Office Administrator; [memb.] Sierra Club, International Society of Poets, various wildlife and environment organizations; [hon.] Deans List, CCCC; [oth. writ.] Free lance articles for local newspapers, especial writings for friends; [pers.] I write poetry whenever I feel the need to express myself in words. My reward in writing lies within myself and on the faces of others when they receive one of my special poems. Inspiration for my poems comes from family, friends, and nature.; [a.] Cobb Island, MD

CATARO, SUSAN
[b.] April 3, 1969, New York; [p.] Jean and Joseph Cataro; [ed.] Centereach High School, S.U.N.Y. at Stony Brook-B.A., Cum Laude; [memb.] Golden Key National Honor Society International Thespian Society; [hon.] Phi Beta Kappa; [pers.] Writing is a deeply personal experience. The mind is a vault and the heart an inkwell.; [a.] Selden, NY

CATLIN, TENNA FAISON
[b.] September 5, 1948, Wewahitchka, FL; [p.] David Faison Sr., Classie Faison; [m.] Dorrill Lee Catlin, August 1, 1970; [ch.] Christopher George, Cenecia Tiere; [ed.] Rosenwald High School, Fayetteville State College, Youngstown State University; [occ.] Histolo-

gist, Salem Community Hospital, Salem Ohio; [memb.] American Society of Clinical Pathology, National Society for Histotechnology, Histology Society of Ohio, Inc., Youngstown State University Alumni Assoc., U.S. Naval Academy Alumni Association; [hon.] Credited for Technical Assistance work on research paper printed in Cancer 35:1236-1242, 1975 A Journal of the American Cancer Society; [oth. writ.] Several unpublished poems, short stories and songs; [pers.] God's creation around me give me my inspiration for writing. By learning to appreciate life, I am able to express it in words and my faith gives me hope that they will be heard.; [a.] Salem, OH

CAUDILL, PHYLLIS A.
[b.] March 23, 1955, Columbus, OH; [p.] William Shaffer and Helen Jarvis; [m.] Donald R., September 24, 1983; [ch.] None by birth. Legal guardians to twin nieces since 1989, due to untimely deaths of both their parents. Melissa Donnetta and Melinda Denise; [ed.] 1 year college; [occ.] Because of disability caused by MS, I do not work outside the home.; [hon.] 1989 Achievement Award, Mid-Ohio Chapter of National Multiple Sclerosis Society, 1991 KEYS Queen (a women's group associated with MS society.), 1993 Super America/MS Walk poster (i.e. billboards in KY); [pers.] I did not get a choice in whether or not to have MS, but I do have the choice in "how" it effects my life.; [a.] Columbus

CEDER, JOHN W.
[pen.] John W. Ceder; [b.] July 21, 1918, Moline, IL; [p.] Hjalmer and Louise Ceder; [ed.] University of Wash. BA, Butler University BS, Indiana University MA, Stockholm's Hogskola (cert.), University of Kentucky MS; [occ.] Retired; [memb.] 88th Infantry Div. Prince of Peace Lutheran Church; [oth. writ.] Butternut The Hook and Eye; [pers.] Thank you for reading my poem. I'd like to send you more.; [a.] Martensville, IN

CESTARE, LYNDA
[pen.] Lynda Conig; [b.] May 29, 1947, Brooklyn, NY; [p.] Ignazio and Marie Conigliaro; [m.] Carmine J. Spatafora J. R., January 17, 1988; [ch.] Peter J. Cestare (son), Carol Ann Cestare (daughter-in-law), Stepchildren: Russell, Terry, Chrissy; [ed.] Farmingdale High School, Farmingdale College, Ultissma Beauty School; [occ.] Stylist, Paul Mitchell National Educator, Innovations, Cape Coral FL; [memb.] National Cosmetology Association, John Paul Mitchell Systems, Educational Program; [hon.] First Place Winner Hairstylist Competition; [pers.] I enjoy writing about "Everyday Reality" within my own experiences, whether it be poetry, short story or a book. I dedicate this poem to my parents and any future writings with alot of love. Both are deceased but always with me.; [a.] Cape Coral, FL

CHANCELLOR, CHARLES EDWARD
[pen.] The Old Cowboy, Dream Painter; [b.] November 5, 1946, Wichita, KS; [p.] William and Stella Chancellor; [m.] Katherine Chancellor (Deceased), July 24, 1965; [ch.] Anthony, Terry, Shenelle; [ed.] High School, Business School Ministerial Degree; [occ.] Retail Manager; [oth. writ.] Breezes of Beauty, Rainbows, A Mothers Prayers, the Beautiful Dancer, the Cowboy, The Beautiful Rose, The Cowboy and the Angel of God, many others; [pers.] I search for the beauty in humanity, Horses, in this earth and ever in the Heavens.; [a.] Umatilla, FL

CHANDLER, LINDA L.
[b.] September 19, 1953, Saint Louis, MO; [p.] Norman Steele, Mary Steele; [m.] Dennis W. Chandler Sr., November 28, 1969; [ch.] Kristina Marie, Dennis W. Jr., Heith Adam; [ed.] Northwest High School; [occ.] Domestic Engineer; [pers.] Each word that I have written is a special part of me.; [a.] Cedar Hill, MO

CHASE, EVE LEWIS
[b.] May 17, Cols, OH; [p.] William T., Doris and Catherine; [m.] Lewis Harry L. Chase, May 16; [ch.] Gizmo the cat; [ed.] Journalism at Ohio State University; [occ.] Secretary; [memb.] International Society of Poets, Former Member San Francisco Press Club, Arizona Press Women, Ohio Press Club and Friday Night Irregulars; [hon.] Editor's Choice in Reflections of Light; [oth. writ.] Features, News Articles and Columns in Piqua Daily Call, Greenville Daily advocate, Parkersburg Daily News, Delaware Gazette, Yuma Daily Sun and Mission Valley News Ohio State Lantern; [pers.] That each offer the other the respect comport and peace He or She wishes for himself or herself.; [a.] San Francisco, CA

CHEARNEY, DONNA JUNE
[b.] June 22, 1937, Connellsville, PA; [p.] Williams and Geraldine Woods; [m.] Herbert Chearney, September 8, 1956; [ch.] Vicky Lynn, Sandra Lee and Laurie Ann; [ed.] Hurst High School; [occ.] Housewife; [memb.] AARP - AAA CWA; [hon.] First prize at fair for my handmade satin photo album; [oth. writ.] A personal collection of inspirational writings, I have written over the years; [pers.] I strive to bring out the innermost thoughts of my heart in my writings.; [a.] Mount Pleasant, PA

CHEATHAM, KATHLEEN T.
[b.] February 3, 1920, AL; [p.] Nina and C. A. Taylor (deceased); [m.] Hebert W. Cheatham, June 23, 1940 (54 yrs); [ch.] Daniel Cheatham, Debby (deceased); [occ.] Retired from Town Council (20 years); [memb.] Eastern Meadows Church of Christ, Cystic Fibrosis Assoc., No Name Club, Arts and Crafts Heritage Festival; [oth. writ.] I have been writing poems for many years, this in first one I have ever submitted for "public" scrutiny.; [pers.] Youth is exciting, maturity is reality, old age is the ability to feel the toy of living, gratitude for my many blessings and a great sense of humor.; [a.] Coosada, AL

CHEN, CHARLIE YEN-CHUANG
[b.] August 26, 1977, Taipei, Taiwan; [p.] Gordon and Amy Chen; [ed.] American High School; [occ.] Student in UCLA; [memb.] D.A.R.E. (Drug Abuse Resistance Education) volunteer/speaker, assistant rum major for school marching band, Amnesty International, Columbia Scholarship Federation, PTSA member; [hon.] Varsity block (letter) in badminton, marching band, and track and field, school block in academics and also in activities, top ten percentile in all four years of high school, first-place in bi-chemathon (State-wide science competition); [oth. writ.] Editor/writer for school magazine, graphics and design editor/staff writer fro school newspaper, writer/editor for school yearbook; [pers.] A truly wise man never plays leap-frog with an unicorn; [a.] Fremont, CA

CHENG, PATRICIA
[b.] June 21, 1979, Sault Ste Marie, Ontario, Canada; [p.] Arthur and Kowling Cheng; [ed.] Grosse Ile High School; [pers.] I dedicate all my work to my closest friends: CV, SR, AP. We are all creators. Writing builds our worlds. Writing breathes lives into our characters. We are all Gods of our own universes. In our works, we live forever. We are immortal.; [a.] Grosse Ile, MI

CHINN, ROBERT E.
[pen.] Bob Chinn; [b.] October 25, 1928, Newark, NJ; [p.] Ernest and Susie Chinn; [ed.] High School Equivalences; [occ.] Retired; [memb.] Director of "Inspirational Choir" at Pilgrim Baptist Church of Newark N.J.; [hon.] Citation from New Jersey Institute of Technology for my autobiography "Dig the Niger Up-Let's

Kill Him Again" which was published in 1976; [oth. writ.] "My Sins", "Criminal Factories", "Loneliness", "To Know", "Dig the Niger Up-Let's Kill Him Again"; [pers.] One need stand amid disaster to truly appreciate the range of one's mental and physical responses, adaptation and survival...; [a.] Newark, NJ

CHISHTY, M. RASHIDUL KABIR
[pen.] Shah Kabir Chishty, Ananda Jeet Kabir; [b.] April 1, 1931, Bangladesh; [p.] Abdul Hakim, Ambia Akater (deceased); [m.] Sajeda Khatun, July 23, 1954; [ch.] Mira, A. Kabir, Nargis, Parvin, Ireen, Masrur Jasir; [ed.] Educated in School, College and University; [occ.] Retired Administrative Officer of University of Dhaka, Bangladesh; [memb.] VIP Member of International Society of Poets, Washington, D.C., Member, Purnima Basar, Anuprash (Poetry Forum of Bangladesh.); [hon.] 1. VIP Best Poet (The National Library of Poetry, Maryland, U.S.A.), 2. Poet of the Year (International Society of Poets, Washington D.C., U.S.A., 3. Editor's Choice Award in 1993, 4. Editor's Choice Award in 1994 (voice) presented by the National Library of Poetry, Maryland, U.S.A.; [oth. writ.] Published A Bengali Poetry - "Sitalakhar Sharat" and fifty other manuscripts for publication in three languages, English, Bengali and Hindi; [pers.] Poetry for peace, freedom, love, light, truth, beauty servitude, sacrifice, salvation and victory.; [a.] Jamaica, NY

CHO, MYONGSU
[pen.] Myonghu Lee; [b.] September 7, 1939, Pusan, Korea; [m.] Mansung Cho, March 11, 1971; [ch.] Eunyoung Cho (daughter), Byonguk Cho (son); [ed.] Kyongnam Girls High. Pusan National University (B. A. Degree in English Literature); [occ.] English Teacher; [memb.] Deaconess of Kwanglim Methodist Church in Seoul, Korea, (Rev. and Dr. Sundo Kim) and St. Mark Church in Arlington, Virginia (Rev. and Dr. Samuel Shinn); [oth. writ.] Several poems published in local newspapers, essays for The Korea Times

CHRISTENSEN, GOLDIE
[b.] March 2, 1909, Indiana; [p.] Maggie and Fred Winkler; [m.] He died 8 yrs. ago we were married 48 yrs.; [ch.] 1 Daughter; [ed.] High School; [occ.] Retired; [memb.] Baptist Church Protestant; [hon.] None but have earned a lot of money thru the years; [oth. writ.] I can't remember them all. I've sold quite a few, I was 15 yrs. old, 1st sold 2 stories I can't possibly remember them all.; [a.] Dearborn, MI

CHRISTOPHER, MAUREEN
[b.] May 1, 1978, Commack, NY; [p.] Eileen Christopher, Jim Christopher; [ed.] Commack High School; [occ.] Student; [memb.] Varsity Track, Varsity Softball, Jazz Choir, Music Honor Society, Caroling Group, Student Council, Singing at Assemblies, Games Pep Rallies and Talent Shows, Student Representative; [hon.] Student Recognition Breakfast, performed solo at ICA concert, won talent shows, writings in literary magazines; [oth. writ.] Poems published in school literary magazines; [pers.] The power to write should not be abused but instead cherished and admired.; [a.] Commack, NY

CHU, CELIA
[b.] October 14, 1930, New York, NY; [p.] George Chin Tai and Lilly Chu; [m.] Divorced; [ch.] Suzan Chu, Penny Chin, Eugene Douglas Yuen; [occ.] Medical Office Manager, A.B.C. Pediatrics, San Mateo, Calif.; [memb.] American Contract Bridge League, U.S. Tennis Association, Chinese American Bridge Club; [pers.] "Do It Now" I expect to pass through this world but once. Any good thing, therefore, that I can do or any kindness I can show to any fellow human being, let me do it now, let me no defer nor neglect it for I shall

not pass this way again.

CHURCH, JERRY
[b.] April 26, 1928, Lone Jack, MO; [p.] Ray and Marie Church; [m.] Peggy, November 25, 1957; [ch.] Melissa, Jonathan, Stephanie, Chad; [ed.] Lone Jack Grade and High School Southwest Baptist College, Bob Jones University; [occ.] Teacher-Muncie Christian School. Church Visitation and Jail Ministry; [memb.] Stony Point Baptist Church; [hon.] Dean's List, English Club President; [oth. writ.] Poems, unpublished but often read in public; [pers.] I have been strongly influenced by the KJV Bible, Hymns, my parents, love of poetry.; [a.] Kansas City, KS

CHURCH, MARILYN
[b.] November 23, 1957, West Virginia; [ed.] Richlands High School, Tazewell Vocational Center, Volunteer State College; [pers.] I am inspired to write by people and events in life. I also believe that words are the magic keys that unlock all doors in life; [a.] Gallatin, TN

CHURCHILL, CABE
[pen.] Blas; [b.] November 23, 1976, Marshall; [p.] Roger Churchill and Alison Yarger; [ed.] Graduated High School - Enrolled in College; [occ.] Mechanic - Auto Service Tech.; [hon.] Homecoming court, Vo-educational succession; [oth. writ.] Hundreds of unpublished works; [pers.] Maria - Thank you for your influence, I love you and I will "never leave your side."; [a.] Marshall, MI

CHUTA, EDITH N.
[pen.] Sister Edith; [b.] February 22, 1956, Nigeria; [p.] Mr. and Mrs. J. W. Chuta; [ch.] Nramdi, Eleanor, Engiona and Nwaka; [ed.] High School-1974, Teacher Grade II-1976, Advance Teachers' College-1982, BSC-Crim-Just, Public Affairs-1992, MA-PAD in progress; [occ.] Publishing, writing and a student at Texas Southern; [memb.] Membet of Fountain of Peace Miracle Church, Owner and President of "All Peoples Missionaries"; [hon.] Dean's List-1985 through 1987, Texas Southern University-Houston, Texas. Awards for founding and running single Landedly all peoples Mission and and "Christian Digest"; [oth. writ.] "All Christian Digest", Divine Alta Call for Missionaries", "Do You Love Me More Than These?"; [pers.] The church may not be our ultimate answer, but I am at reaching the unchurched through my writings of the message of Jesus Christ.; [a.] Houston, TX

CIMINERA, FRANCIS A.
[pen.] Francis A. Ciminera; [b.] October 3, 1918, Waterbury, CT; [p.] Mary and Frank Ciminera; [m.] Margaret Mary (deceased), October 1, 1938; [ch.] Francis L. (first son), Mark A. and Paul J. (twins); [ed.] High School Graduate, One year college; [occ.] Retired - 50 years Retail Jewelry Salesman and Consultant; [memb.] American Legion, Past Comm. Disabled American Veterans Post #9, Favale - General - Flurio Post #8, Member Veteran's Council of Westbury, CT; [oth. writ.] 1 book published "Thoughts on Paper"; [pers.] "Love is an emotion. Of all the emotions that guide our lives. Love is paramount"

CIRILLO, MARIALICIA RYAN
[pen.] Mimi; [p.] John and Mariclare; [m.] Gary; [ch.] Rocco; [occ.] Teacher, Storyteller, Artist; [pers.] Poems are stories, messages, and stories are the best teachers. There is a Hori Indian saying, "Teaching should come from within, instead of without." I can teach best through my writings from within.; [a.] Cinnaminson, NJ

CLAIR, JAMES ROBERT
[pen.] James Robert Clair; [b.] September 5, 1958, Rochester, NY; [p.] Charles and Elizabeth McMaster; [m.] Zeny Clair, September 30, 1994; [ch.] Michael and Jay-ar; [ed.] Fakon Tech. and Ind., B.O.C.E.S. Eastern Monroe Career Center; [occ.] Maintenance Director; [memb.] Rochester Custom Cycle Club; [hon.] Mostly Sport or motorcycle awards; [oth. writ.] Several other poems, this is my first attempt at publication; [pers.] My best poems are not "forced", or written words, but come from the heart and soul as free flowing words.; [a.] Rochester, NY

CLARK, JONATHAN
[pen.] John Clark; [b.] April 20, 1982, Olympia; [p.] Jim and Sandy Randall; [ed.] Chief Moses Jr. High 7th Grade; [pers.] Life's short, have fun.; [a.] Moses Lake, WA

CLARK JR., HERBERT CHARLES
[pen.] He Who Waits; [b.] December 11, 1963, Los Angeles, CA; [p.] Lillian Dorothy Clark; [ch.] Terrance Daniel Clark 3 yrs. old; [ed.] Lynwood S.D.A. Academy Attended: a.) Loma Linda University b.) Oakwood College, Major: Theology/Computer Science; [occ.] Accountant YMCA of Orange County Metropolitan Office; [memb.] The Saints (A Brotherhood of Inter-Racial Activist...Committed to World Order and Peace); [oth. writ.] 25 unpublished poems; [pers.] I think that life is a giant poem...I see myself as just someone that borrows verse from it.; [a.] Lynwood, CA

CLARKE, HYLDA
[pen.] Linsada; [b.] Louisiana; [p.] Rev. and Mrs. S. D. Thomas; [m.] Selwart R. Clarke (Deceased), June 8, 1958; [ch.] Selwart Richard Clarke Jr., Brynne Clarke-Ferguson, Lorna Jill Clarke; [ed.] B.A. - Psychology - Southern University, M.A. Psychology - Teachers College, Columbia University; [occ.] Childcare Supervisor, Brooklyn Family Alliance; [memb.] The Riverside Church - John Donne/ George Herbert Poetry Group, Board Member - The Julius Grossman Orchestra; [oth. writ.] Poetry, Children's Stories, Grant Proposals; [pers.] I am continually amazed by the power of things and events deemed small, comparatively insignificant, to communicate to the spirit in compelling ways.; [a.] New York, NY

CLARKE, MICHAEL
[b.] February 13, 1982, England, UK; [p.] Winsome and Samuel Clarke; [ed.] Presently Attending Junior High 7th Grade; [occ.] Student; [hon.] Honor roll 'A' average since 5th grade. Honorable mention science fair New York City (13th Overall) 1995. Board of Education Science Achievement Award 1994.; [pers.] The mystery of poetry fascinates me.; [a.] Brooklyn, NY

CLAUTHER, JUNIE
[b.] May 20, 1974, Haiti; [p.] Ginette and Charles Clauther; [ed.] College Student at Borough of Manhattan Community Sea College; [occ.] Substitute Teacher; [memb.] Crusade Evangelical of Fisher of Men, In charge of cultural in the youth center; [oth. writ.] Two poems published in my school college discovery book.

CLEMONS, KENNETH L.
[pen.] Ken Clemons; [b.] January 16, 1931, Spring Field, MA; [p.] Charles L., Ethlyn M.; [m.] Marcella J., October 23, 1954; [ch.] 6 - 4 girls and 2 boys; [ed.] Experance; [occ.] Construction Manager; [hon.] A wife, six Children, 3 grandchildren, that love me; [oth. writ.] Looking back, only prepares for what's ahead! We have to build on the past for a better tomorrow; [a.] Spring Field, MA

CLEVELAND, JOHN R.
[b.] December 31, 1951, Houston, TX; [p.] Alfred and Zetta Cleveland; [m.] Jo Dene Cleveland, October 9, 1970; [ch.] Kelly Kathleen, Christi Dawn, Joshua Cade; [ed.] Currently attending University of Houston; [occ.] Retired Locomotive Engineer; [memb.] Brotherhood of Locomotive Engineers; [hon.] Superintendent Safety Award; [oth. writ.] Numerous Christian poetry writings and songs, as well as other contemporary writings; [pers.] In my writings as well as my songs I try to reflect the goodness and mercy of the Lord so that they may be used as schools to further spread the Word of God.; [a.] Houston, TX

CLIFF JR., LLOYD COLLINS
[pen.] Maynard; [b.] March 10, 1973, Wilmington, NC; [p.] Lloyd and Teresa Cliff; [ed.] K-3 Wrightsville Beach Elementary, 4 Bradley Creek Elementary, 5-6 W. Beach Elementary, 7-9 Williston Jr. High, 10-12 E.A. Larvey High, graduated 1991; [occ.] Carwasher; [oth. writ.] 3 years of writing my book - VOICES, and 6 months of writing a second book which remains untitled; [pers.] My pen name is Maynard not Mayvard. Please correct that for me. Send me some notification so that I may know its been corrected.; [a.] Castle Hayne, NC

CLINE, EDYTHE
[b.] May 1, 1916, Buffalo, NY; [p.] Annie and Albert Wouters; [m.] Leroy A. Cline, June 24, 1937; [ch.] 4 daughters, Janice, Joyce, Carol and Glenis; [ed.] High School; [occ.] Retired; [hon.] Never tried, except for having them put in the church bulletin. My poetry is all religious.; [oth. writ.] Lots of them, but none published - never thought myself a good poet!

CLOSSON, JOSEPH LUKE
[b.] November 27, 1983, Fairborn, OH; [p.] Jeff and Karen Closson; [ed.] Going into the 7th grade; [memb.] Eagles Football team; [hon.] I've won many academic and sports awards but I'm proudest of scoring perfect on my BCI test.; [oth. writ.] I've written many other poems such as "Aliens Abducted My Teacher" and "I Gambled My Life Away" but none of them have been published except for a few short stories in a school creative writing anthology; [pers.] The things of the universe life, love, Denver Broncos football. Give me TV or give me death. God bless America.; [a.] Elmore, AL

COAN, ELIZABETH W.
[b.] September 30, 1915, Albany, NY; [p.] Clifford Stanly Woodruff, Anna Waring Woodruff; [m.] William F. Coan, April 10, 1935; [ch.] Constance C. Musa, Alice C. Larsen, Margaret C. Loytty, 7 grandchildren; [ed.] Some College; [occ.] Housewife; [memb.] Corinth Reformed United Church of Christ; [pers.] Since my husband's retirement from the telephone company in 1969 he has on many occasions directed bridge programs on cruise ships. I have enjoyed assisting him.; [a.] Newton, NC

COATS, LILA
[pen.] Lila Coats; [b.] June 10, 1921, Tignall, GA; [p.] Harriet Ledford, William Ledford; [m.] Andrew Dwight Coats; [ch.] Shirley Ebert, Carolyn Crews, Dallas Coats; [occ.] Retired; [memb.] Bethany Baptist Church; [oth. writ.] I have written many poems. One has been set to music; [pers.] This is my way of expressing my thoughts to different occasions in everyday life. I have always loved poetry; [a.] Winston Salem, NC

COBINE, ALBERT STEWART
[pen.] Al Cobine; [b.] March 25, 1928, Richmond, IN; [p.] William and Stella Cobine; [m.] Marian Brown Cobine, September 1952; [ch.] Stewart Thomas, Andrew Jefferson, Ryan William; [ed.] BA Earlham College, MA University of Cincinnati 4 years, Doctoral Program in Political Science, at Indiana University; [occ.] Musician, Band Leader, Music Contractor, Composer; [memb.] Maple Grove Couservancy (Environmental group), Sierra Club A. F. of M. (American Federation of Musicians), Active Democrat, Member of B.M.I; [hon.] Distinguished Alumni Awards from Earlham College and Indiana University; [oth. writ.] I have mostly choral, jazz band and concert band arrangements and composition published from Studio P/R G. Schixmer, Robert King, Columbia Picture, Pub.; [pers.] My philosophy is very Jeffersonian in nature, and in my work for diverse e.g. student of Pol. Sci, but Musician by Profession/Song Writer, Composer, Band Leader but ran Fax Local Gov't Office, elected to Country Council, Tenor Sax Soloist (20 yrs) for late, great Henry Mancini!; [a.] Bloomington, IN

CODDINGTON, MARY
[pen.] Mary Lyons; [b.] April 2 1934, Barre, VT; [p.] William Irene Lyons; [m.] Lyman B. Coddington III, March 11, 1959; [ch.] Peter Coddington; [ed.] Univ of VT., Columbia Univ., New School for Social Research; [occ.] Writer/editor; [memb.] Author's Guild, Pen and Brush Club, Washington Independent Writers; [hon.] Candidate for "Noble" peace prize issued by the Association to Promote Honor in International Affairs my book "Seekers of the Healing Energy" has been in print since 1978 and published in five different editions - most recently translated into Polish.; [oth. writ.] Author of "Seekers of the Healing Energy." Newspaperwoman for Westport News, Brooklyn Heights Press-short stories and poetry in various journals and newspapers; [pers.] I believe that poetry should emphasize clarity and rhythm so that it is easily comprehended by a general audience. Today, obscurity is too often confused with subtlety.; [a.] Washington, DC

COELLO, NARCISO A.
[pen.] Pochy; [b.] December 29, 1972, Brooklyn, NY; [p.] Marta and Narciso Coello; [ed.] Laguarda Community College, New York City Technical College; [occ.] Veterinary Technician; [pers.] My writings and poems reflect the love that I feel for Cynthia Diaz. Cynthia is the woman that I truly love; [a.] Brooklyn, NY

COHEN, ALLISON M.
[b.] April 26, 1967, San Antonio, TX; [ed.] Currently in College (Accounting Major), Attended Beth Jacob High School in Denver, Colorado; [occ.] Part time Medical Assistant; [a.] Brooklyn, NY

COLE, ROBIN M.
[pen.] Robin M. Cole; [b.] March 29, 1970, Chicago; [p.] Donald and Reather Downing; [m.] Ules J. Cole, Jr., August 8, 1992; [ch.] Aaron Scott Cole; [ed.] Associates Degree in Secretarial Science; [occ.] Ward Clerk; [oth. writ.] Several writings published in local, City wide High School paper "New Expression" 1987-1988; [pers.] One can not grasp the mind without touching one's souls.; [a.] Chicago, IL

COLE, ROSE M.
[pen.] Kanni Francis; [b.] August 22, 1964, California, LA; [p.] Roosevelt and Nen Linscomb; [m.] Olesley Cole, August 31, 1990; [occ.] Writer/Police Officer; [oth. writ.] Novels, Manuscripts, Poetry; [pers.] God has blessed me with an incredible Talent to express my thoughts through writing. Now with my partner for life my husband Olesley, we have had the opportunity to combine our literary talents into writing manuscripts for Publication or Movie Production.; [a.] Inglewood, CA

COLEMAN, AARON T.
[ed.] B.S. and Associate Degree Administrative Science, Ohio State University Columbus, Ohio; [oth. writ.] Book name "Streets and Alternatives," a psychology of Street Life and Drugs and alternatives to that life style. Book name - "The Real Revolution," a psychology for success. Book name - "Young Blood Relationships and Common Sense," Common Sense things in ones personal, social and professional life. Book name - "Come Together" reasons why Blacks Should come together and work as one. Book name - "Approaching Spiritually," turning a materialistic outlook into an spiritual discipline to find God and self and ones duty to humanity; [pers.] Change begins from within; [a.] Columbus, OH

COLEMAN, RACHEL A.
[pen.] Rac; [b.] January 28, 1954, Chicago, IL; [p.] Woodrow and Celestia Hudson (deceased); [ch.] Marlon Anthony, Nikkia Cheron, Ronald Lee II; [ed.] Morgan Park High - Chicago; [occ.] Customer Account Specialist - Ameritech; [pers.] Life will be your teacher knowledge will be your guide but education is the key to your success; [a.] Peoria, IL

COLLETTA COMMANDER, EDMOND E.
[b.] April 13, 1927, Philadelphia, PA; [p.] Pasquale and Anna colletta; [m.] Dorothy Trainer Colletta, August 12, 1950; [ch.] Edward Louis Colletta, Stephen Michael Colletta; [ed.] B.S. - U.S. Merchant Marine Academy - 1948, Coombs College of Music 1953; [occ.] Author, Management Consultant; [memb.] USMMA Alumni Association, American Legion, The Retired Officers Association; [hon.] Outstanding Professional Achievement Award, USMMA Alumni Association, Outstanding Public Relations Achievement Award, Boy Scouts of America; [oth. writ.] Japan's Secret Weapon in the Trade Wars (Management Text), The Next Champions (fiction), The Ocean's Roar (unpublished fiction) several hundred poems, songs and song lyrics; [pers.] To improve the knowledge and education of government, management and labor to restore our industrial and economic growth to it's rightful position in the world.; [a.] Newton Square, PA

COLLIER, DARLENE
[b.] Mount Clemens, MI; [ed.] Institute of Financial Education; [occ.] Assistant Branch Manager for Standard Federal Bank, Clinton Township, MI; [memb.] A member of Unity Church of Today in Warren, MI; [hon.] The Institute of Financial Education; [oth. writ.] God's First Little Angel, Fellowship, Marvel, Hang Gliding and many more; [pers.] Our lives are always and forever changing, trust believe and express God's love.; [a.] Detroit, MI

COLLINS, GEORGIA ROSE MCLANE
[b.] November 20, 1925, Grand Rapids, MI; [p.] Virginia and George McLane; [m.] Divorced; [ch.] Woodie, Ernest, Regina, Micheal and Martin; [ed.] Went to Allen Grade School - Kiser High to 12th Grade; [occ.] Poet; [memb.] Easter Stars, The International Directory of Distinguished Leadership, Project Vote; [hon.] National Library of Poetry, Black Writers International Poets Society, World of Poetry, the International Directory of Distinguished Leadership, Easter Stars Worthy Matron, Crossing Guard for the Police Dept.; [oth. writ.] Only poetry; [pers.] If you have a talent don't give up. God will help you. Trust Him persistence always pays off keep the faith.; [a.] Jersey City, NJ

COLWELL, MAREE STOEHR
[b.] June 9, 1956, Ohio; [p.] Gene and Mary Stoehr; [m.] Sonny Colwell, September 19, 1992; [ch.] Shay Danielle and Jeffrey Lee; [ed.] Kennesaw State College, Kennesaw, Georgia; [occ.] Sonny and I own and oper-

ate Soshayma K-9s we import, breed and train German Shepherds for Police K-9s. We are endevouring to specialize in search and rescue dogs for children.; [oth. writ.] Many poems, short stories and philosophical writings enjoyed by family and friends, but never submitted for publication...before now.; [pers.] There is no laughter more joyful, no eyes more trusting, and no love more boundless than that of a child. When we are robbed of even one of our little ones, the world laughs less, trusts less, and loves less.; [a.] Young Harris, GA

COMBS, JENNIFER ALEXIS
[pen.] Jennifer Combs; [b.] March 8, 1982, Denver, CO; [p.] Dean and Lynn Combs; [ed.] 7th Grade; [occ.] Student; [memb.] Girl Scouts of America; [hon.] Orchestra Viola, 1st chair, Metal awarded for Solo Viola ensemble 3rd district festival 2nd place; [oth. writ.] None just a personal journal; [a.] Burton, MI

COMPTON, DEVORAH
[b.] May 5, 1973, Newark, NJ; [p.] Charlice Compton, Frederick Wohl; [m.] Laurence A. Venezia Sr., October 15, 1995; [ch.] Laurence Arthur Venezia Jr.; [occ.] Presently Home maker; [oth. writ.] I have written over 35 poems, and this poem is the first to be published.; [pers.] My inspiration is life! What I feel is what I write. What I believe - I want to achieve I hope one day that my words and feelings will be shared with millions. And I hope that my poetry can bring love, kindness and understanding into the hearts of many.; [a.] Allentown, PA

CONARTY, SHERRY L.
[pen.] Sherry; [b.] December 28, 1943, Muskegon, MI; [p.] Fred and Irene Crawford; [m.] John R. Conarty, March 23, 1963; [ch.] Wendel L. Conarty, Denine R. Burns, Tyrone C. Conarty; [ed.] 10th Grade in school; [occ.] Caring for my 90 year old mother and house wife; [oth. writ.] At the age of 49 years I have written 62 poems. Sometimes I can write 2 or 3 a day. Sometimes it is 2 or 3 or 4 months between them.

CONCEPCION, NELVA
[b.] May 24, 1941, Puerto Rico; [p.] Julia, Alejandro Pizarro; [m.] Divorce; [ch.] Julia, Minerva, Ruben, (Frances Decease); [ed.] 3 yrs College, Far Rockaway High, Cardozo junior High School Manhattan Community College. College Adapter Program; [occ.] Retired. Worked many years as nursing assistant; [hon.] Certificate of Recognition Community College for. Submitting a poem the black musicians ball. Many more poems one publish in the Anthology the edge of twilight. By the National Library of Poetry. Publish letters in daily news voice of the people; [pers.] The sky so blue. The earth so vast. The extremist (so tough) standing at one end. The races (so insecure) at another end. The politician (so engulf) yet at another end. The president (so engrossed) standing alone. Why don't we all join forces, stand together. To make this work altogether (more secure) more engulfing (more engross) Place for humanity.; [a.] Bronx, NY

CONCHIE, PAUL
[pen.] Paul Varjak; [b.] 4-3-64, Liverpool, England; [p.] Kenneth and Doreen Conchie; [ed.] Alsop Comprehensive; City College; [occ.] Freelance writer; [oth. writ.] Poems, short stories, and articles in different readings.; [pers.] I have been influenced by the poems of Robert Frost. "Acquainted with the Night," and "Stopping by Woods on a Snowy Evening," remain my two favorites.; [a.] Liverpool, England.

CONE, JEREMIAH EMIR
[pen.] Floyd Collins; [b.] December 14, 1972, Abadan, Iran; [p.] Richard and Jean Cone; [ed.] 3rd Year College; [occ.] Blues Musician, Chef; [oth. writ.] 3 volumes unpublished poetry, 17 Short Stories, 2 Novels;

[pers.] Life is burnt in an instant, savor the flame; [a.] San Gabriel, CA

CONFORTI, DAVID J.
[b.] August 17, 1971, Oak Park, IL; [p.] John and Linda Conforti; [ed.] Holy Cross High School, B.S. in Accountancy at Northern Illinois University; [occ.] Staff Accountant at Lyon Metal Products, Montgomery, IL; [oth. writ.] Several poems and songs that remain solely in my personal journals; [pers.] My poetry is a product of my emotions towards my surroundings, my friends and family, and this world's battle to "breathe". I also believe that children are the key to our future, and our happiness. We must nature them!; [a.] Saint Charles, IL

CONNER, HEADY D.
[pen.] Dah Dah; [b.] March 10, 1926, Roatan, Honduras; [p.] Randolp Dilbert, Calixta Dilbert; [m.] Edward L. Conner, 1943; [ch.] Calixta, Rosa, Judith Elizabeth, Janeth Judy, Joana Cecilia, Stedmon, Randy, Kike Dilbert; [ed.] School of Christ; [occ.] Missionary; [oth. writ.] Poems and songs, inspirational letters and revelations; [pers.] I'm looking up to the hill from which cometh my strength. I've been inspired by the Holy Spirit to write. I have been born again. It thrills me to be able to touch the heart of so many men and women and cause them to turn to Christ.; [a.] Slidell, LA

CONNOLLY, LOWELL
[pen.] Lowell; [b.] January 20, 1917, Goodland, KS; [p.] William and Hattie Connolly; [m.] Velma Connolly, December 2, 1960; [ch.] Stepdaughter - Joyce, Meddings (deceased); [ed.] One year of High School and many years of working with the public such as Desk Clerk for Motels and Hotels with people here and abroad.; [occ.] Retired but back to writing at the good Samaritan Home where my wife, Velma, and I reside.; [memb.] Our Lady of Perpetual Help Catholic Church and Calvary Gospel Church; [hon.] 1st place for a painting called Pararie Solitude at National Show. This lead to having own studio where I gave art lesson for many years. Painted many canvasses. Also painting now are at places as Paris, San Francisco, Chicago and Kansas.; [oth. writ.] Some published articles; [pers.] Growing up on my father's homestead in Western Kansas, one learns the values and beliefs of one's destiny for the creative minds, the patience to wait until time has taken its course.; [a.] Goodland, KS

CONRAD, DAVID
[b.] January 8, 1961, Canoga Park; [p.] Richard and Charlotte Conrad; [ch.] Kathaleen Elizabeth and Robin Alissa Conrad; [ed.] Class of '79 Canoga Park High School; [occ.] Supervisor at Multi layer Prototype Inc (MPI); [hon.] Graduated High School with Honors, Black Belt Martial Arts, KO'S Taekwondo, West Hills Publication of a poem: Katies Day in "Beyond the Stars."; [oth. writ.] The National Library of Poetry Everyone's Need (not yet published); [pers.] I'd like to dedicate this poem to: My parents and without their proper upbringings, Teachings of Morals and love I wouldn't be who I am. And my daughters Katie and Robin. "Special thanks and love to you Katie: without you there'd be no poem"; [a.] Agoura, CA

CONWAY, JULIE
[b.] October 31, 1977, Florida; [p.] Ed and Kay Conway; [ed.] Finishing 11th Gd. Will be a senior in the coming year.; [occ.] Student; [memb.] Church youth group, Thespian Society, Madrigal Choir, Drama Club; [hon.] Young author's High School drama awards, various choir awards, 2nd place, 1st place, Regency Talent Dance Competition 2rd place; [oth. writ.] Various poems including the loss of her, crying, holiday happiness; [pers.] In my poems I reflect on love, life, loss, and pain. I believe that the best authors are those that write from

their soul, and touch someone else.; [a.] La Grange, KY

COOK, SHARON L.
[pen.] Sharon L. Cook; [b.] September 18, 1940, Fullerton, CA; [p.] Pearl Jefferies; [m.] (Fiance) Fionce Tarry Bluhm; [ch.] 2 Sons David and Robert Bohannon; [ed.] 2 years of Community College, Certification in Drug and Alcohol Studies; [occ.] Real Estate Agent; [oth. writ.] "Woman of Love" a spiritual poem about women, A book on my life of spiritual happenings between 1983 to now which led me on a spiritual search of what was happening to me. None of these have been published. The poem I wrote "Return to the child of Light." Was an appearance that happened to me in 1988 in Palm Springs area in California. A white Light visited me in my apartment.; [a.] Dolores, CO

COOMBS, KEVIN W.
[b.] September 28, 1978, Louisville, KY; [p.] Phil and Kathie Coombs; [ed.] Atherton High, Junior, class of 1996; [occ.] Student; [oth. writ.] Read a few of my poems at three high school poetry readings. I also read at a RANT event at the University of Louisville and twice at twice told coffee shop.; [pers.] Don't let the physical differences separate mankind into classification. Once you do you start to analyze everything until you over analyze it, making the truth into confusion. Allowing the lies to run us.; [a.] Louisville, KY

COOPEZ, ANNELLE G.
[b.] August 23, 1950, Savannal, GA; [p.] Deceased; [m.] Divorced; [ch.] Zelicin Bowe, Kersichia Shelton, Charmell Cooper, Antonio M. Cooper; [ed.] Tompkins High School, James Sprunt Community College and Shaw University; [occ.] Mental Health Specialist, Wake County Mental Health; [memb.] Florence Chittenn Service for Young girls, Charlotte, NC. Christian Faith Center, Creedmoor Noth Carolina; [oth. writ.] Book to be published soon by the Vantage Press; [pers.] I have been inspired to write a book and second this poem that I have submitted. I express my ability and share the uniqueness that God has given each individual; [a.] Raleigh, NC

CORBITT, MICHELLE
[b.] September 24, 1961, Philadelphia, PA; [p.] Eleanor Corbitt and Shannon Corbitt; [ch.] Nadina Michelle and Jhanet Leanore; [ed.] H. H. Davis Middle School, Woodrow Wilson Senior High, Camden County College; [occ.] Assistant Teacher; [a.] Camden, NJ

CORCORAN, MARY ANN
[b.] July 19, 1931, Corning, NY; [p.] John M. Kurchey and Ann K. Kalinich; [m.] Thomas W. Corcoran (Deceased), June 7, 1959; [ch.] Kim M. Corcoran Lesso, Tim T. Corcoran and Sean M. Corcoran; [ed.] Graduate of Jasper Central School - Jasper, N.Y. Class of 1949; [occ.] Retired Acct. Clerk, Typist - Steuben Co. Public Health Nursing Service; [memb.] St. Vincent de Paul's Catholic Church; [oth. writ.] Several poems for friends and family; [pers.] I'm very fortunate to get my inspiration for my poetry from above and for the one's I love.; [a.] Corning, NY

CORDNER, ALTHEA EVELYN
[b.] October 2, 1947, Trinidad; [p.] Muriel and Alstead Fullerton; [m.] Winston Cordner, August 9, 1970; [ch.] Andel Alonn, Beverne Kethura, Cherese Dahlia; [ed.] M. A. Reading Education K-12 Michigan State University, Michigan B. A. Elementary Education Caribbean Union College. Trinidad; [occ.] Principal, Hartford S.D.A. Area School, Hartford, CT; [memb.] 1. National Association of Female Executives (NAFE) 2. Association for Supervisor and Curriculum Development (ASCD) 3. EFG Curriculum Collaborative 4. Northern Conference K-12 Board; [hon.] Alma

McKibbin Sabbatical Award for Excellence in Teaching/Administration 1994; [oth. writ.] Published in the Educational Journal of Trinidad and Tobago, 1990: "Reading Assignments and their Supportive Skills"; [pers.] Climb till you reach your stars.; [a.] Hartford, CT

CORNE, GENIA
[b.] December 12, 1946, Ind.; [p.] Clyde and Mary Lou Mikesell; [m.] Jack W. Corne, December 20, 1991; [ch.] Lisa M. Facemire; [ed.] London High School; [occ.] Secretary; [oth. writ.] Many poems; [pers.] I write from my heart. My family and friends are my inspirations.; [a.] Troy, OH

CORPREW JR., GERALD W.
[pen.] "Spatz"; [b.] April 24, 1956, Stuttguart, Germany; [p.] Gerald W. Corprew Sr. and Helen B. Corprew; [ed.] Central High School, (Phila. PA) '74, Clark Atlanta University, (Atlanta, GA) '78, Temple University (Phila. PA) '87, M.Ed Psycho-Educational-Processes; [occ.] Counselor, Adult Services Program, Temple University (Phila, PA); [memb.] Kappa Alpha Phi Fraternity Inc., (Clark Atlanta Univ./Phila Alumni), Sickle Cell Genetic Diseases Association of America (Phila./Delaware Valley Chapter); [hon.] Who's Who among Students in American Universities and Colleges, 1st Place, Persuasive Speaking (American Forensic Association-Regional Finals Individual Events Tournament (Clemson Univ. S.C.), Gerald W. Corprew Jr. Award for Delicate/Determ/Disc.; [oth. writ.] River of Pain, Flood of Tears, When They Can't Fix Your Pain, Who Do They Think, They Are Fooling, It's Nurses Whom You See, You Look So Good, Sometimes I Get So Mad, The Power of the Spouse, Your Phone Call Saved my Life, Why Am I Cursed; [pers.] It is my dedicated mission, to publish work about Sickle Cell Disease, in order to bring attention to those who must live with this pain. to get individuals with this pain to stand up and express their struggles with the pain, in order to help us all to heal; [a.] Philadelphia, PA

CORRICELLI, BART
[b.] February 4, 1922, Boston, MA; [p.] Giveseppe Corricelli; [m.] Raffaela Corricelli, August 20, 1948; [ch.] Patrick, Mikel, Angela; [ed.] Somerville High School, Radio School - USMC; [occ.] Car Sales, Egolf Auto - No. Manchester - Ind; [memb.] American Legion, V.F.W., Moose Lodge; [hon.] U.S.M.C - 4th Div. - 4th Tank BN Watched Flag Raising on Iwo Jima while in combat; [oth. writ.] Many others, none published; [pers.] I like to write poetry especially for someone close to me that I have deep feelings for.; [a.] North Manchester, IN

COSTELLO, KAREN L.
[pen.] Karen L. Costello; [b.] September 12, 1946, Washington, DC; [p.] Gina Hope and Michael La Rocco (both deceased); [m.] Victor L. Costello, November 11, 1967; [ch.] Rob - age 23; [ed.] AAS Degree in Nursing, Certified HIV/Counselor, many courses in AIDS. Graduated Phi Theta Gamma, Cum Laude; [occ.] Totally disabled since 1978, AIDS Volunteer, Facilitator of Chronic Pain Group; [memb.] One of the founders of the Mid-New York AIDS Coalition; Oneida County Special Commision on AIDS; member "FR Parker Shanti AIDS Project; Founder - St. John The Evangelist "Chronic Pain Support Club"; St. Anthony of Padua Church; [hon.] 1st Place Award Utica Poetry Club, 2nd, 3rd, Honored Place HCCC. Poetry Contest, 1992 Winner J.C. Penny, "Golden Rule Award" for Volunteer of Year, 1993 Oct. (1 wk) Hometown Hero Award have been published in a few small magazines; Clinton High Schl. 30th Reunion Humanitarian Award; [oth. writ.] Kentucky Bluegrass Review Literary Magazine, Vega, A Different Drummer, Arulo; Wrote some short stories;

[pers.] I mostly write about things that upset me. I also write about the beautiful things that most people take for granted.; My greatest inspirations: Gayle Harvey, Laura Detwiler; [a.] New Hartford, NY

COTICH, RUTH F.
[pen.] Felicia Cotich; [b.] Australia; [ed.] Schooled in Australia; [oth. writ.] VALDA, A young adult novel short stories in: Ingenue, Co-Ed, The Antioch Review, Primavera, The Colorado Quarterly, Ante, Raconteur (some works have been re-printed); [a.] Leesburg, FL

COUNTS, TOM
[b.] February 19, 1927, Meade, KS; [p.] John and Elsie (not living); [m.] Linda, December 31, 1985; [ch.] 12 between us and we now have two Haitian children living with us; [ed.] B.A. Ottawa Univ. - Ottawa, KS, M. Div. (Masters of Divinity) Central Baptist Theological Seminary Kansas City, KS; [occ.] Supportive Christian (economical) Missionary in Haiti

COX, MARSHA SOCKWELL
[b.] June 21, 1970, Jacksonville, NC; [p.] Ronald Cardwell, Marie Cardwell (deceased); [m.] Tommy Cox, November 12, 1994; [ch.] Meagan Sockwell and Bryan Cox; [ed.] Garland High School; [occ.] Secretary - Custom Country Homes of Kaufman, TX; [pers.] To anyone who may feel all alone in the world, always remember, that God is always there for you, all you have to do is look.; [a.] Kaufman, TX

COX, OLIVE H.
[pen.] Olive H. Cox; [b.] August 20, 1935, Chicago, IL; [m.] Donald L. Cox, August 6, 1960, Divorced 1993; [ch.] Barbara Jean, Robert John, Ronald James, Deborah Lynn; [ed.] Tavares High—Stetson University—major in Elementary Education and Physical Education; [occ.] Home maker— was (14 yrs.) Teacher, Sub and volunteer Coach; [memb.] St Paul Lutheran Church, Volunteer-Ingells Hospital and St Margarets Hospital, Luther Fast High School Board,; [hon.] Coach of the year "1961", Dean's List, Outstanding essay on "Mothers" and what the word meant to me; [oth. writ.] Poems for Grandchildren, for friends, for thank-you to special people in my life, Divorce and Death; [pers.] I am very sensitive to people and feelings. I express my inner most feelings in poems. Have always liked poetry and asked for poem books for gifts way back in high school; [a.] South Holland, IL

CRAMM, SUSAN R.
[b.] February 10, 1981, Waupun, WI; [p.] Charlotte and Eugean Cramm; [ed.] I will be a Freshman at Cumberland Country High School for the school year of 1995-1996; [memb.] I am the one original members of South Cumberland Elementary School's first Junior Beta Club and of the SCES's Discovery club for two years. I have also been a member of Girl Scouts for eight years and 4-H for six years; [hon.] I have been an honor student for the past two years. I am also going on a Wider Opportunity with the Girl Scouts to Mexico this summer.; [pers.] I think that some people smile the biggest when they're the saddest because they're trying to make everyone think they're happy.; [a.] Crossville, TN

CRAWFORD, NINA M.
[pen.] Nina Marie; [b.] June 30, 1922, Grand Junction; [p.] Warie and Myrtle Peach (Deceased); [m.] Verle Crawford (Deceased); [ch.] Two boys Deceased Grandchild Thomas B. Crawford; [ed.] 6 yrs of College. Was a teacher (primary) 20 yrs.; [occ.] Retired -do some china painting -some writing; [oth. writ.] None that were completed. This was my first-made it for my Christmas card 1994; [pers.] Poem was written because of my attitude of what christmas means today. "All

commercial and not of what it should mean."; [a.] Grand Junction, CO

CRAWLEY, RICK W.
[pen.] Rick Crawley; [b.] May 28, 1958, Connersville, IN; [p.] Chester and Dixie Crawley; [m.] Martha Louise, September 9, 1978; [ch.] Kresha Ann, Lisa Marie; [ed.] Connersville High, University of Rio Grand (1 yr), Ohio University (1 yr.); [occ.] Used car salesman; [hon.] (2) Honorable Distinguished US Navy and various Navy Medals, Honorable Mention for 3rd place in essay contest through Lancaster branch of Ohio University; [oth. writ.] Short Essays, none published; [pers.] Writing is a statement and expression to me. When so many times life keeps me tied down and I feel I can't breath, when there's fields and streams beckoning, I go through the power of pen and ink.; [a.] Trimble, OH

CREECH, JOCELYN RENEE LYLES
[b.] August 24, 1956, LA, CA; [p.] James Franklin Creech and Josephine Belle Creech; [ch.] I am the great grand niece of "Poppa John Creech"; [ed.] Continuing at USF majoring in recording studio engineering; [occ.] Singer/song writer/musician (formally a Aviation Mechanic); [oth. writ.] "A waking dream", "I'm in love someone who's not in love with me" and 12 other songs; [pers.] ...Music opens up the theater of the mind...using words and sound like a paint brush and canvass....; [a.] San Francisco, CA

CRISMAN, SHIRLEY JEANE
[b.] December 25, 1932, Wall Port, OR; [p.] Bert and Daisy Pickens; [m.] Austin R. Crisman Jr., June 4, 1960; [ch.] 1 son Daughter in Law and grandson; [ed.] Forest Grove High School in Oregon; [occ.] Housewife and Artist; [oth. writ.] A Book as yet unpublished and children stories, sci-fic stories; [pers.] I feel very honored to be chosen as one of the semi-finalist, as this was my first poem. Thank you, I'll be writing more now.; [a.] Ebony, VA

CRISP, RUTH JANIECE LANG
[pen.] Ruth L. Crisp; [b.] January 15, 1921, Appleby, TX; [p.] James A. and Dora Evans Lang; [m.] Fred Mauriece Crisp, December 24, 1928; [ch.] Fred Wayne Crisp, Fredora Janiece Crisp Byrd, Richard Bennett Crisp, Linda Kay Crisp Quillin, Kim Lang Crisp; [ed.] High School with honors, Business College; [occ.] Self-employed Electrical Contractor Inc.; [memb.] Fredonia Hill Church, Quest Club, Church Teaching, Favorite (Home-Maker); [oth. writ.] Books of Poems (Family and Friends) Christmas Story - Daily Paper, Articles: Houston Post; [pers.] My life has been richly blessed with my beloved family, my writing began at an early age, influenced by my Dad, and "Poems" in a daily paper by James Metcalf. My writings reflect the lives and activities of my family, friends and especially my grand-children, church and home. I too enjoyed devotions of a religious nature.

CROCKETT SR., DANIEL P.
[b.] December 7, 1966, Wharton, TX; [p.] Corrine; [m.] Veronica Crockett, November 6, 1987; [ch.] Danielle, Daniel Jr., and Mikela; [ed.] 10th Grade-G.E.D.; [occ.] Mini grip/zip-pak manager; [hon.] Medals and Awards for choir; [oth. writ.] I have nine other unpublished poems; [pers.] Good things never die.; [a.] Seguin, TX

CROWLEY, FAYE E.
[pen.] Faye E. Branhof; [b.] Saint Louis, MO; [p.] Elmer S. Branhof and Frances C. Branhof; [m.] J. Matthew Crowley; [ch.] Tracey Lalena; [ed.] Northwest High School - St. Louis with honors and scholarship; [oth. writ.] Several poems published in local newspapers at various times; [pers.] The effects of life's experiences, the finality of death and the afterlife are all

a driving force in my writing.; [a.] Saint Louis, MO

CRUZ, ABIGAIL
[b.] June 21, 1966, Brooklyn, NY; [p.] Guillermo Cruz and Aida Franqui; [ed.] East New York Vocational and Technical High School, New York City Technical College; [occ.] Bus Operator with Manhattan and Bronx Surface Transit Operating Authority; [oth. writ.] "Undeserved Love" published in "Tomorrow Never Knows."; [pers.] My love for Jehovah God has made me a better person. But the love of a woman is what made me a man. Nena, won't you please allow me to stand tall once again.; [a.] Middletown, NY

CULPEPPER, STEPHANIE L.
[b.] December 25, 1975, Westminster, CA; [p.] Aaron and Charlene Culpepper; [ed.] Currently Attending Long Beach City College; [oth. writ.] Several Poems, currently working on my first novel; [pers.] The written word is the tool I use to express feelings I'm too shy to admit to anyone face to face. Look for me in my work.; [a.] Long Beach, CA

CUMMINGS, SHARI
[b.] April 13, 1955, Jola, WI; [p.] Rich and Barb Ogden; [m.] Roger T. Cummings, August 31, 1974; [ch.] Kaylee, Tabitha, Michael, Joshua, Thomas; [ed.] Graduated- W. Delaware Community Schools, Manchester, IA - McConnell Schools Inc, Minneapolis, MN - Iowa haw Enforcement Academy, DSM, IA; [occ.] Retired - Law Enforcement Officer; [memb.] Dubuque, Delaware County Coalition Against Domestic Violence, Delaware County Domestic Violence Victims Services, Iowa Adoptive and Foster Parents Assoc; [hon.] Being a Faster and Adoptive Parent of Special Needs Children; [oth. writ.] "Your Light" -in Famoust Poems of Today, "Diet" -in Inspirations; [pers.] I write about personal experiences and common everyday things. Hoping others can share in the laughter or sadness of the moment; [a.] Earlville, IA

CUNNINGHAM, SUSAN
[b.] April 9, 1947, Washington, PA; [p.] Robert Walters, Sevilla Walters; [m.] Barry Cunningham; [ch.] David Matthew Cunningham; [ed.] Roy J. Wasson High School, Pikes Peak Institute of Medical Technology; [occ.] Writer for the Lord Jesus!; [memb.] Academy Area Christian Women's Club, fellowship Bible Church, Memorial Hospital friend to friend volunteer; [hon.] Love By Christ, what could be a Higher Honor!; [oth. writ.] Chapbook "Journey to eternity"; [pers.] I have the desire to reach hearts for heaven. Love and perseverance should be the hope of man's spirit.; [a.] Colorado Springs, CO

CURNELL, MARY E.
[b.] January 29, 1963, Detroit, MI; [p.] Beatrice and James Curnell; [ed.] High School Graduate Trade School; [occ.] Private Nurse; [oth. writ.] I have written poetry since the late 70's but none of them have been recognized until now.; [pers.] My poetry comes from my environment and experiences, which reflects on all of us.; [a.] Monroe, MI

CURRAN, THOMAS W. BILL
[pen.] Buckshot White and Evergreen Brown; [b.] March 18, 1920, Bakersfield, CA; [p.] Arthur H. and Helen F. Curran; [m.] Muriel E. Curran (Brooks), October 13, 1945; [ch.] Camille Cynthia, Thos. Jr., Billie Marie, Jannette May; [ed.] Bakersfield High, B.J.C., A.B. Univ. Cal Berkeley, B.A. Hons. Cambridge Univ., England (Trinity College); [occ.] Retired Management Consultant, US AFR Ret; [memb.] Kern County Grand Juror's Assoc., TROA, Amer. Legions, DAV's, VFW, 450th Bomb Sqdn.; [oth. writ.] "Personal Effects" (Unpublished 3 Act Play), Poems (Unpublished); [a.]

Bakersfield, CA

CURRY, CHRIS VERNON
[pen.] Chris V. Curry; [b.] January 18, 1951, San Antonio; [p.] Charles V. "Budoy" Curry, Mary Ann Curry; [m.] Paula Ann Curry, March 21, 1981; [ch.] Krystle Dee Curry, Chadwick Vernon Curry; [ed.] G.E.D.; [occ.] Lead Grounds Keeper 17 years; [oth. writ.] I wrote a poem for a co-worker that died. It got copied in main falcon news letter. Also his family contacted me personally, extremely touched!; [pers.] "Proud many" This poem was written to give Billy, Chris, Lynn, Joe, Susie, Tommy, Danny Lou Ann, Lela and Sally Jane. Strength to carry on Life! After the death of our beloved mother on July 12, 1992 proud Mary love the ocean. Fishing and crabbing, especially following the weather about tropical storms and hurricanes.; [a.] San Antonio, TX

D'AMATO, CHARLOTTE
[pen.] Charlotte Browning and Char D'Amato; [b.] May 28, 1940, Brooklyn, NY; [p.] Olga and Charles Browning; [m.] James D'Amato (Deceased) October 1990, December 18, 1964; [ch.] Ted, Christine and David; [ed.] Butler County Community College Butler, PA (Nursing) Nurse May 21, 1975; [occ.] Nurse (LVN); [memb.] Our Lady of Perpetual Help Catholic Church, Eucharistic Minister. Bereavement Ministry. United States Figure Skating Association.; [hon.] Many awards in Modern and Latin International Style Ballroom Dancing, and American Style Ballroom Dancing. Silver Medal in Ice Dancing.; [oth. writ.] Personal and non-published. Poems for my children's birthdays. Poems about my parents. Poem for the birthday of a priest. A personal consolation poem. Poem for a cousins birthday. Writings: for bereavement column in the Good News Bulletin.; [pers.] Love and you will have love. Forgive and you will have peace. Pray and you can endure all things. Be positive and look for the good in people. Be kind and compassionate and you will know beauty.; [a.] El Cajon, CA

DACOSTA, CINTIA
[b.] August 24, 1982, Arengentia, Bouis Aies; [p.] Lucia and Miguel Dacosta; [occ.] 6th grade and baby siting; [memb.] Teen Mag.; [pers.] I enjoy writing poems so I hope you enjoy reading my poem and all my other poems soon.; [a.] Boca Raton, FL

DACRES, AUDREY ADAMS
[pen.] A. V. Adams; [b.] February 22, 1959, Jamaica, WI; [p.] George Adams and Ada Adams; [m.] Richard Dacres; [ch.] Kerry-Ann Kanch, Richard Dacres, Danielle Dacres; [ed.] Trench Twon Comprehensive High, Long Island Beauty School; [occ.] Cosmetologist; [pers.] While some speak to express, with Pen on Paper there is no end to my expression, art and poetry has always been my love.; [a.] Rockaway Beach, NY

DAHL, BERTHA L.
[b.] March 4, 1940, Easton, MA; [p.] Frank H. Dahl Sr. and Flora S. (Eddy) Dahl; [m.] James G. Lincoln, July 24, 1978; [ch.] Annette L. Eddy, Robert E. Eddy Jr.; [ed.] Usual Schooling: Easton and Brockton, MA, Amico's Real Estate School '1968', Taunton Vocational Regional School of Practical Nursing '1972'; [occ.] Real Estate Sales Lady - and Licensed Practical Nurse not working at present; [memb.] Past Member of Enighet Lodge - VASA Order of America Member of Eddy Homestead Assoc. Viking Order of America AARP - Brockton; [oth. writ.] Some poems published locally - write for the Eddy Homestead Newsletter, etc.; [pers.] We must take better care of our world, so it can continue to take care of us. We must get back to basic - renew family values - put priorities where they belong - the family must be our prime concern: Someone must

speak out for the children.; [a.] Raynham, MA

DAKIN, MARCELLE
[b.] August 29, 1938, Plamondon, Alberta, Canada; [p.] Esdras and Melinda Belanger; [m.] Bernard Dakin, October 20, 1956; [ch.] James, Leonel, Kenneth, Laurie-Anne, Michael (Deceased); [ed.] Plamondon High School, North Island College [occ.] Bookkeeper - Tutorer - (North Island College); [memb.] Campbell River Volunteer Society; [pers.] I am greatly influenced by my surroundings as well as my own sense of spirituality.; [a.] Campbell River British Columbia, Canada

DALY, BEAU BRACKNEY
[b.] August 8, 1988, Amarillo, TX; [p.] John P. Daly and Kimberly B. Daly; [ed.] Mamaws Playschool, Sanford-Fritch Elementary 1st grade 94-95; [occ.] Being a kid!; [memb.] Tiger Cub Scouts, Canadian Archery Club; [hon.] 1995 3rd place - coloring contest, nominated into the gifted and talented class 1994-95; [a.] Fritch, TX

DAMIS, EDDY
[pen.] Dady; [b.] May 12, 1962, Pau-Pee, Haiti; [p.] Christian, Amenie Damis; [m.] Angela Damis, October 15, 1992; [ch.] Eddyson, Eddina Chercely, Eddess Ketura Damis; [ed.] Canado Haitian, EFCTEC; [occ.] D.E.T. Student, Deury Institute in Woodbridge; [memb.] "Ecal", "les Etoiles de l'art"; [hon.] Prime Secretary, Drama; [oth. writ.] Several poems published in French, Creole, Spanish and English with "les etoiles de l'art" a group of artists. Dramatist.; [pers.] No matter who you are, where you come from, the important is to be you. By looking at your face in the mirror every day, you are not going to loose yourself in the middle of a sterile garden.; [a.] Elizabeth, NJ

DANIEL, FRANCES MARION
[pen.] F. Marion Daniel; [b.] November 11, 1933, Orlando, FL; [p.] Oscar and Lucille Daniels; [m.] Cabell Walton Daniel, August 10, 1966; [ed.] Jones High School, Orlando, Florida. College graduate, Florida. A&M University 1961 B.S. Degree, work done at Univ. of VA., Longwood College and Lynchburg College; [occ.] Retired Teacher, Owner Dan and Fran's Limousine Service Corner Produce Market; [memb.] Christ Episcopal Church Halifax, Va., Virginia Skyline Girl Scout Council, Inc., G.S. of U.S. America, Lifetime Member; [hon.] Twenty-five years service 1991 Halifax Co. School System. Girl Scouts, Honored at meeting May 18th, 1995. For outstanding service.; [oth. writ.] Started writing family poetry several years ago on family members and friends. Have put together a book of poetry on family members with photos, book has 41 pages, printed by Hedderly in South Boston, VA; [pers.] My past occupation required much writing. Like writing about life in reality, just as how I have known me. Like writing about nature and animals. Wrote a poem on every family member I grew up with.; [a.] Halifax, VA

DANIEL, SALLY EZELL
[pen.] Sally Wells Ezell; [b.] June 10, 1951, Wheeling, WV; [p.] Mr. and Mrs. J. D. Ezell; [m.] Divorce Pending; [ed.] West Liberty State College, W. Liberty, WV, B. S. Communications; [occ.] Sales Coordinator, Choice Hotels; [memb.] Newspaper Institute of America, Mamaroneck, NY; [oth. writ.] Have written several poems, one of which was published in "American Collegiate Poets" in 1985. I am also Marketing a novelette for publication.; [pers.] Writing is a gift, a wonderful talent which should be more encouraged in our schools.; [a.] Wheeling, WV

DAOUD, MIKE
[b.] January 4, 1980, Hartford, CT; [p.] Abe and Lili Daoud; [ed.] Freshmen at Hall High School in West Hartford, CT; [occ.] Student; [hon.] Made Honor Society at Avon Old Farms School; [pers.] I strive to be a good life example to other adolescents, and try to integrate God into all areas of my life, my poetry is inspired by my life experiences.; [a.] West Hartford, CT

DARRINGTON, LOIS ELAIN
[b.] August 24, 1951, Houston, TX; [p.] Herman and Frances Peters; [m.] William C. Darrington, October 5, 1974; [ch.] Charnette Darrington; [ed.] Booker T. Washington H.S., Texas Southern University Prairie View A.M. University; [occ.] ESL-Teacher, Paul Revere Middle School - Houston, TX; [memb.] St. Timothy's United Methodist H.S.P.V.A.'s Theatre Guild, Positive Thinkers Club, PTO, All God's Children Collector's Club; [hon.] Paul Revere's ESL Teacher of the Year 1994; [oth. writ.] Essays and poems; [pers.] Base your life on the fruit of the spirit - love, joy, peace, patience, kindness, goodness, faithfulness, gentleness and self-control; [a.] Houston, TX

DAUGHERTY, MARY J.
[b.] November 7, 1948, Spencer, IA; [p.] Evelyn and Marion Daugherty; [ed.] Spencer High School, Nettleton Business College in Sioux City, Iowa; [occ.] Letter Carrier, U.S. Postal Service, Freno, Calif.; [memb.] Methodist Church, Athletic Club (Clovis), Fresno Community Chorus, Volunteer Work at Fresno Blood Bank; [hon.] Musical (voice) and athletic awards in High School, safe driving awards and United Way Assoc. with work; [oth. writ.] This poem is my first attempt at writing. It is based on my brother's life. I have written articles for U.S. Postal Newsletters also.; [pers.] When life brings you difficult times, remember to pray, and think on this: You could have been born in Russia!; [a.] Fresno, CA

DAUGHERTY, MARY J.
[b.] November 7, 1948, Spencer, IA; [p.] Evelyn and Marion Daugherty; [ed.] Spencer High School, Nettleton Business College, Sloux City, IA; [occ.] Letter Carrier, U.S. Postal Service, Fresno, Calif.; [memb.] Methodist Church, Athletic Club, Eresno Community Chorus Volunteer for Blood Bank; [hon.] Musical (voice) and Athletic; [oth. writ.] This poem is my first attempt at writing. Have written other articles for Blood Bank and Postal newsletters.; [pers.] When life brings you difficult times, remember to pray, think on this: You could have been born in Russia!; [a.] Clovis, CA

DAUPHIN, BUD
[b.] September 23, 1945, Clinton, IA; [p.] Neal and Ree Dauphin; [m.] Marcia Schaaf, October 4, 1990; [ch.] Erwin C. Jr., Tamara Christine; [ed.] B.A. Metropolitan State University, Savanna Community H.S., Savanna, IL; [occ.] Stock Trade and Florist (Schaaf Floral); [memb.] Kiwanis, Raptor Center, Metro State Alumni St. Philips Luth Church; [oth. writ.] Scores of poems given as gifts to very special people; [pers.] It's a gift from God that I use to honor those special people that inspire me.; [a.] Fridley, MN

DAVENPORT, A. F.
[pen.] Al Davenport; [b.] November 1, 1939, Selma, AL; [p.] Albert and Evelyn; [m.] Sheila, November 19, 1982; [ch.] Stefani (11), Karen (23); [ed.] B.S. University of Alabama 1972, MBA Samford University 1979; [occ.] Training Specialist for Bell South Telecommunications; [pers.] I would like for my poetry to reflect good memories of the past, pleasant memories of the present and hope for the future.; [a.] Midfield, AL

DAVIDSON, STAN
[b.] September 8, 1971, Jackson, TN; [p.] Betty and Gerald Davidson; [ed.] Peabody High School, Dyersburg State Comm. College; [occ.] Meat Dept. at Ingram IGA; [memb.] Berea Baptist Church; [hon.] Peabody football Letter Award. Hal Holmes Memorial Scholarship 93-94, 94-95, DSCC Outstanding Chemistry Student Award; [oth. writ.] Several Songs, Poems, and Short Stories; [pers.] I believe that poetry is the lyrical expression of the heart and mind put into words on paper so that others may see what I think and feel. I would like to thank Monica E. Whitsilt for being the inspiration in my Poetry!; [a.] Trenton, TN

DAVIS, BARBARA T.
[pen.] Barbara Toomer; [b.] August 8, 1947, Philadelphia, PA; [p.] Robert and Marion Toomer; [m.] Mondell Davis, August 30, 1975; [ch.] Mara (17), Beandrea (13); [ed.] Philadelphia High School for Girls, Pennsylvania State University, University of Pennsylvania; [occ.] Teacher, Evaluator, Writer; [memb.] Women in Communication, ASTD American Society for Training and Development, Alpha Kappa Alpha Sorority, Beta Eta Chapter; [hon.] Fellowship for Study in Business Administration; [oth. writ.] Historical non fiction articles on religious news. Poetry and short stories, essays, speeches; [pers.] Everyday is a new day that the Lord has made.; [a.] Philadelphia, PA

DAVIS, GWENDOLYN
[b.] February 26, 1948, Turson, AZ; [p.] Jodie and Katie Watson; [ch.] 2 sons (ages 24 and 22); [ed.] High School plus 3 years of College Major Early Childhood Education; [occ.] Manufacturing Specialist; [pers.] I wrote this poem in honor of my mother. She was one of the bravest, and most courageous people. That I have ever known; [a.] Tucson, AZ

DAVIS, PAUL DUKE
[pen.] Duke; [b.] November 28, 1969, Orlando, FL; [p.] Paul and Paulette Davis; [ch.] Brother, Franklin Davis, a most talented young man; [ed.] Univ. Central Florida - Liberal Studies Spirit Life Bible College, Orange County, CA, Brooklyn Law School, School of travel and experience, School of listening (John 10:27); [occ.] Missionary, Law Student, Personal Trainer, Entrepreneur; [memb.] Alumni Spirit Life Bible College My name is written in the eternal book of life! (Revelation 20:15) Miracle Invasion Financial partner with Benny Hinn! (Acts 19:11, Hebrews 2:4, Mark 16:20); [hon.] I have been given the honor to be awarded with two wonderful grandparents, Paul and Beatrice Krotchik. Their names shall be mentioned throughout eternity for the kindness they have shown me!; [oth. writ.] Many other writings and books may be obtained through writing or calling, Paul "Duke" Davis 4601 Larado Place Orlando, FL 32812, (407) 275-1353; [pers.] "They that turn many to righteousness shall shine as the stars for ever and ever!" (Daniel 12:3) "Whosoever calls upon the name of the Lord Jesus shall be saved! "(Romans 10:13) "Life and life more abundantly..." (John 10:10); [a.] Orlando, FL

DAVIS, TOMMIE L.
[pen.] Tommie L. Davis; [b.] March 12, 1933, Montgomery, AL; [p.] Obbie and Lillie B. Davis; [m.] Lena M. Davis, May 23, 1951; [ch.] Tommie L. Davis II, Yvonne Brandel, Michael Davis, Ronald Davis, and Bruce Davis; [ed.] Booker T. Washington High School, University of Minnesota; [occ.] U.S. Army, Retired, First Bank Minneapolis, Retired; [memb.] The Retirement Enlisted Association. The American Legion.; [oth. writ.] A short story: "The Files of Tommie Tuff." A poem published in Women Journal, A private Organization.; [pers.] I am inspired by world events. I try to write with compassion and empathy.; [a.] Minneapolis, MN

DAWLEY, CAROLYN
[b.] October 15, 1957, Kansas City, MO; [m.] Brian Dawley, May 8, 1982; [occ.] Receptionist and Artist; [pers.] I have always loved poetry and writing and hope that others will enjoy reading what I have to say. I have a tremendous respect for the written word and for what comes from the heart.; [a.] West Winfield, NY

DAWSON, MADELINE J.
[b.] August 12, 1952, Brooklyn, NY; [pers.] Life is poetic; [a.] Houston, TX

DE LA ROSA, FRANK
[b.] 1918, Ponce, PR; [p.] Ramona and Abdon; [m.] Lucy, 1948; [ch.] Carmen, Frances, Lucille; [a.] Brooklyn, NY

DEAN, BETTY A.
[b.] October 22, 1922, Mount Morris, NY; [hon.] First poem written January 16, 1988; [oth. writ.] Poor Ajar Journeys End, Parting Vacant Eyes, Solitude, Sands of Time, Afternoon Shadows, Broken Chain, Yester-years, Candle Light, Home, Remember Me, "Stef", Dear Heavenly Father, The Calling (many others); [pers.] My writings display and strong spiritual theme and demonstrate my loving faith. Some tell of loneliness we have all experienced. All come from the heart and are spiritually inspired.; [a.] Mount Morris, NY

DEARING, ANNE
[b.] April 17, 1943, Jackson, TN; [p.] Louis D. Betty (deceased) and Wilsie A. Betty; [m.] Paul C. Dearing, September 1964; [ch.] Ellen Hawkins, Jeff Powell, Robyn Patterson and 3 grand daughters; [ed.] Jackson High, Jackson TN, Hinds Jr. College Raymond MS; [occ.] Sales and Service Associate Barnett Bank, Oviedo Florida; [oth. writ.] Children's stories, as yet unpublished but still hopeful. Essay contest winner for United Way 1994; [pers.] The beauty of art, both written and on canvas, is the medium I use for stress relief.; [a.] Winter Springs, FL

DEEKEN, JOSEPH
[b.] April 18, 1979, Jefferson City, MO; [p.] Alan and Kathleen Deeken; [ed.] Sophomore, High Technology HS; [hon.] Johns Hopkins University Talent Search participant Johns Hopkins Writing Tutorial Ma. Jr. Conservation Camp Information Competition 1st Place; [a.] Keyport, NJ

DEESE, PATTI
[b.] January 2, 1951, Houston, TX; [p.] Bettle M. Proctor, Glenn E. Proctor; [m.] D.R. Johnson, July 16, 1991; [ch.] Nicholas Dartle Deese; [ed.] Stanly Community College, Branell College, Anniston Business College; [occ.] Admin. Asst. Exec. Secretary Collaborator on Novels; [memb.] Stanly Co. Mental Health Association; [hon.] Governor's Volunteer of The Year Award 1980 Dean's List. Regional Debate Champion 1965; [oth. writ.] Several Non Published Writings; [pers.] Love Is Mankind's Salvation, Loved Shared Can Heal Change The Path Of Destruction That The World Is Moving Toward, We Must Truly Share Our Love To Save Mankind, The Planet, The World As We Know It.; [a.] Charlotte, NC

DEFEIS, FREDERIC
[b.] January 6, 1926, Brooklyn, NY; [p.] Mary and Peter; [m.] Carmela; [ch.] Doreen, Danae, Damoh, David; [ed.] B.A. Brooklyn College, MFA. Forum University; [occ.] Executive Director of Arena Players, Assoc. Prof. Theatre - Hofstra; [memb.] Actors Equity Assoc., Long Island Theatre Arts Coalition, Farmingdale Chamber of Commerce, New York State United Teachers; [hon.] New York Teachers Council on the Arts. Suffolk County Forum for the Arts; [oth. writ.] Plays: A

Shadow of Fear the Motel; [pers.] The word is an illusion. Truth can only be found by the theatre.; [a.] Deer Park, NY

DEFILIPPIS, JAMES M.
[pen.] James Micheals Dee; [b.] February 28, 1969, Bronx, NY; [p.] Micheal and Lynn DeFilippis; [ed.] Smithtown High School East; [occ.] Musician/Computer Programmer; [pers.] I would like to thank Dionysus and all who have strived to follow in his steps. You've given me the imagination.

DEGIDIO, CARMELLA
[b.] September 4, 1937, Englewood, NJ; [p.] Palma and Pellegrino Giordano; [m.] Michael R. DeGidio, September 7, 1957; [ch.] Michael Charles, Kevin Peter, Grandchildren Lauren, Kimberly, Nicholas; [ed.] Leonia High School Modern College of Cosmetology; [occ.] Homemaker; [memb.] St. Bernadette's Roman Catholic Church; [pers.] I have been influenced by a life time of pleasant experiences. Memories are the mind's treasure chest.; [a.] Parlin, NJ

DEGRAFF, FRANCESA
[b.] December 6, 1925, Manhattan, New York City, NY; [p.] Mary and Frank DeBella; [m.] Peter DeGraff, July 29, 1962; [ch.] Pier-Marie, Marina and Camille; [ed.] Graduate High School, plus courses in Psychology, Political and Science, Harmony and Counter Point Music, and Sculpture; [occ.] Secretary; [memb.] On May 22, 1994 I was initiated by the Supreme Master Ching Hai and I am an initiate of the S.M. Ching Hai Meditation Association (worldwide).; [hon.] I won a Sculpture Award by the Brooklyn Museum; [pers.] My personal "note" is a song from my heart to have been accepted as a semi-finalist for my poetry. I love to write poetry and inspirations come spontaneously.

DELANCY, IVONNE
[pen.] Ivonne Elliott; [b.] September 24, 1941, Panama Colon, Rep. of Panama; [p.] Albert Elliott, Eunice Brown; [m.] Irvin DeLancy, August 27, 1993; [ch.] Kenneth Parchment Nyoka Parchment; [ed.] Primary School Certificate - Enriquez Heensier Junior High - Abel Bravo Certificate High School - Rainbow City - Canal Zone Center Certificate - How to own and operate a day care; [occ.] Computer Operator, License to care for the disabled do private tutoring at home; [hon.] For been the collector for the Greater New York Fund at work for the telephone Co. 1968. in N.Y; [oth. writ.] Children Books not publish; [pers.] Children in our society, seem to relate better to poetry as a form of expression. Is an excellent form of expressing one's feeling in a brief manner. It's challenging to me because it allows me to reach others especially children; [a.] East Orange, NJ

DELLOVADE, MARY L.
[b.] June 1, 1937, Avella, PA; [p.] Olympia and Joseph Lazzaro; [m.] Robert Dellovade, July 28, 1962; [ch.] Leslie Kristine, Amy Jo Dellovade; [ed.] Avella High School Attended Jefferson Technical College Salutatorian at Avella High School; [occ.] Admitting Clerk Center and Switch Board Oper. - Weirton Medical; [memb.] Friends of the follansbee Library, Brooke Senior Citizens, Brooke County Animal Welfare League, Member of St. Anthony's Church in Follansbee; [hon.] Dean's List, Placed third in West Virginia Beef Cook-off in 1990, Grand Prize Winner, Second Grand Prize Winner, First in Category Winner three times for steubenville Herald Star Cookbook Judge for Annual Steu. Herald Star Cookbook Contest, First in Category Winner for Weirton Daily Times; [oth. writ.] None that have been published as of yet; [pers.] I love to express my feelings in poetry when I am happy or sometime melancholy. I also enjoy writing short stories about my

life experiences and my 19 yr old pet cat - Muffin.; [a.] Follansbee, WV

DELMAR, RON
[pen.] Tully Mars; [b.] April 7, 1949; [p.] Dan and Mary DelMar; [m.] Janice DelMar; [ch.] Lisa Marie, Jessica Lynn; [ed.] Council Rock H.S.; [occ.] Project Manager; [oth. writ.] "Special Tears" written in memory of Nicole Trapanese published by Long Beach Island Sand Paper; [pers.] Treat people the way you want to be treated. Play as hard as you work. Remember you can never get back a good time but you can always make more money.; [a.] Barnegat, NJ

DENAULT, JENNIFER
[b.] March 19, 1981, Framingham, MA; [p.] George and Donna Denault; [ed.] High School; [occ.] Student; [a.] Ashland, MA

DEPINA, ROSALIE
[pen.] Rosalie Hill; [b.] August 30, 1960, Camden, NJ; [p.] John and Myrtle Hill; [ch.] Monique, James; [ed.] Kingsway Regional H.S., Star Technical Institute; [occ.] Shift lead, Heritage Store, Gibbstown, NJ; [hon.] Merit Award - Famous Society; [oth. writ.] Several poems published in Anthology titled Famous Poets of Today; [pers.] Through my poetry I wish to express to others a reflection of hope and a way of survival to better our forever changing times.; [a.] Gibbstown, NJ

DERIENZO, BRENDA
[b.] December 4, 1950, Saint Louis, MO; [p.] Joseph and Betty Funke; [m.] Joseph DeRienzo, shortly after Adam and Eve; [ch.] Tina Renee, Angela Nicole; [ed.] I survived Catholic Private all girls schools; [occ.] Pleasing everyone; [memb.] Motherhood; [hon.] Honored to be considered for your publication; [oth. writ.] Besides grocery lists and checks to creditors nothing much worth mentioning; [pers.] My true passion in my life (next to chocolate, of course) is to write. Escaping to my inner thoughts and emotions brings unmeasurable pleasure to me. Thank God.; [a.] Saint Louis, MO

DERITIS, PAUL A.
[pen.] Anthony Trent; [b.] September 17, 1922, Italy; [p.] Joseph and Gulia; [m.] Angela, October 13, 1959; [ch.] Joseph, Paul, Anthony; [ed.] B.A.N.Y.U., M.A. Graduate School of ED - Fordhan Law Hofstra; [occ.] Retired Teacher; [hon.] Poetry Editor N.Y.U. Literary Magazine Apprentice Published in Blue River Anthology, Reading of "City of Dust" Before Nassau Council of English Teachers; [oth. writ.] "Johanna's Son" - Novel, 3 Plays, 5 Books of Poetry - Editing now for Possible Publication; [pers.] "Preoccupied with Beginnings and ends of everything" enjoy writing as a hobby, Music and Acting.; [a.] Islip, NY

DEROSA, BARBARA
[b.] October 23, 1976; [p.] Steve and Nancy DeCarlo; [pers.] Dedicated to: Daniel Walter; [a.] Long Island, KS

DERRY, JEREMY ALAN
[pen.] J. Alan Derry; [b.] November 14, 1973, Macomb, IL; [p.] Richard and Kay Derry; [ed.] Macomb High, Spoon River College, Western Illinois University; [occ.] Student; [hon.] Phi Theta Kappa; [pers.] I use my writing to help put thing into perspective. The majority of my writings are taken from events in my life my influences range from Poe to King.; [a.] Macomb, IL

DERSCHA, MICHAEL
[pen.] Mikey; [b.] October 8, 1958, Detroit, MI; [ed.] Stevenson High School, Henry Ford Community College, Attending Central Michigan Univ.; [occ.] Systems Analyst, Ford Motor Credit, Disc Jockey; [memb.]

Unity Church of Today; [hon.] Distinguished Honor Graduate NCO Academy U.S. Army; [oth. writ.] Just getting started; [pers.] I write expressions of my inner feelings that I may show them on the outside; [a.] Southfield, MI

DESLOGE JR., JOSEPH
[b.] January 19, 1925, Saint Louis, MO; [p.] Joseph and Anne Desloge; [m.] Martha Seredynski Desloge, June 11, 1966; [ed.] BA Mechanical Engineer; [occ.] President-Founder Population Planning Trust; [a.] Florrisant, MO

DETWILER, DARIUS
[b.] August 20, 1956, Hamburg, Germany; [p.] Philip and Babette Detwiler; [ed.] Souderton High School, Pennsylvania State University, The Art Institute of Philadelphia; [occ.] Artist; [memb.] National Graphic. Artist Guild, the National Chapter of Trout Unlimited, the Guadalupe River Trout Unlimited Chapter; [hon.] Art Institute's Dean's List, Several Addy Awards for Graphic Design and Illustration; [oth. writ.] Several Unpublished poems, unpublished children's book:" The Birth of Butterflies"; [pers.] The fear of writing the simplest Letter is always present in me. As an Artist, Poetry allows me to overcome this fear. It's beautiful, Expressive form prompts me to use, in place of paint, words on paper to Communicate my feelings About myself and the world around me.; [a.] San Antonio, TX

DEVATT, MICHELLE TWINING
[pen.] Sunshine Twin; [b.] July 29, 1969, Easton, PA; [p.] Joan Pysher and Jacob R. Twining; [m.] Married 7 long years; [ch.] Kyle Ray, Roy Oliver, Alisha Lynn, and Dylan Alfred; [ed.] Warren Hills High, Northampton Community College; [occ.] Criminal Justice System, mother of 2 sets of twins; [memb.] Monroe County Mothers of Multiples, Criminal Justice Club; [hon.] Honored to be published in "Beyond the Stars." Dedicating this poem to my 4 beautiful children and to a new start on life.; [oth. writ.] "No tears needed" lullaby hush little one, the day is done. I'll hold you tight, throughout the night. As the clock ticks away, night becomes day. You'll wake up and here I'll be. So now you see, that is why there is no reason to cry. Hush little one.; [pers.] I hope my poems put other peoples thoughts into words, for the world to read and feel. Poems are thoughts written down as away to celebrate life.; [a.] Saylorsburg, PA

DEVINCENZO, MARIO
[b.] November 17, 1928, Newark, NJ; [p.] John and Connie DeVincenzo; [m.] Constance DeVincenzo (deceased), May 19, 1956; [ch.] Diana Otchet and Cynthia Bertuzzi; [ed.] Central High, Newark, NJ; [occ.] Brinks Armored Car, Security Guard; [memb.] United States Air Force 9 Years Service; [hon.] Act of Congress for Permanent Military Rank; [pers.] I'm trying to use poetry to enrich the lives of others and to bring the beauty of poetry back to life.; [a.] Brooklyn, NY

DEVINE, DOUGLAS KENNETH
[a.] Williamsport, PA

DEY, LAUREN
[b.] January 5, 1979, Hackensack, NJ; [p.] Theodore J. Dey and Marlene M. Dey; [ed.] Parsippany High School, Parsippany, New Jersey, St. Peter the Apostle Grammar School, Parsippany New Jersey; [memb.] Parsippany High School Gymnastics Team; [hon.] Varsity Letter in Gymnastics - 1993, 1994 Who's Who Among American High School Students - 29th Edition

DIAMOND, DAWN
[b.] September 3, 1965, New York City, NY; [p.] Linda and Michael Tittmann; [m.] Dean Diamond, August 6,

1988; [ch.] Ryan (6 yrs. old), Kevin (4 yrs. old); [ed.] Richmond Hill High School, Hofstra University, State University of New York at New Paltz; [occ.] Full time mother, will continue with teaching Elementary School in future; [hon.] Dean's List; [oth. writ.] Several children's books awaiting publishing, also co-writing a novel; [pers.] I am endlessly in awe of the great miracles of life - from the rising of the sun to the births of my children. My writing is a reflection of these inspirations.; [a.] Red Hook, NY

DICKERSON, DIANNA
[pen.] Buffy Dickerson; [b.] August 16, 1959, Texas; [p.] Glena Marts; [m.] Rusty Dickerson, November 30, 1985; [ch.] Johnny Lee, Jason Emery, Glena Gayle; [ed.] G.E.D.; [occ.] Home-Health, Hospice Aide; [oth. writ.] A poem published in the Hospice News Letter; [pers.] I try to show people's feelings in my poems.; [a.] Horatio, AR

DICKERSON, EDITH
[b.] July 24, 1950, East Bernard, TX; [p.] Pauline Carr, Farris Dickerson; [ed.] San Jacinto High School, Texas Southern University; [occ.] History Teacher (Paul Reverie Middle School); [memb.] Augustana Lutheran Church, Houston Council of Social Studies, National Education Association, Junior Achievement; [hon.] Perfect Attendance, Character Education, Dean's List; [pers.] I write about things that I feel, or things that I have experienced in life. I believe that a strong faith and belief in God provides a gateway to happiness and fulfillment.; [a.] Houston, TX

DICKSON, ANNE P.
[pen.] Pat; [b.] January 23, 1947, Wilzburg, Germany; [p.] Cornelius De Rooij, Rosemary De Rooij; [ch.] Sonia P. Dickson, Franklin E. Dickson; [ed.] High School EK6 Tech, C. M. Assistant, C. Home Health Aide; [occ.] C. Home Health Aide just started a Financial Business of my own, balancing other peoples Checkbooks and Banking Assistance; [memb.] National Parks Association; [hon.] First Female Vestry Member Christ Church, Pandover, MA. This Publication! I am thrilled to be a part of this!; [oth. writ.] This is the first poem, I have written and actually sent in. It gives me incentive to keep writing.; [pers.] I try the best I can to help our nations elderly. They are so often Mistreated and deserve better. By this work I hope to be judged!; [a.] Lowell, MA

DICRISTOFANO, JOHN
[b.] May 30, 1950, Chicago, IL; [p.] Dominic and Mary; [m.] Divorced, 1975; [ch.] Stacy Lynn (one daughter); [ed.] 16 years (Associates Degree from College of Dau Page and B.S. Degree SIU in Illinois; [occ.] Vietnam Veteran; [memb.] Italian American War Vets; [hon.] 750 hours at Hines VA Hospital and 300 hours at Hinsdale Hospital doing Volunteer work with Ill., 3rd degree Brown Belt and past instructor - Chinese Kenxso; [oth. writ.] Printed book "Aerial" on my own in 1985 and sold about 1,000 copies 2nd book is complete but not a finished product; [pers.] I feel and believe a person, (individual) needs to react and interact with others, not by listening to what they say, just watch what they do.; [a.] Chicago, IL

DIFIGLIA, CONSTANCE J.
[b.] July 30, 1949, Queens, NY; [p.] Basil DiFiglia and Josephine DiFiglia; [ed.] Flushing High Queens College (B.A.), Post-graduate - LI College. Bologna University of Medicine (M.D.), Albert Einstein College of Medicine (Fellow); [occ.] President and Founder: American Association for Professional Ethics (AAPE), President: CJ International; [memb.] American Association for Professional Ethics, Drug Information Association, Non Prescription Drug Manufactur-

ers Association, American Association of University Women. (Numerous others); [hon.] Medicine with laud, NIH Award, MD, Young Investigator's Award, Bolugna, Advances in Neurommurology, Phil PA (Numerous others); [oth. writ.] Numerous publication in Pier Review scientific Journals; [pers.] The period was from 1992 to 1994 that a female doctor refused to sign medical research reports without reading and reviewing them. She was seriously harassed in defending justice and ethics and protecting the safety of American families. In consequences, the American Association for Professional Ethics (AAPE) was founded.; [a.] Hicksville, NY

DIFIGLIA, CONSTANCE J.
[b.] July 30, 1949, Queens, NY; [p.] Basil DiFiglia and Josephine DiFiglia; [ed.] Flushing High, Queens College (B.A.), Post-graduate - LI College, Bologna University School of Medicine (M.D.), Albert Ernstein College of Medicine (Fellow); [occ.] President and Founder: American Association for Professional Ethics (AAPE), President: CJ International; [memb.] American Association for Professional Ethics, Drug Information Association, Non-Prescription Drug Manufacturers Association, American Association of University Women. (Numerous others); [hon.] Medicine with land, Nilt Award, MD, Young Investigators Award, Ferrar, Immunology Award, Bologna, Advances in Neuroimmunology, Phil PA (Numerous others); [oth. writ.] Numerous publications in Pier Review Scientific Journals; [pers.] The period was from 1992 to 1994 that a female doctor refused to sign medical research reports without reading and reviewing them. She was seriously harassed in defending justice and ethics and protecting the safety of American families. In consequence, the American Association for Professional Ethics (AAPE) was founded.; [a.] Hicksville, NY

DILLINGHAM, MATTHEW
[b.] December 11, 1974, Goleta, CA; [p.] Jim and Patti Dillingham; [ed.] Associates Degree Psychology, Amarillo College, Attending Texas Tech. University, Psychology Major; [occ.] Student, Co-owner Utopium and Co.; [oth. writ.] "Twisted Fate," "Christmas Despair," "Daisy Run," "The Going America," "Utopia a Potential Hades," mainly read at local establishments; [pers.] Words are the most extreme face in the Universe. Without words there would be no expression, and without expression there is nothing.; [a.] Amarillo, TX

DILLON, CHRISTA
[b.] November 15, 1979, Livingston, NJ; [p.] Mary Elsa Dillon, Norman Dillon Jr.; [ed.] Columbia High; [occ.] Student; [pers.] All my writings - past, present, and future - are in dedication to all loved individuals in my life. Most important to my mother and my family. I love you all!; [a.] Marplewood, NJ

DIMATTEO, CHRISTINA
[pen.] Christina DiMatteo; [b.] September 6, 1982; [p.] Kim and Andre DiMatteo; [ed.] 7th Grade Our Lady of Angels; [hon.] I earn merit awards in school. M.V.P award for basketball in my rookie year.; [oth. writ.] 4 self written notebooks filled with poems; [pers.] I write poems to express the way I feel my emotions about my personal experiences. I attend Our Lady of Angels School; [a.] Cleveland, OH

DIOSSY, KRISTINA MARIE
[b.] April 6, 1967, Queens, NY; [p.] John W. Diossy and Janet M. Bonelli; [ed.] Attended School of Visual Arts and Queens College; [occ.] Travel Agent; [pers.] To explore and portray the human condition through my insight and experience.; [a.] Glendale, NY

DODSON, THOMAS
[pen.] Thomas Bucket; [b.] May 4, 1957, Toledo, OH; [p.] Marilyn and Vance Dodson; [ed.] Needham High School (Mass.), Museum of Fine Arts, then studied with R.H. Ives Gammell in Boston and later with Giovanni Castano in Needham. I have free-lanced since 1976; [occ.] Pastel Portrait Painter, Teacher (private) and Poet (free-lance); [memb.] Needham Art Assoc. Mass. 1975 to 1979, Weston Art Assoc. Mass. 1985 to 1987. Many "one man shows" - (Wolfeboro Library 1989, Tuftonboro Library 1990, Wolfeboro Library (again) 1991 (all in N.H.); [hon.] Needham Art Assoc. Mass. 1st, 2nd and "Best of Show" (1875 through 1979) "Copley Society Award" received at Sherborn Art Assn. Show "2nd place" 1985, Westboro Art Assoc. - "Best of Show" and 2nd place in 1986 ("poems" were written for many of the pieces and were shown with the works of art.); [oth. writ.] Poems: (none published) "Man/ Woman", "10/17/94", "A Place Called Depression", "In the Wrong Hands", "Amends", "A Carousel Gone By", "Always Another Person", "Unfinished Youth", "Friends"; [pers.] I try to capture the essence and soul of whatever I am painting or writing. All other details are secondary, and will fall into place if I am successful in my attempts.; [a.] Center Tuftonboro, NH

DOHERTY, JOHN COPEN
[pen.] J. Desmond Copen; [b.] January 23, 1968, Ireland; [p.] Hugh Slucy Doherty; [m.] Mary McFadeen, August 27, 1994; [oth. writ.] I have wrote many poems and short stories. But this is the first submitted for a competition or publishing.; [pers.] True lies are so easy to believe but believe them not for a lie cannot be true. Think about it.

DOHERTY, PATRICK
[b.] January 13, 1921, Ireland; [pers.] I was born in the outskirts of the town of Kilkee situated on the Atlantic Oceans West Coast of Ireland. This beautiful old town is the subject of my poem. P.S. I thank you for your kind review.; [a.] Bergenfield, NJ

DOLCE, JESSICA L.
[b.] April 16, 1911, Lakewood, OH; [occ.] Student; [hon.] Hawthorne Award for Creative Writing, National Merit Commended Scholar; [oth. writ.] Published by the National Poetry Society and the Kenyon Writing Institute; [pers.] Poetry elevates one's thoughts, dreams, and desires, reflecting and reshaping them to express a universal truth. I write for know I am not alone.; [a.] Lakewood, OH

DOMEY, MELISSA G.
[b.] December 29, 1963, Poughkeepsie, NY; [p.] Roberta J. Shaw and William R. Shaw (deceased); [m.] Kenneth E. Domey Jr., April 14, 1990; [ch.] Stepchildren Brittany Elizabeth, Jacob Allan; [ed.] Attended Spackenkill Schools; [occ.] Machinist - CNC - Stanfordville, N.Y.; [memb.] Hudson Valley Artisians Guild; [oth. writ.] Several, yet, unpublished poems; [pers.] Influenced by early poets and by mythology; [a.] Fish Kill, NY

DOMINIQUE, LISA
[pen.] Lisa Dominique; [b.] July 5, 1965, Northern England; [m.] September 12, 1990; [ed.] St. Mary's Covenant Hull England; [occ.] Author, Songwriter, Musician, Singer, Producer; [memb.] M.C.P.S. (music publishing), P.R.S. (music sales) England. These are the equivalent of ASCAP in America.; [hon.] M.C.P.S., P.R.S.; [oth. writ.] 2 albums released in Europe. Children's book (as yet unpublished); [pers.] My passion for writing began when I was 11 yrs. old. The magic of walking home from school in the rain, I found what would be my best friend, my imagination and true passion for writing.; [a.] Los Angeles, CA

DONAHUE, CHRISTINE M.
[b.] November 28, 1969, Erie, PA; [p.] Timothy and Barbara Kerwell; [ed.] Pennsylvania College of Technology, Honolulu School of Massage Therapy; [occ.] Registered Nurse, Massage Therapist, Healing Touch Practitioner; [memb.] Hawaii Holistic Nurses Association, Hawaii Nurses Association, American Holistic Nurses Association; [hon.] Academic Award for English, Dean's List, Dedication in Nursing Award; [pers.] Poetry is more than a construction of words. It is a medium for two souls to connect - and a gift to be embraced.; [a.] Williamsport, PA

DONALDSON, CHATHERINE L.
[pen.] C. L. Donaldson; [b.] September 29, 1956, Jacksonville, FL; [ed.] B.A. from Aquinas College in Grand Rapids, Michigan, A.S. from Southeast Center for Photographic Studies Daytona Bch., Daytona Beach Community College, Florida; [oth. writ.] Currently working on a novel and memoirs; [pers.] "The Poet" is my statement about the inner struggle I feel when writing a poem. It is important to me that the reader share in the experience of the poem in some way. I do not want my message to be a mystery but a revelation of understanding between two people.; [a.] Jacksonville, FL

DONZELLA, DONNA
[b.] February 11, 1958, New York; [p.] Mary and Joseph Commisso; [m.] Anthony Donzella, January 29, 1983; [ed.] South Shore H.S., "Precious" graduated 1976, attended Kings Borough Community College 1992-1994 withdraw; [occ.] Housewife Assistant Bookkeeper by profession; [oth. writ.] A Sailor's Retirement Day, Treasured Poems of America 1994; [pers.] Believe in the power of positive thinking. It makes this life a lot easier. Most importantly believe in yourself.; [a.] Brooklyn, NY

DOSS, LISA FINNEY
[b.] April 20, 1963, Reidsville, NC; [p.] Dillard and Betty Finney; [m.] Robert E. Doss, May 14, 1983; [ch.] Joshua R. and Elizabeth E. Doss; [ed.] Rockingham Co. Sen. High, Rock. Comm. College; [occ.] Graphic Artist, the Daily News, Eden, NC; [memb.] Friends of the Oceans; [oth. writ.] Several poems and short stories unpublished as yet; [pers.] The goal of my poetry is to convey the feelings that most of us push aside without thinking. I am influenced by Shakespeare, Masters, Ann Lindbergh. I love the classics.; [a.] Eden, NC

DOUGLAS, RONALD
[pen.] Ron Douglas; [b.] January 1, 1953, Pittsburg, CA; [p.] Agnes and Carl Mann; [m.] Suzanne Belsole Douglas, May 30, 1981; [ch.] Aryan Donovan (9), Adrian Dylan (6); [ed.] High School, Highland Park High, Topeka, KS; [occ.] Remodeling contractor; [oth. writ.] I have files of other writings, but as of this date none have been published. I usually write for myself and friends. This is the first attempt of this nature I have tried.; [pers.] I am a firm believer in the power of the mind. Through the power of prayer and applied faith you can eliminate self defeating limitations and achieve your goals. In my writings I try to motivate and inspire myself and others.; [a.] Mahwah, NJ

DOWNS, ANITA
[b.] April 11, 1963, Tulsa, OK; [p.] David and Rosmarie Beeler; [m.] Dain Downs, October 17, 1987; [ch.] Megan Rose; [ed.] Magazine High School, Northeast Area Vo-tech, Afton, OK; [occ.] Home Payroll Clerk, Seamstress, Teacher and Housewife; [hon.] Miss MHS, Student Council President, Honor Student, Talent Contest Winner in Vocal Duet Competitions; [oth. writ.] Songs "Alba Father", "I'll Praise Him," "The Greatest Gift (to ever hang upon a tree.)" As well as other poems.; [pers.] This particular poem "The Rose" was written for my mother's 50th birthday. She is the "Rose" and this poem is a compilation of her life thus far and the fore sight of more blessings.; [a.] Magazine, AR

DREW, ALLYSAN
[b.] July 1, 1950, Salem, MA; [p.] Margaret and Robert Hillard; [m.] Fernando Dalmau; [ch.] William, Matthew and Carolyn; [ed.] Winnacunnet H.S., University of New Hampshire; [occ.] Real Estate Agent; [memb.] Fort Dauderdale Board of Realtors; [pers.] My children initially, inspired me to write poetry. Their delight in playful rhyming and interest in my thoughts encouraged me to reflect on other aspects of my life, the love joy and sorrow.; [a.] Fort Dauderdale, FL

DRORBAUGH, ELIZABETH THAXTER
[pen.] Elizabeth Drorbaugh; [b.] January 22, 1956, Evanston, IL; [ed.] Ph.D. in process, New York University, Department of Performance Studies; [occ.] College Teacher; [oth. writ.] Plays, performance art, poetry; [a.] Staten Island, NY

DUBOIS, CYNTHIA WILSON
[b.] Brooklyn, NY; [p.] Lavaughn and Lunetta Wilson; [m.] Walter, October 23, 1953; [ch.] Yolanda DuBois Marsh, Michael and Carlton DuBois; [ed.] High School, College; [occ.] Educational Assistant; [pers.] I write like I am talking to people. This way they can see what I am trying to say. Pictures in the mind. (Writing about what I know.); [a.] Brooklyn, NY

DUNAWAY, ROZELLA
[b.] March 7, 1922, Winthrop, AR; [p.] George and Katie Vandyke; [m.] Hubert Dunaway, February 1942; [ch.] Sharon Kay, Jeffus; [ed.] High School and Post Graduate; [occ.] Self Employed; [oth. writ.] Many Christian songs are being sung in several churches in U.S. never presented for publication. These songs reflect great depths and truths that I feel merit publication and would be the fulfillment of a lifetime dream.; [pers.] Variety of poetry for greeting cards and different occasions. This type expresses what I search to find when purchasing a card for a special need.; [a.] Trinity, TX

DUNBAR, JESSIE
[b.] October 10, 1976, Wilmington, NC; [p.] Eartha Allen; [ed.] Brooklyn Technical H.S., Colorado Mountain, Coll., (presently) Clark Atlanta U.; [oth. writ.] Several poems published in the Aspen Times; [pers.] More often than not, my poetry writes itself. The first line of a poem may come to me during an interesting conversation or even while I'm asleep. Once I have a first line, the rest just flows.; [a.] New York, NY

DUNCAN, SALLY L.
[b.] June 14, 1939, Providence, RI; [p.] Walter E. and Catherine S. Horton; [m.] Allen A. Duncan, June 6, 1959; [ch.] James H. Duncan; [ed.] East Providence High School; [occ.] Farming Raise Beef Cattle and Sheep; [oth. writ.] A caption published in Yankee Magazine that accompanied a wildlife photograph, I had taken of a baby raccoon.; [pers.] My inspiration for writing comes from my love of animals, wildlife and nature. Along with the special privilege of working the land.; [a.] Seekonk, MA

DUNN, BARBARA HORN M.
[pen.] Barbara M. Horn Dunn; [b.] September 26, 1940, Lufkin, TX; [p.] Rev. Willie Horn and Barbara Elizabeth Horn; [m.] John H. Dunn Sr., August 26, 1961; [ch.] Angela Micaela Dunn, John Henry Dunn Jr.; [ed.] Wheatley High, VT at Austin (BA), TWU at Denton (MA); [occ.] Retail gift Shop Owner; [memb.] Life Member YMCA, Erma D. LeRoy Life Members Club Outstanding Secondary Educators of America;

[hon.] YWCA Gem, Outstanding Woman-YWCA, Who's Who among High School Educators, Teacher of Yr (Sharpstown SR. High 12 Times) TWU - (Honors Graduate) Outstanding Service Award Mount Moriah Baptist Church; [oth. writ.] A Compilation of Religious Poetry "Sermonettes of Life," (Unpublished to date); [pers.] I strive to reflect God's goodness in my writings and to strengthen others who need a blessing.; [a.] Houston, TX

DUNNING, MARCIA
[b.] January 8, 1937, Cleveland, OH; [p.] Dorothy and Joseph Nocera; [m.] Archie Dunning, August 1962; [ch.] Pamela Ruth Zimmerman-(Wilson), David Alan Zimmerman, Kenneth Charles Zimmerman, Shella Rae Dunning Wolasek and Archie Eugene Dunning; [ed.] Kentucky Elementary School, William Dean Jr. High, West Tech Extension Night School, Tri-C Metro Jr. College; [occ.] House Wife - (Caretaker Husband Dying of Empthazema); [hon.] Dean's List; [pers.] I write for truthfulness and joy. I am a Christian, and I want my work of writing to show it. I hope it will show the compassion and love for the lonely and forgotten.; [a.] Cleveland, OH

DUPREE, SHARON SEAY
[pen.] Sharon Dupree; [b.] February 17, 1959, Bridgeton, NJ; [p.] Mr. and Mrs. John R. Seay (Clara); [m.] Divorced; [ch.] Victoria, Joy Dupree (age 10), Samuel Isaac Dupree (8), Gloria Faith Dypree (age 6); [ed.] Bridgeton High, Lely High Naples, Fla., Shorter College - B.S. - Elem. Ed. - Rome, Ga.; [occ.] Medical Receptionist; [memb.] Served on local Library Board Actively Attends Mt. Paray Church of God; [oth. writ.] Many poems written - none ever published. This poem was inspired by a friend and poetry love Ron Edmonson.; [pers.] I have always loved poetry and feel it reflects the innermost thoughts of the writer. It has the power to open up vast perspectives to its readers.; [a.] Hiram, GA

DURFEE, LISA
[pen.] Lisa Durfee; [b.] February 18, 1980, Meadville, PA; [p.] Harold Durfee, Judith Durfee; [ed.] Student at Conneaut Valley High School; [occ.] Student; [memb.] Student Government at my HS; [hon.] High Honors in Academic Achievement; [pers.] I believe that poetry is a raw reflection of the soul. When I write it comes from my life and experiences that's why its very important to me.; [a.] Springboro, PA

DURKEE, DOROTHY
[b.] March 13, 1916, Drain, OR; [p.] Harvest and Ena Ramsdell; [ed.] University of California, 1939 Decorative Arts; [occ.] Retired; [hon.] Editor's Choice Award for poem (About a Tiger Lily); [oth. writ.] Poem (About a Tiger Lily) published in anthology, "Reflections of Light."; [pers.] I live in Half Moon Bay, a beautiful little coastal town, about 25 miles South of San Francisco, in a senior complex of 58 people. The people in Half Moon Bay are mostly friendly and relaxed and have a wonderful community spirit. My philosophy of life is to keep all the friends I've made through the years, try to be as kind and friendly as I can, to make new friends, keep a positive outlook on life and enjoy the simple everyday pleasures and the beauty of my surroundings and the friendly overtures of these who live here.; [a.] Half Moon Bay, CA

DWINELL, E. MICHELLE ISLAS
[b.] November 2, 1953, Farmington, NM; [p.] Corrine and Eugene F. Islas; [m.] Mike Dwinell, September 25, 1993; [ch.] Joshua Adrian Islas, Michael Justin Islas; [ed.] Farmington High 1973; [occ.] President, EMW Inc. since 1981; [memb.] International Society of Poets - Distinguished Member; [hon.] Marquis Who's Who of American Women 1989/1990 Sixteenth Edition of-

fice of the year 1988 and several Growth Achievement Awards - Uniforce Services Editors Choice Award National Library of Poetry 1994; [oth. writ.] "The Passage" published by Quill Books 1994. "Expectations" published by Quill Books 1995.; [pers.] My poetry is an extension of my life experience and personal growth. I hope to touch other lives by giving them my gift of words for strength, comfort and self realization.; [a.] Farmington, NM

EADY, BERNACE
[b.] November 1, 1955, Raleigh, NC; [p.] Betty eady Gillis; [m.] Walena Cecile Eady, June 12, 1992; [ch.] (Step sons) Mike Batchelor, Patrick Batchelor, Lamont Batchelor; [ed.] Fuquay-Varina High; [occ.] Food Service Assistant at Dorothea Dix Hospital; [oth. writ.] Founded, edit and write a newslatter for the Dietary Dept. of Dix Hospital write articles for the hospital's news paper, the Hillside News; [pers.] I feel that my writing is a God-given gift and because of my gift it should be used to inspire, enlighten, and entertain people.

EADY, JESSIE
[pen.] Jessie Mae Jennings; [b.] March 26, 1933, SC; [p.] Mr. and Mrs. John Jennings; [m.] Paul Edward Eady, June 16, 1957; [ch.] 4 Boys, Roy, Paul Edward Isaiah and Patrick Benson; [ed.] High School Graduate Nursing Sch. Secretarial Business Sch.; [occ.] Home Health Aide; [memb.] AARP, Life-Study Fellowship and Democratic Club; [hon.] Award - Cash in your thought, from chase Manhattan Bk. Voulteer - Working with kids, from Board of Ed.; [pers.] I don't give in, and will not give up.; [a.] Brooklyn, NY

EAGLESHAM, JOHN L.
[b.] October 14, 1924, Irvington, NJ; [p.] Anna McMahon and John Eaglesham; [m.] Anna West, October 21, 1950; [ch.] Anna Marie, Angela, John Joseph, Mary Judith

EASTMAN, LARA MARIE
[pen.] Lara P. S. Eastman; [b.] October 31, 1995, East Lansing, MI; [p.] Robert James Eastman; [ed.] Currently in college earning a B.S. followed by an MS in Behavioral Sciences and Pol. Science; [pers.] For my father, I love you. You never gave up. You are the best. A.J.T. - the man who says, "it won't be done!", this is known and inspired by you. R.L.M. III - stays as pure and honorable as you are to day.; [a.] Reseda, CA

EASTORDAY, DANIELLE
[b.] February 18, 1981, Elyria, OH; [p.] Kerry and Frank Vrettas, Don Easterday; [ed.] Bonita Vista Middle School 8th grade Bi-lingual and computer literate; [memb.] Bonita Althetic Club, Bonita Volleyball, Bonita Karate; [hon.] Award for high Citizanship and Scholarship; [oth. writ.] Many poems in local newspaper, and a short story in Union Tribune, San Diego; [pers.] I'd like to thank my teachers and parents for giving me the opportunity and skills to write great poems.; [a.] Bonita, CA

EBANKS, VERROL K. M.
[b.] January 7, 1952, Jamaica, WI; [p.] Cubie and Mervyn; [m.] Divorced, August 12, 1978; [ch.] Talia, Celene, Bruce; [ed.] Munro College, Jamaica; [occ.] Cost Accountant; [oth. writ.] Several unpublished poems and songs; [pers.] Never worry about the things you cannot change so you'll never have been to worry.; [a.] Far Rockaway, NY

EBERHARD, JILL
[pen.] Jill Eberhard; [p.] Mary and Emmett Mays; [m.] Chris Eberhard, February 15, 1986; [ch.] Courtney Blake Eberhard; [pers.] My all time favorite poems are those for children, such as those by Shel Silverstein. I

was moved to write this poem on an announcement of the adoption of our first child. The poem is only a small reflection of how special she is to me and my husband; [a.] Kearns, UT

EBERT, WILLIAM
[pen.] William Ebert; [b.] November 18, 1974, Pasadena, CA; [ed.] Blair High School, Pasadena City College; [occ.] Student; [memb.] Orpheus Lyric Theatre; [pers.] "I'll steal someone's money, and even someone's food. But never someone's thoughts."; [a.] Altadena, CA

EBONG, THOMAS S.
[b.] April 21, 1952, Nigeria; [p.] Sebastian Ebong and Regina Afangideh; [ed.] Bachelors of Divinity (B.D) Theology Enugu (Urban Affiliate, Rome, 1981, Post Graduate Diploma in Education, Nsukka, Nigeria, 1983, B.A (Radio/TV/Film) Loyola, Chicago M.A (TV prod. Loyola Marymount California, 1994, M.F.A. 1995); [occ.] Doctoral Student - Department of Communication, Wayne State Univ.; [memb.] A Catholic Priest, corporation for Artistic Development - (C.A.D) Detroit; [oth. writ.] Two feature films (unpublished): "Begone", "THE SHATTERED DREAM" and some other poems; [pers.] I love to reflect on things around me, on life and on people.. The most thrilling things in life are those recycled between the eyes and the minds. If we take time to observe and play with the pieces of the puzzles around us, we can create the greatest of funs.; [a.] Detroit, MI

EDDINGS, JENNIFER
[b.] November 19, 1970, Fort Lauderdale, FL; [p.] Joseph and Betty Eddings; [ed.] Ely High, University of Florida; [occ.] English Teacher; [memb.] Delta Sigma Theta Sorority Inc.; [oth. writ.] Poems published in the R and E Journal; [pers.] Always have faith in yourself you will go far.; [a.] Fort Lauderdale, FL

EDGE, CARRIE
[pen.] Sweet; [b.] August 6, 1931, Edgecombe, CO; [p.] Will Hill, Carrie Hill; [m.] John Edge, December 8, 1949; [ch.] Mary, Richard, Marsha, Elmer; [ed.] G. W. Carvey High; [occ.] Retired; [pers.] There are so many positive things, I would like to say to people. This is my way of getting the message to them; [a.] Rocky Mount, NC

EDWARDS, ANGELA MARIE
[b.] October 10, 1979, Indianapolis, IN; [p.] Waymon and Beverly; [ed.] St. Matthew Catholic Grade School, Indianapolis Cathedral High School, Indapolis IN; [occ.] Student, Cathedral High School, Indianapolis, IN; [memb.] Members of the "Pride of the Irish" competition marching band plays: Flute and Piccolo; [oth. writ.] Several poems published in "Poetic License" Cathedral High School's Literary Magazine; [a.] Indianapolis, IN

EDWARDS, CLARENCE JEROME
[b.] September 5, 1948, Evansville, IN; [m.] Sheila; [ch.] Clarence Jr., Kevin, Sheva; [ed.] Benjamin Bosse High, Ind Compton College, Los Angeles Southwest College; [occ.] Manager Service, Master Company; [memb.] Church of Christ Fontana, CA; [hon.] Employer of Year 1994, Los Angeles Project Industry, Employer of year 1995 Los Angeles Urban League; [oth. writ.] "You are the best part of me" Hilltop records; [pers.] I like to write songs glorifying our Lord and Saviour Jesus Christ. I was influenced by rennaissance the greatest accapella group ever.; [a.] Riallo, CA

EDWARDS, ELIZABETH A.
[b.] June 23, 1971, Decatur, IL; [p.] Harry B. and Carol A. Edwards; [ed.] Blue Mound High School, Western Illinois University; [occ.] Paramedic in Factory, Lieutenant on Fire Department; [memb.] Blue Mound Fire Protection Dist., Illinois Fire Protection Association, Decatur Area Emergency Medical Services; [hon.] DAR Citizenship Award Winner; [oth. writ.] Articles for Local Newspaper and School Newspaper; [pers.] Life is what you choose to make of it. You can either it go by and do nothing to help make it better, or you can hitch up your trousers, roll up your sleeves and face it head on, pausing to help ones in need along the way.; [a.] Blue Mound, IL

EDWARDS JR., RICHARD C.
[pen.] Ric Edwards; [b.] May 17, 1930, Muncie, IN; [p.] Richard and Helen Edwards; [m.] Sonia Baspineiro-Edwards, May 20, 1963; [ch.] Richard Carlton Edwards; [ed.] MA in the Performing Arts, Governors State University, BA in English, Olivet Nazarene University; [occ.] Instructor of Speech and English and Speech, Kankakee Community College; [memb.] Kankakee County Historical Society Community Arts Council-Community College Humanities Association-National Federation of State High School Associations- Governors State Alumni Association; [oth. writ.] Several poems published in college literary magazine and in various publications; [pers.] The living of life is a wondrous experience and only we can make it a happy experience. I want the reader to see the smile in my writings.; [a.] Kankakee, IL

EDWARDS, WILBERT F.
[pen.] Wil Edwards; [b.] January 1, 1928, New York City; [p.] Mildred and Bryant Edwards; [m.] Pearl C. Edwards (Divorced), October 14; [ch.] Carlyle M. Edwards and Reva F. Meyers (Edwards) (Common Law); [ed.] George Washington High, N.Y.U. 1 1/2 years, New York School of music 3 years; [occ.] Retired; [memb.] Church of the master, 86 Morning side Ave., New York, NY; [hon.] U.S. Army 1946 to 1948, honorable discharge. Services of 2 1/2 yrs. in Japan.; [pers.] I love good music, and I find life great. I like writing poems and songs.; [a.] New York, NY

EDWARDS, WILLIAM A.
[pen.] Eddie Ranks; [b.] August 25, 1962, Saint Ann, Jamaica; [ch.] Jonathan Edwards, Keyamasha Edwards; [ed.] High School Graduate; [hon.] R.O.T.C., Setptember 79 - June 82, Los Angels High School; [oth. writ.] Many unpublished poems and songs; [pers.] I would like for mankind to come together and clean up the earth (universe and planet.); [a.] Los Angeles, CA

EICHACKER, SHEILA ANN
[pen.] Shelly; [b.] October 13, 1954, Saint Clair County, IL; [p.] John and Maxine Coregony; [m.] Ronald Edwards Eichacker, November 24, 1972; [ch.] Two daughter: Channa Nicole and Erin Michelle; [occ.] Has own Cleaning Business; [oth. writ.] Have many other writings yet to hopefully be published. Is working on a children's story book.; [pers.] I love to write about emotions and experience of everyday life.; [a.] Granite City, IL

EIGENHAUSER, CAROL ANN
[b.] July 21, 1941, Chicago, IL; [p.] Jessie and Martin Jacobs; [m.] Elmer Eigenhauser, August 6, 1960; [ch.] Don, Todd, Sabrina Ann, Eric, Phillip, Rachel Ann; [oth. writ.] Several editorials published in the Chicago Tribune, the Rocky Mountain News, and the Daily Herald Newspapers. Two dedicated poems published.; [pers.] The beauty of nature and my love for all living things inspires my writings in a rainbow you can find happiness, a whispering tree can make music a flowers

fragrance and it's artistic beauty can shower us with joy. Let a birds song bring us harmonious calm. These are by far out most important riches bringing love, contentment and beauty to our lives.; [a.] Hanover Park, IL

EISENSCHMIDT, JAIME LEONA
[pen.] Green Girl; [b.] September 24, 1978, Saint Helens, OR; [p.] Kurt and Christine Eisenschmidt; [ed.] High School; [oth. writ.] Several poems, only known to me; [pers.] Don't let gravity get you down.; [a.] Saint Helens, OR

EKLUND, MARCIA C.
[pen.] Marcia Claire; [b.] Beloit, WI; [p.] Roy and Elsie Norton; [m.] Roger R. Eklund, May 28, 1949; [ch.] Rhonda Rae Eklund; [a.] Rockford, IL

ELIA, DONNA
[pen.] Donna Elia; [b.] July 6, 1945, Rochester, NY; [p.] Thomas and Frances Cannarozzo; [m.] Robert Elia, September 11, 1994; [ch.] Andrea Tauriello, Edward T. Barattini; [ed.] Spencerport High School Rochester Institute of Tech. Eastman School of Music Schuader Realestate Academy; [occ.] Housing Consultant Artist, Poet; [hon.] Scholastic Gold Key Art Awards - Self published "The Honest Profile" Poetry - Art Show - Sedona Arizona; [pers.] Poetry is my core feeling to life experiences "The Song of the heart"; [a.] Tucson, AZ

ELLIOT, ANGELA KAY
[b.] October 24, 1968, Saint Louise, MO; [p.] Velma Pugh, Ronald Matheny; [m.] Ronald James Elliot Sr., September 3, 1989; [ch.] Heather-le Denice (age 5 yrs.), Nicollette Kaylin (age 4 yrs.), Joshua Oscar (age 2 yrs); [ed.] Graduate from Orchard Farm High; [occ.] Home Maker; [pers.] "Count your blessings...not your sorrows."; [a.] Pacific, MO

ELLIS, CHRIS
[b.] May 22, 1975, Springfield, TN; [p.] John Ellis and Jane Ellis; [m.] Tamara Williams (Fiance); [ch.] Kaleshia Williams; [ed.] Springfield High; [occ.] Factory Worker White House, TN; [oth. writ.] Had poems published in school paper, several poems read at my church fairview Baptist; [pers.] I try to express the beauty and tragedy of life and nature in a simple form. Today is a present from God, therefore it's called the present so live it as such.; [a.] Springfield, TN

ELLIS, HOLLY
[b.] September 15, 1977, Allegan, MI; [p.] Roy and Diane Ellis; [ed.] Allegan High School; [occ.] Student, modeling receptionist; [oth. writ.] I have written several poems and short stories that were published in the local literary books and magazines in my school.; [pers.] I carry a pocketful of magical tenderness. I am greatly influenced by the emotions of life.; [a.] Allegan, MI

ELLIS, RAQUEL T.
[b.] December 31, 1976, Torrance, CA; [p.] Lula and Richard Ellis; [ed.] Carson High School, Pepperdine University; [hon.] Distinguished Honor Roll, Appreciation Award for outstanding, Citizenship, Outstanding Award, Excellent Award, and hardest worker award; [pers.] Past experiences inspire my poetry in hope that others will learn from them.; [a.] Carson, CA

ELLIS, TYRONE
[pen.] Tyrone E.; [b.] October 29, 1946, Cleveland, OH; [p.] Fleming and Roberta Ellis; [m.] Alicia T., December 16, 1970; [ed.] East Technical High School, Cleve OH, J. F., Drake Technical College Huntsville; [occ.] Environmental Sanitation; [hon.] Algebra and Social Studies Addison Jr., High Cleveland, Ohio; [oth. writ.] Sanity or insanity an article for "Club 24" message. I have written several other articles on sobriety.

Under the pen name Tyrone E.; [pers.] I wrote this poem as an expression of my loneliness on a particular December weekend. Close to X-mas 1994. A month after my sister came to get my mother and take her to live in South Carolina. Last thanksgiving; [a.] Cleveland, OH

EMRICK, ALLISON LEA
[b.] October 26, 1978, Fort Benning, GA; [p.] Patricia and Roy Emrick; [ed.] Oakwood Academy Private School, Decalb Elementary, Trickim Middle, Parkview High; [occ.] Student; [memb.] Lebanon Baptist Church, Diabetes Association of Atlanta, Mt. Park Athletic Association; [hon.] Student of the month, year. Honor roll, Elementary Honor chorus, Certificate of Baptism.; [oth. writ.] A poem published in the Anthology of Poetry by Young Americans; [pers.] Have faith and encourage the youth of today, let them trace the path of the future. Their eyes portray and reflect the planets horoscope.; [a.] Tucker, GA

ENGELKE, LIBERTY L.
[b.] February 2, 1980, Houston, TX; [p.] Sondra Rhodes; [m.] Lester Engelke, July, 1979; [ch.] Parents had one child; [ed.] Nineth Grade Sam Rayburn High - Pasadena TX; [occ.] Student; [memb.] Volleyball, Pep Club, Drama, Creekmont Baptist Church; [hon.] Drama, National Honor Society, National English Merit Award; [oth. writ.] None that have been published; [pers.] Other Academic Awards, Debate Team Office Aide, Spanish Club

ERB, JENNIFER
[b.] September 18, 1975, Jacksonville, AK; [p.] William Erb, Anna Erb; [ed.] Lake High School, Malone College; [a.] Hartville, OH

ESCOTO, ZONDA LOU DAWN
[pen.] Dawn Escoto; [b.] November 16, 1948, Flint, MI; [p.] Salvador and Ethel Escota (deceased); [ed.] KY Mountain Bible College, Spring Arbor College (MI); [occ.] Teacher, French, Spanish, German, English, Middle School; [hon.] Summa Cum Laude, S.A.C. Valedictorian - KMBC and SAC Who's Who in American Colleges and University; [oth. writ.] (Unpublished to date) 7 religious and 15 sealar collection Forever Fragrant - Poems of Flowers, Going, Going, Gone - Poems on Endangered Species, Bountiful Birds-poems, Precious Gems from Solomon-poems Proverbs, Elem. Russian Textbook, Textbook on Europe, articles.; [pers.] I like to find poetry in everything around me. I experiment with serious elegant, humorous, nostalgic. People need to laugh at their foibles, look seriously at their decadence, and stop to smell, the roses. I admire Emily Dickinson for style; [a.] Farmington Hills, MI

ESKIN, LISA Y.
[b.] August 15, 1961, Rochester, NY; [p.] Howard B. Eskin, Rosemarie D. Eskin; [ed.] Boston University, BS English and Language Arts, Long Island University, MS Educational Technology; [occ.] English Teacher, Huntington Schools, Huntington, NY; [memb.] ASCD, NCTE, LILAC, AFT, PTA, NYSUT, Teaching Tolerance, Klanwatch and Multicultural Action Committee (founder, 1991); [hon.] Boston - 101 Sorority Award, Women's Scholarship Association Stipend, Dean's List and Magna Cum Laude. LIV-Academic, Performance Award and Highest Honors.; [pers.] This poem is dedicated to my nephew, Robert Garis Hess III, who died in the service of his country, aboard the U.S. Coast Guard vessel "Firebush," on December 7, 1992. He was just 22 year old.; [a.] Stony Brook, NY

ESLINGER, ADAM IONAKANA
[b.] March 13, 1980, Honolulu, HI; [p.] Michael and Yolanda Eslinger; [ed.] High School Freshman; [occ.] Student; [hon.] Yuma Union High School A-Team (for

academic performance); [pers.] The declination of man is cause by his own self-deception and misanthropy.; [a.] Yuma, AZ

ESPOSITO, SANDRA
[b.] January 16, 1968; [p.] Richard and Judy Larkin; [m.] Andrew Esposito, July 16, 1994; [pers.] I have been greatly influenced by my husband, whom this poem was written for. Without his love this poem would never exist. And also by my parents who are the greates poets ever.; [a.] Selden, NY

ESTES, JEWELL PFEIFER
[pen.] Jewel Estes; [b.] June 28, 1921, Randlett, OK; [p.] Mr. and Mrs. George L. Pfeifer (Deceased); [m.] Thomas James Estes, January 1, 1944; [ch.] Phillip S. Estes (Engineer), Phyllis A. Estes Cady (Teacher/Speaker); [ed.] Oklahoma Central University - 3 years. Hardin Simmons Univ., Abilene, TX, Richland College, Dallas, TX Medellian School of Sculpting, Dallas TX. American University, Washington, D.C. (Have taught privately, this, an education in itself); [occ.] Homemaker, Writer, Sculptress; [memb.] Poetry Society of Texas, former member of Texas Wing of Women Fliers. Dallas-Walnut Hill Writers' Assn. Methodist Church. WIMSA (Women in Military Service for America)-(Washington, D.C.); [hon.] "Unberibboned" awards are too numerous to mention. I am an artist of several media. I have created 3 bronzes (1 lifesized) whic are in museums. Neil Armstrong dedicated the first one. I take pride in a letter from his mother.; [oth. writ.] Having published my first poems at the age of eight, the innate talent established the very aura of my lifestyle. Participating in the Texas State Poetry Society has afforded me many wins. Entering the Federation of State Poetry Society, I won ther honors. I have two completed novels and Junior High level research textbook on computer ready to edit. I was once engineer in a radio station where I wrote or edited material for airing. I also did tremendous research on the biographies of the 38 Women Airforce Service Pilots who died in service in Wold War II.; [pers.] Writing poetry is an innate talent. It so parallels Nature and the visual arts that their emotional impact is indescernible. Music mimics the soul of poetry. Dance is poetry in motion.; [a.] Dallas, TX

ESTRADA, THOMAS ANTHONY
[b.] September 29, 1975, Santa Clara, CA; [p.] Hugo and Kay Estrada; [m.] Buena D. Estrada, November 22, 1994; [ed.] High School, Naval Technical School; [occ.] Naval air Traffic Controller; [memb.] U.S. Navy/Armed Forces; [hon.] Captain's Safety Art/Poetry Award - NAS Memphis, Various High School Art Awards, Moral/Conduct Recognition-Army Special Forces; [oth. writ.] Several Poems to my wife.; [a.] San Jose, CA

ETHRIDGE, SHARON
[b.] April 29, 1941, Borger, TX; [p.] Herman and Blanche Middlebusher; [m.] Thomas Ethridge, June 2, 1962; [ch.] Jahna, Clark, Boyd; [ed.] High Sch. - Dewey H.S., Dewey, OK, B.S. in Ed, Northeastern State Univ. Tahlequah, OK, MS in Ed, Northeastern State Univ. Tahlequah, OK; [occ.] Retired Elementary Teacher; [oth. writ.] Zack the Vet and His Alphabet (Pre-school alphabet book unpublished); [pers.] The most beautiful and prolific poetry is found in the bible where God communicates with man. What better inspiration to write!; [a.] Leonard, OK

EVAN, DURAND DAN
[pen.] Drum and river of many waters; [b.] April 4, 1947, San Jose, CA; [p.] Dora Doris F. Simpson, John H. Beckmayer; [ed.] Vallejo High - Contra Costa College; [occ.] Special Programs Consultant; [hon.] Numerous public service chairmanships, and committees

and appointments; [oth. writ.] Never published; [pers.] Within the mystery of loving respection the intimacies of our hart gives the spirit purpose and meaning. At times this maybe painful however, let each to the other continue to be true.; [a.] Font Bragg, CA

EVANGELISTA, GREG
[b.] November 22, 1978, Detroit, MI; [p.] Michael and Joanne Evangelista; [ed.] Detroit Catholic Central High School; [occ.] Vocalist of Ska Band, called Aks Mamma, Student, Page at Farmington Hills Public Library; [oth. writ.] Two poems published in my High School Newspaper; [pers.] When you cannot speak it face to face, put it in verse. I have been most influenced by modern rock songwriters.; [a.] Farmington Hills, MI

EVANS, DAVID R.
[b.] March 13, 1948, Holden, WA; [p.] Elza and Vaughn Evans; [m.] Mary E. Evans, April 2, 1971; [ch.] Amanda, Emily, Cortney; [ed.] A.B. Marshall University 70, M.A. Marshall University 78; [occ.] Counselor, Logon High School Logon WV; [memb.] N.E.A. WVEA Scoutmaster Boy Scout Troop 23 Peach Creek WV. Member Crooked Creek Church of Christ, Sunday School Teacher; [hon.] Silver Braver Award Boys Scouts of America; [oth. writ.] None published; [pers.] Ecclesiastes Chapter 3; [a.] Peach Creek, WV

EVANS, WILLIAMS E.
[b.] April 22, 1977, UT; [p.] William E. and Esperanza F. Evans; [ed.] Taylorsville High School; [occ.] Maintenance person - student; [memb.] Race-A-Cop, Taylorsville High School Hockey; [hon.] 2nd place, state National Geographic Geography Bee; [pers.] Always be persistent, listen well and well and never stop trying to improve yourself.; [a.] Salt Lake City, UT

EVERMAN, DONNA
[pen.] Jean Nickles; [b.] August 26, 1937, Portsmouth, OH; [p.] Walter and Olive Nickles; [m.] Widow, 1957-1981; [ed.] High school; [occ.] Retired; [memb.] L.D.S. Genealogy Society Cancer Society Pres. "Shawnee Singles Club; [hon.] Having my poem "Unconquered Love" published by your company; [oth. writ.] Unconquered Love my mother, Myself. Dreams. Compassion things unseen friendships; [pers.] I received my love of poetry from my father, and the talent of writing from my aunt Lorraine Fultzs. "I feel that poetry soothes the best within our hearts"; [a.] Portsmouth, OH

FAGERHOLT, BARRY JAMES
[b.] December 30, 1977, Grafton, ND; [p.] Mark and Linda Fagerholt; [ed.] Valley High School; [occ.] Student; [memb.] First Lutheran Church Senior Choir; [hon.] Who's Who Among American High School, 40 et. 8 Honor Society, North Dakota Boys State Representative; [pers.] Kindness and honesty are the best gifts that you can give.; [a.] Hoople, ND

FAIRMAN, HEATHER
[b.] December 14, 1974, Arcadia; [p.] Debbie and George Fairman III; [ed.] Graduate Temple City High School, 2nd year at Citrus College and will be spending Summer Semester in Paris; [occ.] Pre-school Teacher at Santa Anita Village Pre-school; [pers.] Writing is as necessary as eating for me. I need to release any pent up emotions, memories, or even just sort out my thoughts before they start to make me crazy.; [a.] Temple City, CA

FAIZ, ERIC AMANULLAH
[b.] January 2, 1958, Rangoon, Burma; [p.] Frank Faiz, Fatima Faiz; [m.] Yasmin Faiz, January 13, 1993; [ch.] Hisham Amin Faiz; [ed.] Hamilton High, West Los Angeles Junior College, California State University at Los Angeles; [occ.] Children's Social Worker; [oth.

writ.] More than 50 poems unpublished. Majority of them dealing with romance.; [pers.] Always be patient, kind and respectful to people regardless of race, religion, national origin, status, color, sex and age. Above all, be most kind to one's parents.; [a.] Los Angeles, CA

FARR, JEAN
[b.] October 9, 1957, Alabama; [p.] Ed and Charlotte Glass; [m.] Edward Farr; [ch.] Kelli Edward Corrie; [ed.] High school graduate and two years of early childhood care and guidance; [occ.] Homemaker; [pers.] Secrets was inspired by a fight between my daughter Kelli and her friend Beth; [a.] Ozark, AL

FARR, PAT
[pen.] Pat Farr; [b.] November 14, 1945, Elmira, NY; [p.] Henry J. Pastirk, Lillian J. Morgan Pastirk; [m.] David R. Farr, April 20, 1992; [ch.] John 21, Joy 12, Wendy 21, Ken 22; [ed.] BA Social Criminal from Viltanovall; [occ.] Housewife; [oth. writ.] Fiction - Western - Scifi; [pers.] I am 49 and hope to reach 100 look forward to see 2000; [a.] Elmira, NY

FEDERICO, SHARON Y.
[pen.] Sharon Y. Federico; [b.] October 21, 1963, Jacksonville, FL; [p.] Augustine Woodward and Doris Woodward; [m.] Michael A. Federico, October 1, 1988; [ch.] Augustine White and Sheryl Jones; [ed.] Graduated from Paxon Senior High School Attended Iowa Community College; [occ.] Homemaker; [memb.] Jacksonville chapter Freedoms Foundation Prince of Peace Catholic Church Choir; [oth. writ.] Short story and poem published in monthly news letter of Prince of Peace Catholic Church; [pers.] Through my writings, I pray others will find peace within themselves and the hope and understanding for a better tomorrow.; [a.] Jacksonville, FL

FEDEROFF, TRACY MARDELL
[b.] May 10, 1963, Grosse Pointe, MI; [p.] Virginia and Edward Coonfer; [m.] Sam Federoff Jr., October 20, 1994; [ch.] Sam Edward Federoff Born December 5, 1991; [ed.] Graduate of Warren High School; [occ.] Housewife and Mother; [memb.] We attend Weideman, United Methodist Church; [oth. writ.] I recently starting hand making my own greeting cards with each verse meaning a special something about a special someone.; [pers.] I am inspired by my life's events through my heart, and also by my beautiful son.; [a.] Weidman, MI

FELD, LYNN SANDRA
[pen.] Lynn Sandra Feld; [b.] February 17, 1951, Wilkes Barre, PA; [p.] Max and Reva Oken; [m.] Joel, September 2, 1983; [ch.] Shelby Illysa; [pers.] Life, love and expression should have no boundaries. My family, friends, and animals have taught me this, I'm thankful.; [a.] Syosset, NY

FELICIANO, MARGARET C.
[pen.] Margaret Feliciano; [b.] Puerto Rico; [ed.] High School Diploma, Certificate Monroe School of Business; [occ.] Retired from the New York City Board of Education; [oth. writ.] Poems in the Local City Co-City Newspaper; [pers.] Dedicated to my two grandsons Feliciano brothers, Sgt. Rodney, and Gilbert, M.P. who are presently in the U.S. Army. Poetry, as I see it, is the active mind's distribution of language in the most appropriate and creative manner it can find. "Poetry is not beautiful language, but language beautifully employed."; [a.] Bronx, NY

FELTEN, CHRISTINE
[pen.] Christine (Enor) Felten; [b.] March 27, 1952, Cumberland, MD; [p.] Louise E. Skidmore and the late Peter Enor; [ch.] Matthew J. Felter; [ed.] Fort Hill High School 1970, Allegany Community College 1973; [occ.]

Secretary; [memb.] Lambda Chapter, Beta Sigma Phi; [hon.] Mainly for my volunteering in Scouts, Football, March of Dimes, Fitness Awards from work and I have another poem that won first place in a local contest.; [oth. writ.] I have another poem being published called the "Voyage" it is being published in a book called "Tomorrow Never Knows".; [pers.] Writing poems soothes my spirit, words flow from my mind faster than I can write. I strive to look for the good in my fellowman and have seldom been disappointed.; [a.] Cumberland, MD

FENNELL, STACY UPDYKE
[pen.] Dannie Divins; [b.] August 23, 1973, Franklin, IN; [p.] Linda Updyke; [m.] Gregory Fennell, December 31, 1994; [ed.] Dayton High School, Dayton PA Indiana University of Pennsylvania,, Indiana PA - Bachelor of Science in Fashion Merchandising; [occ.] Sales Associate for Major Department Store; [hon.] Dean's List, Indiana University of Pennsylvania, Summer Happening for Arts; [oth. writ.] Letter published in Rolling Stone Magazine; [pers.] "Do unto others as you would have others do unto you."; [a.] Phoenix, AZ

FERCHAK, SUZANNE
[pen.] Ferchak, Sutton Suzanne; [b.] August 23, 1947, Paterson, NJ; [p.] Robert and Agnes Sutton; [m.] Joseph C. Ferchak; [ch.] Donna Marie Wilson, Lynette Kathryn Cole, Michael Christopher Cole; [ed.] Central High School; [occ.] Horse Breeder; [memb.] American Quarter Horse, N.Y.S. Quarter Horse Assc.; [hon.] Numerous amateur awards in both State and National Level of Equine Competitions; [pers.] My genuine love and life time interest in horses has inspired me to share some of my feelings and experiences with others through my writings; [a.] Cherry Valley, NY

FERGUSON, DOROTHY FRANK
[p.] Judge and Mrs. A. J. Scheineman; [m.] Glen R. Ferguson; [pers.] My poetry has been broadcast in various areas of the United States, parts of South America, Russia, Africa and Europe on both television and radio. It has also been reproduced in hard cover book form, newspapers and magazines such as The Chicago Tribune, Ideals etc. God is the author of my poetry...I am merely a pen within His Holy hand.; [a.] Lyndon, IL

FERNANDEZ, MARIA J.
[pen.] M. M. Fernandez; [b.] June 22, 1961, San Antonio; [m.] Ralph Fernandez; [ch.] Andrea, David, Ralphael and Julian; [ed.] Sam Houston High, San Antonio College - Associates of Arts, University of Texas at San Antonio - BA American Studies; [occ.] University of Texas at San Antonio - Graduate Student; [pers.] "Never stop dreaming and believing!"; [a.] San Antonio, TX

FERREIRA, LUZIA C. R.
[pen.] Tere; [b.] December 13, 1962, Brazil; [p.] Antonio and Filomena Ribeiro; [m.] Regis F. Ferreira, February 08, 1991; [ed.] Civil Engineer Graduated in Brazil; [occ.] Inside Sales; [pers.] This poem is dedicated to my parents, Antonio and Filomena, my husband, Regis, my brothers and sisters, in loving gratitude for the great love and support they have always given me. Also, to all the people that believe in dreams and can reach the skies of imaginations.; [a.] Houston, TX

FERRON, MEGHAN ANN
[b.] February 29, 1988, Madison; [p.] Donald and Kelly; [ed.] Geneva Elementary; [pers.] Due to the fact that see is only 7 yrs. old I do not wish to have her address printed.; [a.] Meghan, Ferron

FETTA, ELIZABETH ANN
[pen.] Seabie Christopher; [b.] January 26, 1931, Rasendale, NY; [p.] Seabie Freeman and Christopher Faisher; [m.] Charles J. Fetta, October 18, 1952; [ch.] Charles J. Fetta Jr., Christopher J. Fetta; [ed.] Kingston High School; [occ.] President of Charbeth's Mase Corp. (Distributor); [memb.] New York Stationery's Asso.; [hon.] Swan in AAA competition back in 45 to 48 never lost a race many trophies; [oth. writ.] Santa came to me golden sunset. Memories lying in a garden etc none published - most are to long to enter in your contests; [pers.] The poem you wish to publish again was written 8 yrs. ago after my husband passed away I was very hurt by the couple's we went places with that sort of ignore my existence; [a.] Hicksville, NY

FEWELL, BETSY
[b.] Altoona, PA; [p.] Elizabeth and Leslie Rinker; [m.] Donald Fewell, August 24, 1974; [ch.] Crystal Virginia; [occ.] Furniture Finisher and Refinisher; [pers.] I just like to share my own feelings that no one else can feel, these days we wait to long to let people know how we feel.; [a.] Cross Junction, VA

FIGGINS, CHELSEA MORRAY
[pen.] CC, Brat; [b.] September 6, 1979, Bountiful, UT; [p.] Teresa Gates; [ed.] Go to Cleveland High a freshman; [occ.] Sales; [hon.] Invited as an alternate to a writing festival; [oth. writ.] Never really done anything like this but I intend to have a lot more published.; [pers.] All I want in life is peace and love, and have fun at it. I write what ever is in my mind then rewrite it so it can be perfect.; [a.] Portland, OR

FILOSO, JAMES M.
[pen.] James De Ville; [b.] May 8, 1945, Newark, NJ; [p.] Lilyan and Louis Filoso; [m.] Gina Sylvester; [ch.] James Jr., Christine, Victoria; [ed.] Oll Graman Verona High; [occ.] Salesman, Automotive; [oth. writ.] Inspired by life family and people. Try to give my children someone to look up to.; [pers.] Morristown, NJ

FINCH, KELLI A.
[b.] September 21, 1963; [p.] Bill Long and Anne Long; [m.] Robert W. Finch, October 26, 1985; [ch.] Bobby Finch age 5 yrs and my daughter Kodi Finch Age 1 yr.; [ed.] JM Hanks High School in El Paso, TX. - Palo Alto College in San Antonio, Tx.; [occ.] Work for Southwest Airlines in Reservations; [memb.] Lythe Meth. Church; [hon.] In the process of working for a black belt in karate, Deans List at Palo Alto; [oth. writ.] Other poems, some writer for school - One published with quill books mostly inspired by my children. I also enjoy writing about life's day to day challenges - I enjoy writing very much. I feel; [pers.] It gives me an opportunity to express my feelings on paper that I cannot express verbally - thank you for publishing this poem, it is always nice to be noticed, this is a dream come true.; [a.] Natalia, TX

FINK, BETTY B.
[b.] September 21, 1923; [p.] Rev. Jehuda and Clara Briskin; [m.] Edwin Wm., September 14, 1952; [ch.] Gary Eliot, M.D., Kenneth Evan, Esq.; [ed.] G.A.R. High, University of Pittsburgh, B.S. Nursing Education, Villanova University, M.A. Ed., Guidance and Counseling Elementary School; [occ.] Retired School Nurse; [memb.] Delaware County School Nurses, Assoc. Kappa Delta Pi (inactive) J.C.C. Travel Club, Folk Dance Center; [hon.] Kappa Delta Pi - honor, Society in Education; [oth. writ.] Poems for Nursing School newsletter Limericks and ditties for School District Socials; [pers.] I try to write "on the lighter side" and to use humor in getting my point across.; [a.] Villanova, PA

FISCHER, HEIDI ELIZABETH
[b.] January 9, 1980, Hutchinson, KS; [p.] Jeff and Gloria Fisher; [ed.] Sophomore, Hutchinson High School; [occ.] Honor Classes, Sophomore, Hutchinson High School; [memb.] Hutchinson Youth Symphony Church Youth Group; [hon.] National Honor Roll Society - 1994, All American Scholar - 1994, Honor Roll Student, Lettered in Band, 1994-95, Hutchinson High School; [a.] Hutchinson, KS

FISCHER, ROBERT F.
[b.] June 22, 1938, Elgin, IL; [p.] Herbert and Ella Fischer; [m.] Josephine Fischer, January 20, 1974; [ch.] Anna Marie, Linda Arlene, Francis George and Vincent Edwin; [ed.] High School Bay City Texas, approx. 2 years of Electronics Training in the Army and Air Force; [occ.] Electronic Technician in Research Laboratory; [memb.] Lifetime member of VFW; [hon.] Served 20 years in the Armed Forces with Two Tours in Vietnam twice awarded the bronze star and retired as CW3 in 1977; [oth. writ.] Short Story about a prehistoric indian. Titled. The Hunter, 100 B.C. also several other unpublished poems.; [pers.] My poetry is about personal experiences and most of it was inspired by my wife Josephine, the source of all my happiness.; [a.] Georgetown, TX

FISHER, J. T.
[b.] October 8, 1983, Madison, WI; [p.] Kim Fisher; [ed.] 5th grade Brisah Elementary; [occ.] Paper Route; [pers.] I love to write but I also love basketball; [a.] Chandler, AZ

FISHER, JASON RICHARD
[pen.] Cupid; [b.] March 7, 1971, San Jose, CA; [p.] Maureen Cerruti; [ch.] Jerrod Fisher, Kayla, Minor and Tyler Zeller; [ed.] Corvallis High, Treasure Valley Community College; [occ.] Student; [hon.] Dean's List; [oth. writ.] Personal; [pers.] I would like to dedicate this to my fiance, Shawna for always believing in me - I Love You!; [a.] Corvallis, OR

FISHER, RACHEL
[b.] November 27, 1978, Chicago, IL; [p.] Murray and Carol Fisher; [ed.] Junior at Niles North High School, Skokie, IL; [occ.] Student; [memb.] Campfire Boys and Girls, Niles North High School Symphonic Wind Ensemble and Jazz Band, Calliope (High School Literary Magazine) Editorial Staff; [hon.] Illinois Music Educators Association - District Band, Bands of America Honor Band, Illinois Junior, Academy of Science - State Science Fair, Winner - top 30 categories; [oth. writ.] Short story Goodnight - in Calliope (High School Literary Magazine); [pers.] "Put on your very green beret and dream of flying..."; [a.] Morton Grove, IL

FITZGERALD, TIMOTHY K.
[pen.] Tim K. Fitzgerald; [b.] January 3, 1946, San Jose, CA; [p.] Ralph and Bernice Fitzgerald; [ed.] San Jose State University (4 degrees), Cal-State Hayward; [occ.] Researcher; [memb.] Sierra Club, Fellowship of Reconciliation; [hon.] Named to "Who's Who in the West" (1996 Edition), Named Outstanding Disabled Alumnus, STSU, 1992; [oth. writ.] Fiction and nonfiction in the Social Sciences - all self-published; [pers.] Favorite poets: Bob Dylan and Robert Frost; [a.] San Jose, CA

FITZPATRICK, JOHN
[b.] October 31, 1984; [p.] John Fitzpatrick, Ilo Fitzpatrick; [m.] Carol Fitzpatrick, May 21, 1969; [memb.] Elk's Lodge - Life Member of the U.S.O. United Servicemen's Organization; [pers.] I strive to bring the events of the past into reality among the confusion of the present that suffers a lack of romance and compassion; [a.] Mannford, OK

FLANAGAN, JON
[b.] February 3, 1971, New Jersey; [p.] Donald Flanagan and Jan Gavzy; [m.] Francesca Flanagan, October 22, 1994; [ed.] Morristown High, West Virginia University and Union County College; [occ.] Branch Manager, World Perfume, Inc.; [oth. writ.] Two unpublished children's books, 1 unpublished movie script, and several lyrics for my former band, mystery; [pers.] My poetry and songwriting are greatly influenced by the works of James Hetfield and Ronnie James Dio.; [a.] Morris Plains, NJ

FLECHEUR, ELYZABETH BAWIEC
[pen.] Crystal Ray; [b.] August 17, 1946, Lansing, MI; [p.] John P. Bawiec and Rev. Dorothy Heinemann; [ed.] Associate of Arts Degree in Psychology with Vocal Music Minor; [occ.] Paralegal/Legal Assistant; [memb.] Choir member of Atlanta Unity Church; [hon.] Took two years of high school French in one year, National Honor Society, ran for State Representative in 1976 as a novice new to my district and secured 20% of my party's primary vote.; [oth. writ.] Two-year newsletter editor of Michigan State University Business Women's Club newsletter where I originated a personality profile column on prominent University people. Various editorial articles published in local newspaper. Numerous articles as assignments for correspondence course in children's literature, as yet unpublished.; [pers.] This poem is part of book entitled "Cosmic Revelations in Prose and Poetry" which I hope to have published later this year. Most of the poems in that book came to me through inspiration while experiencing an unusually testing period in my personal life some 20 years ago. The poems have a spiritual meaning that tie in with my family ministerial background. May all who read those poems be inspired. Both Protestant and Catholic ministers in my family. We are shirttail cousins to the Pope.; [a.] Atlanta, GA

FLECK, LAREE HARMON
[b.] August 3, 1907, Sterling, UT; [p.] R.A.E. and Margretta Musig Harmon; [m.] Joseph A. Cutler (Chemist) and Francis Fleck (Railroad) Mechanic, May 20, 1928, JAC died March 12,1937, Remarried December 3, 1951; [ch.] Estella Dee, LaRene, Thomas, and Glen Cutler; [ed.] Correspondence courses, Art Schools; [occ.] Homemaker, Writer; [oth. writ.] I have in first draft 25 book-length stories and and hundreds of shorter stories and poems.; [pers.] I have on rule: Never write anything of which my children or I will be ashamed.; [a.] Springfield, OR

FLEMING, EILEEN
[pen.] Eileen Fleming; [b.] January 27, 1977, Boston; [p.] Robert and Eileen J. Fleming; [ed.] Amesburg High School Junior, completing; [hon.] Bronze and Gold medal for honor roll, Choir awards for participation; [oth. writ.] Nothing published; [a.] Salisburg, MA

FLORES, ZORAIDA
[b.] August 29, 1954, New York; [p.] Pedro and Bienvenida Arroyo; [ch.] Raul Jr., Tina, and Lizette Flores; [ed.] Julia Richman H.S. Hostos Community College - A.S., City College - B.S. in Nursing; [occ.] Registered Nurse, Morrisonia Diagnostic and Treatment Ctr.; [memb.] New York State Nurses Assoc. DeFenders of Wildlife; [a.] New York, NY

FOLLIS, BETTY J.
[pen.] Betty Jean Woodman; [b.] March 4, 1945, Coldwater, MI; [m.] Chester L. Follis, November 17, 1975; [ed.] Union City High, (Michigan), Indian River Comm. College (Florida); [occ.] Poet and Writer; [memb.] National Assoc. of Female Exec. Poetry Society of America Amer. Institute of Prof. Bookkeepers; [a.] Fort Pierce, FL

FORCINA, VANESSA
[pen.] Ness; [b.] April 8, 1980, Ridgewood, NJ; [p.] Roberta and Sal; [ed.] In June, will finish freshman year in Ridgewood High School; [occ.] Student; [memb.] Lacrosse JV Team; [hon.] High honor for marking periods in high school; [a.] Ridgewood, NJ

FORD, CLARA SMITH
[pen.] Sweet Pea; [b.] April 14, 1938, Oxford, NC; [p.] Nannie Smith, William Smith; [m.] Joseph J. Ford, March 1963 (Divorced); [ch.] Joseph Ford III biological son, 15 - Foster children raised; [ed.] BS in Social Studies 7-12, Adelphi University, B.S. in Elementary Education Adelphi University; [occ.] Social Studies Teacher 7-12, Elementary School Teacher, Part time Production at Estee Lauder Co.; [memb.] New York State Teacher, Mary Potter Academy- NYS Chapter; [hon.] Chancellors Excellent Academic Achievement Award, E.O.C. - S.U.N.Y. at Farmingdale, Deans List - Adelphi University, Perfect Attendance Award (1993-1994) Estee Lauder Co. Certificate of Long Island Writing (BOCES); [oth. writ.] Dreamer; [pers.] You are never to old to learn. One should learn as much as he or she can learn. All that I am and all that I will be I owe to my mother.; [a.] West Babylon, NY

FORDHAM, VONCIEL
[b.] January 22, 1963, Washington, DC; [m.] Benjamin Fordham, August 20, 1987; [ch.] James Howard, William Thomas, Dominique Nicole, Ralynn Renee; [occ.] Waitress-waffle house hwy 74 and 185 Fairburn, GA; [pers.] The greatest gift God give's us (in my opinion) is family. This poem is about my uncle Rocky who died March 1994. Thru all his accomplishments, and our memories we keep him alive in our hearts and minds. And now thru this poem every one will know him.; [a.] Fairburn, GA

FORT, PHYLLIS
[b.] Chicago, IL; [p.] Joseph Fort and Ida Fort; [m.] Deceased; [ch.] Michael, Daniel, Elise, Sarah, Joseph; [ed.] De Paul University, Modesto College of Electrology Pima Community College; [occ.] Raconteur; [memb.] Southwest Author's Association, Anshei Israel Synagogue; [oth. writ.] Fate Magazine, Technical Writing for the Journal of Electrolysis; [pers.] Life is like a chocolate cake. It's only as good as the ingredients you put into it.; [a.] Tucson, AZ

FORTE, ASHLEE
[b.] November 29, 1984, Jacksonville, FL; [p.] Sandi Forte; [ed.] 4th Grade University Christian School; [hon.] Has won Academic Achievement for maintaining straight a honor roll status for - 4th grade; [a.] Jacksonville, FL

FOSTER, MARY KATHERINE
[b.] April 13, 1951, Monterey, TN; [p.] Thomas James Foster and Mary Wayne Hammond; [ed.] Northside High School, Atlanta, GA Dekalb College, Doraville, GA; [occ.] Executive Secretary, AT&T; [memb.] National Speleological Society, The Country and Western Social Club of Atlanta, Tennessee Geneological Society, United Daughters of the Confederacy; [oth. writ.] I began writing at the age of 13, to help vent my frustrations, discover my feelings, and develop my philosophies.; [pers.] For the past few years I have been studying traditional, plains, Native American philosophies, religion and I have discovered the parallels in all walks of life. In researching my families genealogy I have also learned the importance of family, both immediate as well as extended. Now, as always, when I write - it comes from the heart - which is often food for the head.; [a.] Doraville, GA

FOUCAULT, MARY
[b.] March 23, 1951, Everett, WA; [p.] Ingrid Foucault, (Dad Deceased); [ch.] Chastity age 19; [ed.] Finished High School; [hon.] Songwriters Award from Jeff Roberts Publishing Company, and one from NCA Records; [oth. writ.] I've had other poems published in 4 issues My Legacy Poetry of The People, Night Roses Peckerwood, The Advocate, The Caring Connection, Poetry Break, The Acorn, Amherst writers and artists plus more; [pers.] I would like to be a great author someday of poems and songs most of my song's I write about my past.; [a.] Seattle, WA

FOX, CYNTHIA DIANE
[b.] November 11, 1971, Little Rock, AR; [p.] Robert L. Huth and Linda Moody; [m.] Steven L. Fox, March 13, 1993; [ch.] Chase Steven Fox; [occ.] Homemaker-Mother; [oth. writ.] I have recently completed my first book entitled "We must all learn to love". I've also written a children's book and several lullaby's for my son Chase. I am currently looking for a publisher.; [pers.] I look forward to starting the children's guardian angel foundation in the near future. It is the Lords will that the children of this world prosper through his love and it has become my mission here on earth.; [a.] Conway, AR

FOXLEY, DAVID M.
[b.] June 2, 1983, Denver, Co; [p.] Sandra and Bill Foxley; [ed.] I have just completed the fifth grade; [occ.] Student; [hon.] Not applicable for writings. I am on the Scholastic Honor Roll; [oth. writ.] For published writings; [pers.] I think that writing is the best way to express my feelings. My philosophy in life is to experience all that I can and to share my observations through my writings.; [a.] Denver, CO

FRAIMAN, ANITA
[b.] September 4, 1925, Brooklyn, NY; [p.] Bessie and Harry Cohen; [m.] Deceased, September 2, 1945; [ch.] Steven Richard Fraiman, Scott Paul Fraiman; [ed.] Graduated High School, January 1942, (Eastern District H.S.) Brooklyn, NY; [occ.] Retired Sect'y and Computer Operator; [memb.] Sisterhood, Jewish Center of Bayside Hills. Bayside Clear Spring Council (Civic Assoc.) Sect'y Both Organizations; [hon.] Woman of Achievement, Nov. 1993, (from) Jewish Theological Seminary of America; [oth. writ.] Unpublished (you have) Alone, Living Again; [pers.] No matter how dark or how terrible days have become, eventually, there will be better and happier tomorrows, if you let them shine in.; [a.] Bayside, NY

FRANCAVILLA, ANGELA
[p.] Anna Francavilla, John Francavilla; [ed.] Holy Rosary Academy, NYC Central Commercial High School NYC; [occ.] Exec. Secretarial Free Lance Work; [oth. writ.] Covered human interest stories for several Brooklyn newspapers in-house editor for major oil company newsletter, "The Pegasus Pipeline". Have written three plays highlighting the music and times of the 40s, 50s, and 60s performed by Brooklyn theatre groups.; [pers.] Never be afraid to be a late bloomer - you only missed the sun earlier in the day.; [a.] Brooklyn, NY

FRANCIS, GEORGE S.
[b.] October 17, 1947, La Crosse, WY; [p.] Sam Francis and Marguerite Francis; [ed.] U of Colorado - Business Central High - La Crosse, WI; [occ.] Property Manager; [hon.] Extensive 20 yrs. career on Cruise Ships as a Cruise Director has brought me many awards to the soul many awards to the soul making people happy.; [oth. writ.] "Friends" "Death" "Soulmates" "Motorcycling" "The Human" "Clouds" "For Alice" "For Robt and Vera Goulet" "The Opinion" "Twas An Angel" "Send

an Angel" "When I Leave" "Smiles" and More; [pers.] I truly believe my talent for writing is from God. Most of my works have messages of love, hope, peace and happiness contained in them.; [a.] Littleton, CO

FRANKE, WILLARD EARL
[b.] Oakland, CA; [m.] Pearl Young; [ed.] Fremont High of Oakland, Art Editor of the FLAME; [oth. writ.] My best writing wa an assignment from Famous Writer's School of Conn. about the "Sixties" DECADE OF CHICANERY"; [pers.] The utmost insult to Man is the dogma that our Creator's manifistation is "Born in Sin". When Man thinks with his conscious mind - all knowledge bows before him and all things are possible. We are ready to step into a new age and our only obstacle is medievalism, something we make ourselves. In our universe of positive and negative that holds mass together, the power of wrong is equally as strong as the power of right. With three simple qualities - REALIZATION, APPRECIATION, REGULATION, Man is superb! We initials denote Water, Earth, Fire and Few.

FRANKLIN, JACQUELYN LEIGH
[pen.] Leigha Franklin; [b.] November 7, 1980; [p.] Don Franklin and Lynda Cappel; [ed.] Freshman at Nacogdoches High School; [hon.] National Junior Honor Society member, participant in Duke University's Talent Identification Program; [a.] Nacogdoches, TX

FRASER, LESLEY
[b.] July 25, 1959, Bombay, India; [p.] Grant Fraser, Maie Fraser; [ch.] Nicholas Robert; [ed.] John Neilson High, Glasgow University, Scotland, U.K.; [oth. writ.] Prolific Poetry writer with Philosophical bent; [pers.] Lesley passed away in 1990. A great loss.

FRAZIER, OLIVIA MAY
[pen.] Olivia; [b.] January 22, 1952, Brooklyn, NY; [p.] Joseph and Jenese Frazier; [ch.] Xavier, Dawn and Shannon; [occ.] Homemaker, Business Women; [hon.] Community Service Awards 1. Parents Teacher's Association 2. Cheer Leader Coaching. School Broad Dist. 15 Brooklyn, NY plus one club honors, the US Postal System. Dept. of Treasury; [oth. writ.] A number of poems and one short story. Writings on display in Washington D.C., New York City and Philadelphia.; [pers.] The hand that holds the pen, holds also the mind of man.; [a.] Philadelphia, PA

FREEDMAN, MELVIN H.
[pen.] Mel Freedman; [b.] February 25, 1920, Malden, MA; Adoph and Bess Freedman; [m.] Johanna Bafaro ('78); Ruth Glassenberg ('42); [ch.] Niké Lois Speltz; Charles Freedman; Daniel Freedman; [ed.] Harvard College '41; [occ.] Writer (plays, musicals, screenplays, books); [memb.] Dramatists Guild, ASCAP; [hon.] Salutatorian, Harvard '41, CBI and Europe Theaters, USAF '44; [oth. writ.] How to Enjoy This Moment, (S&S); Oh, SoHo! (Monomoy Theatre); Entrepreneurs (musical) - Lincoln Ctr.; Smiling on the Outside (screenplay); [pers.] My parents taught us life, love, laughter. I would like to add new ideas, new songs; treasure old dependables, old friends; and help some "outside" gardens to grow.; [a.] New York, NY

FREELAND, JACK T.
[b.] Superior, WI; [m.] Sharon; [ch.] Shannon - Matti, John - Patrick; [ed.] Superior Central High, Superior Vocational and Technical Institute; [occ.] Stick Built Furniture of Oak; [pers.] Just a country boy who grew up thinking he was a cowboy. I enjoy writing of days of old that time has a way of erasing.; [a.] Gypsum, CO

FREEMAN, ROBERT
[b.] November 24, 1936, Mitchell Co., NC; [p.] W. C. and Stella E. Freeman; [m.] Mavis Leong Freeman,

August 27, 1960; [ch.] Sherri, Garner, Celeste, Jude, Jennie; [ed.] CED, Western Piedmont; [occ.] T.V Technician, Antique Speculator; [memb.] Zilch; [hon.] Zilch; [pers.] To look at life from as many perspectives as possible; [a.] Morganton, NC

FRENCH, KERRY
[b.] May 15, 1951, Louisville, KY; [p.] Bernard and Hazel Wittnauer; [m.] Bruce, May 12, 1973; [ch.] William David; [ed.] I'm still learning; [memb.] Southeast Writers Association; [oth. writ.] Poetry published in Chapbooks through Southeast Writers Association; [pers.] I feel fortunate that I have friends who are more like family, and family members that I consider friends; [a.] Louisville, KY

FRIEND, SHIRLEY
[pen.] Shirley Friend; [b.] August 22, 1927, Long Beach, CA; [p.] Mr. and Mrs. Levi Hugh Wright; [m.] August 30, 1946, Divorced in 1961; [ch.] All dead but one; [ed.] 1 year College - and 12 year self taught. Life experiences.; [occ.] Artist and unpublished writer and a little composing; [oth. writ.] "Short Stories for busy people", it is not published yet.; [pers.] Dreams come true if you persevere.

FROLICH, KRISTEN E.
[b.] August 4, 1988, Pompton Plains, NJ; [p.] Louis Frolich, Barbara Frolich; [ed.] Currently first grade student at our Lady of Holy Angels School Little Fall, NJ; [pers.] Kristen is an excellent student. She enjoys music and singing in the children's choir, reading, playing ball and Aladdin (her cat).; [a.] Little Falls, NJ

FRY, JOE W.
[b.] August 7, 1946, Union City, TN; [p.] Robert and Thelma Fry (divorced); [ch.] Carroll Ann, Katie Lynn; [ed.] Union City High School, University of TN Martin; [occ.] Self-employed sales; [memb.] 1st Baptist Church Union City, TN; [oth. writ.] Personal Book of Poetry not published; [pers.] I am a romantic and nearly all my poems come from experience.; [a.] Union City, TN

FRYE SR., HARRISON L.
[pen.] Harrison L. Frye Sr.; [b.] April 15, 1918, Georgetown Sedalia, MO; [p.] Anderson and Cora Lee Frye; [m.] Gracio M. Frye, June 9, 1962; [ch.] Three Daughters Janice, Winona, and one son, Harrison L. Frye Jr.; [ed.] I attended grade and high school of K.C. and am a graduate of U.M.D.C. Conservatory of Music, Earned Bachelor of Music Degree. Attended speech courses in Modern Creative writing at UMKC; [occ.] Retired Postal Clerk of now Organist for a Church of 26 yrs., Funeral Home and Music Teacher in my own Music Studio, Teaching piano, organ guitar, voice, theory, choir directing, arranging; [memb.] AARP Church of God in Christ UMKC Alumni; [hon.] Formerly Dean of National Music Dept. of Church of God in Christ for 5 years and first state Hm of Music of W. MO, logic for 7 years.; [oth. writ.] I am also a song writer and have written a number of song's, short stories and other poems.; [pers.] I also served as Poetry Editor of the K.C. Call Paper, a weekly paper of K.C., for about 3 years.; [a.] Kansas City, MA

FUHGER, JANE VILLANI
[pen.] Jane Villani; [b.] July 17, 1961, Huntington Long Island, NY; [p.] William and Diane Villani; [ed.] Commack High School South New York Institute of Technology; [occ.] Art Gallery Framing Business Owner Mngr/Director; [hon.] American Long Festival Songwriting Honorable Mention; [oth. writ.] Working on a Boor of Poetry reflecting a female philosophical approach to the greatness and limitation of being alive. In today's society.; [pers.] So much insight into the intricacies of the world such a great need to be heard, so

much feeling have I. To share with open minds. Hear me.; [a.] Kings Park, NY

FULLER, RAQUEL
[b.] San Antonio; [p.] Barbara Jane Dunn; [m.] Divorced; [ch.] Felicia Fuller, Melinda Fuller and Terrence Fuller, whom I love dearly; [ed.] Manual Arts High, L.A. Junior College of Business, West L.A. College; [occ.] Stenographer, LAUSD (Los Angeles Unified School District); [hon.] Crenshaw High School's Martin Luther King Museum Award; [oth. writ.] I had a poem entitled "Holiday Feelings" published in one of your previous Poetry Anthology. I love to write, and have a manuscript of poems, 3 children's books, and I'm working on a novel; [pers.] My poems are deep feelings that I have inside my heart about the world and life in general.; [a.] Los Angeles, CA

FULLERTON II, HARRY D.
[b.] April 5, 1954, Washington, DC; [p.] Harry Fullerton Sr., and Helen; [m.] Betsy A. Fullerton, February 28, 1992; [ch.] Harry III Billie Jo Bowen, Bobbi Jo Bowen; [occ.] Fire Protection Tech.; [oth. writ.] Rolling Thunder; [pers.] I write my poems for you to read. To touch your heart is my deed. If by chance my words get though. Then I shall live with in you too.; [a.] Lusby, MD

FULTON, BRENDA L.
[pen.] Boo-Boo; [b.] January 6, 1961, Mississippi; [occ.] Direct Care Worker

FURMANKOVA, JARMILA
[b.] 1966, Czechoslovakia; [ed.] University of Palacky in Olomouc, Czech Republic, Master of Sciences (1989); [hon.] Second price in Poetry competition (1994, Czech Republic); [oth. writ.] About 200 poems in 10 collections (not published); [a.] Oxnard, CA

GAILEY, CLARE XIMENA
[b.] April 22, 1974, Davenport, IA; [p.] C. K. and Stephanie Gailey; [ed.] Wellesley College Radcliffe Publishing Course; [hon.] Phi Beta Kappa; [pers.] Thank you Becky James, Julie Anne McNary, Olivia Rainsford, Elaine Chin, and all my ones.; [a.] Seattle, WA

GAINER, SCOTT B.
[pen.] Scott Gainer; [b.] March 13, 1980, Elkins, WV; [p.] Harold K. Gainer Jr., Debra L. Gainer; [ed.] At present freshman in high school; [occ.] High school student; [memb.] TIP Program Talent Identification Program from Duke University for Mathematically and Verbally Talented seventh graders, Male Model from John Casablanca Modeling Agency; [a.] Raleigh, NC

GALINDO, JOEL
[b.] August 8, 1959, San Antonio, TX; [p.] Mr. and Mrs. Emilio G. Galindo; [m.] Divorced; [ch.] Vanessa Galindo; [ed.] Antonian (S.A.) High School, graduated from St. Phillips Catholic in Bahle Creek Mich. 1977, San Antonio College of Wise; [occ.] Pedorthist (C. Ped.) 3rd Generation Cobbler; [memb.] American Diabetes Ass., P.F.A. (Pedorthic Footwear Ass.) B.C.P. (Board for Certified Pedorthist P.A.D.I. (Diving Ass.) U.S.A.K.F. (United States of America Karate Federations; [oth. writ.] Adventorial's in S.A. Business Journal and Bulverde Standard newspaper; [pers.] My experience and reflections on life are written in my poem, as are my emotions. I write then for Vanessa and all to read and share; [a.] San Antonio, TX

GALLIGANI, F. J.
[pen.] F. J. Galligani; [b.] November 6, 1938, Cambridge, MA; [m.] May 16, 1959; [ch.] 4 Children; [occ.] General Manager Mfg. plant. My avocation is to work with patients and families experiencing serious medical

problems. I fill this role while working as a Choplain eveing at a large Boston Hospital; [per.] With the years I have remaining, I can only hope in some small way, to repay the love I have experienced as a husband and a father.; [a.] Cambridge, MA

GALLON JR., JAMES
[pen.] Cowboy; [b.] February 9, 1950, Camdew, NJ; [p.] James Sr. Melva Gallon; [m.] Rosemarie, September 30, 1992; [ch.] Rence, Brian, Robin, Jaguway; [ed.] H.S. 3 yrs College, Delsca Rigional H.S., New Mexico University; [occ.] Sponsor; [hon.] Coach of the year football 1979-82

GAMBINO, CRAIG
[b.] April 8, 1972, Arizona; [p.] Susan and Carlo; [ed.] Walt Whitman High School 3 yrs of College Campbell University; [occ.] Delivery Service; [oth. writ.] Just a little binder I've put together in the last few weeks.; [pers.] Find paradise and find yourself, poems like this one can only come from the heart. So I dedicate it to the one I thought of, I've Lisse Rivas; [a.] Huntington Station, NY

GAMBLE, KATIE SOUTHERLAND
[pen.] Mother Katie; [b.] August 13, 1932, Rock Hill, SC; [p.] John and Katie McCright; [m.] Italy Gamble, 1976; [ch.] 5 all grown; [ed.] 10th Grade; [occ.] Full Time in Ministry; [memb.] I am member of the Christian Family. When whiskey was calling the shots in my life. Jesus the Son of God had mercy on my soul. By His grace and mercy. He honored my faith and awarded me with salvation. I have not had a drink of whiskey wine or beer since 1959. Nor have I desired it.; [oth. writ.] Yes, book, songs, 30 mn plays for TV. I am the host of 2 radio broadcast. And only by His help is able to stay on the air.; [pers.] I am in the process of raising money to publish my book. "The Power of God versus sin, witchcraft, and sex." I am praying and looking around. I hope my poem win. It will help me have the money I need for my book. My book will sell by the millions, that will able me to publish my own work. I am sending the #20.00 just hoping for a miracle win. Only because I know with God all things are possible. The name of my radio broadcast is "What God call right is right number 1 (Sat.) and 2 (Sunday).

GAMER, PAUL A.
[pen.] Jericho; [b.] April 5, 1950, Madison, WI; [ch.] Jennifer L. Gamer, Kristopher P. Gamer; [ed.] De Forest High School, De Forest, Wisconsin; [hon.] Beyond the stars; [oth. writ.] Some composition, composing musical arrangements; [pers.] Jericho messages are a labour of Love. Thee Angels.; [a.] De Forest, WI

GARAY, LAURA A.
[b.] September 22, 1967, Utah; [p.] Betty Woodland, E. R. Woodland; [m.] Eric K. Garay, April 10, 1993; [ch.] Jachin Kip Garay; [ed.] Lakeland High, Pierce College, I.S.U.; [occ.] Human Services Counselor; [memb.] American Diabetes Assoc., Relief Society, Human Services Organization; [hon.] Phi Theta Kappa, Dean's List, Desert Storm Appreciation; [oth. writ.] Personal Poetry Portfolio, Children's Music; [pers.] If you want to change a life, let someone unwrap a gift of thought from you. These gifts are reflected in my poetry and music.; [a.] Tacoma, WA

GARBERINO, DENNIS CHARLES
[pen.] Dennis Charles; [b.] February 21, 1956, Saddle Brook, NJ; [p.] Charles and Dolores; [ed.] Fairleigh Dickinson University of New Jersey, USA and Wroxton, England. Business Training Institute; [occ.] Purchasing, Business Consultant; [memb.] National Association of Purchasing Managers, American Management Association, Fairleigh Dickinson Alumni Club; [hon.]

Dean's List, Academic Honors; [oth. writ.] Paper: Morality in the Work Place, Paper Ethnical, Moral, and Social Responsibilities of Corporations; [pers.] "Writing for me has become a friend, that I will carry with me to old age."; [a.] Saddle Brook, NJ

GARCIA, JULIO C.
[pen.] Chacho; [b.] November 24, 1968, Chicago, IL; [p.] Julio B. Garcia, Lupe-Garcia; [ed.] Farragut High School, Daley College; [occ.] Student; [hon.] National Defense Medal, Saudi Arabia - Liberation Medal; [pers.] Inspiration for my poem came from life's experiences, dreams, personal relationships, and a beautiful girl I know named Maria Villagomez; [a.] Chicago, IL

GARCIA, REBECCA
[b.] April 25, 1979, Houston, TX; [p.] Maria A. Garcia, John A. Garcia; [ed.] 9th Grade; [occ.] High School Student; [memb.] American Red Cross Volunteer - for approx. 5 yrs. presently involved with the Youth Leadership Group; [hon.] Honors class in Eng. and History (in high school); [oth. writ.] Many other poems not published; [pers.] I, Rebecca try to make someones feelings positive through my poetry. What influences me most were the times of the 60's (the Hippies) I believe in their way of believe for love and peace for all mankind.; [a.] Houston, TX

GARGUIHO, MILDRED K.
[pen.] Augusta March; [b.] January 20, 1036, Maspeth, NY; [p.] Catherine and John Sheehan; [m.] John J. Garguiho; [ch.] Elizabeth 31 yrs. John and Thomas 29 yrs; [ed.] High School Equiverlansey Diploma; [occ.] Town of Brookhaven Neighborhood Aide; [memb.] U.S. Coast Guard Auxiliary Louis Furco Rep. Club, Girl Scout Leaders, Boy Scout Den Mother. Publicity Person PTO, Patchogue Lioness Club - Several Boards; [hon.] Lioness Club President Award U.S. Coast Guard Auxiliary Commander Flotilla 19-5, Publicity Awards; [oth. writ.] Newspaper and Publicity articles unsubmitted novels and children stories; [pers.] To look beyond one's eyes and hear one's heart and instincts. Then to do what must be done.; [a.] Bellport, NY

GARRETT, JULIE B.
[b.] January 18, 1964, Chester, VA; [p.] Betty Perry and Hugh Burton; [m.] James B. Garrett, November 14, 1983; [ch.] David B. Garrett age 14; [ed.] Thomas Dale High, Institute of Business; [occ.] Teacher's Aid at Bird High School; [oth. writ.] I have not been published before, but I have many poems, and I am currently writing short stories for teenagers.; [pers.] I am striving to write poems from my heart. To all people, no matter what race. That we will put aside our differences, and embrace our a likiness. Thanks to God and Helen Stiner Rice.; [a.] Chester, VA

GARTMAN, MYRTLE I.
[p.] Paul G. and Lillie M. Gartman; [ed.] Roanoke College, Salem, Va. George Washington University, Washington, DC, Berlitz School of Languages, Washington, DC; [memb.] Life Member, International Society of Poets; [hon.] Received from The National Library of Poetry, 1994 - Editor's Choice Award for poem published in At Day's End, 1995 - Editor's Choice Award for poem published in Journey of the Mind; [oth. writ.] Former community columnist for small town newspaper. Poems published by The National Library of Poetry 1994 - At Day's End, 1995 - Best Poems of 1995, 1995 - Journey of the Mind; [a.] Washington, DC

GARZA, DAVINA MARIE
[pen.] Davina; [b.] November 17, 1979, Gilroy, CA; [p.] Sheila and Rick Garza; [ed.] Attending high school as a sophomore this year. Mt. Whitney High; [occ.] Volunteer at a youth community center; [hon.] Public

speaker repressing youth that have been or may starting to be at high risk. Anti-drug, alcohol presentations.; [oth. writ.] Poems, short stories; [pers.] Ever since I was 12 years I wrote poems, though I knew nothing about love. It came to me. I think I was inspired most by my grandmother Mary Ellen Escobar's writings. I would just like to say "Believe in yourself even when you feel like no one else does" I want to thank my Grandpa Frank for believing in me and to Carol brown for never giving up on me and Tim Hernandez for inspiring me!; [a.] Visalia, CA

GARZA, JOSE R.
[pen.] J. R. Garza; [b.] June 26, 1948, San Antonio; [p.] Juanita and Geronimo Garza; [m.] Irma, May 9, 1970; [ch.] Belinda Marie, Jose Jr. Celia Denise; [ed.] Louis W. Fox High, San Antonio Air Force Community College; [occ.] Support Equipment Mechanic; [memb.] NCOA; [pers.] This poem was written about the worries, presented to me by my daughter, Belinda as we prepared for the her wedding in Aug. 1994 I hope I'm inspired more often.

GATES, LAKETA
[pen.] Laketa Green; [b.] February 22, 1977, Philadelphia, PA; [p.] Adelia Gates; [ed.] Burlington City H.S. Diploma AFNA Program at Temple Univ., Phila.; [occ.] Personnel Specialist in the Army Reverse; [memb.] (In school activities) ROTC, Yearbook, Sepia, Spectrum, Student Council, Jr. Achievement, Key Club, Student Helper, Computer Club, Shark Tutor; [hon.] Teen Arts (Poetry), ROTC Athletic, American Legion Award, American Red Cross Award, AFNA Scholar, Honor Roll; [oth. writ.] "Crack" presenting in local contest Teen Arts. "My Commitment to America" and "A Voice in Democracy - What Democracy Means to me" - local VFW Post, America Legion contest.; [pers.] God shall be my hope, my strength, my guide, and a latern to my feet.; [a.] Edgewater Park, NJ

GATO, SERGIO
[b.] May 30, 1979, Havana, Cuba; [p.] Pablo Gato and Ada Balda; [ed.] South Miami High School; [occ.] Student; [hon.] Superior achievement and excellence of performance in Florida Writes 1995; [oth. writ.] Other poems; [pers.] I believe that the civilized world we created was never meant to be. My philosophy is like that of the native American Indians. I believe that the world was meant to exist in nature, not in cities. I try to reflect my beliefs in my writing.; [a.] Miami, FL

GEE, AVERY
[b.] February 28, 1958, Pittsburgh, PA; [p.] Adopted; [ch.] Salina Alesid, Charles Keith, Jashela Renea; [ed.] South Hill High, Pgh PA, The Sawayer School Certificate in Travel and Tourism, Rutledge College Certificate in Business Administration; [occ.] Trade show set up. Also self employed; [hon.] Deans List; [oth. writ.] None published; [pers.] I have always wanted to be a writer, poetry, song, on novel. I write how I feel. I am greatly influenced by black writer like Maya Angelu; [a.] East Point, GA

GEETER, CANDY RENEE
[b.] June 15, 1972, Pontiac, MI; [p.] Rosie and Sam Geeter; [ed.] 2 Associate Degrees in Business Administration and Liberal Arts. I am currently working on a Bachelor's in Education - English Literature.; [occ.] Account Clerk II with the City of Pontiac; [memb.] I am a member of the Pontiac Area Urban League, United Way, and Business Professionals of America.; [hon.] Won the Edje Scholarship Graduated from United Way's Youth Leadership Program. Appeared in local newspapers articles.; [oth. writ.] I have wrote numerous poems and am currently working on a short story/book.; [pers.] I would say that my writings are a key to the door of life.

Also, my writings serve as a translator for the love I have for God and he has for me.; [a.] Pontiac, MI

GELLER, BUNNY
[b.] May 21, 1926, New York; [p.] Shirley and Herman Juster; [m.] Lester R. Geller, July 7, 1946; [ch.] Judy, Robert, Sheryl, Wayne (Six grandchildren also); [ed.] Attended grade schools - NY Jr. High and Senior High School - Calif. UCLA; [occ.] Poet, Artist, Sculptor; [memb.] I was a sculptor associated with Pegasus Mint, Int. Corp. Pennington, N.J., Artists equity Association, Inc., International Society of Artists, Hollywood Art Museum, Sm Ansonian Assoc. (Nat'l. Members) - among others.; [hon.] American Legion Award Excellence for Essay - Balfour Medal, and named Poet Laureate - High School, Sculpture Awards, Art Award - San Francisco World's Fair; [oth. writ.] Poetry published in local Newspaper, poetry in sculpture books; [pers.] I honor the universal human spirit and beauty of the soul. I have faith in the intrinsic good of humanity, that love, compassion, caring, tenderness. Will continue to develop ever stronger on our planet. My poetry and my art express my deep feelings in these beliefs.; [a.] Hallandale, FL

GENET, JULIAN
[b.] February 18, 1951, Miami, FL; [p.] Irving and Sylvia Genet; [m.] Michele Genet, June 1, 1975; [ed.] Coral Gables High, Emerson College; [occ.] Part owner, Dade Paper and Bag Co.; [pers.] "She's as sweet as sugar and calms me so well, happy Twentieth Anniversary I'll always love you Michele"; [a.] Royal Palm Beach, FL

GENTILE, JENNIFER
[b.] September 22, 1980, Bronxville, NY; [p.] Alan and Marianne Gentile; [occ.] High School Student - Pinkerton Academy; [pers.] I've been writing for along time and even though I plan to become an Archeologist after college I will continue to write.; [a.] Derry, NH

GENTRY, LINDSAY
[b.] October 29, 1977, Lawrence, KS; [p.] Ken and Jan Gentry; [ed.] I go to Lawrence High School. I am a junior.; [occ.] Student; [memb.] Lawrence High School Writers Club. Member of Lawrence High School Golf Team; [hon.] On the Lawrence High School Honor Roll, Kansas State Golf Awards from 1992-1995; [pers.] I have always loved reading and writing poetry. I also love to write fiction stories. "If you see through eyes of wisdom of truth."; [a.] Lawrence, KS

GERRISH, DANIELLE
[b.] March 6, 1968, Silver Spring, MD; [m.] Michael E. Gerrish, April 19, 1986; [ch.] Emily Anne Gerrish; [occ.] Homemaker; [oth. writ.] A few children's books, The title book 'True Expressions' from which this poem came. A few song.; [pers.] I feel that I have never 'learned' how to write poetry. But, instead, I was in inspired by life experiences.' The more I experience, the more I'm inspired to write; [a.] Waynesboro, PA

GERVAIS, JOHN J.
[b.] January 18, 1959, Lowell, MA; [p.] Mr. and Mrs. E. Philip Gervais; [m.] Lauren A. Gervais; [ch.] Scott Philip, Erica Redd and Matt Aaron; [ed.] University of Mass.; [occ.] Artist; [oth. writ.] Currently working on a book of poetry and essays; [pers.] Whole heartily be aware of the movement away from that what is actual in myself and all that I do.; [a.] Lowell, MA

GETTRY, JOAN E.
[b.] Jamaica, WI; [p.] Irene and Sylvester Grant, (Deceased); [m.] Martin D. (Deceased); [ch.] 8 yr. old English Springer Spaniel Dog; [ed.] Laguardia Community College Expected Graduation Date, 95 future

goals, Hunter College; [occ.] Homemaker and Student; [memb.] Women's Auxiliary the New York Medical Center. International Society of Poets; [hon.] Dean's List; [oth. writ.] Enrollment in Institute of Children's Literature; [pers.] Life takes twist and turns in everyone's life, no doubt, but the most incredible thing is that no one will develop their hidden Potential until things are ready to click into place. Whenever this occurs, cherish and nurture that knowledge because it's a gift from God. And it's better receiving it late than not at all.; [a.] Beechhurst, NY

GEWARGIS, NAHRAIN
[b.] July 17, 1973, Baghdad, Iraq; [p.] Paul and Juliet Gewargis; [ed.] Mather High School, DePaul University - 1995, Graduate (B.S. Education); [occ.] Elementary Teacher (Chicago, IL.); [memb.] Assyrian Student League; [oth. writ.] A variety of poems that have never been published. This is my first published work.; [pers.] My inspiration for writing comes from my true feelings. By putting my thoughts down on paper, I feel that they have not gone unnoticed.; [a.] Skokie, IL

GIBBS, KELLIE
[b.] January 1, 1961, Independence, MO; [p.] Carole and Hagan Gibbs; [m.] Susan Ramsey, February 2, 1995; [ch.] Erika, Alexander; [ed.] University of Colorado, BA Latin America Studies, Post Graduate Univ. of Colorado; [occ.] Journalist, writer, poet, assistant editor; [oth. writ.] Three collections of poetry, "Wetness Feeds the Fire". "Apathy's Ritual" and "Crossroads", assistant to managerial editor of out front and assistant to Editor Woman's Way; [pers.] Our thoughts are not our own but borrowed from a passing moment yet all the world can be ours if we merely think it—or write it down; [a.] Lakewood, CO

GIBBS, WES
[b.] August 12, 1967, Kentucky; [p.] Martha, Richard; [ed.] BA Indiana University, American University in Paris University of Louisville; [oth. writ.] Poems published in The Paris Atlantic, 1988; [pers.] Extra special thanks to Victoria Moses for her friendship and inspiration.; [a.] Louisville, KY

GIBSON, LAURA ANN
[pen.] Laura G.; [b.] October 24, 1960, Pasadena, CA; [p.] Lester and Lucille Youngblood; [m.] Walter Earl Gibson, July 27, 1991; [ch.] Antoine, Cami, Alisha, Marlene, Brian; [ed.] H.S. Basic, Sub. Abuse Training, Nurse Aide Certified by the State of Michigan; [occ.] Residental Technician, DOT Caring Center Inc.; [memb.] 12 Step Groups; [hon.] Community Groups, First Ward Center Teen Group - Awards, Pre-School Helper Awards; [oth. writ.] Our Family, Life, Grandma, Time, Today, Step-Dad, Moby, Sweetness, Mombo, Two Hearts, Marriage.; [pers.] I write to express the better times ahead. To help others to get through the tough times. I enjoy putting in writing what I feel. And sharing it with my dear friends.; [a.] Saginaw, MI

GIESE, DANA
[b.] February 7, 1982, Chicago, IL; [p.] Debby and Tom; [ed.] 7th Grade at St. Pascal School; [pers.] My poem, Angels, was written for my Uncle David Giese, who died of AIDS in August of 1994.; [a.] Chicago, IL

GIL, MARIO
[pen.] Mr. Gil; [b.] February 2, 1072, North Hollywood, CA; [p.] Catarino Gil, Alberta Gil; [ch.] Christina Gil; [ed.] John F. Kennedy High School; [occ.] Driver, Salesman for arrowhead water; [oth. writ.] I have several poems waiting to be published; [pers.] I have written this poem through deep emotional thoughts which love songs has inspired me.; [a.] Granada Hill, CA

GILBERT JR., PETER A.
[pen.] Peter A. Gilbert Jr.; [b.] May 8, 1964, Ogdensburg, NY; [p.] Peter and Kathy Gilbert; [m.] Fiance - Bobbi Jo Facteau; [ch.] Tiffany Rose Gilbert, Joshua James Facteau; [ed.] Heuvelton Central High School, College - Canton ATC; [occ.] Secured Care Treatment Assistant - 1, Government Employee; [memb.] National Civil War Reenactor - 1st North Carolina State Troops, 4 Battalion, COB Army of Northern Virginia (A.N.V.), Confederate States of America (C.S.A.); [hon.] I receive honors and awards daily in the mail. These come in the form of thank you letters from children whom I have taught and have read my I a member of the sound of America poetry. Honor band and chorus Of the U.S.A.; [oth. writ.] I have three other poems published in various other anthologies. I am also a public speaker on the American Civil War.; [pers.] The poetry I write is meant for young minds as a learning tool. I have young people will learn form my poetry and remember the men who gave their life, north and south, during the civil war so that this country might live.; [a.] Tupper Lake, NY

GILLETTE, MARIE
[b.] February 1, 1954, Texas; [m.] Patrick Allen Gillette, August 14, 1992; [ch.] Samantha Jewel, Olivia Ann; [ed.] Certified Ophthalmic Asst. St. Paul, Minnesota Cullen Eye Institute, Houston, TX; [occ.] Housewife, Certified Ophthalmic Asst.; [memb.] Joint Commission on Allied Health Personnel in Ophthalmology, American Red Cross State of Texas Elder Program Assoc.; [pers.] Through the writings of Herbert W. Armstrong I've learned the meaning of Life and learned not to waste a moment of it, but to instead reflect on purpose and humor in my writings.; [a.] McAllen, TX

GILLIS, ALEC I.
[b.] March 6, 1983, Brooklyn, NY; [p.] Winston and Eileen Gillis; [ed.] Walter Francis Bishop Elementary School, Jamaica Queens NY; [hon.] Valedictorian, Boroughwide Student Attendance Award Winner, Gifted Fair Award Winner; [pers.] Measure ones maturity by his mind not his age; [a.] Jamaica Queens, NY

GILLIS, JAGODA J.
[b.] January 5, 1977, Salem, MA; [p.] Robert G. and A. Krystyna Gillis; [ed.] Triton Regional High, School, Byfield, MA. (Grad. 1995), Salem State College (entering fall 1995); [occ.] Student; [memb.] Business Professionals of America (held position of Historian during Sr. year in high school); [oth. writ.] Publication of a quick quote' in H. Jackson Brown's "Life's Little Instruction Book Vol. III"; [a.] Rowley, MA

GILMARTIN, JAMES
[b.] October 16, 1972, Brooklyn, NY; [p.] Joann Catanese, Jim Gilmartin; [a.] Rockaway Beach, NY

GLASSCOCK, LUCILLE R.
[p.] Mr. and Mrs. G. W. Richardson; [m.] Joe David Glasscock; [ch.] Karen G. Roll; [ed.] Dalton High School, Bachelor of Arts - University GA State, English - Major Sociology - Minor Concentration - Creative Writing; [memb.] Georgia Writers, Inc, Council of Authors and Journalist, Village Writers Group; [hon.] Lambda Iota Tau International Literature Honor Society; [oth. writ.] Poems, short stories, novel unpublished; [pers.] My philosophy of life is to all things well - to reach for the stars.; [a.] Waleska, GA

GLASSMAN, SANDRA
[pen.] Melodee Co; [b.] August 27, 1940, Brooklyn, NY; [p.] Joseph Rae; [m.] Stewart, December 27, 1959; [ch.] Son - Lee, Daugther - Marrah; [ed.] High School Graduate; [occ.] Music Teacher; [memb.] America College of Musician, Nysmata, International Society of Poets America Museum of National History

Smithsonean Washington; [hon.] Two Editors Choice Awards form National Library of Poetry 1993-1994, two published poems IN Journal "Critical Perspectives on Accounting"; [oth. writ.] 3 children stories 250 poems on variety of subjects 2 published songs, 2 poems about Holocaust and a musical composition written for the novel "Take Care of Joseth" by Jacquline Wolf at the Holocaust Archives in Washington DC; [pers.] The eyes are means for us to see but sometimes we need glasses to clarity our aims and goals, if we spend to much time into ourselves, instead of helping others. We have then forgotten, that humanity calls us "sisters and brother"; [a.] Oceanside, NY

GLEASON, SHERRY L.
[b.] December 21, 1952, Dallas, TX; [p.] Mr. and Mrs. Martin L. Burton; [m.] Kenneth D. Gleason, August 12, 1977; [ch.] Kristin Courtney Gleason 11 years old; [ed.] B.A. English from Univ. Texas at Arlington, M. Ed. from Texas, Woman's University; [occ.] English Teacher, Vines High School, Plano, TX; [memb.] TSTA, NEA, PEA, Delta Delta Delta; [pers.] I would like to dedicate this poem to my family, who has always been my support.; [a.] Plano, TX

GLYNN, EMMA
[b.] August 2, 1923, New York, NY; [p.] Ludvig Boyesen, Esther Boyesen; [m.] Charles Glynn, February 14, 1947; [ch.] Laura Beth; [ed.] Walton High School; [memb.] 700 Club, National Anti-Vivisection Society (NAVS); [oth. writ.] Throughout my life, I have written short poems, but unsubmitted.; [pers.] I believe we are in the signs of the end times, and in the ultimate triumph of good over evil.; [a.] Woodbury, NY

GOBEILLE, FRANCINE S.
[pen.] Charlie; [b.] July 17, 1963, Brookhaven, MS; [p.] Fred and Pat Schukis; [m.] Paul V. Gobeille, June 10, 1983; [ch.] Joseph (8), Malinda (6), Bethany and Dalton (deceased); [occ.] Full-time Mom and wife; [oth. writ.] I have written over 100 poems for my still born children. I also have been writing poetry since age 15.; [pers.] There is always someone who can relate to the tragedies life forces on you - Taking and writing are great medications to help heal; [a.] Jacksonville, FL

GODFREY, JULIE
[pen.] O'Brien Deveraux; [b.] September 12, 1974, Akron, OH; [p.] Pamela Grubbs, Larry Godfrey; [oth. writ.] Many unpublished essays; [pers.] Time is consumed instance and occupation.; [a.] Akron, OH

GOLDSMITH, RICHARD A.
[pen.] Rich Goldsmith; [b.] October 28, 1938, Vickburg, MI; [p.] Marlon and Flora Goldsmith; [m.] Susan K. Goldsmith, January 26, 1962; [ch.] Glenn, Laurie, Nathan; [ed.] B.S. Western Mich. U. 1964 Master of Divinity - Grand Rapids Baptist Seminary 1965 - M.S. Georgia State University 1989; [occ.] Teacher, Pastor, Counselor Retreat and Seminar Leader; [memb.] American Association of Christian Counselors, Nat'l Association for Certified Counselors (NBCC); [hon.] Summa Cum Laude Graduate Georgia State University 1989 (MS), Distinguished Service Medal, 2 Brooze Stars (Vietnam 69) U.S. Army Chaplain; [pers.] Victor Hugo once wrote "for great books there must be great readers". I believe the same is true of poetry. The greatness of a poem happens when a reader is taken beyond themself to a rendezvous not only with a greater self, but with the spirit of the poet, and they become friends.; [a.] Martin, MI

GOLSON, RUTH
[b.] July 22, 1903, Pine Bluff, AR; [p.] William Byrd, Mafilda Byrd (Grandmother); [m.] Percy E. Golson (Deceased), 1970 last marriage; [ch.] Adopted daughter Shirley Fleming from Africa; [ed.] Lincoln High in

Arkansas Texas Southern College in Houston, Texas; [occ.] Retired as Primary Teacher from J. Will Jones Elementary School; [memb.] AARR and NBTA Seventh Day Adventist Church since I was eighteen yrs. of age; [hon.] High school awards, awards for God's service as Pianist and Stewardship Leader for many years in SDA Church, college awards during graduation; [oth. writ.] Several poems, but have not been publicized. Most poems refer to church activities. I also have some general poetry referring to Jesus Birth, etc.; [pers.] I have been motivated by chose friends who say I should publish my God given talent through poetry.; [a.] Houston, TX

GOLZ, BARBARA
[b.] July 9, 1962, Arizona; [p.] Bill and Jo Norman; [m.] William Golz - 34, January 8, 1984; [ch.] Brandy Golz - 10, Michael Golz - 7; [pers.] I am greatly influenced by the, love of my husband and children and the love and I have for them. The support that my wonderful husband gives me; [a.] Wiston-Salem, NC

GONGURA, KATHERINE
[oth. writ.] Edited Art Book Editor of a children's Book Authors of two children books; [a.] Forest Hills, WY

GONZALEZ, DEBRA LYNN
[b.] November 14, 1957; [p.] Ralph Williams, Patricia Williams; [m.] Jose Gonzalez, September 11, 1993; [pers.] This poem is dedicated to my husband "Joe" who died Sept. 23, 1994. Our memories are forever, it their kept within the heart.; [a.] Charlottesville, VA

GOOD, ANNETTE K.
[b.] February 23, 1961, Saginaw, MI; [p.] Elmer Larkin and Patricia Uribe; [m.] Jeri Good, September 25, 1982; [ch.] Craig age 12 yrs., Bryce age 2 1/2 yrs.; [ed.] High School (Chesaning) MI; [occ.] Homemaker, Mom and Writer - poet; [pers.] Real life is the best inspiration and always believe in yourself because your dreams start with you!; [a.] Elsie, MI

GOOD, MARGARET
[b.] February 4, 1933, Torrance County, NM; [p.] Claude and Bertha (Crider) Brown; [m.] Paul W. Good; [ch.] Dena Sue Roberts, Edwards F. and Steven W; [ed.] Ewing School, Torrance County NM, Estancia High School, Torrance Co. NM, Harding University, Searcy, Ark (2 yrs); [occ.] Retired Secretary; [memb.] Church of Christ International Society of Poets; [hon.] New Mexico Girls State 1950, High School Salutatorian, Scholarship to Harding College; [oth. writ.] Published in Anthologies: High School 2 yrs and Sermons in Poetry college 1 year, Famous Poets Society, Hollywood, CA, Today's Great Poems, Famous Poems of Today, At day's End Best Poems of 1995 Reflections of Light East of the sunrise at water's edge Sparkles in the sand, and 3 poems in "Vessels", a Christian paper for women by women; [pers.] I credit my 6, 7, 8th grade teacher, Eulah Watson, now deceased, for getting me started writing poetry. My writings generally consist of things with which I am familiar, specific events, people and religion.; [a.] Stephenville, TX

GOODING, BEVERLY
[b.] February 21, 1954, Wyandotte, MI; [ch.] Three sons, Brandon Shane, Barry Sean and Brian Scott; [pers.] This poem was written in honor of my parents. My parents have been such an inspiration in my life. Their love and dedication to each other and their children is the most valuable gift anyone would ever wish for. God has truly blessed all the people who are a part of, or has crossed my parents path in this life.

GOODMAN, KATHY
[pen.] Kathy Goodman; [b.] April 11, 1959, Ellinwood,

KS; [p.] Darold Withrow, Ruby Bruno Withrow; [ch.] Amy Goodman, Brent Goodman, Nicky Goodman; [ed.] Tecumseh High School Tecumseh OK, Grad. 1977, Univ. of Okla., College of Nursing, Grad. 1991, Bach. of Science in Nursing; [occ.] Registered Nurse; [oth. writ.] A poet came to my school in junior high and inspired me to start writing poetry and I have been writing poetry (and reading it) ever since.; [pers.] Inspired by life and people that I come in contact with, and influenced by diverse things my native American heritage for one, the great poets of the past, the wonderfully quirky music of today, and finally the people who are set a part from the rest.; [a.] Tahlequah, OK

GOODSON, ROSE MARY
[b.] July 30, 1945, Little Rock, AR; [p.] Earnest and Eva Schalchlin; [m.] John Goodson, July 28, 1979; [ch.] Four; [ed.] H.S. Robinson High; [occ.] Secretary of Goodson Hauling; [memb.] MADP A. M. Heart Association LR Fitness Center National Geographic; [pers.] I like for my poems to reflect love for one another. Also to respect one another and to consider others hopes and dreams; [a.] Little Rock, AR

GOODWIN, HENRY SAGE
[pen.] Homer Finn; [b.] October 14, 1904, New York City; [p.] Walter L. Goodwin and Elizabeth M. Sage; [m.] Susan T. Sage, March 12, 1939; [ch.] Manning, Rufus, Judy; [ed.] Groton School Groton Mass. grad 23 Yale college B.A. 1927, Yale Architectural school B.F.A. 1930; [occ.] Retired but paint pictures, draw, and do a little writing. Practised Architecture in Hartford CT, for many years best knows works, the Main Hartford Public Library, and restoration of the good speed Opera at E. Haddom CT; [oth. writ.] "A Picture Book for Grown Ups Family Album." This is a fictional History of the U.S.A. in pent ink drugs. With running comments, Pilgrims to WW-2. Characters repeat themselves in different generations. Also other attempts.; [pers.] As a chief petty officer in Seabees, the Naval Construction Battalions, (WW-2, I learn what I didn't learn at school. Ended up Questioning both.; [a.] Avon, CT

GORANSON, KATHLEEN
[pen.] Kathleen Sorte-Goranson; [b.] December 21, 1958, Alexandria, VA; [p.] Donald and Ilo Sorte; [m.] Kevin D. Goranson, July 6, 1985; [ch.] Cory Lawrence and Kelly Conrad; [ed.] Olympia High School, Olympia, WA, Pacific Lutheran Univ. Tacoma WA (BA) U of W - Platteville, Platteville Luisconsin (Master in Counseling Education); [occ.] Social Worker; [memb.] Wisconsin State Counselor Association; [hon.] Child and Family Welfare Scholarship Pacific Lutheran University; [oth. writ.] Too numerous to list, no previous publications; [pers.] To strive for excellence through personal and professional growth, remaining a life long learner.; [a.] Hazel Green, WI

GORDON, SYLVIA LUA
[b.] September 14, 1937, Athens, TN; [p.] Lua Walker and William Snyder; [m.] Bobby W. Gordon, May 12, 1969; [ch.] Danny, Lisa, Becky, Michele; [ed.] Ass. of Science in Social work then attended Univ. North Carolina school of SW, Governors Task Force for status or renders, Hamilton Country Foster Care Review Board, Sub-teacher for Him county; [memb.] Phil Theta Kappa, Vice P, Parole Board's first Offender Program; [hon.] Phi Theta Kappa, Who's Who in America Junior Colleges, National Deans List Student Merit Award - Chatt State TCC 1983; [oth. writ.] Poems published in Southern Baptist Convention, Lutheran Women's Symposium, Unicorn Writers Guild; [pers.] The Bible, Kahlil Gibran, the Tao, and Rod McKuen have helped me to reach inside myself and connect with my hidden feeling.; [a.] Chattanooga, TN

GORMAN, JANET
[pen.] Mary McDonald; [b.] March 5, 1916, Franklin Lakes, NJ; [oth. writ.] Weekly cooking column in newspaper (shopper)-2 years, which also published short articles, commentary, fiction, light verse and poetry, all of used pen name; [pers.] Word relationships are endlessly diverse and fascinating. Nowhere is this more significant than in poetic efforts. Though I want to write prose, my mind and hand often conspire against me.; [a.] Wycroff, NJ

GOSS, DIANE RILEY
[pen.] Reign; [b.] June 17, 1975, Boston, MA; [p.] John Goss - Mary Kate Riley; [ed.] El Dorado High School in California and Ponderosa High School in California; [oth. writ.] Poems published in one local paper (Footsteps). I've written many poems to express inner feelings to family and to friends. It's my way of getting across exactly what I want to say.; [pers.] Writing poetry, for me, is a form of release. A way to reach out or simply a way to show others what I've learned through my eyes. It's how I paint a picture.; [a.] Placerville, CA

GOULD SR., FRANCIS X.
[b.] April 4, 1934, Philadelphia, PA; [p.] Louis and Florence (Deceased); [m.] Rita, Kathleen; [ch.] Francis Jr., Craig Thomas, Samantha, Maria, Grandchildren Justin, Danny, Tommy, Jessica, Frankie III; [ed.] St. Joan of Arc Elementary, John Paul Jones Junior High, Northeast Public High School; [occ.] Driver-Salesman, Stroehman Bakeries Inc; [oth. writ.] "Poppy Copy" (unpublished) stories in rhyme for children of all ages; [pers.] Love to make children laugh.; [a.] Philadelphia, PA

GRACE, CINETREA D.
[pen.] Allahna; [b.] June 19, 1964, Kindley AFB, Bermuda; [p.] Timothy R, Grace Sr., Clarissa A. Grace; [ch.] Jehbreal Muhammed Jackson; [ed.] O.D. Wyatt High Louisiana State University Texas Woman's University B.S. Degree - Journalism; [occ.] Freelance Writer, Producer Actress, Choreographer, Public Speaker; [memb.] Delta Sigma Theta; [hon.] Received H.S. and College writing Awards and Recognition; [oth. writ.] Several poems, editorials and reported stories published; [pers.] I live for the Liberation of All God's Children.; [a.] Fort Worth, TX

GRAHAM, JENNIFER
[b.] February 5, 1979, Harnell; [p.] Lori Graham and James Graham; [ed.] 10th grade at Jasper - Troupsburg Central School; [memb.] Youth to Youth; [hon.] Honor Roll; [oth. writ.] Several poems; [pers.] My poem "My Father" tells a story about how I felt as a little girl when my father left me and my family, all my poems are bases on how I feel.; [a.] Jasper, NY

GRAHAM, KIM STARLENE
[b.] December 17, 1966, Nashville, TN; [ed.] Nashville Christian High School, 1 yr. Computer Programming at Nashville State Technical Institute, Ambassador Institute of Travel; [occ.] Travel Agent; [memb.] Richland Baptist Church, Humane Society of the U.S., and People of Animals; [oth. writ.] Hear My Cry Lord, Angel Wings and two others in the 'Anthology of Christian Poetry', Dear Satan and one other in 'Christian Poet's Pen', two other by world of poetry press, senior class poem; [pers.] My hope is that my generation will overcome all the hurdles of prejudice whether it be racial, musical, religious, physical appearance, personal style, etc. - that have been placed before us and that we, as a unit, will realize that God's love is

GRAHAM, ROSE
[b.] March 14, 1954, Indianapolis, IN; [p.] Fred and Elsie Smerdel; [ch.] 4 Children, 3 Grandchildren; [ed.]

George Washington High School; [occ.] Nursing Assistant, Hime Health Aide; [memb.] Ladies Auxiliary to the Veterans of Foreign Wars #908 Indpls, IN. Arthritis Foundation; [hon.] National Honor Society (High School); [pers.] In light of all the things happening in the world, the poem poses a universal question. I hope someday someone has the answer.; [a.] Indianapolis, IN

GRANHOLM, RICHARD A.
[pen.] Richard A. Granholm; [b.] July 5, 1940, Bronx, NY; [p.] Henry and Caterine Granholm; [ed.] Jamaica High School Marine Corp. GED Beaufort, S.C.; [occ.] Retired postal worker; [oth. writ.] "To be published" East of the Sunrise poems (Say Hello to God throughout the...) 2 Sparkles in the Sand (The Birds Do Sing, To Welcome, the...) 3 Beyond the Stars (...I wish, there was a wishing well...); [pers.] To live and let live and, to inspire, the good in my self and others, is my goal.; [a.] Jamaica, NY

GRANT, JUNITH
[b.] Boston, MA; [p.] Dr. and Mrs. James M. Grant; [ch.] Tonis Shabazz; [ed.] Morgan State Univesity Goergia in State University, Graduate; [occ.] Writer, Dramatist, African America Cultural Documentor, Pret. Culture Heritage Interpreter; [memb.] Mayor's Commision of Women and Minorities, Cultural Art Alliance, Friends of MA Ramey Musuem of the Blues United Methodist Women and Committe; [hon.] Citizen of the Month from Anheuser Bush Company, Plaque for Essay Contest from Columbus Times Newspaper Published Article in Columbus and the Valley Magazine Published feature articles in local newspaper Columbus Times; [oth. writ.] Playwrite "Brewer, Blues" Pruduced and playwrite, "I am" Ply; [a.] Columbus, GA

GRASSO, MEREDITH
[b.] August 11, 1975, White Plains, NY; [a.] Westchester Country, NY

GRAU, MARY F.
[pen.] M. Grau; [b.] February 2, 1918, Col., OH; [p.] Howard and Pearl Sells; [m.] Edw. C. Grau (deceased), November 29, 1936; [ch.] Peggy, Sunny, Donna, Danny and Eddie; [ed.] High School Biewalnut Art Classes; [occ.] Retired; [hon.] Some firsts and honorable mention in art shows; [oth. writ.] Poem "Gone Hunting" and one I lost "The Day After Christmas" and "When I Grow Up"; [pers.] I like music and reading and writing a poem now and then, poems about simple everyday "things" the average person can relate to. Love animals - love life!; [a.] Ashley, OH

GRAVELLE, ENID-ANN
[b.] July 10, 1951, Ontario, Canada; [p.] Raymond Gravelle and Grace Bangs; [m.] Jean-Louis Brouillette, July 12, 1980; [ch.] I daughter Gina; [ed.] H.S. Ontario, Canada, 1 Yr College Montreal, Canada; [occ.] Now work from home doing bilingual commercial correspondence and translation; [memb.] Former (local) C and W band lead singer and guitarist; [pers.] Such humble joy comes with the artistry of mere words as it allows even the simple man to travel and explore the highways of life in grandish style. Yet oftentimes, the most simple treasures, even though within eye's view, sadly remain so foreign to the soul.

GRAVLIN, KAREN R.
[p.] Jack and Terry; [ed.] Bachelor of Science - Penn State; [occ.] Public Accountant; [memb.] PSU Alum. Assoc., Parmi-Nous, Lion Ambassadors, NAFE; [hon.] Parmi-Nous Honor Society Lion Ambassadors; [pers.] Life cannot be defined only lived. If you are able to do this. Then you hold the definition within.; [a.] Philadelphia, PA

GRAY, JASON A.
[b.] July 31, 1973, Jacksonville, FL; [p.] Jo Ann Meehan, Jim Meehan, John Gray; [ed.] Bishop High SFCC, currently attending FCCJ; [occ.] Student; [oth. writ.] Poems and short stories none published; [pers.] Hedonism; [a.] Jacksonville, FL

GRAY, W. RUSSEL
[b.] February 21, 1934, Norristown, PA; [p.] Russel Gray, Margaret Bickings Gray; [m.] Dorothy R. Gray, November 28, 1958; [ch.] Jennifer Claire, Peter Russel; [ed.] Princeton U, U. of Pennsylvania, Temple U.; [occ.] Professor of English, Delaware County Community College, Media, PA; [memb.] National Education Assn, Scriblerus Society, Popular Culture Association; [hon.] Full College Scholarship, Lee Tire Corp., High Honors Undergraduate Thesis, Honorable, Graduate School Research Competition; [oth. writ.] Articles on Orwell, Futuristic Films, International Sports, and Detective Fiction in various Journals and Books; [pers.] I strive to mingles the alternative sonnet structures of cummings, quotidian irony of Macleish, and sixties rhythms of Ricky Nelson.; [a.] Swarthmore, PA

GRAYS, ADRIAN D.
[b.] July 24, 1978, San Diego, CA; [p.] Mr. and Mrs. Stacy and Linda Grays; [ch.] One sister and 4 brothers I'm the youngest; [ed.] In high school 11th grade my age is 16; [occ.] Not working at this time; [oth. writ.] Love to write rap music and music in the future!; [a.] San Diego, CA

GRAYSON, HARVEY L.
[pen.] Harvey L. Grayson; [b.] June 5, 1930, Laredo, TX; [p.] Charles E. Grayson, Audra B. Grayson; [ed.] Phyllis Wheatley High, Portland CC College, Oregon, Ron Bailie School of Broadcasting, Grammar and Reading Teacher; [occ.] Radio and TV Communications; [hon.] Certificate of Recognition for being selected as "Most Inspirational"; [pers.] To say what's in my heart so that others might benefit through my wisdom.; [a.] Seattle, WA

GREASON, JULIE
[pen.] Julie Greason (Julz); [b.] October 7, 1966; [occ.] Artist, musician, writer; [hon.] Performance Painter, HYPHEN-8 Art Gallery and Graphics, Lower Downtown Arts District, Denver, Colorado, Third Place Poetry 1994 National Writer's Association Denver Metro Chapter; [pers.] To me art is a verb, so I dance, paint, sing and write. This brings me happiness, this, and good friends.; [a.] Denver, CO

GREEN, ALICE MAE
[b.] September 21, 1959, Greenville, MS; [p.] Alice Green, Tommy Green, Tennie Lee; [ch.] Antonio Marquette, Myshawna Maeyon; [ed.] Greenville High, Coahoma Jr. College, Miss. Delta Jr. College; [occ.] Non-working-handicap, disabled; [memb.] American Heart Assoc., USO; [hon.] Dean's List; [oth. writ.] Ghetto Child, How Do I Say Thank You published in local newspapers; [pers.] I write solely about situations I've found myself in and my everyday surroundings. I hope that someday someone will read my poems and see whatever situation they are in they are never alone. God is always there. I was greatly inspired by Ruth Porter.; [a.] Los Angeles, CA

GREEN, BENJAMIN DEARDORFF
[b.] February 8, 1974, Fort Wayne, IN; [p.] Charlotte Deardorff and Don Green; [ed.] East Lansing High School Lansing Community College; [occ.] University of Michigan of Art

GREEN, DIANE JACOB
[pen.] Sweet Dee; [b.] December 29, 1945, Los Angeles; [p.] Daniel and Jessie Smith; [m.] Martin D. Green;

[ch.] Fred Jacob, De Carol Jacob Yvette Jacob, Cherri Jacob; [ed.] Centennial High School Compton Jr. College LA City College; [occ.] Accounting; [memb.] Glorybound M B Church, Pastors Aid, First Aid/Church Nurse; [hon.] Best Grandmother 1995; [oth. writ.] Ms. Sweets, Old McAdoo, A Message/Black Woman, and many others - none published; [pers.] I have only two fictional characters in my collection. Mostly, I write about real life issues and spiritual thoughts.; [a.] Compton, CA

GREEN, MELISSA SHIRE
[pen.] Lucy M. King; [b.] February 5, 1978, Houma, LA; [p.] Frank Eulous Green, Vickie J. Arendall; [ed.] Sequoyah High School; [occ.] Part-time cashier; [memb.] National Beta Club, Future Georgia Educators; [hon.] Summa Cum Laude on National Latin Exam, County Level Governor's Honors; [oth. writ.] Several poems published in school literary magazine, the Phoenix; [pers.] When we cannot love, we are locked within the boundaries of our own cold hearts, but when we can, the world is our for the traversing. I owe everything to Clifford J. Edmisten. Without whom I would never have known the joys nor the sorrows to be had. I must say, "Thank you, my dear."; [a.] Woodstock, GA

GREEN, WILLIAM J.
[b.] December 24, 1973, Philadelphia, PA; [p.] William and Linda Green; [ed.] Cardinal O'Hara High School ('91) Currently enrolled at St. Joseph's University; [occ.] Full time student; [oth. writ.] Previously published in "in other words" (Western Reading Service Anthology); [pers.] I write because I enjoy writing, and after, all, the secret to happiness is to do what makes you happy.; [a.] Philadelphia, PA

GREENBERG, MIRIAM
[b.] April 7, 1923, Brooklyn, NY; [p.] Deceased; [m.] Harry, October 30, 1945; [ch.] Susan Beth, Betty Ellen; [ed.] BA Psychology, MA Health Administration (Cert.) Motivation Therapy; [occ.] Retired, Admin. of Resid. for Adult Retardates; [memb.] AWVS (WW II) Vots, NCJW, writer's club, poetry club; [hon.] Love and respect from those I've helped to live a more meaningful life, blind, aged, retarted and depressed.; [oth. writ.] Articles for public in community papers, novel, short stories, poems, asst. writings for writer's club, family, geneology are non-published works; [pers.] Began volunteer work during WW II, continue to do so today. Lead a group in support of visual handicaps.; [a.] Pembroke Pines, FL

GREENE, BURKES GERALD
[ed.] BA VC Long Beach, CA, Graduate work VC Long Beach, CA; [occ.] Writer; [oth. writ.] Fiction in Essence, Black World; [pers.] Beauty does not exist in the abstract, nor is beauty shrouded in mist, beauty attaches to something, to someone. You can touch beauty, then, you are immortal.; [a.] San Pedro, CA

GREENLIEF, ROBERT L.
[b.] May 30, 1946, Glenville WA; [m.] Mabil E. Greenlief, February; [ch.] Robert Jr. and Linda R.; [ed.] High School Grad; [occ.] Retired; [pers.] Having a positive attitude is bathing in the wisdom of life; [a.] Minerva, OH

GREER, DYANNA
[pen.] Dyanna; [b.] June 7, 1962, Texas; [p.] Connie and Cassie Greer; [ch.] Antoino Greer Bianca Ebony Dawn Cooper; [ed.] Palm Springs High; [occ.] Telephone operator; [memb.] Young Adults group at church; [pers.] Though my writing I love to put a smile on others face and a good feeling on the inside.; [a.] Palm Springs, CA

GREGORY, PATRICK
[pen.] Kandy Carter; [b.] November 9, 1969, Panorama City, CA; [p.] Nancy Gregory; [oth. writ.] Lots of poems unpublished or even submitted; [pers.] Poetry, to me, is an expression of emotion, an outlet a vent, a release...Writing it keeps me from going mad.; [a.] Palmdale, CA

GRESHAM, MARVIN
[b.] January 9, 1956, Chicago; [p.] Willie and Florence Gresham; [m.] Diana Gresham, January 22, 1992; [ch.] D'anna - Valre, Trinnetta, Davia, Marcella, Macolm M. Y., Gresham's; [ed.] James N. Thorp Elementary Bowen High School; [occ.] Home Improvement Owner and Store Owner; [memb.] Transformation Baptist Church; [hon.] National Library of Poetry, International Society of Poet of Merit; [oth. writ.] Presently - working on a book of poetry; [pers.] I search for the goodness in mankind and with these emotional feeling within. I wish with all my heart, and help from God to find it. I'm motivated by God and self. To find the true meaning of life.; [a.] Chicago, IL

GRIFFIN, BARBARA JEAN GOOCHER KLABIUS
[pen.] Barbara "Blair" Griffin; [b.] November 7, 1937, Detroit, MI; [p.] Edward P. Goocher and Dora Elizabeth Brainard Goocher; [ch.] Kimberly E. Klabius, Samantha L. Klabius, John A. Klabius; [ed.] Roosevelt High 1955, Anthony Real Estate Schl. - Broker 1967, DeAnza College 1968, CA Life Insurance, CA Fire and Casualty, Second Degree Reiki; [occ.] Owner - "Financial Services" Real Estate Broker, Mortgage Broker, Life and Casualty agent, Real Estate Developer, Prof. Artist, Sculpturess; [memb.] International Sculpture Society, Space and Technology Center of the High Desert, Hi Desert Church of Religious Science, Teaching of the Inner Christ, American Owners and Breeders of Peruvian Paso Horses; [hon.] Peruivan Paso Champion Horse Breeder, Skin Diver of the Year - MI Councel 1964, CEN-CAL Woman Diver of the Year 1967, Who's Who of American Women, Who's Who in the West, Who's Who in Finance; [oth. writ.] Several articles on skin diving events for "Underwater Diver"; presently working on spiritual awakening through channeling.; [pers.] I am on this earth plane to teach that we are all connected to the Oneness and to share the beauty that dwells within all of us and within all creation.; [a.] Applevalley, CA.

GRIZZLE, LINDA MARIE JOHNSTON
[pen.] Linda Grizzle; [b.] Febraury 17, 1941, St. Joseph, Atlanta; [p.] Lewis Johnston and Hazel Johnston; [m.] Frank Grizzle, April 18, 1975; [ch.] Genie Marie Sanderst and Frank Grizzle Jr. 2 Grandsons James and Shane Sanders; [ed.] Went 2 years in Nineth grade took tenth grade subjects in 2 year if ninth except Geography; [occ.] Housewife and Mother-of 18 years old; [memb.] Have been of lost Mountain Babtist and now New Zion Babtist of Acworth; [oth. writ.] I have wrote other poems but nothing ever happen I have other poems. My son Frank thanksgiving and Christmas; [pers.] I love to wite poems in my spare time I love God and I loved writing this poem for him. And I love being a Christain and helping people

GROGHAN, HEATHER
[b.] August 23, 1980, Akron, OH; [p.] Ronald and Franchetta Groghan; [ed.] Freshman at Cuyahoga Falls High School; [occ.] Student; [memb.] People to People Student Ambassadors; [hon.] Two Presidential Academic Fitness Awards. Went to Australia, New Zealand with People to People. Rotary Scholar; [oth. writ.] Two time member of power of the Pen. Poetry competition at Kent State Reading Festival; [pers.] Live up to your greatest expectation, even if you have to fight to get there. Never quit while you on the way there.; [a.]

Cuyahoga Falls, OH

GROSSANO, DEBRA
[b.] July 17, 1960, Montclair, NJ; [p.] Joseph Dorer, Barbara Dorer; [ch.] Timothy, Lisa, Christopher; [occ.] Stained Glass Artist; [oth. writ.] Articles, poetry, and short stories in both local and national magazines and newspapers.; [a.] Phoenix, AZ

GROVES JR., WILLIAM F.
[b.] November 26, 1970, Chas. SC; [p.] William and Patricia Groves; [m.] Karine; [ed.] Bishop England High School, 1 year of College; [occ.] Musician/Composer and Songwriter with Thorn OIL (a band for Chas SC Wich releases their first album "Spaceless" in June 1995 on Zogo Records.); [oth. writ.] I am currently working on an illustrated volume of my poetry entitled "Equilibrium."; [a.] Hanahan, SC

GRUCZKOWSKI, LEAH
[b.] May 17, 1971, Corning, NY; [p.] Irene; [ed.] Notre Dame High School - Elmira, NY Marietta College, Marietta, OH; [occ.] Membership Coordinator, LPGA Tournament Sponsors Assoc. - Stockbridge, GA; [pers.] No matter what you choose to do in life do it with passion.; [a.] Stockbridge, GA

GRUNEWALD, KATHY
[pen.] Kathy Grunewald; [b.] November 7, 1959, Tarzana, CA; [ed.] Taft high School. Received Associate in Arts degree from Los Angeles Pierce College. Currently, in the Honors English program at California State University, Northridge working toward Bachelor of Arts degree in Honor English.; [occ.] Former I was an American Tang Soo Do Karate instructor until I returned to college. I am now a student.; [hon.] I received my first and second-degree black belts within the karate organization The American Tang Soo Do Alliance. I received the English Department Memorial Scholarship Award at Lost Angeles Pierce College twice in two separate years.; [oth. writ.] I have had poems and a short story published in college literary magazines.; [pers.] I am an aspiring English Teacher.; [a.] Woodland Hills, CA

GRZEGORCZYK, EVA MONICA
[b.] August 30, 1977, Poland; [p.] Mary and Stanley; [ed.] Lourdes HS Chicago, IL currently at Loyola University, Chicago, IL pre-med major in Psychology; [occ.] Administrative Asst. at state farm ins.; [memb.] American Cancer Society, National Honor Society, United States Achievement Academy, Who is Who Nomination; [hon.] Creative writings First Place (1995), Honorable Mention (1995), and Second Place (1994); [oth. writ.] Multiple poems published in school senior books; [pers.] Life without love is no life at all love poems are a food for the soul, like bread is food for the body.; [a.] Chicago, IL

GUATELLI, ROSE M.
[b.] December 8, 1920, USA; [p.] Mary and Joseph Sottile; [m.] John L. Guatelli (Deceased), September 7, 1947; [ch.] Susan, John, Debbie and Richard; [ed.] Cuny-BBA, Marin Community College Assoc. Arts Degree, Washington Irving H.S.; [occ.] Retired; [memb.] Noetic Society, Sierra Club, Marin Society of Artists, Elder Hostel, KQED, Center for Attitudinal Healing; [hon.] Wanamaker Award, Marin Society of Artists - Cash Award Beta Gamma Sigma; [oth. writ.] "Time", the Poets' Guild "Windows at the Door" - Sparrowgrass Poetry Forum Inc., "the Waterfront", Poetry Press; [pers.] I agree with Scott Pecks Book on Civility - "A World Waiting To Be Born." Someday we will be a neurosis free generation where the heart rules the head and love will predominate in the world; [a.] San Rafael, CA

GUBERMAN, ALLAN N.
[b.] April 2, 1951, Bronx, NY; [p.] Leon and Lola, both deceased; [ed.] M.S. in Education, Rehabilitation Counseling, Hunter College, N.Y.C; [occ.] Supervisor of (NYS, Mental Health Facility) Rehabilitation Services; [memb.] National Rehabilitation Association, National Rehabilitation Counselors Association, Vocational Evaluation and Work Adjustment Association, Certified Rehabilitation Counselors (CCRCC); [hon.] Undergraduate college dean's list; [oth. writ.] One poem published in Many Voices, Many Lands - Anthology of Poetry (Vol. I, Number 1, Summer 1987 - ISBN 0-940861-00-3), articles in hospital's newsletter; [pers.] Working with a psychiatric population, I tend to write poems which reflect the twists, turns, stumbles and falls a mind can take. Of course, that's not to say my own mind is not encumbered by such false realities. Still, I usually strive for humor using puns and strange imagery to depict situations that may or may not be my own false reality.; [a.] Brooklyn, NY

GUINN, GEORGE C.
[pen.] Cliff Guinn; [b.] March 23, 1945, Yakima, WA; [p.] John Guinn and Helen Guinn; [m.] Jacqueline, July 29, 1989; [ch.] Two; [ed.] Whiteswan High, WA Univ. Maryland, Stuttgart Germany; [occ.] Artist, sculpturist writer; [memb.] Disabled American Vet, 1st Cavalry Assoc., 7th Inf. Assoc. Toastmaster's Int, First Southern Baptist Church; [hon.] Area Toastmaster 1995; [oth. writ.] Invited to recite poetry at numerous local events; [pers.] Look for humor in life, practice humility but never be ashamed or embarrassed of excellence in achievement.; [a.] Salinas, CA

GULLAND, DAPHNE
[b.] July 4, 1953, London; [m.] August 28, 1974; [ch.] 4; [ed.] Virgo Fidelis Grammar School, Bedford College, University of London; [occ.] Writer; [memb.] Friends of the Earth; [hon.] 11+ London for English and German; [oth. writ.] The Penguin Dictionary of English Idioms; the Langenscheidt dictionary of English similes; [pers.] The English language is a great treasure. Let us strive to enjoy it and pass our knowledge and love of reading onto our children.; [a.] Vienna, Austria.

GUNN, ELIZA M.
[pen.] Mae Gunn; [b.] May 15, 1979, Gansville, Fl; [p.] Diane and Kenny Adams; [ed.] 1-6 many different schools, 7th-10th Lecanto (Florida); [memb.] Drama Club; [hon.] My school work is what comes first, I always have academic achievement.; [oth. writ.] All of my poetry is how I felt at the time I wrote it. My poems are basically me. (None ever published); [pers.] My writings are my feelings. Instead of getting angary I get a pin. And always remember you can only achieve what you try for.; [a.] Homosassa Springs, FL

GUTHRIE, ALICE FAY
[pen.] Fay; [b.] November 11, 1941, Walker, CO; [p.] Nora and Lawrence Smith; [m.] Floyd A. Guthrie, February 28, 1974; [ch.] Greg, Joy, Johnny and Vanessa; [ed.] 12th grade Basic EMT (Emergency Medical Technician); [occ.] Home maker and Vol. Rescue Squad - EMT; [memb.] First Baptist Church of Carbon Hill, Carbon Hill, Vol. Rescue Squad National Geneological Society. (AARS) Ala.-Assoc., of Rescue Squads; [hon.] Sec and Trea of our Rescue Squad for 20 yrs., 1st Place in Competition of First Aid in Al., First Aid Team for Rescue Squad, 3rd Place in Quilting Quilts (hand made); [oth. writ.] Have not entered any of my other writings to any one. I just love to sit down and write something. I have songs written but never sent them to anyone; [pers.] I try to help those who don't have what I do. Such as with Vol. work. Food from my garden. I also help with the red cross vol. work.; [a.] Carbon Hill, AL

GUTHRIE, BEVERLY J.
[pen.] B. S. Guthrie; [b.] March 29, 1950, Atlanta, GA; [p.] Dot and Terrell Smith; [m.] Ronald W. Guthrie, July 27, 1974; [ch.] April and Aaron; [ed.] Russell High, Gainesville College, Lanier Tech, Pickens Tech.; [occ.] Deli Clerk; [hon.] Four years honor choir; [oth. writ.] Working on a new children's book; [pers.] I have been greatly infuenced by Elizabeth Barrett Browning and Psalm in the Bible; [a.] Cumming, GA

GUYOT, KATHLEEN
[b.] November 6, 1948, St. Charles, MO; [p.] Mr. and Mrs. Willard and Dolores Paul; [m.] Mr. Paul Guyot, January 8, 1972; [ch.] Sharon, Paul and George; [ed.] High School; [occ.] Housewife; [pers.] I have been greatly influence by my family and faith in God. I really enjoy writing poems, and stories. Although this is my first publish poem.; [a.] DeSoto, MO

HAACK, STEVE
[p.] Raymond and Sarah Haack; [ed.] Cardinal Hayes High School, Bronx, New York, Bronx Community College, Bronx, New York, Franklin University, Columbus, Ohio; [occ.] Electronics' Assembler; [oth. writ.] Commentary in College Newspaper Articles and a Poem in Company Newsletter; [pers.] "May the readers be more accepting of their creativity, of their traumas and the routines of daily life, and hide no longer in the closet of their private world", "Raymond Carver, Robert Bly and Rainer Maria Rilke have been an immense influence in my life and my writings."; [a.] Columbus, OH

HABEEB, WAREETHA
[pen.] Prissy; [b.] January 10, 1948, Buffalo; [p.] Shafeegh and Nafeesah Habeeb; [ed.] Going for my G.E.D. have 17 points to go.

HABER, IRENE
[pen.] Renee Haber; [b.] April 17, 1931, Philadelphia, PA; [p.] Mary Kravil, Walter Kravil; [m.] John Haber, January 27, 1951; [ch.] Jack, Bob, Cindy, Mark; [ed.] O.L.H. of Christians Elementary Nativity B.V.M., Commercial High School; [occ.] Retired Office Manager; [memb.] Certified CCD Teacher, Church Choir; [oth. writ.] Wrote School Play, wrote School Alma Mater Song. Wrote Songs for Recordings, wrote Several Poems; [pers.] I try to reflect in my poetry the true feelings that I cherish within my heart, and which I feel will touch the heart of other when they read it; [a.] Villas NJ

HADLEY, PATTY
[b.] November 17, 1954, Cincinnati, OH; [p.] Anna and Newel Hadley; [ed.] High School Graduate Norwood, Ohio; [occ.] Inventory Control Computer Operator; [memb.] The Humane Society Ladies VFW Victory Baptist Church; [hon.] Customer Care Award's from K-mart G.B.A. Sorority (High School); [oth. writ.] My poems are published in the Local News Paper.; [pers.] I write because it is a talent from God. Through my writing I hope to share hope and the love of Jesus to all. I love Poetry.; [a.] Russell Springs, KY

HAHN, JANET
[b.] March 10, 1961, Saint Louis, MO; [p.] James W. Redington, Teresea E. Long; [m.] Carl Hahn, July 29, 1989; [ch.] Marie Nichole, James Edward, Carl Hugh Jr., - all last names Hahn; [oth. writ.] Poems and Journals; [pers.] I write to express my feelings. To document my experiences. I am inspired by the love I feel for my family and friends and life itself.; [a.] Kirkwood, MS

HALL, JOHN DEE
[pen.] J. D.; [b.] October 12, 1950, Enid, OK; [p.] Frank and Margaret Hall; [ed.] Enid High, N. W University, Alva Oklahoma, University of Central Okla., B.A. Criminal Justice/Sociology, Kensington Univ., Glen-dale, Calif. M.A. Counseling Psychology; [occ.] Supportive Employment, Coordinator, Actor, Write; [memb.] Screen Actors Guild, Eligible American Guild of Variety Artist; [hon.] Certificates in achievement in American Assoc. for Marriage and Family Guidance, L. A. County Probation Department, Juvenile Division, Texas Department of Correction, Peace Officer; [oth. writ.] Several poems published in local newspaper, as well as music and original songs published; [pers.] I write about the tragedies of the struggle of people and about love, the loss of love and try to include the humor of our errors and how we grow as a result of our experiences

HALL, MARY ALICE
[b.] January 23, 1950, Cleveland, OH; [p.] Emma and John Kost; [m.] Frederick P. Hall Jr., March 7, 1970; [ch.] Rachel Marie Hall; [ed.] Graduate of Jane Addams Vocational High School; [pers.] Life is a continuous learning process in which I live one day at a time. Although I take life seriously, I still find time for fun and laughter.; [a.] Cleveland, OH

HAMLIN, KATHY A.
[b.] December 17, 1957, NJ; [p.] Robert and Randy Beebe; [m.] Ronald P. Hamlin Sr., May 14, 1994; [ch.] Al Wilson Jr., Michael Wilson, Lisa Beebe-Hamlin; [ed.] Pennsville High School Salem Community College Gloucester County College Salem County Vocational School; [occ.] Owner of Appliance Repair Business; [pers.] I try to live each day to the Fullest, for tomorrow will come and go, it will only leave memories for us to Carry through this life.; [a.] Sonora, CA

HAMMERS, MARISOL
[pen.] Mari Hammers; [b.] August 15, 1966, San Juan, PR; [p.] Luis Mulero, Ana Molina; [m.] Lawrence Hammers, June 25, 1994; [ch.] Angela Marie, Jorge Luis, Tom Keith; [ed.] West Aurora High, Waubonsee College; [occ.] L.D. Teacher's Assist. Cowherd Middle School, Aurora, IL; [oth. writ.] I have Several fine poems that I have not presented and have not been published; [pers.] As my heart is fulfilled with love that is and love that never was I get inspire to write poetry by the everyday struggle of mankind to share love with one another. Inspire by the beautiful ways of nature taken for granted. Love surpasses eternity; [a.] Aurora, IL

HAMMONDS, SHIRLEY
[b.] August 22, 1935, Porum, OK; [p.] Star and Elsie Largent; [m.] Nathan Hammonds, March 25, 1955; [ch.] Steven Warren, Mark Allen, Kathy Ann; [ed.] McFarland High, Bakersfield City College; [occ.] Homemaker; [oth. writ.] Local newspaper, Church Bulletins

HANLON, SHERRI
[pen.] Sammi Hanlon; [b.] April 8, 1981, Saint Louis, MO; [p.] Tim and Linda Hanlon; [ed.] I attend Wentzville Junior High School in Wentzville Missouri; [hon.] I am an honor student at Wentzville Jr. High; [oth. writ.] I have had one poem published in Anthologies of Young Americans. I have also won writing contests at my school.; [pers.] "If you wake up each morning and all you can think about is writing, then you're a writer, "and that's what I have become!"; [a.] Foristell, MO

HANSON, PETER T.
[b.] July 10, 1973, Biddeford, ME; [ed.] Biddeford High School, B.S. from Franklin Pierce College Major: Leisure Services Management Minor: Philosophy; [hon.] American Collegiate Poets - Special Awards; [oth. writ.] "Alone"; [pers.] The only certainty within this life worthy of attention is death. It is, therefore, the obligation of the living to face death properly, that is without remorse, regret or anxiety.; [a.] Biddeford, ME

HARARY, MERI M.

[b.] July 11, 1969, Brooklyn, NY; [p.] Albert Harary and Chaya Blitzer; [ed.] B.A. in English, University of Hartford, CT, Cum Laude; [occ.] Administrative Assistant, Yale Univ., and Student; [memb.] Principal Flutist, West Haven Symphony; [hon.] 2nd Place in Poetry, University of Hartford's Writing Competition, 1991, Schoen Scholarship, Published in The National Library of Poetry's Reflections of Light, inducted into Sigma Tau Delta, English Honor Society, Plays, Poetry. Research done in the positive effects the arts have on inner city children (and all children).; [oth. writ.] Writing is like a box of chocolates - you never know what you're going to get until after you try it!; [pers.] Hamden, CT

HARAST, RON L.

[b.] January 19, 1969, Chicago, IL; [p.] Lawrence and Julie Harast; [ed.] Morton East High; [memb.] Ballys Chicago Health Clubs; [pers.] I am basically just someone who, when inspired by something, will reach inside and pull out all emotions I'm feeling, and just let the pen keep writing, and I'm usually amazed at what I've done, when I'm finished.; [a.] Norridge, IL

HARDIN, BRET

[pen.] B. H.; [b.] August 24, 1970, Toledo, OH; [ch.] Amber Marie, Ashley Nicole; [ed.] University of Toledo; [occ.] Burlington Air Express; [pers.] Life is a poem; [a.] Toledo, OH

HARDIN, CANDACE

[pen.] Candace Olivia Hardin; [b.] November 8, 1976, TX; [p.] Cecil and Cathy Hardin; [ed.] Graduation pending May 27, 1995 from Stephen F. Austin High in Port Arthur; [occ.] Secretary at Stephen F. Austin School; [memb.] National Honor Society, Business Professionals of America; [hon.] 2nd place in State for poetry and essay in Catholic Daughters of America Contest; [oth. writ.] Several unpublished short stories, manuscript, and poem; [pers.] This particular poem is dedicated to my Grandfather Henry Hardin and to all the loved ones he left behind. We know you'll always be with us.; [a.] Port Arthur, TX

HARDING, CONNIE

[b.] December 31, 1939, New Rome, OH; [p.] Ralph and Pearl Laff; [ch.] 3 children, 5 grandchildren; [ed.] Columbus West High School, self taught in word processing, previous Legal Secretary; [occ.] Semi-Retired and self employed; [oth. writ.] Other poems - non published, I share information through letters printed in American Astrology's "Many Things", including several accurate earthquake predictions documented by them (AA); [pers.] I dabble with herb gardening, make and sell potpourri in a family market, I study and practice the ancient art of astrology and do horoscopes when asked, being published in "Beyond the Stars" would be an honor.; [a.] Columbus, OH

HARMS, BLAIRE

[b.] June 9, 1967, Berkeley, CA; [m.] Stuart Hirstein, June 25, 1994; [ch.] Austin Xavier; [ed.] Bethesda-Chevy Chase H.S., CSU, Chico (undergraduate), Syracuse University (graduate); [occ.] United States Army, Military Intelligence Officer; [pers.] This poem is dedicated to the campers and staff at Copper Creek Camp, Greenville, CA

HARPER, JAMES H.

[pen.] Jim Harper; [b.] September 15, 1949, Gallatin, TX; [p.] Howard and Ila Harper; [m.] Christine Johnson Harper, September 4, 1982; [ch.] Timothy Wright, James Adam; [ed.] Masters Bachelors, Stephen F. Austin State Univ., High School (Rusk, TX), Post Grad., East Texas State Univ.; [occ.] Associate Clinical Psychologist, Risk State Hospital; [memb.] Psi Chi (Na-

tional Honor Society) Psychology, North American Association of Masters in Psychology, Trinity Lutheran Church Usher Board, Board of Directors Cherokee Civic Theatre; [hon.] (Psychology) National Honor Society, College, National Honor Society High School, Best Actor, U.I.C. District; [oth. writ.] Unpublished poetry, published - Journal Aritche in Psychology Journal - (1988); [pers.] I attempt to express the struggle to attend to the passive and quietly beautiful aspects of nature and mankind. I enjoy history and my family.; [a.] Rusk, TX

HARRINGTON, SEAN A.

[b.] July 11, 1976, Baltimore, MD; [p.] Corinthia Johnson, Willie Harrington; [ed.] Edmondson/Westside High, Catonsville Community College; [memb.] National Honor Society, Baltimore Church of God Theater Group; [hon.] Baltimore City Community College Annual Recognition Ceremony Honoree, Member of the National Honor Society, Delegate Scholarship; [oth. writ.] Poem entitled "The Mysterious Woman", novel entitled "Day's End" (both unpublished); [pers.] I feel that writing gives me an emotional outlet to express the way I feel at a certain time.; [a.] Baltimore, MD

HARRIS, AMANDA K.

[b.] July 31, 1974, Philadelphia, PA; [p.] Margaret R. and Daniel P.; [ed.] Germantown Friends School and Bard College; [occ.] College Student, part-time waitress; [memb.] Society of Friends (quaker meeting), planned parenthood volunteer, Rape/Crisis Center Counselor; [hon.] Alum. of PA Governor's School for the arts (in fiction writing), Various Academic Scholarships; [oth. writ.] Letter to editor published in Philadelphia Inquirer; [pers.] I gain strength and inspiration from the voices of women, while striving to achieve what Virginia Woolf terms "The Androgynous Mind of the Writer".; [a.] Philadelphia, PA

HARRIS, CATHERINE M.

[b.] March 8, 1967, Libertyville, IL; [occ.] Administrative Assistant; [pers.] Every poem I have written has been inspired by family and friends. Beauty is always within your reach, you just have to look for it in the things you love most.

HARRIS, DONNA DENISE

[b.] December 30, 1971, Detroit, MI; [p.] Kenneth Harris Sr., Joyce Harris; [ch.] Terrance Scott Jr., Camille A. Yates; [ed.] Frank Cody High, Wayne County Community College; [memb.] Renaissance Baptist Church Youth Dept. Counselor; [hon.] Nominee for The Poet of the year 1995 from the International Society of Poets; [oth. writ.] I have written several poems inspired by people and the emotional/spiritual highs and lows we all face.; [pers.] I have been greatly blessed with this gift to write The secret is to pray for inspiration. So far my prayers have been answered.; [a.] Detroit, MI

HARRIS, ROSSILAND R.

[b.] July 23, 1965, Houston, TX; [p.] Carol J. Chaney (1949-1991); [m.] Carl W. Reed; [ch.] Broderick Antoine, Marcus LeKeith, Kevin Jerome, Carl Wayne; [occ.] Teachers' Assistant, Houston, TX; [oth. writ.] I have a number of poems that have neither been published or received. However, In my opinion are as allusive as the one published here.; [pers.] My poetry travels many different avenues from affairs of the heart to reflections of the mind and soul.; [a.] Houston, TX

HARRIS, STAN

[b.] January 28, 1952, Fresno, CA; [p.] Jack and Leona Rogers; [m.] Cecilia, June 25; [ch.] Sherrie, Heather, David; [ed.] Grey High - Idable Oklahoma; [occ.] Environmental Assistant Saint Agnes Hospital, Fresno Calif.; [oth. writ.] Poems - Songs - Novels unpublished;

[pers.] Accept the challenges of life with an open mind, and a strong heart. Let go of the safety rope long enough to taste the freedom of being you.; [a.] Fresno, CA

HARRISON, BREYANNA SHALIMERE

[pen.] Brey; [b.] October 11, 1982, Columbus, GA; [p.] Mr. and Mrs. John and Francois Duncan; [ed.] Oakcrest Elem. Kettering Middle School; [memb.] Glenarden Church of Christ; [hon.] OM- Perfect Att. Honor roll, instrumental, girl scout, reading, great People to people student ambassador to England, Scotland, Wales, Ireland; [pers.] Strive to make your best better

HARRISON, JANIECE

[pen.] Niecey; [b.] April 18, 1980, Washington, DC; [p.] Larry and Millian Harrison; [ed.] High School (school without walls); [occ.] Student; [memb.] Friends 4 Ever, American Legion, Junior Auxiliary Unit #5; [pers.] I try to let the truth be acknowledge in my poems.; [a.] Washington, DC

HART, PHIL

[b.] July 5, 1977, Raleigh, NC; [p.] Phil Hart Sr., Laurie Ann Hagwood; [ed.] Bunn High School; [memb.] DECA, Bottom Line Writes Group; [hon.] National Deca Leadership Conference; [pers.] I enjoy writing vaguely, it makes the reader think. I believe all things are equal, humans, plants, reptiles and we all have an equal contribution to the world, so we should make the most of it.; [a.] Youngsville, NC

HARVEY, ALFREDA D.

[pen.] Freda Harvey Cook; [b.] November 24, 1947, Philadelphia, PA; [p.] Daniel and Johnnie Mae Harvey; [m.] Thomas Cook; [ch.] Clyde Davis; [ed.] William Penn High School for Girls, Community College for Liberal Arts; [occ.] Certified Nursing Assistant; [memb.] Volunteered at Miquion School Library, Suburban General Hosp., American Red Cross; [pers.] I feel that I'm guided to write by a guardian Angel who in my lifetime can make a change or a difference in the world, my goals are to write something positive, to make a lasting impression on mankind; [a.] Philadelphia, PA

HASTINGS, JEANNE

[pen.] Jeanne Hastings; [b.] July 15, 1909, Osman, IL; [p.] Pauline Held and Walter Hill; [m.] Rufus D. Hastings; [ed.] BFA San Jose State College, CA. entered age 32, Washington University, Seattle, WA, Alfred University, New York, New York University, New York City; [occ.] Painting, writing, enjoying friends; [memb.] LARAC, I was one of five who designed the Lower Adirondack Regional Art Council, Riverside Gallery, and several political organizations; [hon.] Miss Arizona, 1925, BFA, with great distinction and honors in Art, Declared a John R. Silbey Professor at Sandhills Community College Pinehurst, No. Carolina, 1967 Recognized with Appreciation for Excellence in Instruction, 1966-70, 1985-88, "Jeanne Hastings Gallery of Fine Arts"- Sandhills Community College, 1988, Many one-woman shows in Paintings and Crafts; [oth. writ.] So You Want to Paint, The Ness Fairies, Many poems; [pers.] My life has been full of many things. Best of all were my years of teaching, and having dear and caring relatives and friends who have understood my way of life.

HASTINGS, WILLIAM WOODLAND

[pen.] Peacefarmr@ Aol. Com; [b.] January 12, 1960, New York; [p.] V. Stevens, Antoinette P. Hastings; [ed.] Autodidact; [occ.] Environmental and Planning Deputy to an L.A. Councilman; [memb.] Numerous environmental and social justice organizations; [oth. writ.] Self-published Compilations: "Out of the well" "The Pizzocentric Universe and other Revolutionary Theories" "Crumbs from the Poem Jar; [pers.] "Why invent heaven or hell with stars in the sky and water in the well"; [a.] Topanga, CA

HAWLEY, BETH MARIE
[pen.] Beth Marie Reelhorn; [b.] February 10, 1951, Columbus, OH; [p.] Richard and Annabelle Reelhorn; [m.] Robert E. Hawley, August 9, 1986; [ch.] Thane Richard, Darlene, Amy Marie; [ed.] Watkins memorial H.S. Grant Hospital School of Nursing; [occ.] Cardiac Care R.N, CCRN Mt. Carmel East Hosp. Columbus Ohio; [memb.] Peace United Methodist Church, American Association of Critical care Nurses; [oth. writ.] Poems for family and friends; [pers.] My writing is influenced by my faith, my family and twenty-three years of nursing experience.; [a.] Pickerington, OH

HAYNES, LINDA F.
[b.] August 13, 1948, Portsmouth, VA; [p.] Rev. and Mrs. Leroy I. Scott; [ch.] Tracey Hawkins, Julian Roulhac and Crystal Roulhac; [ed.] I.C. Norcom High School, Tidewater Community College; [occ.] Supervisor, Christian Broadcasting Network; [oth. writ.] Other Poetry and Essays; [pers.] I write to express on paper, the emotions that are normally hard to express verbally.; [a.] Portsmouth, VA

HEARN, GLORIA WILLIAMS
[pen.] Gloria Hearn; [b.] April 22, 1934, Greenwood, LA; [p.] James C. Williams and Mary Thelma Robertson Williams; [m.] Dr. George Earl Hearn, June 22, 1956; [ch.] Patricia Gail Hearn Smith, George Eugene Hearn (deceased); [ed.] B.A. - Louisiana Tech. University, Ruston, LA, M.Ed. - LaState University - Baton Rouge, Further Study: Baylor, Tulane, N.S.U., U.S.L., U of Cal. at Pamoner; [occ.] Consultant and Entrepreneur; [memb.] American Association of University Women, Delta Kappa Gamma, Association for Childhood Education International, Matinee Music Club, First Baptist Church of Pineville, Rapides Arts and Humanities Board; [hon.] Special Citation for Outstanding Service - Rapides Parish School Board, England Air Force Base Elementary School, Outstanding Educator Award, Outstanding Service Award Association for Childhood Education International; [oth. writ.] The Fickle Mrs. Whiskers and other Cat Tales, "The Arts, A Tool for Developing the Seeing Eye in Adolescents", Kindergarten Position Paper (for Louisiana ACEI), The Pebble Book - resource book through State Dept. of Education (Louisiana); [pers.] I believe that everyone has the right to become all he/she can become because everyone is valuable and unique. As a teacher I have been dedicated to making sure everyone has his/her turn. Beauty is everywhere if you nurture it.; [a.] Pineville, LA

HEARN, JAMES A.
[b.] January 15, 1975, Long Beach, CA; [p.] Neill Hearn, Barbara Hearn; [occ.] Student; [oth. writ.] This is my first poem taken outside of my room; [pers.] We are all so alone in a billion different ways. In my writing I strive to awaken this fear; [a.] Cerritos, CA

HEFFELFINGER, CHUCK
[b.] July 19, 1951, Freeport, IL; [p.] John and Viola Heffelfinger; [m.] Georgia (Gigi) Heffelfinger, January 18, 1981; [ch.] Stephanie, Charles, Ashley, Michael; [ed.] Morrison Community High School Morrison, Illinois; [occ.] Sign-painter and Musician; [memb.] Calvary Chapel Church; [hon.] In 1970, Placed first in State of Illinois, American Legion Auxiliary Poppy Poster Contest; [oth. writ.] Over 200 poems and writings that are set to music; [pers.] My inspiration for music and art come from personal experiences as I learn to live as a Christian; [a.] Monroe, WI

HEINKE, KATHRYN
[b.] October 5, 1916, Goldhar, WA; [p.] Gladys and George Cross; [m.] Ray R. Heinke, January 24, 1933; [ch.] Ronald R. Heinke, Arlene Miller (5 Grandchildren and 2 Great Grandchildren); [ed.] High School Graduate, Everett High School - Wash. State; [occ.] Retired (Insurance Agent); [memb.] Member - Eastern Star; [pers.] The poem was written and included with Genealogy Papers and information given to my family on Christmas 1994

HEINZ, WILLIAM L.
[pen.] William L. Heinz; [b.] April 25, 1922, Chicago; [p.] Edward and Adeline Heinz; [m.] Virginia L. Heinz, March 17, 1984; [ed.] PH.B Loyola V. (Chicago); [occ.] Retired; [memb.] Currently a student of Ramtha's School of Enlightenment, Velm, Washington; [oth. writ.] Several poems published in The Golden Thread in Velm, WA., A book of Poems and Stories, Called: "Reflections From... The Chairman of the Board"; [pers.] My writings come from a major shift of my consciousness inspired by Ramtha, Conducting school in Velm, Washington; [a.] Rainier, WA

HENRICH, CYNTHIA J.
[occ.] Veterinary Assistant; [pers.] I write to express the contents of my heart, feelings I hold for life, love and spirituality. In sharing my writings, I hope to touch others by expressing what they too feel, but may not be able to express in words themselves.; [a.] Woodstock, GA

HENRY, EDWIN A.
[b.] March 28, 1976, Queens, NY; [p.] Edwin Henry, Phyllis Henry; [ed.] East Islip High School, Suffolk County Community College; [occ.] Student; [pers.] My writings come from my heart. I write what I feel. I feel what I write. My heart is my greatest influence.; [a.] Islip Terrace, NY

HENSLEY, JANICE S.
[pen.] Jan; [b.] September 18, 1943, Flag Pond, TN; [p.] Bruce Shelton, Rosa Lee Shelton; [m.] Seaphus A. Hensley, August 24, 1985; [ch.] Freeman E. Harris, Roger B. Harris, Rose Marie Brown, Barbara L. Sawyer, (step-daughter) JoAnn Hensley, Granddaughter: Sheena Nicole Harris; [ed.] Unicoi Co. High School Graduate, Licensed Practical Nurse, graduate of Tenn. Technical Voc. School, Crossville, Tenn; [occ.] Housewife - Career in Nursing for 20 years, unemployed due to bad health; [oth. writ.] I have a notebook of different writing, which I never sought publishing. "Fallen Nation", however, is being published this year by Famous Poets Society in an anthology called "Famous Poems of Today"; [pers.] I try to show the beauty and value of life, also the tragedy and loss of any loved one. The need for all people to care and always be mindful of others need, pain, and sorrow.

HERRMANN, DENNIS
[b.] March 18, 1943, Saint Paul, MN; [p.] Richard and Gertrude Herrmann; [ch.] Catrina "Laura" Lynn (now residing in 'Heaven'); [ed.] Glendale Comm. College; [occ.] Radiology Darkroom Tech.; [memb.] Former member of Professional Photographers of America, N.A.A.C.P., American Indian Relief Council; [hon.] Associates Degree with High Honors, Phi Theta Kappa, Dean's List; [oth. writ.] Local/National Newspapers and Mags, Poetry Booklet ("Sincerely For Life"); [pers.] "I approach my poetic/philosophical/photographic 'works' thru a 'Fish-Eye' lens. The 'Eye' may be 20/20 or 'jaundiced'. However, the 'Camera of Our Soul' never lies! Thus, I attempt to 'Encompass the Total 'Reflections' of Birth, Life, Death and 'The Hereafter'."; [a.] Phoenix, AZ

HICKS, KATHY
[pen.] K. M. Hicks; [b.] September 15, 1964, Cody, WY; [p.] Don and Evelyn Hicks; [m.] Sharla Hicks, November 21, 1993; [ch.] Kourtney, Age 6, Adrianne, Age 3; [ed.] A.A. Degree in psychology and English from Northwest College, Powell, WY. Attended Eastern Montana College in Billings, Mt.; [occ.] Traffic Control; [memb.] Community spirit; [hon.] Graduated with honors from Cody High School, Glenn Nielson Scholarship, Milward Simpson Scholarship, Honor Chorus Scholarship, Paul Stock Award for writing, Expository Award Scholarship, Progress in writing Award; [oth. writ.] Several poems, two science fiction short stories, expository work on Earl Durand, College Publications; [pers.] Writing has always been my way of freeing my spirit - anything I could ever possibly dream of can come true with words.; [a.] Cody, WY

HIGGINSON, ALLISON ABERNETHY
[b.] October 31, 1969, Vancouver, British Columbia, Canada; [p.] Gail Davies and James Abernethy; [m.] Sam Higginson, July 30, 1994; [ed.] Currently enrolled at University of Massachusetts, Amherst. Matthew McNair High School, Richmond, B.C. Canada; [occ.] Student; [pers.] History, especially personal history, sentiments and feelings are done justice on paper.; [a.] Amherst, MA

HILL, ALLEN A.
[pen.] Allen "Hook" Hill; [b.] April 3, 1921, Lordsburg, NM; [p.] Albert Hill and Fannie Allen; [m.] June Hatch, October 14, 1945; [ch.] Jeanne, Michael, Stephen, Dan, John, Robert; [ed.] Lordsburg, NM High School Utah State College (B.S.); [occ.] Middle school shop teacher, part-time contractor; [memb.] New Mexico Bootheel Cowboy Poets, Lordsburg-Hidalgo County Museum Board Chairman, Teachers Association of Lordsburg, Hidalgo County Literacy Council; [hon.] Phi Kappa Phi; [oth. writ.] Weekly column (5 years) for local newspaper. Col. entitled, "As I Remember. Many poems. Over 125 cowboy poems since 1991; [pers.] We need honest laughter in our society. I enjoy making people laugh, and I am able to accomplish that by reciting my cowboy poetry and through story-telling to many, many audiences. I have read in several cowboy poet gatherings and for all kinds of civic and private groups; [a.] Lordsburg, NM

HILL, BEULAH MAE
[b.] January 17, 1941, Dunn, NC; [p.] Lillie and John Spears; [m.] Rudolph Hill, December 29, 1963; [ed.] Harnett High School Dunn NC and Essex County Tec. in Newark New Jersey; [occ.] Housewife; [memb.] Franklin, St. John's United Methodist Church, a member of United Methodist Women; [hon.] Certificate of Credit Essex County Vocational School (Nurse's Aide; [oth. writ.] This is my second writing; [pers.] To have love and respect for every one; [a.] Newark, NJ

HILL, JODELL R.
[pen.] JoDell Smith, Jo Smith, Jodi, Renee; [b.] April 3, 1970, Medina, OH; [p.] Linda and Andy Anderson; [ed.] Graduated 1988 from Highland High, currently enrolled at Cuyahoga Community College, Parma, Ohio; [occ.] Lab. Tech.; [memb.] Rain Forest Rescue; [hon.] Poet of Merit, Nominated for Poet of the Year, Editors Choice Award for Poetry; [oth. writ.] Published in "Journey of the Mind", "Beyond the Stars", "East of the Sunrise", and "In the Garden of Life"; [pers.] I write with the desire for others to hopefully remember there's good and beauty in all things, no matter how small and insignificant they may seem.; [a.] Medina, OH

HILL, MRS. VIOLA FERN
[b.] August 18, 1928, Denmark, TN; [p.] Louie and Lydia Merriweather; [m.] Divorced; [ch.] (Grown) Vickie, Leah and Myrna; [ed.] Masters degree from De Paul University (Education major) Undergrad-Kentucky, State College Chicago Teacher's College; [occ.] Retired-Chicago Public School teacher 2nd Grade 33 years; [memb.] United Negro College Fund; [oth. writ.] Unfinished Autobiography. And some children's stories; [pers.] "Follow your dreams and help others if you can."; [a.] Chicago, IL

HILL, WENDY A.
[b.] December 25, 1957, Two Harbors, MN; [p.] Harriett M. Walsh; [m.] Timothy K. Hill, May 27, 1978; [ch.] Aaron Timothy, Brandon Michael; [ed.] Cook County High School, Grand Marais, MN, Bethel College, St. Paul, MN, Northwestern Connecticut Community Technical College, Winsted, CT; [occ.] Accountant; [memb.] Boy Scouts of America, Litchfield County Business and Professional Women's Club, Inc.; [hon.] Internship for Litchfield County Bus. and Professional Women's Club, Inc., Phi-Theta-Kappa, Dean's List, Biography Published in "The National Dean's List."; [pers.] My inspiration has been my family and my friends. I have always remembered where I came from and will treasure all my memories.; [a.] Torrington, CT

HILLER, KARL
[pen.] Joe Right; [b.] January 24, 1976, Camden, NJ; [p.] Albert Bruno, Caroline Louise; [ed.] Pennsauken High, Burlington County College; [occ.] Library Worker, Cinnaminson Library; [memb.] American Red Cross, Farragut Sportsman's Assoc.; [hon.] Invited to Recite at Gloucester County College Poetry Center; [oth. writ.] Many poems, several published in local circulars and Pennsauken's 1994 anthology, Images, short stories; [pers.] I am driven by a powerful inner force that must express itself.; [a.] Cinnaminson, NJ

HINCH, CRYSTAL L.
[pen.] Crystal Lenz; [b.] October 9, 1956, Fort Worth, TX; [p.] John W. Lenz, Lillian Jones; [m.] Michael D. Hinch, January 18, 1992

HINES, MARK P.
[b.] August 29, 1954, Orlando, FL; [p.] Ernest and Nancy Hines; [m.] Debra A. Hines, December 30, 1974; [ch.] Amy R. (19), Mark Jr. (17), Laura J. (15), Matthew S. (9); [ed.] BS Math Auburn University 1981; [occ.] Major USMC; [a.] Havelock, NC

HINZ, SHIRLEY ANN
[pen.] Shirley Sorensen Hinz; [b.] September 28, 1942, Denver, CO; [m.] Dale Edward Hinz; [ed.] Denver Lutheran High School, Denver, CO, Fort Lewis College, Durango, CO, Barnes Business College, Denver, CO; [occ.] Section Secretary, USDOI/NBS/MESC; [hon.] Underwood Corporation, "Outstanding Business Education Student", Award of Merit; [oth. writ.] For the past 10 years, I have been writing the story of my life as seen through the eyes of a wife of law enforcement. I hope this writing endeavor will be a tribute to the sacrifice and determination made by those wives of police officers.; [pers.] I enjoy writing for children using a moral, ethical or religious example hoping that children will read about values and begin to practice those values in their early life - our future is our children.; [a.] Ault, CO

HIROSE, NORIKO
[pen.] Aska Hirose; [b.] September 28, 1964, Tokyo; [pers.] Originally, I wished to be a classic pianist. Since I listened to Daryl Hall and John Oates, I have been absorbed in R & B, Pop Music. From several years ago, I started to write lyrics, poem, music. Now my dream is to be a songwriter in America.; [a.] Lost Island City, NY

HIXSON, TRINA K.
[pen.] Trina Kay; [b.] August 16, 1954, Sunbury, PA; [p.] Wilson J. and Evelyn V. Hixson; [ch.] Anthony, William and Christina; [ed.] Penncrest High, Antonelli's Medical and Professional Institute; [occ.] Diagnostic .Tech.; [pers.] I write about what moves me, whether it be nature or political conversations at work. Even with all this inspiration, I never would have started writing had it not been for the confidence brought by my man, Jason.; [a.] Pottstown, PA

HOBBS, MARVELLE
[b.] November 11, 1931, Temple, TX; [p.] Ottie and Jewell Ginn; [m.] Bill J. Hobbs, August 7, 1948; [ch.] Carolyn Ann, Janie Yvonne, Donna Jewell, Bill J. Jr.; [ed.] Lockney High School Watson's Business College; [occ.] Retired; [pers.] I strive to let my life show that I am a Christian, and my work is for the Lord.; [a.] Floydada, TX

HOBSON, MILDRED
[b.] November 9, 1945, Brooklyn, NY; [p.] Kenneth Hodge and Doris Hodge; [m.] Francis L. Hobson, September 10, 1978; [ch.] Katherine, Mary-Ellen, Frank Jr., Kenneth; [ed.] H.S. of Fashion Industries, N.Y., N.Y., Univ. of TX at El Paso (UTEP); [occ.] English; [memb.] The I.O. Foresters, St. Stephen Catholic Church, Rutas Magazine (UTEP), International Society of Poets; [hon.] Dean's list; [oth. writ.] Several published poems and many unpublished poems. Several articles published in the local newspaper; [pers.] In all my writings (past and future) I attempt to address the importance of every human-being. I have been deeply inspired by the satirical writers of Eighteenth Century during the time of the Enlightenment; [a.] El Paso, TX

HOBSON, MILDRED
[b.] November 9, 1945, Brooklyn, NY; [p.] Kenneth Hodge, Doris Hodge; [m.] Francis L. Hobson, September 10, 1978; [ch.] Katherine, Mary-Ellen, Frank Jr., and Kenneth; [ed.] H.S. of Fashion Industries, N.Y., N.Y. Univer. of TX, at El Paso (UTEP), Bachelor of Arts Degree/Educ., minor; [occ.] English Teacher; [memb.] The I.O. Foresters, St. Stephen Catholic Church, Rutas Magazine (UTEP), International Society of Poets; [oth. writ.] Two previous poems published in (A.) Songs on the Wind, (B.) Best Poems 1996, several unpublished poems. Several of my poems have also been published in the local newspaper.; [pers.] I attempt to address the importance and worth of every human being in my writings. I have been deeply inspired by the satirical writers of the 18th Century during the time of the Enlightenment; [a.] El Paso, TX

HOCKEY, KATHY
[pen.] Kathylene Massaro; [b.] November 22, Bay City, MI; [p.] Catherine and David Josephson; [m.] Rolland Hockey, August 11, 1962; [ch.] Mark Allen and Dawn Ann; [ed.] Bridgeport High School Delta College

HODGE, LEON
[pen.] The Kid who wonder; [b.] February 14, 1950, Valdosta, GA; [p.] Walter H. Hodge and Catherine; [ed.] Valdosta High Mt. Zional Elementary; [occ.] Acustodial at a Piedmont Hospital; [memb.] I can only say I'm a part time writer, worker, actor, singer and I loves to writes poem and sing and I got a passion acting especially in comedy; [oth. writ.] The trend, the stranger I a man, the kid who wonder I pity the fool, 'twas time my parent, it a different world stop the war, life, I have always these though; [pers.] My feeling on writing is I tend to bring out the feeling people have on every day life but as for who influenced that have to be the struggle of people life; [a.] Atlanta, CA

HOFRICHTER, LISA
[b.] December 29, 1964, New York City; [ed.] M.A.T. Sacred Heart University, B. A. Sociology Stephens College; [occ.] Teacher, working as a volunteer for special Olympics; [memb.] Council for Exceptional Children; [hon.] Counselor of the Year; [pers.] My words and images are the voice and eyes of my heart. Reading and experiencing many different ideas is my influence. I would like to thank my guide Tom Samose and the Greens, Lazarus, Kiggins, Bett, Chris, Anne, and all my other friends who encourage me to write.; [a.] Norwalk, CT

HOLCK, CHARLOTT L.
[b.] Felton, DE; [p.] Mr. and Mrs. Lott Ludlow; [m.] Bert Holck; [ch.] 2 boys; [ed.] Univ. of Del Newark DE Elem. Ed; [occ.] Guest teacher of Indian Lore; [memb.] Church Boy scouts; [pers.] Traveled a great deal. Much camping and canoeing; [a.] Landenberg, PA

HOLDREN, HEATHER E.
[b.] June 26, 1974, Elko, NV; [p.] Cindy Alvarado, Jim Holdren; [ed.] Dinnba High, MTI Western Business College; [occ.] I own my own sales and marketing firm called Concepts; [pers.] Love is the most powerful emotion known to mankind. It remains the same in life and in death. Love can be carried wherever one goes, whether it be far away or right beside you.; [a.] Reedley, CA

HOLLADAY, BARBARA KAY
[pen.] Barbara Clark Holladay; [b.] October 16, 1941, Pontiac, MI; [p.] Harold and Delight Clark; [m.] Daniel A. Holladay, July 14, 1962; [ch.] Kathy LaBelle and Cheryl Mendham; [ed.] Waterford Township High, Oakland Community College; [occ.] Homemaker/ writer; [hon.] Phi Theta Kappa; [oth. writ.] Poems in New Voices in American Poetry 1986 and 1987; [pers.] Unlike my spoken words, oftentimes forgotten, I have hopes that my written words will, in some small way, by a few... be remembered.; [a.] Waterford, MI

HOLLAND, BETTYE LUDY
[pen.] Lizabeth Hurst; [b.] August 13, 1936, Summerville, GA; [p.] Magnaest V. and Mamie D. Ludy; [m.] Leonard Just Holland, November 28, 1970; [ed.] Summerville High School, Livingstone College, Lewis College of Bus., University of Detroit Mercy; [occ.] Underwriter, Detroit, Michigan, US Dept. of Housing (HUD); [memb.] Fisher Theatre Playgoer, Amez Church Choir, Zeta Phi Beta Sorority, National Society of Poets, Self Trained Painter; [oth. writ.] Poem (copywrited), written for my husband's heroism during the "Battle of the Bulge". Set to the tune of "Trees".; [pers.] Greatly influenced by Michelangelo's willingness to paint what he saw instead of what someone ordered him to paint. My poems must personify my beliefs in life as I know it to be.; [a.] Detroit, MI

HOLLIFIELD, VIRGINIA TIPTON
[b.] August 2, 1942, Mitchell City, NC; [p.] Carl William Tipton, Ethel Marie McFalls; [m.] Ersel Dean Hollifield, October 5, 1977; [ch.] Fred Cook, Audrey Cook, Goldie Lea Hollifield; [ed.] Mill Creek School, St. Augustine, Fla.; [occ.] Care taker for the Elderly - Artist-Marquetry; [memb.] Chamber of Commerce; [hon.] Sent a Marquetry Plaque to the White House/ Desert Rose/to President and Mrs. Bush, it was accepted on behalf of the men and women that fought in the Desert War.; [oth. writ.] "Life in Reverse", "A Sons Prayer" - "A Day of Mourning", "Our Flag Red, White and Blue"; [pers.] I call myself a mood writer, I write happy and sad poems, it's how I feel at the time.; [a.] Sprucepine, NC

HOLMAN, MICHAEL W.
[b.] March 1, 1965, Salem, OR; [p.] Gordon and Virginia Holman; [ed.] McKay High, Chemeketa Community College, Trend Business College; [memb.] American Red Cross (Received Gallon Pin Spring '95); [hon.] Who's who, American High School Students, 1983, Optimist International, most involved in Publications, 1983, Oregon Road Runners, 7 Finisher's Certificates for the Portland Marathon, 1985-93; [oth. writ.] Published in High School and Community College Newspapers (Editor for McKay, Reporter for Chemeketa) and in Salem Oregon's Statesman Journal (letters to the Editor); [pers.] For me, there's always going to be one more finish line to cross and one more point to make with a pen.; [a.] Atlanta, GA

HOLMES, RANDY
[pers.] Randy is originally from Indiana, but now lives in Greenfield, Massachusetts, a small western town nestled at the edge of the Berkshires. Randy lives with his children Angie and Nick, two cats Thelma and Louise, and six fish. Randy has a masters degree in management and psychology from Cambridge College, and owns a company that teaches disabled people work skills and habits. Randy's interest in writing includes fiction, satire, commentary, song lyrics and of course poetry. Randy's ultimate goal with his writing is to collaborate with Elton John, which has been Randy's greatest influence.

HOLT, DE'ANGINAE
[pen.] Nikki Neal; [b.] May 8, 1971, Atlanta, GA; [p.] June Pierce and Calvin Neal; [m.] Gerrard Holt, May 29, 1993; [ch.] Brittani Holt and Brook-lynn Holt; [ed.] Concord High School, Independent Financial Institution Education, Talent Development; [occ.] Aspiring Actress/Model, current waitress; [oth. writ.] This is my first published piece, Thank You!; [pers.] I encourage people to do what they love and the rest will come. I express my feelings through poetry as an artistic outlet. I draw deep on life's experiences.; [a.] Los Angeles, CA

HONG, YOUNG WHA KIM
[pen.] Young K. H.; [b.] May 2, 1958, Seoul, Korea; [p.] In-Gyu Kim, Bong-Sun Lim; [m.] Song Sik Hong, June 20, 1987; [ch.] Jonathan and Joanna; [ed.] Yonsei University in Seoul, Korea (B.A./M.A. in English Literature), Texas A and M; [occ.] Housewife, dreaming to be a good poet; [oth. writ.] Several poems and essays not published, but ultimately will be published in near future; [pers.] As a Mom and Sunday School Teacher, I want to teach my kids how to talk to God and how to listen to Him. And I will do my best not to miss any blinks of their innocent eyes.; [a.] Glendale, CA

HOOVER, ISAAC H.
[pen.] Ike Hoover; [b.] Nashville, TN; [p.] Lillian and Edward Hoover; [ch.] Rosalind, Lillian, Michael; [ed.] B.S. Degree Physical Education - Allen Univ. Class of 1962 Columbia, S. Carolina; [occ.] Management Services Boys and Girls Clubs of Southeastern Mich.; [pers.] I write based on my personal experiences through love, joy, and sadness.; [a.] Troy, MI

HOPKINS, STANLEY C.
[b.] April 27, 1936, Ottawa; [p.] Mr. and Mrs. W. A. Hopkins; [ch.] Stanley, Joshua, Neil, Penelope, Laura; [ed.] Canada; [occ.] Photographer; [pers.] I photograph what I don't want to write about, and I write about what I can't photograph.; [a.] Port Hueneme, CA

HOPWOOD, BILL
[b.] March 6, 1944, Lawrenceburg, TN; [p.] William and Mary Hopwood; [m.] Karen Fehling Hopwood, November 29, 1969; [ch.] Kristin Elizabeth, Michael Benedict, Mary Margaret, Sara Therese; [ed.] Lawrence

County High, Tennessee Technological Univ. (BS), University of Tennessee (MBA); [occ.] Technical Management, Martin Marietta, Oak Ridge, TN; [memb.] St. John Neumann Catholic Church, Institute of Nuclear Materials Management, National Management Association; [hon.] Honorable Discharge - US Army, Math Honor Society (KME); [oth. writ.] Numerous poems for friends and relatives; [pers.] Putting God first is the most important and sometimes the most difficult thing to do.; [a.] Knoxville, TN

HORSLEY, CAROL LOUISE
[b.] August 8, 1950, Lynchburg, VA; [p.] Robert Mosley and Pearl Mosley; [m.] Richard Horsley Jr.; [ch.] Richard Horsley III and Troy Horsley; [ed.] Dunbar High School; [occ.] Repair Operator Ericsson Mobile Communications; [pers.] God has given everyone of us a gift. He has inspired me to write poetry so my desire is to write that God might get the glory and others be blessed from my poems.; [a.] Lynchburg, VA

HOULIHAN, MAVIN
[b.] May 18, 1920, Saint Cloud, MN; [p.] Aaron and Cele Mooney; [m.] Joseph Houlihan, June 16, 1948; [ch.] David Houlihan, Robert Houlihan; [ed.] Huron Universary, 4 year college - BA Degree, Mt. Marty High School; [occ.] Retired Elementary Teacher Dis., Grand Junction, CO; [memb.] Catholic Church, Minister of Praise, Retired Teachers Ass.; [hon.] 24 years Teaching Award; [oth. writ.] Poetry for friends birthdays, anniversaries, baby's births to be used at the requests of others, too. None to be published in papers.; [pers.] After a short retirement from teaching, I went into a 2 1/2 months semi-coma. This was caused by too low potassium and sodium in my body. When I came out of the coma, I had to relearn to eat, write, etc. The poem tells the rest!; [a.] Palisade, CO

HOWARD, GINO A. E.
[b.] September 15, 1960, Inverness, FL; [p.] Amos E. Howard, Roxie A. Howard; [m.] Paula Howard, January 18, 1984; [ed.] Valencia Community College, University of Central Florida; [occ.] Computer Operator. Winter Park Memorial Hospital; [hon.] President and Dean's Lists - V.C.C.; [pers.] This poem is dedicated to my loving wife, Paula.; [a.] Winter Park, FL

HOWARD, THERESA M.
[b.] June 21, 1967, Fort Wayne, IN; [p.] Isiah and Betty Meriweather; [m.] Reginald L. Howard; [ch.] Cheron M. Howard, JaMea L. Howard; [pers.] I believe the Bible is the infallible word of God. I believe in the virgin birth of His son Jesus Christ and the indwelling of the Holy Spirit which empowers and inspires me to write, be a good mother and wife.; [a.] Montgomery, AL

HOWE, KEVIN JAMES
[pen.] KJH; [b.] July 19, Chicago; [p.] James and Elaine Howe; [m.] Kathy; [ch.] Alex, Krystal, Quin; [ed.] Gordon Technical High School; [occ.] Teamster Foreman for Trade shows; [pers.] I try to express the need to remember our young children and elderly in my poems because our future depends on them. My family has a major role in my life; [a.] Joliet, IL

HOWE, LONA BERYL SPAULDING
[b.] March 12, 1910, Baldwinville, MA; [p.] Mr. and Mrs. Lionell Spaulding; [m.] Mr. Harry A. Howe; [ch.] Janet B. Howe, Janice B. Howe, Aurolyn Howe, Jacquelyn D. Howe, Bethelyn A. Howe; [ed.] Templeton High School, Baldwinville Mass. graduated 1928 was our basket ball team for 4 yrs.; [occ.] Retired an 85 years old and live in an elderly housing project in Orange, MA, was divorced in 1943 and remarried my ex-husband November 9, 1969. He died in 1972; [hon.] Never sent in any poem before. Just did it as a past time

and most, are more than 20 lines long.; [a.] Orange, MA

HRUZEK, EMILIE
[pen.] Angel Starre; [b.] May 26, Texas; [p.] Gene and Judy Hruzek; [oth. writ.] (My 1st publication); [pers.] Thanks to my mother, Mrs. Feighny and my "Teddy Bear." "Reach for the moon even if you miss you'll land among the stars!"; [a.] Carrollton, TX

HUANG, JAMES
[b.] December 24, 1968, Kaohsiung, Taiwan; [p.] Luke and Susan Huang; [ed.] Servite High School, Ursinus College, Loma Linda University, B.S., University of California-Riverside, M.S.; [occ.] Medical student at Univ. of Osteopathic Medicine and Health Science DesMoines, IA; [pers.] This poem was written during a critical period of my life in which career, family, aspirations, and love collided. I lost someone who might have been that special person in my life. The poem was written for her when we were on better terms. I doubt matters will ever change. One day, "The One" will know me by the cut of my suit and my soul. My writing attempts to capture the reflections of my heart in order to describe the fragility of the soul and of humanity. I dedicate this poem to my family and close friends who steadfastly believed in me throughout the years.; [a.] Anaheim Hills, CA

HUBBARD, RICHARD
[pen.] Richard Hubbard; [b.] December 9, 1980, NY; [p.] Jean and Tom Hubbard; [ed.] 8th grade student at Elmont Memorial High School; [memb.] Junior High Lacrosse for Elmont Memorial High School; [a.] North Valley Stream, NY

HUBBARD, RICHARD W.
[ed.] B.A. Oakland University, Rochester Michigan, PhD University of Notre Dame; [occ.] Clinical Psychologist, College Professor; [a.] South Bend, IN

HUDSON III, JOHN W.
[b.] October 15, 1974, Torrington, WY; [p.] John W. and Mary F. Hudson Jr.; [ed.] Morrill High School, Morrill NE; [occ.] None to speak of. Writing is my work; [hon.] Awards for acting in One Act Play in high school lettered in band on choir all 4 years of high school; [oth. writ.] Currently working on an unpublished book call A collection of Insanity: Thoughts in The Mind; [pers.] Words are life. Life of meaning. Without words there is no life. My work reflects what I feel, see, hear, an experience everyday. My influence's are insane world of life; [a.] Morrill, NE

HUEBNER, PHIL E.
[b.] October 30, 1947, Waukesha; [p.] Lorraine G. Huebner; [m.] December 11, 1984; [ch.] Phillip Thomas, Joshua Henry, Nicole Marie; [ed.] South Campus H. S., Milwaukee Area Technical College; [occ.] Disabled Vietnam Veteran; [memb.] Disabled American Veteran's; [pers.] Live life in such a manner that when you walk it accents progress and when you turn to look back, that which once there to see, is a mere shadow of what lies ahead.; [a.] Palmyra, WI

HUETSCH, KIMBERLY
[b.] April 1, 1978, Rockford; [p.] Donna and Larry Huetsch; [ed.] High School Junior at Lutheran High School; [oth. writ.] poems published in school newspaper; [a.] Rockford, IL

HUFF, ELIZABETH
[b.] April 25, 1962, Pittsburgh; [p.] Ambrose and Elizabeth Borandi; [m.] Divorced; [ch.] 1 son; [ed.] Graduated High School - College Degree as Paralegal; [occ.] Work for Engineering Firm/Administrative Assistant; [oth. writ.] I have many writings. I write for myself and

for the pleasure of it. Nothing Published.; [pers.] An author once said "We red to know we are not alone." I write to know that there is someone there.; [a.] Springdale, PA

HUFF, FEONA SHARHRAN
[b.] December 11, 1974, Pineville, LA; [p.] Dorothy Huff; [ed.] Norfolk State University, Norfolk, VA Bachelor of Arts, Journalism, Expected May 1997 Journalism GPA:356 Overall GPA:3.3; [occ.] Student and Free-lance writer; [memb.] Association of Black Communicators, Spartan Alpha Tau Honor Society, Imagineers, The Spartan Echo, Student Support Services; [hon.] Les Cygnette Scholarship, Hart Scholarship, The Norfolk Council of Parent Teacher Association, National Association, National Alumni Association Scholarship, NSU Mass Communication Journalism Scholarship, Mildred E. Dudley Scholarship; [oth. writ.] Articles have appeared in The Spartan Echo, The Virginian Pilot and The Ledger-Star, New Journal and Guide (Norfolk, VA), Black College Today (Fort Lauderdale, FL, Black Excellence (Washington, DC); [pers.] My writing is my refuge, my confidant. When no else is there for me, I have my God given-talent of writing, to keep me focused. I advice my young writer to strive for their dream. Never let anyone discourage you. Don't give them the satisfaction; [a.] Norfolk, VA

HUFFMAN, MARLENE
[pen.] Molly J.; [b.] February 29, East St. Louis, IL; [p.] Mary Allen, Deceased (husband); [ed.] Milby High, hargest College, Houston Community College and the Institute of Children's Literature; [occ.] Receptionist, City of Houston, Houston, TX; [memb.] Feed the Children Foundations Greater St. Matthew Chruch, Distributing Education Club of America (DECA) and NHBA; [pers.] I am a firm believer that whatever one holds in the heart, naturalizes into art. Many endeavors in life take something from us. Let us not lose sight of the benefits as we look at our losses.; [a.] Houston, TX

HUGHES, DENISE
[b.] July 10, 1953, Atlanta; [p.] Ouida and Daniel Hughes; [m.] Divorced in 1986; [ch.] Joshua Daniel, Seth Wallace, Amaris Beth; [ed.] Jonesboro Sr. High, Clayton State College, Georgia State University; [occ.] Aviation Magazine, Editor, Writer and Designer; [memb.] Episcopal Church, Atlanta Union Mission, Atlanta Desktop Publishers; [hon.] Past 1st place honors in music, one award for a short story in College, and one for a water color; [oth. writ.] Several stories in an aviation magazine, along with two of my poems; [pers.] I strive to express the depth of human emotion in my poems, both the pain and the joy. I believe every experience contains both, by seeing the good and the negative most of life balances out; [a.] Griffin, GA

HUGHES, JOANNA F.
[pen.] Joanna Moses Hughes; [b.] September 13, 1943, Seattle, WA; [p.] Charles and Vivian Moses; [m.] Divorced; [ch.] Angela Agnes, Kimberly Karol, Charles Donald; [ed.] Gary Edison - St. Joseph, Calumet College, Indiana U.; [occ.] Caseworker Principal, Fulton County Dept. of Family and Children Services; [memb.] Order of Eastern Star, Courtesy Guild Mt. Patmos, Baptist Church. Eastlake Neighbors, GA Conf. on Social Welfare - GCWA; [hon.] Delta Epsilon Sigma - Cum Laude Graduate; [oth. writ.] Poet of the Office; [pers.] I believe poetry should be an emotional experience. Can I really become another Grandmother Moses?; [a.] Atlanta, GA

HUGHES, JONATHAN
[b.] March 11, 1972, Aurora, IL; [p.] Naomi Hughes, Johnny Hughes; [ed.] East Aurora High, University of Illinois; [memb.] Delta Phi Alpha (National German

Honor Society); [hon.] Goethe Award for Scholarship in the Study of German; [pers.] I strive to show the full range of the human experience in modern-day life. Therefore, my writings range from political to romantic.; [a.] Aurora, IL

HUGHES, MEREDITH A.
[pen.] Daisy Hill; [b.] June 25, 1947, Indianapolis, IN; [p.] William L. Bowen and Bertha L. Boyd; [ch.] George B. Hughes II and Benjamin M. Hughes; [ed.] High school and College Writing; [occ.] American Airlines weight and Balance Planner; [memb.] United Way; [oth. writ.] Not yet finished -Movie script The Voice of the Turtle on Popcorn Ridge; [pers.] I love to reach out to mankind and teach them through words of example to think in positive constructive way. By reaching one's own cognitive thought, you can learn of yourself and create a whole and happy person in and for the world; [a.] Hurst, TX

HULL, THELMA LEONE
[pen.] Thelma Hull; [b.] July 5, 1909, Twin Falls, ID; [p.] David Allen and Lucy Stout; [m.] Willard Parker Hull, June 9, 1928; [ch.] Jovita Yvonne and Chloe Marlene Granddaughters, Anita Jo and Sheila McGriff; [ed.] Redondo Beach High Special Drama by Doris Smith of Portland Civic theatre; [occ.] Biblical Studies; [memb.] "Christian Coalition"; [oth. writ.] "God's symphony numerous poems, Autobiography "My Life, My Story, My Song" by Thelma Leone Hull; [a.] Las Vegas, NV

HULSEY, CHRISTINA M.
[pen.] Christine; [b.] November 20, 1967, Tacoma, WA; [p.] Eldon Elliott and Linda; [m.] Phillip Hulsey, November 5, 1987; [ch.] Zachary G. Hulsey; [ed.] Bonner Sprs. High School; Johnson County Comm. College; [occ.] Have my own daycare "The Little Pee-wees"; [hon.] Bowling, writing; [oth. writ.] "That Wind," in Tears of Fire; [pers.] It takes a lot to have me write something with such deep feeling. But my friends and family help a lot. I'm hoping someday I'll get recognized for what talent I think I have.; [a.] Bonner Springs, KS.

HULSTEDT, GRACE
[pen.] Grace Hulstedt; [b.] August 27, 1949, Chicago; [p.] Thomas Elletsen and Gladys Elletsen; [m.] Charles Hulstedt Jr., September 9, 1969; [ch.] Paul Hulstedt, Karin Hulstedt; [ed.] Northern Illinois University DeKalb, Illinois; [occ.] Registered Nurse, B.S.N.; [memb.] Golden Key National Honor Society, Memorial Baptist Church, Rockford, IL; [hon.] Golden Key National Honor Society; [oth. writ.] Poems written for personal basis; [pers.] Poems I have written reflect a spiritual aspect of life and dependence on a Higher Power.; [a.] Rockford, IL

HUMMEL, JENNIFER L.
[pen.] Jennifer L. Hummel; [b.] January 16, 1978, Longview, WA; [p.] Bill and Naomi Hummel; [ed.] Eleventh Grader at Castle Rock - Home School; [occ.] Student, take care of critically ill mother; [memb.] All member St. Paul's Luthern church-C-R WA, CMA (Country Music Association); [oth. writ.] Several other Poem and short stories never published; [pers.] I strive to set a good example as a daughter of God. I am a country music fan! Big time Judd and Reba. Love Books. And the outdoors.; [a.] Castle Rock, WA

HUNTER, ISABELLE
[pen.] Isabelle; [b.] February 16, Penna.; [p.] Alex and Lucy Jackson; [ed.] H. School Communication Bartender Degree; [occ.] Retired; [memb.] Boston Library, Museum of Science, Life Study Fellowship; [hon.] Bible Study Diploma; [oth. writ.] I Dream the Learning

Dream; [pers.] I live day by day; [a.] Boston, MA

HUNTER, KENNETH HENRY
[pen.] Trymutural; [b.] July 10, 1957, New York City, NY; [p.] Eleanor Hunter Robert, Walter Hunter; [m.] Deborah Freemen; [ch.] Kisher Hunter; [ed.] Public School 125, JHS 43, Harlem trail Blazer High school prp, Interboro Institute College undergraduate; [occ.] Off set printer; [memb.] Schomburg Library, Boy scout church of the Master, Church scientology, Urban League, Peew basketball snooky sugarboweh New City Housing Authority Basketball; [hon.] Daily New paper physically fitness 13 Basketball, football, Baseball trophies totaling above and Beyond Requirement statement in Humanities; [oth. writ.] Much more in collection personal and on vertical files 1975 and 1988 Schombage Library on Level 135th street Malcolm Boulevard; [pers.] People are greatest gift on this planet registered for USA Army qualified for score 23 Infantry 1979; [a.] Manhattan, NY

HURT, BONNIE
[b.] October 19, 1949, Hart, CO; [p.] Clarence and Lillie Philpott; [m.] Jerry Hurt, December 15, 1971; [ch.] Jeremy Ray and Jerianna Nicole; [ed.] Graduated Pleasure Ridge Park High School; [occ.] Part-time Nuttin Fancy Antique Shop; [memb.] Path Finders Highland United Methodist Church; [hon.] The National Library of Poetry Editors Choice Award in 1994 nominated for Poet of year 95, A poem in The Reflection of light and Beyond the Stars; [oth. writ.] "Something's Missing Here" to be published in the American Poetry Annual - 1995 Amherst Society; [pers.] Enjoyed Emily Dickinson and Helen Steiner. I've been writing 2 1/2 years. A true gift from God. I enjoy spiritual, everyday life, and nature; [a.] Cave City, KY

HUTT, ALICE M.
[pen.] Madeline; [b.] January 9, 1912, Polk City, IA; [p.] Davie H. Cross, Alpha Kline Cross; [m.] Malcolm L. Hutt; [ch.] Sandra Adams, Rev. John D. Hutt, R. L. Hutt; [ed.] 1928 Graduate Colfax Iowa High School, University of Commerce of Des Moines, Iowa Graduate; [occ.] Retired for 25 yrs., Bookkeeper, Secretary, Office Mgr. during working years; [memb.] Martensdale Community Church, various social and card clubs; [oth. writ.] Lyrics for 2 songs written and published 1963. By Songwriters Assn. Inc. New York but never meant anywhere; [pers.] Most poems were written 30 yrs. ago and mostly are to or about family members like family, nature and patriotic subjects.; [a.] Martensdale, IA

HYDE, STEVE
[pen.] Race Kirin; [b.] May 7, 1962, Portland, OR; [ed.] Bishop Union High School Computer Assisted Daughting cert. 2 semesters at L.I.F.E. Bible College; [occ.] Special Effects; [memb.] Media Fellowship Instructional; [oth. writ.] "Hang `Em All" "The gun"; [pers.] The universe is more than we will ever know.. Abandon preconceptions and discover wonder; [a.] Los Angeles, CA

IANNUCCI, MATTHEW J.
[b.] November 6, 1967, Manhasset, NY; [p.] Anita Iannucci; [ed.] Master of Arts Degree at the State University of New York at Stonybrook, Bachelor of Arts Degree at State University of Stonybrook; [occ.] Social Studies Teacher, Literary Reviewer and Critic; [memb.] Long Island Council for the Social Studies, Long Island Association for AIDS Care; [hon.] Dean's List, Summa Cum Laude; [oth. writ.] Several poems published by the Long Island Quarterly and the local town newspaper.; [pers.] I strive to write unrhymed lyrical poetry. My compositions tend to reflect the discord within my soul which has been brought to the

surface by the Long Island environment. I have been greatly influenced by Walt Whitman, William Carlos Williams, and Maya Angelou; [a.] Port Washington, NY

IMEL, TAULENOH LUCILLE BURKE
[b.] August 20, 1920, Mooreland, OK; [p.] James and Coralee Burke; [m.] John Edward Imel Jr., January 16, 1938; [ch.] Gearld Dean, Jimmie Eward, Garry Don and Lee Dora Lou Imel; [ed.] High School, 9th grade, Turkey - Texas; [occ.] Retired, (Med) from Zebco; [memb.] Grace Baptist Church, Sperry, Okla.; [oth. writ.] Several poems, the last one I wrote - was My Window; [pers.] Being a Christian, I get my inspirations from God and my husband, children and there families, loved ones, and friends, I have 13 grandchildren, 16 great grandchildren, God has been very good to us.; [a.] Skiatook, OK

INGLE, EMILY
[b.] October 1, 1984, Huntington, WV; [p.] Mark and Kelly Ingle; [ed.] 5th Grader Barboursville Elem.; [hon.] 1st Place Cultural Arts Contest (Literature), 1st Place Social Studies Fair, Science Fair - County Winner, Captain Safety Patrol

INGRAHAM, RON
[b.] October 13, 1962, Middletown, CT; [p.] Norman and Maureen; [m.] Diane (St. Paul) Ingraham, October 2, 1982; [ch.] Kristina, Joshua; [ed.] Vinal Tech - Automotive Pratt and Whitney-Machinist Training G.E.D. Adult Education; [occ.] Grounds Keeper, Town of Portland; [memb.] Eagles Club #681 AFSCME, Union Steward - Local 1303 #4, Youth Services Advisory Board, Country Club - 92.5, Safety Committee - Town of Portland; [oth. writ.] Author of "Poets" "Corner" in local newsletter, Country Songs (including) Give Love A Chance to Grow, I Found Love, See With Their Eyes, I Don't Want To Lose Your Love (all published); [pers.] I am influenced most by my wife and kids and my love of country music. I think children are the greatest and should always be encouraged to develop their own creative talents; [a.] Portland, CT

IVINS, DAVE
[b.] December 27, 1948, Augusta, AK; [p.] Harvey Ivins, Ruth Ivins; [ch.] Anthony Thor, Dustin Garth; [occ.] Q.A. Management, STL. Fabrication/Entrepreneur S.D.; [pers.] My greatest endeavor is to separate good and bad and emphasize upon the good. I am greatly influenced by children and nature; [a.] Mounds, OK

JACKSON, DR. CARNEY B.
[b.] August 24, 1951, Clarksburg, WV; [p.] Charles and Ina Jackson; [m.] Beth, May 17, 1975; [ch.] Mark and Luke; [ed.] B.S. Animal/Science at West Virginia University 1973, Doctor of Veterinary Medicine at Oklahoma State University 1977; [occ.] Veterinary Pathologist; [memb.] American College of Veterinary Pathologist, American College of Veterinary Preventive Medicine, American Veterinary Medical Association; [hon.] Maxwell Scholarship Army Achievement Medal, Army Commendation Medal; [oth. writ.] Several poems about life, wife and kids.

JACKSON, JAMES J.
[b.] February 5, 1949, Chicago, IL; [p.] Deceased; [m.] Donna L. Jackson, over 20 years; [ch.] Victoria Teresa Kindra, Jennifer; [ed.] Alumni of Chicago State College; [occ.] State Administrator and Newspaper Columnist; [memb.] Post School Board Chairman, Member County Library Board. Michigan Handicapper Parking Enforcement Task Force; [hon.] Golden Poet Award 1991-94, President's Award for Literary Excellence, 1995 National Author's Registry; [oth. writ.]

Several other poems published in anthologies. Yet unpublished novel, Boiling Rage; [pers.] I love writing in general, but I have a passion for rhyming poetry. I strive to reflect my Christian belief and personal integrity through my writing.; [a.] Lansing, MI

JACKSON, MARTINA BRIDGETTA GEORGE
[b.] September 16, 1975, Chicago, IL; [p.] Sanetta and Wiley Jackson; [ed.] Francis W. Parker High School Western Illinois University; [occ.] Student; [hon.] First prize in the Harvard School of Chicago's writing contest, Junior Citizen of Chicago Honoree; [oth. writ.] Numerous articles in school publications; [pers.] I believe poetry should be universal so that people on different points on the world can all read the same piece and understand the meaning.; [a.] Chicago, IL

JACKSON, NICOLE MONIQUE
[b.] December 1, 1970, Washington, DC; [p.] Deborah Jackson, Ronald Allen; [m.] Allen Young Jr.; [ch.] Rhyan Bree Catherine Jackson; [ed.] Prince Georges Community College Woodrow Wilson High School; [occ.] Records Technician; [oth. writ.] Poems published in local magazines, staff writer for Exase Magazine's and News and Views; [pers.] I write for catharsis! Therefore, every word is heart felt, every line is genuine, and every selection (piece) tells a story.; [a.] Fort Washington, MD

JACKSON, TOD E.
[pen.] Tod Jackson; [b.] May 12, 1960, New York; [p.] Thelma and Bill Pace; [m.] August 16, 1984; [ed.] High School; [occ.] U.S. Military (Navy); [a.] San Diego, CA

JACOBS, OLIVIA DEUTSCH
[b.] September 24, 1925, Chicago, IL; [p.] Matilda and William Sellinger; [m.] Ernest Jacobs, May 29, 1976; [ch.] Barbara Shimberg, Gary Deutsch, Richard Deutsch, Marc Jacobs, Lesley Wagmeister, Grandchildren: Todd Eine, Stephani Fine, Gordy Deutsch, Adam Deutsch, Ryan Deutsch, Tyler Deutsch, Brian Jacobs, Michael Jacobs, Molly Wagmeister, Jason and Ali Shimberg; [ed.] B.A. Soc./Psych—Roosevelt Univ. Minor Education/Journalism Graduate Work - Northwestern Univ. and National College of Ed. in Special Education; [occ.] Retired Director of Resource Room at Middleton School; [hon.] 25 years service award for Teaching. Top 10% of Class - Magna Cum Laude Homecoming Queen.; [oth. writ.] Humorous feature weekly column in college. Co-editor of Teacher's Union Newspaper. Published word puzzle in local newspaper.; [pers.] Writing, especially humor, is rewarding - as is anything that brings a smile to others.; [a.] Oxnard, CA

JAGACZEWSKI, JANIS K.
[pen.] Jan Carter; [b.] March 18, 1950, Phenix City, AL; [p.] Clayton Bartlett, Ida Mae Bartlett; [m.] Edward Jagaczewski Jr., August 14, 1981; [ch.] Tabatha Lynn, Dennis Clayton Nicholas, and Nicole Lee; [ed.] Wilm. High, Belmont Tech.; [occ.] Telemarketer - Insurance Agent; [oth. writ.] Other short writings, and poems, in my journal, I am making for my children. None of which have been published. This is my first publication; [pers.] My writings are on feelings and experiences of myself and people who choose to share theirs with me. My courage to do so comes from a special friends. Nicholas Blatchford.; [a.] Belmont, OH

JAMES, BARBARA W.
[b.] November 4, 1921, Atlanta, GA; [p.] Herbert and Vivian Wallace; [m.] John McKee James, May 27, 1950; [ch.] Audrey James Goff; [ed.] 11 yrs. plus Secretarial School, I got my G.E.D. at Catonsville Community College and took courses there in creative writing, free lance writing and am currently taking a

correspondence course on writing for children and teenagers; [memb.] Leideg Senior Center American Automobile Club; [hon.] I won a poetry contest once for "Drink Deep Of Beauty." Had a narrative poem published in The Evening Capital. No free. I was awarded the title of "Poet Emeritus" by Father Caputo. I considered it a joke.; [oth. writ.] I have written many poems and stories, all unpublished.; [pers.] As Grandma Moses started a career late in life, so should I like to, only in writing, rather than art. Whenever I get discouraged I think of her.; [a.] Baltimore, MD

JAMES, STEVEN
[b.] March 27, 1956, Aberdeen, MD; [ed.] University of Tennessee, University of Delaware, B.A.; [memb.] Alliance Francaise; [hon.] French Honor Society, French Poetry Recitation, 1st prize; [oth. writ.] First Publication; [a.] Wilmington, DE

JAROS, COLLEEN ANN
[b.] June 3, 1975; [hon.] Editors Choice Award from Cynthia Stevens and Caroline Sullivan from the National Library of Poetry for Outstanding Achievement in Poetry. Thank you, I greatly appreciate it!; [oth. writ.] Many unpublished poems, and one poem "I Wish I Could Sing You a Song" published in the Anthology of "Journey of the Mind"; [a.] Holbrook, NY

JARVIS, MARK M.
[b.] October 28, 1970, Canden, NJ; [p.] Edward Jarvis, Margaret Jarvis; [ed.] Attended Drexel University Gloucester County College, now attending Liberty University; [oth. writ.] Numerous poems never before seen by the public; [pers.] My life is bet drops of ink. So I'll continue to write till my pen runs dry.; [a.] Marlton, NJ

JECMENEK, SUSAN LOUISE
[pen.] Susie; [b.] August 29, 1966, Temple, TX; [p.] J.D. and Dorothy Jecmenek; [ch.] Gina Derise Jecmenek, Jefferey Daren Kuhn; [ed.] Rogers High School Rogers TX; [oth. writ.] Poems written to special people in my life; [pers.] I like to write a poem for someone to help sort out their feelings. Sometimes a word or two can make all the difference in the world.; [a.] Temple, TX

JENKINS, JENNIFER
[b.] May 5, 1970, Salinas, CA; [p.] David Jenkins, Ann Mulhern; [ed.] BA English: Literature and Writing Whitworth College Spring 1993; [occ.] Administrative Assist.; [hon.] Outstanding Contribution to the Life of the English Department, 1992-93 Departmentally Honored Senior 1992-93; [oth. writ.] Include my senior portfolio (Poetry) "Salt and Water", various pieces of short fiction, several non-fiction essays and bunches of Poetry; [pers.] I don't write because I love it, though I do, or because I'm good at it. I write because I have to. And nothing in my life is ever easier and more difficult—especially at the same time.; [a.] Seattle, WA

JENNESS, ANGELINE LAURICELLA
[b.] July 6, 1917, N. Girard, PA; [p.] Antonina and Mariano Lauricella; [m.] Howard Chesley Jenness, April 10, 1943; [ch.] Sherril Lynn and Ruth Ellan; [ed.] 1992 attended Kindergarten when there were very few of them Brocton, N.Y., grades and high schools in N. Girard, Girard and Conneautville, Pa. Schools, Penn State and Edinboro State Teacher's Colleges; [occ.] Active Home Maker; [hon.] High School: Top fifth of class Scholarship to Penn State; [pers.] The ice storm that inspired this poem was so strikingly beautiful that the descriptive words flooded my mind, and I felt compelled to share them. I once was given a book on speed reading, which seemed so useless to me, because I like to savor the sounds and various shadings of each word. Why would I want to skip over even one? Words make

prose and poetry! Dedicated to my husband, Howard, our daughters, Sherril and Ruth, and to the dear niece who took me to view the miles and miles of frozen beauty, Norma Hanson.; [a.] Girard, PA

JENNINGS, LILLIAN PEGUES
[b.] May 24, 1926, Ohio; [p.] Deceased; [m.] Deceased; [ch.] Dan and Kim; [ed.] B.S., M.Ed., Ph.D.; [occ.] Retired; [memb.] Mt. Zion Baptist Church, N.A.A.C.P., National Association of Colored Women's Clubs, Inc., Alpha Kappa Alpha Sorority; [hon.] Listed in Who's Who in Black America-1978. Listed in World's Who's Who of Women. Competitive Scholarship to the University of Pittsburgh; [oth. writ.] Professional Publications and Presentations at Academic Association Meetings. Book Reviews.; [pers.] "In the end, I will have done my best."; [a.] Staunton, VA

JERNIGAN, KEVIN L.
[b.] June 8, 1996, Los Angeles, CA; [p.] Melvin Ray and DiAnthia Jernigan; [m.] Angela L. Bell, September 26, 1992; [ed.] Central High of Tuscaloosa, Sheton State Stillman College and University of Alabama; [occ.] Manufactured Home Inspector for Tuscaloosa County; [memb.] United States Marine Corps. American Lergon; [hon.] Honor Graduate, Top five in the class; [oth. writ.] Several poems and short stories also monologues which I have performed; [pers.] This was written in remembrance my grandfather, Dr. Earnest P. Robinson of who past away before he could see me as a man. I feel that in order to build our future, we must save, guide and teach our children.; [a.] Tuscaloosa, AL

JOHNSON, ALEX
[b.] August 26, 1985, Danville, CA; [p.] Francis and Deborah Johnson; [ed.] 4th Grade Student; [occ.] Student; [pers.] Lover of Nature

JOHNSON, ARTHUR MCCREA
[pen.] Mack Johnson; [b.] April 6, 1915, Palouse, WA; [p.] George Jesta Johnson; [m.] Loy M. Johnson, February 27, 1935; [ch.] Alvie, Emma, Tom, Sandy, Tim and Ann; [ed.] Formal education none, by experience, U.S. Marines-WW II, logger, truck driver, Rancher, Steel Mills, Stationery Engineer, Teamster - horses, Heavy Equipment Operator; [occ.] Retired; [memb.] Baptist, Church, Republican, VFW. Presbyterian Reformed Church; [hon.] Elected, Precinct Committeeman, Deacon Elder, Business Agent Local Union, Appointed by Governor: On softy Comm. on Employment Security, Advisory Counsel; [oth. writ.] Poems and short articles in Church and local newspaper; [pers.] America the beautiful is sick from an internal disease called freedom. Social freedoms without moral discipline is a debauchery that will kill any Nation.; [a.] New Plymouth, ID

JOHNSON, AUDREY L.
[pen.] A. L. Johnson; [b.] October 29, 1963, Baltimore, MD; [p.] Barbara Johnson, William Johnson; [ch.] Latoya Johnson; [occ.] Data Processor; [pers.] Writing is my gift from God and not to use it would mean that I have turned my back on the faith that he has in me.; [a.] Baltimore, MD

JOHNSON, BEVERLY J.
[b.] February 22, 1932, Santa Ana, CA; [p.] Joseph and Sophie Zlaket; [m.] Charles J. Johnson, June 2, 1929; [ch.] Roxanne M. Ruhl, Derek C. Johnson; [ed.] Santa Ana High School, Fullerton College Institute of Children's Literature; [occ.] Freelance Writer; [memb.] AARP, Library of Congress Associates, National Trust for Historic Preservation, Menifee Valley Hospital Auxiliary; [hon.] Fullerton College, Dean's List; [oth. writ.] Public Relation Articles - Re: No Idaho Chamber of Commerce; [pers.] I strive to reflect thoughtfulness,

caring, and imagination in my writings for children and teens.; [a.] Sun City, CA

JOHNSON, CHRIS
[b.] March 28, 1979, New Haven, CT; [p.] Joseph St. Onge and Karen St. Onge; [ed.] Currently attending Coginchaug Regional High School, Durham Ct., Grade 10; [occ.] Sales Associate - Filenes, May Company; [oth. writ.] Stories (short), poems, articles, etc.; [pers.] I feel that poetry is a beautiful form of writing, when written from the heart. Therefore, to me, everybody out there has a poetic side.; [a.] Durham, CT

JOHNSON, DAGNEY M.
[pen.] Dagney; [b.] April 25, 1926, Norway; [p.] Tom and Aagot Johannessen; [m.] Arthur W. Johnson, May 24, 1943; [ch.] Karen Keller, Lynn Boucher, Diane Saraceno, Jeffrey, Gary, David; [occ.] Retired; [oth. writ.] Poems published in local newspaper, greeting card words and design; [pers.] My poetry evolves from life-time experience and through these, the words come tumbling.; [a.] Foxboro, MA

JOHNSON, DAVID A.
[b.] April 29, 1930, California; [m.] Joan, October 21, 1958; [ch.] Scott, Mark; [ed.] 2 yrs. college; [occ.] Innkeeper; [memb.] B.P.O. Elks; [pers.] The poem was when I served as U.P.S. Ranger in Alaska 1990.; [a.] Chico, CA

JOHNSON, DWIGHT A.
[b.] March 3, 1928, Storm Lake, LA; [p.] Mahlon and Ardath Johnson; [m.] Jean Fratello Johnson, March 25, 1951; [ch.] Dwight E., Nancy, Linda, Kim; [ed.] BA, Journalism, 1949 U of Wisconsin; [occ.] Writer, Owner, Arlan Communications; [oth. writ.] Book, "Fountain City May Have Talkie Shows - The story of a small Wisconsin town and its weekly newspaper." Book of short stories, "The Last Newspaper"; [pers.] Writing beats working; [a.] Bashing Ridge, NJ

JOHNSON, FLORA M.
[pen.] Peggy Johnson; [b.] February 5, 1930, Atlanta GA; [p.] Robert and Ruby Jordan; [m.] James O. Lynn Johnson, January 8, 1983; [ch.] Debbie Strawn, Charlene Stribling; [ed.] High School; [occ.] Nursing; [memb.] Independent Care Association VFW Auxiliary American Legion Auxiliary; [oth. writ.] Old Cruel World, An Ode to the Soul, Friends, Sands of the Mind; [pers.] I work with terminal cancer patients. I also counsel the family of the patients, if needed.; [a.] Winston, GA

JOHNSON JR., BILLY
[b.] January 6, 1961, Crosbyton, TX; [p.] Billy D. and Mary Johnson; [m.] Divorced; [ch.] Justin, Toni, Tyler; [ed.] High School Graduate, plus many career training schools in the Communications Field; [occ.] Multi-line Phone System and PBX installer; [memb.] Past member volunteer fireman; [oth. writ.] Many poems, which are unpublished; [pers.] I love to write poetry from my heart, everything I write contains my own feelings and dreams.; [a.] Lubbock, TX

JOHNSON, JUDY ANN
[pen.] Judy A. Johnson (JAJ); [b.] January 9, 1948; [m.] Gary Johnson, May 9, 1969; [ch.] Synetra, Damon, Gail, Albert, Michael Gary Jr., Alonzo Benjamen; [ed.] IPS PUblic Schools Clark Office College Sawyer Business College; [occ.] Administrative Secretary CICOA The Access Network; [memb.] Holy Angels Catholic Church The Indianapolis Urban League; [oth. writ.] Book Poetry unpublished; [pers.] To always be able to view myself from within which will allow me to reveal the truths of my surroundings; [a.] Indianapolis, IN

JOHNSON, KIM
[b.] June 8, 1956, New York; [m.] Thomas Wade Johnson, April 26th, 1986; [ch.] Danielle, Travis, Miranda, Douglas, (Granddaughter) Emma; [ed.] 2 years College, Suffolk Community; [occ.] Manager of a Group Home for Disabled Adults; [oth. writ.] Seasons of Life, What a Child Feels, Latch Key Kids, Do and Don'ts, The needle, The Wave, Story of a Sunflower, etc. etc.; [pers.] Living life is always looking forward to the next adventure. Believe in yourself as God believes in you.; [a.] Mastic Beach, NY

JOHNSON, MABLE
[b.] August 16, 1940, Haucock, CO; [p.] Burnard and Lettie Gibson; [m.] Dean Johnson, October 6, 1962; [ch.] Ginger Colleen, Chadwick Keith, Brian Oheal; [ed.] Mulberry Hi-Ged Walter State, Tenn.; [occ.] Farmer and House wife; [memb.] Yellow Branch Baptist Church; [oth. writ.] Several short stories, songs and poems. One poem published in local paper Sneedville, Shopper; [pers.] I have been greatly influenced by my beautiful grandchildren Kendria, Haley and Brianna, most of all by the loving magic of God creations; [a.] Sneedville, TN

JOHNSON, SHEILA
[b.] August 16, 1958, South Carolina; [p.] Julious and Rosa Lee Montgomery; [m.] Bennie James Johnson, May 15, 1979; [ch.] Krestel, Bennie Jr., Rafael, Terra and Felicia; [ed.] Timmonsville High School Several Government Vocational Classes; [occ.] Secretary for Defense Technical Information Center (DTIC); [memb.] National Honor Society at Timmonsville High School; [oth. writ.] I have recently wrote a manuscript for a Novel title (I Saw the Light). God has inspired me to write this novel about visions I am having of the afterlife. When publish it will be a very interesting novel.; [pers.] I would like to give all honor and praises for this poem to my Lord and Savior Jesus Christ. Inspirational note: My family and friends who have been encouraging me not to give up. A special thanks to Mr. Wade Cook my present supervisor, and also a dear friend.; [a.] Woodbridge, VA

JOHNSON, THIERNO ANTHONY
[pen.] Thierno; [b.] January 27, 1971, Washington, DC; [p.] Jeaniece Johnson, William Johnson; [m.] Teri Smith Johnson, August 17, 1994; [ch.] Erik Holloman, Thierno Johnson Jr., Treyvahn Adkisson; [ed.] Wilson High School Missouri Valley College; [occ.] Mental Health Counselor, Youth Counselor; [memb.] Phi Beta Sigma Inc.; [hon.] Deans List, NAIA All American in Football, NAIA All Conference in Football, (MUSE) Minority Undergraduate Student of Excellence in Psychology; [oth. writ.] Co-Author of Thurno and Chante Unmasked Passions and Thierno and Chante she and he both; [pers.] I write from my inner soul and I hope that this sample of my self will touch another soul and inspire them to be creative and open; [a.] Washington, DC

JOLY, TRICIA
[pen.] Tricia Gunning; [b.] December 11, 1948, WV; [p.] Betty and Al Path; [m.] Leo Joly, January 27, 1995; [ch.] Todd Gunning, Tonia Gunning; [ed.] Inglewood High California and the reads of life; [occ.] "Friends In Need" Personal in home care giver for the elderly; [hon.] Minus Academic Achievements - I feel the greatest honor I've received in life is the blessing to meet and enjoy people on all the paths I've walked - that's been an honor!; [pers.] To live life and not share the joys, not to take time to mend the pain and heartache is a selfish thing - the sharing of words and song is good for the soul.; [a.] Carton, GA

JONAS, DAVID L.
[b.] February 15, 1966, Chicago, CA; [ed.] English and History Major, Ripon College, WI; [occ.] Banker; [memb.] New Toen Writers, Chicago; [a.] Chicago, IL

JONES, BRIEON
[pen.] Miss Bre; [b.] October 8, 1986, Flint, MI; [p.] Yvette M. Jones; [ch.] Dyonna, Higi; [ed.] Flint Gundry Elem.; [memb.] Blackwell A.M.E. Zion Church; [hon.] Honor roll Citizen at the week, Eight times, perfect attendance; [pers.] She takes Krate-an Yellow Belt. She sings in the young Adult Choir. Also play the piano she an puppeteer at the Church.; [a.] Flint, MI

JONES, CHRISTINA
[b.] January 12, 1980, Wichita, KS; [p.] Jimmy and Ester Jones; [ed.] Currently Attending Campus High School; [hon.] Honor Roll Student at Campus High School; [pers.] I praise my heavenly father for giving me this talent. I hope that in some way, someone will be reached through my poetry.; [a.] Haysville, KS

JONES, DAVID
[oth. writ.] Many poems, short stories and books; [a.] Vero Beach, FL

JONES, DONNA
[b.] March 6, 1914, Arkansas; [p.] Stella B. (Cates)/ Eugene Masters; [m.] Raymons R. Jones, May 21, 1930; [ch.] 1 daughter; [ed.] High School; [occ.] Retired Garment Worker; [memb.] United Methodist Church, United Methodist Women, Royal Neighbors of America; [pers.] I'm just a silly ole Great Grandma who loves children and all others. I repair all the rips and tears for this little town of ours. Have trouble going up the stairs but time for hugs and listenin'. (Most all call me Grandma Donna who does all the fixin'.

JONES, FREDA ANN
[b.] April 26, 1967, New Kensington PA; [p.] Donna Sweeney, Robert Jones; [ch.] Krystle Jean Jones, 8 yrs. old; [ed.] Currently a Jr. at Concord College, Athens, WV majoring in Social Work; [occ.] Office Manager for Concord College, Beckley, WV; [oth. writ.] Several poems, a couple of short stories - none published; [a.] Beckley, WV

JONES, GEORGIA
[oth. writ.] Journalism, playwriting, short fiction; [pers.] Presently involved in the outline (computer) literary movement hosting a poetry area and with a weekly commentary column on Women's Wire.; [a.] San Carlos, CA

JONES, JACQUELINE ANN MARIA
[b.] June 6, 1980, Cleveland; [p.] Glen M. and Iris Quinones Jones; [ed.] Freshman at Brunswick Senior High School, Ascension of Our Lord Elementary School; [occ.] Secretarial Assistant for Langdon Vertal and Co., Babysitter; [hon.] Academic Excellence Award, Presidential Academic Fitness Award, Cleveland Municipal Clerk of Courts Benny Bonanno Resolution, and the Ladies Auxiliary Polish Legion of American Veterans Essay Citation; [oth. writ.] An essay entitled "What it means to be an American"; [pers.] In my writing, I attempt to illustrate my perceptive on everyday life and the hardships we the youth of today's society must face now, while looking towards a better, more brighter future.; [a.] Brunswick, OH

JONES, JOHN
[pen.] John Jones; [b.] October 7, 1970, Indianapolis, IN; [p.] Edna and Robert Jones; [ed.] GED from Arsenal Technical High School in 1991; [occ.] Assembler; [memb.] Tenth Street Baptist Church; [hon.] Too many to list; [pers.] To make Indianapolis, Indiana a better

place and strive to put its nickname "Naptown" on the map; [a.] Indianapolis, IN

JONES, KEVIN E.
[b.] October 17, 1967, Benton Harbor, MI; [p.] Jacqueline M. Jones, Allen F. Jones; [ed.] Kalamazoo Loy Norrix H.S., Northeast Missouri State Univ.; [hon.] NMSU Dean's List, President's Honorary Scholarship, McNair Scholar, Missouri Academy of Sciences Presenter; [oth. writ.] Smiles are oft denied, Wonder of Maya, Ghetto Bird, Happy Season. All published in windfall literary journal.; [pers.] I am strongly influenced by writers of the harlem renaissance (i.e., Langston Hughes, Claude McKay, Countee Cullen, and Zora Neace Hurston).; [a.] Ypsilanti, MI

JONES, MICHAEL L.
[b.] July 26, 1962, Chicago, IL; [p.] Marvin and Marianne Jones; [m.] Divorced; [ch.] Brianna Dominique; [ed.] Simeon Vocational High Columbia College, Chicago, Austin Peay, Tenn. Daley College Chicago Fort Ben Harrison for Bus. Admin.; [occ.] Mental Health Tech.; [memb.] Work with children and senior citizens, Member of Hull House, also a member for homeless animals; [hon.] High School Treasurer, Year Book Committee; [oth. writ.] My personal poems that I have tucked away; [pers.] Take one day at a time. Believe in God. Believe in yourself. Love you for what you are always.; [a.] Elgin, IL

JONES, PAMELA
[b.] Atlanta, GA; [p.] Ethel M. McLemore; [ed.] B.A. degree in Communications - Clark Atlanta University; [occ.] Public Relations; [memb.] Public Relations Society Association (PRSA), Atlanta Women In Business (Note: I am in the process of joining these two groups. Shall I not be able to join, I will notify you not to publish the piece of information.); [pers.] I want people to know that regardless what happens in life, there's a God and He's there with us until the end. God loves us all.; [a.] Atlanta, GA

JONES, PAULETTE M. MCGEE
[b.] March 28, 1957, Prince George, VA; [p.] Leroy and Alice McGee; [m.] Lesley Jones; [ch.] Juaquina, Keijae, Sedale and Seaira; [ed.] Burlington Twp High Burlington County College; [occ.] Correction Sgt. New Jersey Dept. of Corrections; [oth. writ.] Numerous other writings; [pers.] Within your life time, you must strive to be all you can be. Not what others want you to be.; [a.] Willingboro, NJ

JONES, REV. CLYDE R.
[pen.] Rev. Clyde R. Jones; [b.] September 9, 1923, Wilkesbarrel, PA; [p.] Clyde D. Jones and Mary Wade Jones; [m.] Phyllis McMullen Jones, January 1, 1946; [ch.] Richard Clyde, Bylon Edward, Mary Cellinne Faith Veronica, Timothy Paul, Gerald Nelson, Geraldine Nanette; [ed.] High School, Elim Bible Institute, and Seminars - Ordained. Minister of Assemblies of God. Pastor and Evangelist.; [occ.] Retired, continuing in radio work, Host many times on WH01-1600AM Allentown, Pa.; [memb.] New Life A/G - Tamaqua, Pa. (son Richard is the Pastor), Honorary Member of Sheriffs Dept., Member of "Light for Lost" missionary outreach; [hon.] (Sang at World's Fair) Whole family was honored as "Jones Gospel Singers at World's Fair - 1964-65 - (also on Closed Circuit Television), Honored to be Men's Director for 4 years in East Central Section of Pa-al G. (Retreats etc.), received certificates from governor; [oth. writ.] Have written many articles for Newspaper; [pers.] I endeavor to treat my fellow man, as I would want to be treated. I reach out to those in need.; [a.] Lehighton, PA

JONES-STREETS, URSULLA M.
[b.] December 6, 1962, Jonesboro, LA; [p.] Ruthie Long, Wesley Long; [m.] Virgil Jones, October 20, 1984; [ch.] Onya Aleece, Arrabia Marshay; [ed.] Richard Gahr High, Adelphi Business College; [occ.] Secretary, CBC Naval Base, Port Huenemeca; [oth. writ.] Several poems unpublished; [pers.] For me, expressing how I feel through writing gives me the power to speak with complete thought and confidence. Without interruption. I have the floor.; [a.] Oxnard, CA

JONES, TERRY F.
[b.] November 3, 1964, Alabama; [p.] Jerry Jones and Janet Jones; [m.] Mia Jones, October 15, 1994; [ch.] Ashton Jones; [ed.] Riverdale High, University of Alabama; [occ.] Operations Manager Huntsman Film Products; [pers.] I have been given this life as a loan, how will I repay this debt? For it is a great debt indeed. With the help of my wife, all will be even when the marker is called.; [a.] Murfreesboro, TN

JONES, WILLIAM HENRY
[pen.] William Henry Jones, Bill Jones, Captain J; [b.] April 1, 1924, Black Diamond, WA; [p.] Helenor Jones and John Lloyd Jones (Deceased); [m.] Barbara Jones, May 17, 1960; [ch.] Robert Jones and Denise Williams; [ed.] B.A. San Diego State Graduate Federal Health Care Executives Institute Graduate, Naval School of Hospital Administration; [occ.] Captain MSC USN Ret. (37 1/2 years of Naval Service); [memb.] Fleet Reserve Assn., Alumni Assn.. Federal Health Care Executives Institute; [hon.] Legion of Merit, 15 other Military Awards, Numerous Commendations - All Navy; [oth. writ.] Numerous poems to friends and family with no attempt to publish to date; [pers.] I believed in God and my fellowmen not in materialism. To give assistance where and when appropriate with humor, affection, love and mutual respect with appreciation for the true value and beauty of life; [a.] San Marcos, CA

JOPE, REYNALDO ENCINA
[b.] October 21, 1967, Philippines; [p.] Alejandro Jope, Genoveva Encina; [ed.] Bula Elementary School, Mindanao State University, University of Texas - Pan American; [occ.] Math Teacher, Ida Diaz Junior High, Hidalgo, Texas; [memb.] Filipino - American Association of the Rio Grande Valley, Sacred Heart Church Choir, Edinburgh, Texas; [hon.] 4th Place (National level), Nov. 1990 Professional Board Exam for Teachers (Philippines), 1st Place (Regional level), Oct. 1991 Professional Career Service Exam (Philippines), Distinction Award for Writing (1990), Alay sa Talino Award for Writing (1989); [oth. writ.] "The Journey Of The Heart" (Editors Choice Awardee), published in the anthology After The Storm by the National Library of Poetry; [pers.] In everyone's heart, there lurks a hero awaiting his turn.; [a.] Edinburgh, TX

JOUDREY, BONNIE
[b.] January 30, 1916, Washington, WA; [p.] Thomas and Gertrude Little; [m.] Charles Joudrey, November 14, 1936; [ch.] Charlene, Jack, Linda, Daniel and William; [ed.] Completed High School; [occ.] Retired; [oth. writ.] Poems for holidays, birthdays, events in life, Senior Center Programs; [pers.] I have enjoyed writing poems for a long time. The first one was for my Mother at age ten for Mother's Day. It was placed on her bedroom wall for many years. I will soon be 80 years old.; [a.] Ketchikan, AK

JUILLERAT, RUBY
[pen.] Ruby Juill; [b.] October 12, 1913, Struthers, OH; [p.] Charles and Anna Libert; [m.] Emil Juillerat, February 24, 1932; [ch.] Emil Eugene, Harold Leroy and Richard Roy; [ed.] 2 yr. High School - Poland Ohio, 1 yr. Cleveland Institute of Music., 1 yr. Dana, Young-

stown Ohio., 10 yrs Private Music Study; [occ.] Retired; [memb.]10 yrs as member of Song writers of Youngstown, Ohio, Member of Jehovahs Witnesses; [hon.] Placed 7 years straight in yearly contest of SW of Youngstown, Ohio, 3 1st, 3 2nd and 1 3rd. Never tried for publication for anything; [oth. writ.] A musical play (Nothing Is Forever) both script and music. Submitted poem adjusted lyric from musical - other? Children stories.; [pers.] I almost ignored this but nothing ventured, nothing gained have never tried anything but now maybe my song (Our Ohio Home) which was in the finals for the Ohio States song will be used at State fair. (Only a chance); [a.] Hazlehurst, MS

JUNG, WOONG-SAE JOHN
[b.] November 3, 1977, Seoul, Korea; [p.] Dr. Yun-Joo Jung, Phd, Young-Hwa Jung; [ed.] Strake Jesuit College Preparatory, Paul Revere Middle School; [pers.] We live in a society blindfolded from true realities, in which knowledge corrupts without prejudice and different points of perception go unrealized. I am in constant battle with clockwork oranges, in which two opposite extremes are virtually the same.; [a.] Houston, TX

JUNTUNEN, ARTHUR ERNEST
[pen.] Art Ernest Juntunen; [b.] May 23, 1916, Houghton City, MI; [p.] August, Elma Juntunen (deceased); [m.] Anne Marie Juntunen, July 9, 1976 (my first wife is diceased); [ch.] One step-daughter, one step-son, 6 step grandchildren, 1 step g'grandson; [ed.] Not quite 4 years of College (Roosevelt College, Chicago, Il.); [occ.] Retired from postal service, treasurer of church; [memb.] Victory Christian Assembly, Baraga, MI formerly a member: A.C.L.U. Socialist Party: NAACP, congress of Racial Equality: Some peace organizations; [oth. writ.] Once sent in two poems to Marquette, MI. Mining Journal - one published, '79 or '80. Editor: minority union pepper while in Colorado: handed out "peace" messages of mine to Denver area students and others.; [pers.] Consider myself a left-of-center Christian, was a socialist party member from 1940-1952, in the mild-fifties took to a pacifist-anarchist view. Am still a pacifist in outlook.; [a.] Bavaga, MI

JURNEY, DOROTHY
[b.] September 2, 1927, Dublin, TX; [p.] W. L. (Fat), Alma (Dot) Gee; [m.] Wilber Jurney, April 10, 1976; [ch.] Sue McLeery, Joanie Anderson, Delaine Jurney; [ed.] High School; [oth. writ.] 16 Poems and the history of my life growing up on a farm during the depression. The hard times, the love. Through it all we made it together; [pers.] The poem: Memories like a river flowing, is about the farm where I was born 67 years ago - we still own this farm, which will be in our family 100 years.; [a.] Dublin, TX

KACZMAREK, MAGGIE
[pen.] Alena; [b.] August 27, 1978, Poland; [p.] Wes and Dana Kaczmarek; [ed.] Sophomore in High School; [occ.] Student; [memb.] DECA; [hon.] Honorable Mention in Iliad Press Spring 1995 Award Program; [oth. writ.] "All which never dies" various other poems; [pers.] I feel that love and understanding are the bases on which all of life's relationships are supported. I try and bring this idea out in all of my poems.; [a.] Madison, WI

KALLAND, MATTHEW E.
[b.] October 31, 1976, Torrance, CA; [p.] Eric Kalland, Edita Kalland; [m.] Nichole Kalland; [ed.] Colorado's Finest Alternative High School (CFAHS); [occ.] Telemarketer; [oth. writ.] "Battle for Home" and "The Talking Bear" recognized consecutively in the Young Author's Conference; [pers.] Just give me another sunrise; [a.] Denver, CO

KAMINKOW, SCOTT D.
[b.] August 26, 1977, Baltimore, MD; [p.] Mark and Mary Lou; [ed.] Westminster High School; [occ.] Student; [pers.] The poem "Friends" was written in memory of my best friend Steve whom I will never forget.; [a.] Westminster, MD

KAMMEL, JAMES
[b.] February 12, 1973, Stuart, FL; [p.] James Kammel, Deana Gary; [ed.] Martin County High School US Coast Guard Academy; [occ.] Officer USCG; [memb.] US Sailing Save the Manatees Club, USCGA Alumni Association; [hon.] Graduated Honors, Dean's List, Seven semesters, Most outstanding offshore sailor; [oth. writ.] Numerous unpublished poems and stories. Article for sailing news.; [pers.] I try to take dark thoughts and lighten them with a deeper understanding of the whole picture. We only see a piece at a time, sometimes we need to step back and get a better look.

KAO, KATHERINE
[pen.] Katherine Kao; [b.] July 31, 1984, Taiwan; [p.] Imin Kao and Elarne Chang; [ed.] Currently in Mount School (W.S. Mount), 5th Grade - Kitty Jean Lakatos' class; [pers.] I've enjoyed writing poems since 3rd grade when Ms. Aoyagi taught us the basic principles of writing poetry. After that I felt poetry played an important part in my life.; [a.] Stony Brook, NY

KAPLAN, CAITLIN RAE
[pen.] Rae; [b.] July 12, 1979, Chicago, IL; [ed.] North Shore Country Day School; [oth. writ.] I have written several poems that have been published in surrounding newspapers.; [pers.] Like my friend Bekki once said "I am not sad just existing" I wrote this poem about three of my good friends: Yvette, Chris, and Adi. I love you all! Love is a game that has no rules and can easily be lost!; [a.] Highland Park, IL

KARMIN, ALAN
[b.] September 10, 1960, Brooklyn, NY; [p.] Edward Karmin and Sandra Leibowitz Karmin; [m.] Laura Karmin, February 28, 1985; [ch.] Eddie, Beckie; [ed.] Univ. of Miami, FL; [occ.] Journalism Teacher and Athletic Coach; [memb.] Society of Professional Journalists, International Society of Poets; [hon.] Alpha Epsilon RHO SPJ 1st Place Award for Sports Reporting - 3 consecutive years.; [hon.] Greater Media Newspapers' Journalist of the Year; [oth. writ.] Numerous award-winning news articles, poem published in After the Storm.; [a.] Sayreville, NJ.

KASAKOV, VIVIAN
[b.] April 11, 1931, South River, NJ; [p.] Antonina and Prokop Makarus; [m.] Michael Kasakov (deceased), September 1, 1963; [pers.] My poems are inspired by the deep feelings within my heart, influenced by the people who have touched my life throughout the years, and by the strong faith that has always been a part of me.; [a.] Spotswood, NJ

KAZIMOU, ZEYNEB
[pen.] Zey, Zana; [b.] March 1, 1979, Newark, NJ; [p.] Ferdinand and Arcadia Kazimou; [m.] I have a boyfriend, Joseph, engaged February 26, 1995; [ed.] I'm ending my 2nd year in High School; [occ.] I work in a fast food restaurant, (Burger King); [memb.] I have been attending a dance school, Sussex County Dance and Gymnastics, once a week for five or more years. I've danced since age four.; [hon.] Sussex Dance and Gym. Award; [oth. writ.] I have written lots of poem but this is my first in any type of publication. I am pleased that I now have experience in competing.; [pers.] I was inspired by my English teacher, Mrs. Hill, and my boyfriend, Joe. Without them I would not have entered this contest. I feel writing is the best way to deal with

one's feelings.; [a.] Hopatcong, NJ

KEARNS, JESSICA
[b.] June 9, 1977, Harrisonburg, VA; [p.] Lance Kearns and Joan Eger; [ed.] Harrisonburg High School; [oth. writ.] Poetry published in "Walking On The Sides Of Our Feet," a compilation of poems from poet-in-the-schools program in '94. "Chunk O' Poetry," Creative Writing classes in '95.; [pers.] I once heard poetry, along with any other creative thing, should not be self-absorbed. I strongly disagree with this because everything we do is sprouted from a seed inside. (Whether we are aware of it or not.); [a.] Harrisonburg, VA

KEEN, LAURA K.
[pen.] Reet; [b.] January 18, 1904, GA; [p.] Caesar, Ella Brown; [m.] Bob Lee Keen, December 24, 1922; [ch.] Sarah E. Keen, McGee; [ed.] 8th Grade, I always love reading and writing; [occ.] Retired; [oth. writ.] None published have lot more in Book Form none has been publish all in religious form

KEENAN, CHRISTINA
[b.] November 11, 1954, Illinois; [m.] William Keenan, November 16, 1991; [ch.] Colin Bernard, Trisha Marie; [ed.] Eisenhower High School, Maraine Valley College, Evangelical School of Nursing; [occ.] Registered Nurse; [hon.] May 1994, Tinley Park Writers Group, 2nd Place Poetry. December 1993 N.O.W. Fiction competition, first finalist, short story (entries included 38 states and 6 countries), Nov. 1990, World of poetry, Great Free contest honorable mention; [oth. writ.] Several poems, articles, and personal essays; [pers.] A writer's audience is vast and varied. The common link is emotion. As a writer, I use this link to evoke a deep emotional response in the reader. I try to speak to what is common in every reader, the soul.; [a.] Frankfort, IL

KEGHER, CATHERINE
[b.] August 20, 1980, West Covina, CA; [p.] Donald and Carol Kegner; [ed.] I am in 9th grade, I have enjoyed writing poetry since 7th grade; [hon.] This is my first poem ever published!; [oth. writ.] I have written other poems entitled: Dreams, Flowers, A Mother's Heart, Migration, The Horses of the Wild, and Whales; [pers.] I enjoy writing poetry because it is a beautiful way to describe nature.; [a.] Perris, CA

KELLER, GEORGE E.
[b.] September 23, 1914, Benton Harbor, MI; [p.] Lula May and James E. Keller; [m.] Mary Ann (Siriano) Keller, September 3, 1943; [ch.] George J. Keller (Deceased); [ed.] Benton Harbor High School 1934 graduate; [occ.] Printing, Bookbinding, Computer Software Assembly; [hon.] Senior Class Poet 1934 Grad Cerimony; [pers.] Keep active mentally and physically as you grow older; [a.] Benton Harbor, MI

KELLY JR., DONALD THOMAS
[b.] February 27, 1961, Somers Point, NJ; [p.] Donald Kelly, Peggy Kelly; [m.] Diane Kelly, August 31, 1985; [ed.] Mainland Regional High School, Atlantic Community College; [occ.] Electrician; [memb.] Central United Methodist Church, Local Union #351-IBEW; [hon.] Dean's List, Apprentice of the year 1988 for National Electrical Contractors Association (Local #211); [oth. Writ.] Music: A Lenten Cantata, numerous Sacred Choral Anthems written and performed, numerous songs and classical piano compositions; [pers.] I strive to bring glory to God, and also to acknowledge the beauty of this world, through my art, music and writings.; [a.] Mays Landing, NJ

KENSON, KELLY D.
[b.] March 23, 1974, Cincinnati, OH; [p.] David And Sharyn Kenson; [ed.] High School, currently attending the University of North Florida; [occ.] Car Prep; [pers.] Ugliness has painted me broken; [a.] Jacksonville, FL

KERSEY, HENRY GEORGE
[pen.] Hank Kersey; [b.] October, 1955, Chicago; [pers.] The United States Library of Congress has a statue prohibiting the copying of this material, or any part thereof. Without permission.; [a.] Oak Lawn, IL

KESLING, MARY J.
[pen.] Mary J. Kesling; [b.] May 30, 1925, Dayton, OH; [p.] Robert M. Walter, Ruth M. Walter; [m.] Keith Kesling, May 27, 1944; [ch.] Nancy, Bonnie, Gayle, Sandy; [ed.] Northridge High, University of Dayton, Dayton Art Institute; [occ.] Former librarian at Murlin Heights Elementary School in Vandalia, Ohio. I am presently a free lance writer.; [oth. writ.] Reading to the children in the library, I found a void for certain holidays, so I wrote poems for them. One, "The Lazy Easter Bunny", was the focal point of an Easter Special Show produced by Channel 9, Windsor, Ontario.; [pers.] Let me never fail to do what I think is right, for I shall not pass this way again.; [a.] Shelby Township, MI

KESSLER, CONNIE C.
[b.] February 12, 1942, Latrobe, PA; [p.] Giles and Marion Campbell; [m.] Gary A. Kessler Sr. (deceased), August 22, 1995; [ch.] Scott Alan, Gary Allen Jr.; [ed.] Greater Latrobe High School, WCCC (Westmoreland County Community College); [occ.] Materials Analysis Technician at Kenametal Corporate Technology Center; [memb.] Bethany United Methodist Church, American Diabetes Assoc.; [hon.] Several poems published in Church papers and also newspapers. Received an honorable mention. "Golden Poets Award" for one poem. Presidents list at WCCC.; [oth. writ.] Had a poem written about our new Technology Center printed in our Kennametal Newsletter. Have written poems for friends and graduation gifts.; [pers.] I write how I feel and do this mainly for my enjoyment. My father also wrote poetry. And was very good. I'm much better at poems of thanks than letters. It seems they go together better.; [a.] Latrobe, PA

KESSLER, ERIN MICHELL
[b.] October 15, 1980, Olympia, WA; [p.] Julie, Earl Davidson; [ed.] Middle School; [hon.] Most improved in baseball, Dare Program; [pers.] I get my ideas from events in my life, and I like to read books of all kinds. And I enjoy writing poems.; [a.] Lacey, WA

KESSLER, MARK A.
[b.] July 26, 1967, Illinois; [m.] Lisa L. Kessler; [ch.] Ryan Kessler; [ed.] Highland High School UNM TVI; [oth. writ.] Imagine That (The Book); [pers.] To imagine, is to create!; [a.] Albuquerque, NM

KETZER, STEPHEN ERIC
[b.] July 15, 1974, Aurora, CO; [p.] Steve Ketzer Jr., Delline Ketzer; [m.] Rachelle Duggins (still engaged); [ed.] Palm Desert, High School; [occ.] Operation specialist, in the US Navy; [hon.] Dean's List, Principal's Honor Role, Outstanding Delegate Award for Model United Nations, Senior Best in Vocals, Palm Desert Light; [oth. writ.] Published when I was 10 in the Ssentinel Record Hot Springs, AR, other than that still trying; [pers.] It is my firm belief that all paths, as long as they are positive, end at the same place.; [a.] San Diego, CA

KEYES, BARBARA J.
[p.] Mr. and Mrs. James McCarthy; [m.] Frederick Keyes, May 18, 1968; [ch.] Jeffrey Keyes (son), Jodi Keyes (daughter); [ed.] BA Liberal Arts/Management from Southern Vermont College 1995, Bennington, Vermont; [occ.] Manager - Owner, Barbara's Past Antiques; [memb.] Advisory Board for Southern Vermont College Nursing Programs; [hon.] National Dean's List, Who's Who Among Students In Colleges and Universities 1995; [oth. Writ.] Feature Stories Mountain Press Southern Vermont College student newspaper; [pers.] "The learning process is never ending and each day is a learning experience."; [a.] Williamstown, MA

KHIM, SUNSARY SAMBATH
[b.] September 4, 1983, Forth Worth, TX; [p.] Pot Khim and Nan Yang; [ed.] In 1991 I went to Stevenson Elementary School. Now I am in 6th grade attending Brancroff Middle School; [hon.] I was in the Honor Roll in 6th grade; [pers.] I love to express my thoughts and feeling by writing poem during my free time.; [a.] Long Beach, CA

KIKUCHI, TAKEJIRO
[pen.] Tommy Kikuchi, Jiro-Ga; [b.] May 4, 1969, Tokyo, Japan; [p.] Tokeo Shiga, Kayo Suzuki; [ed.] American School in Japan, Cheshire Academy, Clark University, BA in Economics; [hon.] Several medals 4 trophies in swimming in Connecticut State Championships, New England Championship 4 East-Japan Championship; [oth. writ.] 4 unpublished fiction novels. Currently working in 5th novel.; [pers.] Never had any courage to get any of my work published, hopefully this will change in the near future. Heavily influenced by R. Ludlum, E. V. Lustbader, S. King.; [a.] Sunnyside, NY

KILE, LARRY WAYNE
[b.] June 30, 1964, Louisville, KY; [p.] Curtis Wayne Kile, Wanda Carrol Kile; [m.] Lisa Jean Pearce Kile, July 27, 1985; [ed.] Returned to adult Education System KY, Awarded GED September 25, 1992; [occ.] Hardwood floor installer and finisher; [oth. writ.] Many, many unpublished poems and lyrics. Also paint still life oil paintings and enjoy writing and play in guitar.; [pers.] I write by Gods light in hopes that my poetry and writings may lift the spirits of readers. During there times of need and understanding.; [a.] Louisville, KY

KILGORE, DOLLY
[b.] January 26, 1995, Cullman, AL; [p.] Asa Kemp and Verna Mae Kempa; [ch.] Sabrina Ann Kent; [ed.] Graduated Griffin High School 1973; [occ.] Sewing Machine Operator, Fashion Industries; [oth. writ.] Personal poems to family and friends; [pers.] Thanks to my daughter for the love and inspiration. Thanks to my friends, Lucky, Joy, Jean, Vickie, and Betty for having faith in me.; [a.] Griffin, GA

KILLION, MENROSE ELIZABETH
[b.] March 7, 1959, Detroit, MI; [p.] Walter Lee Spears, Fannye Dargin Spears; [ch.] Terence Lee Randolph; [ed.] Detroit Northern High, Detroit College of Business; [occ.] Owner, Essence of Paris Salon, Customer Care Rep, Ameritech; [memb.] Metropolitan AME Zion Church Stewardess Board, Young Adult Missionery Society, Sisters are doing it for themselves; [hon.] The Detroit News Scholastic Writing Award, Wayne State University's Manuscript Day Award; [pers.] I write from the heart in an effort to touch a soul, touch a mind. An early love for the writings of Nikki Giovanni and Langston Hughes inspired me to express life in words as I view it through my eyes. And my wonderful mother made my life worth writing about.; [a.] Detroit, MI

KIMMEL, CAROL L. ADAMS
[pen.] C-Kim; [b.] May 28, 1935, Oakland, CA; [p.] Ernest Adams, Elinor Adams; [m.] John Paul Kimmel (Divorce 1992), February 14, 1965; [ch.] David L. Cabral, Valerie Lynn Kimmel, Roxanna Marie Kimmel; [ed.] Alameda High, CA, Solano Community CA, Hauser School of Decorative Arts, OK; [occ.] Certif. Art Instructor, Sculptress, Painter, General Office, Receptionist; [memb.] National Assoc. of Female Exec. Business and Professional Women of America National Society of Painters, Member of Nevada and Calif Art Leagues; [hon.] Three times honored for art work now in Smithsonian's National Museum permanent collection yrs '89, '88, '90, Grand champion, first, thru third wards in Colorado, Nevada and Calif; [oth. writ.] Short Stories, Poems, Pen and ink drawings published in San Francisco Examiner; [pers.] Each day is a new beginning. Love for Earth and all mankind has been the spiritual foundation for all sculptures and writings. I strive to make all people feel entwined in togetherness by love in growth, visions, and relationships. Even in grief of love lost, each day is a new beginning given by our creator.; [a.] Springfield, OR

KING, CHERYL ANN
[b.] August 18, 1964, Fitchburg, MA; [p.] Linda Brouillet, Edward Brouillet; [m.] Philip R. King Jr., October 24, 1981; [ch.] Richard Edward, Micheal Philip; [ed.] Fitchburg School Systems Graduated 1983; [occ.] Worked in retail, currently a housewife; [pers.] Thanks to Mrs. Eckfeldt a fifth grade Elementary Teacher for the encouragement to write poems.; [a.] Tampa, FL

KING, GLENNGO A.
[b.] January 19, 1952, Brooklyn, NY; [p.] James A. King, Sara King; [ed.] High School of Art and Design, The Cooper Union School of Art, Hunter College; [occ.] Art Teacher, NYC Bd. of Ed., Actor/Puppeteer; [memb.] Actors' Equity Assoc., Sag and Aftra, the Puppeteers of America, United Federation of Teachers; [oth. writ.] Several Poems Published in Local Literary Art Journals; [pers.] I strive to elevate global consciousness using many local cosmic ingredients, including language, art, music, puppetry, dance, etc. I Have been greatly influenced by a multi-national array of poets and writers, known and unknown.; [a.] Brooklyn, NY

KING, IDA LOIS
[b.] April 16, 1942, Austin, TX; [p.] Fannie Ruth Bolden, Joe T. Bolden; [ch.] Lashawn Jordan, Loinel T. Fisher; [ed.] Thomas Jefferson High, San Antonio, TX., University of Texas at Austin, Mesa College, San Diego, CA; [occ.] Bridal Consultant Dillards, Highland Mall, Austin, TX; [memb.] Texas Temple #1254 IBPO Elks of World, Highland AME Delta Sigma Theta Sorority; [oth. writ.] No other published writings but, I have a notebook full; [pers.] My poems and writings are all spiritual offerings. They have all been given to me to help or comfort others. "God's spirituality, expressed by moritality: Perpetuating positivity and possibility."; [a.] Austin, TX

KING JR., RAYMOND W.
[pen.] Ramon King Jr.; [b.] January 8, 1954, Muskegon; [p.] Ray and Roycine King; [m.] Divorced; [ch.] Chip, Christa and Kari Kin; [ed.] High School Grad., Muskeen High School; [occ.] Self-employed; [oth. writ.] "Left me", American Music Festival no - awards; [pers.] Writing seems to ease the pain of life. Maybe someday the words I write will be shared with someone, somewhere, to ease there pain.; [a.] Montague, MI

KING, MS. MAGGIE EVELYN
[b.] January 31, 1949, Charlotte, NC; [p.] Thomas, Maggie Lee King (Deceased); [m.] Divorced; [ch.] Paula R. Stearns, Marla Patterson, Travis Stearns (grandson); [ed.] GED; [occ.] Ocean/Export Forwarder; [memb.] Friendship Baptist Church; [oth. writ.] In process (Story of my Life), Weight Loss Story was written in The Ebony Magazine about my daughter and

myself September 1994; [pers.] Never fear human, only God who is our maker. And the only one that will accept you as you are.

KING, NADENE C.
[b.] Sumter Co.; [p.] Mr. and Mrs. Leaston S. Cooper Sr.; [m.] John King Jr., November 3, 1960; [ch.] Dr. John D. King, Samuel T. King, Kenneth L. King, Jarvis C. King; [ed.] Staley High School, Savannah State College, BS, Additional Study Fort Valley State College, GA, State University, Master's Degree; [occ.] Retired School Teacher and Writer; [memb.] Lebanon Baptist Church, NAACP; [hon.] Alpha Kappa Mu Honor Society, Graduated Summa Cum Laude; [oth. writ.] Poems published in local newspaper, in other anthologies by National Lib. Poetry, Quill Books, Sparrow Grass Poetry Forum; [pers.] There is some good in every one I look for that and seek to bring out the best in those I'm around.; [a.] Smithville, GA

KING, NELIDA RIOS
[pen.] Nellie; [b.] August 11, 1938, Puerto Rico; [p.] Esteban Rios and Emelina Febus Rios; [m.] Boyd Wendell King, August 27, 1955; [ch.] Wendell Ray King, Sadie Lou Wiltshire, Marilee Ann Ciehoski, Leyla Yvonne Scatt; [ed.] Florencio Santiago High and Northern Virginia Community College. A few courses at George Mason University and other home study course.; [occ.] Housewife; [memb.] Westover Baptist Church; [oth. writ.] Local newspaper (Journal Messenger) published several articles; [pers.] Writing a poem depicts an arduous excavation inside your soul. The more laborious your efforts, doesn't necessarily mean the more value to your treasure. You may find only a handful of dust! But it's best to labor than not to labor at all.; [a.] Manassas, VA

KINNE, MERLE W.
[b.] September 23, 1917, Minnesota; [m.] Patricia Ann, October 12, 1954; [ch.] Kevin W. (38); [ed.] Central High, Minneapolis, Dunwoody Institute, Minneapolis; [occ.] Retired; [memb.] The Heritage Foundation, B.P.O.E. (Demit.); [oth. writ.] Two articles published - Intl. Bow Hunter, 1992-93. Several epic poems of the Old West. Western fiction novel, plus two of foreign intrigue. Sequel in progress. None pub. forty short stories.; [pers.] At 77 I have been writing since penning my memoirs in 1990. An adventurous life is fodder for my PC. Philosophically, I regret weilding a pen so late in life, but hope some readers will find a message in my work.; [a.] Long Beach, CA

KINNEY, WENDELL T.
[pen.] Wen; [b.] November 22, 1961, Uniontown, PA; [p.] Robert and Oliser Kinney; [m.] Pamela E. Kinney, April 14, 1990; [ch.] Wendell and Micaiah Kinney; [ed.] 12th; [occ.] Rehab Aide; [oth. writ.] Poems; [pers.] I can do all things through Christ who strengthens me. Phil. 4:13; [a.] Josephine, PA

KINTAUDI, DELONDI
[pen.] Maleek Kalijh; [b.] January 26, 1976, Los Angeles; [p.] Prudencia and Leon; [ed.] Sophmore at La Sierra University; [occ.] Medical Clerk; [oth. writ.] The Beggar, The Happening, Nikita, Shirley's Gold, Last Laugh; [pers.] Life is a mess ... clear it up. You can do anything in life if you put your heart, soul, and head behind it.; [a.] Montclair, CA

KLEIN, TONY
[b.] January 22, 1967, Iowa City, IA; [p.] Cletus Klein, Jeanne Seaton; [ed.] West High School, Military - US Marine Corps, Kirkwood Community College; [occ.] College Student; [memb.] St. Patricks Parish, North Liberty American Legion, (NAHC) North American Hunters Club; [hon.] Rifle Expert Badge 3rd award,

Letters of Appreciation (2), Sea Service Deployment Ribbon 3rd award, Good Conduct Medal, National Defense Service Medal, South Asia Service Medal with 2 stars; [pers.] Life is a circle. What you do inside of it can never prepare you for the tragedies ahead!; [a.] Tiffin, IA

KLINKHAMMER, TINA MARIE
[pen.] Katie Frost; [b.] May 17, 1966, Rockford, IL; [p.] Marilyn Forrester (Grandmother); [m.] Shawn Klinkhammer, July 8, 1994; [occ.] Aspiring Writer, Loss Prevention Officer; [memb.] I am a member of the American Society for the prevention of cruelty to animals, a member of the international society of poets.; [hon.] Some of my honors include the acceptance of two of my poems to be published in the fall of 1995 and a nomination and acceptance as a distinguished member of the international society of poets; [oth. writ.] A poem titled "Every Now and Then" published in an anthology called "East of the Sunrise". This poem, several articles for newspapers and magazines and I am currently working on a novel.; [pers.] With everything I write I strive to touch the very soul and spirit of the reader. I want my writing to be remembered and carried within the readers heart.; [a.] Rockford, IL

KLIPPENSTEIN, DONALDA
[b.] July 17, 1928, Wheeling, WV; [p.] Donald Layton, Dencie; [m.] Timothy Klippenstein, June 14, 1985; [ch.] Linda Szczypiorski, Cheryl Gordon, Harry A. Miller, III; [ed.] 2 yrs College, Chapman College, Fullerton, 1965, Wheeling, WV, Triadelphia High School 1946, Wheeling, WV, Woodsdale Elementary, 1942; [occ.] Retired, Life Insurance Rep., Secretary 1960-70, Pennsylvania Life 1982; [memb.] Holy Cross Lutheran Church, San Diego, CA, Ecumenical Council of San Diego, (Inter Faith Shelter Network.) ARC Respite Service; [hon.] Salesman of the month, Pennsylvania Life 1982. Grandmother of the Year, 1995, Miss Stardust, 1946; [oth. writ.] I am at present writing a novel "Tomorrow's Dust". I will finish this year, 1995. It has been 50 years in making. Finally my life makes sense.; [pers.] I have lived outrageously without regret and I've learned to trust God to show me the way through protection of God's angelic intervention; [a.] San Diego, CA

KLOTZ, FRIEDA D.
[b.] October 23, 1959, Fairbanks, AK; [ed.] Austin E. Lathrop High School, University of Alaska, Fairbanks, AK; [hon.] Cum Laude, University of Alaska, Fairbanks, AK; [oth. writ.] Other poems published in local west Michigan papers; [pers.] To me, there is nothing more magnificent, more awe-inspiring than the natural wonders of creation and the human spirit. If by my talents, I have shared these treasures, touched your heart and rekindled your spirit, then I have succeeded in my goal.; [a.] Zeeland, MI

KLUMPP, ELIZABETH
[b.] November 11, 1937, Ridgewood, NY; [p.] Paul and Emma Fischer; [m.] Norman Klumpp, March 17, 1963; [ch.] Nanette and Loretta; [ed.] High School (Fort Hamilton-Brooklyn); [occ.] Singer; [pers.] The closeness of love is the substance of life. It is the inspiration of mankind.; [a.] Whiting, NJ

KNAPP, IVO
[b.] July 15, 1923, South Haven, MI; [p.] Henry and Emma Knapp; [m.] Harriet Lockwood Knapp, July 3, 1943; [ch.] Susan Joan; [ed.] 1-6 Lannin Country School, 7-8 Junior High, 9-12 South Haven High School; [occ.] Retired; [memb.] US Army WW II; [oth. writ.] Ancestral poems of our family trees. Numerous other poems plus a centennial poem about the making of a piano (The Everett Epic) published; [a.] South Haven, MI

KNICKERBOCKER, W. E.
[b.] December 28, 1938, Houston, TX; [p.] W. E. Knickerbocker Sr.; [m.] Sandra H. Knickerbocker, January 28, 1962; [ch.] Jon M. Knickerbocker, Amy M. Knickerbocker; [ed.] BA Washington and Lee Univ. (1960), BD Emory University (1965), Ph.D. Emory University (1972); [occ.] Professor of Church History, Memphis Theological Seminary; [memb.] Roman Catholic Church, New York C. S. Lewis Society; [pers.] As a catholic poet, I seek to serve Christ and His church through my poetry.; [a.] Memphis, TN

KNIGHT, REBECCA A.
[pen.] Becky; [b.] September 20, 1948, Kentucky; [p.] Harry W. and Lucille Knight; [ch.] Christy Schroader and Misty Leach, grandchildren: Zachary and Whitney Leach, Dylan Schroader; [ed.] Ohio County High School, Owensboro Jr. College of Business; [occ.] Ins. Agent; [memb.] 20th Century Women's Club; [hon.] Clubwoman of the year 1986-87; [oth. writ.] My first; [pers.] I can reflect memories of childhood in my poems. Being raised in the country can be beneficial. Family values are standards I live by.; [a.] McHenry, KY

KNORR, SASHEEN
[b.] November 9, 1977, CA; [p.] Barry and Christine; [ed.] Ombudsman and Red Mountain High School, I'll soon be attending ASU; [occ.] Full-time student; [hon.] President's Award for Educational Excellence; [oth. writ.] Some more poems, unpublished, "Waterfalling," "Traveling Seat," "Look-out for Purpose," "Look-out for Purpose," "Swirl and World of Thought," also many essays; [pers.] Use the energy that's etched in your soul through motioning nature and beauty's intensified role. I love to feel what's real.; [a.] Mesa, AZ

KNUDSON, RUTH
[b.] April 13, 1937, Harlow, ND; [m.] Kenneth Knudson (Deceased), June 26, 1955; [ch.] Kathy, James, Connie, Coleen, Judy, Kenneth, Randall, Jeffrey; [ed.] Benson County Agricultural School; [occ.] Dietary Cook presently unemployed; [pers.] God has given me many poems through the last few years. As of now none of them are published.; [a.] Litchville, ND

KOENIG, JAMES
[b.] March 6, 1956, Little Rock, AR; [p.] Viola Anna Maria Koenig, Wilbert Koenig; [ed.] Manual High School Indianapolis, Bachelor's and Master of Music from Northwestern University (Dean's List), Goethe Institute in Germany, Studio dell'opera Italiana in Italy, private studies, ad infinitum; [occ.] Opera and concert singer and teacher; [memb.] American Scandinavian Foundation (Past President), Amnesty International, St. Thomas the Apostle Episcopal Church Finlandia Foundation; [hon.] Finlandia Award, Medalist - Tito Gobbi Concorso dell'opera, LoPer Man Poetry Award; [oth. writ.] Poem, Goose-Stepping Through Life... Gallery Series Chicago singing translations of finish songs. A novel - Meter Running Articles Scandinavian Press - on songs of Finland, Art and Ethnicity. Call it a love song there's always one - Cabarets, both one man shows wrote and performed; [pers.] Who cannot respond to the lyrical, the dramatic, the profound, the mysteries, the mystical, the music of it all, be it a song of joy, an elergy, or an "in your face" retort to indignity upon indignity.; [a.] Los Angeles, CA

KOSICH, GEVE FISHER
[pen.] Catherine Cole; [b.] October 12, 1931, Haddonfield, NJ; [p.] Howard Fisher, Ruth Fisher; [m.] Richard Kosich, June 22, 1963; [ch.] Mary Elizabeth, Richard Fisher; [ed.] Haddonfield Memorial High School, The King's College, attented Phila. University of the Arts; [occ.] Professional Artist; [memb.] Haddonfield United Methodist Church, Haddonfield

Club (Tennis), Haddonfort Nightly (Women's Club), DAR, Historical Society of Haddonfield, Tavistook Country Club; [hon.] Poems included in the unsung Vol. II, Awards Won in NJ, Women's Club Writing Contests. Prizes and Awards for paintings, plus have had several man shows; [oth. writ.] I strive to reflect the glory of God and the beauty of creation in poetry and painting. I find most of my inspiration in nature.; [a.] Cherry Hill, NJ

KOVACS, FRANCES
[b.] December 1, 1931, Cleveland; [p.] Emily and John Holowaty; [m.] Gene, May 3, 1952; [ch.] Linda, Cynthia, Christopher, grandchildren: Rochelle, Stephen, Jessica, and Michael; [ed.] High School; [occ.] Professional Cake Decorator. Business called "Custom Cakes by Kovacs"; [memb.] North Coast Sugar Artists, International Cake Exploration Society American Legion Auxiliary, St. Adalbert Catholic Church; [oth. writ.] Published: "The Lonely Heart", "Remembering". Copywrited: "A Loving Farewell". Printed: "Salvations Tree".; [pers.] God gives each one of us talents, but He holds us personally responsible to tap into our own resources. We can then enjoy a life of personal gratification, filled with happiness that can be shared with those we love.

KRAAI, JACK E.
[pen.] E. J. [b.] May 4, 1943, Grand Haven, MI; [p.] Henry and Katie Kraai; [ed.] Coopersville High, Grand Rapids J.C., Michigan State University; [occ.] Retired; [memb.] AAA (member) of Michigan; [oth. writ.] Wrote a children's book: "Patches Goes To Atlantis" (58 Books Sold - Not Published.); [pers.] I enjoy painting, writing, and discussing philosophy. Poem: "Abe" Dedicated to: Family and Friends who have inspired me.; [a.] Allendale, MI

KREITER, EDNA
[pen.] Edna Reeves Kreiter; [b.] February 9, 1937, Greely, MO; [p.] Henry and Georgia Reeves; [m.] Joseph Kreiter Sr. (deceased), April 12, 1966; [ch.] Thomas, Deborah, Marie, John, Daniel and Patricia, stepsons: Joe and Tommy; [ed.] Some Gramer School in MO and AR and Adult Education at Cocoa High at Cocoa, FL; [occ.] Part time telemarkiter and care for disabled daughter; [memb.] Audubon Chapel Baptist Church, 700 Club, VFW Aux. and the NRA; [oth. writ.] Poem in church paper; [pers.] I like to write about a lot of different things. I believe in God and support my country, I was raised in the country and worked with my Dad in timber and the cotton fields; [a.] Merritt Island, FL

KROGER, VIRGINIA ROSE
[b.] May 7, 1972, San Francisco, CA; [p.] Richard Kroger, Madelaine Kroger; [ed.] Terra Nova High, Skyline Community College, San Francisco State University, graduated with BA Radio and Television, magna cum laude; [memb.] Golden Key National Honor Society San Francisco State Alumni; [hon.] Dean's List, Dorothy Dutcher Poetry Award; [oth. writ.] Three poems published in The Talisman (college literary magazine) Second place winner "St. Anthony's Dining Hall", "The Rosary", "Tom Cat"; [pers.] When God shuts a door, he opens a window. And the many windows in life are what inspire my poetry.; [a.] Pacifica, CA

KROLL, MONIQUE GALLOCHER
[b.] June 22, 1926, Angouleme, France; [p.] Etienne Gallocher, Denise Gallocher; [m.] Orville Kroll, August 16, 1963; [ed.] High Education Baccalaureate Level. 6 years of Latin, English and some Spanish. Family of musicians (Operas) Painter (mother) and poets. And a great Hero of the war 1916-1918; [occ.] Just house-wife; [memb.] Member of the "Society of Archeologique at historique de la Charente." France.;

[oth. writ.] More poems in French and English. Wrote my first poem at age 14, during the war 1960, in French: "A La Belgique!" and a short novel at age 15. "Intemperies"; [pers.] Passionate for Archeology and egyptology and ancient civilizations: Egypt, Greece, Pre-Colombian Aztecs, Mayas, and Peruvian Incas, civilizations and Gallo-Romans. "I believe a poet has been in heaven, at sometime, and still remember it...; [a.] Palm Springs, CA

KROUT, HEIDI
[pen.] Heidi Helwig-Krout; [b.] July 6, 1971, York, PA; [p.] Randy and Shirley Helwig; [m.] Douglass W. Krout; [ch.] Kieri P. Krout, Caden Ty Krout; [ed.] Central York High School; [occ.] Housewife and mother; [memb.] American Kennel Club; [hon.] Honorable Mention on other poems; [oth. writ.] Poetry - "Before", "Again", "Until Tomorrow", "Ocean Breeze", etc.; [pers.] My husband Doug, children and animals are my inspiration in life.; [a.] Dover, PA

KRUSE, STEVE
[b.] May 28, 1968, Canton, OH; [p.] Robert Wayne Kruse, Barbara Ann Mitchell; [ed.] Hastinos High School, Houston University of Akron, Akron, Ohio, University of Houston, Houston, TX. Still working toward Baccaulavelate Degree; [occ.] Retail Manager; [hon.] Semi-Finalist Voice of America speech contest, 1985, Published first poem poem submitted, 1995, (National Library of Poetry); [oth. writ.] "Shelter" (1987, poem), "Dig" (1992, poem), "Gerbils" (1992, poem), "Thoughts" (1986, poem), "Intentions" (1990, poem), "Gerbils Cont." (1993, Journal entry), "Expectations" (1991, poem), "Sorrows" (1991, poem), "Sunlight" (1989 poem); [a.] Houston, TX

KRZEMINSKI, MICHELLE
[pen.] Michelle Kane; [b.] February 18, 1971, Detroit, MI; [p.] James and Julie Winter; [ed.] Eastern Michigan University; [occ.] English Teacher; [oth. writ.] Currently working on first novel; [pers.] Being an aspiring, young writer, I hope to gain a following of "new generation readers" that can relate to and appreciate a 90's approach to literature.; [a.] Livonia, MI

KUPLIN, BOB
[b.] December 25, 1964, Scranton, PA; [m.] Shawn (Bates) Kuplin, April 22, 1992; [ed.] BA in Geography, Class of '88, East Stroudsburg University, East Stroudsburg, Pennsylvania; [occ.] Professional Pilot; [hon.] Summa Cum Laude at ESU, awards for distinguished academic achievement in geography; [pers.] Enjoy and appreciate the beauty of nature. Your life can be a truly happy one if you simply make it so.; [a.] Gilbert, AZ

KURGAN, RITA
[pen.] Rita Kurgan; [b.] September 30, Philadelphia; [p.] Nyer and Ethel Kurgan; [ed.] BS Temple Univ., MFA University of the Arts; [occ.] English Teacher, Simon Gratz High School, Phila., PA; [memb.] Philadelpain, Federation of Teachers, Dental Amalgam Mercury Syndrome Organization - Foundation for Toxic-Free Dentistry; [hon.] Graduated Magna Cum Laude — Under-graduate and graduate school; [oth. writ.] Poetry, Short Stories, Non-fiction; [pers.] I am pleased that something positive has come from a negative and painful experience, I never realized that pain could be inspirational.; [a.] Philadelphia, PA

KYLE, LIDI MARY
[b.] May 1, 1915, San Francisco; [p.] Leo Sbrazza, Ida Sbrazza; [m.] Mahlon C. Kyle, December 5, 1943; [ch.] David S. Kyle; [ed.] 8th Grade, Hawthorne School, Oakland, CA; [occ.] Retired, Semi-invalid, living in home; [oth. writ.] Short Verse, 3rd grade hobby; [pers.]

Kindness to all mankind

L'ECUYER, ELEANOR LOVE
[b.] September 18, 1934, Leominster, MA; [p.] Charles Hazzard, Cecelia Hazzard; [m.] Paul H. L'Ecuyer, September 15, 1956; [ch.] Marcella, Paul, Lori and Rochelle; [ed.] Leominster High, Ann Maria College, State College at Fitchburg - (B.A. Anna Maria) State College at (M.ED. Fitchburg); [occ.] Retired Social Studies Teacher - "Out on the Road"; [hon.] Outstanding Alumna Award, Anna Maria College, John F. Kennedy Scholarship; [oth. writ.] Many poems and short stories - never published; [pers.] I write for enjoyment and hopefully to leave a mark to show I have been here, there and every where.; [a.] Kaneohe, HI

LA ROSA, BARONESS ANGELA R. MODICA
[b.] July 12, 1931, Kalamazoo, MI; [p.] Joseph J. and Lucille R. Modica; [m.] Marc Anthony; [ed.] "Cosmetologist, "Char-Del Beauty Coll. Western Michigan College", Bus. Course, Anthony Real Estate School: Real State Broker/Owner of Sophisticated Properties; [occ.] "Real Estate Broker/Owner of Sophisticated Properties" plus Artist and writer. Corporation Pres. of "Angell Exploration and Dev. Corp." and "Angell Mining Corp." Owner of "Angell Printing Co."; [memb.] Nat'l Assn. of Realtors, Western Mining Council, Italian Catholic Fedn. California Assn. of Realtors, San Fernando Board of Realtors; [oth. writ.] "Railroaded by Attorneys and Insurance Company", Billie and the "Yellow Catfish"; [pers.] "My Fanaticism is defined in the children's books I write! While my truth lies, in the happenings of the past and the present! Beyond those writings will bring me back to Fanaticism!"; [a.] North Hollywood, CA

LA VINE, ROCHELLE
[pen.] Rochell La Vine; [b.] February 23, 1940, Chicago; [p.] Thomas and Eve Millis; [m.] John W. La Vine; [ch.] Rene, Tom, Carrie, Tanya; [ed.] 2 yrs. College University of Miami; [occ.] Deputy Sheriff Cook County, IL; [pers.] I write poems for all my children and grandchildren's Birthdays and Special occasions. They too are doing it for their children.; [a.] Palos Park, IL

LABMEIER, MIKE
[b.] August 31, 1950, Cincy; [p.] Catherine; [ed.] 1 Year College; [oth. writ.] Poetry; [pers.] My poetry is about how I feel about real experiences; [a.] Cincinnati, OH

LACKEY, PATRICIA ANN
[pen.] Patricia A. Lackey; [b.] November 25, 1947, Logan, WV; [p.] Noah Frye, Nellie (Knipp) Frye; [m.] William Henry Lackey, May 21, 1970; [ch.] Charlie Adam Frye, William Henry Jr., Randall Noah, Chastity Michelle; [ed.] Logan East Jr. High, Citrus Co. High, (G.E.D.) Calvary High (G.E. Stollings Grade.; [occ.] Homemaker; [memb.] First Pentecostal Church; [pers.] I try to reflect in my writings the Christian values, and Love for people around me. I am greatly inspired by a Loving, unselfish husband.; [a.] Crystal River, FL

LADUE, ROBERT STUART
[pen.] Stu Ladue; [b.] July 9, 1918, Brooklyn, NY; [ch.] Nicole Reslink; [ed.] H.S., 1 year Col (GED); [occ.] Retired, 16 yrs. US Navy, 4 yrs. USAF; [oth. writ.] Writer/Producer Armed Forces Radio Service 1354th Video Production Sq USAF; [pers.] An intense distaste for "Free Verse"; [a.] Santa Monica, CA

LAFFERTY, J. CLAYTON
[b.] June 23, 1928, Detroit; [m.] Lorraine Lafferty, June 29, 1991; [ch.] Craic, Michele, Renee, Lisa, John; [ed.] Ph.D. Clinical Psych Vof Michigan; [occ.] Chair-

man, Human Synergistics International; [memb.] American Psychological Ass'n, Michigan Psychological Ass'n, American Society Training and Dev.; [hon.] Distinguished Alumni, Hillsdale College, Outstanding Psychologist, Mich. Psych. Ass'n; [oth. writ.] 10 Professional Articles.; [a.] Higland, MI

LAKE, MRS. JOANNE MARIE
[b.] September 12, 1945, Waukegan; [p.] Frank and Audree Zalewski; [m.] Gerald E. Lake, September 2, 1967; [ed.] San Jose Community College, Teaching Certificate Religious Education, Reno/Las Vegas Diocese; [memb.] Beta Sigma Phi; [hon.] Won 1st prize in Beta Sigma Phi scrap book contest for the art work that I did; [oth. writ.] I have written poems and verses for the children I taught and I have written music to scripture verses for use by the children. I am currently in the process of writing more children's stories.; [pers.] For the mind to be open to goodness, it must be nourished with input that is good.; [a.] Fall City, WA

LAKSHMAN, BULUSU
[pen.] Bulusu; [b.] July 23, 1967, Uizag, India; [p.] Prof. B.S.K.R. Somayajulu and Smt. B. Sita; [ed.] BS in Computer Science and Engineering, BS in Mathematics from India; [occ.] Software Developer; [oth. writ.] Written 30 poems like "My Dear", "Darling", "Bliss of Solitude", "Look Sharp", "Emotions in Tranquility", "Love", etc., on themes like natural beauty, love, alma mater and the like; [pers.] Dedicated and loves to write and read poetry intensively.; [a.] Newark, NJ

LALITE, YANICK
[p.] Andrea Joseph, Abner Saintus; [ch.] Luis Torres Jr., Daniel Lalite; [ed.] Medgar Evers College, Boricua College 3rd Year-Junior, Major - Teacher Education, Multicultural Education; [occ.] Educational Associate, Part Time Model and Actress

LAMAR, MARIA E.
[b.] December 11, 1952, Philadelphia, PA; [p.] Mildred Barley; [m.] Warren Lamar, July 28, 1979; [ch.] Eric Lee; [ed.] Germantown High, La Salle University, Cheyney University, Gwynedd Mercy College.; [occ.] Teacher; [oth. writ.] Watchful Eyes, Born of a Mixture; [a.] Philadelphia, PA

LAMBRIGHT, MARLENE M.
[pen.] Mar; [b.] March 1, 1955, Columbus, Ohio; [p.] Leo Sr. and Eleanor Robinson; [m.] Divorced; [ch.] Marquisa M. Lambright, Mikka L. Lambright; [ed.] St. Dominic Catholic School, Holy Rosary School, Franklin Junior High, East High School, Ohio Wesleyan Summer College; [occ.] Medical Records, Specialists - Mount Carmel West; [memb.] Volunteer for Columbus Public Schools, Forest Park Elementary School for 5 years; [hon.] Volunteer Awards from Forest Park Elementary; [oth. writ.] School related poetry, never published - new poet. Personal writings collected.; [pers.] Feelings, are silent, the voice is not, feelings are more understood in writing a lot, a heart can move a pen, smooth, silent as the wind, this is why I love to write poems, again and again... My heart is the only author I know, I hope through my poetry, this will show...; [a.] Columbus, OH

LANCY, MELANIA L.
[b.] April 16, 1976, Lake Forest, IL; [p.] Mr. and Mrs. Michael and Randa Lancy; [ed.] St. Mary's Elementary, Lake Bluff Junior High, Lake Forest Academy, Lake Forest H.S., Rhode Island School of Design; [occ.] Student, Studying Architecture; [memb.] Sierra Club; [hon.] Outstanding Score on Trigonometry Final 1994, I won a writing contest in a neighboring community (for each age group) at age five.; [pers.] A solar system of characteristics swarm within me. I live, as if,

I will only live once. Living to experience and learn to expand my universe.; [a.] Lake Bluff, IL

LANDE, IAN B.
[b.] May 29, 1965, Philadelpia, PA; [p.] Richard and Ronda Lande; [ed.] M. Ed CABRINI College B.S. Comm., Kutztown University; [occ.] English Teacher, Story teller; [memb.] Various Teachers Associations; [oth. writ.] Short Stories: New Authors Journal, The Nuthouse, Fade away and Radiate, The Storm, Poetry: The Poet's Attic, Reviews: Voya; [pers.] I have a lifelong fascination with that which exists just beyond the bounds of reality. I am interested in challenging the preconceptions and ideologies that keep us from fully experiencing what it means to be truly human while spinning a good yarn at the same time.; [a.] Drexel Hill, PA

LANDRY, GREGORY P.
[b.] April 11, 1952, Lafayette, LA; [p.] Paul J. Landry and Beatrice C. Landry; [ed.] Northside High; [occ.] Carpenter; [memb.] LA Conference on Water, Waste Water, Hazardous, Waste and Industrial Wastes; [hon.] Viet Nam Service Ribbon; [oth. writ.] 1970 - Los Angeles Poetry Press (Award Edition), 1972 - Los Angeles Poetry Press (Love Poems); [pers.] God Bless America where we are free to express ourselves.

LANE, VIRGINIA TREVILLIAN
[pen.] Jenny; [b.] March 2, 1934, Baltimore, MD; [p.] Mammie and Robert E. Trevillian; [m.] Samuel E. Lane, May 3, 1980; [ch.] Marvin T. Burkindine Jr., Lawrence D. Burkindine and Mitchell Curtis Burkindine; [ed.] Southern High School - Baltimore MD., 11 1/2 years, Got GED Atage 45 and Certificate from Medix School; [occ.] I worked for Dr. Nathen Leonard, of Annapolis, Md. for 10 years until 1992; [oth. writ.] Have more poems.; [a.] Pasadena, MD

LANSING, SHEILA M.
[pen.] 1 of 1 Poetic Artworks; [b.] November 13, 1963, Madison, WI; [p.] Russell and Mary Isaacson; [m.] Robert Lansing, October 22, 1988; [ed.] Oshkosh North High, Fox Valley Technical College of Oshkosh; [occ.] Artist and Poet, Various Clerical Positions with Local Temporary Service; [oth. writ.] I've been writing Poetry and music since the age of 9. I had poetry published in other Anthologies in the past and one article for the local paper. I'm working on a book including all my poems.; [pers.] My life experience is my source of inspiration. I have very profound deep feelings that are only expressed in my poetry and music. Without the ability to express them, I'd be very incomplete.; [a.] Oshkosh, WI

LARSEN, TIMOTHY M.
[pen.] Tim Larsen; [b.] October 5, 1972, Michigan; [p.] Henry A. Larsen, Carol Larsen; [ed.] Detroit Catholic Central H.S., University of Michigan - Dearborn; [occ.] Student; [hon.] Pi Mu Epsilon, Dean's List, Class Honors; [pers.] Any romantic will tell you that it's not the things he says nor the things he does, but the way he feels that makes him a romantic.; [a.] Livonia, MI

LARSON, REBECCA L.
[b.] October 25, 1959, Illinois; [ed.] BA - University of Iowa, JD Mercer University; [occ.] Attorney; [memb.] American Trial Lawyer Association, Phi Kappa Phi, Phi Beta Kappa; [hon.] Distinguished Graduate of 1986, Mercer Law School, Various Awards for Superior Scholastic Achievements; [pers.] Through language and love we can forge a brighter future; [a.] West Palm Beach, FL

LASER, MELISSA ERIN
[b.] May 14, 1981, Lancaster, CA; [p.] John A. Laser Jr., Dixie S. Bahr; [ed.] 8 Years Sacred Heart Catholic, Grade School; [occ.] Student; [oth. writ.] Poems and short stories nothing has ever been published before; [pers.] I like to write about feelings from the heart, thoughts about people and experiences that I know, I will never forget throughout my whole life.; [a.] Palmdale, CA

LASKOS, JOHN M.
[b.] February 13, 1968, Erie, PA; [p.] Mary and Michael Bensur; [m.] Vickie Laskos, July 1, 1991; [ch.] Donovan James, Joshua Alan; [ed.] Girard High; [occ.] Ceramic Artist; [memb.] National Wild Life Federation Audubon, National Geographic, New York Zoological Soc; [oth. writ.] Many poems/short short stories yet to be published; [pers.] Greatly inspired by J. Muir who said "The surest way into the unnerse is through a forest wilderness"; [a.] Fairview, PA

LASSICK, LORNA M.
[b.] June 9, 1929, Homer City, PA; [p.] Elmer W. and Alice M. Cravener; [m.] Michael W. Lassick Sr., June 25, 1947; [ch.] Marlenea Audree, Michael W. Lassick Jr.; [ed.] Graduated Horace Mann (1941), Graduated Junior High 1943, Graduated Senior High 1947, Graduated Technical 1951; [occ.] Retired from Indiana University, Indiana PA. Free Lance Writer; [memb.] Indiana School Employees, Federal Credit Union, AARP - Byzantine Catholic Church, Charter Member of Indiana, County Practical Nurse (Licenced) and Directer for number of years; [hon.] Given recognition for Outstanding Voluntary Contributions to various organisations.; [oth. writ.] Articles published at intervals in various newspapers and pamphlets; [pers.] In the process of writing a novel. Enjoy reading and writing poetry; [a.] Indiana, PA

LASTER, TERRY WAYNE
[b.] October 8, 1961, Spartanburg, SC; [p.] Leon C. Lewis, Jannie Gossette; [ch.] Timmy Wayne Laster; [occ.] All Trista, Zinc Products Co.; [memb.] Loyal Order of Moose No. 692 of Greenville, TN; [oth. writ.] Philosophical, Theological, and as well creative writing; [pers.] I have been inspired to reach other people in their search for solutions to save their relationships - and to bring moral values back within ones heart in my writing.; [a.] Greenville, TN

LATTIMORE III, VERGEL L.
[b.] March 6, 1953, Charlotte, NC; [p.] Vergel Lattimore, Perlia G. Lattimore; [m.] Joy Powell Lattimore, December 16, 1978; [ch.] Vergel Alston, Adam Victor, and Alia Joy; [ed.] North Mecklenburg High School, B.A., Livingstone College, M. Div., Duke University Divinity, Ph.D., Northwestern University; [occ.] Professor of Pastoral Care and Director, M.A. in Alcoholism and Drug Abuse Ministry; [memb.] American Association of Pastoral Counselors, American Association for Marriage and Family Theraphy, Summer Institute of Addiction Studies at the Ohio State University, Anton Boisen Fund Board of the Commission on Ministry in Specialized Settings; [hon.] North Mecklenburg High Student of Year and Hall of Fame, UNCF Scholarship, Alpha Kappa Mu National Honor Society, Personalities of the South, Mover and Shaker Award in Religion, Air Force Commendation MedaL, Who's Who Among Students in American Colleges; [oth. writ.] Articles in Journal Of Pastoral Care, and the A.M.E. Zion Quarterly Review, Article in Revival Hope: Adults Making a Difference; [pers.] Writing provides a vital avenue for emotional and spiritual empowerment. Authentic freedom comes from finding and sharing inner truth.; [a.] Westerville, OH

LAU, MICHELLE
[b.] June 17, 1982, New York City; [p.] Yick and Rose Lau; [ed.] DaMasi Middle School, Van Zant Elementary School; [occ.] Student at DeMasi Middle School; [oth. writ.] Poem published in Anthology of Poetry by Young Americans, Poem published in local newspaper; [a.] Marlton, NJ

LAUER, NANCY C.
[b.] December 25, 1937, Springfield, MA; [p.] Ruth and Francis Towne; [m.] Martin Lauer, February 28, 1987, (2nd marriage); [ch.] Deborah, Beth, Michael, Kathleen, Kevin and Maryellen; [ed.] B.A. - English, Our Lady of The Elms; [occ.] Counselor for sexually abusive youths; [memb.] B.O.M.C., Rosary Altar Society, A.A.R.P., Democratic Town Committee; [hon.] Pope Pius X Award Brightside Volunteer Award; [oth. writ.] Poems; [pers.] My journey is bringing me to an awareness of my false self and to the realization that my life is none of my business.; [a.] Southwick, MA

LAUMEYER, ROBERT L.
[b.] August 31, 1932, Wolf Point, MT; [p.] Joe and Rose Laumeyer; [m.] Kathleen McGlynn Laumeyer, August 31, 1953; [ch.] Rob A. Laumeyer, Jean O'Leary, Barbara Miner, Mary Runkel; [ed.] Nashua High School (MT.), Northern MT. College (Havre MT) Univ. of Missoula MT, Arizona State Univ., Tempe, AZ; [occ.] Retired (and love it); [oth. writ.] Poems published in New Voices in American Poetry 1980 and 1987 and Garden of life 1995, Waters Edge 1996; [pers.] You know you can fail, and yet not a failure be. When a leaf falls it does not kill a tree.

LAURINAITIS, JONAS
[b.] December 5, 1958, Caracas, Venezuela; [p.] Irena Laurinaitis (father died 1960); [ed.] St. Joseph High School 1977 Graduate, Tri-C- Metro College 1977-1979; [occ.] Tradesman, (Carpentry, Plumbing, Electrical, etc.); [pers.] Believe and you will receive... doubt and you will be without; [a.] Willowick, OH

LAWRENCE, TIFFANY
[b.] June 26, 1981, Westboro, MA; [p.] Joseph and Cristenna Lawrence; [ed.] Gibbons Middle School, Westboro High School; [occ.] Student; [hon.] Pop Warner Little Scholars, Honor Roll, Partners in Excellence, Council for Youth Advocacy; [oth. writ.] Nothing Published; [pers.] When I write, I try to reflect my opinions and ideas to those who read it. I think it is important to speak your mind and be heard.; [a.] Westboro, MA

LAWSON, APRIL IONE
[pen.] April Ione Lawson; [b.] May 15, 1983; [p.] Ione and Andrew Lawson; [ed.] K-6th; [occ.] Student; [memb.] 4-H Club, Band, Athena, Soccer team; [hon.] "A" Honor Roll for 6 years, Presidential Academic Fitness Award Superior Rating in Solo and Ensamble; [a.] Conyers, GA

LAYSON, HERMINIA S.
[pen.] Hermie S. Layson; [b.] October 4, 1926, Philippines; [p.] Nicolas and Rosalia San Juan; [m.] Abundio C. Layson, November 15, 1954; [ch.] Manuel, Joseph, Miyet, Bong and Menchi; [ed.] Associate in Arts, Bachelors of Science in Education; [occ.] Housewife and a researcher and a lecture in natural healing; [memb.] Central Filipino Seventh Day Adventure Church, Community Services and Almega Church Choir. Former member of United Nations Women's Group and YWCA; [hon.] Gold Medalist in a Collegiate Oratorical Contest and a Presidential Gold (Phil.) Medal Awardee for Community Services; [oth. writ.] I started writing poems when I was a kid in the elementary grades. In college I had some poems published in the school papers

and a first placer in a literary contest.; [pers.] I give to God all the glory for all my accomplishments and I believe only Service to God and humanity will last through all eternity... "beyond the stars."; [a.] Glendale, CA

LEA JR., GERMANUEL B.
[b.] August 29, 1947, Columbus, OH; [p.] Germanuel B. and Ruth M. Lea; [m.] Laura B. Lea, August 25, 1980; [ch.] Stephen, Shaww, Sammie, Melissa, Sean and Germanuel III; [ed.] Graduated Lincoln Sr High, E. St. Louis, Ill. 1966, Graduated Lincoln, Institute, Cleveland Ohio 1978, Industrial Management; [occ.] Millwright, Bethlehem Steel, Licensed Real Estate Agent and (Salesperson sinse 1989) for Straight Gate Real Estate; [oth. writ.] Flowers of Africa, Death of a Sun Flower, The Party; [pers.] I enjoy reading and playing chess. I find that in a lot ways life is a classic chess game where each move is important to the total outcome and no part of it can be taken for granted.; [a.] Michigan City, IN

LEE, BARBARA R. CALHOUN
[b.] July 26, 1929, Preston Co., WV; [p.] William H. Calhoun, Margaret Pulliam Calhoun; [m.] Ralph M. Lee, April 16, 1949; [ch.] Gregory Clark Lee, Beverley Dianne Lee; [ed.] High School, Secretarial Jobs throughout the years. (School Sec. - Insurance Sec.); [occ.] Retired, Housewife - Part time traveler; [memb.] 1. Daughter's of the American Revolution, 2. United Methodist Women, 3. Quilter's Club, 4. Thursday Sr. Bowler's League; [oth. writ.] A short writing (poetry) published by: Pioneer Press, Terra Alta, WV, Book Name: "Did It Snow In 77?"; [pers.] Many times I feel inspired to write at the time of real life happenings.; [a.] Oakland, MD

LEE, CHARLES
[b.] March 8, 1976, Seoul, Korea; [p.] Soo Bok Lee, Hyun Ja Lee; [ed.] Northern Valley Reg. HS, Massachusetts Institute of Technology; [occ.] Student (Undergraduate) at MIT; [pers.] Desire is the key to excellence. Dream for a miracle, then live to accomplish it.; [a.] Palisades Park, NJ

LEE, COURTNEY
[b.] September 2, 1981, Honolulu, HI; [p.] Hope and Greg Lee; [ed.] Currently attending Lolani 8th grade; [occ.] Student; [memb.] Soccer, Hysa, Ayso, Junior Japanese Club; [hon.] Presidential Fitness Award, John Hopkins University Award Honor Roll, Headmasters; [pers.] Through love and dedication, my parents have influenced my life greatly. They have patterned my life with their wisdom and knowledge. They have helped me to understand and fulfill my potential, and for that I will always be grateful.; [a.] Mililani Town, HI

LEE, STEPHANIE
[b.] August 6, 1976, Palo Alto, CA; [p.] Man Kwok and Vicky Lee; [m.] Marvin the Martian, October 31, 1982; [ed.] Menlo School, Stanford University; [occ.] College Student and Free-lance Population Controller; [memb.] Plunger Liberation Federation; [oth. writ.] Poems published in anthologies; [pers.] We should not live on normality, cuteness, perfection, or breakfast cereal.; [a.] Woodside, CA

LEETE, JASON MATTHEW
[b.] March 3, 1976, Des Moines; [p.] Terry and Linda Leete; [ed.] Graduated from East High School in Des Moines in 1994. Attended UNI in Cedar Falls for a year. Plan to attend Grandview in the fall.; [hon.] Presidential Academic Fitness Award (94) Member of the National Honor Society. Graduate in top 15% of my class.; [oth. writ.] Seasonal Concepts 1993, Tired 1994, A Closer Look 1994, A Repeat of History? 1994, All

published in the Portal High School Literary Magazine

LEIST, JOHN WRIGHT
[b.] April 14, 1919, Columbus, OH; [p.] Joseph and Laura Leist; [m.] Louise Leist, August 7, 1952; [ch.] Patricia, Judith Anne, Andrew, Matthew; [ed.] BA 1940, MD December 1943, Poetry class at Ohio State University, Fall 1976. Music Composition tutoring by Paul Schwartz, Composer, 1987-present; [occ.] Psychiatrist; [memb.] Life Member American Psychiatric Association; [hon.] President Central Ohio Correctional Association 1966, President Neuropsychiatric Society of Central Ohio 1982-1983; [oth. writ.] Several poems. Four of my poems (including To Louise made into songs for voice and piano and one made into a hymn by me as music composer. Two of the songs performed as part of local university music department concert of new music. The hymn was used in church. (I am also composer of other songs for voice and piano (based on poems of others), anthems, church service music, and pieces of piano, for organ, for piano and double bass, etc., Unpublished paper: Determining the Mentally Healthy Qualities (Strengths) in Psychiatric Patients.; [a.] Delaware, OH

LEJUEZ, NANCY
[pen.] Nancy Dale; [b.] December 10, 1922, USA, NY; [p.] Deceased; [m.] Harold, April 23, 1944; [ch.] Jeffrey-Clifford, Jacqueline and Jill; [ed.] Julia-Richman H.S., Certified Course, in Operator-Services Traffic Management School; [occ.] Retired 1980; [memb.] Telephone Pioneers of America, Life Membership American Women's Voluntary Services, Madd, Calvary; [hon.] Celebrated Golden Anniv. to reach the age of 72 and proud of my children and grandchildren.; [oth. writ.] Songs, Poems for Telephone Co. and Jingles; [pers.] We were all born with a gift. Recognize it, use it, and share it with others. Every person is unique.; [a.] Flushing, NY

LELI, TAMMY MARIE
[pen.] Tami Leli, T. Leli, Tam Leli; [b.] January 21, 1969, Buffalo NY; [p.] Frank and Sue Leli; [ed.] St. Mary's High School in Lancaster, Medaille College; [occ.] Mail Clerk; [hon.] NY State, Regents High School Diploma, BS Degree in Media Communication; [oth. writ.] Published, "In a Perfect World I am Gour...", also I am the author of many unpublished poems and short stories; [pers.] Never give up. Thank you Mom and Dad for putting up with me for the last 26 years I Love you Robb, Thank you, Jolie, Bill, Jill, Lisa, Melissa, Mandy, Candy and Johnna.; [a.] Buffalo, NY

LEMON, KAREN
[pen.] Summer Star; [b.] August 30, 1967, Woodbury, NJ; [p.] Norma Maculewicz; [m.] Alfred Lemon, March 18, 1988; [ch.] Jessie and Joshua; [ed.] Green Run High School, Virginia Beach, VA; [oth. writ.] Currently seeking a publisher for a children's book entitled "If only I Could Fly"; [pers.] In my writing I endeavor to reflect the love, the power and the wisdom of our creator, Jehovah God.; [a.] Muse, PA

LEONARDSON, ROYCE E.
[b.] March 13, 1948, Chicago, IL; [p.] H. A. Leonardson, T. E. Leonardson; [m.] Sue H. Leonardson, May 28, 1977; [ch.] Randall Eric, Deena Gayle; [ed.] Maine Township H.S. West Des Plaines, IL; [occ.] Investigator/Inspector, Federal Communications Commission; [memb.] Roswell Street Baptist Church, Marietta, Georgia; [oth. writ.] Numerous poems throughout the years. Penned for fun and the personal satisfaction. Inspired by God to write. A tribute to a friend following the death of my son in 1994 as she was there for me at a time of personal need.; [pers.] God gives us talents to use and we must put them to good use or risk losing them. I am

mostly inspired to write from my daily experiences both good and bad and about those who are a part of my life.; [a.] Marietta, GA

LEOUE, FILIPPA
[b.] September 24, 1946, Italy; [p.] Maria and Francesco; [m.] Divorced; [ch.] Delia Baldwin, Robert Williams; [ed.] Bachelor's Degree in Education 4 years of PhD work in letters, languages, undergraduate and graduate work in other subjects: Business, Marketing, Management, etc.; [occ.] Have worked as a teacher, therapist, counselor, presently, Coordinating and Managing Quality Assurance program in Social Work Service of a hospital; [memb.] Have been limited to animal organizations for the protection, ethical and humane treatment of animals (our best friends); [hon.] YWCA Award for "Outstanding Achievement" several "Outstanding Work Performance" awards, Co-author of article "Serum Prolactin Levels During Extended Cocaine Abstinence" published in the American Journal of Psychiatry, Diploma of Regional Champion of 800 Meters race (Sicily), Panelist in "Call the Experts" program aired on hospital TV - Topic: "Cocaine How much Deception," etc.; [oth. writ.] ICARUS II- The Fall of Modern Man "addresses the drug problem in the United States), The Last Sacred Cow (Expose), Novel (no title yet), Articles and poems, In search of Mr. Right (comical account), Untitled Project addressing common stereotypes and prejudices.; [pers.] "Writing is the best form of communication. I wish to use my talent to inform, educate, entertain and share my ideas".; [a.] Zion, IL

LEVENSON, HARVEY R.
[b.] May 31, 1942, Brooklyn, NY; [p.] Woodrow Levenson (Dec.), Yetta (Levenson) Pearl; [m.] Barbara Levenson, May 29, 1970; [ch.] Damien Levenson, Mark Levenson; [ed.] Ph.D. University of Pittsburgh, M.S. South Dakota State University, B.S. Rouchester Institute of Technology, A.A.S. New York City Community College; [occ.] Professor of Graphic Communication, California Polytechnic State University, San Luis Obispo, CA; [memb.] Technical Association of the Graphic Arts, Graphic Arts Literacy Alliance, Graphic Arts Technical Foundation; [hon.] Distinguished Service Award - U.S. Govn't Printing Office Award of Excellence - Graphic Art Tech. Foundation, Board Member of the Year - Economic Opportunity Commission, San Luis Obispo (CA), Dansforth Associate; [oth. writ.] (Author) "Complete Dictionary of Graphic Arts and Destop Publishing Technology," (Editor) - "Literary and Print Media" "(Author) - "Art and Copy Preparation: An Introduction to Phototypesetting, numerous articles on Graphic Arts Communication, and Literacy; [pers.] Print Media is the most persuasive informative, and detailed form of Mass Communication. This survival of humanity and an informed, educated society, rules on it.; [a.] Amascadeno, CA

LEWIS, ASHAMI
[b.] November 2, 1983, Queens, NY; [p.] Sylvia McInnis, Ashton Lewis; [ed.] Ideal Montessori School, Jamaica, NY, Presentation of the Blessed Virgin Mary, Jamaica, NY; [occ.] Student; [hon.] Science Project Award, Essay Award, Spanish Award, Student of the Month Award, Principal Award, Honor Roll Award, General Excellence Award; [oth. writ.] "Little Butterfly" and several unpublished poems; [pers.] My ability to write poems was greatly influenced by my mother's encouragement and devotion; [a.] Jamaica, NY

LEWIS, DR. ELLEN V.
[b.] February 28, 1936, San Salvador, El Salvador; [p.] Aminta and Dominic Sunseri; [m.] Donald B. Lewis, June 11, 1960, Divorce 1969; [ch.] Kevin Lewis, Nathan Lewis, A.B. 1959; [ed.] Univ. of Cal. Berkeley, 1983 San Francisco State University M.A., 1986, Ed. D

Univ. of San Francisco; [occ.] Retired School Teacher, taught Bilingual Education, Spanish for over 20 years; [memb.] League of Women Voters in San Mateo Country, Commonwealth Club of California; [oth. writ.] Representation of Hispanics in California State Approved Elementary Reading Textbooks, 1986; [pers.] I enjoy good literature and hope to inspire readers.; [a.] San Mateo, CA

LEWIS, JEWELL R.
[pen.] Twin Brothers Lewis; [b.] May 6, Houston, TX; [p.] Charles T. Lewis - Bernice Anderson Lewis; [ed.] Phillis Wheatly High, Texas So. Univ., George Pepperdine Univ., Univ. of So. Calif. New Mexico Highlands Univ.; [occ.] Deceased January 24, 1994 was Psychologist and President J.R.L. Nursery (Landscaping); [memb.] Houston Symphony Chorale, Houston Contemporary Dance Theatre, Am. Speech and Hearing Assn.; [hon.] A certified Master Gardener was proud of his affiliation with the Harris County Master Gardeners Association; [oth. writ.] Poems, journals - unpublished; [pers.] Beauty, cleanliness, excellence - qualities aspired to in life's daily experiences.; [a.] Houston, TX

LEWIS, KATHRYN Y.
[pen.] Kathryn Y. Lewis or Kypol; [b.] March 9, 1960, Pensacola, FL; [p.] Sharnett Harper, James Price (1960-64), Donald Overeem (1965-now); [m.] Daniel K. Lewis, September 8, 1982; [ch.] Brandy Jean, Donald Patrick; [ed.] Roger High Arkansas, US Air Force Jet Engine Mechanic; [occ.] Housewife, mother, childcare, artist; [pers.] The greatest works of art are all around us and in the people we meet and I Love exploring it.; [a.] Tacoma, WA

LEWIS, MARC
[pen.] Marcl; [b.] March 16, 1970, Elizabeth, NY; [p.] Regginald and Carole Lewis; [ed.] BS in Mass Communications, Norfolk State University 1994, Franklyn High 1988; [memb.] AAA and a Rap Group SOS (Scientists of Sounds); [oth. writ.] Several unpublished poems and screen plays; [pers.] My writings reflect my visions through life and also represents the struggle of a modern day blackman in todays society. I have been extremely influenced by the Greatest poet of all, God; [a.] Piscataway, NJ

LEWIS, MONICA L.
[b.] August 19, 1949, Detroit, MI; [p.] Idella and Harvey Flanagan; [occ.] Admin. Asst.; [hon.] Member, National English Honors Society; [pers.] I'm always writing something that usually nobody understands!! My life and me can best be explained by the following: "I'm going, I'm going. I know not where, but only until I'm half way there. There's something I'll do, I know not what, but I'll find out soon — So — wish me luck." I wrote this over 20 years ago and funny, but it still sums up my life today!; [a.] Washington, DC

LEWIS, MR. JON JAIME
[pen.] J. J. L.; [b.] February 8, 1959, New York; [ch.] Timothy Wayne; [oth. writ.] Numerous poems dealing with the ups and downs of personal relationships.; [pers.] I write from the heart whether it's happy, sad, hard or soft.; [a.] New Windsor, NY

LEWIS, ROBERT
[b.] August 16, 1975, PA; [p.] Judith Ann Lewis; [ed.] Bangor High School; [occ.] CNC Operator; [memb.] United States Army Reserves; [pers.] My writing always reflects my personal life. And things that happen around me.; [a.] Portland, PA

LEWIS, SHEILA D.
[b.] July 3, 2966, Martinsville, VA; [p.] Garry Lewis, Betty Lewis; [ed.] Patrick Co. H.S. (Virginia) National Business College, U.S. Army - Honorable Discharge; [occ.] Cashier - Hardee's Clearwater, FL; [memb.] In High School, the Lady's Track and Field team, U.S. Army, and a National Guard unit in North Carolina; [hon.] U.S. Army - Honorable Discharge, Desert Storm Vet., Dean's List at National Business College; [oth. writ.] One poem published (a different one) in The Challenger Newspaper in Wilmington, N.C.; [pers.] I look for nuances that others may overlook. For example, what comes to Your mind when You hear the title "Lavender Lover".; [a.] Clearwater, FL

LEYVA, CYNTHIA J.
[b.] November 23, 1956, Hayti, MO; [p.] Bill Crabtree, Maribelle Crabtree; [m.] Raymond A. Leyva, July 24, 1982; [ch.] James William Leyva; [ed.] Southeast Missouri State University, MA Ed., BS Elementary Ed., AA Child Care and Guidance, North Pemiscot High School; [occ.] Teacher, Anderson Elementary, Houston TX; [memb.] Congress of Houston Teachers, Williams Trace Baptist Church; [oth. writ.] Began writing poetry in 1972. Several poems have been used as lyrics for songs I've composed.; [pers.] Poetry, the music of the spirit, reaching out to touch one's soul.; [a.] Missouri, TX

LICKLITER, CRYSTAL
[b.] July 22, 1981; [p.] Robert and Greta Lickliter; [ed.] 7th grader at Warner Jr. High School; [occ.] Student; [hon.] United States Achievement Academy in English; [pers.] Living on our family farm, watching the animals, inspired me to write this poem. My first poem.; [a.] Xenia, OH

LIEBEL, CHARLOTTE C. L.
[pen.] Charlotte Marie Fawls; [b.] October 28, 1940, New Orleans, LA; [p.] Marie H. Bacon and Claude E. Swaim; [m.] Thomas H. Liebel, February 26, 1983; [ch.] Susanne Michelle Foulk and Deborah Lynne Foulk; [ed.] Francis T. Nicholls HS, New Orleans, LA, Ventura College, Ventura, CA, FCC 3rd Class Radio Telephone Broadcaster 1977 (licensed), California Real Estate Salesperson 1991; [occ.] Ventura College continuing student, storywriter - poet, public relations; [memb.] Publicity Club of Los Angeles 1977 - 1981, California Parents and Teachers Assoc., (PTA) Honorary Life Membership 1974, Hollywood Presbyterian Church 1962 - 1990, St. Rose Roann Catholic Church 1990; [hon.] South Pasadena Delegate to San Francisco, PTA State Convention - Oneonta Elementary School 1974, South Pasadena Jr. High PTA President 1977; [oth. writ.] A Book of Poems Dedicated to the Dream of Love (c) 1979, Astronomy · Creative Flyer 1995; [pers.] All subjects enrich my life. Knowledge brings me happiness. Living near the ocean which I visit often for long hikes has brought calm after the storms of life where I, now, write with passion, and study.; [a.] Ventura, CA

LIM, LEILANI
[b.] January 21, 1977, Philippines; [p.] Joe and Antonette Lim; [ed.] Senior at Earl Wooster High School; [occ.] High School Student; [memb.] National Honors Society, Italian Club President, Teens Against Racial Prejudice V.P., Christian Club V.P., Spanish Club Secretary; [hon.] Most outstanding student of the year, student of the month (March), Senior Class Secretary, USA All American Dancer, NCA Funkiest Dancer, American Cheerleader Magazine Cheerleader of the Month Varsity Dance Team Captain; [oth. writ.] 1994-1995 Yearbook Editor, several articles published in my school hoofprints; [pers.] Every man's philosophy is the power to personalize his style, mold the structure of his words and beautify the nature of his poem. Philosophy Of Every Man.; [a.] Reno, NV

LINDAUER III, JOHN W.
[b.] September 6, 1967; [p.] John and Joan; [ed.] New York University, Bachelor of Fine Arts, Television/ Film Production; [occ.] Television News Researcher; [pers.] Inspired mostly by Musicians/Lyricists like Melissa Etheridge, Cindy Lauper, Peter Gabriel, Aimee Mann, Corey Hart and The Indigo Girls. Also inspired by long train rides, River Views, walks along the beach and rain storms.; [a.] Croton, NY

LINDSAY, DONNA MARIE
[b.] June 21, 1983; [p.] Deborah and Joe Lindsay; [ed.] Oak Valley Elementary School 6th grade; [memb.] Girl Scouts, Safety; [hon.] Honor Roll, Student of the Month, Safety of the Month, Drawing; [oth. writ.] Many others mostly about a holiday; [pers.] When I think of something I try to make a poem out of it.; [a.] Wenonah, NJ

LINES, SHANE
[pen.] Shane Lines; [b.] June 5, 1969, Minneapolis, MN; [p.] William Lines, Pamela Urman; [ed.] Osseo High, Normandale College, Metro State University; [occ.] Security Specialist, First Trust, First Bank Systems; [memb.] Habitat for Humanity; [hon.] Deborah Wells; [oth. writ.] "My Princess", "Simplicity", "Over Cast Days", "Deserving Rose", "Prison People" and "Untitled" writings; [pers.] "Inspiration is self-worth through the hearts of people who bless you with love and interests. I share myself to others as a spiritual being in a physical body pronounce by talents God has given me to express and share. Love is divinely powerful, but not conquering. It is the Human need to be Loved that may conquer."; [a.] Minneapolis, MN

LIPSHAW, LAUREN LEE
[b.] May 9, 1985, Destin, FL; [p.] Doug and Linda Lipshaw and brother Grant; [ed.] I am ten yeas old and just finished fourth grade. I am a student of Addison Mizner, Elementary in their gifted education program.; [memb.] United States Gymnastics, Federation. Competitive level 6 gymnast.; [hon.] Attained honor roll status every grading period since kindergarten. While competing in gymnastics I've won metals, ribbons and a trophy.; [pers.] I wrote my poem "Geese of the 90's", while I was temporarily living in Washington State with my family. At the time I was thinking about the freedom geese have not having to go to school.; [a.] Boca Raton, FL

LITTLE, MOLLY D.
[b.] February 26, 1981, Van Nuys, CA; [p.] Dennis Little, Christy Little; [ed.] Currently an 8th grade student; [hon.] Presidential Academic Fitness Award - 1993, Sportsmanship Award Viking Girls Basketball 1994-95; [pers.] Life is an adventure, live it to it's limits; [a.] Camarillo, CA

LOBB, HAROLD CHARLES
[b.] July 14, 1950, Butte, MT; [p.] Charles and Helen Lobb; [m.] Divorced; [ch.] Jason and Brent; [ed.] Butte High School and Montana State Univ.; [occ.] Horse-Trainer; [memb.] Christian Writers Guild, Victory Fellowship; [oth. writ.] Christian and Cowboy Verses, Poems, and Songs; [pers.] I try to live my life according to a set of Christ like values. I hope my writing brings the readers closer to God and Jesus Christ.; [a.] Butte, MT

LOCKER, DARLENE
[pen.] Darlene Locker; [b.] July 26, 1961, Mount Holly, NJ; [p.] Gene and Charmaine Anderson; [ch.] Edward Locker III; [ed.] Graduated High School 1979 - Maple Shade; [occ.] Scan Coordinator - Acme and Payroll Coordinator - Act Media; [pers.] Children give me great pleasure and influence me in my writing. The love that my son has for life and people he has encourage and

inspired my poems.; [a.] Riverside, NJ

LODEN, KELLY A.
[pen.] Augustina Gray; [b.] April 30, 1962, Wichita, KS; [pers.] It is my endeavor to present whatever topic I choose in the simplest, most direct manner without forsaking the gentle, continuous flow and diction and emotion which constitutes the origination of good poetry.; [a.] Stillwater, OK

LOGSDON, MARY L.
[pen.] Mary Feather; [b.] February 11, 1950, Norfolk, VA; [p.] James E. and Betty L. Feather; [m.] Eddie L. Logsdon; [ch.] Shannon Payton, Jennifer Logsdon; [ed.] Southern High School, Louisville, Kentucky; [memb.] (HSUS) Humane Society of the United States; [pers.] When I write I try to express the happiness, sadness or other emotions I have felt in my own personal experiences.; [a.] Louisville, KY

LOHNER, KATHERINE E.
[pen.] Kay Lohner; [b.] February 1, 1943, Thylor, MI; [ch.] Raoul Lohner, Jodi Cokl; [ed.] B.S. Allied Health Mgt., Madonna Univ., Post-Graduate Studies, Central MI University; [occ.] Environmental Services Supervisor; [oth. writ.] Articles on empowerment and quality assurance for trade journals; [pers.] It's no longer frightening to face death once you've mastered the quality of life, i,e., learning to control negative emotions instead of having them control you!; [a.] Dearborn, MI

LOMBARDI, DORIS I.
[b.] May 25, 1910, Lowell, MA; [p.] Edward and Mae Badmington; [m.] Charles W. Lombardi, February 4, 1945; [ch.] Charlene Lyon; [ed.] Lowell High Lowell Mass New England. Baptist Hospital Navy Nurse Corp.; [occ.] Retired R.N.; [oth. writ.] Poems Published in New Weekly (Chelmsford MA) Dailey News Sun (Sun City AZ) British Porcelain Artist (West Yorkshire, England); [a.] Sun City, AZ

LOOMIS, JANEL LYNN
[pen.] Nellie; [b.] April 15, 1967, Dearborn, MI; [p.] Russell John Rigsby Jr. and JoAnn Rigsby; [m.] William H. Loomis, August 13, 1988; [ed.] Temple Christian High, Baptist Bible College, Springfield, MO; [occ.] Mailroom Supervisor BBC, Teen Youth Worker Baptist Temple; [memb.] Baptist Temple in Springfield, MO, Bill Dowell Jr. Pastor; [hon.] Voted "Most Spirited" in High School; [pers.] I believe a personal relationship with Jesus Christ of the Bible is the one and only way to know that I am going to Heaven after I die. Telling others how to know themselves is my purpose for living.; [a.] Springfield, MO

LOPATKA, ANGELINE
[pen.] Angeline Lopatka; [b.] September 27, 1925, Chicago, IL; [p.] Margaret and Dick Maturo; [m.] Walter (deceased), April 3, 1948; [ch.] Walter Jr. and Joyce; [ed.] (Mitchell), McKinley both Chgo.), Grammer and High School, College Courses, Humanities, and Writing courses (Dupage College Glen Ellyn, IL); [occ.] Retired, Former Deputy Town Clerk, York Township, Lombard, IL; [memb.] Village Garden Club of Villa Park, IL, and currently President. Legislation Chair for Council of Catholic Woman, St. Alexander Church in Villa Park, IL, Committee Woman Republican-District #55, Dupage County, Illinois.; [hon.] Region 7 which includes Illinois, Indiana, Wisconsin and Michigan of the Boy Scouts of America, award for bringing the program of Boy Scouts America to more boys through the organization of scouting units, year 1962. Many Blue ribbons on flowers grown in garden including blue ribbons for flowers and arrangement at Dupage County Fair Wheaton, IL, 1990; [oth. writ.] Many poems and sayings I felt compelled to write - sent

a poem and it was acknowledged by Ideals Magazine. I have written several stories including those of my travels abroad and in the States. (Unpublished); [pers.] My attitude is to enjoy life to its fullest and to use the skills and talents given to me by the Lord.; [a.] Villa Park, IL

LOPEZ, DEBORAH
[b.] September 2, 1962, CA; [p.] Kathie Vines, Ed Vines; [m.] Fidel Lopez, March 18, 1993; [ch.] Christina and Stephanie Mendiola; [ed.] General Education, Graduate of San Jaoquin Valley, College, Honorable Discharge from USAR (United States Army Reserve); [occ.] Housewife and mother; [hon.] General College Awards for Computer Business and Accounting; [oth. writ.] I have many writings from Christ our Lord!; [pers.] Jesus Christ truly gave me the abilities I needed to live. He saved my life in the truest sense. He is my light, life, love, joy, peace, and happiness.; [a.] Fresno, CA

LOPEZ, MARY ALICE PENA
[pen.] Mary Pena, Alegra Pen; [b.] December 20, 1947, Laredo, TX; [p.] Alfonso Pena, Margaret Pena; [m.] Jaime Lopez, August 14, 1993; [ch.] Edward Elvis; [ed.] Martin High, Texas A and I University, Cliff Osmond Acting - Musical Theatre School L.A. CA; [occ.] Social Worker, Substitute Teacher; [memb.] San Antonio Community Theatre, Church of Mt. Calvary Choir; [hon.] Choir, Drama, and Spelling Awards, Miss Hispanic (Suit-Zoot) 1981, Perfect Attendance (Elementary) 6th grade thru High School; [oth. writ.] Books, Crystal Dream and Tribute (unpublished), Also "Songs from the Soul" (unpublished); [pers.] The greatest contribution to Mankind, lies in the simplicity of loving one another, as Christ loved us! Salvation is the ultimate glory. Influenced by life, Emily Dickenson; [a.] San Antonio, TX

LOPEZ, ROSALIE
[pen.] C. Justice Dunn, Rosalie Kidd Lopez; [b.] July 5, 1929, Los Angeles, CA; [p.] Joe Kidd, Grace Kidd; [m.] Ronald E. Lopez, June 20, 1959; [ch.] Karen Baumstark, Patricia Salkham; [ed.] Garfield High School Los Angeles, Chaffey College Alta Loma Calif.; [memb.] Los Angeles, Los Pobladores Ancestoral Heritage Assoc., Los Angeles City Historical; [hon.] 1. Arizona Supreme Court, Foster Care Review Board Member 1992-95, 2. City of Ontario Museum, Charter Member-Docent Ontario Calif., 3. Arizona Criminal Justice Commission 1992-95, Board Member, Victim Witness; [oth. writ.] 1. Political Ghost Writer, 2. Past Editor - El Mensaje, Los Pobladores Publication, 3. 17 Feature Length Articles, Nogales International Newspaper; [pers.] Poetry and writing fulfill a creative need in me to express the power of words in describing our human condition.; [a.] Nogales, AZ

LORD, BRENT N.
[b.] July 28, 1980, Athens, GA; [p.] Bennie N. and Bevelyn G. Lord; [ed.] Jackson County High School; [occ.] Student; [hon.] Two Citizenship Awards, One Leadership Award; [oth. writ.] (None have been published) Variations of Life, Acceptance, The Norm, As Black as the Night, Together We Rise; [pers.] "The answer to any question can be brought to life within the body of poetry".

LOSSON, JO-ANN
[pen.] Jo, Dash; [b.] April 5, 1970, Rolling Meadows, IL; [p.] James and Carolyn Rahn; [m.] George Losson, August 20, 1988; [ed.] Grant High School, Fox Lake, IL; [occ.] Asst. Manager of TCF Financial, Gurnee IL; [memb.] Was Secretary for the Antioch Jaycees in 1993; [hon.] Nominated for Volunteer of the year in Waukegan Park Dist. I am the Asst. Coach for the Waukegan Special Olympics Basket Ball team.; [pers.]

My writings are inspired by my late mother who guides me every day with every thing I do. She is my inspiration and guardian angel.; [a.] Fox Lake, IL

LOUGEE, SONDRA LEE
[pen.] Sondra Lee Gnehm; [b.] August 27, 1960, Paterson, NJ; [p.] Marjorie and Rudy Gnehm; [m.] Jeffrey Lougee, February 14, 1988; [ch.] Jenna Lee and Shawna Lee; [ed.] Midland Park High School, Glassboro State College, Glassboro, NJ; [occ.] Special Education Teacher, Lillian Drive School, Hazlet, NJ; [memb.] NJEA. Middletown Junior Women's Club, Westminster Presbyterian Church; [hon.] NJ Governor's Teacher Grant Recipient 1987, Governor's Teacher of the Year Award 1987, Gamma Tau Sigma, Who's Who Among Students in American Universities, Kappa Delta Pi, Magna Cum Laude GSC 1982; [oth. writ.] "We're Banking On It" behavior management program, several poems for various classes; [pers.] I am grateful to my family for everything they have given me. I strive to express my appreciation and gratitude through my poetry and hope I will give to my children what I was lucky enough to experience.; [a.] Port Monmouth, NJ

LOUK, DONNA JEAN
[pen.] D. J. Louk; [b.] June 2, 1964, Youngstown; [p.] Mr. and Mrs. Edward Korda Sr.; [m.] Ronald E. Louk Sr., October 19, 1985; [ch.] Ronald Jr., Dacia J.E; [ed.] West Branch High School; [occ.] Seamstress; [pers.] The will to accomplish, gives us the strength to survive.; [a.] Salem, OH

LOVETT, LOIS
[b.] October 12, 1954, Miami, FL; [p.] Louie and Anita Buice (both deceased); [m.] Frank (deceased), widowed since March 1984; [ch.] Alex Lovett; [ed.] Currently a student at Barry University - Major: Social Work; [occ.] Funeral Home, Business Office Mgr. - currently on educational leave of absence; [memb.] Dade County Woman's Chamber of Commerce, Florida Funeral Directors Association, COCA Center of Contemporary Art; [oth. writ.] I currently write a local newsletter which is published six times a year for a small business association.; [pers.] I wrote this poem to reflect my feelings at my son's recent graduation from University of South Florida.; [a.] North Miami Beach, FL

LUCKSINGER, ELISA H.
[pen.] Elisa H. Lucksinger; [b.] April 19, 1928, Berlin, Germany; [p.] Milowsky, both deceased; [m.] J. F. Lucksinger (deceased 1985), 2nd January 31, 1981; [ed.] Berlin, Germany, Upper School, Jr. College, 3 yrs Seminar, Nursing in Pediatrics, Emigrate to the USA, June 24, 1952; [occ.] Retired Homemaker; [memb.] Presently not active, belong to the Lutheran Faith, Austin, Tx. German Saengerrunde, Austin Lyric Opera Guild; [hon.] City of Berlin 1945 after May 8, 1945 Germany surrender. Being First to open a state kindergarten, amid's a city of great destruction, Achievement Award; [oth. writ.] Poems for birthdays, anniversary's, etc. To family and friends. Being daily out in nature, a great blessing, absorb a rich knowledge.; [pers.] "Writing a Poem," it start with a glow of one inner feelings to share a smile and laughter and to hold from thee thereafter, nature has beauty and linger in ones mind, let a poem be written in the book of time.; [a.] Austin, TX

LUFKIN, TINA MARIE
[pen.] Cammie Wolfe; [b.] February 13, 1973, Murfreesboro, TN; [p.] Pat Tomlinson and Walter Lufkin, Grandparents Mr. and Mrs. Robert Lufkin and Mr. and Mrs. Joseph Tomlinson; [ch.] Pets: 2 dogs, Rage and Dutchess, 1 cat, Smokey, 1 boa constrictor - Chiba; [ed.] Riverdale High School, Middle Tennessee State University, Tennessee State University; [occ.] Police Officer Trainee, Nashville Metropolitan Police

Department; [oth. writ.] I have written many poems and short stories, but this is my first published work.; [pers.] I want to thank my family and friends, who gave me the confidence to express my inner thoughts and feelings on paper.; [a.] Hermitage, TN

LUND, BARBARA
[b.] May 21, 1964, Salt Lake City, UT; [p.] Jan and Vaughn Smith; [m.] Shawn Lund, July 26, 1986; [ch.] Casey Vaughn, Sarah Elyse; [occ.] Domestic Engineer, (Homemaker); [oth. writ.] I have a collection of thirty poems, one, which is in "Seasons to Come", A national Library of Poetry Anthology.; [pers.] All of my poems are based on events that have touched my heart. I wrote this poem for my father. So there wasn't any questions about what he means to me.; [a.] Salt Lake City, UT

LUND, DANIEL J.
[p.] Lawrence and Patricia Lund; [m.] Vickie Lee Lund; [ed.] Degree in Business Administration from the University of Southern Maine and currently a full time student at Bentley College, Waltham MN; [occ.] Administrative Assistant for a Health Care Provider

LUPO, LUCILLE A.
[b.] April 10, 1928, Detroit; [p.] Mr. and Mrs. A. Bauer (deceased); [m.] Giuliano (deceased), October 10, 1953; [ch.] Thomas, Janet; [ed.] 12 years; [pers.] This poem was written in the 11th or 12th grade. I believe it was for an English subject.

LURIE, RITA
[pen.] Rita Lurie; [b.] June 30, 1921, New York City; [p.] Jennie and David Tobias; [m.] Gustave Lurie; [ch.] Mark Lurie, Dava Jennings; [occ.] Retired from Administrative medical secretarial work in Kissimmee, Florida ad Memphis, Tn. Speak to nursing students on grief, at request of professor. On panels for same subject.; [memb.] RSVP, East Senior Center, MIFA support groups. With husband was part of a nucleus forming a community theater in Kissimmee, Florida 35 years ago. Still very active with productions - theater thrives. Directed and had roles in many popular plays.; [hon.] Heavy into Haiku, Limericks, "Rap" of famous lovers, parodies, matters of local interest; [oth. writ.] Newspaper and magazine articles and poetry, contests, etc. Creative writing for nursing homes, senior newspaper (Active Times), Recognition in various contests - honorable mention, etc. Director of senior writing class in Memphis senior center. (Creative work in poetry, prose, short stories, etc.) Give presentations to other groups around the city and the center.; [pers.] Write for family occasions for friends and seniors, Edit annual book for distribution - same contains the best work of our Writer's Forum class. Capture the imagination of a child then run with it.; [a.] Memphis, TN

LUTTRELL, JEREMY
[b.] December 24, 1982, Anadarko, OK; [p.] Jerry and Karen Luttrell; [ed.] Elementary - thru 6th grade; [occ.] Student; [memb.] Anadarko Karate Institute, Bethel Baptist Church; [hon.] Held 5th Kyu rank in Go ju Ryu Karate; [pers.] I take life one step at a time. My interests are many, so I write about many things.; [a.] Anadarko, OK

LUU, MAI NGOC
[pen.] Mai-Yen; [b.] January 21, 1925, Vietnam; [p.] Lan Luu-Ngoc; [m.] Yen Nguyen, May 29, 1954; [ch.] Thuy Luu, Nuong Luu, Doanh Luu, Thuc Luu, Binh Luu, Luan Luu; [ed.] Commander and Staff Diploma Viet-Nam Republic of Army Forces; [occ.] Lieutenant Colonel, Retiree; [hon.] First Order of National, Croise de guere abec Palme France, Cross of Galantry with Palme, Cross of Galantry with Palme, Cross of galantry with silver star; [oth. writ.] Free Lance Poet; [pers.]

Realistic and Romantic man is trying to find an Ideology of sociality.; [a.] Lemon Grove, CA

LYSY, CRAIG RICHARD
[b.] August 11, 1954, Detroit; [p.] Rose and Richard Lysy; [ed.] Austin Catholic Preparatory School, Michigan State University, University of Chicago; [occ.] Respiratory Care Practitioner; [oth. writ.] Book of Poems "Where Orion Sets...", awaiting publication, "Astrological Symbology of the Minor Planets", awaiting publication, "Symbology of the Tarot" awaiting publication.; [pers.] I strive to follow Kahlil Gibron's precept "In your longing for your giant self, lies your goodness. And that longing is in all of you."; [a.] Glendale, CA

MACK, CAROL JEAN
[b.] 1932; [m.] Dean I. Mack, 1951; [ch.] 6 Living; [ed.] High School Graduate, plus living and rising six kids and being 4 adviser, caregiver, and cashier; [occ.] Retired but still caretaking, writing etc.; [memb.] Methodist Church; [oth. writ.] Published in world poetry anthology in 1987 "I love too," and also recieved honorable mentioned for poem "Youth" in 1987 from world of poetry; [pers.] I have people and life.; [a.] Ostrander, OH

MACK, DEANDRA RIKI
[pen.] Riki Mack; [b.] March 25, 1984, MI; [p.] James and Mary Mack; [ed.] 5th Grade presently; [hon.] Received Award in writing from Oak Montessori School while in 4th grade; [oth. writ.] Written several short stories and poems. Published in school newspaper and yearbook. Is an artist and draws own illustration for poems and stories.; [pers.] Want to enhance and expand the creativity of writing and the pleasure of reading for others, particularly children. Was creating stories and poems she could write.; [a.] Oak Park, MI

MACKEY, DARLENE
[pen.] Jupiter; [b.] November 23, 1977; [p.] Earl and Cynthia Mackey; [ed.] Maurice J. McDonough High School; [memb.] International Thespian Society, Ram Times Staff; [hon.] Who's Who Among American High School Students; McDonough H.S. Theatre Letter; International Thespian Society Letter; [a.] Waldorf, MD.

MACKIN, TINA SWEARINGEN
[b.] August 23, 1968, Memphis, TN; [p.] Bob and Sue Swearingen; [m.] Jay Mackin, October 9, 1993; [ed.] Gibson County High School, Dyer, TN, University of Tennessee-Martin, Martin, TN; [occ.] Owner Words Worth Communications; [memb.] UT Alumnae Assoc, Alpha Delta Pi Alumnae Assoc, St. Agnes Catholic Church, International Assoc. of Business Communicators (IABC); [hon.] Presidential Academic Fitness Award, Who's who among America's High School Student's, 1st in district, 2nd in state historical play contest; [oth. writ.] Article for Today's Woman, Copywriter for several newsletters, brochures and other collateral materials, few plays; [pers.] With God's help, anything is possible.; [a.] Louisville, KY

MACLEOD, PAT
[b.] March 4, 1944, Seminole, TX; [ch.] Sarah Kimberly; [ed.] Lubbock High School, BS Nursing, West Texas A&M, Canyon; [occ.] Registered Nurse, Home Health Care; [memb.] Texas Nurses Assoc., American Heart Assoc.; [hon.] Certifications: IABP Management, Advanced EK6 Interpretation in Coronary Care; [pers.] I strive to reflect the love and compassion shown to mankind by the Lord Jesus Christ. I have been greatly influenced by the wonder of his Love.; [a.] Lubbock, TX

MADSEN, DAVID
[pen.] Turin Turamber; [b.] March 29, 1977, Medford, OR; [p.] Gordon and Linda Madsen; [ed.] Carl Harrison High School, Currently attending Georgia Institute of Technology; [occ.] Student; [memb.] International Thespian Society; [hon.] None worth Mentioning; [oth. writ.] Nothing published; [pers.] My goal is to write poetry which "comes to life" in people's imagination as they read it, to create an image so clear yet fantastic that reader thinks that they didn't read a poem but witnessed an actual event.; [a.] Acworth, GA

MAGEE, TAMIKA
[pen.] Mika, Jupiter; [b.] October 6, 1976, New Orleans, LA; [p.] Karen Magee; [ed.] St. Louise Cathedral Elementary, Mt Carmel Academy, Clark Atlanta University; [occ.] Student; [memb.] Biology Club, Pre-Professional Health Society, Ben Carson Science Academy Council of New Orleans; [hon.] Dean's List, Mathematics Honors Awards, Mentor of the Year of the Atlanta University Center at the Morehouse School of Medicine, Miss Torch of Morehouse College Yearbook; [oth. writ.] Several poems and short stories in the process of being published; [pers.] Writing is a single expression in time recorded and remembered. It is the quintessence of pure thoughts, the untouched idea in a frozen moment of time. I have been influenced by the writers of the Harlem Renaissance.; [a.] New Orleans, LA

MAHONEY, ELLEN LUCAS
[b.] February 23, 1932, Miami, FL; [p.] William and Mary Ellen Lucas; [m.] William David Mahoney (deceased), June 5, 1954; [ch.] Kathleen Marie, William Patrick, David Lucas, James Francis, Mary Ellen; [ed.] Cony High School Augusta, ME, Mercy Hosp. School of Nursing Portland ME; [pers.] Defense of the poet implies that one worthy thought unwritten - dies (E. Mahoney); [a.] Scarborough, ME

MAILLETT, ANDREA
[ch.] Two Children; [ed.] A.A. degree from Harford Community College Presently a Junior at the College of Notre Dame of Maryland; [memb.] Volunteer in the child-at-risk program at the Baltimore County Social Services; [hon.] President's List, Dean's List, Ph: Theta Kappa Alpha Sigma Lambda, Academic Achievement Award; [pers.] Search for the beauty in all things.; [a.] Baldwin, MD

MAJKA, RONALD M.
[b.] September 23, 1946, Philadelphia, PA; [p.] Winifred, Marjan; [m.] Jacqueline, August 17, 1968; [ch.] Ronald Gerard, Robert Anthony and Daniel Cardinal; [ed.] Graduate of Cardinal Dougherty High School - Phila. PA; [occ.] Police Officer, City of Philadelphia, PA; [memb.] Polish Police Association, Sacred Heart Society; [oth. writ.] Several other unpublished poems; [pers.] Most of my poetry is written to reflect the inner and outer beauty of the woman who inspires it, my wife!; [a.] Philadelphia, PA

MAKE, ISABEL ROSE
[b.] October 6, 1947, Philadelphia, PA; [p.] Aaron and Lillian Rose; [m.] Dr. Barry Make, June 14, 1970; [ch.] Jonathan David, Jeremy Simon; [ed.] BA George Washington Univ., Ed. M. Temple University, Doctorate in Progress, West Virginia University; [occ.] College professor, Small Business Owner, Denver, CO; [memb.] Greenwood Village Arts Council, Colorado Council of the Arts, The Denver Social Register, The Metropolitan Club; [hon.] Biography included in: Who's Who in the World, Who's in American Women, Who's in American Education, Distinguished Service Citation (Greenwood Village); [oth. writ.] 1. Child Care in Your Own Home: A Parent's Manual, 2. Reading in the Secondary

Classroom, 3. We're moving to Denver, 4. Several poems published in "The Community News"; [pers.] Throughout history, women have found a voice through their poetry. I am proud to add my voice to theirs.; [a.] Greenwood Village, CO

MALIK, NASIR
[b.] April, 12, 1971, Buchal Kalan, Pakistan; [p.] Muhammad Malik, Rakhmat Malik; [ed.] Millersville University, BS; [occ.] Graduate Student, Department of Pharmacology Pennsylvania State University College of Medicine; [pers.] I conceive of life is its most personal aspect as a dialectical struggle that consists of a multitude of thesis and antithesis all awaiting syntheses that may not exist.; [a.] Lebanon, PA

MALONE, JOHN PAUL
[b.] May 18, 1975, Ireland; [p.] Tony and Mary; [ed.] Marian College High School Dublin; [oth. writ.] All unpublished; [pers.] My humble gift of blue collar poetry is dedicated to my best friend Nathalie Jane Safar. Poetry is .... "JP Malone". Listen! Listen! for youth is opportunity; [a.] Boston, MA

MALTA, JONELLE
[b.] September 15, 1982, Wilkes-Barre, PA; [p.] Linda Malta, John Malta; [ed.] Saint Aloysius School; [memb.] Amnesty International, Cadetted Civil Scouts, Adopt-a-grandparent Program, Junior Youth Group, Mercy Hospital Volunteers, Saint Aloysius Tutoring Program; [hon.] National Physical Fitness Award 1992, National Physical Fitness Award 1993, National Piano Playing Auditions Award, Highest Honors - grade 5, Merit of Academic Achievement; [oth. writ.] "Things Do Not Last Forever," published in the National Anthology of Poetry for Young Americans, 1994 Edition; [pers.] With twenty-five pen pals from around the world, I've been greatly inspired to write about people, life and ways we can improve our living environments.; [a.] Wilkes-Barre, PA

MALUVAC, ROBIN ENGBERG
[pen.] R. L. Engberg; [b.] November 18, 1965, Indiana; [p.] Jean Engberg (father); [m.] Bryon Maluvac, September 25, 1993; [occ.] Administrative Assistant, National Steel Corp.; [memb.] Life time Member of the International Society of Poets, Member of the Center for Marine Conservation; [hon.] Published in The National Library of Poetry's, "Journey of the Mind," "At Day's End," "Whispers in the Wind," and Best Poets of 1995. Received four Editor's Choice Awards.; [pers.] Bryon, every since the day we married, my fondest dreams have been coming true.; [a.] Chesterton, IN

MALVEAUX, ROY L.
[pen.] Roy L. Malveaux; [b.] December 10, 1950, Beaumont, TX; [p.] Vivian and Mamie Malveaux; [m.] Kaffie Loraine Malveaux, November 10, 1984; [ch.] Roy Jr., Latedia, Michell, Tina, Felix and Leslie; [ed.] Hebert High School, Lamar University, Del Mar College, Guadalupe Theology Service School; [occ.] Machine Shop Inspector; [oth. writ.] Other writings in local newspapers, publish book "The Signs of the Times," Vantage Press; [pers.] I have only one life to live...and I will do my best to please God and serve mankind in hopes that my living may not be in vain...; [a.] Corpus Christi, TX

MANCHA, LINDSAY
[pen.] Lindsay La Mancha; [b.] August 8, 1980, Thousand Oaks; [p.] Michael Mancha, Joycelyn Mancha; [ed.] Hillcrest Christian School, Newbury Park High; [occ.] Student/Actress; [oth. writ.] Have been awarded for poetry in minor poetry contests; [pers.] In a time of serious world decay, I believe that true beauty can only be found in two timeless treasures: in the Bible and in

poetry. Alfred Lord Tennyson has inspired me greatly to find release in my writing.; [a.] Thousand Oaks, CA

MANDT, BETTY J.
[b.] February 4, 1924, Champaign, IL; [p.] Frank and Myrtle Pepper; [m.] (Deceased) Almer J. Mandt, Jr., 1949; [ch.] Almer J. III, Susan E., Barbara A., Catharine J., Debra R.; [ed.] General study and courses in Accounting (U. of IL.) IRS Tax Courses. Extensive self-study of literature and history.; [occ.] Retired Accountant (Mandt Tax and Accounting Office); [oth. writ.] I have been writing poetry, especially children's poetry, for fifty years. Have never had them published but working on book. They have been read at schools.; [pers.] I believe there is a place for poetry written simply, from the heart, so it may touch the hearts of everyone, not just those trained to appreciate the classics. Sensitivity and beauty should have no boundaries.; [a.] Freeport, IL

MANGUM JR., GEORGE R.
[b.] September 21, 1956, Cook City; [p.] George and Joan Mangum; [ed.] Columbia College, (1 yr.) Current/Amer. Inst. of Paralegal Studies; [occ.] Unemployed; [memb.] Bally's Health Club and B.E.A.T. Community Rep.; [hon.] Voice of Democracy Awarded me in High School; [oth. writ.] Yes; [pers.] "I can only be sucessful and happy if I have humble but reasonable confidence in my own powers! "Only until I come Full Circle, with myself is when I truly will become happy and contented with thyself.; [a.] Chicago, IL

MANN, ANNA A.
[b.] November 25, 1934, North Adams, MA; [p.] Francis and Anne Trottier; [m.] William C. Mann, November 24, 1990; [ch.] David Lincoln, Daniel Lincoln, Dale Lincoln, Brian Goodell, Kevin Goodell; [ed.] 8th Grade at Freeman School, 9 and 10 at McCanns Vocational, now a Student of Institute of Children's Literature, West Redding Ct.; [occ.] Writer/Disabled; [memb.] Children's Write Columbia Audia Books; [hon.] 1948 - appeared on radio station W.M.N.B. North Adams Mass for essay from picture called the Fisherman's Wife, received book called Trotters Circus on art; [oth. writ.] Today's great poems by Famous Poets Society, Published (A Soldiers, Last Letter) Quill Books, echoed from the silence published (helping hands). Article from local paper enclosed.; [pers.] If you love writing, don't ever give up. Because you never know when you can enter it in competition and become a published poet. Keep right on writing.; [a.] Fallow, NV

MANSHEIM, HELEN C.
[b.] July 26, 1911, Fort Madison, IA; [occ.] Retired, Records Clerk; [oth. writ.] Many poem non published

MANULLA, KRISTOFER
[b.] September 28, 1981, New Britain, CT; [p.] Richard and Donna Manulla; [ed.] 7th Grade, Middle School; [occ.] Student; [hon.] D.A.R.E. Award Recipient; [pers.] In my poems I like to flood peoples hearts with love.; [a.] Torrington, CT

MARAVILLAS, ROSA
[b.] April 8, 1995, Mexico City; [p.] Carlos Maravillas and Mar Elena Maravillas; [ed.] Good Counsel High School, University of Illinois at Chicago; [hon.] Phi Eta Sigma, Alpha Lambda Delta; [pers.] Whosoever seeks to find the truth hidden within oneself will never fell lost and alone.; [a.] Chicago, IL

MARBACH, AMANDA
[b.] July 28, 1975, San Antonio, TX; [p.] Jerome and Betty Marbach; [ed.] Antonian College Preparatory High School -- currently attending University of Texas at San Antonio; [occ.] Child Care Provider at St.

Monica's Catholic School, TX; [oth. writ.] Many poems published in several anthologies/books and in school magazines.; [pers.] I always try to write poems about personal situations other people can relate to. I want people who have similar problems to know they are never alone.; [a.] Converse, TX

MARCUS, NELSON
[b.] Elizabeth, MS; [p.] Benjamin Nelson, Maude T. Nelson; [ed.] Primary and Secondary School, Loop College; [occ.] Playwright, New Concept Theatre, Chicago, IL; [memb.] The Langley Avenue Church of God, The Modern Bookstore Committe; [hon.] Midwest Playwrights Program, Proclamation, The State of Illinois, Governor, James Thompson, Proclamation, The City of Chicago, Mayor, Harold Washington; [oth. writ.] Several Essays Published in The Harambee Shopper, Milwaukee, WI, an article for the Open Dialogue III, Washington, D.C., and some 42 Plays; [pers.] I strive for my Trinity of "C", i.e. Care. Committment. Consideration. I have been influenced by William Shakespeare and Lope de Vega; [a.] Chicago, IL

MARCZAK, THADDEUS S.
[b.] September 13, 1904, Marseille, France; [p.] Deceased; [m.] Deceased- Florentine Marczak, October 29, 1930; [ch.] Florentine Ruesga, William Marczak; [ed.] Studied and worked in Marseille, Paris, Germany worked for Tiffany Studies; [occ.] Deceased; [memb.] Aaron Lodge #49 Fx A.M. Tucson, AZ; [oth. writ.] Stories of many different items many poems; [pers.] Dad would be so happy to know he is finally recognized. I feel honored to present his work. Thank you.; [a.] Tucson, AZ

MARIN, CARMELINA D.
[b.] September 11, 1968, New York; [p.] Juan and Carmelina A. Marin; [ch.] Emmanuel (9), Jonathan (7), and Robert (6); [pers.] I dedicate all that I write and all that I am to my mother, Carmelina A. Marin. She is my inspiration and the wind beneath my wings, and with God's help I'll grow to be just like her. I love you, Mommy.; [a.] Bronx, NY

MARKEL, BARBARA
[b.] October 11, 1938, Augusta, KS; [p.] Clayton and Ellen; [m.] Calvin, January 30, 1980; [ch.] Carol, Christopher, Cindy, Phoebe; [occ.] Housewife and Artist; [oth. writ.] None Published but I have a few stories I would like to see published as I think are amusing for all to read and enjoy; [pers.] I have 8 grandchildren and 6 great grandchildren of the 6 great to two sets of twin's 3 boys and girl; [a.] Douglass, KS

MARSHALL, JOSEPH M.
[b.] January 24, 1977, Brockton; [p.] Henry Marshall and Gidget Marshall; [ed.] High School: New England Baptist Academy. I will be attending Pensacola Christian College in the fall of 1995.; [occ.] Team Captain (head cashier) at shows Supermarket; [memb.] New England Baptist Church; [hon.] Nominated to attend the National Youth Leadership Forum on Medicine in Boston, MA Westside Show's Employee of the Month of August 1993. Honor Roll.; [oth. writ.] I've written a two part poem entitled "Expostulation and Reply" also, I write for a newspaper entitled "The Separatists" and I am in the process of writing a look to educate Christian teens on issue which they face today.; [pers.] This poem is dedicated to my five best friends: Suza Cooper, Keith Brickell, Jennifer Darling, John Watson, and Stephen Deyesso.; [a.] Brockton, MA

MARTIN, BRANDY
[b.] August 23, 1981, Virginia Beach, VA; [p.] Catherine Martin; [ed.] Deep Creek Middle School; [pers.] In all of my poems, I write exactly what I feel inside of myself,

or something that I am longing to feel within I am greatly inspired by Eadger Alan Poe.; [a.] Cheasapeake, VA

MARTIN, JANE
[b.] Chicago, IL; [p.] John and Carmella Martin; [ed.] BA, MA - Xavier University Chicago, IL; [occ.] Social Work

MARTIN, MICHAEL A.
[b.] February 29, 1940, Akron, OH; [p.] Beatrice M. Gorcoff and Albert L. Martin; [ed.] 4 Yr. College Equivilant - Graduated North High (H. S.) - Passed - College GED Military College Courses - Prep Courses/ Received two Major Educational Awards in U. S. Air Force - Strategic Air Command - U. S. Air Force In Europe; [occ.] Professional Security Officer in Las Vegas, Nevada; [memb.] Master Mason (Masonic Blue Lodge) - 32nd Degree Scottish Rite and Shriner - Member Post #8 in Vegas, American Legion, Member of International Society of Poets; [hon.] Presidential Security U. S. Air Force. Selected as a "Best Poet" by "The National Library of Poetry" Received Editors Choice Awards for "Dance on the Horizon" - "Echoes of Yesterday" - Selected for "Best Poems of 1995" - all by The National Library of Poetry". Published Book: "Atlantis Secrets Revealed". Poetry published by you people - Hill Top Records selected "To Eva My Love" for their "America" Album-In "Best Poems of 1995".; [oth. writ.] Poetry published by "The National Library of Poetry" in "Dance on the Horizon" - "Echoes of Yesterday" "Best Poem of 1995" - and Beyond the Stars. "Atlantis Secrets Revealed" published by Gorman Inc. Las Vegas, Nv. Poems published - "A Poem" - "Untitled" - "To Eva My Love" - "Please Give Me A Chance". Hill Top Records selected the poem: "To Eva My Love" for their "America" Album and loved it. They are going to feature it.; [pers.] To strive for perfection in all I do. I go for it and do the best I can. I especially want to make my Book, "Atlantis Secrets Revealed", "The Most Successful of All Books" - I write book - poetry - lyrics for music for enjoyment.; [a.] Las Vegas, NV

MARTIN, RACHEL MAY
[b.] August 19, 1982, Rappahannock Academy, VA; [p.] Live with grandmother, Mary Wilson my parents; [m.] Deceased, December 24, 1954; [ch.] Therea Rose, Judith Lynn, Dianna Lynn, Shirly Larcine; [ed.] Now in Buckingham Middle School 7th grade, next year will attend Cumberland Va.; [occ.] Buckingham Middle School; [memb.] Book Club Shilo Convent Church; [hon.] Safety Patrol, Honor Roll Art, Awards for short stories and power; [oth. writ.] Poems and stories published in school paper at Plum point Md Middle School; [pers.] I am 13 year old I would like to write children books and power and go on to bigger things after college. I want to thank my grandmother Mary Wilson for what and whom I am today for all of her love, support and encouragement and letting me be myself and persue what I like to do. Reading, writing and most of all just being their for me no matter what. I love you grandma Rachel; [a.] Cumberland, VA

MARTIN, SAMANTHA
[b.] June 7, 1984, Turnersville, NJ; [p.] Lisa Martin and Dean Martin; [ed.] Wedgwood Elementary (talented and gifted class); [occ.] Student; [memb.] Girls Scouts an America, National Geographic Society; [hon.] Principal's List, Bowling Awards; [a.] Turnersville, NJ

MARTINEZ, BOB G.
[pen.] Bob G. Martinez; [b.] June 7, 1949, Las Vegas, NM; [p.] Mary Jane Martinez (never knew Dad); [m.] Annette E. Martinez "Luvy", February 10, 1973; [ch.] Lita R. Martinez (18 yrs), She is graduating Valedicto-

rian June 95!; [ed.] I Graduated from Denver North High School in 1968; [occ.] Security Guard at the Denver Merchandise Mart (5 1/2 yrs); [memb.] Recent "Distinguished" Member of the I.S.P.; [hon.] Becoming recognized as a poet by such a Fine Organization as I.S.P. and the National Library of Poets is Quite Honoring!; [oth. writ.] In process of assembling a personal compilation of poems... also looking to have my completed book published, "My Time to Rhyme"; [pers.] My poems bring honor and praise to me.. when others are blessed, I'm happy of course. But I know who gives this ability...suffice it to say, it's higher source.; [a.] Denver, CO

MASON, ELOUISE COLLINS
[pen.] Mary Louise McCoy; [b.] December 17, 1945, Pembroke, VA; [p.] Morrison A. Collins and Hazel M. Collins; [m.] Jery David Mason, June 19, 1978; [ch.] Dennis A. Love, Laura A. Hilton; [ed.] Giles High School New River Community College; [occ.] Disabled; [memb.] Ephesus Free will Baptist Church, Ladies Aux., and Choir, Amherst society and Poet's Guild; [hon.] Certificate of Poetic Achievement Poet's Guild award; [oth. writ.] Poems in a Moment in Time and The Garden of Life. Several of my poems have been published in other books and publications of other magazines and American Annual and Guild; [pers.] Treat God as your best friend talk to him each day. If you talk to him each morning when you awake, and at night before you go to sleep. Everything will be alright!; [a.] Blounts Creek, NC

MATHENY, JENNIFER L.
[b.] February 13, 1967, Danville, IL; [p.] Sandra Waggoner, John McCarty; [m.] James Matheny, May 28, 1988; [ch.] Amethyst Lynn, James Dalton; [ed.] Paris High School; [occ.] Apparel Clerk; [hon.] Musical Awards; [oth. writ.] Other unpublished poems; [pers.] My poems are written from experiences I've had and from my own feelings. I like to read all kinds of poetry.; [a.] Paris, IL

MATHES, MARY L.
[pen.] Forest A. Mathes; [b.] July 27, 1919, KY; [p.] Omega Rodgers; [m.] Joseph Edward Myers, March 27, 1959; [ch.] Linda, Dorn, Betty Mathes, Forest Mathes; [ed.] BS Educ., MA Library Sc, MA - Media Sp., and 72 grad hours, taught 22 yrs; [occ.] Retired - making dolls for homeless children; [memb.] Las Rancheras Rep. Women, UMW - Methodist Church, 3 1/2 yrs WSAF, Boys Club Tutor; [hon.] Rotary Award 5000 hrs - volunteer SMHCCR Assignment by Governor Church Recognition Nomimee - Mrs. Senior Arizone Women of the Year; [oth. writ.] N. Ky Deuta Mag 1940's several opinion articles in local newspaper; [pers.] I have to live with myself and so I have to be fit for myself to know. God doesn't close door without opening a window.; [a.] Scottsdale, AZ

MATSON, SHARON R.
[b.] November 24, 1940, Seattle, WA; [p.] James and K. Lydia Waldal; [m.] "Chuck" Charles R. Matson, July 28, 1957; [ch.] Albert, Audrey, Sylvia, Della, Morris, Linda, Laura, Alyce; [ed.] 9 grades - GED High School, The Institute of Children's Literature ('95 Graduate); [occ.] Homemaker; [memb.] Apostolic Lutheran Church; [hon.] Most Outstanding Student 9th grade, Mother of eight children; [pers.] "My Life With You" is the poem I wrote for my husband's 1995 Valentine. The number one thing in all of life is faith in God.; [a.] Brush Prairie, WA

MATTA, LISA TOMPKINS
[pen.] Lisa Tompkins Matta; [b.] July 22, 1955, Iowa; [ed.] B.A. degree from University of Northern Iowa, currently working on Master of Education degree at

University of St. Thomas.; [occ.] Teacher; [memb.] Assoc. of Texas Professional Educators Houston Museum of Fine Arts, Houston Museum of Science, Greater Houston Area Reading Council; [hon.] Alpha Gamma Delta Scholarship recipient. Grant recipient, 1994-97, Master of Education degree at University of St. Thomas. Teacher of the Year nominee, 1994-95.; [oth. writ.] Am currently working on a collection of poems entitled, Magic Seeds; [pers.] I enjoy writing poetry for people of all ages, however, many of my thoughts and ideas are a result of having worked with children for several years.; [a.] Houston, TX

MATYOK, MARGARET S.
[b.] May 9, 1937, Toledo, OH; [p.] Julius and Margaret Fodor; [m.] Lewis P. Matyok, June 20, 1959; [ch.] Pamela Sue and Lewis Paul Jr., grand children, Alexis and Jacob Lewis; [ed.] Graduated from Waite High School I am a prep. cook. My husband is a Chef, we have been working together now for twenty years. Private clubs, and one Rest. and now Retirement Center.; [occ.] Server at The Parkvue Community Center where my husband is the Chef; [memb.] Chefs Association St. Stephen United Church of Chirst, (Nellie Arthur) My Dearest Friend, encouraged me a lot and inspired me also. She has passed away.; [hon.] Please write this so my husband, children Nellie Arthur, family and friends, and poets, and pootess and the Bible, God, Jesus, inspired me.; [oth. writ.] I have many but never entered them of showed them to many people until now.; [pers.] Right now my grandchildren are the light of my life, my writings help me when I read them, I am inspired from my, past and present life, from my husband, friends, and many famous people, and mist poets, and poetess, and the ones in The Bible, and God, Jesus, inspire me. I gather strength, from people who write poems, the ones of today, and from yesterday, and from the Bible.; [a.] Sandusky, OH

MAY, MELBA
[b.] December 23, 1980, Wadley North, Texarkana, TX; [p.] Dorcas and Chester May; [ed.] In the 8th grade at Nashville Junior High in Nashville, Arkansas; [memb.] A Member of FHA and a Member of Flint Hill C.M.E. Church in Mineral Springs, Arkansas; [hon.] I'm a Superior at Piano. I've been taking for 3 years. I was scholar of the year at my church.; [pers.] I would like to thanks the Almighty God for helping me accomplish such as great task.; [a.] Mineral Springs, AR

MAYORGA, PATRICIA ANN
[b.] March 16, 1952, Sacramento, CA; [p.] Clyde Dunsing, Evelyn Dunsing; [m.] Stephen R. Mayorga, June 20, 1973; [ch.] David, Teresa, Stephanie, Sarah, Linda and Melanie; [ed.] University of Pacific, BA, MA; [occ.] Teacher (Multiple Subject 6th gr.), Taylor Elementary School, Stockton, CA; [memb.] Association of Mexican American Educators, Affirmative Action Advisory Committee Board Member; [hon.] Honors San Joaquin Delta College; [oth. writ.] Poems in local newspaper; [pers.] Believe in the compassion, wonder, fantasies, hopes, and fears than embrace each of us in our journey through life. It is in the journey that the substance of our being is created. May peace and hope always dictate over our human errors.; [a.] Stockton, CA

MAYWEATHER, LATRICE RENEE
[b.] September 10, 1978, Washington, DC; [p.] Candyce R. Nelson, Albert Mayweather; [ed.] Concordia Lutheran School, Duke Ellington School of the Arts High School; [occ.] Student; [memb.] Key Club, DC Youth Orchestra; [hon.] 2 years in Who's Who Among American High School Students; [pers.] Keep true to your heart, never listen to the bad that people tell you, for they might only try and keep you down. Only write

about what you feel in your heart and you can only be happy about yourself.; [a.] Adelphi, MD

MBENG SR., KAFAIN EMMANUEL
[pen.] Kafain Emmanuel Mbeng, Sr.; [b.] December 24, 1956, Cameroon; [p.] Johnson and Mary Mbeng; [m.] Grace Vumah Mbeng; [ch.] Kafain Emmanuel Mbeng, Jr.; [ed.] Southern University, Washington, DC; [memb.] Mt. Vernon Baptist Church; [hon.] Ordained Deacon; [oth. writ.] Even Love Can Hurt You (yet to be published); [pers.] I enjoy turning practical personal or impersonal experiences into abstract issues in fiction style. I only worry about the things that I can change, and adore what I have, not what I want.; [a.] Alexandria, VA

MCADOO, JEANETTE S.
[pen.] Jeannette J. McAdoo; [b.] December 30, 1958, McKeesport; [p.] Steve and Sharon Kossuth; [m.] David Timothy McAdoo, May 21, 1994; [ch.] Timothy Vincent Rump; [ed.] McKeesport High Allegehny Beauty Academy; [occ.] Housewife, Notary; [memb.] PAN- Pennsylvania Association of Noteries American Notery Society; [hon.] Presidential Sports Awards

MCCAIN, G. STUART
[pen.] G. Stuart McCain; [b.] April 6, 1963, San Antonio, TX; [p.] Arther Glenn and Vera Gazle; [ed.] Graduate Kilgore High School, Kilgore, TX, Completed Two Years at Kilgore College, Kilgore, TX; [occ.] O.L. Field Security and Gate Guard; [oth. writ.] "Land of No Relief," "Johnny Lonely" "Wanted: Brothers Who Love One Another" "The Day the Martyrs Cried" "So Long, Mr. No One" "I Ask and He Answers" and "I Am not a Sinless Man" to name a few, all unreleased and unpublished; [pers.] I am a born again son of God, saved by his grace and mercy through faith in his son, the Lord Christ Jesus, who now lives in my heart. And the life I now live, I live by the faith of the son of God, who loved me so much that he died that I might have life and was raised from the dead that I might have life more abundant.; [a.] Kerrville, TX

MCCALL, LYNETTE ELAINE
[pen.] Elaine Monk; [b.] August 18, 1957, Washington, DC; [p.] Mr. and Mrs. Lucas McCall; [ed.] A.A.S. Management Technology; [occ.] Potential Future Author; [memb.] University of District of Columbia Alumnist; [hon.] CPR, Certificate Nurses Aide/Geriatric Aide, V.P. Pre-Alumni Council of U.D.C. 1986 Certificate of Excellence in supervision and training; [oth. writ.] Unpublished manuscripts that solely pertains to the studies related to women in the King James version of the Bible; [pers.] My goal is to enhance women to bring them to their full potential of understanding the Holy Writings of God by Biblical examples that relate directly to women.; [a.] Washington, DC

MCCARTHY, KATHLEEN M.
[b.] May 3, 1954, New York, NY; [p.] Francis P. and Frances E. McCarthy; [ed.] Roosevelt High School, Yonkers New York, Sam Houston State University, Huntsville TX; [occ.] Cashier; [oth. writ.] Writing a series of science fiction and thrillers-trying to get published-all help excepted; [pers.] Life is more than what it seems, It was created that way to make one think, share and grow. Death is just another form of life; [a.] Houston, TX

MCCARTY, CHRIS
[b.] September 25, 1962, Auroa, CO; [p.] Mr. and Mrs. W.C. McCarty; [occ.] Cancer Research; [hon.] Multiple Military Honors and awards, Multiple Military Honors; [pers.] The past is what has made us. I prefer to look at one's ability and what there Capable of, then

look back to to how they got here.; [a.] Boern, TX

MCCHESNEY, HAROLD A.
[pen.] Hal Andrew; [m.] Marian L. McChesney, June 18, 1949; [ed.] B.A., M.A. Gonzaga, University; [oth. writ.] Co-author for technical article "hospitals" journal of the American Hospital Association, article for the "Liguorian"

MCCLAIN, ANDY
[b.] July 8, 1978, Waco, TX; [p.] Scott and Judy McClain; [ed.] High School - Senior; [occ.] Student; [memb.] German and French Clubs, President Student Council (2 yrs), Vice-President National Honors Society; [a.] Waco, TX

MCCLIMON, JUSTINE
[b.] March 10, 1965, Atlanta; [p.] Emily H. Peters; [m.] Patrick J. McClimon; [ch.] Sara Elizabeth; [ed.] GA. State University- B.A. Journalism (1987), J.D. Law (1990); [occ.] Contract Administrator; [a.] Roswell, GA

MCCLOUD, CAROLYN
[b.] March 21, 1952, Southeast, MO; [p.] Raymond and Virginia Crowe; [m.] Divorced; [ch.] James Wayne McCloud II and Tanya Deann McCloud; [ed.] Fot Zumwhalt High, Ofallon, MO; [occ.] Grocery Industry; [pers.] I want to thank all of my friends and Salee Webb at the Ozark Technical College for all their support and encouragement. I feel my poetry is a gift from the Lord from all the influences through out my life because nothing happiness in Gods world by mistake.; [a.] Springfield, MO

MCCLOUD, CAROLYN
[b.] March 21, 1952, Southeast, MO; [p.] Raymond and Virginia Crowe; [m.] Divorced; [ch.] James Wayne McCloud II and Tanya Deann McCloud; [occ.] Grocery Industry; [pers.] I want to thank al of my friends and Sales Webb at Ozark Technical College for all their support and encouragement. I feel my poetry is a gift from the Lord from all the influences, through out my life because; [a.] Springfield, MD

MCCLURE, PATRICIA JEAN
[pen.] Patricia McClure; [b.] January 23, 1935, Houston, TX; [p.] Elmer B. and Ouida A. Miller; [m.] Thomas Alexander McClure, February 23, 1952 to June 29, 1989; [ch.] Michael Timothy; [ed.] Spring Branch High Long Beach City; [occ.] Bookkeeper, Tomball Storage; [memb.] Palestine Organ Club, Holy Sity Strummers, Yaupon Garden Club, Brazosport Sweet Adeline Long Lake Baptist, Teacher, Clerk; [hon.] National Honor Society Spring Branch High, Quill and Scroll Society - Spring Branch High; [oth. writ.] Over one hundred lines printed copy, Spring Branch bear lines facts. Won auto dealership essay contest in Houston.; [pers.] The world is surrounded in beauty. To lose one's self in discovery becomes an unsatable passion. I've always been delighted by poems of love and nature.; [a.] Palestine, TX

MCCLUSKY, HAROLD L.
[b.] December 9, 1928, Shreveport; [p.] Sam J. and Eunice M. McClusky; [m.] Mary Jo. May McClusky, July 2, 1948; [ch.] Judy Lynn and Kelly Ann, grand children Kristen and Stephen; [ed.] Petroleum Explorationist; [oth. writ.] Over 100 other poems mostly religious; [pers.] Member Summer Grove Baptist Church, Adult Sunday School Teacher, Ordained Deacon, Poetry is an outlet for me to express my feelings on various subjects.; [a.] Shreveport, LA

MCCORD, MARGARET M.
[b.] November 20, 1903, Scotland; [m.] John McCord

Deseased, March 4, 1924; [ch.] 3 daughters and 1 son, 10 grandchildren, 10 great; [ed.] Scottish Schools, Business Schools; [memb.] Presbyterian, Homecast Brooklyn, Brooklyn Civic Council, Shepherds Plumb Beach Civic Ass., Inc (founder) precinct council/boys club; [hon.] Congressional Record Honorary Shepherds Historical Society City Council - Boys Club Award New York War Services, Peace Medal many Awards and Honors from Local Association Assembly Community; [pers.] I do volunteer work, covering Community Brooklyn Charities, Public Library I am in 92nd year. And have N.S.E.W. of USA.; [a.] Brooklyn, NY

MCCORMACK, LISA M.
[b.] July 7, 1980, Robbinsdale, MN; [p.] William and LaRae McCormack; [ed.] Currrently Attending St. Francis High School; [hon.] A honor R.roll, in High School; [oth. writ.] I have no previous writings that have been published; [pers.] I would like to thank my grandmother, Janene McCormack, for encouraging me to persue my writing as more than just a personal hobbie.; [a.] East Bethel, MN

MCCOY, WENDY
[b.] May 15, 1972, Lynchburg, VA; [p.] Mitchell and Ann McCoy; [ed.] E. C. Glass High School The University of Virginia; [occ.] Student-University of Virginia, Part-time bus driver University Transit Service; [memb.] Zeta Phi Beta Sorority; [pers.] My poetry reflects the pain that I have suffered from the heartaches of love. I use my writings to ease my mind and express myself. Everyone has the ability to create greatness.; [a.] Lynchburg, VA

MCCUISTION, WILMA CARSON
[b.] Vancouver, British Columbia, Canada; [p.] William H. and Marie A. Carson; [m.] Sam C. McCuistion; [ch.] Linda E. Keen and Lee Carson McCuistion; [ed.] Laura Secord School, Vancouver, B.C., Cordova High School, Cordova, Alaska, University of Washington, Seattle, Washington; [occ.] Writer and Gardener, Retire from Real Estate/Construction Fields; [memb.] Alaska Yukon Pioneers; [oth. writ.] A Collection of Poetry, Short Stories, Autobiography, Ghosted Editorials for Construction Trade Journal; [a.] Galt, CA

MCDANIEL, WARREN E.
[pen.] Beth; [b.] January 21, 1928, Dayton, OH; [p.] Warren and Bessie Mae McDaniel; [m.] Doris Ann, February 23, 1950; [ch.] Five; [ed.] Butler High School, Vandalia, Ohio; [occ.] Artist; [pers.] All his life Warren has been able to entertain children and adults alike with his poetry and ability to draw. His first award was given him in grade school, presented by the artist Milton Caniff, in 1939.; [a.] Valdez, AK

MCDANIELS, JOANN CHEVELLE
[b.] May 10, 1968, Detroit, MI; [p.] Carol A. Hall, Joseph W. McDaniels; [ed.] Kettering High School, graduated in 1986 and Wayne County Community College, graduated with A.A. degree in 1993; [occ.] Machinist; [memb.] United Way; [hon.] Academic excellence award, certificate of appreciation, and certificate of recognition; [oth. writ.] I'm trying to find other publishers who think potential and I want a career in poetry writing.; [pers.] "Dreams" are about your own true feelings.; [a.] Detroit, MI

MCGAHARAN, THURZA I.
[pen.] Terz; [b.] March 29, 1917, Sandusky, OH; [p.] Joseph and Laura Reiter; [ch.] 4-1 Deceased; [ed.] 1st year high school; [occ.] Cleaning; [oth. writ.] Song's Two - Records; [pers.] I have two songs on Records Blue of Tennessee under neath Haurian sky's, have the copyrights; [a.] Sandusky, OH

MCGINNIS, BERNARD W.
[b.] March 18, 1924, Honesdale, PA; [p.] Frank and Florence (Miller) McGinnis; [m.] Divorced; [sib.] Terrence and Valerie; [ed.] AAS-Dutchess Community College B.S. Marist College (Magna Cum Laude) M. B. A. Marist College; [occ.] Retired IBM Staff Engineer; [memb.] VFW, American Legion, USS LST Association, Sampson Navy Vets.; [hon.] 17 IBM Invention Disclosures, 9 US Patents (IBM), 1 Outstanding Innovation Award (IBM), 1st-2nd 3rd Level Invention Achievement awards (IBM), several informal Awards - IBM, VFW County Commander - 1953 US Navy Veteran WW II-Pacific; [oth. writ.] Several unpublished poems; [a.] Poughkeepsie, NY

MCGOVERN, DANIELLE
[pen.] "Evelyn" McGovern; [b.] October 11, 1982, New York; [p.] Kathy and Brian; [ed.] All Honors and class 1st thru 7th grades; [occ.] Student 7th Grade; [memb.] SAG-AFTRA; [hon.] Presidential Academic Fitness Award High Honor Roll Award, N.Y. State School Admin., Gold Medal, All County Chorus, Odyssey of the Mind Spirit Award, Summer Institute for the gifted College Award; [pers.] Life goes so fast, sometimes you have to slow down so you don't miss it.; [a.] Freeport, NY

MCGRAW SR., SHELTON S.
[pen.] "Quick Draw"; [b.] November 4, 1941, Fairdale, TX; [p.] Sim T. McGraw and Helen McGraw; [m.] Mary F. McGraw, July 14, 1962; [ch.] John, Mary Rebecca, Timothy McGraw Jr.; [ed.] High School (12 yrs); [occ.] Self Employed; [memb.] Honorary Member F.F.A., Honorary member Hemphill Fire Dept. Who's Who in Executive of America 1994, President Fire Commission Evadale, TX., Member turkey Call of Texas (replacement of turkeys in the National Forest); [hon.] Lions Club Award (Evadale), Who's Who, World of Poetry Award 1994, F.F.A. Plack Award Honorary Member, Best Working Men from Brown and Root for employees we furnished on Brown and Rott Job; [oth. writ.] Lots of poems. Just Outside My Window - Book, Christmas Cards 1995 - Boxes of 25, Scripture Text - Poems of Christmas inside - To be out in 1995, Cards are completely a McGraw Card; [pers.] All work printed by Shelton McGraw Sr. are in hope that in some way a person may be touched. That a joy in some way may become alive in the person. For to bring Joy and Happiness into a persons life, is in itself rewarding. That a soul may be changed, and that peace in someway may be found. Oh that a smile may be seen, in the face may be a beam, of light that shines to show the way, for others to follow each day.; [a.] Evadale, TX

MCGREW, MYRILE I.
[pen.] Myrile Wills McGrew; [b.] July 11, 1914, Cornwall, England; [p.] Mr. Edward Thomas Pearce Pada Wills; [m.] Mr. Paul K. McGrew, December 11, 1956; [ch.] One adopted daughter Eunice Elizabeth Lonely, 2 grandsons Richard P, Ryan; [occ.] Housewife, Retired; [memb.] Accredited member of the Christian Writers Guild of San Diego County 1991-92 and is entitled to all privileges of the working press Publish a book in 1992 entitled sweet "Aroma Falling in Love" sells for $8.95 Plus Tax. Inspirational thoughts from a county; [hon.] Girl's Diary Consist of My Autobiography in prose plus in verse 62 poems with epilogue

MCINTIRE, JEFFREY W.
[b.] May 7, 1977, Philadelphia, PA; [p.] John Sallis McIntire and Elizabeth Moorhead McIntire; [ed.] Lisle Senior High School 1995 Freshman-Franklin and Marshall College, Lancaster, PA; [memb.] National Honor Society; [hon.] National Honor Society, Illinois State Scholar, Neahaus-Nalley Wrestling Founders Award; [a.] Lisle, IL

MCKENNA, DEBBIE LYNN
[b.] February 10, 1957, Houston, TX; [p.] Marie and Thomas McKenna; [ed.] BA in Philosophy; [occ.] Abstract Expressionist Painter; [hon.] Phi Beta Kappa; [oth. writ.] Too many to mention; [pers.] I don't think twice and I try always to look like I know what I'm doing. Also, I think good poetry is better than no poetry.; [a.] San Diego, CA

MCKINNEY, CAROLE A.
[pen.] C. A. Howard; [b.] July 6, 1949, Longview, TX; [ed.] Pine Tree High School, Longview Kilgore Jr. College, Kilgore, TX; [occ.] Grocery Store Checker Albertsons #4207 Longview, TX; [pers.] My poetry is a reflection of the emotional turmoil in my life.; [a.] Longview, TX

MCKINNEY, KYLE HARRISON
[pen.] Kyle Harrison McKinney; [b.] February 7, 1925, Mascott, TN; [p.] Hubert H. and Arda F. McKinney; [m.] Velma Louise McKinney, November 29, 1944; [ch.] April, Iris, Lisa; [ed.] GED and Technical Schools Trained salesmen in Office Mch. Appointed Sen. SS Teacher COG YPE Oresident several years; [occ.] Retired; [hon.] Winner of Sales and Technician award of year Numerous Sales and technical awards in my vocation NRCC Sen. Citz Poetry Contest New River College; [oth. writ.] Numerous poems published in books of poems published by New River College Dublin, VA; [pers.] I believe firmly in the Holy Trinity for this reason I believe in a much higher calling than we now occupy which I expect to receive by faith I believe my poetry is inspired by the afore mentioned.; [a.] Richmond, VA

MCLAUGHLIN, BONNIE
[pen.] Bo McLaughlin; [b.] May 26, 1966, Paris, TX; [p.] Alana and George Perry; [m.] Edwin E. McLaughlin, February 14, 1992; [ch.] One son, Kody Knight McLaughlin; [ed.] Honey Grove High School, Honey Grove TX; [occ.] Artist, free lance writer, house wife; [oth. writ.] I have been writing for 15 years, all poetry, all poems not one has ever been publish it is a honor for me to have one of my poems in your book (beyond the stars) (L.C. ISBN); [pers.] Anything can be achieve with respect support and encouragement; [a.] Bogata, TX

MCMAHON, AMBER
[b.] March 5, 1981, Orange, CA; [p.] Robert McMahon, Nancy McMahon; [ed.] Currently in 8th grade at Mesa View Middle School; [occ.] Student; [memb.] AYSO Soccer; [hon.] Scholastic awards of merit, principals honor roll, and other academic achievement awards; [oth. writ.] Short stories - Horror, Fantasy, and Non-Fiction; [pers.] My writing comes from the heart. What ever I feel, goes down on paper.; [a.] Huntington Beach, CA

MCMENAMIN, EILEEN
[b.] November 27, 1972, Woodbury, NJ; [p.] Daniel and Barbara Burke; [m.] Patrick McMenamin, August 10, 1991; [ed.] Gateway Regional High School Woodbury Heights NJ; [oth. writ.] Poems published in school newsletters; [pers.] All of my writing pertains to my own life and experiences. I said once that I used to write about a lot of different "Me's". The "Me" I thought I was, the "Me" I'd like to be and finally the "me" I found inside myself.; [a.] Wenonah, NJ

MCMURRY, ERIN COLLEEN
[b.] September 23, 1981, San Antonio, TX; [p.] Irma McMurry-Eilert; [ed.] La Grange Middle School; [memb.] Fox 42 Kids Club Express, Herman Sons Grand Lodge, North Shore Animal League; [hon.] TAAS Mastery Awards, Distinguished Honor Rolls,

U.I.L. Awards, Houston Livestock Show and Rodeo Awards, Bus Safety Award, and Soil Water Conservation Essay and Poster; [oth. writ.] I write poems and short stories. One which was entered in a fiction short story contest in the Houston Chronicle.; [pers.] I only hope the earth will become more peaceful and people will lend helping hands to all.; [a.] LaGrange, TX

MCNAIRY, HAROLD G.
[pen.] Hal; [b.] March 30, 1929, Alberdeen, MS; [p.] Mr. Frank Billips and Miss Valaria Maria McNairy; [ch.] One; [ed.] College Graduate and Higher Hotel and Restaurants Institutes a Lawyer-Degree and Accountant Degree; [occ.] Land owner-retired and a song writer; [memb.] X'Mas Oregem Club, song writer club of Florida and Boston, Mass.; [hon.] The Korea Honors and other, Plus the Purple heart Hero. And Etc.; [oth. writ.] Musical Plays; [pers.] When you want something that is Good, go after it with all the zest you have.; [a.] Saint Louis, MO

MCNICHOLS, STEVEN LESLIE
[pen.] John Leslie French; [b.] August 25, 1971, Whittie-Memorial; [p.] John McNichols, Pamela Mayer; [m.] Wendy "Baby J" Steffan, June 17, 1994; [ed.] Plentywood High, University of Mary; [occ.] Student; [hon.] Dean's List; [oth. writ.] Poetry published in school paper; [pers.] I would like to thank Josephine Nichols Irwin, Frenchy Mayer, Pam Mayer, John McNichols, Moira McNichols, Craig McNichols and God. "Remember that dreams are the voice of the soul."; [a.] Bismair, ND

MCNUTT, IOLA FISHER
[pen.] Iola Fisher McNutt; [p.] Fred and Mabel fisher (deceased); [m.] James C. McNut (deceased); [ch.] Jennifer May, Fredrick James, Laurie Alisa; [ed.] Completed High School and Attended Balfour Girl's College In Regina, Sask. Canada (Business and Music); [occ.] Teacher of beginning piano and writer; [memb.] ASA (American Songwriter's Assoc.) see "Honors"; [hon.] Have been nominated for "Poet of Merit" with the I.S.P. held membership in the IPA (International Platform Association) ASCAP, International Society of poets: Nationally Registered Author; [oth. writ.] Published in many of the leading Anthologies, Standard Publishing, Lorenz Publishers: (Music) and more. Numerous Awards...; [pers.] Life is a wonderful gift, and I hope by example, and by writing I have been able to reflect my appreciation, to our Creator and those around me.; [a.] Memphis, TN

MCPHERSON, MARTHA SUE
[b.] May 25, 1995, Barren Co., KY; [p.] Wallace and Martha Jones; [m.] Bobby Lynwood McPherson, March 20, 1983; [ch.] Paxton, Ashton, Lucas McPherson and Wally Vibbert; [ed.] Temple Hill High School; [occ.] Housewife, Mother; [memb.] Order of Eastern Star #522, Etoile. District 20 Club; [oth. writ.] Several poems never sent for publication; [pers.] It's the best way to express your true inner self. Your heart speaks easier than your mouth.; [a.] Glasgow, KY

MCREYNOLDS, JOHN
[b.] December 15, 1920, Seattle, WA; [m.] Camilla, September 26, 1942; [ch.] Anita Hammett; [ed.] West Seattle High, Vashon WA; [occ.] Retired - Boeing Co. (1940-1982); [memb.] Past-Seattle Power Sqdn., Past-Boeing Supervisors Club; [oth. writ.] Alley Cat and other Cat poems published in Nat. Library of Poetry Editions; [pers.] Enjoy writing for pleasure and memories; [a.] Vashon, WA

MCWILLIAMS, LINDSAY
[b.] May 20, 1979, Joliet, IL; [p.] Shawn and Teresa McWilliams; [ed.] Joliet Central H.S.; [occ.] Student; [memb.] High Honor Roll; [pers.] My writings reflect young love and the problems teenagers go through.; [a.] Joliet, IL

MEESE, DEBBIE
[pen.] Debbie Mees, Debbie Siess; [b.] September 26, 1958, Pensacola, FL; [p.] James and Janet Siess; [m.] Larry Meese, July 16, 1977; [ch.] Sarah Lynn Meese; [ed.] Graduated early from 12th grade; [occ.] Antique dealer and housekeep, wife and Mother; [oth. writ.] Many poems, short stories and even a few theories all unpublished; [pers.] It's been said I was born in the wrong time period. I write mainly for myself and family members. 25 years I've been writing with offers to have my work published. Now it's time to leave my print.; [a.] Kokomo, IN

MEIER, WANDA OWEN
[b.] May 13, 1935, Hagarville, AR; [p.] Ira and Willie Owen; [ch.] Theresa Cheryl, Pamela Sue, Doris Kay, Ross Allen, Arthur Clyde Jr.; [occ.] President and Founder of Miracles of Jesus Ministry - 1994; [memb.] Gospel Music Association; [oth. writ.] Gospel Songs Ministry Material; [pers.] I strive to touch others with "His Glory," that it may shine on them through my poems, songs and writings.; [a.] Burleson, TX

MELLOCH, JUSTINA
[pen.] J. T.; [b.] February 14, 1981, Fort Cauderdale, FL; [p.] Mario and Rena Sanchez; [ed.] Freeport High School, 8th Grade; [hon.] None at the current time. But my family's love for me and my poems, are enough.; [oth. writ.] My Place of Glory, A Place of Torment (based on Slavery). just to name a couple; [pers.] The reason I wrote this poem is because both of my parents are in wheelchairs, and because of that I live with my grandmother.; [a.] Freeport, FL

MELTON, LEE
[b.] February 28, 1957, McAllen, TX; [p.] Jane and Earl Melton; [m.] Peggy Melton, August 2, 1980; [ch.] Aimee, Matthew; [ed.] Gregory-Portland High School, University of Southwestern Louisiana, University of California, Berkeley; [occ.] Software D.development Engineer; [memb.] Boys Scouts of America, Grace Evangelical Free Church; [pers.] Trust in the Lord with all your heart and lean not on your own understanding. In all your ways acknowledge Him and He will direct you paths. Proverbs 3:5-6; [a.] Allen, TX

MENDEZ, ELBA JUNCO
[b.] March 3, 1976, Mexico; [p.] Mr. and Mrs. Junco; [ed.] She studied at the American School foundation of Monterrey, Mexico and is now in College; [occ.] College Student, runs a small business in Mexico; [oth. writ.] I write everything and anything. I love it.; [pers.] There is a story in everything - the problem is to find it and know how to tell it.

MENDOZA, MICHELLE
[pen.] Mickee; [b.] May 16, 1969, Chicago, IL; [p.] Frances and Michael Nares; [ch.] Delia and Iris; [ed.] St. Augustine Grammer, Jones Commercial High School; [occ.] Dispatch Supervisor; [hon.] 2nd Place Certificate for Scary Story Contest in High School; [oth. writ.] Had poetry published in the Westside times; [pers.] I am an amateur poet, I have written a lot of poems, trying to get recognized, yet a little scared. I hope for someday to share my poems with the world.; [a.] Chicago, IL

MENKE, ALEXANDER
[pen.] Alex Menke; [b.] April 1, 1921, New York, NY; [p.] Florence and Ellis Menke; [m.] Virginia B. Menke; [ch.] Laurie and John Milton; [ed.] 2 yrs Univ. Of Penna. 5 years Columbia Univ. (Religion and Ethics); [occ.] Consultant Business (MGEMT. and Finance); [memb.] Lieutenant U. S. Navy 4 years Pacific Theatre, President-United Factors 1978; [hon.] Presidential Citation "Man of Hope" - City of hope Board of Governors- Founder of Diabetic Research City of Hope, Lectured on Ethics Cal. State Los Angeles; [oth. writ.] 30/40 poems (unpublished); [pers.] I believe that God has given us life and the ability to understand the truths that he has created.; [a.] Pasadena, CA

MERRELL, RICHARD I.
[b.] April 5, 1964, Virginia; [p.] Richard and Sally Merrell; [m.] Jill, November 5, 1988; [ch.] Richie (3), Alexandra (1); [ed.] A.S. Degree In Computer Technology, B.A. Degree In Communication; [occ.] Technical Writer for Exectone Information Systems; [hon.] Deans List, Winner of Executone, Information Systems National Slogan Contest; [oth. writ.] Christmas article published in local newspaper. Several unpublished short stories and poems.; [pers.] Do what you feel in your heart is the right thing for you. Do not try to fight it or ignore it because it will never go away. Those who choose to ignore this inner voice die unfulfilled.; [a.] Vista, CA

MERRILL, PETE
[pen.] Doc; [b.] May 20, 1942, Nashua, NH; [p.] Capt Herbert T. Merrill USMC, Lois Merrill; [ch.] Timothy Scott Merrill, Nathaniel Merrill; [ed.] Nashua High School Univ. of N.H.; [occ.] Science Teacher Elm. St Jr High Nashua, N.H.; [memb.] UNH 100 Club; [hon.] "Athletic"; [oth. writ.] "Many" still hiding, New adventure to show! What the hell for $20 I'll take a shot!; [pers.] "Humbleness is the road to compassion", "We do forget how small a babies fingernail is"; [a.] Nashua, NH

MERTZ, STACIE
[b.] March 12, 1972, Kansas City, KS; [p.] Dale Shaw, Linda Brandt; [m.] Dennis Mertz, January 30, 1993; [ch.] Elizabeth Renee, Cole Edward; [ed.] Piper High; [memb.] Business Professional of America; [hon.] Who's Who Among American High School Students; [pers.] I write about how I am feeling and what my life's about. I believe children are the most important thing in the world.; [a.] Kansas City, KS

METCALF, KATIE
[b.] September 6, 1982, Dallas, TX; [p.] Kathy and Bud Metcalf; [ed.] Currently 6th Grade East Cobb Middle School; [occ.] Student; [hon.] State Finalist in Reflections Writing Contest, 2nd place in the Writing Fair. "A" Honor Roll; [pers.] I have a sincere love for nature, and would like to spread that love around the world.; [a.] Marietta, GA

METZ, CAROLYN E.
[b.] July 2, 1941, Detroit, MI; [p.] Louis and Faith Wojcile; [m.] Divorced; [ch.] Carolyn Meredith, Frederick Gerald; [ed.] Lakeview High School, South Macomb Community College, Michigan State University; [occ.] First Grade Teacher Greenwood Elementary School St. Clair Shores, MI; [hon.] Teacher of the Year, 1980 for Greenwood School, (not a district selection), published in who's Who of American Teachers, Lakeview High School Alumni Hall of Fame; [oth. writ.] Have never tried publishing, but have written short stories, poetry, and children's books for my classroom.; [pers.] I love to teach about nature in my classroom and much of my writing has to do with nature or the connectedness of the human heart. I believe that we

are all connected that we are all here for each other.; [a.] Saint Clair Shores, MI

MEYER, DIANA L.
[b.] February 25, 1948, Canova, SD; [p.] Evert and Freda Johnson; [ch.] Shonda Jo, Krista Jo; [ed.] Canova High, Nettleton Commercial College, Sioux Falls College, Richland Jr. College; [occ.] Recovery Specialist; [memb.] 1st Cong. Church; [oth. writ.] Several poems not yet published; [pers.] I find that I am greatly moved and inspired to write by life experiences and by closely observing and absorbing what goes on around me in my space in our world.; [a.] Garland, TX

MEYER, SHERYL L.
[b.] April 21, 1967, Newark, NJ; [p.] Shirley Meyer, Peter Meyer; [ed.] Cooper City High, Broward Community College, Sheridan Vocational Technical Center; [hon.] 2 Outstanding Citizenship Certificates in school. Outstanding student in Home Economics Silver Cup Award, Outstanding Achievement in Home Economics Certificate; [oth. writ.] I've written many poems since I was 8 years old that have been unpublished.; [pers.] My writings reflect the kind of person I am. All of my writings come from deep down inside of me. That is one thing that could never be taken away.; [a.] Cooper City, FL

MEZA, OMAR
[pen.] Gabrielle O. Donald (GOD); [b.] March 24, 1981, San Diego, GA; [p.] Jose and Laura Meza; [ed.] Bonita Vista Middle; [occ.] Student; [memb.] Youth Division of U.S. Soccer Federation; [oth. writ.] Poem for Anthology of Poetry by Young Americans; [pers.] Hope for the best expect the worst. (Or is it be other waa around?) "I dream of her" was influenced by a girl.; [a.] Chula Vista, CA

MICHEL, PEGGY J.
[b.] June 22, 1956, Hicksville, OH; [p.] Dale and Jeanne Michel; [ch.] Heather D. Michel, Hollie J. Gibbs; [ed.] Ross High; [occ.] Buyer for Screen Printing, Retail Store; [pers.] To reach a goal you start with a dream. No matter how far fetched or wild. You dream, you believe, you achieve. Thanks and love to those who believe in me.; [a.] Fremont, OH

MIDDLETON, ALETHA C.
[pen.] Aletha C. Middleton; [b.] November 20, 1904, Georgia; [p.] Daniel W. and Cathrine L. Currie; [m.] Oscar Payne Middleton, May 25, 1923; [ch.] Jay, Joyce, Jimmy Middleton; [ed.] High School, Lyons Georgia, Georgia Normal College, Douglas, GA; [occ.] Housewife; [memb.] Charter Member of Earl of Camden (DAR), Treasurer of Waverly United Methodist Church for 20 years; [oth. writ.] Song writer and poet; [pers.] My love for poetry gave me a great desire to start writing at an early age.; [a.] Waverly, GA

MILLAM, DENNIS
[b.] October 30, 1952, Kansas City, MO; [p.] Charles and June Millam; [ed.] 12 yrs Elementary Clinton High School (9-12), Leesville R-9 Grade (5-8) Seal Martin City Elementary (1-4); [occ.] Plumber; [oth. writ.] None published but do, and have, written several for a special lady; [pers.] This poem was inspired by and written for the one I care so much for... Suzanne Johnson. I love you.; [a.] Clinton, MO

MILLER, BRADLEY
[b.] November 27, 1969, Ellwood City, PA; [p.] Paul and Bonnie Miller; [ed.] Wilmington Area High School, University of Rochester; [occ.] Chemist; [memb.] Sigma Mu Fraternity; [hon.] Bausch and Lomb Scholar; [a.] Rochester, NY

MILLER, BRIAN L.
[b.] March 28, 1974, Sandusky, OH; [pers.] Inspired by: Stephen King, Dean Koontz and Clive Barker. Philosophical statement: When the lightning strikes and the fires start, who will you trust to protect your heart.; [a.] Sandusky, OH

MILLER, COLLEEN
[b.] January 21, 1970, Boston; [p.] Mary E. Gleason, James H. Miller; [ed.] Fontbonne Academy, MT. Ida College; [occ.] Dog and cat groomer dance teacher; [memb.] Grey hound friends; [hon.] Graudated Cum Laude from Mt. Ida College - Deans List Dance Awards, Medals - Certificates Trophies, Enpointe, Top, Jazz, Ballet Drooming Certificates; [oth. writ.] Several collection unpublished - in safe keeping - from poems to short stories - vast aray of subjects; [pers.] Write what you believe, believes what you write... if it's fiction, make others believe.; [a.] South Boston, MA

MILLER, JEAN M.
[b.] May 25, 1955, Lorain, OH; [m.] Divorced; [ch.] April Caroline, Clinton Frederick, and Wesley William; [ed.] Clearview High Lorain Business College; [occ.] Human Resource Secretary, MTD Products Inc.; [pers.] Inspired by a very dear friend, Jeffrey Scott Enderby.; [a.] Lorain, OH

MILLER, ROBERT G.
[pen.] RG; [b.] January 28, 1925, Accident, MD; [p.] Lloyd and Cora Miller, (deceased); [m.] Patricia T. Miller, September 10, 1949; [ch.] Robert Jr., Pamela, Thomas; [ed.] B.S. Univ. of Maryland, M.S. North Carolina State; [occ.] Retired; [memb.] U. of MD Alumni Assoc., Md Farm Bureau, Rockawalkin Ruritan Club, Wicomico Republican Club, Bethany Luth. Church, National County Agents Assoc.; [hon.] Phi Kappa Phi, N.C. State U., Nat. Co. Agents Distinguished Service Award, Delmarva Poultry Ind. "Medal of Achievement" Award; [oth. writ.] Timely Topics (Weekly News Column - Daily Times, 15 yrs) Poetry - (unpublished) "Bugs, "Granddaughter, "An Old Golfers Dream"; [pers.] The world will be a better place when each individual takes full responsibility for his actions.; [a.] Hebron, MD

MILLER, SANDRA D.
[b.] October 30, 1944, Pasadena, CA; [m.] Dr. Scott G. Miller, January 20, 1973; [ch.] 1 daughter - Shannon Senior at Duke University; [ed.] BA, College of Notre Dame, Belmont, California, May 1996, English and Humanities; [occ.] Student, Stanford University; [memb.] Delta Epsilon Sigma, National Honor Society, American Assn. of University Women, San Mateo County Medical Assn. Auxiliary, Amnesty Int'l.; [hon.] Summa Cum Laude, Dean's List, Outstanding Academic Achievement for Humanities Department College of Notre Dame; [oth. writ.] Short Fiction and poetry; [pers.] As I stated in my application essay to Stanford, it is not important when women begin to write but that they begin to tell their tales whenever they can.; [a.] San Mateo, CA

MILLMAN, ALLEGRA H.
[b.] September 21, 1967, New York, NY; [p.] Ianthe Hasler Carpen; [ed.] Lindenhurst High School, S.U.N.Y. at Stony Brook; [occ.] Executive Administrative Assistant; [hon.] Dean's List; [pers.] In my writing, I strive to show that the true fabric of life is seen with the respect, trust and love we give others and others bestow upon us.; [a.] Massapequa, NY

MILNES, JOSEPH G.
[b.] July 4, 1927, Staten Island, NY; [p.] John and Agnes Milnes; [m.] Jean, November 17, 1950; [ch.] Mary Elizabeth, Gordon Douglas; [ed.] High School

(Curtis H.S., S.I. N.Y.), N.Y.U Engineering (2 yrs. Night School); [occ.] Supt. of Construction; [memb.] N.J. Wood Carvers Club Former Rear Commodore Richmond County Yacht Club S.I.; [hon.] Awards in Carving Birds, Golf, Sailing; [pers.] Poetry is beautiful because it comes from the depth of your heart

MINERT, TINA
[b.] May 4, 1969, Flint, MI; [p.] Paul and Ruth Minert; [ed.] Palmer College of Chiropractic Graduate June 1995; [occ.] Chiropractor; [memb.] International Chiropractic Assoc., Palmer Alumni: Foundation, Flushing United Methodist Church, Flushing Michigan; [hon.] PI TAU DELTA Chiropractic Honors Society. Presidential Scholar, Palmer College Palmer Merit Scholarship, Palmer College, Who's Who among America's College Students 93/94, 94/95; [oth. writ.] None published; [pers.] To give is to receive...; [a.] Flushing, MI

MINI, STACY L.
[pen.] S. L. Mini; [b.] February 11, 1970, Boonton, NJ; [p.] Diane J. Mini, Vincent J. Mini; [ed.] Currently Attending Fordham University and Lincoln Center, NY, NY-Studying: Media Studies Creative Writing expected graduate: Spring 96'; [occ.] Full-Time College Student; [oth. writ.] Numerous Articles written for The Fordham Observer; [pers.] "The beautiful people in my life are my inspiration to the union my words embrace. I cherish them, like I cherish my words because they are an expression of all that I am and all that I hope to become..."; [a.] Parsippany, NJ

MINOR, EVELYN LENORA
[pen.] Tiny Tahkeelya; [b.] February 2, 1926, Georgia; [p.] Ezra and Mamie Spear (deceased); [m.] Leonard F. Minor (deceased), December 25, 1954; [ch.] Darryl A. Wooten, Surinder Rapaval; [ed.] AAS Degree in Nursing; [occ.] Retired; [memb.] 1. Ethics Committee Washington Nursing Facility, 2. Pilgrim African Methodist Episcopal Church Washington D.C.; [hon.] Editor's Choice Award 1994 Library of Poetry, Governor's Award State of Maryland; [oth. writ.] Several poems and songs; [pers.] Wait on the Lord and be of good courage, he shall direct your path. My poems are written by the inspiration of God.; [a.] Suitland, MD

MIRABELLA, FRANK
[b.] April 24, 1950, Newark, NJ; [p.] Angelo and Cecelia; [m.] Patricia, October 11, 1970; [ch.] Lisa and Frank Jr.; [ed.] JFK High School - completed Middlesex County College 1 1/2 yrs.; [occ.] Supervisor, at Delta Air Lines; [oth. writ.] This is my first entry in a contest; [pers.] Treat the balance of nature as though it were a snow flake in the palm of your hand.; [a.] Clark, NJ

MIRSCH, VASSILI J.
[b.] August 3, 1918, Philadelphia, PA; [p.] Joseph and Mina Mirsch; [m.] Flora Mirsch (Nee Bogdan), December 12, 1943; [ch.] Vivian Janet Radu, Donald Wesley Mirsch; [ed.] Central High, State Barber School; [occ.] Retired 30 yrs. Service Veterans Administration Past Commander; [memb.] American Legion, Post #847 Romanian Orthodox Church, Elkins Park, PA, Choir Member, and Church Council Member; [hon.] Honorable Discharge U.S. Airforce W.W. II served in C.B.I. Theater. Donated three gallons blood to Red Cross.; [oth. writ.] Compositions, poems and a play, never published; [pers.] I always tried to do my best with what was at hand.; [a.] Philadelphia, PA

MITCHELL, CARTER ALEXANDER
[pen.] Carter Mitchell; [b.] August 2, 1982, Houston, TX; [p.] Felix and Valerie Mitchell; [ed.] Currently attending, Plaza Middle School (6th Grade), Kansas City, MO; [occ.] Student; [memb.] Magna Cum Laude;

[hon.] Best of Show (art), 1st Place (art) - Collin County Art Festival; [a.] Kansas, MO

MITCHELL, JOSEPHA
[b.] October 30, 1930, Renton, WA; [p.] Michael and Margaret Creegan; [m.] Kenneth Deane, April 10, 1951; [ch.] Jeanne, Michael, Teresa, Patrick, Kenneth, Mary, Katherine; [ed.] 12th Grade; [occ.] Retired; [oth. writ.] Poem published in book called, "Sermon's in Poetry" submitted by my English Teacher in 1949; [pers.] It is my ambition to try to write such as "Helen Steiner Rice" who I have admired for so many years.; [a.] Prescott Valley, AZ

MITCHELL, LORRAINE E.
[b.] April 21, 1919, Allentown, PA; [p.] Arden P. and Carrie M. Titlow; [m.] Albert Edgar Mitchell, June 15, 1940; [ch.] Albert Edgar Mitchell Jr., Robin Arden Mitchell; [ed.] Abington High - Editor of "Abington" and contributed poetry and articles to "Oracle."; [memb.] Past member of National Society for the Preservatioin of Covered Bridges and contributed articles to its "Covered Bridge Topics." Our flying family first designated covered bridges on the air chart for "fly-overs" and then followed up using road maps showing their location for "drive-throughs."; [oth. writ.] Presently editor of "Glory Bee," in-house newspaper of Gloria Dei Farms. Some poems have been published in local newspaper and church bulletins.; [pers.] I like to consider my poetry an expression of the heart for family and friends; [a.] Hatboro, PA

MIZGERD, CATHY
[b.] November 15, 1968, Ann Arbor, MI; [p.] Joe and Ann Mizgerd; [ed.] National Cathedral School, Georgetown Day School, The University of Chicago; [occ.] Psychiatric Crisis Assessor, Community Counseling Centers of Chicago; [memb.] WBEZ - FM Chicago Land Public Radio Station; [hon.] Dean's List, Morton Murphy Award for Significant Contribution to University Life; [oth. writ.] This is my first poem to be published; [pers.] If you especially like a drawing someone made for you, you'd frame it, right? And that's what poems do for us with language: They let us frame it. In doing so, they let us "look at" (read: Feel the power of) language just as closely as we please. At last, we can "stare," and it isn't improper!"; [a.] Chicago, IL

MOBLEY, LOUSIE CRENSHAW
[pen.] Lousie Harlin; [b.] July 11, 1921, Thurber, TX; [p.] Orren and Myrtle McAlister; [m.] J. W. Mobley, May 10, 1995; [ch.] Pat Thorn (previous marriage); [ed.] High School and Beauty School; [occ.] Part Time Hairdresser; [memb.] Gordon Church of Christ Overth' - Hill Club, D.A.V. (Lifetime member); [hon.] Published in "World of Poetry" anthology 1989 and "New American Poetry Anthology" 1988; [oth. writ.] Booklet of one-hundred-six poems published in 1989. Copyright 1989.; [pers.] I enjoy reading and writing inspirational poetry. My ambition is to reach those who do not know God and help them learn of this great love for mankind.; [a.] Gordon, TX

MOCH, DAMERON CHEMIESE
[pen.] Sammi Moch; [b.] October 3, 1969, Torrance, CA; [p.] Charlotte Mech Brown, Johnny Jackson; [ed.] Longview High School, Tyler Junior College, Texas Woman's University, B.S., Currently earning M.A. at T.W.U.; [occ.] Graduate Teaching Assistant in History/Government Dept.; [memb.] Psi Phi Pi Sigma Alpha; [hon.] 1st Place - 1st Annual T.W.U. Women's History Poetry Contest, 2nd Place - 2nd Annual T.W.U. Women's History Poetry Contest, Dean's List, National Dean's List; [oth. writ.] Several poems published in campus newspaper, also write scripts and screenplays; [pers.] Poetry is in everything we do, how we live

and in what we see. It transcends time and space and can touch the masses in ways that most things cannot.; [a.] Denton, TX

MONDRAGON, CATHERINE CANDELARIA
[b.] January 25, 1955, Pueblo, CO; [p.] Rupert Joe Valdez and Rose Gloria Valdez; [m.] Mike G. Mondragon, February 14, 1987; [ch.] Rupert Leo and Nicholas Augustine; [ed.] Central High School in Pueblo, Colo. University of Southern Colorado; [occ.] Domestic Engineer; [memb.] Member of Holy Trinity Church; [hon.] Silver Poet Award, awarded to me in 1986, from the World of Poetry, In 1972 I was a contestant in the Miss Colorado Teen-Ager pageant; [pers.] In order to succeed in today's generation, one must know what they want out of life.; [a.] Arvada, CO

MONTARA, THELMA E.
[ed.] English Major, Senior Year - St. Joseph's Univ., BA Spring 1996; [occ.] Histotechnologist - Temple Univ. School of Medicine; [memb.] 1. American Society of Clinical Pathologists, 2. American Society of Histotechnology, 3. The Mayors Commission on Literacy; [oth. writ.] Short Stories; [pers.] I like to paint pictures using words. These pictures appear in vivid colors inside the mind.; [a.] Philadelphia, PA

MOODY, DOROTHY C.
[b.] March 12, 1951, Evansville, IN; [p.] Arthur G. and Myrile M. Neal (deceased); [m.] Joseph N. Moody (deceased 5/89), September 11, 1969; [ch.] Joseph J. Moody; [ed.] High School, Adult ED. Secretarial Course, Cape Girardeau VO-Tech CNA; [occ.] Live on pension; [hon.] In Eight grade wrote on Essay "What American Patriotism Means to Me." My name, Dorothy Neal, is supposed to be in Independence Hall in Philadelphia; [oth. writ.] I have many other unpublished works of poetry, some spiritual; [pers.] Develope and try to use what God gives us, and to thank God everyday for his love, mercy and grace.; [a.] Charleston, MO

MOODY, VON
[b.] September 18, 1959, Richmond, VA; [p.] Melvin Moody, Theresa Moody; [m.] Nita Moody, March 31, 1995; [ch.] Melvin Moody, Hope Moody, Elona Parker, Colt Parker; [ed.] BS Chemical Engineering, Auburn University; [occ.] Chemist Senior, Shaw Industries Cartersville, GA; [memb.] American Association of Textile Chemist and Colorists; [pers.] Don't regret the past, learn from it and pass that knowledge onto others.; [a.] Cartersville, GA

MOON, SHANNON M.
[b.] October 31, 1969, Seattle, WA; [p.] Thomas G. Moon, Eileen M. Moon; [ed.] Kennewick High School, Columbia Basin College, the Evergreen State College; [hon.] Several poetry awards ranging from fair premiums to golden poet; [oth. writ.] Currently six poems published through National Library Poetry and Quill Books; [pers.] These few words here in enscribed for whom my honor's won. Kai Stonebender AKA Carl Turpin; [a.] Pendleton, OR

MOORADIAN, DENNIS
[b.] August 9, 1979, Michigan; [p.] Jack and Judith Mooradian; [ed.] Presently attending Forest Hills Northern High School (Sophomore); [memb.] National Honor Society; [hon.] All Conference Soccer Player, All Regional Team Soccer; [a.] Ada, MI

MOORE, DONNA
[b.] July 27, 1963, New York; [p.] Julius and Sarah Madison; [m.] Ivan Moore, October 19, 1990; [ch.] Dante, age 14; [ed.] Brooklyn Technical High, Medgar Evers College; [occ.] Spiritual Student; [pers.] Our words all come from within, reflections of our inner self,

as we move toward a higher consciousness, we should only speak and write words of healing, words of kindness, words of beauty, words of love. The power of the word is a gift from our creator. Let's use it to elevate ourselves and others.; [a.] Brooklyn New York, NY

MOORE, HEATHER I.
[b.] June 27, 1981, Tampa, FL; [p.] Jennie F. Ellis, and Ronald H. Moore; [ed.] Entering 9th Grade at Tampa Bay Tech., Studying for Physical Therapy Career; [occ.] Student at Eisenhower Jr. High; [memb.] Student Council Peer Pressure Mediator Southside Baptist Church; [hon.] Honor Roll - I have received numerous awards for Academic Excellence; [oth. writ.] Many other poems not published - Pain's River printed in local newspaper; [pers.] I write poetry to express my feelings. I was influenced by my English teacher Mrs. Cavaness. She has taught me to strive for excellence; [a.] Gibsonton, FL

MOOSE, MARY
[pen.] Mirn; [b.] February 25, 1943, Rockester, NY; [m.] Kenneth Moose Sr., July 18, 1959; [ch.] 6 Children - 3 Girls, 3 Boys, 7 Grand Children - 2 Boys, 5 Girls; [ed.] High School, Rush Henrietta Central School; [occ.] School Bus Driver for Rush Henrietta School Dist; [memb.] Rush Henrietta Bus Drivers Association; [hon.] Bus Driver of the year 1993; [pers.] I have several poems written, but this is my first attempt to get anything published. I hope to do a lot more writing.; [a.] Rush, NY

MORA, LEONOR
[pen.] Leonor Mora; [b.] March 8, 1943, Puerto Rico; [p.] Juan Mora, Francisca Mora; [m.] Julio Miranda, December 22, 1962; [ch.] Edwin, Michael, Julio, Mario; [ed.] Kensington High School Phila, PA, BA Turabo University, MA in TESOL Turabo University, Gurabo, PR; [occ.] Teacher (ESL) Pedro Maria Dominicci School, Cidra, PR; [memb.] School Council, PTA; [hon.] Dean's List, BA - Magna Cum Laude, MA - Suma Cum Laude; [oth. writ.] Poetry in Spanish. Several of my poems have been read on special occasions in the school where I work. I'm in the process of compiling my work of publication.; [pers.] In my writings I convey the wonders of nature and creation, the love for my country, and the joy of living in such a beautiful world. I have been greatly inspired by many poets of diverse backgrounds and nationalities.; [a.] Cidra, PR

MORENO, RUDY R.
[b.] October 26, 1956, Los Angeles, CA; [p.] Carlos and Rosie Moreno; [ed.] San Fernando High, Los Angeles Mission College; [occ.] Asset Manager, Pasadena, California; [hon.] San Fernando High Silver Honors; [pers.] This Morose poem was inspired by the untimely death of my beloved Fiancee, Darlene Munoz, whom I love, and will always cherish our short time on this Earth together. She was a native American who loved horses, thus the appropriate title.; [a.] Glendale, CA

MORGAN, PAUL
[pen.] Mustard Irie; [b.] January 12, 1967, Kingstone, Jamaica; [p.] George Morgan, Findalyn McIntosh; [m.] Clarice Tisdale; [ch.] Paul Morgan Jr.; [ed.] Maths, English, Art Craft, Plumbing Pipe Fitting, Social Study; [occ.] Cook; [oth. writ.] The secret; [pers.] To see things that happen now ahead of time and when that time come then it happen from once it happen it can happen again.; [a.] Bronx, NY

MORRIS, CLARIECE
[pen.] Sirrom; [b.] Richmond, VA; [p.] William and Veora Morris (Deceased); [ed.] B.S, Virginia Union University Richmond, VA., MA. Atlanta University Atlanta, GA, Currently enrolled in Ed. D Program

Nova Southeastern University Fort Lauderdale, Florida; [occ.] Consultant, G.A. Dept. Human Resources; [oth. writ.] Thirty four poem included in a book entitled "The Oneness Within"; [pers.] If you are green you can grow. I seek way to grow in my writing and my personal life both of which are interconnected.; [a.] Stone Mountain, GA

MOSQUEDA, KAREN
[pen.] Kay Beth; [b.] September 21, 1964, Brooklyn, NY; [p.] John and Dorothy Hupalo; [m.] Fred M. Mosqueda, November 11, 1989; [ch.] Victoria Lynne, Samantha Elizabeth, Joseph Jesse; [ed.] Carl Sandborg H.S. Morraine Valley College; [occ.] Domestic Engineer; [oth. writ.] Floppy - A Children's Tale, Heard Your Life's Taken Quite a Spin; [pers.] I believe that the only way to reach your goals and dreams is to never say "I've always wanted to ..."But to say" Right now I'm doing..."; [a.] Tinley Park, IL

MOULDS, ROSE M.
[b.] July 29, 1929, Marquette, MI; [p.] Peter Ellis, Lempi Ellis; [m.] James Moulds (Divorced), March 19, 1955; [ch.] Juanita, Michael, Thomas, Laura, Mary; [ed.] Munising High Bay College; [occ.] Retired; [oth. writ.] Some poems and stories sent in but never published; [pers.] Because of my rejections I never thought that my poems were good enough but I never stopped trying to find out.; [a.] Gladstone, MI

MOYER, LARRY W.
[pen.] Larry W. Moyer; [b.] January 18, 1948, Boanoke, VA; [p.] Mary Lee Moyer; [m.] Carole D. Moyer, February 17, 1973; [ch.] Kevin Ernest Moyer; [ed.] Carver High, Salem V.A. Columbus Community College; [occ.] Bus-Driver; [memb.] Church of God; [hon.] Won a Good-Apple award From Columbus Public School, 2nd place in a Piano Competition of VA. 10 years safe driving award; [oth. writ.] A book "Suicide and Teenagers" and an Anthology of Poems, both unpublished as of yet; [pers.] Young Anne Frank, many years ago said, "Inspite of Everything, I still believe that people are good at heart..." God taught me its meaning and my mother taught me its Importance, Life has taught me its true!; [a.] Columbus, OH

MUDGE, STEVEN K.
[b.] December 12, 1971, Manchester, NH; [p.] Doris Lamarche; [ed.] Memorial High, Keene State College; [occ.] U.S. Army, Military Intelligence.; [oth. writ.] I have been influenced only by those individuals who are able to see, feel, and hear, with an aura, which is unseen, unfelt, and unheard of.; [pers.] Fort Meade, MD

MUDRAKOLA, ASHOK
[b.] May 8, 1957, India; [p.] Laxmi, Gandaiah; [m.] Alugu Ushasri, June 2, 1982; [ch.] Harsha Vardhan, Vishnu Vardhan; [ed.] M. S. C. (A9); [memb.] American Heart Association; [hon.] State Merit Scholarship (AP) India, College First (A.P.) India, Dean's List - E.W. Univ. Chicago; [oth. writ.] Published two poems at the age of 14. Started writing after 15 years.; [pers.] I still believe in traditional human values.; [a.] Chicago, IL

MUJA, KATHLEEN A.
[b.] June 24, 1965, Denver, CO; [p.] Thomas R. and Bridget C. Cramer; [ch.] Thomas C. Muja; [ed.] BBA General Business; [occ.] Labor and Employment Specialist II; [memb.] Denver Jaycess, Network Colorado! International Assoc. of Personnel Security; [pers.] Build your staircase to the stars, one step at a time!; [a.] Denver, CO

MUNO, LILA J.
[b.] November 5, 1932, Holly, CO; [p.] Deceased; [m.] November 4, 1950; [ch.] Four adult children, (6 grand); [ed.] Two years college and many hours of home study with library material and textbooks purchased from book stores; [occ.] Aspiring Writer-retired by disability part-time student; [hon.] Twice Golden Poet Awards from World of Poetry-the thank you from people who are touched by me writings is the best award; [oth. writ.] Self published book of inspirational verse in 1989 many poems and verses written for people across the USA. Religious articles for study-privately distributed; [pers.] One's life is made richer or poorer by how one is able to stretch and grow in both adversity and prosperity-but the strength to maintain comes in the time spent alone with the Creator.; [a.] Salem, CR

MUNRO, LINDA FREE
[pen.] Linda Munro; [b.] March 15, 1945, Dallas, TX; [p.] Thomas B. and Frances Free; [ch.] 2 grown children, 1 stepson, 4 grandchildren, 1 step grandchild; [ed.] Graduate of Amon Carter High School, Ft Worth - Part Time Student of Tarrant County Jr. College, Hurst, TX; [occ.] Aspiring Writer and Owner of Limun-Roses where fine old wood furniture is restored; [memb.] More family oriented do not dedicate much time to club and organization - but do have loud voice - socially with periodic readings extended by invitation; [hon.] "B" Honor student, President of Literary Guild in High School; [oth. writ.] "Adrift", "Altered Image", "The Evening News", "A Special Fate", "A Mother's Tribute" - all accepted for publication to appear '95 and '96, 3 short stories in progress 1 novel. Other poems pending "The Harvest of Her Disagree" and "Where Hypocrisy Grows" No Shame in Failure - only in "Not Trying"; [pers.] This year (1995) is the first time I have exposed any of my work for professional review. Response has been wonderful! My parents - who adopted me at age 2 weeks, both departed this life last year. They had great faith in my writing talents and longed for my success. All endeavors are dedicated to their precious memories

MUNSON, WELDON
[b.] February 7, 1920, Hope, TX; [p.] Charlie and Emma Munson; [m.] Esther Haynes Munson, February 14, 1942; [ch.] Rosemary Willingham, Beverly Gomez; [ed.] Bachelor of Science Degree, Master of Arts Degree; [occ.] Retired Medical Technologist M.T. (ASCP); [memb.] YMCA Jeffersonian Club Nazarene Church; [hon.] To Weldon Munson in recognition of 37 years of service 1948-1985 to The Department of Pathology; [oth. writ.] 4 songs published; [pers.] God is the creator of all things He did not create sin for that is rebellion against God. Jesus Christ is both God and man. He is our Saviour, both to save from committed sins and to purify from inherited sin nature. He gives eternal life to man.; [a.] Corpus Christi, TX

MURPHY, DARLENE A.
[pen.] Natasha; [b.] January 13, 1971, Arab, AL; [p.] O.D. and Doris C. Moore; [m.] Thomas Michael Murphy, June 21, 1991; [ch.] Kandi Mikhail Murphy (3), Thomas (Zachary) Murphy (2); [ed.] Tuscaloosa High School graduate, with Scholarship for 2 yrs. Shelton State Community Coll. Computer Science Major; [occ.] Housewife, and Child Care Teacher, or 3yrs old; [memb.] Church of God of Prophacey, Parents Club, for Home Teachers. And my 3 yrs. olds "Road me Mickey Club."; [hon.] 7th grade 1st place in sewing 4-1-D 10th grade class room award for poetry writings. Senior Year, Scholarship for 2 yrs Coll - Dean's list 3 Quarters.; [oth. writ.] Not published in book, but recognized in High School Literature Class for short story and 2 poems written: The Man and Thorns, Death? Just a Whisper, and short story the Eve of Writers; [pers.] I began writing as self theropy and found it was the only way I could relate mind, body and spirit. Nature and man has created poets of us and if were willing to search ourself fruit.; [a.] Green Acres, FL

MURPHY, JEANNE L.
[b.] June 13, 1964, Gouverneur, NY; [p.] Ronald and Shirley Fenlong; [m.] Michael D. Murphy Jr., September 5, 1993; [ch.] 2 Stepchildren, Kaity and Tyler; [ed.] Couvemeur, Jr/Sr High; [occ.] Field Office Manager for Husband's Co., Murphy Bros. Inc.; [oth. writ.] I have a collection of poems about life, love and family; [pers.] My poems are very personal reflections on life, love and family, I am rewarded by helping those whose own feelings they can't put into words.; [a.] Moline, IL

MURPHY, JESSIE C.
[pen.] Ethan Cayne; [b.] January 25, 1936, Duplin Co., NC; [p.] Roland J. and Mamie S. Cottle; [m.] Earl Holmes Murphy, July 4, 1953; [ch.] One daughter, Four sons; [ed.] High School Graduate; [occ.] Retired; [memb.] Bethel Wesleyan Church; [oth. writ.] Shorts Stories, Inserts for weddings; [pers.] I am just beginning my writing career which was postponed to raise my family.

MURPHY JR., WILLIAM
[b.] November 17, 1961, Bronx, NY; [p.] William Murphy Sr. and Mary Murphy; [ed.] Sacred Heart Bronx NY, Dickenson High School Jersey City NJ; [memb.] Duprees Boxing Club JC. NJ; [pers.] This poem is dedicated to my late father William Murphy Sr and to my trainer and friend Jimmy Dupree. Two men who were and are a great influence in my life; [a.] Jersey City, NJ

MURPHY, LAWRENCE J.
[pen.] J. C. Murphy; [b.] March 6, 1942, New York City, NY; [p.] Patrick and Bridget; [m.] Shirley Wong Murphy, November 9, 1985; [ed.] BA, Cath. Univ. of America Wash. D.C., MA New York Univ. N.Y.C.; [occ.] Junior High Teacher; [memb.] Our Lady of the Pillar Catholic Church, Halfmoon Bay; [hon.] Voted the honorary mayor of "Lumpville" 1995 graduating class; [oth. writ.] Short stories, Love letters; [pers.] Firm believer in the power of the spoken and written word. My wife fell in love with me through the written word.; [a.] Halfmoon Bay, CA

MURPHY, SUSAN MARY
[b.] August 24, 1955, Detroit, MI; [p.] James R. Murphy, Mary Lou Murphy; [m.] Divorced; [ed.] High School- Winston Churchill High School- Livonia Michigan; [occ.] Legal Secretary-Katten, Muchin, Zaviz and Weitzman; [memb.] International Association of Scientologists, CCFA-Crohn's and Colitis Foundation of America Inc.; [pers.] Writing poetry is like an gesthetic river that flows out of me in which I can express a thought, view, idea, etc. The greatest compliment to me is when someone understood what I was communicating; [a.] West Hollywood, CA

MURRAY, NORBERT K.
[pen.] Bob Murray; [b.] January 4, 1945, Germany; [p.] Walter and Frieda S. Murray; [ch.] Michael Murray, Michelle Murray; [occ.] Journey Man Meat Cutter; [oth. writ.] (An open heart) American Poetry Anthology Vol. VI, 1986, (My walk thru life) tears of fire, national libraru of poetry 1993, (Heaven sent) famous poetry society Hollywood CA, 1994; [pers.] We only have one life to live, so give your love honestly, and kindness to all that live.; [a.] San Jacinto, CA

MURRAY, PATRICIA
[b.] May 31, 1974, Grayling, MI; [p.] Karen Murray; [ch.] Expecting; [pers.] Every poems I have written comes from my heart and soul. Personal experience is the best poetry; [a.] Lansing, MI

MUSE, BETTY
[pen.] Betty-Lee-Muse BLM; [b.] January 28, 1936, Hospital; [p.] Deceased Harry and Mildred Valega; [m.] Drewy D. Muse, August 30, 1957; [ch.] Dwayne D. Muse, Brian D. Muse; [ed.] 12 years of High School and Elementary, 6 years-Nicolson Elm,-3 years Baton Rouge Jr. High-3 years-Baton Rouge High; [occ.] Housewife; [memb.] WMW at Foster RD, Baptist Church and Joy Club. DRWG Free Club at Bellingraph Elementry school. I also help at Central Food Bank.; [hon.] (To me it was an honor to be able to help) I have done very much, volunteer work, I helped as a volunteer Mother and grand-mother; [oth. writ.] I have a song on rainbow records-called holly wood gold in Hollywood California, "The song is" Named "Throw me something mister" It is a song about mardigrass; [pers.] I hope that I can help others to use their talent, what ever it may be just have plenty of patients.; [a.] Greenwell Springs, LA

MUSSON, ANDREW MARTIN
[b.] February 27, 1954, Grantham, United Kingdom; [p.] Louis Aubrey and Sylvia May Musson; [m.] Ingrid Mary Musson, October, 30, 1982; [ed.] King's Grammar School, Grantham, U.K., Derby College of Art and Technology, Derby U.K.; [occ.] Design Engineer for Automotive Supplies; [memb.] Oread Mountaineering Club - Derby U.K., Notthingham Wind Surfing Club, Nottingham U.K.; [hon.] Distinction in Mechanical Engineering Technology; [oth. writ.] Several other mountaineering poems - none published (so far); [pers.] Try as much as you can, it's better to burn out than it is to rust.; [a.] Port Isabel, TX

MYERS, CATHY D.
[b.] January 22, 1952, Fayetteville, NC; [p.] Lloyd and Katherine Edwards; [m.] Stephen David Myers, October 6, 1990; [ch.] Jenny Hawkins (16), Greg Hawkins (13); [ed.] Cedar Cliff High School, Riverside Hosp. Sch. of Nursing; [occ.] Housewife, Student; [pers.] Currently enrolled in Children's Institute of Literature in West Redding CT; [a.] Linden, VA

NAJAR, CHARLOTTE SNOW
[pen.] Chuckles, Snowflake; [b.] August 7, 1980, Perth Amboy Hospital; [p.] Douglas and Irene Najar; [ed.] Manalapan High School (Freshman); [memb.] Performing Arts, many plays where I've had leads; [hon.] Gold pins and certificates from the National piano guild. Honor Roll Certificates, played Mae Peterson in Bye-Bye Birdie played eulalie McKeknie Schinin Music Man; [oth. writ.] I write many poems and most I will put to music. I write about all different things because it comes so natural to me.; [pers.] I work very hard at everything I do and I strive to be the best that I can writing for me is a way of expressing my feelings and sharing them. It is not something that receives work, but something that I enjoy to do.; [a.] Manalapan, NJ

NASCA, MARY E.
[b.] October 12, 1964, Greenville, MI; [p.] Bert and Elizabeth Lindsey; [m.] Thomas G. Nasca, August 4, 1984; [ch.] Toni E. Nasca; [a.] Greenville, MI

NATOLI, DARRELL
[b.] October 11, 1965, Trumbull, OH; [p.] Joseph and Beverly Natoli; [ch.] Nicholas, Anthony; [ed.] McDonald High School; [occ.] Personnel Systems, Manager, US Air Force; [memb.] Power for Abundant Living Bible Research Silver Key Community Volunteer Service; [pers.] Taking pride in what you do and in who you are is a very important key to success; [a.] USAF Academy, CO

NAUGHTON, DORIS RUTH
[b.] October 9, 1940, Chicago, IL; [p.] Frieda and George Ostertag; [m.] John P. Naughton, September 29, 1989; [ch.] Sheri Lynn Lavish, Kelly Fawn Lavish; [oth. writ.] My first; [pers.] Place your trust in the Lord. He will never forsake you.; [a.] Lombard, IL

NAVE JR., SPENCER DAVID
[b.] February 20, 1944, Carlisle, PA; [p.] Spencer David Nave Sr., Margaret A. (Price) Nave; [m.] Kay A. (Bohrer) Nave, July 15, 1984; [ch.] James Darrell Nave, Spencer David Nave, III; [ed.] High School Diploma; [occ.] Truck Driver; [memb.] VFW Post 10502, American Legion Post 26, OES Chapter 77, Masonic Lodge, AARP; [oth. writ.] Numerous songs written. Recorded original songs, 1st cassette, in Nashville, TN., Have just completed 2nd recording of original songs.; [pers.] I look for the beauty in life, and through my poems and songs I can find it every day!; [a.] Hancock, MD

NEESE, APRIL CHARLOTTE
[b.] March 28, 1979; [p.] Cindy and Kenneth Neese; [ed.] Sophomore at Sunny slope High School, Phoenix, Arizona; [memb.] Sunny slope J.V. Girls Basketball team, sunny slope J.V. Girls Badminton team, Secretary of German Club, Secretary of anyone Club and phone; [hon.] Math Award, Physical Fitness Award, Principals list, Honor Roll; [oth. writ.] "What Memorial Day Means To Me" essay,, 10th Grade first place; [pers.] "Always stay confident and never stop conceiving hope."; [a.] Phoenix, AZ

NEISS, EARL J.
[pen.] Earl Neiss; [b.] August 25, 1922; [p.] William and Phoebe Neiss (deceased); [m.] Mary Ellen Neiss, April 14, 1972; [ch.] Randy, Jess, Del Goudy Brenda Patrick; [ed.] 8th grade; [occ.] Retired; [a.] New Philadelphia, OH

NELSON, CAROL JOHNSON
[pen.] Morning Star; [b.] March 16, 1940, Waterbury, CT; [p.] Thomas Francis Alden Shannon Gertrude Helen Doyle; [ch.] Sheryl Lynne Johnson Neitch Jeffrey Charles Johnson; [pers.] My poetry is dedicated to the God that created me, who is the source of all my knowledge. My life is dedicated to following spiritual principles as taught by the Unity Church, the principles of attitudinal healing based on "A Course In Miracles," and on the teachings of the International University of Meta Physics.; [a.] Las Vegas, NV

NELSON, NIGEL B.
[pen.] 'Nige'; [b.] May 24, 1969, Cardiff, Wales, UK; [p.] Berwyn and Nancy Nelson; [m.] Colleen Nelson, May 29, 1993; [ed.] Christ College Brecon (Wales) Mount San Antonio College; [occ.] Salesman; [hon.] 1st place in english competition in Llandaff Cathedral School (presented by Rohl Dahl) author, none as yet; [oth. writ.] Approximately eighty completed poems. (Unpublished); [pers.] My writings are simply reflections upon life, which on times has seemed, cynical, rewarding, full of love, yet sometimes...haunting.; [a.] Chino Hills, CA

NEMES, ROSA HELEN
[b.] October 5, 1918, Hannibal, MO; [p.] Bela and Mary Nemes; [ed.] Ilasco grade and High School Ilasco, MO, Chillicothe Business College, Chillicothe, MO; [occ.] Retired from the Northern Trust Bank, Chicago, IL; [memb.] Only - Member of Roman Catholic Church and National Committee to Preserve Social Security and Medicare; [hon.] Valedictorian, Senior Class of Ilasco High School 1936; [oth. writ.] One published in the local Hannibal Courier - post titled a ride in the country the bleakness of winter; [pers.] Being one of

eleven children (8 living), growing up in a small country town and the many friends made through my working years gave me the opportunity and inspiration to compose poetry reflecting the joys of various events in our lives.; [a.] Hannibal, MO

NEMZEK, RICHARD SIGA
[b.] June 2, 1968, MD; [p.] Judy Kent, James Nemzek; [ed.] BSA- Francis Marion College; [occ.] Cook; [oth. writ.] Lots of short stories, wanna read some; [pers.] Try not to be in a rush, let the Jone's tire themselves out.; [a.] Columbia, SC

NEUBAUER, SANDRA
[pen.] Sandy Michaels; [p.] Joyce Phelps, Allen Phelps; [m.] Michael Neubauer; [ch.] Kim Lee, Kelly Rachel, Kylean Shannon Joseph Kyle, Michael Cade; [occ.] House wife, part-time singer, songwriter, actress; [hon.] Received "fan mail" for composing music and lyrical verse for television special "Who Will Love This Child" KBYU, Provo, Utah, 1975, Several awards for directing original script and music including "Best Technical Set" for Hunter Central Stake, 1989; [oth. writ.] Collection of poems, country western and spiritual music; [a.] West Valley, UT

NEVIS, EVELYN C.
[b.] February 13, 1911, Nevada City, CA; [p.] Frank and Lottie Naake; [m.] Abner Ruhkala (deceased), January 23, 1931; [ch.] Jo Anne and Jack Ruhkala; [ed.] Roseville High and American River College; [occ.] Retired from McClellan AFB California, (23 yrs. Communications); [memb.] Community Covenant Church, Sierra View Country Club and Sunset Whitney Club. (Both Retired); [oth. writ.] Short Stories - none published; [pers.] Be honest, do not judge, admit it when you are wrong. Don't be afraid to say "I'm sorry". Be kind, have compassion for others.; [a.] Roseville, CA

NEWHALL, DIANA FORRESTER
[b.] December 22, 1923, San Francisco, CA; [p.] George and Marian Newhall; [ch.] Jacqueline Sacville-West Harned Jeannine Wisdom-Forrester Harned; [ed.] BA San Mateo College; [occ.] Realtor; [memb.] Sierra Club, World Wildlife Fund, Humane Society, Arbor Day Foundation, Poromac Valley Borzol Club; [oth. writ.] Several Articles for English Dog Magazines, poem "The Sea" in reflections of light, several short stories in English Publications; [pers.] I am interested in nature and conservation and am an avid reader, love traveling around the world learning new cultures, history, art and music. I have been highly influenced by poets such as Tennyson, Rupert Brooks and De la Mer; [a.] Manassas, VA

NEWSOME, DONALD
[b.] August 16, 1987, Kokomo, IN; [p.] June P. Newsome; [ed.] Columbian School Mrs. McCauley's Class 1st grade; [hon.] This was my first entry; [pers.] The poem really tells how I feel inside. I hope when I grow up I get to work for the city and drive a big tractor.; [a.] Kokomo, IN

NGUYEN, AMY
[pen.] Amy Nugent; [b.] March 26, 1968, Falls City, NE; [p.] Shaaren Zimmerman; [m.] Danny Nguyen, May 23, 1987; [ch.] Nyomi Cheri, Andrew Joseph, Jonathan Daniel; [ed.] Mainland High, Daytona Beach College Professional Career Development Inst.; [occ.] Student, Professional Career Development Institute; [hon.] 1st place, short story FL State Competition, 1982; [pers.] I view all of life, in itself, as a discovery. I often read the needs and emotions of those I come in contact with, compose a sharp impression, and present them as heart felt gifts.; [a.] Houston, TX

NGUYEN, TRI
[pen.] Toson-N; [b.] January 12, 1929, Handi, VN; [p.] Nguyen - Climhi, Nguyen - Thi Giang; [m.] Lan-Thi-Tran (1933), 1955; [ch.] Quod - Khanh, Thien - Tan, Hieu - Hanh; [ed.] College Thang-Long (Hanoi) Ucet-Nam (1948); [occ.] Cook (Marriott Hotel); [memb.] Viet-Namese/Air Force Association; [hon.] A lot of - medals, in Air Force; [oth. writ.] Several poems in Viet-Namese newspapers Tuan-San Tlew Thuyet; [a.] Irvine, CA

NICKAS, JOHN P.
[pen.] John P. Nickas; [b.] January 30, 1940, Newark, NJ; [ed.] Seton Hall Prep, West Orange NJ Seton Hall University, South Orange NJ Drew University, Madison, N.J.; [occ.] Priest, Pastor - St. Rocco's Church, Newark, NJ, 07103 Good Shepherd Aids Ministry; [a.] Newark, NJ

NISHIHIRA, CHRISTINE
[b.] February 7, 1984, San Mateo, CA; [p.] Betty and Frank Rico; [m.] Thomas, December 26, 1969; [ch.] Julia, Lance; [ed.] Diploma - Paralegal Int'l Correspondence Schools also, a diploma in Journalism from same school currently studying for A.A. Degree in speech; [occ.] Accounting assistant; [memb.] Nat'l Notary Assn. Toastmasters Int'l National Speakers Assn. Performing Arts Club; [hon.] Best Student, foreign languages, 1966, Quality Improvement program, Best Idea, Apex Corp. 1982, trophies for 1st and second place speech contests, 1990; [oth. writ.] Three other kitty poems, two humorous short stories, one romantic one, I'm in the process of writing a full-length novel; [pers.] My goal is to illustrate the endearing characteristics of our feline friends and the joy they can bring us.; [a.] Newark, CA

NOBLE, GEORGETTE
[b.] April 5, 1909, Philadelphia, PA; [p.] George and Octavia Lewis; [m.] Ralph Noble; [ch.] Suzanne King, Grace Noble-Jasper; [ed.] High School Drop out; [occ.] Retired; [memb.] Bungalow Park Civic Association - AFTRA-SAG-NAACP-AARP; [hon.] National Library of Poetry (my first); [oth. writ.] Several poems, namely some, I learned..., say what'll, my home town, mice or lice, about Alexander, Friends, Alecia, Peggy, Matt and Wynn, A Mind is a Terrible Thing to Lose, etc.; [pers.] I dropped out of school to go to work. I later passed my GED and studied nursing. Worked at Atlantic City Medical Center for thirty years as Licensed Practical Nurse. Since retiring I write poetry as a hobby and for fun.; [a.] Atlantic City, NJ

NOESSER, JEFF
[pen.] Austacious R. Taldwater; [b.] January 16, 1973, Beach; [p.] Jean Smith, Paul Noesser; [ed.] Sporadic Schooling, Heavy interest in the Arts; [occ.] Wanderer; [hon.] I've been awarded with a mind to express myself; [oth. writ.] Written many short stories and poems, usually shared with close friends only; [pers.] I've tried in my writing to convey that happiness is not a goal to achieve, but an emotion to sustain through enjoyment of life.; [a.] Santa Ana, CA

NORTON, LEE
[b.] July 29, 1935, Utica, KS; [p.] Tom and Juanita (Lehman) Norton; [m.] Delphine (Rogers) Norton, July 31, 1959; [ch.] Randy, D.V.M. and Brenda Dinges (grdch) Brandon and Danielle Dinges; [ed.] Utica High School, Ft. Hays State (2 yrs) U.S.S. Firedrake AE-14, 1956-7; [occ.] Farmer-Rancher; [memb.] Methodist Church; [oth. writ.] The Blonde High Jumper, The Big Game and now time published in your books. Several poems and cards written for friends and family.; [pers.] I enjoy my family, grandkids, church, good neighbors, sports, cows, new born calves, and writing an occasional poem; [a.] Utica, KS

NOUMAN, ANITA T.
[b.] August 8, 1973, Southfield, MI; [p.] Manuel and Beatrice Nouman; [ed.] Clawson High School, Clawson, MI Currently attending Oakland Community College, Auburn Hills, MI; [occ.] Office Manager at Action Metals, Inc. Clawson, MI; [memb.] Association of Women in the Metal Industry; [oth. writ.] I've been writing poetry since age 14 it's become a very important part of my life since each poem I write is an expression of my heart. Two poems were published in my senior yearbook.; [pers.] I believe that happiness starts in believing in one-self. Once that is accomplish, any dream can become reality. It certainly has for me.; [a.] Oakland, MI

NOURSE, JOLIE
[b.] March 19, 1966, Hornell, NY; [p.] Vale Nourse, Mary Nourse; [ed.] Perry High, Washington High Glendale Community College; [occ.] Executive Secretary, Utica Corporation, Utica, NY; [memb.] Future Teachers of America; [oth. writ.] Several poems; [pers.] I'm inspired by the lessons of life. I write when I find it too painful to feel, and feel only after the last word is written.; [a.] Sylvan Beach, NY

O'BRIEN, DAWN
[b.] September 30, 1960, Fort Campbell, KY; [p.] Joan and Tom Hollimon; [m.] Divorced; [ch.] Michael and Daryl; [occ.] Assistant Shipping and receiving coordinator; [oth. writ.] I am currently writing a book and have written over 200 poems in the past 19 years; [pers.] My poems have been inspired by the pain in my and my children's life. I believe there is always something good in everything bad that happens. I would like to write full time; [a.] Niles, MI

O'BRIEN, LISA THOMAS
[b.] January 23, 1967, Watertown, NY; [p.] Lewgene and Flora Thomas; [m.] James P. O'Brien Jr., July 7, 1990; [ed.] Watertown High School; [oth. writ.] How much longer will it be? How young the memory. Taking your first breath, and Forever...are among several that I have written.; [pers.] My hope is that my poetry makes people think and look deep inside themselves. To question and to find answers. My influence is my husband whose love and encouragement makes me believe in myself and who makes all of my dreams come true.; [a.] Adams Center, NY

O'BRIEN, MERRY
[b.] October 28, 1979, Stanford, CA; [p.] Don O'Brien and Becky O'Brien; [ed.] Notre Dame High School; [occ.] Student; [memb.] International Society of Poets member; [hon.] Editor's Choice Award for the National Library of Poetry 1994, Monterey County High School Poetry Competition, Creative Works Award, Cultural Council for Monterey County; [oth. writ.] "The Blaus Circle", "The Memory of Love to Continue", "Red", "A Drop so Deep", "Stinging Sky"; [a.] Gilroy, CA

O'BRIEN, WILLIAM M.
[pen.] Bill O.; [b.] October 11, 1961, Queens, NY; [p.] James and Roseanne O'Brien; [ed.] Watkins Glen High, Oswego State College; [occ.] Medical Supply Sales; [oth. writ.] Society's Trap, Feeling of Love, Your Mother is Always With You and others. All are unpublished; [pers.] Let your spirit run free and climb aboard the soul train.; [a.] Jersey City, NJ

O'DELL, DONALD L.
[b.] November 13, 1942, Indianapolis, IN; [ed.] North Texas State Univ. BA, High Honors Princeton Theol. Seminary M. Div.; [occ.] Management, Adjunct Professor; [oth. writ.] Several manuscripts in search of a publisher; [pers.] My endeavor in verse began (and continues) as a vehicle through which I am able to surface emotions too long hidden from myself.; [a.] Arlington, VA

O'GRADY, TARA
[b.] April 11, 1972, Queens, NY; [p.] Thomas P. O'Grady, Mary O'Grady; [ed.] St. Francis Prep. High School, St. John's University, St. John's Graduate School of Education; [occ.] Performing Arts Teacher; [hon.] Dean's List, St. Vincent College Best Actress Award. Miss New York 1993: "Mary from Dungloe" Irish International Competition.; [pers.] My best writings are ignited by a sudden inspiration in response to observing the simplicities of life for which I hold a passion.; [a.] Queens, NY

O'NEAL, RAY
[b.] January 11, 1932, Trussville, AL; [p.] James and Pearl O'Neal; [m.] Divorced; [ch.] Grandchildren-Jeremy, Heather, Erick, Timothy, Craig and Robert; [ed.] City College, San Diego, CA; [occ.] Retired; [memb.] Christian faith and the International Society of Poets; [hon.] Dean's List; [oth. writ.] Published in "River of Dreams," "Best Poems of 1995," "East of the Sunrise," "At Waters Edge" and "Sparkles in the Sand" recorded in "Sound of Poetry" and "Visions." Other poems pending.; [pers.] Listen to the song of life and share discreetly.; [a.] San Diego, CA

OATES, ALICE S.
[b.] March 29, 1922, North Tiverton, RI; [p.] Edmund and Matilda Durfee; [m.] Joe Joseph Oates Jr., August 1946 (deceased); [ch.] Charles F. Rose Jr.; [ed.] College AA Degree 1984 University of Alaska Tok. AK Bryant College Providence, RI 1940; [occ.] Retired worked for civil service for 30 years and retired in 1980; [memb.] Tok Lions Club, Tok, AK, Ladies VFW Aux. 3629 Fairbanks, AK, Eastern Star 35-Eureka 19 Portsmouth, RI, DAVA Tok AK The National Museum of Women in the Arts, Wash. DC, Charter member the Women's Memorial Wash. DC; [hon.] First Lady's Award from the governor's wife a real celebrity for a year and Governor Hickel gave me the Denali award 1994. Also received the president of the year award from the Ladies Xu Aux VFW of Alaska and my newsletter won State and National Award. I am Vice President of Lions Club. I am an artist.; [oth. writ.] Received a medal from being in Vietnam from the 7th Air Force 1969 employed by civil service with top secret clearance had a poem "Salute to a Colonel" published in a book called "Quiet Thoughts" by Poetry Press A short story print in a book called "Bits Of Ourselves" "Tet Is Here" published in our 20th Century's Greatest poems; [a.] Tok, AK

ODEMS, SONIA Y.
[b.] August 28, 1972, Jackson, MS; [p.] Carolyn A. Odems; [ed.] Callaway High School, B.S. Degree From Jackson State University; [occ.] Computer Programmer, Government, Washington, D.C.; [memb.] Zeta Phi Beta, Sorority, Incorporated; [hon.] Graduated Cum Laude, Who's Who, National Dean's List, 1994 Zeta and Prophyte of the Year; [pers.] "Trust in the Lord with all thine heart, and lean not unto thine own understanding. In all thy ways acknowledge him, and he shall direct thy paths." Proverbs 3:5-6; [a.] Reston, VA

OEKY, EILEEN
[b.] November 4, 1928, IL; [p.] Ida and William Schmitz; [m.] Widowed; [ed.] 12th Grade; [occ.] Retired; [pers.] This is my first attempt at writing. Have always enjoyed reading poetry, so thought it was time to try out my mind and hand. My late husband was my inspiration along with a friend.; [a.] Port Saint Lucie, FL

OFFNER, FRANK
[b.] September 19, 1924, New Orleans, LA; [p.] Deceased; [m.] Genevieve, June 2, 1955; [ch.] Suzanne Marie Offner, Philip Anthony Offner; [ed.] A.B. in English Washington University, St. Louis M.A. in English, San Diego State University; [occ.] Retired Schoolteacher; [memb.] NEA; [oth. writ.] "Flossenberg" (Narrative Pub in Jewish Times Weekly); [pers.] I hope my writing encourages others to reach beyond their narrow self-interest; [a.] La Mesa, CA

OKAB, SANA
[b.] October 22, 1976, NJ; [p.] Al Okab, Susan Okab; [ed.] Cranbrook Kingswood, Colby-Sawyer College; [occ.] Student; [oth. writ.] Several poems, all of which are unpublished; [pers.] I feel that if someone can express their thoughts freely and ignite some sort of firey reaction, they have really accomplished something.; [a.] Troy, MI

OKPE, AUGUST
[b.] August 18, 1943, Port Harcourt, Nigeria; [p.] Nnadi Okpe, Ahuruole Okpe; [m.] Patsy Okpe, June 20, 1967; [ch.] Augustine, Nina, Muka Obinnaya; [ed.] Government College Umuahia School of Instructional Tech Clinton, Ontario, University of Southern California; [occ.] Airline Pilot Douglas DC.10 Captain; [memb.] International Federation of Airline Pilots Assoc. (IFALPA), Military Cross; [hon.] Certificate of Merit and Silver Medal in Literature, Festival of Arts (1961); [oth. writ.] Random Jottings and Philosophical Article in Journals and Periodic; [pers.] Veni, Vidi, Vici; [a.] London, England

OLDENBURG, KEVIN
[b.] June 23, 1976, Poughkeepsie, NY; [p.] Henry and Debby Oldenburg; [ed.] F.D. Roosevelt High School currently Unity College in Unity, ME; [occ.] Student; [memb.] Boy Scout Troop 17 (leader), Unity College Woodsman Team (Vice Pres.), Hudson Valley Classic Car Club; [hon.] Eagle Scout, Member of National Honors Society, Deans List; [oth. writ.] This is my first published writing; [pers.] I feel that you need to live life to the fullest: Take advantage of all opportunities take risks, have fun.; [a.] Poughkeepsie, NY

OLDS, J. WESLEY
[pen.] J. Wesley Olds; [b.] December 5, 1917, Ishpeming, MI; [p.] Joseph and Hilda Olds; [m.] Winifred Breithaupt Olds, February 9, 1951; [ch.] Robert E. Olds, Julia Olds, MacLachlan, Dr. Reid H. Olds; [ed.] Ishpeming High School, University of Michigan College of Architecture; [occ.] Retired Architect; [memb.] Okemos Community Church, Friends of Historic Meridian, Lansing Civic Players, Riverwalk Theatre, Friends of Okemos Library, State Employees Retiree Ass'n, Lansing Art Gallery; [hon.] Blue ribbon for water color in local art show. And many sales of my ink and watercolor work.; [oth. writ.] Editor-Civic Players Newsletter; [pers.] I like to express personal and family experiences in poetry and especially like to read poems aloud when the occasion presents itself.; [a.] Okemos, MI

OLEA, CHRISTOPHER THOMAS
[pen.] Chris Olea; [b.] December 16, 1966, CA; [p.] Eugene and Madeline Olea; [ed.] Bishop Amat High School; [occ.] Musician, Artist; [oth. writ.] I have 20 notebooks filling my top dresser drawer, waiting to be read.; [pers.] I began filling notebooks with words at age 12. It's become a documentation of my life's events. It's very therapeutic and rewarding. I will never stop writing. Inspired by pain-influences are John Lennon, Jim Morrison, Poets of Beat Generation.; [a.] Glendora, CA

OLIVARES, SARA
[b.] August 31, 1980, MO; [p.] Henry Olivares, Corinne Yeager; [ed.] Harmony Middle School; [oth. writ.] Letters to Kansas City Star; [pers.] I believe writing is the best form of communication. It is important the future of knowledge and truth.; [a.] Stanley, KS

OLIVAREZ, NOEL ORLANDO
[b.] September 17, 1960, Harlingen, TX; [p.] Oscar and Nelda Olivarez; [m.] Janie O. Olivarez, September 1, 1985; [ch.] Daughter-Vanessa Olivarez, stepdaughter-Regina Rodriguez, stepson-Tony Rodriguez; [ed.] High School Grad. 1979 (Kennedy High School), Graduate Alamo Area Police Academy 1985; [occ.] Deputy Sheriff with Bexar Co. Sheriffs Dept. (Warrant Officer); [memb.] Special Olympics Torch Runner have helped for last 10 years to raise money and have run in Texas special olympics torch run for special olympics; [hon.] Letter of commendation from Master Judge James Rauch for work done on Child Support Warrants. Award from Commissioners Court Ref: Child Support Warrants executed; [oth. writ.] Many poems written, none ever published, written for own personal pleasure; [pers.] This poem, at the start was written with my daughter in mind. But when it was completed it was clear that only a higher power could have moved my pen to create this. So to God I give this poem and dedicate it to the memory of my mother.; [a.] San Antonio, TX

OLSAK, RUTH
[b.] May 17, 1961, Czechoslovakia; [p.] Ivan and Renata Olsak; [ed.] Bachelor of Science Degree, Palm Beach Atlantic College. The Institute of Children's Literature, and Child Care Certification Psychological Inservice Behavior Modification Training; [occ.] City Parks and Recreation Leader, United Cerebral Palsy RTA; [memb.] Pro-Life, Children's International Sponsor; sing in the church choir; [hon.] Employee Recognition Certificate, Editors Choice Award, HRS Certificate of Appreciation; [oth. writ.] Had several poems published, wrote lyrics to songs; [pers.] Love and respect are the two most important values in life of mankind. They should never be taken for granted.; [a.] West Palm Beach, FL

OLSHAUSEN, VERNEZ C.
[b.] May 19, 1921, Vallejo, CA; [p.] Verne and Ynez Cook; [m.] R. Detler Olshausen, February 15, 1948; [ch.] 6 children, 11 grandchildren; [ed.] B.A. at UC Berkeley (1942) in Music and Public Speaking, General Secondary 1943, UC Early Childhood Certif., SF State U.; [occ.] Part-time teacher for head start, also Child Advocacy Programs; [oth. writ.] Mainly small vignettes of people and nature.; [pers.] Basically, I am interested in just about anything that lives and breathes and takes up space on the earth. I do not look forward to Information Superhighway; [a.] San Mateo, CA

OLSON, MARK H.
[b.] April 5, 1960; [ch.] Sandra, Erika, Amanda; [ed.] Self Taught; [occ.] Dairy Farmer; [pers.] I wish to dedicate this poem to my sister, Laurie I am just a good ol' fashioned Country Boy from North Oak, with an interest in the thoughts and feelings, expressed by the written word.; [a.] Streeter, ND

OMARI, JAHI
[b.] March 18, 1965, Jackson, MS; [p.] John and Mary Jones; [ch.] One son; [ed.] Life, B.S. Ed. Georgia State Univ.; [occ.] Teacher, Facilitator of Inner Wisdom, Science; [memb.] The Khepera School Atlanta, GA. Member-Songhai Institute of Education and Development Atlanta, GA; [oth. writ.] "360 Degrees of life" poetry; [pers.] Live your struggles in love as you live your life in spirit.; [a.] Atlanta, GA

ONNEN, CLAYTON
[b.] May 27, 1966, Vermillion, SD; [m.] Michele Onnen, August 27, 1988; [ch.] Kayla Nicole Onnen; [ed.] Grand Island Senior High Grand Island NE; [occ.] Telemarketing Sales Professional at MCI Long Distance Company; [hon.] Awarded 15 times at Presidents Club for being one of MCI Top Sellers; [pers.] I'm inspired by my wife Michele, my daughter Kayla and life's ups and downs.; [a.] Albuquerque, NM

ORANDAY, EDMUNDO
[b.] September 5, 1964, San Antonio, TX; [p.] Quintin and Maria Luisa Oranday; [occ.] U.S.P.S. Mail Carier; [oth. writ.] Author of Independent Christian Music Cassette, "Otra Vez".; [pers.] God is love (1 John 4:16) and this world needs the healing touch of our Lord who alone can save hurting humanity (Luke 4:18).; [a.] San Antonio, TX

ORLAND, HENRY
[b.] April 23, 1918, Germany; [ed.] Northwestern Univ. Ph.D. 1959, Univ. of Strasbourg (France) 1947; [occ.] Prof. Emeritus, St. Louis Community College; [hon.] WW II Purple Heart, Bronze Star; [oth. writ.] St Louis Post-Dispatch and St. Louis Globe-Democrat. Lit. Critic, Music Critic, Cultural Affairs Writer; [a.] Olivette, MO

ORR, LOIS W.
[b.] August 19, 1923, Mitchell, SD; [p.] Joseph D. and Elizabeth Swenson; [m.] Floyd Robert Orr (deceased), December 11, 1948; [ch.] Mary, Mark, Thomas, Robert; [ed.] Courses at South Dakota State University, General Beadle Teachers College and Dakota Wesleyan University; [occ.] Retired from medical transcription had previously worked as a secretary for Homestake Mining Co. before moving to lead had spent 6 yrs. as a rural school teacher.; [memb.] Shepherd of the Hills Lutheran Church and its Church Women's Group. Past member and Pres. of Women's Aglow Fellowship.; [hon.] Essay and spelling contest winner in elementary school Sec. of SD High School Press Assn., Valedictorian of High School Class; [pers.] Worship is very important to me and as I began to read my morning devotions and work on a Bible study a couple of months ago, this poem (thought I have never been a poet) came to me as fast as I could write it down.; [a.] Lead, SD

ORTEGA, ESTHER LAGE
[b.] November 8, 1918, Havana, Cuba; [p.] Pedro Lage Hidalgo, Italicoo Fernandez; [m.] Nicanor Ortega (died) May 31, 1968; [ed.] Ph.D from Havana University, Music Teacher, both positions won by competitions: Spanish Professor, and Music Teacher in Havana. At Long Island University, a Master of Sciences, Spanish Teacher in New York City, 20 years.; [occ.] Retiree from Board of Education, N.Y.; [memb.] The Interamerican Editor, Academy of Poetry, Horizons, Paterson N. Jersey, The National Library of Poetry, MD, Poetic Academy in Miami. Brujula Compas (Manhattan and Bronx), New York.; [hon.] Diploma from International Society of Poets, several awards from The Library of Poetry (Maryland). Anthologies participations in Poetry.; [oth. writ.] "The Interamerican Editorial House, (poetry)," La Plata, Buenos Aires, Argentina, "Ciculode Cuitura Panamericano", Poetry, "Academy of Poetry in Miami", Flai "Gaceta Lirica." (Anthology). Publishing many poems in newspapers and magazines. Two books of poems: "Light and Shadow", and "Moon in Scorpio" (1988 and 1994).; [pers.] Try to reach and analyze the depths of the human beings, the positive and negative sides. The strength of the destiny, and the environment influences.; [a.] New York, NY

ORTIZ, MARK ANTHONY
[b.] April 3, 1974, San Antonio, TX; [p.] Alfred C. and Blanche M. Ortiz; [ed.] Sharyland High; [occ.] Struggling Student, Assistant Accountant, Advanced Paging; [pers.] Life is a perspective, and until everyone learns to see more than their own perspectives, this world will continue to live in hatred, violence and fear. Keep the peace. Upon your eyes; [a.] McAllen, TX

OTT, NANCY B.
[pen.] "Pouter Burns"; [b.] October 22, 1920, Lyndhurst, NJ; [p.] Anna Dubuy Chay and Henry Chay; [m.] Robert L. Ott, August 11; [ch.] David Bullwinkel and Douglas Bullwinkel; [ed.] Lyndhurst High School, Tulsa University, Napa College, American Institute of Business, Graduate Realtors Institute; [occ.] Semi-Retired Real Estate Brokers and Consultant; [memb.] National Notary Assoc., National Real Estate Assoc., Napa Women's Club National Assoc., "Who's Who in American Women"; [hon.] The nicest honor was having my poem selected by the National Library of Poetry at a time when I am a list discouraged not being able to walk thank you sincerely. It brightened my day!; [oth. writ.] Poetry, articles, newspaper etc. Latin translators.; [pers.] I'm recuperating from being hit by a truck, driven by a very drunk driver who was not insured and not even scratched my injuries were internal, extensive, lasting etc. Lots of time to think! There must be a book inside somewhere. God bless us all!; [a.] Desert Hot Springs, CA

OTTE, ARLENE LEMMEL
[pen.] Arlene Lemmel Otte; [b.] February 16, 1937; [p.] Erwin and Thelma Lemmel; [m.] Carl Otte, October 13, 1956; [ch.] Mary Sue Sandling, Peggy Dittgen, Julie Bailey; [ed.] St. Xavier Commercial High School, on going classes in the school of life; [occ.] Instructor at Diet Workshop, Harrison, Ohio-Homemaker; [memb.] St. John the Baptist Church, various organizations; [hon.] 3 daughters and 6 grandchildren (4 girls, 2 boys); [oth. writ.] Poems and Essays not published; [pers.] My poetry has been a release for me. I started writing earnestly in 1994 after the deaths of my parents.; [a.] Harrison, OH

OUTCELT, FRANK E.
[b.] February 27, 1933, Weiser, ID; [p.] John Outcelt, Opal Outcelt; [m.] Verlyn, December 28, 1962; [ch.] Cheryl, Leslie, ReNee, Kevin Mark, Franklin, Lisa, Cheri; [ed.] High School Graduate; [occ.] 20 yrs. as Church Custodian (Church of Jesus Christ, Latter Day Saints); [hon.] Best Actor of the Year High School Play 1949; [oth. writ.] Published in "The Ensign", Published in "Good Old Days" (True Stories), Local printing book of poetry, music written for several poems. Two requested many times on local radio stations one became a popular local dance number; [pers.] No man should take credit to himself, first, for his talents, it is a God given gift and first credit should go to him from whom it came; [a.] Basalt, ID

OWENS, NORMA JEAN
[b.] November 17, 1934, Muncie, IN; [p.] Ernest J. and Juanita Pearl Dalton; [m.] Ralph W. Owens; [ch.] Chiquita Pearl and Betty Jean; [ed.] 9th grade; [memb.] International Society of Poets, Gospel Music Assoc.; [hon.] Editor's Choice Award, Poem published by The National Library of Poetry. Nominated Poet of the year 1995 by International Society of Poets and awarded free membership in their Society. Poems published in several newspapers and articles; [oth. writ.] I have written several Gospel songs that have been received with great enthusiasm in many churches and large gatherings in Ohio, Kentucky and Indiana.; [pers.] This poem was inspired by my devoted and loving mother Juanita Pearl Dalton. She died after surgery. She said Jesus was

holding her hand and she was going with Him. Many tests and doctors could find no reason for her death.; [a.] Farmland, IN

OXMAN, NANCY G.
[b.] February 8, 1951, Philadelphia, PA; [p.] Joan and Stanley Green; [m.] Stephen Oxman, November 26, 1981; [ed.] Springfield High School, Penn State University "Effective" Non-Fiction Magazine Writing Course, Teacher-Art Spikel; [occ.] Now published poet and consummate dreamer; [hon.] I have continually been singled out for my creative skills but could not find the "brass so and so's" to follow through I just found them!; [oth. writ.] I have 90 other children waiting to bloom.; [pers.] I just about let a burning desire fizzle out! I'm 44 years of age. This is my first attempt toward any form of publication but look out cause here I come... It's never too late!; [a.] Havertown, PA

PACE, LUCY
[b.] September 1, 1952, Altamont, TN; [p.] David Phillips, Rubie Phillips; [m.] Clint Pace, November 23, 1990; [ch.] Davin, Miranda and Allison Johnson; [ed.] Grundy County High, Motlow State Community College; [occ.] Legal Administrative Assistant; [memb.] Gruetli Church of God; [hon.] Dean's List, Office Systems Technology Award; [pers.] My writing comes from the heart-I write about personal experiences and how I feel about certain things. I hope my thoughts and feelings on paper can be used by others to express feelings they have, but cannot express.; [a.] Monteagle, TN

PADGETT, MICKI M.
[b.] April 5, 1951, Shelby, NC; [p.] L. H. McSwain, Sue McSwain; [m.] Stephen H. Padgett, November 21, 1986; [ch.] Jay Speight, Chris Speight; [ed.] Shelby High School, B.A. in Religious Education from Gardner-Webb University; [occ.] Housewife, Mom; [memb.] First Baptist Church of Kings Mountain, NC, Dulcimer Club, Cleveland Country; [oth. writ.] Published in poetic voices of America, Fall 1995 edition; [pers.] God gives the words... I offer the pen. Christianity is not a religion... It is a relationship with Jesus Christ. My writings spring forth from my quiet times of Bible study, prayer, and meditation - time spent with my savior. That I call: "Coffee and conversation... Precious moments with my Savior."; [a.] Kings Mountain, NC

PALOMBO, DARRELL
[b.] July 28, 1945, Abbeville, LA; [p.] Rufus and Gertrude Palombo; [m.] Divorced; [ch.] Douglas Michael, Benjamin John, David Andrew; [ed.] Abbeville High, University of Southwestern LA; [occ.] Insurance; [pers.] I never thought, in my craziest dreams, that I could put together even one stanza of poetry. I don't know where it comes from, but I love it!; [a.] Lafayette, LA

PAMIN, DIANA DOLHANCYK
[pen.] Diana Dolhancyk; [b.] December 13, Cleveland, OH; [p.] Peter Dolhancyk, Diana Dribus Dolhancyk; [m.] Leonard Pamin; [ch.] Louis Peter, Diana Anne; [ed.] West Tech. High, Titus College of Cosmetology; [memb.] Arthritis foundation, International Society of Poets, and I've sponsored a young girl in India for 15 yrs.; [hon.] "Editors Choice Award" for outstanding achievement in poetry, for "The Parting" in journey of the mind", published by the N.L.O.P. "Editors Choice Award" for "Stormy" in "Songs on the Wind."; [oth. writ.] "Burnt by Love" in "East of the Sunrise" and "Shadow Side" in "At Waters Edge". And now "Best Poems of 1996." My poem "The Parting" was in the SUN STAR Newspaper.; [pers.] Always give someone a smile, you'll never known whose heart you might lighten. I wrote my first poem at the age of 12.; [a.]

North Royalton, OH

PAPE, PEGGY B.
[pen.] Lady Jane; [b.] December 14, 1973, West Allis, WI; [p.] Carl and Marguerette Pape; [ed.] Milwaukee Trade and Technical High School, UW-Parkside; [occ.] Graphic Designer; [hon.] National Honors Society, Honorable Mention in the 1995 Iliad Literary Awards Program Public Speaking Awards; [oth. writ.] Poem published in "Voices"; [pers.] The world is full of inspiration for those who take the time to search for rainbows.; [a.] South Milwaukee, WI

PARCELL, JENNIFER B.
[pen.] Junn Hayes Parcell; [b.] February 24, 1974, Gainesville, FL; [m.] Robert B. Parcell Jr., July 18, 1993; [ch.] Jena Renee Parcell; [ed.] Williston High and Miami Southridge Senior High; [occ.] Mother, Wife and Homemaker; [memb.] Future business leaders of America (FBLA), Business Corporative Education (BCE), Key Club and Crime Watch prevention; [hon.] Data Entry and Computer literacy certificates; [oth. writ.] Unpublished Book of Poems; [pers.] My writing is influenced by the struggles and achievements of my life, which have not weakened me but made me stronger.; [a.] Clermont, GA

PARCHETA, JEFFERY JAMES
[b.] March 11, 1976, Buffalo, NY; [p.] Mary and Walter J. Parcheta Jr.; [ed.] Newman Smith High School, completed Freshman year at UTAH - studying business marketing; [occ.] Student at University of Texas in Arlington (Utah); [memb.] Debate Team at Newman Smith High School, Soccer Referee for N. Dallas Soccer Association; [hon.] Scholarships from Carrollton Soccer Association and Newman Smith all sports club; [pers.] My inspiration was my childhood dog "Poochie". I made a very difficult decision to put my best friend to rest... where my road ends.; [a.] Carrollton, TX

PARK, VIOLA
[pen.] Viola SF Park; [b.] August 21, 1979, Wyoming; [p.] Diana Park; [ed.] Sophmore at San Domenico High School Freshman and 8th grade years in International School in Japan; [occ.] Student; [memb.] National Trust Fund in England; [oth. writ.] Several poems published in school newspapers; [pers.] I want to express the goodness of everyday life. I hope to compare the similarities and difference of good and evil. I try to take in nature when I do these comparisons; [a.] Los Gatos, CA

PARK, YOUNG SOAK
[b.] July 3, 1930, South Korea, Chung-Joo City; [p.] Ro-Woon Park and Nam-Ju Kim; [m.] Dr. Chun Soo Park, October 7, 1968; [ed.] (1) College of Education, Seoul National University, (2) "Scuola Superior Alta Moda," Turin, Italy; [occ.] Free Journalist. And (C.S.P., Co. (N.Y.) Manager); [memb.] Member of (1) International P.E.N. Club associate 1960 (2) Korean Literary Society of America U.S.A. (3) Womens Writer Society of Korea (South Korea) (4) Poetess Society of Korea. Coterie Magazine Blue Eyebrow; [oth. writ.] (1) Dai-Han daily newspaper reporter (1959-1980) Europe (Rome, Paris N.Y.) Correspondent (1966-1980) (2) Poems Published "Meditation of Eve" (1959) (3) "Crystal and Rose" 1960 (4) "Contemplation and Eternity" 1962 (5) "Selection of Korean Poets of America 1975 (6) "Essays (single of book) "Communication of America" 1977 (7) "Blue-Eyebrow" (Coterie Magazine Commemoration poem of the thirty years (30 years) anniversary 1993; [a.] Flushing, NY

PARKS, NORMAN L.
[b.] January 19, 1904, Tennessee; [p.] Joseph Wiley and Victoria Parks; [m.] Ella Rae Rupp Parks, September 11, 1930; [ch.] Randolph and Judith Elaine; [ed.] PH. D. Vanderbilt and professor there.; [occ.] Retired. Write mostly now for liberal religious journals.; [hon.] Chosen "Outstanding Professor" at Middle Tennessee, State University in 1969, awarded $1,000. "Freedom Award" conferred by AAUP.; [oth. writ.] Published many articles in professional journals and in N.Y. Times, The Nation, Washington Post, Boston Globe. Chosen to draft elaborate booklet promoting inaugural of Pres. Truman 50,000 copies distributed. Presented programs featuring my love of Romantic poets. Invited to address annual board meeting of AT&T.; [pers.] The poem I submitted was a personal experience with a beautiful college student whose high intelligence and moral standards represented the best in womanhood, now my wife of 64 years. I was her professor. Some poems I have published but never for profit.; [a.] Marfreesboro, TN

PARRISH JR., EMMITT ANDERSON
[pen.] Andy; [b.] August 20, 1958, Savannah, GA; [p.] Emmitt A. Parrish, Shirley Winter Parrish; [m.] Leslie Braswell Parrish, April 18, 1981; [ch.] Audrey Nichole, Vincent Andrew; [ed.] BA Aviation Management Embry Riddle Aeronautical University, Windsor Forest High-Savannah, GA; [occ.] Flight Safety Internat, Gulfstream Marketing Manager; [oth. writ.] Soldiers Daydream, Beyond the Door, Homeless Child; [pers.] Trust in the Lord with all of your heart and lean not on your own understanding. In all your ways acknowledge him and he shall direct your paths. Proverbs 3:5-6; [a.] Savannah, GA

PARSONS, SHALIZA A.
[b.] August 20, 1981, Philadelphia, PA; [p.] Judy Parsons and Mumtaz Ali; [ed.] St. Francis De Sales School, 8th grade Entering West Catholic High School 9/95; [occ.] Student; [hon.] Josephine Connelly Scholarship Award (High School). Obtained certificate for designing cover for the Academy of Music and Arts. Additionally, received (2 certificates from Lincoln University for the Young Scholars Program in Physics and Biology.; [oth. writ.] Composed an article for World Affairs Council at West Catholic High School that was published in the school's newspaper; [pers.] I hope to someday achieve my goals of writing poetry and Art. My poem was a reflection of feeling and mood at the time of composition (mine). I would like to share this with others however, interpreted.; [a.] Philadelphia, PA

PASQUINI, RACHELLE LYLE
[pen.] Rachelle Griffin Pasquini; [b.] December 10, 1963, Manhattan, NY; [p.] Barbara Davis and Richard Griffin; [m.] Anthony D. Pasquini, April 27, 1989; [ch.] Lauren Raye, Ayla Elizabeth; [ed.] Walton Performing Arts High School/Summerville High School, Central Texas College; [occ.] Actor; [hon.] New York womens' Penmanship Award for Narrative Poetry 1980. Dean's List Central Texas College.; [oth. writ.] Articles written for the military press, San Diego; [pers.] My writings and acting and the grace of God, has gotten me through some pretty crazy times. Use your life, and surroundings in your writings. It's usually some pretty incredible stuff.; [a.] San Diego, CA

PATE JR., KENN D.
[b.] June 1, 1979, Waukegan, IL; [p.] Mary and Dave Pate; [ed.] Sophomore/High School; [occ.] Student; [memb.] United Safety Alliance, Pate Mfg. Inc. - Director; [hon.] For short stories, poems, young authors award; [oth. writ.] Many other poems; [pers.] Like to express my feelings through my poems.; [a.] Lake Forest, IL

PATERSON, LESLIE M.
[pen.] Les Paterson; [b.] September 7, 1971, White Plains, NY; [p.] Donald and Luz; [ed.] Walter Panas High, Westchester Community College; [occ.] Auto worker; [hon.] S.Q.A.C. Sportsmanship Scholarship and Mrs. Servinskas Scholarship Awards; [oth. writ.] Several poems in college papers "The Viking"; [pers.] Try to make the negative and depressing beautiful. Strive to find what you do best and do it the best you can. I draw my inspiration from my family and friends.; [a.] Mohegan Lake, NY

PATTERSON, HENRICK
[pen.] Sean; [b.] February 7, 1951; [p.] Verona and Asley Patterson; [m.] Sharon Rosemarie Wiggan; [ch.] Carl and Paula Patterson; [ed.] Ruseas High, Finance and Accounts College of Training; [occ.] Sales (Regional Sales Director); [oth. writ.] Valley of the Swan, Lady of Cathrine House, (bot unpublished.)

PATTERSON, MILTON
[b.] October 27, 1935, Wyckoff, NJ; [p.] Helen G. Patterson and Milton L. Patterson; [m.] Sylvia J. Patterson; [ed.] Entwistle School of Art, Art Students League; [occ.] Artist, Art Instructor; [memb.] American Artist's Professional League, North Shore Art Association; [pers.] Paintings exhibited in several galleries. I have been an artist for forty years and along with the painting there has always been poetry.; [a.] Ringwood, NJ

PATTERSON, MIRIAMA E.
[pen.] Mira Patterson; [b.] November 30, 1962, New Zealand; [p.] Hannah Tatana, Taiti Poareu; [m.] Edwin Dennis Patterson Jr., October 11, 1991; [ch.] Kelly Miriama, Steven; [pers.] You can't change the past, so look to the future and try not to make the same mistakes again. Look for your light at the end of the tunnel.; [a.] Springfield, VA

PAULIK, JUDY L.
[pen.] Judy L. Paulik; [b.] March 17, 1962, Oshkosh, WI; [m.] James Robert Paulik, July 16, 1990; [ch.] Tristy Ann; [ed.] Oshkosh West High; [occ.] Certified Nursing Assistant; [memb.] NRA, National Parks Association; [oth. writ.] Poems for my husband James; [pers.] There's magic in every sunrise and sunset, and beauty in every living thing.; [a.] New London, WI

PEARSALL, ANNA L.
[b.] January 9, 1918, Queens, NY; [p.] Wm. and Louise Nietzold; [m.] Lincoln F. Pearsall, October 1, 1938; [ch.] Linda and Judith; [ed.] High School; [occ.] Retired-Grumman Aerospace Corp.; [oth. writ.] Other poems; [pers.] From 1976-1989 lived on board a 41 ft. sailboat. Did the Intercoastal waters from, Maine to Florida. Spending winters in Florida and Summers in Northport Harbor. Did the Intercoastal Waters 23 times. Parkinson's disease brought us ashore in 1989.

PEARSON, CARYL R.
[pen.] Caryl R. Pearson; [b.] May 9, 1935, Poughkeepsie, NY; [p.] Frank and Olive Pearson; [ch.] Brian, Karen and Craig; [oth. writ.] Collection of poems in process of being edited for possible publication; [a.] Boynton Beach, FL

PEARSON, DAVID W.
[b.] June 17, 1950, Oklahoma City; [p.] Floyd Pearson/Viola Pearson; [m.] Susan Pearson, March 19, 1977; [ch.] Jeff Pearson/Dana Pearson; [ed.] Classen High School; [occ.] Civil Servant, V.A. Hospital, Oklahoma City; [a.] Moore, OK

PECORARO JR., ROBERT MATTHEW
[b.] January 14, 1952, St. Louis, MO; [p.] Robert M. Sr., Patricia J. Pecoraro; [m.] Divorced; [ch.] Seth Matthew, Thaddeus Reuben, and Jonathan Joseph; [ed.] St. Louis Community College; [occ.] Code Official City of Jennings; [memb.] Company G, 11th Mississippi Reenactment Group, Former President of The Jefferson Barracks Civil War Historical Association, Former Historical Advisor to The Historic Daniel Boone Home; [hon.] Facilitator in moving the Zephaniah Sappington Home, and also the Benedict Waumbraught Home to the Daniel Boone Home site, (Defiance Missouri), Civil War Lecturer, Battle Narrator, Movie Extra; [oth. writ.] A personal book of poetry. Over 30 entries chronicle a love affair unsurpassed in my experience and unequalled in the experiences of my peers.; [pers.] The poem Susan Rochelle is a true romantic vignette. I as a Civil War Reenactor saw the opportunity to metaphor concerning injury in love as opportunity for love gained. The action and feelings expressed happened as written as do all my poetic writings.; [a.] Jennings, MO

PEETERS, LILA M.
[pen.] Lila May (Streeter) Peeters; [b.] August 25, 1922, San Bernardino, CA; [m.] Robert Peeters (deceased); [ch.] Roberta Louise (Peeters) Lockwood, grandchildren, Kenneth and Laurie Lockwood; [ed.] AA from San Bernardino Valley College; [occ.] Retired; [memb.] Yucaipa Community Church, Yucaipa Historical Society, Dyslexia Society, City of Hope, VFW Aux., Friends of the Yucaipa Library, and the International Society of Poets; [oth. writ.] Four children books: The Kitten at My House, The Kitten at my House Goes Fishing, The Kitten at my House Plays Hide and Seek, A Different Time and many poems and newspaper and magazine articles; [pers.] I always thought about writing children's books but after my seventieth birthday passed I thought it was time to get started. I joined a creative writing class which has inspired me to fulfill my dream.; [a.] Yucaipa, CA

PELESKA, DAWN
[b.] April 11, 1973, Waukegan, IL; [p.] Roger Peleska, Pat Williams; [m.] Ezell Bell, February 14, 1995; [ch.] Imani Marie, Terin Jamal; [ed.] Stuttgart American High, Last school attended, Earned GED; [occ.] Housewife; [oth. writ.] None published; [pers.] I'm not a perfectionalist I just write about what I see and how I feel about it. It's all in the heart.; [a.] Columbus, GA

PENA, AZUCENA
[pen.] Suzy; [b.] July 31, 1974, Durango Mexico; [p.] Juan Jose Pena, Rita Pena; [oth. writ.] Several poems not published; [pers.] For me poetry is the feeling of a person, the sensibility to let out all over feelings. I personally have never been influenced by other poets, the only thing I do is feel the moment I'm living. And even though my english is not perfect, I can still let come out my best feelings in a language that is not mine.; [a.] West Chicago, IL

PENBERTHY, JENNIFER
[b.] March 3, 1982, Falmouth, MA; [p.] Da Wayne and Robin Penberthy; [ed.] Currently enrolled as a gifted student, 7th grade at MCS Noble Middle School, Wilmington, NC; [memb.] Dancer's Corner Ballet Troupe; [hon.] "A" Honor Roll, currently being tracked by Duke University; [pers.] I believe that everyone should have some form of the arts as a way of expressing themselves.; [a.] Wilmington, NC

PENLEY, DEFORREST A.
[b.] May 20, 1925, Roma, GA; [p.] Deceased; [m.] Deceased, March 15, 1946; [ch.] Ronald Philip Renley; [ed.] U.C.L.A. 1952 B of A Major - English Literature;

[occ.] Retired; [oth. writ.] Nothing published; [pers.] Poetry is a hobby. Most of the poems I write seem brilliant at night, when written, but fade to the mundane by light of day to be crumpled up and discarded, but each one has achieved a step upward on the hopefully endless stairway to increased enlightenment; [a.] Los Angeles, CA

PENNELL, MELISSA LYNN
[pen.] Miggy; [b.] January 2, 1981, Toms River, NJ; [p.] Judy D. Bello, Richard Pennell; [ed.] Memorial Middle School (8th grade); [hon.] Young Authors Conference 1991, winner Ocean County Annual Statewide Alcohol/ Drug Essay Contest - Junior High Div.; [oth. writ.] Personal, unpublished writings (stories, poems, quotes); [pers.] A poet can not feel when he can not write, for he can not write when he can not feel.; [a.] Point Pleasant, NJ

PEPE, CAROLE LYNN
[pen.] Carole Lynn Pepe; [b.] December 12, 1942, Philadelphia, PA; [p.] Michael Sr. and Florence Lillian Pepe; [ch.] Robert Mark Migrone, Sherry and Tricia Sumerford; [ed.] Bartram High School, Temple University B.S. Ed., Temple University M.Ed.; [occ.] Dallas Independent Sch. Dist. Teacher of English as a Second Language Talented and Gifted; [memb.] National Story Telling Association, Classroom Teachers of Dallas (NEA), National Reading Association Scofield Memorial Church; [hon.] DISD has asked me to conduct teacher workshops for ESL teachers across the district.; [pers.] In my career I have taught in Pennsylvania, Louisiana, and Texas and have worked with children from kindergarten to first year of college. I enjoy changing.; [a.] Dallas, TX

PEREZ, LYDIA
[b.] November 7, 1956, San Francisco, CA; [p.] Antonio and Clara Perez; [ch.] Joseph Leo Reiss Jr.; [ed.] Balboa High, Sailing and traveling for 7 years in many countries across 2 oceans was my education; [oth. writ.] "Land Beyond the Sea" a book in the process of being written; [pers.] My inspiration comes from many midnight watches on tiny yachts in a vast ocean and a little vintage Cessna 120. I thank Harry, Michel and David for making it possible to follow my dream.; [a.] San Francisco, CA

PEREZ, ROBERT A.
[b.] March 30, 1959, Brooklyn, NY; [p.] Carlos Perez, Carmen Perez; [m.] Belinda H. Perez, July 23, 1994; [ed.] Pace University, NYC; [occ.] Financial Advisor; [pers.] I strive to reflect the goodness of God in my writing.; [a.] San Antonio, TX

PERIFIMOS, MARY M.
[b.] Queens, NY; [p.] Harry and Georgia Perifimos (deceased); [ed.] BA-Hunter College; [occ.] Administrative Asst. to the Exec. Dir. of a Philanthropic Foundation; [hon.] Dean's List; [oth. writ.] "The Flame and the Fire" which is printed in "Reflections of Light" and an anthology of love poems entitled "Poems from the Heart"; [pers.] As I mentioned in "Reflections of Light" I like to express my feelings of joy and pain through my poems, and lyrics in both English and Greek.; [a.] New York, NY

PERRY, JAMES R.
[b.] September 15, 1975, Miami, FL; [p.] James B. Perry and Peggy L. Turner; [ed.] Studying for Associate's degree of Applied Science in Paramedic at Kankakee Community College; [occ.] Certified Nursing Assistant (CNA) an Emergency Medical Technician (EMT); [memb.] Reddick Fire Dept., Reddick United Methodist Church, Illinois EMT Association; [hon.] Finalist in vocational education as a non-traditional student; [oth.

writ.] Poems written for school and female friends; [pers.] I am a deep-hearted romanticist, dwelling on matters of the heart. I write on my personal feelings at that moment in time.; [a.] Buckingham, IL

PERRY, KIM E.
[b.] March 25, 1961, Chicago, IL; [p.] Mr. and Mrs. W. D. Perry Jr., and Katie Snyder; [ch.] Wesley Perry; [ed.] Woodlands Academy, Aquinas College; [occ.] Accountant Technician, Federal Aviation Administration; [pers.] I want to thank my family for being very supportive of me through the years. Most of my writings come from my own personal experiences.; [a.] Jonesboro, GA

PETERS, JACQUELINE
[b.] April 7, 1964; [p.] Deanna and Carlyle Peters; [ch.] Jason Anthony Primus and Antonia Jasmine Primus; [ed.] George W. Wingate H.S. Oakwood College; [occ.] Legal Assistant; [memb.] Literary Guild, Museum of Natural History; [hon.] Dean's list honor roll; [oth. writ.] Several unpublished materials. A few were printed in school newspaper.; [pers.] Through my interactions with different individuals, I have come to the conclusion that freedom is not liberation of the physical being, but of the mind.; [a.] Brooklyn, NY

PETTIT, MARIE A.
[b.] July 24, 1969, Houston, TX; [p.] Harry and Jean Pettit; [m.] Single; [ed.] BA English and Theatre Education University of Houston; [occ.] 8th grade English teacher, also play guitar in band "Sinister Sirens"; [memb.] International Thespian Society, Oaks Presbyterian Church; [hon.] Dean's list; [pers.] I write because I am in love. In love with life, in love with love, and in love with my boyfriend!; [a.] Houston, TX

PEZZULLO, JOSHUA ANTHONY
[b.] September 19, 1977, Renton, WA; [p.] Barbara Pezzullo, Jim Tobin; [ed.] High School so far 1996 graduate; [occ.] Student; [memb.] FBLA, Science Club; [hon.] Cross Country Letter, Instrumentalist Magazine Merit Award, American Musical Foundation Band, Honors Awards, USAA Scholarship; [oth. writ.] Poems and short stories; [a.] Grandview, WA

PHILLIPS, AARON
[b.] September 11, 1979, Meyersdale, PA; [p.] Stephen Phillips and Rox Wooden; [ed.] Sophomore at Meyersdale Area High School; [memb.] Meyersdale Church of the Brethren; [hon.] 10th grade honors English student; [pers.] You must live to the fullest. Otherwise you will never know how far you can go.; [a.] Meyersdale, PA

PHILLIPS, JANA
[b.] June 30, 1948, Kansas City, MO; [p.] Marion Sapp, Yoland Sapp; [ch.] Aaron Phillips, Tera Phillips-Holland; [ed.] Van Horn High, Kansas City Business College, Central Missouri, State, Center for Degree Studies; [occ.] Engineering Secretary; [memb.] Order of the Eastern Star; [a.] Independence, MO

PHILLIPS, SARAH MICHELLE
[b.] October 9, 1982, Las Vegas, NV; [p.] Michael K. and Katherine A.; [ed.] Nike Middle School; [occ.] Student; [memb.] Nike Middle School K-Club; [hon.] 6 yrs. Principals Honor Roll, Principals Academic Award; [pers.] I attempt to convey my concerns about this beautiful planet we live on, through my writings. In hope that it well reflect the delicate balance of nature.; [a.] Edgerton, KS

PHOTIKARMBUMRUNG, ELMA D.
[b.] February 26, Philippines; [p.] Alfredo Diel and Conception Diel; [m.] Sam Photikarmbumrung, October 14; [ch.] Nate, Nick, Neil; [ed.] Dumangas High

Sch., University of the Philippines, Silliman University; [occ.] Part time lecturer, Office Assistant; [memb.] Pres Byterian Women's Assoc.; [hon.] (1) Class Salutatorian (Dumangas High School) (2) Entrance scholar - (University of the Phil.) Delta Lambda Kappa Phi Omega; [oth. writ.] "It Pays to be Alone at Times" "The Wanton Trail"; [pers.] Faith can move and will move mountains.; [a.] Palatine, IL

PICKETT, ANNETTE M.
[b.] October 8, 1958, Bloomington, IN; [p.] James Eades, Susan Eades; [m.] Charles Pickett Jr., March 23, 1985; [ch.] Charles, Cory, Christopher, Natalie; [ed.] Santa Ana High, Chaffey College; [occ.] Sales Representative; [memb.] Greenpeace; [pers.] I want to share a better way of life with everyone. If I touch one person's heart, they will surely touch another.; [a.] Perris, CA

PIERCE, LEE L.
[pen.] Lee Pierce; [b.] February 26, 1927, New York, NY; [p.] Helen Lee and John T. Lawrence; [m.] Allen Brush Pierce, July 26, 1962; [ch.] W. Shelby and Allen L. Pierce; [ed.] Concord Academy, Barmole College, Univ. of Mexico; and have taken summer courses at the Connecticut College for Women, Tufts, and the Catholic Univ. in Santiago, Chile; [occ.] Currently a storyteller/lecturer traveling with my International DOLL Collection. The dolls share many cultures. (My collection has over 180 dolls from 40 countries.); [memb.] Museum of Fine Arts Boston, Met Museum, NYC, Met Opera, NYC, various theater groups, time share weeks on the Cape, Newport, R12, Sedona, AZ; [hon.] Bicentennial award in 1976 for multi-media historical pageant "Tea and Tyranny" which brought together 6 schls. (public, private and parochial) all ages (8 yrs. to 80) performed at Harvard's Loeb Thtr., now known as the Art, Cambridge, MASS. (AM Repertory Thtr.); [oth. writ.] Poetry, "Friendship," published in the anthology, Reflections of Light; short stories, poetry, and now working on doll stories (true and historical events involving dolls); [pers.] To encourage all ages to share without fear, friendships from the world over - To encourage children to look for beauty in poetry, drama and music.; [a.] Cambridge, MA

PIERNAS, DOMINICK RAMONE
[pen.] Ramone Edgerson; [b.] August 16, 1981, MS; [p.] Sharon and Phillip Jones; [ed.] St. Stanislaus College Preparatory; [memb.] Police Explorers UMXF (United Methodist Youth Foundation) Our Mother of Mercy Alter Boy Society, Slam; [pers.] I base my writing on everyday happenings of my boyhood.

PIETTE, DEBBIE
[b.] July 3, 1956, Neenah, WI; [p.] Robert Smith, Betty Smith; [m.] Michael Piette, August 12, 1989; [ch.] Casey Allen, Salina Allen; [pers.] There is no equivalence to a smile or the love given freely from a child. We must all unite to protect and make this a safer world for them. God bless them all.; [a.] Neenah, WI

PIKE, MARY E.
[pen.] M. E. Pike; [b.] August 26, 1976; [p.] Harvey and Mary Pike; [ed.] Archbishop Prendergast High School, Mercyhurst College; [occ.] Archaeology Student; [hon.] Valedictorian of my High School Class (94); [oth. writ.] Poems, short stories and articles in the Freedom Zone, our campus literary magazine.; [pers.] I wrote this for my mom, because she went back to work at age 44, be me a nurse, and is a great humor. There is no other women I know more deserving the little, "mother." And, my cat, Eric, is the epitome of Armageddon.

PILARSKI, SARA M.
[b.] November 28, 1980, Chesterfield, MO; [p.] Sandy Pilarski, Scott Pilarski; [ed.] Ballwin Elementary, Green Pines Elementary, Rockwood Valley Middle School (A.K.A. RVMS!); [occ.] Freshman at Lafayette High School (fall '95); [memb.] St. Louis Zoo Association, Cornell Laboratory of Ornithlogy St. Louis Pet Search (volunteer); [hon.] RVMS knights of the Round Table, 1994 and 1995. RVMS Student Of The Month for 8th grade red team.; [oth. writ.] Several essays, a few short stories, and poems. One poem is entitled "The Real Reason."; [pers.] There will always be the pattern running through my poems which explains the importance of nature, and how special it will always be to me.; [a.] Ballwin, MO

PILGRIM, LARRY K.
[pen.] Larry Keith Pilgrim; [b.] August 12, 1945, Waco, TX; [p.] Jerry Lee and Catherine Joyce Pilgrim; [m.] Anna Pilgrim, July 29, 1972; [ed.] After many years in business, I have returned to UTSA to finish my degree in elementary education (specialization in reading) - currently a senior.; [occ.] Substitute teacher, student; [oth. writ.] (Unpublished) novel-Teoma Tellus, Supreme Injustice, poems- various, quotes-I especially enjoy creating Larry's quotes; [pers.] I am especially grateful to those special teachers in my childhood that instilled in me a respect of literature and a love of reading and writing.; [a.] San Antonio, TX

PILOTE, MARJORIE
[b.] April 16, 1945, Oakland, CA; [p.] Marjorie and Jack Buettgenbach; [m.] Guy Robert Pilote, November 3, 1976; [ch.] Luke L. Nelson, Mark D. Nelson and Jill A. Nelson-Stockwell; [oth. writ.] The Rose of Jericho, A Diary of Prose and Poetry, penned by A "Kitchen Philosopher" on "Backyard Psychology"; [pers.] My writings are an endeavor from parental concern to nurture acceptance and pride of individuality in a child's evaluation of self.; [a.] Fresno, CA

PINEDA, SERGIO
[b.] September 11, 1978, Bogota, Colombia; [p.] Maria Carrillo and Gustavo Pineda; [ed.] High School; [occ.] Photographer; [pers.] Someone once said to me, "People are not interested in poetry anymore and the world doesn't read poetry anymore". Grief struck me when I heard this for if it's true then the world is losing the greatest and purest form of writing.; [a.] Lodi, NJ

PINKARD, MARCI L.
[pen.] Lynne Landau/Marcy Linnville; [b.] July 11, 1952; [p.] H. M. Pinkard (deceased), Jo Pinkard; [ed.] The College of Charleston; [occ.] Technical/Marketing Communications Writer; [memb.] Sierra Club; [hon.] Academic: Dean's List GPR. Literary: Wilory Farm Poetry Contest Superior Honorable Mention for buddy: to my friend in fur; [oth. writ.] Numerous poems published in literary magazines and anthologies.|; [pers.] In my poetry I specialize in developing mystical, romantic, philosophical and pastoral themes which focus on the outer world as it reflects inner states of being. In my writings I seek to capture the concept of the oneness of all life, the universality of being and feeling.; [a.] Daly City, CA

PINKNEY, SHERRY A.
[pen.] Sherry A. Pinkney; [b.] June 3, 1954, Sumter, SC; [p.] Lillie B. and Albert Pinkney; [m.] Divorced; [ch.] Albert Jermaine and Sonya Michelle; [ed.] Naval Dental Tech. School, San Diego CA. - Georgetown School of Science and Arts - Wash. D.C B+ Average; [occ.] Machine Operator; [memb.] President of Bahlsen Bowling League - Company Union Stewart (Local 204); [hon.] Honorable discharges during Vietnam War and Desert Storm. 1st Place 1990 fall regular season

Billiards. - Monetary award for putting fire out in patient room at V.A. Hospital - Wash. D.C. "1984"; [oth. writ.] Some day want to write my own book of poetry. Has some poems on T-shirts and posters as a business; [pers.] Life is a steady change of feelings, emotions and action, as long as the results are educational and positive life is worth living.; [a.] Raleigh, NC

PIOTROWICZ, BEATA
[pen.] Robert Proniewski; [b.] March 6, 1975, Poland; [p.] Krystyna and Edward Piotrowicz; [m.] Single; [ed.] Union High School, will attend College; [occ.] Student; [memb.] Polish Falcons of America, Nest #281; [hon.] 1-st Runner Up in Miss Polonia Z.P.K.A. contest; [oth. writ.] Several poems in Architects of time, arts magazine, and personal diary from 1988 to 1995; [pers.] We can live our lives happily only after we realize the point of being. Only then we can live in peace within our minds and with other people, and quietly, peacefully die. Because only after finding the sense in lives we also find sense in dying.; [a.] Union, NJ

PIPER, JOANN CHASE
[pen.] Jo Piper; [b.] April 5, 1929, Lake City, IA; [p.] Ella and Wilber Chase; [m.] Charles M. Piper, March 23, 1951; [ch.] Steven, Kevin, Alan; [ed.] BA Education (English) at UNI, Rebuilding Seminars, C of C Workshops, Workshops on Aging, Writing with J. Webb; [occ.] Writer, Volunteer for Aging, Homemaker, Crafts; [memb.] University Honors Societies, Pi Tau Phi Sorority, International Society of Poets, RSUP, Church of Christ; [hon.] 5 Editors Choice from NLP, Distinguished member of ISP, Volunteer Awards, College Honors; [oth. writ.] "Grandma's Psalm", "Intruder", "A Daughter Writes Home", "Retirement Recipe", "Tribute", "Love Letter", "Equinox", "Prodigal Found", "The Word"; [pers.] I am very blessed and still feel humble to have the talent to write. I encourage others in the golden years to use any creative talents they have.; [a.] Loveland, CO

PITALE, VIRGINIA L.
[pen.] Ginger; [b.] May 4, 1946, Hope, AK; [p.] Thelbert and Louise Robertson; [m.] John D. Pitale, May 28, 1988; [ch.] Michaelle, Christopher, Curtis, Brandon, Dylan; [ed.] Albion High, Argubright Business College; [occ.] Chiropractic Asst. Nanny, Singer, Guitarist, Pianist; [memb.] Church, creative writers of battle creek MI; [hon.] First place tie in H.S. Talent show won 2nd place twice in talent shows in atlanta GA 1st place pie selling contest; [oth. writ.] Numerous poems and songs. Poem published in foot prints of battle creek for creative writings; [pers.] I strive to reflect the reality of Jesus Christ and his love in my writings.; [a.] Battle Creek, MI

PLENK, MARGARET
[b.] January 31, 1925, Great Britain; [p.] Joseph Gomm, Mildred Gomm; [m.] Josef Plenk, December 1, 1945; [ch.] Timothy Joseph, Grandchildren Matthew Adam, William Joseph; [ed.] Private Schools; [occ.] Retired; [hon.] Poetry recitations; [oth. writ.] Poems published in local newspapers and church newsletters-bulletins.; [pers.] Something will catch at my soul and a well spring of inspiration arises and captures the moment for all time.; [a.] Lakehurst, NJ

PLOMTEAUX, HEIDI
[pen.] Heidi Plomteaux; [b.] October 3, 1943, St. Wendel, Germany; [ch.] Kevin, James, Candice, Renee; [ed.] College; [occ.] Restaurant-Manager; [pers.] Through my writing I would like to touch people in need and tremendous pain; [a.] Ventura, CA

PLOTZ, TRUDY ANN
[pen.] Saranna Lyndh Tudinsdottir; [b.] November 25, 1956, Cedar Rapids, IA; [p.] William J. Plotz and Helen J. Burton Plotz; [ed.] University of South Florida—BS in Business, Graduate Student in Communication, St. Petersburg Junior College—AA in Music; [memb.] St. Petersburg Writes Club, Southern States Communication Association, Society for Creative Anachronism Inc.; [hon.] Honorable Mention in the 1st Annual International Elvisology Contest for Poetry, Rhetoric Paper Presentation at the 65th Annual Conference for the Southern States Communication Association, 1st and 2nd placements in Public Speaking Contests; [oth. writ.] Several poems published State of Florida newsletter, local magazines, and other anthologies. My one-act play, Ash of Time, performed by Stanton College Prep School. Poem "Unmasked" published in The International Journal of Elvisology and the Elvisian Era.; [pers.] My great-aunt, Isabel Tudeen has always encouraged me to explore writing even when our styles seemed to clash. I have been influenced by Science Fiction, Edgar Allen Poe, Jane Eyre, Icelandic Sagas, classical music, opera, and most of all, college professors.; [a.] Tampa, FL

PLUMMER, ADAM K.
[b.] July 24, 1969, Menomonee Falls, WI; [p.] Kenneth and Sharon Plummer; [m.] Sheryl L. Plummer, July 7, 1989; [ch.] Alexander Kyle Plummer, Zachary Michael Plummer; [ed.] Washington High, Germantown, WI; [occ.] Electronics Technician, US Navy; [oth. writ.] None published; [pers.] I believe our children are the substance of our lives. The greatest gift we can give to them is an atmosphere of unconditional love. Always nurture and protect. They deserve it.; [a.] Orlando, FL

POERIO, RICHARD E.
[b.] February 1, 1964, Greensburg, PA; [p.] Gloria and Richard Peorio; [m.] Lori Poerio, September 30, 1994; [ed.] Oakridge High Valencia C/C; [occ.] Warehouse Manager Barr Display Orlando, FL; [pers.] Although we all live together on the same Earth, our perception causes billions of tiny pockets of reality; [a.] Orlando, FL

POGUE, DOROTHEA L.
[b.] October 3, 1926, Washington, DC; [p.] Bernard Kober, Hazel Kober; [ch.] (4) two boys, two girls, Barbara, Nancy, Chriss, Mike; [ed.] High School, Two years of college..with interest in Nursing. Specializing in care of elderly and terminal ill.; [occ.] Retired; [memb.] Past member of Chula Vista Illiteracy Team; [hon.] Awarded a resolution, of Chula Vista, CA. for participation and Interest in Civic Matters. Resolution #6408 Awarded April 1972, Armed Forces Certificate of Merit for outstanding patriotism (1987); [oth. writ.] Other poems and short stories, yet unpublished; [pers.] My writing comes from my heart. Along with my life experiences...; [a.] Chula Vista, CA

POIRIER, JANICE
[pen.] Janice Poirier; [b.] December 22, 1959, Dorchester; [p.] Wayne and Margaret Scott; [m.] Richard Poirier, January 11, 1990; [ch.] Nicole Diana Miller, John Joseph Miller; [ed.] G.E.D.; [occ.] Disabled; [memb.] St. Edwards Parish Brockton, MA; [oth. writ.] Several poems (non-published at this time); [pers.] I am still searching for my reason for being. As a survivor of 12 years of vicious spousal abuse, I finally freed my children and self. During that time, my only lifeline to sanity and hope was writing my poems.; [a.] Brockton, MA

POLING, CHRISTINA
[b.] July 7, 1980, Barberton; [p.] Weldon Poling, Kim Grim; [ed.] Student at Wadsworth Central Middle School; [occ.] Student; [pers.] Writing poetry has been a dream come true with the inspiration and support from

my close friend Jeromy Straub. He has understood my heart in a way that no body else can, I want to thank Jeromy for always being there, and for being a caring person.; [a.] Wadsworth, OH

POLITE SR., JAMES C.
[b.] February 8, 1947, Jacksonville, FL; [p.] Robert Polite and Edna Polite; [m.] Allie Faye Polite; [ch.] James Jr., Phillip M. Polite; [ed.] New Stanton Sr. High Jax, Fl., City College NYC,; [occ.] Retired NYC Fireman; [memb.] American Red Cross; [oth. writ.] The Woman, Ocean and Red Devil, Red Devil; [pers.] I write and paint. I also raise gold fish; [a.] Jacksonville, FL

POND, MERCEDA RUTH
[pen.] Ruthi Bernard Pond; [b.] October 17, 1933, Portland, OR; [p.] Claire Oliver Bernard, Luella Shaw Bernard; [m.] Leonard W. Pond, April 21, 1950; [ch.] Phyllis, David, Georgena, Leona; [ed.] 7th grade, plus G.E.D. College courses in food service and kitchen management, courses in sanitation; [occ.] Care giver; [memb.] Mount Olive Baptist Church; [oth. writ.] Poem: To My Mother. Published in anthology by World of Poetry. Poem: Let Us Not Forget The Chains, Newspapers Items many published poems; [pers.] We were extremely poor but my father loved poetry and recited to us. He, and the words of the Holy Bible, 'I can do all things through Christ who gives me strength' have prompted me to try and to succeed.; [a.] Dallas, OR

POOLE, PAT
[b.] December 23, 1950, VA; [p.] Clyde and Inez Dye; [ch.] Eric Steven; [ed.] Abingdon High, New River Comm. College; [occ.] Cust. Service Representative; [memb.] BMI; [pers.] Presently have four songs published with Five Roses Publishing; [a.] Las Vegas, NV

PORTAL, NANCY
[b.] July 25, 1936, Habana, Cuba; [p.] Santiago and Adelina Portal; [m.] Octavio Roig (deceased), November 11, 1956 (widowed); [ch.] Lazaro, Ronald (deceased), Fernando, Pedro, Margarita and Nancy Roig; [ed.] San Alejandro Art Academy Havana, Cuba - Bachelors in Fine Arts - Orange Coast College - Costa Mesa, Calif, - 20th century Art; [occ.] Artist; [memb.] Woman's Building L.A., Calif. Los Angeles Art Association Broward Art Guild, Ft. Lavd., FL. Valencia Community College, Orlando Ft. Women in the Arts; [hon.] Los Angeles Art Assoc. 1991 Competition - Second place Stuart Artists Caucees - 1991 Competition - Honorable Mention One woman shows in Calif. Florida and N.Y.; [oth. writ.] Several published honorable mention from world of poetry - 1989 1990, 1993; [pers.] I could not imagine a world without feeling. I use art as a method of expressing my emotions.; [a.] Orlando, FL

POTTER, PATRICK M.
[pen.] P. M. Potter; [b.] June 11, 1973, Baltimore; [p.] Mark and Catherine Potter; [ed.] Penn. State University, G.B.M.C. School of Radiologic Technology; [occ.] Radiographer; [pers.] I find simple things intriguing, the rain on quiet mornings, a bright full moon. We learn a lot from nature, if we take the time to listen.; [a.] Stewartstown, PA

POTYONDY, JULIE GRIFFITH
[b.] July 8, 1966, Oklahoma City, OK; [p.] Susan and Verne Griffith; [m.] David O. Potyondy, September 1, 1990; [ed.] B.A.-Dartmouth College, M.S.-Cornell University 1997, M. Div.-United Theological Seminary of the Twin Cities; [occ.] Candidate for the Ordained Ministry; [memb.] Westminster Presbyterian Church, Dartmouth College Alumni Association of the Upper Midwest; [hon.] Academic Citations in Christian Ethics and Preaching and Worship-UTS, Honors Gradu-

ate-Dartmouth College, Tucker Foundation Honor Society member, Leadership Studies Grant-Nelson A. Rockefeller Center for the Social Sciences; [oth. writ.] "School size and Program Comprehensiveness: Evidence from High School and Beyond" in Education Evaluation and Policy Analysis, summer 1990; [pers.] I believe that we are brought into existence, and we bring God into existence, via relation. Specifically, the only way we may incarnate one another and God, the only way we may live wholly, is in mutual-that is: reciprocal, loving and just relationship.; [a.] Minneapolis, MN

POWELL, KEENETH JEROME
[pen.] Keno; [b.] April 13, 1963, Detroit, MI; [p.] James and Geneva Powell; [m.] Holly Denise Powell, October 29, 1993; [ch.] Armani, Amber, Ashley; [ed.] Pershing High; [pers.] "Knowledge is the key, open up your mind and you'll be surprised at what you'll find inside. Think, it ain't illegal yet."; [a.] Detroit, MI

POWELL, RONDA MARIE
[b.] October 21, 1962, North Hollywood, CA; [p.] Eileen Anderson, James L. Powell; [ed.] Westminster High, Moorpark College; [occ.] Student; [hon.] Moorpark College Dean's List 1982, bowling trophies in high school, ASB Treasurer at Moorpark College in 1983; [oth. writ.] One of my other poems was published in CERA Anthology; [pers.] Thanks to two people Jan Wyma and Gail Wieldraayer for the influence of telling me to continue writing poems. They are special people in my life.; [a.] Simi Valley, CA

POWERS, LADY CAT
[b.] PA; [p.] Jesse and Rhoda Douglass; [m.] Widow; [ed.] College: Psychology and Drama; [occ.] Formerly a professional entertainer-dancer, free lance writer and horse trainer; [memb.] Turf Club (horse racing), Wildlife Groups, Animal Rights Groups; [hon.] Dean's List: College many poetry awards and many articles published; [oth. writ.] On cats and horses songwriter, cat articles, horse articles published nationally and England also: breeder of German Shepherds and Persian cats; [pers.] "Journey not on the path of another, lest you arrive at their destination, and not your own!" Live and let live! The more humans I meet, the more I love my horse! Some people are born cats, others may be lucky enough to achieve "Catness!" Would that humans could learn unconditional love from the animals! My poems and songs come from the Universe, via a form of channelling, a psychic link with the cosmos! All poems and songs come thru automatically and unedited!; [a.] Boulder, CO

PREGENZER, JENNY
[b.] January 8, 1978, Anaheim, CA; [p.] Bill and Dale Pregenzer; [ed.] Rosary High School; [occ.] Student at Rosary High School; [memb.] Surfrider Foundation, National Charity League, Heal the Bay; [hon.] Community Service Award; [pers.] If we could all put our anger, fears, and frustration into words, and put these words on to paper, our world would be a happier and safer place.; [a.] Fullerton, CA

PRESHER, FRANCES TATE
[b.] June 14, 1924, Anderson, SC; [p.] Ruth Eisenman Tate and Curtis Leon Tate; [m.] Deceased; [ch.] Cynthia Diane Hill; [ed.] Anderson Girls High, Various business colleges, Ecole D'Estrangers, Paris, MDME Garibaldi, University of Paris, private student for one year; [occ.] World traveller; [pers.] I have been writing all my life, and have completed many journals of my travels. The first poem was written as a first grader in summer of 1931. Diaries, various reflections of mind, and many poems—which I never submitted for publication. They combine to weave a sort of tapestry of life.

I do not aim to reflect any particular facet of my life, but rather to write as writing presents itself to me. In other words, I don't DELIBERATELY DETERMINE to force the words. The words seem to force me to pick up the pen.; [a.] Columbia, SC

PRETAK, FREDERICK J.
[pen.] "Cook"; [b.] May 6, 1930, Torrington, CT; [p.] Stephen Pretak, Estelle Viscuis; [m.] Dolores Minelli Pretak, August 1, 1953; [ch.] Gerardine, Candace, Lori; [ed.] Sixty-five years of Days of Learning; [occ.] Self-employed, Sign and Airbrush Artist; [memb.] Between reading and writing and painting I find little time for outside membership.; [hon.] Personal satisfaction when a treatise helps another person.; [oth. writ.] Multiple treaties in combining psychology, philosophy and theology in the everyday vernacular of the side street.; [pers.] A caring God. A good wife, three lovely daughters, grand-children to love, a good cigar.... It's been a good life.; [a.] Torrington, CT

PRICE, ALTA E.
[pen.] Alt Rainsberg; [b.] November 28, 1920, Harrison City, OH; [p.] Herman and Olive Rainsberg; [m.] Howar W. Price, June 20, 1939; [ch.] Ruth, Stull, Barbara Renicker, Bobbie G, Todd, Gayle Thompson, and Rhonda Jrover; [ed.] Graduated from, Denison, High School July 1939, and from, Tappan Grade School May 1934. Lived on a farm all my life until 1989; [occ.] Retired Housewife; [memb.] Attend the first assembly of God Christ in Uhrichsville and belong to TS W.M.S. (Womens ministries). Also belong to the Dennison High Alumni Association; [hon.] Editor's Choice Award for outstanding Achievement in poetry from the National Library of Poetry 1994 - Volunteer Appreciation Certificate for outstanding work to aid in the education of local children Trenton Ave. Elem entry children - 1994-95; [oth. writ.] The Bible - God's rainbow - The Thankful Month. Life's Road - Memories My Jesus - and Numerous Small Poems - Do We Care?; [pers.] We are never to old to learn.; [a.] Uhrichsville, OH

PRICE, EDNA
[b.] February 9, 1925, England; [ch.] Virginia Carol, Kenneth Vernon Jr.; [ed.] Parochial School, England; [occ.] Retired Childcare Provider; [pers.] I believe my poems to be a gift of God as I have searched for spiritual truths. My hope is that they will speak to others on the same search.; [a.] Belmont, CA

PRICE, LT. COLONEL WALLACE W.
[b.] March 10, 1921; [p.] Sam and Pennie Price; [m.] Adrienne W. Price, June 5, 1982; [ch.] Wallace W., Catherine A., Sandra Price and Howard; [ed.] Bach. Educ., Southern Ill. Univ., Masters from Univ. Va. State Univ., and Legal Tng. Seton Hall Univ. ECAPT, VP, Germany, Who's Who in Finance and Industry, Who's Who in the East, NAACP National Life Member Past Pres. of National Urban League, Bergen City, NJ, Member Urban League, Bergen County, NJ 20 yrs Former Councilman, Teaneck, N.J., Co-founder of Edges for N.Y. and D.C.; [occ.] Retired; [memb.] Co-founder EDGES Group, NY and DC Member, Alpha Phi Alpha Fraternity American Heart Association, Ill., Congressional Committee, N.J. and D.C. Fair Housing Committee, Bergen County, N.J. (Ret.); [hon.] Community Board Awards, United Methodist Church, Teaneck, N.J.; [a.] Teaneck, NJ

PRICE, MICHAEL
[b.] December 22, 1964, Miami, OK; [p.] Harold and Sandra Price; [ed.] 2 years - Colorado College, 3 years University of California, Santa Cruz, B.A. in Comparative Literature; [occ.] Volunteer at Santa Barbara Art Museum; [memb.] Santa Barbara Art Museum; [oth. writ.] Shades of perception, catharsis through psycho-

analysis. A spring journal, Summer Sojourn, Winter's Lease, Native poems (in progress). The eternal gathering poetic circumstances.; [pers.] The joy of poetic inspiration is developed from both work and leisure. In some sense we are all poets. Life, love and play are our well springs. There is our purpose.; [a.] Santa Barbara, CA

PRICE, RUTH HELEN
[pen.] Ruth Helen Price; [b.] March 5, 1932, Rochester, NY; [p.] Dwight Barry and Alive Barry; [m.] Billie B. Price, October 24, 1978; [ch.] Kathleen England, Linda Lofton and John Cheshire; [ed.] High School; [occ.] Housewife; [hon.] I've had three Golden Poet Awards, several other poetry awards, a certificate of Merit from McFadden Publications. I've also had three poems that were published in poetry Anthology.; [pers.] My love of people and the true Blessings we receive seems to come through in my poetry. I am mostly influenced by the great love between myself and my children. They truly are my greatest blessing.; [a.] Hertford, NC

PRIEST, BEN
[pen.] B. P.; [b.] September 20, 1979, Bangor, ME; [p.] Kerry and Lynn Priest; [ed.] 1 year of High School, now a Sophomore; [occ.] High School Student; [oth. writ.] 2 other poems published in anthologies; [pers.] "Seek not to follow in the footsteps of the men of old, seek instead what they sought."; [a.] Hampden, ME

PROCIDA, JEFF
[b.] May 30, 1964, Bethpage, NY; [p.] Al and Martha Procida; [m.] Michelle Procida, February 10, 1995; [ed.] Observing; [oth. writ.] Nothing published-they sit in a pile in my room. I sent my work to you on a whim and I thank you for your response.; [pers.] Life is an individual experience. Hold yourself responsible for your actions and you can accomplish anything. Self-doubt is as lethal as any drug or abuse.; [a.] Brightwaters, NY

PROTUS, LINDA
[b.] July 2, 1957, Jamaica, NY; [p.] Marion and William Mertens; [m.] Tim Protus - my love, June 5, 1993; [ch.] Kerri Armato - my very special girl; [occ.] Homemaker; [oth. writ.] I have written other poems for pleasure since I was eight years old and have been given a lot of confidence by my two sisters Deb Condon and Judy Docyk.; [pers.] I love to write poetry and express my feelings. I have been inspired by my mother Marion Mertens and my grandmother Marion Paquette

PRPICH, BILLIE PERRY
[b.] September 24, 1912, Yellville Marion, AR; [p.] George H. and Minnie Young Perry; [m.] John M. Prpich, November 24, 1961, Ex-husband Darwin Penney, September 11, 1940; [ch.] Philip D. Penney, Sheri Layne Penney; [ed.] Yellville-Summit H.S. Weber College at Ogden, Utah 2 years. Utah State Univ. Logan Ut. 2 years B.S. degree Univ. of Utah Masters Degree in Educ. minors in fine arts; [occ.] Retired after 30 yrs. of Elem. School Teaching; [memb.] Granite Ed. Assoc. Davis Co. Ed Assoc. U.E.A., N.E.A., U.S.P.S. and National Federation of State Poetry Soc. The L.D.S. Church of which have been a member since I was 8 years old; [hon.] I have won 2nd place awards on Saga of Salt Lake City, the mourning Dove, snowflakes Several at least 5 have won 2nd place a stormy night.; [oth. writ.] I have written at least 80 poems in all some are children's stories in poetry; [pers.] I also am very interested in the political storm - in the U.S. today I have written many poems lately about this situation but haven't had them typed up yet. I have also written many poems, about the environment.; [a.] Salt Lake City, UT

PUGH, COLLEEN
[pen.] Peachies; [b.] September 18, 1981, Pittsburgh, PA; [p.] Thomas and Cheryl Pugh; [ed.] Cornell Elementary and Jr. High School; [occ.] Student at Cornell Jr. High School; [memb.] Cornell High School Swim Team; [hon.] Honor Roll all through elementary, except 5th and 6th grade; [oth. writ.] Poems and stories that I write at home.; [pers.] I strive to do the best I can and I show all my hidden emotions in my writing.; [a.] Pittsburgh, PA

PUSATERI, FRANK C.
[pen.] Jack Christensen; [b.] February 18, 1974, Buffalo, NY; [p.] Ed and Maria Harlukiewicz, Frank E. Pusateri; [ed.] Frontier Central High School; [occ.] Musician; [hon.] Buffalo Music Award; [pers.] I write what I see, feel, and hear of my own mind. For each mind is equally its own - Your own mind is the greatest of all.; [a.] Hamburg, NY

QUARLES, ERIC J.
[pen.] Shadow Man; [b.] July 7, 1968, Detroit, MI; [p.] Earnest and Henrietta Quarles; [ed.] BS - Mfg Sys Engrg, MS - Mfg Sys Engrg, MS - Finance; [occ.] Mfg Sys. Engineer, Chrysler Corp.; [memb.] Omega Psi Phi Fraternity, National Society of Black Engineers, Society of Manufacturing Engineers; [hon.] GMI Engrg and Mgt Inst. Prevost List; [oth. writ.] Several unpublished poems written exclusively for RNB; [pers.] Love to my lady forever and longer still. Love to my brothers since 1911. Peace.; [a.] Detroit, MI

QUEBODEAUX, SCOTT
[pen.] Dylan Scott; [b.] May 12, 1966, Sulphur, LA; [p.] Tracy and Patsy Quebodeaux; [m.] Melissa Quebodeaux, September 26, 1992; [ch.] Dylan Scott Quebodeaux; [ed.] Sam Houston High School; [occ.] Carpenter; [pers.] My writing reflects the truer meanings of feelings, of words, and of life. My influences came from early gothic poets and story tellers the truth always has so many meanings, but only one passion.; [a.] Lake Charles, LA

QUINONES, PAOLA ANDREA
[b.] April 18, 1976, Long Beach, CA; [p.] Gladys Granum, Gilbert Quinones; [occ.] Student; [pers.] Through my writing I pour out my feelings and emotions in which I could never do through speech. It is my gateway to pure harmony and peace.; [a.] Escondido, CA

RACINE, JOHN ALAN
[b.] November 26, 1963, Albuquerque; [p.] Robert and Margaret Racine; [m.] Tonja Racine, September 2, 1984; [ch.] Christopher Robert, Lindsey Nicole, Geoffrey Daniel; [ed.] BA Huntingdon College 1985, MS Navy Post Graduate School 1991; [occ.] Test and Evaluation Manager U.S. Navy Satellite Program; [memb.] American Society of Naval Engineers American Institute of Aeronautics and Astronautics, Home School Legal Defense Association; [oth. writ.] Numerous poems published in the prelude (college poetry collection). Poem published in poetry shell publication.; [pers.] One most strive to find God in all things and remember to love each other as Christ Loved us.; [a.] Landover, MD

RACZ, MARRA
[pen.] Marra Racz of Nagyvarad; [b.] January 24, 1940, Romania; [p.] Sandor and Elisabeth; [ed.] R.N., Cosmetician, Model, Photographer, Writer, Lecturer in Ancient Hungarian Shamanism; [occ.] Freelance writer, Artist photographer, Model; [memb.] American institute of Fine Arts, Whittier Art Association, Collegium Corvinum, Arpad Academy, Cleveland, OH; [hon.] Numerous prizes and Invitational Exhibits, Solo Ex-

hibit, Invited Member of the Arpad Academy of Cleveland, OH, Orientalist; [oth. writ.] Poems, Essays, Newspaper Articles, Lecturers, etc. Ready to Publish:, Life in Callaville, photos and their stories. (English) in publication the same in Hungarian.|; [pers.] Using God given serendipity bring to life flowers and minerals, to give joy and understanding to the reader-viewer, thus helping people to see, beyond mere looking.; [a.] Pasadena, CA

RALPH, CHERYL E.
[b.] June 1, 1948, Panama Canal Zone; [p.] Altha Seymour and Gib Hockett; [m.] Jon K. Ralph, December 18, 1971; [ch.] Shantell Wyers, Cassie Mullins, Jon E. Ralph; [ed.] GED Diploma; [occ.] School Bus Driver, in the Junction City area and secretary in training at the bus barn; [oth. writ.] Children On Probation Clover Of Meadows Green, Dreamcatcher, Shimmering Vine, Lady Slipper Scent, Shrouded Ray's, Frolicking, Entrancing Melody, Tribal Chant, Mystic Mystery, Freedom Soldier, Chilling Decade, Alcoholic's Conscience; [pers.] These are a few of the Poems, I have written and published in a book titled Reflections and Memories, by a self publishing company, I like to write from My dream world, and from the experiences of the, life lines of others, I also enjoy writing, Poems, Regarding the Native Americans, and other Nationalities.; [a.] Junction City, OR

RAMIREZ, AIDEE
[b.] September 18, 1956, Puerto Rico; [p.] Ana Aragonez-Dionicio Ramirez; [m.] Divorce; [ch.] 22 yr. old daughter Brunilda Santiago; [ed.] G.E.D.; [occ.] Housewife; [oth. writ.] 19 poems, none published; [pers.] I'm inspire by my life experience, love and romance.

RAMIREZ, ANNE WALTON L.
[b.] September 22, 1972, Atlanta, GA; [p.] Frank L. Walton, Evelyn S. Walton; [m.] Luis A. Ramirez, April 28, 1994; [ed.] North Fulton High School, AH, GA Georgia State University, Atlanta, GA, Mobile, AL University of South Alabama graduate June, 1996; [occ.] Student, tutor at university to be a translator of Spanish-English; [memb.] Al-Anon Golden Key National Honors Society Alpha Chi-scholarship; [hon.] Dean's list Gabriella Blanco award/scholarship Margaret Pol Stock Award excellence of foreign language study Jeremy Steven Blanton scholarship high scholastic achievement International Baccalaureate degree; [oth. writ.] Poems published by several companies; [pers.] I tend to challenge myself by setting high goals. In this way I always feel that I reach my potential using the gifts that God blessed me with.; [a.] Fairhope, AL

RAMIREZ, JOSE M.
[pen.] Jose; [b.] January 12, 1955, Zacatecas, Mexico; [p.] Maria and Manuel Ramirez; [m.] Maria A. Ramirez, September 22, 1973; [ch.] Analena, Roberto, Flor, Alexandra; [ed.] H.S.; [occ.] Bus Driver; [a.] Brighton, CO

RAMOS, CHRISTINE
[b.] November 23, 1976, NY; [p.] Angel Ramos, Gloria Ramos; [m.] Single; [ed.] Stevenson High School, attending Herbert H. Lehmon Colleges; [memb.] Drama Clubs, Softball Team, Auxiliary Police Face; [oth. writ.] Several unpublished poems short stories and plays; [pers.] I believe to succeed in life a person only has to believe in themselves and keep trying even when the Rd. seem rough and lonely.; [a.] Bronx, NY

RANDT, LORRAINE
[pen.] Lori Raine; [b.] August 27, 1969, Encino, CA; [p.] Frederick Michael Thomas Randt, Maria Randt; [ed.] Miramar High School (Miramar, FL); [occ.] Student; [oth. writ.] I have several unsubmitted pieces;

[pers.] There is no solution for one who can not see beyond the predicament.; [a.] Los Angeles, CA

RAO, KAUSHIKI
[b.] October 14, 1981, Bangalore, India; [p.] V. N. Lalithkumar Rao and Shobini Rao; [ed.] Ashraya, Sophia High School, Rudder Middle School; [occ.] Student; [hon.] National Junior Honor Society, Gifted and Talented School Program, VIL, PREP, Sanskript Level 1 and Level 2; [pers.] I would like to thank Amma, Appa, akka, Ammamma, Tata, Pati, Tata, B. Mami, B. Mama, Dit, Budh and the rest of my family for encouraging me.; [a.] Bangalore, India

RAO, SHARMILA
[b.] October 7, 1964, Manglore, India; [p.] Jaypal Rao, Jayashree Rao; [ed.] B. Arch '87, Univ. of Bombay, M.L.A. '91, Cornell University, M.R.C.P. '94, Univ. of Oklahoma; [occ.] Associate planner/Gis, City of Bryan, TX; [memb.] American Planning Association; [oth. writ.] Master's thesis on campus designs, article for Amateur Astromers' Association, India; [pers.] I write to give form to my thoughts and feelings, those that affect me most intensely.; [a.] College Station, TX

RASCH, STEFANI L.
[b.] January 1, 1977, Derby, CO; [p.] Philip and Rhoby Rasch; [ed.] Graduated from Mary Carroll High School, now attending, Texas A&M University (College Station) Studying Animal Science; [occ.] Student, Kennel Worker at OSO Creek Animal Hospital, TX; [memb.] National Honor Society, German National Honor Society (Delta Epsilon Phi) Texas Scholar, All-American Scholar; [hon.] Co-MVP-District for Soft Ball, Co-Athlete Of The Year in Coastal Bend for Soft Ball, 2nd Team All-state (Softball Captain of Varsity Softball Mup-of Tournament-Bayfront Bash; [pers.] No one ever knows what life will throw their way, therefore one must strive to make the best of what they're given and to live life to its fullest capabilities.; [a.] College Station, TX

RASHID, VICTORIA
[pen.] Torrie Rashid; [b.] July 28, 1965, Providence, RI; [p.] David and Elizabeth Hamlin; [m.] Divorced; [ed.] Rhode Island College; [occ.] Sales person; [memb.] CCD Teacher (spare time), Volunteer for the Smith Hill Center; [oth. writ.] Currently working on a science fiction novel (not yet finished); [pers.] I feel the most important aspect of society tends to be the resource that is all to often overlooked, each other. I strive to portray the aftermath of self-will and indifference in my writing.; [a.] Providence, RI

RASMUSSEN, NORMAN
[b.] January 26, 1920, Brooklyn, NY; [p.] Hans and Elvira Rasmussen; [m.] Marilyn Rasmussen, June 4, 1943; [ch.] Michael, Guy, John, Danny; [ed.] Tilden High School, N.Y. Trade School (sign Painting); [occ.] Retired industrial painter; [memb.] V.F.W., American Legion; [hon.] Honorary Irish Poet (2nd Annual Irish Whiskey Competition); [pers.] I read poetry for pleasure and write poems for fun. Am a book worm and amateur oil painter.; [a.] Lanoka Harbor, NJ

RAVEL, SHERYL
[pen.] Sunshine; [b.] June 10, 1964, Buffalo; [p.] Richard Kruszynski, Alexandra Miller; [m.] Patrick J. Ravel, March 2, 1984; [ch.] Brittney, Jamie, Sydnie, Chelsea, Patric-James Ravel; [ed.] Sweet Home High School Self Study College English and Psychology courses; [occ.] Own small Business (Guzzo's Hot Spot) - Housewife; [memb.] President of our Lady of Czestochowa Home School Association; [oth. writ.] A women in Love... Sunshine...; [pers.] My inspirations come from my husband and five beautiful children, allowing me to

express my feelings on a day to day basis and giving me the time to put them on paper; [a.] Buffalo, NY

RAWHOUSER, DEBBIE
[b.] July 27, 1965, Billericay, England; [p.] Harry James, Alice James; [m.] Brian Rawhouser, September 21, 1985; [ch.] John Michael, Kelly Michelle; [memb.] Audobon Society, The Sierra Club; [pers.] Although I write poetry on many subjects, I concentrate mainly on matters close to my heart, such as the environment, the goodness of humanity and the hope for peace.; [a.] Aumsville, OR

RAY, INIS
[pen.] Inis Danley Ray; [b.] March 27, 1938, Caruthersville, MO; [p.] Myltle and Nelson Danley; [m.] Carl Waymon Ray Sr., October 12, 1958; [ch.] Joy Kerlin, Christi Ray, Carl Waymon Ray, Jr.; [ed.] Caruthersville, MO High, Vo-Tec-Computer, Office Management and Business Courses; [occ.] Office manager/Sec. II at City Hall Inspection Dept. Pine Bluff, AR; [memb.] American Business Women's Assoc, Church Choir and Soloist, American Bolbroom Dance Assoc; [hon.] American Business Women's Assoc. Woman of the year for local Pine Bluff Chapter; [oth. writ.] Local newspaper publishings, and "So Near, Yet So Far" poem in the book "Peaceful Thoughts" a collection of inspirational writings; [pers.] My family and Christian beliefs greatly influence my thoughts for writing. My sister Wanda Koontz of Carothersville, MO, and brother Dr. Walter Elzie Danby of Jackson, TN are an encouragement to me in any literary endeavor.; [a.] Pine Bluff, AR

RAY, JEAN JOHNSTONE
[pen.] Jean Ray; [b.] January 23, 1921, Kansas City, MO; [p.] Dr. Paul N. Johnstone (MD), Cecile Taylor Johnstone (Poet); [m.] Deceased, June 29, 1943; [ch.] Bradley Taylor Ray, William Johnstone Ray; [ed.] AB, BS, (University of Missouri), Masters Education (University of Nebraska), Masters Medical Record Administration, EMORY U., Atlanta, GA; [occ.] Chair-of-Board, Technomed, President, AR/Mediquest, Inc.; [memb.] Professional and business, DAR, Zonta; [oth. writ.] Software for hospitals and medical applications (25 years) children's stories; [pers.] To allow truth to be my guide in all phases of my interaction with people.; [a.] Lansing, MI

RAYBURN, JESSICA
[pen.] Jessica Rayburn; [b.] April 28, 1981, Charleston, MO; [p.] Dorothy Tinnin and Ted Rayburn; [ed.] I will be a Freshman Cornerstone Christian Academy; [memb.] I am a member of Dorena Baptist Church.; [hon.] Honor roll 2nd grade Creative Writing Award; [oth. writ.] I really just like to write poems for myself.; [pers.] I would really like to write about what goes on in this world today. But love poems are my favorite.; [a.] East Prairie, MO

RAZANSKI, NANCY
[pen.] Nancy Razanski; [b.] December 19, 1947, Detroit, MI; [p.] William and Amelia Razanski; [ed.] U.S. Grant High, California State University - Northridge with BA in English, English Teaching Credential; [occ.] Substitute teacher for LA Unified School District Secondary Level; [memb.] Life Member Chatsworth Historical Society, Life Member Santa Susana Mtn. Park Assoc., Life Member Chatsworth Friends of the Library, Chapter Member LA Wild, Sierra Club, SFV Audubon; [hon.] First Place in weekly contest Essay in Valley Times at age 17 section called "Youth Speaks", Sierra Club Angeles Chapt. 1988 Extraordinary Achievement Award, Chatsworth Community Coordinating Council 1989 Exception Service Award; [oth. writ.] Article entitled "Animals of the Santa Susanas"

published in book Over the Pass into the Past in 1973 Santa Susana Mtn. Park Assoc. - Publisher, Article entitled "Ghost Town Resting Peacefully in Nature's Sanct." Publish in smoke signal whats. Hist. Soc. newsletter Apr. 1995, book Swanky The Swan, 1981 illust. by William Razanski; [pers.] Statement: My goal in writing is to inform the mind and uplift the spirit.; [a.] Chatsworth, CA

REDMAN, ANGELA D.
[pen.] Angela D. Redman; [b.] January 16, 1951, Big Spring, TX; [p.] H.C. and Bernice Tidwell; [m.] Justin M. Redman, August 2, 1986; [ch.] Michael Shawn Maderer; [ed.] Forsan High School, Forsan Texas, several hrs. at Jr. College in music and writing; [occ.] Homemaker and Mother; [memb.] American Interstitial Cystitis Assoc., Lupus Assoc., Arthritis Assoc.; [hon.] District and Regional award of merit for Boy Scouts of American; [oth. writ.] Children's stories and poems for friends and family in Oklahoma; [pers.] I have been writing poetry since I was 10 years old. Nature and family are what I draw my inspiration from I mainly write poems for Christmas, Birthdays and special occasions, for people in my community up in a little logging town in the heart of Kiamichi Country, in the Quachita Mountains.; [a.] Wright City, OK

REED, DENNIS T.
[pen.] D. J. R.; [b.] January 23, 1972, Rock Springs, WY; [p.] Gloria Reed and Mother; [ed.] Twelve years; [occ.] Student

REED, LILLIAN MARIE
[pen.] Katie; [b.] April 21, 1938, Taylorville, IL; [p.] Bela and Mary Durbin; [m.] Glenn Franklin Reed Sr., February 10, 1955; [ch.] Glenda Marie Washington Glenn Franklin Reed Jr.; [ed.] 12th grade; [occ.] Domestic Engineer "Tumbling star" Quilt - viewers choice; [hon.] Taylorville Ill Chilefest 1993. "Musical calliope" quilt - 1st place Christian County fair 1994 5th place Ill. State fair viewer choice - Decatus Ill. quit show 1995. Best decorated cake - 2nd place 1989. 8th place 1990 1st place 1990 at St. Louis MO. Christian Academy cookies contest - 1st place 1994 at "Christmas in the park." Mayor Dick Adams proclaimed April 21, 1995 Lillian Reed day in Taylorville Ill. For her outstanding achievements.; [oth. writ.] The christmas lamb" was published in the Breeze Cowries" paper of Taylorville Ill. 1994 also has other unpublished works.; [pers.] Garth Brook's and his music has taught me that you will never know what you can do until you try. I think God for my talent's and Garth for inspiring me to achieve them. Don't let life pass you by. Go against the grain "be original" don't stand outside the fire "take a chance" life is what you make it.; [a.] Taylorville, IL

REED, TAMILIA DENISE
[pen.] Tamilia Denise Reed; [b.] December 20, 1981, Jacksonville; [p.] Eileen King, Rufus Reed Jr.; [ed.] Middle School (James Weldon Johnson); [pers.] I believe the sky is the limit, so what ever you do in life be sure to reach for the stars.; [a.] Jacksonville, FL

REESE, ROSIE
[b.] April 14, 1933, Altoona, PA; [p.] Veronica Joseph Fischer; [m.] Herbert Reese, June 20, 1953; [ch.] Kathy Albright, Michael Reese, Richard Reese, Colleen Irwin; [ed.] Graduation from Altoona Catholic High School 1951 (ACYJS.); [occ.] Retired from Penn. State University 12-91 (Janitorial); [memb.] Mt. Top Fire Co. Aux. AARP Penn State Retirees Chapter Elk's Ladies - Rosary and Altar Society; [hon.] Received Physical Plant Award from PSU-4-90 nominated by Wartik Lab. Building for outstanding work done for the building and occupants; [oth. writ.] Write poems for special occasion of relatives and friends expressing my joy, sorrow or

happiness in a special way. P.S. This poem "Wedding Gown" was written for my husband on our anniversary; [pers.] I love to hear statements how my friends and relatives love being remembered by my poems that is especially reflecting the special occasion for which it is written; [a.] Sandy Ridge, PA

REGAN, LEONORA
[pen.] Leonora Regan; [b.] November 12, 1980, NY; [p.] Barbara Regan and James Regan; [ed.] St. John's Villa Academy; [occ.] High School Student; [memb.] St. John's Villa Drama Club; [hon.] I am a dancer and I have received an award for my many years of dancing; [oth. writ.] Poems published by The National Library of Poetry and poems performed in an School Play; [pers.] I wish to express myself through poetry and a way to vent my emotions; [a.] Staten Island, NY

REGO, DANILE B.
[b.] June 2, 1978, Stockton, CA; [p.] Albert Rego, Gail Rego; [ed.] Santa Margarita High School; [occ.] Student; [memb.] Saddleback Stamp Club, Mandala; [hon.] Model United Nations - WCIMUN, Mission Viejo, H.S. MUN, UCR-MUN, UCLA-MUN. Academic Award - Art 2. First Place Stampt Exhibit, Saddleback Stamp Club Fall Open Competition; [oth. writ.] The short-short story, "The Bells of Santa Margarita", in Mandala 1991, also the article "The Making of a Possible Third World War", in M.U.N. Newsletter; [pers.] Where I am now, there, you may also be.; [a.] Mission Viejo, CA

REICH, ELLEN L.
[pen.] Linnea, Grandma'r; [b.] August 15, 1913, Sweden; [p.] Johan and Agnes Reich; [m.] A. Fredrick Reich (Deceased), June 21, 1936; [ch.] Anne Dickershald B.; [ed.] Commercial Course in Bay Ride High School, Brooklyn worked in Metropolitan Life Ins. Co. for 11 years; [occ.] Retired - Keeps home and garden - church activities; [memb.] Lutheran Church, Babylon Jennylind Rebekah Lodge, 100F, NY City, Women of Evang. Luth. Church Quilters; [hon.] My grandchildren (adults) and my daughter being a dedicated teacher; [oth. writ.] Poems - Economize - Sacrifice, My Fred my hubby etz and others articles in Swedish paper in Swedish and English - always writing letters; [pers.] "If everyone lived by the golden rule" how wonderful it would be; [a.] North Babylon, NY

REILLY, BRYAN
[b.] December 26, 1972, Danbury, CT; [p.] John Reilly, Jeanne Reilly; [ed.] New Fairfield High School, University of Rhode Island; [hon.] 2nd Place in the Nancy Potter Short Story Contest; [oth. writ.] Short Stories, currently writing a fictitious novel; [pers.] Happiness is Mom and Dad, a T-shirt, a pair of worn jeans and listening to the same a dozen or so times in a row.; [a.] New Fairfield, CT

REINAW, PHYLLIS W.
[pen.] Phyllis M. White; [b.] April 21, 1922, Anamosa, IA; [p.] Fred and Susan White; [m.] Charles W. Reinaw, June 28, 1945 (Divorced); [ch.] Charles, Jr, Scott Winslow, and Shelby Susan; [ed.] BA and BS Skidmore College 1943. Equal credits, English, Science/Biology and Music.; [occ.] F.L. Writer, Past VP, Cont. Adv. Agey, Pub Relations; [memb.] A.H.A Board Members, N West Bergen Cty Chapter, Trustee, Emmanuel Baptist Church, Ridgewood, NJ; [oth. writ.] As a public relations writer I have obtained extensive coverage in my metro area medra over the past 20 years, have written for major trade and consumer publication, and have written for almost all media including radio and T.V.; [pers.] Influenced by the greatest writers and poets of one time, I feel important that modern education convey the message of clinical poets to today's

generation. I strangely feel this should be our primary concern.; [a.] Mahwah, NJ

RENO, JUDITH A.
[b.] June 30, 1944, Reno, NY; [p.] Lillian and Emil McMahon; [m.] Frederick E. Reno, September 12, 1964; [ch.] Jennifer Elizabeth Graber, Christine Michele Lowe; [ed.] Reno High School, Utah State University "Word of faith Leadership and Bible Institute Dallas, TX; [occ.] Minister, teacher counselor, wife, mother, grandmother homemaker; [memb.] Women in leadership ordained with faith Christian Fellowship, Women Aglow AACC (American Association of Christian Counselors"); [hon.] Lifetime member "sterling pack jaycees" Pres. "Reston Aglow" founder: "Couples for" Christ "Founder house of Prayer Ministries" it strive to live my life to bring God glory in everything it do, including writing. Ordained 1995 to present; [oth. writ.] Book: "Shout for the victory" Workbook: "The fervent prayers of the righteous men Availeth much" book "words, containers of power"; [pers.] I believe that God sent His only Son Jesus Christ to be born of a Virgin for the express purpose of dying for our sins so that we might live with Him in Heaven for Eternity and that Salvation is a Gift from God. We can give Him the gift of our lives in return his goodness.; [a.] Fairfax, VA

RENSPIE, MARJORIE A.
[b.] March 5, 1943, Collins, OH; [m.] Robert Renspie; [ch.] Catherine, Robert W., Constance, Daniel; [occ.] Receptionist/switch board operator; [pers.] Our short time on this earth must not only be savored... but used to make a difference. My favorite poets are William Wordsworth, Henry David Thoreau, and Robert Frost.; [a.] Columbus, OH

REXRODE, JEANETTE
[pen.] 'Net; [b.] June 12, 1936, Chas, SC; [p.] Nita and Calvin Mole; [m.] Edward Rexrode, February 14, 1990; [ch.] Marty, Linda and Laura Reid; [ed.] North Chas High School, Chas SC Brevard Junior College, Fla., Various other Courses Art in Paris, France; [occ.] Retired; [hon.] Various, All related to profession Business Management; [oth. writ.] Numerous prose and poems, some dating to 30 years ago - Never have submitted any prior to this submittal. I write, print and garden as hobbies.; [pers.] I am Keenly Aware of so many unspoken emotions in everyone I've observed in my travels and day to day experience, I "feel" them, and feel the need to express the emotions through writing or paintings.; [a.] Summerville, SC

REYES, CAROLINA
[b.] April 11, 1978, Santa Monica, CA; [p.] Agustin Reyes, Modesta Reyes; [ed.] McKinley Elementary, Lincoln Middle School; [occ.] Student at Santa Monica High School; [hon.] Varsity X-Country/Trac, Honor List, AP student; [pers.] The people who are closest to me inspire the poems that I write.; [a.] Santa Monica, CA

REYNOLDS, DAVID
[b.] March 29, 1967; [p.] Ellen and Richard Reynolds; [m.] Gloria Bueno-Reynolds, August 26, 1990; [ch.] Under hypothetical discussion!; [ed.] B.A. Education New Paltz College New York; [occ.] Accounts payable clerk; [oth. writ.] Several unpublished poems, essays and short fiction; [pers.] Realize the importance of dreaming Big Dreams, but make sure you wake up long enough to go out and actively pursue them.; [a.] Bensonhurst, NY

RHIND, DAVID B.
[b.] May 7, 1966, Riverside, CA; [p.] Lorrelle K. Rhind and Terence K. Rhind; [m.] Dawn Marie Rhind, April 4, 1992; [ch.] Logan Kendall Rhind; [ed.] Arlington

High, Riverside Community College, California State University San Bernardino; [occ.] Home delivery person; [memb.] PHI KAPPA PHI Honors Society, BETA GAMMA SIGMA Business Honors Society; [hon.] Dean's list, Graduated with High Honors from CSUSB; [oth. writ.] Shame, Untitled, Starry Night; [pers.] My inspiration come from my observations I have made in the world around me. The full spectrum of light and dark within humanity serves as my pallet.; [a.] Rancho Cucamonga CA

RHODES, LINDA D.
[b.] KY; [m.] April 1, 1967; [ch.] Four; [ed.] Twelve; [occ.] School Bus Driver; [pers.] For Marty, my son, all my love. Mom, this poem was wrote around the time you where 16 years old.; [a.] Clermont, KY

RIBAKOFF, ROBERT
[pen.] Reuben Dayog; [b.] October 26, 1925, Kansas City, MO; [p.] David and Rose Ribakoff; [m.] Diana Gubmann Ribakoff, June 19, 1952; [ch.] Alexander Zev, Joseph Meir, and David Baruch Ribakoff; [ed.] Yeshiva - Torus Moshe K.C MO 3 years Kansas City Jr College AA Univ. of Southern Calif B.S. Educ. Univ of Southern Calif. M.L.A.; [occ.] Retired, School Teacher; [memb.] American Fed of Teachers Jewish WAL Veterans of U.S.H. American Jewish Committee Democratic Party; [hon.] Combat Infantry Man's Badge 3 Battle Stars ETO in 2nd World War, Teacher Appreciation Award Selby Grove Parents Club Pico Rivera Calif 1983; [oth. writ.] "Long March", - Poem "AKEDA" - Narrative Poem "Hot Water" Short Story "Kidnapped in Buenos Aires" short story; [pers.] In what work I've done I reflect my own personal experiences and how they reflect on a more universal or at least wider common experience. Privately I believe in God and that each of us is assigned a role in the completion of His unfinished universe, don't know how that if any affects my writing; [a.] Irvine, CA

RICCI, GWEN E.
[pen.] "G" "GG" (Grammy Gwen); [b.] June 19, 1937, Portland, ME; [p.] Mary Jordan Germane; [occ.] Music Educator Hamilton Music School Portland, Maine; [memb.] National Prano Foundation; [oth. writ.] "My Poetry does not come from me, it comes from others, from the people I see" (First line from poem, Dedicated in my unpublished book, Poetry from my heart) Unpublished at this time. My dedication - The Gift Of You - The Color Of Skin - Butterfly - The greatest Show On Earth - Sometimes I think I Would Like To Be...... (This one is a children's book) Friendship - Time - His Greatness - And Many Others.; [pers.] I have been writing poetry for my own pleasure through the inspiration of people that have touched my life. My Philosophy is simple: Every person that touches your life, becomes a part of it. Every minute of each day becomes a memory in your mind. When you open your heart to the people and open your mind to the memories of the day and let them fuse with soul, then your soul, then your inner talents will rise to the top. Talents you otherwise may never know you have.; [a.] Portland, Maine

RICCI, RALPH
[b.] October 10, 1914, Providence, RI; [p.] Raffaele and Concetta (Corbi) Ricci; [m.] Pauline D. Ricci, December 6, 1972; [ch.] Four (Christopher,Deceased) Olive, Elizabeth and Gerald; [ed.] Graduate - Providence Tech High 1931; [occ.] Volunteer - Senior Companion; [memb.] Masonic - Twice past master overseas lodge #40, member. Major General Henry Knox Lodge, 32 degrees Scottish Rite, York Rite, commandery Moslem Grotto, Shriner, Dav - Chapter 1, Retired - Its Printer's Union; [hon.] Award - Paralyzed Vets or America, RI Governor's Citation, Master's Certificate, Purple Heart Veteran; [oth. writ.] Correspondent - US

Army - WW II in Italy, Editor - Book Firm, Wash., DC., Correspondent - RI Freemason, Free Lance Writer for two local Weekly Paper; [pers.] I never write for money. The English language should be enjoyed by all and because of my Masonic Teachings, Charity and The Brotherhood of man are my gifts by choice; [a.] Warwick, RI

RICE, DOROTHY S.
[b.] January 26, 1927, Silverlake, KS; [p.] Berniece and Fred Seeman; [m.] Donald M. Rice, July 18, 1948; [ch.] Barbara and Robert; [ed.] Peoria Central H.S., Peoria Ill., University of Illinois - English, History, Philosophy; [occ.] Homemaker; [memb.] First Unittarian Universalist Church, Columbus, OH, Delta Delta Delta Soc, Sor.; [hon.] National Honor Soc. Alpha Lambda Delta, Deans List Outstanding History Student (high school); [oth. writ.] Effective Letters to Editors - and Washington D.C. Poetry for my pleasure; [pers.] I feel we are all responsible for own actions and reactions for whatever reason, and in the innate goodness of man, which is sometimes emotionally clouded, and that we are all one with a God Spirit. Experience is our difference; [a.] Jackson, OH

RICHARDS, ARLENE
[b.] March 23, 1970, Brooklyn, NY; [ed.] Malverne High School; [oth. writ.] "Correspondence", "All That's Not Done" many other poems, and am currently working on a story "Through a child's eyes"; [pers.] Ignorance is unnecessary and should be wiped out as often as possible.; [a.] West Hempstend, NY

RICHARDSON, DEAN
[pen.] Dean Alexander; [b.] February 21, 1970; [p.] Alden, Helen; [pers.] Marvel at an electric train set in motion, then entertain the possibilities. Let yourself not be distracted by those little puffs of smoke.; [a.] Columbia, SC

RICHARDSON, TOMMY
[b.] August 20, 1943, Granite City, IL; [p.] Clay and Erma Richardson; [m.] Shirley J. Tackett, December 3, 1983; [ch.] Tara M., John F., Danielle K., Rachel E.; [ed.] Granite City High, University of Maryland; [occ.] National Accounts Manager; [hon.] 101st Airborne Division; [oth. writ.] Much poetry; [a.] Lake Oswego, OR

RICHMOND, DAVID F.
[pen.] James Hinton; [b.] June 17, 1924, Hannibal, MO; [p.] W. W. and Mable Richmond; [m.] N. Berniece Riegel, December 22, 1946; [ch.] Meredith, Leah, Brian and Kyle; [ed.] B.S. N.H.S. Univ. MO, Ed. D. Colo. St. U.; [occ.] Retired-Ball Still. professor Muncie, Ind.; [memb.] Am. Psych. Assoc, Am. Counseling Assoc, Am. Fed. Trs. Union, K.A.P., AARP, Etc.; [pers.] We should appreciate all differences and uniqueness which are not hurtful, and strive to be loving and helpful to all whom we can reach.; [a.] Muncie, IN

RICHTER, SHARON L.
[b.] July 3, 1940, San Diego, CA; [ch.] two daughters, Donna Jean and Lisa Kay. Three grandchildren, Ashleigh, Hayleigh and David.; [occ.] Executive Secretary; [pers.] Mother of two, grandmother of three. I have dabbled in poetry most of my life. This is my first entry.; [a.] Tustin, CA

RIDDLEBAUGH, MARAGARET
[pen.] Margaret Campbell Riddlebaugh; [b.] August 5, Newark, OH; [p.] Lloyd and Ann Campbell; [ch.] Rose, Cheri, Jackie, Jennifer, and Kate; [ed.] Attended Utica High and North Central Tech.; [occ.] Personal and Care Giver and at T.O.P. Christian School; [memb.] International Society of Poets. Tabernacle of Praise, Advisory Board for Building Committee. Member of the Praise and Worship Team and Mime Leader of Troubadours'

For The King, Mime Troupe; [oth. writ.] Who Is This Main published in Journey of the Mind, and other printed in church news letter.; [pers.] A big thanks to all my family and friends who continually encourage me in my writing, and to God, who inspires me.; [a.] Bucyrus, OH

RIDEOUT, CATHERINE
[pen.] Catie Rideout; [b.] July 16, 1980, Waltham, MA; [p.] Eugene C. Rideout, Ruthanne Rideout; [ed.] John F. Kennedy Elementary School, Orland S. Marshall Middle School, Billerica Memorial High School; [occ.] Student at Billerica Memorial High School; [memb.] American Shorin-Ryu Karate Association, Billerica High Memorial High School Marching Band (Piccolo Section); [hon.] Billerica memorial High School SUMMA Award of May 1995, Honor Roll; [a.] Billerica, MA

RIDER, TIMOTHY EDWARD
[pen.] Edward Rider; [b.] September 18, 1963, Gainesville, GA; [p.] Lee Rider, Sonja Rider; [m.] Linda Rider, February 14, 1986; [ch.] Desi Ray Lane Rider - 7, Timothy "Levi" Rider - 5; [ed.] East Hall High School; [occ.] Welder; [memb.] I am of the Christian Faith; [oth. writ.] Just Because, Empty Pockets, New Lies for an Old Memory, Broken Fences, The Gift of the Moon and Stars, Runaway Train, Let's Do It Again, Levi's Prayer, Summer Daze with Desi Ray, The Stars are Full of Sky Tonight; [pers.] All my writings or of true life experiences in retrospect. The greatest any man can hope to achieve, is to be a good father.; [a.] Gainesville, GA

RIDLEY, SHANTAE
[b.] September 23, 1978; [p.] Andrea E. Wright; [ed.] High School, Sophomore, Manhattan Village Academy; [occ.] Student; [a.] New York, NY

RIEDY, ADELE RIEDY
[pen.] LAR; [b.] March 24, 1957, Lansing, MI; [p.] Victor A. and Marianne Zucco; [m.] Mark Raymond Riedy, September 6, 1980; [ch.] Brad Raymond Riedy, Brian Victor Riedy; [ed.] Graduation - Michigan State University in College of Nursing in 1979 with a Bachelor of Science in Nursing; [occ.] Pediatric Primary Care Nurse, Clinic Nurse, Public Health Nurse, Consultant. "Retired into motherhood and helping mark start an insurance agency, in Bellaire.; [memb.] Hold a current License as a registered nurse, and badge number as a Red Cross Nurse (volunteer). Chairperson for Antrim County Child Abuse and neglect council (volunteer) PTO Parent teacher Organization - Etracurricular (volunteer) chairperson 3 yrs.; [hon.] 1995 - Scholarship to MSU - "Violence - Free Michigan". Attend - Continuing Education Unit Conferences 3 to 4 times annually (volunteer) attend Antrim County Coordinating Council. (Volunteer) project: S.H.A.R.E; [oth. writ.] Focus on Holistic Health and Wellness first poem published in Junior High School - student paper, from creative writing class (8th grade) 1970.; [pers.] My poetry spans over 25 years revealing a poet's spiritual journey, kept private until now. I live on a river in Northern Michigan, and spend my time with family, volunteer efforts, Kayaking and of course reading and writing.; [a.] Bellaire, MI

RIETZ, FRANCES
[b.] March 15, 1921, WY; [p.] Bessie and James Irvine; [m.] Phil Rietz (Deceased), September 12, 1939; [ch.] Clara Ann Powers and Clayton Rietz; [ed.] High School; [occ.] Retired Rancher still living on Ranch; [memb.] Garden Club, 40 yrs.; [oth. writ.] I have 2 books of Poetry Published by myself. Not well known I have written 3 songs not published.; [pers.] I love the outdoors I write a lot of Western Cow boy. Stuff, I love the Lord and He helps with my writing. I grew up on a Wyoming Ranch with a horse and dog.; [a.] Wheatland, WY

RIGGS, BRENDA
[b.] February 3, 1959, Dallas, TX; [p.] Martha Hunter, Jerry Latimer; [ch.] Jessica Sue, Kyle Walter; [ed.] Forney High School; [occ.] Secretary; [oth. writ.] Gifts of poetry to friends and family; [pers.] I have found that my thoughts and feelings are more fully developed and ready to share when put into my writings. My poetry is inspired by everyday trials and triumphs. The rewards are greatest when my words seem to touch a reader.; [a.] Kilgore, TX

RILEY, DANNY
[b.] December 28, 1977, California; [p.] Jeannie and Brian Riley; [ed.] Senior The Bishop's School; [occ.] Student; [hon.] 1st Place Molly Martinek Creative Writing Award '92, 93, 94; [a.] Rancho Santa Fe, CA

RINALDI, NICOLE JEANINE
[b.] May 25, 1980, Perth Amboy, NJ; [p.] Nicholas and Joanne Rinaldi; [ed.] Currently a Freshman attending Marlboro High School, Marlboro, New Jersey; [occ.] Student; [oth. writ.] Several other poems, none of which have ever been published; [a.] Morganville, NJ

RISER, TOM
[b.] January 9, 1979, Wheeling, WV; [p.] Thomas III and Kimberly Sue; [ed.] Currently a sophomore at Wheeling Park High, with College plans; [memb.] Park Players Club at school; [hon.] Speech Team 6th place - Extemporaneous Speaking/Student of the Month December, 1994 - Performing Arts; [oth. writ.] Began writing short stories and poems in 9th grade. Enjoyed when I was younger. This is the first time to have anything published.; [pers.] I write about what I feel. I try to write things so that others can relate to them. I try to incorporate experiences in my life to my writing. My main goal is to write things I like.; [a.] Wheeling, WV

RITTER, HELEN E.
[pen.] Helen; [b.] September 22, 1934, York, PA; [p.] Mr. and Mrs. Earl Ritter Sr.; [ed.] Certificate in Journalism Attended Penn State, York College Graduated from Yorkstowne Business; [occ.] I am teaching Children Will be teaching children at Harriet Tubman School, Harlem, NY; [memb.] Belong to Ba-hai faith, am an activist and contributor to society; [hon.] Received a letter from Pres. Clinton for contribution to society. Lambda Sorority; [oth. writ.] Truth Is Power and God Talked To Me, Newsletter, Children's Book I am teach children creative writing at the Nepperhan center Yonkers, New York; [pers.] "A broken wing, wing will not work"; [a.] White Plains, NY

RITTERBECK, THERESA A.
[pen.] TR; [b.] August 27, 1953, Akron, OH; [p.] Paul J and Maida (Cogar) Ritterbeck; [pers.] More than face value of words, simile and metaphor. Play a great role in how I express experiences and influences that associate and inspire my writings, my meaning beyond the meaning.; [a.] Camden-On-Gauley, WV

RIVERA, DEBRA
[b.] October 2, 1977, Los Angeles, CA; [p.] Ven and Rita Rivera; [pers.] Kindest and most affectionate regards to David Joseph Wimer, my best friend, with love, and with thanks... for believing in me.; [a.] Glendale, CA

ROAN, CARLOS L.
[pen.] Archer; [b.] December 6, 1965, Jacksonville, FL; [p.] Robert and Pauline Roan; [ed.] Curie High School, Chicago IL; [occ.] Security guard; [oth. writ.] An untitled poem in the anthology Seasons to come; [pers.] I try to convey the message that despite one's own obstacles, that nothing is more enduring than the human spirit for which there are no measure or boundaries. Just one's own imagination.; [a.] Chicago, IL

ROAN, PIERRE H.
[pen.] Old Geezer; [b.] March 28, 1913, New Orleans, LA; [p.] James and Victoria Roan, Dec.; [m.] Elizabeth Strickland Roan, Dec, 1947; [ed.] High school Grad. Architect School self taught poet, song writer, artist; [occ.] Retired; [memb.] U.S. Army, 4 yrs. service Wold War II Palau-Okinawa 1941-45; [hon.] The honor of serving my country-1941-1945 Honorable Discharge-1945; [oth. writ.] Poem published in the Oakland Tribone; [pers.] Do unto others as you would have known unto you; [a.] Los Angeles, CA

ROBBINS, ELIZABETH
[pen.] Liz; [b.] September 26, 1978, Honesdale, PA; [p.] Linda Robbins; [ed.] Sophomore in High School; [occ.] Student, Waitress; [hon.] Honor Roll member; [oth. writ.] Symbol of..., Sauntering Along that Forlorn Road, Turquoise, Black, No Escape, Endless Search of Exit, Evening, and various others; [pers.] Life is too short to waste a day in a bad mood.; [a.] Honesdale, PA

ROBBINS, GLORIA J.
[b.] September 28, 1944; [m.] John Robbins; [ch.] Jeffrey and Dawn; [ed.] Jamestown High School, PA, New Castle Buss. Col. PA; [occ.] Church Secretary; [memb.] Board of Directors, Macon Co. Habitat for Humanity, first presbyterian church; [oth. writ.] Several poems and short stories; [pers.] My writing is influenced by personal feelings and relationship in my life.; [a.] Franklin, NC

ROBERTS, BYRON TERRYL
[pen.] Terry Roberts; [b.] April 19, 1922, Ontario, CA; [p.] Byron S. and Pearl M. Roberts; [m.] Phyllis J. Payne Roberts, August 3, 1952; [ch.] Julie, Tim, Chris and Margaret; [ed.] Greenville HS, (IL), 1940, Univ. of Redlands, (CA), BA, 1948, Koinonia Foundation, Adult Literacy, 1961, California State University at Los Angeles, MA, 1968; [occ.] Retired Educator, Literacy Trainer, CSLA 1989-93, Lect. and Writ, Official in Sport of Athletics (T&F) 1947-95, Comm, AAU, TAC, AOC, SCA, USA T&F, Liaison For & Assigner of Officials 1974-95. Training Official-Starters, CTSA 1973-95. Lecturer And Writer, Personal Travels And The Olympic Movement; [memb.] U.S.A.T.&F., C.T.S.A., C.T.A., A.A.R.P.; [hon.] 1984 L.A. Olympic Games T&F Official. 1988 Mt. SAC Relays Andy and Mary Bakjian Honor Roll of Officials, 1990 U.S.O.C. Delegate to The Interntl. Olympic Acd. at Olympia, Greece.; [oth. writ.] Ungrandfatherly Poems For Grandkids uv bugs and bees and flying fleas, More Poems For Grandkids, Lives Of Olympic Heroes From Which To Learn, Modern Oriental Legends, Ancient Greece As I Saw It, Short Stories Written While Traveling, Anecdotes By T&F, Officials and L.A.O.O.C. Volunteers Who Served During The 1984 Los Angeles Olympic Games, All You Ever Wanted To Know About The Marathon, And Then Some.; [pers.] Recently, The Medical Profession has publicly recognized the value of humor as an extender of life that also enriches it. I understood that long ago and learned to tell stories and jokes so others had an opportunity to smile. I also discovered the best way to assure long life... perhaps the only way ...is to preselect ancestors who lived long and happy lives, laughed a lot, played practical jokes on each other, lived fully and, not the least of all, were willing to share themselves, their knowledge and abilities for the benefit of others around them.; [a.] Calimesa, CA

ROBERTS, ESTHER M.
[pen.] Esther M. Roberts; [b.] March 10, 1959, Fort Worth, TX; [p.] Will J and Marie Roberts; [ed.] M.S. in Critical Care Nursing, UCSF, CA, B.S. in Nursing, Oklahoma Bapt. University, Rift Valley Academy, High School, Kenya East Africa; [occ.] Staff Nurse in a Critical Care Unit at a Medical Center; [memb.] 1. American Assoc. of Critical Care Nurses (Also local chapter) 2. Prior secretary with Local Unit Council of Calif. Nurses Assoc.; [hon.] 1. Advanced Cardiac Life Support Certification, 2. Critical Care Registered Nurse Certification (CCRN), 3. Cited Twice in "Who's Who Among Young American Professionals"; [oth. writ.] Published twice in University of California. S.F. Newspaper "Synapse"; [pers.] Cutting to the chase and describing life with authenticity is my goal. I write out of my experience, but also attempt to portray the human experience as I see it.; [a.] San Francisco, CA

ROBERTS, MARIE
[pen.] Lily Marie; [b.] November 19, 1960; [p.] Frances and George Roberts; [ch.] Danny and Brianna; [ed.] Rockdale Co. High; [occ.] Writer Volunteer Work at Nursing Homes; [memb.] International Society of Poets; [hon.] Editor's Choice Award for Windows of Heaven, 1st Honors in Medical School; [oth. writ.] Working on my Autobiography titled "Absolution" various poems and songs. World's Largest Poem for Peace titled Love and Peace; [pers.] I wish to thank these special people that have touched me someone and inspired my poetry Tim and Neil Finn, Jan, O'Connor, Delayne Gentry Sandy Campbell, Diane and Jay Lozier and Elaine Spears; [a.] Conyers, SA

ROBINETTE, MARTHA
[b.] May 7, 1922, Frostburg, MD; [p.] Alfred and Elizabeth Kelso Hunter; [m.] Paul Robinette, November 3, 1946; [ch.] Carl Eugene, Larry Edward, and George Earnest; [ed.] Fort Hill High School; [occ.] Housewife; [memb.] Zion United Methodist Church, September Singers (Singing group); [oth. writ.] Several Poems - None Published; [pers.] "Doing the tasks you don't like to do, builds character."; [a.] Flintstone, MD

ROBINSON, DOROTHY S. B. B.
[pen.] Othelia Olivier; [b.] April 23, 1939, John's Island, SC; [p.] Richard and Flora Simmons; [m.] Esau Robinson II (Divorced), August 23, 1958; [ch.] Valerie, Esau III and Amy Denise Robinson; [ed.] I attended S. E. State College, Seattle, Trident College, The College of Charleston only, Columbia's University, I am a graduate of Manhattan Medical Assistant School for Roentgen Technologist; [occ.] My occupation, currently is Holy Scriptures, Poetry Writing; [hon.] No honors except that of a Certify Roentgen Technologist; [oth. writ.] I am the Author of Hyllsyde Poems, a collection of poems created by me exclusively with Sweet Ba Ta Touh (God), Interlocking in the Holy Spirit Dr. Jean-Helior Bermingham; [pers.] Summer's Gone (which mean's Summer is Gone) abbreviation style. P.S. Presently I'm an unpublish author but, hope to become it someday soon.; [a.] John's Island, SC

RODABAUGH, SHIRLEY B.
[hon.] I have received awards, and nominated Best Poet of 1995; [oth. writ.] My poetry is published in a View from the Edge, at Days end, beyond the Stars, The World's Largest Peace Poem and The Best Poems of 1995; [pers.] I write to make God's wondrous work visible to the world, the work of Jesus Christ grace and healing love, and the Holy Spirit.; [a.] Williamsport, PA

RODRIGUEZ, ERIN
[pen.] Jo; [b.] August 8, 1979, Mount Vernon; [p.] Diane and Jesse Rodriguez; [ed.] 9th grade High School; [oth. writ.] Only Poetry; [pers.] I have been writing poetry for many years now I have always felt that it was the only way to express. How I feel, a stress reliever; [a.] Lynnwood, WA

RODRIGUEZ, GLORIA M.
[b.] September 5, 1940, Philipsburg, PA; [p.] Felix and Anne Rodriguez; [ed.] B.S. in Architecture; [occ.] Designer/Builder; [memb.] Construction Specifications Institute (CSI); [pers.] Nature is my greatest draw for inspiration and contentment.; [a.] Hercules, CA

RODRIGUEZ, MANUEL
[pen.] Manny Rodriguez; [b.] December 21, 1975, Brooklyn, NY; [p.] Maria Rodriguez; [ed.] F.D.R. High, currently attending Baruch College, Majoring in English Literature; [oth. writ.] Several short stories, music reviews, and articles published in Baruch's newspaper, The Ticker; [pers.] I want to create poetry that will change thought infinitely and represent my peoples. My greatest influences have been hip-hop and the lack of answers that push me deeper.; [a.] Brooklyn, NY

RODRIGUEZ, MARIA OLSON
[b.] December 25, 1945, El Paso, TX; [p.] Conrad and Myrtle Olson; [m.] Benito Rodriguez; [ch.] Rachel, Joseph, and Virginia; [ed.] Graduate of High School and Graduate 1 yr. College for a C.N.A.; [hon.] Safety Cadet, Gold Plaque for Music Soloist for the State of Wisconsin. Honor Art Student in High School; [pers.] God is my personnel guide of life that surrounds me with a world of beauty.; [a.] Milwaukee, WI

ROGERS, CHRISTOPHER
[b.] July 15, 1966, Rochester, NY; [p.] Thomas and Karen Rogers; [m.] Ruth Davis Rogers, October 26, 1991; [ch.] Catherine; [ed.] University of Houston (Clear Lake) M.A. Humanities, Auburn University M.S. Industrial Engineering; [occ.] Engineering Psychologist; [memb.] Space Coast Writers' Guild, Human Factors and Ergonomics Society; [pers.] The verses here express the ideas found in Plato's Symposium. My goal is to dramatized these ideas in a story and in characters. In my recently completed novel (now seeking publication), the contemporary rise from desiring social acceptance and pleasure to desiring Beauty (and that which is higher). We all live these ideas, quietly, the story, however, brings them to life in a romance and adventure.; [a.] Melbourne, FL

ROGOZINSKI, DIANE
[pen.] Deeds; [b.] February 1, 1961, Pittsburgh, PA; [ed.] Carrick High School, Dale Carnegie, and Pennsylvania Insurance Agents' Licensing; [occ.] Commercial Insurance Underwriter, Sweet and Sons, Inc., Mt. Lebanon, PA; [memb.] National Multiple Sclerosis Society; [oth. writ.] "Michael, My Love", sung by Beverly G on the album Now Sounds of Today, "Lost and Found" in the book A Time To Be Free; [pers.] Live to be happy, be happy to life. Believe in the unexpected, but don't expect the unbelievable.; [a.] Pittsburgh, PA

ROHR, CRYSTAL
[b.] April 8, 1980, Beeville, TX; [p.] George Rohr, Ginnie Rohr; [ed.] Freshman - George West High School; [occ.] Student; [memb.] George West 7HA, George West 4H, Three Rivers First Baptist Church Acteens, George West Longhorn Band - 4 years; [hon.] Three years - 1st chair flute, 1993 All American Scholar Award, 1993 US Achievement Academy National Award, 1994-94 George West Band Squad Leader, 1995 VIL Solo and Ensemble Medalist, 1995 - ATSSB All District Band, 1995 - ATSSB All Region Band, 1995 - George West High School Band Outstanding Freshman Bandsman, 1995-96 - George West High School Band Drill Instructor and Second Assistant Drum Major; [pers.] I have been greatly influenced, inspired by the writings of poet Lord Byron. Reflected in my poems are feelings surrounding me at that time.; [a.] George West, TX

ROHR JR., EDWARD J.
[pen.] E. J.; [b.] September 27, 1958, Kansas; [p.] Ed and Charlene Rohr; [occ.] Owner Rohr Studios; [a.] Chicago, IL

ROIZEN, JENNIFER L.
[pen.] Jenny Roizen; [b.] August 3, 1981, San Francisco, CA; [p.] Nancy Roizen and Michael Roizen; [ed.] V of C Lab High School (freshman); [occ.] Student; [memb.] National Lib. Poet, YMCA, AYSO; [oth. writ.] Finally Happy, ?? I forgot what they were called; [pers.] My poetry makes the most important part of myself come alive, my imagination... If it does the same for you, I have found my place.; [a.] Chicago, IL

ROLAND, MELTON MICK
[pen.] Mick; [b.] September 21, 1968; [p.] Melton Roland Sr., June-Ellen Carroll; [ed.] Marmaton Valley H.S. Moran KS; [occ.] Computer Technician; [memb.] VA Army National Guard; [pers.] I would like to dedicate all of my writings in memory of my Mother June-Ellen Carroll. Now God enjoys her wit.; [a.] Winchester, VA

ROLLE, ANDREW S.
[pen.] Steven Andrews; [b.] October 24, 1952, Bahamas; [p.] Florence and Elbridge Brown; [m.] Zelma C., March 30, 1985; [ch.] Livenia, Andrea, Tomeka, Alvilda, Andrew II and Richard; [ed.] A. F. Adderely High Nassau, Bahamas, Bahamas Hotel College and Frec Real Estate, Orlando; [occ.] Real Estate Broker; [memb.] Board of Realtors; [oth. writ.] Many unpublished letters, essays and poems; [pers.] I've been touched by knowledge, through understanding and shaped by wisdom.; [a.] Sanford, FL

ROLLINS, PENNY
[b.] March 25, 1963, Phoenix, AZ; [p.] Viola Carr, Ben Lyons; [ch.] Thomas, Jason, Amber Joey, Jessalyn and Samantha; [ed.] Tempe High; [occ.] Student, Mesa Collage; [pers.] I am greatly inspired by the most important people in my life, my 6 children, family, and my dear friend Cary.; [a.] Tempe, AZ

ROSENBAUM, TANYA BETH
[pen.] Tanya Beth Rosenbaum; [b.] April 16, 1973, Summit, NJ; [p.] Dr. Bernard Rosenbaum and Mrs. Susan Rosenbaum; [ed.] Kent Place School, Rhode Island School of Design, Pre-College Program, Washington University and Drew University; [occ.] Student; [memb.] ASPCA and Kent Place School Alumnae; [hon.] N.J. Governor's School of the Arts Scholarship, 1st place in Newark Academy Juried Art Show, 1990 and 1991, Carol P. Dorian Art Award; [pers.] This poem is dedicated to my Dad.; [a.] Westfield, NJ

ROSINSKI, JENNIFER
[b.] October 21, 1976, New York City; [p.] Eileen and Walter Rosinski; [ed.] Graphic Communication Arts H.S., Emerson College, Boston, MA; [occ.] Summer Operations Intern, Time Inc., New York City; [hon.] Dean's List, Journalism scholarships, Who's Who Among H.S. students U.S. National Leadership Award, Pride of the NY Yankees Award, Outstanding H.S. Journalist, Comptroller's Award, Press Club Award, Best in New Journalism; [oth. writ.] Several poems in various anthologies, every H.S. publication, Jewish Museum Brochure, College newspaper, The Berkeley Beacon - Features Editor/Reporter; [pers.] Life is like chocolate: smooth, rich, and satisfying, but also consequential, satisfying, but also consequential, hazardous to your health, and destructive Make of it what you can!! Writing is the one true way I can express myself - I rejoice in its existence daily.; [a.] New York, NY

ROSS, MARLENE LANETTE
[pen.] M. Lanette Ross; [oth. writ.] This poem has a tune and has also been copy written as a song we have written many other songs and poems, together and separately.; [pers.] We love songwriting and poetry. We hope to have our songs published as well.; [a.] Clinton, IN

ROTNER, MARY J.
[b.] August 15, 1952, Milwaukee, WI; [p.] Dr. Melvin Rotner, Joy Rotner; [ch.] Rosie Rotner, Dan Rotner; [ed.] Our Lady of Peace High School, Providence School of Nursing and Spring Hill College; [occ.] Registered Nurse; [hon.] Judge William V. McDermott Award 1973; [oth. writ.] (A Novella) "Our Love Will Survive", "A Second Chance of Love", "Dreaming", "A New Love Begins" (Short stories), Poems, "Taking The Bear", Short stories, "BIZAK" The Destroyer, "The Road Warrior"; [pers.] Love: The only thing eternal, a gift from God. May it always shine through in my writings and warm those it touches.

ROUNTREE, PAMELA BAINBRIDGE GOODWIN
[b.] November 10, 1956, Montgomery, AL; [p.] L.O. (Pete) Goodwin Jr., Ernestyne (Tyna) Moore Goodwin; [m.] Douglas Boone Rountree, February 26, 1982; [ch.] Boone Goodwin Rountree (step children: Michelle, Cindy, Stephen); [ed.] Autauga Academy, Troy State University Montgomery; [occ.] Self-employed - Business - Goodwin Enterprises, Star Tree Talent Agency; [memb.] 1st Baptist Church, APT Board Member at Prattville Elementary School, Alabama Filmmakers Assoc. - Board Member, Various Volunteer work; [hon.] American Cancer Society, Various community and National Volunteer Organizations; [oth. writ.] Several Poems and Children books (Have not tried to publish yet); [pers.] My poems come from my heart - my children's books from personal experience. We all should carry love in our hearts and a smile on our face.; [a.] Prattville, AL

ROWTON, KATHRYN
[pen.] Kathryn; [b.] June 13, 1979, Wharton, TX; [p.] Mr. and Mrs. Andy Rowton; [ed.] I'm a 10th grader in High School; [memb.] Member of the National Library of Poetry; [hon.] An award in poetry. Honors for grades in school.; [oth. writ.] "Distant" published in Journey of the mind. Others basically describing feelings of all kinds; [pers.] "It's always confusing to get where things seem calm." A saying I thought of that keeps me looking a head instead of behind.; [a.] El Campo, TX

RUDECINDO, SAGRARIO
[b.] October 20, 1973, Bronx, NY; [ed.] Mother Cabrini High School, Marist College; [occ.] Student; [memb.] Sorority Sigma, Sigma, Sigma Inc.; [pers.] I dedicate this poem to my beautiful sister Maribel. We all have guardian Angels, never lose hope.; [a.] Jamaica Estates, NY

RUDLONG, BECKY
[pen.] Ellie; [b.] May 8, 1981, Anoka; [p.] Ron and Lisa Rudlong; [ed.] 7th grade student at Cambridge Junior High School; [occ.] "The Lion King" collector; [memb.] Was a member of D.A.R.E at the age of 12 years old; [hon.] Years ago I entered an invention fair and received a second place award for my "Re Jug" invention. At Saint Cloud, MN.; [oth. writ.] I have other poems that I have written but have never submitted them; [pers.] I love the earth and its surroundings. Together we shall all make it better today and then on. Hopefully!!; [a.] Cambridge, MN

RUIU, ALBERT S.
[pen.] Awaye; [b.] July 16, 1969, Bayonne, NJ; [p.] Bernard and Rolene Ruiu; [ed.] Widener University Chester, PA; [oth. writ.] Volumes sitting on my desk; [pers.] Poetry is a theatre of words we use them everyday to Communicate, Exaggerate, Intimidate, and Misinterpret; [a.] Bayonne, NJ

RUPE, MELISSA R.
[pen.] Marie M. Roop; [b.] January 10, 1976, Roswell, NM; [p.] Michael and Janet Rupe; [m.] Michael A. Hernandez, October 12, 1995; [ch.] Jonathan G. Hernandez; [ed.] Home Schooled by parents; [occ.] Mother, Housewife, Student of life; [hon.] Purple ribbon awarded for my performance on the Balence Beam. Nomination for poet of the year 1995.; [oth. writ.] Unpublished; [pers.] In thanks, respect and tremendous love to the great influences who gave me life.; [a.] Clovis, NM

RUSSELL, KATIE
[pen.] Katie Suzanne Russell; [b.] September 7, 1977, Wilmington, DE; [p.] Anita and Larry Russell; [ed.] Junior in High School Senior 1996 Graduate; [hon.] Who's Who The publication of my poem Pressure; [oth. writ.] Poem - My Turn Book Currently typing up - All the Luck Mother's Day Poem - wrote for my Mom, Anita; [pers.] Don't ever let anyone tell you can't do something. You can!; [a.] Belton, TX

RUSSELL, LINDA L.
[b.] August 7, 1960, Des Moines, IA; [p.] Keith and Edna Eakins; [m.] Anthony Russell, August 26, 1978; [ch.] Anthony, Jessica; [ed.] Urbandale High, Des Moines Area Comm. College; [occ.] CGS Specialist, The Principal Financial Group; [memb.] PTA, Windsor Heights Lutheran Church, LOMA; [hon.] FLMI, ACS; [pers.] I strive to lift readers to a higher plane of thinking and feeling thru my writing.; [a.] Des Moines, IA

RUTH, PENNY L.
[b.] August 7, 1973, Indiana; [p.] Dennis and Deborah Ruth; [ed.] Northern Virginia Community College Pensacola Christian College Moanalua High School; [occ.] Administrative Assistant at SETA Corp.; [oth. writ.] "The Real Me", Interact "I Am", The Source; [pers.] "Quality is never an accident, it is always the result of intelligent effort." John Ruskin; [a.] Springfield, VA

RUTLEDGE, JACK
[b.] September 4, 1911, Mont. Giltedge; [m.] Geraldine, June 30, 1965; [ed.] Graduate Arizona Bible College; [occ.] Semi-retired, Realtor- Bible Teacher; [memb.] First Southern Baptist Church Glendale, Arizona; [oth. writ.] Several poems and anecdotes locally; [pers.] Attitudes, characteristics and nature alone with changing time have always interested me.; [a.] Sun City, AZ

RUTON, MILDRED K.
[pen.] Mildred Marsh Ruton; [b.] November 2, 1906, Kirkwood-Bridgeport, OH; [p.] Jos. Clarence and Pearl Fonner Marsh; [m.] Edgar H. Ruton (Deceased), October 15, 1947; [ch.] Two sons, one deceased (by former marriage); [ed.] Graduate or Wheeling High School, Wheeling West Virginia and self taught thereafter plus travel; [occ.] Stand-up comic, retired, Former Park Mgr. and Operator, Show Business, Many Office Positions, Employment Counsellor etc.; [memb.] Currently - 44 years member Chapter 305 Order of Eastern Start Member and Past President of the Silver Club of Newark, Member of Licking County Acing Program, Distinguished Member 1 SP; [hon.] Editors Choice Award from National Library of Poetry; [oth. writ.] Currently Completing A Children's Book (not yet published); [pers.] Live your life in such away that you'll never be

embarrassed about any truths uttered about you.; [a.] Newark, OH

RUZECKI, VIVIAN
[pen.] Vivian Siegfried; [b.] July 8, 1930, Milwaukee, WI; [p.] Lorraine and Paul Siegfried; [m.] Don Ruzecki (Deceased), June 20, 1964; [ch.] Donald Paul Ruzecki; [ed.] Grammer St Cornelius High School - St. Patrick, Grammer - Von Humboldt, Graduate 1994 June, High School - Tuley High, Graduate 1948, June; [occ.] Retired, Senior Citizen, Job Associate; [memb.] "Many"; [hon.] "Many"; [pers.] I have been greatly influenced by the early romantic poets - (Metcalf) etc.; [a.] Chicago, IL

RZEZNICZEK, JAMES
[pen.] Jim Rez; [b.] December 31, 1944, Chicago, ILL; [p.] Chester and Mary Rzezniczek; [ed.] Foreman High School; [occ.] Retired Former Service MGR. Volkswagen; [memb.] Mystery Science Theater 3,000, Little City; [hon.] Distinguished Service Award from Volkswagen of America; [oth. writ.] A few unpublished poems; [pers.] Try never to lie, if the truth hurts then keep quite or just walk away, sometimes a lie is more painful then the truth.; [a.] Addison, IL

SABUR, TAMI ABDUL
[pen.] James Williams; [b.] December 13, 1958, Tuskegee, AL; [p.] Phillip J. and Eunice L. Williams; [m.] Norma Jean Williams, October 22, 1977; [ch.] Laquanda, Latoya, Tamika, Latterance, and Devosky Williams; [ed.] Trinity Valley Comm. College, Athens, Texas (A. S. Degree) Sidney Lanier High, Montgomery, AL; [occ.] Baker, A/C and Heating Tec, and martial arts instructor; [hon.] Associate in Science, overseas ribbon, several ribbons as from active duty; [oth. writ.] Several other's of which I've written for friends and family to help brighten their days, such as "Dreams of Life," and "With in My Reach."; [pers.] From with in one's self lies the greatest achievements of all, the knowledge of self brings about better judgment of many. Remember one's potential are like rubber if you never stretch it you'll never know how.; [a.] San Antonio, TX

SACCO, TONY
[b.] October 2, 1953, St. Charles, MO; [p.] Joseph and Marie; [m.] Divorced; [ch.] Jared, son 19, Andrea, daughter 14; [ed.] High School Grad; AA Degree from college (community) in Business Administration; [occ.] U.S. Postal Service; [hon.] Two beautiful children who love me, everything else is secondary; [oth. writ.] My own compilation upon request; I have pleased, shocked, staggered and befriended all who have scanned my emotional journey from Penance and Hell-to-Peace; [pers.] I awoke my dormant "skill" while serving a 26 day internment in the custody of the Orange County Jail. I could not "close" a horribly sick relationship. I was diagnosed a "co-dependant." My poetry my escape tunnel.; [a.] Fountain Valley, CA

SADLIER, ROBERT CHARLES
[pen.] Robert Charles Sadlier; [b.] July 11, 1972, Taunton, MA; [p.] Robert and Geraldine Sadlier; [m.] Tammy Sadlier, September 17, 1994; [ed.] Bristol Plymouth Regional Vocational Terminal High School; [occ.] Press Operator; [memb.] International Society of poets; [oth. writ.] A Young Girls Dream, My Children, My Race, Blood, and The Hunter, are several of my other poems that have been published.; [pers.] As a writer I take a lot of letters and stirring them together in such a way that I hope will make sense to whoever reads them. I write what I feel, from the heart.; [a.] Middleboro, MA

SAKAI, MARI
[b.] November 1, 1979, Japan; [p.] Toshinao and Yoko Sakai; [ed.] Freshman at Ridgewood High School; [occ.] Student; [pers.] I want to take this opportunity to thank all of those who encouraged and supported me through writing poems. I strive to write better poems by expressing my true and honest feelings.; [a.] Ridgewood, NJ

SAKATA, GERALD
[pen.] Jiro, Jerry; [b.] September 28, 1948, Stockton; [p.] Frank and Alice Sakata; [ed.] Edison High, S.J. Delta Community College, Sac. St. Univ., Univ. of the Pacific, San Jose St. Univ., Stanislaus St. Univ.; [occ.] Entrepreneur; [memb.] Entrepreneurs exchange, Asian Pacific Islander Political Alliance and Asian-American Alliance of San Joaquin County; [hon.] Bowling Awards, Basketball Awards; [oth. writ.] Pacific Citizen, Karma (Newspaper and Buddhist Temple Newsletter) "Imbibe" moon, willow poetry series.; [pers.] "I've always felt it worthy of others to help one another... and to preach!"; [a.] Stockton, CA

SALERNO, CHARLES
[b.] December 27, 1967, Queens, NY; [ed.] BS (Chemistry) S.U.N.Y. at Stony Brook M.S. (University of Calif., San Diego) Chemistry, Doctoral Candidate; [occ.] Research Assistant, Doctoral Candidate, Univ Calif. San Diego, Chemistry; [a.] La Jolla, CA

SALIS, MIKE
[b.] August 9, 1967, Mount Prospect, IL; [ed.] MFA in painting from Bowling Green State University; [occ.] Independent Artist and Art Instructor; [oth. writ.] Vincent Speaks about the life and art of Vincent Van Gogh, Philosophical essays, and several poems.; [pers.] Through my work, I strive to achieve an understanding of the ultimate reality underlying all things, including humanity's place in the universe.; [a.] Albuquerque, NM

SAMPSON, VIRGINIA P.
[pen.] Virginia P. Farnum; [b.] March 16, 1919, Saginaw, MI; [p.] Ella and Russell Farnum; [m.] Deceased (1978), March 14, 1964; [ed.] 12th Grade High School; [occ.] Retired; [oth. writ.] These poems were written for my 12th grade English Literature class in 1938. I've kept them with my memories all these year.; [pers.] My teacher gave me an A - for the poem I sent in.; [a.] Sandusky, MI

SANCHEZ, ANGEL
[b.] January 10, 1074, Mexico; [p.] Olga Ayala; [m.] Bogaciano Sanchez, October 14, 1995; [ed.] High School (Santa Ana, CA) I will get enroll on College; [occ.] Painter my further plan is to become a computer programer; [memb.] Church's Club - Jovenes Para Cristo; [hon.] A project to help users of drugs and alcohol. (Proyecto Concieneia) Human Relations; [oth. writ.] I haven't published any of my hundred poems. I have them in spanish and english. But as soon I get an opportunity I will show mu talent and skills.; [pers.] I believe that dreams do not create you, you create them. Thus you got the magic to make them come true.; [a.] Atlanta, GA

SANCHEZ, CHANTELL R.
[pen.] Chantell Uhl Sanchez; [b.] September 25, 1968, Stratford, NJ; [p.] Richard and Anella Uhl; [m.] Douglas M. Sanchez, October 20, 1990; [ch.] Danielle C. Sanchez and Douglas M. Sanchez Jr.; [ed.] Overbrook Regional Sr. High; [occ.] Mother/homemaker; [memb.] NJ Licensed Beautician since 1987; [oth. writ.] Overbrook Reg. Sr. High newspaper - Front page headline story and 2 poems.; [pers.] I am inspired by the events in my life, the people I love and the true feelings

of my heart of which none would be possible without God.; [a.] Washington Township, NJ

SANCHEZ, R. F.
[pen.] R. F. Sanchez; [b.] June 5, 1927, El Paso, TX; [p.] Deceased; [m.] Helen, 1947; [ch.] Anita, Victor, Daniel, David; [ed.] B.A. University of Texas at El Paso; [occ.] Author, Newspaper Columnist (El Paso times); [memb.] Lions Club, National Association of Hispanic Journalists, National Turf Writers Assn., University of Texas at El Paso Library board; [hon.] Scripps-Howard awards for (1) Column Writing and (2) Reporting, University of Texas at El Paso Mass Communications Award for Excellence in journalism, El Paso Athletic Hall of Fame, Certificates of appreciation from El Paso County and city of El Paso.; [oth. writ.] Books: The God's of Racing, Haskins: The Bear Facts, El Paso's Greatest Sports Heroes, Basketball's Biggest Upset.; [a.] El Paso, TX

SANDERS, DAVID JOE
[pen.] David Joe Sanders; [b.] September 26, 1946, Sylva, NC; [p.] David and Katy Sanders; [m.] Brenda L. Sanders, September 17, 1975; [ch.] David Joe Sanders Jr.; [ed.] Western Carolina University, Winston-Salem State University, Major: English, Minor: Speech and Theatre; [occ.] Retired, Free-lance writer; [memb.] AMVETS; [hon.] Alpha Psi Omega; [oth. writ.] National High School Poetry Anthology, The western Carolinian, The Nomad, National College Poetry Anthology, Pegasus; [a.] Emerald Isle, NC

SANDERS, LA QUITA
[b.] January 3, 1981, Houston, TX; [p.] Jay and Wanda Sanders; [memb.] Top Teen Sorority, Church Choir; [oth. writ.] Many other poems that have never been published; [pers.] I my self believe that every one has a special gift and thru God the most impossible things can come true.; [a.] Missouri, TX

SANDERSON, D. L.
[pen.] D. L. Sharkey; [b.] 1984, Kansas; [p.] Deceaced; [m.] Landy R. Sanderson, December 31, 1994; [ch.] Hers- Raised 5 (four boys, one girl) Buried 1 his - 4 (three girls, one boy); [ed.] Elementary Kansas, High School Denver, CO, College-Tucson AZ, Professional-Las Vegas, NV; [occ.] Housewife; [memb.] (Former) Red Cross instructor - 9 years, BSA - Adult Leader/ Trainer 12 yrs., R.E.A.C.T. - five years; [hon.] Certified Electronics tech. 1976, M.A. 1987, Red Cross 1993, Editor's Choice Award, 1993; [oth. writ.] Prayer Published in local newspaper, read during morning news-CBS local affiliate, two other poems published in other anthologies, other poems published in church bulletin, "Kids In Action" newsletter, Constitution's Bi-Centennial writing in White House; [pers.] Though it were the last, live every today as love my neighbors and friends as though each were the only one in the world, whatever the task, do it with the best of admit it, go from there, and be sure I forgive me.; [a.] Las Vegas, NV

SANDOVAL, PATRICIA
[pen.] Patty, Tricia; [b.] April 27, 1978; [p.] Mr. and Mrs. Kamiro Sandoval; [ed.] 9 Yrs at St. John Bosco, 3 at Bishop Noll Institute; [occ.] Secretary at St. John Bosco and a cashier; [hon.] Award in finishing workshops in Photography, yearbook and newspaper, awards received in recognition for work being published; [oth. writ.] Acts of Love published in BNI'S, Literary Work in 1994 Call 'Montage', Poems published in Quill, Iliad Press, Sparrowgrass, Poet's Guild, and Amherst; [pers.] Whenever in doubt about others, believe in yourself. You are your future.; [a.] Hammond, IN

SANDY, CORINNE
[b.] November 3, 1978, OH; [p.] Judie Sandy, Lance Sandy; [ed.] St. Peter and Paul Elementary School, Brecksville Broadview Heights High School; [occ.] Student; [memb.] Drama Club, Garfield Heights Softball; [hon.] Honor Roll, Right to Life Poster Winner, M.V.P. of Volleyball Award, chosen to play on a cities all-Star Team; [oth. writ.] Numerous poems and short stories that are unpublished.; [pers.] Capture the time and make it more precious than life. Realize the lucky only understand the unexplained.; [a.] Broadview, OH

SANKS, JEFF
[b.] La Jolla, CA; [oth. writ.] Many collaborations with composers from Norway and Germany; [pers.] I only hope that I see the rewriting of man human and child. Of late I write for "The Children"; [a.] Scottsdale, AZ

SANTA, CHARLOTTE PRESTON
[b.] December 28, 1946, Deland, FL; [p.] Edward Preston and Mary A. Harte; [m.] Joseph Anthony Santa, November 21, 1990; [ed.] Registered Nurse 1969, Certified Addiction Professional 1984, Licensed Clinical Social Worker - 1986 Psychotherapist, Private Practice; [occ.] Psychotherapist, Lecturer, Community Organizer; [memb.] National Association Social Workers, Habitat for Humanity (Partner), Former member Fla. Nurses Association. 3 years tenure on United Way-Family Service Agency Board of Directors.; [hon.] Clinical Excellence Honoree: Fla., Nurses Assn. State of Fla. Student Excellence Scholarship. Awarded several merit scholarships.; [oth. writ.] Self-reflection only.; [pers.] I've spent a lifetime processing personal tragedies into compelling and propelling triumphs. Essentially alone, I've spent untold time in the black abyss between life and death.; [a.] Crescent City, FL

SANTANA, MAYRA DELUCAS
[b.] August 3, 1982, VCMC; [p.] Esther Santana and Mario Delucas; [ed.] I love to learn things everyday. The school in currently attending is Blackstock Jr. High and I am in the 7th grade; [occ.] Right now Im working in future leaders (junior carriers); [hon.] I recently received an award from point Magu Base The Black Employment program committee for a essay on Booker Twashinton, and prejudice; [oth. writ.] In my spare time I sit and if I have any real good or bad feelings and write more poems.; [pers.] I hope you enjoyed reading it because I certainly enjoyed writing it.; [a.] Oxhard, CA

SANTIAGO, ANGELA
[b.] July 21, 1948, Mobile, AL; [p.] Tim Allen, Winnie Allen; [m.] John Santiago; [ch.] Natasha, Cheressa and Nathan; [ed.] Theodore High School; [occ.] Receptionist and Phone Operator; [hon.] Publication's printed in the San Juan Star, Puerto Rico; [pers.] I have just became interested in poetry. I found myself wanting to write poems. I love music and find, it relates to poetry. I play piano and organ.; [a.] Mobile, AL

SAPIA, NATASHA DEA
[pen.] Natasha Briggs; [b.] October 7, 1973, Lubbock, TX; [p.] Nathan and Sonda Baxter; [m.] Nelson L. Sapia Jr., June 29, 1993; [ch.] Katie Bree'ann and Nathaniel Roland; [ed.] Pacific High; [occ.] Mother and Wife; [oth. writ.] I have written many other unpublished poems and short stories.; [pers.] I use the love and support of my husband and children to help me bring out God's wonderful gift, the ability to entertain and move others with my writings.; [a.] Colts Neck, NJ

SAPUTELLI, SHARON
[b.] January 15, 1973, Drexelhill, PA; [p.] Raymond and Marlene Saputelli; [ed.] Archbishop Prendcergast High School, Drexel University (Junior); [occ.] Dietetic Technician and 76 years Cheer leader; [memb.] ADA (American Diatetic Assoc.); [hon.] Dean's Award for outstanding Academic Achievement in Dietetics, Phi Eta Sigma (freshman Honor Society), Dean's list; [pers.] I wrote this poem for a school project to be used as an educational material. They say that necessity is the mother of invention - I guess they were right!; [a.] Drexel Hill, PA

SAUNDERS, AMY
[b.] April 17, 1979, Fairfax, VA; [p.] Howard and Debora Saunders; [ed.] Stonewall Jackson High School; [occ.] Full time student, part time work at Merrifield Garden Center; [memb.] World Wildlife Fund National Wildlife Federation; [hon.] Various academic awards; [oth. writ.] Poetry published in local paper; [pers.] In my poetry, I try to reflect the beauty of nature, as well as the dangers facing wildlife around the world.; [a.] Gainesville, VA

SAUNDERS, KATHRYN R.
[pen.] Kate Routledge; [b.] December 19, 1970, San Antonio, TX; [p.] Ann Saunders Muffeny, Don Saunders; [ed.] Awty International School, William Wood College, San Antonio College, Incarnate Word College; [occ.] Student; [memb.] Delta Gamma Sorority - Delta Omega Chapter, PADI - Scuba diving; [oth. writ.] Various poems that are unpublished; [pers.] I have a learning disability, and I thought that meant that I was not good enough to achieve anything. What I learned was that if you want something and you work hard at it - there is nothing that can stop you from achieving it.; [a.] San Antonio, TX

SAUNDERS, TRACIE
[pen.] Tracie O'Neil-Saunders; [b.] February 22, 1960, Glens Falls, NY; [p.] Terry and Marilyn O'Neil; [m.] Scott Saunders, December 4, 1984; [ch.] Christopher Bartholomew, Benjamin Scott and Alexandra Elizabeth; [ed.] High School, some college, Army Language School - Korean; [occ.] Personal Fitness Trainer, Aspiring Writer; [hon.] Army commendation medal, Good Conduct Medal, Overseas Service Ribbon; [oth. writ.] Children's story poems, Short stories, currently working on a book.; [pers.] I enjoy writing children's stories, using my own children's names. I like writing stories that are fun and capture a child's attention, while providing an ending with a moral standard.; [a.] Springfield, VA

SAYLORS, LAURIE KENDALL
[b.] November 25, 1949, Detroit, MI; [p.] Glen Arthur Kendall, Jane Chamberlin Kendall; [m.] Gene Saylors; [ch.] Bill and Bob Gookin; [ed.] Oxford, Michigan; [oth. writ.] Small personal collection of writings and poems, none previously submitted for publication.; [pers.] I experienced a tremendous tragedy and loss of family in my teen years. It is through recent efforts to write that I have begun to understand and appreciate my past. Some of my strongest feelings have found expression, and the written words have put relief, fulfillment and real pride in place of persistent despair.; [a.] El Cajon, CA

SAYLORS, LAURIE KENDALL
[b.] November 25, 1949, Detroit MI; [p.] Glen Arthur Kendall, Jane Chamberlin Kendall; [m.] Gene Saylors; [ch.] Bill and Bob Gookin; [ed.] Oxford, Michigan; [oth. writ.] Small collection of writings and poems, none previously submitted for publication.; [pers.] I experienced a tremendous tragedy and loss of family in my teen years. It is through recent efforts to write that I have begun to understand and appreciate my past. Some of my strongest feelings have found expression, and the written words have put relief, fulfillment and real pride in place of persistent despair.; [a.] El Cajon, CA

SCARBROUGH, LISA IRIS
[pen.] Lisa Scarbrough; [b.] February 5, 1979, Austell, GA; [p.] Michael and Iris Scarbrough; [ed.] St. Vincent's Academy Savannah GA; [occ.] Lazaretto Creek Marina, Tybee Island, GA; [memb.] United States Power Squadron; [hon.] National Winner Propeller Club Maritime Essay Contest 1995, Poet of the year 1995 nominee for International Society of Poets; [oth. writ.] Mostly short stories about teenagers; [pers.] My brother always told me that if there was ever something I wanted to do, I should do it and not let anyone or anything stand in my way.; [a.] Tybee Island, GA

SCHAEFER, ALICE
[b.] April 10, 1078, Denville, NJ; [p.] Lloyd Schaefer, Barbara Schaefer; [ed.] West Morris Central High School; [oth. writ.] Several unpublished poems and short stories; [pers.] I merely write about my own personal suffering and feelings. I am influenced most by Oscar Wilde and British pop singer Morrissey.; [a.] Califon, NJ

SCHAEFFER, FENELLA T.
[b.] June 4, 1935, Houston, TX; [p.] Mr. and Mrs. Harmand Teplow; [m.] 1st Allen James 1962, 2nd Vernon Schaeffer 1975; [ch.] Robert, David, Calage, Pat; [ed.] Grad. Texas. Univ. College of Medicine 1966; [occ.] I'm a retired Physician, Artist; [oth. writ.] Have written several volumes of poetry-not published; [pers.] As a child of the King, may I always be as the man given 100 talents; [a.] Coleman, TX

SCHAFER, MICHELE
[b.] April 21, 1967, Waukesha, WI; [p.] Greg, Mabel Schafer; [oth. writ.] None this is my first poem. I was inspired by Marcia Clark's brilliance.; [pers.] Writing has given me a freedom I never knew existed. My favorite poet is Edgar Allan Poe.; [a.] Wild Rose, WI

SCHAPER, MARIAH M.
[b.] October 1, 1977, Richland Center, WI; [p.] Christie and Dan Schaper; [ed.] High School; [occ.] Check out at food store; [hon.] 1st place trophy winner for forensics; [pers.] I would like to dedicate my poem to the most wonderful teacher in the world. The one who has made such a difference in my life. Thank you Mr. Hudson for giving me so much.

SCHARFE, PATRICIA M.
[b.] September 4, 1942, Baltimore, MD; [p.] Huey and Nell Riddle; [m.] Ralph M. Scharfe, September 9, 1973; [ch.] Connie, Trish, Louie, Children married, 8 grandchildren; [ed.] Franklin High, Reisterstown MD Grew up in Reisterstown MD, went to Franklin, both grade and high school. College courses at Paradise Comm. College, AZ; [occ.] Office Manager at precious metals company; [memb.] N. Phoenix Baptist Church, Phoenix Az-member; [hon.] Other than data processing school, Bro. Arrow, ok spelling bee championship and school, poem published in school newspaper.; [oth. writ.] First time published expect for poem published in school newspaper. "Maytime Is here"; [pers.] I would like my writing to reflect hope, comfort and inspiration in hearts that have been broken and need mending. May they be used to bless someone in a special way.; [a.] Scohsdale, AZ

SCHAU, ANNETTE J.
[b.] September 29, 1966, Monticello, IA; [p.] Bill OsterKamp, Joyce OsterKamp; [m.] Steve Schau, October 3, 1986; [ch.] Will Alan, Isaac Jordan; [ed.] Midland High School Kirkwood Community College; [occ.] Home maker Hobby Farm; [memb.] Peace Lutheran Church Merry Makers; [hon.] Won at Kirkwood and went to state on the Decision making team in Agriculture Leadership and President of Chorus

and Peer Counseling; [pers.] I enjoy writing poems on special occasions for my family, It lets me show them how much they mean to me; [a.] Coggon, IA

SCHINDLBECK, JANICE
[b.] August 23, 1943, Aurora, IL; [p.] Catherine Nowozelski, Father Deceased; [m.] Daniel W. Schindlbeck, August 29, 1946; [ch.] Steven John, Christine Marie, Stacey Ann; [ed.] BA Communications - Aurora University Registered Radiologic Technologist; [occ.] Executive Secretary; [memb.] Chicago Women in Publishing Society of Radiologic Technologists; [hon.] Aurora University - Presidential Service Award, Employee of Month - Aurora University, Working fulltime - school part time GPA 3.6; [oth. writ.] First Placer Winner - "Arts Alive Contest Tinley Park, IL Non-Fiction, Semi-Finalist - The National Library of Poetry Contest - Spring 1995; [pers.] My Goal is to leave more to this world than I will take out by putting the love of family, fellow Americans and this great country of America always first.

SCHMIDT, BEVERLY
[pen.] Margaret Marshall; [b.] April 19, 1947, Oceanside, NY; [p.] Dorothy and John Uhl; [m.] February 15, 1983; [ch.] Joseph John, Erica Lynn; [ed.] Freeport High School State University at Farmingdale, Mrs. Skinner's Business School, Institute of Children's Literature Long Ridge Writers Group; [occ.] Writer - Mother - Homemaker; [memb.] German Club, Future Nurses of America; [oth. writ.] Article for Freeport Library Essay for Institute of Children's Literature; [pers.] Vanishing Forests and Wildlife - A concern for us all; [a.] Amherst, NH

SCHMITT, CLIFTON C.
[pen.] Clifton C. Schmitt; [b.] March 14, 1937, Savannah, MO; [p.] Lloyd L. and May H. Schmitt; [m.] Joy M. Schmitt, August 30, 1959; [ch.] Cynthia Lee Williams, Cheryl Lane Hundley, Christopher Charles Schmitt; [ed.] B.S. Northwest Missouri State College M.Ed. University of Wyomina Adm. Certification University of Wyo.; [occ.] Director of Planning Boerne Independent School District; [memb.] Phi Delta Kapp; [pers.] My poetry reflects the importance of having God guide my life and the strong moral background influenced by my parents.; [a.] Boerne, TX

SCHNEIDER, PATRICIA ANNE
[pen.] Patricia Clunen Schneider; [b.] March 23, 1952, Alliance, OH; [p.] Wilbur and Margaret Clunen; [pers.] My writings are a mirror that reflects my life. The agony and the ecstasy. It's been a journey, thou at times bitter sweet I find I must share it in my poetry.; [a.] Granada Hills, CA

SCHOLL, MARGIE
[b.] October 24, 1938, Huntsville, TX; [p.] Charlie and Rebecca Moore; [m.] Roger Scholl; [ch.] Terri, Richard and Steve (grandchildren) Mandy, Charlie, Shelby and Trenton; [ed.] Presently in Tomball College for three years; [occ.] Housewife, secretary and bookkeeper for our tractor business; [memb.] Tomball first Baptist Church, Tomball Sports Center, and Tomball Library; [pers.] Writing poetry gives me a lot of pleasure because it is an expression of my true feelings.

SCHRADER, LAURA ELAINE
[pen.] Elaine Emmett; [b.] December 21, 1973, Oscoda, MI; [ed.] Port Huron Northern High School, St. Clan County Community College (SC4); [occ.] Circulation Technician Assistant, SC4 Library; [oth. writ.] Many other rhythmical poems and songs; [pers.] I believe that in order to live effectively, we must always look for the beauty in ourselves, others and our surroundings. Greatly influenced by: Jim Morrison, ans American

Poet.; [a.] Port Huron, MI

SCHRECK, BREANNA MARIE
[pen.] Bree Schreck; [b.] March 17, 1981, Chillicothe, OH; [p.] Jeffrey and Alisha Schreck; [ed.] Paint Valley H.S.; [occ.] Student; [pers.] All of my poems always comes from he heart. I put all of my emotions and feelings that I feel at that time, I just put it into words.; [a.] Bainbridge, OH

SCHROEDER, PENNY
[b.] February 12, 1964, Toucson, AR; [p.] James and Ramona Osborne; [ch.] Ramona Schroeder and Jennifer Downes; [ed.] Springfield High School Springfield Ill.; [occ.] House mom; [pers.] I dedicated this poem to the love of my life and to my "momo" who I miss dearly Ramona May Osborne died October 26, 1988; [a.] Fort Worth, TX

SCHULTZ, HAROLD
[pen.] "Happy"; [b.] February 9, 1953, Fairborn, OH; [p.] Gregory (deceased), and Ann; [ed.] High School Graduate have read books all my life; [occ.] Janitor; [memb.] BBT - Bhaktivedanta Book Trust; [oth. writ.] A few other poems published by world of poetry contests; [pers.] I believe very highly in being a vegetarian and freeing my self from the chains of Kasmic reaction; [a.] Albuquerque, NM

SCHULTZE, CHESTER L.
[b.] March 5, 1968, White Fish, MT; [p.] Rev. and Mrs. Schultze; [ed.] Kokomo High School, Ivy Tech. State College; [occ.] Soda Fountain Worker; [memb.] Kokomo Christian Fellowship; [oth. writ.] One poem published in "At The Water's Edge," and "The Sound of Poetry."; [pers.] I believe that God can be seen in all, around us. And if you were adopted as I was, don't let anyone try to kill your dreams.; [a.] Kokomo, IN

SCHULZE, MICHAEL
[b.] May 24, 1980, Conroe, TX; [p.] Lea and Ernest Sepulveda; [occ.] Student; [pers.] It is always the adventurers and dreamers who succeed, it is the dictators and the narrow minded who hold us back.

SCHWABEN, JODI NICOLE
[pen.] Connie Lee; [b.] August 9, 1985, Oklahoma City, OK; [p.] Dana J. Schwaben (mother); [ed.] 3rd Grader at Lakeview Elementary, Coventry, OH; [occ.] Student; [memb.] South Akron Church of Christ; [hon.] Softball, Baby Beauty Pageant, Cheer leading, Honor Roll, Violin, Creative Composing; [oth. writ.] Pop Corn, Pop Corn.; [pers.] The person who actually helped me was God. My influence was William J. Smith he's a great, funny poet!; [a.] Akron, OH

SCHWARTZ, KIMBERLEE
[b.] May 7, 1983, Long Island, NY; [p.] Pearl and Alan Schwartz; [ed.] Grades 1-6 went to Birchwood Elementary (Hunt, NY) Grade 6 Stimson Middle School 1 (Hunt. NY) High Honors student; [memb.] Belong to dance studio and a baseball team; [hon.] Math Olympiad trophy, 9th highest scorer in school on the suffolk County Math test; [oth. writ.] Many unpublished poems and stories; [pers.] I love to write because it takes me into the world of imagination. I can control what happens bad or good.; [a.] Huntington Station, NY

SCHWARTZENTRUBER, CARRIE A.
[pen.] Carl Anthony Sanders; [b.] Lowville, NY; [p.] Nelson K. and Bernadine Schwartzentruber; [ed.] Lowville Academy; [hon.] Xerox Award in the Humanities and Social Sciences; [oth. writ.] "Christine" (short story); [pers.] There come times in life when you must dive off the high diving board in the dark, without knowing if there's any water in the pool. If there is

water, will you swim - or drown?; [a.] Tug Hill, NY

SCISM, DARIN
[b.] August 16, 1965, Kings Mountain, NC; [ed.] AA, Gaston College. BA, University of North Carolina-Charlotte; [pers.] Belief always preceeds understanding.; [a.] Lancaster, TX

SCOTT, CAROL L.
[b.] October 23, 1946, Doylestown, PA; [p.] Lewis and Kathryn Scott; [ch.] Jude Scott-Fowler (deceased); [ed.] Central Bucks High School, Temple University, Carlow College; [occ.] Manager Human Resources; [memb.] National Peace Corps Association (Returned Peace Corps Vol./Nepal), Society for Human Resource Management; [a.] Bozeman, MT

SCOTT, CHERYL FELDER
[b.] March 4, 1948, Baltimore, MD; [ch.] Blair Cameron Scott; [ed.] Kent State University; [occ.] Pursuing Doctorate in Organizational Behaviour at Western Reserve University; [oth. writ.] Unpublished prose and essays, only so far. None submitted. I was once employed as a reporter for campus newspaper.; [pers.] The poem published here, Historic Tree, was adapted from my son, Blair's, Reflections after his visit to a Landmark Ohio Park.; [a.] Cleveland, OH

SCOTT, LILLIAN E.
[b.] September 25, 1915, Coalport, PA; [ed.] Eight years - Grade School; [occ.] Retired; [oth. writ.] Approx. 1500 poems

SCOTT, PATRICIA JACQUELINE
[b.] August 1, 1976, Philadelphia, PA; [p.] Donald and Patricia Scott; [ed.] Downington Senior High School; [occ.] Student at Georgetown University; [pers.] Take what God gives you and make the most of the opportunities. Much love and thanks to my Family and friends.; [a.] Downington, PA

SCOTT, PEGGY
[pen.] Marquease Scott; [b.] June 23, 1943, Sumner County, TN; [p.] J. W. Cron, M. R. Cron; [m.] P. D. Scott, September 9, 1962; [ch.] Son, daughter, four grandchildren; [ed.] Graduate of Portland High School 1962. Completed home writing course Writing To Sell Non-Fiction, in 1994 with Writers Digest School.; [occ.] Employee of Sunbeam Outdoor Products 1970, like to become a published writer with income; [memb.] Portland Creative Writers; [oth. writ.] "The Little Red Wagon," "Christmas Treasure" stories published in local newspaper seasonal pamphlet.; [pers.] I am honored to have been asked to print my poem in the book.; [a.] Portland, TN

SCOTT, RAY MARCEL
[pen.] Ray-Dia-Tion; [b.] August 25, 1973, Detroit, MI; [p.] Rayfus Scott and Marion Scott-Williams; [ch.] De Ante Marcel Baker; [ed.] MacKenzie High School, Detroit, MI, Central State University, Xenia, OH, Major: Engineering; [occ.] Deceased; [memb.] Deceased; [hon.] 1988: Oratorical Award received for The Boys Club of America. Letter in Track-MacKenzie High School 1989-90.; [oth. writ.] Ray wrote many poems in his eighteen years. I have preserved most of his writings.; [pers.] Ray Marcel Scott was killed in October of 1991 by a deranged student in the state of Ohio. One of Ray's goals was to publish as many of his writings as he could.; [a.] Southfield, MI

SCOTT, SUSAN GAYLE
[pen.] Susan Scott; [b.] April 5, 1961, Dallas, TX; [p.] William and Gavy Lumpkin; [m.] Delroy E. Scott, July 9, 1988; [ed.] Mesquite High School, Eastfield Jr. College; [occ.] Aspiring writer; [memb.] International

Society of Poets; [hon.] Editor's choice award for out-standing achievement in poetry 1994; [oth. writ.] My poem sometimes in my darkest hours was published in the anthology Reflections of light. I have also written a manuscript for a horror/sci-fi book.; [pers.] Each time I write a poem, I always feel God's help. It's as though my poetry is spiritual, while my stories are for human fun.; [a.] McMinnville, OR

SCOTT, TERRI L.
[b.] August 12, 1953, Ashtabula, OH; [p.] Edward L. and Jean Scott; [m.] Divorced; [ch.] Chad E. White, 17 years old; [ed.] Sterling High School, Lee College; [occ.] Developing seminar to release women from abuse; [memb.] Unity Church and Chapel of Prayer, Houston; [hon.] Peer Recognition Award - Exxon Chemical; [oth. writ.] (This is the first time I've tried to publish!); [pers.] I strive to offer the higher lessons of life experiences. "The universe is perfect -there are no mistakes, only learning experiences." I enjoy expressing the spiritual suggestion; [a.] Baytown, TX

SCOTT, TONI
[oth. writ.] Currently, I am writing an innovative book of inspirational poetry for publication.; [a.] Philadelphia, PA

SEAMAN, THOMAS
[b.] July 6, 1951, Washington, DC; [p.] Frederick and Rozella Seaman; [m.] Ana L. Seaman, May 19, 1980; [ed.] High School Oxon Hill Md., Opera lessons and guitar theory; [occ.] Musician; [hon.] Winner of various singing Competitions, Honorable Mention American song Festival; [oth. writ.] Many songs and poems from the time period 1974 (1974) until (1995); [pers.] True life mystery is inspired by continued suffering of women and children in conflicts in the past and today; [a.] Charlotte, MD

SEGARS, MARCI
[b.] August 6, 1980, Huntsville, TX; [p.] Jim and Mary Segars; [ed.] Freshman-Kermit High School; [hon.] National Junior Statesmen Candidate; [oth. writ.] Four other poems and three short stories (all unpublished); [pers.] Hunger creates art.; [a.] Kermit, TX

SEGRAVES, SHEILA A.
[b.] January 2, 1948, Alton, IL; [p.] Nelson and Virginia Segraves; [ed.] Assoc. Degree - Science; [occ.] Production Planner for Owens-Brockway Glass Container; [memb.] Saturday Night Ladies Art League; [hon.] The S.N.L.A.L. won 1st place in the Alton Halloween Parade in 1988 for their float's rendition of "Don't Worry Bee Happy." Alton has the oldest and largest Halloween Parade in the nation.; [oth. writ.] "Conversation with Myself," in Treasured Poems of America - Fall/1990.; [pers.] I like to think that I have become who I am because of everyone I have ever met and I hope I have left a little part of me with them. This poem was inspired by my late grandfather, W.O. Segraves and is dedicated to his memory.; [a.] Elsah, IL.

SEIDER, SUZANNE MARIE
[pen.] Suzanne Seider; [b.] January 15, 1975, Richmond, IN; [p.] John and Pamela Seider; [ed.] Graduate of James Bowie High School, attended Xavier University, now attending Texas Christian University; [occ.] Student; [memb.] NAFE; [hon.] 1991 Third place North Texas Children's Book Writer's Contest, 1991 Remember of Presidential Classroom; [oth. writ.] "Gentle in Spirit" published by The Anthanaeum of Xavier University.; [pers.] It is through our own words that we find the purpose and beauty of our lives.; [a.] Arlington, TX

SEIGLER, DESSIE ANNE
[b.] August 26, 1916, Pendelton, SC; [p.] Thomas Luther and Erco Whitman; [m.] Rev. John E. Seigler (deceased); [ch.] Dot Davis, John Ernest Seigler Jr, Louise Bowen, Edith Miller, Joyce Burton, Mary Jensen; [ed.] Grade 6; [occ.] (Deceased) April 2, 1995; [memb.] Member of Gods heavenly Angels in a land of Peace and Love; [hon.] Many stars in her Crown, A new body, walks on streets of Gold. Before she died she saw beyond the stars and she said "It's unbelievable"; [oth. writ.] My Bible and I, Some Morning Fair; [pers.] Mother read us, "sheltered by the Blood" on Christmas of '94 shortly before being told she had terminal Cancer, she went home to be with Jesus on April 2, 1995; [a.] Pelzer, SC

SERRANO, JOSE R.
[b.] June 3, 1961, Mexico; [p.] Alfonso and Olga Serrano; [m.] Lorena Serrano, June 16, 1990; [ch.] Eveleen, Andy Ray; [ed.] Huntington Park High - University of Phoenix; [occ.] Transit Operations Supervisor; [pers.] This poem is dedicated to my beautiful daughter who gave me the inspiration of putting together these special words. Love you always - your Dad.; [a.] San Bernardino, CA

SEVIER, MARCIA R.
[pen.] Marcie; [b.] July 28, 1944, New Orleans; [p.] Hattie Reed and Jesse Reed; [m.] Ronald Sevier (deceased), June 25, 1968; [ch.] Ronald L. Lewis, Jr., Allison Sevier; [ed.] Walter L. Cohen Sr. High, Delgado Jr. College, A.A. Degree Library Science, Loyola University Liberal studies - with concentration in behavioral science.; [occ.] Unemployed, Library-assistant, Clerical (Temporary Disabled); [memb.] None at present, 1984-85 Member of Loyola University Support Staff Council, Den Mother of Cub Scouts 1979, Drama Club (High School); [hon.] I made high School Honor Roll, my poem "God make Me New" Won on Honorary mention in American Collegiate Poets Anthology 1983, Award of Merit Certificate 1991 in World of Poetry, Sacramento, CA; [oth. writ.] Other poems published in poetry press, Pittsburg, TX, American Collegiate Anthology, "God Make Me Now" The stillness of the waters" and other poetry writings; [pers.] Because I had a wonderful english professor in college who loved all literary writings, I began a love for poetry during that time around 1981.; [a.] Santa Ana, CA

SEWARD, BARBARA GOODRUM
[b.] April 17, 1951, Bayou La Batre, AL; [p.] Harold and Marian Goodrum; [m.] Ernest L. Seward, August 2, 1968; [ch.] April Seward, Scott, Ricky Seward, Sandra Seward Deceased; [ed.] Alba High School Bayou La Batre Alabama; [occ.] Teachers Aide, Big Sandy ISD Dallardsville, TX; [oth. writ.] Just poems and stories at home.; [pers.] There is a lot you can write about, when you look at the wonders and beauty of the world. I want to thank my Precious Jesus for love of my family, friends and my life. Without him I wouldn't be writing anything.; [a.] Livingston, TX

SHALLBETTER, RAYMOND J.
[b.] September 4, 1917, Chicago, IL; [p.] Arthur and Anna Shallbetter; [m.] Alethea Harvey Shallbetter, May 12, 1943; [ch.] Raymond, Rinda, Jaman, Karl and Alethea; [ed.] High School, Attended Chicago Art Institute, Colorado Spring Fine Arts Ctr. Chicago Tech. College; [occ.] Retired, Weapons Quality Engineering Ctr. U.S. Navy- Mech. Design; [memb.] Church of Jesus Christ of Latter-day Saints, Boy Scout of American, Siskiyou County Vetran's Advisory Comm. And American Legion and Siskiyou Writers Club; [hon.] Third place, International Tech. Illustration show, Commendation from President Ford, Legion of Merit and Silver Beaver- B.S.A., Bronze Star Medal and the Purple Heart - U.S.Army WW II; [oth. writ.] Tech. writing for manuals, Introductory Poem and Illustrations for Natural resources Conserve program Newspaper writings while serving as a public Communication Missionary for the L.D.S. church.; [pers.] I believe in being honest and true in all dealings with my fellow men looking for the good in life. In composing poetry I find myself to be inspired by my family, church, animals, mountains and all of nature.; [a.] Etna, CA

SHANE, DICK
[b.] August 8, 1936, Philadelphia; [p.] Deceased; [m.] Gai Shane, October 16, 1966; [ch.] Rebecca; [ed.] Theater Arts Degree, Pasadena Playhouse, Calif.; [occ.] Casino Manager; [memb.] 3rd Mamne Division Association, American Legion; [oth. writ.] 2 Poems Published in "Leatherneck" magazine; [pers.] Hitchhiked Award the world for 3 years, lived past 21 years in Australia.; [a.] Edgewater, CO

SHANEYFELT, J. L.
[b.] December 28, 1932, Leachville, AR; [p.] Eugene and Pauline Shaneyfelt; [m.] Joy, October 5, 1952; [ch.] Bill, Debbie, Jan, Jamie; [ed.] Osceola High School, Osceola, Ark, BSE - Arkansas State University, Memphis State University, D.D.S. University of Tennessee School of Dentistry; [occ.] Dentist; [memb.] American Dentist Assoc., MO State Dent Assoc., S.E. Mo. Dist. Dentist Assoc., Evangelical Methodist Church; [hon.] First place: Humorous Verse State of Ark. High Schools 1949; [oth. writ.] Numerous other poems; [pers.] "And whatsoever ye do, do it heartily, as to the Lord, and not unto men" Colossians 3:23; [a.] Kennett, MO

SHANNON, EMILY FRANCESCA
[b.] September 20, 1982, Mountain View, CA; [p.] Vincent J. and Joan R. Shannon; [ed.] 7th grade; [occ.] Student; [memb.] California Youth Soccer Association, Golden State Track Club; [hon.] First Academic Honors 2nd, 3rd, and 4th periods, 2nd place St. Nicholas science fair, 1st place Santa Clara, Valley science and Engineering fair in the Biology category.; [pers.] I am very honored by your interest in my poem.; [a.] Los Altos, CA

SHANNON, STEVE
[b.] January 10, 1966, New Braunfels, TX; [p.] Leon Shannon, Esther Shannon; [ed.] Blanco High; [occ.] Rancher; [memb.] GPAA; [oth. writ.] Various other poems and songs; [pers.] This poem, "A Rose," is meant to be sent to a significant other in place of a real rose. As inspiration of the heart can inspire the world.; [a.] Hiawatha, KS

SHARPE, SANDRA L. ROBAR
[pen.] Sandy Sharpe #1 daughter; [b.] October 12, 1955, Potsdam, NY; [p.] Dale A. Robar and Dorothy A. Tuper Gardner; [m.] David E. Sharpe, July 4, 1988; [ch.] Phillip E. Swinyer 20 yrs. Selena A, Swinyer 18 yrs, Krystal M. Sharpe 5 yrs; [ed.] Colton - Central High School; [occ.] School Bus Driver Colton - Pierrepont Central School; [memb.] Fish and Game Club - Raquette Valley; [hon.] Special Mention Award for Poem "Silent Prayer" - John Campbell, Editor and Published Adirondack Long Rifle - 3rd Place women's Competition - Boonville, NY; [oth. writ.] Several poems not yet recognized, waiting to be heard, Also one Poem by National High School Poetry Press - Young America Sings - Title of Poem - I'm sitting here wondering why - Sandra L. Robar/Sharpe; [pers.] With every sunrise, there is a sunset - with every new day, a new tomorrow - Every tomorrow, a new Hope - Yesterday can be forgotten - therefore, I live for today and tomorrow - not for what is past. Thank God, for that.; [a.] South Colton, NY

SHARPTON, STACEY M.
[b.] September 28, 1968, Tulsa, OK; [p.] Wendell and Connie Sharpton; [ed.] Bachelor of Science in Education - Oklahoma State University, 1990; [occ.] Early Childhood teacher or Sp. Ed. teacher; [memb.] O.S.U. Alumni Association; [hon.] Kappa Delta Pi, Phi Kappa Phi, President's Honor Roll (1 sem.), Dean's Honor Roll (9 sems), Various college scholarships, nominated for "Teacher of the Year" 1st yr of teaching; [pers.] It's as simple as this... "follow your heart and doors will open!"; [a.] Austin, TX

SHASKEVICH, HELENA
[b.] January 23, 1986, Chicago; [p.] Anna and Michael; [ed.] Preschool, Kindergarten 1-2, and 3rd grade; [occ.] Student; [memb.] Girl Scout; [pers.] If we didn't have writing everybody would be sad because there wouldn't be any stories or poems to read.; [a.] Chicago, IL

SHAW, AMANDA
[b.] July 4, 1980, Hudson, MI; [p.] Naomi Brenner; [ed.] Kindergarden - 8th Grade; [occ.] School; [memb.] I am member of a peerlistening, It is someone who listen's to other peoples problems without spreading it around, and someone who can keep things to themselves; [hon.] I got an award for, National Physical Fitness. I got 3 awards for my athletic in Track, Volleyball, and basketball and a awardin academic achievement for being an play.; [oth. writ.] I wrote a poem about "Elvis Presley" in 6th grade I was suppose to send it in for a poetry contest for Social Studies but never did.; [pers.] I will continue to write Poetry in my future and make sure I put all my Good effort into it, and also write the best I can write.; [a.] Addison, MI

SHEEDY JR., THOMAS ALVA
[b.] October 13, 1953, Brooklyn NY; [p.] Thomas and Marjorie Sheedy; [ed.] John Glenn H.S. Westland Mi Washtenaw Comm. College, Ann Arbor Ford Vo-Tech Westland Eastern Michigan University, Ypsilant; [occ.] Plant Engineer; [memb.] UAW Journeyman Machine Repair; [hon.] First Congregational, Church of Wayne, Boy Scouts of America Alpha Sigma Phi Fraternity Fraternal Order Eagles; [pers.] Accept the Holy Spirit and let the Devil pass you by may all your love comeback to you and no one ever see you cry.; [a.] Canton, MI

SHEPARD, VIRGINIA A.
[pen.] Ginger; [b.] May 7, 1956, Fort Banning, GA; [p.] Mildred A. and Phillip N. Shepard; [m.] Franklin D. Kellar, February 14, 1993; [ch.] Jesse Lee; [ed.] Nathan Bedford Forrest High School; [occ.] Home Maker and raising and breeding Australian Shepherds; [pers.] I've been writing poem's since childhood. They are a release of my innermost feelings. I was influenced by my mother Mildred Shepard.; [a.] Jacksonville, FL

SHEPPARD, MARTHA
[b.] October 8, 1928, Shingleton; [p.] Lester and Lucy Livermore; [m.] Delbert Sheppard, January 10, 1947; [ch.] Three boys, one girl; [ed.] High School Graduate; [occ.] Housewife; [pers.] I do all to the glory to God.

SHERIDAN, MARYANN
[pen.] M. A. Sheridan; [b.] March 20, 1961, Bayshore, NY; [p.] William Sheridan, Lydia Sheridan; [ed.] Brentwood High; [occ.] Binderly Assistant; [pers.] My basis for writing stems from the beauty and sadness of lifes great experiences. Poetry is the music within me which guides me to achieving my ultimate goal of songwriting.; [a.] Lake Worth, FL

SHERMAN, DONNA B.
[b.] May 29, 1953, Canada; [p.] William and Ruby Sherman; [m.] L. J. White, April 7, 1987; [ch.] Nikki Lynn Sherman; [ed.] Rincon High School, Mesa Community College, Arizona State University; [occ.] Disabled writer-artist; [memb.] Mesa Community College Honors, Golden Key National Honor Society; [hon.] Cum Laude; [oth. writ.] Book: Looking for Mercy; [pers.] I value kindness and compassion to others.; [a.] Mesa, AZ

SHERRARD, BURTON
[b.] September 17, 1949, Detroit, MI; [p.] Robert and Georgia Sherrard; [ed.] Ferndale High School, Syracuse UMV, BA degree Oakland University, William Tyndale; [occ.] Manufacturing - Chrysler Corporation; [pers.] If my poetry can elicit a great emotional response from those who read it, then I have accomplished my purpose, for poetry, like music, comes from the soul; [a.] Ferndale, MI

SHERRILL, DEBORAH L.
[b.] May 28, 1972, Anderson IN; [p.] William Sherrill, Kandace Sherrill; [ed.] Hamilton Southeastern High School graduated 90. Attend Anderson University, Major: Mass Communications, Journalism. Est. Graduation date, 1996.; [occ.] Student; [memb.] Xi Theta Chi; [hon.] Fund raising Director, 93, Xi Theta Chi; [oth. writ.] 1st writing published wrote for A.U. Newspaper, "Andersonian"; [pers.] Always criticize, think and evaluate life challenges: Then follow your dreams. Love, peace, happiness.; [a.] Lapei, IN

SHETH, SACHIN
[b.] November 7, 1971, Bombay, India; [p.] Dinesh and Shakuntala Sheth; [ed.] Bachelor's in Petrochemical Engineering, (India); [occ.] Student (working towards my master's degree in Chemical Engineering (U.S.A); [memb.] American Institute of Chemical Engineers, Literary Circle; [hon.] First prize in the musical talent contest (Instrumental category), Distinction grade throughout my academic career.; [oth. writ.] Heat and Dust, Kurukshetras Galore, The unfinished sketch, Equality in question, Today (and others); [pers.] I like to write about the beauty of nature, relationships and about little things which go unnoticed. I have learn a lot from my family members and friends to whom I am very grateful.

SHIELDS, BETH
[pen.] Tina Lovitt; [b.] December 31, 1974, Torrance, CA; [p.] Linda Shields, Richard Lovitt; [m.] Robert Scism (fiance); [ed.] San Pedro High; [occ.] House Wife; [oth. writ.] Poetry contests in High School; [pers.] I love to bring my feelings and other peoples feelings out by enhancing them with the beauty of nature; [a.] San Pedro, CA

SHINSATO, EMILY Y.
[b.] January 11, 1977, Hawaii; [p.] Shige and Lisa Shinsato; [ed.] Moanalua High School; [occ.] Student; [memb.] Power Rangers Fan Club, X-Files Fan Club; [hon.] Joe Blasco Make-Up contest Semi-Finalist, Who's Who Among American High School Students, Leeward Community College Film Experimental Video Award; [oth. writ.] Unpublished screen plays seniors Portfolio; [pers.] Heather Langen kamp, Gillian Anderson, Yancy Butler, Tawny Kitaen, Charlie's Angels and Mitzi Kapture: You inspire me when I have writer's block. Ms. Karen Kirk and Susan Yokota (Shimizu), the coolest English teachers! Thanks!; [a.] Waipahu, HI

SHIPMAN, ROBERT OLIVER
[b.] February 13, 1920, Flushing, NY; [p.] Bertram Shipman, Elydia Shipman; [m.] Jeanille Hadden Shipman, November 2, 1944; [ch.] Robert H. Shipman, Anne Shipman Brennan, Gary Shipman, Bertram F. Shipman; [ed.] A. B. Bowdoin College 1947, MS Journalism Columbia University, 1948; [occ.] Retired educator; [memb.] Past: Society of Professional Journalists, Sigma Delta Chi, Society of Weekly Newspaper Editors, Minnesota Press Association, Association for Education in Journalism, American Councilor Education, National Education Association, Goodwill Associates founding president, Society of Poets, Southern Minnesota; [oth. writ.] A Pun My Word: A Humorously Enlighted Path to English Usage. Numerous poems and short stories.; [pers.] Language and the love of words has been a lifetime passion. That has found fulfillment and gratification in print.; [a.] Mankato, MN

SHIREY, BETTY DELORES
[pen.] Betty Bromm; [b.] May 9, 1921, Scottdale, PA; [p.] Dorothy and Frank Browm; [m.] Clare W. Shirey (deceased), March 25, 1940; [ch.] Terrance Lane, Kitrick Alan, Marcy Lee; [ed.] High School, Mott Adult Education, Secretarial; [occ.] Retired; [memb.] AARP American Legion, St. Helen Community Baptist Church; [hon.] 1991 Quilting Awards - Blue Ribbon, Gold State Ribbon and Trophy Ike Award, Hand-dipped Chocolate Awards; [oth. writ.] "Essence Of Life", "The Days Of Spring", "His Hand", "Something", "My Tree Of Christmas"; [pers.] I look for the beauty and wonder of the world, ("something don't make a sound, so they may be heard"); [a.] Saint Helen, MI

SHIRK, VIOLET GEMBERLING
[b.] April 17, 1913, Union County, PA; [p.] Mr. and Mrs. F. S. Gemberling; [m.] Samuel S. Shirk; [ch.] Juanita and Larry; [ed.] Bloomsburg College; [occ.] Retired; [memb.] United Methodist Church PA, Retired Public Schools Northumberland County Retired Teachers, Local Missionary Societies, many Charitable institutions:; [oth. writ.] Many poems, too numerous to mention

SHOAF, SALOME E.
[b.] November 13, 1970, Bloomsburg, PA; [p.] Anna and Frank, Werkheiser; [m.] Orville S. Shoaf, September 21, 1933; [ch.] Gail Anne, Richard David, Carole Louise and Gerald H.; [ed.] Bloomsburg High School, Geisinger Memorial Hospital; [occ.] Retired; [memb.] First Methodist church of Media, PA Past president of council of Evangelical Manor; [oth. writ.] Several poems published in various church leaflets; [pers.] My life has revolved around my family and my faith and my poems tend to reflect this I find much inspiration in the Bible.; [a.] Philadelphia, PA

SHOLEY, JEFFERY D.
[b.] October 26, 1963, Sewanee, TN; [p.] Dwight and Vickie Sholey; [ch.] Dona Nicole Sholey; [ed.] 1-6 Sewanee Public, 7-9 South Jr High, 10-12 Franklin Co. High School; [occ.] Grundy Co. Board of Ed.; [pers.] Let the light of the rising son be your inspiration for the day.; [a.] Tracy City, TN

SHORT, DOLORES E.
[pen.] Dede Short; [b.] December 19, 1940, Longmont, CO; [p.] Margaret and Oliver Travis; [m.] Norman Short, May 15, 1983; [ch.] Jack Beckingham, Scott Short and Daren Short; [ed.] High School Graduate 2 years College, Marinello Cosmetology School, Marinello Teacher's Academy, Creative writing courses; [occ.] Apartments Manager, Management Instructor, Writer; [memb.] Crossroads Church Onesmis Ministries (Prison Ministry); [hon.] Licensed Cosmetology Instructor, (4) Apartment Management Awards; [oth. writ.] "Seasons" a true to live humorous novel. "Your career in rental Management" several unpublished poems; [pers.] This poem was a gift ot Jesus. He alone will profit from it. I love him.; [a.] Garden Grove, CA

SHORTER, GERI COOPER
[pen.] Geri Cooper Shorter; [b.] April 9, 1950, Inkster, MI; [p.] William and Cassie Cooper; [m.] Divorced; [ch.] Nakita L. Shorter, Hakiem S. Shorter; [ed.] Robichaud High, UCLA, Wayne County College; [hon.] Magna Cum Laude, Dean's list; [oth. writ.] Numerous poems, and papers.; [pers.] It is up to us to let God know there is still hope.; [a.] Detroit, MI

SHUTTLEWORTH, WILLIAM H.
[b.] May 6, 1937, Philadelphia, PA; [p.] William and Irene Shuttleworth; [ed.] Dobbins Voc. Tech. High 1955, Cheyney State College, 1 yr., Phila. College of Bible 1 yr.; [occ.] Furniture Finishing and Repairs; [memb.] Art League of Jacksonville, International Society of Poets; [hon.] Exhibitor in Arts Mania 1994, International Poet of Merit Award 1994 (ISP), Editors Choice Award 1994 (Nat. Lib. of Poetry). Ordained (American Rescue Workers) Minister 1967; [oth. writ.] Last year a local paper published one of my poems and then an article I wrote. I'm also excited at having my own first book of poetry available from a publisher in a few months.; [pers.] In a word full of trouble I hope to communicate with my pen, the unfailing promises of God found in the Holy Bible, "An anchor of the soul, both sure and steadfast" (Heb. 6:19).; [a.] Jacksonville, FL

SHVEYTSER, KAROLINA
[b.] December 2, 1976, Odessa, Ukraine; [p.] Victor, Shveytser, Lyubov Shveytser; [ed.] Fair Lawn High School, Rutgers University; [occ.] Student at Rutgers University; [hon.] Dean's List, National Council of Jewish Women - Jewel Pekelney Creative Writing Award; [oth. writ.] Several poems published in High School poetry magazine, articles for High School Newspaper; [pers.] Literature is the looking glass into the past and the key to the future; [a.] Fair Lawn, NJ

SICKLE, MARIANNE J.
[p.] George and Teresa Pope; [m.] James Allen; [ch.] Brenda Jeanne; [pers.] Fulfilled a promise - owing it all to my beautiful and caring daughter who never ceases to amaze me. Thank you for making the difference in my life.; [a.] Hilliard, OH

SIDES, LUANN ALLEN
[b.] October 28, 1946, Lufkin, TX; [p.] Flora Beele and Alton Allen; [m.] William Sides, May 7, 1965; [ch.] Yvonne DeReigh and Vanessa DeLane; [ed.] H.S. Graduate and some College; [occ.] Homemaker, and DJ; [oth. writ.] Poems, short stories and songs; [pers.] The Singer was written in house of Rev. Kenny Hinson singer/songwriter of Nashville, TN after and found out he had been diagnose with cancer. I wanted to tell him in some small walk how much his music had touched my heart and life.; [a.] Lufkin, TX

SIKES, ARIANNA
[pen.] Ari, Lil' Bit, and Danne'; [b.] November 1, 1979, Atlanta, GA; [p.] Dann and Janice Spikes; [ed.] Oglethorpe Elem, Inman Middle, and Northwest Junior High; [occ.] Student; [memb.] Northwest Georgia, Girl Scout Council; [hon.] Performing Arts Award, Georgia Tech. Award for Architecture, Georgia Tech. Summer Camp for Environment, and Science; [oth. writ.] What is a best friend? Meeting The Grim Reaper, That Night, My Broken Heart, and Feelings; [pers.] Life is full of hopes and dreams, you can get over obstacles, no matter how hard it seems.; [a.] Meridian, MS

SILEO, STEFANIE
[b.] May 3, 1983, New York; [p.] James Siko and Janis Sileo; [a.] Massapequa, NY

SILLER, MARGARET STEPHENS
[pen.] Margo; [b.] December 20, 1953, South Carolina, FL; [p.] Mr. and Mrs. Allen Stephens; [m.] Separated; [ed.] St. George High School, St. George S.C. Claflin University, Orangeburg, S.C. Florida, Institute of Technology Melbourne, Fla.; [occ.] Supervisory Contract Officer, Department of Housing and Urban Development, San Francisco, CA.; [memb.] Alpha Kappa Alpha Sorority, Vice-Pres. National Association Procurement Professionals, West Coast Chapter Regional Advisory Council for American Charities, Northwest Region; [hon.] Dean's List, English Award, Who's Who in Out Service Employee of the Year Award; [oth. writ.] Poetry, poems, several poems published in local newspapers; [pers.] Life is full of opportunities, I pray, reach and seize the day, if you set your limitations, you get to keep them.

SILVER, SCOTT
[pen.] Louis Trent; [b.] January 2, 1970, New York City; [ed.] School of Visual Arts, Nassau Community College; [hon.] Rickey Hernandez Scholarship; [pers.] I write an astronomy of lipid words like pieces of an emotional puzzle for the reader to conclude and or possibly associate within themselves.; [a.] Flushing, NY

SILVEY, MICHAEL
[pen.] Mickey J. Woods; [b.] June 30, 1960, Akron, OH; [p.] Patricia Wilson; [ed.] 1978 Kenmore High Graduate Weber State College - 2 years, (working towards PhD in Bovine scatology); [occ.] Entrepreneur; [memb.] National Academy Of Song Writers; [oth. writ.] Poems, songs and chants vol.1 In my room - short story reflections of a distorted mind; [pers.] People - why cant we learn to love together???; [a.] Akron, OH

SILZER, VICTOR
[b.] July 25, 1920, Obermetzenseifen; [p.] Anna and Julius Silzer; [m.] Dorothy Grace Silzer, April 28, 1945; [ch.] Elizabeth Ann; [ed.] B.E.E. degree Polytechnic University, Shrivenham American University (England), Post Graduate Pratt Institute El (Power Engineering); [occ.] Senior Electrical and Electronics Engineer-retired; [memb.] Life Member, IEEE (Institute of Electrical and Electronics Engineers), Polytechnic Alumni Association; [oth. writ.] Wrote sixty one English and eleven German poems i.e. 72 poems some published. Am influenced by the great German poets Friedrich Von Schiller, Johann Wolfgang Von Gothe, Heinrich Heine etc.; [pers.] Have great reverence for Life. Marvel at the mystery of the Universe. Was Communications Engineer and Group Leader on the Lunar Module (LM) Television, and Senior Engineer on Space Station and Navy Air Craft in WW II taught Radar in USAAC knew Dr. William Shockley inventor of Transistor also Dr. Lee De Forrest-Father of Radio. Dr. Wernher V. Braun designer of moonship rocket astronaut Glenn, and many others. Hobbies: ham radio, medicine, photography; [a.] Woodbury, NY

SIMMS, TRACY
[pen.] Trace; [b.] July 25, 1972, Yonkers, NY; [p.] Lucille Downes; [ed.] Charles E. Gorton High, The College of Mt. St. Vincent; [occ.] Graduate student, Wheelock College, Boston, MA; [memb.] Psi Chi National Honor Society (Psychology), Modern Foreign Language Honor Society (Spanish), International Student's Assoc.; [hon.] President's Academic Honor roll Award, Montefiore Medical Center, Volunteer Award, Club President Award, Honorable Mention for Mt. St. Vincent Moral contest; [pers.] I strive to reflect what I see in everyday life. My writing comes from my heart and soul.; [a.] Yonkers, NY

SIMON, NEIL W.
[pen.] Neil W. Simon; [b.] September 3, 1975, Blue Island, IL; [p.] Bill and Arlene Simon; [ed.] Victor J. Andrew H.S., Moraine Valley Community College and Future student of Eastern Illinois University; [occ.] Student; [oth. writ.] Several song lyrics.; [pers.] My writings and songs express my experiences and thoughts of things that mean so much to me.; [a.] Tinley Park, IL

SIMPSON, WILLIAM D.
[pen.] Penguin; [b.] October 22, 1956, Key West, FL; [p.] Charles Simpson, Dorothy Simpson; [m.] Lucille Simpson, July 23, 1988; [ch.] William D. Simpson III, Meagan A. Simpson; [ed.] Palm Beach Gardens High, Palm Beach Community College; [occ.] Safety Coordinator, Tiara Condominium; [hon.] Dean's list, Good Conduct Medal; [pers.] My poetry efforts display a type of fictional literary composition (story). My influence was inspired by the lyrics of singer and songwriter Elton John.; [a.] West Palm Beach, FL

SINGER, MARIANNE J. G.
[pen.] Marianne Davidson; [b.] March 7, 1938, Windsor, Ontario, Canada; [p.] Johnathan and Mary Davidson; [m.] Divorced; [ch.] Christina Marianne, Cheryl Lynn, Louis Johnathan, Randall Matthew; [ed.] W.D. Lowe Vocational, St. Clair College; [occ.] Home Support Worker II, Para-Med Health Services; [pers.] I love how the soul expresses itself in poetry. One of the highest achievements: Emily Dickinson; [a.] Windsor Ontario, Canada

SINGS, VALERIE
[b.] August 20, 1982, Walnut Creek, CA; [p.] James Sings and Betsy Sings; [a.] Danville, CA

SIRKIN, ESTELLE
[pen.] Estelle; [b.] March 25, 1928, New York; [ch.] Nancy Sue Sirkin, Lloyd and Bathia Sirkin, grandchildren: Asher and Aliza Sirkin; [ed.] Evander Childs H. S. - Grad., 1945, Phoenix Community College, Grad., 1992, Arizona State University - Grad., 1995; [occ.] Retired - worked as secretary for 48 years; [oth. writ.] Developed newsletter for Tom Jones love circle wrote for Arthur Andersen newsletter; [pers.] Are a free-lance writer, I hope to affect some urgent issues facing our country today. I have plans for two novels in the hat-to-distant future.; [a.] Phoenix, AZ

SISK, BARRY C.
[b.] October 2, 1960, Sikeston, MO; [p.] Charles and Mickey Sisk; [ed.] Charleston High School; [pers.] I seem to have a unique writing style all my own. This pleases me, for I have always felt that original is essential to all art forms; [a.] Bertrand, MO

SKALNEK, DIANNE
[b.] November 6, 1942, Detroit; [p.] Hans and Mary Hill (deceased); [m.] James Skalnek, November 20, 1971; [ch.] Mark, Betsy, Eric; [ed.] St. Jude Elementary St. Bernard, Detroit Sacred Heart, Roseville S. Macomb College (1 yr.); [occ.] Housewife, Poet Part time; [memb.] St. Dorothy Church; [hon.] Won CSA contest in High School with poem about Cardinal Mooney, 9th grade I wrote a playlet which a received a standing ovation. Straight A's in 3 subjects, 11th grade Points-Magna Cum Laude in 11th grade; [oth. writ.] Many other poems unpublished: Angel, Flowers, Black vs. White Women, Love, Family Types, Humming Bird, Dreams, Mother's Day; [pers.] I like to feel what I say to others inside myself. I have an ability to think or act a child who is an adult having fun.; [a.] Roseville, MI

SKIOLD, S. ANN E.
[b.] November 15, 1955, Malmo, Sweden; [p.] Manilyn Muckenzie Skiold, Olof Skiold; [ed.] Soderstatts gymnasiet, Sweden Lund's University Swedeu, University of California Santa Barbara, Flinders University. S. Australia, Bradley University, Illinois; [occ.] Graduate Student - Will begin working on my M.F.A. in Aug 5, painting. (Bradley Univ. Ill.); [memb.] Santa Barbara Museum of Art. (C.A.), Contemporary Arts Forum (C.A.), Amnesty International, (C.A.) Ojai Center for the Arts (C.A.); [hon.] Rotary Exchange Student (high school) Rotary Foundation Scholarship S. Australia, Second place 1/2 marathon, horse jumping (1-4 places); [oth. writ.] Art critic for the Santa Barbara Independent CA; [pers.] I want my poems (and paintings) to be like a window into the world we seldom visit, that of imagination, overcoming obstacles and most of all hope. There are no limits in the universe of art. We set our own horizons; [a.] Santa Barbara, CA

SLANE, MELANY
[b.] June 6, 1953, Columbus, OH; [p.] Mimi Alice Slane, Ernest Eldon Slane; [ed.] Creighton Elementary School, Camelback High School Graduate (Both in Phoenix); [occ.] Early Retiree-Having held computer operator position at Phoenix Motorola Plant, At one time was recording artist, songwriter, performer; [memb.] Former member of ASCAP and ASPCA - Former is: American Society of Composers, authors and publishers, latter is: American Society for prevention of cruelty to animals.; [oth. writ.] Several songs that I had recorded in Nashville, Tenn, and quite a few more that had not been recorded by myself or any artist-had not been writing song/poems or any poetry for about ten years prior to my entry; [pers.] "The ways in which the eternal spirit of all living beings manifests itself are many and varied. One must develop and open mind in order to fully appreciate and benefit from the experience."; [a.] Phoenix, AZ

SLAPINSKI, PAT MCINERNEY
[b.] March 15, 1929, Chicago, IL; [p.] John and Katherine Doran McInerney; [m.] Chester V. Slapinski (RIP), November 19, 1955; [ch.] Paul Slapinski, Mike Slapinski, Rob Slapinski, Ann Grys, Peggy Bulatek, Mary Beth Meyers; [ed.] St. Mel Grammer, Providence High, and Loyola Univ. All of Chicago; [occ.] Retired; [oth. writ.] Essay, letters, poetry in local publications. Geneology research

SLONE, RENEE DELEE
[b.] December 26, 1980, Fort Wayne, IN; [p.] Bennie and Christine Slone; [ed.] I am in Junior High at Rome City School; [oth. writ.] What Indiana Means To Me, several unpublished poems; [pers.] When I write I say things that I can't say any other way. I try to make every word touch the heart of it's reader.; [a.] Kendallville, IN

SMALLWOOD, SUSIA
[b.] July 5, 1951, NC; [p.] Mr. and Mrs. Andersor and Eula Pugh; [m.] September 23, 1968; [ch.] Arretha, Michell, La Royal, Chris-Grandson; [ed.] BSN - Nurse, Bowie State University; [occ.] RNC Case Manager, St. Elizabeth Hosp.; [memb.] DCNA; [hon.] Certified Mental Health and Psychiatry, Pioneer in Nursing Award, Bowie State Univ, 1995; [pers.] I am making a deliberate and conscious effort to present my person life experiences in a humane and therapeutic manner. Poetry is the channel that serves this objective.; [a.] Temple Hills, MD

SMART, TERRE
[b.] January 8, 1957, Huntington, WV; [p.] Marvin and Martha Thacker; [m.] Richard Smart, July 11, 1975; [ch.] Christopher C. Smart; [ed.] Graduate of Prince George High 1975; [occ.] Self employed; [hon.] In

Junior High my poetry won honorable mentions; [pers.] My feelings of life prompt me to write poetry. It helps me understand our world and how I can fit in. It gives me spiritual healing.; [a.] Chesterfield, VA

SMENTEK, INGE
[b.] September 12, 1949, Copenhagen, Denmark; [p.] Ellen and Holger Mogensen; [m.] Marius Smentek; [ch.] Heidi Mogensen; [ed.] The academy of Art's, Aarhus, Denmark, Institute of Psychology Aarhus, Denmark.

SMILEY, SARAH
[b.] Los Angeles, CA; [p.] Geraldine and Porter Hall; [ed.] The Bishops School, Pomona College, Claremont Graduate School; [memb.] Earth Save, Greenpeace, People for the Ethical Treatment of Animals, Sierra Club, Vegetarian Society, Inc.; [pers.] I write to heal myself, others, and Earth.; [a.] Los Angeles, CA

SMITH, AMANDA LEE
[b.] March 7, 1979, Benson, AZ; [p.] George Smith and Donna Smith; [ed.] Benson Union High; [oth. writ.] Several other poems.; [pers.] I just write what comes to mind. Mainly on my emotions and feelings.; [a.] Pomerene, AZ

SMITH, CAROLINE C.
[b.] July 1, 1938, Chicago; [p.] Arthur and Agnes McAfee; [m.] Jack C. Smith, February 18, 1955; [ch.] Jackie, Shirley, Sandy, Robert, Jason, Jillian, Ashley, Rachel and Adam; [occ.] Housewife; [pers.] My Poem is dedicated to: Jack, Jackie, Shirley, Sandy, Robert, Jason, Jillian, Ashley, Rachel and Adam, with Love; [a.] Osage Beach, MO

SMITH, GERTRUDE M.
[b.] November 3, 1934, Follensbee, WV; [p.] Roscoe N. Brady and Mary Brady (Deceased); [m.] Bernard C. Smith, November 5, 1950; [ch.] Pamela, Melody, Bernard Jr., Robert and Pete; [ed.] Weston High School, Weston WV; [occ.] Home Maker, (Widow); [memb.] Extension Home Makers Club Doddridge County WV, St Johannas Lutheran Church Woman's Bowling Association of Clarksburg WV; [hon.] Just community Honors as a member of a Clubs I belong to; [oth. writ.] I have had several poems published in the local Newspapers. The Herold Record, West Union WV. I have my poems saved in an album; [pers.] I only write poems as a hobby. I sometimes write poems about local people in our community if someone is getting married, or having a baby, or a birthday (etc); [a.] New Milton, WV

SMITH, GORDON N.
[b.] October 9, 1962, Lexington, KY; [p.] Gordon Smith, Evelyn Smith; [m.] Cathy M. Smith, May 26, 1984; [ch.] Allyson Marie, Haley Kathleen; [ed.] Lafayette High, University of Kentucky, BA; [occ.] Studio Supervisor, WKYT-TV Lexington, KY; [memb.] 7th Kentucky Infantry (Union re-enactment/Civil War); [hon.] University of Kentucky, Dean's List, Golden Key National Honor Society; [pers.] Through my writing, I seek to honor my Lord and my family by expressing the great love and respect I have for both.; [a.] Winchester, KY

SMITH, HEATHER L.
[b.] April 21, 1970, Stamford, CT; [p.] Karen L. Bennard (mother); [m.] Dennis J. Smith, June 28, 1991; [ch.] Ryan 4, Holly 2 1/2; [ed.] Platt Regional Vo-Tech, Milford, CT, currently completing a course in Children's Literature from Institute of Children's Lit. - in Ct.; [occ.] Home-maker; [hon.] Awarded 3rd place in Panhandle Writer's Guild spring poetry, contest as for 'The Secret', Honorable Mention Awarded, Panhandle Writer's Guild; [oth. writ.] Poem entitled - 'All Of What

You Are To Me,..." published in 'Dusting Off Dreams' - anthology of poetry by Quill Books, Harlingen, Texas; [pers.] People tell me the eyes are the 'Windows to the soul'.... My poetry conveys much more of my soul than meets the eye.; [a.] DeFuniak Springs, FL

SMITH, JEFFERY STEVEN
[pen.] Randor Krill; [b.] January 30, 1971, Indianapolis, ID; [p.] Ronald Smith, Sandra Smith; [ed.] Timber Line High School, Seattle Washington; [occ.] Cook, Pizza Hut; [oth. writ.] None published, only school writings, short stories and essays. All of which I received A's and B's.; [pers.] For what I lack in experience, I make up with a passion for writing and a Romantics Heart. Creativity is something you're born with. Use it well, and there is nothing you cannot accomplish.; [a.] Callaway, FL

SMITH, JOAN R.
[b.] April 15, 1942, New Haven, CT; [p.] Raymond Buckner, Bertha Orange; [m.] Anthony I. Smith, March 7, 1970; [ch.] Six sons, one daughter, six grandchildren; [ed.] Girls High School B'klyn NY., North Tech. Ed. Ctr. LPN Course Riv. Bch. FL. Graduated December, 1986; [occ.] LPN; [memb.] R.V. Bch. FL., Daughters of I.R.P.O.E. Eastern Star River. Bch. Fl. Riv. Beach Senior Services Coalition; [hon.] Outstanding Volunteer of sickle cell foundation 1986 State of Conn. Unsung Heroine Award August 6, 1988 Cert. of appreciation Sickle Cell foundation 1988, Cert. of appreciation Riv. Bch. Senior Sucs. 1994; [oth. writ.] Many poems since age 15; [pers.] All my poems come from deep within my heart and are usually attributed to something or someone special who has touched my life.; [a.] Lake Park, FL

SMITH, LAYNA
[pen.] Layna Smith; [b.] September 7, 1973, Englewood, CO; [p.] Carol Phipps; [m.] Scott J. Smith, June 5, 1993; [ed.] Roosevelt High School, Augustana College; [occ.] Child care worker; [hon.] United States Navy Spouse Award; [oth. writ.] I have written several other pieces of poetry. "The Candle of Love" is the only piece that I have released to the public.; [pers.] I enjoy writing poetry in my space time. I am inspired by family, friends and the occurrence of everyday life.; [a.] Saint Marys, GA

SMITH, MICHELLE
[b.] May 29, 1963, Middletown, NY; [p.] Antoinette, Roger Smith; [ch.] Jennica Smith; [ed.] Graduated from Middletown High School; [occ.] Machine Operator at Genpak; [hon.] Editors choice Award and International society of Poets.; [pers.] Be happy, do your best and live each day to your fullest potential; [a.] Middletown, NY

SMITH, MINETTE
[pen.] "The Missionary Poet"; [b.] December 16, 1949, Saint Louis, MO; [p.] Fred and Clendell Henry; [m.] Divorced twice; [ch.] Johnny Johnson Jr., Michelle Smith, Melodie Smith-Wells; [ed.] I am a graduate of O'Fallon High. Student Mt. Airy Sunday School Student of Westside Leadership School. Student Mt. Airy Wednesday Night Bible Class.; [occ.] Homemaker; [memb.] Mt. Airy Mission Society, Mt. Airy M.B. Church, Pastor Charles J. Brown Sr., Berean District Missionary Baptist Asso., Berean District Women and Mission Union Auxiliary International Society of Poets Distinguished Member; [hon.] Substitute Sunday School Teacher Award, The Editor's Choice Award, Poet of Merit Award, International Society of Poets Distinguished Member Award; [oth. writ.] "Jesus Christ", published in "Reflections of Light". "Inherited Punishment", published in "At Water's Edge." Many unpublished poems. A Christmas play, and a song which are also unpublished.; [pers.] I enjoy writing poetry that

sow God's righteous seed, the word, with hopes that it will reap a fruitful harvest, which is Christian souls.; [a.] Saint Louis, MO

SMITH, PATSY J. WILSON
[b.] October 10, 1948, Hobbs, NM; [p.] Willie-Lee and Allamae Wilson; [ch.] Shannon L. Greene, Brent M. Smith; [ed.] Elementary - Will Rogers - Hobbs High; [occ.] Telephone Operator; [memb.] My father is a Choctaw Indian, Mother-English, Scott, both deceased, Choctaw Indian Nation Idabell, OK; [oth. writ.] Yes, I have many poems - for others to read and enjoy.; [pers.] I feel I can show others and let them see - where they haven't and look up into the sky and say yes - I know now. I want to write to all - to know.; [a.] Wentzville, MO

SMITH, RAYMOND
[pen.] Ray Smith; [b.] New York City; [p.] Edward and Dorothy Smith; [m.] Claire Virginia, January 30, 1979; [ch.] Raymond, Edward, Elizabeth Lindgren, Kathryn Hayword; [ed.] Williamsburg High School New York Tech; [occ.] Retired technical writer and design draftsman; [memb.] Library of Congress Associate Veterans of Foreign Wars Nassau County Board of Elections; [oth. writ.] "Doorway To Space" published in American Heritage (November, 1990) Various poems in local publications Technical Manuals; [pers.] I am one of those who believe poetry to be a much more powerful means of expression than prose. I have written poems about storms at sea, Bowery bums, dishonest auto mechanics, walking on the beach by the sea, lost loves, the joy of a newborn child, a scandalous divorce suit filed by Santa Claus's wife, etc.; [a.] Oceanside, NY

SMITH, REVIS DALE
[b.] April 26, 1963, Highland Park, MI; [p.] Revis Smith, Josephine Farris; [ed.] Robert S. Tower High School, Macomb Community College, Oakland University, Walsh College; [occ.] Starving Writer; [memb.] America on Line RSMITH0463; [oth. writ.] Book, Waxing Poetic, A View from The Chair; [pers.] J. R. R. Tolkien, and Edgar Allan Poe have influenced me. I believe that to write well about a subject, you must draw from own life experience.; [a.] Sterling Heights, MI

SMITH, RICKY DOUGLAS
[pen.] R. Douglas Smith; [b.] March 2, 1952, Greenville, SC; [p.] Henry S. and Dorothy O. Smith; [ed.] Berea High, North Greenville College, (Assoc. General Studies) Greenville County Museum School of Art. (Assoc. Applied Arts, Assoc. Fine Arts); [occ.] Retail sales, Freelance artist; [memb.] American Rose Society, Greenville Chorale, PCA Musician Association, SC Chapter, Second Presbyterian Church Centennial Historical Committee; [hon.] Gamma Beta Phi Society, Faber Castel Advertising Award. The best of Poets 1996 The National Library of Poetry.; [pers.] Strive to write from the heart.; [a.] Greenville, SC

SMITH, RYDER E.
[pen.] Ryder Aynde; [b.] October 27, 1963, New York, NY; [p.] Ed Smith, Gail Gregory; [m.] Julie Ann Smith, October 30, 1993; [ch.] Elyse Ariana Smith; [ed.] Carleton College (BA 1985), The Ohio State University (MHA 1990); [occ.] Health Care Consultant, Freelance Writer, Chicago, IL; [memb.] Diplomate, American College of Health Care Executives; [hon.] Huntington Poetry Price, Association for Conservation Information; [oth. writ.] Poems in chapbooks and regional writers mags, text for broadcast and print media; [pers.] Thanks to friends, family, T.S. Eliot, and W.C. Williams.; [a.] Naperville, IL

SMITH, SHELIA R.
[b.] October 1, 1952, Hawkins Co, TN; [p.] Elzie Carpenter, Joe Gilliam; [m.] Larry M. Smith, September 17, 1983; [ch.] Angela and Mark Carpenter, Joshua Smith; [occ.] Bristling operator anchor Brush Company Morristown, TN; [oth. writ.] Poems published in local newspaper. Received awards for being a Lyric writer at age 12; [pers.] Each word that I write comes from my heart and is inspired by my higher power. "God," I try to show his love in everything I do.; [a.] Russellville, TN

SMITH, STACEY
[pen.] Tay; [b.] October 28, 1978, Jamaica; [p.] Hugh and Marjorie Smith; [ed.] Senior at Miramar High School; [oth. writ.] I have written several other poems one of which was published in the Caribbean Lifestyle Magazine entitled "A Women Worth Respect".; [pers.] Motto to live by, if you fall, stand tall and come back for more; [a.] Miramar, FL

SMITH, WILLIAM HENRY
[pen.] Willis, Smitty, Shorty; [b.] August 21, 1943, Sontag, MS; [p.] Jesse Smith (D), Mary Alice Smith-Brown; [m.] Gloria Ann, June 21, 1964; [ch.] Angelia Rene, Bridgetta Schran; [ed.] Wisner-Gilbert High, Wisner, LA Association Degree, St. Leo College, FL (Business) with special studies - Human Resources and Counseling; [occ.] Administrative Assistant Drug Testing Lab, Brooks AFB, TX; [memb.] AARP, African-American Cultural Association; [hon.] Nominated: Civilian of the Quarter (January-March 1995), 1995 "Angel" of the Year Award, 1995 Federal Employee of the Year, Painting - "Old House In Phebus (VA) won 1st place in The All Army Art Contest - 1977; [oth. writ.] Article - "I Stand Accused" (1994); [pers.] Retired (US Army) (24 years), enjoys paintings with oils, fishing and hunting, very active in a local church, works extensively with youths. Have a desire to write a book for children - title "SHORTLY" in series/volume. Growing up in MS and LA was a unique experience for me. Remember the movie "ROOTS" - I lived ROOTS.; [a.] Converse, TX

SNAPP, COSTELLA HARPER
[b.] August 7, 1959, Tallahassee, AL; [p.] Eula Williams; [m.] Perry Snapp, September 3, 1992; [ch.] James Timmons, Jason Timmons and Erica Snapp; [ed.] Wakulla High School; [occ.] Secretary III, Apalachee Center for Human Services Tallahassee, FL; [pers.] When you have the opportunity to follow your dreams, don't pass it up. We have only one life to live so why not make the best of it.; [a.] Tallahassee, FL

SNIDER JR., MICHAEL
[pen.] Wonder; [b.] January 22, 1976, Arkansas; [p.] Michael Snider; [m.] Rose Snider, August 1, 1977; [ed.] Still in High School, plan on pursuing College and Joining sports program; [occ.] Athlete; [hon.] 3 year varsity track state Competitor in Hurdles.; [oth. writ.] School news paper, write for my friends.; [pers.] I write my poetry based on experience. Love, sensitivity, loneliness, commits to my thoughts. I strive my thoughts on paintings, certain things I see attract my attention, walks threw certain places and areas. I write to calm and realize pain can be felt even in literature; [a.] Lompoc, CA

SNYDER, GLORIA J.
[b.] March 9, 1960, Fort Campbell, KY; [p.] Roy and Evan Jean Rohrbaugh; [ch.] Justin Michael Snyder 12, Savannah Rae Elise Snyder 10; [ed.] Central York High School, Advanced courses at York College, and Penn State; [occ.] Shipping Supervisor, General Graphic Services, York, PA; [memb.] Living Word Community Church; [oth. writ.] This was my first submission of my writings and my first publication.; [pers.] In some form we all share similar dreams, feelings and emotions. The heart of everyone has something to say and we should take time to listen. I strive to put these things on paper. By doing so, there is a realization that we really are, never alone.; [a.] York, PA

SNYDER, LOUISE BROOKS
[b.] April 5, 1932, NC; [p.] Walter and Carrie Conner Brooks Owen; [m.] George Snyder (divorced), November 16, 1947; [ch.] Seven; [ed.] G.E.D. Creative writing course my books, I love, self-taught poet; [occ.] Retired; [memb.] V.F.W. As a Gold Star Mother., A.A.R.P., Baptist church; [oth. writ.] I have had two articles published in our local paper. One on my Pioneer family, one on my son who died in Vietnam.; [pers.] I try to live by the Golden Rule. I'm very loyal to my God, Country, Children and all my Family.; [a.] Waynesville, NC

SNYDER, MILDRED REX E.
[b.] March 28, 1912, Near Syracuse, IN; [p.] Walter and Jessie Warble Rex; [m.] Richard E. Snyder (Deceased), January 1, 1933; [ch.] Richard Rex Snyder, Mary Gail Snyder, Ridenour; [ed.] Avilla, Ind. High School, International Business College Ft. Wayne, Ind.; [occ.] Retired; [hon.] Salutatorian of 8th Grade classes of Noble Co., Ind. 1926, Salutatorian and class President of 1930 High School Graduating Class Treasurer of Resident Council of Concord Village; [oth. writ.] None published but I have a warped sense of humor and can taught at myself and love to write limericks; [pers.] Of course the "Beau" in my poem was the man I was married to for nearly 54 yrs until his death in 1986. My mother was an organist, pianist, poetess, a cousin is an artist and I am an organist and pianist. Poetry and music add that special dimension to life that makes it more enjoyable. I'm an incurable romantic. The poem is a true story.; [a.] Fort Wayne, IN

SNYDER, WILLIAM L.
[pen.] Sweet William; [b.] January 18, 1933, Wichita, KS; [p.] William Mathew, Maxine Virgina; [m.] Lahoma Faye, October 28, 1951; [ch.] Mark Stacy, Pamela Faye, Malinda Lee, Rebecca Michelle; [ed.] Long Fellow Grade, Allison Jr. USMC GED-High Equivalent, Law and Layman Fullerton College, Graduate Police Academy.; [occ.] Self employed retired Commander American Legion Post 383; [memb.] American Legion Lions, Kiwanis Marrage Encounter President's Club, City Fact Finbers Chamber of Commerce, Past Pres, 84-95; [hon.] Santa Claus yearly 73-95 Man of Year City of Stanton 86-89 Planning Commission 80-81 Kiwanis Man of Year 86-87, Community Safety Commission Vise Chair Orange country supervisor Rep, Highway super Blvd Project; [oth. writ.] Fine Collection of Untyped-Unpublished Poetry one poems painted in Wichita Earle, August 30, 1990 C.E., McCune, Family Writings, Eulogy for service men of American Legion, may God's hands hold them.; [pers.] Birth to Korean War 1950 Writerless-Letters, then to my love, nothing til-1996 Marrage Encounter, an openness of mind-heart, I wrote visions seen in eyes beautiful words of our earth-sunrise, evening hubs midnight rainbows upon deserts moon, but most beautiful-life as it flows among 45.; [a.] Stanton, CA

SNYDERS, CLARISSA EILEEN
[pen.] Clarissa Cyrils; [b.] November 12, 1922, Batchtown, IL; [p.] Walter and Minnie Grigsby; [m.] Cyril Melvine Snyders, August 26, 1939; [ch.] Eileen, Brenda, Karen, Ruth, Curtis, Cyrild; [ed.] Elementary Calhoun County, Illinois, Batchtown and Hardin; [occ.] Housewife, Widowed; [hon.] Poet 1988. "The Journey." Golden Poet Award 1990. Silver Poet Award Eddie Lou Cole, Poet Editor John Campbell Editor and Publisher. Published in local church and news paper,

"Far One So Small as I"; [oth. writ.] I have written most of my poems about God and being a Christian. But have also poems, like "Tears in My Candy" and many more. When I hear the words of my poems from God I write them as fast as I can write.; [pers.] I am one of ten children. A twin. A brother. Calvin Abraham Grigsby. I am a Born Again Christian. A Catholic. Poetry is a family trait. I have lived here for ten years in a more noble home.; [a.] Prosser, WA

SOBERANIS, SUMMER
[b.] July 2, 1979, Houston, TX; [p.] Maria D. Soberanis, Miguel Angel Soberanis; [pers.] I believe that if we put God in all that we do first and believe in ourselves anything can happen; [a.] Houston, TX

SOLEAU, KELLY H.
[b.] March 4, 1984, Hartford, CT; [p.] Chris and Bob Soleau; [ed.] Hopewell School, Glastonbury, CT, The Ethel Walker School Simsbury, CT; [occ.] Student; [memb.] American Horse Show Assoc., Connecticut Hunter and Jumper Assoc., Green Mountain Horse Assoc.; [hon.] Short Stirrup Hunter Champion - 1992 - Children's Hunter Reserve Champion - 1993 Children's Hunter Champion - 1994; [a.] Glastonbury, CT

SOLIS, ELSA D.
[b.] July 14, 1944, Oilton, TX; [p.] Gertrudis and Bonifacio Davila (Deceased); [m.] Divorced; [ch.] Ruben S. Solis, 23 yrs., John G. Solis, 21 yrs.; [ed.] Bruni High School Bruni, TX, 5/62 some College - San Antonio College, San Antonio, TX; [occ.] Social Worker - TX Department of Human Services - Community care to aged and disabled program; [oth. writ.] Several writings - new publisher yet to be published in a book to be entitled Inner Pearl refreshing thoughts for a thirsting soul; [pers.] I reflect the compassion heavenly father has give me in my writing - The writing given me have been to encouraged me and others - Have written for past 19 years. Have written about moral and spiritual values; [a.] San Antonio, TX

SOLOCINSKI, MICHELLE L. MIENTEK
[b.] October 4, 1967, Warren, MI; [p.] Mike and Rene Mientek; [m.] Alan H. Solocinski II, August 1, 1988; [ch.] Jeremy M. Mientek, Matthew David Solocinski, Daniel J. Solocinski; [ed.] Graduated Hazel Park High School; [occ.] Wife, Mother and child care provider; [memb.] International Society of Poets; [oth. writ.] The last goodbye (East of the Sunrise), Night Sky (Poetic voices of America).; [pers.] I would like to thank my family for their love and support, and a special thanks to my husband and children for their love, support and encouragement.; [a.] Jacksonville, FL

SORENSEN, BORGNY
[b.] September 17, 1917, Bergen, Norway; [p.] Olaf, Karen Bakke; [m.] Vincent Neil Sorensen, September 29, 1946; [ch.] Linda-Lee, Roger, Jonathan, David, Karen; [ed.] Bay Ridge High School, Brooklyn, N.Y., Methodist Hosp. School of Nursing; [occ.] Retired and ailing, but trusting the Lord; [pers.] I desire to tell young and old that we may have eternal life by looking to Jesus, who loves us all. The Holy Bible explains (John 17:3 - the book after Luke). "Him that cometh to me I will in no wise fast out" Jesus says.; [a.] Huntington Station, NY

SORENSEN, KATHLEEN
[pen.] Kathy Robertazzo; [b.] September 12, 1951, Chicago; [p.] George and Caroline Robertazzo; [m.] Randy Sorensen, February 16, 1991; [ch.] Stepson - Joseph Robert Sorensen; [ed.] Associate's Degree Steinmetz High School, MacCormac Junior College, Chicago College of Commerce; [occ.] Court Reporter; [memb.] National Court Reporter Association NCRA,

Illinois Shorthand Reporters Association ISRA; [a.] Hoffman Estates, IL

SORGE, ARTHUR L.
[pen.] Arthur L. Sorge; [b.] May 24, 1921, PA; [p.] Deceased; [m.] Deceased; [ch.] Thelma H. Sorge, (Lorentz); [ed.] Graduated Altoona Sr. High School 1940, I pass Th' Key To You; [occ.] Retired; [memb.] American Legion, 82nd Airborne Asso.; [hon.] Decorated World War II Purple Heart, Bronze Star, Central European Theatre Campaign Medal, Three Spearheads; [oth. writ.] I Want To Go Back; [pers.] The Bible: Is, in my view, a bulwark against human savagery. It reached it's peak with the arrival of the Pilgrims, and is now on the decline.; [a.] Cleveland, OH

SORRICLE, STEPHANNIE
[b.] February 28, 1980, Hanford; [p.] Stephen and Sandra; [ed.] Freshman (H.S.); [occ.] Student, Maintenance Engineer; [hon.] 8th Grade Scholastic Award - 100% - 1994; [oth. writ.] 1st Place Winner in High School Writing Contest 1995

SOTTILE, CHARLOTTE L.
[pen.] Jade Archer; [b.] February 22, 1951, Charleston, SC; [p.] Salvador V. Sottile, Louise W. Sottile; [ed.] Clemson University-BA in Liberal Arts, 1972; [occ.] Senior Producer and Deputy Director of News and Public Affairs, South Carolina ETV; [memb.] Helpline of the Midlands, Delta Delta Delta, Clemson University Alumni Association, Clemson University Women's Council, The ETV Endowment of South Carolina, Friday the 13th Club; [hon.] 1989-Profiled in The State, Columbia, SC, 1980-Outstanding Young Women of America, 1970-73 The National Student Register; [oth. writ.] Several poems published in the spring-summer 1994 issue of Kaleidoscope of Carolina, (Columbia, SC); [pers.] I credit my sister Bette with teaching me that poetry need not rhyme to be effective. My inspiration comes from the visual and the emotional including several relationships which didn't last as long as the poetry!; [a.] Columbia, SC

SOUCY, SANDY
[b.] November 14, 1953, NH; [m.] Daniel Soucy, November 14, 1975; [ch.] Two children Holly and Heather; [ed.] Milford, NH Area School Attended Keene State College; [occ.] Paraprofessional, Fairgrounds Elementary School; [oth. writ.] "A place where we can go", "Forever her song", "Reflections", "You'll soon be on your way"; [pers.] "To enrich one's life is to fulfill a dream within and share it with the world through love, song and writing."; [a.] Nashua, NH

SOUTHERN, MARTHA
[b.] March 3, 1978, Queens, NY; [p.] Arnetha and John Southern (both Deceased); [ed.] P.S. NQ, J.H. 5#8 Graphic Arts Communication High School Specialized for writing; [occ.] Student; [memb.] The National Sorority of PHI Delta Kappa, Inc. An Organization of Women in Education. Chapter Beta - Omicron, Tabernacle of Joy Ministries Church.; [hon.] Excellence in Poetry, a Publication from the National Library of Poetry; [oth. writ.] The dark, he's taken my depression away, transition; [pers.] I write the truth trying to create beautiful words even when its painful. I was greatly influenced by my mother, my sister Georgia Southern, my former English teacher Carla Carter.; [a.] Jamaica, NY

SPAINHOUR, POLLY L.
[b.] June 2, 1945, NC; [p.] Cecil Lynch, Rena S. Lynch; [m.] Kenneth C. Spainhour, September 3, 1966; [ed.] Pinnacle High School Winston, Salem Business College; [occ.] Employed at Winston-Salem, NC. N.C. Baptist Hospital in Data Audit; [oth. writ.] Poems

published in local newspapers "The Pilot"; [pers.] I enjoy writing about the beauty that I see and feel about nature and the people around me.; [a.] Pinnacle, NC

SPEARS, AARON D.
[pen.] Erno; [b.] July 10, 1971, Washington, DC; [p.] Richard and Veronica Spears; [ed.] Oxon Hill Senior High, Clarion University, Delaware State University; [occ.] Computer analyst, aspiring actor and writer; [memb.] Kappa Alpha Psi Fraternity Inc., NSBE; [hon.] Graduated Summa Cum Laude 3.4 GPA, Dean's List, Who's Who Among American Colleges and Universities, Who's Who Among American High Schools, 5 yrs. Letterman in Football and Track and Field, BS in Computer Science; [oth. writ.] Romance, Mystery, Drama, and thought provoking topics of great interest may also be obtained through contacting me.; [pers.] Success is determined by the contents of your heart and mind, not by the social acceptance plagues that are hung upon the atmosphere that you inhibit.; [a.] Oxon Hill, MD

SPEARS, GLENDA
[pen.] G. Chase; [b.] June 11, 1946, Cincinnati, OH; [p.] Cecil and Eva Spears; [ch.] Eva, Shandra and Alton Faile, Shirley, Scott, John Spears; [ed.] High School, and am now a college student, majoring in computer science; [occ.] I was an off shore cook until inherited 3 small children - single foster mom of 4; [hon.] My honors are the love and respect I see in the children's eyes that I have raised, by the sweat of my brow.; [oth. writ.] I have other writings I would love to publish. It is my prayer, so that I might provide college for three children I have fostered, which are my neice and nephews.; [pers.] I do not know who said it fist or last "Every journey begins with the first step." Believe in yourself and keep trying.; [a.] Oak Harbor, WA

SPINNEY, JONATHON RAY
[pen.] Jonathon Ray; [b.] May 27, 1955, Texas; [ch.] Jason Spinney, Jonathon Spinney; [ed.] 4 yrs. University of Maine; [occ.] Artist, Writer, Musician, Sculptor; [hon.] Art work has been featured in Maine and New Mexico; [oth. writ.] Book - 'Awakening of Red Feather' Journalist for Odyssey in Southern Maine writer for various monthly publications; [pers.] 'Humanity must embrace the Goddess and the feminine ways of knowing and being if this planet is to fully heal'; [a.] La Grange, ME

SPIVEY, TERESA
[b.] March 6, 1961, Fort Stewart, WA; [p.] Jack and Rose M. Marsh; [m.] Randall Spivey, February 12, 1980; [ch.] Mathew Spivey, Daniel Spivey; [ed.] Bradwell Institute; [occ.] Recreation Aide: At youth center; [hon.] Who's who, among American High School Students. 1978/79; [pers.] I believe, everything happens, for a reason, and only god knows what that reason is. It's up to us to find out and deal with it.; [a.] Kingsland, LA

SPOHN, ALMA
[b.] August 31, 1957, Harrisonville, MO; [p.] Flora Jordan, Ron Jordan; [m.] Richard Spohn, July 4, 1976; [ch.] Johnny Ray, Angela Marie, Gypsy Christine, Benjamin Arnold; [ed.] High School Graduate from Harrisonville Senior High; [occ.] Housewife and full time Mom; [memb.] Freedom of Road Riders, Local #14 in Independence, MO; [pers.] When a child's innocence is combined with the love and wisdom of the elderly, something magic occurs. I hope to project a little bit of this magic through my writing and , with luck, make other people more aware of the elderly people around them.; [a.] Sugar Creek, MO

SPRAGUE, BECKY
[b.] November 20, 1945, Iowa City, IA; [p.] Earl and Violet Frauenholz; [m.] Louis Sprague; [ch.] Terri Lynn, Scott Ryan, Mark and Jane, Steven Wayne, Teresa and Kevin; [ed.] L-M High School; [occ.] Homemaker; [oth. writ.] Several more poems and numerous short stories; [a.] Muscatine, IA

SPRANGER, ANGELA M.
[b.] April 1, 1979, Wausau, WI; [p.] Susann and James Spranger; [ed.] D. C. Everest Senior High School; [occ.] Student; [memb.] D. C. Everest Senior High Marching Band, Symphonic Wind Ensemble, Concert Choir, Varsity Football Cheerleading, Varsity Wrestling Cheerleading, Peer Helpers; [hon.] Presidential Academic Fitness Award, Renaissance; [oth. writ.] Why Did You Go Away?, The Truth, You Said (These have been approved for publishing); [a.] Wausau, WI

SPROUSE, LINDA
[b.] June 24, 1943, Peoria, IL; [p.] Walter and Fran Ulrich; [m.] Thomas Sprouse, July 29, 1962; [ch.] Kevin, Keith, Craig, grandson, Nicholas; [ed.] Peoria High School, Illinois Central College; [occ.] Freelance Artist, Independent Consultant for Mary Kay Cosmetics; [memb.] Illinois Art League, Art Guild, Lakeview Museum; [hon.] Numerous awards for Art Competitions; [pers.] I work in many art forms, both written and visual. I believe with positive thinking you will reach your goals.; [a.] Peoria, IL

SROK, BEN
[pen.] Ben Srok; [b.] July 12, 1981, Atlanta, GA; [p.] Ed and Dawn Srok; [ed.] Ooltewah Middle School, Gowana Jr. High School (Present); [occ.] Student 8th Grade; [memb.] Boy Scouts of America, Tennessee Valley Herpetological Society; [hon.] 1994 - 1st place on the class, school, and loval levels of the Optimist Oratorical Speech, Contest, 2nd place on the regional level numerous Star Rolls and Honor Rolls in school; [oth. writ.] One poem published in "Anthology of Poetry by Young Americans"; [pers.] If you live in the woods, don't make fun of bears.; [a.] Ballston Lake, NY

ST. JEAN, MELISSA M.
[b.] January 13, 1984, Anchorage, AK; [occ.] Currently in the 5th grade at Griswold Int. School; [memb.] Member of Smithsonian Institute, and Audubon Society; [hon.] First place winner in a school wide essay contest; [pers.] I think women, men, and all living things should be treated with respect.

STAHL, SHEILA
[pen.] Austin McKinsey; [b.] December 1, 1968, Lubbock, TX; [p.] Judy Stahl; [ed.] Baylor University; [occ.] Bartender, Outback Steak house; [memb.] USTA; [hon.] National Honor Society; [pers.] I attempt to Express with a pen that which many only feel and dream.; [a.] San Antonio, TX

STALLARD, ROBERT R.
[b.] July 10, 1946, Esserville, VA; [p.] Harley and Bunnie Stallard; [m.] Nell K. Stallard, January 17, 1970; [ed.] Powell Valley High, Southwest VA Community College, VA Tech.; [occ.] Self-Employed; [memb.] President - Montgomeny County Kiwanis Club, Roanoke Moose Lodge, President - Stallard Family Association; [oth. writ.] Many poems; [pers.] My poetry is an expression of my being. My favorite poem is how do I love thee? Let me count the ways by Elizabeth Barrett Browning. My favorite Poet is Poe.; [a.] Blacksbury, VA

STAMATIOU, KIKI
[pen.] Kyriakh; [b.] July 4, 1969, Kalamazoo, MI; [p.] Toula and Odysseus Stamatiou; [ed.] Mattawan High School, Kalamazoo Valley Community College, Western Michigan University; [memb.] Songwriter Club of America, National Authors Registry International Society of Authors and Artist, International Society of Poets, National Poets Association Kalamazoo County Historical Society; [hon.] Recognition Award for Poem "Colesion" from Creative Arts and Science Enterprise (1945) Honorable Mention Award in for prose "All In A Days Work" in full 1994 Iliad Awards program, it also got 1995 President Award from National Authors Registry; [oth. writ.] `Ode to Ancient One' (The Spare Between - National Library of poetry), `Ode to Greek Pioneers" Pub in "New Voice" by JMW Publishing; [pers.] Soft winds burn inside a jilted fire; [a.] Kalamazoo, MI

STAMP, CHARLES
[b.] December 1, 1970, Hackensack; [ed.] Montclair State University English and Marketing; [occ.] President of "Lyrics That Hit!"; [oth. writ.] Song Lyrics "The City". Advertising and Marketing, Slogans. Some journalism, prose, "Religious vast and vanished"; [pers.] Would like to someday begin working on a philosophical work titled: "Corrupted from birth. Disillusioned by Pride".; [a.] New Milford, NJ

STANLEY, CHARLES KEITH
[b.] December 10, 1956, Indianapolis, IN; [p.] Robert and Carol Stanley; [m.] Brenda Stanley, October 18, 1979; [ch.] Marshall Aron, Joseph Logan; [ed.] Whiteland High, Lake City Community College, FL; [occ.] Aerospace, Defense, Northrop, Grumman; [oth. writ.] Several Commemorative and private poems. No attempts to publish, writer of proverbs.; [pers.] Art is more than expression of the heart. "Art" is such, only when the creator of the creator is glorified, and thus, the results of expression are truly beautiful.; [a.] Azle, TX

STANLEY, CHRISTINA
[b.] May, 18, 1995; [p.] Mr. and Mrs. Stanley; [ed.] I'm in my second year of high school; [occ.] Student; [pers.] This poem is an extension of my life and my heart, and how it's been broken by the twisted nature of some people.; [a.] San Dimas, CA

STANLEY SR., FRANK L.
[b.] August 27, 1949, West Chester, PA; [p.] Jess Stanley and Dorthy Stanley; [m.] Mary Irwin (divorced), April 9, 1969; [ch.] Mary J. Stanley (Stern), (Frank L. Stanley Jr.), (Aaron M. Stanley); [ed.] 7th Grade Unionville High, Unionville, PA. Chadsford Elementary, Chadsford, PA; [occ.] Disable; [memb.] American Heart Association, The Top Records Songwriters Association, Songwriters Club of America; [oth. writ.] In the process of trying to get a book published titled "A Whisper In the Wind and Selected Poems" I also write lyrics for country and western song sand have copy's of demos from eight of them that is being promoted in hopes of getting published, and I am working on four more at this time!; [pers.] I like to think that despite day-to day problems, life still contains many blessings. But most of all I want to thank Josephine Alexander who lives in Trinidad, West-Indies and my son Aaron who has given me a lot of encouragement to continue to write poetry.; [a.] Lafayette, IN

STARACE, THOMAS
[pen.] "Star" or Pied Piper; [b.] September 24, 1968, New York; [p.] Thomas and Carmela; [ed.] St. Patrick's (Elementary) Glen Cove (High School) Nassau Community College AA Degree; [occ.] Golf Pro, for Piping Rock Club (Locus Valley) Long Island; [memb.] Worked Piping Rock Club; [hon.] Played National Tournament of Junior Colleges, Region 15 Champions for 2 years, there is a trophy given in his name by Met PGA Jr.; [oth. writ.] Enclosed is what Tom wrote about his family and happenings, also Tom wrote sports for the local newspaper in Glen Cove.; [pers.] Thomas died at age 24. He was a caddy for Jim Albus. 1991-1992 Senior Tour, may the love Tom had for the game of gulf be passed down to other youths and his memory shine like a "star" for years to come.

STAVE, BONNER
[b.] May 21, 1985, Wickenburg, AZ; [p.] Robert and Pam Stave; [ed.] 4th Grade Gifted Program; [occ.] Student; [hon.] Abbit honor roll new windows 95, technology, certificate of scholarship June 7, 1995; [oth. writ.] "The Quest", "Everyone", "Hero of my heart"; [pers.] I live on a boat with my Mom and Dad, a dog named Lola and a cat named Sam. I have a good life.; [a.] Key West, FL

STEAVENSON, CRAIG A.
[b.] February 13, 1963, Denner, CO; [p.] Dan and Katie Steavenson; [ed.] Montbello Jr. Sr. High, Northwest Schools Port. OR. Denver Business College; [occ.] Fry Cook and food prep, Trainer Apple bees Mesa, AZ; [memb.] At one time - Smithsonian Institute and Literary Guild; [hon.] In 1986 I was offered nomination into the Republican party inner circle society by Senator John Tower; [oth. writ.] "Dreams," "What is it," "The winds of change," all non published works that I am very proud of.; [pers.] In my writings I strive to help others look into themselves and find peace and compassion for all beings in both humanity and the animal kingdom; [a.] Mesa, AZ

STEGALL, DORIS
[b.] July 26, Los Angeles, CA; [m.] Ben Stegall, March 4, 1962; [ch.] Wendy Lauren, Sheri Dawn; [ed.] Los Angeles High School, Santa Monica College; [occ.] Instructional Assistant, Grant Elementary School, Santa Monica; [memb.] Kehillath Israel Synagogue Choir, Red Ribbon Square Dance Club, Past President "Ethnos" Dance Performance Ensemble; [hon.] "Golden Girl" in 1960 Democratic National Convention and Personal thank you letter from John F. Kennedy; [pers.] I love teaching and helping children develop a love for learning new skills that will enable them to be successful citizens in today's world so they can make a positive contribution ot their society.; [a.] Santa Monica, CA

STEINBERG, DONALD
[b.] August 12, 1922, Toledo, OH; [p.] Sarah and Julius Steinberg; [m.] Janet Ann Steinberg, April 4, 1971; [ch.] Steven, Laurie, Daniel, Stephanie; [ed.] B.S., M.D. Ohio State Univ. Seven years post graduate study; [occ.] Retired General Surgeon; [memb.] Amer. College of Surgeons, American Medical Association, Ohio State Univ. Alumni Assoc., Ohio State Univ. "Varsity O", numerous local clubs and associations; [hon.] 1945 Outstanding Athlete and Scholar in Big Ten Conference "Hall of Fame" Lucas County, Oh, Pres. Toledo Surgical Society, Honorable Mention 1942 Big Ten Football; [oth. writ.] Numerous articles in surgical magazines and books., "Expanding your Horizons" published 1992, Dorrance Publishing Co., Currently writing a scientific novel, "Anthropomorphia" an unpublished anthology of philosophical poetry; [pers.] Have a love affair with life and an unblemished name.; [a.] Toledo, OH

STEINHAUSER, MARY JEAN D.
[b.] August 18, 1961, Buffalo, NY; [p.] Pasquale and Ida De Nora; [m.] Daniel F. Steinhauser, August 22, 1992; [ed.] Archbishop Carroll High School Erie Community College-North Campus Daemen College; [occ.] Medical Technologist and Utilization Coordinator; [memb.] American Society of Clinical Pathologists, CPR certificate, Eucharistic Minister for St. Lawrence R.C. Church; [pers.] I write what I feel from the heart

and I try to balance my talents in the scientific and artistic fields of interest.; [a.] Kenmore, NY

STEMBRIDGE, KERRI
[b.] August 21, 1969, Tyler, TX; [p.] Betty Deslatte, Joe Deslatte; [m.] Greg Stembridge, May 23, 1992; [ed.] Pine Tree High School, Kilgore Jr. College, Stephen F. Austin State Univ.; [occ.] Telephone Operator; [hon.] Volunteer Award, Who's Who (high school); [oth. writ.] Eleven year daily Journal, several non-published stories and poems; [pers.] Imagination feeds the mind and soul. My imagination takes me to places beyond the realms of dreams. I reflect this in my writings.; [a.] Gladewater, TX

STEPHENSON, CHERYL
[pen.] Lou-Lou; [b.] November 15, 1973, Huntington, WV; [p.] Sharon and Mike Stephenson; [ed.] Attending Marshall Univ.; [occ.] Struggling member of generation "X"/full-time data entry for government/ part-time retail; [memb.] MUFON, Humane Society; [oth. writ.] Other poems published in school anthologies; [pers.] Writing is my most gratifying therapy.; [a.] Huntington, WV

STERLING, ANNE MARIE
[b.] June 29, 1970, North Miami, FL; [ed.] DeLand Sr. High School, Stetson University, DeLand FL-BA Degree Political Science; [occ.] Executive Secretary; [memb.] Hospice of Central Florida, St. Stephen's Catholic Church, Village Players of Oviedo; [hon.] Editor's Choice Award in Seasons to Come from National Library of poetry Contest 1994-1995; [oth. writ.] Dozens of poems, some published in school-college publications, 'Lonesome' published in National Library of Poetry's Anthology of Poetry, 'Seasons to Come' 1994-1995, working on a book of poetry and an autobiography.; [pers.] The two ways in which the Lord has blessed me with the gift of self-expression are through my voice and my poetry, and I am forever grateful.; [a.] Oviedo, FL

STETTER, YVONNE
[b.] February 21, 1960; [p.] Mr. and Mrs. John McGuire; [m.] Richard Alan Stetter, April 20, 1980; [ch.] Jami, Jered, Jesica; [ed.] Attended Sullivan - Louisville, KY, Vincennes University Jasper Center; [occ.] Clerk; [memb.] International Society of Poets; [hon.] Editors Choice, Poet of Merit; [pers.] Poetry is an adventure through the paths of the internal soul.; [a.] Dubois, IN

STEVENS, ROBERT L.
[pen.] Bob Stevens; [b.] December 26, 1933, DeLand, FL; [p.] John M. and Cordia Belle Stevens; [m.] Faye Townsend (not Stevens), November 14, 1992; [ch.] Bob's children by a previous marriage Samuel, Aaron and Daniel Stevens; [ed.] B.S. in Business Administration from Stetson University, and Master of Divinity (M. Div.) from Columbia Theological Seminary; [occ.] Supervisor, Palmetto Center, Florence, SC (Inpatient addiction treatment Center); [memb.] American Motorcyclist Association, People For The American Way, and Parents and Friends of Lesbians and Gays (PFLAG); [hon.] Selected as a member of the Prime Study Committee by the Institute of Rehabilitation Issues (1967 and 1992), Invited to introduce the course, "Vocational Rehabilitation of Alcoholics", into the curriculum of the Rutgers University Summer School of Alcohol Studies (1967); [oth. writ.] Articles on addiction published in publications circulated within the field of addiction treatment, Informational "handouts" and brochures written for Palmetto Center, where I work, unpublished poetry.; [pers.] The older I become, the fewer absolute truths I believe in. I do believe that loving is more important than "morality". We use too many principles to separate ourselves from other people.; [a.] Florence, SC

STEVENSON, ANIKA E.
[pen.] Anika; [b.] March 11, 1981, Redwood City, CA; [p.] Annerieke Green and Ed Ollie Stevenson; [ed.] Attending 8th grade, Bowditch Middle School; [occ.] Student; [hon.] Honors student in Junior High and attending honor classes as a freshmen next year.; [oth. writ.] Personal collection of poems I wrote in my spare time.; [pers.] I feel that people like myself can express their feelings and emotions through poetry in an unique and personal way.; [a.] Foster City, CA

STEWART, LUCRECIA
[b.] May 8, 1956, New York; [p.] George Stewart, Christine Stewart; [ed.] The Brearley School Utica College of Syracuse Univ. (B.A.) Univ. of West Florida - (M. A.); [occ.] Elementary School Teacher, Bronx, NY; [memb.] Alpha-Kappa-Alpha Sorority, Unity Church of New York City; [hon.] Who's Who among Students in Amer. Colleges and Universities 1980-81; [pers.] I believe that to love myself, other people, and all of creation is my true goal in life. My ultimate mission to radiate this love wherever I go.; [a.] New York, NY

STEWART, MR. DALE T.
[b.] September 21, 1922, Virden, IL; [p.] Mr. and Mrs. Herbert E. Stewart; [m.] Maxine K. Steward, September 27, 1952; [ch.] Dianne, Mike and Ronnie; [ed.] 12 years and Ft. Belvoir Engineering School, Ft. Belvoir, Va.; [occ.] Retired, Technical Illustrator. Currently selling wholesale and doing several medias of Art.; [memb.] Brighton Heritage Group Museum. American Legion; [hon.] Over 800 Art awards sculpture award "1st. International Art Show" NY City, 1970. In 1961 exhibited an empty frame, titled "Nothing" made AP and API news.; [oth. writ.] 4 songs, one published "World War II" about House cat "Socks" published. My poem "Tall Tale" probably the first ever written with only one word in each line.; [pers.] I keep busy with my paintings, designs and writing. I especially want to be known for my variety of Art that I have pursued the past 40 years.; [a.] Brighton, IL

STEYER, SAMUEL DENISON TAYLOR
[b.] May 5, 1988, San Francisco, CA; [p.] Tom Steyer and Kat Taylor; [ed.] The Little School, 1993, Marin County Day School, 2002; [occ.] Student; [a.] San Francisco, CA

STOLL, NATASHA LATOJA
[b.] June 7, 1976, Guyana; [p.] Stephen and Leila Stoll; [ed.] Richard Ishmael's Secondary School Guyana, South America; [oth. writ.] Darkness of night. Where has it gone. Trust and forgive paradise.; [pers.] My inspiration came from my father who is a poet and from the people of my country Guyana. Who are friendly and loving people. Of whom I am proud of being a part of.; [a.] Georetown Guyana, South America

STONE, DEBBE
[pen.] Debbe; [oth. writ.] Newsletter articles co-author of the booklet 'Express Who You Are' and several poems; [pers.] Our journey here is short, remember to laugh in trust, to play in faith and to find the joy in every moment. Remember to, Eat your desert first.; [a.] Troy, NH

STONE, SARA E.
[b.] Philadelphia, PA; [m.] Jesse, 1949; [ch.] Dawn, Tracey, Vicky, Linda, Wanda Joy, Jesse P. Stone; [occ.] Retired, sew and selling doll cloths at craft; [oth. writ.] I keep myself busy writing poems and short stories. I have had several published in mags. and newspapers over the years.; [pers.] I love life, and enjoy my family, friends and my dog, four cats and a rabbit.; [a.] Mount Laurel, NJ

STONEKING, VERNIE V.
[b.] October 3, 1924, Gin Ridge, IL; [p.] Bert Stoneking, Josephine Babb Stoneking; [m.] Widow; [ch.] Judith, Dennis, Deborah; [ed.] High School; [occ.] Retired; [hon.] WW II Air Force Air Medal with 3 battle stars and 6 Oak Leaf Clusters; [oth. writ.] Numerous poems and songs; [pers.] I loved poetry as a child and have been writing poems and songs all my life.; [a.] Galesburg, IL

STOTLER, MELISSA DAY
[pen.] Melissa Day; [b.] August 4, 1976, Kinston, NC; [p.] Cindy Stotler, Nelson Stotler; [ed.] South Lenoir High School; [occ.] Full time student at Lenoir Comm. College; [memb.] First Pentelostal Holiness Church of kinston, in high school, member of Science club and vice president of Library club, and photographer for Vica Club; [hon.] Who's who among American High School students, National Junior Honor Society; [oth. writ.] Few poems and short stories never before published; [pers.] A few words of wisdom are the fact that, "knowledge comes, but wisdom lingers," (tennuson) "Success is a journey, not a destination," but, "Don't confuse fame with success. Madonna is one, Helen keller is the other," (Erma Bombeck) and remember. Begin each morning with a talk with God.; [a.] Kinston, NC

STOWE, ROBERT L.
[b.] January 5, 1921, GA; [p.] Joe and Frances Stowe; [m.] Madge Stowe, February 16, 1990 (2nd); [ch.] Jane, Joyce and Robert; [ed.] High School Some College; [occ.] Retired; [memb.] Society of American Inventors; [hon.] Presidential Lecion of Merit; [oth. writ.] Other Poems published by National Library

STRACCIONE, CARMELA
[b.] April 5, 1944, Philadelphia, PA; [p.] Ann and Dave Roccia; [m.] David Straccione, March 25, 1970; [ch.] David and Michael Wagner, Anthony, Carmen and Lisa Straccione; [ed.] Bishop McDevitt High; [occ.] Secretary, Bookkeeper, Baiocco Development Co.; [hon.] First prize winner in People Category in Florida Keys Magazine's, 2nd Annual Photo Contest; [pers.] My poems are inspired and written with the help and guide of my guardian angels.; [a.] Media, PA

STRAKA, MICHAEL
[pen.] Michael Strake; [b.] October 10, 1969, Newark, NJ; [p.] Frank and Elizabeth Straka; [ed.] Monsignor Donovan High School Toms River, NJ - Rutgers University BA English, Drama and Bobby Lewis, Theatre Workshop; [occ.] Actor, NYC and Newsman/writer CBS News; [memb.] Screen Actor's Guild (SAG) Actor's Equity Association (AEA), American Fed of Radio and TV Artist (AFTRA), Writers Guild of America (WGA), US Tae Kwon Do Union; [hon.] 1991 National Taekwon Do Champion, 1992 NJ and NJ State TKD Champion, 2nd Degree Black Belt, Varsity Wretler at Rogers Univ.; [oth. writ.] Television Drama and News - more poems - an off - Broadway Autobiographical One-Man Show "On The Mat"; [pers.] I put my thoughts on paper in the form of poetry, to better understand, my struggles for happiness, and for the craft of acting; [a.] New York, NY

STRICKLETT, TANDI
[b.] May 29, 1970, Omaha, NE; [p.] Mark, Sharon Stricklett; [ed.] Mercer Univ.; [occ.] Nursing student; [pers.] Dedicated to all the souls searching the earth for their destiny.

STROMMEN, JOHN A.
[b.] December 13, 1924, Milwaukee; [p.] Hjalmar and Hildegarde Strommen; [m.] Helen Strommen (Deceased), June 12, 1952; [ch.] Linda, Stephen, Mary, and Scott; [ed.] Masters Degrees Mechanical Engineer-

ing Univ. Wisconsin, Mathematics Marquette Univ.; [occ.] Retired; [memb.] American Legion, Mt. Hope Lutheran Church; [hon.] Air Medal WW II Notary Public; [oth. writ.] J-Factor for Gears. American Gear Manufactures Assoc. Fatigue Life at Materials Machine Design Magazine; [pers.] The pride of my life is the accomplishments of my 4 children. Some are youngest actually Stephen, Fiddeling champion of World Mary.; [a.] West Allis, WI

STULCE, HELEN M.
[pen.] War Kloud; [b.] March 8, 1944; [m.] Lee E. Stulce Sr., October 12, 1960; [ch.] Lovie, Lee, Francis, James, Lee (foster child); [ed.] Lincoln School of Practual Nursing; [occ.] Med-mentor on bus for severely handicapped children; [memb.] Life member VFW AUX Post 1699. Life member of St. Marys Hospital Aux-of Jeff City. Fraternal Order of Eagles -AERle #3015 twice past president of P.T.O. for Henery Kreschner State School for severely handicap; [hon.] 2nd place short story contest, Rtd Systems-Lemon twest Honorable Mention in Poets Guild. Presidents Award; [oth. writ.] Camp Fires Brite, Grandmas Hugs. I dream. In your dress so very Different. "Gene", Tender Love; [pers.] I am an native American, been married 35 years. Have 4 children, one foster son, and am so proud of my grandchildren, Jessica Soma and Tyler Soma and Matt, Ashley, Taylor Vineyard. And I live in Beautiful; [a.] Jefferson City, MO

STUTLER, LENNEL ANN
[b.] March 15, 1912, Harrison, WV; [p.] Dauphin Altice and Della (Furby) Stutler; [ed.] Grade High School and Rededicated to be a Librarian; [occ.] Retired after 41 years, 31 of those a Head Librarian of Louis Bernnetthem Library; [memb.] First United Methodist Church West Va. Library Association A.A.R.P.; [hon.] I've had a few but they are not important to my Biography; [oth. writ.] I've only allowed one other poem and a piece of writing to be published. I've always been shy about showing my poems, even to friends; [pers.] I can only write when inspired by a person, place, or even it. I'm unable to put words together to make a poem; [a.] Jane Lew, WV

SULLIVAN, CAROLYN DENTREMONT
[pen.] Carolyn Dentremont; [b.] August 4, 1949, Exeter, NH; [p.] Rachael E. Hussey my mother; [m.] Divorced; [ch.] Hillary Blackwood Sullivan, Morgaine Hayes Adair; [ed.] York High School, York, ME, Becker College, Worcester, MA; [occ.] disabled - severe rheumatoid arthritis; [memb.] South Congregational Church, Concord, NH; [hon.] N. H. Bad Association 1979 top award for investigative series published in Nashua, N.H. telegraph on N.H's weak medical examiner system; [oth. writ.] N.E. Business Magazine, Former Editor, Rockingham County Newspapers, Columnist, Nashua telegraph, Staff Writer, Nashua telegraph, Nashua, N.H's Foster's Daily Democrat, Dover, N.H.; [pers.] I believe nature is our greatest teacher and tonic. Our oneness with the earth will help make the world a more peaceful planet; [a.] Concord, NH

SULLIVAN, HELEN D.
[pen.] Dorothy Cushing; [b.] October 6, 1910, Boston, MA; [p.] Deceased; [m.] Deceased, October 30, 1927; [ch.] Warren, Charles, John, Paul, Carol; [ed.] St. Gregory High ; [occ.] Retired; [memb.] Women's Educational Industrial Center Boston, Ma. Member of "The Wilderness Society" and Auderbon Society; [hon.] Golden Awards for poems, The wonder of it all and along the lane; [oth. writ.] Happy Thoughts for Little Tots, In My Leisure Moments Children Story Book (2) The Cub who didn't want to hibernate little hoots strange Christmas; [pers.] I have written articles for the Mattapan tribunal. I am interested in saving our nations precious wild lands from destruction, and save the trees as they purify the air we breath.; [a.] Weymouth, MA

SULLIVAN, KAYDEE
[b.] August 8, 1971, Washington, DC; [p.] Judy and Bill Sullivan; [ed.] Pilgrim High School Community College of R.I.; [occ.] Manager of a Group Home, CPR Instructor; [pers.] I try to meet as many people as I can and grow from everyone of them.; [a.] Cranston, RI

SULLIVAN, LAURI MICHELLE
[b.] June 11, 1971, Mount Kisco, NY; [p.] Angela and Michael Sullivan; [ed.] John Jay High School in Hopewell Jct, NY and Dutchess Community College, Poughkeepsie, NY; [occ.] Customer Representative for Therapeutic Pain Rub International; [memb.] St. Jude's Hospital Foundation, Muscular Dystrophy Foundation. I have donated money to both these reputable charities.; [oth. writ.] A fictional human interest story was published in a local newspapers located in New Windsor, NY; [pers.] I believe that winning not only comes from the mind but from the heart. If you do not strive for extraordinary feats, you will never be aware of the possibilities of being alive and being a success.; [a.] Tampa, FL

SUMMERS, ANGELA
[b.] January 29, 1979, Martinsville, IN; [p.] Mr. and Mrs. Earl Summers; [ed.] Smith Elementary, West Middle School, I am now in my first year in Martinsville High School, Martinsville, IN; [hon.] Having my poem published in the National Library of Poetry is the greatest Honor I have had in my 16 years of life. Thank you; [pers.] I have written two other poems since this one. I feel more confident about my writing now. who knows, maybe someday I will have another poem published.; [a.] Paragon, IN

SUTOR, JACKSON B.
[pen.] J. B. Sutor; [b.] March 10, 1942, Mount Pleasant, PA; [p.] R. Orland Sutor, Evelyn P. Sutor; [m.] Divorced; [ch.] Ms. Deborah Huling 23 February 1963; [ed.] High School Graduate, Two years college; [occ.] Self employed contractor, also retired U.S. Navy; [memb.] Masonic lodge, Ionic 101, Moose Lodge, 2020 Lake shore, fleet reserve association; [oth. writ.] "Have you listened to the wind"; [pers.] Hope always that my writing will enlighten another life

SUTTON, CASEY M.
[b.] March 31, 1981, Alexandria, LA; [p.] Michael and Charlotte Sutton; [ed.] Elizabeth High School; [occ.] Student; [memb.] NRA; [a.] Elizabeth, LA

SWANCEY, GARY GENE
[b.] January 8, 1953, Atlanta, GA; [p.] William and Betty Swancey; [ch.] Elethia Denise, William Gary and Dell Allene; [ed.] Southwest DeKalb High, Purdue University; [occ.] HVAC Contractor, Swancey Services Inc.; [memb.] Condition Air Association of Georgia, American British Business Group, Atlanta Shakespeare Company; [hon.] Boy Scouts of America, Scout Master National Quality Award 1986, BOMI Teaching Award; [oth. writ.] Numerous Epices, Children Stories and Poetry ot published yet.; [pers.] I attempt to convey a meaning about real life events savored with a basic style for flavoring; [a.] Stockbridge, GA

SWANSON, CHARLES A.
[b.] April 2, 1930, Sioux Falls, SD; [p.] Elmer and Edna Swanson; [m.] Elsie Swanson (divorced), November 27, 1954; [ch.] Julie, Charles Jr. and Craig; [ed.] Two years College (science); [occ.] Just retired - previously hospital work (credit); [memb.] YMCA, Red Cross, Churon, Timely employment awards, Light house award (missions); [hon.] Armed services awards, Gospel missions award; [oth. writ.] Poems of various subjects for selected reasons and occasions, some of which are published.; [pers.] Through my poety I wish to enhance human understanding and feeling to appreciate the good, beauty and positive in a manner of communication to touch each and everyone.; [a.] Chicago, IL

SWANSON, DENISE A.
[b.] August 31, 1959, England; [p.] Audrey and Peter Knowles; [ch.] Sebastian Lee Swanson; [occ.] Homemaker; [pers.] All poetry dedicated to the husband who helped me to be the person I am. And to my son who inspired me.; [a.] West Palm Beach, FL

SWANSON, MARY
[b.] November 14, 1941, Madison, WI; [p.] Al and Marjorie Satterfield; [m.] Cyril B. Swanson; [ch.] G. Eric Webster, Tara Lynn Webster; [ed.] West H.S. Madison, WI, Arizona State Univ - BS, Arizona State Univ MA, Arizona State Univ MC; [occ.] Counselor/Instructor, Eastern Arizona College, Payson, AZ; [oth. writ.] Ballads and Folk songs; [pers.] I write about the two things I know best—the natural world and the human world—and the interconnection between the two.; [a.] Payson, AZ

SWEENEY, SARA E.
[pen.] Sallie; [b.] June 10, 1917, Pitman, NJ; [p.] Edward Drew, Lillie Drew; [m.] John F. Sweeney, June 24, 1939; [ch.] John Iroin, Sheila Gay, William Patrick, Michael Frances; [ed.] Cape may High School Cape May, N.J.; [occ.] Retired; [memb.] Catholic Daughters St. Peter's, Riverside N.J. V.F.W. Aux. Hightstown N.J.; [oth. writ.] "After The Storm" published in "Reflections Of Light"; [pers.] Very proud of my granddaughters - Kellie Anne, Kath-Leen, Kollen Sweeney of riverside, N.J. and Jennifer Ann, Bridget Lynn, Seeney of Manahawkin, N.J.; [a.] Burlington, NJ

SWENEY, TANYA D.
[b.] November 13, 1965, Los Angeles, CA; [ed.] George Washington Preparatory High School, B.A.-Psychology, Sacramento State, M.A.-Counseling, CSU, Dominguez Hills (CSU= California State University); [occ.] Supervising Counselor for Developmentally Disabled Adults; [memb.] Order of the Eastern Star; [hon.] Sacramento State, Honors at Entrance, CSU, Dominguez Hills, Dean's list; [pers.] Education is the key to open many doors, but there are those who have the key and still find themselves locked out. Never stop learning; [a.] Los Angeles, CA

SWENSEN, CAROLINE
[b.] September 26, 1978, Somerville, NJ; [p.] Linda Conaty, Scott Swensen; [ed.] Bridgewater - Raritan Regional High School; [occ.] Student; [memb.] Blessed Sacrament Church, Drug Abuse Resistance Education (DARE); [hon.] Varsity Tennis, Varsity Basketball, Choir, Band; [pers.] All I do is write what I feel. And when I know what I feel, it's easy to write.; [a.] Bridgewater, NJ

SZEKELY, GINNY LYNN
[b.] October 6, 1955; [p.] Edward and Sarah Marshall; [m.] Rudolph S. Szekely, June 19, 1989; [ch.] Traci Heather, Jordana Jean, Sarah Ann and Rudolph Stephen II; [ed.] Attending College presently to obtain a degree in Nursing; [occ.] Domestic Engineer; [oth. writ.] Several poems published in local newspapers.; [pers.] My hope is to convey, through my writings that regardless of race, creed, gender socio economic background we are all born of the human condition and that love is the key to our recovery. I am influenced by my "Higher Power" and my angel Christine to whom I give thanks.; [a.] N. Braddock, PA

TAASEVIGEN, CALVIN M.
[pen.] C. M. Taasevigen; [b.] September 11, 1929, Fairview, MO; [p.] Emil and Viola Taasevigen; [m.] Darlene Taazevegen, December 31, 1972; [ch.] Two Boys and Three Girls; [ed.] Eight Grade; [occ.] Electronic Tech Retired; [memb.] AARP, BPOE, Good SAM Club, Hunting and Fishing I grew up on a Farm; [hon.] Graduate from Spokane Tech and Vocational School (1958) spokane Wash several other degrees.; [oth. writ.] Many; [pers.] I enjoy wrting poetry making Home Brew in the Dakotas in 1929.

TACTO, CAMILA ESTEVES
[pen.] "Camille"; [b.] May 17, 1967, Philippines; [p.] Feliciano Tacto Sr. and Emilio Esteves Tacto; [ed.] Saint Marys Academy Phil. Baguio Colleges Foundation Phil.; [occ.] Laboratory Technician; [pers.] I consider poetry as a positive results of my daily activities.; [a.] Carson, CA

TANNER, EVA-MARIE
[b.] February 27, 1985, La Mesa, CA; [p.] Richard E. Tanner, Paula M. Tanner; [ed.] 4th grader Flying Hills Elementary School - GATE (Gifted and Talented Education) Program; [occ.] Student; [hon.] 3rd grade El Cajon Historical Society Essey Contest, Best of School Award; [oth. writ.] Wrote short story and won the opportunity to meet Save Wilson, children's author.; [pers.] Love life and am an avid competitive gymnast. I love to read and write. I also love my pet dogs, Tasha and Knight, and my cats, Shadow and Opposite.; [a.] El Cajon, CA

TANTON, KATHY
[b.] October 24, 1995, Rochester, NY; [m.] Divorced; [ch.] Paul Donald; [ed.] Alhambra High, Phoenix College; [occ.] Bookkeeper/Legal Assistant; [memb.] Legal Assistants ot Metropolitan Phoenix (LAMP), Arizona Lawyers Committee on Violence (ALCOV); [hon.] 1994 Valedictorian for Phoenix College; [oth. writ.] This is my first publication - although I've written other poems.; [pers.] I started college at the age of 36. My new - found love of poetry started in Eng. 101 and continued into Humanities 204.; [a.] Phoenix, AZ

TARRANT, DANIEL T.
[b.] March 3, 1975, Abington, PA; [p.] Mary and Dan Tarrant; [ed.] Archbishop Wood HS, Elizabethtown College; [oth. writ.] Three books of poems, currently writing a fourth, all unpublished and shared only with a number of kindred spirits.; [pers.] These poems stem from a deeper awareness and an ever intensifying relationship with God. I consider each one a blessing.f; [a.] Warminster, PA

TAUTE, MISS. EVELYN RUTH
[pen.] Eve; [b.] January 4, 1933, Hastings, NE; [p.] Wilter R. and Emille B. Taute; [ed.] AYR School AYR NE, Blue Hill High School Blue Nill, NE, Hastings College Hastings NE, Grand Island Business College One Year and Christian School; [occ.] Volunteer Work; [memb.] Peace Luthern Church, YWCA, Adult Eastern Care Sponsor 20 years; [hon.] 4-H District Speech Contest, 4-H Ribbons and Cash for Displays.; [oth. writ.] Several at Christian nature - short stories, poems; [pers.] I have been influenced and inspired by several people both local and also some that now inside in other locations a elderly lady by the name of Marie Kruse inspired me to write the poem, "Who it comes to sweetheart". I have been inspired to write due to a long period of stressful struggles in my life. Marie Kruse lives at a apartment at a retirement village in Hastings, Nebraska.; [a.] Hastings, NE

TAYLOR, DEANNA JOY
[pen.] Dee Taylor; [b.] September 22, 1938, Chicago; [ed.] B.A. Astrology in History/Astrology in Psychology - 1st ever awarded; [occ.] Former practicing astro-psychologist, lectures on philosophy and science, political campaign work, work with artist's coalitions, community service with children and young adults, sometimes radio-TV guest.; [oth. writ.] I was iconologist for Dr. Jean Gillies, Art Chair/Northeastern University - on her dazzling research on Botticelli's PRIMA VERA, Learning Disabilities in Children with Dr. Juan Morales, Mexico.; [pers.] (U.S., Mexico, Puerto Rico) poetry, psychology, philosophy, social criticism and athletes. Other writings: an epic poem and a collection, 2 novels, 1 play. My lifelong passion is the human mind and the nature of time, desire, will and choice. My dream: a philosophical opus on THE NATURE OF CHOICE.; [a.] Chicago, IL

TAYLOR, DONNA L.
[b.] July 15, 1945, Tacoma, WN; [p.] Dan Taylor, Lucille Kidd; [ch.] Denese Weatherly, Tammy Taecker; [ed.] Lathrop Sr. High, Alaska, Tacoma Voc. Tech. Inst., Washington; [occ.] Nanny, Yardely, Pa.; [memb.] Delaware Valley Professional Nanny's Association; [pers.] When I truly feel something from the heart, I try to write it down to make it last forever.; [a.] Yardley, PA

TAYLOR, J. FREDERICK
[b.] October 11, 1951, San Bernardino, CA; [p.] Jack F. Taylor, E. Lavern Taylor; [ch.] Rachel Ellen, Matthew Aaron, Thomas Ian; [ed.] Scottsdale Community College, Arizona State University - BFA, Painting 1982 - Cum Laude U.S. Army 1971-1974; [occ.] Artist, Illustrator; [memb.] International Friends of Transformative Art; [hon.] Dean's List, the award for Excellence in Drawing 1982, Realism V Leslie Levy Gallery, National Show 1992, Other Visual Art Awards. Edition's Choice Awards, National Library of Poetry 1994; [oth. writ.] Horton Springs, Poem, Season's To Come, National Library of Poetry, 1995, In House Publication "The Sentinel", Salt Riven Project. Scottsdale Community College Literary Pub. 1974. Illustrations: Expanding Your Child's Horrors, Dr. Art Atwell, Blue Bird Publishing, Tempe, AZ. 1994. The Greatest of these, L. Myecke Kesner, Blue Bird, publishing, Tempe, AZ. 1993. ASU West Literary Publication 1993.; [pers.] Looking into ones experience images and metaphor's spring. Some it is hoped, touch the universal, could I catch the moment frozen, then be gone? I visualize now the American School, Writers Musicians and painters.; [a.] Mesa, AZ

TAYLOR, RYAN
[pen.] Taylor, R. T.; [b.] May 6, 1976, Atlanta, GA; [p.] Rose Taylor; [ed.] St. Thomas More Grammar School, St. Pius Catholic High School; [occ.] Restaurant Service; [oth. writ.] Tilt, Eneray Boy, Flathead, Catatonic Company (all unknown) etc.; [pers.] Most of my poems are based on turns life and unfairness of authority looking down on us. "You Without Yourself Is Lost," "I Jump To Call It God".; [a.] Lawrenceville, GA

TEAL, JOYCE W.
[pen.] Joyce W. Teal; [b.] March 24, 1952, Vernon, TX; [p.] Riley and Essie Willard; [m.] Prince O. Teal Jr., June, 1964; [ch.] Rodney and Geisel Teal; [ed.] Washington High School, College - Prairie View A and M University, TX; [occ.] Classroom teacher of language arts and mathematics; [memb.] Alfred St. Baptist Church Zeta Phi Beta Sorority, Inc., Poet's Guild, American Black Book Writer's Assoc.; [hon.] Numerous awards and certificates for excellency in teaching. Teacher of the Year Honor in Atlanta at Long Middle School, Crawford Long Middle School Teacher of the Year, 1989-90; [oth. writ.] Grammar Rapp, Copyright,

1990 "The Yield" (publication pending), "The Point System" (unfinished manuscript); [pers.] In my writing I strive to enlighten and inspire. I desire to reflect and reveal. I want to reflect mankinds innate goodness. I desire to reveal injustices inflicted, especially on those at a disadvantage.

TEASLE, LOUISE L.
[b.] June 25, 1974, Monroe, LA; [p.] Elizabeth McJimsey, David McJimsey; [m.] Danial L. Teasle, February 14, 1995; [ch.] Cassia Rea, Aubrey Victoria; [ed.] Vidalia High Northeast Louisiana University, University of Texas of the Permian Basin; [occ.] House wife; [hon.] Dean's List; [pers.] I owe much of my success to my friend and advisor, Dr. Jeff Galle. His support influenced me to bring my work out into the view of the public eye.; [a.] Odessa, TX

TEEGARDEN, CAROLYN
[b.] May 14, 1954, Wichita, KS; [p.] Frank Sanders and Dorothy (Sanders) Phillips; [m.] Ben Teegarden Jr., June 28, 1980; [ch.] Three step children, two step grandchildren; [ed.] Calico Rock Public School, GED, Early Childhood Credential, Diploma on Writing Children's Short Stories; [occ.] Head Start Assistant Teacher; [memb.] ACEA; [pers.] I especially enjoyed poetry in high school. This is my first contest and chance to be published. Though borne in a city, I've spent my life on a farm.; [a.] Pineville, AR

TELTHOESTER, AUDREY L.
[b.] May 10, 1962; [p.] Lester and Doris Telthoester; [ch.] Jessica L. Klitzke, Kelli J. Klitzke; [ed.] Graduated High School; [occ.] Homemaker; [oth. writ.] Many - nonpublished; [pers.] I am moved by the Spirit to spread glad tidings, and inspire hope. Having once been entirely at the other end of that spectrum, and freed - it is my heart's cry.; [a.] Mankato, MN

TENERIO, VICKI
[b.] December 30, 1974; [p.] Margarito Sr. and Julia Fe Tenorio; [ed.] Albert G. Lane Technical High School, Wilbur Wright College; [occ.] Ward Clerk; [pers.] Whenever my world is spun out of orbit, I always travel to the imaginative underworld of poetry.; [a.] Chicago, IL

TENNEY, JEANNE MARIE
[b.] November 24, 1937, Portland, ME; [p.] Charles and June Norman; [m.] Melvin Tenney, (second marriage) February 14, 1987; [ch.] Michael, Patrick, Timothy and Thomas (twins), Susan and Julie; [ed.] Naples Elementary Naples, Maine and Bridgton High School, Bridgton, Maine; [occ.] Homemaker; [memb.] Christian and Missionary Alliance Church, South Casco, Maine; [oth. writ.] Poems published monthly in my church newsletter, "The Antenna". Poem submitted to the "Songtime U.S.A. radio program, with Dr. John DeBrine; [pers.] I have only been writing poetry for approximately a year. It is inspired by my love and appreciation for our Creator. I write to bring honor and glory to His magnificence.; [a.] Naples, ME

THAYER, HOLLY SWEET
[b.] January 13, 1956, San Jose, CA; [p.] Gaynell Elaine Sweet and John Robert Sweet III; [m.] Monty Thayer, December 1, 1979; [ed.] AA, (1990) Liberal Arts, DeAnza College, Cupertino, CA, BA, Elementary Education, University of North Carolina at Charlotte - 1996; [occ.] Office Assistant/Word Processor/Student; [memb.] Golden Key National Honor Society, Kappa Delta Pi, North Carolina Council of Teachers of Mathematics, Fremont High School Alumni; [hon.] DeAnza College Academic Achievement Award, National Dean's List, UNCC Dean's List/Chancellor's List; [oth. writ.] This is my first published work; [pers.] My

interest in poetry has been influenced by my Grandmother, Elsa Schroeder, who on rainy melancholy days would read to me Jabberwody and Hiawatha, and my Mother who always encouraged my creative endeavors.; [a.] Charlotte, NC

THISSE, MARILYN VENITA
[b.] April 8, 1953, Wyandotte, MI; [p.] H. B. and Lillian Chavis; [m.] Laurence C. Thisse, September 7, 1973; [ch.] Michael, Matthew, Mark; [ed.] Taylor Center High; [occ.] Homemaker Sunday School Teacher.; [oth. writ.] Several poems published in Companions, a Christian teen publication; [pers.] The most important thing for me in my poetry is that the reader see God. As he touches every part of my life, I pray He touches yours through this poem; [a.] Taylor, MI

THOMAN, CYNTHIA A.
[pen.] Cindy Thoman; [b.] August 18, 1965, Providence, RI; [p.] Charlie H. Tucker and Jessence; [m.] Roger B. Thoman, October 26, 1991; [ch.] Randy, Kevin and Aaron; [ed.] High School; [occ.] Housewife; [memb.] New Members to National Audubon Society; [oth. writ.] None published I have a few in the works.; [pers.] I try to put into words my feeling. I want to make a change in the world for the better. This poem is for my Dad who die this May. To Charlie H. Tucker.; [a.] Foster, RI

THOMAS, ASAYO OKUMURA
[pen.] Asayo Thomas; [b.] January 1, 1961, Tokyo, Japan; [p.] Shuichi Okumura, Seisuko Okumura; [m.] Rodney Thomas; [ch.] Miya Angelica Thomas; [occ.] Essayist, Musician, Artist; [memb.] Founder of half and half, Global Family Club; [pers.] I would like to pursue the pure spirit of human beings and the preciousness of nature. At the same time I want to purify myself by writing and devote myself to make real harmonious and peaceful world.; [a.] New York, NY

THOMAS, CHAD A.
[b.] April 2, 1975, Des Moines, IA; [p.] Terry and Marry Thomas; [ed.] Bondurant-Farrar High School, Drake University undergrad.; [occ.] Student; [oth. writ.] Stage plays performed by high school drama dept. junior and senior year, quarterly newsletter for local building materials wholesaler; [a.] Bondurant, IA

THOMAS, GREGORY O.
[pen.] Peter Damion Boyd; [b.] June 25, 1975, Durango, CO; [p.] Owen and Virginia Thomas; [ed.] Kirtland Central High School, San Juan College, University of New Mexico; [occ.] Sales Representative; [memb.] Church of Jesus Christ of Latter Day Saints, Boy Scouts of America; [hon.] National Honors Society, Who's Who In America, Star Scholar Award from UNM, Honor Scholar Award from New Mexico State University; [oth. writ.] Pesonal Collection, Beginning Writer; [pers.] Everyday brings forth a new horizon to excel, there is no such thing as failure, if your heart has done it well!; [a.] Kirtland, NM

THOMAS, MARK
[pen.] Mark Thomas; [b.] May 16, 1965, Oklahoma City; [p.] Paul R. Thomas, Joyce Thomas; [ch.] Joshua Thomas, Nicholas Thomas, Shanna Thomas; [ed.] Moore Okla. Public Schools, Moore High School, Hvac Trade School; [occ.] Sheet metal worker; [oth. writ.] Numerous poems and Sony lyrics - guitar compositions. Too many to list.; [pers.] I try to write in ways that will make people think. If I can write a poem or a song and one person says "I can celebrate to that," then I have achieved what I set out to words are powerful, they can change lives...; [a.] Moore, OK

THOMAS, PATRICE
[pen.] Clarke Elaine Glover; [b.] October 22, 1957, Atlanta, GA; [p.] Betty C. Culpepper and Dr. Ridley Glover; [m.] Dewey C. Thomas, September 22, 1992; [ch.] Adam J. Thomas (Stepson); [ed.] RN - LaGrange, College School of Nursing, LaGrange, GA; [occ.] Registered Nurse, Labor and Delivery - St. Joseph's Hospital, Savannah, GA; [hon.] Magna Cum Laude, 1977 - LaGrange College School of Nursing; [oth. writ.] Published in: The Poetic Voices of America, Savannah News, photographer for Baby By Appointment, (Education film - Candler General Hospital), Savannah Magazine, Border Contest Winner, Super Game Boy (Nintendo), Video Games, Magazine, and Electronic Games Magazine; [pers.] My inspiration comes from God the original author, poet and artist of us all.; [a.] Savannah, GA

THOMAS, SANDRA E.
[pen.] Sandy; [b.] June 15, 1938, Winston-Salem, NC; [p.] James Garner, Hattie Garner; [m.] Jake Thomas, June 19, 1995; [ch.] Lionel Jay Thomas, Monique Alicia Thomas; [ed.] Atkins High Kate Bitting Reynolds School of Nursing Winston-Salem, NC., R.N. Diploma BS. Nursing Adelphi University Garden City NY., MA Nursing Completing Dissertation Administration NYU. Prof. Diploma CW East Brookville, NY; [occ.] Health Teacher Prospect and Margarite Golden Rhodes Hempstead, NY; [memb.] American Heart Association American Nurses Association, Holy Ghost Tubenacle Glorious Church of God. Life time member National Alliance of Black School Educators; [hon.] Delta Sigma Theta Sorority Scholarship to Kate Bitting Reynolds School of Nursing, Dean's List Adelphi University Traineeship.; [oth. writ.] Tribute to My Mother, The Crossing Guard.; [pers.] I like to put children first by setting an example. I must live with myself and so I must be fit for myself to know so that others may see the great person I am striving to be.; [a.] Hempstead, NY

THOMAS, VAUDALINE
[pen.] Virginia Rogers; [b.] February 22, 1916, Sweetwater, TX; [p.] Claude and Marguerite Rogers; [m.] T. T. Thomas, July 1, 1934; [ch.] Toby (Deceased), Mondelene, Cleckler, James; [ed.] B.S. and Master's degrees, Texas Tech. University, Lubbock, TX; [occ.] Retired Teacher; [memb.] AARP-3591, Retired Teachers, Lubbock County Member, Church of Christ, Member of International Society of Poets, Volunteer Texas Department of Human Services; [hon.] Certificates: Lubbock Retired Teachers, Human Services, Plaque: Poem "Government Butter and Cheese", Articles for Church Bulletin; [oth. writ.] "Plum Creek", "Memorabilia", "Straightway to Heaven", "Term Related the Exceptional", "Legacies #1, #2, #3", Articles for Lubbock Avalanche-Journal.; [pers.] I accept life and try to make the best of it. I try to be wise, calm, reasonable, to be philosophic in defeat.; [a.] Lubbock, TX

THOMPSON, KATHLEEN
[pen.] Kay Thompson ("Katie"); [b.] October 23, 1951, Syracuse, NY; [p.] Jim and Rosemary McJury; [m.] Tom E. Thompson, May 19, 1973; [ch.] Sheri, Diane, Bill, Kathleen, Joey, Maureen; [ed.] BA Univ. of MD Bremerham, Germany, MS Chapman Univ., Seoul, Korea, (Human Resource Management and Development); [occ.] Housewife, Story teller; [memb.] Secula Franciscan Order (1980); [a.] Alexandria, VA

THOMPSON, VERA
[b.] May 16, Monty, AL; [p.] Andrew and Manola Thomas; [m.] Felton C. Thompson, August 24, 1969; [ch.] Chasity Quianna Thompson and Felton C. Thompson II; [ed.] AIA State Laboratory High BS and MED - Alabama State University MED - Auburn University; [occ.] Principal - Cotoma Elementary; [memb.] Alpha Kappa Alpha Sorority National, State Education Association; [hon.] Graduated - Magna Cum Laude Working woman of the year Recognition honor roll - Church Youth Advisor; [oth. writ.] Several skits for Church and School performances; [pers.] I can do all things through Christ who strengthens me my writings are usually of tribute.; [a.] Montgomery, AL

THOMSON, DAVID C.
[b.] July 8, 1943, Warren, PA; [p.] David A. and Vernice M. Thomson; [m.] Divorced; [ch.] Three girls; [ed.] Warren Area H.S. and one year at Edinboro State University, Warren Off Campus Center.; [occ.] On Social Security Disability (SSI); [memb.] Trinity Memories Episcopal Church I endeavor to bring as much "reality" to my work as possible.; [oth. writ.] In the past I have had poems published by POEM Magazine and Sparrowgrass Poetry Forum, Inc.

TIGHE, WILLIAM D.
[b.] June 19, 1936, New York, NY; [m.] Lise Paquin; [ed.] University of New Hampshire Hofstra College; [occ.] Retired; [memb.] Amer. Soc. Mech. Engrs., Toast Master Intl., P. Kappa Alpha; [hon.] Toastmasters CTM, ATM; [oth. writ.] Poems published in local newspaper; [a.] Sunapee, NH

TILLERY, AMY
[pen.] Shantel; [b.] November 29, 1976, Dumas, TX; [p.] Terry and Janis Tillery; [ed.] High School Diploma Stratford High School Stratford TX 79084 Graduated one year early; [occ.] Clerk at 7-11 midnight shift; [memb.] Credit Union, FHA; [oth. writ.] Mostly of all my poems are all just doodles that I write for myself. It helps me to see life for what it is.; [pers.] I want to thank Al Morgan he is my inspiration.; [a.] Bush, CO

TIMBIE, MEGAN
[b.] January 15, 1980, Honolulu, HI; [p.] Donald S., Darlene Timbie; [occ.] I am an eighth grade student.; [pers.] My poem reflects my view of the world. I am a fifteen year old that drives an electric wheel chair.; [a.] Mill Valley, CA

TINSTMAN, CARL
[b.] February 1, 1922, Ford City, PA; [p.] Carl C. Tinstman and Irene Mechling Tinstman; [m.] Caroline Marvin Tinstman, May 1, 1943; [ch.] Carl Clinton III, Barbara Laine, Tinstman Cluster, Jeffrey Lee; [ed.] B.S., Electrical '42 Engineering Case School of Engineering, Case Western Reserve University, graduate School Studies, Clinical and Industrial Psychology, Kent State University (and Western Reserve); [occ.] (Retired) Vice President, The McCommon Company, Career Transition Consultants, Serving Nationally Prominent Corporations.; [memb.] Past Officer and Committee Chairman of Management Development Forum, Local Level Chambers of Commerce, United Fund, Scouting USA, and PTA. Workshop Chairman and Seminar Speaker, American Management Associations, Member of IACMP (International Association of Career Management Professionals); [oth. writ.] (Key Contributor) and Editor of Guidelines For Managing, published as Chapter VI of Conference Board Study #212: Managing by-and-with objectives; [pers.] As a managememt consultant and trainer, coach, and mentor of managers and executives - I am both thankful for and proud of helping individuals and their organizations become more productive in the achievement of operational and personal goals.; [a.] Winfield, IL

TIPPS, LOU ANN
[pen.] Ellis (at times); [b.] February 2, 1949, Shawnee, OK; [p.] Dr. Bill D. and Mattie O. Ellis; [m.] Ronnie R. Tipps, October 10, 1969; [ch.] Chad R. Tipps and Rod

R. Tipps; [ed.] Ardmore High School, Ardmore, OK Southeastern Oklahoma State University, Durant, OK; [occ.] Executive Secretary for the Director of Special Services at Ardmore City Schools, Ardmore, OK; [memb.] Court Appointed Special Advocate (CASA), First Baptist Church, National Author's Registry, Educational Support Personnel Organ. (ESPO); [hon.] 1991 CASA of the Year; [oth. writ.] Treasured Poems Of America, Fall '94 published "A Fire" and "October," Treasured Poems Of America, Winter, Winter '95 published "Child of a Darker World," which also received an Honorable Mention in the Ilead Awards Program, 1995 and will be published in voices.; [pers.] Writing is a release for me. But more than a personal self-satisfaction, I try to express thoughts that make a difference to someone else, or to paint a picture in words. I write in clear concise messages for the heart. I can see in everything. I hope to some day write lyrics for songs.; [a.] Ardmore, OK

TIPTON, JENNIFER C.
[b.] August 25, 1977, Baytown, TX; [m.] Patrick G. Tipton, March 12, 1994; [ed.] I am a college student at Northwestern State University in Louisiana. My major is Nursing; [occ.] Full-time student; [pers.] Be thankful for what God has given you. Some kids say "I wish I was an only child," but I always prayed for a sister/brother. My sister, Bonnie-Christine, Nicole Hyphenated Hess was born Oct. 17, 1989 and died 17 months later. I am thankful for the 17 months we shared.; [a.] Leesville, LA

TIPTON, NELL
[b.] May 27, 1912, KY; [p.] Jesse and Leva Marcum; [m.] Wesley Tipton, July 29, 1932; [ch.] Jim, Tom, Mary, Tippy and Russell; [ed.] Elementary and one term at Berea College at Berea, KY.; [occ.] Just a grandmother and great mother; [oth. writ.] Poems and other observations, none published; [pers.] I'm strictly amature, but words and phrases tascinate me... Wish I had enough education to be a "real" writer.; [a.] Ravenna, KY

TODARO, DIANA A.
[b.] March 28, 1930, Brooklyn, NY; [p.] Domenico and Emilia Andreana; [m.] Carl Todaro, June 21, 1958; [ch.] Ronald J. Todaro, Vivian R. Schaufler; [ed.] High School; [occ.] Wage Hour Assistant, U.S. Department of Labor; [memb.] Three years President of The Association for the help of Retarded Children (AHRC). Valley Stream - No Woodmere Auxiliary; [hon.] United States Department of Labor Distinguished Career Service Award. Special Achievement Award.; [oth. writ.] One song about Long Island, Several Poems, one of which was published in my High School year book New Utrecht H.S. 1947; [pers.] I value Decency and honesty, and write when inspired by everyday experiences.; [a.] Valley Stream, NY

TOFSON, ROBERT L.
[pen.] "Fireball"; [b.] October 12, 1941, Los Angeles; [p.] Lester N. Tofson, Kay A. Tofson; [m.] Sandra J. Tofson, November 29, 1963; [ch.] Eric M. Tofson, Carolyn J. Tofson; [ed.] RM-O-World High School Lake Arrowitead, California, San Bernardino Valley College San Bernardino, California; [occ.] Area Fire Marshal, W.S. Navy; [memb.] International Association of Fire Chiefs, Navy and Marine Corps. Fire Protection Association; [pers.] "Fly Away, Fly Away to be Free" Is dedicated to my mother, my wife and two children.; [a.] Hantero, CA

TOKUMINE, WADE
[b.] December 7, 1975, Honolulu, HI; [ed.] Roosevelt High School, University of Hawaii at Manoa

TOLEDO, MARLENE
[pen.] Citi; [b.] May 29, 1975, New York City, NY; [p.] Israel Toledo, Maria Toledo; [ed.] Philippa Schuyler School for the gifted and talented, Grover Cleveland High School, La Guardia C.C.; [oth. writ.] Several other poems unpublished; [pers.] My inspiration came from life, solitude and Rock Music. My mentor is Bono from the group U2. His lyrics are deep and full of emotion. He inspired me to write from within me. Someday I would like to learn to write songs like his.; [a.] Queens, NY

TOLER, JAMES OLIVER
[b.] September 9, 1942, Detroit, MI; [p.] James and Dorothy Toler; [m.] Genevieve Nolan, January 25, 1985; [ch.] Carrie, Lupini, Dana Toler, Nolan Toler and stepdaughter Shellie Doell; [ed.] Macomb County College, Highland Park High School, Highland Park Junior College, Wayne State University; [occ.] Teacher for special education students; [oth. writ.] You, My Heroes, On Call, Speak, Beacon, Pure, Eagle, Antibiotic, Thallophyte, Mind, The Garden, A Speck of Time, Here, The Message, New Set of Friends, Categorize, English Travel Memories - 1993, Mom, Georgie and Me, Waters, Lost; [pers.] Let's not kill and hate for perspective is the key to how we think.; [a.] Rochester Hills, MI

TOLLEY, DAVID V.
[b.] March 25, 1951, Charleston, WV; [p.] Roy Tolley, Minnie Tolley; [m.] Janet Wolverton, September 16, 1973; [ch.] Omega lea, Stephanie Lynn, Jennifer Ann; [ed.] Canton South High School; [occ.] Danner Press Corp.; [a.] East Sparta, OH

TOMLINSON, DAWN-MARIE
[b.] October 19, 1962, Brockton, MA; [p.] Nancy Gurley; [m.] Divorced; [ch.] Jade 10 yrs., Jasmine 9 yrs., Chloe Dawn 5 yrs.; [ed.] Some College Medical Legal; [occ.] Day care provider; [pers.] Writing helps me to get in touch with my spirit and peace of mind.; [a.] Brockton, MA

TONKS, SALLY MORRIS
[b.] April 19, 1944, Milford, CT; [p.] Helen Swift and Willoughby Lay; [m.] Richard Tonks, April 27, 1991; [ch.] Alicia, Jeffrey, Curtis, Joel, Benjamin and Jared; [ed.] Attended Harlt College of Music - graduated 1966 from Southern Conn State University, Attended Middlesex Community College 1989-92; [occ.] Sales, Oscar J. and Co.; [hon.] Deans list, Southern Conn 1965, Middlesex College 1990; [a.] Chester, CO

TOOKER, G. CALVIN
[pen.] Cal Tooker; [b.] August 1, 1924, Wetonka, SD; [p.] Grant and Elizabeth Tooker; [ed.] Master of Science in Library Science from U.S.C.; [occ.] Retired; [oth. writ.] The Hoarfrost. This is nuts, teddy bears, soul mates.; [pers.] From fundamentalist Christian background to bouts with metaphysics and agnosticism, I've come to generally accept life "as is", appreciate my "Dust Bowl" heritage, beginning to have fun and let others have their beliefs and faiths so long as that don't harm me and mine.

TOOLE, DIANA L.
[b.] November 22, 1970, Ann Arbor, MI; [p.] Janet Alford, Thomas Sherred and Bob, Velma Neau; [occ.] Receiving Clerk at Waldenbooks and second time student; [oth. writ.] Not previously published in anything serious. Mainly a short story/novel writer. Like dabbling in poetry, and play wrighting.; [pers.] Through the power of words, you can mean much more than the words say. Everyone has something important enough to convey to the world, they just need to find their words with which to say more.; [a.] Indianapolis, IN

TOOMEY, KERRY
[pen.] Kerry 2me!; [b.] July 22, 1972, Bellevue, WA; [p.] Darrell 2me and Diane Cramer; [m.] Tom Bernhardy; [ch.] Darrell Jacob Toomey, one unborn due Jan 1996; [ed.] Kamiakin Jr. High; American Schl. (correspondence); [occ.] Home Maker; [memb.] F.O.E. #2681 Fraternal order of Eagles, Kirkland, WA; I.J.A. International Jugglers Assoc. Life member; [oth. writ.] Poem in The Coming of Dawn and a poem in Treasured Poems of America (winter 1994); [pers.] If there is something you want out of life you have to go for it no matter what others say, follow your dreams.; [a.] Bellevue, WA.

TORGERSON, KRYSTEN M.
[pen.] C. J. Nicholes; [b.] March 4, 1970, Westminster, CA; [p.] Bonnie and Dvane Torgerson; [m.] Steve Livingston, November 9, 1993; [ch.] Tyler Livingston; [memb.] World Wildlife Federation, People for the ethical treatment of Animals; [a.] Mesa, AZ

TORRES JR., RAUL G.
[pen.] Raul G. Torres Jr.; [b.] April 11, 1956, San Antonio, TX; [p.] Raul H Torres Sr. and Mary A. Torres; [m.] Estella R. Torres, August 11, 1983; [ed.] Sidney Lanier H.S., St. Philips College, Our Lady of The Lake University; [occ.] Civil Service, KAFB; [pers.] My philosophy in life is, there's always someone better than you are, but try to be that someone yourself... RGT; [a.] San Antonio, TX

TOWE, ERIC SAMUEL
[b.] May 24, 1966, Dayton, OH; [p.] Samuel A. Towe, Dorothy M. Jones; [m.] Carmina A. Towe, November 13, 1995; [ed.] B.A. History from Ohio, Wesleyan University 1988, Cum Laude; [occ.] Naval Aviator, U.S. Navy; [memb.] PI Sigma Alpha National Political Science Honor Society - Phi Alpha Theta International History Honor Society - Omicron Delta Kappa National Honor Society; [hon.] 2 Time Who's Who among American High School, students - 2 time National Dean's List - Outstanding Young Men of America 1988 - Honors Graduate with distinction from Navy advanced helicopter training; [oth. writ.] One article published in "approach" magazine, a naval aviation safety publication; [pers.] Believe you can do anything, and you will.; [a.] Corpus Christi, TX

TRAGUS, MARY
[p.] William Francis Dougherty, Mary Crawford; [ch.] Theodore Tragus, Rachael Lovern, Mary Ann Holt (Grandchildren) Kevin Scott Lovern Jr., Amanda Lovern, Mary Beth Tragus and Sabrina M. Tragus; [ed.] Sacred Heart Academy, Studio School of Art and Design - University of PA, Pre-Vet Program, Philadelphia, PA.; [occ.] Former Art Manager of Publication at University of PA, Foremer 3rd grade teacher in Swaretmore, PA.; [hon.] Mother, Honorary, Stepmother and Grandmother to a four wonderful grandchildren called a friend by many. A Sister, A Child of God, Dean List in School; [oth. writ.] High School Class Poem; [pers.] Diagnosed with colon cancer in 1992. I belong to the Lankenag Hospital General Cancer support group and other community support groups. "The sadness of saying good-bye to old and new dear friends overwhelms me at times. When the depression hits it lowest I find myself dreaming a type of prose about my friends.; [a.] Philadelphia, PA

TRAN, CHRISTOPHER
[b.] December 25, 1982, Pittsburgh; [p.] Judith and Steve; [occ.] Student at Waldrow Mercy Academy; [pers.] I would like to be writing more and more things. Don't ever say, "I can't write."; [a.] Philadelphia, PA

TRAVES III, DONALD E.
[b.] April 17, 1972, Albuquerque, NM; [p.] Charlotte Rowan, Donald Traves Jr.; [m.] Jolene E. Traves, December 16, 1994; [ch.] Aaron M. (Traves), Joshua M.; [ed.] Thompson Valley High, Chaminade University of Honolulu; [occ.] United States Marine Corps., Kaneohe Bay Hawaii; [memb.] National Rifle Association; [hon.] 1994 Pacific Division, 1. Marine Corps. Pistol Team Champion, 2. 1994 Bronze Medalist USMC Rifle Comp. 3. 1995 2nd Place Rifle Team Competition Marine Corps. Matches 4. 1995 3rd Place Rifle Team Comp, Okinawa Japan, Far Eastern Division; [pers.] Writing is the only way to truly escape into one's true self.; [a.] Delta, CO

TRAVIS, MARK A.
[b.] December 16, 1958, West Palm Beach, FL; [p.] Jerry Travis, Bertie Travis; [m.] Mark A. Travis; [ed.] Martin County High, Stuart, Fla Palm Beach Jr. College, W.P.B. Fl. Florida State University, Tall Ahassee, Fl; [oth. writ.] The book of poetry "Time" will be published soon by Vantage Press. There's A time and Place for Everyone is not printed in the book "Time" It has never been published.; [pers.] Mark received a Bachelor of Science degree from Fla. State University. Mark wrote many poems and journals. He died March 31, 1987. There's A Time a place for everyone was the last poem Mark wrote before he died.; [a.] Stuart, FL

TROPP, TRUDI
[b.] May 7, 1946, Brooklyn, NY; [ch.] Robert James (Son), Anthony James (Grandson); [occ.] Legal Records Manager; [memb.] GLA-ARMA (Greater Los Angeles Adm-Records Managers Assoc.) and LRMA (Law Records Management Assoc.); [hon.] Received various certificates of appreciation for volunteer work, GLA-ARMA, B.I.L.Y. (Parent support group), Sunday School Teacher - 2 years; [oth. writ.] Started writing poems and riddles in elementary school.; [pers.] Between yesterday and tomorrow is the most important day.; [a.] Studio City, CA

TROUTZ, MARGARET EILEEN
[pen.] Eileen Corey Norwood; [b.] October 14, 1920, Marquette, MI; [p.] Ronald M. and Lily Mae Corey; [m.] Thomas Troutz, Sgt. (deceased), December 21, 1982; [ch.] Jeanine M. Conroy, Sharon E. Beene and Richard Freeland; [ed.] Graduated and 1/2 year of Psychology. Have studied and taught Psychic Phenomena.; [occ.] Retired from G.M. Co. National Psychic Retiree.; [memb.] Veterans of foreign wars Aux. Past president of Fleet reserve Auxiliary Br 21. Mich. N.R.A., AARP, Writer's Digest.; [hon.] For drug free America. Youth Athletic Awards. 2 times ordained for ministry. I can not count my awards. "I was honored by translates of Kahlil Gebrans Works, Anthony Ferris."; [oth. writ.] 7 Booklets of poetry titled "Universal Eye, Inspirational wisdom." Wrote columns in newspapers." Detroit, MI. Naubinway, MI. and Fairfield, TX."; [pers.] The smallest church in the world, is the one that I attend daily, "The Bible" I believe we are "all" made of one spirit. The Holy Spirit.; [a.] Fairfield, TX

TRULL, YVONNE
[pen.] Yvonne Orman Trull; [b.] May 15, 1919, Ottumwa, IA; [p.] Riley and Emma Orman; [m.] Willis Trull (Deceased 1986), January 21, 1946; [ch.] Edward; [ed.] Graduated 1937 from East Des Moines High School; [occ.] Retired; [oth. writ.] I have found satisfaction from a very early age in writing poetry as a form of expression and for relatives and friends on special occasions.; [pers.] I feel it a privilege to find inspiration, comfort or entertainment from poets and poetry old and new.; [a.] Portland, OR

TRUXAL, NELLIE LUCHSINGER
[b.] October 16, 1906, Blairsville, PA; [p.] Knox and Emma Luchsinger; [m.] Karl M. Truxal (Deceased), July 6, 1926; [ch.] Dorothy Scoyec; [ed.] Master of Education Indiana U. of PA. plus additional past graduate work at Univ. of Pittsburgh and Univ. of Dayton (OH.); [occ.] Retired Teacher. Experience from 1 room school to head of Math Dept. in Jr. High School; [memb.] National Education Assoc., PA. State Education Assoc., Historical Society of the Plairsville Area (PA.), Hernando Co. Museum (Fla.); [hon.] Certificate of Appreciation for work as a volunteer at the Hernando Co. Historical Museum in Brooksville, Fl.; [oth. writ.] Contributed articles to two books of Memories published by the Historical Sec. of the Blairsville Area, Researched and wrote a study of early schools in W. Central Fl. for Hernondo Go. Hist. Museum, two articles published by the Tampo Tribune "I Remember it Well"; [pers.] I have written poetry for children which I used in my class room and for entertaining groups of children, I was a private teacher of violin for 50 years and played in an orchestra for silent movies. My love of music translates to poetry.; [a.] Tampa, FL

TSAI, EDWARD S.
[b.] June 2, 1980, Daly City; [p.] Raymond Tsai and Anita Tsai; [ed.] 9th Grade; [occ.] Student; [memb.] Have of Christ; [hon.] Award of Honor in Spanish, Principals Honor Roll, Science Bowl, 1st place, Award of Honor in History; [oth. writ.] National Library of Poetry; [pers.] I believe that Jesus is Lord. I believe that God raised Him from the dead. I have been greatly influenced by the Bible.; [a.] Union City, CA

TUBBS, BOBBYE
[b.] January 12, 1930, Bay Springs, MS; [p.] Earl and Fleeta Vanderslice; [m.] Pascal Brooks Tubbs, August 11, 1984; [ch.] Johnny read, Sherry Williams, Marsha Bankston, 8 grandchildren, and 3 great-grandchildren; [ed.] Bay Springs High School; [occ.] A child of God, wife, and mother, crafter, Poet, Writer, make baby clothes and burial gowns for NEO-natal I.C.U. for UMC hosp. in Jackson Ms.; [memb.] Sylverena Baptist Church, Care-Wear Volunteers, International Society of Poetry.; [hon.] To be loved by family and friends. Poem published in Journey of the Mind, Many Blue ribbons at exhibits for handwork, crochet items, oil paintings, crafts, knitted sweaters that went to the state fair and won grand prize, and miniature quilts. I received The Editor's Choice Award and was nominated Poet of the Year by National Library of Poetry.; [oth. writ.] Poems published in local and out of state newspapers. A poem to be pub. in Sea of Treasures and one in Best Poems of 1996 by Nat. Lib. of Poetry. Also one in Voices of America by The Sparrowgrass Poetry Foram. I have written a short story, childrens's story and book entitled: Tender Comrade.; [pers.] I find it easier to express my feelings through my writings. I sometimes find hidden places in my heart that will only surface with pen in hand in the darkness of the night.; [a.] Bay Springs, MS

TUCKER, DANETTE C.
[pen.] Dani; [b.] February 7, 1970, Washington, DC; [p.] Kenneth and Cynthia Tucker; [m.] Rahim Hooper; [ch.] DeVaughn Marquise Hooper; [ed.] Benjamin Banneker Academic High School, Howard University; [occ.] Secretary, Department of Commerce; [memb.] American Federation of Government Employees (AFGE-AFL-CIO), Toby Palmer and Chosen Generation (choir-alto); [hon.] 1988-1989 - Executive Editor - Youth Leader Newspaper - Wash, DC, 1986 - Youth Ambassador to Israel, 1987 - Presidential Honoree for Volunteer Work (Volunteer Clearinghouse); [oth. writ.] Articles published in agency newsletter. Articles published in Youth Leader Newspaper.; [pers.] "Life is

walking a path, and decisions are just forks in the road... choose a path and follow your heart...that's what I do in my poetry".; [a.] Capitol Heights, MD

TUCKER, IRIS CAYWOOD
[b.] December 15, 1910, Sapulpa, OK; [m.] Widow; [ed.] Guthrie High School, Guthrie, Oklahoma, graduated 1929, Wichita Bussiness College, graduated 1930, Special Studies - Oil Painting, Carmel, California, 1978-80.; [occ.] Bookeeper at Boeing United, (Retired in 1972); [oth. writ.] Other published works: Poems — "First Time," Wichita U. paper, 1972, "Stunned Silence," Wichita U. paper, 1975, "Sands of Time," Monterey Peninsula Herald, 1990, "Tears," Monterey Peninsula Herald, 1980.; [pers.] "I have been more or less a world traveler since retiring and widowed in 1977. Raised two daughters, spend my time writing short stories, painting and crafts."

TUCKER, M. CASEY
[pen.] Casey Tucker; [b.] June 20, 1980, Marietta, GA; [p.] Kevin Poole, Sally Tucker; [ed.] Marietta Middle School; [occ.] Student; [oth. writ.] Lots of poems I have never had any published or printed.; [pers.] I write poems to express my feelings about things that happen in my life. This poem was written after the death of my great-grandmother.; [a.] Marietta, GA

TUCKER, PAUL B.
[pen.] The Word Farmer; [b.] October 4, 1933, Robinson, IL; [p.] Koley and Blanche Tucker; [m.] C. Maxine Tucker, Feburuary 7, 1958; [ch.] Paula, William and Sandra; [ed.] High School Graduate; [occ.] Semi Retired; [hon.] Was born to make a difference in the world. Am happy to say I've been a success and now I plan to teach what I've learned thru poetry.; [oth. writ.] In the past two or three years I've only past my work to a few friends and the local newspaper, they are greatful and encouraging.; [pers.] I flung my hut into the floor for to jump on and to goar. Another lotto purse has come and went and left me without one real out.

TUCKER, SHEILA
[pen.] Sheila Tucker; [b.] May 18, 1966, Grantsburgh, WI; [p.] Mary Matrious and Gary Kerns; [m.] Christopher Tucker, February 20, 1991; [ch.] MaryJane Tucker; [ed.] High School Graduate; [occ.] Homemaker; [pers.] I really enjoy writing poems. It makes me think about so many things; [a.] Forth Huachuca, AZ

TUCKER, SONYA V.
[pen.] Jessi Louise; [ed.] Univ. of Georgia; [occ.] Realtor, Jennings Mill Real Estate Co.; [memb.] Georgia Association of Realtors, Bethany Methodist Church; [pers.] My poems through out my life have helped me to understand myself and are reflections from my heart.; [a.] Watkinsville, GA

TUCKER, WALTER
[b.] July 14, 1971, Hartwell, GA; [p.] Jewel and Walter Tucker Sr.; [ed.] Hart County High, PSI Junior College; [occ.] Assistant manager, crown books, silver spring, MD; [memb.] American Heart and Lung Association, member of Rhema Christian Center; [hon.] (MVP) Received most Valuable Player Award and Trophies; [oth. writ.] Quit a few poems published in local newspaper. Poetry readings, Bethesda MD.; [pers.] It shall not be said, for one to be mislead, subconscious thinking instead, of allowing the mind to be feed, what belongs in the head.; [a.] Hyattsville, MD

TURNER, BEVERLY LEE
[b.] December 20, 1958, Seneca, SC; [p.] Rev. Marvin and Patsy Lee; [m.] Thomas A. (Tony) Turner, November 5, 1977; [ch.] Paul Anthony, Candance Lee; [ed.] Seneca Sr. High; [occ.] CSR, Northland Cable; [memb.]

Oconce Sertoma Club, SHS Jr. and Sr. Beta Club Member; [oth. writ.] Several poems written as gifts to family and friends. Author of my 9th grade English Class Play.; [pers.] My best poetry is inspired from emotional events experienced in my own life. My greatest encouragement came from my 9th grade English teacher, Mrs. Carolyn Ross. My mother is a very talented writer also.; [a.] Seneca, SC

TURNER, EMMA P.
[b.] Philadelphia, PA; [p.] Charles A. Turner; [ch.] Charles, Raymond, Warren, Marcia, Bonnie, Jeanne Marie; [ed.] William Penn. - High Phila, PA Mercy - Technology Phila, PA; [occ.] Retired, reading teacher; [memb.] Willingboro Art Alliance; [pers.] I believe hard work and perseverance is the key to attaining your goals. I am influenced by the writings of Shakespeare and Lord Jennyson; [a.] Willingboro, NJ

TWISDALE, MARVENE K.
[b.] March 17, 1943, Gulfport, MS; [p.] Marvin Kinney, Odell Kinney; [m.] A. B. Twisdale, November 21, 1963; [ch.] Alysia T. Lavelle; [ed.] Byars - Hall High School; [occ.] Wife, Homemaker, Calligrapher; [memb.] Fbenezer Cumberland, Presbyterian Church; [oth. writ.] Short stories, the most recent: about a congregation helping victims of the Flood of 1993, published in the December issue of the Missionary Messenger.; [pers.] "To make a difference in life" I believe that the (written word) of thoughts, insights, and experiences are lasting for future generations. To help focus one, toward God and his goodness, mercy peace and blessings is my goal and legacy.; [a.] Mason, TN

TZERMAN, SUZANNE
[b.] May 3, 1963, Queens, NY; [ed.] Bay Ridge High School, Borough of Manhattan Community College; [pers.] I dedicate this poem to my Mother, Florence. She took the time to read for me when I was a child. It will never go forgotten.

UHLMAN, STEPHANIE
[b.] December 18, 1975, Staten Island; [p.] Josephine and Robert Uhlman; [ed.] Currently attending Rutgers College, Majoring in Administration of Justice And Sociology; [memb.] Rutgers College Honors Program, Rutgers College Program Council, Off-Campus Students Association; [hon.] Dean's List, Certificate of Academic Achievement; [pers.] I don't reach for the stars but beyond them. I never settle for anything but the best.; [a.] Staten Island, NY

ULLOA, ERLINDA ROSE
[pen.] Chulie Ulloa; [b.] February 16, 1981, Orange; [p.] Sylvia B. Gonsalez; [ed.] Bonita Vista Middle School, Bonita Vista High School; [occ.] Student; [memb.] ASB Freshman President. Tall Flags Officer, JV Cheerleader, Mecha secretary; [pers.] Never underestimate yourself always give 100% in anything you do. Follow your heart and your dreams will come true.; [a.] Chula Vista, CA

UPCHURCH, AIMEE LEE
[b.] January 29, 1981, Denver; [p.] David Upchurch and Linda Van Valkenburg; [ed.] Eigth grade - student; [memb.] 4-H, Royal Egeria; [hon.] Lettered in all school sports; [hon.] Certificate of merit in English; [oth. writ.] Work has been published in school newsletters and church plays.; [pers.] If you have a dream, go out and do it. Poetry has been an interest (goal) of mine since I can remember. I believe I've accomplished a portion of this and hope to explore more in this area.

UPTHEGROVE, CLAUDE S.
[b.] November 3, 1928, Okeechoha, FL; [m.] Pansy Cain, March 23, 1928; [ch.] Sheldon Jr., John David,

Brenda, Lynn; [ed.] B.A at Bible training school in Siville Tenn-Medical Corp in the navy taught school in Miracle Valley Ariz; [occ.] Minister; [hon.] Ran the longest revival in the history of any evangelist, in detroit beginning Jan 1st 1969 until June 1972 Pastor Ralph Hart have built three churches; [oth. writ.] Many poem have been written to Pastors and friends, now for 50 years. Some have been published in church magazines.; [pers.] The beauty of poetry has many times, brought tears to my eyes - when I write a personal poem to some one or a group, it is from my heart. Poetry speaks as nothing else in the world; [a.] West Palm Beach, FL

URIBE, ROBERT R.
[b.] April 5, 1976, Flint, MI; [p.] Robert W. Uribe, Debra Moretto; [m.] Jessica Uribe, July 9, 1994; [ch.] Brandon Robert Uribe; [ed.] Naperville North HS (IL) currently working towards a business degree at Michigan State University; [occ.] Manager at a local movie theatre; [oth. writ.] Personal collection of poems and short stories; [pers.] I like to write poetry to reveal things about myself. It's easier to deal with emotions and life's complications when I create visual images with my writing. More than anything it's fun to create this kind of art.; [a.] East Lansing, MI

URSRY, MELISSA
[pen.] Cricket Ursry; [b.] September 1, 1981, Florida; [p.] Donna and Randy Ursry; [ed.] Kindergarten through 8 St. Patricks; [occ.] Students; [oth. writ.] Family, love, life; [pers.] I would like to think my family, Norma, Harold, Jan, Donna and Randy for all there support.; [a.] Jacksonville, FL

UY, JERRY ENRIQUEZ
[pen.] Jeremiah Hastings Whitman; [b.] November 14, Laguna, Philippines; [p.] Uy Ching Sio, Luz Enriquez; [ed.] Lyceum of the Philippines, BA in Literature, University of the Philippines MA in Communication Research, Beaver College, M Ed in Written Communication; [occ.] Technical Writer, Advanced Logic Research; [memb.] American Freestyle Association; [hon.] Resident Scholar, Lyceum of the Philippines, 1992 World Champion, Bicycle Freestyle, Team Manager, Trier Germany, First Place - Poetry writing, Lyceum of the Philippines; [oth. writ.] "Hanggang Langit" - Lyricist, Metro Manila Music Festival, poetry for Decision Magazine; [pers.] "For our light and momentary afflictions are achieving for us an eternal glory that far outweighs them all."; [a.] Aliso Viejo, CA

VACIK, KATHLEEN
[b.] March 18, 1964, Rantoul, IL; [p.] Ernest Keith, Marian Keith; [m.] Michael Vacik; [ch.] Robert Erik Korson, Rachel Kathleen Vacik; [occ.] Office Automation Specialist; [a.] Gainesville, FL

VAGUE, FRED J.
[b.] December 2, 1932, Brooks, MN; [p.] Leroy W. and Anna M.; [m.] Joan M., May 18, 1957; [ch.] Jeff, Kathy, Karen, Bill; [ed.] H.S., 3 yrs College Major in Industrial Education; [occ.] Retired; [oth. writ.] Several poems published that won contest and placed in book similar to yours mag winners - also write short stories for young adults; [pers.] My story telling is reflected in my poems all I write about is true life experiences.

VALDEZ, CATHERINE GAIL
[pen.] Kate; [b.] April 18, 1959, IL; [p.] Douglas and Mary Sletten; [m.] Daniel, March 27, 1976; [ch.] Danny, Jeremy; [ed.] Frank Borman Jr High, Maryvale High Glendale Community College; [occ.] Homemaker; [hon.] The last line of the poem What is real love was put on Aids Guilt; [oth. writ.] Partnership, Friends, Came to Believe, These Rooms, Mary Smiles Mama Doesn't

Cry; [pers.] Writing is the way to become immortal. It is one soul talking to another soul.; [a.] Scottsdale, AR

VALENTINE, TREVOR
[b.] March 7, 1954, Jamaica; [occ.] Physician; [memb.] American Academy of Pediatrics, Massachusetts Medical Society; [pers.] This poem is dedicated to my son Neil; [a.] Rockland, MA

VAN CLIEF IV, JEFFERY T.
[pen.] Warren Parker; [b.] May 4, 1956, Brooklyn, NY; [p.] Jeffery T. Van Clief; [m.] Deborah Van Clief, December 16, 1988; [ch.] Warren and Jeffery Van Clief; [ed.] George Westinghouse H.S.; [occ.] Oven Operator-Quaker Oats Company; [oth. writ.] Dead Time stories. Currently Being written. The Adventures of Homey D. Elf not yet published.; [pers.] Family togetherness is the only key to success and happiness.; [a.] Manhathan, KS

VANDERHOOF, VICKIE L.
[b.] April 10, 1954, Indiana, PA; [ed.] University of Pittsburgh-B.A., Tri-State Computer Institute-diploma; [occ.] Unemployed seeking to become self-employed; [oth. writ.] Poem published in National Library of Poetry anthology "At Water's Edge" editorial letter(s) and other works knocking on publisher's doors; [pers.] Life is tough-love is tougher-faith is the toughest of all. God's "retirement plan" is worth it!; [a.] Fairview, PA

VANFLEET, ROXANN
[pen.] RJ Vanfleet; [b.] September 1950, Illinois; [p.] Doris and O.C. Henson; [ed.] Valley High School, West Des Moines Iowa/ Graceland College, Lamoni Iowa; [occ.] Self Discovery Thru Painting and Writing; [pers.] I try consciously to influence no one other than myself thru experience what I dread and what I love each day. That which I express on paper or canvas is for concrete personal reflection.; [a.] Mission Hills, KS

VANNORDSTRAND, JENNIFER JO
[pen.] L. M. Palmer, Blu Trip; [b.] December 12, 1970, Atlanta, GA; [p.] W. J. Vannordstrand and Anne Smith; [ed.] Self-educated; [occ.] Incredibly intelligent waitress; [hon.] Being a true poet is my only honor; [oth. writ.] Daffodils and dreams many poems short stories and a start on a novel; [pers.] Life is just a shadow of what we see I am Lord Byron Reincarnated; [a.] Charlotte, NC

VARGAS, VICTORIA H.
[pen.] Vicky H. Vargas; [b.] Peru, S. America; [p.] Dr. Victor M. Amesquita and Luzmila Ymana; [m.] Miguel V. Vargas; [ch.] Margarita, Nancy, Miguel, Lucy, Richard, Steven; [pers.] ("This is the country of my children and in projection my own:) Her love for poetry goes back many decades, has won several awards in amateur contests and is now working for the publication of a selected number of her poetry in Spanish. The insertion of "Healing" in your book Beyond the Stars" Touches her deeply.

VARGO, JUNE K.
[b.] June 5, 1931, PA; [p.] Michael and Susan Kanyan; [m.] Michael H. Vargo, June 30, 1951; [ch.] Susan DeNora, Elizabeth Masia, Michael P. Vargo; [ed.] Blairsville High School, attended Indiana Hospital School of Nursing, Indiana, PA; [occ.] Retired-Nursing Division of School Health-Monroe County Health Dep't; [memb.] United Methodist Women, Gradell, Girl Scouts of America, P.T.A. In Service Planning Committee for M.C.H.D.; [hon.] American Legion School Award, President Usher's Club, President Latin Club; [oth. writ.] As a senior in High School Co-wrote 122 poems for class day. Representative for Bell Breeze - Co. Magazine. 2 completed adult fictional Novels. 8 Copy

right in Lib. of Congress for Musical scores. Many, many poems. Some published, children's stories.; [pers.] I constantly strive to create a mirror effect of myself and my characters. As with Longfellow, Emerson, Wilcox and Kipling, I try to use loving, caring words to help unite a bond with friends around the world.; [a.] Rochester, NY

VARNER, CONNIE L.
[pen.] Constance L. Ourada; [b.] July 30, 1942, Boise, ID; [p.] Nick Ourada, Colleen MacIntosh; [m.] Mitchell L. Varner, August 5, 1961; [ch.] Ladeed Ann, Cora LeAnn, Mitchell Leroy; [ed.] Boise, Idaho High School; [occ.] Housewife; [memb.] Nazareno Church of Grandview, WA; [pers.] The Lord gave me these poems. One night I woke up and these words were coming so fast. I just put them down on paper; [a.] Grandview, WA

VAUGHN, JANET A.
[pen.] Janet A. Tedford; [b.] October 21, 1946, NJ; [p.] Gloria Palladino and John Dubeski; [ed.] William Allen High School Allentown, PA; [occ.] Disabled; [hon.] Certificate for penmanship in Skillman, NJ; [pers.] I believe we are reincarnated to a higher power then ourselves. That's why God made an angel from up above.

VAZQUEZTELL, CARMEN A.
[b.] February 25, 1952, Cabo Rojo, Puerto Rico; [ch.] Lizette; [ed.] B.S. in secondary education and foreign languages and an M.A. in Educational Administration from New York University, a professional diploma in reading from Hofstra University, currently pursuing a doctorate in reading, language, and cognition from Hofstra; [occ.] Principal-Adult Continuing and Occupational Education, Western Suffolk BOCES; [memb.] Member International Reading Association, NYS Association for Bilingual Education, NYS Teachers of English to Speakers of Other Languages, Teachers of English to Speakers of Other Languages, National Association for Bilingual Education, American Vocational Education Association, Association for Supervision and Curriculum Development, Supervisors and Administrators Association of New York State, Council of Administrators and Supervisors; [hon.] Recipient of the Dr. Martin Luther King Scholarship Award, US Office of education Title VII Fellowship, Frank D. Whalen Outstanding Citizenship Award, Outstanding Achievement Award in the Study of Foreign Languages and International Education, Member Sigma Delta Phi; [oth. writ.] Stolen moments. In Edge of Twilight. NL of P, If I were a flower. In East of Sunrise. NL of P; [pers.] Dedicated to all who have helped me discover the inner strength and peace that allows me to write poetry.; [a.] Jackson Heights, NY

VEALE, LORNE D.
[b.] September 25, 1931, Toronto, Canada; [p.] Edith and Wlm Veale; [m.] Divorced; [ch.] Joan Lorna; [ed.] Public School; [occ.] Cottage Court Owner Singer and M.C. For C/W Jamborees; [memb.] C.K.N.X. Barn Dance Hall of Fame, Completed Public Speak. and Sales Coarses; [hon.] Sang at Nashville Palace Nash Tenn. Also Renfro Valley Barn Dance Appeared on Toronto's W5 T.V.; [oth. writ.] Written four songs including Tribute to Roy Acuff, M.C. of Grand Oldopry also other poems; [pers.] Judge me not by my type or skin nor by my country, or my kin judge me alone on strength of merit this a man does not inherit; [a.] Wasaga Beach Ontario, Canada

VELASQUEZ, MARIA
[pen.] Raven; [b.] April 27, 1966; [p.] Juan Velasquez, Catalina Velasquez; [ed.] Bassett High School, ELAC (East Lost Angeles College), FIDM (Fashion Institute of Design and Merchandising); [occ.] Administrative Assistant; [hon.] Dean's List; [pers.] As a romantic, I am free to explore the many possibilities of feelings in my writing. The early romantic poets were always an inspiration to me.; [a.] La Puente, CA

VELLA, ERIKA
[pen.] Erika; [b.] October 20, 1983, San Diego, CA; [p.] Tony and Maria Vella; [ed.] 6th Grade; [occ.] Student; [a.] El Cajon, CA

VERNON, CYNTHIA L.
[pen.] C. L. Vernon; [b.] June 18, 1958, Newark, NJ; [p.] Liba and Margaret Vernon; [ed.] High Sch. graduate-1976, Tioga Central High School Tioga Center, NY; [hon.] Editor's Choice Award 1994-the National Library of Poetry; [oth. writ.] Poem-"The Key" published 1994, Reflections of light - The National Library of Poetry additional poetry - ghostwrite short stories with my sister Lisa Vernon; [pers.] Poetry is an outlet for me. An enjoyable break in the hassles of life.; [a.] Binghamton, NY

VILLEPIGUE, JAMES CHARLES
[pen.] J.C.V. Soul Lifter; [b.] May 20, 1971, Manhasset, NY; [p.] James Sr. and Nancy Villepigue; [ed.] Roslyn High, University of Bridgeport, CT. Wassau Comm. College, The New Center for Wholistic Health Care and Research; [occ.] Student of Orient medicine and fitness trainer; [memb.] AFAA (Aerobic and Fitness Association of America); [hon.] I recently won an award for a Biography contest, in which I was photograph and written about in American Fitness Magazine, as the youngest trainer, ever to win and ever published; [oth. writ.] I have written several poems, although this is the first one we ever submitted. I hope to submit others and gain recognition as a professional writer.; [pers.] I feel many individuals have the knowledge and the talent to be poets. Though I feel it is not the talent alone that counts. It is the talented poet who can reach in, search their souls, take in, and pass on the lively they hold in their hearts. That is a treasure in itself.; [a.] Roslyn, NY

VIRNELSON, BETSY
[pen.] Betsy Winters Virnelson; [b.] April 28, 1944, Cleveland, OH; [p.] Ed and Ferne Winters; [m.] Craig Virnelson, August 28, 1965; [ch.] Wesley Craig, Kevin Michael; [ed.] Euclid High School, Mount Union College, St. Luke's Hosp. School of Nursing; [occ.] Parish Nurse, Mayfield United Methodist Church; [memb.] Health Ministry Association; [pers.] I believe that God has given me a deep compassion for people, which for me finds its primary and truest expression in my nursing and writing. I write from my heart.; [a.] Chesterland, OH

VISBAL, RICHARD LEE
[pen.] Ric Lee; [b.] May 12, 1957, Cincinnati, OH; [m.] Ramona P. Visbal, February 23, 1979; [ch.] Richard, Michelle, Christina; [pers.] The writing was inspired to me by the love and compassion of family and friends of Ramona Wilma Leoda Kidd in her final moments, May 20th 1994.; [a.] Cincinnati, OH

VITALONE, JENNA
[b.] January 20, 1989, Dallas, TX; [p.] Joe and Joanne Vitalone; [ed.] I am 6 years old and I am in kindergarten; [occ.] Student; [memb.] Brownie Girl Scouts of America, Taekwondo, Piano, T-ball; [pers.] I love animals. I love to write about them and draw them. When I grow up I would like to be a Veterinarian.; [a.] Flower Mound, TX

VIVERETTE, MARYANN
[b.] May 13, 1960, Evanston, IL; [p.] Edward and Lena Campbell; [m.] Dennis Viverette, February 14, 1990;

[ch.] Sarah Rhiannon, Melissa Dawn, Jeremy Ray; [ed.] Herndon High School (Herndon VA) Computer Processing Inst. (Hartford CT); [occ.] Corporate Executive Secretary - Consolidated Exe Care-Rocky Mt. NC; [hon.] I have had the honor of being asked to write for friends and family in certain emotional times - e.g. weddings and funerals. This has meant a lot to me and has brought me great joy.; [pers.] To Me: Poetry is the rhythmic thoughts and emotions of song, only without music. When one is emotional, they say it's best to talk about it - it'll make you feel better. Well, I know only to write about it, it does make me feel better. I only hope, by my writings, I may touch the heart of someone and maybe they'll feel better too.; [a.] Rocky Mount, NC

VOGELSANG, JACQUELINE
[pen.] "A Lady Of A Certain"; [b.] August 30, Jax, FL; [p.] Basil and Birdie Davis; [m.] 1977, EDW Hopkins (Divorced); [ch.] Crystal and Michael; [ed.] High School, Reading and travel around the world for many years. I love to sing. And sometimes sing with a Club Group with friends and am writing songs.; [occ.] I am Retired from Yacht Supply Business, South Side N.C. Club; [memb.] I am a member of The Southside newcomers club for two years, Sherrill Wilsons piano Bar Group, Baptist Church; [hon.] I like to travel I am new at writing but have had poems accepted by The National Library, Three of them and am published by The mandarin News, Opinions mostly; [a.] Mandarin Florida, FL

VOGLE, MICHAEL D.
[pen.] David Steinburg; [b.] December 22, 1950, Los Angeles, CA; [p.] George Edgar and Mary Louise; [m.] Joan Helen Vogle, June 2, 1984; [ch.] David Paul Vogle; [ed.] Long Beach City College, Catholic University, Old Dominion University and Georgia Tech.; [occ.] Import/Export and Author; [memb.] International Traders Worldwide, National Arbor Day Association, World Wildlife Federation, North American Hunting Club, The Wilderness Society, The National Trust for Historical Preservation and the IA Zoo Association, National Parks and Conservation Association; [hon.] Distinguished Heroic Citizen Award (1967), Catholic Confermation of the Christian Doctrine (Lay Teachers) Award (1971), The United States Department of Labor Certification of Recognition for the Training of men in the field of Building and Carpentry (1977); [oth. writ.] The inner rebellion and a short story called an Unlikely Killer, The Complete Corporate Evaluations Service Manual/for Corporations Large and Small; [pers.] "I believe that if we are to be able to keep all that God has given each and all of us, we Must give it all away!" Also," If we are to live in peace admit the Evil around us, we must let Love pour from the depths of our souls toward all who we come in contact with!"; [a.] Long Beach, CA

VOORIS, MARIE L. PACACHA
[pen.] Maria Taylor; [b.] June 10, 1931, New York City; [p.] Felice and Joseph Genzardi; [m.] Charles R. Vooris, January 10, 1959 and July 17, 1991; [ch.] Frank E. Pacacha, Ellen Marie Pacacha; [ed.] Bachelor's Degree Cum Laude; [occ.] Retired Payroll and Health Benefits Admin.; [memb.] Past President, Sons of Italy in America, Palm Beach Gardens Women's Club, Scholarship Awards Ceremony Chairperson; [hon.] Children of Columbus Award, Staten Island College, 4.0 GPA AA Degree Adelphi University, Palm Beach Garden Women's Club; [oth. writ.] Character studies and short stories. Articles published in local newspapers organizational newsletters; [pers.] Poetry speaks from the heart of our inner most dreams and touches us all.; [a.] Palm Beach Gardens, FL

VOROS II, JOSEPH PAUL
[b.] February 5, 1961, Pittsburgh, PA; [p.] Joseph Paul Voros, Rita Voros; [ed.] Central High School, Villanova University; [occ.] President, Voros Holdings; [hon.] Barnwell Honor Roll, Who's Who in the East, 24th Edit., Men of Achievement, 16th Edit., Sterling Who's Who, Who's Who Registry of Business Leaders 1994-1995; [oth. writ.] Love Poems and sonnets Panda Bear Mountain, The Grandmother's Blessings (short stories); [pers.] My writing connotates my inspiration and love for life and others.; [a.] Cheltenham, PA

VOSS, BARBARA
[b.] June 5, 1949, Allegan, MI; [p.] Argyle Read, Florence Read; [m.] Kenneth Voss, August 17, 1968; [ch.] Joshua Matthew, Larissa Kathryn, Jordan David; [ed.] Allegan High School Michigan State University; [occ.] Small Business Owner; [oth. writ.] I am currently working on a collection of poetry; [pers.] I write for the sheer love of the art and began composing poetry in 1993. I don't know where my writing will take me but while constantly striving for excellence, I want foremost to enjoy the journey. If along the way, I can bring something positive to others, that would be the ultimate reward.; [a.] Eureka, CA

VOSTERS, LARRY
[b.] December 2, 1946, Douglas, AZ; [m.] Barb, 1967; [ch.] Kenyan, Shoshana Craig; [occ.] Training Coordinator-Food Motor Co; [memb.] WAW, Washtenaw Education-Work Consortium; [a.] Chelsea, MI

VU, HOAL D.
[pen.] Ducminh; [b.] May 15, 1932, Hanoi; [p.] Tan Vu, Can Vu; [m.] Nga Pham, December 1, 1965; [ch.] Ngoctuyen Vu, Dung D. Vu; [ed.] Jean Dupuis High, Law Faculty College; [occ.] Retired; [memb.] Rotary Club, Lions Club; [oth. writ.] Some poems of novels published in local magazines; [pers.] Human love and country love; [a.] Valinda, CA

VU, ROY
[b.] March 25, 1976, Houston, TX; [p.] Anquan Kien Vu, Dung Tran Vu; [ed.] J. Frank Dobie High, Texas Christian University; [occ.] Business Major, International Relations Minor; [memb.] High school-National Honors Society, French Honors Society, and Latin Honors Society, United Asian Community, Amnesty International; [hon.] TCU Faculty Scholarship; [oth. writ.] Several poems published in High School magazine, Unity; [pers.] Do not ever let the flowers of your heart die, even as they are placed upon your grave. I have been greatly influenced by the likes of Lord Byron, and Keats.; [a.] Houston, TX

WAGNER, BRIDGET
[b.] January 11, 1960, South Africa; [ed.] London University, U.K.; [occ.] Research; [a.] San Francisco, CA

WAGNER, HAROLD E.
[b.] April 11, 1917, Waldo, KS; [p.] Frank and Mary Altena Wagner; [m.] Olive Wagner, June 15, 1947; [ch.] Tamara Wagner Steen, Mark Wagner, Debra Wagner Miller; [ed.] 2 years Completed Business College Certificate, 4 year College - B.A. Degree in History, 3 year Seminary - Master's Degree in Theology; [occ.] Retired Senior Citizen with avocation of photography and research of pioneer structures across America (Barns, Soddies, etc.); [memb.] Garson Art Gallery/Yakiwa, WA., Central Washington Agric. Museum/Yarima, Writer's Club of Yakima, WA., Prairie Museum of Art and History/Colby, KS., Presbyterian Church/Grandview, WA; [hon.] Mint (AG) Industry Man of the Year Award, Realtor of the Year Award, U.S. Navy Honorable Discharge, U.S. President Cer-

tificate for Youth Counselling/Leadership; [oth. writ.] Former writer/reporter for WA, Mint industry plication, "Mint Drops." Author of book Barns on Parade Across America, (1993), Poet of poetry published Internationally by East and West Literary Society.; [pers.] "A person's positive attitude and true wealth are the good deeds a person does in this life."; [a.] Grandview, WA

WAGNER, KEN
[b.] March 23, 1979, Alabama; [p.] Doug and Alice Wagner; [ed.] High School student in Chambersburg, PA; [occ.] Student; [pers.] As my life is really just beginning, I hope this is the first of many poems on what life will bring to me; [a.] Chambersburg, PA

WALCZAK, PAMELA K.
[pen.] Pam; [b.] March 9, 1962, Biloxi, MS; [p.] Divorced; [ed.] Taunton High, '76-'79, Norton High, '79-'80; [occ.] Volunteer, Sturdy M. Hospitable Attleboro, MA; [hon.] Sturdy Memorial Hospitable volunteer 100 hour, 500 hour and 1000 hour award pins; [oth. writ.] Poem published in my senior year in High School magazine and in local newspaper, article for the Sun Chronicle; [pers.] I've liked reading and writing poems since childhood. I hope to write poems as excellent as the most famous poets. Writing good poems as long as possible is fun to me.; [a.] Norton, MA

WALDMAN, STACI
[pen.] Staci Hope; [b.] September 13, 1977, Brooklyn, NY; [p.] Steve and Sharon; [ed.] Sheepshead Bay H.S., Hunter college; [occ.] Student; [pers.] Poetry helps me to express my deepest feeling without actually having to speak them.; [a.] Brooklyn, NY

WALDRON, MADELINE
[b.] March 10, 1971, Plainfield, NJ; [p.] Marie and James Regan; [m.] Robert E. Waldron, October 12, 1941; [ch.] Lynn Waldron Walker, Robyn Waldron Massey; [ed.] High School; [occ.] Retired, Restaurant Owner; [memb.] Smithsonian Inst.; [pers.] All my writing, up till now mainly a hobby. (Letters - Philosophical Musics, Poems ect. Serving the ever present urge to write thru the years.; [a.] West Stockbridge, MA

WALKER, GLADYS E.
[pen.] Ann; [b.] March 18, 1927, NJ; [p.] Deceased; [m.] George C. Walker Sr. (deceased), November 7, 1950; [ch.] Penny Roxann, Maryann, George Jr., Susanne L., Georgeann C., Nancy, Cathy; [ed.] 8th Grade; [occ.] Housewife (disabled); [pers.] Only poetry I wrote was on relative's birthday cards and Christmas cards. They told me to go on with it. Higher, I decided to try writing it for others Good or Bad I will.; [a.] Phillipburg, NJ

WALKER, HELEN, C.
[b.] April 7, 1924, Virginia; [p.] Mr. and Mrs. William Daniels; [m.] Charles W. Walker, September 7, 1940; [ch.] Four lovely daughters; [ed.] High School; [occ.] Retired; [hon.] Four honorable mentionables in "The American Song Festival" an International songwriting competition; [pers.] I seem to express every day happenings, whether it be a holiday, special occasion or traumatic experience, in poetry or song.

WALKER, JANE R.
[b.] October 1, 1952, Woodland Hills, CA; [occ.] Owner/publisher "Realistic Extremes" a publishing house, writer Screenplays, Novels, Essays; [memb.] "NAACP, Organization of Black Screenwriters"; [oth. writ.] "From the Eyes of Joshua" a novel - published work: Includes exclusively for the jet sitter, "1st Edition" a book of humorous satire on the airline industry and" ...And Still We Rise" a monthly newsletter; [a.] Woodland Hills, CA

WALKER, KYOTO
[p.] Bernice and Walter Walker; [pers.] Love and honor thy parents, and above all, let God order thy steps. Thanks mom and dad for all of your support.

WALKER, PATRICIA MALYNN
[b.] March 27, 1961, Detroit; [p.] Dorothy Etchison; [m.] Jerry Lee Walker, June 25, 1993; [ed.] Got GED back to Cambridge Business School, got Certified as Nurse Aide; [occ.] Nurse Aide, take care of disable people; [oth. writ.] Thank you very much, when I was young I lost my self-esteem put God first the love for Him and I believed in myself.; [pers.] I wrote this poem and a lot more other poems of the feeling, gift and downfalls of life to give myself and others that things will happen good and bad just believe in yourself first.

WALL, COREY MICHELLE
[b.] May 12, 1986, Demorest, GA; [p.] Deborah and Tony Purcell, John Wall; [ed.] Merion Elementary School (Merion, PA); [occ.] Student - 3rd Grade; [hon.] Third place in school relays; [pers.] Writing is fun to me and I think other children should write poems too.; [a.] Carnesville, GA

WALL, LUCILLE MILBURN
[b.] August 29, 1920, Oklahoma; [p.] Harold and Marquerite Milburn; [m.] Ed, one week before Pearl Harbor 1941; [ch.] 3 Adult children, 6 grandchildren, 2 grandchildren; [ed.] 3 to 5 years of Adult and Jr. College Creative Writing, 1 Semester University Irvine. Also attended many Writers Seminars.; [memb.] Orange County Spellbinders Writers (and Contest Chairman for spellbinders Orange County Writers Contest), Society of Children's Book Writers; [oth. writ.] Published (Full Page Poem) in Parents Magazine, Listen Magazine, Farm Wife, El Vivaz (Santa Ana College) Magazine. Four years Publicity Chairman for Human Interest Stories, PTA, Cub Scouts and A.F.S., and Scout and Church programs.; [pers.] "...I write Because I Have To!" God has given me an `overdose of Motherhood' and an Empathy that lets me enter the pains and joys of other peoples hearts.

WALLACE, DOROTHY A.
[b.] September 11, 1942, Wright Country, MO; [p.] Stephen Foster Dudley, Lois Breman Dudley; [ch.] Michael Huckaby, David Wallace; [ed.] Mansfield High School, Mansfield, MO, Drury College and Southwest Missouri State University, Springfield, MO; [occ.] Director of Special Services, Mansfield Schools, Mansfield, MO; [memb.] Missouri State Teachers Association, Council of Administrators of Special Education, American Salers Association, International Society of Poets; [oth. writ.] Several poems published, articles for local newspapers, family histories for county history books; [a.] Mansfield, MO

WALLACE, VICTOR S.
[b.] November 30, 1924, Harrisburg, IL; [p.] William and Verba Wallace; [m.] Ruby V. Wallace, February 3, 1964; [ch.] David Wallace and Linda L. Bishop; [ed.] High School Grad., Plus Grad. as a Physical Therapist; [occ.] Retired with plenty of work. Take some time to fish with good luck. I was in WW II European Theater, 27 month overseas, in the front lines 24 months. Africa, Italy, France, Germany and Austria. (2nd Field Artillery Observation Battalion); [memb.] The American Legion; [hon.] Oh, a good conduct metal in the Army!!! and 5 bronze Battle stars. European Theater of Operations.; [oth. writ.] I have written twenty-three short stories ranging in topica from: Love to Adventure, to Surprise, Romance, Mystery, Murder, Torture, Ghosts, Rape, Specters, Sex, Joy, and etc., My manuscript is ready for Publishing and totals Five Hundred and Seventy-Five pages, double-spaced and in good form. ——

I have also written twenty-seven songs, ranging in: pop, country blues, Hawaiian, the Island sound, gospel, trucking, rap, and patriotic. I have written some poems also.; [pers.] If you start down the road and come to the end of that road, don't turn and go back. Go ahead, the trial that you blaze many some day turn a Super-Highway. We may get hurt,.. and we will have pain,.. then we heal,.. With God's help. If we look, we will see things to do. Do them, usually they turn out to be worthwhile. We get hurt,..... and we feel pain,... then we heal,... with God's help.; [a.] U.S.A.

WALLEN, ALFHILD
[pen.] Stina Strom; [b.] February 5, 1915, St. Paul, MN; [p.] Efraim and Malin Ahlstrom; [m.] Arnold F. Wallen (deceased), 1938; [ch.] 4 daughters 2 grandchildren Lynne, Christine, Nancy, Lisa; [ed.] Through Junior College/Business School Numerous U. of California Extension Courses in Literature. (Night classes in San Francisco, Berkeley, Hayward University.; [occ.] Partner - Art Gallery (Christopher Queen Galleries); [memb.] 20 years Poetry Society of America California Writer's Club - 40 years Smithnian Institute - Contributing Membership Sonoma Co. Museum - Benefactor California Historical Society St. Mary's College - Benefactor Academy of American poets - Member Inc. Cool brith Circle. (California Poetry Society) Bay area Poet's Coalition; [hon.] Works in numerous anthologist Co-authorship of 2 books. Historical Literary One hard-cover book of poetry. Prize winner in 29 states Grand prize. State of Pennsylvania over one hundred prize awards (grand prize judge for major competitions.); [oth. writ.] Numerous articles, essays in regional magazines and newspapers; [pers.] In all things strive for perfection "Fall down 7 times - Get up 8, "Chinese Proverb Speak to one's Truth. Love, but not blindly.; [a.] Duncans Mills, CA

WALLS, JIMMY
[pen.] Jimmy Walls; [b.] April 18, 1926, Bronx, NY (deceased); [p.] Anna and James Walls; [m.] Dorothy Walls; [ch.] Had two families. Two sons named James Patrick, a daughter named Kathy, a grandson James Patrick, granddaughters Jaime Lynn and Jessica, a great grandson named Lyle; [occ.] Served on USS, Pennsylvania during World War Two. [ed.] James Monroe High School Bronx, NY; [oth. writ.] Wrote Poems in the Navy while on the USS, Pennsylvania common law ex-wife has book of poems, not published; [pers.] Loved NEW YORK, loved words and was a great poet. He loved Shakespeare and Edgar Allen Poe; was a great Scrabble player. He was memorizing the dictionary when he passed away.

WALLS, WILLIAM J.
[b.] January 28, 1939, Memphis, TN; [p.] Willie Walls, Anna Bertha Walls; [m.] Betty L. Walls, December 25, 1983; [ed.] Dusable High, Radio Communication (USAF), Chicago Baptist Institute, Ordained Minister; [occ.] Bus Driver (Chicago Transit Authority) 27 years; [oth. writ.] Essay on life. Religious poems (none ever published or sent in); [pers.] Once we as Human being accept responsibility for our actions toward ourselves and others, then can we appreciate and benefit from what life has to offer.; [a.] Chicago, IL

WALSH JR., HERBERT JAMES
[pen.] Herb Walsh; [b.] August 18, 1918, Chicago, IL; [p.] Herbert James Walsh Sr. and Estelle Nathan; [ch.] Dale, Tarilynn, Dean, Reed; [ed.] Senn High School (Grad) Chicago IL; [occ.] Retired Orchestra Conductor; [memb.] Musicians Union - local #47 (L.A.) also local #10 - Chicago IL

WALTER, JOYCE
[b.] August 24, 1940, Lansing, MI; [p.] Cari and Luna Casler; [m.] Wayne Walter, June 30, 1961; [ch.] David, Darin, Duain, (Dale died at age 20); [ed.] J.W. Sexton High School, Lansing Community College; [occ.] Owner of "Me and Thee Floral", take care of 2 year old granddaughter and care for my 90 year old mother-in-law who lives with us; [memb.] Lansing Seventh Day Advantist Church, Women's Ministry, Garden Club; [oth. writ.] Short Stories, poems; [pers.] Look for good and you shall find it believe in people and they will not let you down. Hope and you will not despair; [a.] Lansing, MI

WALTON, GREGORY
[pen.] Sweetdaddy Walton; [b.] November 1, 1951, Wash., DC; [p.] Ethel Walton; [ed.] Three years college; [occ.] Drywall Finisher; [memb.] Capital Hill Seventh Day Adventist Church; [oth. writ.] I have finished writing a Christian love story called (Claudette); [pers.] To Glorify God and to bring forth the lovelyness of being in love. In my writings, for (God) made a woman the most tenderest creature alive; [a.] Washington, DC

WALTON, RICHARD L.
[b.] July 12, 1953, Tucson; [p.] Clem and Obal Walton (Deceased); [ed.] Catalina H.S.; [pers.] Dedicated to those who have never forgotten their first and or only true love; [a.] Tucson, AZ

WARD, JODI MABEL
[pen.] Jo-Jo; [b.] November 10, 1980, Bronx, NY; [p.] Gloria and Joseph Ward; [ed.] Just promoted to the 10th grade at Harry S. Truman H.S; [hon.] Award for the Honor Roll at School, Awards and Trophies for Softball all Stars, Bronx Boro Pres Fern and Ferrier Award; [oth. writ.] Short Stories for School Classes; [pers.] Success is when you've done the very best you can

WARD, MYROU R.
[b.] December 16, 1949, USA; [p.] Joseph and Mabel Ward; [ed.] NYC Community College '72 Bernard Baurch College Major: Business, Current; [occ.] Electrical Designer Consolidated Edison La. of N.Y.; [memb.] Sigma Alpha Delta Night Honor Society at Baruch College; [hon.] Dale Carnegie Class: Effective Speaking and Communication Award: Outstanding Performance Award: Personal Achievement; [oth. writ.] Articles for school newspaper, "The Ticker"; [pers.] I strive to be a better person, for each day brings about new feelings, new adventures, new knowledge. We are never the same person we were yesterday.; [a.] Ossining, NY

WARDWELL, LOREE
[b.] January 23, 1980, Beaumont, TX; [p.] Craig Wardwell, Carrie Page; [ed.] In ninth grade right now, about to be in tenth; [memb.] High School Choir, High School Drill Team Member of Journalism Dept.; [hon.] Science Honor Award, Algebra Honor award, Modeling Awards; [oth. writ.] Book of almost one hundred poems, articles in my High School Paper, Short Stories; [pers.] My poetry reflects all my deepest thoughts and feelings. The best poet to me is Giuseppe Belli who I have been reading since I was 13.; [a.] Houston, TX

WARNER, ANGELIQUE ANNE
[b.] June 21, 1978, Scow, OH; [p.] Thomas and Pamela Warner; [ed.] Eleven years of homes school education; [occ.] High School Student St. Christian Liberty Academy Satellite School; [pers.] In poetry, the ages of man's past Carnality Falls away, and the true beauty of his everlasting spirit is seen. This is what I strive to illuminate in my poetry; [a.] South Euclid, OH

WARNER, BRIDGET
[b.] January 11, 1960, South Africa; [ed.] University of London, England; [occ.] Physician (Research clinical); [oth. writ.] Short Stories; [pers.] US resident for 9 years; [a.] San Francisco, CA

WARNER, RUTH
[b.] October 6, 1923, Toledo, OH; [p.] Pearl (Beyer) and David Edwards; [m.] Neal E. Warner, October 27, 1945; [ch.] Craig A. Warner; [ed.] Woodward High School, Stautzenberger Secretarial School; [occ.] Housewife, Former Secretary; [memb.] The National Authors Registry Int'l. Society of Authors and Artists; [hon.] Editor's Preference Award of Excellence 1994, Editor's Choice Award 1995 President's Award for Literary Excellence 1995; [oth. writ.] "Zest for Living" Published in treas. Poems of American Fall 1994. "Which Mask" Published in Remembrances 1994, "Aunt Laura" published in seasons to come 1995; [pers.] Newspaper articles and personal human relationships are the main sources for my poetic inspirations. Poetry can be wonderful therapy.; [a.] Northwood, OH

WARREN, MICHAEL
[pen.] The Lefthanded Boy; [b.] November 3, 1963, Omaha, NE; [p.] Jeanette Warren, David King; [ed.] Prairie View A. and M. University, B.S., University of Michigan, M.S.; [occ.] Mechanical Engineer; [memb.] Brotherhood Society of the New Life Baptist Church; [hon.] National Dean's List, Who's Who; [oth. writ.] Several poems of love, religion, and life that are anxiously awaiting to be published; [pers.] Let me do good while yet I still can, and be a fitting example of what it is to be a man.; [a.] Cincinnati, OH

WASHINGTON, CHALETTE RENEE
[b.] April 23, 1970, Philadelphia, PA; [p.] Harold R. Washington Jr. and Jeanette Washington; [ed.] Glassboro High (88), Fairleigh Dickinson University (90), Lincoln University, PA (94); [occ.] Order Picker at Inacom Logistic Center in Swedesboro, NJ; [memb.] Mt. Zion Baptist Church; [hon.] Lincoln University Scholarship Award, Contribution to Brotherhood Award; [pers.] Writing allows my mind to explore the ideas of truth, the depths of fantasy, and the realm of insanity. Eighteenth Century literature, particularly, Edmund Burke's "Philosophical Enquiry", dominates my train of writing.; [a.] Glassboro, NJ

WATSON, CHUCK
[b.] October 13, 1969, Amityville, NY; [p.] Kenneth and Lillian Watson; [ed.] Tucker Avenue Elementary School West Babylon Junior and Senior High Schools State University of New York at Farmingdale; [occ.] Clerk; [memb.] Center for American Valves, United Seniors Association, Inc., National Republican Senatorial Committee, Media Research Center, Council for Government Reform, Help Hospitalized Veterans, Hentor Foundation, the Senior Coalition, we the people, GUPAC, Citizens for a Sand Economy, US Tern Limits. BAMPAC center for the study of popular culture, Club ABC Tars.; [hon.] National Republican Senatorial Committee Senate Majority Certificate, Capital/ Watch 1994 Conservative Leadership Award, Veterans of Foreign Wars of the United States 1995 Certificate of Appreciation, Abraham Lincoln Foundation 1995 Certificate and Appreciation, The Leadership Institute Youth Leadership School Certificate of Achievement, National Republican Senatorial Committee Order of Merit, Suny Farmingdale Rambler Certificate of Appreciation American for Responsible Television Certificate of Achievement American Media media Network Certificate of Appreciation; [oth. writ.] Visions of Peculiarity (1991 Raynor Wallace Poetry Award - Runner Up), Zuzana (Sparkles in the Sound), various lyrical works; [pers.] Intolerance in the defense of

sanctity is no vice.; [a.] West Babylon, NY

WATSON, JULIE
[b.] October 1, 1975, Tuscaloosa, AL; [p.] Slade Watson and Myra Rheaume; [ed.] S.S. Murphy High School; [occ.] Student at Auburn University at Montgomery; [hon.] Phi Eta Sigma, Dean's List; [oth. writ.] None Published; [pers.] Love is something you will never lose. The pain and heartache of love cannot take away from the irreplaceable joy love gives.; [a.] Mobile, AL

WATSON, MICHELLE COLETTE
[b.] February 9, 1971, Cleveland, OH; [p.] John and Ruth Watson; [ed.] Aviation High School Air Traffic Control Student Class of 1989; [pers.] Having no children of my own as of yet, I look to my siblings children to give me inspiration. They are my greatest source of strength. Thanks, to all of you.; [a.] Cleveland, OH

WEAR, MARY ANN
[b.] August 26, 1939, Covington, KY; [p.] John and Margaret Dunn; [ch.] John, Joseph, Lisa, Leanne, Danny Lee; [ed.] Graduated, St. Mary High School, Alexandria, Kentucky 1957; [occ.] Nurse Companion; [oth. writ.] Masterpiece 1989, Secrets of My Heart 1990, My Captain 1990, My Precious Lord Hold My Hand Today 8/90, The Present 1990; [pers.] "The Lord is my Shepherd", Living with the Psalms, the key to life. The Book of Psalms, sometimes called, The Psalms of David. Anthology of David, a collection of the lyric poetry of his people. The Book of Job. It is a didactic poem with a historical basis. The key to knowledge.; [a.] Englewood, FL

WEAVER, CECELIA
[b.] October 7, 1899, Waterville, MN; [p.] S.P. and Julianna Weaver; [ed.] B.S. - 1929 - Univ. of MN (Music Major), B.S. - Certificate of Elementary Education; [occ.] Retired - 33 years of teaching experience, 25 years in the St. Paul Elementary Schools; [memb.] Life Memberships in National PTA, American Federation of Teachers, League of Minnesota Poets, Southern Minnesota Poets Society and National Federation of State Poetry Societies.; [hon.] "Cecelia Weaver Day" by Mayor Proclamation in Mankato, MN, May 10, 1980. Many awards for published poetry since 1955, including Best Poem of Year, "The Last Hunt" by Parnassas Literary Journal and Honorable Mention, May 8, 1995 - League of Minnesota Poets Seminar; [oth. writ.] "Using chord method in Teaching Piano to Beginners" (Unpublished); [pers.] My philosophy is expressed in my poem, "But That Was Yesterday".; [a.] Mankato, MN

WEBB, CHRISTINE
[pen.] Christine Webb; [b.] September 1, 1926, Joliet, IL; [p.] Ed Lewis and Effie Yarns; [m.] Robert I. Webb, May 12, 1946; [ch.] 12, 9 Living Robin, Robinann, Lynda, Janet, Robert, Susan, Denny, Michael, Richard, Christopher; [ed.] I attended Joliet Public Schools, J.T. H.S. Dist. 204 Joliet Jr. College and Lewis Univ.; [occ.] Employment Security Service Rep. and Acct. Executive; [memb.] ARRP, American Cancer Assoc., NWACP, St Thaddeus Alter Society, IAPES Professional Assoc.-International Chgo. Chapter of Adpidecation Assoc.; [hon.] 4 Awards for other Poetry Golden Part Award, Honorary Mention for 3 poems., Key Note Speaker for Girl Scouts and Martin Luther King 10th year Celebration; [oth. writ.] Compeled a list of my poems, speeches, themes and philosophy, "A Black Women Point of View" Speeches poems and philosophy several poems published in Joliet Time Newspapers.; [pers.] We all have a highest power one who shares our loads in life. The greatest cross we have to bear is love. I feel love is the answer to inner peace.; [a.] Joliet, IL

WEBB, SARA A.
[b.] November 4, 1977, Redding; [p.] Paula Webb, Norman Webb; [ed.] Shasta High School Shasta College; [occ.] Associate at Montgomery Ward; [memb.] Shasta Cascado Riders Future Farmers of America (FFA); [hon.] Public Speaking CARRCDS in San Diego State Competition 5th place. Excepted into program called College Connection. FFA won Star Chapter Farmer and Star and Star Green hand awards.; [oth. writ.] All unpublished; [pers.] Being only seventeen years old, I absorb the things that react around the world I live in and bring them down in writing poetry. My poem the lights. I wrote when I was fifteen years old. Describing pollution taking beauty away.; [a.] Igo, CA

WEI, WANG
[b.] May 30, 1952, Beijing, P.R. China; [ed.] B.A. in English, Jilin University, P.R. China, 1982, M.A. in English, Texas A&M University, 1990; [occ.] Accounting Dept. Clipper Americans, Inc.; [hon.] Prose in Creative Writing, Jilin University, 1982; [oth. writ.] Poetry, prose, news reports in local newspapers, P.R. China. B.A. Thesis: Comparative Study of Nature Poetry in the Works of Tao Yuan-ming and William Wordsworth, China, 1982, M.A. thesis: Chinese Ideograms in Ezra Pound's Canto 85, Texas A&M University, 1990.; [pers.] The language of poetry should have no boundaries. I pursue a harmony in the eastern and western cultures, languages, ideologies, poetics, and poetical forms.; [a.] Houston, TX

WEICHAL, MARJORIE F.
[pen.] Marj; [b.] March 27, 1929, Minneapolis, MN; [p.] Roy Lee and Gertrude Chapel; [m.] R. Allen Weichal, April 7, 1949; [ch.] Vicky Telfer, Laureen Young, Christine Weibel, Darla Minor; [sib.]; [ed.] B.A. Pacific Christian College, B.A. California State University Long Beach, M.A. Pepperdine University, Los Angeles; [occ.] Artist, Faculty of Pacific Christian College, Part-time; [memb.] Brea Art Association, CA, School Board Member, Eastside Christian School, Fullerton, CA, Pacific Christian Women's Association Education Committee, Fullerton Chamber of Commerce; [hon.] Honor Scholarship Society, Coe Fellowship; [oth. writ.] Format for Fitness: One way that Works, Inside out: a way to grow (poetry collection), Yes you can do and teach watercolor - 20 lessons for the classroom teacher. Articles for the look out, Cincinnati, OH.; [pers.] My poems speak to me out of a full life, I have to be willing to write them down; [a.] Fullerton, CA

WEINER, SHERRI E.
[b.] May 6, 1975, Akron, OH; [p.] Dr. Dennis Weiner and Phyllis Weiner; [ed.] Graduate from Revere High School in Richfield, Ohio and now a junior at the College of Wooster in Wooster, Ohio, Pre-Law, Psych. major; [hon.] Dean's list; [pers.] The freshest breath one can take is that of love, writing poetry makes me feel as though I've taken that breath.; [a.] Akron, OH

WEISS, DANNY L.
[b.] May 26, 1948, Eureka, CA; [p.] Helen M. Weiss; [ch.] Daughter, 19 yrs. old, Zephera A. Weiss; [ed.] San Lorenzo Valley High School, Felton, CA; Cabrillo College A. A. Degree; Computer Technology, Networking; [occ.] Computer Tech, Property Management; [memb.] Rosicrucian Order, AMORC, Ancient Mystical Order of the Rose Cross); [oth. writ.] Publish quarterly, newsletter called ISCE, "about ancient legends that relate to UFO's; membership conducting expedition to North Pole, Reenactment of Admiral Richard E. Byrd; Book: Nordic Connection; Produced/sold video called "Journey to the Hollow Earth"; [pers.] Paradise is a world within us and the world where the human race resides. It is the latter that I am deeply concerned with.; [a.] Felton, CA

WEST, DENNY ANN
[b.] January 13, 1972, San Antonio, TX; [p.] Billy D. West and Patricia A. Dixon; [ed.] High School, National Education Center for Business Diploma; [occ.] Telephone Service Representative - Utility Company; [pers.] I believe that when I am writing it is coming from my heart. I mostly write about my family that I love very much, my best friend, my Mom, my Dad, and my twin brother Danny, but that's another poem.; [a.] San Antonio, TX

WHEELER, GAYLE R.
[b.] March 7, 1947, Mass.; [p.] Both dead; [m.] James (divorced), single mother; [ch.] Tina 26, Annette 25, Theresa 22, James 12 and raising 2 grandsons while daughter works, ages 4 Tylor and Matthew 5; [ed.] Graduated Catalina High School in 1966; [occ.] Transportation monitor on a bus for special needs students; [memb.] First Free Will Baptist Church; [hon.] Had a poem published in a Christian Book my church subscribes to called "Co Laborer"; [oth. writ.] I've written other poems for my family and friends but its mostly a hobby. I have 115 poems so far, I just want to share them.; [pers.] I'm a born again Christian and I just try to live for the Lord and let my poetry and my life reflect that in doing my best to love others. I work with children and adults trying to make a difference in their lives and finding the greatest joy is just being able to love them. Our greatest gift is God's love, and our greatest task is sharing it with those no one else can love.; [a.] Tucson, AZ

WHITAKER, CAROLE E.
[b.] December 29, 1953, Doncaster, England, UK; [p.] Mallie Clarke; [m.] R. Iain Whitaker, October 19; [ch.] Katy and Jonathan; [ed.] Willowgarth High School Brentford College, London, England; [occ.] Housewife; [hon.] Diploma of the National Institute of Housecraft; [oth. writ.] Manuscript of Poems; [pers.] The influence and memories of my life I left behind in England stimulated my desire to record my memoirs inverse. My writings may encourage others to remember where they originated from and not to forget their own pasts.; [a.] San Antonio, TX

WHITAKER, GLORIA J.
[b.] June 11, 1961, Rocky Mount, NC; [p.] Annie Mae and William H. Whitaker; [ch.] Shanisha, Jeffrey, Tybree, David, Ashley, Whitaker; [ed.] High School Graduate Kane Business Ins., Vocational School Certified Nursing Assistant; [memb.] World Harvest Christian Center; [oth. writ.] Poems and Poetry writer, songwriter; [pers.] I thank God for blessing me with this talent. All the Glory and Praise I give to Him. Because He's good all the time.; [a.] Camden, NY

WHITCOMB, MARY BURG
[b.] April 25, 1909, Berkeley, CA; [p.] Edward J. and Beatrice Burg; [m.] S. L. Whitcomb, September 2, 1930; [ch.] Jackie, MaryBea, Richard, Felicia, Frederick and Melody, Grandchildren: 19 Great, and 1 Gr. Gr.; [ed.] 2 yrs. University of California, Berkeley. Resumed in 1955 now out on Honorable Leave.; [occ.] Writer. Mary Burg Whitcomb, Western Pub. Co. Racine, Wis.; [memb.] Sacramento Valley Astronomical Society, Sacramento, CA; [oth. writ.] Author of Tee-Bo and the Persnickety Prowler and Tee-Bo in the great Hort Hunt, 1975/1979 and Where The Sea Moans, Young Adult. Carlton Press, N.Y. 1994.; [pers.] I live on the shore of a beautiful wild river where the air is fresh and wildlife abounds. As close to Nature as Adam and Eve. Where the skies are magnificent. And swimming a totally great adventure.; [a.] Somerset, CA

WHITE, JASON MARK
[pen.] Jason M. White; [b.] November 2, 1974, NC; [p.] Richard and Linda White; [ed.] Attending Mount Vernon Nazarene College; [memb.] Church of the Nazarene; [oth. writ.] Published in "Windows Within", MVNC Literary Magazine; [pers.] Poetry liberates the mind and frees the soul.; [a.] Centerville, IN

WHITE, PATRICK
[occ.] Cemetary Caretaker; [pers.] An intelligent person is one who notes and understands that which is obvious; [a.] Pinehurst, TX

WIEDECKER, BRETT
[b.] March 6, 1978, Rahway, NJ; [p.] Linda and Robert W.; [ed.] Home schooling; [occ.] Student; [hon.] Black Belt in Taekwondo and Karate; [oth. writ.] Fiction and Prose; [pers.] "My poetry, if it may even be so honored as to be called such, is not a record of who I am or how I feel, but who I wish I wasn't."; [a.] Highland Park, NJ

WILENSKY, SYLVIA T.
[b.] October 14, 1937, B'klyn, NY; [p.] Lempi and Hjalmar Halikka; [m.] Irv Wilensky, February 9, 1957; [ch.] Jesse, Chris, Adam, Mark, grandchildren: Simon, Erin, Eric, Jon; [ed.] Phillips Jr. College, Melbourne, FL Bus/Accounting Degrees, 3.9 GPA, 1 year Brevard Comm. College; [occ.] Housewife; [hon.] Student of the Quarter Summer, 1991 Phillips JC Presidents, List (7) quarters 4.0 average; [oth. writ.] "Beauty" was recently published in "After the Storm". Eventually, I hope to have more of my poems published.; [pers.] I am basically new at writing poetry for publication. It comes easy, to me, writing poetry is life itself. Feelings are kept alive thru poetry, otherwise lost in thought.; [a.] Sebastian, FL

WILEY, REBA JUNE REEVES
[pen.] June Wiley; [b.] March 8, 1944, Reynoelds Co., MO; [p.] Henry and Georgia Reeves; [m.] Darryl Lynn Wiley, March 22, 1964; [ch.] Kathryn and Amanda; [ed.] Cocoa High Adult Ed. 1980, El Reno Jr. College 1983-84; [occ.] Waitress; [memb.] Clearlake Baptist Church, Girl Scout Coleader; [hon.] National Dean's list 1984; [oth. writ.] Poems for Church paper; [pers.] I have 4 grandchildren Amanda, Scarlett, Kenny and Erik. I love nature and people. God is the most important being in my life also family me and everything; [a.] Merritt Island, FL

WILHELMY, GUS
[b.] February 17, 1935, St. Paul, MN; [p.] George and Emily Wilhelmy; [m.] Mary Vallely, September 1, 1990; [ch.] Rebecca, Rochelle, Todd; [ed.] Good Counsel High, Passionist Academic Inst. Univ. of MI, Univ. of WI; [occ.] Fund Raising Consultant; [memb.] National Society of Fund Raising Executives, American Marketing Assoc., American Management Assoc., Chicago Assoc. of Technical Assistance Providers; [hon.] Martin Luther King Community Leadership Award, Young Man of American; [oth. writ.] Published articles "My Sunday Visitor", "Business Horizons" of Univ. of Indiana, "Spirit" magazine; [pers.] My poetry reaches deep down into my innermost self and allows me to reveal what is unique, yet tragically wonderful about each of us.; [a.] Chicago, IL

WILKERSON, DIANA
[b.] November 1, 1951, Alabama; [p.] George and Esther Williams; [m.] Widowed, September 6, 1971; [ch.] Kenyon, Diarra; [ed.] River Rouge High School Grad. - 1969, Wayne State University; [occ.] Senior Membership Consultant (Blue Cross Blue Shield of Michigan); [memb.] United Citizens S.W. Detroit, Southpointe CB Patrol, Wm A. King Scholarship Fund,

BCBSM HAP/PAC, National Management Assoc.; [oth. writ.] Editor - The Council (Community Newsletter); [pers.] My talent is a gift from God, He is worthy of all praises. My work reflects His love and divine grace.; [a.] Detroit, MI

WILKS, MARY COOKSEY
[b.] June 26, 1948; [p.] Carlos Cooksey, Marian Meehan Cookey; [ed.] Graduate of Verona High School; [occ.] Owner of Tailwaggers Pet Sitting Service, Part Time School Crossing Guard, Part Time Dental Receptionist; [memb.] Chairman of Verona Recreation Advisory Committee, Sub Committee Chairman of Verona Community Center/Member of Handgun Control, National Wildlife Federation; [oth. writ.] Poem "New Friends" published in National Library of Poetry anthology Journey of the Mind - Poem "Life's Simple Treasures" published in National Library of Poetry Anthology A Moment in Time; [pers.] I hope someday to be able to spend more time writing but for now thoroughly enjoy spending my time working with children, caring for animals and service on local committees.; [a.] Verona, NJ

WILKUM, PAULA
[b.] July 22, 1965, Oshkosh, WI; [m.] David Wilkum, June 18, 1988; [oth. writ.] Favorite writing subjects include: Nature, Environments, Relationships and History; [a.] Oshkosh, WI

WILLIAMS, ANN BLESSING
[pen.] Margaret Arthur; [b.] May 8, 1951, Russell, KS; [p.] Art and Lorene Blessing; [m.] Martin S. Williams, April 6, 1993; [ed.] Russell High School, Ft. Lewis College - B.A., Ft. Hays State Univ. - M.A.; [a.] Hays, KS

WILLIAMS, DANIELE
[b.] August 28, 1974, Manhattan, NY; [p.] Marion E. Williams; [ed.] A. Philip Randolph Campus High School, Hartwick College, Katharine Gibbs School; [occ.] Receptionist; [memb.] Peoples Baptist Church; [hon.] The Langston Hughes Award for Writing, Deans List, President's List; [pers.] I will trust in the Lord all the days of my life, for: "...In all things God works for the good of those who love him, who have been called according to His purpose." -Romans 8:28; [a.] New York, NY

WILLIAMS, EDGAR
[m.] Helen Turner, 1951; [ch.] We have three sons and seven grandchildren; [occ.] Working in factories, traveling on high seas during war times, plus battling court cases, some winning, some lossing. My right hand is one hundred percent disabled from a microwave oven burn of ten years. I trained my left hand to write which I do for pain control therapy.; [oth. writ.] My poetry songs and stories cover a wide range of events and imagination.; [pers.] Being raised on a farm near the small town of Fayetteville, Ga., surviving on what nature provided.; [a.] Fayetteville, GA

WILLIAMS III, HAROLD I.
[b.] July 31, 1963, Weymooth, MA; [ch.] Elizabeth Mae Williams (My beautiful daughter is 4 years old); [ed.] Bachelor's of Business, Bridgewater State College, Dean's List; [occ.] Merchandise Manager Costco Wholesale Co, Avon, MA; [hon.] Dean's List in College isn't test of service of Merchandising; [pers.] I believed writing and poetry should be used to bring to light the shortfalls and areas of society that those of us who are better off should concentrate and contribute to.; [a.] Abington, MA

WILLIAMS, JAMES EDWARD
[b.] July 14, 1956, Thonotosassa, FL; [ed.] Self-Educated; [occ.] Construction; [memb.] Mental Health Ass.; [oth. writ.] Working on first book. Title: Understanding, Tragedy and Human Misery. Special to No One, The Same Old Fool, From Children's Hour, Somebody Tell Me When, A Shattered Dream, Am I wrong to Hunger, If I Should Even Flounder; [pers.] Only through Truth, Understanding, and Rightousness can we find our way.; [a.] Atlanta, GA

WILLIAMS, JANICE E.
[pen.] Jan; [b.] August 21, 1958, Nashville, TN; [p.] Elzie Williams and Percy Williams; [ch.] Tamara Michelle Williams; [ed.] Graduated Hillwood HIgh School, Graduated: Area Vocational School in Nashville, Attended: Nashville Area Technical School; [occ.] Administrative Clerk for the State of Tennessee Dept. of Commerce and Insurance; [memb.] Corinthian Missionary Baptist Church Young Adult Choir; [hon.] 17 years of continued Public Service with the State of Tennessee; [oth. writ.] First publication with the National Library of Poetry; [pers.] I thoroughly enjoy the fulfillment of creating poetry. I have tremendously been influenced by Dr. Maya Angelou.; [a.] Nashville, TN

WILLIAMS, JIM
[pen.] Jim Williams; [b.] October 21, 1954, Cleveland, OH; [p.] Amos and Dorothy Levert; [m.] Terry H. Williams, August 27, 1988; [ch.] Nichole D. Hine, Brandon R. Jackson, goddaughter Tiaira D. Harris; [ed.] East Technical High, Dyke Business College; [occ.] Computer Operator; [memb.] Salem Baptist Church Atlanta, Georgia; [pers.] Dedicated to Darryl Phillips, Will A. Mills, Oise P. Tabbs, Tyrone S. Gillum, Jerome Dowell, Adrain Saddler and James Mitchell. These words will last an eternity and my prayers are, so will our friendship. Thanks for being my friends I'll always be yours.; [a.] Lithonia, GA

WILLIAMS, JOEY
[b.] March 19, 1978, Sunnyside, WA; [p.] Joe and Mary L. Williams; [ed.] Prosser High School; [occ.] Full time student; [a.] Prosser, WA

WILLIAMS JR., MR. STANLEY
[pen.] Mr. Stanley Williams Jr.; [oth. writ.] Please see other copies sent-previously for both poems, "The Working Maid" and "To Be Poor." I'm sending $20.00 more just in case, If not please use this $20.00 towards purchase for Beyond The Stars etc.. The Biographical Data Form, same as this one was filled and sent to your office along with two (2) Author's Release Form also filled with proof only of my original work by me only.

WILLIAMS, LAUREN M.
[pen.] Lauren Marie; [b.] August 27, 1972, Chicago, IL; [p.] Adrienne and Charles D. Williams; [ed.] Associates in Arts Harper College current: Columbia College in Chicago studying Journalism for T.V. Broadcast; [occ.] Student/Retail; [hon.] Student of the Year '90, Australian Exchange Student, Dean's List Honors, FHA Hero 1st place, 1st in State in Fashion Design, Girl Scout of the Year 1989, 1st place in District 214 Art Festival; [oth. writ.] This is my very first poem I ever wrote except for when I was in grade school; [pers.] "Everything in life happens for a reason. We may not know why now and we may be hurting, but someday it will click and we will know why. So keep your head up and don't let it down."; [a.] Chicago, IL

WILLIAMS, MARIE B.
[pen.] Marie E. Barthel; [b.] U.S.A.; [p.] Elizabeth and Charles; [m.] Broughton M. Williams, April 1945;

[ed.] Through College; [occ.] Retired; [memb.] WWCA Gymnastics; [hon.] (Medals and Diplomas and Cups); [oth. writ.] Lots, just never tried to publish; [pers.] Was robbed, shot in 1978. Reflects arm and ride not completely functioned - none leukemia, destroyed left eye. Heart and Disc. handicapped to spins. I'm bad shape but still write.; [a.] San Francisco, CA

WILLIAMS, MEGHAN K.
[b.] February 21, 1979, Morrisville, PA; [p.] Eileen Corney and Robert Williams; [ed.] Sophomore at Morrisville High School; [occ.] Employed part time at the Dairy Queen of Morrisville; [memb.] Volunteer at Mercy Hospital, volunteer at Soup Kitchen, Senior Citizen Aide, 2 years Christiphony participant, participant and soloist in the Morrisville Senior High Chorus and PYEA; [hon.] Honor Roll, Achievement Award, participation in Sign Language Class Award, participation in "Bring Our Daughters to Work Day" Award; [oth. writ.] Published in 1994 Treasured Poems of America and in the 1995 Treasured Poems of America; [pers.] I am greatly influenced by the best poet in the world (in my opinion anyway), my Dad. Our poetry is simply what's inside our hearts.; [a.] Morrisville, PA

WILLIAMS, PATRICK SHAWN
[pen.] Rickshaw Greeting Cards; [b.] April 1, 1963, Grand Junction, CO; [p.] Wendell and Betty Williams; [ed.] High School Graduate; [occ.] Part owner company: The Antlershed. Makers of Fine Handcrafted Antler Furnishings.; [memb.] Seventh-Day Adventist Church, A.C.A.P. (Adventist Composers, Arrangers, and Poets); [oth. writ.] A few poems printed in Acapella Magazine, personalized greeting cards for friends and family; [pers.] My poetry is a reflection of my own personal experiences, feelings, and views born of a growing relationship with Jesus Christ. It is my goal to write that which will lead others to seek him out.; [a.] Grand Junction, CO

WILLIAMS, RICHARD D.
[pen.] Weldon Faulmann; [b.] May 23, 1939, San Francisco, CA; [p.] Juan Manuel Reposa and Grace Faulmann; [m.] Margaret J. Williams, January 31, 1976; [pers.] This is from a small collection of poems entitled "The Catharsis". Written mostly in Haiku and Tanka style of 17 and 31 syllables per stanza, it reflects feelings as he found his anemia both in nature and other people.; [a.] Clovis, CA

WILLIAMS, SHAWNTA R.
[b.] October 16, 1975, Elizabeth, NJ; [p.] Mary Sheffield; [ed.] Elizabeth High School Graduate, and 2 years at Bloomfield College; [hon.] 1 Nursing Award; [oth. writ.] I have written one or two songs; [pers.] When you set your sites on doing any thing, believe in what you are doing and you will succeed.; [a.] Elizabeth, NJ

WILLS, SUSAN J.
[pen.] Chelsie Wilder; [b.] April 9, 1968, Philly, PA; [p.] John Buckley and Fran Piotrowski; [m.] Jeffrey A. Wills, June 30, 1990; [ch.] Tiffanie Jenna, Brittaney Justine; [ed.] Margate Middle School, Coconut Creek High School, Atlantic Vocational School; [occ.] Entrepreneur, Writer-Poet and Housewife; [memb.] Calvary Chapel Church, Ft. Lauderdale, Fla.; [hon.] Drama Award 1984; [oth. writ.] Several poems written over the course of the past thirteen years; [pers.] I have found healing through my poetry and my hope is that all who read it will be inspired. My ability to write is not that of my own, but, is a gift that comes from the hand of my Lord and Savior, Jesus Christ!; [a.] North Lauderdale, FL

WILSON, ELIZABETH M.
[pen.] E. Linda; [b.] February 12, 1965, Washington, DC; [p.] Cannon Eugene Wilson, Virginia Manning; [m.] Kenneth R. Townsend (fiance); [ch.] Barry J. Bungo Jr., Tiara K. Townsend; [ed.] Newark High School, Salem Community College, attended college 2 years, currently going to Votech for Drafting; [occ.] Attending school for Computer Assisted Design and Drafting; [oth. writ.] I have no other poems published, but I've written quite a few for people or special events.; [pers.] My poems comes from my own experiences, as well as the very special people around me. I am inspired most by Deloris Bowen, (my son's grandmother) my one true friend, my heart.; [a.] Penns Grove, NJ

WILSON, JUDITH A.
[b.] April 7, 1946, Trenton, NJ; [p.] Frank Nutt Jr. and Jane V. Nutt; [ch.] Richard Lloyd, David Andrew; [ed.] Notre Dame High School, Trenton State College; [occ.] Special Education Teacher Mutt School, Trenton NJ; [memb.] National Education Association, Trenton Education Association; [hon.] Governor's Teacher Recognition Award, 1994, Dean's List-Trenton State College; [oth. writ.] Poems - "Changed?", "The Club" "Me, You Probably Lots of Others", "Ebony Pearl", "You" - not yet submitted but planning to submit; [pers.] My writings are inspired by those people and processes that have impacted my life and upon whom my life changes have impacted.; [a.] Trenton, NJ

WILSON, MICHAEL D.
[b.] May 3, 1953, San Antonio, TX; [p.] Eileen Matticks, Burke Wilson; [m.] Roulette La Gardner, October 9, 1079; [ch.] Eudocia Elvina; [ed.] 10th Grade; [occ.] Recovering Disabled vet (P.T.S.D.), Artist (Painter) Poet, Author; [memb.] Veterans of Foreign Wars, Disabled American Veterans; [hon.] Combat Infantry Badge, Vietnam Service Ribbon; [oth. writ.] A 205 page Book "Moments in Time" of war, Life and conditions in the world in 25 oil paintings and poetry completed and self taught in 18 months, several poems published in Kentucky New Readingston, Spokane, Wa., for Veterans Day; [pers.] Should we destroy ourselves, it is only because we believe in our own destruction: We are a people with the power to lead, but, choose to be led; [a.] Spoken, WA

WILSON, MIKE
[pen.] Mike Wilson; [b.] April 11, 1979, Westlake Village, CA; [p.] Maurine and Bob Wilson; [ed.] Newbury Park High School; [occ.] Student, part-time worker; [hon.] Honor Roll, Eagle Scout; [oth. writ.] Some other poems somewhere; [pers.] I tried to show insecurities of our world.; [a.] Newbury Park, CA

WILSON, ROSALEE
[b.] December 20, 1955, Nashville, TN; [p.] Frank Sweatt, Nellie Sweatt; [m.] William David Wilson, November 19, 1994; [ch.] Lisa Marie Neighbours, James Neighbours Jr., Michael David Wilson; [ed.] Conn High School; [occ.] Accountant American General INS Comp.; [pers.] I try to express in my writing how I view nature and how I feel about life in general.; [a.] Nashville, TN

WILSON-SMITH, GLORIA J.
[pen.] Soliloquy Swift; [b.] October 10, 1957, AK; [p.] Jessie and Effie Wilson; [m.] Divorced; [ch.] Correy; [ed.] B.A. Speech Communication, MSOCED; [occ.] Teacher; [memb.] Zeta Phi Beta Sorority, Queen Esther Chapter 5 Order of the Eastern Stars; [hon.] National Dean's List. I've written the 1st Comprehensive Study on Adolescent Suicide in Chicago since 1929. Syndicated Author, new release "The Tootsie Roll Man"; [pers.] Seek God first, then, have faith in Him to direct your path.; [a.] Chicago, IL

WILSON, STEVEN D.
[b.] November 28, 1950, Kansas City, KS; [p.] Richard A., Evelyn J. Wilson; [m.] Trina A. Wilson, April 12, 1982; [ch.] Steven, Steffanie, Mary, Stephanie, Christy; [ed.] Chancellors Certificate UMKC; [occ.] Freelance Writer; [oth. writ.] Specializing in comedy. Has written for Bob Hope and Joan Rivers. Also writes and produces scripts for video and television.; [a.] Mission, KS

WINLAND, AUDREY HANSEN
[b.] July 24, 1924, Jersey City, NJ; [p.] Deceased Anna and Howard S. Hansen; [m.] Deceased James Edward Winland, November 2, 1947; [ch.] Daryl L. Winland, Denise L. Winland, Bruce E. Winland; [ed.] Abraham Clark High, Roselle, NJ; [occ.] Retired Educational Secretary - Roselle Board of Education having worked 34 1/2 years; [memb.] Member Elmora Presbyterian Church, Member Women's Council, Former Church Elder, Deacon, Sunday School Superintendent, Member N.J.E.A., National Association of Educational Personnel, N.J. Association of Educational Personnel, Union County Retired Educators Association, Friends of the Linden Library, American Society of Notaries, American Association of Retired Persons, Mental Health Association, Order of the Eastern Star - Emmanus Chapter #183, Linden, Deborah - Hilda Gould Chapter, Linden; [hon.] Golden Poetry Award Certificate 1988, Merit Certificate - 4th place 1988, World of Poetry; [oth. writ.] Poem printed in PTA Bulletin Poem used for Rainbow Girls and Church; [pers.] Poetry has always been a way of expressing myself; [a.] Linden, NJ

WINN, BETTY
[b.] September 11, 1945, Victoria, British Columbia, Canada; [m.] Divorced; [ch.] One son, grandchildren: Two grandsons; [ed.] High School Graduate, some College; [oth. writ.] Two poems published in Christian Newsletters. One article published in a local newspaper. Another published in a newsletter for The Tucson Centers for Women and Children.; [pers.] In each poem or article I write, I strive to write from the heart.; [a.] Tucson, AZ

WINSTEAD, SANDRA CHESHIRE
[pen.] Molly Pond; [b.] June 19, 1944, Rocky Mount, NC; [p.] Thomas and Helen Cheshire; [m.] Robert, November 29, 1963; [ch.] David, Mathew, Valerie; [ed.] Rocky Mount Senior High School, Hard Barger Business College, University of NC at Chapel Hill, Work Forest University; [occ.] Property Tax Assistant, Hardee's Food Systems, Rocky Mount, NC; [memb.] United Daughters of the Conferacy, First Baptist Church; [hon.] Whos Who in Church Music '90-'94, Best of show in Photography - Art 1991, Rocky Mt. Fair, Several 1st place ribbons for water color Photography '92-'94; [oth. writ.] Several poems published in 'Poetic Voices of America'; [a.] Rocky Mount, NC

WION, JILL SUE
[b.] January 6, 1959, Korea; [p.] Donald and Eunice Mast; [ch.] Stephanie, Jennifer and Jeffrey Wion; [occ.] Family Resource Worker: For AKA Head-Start; [oth. writ.] Collection of poems published in college papers. Manuscript (fiction) "Blame Someone." (1982); [pers.] My mother's last words to us before she passed away, "Go out into this world and make a difference." (1994); [a.] Spring Valley, CA

WISNESKI, KATHLEEN
[b.] October 20, 1985, NY; [p.] Walter and Jane Wisneski; [ed.] Blessed Sacrament School; [occ.] Student; [memb.] 4 H, School Select Choir; [hon.] First and Fourth Place in School Art Contest and 4H Achievement Awards; [pers.] I write my poems mostly to cheer someone up. Although they have not been published they have served their purpose.; [a.] Valley Stream, NY

WISSERT, PATRICIA RUTH
[b.] July 10, 1956, England; [p.] Othon and Betty Hagan; [ch.] Timothy Killebrew, Delilah Wissert and Nicholas Wissert; [ed.] A.A. degree in Clerical Office from Merced College; [occ.] Typist Clerk II; [memb.] Member of Atwater's Ladies Auxiliary VFW Post #9946 Since 1984; [hon.] 'B' Honor roll in Merced High School and Merced College; [pers.] A hard lesson I've learned: Life is not a punishment, but a lesson to be learned.; [a.] Merced, CA

WISSNER, ILSE E.
[pen.] Ilse Wissner; [b.] August 10, 1925, Germany; [m.] Earl W. Wissner (Deceased 1961), December 23, 1950; [ch.] 2 sons; [ed.] H.S., Coll. of Ed., Germany, Madonna University (B.A.), Livonia, Mich., Wayne State University (M.Ed.), Detroit, Michigan; [occ.] Retired Teacher; [memb.] Lifetime member of the International Society of Poets; [hon.] Lambda Iota Tau, International Literature Honor Society, several Editors's Choice Awards, One Third Place Award, poem chosen for Best Poems of 1995. All poems published in anthologies by The National Library of Poetry; [oth. writ.] A number of unpublished poems, short stories, Authobiography in Verse; [pers.] My poems are inspired by personal experiences, feelings, and reflections. I like sharing them with others, especially those who hardly ever read a poem before but now enjoy rading my verses as well as other poems.; [a.] Livonia, MI

WOITHA, KAY
[b.] July 27, 1957, Detroit; [p.] Roland and Joyce Forsmar; [m.] Jeffrey, August 20, 1977; [ch.] John, Jason, and Katie; [occ.] Wife and mother; [oth. writ.] I write poems on life and people.; [pers.] I hope my writings encourage others while we are together on this planet called earth.; [a.] Perrysburg, OH.

WOJTANOWSKI, NORA LOUISE
[b.] December 8, 1977, Harvey, IL; [p.] Joseph Wojtanowski; [ed.] Highschool student as of now; [occ.] Student; [hon.] A-B honor roll, 3 Consecutive as a Junior; [pers.] I write to make the human mind think; [a.] Vernon Hills, IL

WOLFF, JEFF
[pen.] Jeffrey A. Wolff; [b.] February 3, 1966, Baldwin, WI; [m.] Jodi Wolff, September 12, 1992; [ed.] Oshkosh North High, U.S. Army; [occ.] Drywall, Carpentry; [memb.] Timber Wolf Alliance; [oth. writ.] Newspaper Publishings; [pers.] Always been a writer, but my wife has been a true inspiration. I wouldn't have made it without her.; [a.] Eureka, WI

WOMACK, YOLANDA
[b.] January 23, 1979, Dode City, FL; [p.] Richard and Lillie Womack; [ed.] 10th gr. at Pasco High School; [occ.] Musician at New Bethel A.M.E. Church; [memb.] New Bethel A.M.E., Church Youth Department, Jr. Choir, National Honor Society, McKnight Achievers Society, Pasco High School (PHS) Marching Band, PHS Track Team '94; [hon.] National Honor Society, Assault on Illiteracy, Honor Student, Most outstanding Athlete award for the 1994 - 95 Track season; [oth. writ.] A poem entitled "To Be Black" and "Africa"; [pers.] I strongly express my heritage, tradition, and what's going on in today's society in my writings.; [a.] Lacoochee, FL

WOOD JR., CHARLES U.
[b.] February 9, 1948, Baltimore, MD; [p.] Charles and Ida May Wood; [m.] Brigitte Erika Wood, July 30, 1975; [ed.] Mt. St. Joseph College - Diploma 1966, The Johns Hoplins University, BA 1970, George Washington University, Graduate Studies in Business, Market-ing Management 1978-79; [occ.] Senior Analyst - ACIST Corporation, Alexandria, VA; [memb.] American Management Association Defense, American Preparedness Assn., Pension Ritlas, Various Scholastic Organizations, Hollow Orly Community Association; [hon.] Honor Graduate, Mt. St. Josephscholarship alters/awards, Distinguished Military Student/ Graduate - Army ROTC, Army Commendation Medal, other certs.; [oth. writ.] Numerous articles as Reporter/ Editor "The Quill" - Mt. St. Joseph, various articles as reporter for JHU newsletter, Editor - "Spearhead Alter Hours" - 3d Armored Division, Technical/Management courses a publications as part of professional services, Advertising Copy; [pers.] Writing is an extremely satisfying creative effort. I instead to expond my horizons as a professional writer and become successful at it.; [a.] Columbia, MD

WOOD, MICHEAL
[b.] November 22, 1966, Albion, MI; [ed.] Butler University, Indianapolis IN, University of Florida, Gainesville, FL; [occ.] Activity Leader, Lake Forest Elementary/Artist; [hon.] Purchase Award Winner, Smalls Works Exhibition, Orlando, FL, Dean's/Presidents List Kendall College; [pers.] I have been fascinated for a long time with the small moments that weight with a certain gravity or that change the events of your life. The simple passions of Eudora Welty and Maya Angelou have influenced me.; [a.] Gainesville, FL

WOODARD, MERRY G.
[b.] December 14, 1953, Kenosha, WI; [p.] George and Dorothy Broughton; [m.] George W. Woodard, April 8, 1989; [ed.] B.A. Modern Foreign Language from Indiana University in 1977, currently working on BSED in Elementary Education from Western Carolina University (WCU); [occ.] Program Assistant IV at The Reading Center/WCU; [memb.] Recording Secretary - Support Council for Office Personnel Enhancement (SCOPE), Treasurer - Western Carolina University Association of Educational Office Professionals, North Carolina Association of Educational Office Professionals, student member of the National Council of Teachers of English, member of the Southeast Writers Association; [hon.] Presented paper at the 1994 National Conference on Undergraduate Research, I hold a 4.0 average but am not on the Dean's List because I am only a part-time student; [oth. writ.] Poetry and children's books, all of which are unpublished, Addendum: poem entitled "Moon Rise" to be published in chapbook series "New South Poetry" by The Southeast Writers Association 9 or 10 1995; [pers.] For me, writing is the lighting of a fire and the realization of a dream. Without my writerly life, the world would lose its vital vividness and my dreams would fade to black.; [a.] Sylva, NC

WOODY, TISHA
[b.] December 5, 1979, Galveston, TX; [p.] Tony Woody, Brenda Darn; [occ.] Student; [a.] Deer Park, TX

WORKMAN, TAYLOR
[b.] November 6, 1982, Craig, CO; [p.] Beth Eschenburg, David Workman; [ed.] Craig Middle School 6th grade going into 7th grade; [hon.] I got my Dare Award for being drug free and Citizenship Honors Award; [oth. writ.] I've never been published, but all my writing teachers, friends, and family love my poems; [pers.] I have poems, when I'm felling down I write and write. Its just another way of me saying my fellings, of people, earth, me just life things.; [a.] Craig, CO

WRIGHT, ELENA DIANE
[b.] December 29, 1981, Atlanta, GA; [p.] Sharron and Jack Wright; [ed.] 7th Grade at Garrett Middle School Austell, GA 30001; [occ.] Student, Garrett M/S; [pers.] I was born without a left hand, but my feelings are, "I can do all things, through Christ, who strengthens me".

WRIGHT, ROBERT L.
[b.] March 6, 1995, Charleston, SC; [p.] Mr. Willie Stanley, Mrs. Dorothy Wright; [m.] Mrs. Rozita P. Wright, April 12, 1980; [ch.] Mr. Robert L. Wright Jr., Donnelle, Michelle (Twins), Shawntelle, Laquetta, Kimberl Wright; [ed.] Associate Degree in Criminal Justice, Graduate Aug. 1980 Trident Technical College, Charleston (Palmer Campus); [occ.] Delivery Leadman, Charleston County School District; [memb.] Azalea Drive Church of Christ Bible School Teacher..., National Arbor Day Foundation... Baptist Haiti Mission (An Independent Mission Society); [hon.] Classified Employee of the Year, Volunteer Service Awards from Juvenile Court System, OAK, Grove Orphanage Big Brother/Big Sister, USMC Outstanding Service Award; [oth. writ.] Other non-published poems... one published short story entitled, "A Society That Made A Good Man Go Bad..." Stars and Stripes 1971, gist of story: A young man falsely accused and jailed a crime, once released, he retaliates.; [pers.] In short and long range planning one future has many locked doors waiting to be unlocked... Well, what and you waiting for? You are its key... The very essence to one's survival as a human being depends on one's self-drive and stamina.. one must feel this way in one's quest to succeed in life!!!; [a.] Charleston, SC

WRIGHT, STEPHANIE M.
[b.] April 1, 1971, Oil City, PA; [p.] Grace and Sam Arnold, Harold Nancy Wright; [ed.] Parkersburg South High, Washington County Career Center Studied to be an Automotive Technician; [occ.] Parts clerk at a dealership; [pers.] My family is a big inspiration to me. We've had a lot of hardships but good things are around the corner. Love is precious and family is priceless, both are dear to me.; [a.] Walker, WV

YAGHMOUR, BANOMATEE N.
[b.] August 19, 1960; [p.] Mr. and Mrs. Dharmu M. Nath; [m.] Khalid Yaghmour, March 1, 1985; [ch.] Almaza, Nidal and Sammy; [ed.] BS in Elementary Education, MS in Guidance Counseling (Brooklyn College); [occ.] Teacher; [memb.] Wildlife Conservation, The Journal of National Association for the Education of Young Children, The Brooklyn Children's Museum; [oth. writ.] Short Stories "Mom 9 Feel Sick" (in press for publication); [pers.] Most of my making hours are spent among children. My every thought is about them. I feel the joy and sadness with them. My writing expresses my most inner feeling about children.; [a.] Brooklyn, NY

YANG, ANDREW C.
[b.] February 3, 1982, New York City; [p.] Tay Ing Yang, Ling Wang Yang; [ed.] Iolani School, 7th Grade, Honolulu Hawaii; [occ.] Student; [pers.] My poems are greatly influenced by my mood. If I'm cranky, my poems reflect that.; [a.] Kaneohe, HI

YAROSLAWSKI, MARY FRANCES
[pen.] Mary Frances Yaroslawski; [b.] February 14, 1938, Jacksonville; [p.] Menzo Willis, Hattie Willies; [ch.] Orusilla Davis; [memb.] Moncrief Missionary Baptist Church; [a.] Jacksonville, FL

YERKES, AMY
[b.] May 9, 1977, Passaic, NJ; [p.] Elizabeth Yerkes; [ed.] Parsippany Hills High School, attending University of Maryland as a freshman, fall 1995; [occ.] Hostess at Chili's Restaurant; [hon.] National Honors Society, Garden State Scholar, All State Coaches Award-Tennis, "Who's Who Among American High School Students, All American Scholar, President Scholarship

from Univ. of Maryland; [oth. writ.] Poem entitled "Black" published in Treasured Poems of America Anthology by Sparrow grass Poetry Forum, another published by Creative Communication in the anthology A Celebration of New Jersey's Young Poets; [pers.] Whenever I get depressed by my small size (5'2") I remember this philosophy: "I hope if dogs ever take over the world, and they choose a king, they don't just go by size, because I bet there are some shitzus out there with some good ideas."; [a.] Denville, NJ

YOAKUM, DIANA
[b.] July 7, 1946, Indianapolis, IN; [p.] Gaspord and Ione Ricketts; [ch.] Kevin Lewis, Carolyn Lewis; [ed.] Rockville High; [memb.] Loyal Order of the Moose and Loyal Order of the Eagles (Aux.); [hon.] Company excellence award; [oth. writ.] Poem published in a local community newspaper; [pers.] In my writing, I strive to create an Aurora of Warmth, and imagination. Reflecting reality and true emotions.; [a.] Jupiter, FL

YOLMAN, JONAH BOLT
[pen.] Jonah Bolt; [b.] January 1, 1979, Avon Park, FL; [p.] Ken Yolman; [ed.] I attend Boca Raton High School; [occ.] Student; [oth. writ.] "The Time Has Come" published in echoes from the silence, by Quill Books; [pers.] I hope my writings make a positive difference living in this CD-ROM Society.; [a.] Boca Raton, FL

YOSHIDA, IKUKO
[pen.] Kagami; [b.] March 15, 1972, Tokyo, Japan; [p.] Mr. Shutoku Yoshida, Mrs. Kazuko Y.; [ed.] Jiyu-Gakuen High School Tokyo National University of Fine Arts and Music; [occ.] Student; [pers.] Ich empfinde die Begreiflichkeit der Weltals Wunder oder ewiges Geheimnis. By Albert Einstein.; [a.] New York, NY

YOUMANS, BECKY
[b.] July 24, 1979, Danville, IL; [p.] Rick and Kathy Youmans; [ed.] Monrovia High School Monrovia, IN; [occ.] Student; [memb.] National Junior Honor Society - 1 year, National Honor Society - current, Numerous Academic Competition Teams, Envirothon Team, Gasburg Baptist Church and Youth Group, Marching Band; [hon.] 3 Academic Achievement Awards, Presidential Academic Fitness Award 1989/1990, Member of Top 10 Showband in State of Indiana in 1992, 1993 and 1994; [pers.] I believe that anything's possible with the help of God.; [a.] Mooresville, IN

YOUNG, CODY
[b.] December 10, 1975, Redding, CA; [p.] Cindee Totherow, Robert Young; [ed.] Fortuna Union High School, starting my first semester of college, attending College of the Redwoods - Humboldt Co.; [occ.] Lumber Handler, Planner/Pacific Lumber Co.; [memb.] Pending; [hon.] Yet to come!; [oth. writ.] Personal writings, and poems, views, and ideas.; [pers.] I speak from the heart, soul, and mind. I represented the sun, and the earth. Linked as one, they create an engulfing philosophy, greater than life itself.; [a.] McKinlyville, CA

YOUNG, DEBORAH A.
[b.] December 26, 1973, Marlboro, MA; [p.] Nancy and Kenneth Young; [ed.] Tantasqua High School in Sturbridge Mass.; [occ.] Hyde Mfg. Company in Southbridge Mass.; [memb.] SADD (Students Against Driving Drunk), IFAW (International Fund for Animal Welfare); [oth. writ.] Several poems published in "passages" and in local newspapers. Two short poetry books printed on my own, "Paths Into My Mind" and "As Time Goes By."; [pers.] I hope to one day be a well known poetry writer or to have at least wrote something that sparked a memory in someone's heart, for they could release to it.; [a.] Sturbridge, MA

YOUNG, GWEN M.
[b.] July 14, 1957, Newport News, VA; [p.] Judy and Ted Miller; [m.] Derris S. Young, May 2, 1985; [ch.] Shasta Autumn (age 8) and Shannon Jesse Miller Young (age 15); [ed.] High school graduate in 1975 at Rogers Senior High School in Michigan City, IN; Junior College for 1 semester in Lancaster, CA; [occ.] Boookkeeper Albertson's Groc. Rosamond, CA; [hon.] In Junior High School I won 2nd prize in a talent contest -- I sang "Gypsies Tramps and Thieves" by Cher; [oth. writ.] A poem called "Only in God's Time" printed in the local newspaper, many poems and a few songs that I've never tried to have published as of yet.; [pers.] I recently went through a battle with breast cancer and I thank God I won. I realize that life and the quality of life is way too short. In no time at all we're gone. However, there is comfort in knowing that a person may be remembered for their works, efforts and artistic contributions for generations to come.; [a.] Castaic, CA.

YOUNG, MATHEW GLENN
[b.] December 2, 1967, Bremerton, WA; [p.] Glenn A. Young, Margaret R. Dives; [m.] Kazuko, Fujii Young, January 19, 1992; [ch.] Jonathan and Christine; [ed.] Malad High School, Malad, ID. Idaho State University; [occ.] U.S. Navy, Weapons Technician on board USS Ford FFG 54; [oth. writ.] Several poem written to my wife, many other poems, most of which relate to the sea, or life on the sea; [pers.] My inspiration derives from, my love for my wife and family, my love for my country, and my respect for the sea. I wrote "Another Day Turns Into Night" shortly after participation in a 21 gun salute during a burial at sea.; [a.] Marysville, WA

YOUNG, MR. DIDESHE
[pen.] Desharne; [b.] October 17, 1975, Little Rock, AR; [p.] Linda Whitley; [ed.] Parkview High, University of Arkansas at Little Rock; [occ.] Reservationist, Fairfield Communities; [pers.] Ordinary people dream about how they live extraordinary people live their dreams; [a.] Scott, AR

YOUNG, VILMA CLARK
[b.] Belize, CA; [p.] Branstan S. Clark; [m.] Keith Young, July 25, 1964; [ch.] Lionel B. Young; [ed.] Brooklyn Conservatory Music of Brooklyn College, Empire State College, New York University. State University of N.Y., A.A., B.A.; [occ.] Private tutor music teacher private; [memb.] Com. board 12 youth committee, founder - Director Christian Children's Assn. Belizean Youth Congress; [hon.] American Women of Today by American Biographical Institute; [oth. writ.] Belize, New York A Cultural Diversity, The Caribbean Anthem; [pers.] I intend to promote friendship and understanding between the varied cultures of the international community in my poetry and music.; [a.] Bronx, NY

YOUNG, WILLIAM A.
[b.] August 23, 1946, Hamilton, OH; [p.] Helen Young (deceased), Murray A. Young Sr.; [ed.] Graduated 1965 from Hamilton Taft Sr. High, Graduated 2 yrs Business School Miami Valley Institute of Technology; [occ.] Manpower Temp., Svcs., Employee doing whose work; [memb.] At present I'm a Volunteer Scorekeeper, Chaperone with the Hamilton Handicapped Bowling League. I've been doing this since September 79. (Mentally Retarded); [oth. writ.] I have written several others (none published); [pers.] I believe in God to the fullest and believe the sooner everybody comes back to Him the better!! Many thanks for the publishing of my poem!!; [a.] Hamilton, OH

YOURS, LORINE CAROL
[b.] December 27, 1972, Charlston, WV; [p.] Ayrest Yours and James Oscer Yours Jr.; [ed.] Graduated from

Milton High School; [occ.] Writing and taking care of my health and mother with lots of problems; [memb.] Hurcan Bible Church; [hon.] Trouble much for a short store in the Yours Writers Contest when I was a soft more in high school; [oth. writ.] A couple short stories some songs one, book working on another all unpublished; [pers.] I couldn't do anything without God. He give me that talent and strength to write.; [a.] Culloden, WV

ZAMORA, JULIO S.
[pen.] Julio S. Zamora; [b.] April 12, 1929, San Antonio, TX; [p.] Manuel D. Zamora and Soledad Sotomayor Zamora; [m.] Maria Delos Angeles Zamora, 1990; [ch.] Two, Anita and Angie Zamora; [ed.] High School G-1947 (Sidney Lanier) SA, Tx.; [occ.] Retired; [pers.] May the beauty of nature be forever for the enjoyment of all mankind; [a.] San Antonio, TX

ZAMORA, TRICIA A.
[b.] September 29, 1982, Corpus Christi, TX; [p.] Mary Ellen Martinez; [ed.] Paul Haas Middle School 6th grade; [occ.] Student; [memb.] Haas Spirit Club; [pers.] Just try hard at what you like best an don't let anyone stop you from reaching yours goals.; [a.] Corpus Christi, TX

ZELLO, VICKIE
[b.] February 24, 1957, Ann Arbor, MI; [p.] Donald and Bernice Goethe; [m.] Fred Zello, February 9, 1980; [ch.] One; [ed.] Huron High School Lansing Community College, Washtenaw Community College; [occ.] Hospital Unit Clerk; [memb.] Zoning Board of Appeals for the Village of Pinckney; [hon.] 1st place n short story, poetry contest Hamburg Township Library 1995; [oth. writ.] Currently writing a science fiction novel.; [a.] Pinckney, MI

ZIMMERMAN, JASON
[pen.] Z-man; [b.] September 17, 1976, Tulare, CA; [p.] Marilyn Cunning, Robert Zimmerman; [hon.] 1995 Western Regional Waltz Champion/Teen Division, 1995 2nd in the World of 2-Step/Teen Division, Sharpshooter Medal in CACC, and Gold Medal in State Rifle Championships for CACC; [oth. writ.] This poem was inspired by and dedicated to the Danieli's and the folks at Jazzy-D, thanks for everything.; [a.] Clovis, CA

ZIPPRICH, THERESA
[pen.] Theresa Zipprich; [b.] November 23, 1971, Jerseyville; [p.] James and Wanda Vahle; [m.] William Zipprich, November 05, 1993; [ed.] Jerseyville High School, Lewis and Clark College; [occ.] Certified Nurses Aid Jersey County Health Dept.; [memb.] Fraternal Order of Eagles Aux 2747; [hon.] National Achievement Academy Award; [oth. writ.] Several poems written for myself and friends; [pers.] The words I write come from loved ones in mind, and about the happiness we find. I wrote "Forever Together" for the front of my wedding invitation.; [a.] Jerseyville, IL